THE
NATURALIST'S NOTE BOOK.

THE NATURALIST'S NOTE BOOK

FOR 1867.

A MONTHLY RECORD

OF

ANECDOTES, THEORIES, AND FACTS RELATING TO NATURAL SCIENCE.

TOGETHER WITH

NOTICES OF NEW BOOKS, REPORTS OF THE MEETINGS OF LEARNED SOCIETIES, ORIGINAL CORRESPONDENCE, AND DESCRIPTIONS OF NEW INVENTIONS.

Think nought a trifle, though it small appear;
Small sands the mountain, moments make the year,
And trifles life.　　　　　　　　　　YOUNG.

OFFICE:
1, RACQUET COURT, FLEET STREET,
LONDON.

PREFACE.

ON the completion of this our First Volume we wish to return our thanks to those editors from whose papers, periodicals, and magazines we have largely extracted, amongst which we may mention "Once a Week," "Chambers's Journal," "The Field," "Land and Water," "Gardener's Chronicle," "The Popular Science Review," "Quarterly Journal of Science," "Zoologist," "Entomologist," and, not least, "The American Naturalist," (a publication we hope some day to see as popular in this country as we have no doubt it is in the land of its birth). Our thanks are also due to the following publishers—Messrs. Murray, Longmans & Co., Hardwick, Lovell Reeve, Churchill, Routledge, Sampson Low & Co., and Smith & Elder; together with many other gentlemen who have favoured us by permission to extract from their works.

We also beg to thank our numerous Subscribers who have supported us during the past year. Our endeavour has been to make the NATURALIST'S NOTE BOOK a complete record of new facts, theories, and anecdotes connected with all branches of Natural Science. If we have not succeeded entirely to our own and our readers' satisfaction, it has been because of the limited space at our command and the vast quantity of new matter always before us. Still we trust we have gathered together much information worthy of preservation, and which will always be found entertaining.

Of the future we have little to say. Our exertions will be continued to make the "Note Book" as interesting as possible, and to add in any way to its utility, by the addition of any new feature that will be likely to make it more acceptable to our readers.

January, 1868

INDEX.

ASTRONOMY, METEOROLOGY, and the WEATHER.

Aërolites, Meteors, and Shooting Stars, 325.
Atmosphere, the, 72.
,, in its relation to heat, 136.
Clouds, up in the, 83.
Comets, 15.
Dew, 234.
Earth's Motion, on the, 31.
Eclipses, Ancient, 75.
Fogs, Electrical, 25.
Hailstones in China, 139.
Jupiter, 210.
Jupiter's Satellites, 85.
Light, Waves of, 226.
Lightning, Effects of, 337.
,, Figures, 39.
Mars, 167.
Meteors, 36, 310, 325.
,, Colours of, 56.
,, The November, 196.
Meteoric Showers, 6, 111.
Meteorology and the Garden, 94.
Moon, Volcanoes in the, 249.
Rain, 146.
,, Black, 289.
,, Coloured, 37.
Rainbows, 307.
Snow, 124.
Sound, 54.
Stars, 52.
Star Showers, 118, 325.
Stars, Message from the (A), 18.
,, Spectrum Analysis of, 18.
Sun, the, 100.
,, Heat of the, 153.
,, Light of the, 24.
Sunrise and Sunset, 319.
Thunderstorms, 156.
,, the August, 288.
Weather, the, 298.
,, How to Forecast, 74
,, Signs, 40.

BOTANY.

Agave, the Mexican, 32.
Aloe Tree, Great, 26.
Aralia papyrifera, 100.
Bamboo, the, 126.
Banyan Tree, the, 28.
Baobab ,, 8.
Beech, the, 319.
Beet-root Sugar, 137.
Berberry the, and its uses, 110.
Betel Nut, the, 165.
Borage, 23.
Brownea Grandiceps, 111.
Bullrush, Flock from the, 111.
Camelias as Climbers, 167.
Centurea Babylonica, 290.
Cinnamon, 25.
Cocoa Nut, the Double, 244.
Coffee Plantations, injury to, 353.
Cypress, the Deciduous, 90.
Daisy, the, 120.
Dionæa Muscipula, the, 25.
Esparto, 145.
Ferns, 18.
,, How to grow, 175.
,, Norwegian, the, 212.
,, Raising from Spores, 25.
Fungi as food, 150.
Flora, Arctic, 111.
Flowers and Birds of Iceland, 87.
Forest, a Petrified, 320.
Forests of Russia, 135.
Fruit, an edible, 19.
Fruits, Dessert in 1256, 19.
Fushia, the, in Valentia, 25.
Garden, Meteorology and the, 94.
,, Productions, 109.
Ginseng, 165.
Grapes, a large bunch of, 320.
Grasses, Ornamental, 173.
,, of New Zealand, 71.
Horse Chesnut, the, 28.
Lastrea Œmula, 250.
Leaf, Fall of the, 28.
,, Parasites, 184.
Leaves, Autumn, 353.
,, and Bark, 43.
Lotus, the, 23.
Mammoth Tree, the, 76.
Maple in Canada, the, 25.
Mosses, 304.
Mulberry Tree, the, 44.
Orange Flowers, 27.
Orchards, Hereford, 27.
Orchids, 84.
Ordeal Bean of Calabar, 174.
Oriental Mysteries, 14.
Palm, the Date, 269.
Panicum Spectabile, 249.
Parasitic Plants, American, 209.
Pear, the China, 346.
Plant Architecture, 135.
Plants and Birds at Christmas, 1866, 55.
,, and their leaves, 319.
,, colours in, 181.
,, diseases of, 76.
,, evaporating power of, 320.
,, hardy Fern like, 83.
,, Minerals in, 26.
,, number of, on the Globe, 56.
,, of Ancient Egypt, 24.
,, of New Zealand, 16.
Plums as Orchard Trees, 17.
Potatoe, the, 101.
Potatoes, new use for, 194.
,, Mites in, 166.
Rice growing in Japan, 290.
Roses, new, for 1867, 98.
,, Rumelian, 194.
Saffron, 28.
Seeds, Vitality of, 19, 259.
Sensitive Plant, the, 53, 256, 290, 311.
Shrubs suitable for Shrubberies 84.
Sorghum, 249
Sub-tropical Plants, 73.
Sugar Cane, the, 102.
Thorn, the double Crimson, 128.
Tree Ferns, 289.
Trees of Missouri, 289.
Vegetation, Brazilian, 203.
Vine, a large, 26.
,, Growth of the, 59.
Vinery, uses of a ground, 47.

ETHNOLOGY.

Abyssians, 23.
Andaman, Natives of, 109.
Egyptian Fellah, the, 56.
Esquimaux in Europe, 13.
Krooman, the, 83.
Man in the early ages, 306.
Man's Work and Waste, 46.
Men, animals, and plants, 38.
Natives of the Zambesi, 51.
Saxons, 55.
Wild Tribes of India, 155.

GEOGRAPHY.

Abyssinia, Geography of, 17.
African Village, an, 99.
Amazon, the, 97.
America, the Uplands of, 111.
American Lakes, the, 320.
Equatorial Africa, 53.
Geography, Ancient, 101.
Greenland, Exploration of, 184.
Gulf Stream, the, 288.
Indian Scenery, 256.
Lago Maggiore, 196.
New Siberia, 54.
Oceanic Currents, origin of, 266.
Santorin, 258.
Sea, encroachment of the, 123.
Sweden, Sea marks on the Coast of, 139.
Zanzibar, 166.

GEOLOGY.

Agate Mountain, 28.
Artesian Wells of Grenelle, 42.
,, ,, in Algeria, 195.
Atom, an, 53.
Atoms in a piece of Iron, 55.
Cave in a Limestone Quarry, 291.
Coal Fields, 225.
Corals, Stoney, 305.
Cists, discovery of, 103.
Earthquakes, 111.
Egypt, Geology of Upper, 19.
Geology and the Microscope, 296.
,, of America, 68.
,, of Hampshire, 235.
Geological Curiosity, a, 290.
,, Theory, a new, 307.
Glaciers, What are they, 65.
Glacial or Northern Drift, the, 33.
Granite, 27, 45,
,, Garnets in, 28.
Mountains, How they are made, 1.
Madrepores, 245.
Peat Bed, a, 104.
Pebble, a curious, 56.
Peruvian Silver Mines, 24.
Rivers, what they are doing, 26.
Sulphur Mountains, 138.
Tiberius, the Hot Salt Springs of, 10.
Volcano (a new) in the South Seas, 227.
Well, a Burning, 256.

ZOOLOGY.

Alligators, 44.
Animal Life, Geometrical Forms in, 9.
Animals, Distribution of, 224.
,, Feeling of Beauty among, 12.
,, Extinct, 339.
,, Influence of Sound upon, 341.
,, Increase in size of, 127.
,, (Moss) or Fresh Water Polyzoa, 148.
,, Winter dress of, 103.
Ant, the Driver, 54.
Ants, 155.
,, African, 28.
,, Mushroom Hived, 64.
Arvicolea (British) or Voles, 204.
Avoset, the, 136.
Bear, the Indian, 206.
Beaver, the, 193.
Beavers and their Camps, 143.
Bee, the Carpenter, 297.
,, Funeral of a, 291.
,, Keeping in California, 197.
Bees, Wild, 95.
Beetle, the Burying, 197.
Beetles Assemblage, 195.
Birds, Colouring the plumage of, 56.
,, Destruction of, 300.
,. Food of, 302.
,, and Flowers of Iceland, 87.
,, in China, 52.
,, Migratory, 256.
,, Nest, (Double) 198.
,, Notes on rare, 165.
,, of Passage, do they steer by the Sun? 23.
,, of Polynesia, the, 6.
,, of the East, 261.
,, ,, Isle of Man, 125.
,, Rare, 139, 226.
,, Small, 317.
,, Song of the, 171.
,, Why they fly, 52.
Bird's Perseverance, a, 195.
Bittern, the Little, 26.
Bombyx Cynthia, 109.
Borer, the, 353.
Butterfly, the Brimstone, 182.
Camels, 16.
Canaries, Young, fed by an old nestling, 198.
Cat, the, 27, 138.
,, Ring Tailed Civit, 320.
,, Extraordinary fecundity in a, 196.
,, Fish, 138.
Centipede, the, 55.
Chickens, Curious, 290.
Clothes Moth, the, 335.
Cobra attacked by a Hen, 225.
Cockroaches, 34, 251.
Coral Fishery, 46.
Crabs, Burrowing, 263.
Crocodile Pond, a, 301.
Crow, the Carrion, 135.
Cuckoo, the, 288.
Decapod Crustacea, hearing of, 110.
Deer Hunt, extraordinary, 318.
Dog, Story of a, 291.
,, a Wise, 319.
,, a Knowing, 111.
Diatomaceæ, 47.
Diatoms, on Cleaning, 223.
Doves breeding in a Church, 136.
Eider Ducks, 72.
Elephants, Intelligence of, 67.
,, 43.
Elephant Hunt, an, 174.
Falcon, Nesting of the Peregrine, 183.
Fish, a curious, 167.
,, Culture, 167.
,, in Ceylon, 76.
,, in the Amazon, 139.
Fishes, Reproductive power of, 139.
Foxes, 138.
Guinea Fowl, the, 353.
Goat, the Wild, 75.
Grasshoppers, Plague of, 55.
Hare, Reasoning in a, 226.
Hedgehog, Habits of the, 27.
Hen and Duck, the, 55.
,, the, a Tactician, 291.
Herring, the, 273.
Horses, Sympathy among, 225.
Humming Bird, the Ruby Throated, 340.
,, ,, Food of the, 223.
Hydrophila, Larvæ of, 197.
Insects in Australia, 81.
Jackdaw, the, 109.
Jellyfishes, something about, 239.
Kangaroos, 70.
Kingfisher, the, 215.
Lady Bird, the, 56.
Lark, Song of the, 111.
Leopards, 9.
,, the Snow, 54.
Limpet, the, 213.
Lion's Life, the, 56.
Locusts, 47, 248.
,, a flight of, 196.
Lyre Bird, the, 136, 251.
Macaw, the, 109.
Mice breeding in a dove's nest, 110.
,, in a corn bin, 258.
Mites in Potatoes, 166.
Mocking Bird of America, the, 271.
Monkeys stealing Spectacles, 196.
Monster Eel, 354
Mouse's Store, a, 198.
Nightingales, 258.
Opossum, the, 75.
Oriole, the Golden, 167.
Owls, 136.
Panther, the, 317.
Parrots, food for, 257.
,, Age of, 226
Phosphorescence, 291.
,, of the Sea, 27.
Pied Sparrow, a, 166.
Pigeons at Sherwood, 344.
Pike, Instinct in a, 76.
Pipe Fishes, 93.
Plesiosaurus, new Species of, 99.

INDEX.

Pony, a Clever, 166.
„ and Dog, the Milkman's, 196.
Poultry and their Eggs, 136.
„ for a Farmyard, 110.
„ keeping in London, 25.
„ newly imported species of Indian, 290.
Potamogale Velox, the, 84.
Rabbit Breeding, 28.
Rattlesnake at large, a, 255.
Rat, a curious, 165.
Rats, 246.
„ and Mice in India, 311.
„ Sagacity, 45.
„ in Africa, 53.
„ Musk, 224.
Raven, the, 139.
Reindeer, the, 52, 342.
Rhinoceros, the, 151.
Ring Ouzel, the, 166.
Rodentra, 258.
Robin, food of the, 331.
Roebuck, Horns of the, 195.
Rooks, 116.
Sand Martin as an Engineer, the, 10.
Sand Martins, 193.
Saurians, Marine, 97.
Sciara, 250.
Scorpions, 55.
„ of Texas, 215.
Sea Gulls, 354.
Seedfinch (a St. Helena) near London, 166.
Sharks, 293.
„ Mode of capturing, in Polynesia, 17.
Shrew-mice, British, 88.
Silkworm Disease, the, 25.
Silkworms from Natal, 345.
Skylark in Australia, the, 320.
Slugs, 302.
Snails, 123.
Snakes, 243.
Starfish, the, 224.
Starlings, 102.
Stickleback, the, 151.
Sparrows in America, 225.
Sparrows, House, 60.
Spiders, Burrowing, 56.
„ and Beetles, Indian, 212.
„ „ Wasp, 259.
Squirrel, the Californian Ground, 48.
Swallow, the, 254.
Tarantula Killers, the, of Texas, 180.
Terrier Dog, 27.
Testacella, the, 316.
Toads, 257.
Tomtits nesting in a Letter Box, 194.
„ „ „ Pump, 167.
Trichina Spiralis, experiments with, 84.
Tumblers, 238.
Volvox, the, and its Parasite, 257.
Vultures in India, 129, 256.
Walrus, the, 343.
Wolves in Ireland, 128.
Wapiti, 54.
Water Blackbird, the, 126.
Woodlarks, 223.
Woodpeckers, 214.
„ Do they Migrate? 214.
Worms, Hair, 197.
Yellowhammer, the, 167.

CORRESPONDENCE.

Animals, Change of the Habits of J. S., 80.
Animals, Health of Wild, J. S., 134.
Birds, Names of, J. A. H., 255; W. W. Spicer, 316; H. H. Ulidia, 316.
Birds of Passage, Alpea, Leigh Hunt, 163; H. H. Ulidia, 287; Arthur G. Harvie, 315.
Earth's Orbit and our Seasons, the, H. H. Ulidia, 133; Gulielmus, 163.
Glacial Action, Gulielmus, 221.
Horse Chesnut, W. H. Ade, 51.
Ice Floe in the North Atlantic, Col. H. E. Austen, F.M.S., 134.
Insect Life, T. A. H., 107; Arthur G. Harrie, 107; T. P. Bellingham, 108.
Insects, Migrations of, R. W. B., 221; H. H. Ulidia, 287.
Mole and Mouse, J. R., 108.
Naturalist's Museums, a Juvenile Member, 287; W. F., 316; Walter Wallis, 317.
Potato Disease, the, R. R., 106; J. R., 107.
Poultry, J. D. S. W., 165.
Shooting Stars, what are they? a Country Rector, 22; F. A. A., 51.
Spiders, Arthur G. Harvie, 193.
Squirrel, Habits of the, Schoolmaster, 51.

MEETINGS OF LEARNED SOCIETIES.

Astronomical, 350.
Anthropological 350.
British Association, 275.
Bristol Naturalist's Society, 350.
Botanical Society of Edinburgh, 132, 160, 190, 220, 313.
Entomological, 188, 219, 351.
Ethnological, 132, 162, 187, 219, 351.
Geological 160, 188, 219, 350.
Geologists' Association, 350.
Linnean, 132, 160, 190.
Queckett Microscopical, 224, 254, 313, 351.
Royal Geographical, 131, 162, 188, 219, 354.
„ Horticultural, 132, 159, 188, 351.
„ Microscopical, 161, 189.
Zoological, 132, 162, 188, 218.

MISCELLANEOUS.

Amber, 16.
Aviaries, Orchard House, 345.
Cameo Shells, 28.
Dean in Difficulties, the, 289.
Egg, a wonderful, 289.
Good Old Times, the, 222.
Grass Sponge, 320.
Hard Winter, Signs of a, 308.
Infusoria and Mycelium, 121.
Instinct, 268.
Ivory, 2.
Luminosity of the Sea, the, 332.
Magnetic Attraction, 220.
Nature, Imitation in, 201.
„ Protection in, 272.
„ Mimicry in, 231.
„ How it preserved a record, 291.
Naturalist in India, the, 206.
„ in the China Seas, the, 115.
Naturalists' Field Clubs, 295.
Ocean Currents, the, 45.
Pearls, 177.
Rubies and other Precious Stones, How to make, 111.
Silk Mountain of North China, 15.
Sponge, a beautiful, 56.
„ (Fishery) the West India, 18.

NOTICES OF BOOKS.

AMERICAN.

American Naturalist, the, a Popular Illustrated Magazine of Natural History. No. I. 131.
Annual of Scientific Discovery; or, Year-book of Facts in Science and Art for 1866 and 1867. Edited by Samuel Kneeland, A.M., M.D. 217.
First Annual Report of the Geological Survey of Iowa. By C. A. White, M.D., State Geologist. 131.
First Annual Report of the Geology of Kansas. By B. F. Mudge, Professor of Geology, &c. 131.
Geological Survey of Illinois. Vol. I. Geology; Vol. II. Palæontology. A. H. Worthen, Director. 348.
Influence of Climate in North and South America. Compiled by J. Disturnell. 348.

Meteoric Astronomy: a Treatise on Shooting Stars, Fire Balls, and Aërolites. By Daniel Kirkwood. 312.

Mind in Nature; or, the Origin of Life, and the Mode of Development of Animals. By Henry James Clark, A.B., B.S. 217.

On the Rock Salt Deposit of Petit Anse, Louisiana Rock Salt Company. Report of the American Bureau of Mines. 131.

Ornithology and Oology of New England. By Ed. A. Samuels, Curator of Zoology in the Massachusetts State Cabinet. 252.

Seaside Studies in Natural History; Marine Animals of Massachusetts Bay—Radiates. By Elizabeth C. Agassiz and Alexander Agassiz. 253.

Sorghum and its Products. By F. Stewart. 252.

Preliminary Report of the Geological Survey of Kansas. By. G. C. Swallow, State Geologist. 13.

Report of the Progress of the Geological Survey of North Carolina, 1866. By Professor W. C. Kerr, State Geologist. 131.

ENGLISH.

Astronomy without Mathematics. By Edmund Beckett Denison, LL.D., Q.C., F.R.A.S. 157.

Australia as it is; or, Facts and Features, sketches and Incidents of Australia and Australian Life, with Notices of New Zealand. By a Clergyman. 105.

Bacon's Descriptive Handbook of America. By G. W. Bacon, F.R.G.S., and W. G. Larkins, B.A. Crown 8vo. With numerous Maps, Engravings, etc. 79.

The Birds of Norfolk, with Remarks on their Habits, Migrations, and Local Distribution. By Henry Stevenson, F.L.S., Member of the British Ornithologists' Union, vol I. 130.

British Butterflies and Moths; an Introduction to the Study of our Native Lepidoptera. By H. T. Stainton, F.R.S. 312.

British Grasses; an Introduction to the Study of the Gramineæ of Great Britain and Ireland. By Margaret Plues. 217.

Chemistry, Inorganic and Organic, with Experiments, and a Comparison of Equivalent and Molecular Formulæ. By Charles Loudon Bloxam. 158.

Contributions to the Flora of Montone. Parts I. and II. By J. Treherne Moggridge. 22.

Descriptive Astronomy. By George F. Chambers, F.R.A.S. 105.

Dogs of the British Islands, the, being a Series of Articles and Letters by various Contributors, Reprinted from the FIELD Newspaper. Edited by "Stonehenge." 252.

Edible Mollusks, the, of Great Britain and Ireland. By M. S. Lovell. 186.

Explanation of the Popular Prognostics of Scotland, an, on Scientific Principles. By the Rev. Charles Clouston. 252.

Fern Book for Everybody, a, containing all the British Ferns, with the Foreign Species suitable for a Fernery. By M. C. Cooke. 185.

The Fishes of Zanzibar. By Lieut. Col. R. L. Playfair and Dr. Albert C. Gunter. 130.

Geology for General Readers: a Series of Popular Sketches in Geology and Palæontology. By David Page. Second and Enlarged Edition. 48.

Handbook of Vine and Fruit Tree Cultivation under Glass, a. By Samuel Hereman. 348.

Handy Book, a, to the Collection and Preparation of Freshwater and Marine Algæ, Diatoms, Desonids, Fungi, Lichens, Mosses, and other of the lower Cryptogamia, with instructions for the formation of an Herbarium. By Johann Nave. Translated and edited by the Rev. W. W. Spier, M.A. 219.

Heavens, the, an Illustrated Handbook of Popular Astronomy. G. Amedée Guillemin. Edited by Norman Lockyer, F.R.A.S., &c. 49.

Hog-hunting in the East, and other Sports. By Captain J. T. Newall, Author of "The Eastern Hunters," "John Neville," &c. 274.

Home in the Wilderness, at. By John Keast Lord, F.Z.S., late Naturalist to the British North American Boundary Commission. 158.

Journal of Anatomy and Physiology, the. No. 1. November, 1866. 49.

Journey to Ashango Land, a, and Further Penetration into Equatorial Africa. By Paul B. Du Chaillu. 77.

Lecture Notes for Chemical Students, embracing Mineral and Organic Chemistry. By Edward Frankland. 49.

Letters Home from Spain, Algeria, and Brazil. By the Rev. Hamlet Clark, M.A., F.L.S. 312.

Light; its Influence on Life and Health. By Forbes Winslow, M.D. 157.

Lima: Sketches of the Capital of Peru, Historical, Statistical, Administrative, Commercial, and Moral. By Manuel A. Fuentes, 79.

Loudon's, Mrs., Entertaining Naturalist; being Popular Descriptions, Tales, and Anecdotes of more than 500 Animals. A new Edition. By W. S. Dallas, F.L.S. 311.

Meteoric Theory of Saturn's Rings, The, considered with reference to the Solar Motion in Space. By S. M. D., R.A. 130.

Mushrooms and Toadstools. By W. G. Smith. Pp. x. and 64; with two large sheets containing figures of Edible and Poisonous Fungi. 274.

Nile Tributaries of Abyssinia, the, and the Sword Hunters of the Hamran Arabs. By Sir Samuel W. Baker, M.A. F.R.G.S. 346.

North West Peninsular of Iceland, the, being the Journal of a Tour in Iceland in the Spring and Summer of 1862. By C. W. Shepherd, M.A., F.Z.S. 104.

Open Polar Sea, the, a Narrative of a Voyage of Discovery towards the North Pole in the Schooner United States. By Dr. I. I. Hayes. 79.

Orchard and Fruit Garden, the. By Elizabeth Watts. 274.

Physical Geography. By Professor D. T. Ansted, F.R.S., F.R.G.S., F.G.S., Honorary Fellow of King's College, London, and late Fellow of Jesus College, Cambridge. 21.

Pigeons, their Structure, Habits, and Varieties. By W B. Tegetmeier, F.Z.S. 159.

Polynesian Reminiscences; or, Life in the South Pacific Islands. By W. T. Pritchard, F.R.G.S., F.A.S.L., formerly H.M. Consul at Samoa and Figi. Preface by Dr. Seeman. Illustrations. 21.

Poultry Book, the, comprising the Breeding, Management, and Characteristics of Profitable and Ornamental Poultry. By W. B. T. Tegetmeier. F.Z.S. 185.

Practical Poultry Keeper, the. By L. Wright. 252.
Principles of Geology, or the Modern Changes of the Earth and its Inhabitants. By Sir Charles Lyell, Bart., M.A., F.R.S. Tenth Edition. Vol 1. 20.
Reasoning Power in Animals. By the Rev. John Selby Watson, M.A., M.R.S.L. 79.
Routledge's Illustrated Natural History of Man in all Countries of the World. By the Rev. J. G. Wood, M.A., F.L.S., &c. With Illustrations by Wolfe, Zwecker, Keyl, Houghton, &c. 158.
Scientific Works published in England and America during the year 1866. 48.
Silkworm Book, the, or, Silkworms Ancient and Modern, their Food and Mode of Management. By W. B. Lord, R.A., 186.
Sunshine and Showers, their influence throughout Creation, a Compendium of Popular Meteorology. By Andrew Steinmetz, Esq. 105.
Twin Records of Creation, the; or, Geology and Genesis, their perfect harmony and wonderful concord. By George W. Victor Le Vaux. 105.
The Vegetable World. By Louis Figuier. Translated by W. S. O., 8vo, pp. 574, with numerous Illustrations. 21.
Wanderings of a Naturalist in India, the Western Himalayas, and Cashmere. By Andrew Leith Adams, M.D., Edinburgh. 216.
Wild Elephant, the, and the Method of Capturing and Taming it in Ceylon. By Sir J. Emerson Tennent, Bart. 78.
Wild Life among the Pacific Islanders. By E. H. Lamont, Esq. 129.
A Winter with the Swallows. By Matilda Betham Edwards. 21.

FRENCH.

Chaleur, La. Par Achille Cazin. Ouvrage Illustré de 92 vignettes, par A. Jahandier. 151.
Elements de Botanique, etc. Par P. Duchartre, de l'Institut. 2de partie. Paris and London. 131.
Essai sur l'unite des Phenomenes Naturels. 253.
Etudes et Lectures sur l'Astronomie. Flammarion. 253.
Grottes et Cavernes. Par Ad Badin. (Bibliotheque des Merveilles.) 159.
Insectes, Les. Par Louis Figuier, Ouvrage Illustre de 605 Figures, &c. 131.
L'Année Scientifique et Industrielle. Par L. Figuier. 11e Année. 159.
L'Eau. Par Gaston Tissandier, Bibliothèques des Merviles. 312.
L'Oiseau. Par J. Michelet. Hutième édition, illustrée de 210 vignettes sur bois, dessinée par H. Giacomelli. 159.
Monde de Papillons, Le. Texte et Dessins de Maurice Sand. Avec une Preface de G. Sand. Paris, Rothschild. 130.
Navigations Françaises, Les, et la Révolution Maritime du 14e au 16e Siècle, d'après les Documents inedits tirés de France, d'Angleterre, d'Espagne et d'Italie, par Pierre Margry. 349.
Rapport sur les Progrès de l'Anthropologie. Par A. de Quatrefages. 349.
Rapport sur les Progrès de l'Astronomie. Par M. Delaunay. 349.
Saisons, Les, Etudes de la Nature. Par L. Hoefer. Paris and London. 159.
Vie Souterraine, La, ou les Mines et les Mineurs. Par L. Simonin. Ouvrage Illustre de 160 Gravures sur bois, &c. 131.
Volcans et Tremblements de Terre. Par Zurcher et Margolle. Ouvrage Illustre de 62 Vignettes, par E. Riou. 131.

GERMAN.

Abhangikeit der Insecten, Die, von ihrer Umgebung. Von Dr. L. Möller. Leipzig. 253.
Allgemeine Missions-Atlas nach Originalquellen. Bearbeitet von Dr. R. Grundemann. 159.
Bibliographia Geographica Palestine, Zunächst kritische Uebersicht gedruckter und ungedruckter Beschreibungen der Reisen ins Heilige Land. Von Titus Tobler. 312.
Beiträge zur Ethnographie and Sprachenkunde Amerika's zumal Braziliens. Von Dr. C. P. F. von Martius. 2 Bde. 349.
Geschichte der Arier in der altenzeit, Die. Von Max Duncker. Leipzig: Duncker & Humblot. 253.
Reisen und Jagden in Nord-Ost-Afrika, 1864-1865. Von Carl Graf. Krockow von Wickerode. Th. I. 312.
Ueber die Polarländer. Von Dr. Oswald Heer. Zurich: Schulthess. 253.

REMARKS, QUERIES, &c.

American Society for the Advancement of Science. 355.
Atoms, 86.
Bark of Trees, 292.
Barn Owl, the, 260.
Bees, 114, 168.
Beetle, a curious, 323.
Birds and their young, 355.
   ,, Counterfeiting Lameness, 230.
   ,, near London, 112.
   ,, that Sing during January, 29.
Blood Stains, 142.
British Shrews, 199, 230.
Butterflies, 200, 228.
Chelifer, the, 355.
Colias Palæno, 57.
Common Mouse, the, 356.
Curious position of a Flycatcher's nest, 260.
Duck, the, 229.
Early Moorhen's nest, 114.
Egg Collecting, Aids to, 112, 140, 198.
Entomological Notes, 227.
   ,, ,, for June, 167, 200.
Esquimaux in Europe, 142.
Ferns, growth of, from Spores, 355.
Fleas in Dogs, 141, 200, 230.
Flora of Bucks, 323.
Flower Garden, 29.
Forest Trees, 292, 322.
Frogs and their Food, 324, 356.
Gold Fish, 141.
   ,, Diseases in, 199.
Golden Eagle, 57.
   ,, Oriole, 200.
Gooseberry, origin of the word, 86.
Granite in Devon and Cornwall, 142.
House Sparrow, the, 355.
Hydrophobia in Dogs, 292.
Insect Destroyer, an, 321.
Insects, Preservation of, 200.
Instinct in a Rook, 170.
Irish Elk, the Ancient, 324.
Jackdaw, 229.
Juvenile Museums, 260.
Kestrel, the, 169.
   ,, and Sparrowhawk, 355.
Kitchen Garden, 29.
Last Irish Wolf, the, 321.
Lawson's, Dr., New Microscope, 321.
Life at the bottom of the Atlantic, 27.
Little Bittern, the, 170.
Lizard, the common green English, 199
Lizards, 323.
Lepidopteræ, how to distinguish, 324.
Merlin, the, 57.

Mice as Cannibals, 323.
Milk, how to preserve, 292.
Minute Animals, 58.
Mouse, an audacious, 228.
Natural History of New Zealand, 356.
Nests, 323.
New Plant Club, 114.
Notes from Maidstone, 140.
Old birds fed by young, 230.
Ornithology of Berks and Bucks, 356.
Pied Wagtail, 113.
Pike, the, 57.
Plants, hardy bedding, 29.
Population of the Sea, 141.
Potatoe and its Parasites, the, 57.
    „   Disease, the, 86.

Rain water, 356.
Rare birds in Leadenhall Market, 85.
Rats on their rambles, 292.
Remarkable Fecundity in a Dove, 259.
Ring Doves, 259, 324.
Roses, some good, 29.
Skins, preservation of, 170.
Smoke from a lamp, 113.
Smoking Birds, 230.
Snake Story, a curious, 229, 259.
    „   and Toad, 259.
Sparrowhawk, the, 85.
Strawberries, good, 30.
Summer Migrants, 140, 169.
Swallow's nest, 57.
Tallow Tree, the, 57, 259.

Trout living in Salt Water, 169.
Turt e Dove, 57.
Vitality of Wasps, 142.
Waxwing, the Bohemian, 57.
White Swallow, a, 230.
Winter Aconite, 57, 86.
Woolhope Naturalists' Field Club, 259.
Wren, the, 114.
Wren's nest, 142.

WEATHER TABLES.

Pages 30, 58, 86, 114, 142, 170, 200, 230, 266, 292, 324, 356.

THE NATURALIST'S NOTE BOOK.

ADDRESS.

THE NATURALIST'S NOTE BOOK will be essentially what its title indicates—a Collection of Notes gathered from many sources on subjects of Natural History—not confined to one branch only, but extending to all, so that Astronomers, Botanists, Ethnologists, Geologists, Geographers, Meteorologists, Mineralogists, Zoologists, &c., will find matters of interest in its pages.

It is our intention to select facts interesting to every lover of Nature, not from periodicals only, but from all new works that appear during the month; and in gathering these *pearls* we shall candidly and fairly, in every instance, acknowledge their source. While thus much is due from us to those who supply us with information, it will at the same time enable those of our readers who may desire it to obtain further particulars upon any special subject in which they take an interest. Space will be reserved for original correspondence and remarks, and we shall, at all times, be glad to receive communications, interesting to the general body of our readers. It will be our endeavour also to answer to the best of our ability any inquiries under the head of *Queries*, which may be made to us.

The multiplicity of things in Nature worthy of our greatest admiration and constant study, unknown to the many, which are about us on every side, and the continued fresh revelations from day to day made known to us by science—Nature's handmaid—induce us to launch our little bark in the confident belief that our efforts to instruct and to amuse will be appreciated by the public. The aim of THE NATURALIST'S NOTE BOOK will be accomplished if it succeeds in advancing the growing desire for a further acquaintance with Nature's handiwork.

No. 1.—Vol. I.

HOW MOUNTAINS ARE MADE.

IN examining the outer crust of the earth, endeavouring to discover signs of movement, and the nature and causes of the movements which take place, suppose, that, after traversing the mountains and plains of Europe, you at length set off to look at the most extensive of all mountain ridges, which is that which extends almost from pole to pole along the western coasts of North and South America. You traverse the pampas, where the land is for the most part slightly undulated, so that in riding over it the horizon is constantly changing, and the eye is ever on the alert as objects appear or vanish in the distance. After passing San Luiz you traverse a series of undulations, which give to the country the appearance of a succession of huge ocean rollers pressing forward in parallel lines toward the mountains. You cannot fail to be struck with the peculiarity of the scene, They are a series of undulations upon a much greater undulation, for the land falls again before reaching the mountain. When yet two hundred miles east of that mountain-range you may catch sight of it, as its snow-covered peaks fling back the rays of the rising sun. You pass through the ruins of the city of Mendoza, which but five years ago was destroyed by a comparatively slight movement of the outer crust of the earth. At length you commence to mount the eastern slope of the huge mountain-ridge. You may glance eagerly from mountain to mountain—from valley to valley—districts of gravel, districts of sand, districts of earth, stratified masses, and unstratified masses. You may glance at all, vainly endeavouring by inductive steps to learn the process of their formation; all appears crude disorder and confusion. As the keen winds rush by perchance they laugh a derisive laugh, and the vast mountain-ranges—rugged, stern, and inhospitable—frown in silent majestic disdain. Here man is scorned. The rude mountains frown and the angry winds rage, as if threatening destruction to all who dare to venture here. But man shall triumph yet; for as you stand upon a narrow ridge which rises like a wall fourteen thousand feet above the sea, and on your right and left snow-covered peaks tower upwards nine or ten thousand feet higher, there stung by the failure of your efforts by the paths of induction, you boldly rush upon the dizzy-heights which are traversed by the dangerous paths of deduction. With a vigorous effort you fling imagination back through time, and let it place you in an age between which and the present countless ages have intervened. You then find that not only the mountains but the whole continent has fallen away from beneath you, and there now lies before you one vast expanse of water. The water is deep, but below there is a hard stratified ground, beneath which the interior of the earth is in a state of liquid heat, but gradually cooling, and as it cools the hardened surface is compelled to bend in graceful curves in order to suit the decreasing size of the globe. By this bending the water becomes of unequal depths, deepening in parts as it becomes shallow in other parts. At length immediately below you a ridge of dry land appears; this, then, is the birth of the South American Continent—it continues gradually to rise, throwing off the water to the east and west. There then lies the Pacific and there the Atlantic Ocean. The bending upwards and downwards in the same easy graceful curves continues as long as the surface remains sufficiently pliant; but at length becoming more hard and brittle as the strain still continues, it cracks with a tremendous crash, the rent extending north and south, almost from pole to pole. Up to this moment the surface has yielded gradually to the power of gravitation, offering great resistance. But once broken, this resistance is gone, and gravitation acting with unchecked power, crushes and grinds the broken edges together with a force scarcely conceivable by the mind of man. Enormous masses of what had once been horizontal strata are now perpendicular or even reversed. The smashing and grinding of the broken edges by the overwhelming lateral pressure caused by gravitation, leaves scarcely a trace of the former stratified order, but leaves mass piled on mass in vast confusion, forming this huge mountain range along the course of the crack. And more than this, the outer crust of the earth had hitherto been in a great measure self-supporting, its weight resting upon itself laterally in all parts, so that the interior parts of the earth were in the same measure relieved from the weight of its inward pressure. That is, inward pressure had been changed to lateral pressure in proportion as the hardening surface of the earth offered increased resistance to the power of gravitation. But when the hardening surface of the earth becoming more brittle had bent upwards as far it could without breaking, it at length breaks along the top of the ridge, and in proportion with the loss of lateral support thus caused, the weight of the adjacent parts of the surface press inwards, and the inner parts of the earth being in a state of liquid heat, the increased weight pressing upon the fluid part forces the fluid matter upwards through the fissures in the crack, and thus in some places mountain ranges of unstratified rock are formed as the fluid hardens on the surface; but here the accumulation of broken masses of stratified matter is so enormous that this part of the range seems to consist of nothing else. The stratified surface to the east of the crack has here overlapped that to the west. So that on the west the Pacific ocean rolls against the disjointed masses that have been piled up abreast of it, whereas on the east, the elevated strata slopes away gradually to the Atlantic Ocean. That slope is itself undulated by pressure, but those undulations are probably precedent to the occurrence of the crack which led to the piling up of the Andes, most, if not all, subsequent readjustments of the surface having been arranged by movements along the still uniformly placed edges of the crack. The sudden movements in this neighbourhood even now cause at times a shock or earthquake sufficient to overwhelm cities. In these movements also, either by direct pressure of the surface downwards, or oftener probably by water or other matter being suddenly brought into contact with intense heat, matter from below the stratified surface is, in a state of liquid heat, forced upwards through openings in the crack, thus forming, as the matter hardens on the surface, those high volcanic peaks which are here so numerous. Or in other places the same expansion, not having sufficient force to burst through the surface, simply raises it in the form of an evenly rounded hill.—*The Elements, by William Leighton Jordan*. Vol. I.—Longman.

IVORY.

THE elephant is a tolerably large animal, but he is of little use to mankind unless he deposits his tusks in some convenient place where an enterprising Yankee or a roving Englishman may find them. It is the tusks of this lively beast, who generally travels with a circus in this country, that supply the ivory in commerce. The hippopotamus, the walrus, the narwhal, and a few other animals, make annual contributions to the ivory market, but the quality of the article they furnish is inferior to that supplied by his royal highness the elephant. This is unfortunate for the elephant, for the superior quality of the ivory he carries in his mouth tempts greedy hunters to slay him, that they may thereby derive much profit. Consequently, where elephants do most abound, there dwells also the ivory-hunter. The western coast of Africa is well supplied with elephants, and their tusks yield the finest and best quality of ivory. Other portions of Africa abound in elephants, but their ivory is not so transparent as that found in the west coast elephants. The principal supply of ivory is derived from Bombay, the Cape of Good Hope, Calcutta, Singapore, and other East India ports.

The tusks vary in size, weighing from six ounces to one hundred and sixty pounds. A German writer mentions having seen them weighing one hundred and eighty-six pounds, and ten feet in length. The number of elephants annually killed for their ivory alone can scarcely be estimated, but some idea may be formed when it is known that the slaughter of 22,000 elephants a year is required to supply the cutlery establishments of Sheffield with handles for the knives and other cutlery made there. Dealers in ivory express considerable alarm lest the supply of elephants should run short in a few years, and so throw them out of business. African tusks are the most transparent and the freest from cracks. The straightest tusks are considered the best; they are covered with a thin rind, which has to be removed previous to being worked, and are usually hollow for a portion of their length, the cavity sometimes extending half way to their middle. The tusks are imported in their full proportions by the manufacturers or workers in ivory.

Ivory is susceptible of receiving a very high polish, and is easily worked with proper tools in the hands of skilful workmen. It is principally used in the manufacture of handles for cutlery, billiard balls, gambling checks, chessmen, napkin-rings, and ornaments for ladies' wear. Some sets of chessmen are most elegantly carved by Chinese workmen, who are famous for their skill and dexterity in producing fancy articles from this material. In this country the principal use found for ivory is in the making of billiard balls. The immense popularity of this game in America renders it almost impossible to keep up the supply of balls. Ivory is apt to shrink considerably, and it is necessary to cut out the balls in the rough and hang them up to season for a long time before they can be turned exactly round and true as required. When the ivory is properly seasoned, a section is put in an ordinary turning-lathe, when, with a proper tool, a skilful workman speedily turns it down to the required size. He commences in the centre of the ball, and passes his tool rapidly to the pole, throwing off a complete ring. This is repeated until the ball is perfectly accurate in all its proportions. Other articles are made, either in the turning-lathe or with tools similar to those used by carvers of wood. Designs of almost any kind can be carved in ivory, but there are but few workmen in this country capable of producing the finest work. Indeed, the Chinese may be said to monopolise the fine work in ivory carving, and specimens of their skill are often seen in the handles of ladies' fans. Labour being so cheap with them, the artists of this and other countries are unable to compete with them. The writer of this once "took a chance" in a raffle for a set of chessmen carved in China, each piece being of most exquisite workmanship. The set was valued at 500 dollars, but could not have been done in this country for five times that sum. Napkin-rings, next to billiard balls, are the most saleable articles manufactured from ivory. They are turned in an ordinary lathe, and some of them are subsequently ornamented with carved work done by hand. The process of colouring these and other articles is a secret of the trade which is carefully guarded. They are subjected to the action of chemical dyes until the desired colour is produced. A French gentleman in America has invented an ivory dye which is said to be the best and most lasting in use. He is very ready to tell how to use it, but does not mention the ingredients of which it is made. As he has the article for sale, he cannot be blamed for his reticence. There is a great demand for gamblers' checks, also. These are simply little round or octagonal bits of ivory, about the size of a silver dollar, of various colours with figures cut upon them. In a gambling saloon these represent dollars, and are issued by the "bank" on payment of greenbacks.

There is no waste of any account in the ivory manufactory. All the scraps and shavings are put to some use. Pianoforte keys, penknife handles, sleeve-buttons, and numerous other small articles are made from the scraps, and a very good article of jelly is made from the dust and shavings. From the unclean refuse an article known as ivory black is made, which enters into the composition of ink used by copper-plate printers. Ivory can be cut into exceedingly thin sheets, and is frequently used for veneering purposes. To do this a portion of a tusk is put into a lathe, and a thin, continuous sheet turned off with a very delicate tool. It is then placed in a chemical solution to destroy its earthy substance, after which it will retain the form in which it has been placed. At the London Exhibition of 1851, a piece of ivory veneering, one foot wide and forty feet long, was exhibited in the United States' Department.

Ivory is used to a considerable extent in the taking of portraits, and was formerly used to a great degree by painters and sculptors. Many mathematical and other instruments, and a great variety of toys and ornaments, are made from this material. For some articles—billiard balls, for instance—made from ivory, no substitute has been found. A large dealer in billiard stock has offered a reward of several hundred dollars to any person who will produce a substance from which billiard balls can be made as durable and cheaper than ivory ones. As yet no one has responded.—*Building News*, Dec. 14.

THE BIRDS OF POLYNESIA.

THE most rare and, when in full plumage, one of the most graceful of Samoan birds is the Dodo-like Manumea (*Didunculus Strigirastis*). Its plumage is a brilliant dark blue, with just a tinge of brown on the edge of a feather here and there; its size about that of a common house pigeon, its legs pink, its bill dark, with a tinge of pink. Its habits are nocturnal, and with its diminutive wings it travels by long hops or jumps. When at rest it perches on the low branches of the bushes, to which circumstance the natives attribute its extinction, as it is so easily caught by the wild cats and monster rats which infest the wood.

The Punæ (or springer-up) is another remarkable bird, which is now also nearly extinct from the same cause. The natives state that it burrows in the ground, feeds on grubs, worms, and insects, runs very fast, and, when first starting from its burrow, makes a long spring upwards from the ground, but having very small wings it cannot fly.

The Manu-ma (or bashful bird, *Ptilonopus Mariæ*) is a very beautiful and resplendent dove, closely allied to the Manu-tagi (tangi) or crying bird (*Ptilonopus fasciatus*). The first has the crown of the head a bright purple; back, wings, and tail, a pale green; breast, white, purple, and yellow, intermingled; and the under part of the body a very pale grey or stone colour; under the tail is a little tuft of yellow feathers fading into the pale green of the tail. The second has the head a very pale crimson; back, wings, and tail a light green; breast and lower part of the body a pale yellow intermixed with pale green. Both feed on berries, and are very shy in the bush, but soon become quite domesticated when caught, and, like the pigeon, eat freely from the hand. They are also trained to fly round the Maloe, with a long string, like the pigeon, and, at the call, to return and perch on the finger. Another beautiful dove is the Manu-lua, or double bird, not unlike the Manu-tagi in plumage, and similar in habits. The Tu, or Tu-aimeo, are very pretty little birds of the dove family, with plumage of a dark chocolate brown, which varies in its tinges according to the light thrown upon it, and a yellow bill; they hop and fly about very actively on the lower branches of the small trees, and run on the ground very swiftly. The Lulu is a species of owl (*Strix delicatula*), is very common, and preying as it does on the chickens, even at the house door, it is destroyed whenever the opportunity offers.

The Manu-ao, or morning bird, is perhaps the best songster the Samoans have; it possesses a very melodious voice, ranging from the lively to the plaintive in one breath, and is always heard in the early dawn. Its plumage is something between a black and a brown, with a tinge of blue, and is about the size of our nightingale. The Fuia reminds us of our blackbird in colour and size, but its song is inferior, though I think it ranks next to the Manu-ao among the few song-birds of the Samoa. The Tutu-malili is also like our blackbird, but without its song. The Tiotali (*Dacelo albifrous*) very much resembles our kingfisher in appearance, and feeds on grubs and worms, and has no song. The Sega is a beautiful little parroquet, with a deep green plumage and red breast. It sucks the honey found in the blossoms of the cocoa nut and the gatae (ngatea). The little boys climb the cocoa-nut trees, and, as it feeds, slips a noose made of the fibre of the cocoa-nut husk, over its head; but, unlike the parroquet of Fiji, it does not live many weeks when caught. The Iao, another honey eater, with a light brown plumage, is an active, saucy little bird, whose chief delight is to join with its mates to tease and worry the Oleoa, a timid, stupid bird, very much like our cuckoo. The Tolai or Tolai-ula is a delicate little bird, with a bright black plumage, a brilliant scarlet breast, and long black bill and legs. The Pea-pea is a bold little swallow, always playing about one's head in the evenings, feeding on gnats and other insects. The Sega-mauu is a handsome bird, with a plumage of bright green, feeds on seeds, and has no song.

The Tuli is a species of plover, found at low tide seeking its food along the sandy beaches, and is very good eating. Another seashore bird is the Matuu, or crane, of which there are three varieties, distinguished as they stalk about the sandy beaches, or over the mud flats, by their plumage—lead-colour, pure white, and speckled—the first is the most common. The Manu-lii is a very handsome bird, with a brilliant blue plumage, a bright red cap on the head, red bill, and long red legs, and makes a very hideous screeching noise. It lives and feeds in the marshes and swamps, where the natives plant the water-taro, which it destroys by scraping up the young roots. It is readily domesticated, and learns to follow its master like a dog. The Soloa is a species of teal, is found in goodly numbers about the taro swamps just outside the villages as well as up the valleys, and about the banks of the rivers.—*Polynesian Reminiscences*, by *W. T. Pritchard.* Chapman and Hall.

THE NOVEMBER METEORIC SHOWER.

THE fiery shower foretold by the science of America and Europe for the night of the 13th-14th November, 1866, was seen in full splendour. From about eleven o'clock occasional meteors might be seen gliding along the sky, from east to west, but these were only the *avant-couriers* of the great legion that followed at a later hour.

The numbers increased after twelve o'clock with great rapidity. From Paddington Green, a fairly open position, 207 meteors were counted between 12 and 12.30, and of these the greater number fell after 12.20. The next hundred was counted during the six minutes that succeeded the half-hour. Soon after this it became impossible for two people to count the whole that were visible from this station; and doubtless from positions with a purer atmosphere, and a wider horizon, the spectacle must have been one of surpassing splendour. Indeed, from a window at Highgate, looking N.N.E., but with a circumscribed view, an observer counted 100 meteors in the four minutes between 12.32 and 12.36, and no less than 200 in the two minutes between 12.57 and 12.59.

As the constellation Leo rose over the houses north of Paddington Green and cleared itself of haze, the divergence of the meteor-paths from a point within it became obvious, not merely in the directions of the streams that shot from or through the zenith, but in those that left their phosphorescent-seeming trails in the sky towards every point of the compass.

Sometimes these rocket-like lines of light would glide out like sparks flying from an incandescent mass of iron under the blows of a Titanic hammer, but with the distinctive features, first, of those lingering lines of illuminated haze in their track, and secondly of their rarely appearing as if they originated in the region of the sky from which their courses evidently diverged.

Sometimes the meteor was orange and almost red in its colour, whereas the luminous trail seemed almost always, probably by contrast with the surrounding light, of a bluish hue. In one splendid instance the trail, after having nearly disappeared, together with the rocket-head that had produced it, became again lit up and visible coincidently with a sort of resuscitation of brightness in the body of the meteor. Now and then a little illuminated puffball would appear in the middle of the constellation Leo, generally more or less elongated or elliptic in form, as it seemed to be more or less distant, and at the same time convergent from an imaginary point that seemed about thirty degrees S. by E. of the star γ Leonis; and one as near as could be estimated to such a point, was simply a star that waxed, and waned, and disappeared as one looked at it.

Sometimes a minute point of light, like a firefly, would dart with an angular jerking motion and zigzag course hither and thither, but still as if away from Leo.

Only about three meteors were seen during an hour and a half to take a direction manifestly opposed to that of these diverging multitudes. The meteors which shot towards the western horizon seemed more brilliant and larger in their courses than those which dropped into the eastern; indeed, very few seemed even to reach the roofs of the houses from behind which Leo had arisen. This was possibly only an effect of perspective, or it may have arisen from the curtailment of the view. As regards the long lines of light that lingered in the paths of the meteors it seemed that generally they were more dense and brightest towards the middle of the visible path of the meteor, while the meteor itself seemed brightest just before its extinction, an effect possibly due to an obscuration in the middle of its course by matter thrown off from it. The meteors seemed also to lose velocity as they went, but this might have been the result of perspective in those passing through the zenith.

One singular feature in these celestial fireworks was the rapidity with which the *maximum* of frequency came on and went off again. About two o'clock the meteors seemed to have become as scarce as they were at twelve, though they continued in smaller numbers till the verge of daybreak.

From half-past twelve or a quarter to one, until about a quarter-past or half-past one the heavens seemed veritably alive with stars rushing in many parts of the sky, in groups of two or three together, or in immediate succession on each other, seeming as though racing over the blue vault, except that their courses so rapidly diverged.

The cloudless beauty of the night near London was a happy circumstance, on which we may congratulate every "watcher of the skies," not only as allowing the forecasts of the astronomers to be thus signally and splendidly verified, but still more as having, we trust, enabled them to take such a store of facts regarding the nature of the light, and of the motion of meteors, and so many simultaneous observations of them in different parts of our islands, as may lead to some accurate knowledge of their laws and their nature, and add one more chapter to the sublime volume of astronomical physics.—*Times, Nov. 15th,* 1866.

TO THE EDITOR OF THE TIMES.

SIR,—The predicted shower of meteors has been witnessed here during the past night under very favourable atmospheric circumstances. In addition to Mr. Wiss and myself, our observing force included M. du Chaillu (who kindly volunteered his assistance on this occasion) and Dr. Hampshire. From midnight to one o'clock a.m., Greenwich time, 1,120 meteors were noted, the number gradually increasing. From 1 a.m. to

1h. 7m. 5s. no less than 514 were counted, and we were conscious of having missed very many, owing to the rapidity of their succession. At the latter moment there was a rather sudden increase to an extent which rendered it impossible to count the number, but after 1.20 a decline became perceptible. The *maximum* was judged to have taken place about 1.10, and at this time the appearance of the whole heavens was very beautiful, not to say magnificent. Beyond their immense number, however, the meteors were not particularly remarkable, either as regard brilliancy or the persistence of the trains, few of which were visible more than three seconds; indeed, M. du Chaillu observed that in these respects the meteors fell far short of those of the April period, which he had witnessed under a fine sky in equatorial Africa. From 1.52 to 2.9 300 were registered; from 3.9 to 3.24, 100; from 4.42 to 5 the number seen was 12, and these mostly faint; and from 5.45 to 6 only five were counted.

No person acquainted with the constellations, who carefully watched the display of last night, could have any doubt as to the accuracy of the astronomical theory relative to these bodies. The radiant in Leo was most strikingly manifested; while the meteors in the opposite quarter of the sky traversed arcs of many degrees; in the vicinity of the diverging point they shone out for a few seconds without appreciable motion, and might have been momentarily mistaken for stars by any one to whom the configuration of the heavens in that direction was not familiar.

Several very vivid flashes of lightning were remarked during the night. The last, at 3.54, was particularly brilliant, of a deep orange colour, and apparently emanated below the radiant in Leo. The horizon in that quarter was occupied by a pale glow, resembling what has often been remarked during exhibitions of the aurora borealis.

A telegram from Mr. Bishop, who watched the phenomenon during the night at Weymouth, mentions one a.m. as the time of *maximum*, which is in accordance with the determination made here.

I am, Sir, your obedient servant,
J. R. HIND.

Mr. Bishop's Observatory, Twickenham,
November 14th.

THE BAOBAB TREE.

THE Baobab (*Adansonia digitata*) is a tree of tropical Africa, which has been transplanted by man into Asia and America. It may be ranged among the marvels of nature. Its trunk does not exceed fifteen or eighteen feet in height, but its girth is enormous, attaining, as it sometimes does, the circumference of thirty to forty feet. This trunk separates at the summit into branches fifty to sixty feet long, which bend towards the earth at their extremities. The trunk being short, and the branches thus curving towards the earth, it follows that the baobab presents at a distance the appearance of a dome, or rather a ball of verdure over a circuit of a hundred and sixty feet. Adanson concluded, from the observations he made, and from his calculations upon their growth, that some of the specimens which he studied could not have been less than 6,000 years old; but it is the general opinion of botanists that this estimate was enormously overrated. This colossal vegetable was first observed by Adanson on the Senegal, and after him the genus was named Adansonia. The baobabs have since been discovered in the Soudan and Darfour, and in Abyssinia.

The bark and leaves of the tree possess considerable emollient properties, of which the natives of Senegal take advantage. Its flowers are proportionate to its gigantic trunk; they reach the length of four and a half and five inches, their breadth being from seven to eight. The fruit, called by the French settlers in the Senegal *monkey's bread*, is an ovoid capsule pointed at one of its extremities, and from twelve to twenty inches long, by six to seven broad; that is, the fruit is about the size of a man's head. It encloses in its interior from ten to forty cells, containing several kidney-shape seeds, surrounded by mucilaginous pulp. The natives make daily use of the dried leaves of the baobab. They mix them with their food for the purpose of reducing excess of perspiration, and modifying the ardour of their fiery climate. The fruit is eatable, its flesh is sweet, and of an agreeable flavour; the juice, when extracted and mixed with sugar, forms a beverage very useful in the putrid and pestilential fevers of the country. The fruit is transported into the eastern and southern parts of Africa, and the Arabs pass it on into the countries round Morocco, whence it finds its way into Egypt. The negroes take part of the damaged fruit and the ligneous bark, burn them for the sake of the ashes, from which they manufacture soap by means of palm oil. They make a still more singular use of the trunk of the baobab. They expose upon it the bodies of those they consider unworthy of the honour of sepulture. They select the trunk of some baobab already attacked and hollowed out by insects or fungi; they increase the cavity, and make in the trunk a kind of chamber, in which they suspend the body. This done, they close up the entrance of this natural tomb with a plank. The body becomes perfectly dry in the interior of this cavity, and becomes a perfect mummy without further preparation. This kind of sepulture is especially reserved for the *Guerrots*. The Guerrots are the musicians and poets who in the tombs of negro kings preside at all fetes and dances. During their life this kind of talent gives them influence and makes them respected by other negroes, who look upon them as sorcerers, and honour them under the title; but after death this respect is succeeded by a kind of honour. These superstitious and infantile people imagine that if they consigned the body of one of these sorcerers to the earth, as they would the bodies of other men, that they would draw upon themselves the celestial malediction. Hence the monstrous baobab serves as the resting place of the Guerrot. There is a strange poetry in this custom of a barbarous people, which leads them to bury their poets between heaven and earth in the side of the vegetable king.—*The Vegetable World, by Louis Figuier.* Chapman and Hall.

GEOMETRICAL FORMS IN ANIMAL LIFE.

WE may observe that while certain plants and flowers suggest by their form of construction various crystalline forms, certain animals (insects especially) work in similar conformity with geometrical principles. The cells of bees, for instance, are a notable exercise in this way; they are so built as to present a double front, although not set precisely end to end, their bases consisting of three sides, and the upper side of one base coinciding with the lower division of its opposite base. The other two of each reciprocally corresponding, now with a view to the least possible expenditure of wax, it is required that those six sides should be inclined at angles which were determined by a celebrated mathematician to be almost inappreciably less than the bees had made them. On further investigation, however, it appeared that several small quantities had been neglected in the analysis, which, on being taken into account, proved the architecture of those accomplished insects to be unimpeachable.

The web of the spider may be regarded as another example of that geometrical government which is of such extensive operation throughout the universe. The artist begins his work like a skilful engineer, fixing the threads which form the basis of his operations with the utmost mechanical skill; and what deserves notice is that all such arrangements necessarily depend upon the form and conditions of the locality he selects. There is always a logical reason to be rendered for the attachment of this line and of that. The state of his premises require a considerable length in a third line, and as he is aware (or seems to be so) that the curve named the catenary might be incidental to it, he secures its due tension by joining to it a fourth line midway between its extremities, which he fixes to its right support in a manner that is truly knowing. In the structure of the web he lays his threads parallel to one another, and carries them round the circle, fastening them as he goes without deflecting from his ideal a hair's breadth. He must know, one would think, that what he has been so ingeniously contriving is neither more nor less than a snare to catch flies, though he might possibly not go to the length of reflecting that of all the artifices that could be ordained for such a purpose there never was anything under the wide heaven equal to it.

The star fish, which belongs to the highest class of Radiata, is extended into five triangular rays, disposed with mathematical accuracy, the base of each triangle being opposite to the angle formed by two others. In the pentagon of the centre, moreover, a circle is inscribed, from which five bundles of fibres are given off, one to each ray. This is the star fish's nervous system, and the manner in which those nerves originate cannot fail to remind you of the setting of stamens in a flower. But there is a display of higher geometry still in very humble life—in that, namely, of the shell tribes, many of which are developed into whorls and spirals which might try the skill of an analyst to investigate.

It is very singular that the surfaces which are presented by the eye of the bee are all hexagonal, like its cell. This construction, however, is not confined to the eyes of bees, but is found in very many other of the articulates. In the Mordella beetle 25,000 have been counted, in a butterfly 17,000, and in a dragon fly 12,500.—*The Key to the Universe.* Chapman and Hall.

LEOPARDS.

IN common with other spotted cats, the leopard is an animal which varies a good deal in its markings, and also in depth of hue. Much diversity is observed in examples from the same neighbourhood. In general, those from temperate and cold countries run very pale, and have longer fur. Such are the leopards from Persia and Afghanistan, and from the higher Himalaya. We never see black or blackish (melanous or melanoid) individuals from those countries. In Southern India and Burmah, and over the Malayan region generally, wherever this animal extends its range, it is commonly of a deep ground colour, and in Bengal and Central India, both pale and deeply coloured individuals are common, as also generally over Africa. There is no constant difference whatever between Asiatic and African leopards, however individuals may vary, although a distinction between the so-called panther and the leopard has often been sought to be made out; but this animal attains an unusual size in Barbary, or at least in Morocco, and becomes formidable in proportion to its magnitude. A huge Morocco leopard may now be seen in the Zoological Gardens.

We do not remember seeing a black leopard from any part of Africa, but have seen many black or blackish individuals from Central India, Malabar, Assam, the Tennasserim provinces, Malacca, and Java; and we once saw a litter of four cubs, three of which were of the usual colouring, and the fourth deep black. Intensely black individuals sometimes occur, in which the usual black spots can only be seen at particular angles of reflection; but more commonly the ground hue is more or less brownish, and the spots are tolerably conspicuous.

Such animals are commonly designated as black tigers, but a genuine black tiger we never saw, nor the skin of one. In M. d'Almeida's "Life in Java," however, we find a notice which should apply to a real black tiger. This author remarks, "We stopped to see a couple of fine tigers in two separate cages, or inclosures made of palisades fixed close together. One of these formidable animals was what they call the *macham itam*, or black tiger, which has a very dark, silky coat, the black streaks of which are less distinct than those of the common kind. Both of these wild beasts had been entrapped in one of the neighbouring forests, and, with the wild buffalo, were to form the chief amusement at the coming election of his excellency the young regent, to whom we had been introduced. The natives are very fond of the sports in which these dangerous animals are introduced; and it is the custom of the chiefs to preserve tigers, &c., for occasions of rejoicing."

In this notice the *stripes* of the skin are distinctly mentioned; but we have often been disappointed upon inspection of animals which had been as positively denominated black tigers and not leopards; though, of course, there is no reason why a black tiger should not also sometimes occur. The Javanese tiger is less brightly coloured than that of Continental Asia, and the fluvous colour suffuses the white of its underparts, which therefore do not contrast so brightly as in tigers from the mainland.—*Land and Water*, Dec. 1.

THE HOT SALT SPRINGS OF TIBERIAS.

These springs, which have been noticed from a very early period, are about a mile from the city. Josephus often mentions them under the names of Emmaus and Ammaus, probably a Greek form of the Hebrew *Hammath*; *i.e.* warm baths. The Arabic word Hammam, by which they are now generally known, is a corruption of the Hebrew. Seetzen thinks that if these springs were in Europe, they would form one of the most attractive bathing places of the world. Burckhardt found a bathing-house erected over the one nearest to the city, and furnished with two apartments. The spring which is used is the largest of the four hot ones, and the supply of water is great enough to turn the wheels of mills! The three other hot springs, or really four, if one counts two smaller ones lying side by side, are two hundred steps farther south, and the most southern one, which is so shallow that the hand can scarcely be dipped into it, is the hottest of all. These baths are much resorted to by persons afflicted with rheumatism, scurvy, and leprosy, from many parts of Palestine and Syria.

Von Schubert found the hot springs to have a temperature of 48 deg. Reaum., and to contain salt and a solution of iron. He compares the waters with those of Carlsbad: at the bottom he observed sulphur and lime globules, coloured red with the oxide of iron. Not merely the warmth of the springs themselves seemed to be favourable to the persons afflicted with palsy, who use their waters, but the warmth of the nights there also seems beneficial. There prevails around Tiberias a true hothouse climate, and the palm flourishes there as well as in Akaba and Alexandria. On the north side of the city of Tiberias also, at Szermadin, there is a warm brook of about 20 deg. Reaum., which rushes forth from a cavernous outlet in the rock, and whose waters taste of salt and iron. Its banks are abundantly overshadowed with the beautiful evergreen oleander, with its rose-like blossoms, a true delight to the eyes. Still further to the north are found copious warm springs issuing from the basalt rocks, and forming brooks of considerable size, that dash down the steep declivity leading to the sea. The great number of these springs, and the abundant supplies of water which issues from them in a region very scantily supplied with springs of fresh water, hint very strongly at volcanic activities once at work there, to which probably they owe their existence.—*Comparative Geography of Palestine*, by C. Ritter. T. & T. Clark.

THE SAND-MARTIN AS AN ENGINEER.

The *Quarterly Review*, in an interesting article on the building powers of birds and insects, says—"Among birds the little sand-martin, with its slender feet and minute bill, seems at first sight but ill fitted for engineering operations. "Few would suppose," as Mr. Wood remarks, "after contemplating its tiny bill that it was capable of boring tunnels into tolerably hard sandstone.

Such, however, is the case, for the sand-martin is familiarly known to drive its tunnels into sandstone that is hard enough to destroy all the edge of a knife." The mode in which this little miner excavates its gallery, at the end of which it places his nest, has been carefully observed and well described by Mr. Rennie, in his "Insect Architecture," whose name is well known to every naturalist as an admirable observer of the habits of animals. "The bird works with its bill shut. This fact our readers may verify by observing their operations early in the morning through an opera-glass, when they begin in the spring to form their excavations. In this way we have seen one of these birds cling with its sharp claws to the face of a sandbank, and peg in its bill as a miner would do its pickaxe, till it had loosened a considerable portion of the hard sand, and tumbled it down amongst the rubbish below. In this preliminary operation it never makes use of its claws for digging; indeed, it is impossible it could, for they are indispensable in maintaining its position, at least when it is beginning its hole. We have further remarked that some of these martin's holes are nearly as circular as if they had been planned out with a pair of compasses, while others are more irregular in form; but this seems to depend more on the sand crumbling away than upon any deficiency in the original workmanship. The bird, in fact, always uses its own body to determine the proportions of the gallery, the part from the thigh to the head forming the radius of the circle. It does not trace this out as we should do by fixing a point for the centre around which to draw the circumference; on the contrary, it perches on the circumference with its claws, and works with its bill from the centre outwards; and hence it is that in the numerous excavations recently commenced which we have examined we have uniformly found the termination funnel-shaped, the centre being always more scooped out than the circumference. The bird consequently assumes all positions while at work in the interior, hanging from the roof of the gallery with its back downwards as often as standing on the floor. We have more than once, indeed, seen a bank-martin wheeling slowly round in this manner on the face of a sandbank, when it was just breaking ground to begin its gallery. All the galleries are found to be more or less tortuous to their termination, which is at the depth of from two to three feet, where a bed of loose hay and a few of the smallest breast feathers of geese, ducks, or fowls is spread with little art for the reception of the eggs. It may not be unimportant to remark also that it always scrapes out with its feet the sand detached by the bill; but so carefully is this performed that it never scratches up the unmined sand, or disturbs the plane of the floor, which rather slopes upwards, and of course the lodgment of rain is thereby prevented.

HOW TO MAKE RUBIES AND OTHER PRECIOUS STONES.

IN 1814, Davy first showed the elementary nature of the diamond by burning it in oxygen, and subsequent analyses have made known the very ordinary materials which compose most other precious stones. Thus rubies and sapphires are nearly pure alumina, with a little oxide of chromium, to which they owe their colour; garnet consists of silica, oxide of iron, and alumina; emeralds of silica, alumina, and glucina, *et cetera;* and similar ordinary constituents form most gems.

But, unfortunately, the mere knowledge of the composition of these gems is only a small step towards their production. The real difficulty is to cause their elements to unite and assume the crystalline form and properties to which they owe their beauty and reputation, and to effect this with substances that do not admit of the application of the usual means of producing crystallisation, appears at first sight an impossibility, since neither the gems nor the materials of which they are composed are soluble in any liquid, or are capable of being volatilised. But the circumstance of their being found native shows the possibility of forming them by natural means, for, to quote Leibnitz while advocating this very subject, "Nature is only art on a grand scale." In the laboratory of the earth long continued high temperature with steam and other vapours at enormous pressure are probably very frequent conditions; and, indeed, these internal phenomena make themselves apparent to us at the surface by volcanic eruptions, boiling springs, &c., facts whose frequent occurrence we are somewhat apt to disregard. But while these internal conditions doubtless occur on the grandest scale, there is no reason for supposing their essential effects cannot be imitated by means at our command. The success already achieved in the attempt to obtain natural productions by artificial means not only possesses an intrinsic reward, but has also thrown much light on the operations of Nature herself.

Seventeen years ago Ebelman perceived that the high and long-continued heat of the porcelain kilns of Sèvres offered probably the necessary conditions for the production of some natural minerals, and proceeded to make a series of most ingenious and successful experiments with this view. He put together certain portions of alumina, magnesia, and a little colouring oxide, with a considerable amount of boracic acid, and exposed the whole mixture to the long-continued heat of the furnace. The acid melted and dissolved materials, and at length in part evaporated. When the mixture was finally examined, Ebelman found in place of the original substances—perfect crystals of spinelle ruby.

By proceeding on this principle, and varying the materials and solvent, he succeeded in producing true rubies and emeralds of perfect form, which it was impossible to distinguish from the natural ones. Size was the only advantage which the workmanship of nature had over that of art; some of Ebelman's stones, however, had crystalline facets of an eighth of an inch across.

These were the first successes in the artificial production of minerals, but more lately many other methods have been discovered, which are of wider and more ready application. These processes are of the highest interest to the geologist, since they serve to explain the natural formation and occurrence of many minerals. But we will continue our original alchemical view of the subject, and disregarding the methods by which the meaner minerals have been formed, consider only the case of the precious stones. Malachite was formed by Senarmont by acting upon chalk with a solution of chloride of copper at a high temperature and pressure. Perfect topazes have been made by passing the gaseous fluoride of silicon over red-hot alumina. But perhaps the most prolific method yet discovered is that which we owe to the labours of M. Deville; it consists in making the vapours of metallic fluorides act on oxides at a very high temperature. By this means rubies of great beauty were obtained of exactly the same colour and properties as the natural ones, and of a size moreover that entitled them to be really called jewels. In the same manner sapphires were prepared of the true oriental tint, and chrysoberyls precisely resembling those from America, having the same peculiar convergent striæ which are characteristic of that gem.

It was not a little remarkable that the same process occasionally produced rubies and sapphires side by side, the two gems appearing to differ only in the condition in which the colouring oxide existed, the same substances apparently producing a blue or a ruby-red according to its state of oxidation.—*Once a Week*, Nov. 3rd.

FEELING OF BEAUTY AMONG ANIMALS.

Tynron, Dumfrieshire, Nov. 19, 1866.

FROM the ancient references in Eastern literature to the serpent charmers down to modern times, the facts showing that certain animals are gratified by music have been accumulating. He would be a bold man who should say that birds have no delight in their own songs. I have been led to conclude from experiments which I have made, and from other observations, that certain animals, especially birds, have not only an ear for fine sounds, but also a preference for the things they see out of respect to fine colours or other pleasing external features. To begin with ourselves, the pleasure which we derive from a certain class of objects is universal and well marked; even when man becomes animalized this instinct is never lost, but only undergoes modification. Christian babes and cannibals are equally vain of fine clothes, and have a similar passion for beads and glittering toys. Carlyle suggests that the love of ornament rather than the desire of comfort was at the origin of clothes. It is chiefly among birds, when we consider the case of animals, that a taste for ornament and for glittering objects, often very startling and human-like, is to be found. The habits of the pheasant, peacock, turkey, bird of paradise, several birds of the pigeon and crow kind, and certain singing birds, are evidence. The Australian satin bower-bird is the most remarkable of that class which exhibit taste for beauty or for glittering objects out of themselves, that is, beauty not directly personal; collecting, in fact, little museums of shells, gaudy feathers, shining glass, or bits of coloured cloth or pottery. It will be found with many birds that fine plumes, a mirror, and an admirer, are not altogether objects devoid of interest.

Another consideration leading me to the same conclusion, is the fact that beauty in animals is placed on prominent parts, or on parts which by erection or expansion are easily, and at the pairing season, frequently rendered prominent, such as a crest or tail. A spangle of ruby or emerald does not exist, for instance, on the side under the wing, which is seldom raised, of our domestic poultry. Such jewels are hung where man himself wears his, on the face and forehead, or court attention, like our own crowns, trains, shoulder-knots, breast-knots, painted cheeks, or jewelled ears. I cannot account for the existence of these gaudy ornaments to please man, for nowhere are they more gorgeous than in birds which live in the depth of the tropical forest, where man is rarely a visitor; I cannot account for them on the principle that they do good to their possessors in the battle for life, because they rather render them conspicuous to their enemies or coveted by man. But when I consider that the beauty of these beings glows most brightly at the season of their love-making, and that most observers agree that the female is won partly by strength, partly by gesture, and partly by voice, and that the male, whose interest it is to be most attractive, is often in his wedding-suit, the most gaily decorated, it seems to me that beauty, through a wider range than has yet been generally acknowledged, is accessory to love.

Butterflies, it is true, have gay patterns on the under wing, but this rather strengthens than diminishes the force of my argument, for with them, in a state of rest, the wings are folded erect, whereas others of that class, as moths and hawk-moths, whose wings, when at rest, are either inclined, horizontal, or wrapped round the body, have only the upper side of the wings beautiful. It is to be noticed also that these creatures, out of the three states in which they exist, are only remarkable for beauty in that state which they seek their mates, and whoever compares many of their males (as that of the orange-tip) to the females will find that gaudy colouring also favours the former. These delicate and ephemeral creatures are often to be observed flying lazily, as if aware of their splendour, and as if giving time that it might be seen.

Among fishes it is amusing to watch the combats of male sticklebacks for the females, which can be witnessed in an aquarium, and to note how the victor waxes brilliant in hue, and the vanquished, if he survive, wanes greatly in splendour. Fishes, and more especially insects, are often destroyed through the strange attraction which light has for them.

Birds are sometimes caught, especially larks in France, through the same allurement; and those very fire-flies, whose luminosity is so pretty to us, I have no doubt find it attractive to themselves. They are caught by means of their eagerness for light by those West Indian ladies who use them as jewels for their head-dress at a dance.

I am much strengthened in the conclusions at which I have arrived on this subject by the reference made to it by Mr. Darwin in the fourth edition of his work on Species, a copy of which has just now reached me. The selection of beauty in their mates by some animals is there made to follow from their appreciation of it, so that effect and cause mutually throw light on each other. Some profound and interesting remarks are further added by the author, explanatory, on scientific grounds, of the origin of flowers, which strike me, although the remarks are very brief, as being the first likely solution of what has been for ages an inscrutable problem. J. Shaw.—*Athenæum*, Nov. 24th.

ESQUIMAUX IN EUROPE.

WHILE the archæologists were working backwards in time, through the antecedent civilizations of Europe, the geologists, in tracing life from its first appearance on the earth and unfolding its progress, suddenly lighted upon the evidence of man's co-existence with many of the extinct animals in the latest deposits of which they took cognizance—in the river-gravels of Gaul and England, and in the bone caves of England and Belgium. He is proved by his implements and weapons to have been a savage of the lowest grade, unacquainted with the use of pottery, and even ignorant of the art of polishing or ornamenting the splinters of bone or the rough flint that he used. So far from having discovered the metals, he had not even found out that other stones, of different hardness, toughness, and elasticity, were better fitted for some of his purposes than the untractable flint or chert. He had, however, mastered the use of fire; and armed with the bow, the spear, and the sling, made good his foothold in a fauna which comprised the cave-lion, bear, and hyæna. The climate also under which he lived was so much more severe than those now found in the same latitudes, that against its effects the rhinoceros and mammoth, then living in Northern Europe and Asia, were clad in long hair and fur; while the musk-sheep and the reindeer, now confined to the extreme north, were able to range as far south as the Alps and Pyrennees. Glaciers descended from the mountains of Wales, Cumbria, and Scotland, and the winter cold was sufficiently intense to form ice in the rivers thick and strong enough to transport great stones, which are frequently found among the finer gravels in their ancient beds. Geographically, also, Europe was altogether different from what it is now. The Rhine, the Elbe, and the Thames, instead of discharging their waters along the present coast-line, joined to form one great estuary which, after flowing through a plain, entered the North Sea near the latitude of Berwick. The British Channel had no existence, and Britain formed part of the mainland extending far into the Atlantic.

. . . .

The sum of the evidence proves that man, in a hunter state, lived in the south of Gaul, on reindeer, musk-sheep, horses, oxen, and the like, at a time when the climate was similar to that which those animals now inhabit. To what race did he belong? In solving this, the zoological evidence is of great importance. The reindeer and musk-sheep now inhabit the northern part of the American continent, and are the principal land animals that supply the Esquimaux with food. The latter of these has departed from the Asiatic continent, leaving remains behind to prove that it shared the higher northern latitudes of Asia with the reindeer, and this latter has retreated further and further north during the historical period. May not the race that lived on these two animals in Southern Gaul have shared also in their northern retreat, and may it not be living in company with them still? The truth of such an hypothesis as this is found by an appeal to the weapons, implements, and habits of life of the Esquimaux. The fowling-spear, the harpoon, the scrapers, the marrow-spoons, are the same in the ice huts of Melville Sound as in the ancient dwellings of Southern Gaul. In both, there is the same absence of pottery; in both, bones are crushed in the same way for the sake of the marrow, and accumulate in vast quantities. The very fact of human remains being found among the relics of the feast is explained by an appeal to what Captain Parry observed in the Island of Igloolik. Among the vast quantities of bones of walruses and seals, skulls of dogs and bears, found in the Esquimaux camp, were numbers of human skulls lying about among the rest, which the natives tumbled into the collecting-bags of the officers without the least remorse. A similar carelessness for the dead was also observed by Sir J. Ross and Captain Lyon. This presence, then, of human remains in the south of Gaul is another link binding the ancient people then living there to the Esquimaux. Their small size also is additional evidence.

The only reference that can be drawn from these premises is that the people in question were decidedly Esquimaux, related to them precisely in the same way as the reindeer and musk-sheep of those days were to those now living in the high North American latitudes. The sole point of difference is the possession of the dog by the latter people; but, in the vast lapse of time between the date of their sojourn in Europe and the present day, the dog might very well have been adopted from some other superior race, or even reduced under the rule of man from some wild progenitor. By this discovery a new people is added to those which formerly dwelt in Europe. The severity of the climate in Southern Gaul is proved by the northern animals above mentioned. As it became warmer, musk-sheep, reindeer, and Esquimaux would retreat further and further north, until they found a resting-place on the American shore of the Great Arctic Sea. Possibly, in the case of the Esquimaux, the immigration of other and better-armed tribes might be a means of accelerating this movement. We know nothing of the date of his dwelling in Europe, except that he succeeded the earliest race of man, and was himself followed, after an unknown interval of time, during which great climatic changes took place by the polished-stone-using-folk. In the scale, then of the former occupants of Western Europe we have, first, the flint-folk of the geologists, then the reindeer folk, or the Esquimaux, then the polished-stone-using-folk, then the Celts, and lastly the Teutons.—*Saturday Review*, Dec. 8.

ORIENTAL MYSTERIES.

THESE are sold in envelopes or packets at 1s. per packet, each of which contains 25 "mysteries." In the state in which they are purchased they are of no apparent shape or make. Some appear like pieces of a common lucifer match; others like little dirty, irregular chips of a soft wood; and others, if I may so express myself, like nothing at all. In this state they appear quite useless, and certainly are not worth 1s., but immediately upon dropping one of them into a cup or saucer of hot water, it changes into a star, a fish, a flower, or some other tangible form. The change is instantaneously effected by coming in contact with the water, and the worthless-looking splinter of dried wood expands to many times its original size, and, what is more, the specimens, when so enlarged, are many of them highly coloured, representing, more or less accurately, not only the form but the colour of the objects for which they are intended. As might be supposed, the quickness of the expansion and the power of increasing to so many times the original bulk, has caused many inquiries to be made as to what the material could be of which these " mysteries " are made, and whether that material, whatever it might be, is treated chemically. I was fortunate enough to have put into my hands a "mystery" of large size, containing more solid material than those sold in the London shops, and on close examination I was enabled to determine the nature of the substance, which is simple vegetable tissue without any preparation whatever. The plant yielding it is a common one in the East, and is known as the Shola (Æschynomene aspera), belonging to the Leguminosæ or Pea Family. It is a marsh plant, and grows in abundance in the lakes and jheels of Bengal, as well as in other parts of India. If the objects are veritably of Japanese manufacture, it would seem that the stems of the Shola must have been obtained in the first place from the East Indies, as the plant is not known to grow either in China or Japan. It seldom attains a greater height than 8 or 10 feet, and the diameter of its stems is not more than $2\frac{1}{2}$ inches. The wood is remarkably soft and light—so light indeed as to appear nothing more than a mass of cellular tissue, and might readily be mistaken for pith; but upon microscopic examination, the annular rings and medullary rays are distinctly visible, though exceedingly fine. It is the large amount of cellular tissue present which causes so great a degree of expansion to take place. When dry, and submitted to pressure, the cell walls collapse, and are pressed against each other, but upon coming in contact with heat and moisture when placed in hot water, the cells immediately absorb the moisture, and regain their natural bulk; the effect of the moisture also expands the vascular tissue or woody fibre, and in that way causes the instantaneous opening of the chip-like objects. The material is in common use amongst the natives of the East Indies for the manufacture of various articles, both of dress and domestic use; its extreme lightness recommends it for many purposes, such as fishing floats, swimming jackets, bottle cases, but more especially for hats, as it is a bad conductor of heat, and the hats can be made of almost any thickness, and still be exceedingly light. For modelling it is a favourite material with the natives, who turn out some really beautiful articles with it. There is a very fine model of a temple made of the Shola in the East Indian Museum, and another in the Kew Museum. The stems are usually cut about the months of April and May, and are commonly sold in the bazaars at Calcutta. From the foregoing description it will be seen how simple in structure these startling "mysteries" are, and how easily and cheap they may be made. From a very thin slice of the wood a large number could be produced, and many such slices could be cut from one stem. I believe that the "mysteries" hitherto sold in London have all been imported from India or Japan, but there is no reason why they should not be made in this country, and perhaps at a cheaper rate than purchasing them of the Eastern manufacturers. The material, if the demand for the articles continued, could be imported in almost any quantities from the East Indies, and by cutting the stem up into thin slices, and then stamping the objects out with a kind of die, thousands could be produced and rolled into a small compass in a very short space of time. *F.—Gardeners' Chronicle, Dec. 15th.*

COMETS.—On the 27th February, 1826, Professor Biela, an Austrian astronomer of Josephstadt, discovered a small comet. When its motions were carefully studied, it was found by M. Clausen, another of those indefatigable German computists, that it revolved in an elliptic orbit in a period of 6 years and 8 months. On looking back into the list of comets, it proved to be identical with comets that had been observed in 1772, 1805, and perhaps in 1818. Its return was accordingly predicted, and the prediction verified with the most striking exactness. And this went on regularly till its appearance (also predicted) in 1846. In that year it was observed as usual, and all seemed to be going on quietly and comfortably, when, behold! suddenly on the 13th of January it split into two distinct comets! each with a head and coma and a little nucleus of its own. There is some little contradiction about the exact date. Lieutenant Maury, of the United States' Observatory of Washington, *reported officially on the 15th having seen it double on the 13th,* but Professor Wichmann who *saw it double on the 15th* avers that he *had a good view of it on the 14th,* and remarked nothing particular in its appearance. Be that as it may, the comet from a single became a double one. What domestic troubles caused the secession it is impossible to conjecture, but the two receded farther and farther from each other up to a certain moderate distance, with some degree of mutual communication and a very odd interchange of light—one day one head being brighter, and another the other—till they seemed to have agreed finally to part company. The oddest part of the story, however, is yet to come. The year 1852 brought round the time for their reappearance, and behold! there they both were, at about the same distance from each other, and both visible in one telescope. The orbit of this comet very nearly indeed intersects that of the earth on the place which the earth occupies on the 30th of November. If ever the earth is to be swallowed up by a comet, or to swallow up one, it will be on or about that day of the year. In the year 1832 we missed it by a month. The head of the comet enveloped that point of our orbit, but this happened on the 29th of October, so that we escaped that time. Had a meeting taken place, from what we know of comets, it is most probable that no harm would have happened, and that nobody would have known anything about it. It would appear that we are happily relieved from the dread of such a collision. It is now (February, 1866) overdue! Its orbit has been recomputed and an ephemeris calculated. Astronomers have been eagerly looking out for its reappearance for the last two months, when, according to all former experience, it ought to have been conspicuously visible, but without success, giving rise to the strangest theories. At all events, it seems to have fairly disappeared, and that without any such excuse, as in the case of Lexell's, the preponderant attraction of some great planet. Can it have come into contact or exceedingly close approach to some asteroid as yet undiscovered; or, peradventure, plunged into and got bewildered among the ring of meteorolites, which astronomers more than suspect?—*Herschell's "Familiar Lectures."*

MOUNTAIN SILK OF NORTH CHINA.—Mr. Consul Meadows, whose consular district includes Manchooria and Eastern Mongolia, reports that mountain silk remains as yet the one article which the district is likely to furnish to England. There are two crops of the mountain cocoon, a spring and an autumn; the autumn much the largest, but the spring greatly superior in quality. In the autumn the cocoons intended for the spring crop are placed in baskets, which are hung up in Chinese dwelling-rooms facing the south, but still having a temperature in the greater part of the winter considerably below freezing-point. The natural heat of spring suffices to bring the chrysalis out of the cocoon in the butterfly state. The butterflies then couple, eggs are produced in four or five days, and are laid on paper spread upon mats and tables. In a few days each egg produces a very small black worm, which is nourished by young oak leaves that are gathered and scattered over the paper. After some days the worms are transferred to the oak bushes on the hill slopes. After its first sleep or torpor of a couple of days, the worm becomes green in colour and larger in size. For its fifth sleep it prepares by spinning itself into a cocoon, in which it assumes the chrysalis shape. When the worm begins to make its cocoon, it selects two or more oak leaves, more or less facing each other, and joins them together by a network of the silk thread, which keeps issuing from its mouth as it moves its head from the one leaf to the other, holding on by its back claws to the twig from which the leaves grow. When the leaves are sufficiently joined to form a sort of cup or basket under the twig, the worm drops into the receptacle it has thus formed, first quite surrounds itself with the loose, flossy-like, silk which forms the outer portion of the cocoons as they come to market, and then proceeds to thicken the inner surface by further thread-spinning, till its bulk is sufficiently decreased for its turning into the chrysalis shape. The best silk is produced by nourishing the worms on the leaves, not of the oak, but of the "Tseen-tso-tsze," which exists, however, only in small quantities. The chrysalids which are not kept for breeding are used by the Chinese as an article of food. Not a tenth of the hillsides suitable for the oak bushes are at present planted with them. But considering the quantity of silk already produced, it may be taken that the trade could be developed into one of appreciable importance even for our great manufacturing interests, unless exactions and jealousies of the local mandarins interposed to repress it.—*Gardeners' Magazine Nov. 24th.*

THE CAMEL.—The popular notion of a camel connects it with the burning sands of the Arabian or African desert; but the one-humped race of Turkistân, equally (it would seem) with the two-humped or Mongolian species, is capable of enduring the opposite excess of cold. The Abbé Huc describes the two-humped kind, when the temperature was at zero of Fahrenheit, standing on the brink of a precipice and inhaling, with apparent satisfaction, the bitterly cold gusts from the north; and in Mantchuria, it seems that the loads are annually transferred from the backs of these two-humped camels to those of rein-deer, who convey them a further distance poleward. The one-humped camel of Turkistân is, in like manner, capable of withstanding the terribly severe winter of the Khiva steppe, as described in Col. Abbott's narrative of his winter journey over that desolate region, from Herât *via* Khiva to the Caspian. Near the Aral he met with "a double-humped camel," which he then regarded as a curiosity; and it follows, therefore, that his own train of camels must have been single-humped; and he remarks of them—"The magnificent camels, in their long, shaggy fur, hardly heed the weather. The icicles hang from their beards, and hoar-frost garnishes their heads. Their large, full, lustrous eyes seem acquainted with hardship, but not with trouble. They are the very philosophers of patience, who conquer all things by tranquillity of spirit." Still accompanied by them, he observes: "The cold is now excessive; the intense chill of the north wind, in these parts, cannot be imagined by any who have not so wintered on an extensive continent. The breath clings in icicles to the pillow and bed-clothes within the tent. Towels hung up to dry in a close room with a fire, or in the sun, are instantly stiffened into ice; and water freezes hard within three feet of a charcoal fire." Yet he says nothing of his camels suffering; and he observed "wild asses" (*ghor-khurs*) in abundance, and flocks of the saiga antelope, there termed "kaigh." He counted eight hundred *ghor-khurs* in a single herd. This was after passing the solitary individual of the double-humped species, which was a stranger in that part of Khorâsân, and a novelty to him, clearly indicating that his own camels (which withstood so severe a temperature) were single-humped.—*Land and Water*, Nov. 17th.

PLANTS OF NEW ZEALAND.—The following communication was read at the Botanical Society of Edinburgh, *Nov.* 8, Prof. Balfour, Hon. Sec., in the Chair. I. *On plants collected at Otago, New Zealand.* By Dr. W. Lauder Lindsay. 1, Fungi; 2, Mosses; 3, Hepaticæ; 4, Ferns. In speaking of Tree Ferns, the author remarked that 6.81 per cent. of Otago Ferns were arborescent. These Tree Ferns rank, as regards beauty, and frequently as regards height, girth, and usefulness, with the exogenous forest trees with which they are generally more or less intermixed. Cyathea Smithii is the most common species in Otago. Dicksonia squarrosa and D. Antarctica are also marked Tree Ferns of the district. In the South Island of New Zealand, Tree Ferns are associated with glaciers, snow, and other evidences of an alpine and rigorous climate. There are also found bordering on glaciers Fuchsia trees and Cabbage Palms associated with Araliaceæ, Myrtaceæ, and other trees usually regarded as denizens of comparatively warm climates. The largest glacier, Mount Cook (13,000 feet elev., in lat. 43½ deg.), which gives rise to the Waivan river, descends as low as 500 feet above the sea level on the west coast of Canterbury, and within eight miles from the sea. On both sides of this glacier luxuriant forests of Tree Ferns; Cordylines, Myrtaceæ, and other temperate and sub-tropical types are found. And no great distance from these glaciers are found true Palms (Areca sapida). In the mountainous forests and ravines of Nelson Tree Ferns ascend to 2,000 feet. The acclimatisation of New Zealand Ferns in Britain has been lately attracting the attention of horticulturists. Dr. Lindsay, however, doubts whether these plants will be hardy enough to stand the severest British winters without protection. The classification and nomenclature of New Zealand Ferns furnish us with some notable instances of the proneness to error in reference to climate, and in the definition of genera, species, and varieties. Dr. L. states that 30 species have been made out of Ophioglossum vulgatum, 20 different names are given to Pteris aquilina (the common Bracken), and about a dozen species have been manufactured out of Lycopodium clavatum. The variability of the species of New Zealand Ferns is remarkable. This is illustrated by species of Asplenium, Lomaria, Aspidium, Hymenophyllum, &c.

AMBER.—This word is derived from the Arabic:— "The well-known substance so called is a fossilized resin of certain unknown coniferous trees, of the fir or pine genus. Great virtues were attributed to it by the ancients. Pliny tells us that Sophocles held amber to be the petrified tears which the birds of Meleager dropped to the memory of that great hero of mythology. Amber has been among the moderns a subject of great discussion. The mystery in which it was involved was increased by the circumstance that Hebrew and Arabic characters were often found engraved upon it, in a perfectly legible state. Dr. Thomas, of Kœnigsburg, has given us the explanation of this singular fact by stating that the pieces of amber so engraved were neither more nor less than seals. Many of them are preserved in the Museum of Portici, but chiefly brought thither from Herculaneum. The largest known deposit of amber lies on the Prussian coast of the Baltic; it is found in a bed of lignite, which is supposed to extend far under the sea. Another deposit of amber lies almost horizontally on the outskirts of Dirschheim, at a depth of only four feet from the surface. Pieces of amber are often found lying on the coast after a storm. Thus, on the first of January, 1848, upwards of 400 kilos. of this substance were thrown out of the sea within a very small space. Amber has been known from the highest antiquity, and important medical properties were attributed to it; even now it maintains its place in our pharmacopœias, together with the oil distilled from it, as a stimulant, an astringent, and an antispasmodic. Amber necklaces have been found in Celtic tombs both in England and Brittany. Regnard tells us that in his time the Margrave of Brandenburg presented the Emperor of Russia with an arm-chair entirely of amber, and the Dauphin with a mirror of the same material. In 1599, a block is said to have been found on the coast of Melinda so large that a man was able to hide himself behind it. Amber has this curious property, that when it is slightly warmed by friction on a piece of cloth or any other woollen stuff it will attract straw or grasses. Hence the science of electricity has its name from "electon," its classic name; and it is thus that dealers are enabled to distinguish between the real and imitation article.— "Varia," in *La Liberté*.

MODE OF CATCHING SHARKS IN POLYNESIA.— Perhaps as remarkable a mode of catching sharks as any, is that I have heard narrated by Rarotonga men, as practised by their neighbours on the island of Aitutaki, one of the Harvey group. At one end of the island is a large lagoon, formed by the reef that runs round it, stretching far out from the land, and there the sharks breed, and are regularly fed. As they are very prolific, I have seen as many as twenty-five and sometimes thirty little ones taken out of a shark; they increase rapidly. When any feasting is going on amongst the natives, sharks being held necessary to complete the variety of food, parties are sent out to catch them in the lagoon. Provided with a strong rope and a supply of bait, two or three young men start off in a canoe, and, taking up a position over the haunts of the sharks, throw over bait after bait, until the greedy monsters have eaten to repletion. Waiting quietly in their canoes, the fishermen soon see the sharks stretching themselves lazily on the sand, with their heads just out of the caves formed by the overhanging rocks that rise from the bottom of the lagoon. With a noose in the end of the rope, which he holds in his hand, a man quietly slips from the canoe into the sea, dives down to a shark, slips the noose over his tail, and, as with the jerk of the rope he tells the men above the prey is fast, he himself, with a strong spring from the ground, swiftly rises to the surface. All pulling away at the rope together, the shark is soon brought to the water's edge, and, as the tail is raised out of the sea, he becomes almost helpless; then, with a strong pull together, after a moment's spell, the shark is suddenly bounced into the canoe. Frequently, as the shark lies at the mouth of a cave, with only his head out, the tail cannot be reached. The diver then has to tap the monster gently on the head, who, lazy and drowsy after the good feed just supplied from the canoe, quietly turns his tail to the intruder—and, by Jove, on slips the noose before he knows it is there.—*Pritchard's Polynesian Reminiscences*.

PLUMS AS ORCHARD TREES.—The Diamond Plum originated at Brenchley, in Kent; and was named after the raiser, who was foreman to Mr. Hooker, of the (then) Brenchley Nurseries. There is also one in cultivation called the "Dummer," which is the same kind. The Diamond is in great demand, being a showy market plum, and if gathered a few days before ripening it retains a fine bloom and travels well.

The Prolific Damson is a very abundant bearer. We have seen young trees with as many fruit as leaves, and in many places the shoots were completely hidden by the clustering fruit. It is also called locally the "Cluster Damson," "Farleigh Damson," and "Crittenden's Damson." We have had fruit on maiden trees in our nursery gardens. It has been but four or five years in the trade, and is not so widely known as its merits deserve. A vast quantity of these and other damsons find their way into cheap port wine.

The Cheshire Damson is largely grown, and the old sort with bullaces, is generally planted at the edges of plantations for shelter, to "break the wind" as the farmers say. Besides those named by Mr. Robson, the following are coming into repute with fruit-growers:—

Prince Englebert.—A sturdy grower, and a free-bearing kind; its upright growth is greatly in its favour, and the fruit, though large, is not liable to crack.

Mitchelson's Damson.—As large as a small plum, a free grower, and a heavy cropper. It will take first rank as a market plum; though it has been known in the London markets for some years, it was only recently introduced here by us.

Rivers's Early Prolific and Rivers's Early Favourite are being more planted every year. They are most valuable sorts; the fruit finds a ready sale at a long price, and the trees, though fine-wooded, are pretty strong in a few years, and bear well.

Bush Plum.—A very valuable marked plum; its late season and abundant cropping make up for its deficient flavour. It is largely grown in some parts of Kent. A sturdy grower, and not so liable to split and break as many plums are. It is a good kitchen plum; medium-sized fruit.—*Cottage Gardener*, Nov. 13th.

GEOGRAPHY OF ABYSSINIA.—The geographical position of Christian Abyssinia, its political institutions, its religious condition, are fully described in a singularly able paper, enclosed in Mr. Plowden's despatch of the 20th June, 1852. The first of these is simple and easily defined. The northern boundaries do not reach within a hundred miles of the Red Sea at any point; and the interval is occupied by various savage tribes, all Mohammedan, all except the Gallas, totally without government, living by their flocks and camels, and engaged in incessant feuds. The only good harbour in the Red Sea is Massowah; and the Turks own the island, and claim the coast for sixty miles inland. So much for the north. The western boundary is the pashalic of Sennaar. To the south-west, vast forests, frequented by wild beasts, or hot plains inhabited by negro races, exclude Abyssinia from the navigable part of the Blue Nile, whose impetuous torrent, on the other hand, protects the country from the daring and dauntless Gallas, a fine race, whose men are brave and honest, and whose women are beautiful. On the east and south-east are various tribes of fierce and fanatic Mohammedans, who are themselves barred from the sea by the savage Adaiel, by whose hordes, led by the famous chief, Mohammed Grayne, Abyssinia was nearly destroyed, when Portugal interposed, and saved it by the introduction of firearms. Stretching all along the eastern boundary, again, to join the north, are other savage tribes, once Abyssinian, and still speaking the ancient Ethiopic tongue, but all lawless and inimical. The country which lies within this pleasant border is a range of vast table-lands and fantastic mountains, varying from four thousand to fourteen thousand feet above the level of the sea. Deep valleys, the beds of the larger rivers, intersect this, but however circuitous their course, all these streams finally join the Blue Nile. They are nowhere navigable, and only a few mountain-torrents, swollen by the rain, find their way to the Red Sea. The valleys teem with the richest produce; and the soil is capable of growing everything which will grow anywhere; but there is little cultivation in proportion to the extent of territory. The scenery is varied and beautiful, and the country combines mineral resources, a delightful climate, tropical luxuriance, and such salubrity that no waste of European life need be apprehended from frequenting it.—*Chambers's Journal*, Nov. 17th.

FERNS.—Though ferns now occupy a conspicuous place in our gardens, and are in high favour with cultivators, it is only in comparatively recent times that they have been brought into notice. During the last century certain classes of plants came into fashion, and after a season of popularity again fell into disrepute. Thus: Tulips were once the rage. At the time of the establishing of the several provincial Botanic Gardens, all of which were founded upon a strictly botanical footing, though many of them have now, to a greater or less extent, degenerated into places of amusement, the plants in greatest demand were those of our New Holland and Cape colonies, principally the Heaths, *Proteas*, *Aloes*, and their kindred. In after years dealers obtained large prices for cactuses; but, with the exception of a few of the easily-grown and most showy kinds, these are now scarcely saleable. Still more recently the magnificent flowering orchids were promoted to the first place in our gardens; and though these may still be said to maintain their position, the expense attending their cultivation is so great that they are for the most part confined to the gardens of the wealthy. Ferns, on the contrary, may, as a general rule, be grown in a comparatively inexpensive manner. The discovery made by Mr. N. B. Ward, that these plants can be grown to great perfection in small ornamental closed cases (now well-known as "Wardian Cases"), suitable not only for the drawing-rooms of the wealthy but for humbler dwellings, renders it possible for amateurs to indulge their love of ferns without going to the expense of erecting hothouses and employing a staff of gardeners; and it is to be hoped that this will be the means of retaining them in favour and spreading them still wider. The enumeration shows that at the present time above nine hundred exotic species of ferns are cultivated in the various public and private gardens in this country; and of these by far the greater number have been introduced during the last quarter of a century.—*Smith's Ferns, British, &c.*

THE WEST INDIA SPONGE FISHERY.—At present, perhaps owing to the large reduction in the collection and exportation during the late war in the United States, the supply of Bahamas sponge is not equal to the demand, and prices rule high. In the ten years ending 1864 the average export was 3,330 cwt. per annum, valued at £17,369. But four or five years ago as much as 5000 to 6000 cwts. were shipped from those islands. Bahamas sponge is inferior to the Mediterranean kinds, and a quarter of a century ago it was of little value. It was simply classed as coarse and fine, the former including the qualities now known as velvet, sheepwool, and grass, and selling for four to five dollars the cwt., the fine, or glove sponge, at 10 dollars. Now it is divided into the eight following classes, to each of which is affixed the average price per pound which it fetched in 1864:—1st, common, or boat sponge, with white or yellow tissue, called in the island sheepwool, and in America carriage sponge; 2nd, common, or velvet sponge, with brown tissue; 3rd, large fine brown (fine hard-head), all these three 1s. 8d. per pound; 4th, large coarse brown (coarse hard-head), 10d. per lb.; 5th, common coarse, or grass sponge, 4d. per lb.; 6th, large fine, soft tissue, not strong, called glove sponge, 4d. per lb.; 7th, small fine, soft tissue and good forms, called beef sponge, 2s. 6d. per lb.; 8th, small fine, hard tissue (small fine, hard-head, or hard brown), best quality, also often called beef sponge, 1s. 3d. per lb. Of late years sponge has been applied to a great many new purposes. The price of some qualities has doubled, of others quadrupled, and of some, such as velvet and sheepwool, for which apparently there could have been no foreign demand, the price is ten times greater than formerly. Large quantities of all the above kinds are sent to the United States, of the velvet and glove sponge to England, while France takes the finest qualities. There they undergo a final operation of cleaning and dyeing.—*Queen*, Nov. 10th.

SPECTRUM ANALYSIS OF STARS.—The results of spectrum analysis as applied to the heavenly bodies were discussed at considerable length by Mr. William Huggins, F.R.S., in a lecture read before the British Association in August last. Mr. Huggins concluded by summing up the new knowledge that has been

gained from observations with the prism, as follows:—
1. all the brighter stars, at least, have a structure analogous to that of the sun; 2, the stars contain material elements common to the sun and earth; 3, the colours of the stars have their origin in the chemical constitution of the atmospheres which surround them; 4, the changes in brightness of some of the variable stars are attended with changes in the lines of absorption of their spectra; 5, the phenomena of the star in Corona appear to show that in this object at least great physical changes are in operation; 6, there exist in the heavens true nebulæ: these objects consist of luminous gas; 7, the material of comets is very similar to the matter of the gaseous nebulæ, and may be identical with it; 8, the bright points of the star clusters may not be in all cases stars of the same order as the separate bright stars. It may be asked, Mr. Huggins adds, what cosmical theory of the origin and relations of the heavenly bodies do these new facts suggest? It would be easy to speculate, but it appears to me that it would not be philosophical to dogmatise at present on a subject of which we know so very little. Our views of the universe are undergoing important changes. Let us wait for more facts, with minds unfettered by any dogmatic theory, and therefore free to receive the obvious teaching, whatever it may be, of new observations.—*Mechanics' Mag.*, Nov. 24th.

ERUPTION OF THE STROKKUR.—While the travellers were engaged in collecting these delicate formations, they were surprised and delighted by a sight which has fallen to the lot of but few previous visitors to Iceland—a gigantic and voluntary eruption of the Strokkur. Behind them a subterranean thunder suddenly began rolling, and a pillar of dense white steam shot up from the Strokkur into the air with the speed of an arrow; this steam contained in its centre a cylindrical jet of water, at least ten feet in diameter, which at the top parted like a gigantic pine tree into various arms, whose ends, dissolving into dazzling white mist, flew away in all directions. The jet had scarce sunk again to half its length, with the same speed as it ascended, ere it rose again with astounding rapidity and a deafening roar, so that it could scarce be followed with the eyes. Countless other jets shot forth from the steam-like rockets, with a hissing sound, and also dissolved into a fine dust rain, whose pearls slowly fell to the ground, while immeasurable steam-clouds brooded over the whole scene. Ere long it seemed as if the giant's strength were exhausted, and the fatigued pillar were about to break down, but it rose again to a height not before reached, with even greater speed and louder thunder. So great was the power of the steam that although there was a strong breeze blowing, the jet was not at all driven out of the perpendicular. This wondrous spectacle lasted for fifteen minutes, until the fury was spent and the pillar of water fell back not to rise again; the greatest height which it attained was 140 feet.—*Day of Rest*, Dec.

DESSERT FRUITS IN 1256.—The only kinds of fruits named in the Countess of Leicester's expenses are apples and pears. Three hundred of the latter were purchased at Canterbury, probably from the gardens of the monks. It is believed, however, that few other sorts were generally grown in England before the latter end of the fifteenth century; although Mathew Paris, describing the bad season of 1257, observes that apples were scarce and pears scarcer, while quinces, vegetables, cherries, plums, and all shell fruits were entirely destroyed. The shell fruits were probably the common hazel-nut, walnuts, and perhaps chesnuts. In 1256, the sheriffs of London were ordered to buy two thousand chesnuts for the King's use. In the wardrobe book of the 14th of Edward the First we find the bill of Nicolas, the Royal fruiterer, in which the only fruits mentioned are pears, apples, quinces, medlars, and nuts. The supply of these from Whitsuntide to November cost £21 14s. 1½d. This apparent scarcity of indigenous fruits naturally leads to the inquiry what foreign kinds besides those included in the term spicery, such as almonds, dates, figs, and raisins, were imported into England in this and the following century? In the time of John and of Henry the Third, Rochelle was celebrated for its pears and conger eels. The sheriffs of London purchased a hundred of the former for Henry in 1223.—*Timb's Nooks and Corners of English Life.*

VITALITY OF SEEDS.—In a paper addressed last week to the Academy of Sciences, M. Pouchet, the celebrated physiologist of Rouen, gives an account of some experiments of his on the vitality of the seeds of the *Medicago Americana*, a sort of clover. A vast quantity of wool is received at Elbœuf, from Brazil; but it is in a very dirty state, and contains amongst other impurities, the seeds of various plants. M. Pouchet was told by several credible witnesses that the seeds mixed up with this wool would strike root and grow up into plants even after undergoing a four hours' ebullition during the various operations of dyeing. This was a startling assertion, it being admitted on all hands by physiologists, from Spallansani downwards, that the vitality of seeds is utterly destroyed in boiling water. M. Pouchet resolved to verify the truth of this alleged fact, and accordingly boiled some of these seeds for exactly four hours without any interruption. After this operation the seeds of the Medicago were found to be enormously swollen; the water had become mucilaginous, and it was with no great faith in the success of his experiment that our author put these disorganized seeds into flower-pots containing earth utterly free from any seeds of the same kind. Nevertheless, in the course of from 10 to 20 days, several roots sprang up; and this experiment was repeated more than 20 times with equal success. After minutely examining all the circumstances, M. Pouchet at length found that among a large number of seeds in a state of utter disorganization there were yet a few that had successfully resisted the action of boiling water. They had, indeed, borne the temperature of 100 deg. Centigr. for the space of four hours, but their outer tegument had proved watertight by some unexplained circumstance. Our author immediately concluded that such must also be the case with other seeds, and he accordingly tried with wheat, barley, millet, &c., but without success; for the present the seeds of the Medicago are the only instance of this wonderful vitality.—*Galignani.*

GEOLOGY OF UPPER EGYPT.—At the first cataract the Nile flows over crystalline rocks consisting principally of quartz, felspar, and hornblende, combined in various proportions, and then appearing under the forms of syenite, greenstone, hornblende, and mica-schists, or else occurring in separate masses. In the bed of the river the surface of the harder portions of these rocks is beautifully polished. The whole district is traversed by dykes of greenstone, of which the prevailing direction is E. and W. The crystalline rocks forming the bed of the river are overlain by a sandstone, sometimes coarse and gritty, and at other times fine-grained and compact. The prevailing colour is light-yellow, but in places it is dark-purple and even black, owing to the presence of iron. As yet no organic remains have been discovered in it. This sandstone rest on the uneven surface of the syenite in slightly inclined strata, dipping N.N.E. It is nowhere altered at its junction with the syenite, nor is it anywhere penetrated by dykes. To the eastward of the first cataract in a wide valley, commencing opposite the Island of Philæ, and joining the Nile valley again about three miles below Assouan. Through this valley the Nile may have formerly flowed, as freshwater shells and deposits of Nile-mud are found at a considerable height above the present level of the river. To the westward of the first cataract the crystalline rocks disappear below the sandstone, and the country is almost entirely covered with sand of a rich yellow colour, composed of fine rounded grains of quartz.—*Paper read at the Geological Society, Dec. 3.*

New Books.

[*Our limited space must of necessity compel us to give but very short notices of new books, but they will perhaps serve as a guide as to what books our readers may ask for at their libraries.*]

Principles of Geology, or the Modern Changes of the Earth and its Inhabitants. By Sir Charles Lyell, Bart., M.A., F.R.S. Tenth Edition. Vol. I. London: John Murray.

After a lapse of thirteen years and a half Sir Charles Lyell has reissued his celebrated "Principles of Geology"—a long interval, as he says, in the history of the progress of a science. As our readers may expect, he has found it necessary to re-write some chapters and recast others, introducing a large quantity of new matter.

The Principles (to quote from his preface) treat of such portions of the economy of existing nature, animate, and inanimate, as are illustrative of geology, so as to comprise an investigation of the permanent effects of causes now in action which may serve as records to after ages of the present condition of the globe and its inhabitants. Such effects are the enduring monuments of the ever-varying state of the physical geography of the globe, the lasting signs of its destruction and renovation, and the memorials of the equally fluctuating condition of the organic world. They may be regarded, in short, as a symbolical language, in which the earth's autobiography is written.

When the work first appeared in 1830 it embraced, not only a view of the modern changes of the earth and its inhabitants, but also some account of those monuments of analogous changes of ancient date both in the organic and inorganic world. This last part was in 1838 omitted, and enlarged into a separate treatise, and called the "Elements of Geology," of which there has been six editions, the last in January, 1865. In separating the works much matter was retained in the Principles which might be regarded as common to both, such as the historical sketch of the early progress of geology, &c. In 1863 was published the "Antiquity of Man," the subject matter of which coincided in part with the fossil remains of man and his works in both the Elements and Principles, but in the former it was more expanded. The manner in which the origin of species is handled in the "Antiquity of Man," the author tells us, will be found to be different in many respects from that in which he will view the same subject in the concluding volume of this work.

For the benefit of such of his readers as are acquainted with his earlier editions, he gives a list of the chief additions now made, from which we give the following on

ARTESIAN WELLS.—An analogous phenomenon is recorded at Reimke, near Boctumi in Westphalia, where the water of an artesian well brought up from a depth of 156 feet several small fish three or four inches long, the nearest stream in the country being at the distance of some leagues. In some artesian wells sunk by the French in the north eastern part of the desert of Sahara small fish have been frequently brought up alive with the first gush of the water from a depth of 175 feet. M. Desor informs us that in January, 1863, he saw some of these fish in a well in the oasis of Ain Tala. They were of the genus Cyprinodon, not blind like those taken from the underground caverns of Adelsberg or Kentucky, but with perfect eyes. The nearest ponds or lakes were at a great distance on the surface of the desert, and in this and the other cases before mentioned of the subterranean transportation of shells, fish, and fragments of plants we see evidence of the water not having been simply filtered through porous rock, but having flowed through continuous underground channels. Such examples suggest the idea that the leaky beds of rivers are often the feeders of springs.

It would seem very like presumption for us to attempt to speak highly of a book that is known to all the world. The learned author has made for himself a reputation which will last until that time when perhaps the earth shall undergo one of the many changes it has undergone before, and with mighty volcanic action sweep us poor helpless mortals off the face of it. As other works from his pen have grown and grown until a few pages have become volumes, so this edition has increased and improved upon all former ones. We hope at some future time another edition from him will improve and enlarge upon this.

Polynesian Reminiscences; or, Life in the South Pacific Islands. By W. T. Pritchard, F.R.G.S., F.A.S.L., formerly H.M. Consul at Samoa and Fiji. Preface by Dr. Seemann. With Illustrations. Chapman and Hall.

This is a very interesting account of fifteen years' residence in Tahiti, Samoa, and Fiji, the first two chapters containing a brief account of Tahiti, and the remainder giving the author's experience and observations as consul of Fiji and Samoa. It contains much useful information about Polynesian manners and customs, and is worthy, in the estimation of Dr. Seemann (who writes the preface) of being ranked with "Ellis's Polynesian Researches" and "Mariner's Tonga," the two standard works on the subject.

There are many curious legends of the religion and mythology of the native Fijians and Samoans, who, at the present day, are pretty much alike, but who seem formerly to have been of different origin, the first inhabitants of Fiji, according to Mr. Pritchard, having been Papuans, black skinned, rough, and very muscular, with short bushy hair; while the Samoans were of Malay parentage, with reddish brown soft skins, long straight hair, of larger build than the Fijians, but with much less energy.

There are also many pages of matter relating to the natural history of the Islands, written in a pleasing and readable manner, which will well repay perusal.

Physical Geography. By Professor D. T. Ansted, F.R.S., F.R.G.S., F.G.S., Honorary Fellow of King's College, London, and late Fellow of Jesus College, Cambridge. London: W. H. Allen and Co.

We are glad to welcome this volume of Professor Ansted's, and to have the opportunity of calling attention to it in this our first number. The Professor's object seems to be to enable the general reader or the student to obtain an outline of the main facts, in language as simple and definite as possible, and, as far as we can see, this is admirably carried out. Physical geography regarded as a science, although of deep interest to us all, cannot be treated of so as to make light reading; but the statement of numerous facts, and the close reasoning necessary on such a subject, are so handled and classified by the author as to render the whole far from difficult or tedious. The Professor is careful to tell us that he does not claim the present volume to be complete; and while in some cases "the conclusions arrived at differ most from popular notions," he believes "they are not inconsistent with the views of those who are recognised, both in England and on the continent, as the ablest pioneers of science." This is a question we cannot pretend to determine. The volume is divided into six parts, comprising, first, a General Introduction; then Earth; thirdly, Water; fourthly, Air; fifthly, Fire; and, lastly, Life; and altogether will, we believe, supply a serious want, often felt.

The Vegetable World. By Louis Figuier. Translated by W. S. O., 8vo, pp., 574, with numerous Illustrations. London: Chapman and Hall.

A handsome volume, translated from the French of M. Figuier, the well-known author of the "World before the Deluge." It is beautifully printed and illustrated, containing over 400 woodcuts and 24 full-page illustrations, the majority drawn from nature by M. Faquet. It is intended to place before the reader a popular and entertaining work on the vegetable world, combining instruction and amusement; and so far the object seems well attained, for the multitude of good examples of the different varieties of plants and the graphic way in which they are placed before the reader, with the illustrations picturing them, must make the subject interesting even to those who look upon the study of botany as dry and tedious.

It is divided into four parts, the first treating of the Physiology; second, Classification; third, the Natural Families; and the fourth, the Geographical distribution of plants.

A Winter with the Swallows. By Matilda Betham Edwards. Hurst and Blackett.

A cheerful and spirited account of a winter spent in Algeria. As a fair specimen of the author's style, we extract the following from her excursion into Kabylia:—

Soon after leaving Tiziozou we crossed a broad river-bed, and then entered a wholly new and beautiful region. The road—such a road as only French military roads can be—wound corkscrew fashion about the hills, which were verdant from base to summit. Now we passed under a natural arch of olive boughs; now we came upon a sunny plateau with fields of corn and orchards of the fig-tree, the wild plum and the almond on either side. Everywhere smiled a happy nature; everywhere was the evidence of peace and plenty. As we advanced more and more into the country, traces of French civilization disappeared, and instead of the straight little houses with their rows of carob-trees, new church and handsome drinking fountain, we saw on every crest and mountain-top a Kabyle village, looking, I dare say, precisely as a Kabyle village looked a thousand years ago. Anything more picturesque and poetic than the scenery of Grand Kabylia cannot be conceived. The lovely hills, purple or green or golden as the light made them, each crowned with a compact mass of tiny stone houses, the deep valleys of tender green, the lofty rocks bristling with wild cactus, the groves of majestic olives, the distant panorama of blue snow-tipped mountains—all these features made a picture not easy to forget. . . . . The journey from the Metidja and ascent of Fort Napoleon reminds one of the long ride across the Campagna to Tivoli. The road wound round the mountains like a thread twisted about a sugar-loaf. We looked up, and said, "Oh, it is impossible that we can get there." We looked down, and said, "Have we really climbed so high?" And still we climbed higher and higher and higher. Everywhere were signs of cultivation; and it was quite touching to see how laborious, and often ineffectual was the system of it.

Contributions to the Flora of Mentone. Parts I. and II. By J. Traherne Moggridge. London: Reeve and Co.

Mr. Traherne Moggridge, with the assistance of M. Ardonio (who is preparing a flora of the Alpes Maritime) has produced two parts of an illustrated work on the flora of Mentone, each part containing twenty-five beautifully executed coloured illustrations, artistic and very true to nature. In the letterpress which accompanies them the characters of the plants are given, with references to authors, and able comments of his own.

The following works likely to interest our readers have appeared during the past few weeks:—

A Dictionary of British Birds. Reprinted from Montagu's *Ornithological Dictionary*, with additions. Compiled and edited by Edward Newman, F.L.S., editor of the *Zoologist*. Van Voorst.

Occasional Essays. By Chas. Wren Hoskyns, author of "Talpa; or, the Chronicles of a Clay Farm," "Inquiry into the History of Agriculture," &c. Longmans, Green, and Go.

The States of the River Plate; their Industries and Commerce. By Wilfred Latham. Longmans and Co.

On the Jostedal-Bræ Glaciers in Norway; with some General Remarks, and a Plate. By C. M. Doughty. Stanford.

A Naturalist's Ramble to the Orcades. By A. W. Crichton, B.A. Van Voorst.

Lectures on Animal Chemistry, delivered at the Royal College of Physicians. By William Odling, M.B. Longmans and Co.

Le Jardin Frutier du Muséum, ou Iconographie de toutes les Espèces et Variétés d'Arbres Frutiers cultivés dans cet Etablissement, avec leur Description leur Histoire leur Synonymie, &c. Par J. Decaisne, Membre de l'Institut, Professeur de Culture au Muséum d'Histoire Naturelle. Paris: Firmin Didot and Co.

The Sea and its Living Wonders. A Popular Account of the Marvels of the Deep. By Dr. G. Hartwig. Third Edition, Considerably Enlarged and Improved. (Longmans.)

The Tropical Resident at Home. Letters addressed to Europeans returning from India and the Colonies on Subjects connected with their Health and General Welfare. By Edward J. Waring, M.D. (Churchill & Sons.)

Lessons in Elementary Physiology. By Thomas H. Huxley, LL.D., F.R.S. (Macmillan and Co.)

Buckmaster's Elements of Animal Physiology. By John Angell. (Longmans & Co.)

Correspondence.

[*Under this head we shall be glad to insert any letters of general interest.*]

WHAT ARE SHOOTING STARS.

Sir,—I was an admiring beholder of the November meteors, and I read with interest the various accounts of other observers given in the public prints. The precision with which our astronomers calculated the visitation of these vagrant lights does them infinite credit. But having seen, I wish to know more about them. The spectrum analysis does not in this instance appear to have seconded the endeavours of our scientific men to discover the composition of the celestial fireworks. Whatever they may be, I do not believe in the cloud of stones revolving round the sun, in which our earth periodically becomes involved. If these meteors were stones which became incandescent in consequence of the friction produced by their being projected through our atmosphere at an amazing velocity, surely some of them would come to earth. We have many authentic accounts of isolated meteors which have burst or exploded with a loud report, and the fragments have been seen to fall and plough up the ground. These are well known as aerolites. That none of the November meteors fell to the earth I think proves satisfactorily that they are not stones in the ordinary acceptation of the word; but I see no reason why they should not be composed of some phosphorescent substance which becomes ignited either by friction or contact with our atmosphere, and is entirely consumed during its brief visible existence.

I offer this merely as a suggestion, hoping that some one more learned in the stars will take up the subject in the NATURALIST'S NOTE BOOK. I am, Sir, yours, &c.,

A COUNTRY RECTOR.

TO CORRESPONDENTS.

The Curiosity Hunter (Leeds)—Please specify the receipts you require. We shall be glad to introduce an exchange column if desired.

J. W. S. (Hastings)—Woodward's Manual of the Mollusca will suit you. Messrs. Virtue, Ivy Lane, have just published a new edition at 5s. 6d.

W. Crisp (Holloway)—Mr. Stevens, King Street, Covent Garden, sells such things every Friday. By watching his sales you will probably get what you want at a low figure.

C. R. (Maldon)—Wood's Natural History is published by Routledge, in 3 volumes, at 18s. each.

Short Notes.

ABYSSINIANS.—The people of Abyssinia possess in their own land all the necessaries, and many of the luxuries of life in profusion; they have great freedom of speech and action, and they are constitutionally and systematically gay. They meet misfortune and death with perfect fortitude; they are not violent or emotional; when it suits their interests or convenience to commit what we should consider very serious crimes, they go and do it, and tell all the particulars with good-humoured laughter. It is difficult to our minds to realise all the influences and results of a social system in which neither crime, detection, or punishment is recognised as disgraceful, in which, in fact, there is no such thing as disgrace, and consequently no susceptibility, sensitiveness, or shame; but if we could succeed in realising these influences and results, we should understand the people over whom King Theodore assumed his sway, and the wonderful work he is doing. They are sensible, witty, superstitious, dirty, proud, litigious, intensely obstinate, and singularly averse to new ideas. The Jewish origin of many of their institutions is unmistakable, and several of their characteristics are strongly Jewish. They have a written language, but they never use it; all affairs are transacted verbally; in the rare case of a letter being written, it is neither signed, sealed, nor dated. Marriage is a civil contract, dissolved at pleasure, and no distinction is made, in station or provision, between legitimate and illegitimate children. The ties of relationship are strong, from interested motives, as a barrier to the exactions of rapacious governors, and the violence of the soldiery. They do not carry their sentiments to the practical point of sharing their means; on the contrary, incessant lawsuits are carried on between relatives, for land and property; and they will muster in thousands to bewail and avenge the death of one whom they would cheerfully have permitted to starve.—*Chambers's Journal*, Nov. 17.

BORAGE.—Borage is a rough plant, with fusiform roots, oblong or lanceolate leaves, and blue panicled or drooping flowers. The plant came originally from Aleppo, but is now naturalised in most parts of Europe and America. It is frequently found on dunghills and heaps of rubbish. Parkinson, who died about 1640, states that it grew plentifully in Kent in his day. Borage was formerly in great request, being reckoned one of the four cordial flowers. "Very light," says an ingenious author, "were those sorrows which could be driven away by Borage." Yet Borage flowers are at least innocent, which is more than can be said of many other general remedies for care. The whole herb is very succulent, and very mucilaginous, having a peculiar faint smell when bruised. The plant is now seldom taken inwardly. The young tender leaves may be used as a salad, or as a pot herb. The flowers are one of the chief constituents in the composition of a cool tankard. Borage is a pretty annual, and is raised from seeds, and in order to have it young all the year, it should be sown in spring, summer, and autumn, either in drills, or broadcast, from March to May. When the plants come up thick, they must be thinned to nine inches asunder. They will not bear transplanting, in consequence of the length of their tap roots: at all events, if the operation be attempted, it must be done when the plants are very young. It sows itself in autumn, and likes a dry soil. Borage ought to be cultivated in the vicinity of every apiary, as it is a plant to which the bees resort with great avidity, it being excessively rich in honey.—*Journal of Agriculture*, N. S.

DO BIRDS OF PASSAGE STEER BY THE SUN?—Sir, to this question by "Philornis" a decided negative must be the answer, for it appears that migration is chiefly performed by night. When the season arrives for their departure, our various small migratory birds, as observed in confinement, become restless after dark, fluttering their wings, pointing the beak upwards, and frequently springing up to the roof of their cage, to the injury of their plumage if this be not carefully provided against. They continue to evince this restlessness for some weeks; and I have known it, in one instance of a blackcap (*Sylvia atricapilla*), to be manifested throughout the winter, till in spring the bird has fairly worn itself out and died, though it had been caged for three or four years. The most curious fact is, that the same birds return, year after year, to the same haunts, and the young to the place of their nativity. A lame redstart was observed to return for eleven successive seasons to the same garden. Nightingales reared from the nest are found not to sing like wild birds of the species, but to pick up a medley of notes, mixing up whatever they may chance to have heard. A bird of this sort was turned loose by Mr. Sweet, a well known writer on cage-birds, in the course of the autumn, and returned the next season to his garden, being at once recognised by his peculiar song. Other instances might be adduced. How a bird that migrates by night should thus be guided in its course is a mystery seemingly beyond explanation; and equally the means by which other animals have been known to find their way home from vast distances, of which so many anecdotes are recorded.—B.—*Land and Water*, Dec. 1st.

THE LOTUS.—Drawings, both of the flower and the fruit of the Nelumbium, appear upon the ancient coins, mosaics, and monuments of the countries in which it was either indigenous or cultivated, often with ears of corn interspersed, then to form the insignia of Isis. Notices of it occur repeatedly in oriental poetry and legend, and, doubtless, it was some wandering Indian tale that gave origin to that beautiful fable in

Ovid, where he recounts the metamorphosis of the nymph Lotis, in the flower which, he tells us, "in the water preserves her name." To see as I have done, that glorious Chatsworth plant, not alone in the brightness of day, but lost in the sweet mystery of September moonlight, which disclosed, at the same moment, the green islands made by the floating leaf-trays of the Victoria, with, in the centre, a livid miracle of floral sculpture, white and rose-colour, like alabaster; and tall Papyrus stalks, bearing at top great green globes of bending hair; and broad leaves and lustrous bloom of many another princely exile from the far east, all, as it were, asleep, like the water, in the fragrant and luminous stillness—to see that glorious Chatsworth plant, I say, as then, was enough to re-invest it with all the ancient sanctity, and to make one feel how deep and reverent was that ancient flower-worship, and that if *this* were the plant that charmed Ulysses' ancient mariners, well might they "no longer wish to return, but prefer to remain in that country, and with the lotus for ever."—*Leo H. Grindon, in Country Words.*

PERUVIAN SILVER MINES.—Silver and gold are extracted in various places in Peru; but the only mines of importance are the silver mines of Pasco. Silver sometimes is found in native state, but most often in sulphides of silver, in argentiferous pyrites, carbonates and sulphates of copper. The processes made use of at Pasco are primitive; the wet ore is crushed by means of machinery put in motion by water power. From thence it is placed on the circo, basins of masonry within low walls. It is mixed with 10 to 11 per cent. of sea salt and turned with a shovel, and horses or mules are driven round upon it for several hours; quicksilver is then added and afterwards lime. This mixture is allowed to rest for two or three months, then it is put into bags, and an amalgam of silver and mercury is obtained free from any foreign matter. The amalgam is enclosed in large earthern jars; at the mouth of which a gun barrel or iron tube is fixed, that leads to a vessel full of water for condensing the quicksilver. It is then heated, the mercury evaporates, and the silver remains. A great loss is caused by this rough process; 75 per cent. of the mercury employed disappears. The slowness of this process, the loss that it causes, the scarcity of labour, all these have greatly diminished the working of the Pasco mines, and Peru scarcely yields annually gold and silver to the value of six million piastres.—*Journal of Society of Arts,* Dec. 7.

PLANTS OF ANCIENT EGYPT.—Professor Unger, in a paper communicated to the Imperial Academy of Sciences at Vienna, shows that Egyptian bricks contain a variety of evidence, preserved, as it seems, in an imperishable form. He has examined a brick from the pyramid of Dashour, which dates from between 3400 and 3300 B.C., and found imbedded among the Nile mud or slime, chopped straw, and sand, of which it is composed, remains of vegetable and animal forms, and of the manufacturing arts, entirely unchanged. So perfectly, indeed, have they been preserved in the compact substance of the brick, that he experienced but little or no difficulty in identifying them. By this discovery Prof. Unger makes us acquainted with wild and cultivated plants which were growing in the pyramid-building days; with freshwater shells, fishes, remains of insects, and so forth, and a swarm of organic bodies, which, for the most part, are represented without alteration in Egypt at the present time. Besides two sorts of grain—wheat and barley—he found Teff (Eragrostis abyssinica), the Field Pea (Pisum arvense), the common Flax (Linum usitatissimum), the latter having, in all probability, been cultivated as an article of food, as well as for spinning. The weeds are of the familiar kinds—Wild Radish (Raphanus Raphanistrum), Corn Chrysanthemum (Chrysanthemum segetum), Wartwort (Euphorbia helioscopia), Nettle-leaved Goosefoot (Cheriopodium murale), Bearded Hare's-ear (Bupleurum aristatum), and the common Vetch (Vicia sativa). The relics of manufacturing art consist of fragments of burnt tiles, of pottery, and a small piece of twine, spun of flax and sheep's wool, significant of the advance which civilisation had made more than 5,000 years ago. The presence of the chopped straw confirms the account of brickmaking as given in Exodus and by Herodotus.—*Journal of Botany.*

LIGHT OF THE SUN.—Let me say something now of the *light* of the sun. The means we have of measuring the intensity of light are not nearly so exact as in the case of heat; but this at least we know, that the most intense lights we can produce artificially are as nothing compared *surface for surface* with the sun. The most brilliant and beautiful light which can be artificially produced is that of a ball of quicklime kept violently hot by a flame of mixed ignited oxygen and hydrogen gases playing on its surface. Such a ball, if brought near enough to appear of the same size as the sun does, can no more be looked at without hurt than the sun; but if it be held between the eye and the sun, and *both* so enfeebled by a dark glass as to allow of their being looked at together, it appears as a black spot on the sun, or as the black outline of the moon in an eclipse, seen thrown upon it. It has been ascertained by experiments, which I cannot now describe, that the brightness, the intrinsic splendour, of the surface of such a lime-ball is only 146th part of that of the sun's surface. That is to say, that the sun gives out as much light as 146 balls of quicklime *each the size of the sun*, and each heated *all over its surface* in the way I have described, which is the most intense heat we can raise, and in which platina melts like lead.—*Sir John Herschell's Familiar Lectures.*

THE MAPLE IN CANADA.—The tree which specially attracts the stranger's attention, from the beauty of its form as well as of its foliage—the maple tree—is also a source of wealth to the farmer, and every farm of any consequence has attached to it its "sugar-bush." My attention was first attracted to the maple tree by seeing a bucket attached to one of them about three feet from the ground; upon inquiry, I learned that it was for the purpose of catching the juice as it flowed from the tree, and from which a very excellent sugar is manufactured. The operations usually commence in the latter end of March, when the great cold has disappeared, and the sap commences to ascend the tree. A hole is bored about 1 in. in depth, with ¾-inch augur, some 3 ft. or 4 ft. from the ground, a little tin spout is put in, and a bucket suspended from a nail above receives the sap as it falls. The sap, when collected, is taken to the sugar-house and boiled down to a proper consistency, which is ascertained by taking a birch twig and twisting it together so as to leave a hole about the size of a shilling; this is dipped into the boiling sap, and if upon being taken up and blown through the sap will fly away in particles like feathers, the sugar is done; but should the sap, on the contrary, fall to the ground in a thick heavy substance, the boiling must be continued. When properly boiled, and allowed to get cold, it becomes crystallised, and is used for various household purposes. In its liquid state it has the appearance of molasses, and is used like honey. This season I heard one farmer made over 1,300 lb. of maple sugar, which was worth a York shilling (7½.) per lb. The whole operation is over about the middle or end of April, as the sap ceases to run when the buds begin to form.—*Land and Water*, Nov. 10th.

RAISING FERNS FROM SPORES.—Half fill a pot or pan with pieces of broken pots, and fill to the rim with peat two-thirds, and loam one-third, adding one-sixth of silver sand. Make the surface smooth and firm, and give a good watering. Whilst wet scatter the powder or spores of the Fern over the surface; or, holding a frond with ripe spore-cases over the pot, rub the hand against the back or under side of the frond, and the yellow or brown powder-like spores will settle upon the surface of the soil. Gently pat the surface with the hand and cover the pot with a bell-glass, its rim fitting exactly within the rim of the pot and resting on its soil. Place the pot in a saucer, and fill the latter with water, always keeping it full, and put all in a house with a temperature of from 60° to 65°, the house being shadowed from bright sun, or if not, a paper cap made to fit on the upper part of the glass, and put on during bright sun, will answer every purpose of shade. The surface of the soil must always be kept moist, and the glass should be kept on closely until the soil becomes green; then tilt the glass a little on one side by night, and increase the amount of air by day, and as the surface becomes more green. Continue the bell-glass over the pot until the plants have formed two or three fronds, and then gradually harden off and pot the seedlings when large enough to handle, keeping them moist and carefully shaded.—*Journal of Horticulture*, Nov. 24.

THE DIONŒA MUSCIPULA is originally from South America. Its leaves, which are spread out on the soil near the roots, are composed of two parts, the one elongated, which may be considered as a sort of petiole, the other, larger and broader, and nearly circular, formed like two trap-nets, which are united at the base by a nervure, fashioned like a hinge, and furnished round the edge with rough hairy cells in the upper surface, these plates are furnished with certain small glands, whence exudes a viscous liquid which attracts the insects. If a fly lights on this singular apparatus the trap raises itself quickly by means of its long hinge. They approach and it closes rapidly, crossing its long cilia, and the insect is a prisoner. The efforts of the fly to escape increases the irritability of the plant, whose fangs only open when the movements of the animal have ceased with its life.—*The Vegetable World by Louis Figuier.*

KEEPING POULTRY IN LONDON.—I know there are some people who say this is impossible, but I have done so for two years and wish to state my experience. Having formerly lived in the country, and having there been a poultry fancier, when I came to London I naturally had the desire to keep my old friends—fowls. Now, I have a garden which is about 120 feet long and 40 broad, and at the bottom of it I have put up a fowl-house, a good-sized court, in which I keep half a dozen hens and a cock. They have for about five months of the year the run of the garden, but are shut up in the court during the remaining months. In looking over my accounts I find I have suffered no pecuniary loss by them, for taking the eggs at London prices I find I have gained 2s. 6d. I have found out that one breed does not thrive in London, and so have adopted a cross between Dorkings and barndoor fowls.

The following is the number of eggs laid by the six hens in the year:—

January	24	August	80
February	70	September	3
March	47	October	0
April	62	November	3
May	94	December	16
June	65		
July	34	Total	448

Journal of Horticulture, Nov. 3.

ELECTRICAL FOGS.—Sudden changes sometimes take place in the electrical conditions of fogs. A remarkable instance of this is mentioned by Mr. Crosse. One day, while there was a dense driving fog from the south-west he repeatedly tested his atmospheric exploring wire without detecting any electricity. "But all at once," he says, "about four o'clock, I suddenly heard a very strong explosion between the receiving-ball and the ball connected with the atmospheric conductor, the two being an inch apart. Shortly the sparks became one uninterrupted stream of explosions, which died away, and then immediately recommenced with the opposite electricity. The stream of fire was too vivid to look at for any length of time, and the effect was most splendid, continuing for five hours, when it suddenly ceased. . . . The least contact with the conductor would have occasioned instant death, and in every acre of fog there was enough of accumulated electricity to have destroyed every animal within that acre."—*Land and Water*, Nov. 24.

THE FUCHSIA IN VALENTIA.—Friends who have lately visited me here (Valentia, South of Ireland) encouraged my conceit about the size of my fuchsias. I have just mentioned one plant of Riccartoni which was planted in the year 1854, on a sloping grass bank in my flower garden. It measures just 90 feet in circumference, taken round the extremities of the branches. It would certainly have measured 8 or 10 feet more if it had not been cut away, to prevent it from encroaching on a gravel walk. The garden slopes to the sea with an easterly aspect. The plant in question stands 10 or 12 yards from the edge of the sea bank. It is estimated to stand 16 or 18 feet high, but of this I cannot be positive. There never has been anything done for this fuchsia, either in the way of protection or of manuring, since the day it was planted. —*T. Fitzgerald, Knight of Kerry, in the "Journal of Agriculture."*

THE WATER BLACKBIRD.—There is a little bird inhabits the shores of the lake, and feeds at the bottom; the inhabitants call it Aderyn du cwr; in English, "water blackbird" (Turdus cinclus, Linn.; Cinclus aquaticus, Macg.) The feathers are jet black, except the breast, which is as white as snow. It is a trifle larger than a sparrow, and makes a similar noise. As I stood on the bridge that crossed over the Dee, looking at the waters rushing from the lake to the river (the Dee runs through the lake, and the inhabitants of the neighbourhood tried to persuade me that the waters do not mix, and they pointed out the rapid current in the middle), the bird flew from a bush and sat upon a stone, the top of which was just out of the water. I thought it had taken a very dangerous position, and must get washed off, but in a minute he walked off the stone into the water, and ran along on the bottom as if trying to commit suicide. I ran to the other side of the bridge to see him come under. He kept under water about half a minute, just coming to the surface and then dipping under again. He travelled with the stream, and would travel about twenty yards at a time. I watched this little creature for at least 150 yards down the river; its white breast made it visible such a distance.—*Gardeners' Mag.*, Nov. 24.

GREAT ALOE TREE.—To observe its character more closely I turned aside towards the largest tree, and to my astonishment saw that it was in reality a gigantic Aloe. Kneeling down so as to bring my arms low enough to embrace the solid trunk I found the circumference to be nearly twelve feet. Above this it divided into five stems, each of which about four feet higher was subdivided into four or five more, and from these arose branches nearly as thick as my arm, and of uniform size even to the very top, where each was crowned by the star of Aloe leaves, short, thick, tapering to a finely hardened point, and curving gracefully upward, and each surmounted by three or more magnificent spikes of yellow flowers showing with more than golden lustre above the fresh green of the succulent leaves. The stems were smooth, round, and externally of a light cream colour; upon the smaller branches, immediately below the leaves, thin annular flakes, easily detachable, marked, I suppose, the position of those that had been most lately shed, and near the base of the main trunk the bark seemed to burst and curl off as if very thin veneers of fine satin wood had warped off the foundation they were laid upon. The effect of this magnificent crown of leaves and flowers, more than fifteen feet from the ground and twenty in diameter, growing from sterile ridges of rough red rock, strewed with many coloured pebbles and quartz crystals in flashing back, like diamonds, the intense sunlight, was lovely in the extreme. —*Nature and Art*, Dec. (Accompanying the above is a beautiful Chromo-lithograph of the tree.)

THE LITTLE BITTERN.—On the continent of Europe the little bittern is a bird of passage, but the direction of its migrations has not been clearly made out; the accepted theory of migration would make it go northwards to breed in May, and southwards in August and September; but there is an absolute absence of observation to prove this to be the case. On the contrary, the theory of a lateral migration, from east to west in spring, and from west to east in autumn, seems to have some support from facts; but the bird appears to move only in the night, and on the continent of Europe to take the course of the great rivers. In May and September it is most abundant in Holland, and is of frequent occurrence in Central Germany. It is particularly abundant in the marshes of Essone, near Paris, in September, and it is said that if a gun be fired the whole valley re-echoes for many minutes with the cries both of the old and young birds. It occurs in the same locality in May; it stands on the tufts of carex and aira, waiting motionless for the appearance of its prey, which is said to consist entirely of small fishes. I cannot find a single record of its breeding in these marshes; it come no one knows whence, and returns no one knows whither. It therefore seems highly probable that some individuals during their migratory movements should be observed in the southern counties of England, both going to and returning from their breeding places.—*Field*, Nov. 17.

WHAT RIVERS ARE DOING.—What the sea is doing the rivers are helping it to do. Look at the sand-banks at the mouth of the Thames. What are they but the materials of our island carried out to sea by the stream? The Ganges carries away from the soil of India, and delivers into the sea, twice as much solid substance *weekly* as is contained in the Great Pyramid of Egypt. The Irawaddy sweeps off from Burmah 62 cubic feet of earth in every second of time on an average, and there are 86,400 seconds in every day, and 365 days in every year; and so on for the other rivers. What has become of all that great bed of chalk which once covered all the weald of Kent, and formed a continuous mass from Ramsgate and Dover to Beechy Head, running inland to Madamscourt Hill and Seven Oaks? All clean gone, and swept out into the bosom of the Atlantic, and there forming other chalk-beds. Now, Geology assures us, on the most conclusive and undeniable evidence, that ALL our present land, all our continents and islands, have been formed in this way out of the ruins of former ones. The old ones which existed at the beginning of things have all perished, and what we now stand upon has most assuredly been, at one time or other, perhaps many times, the bottom of the sea.—*Herschell's Familiar Lectures*.

MINERALS IN PLANTS.—So undetermined are the three great kingdoms of Nature, that animal existence cannot in many instances be altogether distinguished from vegetable nor vegetable from mineral. There is for examble a medicine very popular in the East named Tabasheer, which is extracted from the stems of the bamboo, and has been ascertained by analysis to be flint. In the same plants crystals have been discovered as hard as the diamond. Flint is contained also in the cuticle of straw, and on the leaves of the Deutzia it crystallizes in beautiful star-like points. Oxalate of lime is found in the roots of the garden rhubard and in all the species of Cactuses. Corallines and various marine lichens are in a manner petrified by the diffusion throughout their tissues of carbonite of lime, which on being dissolved out by means of acid leaves the vegetable texture of those orders clearly defined.—*The Key to the Universe.*

GRANITE.—Granite is the hardest of our native stones, and as a natural consequence, the most lasting. The Egyptian monuments formed of it, show no signs of decay after a lapse of three thousand years. The same cause has contributed in no small measure to the preservation of the old way-side crosses which so frequently meet the traveller in Cornwall. Should felspar, however, predominate, there is danger of its soon crumbling to pieces ; in fact, the more felspar the less durable is the block. If pyrites or iron occur in granite they disqualify it for building purposes, as they form centres of decay under the influence of weather. After it has been quarried for some time it becomes refractory to work ; and when intended to be used in the manufacture of ornamental objects, it is usual to keep it under water to soften it. The mode of extracting it from the quarry is by an iron bar tipped with steel, called a *jumper.* It is also split out in masses along the line of fracture by boring holes and inserting wedges. Owing to the demand for granite it becomes an important source of revenue to the districts formed of it. Thus the famous Peterhead quarries in Aberdeenshire give employment to some 500 workmen and 50 horses, and about 50,000 tons per annum are extracted. Although they had been worked for two centuries and a-half, much granite had never been quarried until 1741, when a large fire at Aberdeen elicited a municipal order that the fronts of the houses should be built of stone instead of wood, as hitherto.—*Once a Week,* Nov. 17.

TERRIER DOG.—A Staffordshire gentleman used to come twice a year to town on horseback, accompanied by his terrier ; but, for fear of losing it in the metropolis, he always left it in the care of his landlady, at St. Albans. Once, however, the house-dog of the inn and the terrier guest having a quarrel, the latter was so much overmatched that it was with difficulty he could crawl out of the yard, and for a week no one knew what was become of him. He then returned, and brought with him a larger dog than that by which he had been beaten ; when both of them fell on the former victor, and bit him most unmercifully, leaving him half dead. The terrier and his friend again disappeared ; and as all this happened while the gentleman was in London, when he called on his way home at St. Albans, he had the mortification to hear the above particulars, and gave up his dog for lost. On arriving at his home, however, he found his terrier safe ; and, on inquiry into the circumstances, was informed that he had returned upon his being first missed at St. Albans, and had coaxed away the great house-dog ; with which he proceeded to avenge the injuries he had received, and then came home in quiet with his companion.—*Notes and Queries.* Nov. 10th.

A LARGE VINE.—This vine, which is growing at Kinnell, in Perthshire, is described as being 36 years old, and fills a lean-to vinery, which is 89 feet long from east to west, and has a perpendicular front elevation of 5 ft., and a sloping roof of 18¼ ft., equal to about 229 superficial yards of glazed surface. It covers the whole house, and its stem before branching off is 6 feet long by 16 inches in circumference. It is in healthy vigorous growth, produces highly-coloured fruit of sufficient excellence to carry of first prizes, and has for the last four seasons borne an average crop of about 600 bunches.—*Gardeners' Chronicle,* Dec. 1.

HABITS OF THE HEDGEHOG.—Let me give you an instance of the agility and appetite of a hedgehog. On Monday last I saw a young one (the size of a rat) eating ravenously of the Indian corn that I had strewn for my pheasants in front of my house. After watching it eating for some time, I turned my poodle dog out to see what he thought of him. After a little time I brought him in again, and the hedgehog made away at a rapid pace. Within half an hour after that, and close by, I found him actively engaged in eating a young rat (about double the size of a large mouse.) I touched him with my stick, and at once he rolled himself up, but retained his hold of the rat. I took it from him, and felt that it was warm and just killed. I then threw it down beside him and left. Shortly after I returned, and found that he had eaten all but the tail and hind legs. Next morning there was not a vestige left. How did he succeed in catching so agile a thing as a young rat?—QUAIL.—*Field,* Nov. 10.

THE CAT.—The cat was worshipped in Egypt as a symbol of the moon, not only because more active at night, but from the priests conceiving that the contraction and dilitation of the eye afforded an emblem of the increase and decrease of the moon's ever-changing orb. In the British Museum may be seen several figures of the cat-headed Goddess Pasht, under which name the moon was worshipped by the Egyptians, Pasht signifying the face of the moon. Pasht is compounded of the consonants P, SH, T ; T is the Coptic feminine article, which, being omitted, the name is reduced to P,SH, but the aspirate SH, should be the tenuis S. and then the word would be P S, as in Hebrew, which may be pronounced "Pas" or "Pus" (Puss). It thus appears that our familiar name for the cat can boast of a very high antiquity.—*London Review,* Nov. 24.

PHOSPHORESCENCE OF THE SEA.—The cause of the phosphorescence of the sea has long occupied the sagacity of our savans. In the opinion of Dr. Yvan and others, it is caused solely by the molluscs swimming in the water, and more especially by microscopic molluscs. "Every time," says the doctor, in a new work, "I threw a net into the water, I withdrew it full of biphores, beroes, and medusæ. In one single drop I discovered myriads of small beings moving rapidly about, and at every contraction of these animalculæ the emission of light became more intense ; so that it may be supposed that their muscular movements develop certain electric properties of which the action is extremely visible. Besides, it is so with the larger ones. I had placed in a glass vase some gigantic biphores ; I saw them alternately rise and fall in the water, and all their movements were accompanied by a jet of fire, which increased the luminous intensity of the liquid fourfold."—*Queen,* Nov. 10.

ORANGE FLOWERS, A BRIDE'S DECORATION.—The orange blossom was adopted as an emblem of fruitfulness. Formerly this was considered a good quality in a wife, but one scarcely appreciated in these days. I have a note that the use of orange flowers at weddings is derived from the Saracens, amongst whom they were emblems of a prosperous marriage; and this is partly to be accounted for by the fact that orange trees in the east bear, I believe, ripe fruit and blossom, on the same tree at the same time.—*Notes and Queries*, Nov. 10.

RABBIT BREEDING.—Having read the different opinions of people as to whether tame rabbits would pay for breeding on a large scale, I can say, from great experience, that with good management they will pay much better than sheep; for instance, 800 breeding does, with their young, will consume upon an average about the same quantity of food during the year as 100 ewes and their lambs. The first outlay for purchase of stock: 100 ewes at 50s., £250; does, 800 at 2s. 6d., £100. The produce of the ewes during the year, say 100 lambs and wool, £250; the produce of the does at three months old would fetch in the London market during the same period at least £1000. I have now 150 does; stock, including young and old, about 1000. Any gentleman wishing to see them can do so. Address, "H. R., Post-office, Kingsclere, Hants."—H. BUCKERIDGE.—*Field*, Nov. 10.

AFRICAN ANTS.—The Scientific journal *Cosmos* has some remarks upon ants. This paper says it has often been asked what these insects are good for, especially the termites, which are the terror of the inhabitants of the tropical countries? On the strength of the testimony of a traveller recently returned from Western Africa, *Cosmos* says that the equatorial regions would be uninhabitable were it not for the ants, who are constantly engaged in clearing away all putrescible matter; their number is incalculable, and their voracity prodigious. The hives which they construct for themselves are, according to this West African traveller, far superior in appearance to the huts of the Liberian negroes, in an architectural point of view; they are built in the shape of a pyramid, and sometimes are as high as 30 feet.—*Cosmos*.

BANYAN TREE.—The famous Banyan Tree on the Herbuddah is said, by the late professor Forbes, to have 300 large and 3,000 smaller roots,—ærial roots as they are sometimes called. It is capable of sheltering 3,000 men, and thus forms one of the marvels of the vegetable world.—*The Vegetable World by Louis Figuier*.

GARNETS IN GRANITE.—In the Museum of Practical Geology, Jermyn Street, is a series of 293 specimens of granite and its constituents. The true rock is here seen passing into all its schoralceous and porphyritic varieties. Amongst other curiosities is part of a granite boulder from the bank of the St. Lawrence, containing numerous garnets, and a specimen of granite with black mica. The felspar is here seen in process of decomposition, passing into *kaolin*. It is superfluous to recommend every geological student to visit this superb collection.—*Once a Week*.

CAMEO SHELLS.—The several varieties of the so-called conch shells (species of cassis and strombus) with which the stores of the Bahamas Islands abound, form an important article of export, and their collection affords a useful means of employment to the maritime and littoral population. They are chiefly sent to France. In the last three or four years the collection was somewhat interfered with by the more stirring trade carried on from Nassau during the American civil war, and the quantity shipped was reduced to one-half. From 1855 to 1860 the average value of the shells exported was upwards of £2,600, but from 1861 to 1865 the annual average was below £1000.—*Queen*, Nov. 10.

SAFFRON.—Saffron was one of the perfumes most in favour with the Romans. They not only had their apartments and banqueting-halls strewed with this plant, but they also composed with it unguents and essences which were highly praised. Some of the latter were often made to flow in small streams at their entertainments, or to descend in odorous dews over the public from the *velarium* forming the roof of the amphitheatre. Lucan, in his "Pharsalia," describing how the blood runs out of the veins of a person bitten by a serpent, says that it spouts out in the same manner as the sweet-smelling essence of Saffron issues from the limbs of a statue.—*Rimmell's Book of Perfumes*.

HORSE CHESNUT.—The etymology is not a settled mattter, but if you are disposed to investigate it, no doubt you will find it amusing. The horse shoe and nails are to be found at the foot of the leaf-stalk when it has just fallen, or when it can be detached by a mere touch. Probably many stalks bearing the insignia may be found under any chesnut tree now, though a month ago they should have been looked for. The articulation of the leaf-stalk to the stem is in a horse-shoe form, and when the stalk parts from the stem the fanciful nails are quite conspicuous. The leaf-stalk of the Ailanthus glandulosus is articulated in a similar manner, and also exhibits similar resemblances to the horse shoe and nails.—*Gardeners' Magazine*, Nov. 24.

AGATE MOUNTAIN.—The Reese River (California) *Reveille* says that about three miles north of Ione there is an isolated mountain, some 500ft. high, which is called Agate Mountain. Its entire surface upon all sides, from summit to base, is covered with agates and concretions, and on digging into the soil they are found like potatoes in a hill. The agates are usually oval and sometimes globular in form, and varying from 1in. to 4in. in diameter, and are beautifully banded and striped.—*Mechanics' Magazine*, Dec. 17.

FALL OF THE LEAF.—Several independent observers, among whom Dr. Inman, of Liverpool, is one, have arrived at the conclusion that the fall of the leaf is due to the formation of a layer of cells, arranged in a plane different from that of the rest of the tissues, thus gradually severing the leaf from its support, much as a knife-blade would do, and moreover serving as a thin skin to protect the surface of what would otherwise be an open wound.—*Gardeners' Chronicle*, Nov. 24.

Remarks, Queries, &c.

(*Under this head we shall be happy to insert original Remarks, Queries, &c.*)

FLOWER GARDEN.—All bulbs that have not already been planted should be put in the ground at once. Tulips kept from frost, if possible. Auriculas cleared of dead leaves and kept moist, taking care not to give too much water. Hyacinths in borders should be protected by matting or litter. Pinks and pansies covered with litter, but not sufficient to deprive of light and air. Cuttings should be taken of chrysanthemums and put into thumb-pots; those that are struck should be shifted. Plants in greenhouse or pits should be carefully protected from frost and seldom watered. Hedges should be cut and trimmed, and mended with new plants if requisite. Box-edgings and gravel-walks should be attended to, and all contemplated alterations made.

KITCHEN GARDEN.—Sow early dwarf peas in rows a yard apart; earth up any that are forward enough. Plant out cabbage in vacant spaces a foot apart in rows, eighteen inches from row to row. Autumn sown broad beans should be protected, and more early kinds sown in beds for transplanting. Cauliflowers under glass must be protected by extra covering. If mild and dry, hoeing and earthing-up round the stems of winter crops should be attended to. Earth up celery, and if very frosty protect with litter. Rhubarb or seakale may be forced by covering with a pot and surrounding with hot dung. Prune all fruit trees left undone. Plant trees, if any are wanted. Cut away old raspberry canes, and reduce the new ones. Repair the fastening of all climbing plants if necessary.

SOME GOOD ROSES. — *Crimson*—Senateur Vaisse, Louise Carique, Adolphe Noblet, Eugene Beauharnais. *Pink*—Baronne Prevost. *Yellow, buff, and white*—Solfaterra, Triomphe de Rennes, Gloire de Dijon, and Souvenir de Malmaison. For planting against a house or verandah. *South aspect*—Solfaterra, Gloire de Dijon, Triomphe de Rennes, Celine Forestier, all shades of yellow. *East and west*—General Jacqueminot, Senateur Vaisse, Jules Margotten, and Charles Lefebre, all shades of crimson, *North and exposed situations*—Paxton, Baronne Prevost, and Louise Carique, two first pink, the latter crimson. The cost from a large grower is, 1s. to 1s 6d. a plant.

HARDY BEDDING PLANTS.—A correspondent in the *Gardener's Chronicle* suggests substituting the hardy herbaceous and alpine plants in the place of geraniums, calceolarias, &c., so much used at present. Amongst others he names the following as well adapted—Viola cornuta, Achillea aurea, Polemonium cœruleum varigatum, Dactylis glomerata variegata, Sempervivium californicum, the silvery Saxifragas Gnaphaliums, and Cerastiums the new Poa, variegated Daisies, dwarf Autennaria tomentosa Tritomas, Cliveden pansies, Anemone japonica, and Rudbeckia neumanni.

DURING January the following birds sing:—Redbreast, missel thrush, hedge sparrow, great titmouse, thrush, wren, skylark, woodlark, chaffinch; and the blackbird whistles.

ROOKS come back to their nests. The house-sparrow and white wagtail chirps. Earth worms lie out. Ivy casts its leaves. Jackdaws frequent churches. Gnats play about. Insects swarm. Slugs, bees, chaffinches, bats, nettle butterflies, and yellow wagtails appear. Larks and linnets congregate. Spiders shoot their web. Nuthatch is heard, and latter end of the month shell-snails appear.

THE following were noticed by White at Selborne to flower during the month:—Winter aconite, bear's-foot, polyanthus, double daisy, mezereon, pansy, red dead nettle, groundsel, hazel, hepatica, primrose, firze, wallflower, stock, black helibore, snowdrop, white dead nettle, trumpet honeysuckle, common creeping crow's-foot, dandelion, crocus, hazel, honeysuckle.

PLANTING CHURCHYARDS.—There has been some interesting correspondence in the *Gardener's Chronicle* during the past month about beautifying churchyards. A gentleman in the number for December 13th writes the following:—I beg to recommend for such places Cypress, Deodars, Irish Yew, Chinese Arborvitæ, Cedar of Lebanon, Weeping Ash, Weeping Willows, and variegated Hollies; and if trees which shed leaves are not objected to, Red Beech. For binding unsightly walls I would recommend Irish Ivy, and a still handsomer Ivy with broad and large polished leaves, called Hedera Rœgneriana. Cotoneaster, when in berry, is also good for the purpose and highly ornamental. The stoneless Barberry, so valuable for preserving, is likewise a very ornamental tree. I am likewise in favour of Roses, of which the following are strong growers and abundant bloomers, viz.:—*White*: Acidalie. *Yellow*: Gloire de Dijon. Triomphe de Rennes, and Céline Forestier. *Rose colour*: Anna Alexieff, Baronne Prevost, Souvenir de la Reine d'Angleterre, John Hopper, and Madame Clemence Joigneaux. *Salmon-rose*: W. Griffiths. *Silvery rose*: Cecile Chabrillant. *Dark crimson*: Charles Lefebvre, Duc de Cazes, and Vicomte Vigier. *Very dark crimson*: Prince Camille de Rohan and Empereur de Maroc. *Vermillion-red*: Duc de Rohan, and Maurice Bernardin. *Scarlet-crimson*: Senateur Vaisse. *Clear red*: Madame Louise Carique. *Purple-crimson*: Triomphe de Paris. *Blush*: Souvenir de la Malmaison. These are beautiful and very hardy. It is of no use to plant less hardy and less vigorous growers in exposed churchyards. They should be on the Manetti Stock. Briar Roses are unsightly objects.

GOOD STRAWBERRIES.—A correspondent of the *Journal of Horticulture* gives the following list of good strawberries for the market :—*For Early Crop.*—Princess William of Prussia is very early, a good bearer, but the fruit is rather small after the first picking, but it makes up for this by being about a fortnight earlier than any variety which we have. We grow this on the fruit borders for one-year croppers.—Alice Maud is our standard. General Havelock is a very good early variety, large, and hard ; to be grown in rows ; comes in about a week later than the last. We have a new kind called the Princess of Wales, which is earlier than Princess of Prussia I believe.—*Second Crop.*—Kitley's Goliath is an old standard variety, a good bearer and medium hard. Caroline Superba is a very good bearer, hard, and would be better with more colour. It will sell after the people know it. Sir Harry is a good bearer, and very large. It must be gathered before ripening when sent to a distance. Sir Charles Napier is very good but rather sharp. Myatt's Eliza is one of our best market strawberries. We sell it mostly for preserving. It is much better than Elton, of which we grow a few.—*Late Crop.*—Frogmore Late Pine is, as I have said before, everything that can be desired. Myatt's Eleanor is very good. It must have plenty of sun and air.

NOTICE.

All communications should be addressed to the Office of the "NATURALIST'S NOTE BOOK," No. 1, Racquet Court, Fleet Street.

The Annual Subscription is 5s. free by post.

The charge for Advertisements, which should be forwarded not later than the 20th of each month is ;

	£	s.	d.
Five lines	0	2	6
Every additional line	0	0	6
Column	2	2	0
Page	4	0	0

STATE OF THE WEATHER NEAR LONDON.

Nov. and Dec.	Moon's Age.	Barometer. Max.	Barometer. Min.	Temperature. Of the Air. Max	Min	Mean	Of the Earth 1 foot deep	2 feet deep	Wind	Rain.	Remarks.
Thurs. 15	☽	30.121	29.788	56	43	49.5	50	49	S.W.	.02	Slight frost early A. M.; uniformly overcast; slight rain.
Friday 16	9	29.441	29.313	57	27	42.0	50	49	S.W.	.00	Overcast; cloudy and boisterous; slight frost at night.
Satur. 17	10	30.237	30.072	49	22	35.5	50	49	S.W.	.00	Clear, quite cloudless, and very fine; Barometer very unsteady for a week past.
Sunday 18	11	29.835	29.793	52	30	41.0	48½	48	S.	.14	Partially overcast; cloudy; overcast; slight frost; rain.
Mon. 19	12	29.960	29.837	54	23	38.5	48	48	N.W.	.00	Rather boisterous; fine; very fine; clear; frosty at night.
Tues. 20	13	30.117	29.960	45	19	32.0	47	48	N.W.	.00	Clear and frosty; very fine; cold wind; sharp frost at night.
Wed. 21	14	30.119	30.041	48	24	36.0	46	46½	N.W.	.00	Fine, clear with bright sunshine; very fine; frosty.
Thurs. 22	○	30.160	30.095	46	37	41.5	45	45	S.W.	.04	Light clouds and fine; overcast; rain at night.
Friday 23	16	29.893	29.644	50	30	40.0	45	45	W.	.01	Overcast; lightly overcast; fine, slight shower at night.
Satur. 24	17	29.885	29.712	49	39	44.0	46	45	N.W.	.01	Fine throughout; overcast; slight rain at night.
Sunday 25	18	29.516	29.427	53	30	41.5	46	45	W.	.00	Fine; cloudy; fine at night.
Mon. 26	19	29.939	29.803	49	36	42.5	46	45½	N.W.	.01	Cloudy; clear and fine; overcast at night.
Tues. 27	20	30.035	29.848	50	23	36.5	46½	45½	N.W.	.00	Overcast; clear, with a few white clouds; very fine; frosty.
Wed. 28	21	30.233	30.164	47	24	35.5	45½	45	W.	.00	Hoar frost; clear; cloudless and very fine; foggy; frosty.
Thurs. 29	☾	30.214	30.158	51	26	38.5	44½	45	W.	.00	Foggy; clear and very fine; overcast at night; slight frost.
Friday 30	23	30.092	29.885	45	30	37.5	45	44½	S.E.	.00	Light hazy clouds; clear, very fine.
Satur. 1	24	29.789	29.730	36	31	33.5	43½	43½	E.	.20	Overcast; cold uniform haze; overcast; rain.
Sunday 2	25	29.798	29.747	50	25	37·5	43½	43½	S.W.	.08	Hazy, with slight drizzle; overcast; rain at night; frost.
Mon. 3	26	29.788	29.703	55	48	51.5	44	43	S.W.	.10	Overcast; rain; drizzly; rain.
Tues. 4	27	29.693	29.669	56	50	53.0	45	45	S.W.	.14	Rain; overcast and boisterous; much vapour driven by warm S.W. wind.
Wed. 5	28	29.799	29.745	56	44	50.0	45½	46	S.W.	.48	Densely clouded; rain; rather boisterous and wet throughout.
Thurs. 6	29	29.854	29.529	57	45	51.0	45	45½	W.	.16	Rain through the day; boisterous at night.
Friday 7	●	29.717	29.458	51	29	40.5	46	47	W.	.00	Uniformly overcast; boisterous and showery; fine at night; slight frost.
Satur. 8	1	30.429	30.136	49	20	34.5	44	47	N.W.	.00	Clear and very fine, with bright sun; frosty at night.
Sunday 9	2	30.355	29.904	55	31	43.0	43½	46½	S.	.06	Uniformly overcast; overcast; rain at night.
Mon. 10	3	30.128	29.495	53	24	38.5	44	45½	N.W.	.02	Partially overcast; very fine; fine at night; frosty.
Tues. 11	4	29.230	29.152	52	28	40.0	45	45	S.E.	.02	Foggy; hazy; rain at night; slight frost.
Wed. 12	5	29.813	29.451	56	44	50.0	44	45	S.W.	.00	Densely clouded; cloudy and windy; overcast; heavy rain at night.

ON THE EARTH'S MOTION.

THE earth rotates on its axis and revolves in its orbit; and this twofold motion secures to it those alternations of light and darkness, as well as that succession of seasons, without which, organised as we are, our very existence would be impossible. That this beautiful combination of motions is not due to accident is proved by the admirable harmony which prevails throughout creation; by the wonderful adaptation of means to the end proposed, which is everywhere perceptible; by the skilful balance of antagonistic forces, so as to establish a constant equilibrium; and by the production of good from seeming confusion and evil.

The relations between the earth and sun are such that they would scarcely admit of any modifications compatible with those forms of animal and vegetable life that are known to us. If the earth had been left in a state of rest, how different would have been its condition from that which exists at present! If it did not revolve on its axis, or if, like the moon with regard to the earth, it always presented very nearly the same surface to the sun, on account of its diurnal and annual revolutions being performed in the same time, there would be no distinction between day and night, the happy alternations of which are so well adapted to those successive periods of exertion and repose that are a necessity of our nature. Changes of temperature, winds, and tides, which are indispensable to the purification of the atmosphere and the waters, could not occur. Half the earth's surface would be shrouded in perpetual darkness, and consigned to eternal cold; and half of it would be exposed, from the endless duration of its day, to a temperature such as neither animals nor plants could endure.

Any spontaneous change in the axis of the earth's rotation would be fatal to us; but such a change is rendered impossible by its revolving on its shortest axis. This is a necessary consequence of the laws by which it has been decreed by Providence that matter should be governed. Being at first, most probably, in a gaseous state, the earth assumed the spherical form, on account of the attraction of gravitation; and the centrifugal force generated by its revolution changed it into an oblate spheroid—that is, a spherical body flattened at the extremities of its axis of rotation, and bulged out at its equator.

The mere diurnal rotation of the earth would not suffice to render it capable of maintaining organised beings on any considerable portion of it. The days and nights would remain constantly equal in length; the solar rays would fall too obliquely, and for too short a period during each day, on a large part of its surface. It has been made, therefore, to revolve round the sun in a plane which makes an angle with the plane of its equator. This simple arrangement produces the most important results; for to it is due the constant succession of the seasons, with all the advantages we derive from them. By means of it the sun, during its *apparent* annual revolution, is found alternately north and south of the equator. The days are longer than the nights in that hemisphere in which it is; and, as it rises to a greater height above the horizon than it would have done were it to remain constantly over the equator, its rays descend less obliquely, and therefore a larger amount of them fall upon a given surface of that hemisphere. Both the length of the day and the sun's altitude increase as the distance from the equator increases—that is, the sun becomes, in other respects, less powerful. But, when the day is longer, there is more time for the sun's rays to accumulate, and less for them to pass off by radiation. Since the temperature of a place depends very much on the duration of its exposure to the sun's rays, the increasing length of the summer day, as either pole is approached, makes up to a great extent for unfavourable position with reference to the sun; and hence the hot summers which are found even in very high latitudes. If the obliquity of the ecliptic, that is, the angle its plane makes with the plane of the equator, were less than it is, the seasons would not be sufficiently varied; if it were greater than it is, there would be extremes of temperature incompatible with organic life.

That the earth's orbit should be an ellipse, and not a circle, is a consequence of the general law of gravitation. It has been supposed that this ellipticity causes some modifications in the relative temperatures of the northern and southern hemispheres; and the more severe cold experienced in high southern than in high northern latitudes has been ascribed to the sun being nearer to the earth during the northern than the southern winter.

This difference of temperature is, however, fully accounted for in another way. The climate of any place depends, not only on the number of solar rays which it receives, but on the relative amount of land and water, on altitude above the sea, on proximity to the ocean, &c. It makes a great difference, if, as is the case in the southern hemisphere, the surface consists of water, into which the heat rays penetrate, instead of being, as in the northern hemisphere, chiefly land, which reflects the heat rays into the atmosphere, so as to raise its temperature.

The elliptical form of the earth's orbit produces in reality no effect on the seasons; for the supply of heat to any place depends not only on the amount imparted to it in a given time, but on the length of time during which it continues to be received. Now the time during which the sun shines on any place is modified by the velocity of the earth in that part of its orbit in which it happens to be; because, as the earth's distance from the sun increases, its angular velocity diminishes; and thus the time during which the heat is communicated is increased, the injurious effect of the sun's augmented distance being exactly counterbalanced by the diminished velocity with which it travels through a given distance, and the resulting greater length of time during which its rays are received. This is a consequence of one of the laws discovered by Kepler. According to this law " the spaces described by a line joining the centres of the sun and the earth or any other planet, are equal in equal times," no change being caused by any alteration in the planet's position in its orbit, the angular velocity being least when the distance from the sun is greatest, and *vice versâ*. The rays of the sun, intercepted by the earth, in equal times, no matter where it may be in its orbit, are therefore always equal in quantity.

But for this admirable compensation the difference between summer and winter would be greatly augmented in the southern and lessened in the northern hemisphere, since the earth's distance from the sun fluctuates to the extent of nearly the one-fifteenth of its entire amount. The direct impression of the solar heat is, however, in the height of summer, under a perfectly clear sky at noon, greater in a southern than in a corresponding northern latitude; and hence the sufferings of travellers in the thirsty deserts of Australia are greater than in those of Africa.

The earth is retained in its orbit by two forces one of which—centripetal—prevents it from flying off into infinite space; and the other—centrifugal, which was originally that of projection—prevents it from being precipitated upon the sun. And, just as the former of these, during the earth's revolution in its orbit, is increased by the earth's approximation to the sun, the latter, which is required to counteract it, is increased also. Each becomes predominant alternately, but neither retains its superiority long enough to produce an injurious effect. The very velocity with which the earth, in one part of its orbit, rushes towards the sun, generates a force which carries it away from that body; and the velocity with which it flies from the sun is gradually lessened by centripetal force, until at length the latter becomes sufficiently powerful to turn it back again towards that luminary. If the direction and amount of the force with which the earth was first projected, so as to cause it to revolve round the sun, had been such as to produce an elliptical orbit of great eccentricity—that is, a very long and narrow ellipse—the earth, during part of its revolution in such an orbit, would be so far from the sun as to derive but little benefit from it.

The rotation of the earth on its axis is necessary to produce alternations of day and night; and the revolution of the earth round the sun, in an orbit oblique to the equator, is required for the changes of the seasons. Were the variation of this orbit from the circular form not compensated by a change of velocity depending on the mutual action of the centripetal and centrifugal forces, or were the obliquity of the ecliptic either greater or less than it is, we should be subjected to extremes of temperature which, if not fatal to our existence, would greatly affect our comfort.

Thus, in these, as in all other circumstances connected with this earth and whatever it contains, not only our preservation, but our happiness has been carefully provided for.—*The Scientific Review*, January, 1867.

THE MEXICAN AGAVE.

The American Aloe (*Agave americana*) is a native chiefly of Mexico, but it is found in other parts of America. The precise date of its introduction into this country is not known, but it is recorded that one flowered in Lambeth in 1698. It grew to a height of from 12 to 15 feet, and was considered very choice and rare. The plant appears to have flowered in Paris in 1663, and at Leipsic in 1700. In 1729, and again in 1743, two plants flowered at Hampton Court, it still being considered a great rarity.

There is a popular notion regarding the agave that it flowers but once in a hundred years. The plants cannot be said to flower more than once during their life, but this flowering period may be at any age, and is influenced by the soil and position in which they grow. After flowering the plants die, but new ones are produced by suckers. Though the agave itself is of comparatively slow growth, the flower spike, which shoots up from the centre of the tuft of leaves, on the contrary, grows very rapidly, gaining a height of from 20 to 30 or even 40 feet, from the upper portion of which small branches are given off, which are crowded with the yellowish-green flowers. At the base these flower spikes are nearly as thick as the wrist; the longest one ever recorded was 40 feet, and grew in the King of Prussia's garden. The flower spike which runs to this great height is a very striking object, being of a remarkably straight growth, and remaining in flower for several weeks; it contrasts favourably with the great fleshy, rigid leaves, which apparently spring from the ground without any stem intervening; these leaves sometimes grow to a length of 6 feet, and remain perfect for many years. Interspersed through the fleshy substance of these leaves is a large quantity of strong fibre, much used for a great variety of useful purposes in all countries where the plant grows. It makes excellent twine and cord of any thickness, and is exceedingly strong and of a very clean appearance; the fibres themselves are very regular and even. Hammocks are constantly made of this twine, and very strong and durable articles they are. The fibre has also been imported into this country of late years under the name of Mexican fibre, and it is much used in the manufacture of nail brushes, scrubbing brushes, and similar articles. Humboldt speaks of a bridge in Quito over the Chimbo, the span of which was upwards of 130 feet, and the principal ropes, which were four inches in diameter, were made of this fibre. It is separated from the fleshy part of the leaves by bruising them, then macerating them in water, and afterwards beating them. This fibre has also been used for paper making. Important as is this product of the plant, the most valued of all is the sap, which, when fermented is known as pulque in Mexico, where it is much used as a beverage.

There are three or four species of agave, all of which yield a vinous sap, but *A. americana* is the most important; of this, however there seems to be many varieties, for in a very lengthy report received at the Foreign Office from the consul at Mexico, upon the cultivation and uses of the plant, he says that as many as ten varieties yield neither juice nor fibre, and are consequently of no other use but for making hedges; he then enumerates twenty other varieties, each yielding juice in greater or less abundance, or of different degrees of quality.

The introduction of the use of pulque into Mexico is said to have been "between the years 1045 and 1050, in the reign of the eighth king of the Taltec tribe, named Tepancaltzin, at whose court a relation of his, named Pepantzin, presented himself, and informed him that his daughter had discovered that a sweet and aromatic liquid sprung forth from the Metl plants in her garden. The king ordered her into his presence, and she brought him a 'Tecometl,' or vase of the liquid she had discovered, which he tasted and then ordered her to bring him more; and subsequently becoming enamoured of the maiden, whose beauty was great, and whose name was Xochil, or 'flower,' he married her; of which union a child was born, to whom was given the name of Meconetzin, or 'son of the Metl,' or Maguey, in allusion to the circumstance which was the origin of his parents' first interview.

"Whether the discovery of the use of the juice of the Maguey be really attributable to the god Izquiticatl, or to the queen Xochil, there is no doubt that the divers properties of the plant itself were known many years before the discovery of Mexico by the Spaniards, for not only is it mentioned as furnishing thorny scourges as well as whips made of the fibres of the plant's leaves, for the multitudes who annually met to celebrate a festival in honour of the good Texcatlipuca, in the great Temple of Tenochtitlau (the modern Mexico), but the use of the juice became so general that many severe laws against the drunkenness resulting from it were issued by the ancient Mexican kings, mention being made of a widow who sold it promiscuously having been put to death by order of the king Netzahualcoqatl; only women suckling infants, old people, and soldiers upon the march, being allowed to drink it.

"To the various uses to which the Maguey plant was turned by the ancient Mexicans, and which were so much commented upon by the writers of the period, may be added that of making of paper from the skin of the leaves, many curious old documents still existing of that material, as well as the manufacture of a kind of soap from the root. As to the extent of the lands appropriated to the culture of the plant, the writers in question give scanty information, but still sufficient to show that it was cultivated on an extensive scale in various districts of Mexico, where the vassals paid a great part of their tribute money in clothes and sandals made of 'ixtli,' or Maguey fibre, and it is worthy of observation that the districts in question were the most thickly populated of the ancient Mexican territory, which is stated, perhaps somewhat vaguely, by the old Spanish writers to have contained more than thirty million inhabitants."
—*Gardeners' Chron.*, Dec. 29.

THE GLACIAL OR NORTHERN DRIFT.

THIS is a layer of loose materials—gravel, clay, mud, pebbles, and angular stones, which is found spread at intervals all over Northern Europe, and is very common in the valleys and upland slopes of North Wales. It is very abundant all round the town of Dolgelly, where it forms undulating slopes, mounds, and hummocks in most of the valleys, filling up the space between the flat alluvial meadows on the river side and the steep rocky slopes of the adjacent mountains. Wherever this is cut through in making roads or railways, it is seen to be full of blocks of stone, pebbles, and large masses of rock distributed through it without any order or arrangement, the top, middle, and bottom being alike in composition. From the contour of the surrounding mountains, it can be often seen that this deposit is of great though very variable thickness, probably often exceeding a hundred feet, and it certainly covers many hundred square miles of country in North Wales alone. On ascending the mountains it is often found on their less precipitous slopes, and in the upland valleys at more than a thousand feet elevation, and it has even been traced around Snowdon, by Professor Ramsay, to a height of more than two thousand feet. The materials of which the drift is composed are various. Sometimes the rocks are nearly all those of surrounding mountains; at other times they are such as must have been brought from a great distance. The geological age of the drift is determined by its overlying all, even the most recent formations, and by its containing occasionally marine shells of an Arctic type, and of species which are all now living.

Here we have materials of a loose and miscellaneous nature, which were deposited *in* the sea, but not *by* the sea. That the drift was deposited in the sea is proved by the marine shells which have been found in it up to the height of 1,300 feet, on some mountains in Carnarvonshire; and we have thus a proof that North Wales, was, at a very recent epoch, sunk to at least that depth beneath the ocean. The presence of the drift itself, however, at a height of more than 2,000 feet would prove a much greater submergence. That the deposit could not have been made by the sea is shown by the want of arrangement of the materials, and the abundance of large angular fragments of rock. Water always sorts the materials it deposits. The rocks, the pebble, the shingle, the sand, the mud are carried different distances, and deposited in different places or in different layers. Water deposits are stratified. Neither can rocks be carried far by water and retain their angles and clean-fractured surfaces. They get rounded into boulders or pebbles, whereas many of the rocks and stones found in the drift are as sharp, angular, and irregular as the blocks and masses which are detached by the winter's frost, and lie under an inland precipice.

The solution of this curious problem of the origin of the drift is to be found in the history of glaciers and icebergs. When a valley is filled with ice the rocky *debris* from its slopes and precipices fall upon the surface of the glacier. A quantity of earth and stones of the bottom of the valley is also forced into the crevices, or frozen to the bottom of the icy mass. Now, when the ice-filled valley terminates in the sea, large fragments of the glacier break off and become icebergs, and floating away, carry with them their load of earth and rocks, which are, deposited where they melt, or topple over, or are stranded. In the North Atlantic, as far as icebergs float there must be an annual deposit of matter, on its bottom exactly of the same nature as the drift; while in Hudson's Bay and the gulf of St. Lawrence it must be accumulating still more rapidly. When North Wales was one or two thousand feet lower than at present, it must have formed a group of islands, among which icebergs would frequently become entangled, and deposit their loads of foreign matter. Bt the same time Snowdon and Cader Idris would have been sending down glaciers into the sea, which would spread the *debris* of their precipices and valley bottoms on what are now the upland slopes and low valleys, but which then were submerged banks and ocean straits. As the land rose above the sea to its present elevation, rivers, floods and glaciers would more or less furrow and clear away the drift from the valleys, and leave it distributed in the irregular manner in which we now find it. The mere presence, therefore, of this unstratified mass of earth, rocks, and boulders would of itself prove a recent glacial period, since it clearly indicates the existence of icebergs and glaciers in seas and countries where they are now never found.—*The Quarterly Journal of Science*, January. John Churchill.

COCKROACHES.

Of the "gentlemen of England who live at home at ease," very few, I suspect, would know a cockroach, although they found the animal in their soup—as I have done more than once. Cockroaches are of two principal kinds—the small, nearly an inch long; and the large, nearly two and a half inches. Let the reader fancy to himself a common horse-fly of our own country, half an inch in breadth, and of the length just stated, the body, ending in two forks, which project beyond the wings, the head, furnished with powerful mandibles, and two feelers, nearly four inches long, and the whole body of a dark-brown or gun-barrel colour, and he will have as good an idea as possible of the gigantic cockroach. The legs are of enormous size and strength, taking from fifteen to twenty ants to carry one away, and furnished with bristles, which pierce the skin in their passage over one's face; and this sensation, together with the horrid smell they emit, is generally sufficient to awaken a sleeper of moderate depth. On these legs the animal squats, walking with his elbows spread out like a practical agriculturist writing an amatory epistle to his lady-love, except when he raises the forepart of his body, which he does at times, in order the more conveniently to stare you in the face. He prefers walking at a slow and respectable pace; but if you threaten him by shaking your fist at him, or using opprobrious terms to him, it is very funny to see how quickly he takes the hint, and hurries off with all his might. What makes him seem more ridiculous is, that he does not appear to take into consideration the comparative length of your legs; he seems impressed with the idea that he can easily run away from you; indeed, I have no doubt he would do so from a greyhound. The creature is possessed of large eyes; and there is a funny expression of conscious guilt and impudence about his angular face which is very amusing; he knows very well that he lives under a ban—that, in fact, existence is a thing he has no business or lawful right with, and consequently he can never look you straight in the face, like an honest fly or moth. The eggs, which are nearly half an inch long, and about one-eighth in breadth, are rounded at the upper edge, and the two sides approach, wedge-like, to form the lower edge, which is sharp and serrated, for attachment to the substance on which they may chance to be deposited. These eggs are attached by one end to the body of the cockroach; and when fully formed, they are placed upon any material which the wisdom of the mother deems fit food for the youthful inmates. This may be either a dress-coat, a cocked-hat, a cork, a biscuit, or a book, in fact, anything softer than stone; and the egg is no sooner laid, than it begins to sink through the substance below it, by an eating or dissolving process, which is probably due to the agency of some free acid; thus, sailors very often (I may say invariably) have their finest uniform coats and dress-pants ornamented by numerous little holes, better adapted for purposes of ventilation than embellishment. The interior of the egg is transversely divided into numerous cells, each containing the larvæ of I know not how many infant cockroaches. The egg gives birth in a few weeks to a whole brood of triangular little beetles, which gradually increase till they attain the size of huge oval beetles, striped transversely black and brown, but as yet minus wings. These are usually considered a different species, and called the beetle-cockroach; but having a suspicion of the truth, I one day imprisoned one of these in a crystal tumbler, and by and by had the satisfaction of seeing, first the beetle break his own back, and secondly, a large winged cockroach scramble, with a little difficulty, through the wound, looking rather out of breath from the exertion. On first escaping he was perfectly white, but in a few hours got photographed down to his own humble brown colour. So much for the appearance of these gentry: now for their character, which may easily be summed up: they are cunning as the fox; greedy as the glutton; impudent as sin; cruel, treacherous, cowardly scoundrels; addicted to drinking; arrant thieves; and not only eat each other, but even devour with avidity their own legs, when they undergo accidental amputation. They are very fond of eating the toe-nails; so fond, indeed, as to render the nail-scissors of no value, and they also profess a penchant for the epidermis—if I may be allowed a professional expression—of the feet and legs; not that they object to the skin of any other part of the body, by no means; they attack the legs merely on a principle of easy come-at-ability.

In no way is their cunning better exhibited than in the cautious and wary manner in which they conduct their attack upon a sleeper. We will suppose you have turned in to your swinging cot, tucked in your toes, and left one arm uncovered to guard your face. By and by, first a few spies creep slowly up the bulkhead, and have a look at you; if your eyes are open, they slowly retire, trying to look as much at their ease as possible; but if you look round, they run off with such ridiculous haste, and awkward length of steps, as to warrant the assurance that they were up to no good. Pretend, however, to close your eyes, and soon after, one bolder than the rest, walks down the pillow, and stations himself at your cheek, in an attitude of silent and listening meditation. Here he stands for a few seconds, then cautiously lowering one feeder, he tickles your face: if you remain quiescent, the experiment is soon repeated; if you are still quiet, then you are supposed to be asleep, and the work of the night begins. The spy walks off in great haste, and soon returns with the working party. The hair is now searched for drops of oil; the ear is examined for wax; in sound sleepers, even the mouth undergoes scrutiny; and every exposed part is put under the operation of gentle skinning. Now is the time to start up, and batter the bulkheads with your slipper; you are sure of half an hour's good sport; but what then; the noise made by the brutes running off brings out the rest; and before you are aware, every crevice or corner vomits forth its thousands, and the bulkheads all around are covered with racing, chasing, fighting, squabbling cockroaches. So numerous, indeed, they are at times, that it would be no exaggeration to say that every square foot contains its dozen. If you are wise, you will let them alone, and go quietly and philosophically to bed, for you may kill hundreds, and hundreds more will come to the funeral feast. So the sailors say: "Let them sweat," and sweat they do, and the least said about *that* the better. Cockroaches are cannibals, practically and by profession. This can be proved in many ways. They eat the dead bodies of their slain comrades; and if any one of them gets sick or wounded, his companions, with a kindness and consideration which cannot be too highly appreciated, speedily put him out of pain, and, by way of reward for their own trouble, devour him. They have a decided relish for port wine. Seeing a large cockroach one day standing on the top of a bottle of wine, part of which had been recently used, engaged in sipping what still adhered about the mouth, I pinned him to the cork by means of a fine needle. At first he spun madly round and round on his pivot, but very soon tiring of this exercise, and no doubt giving himself up for lost, he seemed to think he could not do better than drown his misery in the wine-cup, and in fact die drunk. Accordingly, he recommenced the imbibition of the vinous fluid, as cooly as though nothing had occurred to interrupt his enjoyment. I was just thinking of extracting the needle, when another cockroach, who had no doubt observed his helpless condition, and determined to profit by it, crawled up, and attacked him in the rear. The other wheeled about, and stood on the defensive, and a very interesting and exciting fight took place; the attacking party endeavouring to get up behind, and the attacked wheeling round on the needle, in order to keep his front to the foe, and dealing the assailant such powerful blows as to keep him for the time effectually at bay. Round and round the bottle's mouth whirled the couple, fighting with such determination and spirit, that there seemed little likelihood of the fight coming to a speedy termination; and there is no knowing how the battle *would* have been decided, had not other two brave and warlike 'roaches, scenting the battle from afar, suddenly appeared on the field, and taking part against the unhappy wine-bibber. He was now simultaneously attacked in front and rear, and very soon his struggles were over. His wings were rent in ribbons; then one leg, then another, was torn off; and he was in a fair way to be eaten alive, had I not at that instant placed the bottle gently in a basin of water, and pouring a tumbler of the same fluid on them, and drowned the whole three, and thus ended the unequal and unnatural contest.—*Chambers's Journal*, Dec. 22.

METEORITES.

Stony or metallic masses are projected from a large class of luminous meteors, to which the term meteorites—including aërolites, siderolites, and siderites—has been applied. Of such bodies, a catalogue, contained in a recent work by P. A. Kesselmeyer, on the "Origin of Meteorites," supplies the dates and places of fall of between six and seven hundred individuals. The pamphlet, although singular in its object in attempting to uphold a theory of the terrestrial origin of meteorites, is yet a very valuable essay on the subject of the geographical distribution of meteorites. From the maps of the continents, upon which the place of each fall, up to the year 1860, is faithfully laid down, it appears that 130 stone-falls of the list, since the beginning of the last century, belong to Europe alone; a rate of sixty a year, if extended uniformly over the whole surface of the globe. This computation of the number of meteorites fallen in with by the earth is certainly far below the mark. Von Schreibers reckons the number at 800; and other writers at even a higher figure. *One meteorite in a day* is, therefore, not an exaggerated estimate.

The height of the fireballs from which they fall, and their speed, greatly resembles that of the November meteors. A striking example of this was recently presented by the luminous meteor, which scattered a shower of stones, on the evening of the 14th May, 1864, in the neighbourhood of the town of Orgueil, in the South of France. The fireball shot from a height of between thirty and sixty miles above the earth, to a height of ten or twelve miles above Nohic, near Orgueil, where it disappeared, with a speed rated at twelve to thirteen miles in a second. Humboldt termed aërolites "pocket planets," partly on account of their distinct petrological character, and partly because the speed of their arrival from a foreign locality, makes known that, like the planets, they roam in wide and spacious orbits around the sun.

Aërolites are fragments, evidently of larger rocks; generally heavier than granite, sometimes compact, like marble, or trap, resembling in structure trachitic porphyry; at other times possessing a loosely coherent, almost earthy, texture, with considerable varieties of mineralogical composition. They consist of a flinty-grey cement, or a breccia-like volcanic tufa, in which is imbedded a multitude of fragments of broken crystals, spherules, metallic iron in grains, and here and there a small nest or spangles of yellow iron pyrites. The usual grains of metallic iron are sometimes wanting in the aërolites of Juvenas and Stannern, whilst in the siderolite of Hainholtz they exceed the stony part in bulk; and the mass of meteoric iron which fell at Agram, in Croatia, on the 26th of May, 1751, was capable of being forged into nails, so entirely free from earthy admixture is the iron of which the siderite is composed. Pure siderites, or masses of meteoric iron, have rarely been seen to fall, but specimens of native iron, occasionally met with upon the surface of the earth, are evidently of meteoric origin, deposited there by meteors, the antiquity of whose fall is unknown. The metals nickel, chromium, cobalt, tin, copper, and lead, and others, have successively been discovered in meteoric masses. Carbon occurs in the form of graphite; and phosphorus and sulphur in combination with iron. Alkaline and the other earths, especially magnesia, form, with silica and iron, the flinty part of the structure, almost identical with certain volcanic lavas, but strikingly distinguished from all terrestrial scoriæ by the occurrence of iron, in meteorites, in the metallic state. So great is the heat to which their exterior surface is exposed, in the fireball that attends their passage through the air, that a thin black crust, or molten substance of the mineral, envelopes them completely; and they not unfrequently reach the ground so hot, that one which fell at Eichstadt, in Bavaria, on the 19th of February, 1785, was first cooled in snow before it could be handled.

The first chemical analyses of meteorites, by Edward Howard and the foreign chemists already named, at the beginning of the present century, which made known the existence of the metal nickel as a characteristic ingredient of meteoric iron and stones, and those of Berzelius, Wohler, and others, in later times, succeeding in establishing the fact that no elementary substances have hitherto been found in meteorites which are not already known to exist upon the earth. Whether this is true regarding the mode of their chemical combinations, is a matter not yet sufficiently ascertained. The meteorites of Orgueil, besides the usual inorganic constituents, contains six per cent. of a black amorphous organic substance, composed of the organic elements, carbon, hydrogen, and oxygen, in proportions quite similar to those in which they occur in lignite and peat; in other words, a veritable *humus*. M. Wohler infers from all the facts, that wherever meteorites originate, organic matter—and hence probably, also, organised matter—*organism* in fact—must have an existence. The various annals of science, and the journals and proceedings of philosophical societies, contain many such researches. Indeed, the literature respecting meteorites, constitutes already a branch of study by itself, which, under the name of "Aërolitics," has for its theme the splendid collections of meteorites at present to be found in the galleries of most of the great mineralogical museums. A work, entitled "An Index to Aërolitic Literature," has lately been published by Dr. Otto Buchner, by means of which the original accounts of meteorites may be consulted, and the facts are collected.—*Edinburgh Review, January,* 1867.

COLOURED RAIN.

THE first illustration which we shall quote is that memorable example of red rain known to have fallen at the Hague in the year 1670. It has been related by Swammerdam, that, early one morning in that year, the whole population was in an uproar. It was soon discovered that the commotion arose from a mysterious rain of blood, as it was considered by all. This rain must have fallen during the night hours, for the lakes and ditches were known to have been full of water on the preceding evening. People of all classes, high and low, were affected by this apparent miraculous act of Providence, foretelling scenes of approaching war and bloodshed. There happened, however, to be a certain physician in the town, whose scientific curiosity urged him to inquire into the cause of this wonderful phenomenon. He obtained some of the water from one of the canals, analysed it with a microscope, and found that it had not really changed colour, but that the blood-like red was produced by swarms of small red animals or insects, of perfect organization, and in full activity. This scientific physician immediately announced the result of his examination of the water; but though the Hollanders were convinced of the accuracy of his discovery, they did not appear to be anxious to divest the occurrence of its prophetic character. On the contrary, they concluded that the sudden appearance of such an innumerable host of red insects was as great a miracle as the raining of actual blood would have been; and, in after years, there were many who believed this phenomenon to have been a prediction of the war and desolation which Louis XIV. afterwards brought into that country.

It has been supposed that the insects alluded to above, and the cause of such a universal panic, were a kind of water-flea, with branched horns, called by Swammerdam *Pulices arborescentes*. How they became so suddenly multiplied has never been explained, except by the rational supposition that they were brought from a distance by the wind, and then deposited with the rain.

Something analogous to this came under the eye of the writer a few years ago. During a very gloomy rain which fell at Greenwich, a universal deposit of small black flies was found to have taken place. The plants and shrubs in the writer's garden were covered by hundreds of thousands of these insects, in some instances completely hiding the plant from view. Before the rain began not one was noticed. We have been lately informed that a similar deposit occurred at Cambridge about eleven years ago.

On the 14th March 1813, the inhabitants of Gerace, Calabria, perceived a terrific cloud advancing from the sea, the wind having blown from that direction during the two preceding days. At two o'clock in the afternoon this dense cloud, which gradually changed from a pale to a fiery red, totally intercepted the light of the sun.

Shortly after, the town was enveloped in a darkness sufficiently great to excite timid people, who rushed to the cathedral, thinking that the end of the world was approaching. The appearance of the heavens at this moment was unspeakably grand, the fiery red cloud increasing in intensity. Then, amid terrific peals of thunder, accompanied by vivid flashes of forked lightning, large drops of red rain fell, which were hastily assumed by the excited populace to be either drops of blood or fire. The rain more or less coloured, continued to fall until the evening, when the clouds dispersed, and the people were again restored to their ordinary tranquillity.

Some coloured rain, which fell under similar circumstances to the above, in another part of Italy, was subsequently analysed by M. Sementini, who found that the colouring matter consisted of light dust of a marked earthy taste. By the action of heat he discovered that this earthy deposit became brown, then black, and finally red. After being thus calcined, numerous small brilliant particles of yellow mica could be perceived by the naked eye. M. Sementini concluded from his analysis that the deposit was compounded principally of silica, alumina, lime, carbonic acid, and oxide of iron. A yellow resinous substance was also found to be a part of its composition. It is very probable that these, and similar specimens of coloured dust, were first emitted from an active volcano, and afterwards carried a considerable distance through the upper regions of the atmosphere, finally descending in the form of rain.

A coloured deposit, resembling brick-powder, took place in the valley of Oneglia, Piedmont, during the night of the 27th October, 1814. This powder covered the leaves of the trees, grass, etc. On the following day a very fine rain fell, which, on being evaporated, carried away the more soluble and less coloured particles. The remainder, accumulating in the cavities of the leaves, produced the startling appearance of blood-spots, and created the utmost consternation amongst the peasantry. The deposit was of a decided earthy flavour, and was supposed by M. Lavagna, a resident physician, to have been of volcanic origin, brought from the south by a high wind which had blown from the quarter during the night. The celebrated French philosopher M. Arago, referring to this phenomenon, has remarked, "Is not this an example of those pretended rains of blood which were always considered by the ancients to be such fatal omens?"

In an analysis of some coloured rain of this description, which fell in the Netherlands in 1819, it was discovered by MM. Meyer and Stoop, chemists of Bruges, that the colouring matter was principally chloride of cobalt. On another occasion, in Tuscany, a quantity of the coloured matter deposited on the leaves of plants was collected in the Botanical Garden at Siena, and subjected to analysis by Professor Giuli. It was found to be composed of some vegetable organism, in addition to carbonite of iron, manganese, carbonate, of lime, alumina, and silica. In a remarkable fall which occurred on the 19th February, 1841, in the district between Genoa and the Lago Maggiore, the earthy deposit consisted of talc, quartz, carbonate of lime, bituminous matter, and also some remains of the seeds of different plants.—*Edwin Dunkin, in Leisure Hour*, Jan. 5.

MEN, ANIMALS, AND PLANTS.

ARISTOTLE was one of the first to notice the resemblance between man and animals, but his remarks on this subject are of various value, but he wisely recognises the great importance of physiognomical observations. Some of his statements are most true, and all are interesting, as occurring to one who lived so long ago. He said that no man was entirely like a beast, although some of his features indicated occasionally a brutal character. He remarked that weak hair had cowardice, and strong hair courage. Thus the deer, the hare, and the sheep, which have soft hair, are less courageous than the ox, the boar, or the lion, which have coarse hair. Also, that birds having firm and rough feathers were in general more courageous than those with soft feathers. He applied the same principle to man. Thus, those men who have strong hair were courageous, and those who have weak hair were relatively wanting in courage. Animals distinguished for courage or nobleness have clear and sonorous voices, which they vent in a distinct, slow, and measured manner, while those with prattling voices are weak and mean-spirited. Aristotle's remarks on the character of the men who resemble animals are of less value. Porta, Haller, Versalius, Camper, Buffon, and Lavater—all have written on the resemblance between man and animals; but the remarks of some of these writers are very fanciful, and contain amongst the few embers of truth much that is best consumed. What Camper, Haller, and Lavater state from their own observation is, however, of great value. After having studied these subjects for some years, I was made acquainted with the researches of these great writers, and was much pleased to find that in many cases my observations were confirmed, which is doubly valuable as the confirmation of impartial authorities.

The resemblance and difference between man and animals has always appeared to me to be a subject of vast importance, for by its just appreciation the position of man in the scale of being is defined. Extended researches into every branch of science have convinced me that man is the "Microcosm," the epitome of creation. The axis of creation turns on man; for nature in her lowest, as in her highest forms, affords illustrations of man, both as a being and as an individual. He who understands this but interprets the universal language of nature. But there are various ways in which man illustrates lower forms of life. The first, and most extensive, is by analogy; the second, or more confined, is by the actual resemblance which creatures bear to the head of the animal creation.

"Like master like man" is an old proverb, this should be like master like dog, horse, or pig, for animals through the influence of sympathy—true "animal magnetism," acquire the qualities to a certain limited extent—of the men they are with; but I shall in this paper confine myself principally to the actual resemblance that some animals bear to man. Had I space, it would be easy to point to the marvellous way in which animals and plants by analogy illustrate man; and how, even the inorganic world in its varied elementary system, points to the qualities of his mind, and how the races of man by their geographical distribution harmonise with the qualities and peculiarities of their various habitats, and how the history of man is typified in that of the earth with its rocks and fossils, which are but the antitypes of great deeds, and of their producers—heroes.

In plants, the lower division of organisms, we see many types of man—I could name hundreds, but shall at present only mention a few, whose appearance and qualities remind us of his. Red apples have mostly a sharp flavour, as have red currants, berberries, and many other red fruits. Black fruits have an intensely strong flavour, as black currants, black grapes, and black elderberries. Very light coloured fruits, as white-heart cherries, white currants, and light coloured plums, have a more delicate flavour than the red or black of the same family. White strawberries have much less taste than the red, as have light coloured gooseberries. Yellow fruits are commonly sweet and luscious, with less flavour than red or black; as for instance yellow gooseberries, yellow plums, and yellow apricots—for the best flavoured apricots are streaked with carmine. The sweet, rich, and sustaining grain is golden, as is the basis of our nation's credit. These various colours point to the various qualities of the fruits of the earth; they are not less significant of those of the sons of Adam. Red haired races are fiery, impetuous, and have strongly marked qualities, as in red skinned peoples. The black-haired have even a greater extreme of qualities, but are less susceptible of improvement than the yellow and lighter brown. Black skinned races likewise have intense peculiarities, and their types are usually extremely permanent; how difficult it is for instance, to eradicate the traces of negro blood; one drop of ink will discolour a glass of clear water.

The Scandinavian, the most precious race on earth, has often golden hair; sweetness and equanimity of temper is more commonly found amongst them than in other divisions of mankind. The different combinations of colour in fruits point not merely to a union of various qualities, but typify similar combinations in men. Thus the yellow and red apples, mangoes, tomatoes, and the woody nightshade, are both sweet and sour, or have other divers qualities. Similar remarks may be made with regard to streaked gooseberries, variegated strawberries, melons, and a vast variety of other fruits, which have their prototypes amongst men with yellow hair and dark skins, black hair and fair skins, or dark hair with bright complexions. Fruits which longest retain their good qualities are seldom black or red; and dark and red-haired races have generally less evenly-balanced frames, and consequently do not live so long as those of more mixed colours.

Lastly, those fruits which show great paleness of colour and a want of flavour have analogy with albinos, or those who, from extreme fairness, have a bleached appearance. Such are generally characterized by a want of vigour.—*Land and Water*, Dec. 22.

LIGHTNING FIGURES.

It is related that Benjamin Franklin was often heard to speak of a man who was standing near a tree when it was struck by lightning, and that an exact representation of the tree was afterwards found on the man's breast. We have not been able to find this statement in any of Franklin's printed works, but similar statements are made in the newspapers every year. Thus we read that in August, 1853, a little girl was standing at a window before which was a young maple tree, and a complete image of the tree was found impressed on her body after a flash of lightning. Again—a boy climbed a tree to steal a bird's nest; the tree was struck by lightning, and the boy thrown to the ground. "On his breast the image of the tree, with the bird and nest on one of its branches, appeared very plainly." An Italian lady of Lugano was sitting near a window during a thunderstorm, and had the portrait of a flower permanently impressed upon her leg. A case is recorded in which some sheep were killed by lightning. The animals were skinned, and the fellmonger found "a very accurate representation of the tree and a portion of the surrounding scenery on the inner surface of each skin." During the year 1866, two such cases have been reported.

A few years ago a scientific man, M. Poey, attempted to prove that these curious figures were really photographed by the lightning; that the surface of the human body might, in fact, be so sensitive to the intense light of the discharge, that a picture of a tree might be impressed on the body of a person standing near it. M. Poey forgot to explain how a reduced image of the tree is formed, or what performed the office of the lens which in photography converges the rays of light which proceed from the object, so as to formed a small optical image on the sensitive plate. As long back as 1786 a report was made to the Academy of Sciences of Paris, on some tree-like figures found on the body of a man who had been killed by lightning. These marks were accounted for on the supposition, that the lightning, in passing through the body, had forced the blood into the vessels of the skin, so as to make all their minute ramifications visible on the surface. We read in the *Lancet*, July 30th, 1864, that some boys had been struck by lightning, and the medical man who reports the case says of one of them, "The figures on either hip were so exceedingly alike, and so striking, that an observer could not but be impressed with the idea that they were formed in obedience to some prevailing law."

Our knowledge of these occurrences is chiefly derived from the remarks, not of trained observers but of ordinary bystanders, who, seeing a tree-like figure on the body of the person struck by lightning, naturally associate it with the tree. To make their narration more surprising, they call the image "a true picture," or "an exact representation of the tree." A blur in the image will pass for the bird's nest; another blur for the bird, and so on. Nothing is more difficult than to observe and report a fact correctly, especially when the theory which apparently explains the fact is already in circulation. It is popularly admitted that lightning has this wonderful property of imprinting a copy of a tree on the body; and when a ramified figure is seen on the skin, an unskilled observer concludes that it is a copy of the tree; and if the figure have a number of small branches, he will declare the copy to have all the minute details of a photograph, as indeed was said in a case reported in the *Times* of the 8th of September, 1866. The true explanation was given in a paper read by Mr. Tomlinson before the British Association, in 1861, by whom it was shown that common electricity, in passing between two conducting surfaces, actually forms a tree-like figure, which can be made visible.

* * * * * * * *

In imitating these effects with electrical apparatus, a Leyden jar may be conveniently used, in which electricity has been accumulated by the usual process. If the jar be discharged by means of a bent wire, with a knob at each end and a glass handle in the middle (called a discharging rod), the two electricities will rush together without passing through the body of the operator, and there will be a dazzling spark of light, and a loud crackling noise—the one representing the lightning, the other the thunder. If we hold, between the upper knob of the discharging rod and the knob of the Leyden jar, a piece of window glass about four inches square, the discharge will pass over the glass, turn round the edge, and so get to the conducting knob of the discharging rod. On holding the pane of glass up to the light nothing is seen, but on breathing on the glass a remarkable tree-like figure becomes developed; consisting of a trunk, and a number of branches and twigs, the manner of producing which may be thus explained. All objects exposed to the air become covered with an invisible organic film, which no dusting or ordinary cleaning will remove. Wherever this electricity touches this film it burns it away, and leaves the glass chemically clean; so that, on breathing on the surface, the breath condenses in continuous streams wherever the electricity has been; while in other parts of the plate, where the film still remains, the moisture condenses in minute globules or dew.

The electric figures consist of a main trunk of a somewhat rippled character, representing the line of least resistance along which the principal discharge travels. This trunk is evidently hollow, and reminds one of those lightning-tubes sometimes found in sandy districts, formed by the lightning striking the ground, penetrating it, and fusing the sand into a tube, twenty, thirty, or forty feet long. These tubes are called fulgurites, and specimens may be seen in the British Museum. They are often branched, showing that the lightning divided, or *bi-furcated*, as it is called, and when there are three branches, *tri-furcated*. This is exactly what sometimes takes place when a building is struck. The discharge may fall at the same moment on two or even three parts of the building, or it may strike the building and then divide into two or three branches. In like manner the figures on our glass plates sometimes give admirable examples of bifurcation and trifurcation. But whether each trunk be single or divided, it is accompanied by a number of smaller branches.

It is a remarkable circumstance, that in

the formation of this tree-like figure, the trunk is not the first to be produced. The electricity sends out feelers, which find out, as it were, and prepare the line of least resistance, along which the principal discharge can most readily take its way. It is a common observation among sailors, that before a ship is struck they experience a tickling sensation, as if spiders' webs were being drawn over the face. This is exactly what takes place if a glass tube be rubbed with a dry silk handkerchief, and moved up and down before the face. A similar sensation is felt by some persons if an electrical machine be worked in the room where they are sitting. We have proof in our glass plates that the branches and spray precede the main discharge; for if the glass be so thick as to oppose too much resistance, the jar is not discharged; but upon breathing upon the glass plate we get the spray, and some of the smaller branches of the figure, but not the trunk.

A singular confirmation of Mr. Tomlinson's theory may be found in the fact that when a tree is struck by lightning, and portions of the bark are torn off, the passage of the discharge may be sometimes traced by ramified lightning figures impressed on the inner surface of the bark. Dr. Pooley has communicated to the writer such a case, which occurred in 1857, at Oakley Park, near Cirencester. The lightning first fell on a branch north-west of the tree, which it barked, and shivered to pieces; it also passed through the fork of the tree, and descending the south-west side, cut a clear line, about one inch and a half in width, out of the bark, and loosened other portions of the bark to the extent of one foot and a half on each side. The seam gradually widened as it reached the knotty roots. The chief lines of the figure were gouged out, roughened, and slightly charred at the edges; but such figures whether on the bodies of men or on the bark of trees, are not very permanent. They fade in a few days, or even hours.—*People's Magazine, Jan. 19th.*

WEATHER SIGNS.

CHANGES of weather may be foreseen, often by long intervals, by other aids far more efficacious than those of the moon, or of weather cycles; a moon's changes' rivalry even may be established with the meteorologists of Whitehall. The apparatus required may, with the exception of a barometer and the clouds, be all found in the animal kingdom, a careful observation of the habits of some of the denizens of which is the sure road to successful weather wisdom. There seems to be a sensibility to atmospheric change in the lower orders of creation which answers them as instincts, and directly gives them information which man only arrives at by the longer road of reason. The scent of the hound is an instance of a delicate sense, which we cannot form an idea of, though it may help us to conceive the possibility of "pigs seeing the wind," or of horses and cattle "sniffing a distant storm." A sow carrying straw in her mouth to make her bed is as sure an indication of coming foul weather as any the barometer can give; and when puss turns her tail to the fire, and in that position commences to wash her face, it is said the same event is predicted. It is as true of the skies as of domestic affairs, that when the hen crows a change for the worse is at hand; and, as to the lord of the poultry yard, we have the old saying, that—

"If the cock crows going to bed,
He'll surely rise with a watery head."

Robin Redbreast singing in the midst of rain on the top twig of a tree is an infallible index of a beneficial change to fair for a few days at least; and the screech of the owl under similar circumstances is said to have the same meaning, though the peacock's screech at all times denotes ungenial weather. Frogs also furnish their signs, becoming brown on the approach of rain, but remaining yellow so long as it is absent. There is a curious weather-glass made in Germany, the materials entering into the composition of which are two frogs, two small ladders, and a cylindrical vessel of water. Frogs and ladders being duly put into the water, if the froggies climb their ladders and look over the vessel's side, foul days are at hand; if they remain below, the sky will continue fine. Leeches in water furnish similar indications; but spiders and snails are the most remarkable of all the weather prophets. When the former make their webs at night, the morning is sure to be fine; if they make them in the morning, the coming day may be relied on for a drive or walk. Hence the saying:—

"When you see the gossamer flying,
Be you sure the air is drying."

An instance is on record of a French officer, confined in a prison in Utrecht during the wars of the French revolution, having so closely and accurately observed the habits of some spiders that were his sole companions, that he was able by their movements, to foretell a frost fourteen days before it came, and thereby turn the certain defeat of the French army into a glorious victory. But snails are remarkable weather indicators. Like frogs, their colours change on the approach of rain, and some species indicate rain so much as ten days before by tubercles, which appear on their bodies, and seem intended for the purpose of imbibing the approaching moisture. As a general rule these creatures, according to their habits, two or three days before rain, may be seen climbing the trunks of trees, or seeking shelter under leaves, or making their way to open places. We thus see that by a careful assortment of spiders, snails, frogs, and leeches, and a few domestic animals, combined with a good barometer, and accurate observation of the language of the clouds, and the song and cries of birds, any person may easily become a weather prophet of no mean practical wisdom.—*London Review*, Dec.

THE ARTESIAN WELL OF GRENELLE AT PARIS.

THESE wells were first known in Europe in the province of Artois, in France, from whence they take their name. Centuries before they were prevalent among what is called civilized nations, the "barbarian" Chinese knew their value, and they have been in use in China from a date beyond record. It is said that ten thousand of them may be found in one Chinese province; this is probably an exaggeration.

The principle of these artesian wells is the same as that of a fountain. *Everywhere water finds its own level.* Supposing the spring takes its rise in a mountain, it penetrates through sand or porous earth to a great depth into the valley below, and which is situate, perhaps, miles from the source of the spring. By boring into the valley to the depth of the water, the latter rises of its own impetus to as high as the mountain stream from whence it sprung. Below this sand and porous earth there is sometimes a bed of clay to be perforated to the underlying chalk. This was the case with the Artesian well at Grenelle. Upwards of 194 feet had to be bored below the spot where it was said water would be found.

The statistics given of this well are very interesting. It was commenced in 1833, and completed in 1841. The borer weighed 20,000lbs., and was three times the length of the height of the Hôpital des Invalides in Paris. When the boring had been successfully performed to within 548 feet of its completion, the great chisel attached to the borer fell, with 262 feet of rods, to the bottom, the whole of this fallen mass weighed five tons. The engineer, M. Mulot, nothing daunted, put a screw on the end of the fallen rods; attached others of sufficient length to them, and, after fifteen months of labour, drew up the chisel. At another time, to give impetus, the chisel was raised with great force, and sunk at one stroke, into eighty-five feet of chalk. The depth of the Grenelle well is four-and-a-half times the height of St. Paul's, and nine times that of the monument in London. If Strasburg Cathedral, the Hôpital des Invalides in Paris, St. Peter's at Rome, St. Paul's and the Monument in London, were piled one upon the other, they would not be so high as the well of Grenelle is deep by more than eleven feet. Astoundingly deep as this is, there is an Artesian well in the Duchy of Luxembourg which is upwards of 1,000 feet deeper than that of Grenelle.

The water of the Grenelle has its source in a stratum of sand, which lies considerably higher than the level of Paris, but it had to be bored for, first beneath the clay, and into the chalk which forms the subsoil on which Paris stands. The peculiarity of this water is that it is not *aërated*, and being consequently unfit for drinking, a tower had to be constructed, in the centre pipe of which the water is forced up, and descends on the outside in innumerable threads, so as to expose as much of its surface as possible to the air.—*Ladies Treasury*, January.

LEAVES AND BARK.

LEAVES.—When the leaves have accomplished their physiological functions, they fall, even in the year which witnessed their birth. But there are some which are not detached till the following year, while others remain for many years attached to the stem. The leaves of most of the conifers, those of the box (*Buxus*), the holly (*Ilex*), of the orange-trees (*Citrus*), do not shed them in the year in which they are developed, but are met by a continual growth of new leaves. These plants are never seen naked; they constitute the plants commonly known as evergreens. In the first of these states the plant is said to be deciduous, from *de*, down, and *cado*, I fall, when the leaves fall before the next spring. They are marcescent from *marcesco*, withering, when they wither before falling, as in the oak and beech. They are persistent, from *persistens*, remaining, standing, when they remain longer than a year.

In some plants, as the cactus, the leaves are shed almost as soon as they appear. These are said to be *caducans*, from *Cado*, I fall. The leaf thus dies, like all created beings, when the purpose for which it was created is accomplished. The immediate cause of death seems to be this: the cells of which it is composed have become encrusted with foreign matter, deposited during the processes of digestion and evaporation carried on by the organ, which then becomes incapable of further action.

On the subject of the distribution of evergreen trees, August de St. Hilaire makes the following remarks:—" As we retire from the tropics, the number of evergreen trees goes on diminishing in rapid succession. At Porto Allegra, near latitude 30 deg. south, I found in the coldest season that the trees nearly all changed their leaves. At San Francisco de Paula, near the Rio Grande, in 34 deg., nearly one-third of the ligneous vegetation had lost their leaves; and finally, at two degrees further south, a tenth of the trees only preserved their foliage. At Montpellier, the fields in winter are not yet deprived of verdure; and Lisbon, Madeira, and Teneriffe present a still more considerable number of trees always green. It must not be supposed, however, that in the tropics all the trees are evergreens. Even in the vast forests which occupy the Brazilian coast, and where vegetation is maintained in continual activity by its two principal agents, heat and moisture, there exist trees, such as some of the Bignoniaceæ, which lose every year, like European trees, all their leaves at once, but immediately after, they are covered with flowers, and in a very short time these are succeeded by new foliage. I speak here of woods growing in equinoctial regions, where, as with us, rain and drought have no determinate period. In countries, on the other hand, where six months' continual rain is succeeded by uninterrupted dry weather, there are woods which every year remain for a considerable time destitute of verdure, and the traveller who traverses them is scorched by the ardent blaze of the equinoctial zone, while he has before his eyes the leafless image of European forests during winter. We have even seen this excessive drought continue during two years, and the trees remain for two years without their foliage."

BARK.—The *bark* of trees is essentially composed of fibrous and cellular tissue; but it is easy to understand how varied are the forms, disposition, and structure of these substances, when we consider the extraordinary variety in the appearance of the bark of trees, and the diversity of their products. To explain everything which relates to the structure of the bark, would lead us into details which our space does not admit. We must therefore limit our remarks, and content ourselves with pointing out the principal characteristics of bark. Briefly, the young stem is invariably covered with a thin cuticle, the *epidermis*. As the stem increases, new bundles of woody fibres are deposited in regular annular layers one in each year, the new layers being deposited outside those already formed. The new layers of bark and wood are thus formed almost in contact. The epidermis covers the bark, as it does every other part of the vegetable, but its existence is altogether ephemeral. It is destroyed at an early stage as much by the growth of the vegetable as by the action of external agents. It is otherwise with the *suber*, which forms the next layer, the cells of which are of a cubical form, and are closely united to each other with thin walls or partitions, without colour at first, but afterwards they acquire a brownish hue.

In many trees the *suber* is very slightly developed. But this is not the case with the Cork-oak (*Quercus suber*). In this beautiful tree, which furnishes man with one of his most useful commercial products, the *suberous layer* acquires an extraordinary thickness; it is, in short, the substance known as cork, in Latan *suber*, whence the specific name of the tree. When about five years old the *suber*, which constitutes the greater part of the bark in the cork-tree, begins to make a remarkably quick growth; then all the energy of its vegetation seems to concentrate itself on this part of the tree. New cells appear on the internal face of the primitive zone, pressing upon the exterior cells which preceded them. Independently of these cells, the successive accumulation of which constitute the mass of cork, others are formed which are shorter, darker in colour, of a flat or plate-like form, which divide the mass of cork into successive zones of growth. This mass attains by degrees to a considerable thickness. If left to itself, it would crack so deeply as to become unfit for the uses to which cork is applied. It is necessary, therefore, to strip it off before it acquires this hard and fissured appearance.—*Louis Figuier's Vegetable World*.

ELEPHANTS.

Having related the modes of capturing elephants practised in India in the present day, perhaps my readers may not be unwilling to compare them with the ancient methods of taking these huge animals; and the following account, taken from Arian's book on India, will doubtless prove interesting. Arian was a Greek writer, and lived in the second century of our era. He derived his information chiefly from memoirs left by Alexander's generals, and from other Greeks who visited India about the period of its invasion by this great monarch. "The Indians hunt other wild animals, just as the Greeks do; but their mode of taking the elephant is quite peculiar, as indeed, the animal itself resembles no other. Having picked out a level piece of ground open to the sun, they enclose by a ditch a circular space large enough for the encampment of a considerable army. The width of the ditch is about thirty feet, and the depth about twenty-four. The earth that is dug out is heaped up on each margin of the ditch, and serves as a wall. In the exterior wall thus formed, they make excavations which serve as hiding-places, from which, through certain holes that are left for supplying light, they watch the elephants as they approach and enter the enclosure. Then, having placed three or four very tame female elephants within the enclosure, they leave one entrance, which is made by bridging over a part of the ditch; and, that the elephants may not have any suspicions, they throw a quantity of earth and grass on the bridge, to prevent the animals from seeing what it really is. Having done this, the hunters hide themselves in their holes. Now the wild elephants never come near inhabited spots in the daytime, but when it is night they ramble about in all directions, and feed in herds, following as a leader the largest and boldest of their company, just as cows follow the bulls. When the elephants have come near the enclosure, they discover the females, both by their noise and smell, and, hastening towards the spot, they run round the ditch till they find the bridge, over which they all try to push into the enclosure. The huntsmen, on seeing the elephants within the ditch, quickly take the bridge down, while others of the party run to the neighbouring villages to let the people know that the elephants are caught. A large party now mount all their strongest tame elephants, and ride straight to the enclosure, where they wait till the wild elephants are much weakened from want of food and water. When the hunters think the elephants are thus sufficiently subdued, they set up the bridge again, and the tame elephants, entering the place, commence a fierce contest with the wild ones, which naturally terminates in favour of the tame animals, as their opponents are quite exhausted by what they have suffered. The riders now, getting down from their elephants, tie the feet of the wild ones while they are in this helpless state, and then urge the tame animals to beat them till they fall down. The next process is to put ropes round their necks and mount them as they lie on the ground. To prevent the elephants, however, from throwing off their riders, or doing any other mischief, they make an incision with a sharp knife in the skin of the neck all round, and fit the rope into it, that the pain from the sore may make the animals keep their heads steady. The elephants being thus compelled to remain quite, and feeling that they are subdued, are led by a rope, which is attached to the tame ones.—*Land and Water*, Dec. 22.

GRANITE.

I have been much struck by the numerous instances, in the Highlands of Scotland, in which pieces of hornblende, having the shape of water-worn pebbles, are found in granite. Autumn tourists will find a flattened specimen in the first pier of the wall of Lord Seaforth's park-wall, on the road from Grantown, and a triangular one, rounded at the angles, on the bevelling of the left-hand pier of the park gate. I have also several specimens in my possession. In shape, they resemble the specimens of granite found in the lower series of the Old Red Sandstone. Rolled pieces of the same kind also occur in red granite. There is nothing inconsistent with what is now going on in Nature in supposing these to have been first water-worn and then inclosed in their granitic bed on the solidification of the latter in an age when silica and alumina appear to have been very abundant,—as much so as lime at a later period—for the deposition of siliceous matter is now going on in New Zealand. "Grand and beautiful geysers, ejecting water two degrees above the boiling-point of pure water, and holding various silicates in solution, are found around the lakes of Rotomahana and Rotorna. This water on cooling incrusts every substance it comes in contact with, and birds thrown into it are brought out like pieces of flint. On looking down through the clear, smooth water of the Te Tarata geyser on Lake Rotomahana, the siliceous matter is observed deposited at the bottom, like the hills on the eastern side of Lake Taupo—a formation which, when seen from a canoe on the lake, suggests to the eye waves of lava suddenly cooled." (Thomson's "New Zealand," vol. i., p. 12). Silicates thus deposited would, on crystallizing, discharge any superfluous matters. The particles of hornblende, &c., thus ejected, unable to escape from the overwhelming mass of siliceous matter have arranged themselves so as to give granite its spotted appearance, and, under some circumstances, have given rise to the stratified appearances so prominently seen in gneiss. The former would occur when the crystallization took place in masses, or when the liquid was in a state of agitation,—the latter when the siliceous matter was deposited in layers.—JOHN JOS. LAKE.—*Athenæum*, Jan. 12.

THE MULBERRY TREE.

The following information on the cultivation of the mulberry tree in the kingdom of Siam will not be without interest. It is chiefly in Laos, or the kingdom of Lieng-Mai, a tributary to Siam, that the rearing of silkworms is carried on on some scale. The greater part of the silk produce is employed on the spot by native industry, so that very little of it comes to the Bangkok market. The annual export of this product does not exceed 50,000 kilogrammes (50 tons). Of late years several lots of it have been shipped for Europe. The Laos silk is of an excellent quality, but the means used for spinning are very imperfect, so that this product is placed amongst the inferior qualities. The Anamese, who are established in the neighbourhood of Bangkok, rear silkworms, but in small quantities. They understand the method of their treatment better than the inhabitants of Laos and Cambodia, and their products are better able to compete with the good qualities of China and Japan; but the whole of the silk produced by them is used for domestic purposes, and none is found in commerce. The mulberry is the object of special care in Laos and Cambodia; but it equally succeeds in all the Siamese provinces, and the rearing of silkworms might be successfully carried on there, as proved by the attempts at Bangkok, which is less advantageously situated. It appears up to the present time that no epidemic disease has made its appearance either in Laos or in Cambodia. The Anamese employed in the rearing of the silkworms from eggs from Laos have observed that after that they have been reproduced three or four times a fresh stock should be obtained; this, however, seems to indicate a germ of disease. Should the worms a few days after hatching seem ill and not likely to succeed, the air is changed by taking them somewhere else; this often produces the desired result. If some crops are lost it is not due to the epidemic. The eggs are transformed into cocoons at the end of a month. Three or four crops of silk are usually produced yearly, during the months of May, June, July, and August. They can be reared during other months of the year, but with less success.—*Journal Soc. of Arts*.

ALLIGATORS.

Most of the streams of tropical Africa abound with alligators. They are apparently of the same species as those of the Nile, and, so far as I can see, very similar to those of the Victoria and other rivers of North Australia. But it is singular that, while the rivers of Natal on the east or coast side of the Drakensberg contain great numbers of these reptiles, not one is to be found in the tributaries of the Vaal or Orange rivers; or in any of those streams of the elevated plateau of the interior, on the west, which lie nearly in the same latitude (from 27° to 30° south), while the Limpopo, which rises but a short distance further north, or in about 26° south, is expressly called Krokodil River by the Dutch colonists of the Transvaal country.

On the shoals of the Zambesi, from the sea to Tette and Kabrabasi, in fact, all the way to the Victoria Falls, and in the Bo-tlét-le River and Lake Ngami, they may be seen basking on the sands or rocks, or floating like shapeless logs in the quiet reaches.

In the dry ravines that carry off the occasional torrents of Namaqualand, no one would expect to find them; and, though I certainly must confess to having dreamed of alligators there, it was during the delirium of fever, and I still had sense enough to picture them all dead of thirst, lying for many days' journey along the borders of the waterless gully. Here, again, only a few degrees to the north, the Okovango River, discovered by C. Andersson in 17° 30' S., is full of them; but in this case the permanence of the deep and slowly flowing stream is sufficient reason for it. I can only surmise that perhaps the difference of temperature, caused by the elevation, may prevent them inhabiting the rivers of the plateau, and invite them to those of the lower regions on the coast from Delagoa to Natal.

To fire at them is in general of little use; for, though they lie sufficiently exposed, their position is invariably such that, if life enough is left to make but one convulsive motion, that motion launches them from rock, or shoal, or sloping mud-bank toward the water, in the depths of which they lie till either they regain strength enough to escape, or the generation of gas causes the dead bodies again to float upon the surface. Sometimes, indeed, they are torn to fragments in the interim by their fellows, who will even drag down the carcass from the shore, as they did with one killed high and dry by Mr. Baldwin, near Natal, a few years ago.—S. BARNES, F.R.G.S., in *Leisure Hour*, Jan. 26.

THE OCEAN CURRENTS.

Professor Grimes, of Philadelphia, made the following remarks upon the subject of the Ocean Currents, at a recent meeting of the American Institute—Polytechnic Branch, the president, Professor Tillman, being in the chair;—Columbus, during his first voyage, discovered in the midst of the ocean an immense stream moving with great velocity and superior in its proportions to the largest continental river known. Since the announcement of the existence of this, the Gulf Stream, similar currents have been traced, both in the Pacific and Indian Oceans, and now physicists recognised five, one each in the North and South Atlantic and Pacific, the remaining one in the Indian Ocean. The six continents of the world are arranged in pairs, as a glance at any map will show. Hence, from this and many other points of similarity, it is evident that whatever force caused the one repeated itself in forming the others. The hypothesis advanced by Professor Grimes refers the question back to the age when the entire earth was covered with water, at which time six elliptical currents were formed. Five now remain; the sixth one was formed in the North Indian, an ocean which, owing to the elevation of land, no longer exists, but the Caspian and Aral seas, and the large lakes of Asia furnish proof of its former reality. By a simple mechanical problem we can demonstrate why these ellipses were formed. If near the edge of a disc revolving rapidly on its centre a ball is placed, and caused by any means to pass alternately back and forth on the radius, its motion will not be in a straight line, but it will invariably traverse an ellipse. To make an application: when the waters in the Gulf of Mexico have become heated by the sun, the tendency will be to pass north until cooled, then to return to the equator, and such would be the only motion were the earth at rest; but the revolution of the earth is a constant force acting upon the current of water and gradually overcoming this northernly motion, and turning it to the east, by the coast of Ireland. Becoming cool, it seeks the warmer regions, and the easting is transferred into a general southernly direction, but as it nears the coast of Africa, its velocity is lost, and as the earth moves more rapidly than the current, the latter is left behind, or is giving an apparent westward motion, till the Gulf of Mexico is again reached and the circle is completed. During the Creation the land appeared on the margin of, and between, the circles; in proof of which the pointing of the three southern continents to the south east—features first pointed out by Humboldt—the accumulation of lands toward the north, rather than the south, and the direction of the glacial markings during the drift period—these all bear witness to and are explained by this theory.—*Mechanics' Mag.*, Jan.

RATS AND THEIR SAGACITY.

Among many instances of these, the following may be worth recording:—Captain ———, one of the passengers to Bombay in the Peninsular and Oriental steamship Jeddo, 1862 (since wrecked), missed several small articles from his cabin table—his toothbrush, a bunch of keys, and several other things. The peculation being continued, his suspicion fell upon the steward, until one day some things tied with a long string were taken. This string the captain found hanging over the corner of a beam near the ceiling of the cabin, and following the clue, discovered a varied assemblage of his missing things and others. His keys, toothbrush, &c., were recovered, but some of the articles had been carried out of reach. That rats had stolen them was proved by some papers being nibbled up to form their nests no doubt. Another instance occurred in a store-room in Ireland some few years since. Butter and eggs, &c., were missed, which led to the place being watched, and it was discovered that some rats had fixed their dwelling in the stopping of a chimney, stuffed, just above the fire-grate, with old carpets, &c. In these a store-house had been formed, and several pats of butter were found neatly placed together; while in another direction were a number of eggs, some bones, and meat. As the nest was two feet or so from the ground it became a question how the rats succeeded in getting the eggs into it; so means were used to observe, and our informant soon saw the thieves at work again. A basket containing something not for them was hung by a cord from a horizontal bar, along which one crept, cut the string, and when it fell, they all commenced to rifle it, carrying off the contents. Now, however, some eggs, placed in their way, attracted attention, and the mystery of the transport was solved. One fellow, throwing himself upon his back, clasped an egg firmly between his claws clinging to it with all four legs, while his companions triumphantly dragged him and his egg up into the nest. Rats will cut through lead pipes to get at water; yet sailors who tame them so that they come to a call or whistle, say that they never cut through a ship below the water line, lest their home should sink. Indeed, we have heard of one which, choosing to leave his ship by going through her side; and, as if aware that she was coppered to the water-line, made his exit through her planking within a couple of inches of the copper. Such tales as these would almost incline one to believe in a tale which was told as true, of a thirsty rat, having got upon the edge of a jar, the water in which was just beyond his length of neck, promptly reversing his position, he let his tail down into the vessel, then withdrawing it, licked the water off, and repeated the operation.—*Land and Water*, Jan. 12.

THE INDIAN BEAR.

The bear, like other wild animals noxious to man, is, for its own safety, obliged to roam about in search of food at night. But it will commence its rambles at sunset, unless too near human habitations, and is of a more open and fearless nature than other feræ. I have often watched them from a moderate distance in quiet places, open glades in forests, of turf scattered over with bushes, during the brief twilight of an Indian evening. They then move busily about; sometimes a grown-up couple, sometimes a she bear with one or two half-grown cubs, silently eating the bairberries, or if they come across an anthill, vigorously scratching up the soil and sucking the ants out of their cells with loud puffs that may be heard of a still evening for nearly half a mile. Their senses seem at all times rather blunt, and I have frequently found them on these occasions approach me to within fifty or sixty yards, unconscious apparently, of my presence. When they perceived me they would pull up at once with an abrupt snuff, or snort, sometimes rear, give a short, angry puff, and then, dropping on all fours, turn suddenly round and make oft in a lumbering gallop, occasionally stopping and looking round, and then, with a peculiar barking moan, as if protesting against all intruders, continuing their retreat into the jungles. It is not always, however, that they depart so peaceably; they will sometimes, after a partial retreat, appear to think better of so quietly relinquishing the ground, and return moaning and barking, stopping and rearing, and shaking their huge shaggy heads, and at last perchance fairly charging at the observer with prodigious uproar, uttering loud, hollow grunts, which try the strongest nerves. Of course, a person venturing at such hours into places infested by bears is supposed to be well armed. A shot will usually turn one, but not always, and should both barrels fail to do so, there is nothing for it but to exercise the better part of valour and take to one's scrapers. Happy he, at such a moment, whom Nature hath endowed with a light pair of heels.—*Field*, Jan. 5.

MAN'S WORK AND WASTE.

Suppose a chamber with walls of ice, through which a current of ice-cold air passes, the walls of the chambers will of course remain unmelted. Now, having weighed a healthy living man with great care, let him walk up and down the chamber for half an hour. In doing this, he will obviously exercise a great amount of mechanical force; as much, in fact, as would be required to lift and push his weight through the distance which he has raised himself at every step, and transported himself by all his steps. But in addition, a certain quantity of the ice will be melted or converted into water, showing that the man has given off heat in abundance. Furthermore, if the air which enters the chamber be made to pass through lime-water, it will cause no cloudy white precipitate of carbonate of lime, because the quantity of carbonic acid in ordinary air is so small as to be inappreciable. But if the air which passes out is made to take the same course, the lime water will soon become milky, from the precipitation of carbonate of lime, showing the presence of carbonic acid, which, like the heat, is given off by the man. Furthermore, even if the air be quite dry as it enters the chamber, that which is breathed out of the man, and that which is given off from his skin, will exhibit clouds of vapour: which vapour, therefore, is derived from the body. After this experiment has continued for a longer or shorter time, let the man be released and weighed once more. He will be found to have lost weight. Thus, a living active man constantly exerts mechanical force, gives off heat, evolves carbonic acid and water, and undergoes a loss of substance.—*Huxley's Elements of Physiology*.

CORAL FISHERY.

Coral is obtained in large quantities in the Mediterranean. The French have, from time immemorial, carried on the fishery for this precious zoophyte off the Algerian coasts. Coral is also an important branch of industry and commerce in Italy. That which is obtained from the Sardinian coasts is chiefly found in the shallow waters near Carloforte; Alghero, a province situated on the west coast of the island; and the island of Maddalena. At Alghero, where the growth of coral is the most plentiful, it may be estimated that 190 vessels, of which 150 are Neapolitan, 20 Tuscan, and 20 Sardinian—manned by 1,930 sailors—are employed in this fishery, which begins in the month of March, and ends during the month of October. The rose coral, which is the most prized, is sold at very high prices, as it is entirely a fancy article. £80 was paid a short time ago for a piece of uncommon beauty weighing nine ounces. The ordinary price is about £24 per kilogramme. The price of red coral is about £6 per kilogramme. The white coral, the quality of which is often deteriorated by being worm-eaten, is sold at about £2 8s. per kilogramme, and the *ferraglio* at 5s. per kilogramme. The greater part of the coral is brought to Torre del Greco, near Naples. The Sardinians and Tuscans send the produce of their fishery principally to Genoa and Leghorn. The value of the coral obtained each year amounts to £60,000. From this must be deducted £45,800 to defray the expenses of the fishery, so that there remains a net profit of £13,000.—*Journal of the Society of Arts*, Jan. 5.

DIATOMACEÆ.

Nowhere is ornament more richly given, nowhere is it seen more separate from the use, than in those organisms of whose countless millions the microscope alone enables a few men for a few moments to see a few examples. There is no better illustration of this than a class of forms belonging to the border-land of animal and vegetable life called the *Diatomaceæ*, which, though invisible to the naked eye, play an important part in the economy of nature. They exist almost everywhere, and of their remains whole strata, and even mountains, are in great part composed. They have shells of pure silex, and these, each after its own kind, are all covered with the most elaborate ornament—striated, or fluted, or punctured, or dotted in patterns which are mere patterns, but patterns of perfect, and sometimes of most complex beauty. No graving done with the graver's tool can equal that work in gracefulness of design, or in delicacy and strength of touch. Yet it is impossible to look at these forms—in all the variety which is often crowded in a single lens—without recognising instinctively that the work of the graver is work strictly analogous—addressed to the same perceptions—founded on the same idea—having for its object the same end and aim. And as the work of the graver varies for the mere sake of varying, so does the work on these microscopic shells. In the same drop of moisture there may be some dozen or twenty forms, each with its own distinctive pattern, all as constant as they are distinctive, yet having all apparently the same habits, and without any perceptible difference of function.—*Duke of Argyle's Reign of Law.*

USES OF A GROUND VINERY.

In the largest gardens in the land they will be found most useful during our wretched winters and cutting springs for the protection of such stuff as small salading, &c., and not a few other uses which will soon suggest themselves to the amateur when once he makes the acquaintance of this simple ground vinery. Parsley, for instance, is often taken up and potted, to ensure having a supply in case of hard weather; but placing one of these over it will quite suffice for the usual run of our winters, while numerous batches of seedlings and half hardy things will be the better for their protection; and of course they may be taken off the vines when they have had their fruit removed and wood ripened in autumn, if it be desired to do any of these things with the ground vinery. Passing through the grounds of a large market grower of strawberries on the south side of London the other day, we observed Black Prince, the earliest kind, planted three rows rather close together, not more than 8in. between them, and then an alley of 15in. or so left between each set of rows. This grower sells his Black Prince strawberries very early at a high price; but he or anybody else may very nicely accelerate the earliest variety by placing one or more ground vineries over the rows, which their size just adapts them to fit. They seem, in fact, as well adapted for gently forwarding the strawberry as for the sure fruiting of good grapes without artificial heat; and most people will agree with us that the longer we can prolong the season of the strawberry the better. Lettuce, and endive too, in winter will be very thankful for the protection, and, with the aid of the ground vinery (by keeping snails and such vermin from devouring them), we may enjoy salad, which in winter is usually only for those who have pits and frames to spare, and who, moreover, manage them well.—*Field*, Jan. 5.

LOCUSTS.

I have just noticed "Firefly's" note on "the Carob tree, or St. John's bread," in *Land and Water* of December 8, *apropos* of which I send you the following extracts on the subject of locusts and the carob tree. The first is taken from Dr. Thomson's very interesting work on the Holy Land, entitled "The Land and the Book." Dr. Thomson is an American missionary, living at Beirut. His work is based upon twenty-five years' experience in Syria and Palestine. He thus writes:—"Do you suppose that the meat of John the Baptist was literally 'locusts and wild honey?' Why not? By the Arabs they are eaten to this day. The perfectly trustworthy Burckhardt thus speaks on this subject:—"*All* the Bedouins of Arabia, and the inhabitants of towns in Nejd and Hedjary, are accustomed to eat locusts.' 'I have seen at Medina and Tayf *locust shops*, where these animals were sold by *measure*. In Egypt and Nubia they are only eaten by the poorest beggars.' 'The Arabs, in preparing locusts as an article of food, throw them alive into boiling water) with which a good deal of salt has been mixed. After a few minutes they are taken out and dried in the sun; the head, feet, and wings are then torn off; the bodies are cleansed from the salt and perfectly dried, after which process whole sacks are filled with them by the Bedawin. They are sometimes eaten boiled in butter, and they often contribute materials for a breakfast when spread over unleavened bread mixed with butter.' Thus far Burckhardt. Locusts are not eaten in Syria by any but the Bedawin on the extreme frontiers, and it is always spoken of as a very inferior article of food, and regarded by most with disgust and loathing, tolerated only by the very poorest people. John the Baptist, however, was of this class, either from necessity or election. He also dwelt in the desert, where such food was, and is still used; and therefore the text states the simple truth. His ordinary 'meat' was dried locusts, probably fried in butter, and mixed with honey, as is still frequently done."—*Land and the Book*, part ii., pp. 419, 420.—*Land and Water*, Dec. 29.

New Books.

[*Our limited space must of necessity compel us to give but very short notices of new books, but they will perhaps serve as a guide as to what books our readers may ask for at their libraries.*]

Geology for General Readers: a Series of Popular Sketches in Geology and Palæontology. By David Page. Second and Enlarged Edition. (Blackwood and Sons.)

This is a second and improved edition of a little work that has already taken the position of best elementary work on geology for students. Most of our readers have no doubt an old acquaintance with it; for those who have not it is only necessary to say that the arrangement is so admirable, and the language so felicitous, that the increasing number of persons who are making this science their study cannot rise from an attentive perusal without feeling a still deeper interest in it.

The additions made to the present volume consist of a short chapter on the Origin of Veins, another on our Coal Supply, and several pages on Metamorphism, the introduction to which we subjoin :—

This conversion, or *metamorphism*, as it is technically termed, by which chalk, for example, can be changed into crystalline marble, or clay into glistening roofing-slate, forms one of the most abstruse problems in geology. As it is often referred to in geological writings, it may be of use to the general reader to indicate the principal causes which seem to be concerned in its production. These are—1. *Heat by contact*, as when any igneous mass, like lava, indurates, crystallizes, or otherwise changes the strata over or through which it passes. 2. *Heat by transmission, conduction, or absorption*, which may also produce metamorphism, according to the temperature of the heated mass, the continuance of the heat, and the conducting powers of the strata affected. 3. *Heat by permeation* of hot water, steam, and other vapours, all of which, at great depths, may produce vast changes among the strata, when we recollect that steam, under sufficient pressure, may acquire the temperature of molten lava. 4. *Electric and galvanic currents* in the stratified crust, which may, as the experiments of Mr. Fox and Mr. Hunt suggest (passing galvanic currents through masses of moistened pottery clay), produce cleavage and semi-crystalline re-arrangement of particles. 5. *Chemical action and reaction*, which, both in the dry and moist way, are incessantly producing atomic change, and all the more readily when aided by an increasing temperature among the deeper seated strata. 6. *Molecular arrangement by pressure and motion*—a silent but efficient agent of change as yet little understood, but capable of producing curious alterations in internal structure, especially when accompanied by heat, as we daily see in the manufacture of the metals, glass, and earthenware. Such are the more general and likely causes of rock metamorphism; and as it is possible that several of these may be operating at the same time, the reader will perceive that no hypothesis that limits itself to any one agent can be accepted as sufficient and satisfactory.

Scientific Works published in England and America during the Year 1866.

In a literary supplement issued with the *London Review* for Jan. 5, 1867, the following interesting account of scientific works published during the past year in England and America is given :—

We have had two volumes of Professor Owen's work on "The Anatomy of the Vertebrates," including fishes, reptiles, birds, and mammals; Mr. Samuel Laing's "Prehistoric Remains of Caithness," to which Professor Huxley has added notes on the human remains of that district; Lieut.-Colonel Forbes's "Early Races of Scotland, and their Monuments;" a translation of Dr. Ferdinand Keller's work on "The Lake Dwellings of Switzerland;" Dr. Hartwig's "Harmonies of Nature, or the Unity of Creation;" Mr. Charles Bray's work "On Force and its Mental and Moral Correlates;" Mr. Evan Hopkins's "Geology and Terrestrial Magnetism;" a further volume of the "Memoir of the Geological Survey of Great Britain;" translations of M. Louis Figuier's "World before the Deluge" and "Vegetable World;" Professor Stephens's "Old Northern Men of Scandinavia;" Sir John Herschel's "Familiar Lectures on Scientific Subjects;" and Mr. Fairbairn's "Treatise on Iron-Ship-building" and "Useful Information for Engineers," the latter consisting of lectures on the applied sciences, with treatises on the merits of the Paris and London International Exhibitions, the Atlantic Cable, the effect of impact on girders, &c.

Among works of science in America one of the earliest of the year was by Professor Agassiz on "The Structure of Animal Life," which, although it presents nothing new to the adepts of science, is a remarkably clear statement for the ordinary student of the Principles of zoological classification. "Geological Sketches," from the same distinguished naturalist, is a finely-illustrated volume of 311 pages. In both of these works the Professor repeatedly expresses his dissent from the theory of Mr. Darwin. Of the opposite school is Professor Clark, of the same University (Harvard) as Agassiz, who has given to the world a work of originality and learning, under the title "Mind in Nature; or, the Origin of Life, and the Mode of Development of Animals." The author holds that the old doctrine *Omne vivum ex ovo* is exploded by the fact of the origination of some animals by budding and self-division, and defends the theory of spontaneous generation. "Coal, Iron, and Oil, or the Practical American Miner," &c., &c., is the joint production of Messrs. Daddon and Bannan, who are both well acquainted with their subject, and have given a comprehensive account of the statistics, &c., of mining in America for thirty-five years. With this may be mentioned a "Special Report on Coal," by S. H. Smeet. Mr. Smeet estimates the coal resources of North America at 7,669,900,000,000 tons. "New Physiognomy," &c., by S. R. Wells (containing more than 1,000 illustrations), is a valuable book, as giving a complete encyclopædic account of nearly all that has been thought and said on this shadowy science from the time of Lavater. "Comparative Physiology, or Resemblances between Men and Animals," by J. W. Redfield, M.D., (with 300 illustrations), is a very curious book, and one of much research. We must pass over several scientific works of value. From the Smithsonian Institution we have received during the year among many useful publications, "Check List of the Invertebrate Fossils of North America, Eocene and Oligocene," by T. A. Conrad; "Check List of the Invetebrate Fossils of North America, Cretaceous and Jurassic," by F. B. Meek; "New Species of North American Coleoptera, by J. L. Leconte, M.D.; and from Philadelphia, "Observations upon the Cranial Forms of the American Aborigines, based upon Specimens contained in the Collection of the Academy of Natural Sciences in Philadelphia," by J. A. Meigs, M.D.

The bookseller gives the number classified published in England as follows:—

Medical and Surgical 160
Travels, Topographical and Geographical 195
Agriculture and Horticulture 64
Science, Natural History, etc.......... 147

The Journal of Anatomy and Physiology. No. 1, November, 1866. London: Macmillan.

This is the first number of a new quarterly journal devoted to the study of anatomy and physiology. It is conducted by G. M. Humphry, M.D., F.R.S.; Alfred Newton, M.A., F.L.S.; William Turner, M.B., F.R.S.E.; E. Perceval Wright, M.D., F.L.S.; and as Editor, J. W. Clark, M.A.

The first number is very rich in subjects of interest—containing an address on Physiology, by Prof. Humphry; the Anatomy of the Cornea, by Dr. Lightbody; the Comparative Anatomy of the Muscles of the Shoulder, by Mr. Wood; the Human Crania, by Prof. Huxley; on the Gestation of Arius, by Mr. Turner; Variation in Buccal Nerve, by the same; the Action of Muscles, by Dr. Cleland; the Retina of Amphibia, by Mr. Hulke; Amylotic Ferments, by Dr. Foster; Rigor Mortis, by Dr. Harris; together with reviews, analytical, critical and other notices, letters, etc., etc.

The Heavens. An Illustrated Hand-book of Popular Astronomy. G. Amedée Guillemin. Edited by Norman Lockyer, F.R.A.S., &c. London: R. Bentley.

A second edition of one of the most complete and useful treatises on the science of astronomy. It has been highly praised and recommended by M. Leverrier, Director of the Imperial Observatory in Paris, Mr. Warren de la Rue, of the Royal Astronomical Society, and Sir J. Herschel —names a sufficient guarantee of its merit. The author says:—"In order to make astronomy accessible to all, it is necessary to banish from the work the mathematical portion of the science, which forms the essential element in the special treatise on the subject. But, on the other hand, the most interesting details relating to the constitution of worlds which people space, the more recent observations made by the magnificent instruments now erected in the observatories of Europe and America, occupy a large place in the physical description of the universe."

Lecture Notes for Chemical Students, embracing Mineral and Organic Chemistry. By Edward Frankland. Van Voorst.

The above seems to be an accurate outline of the author's lectures delivered at the Royal College of Chemistry, and consists principally of chemical formulæ. It is likely to be of great interest to many.

The following works likely to interest our readers have appeared during the past few weeks:—

The Art of Fishing, on the Principle of Avoiding Cruelty. By the Rev. O. Raymond, LL.B. Longmans & Co.

Familiar Lectures on Scientific Subjects. By Sir J. Herschel, Bart. Strahan.

Revue des Cours Scientifiques de la France et de l'Etranger. Germer. Ballière.

Chemical Handicraft. By John Joseph Griffin. Griffin and Sons.

The Elements: an Investigation of the Forces which determine the Position and Movements of the Ocean and Atmosphere. Vol. I. By W. L. Jordan. Longmans & Co.

A First Book of Botany, for the Use of Schools and Private Families. By William Rossiter. Allman.

An Elementary Treatise on Heat. By Balfour Stewart, LL.D. Oxford: Clarendon Press.

A History of Geography—[*Geschichte der Erdkunde,* von Oscar Peschel]. Munich Cotta. London: Nutt.

A Dictionary, Geographical, Statistical and Historical, of the various Countries, Places, and Principal Natural Objects in the World. By. J. R. M'Culloch. New edition, carefully revised by Frederick Martin. Longmans and Co.

The Student's Text-Book of Electricity. By Henry M. Noad. Lockwood and Co.

Terrestrial and Cosmical Magnetism. The Adams Prize Essay for 1865. By Edward Walker, M.A. Bell & Daldy.

Correspondence.

[*Under this head we shall be glad to insert any letters of general interest.*]

WHAT ARE SHOOTING STARS?

Sir,—I cannot at all agree with "A Country Rector" in considering shooting stars as merely gaseous bodies, and in doubting the theory of the regular orbits and periodic revolutions of aërolites. The very fact of the periodic recurrence of the fiery showers, often upon the same night, seems to prove that, as they are met with in certain portions of space at stated periods, they must be controlled by some fixed laws, and proceeding upon some regular orbit. Curiously enough, in the very number in which "A Country Rector" expressed his incredulity concerning the regular movements of the "clouds of stones," as he calls the meteors, a passage from Herschel's "Familiar Lectures" is quoted, which speaks of the "*ring of meteorolites, which astronomers more than suspect.*" Surely the name of Herschel carries weight on any matter pertaining to astronomy. "A Country Rector" bases his denial of the solidity of shooting stars upon three points; *i.e.*, the failure of the spectrum analysis to dissect their light, and discover in it traces of solid matter; the supposed general fact that shooting stars never fall to the ground; and the secondary one that none of them did fall on this particular November night.

As to the first objection, I suppose it would be extremely difficult to apply the analysis to the light of so fugitive a body as a meteor, which rarely remains in view more than a few moments: but if it could be done, probably the case would remain analogous to that of the comets, the larger ones showing traces of a solid nucleus, but the smaller seeming to be merely gaseous. I dispute the fact that shooting stars never fall to the ground. "A Country Rector" attempts to place meteors upon a different footing by calling them "isolated," but this is by no means a distinguishing characteristic of falling stones, for several instances of *showers* of these bodies exist; that, for instance, at L'Aigle, in Normandy, in 1803, when two or three thousand aërolites fell over an extended area. Indeed, the dark cloud from which these falling stones invariably debouch would, it is strongly suspected, be luminous by night, and thus a fall of many of these would present the exact appearance of a fall of shooting stars.

Finally, "A Country Rector" illustrates his assertions by citing the night of the 13th of last November, in which he states that no solid bodies fell. The unaccountable case of the policeman drowned in Loch Katrine on the night of the display has been plausibly explained by supposing the man to have been struck by some falling stone, and if this surmise were capable of proof it would rather invalidate the argument; but of course the shooting stars which come to the ground as meteors are the exceptions, and not the rule. I would venture to suggest that they are generally reduced to powder by the fierceness of their combustion, and shed on our earth in imperceptible powder, only the very large ones reaching the earth, and then in a mutilated and incandescent state. The ignition of meteors cannot be explained wholly by atmospheric causes, but is probably owing rather to electric and magnetic agency, since the height at which many of them are seen is far superior to that of the earth's atmosphere.

I am, &c., &c.,
F. A. A.

HABITS OF THE SQUIRREL.

Sir,—Perhaps no department of natural history is of so much popular interest as the one which relates to the habits of animals. But the very popularity of this interest admits of a motive for fallacy, since exaggeration seems to add season to the dish; and with people cultivating a taste for reading, what is wonderful or out-of-the-way catches attention more readily than what modestly and soberly fits into all the other facts of the case.

There has reached me for perusal a book entitled the "Young Reader," published by Nelson and Sons. At page 93 there is a pretty enough picture of grey squirrels crossing a river, each on a canoe of its own launching, the material being the bark of a tree, "with their bushy tails spread out to catch the wind." The "lesson" accompanying the picture relates the story as if it were a common enough occurrence, and with no remark in the least modifying the extraordinary statement. Then follows a poem, by Mary Howitt—a nice poem in its way—containing the same assertions, and attempting to engrave them on the young mind by the aid of rhyme.

I have traced the story back to *Goldsmith's Earth and Animated Nature*, where it is given on the authority of Linnæus, but highly-respectable modern articles on the squirrel do not mention the habit. One of the most characteristic of man's inventions is that whereby he masters the waters:—

"He made him a boat of a hollow tree,
And man became lord of the awful sea."

When I am told the squirrel is in possession of a secret so important for the dignity of our species, I naturally regard the statement with some degree of credulity, and don't at all feel disposed to stamp it as an indubitable fact, or allow it quietly to drop, like an acorn in a crevice, on the fruitful soil of a young child's mind. I wish to know if any of your readers could help me either by confirming so remarkable a circumstance or by exploding it.

SCHOOLMASTER.

Dumfriesshire, 7th Jan., 1867.

THE HORSE CHESTNUT.

SIR,—Referring to a "Note" in No. 1 of the N. N. B., upon the etymology of "Horse Chestnut," it seems to me that the name *Horse* Chestnut was employed merely to indicate its strong, astringent flavour, and consequent fitness for horses and other cattle, in contradistinction to the "Sweet Chestnut" eaten by man, and perhaps given by our forefathers from a notion that horses really ate them as cows and deer do.

To show the plausibility of this derivation, I can point to "Horse Radish" as one instance where the prefix "Horse" is used to indicate strength and coarseness of flavour; and possibly others might be found.

While on the subject of derivation, I shall be glad to have the opinions of any of your readers on the origin of other of our popular names—among others of Gooseberry, Strawberry, Raspberry, Cranberry, Whortleberry, &c.

That all these names and probably most popular descriptions when given were eminently descriptive and characteristic I have no doubt—Blackbird, Blackberry, Dewberry, for example, but corrupted in spelling and pronunciation in coming down to us; and it is only reasonable to suppose that the names of doubtful origin are so to us only because of corrupted orthography, or because the descriptive prefix has now become obsolete as a separate word, and thereby its meaning and force are hidden from us in these days.

I have ideas of my own on the derivation of some of the words named in my query, but shall nevertheless be pleased to hear what some of your correspondents may say about them.

I am, sir, yours respectfully,

W. H. ADE.

Worcester.

TO CORRESPONDENTS.

W. Q. Cubitt—Many thanks for your kind wishes. You will see the advertisements are not paged in the present number; it was noticed in No. 1, but too late.

William Clark—See answer to W. Q. Cubitt.

F. Wilkinson—We approve your suggestion, but think it advisable to wait a few months.

D. E. S.—There is a long article upon the subject in *Land and Water*, Nov. 24, but no mention is made as to where the experiments took place.

R. W. T. S.—There are several respectable men in Leadenhall Market, who will give you all particulars. We know of no work on the subject.

Short Notes.

THE RHINOCEROS.—The Rhinoceros of the Terai appears to be somewhat larger than the same animal as found in the Rajmhahall Hills and the Bengal Soonderbunds, but I much doubt his being of a different species. As this rare and interesting animal does not appear to be well known in Europe, a few remarks on his appearance, character, and habits may not be out of place. The Indian Rhinocerus (Rhinoceros Indicus) is at least as large as his African brother, whether white or black: but the "horn," as it is generally but erroneously called, is much shorter in the Indian than in the African variety, and is composed not of horn, but of numerous small hairs, forming a hard compact protuberance growing from the thick skin of the snout, and which, so far as my experience goes, is seldom more than a foot in length. The stature of this singular animal is not nearly so great as that of the elephant, but in girth and in the colossal thickness of his limbs he is nearly equal to the latter, and in the combats which not unfrequently take place between these monsters the rhinoceros is said to be usually the victor. The rhinoceros is a stupid, solitary, and ferocious animal, and loves to haunt the deepest and most mysterious depths of swamps and thickets, where he feeds on the young roots of trees, leaves, &c. His great strength, and the thick armour plates which protect his shoulders and haunches, render him almost invincible against the attacks of any other denizen of the forest, and he seems to treat the rest of the *færæ naturæ* with a sort of calm disdain; but when once his haunts are invaded he becomes enraged at the slightest sound, and woe to the luckless wight who is within reach of his irresistible charge. The hearing of this animal is wonderfully acute, but his little pig-eye, has but a limited range of vision, and in favourable situations, and by the exercise of great caution, he may be stalked. In the Terai, however, he is generally shot from the backs of elephants. No timid man should ever try to shoot rhinoceros on foot; the work is fearful, and the danger very great. In a state of captivity this strange animal is easily tamed, and becomes as remarkable for docility as he was when in a wild state of ferocity—*Field*, Dec. 22.

NATIVES ON THE ZAMBESI.—They were magnificent fellows, but had the look of unmitigated savages. They wore a kind of kilt made of monkey skins, and their loins were covered with strips of monkey skin and buckskin alternately arranged. It is a far more picturesque attire than the bit of dirty calico I had hitherto seen worn by the natives. Their necklaces were made mostly of the horns of a diminutive antelope, strung through the roots, though one fellow, the medicine man, had a forest of chips about his neck. He also had at least twenty bracelets of steel wire on each arm, and on the fingers of each hand were many rings of the same material. Their snuff-boxes were made of a section of bamboo or reed; they were about a foot long, an inch in diameter, and ornamented with elaborate carving, very skilfully executed. One man carried his snuff-box in a hole made in the lower lobe of his ear. They were well pleased with their visit to us, for Dr. Livingstone conversed with them freely, and gave them trifling presents. There was nothing servile in their bearing; indeed, they regard all the natives around as their servants and slaves. They do no work, but quarter themselves upon the tribes they have subjugated. Those who visited us were, with many others, living upon the villagers near to Shupanga, and they assumed the air and manners of lords and masters. They carry off the stalwart lads as recruits, and the young women as wives. The Portuguese are really unable to do anything with them. Once, when repelling an invasion of these people, they captured two of them, and carrying them to Quilimaine, did their best, by flogging, &c., to subdue their spirit. But they only evoked threats of vengeance and defiance. Until death they breathed out threatening and slaughter against their captors. They were as little moved to supplication as the North American Indian.—*Rowley's Story of the Universities' Mission to Central Africa.*

BIRDS IN CHINA.—Their mode of taming is somewhat quaint and peculiar, being effected by dipping the bird into a pail of cold water, holding it at the same time carefully in the hand. After this process, whether from the shock of the sudden immersion and cold, or from a feeling that the hand of its owner has protected it from danger, it seems to be quite under control, and ceases to attempt its escape from the cage, or to be the least afraid of the human face and voice. It will ere long be taught to know its master's call, and after enjoying full liberty in the open air for hours, will return instantly at the sound of his voice. The golden oriole is a tenant of the northern woods, as are also several varieties of the thrush tribe (one of which was brought to England by Mr. Fleming), the blue-throated warbler, the gorget warbler, the red throat, and the North China lark. The latter is a good mimic, and when it has been educated to imitate successfully the mewing of a cat, it is considered highly accomplished, and will command a high price. It is called the pe-ling, or "hundred-spirited bird," and to the poorest Chinese, its sweet natural strains, which are lively and constant, will afford amusement and consolation in the midst of many hardships and sorrows. The crying thrush too, is highly prized, and when pouring out its evening ditty, which is peculiarly sweet at the fall of day, a melodious concert may be frequently enjoyed, for the owners of these birds love to bring them together in competition, and many delighted hearers will assemble to listen to the simple harmony.—*Land and Water, Jan. 5.*

THE REINDEER.—The ease with which the reindeer makes its way through the masses of snow is wonderful. It seems scarcely credible that so small an animal can wade up to its belly in the snow, and yet be able to drag a pulk containing a good weight (I am fourteen stone without my boots) after it. Often my pulk would sink so deep that it was exactly as if one was passing through a snow cutting, the sides of which towered far above one's head. Often, too, it made me grieved to see what hard work it was for the poor patient beast, and yet how obediently it would obey the rein attached to its left horn—how meekly it would receive a whacking, giving utterance perhaps to a grunt, while its tongue would hang down out of its mouth—a sure sign of distress. To say nothing of their numberless enemies in the summer, in the shape of all kinds of insects, and not to speak of their winter foes, the wolves, it is often terribly hard work for them to provide provender during this latter season; for the moss on which alone they feed is frequently at a depth of several feet below the surface of the snow, and this they have to scratch on one side, and bore a deep hole till they find it; and it frequently happens that when they have worked hard for a length of time, their mining operations prove fruitless, for there is no moss. But the young calves, how do they manage? They are not strong enough to scratch the snow aside, like the old ones; so they stand around, waiting for the pieces of moss to be scratched up, which the old deer in its burrowing scatters, far and wide.—*Chambers's Journal*, Dec. 29.

WHY BIRDS FLY.—In the first place it is remarkable that the force which seems so adverse—the force of gravitation drawing down all bodies to the earth, is the very force which is the principal one concerned in flight, and without which flight would be impossible. It is curious how completely this has been forgotten in almost all human attempts to navigate the air. Birds are not lighter than the air, but immensely heavier. If they were lighter than the air they might float, but they could not fly. This is the difference between a bird and a balloon. A balloon rises because it is lighter than the air, and floats upon it. Consequently it is incapable of being directed, because it possesses in itself no active force enabling it to resist the currents of the air in which it is immersed, and because, if it had such a force, it would have no fulcrum, or resisting medium against which to exert it. It becomes, as it were, part of the atmosphere, and must go with it where it goes. No bird is ever for an instant of time lighter than the air in which it flies; but being, on the contrary, always greatly heavier, it keeps possession of a force capable of supplying momentum, and therefore capable of overcoming any lesser force, such as the ordinary resistance of the atmosphere, and even of heavy gales of wind. The law of gravitation, therefore, is used in the flight of birds as one of the most essential of the forces which are available for the accomplishment of the end in view.—*Duke of Argyle's Reign of Law.*

STARS.—Prof. Zollner, of Leipzig, who has been working at some of the most important questions which have of late occupied the attention of astronomers, finds from his photomeric investigations that the star a Centauri seems to be equal to our sun. If the sun were at such a distance that $3\frac{3}{4}$ years would be required for its light to travel to the earth, it would then appear similar to Capella, and have a parallax of 0·874 seconds. Consequently, if light undergoes no absorption in its passage through space, the light of Capella must be much more abundant and intense than that of the sun. Data are given for a comparison of intensities, and of the reflection from different terrestrial and artificial surfaces; and the Professor throws out certain theoretical views which will, perhaps, be put to the test by those who have watched the recent progress of cosmical science. Every star-sun, to use his own term, has a history divisible into five periods; the glowing gaseous, the glowing liquid, the slag, the eruption, and the complete refrigeration period. Then applying this theory to actual phenomena, he finds the first period represented by planetary nebulæ; the second, by the invariable stars; the third, by our sun; the fourth, by new stars; and the fifth, by Bessel's dark stars. All the periods may be traced in the cosmical history of the earth. The non-planetary nebulæ occupy a place between the first and second periods. The third, or slag period, is that in which a cool non-luminous surface was developed; and in the fourth, or eruption period, the surface was vehemently disturbed and broken up by frequent outbursts of heated matter from the interior.—*Athenæum*, Dec. 29.

EQUATORIAL AFRICA. – Equatorial Africa for about ten degrees on both sides of the Line, and nearly quite across the Continent, still remains almost a blank unknown to explorers. One brilliant track has, within the last ten years, been broken through this vast belt. It is the route between the East Coast and the Nile, advocated by Dr. Beke in 1846; and pursued under the direction of the Royal Geographical Society, by Burton and Speke in 1857-8, from Zanzibar to Lake Tanganyika, and by Speke alone to Muanza. Again in 1860-63, Speke and Grant penetrated along the same track to Kazeli, and onwards to the Nile. In the reverse direction, Mr. and Mrs. (now Sir Samuel and Lady) Baker, ascending the Nile with supplies for Speke and Grant, met them at Gondokoro; and pushing on against desperate obstacles, forced a passage southwards, until they discovered the great Lake Albert. Between the great lakes and the confluence of the Sobat on the north, some western affluents of the Nile have been made known by Mdlle. Tinné, Mr. Petherick, M. Poncet, Dr. Penney, and other distinguished explorers. On the west coast, M. du Chaillu had made some progress towards the interior from the neighbourhood of the Gaboon, when he was compelled to retreat. On the east coast, Baron von Decken attempted to ascend the Jubb River, and was killed by the natives. Thus the Nile routes form the only important part of Equatorial Africa at present explored.—*Reader*, Dec. 29.

AN ATOM.—Let a man but know one single atom perfectly, with all the tendencies and forces animating and controlling it—and just as another who should know all the capacities and tendencies of a single human being might out of them construct the full idea of society, so he, pursuing all these forces to their natural results, would range at will through the whole circle of the sciences. He would have the key to all the secrets of astronomy, for they depend upon the law of gravitation, or attraction between atoms at a distance. He would have the key to all the phenomena of solids, liquids, gases—strength of material, friction, elasticity, and a hundred other subjects, for these depend upon the various attracting and repelling forces existing betweeen atoms near to one another. He would have the key to all the phenomena of growth, decay, and change of form and substance apparent, whether in living bodies or in inorganic substances, for these depend upon the chemical affinities and forces resident in atoms. He would have the key to all the phenomena even of electricity, I suppose, and magnetism, for these depend upon mysterious forces which can be studied only in connection with the atoms which they influence. And though he should not solve the question—What is life? he would approach the answer nearer than any other man, for knowing the behaviour of a living atom, and knowing all the forces which affect a dead one, he could discern with clearness, and separate, eliminate with accuracy all that was distinctly due to life alone.—*Gardener's Journal, Jan. 12.*

RATS IN AFRICA.—There are several species of rat, and the bewa, the field rat, a harmless looking creature, small in size, slender of form, and of the colour of lavender, is regarded by the natives as the best of all meat. At certain seasons of the year there is a regular rat harvest, the boys being the reapers. You see them coming home with dead rats on a reel, like larks on a skewer. They dry them, smoke them, and hang them up in bundles, like sprats at Billingsgate, and eat one now and then as a dainty. One evening my boy Juma (one of the boys now with Dr. Livingstone) came into my hut with his supper, a lump of Nsima, and something like a burnt sausage. "What is that, Juma?" said I. "Bewa," said he. "Is it good?" "It is good. Better than sheep, better than goat, better than bird or fish, better than all other meat. Shall I roast one for you?" And he pulled out a fine rat from his bag, and held it up for admiration. I nodded assent, and off he ran delighted. He returned with the rat frizzled and black, cooked to a turn. Its odour was savoury, but it was rat, and I hesitated, "Did you skin it, Juma?" "No." "Did you take the entrails out, Juma?" "No; they are the best of it—the fattest," said he, in surprise at my want of power to appreciate what a rat was. I did not taste it, though I afterwards thought myself weak to allow prejudice to interfere with my taste, for I have no doubt the boy was right, and that rat was pleasant food, and the method of cooking it was no worse than our method of dressing snipe."—*Rowley's Story of the Universities' Mission to Central Africa.*

THE SENSITIVE PLANT.—In a letter of Dr. Sigerson's to the *Athenæum*, he states that the folioles of the sensitive plant were touched by him with a non-conductor, and exhibited no movement. The sensitive plant is a common weed here, and is at present, as in his experiments, in flower. I touched it with glass, sealing-wax, iron, and the hand, and in all cases found the usual movement, which also took place when the plant was gently blown on with the breath. No such difference as, on any electrical hypothesis, we should expect, existed between the sensitiveness of the ends and middles of the folioles. Another fact about the sensitive plant, which the electrical theory does not explain, is the closing of the leaves at night. Perhaps the more hopeful question would be, not "why do they shut?" but "why do they open?" And I may be permitted to guess that the solar rays in the morning, or the solar diffused light, throws the molecules of the folioles into some new condition, the result of which is their opening, and that such a molecular condition is destroyed by the vibration caused by touch. What this molecular condition is, perhaps we shall never know, or, if ever, through microscopic analysis. Dr. Sigerson's observation, that children affect the sensitive plant more than adults, I confirmed by comparing the effects of my own touch with that of a child of seven years old, who affected the plant more powerfully than I could do.—W. E. HAMILTON.—*Athenæum*, Dec. 29.

THE SNOW LEOPARD.—The snow leopard is represented by Colonel Markham and Mr. Wilson as being found in considerable numbers in the upper parts of the mountains, but though tolerably numerous, it is so shy and cautious in its habits as to be very rarely seen. Mr. Wilson only shot one specimen, and that a half-grown cub, during his sojourn in the hills, which extended over a considerable period of time, and during which he collected nearly all the rarer Himalayan mammals and birds. The *Felis irbis* above referred to exists also, I believe, in some of the Persian mountain ranges, being most probably the animal alluded to by Tennyson in his exquisite poem of "Œnone," where he so accurately describes the deep yet muffled voice of the animal as being heard from the pine-fringed mountain glens during the twilight of early morning. This peculiar sound emitted by the leopard has been noticed by the natives of Eastern Africa, who have a machine for grinding, or rather crushing corn, which causes a similar noise, and is called by the same name, "nyalugwé." The voice of the leopard consists of three or four loud, harsh growls, repeated rapidly in succession, more resembling the sawing of large, dry boards than anything else I can compare it to, while the jaguar of South America (*Felis onca*) commences by uttering a short roar like that of a tiger, followed by several grunts, dying away gradually in long-continued sighs. The puma (*Felis concolor*) on the contrary mews like a magnified tom-cat, there being none of the majesty and consciousness of physical power so conspicuous in the roar of the tiger or lion.—*Land and Water*.

NEW SIBERIA.—New Siberia and the Isle of Lakon are, for the most part, only an agglomeration of sand, ice, and elephant's teeth. At every tempest the sea casts ashore fresh heaps of mammoth tusks, and the inhabitants are able to drive a profitable trade in the fossil ivory thrown up by the waves. During summer innumerable fishermen's barques direct their course to this isle of bones, and in winter immense caravans take the same route, all the convoys, drawn by dogs, returning charged with the tusks of the mammoth, weighing each from 150lb. to 200lb. The fossil ivory thus obtained from the frozen north is imported into China and Europe, where it is employed for the same purposes as ordinary ivory, which is furnished as we know, by the elephant and hippopotamus of Africa and Asia. The isle of bones has served as a quarry for this valuable material for export to China upwards of 500 years, and it has been exported to Europe for upwards of 100 years; but the supply from these strange mines remains undiminished. What a number of accumulated generations does not this profusion of bone and tusks imply!—*Mechanics' Magazine*.

WAPITI.—There are few prettier sights to a naturalist than to watch a herd of wapiti, five or six in number (they seldom assemble in larger bands), browsing in some quiet gorge. The king of the herd, ever on the watch for the slightest sign indicating the approach of danger, twists about his long ears to catch the faintest sound, anon elevating his dewy nose, sniffs the breeze, to discover if it bears along with it the scent of a lurking foe. Round about him some of the does are lying down beneath the shadow of the trees, half hidden by the grass and wild flowers, whilst others are lazily cropping the succulent plants, or in dreamy enjoyment chewing the cud. Let a stick crack sharply beneath your foot, or a gust of wind blow from the hunter towards the herd, or a displaced stone go rolling down the hill-side, then, quick as thought, the antlered monarch sounds the shrill note of alarm, and leading off at a jog-trot, is at once followed by his wives and subjects.—*Leisure Hour*, Jan. 5.

THE DRIVER ANT.—Sometimes, as is usual in tropical countries, the rain descends like a flood, converting in a few minutes whole tracts of country into a temporary lake. The dwellings of the driver ant are immediately deluged, and, but for a remarkable instinct which is implanted in the insects, most of the ants, and all the future brood, would perish. As soon as the water encroaches upon their premises, they run together and agglomerate themselves into balls, the weakest (or the "women and children," as the natives call them) being in the middle, and the large and powerful insects on the outside. These balls are much lighter than water, and consequently float on the surface, until the floods retire and the insects can resume their place on dry land. The size of the ant balls is various, but they are on an average as large as a full-sized cricket ball. One of these curious balls was cleverly caught in a handkerchief, put in a vessel, and sent to Mr. F. Smith, of the British Museum, who has kindly presented me with several specimens of the insect.—*Homes without Hands*.

SOUND.—The waves of sound go only 377 yards in a second, while the earth itself goes eighteen and one-third miles, and light ten thousand times faster than that; while electricity (which again is probably another kind of vibration of the solid atoms of bodies, and certainly not a fluid) runs along a wire about half as fast again as light. So says Mr. Denison, in his "Astronomy without Mathematics," if the earth were a cannon ball, shot at the sun from its present distance, with the velocity it now travels with, and the moment of explosion telegraphed to the sun, they would get the telegram there in about five minutes, and see the earth coming in eight minutes, and would have nearly two months to prepare for the blow, which they would receive about fifteen years before they heard the original explosion. This is merely taking the sun as a target to be shot at, without regard to his power of attracting the earth at the final rate of 90 miles a second.—*Mechanics' Magazine.*

SAXONS.—The Saxons seem generally to have settled in the open country, not in the towns, and to have built timber halls and cottages after their own custom, and to have avoided the sites of the Romano-British villas, whose blackened ruins must have thickly dotted at least the southern and south-eastern parts of the island. They appear to have built no fortresses, if we except a few erected at a late period to check the incursions of the Danes. But they had the old Roman towns left, in many cases with their walls and gates tolerably entire. In the Saxon MS. Psalter, Harleian 603, are several illuminations in which walled towns and gates are represented. But we do not gather that they were very skilful either in the attack or defence of fortified places. Indeed, their weapons and armour were of a very primitive kind, and their warfare seems to have been conducted after a very unscientific fashion. Little chance had their rude Saxon hardihood against the military genius of William the Norman, and the disciplined valour of his bands of mercenaries.—*Art Journal*, January.

CENTIPEDE.—But a worse adventure befell an engineer of ours. He was doing duty in the stoke hole, when one of these loathsome creatures actually crept up under his pantaloons. He was an old sailor, and a cool, and he well knew that if he attempted to kill or knock it off, the claws would be inserted on the instant. Cautiously he rolled down his dress, and spread a handkerchief on his leg a short distance before the centipede, which was moving slowly and hesitatingly upwards. It was a moment of intense excitement, both for those around him as well as for the man himself. Slowly it advanced, once it stopped, then moved on again, and crossed on to the handkerchief, and the engineer was saved; on which he immediately got sick, and I was sent for, heard the story, and received the animal, which I placed beside the other.—*Chambers's Journal*, Dec. 22.

PLAGUE OF GRASSHOPPERS.—A curious story comes to us from across the Atlantic, nothing less than the stoppage of a railway train by grasshoppers. Letters from Kansas, U.S., refer to a widely extended and destructive plague of these destructive insects. Some idea of their numbers may be had from their taking three weeks to pass Lauenworth, in a stream about twelve miles wide and 300 miles long. And from another fact that, having got on the railroad track of the Union Pacific road in such numbers as to cause the wheels to slip on the rails, and the freight train at Wyandotte was detained several hours beyond its time by the impossibility of penetrating the massive crowd of the insects, the slipping of the engine wheels, and the almost total darkness caused by their numbers.—*Mechanics' Mag.* Dec. 22.

THE HEN AND DUCK.—A paper has been received by the Paris Academy of Sciences from M. Comaille on the comparative value of the hen and duck as egg producers. His observations were limited to three hens and three ducks, all fine animals, hatched at the same time in the month of February. During the following autumn the ducks laid 225 eggs; they recommenced laying in February, and continued to do so until the middle of August. The hens laid no eggs during the autumn, but began in January, and left off about the middle of August. The totals of each at the end of that time were—the hens, 257 eggs; the ducks, 617. M. Comaille next examined the nutritive value of each kind of egg, and found them nearly equal in that respect. Hence the duck is more profitable than the hen by far.

PLANTS AND BIRDS AT CHRISTMAS.—In south Devon, on the shortest days of 1866, there are violets and primroses plenty in bloom, snowdrops showing their buds, mignonette, tropæolum, canariensis, wallflowers, rhododendrons, scarlets and pinks in variety; humble bees and wasps humming and buzzing about the arbutus trees in flower; the wild wood bee, mason wasp, bluebottles, and other varieties of flies and gnats swarming about the ivy in blossom on the sunny side of old walls and trees. Our songsters are the missel thrush or stormcock, the common grey thrush, and the woodlark; while the hedge-sparrow, robin, and little jenny wren are also to be seen. Thermometer at five a.m., 45 deg., wind south.—JAS. BARNES, *Field*, Dec. 29.

SCORPIONS.—In my cabin, besides the common earwigs, which were not numerous, and were seldom seen, I found there were a goodly number of scorpions, none of which, however, were longer than two inches. I am not aware that they did me any particular damage, further than inspiring me with horror and disgust. It *was* very unpleasant to put down your hand for a book, and to find a scorpion beneath your fingers—a hard scaly scorpion; and then to hear him crack below your boot, and to be sensible of the horrid odour emitted from his body—these things were *not* pleasant. Those scorpions which live in ships are of a brown colour, and not dangerous; it is the large green scorpion, so common in the islands of East Africa, which you must be cautious in handling, for children, it is said, frequently die from the effects of this scorpion's sting.—*Chambers's Journal*, Dec. 22.

ATOMS IN A PIECE OF IRON.—M. A. Gaudin, who fancies that he has ascertained the exact forms of the molecules of many organic and of some inorganic compounds, believes that he has also determined the size and weight of the ultimate atoms of some of the elements. His calculation of the number of atoms in a piece of iron of the size of a pin's head will afford an example of his notions on this latter point. He makes the result twenty million times twenty million times twenty millions—a number expressed in 8 followed by twenty-one cyphers, and so inconceivably great that, as M. Gaudin points out, it would take two hundred and fifty years to count it, even at the rate of *sixty thousand millions a minute*, being at the rate of as many per minute as there are grains in fifty thousand bushels of barley. The atoms may be,—probably are,—as infinitely minute as this, but we may be excused for doubting the absolute accuracy of M. Gaudin's measurements of them.—*Mechanics' Magazine.*

THE EGYPTIAN FELLAH.—The size of a "fellah's" house varies from nine to eighteen feet square, and in height a little more than three feet. The sides of this hut are composed of marsh reeds, plastered with cow's dung, the top covering being a flat earthern roof; a hole in the reeds of about four inches diameter represents a window, and there is a large aperture typical of a door by which the fellah enters "on all fours." In this unpartitioned wigwam sleep the fellah, his wife (or wives) and children, and frequently his children's husbands or wives and their children. Here also about half a dozen fowls, and probably two or three goats, nightly seek shelter. The furniture is quite in keeping with the dwelling. The hallah (a kind of saucepan), three or four wooden spoons, a straw mat, a primitive Egyptian handmill used by the women in grinding Indian corn for food, the gulleh or earthen drinking vase, and a larger one for carrying water, as in the days of Rebecca; a rude cushion, a quilt, and a looking-glass the size of one's hand complete the inventory. There are no such things as village schools, and the fellah has no means of instruction within his reach, and consequently possesses no knowledge whatever beyond the animal instincts of a savage.—*Standard*.

BURROWING SPIDERS.—Many of the true spiders are among the burrowers; and even in our own country it is possible to see a sandy bank studded with their silk-lined tunnels. There is such a bank that skirts a fir wood near my house, the material being the loosest possible sandstone, scarcely hard enough in any place to resist a pinch between the fingers and thumb. About an inch or two beneath the soil this sandstone is quite excavated by the spiders; and as the sandy sides of their tunnels would fall in were they not supported in some manner, every tunnel accordingly is lined by a coating of tough webbing, very strong, very elastic, very porous, and yet not suffering one particle of sand to pass through its interstices. From the opening of each burrow a web is spread, looking very much like a casting net, with a hole through its middle. From this, again, radiate a number of separate threads, which extend to a considerable distance from the entrance. At the very bottom of its silken tunnel the living architect lies concealed, its sensitive feet resting on the web, so that it is enabled to perceive the approach of the smallest insect that crosses the spot which it has so elaborately fortified.—*Homes wihout Hands*.

COLOURING THE PLUMAGE OF BIRDS.—The Indians have a curious art by which they change the colours of the plumage of many birds. They pluck out a certain number of feathers, and in the various vacancies thus occasioned infuse the milky secretion made from the skin of a small frog. When the feathers grow again they are of a brilliant yellow or orange colour, without any mixture of green or blue, as in the natural state of the bird; and, it is said, the yellow feather will ever after be reproduced without a new infusion of the milky secretion.—*Fletcher and Kidder's Brazil*.

THE LION'S LIFE.—The career of a lion is not without its lesson. At two years he is equal to an ox; at eight years he is full grown—teeth, claws, and talons in perfection; at twenty his powers begin to fail—he dares not encounter the buffalo-bull, but shirks the contest, and prefers the kraal, where he can steal a kid or some heedless child or woman. He grows mangy and lean, and even the field-mouse is a victory. A cowardly hyæna or two, or some valiant sportsman finds him, and glories in his destruction.—*Land and Water*, Jan. 5.

COLOURS OF METEORS.—A word or two as to colours of meteors. These appear to differ, at least the observations differ. Thus (Humboldt's *Cosmos*, chapter on Shooting-stars), of 4,000 observations collected during nine years, two-thirds were white, one-seventh yellow, one-seventeenth yellowish-red, and one thirty-seventh green. Now, of 271 meteors observed at the Royal Observatory, Greenwich, on the night of November 12, 1865, 197 were blue, 34 white, 34 bluish white, the remaining 10 being, some yellow, some red, and some green.—*Chambers's Journal*, Dec. 22.

LADY BIRD.—We cannot conclude our article without a word of praise for the farmer's active little friend, the lady bird, whose true character requires vindication, since it is not unfrequently condemned by the ignorant as an enemy, and we well remember an otherwise intelligent farmer attributing the loss of his turnips "to them earrwigs and lady cows," one, if not both, of which were doing all they could to clear the crop of its real enemies. The lady bird is most voracious in her tastes, and both in the imago and larva state wages war upon lice, bugs, &c.—*Field*.

CURIOUS PEBBLE.—A pebble (pure silex), was recently picked up at Eastbourne by the son of a lapidary of Terminus-road. This stone, on being cut and polished, was found to contain the profile of a dog's head, as perfect, it is said, as if drawn by an artist. No less than 20 guineas had been refused for this great curiosity, which is now mounted as a brooch, and is valued at 50 guineas.—*Building News*.

NUMBER OF PLANTS ON THE GLOBE. —Let us establish, before going further, the approximate number of vegetable species which inhabit our globe. The appreciation of the statistics of plants is necessarily very varied in this sort of estimate. Linnæus, in 1753, was acquainted with 6,000 species. Persoon, in 1807, reckoned 26,000. In 1824 Stendel carried the number up to 50,000, and in 1844 to 95,000. The most recent works contain about 120,000 species. From the species described botanists have been able to form some approximate estimate of the total number of existing species. By an ingenious calculation of the space occupied by an average-sized plant, Alphonse de Candolle thinks he may infer that the number cannot be less than from 400,000 to 500,000.—*Louis Figuier's Vegetable World*.

BEAUTIFUL SPONGE.—The British Museum has lately received a series of specimens of the beautiful sponge called Venus's Flower Basket (Euplectella Speciosum). It is more like the work of the lacemaker than a congeries or republic of minute jelly-like animals; and the thread of which it is woven is so hard that it will scratch glass.—*Athenæum*.

Remarks, Queries, &c.

(*Under this head we shall be happy to insert original Remarks, Queries, &c.*)

THE MERLIN, or Blue Hawk, is said, as a rule, to build its nest on the ground. I think there is no foundation for this statement. Out of three nests taken not long since, not a single nest was built on the ground, one being in a hollow in a larch, the other two being up fir-trees.   C. E. M.

LIFE AT THE BOTTOM OF THE ATLANTIC.—At the Natural History Society of Glasgow, a series of *foraminifera* was exhibited, obtained from mud brought up from the Atlantic sea bed, in the soundings made by Captain Anderson, of the Great Eastern, at a depth of 2,000 fathoms. The series embraced about fifteen different species. The *foraminifera*, are minute marine animals, with calcareous shells of a spiral form. They are very elegant in appearance.

WINTER ACONITE.—What colored flower has the Winter Aconite, and what does it grow best in?   AMATEUR.

[Eranthis hyemalis, or winter aconite, is a small stemless, tuberous, herbaceous plant, inhabiting shady places in the midland parts of Europe. The flowers are cups of bright yellow; it has pelate, many cut pale green smooth leaves, and a single-flowered scope only a few inches high. Perhaps some of our readers can tell you what it grows best in.—ED.]

THE PIKE.—Although the most voracious, and one of the largest of our British fresh-water fish, is sometimes killed in a very peculiar way. A large pike was seen to snap at a frog, when the frog sprang upon the head of the fish and fixed its claws into its eyes, and in spite of the endeavours of the pike to rid himself of it, maintained its position until the fish died. The pike weighed 15 pounds, the frog three-quarters of an ounce.   C. E. M.

COLIAS PALÆNO—May Colias Palæno be regarded as a British species, or is there any record of its being taken in England. It is figured by Wood in the "Index Entomologicus," pl. 53. fig. 11. and introduced there amongst the list of doubtful British Butterflies.
   F. WILKINSON.

The BOHEMIAN WAXWING.—Mr. Charles Norris, Buston Vicarage, writing to the *Standard*, Jan. 7, 1867, gives an account of his having shot one of these birds. He says: my bird measures nearly nine inches, has eight tips on one wing, seven on the other; four feathers in the tail are also slightly wax-tipped, and like all the specimens I have seen in Norfolk, numbering forty-five, has the tawny-brown feathers under the tail. More than a hundred have been shot in Norfolk this year. I believe they come over in largs flocks, and disperse in knots of ten to twenty.

THE TALLOW TREE.—Having lately heard that the tallow tree of China, which gives rise to a vast trade in the northern districts of the celestial empire, has been introduced into India, can any of your readers favour me with an account of this tree, or inform me where I can obtain a full description of it?   I. S.

SWALLOW'S NEST.—The following may interest some of your readers:—There was an arch over the front door of our house, with ledges in the interior. A swallow thinking that this would be a convenient spot to build a nest commenced operations, using mud only. While so doing particles fell and stained the flag at the front door; upon which my brother thinking the bird a nuisance pulled it all down, when nearly completed. But the bird, not to be outdone, recommenced operations, building a second nest, which shared the same fate. The bird then flew away as if to consider what was best to be done after the ruin of her second house. She returned and began a third time, this time mixing hay and other litter with the mud to render it more adhesive. With these materials she constructed her nest, which for pity's sake was allowed to stand; and here she spent her summer and hatched her young.   J. A. SLATER.
Rushton.

THE POTATO AND ITS PARASITES.—Under this head in the *Times* of Jan. 10th, is the following:—" It is stated in *La Patrie* that the microscope reveals to us the existence of a small black spot of the diameter of a pin's head, in the potato. In this small space can be detected some 200 ferocious animals of a coleopteric form, which bite and tear each other with continued fury. It is easy to comprehend the potato disease when such an intestine warfare is raging."

Quite as easy we should say as to comprehend this account of the intestinal condition of "the potato," presumably by the context of potatoes in general. The arena of the combat, it is true, is very limited, the diameter of a pin's head even of the largest size would afford no room for the combatants to have fair play, and we might expect that in such a general fight as would ensue among "ferocious creatures" in proximity there would be nothing left but fragments of the "coleopteric forms." But clearly these atomic monsters are not like the famed Kilkenny cats; they not only live to eat, but live in spite of being eaten, and accomplish the purpose of their being by causing the potato disease. Prodigious! Nature maximé miranda in minimis. We wish the observer with the microscope had conveyed more definitely what he means by "the coleopteric form." The *coleoptera* of ordinary entomologists have hardy horny coverings, and vary in form from globular to cylindrical or multiangular,

and are often beset with long spines; what then is the coleopteric form? But is not the whole story one of the pseudo-scientific statements which are put forth from time to time to excite the wonder and talk of a credulous unobservant public? W. DOUGLAS.
Lee, 10th Jan., 1867.

TURTLE DOVE.—In an aviary at Knowlsley there is a turtle dove which hatched two young ones in a tree in the open ground on Christmas day morning. The same pair of doves hatched on Christmas day last year, in the same tree, and on New Year's day the year before.—*The Liverpool Albion.*

THE GOLDEN EAGLE.—A fine specimen of this bird, a female, was shot on Saturday, December 29th, close to the sea beach, at Kunkel Cave. The bird is in excellent plumage, and measures about eight feet from tip to tip of the extended wings: it is a very rare bird here, and is supposed to have come from Norway. It was exhibited at the town hall during the week.
J. M. (St. Andrew's.)

MINUTE ANIMALS.—It has been found that in certain Bohemian schists there are fifty-one millions of animalcules to the cubic inch; each skeleton weighing no more than the two hundred-millionth of a grain.

STATE OF THE WEATHER NEAR LONDON.

Dec. and Jan.	Moon's Age.	Barometer.		Temperature.					Wind.	Rain.	Remarks.
				Of the Air.			of the Earth				
		Max.	Min.	Max	Min	Mean	1 foot deep	2 feet deep			
Thurs. 13	6	29.521	29.335	56	35	45.5	45½	45½	S.W.	.20	Rain; cloudy; slight rain; fine at night.
Friday 14	7	29.470	29.377	50	28	39.0	46	45	W.	.00	Overcast; very fine; slight frost.
Satur. 15	☽	29.452	29.372	51	38	44.5	46	45	W.	.15	Fine; constant rain; showery at night.
Sunday 16	9	29.892	29.662	50	25	37.5	46½	45	S.W.	.00	Fine; overcast throughout; slight frost.
Mon. 17	10	30.186	30.142	52	42	47.0	45	44	S.W.	.01	Hazy; slight rain; very fine at night.
Tues. 18	11	30.219	30.123	53	40	46.5	46	45	S.W.	.00	Hazy clouds; densely clouded; very fine.
Wed. 19	12	30.284	30.215	56	20	38.0	48	43	N.W.	.00	Exceedingly fine, very mild for the period of the season; frost
Thurs. 20	13	30.436	30.367	39	29	34.0	45	45	W.	.01	Frosty and foggy; foggy throughout; slight frost.
Friday 21	●	30.288	30.279	40	26	33.0	45	45	W.	.00	Hazy; fine; foggy; very fine at night; slight frost.
Satur. 22	15	30.340	30.301	42	32	37.0	43	43	S.W.	.01	Foggy throughout the day.
Sunday 23	16	30.333	30.313	45	31	38.0	44	43	W.	.00	Hazy; overcast; fine at night.
Mon. 24	17	30.244	30.222	43	28	35.5	45	43	S.W.	.01	Hazy and very mild for the season; drizzling rain; slight frost
Tues. 25	18	30.192	30.073	43	34	38.5	45	43½	S.W.	.00	Very fine; overcast; very fine throughout.
Wed. 26	19	29.988	29.912	53	37	45.0	46	44	S.	.10	Densely overcast; remarkably fine; boisterous; rain at night
Thurs. 27	20	29.831	29.742	54	40	47.0	46	44	W.	.00	Boisterous; cloudy; starlight at night; but without frost.
Friday 28	☾	29.850	29.865	55	40	47.5	47	45	W.	.00	Overcast; fine; warm for the season.
Satur. 29	22	29.788	29.404	51	30	40.5	47	45½	S.W.	.04	Fine; very fine; boisterous, with rain at night.
Sunday 30	23	29.850	29.213	45	19	32.0	47	45	W.	.00	Flear, quite cloudless; very fine; frosty at night.
Mon. 31	24	29.270	29.247	35	19	27.0	44	44	S.W.	.00	Frosty; partially overcast; fine; frosty; barometer very low
Tues. 1	25	29.342	29.250	35	15	25.0	43	43½	N.E.	.00	Clear and frosty; exceedingly fine; severe frost.
Wed. 2	26	29.600	29.004	30	(-)4	13.0	43	43	N.E.	.00	Heavy snow storm; drifting snow; intense frost; thermometer at night 4 deg. below zero—(36 deg. below freezing.)
Thurs. 3	27	29.810	29.650	33	2	17.5	40	40	N.E.	.00	Hazy; densely overcast; snowing; overcast; severe frost.
Friday 4	28	29.960	29.888	30	11	9.5	40	40	S.W.	.00	Intense frost continuing throughout the day; 11 deg. below zero at night.
Satur. 5	29	29.974	29.902	30	16	23.0	40	40	N.E.	.54	Hazy; overcast; cold wind at night.
Sunday 6	○	29.878	29.336	49	30	39.5	39½	40	S.E.	.00	Hazy; with slight rain; fine and rather mild.
Mon. 7	1	29.230	29.026	53	44	48.5	35.	40	S.W.	.46	Rain; cloudy, with mild temperature; very boisterous at night.
Tues. 8	2	29.114	28.760	52	36	44.0	35	40	S.W.	.01	Boisterous, with rain; very boisterous; fine at night.
Wed. 9	3	29.046	28.832	48	36	42.0	40	42	S.	.29	Boisterous, with rain; fine at night.
Thurs. 10	4	29.426	29.070	43	26	34.5	40	40	W.	.00	Very densely clouded; cloudy and damp; overcast.
Friday 11	5	29.680	29.584	38	16	27.0	40	42	N.E.	.00	Fine throughout; sharp frost at night.
Satur. 12	6	29.660	29.518	34	14	24.0	39	39	S.	.00	Dry and frosty; snow falling thickly in broad flakes; overcast.
Sunday 13	☽	29.700	29.460	35	3	19.0	39	40	N.	.00	Clear and frosty; very fine; frosty; within 3 degrees of zero at night.
Mon. 14	8	29.788	29.760	33	7	20.0	39	39	W.	.00	Severe frost; clear and frosty; as low as 7 deg. at night.
Tues. 15	9	29.844	29.708	36	20	28.0	38	38	N.E.	.00	Severe frost; uniformly overcast; cold frosty wind.
Wed. 16	10	29.840	29.640	38	25	31.5	39	39	N.E.	.00	Clear and frosty; slight snow; overcast. Notwithstanding the low temperature of the air, that of the earth, it will be observed, has been, and still continues, unusually high for the season, and has been parting with heat from a source of about 40 deg. for nearly a fortnight, to act constantly night and day on the under surface of the rapidly formed ice, which from this cause must have been rendered fatally weak.

GROWTH OF THE VINE.

THE reciprocal action of Root and Branch is a fact so fully recognised by physiologists that to enter more than cursorily on its discussion would be a waste of words; but as some may not fully understand what is meant by this reciprocal action, it may be necessary to give a little explanation. Taking an Oak, Elm, Ash, or any other kind of forest tree, it has been ascertained by experiment, and is now an admitted fact, that however far the branches of a fully exposed tree may extend laterally, however great the diameter or circumference of the branches may be, the superficial area covered by the roots, impediments apart, will be the same, if not more. The roots of some trees, as for example the Elm, Ash, Poplar, &c., will travel a considerable distance in search of nutriment; indeed these might, as compared with the Oak, be called predatory plants, ever ready to plunder the soil which surrounds them. In recently making some alterations we found that the roots of an Elm and an Acacia, forming part of a neatly clipped hedge close by, had extended through some Asparagus beds more than 90 feet. But taking a plant in good soil, and fully exposed on all sides, the roots rarely extend beyond the circumference of, or area of, the branches, and if they do it will almost invariably be on the windward side, so as to act as a counter strain against the leverage of the branches when pressed by severe storms of wind. Such is the provision which Nature uncontrolled provides for plants left to her control; but when her journeyman, the gardener, steps in, he too frequently thinks to improve upon Nature's teachings, and sometimes sets about it in a very singular manner.

Hence, in the management of the VINE, what do we do? We provide a border of considerable area and rich material, draining it thoroughly—sometimes paving, concreting, and even warming the bottom, and generally making the border from 18 inches to 3 feet deep, and occasionally more. Thus we provide a rich pabulum for the plants to feed upon, and what do we do next? Why, so soon as the plants get into free luxuriant growth we commence pinching and 'thumbscrewing' the young branches—the laterals, as we call them in Vine management—some cultivators in fact pinching them out altogether. Now, if the action of the root and branch is reciprocal, and there can be no doubt of it, this pinching or removal of the branches is a direct and constant check upon the progress of the roots, and hence while we invite growth at the root, we prevent it by the injudicious management of the branches. Of course under artificial treatment it would be wrong to retain more branches than could be exposed to the full action of light, and thus enabled to perform their proper functions; but in the case of a young Vine trained for the first season on the single-rod system and growing vigorously, it is exceedingly questionable if, so long as the leading shoot was not checked, it would not be better to train the lateral shoots out 18 inches on each side than to follow the present denuding system. If there is any truth in physiology it is quite certain that by such a system more roots would be formed, and as the first object of the Vine planter should be to secure healthy and extended root action, this appears to be the only natural means of doing so.

Some years back we were consulted by a gentleman who had built Vineries extensively. His largest house was 190 feet long by 30 feet wide, with a span-roof of Hartley's plate glass. At right angles at each end, thus forming three sides of a square or parallelogram, were two other Vineries, each 100 feet by 30 feet, and hence, as the borders were all outside, there was 30 feet of space at each end of the longest house where no border could be formed, and where consequently no Vines had been planted. We were asked to suggest a remedy for this empty space, and we did so by carrying the two end Vines horizontally along the wall plate, taking up from each, at intervals of about 3 feet, shoots perpendicularly to the top of the house. At the same time the fellow Vines, then two years planted, and very nice rods, were cut back to about 8 feet, and each was allowed to carry six or eight bunches of Grapes. Now it would perhaps be expected by many, that the two Vines trained horizontally, and from each of which nine shoots or rods were trained across the house, would not make such wood as those which carried a few bunches of Grapes and had only one shoot to make. But such was not the case; the nine rods from the single Vine were quite as good as the single rod from the Vines that had borne fruit—a result scarcely anticipated, and much more gratifying than had been expected. The kinds were Royal Muscadine and Black Hamburgh, and of each variety the growth was about equal.

The growth of these two Vines we regard as supplying two exceedingly strong facts. If a Vine of a certain age and strength will carry nine shoots, just as well as another Vine of the same age carries one shoot and a few bunches of Grapes—certainly not equivalent to the work of the other Vine, it only shows how accommodating plants are, and how much more work they would do, under artificial treatment, if they were only allowed to do it. We regret that after the time specified, the end of the season when the growth before alluded to was made, we had not an opportunity of seeing the progress the plants made, but we can scarcely imagine a growth so well begun could have had anything but a good ending.

The Vine, it should be observed, when allowed full freedom of action is not a profuse root producer; that is, in the open border it does not produce that multiplicity of roots so characteristic of it under pot or artificial treatment. Such being the fact, it is essential in planting a Vinery to make a narrow border at the commencement say 6 feet wide, and then, as soon as that space is filled with roots, to extend the border 4 or 6 feet wider. In this way it is fair to infer a much larger quantity of roots will be formed at home, that is near to the house, and once formed there, they are sure to spread and ramify through the border as it is provided for them.

That a properly planted and developed Vine will do much more work, and carry a very much heavier crop than hitherto has been considered right, is no longer a matter of speculation. The success of the Vine at Finchley is positive evidence of the fact; and Mr. Norman, in his testimony respecting the Muscat Vine at Bromley Common, supplies another very gratifying fact, viz., that *the berries of former days were much smaller than those of the present,* so that now a Vine, say 100 years old, not only continues in perfect health, but has been improved, the berries not being so small as in former days. What evidence do the Vines of modern planting supply? As a rule, splendid bunches and berries for the first five or seven years after planting, and then they sink gradually but certainly into comparative mediocrity. This is the history of all the Vines from which the splendid Grapes for the London exhibitions have been cut for the last 20 years. Vines in robust youth produce fine bunches for a few years under the restrictive system of development, but left to themselves comparatively, and allowed to send their roots and branches far and wide, they not only continue to produce fine branches and berries, but, according to Mr. Norman's experience, after 100 years the berries may be had larger than they were when the Vine was younger. These are facts which should make us pause; and if we look philosophically into the matter we shall perhaps find that we have for years been working in the wrong groove, and that to bring the Grape to the greatest perfection, we must allow the Vine more room to develop itself both by root and branch. If any proof of this be wanting, select two common trees of any kind, and as nearly alike as possible. Next spring as soon as they start into growth, stop the shoots of one weekly, just as the shoots of the Vines are stopped in our hothouses, and if, by the end of the season, it is not evident how effectually the growth of the plant operated upon has been dwarfed as compared with that left to Nature, we shall be much mistaken. All evidence is in favour of allowing Vines to take a much wider range of growth than has been customary for many years past, and by doing so, and inducing constitutional vigour, we not only reduce the chances of the plant suffering from a temporary check, but we also place it, in a great measure, beyond a check of any kind. With a large growth of branches there must be an equally large development of roots, and hence the plant, by the number and activity of its feeders, is placed beyond the power of seasonal changes or slight accidents.

Nor is this evidence confined to the sunny south or the range of the Grampian Hills. There are Vines quite as large and as fruitful as those which have lately been alluded to. It is therefore worth while for gardeners to consider how they will read this lesson of Nature's teaching, and utilise it for the improvement of their Grape crop. Practically, especially in early forcing, we have always looked upon a strong main stem as a reservoir or store of nutriment upon which the young branches could feed until the roots got into active growth, and without this store, especially in the case of cold borders, we should have more failures than we have had hitherto. What is the cause of the incipient bunches of Grapes going blind? Let the young gardener study what we have written, and if he cannot find the answer to this question, we will try to find it for him.—*Gardeners' Chronicle*, Feb. 9th.

HOUSE SPARROWS.

Of all our native birds not one is so well known or so universally distributed throughout the British Isles as the House Sparrow (*Passer domesticus*). Town and country, smiling fields and barren moorlands, wherever there is a human habitation, however humble, all are the same to him, for he is always at home. Everywhere he is the same fearless, independent bird; but the town sparrow is a much more pert little fellow than his brother of the country, and of the former class the London bird is the *beau-ideal*—he seems to have borrowed all the forwardness and impudence of the London *gamin*, and, as for fear or timidity, it has no place in his disposition. But it is with country sparrows that we have now to do; and though they are rather more unsophisticated than those inhabiting our towns, they are still a fearless tribe, and very amusing with their consequential and impudent airs.

But notwithstanding all that can be alleged against them, they are eminently serviceable to man, and certainly do not deserve the indiscriminate attacks which are made upon them. I believe the benefits they confer in the destruction of caterpillars and other insects injurious to our various crops outweigh tenfold their consumption of corn and other seeds, and I have found them most valuable assistants in my garden in clearing my gooseberry and currant trees of caterpillars; one pair of sparrows, during the season of feeding their young ones, will kill in a week 3,400 caterpillars. I am convinced that the sparrow suffers unjustly from the many accusations brought against him by those who have not closely watched him feeding from one year's end to the other, but have formed their judgment from seeing, perchance, a flock revelling on the corn where laid by the wind, or even on the gathered sheaves.

The nest of the sparrow is a loose, careless structure, and it is amazing to see in some cases the quantity of materials of which it is composed without any apparent necessity for such an accumulation. The mouth of a cast-iron pipe, about six inches in diameter, proceeding from a stove in a laundry attached to my father's house was, singularly enough, chosen every year, and sometimes twice in the season, as the site for a nest. The stove was only used every fortnight, and in this time the nest was built and some eggs always laid, but I never knew the parents bring up a brood, for the smoking of the stove always led to the obstruction being discovered and removed; and sometimes I have found the eggs quite baked with the heat.

The space underneath the tiles of my own house was generally occupied by a pair or two of sparrows, and hearing one day a very noisy commotion on the roofs, and seeing numerous birds flying to and fro in apparent trepidation, as if some calamity had befallen them, I was convinced something was the matter, and procuring a ladder I mounted to the spot, and at once discovered the reason for all the outcry. One of the owners of a nest underneath the tiles—the female—in passing through the small aperture leading to her domicile, and which at the lower end tapered quickly, had evidently slipped, and her neck had become so securely wedged between the tiles that escape was impossible. Her dying struggles attracted her neighbours, who with great good will had done their best to extricate her from her unfortunate position; their zeal, however, was greater than their discretion, for they had pulled and tugged so earnestly that, when I arrived on the scene, hardly a feather was left on the body, which of course was lifeless.

I remember another similar instance, and on the same roof too, where a young one in leaving the nest had got its leg entangled in a loop of a piece of worsted which was amongst the materials composing the nest. It vainly tried to free itself, and, as in the former instance, a great crowd assembled to assist their unfortunate companion; but their efforts did more harm than good, for, as it hung halfway down the tile, suspended by the thread, they had tried to release it by pulling it, and with the same result as in the other instance, for by the time I reached it it was half stripped of its feathers, and its little life was almost gone.

In both these cases I feel convinced that the efforts which were made by the companions of the luckless sparrows were prompted by a feeling of compassion and a real desire to alleviate their misfortunes; their anxious hurrying to and fro, and the distress expressed in their cries, clearly indicated this. I have seen similar feelings of alarm and sympathy shown by domestic poultry, when on one occasion a cock was flying to the top of a fence in my own yard, but missed his aim, and fluttering down, his head slipped between two of the palings; the hens hurried to help him, but of course unavailingly, and he would soon have been strangled if I had not gone to the rescue.

I have often been amused to see a sparrow take possession of the nest of a house martin (*Hirundo urbica*). The eaves of a house near my own were always selected by the martins year by year for their erection, and rarely has a season passed without one of the aggressions occurring, which I have watched from my windows with much interest.

It always appears to me that this forcible taking possession of their neighbour's house by the sparrows was never done with any intention of making it their own residence, but from sheer mischief, and a desire to tease and tantalise the poor martins. These invasions always took place when the nest was empty, either before any eggs had been laid, or after the young had gained sufficient strength to take wing. I have watched the sparrow sitting quietly on the tiles above the nest, as if he was the most innocent creature possible, intent only upon his own affairs, and had not the slightest thought of intruding upon his neighbour's; but the moment he became assured that the nest was unoccupied, he fluttered down, and popping in, turned himself quickly round, and sat with his head peeping out of the opening. Great, of course, was the consternation and distress of the martins on discovering the intruder; but though I have seen the incident dozens of times, I never saw any attempt to attack or eject the sparrow, nor, as it is asserted has been done, to stop up the hole with clay, and thus to inclose him, as the erring nuns were of old,

Alive, within the tomb.

I have always been inclined to disbelieve this story altogether, for I thought that the sparrow was too bold a bird to sit quietly and allow itself to be thus immured, when a few strokes of its strong beak would speedily demolish its prison walls, but M'Gillivray adduces three such well-authenticated instances of such an occurrence that I am compelled to abandon my doubts in the face of such an authority. One of these instances he thus relates:—

"A few years ago, in the window of a second storey of a house in Linlithgow, inhabited by Mr. James Brown, buckle-maker, a pair of martins built a nest, which was taken possession of by a female sparrow. In attempting to dislodge this bold intruder, a dozen of their companions came to their assistance, but after many severe struggles they were unable to effect their object. For her rash conduct, however, they were determined to make her suffer. They agreed to entomb her alive by closing up the entrance with the mortar which they use in building their nests, and in this they succeeded. Mr. James Douglas, slater, with whom I have been a long time acquainted, and upon whose veracity I can depend, assured me that he was a spectator of the occurrence, and that he in the presence of several individuals, some of whom he named, took the dead bird out of the nest. The truth of it is further confirmed by Mr. John Ray, nailer, in Linlithgow, who told me he was also present when it happened."

He also mentions two other instances that came within his knowledge.

What I have said about its boldness is well proved by the following incident, which occurred at the vicarage of Beeston, near Nottingham, in August, 1859. Numerous flocks of sparrows had frequented the grounds, and the cat belonging to the house had been watching their arrival, and seized every opportunity of pouncing upon them. She was at the foot of a tree one day, looking up at the sparrows, and doubtless on murderous deeds intent, which they seemed to divine, for in a few minutes they descended *en masse*. As the birds came within reach the cat made a spring at them; but the tables were now turned, for so fierce and pertinacious was their attack, so closely did they follow up their enemy, hemming her in on all sides, that she was perfectly cowed, and compelled to seek safety by springing through a window, leaving the victory to her brave little assailants.

I know a few years since an instance of the power of imitation which the sparrow possesses. A young one was brought up by a person at Newark from the nest, its place being always in a cage by the side of a skylark. Here it learnt the song of the lark, and would repeat it so accurately, that if you did not see the bird it was impossible for a time to tell whether it was the lark or the sparrow that was singing. Often have I heard and admired its surprising imitation, when suddenly it would cease its song and utter the usual harsh chirrup of its race. Sometimes its sweet song would be frequently interrupted by this natural note, while at others it would sing for a long time without giving vent to it.

Variations of the sparrow's plumage are not uncommon, being chiefly interminglings of white. In December, 1859, one was shot at Ollerton which had the whole of the plumage white, the head and back merely having a slight tinge of brown, giving the white on those parts a dirty appearance.

I have seen a singular place selected for the nest of a sparrow—viz., the ornamental iron brackets supporting the roof over the platforms of several of the stations on the Liverpool and Manchester Railway, and where they seemed quite unconcerned by the passage of the trains. —*Field*, Jan. 26th.

TREE-FERNS.

TREE-FERNS form one of the most striking and conspicuous, and at the same time elegant, features in the landscape of certain tropical regions. They would seem to unite in themselves the majestic growth of palms, with all the delicacy of the lower ferns, and thus attain a beauty to which nature shows nothing similar.

They are confined to districts within the torrid zone, at least in the northern hemisphere; though in the southern they are found in as high a latitude as the farther extremity of Van Dieman's Land, and at Dusky Bay, New Zealand—*i.e.*, nearly the forty-sixth parallel. This difference is due in all probability to the greater amount of moisture in the atmosphere in the southern hemisphere; inasmuch as a moist and damp climate is such as is especially favourable to their development. Indeed, wherever the tree-ferns appear within the tropics, from the plain to the height of 3000 or 4000 feet, the soil and atmosphere are full of moisture; whereas, on a barren soil, or where the atmosphere is very dry, they are entirely wanting. On tropical mountains of South America, they are found at an elevation varying between 1900 and 3800 feet, the palms and bananas taking their place at a lower elevation. As might be inferred, islands would be expected to abound with these noble creations; and such is the case. The coasts of the Sandwich, Cape de Verd, and Ladrone Islands, as well as New Caledonia, the Isle of France, the

Isle of Bourbon, and the most southern of the Friendly Islands in the southern hemisphere, possess, particularly in summer, almost the same climate as is found at the equator, and consequently the same vegetation prevails there as in equatorial regions, only somewhat less luxuriant, since there is generally a deficiency of soil and water. But, in these islands, the palms and bananas quickly disappear when we ascend above the level of the sea; and at the height of 300 or 400 feet, we enter the region where the shrubby and arborescent ferns predominate.

In the Brazils, Von Martius observed trees of the handsome *Alsophila excelsa*, and of *Didymochlæna*, upwards of twenty-five feet in height, and six or eight inches in diameter.

In the eastern hemisphere, Dr. Hooker met the species *Alsophila gigantea* ascending nearly 7000 feet in elevation on the outer (Sikkhim) Himalaya. The black trunks of these ferns are rugged in comparison with those of other species of many other countries, and seldom reach the height of forty feet. Another species, *A. spinulosa*, of which the soft pith is eaten by the native Lepchas in times of scarcity, is very abundant in East Bengal and the peninsula of India; while the last-mentioned *A. gigantea* is far more common from the level of the plains to 6500 feet elevation, and is found as far south as Java.

The most luxuriant specimens visited by Dr. Hooker were at Silhet, where "in the narrow parts of the valleys, the tree-ferns are numerous on the slopes, rearing their slender brown trunks forty feet high, with feathery crowns of foliage, through which the sunbeams trembled on the broad and shining foliage of the tropical herbage below." Similarly, on some of the East Indian Islands, the tree-ferns grow in such numbers that their stems are as close to each other as the slender firs and pines of our plantations.

Beyond the extreme elegance of form, and the beauty of their foliage, tree-ferns possess little or no economic value. The remarkable nature of their wood renders them totally unfit for any purposes to which our ordinary timber trees can be applied.

The mass of it consists of soft pith of a brown colour, through which are scattered, about the centre, isolated bundles of hard woody fibres, while near the circumference curiously curled or waved plates of wood occur. These touch one another at different places up the stem, and unite at those points. They separate again, to reunite at some higher place up the stem. From these points, where the woody plates unite, bundles of wood pass off externally into the leaves (fronds), and go to form the "ribs" and "veins" which constitute their "skeleton" or framework.

A remarkable difference exists between these plates of wood and that of our own forest trees. In the latter a cross section exhibits a series of concentric circles; these really being transverse sections of cylinders of wood, continuous throughout the tree, and of which the outermost layer is the youngest, one cylinder being formed annually outside that of the preceding year. Moreover, the whole is encased in a separable bark which continues to increase in thickness by yearly additions to its inner surface. But in tree-ferns there is nothing of the sort. The plates of wood, once formed, never increase in size laterally. They grow only at the summit, and thus become elongated as the tree itself increases in height. Again, there is no true bark, as, *e.g.*, in the oak. There is a sort of rind, principally formed by the bases of the leaves, which, as they fall, have diamond or lozenge shaped scars arranged more or less in a spiral manner upon the exterior surface of the stem. The lower part frequently throws out an innumerable quantity of fibre-like roots, giving it somewhat the appearance of an old branch of ivy, and which completely invest the trunk, forming a covering several inches thick; this covering, in fact, being often nearly, if not quite, as thick as the whole diameter of the trunk itself.

Another point of interest is the method of propagation, which is similar to that of any of our ordinary English ferns. If, for instance, a full-grown frond of the common "male shield fern" (*Aspidium Filix mas.*) be examined, there will be found on the under surface what appear at first sight as minute brown patches, or spots, each being covered by a little disk-like scale. These patches are called *sori*, and constitute the reproductive organs of ferns. The sori of *Alsophila nigra* consist of a number of little "sporanges," supported by short stalks, and growing from a small cellular cushion from which spring a quantity of delicate-jointed hairs. These "sporanges" have strong elastic borders, which, on their becoming mature, contract and cause them to burst; when out fall a number of seed-like bodies of a somewhat rounded or angular form, called spores. These, like seeds, fall to the ground, germinate, and give rise to young fern-plants. They are not true seeds, because these latter can only be produced by the agency of flowers, or at least certain elements of them, which are essential to their production; and it must be borne in mind that ferns never blossom. Our "royal fern" (*Osmunda regalis*) is sometimes called the "flowering fern," but it is a misnomer, the fact being that, when about to produce its fructiferous organs, it sends up a tall frond of different construction from the rest, and entirely covered with sporanges, few or no green parts accompanying them. Hence it presents some general appearance to a stem crowded with minute blossoms, but its construction is essentially the same as that above described.

A vast diversity obtains amongst the fronds of different ferns, as well as considerable variety in the form of the indusia, or scales over the sori, as well as in other points. Upon these distinctions the different groups of ferns are made, and receive different names accordingly. Nevertheless, there is a remarkable uniformity in all essential particulars throughout the class. One more particular is, perhaps, worth noticing; namely, that these gigantic tree-ferns come very near in point of structure of their organs of fructification to a minute but rare English fern (*Woodsia ilvensis*), in possessing peculiar hairs or bristle-like processes which rise from beneath the sori.—Rev. G. Henslow in *Leisure Hour*, Feb. 16th.

MUSHROOM HIVED ANTS.

LET us begin with the species that builds the mushroom-shaped edifice. These singular hives, shaped like gigantic mushrooms, are scattered by tens of thousands over the Otando Prairie. The top is from twelve to eighteen inches in diameter, and the column about five inches, the total height is from ten inches to fifteen inches. After the grass has been burnt they present a most extraordinary appearance; near Máyolo they are met with almost at every step. They are not all uniformly built, as they appear at a distance, but differ in the roundness or sharpness of their summits. I opened a great number of these, and followed up my researches, day after day, into the habits of their inhabitants. These, and all similar edifices, are built to protect the White Ants against the inclemencies of the weather and against their enemies, which are very numerous, and include many predacious kinds of fellow ants.

The mushroom shaped hive is not so firmly built in the ground but that it can be knocked down by a well planted kick. It is built of a kind of mortar after being digested in the stomachs of the ants. When felled, the base of the pillar is found to have rested on the ground, leaving a circular hollow, in the middle of which is a ball of earth full of cells, which enters the centre of the base of the pillar, and the cells are eagerly defended by a multitude of the soldier class of ants, which I took to be males, all striving to bite the intruder with their pincer-like jaws. On breaking open the ball, which, when handled divided itself into three parts, I always found it full of young white ants, in different stages of growth, and also of eggs. The young were of a milky white colour, while the adults were yellowish with a tinge of grey when the abdomen is full of earth. Besides these young ants, there were a great many full grown individuals, whom I took to be females, and who appeared to be the workers or labourers described by entomologists. These have not elongated nippers, like the soldiers, but have very bulky abdomens, and they are inoffensive. Besides these soldiers and workers, I always saw, whenever I broke a hive, a very much larger specimen than the other two, which came in from the inner galleries, looked round and went away again. These large ants were very few in number. There were therefore three distinct sets of individuals. To these large ones I shall give the name of head men, or chiefs.

In order to examine the rest of the structure, I often took an axe, and broke the rest into several pieces; but the material was so hard, that it required several blows before I succeeded. I tried then to make out the structure of the chambers and galleries of which the interior was composed. But before I could do this, I was somewhat perplexed at discovering that there was another distinct species of white ant, mixed up with the proper architects of the edifice. The soldiers of this other species, were much smaller and more slender, and as I brake the pieces, these two kinds fell too fighting one another. On close inspection, I found that these slender fellows come out of cells composed of yellow earth, whilst the others inhabited cells of black earth. The yellow colour was due to a coating of some foreign substance on the walls of the cell. The chambers inhabited by the slender species did not communicate with those peopled by the lords of the manor, they seemed rather to be inserted into the vacant spaces, or partition walls, between the other cells. No doubt they had intruded themselves after the building had been finished, from under the ground. In the fight the larger kind showed no mercy to the smaller. It was quite marvellous to witness the fury with which the soldiers of the one kind seized the bodies of the others with their powerful pincer jaws, and carried them away into their own chambers. The soldiers of the slender kind also possessed long pincer like jaws, and I noticed in one instance, when a worker of the larger kind had seized a small worker who was in her last struggle for life, that one of these slender soldiers flew to the rescue and snapping into the soft abdomen of the assailant twice its size, let out its contents. The slender one then fell from the pincers that had gripped her, but life was extinct. The rescuer came, examined the body, and seeing that she was dead went away and disappeared. If she had been only wounded, she would probably have been carried away as they do the young. I may here remark that with the exception of the head, the body of the termites is exceedingly soft. On examining the structure of the soldiers it is evident that their powerful pincer jaws are made for wounding and piercing, while the structure of the workers shows that their pincers are made for the purposes of labour. Nothing astonished me more than this impetuous attack; my attention was intense on this deadly combat. The weaker species knew the vulnerable point of his formidable enemy who was too busy to protect himself. A further examination showed me that the mushroom-like cap of the whole edifice was composed of both black and yellow cells. This curious mixture of two species, each building its own cells and yet contributing to form an entire and symmetrical edifice, filled me with astonishment. The wonder did not cease here; for in some of the mushroom-like heads there was still a third kind quite distinct from the other two, not a white ant.

The mushroom nests are built very rapidly, but when finished they last in all probability many years. The ants work at them only at night, and shut out all the apertures from the external air when daylight comes, for the white ant abhors daylight, and when they migrate from an old building to commence the erection of a new one, they come from under the ground. Sometimes they add to their structures by building one mushroom head above another. I have seen as many as four, one on the top of the other. The new structures are built when the colony increases; new cells must be found for new comers. The shelter is quite rain proof.

I passed hours in watching the tiny builders at work. Their daily labours in the cells, which I was enabled to do by laying open some of their cells, and then observing what went on after all was quiet. So soon as the cells are broken a few head men or chiefs are seen, each one moves his head all round the aperture and then disappears into the dark galleries, apparently without leaving anything. Then the soldiers come; these do no work, but there must be some intention in their movements, they no doubt were on guard to protect the workers: I was never able even with my magnifying glass to see them do anything. The workers then come forward, and each of them turns round and eject from behind a quantity of liquid mud into the aperture, and finally walls it up. They come one after the other and all of them leaves their contributions. This is done first in a row, from one end of the aperture to another, then each ejection is put on the top of the other, with a precision that would do honor to a bricklayer or stonemason. The question to me was to know if the ants went away to eat more earth and came again. How much would I have given to be able to see into the dark recesses of the chambers, but I do not see how this will ever be done. The apertures of the cells were only closed during the day, and during the following night the part of the structure which I had demolished was rebuilt in its original shape. Some of them brought very small grains of sand, or minute pebbles, and deposited them in the mud. When demolishing their shelter, I saw several cells filled with these little pebbles which I had also collected and preserved. Soon after others came and closed up the cell. The earth which they eat, can be seen shining through the thin skins of their bodies, but I was unable to see where it was stored in the interior of the edifice. The mud is mixed with gluey matter through the digestion when it is ejected, and with this material the little creatures are enabled to build up the thin tough walls which form their cells, and in course of time the firm and solid structure of the entire nest. Sun and rain are equally fatal to the white ants; thus it is necessary that they should build a hive impervious to light, heat, and rain. I have put white ants in the sun, and they were shortly afterwards killed by its heat. I thought each cell was perhaps inhabited only by one ant, but the great number I saw in each mushroom-like edifice, made it quite improbable that it should be so.—*Du Chaillu's Journey to Ashango Land.*

WHAT ARE GLACIERS?

RENDU first observes the piling-up of the mountain snows. The snow falling upon the mountains is partly converted into water, which runs away to the river and through the river to the sea. The ice thus formed Rendu estimates to equal in the Alps fifty-eight inches annually, which would make Mont Blanc four hundred feet higher in a century, and four thousand feet higher in a thousand years.

"Now it is evident," observes he, "that nothing like this can occur in nature. This ice must be removed by the operation of some natural cause;" and observations having shown that this actually takes place, Rendu occupies himself with methods to discover how Nature has performed the task; and he comes to this very rational conclusion—that the glacier and river are in effect the same, that between them there is a resemblance so complete that it is impossible to find in the latter a circumstance which does not exist in the former, and as the river drains the *waters* which fall upon the hillsides to the ocean, so the glacier drains the *ice* which forms from the snows on the mountainsides down to the same level.

And he closes his argument with declaring the law—"The conserving will of the Creator has employed for the permanence of His work the great law of *circulation*, which strictly examined is found to reproduce itself in all parts of Nature."

And in illustration of this law we see that the waters circulate from the ocean to the air by evaporation, from the air again to the earth in the form of dews, rain, and snows, and from the earth back again to the ocean through the great rivers which have gathered up the little streams from every hillside and valley.

Now this law of circulation is in the icy regions of the Alps, of the lofty Himalayes, of the Andes, of the mountains of Norway and of Greenland, the same as in the lower and warmer regions of the earth where the rivers drain the surface-water to the sea.

A glacier is in effect but a flowing stream of frozen water, and the *river systems* of the temperate and equatorial zones become the *glacier systems* of the arctic and antarctic.

We have now seen that a part of the snow which falls upon the mountains is converted into ice, and this ice, strange though it seems, is moveable: by what exact principle of movement has not yet been decided to the satisfaction of the learned, but it is nevertheless true. Rendu truly remarks—"There is a multitude of facts which would seem to necessitate the belief that the substance of glaciers enjoys a kind of ductility which permits it to mould itself to the locality which it occupies, to grow thin, to swell, to narrow itself like a soft paste."

And this, true of the Alpine passes, is true also of the Greenland valleys. A great frozen flood is pouring down the east and west slopes of the Greenland continent; and, as in the Alps, what is gained in height by one year's freezing is lost by the downward flow of the mobile mass.

And this movement is not embarrassed by any obstacle. The lower chains of hills do not arrest it, for it moulds itself to their form, sweeps through every opening between them or overtops them. Valleys do not interfere with its onward march, for the frozen stream enters them and levels them with the highest hills. It heeds not the precipice, for it leaps over it into the plain below—a giant frozen waterfall. Winter and summer are to it alike the same. It moves ever forward in its irresistible career, a vast frozen tide swelling to the ocean. It pours through every outlet of the coast, ranges down every ravine and valley, overriding every impediment, grinding and crushing over the rocks, and at length it comes upon the sea. But here it does not stop: pushing back the water, it makes its own coast-line, and moving still onward, accommodating itself to every inequality of the bed of the sea as it had before done to the surface of the land, filling up the wide bay or fiord, expanding where it expands, narrowing where it narrows, swallowing up the islands in its slow and steady course, it finally reaches many miles beyond the original shore-line.

And now it has attained the climax of its progress.

When long years ago after pouring over the sloping land it finally reached the coast, and looked down the bay which it was ultimately to fill up, its face was many hundreds of feet high. Gradually it sank below the line of waters as it moved outward, and finally its front has almost wholly disappeared.

In a former chapter I have mentioned that a block of fresh-water ice floating in sea water rises above the surface to the extent of one-eighth of its weight and bulk, while seven-eighths of it are below the surface. The cause of this is too well known to need more than a passing explanation. Every schoolboy is aware that water in the act of freezing expands, and that in the crystal condition fresh water occupies about one-tenth more space than when in a fluid state, and hence when ice floats in the fresh water from which it was formed one-tenth of it is exposed above, while the remaining nine-tenths are beneath the surface. When this same fresh-water ice (which it will be remembered is the composition of the glacier) is thrown into the sea, the proportion of that above to that below being changed from *one* and *nine* to *one* and *seven* is due to the greater density of the sea water, caused by the salt which it holds in solution.

Now it will be obvious that as the glacier continues to press further and further into the sea, the natural equilibrium of the ice must ultimately become disturbed; that is, the end of the glacier is forced further down into the water than it would be were it free from restraint, and at liberty to float according to the properties acquired by congelation. The moment that more than seven-eighths of its front are below the water-line, the glacier will like an apple pressed down by the hand in a pail of water have a tendency to rise, until it assumes its natural equilibrium. Now it will be remembered that the glacier is a long stream of ice many miles in extent, and, although the end may have this tendency to rise, yet it is for a time held down firmly by the continuity of the whole mass. At length, however, as the end of the glacier buries itself more and more in the water the tendency to rise becomes stronger and stronger, and finally the force thus generated is sufficient to break off a fragment, which once free is buoyed up to the level that is natural to it. This fragment may be a solid cube half a mile through, or even of much greater dimensions. The disruption is attended with a great disturbance of the waters, and with violent sounds which may be heard for many miles; but, floating now free in the water, the oscillations which the sudden change imparted to it gradually subside, and after acquiring its natural equilibrium the crystal mass drifts slowly out to sea with the current, and is called an ICEBERG.—*Dr. I. I. Hayes' The Open Polar Sea.*

INTELLIGENCE OF ELEPHANTS.

IT is most interesting to observe the elephant, as it is to observe any other animal, not when it is practising tricks taught it by man, or acting under the influence of habits acquired in confinement, but when it is acting from its own impulse, and using its own natural sagacity. A person who has never seen an elephant except in a cage, kept quiet under the control of its keeper, can have but a faint notion even of its corporeal powers. For my own part I had no conception of the effect with which an elephant can use his trunk till, several years ago, in the Regent's Park Zoological Gardens, I saw one, that had been led out for exercise and left standing by its keeper for a few moments under a tree, whisk its proboscis perpendicularly up among the branches, twist off a leafy bough, with the utmost ease, in a moment, convey it to his mouth. Nor do we form any due estimation of the elephant's ingenuity and intelligence until we see him exercising it of his own accord.

"It is a usual part of the performances of an elephant at a public exhibition to pick up a piece of coin, thrown within his reach for that purpose, with the finger-like appendage at the extremity of the trunk. On one occasion a sixpence was thrown down which happened to roll a little out of the reach of the animal, not far from the wall; being desired to pick it up, he stretched out his proboscis several times to take it, but it was even yet a little beyond his reach; he then stood motionless for a few seconds, *evidently considering* (we have no hesitation in saying *evidently considering*) *how to act;* he then stretched his proboscis in a straight line as far as he could, a little distance above the coin, and blew with great force against the wall; the angle produced by the opposition of the wall made the current of air act under the coin, as he evidently intended and anticipated it would; and it was curious to observe the sixpence travelling by these means towards the animal till it came within his reach, and he picked it up. This complicated calculation of natural means at his disposal was an intellectual effort beyond what a vast number of human beings would ever have thought of, and would be considered a lucky thought and a clever expedient, under similar circumstances, in any man whatsoever. It was an action perfectly *intelligent,* and one that had no relation either to self-preservation or propagation."

"I was one day," says Mr. Jesse, "feeding the poor elephant (who was so barbarously put to death at Exeter Change) with potatoes, which he took out of my hand; one of them, a round one, fell on the floor, just out of reach of his proboscis. He leaned against the wooden bars, put out his trunk, and could just touch the potato, but could not pick it up. After several ineffectual efforts he at length *blew* the potato against the opposite wall with sufficient force to make it rebound, and he then without difficulty secured it. Now it is quite clear, I think, that instinct never taught the elephant to procure his food in this manner, and it must, therefore, have been reason or some intellectual faculty which enabled him to be so good a judge of cause and effect; indeed, the reflecting powers of some animals is quite extraordinary."

The male elephant called Jack, which was in the Zoological Society's Gardens in the year 1840, used to be made to fast the whole of Sunday, like the carnivorous animals, with the exception of a slight breakfast. But after enduring this weekly privation for a time he came to a resolution to submit to it no longer. Accordingly he made such disturbances on several successive Sunday nights that the keepers had little repose. But as this procured no relief to his hunger he at length proceeded further, and made on one occasion such a determined attack on his door that the people were glad to get up in the night to feed him. After this energetic demonstration he was allowed his full meals on Sundays, and continued quiet.

This elephant gave a remarkable proof of ingenuity by certain operations on the ceiling in front of his apartment. It was a ceiling formed of boards, and considerably lower than that of the room within, but thought to be sufficiently high to prevent him from injuring it, and its surface was made perfectly smooth, so as to afford him no means of effecting a hold on it. But, wanting something to do in the monotony of his confinement, he appears to have sounded it and concluded it was hollow; then, raising his head suddenly, he drove one of his tusks through a board, and next, setting to work with his trunk, he broke away the edges of the hole thus made and gradually enlarged it; putting his trunk through and tearing down board after board, until his proceedings were observed and means taken to stop them.

Of the elephant's sense and judgment, the following is given as a well-known fact in a letter of Dr. Daniel Wilson, Bishop of Calcutta, to his son in England, printed in the life of the Bishop, published a few years ago.:—An elephant belonging to an engineer officer in his diocese had a disease in his eyes, and had for three days been completely blind. His owner asked Dr. Webb, a physician intimate with the Bishop, if he could do anything for the relief of the animal. Dr. Webb replied that he was willing to try, on one of the eyes, the effect of nitrate of silver, which was a remedy commonly used for similar diseases of the human eye. The animal was accordingly made to lie down, and when the nitrate of silver was applied uttered a terrific scream at the acute pain which it occasioned. But the effect of the application was wonderful, for the eye was in a great degree restored, and the elephant could partially see. The doctor was in consequence ready to operate similarly on the other eye on the following day; and the animal, when he was brought out and heard the doctor's voice, lay down of himself, placed his head quietly on one side, curled up his trunk, drew in his breath like a human being about to endure a painful operation, gave a sign of relief when it was over, and then, by motions of his trunk and other gestures, gave evident signs of wishing to express his gratitude. Here we plainly see in the elephant memory, understanding, and reasoning from one thing to another. The animal remembered the benefit that he had felt from the application to one eye, and when he was brought to the same place on the following day and heard the operator's voice, he concluded that a like service was to be done to his other eye.

The two following stories are of a similar character. The second especially shows the sagacity of the animal:—

"During one of the wars in India, many Frenchmen had an opportunity of observing one of the elephants that had received a flesh-wound from a cannon-ball. After having been twice or thrice conducted to the hospital, where he extended himself to be dressed, he afterwards used to go alone. The surgeon did whatever he thought necessary, applying sometimes even fire to the wound; and though the pain made the animal often utter the most plaintive groan, he never expressed any other token than that of gratitude to this person, who by momentary torments endeavoured, and in the end effected, his cure."

"In the last war in India, a young elephant received a violent wound in his head, the pain of which rendered it so frantic and ungovernable that it was found impossible to persuade the animal to have the part dressed. Whenever any one approached it ran off with fury, and would suffer no person to come within several yards of it. The man who had the care of it at length hit upon a contrivance for securing it. By a few words and signs he gave the mother of the animal sufficient intelligence of what was wanted; the sensible creature immediately seized her young one with her trunk, and held it firmly down, though groaning with agony, while the surgeon completely dressed the wound, and she continued to perform this service every day till the animal was perfectly recovered."—*The Reasoning powers of Animals*, by the Rev. J. S. Watson. Reeve and Co.

GEOLOGY OF AMERICA.

IF we draw a line from New York to the east end of Lake Ontario, the Peninsular lying north-east between the St. Lawrence and the sea, consists of primitive interspersed with some patches of secondary rocks. From this line southward the country has a different geological character. A belt of alluvial soil, beginning at Long Island, extends along the shore of all the Southern States to Natchez, on the Mississippi, having an average breadth of a hundred miles, and probably including all Florida, except some high ground in the interior. It is everywhere penetrated by the tide-water in the rivers. On the west side of this is a region of primitive rocks from 100 to 200 miles broad, in which gneiss predominates. It embraces the eastern ridges of the Alleghanies with the rolling country at their foot. On the west side of this again is a long narrow zone of transition-rocks, including the western ridges of the Alleghanies, and extending from Lake Champlain to the north-west angle of Georgia.

One of the most remarkable circumstances connected with the primitive rocks is the granite ridge which forms the boundary between the primitive and the alluvial regions. This ridge seems to have been the ancient line of the sea-coast in the Southern and Middle States, and very probably through Connecticut.

New England rests on a bed of granite and marble, the Middle States on sandstone and freestone, and the greater part of the Ohio region has a foundation of limestone.

The oldest-known strata in the crusts of the earth, the Laurentian series, consisting of gneiss more or less of granitic, quartz rock, limestones, dolomites, conglomerates, and in the upper portion of feldspathic rocks, occur in the Adirondac region of Northern New York. The Green Mountains, the White Mountains, and a greater portion of the New England States, consist of crystalline formations of a more recent date, marked by the absence of argillaceous, talcose, and chloritic schists, and by various other characteristics.

The next overlying series, known as the Huronian, and regarded by Murchison as the equivalent of the Cambrian sandstones, is formed in Michigan and the southern shores of Lake Superior. Though these rocks have been classed as azoic, indications are found of their having been originally sedimentary deposits, abounding in organic bodies, the forms of which have been dislodged by the metamorphic action to which they have been subjected.

In Massachusetts, the central portion of North Carolina, and in Georgia, occur the oldest fossiliferous rocks, known as the "Taconic system," and characterised by ancient genera of trilobites. Some geologists maintain that some of the sandstones in Iowa and Minnesota should, by reason of their fossils, be placed in this system.

The crystalline and schistose strata of New England, the highlands of New York and New Jersey, and extending through the Appalachian chain to Alabama, have been variously classed, some considering that as they consist of feldspathic gneiss, quartz rocks, talcose, and chloritic slates, they form the base of the Appalachian system. Others consider them as the metamorphosed sandstones, etc., of the lower Silurian series.

From this range westward, the whole country to the rocky mountains, with the exception of the Ozark mountain region, in South Missouri, and a few localities in Wisconsin and the northern peninsula of Michigan, contain no crystalline rocks.

The lower silurian limestones come up to the surface at Cincinnati, Ohio, at Frankfort (Kentucky), and at Nashville (Tennessee). The carboniferous series whenever met with is the uppermost formation, except in Illinois, Iowa, and Kansas, where the Permian strata have been recognised. The great plains that extend from the Missouri and up the valleys of the Akansas, Red River, to the Rocky Mountains, are almost exclusively occupied by cretaceous rocks, sometimes overlaid with those of the tertiary age. Florida, Louisiana, and the coasts from Texas to Martha's Vineyard, are composed of the tertiary, the older strata cropping out inland.

The cretaceous formation rests principally on the metaphoric belt of the Appalachian, rising to the higher platform of those rocks, the ascent south of New York being marked by the first or lowest falls of the rivers, and determining the head of their navigation. This formation passes across New Jersey and the Northern Delaware, from New York Bay to the head of Chesapeake Bay, occurs at a few points in Virginia, near Wilmington, North Carolina, and through Central South Carolina and Georgia; thence it stretches in a broad continuous belt through Central Alabama, Northern Mississippi, and Western Tennessee.

A narrow belt of red sandstone occurs along the valley of the Connecticut, continued through New Jersey, across Pennsylvania, into Virginia.

The newer phiocene is met with in only a few localities in the southern part of Maine, and on the borders of Lake Champlain.

The drift formation covers all the northern part of the United States, the limit southward being lat. 40. The deposits of alluvium are mostly confined to the borders of the rivers and lakes, the most extensive and remarkable alluvial tract being that around of the mouth of the Mississippi, where it spreads out into a delta of broad area.

In the Rocky Mountains the metamorphic rocks of the Appalachian are repeated on a grander scale. Between the numerous ridges are wide belts of the cretaceous strata and modern tertiary deposits. These form the plains and slopes which stretch out towards the Pacific. In the mountainous districts are found all the formations from the lower crystalline groups to the coal, often traversed by great dikes of trappean and other eruptive rocks.

Beyond the Sierra Nevada and Cascade Mountains, and on the Colordo River, is a volcanic district, extending to the Pacific. It consists chiefly of tertiary strata, which have been so broken up by movements of the crust and volcanic eruptions, as to present an excessively rugged and diversified structure.

The metals of the United States are principally found in the crystalline rocks, the exceptions being the copper regions of Lake Superior, and some of the western lead and iron mines, frequently in sandstone.

In the Atlantic division the metals follow the Appalachian range. In the Pacific division they follow the Rocky Mountain and Sierra Navada ranges, the *débris* from which, swept down into the tertiary strata, have furnished these with the precious metals in large deposits.

Except a few insulated fields, all the bitumous coal in the United States lies west of the Appalachian chain, where a vast series of coal-beds stretch from the mountains westwards through Ohio, Indiana, and Illinois, parts of Kentucky, Tennessee, and Alabama, into the State of Mississippi, and even as far as 200 miles beyond the Mississippi River. Anthracite coal, or that best suited for manufactures, lies at the northern extremity of this great field, in Pennsylvania, in the western parts of Virginia, in part of Ohio, and in Illinois. In the central portion of the lower peninsula of Michigan is a coal-field of some extent, and another and larger one spreads over nearly the whole of Iowa, Northern Missouri, and a large part of Kansas.—Bacon's *Descriptive Handbook of America*. G. W. Bacon and Co.

KANGAROOS.

I HAVE lately passed a few days in the agreeable society of a well-informed and intelligent gentleman, the proprietor of a large estate in what is called Gipp Land, and another in the western district, two of the most productive in the colony of Victoria. In the extensive provinces of this district, bounded on one side by a river, his numerous herds of cattle depasture, and become fat in a very short space of time. Their grass was, however, much diminished by the quantities of kangaroos, which also fed on the productive grass. To give some idea of their extraordinary number, I may mention that one gentleman, a squatter, shipped to England in the year 1863 no fewer than 30,000 skins taken from those animals killed on his run, but which, it is to be regretted, were of but little value in this country. Extraordinary, however, as it may appear, after this large quantity had been destroyed, their number did not seem perceptibly diminished. My informant said, that in driving along the roads he had seen them as thick together as a flock of sheep. In order to show the injury they do to the cattle browses, it may be mentioned that they feed on the best part of the native grasses, where it is the shortest and sweetest. Their increased numbers may be accounted for by the destruction, by poison, of the native dogs which formerly killed many of the kangaroos, and also by the blacks being at present so few in number that they do not procure them for food as formerly was the case when they were so numerous.

The English settlers do not prize the flesh of the animal, except the tail, which is made into soups, and considered as good as ox-tail soup, although rather more glutinous.

The kangaroo is hunted by dogs which are a cross between the deer or stag-hound and the English greyhound, for it requires a very fast dog to overtake them in the chase; in fact, speed with strength. One dog by himself is no match for an old kangaroo, for it will take one of these large dogs in his forearms and run away with him with the greatest possible ease. The claws on the hind legs of the kangaroo are formidable weapons: with them they can rip up a dog, and even a man, if he happens to come in too close contact with it. The supposition that they spring from their tail is quite a mistake: they only use the tail in order to balance themselves, and also as a rudder. While running at full speed, a fence four feet six inches in height will not stop them: they will clear it with as much speed as a horse could, or perhaps with more ease than a horse.

The kangaroo, like the opossum, has an abdominal pouch. This singular animal was discovered by that great navigator, Captain Cook, in the year 1770, in New Holland, as it was then termed. Its principal progress when in motion is by leaps, and these have been ascertained to exceed twenty feet at a time; and thus it will elude the swiftness of the fleetest greyhound. The kangaroo is now known to feed standing on its fore feet, like other quadrupeds. The female has two breasts in the pouch, on each of which are two teats; and yet, strange to say, she has generally but one young one at a time. It is then excluded from her uterus and placed in the pouch, but by what process has, I believe, never yet been satisfactorily ascertained. It then scarcely exceeds an inch in length, and weighs about twenty grains. At this time, according to some naturalists, its mouth is only a round hole, only large enough to receive the nipple. It has been supposed that in the first instance it is attached to the teat by a glutinous substance which is found in the uterus. At this time, fable as it may appear (I quote from Philosophical Transactions), the forepaws are comparatively large and strong, and the claws extremely distinct, in order to facilitate the motion of the little animal during its residence in the large pouch; while the hind legs, which are afterwards to become very long and stout, are now both shorter and smaller than the others. The young one continues to reside in the pouch till it has attained its full maturity, occasionally running out for exercise or amusement; and even after it has quitted this maternal retreat, it often runs into it for shelter on the least appearance of danger.

I have been assured by an eye-witness of the fact, that when a female kangaroo, with a young one in its pouch, has been hard pressed by dogs, she has been seen to take the young with her fore feet and throw it as far as she was able on one side, so as to lighten her own burthen and thus to facilitate her escape. It has been supposed from this fact that she has but little regard for her young; but such probably is not the case, but more likely that, having evaded the pursuit of the dogs, she returns to seek her young one.

Kangaroos live entirely on vegetable substances. In their native state they are said to feed in herds of thirty or forty together, and one is generally observed to be stationed, apparently on the watch, to give alarm of approaching danger, at a distance from the rest, similarly to what gregarious birds are known to do. One writer (Labatrardière) has been of opinion that they live in burrows which they form in the ground, but I am not aware that there is any authority for this supposition. There is a smaller species of kangaroo in New Holland, about the size of a badger, which certainly burrows in the ground. Not so the larger one, which frequently is found to be as tall as a man.

The hair of the kangaroo is of a greyish-brown colour, similar to that of our wild rabbit. It is thick and long when the animal is old, but it is late in growing, and when only begun to grow is like ashy down.

The teeth of the kangaroo are so singular, that, according to the celebrated naturalist John Hunter, it is impossible from them to say to what tribe they belong. They are not ruminating animals.—Edward Jesse in *Once a Week*, February 9th.

GRASSES OF NEW ZEALAND.

In this paper the author included the natural orders Juncaceæ, Restiaceæ, Cyperaceæ, and Gramineæ, and enumerated the different genera and species he met with, and recorded the localities in which they occur. Buchanan is of opinion that some of the more fibrous Grasses (species of Triticum, Agrostis, Arundo, Danthonia) which abound on the lower hill ranges, at elevations over 1,000 feet, might be used as a source of supply of paper material. But there are various strong reasons why it is extremely unlikely these native Grasses should be able successfully to compete with other paper materials which are both much more abundant and cheaper. Several Grasses are recorded as indigenous by Dr. Hooker, which are also British: not a few British Grasses have, undoubtedly, been introduced, and are now, more or less, extensively naturalised; while some are probably both indigenous and introduced. The problem here offers itself for solution to the local botanist— viz., whether, or how, it is possible to distinguish the native from the naturalised condition of the same species? for, on one hand, Grasses regarded by Dr. Hooker as introduced occur under circumstances in which it is, to say the least, extremely difficult to conceive of their diffusing from remote stations; while, on the other, those recorded as indigenous are found in localities which give rise to the legitimate conjecture that they have been introduced. For instance, two British species of Festuca occur in Otago (F. duriuscula, and F. bromoides). The former is recorded by Dr. Hooker as native; the latter as "certainly introduced and nowhere native." I found them growing in the same habitats, and intermixed; it was impossible to determine that the one was native and the other introduced. So far as regards their botanical characters, they appear identical with British specimens, and from their occurrence on the sheep and cattle runs of settlers were probably introduced rather than indigenous. Again, Kœleria cristata is recorded in the Hand-book. Fl. No. 3 (p. 335), as native, though Dr. Hooker adds, it is "probably introduced only." But in a letter [Jan. 31, 1865] he says of it, "I have increasing reasons for considering it introduced. Nevertheless the plant occurs high on the Alps (4000 feet) of Canterbury and Otago, most remote from cultivation or settlements. Poa annua is regarded as introduced, but it was the most extensively distributed Grass I met with in Otago, growing in a great variety of habitats, and in a corresponding multiplicity of conditions. Phalaris canariensis was gathered by Foster in 1772, being before the colonisation of New Zealand (Otago was colonised so recently as 1847), but three years subsequent to Cook's first voyage (1769). It is difficult in such a case to understand how it came to be introduced, and yet it is included in Dr. Hooker's list of naturalised Grasses. I found it growing in Otago apparently as wild as those British Grasses to be hereafter mentioned, which are considered truly indigenous. Anthoxanthum odoratum has been gathered at elevations of 3000 to 4000 feet on the glacier Mount Cook (13,000 feet high). It is extensively distributed throughout New Zealand, and it is one of the Grasses I found growing in great profusion and luxuriance in several parts of Otago. Specimens indistinguishable as to size and general aspect from my Otago plant were collected by myself in 1850 on the meadows bordering the Elbe, Holstein. It is included, however, in Dr. Hooker's category of naturalised Grasses, as is also Bromus mollis, which has been found on the Canterbury Alps at 4000 feet. On the other hand, the following are recorded by Dr. Hooker as native:—Agrostis canina, Alopecurus geniculatus, and Deschampsia cæspitosa. I do not think the problem is now capable of satisfactory solution in all cases. In certain cases there may be a strong probability that the plants were introduced, such as Lolium perenne, Anthoxanthum odoratum, or Poa annua, but I do not admit the conclusiveness of the evidence according to which certain British species of Festuca, Agrostis, Alopecurus, and Deschampsia are determined to be native, and those of Kœleria, Phalaris, Bromus, and Festuca to be merely naturalised. It is equally impossible to assert that the former are not native, or the latter also native; all that I hold is that in the present stage of colonisation—in the present state of our knowledge of the botany of New Zealand—proof of a sufficient or satisfactory kind to establish either one set of propositions or the other, is probably impossible of attainment. The New Zealand Gramineæ illustrates well that continuity of variation, so characteristic of New Zealand plants in general, which so frequently sets at defiance all the efforts of the systematist to classify particular plants or forms, whether as variety, species, or even genus. It seems to me a fruitless and absurd effort to name separately the infinite and inconstant variation forms of the supposed species or type, while the supposed book species, and even in certain cases genera themselves, are much too numerous for the proper purposes of science or the student.—*Paper Read by Dr. Lauder Lindsay at the Botanical Society of Edinburgh*, Jan. 10th.

EIDER DUCKS.

The greatest favourites and the most valuable of all the feathered tribes here are the eider ducks. Their down is the lightest and softest of animal coverings, probably the worst conductor of heat, and therefore the warmest clothing that is known. The eider down has long been one of the most important products of Iceland, and, until lately, has usually sold at several dollars a pound. The kings and princes of the north of Europe do not sleep on the down of the cygnets of the Ganges, but on and under the down of the eider duck. The increased products, the varied manufactures, and the widely-extended commerce of the world have brought into use other materials more conducive to comfort and health than the eider down; and the consequence has been, the price has greatly fallen, so that now the poor peasant can sleep on down, and it can be purchased for less than 50 cents a pound. The eider duck (*Somateria mollissima*) is a large and fine-looking bird. The male is over two feet in length, and weighs six or seven pounds. His back, breast, and neck are white, inclining to a pale blue; the sides white; the lower part of the wings, the tail, and the top of the head, black. On the water he is as graceful as a swan. The female is much smaller than the male, and differently coloured. The female is pale yellowish-brown, mottled with both white and black. The tips of the wings are white, the tail a brownish-black. But a poor idea is given, however, of the looks of these birds by an enumeration of their colours. The down is a sort of brown or mouse colour. These singular birds have both the character of wild and domesticated fowls. In the winter they are so wild that it is difficult to come near them; but in the breeding season—the month of June—they are tamer than barn-door fowls. On the islands all round Iceland, and many parts of the main shore, they cover the land with their nests. When left to themselves, the brood of the eider duck does not exceed four; but remove the eggs daily, and she will continue to lay for weeks. The drake is a very domestic husband, and assists in all the little household arrangements previous to the advent of the little ducklings. They build not far from the water, making the nest of seaweeds and fine grass, and lining it with the exquisite soft down which the female plucks from her breast. If you approach the nest—which is always near the water—the drake will give a hostile look at you, then plunge into the sea with great violence; but the female stands her ground. If in a gentle humour, and used to seeing company, she will let you stroke her back with your hand, and even take the eggs and down from under her. Sometimes she will fight and strike with her sharp beak, and she gives a blow in earnest. On finding the down gone from her nest, she plucks off more; and when the supply fails, the drake assists in furnishing it. I have been told if their nests are robbed of the down more than twice, they abandon the place and will not return there the following season. Half a pound is the usual quantity taken from a nest, and this seems a great deal, for the domestic goose, at a single picking, rarely yields more than a quarter of a pound of feathers. A greater quantity of down is gathered in wet seasons than in dry. What immense quantities of these birds come around Reykjavik and spend the breeding season, particularly on the islands of Engey and Vithey, in the harbour. Around the houses, and frequently all over the roofs, their nests are so thick that you can scarcely walk without treading on them. The inhabitants get eggs enough to half supply them with food. The eggs are the size and about the colour of hen's eggs, though not quite so white, rather inclining to a yellow. They are nearly equal in quality to those of barn fowls. After the young are hatched their education commences immediately. They graduate after two lessons. The old duck takes them on her back, swims out into the ocean, then suddenly dives, leaving the little mariners afloat. The flesh of these birds is excellent, better than any other sea-fowl. In Iceland their value is so great for their eggs and down, that there is a law against shooting them. For the first offence a man is fined a dollar, and for the next he forfeits his gun. They are greatly alarmed at guns, and, if often fired among, they quit the coast. So, with kind treatment, they give a good return; but treat them unkindly, and they will not return at all.—*Rambles in Iceland*.

The Atmosphere.

The atmosphere, or, in more familiar terms, the "element we live in," may be described as a thin, transparent, invisible, and elastic fluid. It surrounds the earth, covering the sea and land, revolves with it, and extends to a considerable height above the summits of the highest mountains. It is fluid always, from one known extreme of temperature or pressure to another. It is ponderable, and possessed of a degree of elasticity that no compression can remove or lessen. When confined, it may be reduced into any part of its ordinary bulk, however small; and when again released, it will expand to any volume, however large. When compressed it is dense, and its elasticity, or elastic force, is in direct proportion to its density, supposing its temperature to remain unchanged. If the temperature be increased, its elastic force increases; and if it be decreased, it diminishes,—in both cases at the same rate.

The atmosphere is compounded of many constituents, and is the most subtle and penetrating of the elements. Its laws have a direct bearing upon human life, and the products of the soil. Under ordinary conditions, it is the breath of our life; but when contaminated, it generates disease, and carries with it a mortal pestilence. The evil effects of impure air may be witnessed every day in the crowded habitations of the London poor: when joined with neglect and filth, the "element we live in" becomes a living poison. I have myself too often witnessed the evil-operation of air defiled by the respiration and re-respiration of individuals, confined to a small apartment.

The air so breathed is deteriorated, and deprived of the healthy properties belonging to it in nature. Inured to the morbid action of its poisonous breath, the inhabitants of a district thus defiled attest its influence in their weakly frames and pallid faces; but no outraged perceptions of taste and smell warn the sufferers of its pernicious influence, and they inhale, with blunted consciousness, an atmosphere rife with the germs of fever and premature decay.

But the same atmosphere, unsullied by human neglect and sordid necessity, exists in its fullest purity for miles as we ascend, to a height greater than man has yet gone or can go. Colourless when near, its transparent depths are the medium of reflected colour, which, as we ascend beyond the influence of earthly vapours, deepens to an intensity of blue we know nothing of below.

The air is a blending of subtle gases, of which more than 99 per cent. consists of oxygen and hydrogen, a great part of the remainder of aqueous vapour and carbonic acid, with other gases in very small proportions. These quantities prevail at all elevations, whether among mountains, or vertically in space, up to the greatest height which has yet been attained. With these aëriform fluids the waters of the earth mix in alterable proportions, according to the process of evaporation. Invisibly suspended, the aqueous vapour of the atmosphere varies in quantity according to the season of the year and the hour of the day; its regulating power is temperature, which, as the air becomes cooled, condenses vapour into visible form and substance.

For miles above the earth a variable quantity of water is mixed with the air. It is this union of two dissimilar fluids, which produces the whole visible phenomena of cloud, haze, fog, &c. Whenever the temperature of the air declines from any cause, the moisture which at the higher temperature was in the invisible form of vapour, is condensed, and assumes the visible shape of clouds.—*James Glaisher, F.R.S., in Good Words*, Feb.

SUB-TROPICAL PLANTS.

The taste for this class of plants, though but of recent devolpment in this country, is increasing, so that it may be as well to specify those kinds which may be quickly raised from seed, and are likely to produce a satisfactory effect. Unquestionably the most effective and the cheapest of all are the rather numerous form or varieties of the castor oil plant, Ricinus communis They are cheap, and may be raised on heat as freely as pickling cucumbers, while the fine effect they produce must be remembered by every visitor to Battersea Park sub-tropical garden. Next in importance come the numerous kinds of Cannas, so extensively employed in Paris, and of late years about London. Nothing can be better adapted to relieve the monotony of the flower garden and diversify it with graceful verdure than these. They should be raised on a brisk hotbed, pit, or warm stove in early March, and encouraged to grow freely and without check in every way, till turned into a cooler structure about May to "harden off" a little previous to being turned out in rich beds in a warm-sheltered situation in June. After these the best are Artemesia annua, a green and graceful bush, quite a free growing annual, grows six feet high or more in good ground; Aristolochia Sipho, a hardy, great-leaved climber, fine for covering arbours, high trellis work, &c.: Carduus marianus, the milk thistle; Onopordon acanthium, the great cotton or Scotch thistle, fine when seen isolated among green shrubs. Numerous kinds of Cucurbita or gourd, both large and small kinds, as nothing can be better adapted for running over trellis work, banks of rich ground, pyramidal beds, or many positions, while the fruit of all is ornamental and of most edible. Ferdinanda eminens, the tall plant, used so much at Battersea; Gynerium argentum, the pampas grass, surely as "sub-tropical" in effect as anything can be; the stripped Japanese maize, for choice positions, and for placing among not over-vigorous neighbours; the Virginian tobacco, which is very effective in leaf when grown in rich ground, and not by any means to be despised as a flowering plant; the summer cypress (Kockia scoparia), which forms a neat little green pyramid; Salvia argentea, a hardy, free-growing thing that forms very large silvery leaves spreading flat upon the ground; Solanums in variety, and particularly robustum, marginatum, macrophyllum, and verbascifolium; Wigandia caracassana, a magnificent thing, requiring, however, good culture; and Chamapeuce diacantha, a very extraordinary thistle-like subject.

Along with these we will enumerate the best of the bedding plants that furnish effect in our parterres from their leaves alone, or at least those of them that may be raised from seed. They are as follows:—Amaranthuses, and particularly A. melancolicus ruber, Artemesia argenta (not much used, but good—raise in heat, and preserve over the winter). Atriplex hortensis rubra (good, but rather coarse), the two Centaureas, ragusina and gymnocarpa. These may not be fit for much the first year of raising unless sown early, and they are now pretty cheap as plants; but it is as well to state that they may be raised from seed. Cineraria maritima (a well-known silvery edging plant), Chenopodium atriplices (a free-growing annual, with a peculiarly pleasing tint over the tops of the shoots), Perilla, Oxalis tropæoloides (a low, dark-leaved trailer, very useful), Santolina inanca, and Cerastiums Biebersteini, and tomentosum.—*Field*, Jan. 26.

How to Forecast the Weather.

The following were among the maxims of the Meteorological Department in determining their forecasts. They are selected and re-arranged from the digest made by the committee and appended to their report. It is to be hoped that meteorologists will both amend and add to this imperfect list, on which the committee remark:—"Some of these maxims rank among the long-established truths of meteorological science, while others are clearly open to considerable doubt." I. Atmospheric or air currents.—In the latitude of the British Isles, and of North-Western Europe generally, there are two, and only two essentially different atmospheric currents—one S.W., running from the equator towards the pole, and the other N.E.; running from the pole to the equator. The characteristics of the S.W. current lie not only in its general direction, but in its quality; for it is light, warm, and moist. In other words, its presence is shown by a low barometer, by a high thermometer, and by a small difference between the wet and dry bulb thermometers. The characteristics of the N.E. current, in a similar way, lie not only in its general direction, but also in its quality, for it is heavy, cold, and dry. In other words, its presence is shown by a high barometer, a low thermometer, and by a large difference between the wet and dry bulb thermometers. The weather in this country depends almost wholly on the conflict, combination, alternate preponderance, or alternate succession, of portions of these opposite currents. Not only is the actual presence of either current shown by its corresponding instrumental tests, but an approaching change from one current to the other is foretold by the instruments beginning to change their indications. (Hence, as changes of weather must necessarily commence at some places earlier than at others, there is great advantage in receiving by telegraph information of the state of the weather, and of the instruments at many stations.) When S.W. and N.E. currents alternately prevail, the wind blowing over any station has a strong tendency to "veer," and not to "back." That is to say, the general order of the changes is N.E.S.W.N,, and not N.W.S.E.N, II. Weather changes—Gradual changes of weather are shown by a gradual rise or fall of the barometer; for instance, at the rate of one-hundredth of an inch in an hour. Great differences of temperature at the same, or adjacent places, are followed by changes of weather. Rapid changes of all kinds commonly presage violent atmospheric commotion. The result of all rapid changes in the weather, or in any of the instrumental indications, is brief in duration; whilst that of a gradual change is more durable. III. Direction and Force of Wind—The wind usually blows from a region where the barometer is high to one where the barometer is low. The force of the wind is usually proportionate to the differences of barometric pressure at adjacent places. In other words, the greater the barometric tension the stronger the wind. Strong winds are far more steady in duration than light or moderate winds. IV. Gales or Storms—Great storms are frequently preceded by excessive meteorological disturbance, as by heavy falls of rain or snow, by much lightning, by unusual cold, or excessive heat. Sea disturbance often precedes gales. Great storms are usually shown by a fall of the barometer exceeding one inch in 24 hours, or by a fall of nearly one-tenth of an inch in an hour. The barometer frequently continues high during a N.E. storm, but there is a fall of the thermometer. Most of our violent storms travel bodily in a N.E. direction. V. Calms—Calms may be due to either of three different states of weather—1, the appulse of winds coming together from opposite quarters; 2, the divergence of winds going towards opposite quarters; 3, the centre of cyclonic storms. The barometer rises in 1, and sinks in 2. It is extremely low in 3. When the S.W. and N.E. currents intermingle, water is precipitated in the form of cloud, rain, or snow.—*Gardeners' Chronicle*, Feb. 2nd.

The Wild Goat.

The best modern account of the wild *C. ægagrus* is by Captain T. Hutton (in the second volume of the "Calcutta Journal of Natural History") who observed it in Afghanistan, where he possessed a tamed buck, which he figures in outline from the living animal, and we are indebted to him for a coloured figure of the same individual, which few persons would hesitate to refer to a domestic goat of some kind, by no means extraordinary in its appearance. This animal stood 3ft. 1in. at the shoulders, and the horns of a particularly fine specimen in the British Museum measure 50in. round the arched curvature, and would have grown at least six inches more; they were in their ninth year of growth: beard about 1in. long. "The shoulder," remarks Captain Hutton, "has every appearance of great muscular power, and is, what in a horse would be termed heavy. The neck also is massive, doubtless for the purpose of enabling it to support the enormous horns which grace its head. The hind-legs are generally kept somewhat in a crouching attitude, as if ready for a sudden spring in case of alarm. This attitude imparts a wildness to the general character of the animal, and at the same time gives it the appearance of being much higher at the withers than at the croup, and the back consequently appears to slope gently from the shoulders to the hind-quarters. This feature is much heightened by the occurrence along the back of the neck and shoulders of long hair, which stands up erectly, so as to form a well-marked mane, which, when the animal is alarmed or angry, becomes a very prominent character. This mane is dark-coloured, and forms part of the black dorsal line. The head is usually kept stretched out, as it were, and the expression of the face is gentle though somewhat wild. The attitude when on the alert, and springing fearlessly from crag to crag in the rocky fastnesses, where it delights to roam, is bold and haughty, giving an idea of great muscular strength and agility, which indeed the animal possesses in no ordinary degree, but its speed is not sufficient when it descends to the plains to preserve it from the greyhound. It is, however, only when driven from his haunts by the intensity of the winter that he condescends to visit the lowlands, and that but rarely happens. The usual pace of this animal is a kind of canter, which among the hills enables it rapidly to evade pursuit, but is not nimble enough, nor is the stride sufficiently long to suit it to the plain lands, though for scaling mountain heights it is admirably adapted. The leaps which they take are tremendous, and almost pass credibility."—*Land and Water*, Feb. 2nd.

Ancient Eclipses.

A short time before his decease the late Dr. Hincks communicated to the Royal Academy of Sciences at Berlin a paper "On a newly-discovered Record of Ancient Lunar Eclipses," which has just been published in the *Monatsbericht* of the Academy. He made the discovery in the last volume of the "Cuneiform Inscriptions of Western Asia," published by the British Museum, during a particular search for all the inscriptions that appeared to have an astronomical character. Among a great deal which he confesses he does not understand in plate 39, No. V., described as part of an astronomical tablet, he met with three statements, "the meaning of which appeared to him absolutely certain." They are as follows :—"In the month Nisan, on the fourteenth day, the moon was eclipsed." "In the month Tisri the moon was eclipsed." "In the month Sabat the moon was eclipsed." To the second of these statements a sentence is added in the original, explaining that "the moon emerged from the shadow while the sun was rising." Having published in the *Transactions of the Royal Irish Academy* a table by which the commencement of each Assyrian year might be ascertained, Dr. Hincks set himself to a careful investigation of these eclipses, with a view to fix the date of their occurrence. If that could be done, highly valuable conclusions would be obtained, of which astronomers would be only too glad to avail themselves. After an elaborate calculation, the details of which are given in the paper, he satisfied himself that the three eclipses had been seen as described, that the second occurred about the time of sunrise, on the 13th of September, 701, at the beginning of the reign of Sennacherib. Such an eclipse is so very unusual, that, if seen, Dr. Hincks assumes it would certainly be recorded, and he asserts that at the date above given, "this phenomenon was visible *somewhere* under the parallel of Nineveh." And he continues, "According to Hanson's Tables, the moon would be very far, perhaps half a degree, beyond the place which would allow the phenomenon to appear in the longitude of Nineveh. If, then, it be a fact that it was observed there, it furnishes astronomers with a most important datum for correcting the lunar tables." Dr. Hincks expresses his belief that professed astronomers will find it possible to reduce all the observations of the eclipses which he has mentioned to harmony with calculations by adopting the values of certain specified coefficients of Prof. Adams; and by computing all the elements of the eclipse for a time later than that of the actual time of observation by a small fraction of a day, multiplied by the square of the number of centuries from A.D. 1800. He points out that this last correction, which acts in the opposite direction to Adams's, is due to the retardation of the diurnal motion caused by the tides. These are the leading facts of this interesting communication; for the profound technical arguments by which the author's views are supported, we must refer the reader to the paper itself. Who would have expected when Mr. Layard began his excavations at Nineveh that they would give up particulars of eclipses which happened 700 years before the Christian era, and supply to astronomers of our day a means of rectifying one of the most important questions in their favourite science?—*Athenæum*, Feb. 9th

The Opossum.

The Opossum is another extraordinary animal, with a pouch for the reception of its young. Mr. Hunter tells us that he was so fortunate as to ascertain the size and weight of several embryos immediately after their exclusion from the uterus. One of them only weighed a grain. The weight of the six other young ones was but little more than this. The young opossums, unformed and perfectly without sight as they are at this period, find their way to the teats by an invariable instinct. They continue about fifty days in the pouch, when they attain the size of a common mouse; then they begin to leave the teats occasionally, but return to them again till they are about the size of rats. Their eyes open about the end of fifty days from their first reception in the pouch. The animal attains its full growth in about five months.

The opossum is distinct from all other animals, for there is not one that it can be immediately classed with, except it is a second degree from the monkey. It is supposed that they pair. They eat fruits of all kinds. It is about the size of a small cat, and when on the ground it appears to be very helpless, but it is able to ascend trees with great facility. It hunts after birds and marmots, and is destructive to poultry. It will put on a semblance of death when in danger. They are very tenacious of life: there is an old saying, "If a cat has nine lives the opossum has nineteen." Their flesh is white and well tasted, and is by some preferred to pork.

There is something in the mode of propagation in this animal that deviates from all others. It is known to be extraordinary, but the investigation has never been completed. Mr. Hunter tells us that he has endeavoured to breed them in this country, having brought a great many, and had friends who assisted him by bringing them or sending them alive, yet he never could get them to breed.

As the female opossum has a false belly, it may be supposed that she does not make any nest for her young, but carries them from place to place. The male opossum has a small tendency to a pouch on the belly.

It is to be regretted that we have not more decisive knowledge of the animals of New South Wales; as they are, upon the whole, like no others that we are acquainted with. They occupied much of Mr. Hunter's attention, but he evidently failed in classing them to his satisfaction.—*Once a Week*, Feb. 9th.

Diseases of Plants.

If we now examine the first deviations from normal phenomena which are exhibited in the occurrence of internal diseases, as for instance in smut (Uredo segetum), in decay, as in the stems of Cacti, juicy fruits, &c., or in the potato murrain, we find in every case that the nitrogenous lining of the cells first becomes discoloured, assumes a darker tint, a firmer consistence, a more evident granulation, and that it begins at the same time to percolate and saturate the cell-wall, so that it ceases to exhibit its pure reaction on the cellulose. These phenomena are so general that we may well suppose that all inward diseases of plants actually derive their origin from an abnormal condition of this coat, and inasmuch as the peculiar power of the chemical process in the cells is apparently concentrated there, its deprivation first calls into existence the symptoms of disease which are perceptible at a later period in the other portions of the cells. The comparative luxuriance of plants depends upon the inorganic matters presented to them in the soil. The proportional rarity of phosphates in most geological formations, and also in the soils which are wholly or principally formed from them, is well known ; on the contrary, they are accumulated in soils principally formed of decomposed vegetable matter, after being slowly collected by the plants. Animal excrements are very rich in these salts, and therefore manured fields, and especially gardens, contain a greater proportion than is normally present in plants, or can be consumed by them. But the influence which inorganic substances in the soil exercise on vegetation depends upon their being generally present. For since plants have not the power of choosing their own nutriment, and since the proportions in which soluble substances present themselves for absorption can be altered by endosmose within very narrow limits, it is equally important that the substances which are requisite for plants should be contained in the soil in something like the proper proportions, since the plants are otherwise compelled to receive matters in greater quantities than is agreeable to their normal structure, and in consequence inevitable anomalies take place in their vital action. The sum of what has been said may be stated thus :—The more phosphates are relatively increased in any soil in consequence of its mode of formation or cultivation, the more will the plants which it sustains have a tendency to deviate from their original type, to form sub-species and varieties, and finally to be attacked and destroyed by internal disease.—*Journal of Agriculture for Nova Scotia.*

Fish in Ceylon.

Ceylon, rich in forms of animal and vegetable life, continues to afford fresh instances of novel characteristics worthy of note ; for example :—recent observation confirms the fact of the natives being in the habit of digging for fish ; a place is selected on comparatively firm ground, where swampy land is covered with a rank vegetation for some years ; and having heard the fish beneath his feet breathing (for they are an air-breathing variety of *Ophiocephalus* and *silurus*—three species in all), the native proceeds to break down the soil for some little distance all around the place, filling up the belt he makes, with the tall reed-stems, and so making a kind of barrier, through which the fish don't escape, as it seems they might if they tried. Then he proceeds to thicken the swampy soil by the addition of some dry earth, till it becomes of the consistency of thick mud, thicker than the liquid part, and nearly as thick as that lying below. He also places layers of reeds at right angles, to make a kind of network horizontally ; and nothing then remains to be done but to wait for the fish, whose coming is indicated by bubbles of air rising to the surface, each fish making bubbles peculiar to its species. Presently the *silurus'* head appears, and then the native catches him, as he cannot withdraw, owing to the network through which he has just forced himself. At Callura there is a *siluroid* fish (water-breather), whose eggs, about the size of small grapes, are sold as food to the villagers ; and these eggs are emitted from the mouths of captured fish, where they are carried during the process of hatching ! The Rev. Mr. Boake, long resident at Ceylon, has given the most patient attention to these facts, and has collected specimens from the mouths of the parent fish. The eggs are produced in the ordinary way. The parent-fish are plump, and good to eat at the commencement of the season, but soon grow lean and ill-conditioned, from the want of power to feed for so long a time. One fish, nine inches long, had thirteen eggs, in which some were more advanced than others. The embryo's blood-vessels in the umbilical sac is plainly seen in some ; the head and tail have already escaped from others ; and besides this, the fish carrying these mouthfuls of eggs are all males. Dr. Günther describes a South American species of *Arius*, to which the Ceylon species belongs, as identical in this peculiar habit of carrying the ova in the mouth. Dr. Boake tried several experiments to test the vitality of air and water breathing fishes with fatal success.—*Land and Water*, Jan. 12.

Instinct in a Pike.

When Dr. Warwick was residing at Durham, the seat of the Earl of Stamford and Warrington, he was walking one evening by the side of a fish-pond in the park and observed a large pike of about six pounds' weight, which darted hastily away, and in so doing struck its head against a tenter-hook in a post and fractured, as it afterwards appeared, its skull and turned aside its optic nerve. It seemed to be in great agony : it first rushed to the bottom of the water and bored its head into the mud, thickening the water so that it was for a time lost to sight ; afterwards it plunged about hither and thither, and at last threw itself completely out of the water upon the bank. The doctor examined it and found that a small portion of the brain was protruding from the skull, and succeeded with the aid of his toothpick in replacing it, and then put the fish into the pond again. At first it seemed relieved and was quiet, but in a few minutes darted about again till it threw itself out of the water a second time. Again the doctor did what he could for it, and put it back into the water ; but it was still furious with pain, and afterwards threw itself out of the water several times. At last, with the assistance of the keeper, the Doctor contrived a bandage for its head, and left the fish in the water to its fate. He, however, took care to visit the pond on the following morning, when the pike came up towards him close to the edge, and, as he said, actually laid its head on his foot. He examined the fish's skull and found it likely to do well. Afterwards he walked backwards and forwards along the bank of the pond for some time, and the fish continued to follow his movements, turning as he turned. Next day he took some friends to see it; it came up to him as before: and at length it grew so docile that it would approach whenever he whistled and feed out of his hands, though to other persons it continued shy.—*Rev. J. S. Wanson's Reasoning Power of Animals.*

Mammoth Tree.

A great wonder of the vegetable world is the mammoth tree in California. A grove of 427 trees, the largest of which are 30 feet in diameter, and 300 feet in height, is in Mariposa county. It is the largest species of tree in the world, and this is the largest collection. The grove is about 20 miles from the Gosemite Valley, and about 4,500 feet high, on the western slope of the Sierra Nevada. When the traveller enters the grove he sees on all sides of him these huge giants of the forest, varying from 20 to 34 feet in diameter, and from 275 to 325 feet in height. The grove covers a space half-a-mile wide and three-quarters of a mile long. There is one tree 34 feet in diameter, two trees of 33 feet, thirteen between 25 and 33 feet, thirty-six between 20 and 25 feet, and eighty-two between 15 and 20 feet. One very large tree has fallen, and a considerable portion of it has been burned, but appearances indicate that it was nearly forty feet in diameter, and 400 feet high. The mammoth tree is found only in a few small groves, of which six or seven are known, though probably there are others in unexplored parts of the Sierra Nevada. The Calaveras Mammoth Grove was the first discovered, and attracts the greatest number of visitors. There are in this grove ten trees 30 feet in diameter, and eighty-two between 15 and 30. One of the trees which is down must have been 450 feet high, and 40 feet in diameter. The Horseback Ride, one of the notabilities of the place, is a hollow tree which a man on horseback can ride through. One tree which was stripped of its bark for a height of over 100 feet continued green and flourishing two and a half years, and some of its branches remained green seven years late.—*Bacon's Guide to America.*

New Books.

[*Our limited space must of necessity compel us to give but very short notices of new books, but they will perhaps serve as a guide as to what books our readers may ask for at their libraries.*]

A Journey to Ashango Land, and Further Penetration into Equatorial Africa. By Paul B. Du Chaillu. London: John Murray.

The above volume has no doubt been anxiously looked for, and accounts of the wonders therein contained has probably by this time afforded amusement and instruction to many. Such a work would require many pages of our magazine to do it justice, therefore we can do little more than inform those of our readers who are not already acquainted with the fact that it is now to be obtained at all libraries.

Most of the supposed fables detailed in M. Du Chaillu's "Equatorial Africa" have been corroborated by other eminent men, so that the present work, if it does not create as much excitement as the previous one, will at all events be read as a truthful description of a strange and wonderful country. Those who endeavoured to detract from the truth of M. Du Chaillu's former work will do well to read the manly and excellent preface to the present volume.

The gorilla is here again described in his native home. Also a further account of the curious potamogale velox, which we give on another page; as also the nest of the mushroom-hived termes. It may interest many of our fair countrywomen to learn that the present beautiful fashion of adorning the head was in vogue during M. Du Chaillu's visit, as may be seen in the following description of an African tribe—

The Ishogos are a fine tribe of negroes; they are strongly and well built, with well-developed limbs and broad shoulders. I consider them superior to the Ishiras in physique, and I remarked that they generally had finer heads—broader in the part where phrenologists place the organs of ideality. With some of them their general appearance reminded me of the Fans. The women have good figures: they tattoo themselves in various parts of the body—on the shoulders, arms, breast, back, abdomen; and some of them have raised pea-like marks, similar to those of the Opono women, between the eyebrows and on the cheeks. Both men and women adopt the custom of pulling out the two middle incisors of the upper jaw, but this mode of adding to their personal attraction is not so general as among the Aponos; many file their upper incisors and two or three of the lower ones to a point.

The men and women ornament themselves with red powder, made by rubbing two pieces of bar wood together: but their most remarkable fashions relate to the dressing of the hair. On my arrival at Igoumbié I had noticed how curious the head-dresses of the women were, being so unlike the fashions I had seen among any of the tribes I had visited. Although these modes are very grotesque, they are not devoid of what English ladies with their present fashions might consider good taste; in short, they cultivate a remarkable sort of chignons. I have remarked three different ways of hair-dressing as most prevalent among the Ishogo belles. The first is to train the hair into a tower-shaped mass elevated from eight to ten inches from the crown of the head, the hair from the forehead to the base of the tower and also that of the back part up to the ears being closely shaved off. In order to give shape to the tower, they make a framework generally out of old pieces of grass cloth and fix the hair round it. All the chignons are worked up on a frame. Another mode is to wear the tower with two round balls of hair, one on each side above the ear.

A third fashion is similar to the first, but the tower instead of being perpendicular to the crown is inclined obliquely from the back of the head, and the front of the head is clean shaven almost to the middle. The neck is also shorn closely up to the ears.

Those who procure the book will find illustrations of the different styles of chignons.

The Wild Elephant, and the Method of Capturing and Taming it in Ceylon. By Sir J. Emerson Tennent, Bart. London: Longmans and Co.

Everyone who takes an interest in one of the most intelligent and sagacious of animals should possess the above little work, issued at a price to suit most pockets. The author says: " In this volume the chapters descriptive of the structure and habits of the wild elephant, are reprinted for the sixth time from a larger work published originally in 1859. Since the appearance of the first edition, many corrections and much additional matter have been supplied to me chiefly from India and Ceylon, and will be found embodied in the following pages."

It would appear that the elephant found in Ceylon is identical with the one found in Sumatra, which differs in many material points from those found in India and Africa—for particulars of this curious problem we must refer our readers to Sir Emerson Tennant's preface, where also is related the curious fact of an elephant leaping a barrier nine feet in height, an extraordinary leap for such a weighty and unwieldy animal.

The work is divided into two parts of three chapters each, the first describing its habits in a state of nature; the first chapter of which relates to its structure and functions; the second, its habits when wild; and the third to elephant shooting. The second part treats of the mode of capture and taming. Subdivided, the chapters are—1st, an elephant corral; 2nd, the capture; 3rd, taming, and conduct in captivity.

Upon another page will be found some anecdotes collected to show the reasoning power of the elephant. The following account as witnessed by Major Skinner may be well added to those facts:—

The case you refer to struck me as exhibiting something more than ordinary brute instinct, and approached nearer to reasoning powers than any other instance I can now remember. I cannot do justice to the scene, although it appeared to me at the time to be so remarkable that it left a deep impression upon my mind.

In the height of the dry season in Newera Kalawa, you know, the streams are all dried up, and the tanks nearly so. All animals are then sorely pressed for water, and they congregate in the vicinity of those tanks, in which there may remain ever so little of the precious element.

During one of those seasons I was encamped on the bund, or embankment, of a very small tank, the water in which was so dried that its surface could not have exceeded an area of 300 yards square. It was the only pond within many miles, and I knew that of necessity a very large herd of elephants which had been in the neighbourhood all day must resort to it at night.

On the lower side of the tank, and in a line with the embankment, was a thick forest, in which the elephants sheltered themselves during the day. On the upper side, and all round the tank, there was a considerable margin of open ground. It was one of those beautiful, bright, clear moonlight nights when objects could be seen almost as distinctly as by day, and I determined to avail myself of the opportunity to observe the movements of the herd, which had already manifested some uneasiness at our presence. The locality was very favourable for my purpose; and an enormous tree, projecting over the bank, afforded me a secure lodgment in its branches. Having ordered the fires of my camp to be extinguished at an early hour, and all my followers to retire to rest, I took up my post of observation on the overhanging bough; but I had to remain for upwards of two hours before anything was to be seen or heard of the elephants, although I knew they were within 500 yards of me. At length, about the distance of 300 yards from the water, an unusually large elephant issued from the dense cover and advanced cautiously across the open ground to within 100 yards of the tank, where he stood perfectly motionless. So quiet had the elephants become (although they had been roaring and breaking the jungle throughout the day and evening) that not a movement was now to be heard. The huge beast remained in his position still as a rock for a few minutes, and then made three successive stealthy advances of several yards (halting for some minutes between each with ears bent forward to catch the slightest sound) and in this way he moved slowly up to the water's edge. Still he did not venture to quench his thirst, for though his fore-feet were partially in the tank, and his vast body was reflected clear in the water, he remained for some minutes listening in perfect silence. Not a motion could be perceived in himself or shadow. He returned cautiously and slowly to the position he had at first taken up on emerging from the forest. Here in a little while he was joined by five others, with which he again proceeded as cautiously, but less slowly than before to within a few yards of the tank, and then posted his patrols. He then re-entered the forest, and collected round him the whole herd, which must have amounted to between 80 and 100 individuals—led them across the open ground with the most extraordinary composure and quietness, till he joined the advanced guard, when he left them for a moment and repeated his former *reconnoissance* at the edge of the tank. After which, having apparently satisfied himself that all was safe, he returned, and obviously gave the order to advance, for in a moment the whole herd rushed into the water with a degree of unreserved confidence so opposite to the caution and timidity which had marked their previous movements, that nothing will ever persuade me that there was not rational and preconcerted co-operation throughout the whole party, and a degree of responsible authority exercised by the patriarch leader.

The Reasoning Power in Animals. By the Rev. John Selby Watson, M.A., M.R.S.L. London: Reeve and Co.

Mr. Watson has here given us a wonderful collection of anecdotes illustrating the intelligence of animal life, showing how very near (if they do not really possess) they approach to what man alone believes himself to be master of—the power of reason.

Descartes and many others were of opinion that all the lower animals are mere unreasoning machines, as much as a clock or watch; that all their actions may be explained by the laws of mechanism; that many things doubtless they do better than man could do them, but that they do these things only, and cannot learn to do others; showing that they do not act from thought or judgment, but from mere instinctive use of their organs. Our author is not of the same opinion, and after reading his volume most people will agree with him that there is often something more than instinct, wonderful as that power is, in many of the ways of animals.

Of the examples selected for illustration the dog, as we may suppose, stands pre-eminent, there being no less than fifteen chapters devoted to him: next in importance is the elephant, about which there are five chapters. The two occupying half the volume, the rest—some eighteen chapters—contain a motley collection of beasts, birds, and fishes: amongst which are the lion, tiger, glutton, racoon, beaver, ox, sheep, pig, hare, wolf, cat, fox, rats, mice; robins, tomtits, swallows, parrots; carp, mullet, salmon, eels, walrus; bee, ants, spiders, butterflies, &c.

Bacon's Descriptive Handbook of America. By G. W. Bacon, F.R.G.S., and W. G. Larkins, B.A. Crown 8vo. With numerous Maps, Engravings, etc. London: Bacon.

The above contains in a small volume a quantity of matter suitable to the tourist, capitalist, or emigrant, and those who remain at home but take an interest in the welfare and success of the great nation across the Atlantic. Everything peculiar to the country and the people is here collected, condensed, and arranged in such a form as to make it a complete *vade mecum* of information, and in a way that deserves the highest praise and commendation.

In its pages will be found a description of the early settlement, physical and political geography, agriculture, manufactures, commerce, finance, education, religion, laws, institutions, characteristics, etc. The maps consist of a large one of the whole country (size 18 by 28 in.) and four smaller ones, illustrating the physical features, the geology, the agriculture, and the six groups of states.

The Open Polar Sea: a Narrative of a Voyage of Discovery towards the North Pole in the Schooner United States. By Dr. I. I. Hayes. London: Sampson Low, Son, and Marston.

A personal narrative of a voyage to the Arctic regions, in order to complete the survey of the north coast of Greenland and Grinnell-land, and to make such explorations as might be found practicable in the direction of the north pole. The volume forms a valuable addition to our works on the Arctic regions. The scenery is well described, and the physical forces which characterise that portion of the globe ably explained. The purpose of the voyage being scientific, it may be imagined that much valuable information has been collected. It is written in a lively and spirited manner, and the author carries the reader interested with him to the end, and leaves him to regret that there is no more.

Lima: Sketches of the Capital of Peru, Historical, Statistical, Administrative, Commercial, and Moral. By Manuel A. Fuentes. London: Trubner.

The above is intended to place before the reader an accurate and faithful description of the capital of Peru and its inhabitants. A fairy land (the author says), whose very name has become a proverb, but which has been constantly misrepresented by the narratives of fantastic voyagers, who, being thoroughly ignorant of the country, have mistaken mere accidental circumstances for the general characteristics of its inhabitants.

The volume is full of illustrations, depicting the principal buildings, gardens, etc., and a goodly number of portraits of the *belles* of Lima.

The following works, likely to interest our readers, have appeared during the past few weeks:—

A Companion to the Weather Glass, designed to record, Numerically and Graphically, the Natural Phenomena presented by the Barometer, Thermometer, Rainguage, Clouds, Winds, &c., with Calendar, Plates, and Engravings. By Rev. R. Tyas, M.A., Cantab., F.M.S., &c. London: Bemrose and Sons, 21, Paternoster-row.

The Royal Atlas of Modern Geography. By A. Keith Johnston, LL.D., F.R.S.E., &c. Dedicated by Special Permission to Her Majesty. Imperial folio, half bound in russia or morocco, £5 15s. 6d. With Index of 150,000 Names contained in the Atlas. William Blackwood and Sons, Edinburgh and London.

Descriptive Astronomy. By George F. Chambers, F.R.A.S., of the Inner Temple, Barrister-at-Law. 21s. Macmillan and Co., London.

The Past and Future of the Kaffir Races. In Three Parts. By the Rev. William C. Holden. With Map and Illustrations. (Published for the Author).

The Elements: an Investigation of the Forces which determine the Position and Movements of the Ocean and Atmosphere. Vol. II. By W. L. Jordan. 4s. 6d. Longmans and Co.

The Heavens: an Illustrated Handbook of Astronomy. By Amédée Guilleman. Edited by J. Norman Lockyer, Esq., F.R.A.S. Royal 8vo, 200 Illustrations, 21s. London: R. Bentley.

Episodes of Insect Life. By Acheta Domestica. Edited by the Rev. J. G. Wood. 21s. London: Bell and Daldy.

Transactions of the Zoological Society of London. Vol. VI., Part II., price 36s., containing Professor Owen's Paper "*On the Osteology of the Dodo.*" With Ten Plates. London: Longmans and Co.

The Open Polar Sea: a Narrative of a Voyage of Discovery towards the North Pole. By Dr. Isaac I. Hayes. With Illustrations. 8vo., cloth, price 14s. London: Sampson Low.

New America. By William Hepworth Dixon. Third Edition. 2 vols., demy 8vo. With Illustrations, 30s. London: Hurst and Blackett.

Practical Chemistry. By Stevenson Macadam, Ph.D. London: Chambers.

[NOTE.—During the past month we have received several letters asking us to give prices to the books we publish a list of; it is not a usual course, but we see no reason why it should not be adopted if of benefit to our readers.—ED.]

Correspondence.

[*Under this head we shall be glad to insert any letters of general interest.*]

CHANGE OF HABITS OF ANIMALS.

SIR,—In 1801 the population of Glasgow was 84,000, in 1861 it amounted to 446,000, and now it is estimated at half a million. One consequence of this enormous increase in population, is, that the filth and stench of the river Clyde is in summer almost intolerable, and a large margin of flat sandy shore is exposed at low water, from Bowling to Greenock, more or less covered with deposits of slime mixed with garbage—organic matter in every stage of decay, excellent food for the gull, which picks up almost anything animal.

Within my own recollection the gull and birds of like feather have augmented in numbers on the Shores of the Clyde, almost, it seems to me, at the same ratio as that of the great city itself. Here, then, is a new feeding ground for this animal, and a new kind of food. At best it is a poor diver, and this new kind of food will not make it any more expert at diving, but rather tend to enfeeble, by disuse, muscles formerly so employed.

In consequence of its numbers increasing so much on the banks of the Clyde, I have observed it of late much more frequent on the tributaries of that river; for instance, on the Cart to Pollockshaws and upwards, and on the Brock, a small tributary of the Cart.

These waters are so polluted by chemical dye-stuffs that no trouts are to be found in them, scarcely even eels, so that their bill of fare must differ considerably from that afforded by clearer and purer streams; but, pressed by numbers, worms on the adjoining parks and any dead floating garbage on the rivers are thankfully received by the emigrants. Yarrell records that when this bird was fed on corn the walls of the stomach were found, on dissection, to be thickened, and I can easily allow of some slight change of organization incident on any animals' change of food or of habits. Thoughtless persons tell us that the fauna and flora, remains of which are found in the pyramids of Egypt, are the same as those found now. I do not think they are likely to be quite the same if the circumstances be much altered. The beaver loses its building habits and becomes solitary, where much persecuted, just as man himself does. Animals when pressed apply to new sources of subsistence, like individuals of our own species. The crow took to turnips during the severe winter of 1826, some *genius* among them having likely led the way, for every bird fancier knows that there are differences in the mental constitution of birds.

I know a case where weasels having multiplied considerably and being pressed by the wants of their large families, after having stocked their nests to no purpose, the mouths were so many, (for weasels have foresight often in stocking their larders,) dared in their hunger to venture on the untried; and fixing themselves on the cheek, nose, and underneck of the minister's cows at night, damaged them considerably. Their blood-thirsty new invention was discovered, cartfulls of dried whins were set fire to around or above their supposed nests, and the whole country was up, each rustic armed with a bludgeon, and hundreds of the little philosophers were sacrificed over the head of their selfish and daring discovery.

J. S.

Dumfriesshire, 13th February, 1867.

INSECT LIFE.

Sir,—Deriving much pleasure from the contemplation of insects and their habits, I, as an "Entomophilist," shall be glad of occasional information concerning them, from yourself or such of your readers as claim to be Entomologists.

While strolling in a garden in Suffolk one pleasant day last summer, my attention was arrested by the sight of an insect emerging "tail-first" from a hole in the sandy path at my feet. When clear of the hole, my little miner instead of flying off as I expected, merely made a dart of a few inches from the ground, at the same time throwing from him, or dropping, quite a shower of grains of sand and dirt, which he had evidently been excavating in the hole. On thus ridding himself of his load, he (taking no notice of me, although I had stooped to within a foot or so of the ground) as quickly returned, and plunging head first into the narrow opening was quickly out of sight. In a few seconds he again emerged with another load, which he discharged as before. Thus he continued to labour for some minutes, during which time the surface of the surrounding path was becoming strewn with the granules of earth, so laboriously "brought to light." I watched the industrious fellow carefully, to detect if possible how he contrived to bring up so many of these little dry detached masses at a time as he did, but could make nothing of it beyond seeing that his legs were crossed or bent under him, so as to form a sort of basket. His flight was so quick and so sudden that it was difficult to perceive the exact arrangement. Having bored the hole to the required depth and deposited an egg or eggs on the bottom thereof (I presume), this female miner or civil engineer flew off once more, this time to a short distance, and on her return brought with her a stone or lump of dry earth, which she placed over the mouth of the scene of her labour and her love; this piece was presently supplemented by other and smaller pieces, until the opening was so completely and cleverly closed and hidden that I could with difficulty discern it after taking my eyes off the spot. And now for a few words upon the labourer herself. And here I now regret that I did not at the time take more accurate notes of her size, formation, &c. The general appearance of the creature was that of a common wasp, but considerably larger and more slender. It had the same yellow and black banded body, the same narrow and strongly nerved wings, the same fierce and defiant looking eyes, and strong mischevious jaws. I did not attempt to catch it, and so cannot say whether it had a sting or not. In length it was nearly or quite an inch, the body being slender and the abdomen elongated. It would seem to be carnivorous, for I afterwards saw one of the species with a fly which it had caught in its jaws. Perhaps some of your scientific readers may be enabled from this meagre description to determine the genus and species, and inform me through your pages.

Worcester.   W. H. ADE.

DERIVATION OF WORDS.

Sir,—Referring to Mr. Ade's letter (N.N.B. p. 51), there is, I think, little doubt, that the prefix "horse" was originally used to denote size or coarseness in a species, by way of distinction from the ordinary species.

In Todd's Johnson's Dictionary, 2nd edit., 1827, it is stated, under the title "Horse":—"Joined to another substantive it signifies something large or coarse. The prepositive 'horse' is applied to denote several things large and coarse by contradistinction. Thus in the vegetable kingdom we have horse radish, horse walnut, horse chestnut. In the animal world there is the horse emmet, horse muscle, horse crab."

The same Dictionary gives us: "horse cucumber; a large green cucumber,"—"horse emmet; a species of large ant."—"horse mint; a large coarse mint,"—"horse muscle; a large muscle or shell fish." Webster's Dictionary gives these words also.

In addition to these instances, I may mention that the horse mackerel is described in Maxwell's Wild Sports of the West as a coarse species of mackerel, often caught with the common mackerel, off the coasts of Mayo.

There is also a fungus, called in many parts of England the horse mushroom. It is a larger species than the common mushroom, and, I believe, not fit to eat.

A large species of leech, found in some of our ponds, is called the horse leech. Possibly, in this instance, however, the name may be thought to refer to the notion that the creature sucks the blood of drinking horses.

Finally, I may mention that the original main channel to the Port of Liverpool was sometimes called the Horse Channel. No large ship could, in former times, enter the port, except by that channel, and I fully believe that the prefix "horse" was, in this case, used to denote size, in contradistinction to the other channel, which admitted small craft only.

I am, Sir, &c.,

Esher, 18th Feb.   T.

Sir,—Upon seeing the letter of W. H. Ade, in the 2nd number of the "Note Book," I have great pleasure in sending you the following probable derivations of the words "Gooseberry, Strawberry, Raspberry, Cranberry, and Wortleberry." The following *derivations* are taken from Richardson's English Dictionary.

(1.) *Gooseberry.* — Perhaps *gorse-berry;* so named from the prickliness of the wood. Skinner thinks so called, because the juice of these *berries,* when half ripe, are the best sauce to a *goose.* Junius suspects that the name was original *groisberrie,* corrupted from the French *groiselle,* and that by a further corruption our *gooseberry* was formed. English gardeners say from its thick skin.

(2.) *Strawberry.*—All that I can find about this word, is that it means " to scatter *seed.*"

(3.) *Raspberry.*—The fruit is so called, perhaps from the *rasping* roughness of the wood (*rasp* meaning to *rub*).

(4.) *Cranberry.*—Of the derivation of this word I cannot find anything.

(5) *Wortleberry.*—The word *Wort* applies to any plant that rises out of the ground.

I hope the above may be of use to Mr. W. H. Ade ; and,

I remain, Sir, yours, &c.,
ALEXANDER W. M. CLARK-KENNEDY.
Eton, Feb. 14th, 1867.

SIR,—Referring to a query in No, 2 of the " N. N. B.," by W. H. Ade, concerning the etymology of the words Gooseberry, Strawberry, Raspberry, Cranberry, and Wortleberry, I beg to offer the following opinions :—1st. In Gooseberry, the prefix goose is a corruption of gorse, prickly, so called from the prickly nature of the shrub. 2nd. Straw in Strawberry is analogous to our word strew, so called from the creeping nature of the plant. 3rdly. Rasp in Raspberry means rough, so called from the roughness of the fruit. Wortleberry is derived from the Saxon Heortberg. Hartberry, called Hartberry, I suppose, because the stags used to feed upon it. Cranberry is Crane berry. Hoping these answers will meet with W. H. Ade's approval,

I remain, &c.,
E. A. D.

WHAT ARE SHOOTING STARS.

SIR,—The following, which appeared about three months ago in an Australian paper, tends to confirm the suggestion made by F. A. A. in No. 2 of the N. N. B. that meteors usually reach this earth in a state of powder :—

"Increase in the size of the earth. Some very curious speculations have lately been put forth by M. Dufour concerning the increase in the size of the earth. Will it be believed that the size of our globe is increasing in bulk year by year, owing to the quantity of meteors (falling stars) which are projected into it from the regions of space ? M. Dufour has made calculations showing that the earth sustains an annual increase equal to 114,400,400th of its weight. It appears that nearly two cubic metres of meteoric dust fall upon every acre of the earth's surface in the course of a single year. It is stated that in some parts of England this meteoric dust may be found in accumulation nearly a foot deep.

"The French Stire or Cubic Metre is equal to 35·3174 cubic feet."

I am, &c.,
D. C. STEWART.

HABITS OF SQUIRRELS.

SIR,—I find that the story of the squirrels crossing the river on their bark canoes is given in Cassell's Popular Natural History, vol. 1, p. 30. "Scheffer in his 'History of Lapland' cites Olaus Petri as witness" to the fact. The common squirrel, however, which in the winter changes to a light steel grey, seems to have been mistaken for the grey squirrel which is only found in North America.

The story, no doubt, may be classed with that of the Nautilus ; which in the main is true, though it has been adorned with some poetical embellishments.

I am, Sir, yours truly
GULIELMUS.
Faversham, Kent.
Feb. 15th, 1867.

TO CORRESPONDENTS.

J. S. CALDWELL (Studley),—Wells' New Physiognomy is published at 14s., and Redfield's Comparative Physiology at 25s. ; you can obtain them at Messrs. Trübner's, 60, Paternoster Row.

COCK ROBIN.—The prices are given where possible. The best weekly papers are the *Field* and *Land and Water ;* monthly: *The Intellectual Observer,* 1s. 6d., *Nature and Art,* 1s., *The Zoologist,* 1s., and, occasionally, *The Annals of Natural History,* 2s. 6d.

R. K.—Dr. Ecklow, a Cape botanist, when shown the aloe tree, considered it to be the kakir boom, or quiver tree (*Aloë dichotomo*), but Dr. Hooker thinks it a new species.

A CHESHIRE BEE-KEEPER.—Many thanks for your letter ; the question of feeding is a vexed one ; with regard to covering you cannot do better than place a common earthenware pan over the hive. It is too late to open a discussion upon the subject.

S.B.—The question is more suitable for a debating society ; we should think iron.

A LOVER OF FLOWERS.—Many thanks for your interesting letter.

W. M. STEPHEN.—Too late for insertion in this number, shall appear in the next.

Short Notes.

UP IN THE CLOUDS.—We had risen to a height of three miles; our boots were sheathed with ice. Sound was sharp and clear, and divided the keen moist air with a ringing echo. Stratus below, cirrus above; a sea of clouds around, 1000 feet in depth, and underneath, the surface of the earth, without a ray of sun, murky and dim. The scene around possessed elements of grandeur which bore no relation to the sun-rise of earth. Grouped around the car, above and below our level, were summits of Alpine cloud, sloping to their base in glistening plains of light, or towering upward from sheets of stratus which descended to earth, or the more simple form of mist and haze, which still clouded the atmosphere below. High overhead floated the cirrus in the deepening azure of the morning light. Thus we were conscious of height and distance, in the position of the clouds, their structure, and the true bulk which they attain. Light and colour helped us to explore their territory; and in the kingdom of illusive forms we realised the finest applications of the principles of colour and the force of contrasted shadow. Colour has always seemed to me a distinctive beauty in a field of vapour. Clothed in hues of neutral grey, the clouds are tinged with the prevailing blue of the atmosphere. Immersed in a transparent medium, they receive upon their surface remote modifications of the reflected glories of sunrise and sunset. Without traces of local colouring, a field of cloud looked down upon from above is diversified with hues allied to the tertiary divisions of the chromatic scale. In one glance I have seen olive, russet, and citrine, together deepening into grey or bluish shadows. Should the sun be setting, it gilds the brown, pale shadows of the topmost clouds, and will show probably wreaths of newly-forming vapour, ready to descend, and crown the topmost summit of Alpine peaks, which rear themselves from a mass of dense shapeless shadows in the grey obscurity of formless clouds. I am speaking now as an observer among the clouds, where the line of the horizon is the circumference of a circle, of which the balloon itself marks the centre.—*Good Words*, Feb.

THE KROOMAN.—In the first place, the Krooman is free, and is deeply insulted by the term "nigger," for on this coast nigger means slave. During his term of service in the capacity of "boy," a large proportion of his pay is appropriated by his "headman" and relatives. When he at length gains age and experience enough to be employed as headman himself, he in his turn receives from those under him a proportion of their wages; and, after a few voyages in this capacity, will have gained enough to stay at home with his wives and family. There he is the laziest being in existence, lies by the fire smoking and drinking when he can get rum and tobacco, and sleeping all day long when these luxuries are not attainable. His only excitements are the arrival of a ship from which he may get a "dash" or present for hiring his boys; and the quarrels in which he is either politically or privately engaged. For the villages all along the Kroo coast (or Grain coast) are in a state of perpetual feud, and make war ferociously on one another in the cruel and treacherous African style, showing no mercy, and expecting none. Their private quarrels, like these of the more civilized portion of mankind, are almost always about women or money. In a country where polygamy is the rule, and no guarded harems exist as among the Turks; where the old man is rich and buys many wives, and the young man is poor and cannot buy any, the marriage vow, as may readily be imagined, is very often broken. The punishment is a fine, but no divorce follows, the wife being a valuable chattel, and not an expensive luxury; and the result of the *liaison* (being also valuable) is adopted by the owner of the frail spouse. There is also another rock on which a Krooman may split. If he outstrips his fellows in the race, if he is rich and prosperous, and in the vanity of success becomes purse-proud and overbearing, envy and malice enter into the hearts of his neighbours, and the first case of death by disease is used as a pretext "to make witch palaver for him"—*i.e.*, to acuse him of witchcraft. He is arraigned before a tribunal of enemies thirsting for his death and their share of his effects. The fatal trial poison is administered with no doubtful result, and his wives, children, cattle, and goods are divided among his judges.—*Land and Water*, Feb. 9th.

HARDY FERN-LIKE PLANTS FOR THE FLOWER GARDEN.—I have more than once drawn attention to several good things in this way, and particularly to Thalictrum minus, which, while growing freely in ordinary soil in the full sun, and being perfectly hardy and permanent, I have proved affords us a beauty almost identical with that of Adiantum cuneatum, and which may be made the nicest use of by the flower gardener. In consequence of recommending it so strongly through various channels, there have been many demands for the plant which nurserymen are not at present able to comply with, though I learn that somebody has lately got a stock. The plant is to be had in abundance in some parts of Britain, particularly in the north and northwest. It is also freely found in Ireland, and is abundant in the Lake District, growing high up amongst T. alpinum, and a taller and coarser species. Once established, the only thing that need be done is to pinch off the growing flower stems, and thus keep the poor little flowers out of sight. The Italian Isopyrum thalictroides is dwarfer in growth and with a similar aspect, though the leaflets are larger. It is grown in most botanic gardens, and may doubtless be had in profusion in its native country. It would form a graceful dwarf Fern-like fringe, but is not equal to my favourite T. minus when once firmly established in nice cushionary tufts. I doubt if we shall ever surpass or equal that as a nice Fern-like plant for the flower-garden. The Isopyrum must also have its young flower shoots pinched carefully off. But I now write to particularly recommend another Fern-like plant for the flower-garden, quite distinct in aspect from either of the foregoing, but likely to furnish a most useful Fern-like effect. It is Spiræa Filipendula, the Dropwort—either the single or the double kind will do—and the plant is rather frequent wild in England. The leaves are cut into deeply toothed segments, will of course stand any amount of exposure, are pleasing in outline, lasting in character, and certain to produce a capital Fern-like effect of the pinnated type. Pinch off the stems and you will then have no further trouble in producing a dense green margin with this plant. The leaves will grow from 5 to 8 inches long according to the soil. The flower gardener who is at all inclined towards variety and interest, can of course make a tasteful use of these plants. I may add that I have used the leaflets of T. minus among flowers with good effect; they are of a more lasting character than those of the Fern.—*Gardeners' Chronicle*, Feb. 9.

THE POTAMOGALE VELOX.—The 28th of December was a happy day to me, for I succeeded in what I had been long wishing for, the acquisition of specimens of the curious otter-like animal *Potamogale velox*. It was one of my most interesting discoveries on my former journey, and I had given a description of it which was published in the *Proceedings of the Boston Society of Natural History for* 1860 (vol. vii. p. 353). I had been unable to bring home more than a skin of this animal; and when it was made the subject of one of the ungenerous attacks made at that time upon me, I was unable to produce evidence, in a skeleton or specimen of the perfect animal, of the truth of the account I had given of it. I had examined the living animal, and had described it from remembrance as allied to the otters. But my critic, from an examination of the skin, only ridiculed my statement, and declared that it did not even belong to the order under which otters are classed, but was a rodent animal. He proposed even to do away with the name I had given it, and to call it Mythomys, in commemoration of my supposed fabulous statement. It may be imagined, then, how glad I felt in obtaining two specimens of the Potamogale. I preserved the skeletons as well as the skins of both, and wished that I could at once have sent them to London to vindicate my statements. Some weeks afterwards, when at Máyolo, I obtained four more specimens. The Potamogale lives in many of the shady and rocky streams near Olenda, gliding under water with great velocity after its prey. On opening the stomachs of all my specimens, I found only freshwater crabs in those I found at Olenda. At this season of the year, the waters are all turbid with the floods, and I imagine that the Potamogale, unable to find fish, which are his ordinary food, has to content himself with crustacea, which he finds about their holes, under the rocks and stones on the banks of the rivulets. Three of those found at Máyolo had fish in their stomach, and one had crustacea. The animal is not found in the Ngouyai or other large rivers of the country, but is confined to the smaller streams. In the dry season it is seldom to be found anywhere.—*Du Chaillu's Ashango Land*.

EXPERIMENTS WITH TRICHINA SPIRALIS.—The experiments made with birds were negative, and this so far agrees with the experience of continental observers, Professors Pagenstecher and Fuchs, who, though they found that the ingested muscle Trichines acquired sexual maturity within the intestinal canal of their avian hosts, yet never found young Trichinæ in the muscles of the birds, nor any evidence of an attempt on the part of the escaped embryos to effect a wandering or active migration on their own account. Carnivorous mammals, and especially those which subsist on a mixed diet, appears to be the most liable to entertain Trichinæ. It is, however, possible to rear flesh-worms in herbivora; though on account of the expense comparatively few experiments have been made in this direction. "It is quite clear that in their natural state herbivorous animals can seldom have an opportunity of infesting themselves, whilst the reverse is the case with swine, carnivorous mammals, and ourselves." Looking at the subject in relation to the public health, the author observed, that he had no hesitation in saying that a great deal of unnecessary fear had been created in this country. English swine are almost entirely, if not absolutely, free from this so-called disease, and not a single case of trichiniosis in the living human subject has been diagnosed in the United Kingdom. Some 20 or 30 have been discovered *post mortem*, and it is highly probable that most, if not all of these individuals, have contracted the disease during life, by eating German pork sausages or other preparations of foreign meat.—*Paper read by Dr. Cobbold before the Linnaen Society, Jan. 17th.*

ORCHIDS.—The family of Oncidium has a wide geographical distribution in the New as well as in the Old World. The only genus that bears comparison at all with it in this respect, is that of Epidendrum. There is scarcely a field of importance that has come under the investigation of our enterprising and intrepid collectors but has furnished some individual of interest or beauty, to our rich European stores. It may have been found in close proximity to the snow-capped ridges of the almost inaccessible mountains that dot the surface of Central America, which are within the icy grasp of a polar atmosphere, many of them remarkable, as is well known, for their tremendous volcanic eruptions. That the family connection is a large one may be taken for granted when we know that one or other of them are found in Brazil, Mexico, Oaxaca, Guatemala, New Granada, Ocãna, Peru, Panama, Surinam, Jamaica, and Tropical America generally—a range which includes such a variety of climate, verging upon the line of both extremes of a polar and tropical temperature, as to demand something like a systematic arrangement in our endeavours to naturalise them. There is this difficulty—and it is one that is not easily bridged over—the want of complete data for cultural purposes. Any one possessing the slightest knowledge of the geography of the earth can well understand the dilemma of a cultivator, who is handed half a dozen species or varieties of Orchids, and simply told they were found in Mexico. He introduces them into a "convalescent home," and is expected, with the knowledge he may already possess of plants in general, to be able, by wise means, to recruit subjects exhausted to the last degree of physical energy, and restore them to their wonted health and vigour, so that they may increase in bulk and periodically produce flowers. The gardener may probably succeed, but don't abuse him if he lamentably fails; for most of the climates of the earth are to be found on the surface of Mexico.—*Gardeners' Chronicle*, Jan. 26.

SHRUBS SUITABLE FOR SHRUBBERIES.—Those that I am about to describe are very hardy, evergreen, good growers, even under shade and under the boughs of deciduous trees. They are all three very ornamental, and I think I could make a beautiful fox or game covert out of them. The first I name is the Berberis vulgaris; it is the most shrubby of all known plants. It is easily propagated by cuttings, layers, and distribution of the roots. It gives yellow flowers in May; its leaves are like ash leaves. The next I mention is Cotoneaster, with box-like leaves, white flowers, and coral red berries. This is the best of all trailers, and quickly grows, and propogates itself by layers and also by seeds. I should think it would help to make up a famous jungle. The last is common Aucuba, with splotched, laurel-like leaves. This also is propagated by cuttings, layers, and division of roots. The first and last are here; the second I made use of at my late residence at Rushton to ornament an unsightly wall, by allowing it to grow up behind a wire trellis, and very well it answered the purpose. The first and last will grow eight feet high, and the other will trail almost any length, and spread in all directions. I should not think that rabbits or hares would eat either of them. The aucubas and plants of the Berberis vulgaris here do not appear to be affected by this severe weather. The thermometer in my cold vinery to-day (Monday) was two degrees below zero; and in seven minutes from the time that I placed it out of doors, six feet high, the quicksilver fell to six degrees below zero.—*W. F. Radclyffe.*—*Field*, Jan. 26.

JUPITER'S SATELLITES.—An astronomical phenomenon, of which two observations only are on record, will occur during the present year—namely, the simultaneous disappearance of Jupiter's four satellites. On August 21st the planet will appear to lose its moons for nearly two hours; three of them disappear by passing across its face; the fourth will be masked by its shadow. If the weather be favourable, the disappearance and re-appearance may be witnessed in this country.—*Athenæum*, Jan. 26.

Remarks, Queries, &c.

(*Under this head we shall be happy to insert origina Remarks, Queries, &c.*)

THE SPARROWHAWK.—The sparrowhawk (*accipiter nisus*) belongs to the order of Raptores or prey catchers, and to the family Falco; he is No. 15 on the list of British birds.

Comparatively few people know the sparrowhawk by sight, but almost all who do know him like to see him. A few months since while walking along the road I saw a lark flying towards the road, about 50 yards before me, closely followed by a brownish bird with a speckled breast, which I recognized as a sparrowhawk. Just as the lark was flying over the wall of the road and within a foot of it, the sparrowhawk seized him in his talons, and making a most beautiful curve upwards soared back over the oat field. But finding apparently his prey too heavy he settled on the ground to examine it, when either dissatisfied with it or frightened by me he flew off indignantly to the nearest wood, and the lark fluttered along and hid in a sheaf of oats.

Unlike the kestrel, the sparrowhawk is a very silent bird; only once do I remember hearing his harsh, shrill, short cries.

One evening last spring I went birdnesting, or (as it is the fashion to call it now) to seek specimens of oology for my cabinet. I went to L—a—e Dene, and on getting about 500 yards down it I saw up a fir tree what I thought was a ringdove's nest; on climbing up, however, I found it was a sparrowhawk's. The following are the notes I took at the time:—

"Took a sparrowhawk's nest composed entirely of dry twigs of the fir from a fir tree in L—a—e Dene, which contained 5 eggs. Three of them are blueish white, blotched with a ring of brown round the large end; the fourth has the ring round the small end; and the fifth has a broad band of light reddish brown round the middle." The nest as stated above is made entirely of fir twigs, without any other material, its dimensions are diameter 2 feet, hence $(7 : 22 :: 2 :)$ $6\frac{2}{7}$ feet is the circumference, and its depth is 10 inches, the cavity in which the eggs lay is 5 inches in diameter, its depth half an inch.

From the above it will be seen that the nest is a large structure. Now, in all the Ornithological Works I have seen the sparrowhawk is described as either taking a crow or magpie's nest for its home, or building one "like a ringdove's, flat and shallow, in low trees." Can any one give me any information on the subject.?

BADGER.

RARE BIRDS IN LEADENHALL MARKET.—During the past few months I have obtained several *rare birds* in the Leadenhall Market, which have been sent up from the country with the game and poultry, viz.:—

Spotted Crake, Temmincks Stint (Tringa Temminckii), several specimens of the Goosander (Mergus Castor), and a few Bitterns (Botaurus stellaris), which most likely come from Holland. I also obtained 2 specimens of pied Blackbird, male and female, both in good plumage. I think that anyone living in the neighbourhood of London would have a good chance of collecting some very rare spimens of birds in the market, and at a very little cost, as the poulterers are often ignorant of the value of these birds.

Perhaps it would be worth mentioning that the Tringa Temminckii was sold to me for a snipe, for a few pence. ORNITHOLOGIST.

"E. S." sends us the following queries for solution:—1st.—"If you look at a lamp burning clearly, you can see no smoke issuing distinctly from the chimney; but viewing the reflection of it in a looking-glass you can see the vapour ascending to a considerable height." 2nd.—"In Australia it is said that the barometer *rises* before bad weather and falls before good; the reverse of what takes place in England." If this is true what is the cause of this difference?

As they are both interesting subjects, perhaps some of our readers may like to send us their opinions.

ATOMS.—Referring to the extract "An Atom," on p. 53 of N. N. B., the words, "for, knowing the behaviour of a living atom, and knowing all the forces which affect a dead one, &c.," seem to me misleading. I would ask, can atoms, as such, be considered as either alive or dead absolutely; are they not simply indifferent? that is, can only be considered alive or dead, as they form portions of live or dead masses. I hold that atoms are, as far as we can test or conceive, always active, for we find that in a dead mass the activity of the atoms is displayed as powerfully and incessantly as in a living mass, only, acting and re-acting under a new set of conditions. I am aware how difficult it is to discuss or examine such a subject in brief, but have thought it well to at least draw attention to the implied erroneous notion, as I think.

Mr. A. Gaudin's ingenious but, I fear, fallacious calculations on the number and size of the ultimate atoms, &c., is very provocative of remark, but I dare not venture upon criticism, beyond briefly saying that there can be little doubt that the "*ultimate* atoms" of *all* the elements are of the same size, in short identical, and that the differences we observe are due entirely or mainly to the varying rates of movement and systems of combination existing therein. W.H.A.

WINTER ACONITE.—"Amateur" will experience no difficulty in cultivating the Winter Aconite, as it grows freely in common soil. That in which it grows best is a moderately rich and slightly tenacious loamy soil. R. K.

I think "Amateur" will find no difficulty in growing the winter aconite in any ordinary garden soil, as I have seen them grow and flower freely in various parts of the country. They would *prefer* a light, free soil, loam, or otherwise; in short, anything but a cold, wet, heavy soil would suit them. W. H. ADE.

The winter aconite is very common, and likes almost any soil. It thrives best when *not moved* for many years, like the Christmas Rose it is one of the few things that may be moved while in blossom. A LOVER OF FLOWERS.

ORIGIN OF THE WORD GOOSEBERRY.—In Timbs' Nooks and Corners of English Life, gooseberries are said to have derived their name from being used for stuffing roasted geese.
D. C. S.

POTATO DISEASE.—"A Lover of Flowers" wishes to know if any of our readers can give any information as to the potato disease.

STATE OF THE WEATHER NEAR LONDON.

Jan. and Feb.	Moon's Age.	Barometer.		Temperature.					Wind	Rain.	Remarks.
				Of the Air.			of the Earth				
		Max.	Min.	Max	Min	Mean	1 foot deep	2 feet deep			
Thurs. 17	11	29.536	29.430	34	20	27.0	38	38	N.	.00	Partially overcast; frosty; snow flakes falling; fine.
Friday 18	12	29.636	29.447	34	11	22.5	38	38	N.	.00	Hazy, with small granular snow; slight haze; very fine.
Satur. 19	13	29.810	29.636	35	16	25.5	37	38	N.E.	.00	Hazy and frosty; hazy; fine at night.
Sunday 20	○	29.865	29.832	32	25	28.5	37	38	N.E.	.00	Frosty; overcast; frosty wind; overcast throughout.
Mon. 21	15	29.860	29.815	30	20	25.0	37	37	N.E.	.00	Frosty and stormy; boisterous; overcast at night.
Tues. 22	16	30.000	29.810	45	21	33.0	37	37	E.	.12	Overcast; frosty; densely overcast; drops of rain at night.
Wed. 23	17	29.650	29.525	52	34	43.0	37	37	S.	.01	Densely overcast; hazy; fine; slight rain.
Thurs. 24	18	29.442	29.437	54	34	41.0	37	37	S.W.	.00	Densely overcast; fine; with clouds; fine.
Friday 25	19	29.766	29.398	52	44	48.0	36	37	S.W.	.00	Foggy; hazy clouds; very fine.
Satur. 26	20	29.993	29.840	53	38	45.5	37	38	S.W.	.14	Hazy; uniformly overcast; rain at night.
Sunday 27	☽	29.955	29.845	56	47	51.5	38	39	W.	.02	Densely overcast; cloudy; overcast; slight rain.
Mon. 28	22	29.962	29.797	53	34	43.5	40	42	S.W.	.00	Clouds in strata; cloudy and rather boisterous; fine.
Tues. 29	23	29.793	29.789	52	45	48.5	42	42	S.W.	.00	Fine; densely clouded; boisterous and overcast.
Wed. 30	24	29.959	29.851	51	34	42.5	46	42	S.W.	.47	Fine; showery; heavy rain in afternoon.
Thurs. 31	25	30.122	29.985	45	32	38.5	46	43	W.	.10	Fine; very clear; overcast; rain at night.
Friday 1	26	30.062	30.031	48	40	44.0	45	43	S.W.	.00	Hazy; drizly and foggy; overcast.
Satur. 2	27	30.413	30.176	48	25	36.5	46	43	W.	.00	Fine; exceedingly fine throughout.
Sunday 3	28	30.457	30.195	50	29	39.5	45	43	S.	.01	Clear and frosty; very fine; overcast.
Mon. 4	●	29.700	29.482	51	32	41.5	45	43	S.W.	.08	Densely clouded; very boisterous and wet; fine at night.
Tues. 5	1	29.417	29.014	50	33	41.5	45	43	S.	.14	Fine; rain; boisterous; hurricane in the night.
Wed. 6	2	29.056	28.808	51	31	41.0	45	43	N.W.	.04	Boisterous and wet; clear, cold, and boisterous; fine.
Thurs. 7	3	29.406	29.626	54	36	45.0	44	43	W.	.22	Clear, with scattered white clouds; rain at night.
Friday 8	4	29.981	29.328	53	40	46.0	45	43	W.	.02	Very boisterous and showery; fine; lightning at night.
Satur. 9	5	29.971	29.768	55	42	48.5	46	44	S.W.	.06	Fine; very fine; densely overcast.
Sunday 10	6	30.161	29.943	55	35	45.0	46	43	S.	.21	Cloudy; overcast; boisterous; with rain at night.
Mon. 11	7	30.166	29.911	53	40	46.5	46	44	W.	.02	Quite clear; fine, with clouds; slight rain.
Tues. 12	☾	30.168	30.152	55	42	48.5	46	45	W.	.00	Overcast; uniformly overcast; cloudy.
Wed. 13	9	30.324	30.164	52	43	47.5	47	44	S.W.	.00	Slight drizzle; hazy; densely overcast.

ICELAND: ITS BIRDS AND ITS FLOWERS.

HE central deserts of Iceland are unexplored. A man must be bold, and singularly favoured by weather, to investigate their mysterious recesses and to return with life. One region, part wild tumbled snow and glacier mountains, part plains of bristling lava, is as unknown as the heart of Africa. The glimmer of silver peaks has been seen from afar, across an impassable arm of lava; the confines of the great sea of molten matter has been skirted; but those billows of black, ragged stone have never been traversed, even in the old venturesome days of Iceland. Sometimes violent shocks and a rising column of black cloud warn distant settlers that volcanic fires are still active in the heart of that fearful wilderness; then the one great river Jökulsá, which flows from its mysterious depths, is tinged with volcanic ash, and swollen with melted snows; then, too, the night sky gleams scarlet over some unvisited, unknown, yawning crater, which is pouring forth its flood of molten rock.

This sea of lava sweeps up to the roots of a chain of snow mountains perfectly unexplored, themselves volcanoes ready to toss aside their mantles of white, and spread destruction for miles round.

To the west of this vast region of lava and snow, lies an upland desert of black sparkling sand, stretching completely across the island. This sand is volcanic, and has been deposited during outbursts of the neighbouring mountains, when the clouds rain down sand till the ground is covered many feet deep, and every particle of vegetation is destroyed. I had an opportunity of observing a cutting made by a stream in this district, and I found traces of three several depositions of volcanic dust, the last as much as thirteen feet deep. Vegetation advances in Iceland with none of that rapidity with which it covers the flanks of Vesuvius, and sand in Iceland is many hundreds of years old before it becomes covered with a scanty growth of marram and moss campion.

Part of this elevated table-land of desert is studded with countless lakes of all shapes and sizes,—disconnected, landlocked; some, quiet tarns of crystal clear water, others winding among the hills, ruffled and tossed into angry waves by the cutting blasts which howl over the waste. This wild region is utterly barren. The hills are bare, exposed stone, broken into angular fragments, and torn into gullies by the melting snows of spring. The elevated plains are masses of splintered trap and black mud, into which a horse will flounder to its belly. The dales are occasionally grey with moss, and partially clothed with stunted willow.

But every spring-thaw helps to destroy the little amount of vegetation which exists, as the icy water tears down the hill slopes and rips up the moss, or bears away the sandy soil in which the willow found root.

It must not be thought that a mossy, willowy bottom is common. You may travel all day without coming to one, but a few do exist, known only to certain individuals who haunt the waste during the summer, gathering the *lichen islandicus*, or seeking swans. This region bears some resemblance to the Siberian tundras, but it is more barren. The tundras are moss-covered, and nourish herds of reindeer; but the "*heidis*" of the centre of Iceland could not support any quadruped. For the most part this desert is devoid of living creatures, for birds will not frequent spots where there is no vegetation.

Wherever a morass of moss, blaeberry, and willow is to be found, however, multitudes of wild fowl congregate. The lakes teem with red-fleshed alpine trout and magnificent char, and where the fish are, there are to be found the swan and the diver. Swans breed in considerable numbers among these lakes, unmolested except by a hardy native who may venture into the wilds to shoot them for their feathers. The swan is of only one species, the *cygnus musicus*: some naturalists have asserted that another species is to be found in the island, but the natives are very positive that one kind only visits the island, and certainly amongst those which I saw, I noticed none but the Hoopers. Glorious, indeed, is the note, shrill as a trumpet-call, uttered by this majestic bird, when the labours of incubation are completed, and it sings its pæan of triumph over its fledglings. The swans generally are in pairs in a lake: among these tarns it is rare to find more than one couple to each sheet of water. An attempt on the part of a second pair to intrude is resented as an intrusion, the swans regarding the lake, as an Englishman regards his house—as a castle. But this is not the case always. I counted some eighteen swans on the great lake in the Vatnsdalr; but there the sheet was extensive. Perhaps the reason of the tenacity of the swans on the *Arnarvatn heidi* to their rights is the scarcity of provender, and they may be aware that what is enough for two, would be starving for four.

Another bird frequenting these lakes, also in couples, is the Great Northern Diver, a magnificent fellow in gorgeous metallic glitter of green and black, his wings and back sprinkled with white, and his breast of spotless purity. The size of the bird is great, his neck and head well-proportioned, the latter narrow and armed with a pointed dark-coloured bill, and furnished with bright crimson eyes, like rubies. The diver is a heavy bird, and a clumsy walker: but he flies well, though low, rising when alarmed from his lone dark pool with a weird cry, mingled with gulping whoops, like the laughter of a fiend. The diver is a very powerful swimmer, and it is difficult for a boat to keep up with him. He laughs at a storm, dancing like a cork on the waters, plunging through the waves, and appearing on the other side with a fish in his mouth, which he swallows with a toss of his head.

In the neighbourhood of the lakes where there is vegetation the wimbrel stands on his long legs, uttering his wild sad cry, and seeming quite unconcerned if you present your gun. Have him we must, for we depend entirely for provisions in these wastes on what we shoot; and wimbrel, though stringy and tasteless, is not to be despised when little else is to be got. Ah! we have disturbed a covey of ptarmigan. They looked like grey stones, crouching so unconcernedly on the ground as we rode by. But the ptarmigan is sure before long to give notice of his presence, for he is proud of his voice, and one might pass within a few feet of the bird without noticing him, but for his tell-tale call—riö, riö, riö—which has given him his name in Iceland of Rjupr. We catch the zick-zack of the snipe in yon morass, and the cease-less melancholy pipe of the golden plover sounds from every stony hill around the tarn. Just here there is abundance of life; a gun-shot beyond the top of the rise you will not see or hear a bird. If you are lucky, you will catch sight of the great snowy owl, like a snowball sailing by, uttering its solemn note. Its haunts are somewhere among the unvisited, unknown recesses of the vast Jökulls which close the view on the south.

Here, close to us, is a little snow bunting, sitting wagging its tail and cheeping; lucky bunting that you are! had the owl but seen you, you would not be perched so unconcernedly there. How tame the little being is, or rather how stupid; you have only to steal up softly whilst it is occupied cheeping, and you can catch it in your hand. These rocks around us harbour countless buntings, but their nests are so far in among the crevices that it is a difficult matter to obtain an egg.

Have done with the birds: let us take a glance at the flora of this wild spot. This is scanty. The very moss in some places is turned black as coal by the icy tricklings from the snow, and it is only where there is a dry sheltered spot that any flowers can blossom. There are a few. The pale blue butterwort (*Pinguicula alpina*). on its sickly leaves, trembles timorously in the piercing blasts which roll over the Jökulls, and yet bravely endures them. I do not think the little flower has as cheerful a hue here as in the south. It seems blanched with cold. The grass of Parnassus is also to be found, but the little bullet heads are not yet unfolded. On a southern slope of volcanic ash a scanty growth of creeping azalea may be discovered, and a few varieties of heath which I cannot identify just now, as they have not yet flowered. In the marsh at the head of this tarn, in which my poor ponies are wading after the young willow tops, I find the bog-whortle and the blaeberry, now coming into flower (*Vaccinium myrtillus, V. uliginosum, V. vitis idæa*), and I light upon a bunch of *Bartsia alpina*, its rich plum-coloured flowers just beginning to open. On the lava rocks, especially when old, may be seen masses of pale *Dryas octopetala*—a glorious flower, with its eight delicate milky petals and its sunny eye. Nowhere have I seen this plant in such perfection as in Iceland; the blossoms are larger there than I have seen in the Alps or the Pyrenees, but probably the volcanic constituents of the rock on which it lives are those best suited for its development. We may find a few saxifrages also, but they are more plentiful elsewhere than upon this desert. However the *Saxifraga hirculus, S. aizoides, S. nivalis, S. hypnoides, S. cæspitosa*, and *S. tridactylites*, may be discovered with a little trouble. One flower, however, which is sure to attract the eye, is the dwarf campion (*Silene acaulis*), of all gradations of colour, from pure snow-white to carmine pink, in dense masses of little blossoms, studding the sand, and growing where nothing else can grow. Brave, bonny little plant! I have become attached to it from association, as it has cheered my eye, wearied with the unrelieved monotony of black wastes for miles and miles in Iceland. —*Good Words.*

BRITISH SHREW-MICE.

These curious little animals are regarded by some persons as being actually mice, on account of their somewhat mouse-like form, though they belong in reality to the insectivorous order, which in Britain comprehends the shrews, the hedgehog, and the mole, and has not the slightest affinity to any of the rodent types. The genus *Sorex* is characterised by having the ears and eyes small, the snout singularly elongated, and tapering to a point; the tail long, slender, and somewhat quadrangular in form; the feet short, with five toes, the claws being compressed and acute. The dentition consists of two incisors in each jaw; the upper ones are curved and notched at the base; the lower ones are elongated and almost horizontal, the upper edge being serrated in some species; these are followed by three, four, or five præmolars on each side above, and two below. These teeth have been regarded as lateral incisors by some zoologists. The true molars are four on each side above, and three below. The shrews are all plantigrade, and possess clavicles.

The common shrew (*Sorex araneus* of most authors) is extremely common in most parts of England, frequenting hedges and moist pastures, and feeding on worms, the larvæ of insects, and young frogs and lizards. In procuring the former, its long, flexible snout is of great service for burrowing and rooting in the loose soil. This species breeds in the spring and summer, producing two litters of from four to seven each. There is generally, from some hitherto unexplained cause, a periodical mortality among these little animals in August or the beginning of September, at which period numbers are found dead along pathways and the sides of roads, in most cases displaying no external injury. Many hypotheses have been started to account for this sudden death of so many, the real reason being, in my opinion, the want of water. It is well known that the insectivora are more impatient of hunger and thirst than any other class of mammalia, dying if deprived of food and water for four or five hours. I believe, therefore, that this annual mortality must principally be referred to this cause, as during a wet season few, if any, dead shrews are to be found, and in many specimens I have dissected at this period I could find no trace of external or internal injury.

The male shrews, are, as is also the case with the mole, much more numerous than the females, and in the spring they seldom meet without fighting. Besides this species, another kind, the chestnut shrew (*Sorex castaneus*), is described by Mr. Jenyns. I believe it merely to be the common shrew in its summer fur, which at that period is light reddish brown, varying in shades in different individuals. Its winter and spring coat is longer and thicker, and is dark brown above, and grey beneath. In many specimens the tints vary, and I am inclined to think that both the so-called *Sorex castaneus* and *hibernicus*, to be merely specimens deviating slightly from the ordinary tint. Two species of shrew have been discovered in a mummied state in the catacombs of Thebes and Memphis. Of these, one is the *Sorex giganteus* of Isidore Geoffroy;

the other is a small species, termed *Sorex religiosus* by the same author. Of this species several well-preserved specimens existed in M. Passalaqua's collection of Egyptian antiquities in Paris. A shrew, probably this species, was especially held sacred in the athrilitic district of ancient Egypt.

The water shrew (*Crossopus fodiens*) closely resembles the common species in form, the snout being lengthened in the same manner, and the fur having the same velvety softness of texture. In size, however, it is superior—a full-grown specimen measuring more than five inches in length, while the common shrew rarely exceeds four. The colour above is principally deep glossy black, and pure white on the sides and under parts, the line of demarcation being very distinctly defined. There is also a small tuft of white hairs at the opening of the ear. The water-shrew, as its name implies, is usually found in the vicinity of pools and rivulets, forming in the banks long and winding burrows, which penetrate for a considerable distance into the soil, and end in a small chamber furnished with a bed of moss and dry grass. In this secluded retreat the young are born about the beginning of May, there being commonly from six to ten in the litter. When first born, they are curious pinky-white little animals, with round blunt noses and semi-transparent bodies, bearing as little resemblance as possible to their parents. A small colony of these shrews frequently inhabit the same spot, and towards the cool of the evening may be observed searching for food and sporting with each other in the water—now hiding behind stones or large leaves, to elude their companions, and then darting out to engage in a general skirmishing chase, diving and swimming with the greatest activity. By constantly traversing the same ground, in entering and returning from their burrows, they gradually tread down a path among the grass and herbage, by means of which their presence may be readily discovered. When under water, their fur is covered by multitudes of tiny air-bubbles, that shine like silver, and have a beautiful effect when seen in contrast to the dark surface of the body. Spots where the stream, in some bend of its course, forms a small pool, are the favourite resorts of this pretty little creature; and though easily startled by the slightest noise, their range of vision seems to be far from extensive, as, by approaching as quietly as possible, I have often succeeded in watching their gambols without causing alarm among the community. The food of the water-shrew includes insects, worms, frogs, and small fish, which latter it pursues and captures with all the grace and agility of the otter. I am enabled to speak with certainty as to this fact, having kept a pair in confinement myself, and the account of whose habits I hope will not prove uninteresting. The cage I kept them in was made of wire, being twelve inches in height by eighteen in length, a zinc tank for water being adapted to hook on to the doorway. The shrews made themselves quite at home in their new quarters, feeding freely on worms, raw meat, and insects. When minnows were placed in their bath, they instantly plunged into the water, and seized the fish with great eagerness. I remarked that, while feeding, they held the fish firmly between their fore-paws, and commencing at the head, ate gradually downwards. They frequently ate three or four minnows each in a day. Your correspondent "Nooe," in a former number of *Land and Water*, remarked that many of his young trout had been killed by them, and a more destructive little beast to small fish than the water-shrew could scarcely be found. When running about their cage, these shrews often uttered a shrill sibilant chirp, resembling the note of the grasshopper lark. They would also play with each other in the water, rearing half up, and striking with the fore-paws, or rolling over each other on the surface.

Besides the water-shrew, another species, the oared shrew (*Crossopus remifer*) is found in Britain. For some time this animal was confounded with the water-shrew, as its habits are similar, and it frequents the same situations. It differs, however, in colour, the black on the back and sides being flecked with white hairs, the throat and abdomen blackish grey tinged with yellow; though scarcer than the other two kinds, the oared shrew is more abundant than is often supposed by naturalists, as I have several times taken it in different part of Hertfordshire and Surrey. I must here notice that the ears of both the oared and water-shrews are furnished with a peculiar and beautifully-contrived apparatus, by which the water is excluded from those organs; it consists of three small valves, which fold together when the animal dives, effectually preventing the entrance of a single drop of moisture. As soon, however, as the pressure is removed on the shrew rising to the surface they re-open spontaneously. Without this provision of nature, the animal would constantly be annoyed by the water filling the cavities, and irritating the delicate membranes of the ears.—N. L. AUSTEN, F.R.S., *Land and Water*.

THE DECIDUOUS CYPRESS.

ALL trees have an individual character of their own. Some have it so marked that they impart a character to the whole scenery in which they occur, but few have it in such a degree or of such an impressive nature as the Deciduous Cypress. The gloomy brakes in which it stands up to the "knees" in water combine with it to make a scene of desolation and awe overpowering to the human mind. We remember a collector who went out to Brazil, and was exceptionally unsuccessful. The forests which yielded so much to others seemed to yield nothing to him. It was a puzzle at the time, but long afterwards (long after the poor man was in his grave) we learned the cause from one who had met him in Brazil. He could not stand the Brazilian forests. There was nothing in them to harm him, and he knew it, but they frightened him; their awful silence, dim obscurity, and impressive height took possession of his soul, and filled it with fear and trembling. With a companion he did well enough, but alone they scared him. If that is the impression left by the Brazilian forests, we may guess how much more the gloomy Cyprières, with their alligators, and countless creeping and slimy accessories (imaginary or not) must weigh upon the spirits. To form an idea of these regions we are told we must visit the spot itself; we may imagine but we cannot realise their oppressive silence, their awful lonesomeness, and their dreary aspect. Animated Nature is banished, life itself seems dead, until the sullen splash of the alligator wakens the echoes through the long canals, arched over like lofty aisles by the gloomy canopy of thick boughs of the Cypress. Not that natural beauty is wholly wanting: "The varied windings and intricate bendings of the lakes," says Darby, "relieve the sameness, whilst the rich green of the luxuriant growth of forest trees, the long line of woods melting into the distant sky, the multifarous tints of the Willow, Cotton, and other fluviatic trees, rendered venerable by the long train of waving moss, amaze the fancy."—Darby's "Louisiana," p. 69.

One not unfrequent incident in the life of the Swamp Cypress is its growing on floating islands in the creeks connected with the Mississippi, and by its long roots anchoring them and converting them in time into stationary land. "One of my fellow passengers," says Sir C. Lyell (Second Visit, ii., p. 186), "urged me to visit Lake Solitude, 'because,' said he, 'there is a floating island in it, well wooded, on which a friend of mine once landed from a canoe, when to his surprise it began to sink with his weight. In great alarm he climbed a Cypress tree, which also began immediately to go down with him as fast as he ascended. He mounted higher and higher into its boughs, until at length it ceased to subside, and looking round he saw in every direction, for a distance of 50 yards, the whole wood in motion. On inquiry Sir Charles learned the explanation of this marvellous tale. It appears that there is always a bayou or channel connecting during floods each deserted bend or lake with the main river, through which large floating logs may pass. These often forms rafts and become covered with soil supporting shrubs and trees. At first such green islands are blown down from one part of the lake to another by the winds; but the deciduous Cypress, if it springs up in such a soil, sends down strong roots, many feet or yards long, so as to cast anchor in the muddy bottom, rendering the island stationary."

It is to such a locality as this that M. Bossu refers when one day he had the misfortune to see his boat hemmed in by the branches of a tree that was set under water; he was benighted in this disagreeable situation, and obliged to wait for the break of day. But as this river rises and falls by the floods, he found himself quite in the air in his boat. They were 25 leagues from the mouth of the river, but the Mobilian savages that accompanied him comforted him by the hope that the next tide would set him afloat again, and really the tide mounting up the river from Mobile Bay delivered him from his disagreeable situation (Bossu's "Travels through Louisiana," p. 227, 1781.)

Mr. Darby's description of the great raft, 10 miles in length, which choked the Atchafalaya, gives us a more pleasing idea of such an island than we should have expected :—" In the fall season," says he, " when the waters are low, the surface of the raft is perfectly covered by the most beautiful flora, whose varied dyes, and the hum of the honey bee, seen in thousands, compensate to the traveller for the deep silence and lonely appearance of Nature at this remote spot. The smooth surface of that part of the river unoccupied by the raft, many species of papilionaceous flowers, and the recent growth of Willow and Cotton trees, relieves the sameness of the picture. Even the alligator, otherwise the most loathsome and disgusting of animated beings, serves to increase the impressive solemnity of the scene."

But it must not be supposed that in all these Cyprières the ground is perpetually a swamp; some are, but many are so only for a portion of the year. Darby tells us that "the lands that are inundated by the spring freshes in the low lands of the Atchafalaya remain almost entirely devoid of water on the retiring of the floods. No portion of wood-land in America is more completely without water in the fall season than this. Miles in succession of those regions that we have in former times consigned to eternal submersion, are, in fact, eight months of the year almost totally deprived of water for the ordinary necessities of animal existence. This observation will be found circumstantially correct in all the range that divides the delta from the prairies, or heights, to eight or ten miles distant from either." At the other season all is changed, and one universal inundation covers everything. From the mouth of the Courtableau to the head of the Cow Island, the breadth of the overflow between the Atchafalaya, Opelousas, and Allacapas is about eight miles wide. This space is an immense lake for many months; the currents of the smaller bayous are lost in the maze, and only remain distinguishable by the openings of their channels. The many lakes that mingle with the outlets of the river, and with each other, render this region most inconceivably intricate. It is with the utmost difficulty that the real channel of even the river can be distinguished from the number of outlets and inlets that wind in every direction.—A. M.—*Gardeners' Chronicle*, March 2.

INSECTS IN AUSTRALIA.

THE entomologist would reap a rich harvest of delight in Australia. The whole ground, and much of the vegetation, in summer, are literally alive with insects of very great variety, differing in different places, affording another remarkable contrast to New Zealand, where there are very few insects, and where one may lie on the ground with as little fear of them as he would on his bed. There are great numbers and varieties of centipedes. The tarantulus, a poisonous spider, and the scorpion, have no doubt some great purpose in the economy of creation here, and are useful in their place. The greatest amount of harm the insects would seem to do is to create an uneasy feeling whilst resting one's-self on the ground, which it is almost impossible to do without the knowledge of the certainty of smothering hundreds of them. The centipede, however, is quite able to resent an injury of this kind. In lifting firewood, fear is always entertained of some poisonous insect.

Ants are spread all over the surface, and they live as if they claimed to be the sole and rightful owners of the soil. The branches of the highest trees are not exempt from their excursions and marauding expeditions. There are many varieties of them, one of which, the Soldier Ant, about an inch in length, will stand up on its hind legs, and in this threatening attitude face a man on horseback as if disputing the right of way. They have settlements all over the bush, with paths leading to them, beaten hard and plain like a great public highway. Some of these settlements are very conspicuous objects, and the stranger is sadly puzzled in endeavouring to guess what they are—assuming, as they do, the shape of conical shaped mounds of red earth occurring at intervals, some of which are as large as small haycocks; these are called ant-hills. There are also ant-beds of greater or less size, all teeming with life, and not much elevated above the level of the ground. There is a species which is provided with wings at a certain period, said to be females. The wings drop off after they have flown about for a short time, and the ground seems strewn with them. The ants are proverbial for their untiring labour and industry, and their thoroughfares through the bush are crowded with them, going to and fro, from the early dawn of the morning till late in the evening, those returning to the settlements carrying spoil of some kind or other. In the manna country and season, they appear as if conveying bags of flour on their backs. They are the great bush scavengers, and make prey of all the dead animal matter and all the insects which they can get hold of. Great numbers of them may be often observed engaged in a conflict with a live butterfly or beetle, which they are careful at first sight to denude of the wings. Unable to draw it along whole, it is cut or sliced into small pieces, to admit of easy and speedy carriage. The law of co-operation seems to be well understood by them, help being always rendered where help is required; and if one of them is unfortunate in laying hold of too large a piece for carrying, there are always plenty ready to give a helping hand. They have evidently some means of communicating information to one another—a language of signs—and they may be frequently observed on their journeys to put their heads close together, as if receiving and imparting intelligence. The very diminutive black ants are the most troublesome. They have settlements under ground, and come out in myriads when the scouts have discovered some delectable stuff, such as honey or sugar, in any part of a house. They are always seen in a line, like a train of gunpowder, following one after the other, passing and repassing. Every conceivable expedient is resorted to for keeping sugar, preserves, and other sweets, out of their reach. The white ant would seem to be one of the principal agents in earth-making in Australia, causing the trees to supply a vegetable mould from the trunks and branches which is not done with the leaves: in fact, they may be very serviceable in this way, as they will make a heap of dirt in a very short time. It is not so agreeable, however, when they effect a lodgment in the pine flooring and the other timber of a finely painted and furnished dwelling-house.

There is a great abundance and variety of spiders, butterflies, beetles, and moths, and some of the last are very large and beautiful. Every one complains of the common house fly being far too plentiful in summer, and a very great annoyance; the March-fly, the same as the gad-fly, is very tormenting to horses and cattle; the blow-fly occasions immense anxiety, and though a great foe to strivers after domestic economy, is a great friend of hungry dogs. It is remarkable that sheep never seem to suffer from it, not even when newly shorn, and when the Australian sheep-shearers appear almost indifferent as to shearing the skin off with the wool. No doubt the great dryness of the climate will account for this.

Mosquitoes, from the bites of which new-comers complain so much, are not much known in the interior; sandy, bushy, low-lying parts of the country, where there is water, being their favourite place of resort. It is only when first bitten that their bites are attended by very disagreeable eruptions upon the hands and face. The sand-fly in New Zealand is almost as annoying, but neither of them are much worse than midges. There is a large fly called a locust, which comes out of the ground in summer, leaving its grave cerements generally at the grave's mouth. In some districts the trees are completely covered with them, and they make a most deafening noise.

There are none of the flying insects so much deserving notice as the bees. The native bee has no sting, is dark in colour, slender in body, and not much larger than the common house-fly. The aborigines adopt a very ingenious method of discovering their hives: catching one, which they can always readily do where there is water, they fix with gum, which is easily obtained from any of the trees beside them, a small particle of white down upon its back, let it fly away, and keep running after, holding their eyes intently upon it, till they see it alight at its hive, which is always found in a hole in an upstanding tree. One native, with a tomahawk or stone adze in hand, cuts notches in the trees for his big toes to rest upon, and in this way, making notches as he ascends, using them as steps in a ladder, and holding by the tree with one of his hands, he mounts, and very speedily cuts out the honey-comb at the place where the bee was seen to enter. The bark from the knot of a tree serves for a dish to hold the comb, and it is soon devoured at one meal. Hives of English bees were regarded, until a comparatively recent period, as great curiosities. It is most surprising how fast these bees have multiplied here, and how rapidly they have spread. Farther and farther every year they are found making their way into the interior, to the great delight of many who had not anticipated the arrival of such welcome visitants. With the countless numbers of milch kine and the honey lodged in the trees, it almost ceases to be a figurative expression to say of Australia that it is a land flowing with milk and honey. There are none who have benefitted so much from the introducrion of English bees as the shepherds and their families. Out all day with their flocks of sheep, and straggling after them amongst the trees, it is a pleasant recreation and a profitable way of spending their superabundance of spare time, to look for the treasures of honey. There was one hut which I entered where the man employed as hut-keeper had been very industrious in laying up a large store of it in casks for sale. The atmosphere in some quarters is strongly impregnated at a certain season with the smell of honey, and this is the case especially where a heath, much resembling the Scottish heather, abounds. The mamosa tree is one mass of sweet-scented golden blossoms and sprigs, and there are other flower-bearing trees of a larger kind, furnishing no end of pasturage for bees. The climate would also appear to be highly favourable to their increase and spreading. There are many of the trees hollow in consequence of the destruction effected by the white ant, and these hollow upstanding trees are as excellent places of shelter for bees as they are for opossums.—*Australia as it is.* Longmans.

PIPE FISHES.

THERE is a small group of fishes which are called, from their structure, Pipe, or Bill Fishes. They are among the oddest of the finny race and are well worth a careful examination. Fortunately, they are very plentiful, so that there is no difficulty in obtaining specimens for investigation.

In this group there exist so many peculiarities that it is difficult to describe them in their proper order. We will, however, begin with the structure from which they derive their name. They are among fish what the snipe and woodcock are to birds, their jaws being greatly lengthened and attenuated. But they differ from the snipe in the fact that the jaws are united throughout their whole length, and have but a very small mouth at the extremity. The structure of the jaws and mouth is almost exactly similar to that which is found in the Echidna, or Spiny Anteater of Australia, and it is impossible to compare the two creatures together without seeing that the same principle has been carried out in a denizen of the land and a dweller in the water.

The gills of the Pipe Fish are not in the least like those of the fishes which have been already described, and which are familiar to us by means of the fishmongers' shops. Instead of the scarlet fringes which deck the branchial arches, the Pipe Fishes have a number of little round tufts set closely together.

The body is long and snake-like, and in one species, which is scarce, and not likely to be taken near the shore, the body is not thicker than a goose quill, though a foot or fourteen inches in length, and tapers away almost to nothing at the tail. The end of the tail is prehensile, and is used exactly as are the tails of the various prehensile mammalia. These animals inhabit trees, and use their tails as a means whereby they can suspend themselves from the branches, or more firmly maintain their position, whereas the Pipe Fishes use them in order to grasp the seaweed and anchor themselves in safety while the restless tide is passing by them.

Pipe Fishes are very interesting inhabitants of an aquarium. They are restless, inquisitive beings, poking their long snouts into every crevice, and assuming the most extraordinary attitudes. Sometimes four or five of them will be seen quite perpendicular in the water, all having their tails twisted round the same object, and all holding their odd little mouths close to the surface, as if to capture any small insect that might be unfortunate enough to fall into the water. Sometimes they will assume a perpendicular attitude, but in just the opposite direction, their tails being near the surface and their mouths at the bottom of the aquarium.

These curious positions are maintained by means of the dorsal fin, *i.e.*, that fin which runs along a portion of the back, and which is in itself a really wonderful piece of mechanism. Practically, it is a screw propeller, which undulates instead of revolving, and which causes the fish to advance or recede in precisely the same manner as the undulations of a snake in the water enable it to swim. If any of my readers are experienced in boating, they will understand this movement better by comparing it with the familiar method of propelling a boat by working backwards and forwards an oar passed over the stern. Even the rudder of a boat will act as a screw propeller, if worked steadily backwards and forwards.

The undulations of the dorsal fin are so rapid, that a somewhat quick eye is needed to discern them, or even to see the fin at all, which seems to disappear like magic, and which can only be detected by the reflection of light from the successive waves that ripple over the fin. The fin itself is exceedingly thin and delicate, and when the fish is taken out of the water the fin collapses so completely that it is scarcely recognisable.

Another of the oddities of the Pipe Fish is the method by which its body is protected. Instead of being covered with scales, as is the case with the generality of fishes, it is armed with a number of hard flat plates, rather variable in number according to the particular species. The reader will remember that a somewhat similar armature is found in the sticklebacks.

But by far the most curious portion of the Pipe Fish's economy is the pouch in which the eggs are hatched, and in which the young are sheltered for some time after they have left the egg. We are familiar with a terrestrial example in the kangaroo, and all the marsupial tribe, and would naturally expect that certain inhabitants of the waters might be furnished with a similar apparatus. In the Pipe Fish, however, the pouch belongs, not to the female, but to the male fish, and, in consequence, was the cause of sore perplexity to those who first investigated it. The pouch is composed of two long flaps of skin, which run from the tail along the under side of the body, and are several inches in length. Between these flaps the eggs are deposited. There they are preserved from the merciless jaws of other fish, until they are large enough to encounter with safety the dangers of the seas.

Mr. Yarrell mentions that the fisherman told him of a curious fact with regard to the Pipe Fish. If they take a Pipe Fish, open the pouch, and shake the young into the sea, the little creatures do not swim away, but hover about the spot, as if waiting for their parent. Then, if they hold the fish in the water, the young will swim to it, and immediately re-enter the pouch. Some young that were found in the pouch of a male fish by the above-mentioned author measured rather more than an inch in length.—Rev. J. G. Wood in *Routledge's Magazine for Boys*, March.

METEOROLOGY AND THE GARDEN.

THERE are five plants which have been observed from time immemorial for the signs of the weather. The dandelion, the trefoil, the pimpernel, chickweed, and the Siberian sowthistle.

The dandelion is a very common plant, which flowers early, and remain in bloom more or less all the year. The general flowering, however, takes place about the 8th of April, and for a month it bespangles the fields, mixing agreeably with the daisy. The down of the dandelion closes for bad weather, but expands for the return of sunshine; the down of other plants may be observed for the same indications.

The trefoil, according to the observations of the great Lord Bacon, grows more upright with a swelling stalk against rainy weather, and the same may be said of the stalks of most other plants, though not so conspicuously as in the trefoil. Before showers the trefoil contracts its leaves, as does the convolvulous and many other plants.

The pimpernel is the *anagallis arvensis* of Linnæus, and is found in our stubble fields and in gardens flowering in June, and continuing all the summer. When this plant is seen in the morning with its little red flowers widely extended, we may generally expect a fine day; on the contrary when the petals are closed rain will soon follow. This is the plant which Lord Bacon seems to refer to under the name of *windcope*, and which has also been styled *the poor man's weather glass*.

Chickweed is said to be an excellent weather guide. When the flower expands freely no rain will fall for many hours. If it so continue open no rain for a long time need be feared. In showery days the flower appears half concealed, and this state may be regarded as indicative of showery weather. When it is entirely shut we may expect a rainy day.

If the flowers of the Siberian sowthistle remain open all night we may expect rain next day.

We have no doubt that if the subject were systematically studied in daily observation almost every plant would be found to indicate more or less conspicuously all coming changes of the weather; and so it is obvious that a new charm or interest might be given to our gardens, an examination or passing inspection of which in the morning before leaving for town would lead us to infer whether "we had better take an umbrella or not;" a matter of frequent doubt in our changeable climate.

Besides being natural meteorological instruments, plants have also shown themselves capable of serving as clocks and watches. The term Flora's clock has been applied to this curious phenomenon denoting the periodical opening of flowers, whereby the hours of the day are indicated.

As the opening of flowers depends upon temperature, the main fact need not surprise us; but it is very curious to discover that the degree of temperature required in every case is so accurately measured by nature as to take place at fixed periods of the twenty-four hours.

Accordingly we find that the flowers of one country do not open at the same time as in others. Thus an African plant which opens at 6 o'clock, if removed to France will not open till 9, nor in Sweeden till 10, that is until it gets the requisite temperature; those which do not open in Africa till noon do not open at all in Europe, because of course their requisite temperature is never attained.

The goat's beard opens at sunrise and closes at 10. The garden lettuce opens at 7 and shuts at 10. The yellow star of Jerusalem (*Tragopogon pratensis*) and the purple star of Jerusalem (*T. porripolius*) close their flowers exactly at noon. The mouse ear closes at ½ past 2. The cat's ear closes at 3. The princes-leaf, or four o'clock, opens at 4. The evening primrose (*Ænothera biennis*) opens at sunset, and closes at daybreak; it opens with a snapping noise.

A species of serpentine aloes without prickles, whose large and beautiful flowers exhale a strong odour of the vanilla during the time of its expansion, is or was cultivated in the Imperial Gardens at Paris. It does not blow till towards the month of July, and about 5 o'clock in the evening, at which time it gradually open its petals, expands them, droops and dies; by ten o'clock the same night it is totally withered, to the great astonishment of the spectators. The cerea, a native of Jamaica and Vera Cruz, expands a beautiful coral flower, emitting a fragrant odour for a few hours in the night, and then closes to open no more. The flower is nearly a foot in diameter, the inside of the calypse of a splendid yellow, and the petals of a pure white. It begins to open about 7 or 8 o'clock in the evening, and closes before sunrise in the morning.

The dandelion must be mentioned again, it opens in summer at half-past five in the morning, and collects its petals towards the centre about 9 o'clock. It also possesses the very peculiar means of sheltering itself from the extreme heat of the sun, as it closes whenever the heat becomes excessive.

Such are a few of the most remarkable horary flowers; but no doubt most flowers are more or less "particular" in their hours of opening, depending as the fact does on the requisite temperature, and therefore such observations may be turned to meteorological account in connection with the daily temperature and the seasons.

Other conditions, however, besides temperature are required for the time of blooming; and of all the propensities of plants none seem at first more unaccountable than the different seasons in which their blossoms appear. Some produce their flowers in winter, as the Christmas Rose; others in February, as the elegant snowdrop; in March the crocus; in April the sweet-scented violet peeping through the thorn; in May the cowslip perfumes our meads; and June is crowned with all the varieties of the unrivalled rose. Thus throughout the varying year, till after most plants have formed their seeds, fade, and decay, appears the beautiful leafless flower, the winter crocus. This common circumstance is amongst the wonders of creation, and it would perhaps be as difficult satisfactorily to explain it as the most rare or stupendous phenomena of nature.—*Andrew Steinmetz's Sunshine and Showers*. London: Reeve and Co.

WILD BEES.

THERE is no genus of wild bees so generally known, in this country, as that of Bombus: it contains the humble bees, known to us even in childhood; the schoolboy is familiar with them, and but too frequently ruthlessly robs them of their stores; the artless rhyme that he lisped in childhood taught him that the bee " gathers honey all the day from every opening flower," and he fails not to avail himself of that knowledge.

The Bombi are among the first bees that are tempted forth from their winter hybernaculum, and those that first appear are the females that were reared in the nests of the previous year, and which have just awoke from the state of torpidity in which they have passed the winter months; their hum is one of the most joyous notes that greet us in early spring. Humble bees are to be found almost everywhere: they are seen in every sunny nook, they are on the hills, they are in the valleys; and if we are tempted to wander over trackless moors, far from the haunts of man, these bees are there also.

There are no bees that have a wider geographical range: nineteen species inhabit this country, and nineteen additional ones are found in other parts of Europe; eighteen are known from North America and the regions within the arctic circle; India, China, and the islands of the Eastern Archipelago, have at present furnished twenty species, and many more no doubt will be discovered in the northern parts of the great continent; but in Australia, New Zealand, and Africa the Bombi are not found, if we except two or three European species that have been observed to penetrate the north of the latter country: as yet only five or six species have been discovered in the new world, but the above enumeration will show how widely they are distributed.

Of the species found in this country the majority are generally distributed, but a few are extremely local, being confined either to the mountainous or extreme parts of the north, two species having hitherto been found in Shetland only.

During a series of fine, hot, and dry summers, these bees multiply in great numbers, whilst a succession of cold and wet seasons reduces them; indeed, so greatly were those species that build their nests on the surface of the ground reduced by the continued rains of the summers of 1859-60, that at this time they have by no means regained their usual maximum of abundance.

Their numbers are also greatly reduced by various enemies, and parasites of their own order: field-mice and weazels are said to devour the contents of their nests; such a circumstance has not, however, fallen under my notice. Of insect-parasites various species of Diptera are the most destructive to our native species: some nests are infested by species of Volucella, which destroy a considerable portion of the larvæ. A fossorial insect, Mutilla Europea, is occasionally found, in the larva state, feeding on the young brood of these bees: M. Drewsen reared from a nest of Bombus Scrimshiranus, taken near Copenhagen, no less than seventy-six of this Mutilla; the parasite is, however, too rare in this country to cause any great diminution of their numbers. Acari occasionally render their nests almost untenantable by their numbers; they devour the honey and wax. I have also frequently found Coleoptera in nests, but not in such numbers as to render it at all probable that they cause any great destruction of the inhabitants; Anobium panicium, Antherophagus nigricornis, and one or two species of Brachelytra, are among the number.

The nests of the Bombi are constructed either on the surface or under ground: such is the normal habit of the species, but numerous departures from their normal habits have been observed. One or two species frequently construct nests under stones, in crevices of rocks, and in other situations adapted to their purpose; others avail themselves of the nests of birds; and I have observed one instance in which Bombus senilis had taken posession of the nest of a fieldmouse, and I am inclined to believe this to be a not unfrequent occurrence. I have recorded one instance of Bombus Pratorum having taken possession of the nest of a robin, built in the porch of the cottage of my friend Dr. Bell at Putney; and Bombus Muscorum was observed entering the nest of a wren at Holmbush, near Brighton: the eggs of the wren were embedded among the waxen cells of the bee. A lady of my acquaintance, some years ago, observed Bombus Muscorum collecting horsehair in the latticed window of a stable, and, by watching her when conveying a load, discovered the nest, composed entirely of that material. These are a few instances sufficient to show that these bees, like those of other genera, as I shall have occasion to record, sometimes depart widely from the normal habit of their species.

Those species that build on the surface of the ground have received the popular cognomen of moss-builders, a term by no means appropriate, since, of the number of nests that I have examined, not more than one in a dozen has been constructed of that material. As well as my experience enables me to judge, the Bombus Derhamellus more frequently selects moss than any other species: this bee very frequently selects some cavity in a hedgerow-bank where moss is growing, and under such circumstances chooses that material; but in Yorkshire, where the species is much more numerous than in the South, its nests are of very frequent occurrence in hay fields, and in such situations they are principally constructed of blades of grass and small leaves of various plants, &c. The nests of Bombus Sylvarum are also usually composed of grass and the fibres of plants.

The name carder-bees has also been applied to the surface-builders: they are said to comb or card the moss used in constructing their nests. A very interesting account of their proceedings is given by Réaumur; Kirby has given the same history of them, and Shuckard has repeated the account in his recent work on the "British Bees." A representation of a number of humble bees at work will be found in Réaumur's "Mémoires." The account is in substance as follows:—"A worker bee takes a small portion of moss, and with its maxillæ and fore legs proceeds to card and comb it; when the pieces are sufficiently disentangled they are placed under the body by the first pair of legs, the intermediate pair receive them and deliver them to the last, which push them as far as possible beyond the anus. When, by this process, the insect has formed behind it a small mass of moss well carded, either the same or another insect, who takes her turn in the business, pushes it nearer to the nest. Thus small heaps of prepared moss are conveyed to its foot, and in a similar manner they are conveyed to its summit or wherever they are most wanted. A file of four or five insects is occupied at the same time in this employment."

The entrance to the nest is also described as being through "a long gallery or covered way, sometimes a foot or more in length." Although I have on several occasions observed these bees at work, I never detected this co-operative process of building: I watched a nest of Bombus Sylvarum last summer, and saw working bees dragging pieces of grass towards the nest, but each bee worked alone; and some years ago I saw a colony of Bombus senilis, in which three or four working bees were dragging pieces of moss on to the nest, not, as described by Shuckard, in the form of pellets, but simply sprigs of moss, which the bees had apparently just cut off, close to the nest. Neither have I ever been able to detect the covered ways; probably these are only occasionally constructed: all the nests that I have examined had entrances at the basal margin of the nest. Réaumur found nests with the "interior surface or roof cased or sealed with a kind of coarse wax, in order to keep out the wet:" this is a process that none of the nests that I have taken had undergone; I have in wet seasons found nests containing a mass of comb covered with mould, all the grubs having perished, and apparently the entire community had shared the same fate.—Frederick Smith, in the *Entomologist*, March.

MARINE SAURIANS.

THE Ichthyosaur, Teleosaur, Pliosaur, and Plesiosaur, were the most terrible and monstrous creatures that ever inhabited the "vast oceans" of earth; and although great and abundant monarchs of a world of water, they were still but a "powerful few" amongst the numerous families of reptiles whose aquatic habits have caused the lias formation to be so rich with their fossil remains. The teleosaur resembled the modern crocodile, and was more abundant during succeeding ages. These various genera of marine monsters were all of huge proportions. Those of the ichthyosauria tribe were upwards of fifteen yards in length, their eyes were usually about ten inches in diameter, and their huge lizard-like heads and crocodilian teeth contrasted strangely with their long fish-like bodies and short intervening necks. The bodies of the ichthyosauri and pliosauri seem to have been attached directly to the head, without the intervention of anything that could be called a neck. Their fins, or paddles, were admirably adapted to their habits, being of enormous dimensions, although in proportion to their bodies, and of herculanean strength. With one stroke of their mighty fins they could shoot along through the deep with incredible velocity, and overtake, kill, and devour the largest and most powerful sharks, in consequence of their greater strength and activity. The ichthyosaur was truly a most ferocious and predacious creature, and its structure was such as to lead us to conclude that a regular periodical or intermittent ascent to the surface for the purpose of breathing air was necessary to an existence.

Prowling about far below the surface, says the learned Professor Ansted, but with an eye glaring upwards like a large globe of fire, the ichthyosaur may be supposed to distinguish the work going on above, and watch the plesiosaur in its search after prey. Suddenly, and with one stroke of its powerful fore paddles, and the powerful action of its huge tail-fin, it rises to the surface with the velocity of lightning. Its vast mouth, lined with formidable rows of teeth, opens wide to the full extent; it overtakes the object of its attack, and with a motion quicker than thought the jaws close, and perhaps some plesiosaur falls a prey. Not always, however, would it fall a resistless prey, or die unrevenged; for there can be little doubt, that with the advantage of position, the stroke of the head of this slight but active reptile might occasionally reverse the picture, and insure victory to the less powerful of the combatants.

The plesiosaur was a very formidable creature, usually from eight to twelve yards in length, whose fins, or paddles, were like those of a whale, and its teeth similar to those of a crocodile. It was, of course, an air-breathing animal. It had the head of a lizard, and a flexible neck of enormous length, arched like that of a swan, and somewhat like the body of a serpent, which, as it generally swam at the surface of the waters, it thrust downwards or upwards to seize the fishes or birds that might happen to come within its reach. This monstrous creature was one of the most voracious, predacious, and formidable animals that ever existed within the wide precincts of our globe. It was, truly, the tyrant of the deep—of the more shallow seas in particular—during the days of its existence, and well was it for its contemporaries that its increase was checked, and its numbers kept within bounds by the deadly ravages of the still more ferocious ichthyosaur, who, it seems, had a strange feeling of delight in feeding on the body of its less powerful rival.

How strange must have been the plesiosaur's appearance on the waters as it paddled rapidly along, raising betimes its strange, wedge-shaped head high in the air, then plunging into the deep, and then, with an inconceivable velocity, darting to and fro on the waters like the fabled sea-serpent, pursuing, seizing, and devouring its prey, or perhaps occasionally seeking shelter from the deadly jaws of the monstrous ichthyosaur. When attacked in the deeper seas, it fled to the shallow waters near shore (as it could swim on the surface, and was exceedingly brave and active), it had the advantage of its colossal foe, and generally compelled him to beat a hasty retreat.—*Victor le Vaux's Twin Records of Creation*.

THE AMAZON.

THE whole extent of the area of the valley is covered by forests, and is not, like other plains under the tropics, partly desert and partly covered by vegetation. The whole of the Amazon valley is covered with luxurious vegetation, and this vegetation is sometimes so dense that it is almost impenetrable, and of its characteristics in this respect, he would give some account. The river Amazon runs through three different regions, each presenting a different aspect and characteristics from one another. In the lower part of its course two tributaries join the Amazon —one of them rising in the high table land of Guayana, the Rio Negro on the northern shore, and which latter has its source in the mountains of Bolivia. These tributaries are of great dimensions, and the whole basin of the Amazon is full after having received their waters. It is from the junction of these rivers that the great river itself receives its name, and from thence extends to the Atlantic Ocean. That part of the Amazon which occupies the middle tract of the continent is called Solemock. The southern shore of the Amazon, below its junction with the Madeira, receives other rivers, three of which flow from the southern slope of the table land of Brazil. To the east of the Rio Negro there are a number of other rivers flowing into the Amazon, hardly known among us by name, and yet of very great importance, and remarkable for their peculiar character. There are among those tributaries four rivers so broad that we have hardly any river so broad, though their courses are not very long. These at their mouths are over thirty miles wide, and some of them over sixty miles wide. Following the southern shore of the Amazon to its mouth, you behold an entrance so wide, that it is as if the wide ocean were spreading before you, and you were passing from a river to the open sea. These rivers are comparatively shallow, and their current is very light: the natural consequence is that they carry little material in suspension, and their waters are therefore clear and transparent, but somewhat tinged by vegetable substances to a greenish hue. Others of these waters are tinged with gray, and others again are yellowish. The river Madeira is totally different in its character from those. It is a very deep river, flowing rapidly, and carrying with it a large amount of loose material, giving the water a whitish colour, from which circumstance the Madeira is called "White Water River." There are three tributaries called "White Water River," but they differ materially from the Madeira, though, like it, very deep. They are very tortuous and meandering, and destitute of islands, while the Madeira has numerous islands. The consequence is, these rivers can be navigated to a distance of five hundred miles by large vessels drawing fifteen or eighteen feet, with as much ease as they could in the main stream of the Amazon. The Rio Negro presents a very different aspect; it is very wide, but less deep, and has a very slow course, and is dark and transparent, owing to the large amount of vegetable matter held in solution in the water, and when seen from above it looks as dark as ink. Therefore, not only in the width, and depth, and bulk of water, but also in the characteristics of the water, every region of the Amazon has its peculiar character. The Amazon, as a whole, is a white water river. The mouth of the Amazon, where it enters the Atlantic, is one hundred and fifty miles wide. It is the widest, largest, and of the greatest volume of all known rivers. The lecturer then proceeded to give a brief description of the productions of the region of the Amazon, enumerating the costly dye-woods, medicinal plants, and the valuable timber which grows in great abundance in the valley, and which at present forms but a small and meagre source of traffic. The liberal policy of the Emperor of Brazil would, however, change all this, and he expected ere long to see the whole country of the Amazon and the Andes opened by the enterprise of the American people.—*From a Lecture delivered by Professor Agassiz, at the Cooper Institute, New York*, Feb. 18, 1867.

NEW ROSES FOR 1867

HYBRID PERPETUALS. Alba Carnea (*Touvais*), white, lightly tinged with rose, the under side of the petals pure white, the flowers are of medium size and beautifully formed, habit moderately vigorous. Antoine Ducher (*Ducher*), brilliant red, very large, double, and superbly formed, robust and vigorous habit: a seedling from Madame Domage. Charles Verdier (*Guillot père*), fine rose colour, with whitish edges, very large, very double, and well formed, habit very vigorous: a seedling from the esteemed variety Victor Verdier. Comte Litta (*E. Verdier*), brilliant velvety purple, edged with violet, growth vigorous, flowers large, full, and well formed, having large undulating petals. Comtesse Félicie Morguès (*Pernet*), brilliant rosy red, the centre petals edged with white, habit robust, flowers large and full: a seedling from Victor Verdier. Eugene Scribe (*Gautreau*), brilliant dazzling red, extra large, full, and well formed, growth very vigorous. Francoise Treyve (*Liabaud*), fine deep shining scarlet, quite a new colour, large and double, very vigorous grower. Gloire de Monplaisir (*Gounod*), lively red, large double, and of excellent form, habit very vigorous and free flowering. Horace Vernet (*Guillot fils*), velvety reddish purple, shaded with deep crimson, flowers of extra size, with very large petals, making a very effective appearance on the plant, a vigorous grower. Madame Anna Bugnet (*Gounoa*), tinted white, changing to marble rose, large, full, and imbricated, a vigorous grower, producing large clusters of flowers. Madame Bellenden Ker (*Guillot père*), superb pure white, medium sized, fine, and double, of moderately vigorous habit. Madame George Paul (*E. Verdier*), brilliantly tinted and shaded rose, with whitish edges, large, full, fine imbricated form, vigorous and distinct. Madame Rival (*Gounod*), delicate, satin-like rose, large, double, and well shaped, habit very vigorous: a seedling from Auguste Mie. Madeleine Nonin (*Ducher*), rose, lightly tinged with salmon, medium sized and very double, flowers excellently formed, habit vigorous, a fine autumnal rose. Mademoiselle Annie Wood (*E. Verdier*), clear brilliant red, large, very full, and perfectly imbricated, habit very robust, a most distinct and remarkable rose. Mademoiselle Eleanor Grier (*E. Verdier*), deep rose, large, full, and of perfect form, fine robust habit. Mademoiselle Marie de la Villeboisnet (*Trouillard*), fine delicate rose, very large, very double, and slightly imbricated, good habit and vigorous grower. Mademoiselle Jeanne Marix (*Liabaud*), bright rose marbled with purple, very large, full, and cup shaped, a remarkably vigorous grower. Monsieur Chaix d'Est-Ange (*Leveque*), brilliant vermillion red, large, full, and excellently formed, a vigorous grower and profuse bloomer. Monsieur Noman (*Guillot père*), delicate rose colour, the edges of the petals being almost white, large and double, a good grower and abundant bloomer: a seedling from Jules Margottin. Monsieur Theirs (*Trouillard*), fine brilliant red, large and very double, the outer petals very regular, those towards the centre slightly incurved, good habit. Napoleon III. (*E. Verdier*), brilliant scarlet and deep violet, large and double, a very distinct and remarkably rich rose, fine robust habit. Paul Verdier (*C. Verdier*), magnificent bright rose colour, large, full, and perfectly imbricated form, vigorous habit, producing several fine flowers on a branch. Souvenir de Mons Roll (*Boyan*), fine reddish cerise, richly tinged or shaded, a large and beautifully formed rose, making a vigorous and very effective plant. Thorin (*Lacharme*), pure brilliant rose, large, full, and of excellent form, habit remarkably robust.—TEA SCENTED. Bouton d'Or (*Guillot fils*), superb deep yellow, reverse of petals white, medium sized double flowers, an excellent variety, with a fine style of growth. Isabella Sprunt (*Verschaffelt*), delicate yellow, lighter towards the edges of the petals, good habit, and very free. Madame Bremont (*Guillot fils*), fine reddish purple, varying to deep purple, large and double, vigorous habit and fine style of growth, very distinct. Madame Margottin (*Guillot fils*), fine deep citron yellow with rosy peach centre, the edges of the petals white, flowers of good size, very full, and rather globular; this is a most distinct variety, of vigorous and pleasing habit. Monsieur Furtado (*Laffay*), bright sulphur yellow, medium size, very double, and well formed, a hardy and vigorous grower.—BOURBON. Œillet Flamand (*Ogar*), brilliant rose, delicately striped with pure white, a medium sized compact and double flower, habit robust, quite a distinct variety.—*Floral World*, March.

NEW SPECIES OF PLESIOSAURUS.

A fine addition has recently been made, by purchase, to the remains of *Plesiosauri* in the British Museum. This specimen is from the Lower Lias, near Charmouth, and was obtained by E. C. H. Day, Esq., F.G.S., the fortunate discoverer, in the same locality, of the larger specimen of *Plesiosaurus rostratus*, described and figured by Professor Owen in the "Palæont. Soc. Mon." for 1865. The fossil has been skilfully developed from its matrix by Mr. Isaac Hunter, of Charmouth. The entire skeleton measures nearly fourteen feet in length, and has almost all the vertebræ in their natural sequence and position, a few only of the caudle series being displaced. The neck, which is slightly curved, is long, and gradually tapered to rather slender proportions at its connection with the head. A large portion of the cervical, and the whole of the dorsal vertebræ, with their spinous processes, and the ribs, have been partially cleared from the rock in which they were embedded; thus giving an upper and under view of the skeleton, which is placed in a frame, with its ventral surface towards the observer. A plaster cast of the dorsal region, which would otherwise have been hidden, has been made and fixed above the specimen, to show the continuity of the series of vertebræ, which are entire, having their lateral processes and neural spines attached; the ribs are also preserved. This ventral view shows well the very large, perfect, and strong sternal and pelvic bones, with their broad surfaces, for the attachment of the powerful muscles of the paddles; these are, however, imperfect, for, of the numerous bones of which they were composed, only the right humerus and femur, and portions of those of the left side are preserved. The head, which has lost the anterior portion of the muzzle, was, with a part of the neck, turned over when the animal was deposited in the mud of the Liassic sea, and is, therefore, seen from above. It is much larger in proportion than in *P. homalospondylus*, Ow., or *P. dolictrodeirus*, Conyb., but not so large as that of *P. rostratus*, Ow. The neck is much longer than that of the latter species. The present specimen has been named by Professor Owen, *Plesiosaurus laticeps*.—W. D., in the *Geological Magazine* for March.

AFRICAN VILLAGE.

The village of Mokaba is large and well arranged; its site, as I have before remarked, is picturesque, and, in short, it was the prettiest village I have ever seen in Africa. There are upwards of 130 houses or huts, which, as in other West-African villages, are so arranged as to form one main street. But, in Mokaba, several houses are connected so as to form a square, with a common yard or garden in the middle, in which grow magnificent palm trees. Behind the houses, too, are very frequently groups of plantain and lime trees. The village being thus composed of a series of small quadrangles and back gardens, containing trees with beautiful foliage, the whole effect is very charming. In the rear of the houses, amidst the plantain groves, they keep their goats, fowls, and pigs. This is the only village where I saw tame pigs. I was struck with the regularity of the main street; but, besides this, there was another narrower street on each side of the village, lying between the backs of the houses and the plantain groves, and kept very neat and closely weeded. Each house has in front a verandah, or little open space without wall, occupying half the length of the house; the other half, in equal portions on each side, forms apartments in which the owners sleep and keep their little property. When a man marries, he immediately builds a house for his new wife; and, as the family increases, other houses are built, the house of each wife being kept separate. The palm trees in the quadrangles are the property of the chief man of each group of houses; and, being valuable property, pass on his death to his heir, the next brother or the nephew, as in other tribes. Some of these palm trees tower up to a height of fifty feet, and have a singular appearance in the palm-wine season from being hung, beneath the crown, with hollowed gourds receiving the precious liquor.

The large quantity of palm trees in and around the village furnish the Aponos of Mokaba with a ready supply of their favourite drink, palm-wine; for, as I said before, they are a merry people, and make a regular practice of getting drunk every day as long as the wine is obtainable. I often saw them climb the trees in early morning, and take deep draughts from the calabashes suspended there. Like most drunken people they become quarrelsome, and being a lively and excitable race, many frays occur. Happily the palm-wine season lasts only a few months in the year: it was the height of the drunken season when I was at Mokaba. I saw very few men who had not scars or the marks of one or more wounds, received in their merry-making scrimmages. Their holidays are very frequent. Unlimited drinking is the chief amusement, together with dancing, tamtamming, and wild uproar, which last all night. They are fond of the *ocuya* performances. The ocuya is a man supporting a large framework resembling a giant, and whimsically dressed and ornamented, who walks and dances on stilts. In Mokaba he appears in a white mask with thick open lips, disclosing the rows of teeth *minus* the middle incisors, according to the Apono fashion. The long garment reaches to the ground, covering the stilts. It struck me as a droll coincidence that his head-dress resembled exactly a lady's bonnet—at least the resemblance held good before chignons came into vogue—it was surmounted by feathers, and made of the skin of a monkey. Behind, however, hung the monkey's tail, which I cannot say has its parallel in European fashions, at least at present.—*Du Chaillu's Journey to Ashango Land.*

ARALIA PAPYRIFERA.

The Chinese Paper-plant, as this Aralia is commonly called, is a plant of regal aspect, and may, I think, be considered as the most strikingly beautiful of all the fine foliage plants used for the decoration of the sub-tropical garden. It has been used for several years past in the public gardens of Paris, where it attains such a degree of vigour and size of foilage, as was never seen during the period it occupied a place in our stoves. Though a native of the island of Formosa, the stove is not its proper place. In such a situation its leaves are always a rendezvous for the mealy bug; and there it also lacks that robustness of character which is constantly observed when it is grown in the sub-tropical garden, in which its leaves are perfectly free from that abominable pest of our stoves, and where moreover it appears to revel in all its native luxuriance. In the autumn of 1864 I saw beds of this plant in the gardens of Paris; they were of all sizes, from 3 feet to 8 or 9 feet high. In all cases they stood alone for beauty of foliage and nobleness of aspect, the leaves often measuring 1 foot 6 inches in diameter.

I was delighted last summer (despite the unfavourable weather) to see these plants growing in the sub-tropical garden at Battersea Park, almost as vigorously as in the Paris gardens; and a few small plants turned out in the Horticultural Society Gardens at South Kensington, grew vigorously, and quite covered the bed with their healthy leaves early in the autumn. It must be most gratifying to all lovers of sub-tropical gardens to know that this beautiful plant can be grown successfully in this country.

Sir W. Hooker informs us in the "Journal of Botany" that this Aralia was sent to Kew by Sir John Bowring, then Governor of Hong-Kong, and that a plant 5 feet high produced blossoms in December, 1855, but owing to the unfavourable season of the year the flowers damped off, and did not develop fruit. Sir John Bowring describes a plant in Hong-Kong as being 7 feet high, with a circumference of terminal branches of 20 feet, throwing out from 12 to 14 panicles of flowers, drooping in magnificent plumes and in regular form over its dark palmate leaves.

I am not aware that the plant produces its flowers in the summer season in Europe. As soon, however, as they are lifted in the autumn and placed in the houses they throw up a number of flower-stems, but I fear, from the unfavourable season of the year, that the flowers rarely become developed. A greenhouse temperature is all that is requisite during the winter months; indeed, the plants look much healthier in a greenhouse than in the stove. It is readily increased by cutting up the roots and planting them in rich light soil in heat; the young shoots will also take root freely. The plants should be strong and well hardened off before turning out, and the soil in the bed should be of a light and rich character.—E. in *Gardeners' Chronicle*, March 9.

THE SUN.

The consideration of the comparative lightness of matter composing the sun has led Sir J. Herschel to think thet it is highly probable that an intense heat prevails in its interior, by which its elasticity is reinforced and rendered capable of resisting (the) almost inconceiveable pressure, (due to its intrinsic gravitation) without collapsing into smaller dimensions.

The sun is a sphere, and is surrounded by an extensive and rare atmosphere, and is self-luminous, emitting light and heat which are transmitted certainly beyond the planet neptune, and therefore more than 2,700 millions of miles. Of the sun's heat it has been calculated that only $\frac{1}{2381000000}$ part reaches us, so that the whole amount of it must be past human comprehension, like many other things in science. Our annual share would be sufficient to melt a layer of ice all over the earth 38 yards in thickness, according to Pouillet. Another similar calculation determines the direct light of the sun to be equal to that afforded by 5,563 wax candles of moderate size, supposed to be placed a distance of one foot from the oberver. The light of the moon being probably equal to that of only one candle at a distance of 12 feet, it follows that the light of the sun exceeds that of the moon 80,1072 times according to Wallaston. Zöblner's ratio is 618,000.

When telescopically examined, the equatorial zones of the sun are frequently found to be marked with dark spots, or *maculæ*, each surrounded by a fringe of lighter shade called a *penumbra*, the two not passing into each other by gradations of tints, but abruptly. In the few cases in which a gradual shading has been noticed, Sir J. Herschel believes the circumstance may be ascribed to an optical illusion arising from imperfect definition on the retina of the observer's eye. It is not however always the case that each spot has a penumbra to itself, several spots being occasionally included in one penumbra. And it may further be remarked, that cases of an umbra without a penumbra, and the contrary, are on record, though these may be termed exceptional, and considered as closely relating to material organic changes. A marked contrast subsists in all cases between the luminosity of the penumbra and that of the general surface of the sun contiguous. Towards their exterior edge the penumbræ are usually darker than nearer the centre. The outlines of the penumbræ are usually very irregular, but the umbræ, especially in the larger spots, are often of regular form, (comparatively speaking of course), and the nuclei of the umbræ still more noticeably partake of a compactness of outline. Spots are for the most part confined to a zone extending 35° or so on each side of the solar equator, and are neither permanent in their form or stationary in their position, frequently appearing and disappearing with great suddenness. The multitude of facts concerning them, accumulated from the journals of many observers extending over long periods of years, is so great as to bewilder one.—*Chambers' Descriptive Astronomy.*

POTATO.

Notwithstanding the whimsical objection to potatoes urged by the Puritans, who denied the lawfulness of eating them because they are not mentioned in the Bible, this vegetable must ever be ranked among the best gifts of Providence. The introduction of the potato into England may be thus succinctly stated, It first entered Europe by two different routes. It was introduced from Peru to Old Spain, and thence made its way to Italy and Germany, where special laws were enacted to compel the cultivator of the soil to grow, at least, a certain annual quantity.

Some authors have asserted that Sir Francis Drake first discovered the potato in the South Seas; and others that it was introduced into England by Sir John Hawkins, A.D. 1563. But the plant here alluded to was evidently the sweet potato (*Batatas*), which was used in England as a delicacy long before the introduction of our potato (the *Solanum tuberosum*). The sweet potato was imported in considerable quantities from Spain and the Canaries, and was not considered amiss in restoring decayed vigour. The kissing-comfits mentioned by Shakspeare, Webster, and Massinger, were principally made of these and Eringo roots. At length the Virginian potato (the *Solanum*) both became a substitute for it and appropriated its name.

In 1584 Queen Elizabeth granted a patent "for discovering and planting new countries not possessed by Christians," and under this sanction some ships, principally equipped by Sir Walter Raleigh, sailed to America. In 1585 the first body of colonists landed, under the government of Mr. Lane, in Virgina, so called in honour of the virgin queen. Harriott, a celebrated mathematician of the day, went out to survey the colony; his survey and report, and the introduction of the potato and the tobacco-plant into England for the first time, were almost the only fruits of this attempt. The misconduct of the colonists brought the hostility of the Indians upon them; and they were glad to re-embark within a year on board a vessel of Sir Francis Drake, who was returning from an expedition against the Spaniards in North America, and had been commanded by the Queen to visit this plantation in his way, and see what encouragement or assistance they wanted. In Drake's ship was most probably brought home our potato, since in Harriott's report of the country, printed in De Bry's *Collection of Voyages*, he describes (vol. i. p. 17) under the article "Root," a plant called openawk, which is considered identical with the potato. Gerard, in his *Herbal*, mentions that he had the plant from Virginia; that he had grown seedlings of it in 1590; that it grew admirably in his garden, and recommends the root as a delicate dish, but not as a common food.—*Notes and Queries*, March 9th.

ANCIENT GEOGRAPHY.

The French exert themselves in the publication of geographical matters. It is known that Napoleon the First, who was a special admirer of Strabo, the sage of Amasia, caused a French translation to be made by MM. La Porte du Theil and Coray, which was, however, only completed in 1819 by M. Letronne. This superb work is, by its costliness, not within reach of the majority of readers. Since its appearance so much has been done for the text of Strabo, that the want of a new translation, in a more accessible form, was felt. This has been undertaken now by M. Amédée Tardieu, sub-librarian of the Institute, with the assistance of his colleague, M. Thoulin, Librarian of the Institute. The first volume of this new translation has just appeared at M. Hachette's, the well-known Paris publisher. "La Géographie de Strabon" will form three volumes, and will follow in its arrangement the Greek edition of Meineke, in order to faciliate the use of the original and the translation. All the results of modern learned inquiry have been carefully used, and thus the work promises to do credit to French diligence.—M. Renan, in the *Journal des Débats*, reports on another interesting novelty in this branch of science; it is a photo-lithographic reproduction of a manuscript of the geography of Ptolemæus, which is in the possession of the Vatogedi Convent, at Mount Athos, and which has been published by M. Firmin Didot. The maps which accompany this manuscript are very valuable as copies of old maps. This manuscript was discovered in 1840 by a Russian traveller; it was described in 1846 by the

Russian Bishop Uspensky, and every page photographed in 1857 by M. de Sewastianow. Unfortunately, the manuscript has suffered cruel mutilations during the years from 1840 to 1857. M. Renan does not say who crippled it in this way. These photographs have been drawn on stone in the Poitevin manner, and are accompanied by an introduction from the pen of M. Victor Langlais, treating on Mount Athos. M. Renan strongly recommends this photo-lithographic manner of Poitevin for the reproduction of old geographical works.—Another geographical work has just appeared at M. Didier's, "L'Empire du Milieu," by the Marquis de Courcy, who lived for six years in China as French Chargé-d'Affaires, and who deserved the thanks of his country for his exertions in the diplomatic negotiations which ultimately resulted in the throwing open to France of this vast and important market. This work is meritorious, for not only had M. de Courcy his eyes open during the six years of his abode, but he has carefully read up the books of English authors and of his countrymen on China. M. de Courcy describes the topography, the manners and religions, government and administration, agriculture, industry and commerce of China; and, finally, gives a sketch of the history of occidental relations with the empire.—*Athenæum*, March 2.

STARLINGS.

The starling (*Sturnus vulgaris*) frequents the old oaks in the forests by thousands and tens of thousands. Every tree during the summer has its several pairs of birds, who build their nests in the holes and decayed cavities in company with the jackdaws. In the autumn they collect together in immense flocks, and leave the district for the winter, resorting to the reed and osier beds on the Trent. Their return to us is very gradual, a few pairs being seen in some years as early as the middle of January, in others not until some weeks later.

Pairing has already taken place in those who reach us the earliest, and their peculiar guttural breeding-call I have heard at the beginning of February. Every week adds to the number until we receive our full complement, and the woods resound with their prolonged plaintive whistle, alternating with an oft-repeated gurgling note.

The starling is not only subject to local migrations, but I believe large flocks leave us for the Continent in the autumn and return in the spring; indeed, the fact that on one occasion seventeen dozen were picked up near the lighthouse on Flamborough Head, which had been killed, lamed, or stupified by flying against the lantern of that brilliant light, seems to leave no doubt on the question, as they were evidently approaching our shores from the Continent.

The great abundance of old decaying oaks in the forest leaves the starlings little to desire in the choice of a nesting place, and with us other sites are but seldom selected; but in 1853 I met with several pairs which had appropriated some deserted holes of the sand-martin at Robin Dam, near Rufford. Pigeon cotes are also chosen; but in these cases the poor starlings become the victims of an ignorant prejudice, the common idea being that they suck the eggs of the pigeons. I fully believe them guiltless of such a habit, and that they are prompted to resort to such places only by a natural instinct to secure a comfortable domicile for their young. The stove-pipe, which I have mentioned as generally occupied by the sparrow, was once selected by a starling for its nest, but its eggs shared the same fate of being half baked.

Insects form the staple of the starling's food, and I think are always preferred when attainable. I have occasionally seen the birds seize insects on the wing, although it is not a common habit, and the first time it came under my notice it struck me as very unusual. A pair had a nest in the hollow of an old oak in the forest, which at the time contained young ones; one of the parent birds flew out of the hole, which it had just previously entered, and was rapidly departing for a fresh supply of food, when it suddenly deviated from its course and seized a large insect which was flying near, and then darted to the other side and captured another. I was within four or five yards at the time, and had a distinct view of what was to me then a novel proceeding; but I have since observed it several times, and particularly so on the 20th of May, 1856, when I saw a number of them hawking for flies in the manner of the swallows. In this case it was no momentary impulse that prompted the habit, as in the first instance, but they were steadily making a business of it, and continued thus employed for some time.—W. J. Sterland (Sherwood) in *The Field*, March 9.

THE SUGAR CANE.

The Sugar Cane is one of a genus of many species of tall Grasses. Like most cultivated plants, it consists of several permanent varieties, differing in size, in the colour of the epidermis, and in the proportion of saccharine matter they contain. Like most of the cereals, the Sugar Cane has not been traced to its wild state. In its cultivated state it has been found in many independent places, often remote from each other, and bearing independent names. Its geographical limits are nearly the same as those of Cotton; that is, extending from the equator to about the 30th degree of latitude. Like Cotton, its culture has been pushed up to the 40th degree, but even with less success, for the cane takes a year to arrive at maturity, and is therefore liable to be cut off by severe frosts. In what country the Sugar Cane was first cultivated it is out of our power to discover; but, as far as we know, it has been immemorially cultivated in the tropical and subtropical parts of Hindustan, in the Hindu-Chinese countries, in the tropical and sub-tropical parts of China and Japan, in the Malay and Phillippine Archipelagos, and in the tropical islands of the Pacific. There is no evidence of its having been cultivated in any country west of the Indus. It was unknown as a wild plant in Australia and New Zealand, and is unquestionably an exotic in America. The Greeks and Romans knew nothing of sugar but as an article of trade. They were uncertain about the country which produced it, and ignorant of the plant which yielded it. The Arabs, on the contrary, brought the plant itself from India, with the Indian name of its produce, cultivated it in Syria, in Egypt, in Greece, in North Africa, in Spain, in Sicily, and in Southern Italy, manufacturing sugar from it in all these places. At what time the Arabs introduced the culture of the Cane and the manufacture of sugar into Syria and Egypt is unknown, but it is ascertained that sugar was imported into Venice from the countries enumerated at the end of the 10th century. The Crusaders found the Cane cultivated in Syria as early as the beginning of the 12th century. In the year 1420, or 72 years before the discovery of America, the Portuguese carried the Sugar Cane to Madeira. In the 15th century the Spaniards carried the Cane and manufacture of sugar to the Canary Islands, from whence they were conveyed to tropical America and its islands. In 1503, or about 11 years after its discovery, the culture and manufacture were fully established in Hispaniola. Sugar was, however, an article of consumption in Western Europe long before the discovery of America. England was supplied from the emporia of Venice and Antwerp, and in the time of Shakespeare the name of the article was so familiar as already to have its secondary or figurative meaning, as in the expression, "sugared words."—*Mr. Craufurd on the Migration of Plants.*

DISCOVERY OF CISTS.

Mr. Stuart read two papers communicating the discovery of a singularly-interesting group of Cists at Broomend, in the parish of Inverurie, Aberdeenshire. The first was sent by Mr. James Hay Chalmers, a Fellow of the Society, detailing the discovery of the first Cist; and the second by Mr. Charles Brown Davidson, also a Fellow, with a notice of those subsequently discovered. Broomend is about a mile from the town of Inverurie, and the cists were disturbed in the course of cuttings in a natural sandbank made by Mr. Tait for his paper-mill. The first cist which he discovered was empty and attracted little notice. The next contained two skeletons laid on their sides in a doubled-up position, with the two urns much ornamented placed at the back of the necks. A few flint flakes and pieces of charcoal were in the cist, the bottom of which was laid with a bed of water-worn pebbles, about ten inches in depth. The cist was about five feet three inches in length. There was found in it a large finger ring formed of bone, and a fragment of oak, the cross cutting of which was remarkably smooth.

The cist described by Mr. Davidson was within a few feet of the last. It was 5 feet 5 inches long, formed of stone slabs, of which the joints were cemented with clay (as was the case in the previous cist), and the bottom was formed of small pebbles, below which was a slab. The cist was found to contain a large male skeleton and a young female skeleton. The large one was laying on its left side, with the knees drawn up to the chin; at its back was a large urn much ornamented. The female skeleton was in the north-west corner, in a sitting posture, and behind it was a small urn, also ornamented. Two flint flakes were found behind the shoulder of the large skeleton, and a good many pieces of charcoal appeared among the pebbles at the bottom of the cist. The large skeleton and part of the small one were covered with the skin of an ox of tawny colour. Hanging into the large urn, a lamp of stiffened leather, with a tag of the same substance for suspending it, was found. A miniature cist, containing only a skull and an urn, was also found in the same locality.

Mr. Stuart expressed an opinion that the present find was one of the most valuable which had been recently made, as affording new and carefully observed facts illustrative of the burial usages of our early races, and thus giving us a key to their thoughts and condition. A finger ring seemed to him to be a new feature in deposits of this early character, and the leather lamp, which probably was connected with the burial rites, was also a novelty. Mr. Stuart described a cist recently discovered in the neighbourhood of Elgin, in which a skeleton was found which seemed to have been at least partially enveloped in ox-skin, and along with it the fragment of a bronze dagger, which he exhibited.—*Paper read before the Society of Antiquaries of Scotland.*

WINTER DRESS OF ANIMALS, ETC.

North and North-Western America furnish seven well-marked species of stoat, classed under the general term of weasels, some of which, if not the whole of them, turn white in winter. It is, however, very questionable whether the ermine (*P. erminea*), common to the northern parts of Europe and Asia, is ever found in America; my own experience leads me to think that it is not, although two of the North-Western American species are very closely allied to it. In the neighbourhood of Hudson's Bay the ermine taken is *P. agilis* of Audubon and Bachman; it usually frequents the barren grounds and open plains. I have said that the summer-dress of the ermine weasel is brown, but in northern regions the hairs become milk-white during winter; hence we may describe the ermine as a stoat in its winter costume. It would be very difficult, if not impossible, to discover in the animal world a more beautiful example of God's all-wise providence—displayed in adapting the creature to resemble in colour the various habitats it is compelled to live in, changing, too, in exact accordance with altered conditions of temperature, that concealment, for whatever purpose it may be resorted to, shall be rendered as easy and perfect as circumstances will admit of—than is to be found in the transformation both birds and animals undergo in all high latitudes, from brown to snowy white. We have two admirable instances of this change in the ptarmigan and ermine, although the northern hare, and many other analogous instances of this change might be related if it were desirable. All who have been fortunate enough to see ptarmigan in their summer plumage, amidst the brown heather, hill plants, and lichen-clad rocks and boulders of their favourite hills must have been struck with the close similitude the mixture of colours marking the feathers of the backs and wings, bore to the surrounding rocks and foliage. In a like manner, the brown jacket of the ermine exactly corresponds in colouration with the dried-up vegetation, seen on the sunburnt barren plains over which it loves to roam. But when snow buries all the rocks and leaves, settling on the tops of the pine-tree until they bend beneath its weight, and covering the ground with a carpet of dazzling white, on which any living thing having a trace of dark colour in its clothing would be most conspicuous, then the animals and birds destined to winter amidst such desolation, change, as if by enchantment, from brown to white, and this, not by an actual shifting of the clothing, whether fur or feathers, but to a great extent by the absorption of the colouring-matter, leaving the hair or fur so deprived of the summer tint, white.—J. K. Lord in *Land and Water*, March 16th.

PEAT BED.

A section of the bed appeared in a bank cut through by a small stream near the village of Southend. The bank appears to belong to the "Old Coast Line," which is so well-marked a feature around most parts of the west coast of Scotland. The peat at the point described is 3 feet 9 inches thick; above it is a bed of fine clay, from 13 to 14 inches thick, containing hazel-nuts, followed by a bed of fine yellow sand, 4 feet thick, which is succeeded by a bed of coarse gravel, with small boulders of the thickness of 14 feet. About 400 yards further up the stream there is a bed of fine black-blue clay with mussel-shells. These beds appear to furnish evidence of some five or six different changes of level. (1) The peat-bed has been depressed under shallow and very muddy water, depositing the bed of fine clay; (2) a further depression has subjected this mud to an inroad of the sea, bringing with it the sand which overlies the clay; (3) a further depression, or, possibly, a partial elevation, exposing the same surface to some strong current or littoral action, has brought down upon it the bed of coarse gravel; (4) all these beds have been consolidated and re-elevated above the sea; (5) another depression has enabled the sea to erode the valley of which the "Old Coast Line" forms the boundary, and in which this section is exposed. A long period seems to have followed, during which this old coast-line formed the coast of Scotland, and during that period the upper mussel-bed seems to have been deposited; (6) a final elevation of the land has determined the present coast-line, and left the old one as it now appears—subsequently modified by atmospheric action, and cut through by streams. All these changes have occurred during what, geologically, must be called the existing period, as the vegetable remains in the peat and in the clay seem to be all referable to existing species.—*Paper read by the Duke of Argyle before the Geological Society.*

New Books.

[*Our limited space must of necessity compel us to give but very short notices of new books, but they will perhaps serve as a guide as to what books our readers may ask for at their libraries.*]

The North West Peninsular of Iceland, being the Journal of a Tour in Iceland in the Spring and Summer of 1862. By C. W. Shepherd, M.A., F.Z.S. London: Longmans & Co.

Ornithologists will welcome this little volume with pleasure, and the general reader will find much that is interesting and amusing in its pages. It is an account of a second journey with the intention of exploring the north-west peninsula and the Vatna Jökull, and also of settling some vexed questions in Ornithology. Seldom have we taken up a more genial or pleasant work; and if, after having read it carefully through we find a fault, it is that there is not more of it; small as it is it will be found a good companion to the works of Mr. Baring Gould, our chief informant hitherto.

The manners and customs of the inhabitants are pourtrayed in a very happy and homely style, while the accounts of the various birds will gladden all those who make Ornithology their chief study. Iceland would seem to be the very paradise of ducks; so many were there in some parts that it it was difficult to walk without treading upon their nests. Some idea of their quantity may be gathered from the following:—

The island being but three-quarters of a mile in width, the opposite, or southern shore was soon reached. On the coast was a wall built of large stones, just above the high-water level, about three feet in height, and of a considerable thickness. At the bottom, on both sides of it, alternate stones had been left out, so as to form a series of square compartments for the ducks to make their nests in. Almost every compartment was occupied, and as we walked along the shore a long line of ducks flew out one after another. The surface of the water also was perfectly white with drakes, who welcomed their brown wives with loud and clamorous cooing. When we arrived at the farm-house we found that the haymakers had apprised their mistress of our approach. She gave us a cordial welcome. The house itself was a great marvel; the earthern walls that surrounded it, and the window embrasures were occupied by ducks. On the ground the house was fringed with ducks, on the turf slopes of the roof we could see ducks.

A grassy bank close by had been cut into square patches like a chess board, (a square of turf of about 18 inches being removed and a hollow made, and all were filled with ducks). A windmill was infested, and so were all the out-houses, mounds, rocks, and crevices. The ducks were everywhere; many of them were so tame that we could stroke them on their nests, and the good lady told us that there was scarcely a duck on the island which would not allow her to take its eggs without flight or fear. On entering the house we were shown into a little room, whose furniture was very grand for Iceland. Four maidens soon came in, each bearing a large bowl of milk. Each in turn approached the table, and taking a sip from her bowl, placed it before us. Our hostess told us that, when she first became possessor of the island, the produce of down, from the ducks, was not more than 15lbs. weight in the year, but, that under her careful nurture of 20 years, it had risen to nearly 100lbs. annually. It requires about $1\frac{1}{2}$lbs. to make a coverlet for a single bed, and the down is worth from 12s. to 15s. per pound; most of the eggs are taken and pickled for winter consumption, one or two only being left to hatch.

Mr. Shepherd says to intending visitors the Ornithologist should visit Iceland in the spring, and endure with what patience he can the storms of that season. The tourist will do well to delay his visit till the summer, as the weather is charming from the middle of July to the middle of September.

There are several coloured illustrations in the volume, taken from sketches drawn on the spot by Mr. G. G. Fowler.

Sunshine and Showers, their influence throughout Creation, a Compendium of Popular Meteorology. By Andrew Steinmetz, Esq. London: Reeve & Co.

Mr. Steinmetz has endeavoured, in the present volume, to exhaust the subject of the weather in all its meteorological bearings, and, so far as we can judge, seems to have done so with complete success. As the weather is the principal topic of conversation with our countrymen, they will, no doubt, be well pleased to obtain a work that will give them more information upon the subject, in a readable form, than any that has hitherto been issued for that purpose.

In addition to the very pleasant reading, there is much to be learned from the present volume, and we would more especially call our readers' attention to the chapter on lightning, upon which subject it would be well for all of us to have some acquaintance. Mr. Steinmetz says :—

"From a note presented to the French Académie des Sciences, by M. Boudin, it appears, that during the period elapsed between 1835 and 1863, that is 29 years, no less than 2,238 persons were struck dead by lightning. The annual maximum has been 111, the minimum 48; but if we add the number of injured to that of the dead, the total number of the victims exceeds 6,700, and the average per annum is 230."

And further on he says :—

"Out of 6,714 persons struck by lightning, it is not surprising to find that, about one-fourth have been struck *under trees*. In spite of the everlasting warning as to the avoidance of that fatal neighbourhood during thunderstorms, obviously people rush under trees to get shelter from the rain; but, when the terrible danger is known, we apprehend that few will do so. It is quite certain from present statistics, that 1,700 persons out of 6,714, would have escaped death, or severe wounds, by avoiding the vicinity of trees during a thunderstorm."

It appears that females are much less likely to be struck than males; that out of a number of 880 victims, there were only 233 females, only a few more than a fourth; another curious fact is, that some persons are more liable to be struck than others, and one man is spoken of who was struck three times in three different dwellings. This information and a great deal more, is of the most important value to the public, and we therefore hope Mr. Steinmetz's book will meet with a very large body of readers. It certainly deserves to be in the hands of everyone, both as a source of amusement and profit. The many who affect to be weather wise, will probably find their wisdom of a more reliable kind after a perusal.

Descriptive Astronomy. By George F. Chambers, F.R.A.S. Oxford: The Clarendon Press.

A very valuable work on Astronomy, the aim of which is to be generally useful, scientific without being technical, and popular without being vapid. The author says "preferring facts to fancies, I have confined, within very moderate limits, theoretical considerations, and especially have I avoided chronicling any of those mischievous speculations on matters belonging to the domain of recondite wisdom, which have within the last few years borne such pernicious yet natural fruit. The latest information is given on all branches of the science, carefully arranged, and plentifully illustrated with woodcuts, executed under the author's own superintendence. The volume is beautifully printed, and well deserves a place in every gentleman's library.

The Twin Records of Creation; or, Geology and Genesis, their perfect harmony and wonderful concord. By George W. Victor Le Vaux. London: Lockwood & Co.

A nicely printed little volume, with excellent illustrations, in which the author endeavours to prove the affinity between the two records, Genesis and Geology. The various phases of geology are arranged to correspond with the seven days of scripture, and the progress of the earth is represented as agreeing with the mosaic narrative. Our readers must judge for themselves how far they agree with the author, as such a subject is scarcely fit for discussion in our pages; but we may add that those who procure the volume will find much interesting matter written in anything but a dry manner.

Australia as it is; or, Facts and Features, sketches and incidents of Australia and Australian Life, with notices of New Zealand. By a Clergyman. London: Longmans & Co.

An unbiassed description of Australia, containing a multitude of facts collected during a residence of thirteen years. What the author saw and heard has been treasured up for the benefit of those who wish to become acquainted with details of the country. The volume will be found interesting to many besides those who seek for descriptions of nature; as the author has devoted a portion to the consideration of manhood suffrage in Australia, in a chapter headed "Democracy and its results," to which he especially calls attention.

The following works, likely to interest our readers, have appeared during the past few weeks:—

An Elementary Treatise on Quartz and Opal. By George William Traill, F.G.S.E. 4s. Edinburgh: Maclachlan & Stewart.

A Memoir of Thomas Bewick. Written by Himself. With numerous Woodcuts of Fishes and Vignettes by the Author. 1 vol., cloth, 13s. 6d.—Also, *A History of British Birds.* By Thomas Bewick. 2 vols., cloth, 31s. 6d. London: Longmans & Co.

Illustrated Natural History of British Moths. By Edward Newman, F.L.S., F.Z.S., &c. In Numbers, price 6d. each. Nos. I. to V. now ready, the others to follow monthly. W. Tweedie, 337, Strand.

A Book of Angling, a Complete Treatise on the Art of Fishing in every Branch. By Francis Francis. With 15 Plates. Post 8vo, 15s. London: Longmans.

Domestic Medicine: Plain and Brief Directions for the Treatment requisite before Advice can be obtained. By Offley Bohun Shore, Doctor of Medicine of the University of Edinburgh, &c. 2s. Edinburgh: William P. Nimmo.

Correspondence.

Under this head we shall be glad to insert any letters of general interest.]

POTATO DISEASE.

Sir,—I beg to inform "A Lover of Flowers" that the potato disease is occasioned by a minute fungus, *Botritis infestans*, and was first known in this country in the year 1845. This parasitical fungus, or mould, at first preys upon the tissue of the leaves, those brown spots on them being the primary visible results of its presence. It speedily spreads over them and the stems, and by the latter descends to the tubers, on which it too often feeds greedily, leaving behind disorganized tissue, which generally soon becomes converted into a mass of putridity. In the diseased tubers, before they become rotten, the starch is wholesome.

The cause of the fungus attacking the potato we know not. The only thing we do know respecting it is, that whenever the plants have attained a certain development, and the season sufficiently advanced, it makes its appearance, and according to circumstances, preys on leaves, and stems, and tubers, more or less. From what I have seen of its effects upon varieties differing in degree of vitality, all cultivated in the same plot, I am of opinion that the *constitution* of the variety has a great deal to do with it. By this I mean, that varieties of a weak constitution and habit are more easily preyed on by the fungus than those having a stronger constitution, such as robust habit, firmness of tissue, &c.

In order to prevent, or at least lessen, the chances of the disease, some plant early, while others dust the sets with sulphur—both of these remedies have their advantages. The early planting is decidedly of great importance, for by it the tubers will have reached to maturity before the disease appears, or, at least, to an almost complete state of organization, when it seldom attacks them. For a similar reason some often employ tolerably precocious varieties, and though the produce is small, yet, in moist unfavourable seasons it often escapes the ravages of the disease, and outweighs the sound crop of late varieties. The sulphur being poisonous to the parasite, sometimes materially retards its progress. As, however, it establishes itself primarily in the interior of the living tissue, and subsequently fructifies externally, it is exceedingly difficult, if indeed possible, to apply a remedy. It is difficult for us to defeat these minute fungi, or moulds, and this difficulty arises from our imperfect knowledge of their sudden and mysterious appearances and development. We can understand and have control over the higher organized forms of vegetable life; but the lower, alas! are often incomprehensible and uncontrollable. We see them, but know not how nor whence they came, and being ignorant of their origin, we are also ignorant of their exit.

Besides the *Botritis infestans*, the potato is subject to the parasitism of another mould, *Fusisporium solanii*, which likewise is very destructive to the unfortunate *Solanum tuberosum*, in bringing on decay to all the parts preyed upon by it.

Hoping that a "Lover of Flowers" may receive information from other sources,

I am, Sir, yours &c.,

Kew.   R. K.

Sir,—On reference to "A Lover of Flowers'" inquiry regarding the "potato disease," in No. 3 of your magazine, I think I can enlighten him a little. In the district of which I speak (which is in Dumbartonshire) it appeared, in or about 1845, as a small dark-brown spot on the under part and sometimes in the "eyes" of the potato, which spread all over; and on being housed, even if quite good, in two or three days the smell became unsufferable. About the end of August and beginning of September, when a *mist* hung over the field at nightfall, in which the "mischief" was supposed to lurk (same theory as that of Mr. Glashier, the aeronaut, and others on the "cholera mist"), the *leaves* were afterwards invariably found to be spotted, similar to the potato itself, which diverged over the leaf and came down the stalk in a yellowish autumnal hue. Its ravages were greater in low-lying damp ground, and the potatoes worse tasted. Lime and other preventatives were tried, but were of no material use, and, as far as I can learn, about the half of a crop was usually useless, although it may not have been so destructive in other parts. On one or two occasions when the ground above the planted potatoes was tramped firm, by mere chance, there was scarcely a diseased one to be found.

Greenock.   J. R.

INSECT LIFE.

SIR,—The insect mentioned by Mr. Ade in his letter contained in your last number, is, I think, *Mellinus arvensis*, a species of burrowing wasp, which is very common in the country, particularly in autumn. The female is larger than the male. The object of the *hole*, or *burrow*, is to provide a home for the education of the young Mellini. The construction of the habitation itself appears to have been accurately observed by your correspondent—the subsequent part of the insect's labour he appears not to have seen. This I shall endeavour to describe in as few words as possible. Having made the burrow, it next proceeds to catch flies, which it brings to the hole one at a time. Removing the clay or pebble from the entrance, it thrusts the fly to the bottom, and having deposited an egg on it, re-closes the entrance. The Mellinus then goes away again for another fly, and returns to the burrow as before, and this it does until a sufficient number of flies has been collected. According to Wood, each larva requires six flies, on an average, eating all but the head, limbs, and greater part of the thorax. When full grown it spins a cocoon, and passes into the chrysalis state in the burrow. The common sand-wasp (Ammophila gabulosa), which is rather longer and more slender than Mellinus arvensis, and has not so many *bands* on the abdomen, also makes a burrow in the same way, storing it with caterpillars instead of flies, and *Philanthus triangulum* (so called from the triangular marks on the abdomen), about the same size as Mellinus arvensis, stores its burrow with honey-bees, which it previously stings to death. The small *Pemphredon lugubris* (so called from its funereal aspect), great numbers of which I saw and watched last year, make a burrow in decayed wood, which it stores with aphides. All these insects have stings. For further information respecting these, and other mining and boring hymenoptera, I may refer to Kirby and Spence's "Entomology," cheap edit., p. 159; Rennie's "Insect Architecture;" and Wood's "Garden Friends and Foes," which book I would strongly recommend to the *Entomophilist* who wishes to become acquainted with the names and habits of our common insects without proceeding to much scientific detail.

I am, &c.,

Milesdown, March 11.   T. A. H.

SIR,—Although I cannot lay claim to being anything more than an "Entomophilist," like Mr. W. H. Ade, I think I can give him an answer to his query respecting the insect of which he gave a description in your last issue. From the various authorities I have searched, and from my own observation, I imagine this insect to be the mason wasp (*Odynerus muraria*, Latreile). It is so called from its habit of boring a cylindrical hole from two to three inches deep in the ground (generally of a sandy nature) for the purpose of depositing its egg in it. At the same time it siezes a large caterpillar or maggot, which it also deposits in the cavity with the egg, and closes the mouth of the hole, as your correspondent observes, with a small stone or piece of earth. At certain periods she revisits the nest and lays in another stock of food for her progeny.

What wonderful instinct does this little worker display, both in the formation of her nest, the knowledge of the exact time when the food of the larva will be exhausted, and the remembrance of the exact situation of the nest! The wasp is also extremely careful about closing the mouth of the cell, to prevent ichneumons from laying their eggs in the larva, which would soon cause its death. As far as I can learn, the mason wasp stings, and has the same members with the other members of the same family. Hoping this most imperfect account will be satisfactory to your correspondent,

I remain, Sir, yours, &c.,

ARTHUR G. HARVIE.

London, March 2, 1867.

SIR,—The insect Mr. Ade refers to in your last number of the "N. N. B." belongs to the genus Odynerus, generally called mason wasps. A male and female usually work together—the female, however, does the greatest part of the work connected with their lonely hive. After the nest is formed in a bank, or soft stone or brick wall, the female generally supplies the young with a stock of caterpillars, which the grubs manage to consume before they enter into the pupa state, or winter sleep. The entrance to the nest is concealed, to secure the young wasps from ichneumon flies. I do not think that any of the family of insects are carniverous; but there is one kind of mason wasp (*Mellinus arvensis*) that feeds its young with living flies—it is probable that Mr. Ade saw some of that family.

I wish some student of the hymenopterous branch of entomology would favour your readers with information on the various species of the genus Odynerus. I should be pleased to see some good articles on entomology in your journal.

I am, Sir, yours, &c.,
I. P. BELLINGHAM.

Redruth, March 4.

WHAT ARE SHOOTING STARS?

Sir,—Perhaps the following facts and suggestions respecting the nature of shooting stars may prove of interest to your readers.

Dr. Reichenbach, of Vienna, has shown that the tops of mountains are covered with a dust which contains nickel, cobalt, phosphorus, and magnesia, the usual constituents of meteoric stones, in considerable quantities. He believes that this dust pervades all space and reaches the earth in the form of an impalpable powder, which sometimes agglomerates so as to form meteoric stones of different sizes.

Again, it has been found, by M. Schiaparelli, an Italian astronomer, that the elements of the orbit of the August meteors agree with those of a moderately large comet observed in 1862.

Putting these facts together, would it not seem that the meteors observed periodically are neither more nor less than *comets* revolving in an orbit nearly coincident with that of the earth, and that meteoric stones are in no way connected with those appearances? This would account for the fact that none of the November meteors reached the earth, as their density would not be sufficient to enable them to penetrate the atmosphere to any great distance.

I am, Sir, yours truly,
Faversham, March 14.   GULIELMUS.

MOLE AND MOUSE.

Sir,—In the summer of 1858 I discovered a small quadruped resembling a mouse at first sight, but examining, it seemed a cross between a mole and a mouse. The body, slightly elongated, legs and feet, long hairy tail, were those of a mouse, but the entire head was a mole's, as neither ears nor eyes were prominent. It possessed the real snout for excavating, and the soft, velvety, black fur too. I caught it with little difficulty, and had it for several hours. On being allowed down, it seemed exceedingly anxious to be out of sight by burrowing. I eventually let it go "on its way, and I saw it no more." If such a combination was possible, it is surely a singular coincidence. It is not the shrew-mole (Scalops aquaticus), as it is about the size of the common mole, and its colour bright lead, and only to be found in North America.   Yours. &c.,
Greenock.   J. R.

TO CORRESPONDENTS.

ERRATA.—Page 73, in an article on the Atmosphere—"The air is blending of subtle gases, of which more than 99 per cent. consists of Oxygen and Hydrogen;" for *Hydrogen* read *Nitrogen*. This mistake also occurs in the number of *Good Words* for February, from which it was copied.

W. H. A.—1. The words stripped for striped is an error, also melancolicus for melan*ch*olicus, the remainder are correct.—2. The tree *is* the Wellingtonia gigantea; Mr. James Smith, Darley Dale nurseries, near Matlock, has one, of which he says:—"We have a plant of Wellingtonia gigantea that was planted out of a thumb pot, being then one year old, about 2in. high, in the summer of 1853. It measures now as follows: at the ground, 4ft. in girth; at 6in. from the ground, 3ft. 7in.; at 12in. ditto, 3ft. 6in.; at 36in. ditto, 2ft. 5in. Its height is 19ft. 3in., and the space covered by the branches is 30ft. in circumference."—3. Will try and put your letter on the "Derivation of Words" in our next.

M. L. A.—We have not room for your letter in the present number. If the subject is re-opened in our next, will insert.

Short Notes.

THE MACAW.—I do not know whether the capricious nature of the macaw is well known. Possessing a most handsome orange and blue macaw, on whom I bestow a great deal of attention, either feeding him from the hand or placing the food in his pan myself, many opportunities are afforded me of witnessing his extremely variable disposition. To day he will devour with avidity that food which to-morrow will be refused by him; and although I have given him many kinds of food, yet, after the lapse of three months, I am unable to determine which food he appreciates most. One incident is worthy of record, as it shews he is susceptible of grateful feelings. Being confined to my room through illness, the macaw made known his regret at my absence by loud and piercing shrieks, by refusing his food and overturning his pan. He resisted, by unmistakeable signs, the efforts of those who tried to pacify him; the bird, at other times tractable enough, was now pronounced "an ill-natured creature." At first when I was able to visit him he did not appear to know me, but, on hearing my voice he instantly recognised me, and allowed himself to be fondled, uttering a low chirp, far different from the horrid shriek, raising his wing and holding out his leg, thus demonstrating his pleasure at seeing me again. I was positively told that it would be of no avail offering him any food, as he would certainly refuse it; such, in fact, was not the case, for he ravenously ate the proffered food. It is stated by Bechstein that this bird is remarkable for imitating the barking of dogs, mewing of cats, &c.; but although he imitates the human voice distinctly, I have not found this to be the case. Perhaps, however, the experience of some of your readers may be different from mine on this point.—*Philopsittacos.—Field.*

NATIVES OF ANDAMAN.—The Andaman is rather the negro of Africa, the true woolley-headed negro in every particular but one, he has no excessive projection of the heel. He is a small specimen of humanity—being only four feet nine or ten inches in height, but well-made, lithe, and active; he wears no clothes of any kind, is armed with a singular bow of great power and a bunch of arrows, is quick and intelligent, and as a proof of his docile nature he is tender towards children, caressing them with as much gentleness as the most civilized people manifest for infant helplessness (at least such was the conduct of the only Andaman islander we have any account of, a young Andamaner, who was captured in the year 1858, and taken to Calcutta, where unfortunately he died in a short time; he behaved with decorum, he recognized his photograph—a trifling fact apparently, but significant of mental powers above other savages, and had the quick joyous laugh of the negro races; they occupy their time in seeking food and the manufacture of nets, boats (to contain eight people) with an outrigger similar to the native boats of Ceylon, arrows, and hard-wood arrow heads, their simple huts in which they always set up the skull of a hog, on the forehead of which they make certain marks in red earth, a custom that can be traced to nearly all the islands of the Indian Archipelago as far north even as Jesso, as we saw lately in some Japanese drawings, illustrating these curious hairy people, in which is a bear-skull on a pole near to their huts, whatever the symbol may mean.—*Land and Water.*

BOMBYX CYNTHIA.—Dr. Wallace exhibited numerous specimens of the cocoon and imago of Bombyx Cynthia, and the silk thereof. One was a double cocoon, the joint work of two larvæ. Another cocoon, formed in 1865, and which in due course ought to have produced a moth in 1866, contained a still living pupa, which would probably hatch in 1867. He mentioned that though the moths were greedily eaten by fowls and other birds, the larvæ, though not hairy, were rejected; and that when Ailanthus leaves were not procurable the larvæ had been found by Captain Hutton to thrive on honeysuckle. The moths of B. Cynthia were subject to considerable variation in size and coloration. He had invariably found that at the commencement of the hatching out of a brood the males greatly outnumbered the females, whilst at the end the reverse was the case: he argued that in proportion as the individual was finer the time required for its metamorphosis was longer; hence in general the female, which was the larger and heavier insect, was preceded by the male, which was smaller and had less to mature. He thought Bombyx Guerinii and B. Ricini were probably only varieties or local forms of B. Cynthia. Lastly, Dr. Wallace mentioned that he had frequently observed a sound to proceed from the eggs of B. Cynthia, "a sort of click, a single sound generally in the second week," which was attributed to "the parchment-like shell being pressed out with a spring by the effort of the larva within, and returning to its concave form."—*Paper read before the Entomological Society.*

THE JACKDAW.—There is in the parish in which I reside (Melbourne) a somewhat remarkable character. He ought to be more honest than he is, for he resides with a policeman. This character is a jackdaw. One morning a lady in the place lost a gold watch and chain and several valuable rings. Many were the conjectures about the loss, but at last it was pretty correctly ascertained that Master Jack had carried them away. The watch proved too heavy for him, and he dropped it about fifty yards from the house. One morning he paid a visit to my house and he was watched very closely. He entered a bedroom through an open window and eyed the contents of the room. Then he placed himself before a mirror on the dressing table, and walked backwards and forwards with great self-conceit, evidently thinking that no bird in the universe had a coat half so glossy as he. The pincushion caught his eye, and he immediately amused himself by picking every pin out of it and strewing them about very adroitly, taking care that not one of them should prick him. That finished he set to work to pull the bottom of a chair to pieces, very much to his own satisfaction and to our annoyance. At this juncture our patience was exhausted and in we rushed, but Jack was too sharp for us and flew away through the window, chattering at us a provoking "caw, caw."—JOHN JOSEPH BRIGGS (King's Newton, Swarkeston, Derby).—*Field.*

GARDEN PRODUCTIONS OF NATAL.—Most of the European vegetables can be grown in the uplands of Natal. The beetroot and turnip thrive in many districts. Beans, peas, onions, cucumber, cauliflower, cabbage, and lettuce, in every variety, are common in the gardens. The pumpkin flouriehes like a weed, and yields the most astonishing crops. The tomato and capsicum ripen in luxuriance. The capsicum is grown for commercial purposes; 18cwt. of cayenne pepper, worth £86, was exported from Natal last year, in addition to the quantity consumed in the colony. The pine-apple, papaw, and banana are common everywhere on the coast. The orange is found in great plenty in certain districts; there are individual trees in the colony that yield 45 bushels of fruit. The gardens of Maritzburg furnish peaches, apricots, nectarines, apples, mulberries, medlars, grapes, raspberries, figs, guavas, the granadilla, loquat, and St. Helena peach. Ginger and turmeric are common productions in many gardens. The tea-plant grows readily in the lands that are suitable to the coffee. It has not hitherto been planted in any quantity, and a gentleman near Durban is now making arrangements to see what may be done with it on a somewhat large scale. Indigo grows everywhere. Arrowroot has long been manufactured in some quantity in the coast district, and would be very largely produced but for the limited and uncertain market that it commands. Natal arrowroot is now known in the English markets as being of unexceptionable quality.—*Natal Land Settlement Pamphlet.*

HEARING OF DECAPOD CRUSTACEA.
—Sir John Lubbock, in his address to the Entomological Society, says:—"We do not yet thoroughly understand how they [Crustacea] see, smell, or hear; nor are entomologists entirely agreed as to the function or the structure of the antennæ. This interesting subject offers a most promising field for study, and I would particularly call the attention of entomologists to a remarkable memoir by Hensen on the auditory organ in the decapod Crustacea. Henson has shown that the [supposed] otolithes in the open auditory sacs of shrimps are foreign particles of sand, *introduced into the organ by the animal itself*. He proved this very ingeniously by placing a shrimp in filtered water without any sand, but with crystals of uric acid. Three hours after the animal had moulted he found that the sacs contained many of these crystals. M. Hensen has also shown that each hair in the auditory sac is susceptible of being thrown into vibration by a particular note, which is probably determined by the length and thickness of the hair. It may be experimentally shown that certain sounds throw particular hairs into rapid vibration, while those around them remain perfectly still."

THE BERBERRY AND ITS USES.—The Berberry (Berberis vulgaris) is a deciduous shrub, a native of Britain in woods and hedges on dry soil, and sometimes planted in gardens for its fruit; which is not eaten raw but is excellent when preserved in sugar, in syrup, or candied. The berries are also made into jelly and rob, both of which are not only delicious to the taste but extremely wholesome, and they are pickled in vinegar when green, as a substitute for capers. They are also used instead of lemon for flavouring punch, for garnishing dishes, and for various other purposes, independently of their medicinal properties. When the fruit is to be eaten, there is a variety in which it is larger and less acid, B. vulgaris, var. dulcis, of which there are plants in the Horticultural Society's Gardens, from which scions may be procured for budding or grafting on the common berberry. For all the other purposes the species may be taken, though for the curious there are varieties with yellow, white, purple, and black coloured fruit; and there is one also without seeds, B. v. asperma, of which the delicious *confitures d'épine vinette*, for which Rouen is so celebrated, are made.—*Loudon's Horticulturist.*

EARTHQUAKES.—The cause of earthquakes is very obscure, and many theories have been brought forward to account for them. All agree as to their connection with volcanoes, and that they are produced by the same subterranean agency. Sir H. Davy, when he discovered the metallic bases of the alkalies, suggested the idea that those metals might abound in an unoxidized state beneath the crust of the earth, and that when water came in contact with them, gaseous matter would be set free sufficient to produce the earthquake; the metals would combine with the oxygen of the water, and the heat evolved melt the surrounding rocks. When an eruption takes place at the bottom of the sea, large fissures are opened, through which the water pours on the heated surface beneath. The trembling which precedes the shock is then felt; a vast volume of steam is raised in the cold water above; the force is transferred in all directions, at the rate of thirty miles an hour and in amplitude for several miles. The Lisbon earthquake was felt at Finland, Canada, the West Indian islands, an area of 7,500,000 miles: 150,000,000 cubic miles of water was displaced, and the returning wave at Cadiz was sixty feet high.—*Land and Water.*

POULTRY FOR A FARMYARD.—We have seldom seen a farmyard that had not half a dozen poultry houses already made. Any house that possesses the following qualifications is a poultry-house:—Height from 5 to 8 or 9 feet; water-tight roof of any kind; ventilation just under the roof or within a foot of it; door at one end; earthen or gravel floor; if opening into the yard, and near to stacks and ricks, so much the better. The floor of the house should be higher than the level of the yard, and should rise in all directions from the door. A calf-pen often makes a good fowl-house. Roosting on carts and waggons and under sheds and lean-to's is often more favourable to health than a well-appointed house with all modern appliances. If, therefore, the birds are safe from thieves or from foxes, we advise you to let them roost at will. You will have to look after their eggs. Dorkings do well in a farmyard; it is their place. Brahmas and Cochins are hardier, and very good layers. Hamburghs, La Flèche, Houdans, and Crève Cœurs are excellent layers but do not sit. All the latter lay larger eggs than Hamburgs.—*Journal of Horticulture.*

MICE BREEDING IN DOVES' NESTS.—A correspondent of *Land and Water*, relates the following curious fact upon this subject:—"A pair of doves confined in a wicker cage, which was suspended in the hall of a lady's residence in this parish, prepared their nest and produced two eggs, the ordinary complement. During the process of incubation two young dead mice were one day observed lying at the bottom of the cage, but they disappeared in the course of the night. Upon the ensuing morning an examination was made, when it was discovered that a mouse had taken possession of the doves' nest, which contained three live, and it is presumed, the two dead mice. This joint possession had been enjoyed apparently without conflict; I say apparently, because although the female dove remained tenant in occupation, one of the eggs was found broken; the hand of fate was not slow to overtake the invaders, and the parent mouse having been presently entrapped, all suffered the punishment of death for the unhallowed intrusion; humanity recoiled from the massacre, but the predatory habits of the 'varmen' forbade a mitigation of the penalty."

THE METEORIC SHOWER.—The meteoric shower of November last forms the subject of contributions from nineteen different observers to the *Monthly Notices* of the Royal Astronomical Society. Two observers in Kent report that in three hours of the night of the 13th—14th they counted 5,600 meteors, of which number 1,600 streamed past in eight minutes. The time of this great stream was from two to ten minutes past one A.M. Sir John

Herschel, from careful observation, fixes the radiant point of the meteors less near the star γ Leonis than other observers, and in longitude 142° 20' and in latitude 10° 15' north. The Astronomer Royal remarks that the meteors had not much motion towards or from the sun; but were moving perpendicularly to the plane of the ecliptic, from north to south, with an absolute velocity nearly one-fifth part of the velocity relative to the earth in the direction of the earth's motion. And he concludes that the inclination of the orbit of the meteors to the ecliptic is less than nineteen degrees.—*Athenæum.*

ARCTIC FLORA.—A beautiful valley lay there nestling between the cliffs and rich in arctic vegetation. It was covered with a thick turf of moss and grasses, among which the *Poa arctica, Glyceria arctica,* and *Alopecurus alpinus* were most abundant. In places it was indeed a perfect marsh; little streams of melted snow meandered through it, gurgling among the stones, or dashing wildly over the rocks. Myriads of little golden petalled poppies (*Papaver nudicule*) fluttered over the green; the dandelion (*Ranunculus nivalis*), with its smiling, well-remembered face, was sometimes seen, and the less familiar *potentilla* and the purple *pedicularis* were dotted about here and there. The saxifrages—purple, white, and yellow—were also very numerous: I captured not less than seven varieties. The birch and crowberry, and the beautiful *Andromeda* (the heather of Greenland) grew, matted together, in a sheltered nook among the rocks, and, in strange mimicry of southern richness, the willows feebly struggled for existence on the spongy turf: with my cap I covered a whole forest of them. —*Dr. I. I. Hayes, The Open Polar Sea.*

UPLANDS OF AMERICA.—In these uplands Nature is lord and king. Snipes and plovers abound; blackbirds, carrion crows, ravens and vultures are also seen. Flowers are still common; most of all, the dwarf sunflower, which is sown so thickly through the landscape as to give it a shimmer of burning gold. The dwarf sunflower is, in fact, *the* prairie flower, lighting up the face of nature everywhere in our route, from the Missouri river to the Great Salt Lake; in some parts growing low and stunted, the stalk not one foot long, the flower not higher than a common marigold, in others rising ten or twelve feet high, with clusters of flowers each as big as a peony. Ants are toiling in the ground; the little prairie-dogs, comedians of the waste, sit crowing on their mounds of earth until we drive close up to them, when they utter a quick laugh, and, with a shout of mockery, plunge into their holes, head downwards, disappearing from our sight with a last merry wag of their tails. Owls, prairie-dogs, and rattlesnakes live on the most friendly terms with each other; the owls and snakes dwelling in the prairie-dogs' holes, and sometimes, I fancy, eating the dogs when they happen to be short of food.—*Hepworth Dixon's New America.*

SONG OF THE LARK.—A correspondent of the *Field* suggests that larks sometimes sing from joy and sometimes from the contrary, and in corroboration of the latter, relates the following:—"I was walking yesterday in the fields, when I noticed a small hawk rapidly skimming the ground and dipping over the hedges as they do when bent upon mischief. I therefore watched, and soon saw him encounter some larks, one of which being singled out, immediately took to soaring, after its idea of safety. The hawk rising likewise, was making rapid passes, and the bird eluding them, when I heard the air filled with the well-known gush of song of the lark, which seemed to come just after a swoop was missed. I think I am not mistaken in attributing the notes to the terrified bird that was being chased. The songsters of the neighbourhood (and I have heard none before) would have been surely silent with a hawk in their midst, and I could scarcely be wrong about the direction of the sounds."

BROWNEA GRANDICEPS.—A magnificent head of flowers of Brownea grandiceps was shown from the garden of Sir Hugh Williams at Bodelwyddan. The tree which produced it was stated to be of considerable age and of large size, so much so indeed that the house in which it is growing has had to be enlarged once or twice, in order to give it sufficient room. It has long pinnate leaves with about 12 pairs of leaflets, and axillary or terminal bright crimson flower-heads 6 or 8 inches in diameter. The flowers are very numerous, and are arranged in tiers, as it were, round a conical axis, the outer ones expanding first. This species is a native of Venezuela, where it is called Rosa del Monte or Palo de Crux, and was introduced into this country some 40 years ago. It is nearly related to Amherstia and Jonesia, and besides flowering with Sir Hugh Williams has also blossomed at Chatsworth, Glasnevin, and other places, in which for its great beauty it has been much admired.—*Royal Horticultural Society,* March 5th.

FLOCK FROM THE BULRUSH (TYPHA LATIFOLIA).—I think it would be useful for many poor people to know that the common Bulrush is excellent for stuffing beds, pillows, &c. My attention was called to this by our upholsterer, Mr. Read, who has been using it through the winter himself upon trial, and who speaks highly of its usefulness. I send a portion, and I think it will surprise you to find the quantity that one head produces. I should not think it required anything beyond gathering when fully ready in the autumn, and well drying, when it will come easily from the stem—at least this is all that has been done with the sample I send. When we consider how plentiful this plant is in our lakes and rivers, in all the three kingdoms, there cannot be any doubt it would prove a great boon to many poor people, if used for purposes of this sort.—*J. F. Cliveden.—Gardeners' Chronicle.*

A KNOWING DOG.—A lady, residing near Ayr, has a pet terrier, which, among other accomplishments, performs the duty of domestic letter-carrier. The other morning his task was easy, for there was only one letter, and away he trotted with it as usual. His mistress was returning to the house, and, passing the window, was alarmed at seeing Fido, instead of laying the letter on a chair, toss it into the fire. Rushing into the room, the lady rescued the epistle, with only one corner singed. Judge of her surprise (and account for the fact, ye sceptics, as best ye can) to find that the letter the indignant Fido had tried to commit to the flames was a tax paper, with a charge of 12s. for himself! The incident is the more singular as he never previously took any such liberty.—*The Queen.*

Remarks, Queries, &c.

(*Under this head we shall be happy to insert original Remarks, Queries, &c.*)

BIRDS NEAR LONDON.—I forward you a list of *some of the birds observed in and near Leytonstone, Essex,* for insertion in your next number. As we are only *seven miles from the metropolis*, perhaps this may be interesting to some of your readers:—

Peregrine Falcon (falco peregrinus), one specimen of this bird obtained here in 1837.
Hobby (falco subluteo), several noticed.
Kestrel (falco tinnunculus), common.
Sparrowhawke (accipiter Nisus), occasionally.
Long-eared Owl (otus vulgaris), rare.
Short-eared „ (otus brachyotus), common.
Barn „ (Strux flammea), ditto.
Tawny „ (Syrnuim stridula), rare.
Red-backed Shrike (Lanuis collurio), occasionally.
Stone Chat (Saxicola rubicola), common where furze abounds.
Whin Chat (Saxicola rubetra), ditto.
Nightingale (Philomela luscinia), occasionally.
Wood Warbler (Silvia sibilatrix), several obtained.
Golden-crested Wren (regulus cristalus), common.
Willow Warbler (Silvia trochilus), ditto.
Chiffchaff (Silvia hippolais), ditto.
Grey Wagtail (motacilla borula), frequently observed.
Ray's Wagtail („ fluva), ditto.
Cole Tit (Parus uter), common.
Marsh Tit (Parus palustris), common.
Long-tailed Tit (Parus caudatus), ditto.
Bullfinch (Pyrrhula vulgaris), ditto.
Bramblefinch (fringilla montifringilla), several obtained.
Hawfinch (coccothraustes vulgaris), ditto.
Meadow Pipit (authus pratensis), common.
Crossbill (Loxia curvirostra), a few of these birds were obtained about eight years ago from some fir trees in the neighbourhood.
Jay (Garrulus glaudarius), common.
Magpie (Pica caudata), ditto.
Hooded Crow (corvus cornix), several obtained.
Green Woodpecker (picus vividis), occasionally.
Great Spotted Woodpecker (picus major), a few of these birds obtained every winter and spring.
Less Spotted Woodpecker (picus minor), ditto.
Nuthatch (Sitta Europæa), common in spring.
Wryneck (Yunx torquilla), ditto.
Cuckoo (Cuculus canorus), ditto.
Kingfisher (Alcedo ispida), common.
Nightjar (Caprimulgus Europæus), ditto.
Turtle Dove (Columba turtur), several.
Heron (ardea cinerea), common.
Woodcock (scolopax rusticola), occasionally.
Common Snipe (scolopax gallingo), common.
Jack Snipe (scolopax gallinula), ditto.
Land Rail (crex pratensis), several met with.
Water Rail (rallus aquaticus), ditto.
Sclavonian Grebe (podiceps cornutus), one specimen.
Little Grebe (podiceps minor), common.
Cormorant (Phalacrocorax carbo), one specimen at Wanstead Park.

ORNITHOLOGIST.
Leytonstone, March 18, 1867.

AIDS TO EGG-COLLECTING. — In collecting eggs the three chief points to be observed are—Identification, Authenticity, and Preservation; for the better these are established the more valuable the egg is.

Of the first, to ascertain what kind any egg is, it is best to apply to some experienced oologist, to any public collection of eggs, or to some work on eggs. In these cases it will be a great help to know also something about the nest, its situation, &c., and notice should always be taken of any circumstance connected with them. Every nest taken should be recorded in a note-book.

This plan will also be very useful in establishing the authenticity of eggs. On getting them home, if the egg is large enough, it is best to mark on it with ink its kind, if liked where it was taken, and the date—in three lines. If it is small this may be done on paper, and then gummed on. If similar eggs are taken on the same day as owls' and ringdoves', a small pencil-mark is the safest method of preventing their being mixed.

The preservation of eggs includes blowing, conveying them home, and mounting them. There are many ways of performing the first of these operations, (which all dread) a hole to be made in the shell, this may be done in many ways. The country boy takes a thorn out of the hedge, or uses a pin or needle; but the egg-collector wants something that will make a hole any size and always circular; sail-makers' needles are very good and cheap, but the most effective thing is a small drill, or bar of steel, round, and having at one end several faces (mine has 8) coming to a point, which is used by being twirled between the finger and thumb.

The first and commonest method of blowing an egg is by making a hole in each end and blowing through; except making the holes at opposite sides, which is the second method: this is, I think, the worst way there is. The third is to make a hole in the small end, and another in the larger diameter; this shows even when the eggs are mounted. The fourth is the same, but that one hole is made in the large end which does not show when mounted; but still it disfigures the egg much more than the fifth, which is, I think, the first good one. In blowing a curlew, for instance, by this method, I should make a hole in the greatest diameter, and another in a line with it and two-thirds of the distance between it and the small end. In all these methods one of the holes can be very small. I have a goose's egg blown by the fifth way, where the small hole will just admit a pin, and the large hole is less than one-fifth inch diameter.

In the next methods a blowpipe with as small a nozzle as can be had (very good ones, half brass and half tin, can be had for 6d.), or what chemists call a pipette, and which can also be had for 4d. or 6d., is necessary, as only one hole is made in the egg, into which the end of the blowpipe or pipette is inserted, and by blowing or sucking the contents are forced out, or into the bulb of the pipette. There are also some methods of cleaning eggs when they have been sat on, entailing the use of several instruments, with which I am not acquainted.

Eggs are conveyed in safety by being placed in boxes lined with and having some loose cotton wool in them. For long journeys pack each egg separately in a piece of wool, and never send them loose in bran or sawdust or they will be broken.

In mounting eggs and forming a collection, they may either be stuck on cardboard or laid in cotton wool, and each kind labelled. Complete lists of British birds for this purpose can be had at Mr. J. Gardener's, 195, Oxford-street, London. I have been trying some experiments in mounting eggs in plaster of Paris, but without enough success to enable me to recommend it.

Any one who will send any hints on mounting or any methods of blowing birds' eggs (through this paper) will greatly oblige

KELLICK.

Smoke from a Lamp.—In reply to the query of "E. S.," anent the lamp, the following considerations will, I think, explain the phenomenon to which he refers:—

In all burning lamps, candles, &c., there is a column of heated air, &c. (the products of combustion) rising with considerable velocity through the chimney-glass; added to which there is a variable quantity of unconsumed carbonaceous matter, which in low temperatures is recognised as smoke. This column of heated matter on leaving the mouth of the chimney is met and resisted by the mass of colder air outside (above and around it), and is thereby affected in two ways: first, mechanically, by simple pressure or resistance which tends to check and divert the upward hot current; and secondly, chemically, by abstracting heat from the rising mass of vapour, and causing it thereby to become denser, more visible, or in simple language more smoke-like. Now this takes place in all similar cases of combustion, and is in all (in theory) equally evident; but the reason the phenomenon is not perceived under ordinary circumstances is this: one effect of this mingling of the cold and hot airs is to cause the air (as a medium of light) to be unable to convey a perfectly clear and steady impression of objects seen through it; and as the background (being the distant wall or ceiling) is not usually of a character to allow us to notice the distortion, it is only when we place a mirror or something analogous (as a background) that we are enabled to detect it: the face of the mirror being smooth and bright enables us by contrast to see the smoke and heated currents of air rise in front of it. This explanation will, I hope, prove satisfactory both to "E. S." and to your scientific readers generally. I hope I have made myself understood. I have tried the experiment with a moderator lamp, but did not perceive the phenomenon. Perhaps the combustion was too perfect to allow enough smoke to be formed.

W. H. A.

PIED WAGTAIL.—Two correspondents of *Land and Water* speak of the pugnacity of the pied wagtail, which we quote:—

"The snow was on the ground, the frost was severe, and a flock of chaffinches and greenfinches had congregated on a small spot of ground where some crumbs and grains had been recently thrown down. Three pied wagtails made their appearance amongst the flock of finches, and most vigorously attacked them whilst feeding, and one wagtail especially flew at a chaffinch which had perched on the handle of a wheelbarrow, which was standing near, and knocked it completely off. This was repeated several times on the chaffinch attempting to regain his post."

The other account says: "During the severe frost and snow we always threw crumbs out before our breakfast-room windows, which soon attracted a goodly number of sparrows, chaffinches, robins, and a thrush. They were not, however, allowed long to eat their meal in peace, for, almost immediately, a female pied wagtail (*Motacilla alba*, Linn.) popped in and sent them flying in every direction. The curious part remains to be told, for, having satisfied her own hunger, she placed herself in the midst of the largest heap, and, like the dog in the manger, drove off every bird that attempted to pick up a stray morsel."

THE WREN.—I have observed great differences in the formation of the nest of this little bird. One I found was like a tube built into the ground at the foot of a bush of broom, and another was completely round, with a small opening to allow the occupant to pass in and out. It was built beneath a bank of sand; and as I approached, the wren flew out. Can any one inform me whether this was a different species, or the same bird accommodating itself to circumstances?   FOX.

BEES.—Having last autumn failed in attempting to take honey from a hive of bees, by means of fumigating with fungus, I am anxious to learn how. Could any of your readers oblige me with an account and full particulars how to do it? I used Neighbour's fumigator (No. 12). The hive was full of bees, but only the bottom ones seemed to be affected by the smoke. A. B.

EARLY MOORHEN'S NEST.—A correspondent of the *Field* says: "A moorhen has already constructed her nest on the surface of a small pond at the foot of the ancient elms which the rooks love to frequent, and on the 5th of March had laid six eggs. Is she not very early?"

NEW PLANT CLUB.—Many of my flower-loving lady friends have formed a club or association, with rules hitherto strictly abided by, through which we are enabled to obtain many novelties that otherwise, from the high prices they bear, we could not hope to possess; and since it has proved so eminently successful, I am authorised to communicate with such other ladies as may desire to proceed on the same footing as ourselves, but I beg leave to observe, it will be left to our option to forward our rules only where we can, through the means of friends, ascertain from whence and from whom the applications proceed. I have only to remark that by the combination of friends we are enabled to procure such plants and seeds as are most desirable, and which by propagation and division we can all participate in; and thus we all become possessed of new and choice varieties at very trifling cost, some of our gardeners being, I should say, good propagators, and soon getting up the required number of plants. Should any of your numerous friends feel desirous of following our example, they will please apply through you.—*Isabella, Salisbury.*

[The above appeared in the *Gardeners' Chronicle*, March 16th. Should any of our readers feel disposed to interest themselves they will please direct to the Editor of the *Gardeners' Chronicle*, 41, Wellington-street, Strand.]

STATE OF THE WEATHER NEAR LONDON.

| Feb. and March. | Moon's Age. | Barometer. | | Temperature. | | | | | Wind | Rain. | Remarks. |
| | | | | Of the Air. | | | of the Earth | | | | |
		Max.	Min.	Max	Min	Mean	1 foot deep	2 feet deep			
Thurs. 14	10	30.281	30.194	54	34	44.0	48	44	E.	.00	Foggy; hazy; very fine at night.
Friday 15	11	29.998	29.710	58	45	51.5	47	44	S.E.	.10	Fine; very fine; cloudy; rain.
Satur. 16	12	29.774	29.719	59	40	49.5	49	46	S.W.	.38	Rain; fine; heavy rain at night.
Sunday 17	13	30.138	29.879	53	36	44.5	50	46	E.	.00	Foggy and mild; fine; cloudy.
Mon. 18	●	30.412	30.061	48	42	45.0	49	46	E.	.00	Dense fog; hazy; overcast at night.
Tues. 19	15	30.368	30.289	54	45	49.5	49	46	S.E.	.00	Hazy and damp; fine; overcast and mild.
Wed. 20	16	30.479	30.407	58	41	49.5	49	46	W.	.00	Hazy; fine; slightly overcast and fine at night.
Thurs. 21	17	30.485	30.428	57	37	47.0	49	46	S.W.	.00	Uniformly overcast; overcast throughout.
Friday 22	18	30.412	30.328	52	36	44.0	49	46	S.W.	.00	Overcast; densely overcast at night.
Satur. 23	19	30.456	30.406	56	30	43.0	49	46	N.W.	.00	Fine throughout; mild at night.
Sunday 24	20	30.216	30.133	54	35	44.5	48	46	S.W.	.00	Densely overcast; fine throughout.
Mon. 25	21	30.146	29.965	50	38	44.0	48	45	W.	.01	Fine; very fine; densely overcast; rain.
Tues. 26	☾	29.990	29.960	45	35	40.0	47	45	W.	.04	Drizzly; fine; overcast.
Wed. 27	23	30.017	29.990	44	32	38.0	47	45	N.E.	.00	Hazy clouds; dry haze; overcast at night.
Thurs. 28	24	30.344	30.162	45	23	34.0	46	45	E.	.00	Cold haze; dry, slight haze; very fine; frosty.
Friday 1	25	30.565	30.472	45	28	36.5	44	44	N.E.	.00	Partially overcast; dusky clouds; overcast.
Satur. 2	26	30.687	30.655	40	25	32.5	43	43	N.E.	.00	Foggy; cold hazy clouds, with dry easterly winds.
Sunday 3	27	30.666	30.518	45	30	37.5	42	42	N.E.	.01	Dry and frosty; fine; overcast; slight rain at night.
Mon. 4	28	30.438	30.233	47	33	40.0	42	42	N.E.	.00	Hazy and cold; fine, but cold and dry; overcast.
Tues. 5	29	30.125	29.974	49	25	37.0	41	42	N.E.	.00	Densely overcast; fine; very fine; slight frost at night.
Wed. 6	●	29.810	29.657	42	27	34.5	42	42	N.E.	.00	Overcast; sky of gloomy dusky hue; sun eclipsed, at times distinctly visible; clouds in strata, the lower floating dark and low; the upper stationary.
Thurs. 7	1	29.593	29.583	37	28	32.5	42	42	N.E.	.00	Hazy; snow in broad flakes; snow at night.
Friday 8	2	29.570	29.486	40	26	33.0	42	41	N.E.	.08	Snowing in broad flakes; cloudy and cold; overcast.
Satur. 9	3	29.518	29.202	44	35	39.5	45	41	N.E.	.46	Slight haze; boisterous; heavy rain at night.
Sunday 10	4	29.456	29.121	45	33	39.0	42	42	N.E.	.03	Hazy and damp; drizzling rain; densely overcast at night.
Mon. 11	5	29.682	29.561	41	32	36.5	42	42	N.E.	.04	Hazy throughout; drizzly rain at night.
Tues. 12	6	29.741	29.646	39	27	33.0	42	42	N.E.	.06	Sleet; boisterous; overcast at night.
Wed. 13	☽	29.891	29.633	34	30	32.0	40	41	E.	.40	Frosty; cold and overcast; snow at night.

THE NATURALIST IN THE CHINA SEAS.

N Monday morning, April 30th last, Capt. Bullock and I, with Mr. Sutton, chief engineer of the SERPENT, visited the island (Pratas) two hours' pull from the ship; and I spent the whole day in exploring its character and natural history features. It is formed entirely of coarse coral sand or debris, generally shelving gradually, but in some parts having a steep bank, about 3 feet high. The interior is rough and hilly from accumulations of similar white sand blown up from the shore, and so overgrown is it with shrubs as to be in some parts almost impenetrable, though the soil might be supposed to be anything but favourable to vegetable growth, nothing but sand being anywhere visible, and that of the coarsest and loosest description. The bushes in some places approach very near the sea, and between them and the water's edge various flowers not unfrequently peep out from the inhospitable soil, including a patentilla, an anemone, a plantago, and some grasses. On the west side of the island is a deep indentation into which the sea enters, forming a shallow lagoon or bay, on the banks of which the vegetation assumes quite a park-like aspect, bushes and even small trees with spreading branches springing forth close to the ground producing a scene of great luxuriance and some beauty. Amongst the bushes immense orthopterous insects (grasshoppers) flew, about exhibiting a deep red underwing, and looking very much like small birds. To the shrubs also were attached numerous geometric webs, which were occupied by a species of spider belonging to the division *Acrosoma*, having a squareish abdomen, from the upper surface of which projected several spike-like processes. This was the only species of spider which came under my notice, and in its web there appeared to be as often another spider of the same species, as any other kind of insect, the paucity of insect life on the island apparently driving them to cannibalism. A moth whose expanse of wing was about an inch, and having small red and black spots upon the wing, was pretty numerous, and appeared to be the only lepidopterous insect, with the exception of a large clear-winged species, which was captured but unfortunately escaped again. These, with some ants and a few carrion beetles, constituted the insect fauna as far as could be determined during our single visit.

Among the coral debris upon the beach were numerous masses of various sizes, consisting of rolled Astræas madrepores, etc., and mingled with them were fragments of shells of a great many species of consus, cypræa, turbo, ponna, hippopus, &c., but none of them entire. Innumerable little hermits (paguri and cœnobitæ) occupied the deserted shells of noticæ and neritinæ, and larger ones those of good-sized turbines; but I saw no live shells upon the beach except a few insignificant ones, such as litorinæ and purpuræ; nor, though the water was bright and clear and I waded out as far as I could go, could I anywhere see any traces of annelids or echinoderms. The harder parts of the sand were harrowed with deep holes of various sizes from which emerged from time to time wary and swift-footed crab (ocypoda) which scuttled nimbly down to the sea upon the first sign of approaching footsteps, and appeared to be aware of us at least at fifty yards distance. Nor was it easy to capture a specimen, for while on the one hand they never made the mistake of running *away from* the sea, on the other hand, if cut off, they fled so quickly and *doubled* so nimbly, suddenly running the opposite way without the clumsy process of turning round, that they afforded great amusement and not a little exercise and exertion.

The sea in the neighbourhood of the Pratas Island has a very variegated appearance, from the alternative of bare white sandy bottom with patches of ulva and zostera, both of which are very abundant. The ulva is a very beautiful reticulated species, and the zostera leaves float about in all directions, and in all stages of decay, generally bearing upon them minute dendritic polyzoa, lurnilites, spirorbis, &c., with which the towing net from the ship was replenished. Besides the ulva, I obtained several other species of seaweed washed up on the beach, and conspicuous among them a species of padina, very abundant everywhere in these seas, and a sargassum.

Although some classes of animals were poorly represented upon Pratas Island, there were plenty of birds, and of several species; bush, sea, and land birds. A buzzard I noticed several times, but it was too wary to allow me to come within gunshot, although it offered a tantalizing mark just out of range. I observed a very handsome shrike, with an ash coloured head and black moustache; the blue-jackets reported that they had seen a canary, and I afterward saw myself a yellowish bird, resembling the English siskin, which was, probably, the bird they had noticed. Another bird, about the size of a blackbird, was of a glossy metallic blue above, and fawn coloured beneath; its stomach contained the clytra of beetles. A fifth species presented all the appearance of a veritable blackbird, but I could not get near enough to examine it closely. A species of swallow, with glossy bluish back, chesnut neck, and with a speckled fawn colour underneath, was flying about in considerable numbers; and, on the banks of the shallow inlet, I saw a bright coloured kingfisher, very similar, in appearance and size, to our own species. There were also, some small birds which crossed our path from time to time with the jerking flight and the chirrup of the hard billed passeres. Large flocks of Tringas, (sandpipers) of at least two species, were visible on the sandy flats of the inlet which were left uncovered in the afternoon, and also upon some parts of the seaward shore of the island, where it was inclined to be soft and marshy. There was also two species of plover; the one of a reddish brown colour, with orange red legs, and a godwit, (Limosa) speckled grey and brown, with greenish legs and a remarkable beak. A large rapacious looking bird, which came sailing majestically within gunshot, was brought down, and turned out to be the frigate bird (Tachypetes aquilus), a bird confined to tropical regions, but having a wide range throughout them, being not uncommon both in the Atlantic and Pacific Oceans. When it fell, a strong guano smell pervaded it, which was very disagreeable. I measured its expanse of wing, which proved to be nearly seven feet from tip to tip; and on opening its stomach I found, in a partially digested state, three large flying fishes and two squid. Small flocks of a pretty species of white egret frequently flew along the shore, and indeed, with gannets, made their appearance about the ship immediately upon her anchoring off the shoal. I shot one from the ship for examination, and found it to be twenty inches long from tip of beak to end of tail, and of a pure white colour, with the exception of a few orange feathers over the base of the beak, which formed a sort of crest, bill yellow, and legs greenish brown. It was not provided with any of those special feathers which adorn our British species; the stomach contained a few remains of beetles.

But the dominant and characteristic bird of Pratas Island, is the gannet. These birds measure 4ft. 10in. from tip to tip of wing, and 2ft. 9in. total length from beak to tail, which is wedge-shaped. The head, neck, back and tail, are fuscous; breast and belly white; legs and feet yellow, and completely webbed. They are common birds on most of these islands, and are well known to seamen. They fly heavily, and usually low, fearlessly approaching within gunshot and even stonesthrow, and some of the men amused themselves with throwing lumps of coral at them as they flew by, the same bird returning again and again at the risk of being knocked down.

A walk through the interior of the island among the shrubs and bushes revealed to me the domestic economy of these birds. In the open places and under the shelter of the bushes, the mother gannets were sitting upon their nests and eggs. The nests were mere hollows in the coral sand strewn with a few bits of grass, with some admixture of feathers, and perhaps a bit of seaweed, forming at best a very rude cradle in which were deposited two eggs. These eggs were about the size of goose eggs, white, with a suspicion of a blue tinge, not smooth and glossy like hens' eggs, but more or less scratched as though the scratches were made when the external coat was soft and had afterwards dried, preserving the marks. One nest contained four eggs. The poor bird sitting upon this nest would show symptoms of uneasiness as I approached, pecking the ground or coarse grass fiercely with its long straight beak, but did not offer to quit the nest until I was within two or three yards of it or even less. Then placing the end of its bill upon the ground, with a gulping effort it vomited up its meal, depositing it beside the nest, and floundering forward took wing and rose into the air. This was the proceeding at nearly everyone of the hundreds of nests which I disturbed. It was evident that the birds had just gorged themselves with food and then sat upon their eggs (unless indeed the mate had brought them food, a circumstance which I did not see myself) and that they were unable to raise themselves off the ground until they had got rid of the superfluous weight in their stomachs. On examining the vomited food, I found it to consist invariably of flying fish generally of a large size and usually but slightly digested. There were sometimes six or seven of these fish, in other instances only three or four, and in two or three cases a squid or two intermixed with them. But what numbers of flying fish must exist in the neighbourhood to afford such a daily supply to so large a number of birds, and yet we did not see a trace of flying fishes about the island, and might otherwise have supposed there were none. Meanwhile the gannets formed a thick cloud over head, the noise of whose screams and the rustling of whose wings formed a wild accompaniment of sounds. They flew so close over head that I could have knocked them down with a stick in any numbers, and was obliged to wave my gun about as I walked along, in order to keep them from carrying away my hat. By degrees the birds rose higher, and those I had disturbed returned to their nests as soon as I had passed a few yards.—*The Quarterly Journal of Science, London.* JOHN CHURCHILL & SONS.

ROOKS.

THE Rook (Corvus frugilegus), with perhaps one exception, is more numerous than any bird in our district; that exception is the jackdaw, which, though it does not assemble in immense flocks like the rook, yet, I think, equals it in numbers. Rookeries, great and small, are scattered all over our neighbourhood, those in Thoresby Park being the largest and most thickly populated. One of these, in a grove of Scotch fir and oak about a quarter of a mile from the mansion is of immense extent, and its occupants must be counted by thousands.

I have seen them in an evening when they were returning to their nests quite darken the air with their flight, and on one or two occasions, when the turf has been infested more than usual with the larvæ of the cockchafer, they have literally blackened a patch of ground about a quarter of a mile square; and never shall I forget the amazement with which a relative of mine, fresh from a town residence, gazed on their countless numbers.

Their partiality for the grub of the cockchafer is productive of the most beneficial results. But I have seen long patches of sward in the forests and parks so thoroughly and uniformly dug up in their search for them that it was greensward no longer; not a patch as large as the hand had escaped being uprooted.

I do not agree with the opinion so commonly expressed, that the bare space around the base of the bill of the rook is produced by its habit of grubbing in the ground; I have watched them very closely when they have been engaged in upturning the turf as I have described, and I never saw the bill plunged beyond its length. Even when they are searching the newly-ploughed ground, when they approach so closely, I never observed any action which could produce the abraded appearance. I admit it is very natural to attribute it to such a cause; but is it not a singular fact telling strongly against this theory, that in the extent of this bare skin there should be no appreciable difference in one bird over another, but all are equally denuded? Surely, if it was produced by digging, some variation in this would be noticeable, but I never saw such; the jackdaw, too, is as great a digger as the rook, and has a shorter bill, and yet the base is clothed with feathers which bear no trace of injury from such a cause.

Though naturally insect feeders, yet there are times when, pressed by hunger, rooks levy their contributions on the newly-springing corn, and in hard winters they will even frequent stackyards. They are very partial to potatoes, at least they are much addicted to digging up and carrying off those freshly planted, but it is chiefly at the time when their young are clamorous for food, "when there is little to earn and many to keep;" indeed they often suffer greatly from want at this time of the year. Macgillivry doubts the assertion that the rook pilfers freshly-planted potato sets, but I have seen them do so hundreds of times.

Though in our neighbourhood the corn is always tended by boys, from the time of sowing until it is well out of the ground, in order to drive off the rooks, who would otherwise commit great havoc, yet I think the cultivators of the land have a pretty correct idea that, on the whole, the labours of these birds are productive of great benefit to the crops, and no greater destruction is made than of an occasional one who, with wings extended by two split sticks, is placed *in terrorem* in the centre of a corn or potato field; and a very effectual scarecrow he makes —his constrained attitude is understood at a glance by his wary brethren, and they need no other hint. In some parts of the country the agriculturists are not so conversant with the habits of the rook, and I know that in one locality in an eastern county a large rookery was destroyed under the belief of the farmers that its inhabitants were hostile to their interests, and consumed a large quantity of corn. But mark the result. Two years passed away, and the farmers congratulated themselves on being rid of their winged foes, little thinking that they had other foes in their place whose approach was more difficult to detect. In the second year many fields of wheat suffered from wireworm; but in the third their ravages had become so general throughout the district as to occasion serious alarm. Little could be done to suppress their numbers until the rooks were again thought of, and the evil was traced to its true course. The rookery was permitted to be re-established by the return of many who had escaped the massacre, and who still cherished a partiality for their native trees, but who had hitherto been continually driven off. Their rapidly increasing numbers soon reduced the insect pest, leading the farmers to acknowledge the error into which they had fallen, and hence forth to look upon the rook as a friend instead of an enemy.

When rooks are feeding they always station several of their number as sentinels, and very faithful they are in sounding the alarm on the approach of a foe; they are not only vigilant in their watch, but evince a large amount of sagacity, an amusing instance of which was communicated to me by a friend on whose statement I can rely, and who witnessed the occurrence.

A very large field had been sown with wheat, and in the centre a little hut had been erected to shelter the boy who had to tend the field, and to enable him to reach all parts of it. A gentleman who wished to obtain a few birds to hang up in his own fields thought this would be a good opportunity of procuring them, for they thronged around in great numbers, and kept the boy actively employed to drive them off. So taking his gun, he went into the hut accompanied by the boy, and through some holes in the sides prepared to pour a volley on the invaders. But he reckoned without his host. The watchful sentinels seemed instinctively to divine the plot, their warning "caw" was loudly uttered, and the presence of the ambushed foe made known. They circled round and round and settled in the surrounding field, but not one of them would trust themselves within gunshot of the hut. For some time the gentleman waited in vain, and then sent the boy away with directions to walk straight out of the field; but this ruse did not succeed. The rooks still refused to "come and be killed," so he left the hut and followed the boy, but no sooner had he gone out of the gate of the field than the sentinels gave the signal, and scores of their fellows at once descended and commenced their foray. The sportsman determined not to be outwitted in this way, so he immediately took two persons with him into the hut and resumed his ambush, the rooks having taken flight on his reappearance. After a short time had elapsed he sent one of the persons away; and after another interval the second, expecting that as soon as they both left the field the rooks would return; but he was again doomed to disappointment; "beware" cawed the sentinels in the most sonorous tone, and none ventured to disregard the warning. Determined still further to test their powers of numeration, he again left the hut and returned with three persons, all four entering together. Again, one by one, the companions were sent away, and the plan was at last crowned with success; the rooks could count as far as three, but four was beyond their powers, and no sooner had the third person left the field than they hurried to the spoil, but only, alas! to leave two of their number dead on the field, victims to the want of a knowledge of numeration.

I met with an interesting account of the sagacity of the rook in the *Dundee Courier* a few years since. Its truthfulness was vouched for by the gentleman who communicated it, and by the editor:—On Saturday week a very curious scene occurred in the colony of crows on the South Inch, Perth. One of the black denizens had been laboriously occupied in conveying sticks from the opposite side of the river, wherewith to build his nest, when something seemed to strike him that he was making no progress in his erection, and that he was the victim of some thievish neighbour. That his suspicions were correct he soon discovered, and evidently adopted the following plan to detect the culprit. He set off apparently to cross the river, and kept his usual way, but on reaching the island he suddenly wheeled round, and sweeping behind the lime sheds he reached his nest just in time to catch the suspected rogue in the very act of robbing him of a stick. A fierce engagement ensued, lasting several minutes, when the thief clearly having the worst of the fight, was compelled to render justice to his injured neighbour by restoring his stolen property, as for nearly half an hour after the latter was seen to carry stick after stick from the other's nest without any molestation, and apply them to his own.

I can quite give credit to this anecdote, for I have known two similar cases, in which one rook was detected stealing sticks from another; in both instances, however, the punishment was inflicted by more than the injured bird, and in one case with such severity that the offender's life was forfeited. I have more than once seen a rook chased from a rookery by a number of its inhabitants, but whether the hostility was shown because it was a stranger or a criminal I could not discover.

Lord Campbell, in his "Lives of the Chancellors," says that "in Scotland the crows, who take such good care to keep out of gunshot on every 'lawful day,' on the Sabbath come close up to the houses, and seek their food within a few yards of the farmer and his men, discovering the occurrence of the sacred day from the ringing of the bells and the discontinuance of labour in the fields, and knowing that while it lasts they are safe."

I am not aware whether rooks ever indulge in eating eggs, but I once saw a pair on the 4th of June actively engaged for some time in chasing a pair of green plovers in a field on the verge of the forest. They were evidently bent on driving them away from a particular spot, which the plovers seemed as determined not to leave, and from their pertinacity I concluded that their nest was thereabouts, and that they suspected the rooks of a wish to plunder it; I must say the conduct of the latter was very suspicious.

The rook is occasionally subject to variations of plumage, and the saying as "black as a crow" is not always applicable. In March, 1860, one was killed near us which was uniformly speckled all over with white.—*Field*, March 30th.

STAR SHOWERS.
FROM the interior richness and brilliancy of the recent star-shower as compared with that described by Humboldt and others in 1799 and 1833, it has been suggested by M. Coulvier Gravier that the late display is but the precursor to the fuller and really periodical phenomenon which may be expected at the same period of the current year. Be this as it may, the law of periodicity has been sufficiently established to remove all doubt from the theory that these flights of meteors are due to the existence of a ring or rings of cosmical matter revolving round the sun. As early as the year 1835, Arago was led to enunciate the belief that there exists a zone composed of millions of small planetary bodies with the sun for their centre, whose orbit

cuts the plane of the ecliptic at about the point which the earth annually occupies between the 10th and 14th of November. The period from the 10th to the 14th of August was first noted by M. Quetelet, of Brussels, and has been determined by Mr. Alexander Herschel to be one of eight years. It is now supposed by German, English, and American observers, that star-showers recur, though less regularly, in January, twice in April, in July, October, and December. But, earlier than all, Cassini had stated his theory of the zodiacal light, which referred that phenomenon to a ring of nebulous or gaseous matter, or of innumerable small planetary bodies, revolving round the sun. And he went so far as to suggest that the fall of meteors might be connected with the passage of our planet through this ring. There have, indeed, been some who, regarding the zodiacal light as a ring of the same sort of matter, have assigned it to the earth, instead of the sun, as its centre. But this hypothesis may be set aside by the most simple geometrical consideration. The form of the luminous cone is unmistakably such as, if prolonged, would describe an ellipse with the sun in one of its foci. And, notwithstanding the opposition of Olbers, the general opinion of astronomers has gone with Olmsted and Biot in definitively connecting this phenomenon with the November meteors, of which the radiant point is in Leo. The discovery of additional radiant points in Perseus, Hercules, and other constellations, may fairly be taken to indicate additional rings inclined at different angles with the ecliptic between the orbits of Venus and Mars. The nodes of the August ring seem to be stationary, while those of November have a direct proper motion retarding the star-shower year after year. It appears probable that the matter of which these rings are composed is by no means equally diffused in space, but may be scattered in sporadic groups or masses, more or less dense at different portions of their orbits. The so-called planetoids, which have been discovered to the number of seventy and more, may not improbably be taken to represent larger members of a series such as this. Mr. Herschel even goes so far as to consider it certain that not only periodical meteors, but ordinary shooting-stars, such as may be seen at any time of the year upon clear nights, belong to rings having a determinate orbit; and not fewer than fifty-six such rings he believes to be as well determined as those of August and November.

Besides this, which may be termed the "planetary" hypothesis, there has also been suggested the "satellite" theory of meteors. According to the latter view, we are to suppose a flattened ring or rings circling the equatorial regions of the earth, analogous to the system of Saturn. We have seen that no such theory as this can be connected with the zodiacal light. But there is nothing to prevent its being accepted on grounds of its own, and it may well takes its place in perfect harmony with the other. Both the sun and the earth, that is, may have their hosts of indefinitely smaller bodies. M. Petit, of Toulouse, has in fact satisfied himself of the existence of one such revolving body, having an orbit round the earth of three hours and a half, at a mean distance of 5,000 miles from the earth's surface. To the same category we may, perhaps, refer the dark spots which are occasionally seen to cross the sun's disk. On the 4th of October last a dark mass was observed by M. Heis to traverse the sun through eleven degrees of right ascension. A similar spot was seen by M. Aristide Coumbary at Constantinople, on the 8th of May, 1865, to cross the sun's lower limb (reversed) in forty-eight minutes. And the astronomer Meissier, on the 17th of June, 1779, as reported by Arago, witnessed, for about five minutes, a "prodigious number of black points passing across the sun." May we not, in fact, consider our magnificent secondary, the moon, as but the chief of a series of meteoroid masses of this kind? Saturn, we know, in addition to his belts, has eight attendant moons or satellites. Our planet, less richly endowed, has but one on a like scale of magnificence. Conceiving the planetary system at large to have been condensed and solidified from the cooling down of the sun's atmosphere, we may suppose certain minor masses or particles of the same cosmical matter to have been left out from the major masses of the earth and moon, and to have been scattered on the path along which those bodies held their way. We are thus led to the conclusion, graphically put by Dr. Phipson, that our earth circulates round the sun "in or near a continuous cloud of its own dust." On the supposition that the largest aerolites fall in the day-time, while detonating bolides or fire-balls occur about the period of sunset, Mr. Herschel has conjectured that the larger fragments have their orbit inside that of the earth, and that the size of these bodies gradually decreases, the meteoric dust or shooting stars lying beyond the earth's orbit, so as to be seen only by night. Seen thus from some imaginary point in space beyond the earth's orbit, the spectacle we might conceive our system to exhibit would be that of a composite group—earth, moon, and meteoric rings—moving round the sun at about the same mean distance as the sun's ring or rings before descrebed. Its orbit being one of greater eccentricity, our system would be seen annually to draw near, and possibly every thirty-three years to break through, one at least of the solar rings. Thus the regularly recurring flights of meteors would be accounted for. At the same time, the earth's superior attraction for the moment might be supposed to steal away, so to say, sundry of the sun's tributaries, and to attach thenceforth these stragglers to her own train. From the mass thus accumulated round her central regions, occasional bodies, jostling each other in their flight, or getting entangled in the earth's atmosphere, would be precipitated in those solid forms which are accumulating so rapidly on the shelves of our museums. With this view concurs the fact of meteoric falls being observed to be more frequent towards the tropics than towards the poles.—*Saturday Review, April* 6.

THE DAISY.

THIS very humble evergreen herbaceous plant, the *Bellis perennis* of botanists (from *bellus*, pretty), was the delight of my boyhood; for I cultivated the Daisy for an edging, when my father alloted me a patch of ground about 12 feet by 6, for floriculture. As I advanced in years I found to my cost that this friend of my youth was a troublesome lawn weed, and that it had been rightly named perennial, for it proved remarkably tenacious of life. Every gardener has been tormented with its fine healthy appearance, in full bloom all over the lawn in little more than a day after mowing; and, as the following quaint epitaph from an Irish churchyard indicates, it is destined to get the upper hand at last :—

"Here I'm arrived, and my burden is aises,
    With the point of my nose, and the tips of my toes,
Turned up to the roots of the Daisies."

This pretty composite flower, with its coronet of rosy florets, seems as if its involurated head had been brow-bound with a reversible garland, for when the wild daisy is expecting rain or heavy dews, we find it forming an elegant bud, beautifully tipped with pink; but when the sun shines, and the sky is serene, it shows the white star spreading from its golden centre, and in this state, wherever the highly-kept lawn is respected, the gaudy little weed is sure to be detested. In botanical works the daisy is said to flower from March until August. I saw some in flower in January this year, and the previous weather had certainly not been by any means forcing—in fact, the daisy was only a few days behind the snowdrop in showing blossoms, and we may safely reckon upon its blooming in favoured localities until the end of October.

The large double garden variety not being a perfect flower, but a very beautiful transformation, is more shy of blooming, and seldom shows fine flower buds excepting in spring. The double quilled kinds seem to have carried the transformation still further, and piped each floret, so that the style and character of the original type become altogether changed. Under ordinary circumstances these double flowers are barren, and consequently have to be propagated by division of the roots. There is a proliferous kind called the Hen-and-Chicken Daisy, which forms lateral flower heads around the parent head—a mere oddity, and by no means ornamental like the garden varieties above noted. The daisies have one very important point in a business point of view—they sell very well, having a good deal of decided character about them, and making pretty little presents for children; but the daisy, as an ornamental flower, is not to be confounded with the lawn weed, nor with the Hen-and-Chicken varieties. There is a kind—*aucubæfolia*—having beautifully variegated leaves, and where the variegated leaf is required the plant is seldom allowed to flower, as the blossoms take away from the effect of the foliage.

In planting daisies do not be alarmed about dividing them, only take care that some little rootlets be attached to each crown. If planted for edgings, about six plants should go to the foot; be careful to dip the roots of each plant into some rich mud, of about the consistency of thick paint, before planting; and if planted in finely pulverised soil and watered they will not fail to grow, for the daisy is a sure cropper. I have mentioned this way of planting daisies for edgings for the sake of the veriest beginners in floriculture, who, like myself, may have to start with the fourth part of a perch of garden ground. Let no one cheat the child out of such a harmless hobby as this, for I speak from experience when I say that I found great happiness in that small spot of black earth. It is, however, to the oft-recurring little patch of daisies all along the sheltered border that I would particularly direct attention, for they are among the cheapest flowers we have, and never fail to bloom freely under very ordinary culture. In order to have them looking neat, let me advise that all the flower-heads should be constantly plucked off as they begin to tarnish in any way, either with soil from dashing rains, or from decay. It is surprising what newness of life will be imparted to pet plants by this slight attention. There is nothing either first or last in floriculture. The cedar on the lawn, and the daisy on the common, are limited according to the measure meted out to each.

It is quiet disheartening to a young cultivator to begin growing good flowers, as they are called, for if they suffer the least neglect, they are done for; and there are a great many more bunglers in floriculture than it would be desirable to name. A few pence, however, well laid out on daisy plants will do more for a permanent display of neat and very showy spring flowers than can be had from any other genus that I know of. Daisies neatly dotted round a curve at distances of about six feet, or in straight lines at the same distance apart, will give the early-spring border a charm quite peculiar, as the flowers are so well thrown up above the foliage, and there is such a dense mass of flower-heads if the plants have been well fed.—Alex. Forsyth in *The Florist and Pomologist*, April.

INFUSORIA AND MYCELIUM.

The infusoria (so called from their occurrence in infusions of vegetable matter when exposed to the air) are found in enormous numbers in every stagnant pool, and form a large class of varied types of animal life; some possessing a complicated system of stomachs and digestive organs; others, again, being bags of jelly-like substance with an opening or mouth through which the food is taken up, whilst the simplest form of such beings as the amoeba, or protent animalcule, consists of a mass of clear jelly, possessing neither stomach nor mouth. Observed under the microscope, the amoeba may be seen gradually to move its gelatinous body into various shapes, and should it come into contact with the decaying vegetable or animal matter, which serves as its food, the jelly is seen to spread over and enclose the decaying particles, which then become digested as if the animal possessed a complete mouth and system of stomachs. Most of the infusoria, however, have funnel-shaped openings or mouths, and are covered by hairs or celiæ, by the vibration of which food is brought into the mouth, and the animal is enabled to swim about. These polygastric infusoria, as Owen tells us in Hunterian Lectures, "are the very type of the digestive function, assimilating and reorganising the decomposing particles of animal and vegetable matter with a hundred-stomach power. That low delight, the bliss supreme of the civilised gourmand, is given most liberally where it ought to be, to the creatures at the lowest grade of animality." The smallest of these infusoria, and those which make their appearance first in the vegetable decoctions exposed to the air are called *monads;* they appear, under the microscope, usually as mobile points, possessing, as a rule, a diameter of about $\frac{1}{50000}$ part of an inch. Lower still in the scale of animal life come the *vibrios;* these are jointed animalculæ, each individual consisting of a very thin filament which splits off from the parent. They possess neither head nor tail, nor do they show any trace of structure, and except that they exhibit a power of apparently voluntary ciliary locomotion, they might be classed amongst the vegetable world.

These creatures are always present in infusions, and are distinguished as vibrios when existing in the pliable filaments, as bacteriums when the corpuscles are connected together by a thread-like, more or less, inflexible chain, and as spirillums when they have a corkscrew shape and move in a spiral direction. Some idea may be formed of the difficulty of making observations respecting the structure and habits of these creatures owing to their extremely minute size, when we learn from the observations of Ehrenberg that eight hundred thousand millions of these animalculæ may be contained in one cubic inch of water, and yet occupy but one-fourth of its space.

Doubts have been expressed by some of our leading microscopists even as to the animal nature of these organisms. Certain decided forms of vegetable life are well known to possess a power of ciliary locomotion, and it is in fact still an open question whether the organisms which are classed as monads, vibrios, and bacteriums do not often consist of the spores of plants. The mode of propagation and distribution of these minute creatures is thus well described by Professor Owen:—"The act of oviparous generation—that sending forth of countless ova through the fatal laceration or dissolution of the parent's body—is most commonly observed in the well-fed polygastria, which crowd together as their little ocean evaporates, and thus each leaves, by the last act of its life, the means of perpetuating and diffusing its species by thousands of fertile germs. When the once thickly tenanted pool is dried up, and its bottom converted into a layer of dust, these inconceivably minute and light ova will be raised with the dust by the first puff of wind, diffused through the atmosphere, and may there long remain suspended, forming perhaps their share of the particles which we see flickering in the sunbeam, ready to fall into any collection of water, beaten down by every summer shower into the streams or pools which receive, or may be formed, by such showers, and, by virtue of their tenacity of life, ready to develope themselves wherever they may find the requisite conditions for their existence."

The lowest forms of growth of the vegetable kingdom are the peculiar organisms which make their appearance in widely different situations, producing disastrous effects upon crops of every kind. To these microscopic fungi the botanical name of mycelium is given, but they are more generally known by the common names of mushroom spawn, mould, rust, smut and mildew. The material of which these several kinds of fungi are composed possess an extraordinary amount of vitality; it may be dried and kept for years, and even heated to the boiling point of water, and still, when again exposed to moisture and to a moderate temperature, it revives and grows. The edible part of the mushroom and visible portions of the larger fungi are, in reality, only the organs of fructification of the plant. They contain the seeds, or spores, consisting of millions of the most minute particles, which fall out when the plant is ripe, and are carried by the wind to far distant spots, there to form new mycelium and new spores. A beautiful natural photograph of the mushroom, or fungus, may be obtained from these sporules, as Sir John Herschel has shown, by allowing the ripe mushroom, having the stalk end off, to lie for twelve hours upon a clean glass plate; the spores then drop out from the radiating folds of the mushroom in which they are contained, and, adhering to the surface of the glass plate in the place upon which they fall, leave a most delicate and exact tracery of the plant. The same mode of propagation is found to exist among all fungi, whether microscopic or not, and of the latter class we now find no less than 2,479 distinct species enumerated in the "Index Fungorum Britannicorum."

It is the existence of sporules of these various species of fungi, floating about in the air, that gives rise to the common phenomenon of "mould," which we observe in bread or in cheese. The sporules fall upon the moist bread, find there circumstances to suit their growth, and gradually develope into a tree-like form bearing sporules, which in their turn are dropped, float in the air, and form the origin of a new fungoid colony. This particular fungus is termed by mycologists *Penicillium glancum*, and it possesses characters of as specific a kind as those of the edible mushroom. The number of distinct species of moulds already recognised is very large; they are generally parasitic; and cultivated plants of all kinds, and even the bodies of animals, are more or less subject to their ravages. No less than thirty species are known to infest plants of the corn tribe, whilst ten different fungi inhabit the potato and produce the dreaded disease. The vine disease and hop blight, the black rust on standing corn, and the mildew which rots cotton, cloth, and causes so much trouble to the merchant and manufacturer, as well as the green mould, which the epicure values on a Stilton cheese, are all produced by this fine microscopic fungoid dust which is constantly present in the air, and being of so minute a kind cannot be in any way excluded. It is rendered visible as motes in the sunbeam, and only requires to find a suitable position to sow itself and produce its kind.—*Edinburgh Review*, April, 1867.

ENCROACHMENT OF THE SEA.

IN 1864 I published the following account in a "Sketch of the Geology of Norfolk," printed in White's *Gazetteer* of the County, page 180:—"It is very difficult to obtain precise and accurate information respecting the amount of land washed away in a given number of years. We, therefore, gladly avail ourselves of a communication on the subject by a very intelligent as well as interested observer, Mr. William Cubitt, of the Bacton Priory Farm. He states that, at Bacton, where he and his predecessors have carried on the business of coal-merchants during the last thirty-five years, he has seen four coal-yards successively, a small farm-house with a barn, outhouses and garden used as a bowling-green washed away, measuring at least ninety yards to the present cliff; and that vessels can now sail at high water where the land was then cultivated." The substance of this account was detailed by me at a meeting of the Norwich Geological Society.

The following notes and observations, which I have from time to time made, of the encroachments of the sea, and of the process by which the waste of the coast is effected, may serve the purpose of illustration. The high seas, aided by land springs, undermine the cliffs very rapidly where the base of them is of sand, or any loose material; and more gradually where it consists of hard clay or chalk; and when the cliffs are levelled to the beach, the beat of the waves near the shore scoops out and clears away even the hard iron pan of the so-called "elephant bed," which prevails at Bacton to the depth of four or five fathoms, so that ships can sail over it. At Bacton the present coal-yard is within a few feet of the edge of the cliff, and the ground where the artillery practised three years ago is washed away. Beyond Cromer several pinnacles of chalk, enveloped in the glacial beds figured by Sir C. Lyell in his 'Elements of Geology,' are either entirely removed, or so reduced and altered in form as to be scarcely recognizable. One of the three bluffs of chalk at Trimingham, the sole known surviving remnants of an upper bed of chalk, has entirely disappeared; another is reduced to a mere shell, and the third is much wasted. At Cromer, the old lighthouse, on the step of which was the broad-arrow, marking the highest spot in Norfolk, noted in the Ordnance Survey, namely 248 feet 10 inches, was last December precipitated to the beach, some say buried in the debris of the cliff, others crumbled to pieces by the fall, and since entirely washed away. After long search, about a month ago, I was unable to find a vestige of brick or stone remaining. At Mundesley, during the last three or four years, the walls raised round Mr. Wheatley's house have been nearly demolished; on the south side of it several cottages have been either removed or destroyed; and on the north side of it, about eight yards inland of the river-bed described by Mr. Prestwich (*Geologist*, No. 38) have been carried away, together with a Carpenter's shop and a footpath on the summit of the cliff. This river-bed was considered by that geologist to be coeval with the Hoxne brick-pits; and it was satisfactory to obtain from it a tooth and several bones of the *Elephas antiquus*, corroborative of that opinion. At Happisburgh the encroachments of the sea have been no less remarkable. The Preventive Service Station, which had been built not many years since in a more secure position than its predecessor, is now endangered. At Eccles, the tower of the old church, till lately enveloped in the Marram hills, now stands upon the beach, occasionally surrounded by waves; at least, such was the case in 1865, when breakwaters were erected, which have resisted and repelled the onslaught of the sea. In 1863, in one night about twenty yards inland of the sand-hills were washed away, and the old marks of cultivation—hedges, tracks of wheels and of horses, probably 200 years old—were laid bare. If we search historical records, we find that Eccles suffered from time to time such inroads that in 1644, only 100 acres remained out of 2,000; that several parishes, or such portions of them, have been destroyed as to leave scarcely more than their names, as little Waxham, Whimpwell, adjoining Happisburgh, Shipden, near Cromer, and Keswich, adjoining Bacton. I trouble you with these particulars because they prove that Mr. William Cubitt's statement, which has attracted considerable notice, is by no means exceptional.—JOHN GUNN, *Athenæum*, *April 6th*.

SNAILS.

THE snail has no power to leave its shell, as many suppose. The shell is as much a part of the animal as is the hard crust of a beetle a component part of the insect, and not only this, the snail is attached to the shell by a permanent muscular attachment, and cannot be withdrawn from it alive. In order to clean the shell of its contents, it is customary to scald it in boiling water, when the muscular attachment becomes separated from the shell and the soft parts can be easily removed. The finding of empty shells in the woods has oftentimes been cited as a proof that the snail can leave its shell, and the occurrence of certain species of snails which have no visible shell, has served to strengthen a belief in this error. When the creature dies, the soft perishable parts are soon decomposed, or else devoured by insects, leaving the more enduring shell as a monument to its memory. On the approach of winter, or the continuance of a severe drought, the snail hibernates; that is, it ceases to feed, and withdraws itself far within its shell, leaving at the same time, several barriers within the aperture of the shell composed of the mucous secretions of the animal. In this condition it remains motionless, and apparently lifeless; the mode of forming the partitions is quite curious, and will interest the observer. As the snail withdraws within the shell it inspires a certain quantity of air; the creeping disk and the parts of the animal bordering the aperture of the shell, pour out a certain quantity of mucus, which stretches completely across the aperture of the shell. This soon hardens, and the snail, by expiring most of the air in its lungs and thus reducing its bulk, retires still farther within its shell, and again forms a barrier similar to the one just formed, and oftentimes several partitions are formed in this way, one behind the other, affording a complete protection against the inroads of cold and water, and apparently of heat as well, since they always do this when confined in a dry or hot place. In a certain foreign species, this partition partakes of a calcareous nature, and thus affords a more enduring barrier. In the spring time the snail resumes its activity; the barriers are forced through by the tail, and frequently the snail devours them as if famishing after its long continued fast. All species of land snails, with a few exceptions, are oviparous; that is, the young are hatched from eggs laid by the parent. The sexes are united in each individual, though the mutual union of two individuals is necessary to fertilize the eggs; they lay from fifty to one hundred eggs at a time. The eggs of most species are very small, white in colour, and resemble homœopathic pills. If the conditions are favourable, the young issue from the eggs in the course of two or three weeks, furnished with a shell composed of one whorl and a half. The shell is increased in size by the addition of calcareous matter round the margin of the aperture, the successive lines of growth can be easily traced on the shells of most species. They attain their complete growth in from one to two years. The numbers of eggs produced by an individual varies in proportion to the greater or less protection afforded to the animal; thus in the common slug limax and allied genera having no exterior shell into which they may withdraw in times of danger, the number of eggs produced is much greater; and, according to Dr. Leach, who kept two specimens of the common garden slug in confinement, seven hundred and eighty-six eggs were laid in one year.

The vitality which the snails' eggs possess surpasses belief. Certain French naturalists assert that they have been so completely dried as to be friable between the fingers. In this dried condition they have been kept for a long time, and yet a single hour's exposure to humidity and warmth has been sufficient to restore them to their original form and elasticity. They have been dried in a furnace eight successive times, until they were reduced to an almost invisible minuteness, yet in every instance have they regained their original bulk in a moist situation. In all these instances the young have been developed in the same manner as other eggs, not subjected to this experiment (Binney). This wonderful vitality extends to the snail in all stages of its existence. We have seen certain species frozen in solid blocks of ice, and yet regain their activity when subjected to the influences of warmth. The dependence on moisture naturally places them in moist situations. Yet we have seen certain species attached to leaves where the sun had shed its scorching rays for weeks, crisping the leaves and baking the ground as dry as potter's ware, and yet the conditions not affecting in the least their vitality. They have been kept for years in pill boxes, and yet on subjecting them to moisture, have crawled about appearing as well as ever. In Woodward's "Manual of Shells" is the following, chronicled by Dr. Baird regarding the resuscitation of a desert snail:—"This individual was fixed to a tablet in the British Museum on the 25th of March, 1846, and on March 7th, 1850, it was observed that he must have come out of his shell in the interval (as the paper had been discoloured apparently in his attempts to get away) but finding escape impossible, had again retired, closing his aperture with the usual glistening film. This led to his immersion in tepid water and marvellous recovery." The power possessed by the snail to reproduce certain portions of its body removed by violence, has long attracted the attention of zoologists. The horns or tentacles, and even portions of the head, have been cut away, and in due course of time these lost parts have been restored by a new growth. The whole head has been cut away, and though in many cases terminating the life of the victim, yet in some instances the parts removed have been fully restored. This seems the more wonderful when we consider the complicated character of the head and mouth. The shell may be broken, and even portions of it removed, and yet, after a certain lapse of time, the injured parts will be repaired by a deposition of shelly matter at the fractured parts.—*The American Naturalist*, March, 1867.

SNOW.

SNOW not only constantly changes in character while falling, but after it has fallen. In our climate the snow is generally moist, and cakes together, as every one knows who ever made a snowball. At lower temperatures than are common in this country the snow is fine and dry as a powder. In Lapland it is often like sand, crisp to the tread, and suitable for skating on with those long narrow pieces of wood attached to the feet, and called *snow skates*. Should very cold weather ensue, the snow beneath the surface forms into irregular hexagonal lumps, which the Laplanders prize, and will dig out from under the recent snow to fill their kettles, as it yields more water than fresh snow. The Laps prefer the dry or sand snow for lying upon, as it does not yield so much to the weight, nor get into the folds of the dress, nor melt in the fur. It does not become sloppy before a fire, but seems to disappear by evaporation. Fresh flakes of snow contain a great deal of air, so that a depth of twenty-seven inches of snow will not give more than three inches of water. It is to this entanglement of air with minutely divided water that the snow owes its whiteness. White foam is similarly produced, as when the top of a wave is broken up, and the air rushes in between the drops. But where the sun strikes upon the snow and melts a portion of it upon the surface, the water sinks through and forms ice with the lower portions, and as this process is constantly going on; in the Swiss Alps for example, we get that peculiar kind of snow called *neve*, which is ice of a whitish colour, containing a large number of air-bubbles. As this ice becomes compressed by the over-lying mass of snow, the air-bubbles are squeezed out, and we get the ordinary ice of the glacier.

The snow that forms the caps of high mountains is permanent all the year round. In ascending the mountains we come to a point called the *snow-line*, beyond which the snow does not melt. This line varies in height, according to the climate, from many thousand feet to the level of the sea. The accumulation of the mountain snow is got rid of by the caps becoming top-heavy, as it were, and slipping off form the *avalanche*, "the thunderbolt of snow." The snow thus shot down fills up the valleys with glaciers, which, like a river, move slowly on to the lower valleys under the pressure of the accumulating snow in the upper valleys. The waste of snow and ice in melting forms the sources of many noble rivers.

The snow of the Alps at different altitudes is of various colours, or rather the colour of the light in cavities in the snow varies, a common tint being a lovely *blue*.

Snow of a *red* colour has been seen even when falling, although the red colour is usually seen on old snow. In the celebrated "Crimson Cliffs" of the Arctic regions, the red colour was found to extend to the depth of about a foot.

The colour seems to be due to minute vegetable and animal life.

Lastly, *luminos snow* has been observed. A party on Loch Awe, in Argyleshire, overtaken by a snow shower, were astonished to find the flakes luminous, and that they continued to be so after setling on the sides of the boat and on persons' dresses. The effect was probably due to electricity.

We have already referred to the disappearance of snow by evaporation. One hundred grains of light snow have been found to lose sixty grains in weight in one night. when the temperature was below 25 deg.

The use of snow in affording a warm covering to the surface of the earth is well known. The air may be 30 deg. or 40 deg. below the freezing point of water while the ground below the snow will be only *at* the freezing point. Mr. Glaisher placed a thermometer on long grass one cloudless night in February, and found the temperature to be—6 deg., or 38 deg. below the freezing point, while a thermometer on grass covered only by three inches of snow marked 28 deg., or only 4 deg. below the freezing point. Some time after a thermometer *on* the snow gave—12 deg.; so that there was actually a difference of 40 degrees between the surface of the snow and the grass three inches below it. Facts like these are as wonderful, and prove *design in creation* quite as much, as the astonishing conditions connected with the freezing of water. It is to this circumstance, that the ground is kept warm by snow, that we have the fine healthy colour of young wheat and grass after the snow has melted in the spring. So also in the Alps there are numerous beautiful and somewhat delicate plants, such as auriculas, saxifrages, &c., which delight the eye when the snow has disappeared, but which would have perished but for the white winter coverlid.

Snow, like ice, makes good roads in countries where the winter is long and severe, and where people ride about in *sleighs*, or carriages without wheels. As the road is noiseless the sleigh horses are hung with merry jingling bells. Snow shoes and snow skates are worn by the pedestrians, and these presenting flat surfaces to the snow, enable them to get over the ground quickly. The Esquimaux build their houses of snow, and in the Apennines there is a harvest of snow sufficient to supply all classes in Naples with the means of cooling their summer drinks.—*People's Magazine, April 20th.*

BIRDS OF THE ISLE OF MAN.

THE following are a few remarks upon the presence and habits of some of the birds of the Isle of Man, which I trust may not be altogether uninteresting to those who find pleasure in the pursuit of natural history. They are but a few and feeble attempts to make known the history of a part of animated nature in a small and isolated fragment of Great Britain; but I hope that the backwardness of better and abler pens to diffuse this knowledge may be sufficient to shield me from the imputation of presumption.

The golden-crested wren (*Régulus cristatus*), the most minute and one of the most beautiful of British birds, frequents our edges and plantations through all the seasons of the year. At this time it seems to be especially abundant; but it may be that at other seasons, when the trees and edges are loaded with leaves and blossoms, this creature escapes detection through its minuteness. Its favourite haunt is the plantations of fir, where, on the fine sunny days that occur here even in mid-winter, its habits and antics may be observed with pleasure and not without instruction. Darting about in short flights, from branch to branch, and crossing the sunbeams that are broken into shafts among the trees, its wings and little crest sparkles with golden scintillations among the dark green verdure of the fir. I have always observed most of these birds to remain in pairs through the entire year. A beautiful blackbird, with several white feathers in its left wing, has frequented a corner of my garden for more than twelve months. I have on many occasions observed others marked with white in different manners. A perfectly white specimen has been shot by a gentleman near here some time ago. Pied crows also are not unfrequently seen on Douglas Head.

The ring-ouzel finds a home far up among the lonely rocky glens which wind among our mountains to the sea. Several water-ouzels, too, one of which I shot, frequented a little trout-stream some time since in this neighbourhood.

There are two remarkable cases here of a gradual extinction of species from no obvious cause whatever. Formerly the chough (*Frégilus graculus*) was so abundant that its eggs were used as an article of food, and even in later times it was by no means an uncommon bird among the hills and upon the sea coast. Now I may safely assert that it is an extinct species, well known indeed in the memories of the present generation of men, but itself very rarely if ever seen. The precipitous and rocky cliffs of the Calf of Man were once the homes of immense swarms of puffins, so numerous indeed that they waged a successful war against the rabbits, that found a shelter in the holes and crevices among the rocks. Now the rabbit is the sole tenant of this dreary coast; he occupies without a rival his desolate habitation, and hears alone and undisturbed for ever the roar of the sublime ocean below. This extinction of the species was so apparent and so rapid, that many reasons have been invented for it by the ancient Manx, a race of men who took no thought of the operations of nature around them, save only such as excited their fears, or aroused their superstition. Among many others, the most sensible seems to be, that they were suddenly extirpated by a swarm of brown rats, which were cast ashore from the wreck of a Russian vessel.

The stormy petrel finds sometimes a congenial home here, on that turbulent element which rages among the scattered rocks in this locality. Along the coast, but especially at such parts as are most steep and precipitous, are found the shag in great plenty, the cormorant, the curlew, several species of gulls and *Tringæ*, and among them the skua. The gannet may often be seen rising high over our bays, and dropping down straight like a bolt at the fish below. Many species, not only of birds but of other animals and plants, which in the surrounding countries are very common, are here altogether wanting. Of the rarer British birds the only ones which we can lay claim to as occasional visitants, are the kingfisher, the crossbill, the great grey shrike (*Lanius excubitor*), the hoopoe, and the roller. Of the smaller birds the goldfinch and the linnet tribe are very numerous. The bullfinch is not found, the greater titmouse is very common, the woodlark and the various species of woodpecker are not found, and the nightingale was never heard to break the solitude of Mona's nights.

Partridge and moor-hen were formerly very abundant—the latter is now extinct, and the former only just remains to remind us of our present poverty. We have several common species of hawk, the raven, the hooded crow, and some others of the carrion tribe. The sharp frosts of winter generally send us various birds of passage. The wild swan is said to have been shot in the bogs of the north, and long files of wild geese are annually observed crossing the island in their flight from the frozen regions. But these mysterious voyagers only occasionally alight as a rest in their journey to more sunny climes.

Woodcock, teal, land-rail, quail, and widgeon are generally plentiful in their proper seasons. Snipe in hard weather are sometimes very abundant, a considerable number, too, remain with us during the whole year. The common and the golden plover are not at all uncommon, but are not seen in very large flocks. The swallow comes true to its season, but unaccompanied here by any of those others of its tribe, which are so common in England. The martin is unknown. The goatsucker is so rare that I can only say that it has been seen. The heron is found commonly in summer upon the rocks of the coast, and when the storms of winter drive him from thence he wanders among the streams and ponds in the interior.

The rock pigeon does not occur in great numbers, but a few are found in the caves along the coast. In those sheltered creeks and bays which occur in many parts, may be seen calmly riding on the water after a storm, several of the diver kind, the little auk very rare, and at certain seasons innumerable flocks of wild duck. As civilization advances, and man and his works multiply, in every region the wild beast of the field and the fowl of the air are ever found to diminish.

One by one they either sink under the oppression of his tyrannies; or move away to remoter regions, where either his curiosity has not urged him, or his avarice has not been tempted. Even here, when men were few and their manners simple, animated nature existed in every variety —unawed by those terrible engines which human ingenuity has created. Eagles formerly reared their young among the rocks of Sneefell, but their memory now only exists in local traditions; though even still, the peregrine falcon, mentioned in Sir Walter Scott's "Peveril of the Peak," haunts the cliffs on the sea-coast, though it is of rare occurrence. Lately a canary-bird has lived in this neighbourhood for nearly two years, and is now in a perfectly wild and naturalized state. It resorts with that numerous flock of small birds, which at this season of the year congregate for support around the habitations of man, and of which happily neither his indifference nor his avarice is able to deprive them.—PHILORNIS *in Land and Water, April 6th.*

THE BAMBOO.

The bamboo, from its first existence until its decay, never ceases to furnish something useful to man. Every part of it is useful, of whatever species it may be. It is said that the numerous mines of the vast empire of China are of less value to the Chinese than the precious bamboo. Rich and poor neighbours all alike benefit in some way or other from it.

The bamboo is a native of the warm climates of the east, where it grows wild. It oftentimes rises to the height of 60 or 80 feet, with a hollow stem, shining as if varnished. Little stalks, with narrow-pointed leaves, spring from the joints, and give it a graceful feathery appearance as it waves in the wind. It sometimes grows three or four inches in a single day. Persons who have closely watched it say that they have seen it rise 20 feet, and as thick as a man's wrist, in five or six weeks; it has been known to reach 30 feet in six months.

As soon as the young shoots appear, the bamboo begins its life of usefulness. The soft juicy shoots are cooked in various ways, and used as food. Many of the poorer classes live upon it in times of scarcity. It is recorded in Chinese history that its seed has preserved the lives of thousands. As the plant grows older a sweet juice gradually collects in the hollow joints, affording a very pleasant drink. If allowed to remain in the reed this juice becomes solid, and from it is formed a kind of glass, said to be indestructible by fire. Other parts of the bamboo—as the leaves, buds, bark, and roots—are used as medicine.

Upon bamboo rafts the Siamese love to build their floating-houses; the carpenter uses the stem as posts and supports; split up it serves for floors and rafters, or as lattice-work for the sides of rooms, while the leaves form the thatching for the roof. The shipwright forms the hull of his vessel from the stem of one species, which is easily split into planks, while smaller plants supply the masts and yards; ships with masts, sails, rigging, and cables complete are fitted for sea from the wonderful bamboo.

The farmer uses the bamboo for his fences, windmills, waterpipes and wheels, ploughs, carts, wheelbarrows, spades, and all other agricultural implements; his wife's furniture, baskets, and numberless articles for domestic use, and his children's toys are all made from the same plant. It is also manufactured into umbrellas, hats, musical instruments, cups, brooms, soles or shoes, sedan chairs, and wicks of candles. The bark bruised and steeped is formed into a pulp from which paper is made; and in some parts of Asia a certain species supplies writing pens. Its fine fibres are made into twine; its shavings form stuffing for pillows, and its leaves are employed as a kind of cloak for wet weather. From the bamboo the fisherman makes his boat, with sails and oars complete; his ropes, floats, basket-cages, and other articles used in fishing. From it the hunter obtains his bows, arrows, spears, and other weapons.

In the jungles of India tigers and other wild beasts are captured in a curious manner by the help of the bamboo. When hard pressed by hunger the savage animals leave their haunts in the forests and jungles, and stealthily prowl about the villages, carrying off fowls, sheep, and sometimes even human beings. The enraged villagers meet in a suitable place, and, choosing a strong young bamboo, they bend its stoutest and tallest branches, and bury the ends many feet in the ground. A kid or a bird is fastened amongst the leaves, close by a slip noose of stout rope. The hungry beast, attracted by the cries of the decoy, rushes into the snare; the noose tightens round its throat, and in its struggles to escape loosens the buried branches, which swing aloft with mighty force, carrying up into the air the savage thief, who is there left to swing until its cries attract the watchers.

We cannot describe half the purposes to which the bamboo is applied. Indeed, it would be nearly as difficult to say what it is *not* used for as what it is. "It is in universal demand in the houses, in the fields, on water and on land, in peace and in war. Through life the Chinaman is almost dependent upon it for support, nor does it leave him until it carries him to his last resting-place on the hill-side, and even then it waves over and marks his tomb."—*The Cottager and Artisan*, April.

INCREASE IN SIZE OF ANIMALS.

At the sitting of the French Academy, on the 18th of March, M. Em. Blanchard presented a memoir "On Increase in Size amongst Cold-blooded Animals." Warm-blooded animals, that is to say, mammals and birds, ceased growing upon attaining to the adult state; and insects, whose life is very short, follow the same law. The greater part of the animals belonging to the other groups differ in this respect. Reptiles, fishes, crustaceans, and mollusks, continue to grow after fully arriving at the adult state. This growth, however, takes place with extreme slowness; yet, individuals placed in favourable conditions, and abundantly supplied with nourishment, can acquire a surprising magnitude if they attain to a very advanced age. We know that the writings of the ancients cite examples of the enormous size attained by fishes which we at the present day are accustomed to see of very moderate dimensions. And it is certain that, at a time when there was but little activity shown in fishing the rivers in France, old fishes were occasionally captured of a size greatly in excess of that of ordinary individuals. Amongst crustaceans, also, many facts prove the exceptional growth occasionally attained by some individuals. At a former date, when the creatures inhabiting the coasts of the United States were not pursued by man, the American lobster attained a large size. Two in the Museum at Paris may be termed gigantic, and led to the belief that the American lobster was much larger than the European. At the present day in the same localities the American lobster does not surpa s in size its European congeners. A Japanese crab brought to Europe by M. Siebold, and recently placed in the Museum of Natural History at Paris, measures, when the claws are extended, 2·6 mètres (8 ft. 6⅜ in.), each of the anterior claws measuring 1·2 mètres (3 ft. 11⅜ in.). The same phenomenon of excessive growth has been observed in mollusks fished in unfrequented regions. The common edible mussel was found by M. Nordmann of almost incredible dimensions on the coast of the island of Edgecombe, near Sitcha, in Russian America. Oysters also have been found of gigantic size in unexplored localities. We have no definite knowledge as to the possible duration of life amongst fishes, crustaceans, and mollusks, the means to determine the point being wanting. We have, however, every reason to believe that the existence of these animals may prolong itself to an extreme old age. This is indicated by the continuance of their power of growth whilst growing old, so different from the diminution in vital vigour which age always produces in mammals and birds. Amongst the fossils of divers groups of the animal kingdom, species closely allied to species now living have been met with, but greatly exceeding the latter in size. Must we not in many cases attribute this superiority in size to the extreme old age attained by certain creatures before the appearance of man on the earth?

HEREFORD ORCHARDS.

Duncomb, in his "Agriculture of Herefordshire," quoting Evelyn's "Pomona," (A.D. 1679), said:— "The plantations of Herefordshire acquired the peculiar eminence they still retain in the reign of Charles I., when, by the noble exertions of Lord Scudamore, of Holme Lacy, and other gentlemen, Herefordshire has become in a manner one entire orchard." In this opinion I cannot agree. Indeed, Dr. Beale, in his "Herefordshire Orchards," says:—"From the greatest persons to the poorest cottage all habitations are encompassed with orchards and gardens, and in most places our hedges are enriched with rows of fruit trees, Pears or Apples, Ginnett, Moyles, or Crab trees." The same writer adds: "One reason why fruit do so abound in the county is for that no man hath of late years built him a house but with special regard to the proximity of some ground fit for an orchard, which should be some depth, as is commonly towards the foot of a descending ground, and frequently with a proclivity towards the south, and the land not too friable or hollow, but somewhat tough, binding, and tenacious, lest the winds root up the stock; and many times servants when they betake to marriage seek out an acre or two; for this they give a fine or double value for years or lives, and thereon they build a cottage and plant an orchard, which is all the wealth they have for themselves and their posterity." He also remarks upon the great size to which the fruit trees grow, and expresses an opinion that some sorts live a thousand years, in support of which he mentions, "an Apple tree at Ocle Pitchard, which one year yielded 5 hogsheads of cider without water, and never faileth of 3 hogsheads of 64 imperial gallons, which tree had not been noticed to vary in size by the owner, who was then 80 years of age." The difficulty of propagating the old fruits is treated upon at some length, and French fruit is more than once alluded to. Therefore I think Mr. Duncomb would have been more nearly correct had he said Lord Scudamore zealously applied himself to the improvement of orchard cultivation, particularly of the red-streak Apples, and probably was the introducer of French fruits; but there is abundant evidence that the art of cider-making, and the knowledge of the strength of cider, were well understood in England and in the county of Hereford several centuries before his day. Be this as it may, I believe I am right in stating that the cider made in the county is unsurpassed in strength by that produced in any other county; and not only so, but the strength is very long retained; indeed, I have myself drunk some which, after having been in bottle 56 years, left a pleasant dry roughness on the palate without acidity.—*Duckham on the Farming of Herefordshire.*

DOUBLE CRIMSON THORN.

THERE are before you plants of the new Double Crimson Thorn. Strange as it may seem this is descended from the common White Thorn, or May of our hedges. But this has not happened suddenly, but by a gradation of changes. Most observers will doubtless have noticed in our hedges that some of the plants produce flowers of a pink tinge, though still with single flowers, This is the "break" previously explained: this was step I. Some of the seedlings raised from these would give flowers of a still deeper colour. This was step 2, which we recognise in the single Rose-coloured Thorn, a variety found growing in a hedge at Guddington, in Northamptonshire. Some of the offspring of this would be of a still deeper colour, step 3, the new Scarlet Thorn. A seedling, or a sport from this or the original May of our hedge-rows would produce double flowers, and here was step 4, the Double White or new Double Pink Thorn. Now, I am not asserting that all these steps are authentically recorded, but it is well known to those who are practically engaged in these matters, that such is the rule of progress. But the origin of this new Double Crimson Thorn we do not know. It is not a seedling, but what is called a sport from the Double Pink Thorn, that is, a branch of the Double Pink produced flowers of this deep and beautiful hue. The branch was budded and grafted, and the young plants so obtained produced flowers of the same vivid colour. In the same way have been produced the many varieties of the common Hawthorn, one of the most notable, the Weeping Thorn, having been selected from a bed of seedlings by General Monkton; the upright growing variety was selected from a bed of seedlings by Mr. Ronalds, of Brentford. Now, it is the same with leaves as with flowers. Take the Pelargoniums before you. They are all originally produced from green-leaved varieties, either from sports of the branch, or later in their history from seeds of the sports so fixed. The first variegated Pelargonium originated by a branch of a green-leaved variety producing variegated leaves. This branch was cultivated till the habit became fixed. The seeds of these were saved and sown, and a brood of young plants was produced, retaining the variegation of the parent. The plants before you, which are seedlings, show this tendency; on some there are both green and variegated leaves. Now, to fix either character is the problem. If we wish to retain the green character, we nip off all the variegated leaves; if we wish to retain the variegated character we nip off all the green leaves from time to time as they appear, till the plant produces leaves of the one character only. It is the same with the Acubas. The green-leaved variety is the normal form; the variegated kinds are sports, either from branches or from seeds. This is, in brief, the process that has been worked out in all cultivated plants where leaves or flowers show a wide divergence from the normal form.—*Proceedings of the Royal Botanical Society.*

WOLVES IN IRELAND.

In a recent communication, "C. T. W." called attention to "the last British wolf" killed in Scotland, as being probably still in preservation in some country mansion, secured from injury in its glazed case; and he referred to wolves having existed in Ireland to a much later period. In the first volume of the "Journal of the Geological Society of Dublin," Dr. Scaulin brought together the ascertained facts connected with the extirpation of the wolf in the sister island, which you may deem worthy of reprinting in your journal. "Great numbers of wolves," remarks Dr. Scaulin, "formerly existed in Ireland, and they maintained their ground in this country [Ireland] for a longer period than in any other part of the empire. Campion, whose 'History of Ireland' was published in 1570, informs us that wolves were objects of the chase. 'They' (the Irish) 'are not,' he says, 'without wolves or greyhounds to hunt them; bigger of bone and limme than a colt.' A century later they appear to have been equally abundant, for we find by the journals of the House of Commons that, in 1662, Sir John Ponsonby reported from the Committee of Grievances, that a bill should be brought in to encourage the killing of wolves and foxes. Effective measures for this purpose appear to have been taken, and the wolf was at last extirpated about the year 1710. Dr. Smith, in his 'History of Kerry,' when speaking of certain ancient enclosures, observes that 'many of them were made to secure cattle from wolves, which animals were not finally extirpated till the year 1710, as I find by presentments for raising money for destroying them in some old Grand Jury books.'" Referring to Thompson's "Natural History of Ireland," I find that he cites the foregoing notice, adding that "Three places in Ireland are commemorated, each as having the last Irish wolf killed there, viz., one in the south; another near Glenarm; and the third (Wolf-hill) three miles from Belfast." Fortunate are we that our insular boundaries permitted of the extermination within their limits of so formidable and destructive a beast of prey, which is still occasionally not a little troublesome in hard winters to some of our continental neighbours. AGRICOLA.—*Land and Water.*

VULTURES IN INDIA.

A large black vulture (*Vultur calvus*), with conspicuous bare red head and neck, having a lappet of skin on either side, occasionally makes its appearance, always in pairs only, never flocking; it has a much more formidable beak than the others, which invariably give place to it, and hence it is known to Europeans as the king vulture—a name which is here bestowed upon a South American species. All of these vultures build great nests upon high trees, without affecting concealment: the social species more or less in company. They are almost voiceless birds, which merely utter a low snorting and cackling in their eagerness over their carrion, being as devoid of proper voice as are the storks and adjutants.

A small white vulturine bird (*Neophron ginginianus*), nearly akin to the "Pharoah's chicken" of Egypt, or "Ráchamáh" of Bruce, from which it has only recently been discriminated, is very common in most parts of India, but is never seen on the alluvium of Lower Bengal below the tideway of the rivers. Elsewhere it often comes into the streets, or about the open places of towns; and it is about the most disgusting of feeders, being greedy of human ordure, like the corresponding genus *Cathartes* in the New World —the so-called "turkey buzzards" and "carrion crows" of America. Hence it commonly abounds about camps, following the marches of armies. This bird is white, with black wing tips, and a yellow face; and the young are dark brown, with the bill and claws fleshy white; whereas in the African "Ráchamáh" they are black. It is often miscalled a kite by Europeans.

Towards the Himalaya, both of the great European vultures make their appearance (*Vultur monachus* and *Gyps fulvus*); and the læmmer-geyer (*Gypaëtos barbatus*) is common about some of the Himalayan stations, being the reverse of shy, from not being persecuted, as in the Swiss Alps. In the menagerie of the Zoological Society, in the Regent's Park, there is now every known species of vulture, except one South American *Cathartes*, and the three commonest vultures of India, *Gyps indicus, G. bengalensis*, and *Neophron ginginianus*, which are so exceedingly abundant that nobody can be induced to fancy them worth sending.—*Leisure Hour*, April 20.

New Books.

[*Our limited space must of necessity compel us to give but very short notices of new books, but they will perhaps serve as a guide as to what books our readers may ask for at their libraries.*]

Wild Life among the Pacific Islanders. By E. H. Lamont, Esq. Hurst and Blackett.

This is one of the most amusing books we have read for a very long time, and we heartily recommend it to all who would study nature under some of its wildest aspects. It is full of strange adventures, that would seem to belong more to the realms of fancy than to sober reality. Mr. Lamont has, we think, made one little mistake; we allude to the absence of dates, throughout the volume. It would have been better had they received greater attention at his hands. Notwithstanding, the volume will be found to be the best record of life among the inhabitants of the Coral Islands of the Pacific.

Mr. Lamont, with an adventurous crew, sailed from California on a trading voyage among the Pacific Islands. He was unfortunate in starting, finding his captain a drunken, dissipated gentleman, with whom he had much trouble. For several months they got on pretty well, then the vessel was wrecked, and he and his companions were forced to make the best shift possible amongst the natives. Mr. Lamont seems to have soon made himself at home, readily falling in with their customs and habits. Several times did he take unto himself a wife, apparently more from compulsion than fancy. Perhaps, it would have been as well if he had not given so much space to these ceremonies. Details of the Polynesian code of morals is none of the most welcome to Europeans, and many may think the volume would have been quite as valuable had they been left out.

The life must have had many charms, for at one time, we find, our author had thoughts of taking possession of one of the islands, and setting up a kingdom on his own account. His appearance about this time he describes as follows: " My hair was now very long, my beard thick and bushy. My trousers were in a very dilapidated condition, only kept together by the help of my fish-bone needle and bark thread, but in so coarse a fashion that I was fain to wear my nondescript coloured shirt over them as a tunic.

My costume, however, was greatly admired by these people, whatever might have been thought of it by those who were accustomed to garments of a more civilized fashion."

Of matters relating to the natural history of the islands, we have not a great deal, but what there is is very interesting. We may call attention to the native method of capturing flying fish, of which there is a picture on the outer cover, also, the description of various kinds of cocoa nut palms, and a short bit about land crabs and lobsters, which we subjoin:

The only residents of this dreary place were hosts of tupas (land crabs) and cavios (land lobsters). They are held in the greatest abhorrence by the natives, because they eat filth, and nothing could exceed their disgust, when I made them understand that these animals were much esteemed in other countries. The land crabs, some nearly a foot long, are so tame that they dispute the footpath with you, viciously spreading out their great claws. The lobsters, although of the most brilliant colours, scarlet, orange, blue or green, marked with white, are the most disgusting things imaginable, and are generally to be seen in the evening stealthily crawling towards the beach. On the approach of an enemy they hurriedly retreat, stern foremost, pulling themselves back by their toes, and pushing at the same time with their enormous claws. If molested they will start up a tree in this manner; their retreating motion when ascending having a most absurd appearance. When they cannot readily escape they prepare for combat and look very formidable. Though measuring about two feet in length, however, they are not really dangerous, and a blow with a stick soon finishes them.

The Birds of Norfolk, with Remarks on their Habits, Migrations, and Local Distribution. By Henry Stevenson, F.L.S., Member of the British Ornithologists' Union, vol. I. London: John Van Voorst, 1, Paternoster Row. Norwich: Matchett and Stevenson.

AN highly interesting account of the Birds of Norfolk, a county that has been long celebrated for its ornithology. This, the first volume, treats of the land birds. There is a good descriptive introduction, consisting of some 74 pages, surveying the county, from an ornithological point of view, the land birds number 142, inclusive of stragglers, and the pheasant, black grouse and red legged partridge, which have been introduced. For full particulars and details, we must refer to the volume, as our space will not permit us to review it in detail.

The Meteoric Theory of Saturn's Rings, considered with reference to the Solar Motion in Space. By S. M. D., R.A. Dublin: Hodges, Smith, and Co.

Our author, in this little pamphlet, suggests that "Saturn, with a magnitude but little inferior to that of Jupiter, and moving much more slowly in his orbit,—scarcely with two-thirds the velocity of the latter planet,—has, perhaps from this cause, accumulated the magnificent assemblage of satellites attendant on him. The velocities of the meteorites themselves, falling in from extra-planetary space, would, at Saturn's distance from the Sun, be infinitely less than at Jupiter's distance; and this, coupled with Saturn's own slower orbital motion, would expose them, notwithstanding his inferiority in mass, for a longer period to his disturbing influence, and thus, I think, would account for the formation of his rings."

The Fishes of Zanzibar. By Lieut.-Col. R. L. Playfair and Dr. Albert C. Gunter. London: John Van Voorst.

The rivulets of Zanzibar are small, and contain but two species of fish. To compensate, there have been some 400 distinct species of salt water fishes, &c., caught off its coasts, many are found elsewhere, but the majority are peculiar to this district. This is the first description of fishes found on the part of the African coast, extending from the Straits of Babel Mandeb to the Mozambique Channel. The volume is very expensively got up and profusely illustrated; the engravings having been executed by Mr. Ford; several are coloured, and display to advantage the gorgeous hues that characterize the fishes of tropical seas.

The following works, likely to interest our readers, have appeared during the past few weeks:—

Old and Remarkable Trees. Printed for the Highland and Agricultural Society. W. Blackwood & Sons.

The Development of Science among Nations. By Baron Justus Liebig, F.R.S., &c. Edinburgh: Edmonston & Douglas, 1867.

FRENCH AND AMERICAN WORKS.

Elements de Botanique, etc. Par P. Duchartre, de l'Institut. 2de partie. Paris and London: Bailliere, 1867.

When the first part of this work appeared, it was considered by many to be the most complete text book on Structural and Physiological Botany. In this part the anatomy of plants is resumed, with a description of the various kinds of fruits, and the changes they undergo during the transition from the immature to the ripe condition. In succeeding chapters, M. Duchartre treats of the general phenomena of vegetation or those manifested especially in the nutrition of the plant.

Le Monde des Papillons. Texte et Dessins de Maurice Sand. Avec une Preface de G. Sand. Paris: Rothschild. London: Nutt.

This work (The World of Butterflies) consists of two parts; the first containing a full treatise on the butterflies in Europe by the learned naturalist, M. Depuiset, and the second giving a general description of the history, classification, breeding, and preservation of butterflies. The illustrations are by the lamented Maurice Sand himself.

La Vie Souterraine, ou les Mines et les Mineurs. Par L. Simonin. Ouvrage Illustre de 160 Gravures sur bois, &c. Paris et London: Hachette.

A pleasant description of mines and miners, suitable for general readers. The first part treats of coal, the second of metals, and the third and last of precious stones. It contains one hundred and sixty woodcuts and thirty coloured maps.

Les Insectes. Par Louis Figuier. Ouvrage Illustre de 605 Figures, &c. Paris et London: Hachette.

An exhaustive treatise on insects, written in the most popular style, full of illustrations executed with great care and exactness, especially the designs illustrating the scientific part.

Volcans et Tremblements de Terre. Par Zurcher et Margolle. Ouvrage Illustré de 62 Vignettes, par E. Riou. Paris et London: Hachette.

A scientific and historical account of the volcanic action of the earth, written in a very popular style.

La Chaleur. Par Achille Cazin. Ouvrage Illustré de 92 Vignettes, par A. Jahandier. Paris et London: Hachette.

An interesting work on the science of heat, treated in accordance with the recent investigations of Prof. Tyndall.

The American Naturalist, a Popular Illustrated Magazine of Natural History. No. 1. 56 pp., 8vo. Salem, Essex Institute.

The first number of a new magazine on Natural History, published monthly, edited by A. S. Packard, Dr. E. S. Marse, A. Hyatt, and F. W. Putnam. The contents are varied and highly interesting. The principal articles are the Land Snails of New England; the Volcano of Kilauea, Hawaiian Islands, in 1864-5; the Fossil Reptiles of New Jersey; the first part of a Paper on the American Silkworm and Winter Notes of an Ornithologist, together with miscellaneous notes on Botany, Zoology, and Geology, Correspondence, &c. Among its illustrations are two plates, one of the crater of Kilauea, and the other the structure of the Land Snails, from which article we have given an extract on another page.

Preliminary Report of the Geological Survey of Kansas. By G. C. Swallow, State Geologist. 198 pp., 8vo.

Contains the results of an examination of Eastern and Central Kansas made in 1865, and includes the reports of Dr. C. A. Logan on the sanitary relations of the State, and that of Dr. T. Sinks on its Climatology, and report of the Assistant-Geologist, Major F. Hawn, together with a chapter on Economical Geology.

First Annual Report of the Geology of Kansas. By B. F. Mudge, Professor of Geology, &c., in the Kansas State Agricultural College, Lawrence. 56 pp., 8vo.

Contains facts of general interest to the people of Kansas, especially in regard to saline springs and the manufacture of salt.

First Annual Report of the Geological Survey of Iowa. By C. A. White, M.D., State Geologist. 4 pp., 8vo. Des Moines.

A preliminary notice of the organization and commencement of the present survey during the past year. A brief report by the State Chemist, Professor Hinrichs, is appended.

Report of the Progress of the Geological Survey of North Carolina, 1866. By Professor W. C. Kerr, State Geologist. 56 pp., 8vo. Raleigh.

A brief report; contains information on the Geology of the State.

On the Rock Salt Deposit of Petit Anse, Louisiana Rock-Salt Company. Report of the American Bureau of Mines. 36 pp., 4to. With Maps.

This Report is based on the investigations of Dr. C. A. Goessmann. Dr. Goessmann obtained for the composition of the salt of Petit Anse chlorid of sodium 98·8823, sulphate of lime 0·7825, chlorid of magnesium 0·0030, chlorid of calcium 0·0036, moisture 0·3286 = 100.

Description of Fossil Plants from the Chinese Coal-bearing Rocks. By J. S. Newberry, M.D., being Appendix No. 1 of Geological Researches in China, Mongolia, and Japan, by Raphael Pumpelly. 5 pp., 8vo, with a Plate. Smithsonian Contributions to Knowledge, 1867.

Geological Survey of Canada. By Sir Wm. E. Logan, Director. Report of Progress from 1863 to 1866. 322 pp., large 8vo. Ottawa.

Meetings of Learned Societies.

ROYAL GEOGRAPHICAL SOCIETY.

At the meeting of the above society on Monday evening, April 8th, Sir R. J. Murchison asked the public to suspend their belief in the death of Dr. Livingstone until further testimony could be received. He also stated that the council of the society had passed a resolution that it was desirable that an expedition should proceed to Lake Nyassa to ascertain the fate of Livingstone, and hoped for the assistance of the Government. Lieut. J. B. Bemsher read a paper on part of Mesopotamia. The author confined his remarks to the ruins, streams, and artificial navigable canals, and to the identification of the sites of ancient historic records. The town of Kathemain contains the tomb of Fatima, daughter of the Prophet, domed, covered with gilt tiles, minarets, and pretilly built with enamelled tiles. There are 15,000 inhabitants; four miles away is the tomb of Zobeyda, wife of Haroun-al-Rasheed—familiar name to all readers of the "Arabian Nights." In Xenophon's account of "The Retreat of the Ten Thousand," we learned all about Kunaxa; what then was our author's surprise to hear an Arab mention the name of "Kunassa," a mound of some thirteen miles long and eighty feet high, and a pebly ridge confirmed his opinion, as such a ridge is expressly spoken of as the halting-place of Artaxerxes. The patient examination, care, and research given to this work deserve, and won the highest praise from the various travellers in Mesopotamia, amongst whom are Mr. Felix Jones, Mr. Lynch, Sir H. Rawlinson, and others.

ZOOLOGICAL SOCIETY.

At a meeting on 11th April, Professor Huxley read a paper on the Cranial Characters of Birds. Not satisfied with the clumsy classification of Cuvier, which was by Dr. Gray stated to have been the work of the great master's pupils, and repudiated by Cuvier himself, Professor Huxley, looking for a sounder basis on which to form a surer system of classification, and seeing how constant was the law of cranial structure amongst mammalians, was directed to the study of the palate-bones of birds, rather than to the sternum or tarsal and metatarsal bones, from a more strikingly constant law pervading the families which came under his observation, and hence the system of palatine structure as a mark of classification. By a series of beautifully drawn diagrams of the palates of various genera, and wonderfully simple tables of gradation, he was able to clearly illustrate the result of his most valuable contribution to science.

Dr. J. Murie read a paper giving a description of the tracheal pouch found in the Emu.

Mr. E. P. Ramsay, of Dobroyde, Sydney, N.S.W., communicated some notes on the nidification of *Baja subcristata*. This rare bird was seen by Mr. Ramsay while on a trip to the North Richmond and Clarence rivers; the most favoured spots seemed to be the edges of the scrubs on these rivers, from whence they would sally out to the more open parts in the mornings and evenings in search of food. The sexes are alike, except that the male has the occipital crest more developed. The nest is a comparatively small structure, composed of sticks, and placed on a horizontal bough at a considerable distance from the ground, the eggs have a ground-colour of greenish-white sparingly smeared and spotted with light brown; in shape, very much rounded at the larger end, short upon the whole, the thin end pointed abruptly, average length 1 7-10 inch by 1 4-10 inch in breadth.

Dr. J. E. Gray read some notes on certain species of Cats in the collection of the British Museum.

LINNEAN SOCIETY.

At the meeting of the Linnean Society, held April 4th, G. Bentham, Esq., in the chair, Dr. Hooker exhibited a series of most interesting photographs of the Botanic Garden (*Peredenea*) of Ceylon. A very remarkable fruit was likewise exhibited of *Zanonia macrocarpa*, a new species belonging to the gourd family (*cucurbitacea*), and of the order *Nhandirobeæ*. Its size is about that of a cocoa-nut, the pericarp, which is hard and tough, encloses a number of most remarkable seeds, strangely and wonderfully constructed to wing their way, bird-like, to localities far away from the parent plant. The seed is nearly round, about the size of a shilling, brown in colour, and surrounded by a satin-like membraneous structure, shaped somewhat like a bow, but so beautifully light and buoyant that the slightest breeze bears it off with its freight as though it were thistle-down. These singularly winged seeds bear a striking resemblance to the seeds of the *Bigononæ*, although there is not the slightest kinship between the plants. The *Zanonia* is a native of Java.

Mr. J. G. Baker read an interesting and valuable paper on the geographical distribution of ferns.

ETHNOLOGICAL SOCIETY.

At the above society Dr. Hyde Clarke read a paper on iron metallurgy as practised by the ancient races, the Calybees and the Gipsies, though these people were not ethnologically identical, and described the route they took from the far East to the extremes of Europe, settling on such places as they found containing surface iron, until they exhausted it in their operations. Mr. Crawfaurd read a paper "On the Classification of the Races of Man according to the Form of the Skull," which was followed by a most interesting discussion.

ROYAL HORTICULTURAL SOCIETIES.

On April 6th, the second of Dr. Master's lectures on Plant Architecture was given, and was devoted to the consideration of the roots, which the lecturer compared in some respects to the basement story of a house. The primary root springs directly from the seed, but secondary or adventitious roots may be produced from any portion of the plant, when required for purposes of support or of nutrition. Gardeners are thus enabled to propagate by cuttings, or by portions of the leaves, and in some instances even the fruit will emit roots, as had been proved in the case of catcuses, cucumbers, &c. They may also be formed in the soil, in the air, or in water, but the root formed say from a cutting in water, seems useless when planted in earth; new roots have to be formed when the medium in which the plant is to grow, is changed. Wherever and under whatever circumstances produced, the original form of the root is that of a fine thread with a pointed conical end, the thicker portion being the body or base, which usually divides after a time into a number of branches or fibres.

BOTANICAL SOCIETY OF EDINBURGH.

At the meeting on March 14th, Isaac Anderson Henry, Esq., read a most interesting communication on the Hybridisation or Crossing of Plants. Referring to the blue dahlia he says:—"Some of my earliest efforts were among what have been since denominated 'florists' flowers,' such as the calceolaria, the dahlia, the fuchsia, &c. At that time every colour had been brought out in the dahlia save blue; and some began to speculate upon such a colour being realised, though none, so far as I was aware of, ever suggested the means of accomplishing it. This, however, seemed to me no great matter to achieve. I looked over the tribes bearing the nearest affinity to it, among its natural family, the compositæ, having the desired colour, and I found many flowering plants, such as aster, agathæa, kaulfussia, &c., having various tints of blue, sufficient, as I thought, for my purpose. With the pollen of these upon a white dahlia, a blue might, I believed, be obtained; but it was calling spirits from the vasty deep, for neither blue nor even white, not even a ripened seed, ever came of it. Unvarying failure damped my zeal bit by bit, and I began to see that I could not transfer a colour alien to any one genus from another genus remotely akin to it, to which such colour was common.

Correspondence.

Under this head we shall be glad to insert any letters of general interest.]

THE EARTH'S ORBIT AND OUR SEASONS.

SIR,—In page 31, No. 2 of the "Naturalist's Note Book," an extract from the *Scientific Review* says :—"*The elliptical form of the earth's orbit produces in reality no effect on the seasons.*" What do your scientific correspondents say to this proposition?

Writers on physical geography tell us that on account of the elliptical form of the earth's orbit, the sun is eight days longer in the northern than in the southern hemisphere; and hence a modification of temperature, and consequently, an effect on the seasons. I hope, Sir, some of your scientific correspondents will take up the subject and give it a full investigation.

I am, Sir, yours, truly,
H. H. ULIDIA.

Dromore, April 8, 1867.

THE ICE FLOE, 200 MILES LONG, IN THE NORTH ATLANTIC—CAN IT AFFECT OUR CLIMATE?

Sir,—The following paragraph appeared in the *Jersey British Press* of the 10th April, 1867 :—

UNPRECEDENTED QUANTITIES OF ICE IN THE NORTH ATLANTIC.—It has been asserted that the severe weather recently experienced in Great Britain and France was due to atmospheric disturbances in the North Atlantic Ocean, and all arrivals at Liverpool from New York and other ports in the United States and Canada report unprecedented quantities of ice *in the mid ocean*, about 44 N. lat. and 53 W. long. One vessel had to sail for nearly 200 miles in a southerly direction alongside a *perfect continent of ice;* while others passed icebergs of enormous size, all much further south than is common at this season.

When I read this paragraph on Wednesday last which told of an ice floe in *mid ocean*, 200 miles long, I was certainly startled at so abnormal a phenomenon, for the map in that charming work, *The History of the British Seas*, by the late Professor Forbes, and Mr. Godwin Austen, F.R.S., had led me to believe that no field ice from Davis' Straits could be found east of longitude 50°, at the latitude stated, viz., 44° north. On referring to a large marine chart of Findlay's for the locality of this ice island, I find that it bars the passage completely of the outward bound vessels going to Portland, Boston and Halifax. Can your readers conceive such a mass of ice as this described as the coast of a floating continent, as it well may be? In extent, indeed, it stretches as far as Cowes is from Land's End—or as Cowes is from Liverpool—or as Yarmouth is from Sunderland—and would completely obstruct the chops of the English Channel, were it floating there! Captain Maury, of the American Navy, states, in his great work on the sea, that Lieut. de Haven, when in command of the American Arctic Expedition, was floated bodily along with the ice floe in which his vessel was wedged, 1,000 miles to the South, from the Wellington Straits; and that this same mass of pack-ice *was six times the size of all England!* or, 300,000 square miles, in surface area ; (as the English exploring ship *Resolute* had found previously—when abandoned by Capt. Kellett). These ice islands melt rapidly when they reach the gulf stream, however, the temperature of those waters being about 80° Fah. As to the influence of this said ice floe on our present spring weather, I greatly doubt any such effect. 'Tis true the late Admiral Fitzroy endeavoured to account for the ungenial summer of 1860, from the great quantity of ice, from Spitzbergen, then afloat, between W. Long. 20° and N. Lat. 65°, (or about from 6 to 700 miles to the *North* West of the Hebrides); whereas this ice floe, from Davis' Straits, is over 400 miles to the south of our lowest English latitude of the Land's End, and fully 1,700 miles to the west of the westermost point of Ireland. Furthermore, I see by the same map, that the Gulf Stream does *not* extend beyond the longitude of the Azores—or 27° west—and therefore the precipitation which such a mass of ice may have caused in the vaporous atmosphere that overhangs that river of the Ocean—as Maury happily calls it—so far to the west, and so far to the south of our latitude—is *not* likely to have made *our* spring so unpropitious, and so ungenial; especially as *easterly* winds, and *not* westerly ones, have been so over prevalent for some time past. I shall be curious, however, to learn from my brother officer, and fellow Meteorologist, at Halifax, Nova Scotia, how *his* climate has been affected by this said ice-island.

COL. H. E. AUSTEN, F.M.S.
Jersey, April 12, 1867.

HEALTH OF WILD ANIMALS.

AN opinion obtains that man is eminently the subject of disease; and this opinion is advanced by the social reformer, the politician, or the theologian, whenever it seems to fall in with any particular proposition each maintains. When you point out the diseases of the domestic animals, it is urged in reply that these diseases are incident to the artificial habits which they have acquired and to the manner in which man, their master, treats them. In a recently published sermon I have seen the following: "For, remember man alone is subject to disease. The wild animal in the wood, the bird upon the tree, seldom or never know what sickness is; seldom or never are stunted or deformed. They live according to their nature, healthy and happy, and die in a good old age." There is great obscurity necessarily in investigating this subject with regard to wild animals. Health seems in many cases so essential to their very existence, that sickness and death become synonymous terms." That they die at a good old age may reasonably be disputed by every one acquainted with the habits of that vast order which lives by destroying the lives of others. That they live happy is extremely questionable, since one can scarcely walk in the country without hearing the screams of terror of the wild birds, or witnessing the start and flight of the wild quadrupeds. In "Prehistoric Times," Sir John Lubbock quotes an authority who states that wild beasts lead unhappy lives; that the antelope has a run for its life once every two days on an average, besides many false starts. Notwithstanding the fecundity of some animals, they are scarce, and it is accounted for on principles which are not calculated to make us envy their condition. Extraordinary plagues visit whole species at a time. The wild cattle at Hamilton were terribly scourged with rinderpest. During the extremely hot weather of June last, fishes were caught in the pools in the shallow shores of the Solway, half dead, as if from sunstroke, in such abundance as to be of service to the cotters living by the shore. I remember eight years ago seeing the Ayrshire coast, West Kilbride, covered with dead sea-birds, rotting in such numbers that I was glad to make a detour to avoid the stench.

The poet Moore alludes to an Eastern opinion when he alludes to—

"The rain from the sky,
Which turns into pearls as it falls in the sea."

But the pearl is obtained by the endeavour to avoid abnormal irritation on the part of certain sea and fresh-water shell-fish, and the precious secretion wherewith they coat the irritating particle of sand which has accidentally entered the shell may be regarded as the product of disease. I have shot and dressed rooks, and found them dreadfully invested with parasites; but yesterday I saw worms procured from the intestines of a wild or mountain cat shot in Invernesshire. Animals in their wild state have been found stunted and deformed. the Rev. J. Wood in "Common Objects of the Country," instances the case of a crippled butterfly (Atalanta), which he discovered wriggling in the grass, the wings on one side not having been developed. A friend of mine shot a rat, which had an enormous development of the canine teeth projecting like tusks from his mouth, and affording him a good mark for his shot. The wild elephant, by employing one tusk more than another in rooting plants, &c., often breaks that tusk and renders it of less commercial value. Age, with its symptoms of second childhood, creeps apace on those mammals and birds which survive in the struggle for existence. The old lion becomes lean, timid, mangy, and is thankful for prey that he would have disdained in his prime. Many beasts to their dying day bear the mark of bites or fierce battles with hoof and horn received from their own species (chiefly at the rutting season) or from those species that are their natural enemies. Bees are said to die a lingering death after the loss of their sting.

Many quadrupeds are half-drowned by floods, and half-starved by long-continued frost. Leaving out the case of the domestic animals altogether, man has no monopoly of the ills that flesh is heir to, but rather seems to be the most enviable being in creation when good luck and his own wisdom combine to assist him.

It would be interesting to compare the longevity of wild and domestic animals having close affinities, as, for instance, those of the family *Phasianidæ*. In this case I have no data as to the length of life of the wild birds; but Mr. Imrie, of Aulgirth, has at present a cross between the golden Hamburgh and common hen of the great age of twenty-nine years. It is both plump and lively. For seventeen years she was an excellent layer, but for a dozen years she has passed beyond the cares of maternity, and changes her plumage occasionally, when her tail-feathers resemble those of a cock. I kept a caged thrush twelve years. I know a cat at present of sixteen years, and a horse of thirty. To obtain the age of a wild animal is more difficult, although it has been approximated from dentition, &c., and where the weapon (harpoon, for instance) has known to have been lodged in them years before; and I have known cases of the same red-breast resorting to the hand that fed it in winter for four or five successive seasons.

J. S.

Thornhill.

TO CORRESPONDENTS.

ERRATA—In our last month's answers to correspondents under "W. H. A.," a description of the Wellingtonia gigantea, Mr. Smith, Darley Dale Nurseries, near Matlock, writes to say the tree was planted out of a thumb pot in the year 1856 instead of 1853.

A LOVER OF FLOWERS.—Communication received too late for insertion in our present number.

M. L. A.—*Land and Water* is published weekly, price 6d., the Office is 80, Fleet Street.

KELLICK.—We have mislaid your address; please forward, as we have a valuable Catalogue of Birds for you, forwarded by Rev. S. C. Malan. See under "Remarks, Queries, &c."

REV. R. BINGHAM.—Monogram received with thanks.

M. H.—Will answer your inquiries in next number—not sufficient space in present one.

Short Notes.

PLANT ARCHITECTURE.—In a paper read before the Royal Horticultural Society, March 30, the lecturer began by stating that the subject was chosen as one by means of which a general idea of the conformation of the higher plants could be obtained without the necessity of going into minute detail or employing many technicalities. After a passing notice of the "cells" or living bricks of which the plant is made up, the lecturer proceeded to show how, on a "foundation" of cellular tissue, of which alone the simplest plants are built, the more complex plant structures, such as the leaves, flowers, and fruit, are gradually erected, these several parts being set apart for distinct purposes, just as the rooms of an ordinary house are devoted to special uses, the several organs being connected one with another, by the medium of the root and stem or "axis," in somewhat the same way that the rooms of a house are brought into communication one with another by means of the staircase. In the simplest plants, one cell, or an aggregation of such, sufficed for all the business of life, just as in uncivilized countries a hut or a wigwam served for many purposes, for which, in other climes, and under other circumstances, separate rooms were set apart and so arranged and modified as to suit the varied requirements of the possessor. In the case of plants, it was shown that the possession of separate organs, and the form of these latter, were specially dependent either on adaptation to particular purposes and to external circumstances, such as mutual accommodation, the necessity for light, air, increased supply of nutriment, etc., or to the hereditary transmission of the form and attributes of the parent plants to the offspring. Plant architecture, or the plan upon which plants are built up, is thus in great measure the result of a compromise between these two agencies. In the case of the flowering plant, all the numerous and seemingly different organs may readily be referred to two primary ones, the axis and the leaf, the differences in form, etc., being brought about by the action of the causes before mentioned. Except for convenience sake, the axis and leaf could hardly be considered as intrinsically different, but for practical purposes it was necessary to consider these two as distinct elements in plant construction. The principal forms and modifications of these, it was intimated, would be treated of in the following lectures.

THE CARRION CROW.—A correspondent of the *Field* writes:—"The craftiness of the crow is very interesting to the observer, and I have good opportunities of watching the habits of these birds. Not far from my house, and near to a lake, there is a plantation containing some fine old Scotch firs, which tower above the surrounding trees, and have boles many feet in height before there is a bough. In those firs I have for many years observed a pair of crows. If one pair is trapped or shot, and their nestlings destroyed in the season, another pair very soon arrive to take their place. These birds I have always observed live pretty sumptuously throughout the year. At the present season, just as the rooks begin to lay, the crows visit their nests and pillage their eggs. March 11 was with us the first day they commenced rummaging over the rookery. On coming near the rookery that morning I saw that the poor rooks were in great trepidation, cawing, fluttering, and flying round and round, and there were the pair of crows as unconcerned as possible, hopping from one nest to the other, rummaging and peeping into all. Soon one of them flew off with an egg to a high piece of ground in the park. I have observed similar proceedings for years, and the most astonishing thing to me is that a pair of crows should be allowed to strut over and rob a rookery in such a bold, independent manner, amongst hundreds of rooks, not one of which has the courage to give battle or offer to defend its own. There is not a vast difference in the size and weight of the rook and crow, and as to numbers the rook is a thousand or more to one. As soon as the pheasants begin to lay the crows commence seeking out their nests, and they are not at all particular as to the state the eggs are in, whether fresh laid or about to hatch. On a high piece of ground of some extent, away from all trees and fences, out of gun shot, where they have a famous position of observing from a distance any approaching enemy, I have seen scores of empty shells, and it is easy to observe by their colour and the streaks of blood that they have been pillaged in every stage of incubation.

THE FORESTS OF RUSSIA.—Amongst the sources of wealth, unproductive as yet, are the forests of Russia, and which, for the most part, have the appearance of virgin forests. The forests of Prussia, which are not to be compared with those of Russia, are, thanks to a model management, the source of considerable revenue to the State, whilst those of the latter are at present only an expense. Forest economy in Russia is in its infancy: its importance is reserved for the future; and the numerous railways now in the course of construction will contribute largely to its extension. The western part of Northern Europe is poor in forests, whilst, on the contrary, the east is rich. Finland, the governments of Olonetz, Wologda, Kastroma, and Archangel all possess immense forests. On the 80,269,375 deciatines (1 deciatina = 2 acres, 2 roods, 32 perches) that form the government of Archangel, 30,312,209 deciatinas are covered with forests, of which 1,151,088 are the property of the Admiralty, as they furnish excellent timber for ship-building purposes. One district alone (Misen) contains 14,865,872 deciatinas of forest land; and the districts of Pinega, Kemi, Cholmogory, Onega, and Archangel are equally rich in timber. The Scotch Fir (Pinus sylvestris) is found in great abundance, and the forests of the governments are principally composed of this tree; however there is no scarcity of the Spruce Fir, the Siberian Cedar, the Birch, and the Poplar. The first exportation of timber from Archangel appears to have been in 1761. During the last ten years the value of the timber exported from the ports of Archangel and Onega amounted to 346,978 roubles (£54,215), a small sum as compared with the riches of the forests of the country; and the Grand Duchy of Finland, though much smaller in extent, exports annually timber to the value of upwards of two millions of roubles (£312,500). Better results may be predicted for the future, now that the Petchora, and especially its mouths, are navigable.—*Correspondance Russe*.

DOVES BREEDING IN A CHURCH.—You will be interested to hear of an unusual situation for a stock dove's nest. The spire of the old village church here is a wooden one, and has for many a day given shelter to a loving couple of white owls and several pairs of starlings, not to mention the noisy sparrows which have taken possession of the waterspouts. During the summer of 1865 I often remarked a pair of pigeons flying out from a good-sized hole at the base of the spire. They looked like stock doves, but the scarcity of this species here in the breeding season, as well as the unlikely situation which they had selected, caused me to think at the time that they could be only a pair of escaped blue rocks. I could easily have shot one of the birds as he flew out, and thus settled the question, but I was anxious to prove something more. An inspection of the interior of the church, which I unfortunately delayed until the summer was far advanced, showed that a nest, evidently that of a pigeon, had been built upon a cross beam above the bells. I was too late then for the eggs; the young had flown. There was nothing for it, therefore, but to wait until the following spring, and then endeavour to secure a pair of young birds. Accordingly, jotting down a memorandum in my notebook, and resolving to keep the fact of there being pigeons in the church spire to myself, I waited patiently for another nesting season. My patience has been so far rewarded that, after watching a pair of birds take up their quarter in the same site as that selected the previous year, and after several anxious visits of inspection, I was at length enabled, in July, 1866, to carry off a pair of fine young pigeons, which were almost ready to fly. The "coo" of the stock dove is very peculiar, and by this time I had heard and seen enough of the birds in question to convince me that they belonged to this species. Their young, which I had secured, after being fed for some time in a cage in the house, were transferred to my aviary. They are now in fine plumage, and have proved, as I suspected, to be undoubtedly the young of *Columba œnas*.—*J. Edmund Harting (Kingsbury, Middlesex), in Field*, March 30.

THE ATMOSPHERE, IN ITS RELATION TO HEAT.—The movable and transparent element by which we are surrounded, not only furnishes the gases necessary to the respiration of living creatures, but it moreover acts in a manner essential to the general distribution of the light and heat dispensed by the sun. The winds diffuse over the surface of the earth the heat they bring from the burning soil of tropical regions. And the operation of the atmosphere is not limited to that effect. It serves as a vast fire-screen interposed between the earth and the sun; it retains or absorbs a part of the rays which the latter transmits to us; and while it moderates the original warmth and splendour of that luminary, it reverts those calorific rays which escape from the sun, and which without this kindly barrier would be lost in the celestial spaces. The solar rays, taken together, undergo such an absorption in the atmosphere, that about a half is lost by the way; and this loss is shared by both the visible and the obscure rays. The radiation from the ground, on the other hand, is composed exclusively of obscure heat; it experiences from the atmosphere a much greater resistance than luminous heat does; a tenth only of the terrestrial radiation traverses the thick protecting mantle formed by the air around the globe. This result may be compared with that of our glazed structures. The sunshine passes freely through the glass and warms the soil which it covers; but the heat which the latter throws off in the way of radiation cannot now pass outside, because glass is opaque to obscure heat, and that heat is accumulated within the glass. The atmosphere, therefore, produces the same effect as if the whole earth was inclosed in glass; it transforms it into a hothouse; the sun effects an entrance, but its exit is barred. Such is the function of the air in respect to the calorific rays of the sun.—*P. Radau, Revue des Deux Mondes*, tome lxvi. p. 223.

THE AVOSET.—In *Land and Water*, April 6th, the following accounts of three of these birds having been shot appears:—1. A very unusual bird was shot on Tuesday, the 19th ult., by Captain Pretor, near the Portland Ferry Bridge. It is called the "avoset," and we are informed it is many years since a specimen has occurred in this locality. In Yarrell's "British Birds" it is thus described:—"It is a singular looking bird, both in reference to its beak, as well as its feet. The beak is curved upwards, is slender, pointed, and flexible, having much the appearance of a thin piece of elastic whalebone. The semi-palmated feet seem only intended to support the bird on soft mud, as it never attempts to paddle or swim when out of its depth. The bird is a great rarity now, the last being heard of in 1837. Four are recorded as having been obtained in Devonshire, and one or two in Dorsetshire." 2. "It will probably interest some of your readers to be informed that a beautiful specimen of that rare British bird the scooping avoset (*Recurvirostra avocetta*) was recently killed in the estuary of the River Exe. It has been sent for preservation to Mr. Tucker, of Queen-street, Exeter, and is to be presented to the Albert Museum of this city. I am not aware that the avoset has ever previously been obtained in our western county." 3. "When at Christ Church a few days since, Mr. Hart, the well-known taxidermist of that town, showed me a very fine specimen of the avoset, shot near the entrance of the harbour. Thus we have this week a record of three specimens of this most interesting and curious bird, which, as Mr. Wood informs us, is sometimes called the "cobbler's awl bird," the beak being very much the shape of this instrument. These poor birds formerly bred in this country; 'the eggs are yellowish brown, with black marks.'—*Frank Buckland*.

BEET ROOT SUGAR.—An experiment has recently been made of growing beet-root for the manufacture of sugar in Illinois. About 400 acres of fresh prairie were planted, and 4,000 tons of beet raised, which is in course of being worked up, and is expected to reach nearly 400,000lb. of refined sugar. The United States have been like ourselves, the most important consumers of cane-grown sugar, the continent generally having long accepted the beet as the raw material of their supply. But if the Americans and the Germans and French can grow their own sugar, why should not we do so? Beet-root is not like sugar-cane, an article only to be reared in tropical or semi-tropical countries. We raise it in England of excellent quality, and not only do we raise the crop, but of the sugar we consume, about one-sixth part—according to the *Produce Markets Review*—is beet-root sugar imported from the continent. There seems no reason why this additional branch of industry should not be added to the many enterprises of the country. While the beet has been planted for purposes of sugar-making on the prairies of the West, the cane is being vigorously cultivated in the colony of Queensland. It is estimated that upwards of a thousand miles of alluvial soil on the coast line of that colony is in every way adapted to the cultivation of the cane. The attention of all countries seems to be directed more and more to the supply of sugar. We used to be dependent for our supply upon the West Indies, just as we were upon America for our cotton; but every day the sugar question is becoming better understood, and in spite of our scale of duties, the West Indians will be compelled to feel more and more the influence of competition, and the necessity for exerting themselves accordingly.—*Mechanics' Magazine*.

POULTRY AND THEIR EGGS.—Mr. J. D. Mechi, writing to the *Gardener's Chronicle* upon this subject, says:—"An old shoemaker in this neighbourhood, too blind to work at his trade, has devoted his workshop to chicken-rearing, keeping a fire in the grate all winter. The consequence was an abundant supply of eggs at 1½d. each wholesale, and young chickens that in a month's time will bring 7s. per pair wholesale. He has thus realised exceptional and profitable results, and escaped that competition of cheapness and abundance which is produced by mild or summer weather." Another gentleman, a Mr. Burr, writing to *Land and Water* upon the same, says:—"Whilst on a visit at a country house near Ballinasloe early in February, a few years ago, I used to view with great admiration a splendid supply of eggs, which the mistress of the mansion was proud of producing daily at breakfast. On my venturing to inquire what valuable breed of fowls she possessed, to produce such gratifying results, she informed me that the poultry were of no particular sort, but the hens were induced to lay perpetually by having their roosting house warmed with a flue during the winter months. I had often heard of this, but had never witnessed its practical results before. Soon after my return home from this visit, application was made to me to have our fowlhouse repaired; and finding it in a very dilapidated state, I at once resolved to build a new one, which I have had warmed with a flue, and it has answered most admirably. During cold weather a fire is lighted about two or three o'clock p.m., which is not required to be kept up, and this keeps the place comfortable until the following morning. The fowls are of no particular breed, but I hear the black hens are considered the best layers.

THE LYRE-BIRD (*Menura Superba*).—A fine healthy specimen of this bird has been received at the Zoological Gardens, Regent's Park. We believe it is the first that has been imported alive into Europe. Mr. Gould, in his "Birds of Australia," says:— "The lyre-bird is of a wandering disposition, and although it keeps to the same brush, it is constantly traversing it from one end to the other, from mountain-top to the bottom of the gullies, whose steep and rugged sides present no obstacle to its long legs and powerful muscular thighs; it is also capable of performing extraordinary leaps, and I have heard it stated that it will spring to the ledge of a rock or the branch of a tree ten feet perpendicularly from the ground. It appears to be of solitary habits, as I have never seen more than a pair together, and these only in a single instance; they were both males, and were chasing each other round and round with extreme rapidity, apparently in play, pausing every now and then to utter their long, shrill calls; while thus employed they carried the tail horizontally, as they always do when running quickly through the bushes, that being the only position in which it could be conveniently borne. Among its many curious habits is that of forming small hillocks, which are constantly visited during the day, and upon which the male is continually trampling, at the same time erecting and spreading out his tail in the most graceful manner, and uttering his various cries, sometimes pouring forth his natural notes, at others mocking those of other birds, and even the howling of the dingo. The early morning and the evening are the periods when it is most animated and active."

OWLS.—"I do not know many sights more engaging to a naturalist than one which often presents itself on peering into a thickly-growing Scotch fir-tree. A family party of some half-dozen long-eared owls may be descried perched in close proximity to the observer's head. Their bodies are drawn up perpendicularly and attenuated in a most marvellous manner, the ear-tufts nearly erect, or, if not exactly parallel to one another, slightly inclined inwards. Except these, there is nothing to break the stiff rectangle of the bird's outline. There they sit, one and all, swaying slowly upon one foot, and gravely winking one eye at the intruder. Underneath such an owl-roost as this is certain to be found a large quantity of the pellets ejected by its frequenters, and a good notion of their usual food is to be gathered from an examination of the same. Half-grown rats and mice, chiefly the former, constitute the staple, but small birds contribute no small share, and I have recognised among the remains unquestionable bones of the wheatear, willow wren, chaffinch, greenfinch, bullfinch, and yellow bunting. How the owls catch them I am unable to say, but I am bound to mention that never in a single instance have I discovered a trace of any game bird; and I feel assured that the keepers, who wage war against the long-eared owl for the protection of their young pheasants and partridges, are not only giving themselves unnecessary trouble, but are also guilty of the folly of exterminating their best friends, for the number of rats destroyed by this species is enormous, and I look upon the rat as the game-preserver's worst enemy."—*Stevenson's Birds of Norfolk.*

CATFISH.—SIR: I enclose an extract from a private letter, containing some very interesting particulars of the capture of two catfish.—T. D. P. "It was in August, when we were returning from Norway. The yacht's course was from Christiansand to the North Coast of England. We had splendid weather, and hardly breeze enough to sail sufficiently fast for fishing; however, we had the trawl overboard, and, to the surprise of the sailors, all at once the net got fast on something (for we were in the middle of the North Sea, miles and miles from land, and no ship in sight). Almost as soon as the net got free the trawl was hauled on board with a very fair catch of fish, and among them were two horrid catfish, which snapped at everything near them. I begged to have them thrown overboard. So, putting the handle of a mop near one, it seized the stick with such strength and fury that it was lifted up and put into the sea again, leaving, however, one of its teeth broken off in the mop-stick by the violence of its bite. The other fish was killed and its head brought home and given to a museum. The teeth are most curious, some are canine, and some calculated for vegetable diet. The sailors said that no doubt the net had caught on part of a wreck, and that the catfish haunted the remains of a vessel, for they generally are in pairs, and are very fond of playing at 'bo-peep' among pieces of timber, &c. They must have been only just caught when the net was hoisted up, as none of the other fish were bitten. They certainly would have attacked them had they been any time together. The sailors told me that the jaws of a catfish are so powerful that they can bite off a man's arm. This may be the fact or not; but they look vicious enough for any atrocity."—*Land and Water,* March 30.

FOXES.—Eight species, or perhaps it will be safer to say different varieties, of foxes contribute their jackets to supply the fur market—the black or silver, the cross, the red, the white, the blue, the kitt, the grey, and the Corsac fox. The family *Canidæ* includes animals characterised by having the jaws somewhat produced, the legs of equal length, the anterior furnished with five, and the posterior with four toes. The claws are not retractile; and from walking, as it were, on tiptoe, the term "digitigrada" (Lat. *digitus,* a toe, *gradus,* a step) is applied to all members of the group. The foremost feet have each a rudimentary toe or thumb, placed some little distance up the leg, to which a claw is generally, though not invariably, attached. Foxes belong to the sub-family *Vulpinæ.* Professor Baird ("N. Am. Mam.") says: "It is in this group of the *Canidæ* that we find animals known in North America and the Old World as foxes, several species of which belong to this continent. Among these there are many very distinct types, with one or more species in each." In the one type the tail is uniformly bushy all round, composed of long hairs, mixed in amongst a shorter fur. The skull, very wolf-like in character, has the temporal crests strongly developed, and extending somewhat beyond the parieto-frontal suture; the muzzle is much produced and particularly sharp. To the group of foxes thus characterised the Professor says the name of *Vulpes* ought to be applied.

FLIES IN AMBER.—Of the dipterous flies in *amber* 850 species have been counted, and all these are proboscidians. The amber period reveals to us much information, as we can by the mummies so entombed in this substance, arrive at certain knowledge that the animal life of the time was identical in some respects with our own. Swarms of one kind preying on others, and insects depending on mammals for support, and even at that time the frequent victims of spiders. The flora, too, was rich in species, and then as now, certain kinds were common to America and to Europe. Diptera are more generally distributed, and even as civilization extends, these creatures find their way into localities where they had formerly no habitation. Cheese and dried meat is one vehicle for their transport, and a kind now common in Egypt, the Gallopagos islands, and Greenland, have accompanied man in his intercourse with these far distant lands. The horse and the sheep have also carried with them flies, to lands where these animals are acclimatised; one unwieldy fly is carried over the seas by the heron, another by the swallow, wherever she builds her nest. Cultivated plants bring their share of living flies; the orange, and lemon, and the olive, have each their little winged companion. Such testimony, humble as it seems, is an invaluable agent in palæontological investigation.

SULPHUR MOUNTAINS.—The sulphur mountains on the east of the lake Mý-vatn, in Iceland, were recently described by Mr. C. W. Shepherd; they are very wonderful, being of various colours, a variety of mixtures of red and yellow; from their sides are emited numerous jets of steam, and masses of bright yellow sulphur are strewed all around them; at the foot, on the eastern side, one of the mud geysers—huge cauldrons of blue mud, in different stages of solution—some bubble and spurt like filthy water, others are so gross that they can scarcely heave the massive bubbles to the surface. All around the soil was very treacherous, consisting of hot mud with a covering of sulphur about an inch in thickness; the clouds of steam, the roaring, the spluttering, and the splashing of the loathsome pits, the sickening smell and the desolate country had an awe-inspiring effect on the beholders. Not far off was the Obsidian mountain, where the sides are covered with shining polished surfaces of the mineral, resembling broken wine-bottles in appearance, and presenting the greatest difficulties to the explorer, as their edges were equally sharp and dangerous to walk upon.

HAILSTONES IN CHINA.—On Tuesday at six p.m. on June 5, 1866, a thunder storm came from the north-east, and broke over Peking with great violence. The hailstones soon followed the first dash of rain, and increased in size and quantity till the rain almost seemed to cease. The shower lasted 40 minutes, leaving the yards white with hailstones, but as the wind was light no damage was done. The very largest stones were 4 to 4½ inches in circumference; the prevailing shape was conical, and almost all the stones exhibited a kernal of clear ice enclosed in frozen snow, with a covering of ice outside. The strata of air through which they passed in their descent must have been of very different degrees of temperature to produce such distinct layers of ice and snow in the stones. Such hailstorms are not frequent in the North of China, and the people say that this one is the most remarkable since July, 1838, when the stones were like oranges and apples and melons for size, and did great damage to dwellings and trees.—S. W. Williams in the *American Journal of Science and Art*, March.

SEA MARKS ON THE COAST OF SWEDEN.—The Earl of Selkirk has communicated to the Geological Society certain conclusions at which he has arrived after an examination of ancient sea-marks on the coast of Sweden. Sir Charles Lyell, who saw those marks thirty-two years ago, has endeavoured to show that they indicate a gradual rise in the land of about three feet in a century. The Earl, on the contrary, argues that no certain proof of such a rise is afforded by the marks, for the fluctuations in the level of the water are so great from day to day and week to week, that to institute a comparison of difference of level is difficult if not impossible. The strongest indication of a change of level was shown by the marks off Gefle; but even in them there were elements of uncertainty. The question thus opened is important and interesting. Sweden has a staff of able geologists; will they set themselves to work and settle the question?—*Athenæum*, April 13th.

THE CAT.—Lieut.-Colonel W. A. G. Wright, Royal Marines, has been recently transferred on promotion from Plymouth to the division at Portsmouth. On Saturday, the 30th of December, a favourite cat was secured in a basket, and forwarded by the South Devon Railway to Portsmouth, when it was received in the colonel's new residence. The cat remained the Saturday night, but was missed on the Sunday. On Wednesday, the 3rd of January, it was observed in the garden in the rear of its master's former residence at Stonehouse (Plymouth), now unoccupied, and has since been fed by an officer of the corps, who lives adjoining. The animal is a large, strong male; it was born in Stonehouse, is only twelve months old, and never before quitted the town. How it managed to find its way back so great a distance in so short a time seem inexplicable.—*Our Own Fireside*, April.

RARE BIRDS.—A correspondent of *Land and Water*, writing from Henley-on-Thames, says:—"The 'little auk,' or rotche, was shot in a pond near here the last week in December, 1866. Bramblings, or mountain finches, have been abundant; I have had several fine specimens. A fine specimen of the oyster-catcher was shot at Mill-end last Wednesday. I have sent it to Gardiner to preserve for me. It was in very clean, neat plumage. I fancy this must be far inland for it to wander. A few sea-gulls and two curlews have been obtained this winter. Fieldfares and redwings very abundant; moorcocks more so than usual. I saw a very large otter that was shot up the Loddon last Friday, the 8th; it weighed 23½lb. Young Parrot shot it. It was feeding on a large chubb, and had a fine set of teeth. Otters are now becoming very rare around here.

FISH IN THE AMAZON.—In the lecture on the Amazon, of which we gave a portion in our last number, Professor Agassiz says that he has not found one fish in common with those in any other fresh-water basin; that different parts of the Amazon have fishes peculiar to themselves; and as an instance of the teeming variety of the Amazon, he adds, that a pool of only a few hundred square yards showed 200 kinds of fish, which is as many as the entire Mississippi can boast. In the Amazon itself 2,000 different kinds exist, a great proportion of which are most excellent eating. Several are extremely curious, one especially, which has the power of walking or creeping on dry land, and of worming its way up the trunks of trees.

THE RAVEN.—The following account of a raven appears in a recent number of *The Field*:—Many years ago the landlord of the Black Inn at Mansfield had a tame raven in his stable-yard. I always frequented this inn when I had occasion to go to Mansfield, and whenever I drove or rode into the yard, Tom, the Raven, was sure to be about; and if the ostler was not in sight, he invariably called out with a hoarse but distinct voice, "Ostler, come and take the gentleman's horse!" bustling about all the time in a pompous, amusing manner, as if he had sole charge of the yard.

REPRODUCTIVE POWER OF FISHES.—The great reproductive power of fishes certainly seems, *a priori*, to negative the probability of any permanent diminution of their numbers being affected by any appliances devised by the ingenuity of man. Terrestrial animals give birth as a rule to but one or two young at a time; some fish produce thousands, others millions of ova, a large proportion of which are probably matured into life. A female cod has been found to contain 3,400,000 eggs; a flounder, 1,250,000; a sole, 1,000,000; a mackerel, 500,000; and a herring, 36,000.—The *Quarterly Review*

Remarks, Queries, &c.

(Under this head we shall be happy to insert original Remarks, Queries, &c.)

SUMMER MIGRANTS.—The following notes, showing the time of arrival and places where seen or heard, have been collected from the *Field* and other papers:—

The Sand Martin—Chudleigh, Devon (one shot), March 12th. St. Austells, March 20th. Shaine's Castle, co. Antrim, March 25th. East Retford, Notts, March 26th. Twickenham; Wellington, Salop; Birmingham; Petworth, Sussex, March 27th. Wistastor, Nantwich, March 28th. Dorchester (40 or 50 flying in N.W. direction), March 29th. Saltburn-on-the-Sea, March 30th. Maidstone, April 16th.

The House Martin—Wellington, Salop (two) March 29th.

The Swallow—Isle of Anglesea, March 23rd. Emlyn, Carmarthenshire, March 24th. Wellington, Salop, March 27th. Dorchester, April 1st. Dunster, Somerset (about twenty), April 1st. Boxted, Essex, April 2nd. Islip, Oxon, April 8th. Dorking, April 8th. Petworth, April 10th. Southampton, April 12th. Meldreth, April 10th. Berwickshire, April 14th. Maidstone, April 16th.

The Wheatear—Crumbles, Eastbourne, March 19th and 20th. St. Austells (plentiful), March 20th. Dorchester; Kington, Herefordshire, March 22nd. Ratham, Chichester, March 24th.

Chiff-chaff—Ratham, Chichester, March 21st. Dorchester, one on the 26th, plentiful on 28th. St. Austells, March 27th. Seaham Harbour, Sunderland, April 1st. Saltburn-on-the-Sea, April 7th.

The Wryneck—In Suffolk on March 28th. Meldreth, April 10th. Southampton, April 15th. Maidstone, April 16th.

The Willow Wren—Petworth, March 26th. Seaham Harbour, Sunderland, March 27th.

The Hoopoe—St. Austells (one shot), March 27th.

The Corncrake—Hornsey, March 26th (one heard).

The Skylark—Kington, Herefordshire, March 17th.

The Cuckoo—Southampton, April 15th.

The Nightingale—Winchester, April 9th. Ipswich, April 13th. Maidstone, April 14th. Windsor Forest, April 17th. Cheltenham, April 18th.

The Water Wagtail—On March 15th a pied wagtail was seen in the most complete summer plumage, and on the 18th one with back perfectly black.

NOTES FROM MAIDSTONE.—*January* commenced in this district with a heavy fall of snow, beginning and terminating on the 2nd. About the middle of the month snow fell again, followed by a severe frost, lasting nearly ten days. I noticed in the Earl of Romney's park a red-skinned mouse run from the bank by the road, and career round and over the foot of a gentleman passing at the time. The mouse paid no attention to our watching, and at last leisurely ran off. The snow being thick at the time, the little animal was probably tamed by hunger.

Snow was much deeper in East than West Kent, and the London, Chatham, & Dover and South-Eastern Rails were for a short time blocked, and beyond Margate for about a mile the snow was piled 17 feet. Sunday (20th) was unusually cold, with a dead N.E. wind. (22nd) Rain and sleet fell at night, freezing upon the pavement, covering the streets with ice; and a gentleman at Chatham was enabled to use his skates. The 23rd brought a "thaw," and the snow quickly went. (29th) Found the primrose (primata vulgaris) on Yalding Hill.

February (3rd) Fine and mild; gnats about. (White—Feb. 3rd). Furze, fl. (ulex europæus). (White—Feb. 1st). On 17th observed an owl fly over the Ashford-road at Roseacre. (20th) A beautiful day, sunny and warm; lambs in the fields; gnats and bees. Saw a couple of Bats at Harrietsham. (24th) Wood anemone (anemone nemorosa), fl. The violet (viola adorata) has been out some time. Helleborus fœtidus fl. on the Boxley Hill. (27th) Cold weather again. Snow fell a few mornings since.

March (7th) An anular eclipse of the sun observed about 10.15; (8th) snow, the third time this winter we have had "white weather" (9th) rain; (10th) dull, cloudy, and wet; (30th) an extraordinary mixture—fine, cloudy, windy, rain, snow, hail, lightning and thunder. March has not been so characteristic in the way of wind this year as is usual, I think. (31st) fine. The woods are painted with flowers. Bittercress (cardamine pratensis); Lesser Perriwinkle (vinca minor), primrose, anemone, violet, &c.

Maidstone.   T. F., Jun..

AIDS TO EGG-COLLECTING.—Your correspondent "Kellick" is, I fear, wide from the mark in his egg-collecting. As I have some experience in this branch of natural history, he will perhaps allow me to give him a few hints:—

(1) Strictly speaking, no egg is worth anything that is not taken in the nest. Few, if any, dealers are to be trusted: turkeys' eggs for golden eagles'—the commonest terns' and gulls' eggs for some of the rarest, &c., are among the early chances of a young inexperienced oologist. As it is impossible to find very many eggs oneself, except by devoting one's existence to the pursuit, the next best thing is to be very wary in the purchase, and intelligent in the identification of eggs purchased or exchanged; for a collection of eggs is valuable only in proportion of its authenticity.

(2) There is only one way of blowing an egg, and that is through a hole made on one side of the egg at its largest circumference. This hole should be made not with a drill—that is sure in most cases to crack the egg—but with a small round (rat-tail) file, the end of which has been sharpened into a three-faced point; the great advantage of this is that the file bores a hole into the shell without cracking it. But care must be taken not to push the file in too abruptly, but only by degrees, twirling it all the while between the thumb and the index. By this means I have drilled a hole in scores of the smallest eggs—as, for instance, those of the golden-crested wren—without breaking one.

(3) When the hole is made, then take a blow-pipe, draw with your mouth water into it, and blow that water back into the egg through the hole made. The water will thus bring out the yolk, and at the same time wash the inside of the egg clean.

(4) Then let the egg rest on the hole, on a towel, or handkerchief; all the wet will run out into the cloth, and the egg will soon be dry.

(5) Eggs should never be "mounted." If they be collected for a scientific purpose, nothing short of the number laid by the bird (if that be attainable) should be procured. A small round piece of paper is then gummed over the hole, and a number referring to the catalogue is then written over it. I send you a copy of it for Mr. "Kellick's" acceptance. No labels should be glued on the egg, nor any name written in ink. The way I mention is by far the best, and the most satisfactory.

(6) It sometimes happens that the egg is brooded, so that the water will fail to bring out its contents. In that case, if the egg be a common one, the best way is to throw it away; if, however, it be worth keeping, then make no hole with the drill-file, but with a sharp penknife cut off slowly a square bit of the shell—put it by, take out the contents of the egg, and then gum the bit of shell back into its place. Various liquids are recommended for the purpose of dissolving the brooded yolk, but they all injure the shell. S. C. MALAN.

Broadwindsor Vicarage, April 8th.

Having read in your last number of the "Naturalist's Note Book" that "Kellick" would be greatly obliged by any hints regarding the blowing of eggs, I send him an account of the following method, which I have used for a long time with great success:—

Take a clear straw—or a fine stem of grass is best—and, making a hole in the centre of the egg rather larger than the straw, blow gently through the straw, when the yolk and white will both come out of the hole, and leave the egg empty.

This method is preferable to any other, because it only makes one hole in the shell instead of two, and consequently weakens the egg much less. Also, when the egg is placed on card the hole is covered, and the egg presents to all appearance a perfect shell; it also prevents insects getting into the egg. M. L. A.

Redhill.

The method of mounting eggs on cardboard, &c., is seldom resorted to, cabinets being employed where good collections are made. Would some of your correspondents inform me what size a cabinet must be, and in what manner constructed so that a moderate collection of all the British birds' eggs may be arranged according to a scientific classification, and not mixed up according to size, as is generally the case? I should like also to know the probable cost.

"AQUILA."

St. John's Wood, N.W.

POPULATION OF THE SEA.—If the sea is prodigal of life to a degree that baffles our powers of conception, it is no less a scene of boundless destruction. The life of all fishes is one of perfect warfare, and the only law that pervades the great world of waters is that of the strongest, the swiftest, and most voracious. The carnage of the sea immeasurably exceeds even that which is permitted to perplex our reason on the earth. We know, however, that without it the population of the ocean would soon become so immense that, vast as it is, it would not suffice for its multitudinous inhabitants. Few fishes probably die a natural death, and some seem to have been created solely to devour others; there is probably none which does not feed on some other species or on its own. Many of the monsters that swim the watery plains are provided with maws capable of engulphing thousands of their kind in a day. A hogshead of herrings has been taken out of the belly of a whale. A shark probably destroys tens of thousands in a year. Fifteen full-sized herrings have been found in the stomach of a cod. If we allow a codfish only two herrings per day for his subsistence, and suppose him to feed on herrings for only seven months in the year, we have 420 herrings as his allowance during that period, and 50 codfish equal one fisherman in destructive power; but the quantity of cod, and of ling, which are as destructive as cod, taken in 1861, and registered by the Scotch Fishery Board, was, says the commissioners, over 81,000 cwts. On an average 30 codfish make 1 cwt. of dried fish, and 2,400,000 will equal 48,000 fishermen. In other words, the cod and ling caught on the Scotch coast in 1861, if they had been left in the water, would have devoured as many herrings as were caught by all the fishermen of Scotland and six thousand more in the same year; but as the cod and ling caught were certainly not one-tenth of those left behind, we may fairly estimate the destruction of herrings by those voracious fish alone as at least ten times as great as that effected by all the fishermen in Scotland—*Quarterly Review*, April, 1867.

GOLD FISH.—Perhaps one of your numerous readers can favour me with an explanation of the following case:—

For some years I have kept a small aquarium, confining my attention chiefly to gold and silver fish. Up to the present time they have been very healthy; but a short time ago the largest gold fish (about four inches in length) was attacked with a kind of fungus, or film, which made its appearance on its tail and dorsal fin, when all the firmness of those parts seemed to give way. The tail came off, and the dorsal fin stuck quite firmly down to its back. The film continued spreading towards the head, till about a fortnight after the fish had been attacked the fungus had so enclosed the whole of its body that it could hardly move, and soon afterwards died.

Mr. Frank Buckland, in his "Curiosities of Natural History," mentions the disease as one from which fish do not recover. I find two or three other writers on aquariums, &c., mention it; but no person has given any clear account of it.

If one of your correspondents or readers could give me some account of this disease, or its prevention, he will greatly oblige,

London. AQUARIAN.

FLEAS IN DOGS.—Can any of your readers give a harmless, and, at the same time, effectual remedy for destroying fleas in dogs—something that will not injure them if they lick themselves after the application?

J. L.

[Persian insect powder, to be had of Messrs. Butler and M'Culloch, Covent Garden Market, in 1s. and 2s. 6d. packets, is the best we know of.—ED.]

VITALITY OF WASPS.—I will feel obliged if some of your correspondents will state the cause of the extraordinary vitality of wasps after having been decapitated. I lately caught a large one in the greenhouse; I severed his head, and also the bag or hinder part from the body, making three separate parts; the head lived for about sixty seconds, opening and shutting the jaws, and moving the feelers; the remaining two parts showed strong signs of vitality for thirty minutes after being severed, the legs and wings in the one moving actively and almost constantly; and the hinder part was also very active, darting out the sting when merely touched. I cannot help thinking this activity, after such complete severation, as very strange.—J. L.

ESQUIMAUX IN EUROPE.—Your article on "Esquimaux in Europe," page 13 in the January number, extracted from the *Saturday Review*, has attracted my attention in an especial manner. Surely the period when the Esquimaux and the reindeer were indigenous to South Gaul, when the Thames, the Rhine, and the Elbe flowed into *one common* embouchure, or basin, or bay, and when the Straits of Dover scarcely existed, must have been some ages *preadamic*. In this case, what becomes of the miserable theory that "man" existed on the earth only A.M. 5,871 years ago?—viz. A.C. 4,004, P.C. 1,867 = 5,871.   E. WARD.

WREN'S NEST.—The nests "Fox" mentioned in last "Naturalist's Note Book" were those of the common wren in both cases.

They love especially the root of a broom-bush, on the ground—the turf in a hole of the wall, or beneath the trunk of a tree—for their nest, which has quite a rough exterior, but a nice feathery inside, and always the same small aperture in the side for entrance and exit.   J. R.

GRANITE IN DEVON AND CORNWALL.—Can any of your numerous correspondents give me any information respecting the large beds of disintegrated granite found in Devon and Cornwall, and from which the China clay is obtained?

Plympton.   A. WENTZL.

BLOOD STAINS.—Could some of your readers be so kind as to inform me how to detect spots of blood upon any article?

The reason I wish to know is because I have an Indian arrow which has some red spots on it, and I have an opinion that it is spots of blood.   MATTIE.

STATE OF THE WEATHER NEAR LONDON.

March and April.	Moon's Age.	Barometer.		Temperature.					Wind	Rain.	Remarks.
				Of the Air.			of the Earth				
		Max.	Min.	Max	Min	Mean	1 foot deep	2 feet deep			
Thurs. 14	8	29.622	29.512	41	28	34.5	40	40	E.	.00	Snow and sleet; overcast; snow in broad flakes; overcast.
Friday 15	9	29.778	29.692	40	25	32.5	40	40	N.E.	.11	Snowing; uniformly overcast; fine at night.
Satur. 16	10	29.985	29.875	38	20	29.0	40	40	N.E.	.00	Clear and frosty; fine, with white clouds; frosty at night.
Sunday 17	11	29.995	29.678	38	30	34.0	39	39	E.	.00	Frosty, with slight haze; cloudy and fine; boisterous.
Mon. 18	12	29.496	29.445	35	30	32.5	40	39	E.	.06	Very cold and boisterous; snowing; densely overcast.
Tues. 19	13	29.370	29.272	36	32	34.0	39	39	N.E.	.25	Overcast; heavy fall of snow and sleet; drizzling rain at night.
Wed. 20	○	29.744	29.409	43	27	35.0	39	39	N.E.	.00	Densely clouded; cloudy and cold; overcast at night.
Thurs. 21	15	29.816	29.644	44	30	37.0	39	39	N.E.	.28	Partially overcast; cold, with dry air; fine at night.
Friday 22	16	29.730	29.631	49	36	42.5	39	39	E.	.02	Heavy fall of snow; hazy; foggy at night.
Satur. 23	17	29.722	29.460	57	43	50.0	40	40	S.	.04	Uniformly overcast; rain; overcast at night.
Sunday 24	18	29.596	29.495	59	43	51.0	41	41	S.W.	.00	Fine; very fine; overcast.
Mon. 25	19	29.697	29.446	53	47	50.0	43	43	S.	.12	Cloudy; rain; fine at night.
Tues. 26	20	29.397	29.335	57	40	48.5	45	43	S.W.	.00	Very boisterous; fine, with low white clouds; fine.
Wed. 27	21	29.421	29.299	57	29	43.0	45	44	S.W.	.00	Cloudy; fine, dry air, overcast; fine at night.
Thurs. 28	☽	29.456	29.370	55	30	42.5	46	44	S.W.	.00	Very clear, quite cloudless; fine at night.
Friday 29	23	29.652	29.543	52	31	41.5	46	44	W.	.00	Fine; cloudy and cold; fine; very slight frost.
Satur. 30	24	29.745	29.738	50	31	40.5	46	44	N.W.	.01	Fine; showery; storm of thunder; lightning, with hail at night.
Sunday 31	25	30.331	30.020	58	23	40.5	46	44	N.W.	.00	Cold and exceedingly clear; fine; very fine at night; frosty.
Mon. 1	26	30.393	30.297	59	46	52.5	46	44	W.	.00	Fine; sunshine, with dry air; densely overcast.
Tues. 2	27	30.136	30.081	62	35	48.5	48	44	W.	.00	Overcast; cloudy; fine at night.
Wed. 3	28	30.215	30.097	64	45	54.5	48	45		.00	Fine; very fine throughout; occasionally rather boisterous at night.
Thurs. 4	●	29.857	29.792	59	40	48.5	49	46	N.W.	.02	Cloudy; boisterous and showery; fine at night.
Friday 5	1	30.033	29.945	62	40	51.0	50	46	W.	.01	Slight haze; very fine, with dry air; very fine at night.
Satur. 6	2	29.992	29.979	62	45	53.5	50	46	W.	.00	Overcast; cloudy; fine at night.
Sunday 7	3	29.972	29.644	58	40	49.0	50	47	S.W.	.02	Cloudy; overcast; densely overcast at night.
Mon. 8	4	29.527	29.331	53	39	46.0	50	47	S.W.	.14	Cloudy; boisterous, with rain; very boisterous at night.
Tues. 9	5	29.755	29.545	59	29	44.0	50	47	N.W.	.02	Cold and boisterous; fine; thunder, vivid lightning and some hail.
Wed. 10	6	29.899	29.511	54	40	47.0	49	47	S.W.	.02	Fine; overcast; boisterous, with rain at night.
Thurs. 11	☽	29.967	29.516	57	26	41.5	49	46	N.W.	.00	Boisterous and stormy; very boisterous, with dense dusky clouds; fine at night.
Friday 12	8	30.158	30.066	58	38	48.0	49	46	S.W.	.03	Clear and very fine throughout.
Satur. 13	9	30.057	29.799	55	46	50.5	49	47	S.W.	.09	Rain and rather boisterous; densely overcast at night.
Sunday 14	10	29.607	29.295	49	41	45.0	50	46	S.W.	.30	Boisterous, with rain; very wet and boisterous.
Mon. 15	11	29.695	29.415	62	40	51.0	50	47	W.	.04	Boisterous; showery and boisterous; fine.
Tues. 16	12	29.722	29.608	56	41	48.5	50	47	S.W.	.06	Rain; showery, drizzly; overcast at night.
Wed. 17	13	29.901	29.742	62	37	49.5	50	47	N.W.	.01	Hazy and drizzly; exceedingly fine throughout.

BEAVERS AND THEIR CAMPS.

HE vicinity of a large beaver camp very much resembles that around an Indian camp, so much so that a person unacquainted with and unprepared for the animal might readily mistake the former for the latter. I will try and describe one that I found on the head of the Metapedine.

The stream was some fifteen or twenty feet in width, with a considerable fall. Four dams had been constructed at intervals of about a hundred yards. The pond formed by the upper dam but one was probably about an acre in extent, of a depth of eight feet in the centre, shoaling off towards the edges. The place was thickly wooded; but, as it was an old colony, the trees in the pond had all been killed by the water—some remained standing, others had fallen and lay on the surface. The dam was semicircular, convex to the stream, and about a hundred and fifty yards in length; in an irregular way it surrounded the upper half of the pond. The spot for building this dam had been chosen, as is invariably the case, with remarkable judgment; and all natural features, such as little islands, rocks, stumps of trees, &c., had been turned to good account. The centre of the dam was about five feet in height, and eight or ten in width at the base, and so compact that it took two men with axes the greater part of an hour to cut through it an aperture six feet wide. The camp was situated near the centre of the pond on the original bank of the stream. It was about the size and shape of an ordinary haystack, a little flattened down; rather more than two-thirds showed above the water (about eight feet). Internally it contained one large circular apartment, about six feet six inches in diameter; the roof, which was arched or dome-shaped, being two feet three or four inches in the centre, and gradually sloping downwards to the edge. The floor was ten inches above water-mark, and contained four beds made of chips of wood cut very fine. The walls were from four to five feet thick, and made altogether of earth and wood. There were three entrances, all under water. Close to the camp was the storehouse—an accumulation of fresh logs and branches submerged in the water for winter use; I calculated that there must have been half a dozen ordinary cartloads, and the pile was not completed. The peeled boughs had been piled on the house and dam. Some of them had been hauled a distance of sixty yards by land, and twice that distance by water. There were six well-made roads, twelve or fourteen inches in width, and worn quite smooth and hard, running into the woods in different directions. Trees of all sizes, from a foot in diameter downwards, that had been felled by the beaver, lay scattered all round the pond and in the water—some freshly cut, others decayed and covered with moss. The boughs of the larger ones had been lopped off and carried to the storehouse, the bark of the stems being eaten on the spot. Smaller trees had been felled, cut into logs, and carried bodily off. Saplings of the size of an axe-handle had been cut as with one slanting blow of an axe; but the larger trees were gnawed all round. Dry sticks and roots that obstructed their roads had been cut neatly off at the proper breadth, and the piece thrown aside.

* * * * *

The beaver selects a little island, or shallow spot near the centre of his pond, for building on. A dry bed close to deep water is essential; this is one of the ends secured by dam building, which keeps the water much on the same level throughout the year. In its earlier stages the house resembles a gigantic bird's nest, made of mud, sticks, and stones; branches are then laid across to serve as rafters, more sticks and mud being piled on the top of them to complete the edifice. The beavers then burrow into the pile, cut off projecting sticks, and fashion out the apartment or apartments—for there are frequently more than one. The walls and roof are made of great thickness—four or five feet, to resist the frost; and for the same purpose the roof gets a fresh plastering of mud every fall, just before the frost commences. When a house is inhabited by a large family of beavers the heat they generate is so great as to melt the snow on the roof, which is but partially frozen.

I never could perceive that beavers use their tails as trowels, though they have got the credit of it. I have little doubt, however, but that this appendage is made to serve some useful purpose in the plastering line, else why should it, unlike other amphibious animals, have the tail flat horizontally. If of no other use, it certainly makes a comfortable seat for them.

Beavers do not inhabit the same house for more than three or four successive years. The reason of this is obvious. It is easier to build a new house, where wood is plenty, than to haul their provisions a long distance to the old one. Hence, on streams and lakes inhabited by beavers there are always a great number of camps in all stages of repair and dilapidation, also dams without end; but these latter are always kept in repair within half a mile or so of the dwelling-house. The series of ponds thus formed gives them a greater extent of feeding ground, and enables them to haul wood up stream. Sometimes beavers, driven away by a feeling of insecurity or some other cause, will leave a new house and take up their abode in an old shanty, returning to their deserted abode every night for provisions.

The materials used for building the dams are the same as for the houses. I have never seen the beaver actually at work at the building. I do not think they build in the daytime. The sticks they use vary in size, from the thickness of a man's finger to that of his leg, and in length from one foot up to five or six. Most of them are peeled previous to being worked up. Dead wood also and stones are used. I have seen the latter as big as a man's head, that must have been carried some little distance. Stones and mud they carry with their fore paws or hands, pressing them against their chest and walking on their hind legs. Some sticks lie horizontally, others in a slanting position, with the branchy end pointing up in the air and the butts down stream, and some short ones are in a perpendicular position. The chief difficulty must be with the foundation; when once that is laid it is comparatively easy to lean boughs against it as I have described, place others crossways, weigh them down with stones and plaster them with mud. Often they take advantage of a windfall, or a little chain of rocks, for they are capital engineers. The slope on the upper side of the dam is much less than on the lower, and the top is accurately levelled.

I will briefly enumerate their reasons for dam building. 1st. To deepen the water around their camp, enabling them to dive and defy pursuit. 2ndly. As a protection from the frosts of winter, which would freeze shallow water to the bottom. 3rdly. To equalise the height of the water throughout the year, and prevent their beds from being flooded. 4thly. To enable them to haul wood with greater ease. In addition to these I really believe that beavers like dam building for the amusement it affords them. I am aware that in this opinion I differ from other writers. But, if they are right, how is it that on lakes having streams running into or from them, such streams are invariably dammed by the beavers of the lake? At the head of a lake two or three miles in circumference I have seen a beaver house; at the outlet of the same lake, a mile off, a dam built and kept in perfect repair by the beavers. Now I cannot see what use this could have been; it would scarcely raise the level of the water as many inches as the lake was fathoms in depth.

On the Miramichi, New Brunswick, I found a small brook—a rapid stream with a great fall. One family of eight or ten beavers lived on it, and in the course of little more than half a mile they had constructed no less than thirteen dams, each about three feet high. The effect of this in winter time was curious enough; the ponds, frozen over and covered with snow, formed a series of tolerably regular steps or terraces.

* * * * *

Although the principal food of the beaver consists in the bark of certain trees, it is lucky for them that they are not wholly dependent upon wood, else they would die of starvation when large fires sweep over the land. They dive for and eat with great relish the large cucumber-shaped roots of the water-lily and other stalks and roots that grow in the water. The barks they eat in order of preference are those of the popple, or American poplar (a soft, sappy tree of very rapid growth), white birch, alder, rowan tree, moose wood, white maple, willow, spruce, and cedar; the two latter only when no other can be procured. In summer they wander about, stopping here and there to feed. I have heard of their visiting a deserted camp and eating potatoes that they found therein; and it is not an unusual occurrence to find an old mocassin or the lid of a kettle worked up in a beaver house or dam. In winter they pay a daily or nightly visit under the ice to their stores, which are close at hand, and carry off a stick to camp, where they eat the bark at leisure. They are very cleanly in their habits, never making a mess in the camp, which, together with their beds of chips and savings, they keep scrupulously clean. Periodically they have a cleaning-out day, when the *débris* of peeled sticks, &c., are thrown out of camp. In thaws and on very mild days they come out from under the ice for a "constitutional" and a little bit of fresh bark. Their tracks in the snow resemble those of an enormous goose, the marks made by the little fore feet or hands being entirely obliterated by the webbed hind ones.

In no way do the beavers show their superior intelligence over the rest of the brute creation more than by their knowledge of the power of combined efforts. Thus two or more beavers will work at the same tree, chopping away at different sides till the scraps meet and the tree falls. They cut trees about a foot and a half from the ground, sitting on their haunches and tails, their arms against or round the trunk. The chips they take out vary from half an inch to two inches in length, chopped at both ends. I have seen several trees of five or six inches in diameter cut by a small family of beavers in the course of one night. The hunter tells the age of the beaver by the tooth marks, and from this can give a very shrewd guess of the number in the camp. I measured the stump of a birch tree freshly cut by beavers on the Memoyckel, New Brunswick; it was between thirteen and fourteen inches in diameter. The boughs had been neatly lopped off as with an axe, and nothing remained but the trunk, which supplied me and my party with back logs for the night.—*Field*.

ESPARTO.

WHO has not heard of the lamentations of the paper-makers, whose wailings on the paucity of rags, and the total absence of fibre suited to their requirements, were followed by mortuary dirges on the decline and fall of their beautiful manufacture; whilst, as a contemporaneous fact, there continued to bloom and die on the arid plains bordering the sunny Mediterranean, a perennial plant, containing within its wiry stem no less than 70 per cent. of fibre, eminently suited to their wants? This plant is the *Gramen spartum*, Plinii, *Stipa tenacissima*, Linn. By the Spaniards it is called Esparto, and by the French Alfa. It is placed by botanists among the sedges, and is indigenous to the southern shores of Portugal, Spain, and Italy, as well as to the coast of Northern Africa, from Algeria to the confines of Egypt. It grows in tufts like a rush, is perennial in habit, attains a height of from 18 to 30 inches, according to situation, and, having a basis of silica and iron, flourishes on arid soil. Its principal *habitats*, however, are Spain and Algeria, from which countries a supply sufficient for all present demands may be drawn with ease. There is probably no plant within our knowledge which possesses so remarkable a history as that now under review. Pliny, that most careful and observant of naturalists, gives a surprisingly accurate description of the *Spartum*, and enumerates the uses to which it was put in his day. He speaks of it as a morbid production—"confined to a single country only; for in reality it is a curse to the soil, as there is nothing whatever that can be grown or sown in its vicinity." He describes the species of spartum found in Africa as of stunted growth, of no use whatever for practical purposes; and, altogether, he seems to entertain a very poor opinion of the African variety. It is interesting to note the similarity of uses found for the plant in the days of Pliny, to those prevailing in our own. Then, as now, the peasantry stuffed their beds with it, and, no doubt, obtained as springy a couch as is yielded by our own native heather. It was used as fuel made into torches, woven and plaited into summer garments for the shepherds, and manufactured into shoes which, under the name of Alpargates, are still extensively used by the poorer inhabitants of the Iberian peninsula. It was also very largely used for cordage; and we have the authority of Mr.. M'Culloch for the statement that cables made from Esparto were some years ago—if they are not still—preferred in the Spanish navy to similar stores made from hemp. Merely to enumerate the articles of utility into the construction of which Esparto entered, would in fact be a recapitulation of the utensils and appliances appertaining to the domestic economy and manufacturing industry of the Spaniards and Carthagenians. Pliny most appropriately designates his *Gramen spartum* a marvellous plant; and the reflection is by no means a flattering one that, notwithstanding his painstaking researches, and the uninterrupted use of the plant in the same districts through centuries of time, we should have failed to bring our chemical knowledge to bear on its constitutional difficulties, until our need became so *exigeant* as to render further neglect well-nigh impossible.

During the past ten years the French have been indefatigable in the prosecution of researches in the utilization of Alfa as a paper-making fibre, and it is to the *savans* of that country that we are primarily indebted for a knowledge of the economic conditions of the plant; possibly because it grows abundantly on a portion of their own territory, the natural resources of which the French Government are most anxious to develop. The province of Oran, in Algeria, is that in which the traffic Alfa is mostly concentrated. There it alternates with the Dwarf Palm and Asphodel, and it grows luxuriantly from the coast up to the minor peaks of the contiguous mountain ranges. The crop should be gathered in the months of April, May, and June, varying according to the forwardness of the season; the object being to secure the plant while yet green, yet as near as possible to ripeness. If gathered too green, the fibre is deficient both in quantity and strength, whilst if allowed to ripen fully, the constituent elements of silica and iron are established too securely in its structure. The best time for collecting, according to Pliny, is between the Ides of May and those of June, a statement which has been fully confirmed by modern practice. On the best method of gathering, the ancient philosopher is equally in accord with our own observations. The plant, he says, is twisted round levers of bone or holm oak, to get it up with the greater facility. It has been proved experimentally, that this is the best mode of reaping the crop, having a due regard to the succeeding harvest, as cutting not only injures the plant, but altogether endangers its vitality, thus rendering the labour of collection exceedingly severe, as the workmen must both pull and stoop as he traverses the ground. The *modus operandi* is very simple. Providing himself with a stick of moderate thickness, the labourer grasps a handful of Alfa, twists it round the stick, and, by a sharp pull with both hands, disengages the stalks at the articulations. Securing the bunch under his left arm, he pulls away until, no longer able to hold the produce, he throws it down to be tied into a bundle called a *Manada*, and proceeds with his work *de novo*. These bundles are then ranged in the field to dry, a result which is usually attained in a week, during which time the Alfa looses about 40 per cent of its weight. The bundles, or *Manadas*, are then packed into bales and carried to the port of shipment. It is not improbable that, in course of time, the propagation of Alfa with a view to increased supply may be requisite in places suited to its growth, as it is only in particular areas that its preparation for export can be conducted, on account of the cost of carriage to practicable shipping points on the seaboard. At present the demand from England and France is exclusively on behalf of the paper manufacture; but should application of the fibre be extended—and there is no reason why it should not be so with great advantage, its culture will become an important branch of Algerian husbandry. Arrived in this country and stored at a paper-mill, the *Manadas* should be ranged so as to allow of the roots and tops being pulled, an operation which clears the Alfa from a good deal of waste substance adhering more or less to the stalks. It has now the appearance of dried rushes, firm and wiry to the touch, and as unlikely-looking a material from which to manufacture white paper as can well be imagined. Nothing, however, can be simpler. After having been opened and well shaken out, the stalks are thrown into a boiler containing a strong solution of caustic alkali, and are boiled until a handful can be twisted asunder with ease. It has now parted with a good deal of colouring matter, and is ready, after having drained sufficiently to be broken and washed—operations which are carried on simultaneously in what is technically known as a "washing engine," an elliptical trough having the machinery on one side of a partition, placed down the centre of the engine, but terminating at some distance from either end; the effect of this arrangement being that the material in the engine is made to flow round the partition or "midfeather," by the rotary action of the machinery. The Alfa now gradually assumes a light yellowish tinge, and with the introduction to the engine of a quantity of chloride of lime the process of bleaching commences. Meanwhile the Alfa is being drawn out into fine short filaments by the triturating action of the machinery. Gradually all colour departs, and, as it flows round the engine, the stuff more nearly resembles a duct of snow-white cream than anything else to which it can be likened. Now the shutters of the washing cover are withdrawn, in order to thoroughly eliminate the "bleach." That done, and the stuff finished as regards sizing and tint, a valve in the bottom of the engine is drawn, the prepared Alfa plunges into the stuff chest at the head of the paper-machine, and, in less time than is consumed in recording the fact, is ready for the hands of the printer.—*Nature and Art Magazine*, May, 1867.

RAIN.

ONE of the most curious things about rain is the inequality of its distribution. The reader is of course aware that rain may be measured in inches in almost any vessel set out to catch it. If a pail, for example, be put out in an open space on the ground, it will catch as much rain as would otherwise have sunk into the ground on the space occupied by the bottom of the pail. If we visit the pail after every shower, we may, by means of a two-foot rule, tell what depth of rain has fallen. This is the principle of the rain-gauge. In practice better means are of course adopted, so as to prevent evaporation and to measure the depth. Now it is of great consequence where we place our rain-gauge. It might be supposed of no importance whether it were on the top of the house or in the garden close by. And yet, strange to say, a gauge in a garden near Westminster Abbey caught twenty-three inches of rain in the course of the year, while one on the roof of a house caught only eighteen inches, and one on the top of the Abbey only twelve inches. The fact is, rain forms at a very low elevation, much lower than is generally supposed; or, if not actually formed at a very low elevation, it increases the size of the drops which come from higher levels. Thus, while Mr. Glaisher was descending in a balloon, he passed through a dry, and then through a wet fog, when the drops of rain were exceedingly fine, covering his note-book like pins' points. These increased in size on approaching the earth, but more rapidly when very near the earth.

The average quantity of rain which falls at Greenwich every year is rather more than twenty-five inches; but it varies in a remarkable manner even in different parts of London. Thus, in 1863, 17·42 inches of rain fell in Spring Gardens, 20·10 inches at Guildhall, 21·07 inches in Bryanstone Square, 19·09 inches in Chiswell Street, and 21·49 inches in Camden Town. The variation is still more remarkable if we extend our observations to different parts of England. Cold, high lands, for example, act as condensers to moist air, and precipitate rain which would otherwise have passed without falling. This must not be confused with a less amount of rain at the top of a tall building than on the ground, for the tall mountains stop the moist air and squeeze out its contents. Hence in some parts of North Wales the annual rainfall amounts to one hundred inches; and in Cumberland, at one remarkably wet spot, the Stye, at the head of Borrowdale, to nearly two hundred inches. In the flat districts of Bedfordshire, Lincolnshire, and the east coast, on the contrary, the rainfall scarcely exceeds twenty inches per annum.

The reader is aware that what is called a *low barometer* is generally a sign of rain, as a *high barometer* is of fine weather. That is the general rule, although there may be rain when the mercury stands high, and it may be fine when the mercury is low. The barometer represents the weight of a column of air from the spot where it is placed to the top of the atmosphere, which may be about fifty miles in vertical height. If water were used in the barometer instead of mercury, the barometer tube would have to be upwards of thirty-five feet in length, since mercury is about thirteen and a half times heavier than water. A column of mercury thirty inches high, in a tube of one square inch section, weighs about fifteen pounds. A similar column of water, thirty-four feet high, weighs the same; and as these columns of mercury and of water are supported by the air, a similar column of air about fifty miles high must also weigh about fifteen pounds. This is what constitutes atmospheric pressure. We also see that it is a varying quantity; for as the barometer observed at the same spot is sometimes high and sometimes low, sometimes at nearly thirty-one inches, and at other times a little above twenty-eight inches, this shows an increase of atmospheric pressure at one time and a diminution at another.

Now the atmosphere is made up of a number of ingredients, the two principal of which, the oxygen and the nitrogen, are in fixed quantities, *i. e.*, about one-fifth of oxygen and four-fifths of nitrogen. The other ingredients are found in varying quantities. Omitting all notice of accidental impurities, such as smoke and sulphur acids, which depend on locality, there are two ingredients which are found in the air in varying quantities at every part of the earth's surface, and at every elevation. These are carbonic acid, one of the products of the respiration of animals, and the burning of coals, gas, candles, &c.; and aqueous vapour, or vapour of water, the result of the evaporation of the waters of the earth, whether salt or fresh, whether from the surface of water or of moist earth.

Now all these ingredients are concerned in supporting the mercury column in the barometer. The oxygen atmosphere raises it a certain number of inches; the nitrogen atmosphere a still larger number; the carbonic acid atmosphere a small varying fraction of an inch; the aqueous vapour atmosphere a larger but still varying fraction of an inch; and the sum of all these quantities is what we call the height of the barometer.

Now let us attend only to the aqueous vapour atmosphere, dismissing the other three atmospheres. Suppose, for example, the air were entirely composed of aqueous vapour; its quantity, elasticity, and pressure would, as it now does, depend entirely on its temperature. At sixty degrees Fahrenheit the mercury would stand in the barometer at the height of rather more than half an inch; at seventy degrees, at about three-quarters of an inch; at eighty degrees, at one inch; at one hundred degrees, at nearly two inches. At the temperature of boiling water, however, the vapour would have sufficient force to support thirty inches of mercury, which is the same as the mean atmospheric pressure of the whole atmosphere. Of course we never get such a natural temperature, so that, in endeavouring to explain the formation of rain, we must keep to temperatures actually observed.

Bearing in mind what was said about the quantity of vapour depending on temperature, let us inquire what would take place, supposing a cold air charged with vapour at forty degrees were to blow into an air charged with vapour at sixty degrees. In the absence of experiment, almost any thoughtful person would say that it would be like mingling equal quantities of water at forty and sixty degrees, the result of which, we know, is the mean temperature of fifty degrees. So he would say, in the present case, the moist air at forty degrees mingling with the moist air at sixty degrees would produce a mean, both as respects temperature and moisture, and matters would remain unchanged; except that the cold moist air would have become a little warmer, and have taken up more moisture, while the warmer moist air would have become a little cooler, and have given up a little of its moisture to the air that was at forty degrees. Any one would say that the air at fifty degrees would, as respects its moisture, represent the mean of the two quantities of air at forty and at sixty degrees, and there would be no rainfall, or *precipitation*, as it is called. Nevertheless, this reasoning would be all wrong; for by another of those admirable adjustments, which mark design as clearly as the sun at noonday, it has been ordained that the elasticity of aqueous vapour shall diminish much more rapidly than its temperature; so that the air at fifty degrees holds less than the mean quantity of vapour contained in air at forty degrees and air at sixty degrees.

For example:—Vapour at forty degrees will support nearly a quarter of an inch of mercury, at sixty degrees about half an inch of mercury;

or, more accurately, the quantities are 0·24 and 0·52; add these two together, and divide by 2, and we get 0·38 as the mean quantity of vapour in the two temperatures. But it is proved by experiment that vapour at fifty degrees will support only 0·36, so that there is a difference of 0·02 inch of mercury, which represents the quantity of vapour which cannot be taken up by the mean temperature, and it is this which falls as rain.—*People's Magazine*, May.

MOSS-ANIMALS, OR FRESH WATER POLYZOA.

Among all the creatures found in our pools and lakes, none are more pleasing to the eye when carefully examined than the moss-animals. These delicate animal flowers may be found in communities expanding their shadowy plumes in the darker recesses of our ponds, attached to the under side of submerged sticks, logs and stones.

The moss-animals of our fresh waters are, with two exceptions, all members of one group, called phylactolæmata, or animals with guarded throats; that is, having a little flap outside of the mouth which guards this aperture. The two exceptions mentioned have not this characteristic, and, therefore, belong to the same division as their marine relatives, the gymnolæmata, or polyzoa with unguarded throats. Notwithstanding their harsh scientific name, the phylactolæmata are light, elegant, mossy growths, and, when placed under a low power of the microscope, are even more beautiful than the flowers they resemble.

Their plant-like aspect, however, is a mere semblance, notwithstanding the branching mode of growth. If we examine any one specimen of the genus Fredericella, we speedily learn that the trunk is not a single, straight, solid stem, as in the plants, but made up of a series of minute, dark brown, tubular cells, arranged in a line, with the main branches and shorter twigs, also constructed of cells, arranged in a similar manner. Each cell is a single animal, and contains the organs and muscles of one being, though so intimately attached to others, and so merged in the general life of the community, that it cannot, strictly speaking, be called an individual. An individual is but one animal, freely following the bent of its own will, and containing within itself an isolated, independent system of organs.

The lower portion of every cell is straight, being the continuation of the axis of the trunk, or branch of which it is a part; but the upper portion turns out of the direct line with an elbow-like bend, elevating one end above the stem. This end is free, and is surmounted by a transparent tube, which is closed by a round disc, perforated by the mouth, and bearing a crown of translucent, slender threads, called tentacles, which gracefully curve upwards like the petals of a lily. The tongue-like flap overhangs the mouth, and is continually jerked downward, instantly resuming its upright position, as if it were hinged on springs. This is a most curious organ, and although situated outside of the mouth, it seems to answer many of the ordinary purposes of a tongue. It evidently discriminates between the different kinds of food, but is oftener employed to close the mouth over some struggling animalcule which obstinately refuses to be swallowed. It is a fleshy semicircular prominence formed by a fold of the disc, and is both the door of a trap and an organ of taste combined.

The crown is interesting, not only on account of its beauty and delicate transparency, but from the dreamy outline of each little thread, caused by the movements of the innumerable hairs investing them. The hairs or cilia themselves are not visible, owing to their extreme tenuity, but the waves they make in the water can be plainly seen. So many thousands of these cilia are simultaneously moving upward on the outer sides of the threads, and downward upon their inner sides, that they force the water along in strong currents from the exterior down toward the bottom of the open-work vase where the mouth lies. The meeting of these currents coming from all sides at once creates a whirlpool, in which hundreds of careless animalcules are continually caught and transported to the mouth. This being placed at the centre of the vortex catches all the objects entrapped by the current above, and it has also, unfortunately for its helpless prey, a stomach beneath, which is indeed "an abyss no riches can fill." The thousands of sleepless cilia are day and night constantly in motion, drawing into the throat an endless stream of food. The stomach below is equally active, and thus all the organs work harmoniously, like machinery driven by steam, untiringly capturing and digesting the food, which, when assimilated, supplies the waste occasioned by the great activity of these parts. The threads or tentacles also prove useful in many other ways. They can twist together with incalculable rapidity, barring out any objectionable animal which may manifest a disposition to pry into the crown; or each one can by itself bend over and eject annoying particles; or, if the throat need a little cleaning, force its way down the tube and clear it, by pushing into the stomach whatever may be clinging to the sides. They are most amusing, however, in the angry pettishness they occasionally exhibit toward intruding neighbours. First comes an admonitory push, then a harder one, if the first is not successful, and lastly, unmistakeable blows administered with vicious rapidity by many threads in unison. Sometimes a "big fish" enters the crown in the shape of an animated speck, perceptible only when magnified twenty or thirty times its own size ; then the sensitive tips of the threads curve together and imprison the coveted morsel. Caged thus in a living net, and unable to break through the bars, it is soon exhausted by the power of the miniature maelstrom, and swept, in spite of many fruitless struggles, down into the gaping mouth.

On the exterior of the tentacles, reaching about halfway up their sides, is a thin veil, looped up and hanging gracefully between them like a delicate ruffle with pointed folds. Between this veil and the dark brown cell is the pellucid tube, and through its walls we can examine the internal organs. Directly under the tongue-like projection of the disc or epistome is the nervous mass, which takes the place of a brain in all the polyzoa. It has nerves leading to the throat, the stomach and intestine, besides two branches that go to the disc, and distribute those minute nervous tendrils which endow them with such acute sensibility. The epistome, or false tongue above the mouth, being only a fold of the disc, is hollow. The nerve-mass retreats into this cavity at will, probably by means of minute muscular fibres ; and in this position also seeks security from injurious pressure, while the polyzoon is crowded within the shelter of its cell. Thus the epistome, in addition to its other multifarious uses, serves at times as a brain box.

The organs of digestion hang from the disc above, occupying the centre of the tube, and floating freely in the rapidly moving blood. The throat is closed at the lower end by a valve, which opens into a gourd-shaped sack, the stomach ; close by this is another valve which opens from the stomach into the intestine. The last is a canal leading up, side by side with the throat, for a short distance, but finally bending away from it, and opening externally through an aperture in the pellucid tube, just below the base of the ruffle, and not far from the mouth.

Though the walls of these organs are variously tinted, they are not opaque, and, therefore, while not interfering materially with the view through the clearer substance of the tube, add greatly to its beauty. The yellowish throat, the stomach striped with dark brown, and the intestine, also dark brown, form a coloured axis, giving a lifelike warmth to the airy delicacy of the surrounding film.

We have seen by what strange methods the food is captured, but this is not more curious than the way in which it is digested. A throatful, for we cannot say mouthful, is no sooner admitted to the stomach than it is rolled up and down from one end to the other with great violence. The walls of this organ take on a circular constriction, which pursues the morsel without intermission, forcing it first to one end and then back again to the other, from which it entered, until the particles are all crushed and reduced to a pulp. These violent convulsions also serve another purpose ; they squeeze the nutritious matter, resulting from digestion, out through the membranes of the stomach into the cavity of the tube and cell, where it becomes mingled with the blood, and is carried off to give health and strength to the body.

We have spoken of the plumes being withdrawn in one of the colonies, and, though it has been only casually mentioned, this habit is the greatest obstacle to the observer while endeavouring to study their form. If the table be shaken ever so lightly, every unfolded crown vanishes, and often half-an-hour or more elapses before continued quiet allures them forth.

All the finely proportioned transparent parts are balanced upon a fold of the wall of the tube, which is retained in its place inside of the cell by many muscles, like fine hairs, attached by one end to the fold, and by the other to the cell wall. A continuation of the fold-membrane carpets the whole interior of the cell, and to it are attached near the lower end the muscular fibres which drag the crown and the more delicate external parts into its shelter at the approach of danger. The muscles are arranged in great broad bands rising in two trunks, each one spreading out above into numerous smaller branches. These branches are attached to the stomach, throat and disc near the mouth, and one of them to the wall of the tube not far from the base of the veil. They are diaphanous, but their delicate aspect is no measure of their strength. They jerk the crown and outer tube within the cell quicker than the eye can follow them ; and it is a curious fact, that after the movement is completed and they are safely ensconced, the fibres are not content to rest, but still keep up a lively motion, writhing and twisting like bundles of minute worms.

The tentacles all the while lie gathered closely together in the sheath, formed for them by the tube, which has been doubled upon itself inside of the cell like the finger of a glove inverted within the empty palm. When once more ready to emerge, the opening of the cell, which has been contracted by a circular band of muscle, like the mouth of a bag drawn up with a string, relaxes and permits the ends of the tentacles to protrude. These warily search for the cause of the previous alarm, and, if no hostile movements betray the presence of an enemy, the whole bundle slowly and cautiously follows, halts a moment, and then confidently unfolds its circlet of sentient threads. The polyzoon reasons from the impression made upon these feelers, and cannot be induced to expose itself until thoroughly satisfied, by their exquisite sense of touch, that no danger lurks near its retreat.

Strange to say these plant-like creatures, singly mere animated pouches containing stomachs, show greater nervous sensibility than many more highly organised animals. They continually surprise us by actions which exhibit caution, fear, and anger to a remarkable extent, and imply a degree of complication in their relations, both social and physical, which the simplicity of the organisation, and the limited sphere of its exercise render doubly interesting to the philosophical observer.—*American Naturalist*, April, 1867.

FUNGI AS FOOD.

THE Mouceron may well be placed at the head of our list, as it is one of the earliest and the best of the Mushroom tribe. It usually appears the first week in May on Grass downs, and in poorer meadows growing in rings which vary in size to more than 30 yards in diameter, as we have seen on Salisbury Plain. At this season no other "fairy ring" Agaric has made its appearance, so that it is next to impossible to confound it with any other species. It occurs plentifully in the meadows in front of the Agricultural College at Cirencester, and is the one upon which Professor Way experimented for his paper on Fairy Rings, though the species was erroneously referred to as the A. Georgii.

While at the College I was much interested in the subject, and yearly watched the coming of the Fungus with some anxiety, and seldom for as many as fifteen years was it later in making its appearance than the end of the second week in May, its most usual time being the first week. I soon saw that the species was the A. prunulus, so well described by Dr. Badham, being identical with the Italian plant of which he quaintly observes that little baskets of the earlier examples are sent as "presents to lawyers and fees to medical men," and that its Italian name of Fungi de Genoa denotes superior excellence, as with our Kentish Cherries, Battersea Asparagus, &c.; and further, that in the dried state it is sold at Italian warehouses at the enormous rate of 6d. per ounce. Seeing, then, that it was described as so good, we procured a dish, and got them cooked for the Professor's table, and, as in the case of the burnt pig so admirably described by Charles Lamb, the perfume was so agreeable, that the whole College was seduced into eating them; the students gathered them, and prevailed on the cook to send them up for supper; and so plentiful were they that enough were gathered for near upon 100 people, all whom ate of them heartily without a single case of indigestion.

In 1849 the Cotteswold Naturalists' Club May Meeting was fixed for Swindon Station; to this I took a basket of this A. prunulus, which were there cooked for breakfast, and in such perfection that the tempting smell wooed all to partake of them, though for the first time in their lives—all except myself, who was so busy making tea that the dish was emptied before that important process was over. I afterwards learned that at this establishment was an Italian cook, who, upon seeing my funguses, gave vent to his joy in the kitchen, and went into rhapsodies upon "verdant Italy."

From this time the members of the Club and others in Gloucestershire and elsewhere amongst my old pupils, ate this Fungus freely. I know of no better way to cook them than with a little butter, pepper, and salt, to grill them like the common Mushroom; or they may be fried with thin slices of bacon. A lady friend of mine once directed some to be stewed; how the process was performed I cannot say, but the result was that the Fungus had the appearance of bits of soddened leather breeches; and so it is to be feared that the difference between the provider of meat and of cooks, will cause the party who thus tried to partake of them to consider them mere toadstools as long as they live.

The Champignon is also a fairy ring species, making its appearance from August to October, and even until near Christmas in mild weather. It is common on lawns and in pastures and sometimes occurs in clusters on banks. Its rings are usually small, but, as I have this year seen, are so thick that many pounds may be gathered in a small space of time; and the Rev. M. J. Berkeley says of it no more than I have constantly experienced:—"When of a good size and quickly grown, it is perhaps the best of all Fungi for the table, whether carefully fried, or stewed with an admixture of finely minced herbs, and a minute portion of garlic. It is, at the same time, tender and easy of digestion: and when its use is known, and character ascertained, no species may be used with less fear. It is so common in some districts that bushels may be gathered in a day." They are exquisite if served on buttered toast with game, or poultry of all kinds.

The Common Mushroom is so well-known that, in spite of all that may be said to the contrary, I have never known the veriest bumpkin make a mistake in regard to it. Its flavour is so rich that all classes of people in this country esteem it as a rare "dainty dish even " to set before a king," and in its favour, except with a few, all other Funguses are cast aside. It is, however, a curious fact that it is despised on the Continent, so much so as not to be permitted to enter the fungus market. I recollect questioning the Prince of Canino on this matter, at one of the meetings of the British Association, when he informed me that it really was a poisonous species; and that it is so with some people, perhaps in peculiar conditions of the digestive system, I can fully confirm.

Few amongst us but have noticed towards autumn the ominous newspaper paragraph— "Poisoned by Toadstools." Now in some of these cases I have inquired into the species, and never did I detect an error; but take an example of the present season: A farmer and his wife partook heartily of Mushrooms for their supper, of which I found the former had taken the "lion's share." He thought himself dying in the night, as he supposed from eating toadstools, but in this case I not only ascertained that his fungus was the best variety of this Mushroom, but I partook of them with great relish, as his wife had done, without any ill-effects. I conclude then with regard to this fungus that it should always be taken with moderation, and only during the period that its gills preserve their fresh pink hue. The smaller pickled "buttons" are always good, and I have never heard of ill-effects from them.—J.B., *Gardeners' Chron.*, May 4th.

THE STICKLEBACK.

The Stickleback is one of our commonest British fishes, and is known in different parts of England under the names of tittlebat, pricklefish, and sharplin. It belongs to the vast order of the spine-finned fishes.

It is a most bold and lively little fish, hardly knowing fear, pugnacious to an absurd degree, and remarkably interesting in its habits. Even more voracious than the perch, it renders great service in keeping within due bounds the many aquatic and terrestrial insects which, although performing their indispensable duties in the world, are so extremely prolific, that they would render the country uninhabitable were they allowed to increase without some check.

Any one can catch a stickleback without rod, float, or even hook. All that is needful is to repair to the nearest streamlet, armed with a yard or two of thread and a walking-stick. Thin twine will answer very well instead of the thread, and even the stick is not absolutely needed. Having proceeded, thus equipped, to the bank of the stream, a worm may be picked out of the ground, tied by the middle to the thread, and thrown quite at random into the water.

The sticklebacks will not be in the least frightened by the splash, but rather rejoice in it, as calling their attention to food. In a moment the worm will be the centre of a contending mass of little fishes, rolling over and over, struggling to the utmost of their power, and entirely hiding the worm from sight. Now let the angler quickly lift the bait out of the water, swing it on shore, and he will almost certainly find that he has captured two sticklebacks, one hanging to each end of the worm and retaining its hold so perseveringly, that it can hardly be induced to relinquish its gripe. This process may be repeated at pleasure, and as the sticklebacks never seem to learn wisdom, a large store may soon be accumulated. This is a good way of stocking an aquarium, as the strongest and liveliest fish are sure to be caught first.

"I have caught them," writes Mr. Wood, in his invaluable "Natural History," "by hundreds in a common butterfly-net, by the simple stratagem of lowering the net into the water dangling the worm over the ring, and by degrees lowering the worm and raising the net until I had the whole flock within the meshes." Mr. Wood continues: "Should my reader be disposed to place his newly-captured specimens in an aquarium, he must make up his mind that they will fight desperately at first, and until they have satisfactorily settled the championship of the tank their intercourse will be of the most aggressive character. Never were such creatures to fight as the sticklebacks, for they will even go out of their way to attack anything which they think may possibly offend them, and they have no more hesitation in charging at a human being than at one of their own species. I have known one of these belligerent fish make repeated dashes at my walking-stick, knocking his nose so hard against his inanimate antagonist, that he inflicted a perceptible jar upon it, and, in spite of the blows which his nose must have suffered, returning to the combat time after time with undiminished spirit. These combats are most common about the breeding season, when every adult stickleback challenges every other of his own sex, and they do little but fight from morning to evening. They are as jealous as they are courageous, and will not allow another fish to pass within a certain distance of their home without darting out and offering battle."

Any one may see these spirited little combats by quietly watching the inhabitants of a clear streamlet on a summer day. The two antagonists dart at each other with spears in rest, snap at each other's gills or head, and retain their grasps with the tenacity of a bulldog. They whirl round and round in the water, they drop, feint, attack, and retreat with astonishing quickness, until one confesses himself beaten, and makes off for shelter, the conqueror snapping at its tail, and inflicting a parting bite.

"Then is the time to see the triumphant little creature in all the glory of his radiant apparel; for with his conquest he assumes the victor's crown; his back glows with shining green, his sides and head are glorious with gold and scarlet, and his belly is silvery white. It is a little creature certainly, but even among the brilliant inhabitants of the southern seas, a more gorgeously coloured fish could hardly be found. If the conqueror stickleback could only be enlarged to the size of a full grown perch or roach, it would excite the greatest admiration. It is curious that the vanquished antagonist loses in brilliance as much as the conqueror has gained; he sneaks off ignominiously after his defeat, and hides himself, dull and sombre, until the time comes when he too may conquer in fight, and proudly wear the gold and scarlet insignia of victory."

These struggles are not only for mastery, but are in so far praiseworthy, that they are waged in defence of home and family.

As a rule, fishes display but little architectural genius, their anatomical construction debarring them from raising any but the simplest edifice. A fish has but one tool, its mouth, and even this instrument is of very limited capacity. Still, although the nest which a fish can make is necessarily of a slight and rude character, there are some members of that class which construct homes which deserve the name; and the sticklebacks certainly furnish the best instances of fish architecture.

They make their nests of the delicate vegetation that is found in fresh water, and will carry materials from some little distance in order to complete the home. They do not, however, range to any great extent, because they would intrude upon the preserve of some other fish, and be ruthlessly driven away.

When the male stickleback has fixed upon a spot for his nest, he seems to consider a certain area around as his own especial property, and will not suffer any other fish to intrude within its limits. His boldness is astonishing; for he will dash at a fish of ten times his size, and, by dint of his fierce onset and his bristling spears, drive the enemy away. Even if a stick be placed within the sacred circle, he will dart at it, repeating the assault as often as the stick may trespass upon his domains. Within this limit, therefore, he must seek materials for his nest, as he can hardly move for six inches beyond it without intruding upon the grounds of another fish. This right of property only seems to extend along the banks and a few inches outwards, the centre of the stream or ditch being common property. Along the bank, however, where vegetation is most luxuriant, there is scarcely a foot of space that is not occupied by some stickleback, and jealously guarded by him.

Although the nests of the stickleback are plentiful enough, they are not so familiar to the public as might be expected—principally because they are very conspicuous; and few of the uninitiated would know what they were, even if they were pointed out. Being of such very delicate materials, and but loosely hung together, they will not retain their form when removed from the water, but fall together in an undistinguishable mass, like a coil of tangled thread that had been soaked in water for a few weeks.

The materials of which the nest is made are extremely variable, but they are always constructed so as to harmonize with the surrounding objects, and thus to escape ordinary observation. Sometimes it is made of bits of grass which have been blown into the river, sometimes of straws, and sometimes of growing plants. The object of the nest is evident enough when the habits of the stickleback are considered. As is the case with many other fish, there are no more determined destroyers of stickleback eggs than the sticklebacks themselves; and the nests are evidently constructed for the purpose of affording a resting-place for the eggs until they are hatched. If a few of these nests be removed from the water in a net, and the eggs thrown into the stream, the sticklebacks rush at them from all sides, and fight for them like boys scrambling for half-pence. The eggs are very small, barely the size of dust-shot, and are yellow when first placed in the nets but deepen in colour as they approach maturity.

Sometimes the stickleback becomes rather eccentric in its architecture, and builds in very curious situations. Mr. Couch, the well-known ichthyologist, mentions a case where a pair of sticklebacks had made their nests "in the loose end of a rope, from which the separated strands hung out about a yard from the surface, over a depth of four or five fathoms, and to which the materials could only have been brought, of course in the mouth of the fish, from a distance of about thirty feet. They were formed of the usual aggregation of the finer sorts of green and red seaweed, but they were so matted together in the hollow formed by the untwisted strands of the rope, that the mass constituted an oblong ball, of nearly the size of the fish, in which had been deposited the scattered assemblage of spawn, and which was bound into shape with a thread of animal substance, which was passed through and through in various directions, while the rope itself formed an outside covering to the whole."—*Our Own Fireside.*

HEAT OF THE SUN.

YOU will find in Herschel's Astronomy an account of the curious speculations which have been made as to the generation of heat in the sun, and also some calculations of the amount of heat which it sends out in any given time. One is that each square yard of surface gives out every hour rather more than would be got by burning six tons of coal, and from that you may deduce the following calculation. Six tons of coal weigh about as much as seven cubic yards of the sun's average substance; that is, if the sun were a great coal he would have to burn down seven yards an hour to give out the heat that he does, or thirty-five miles deep would be burnt off him in a year, which is about a 4,000th part of his whole bulk. The consequence is that the sun would have been burnt away into ashes, which would burn no more (though all his weight would remain there) in 4,000 years. We may be quite sure then that the sun's heat is not kept up by the burning of his own substance, at any rate. Another mode of keeping up the sun's heat has lately been imagined, which is remarkable for its ingenuity, if not for its probability. It is that the heat is due to a constant shower of meteoric stones falling all round the sun with the velocity they would fall with, if they once got near enough for his attraction to overpower their velocity in another direction. You may soon satisfy yourself that blows will produce heat by holding a nail in your finger while you hammer it well on an anvil, in fact, it can be hammered hot enough to light a match. It is calculated that if stones as heavy as granite fell all over the sun twelve feet thick in a year, with the greatest possible velocity (384 miles a second) from the sun's attraction, they would maintain the actual heat; or if they fell with the more probable velocity of small planets dragged out of their orbits sideways into the sun, or 270 miles a second, 24 feet of thickness a year would be required; and as granite is about two and a half times as heavy as the average matter of the sun, that would be equal to an addition of a mile to the sun's diameter every fifty years, or an increase of the sun's weight or mass by about a 7,000th part in the 2,000 years since tolerably accurate astronomical observations began to be recorded. And that is enough to have shortened the year by more than half-an-hour, according to the law by which the length of the year depends on the sun's mass and distance. But the year has not shortened, for even the four seconds mentioned are no shortening of the absolute revolution of the earth, but only a slow increase of precession of the equinoxes. This last objection certainly would fail so far as the earth is concerned, but would still hold as to Mercury and Venus if the whole store of meteors, or little planets, or asteroids which fall in the sun, is equally scattered round the sun within the orbit of the earth, because then the attraction of the meteors and sun together, or bodies outside them all, is the same as if they were concentrated in the sun. Accordingly, it is next supposed that this store of meteors is a certain nebulous and faintly luminous mass called the zodiacal light, sometimes looking like the milky way which surrounds the sun in the form of a lens or very flat spheroid, extending nearly or quite as far as the orbit of the earth. Then it is assumed that a sufficient number of the asteroids are continually missing their way (as we may say) and getting dragged into the sun and swallowed up for food to maintain his heat by their concussion. The cause of their so missing their way is imagined to be a certain resisting medium called æther, which there really is reason to believe fills all space, and must in time gradually contract the orbit of everything which moves in it. Not that there is the least evidence of any solid body in the universe having yet been at all affected in its orbit by such resisting medium, though one comet is believed to have had its period shortened in that way. You will see how extremely unlike comets are to granite or meterotic stones in density. Nor do the comets themselves, though very sensitive to disturbance by reason of their lightness, appear to be ever disturbed by passing right through that mass of zodiacal light, about 180,000,000 miles wide, full of real or supposed meteors or asteroids. The crossing of two streams of meteors by the earth every August and November, gives no help to the theory of the sun being supplied from a store within the earth's orbit. Those are revolving round the sun in periods not very different from the earth's. Every now and then there have been great flashes of light in the sun, which may possibly have come from some such concussion. Otherwise there are no visible indications of this rain of stones upon the sun, but perhaps that could hardly be expected, for if a whole year's supply came in one piece, it would be smaller than the moon, which could not be seen at that distance in the brightness of the sun. In this state of things it is not surprising that the meteoric hypothesis is not yet accepted by astronomers as the real explanation of the sun's heat, though no more probable one has been invented.

Leaving these speculations into unknown causes, Sir J. Herschel gives us another measure which has been experimentally obtained of the quantity of the sun's light and heat by himself and others, viz., that the light of any piece of his surface is 146 times greater than that of an equal surface of lime under the oxy-hydrogen flame, which gives the most intense light and heat we can make, and that the heat is enough to melt fourteen yards thick of ice laid all over the surface of the sun in a minute. From this you may easily calculate that that shell of ice round the sun would be about three-fifths of the size of the earth, and, therefore, the whole heat of the sun is enough to melt an earth of ice in less than two minutes; and it would boil all that water in two minutes more and turn it all into steam in a quarter of an hour from the time it was first applied to the ice. Of course the earth receives only a very small part of all the heat sent off by the sun. Indeed, less than the 2,000-millionth part, all the planets together only a 227-millionth. So although we have so much difficulty in finding out how the sun's heat is kept up, he can afford to waste (as far as we know) many million times as much as all his satellites can use. The earth receives as much heat in a year as would melt 100 feet thick of ice, or boil 66 miles deep of water all over the globe.—*Denison's Astronomy Without Mathematics.*

ORDEAL BEAN OF CALABAR.

THE Calabar ordeal bean, *Physostigma venenosum* of Professor Balfour, comes to us, as its name intimates, from Calabar, a name by which Europeans designate a small but influential tribe of negroes inhabiting the left bank of the Old Calabar River, which flows into the Bight of Biafra, west coast of Africa, immediately to the north of the island of Fernando Po. By the natives of Calabar the bean is called *esere*—has long been known to them, and has long been used by them as an ordeal, for the purpose of detecting and extirpating the superstitious crime of witchcraft.

The plant from which the beans are obtained is a *climber*, attaining often to very considerable dimensions, and frequently found growing on the banks of the river, at the water's edge, where it climbs the overhanging trees, almost entirely masking their foliage with its own rich festoons. About the month of August it makes an abundant display of pretty pink and white papilionaceous flowers, of which, however, comparatively few come to maturity. The fruit which is ripe in November is a pod not unlike that of our own horsebeans, containing rarely three, commonly one or two beans. On the 29th October, 1862, rather too early in the season, perhaps, I gathered the fruit of two considerable plants, one of them having a stem an inch and a half or two inches in diameter, and at its lower part towards the root so twisted upon itself as to simulate a cable of three or our inches in diameter. From the first of these plants 230 pods were procured, representing about 170 clusters of flowers, and yielding exactly 375 beans. From the other plant the number of pods obtained was 261, representing at the same average about 190 clusters of flowers, and yielding exactly 430 beans. These beans when gathered were still full of moisture, nearly as large again as the dry bean, of a dark grey colour—not the dark chocolate brown which they ultimately acquire—and they averaged in weight 54 beans to the pound.

The natives of Calabar obtain their supply from the shores of the river, where the beans are cast up in sufficient quantity to serve their purpose. In former days every free man of the least consequence in his village kept a stock in hand, so as to be able to contribute his quota as occasions of public trial by the ordeal might require; or to test the loyalty of suspected wives or slaves of his own; or even in case of his being threatened with a public trial, to put himself quietly to the proof, with proper remedies at hand, so as to obtain a prognosis that might encourage him to face the ordeal with hopes of an honourable acquittal, or else warn him in time to flee from certain and ignominious death. And yet it is a curious fact, that hardly any of these people know anything at all of the plant; indeed, one may safely venture to say that none of them are able to identify the plant in new situations, except by the aid of the fruit.

According to Dr. Fraser, of the Edinburgh University, who has written on the subject, the dry bark of the plant is quite harmless, though the sap which exudes from it when a fresh part is wounded, is first astringent and then acrid to the taste. The leaves also are quite harmless. Goats devour them greedily without any deleterious effects ensuing.

In publicly administering the Calabar bean as an ordeal, it is commonly given both by the mouth and in the form of a clyster. The suspected person has some entire beans handed to him, which he is compelled to eat up in this condition. Meanwhile, others are bruised in a mortar or on a slab, and being well mixed with water, one part is taken as a draught and the rest administered as an enema. If, after vomiting and purging, when the ordeal has been given in both forms, the person recovers, he is declared to be innocent and harmless, if not he is pronounced guilty, and the community congratulates itself on having thus avenged past and prevented future mischief.

It would be very gratifying indeed to be able to say, though it were only now after the presence of missionaries amongst them for some twenty years, that the negroes of Calabar have quite abandoned this stupid and most fatal custom—a custom by which formerly hundreds of lives were sacrificed annually, and by which many still occasionally perish.—*Dr. E. Watson in the Edinburgh Medical Journal for May,* 1867.

Wild Tribes of India.

The most remarkable of all the wild tribes of India are those inhabiting the mountain-range of Southern India, well known as the Nilgharries, a Sanskrit compound which signifies "Blue Mountains." The Nilgharries lie between the tenth and eleventh degrees of latitude, embrace an area of about six hundred square miles, contain plateaus, some of which attain the elevation of from five thousand to seven thousand feet, while the highest mountain peak is eight thousand seven hundred feet above the sea-level.

The inhabitants of the range consist of five different tribes, four of which have each their own separate and independent language, while the fifth, the most numerous and the most industrious, speaks the Cenarese tongue, that of their nearest civilised neighbours; a fact from which we may be disposed to consider them as stranger immigrants. It is this tribe alone which has adopted the manners, institutions, and religion of the Brahmins. All the five tribes possess the usual features and bodily form of the Hindus of Southern India; but this character is most remarkably pronounced in the small tribe called the Todars, whose number is computed not to exceed six hundred, and who occupy the highest of the mountain uplands. They are herdsmen, as their name, which is the corruption of a Tamil word having this meaning, implies; their only cattle being the buffalo, the milk of which forms their chief ailment. All European observers agree in considering the Todars as a handsome race, above the average stature of Hindus, with regular features and elevated countenances—in short, Greeks with black skins. But the same account might be very faithfully given of several other Hindu peoples; such, for example, as the Seiks and the Cashmirians.

The believers in the Aryan theory are much puzzled by the Todars. They ought, were they aborigines, to have, according to the theory, Negroid features; but, on the contrary, they happen to have European, and therefore, in despite of their small numbers, their low social status, and their geographical position in a remote corner of India difficult of access, they pronounce them to be a race of foreign Caucasian conquerors, without being able even to guess of whom they came, where they came from, or when they settled in the upper plateau of the isolated Nilgharri mountains.

It is an opinion very generally entertained by Indian ethnologists, that the races which they suppose to be the aborigines of India partake of a negro character, in contradistinction to the civilised people of the low lands; but this is a notion for which I am satisfied there is no ground whatever. Throughout the continent of India—indeed, throughout the entire continent of Asia—no Negro or Negroid race has ever been found to exist, the only exception being a few pigmy Negroes in the interior of the Malay peninsula, which is rather a portion of the neighbouring archipelago than of the Asiatic continent. Wherever Negritos or Negroid races really exist, their presence is unmistakably pronounced, as in the case of the Andaman islands, in the mountains of the Malay peninsula, in several of the Philippine islands, and in the long range of islands which extends from New Guinea to the Fiji groupe in the Southern Pacific. Everywhere their peculiar physical character is clearly indicated. Sometimes they have whole islands to themselves, as in the instances of the Andamans, New Guinea, and some of the islands of the Southern Pacific; but even when they are joint occupants with other races, as in the Malayan peninsula and the Philippines, they dwell isolated in the mountains, never intermixing with the fairer and more highly endowed races their neighbours. All, it will be seen, that so careful and faithful an observer as Colonel Dalton can say of his most ill-favoured race of mountaineers, the Oraons, is that he has "seen amongst them heads that in woolly crispness of the hair completed the similitude of the Oraons to the Negro." He finds no such resemblance in the better looking Moondah tribe. "When," says he, "it varies from the Aryan or Caucasian type, it appears to me rather to merge into the Mongolian than the Negro." No doubt such heads and features as Colonel Dalton describes would be found among the Kols; but they are also to be found in every race of man. Thus Colonel Dalton would certainly find occasionally among his own countrymen heads and faces that, with the addition of a black skin, would bear a considerable resemblance to an African Negro, and other heads which, with a yellow skin superadded, might readily be mistaken for Mongols. Rules are not to be deduced from exceptions.—*Paper read before the Ethnological Society.*

Ants.

The females, who usually occupy a special part of the colony, seem, contrary to the views of those who slander the gentler sex, to live together in the most perfect harmony. In course of time they lay a number of extremely minute, white, spherical eggs, and with this operation end their duties to the colony. To the workers is consigned the important labour of incubating the eggs, and rearing and nursing the young. They take charge of the ova the moment they are laid, and remove them to chambers specially arranged for their reception. A certain amount of warmth is required for the development of the eggs into larvæ, and this is procured by removing the ova in fine weather from the cells, in which they have been detained, into the open air. There they are exposed to the sun's rays—care being taken that too high a temperature is not imparted to them—for some time, and then the ever-active workers remove them to the nurseries. It is this process we see going on in summer time when we disturb an ant-hill. Myriads of the busy little insects may be seen rushing about laden with little white grain-like bodies, of which they take the greatest care, and eventually succeed in carrying beneath the surface. These white, grain-like bodies are the larvæ, and as some of the earlier observers fancied they were grains of cereals, seeds, and such like, the ant acquired a reputation for thriftiness and providence which it certainly does not deserve. In about fifteen days the eggs are hatched, and the larvæ make their appearance as little whitish, semi-transparent, ovoid worms. They possess a head and body, the latter being divided into a number of rings or segments which are unprovided with feet. Their mouth is a sort of retractile proboscis, in which we may see the rudiments of the future mandibles, but at this period of their existence it is only employed for sucking. They feed upon the peculiar honey-like fluid provided for them by the workers, who prepare it in their stomachs, and then disgorge it for the nourishment of the young. The most sedulous attention is paid by the worker-nurses to the larvæ, the latter, as we have already stated, being constantly removed from their underground chambers to the outer surface of the ant-hill, where they receive the genial influence of the sun, and thus further metamorphosis. The nurses, too, advance this phenomenon by gently irritating, rubbing, and distending the skin of the larva with their palpi. Soon this metamorphosis takes place. The little larva spins its temporary greyish-yellow silken coffin, and becomes a nymph, or pupa. Gradually beneath the veil under which Nature conceals her mysterious operations, the larva is transformed into a nearly perfect ant, the proboscis disappears, and is replaced by a set of horny jaws, the skin changes its colour, assumes a reddish-brown tint, powerful and strangely organized limbs are formed, and the head and appendages increase in complexity of structure. These singular changes all take place, and yet the creature remains motionless and death-like, and when the metamorphosis is complete, the nurses once more commence their labours. They now tear away the curtain and disclose the perfect insect or *imago*, as it is scientifically termed. Nor do they cease their tender exertions. They still continue to watch over the welfare of the new-born, till they are able to take their own place in their own little sphere of existence.

THUNDERSTORMS.

A fearful hailstorm passed over Wakefield on Monday night, May 6th, a little past eight o'clock. It was preceded by singularly vivid and beautiful lightning and by rumbling thunder. The downfall of hail lasted only about ten minutes, but with such impetuosity as has never been remembered. Hailstones the diameter of an inch were far from uncommon, and after the storm was over the ground was covered with others the size of marbles.

At sunset on Friday, May 10th, and at daybreak on Saturday two thunderstorms broke over London, which, although they lasted a short time, were very violent. About seven o'clock on Friday evening the sky became very dark towards the south and west, and was suddenly lighted up by vivid flashes of lightning. They were followed by heavy peals of thunder and gusts of wind and rain. Between eight and nine the storm had cleared away, but a dark cloud stood out in the north-west against a clear sky, and was lighted up at intervals with the most dazzling flashes of sheet lightning. Towards the east and south, where the sky remained cloudy, lightning was also visible, and slight peals of thunder were heard throughout the night. The second storm, which was also accompanied with wind and rain, broke out about five o'clock in the morning of Saturday. The lightning was very brilliant, and was followed by several frightful crashes of thunder; but it does not appear to have caused any serious damage.

In Buckinghamshire the storm of Friday evening was very violent. The goods station at Winslow was partly unroofed by the wind, and 86 panes of glass were broken by the hailstones, some of which, when measured by the police, proved to be five inches in circumference. Similar damage was done at the Swanbourne and Claydon stations. The storm extended to Aylesbury, while it blew down trees and walls and flooded the streets. But it was in the vicinity of Buckingham that most damage was done. In Castle-street and High-street panes were broken in every window.

At Cambridge the storm commenced about eleven o'clock on Friday, and continued at intervals during the day and night. The lightning was very vivid, and many of the by-roads were rendered impassable by the floods. At Barrington, Cambridgeshire, a labourer named Patman was struck by the lightning and killed. He was in a field ploughing with his master's son and four labourers, and when the storm came on, about one o'clock, they all took shelter under an adjacent straw stack. One flash of lightning rendered them all insensible. The others, upon reviving, went to their companion Patman, and found him lifeless, with his shoes, leggings, and hat torn to atoms. He was removed to his lodgings in the village, where an inquest was held in the evening. The deceased was a widower, fifty-six years of age, and had been in Mr. Coleman's employ for about forty years. A boy at work in the same field had the upper portion of one of his shoes cut clean out by the lightning, and a piece of flesh, about the size of a shilling, from under his great toe. A horse was killed by the lightning at Walton's coprolite diggings, near Coldham's-lane, Cambridge.

On Friday evening a sharp storm visited Newcastle and the lower reaches of the Tyne. The lightning struck West House, St. Anthony's, the residence of Mr. Cook, chymical manufacturer. A huge stack of chimneys was knocked down and fell through the roof. It broke the furniture in the rooms through which it passed, and a little girl who was sitting in the drawing-room had one of her shoulders dislocated. Considerable damage was done. Rain fell heavily in the north on Saturday, and in the evening the wind got round from the north and blew somewhat cool.

New Books.

[*Our limited space must of necessity compel us to give but very short notices of new books, but they will perhaps serve as a guide as to what books our readers may ask for at their libraries.*]

Light; its Influence on Life and Health. By Forbes Winslow, M.D. London: Longmans and Co.

In his preface, Dr. Winslow says, the object of this work is to demonstrate the inestimable value of light as an hygienic agent, and to analytically examine its physiological influence in the development of vital phenomena as manifested in the animal and vegetable kingdom. How well the author has fulfilled his task, will be best seen by reading the volume. The reader need not fear any dry disquisition upon the subject. The work from beginning to end is cheerful and lively, and full of information of the greatest value and interest, gathered with great care from a variety of sources.

The first chapter opens with the origin of light, its effects upon the animal and vegetable kingdom. As to its effects upon mankind, we find that where light is not permitted to permeate are to be found bodily deformities, intellectual deterioration, crime, disease, and early death. The total exclusion of the sun's beams from the body (says Dr. Winslow) induces the severer types of green sickness and other anæmic conditions depending upon an impoverished and disordered state of the blood, the general health becomes vitiated, and specific diseases generated—these consequences have been observed in those who labour by night and sleep by day, such as bakers, police-constables, compositors, and more especially amongst miners. We have some facts as to the action of solar light on the discoloration of the skin. Black, brown, and copper-coloured skins are observed amongst those who reside in tropical climates in proportion to the intensity of the solar light, and the degree to which the body is exposed to its influence. It is not perceived amongst those who live in colder regions. Nearer to the pole it assumes a browner cast, as amongst the Laplanders, Esquimaux, and Greenlanders. It is noticeable that the African negroes who live for many months of the year in the shades of the forest lose some of the intense blackness. It is said that the black colour of the negro is less permanent than red or olive tints; the children of copper-coloured parents are so from the moment of birth, whereas with blacks it is six, eight, or ten months before the dark pigment is fully secreted; in some cases the pigment cells are not matured, and then we have what are called spotted negroes; in illness too it may be entirely absorbed, and a white pigment cell developed in its place, thus affording a remarkable illustration of a black person suddenly bleached into a white man. In the "Transactions of the Royal Society" is an account of a woman whose left shoulder, arm, and hand were as black as an African negro's, whilst all the rest of the skin was perfectly white. Upon animals the exclusion of the solar beam produces organic alterations in the visual organs. Certain animals whose natural hue is white, if bred and brought up in darkness become completely altered in texture and colour. The cockroach in its normal state is intensely black; if this insect is taken at an early stage of its existence and carefully reared in darkness, instead of assuming an inky hue, when it arrives at full growth becomes nearly white; the larvæ of most insects that burrow in the earth, plants, or animals, are white from the same cause. Of its influence upon vegetable life some curious facts are recorded. In the spring a potato was left behind in a cellar where some tools had been kept during the winter, and which had only a small aperture at the upper part of one of its sides; the potato which lay in the opposite corner shot out a runner, which first ran twenty feet along the ground, then crept up along the wall and so through the opening by which light was admitted. Some flowers are seen inclining their flowers towards the quarter of the heavens in which the sun is shining. If a leafy shoot of any plant is bent down without injury so as to reverse the usual position of the face of the leaves, the latter will twist upon their petioles and turn their upper surfaces to the light. Plants trained in a dark recess will turn their growing point backwards on the older part of the stem, also twisting round to face the light; plants nurtured in darkness never acquire their natural colour; the rich colour of seaweed found on the surface of the water is owing to its free exposure to light. The second part treats of the lunar ray, the third on the alleged influence of the moon on the insane, the fourth finishes with the hygiene of light.

We have gathered these few notes together to give the reader some idea of the contents of the volume.

Astronomy without Mathematics. By Edmund Beckett Denison, LL.D., Q.C., F.R.A.S. London: Society for Promoting Christian Knowledge.

This is a third edition, considerably enlarged, and going deeper into the subject. The additions chiefly relate to meteors, nebulæ, and stars, the moon's acceleration and other disturbances, the tides and the calculations for Easter in all ages, and a fuller account of the methods of weighing the sun, moon, and planets. The chapter on telescopes has also been enlarged. In this little work the study of astronomy is made as easy as it can be made; and the sale of some 3,000 copies in little more than a year points out the fact that a really popularly-written scientific work is certain to prove a success.

Chemistry, Inorganic and Organic, with Experiments, and a Comparison of Equivalent and Molecular Formulæ. By Charles Loudon Bloxam. Churchill and Sons.

Undoubtedly one of the most useful works that has been issued for some time. The description of the elements and their compounds is given in a very clear and simple manner. Mr. Bloxam has adhered to the simple rule of explaining the chemical changes by symbols, representing the combining weights of the elements. In nearly every case the student is referred to an illustrative experiment, and is greatly aided by many excellent illustrations, displaying the apparatus employed and mode of manipulation.

At Home in the Wilderness. By John Keast Lord, F.Z.S., late Naturalist to the British North American Boundary Commission; author of "The Naturalist in Vancouver Island and British Columbia." Hardwicke, 192, Piccadilly.

Mr. J. K. Lord has here given us a capital little volume, which will be found to be of the greatest value as a hand-book for emigrants, and indeed for all, who whether for pleasure or business, are likely at any time to find themselves in the wilderness—nor are these the only ones who will derive benefit from a perusal—there are many hints and suggestions that will be found as valuable to the country gentleman as the traveller. It is nicely got up, well illustrated where requisite, and published at a price that will suit most pockets.

NEW PERIODICALS.

Routledge's Illustrated Natural History of Man in all Countries of the World. By the Rev. J. G. Wood, M.A., F.L.S., &c. With Illustrations by Wolfe, Zwecker, Keyl, Houghton, etc. Part I. Monthly. Price 1s.

This very handsome work is intended to form a companion to the well known and popular "Natural History" already published. It will treat of mankind geographically, commencing at the great southern points of the world, and proceeding northwards through each country. Abstract, ethnological, or anthropological theories will be avoided. The present part commences with a description of the great Kaffir race, and is extremely interesting. The following is a description of Goza, the well-known Zulu chief:—

He is one of the most powerful chiefs of the Zulu tribe, and can at any moment summon into the field his five or six thousand trained and armed warriors; yet in ordinary life he is not to be distinguished from the meanest of his subjects by any distinction of dress. An experienced eye would, however, detect his rank at a single glance, even though he were not clad in his "tails." He is fat—and none but chiefs are fat in Kaffirland; in fact none but chiefs have the opportunity, because the inferior men are forced to such constantly active employment, and live on such irregular nourishment, that they have no opportunity of accumulating fat.

But a chief has nothing whatever to do except to give his orders, and if those orders are within human capacity they will be executed. Tchaka once ordered his warriors to catch a lion with their unarmed hands, and they did it, losing of course many of their number in the exploit. The chief can eat beef and porridge all day long if he likes, and he mostly does like. Also he can drink as much beer as he chooses, and always has a large vessel at hand full of that beverage. Panda, the King of the Zulu tribes, was notable for being so fat that he could hardly waddle.

As to Goza, he is a wealthy man, possessing vast herds of cattle, besides a great number of wives, who as far as can be judged by their portraits are not beautiful, according to European ideas of beauty, but are each representatives of a considerable number of cows. He wields undisputed sway over many thousands of subjects, and takes tribute from them; yet he dresses on ordinary occasions like one of his own subjects, and his house is just one of the ordinary huts of which a village is composed. When he wishes to appear officially he alters his style of dress, and makes really a splendid appearance in all the pomp of barbaric magnificence. Also when he mixes with civilization he likes to be civilized in dress, and makes his appearance dressed as an Englishman in a silk hat, a scarlet coat, and jack boots, and attended in his rides by an aide-de-camp dressed in a white-plumed cocked hat and nothing else.

Pigeons, their Structure, Habits, and Varieties. By W. B. Tegetmeier, F.Z.S. Parts I. and II. London: Routledge and Sons.

This work is intended to give an account of the structure, habits, and food of the wild original of our domestic breeds; the consideration of the pigeon as a domestic animal, including characteristics of all the varieties, the practical management of the several breeds will be fully treated. It is beautifully illustrated in colours, drawn from life by Harrison Weir. The first and second parts contain pictures of eight different sorts—turbines, jacobites, nuns, swallows, fullbacks, fantails, blue brunswicks, and black priests. It will be completed in eight shilling parts, and when finished will form a very handsome volume similar to Mr. Tegetmeier's well-known poultry book.

The Laboratory. A Weekly Record of Scientific Research. Weekly. Price 6d.

FRENCH AND GERMAN WORKS.

Les Saisons, Etudes de la Nature. Par L. Hoefer. Paris and London: L. Hachette and Co.

In this work Dr. L. Hoefer has collected together, and published under the title *Les Saisons*, various natural-history sketches which came out in the *Cosmos*, the *Magasin Pittoresque*, and other popular scientific journals. It is of a strictly elementary character. Each of the four divisions forms, in its turn, two sections, which take the observer successively to the realms of astronomy and to those of natural history properly so called—the latter supplying observations for four different days.

L'Année Scientifique et Industrielle. Par L. Figuier. 11e Année. Paris and London: L. Hachette and Co.

A *résumé* of scientific literature for the year. The several items of astronomy, natural philosophy, meteorology, chemistry, nautical science, statistics, natural history, hygiene, and agriculture—the transactions of learned societies, and a very complete meteorological list—supply M. Figuier with ample materials for his useful volume.

Allgemeiner Missions-Atlas nach Originalquellen. Bearbeitet von Dr. R. Grundemann. Gotha: Perthes. London: Asher and Co.

A general atlas of missionary stations all over the world, with an accompanying text descriptive of their situation and present condition. It is one of the many valuable contributions for which science is indebted to missionary enterprise. The first part contains seven maps, comprising the western coast of Africa from the Gambia to the Gaboon.

L'Oiseau. Par J. Michelet. Hutième édition, illustrée de 210 vignettes sur bois, dessinée par H. Giacomelli: Librairie de L. Hachette et Cie. 1867.

This is the eighth edition of *L'Oiseau* by Michelet, illustrated by H. Giacomelli, whose ornamental designs in the columns of Doré's Bible have been favourably noticed. In the present work he has been particularly happy in his choice of subjects, and the reader will gaze with pleasure upon meadows, wayside brooks, and sunny cottage gardens, made more lively by the presence of some of the best known specimens of the feathered tribe.

Grottes et Cavernes. Par Ad Badin. (Bibliotheque des Merveilles). Paris and London: L. Hachette and Co.

An interesting work on the most celebrated grottos and caverns throughout the globe, giving a clear account of the natural and scientific phenomena which may be observed in them—stalactites, fossils, ice deposits, chemical formations, &c. Woodcuts are plentifully supplied, and are remarkable for their neatness and accuracy.

WORKS RECENTLY PUBLISHED—

The Management of Bees. By W. J. PETTITT. Second and enlarged edition, with a catalogue of the most modern and approved Hives and Bee-Houses. Copiously illustrated. 8vo, cloth gilt, 1s 6d. Dover: W. J. Pettitt, Snargate Apiary.

A Manual of British Butterflies and Moths. By H. T. Stainton, F.L.S. Containing Descriptions of nearly Two Thousand Species, interspersed with "readable matter," and above two hundred woodcuts, fifth edition, 2 vols, fcap. 8vo, cloth, 10s. John Van Voorst.

Brande's Dictionary of Science, Literature, and Art. Reconstructed by the Author and the Rev. G. W. Cox, M.A. 3 vols, 8vo, 63s. London: Longmans.

Ure's Dictionary of Arts, Manufactures, and Mines. Rewritten and enlarged by R. Hunt, F.R.S. With 2,000 woodcuts. 3 vols, £4 14s 6d. London: Longmans.

Holiday Excursions of a Naturalist., forming a Guide Book to the Natural History of the Inlands and Littorals. Crown 8vo, cloth, price 7s 6d. London: Robert Hardwicke, 192, Piccadilly.

Meetings of Learned Societies.

ROYAL HORTICULTURAL SOCIETY.

On Saturday, April 30, Dr. Masters continued his Lectures on "Plant Architecture;" the subject this day was "The Leaf and its Modifications." After alluding to the points of distinction between it and other organs, to its parts, and to the principal heads under which the exceeding numerous variations in its conformation might be grouped, the lecturer passed on to the consideration of the arrangement of the leaves on the stem and branches—a matter of more importance than the mere shape. The different ways in which the leaves emerge from or are attached to the stem and branches, were explained and illustrated. In all cases, whether the leaves are arranged in pairs, in whorls, or in spiral cycles, care seems to be taken that one leaf shall not interfere with the growth of its neighbours, so that in the case of two adjacent leaves, the one never completely overlaps the other, however crowded they may be, and in this manner every leaf has a fair chance of due exposure to light and air. The same end is sometimes attained by the development of a larger leaf at the base of a spiral cycle than elsewhere, so that the upper smaller leaves only partially overlap the larger one below. The lengthening of the stem between the leaves, and the consequent separation of these organs one from another, tends to the more free exposure of leaf surface; on the other hand where, as in the case of the House-leek, (*Sempervivum*), the stem is very short and contracted and the leaves numerous, the individual leaves are small and comparatively imperfectly developed. Here the number compensate for the diminished extent of surface in the case of separate leaves. The curious way in which the leaves are often bent so as to get out of one another's way, in cases where if they retained their original direction they must necessarily interfere with their neighbours, was also alluded to as offering another instance of the way in which the arrangement of these parts is subordinated to the offices they have to fulfil as the main organs of respiration, exhalation, and digestion, functions which demand free exposure to light and air for their due accomplishment. Where leaves have to perform the duties of protectors, as in the case of the scales of the leaf-bud, the outer portions of the flowers, &c., there is less need of a widely expanded surface, and the object is attained by the close approximation of a number of imperfect or rudimentary leaf-scales.

Saturday, April 27.—The last of the series of short lectures on "Plant Architecture" was given on this day, and was devoted to the consideration of "The Flower," the various parts of which were pointed out, some seeming to be useful for protection, or for attracting insects, while the stamins and pistils are exclusively devoted to the formation of the seed. The numerous forms which the flower assumes may partly be explained by reference to the principles upon which the leaves are arranged on the stem, as explained at a former lecture, the same principles holding good in the flower. If the parts of a flower are few and even in number, they are usually arranged in pairs, which cross one another or decussate as in the case of "opposite" leaves; the pairs of organs are in this case formed simultaneously, but if the number of parts in the flower be large, or if the number be *odd*, say 3 or 5, or some multiple of those numbers, then the arrangement is spiral, and the development successive. In both instances, as a rule, the organs are so placed as not to interfere with one another, and where, as in the case of Sabia, &c., the "law of alternation" is departed from and stamen stands before petal, petal before sepal, and so on, instead of one petal between two sepals, &c., it will be found that either there is great disproportion in the size of the organs, so that they scarcely impede one another at all, or else that the direction of the parts is different, one being erect, another reflected or bent out of the way, and so forth.

BOTANICAL SOCIETY OF EDINBURGH.

The Monthly Meeting of this Society was held on Thursday, 11th ult., Isaac Anderson-Henry, Esq., President, in the chair. The following communications were read:—1. "On Silicified Vegetable Structures from the Zambesi." By Dr. John Lowe, Lynn.—2. "On the Progress of Cinchona Cultivation in India." By an Indian Correspondent. Communicated by Professor Balfour.—3. "Notice of Cinchona Planting in the Kangra Valley." By William Coldstream, Esq., B.A.—4. "On New Zealand 'Carrageen.'" By W. Lauder Lindsay, M.D.—5. "On the Botany of the 'Jardin' of Mont Blanc." By Dr. Buchanan White.—In this communication the author gave an account of an excursion which he made to the "Jardin" on Mont Blanc, in September, 1866. He remarked:—"The height above the sea is between 9000 and 10,000 feet. A flock of ptarmigan seems to be the only feathered colonists of the place; while a few insects, including among others the common tortoiseshell butterfly (*Vanessa Urticæ*), one or two species of the genus Erebia, the larva of an Argynis, completed the zoological list. The flora has been several times investigated, and, among others, by Mr. Percy, who recorded the plants he found at a meeting of this Society. In a paper by Professor Martins in the Memoires for 1865 of the Academy of Sciences of Montpellier, the Phanerogamia he stated to be 87 in number; Musci, 16; Hepaticæ, 2; Lichens, 23—making a total of 128 plants. In my visit I found in flower 45 of the species given in Professor Martins's list, and 4 species not mentioned therein; one Fern, Allosorus crispus (not mentioned by him), and one species of Agaricus. The Mosses and Hepaticæ I have not yet examined, but of the former I have at least 26 species, and of the latter 3." The paper was illustrated by specimens of the plants collected, and photographs of the "Jardin."—6. "Notes on Grimmia subsquarrosa of Wilson's M.S." By Dr. Buchanan White.—7. "Note on the Occurrence of Buxbaumia indusiata in Aberdeenshire." By Professor Dickie.—8. "Extracts from Botanical Correspondence." By Mr. John Sadler.—9. "Report on the State of the Open-Air Vegetation in the Royal Botanic Garden." By Mr. M'Nab.—10. "Miscellaneous Communications." 1. Mr. Isaac Anderson Henry, Hay Lodge, exhibited a growing plant of Draba violacea, which he had raised from seeds transmitted to him by Dr. Jameson, of Quito. 2. Mr. R. M. Stark exhibited growing specimens of American plants in flower.

LINNEAN SOCIETY.

April 18.—G. Bentham, Esq., in the chair. Abbotts Smith, M.D.; and W. E. Williams, jun., Esq., were elected Fellows. The papers read were:—
1. "On the prevalence of Entozoa in the Dog, with remarks on their relation to Public Health." By T. S. Cobbold, M.D.—2. "Fungi Angolenses: a description of the Fungi collected by Dr. Fredrich Welwitsch in Angola during the years 1855-61." By Dr. Welwitsch and F. Currey, Esq.

On Wednesday, May 1st, the President gave a Soirée at Burlington House. Mr. A. Wallace, F.Z.S., etc., exhibited a case containing fourteen specimens of an eastern butterfly (*Kallim anachis*). The singularity of this butterfly consists in its exact similitude to a dead leaf, when the wings are folded and the insect at rest. To illustrate this, the butterflies are fastened to a spray, and thus represent its foliage, and so close, even to the minutest detail, is the resemblance to leaves, that the keenest eye can scarcely detect the difference, or say they are not leaves he is looking at. Major Owen, F.L.S., exhibited some exquisite specimens of Pteropoda, skimmed from the surface of mid ocean. Examples were shown obtained from the Indian Ocean, and South and North Atlantic Oceans, which were taken with a net towed after the ship. The forms of some of these singular and delicately fragile creatures, were beautiful beyond all power of description. Major Owen also exhibited some new microscopic forms of *Thalassicolla*. Mr. Leadbeater, F.L.S., exhibited some very admirable examples of bird stuffing. Mr. W. Rich, of Great Russell-street, showed a remarkably fine specimen of *Echinocrinus*, from the carboniferous limestone obtained at Clevedon, near Bristol. Also a case of shells (*Fusus*), showing how singularly alterations of form may arise from change of *habitat*. Mr. Stevens showed some good specimens of *Euplectella*; and a case of curious crabs, from Malden Island, South Pacific, were exhibited by Mr. H. Deane. Arranged on the side wall was a fine series of illustrations, about forty-three in number, of Cretaceous echinidæ, Liassic reptilia, Liassic corals, Silurian brachiopoda, trilobites, and recent corals, exhibited by the Rev. Thomas Wiltshire, F.L.S. Mr. Bull, F.R.H.S., exhibited a great variety of new and rare plants. Amongst the orchids we may specify *Anthurium Schertzerianum* a brilliant scarlet flower, with a kind of crumpled horn growing from its upper edge; *Uropedium Zindenii*, a most grotesque flower, having three of the petals in each flower extended to eighteen inches in length, and drooping like slender pennants from a mast-head during a dead calm; *Cypripedium villosum*, and *Sarracenia Drumundi*, as being singularly rare, grotesque in form, and as unlike each other, as they are unlike every other kind of flower. A plant of *Aucuba Japonica* was exhibited, curious, inasmuch as it had fertile seeds. The female plant has been long common, but the male has only been obtained very recently. Mr. Saunders, V.P.L.S., exhibited a series of very rare and certainly very lovely plants. A begonia (sp. *nov.*) peculiar for growing its flowers up the main stem; a very splendid orchid (*Saccoladium ampellaceum*) remarkable for the bright pink colour of its flowers.

Geological Society.

April 17th.—Sir Charles Lyell, Bart., M.A., F.R.S., Vice-President, in the chair. The following communication was read:—"On the Physical Structure of North Devon, and on the Palæontological Value of the Devonian Fossils." By Robert Etheridge, Esq., F.R.S., F.G.S., Palæontologist to the Geological Survey of Great Britain. The Lower, Middle, and Upper groups of sandstones and shales of West Somerset and North Devon were described in this paper as occurring in a regular and unbroken succession from north to south, namely, from the sandstones comprising the promontory of the Foreland, at the base, to the grits and slates, etc., overlaying the Upper Old Red Sandstone of Pickwell Down to the South. The author was unable to see any traces of a fault of sufficient magnitude to invert the order of succession, or that would cause the rocks of the Foreland at Lynton to be upon the same horizon as those south of a line of high ground that passes across the county from Morte Bay on the west to Wiveliscombe on the east. The Foreland grits and sandstones are overlain by the Lower or Lynton slates, and form a group equal in time to the Lower Old Red Sandstone of other districts, but deposited under purely marine conditions. The author then showed that above the Lower or Lynton slates there is an extensively developed series of red, claret-coloured, and grey grits, from 1500 to 1800 feet thick; these form a natural and conformable base to the Middle Devonian or Ilfracombe group. The highest beds, containing *Myalina* and *Natica*, insensibly pass into the gritty and calcareous slates of Combe Martin, Ilfracombe, etc.; this Middle group Mr. Etheridge unhesitatingly regarded as the equivalent of the Torquay and Newton Bushel series of South Devon. The author compared the whole of the Devonian fauna of Britain with that of the Rhine, Belgium, and France, by means of a series of Tables based upon the British types. These marine Devonian species were compared with those of the Old Red Sandstone proper, the Silurian, and Carboniferous, and analyses were made of all the classes, orders, genera, and species, with relation to the groups of rocks in which they occur—the result being the conclusion that the marine Devonian series, as a whole, constitutes an important and definite system.

At the Meeting on May 8th, Sir William Logan read a paper on new specimens of eozoon discovered by him; these specimens were from explorations made by the Canadian Geological Survey, and afforded Mr. Dawson who followed with a paper on the fossils recently obtained from the Laurentian rocks of Canada and on objections to the organic nature of eozoon, conclusive evidence of their organic character, opinions shared by Dr. Carpenter who also had the opportunity afforded him of their investigation, and of testing their organic nature by the long and accurate attention he has paid to such organisms with the microscope.

Royal Microscopic Society.

On Wednesday, April 24th, the Soirée of the above society was held at King's College; more than a thousand guests attended. Between two and three hundred instruments were shown in the different rooms. Mr. Baines detailed some of his African adventures, which were illustrated by himself and projected upon a screen by one of Hou's oxy-hydrogen lanterns. The evening passed away very pleasantly.

On May 8th, a very interesting communication from J. B. Sheppard, Esq., M.R.C.S., of Canterbury, was read by the Rev. J. B. Reade, "On an example of the production of a colour possessing remarkable qualities by the action of monads (or some other microscopic organisms) or organized substances." Mr. Sheppard recently found on submerged stones, in a pool in East Kent, some olive-coloured confervoid filaments, resembling those of oscillatoria or diatoms. Being unprepared with bottles or other collecting apparatus, he wrapped some of these fibres in paper which was greasy with the fat of some sandwitches provided for refreshment. On arriving at home, he was astonished to find the paper stained red and purple by gelatinous globules looking like coagulated blood, and that on placing these globules in water, the liquid became of a red, Magenta colour when the light was reflected from it, and of a lambent blue when viewed by transmitted light. He made a variety of experiments to ascertain whence the colour was derived. From an offensive odour arising from it (so powerful as to occasion headache and sickness), he was, at first, disposed to attribute it to decaying vegetable matter, but he at last satisfied himself that it was caused by the action of some form of animal life, such as vibrios or monads, on some form of soluble albumen. It was not attributable to the vibrios themselves, for they were colourless. The colouring matter can be separated from the animals which produce it; and it appears to be identical in its properties with the aniline colour known as "Magenta." Not the least remarkable circumstance connected with this solution is the spectrum it exhibits when submitted to the analysis of the micro-spectroscope. Mr. Browning pronounces it to be the most curious he has ever seen. A strong, dark band appears between the red and orange, with a trace, also, of the characteristic band of the blood spectrum. Several important subjects for future thought and investigation are evidently involved in this singular discovery.

ETHNOLOGICAL SOCIETY.

At the meeting held of this Society, Mr. Crawfurd, president, in the chair, a short and interesting paper was read by Dr. Collingwood on "Some Natives dwelling in the North-eastern end of the Island of Formosa." In the walled village called Kibalon, in the Sano Harbour, he had an opportunity of comparing these natives with some Chinese who occupied another portion of the bay, who had come from Amoy, and the contrast was greatly in favour of the Formosans; they were a fine, tall, musical race, open and frank in bearing, and their children and young people merry, full of fun and enjoyment. On ordinary occasions these people go perfectly naked, but in the presence of visitors they adopt the Chinese drawers, and the women, who are exceedingly fine and handsome in appearance, assume an appropriate garment; their engaging manners, free from awkwardness and the restraint imposed on women so universally in China, their flushed cheeks and love for finery were most noticeable; they possess also a higher natural refinement than the Celestials. There was still another race of natives in the interior, a wild and lawless set, of which the dwellers in the village had the greatest fear, and it was with difficulty one could be induced to serve as guide to the explorers.

The Chairman read his paper on "The Skin, the Hair, and the Eyes as Tests of the Races of Men." He proceeded to survey the conditions of man geographically distributed, and after a clear and rapid survey of the whole human race in respect to the subject of his paper, he concluded by stating as to the question of variety of colour in the skin in the races of man, its apportionment is evidently a mystery beyond our reach, just as much as are the variety and distribution of colours in the different species of the same genera of the lower animals. Some have fancied that colour in man depends on climate, or that a powerful sun makes the complexion more or less black, while a weaker one leaves it to improve in fairness in proportion to its feebleness. This popular error arose out of the narrow experience of our ancestors. It is a fact that the races of Southern Europe are generally of darker complexion than those of the north. Dark complexions diminish until we reach the people of Scandinavia, when the fair skin attains its acmé. After this, however, it becomes darker as we leave the sun, up to the polar circle.

Mr. Dunne stated his views had undergone no change since he read his paper some nine years ago on the subject, and read a portion of it.

Mr. Carter Blake spoke of the discoveries of M. Pruner Bey as tending to divide all the human family into three classes; the transverse section of whose hair fell into the category of circular tubes of the great European race, the elliptic tubed hair of the American, the Mongolian, &c., the ovoid contour of the true negro. He congratulated the Chairman on the important bearing of his paper, in which he clearly overthrew the old idea that climate influenced colour.

Mr. Mackay said the hair of the negro was reniform, and hence its spiral form; he appeared to think that light was the main influence in affecting the colour of the skin.

A paper by Dr. Cullen on "The Darian Indians, their Habits and Customs, and their Longevity, their Domestic Occupations, and the Natural Productions of the Country," was read.

Mr. Jon A. Hjaltelin read a paper on the "Civilisation of the first Icelandic Colonists, with a General View of their Manners and Customs." The author told of the coming to the island in the 4th century of a band of Irish missionaries whose remains were found in later times by a host of Norwegian exiles who, from political causes, were either obliged to leave Norway, or sought for the freedom denied them in their own country in this distant region. Of these early colonists there are abundant records, both in Irish and Norwegian ancient literature. Celtic remains are accurately described in the early manuscripts. These people had even in remote times attained to a degree of civilisation hardly to be realised without study of their writings.

The Hon. A. Dillon, who had visited the island, gave his opinion of its present condition, and having devoted much attention to the Icelandic literature, spoke favourably of their early attainments in laws, astronomy, and navigation.

Mr. Crawfurd stated that Iceland is one of the few localities destitute of aborigines, and while he doubted the Irish colony, he had equal misgivings of the value of the contents of the Sagas and Eddas, so much spoken of by literary people.

Dr. Lamprey read further remarks on the "Chinese Ethnology, and Notes on the Comparative Ethnology of the Chinese Race."

Dr. Lamprey exhibited the skulls of Chinese, and Hottentots from South Africa, with illustrations of these latter people by Mr. Baines, the African traveller.

ZOOLOGICAL SOCIETY.

May 9. G. Busk, Esq., in the chair. Mr. P. L. Sclater made some remarks on recent additions to the society's menagerie, amongst which were particularly noticed a pair of Kaka parrots (*Nestor hypopolius*), presented to the society by the Acclimatization Society of Canterbury, New Zealand; Mr. Sclater also exhibited a skull of Baird's tapir (*Tapirus Bairdi*), from Nicaragua, which had been forwarded to him by Capt. J. M. Dow. Prof. Owen communicated a letter addressed to him by Sir W. Elliot, containing a correction of an error made in Prof. Owen's recent memoir "On Indian Cetacea collected by Sir W. Elliot." A communication was read from Mr. G. Krefft, containing a description of the same bird of which a specimen had recently been received by the Sydney Museum. Prof. Owen communicated some notes, by Mr. E. S. Hill, on the mode of passage of the young kangaroo to the pouch at the time of birth. A communication was read, from Dr. Macalister, on some points in the anatomy of a cetacean (*Globiocephalus*), lately captured off the coast of Ireland. A communication was read, from Dr. F. Day, containing descriptions of ten new or imperfectly known fishes of the Madras Presidency. Dr. Baird and Mr. H. Adams communicated some notes upon some interesting Chinese shells, together with descriptions of some new species of Unionidæ, collected at Shanghai by Dr. J. Lamprey. A paper was read, by Dr. J. E. Gray, containing notes on the arrangement of sponges, with the descriptions of some new genera of this order. Dr. Murie read a memoir on the dermal and visceral structures of the kagu, sunbittern, and boatbill, as observed in examples of these birds recently deceased in the society's menagerie. A communication was read from Dr. A. L. Adams, containing a description of a new fossil dormouse from the quaternary formations of Malta, proposed to be called *Myoxus Melitensis*. Mr. E. Blyth exhibited a skin of a quail, shot near Mussouree, new to the Fauna of Continental India, but already described by Dr. Gray, under the name *Rollulus superciliosus*.

ROYAL GEOGRAPHICAL SOCIETY.

At a meeting of this society on the 13th inst., Sir R. I. Murchison, who presided, said he was happy to inform the meeting that at the solicitation of the society the Government had, with great liberality, granted a certain sum of money towards an expedition in search of the only fact which it was desirable to set at rest, whether Dr. Livingstone had been killed at the spot described by the Johanna men, about thirty miles from the northern end of Lake Nyassa. To send an expedition into the interior of the country would be a search in vain, because Livingstone, if he once succeeded in getting through the difficulty which he met with in the first instance, would be in comparative safety, and would be on his way to the lake Tangyanika, which was the great object of his journey, with the view to determine whether that lake had a northern outflow, and whether it might not be one of the ultimate sources of the Nile. The expedition would be under the command of Mr. Allen Young, who for two years served under Livingstone, in charge of the Pioneer on the Zambesi. The Admiralty were building a steel boat capable of being taken to pieces and carried up the rapids of the river Shire by the three men who would accompany Mr. Young; and thence they would advance to the north end of Lake Nyassa, where they would ascertain completely whether the story of Livingstone's death was a fable or the truth. With regard to the possibility of his being in the interior, a caravan of Arab traders, a month or two after his reported death, left a spot within ten miles of where Livingstone was said to have been killed, and upon their arrival at Zanzibar they declared that they had heard nothing of the event; on the contrary, that he had passed on into a friendly country. He had also received only that morning a letter from Dr. Kirk, reporting that a trader had recently arrived, coming direct from Lake Tangyanika, who averred that he had seen and spoken with a white man. Dr. Kirk said he had not then found this merchant, he had only heard the report of what he had said. Now, if this report were true, what white man could it be but Livingstone? for no other European, he could affirm, had gone into those regions of late years. The report, so far, was consolatory, and it was a justification of the propriety of the search which the society had set on foot.

Captain Sherard Osborn exhibited a diagram from surveys made by the Russians in Eastern Siberia, and from maps of the caravan routes in Central Asia by Colonel Walker, of the Hindostan survey, and by means of these and such geographical information as he could gather from Du Halde and others, he was enabled to explain in a clear and intelligible manner the present actual condition of the Russian possessions now nearly advanced to our own frontiers of Western British India.

Mr. Ley, Commissioner of Customs formerly, gave a sketch of the progress of the Russians in Northern and Central Asia since the year 1640. Sir H. Rawlinson commended the paper as a *résumé* of the information we possess regarding Central Asia, put in a popular point of view.

Correspondence.

Under this head we shall be glad to insert any letters of general interest.]

BIRDS OF PASSAGE.

SIR,—The remarks of "B," in the *Naturalist's Note Book*, page 23, quoted from *Land and Water*, relative to the passage of migratory birds, are curious in the extreme. "B" is of opinion that birds of passage leave by night, and the reasons he assigns for this, drawn from certain observations alleged to have been made by him, are scarcely less remarkable. His theory seems almost as wild as that of the naturalist who fancied that swallows become fish during the winter months, and live in the water. I think that a far more reasonable and feasible theory is, to believe that the passage of migratory birds from one country to another is directed by a simpler and more natural cause. My own opinion is that they follow the insects upon which they evidently live, and that as the great horde of insects change their position according to the temperature of the atmosphere—the same temperature (or nearly the same), being always essential to their existence—so the ordinary birds of passage change theirs in pursuit of their prey.

The naturalist can scarcely have failed to observe, during the summer months, that the altitude at which the martin and the swallow flies, is solely referable to atmospheric causes.

When clouds obscure the sun, and the air is humid, and the temperature is low, it may always be observed that these birds, so to speak, "hug the earth," that is to say, they invariably fly at the lowest altitude. On the contrary, when the temperature is raised, and the sky is clear and dry, they frequently soar so high that they are scarcely visible to the naked eye. The reason for this changing position may safely, I think, be said to be the same as that to which I have before alluded. The insects upon which these birds habitually feed are influenced entirely by atmospheric changes, and undoubtedly much the same temperature is essential to their existence.

It would hardly seem wise in these days of science and common sense, to suppose that the myriads of tiny insects that fill the air during the summer months, all perish at the approach of winter. Is it not far more reasonable to believe that they change their position horizontally as well as perpendicularly, with the change of the seasons, and that they also are migratory? At least I know of no better theory than this, but I should not be averse to learn if a better one really does obtain,

I am, Sir, yours faithfully,
ALFRED LEIGH HUNT.

THE EARTH'S ORBIT AND OUR SEASONS.

SIR,—The following considerations will, I think, satisfy your correspondent H. H. Ulidia, that the writer in the *Scientific Review* was correct in his assertion that "the elliptical form of the earth's orbit produces in reality no effect on the seasons."

As your correspondent observes, the sun is about eight days longer in the northern hemisphere than in the southern. The northern spring and summer are, therefore, longer than the southern.

But the sun passes his aphelion, or is at his greatest distance from the earth on the 1st of July, that is during the northern summer.

Thus, although the northern spring and summer are longer than the southern, they are at the same time, somewhat colder, owing to the sun's greater distance, and these two effects exactly counterbalance each other,

I am, Sir, yours truly,
GULIELMUS.

POULTRY.

SIR,—"Who would keep poultry?" are the words of not a few persons who are either ignorant of poultry matters, or have some different fancy which runs counter to a love of fowls as domestic favourites. Such a sentiment indeed cannot be entertained by an intelligent amateur, or experienced farmer. It is generally supposed that poultry, if allowed the run of fields where corn is planted, will rake up and devour it. This, in my opinion, is a great mistake, for it has been proved by much experience, that fowls, both by destroying noxious insects, and enriching the soil with their dung, do much more good than harm; if the seed corn be well ploughed into the ground, the fowls will not take the trouble to root it up, since they can obtain insects, which they greatly prefer, with much less difficulty. When the corn begins to appear above ground they certainly destroy a little at first, but they soon tire of it, and leave it for grass which is much more tender.

Fowls require animal food, and will not thrive without it, and in summer it is a great save of expense to let them find it for themselves. The exercise also is very good for them, and it is well known that fowls confined in yards lay very few eggs compared with those that have free access to the fields. Fowls kept either on a large or small scale, if managed properly, are both interesting and profitable. Some people indeed, make nothing by them, and just because they deserve nothing better. Laziness or greed, is in such cases generally visible; one of these unlucky beings packs a pretty large stock into a small hole, where every passer-by is offensively met by the strong fumes rising from the accumulated droppings of the unhealthy inmates. Another feeds them on boiled potatoes tainted with disease, or with any other unwholesome food that comes to hand, thinking "any slobber is good enough for hens." To advise such persons to give up keeping poultry, would be an act of humanity, for no one I think could wish success to persons so cruel and greedy. There is at present a great demand for the Cochin, Brahma, Pootra, and other foreign fowls, but having had great experience both in these and our best British fowl, the Dorking, I greatly prefer the latter, it being an excellent layer, a good sitter, and the finest fowl for the table. In conclusion, I would advise all country gentlemen to keep at least a few fowls of *one kind;* to see that their houses are not over-crowded, well ventilated, and cleaned daily, to change their food occasionally, and never withhold sound grain as a portion of their daily fare. They will find this a source of great amusement, and very little trouble.

I am, yours truly,
J. D. S. W.

Short Notes.

GINSENG.—The Foreign Commissioner at the treaty port of Newchwang reports that ginseng maintains its great repute in China. Every native from the Emperor to the humblest coolie, places implicit faith in the efficacy of this strange root, which for ages has been extolled as a universal medicine or panacea. The genuine Manchurian ginseng consists of a stem from which the leaves spring, of a centre root, and of two roots branching off at the same point from each side of the centre root; the stem somewhat resembles the head and neck, the side roots the shoulders and arms of a man, the main root represents the body, and a fork which the main root frequently forms supplies the legs. The Chinese, with a not ungraceful feeling, believe that a plant which thus expands into the human form, amid thickets and jungles on which the foot of man never trod, must be intended to alleviate the sufferings of the human race. For ginseng loves the moist dense forests which cling to the slopes of the hills; it nestles in recesses which are as pathless now as in the days when the Golden Tartars were dwelling in the plain. Fine Manchurian ginseng is only found in the upper valley of the Usuri, where ruined towns and forts mark the cradle of the race which occupies the Imperial throne. The precious qualities of ginseng are increased and intensified by age, and a plant is of no great value until it has been growing and gathering strength for at least an ordinary lifetime. The upper portions of the root possess the healing power; the stem which appears above ground ought not to be eaten. Formerly the collection of ginseng was in the hands of some 40 merchants, who obtained the necessary authority from the Tartar General of Kirin on payment of a heavy fee, handing over to Government also a certain weight of the product of the search. The merchants employed outlaws, whom the fear of punishment had driven to take refuge in these wilds, and who underwent great hardships in the task, menaced by starvation, and by the wolf, the tiger, and the leopard. But in the time of Taukuang ginseng was becoming yearly more scarce, and plants of any great age were rarely found. In order to arrest their utter extinction, the collection of the wild root was prohibited by Imperial edict. Nevertheless a very small quantity is still clandestinely collected—to a considerable extent, however, in Russian territory. The cultivation of ginseng, though allowed, is not encouraged. It is cultivated in Manchooria, and in the Corea.

THE BETEL NUT.—The trade in this curious article of consumption is of vast extent throughout the Eastern seas, and the ports of Sumatra, Cochin China, and some other localities, are annually visited by the merchant fleets for its collection. The sea-board of the Acheen country, which is under the government of the Rajah of Acheen, is perhaps the most important trading point, and is pretty generally spoken of as the "Betel-nut Coast;" and the inhabitants of many towns and villages of considerable local importance trade in betel-nut exclusively, not only furnishing cargoes to ships, from the continent of India, but indirectly supplying the Chinese markets (where these nuts are valued at from three to four dollars the pecul, according to quality), through Penang, whither the cargoes are first sent. The export from one of these Acheenese towns amounts to about sixty thousand peculs annually; the total supply collected from the various ports of shipment on the whole line of the Betel-nut Coast is estimated at ninety thousand peculs per season, commencing in May and ending in August. The nut is the produce of the Areka palm (*Areka Catechu*), which is one of the most beautiful members of the palm family, shooting its slender stem straight up to the height of from fifty to sixty feet, when a splendid mass of dark green leaves is thrown out like a huge plume of feathers. These palms produce their nuts but once during the year, at which time they present the most beautiful and attractive appearance that can well be imagined; the fruit hangs in clusters at the ends of the long, tough stems from which it is suspended. It is of an elongated oval form, about the size of an egg, and of orange colour, contrasting charmingly with the rich green of the palm leaves. Each nut is enveloped in a thick fibrous coat; on removing which the kernel is found within, covered with a much slighter and more delicate integument, each husk containing one nut only. These, when removed from their coverings, are usually of an irregular conical form.—*Nature and Art*, May.

A CURIOUS RAT.—By the kindness of Mr. Taylor, the civil and intelligent official at the Waterloo Railway Station, I have received the most remarkable rat it was ever my luck to behold. The poor thing has a bone collar round its neck; this collar is evidently a section of pig's thigh-bone. It is a little larger than a gentleman's full-sized finger-ring, but a little broader. The only way I can account for the ring being on the rat's neck—unless it was put there by human hands—is that when he was young he has been stealing and gnawing at a rasher of ham. During his work he has, unfortunately for himself, thrust his head through the ring-shaped bone, the set of his ears and the size of his head not allowing him to pull it off again. As the rat grew larger (he is now about half-grown) of course the bone got tighter, and now his neck is considerably diminished and elegantly fashionable. The neck, I observed, was in a considerable state of inflammation; but as the rat ran about his open wire cage, I poured warm water on it with a large sponge. The poor little animal stood still, raising himself on his hind legs, and seemed to much enjoy the ease the fomentation evidently afforded. Having fomented him a while, I caught him, and, placing him in a cloth, operated with a sharp lancet on a swelling under his jaw, caused by the pressure of the ring. The poor thing was very much relieved by what I had done for him, and the ring seems certainly looser. By judicious treatment I hope to keep this rat alive with the collar round its neck, and make a "perfect cure" of him. It will be curious to see how far Nature will adapt herself to this most singular accident.—FRANK BUCKLAND.—*Land and Water*, May 11.

NOTES ON RARE BIRDS.—A gentleman writing to *Land and Water*, May 11th, says Black Kite (*Milvus migrans*, Linn.) A very fine full-grown male of the black kite was taken in a trap by Mr. Foulger, the Duke of Northumberland's head gamekeeper, at Alnwick, in May, 1866. The plumage was in good condition, except on the lower part of the body, where it had been injured by the trap. This is, probably, the first occurrence of this bird in Britain.—The Waxwing (*Bombycilla garrula*, Linn.).—This bird has appeared in considerable numbers in the northern counties of England this winter. In the last weeks of November several specimens were shot in the neighbourhood of Rothbury and Stanhope. Again, in the early part of December, Mr. Embleton shot six in the neighbourhood of Broomhouse, in Northumberland. About the same time seven was shot at Berwick, three at Norton Cross near Darlington, sixteen at Stanhope, and eight at Alnwick. Ten are reported as having been shot on the Tyne, a few miles above Newcastle, in the latter half of December. The death of others is reported in January. Altogether eighty-two specimens are known to have been killed in Durham and Northumberland.

ZANZIBAR.—Zanzibar is the chief market of the world for the supply of ivory, gum, copal, and cloves. The export in the single year was 488,600lbs. of ivory, worth nearly £147,000, gum is dug from the earth in places where no trees are found, and is supposed to be in inexhaustible quantity, but from the indolence of the African negro only about £37,000 worth was sold in a year, while the cloves produced nearly £56,000. These clove trees of Zanzibar have been only introduced about thirty years, having come from the Mauritius, (a fact well worthy the notice of our Acclimatisation Society). Cowries worth £52,000 were sent to Africa with sesamum, red pepper, cocoanuts, cocoa-nut oil. Sesamum is also of very recent cultivation, and arose out of a demand for this production for the French market in 1859: the receipts for it exceeded £20,000. The value of the trade for the year altogether, was £1,664,577; and in 1834 the government report of the commander of the Imogene stated that "the trade of Zanzibar is very trifling," a few cloves, a little gum and ivory being all that the place produced.

MITES IN POTATOES.—The unusually wet weather experienced in France last year was found to produce a very serious effect upon potatoes. Myriads of mites, of the species described by zoologists as the *Tyroglyphus feculæ*, covered them in a few days, presenting the appearance of an animated gray dust. This dust, which could be collected in large quantities by means of a feather, consisted of the insects in every period of their existence. As might be expected, it attracted great numbers of other insects, who thus obtained an abundant feast, but presented a very strange appearance, becoming coated all over with the dust, so as to be no longer recognisable. Even those potatoes which were apparently sound were covered with the mites, and the very pavement on which they are laid became in a short time overspread with them to a very considerable thickness. It is not yet known whether they are the cause or the consequence of the potatoe disease, which at a later period makes its appearance.—*Scientific Review*, April.

RING OUZEL.—The ring ouzel has been known occasionally to nest in this county, and although probably overlooked, from its general resemblance to the common blackbird and the similarity in the eggs of the two species, it is not improbable that a few pairs may do so nearly every year in favourable districts, and I have reason to believe that such is the case at Holkham. Mr. Spalding, of Westleton, who has paid much attention to their habits in Suffolk, assures me that he has himself taken several nests and eggs in his neighbourhood, where they remain till late in May, should the winds be contrary, and then frequently nest and lay; but he has never known the young to be hatched, as the old birds appear at once with the first favourable wind for more northern localities. They build on the stubs in low damp cars, both at Westleton and Yoxford, where the birds have been watched, and would appear to remain in all cases at no great distance from the coast. About thirty years ago a nest of this species, with the old bird sitting upon it, was found by Mr. Rising in his garden at Horsey."—*Stevenson's Birds of Norfolk*.

A CLEVER PONY.—Sir Emerson Tennent gives in *Land and Water* an interesting account of a pony, the property of Mr. Field, of 47, Warwick-street, milkman, which brings milk to Sir Emerson's door daily. The little animal was bought cheap by Mr. Field some five years since, on account of the evil character which it bore as a jibber. By means of bread, sugar, and chestnuts it has been tamed, and it now moves from door to door of its own accord, preceding the milkman in charge of it; so that whilst he is settling with the servants at one house, the servants of the next house, warned by the sound of the stoppage of the cart, may be in readiness to take in the milk when the man arrives. More than this. At certain doors, where the pony is in the habit of being regaled with doucers of bread, apples, &c., the sagacious little animal contrives, without upsetting the cart, to raise the knocker with its nose and rap twice.

ST. HELENA SEEDFINCH NEAR LONDON.—A very perfect specimen of this beautiful finch, the Cythragra butyracea of scientific authors, was brought to Mr. Ashmead's, of Bishopsgate-street, last week, for preservation; it was observed consorting with greenfinches several weeks previously, and was taken alive and caged; it soon grew tame, and evinced a very familiar disposition. Examples of this interesting bird have frequently been in our aviary at the Zoological Gardens, and one year a pair of them bred. It is not only valuable as an ornamental cage bird, its colour being a most vivid yellow-green, but has very engaging manners, and a sweet song. There is no reasonable doubt that in this instance the bird had escaped from confinement, but from its very perfect condition had evidently been long at liberty, and felt itself quite at home with its cousins, the greenfinches.—EDWARD NEWMAN.—*Field*, May 11.

PIED SPARROW.—A correspondent of the *Field* in a recent number says: We have a very curious specimen of a house-sparrow with us (a hen bird). Last year the head and beak of the bird were perfectly white after moulting; in the autumn the neck, back, and wings, including flight feathers, also became white, with the exception of three or four feathers of the ordinary colour, which gives the little bird a spangled and very pretty appearance. No doubt after the next moulting season it will be a perfect little snowball; the breast and tail feathers now only remain their natural colour. It is constantly about our station, and last brought up a brood of young in the goods warehouse; it is now preparing for a second offspring in one of the water pipes outside the same building. It is very tame, is a great pet, and feeds with my poultry daily.

CAMELLIAS AS CLIMBERS.—The following interesting note appeared in the *Field*, May 4th: Will you permit me to say a word in favour of camellias as climbers? If you have climbers you probably have a shady wall where few things will grow. I have a small vinery, and at the back wall I train up a trellice, camellias. They grow luxuriantly, and produce many hundreds of bloom annually. The border is 18in. wide and about 12in. deep, confined by slates and border tiles. Their peculiar advantage is that they require little sun. Secondly, they require so little water when once the buds are set. They do not materially interfere with the preservation of the grapes. I have a couple of bunches of Lady Down's seedling now hanging in the house, in which my camellias have freely bloomed, and surely no flower is more worthy of a place.

A CURIOUS FISH.—The *Courrier de Saigon* brings, as a contribution to Natural History, the not very credible-sounding description of a fish called "Ca-oug" in the Anamite tongue, which is said to have saved the lives already of several Anamites; for which reason the King of Anam has invested it with the name of "Nam hai dui bnong gnan" (Great General of the South Sea). This fish is said to swim round ships near the coast, and, when it sees a man in the water, to seize him with his mouth and to carry him ashore. A skeleton of this singular inhabitant of the deep is to be seen at Wung-tau, near Cape St. James. It is reported to be 35 feet in length, to have tusks "almost like an elephant," very large eyes, a black and smooth skin, a tail like a lobster, and two "wings" on its back.

THE GOLDEN ORIOLE.—On the 6th inst., when driving through some marshes near the S.E. coast of Kent, I met with a single oriole in full plumage, which kept before me for about a quarter of a mile, flying from tree to tree, where the hawthorns are rather thick and numerous. The day was unusually hot and bright, and the reflection on his yellow plumage made him (what he really is) comparatively a rare sight in this country. I hear or see one or two, nearly every year, of immature plumage, but the date of the above-mentioned bird is, I think, very early. I have never heard them before the end of this month. The bird I have recorded in this instance I am sure had not long arrived, as he was by no means shy, which is contrary to their general habit.—W. B. D.—*Field*, May 11.

TOMTITS NESTING IN A PUMP.—A pair of tomtits (parus cœruleus) have nested in an unused pump, three yards from the window of a room with numbers of people in it. The birds fly in and out of the slit in which the handle works, and the nest is about twenty inches from the top of the piston rod. The most curious and interesting part is that this is the fifth year in which these birds have built, or rather added to their nest, and hatched from six to eight eggs every year, in the most undisturbed appearance of perfect security, though a path to the garden passes the pump. Can they be the same pair of birds, or their "heirs, executors, and assigns," who have occupied the entailed estate from year to year? I confess this puzzles me, and I should like an explanation on the subject.—*Unus, Field*, May 18.

FISH CULTURE.—The *Mémorial de la Loire* says:—"In the Lake of Bouchet, belonging to the department of the Haute-Loire, an establishment of pisciculture has been founded, with the double object of turning the waters to account and of introducing into the rivers connected with it certain valuable kinds of foreign fish whose growth is very rapid. The operations, which commenced this winter, have perfectly succeeded, the hatching is terminated, and the small fry have already attained a size which allows them to be successively set loose in the water. Last week 10,000 young fish were put into the lake, consisting of salmon of the Rhine, graylings, trout of St. Front, others of the common sort, &c."

MARS.—Not a few astronomers have taken advantage of the recent opposition of Mars for study of some of the interesting phenomena of that planet. The ruddy colour has been ascribed to a peculiar absorption prevailing in its atmosphere; but Mr. Huggins, after careful examination with his spectroscope, is of opinion that the colour is produced by the material of which certain parts of the surface of Mars are composed. He finds, too, that Mars and the Moon have much in common as regards surface, and that the former absorbs a large proportion of the light which falls upon it.—*Athenæum*, May 18.

YELLOWHAMMER.—"As a cage-bird the yellowhammer, though looking a giant amongst the smaller finches, is exceedingly gentle in manner, maintaining his own rights with a quiet dignity that brooks no insult, though he never interferes with others. In fact, a feathered gentleman, and graceful in action, he floats, rather than flies, from one perch to another, or amuses himself by repeatedly springing into the air, and with a rapid turn of the wings alighting again on the same spot."—*Stevenson's Birds of Norfolk*.

Remarks, Queries, &c.

(*Under this head we shall be happy to insert original Remarks, Queries, &c.*)

ENTOMOLOGICAL NOTES FOR JUNE.—I have strung together the following notes, thinking they may be of use to those of your readers who have only recently commenced this interesting study. Amongst COLEOPTERA we have (during the month of June):—
Necrophorus Humator.—This is one of the species of burying-beetles, so named from their habit of entering

small animals after death as a receptacle for their eggs. Having found a mole, or mouse, or any other animal dead, they creep beneath the body and scratch away the earth until they have made a pit, into which the animal sinks; when of sufficient depth, the earth is thrown over it, and the young larvæ when hatched find themselves in the midst of food. This species is brownish-black; the three last joints of the antennæ orange-yellow, the elytra are deeply punctured, and each has three slightly elevated lines; the breast and legs are covered with yellowish hairs. *Geotrupes stercorarius* is entirely black above, tinted with violet; the thorax is without punctures on the disc, but has a few at the sides, and a short line in the middle; the elytra are marked with deep grooves, the spaces between being smooth and convex; the under side and legs are steel-blue, glossed with purple or green. *Lucanus Cervus*, called the stag-beetle, is about two inches in length, is entirely of a brownish-black colour, shining surface covered with small punctures, near the fore-leg a patch of golden-coloured hair; the female is smaller than the male. The formidable mandibles of this beetle are employed in wounding the bark of trees in order to feed on the sap. *Cetonia aurata*.—This, the rosechafer, is one of the most beautiful of British beetles; colour a golden green, very shining above, and a bright coppery hue beneath, elytra ornamented near the tips with transverse white marks, form of body rather obtuse. *Rhynchites populi*. —The body golden, green, or bluish tint on the upper side, and dark violet beneath; antennæ black, elytra punctured. *R. pubescens*, somewhat longer than the preceding, of deep violet colour, clothed with long hairs, elytra marked with punctured lines. *R. Bacchus* is a beautiful species, found chiefly in Kent on the vine. *Necrodes littoralis*, entirely black, three termal joints of the antennæ, yellow, three elevated lines on each elytron; spaces between thickly punctured; hind legs thick and toothed on the under side; it is found on the sea-shore and banks of rivers. *Dermestes lardarius*, a dirty ash-colour, with three small black spots; it infests bacon. DERMAPTERA.—*Forficula auricularia*, or earwig, is too well known to need description. TRICHOPTERA.—*Phryganea grandis*, upper wings brownish grey, with longitudinal black ray, and two or three white joints at the extremity; these are found near water, and are known as Caddice Flies or water-moths, and the larvæ Caddice worms, in which state they reside in the water, in cases made of sand, shells, &c. LEPIDOPTERA.—Under this head I fear I cannot do more than give the names, as a full description would take up too much of your space. *Hipparchia Galathea* (Marbled White); *H. Tithonus* (Large Heath); *H. Pamphilus* (Small Heath); *H. Janira* (Meadow Brown); *H. Hero* (Silver Ringlet); *Melitæa cinxia* (Glanville Fritillary); *Argynnis Adippe* (High Brown Fritillary); *A. Aglaia* (Dark Green Fritillary); *Vanessa urticæ* (Small Tortoise-shell); *V. Calbum* (Comma Butterfly); *Polyommatus agrestis* (Brown Argus); *Pieris cratægi* (Black-veined White or Hawthorne Butterfly); *Smerinthus ocellatus* (Eyed Hawk Moth); *Deilephila euphorbiæ* (Spotted Elephant Hawk Moth); *Macroglossa stellatarum* (Humming-bird Hawk Moth); *Lasiocampa quercus* (Oak Egger Moth); *Hyperacampa dominula* (Scarlet Tiger Moth); *Cerura vinula* (Puss Moth); *Thyatira Batis* (Peach Blossom Moth); *Melanippe hastata* (Mottled Beauty); *Ourapteryx sambucaria* (Swallow-tail Moth); *Hylophila prasinana* (Green Silver Lines); *H. quercana* (Scarce Silver Lines); *Abraxus grossulariata* (Gooseberry Moth). HOMOPTERA.—*Cicada spumaria*, is of a brown colour; with two white spots on the upper wings; the larvæ of this insect discharges a kind of frothy matter called cuckoo spit. DIPTERA.— *Œstrus equi*; head, yellowish white; thorax yellow, with elevated hairs on a bluish point; end of body reddish, with two black spots; the wings have a band in the middle, and two small black points at the extremity. These insects have the appearance of large flies; their habits are remarkable, each species being confined to its own quadruped, the horse, ass, ox, etc.: the larvæ reside either in the stomach or beneath the skin of cattle; the œstris of the sheep is small, and of a greyish colour; it places its eggs in the nostrils of that animal, whence the larvæ ascends into the head, and, when full-grown, falls and assumes the pupa state on the ground. *Tabanus bovinus*: head, greyish white; eyes, of shining green; thorax and body blackish brown, with spots of a red tinge; wings transparent, and veined with brown. *Musca domestica* (common fly); *M. Vomitoria* (Bluebottle Fly); *M. carnaria* (Blow Fly). The *Chironomus plumosus*, or Midge, finishes the list of insects and moths that may be looked for. This list may not be quite perfect, but will be useful to the young beginner.

E. G. S.

BEES.—A lover of flowers sends us the following in answer to A. B.—Your correspondent will find full, exact, and all possible information on bees in "My Bee Book," written some few years since, by the Rev. W. C. Cotton, son of the late excellent governor of the Bank of England. Mr. Wood, also, has published a little work, on their "habits, management, and treatment;" but all those who desire to read a very interesting and well-written, as well as amusing volume, should decidedly either get or borrow "My Bee-Book,"—and if they cannot afford this, "A Letter to Cottagers, the first on Bee-Keeping, and second on Bee-Observing," by the same author. Mr. Cotton, like all those who study and observe closely the habits of animals, made his bees quite his friends; and I well remember an account of his going down to Sydenham with some bees in his pocket, much to the astonishment of his host. In answer to A. B.'s query as to fumigating, &c., I will make an extract or two, from the work itself. Mr. Cotton advises all people, cottagers especially, to keep bees, well observing that it is economy to do so, and that many a good example of patience and industry do they afford, as well as employment of time. This "book" contains a voluminous list of treatises on bees, Huber's writing, and observations upon them, Sypendort's, &c., and, above all, he deduces from their habits the one great object of the study of all works of Nature, and which everyone should keep in view, that of "looking thro' Nature, up to Nature's God," dedicating the work to his father, who, he says, "first gave me a love for bees, and made me an observer of the wondrous works of our heavenly Father." The following is a short extract from the book:—"In the first place, then, *never kill your bees*. Many will say, my father did so, why should not we? This is a very good rule, generally; but I hope to show you that the new path is better, and straighter, too, and the plan of learning is very well for those who know no better; but, I am sure, you must all feel sorrow when you murder those in the autumn who have worked hard for you all the summer, and are ready to do so again. In taking a hive, first, then, get everything ready beforehand, and sit up all night when ready. You will find in damp meadows a fungus, which is commonly called "puff-ball," the proper name being "Fungus Maximus," or larger mushroom, or "Fungus Pulverulentis." When quite ripe, a dirty powder, like smoke, comes out (this powder will stop bleeding). Pick them, when half ripe, put them in a bag, and when you have squeezed them to half the size, dry them in an oven, after the bread is drawn, and if fit for use, and properly done, they will hold fire, like tinder. When the fungus cannot be had, rag soaked in nitre will do; but this costs money. Second, mark your hives, having, I presume, weighed them when empty; get a little tin-box fitted to the nose of your bellows, having a spout coming from it, which fits the door of your beehive. (The stocks should, if possible, stand next to good, heavy ones, to which you may join the bees by this process.) Take a piece of fungus, twice the size of an egg, light it, and when it burns freely, put it into the box, fit it into your bellows, and blow the smoke into the hive. Stop that part of the door up with wet clay, which the tin spout does not fill, that none of the smoke may get out. The bees, at first, will make a great buzzing; in about five minutes all will be still as death. Lift the hive gently off, and turn those bees which have fallen on to the bottom board into a large white dish. They will be quite harmless and still, as if they had been burned with brimstone; but the fungus does them no harm, it only makes them drunk, which is very good for bees, though bad for men, as they get well in twenty minutes, have no headache the next morning, and all the merrier afterwards, and it was not their fault they were so overtaken. Look for the queen bee, and let some one help you as also to cut out the combs, and sweep the bees off, for many hands, as well as eyes, are better than one. Put her softly on one side, and sweep all the other stupid bees with a feather into the dish. Then cut the combs carefully, and if you have not found the queen, look sharp on each comb. Nine times out of ten she does not fall down, but holds fast to the top of the hive, in the very middle. When you have found her, use *her tenderly*, for on her the lives and happiness of thousands depend; then go on with your work. Pour the bees all back into the hive, and set it in its old place till the evening, leaving little bits of comb sticking to the top of the hive, as they will cluster round this, like a new swarm, and will set about clearing out the wax, and putting the hive straight as fast as they can. In the evening blow a little smoke into the strong hive, which stands next to them; when the bees are quiet, turn it up gently, and pour some honey and water into the combs. Put three breaks on the bottom board, so that when you set the hive down again no bees may be crushed; then take the hive from which you took the combs in the morning, and, with one smart blow, knock all the bees out upon the bottom boards of the hive whose bees you have sugared. Set their hive gently in its place, on the bricks, over the bees you have just knocked out; they will begin to lick the first drops of honey which trickle down, and will be led up by the scent of that which you have poured into the combs, to mix themselves with the other bees."

SUMMER MIGRANTS.—Our first swallows reached here on 9th April, and the cuckoo on 17th April, *Jeune Duprez*, hybrid perpetual, roses in bloom on an open wall here, on 20th April.

Jersey.　　　　　　　　　　　　H. E. A.

DISEASES OF GOLD FISH.—In answer to your correspondent respecting the fungus on gold or other fish, I have often lost by this well-known disease hundreds of fish; one of my customers at Louth, in Lincolnshire, has written me a long account of how he has treated the disease: First, he took the fish out of the aquarium, and carefully washed it all over with brine or very salt water; he then introduced them into a large cistern of fresh water, and has found them recover; I have often taken out carp and given them a swim in one of my large marine aquariums, then by putting them into plenty of fresh water, and keeping them in a dark cellar, they recover. I had a customer whose little goldfish lost its tail, and every fin twice in eighteen months, and it recovered by changing the water each day. I have a pond in Sussex which has a iron spring at the head of it; this, I fear, is one of the causes of disease, for if a bough or a few leaves fall in, the fungus grows on it wonderfully fast. I fear that the disease is promoted by the water passing through the iron pipes of London. If the aquarium is well stocked with suitable plants, and a little boiled water is introduced once in one or two weeks to keep up the evaporation, and the water is not changed for five or six years, so much the better. No disease will appear if the food and decomposed vegetation is removed.　　　　　　　　　　　　G. H. KING.

THE KESTREL (*Falco Tinnunculus*).—This is the commonest of our British hawks, and may be found in all parts of our country, as well as in every quarter of the globe. It builds no nest, but lays its eggs, which are four or five in number, and of a light colour speckled and blotted with red, in holes in rocks, and sometimes in the deserted nests of crows and magpies. This bird, though naturally bold and fierce, is easily tamed. One that I kept for some time, after having obtained its liberty, would not leave the place, but, when hungry, flew down and took food from the hand, which it carried to some neighbouring tree to eat at its leisure. In June, 1866, I found a dead chicken in a nest containing four young, which proves that the kestrel is occasionally guilty of depredations in the poultry-yard, as well as the sparrow-hawk. A sparrow-hawk that I kept in confinement allowed a small turtle-dove to roost on the same perch without offering to offend it.　　　　　　　　　　　　R. W. B.

TROUT LIVING IN SALT WATER.—Accidentally in showing a trout to a customer (Mrs. Tidcombe) let it fall in the yard into a cistern of salt water, 5 feet deep and 5 feet long, containing about 500 gallons—it had come up the day before in barrels fresh from the sea. The trout lived in the water three days and nights. It was shown to several persons alive in the sea water, and the third day Mrs. Tidcombe and friend saw it. I have had a plaster cast taken of the trout, which was exhibited with some young trout of my own breeding to a Natural History Society, and proved of great interest. I mention this, as the air-bladders in different fishes is one of the causes, I believe, of their living in sea-water. It is very easy to acclimatize sticklebacks, adding sea-water gradually; but carp I could never succeed with, though I have often tried them.   G. H. KING.

Aquaria Establishment, 100, Gt. Portland St.

THE LITTLE BITTERN, AND PURPLE CRESTED HERON.—This little heron is so rarely met with in Cornwall that its occurrence deserves a record. Since 1833 I have not succeeded in procuring a specimen, although pretty much on the watch for rare birds. Last spring, however, I had the good fortune to obtain a perfect plumaged male bird from one of the Scilly Isles; last month a bird in similar plumage was obtained from this immediate neighbourhood, and last evening I received a note from Mr. F. V. Hill, of Helston, reporting the capture of an adult female found in an exhausted state on a beach near the Lizard; near the same spot was shot, a few weeks since, a female purple-crested Heron, with the ovarium full of eggs.

Golden Oriole at Scilly.—Three of these birds have been observed together, one in very bright plumage, on the grounds of the lord proprietor, during the past week.

Hoopoe at the St. Michael's Mount.—These birds are seen every spring in the Land's End district; one was obtained this spring at St. Michael's Mount.—
EDW. HEARLE NOAD, Penzance.
May 14, 1867.

INSTINCT IN A ROOK.—A labourer on the estate of a relation of mine, caught a young squab which had been blown out of its nest during a gale of wind. He took it home and reared it: and it now lives, with its wings clipped, in his cottage. Regularly every building season Mr. Rook brings in a lot of straw twigs, pieces of cloth or rags—in fact, anything it can get hold of, and essays to build a nest on the bars under the seat of a chair, where it gravely sits till dislodged by the "missus," who objects to the litter without looking at the performance from a scientific point of view.   A. G. H.

PRESERVATION OF SKINS.—Corrosive sublimate dissolved in alcohol (strong whisky or brandy) is a very effectual, as well as simple, preparation for preserving the skins of birds and quadrupeds; it also excellently preserves insects. It gives a peculiar odour very like that of apples to the object preserved.
R. W. B.

STATE OF THE WEATHER NEAR LONDON.

April and May.	Moon's Age.	Barometer.		Temperature.					Wind	Rain.	Remarks.
				Of the Air.			of the Earth				
		Max.	Min.	Max	Min	Mean	1 foot deep	2 feet deep			
Thurs. 18	○	29.878	29.672	64	47	55.5	51	47	S.	.00	Very fine; densely clouded; overcast.
Friday 19	15	29.586	29.460	65	50	57.5	52	48	S.W.	.01	Very fine; strong S.W. wind; overcast.
Satur. 20	16	29.331	29.015	59	37	48.0	54	49	S.	.32	Cloudy and rather boisterous; densely overcast; boisterous, with rain.
Sunday 21	17	29.546	29.305	54	37	45.5	53	49	S.W.	.01	Low dusky clouds, and boisterous; very stormy at night.
Mon. 22	18	29.790	29.714	61	42	51.5	52	49	S.W.	.05	Clear, with cold wind; overcast; rain at night.
Tues. 23	19	29.735	29.712	64	44	54.0	52	49	S.W.	.12	Overcast; showery; fine; strong S.W. wind.
Wed. 24	20	29.659	29.580	63	43	53.0	53	50	S.W.	.18	Heavy clouds; with showers; masses of dark and white clouds; rain.
Thurs. 25	21	29.818	29.693	53	42	47.5	53	49	N.	.01	Hazy and damp; overcast; densely overcast at night.
Friday 26	22	29.760	29.646	57	42	49.5	51	49	E.	.02	Hazy; overcast; slight rain at night.
Satur. 27	☽	29.523	29.484	60	29	44.5	52	49	S.W.	.03	Cloudy; masses of white clouds; very fine at night.
Sunday 28	24	29.727	29.370	61	30	45.5	52	49	E.	.00	Foggy; overcast; very fine at night.
Mon. 29	25	29.830	29.786	65	32	48.5	51	48	N.	.04	Fine; exceedingly fine throughout.
Tues. 30	26	29.747	29.664	64	36	50.0	52	49	W.	.12	Cloudy; white and dusky clouds; rain at night.
Wed. 1	27	29.954	29.870	62	33	47.5	52	49	N.W.	.00	Cloudy and damp; cloudy; very fine at night.
Thurs. 2	28	30.051	30.027	65	40	52.5	52	49	N.E.	.00	Very fine; overcast; fine at night.
Friday 3	29	30.116	30.072	70	37	53.5	53	50	E.	.00	Overcast; cloudless and very fine; fine.
Satur. 4	●	30.125	30.003	68	39	53.5	54	50	S.E.	.00	Very fine throughout.
Sunday 5	1	29.965	29.889	75	47	61.0	55	51	S.E.	.00	Very fine throughout; warm at night.
Mon. 6	2	29.905	29.878	81	49	65.0	56	52	S.E.	.00	Very fine; exceedingly fine; masses of black clouds.
Tues. 7	3	29.958	29.880	82	51	66.5	56	52	S.E.	.00	Exceedingly fine; cloudless and hot.
Wed. 8	4	29.866	29.842	82	42	62.0	57	53	S.	.00	Very fine; hot and dry; fine at night.
Thurs. 9	5	29.952	29.825	75	47	61.0	57	53	S.	.00	Cloudless and very fine; exceedingly fine throughout.
Friday 10	☾	29.778	29.597	79	47	63.0	57	53	S.	.52	Cloudy and hot; thunder shower in forenoon; overcast.
Satur. 11	7	29.776	29.461	69	48	58.5	58	54	S.W.	.00	Heavy thunder-storm 4—5 A.M., cloudy; fine at night.
Sunday 12	8	29.444	29.341	58	43	50.5	59	54	S.E.	.07	Slight rain; densely overcast throughout; rain.
Mon. 13	9	29.685	29.523	51	44	47.5	58	54	N.E.	.01	Overcast; hazy; densely overcast at night.
Tues. 14	10	29.803	29.723	52	40	46.0	55	53	N.E.	.00	Overcast and cold; cloudy; cold at night.
Wed. 15	11	29.916	29.620	53	40	46.5	54	52	N.E.	.00	Overcast and cold; cloudy, cold, and dry; overcast at night.

THE SONG OF BIRDS.

IN some simpler age, poets may go back, like the old Minnesingers, to the birds of the forest, and learn of them to sing. And little do most of them know how much there is to learn; what variety of character, as well as variety of emotion, may be distinguished by the practised ear, in a 'charm of birds' (to use the old southern phrase), from the wild cry of the missel-thrush, ringing from afar in the first bright days of March, a passage of one or two bars repeated three or four times, and then another and another, clear and sweet, and yet defiant (for the great 'storm-cock' loves to sing when rain and wind is coming on, and faces the elements as boldly as he faces hawk and crow)—down to the delicate warble of the wren, who slips out of his hole in the brown bank, where he has huddled through the frost with wife and children, all folded in each other's arms like human beings, for the sake of warmth—which, alas! does not always suffice; for many a bunch of wrens may be found, frozen and shrivelled, after such a winter as this last. Yet even he, sitting at his house-door in the low sunlight, says grace for all mercies (as a little child once worded it) in a song so rapid, so shrill, so loud, and yet so delicately modulated, that you wonder at the amount of soul within that tiny body; and then stops suddenly, as a child who has said its lesson, or got to the end of the sermon, gives a self-satisfied flirt of his tail, and goes in again to sleep.

Character? I know not how much variety of character there may be between birds of the same species, but between species and species the variety is endless, and is shown—as I fondly believe—in the difference of their notes. Each has its own speech, inarticulate, expressing not thought but hereditary feeling; save a few birds who, like those little dumb darlings, the spotted flycatchers, who have built under my bed-room window this twenty years, seem to have absolutely nothing to say, and accordingly have the wit to hold their tongues; and devote the whole of their small intellect to sitting on the iron rails, flitting off them a yard or two to catch a butterfly in air, and flitting back with it to their nest.

But listen (to return) to the charm of birds in any sequestered woodland, on a bright forenoon in June. As you try to disentangle the medley of sounds, the first, perhaps, which will strike your ear will be the loud, harsh, monotonous, flippant song of the chaffinch, and the metallic clinking of two or three sorts of titmice. But above the tree-tops, rising, hovering, sinking, the woodlark is fluting, tender and low. Above the pastures outside the skylark sings—as he alone can sing; and close by, from the hollies rings out the blackbird's tenor—rollicking, audacious, humorous, all but articulate. From the tree above him rises the treble of the thrush, pure as the song of angels: more pure, perhaps, in tone, though neither so varied nor so rich, as the song of the nightingale. And there, in the next holly, is the nightingale himself: now croaking like a frog; now talking aside to his wife on the nest below; and now bursting out into that song, or cycle of songs, in which if any man finds sorrow, he himself surely finds none. All the morning he will sing; and again at evening, till the small hours, and the chill before the dawn: but if his voice sounds melancholy at night, heard all alone, or only mocked by the ambitious blackcap, it sounds in the bright morning that which it is, the fulness of joy and love. True, our own great living poet tells us how—

> In the topmost height of joy
> His passion clasps a secret grief,—

and Coleridge may have been somewhat too severe when he guessed that—

> Some night-wandering man, whose heart was pierced
> With the remembrance of a grievous wrong,
> Or slow distemper, or neglected love
> (And so, poor wretch, filled all things with himself,
> And made all gentle sounds tell back the tale
> Of his own sorrow)—he and such as he,
> First named these sounds a melancholy strain,
> And many a poet echoes the conceit.

But that the old Greek poets were right, and had some grounds for the myth of Philomela, I do not dispute, though Sophocles, speaking of the nightingales of Colonos, certainly does not represent them as lamenting. The Elizabethan poets, however, when they talked of Philomel, 'her breast against a thorn,' were unaware that they and the Greeks were talking of two different birds—that our English Lusciola Luscinia is not Lusciola Philomela, which (I presume) is the Bulbul of the East. The true Philomel hardly enters Venetia, hardly crosses the Swiss Alps, ventures not into the Rhine-land and Denmark, but penetrates (strangely enough) further into South Sweden than our own Luscinia: ranging meanwhile over all Central Europe, Persia, and the East, even to Egypt. Whether his song be really sad, let those who have heard him say. But as for our own Luscinia, who winters not in Egypt and Arabia, but in Morocco and Algeria, the only note of his which can be mistaken for sorrow, is rather one of too great joy; that cry, which is his highest feat of art, which he cannot utter when he first comes to our shores, but practises carefully, slowly, gradually, till he has it perfect by the beginning of June; that cry, long, repeated, loudening and sharpening in the intensity of rising passion, till it stops suddenly, exhausted at the point where pleasure, from very keenness, turns to pain.

How different in character from his song is

that of the gallant little black-cap in the tree above him. A gentleman he is of a most ancient house, perhaps the oldest of European singing birds. How perfect must have been the special organisation which has spread, seemingly without need of alteration or improvement, from Norway to the Cape of Good Hope, from Japan to the Azores. How many ages and years must have passed since his forefathers first got their black caps? And how intense and fruitful must have been the original vitality which, after so many generations, can still fill that little body with so strong a soul, and make him sing as Milton's new-created birds sang to Milton's Eve in Milton's Paradise. Sweet he is, and various, rich, and strong, beyond all English warblers, save the nightingale: but his speciality is his force, his rush, his overflow, not so much of love as of happiness. The spirit carries him away. He riots up and down the gamut till he cannot stop himself; his notes tumble over each other; he chuckles, laughs, shrieks with delight; throws back his head, droops his tail, sets up his back, and sings with every fibre of his body: and yet he never forgets his good manners. He is never coarse, never harsh, for a single note. Always graceful, always sweet, he keeps perfect delicacy in his most utter carelessness.

And why should we overlook, common though he be, yon hedge-sparrow, who is singing so modestly, and yet so firmly and so true? Or cock-robin himself, who is here, as everywhere, honest, self-confident, and cheerful? Most people are not aware, one sometimes fancies, how fine a singer is cock-robin now in the spring time, when his song is drowned by, or at least confounded with, a dozen other songs. We know him and love him best in winter, when he takes up (as he does sometimes in cold, wet summer days) that sudden wistful warble, struggling to be happy, half in vain, which surely contradicts Coleridge's verse:—

In nature there is nothing melancholy.

But he who will listen carefully to the robin's breeding song on a bright day in May, will agree, I think, that he is no mean musician; and that for force, variety and character of melody, he is surpassed only by black-cap, thrush, and nightingale.

And what is that song, sudden, loud, sweet, yet faltering, as if half ashamed? Is it the willow wren, or the garden warbler? The two birds, though very remotely allied to each other, are so alike in voice, that it is often difficult to distinguish them, unless we attend carefully to the expression. For the garden warbler, beginning in high and loud notes, runs down in cadence, lower and softer, till joy seems conquered by very weariness; while the willow wren, with a sudden outbreak of cheerfulness, though not quite sure (it is impossible to describe bird songs without attributing to the birds human passions and frailties) that he is not doing a silly thing, struggles on to the end of his story with a hesitating hilarity, in feeble imitation of the black-cap's bacchanalian dactyls.

And now—is it true that

In nature there is nothing melancholy?

Mark that slender, graceful, yellow warbler, running along the high oak boughs like a perturbed spirit, seeking restlessly, anxiously, something which he seems never to find; and uttering every now and then a long anxious cry, four or five times repeated, which would be a squeal, were it not so sweet. Suddenly he flits away, and flutters round the pendant tips of the beech-sprays like a great yellow butterfly, picking the insects from the leaves; then flits back to a bare bough, and sings, with heaving breast and quivering wings, a short, shrill, feeble, tremulous song; and then returns to his old sadness, wandering and complaining all day long. Is there no melancholy in that cry? It sounds sad: why should it not be meant to be sad? We recognise joyful notes, angry notes, fearful notes: They are very similar (strangely enough) in all birds. They are very similar (more strangely still) to the cries of human beings, especially children, when influenced by the same passions. And when we hear a note which to us expresses sadness, why should not the bird be sad? Yon woodwren has had enough to make him sad, if only he recollects it; and if he can recollect his road from Morocco hither, he maybe recollects likewise what happened on the road—The long weary journey up the Portuguese coast, and through the gap between the Pyrenees and the Jaysquivel, and up the Landes of Bordeaux, and through Brittany, flitting by night, and hiding and feeding as he could by day; and how his mates flew against the light-houses, and were killed by hundreds; and how he essayed the British Channel, and was blown back, shrivelled up by bitter blasts; and how he felt, nevertheless, that 'that was water he must cross,' he knew not why: but something told him that his mother had done it before him, and he was flesh of her flesh, life of her life, and had inherited her 'instinct' (as we call hereditary memory, in order to avoid the trouble of finding out what it is, and how it comes). A duty was laid on him to go back to the place where he was bred; and he must do it: and now it is done; and he is weary, and sad, and lonely; and for aught we know thinking already that when the leaves begin to turn yellow, he must go back again, over the Channel over the Lands, over the Pyrenees, to Morocco once more. Why should he not be sad? He is a very delicate bird, as both his shape and his note testify. He can hardly keep up his race here in England; and is accordingly very uncommon, while his two cousins, the willow-wren and the chiff-chaff, who, like him, build for some mysterious reason domed nests upon the ground, are stout, and busy, and numerous, and thriving everywhere. And what he has gone through may be too much for the poor woodwren's nerves; and he gives way; while willow-wren, black-cap, nightingale, who have gone by the same road, and suffered the same dangers, have stoutness of heart enough to throw off the past, and give themselves up to present pleasure. Why not?—who knows? There is labour, danger, bereavement, death in nature; and why should not some, at least, of the so-called dumb things know it, and grieve at it as well as we?—Rev. C. Kingsley in *Frazer's Magazine*, June.

ORNAMENTAL GRASSES.

OF late years public taste has been turned to the advantageous effect of grasses in landscape gardening. Ferns had the credit of first winning attention from colour to form, and grasses next stepped in to confirm the preference for grace and elegance over gaudy colouring. We seldom now find a velvet lawn without its suitable contrast of a clump of Pampas-grass, either standing as an object of solitary beauty, or grouped with shrubs in a verdant background.

This beautiful plant is now so thoroughly established as a general favourite, that we offer remarks on its culture, culled from the *Gardeners' Magazine*, with a full confidence in their general acceptability.

The seeds must be sown in pots, and covered very lightly with sandy loam and peat. Then the pots must be placed in a slight heat till the blades are well developed. The young plants must next be separated, and only a few put into each pot; a cool frame is best adapted to them in this stage, and they require to be well watered. On being finally planted out, the place must be prepared for them with plenty of mellow loam, and must be in a moist situation. This grass has the male and female flowers on different plants. The latter is the one generally preferred, as best suited to our climate. It soon developes a large circular tuft of leaves, which attain a length of several feet, and bend outwards in the style so much admired in the coronal ferns, until the abundance of arching foliage resembles the graceful streams of a fountain. From the centre of this arching group arise a number of perpendicular culms, the apices at first seeming only thickened, but shortly developing a folded sheath, within which reposes the close-packed flower-buds; these culms shoot upwards with such rapidity, that they have been known to grow an inch in twenty-four hours, and they attain their full height of from five to seven feet in September. Then the sheath opens gradually, and the inflorescence emerges by degrees, at first as a closely-packed head, then exhibiting its complex structure of branches and buds, and by the end of October developing its full glory of spreading panicle a foot long, and numerous feathery flowers, so white and glossy as to shine like silver, and so lightly mounted on the slender branches that they wave and tremble in every zephyr. The male plant differs in the foliage, being less graceful and the inflorescence later in opening. The latter habit unfits the plant for out-door culture in Britain, for it leaves little chance of the flowers being perfected before the early frosts; and the culms, being then full of sap, are unable to stand the cold, and so perish before the flowers can expand. The best way of utilizing the beauty of the male plant is to cut the unopened panicles before the coming of the frost. The heads should then be dried, and the sheaths carefully stripped off; the young florets lying snug within seem made of frosted silver, but so closely packed that they present the appearance of a solid body. But when this compressed crowd of silver blossoms is shaken gently and repeatedly, they separate, and the true form of branching rachis soon becomes developed. Thus treated, the heads which would have perished in a night, leaving their latent beauty undeveloped and almost unsuspected, become the most lovely objects for drawing-room decoration possible. Mr. Johns recommends this treatment most highly.

In the *Cottage Gardener's Magazine*, the botanical name of the Pampas-grass, *Gynerium argenteum*, is said to be derived from two Greek words, *gyne*, female, and *erion*, wool, because of the woolly stigma. The writer of the article takes great umbrage at the popular name Pampas-grass, for he says it is found in no part of the Pampas, but only upon the banks of the Parana and other rivers in South America.

The roots of this grass are wide-spreading, fibrous, and very numerous. The leaves are hard and spiny at the edges; they are about half an inch broad, and from six to eight feet long. So sharp are the spines, and the leaves of such strong texture, that they inflict severe cuts upon any hand rash enough to attempt to gather them.

Mr. Moore introduced the Pampas-grass into Britain, and Messrs. Henderson were among its first cultivators. It is quite hardy, but these experienced nurserymen find it advantageous to tie the leaves together at the end of autumn, so as to enclose the heart of the plant, and to wrap a mat around. This they open on favourable occasions, and remove it entirely in March. By this means the plant is able to produce its culms earlier, and the grower has the advantage of the beautiful panicles for a longer period.

Clumps of the Sugar-grass (*Holcus saccharatus*) form desirable objects in a landscape garden. This grass was introduced into Belgium from Shanghai, and thence into England a few years ago. It is extensively cultivated in the United States, attaining there a height of from eight to sixteen feet, but in Europe it seldom exceeds eight feet, and a dull or cold season dwarfs it greatly. The culm is straight, the leaves flag-like, flexuous, drooping and bending most gracefully in the manner of those of the *Zea Mays*. The panicle is cone-shaped, the flowers densely crowded; the flowers are green at first but soon become tinged with purple, and very elegant. It can bear the frost very well after the flowers are expanded, but if the frost come before, the sap is still flowing, and the culms perish as certainly as those of the male Pampas grass. But with care in early sowing there is no danger of this, as it attains its growth quickly, and in a favourable season two crops may be obtained.

The Maize is well worth cultivation for its beauty and unique habit of growth; its more sterling qualities are enumerated in the chapter on Cereals.

The Panick-grasses include a number of very beautiful species, some of considerable size and fitted for distant grouping, and many of smaller stature, well adapted for flower-borders, pots in the conservatory, and bouquets.—*British Grasses*, by Margaret Plues. London: Reeve & Co.

AN ELEPHANT HUNT.

WE halted after eight miles and a third of travel by trochiameter, and Chapman walking onward to the vlei a quarter of a mile further, found himself face to face with an elephant, and with nothing but a charge of shot in his gun. He returned at once for his rifle; the hut we had commenced to shelter the ivory from the unloaded waggon was left to finish itself; the sketch I was busy with was put away at once, and we started at once in search—the Damara servants holding the dogs in leash while we beat the bush in all directions till elephants were seen to the eastward; these proved to be a troop of cows, bearing only small ivory, and we returned to take up the spoor of the first that had been seen. A tempting shot at a duikerbok, was, of course, disregarded, and we pressed on to the northward over sandy ridges covered with shrub and bush, thorny or thornless as it happened. Chapman ran faster than I, and was beside less heavily loaded, and as we descended into the next valley I heard three shots in rapid succession, followed by the wild shrill scream of the enraged elephant and the angry baying of the dogs. Next minute I cleared the bush, and before me in the open hollow lay a broad pool, a very gem of the wilderness bordered by rich grass, and enclosed by an amphitheatre of forest—on the further side the people were rallying from the confusion into which the headlong charge of the elephant had thrown them, and the giant form of the huge animal was visible for a moment as he forced his way through the yielding bush beyond. Chapman who was loading his rifle shouted to me to take care, as the beast was savage; and taking the track marked by his huge footsteps I followed into the bush. Chapman came up as soon as he had reloaded, but the dogs had been dispersed, and it soon became evident that we were on the spoor of an unwounded bull—the bushmen followed at full speed, and one of the Damara boys (Bill) joined them—with a nimbleness and hardihood which, had it only been supplemented by skill in the use of the gun must have successfully terminated the chase, but, for a white man on foot to keep up with these naked children of the desert was an impossibility, and both of us were soon distanced.

I held on for about ten miles, but finding that no one else was following, and that the elephant was most probably many miles ahead, and going at a rate that would render pursuit hopeless, I lay down after sunset from sheer weariness, and waited till the moon and stars shone through the clouds sufficiently to allow of my shaping a course homeward. After a time I heard the faint reports of guns fired by the Damaras sent out by Chapman to meet me, but at length these ceased, and darkness coming on, I was no longer able to avoid entanglement in the low, invisible grey thorn bushes; I therefore spread a couch of grass, and as the night was not cold enough to make a fire necessary I slept very comfortably till daybreak enabled me again to see my way. During the night I had, of course, been unable to distinguish tracks, and had merely held a tolerably correct course across country, but now I crossed a spoor, which I knew to have been formed yesterday, and soon met some of our Damaras coming from the waggons. Kalokolo and a bushman relieved me of my gun, and I reached our outspan just as the cattle were being milked for early coffee. I learned, to my surprise, that Chapman himself had fired the guns that I had heard the previous night, the immense charge of powder—no less than fourteen drachms—accounting for the distance at which they were audible. He had, of course, been anxious, but the bushman had spoken up for me. "He has a beard like you, he cannot lose himself." The poor fellow little thought that the hirsute appearance of an Englishman was no guarantee of ability to find his way in the bush.

I was also told that the elephant on entering the hollow had been met by another, coming, all unconscious of the chase, to refresh himself at the water, and Chapman, keeping back the people as much as possible, had been obliged to fire across the vlei at the second, between one and two hundred yards distant, although the ivory of the first, notwithstanding a broken tusk, seemed forty pounds heavier than that of the intruder. At the second shot the people had run past him, and exposed themselves to a furious charge, Bill, after firing his shot, escaping with marvellous alacrity, but subsequently proving himself as bold and eager in pursuit as could be wished. The wrong elephant, however, was followed, and it was only when Chapman had given up the chase and was returning that the bushmen suddenly pointed to some object, and handed him his gun to shoot it, but another glance showed that it was the carcase of the first elephant lying within a few hundred yards of the spot where it had been wounded.

Breakfast was soon over, and collecting my drawing materials I started with Kalokolo and the bushmen, regretting only that my friend for want of his bath and other photographic apparatus, could not accompany me. Wanting the excitement of the chase, the length of hill and dale we traversed now seemed wearisome enough; the wild ducks on the placid surface of the vlei, scarcely noticed us as we passed, and a few hundred yards beyond it we first saw the gigantic carcase of which we were in quest, looming like a grey granite boulder above the bush. Of course I had seen elephants, but it had always been at my home and not theirs, and neither picture nor well-groomed black-skinned show specimen from India, had quite prepared me to stand for the first time, without a feeling of awe and wonder beside the mighty African thus fallen in his own domain. Masses of earth had been upturned by his broad feet, his column-like legs were stiffened in his tracks, the tusk on the lower side was buried in the soil. The head and curling trunk extended forward, leaving the broad forehead (flat or even convex and not indented like the Indian) nearly in a line with the body.

The ears which in the African are of enormous size, covered with their upper part nearly half the neck, the lobes actually meeting above the spine, the hinder part reaching to the "death spot" behind the shoulder, and the lower descending nearly to a level with the chest. The rough grey side deeply marked with wrinkles crossing each other like a network, and destitute of hair except a few solitary bristles, rose more like a rock than the skin of a lately living animal, so high that I could barely see the head of a man beyond it. A dark purple stain upon the lower side of the chest alone indicated the cause of death, the bullets having entered the shoulder now in contact with the ground. I wished at the moment for the companionship of Wolf, the artist of the beautiful illustrations in Anderson's "Lake Ngami," or some other artist more competent than myself to give in all their integrity the characteristics of the mighty animal; but only the Damara and bushmen were there, and their impatience I checked peremptorily till I had made a careful outline, allowing them to open the abdomen while I was working in the colours. The sun was just beginning to be warm, and the carcase had not swelled much; nevertheless the Bushman approached the flank with the caution of a practised fencer, springing aside with marvellous agility when he had made his blow. Nor was the caution vain, for the discharge of a fire-engine was nothing to what followed and I can easily believe in the cannon-like explosions I have been told of when the carcase that has been all day under a vertical sun is pierced for the first time. Before long the fat and sheets of the intestines were spread like blankets over every bush, tit-bits were broiled and eaten among the garbage in which the savages were revelling and delighting, especially in the wild songs that issued in sepulchral tones from the cavernous interior until the ribs were sufficiently bared to reveal to view those who were detaching the dainty morsels within them; but to me, I must confess, the most disenchanting sight of all was the flock of lovely butterflies with all their spiritual and Psyche-like associations fluttering fearlessly among them and feeding greedily as they on the most offensive portions.

I made another sketch while the hide, more than an inch thick, was being torn in planks from the ribs, and was just beginning to enjoy a bath in the vlei when the bushmen came down for the same purpose, the Damara alone thinking a wash a work of supererogation. At night we supped on steaks which were really superior to much of the beef we had latterly eaten, and as this was the first elephant at whose death I had been present, I asked Chapman to relinquish in my favour his right to the tail, which I preserved as a memento of the scene.—Thomas Baines, F.R.G.S., in *Land and Water*, June 8.

HOW TO GROW FERNS.

No plants are so suitable for indoor or town culture as ferns, hence no others are so popular, and those who have not had much experience in their treatment will not object to a few hints on the subject. There are two methods in which ferns may be cultivated, viz., in an open fernery, or in closed cases; but before adverting to either, it may be advisable to give a hint or two on raising ferns from spores. The German gardeners take a cube of turfy peat, about 1½ inch square, and this they dip in boiling water in order to destroy all the animal life which it contains; it is then laid in a flat saucer, and the spores are sprinkled upon the upper side. A small quantity of water is poured into the saucer, and the whole is covered with a bell-glass. A little water is required to be added from time to time, to compensate for evaporation, but great care must be taken to pour it in without washing the spores off the turf, and in five or six weeks a green moss-like substance will cover the turf, and the young ferns will gradually develope themselves.

Mrs. Helen Watney informs us that it is a curious fact that fern spores which have been gathered and dried three or four years, will, when sown, germinate more quickly than fresh spores.

Some persons employ a porous sandstone in the place of peat, and the lady to whom we have already alluded recommends cinders, for the following reasons:—"Sandstone almost invariably contains the germs of fungi, which hinder, and very frequently prevent, the development of the fern spores, and peat, unless prepared by dipping in boiling water, and thus destroying all life, is open to the same objection. Now, if cinders (which, if fresh, contain no fungi) are used, mixed with a suitable quantity of peat, subjected as above, the ferns will have a fair chance of proper development, for it is highly improbable that fungi will obstruct their growth. I have found that peat, if used alone, becomes soddened; and as ferns, like all other plants cultivated in pots, require good drainage, that essential is obtained by the use of cinders mixed therewith." Many gardeners raise their ferns by sowing the spores on silver sand. We have known of many successes from the employment of sandstone, and some failures through the prevalence of fungoid growths; but of the admixture of cinders and peat, as above recommended, all the testimony has hitherto been favourable.

The cultivation of ferns in the open air demands but little special comment. A sloping bank, shaded from the direct rays of the sun, in a sheltered situation, and where possible in the neighbourhood of a pond, stream, or ornamental water, is the first object to be regarded. If these conditions cannot be fulfilled, the situation should, at the least, be damp and shady. It is customary to plant ferns in an artificial rockwork; but, when this is done, the mound should *not* be so constructed that every drop of moisture is carefully drained away, but rather to be the face of a slope from higher ground, so that the drying winds do not whistle all around it, and extract every atom of water. If the spot is carefully selected, and a light soil provided for the interstices of the stone-work, there is very little to fear. The most luxuriant plants of the Royal Fern which we have ever seen under cultivation were placed amongst the rough stone-work of a large rustic fountain, and here they flourished apparently as well as in their native "homes and haunts." Many a window, in towns, from which the prospect is only a blank wall, might be made to look cheerful and comfortable by raising an outdoor fernery of the hardiest species around it. Under such conditions, a humble imitation might be made of the fernery windows on the ground floor of the South Kensington Museum.

Ferns may be grown in pots with great success. The common deep flower-pots are as good as any for the purpose, and it is as injurious to put in too many "crocks" for drainage as too few: moderation is best, and, as a rule, what would be considered good drainage for ordinary pot plants will answer very well for ferns. From whatever soil they may be taken, it is surprising how soon ferns will accommodate themselves to the loam and peat in which they are usually grown. The rock-loving species are best grown in a mixture of broken brickbats, old mortar, and sandy loam, taking care that they are not stinted of moisture in the summer, and but slightly moistened during the winter. Many species are very impatient of any moisture at their crowns, so that it is a good plan to keep the crowns elevated to the level, or a little above the level, of the pot. We have found that all the plants which required to be transferred to larger pots—an operation which becomes essential every two or three years—may be removed as well in the early spring as at any other season of the year, and much better than during the winter. A great deal is said and written about plenty of light and air, but too much of either is certainly a disadvantage in fern culture. At all times of the year, except about three months in the winter, we should certainly recommend shading them more or less, according to the strength of sunlight. Water is another point on which theory and practice often differ. Ferns will certainly never flourish in a dry powdery condition of the soil, nor will they continue to do so when it is permanently saturated with moisture. A moist atmosphere is better than all the syringing in the world: in fact, the continual squirting of water over the foliage and crowns of many ferns, except the hardiest, is simply dooming them to death. Rain-water in moderation, no direct glare of sunlight, gradual admission of air when the temperature is too high, and the careful des truction of small slugs and all similar pests, are the best rules to remember.

For the introduction of the method of growing plants in closed cases we are indebted to Mr. N. B. Ward, from whom such cases are generally denominated Wardian cases. There are two errors commonly entertained with regard to the growth of ferns in closed cases. One error exists in the belief that the cases must be airtight; and the other, that it is quite sufficient, at stated intervals, to let in upon them a deluge of water.

The form of the case may be accommodated to individual taste. Some prefer the octagonal, some the quadrangular. Let each consult his or her peculiar taste; and we will describe one to serve as a model either to imitate or shun, as taste may prompt, the object being rather to illustrate the principle of construction, &c., than to establish any orthodox standard.

First of all construct a strong wooden box, 30 inches in length, 17 inches in width, and 5 inches deep. Cover it well inside with pitch, and outside with paint. At one end, and on a level with the bottom, insert a small stop-cock or a wooden plug, so as to draw off, if necessary, any superfluous water. Lay on the bottom, to the depth of one inch, any drainage material. Then fill to the top with soil. Some will prefer sifted cocoa-nut refuse and charcoal, others a mixture of fibrous peat and sand, whilst others will be content with a light loam. In this the ferns may be planted, according to taste. The upper portion, which consists of a zinc framework glazed, may rest upon a ledge, half an inch below the level of the top in the interior of the wooden box. Or if the case is smaller than the above dimensions, and the top not too heavy, it may rest on the soil, leaving a space of half an inch all round between the box and the cover: by this means the external air passes and is filtered through the soil before it enters the case. Whatever may be the form of the upper portion of the case, it is always advisable to have at each end, at the top, a strip of perforated zinc, about an inch in depth, and extending across the case. This should be furnished with a shutter inside, so contrived that it may be opened or closed at will. This arrangement will obviate the cloudy appearance of the glass, which in perfectly closed cases often prevents the contents being seen, and will, moreover, be advantageous to the ferns. As the consumption of water is small, such a case *seldom* will require its addition, and *never* improve under a deluge. Any excess of water which may have been supplied may be drawn off by the plug or stopcock at the end.

Planting the case may next occupy attention; and this may be done either by inserting potted ferns, and covering the pots with the soil, or employing only cocoa-nut refuse for the purpose; or the ferns may be transplanted directly into the soil. Special precautions must be taken with species having creeping rhizomes, which must be provided with little elevations on which to be planted.

The selection of species must depend greatly on the localisation of the fernery when completed. If it is to be placed in a room in which a fire is constantly kept during the winter, more tender species may be cultivated than if the case is intended to take its chance in some room whence fires are generally excluded. Many foreign species may be added with advantage to those which are natives of this country, half of which, at the least, are too large for any moderate-sized fernery.

In placing this fernery, when completed, the full glare of sunlight should be studiously avoided: a northern aspect is good, north-western is perhaps the best. When travelling through North Wales in search of ferns, we ascertained the aspect of a great number of flourishing fern patches by means of a pocket compass, and found invariably that it was northwest; a fact which we have taken care to remember.

It is by no means essential that an elaborate fern-case should be constructed at a great expense to cultivate a few ferns. For a few shillings a very respectable cottage fernery may be established. Two or three ferns may be planted in a common flower-pan, which is naturally porous, not being glazed either inside or out. This may be placed in a round earthenware dish, with the space of an inch all around between the outside of the pan and the inside of the dish. This intervening space may be filled with bog moss (*Sphagnum*), and a bell-glass over all, or only over the inner pan. The common hand-glass, with a greenish tint, are preferable to those which are colourless, and whose sole recommendation lies in their higher price. A hole may be drilled with advantage through the handle at the top of the glass, for ventilation. A piece of soft wood will easily stop it if desired. When water is added, it should be poured over the bog moss in the outer circle only, enough moisture will then find its way through the porous sides of the inner pan; and a very convenient and economical little fernery, wanting scarcely any attention, will be the result.—*A Fern-Book for Everybody*, by M. C. Cooke. London: Warne

PEARLS.

PEARLS are occasionally found in the common mussel, and also in the oyster, scallop, cockle, periwinkle, and pinna; but they are generally inferior in size and quality to those of the fresh-water pearl-mussel (*Unio margaritiferus*); and Mr. Beckman, in his "History of Inventions," states that real pearls are found under the shield of the sea-hare (*Aplysia*), as has been observed by Bohadsch, in his book, "De Animalibus Marinis" (Dresdæ, 1761.) Our Scotch pearl-fishery has, within the last few years, been most successfully revived, and in 1860 Mr. Moritz Unger, a foreigner, on making a tour through the districts where the pearl-mussel abounds, found that the pearl-fishing was not altogether forgotten, many of the people having pearls in their possession, of which they did not know the value. He purchased all he could obtain; consequently, in the following year, many persons devoted their spare time to pearl-fishing, and during the summer months made as much as £8 to £10 weekly. The summer of 1862 was most favourable for fishing, owing to the dryness of the season, and the average price was from £2 6s. to 10s., £5 being a high price. They now fetch prices varying from £5 to £20. The Queen purchased one Scotch pearl for 40 guineas, others at high prices have been bought by the Empress of the French, and the Duchess of Hamilton, and Mr. Unger has a necklace of these pearls, valued at £350. Pearl-mussels are found in Lochs Earn, Tay, Rannoch, and Lubnaig, and in the Don, the Leith, and in many of the other Scotch streams; also in some of the Welsh rivers, from whence I have received fine specimens; in Ireland, near Enniskillen, and in the river Bann, which is noted for its fine pearls. They wade for them in the shallow pools, or take them by thrusting a long stick between the valves when the shell is open. When a number have been collected, they are left to decompose, when the pearls drop out. They may also be found in Kerry, in Donegal, in the Moy, near Foxford, and in many of the Irish rivers; and Mr. Buckland states in the "Field," December 10th, 1864, that they abound near Oughterard, and that a man called "Jemmy the pearl catcher," told him he knew when a mussel had a pearl in it, without requiring to open it first, because "she (the mussel), sits upright with her mouth in the mud, and her back is crooked," that is, it is corrugated like a cow's horn. Bruce in his "Travels," observes that the pearl-fishers of Bahrein informed him that they had no expectation of finding a pearl when the shell was smooth and perfect, but were sure to find some when the shell was distorted and deformed, and he adds, that this applies equally to the Scotch pearl-mussels. In France they also collect from the pearl-mussels, and they generally sell them as foreign pearls. At Omagh, in the north of Ireland, there was formerly a pearl-fishery, and Gilbert, Bishop of Limerick, about 1094, sent a present of Irish pearls to Anselm, Archbishop of Canterbury. Scotch pearls were in demand abroad, as early as the twelfth century. Suetonius says that the great motive of Cæsar's coming to Britain was to obtain its pearls, and states that they were so large that he used to try the weight of them by his hand, and dedicated a breastplate made of them to Venus Genetrix. According to Pliny, the island of Taprobane (Ceylon), was most productive of pearls, and he considers that the most valuable were those found in the vicinity of Arabia, in the Persian Gulf.

Oriental pearls are found in the *Meleagrina margaritifera*, or pearl oyster; and Chares of Mytilene, in his seventh book of his "Histories of Alexander," tells us that, "in the Indian Sea, and also off the coast of Armenia, Persia, Susiana, and Babylonia, a fish is caught very like an oyster, large, and of oblong shape, containing within its shell flesh, which is plentiful, white, and very fragrant, and from it the men pick out white bones, called by them pearls, and of these they make necklaces and chains for the hands and feet, of which the Persians are very fond, as are the Medes and all Asiatics, esteeming them as much more valuable than golden ornaments." Occasionally, they are called stones and bones by Greek authors, and Tertullian calls them maladies of shell-fish and warts—*concharum vitia et verrucas*. Pliny states that when pearls grow old they become thick, and adhere to the shell, from which they can only be separated by a file; again, that pearls which have one surface flat and the other spherical, opposite to the plane side, are for that reason called tympania, or tambour-pearls, "quibus una tantum est facies, et ab ea rotunditas, aversis planities, ob id tympania mominantur." The "tympana," or hand-drums of the ancients, were often of a semi-globular shape, like the kettle-drums of the present day. Shells which had pearls still adhering to them were used as boxes for unguents. Long pear-shaped pearls, called elenchi, had their peculiar value, resembling the alabaster boxes in form, which were used for ointments. Ear-rings were invented by the Roman ladies, called "crotalia, or castanet pendants, from the pearls rattling as they knocked against each other."

The story of Cleopatra swallowing the pearl, in order that she might say she had expended on a single entertainment ten millions of sesterces, is too well known to require repeating here; suffice it to say, that Pliny informs us that before the time of Antony and Cleopatra, Clodius, the son of the tragic actor, Æsopus, had done the same at Rome; "he having dissolved in vinegar (or at least, attempted to do so), a pearl worth about £8,000, which he took from the earring of Cœcilia Metella." Pliny further adds, that, by way of glorification to his palate, Clodius Æsopus was desirous of trying what was the taste of pearls, and as he found it wonderfully pleasing, that he might not be the only one to know it, he had a pearl set before each of his guests for him to swallow." It was not unusual for the Romans to adorn their horses and other favourite animals, with splendid necklaces; and we are told that Initatius, the favourite horse of the Emperor Caligular, wore a pearl collar. The Roman ladies even wore pearls at night, that in their sleep they might be conscious of the possession of these valuable gems. Julius Cæsar prohibited the use of purple and pearls to all persons who were not of a certain rank, and the latter also to unmarried women. From the twelfth to the sixteenth centuries, extravagance in jewellery was carried to an unlimited extent at the Courts in Europe, and from the reign of Francis I. to that of Louis XIII., the greater part of the jewels worn were set with pearls, and these latter were worn in preference to all other ornaments, until the death of Maria Theresa of Austria. The French call irregular-shaped pearls " Perles barroques," and these malformations were ingeniously utilised by the fanciful taste of the Cinque Cento period. No doubt many of my readers will remember the specimens exhibited in the loan collection at the South Kensington Museum. One was a Cinque Cento pendant, in the form of a siren; the head, neck, and arms of white enamel, the body made of a very large " pearl barroque," and a fish's tail enamelled and set with rubies. It belonged to Colonel Guthrie, and is of fine Italian work of the sixteenth century. Another, in the possession of Messrs. Farrer, was a gold pendant jewel in the form of a ship with three masts, a large pearl barroque forming the hull, &c. The wedding dress of Anne of Cleves was "a gown of rich cloth and gold, embroidered with great flowers of large orient pearls." The unfortunate Mary, Queen of Scots, possessed pearls which were considered the finest in Europe, and these were purchased in a most iniquitous manner by Queen Elizabeth from the Earl of Moray, for a third part of their value. Miss Strickland (in her " Lives of the Queens of Scotland," pages 82 and 83, vol. vi.), says that if anything further than the letters of Drury and Throckmorton be required to prove the confederacy between the English Government and the Earl of Moray, it will only be necessary to expose the disgraceful fact of the traffic for Queen Mary's costly parure of pearls, her own personal property, which she had brought from France. A few days before she effected her escape from Lochleven Castle, the Regent sent these with a choice selection of her jewels, very secretly, to London, by his trusty agent, Sir Nicholas Elphinstone, who undertook to negotiate their sale with the assistance of Throckmorton. Queen Elizabeth had the first offer of them, and the French Ambassador thus describes them:—" There are six cordons of large pearls strung as paternosters, but there are five-and-twenty separate from the rest, much finer and larger than those which are strung. These are, for the most part, like black muscades" (a very rare and valuable variety of pearl, with the deep purple colour and bloom of the muscatel grape.) They were appraised by various merchants, but Queen Elizabeth was determined to have them at the sum named by the jeweller, though he would have made his profit by selling them again. Others valued them at three thousand pounds sterling, some Italian merchants at twelve thousand crowns, and a Genoese at sixteen thousand crowns, but twelve thousand was the price Queen Elizabeth was allowed to have them for, and Catherine de Medicis was quite as eager to purchase these pearls as her good cousin of England, knowing they were worth nearly double the sum at which they had been valued in London, having presented some of them herself to Mary. She therefore used every endeavour to recover them, but the French Ambassador wrote to inform her that it was impossible to accomplish her desire of obtaining the Queen of Scots' pearls, " for as he had told her from the first, they were intended for the gratification of the Queen of England, who had been allowed to purchase them at her own price, and they were now in her hands." The possession of wealth and jewels is not always a source of happiness or benefit to their possessors, if we may judge " from the above mentioned fact in history, and, indeed, it is even more clearly exemplified in the case of the eminent Mogul, who died of hunger during a grievous famine, which depopulated part of Guzerat. A large mausoleum or Mahometan tomb was erected to his memory in the suburbs of Cambay, with an inscription, telling us that during this terrible scarcity the deceased had offered a measure of pearls for an equal quantity of grain, but not being able to procure it, he died of hunger."

A pearl is described by Madame de Barrera, as nearly the size of a pigeon's egg, and pear-shaped, it weighed 250 carats, and was known as " La Peregrina," and belonged to the crown of Spain. It was brought from Panama in 1560, by Don Diego de Temes, who presented it to Philip II. " It was then valued at fourteen thousand ducats, but Freco, the King's jeweller having seen it, said it might be worth £14,000, £30,000, £50,000, or £100,000, as such a pearl was priceless." In 1779 a pearl, which from its shape was called the Sleeping Lion, was offered for sale at St. Petersburg, by a Dutchman, it weighed 578 carats, and was bought in India for £4,500. The largest pearl known, I believe, is the one which was exhibited at South Kensington Museum, in the loan collection, in the possession of A. J. B. Beresford Hope, Esq. It weighs 3 oz., is 2 inches long, 4½ inches in circumference, and is set as a pendant.—*Edible Mollusks of Great Britain*, by Mr. Lovell. Reeve & Co.

THE TARANTULA KILLERS OF TEXAS.

AN investigation of the extensive family of Mud Daubers would be an interesting and instructive study. It would necessarily include that of the various types of spiders, from the great hairy Mygale Hentzii, down to the smallest, almost microscopic species; for nearly every type of spiders has its special enemy among the Mud Daubers.

The large, red-winged "Tarantula Killer" (the *Pompilus formosus* of Say) is, as far as I know, the largest of the dauber group. It takes its prey by stinging, thus instantly paralysing every limb of its victim. The effects of the introduction of its venom is as sudden as the snap of the electric spark. The wasp then drags it, going backwards to some suitable place, excavates a hole five inches deep in the earth, places its great spider in it, deposits an egg under one of its legs, near the body, and then covers the hole very securely. A young Tarantula Killer will be produced from this egg, if no accident befalls it, about the 1st of June of the ensuing year.

This large and conspicuous insect is everywhere in Texas called the Tarantula Killer, and is over two inches in length; the head, thorax, abdomen, and long spiny legs are all black, while the wings are sometimes of a bright brown, with black spots at the tips. It is armed with a formidable sting, which it invariably uses in taking its prey. This sting does not kill the Mygale, but paralyses it—suspends all animation—and in this state, in a dry place, and at the proper temperature, it is in a condition to resist decomposition a long time. The entire group of Mud Daubers possess the power of paralysing their victims, and in that condition they store up their spiders, caterpillars, and other insects, which are to serve as food for coming generations.

The Tarantula Killer pursues several other species of the large ground spiders, but the Mygale Hentzii, or Tarantula, is his favourite.

I have sometimes found under shelving rocks, and other sheltered places, dauber's nests that were doubtless several years old. In some of the cells, where the egg had proved abortive, the spiders were there, still limber, with no signs of decomposition about them. They did not seem to be dead, but looked as if they could almost move their legs, and were perhaps not unconscious of their deplorable condition. I should be frightened at the prospect of being stung by any of the larger types of this group of insects. I have, however, known but a single instance of this kind. Several years ago a person was stung by a common black dirt dauber on the shoulder near the neck; he complained of numbness in the part for a distance of some inches around the wound, but of no pain. Its effects lasted about twenty-four hours. I think it quite probable that the large Tarantula Killer would produce a more serious inconvenience, and perhaps paralyse the whole system. The Pompilus, however, is a good-natured insect, showing no signs of pugnacity, except when she has a fine fat Tarantula in hand, and then she only threatens violence by spreading out her red wings, and running a little way towards the intruder. She is quite tame, and will come familiarly in and about one's yard and house, dragging the prostrate Mygale under the floor, where she hides it from the intrusion of other Tarantula Killers, who would, if they could find it, take out the egg and put one of their own in its place, as they are remarkable for such thieving propensities.

The Mygale Hentzii, on the other hand, sometimes succeeds in capturing his great enemy, as I once noticed. When first observed, the Mygale had the Tarantula Killer, still alive, in his mouth, holding it by the back. The Tarantula seemed to be greatly elated at its success, which it manifested by capering about, and performing various other antics, such as running suddenly at anything or person that came near it, holding on to his victim all the time. The Tarantula Killer appeared to be conscious of her condition, and was, as far as I could discern, fully resigned to her fate, remaining perfectly quiet. I regretted that I could not wait to witness the finale of this affair: such cases do not often occur.

The Tarantula Killers have severe fights with each other. It occasionally happens, when one of them succeeds in capturing a Tarantula, that another one, or more, flying around in that vicinity, and smelling the odour that arises from the Tarantula Killer when she uses her sting, which resembles the odour of the paper-making wasp (Vespa), only much stronger, takes the scent like a dog, tracks the Tarantula, following it up closely, and makes a violent effort to get possession of the paralysed spider. A fight ensues, which occasionally terminates in the death of both parties; at other times the contest lasts but a little while, as the stronger party drives off the weaker, and takes possession of the prey.

It is surprising to one who has been educated to believe that the faculty of reason belongs alone to man, to contemplate the consummate ingenuity which is displayed by these insects in their efforts to secure their eggs from the observation of their own thieving sisters, and to hide the food they have provided for their young during the period of its existence under ground.

The Tarantula Killer feeds upon the honey and pollen of the flowers of the Elder, and of *Vitis ampelopsis*, the Virginia Creeper; but its favourite nourishment is taken from the blossoms of Asclepias quadrifolium. This species of Asclepias blooms through the summer, and the Tarantula Killer seems to know the locality of every plant. If one finds on the prairie a plant of Asclepias quadrifolium in bloom, and watches ten or fifteen minutes, he will be almost certain to see a Tarantula Killer come to it. This insect requires considerable food, as its period of life extends from the 1st of June until November, or till the frost destroys all the flowers, when it seems to die for want of food, as it is often seen at this time crawling about in a very feeble state. I do not think any of them ever survive the winter, as they never appear earlier than June.—*The American Naturalist*, May.

COLOURS IN PLANTS.

Nimium ne crede colori is one of those many aphoristic sayings which people now-a-days take the liberty of heeding or of disregarding at their own sweet will and pleasure, and wholly independently of the sayings or doings of poets or philosophers; and when the soft velvety pile of a pansy, or the exquisite tints of a rose are in question, it is too much to expect one to heed the admonitions of those botanists who are apt to pooh-pooh colour in plants as beneath their notice, or at any rate as being insufficient to "furnish specific characters." In this latter point, indeed, we feel compelled to concur, not, however, without an impression that when more is known as to the mode of production of colour, its disposition in certain portions of the plant to the exclusion of others, and when the curious relations that exist between colour and form, as pointed out some years since by Dr. Dickie, are sufficiently worked out, then the botanists will have to alter their opinions; and colour, like the other attributes of the plant, will furnish its quota towards the sum of characters by which one set of plants is distinguished from another. It does so now to some extent, notably so in the case of seaweeds, but by-and-by its services in this way will, we doubt not, be better appreciated. In the meantime the increasing popularity of plants with brilliantly coloured foliage necessarily leads to the consideration as to how these varied hues are produced, and induces the cultivator to reflect on the power that he has to produce, modify, or obliterate these tints at will. The principal facts relating to the colouration of leaves are pretty well known to our readers, or, if not, they are readily accessible. Mr. Berkeley alluded to some of them at the last meeting of the Royal Horticultural Society, and our main object at present is to supplement his remarks by calling attention to some facts, not novel, indeed, but still worthy the consideration of the gardener, and which we have lately had the opportunity of testing by the examination of specimens kindly furnished to us by Mr. Wills.

We would specially call attention to the localisation of the colour in particular cells. Thus, in the Zonal Pelargoniums, not only is the colour distributed in a somewhat semicircular zone, but a microscopic section reveals that the coloured cells are almost entirely to be found just under the epidermis, especially on the upper surface of the leaf; no doubt in some cases they may be found elsewhere, but the spots mentioned are, so to speak, the head-quarters of the coloured juices, and the same thing holds good in the red cabbage and many other brightly coloured plants known to us.

This may be due to the more intense action of light on the surfaces of the leaf, though there are many difficulties in the way of accepting such a solution to which our space now forbids us to allude. Again, the anatomical structure of the leaf, so correctly described by Mr. Berkeley, does not fully explain the localisation of the colour; for while it is undoubtedly true that in most cases the coloured fluids are to be found in the prismatic cells to be found just beneath the upper skin of the leaf, yet they are not confined to those cells; and some of the Pelargoniums are destitute of cells of this form. But perhaps the leaf-stalk shows the greatest peculiarities in the position of the coloured juices. On submitting to the microscope a longitudinal slice of the pink leaf-stalk from one of Mr. Wills' seedlings we saw, what we had often seen before in other plants, that the coloured cells were arranged in longitudinal rows throughout the stalk, the rows being separated one from the other by colourless cells, so that the appearance was not unlike that of a ribbon border, so regular was the arrangement. It is very difficult to account for this arrangement, and we shall not attempt to do so at present.

There is one point upon which we should be glad to have further information, as we think probably there are more exceptions to be met with than we have ourselves encountered, and that point is as to the precise part of the cotyledons or seed leaves in which the red tint first makes its appearance. As far as we have seen in seedling plants of red zoned varieties, while in the perfect leaves the red tint first shows itself in the median zone of the leaf, in the case of the seed leaves and also in the case of the stipules, the red tint is first perceptible at or near the edges, and specially as regards the stipules near their points.

Other matters revealed, by an examination of Pelargonium leaves, not without significance for the thoughtful cultivator, are these:—

The pure white spots are due to the entire absence of chlorophyll, hence it is no wonder that if a seedling show itself with two wholly white seed-leaves that it speedily dies, because the due production of chlorophyll or leaf-green is well known to be intimately associated with the healthy development of the plant. Hence, as Mr. Wills says, "if the white is allowed to have its course, the plant will do no good for itself." Indeed, specimens sent to us by Mr. Wills show this conclusively; the green leaves having been removed and only the white ones suffered to remain, the effect has been to check the growth; and had the experiment been pursued longer, death must have ensued. This absence of chlorophyll, and attendant loss of vitality in the cells, as Mr. Grieve well remarked accounts for the puckered convex leaves of so many of the Silver Tricoloured Pelargoniums. To us it has also appeared, though in this matter our experience is in some degree opposed to that of others, that the red colouring matter is not produced unless there be at least some chlorophyll in the leaf; in other words, we have never seen a trace of pink colouring matter in leaves that are *absolutely* white, though in those that have even the faintest tinge of yellow, indicating the existence in small proportion of chlorophyll, the reddish tint may very often be met with. But while we have not satisfied ourselves of the existence of red colouring juices (or we may add of starch grains) in leaves which are entirely destitute of chlorophyll, we have frequently seen clusters of crystals or "raphides" in the colourless cells of the white leaves. If this be borne out, it will furnish an additional argument to those who look on rhapides as mere excretions. But this is running away from the subject of colour, and in order not to weary the patience of our readers, we dismiss the subject for the present, merely adding a record of a circumstance which has been made known to us by the courtesy of Mr. Bull, and which is very significant, and that is, that a pink tint may readily be produced in the silver-edged ivy-leaved Pelargoniums by placing the plants near to the glass, and thus exposing them fully to the action of light. In this plant the coloured juices may be seen to be contained in spheroidal or polygonal, not prismatic cells, and, in some parts of the leaf at any rate, to be as abundant on the lower as on the upper surface of the leaf.—*Gardeners' Chronicle*, June 8.

THE BRIMSTONE BUTTERFLY.

THIS delicate butterfly is, wherever it occurs, one of the most common of British insects; it is by no means rare upon the Continent, and may be met with in great numbers in some parts of India. Few insects can be more attractive to the eye than this species when upon the wing; its flight, though rather more rapid and powerful, very much resembles that of the well-known *Pieris Brassicæ*, or common white butterfly of our gardens; like it, the Brimstone has a habit of repeating the same regular journey over and over again for hours together, therefore, though the collector should miss his insect the first time it passes him, he need not despair of eventually capturing it, if he but remains in the same place for a few minutes. Of this fact we had practical proof the very first time that we saw the insect alive, and in the neighbourhood of London.

The Brimstone is at its prime towards the middle of August. In order to see it to perfection it is necessary to leave the noise and bustle of town, and choosing, if practicable, a clover field in the vicinity of some large wood, we are not long in detecting its golden glories upon the wide-spread purple carpet, for in such spots as these our yellow friend especially delights.

What luxury, whilst scenting the delicious perfume of the clover, to watch those sulphur-coloured fairies fluttering from flower to flower in search of their sweet food!

Having taken our fill at the Brimstone's restaurant, we may enter the wood where we again perceive these butterflies in pursuit of beauty. The charm of the female of this species depends upon its greater delicacy of colouring, the male having the advantage in richness of hue.

The males far exceed the females in number (this seems to be usually the case with common species), and consequently the competition in matrimonial affairs is something dreadful. We have taken seven Brimstone butterflies at one stroke of the net, and six of them proved to be males. The genus *Rhodocera*, to which this species belongs, contains a great variety of beautiful forms, in all of which the prevailing colour is yellow. A figure of this species, showing both sides of the wing, will be found in the "Proceedings of the Zoological Society" for 1865, under the name of *Gonepteryx Urania*. The eggs of the Brimstone butterfly are of a conical form, with ribs sculptured on the sides. The caterpillar, when fully grown, is green, finely speckled with black, and with a pale lateral line; it may be found upon buckthorn (*Rhamnus catharticus*) and alder buckthorn (*R. frangula*). The curiously-shaped chrysalis is suspended by means of a central girdle and a web of fine silk at the extremity of the tail; its colour is bright green varied with yellow.

The only well-known variety of the Brimstone is found in the south of Europe, India, Madeira, &c.; it differs from the common form in having the greater portion of the front wings suffused with orange. It has, however, been described as a distinct species under the name of *Cleopatra*, but the fact of its having been bred from the same batch of eggs with *R. Rhamni* has effectually proved its identity with this common species.

The arrangement of the veins upon the wings of this insect differs considerably from that in the swallow-tailed; the nervules of the front margin (*costa*) of the upper wings being all widely separated, whilst in *Papilio Machaon* they lie close together. Again, the termination of the cell is in this species concave instead of convex, but a careful eye will readily detect these and many other points of distinction between the two insects; so we need not enter into a more detailed description of them here.

The scales are somewhat variable in shape, but not nearly so much so as in the preceding species; this may be partly owing to the uniform colouring of the insect. The legs are short, hairy, and thickly clothed with scales: as in the swallow-tailed, they are all made use of in walking. The antennæ (horns) are flat, and in form something between a cricket-bat and a canoe-paddle; the annulations are not very distinctly marked and are rather wide apart. The proboscis is black and flattened; it coils up very much like a watch-spring, and is protected by a pair of moderately large palpi, which when strongly magnified, form beautiful microscopic objects; they are clothed with long yellow scales, excepting at the upper outer margin, where the scales are short, and of a blue-grey colour, varied with red points.

The caterpillar of *Rhodocera Rhamni* may be found from May to July; the perfect insect leaves the chrysalis during the following month, and may be met with until towards the end of October, when it hybernates, and appears again in February, the females then continuing until May. The males, if taken in the spring, are frequently so much shattered and chafed, that they are utterly useless as specimens for the cabinet, although they may still be of value to cut up for microscopic objects. This beautiful insect is common and generally distributed in the south of England; it is scarce in the midland counties, and does not occur in Scotland.—Arthur G. Butler, F.Z.S., in *Nature and Art*, June.

Nesting of the Peregrine Falcon.

Mr. H. W. Fielden, writing in the June number of the *Zoologist*, says:—"I wrote to a friend in Stirling, in the beginning of April, to inquire whether the falcons had made their appearance this spring in the hilly districts that lie to the south of the villages of Hippen and Gurgunnock, in Stirlingshire, a locality at least thirty miles in any direction from the sea. In a few days I received a reply, to the effect that he had seen a pair of peregrine falcons sailing around a precipitous mountain-side, from which, in 1857, I had taken a nest. Begging him to watch carefully for the nesting-places, and to get ready a sufficient amount of rope, I waited till the 26th of April, and then went to Stirling. The morning of the 27th saw us at early dawn at the base of the precipice, and I immediately—directed by his barking note—descried the tiercel sailing high overhead: my companion pointed out a spot where he thought he had marked the nest, but, after a severe climb, there was no hole or trace of a nest to be found. Rather disappointed, but still hoping that the female was sitting close somewhere in the rock, I walked along the base of the crag, shouting out, and every now and then striking some rock with my stick: suddenly from behind me the female bird started forth from the rock with a wild cry, and began circling round our heads, apparently in great anger. Not having discovered the exact situation of the nest, we withdrew about a quarter of a mile, and hid ourselves behind a boulder rock, watching every movement of the falcons through a glass: as soon as we were out of sight the female began wheeling around that portion of the cliff where evidently the nest was. The tiercel came down and joined her, both sailing backwards and forwards across the face of the cliff, with a flight not unlike that of swifts. In a quarter of an hour or so the female bird alighted on a small projection of the rock, stretched her pinions to their full extent, then gracefully closed them and commenced preening her wing-feathers: her toilet being arranged she turned round and popped into a small hole behind her in a most undignified manner, bobbing her head and waddling in after the manner of a pigeon entering a dovecote. I felt confident this must be the nest, but walking back again to the base of the rock, struck with my stick, and out she flew, screaming wildly and hovering about thirty feet over my head: the tiercel again joined her, and both of them displayed great indignation at my intrusion, circling round my head and uttering sharp cries, the tiercel, however, always keeping at a far greater distance than the female, which I could have shot with the greatest ease. To get at the nest was a matter of some difficulty: the precipice, a straight up and down slippery trap rock, was at least a hundred and fifty feet high, and the nest about fifty feet from the bottom: our best plan was to let a rope over until it touched the ground, and then with its aid climb up to the nest, but to accomplish this required more rope than we had with us, so we returned to Stirling. Sunday intervened, but the 29th of April saw us out again with an extra hundred feet of rope: letting the rope over, attaching it to a post at the top, constructing a rough ladder to ascend by, took us some hours, and it was six in the evening when my companion got up and took four eggs out of the hole: the eggs were lying on the bare rock, not a bit of material of any kind underneath them: during the time my companion was ascending the rope the female bird made most vicious attempts to strike him, sometimes coming within five or six feet of his head. I must mention what occurred when my companion was within ten feet of the nest: a pair of wild ducks, going to their lowland feeding-ground, came down the glen; the tiercel, as they passed the cliff, dashed off in pursuit, singling out the mallard, who with loud quackings attempted to rise above the hawk; the sight seemed too much for the female falcon; for a few moments she forgot her maternal instincts and joined her partner in the chase; making one dash at the mallard, which he eluded, she returned again to hover over our heads: a thick fog rolling up the glen shut out the tiercel from my view, and I could not see whether he killed his quarry or not, but I expect he did, as the ground at the base of the precipice was strewn here and there with grouse and duck bones and feathers. After withdrawing the rope, the falcon re-entered the hole, and as long as we were there did not leave it, and as it was getting dark I fancy she would remain seated in the nesting-hole till next morning. The eggs were deeply sat on, and gave me some trouble in emptying. These falcons will doubtless raise a second brood, unless some keeper gets his eye on them. I was so interested in their magnificent flight, courage and beauty of plumage and shape that, easily as I could have shot them, I refrained from doing so, hoping that they will hatch their second clutch of eggs and rear their brood in safety.

Exploration of Greenland.

Mr. Edward Whymper, the renowned Alp climber, who has started on his journey to Greenland, sends the following interesting letter to the *Athenæum*, June 15th:—

Copenhagen, 1867.

I shall be landed at the small Danish settlement of Jakobshavn (on the 69th parallel), and that place will be my head-quarters, at which I shall make my depot, and from which my journeys will be made. I have selected this point of departure, because there are greater facilities of communication between it and the other settlements than I could find at other stations, and also because I have reason to believe that the chances of getting into the interior will be greater for a party starting from there, than from any point in the neighbourhood.

I intend to travel by means of dog sledges, but I expect considerable trouble in getting them over the rough country which intervenes between the coast and the inferior snow. The latter, when once reached, I expect will prove comparatively easy travelling.

My system of travelling will be to do without depots *en route*, carrying as little weight and moving as rapidly as possible. In the first instance some time will be spent in preliminary trials and reconnoitering, and I shall then start for a month or five weeks' journey, taking at first a north-easterly direction, then coming south, and returning due west. I shall, if this journey is not entirely unsuccessful, then go for a similar amount of time to the south-east, returning to Jakobshavn by a more northerly route. The remaining time, if any, will be spent in exploring the island of Disce, and in examination of the fossil remains which are found in the neighbourhood, particularly on the shores of the Waigat Strait. I expect to leave for England in September, and to be home by the end of October or early in November.

The interior of Greenland is at present entirely unknown, and no serious attempt has ever been made to explore it. The two or three excursions which have been made by Danes towards the interior during the present century have experienced no greater difficulties than might be expected from inadequate time and imperfect means. Dr. Hayes (U.S.) has, however, on more than one occasion, made excursions towards the interior with considerable success, and has managed to travel occasionally as much as thirty-five or forty miles in a day. There is no reason to suppose that the interior presents extraordinary difficulties for travelling, and there is good reason to believe that it is something better than a dreary waste of ice and snow. Not only are traditions to be met with on every hand among the Greenlanders that the interior is a fertile country, but it is made almost a certainty by the fact that the countless herds of reindeer which occasionally visit different parts of the coast always retire towards the interior, where they are not followed. These herds of reindeer are so vast in numbers that they must require for sustenance a considerable amount of food; and hence it is believed by many who are best acquainted with the subject that the interior, if not a fertile, must be very far from a barren, country.

The unconquerable aversion of the natives to travel over the snow has proved hitherto the greatest difficulty in the way of visiting the interior. They have traditions of a savage, cannibal people living on the other side of the range of mountains which bounds the view from Davis's Strait; and others of a ferocious wild beast, the "Amarok," which has never, however, been known to be seen, much less taken. But the largest part of their aversion to travel over the snow is derived from their fear of the crevasses which it covers and conceals, and into which they have oftentimes fallen. I shall probably get no assistance from the Greenlanders, but I reckon on some from the half-breeds.

I cannot close this letter without a recognition of the kindness I have received at the hands of the Danes. Great and unexpected as the assistance has been which I have received in England, I must say that it has been surpassed by that which I have received from total strangers, who have not and who cannot receive any return.

Leaf Parasites

A letter has just been received from Professor Passerini, in which he alludes to two leaf parasites which have lately been observed in Italy. Of the first he says—"It may perhaps interest you to know that I have lately published and described, under the name of Uromyces Amygdali, in 'Erbario crittogamico Italiano,' No. 1373, a new fungus which has been gathered on peach leaves at Lago Maggiore; and in the fasciculus of that work just published I have given specimens and a description of another new fungus, which has been named Zythia Rabiei, from its being found on cicer arietinum (the chick pea) when attacked by rabbia, a disease which causes great injury in our fields to the crops of that plant. Though I have long been acquainted with the disease, I have not hitherto been able to detect the immediate cause, which perhaps is not dependent on the zythia, though it seems at least to be a constant attendant on the malady."

We touched on a similar subject in this journal (Nov. 26, 1864) on receiving some diseased peach leaves from an unknown correspondent, "W. W." These peach leaves were attacked by a little fungus, puccinia pruni, which in an early stage of growth is lecythea pruni spinosæ of Léveillé. We had, however, previously received from different parts of the world a distinct though nearly allied parasite on peach leaves, of which also we gave a figure. We have specimens of this from Madeira, sent by Mr. Salwey; from South Carolina, by Dr. Curtis; from Port Louis, Mauritius, by the late Dr. Ayres; from Valparaiso, by Mr. Bridges; and on apricot leaves from Marseilles, by Monsieur Castagne—so that it has a very wide geographical range; and like puccinia pruni, which occurs on apricot and peach leaves occasionally, as well as on those of the plum, seems to travel wherever the tree which produces it is carried. It becomes, therefore, a matter of some interest to ascertain exactly what Signor Passerini's parasite is, and we hope, therefore, to obtain specimens of that as well as of the zythia.

It is curious to see several of our leaf parasites so widely distributed. Both smut and wheat mildew occur wherever our common cereals are cultivated, and seem quite indifferent to climate. We are prepared to meet with the same species of fungi in similar climates, but scarcely in such different localities as Northern Europe and the hot plains of India. We might perhaps attribute this to the extreme simplicity of their organisation, which enables them to adapt themselves to very diverse conditions, were it not for the fact that some plants, as the common hollyhock, which are free from parasites here, are martyrs to them in other countries.—*M. J. B.*—*In Gardeners' Chronicle, May 25th.*

New Books.

[*Our limited space must of necessity compel us to give but very short notices of new books, but they will perhaps serve as a guide as to what books our readers may ask for at their libraries.*]

The Poultry Book, comprising the Breeding, Management, and Characteristics of Profitable and Ornamental Poultry. By W. B. Tegetmeier, F.Z.S. Routledge and Sons, The Broadway, Ludgate.

Although the mania for poultry has somewhat subsided, most persons with the smallest pretence for a yard have the fit come over them and think it would be so nice just to keep a few fowls. Unfortunately, want of knowledge, or want of proper attention to cleanliness, often compels the amateur to give up the attempt at some loss. The rule generally is to procure your stock and gather your knowledge with as little trouble as possible afterwards. If many would only study the various breeds and their qualification first there would not be nearly so many failures. For those who care to do this the present volume is published, and will be found to contain every possible information both as to keeping poultry for eggs and the table and breeding for show. We fear even with this knowledge there are few who will supplement it with a little careful thought, and recollect that fowls like children are the nicer the cleaner they are kept. There is practically no reason why fowls should not be kept in small spaces, but it is essential that they should be *kept clean*. Very few who keep pet canaries or other birds would think of letting their cages remain in a state of filth for weeks, yet many of these same persons would let their fowl-houses and runs go for months, until in fact they become such a nuisance that they must be done away with. As they are cleanly with their small birds, so should they be with their fowls; whatever space they occupy should be looked upon as a large cage and kept clean and wholesome. If this was properly attended to, we are convinced that every house with its few feet of yard might keep a few fowls. For those who live in the country there is positively no excuse; for where fowls can procure fresh air, fresh grass, and fresh ground they are naturally strong and healthy, and require very little looking after.

The volume before us is certainly most handsome, with beautiful illustrations printed in colours, and bound in crimson and gold; it looks like a book got up solely for the purpose of laying on the table to be admired; yet the contents are valuable and practical. Each variety of breed is described by its most successful cultivator, and this gives us such names as Hewitt, Teebay, Douglas, Zushorst, Jones, Horner, Ballance, and Brook as contributors to the volume. A careful study of such a book as this is absolutely necessary to those who intend keeping fowls in confinement, as there are many sorts that will not bear it at all, as Hamburghs, Dorkings, and Game Fowls. Cochins and Brahmas, on the contrary, are equally content in confinement and at liberty. Honduras are hardy birds, but intolerant of confinement, while Polish, Spanish, and Creve Cœurs are amongst the less hardy. The Polish cannot endure damp, and rot under it like sheep; Spanish are very fragile; and Creve Cœurs subject to roup, gapes, and throat affections.

In conclusion, we would suggest those who wish to keep fowls to commence with Brahmas, about which we extract the following:—

Respecting the Brahmas as profitable fowls Mr.

Teebay has favoured us with the following communication: "There is no variety so suitable for a wet, cold situation as this; they even appear to enjoy being out in a drizzling rain searching for insect food round the edge of any small piece of water they meet with. If they have an unlimited range they are great ramblers, remaining out later at night than any other variety that may be in the same run; they are good layers, especially during the cold winter months; they, however, do not want to set so often as the Cochins, and are far more easily cured of their broodiness. When allowed to hatch they cannot be surpassed as mothers, no fowls being more careful not to step on their children, brooding them better, or searching more diligently for insects for their food.

"Brahmas are good table-fowls, the pullets being remarkably full of white meat on the breast, and they lay on flesh very quickly when put up to fatten. The chickens grow with great rapidity, and are very easily reared. I have weighed a cockrel at seven months and two weeks old that weighed 10 lbs. 4 oz., and have seen several cocks under two years old that weighed 15 lbs. each. At four or five years old these large cocks become so heavy that they are generally to be seen resting on their hocks or lying sideways upon the ground, although at the same time in the best possible health; if in this state they are supplied liberally with soft food they will gain weight very fast, and make enormous birds. The average weight of the pullets at five months old is 7 lbs. I may remark that weight is not a good criterion as to the size of Brahmas; for if taken from an open run and confined in a very small place, and liberally fed, they lay on flesh so fast that they will occasionally add from one-fourth to one-third of their weight in three weeks. There is no variety of domestic fowls that breed more true to colour than the two kinds of Brahmas, if they are kept distinct; but should there be the slightest intermixture of the two varieties in the birds that are bred from, few of the pullets will be fit for exhibition, and there will be but seldom two alike in colour or markings in the same brood."

A Fern Book for Everybody, Containing all the British Ferns, with the Foreign Species suitable for a Fernery, By M. C. Cooke. London: Frederick Warne and Co.

It is surely a healthy sign of the times when we find our children taking a delight in the study of animal and vegetable life, and thereby not only amusing and instructing themselves, but also causing our older heads to become interested in subjects that not many years ago were confined only to scientific professors. And how delightful to find these self-same professors whom we had been in the habit of looking upon as persons to be kept at a distance, who, as we thought, could only talk barbarous words in an unknown tongue, and who we consequently avoided as mortals beyond our ken—how delightful to find these men condescending to write and lecture to us and for us in a plain and simple manner. How pleasant to find men who have spent half a life perhaps in the study of one particular subject taking pains to make such a subject popular, and so that we can comprehend and appreciate. Scientific men in these days can see how useful they may become to mankind at large, and do not shut themselves up with all the mystery of alchymists of old. And we are beginning to see the results. The aquarium, the fern-case, and the microscope are taking the place of tops, marbles, and Skelt's halfpenny sheets of characters amongst our children, while we have found new and cheerful amusements for our leisure hours.

Few of us but think we should like to have an aquarium. We get one, but through want of patience or something else we are not successful. Our fishes die, our green stuff will not do as it ought; big beetles eat up little beetles, and large fish as well, and then having nothing else commence upon each other; and our water will smell very nasty. What shall we do with it? It stands for some time empty and useless, and eventually gets smashed; or some one walks in and suggests a fernery. This is not the case with all. Some have patience—some do persevere until they find out wherein they have failed; but many do not, and hail with pleasure the idea that they can turn their monster bell glass upside down and convert it into a miniature fairy land, and that with very little trouble or expense.

For such persons as these, and all others who take a fancy to fern-growing, this little volume is written. It is simple and popular, and is emphatically a "Fern Book for Everybody." In it all the British species are described and figured, and such foreign species as are likely to come under the fern-grower's notice. It would be impossible to have the subject treated in a more pleasant manner, while the well-known name of the author is sufficient guarantee of its accuracy. It is illustrated with plates, each plate depicting two or more varieties. It forms a companion volume to "Common Shells of the Sea Shore and Common Sea Weeds," and is published at one shilling. What more need we say? The price, quantity, and quality are its best recommendations, and indeed will do more to insure its success than anything else.

A Handy Book of Meteorology. By Alexander Buchan, M.A., Secretary of the Scottish Meteorological Society. 12mo. Pp. 204. William Blackwood and Sons.

This handy little volume gives a short history of meteorology. Beginning with a sketch of its history and scope, the author in different chapters treats of the pressure of the atmosphere, its temperature, solar and terrestrial radiation, distribution of temperature, moisture, &c. It is clearly arranged in paragraphs under separate headings.

The instruments used are described and figured, and woodcuts interspersed where necessary, together with five charts. It is by no means dry, notwithstanding the show of dates, measurements, and tables. The observations on storms are very interesting, as is also the description of the various kinds of clouds. Those of our readers who desire a handy book of meteorology cannot do better than procure this little work. As a specimen, we select the following extract on—

Increase of Temperature with Height in Cold Weather. —"This takes place invariably in dry, calm, clear weather during the night, and in winter, when the temperature of the air falls by contact with the chilled surface of the earth (Proofs from the observations of Mr. Glaisher and Mr. Ch. Martins). But the rate at which the temperature rises with the height is modified to a very great extent by the physical configuration of the surface—that is, whether that surface be level, undulating, or mountainous. Suppose an extent of country, diversified by plains, valleys, hills, and table lands, to be in circumstances favourable to radiation, and each part under the same meteorological conditions, except in the single point of position, radiation will proceed over the whole at the same rate, but the effects of radiation will not be felt everywhere in the same degree and intensity. For as the air in contact with the declivities of the hills and rising grounds becomes cooled by contact with the cold surface of the ground, it acquires greater density and weight, and consequently slips down the slopes, and accumulates in the plains below. Hence places situated on rising grounds are never exposed to the full intensity of frosts; and the higher they are relatively to the surrounding ground, the less are they exposed, because they are protected by their elevation providing, as it were, an escape for the cold almost as fast as it is produced. On the contrary, valleys more or less environed by hills or eminences, not only retain their own cold of radiation, but also serve as reservoirs for the cold of neighbouring heights. Hence low-lying places are peculiarly exposed to intense cold. Plains and table lands are similarly affected by their own radiation. This explains why vapour becomes visible so frequently in low places, whilst adjoining eminences are clear; and the same fact instinct has made known to cattle and sheep, which generally prefer to rest during nights on knolls and other eminences. Along most of the watercourses of Great Britain, during the memorable frost of Christmas, 1860, Laurels, Araucarias, and other trees growing below a certain height, were destroyed, but above that height they escaped, thus attesting by unmistakeable proof the great and rapid increase of the temperature with the height above the lower parts of the valleys.

The Edible Mollusks of Great Britain and Ireland. By M. S. Lovell. 8vo, pp. 208. 9s. London: Reeve and Co.

Mr. Lovell deserves many thanks for endeavouring to make popular in the present volume a class of food that has hitherto been lamentably neglected. On our coasts are to be found many edible species of mollusks with which an acquaintance may be made with advantage. Mr. Lovell is here kind enough to introduce us to all the species found in Great Britain, not only marine, but air-breathing. The volume is very readable, as well as valuable in a gastronomic sense, giving the history and employment of the different species, which is followed by directions for cooking and preparing for human food. There are many coloured illustrations which serve to impress them with certainty upon the reader's mind.

The Silkworm Book; or, Silkworms Ancient and Modern, their Food and Mode of Management. By W. B. Lord, R.A., Author of "Sea Fish, and How to Catch Them," &c. Demy 8vo., price 2s. 6d., cloth gilt. London: Horace Cox.

This work treats of all the known kinds of silk-producing worms, the food that should be given them, and the way they should be managed. It is well illustrated with engravings of the caterpillar, moth, and cocoon of the Oak-leaf Silkworm (the Yama Mai), the Ailanthus, &c.; and illustrations descriptive of the apparatus, &c., used in the management of the worms, and the preparations and winding off of the silk from the cocoons.

BOOKS RECENTLY PUBLISHED.

On the Management and Preservation of Game and Ornamental Birds, and the Laws Relating Thereto. With numerous Illustrations. Price 1s. 6d. London: Bemrose.

The Apiary, or Bees, Bee-hives, and Bee Culture. With numerous Illustrations. By Alfred Neighbour. Price 5s. Geo. Neighbour, and Sons, 149, Regent-street, 127, High Holborn.

The Salmon: Its History, Position, and Prospects. By Alex. Russel, Editor of the *Scotsman*. 1 vol. demy 8vo., 7s. 6d. Edmonston and Douglas, 88, Princess-street, Edinburgh.

An Angler's Rambles, and Angling Songs. By Thos. Tod Stoddart, 1 vol. 8vo., price 9s. Edmondston and Douglas, 88, Princess-street, Edinburgh.

Meetings of Learned Societies.

ETHNOLOGICAL SOCIETY.

At the meeting of this society, held May 21st, J. Crawfurd, Esq., president, in the chair, the Report of the Council and of the Treasurer were read. The number of new members during the past year was greater, and the balance at the bankers larger, than on any previous occasion. The following officers and council were elected for the ensuing year:—*President*, J. Crawfurd, Esq.; *Vice-Presidents*, R. Dunn, Esq., Sir J. Lubbock, Bart., Prof. Busk, and General Balfour;

Hon. Treasurer, F. Hindmarsh, Esq.; *Hon. Secretaries*, T. Wright, Esq., and D. W. Nash, Esq.; *Hon. Librarian*, L. J. Beale, Esq.; *Council*, Lord Milton, W. Blackmore, H. G. Bohn, Dr. A. Campbell, T. F. D. Croker, Sir W. A. Clavering, Bart., J. Dickinson, Sir J. Shiel, Dr. H. Tuke, Dr. Beddoe, Sir M. Wells, Rev. F. W. Farrar, Prof. Huxley, J. Mayer, Sir R. I. Murchison, Bart., Sir C. Nicholson, Bart., Sir E. Ryan, Lord Strangford, J. Thrupp, and Sir J. Davis, Bart. A special vote of thanks to the President for his zealous and valuable services to the society, both in respect to the active management and the able and numerous papers contributed to its evening meetings, exhibiting, as they have done, the most mature deliberation and extended research and experience, was appropriately and deservedly proposed by General Balfour, and carried by an acclamation and accord significant of the heartiest personal attachment of the fellows to their veteran chief.

ENTOMOLOGICAL SOCIETY.

At the meeting May 6th, Prof. Westwood, V.P., in the chair. Mr. J. Sidebotham was elected a member, and M. S. C. Snellen van Vollenhoven, of Leyden, corresponding member.—Mr. S. Stevens exhibited a number of Coleoptera from the Cape York district. —Mr. Stainton exhibited larva-cases of *Coleophora lixella*, which when young was found to feed on thyme, but afterwards transferred itself to a species of grass; also the larva of *Hyponomeuta egregiella*, found at Fontainebleau on *Erica cinerea*.—Professor Westwood had recently received some Cimicidæ (*Enicocephalus Tasmanicus*) which possessed a pleasant musk-like scent, which communicated itself to the letter in which the insects had been forwarded.— The Secretary read a letter from Mr. R. W. Fereday, corresponding member in New Zealand, in which he says: "I have much satisfaction in communicating to the society the capture of a specimen of Cynthia Cardui, in the province of Canterbury, on the 5th of January last. The plains of Canterbury are separated from the west coast of the island by a range of mountains, one of these is named Mount Torlesse, and is about 6,000 feet above the level of the sea; immediately adjoining are some lower hills, and it was at the summit of one of these, about 3,000 feet above the sea, that I met with this butterfly, and made the capture. It was flying about and settling on a piece of rock, the herbage up to the top of the hill being tolerably luxuriant amongst the stones. It is the only specimen I have seen, and have not heard of any one else having seen one in this colony. It is so precisely like my English specimens in size, colour, and markings, with one exception, that I entertain no doubt of the identity of the species. I attribute the exception to a local variation; it is with respect to the round spots on the hind wings, which in my British specimens have no distinct centres, whilst in this specimen ocelli take the place of mere spots; it is, as it were, a spot of bright light blue, the same colour as the small blue marks at the anal angle of the hind wings, introduced into the centres of the normal spots of the English specimens. I enclose a photograph of it. I do not recollect whether any of the British examples have the blue centres to the spots. If the insect is Cynthia Cardui, of which I do not entertain a doubt, this capture is important, as it will add the link which will complete the circuit of the globe in the range of this species." A letter was also read from Mr. C. A. Wilson, corresponding member at Adelaide, in which the writer gave an account of a centipede having been killed by the excessive heat of December last in Cockatoo Valley, and announced the discovery on the Gawler River of a stylops, the first time that a strepsipterous insect had been detected in Australia.—Mr. F. Smith added some further information respecting this stylops, and exhibited specimens of the wasp, *Paragia decipiens*, upon which it is a parasite.—Mr. Bates read a paper "On a Collection of Butterflies formed by Thomas Bell, Esq., in the interior of the Province of Maranham, Brazil."

On June 3rd, Sir John Lubbock, Bart., president, in the chair.—Mr. Pascoe exhibited a collection of Coleoptera from Graham's Town.—Mr. T. W. Wood exhibited specimens from British Columbia of a Vanessa allied to *V. Urticæ*.—Mr. Stainton exhibited the larva, pupa and imago of *Earias siliquana*, a moth which was described as having almost destroyed the cotton-crops in both Upper and Lower Egypt; the larva eating into the ovary of the flower, and changing to a pupa in the cotton-ball.—Mr. Bond exhibited a Tortrix, captured by Mr. Meek at Darenth Wood, and believed to be new to this country.—Mr. F. Smith exhibited a razor-case, in an empty compartment of which, entered through a hole at the bottom, the wasp *Odynerus quadratus* had constructed its nest, from which Mr. Smith had bred ten male and four female wasps.—The President exhibited *Epidapus venaticus*, found in Kent, under bark.—Several instances were mentioned, in which, after the heavy rain of the previous night, numerous specimens of Gordius were observed. Mr. S. Stevens had noticed them at Kennington, on the ground, and a nephew of his, at Ashford, on rose-bushes; Mr. Weir, at Brixton, and Mr. Broad, near Regent's Park, also on bushes.

ZOOLOGICAL SOCIETY.

At a meeting of the above Society of London, held at Burlington House, on Thursday, May 23rd, Dr. J. E. Gay, vice-president, in the chair, Mr. E. Blyth exhibited some tracings and photographs of horns of different Indo-Chinese deer, also two fine specimens of *Corvus*, from Australia.—Mr. E. P. Ramsay, of Sydney, New South Wales, communicated a note "On the nesting of the Australian Stilt-plover" (*Himantopus leucocephalus*) as observed by himself in the neighbourhood of Grafton, N.S.W.—Messrs. P. L. Sclater and O. Salvin read a paper on the birds collected by Mr. Wallace on the Lower Amazon and Rio Negro. The total number of species collected by Mr. Wallace in the neighbourhood of Para was stated to have been 240, three of which appeared to be new to science. The chief result arrived at from the examination of this collection was, that the district of Para, as regards its birds, belongs strictly to the same province as Guiana, and is broadly distinguishable from the wood region of South-Eastern Brazil. Another paper was also read by the same gentleman on some new American pigeons of the genus *Leptoptila*.—Dr. Murie read a paper on the osteology of the wombats.

—Dr. J. E. Gray communicated two papers, one on a new species or variety of lemur, in the Society's gardens, the other on the variegated or yellow-tailed rats of Austral Asia.—Dr. Edwards Crisp read a paper on certain points in the anatomy of the hippopotamus, and exhibited some casts and drawings of the same.—Mr. F. Moore read a paper on the lepidopterous insects of Bengal, being the third and final part of a memoir upon this subject.

ROYAL HORTICULTURAL SOCIETY.

May 21st, W. Wilson Saunders, Esq., in the chair. —After the election of 17 Fellows, and the affiliation of the Wolverhampton Horticultural Society, the Rev. M. J. Berkeley remarked, that as the meeting was chiefly devoted to tricolour-leaved Pelargoniums, he would call attention to the principles on which their colouring depended. The original species from which they were all derived was the old Cape species Pelargonium zonal, of which he produced a specimen, in which the leaves were only slightly zoned. The first improvement on this was Fothergillii, which was a seedling, from which all the improved varieties around him had emanated. Variegation, he said, was really a disease; and in the vegetable kingdom everything abnormal in structure may be considered as the result of disease. Kohl Rabi, the useful portion of which results from an overgrowth of the stems, Radishes, &c., were cited as illustrations of this fact, even blanching was stated to be a species of disease, as was also the variation in Tulips and other matters of that description. Diagrams showing the structure of the leaf of one of the best showy zoned Pelargoniums were then exhibited. Beautiful, he said, as were the plants exhibited, it might, however, safely be concluded that perfection in regard to these Pelargoniums had not yet been attained; and in illustration of this he exhibited the drawing of a leaf, in which occurred distinct zones of yellow, red, and green, without radiation, which he said it has been proposed by Mr. Moore should in future form a criterion by which the merits of these plants should be judged.
The Rev. Joshua Dix congratulated the meeting on the success of the Exhibition, the idea of holding which had first originated with Major Trevor Clarke. —Major Trevor Clarke said, that when he had put together a few notes on the general phenomena of variegation in plants, he was not aware that the subject would be taken up by Mr. Berkeley; but as his own views were different from those of the reverend gentleman, he would state them. Mr. Grieve, gr. at Culford Hall, near Bury St. Edmund's, was introduced by Major Clarke, and to whose indefatigable industry we owe the first and best of the fine forms of tricoloured Pelargoniums which now grace our gardens, who then read a very interesting paper.
At the Meeting held June 18th, Sir R. Murchison, Bart., in the chair. After the election of five new members and the affiliation of three societies, the awards of the Floral and Fruit Committees were announced, and Mr. Shortt, gr. to Lord Eversley, at Heckfield, was called upon to offer a few remarks in reference to two fruits of what was called Passiflora macrocarpa, which he exhibited.
The Rev. M. J. Berkeley, in his remarks on some of the plants exhibited, first directed attention to Gordonia javanica, which belongs to the same natural order as the Tea plant. Gordonias, he said, are bog plants, the bark of which is used in North America for the purposes of tanning.
Mr. Bateman said, that though all knew the splendid specimens of orchids which Mr. Anderson, Mr. Dawson's gardener at Meadow Bank, was in the habit of exhibiting from time to time, yet he had never sent finer than those which he exhibited on this occasion. Beautiful as was his bunch of Odontoglossum Pescatorei, it only represented a fraction of the blossom on the plant from which it was cut, and on which no less than 300 flowers were counted. Coming to the immediate subject of his lecture, Lælia majalis or Flor de Maio, it was, he said, one of the few orchids which was fortunate in having a history as well as a name—in fact, many names, the native one being Itzumaqua; besides which it had two or three Spanish, and three or four Latin names. He approached, and not without perplexity, the subject of the treatment best adapted for this beautiful Lælia, the more so as it perhaps ought to be considered typical of the proper *régime* in what was called the "Mexican," as contradistinguished from the Peruvian and other cool houses.
The chairman, in returning Mr. Bateman the thanks of the meeting for his interesting lecture, said that though a fossil orchid had never yet been discovered, he would endeavour to stimulate geologists to search after such, and did not despair of finding such a thing when the geology of the countries where orchids now most abound was thoroughly investigated.

GEOGRAPHICAL SOCIETY.

May 27th.—Anniversary Meeting.—Sir R. I. Murchison, Bart., in the chair.—The Report of the Council showed that during the year 147 Fellows had been elected; 19 paid life compositions; and 45 Fellows, neglecting to pay subscriptions for three years, had been struck out of the list. The excess of income over expenditure was £1,032 13s. 3d., £1,000 being added to the funded property. The library received during the year 1,068 volumes of books and pamphlets, and the librarian had, since his appointment, arranged the various works according to their subjects as far as possible, and had also made some progress in a systematic catalogue of subjects and authors. The map-room had also received 2,426 additional maps and charts, some being of the greatest value and interest. A sum of £200 was devoted to the Leichardt search fund; a further sum of £50 to promote the search for M. G. Rohlfs, last heard of at Lake Tshad; a set of instruments for Mr. Whymper, for his exploration of Greenland; and also a set for Mr. H. Whitely, who is at present on the eastern slopes of the Andes in Southern Peru.—This year the royal medals for the encouragement of geographical discovery were awarded to the Russian Admiral Boutakoff, who launched a steamer on the Sea of Aral and established steam communication between that sea, through the river Jaxartes, with Central Turkestan; by this means land communication is established between China and St. Petersburg. Captain Crown, Russian Navy, in accepting the gold medal of the founder on the part of his friend, stated that Russian works hitherto published in that difficult language would be for the future issued in a form more accessible to English readers. The Victoria medal was handed to the American minister to be forwarded to Dr. Kane's fellow-traveller in the far north, and Dr. J. J. Hayes adds this fresh acknowledgment of the world's esteem for his courage, endurance, and fortitude in penetrating further north than any civilised man, as may be readily seen by reference to Peterman's recent comparative maps, showing in one sheet the work of Batfin, 1616, Ross, 1818, Englefield, 1852, Kane, 1855, and our hero, 1861. "The Open Polar Sea" will be a favourite work for many years to come, and in accepting the reward Mr. Adams said the discovery of his own country by Columbus was due to the same spirit of enterprise which stimulated his countryman; how often, he remarked, was the reward for the endeavour greater than the value of the object sought; and he was happy to state that in his country enterprise was applauded and emulated when our efforts were being made with the same hearty good fellowship, he was proud to see actuated ourselves. The United States still see that Arctic expeditions are worthy the attention of even that sensible nation, and it is a pity that an enterprise so long prosecuted by Englishmen is likely to have its last chapter written by American hands, after nearly three centuries have been spent by us in this noblest field of scientific research.

The President then gave his address, and in the evening the Fellows dined at Willis's Rooms.—The following officers were elected:—*President*, Sir R. I. Murchison, Bart.; *Vice-Presidents*, Vice-Admiral Sir G. Back, F. Galton, Esq., Major-Gen. Sir H. C. Rawlinson, and Major-Gen. Sir A. Scott Waugh; *Trustees*, Lord Houghton and Sir W. C. Trevelyan, Bart.; *Secretaries*, C. R. Markham, Esq., and R. H. Major, Esq.; *Foreign Secretary*, C. C. Graham, Esq.; *Councillors*, Hon. H. U. Addington, J. Arrowsmith, Major-Gen. G. Balfour, Sir S. W. Baker, T. H. Brooking, J. Crawfurd, Right Hon. Lord Dufferin, Commodore A. P. Eardley Wilmot, J. Fergusson, A. G. Findlay, Right Hon. Sir T. F. Fremantle, Bart., W. J. Hamilton, Capt. F. Jones, Sir W. S. Maxwell, Bart., H. Merivale, Sir C. Nicholson, Bart; L. Oliphant, Capt. S. Osborn, Capt. G. H. Richards, Viscount Strangford and T. Thomson; *Treasurer*, R. T. Cocks, Esq.

At a meeting, June 3rd, Sir Roderick Murchison, K.C.B., in the chair. The following new Fellows were elected: H. A. Glass, E. T. Higgins, J. Johnson, R. Eadie, A. Seymour, M.P., and J. E. Wilkins, H.M. Consul Chicago. A paper was read by Mr. G. A. Findlay, "On the last Journey of Livingstone in relation to the Sources of the Nile;" the careful, elaborate, and exhaustive investigation of the accounts of every previous explorer of the great lakes of central Africa, given by the learned author of the paper was listened to with marked attention, and the number of charts and diagrams exhibited afforded the audience every facility in following the narrative. Dr. Kirk's opinion was that Livingstone had settled the northern termination of Lake Nyassa, and that any streams met with beyond flowing to north-west were tributaries of Lake Tanganyika, and this lake in all probability communicated with the Albert lake and the Nile. This opinion, strengthened by the harmony in the known levels of these waters, confirmed the deductions arrived at by the author. Mr. Petherick expressed his entire disbelief in the reported death of the illustrious traveller; Mr. Baines, Mr. Waller, and the President also expressed their hopes for his safety.

Mr. Young and his companions, who left London on Thursday for Southampton, to solve this grave doubt as to the fate of Livingstone, were present at the meeting. A beautifully bound volume of photographs of Fellows, presented by Maull and Company, has been added to the library of the Society.

GEOLOGICAL SOCIETY.

The following papers were read at the ordinary general meeting of this Society on the 22nd inst., J. Carrick Moore, Esq., M.A., F.R.S., Vice-President, in the chair:—

1. "On the Bone-caves near Crendi, Zebbug, and Melheha, in the Island of Malta." By Captain T. A. B. Spratt, R.N., C.B., F.R.S., F.G.S. The Crendi (or Mahlek) Cavern is situated on the south coast of Malta. The flooring consisted of two distinct deposits, the lower being a stratum composed of a hard stalagmitic clay with rounded pebbles, and containing teeth and bones (unworn) of the hippopotamus (H. Pentlandi). The upper stratum, also a stalagmitic deposit, contained bones of the *Myoxus Melitensis*, and of birds, with some recent land shells. The Zebbug cavern, in the interior of the island, was, when discovered, filled with sandy clay containing subangular fragments of the rock, and bones of at least two species of elephant, comprising a complete set of the teeth and tusks of the pigmy elephant, representing animals in every stage of growth, and part of the tusk of a much larger elephant. No remains of hippopotamus were met with in this cavern; but a few bones of *Myoxus* (2 sp.), of birds, and of a chelonian, were discovered in it. The Melheha Cavern, at the north end of the island, contained a deposit with remains of the teeth and bones of the hippopotamus only, and seemed therefore to represent the lower stratum of the Crendi Cavern. From the fact that the deposits containing remains of the hippopotamus were so distinct from those including the elephant remains, Captain Spratt inferred that these two mammals belonged to distinct geological epochs, the elephant being the more recent. As Malta and Gozo were probably elevated above the sea at the close of the Miocene period, it is very possible that the caverns, formed by the long action of the sea upon its cliffs, may contain the relics of animals of more than one, if not of each, subsequent geological period.

2. "On the Lower Lias of the North-east of Ireland." By Ralph Tate, Esq., A.L.S., F.G.S. The author described the Lias of Ireland as consisting of (1) the Avicula-contorta series, including a well-developed zone of *Avicula contorta* and the White Lias; (2) the lower Lias, embracing the equivalents to the zones of *Ammonites planorbis*, *A. angulatus*, and *A. Bucklandi* of Great Britain; and a fourth zone (that of *Belemnites acutus*), representing that portion of the Lower Lias superior to the zone of *Ammonites Bucklandi*. Mr. Tate stated that the principal portion of

the Lias belongs to the zone of *Avicula contorta*, and that the greater portion of the Lower Lias is comprised in the zone of *Ammonites angulatus*. The remarkable and isolated mass of metamorphosed Lias at Portrush was referred to the "Planorbis series."

3. "On the Fossiliferous Development of the Zone of *Ammonites angulatus* in Great Britain." By Ralph Tate, Esq., A.L.S., F.G.S. In this paper the author recorded the discovery of a fauna, hitherto imperfectly known in this country, characterising beds below the Limestone-series of the Lower Lias. It is exceedingly rich in fossils. Cephalopoda are few in number (about eight species); Casteropoda are very numerous and characteristic, there being about fifty species, the majority of which are new to Great Britain; the Corals are abundant and peculiar. *Ammonites angulatus* was stated to occur at various places in Ireland; at Marton, Lincolnshire; in Warwickshire; in North Gloucestershire; at Brocastle and Sutton, in Glamorganshire; and in Dorsetshire.

4. "On the Rhætic Beds near Gainsborough." By F. M. Burton, Esq., F.G.S. Beds of the Rhætic series were stated to occur at Lea, two miles to the south of Gainsborough, and were described as consisting of more or less indurated and highly micaceous sandstones, alternating with black shaly clays, and containing two bone-beds. The fossils are very abundant, and are those which are usually met with in the *Avicula contorta* zone of other parts of Great Britain. However, the right *ramus* of the lower jaw of an *Icthyosaurus* was found in the lowest bed, lying on the blue Keuper Marl. Two interesting additions to the vertebrate fauna of this series are *Trematosaurus Alberti*, and *Lepidotus Giebeli*. The author pointed out the correlation of these beds with those at Aust Cliff and other well-known localities in England, and their probable connection with similar deposits in Ireland and on the Continent; and he concluded by defining the surface-extent of this the most northern English deposit of Rhætic age as yet discovered.

On June 5th, W. W. Smyth, Esq., in the chair. The following addition to the bye-laws was proposed by Mr. S. R. Pattison, seconded by Mr. J. W. Flower, and adopted by ballot, with one dissentient: "Section XIX. 5. The Society shall not and may not make any dividend, gift, division, or bonus in money, unto or between any of its members."—Mr. A. W. Franks was elected a Fellow.—The following communications were read: "The Alps and the Himalayas, a geological comparison," by Mr. H. B. Medlicott. The views of the author did not coincide with those expressed by Sir Roderick Murchison, Sir Charles Lyell, or Professor Ramsay, and at the conclusion of the paper, Sir Roderick, Sir Charles, and Professor Ramsay spoke to the subjects to which their attention was particularly drawn. Sir Charles spoke at great length in support of his views of the depression, upheaval, and contortion of the Alpine range, and explained the actual condition of the fresh water, brackish, and sea deposits in the locality, he did not agree with the writer, and was under the impression that the writer had misunderstood him. Sir Roderick, whose writings and observations on the Alpine and Jura range had been long since generally accepted, was at a loss to understand the system of the writer, and still held to his opinion. While he expressed his admiration of the industry bestowed on the paper he refrained from going into the subjects treated of, as he believed they each were worthy of separate discussion, and Professor Ramsay having by means of a rapidly sketched diagram elucidated the accepted theory of the structure and condition of the Righi, and the position and direction of the various beds composing the elevated portion of the district and accounted for the position of the strata, avoided touching upon the other theories advanced. Mr. Blanford, lately returned from India, explained the views held by his friend Mr. Medlicott, whose labours in the Himalaya were worthy of perfect confidence, as he had devoted many years to the study of their geologic structure; he feared the scope of Mr. Medlicott's paper, owing to an abstract of it only having been laid before the society, would fail to be appreciated by the members at its full value. In recent volumes of the society's transactions the details of Himalaya geology were recorded by the author, and his object in instituting a comparison with the Alpine range in Europe, was simply because he thought he saw in a recent visit to the Alps, a sufficient similarity of structure to justify him in laying the two subjects side by side for comparison by those who had only opportunity to visit the European range.

Mr. Woodward, alluding to a passage in the paper, in which it was stated that the vaults in the British Museum contained the Indian geological specimens, stated that his late brother had carefully set out in the Museum the collection from the Himalaya range, and the valuable series added to by the many contributors, whose names he mentioned, were accessible at all imes.t—"On some striking Instances of the Terminal Curvature of Slaty Laminæ in West Somerset," by Mr. D. Mackintosh.

ROYAL MICROSCOPICAL SOCIETY.

The meeting of this society on the 12th instant (Dr Arthur Farre, F.R.S., Vice-President, in the chair was the best as well as the last of the session. Dr W. B. Carpenter described two microscopes by Nachet of Paris, who was the first to successfully work on the principle of stereoscopic binocular microscopy.— Professor T. Rymer Jones read a paper on the Larva of *Corethra plumicornis*. The creature has hitherto been very imperfectly described, and has, in fact, only been figured as a serpentine larva, with a hook at the end of its tail. Its really wonderful structure, and the startling rapidity with which its tracheal system is developed, were explained by the professor in his peculiarly eloquent and lucid manner; and he concluded by observing, as a useful hint to those who would preserve it as a permanent object for the cabinet, that it must be mounted neither in spirit nor glycerine, but merely in distilled water, in a cell hermetically sealed in the usual way.—The Rev. J. B. Reade made a few remarks (which were confirmd by Mr. Browning) supplementary to the paper read by him at the preceding meeting to the effect that the dichroic solution then described was found to yield a different spectrum when viewed by reflected light from that produced by rays transmitted through it.—

Various presents of books and objects were acknowledged, and eighteen gentlemen were elected Fellows of the Society.

LINNEAN SOCIETY.

At the meeting on *June* 6.—G. Bentham, Esq., president, in the chair. The President nominated J. J. Bennett, Esq., Dr. J. D. Hooker, Sir J. Lubbock, Bart., and W. W. Saunders, Esq.; Vice-Presidents for the year ensuing: Messrs. T. C. Allbutt, J. Colebrook, E. Newton, and Dr. C. Meller were elected Fellows. —Living specimens of *Mermis nigrescens* were exhibited by Dr. Iliff, which had suddenly appeared in great abundance in gardens near Epsom, after heavy rain and thunder. The occurrence of the same worm, under similar circumstances, and about the same time, in other localities, had been observed by several of the Fellows present. Dr. Cobbold exhibited specimens of *Lepidium ruderale*, which he had gathered at Southall, Middlesex.—The following papers were read, viz., "Further Observations on *Cygnus Passmori*, and *C. Buccinator*," by the Rev. W. Hincks. "Notes on the Thysanura, Part III.", by Sir John Lubbock, Bart. "Notes on some Insect and other Migrations observed in Equatorial America," by Mr. R. Spruce. "On the Mechanical Appliances by which Flight is attained in the Animal Kingdom, by Dr. J. B. Pettigrew.

BOTANICAL SOCIETY OF EDINBURGH.

The monthly meeting of the Society was held on the 9th ult., in the histology class-room at the Royal Botanic Garden; William Gorrie, Esq., Vice-President, in the Chair. The following communications were read:—1. "On Submarine Forests and other remains of Indigenous Wood in Orkney." By Dr. William Traill, St. Andrew's.—With the exception of the island of Hoy, where bushes of Mountain Ash, Birch, and Aspen Poplar are found in some sheltered nooks, no natural wood now grows in Orkney, nor is there any reliable account of trees having existed there in former times. Nevertheless there are submarine forests in Orkney, and while history is uncertain, we are fortunately in possession of other silent records of the past, which enable us to affirm that at some period anterior to the Norse invasion these islands were inhabited by a rude race of men who appeared to have obtained a part of their subsistence by hunting deer and other wild animals in the forests. This is clearly proved by numerous remains of human habitations, constructed of stone, found on nearly all the islands, which generally contain horns and bones of the red deer, and of a species of ox, Bos longifrons, along with bones of the hog and other smaller quadrupeds and birds, including the Alca impennis, or great auk, which has become extinct in Orkney only during the present century. The specimens of antlers and bones of red deer are interesting, not only as relics of a fauna locally extinct, but they are also valuable as enabling us to connect the period at which these forests grew with undoubted marks of the presence of human inhabitants; so that it is evident that before the epoch of the forests and their fauna had terminated, that of the human inhabitants had commenced. Most of the principal islands of Orkney show remains of trees in their peat mosses.

During last summer I visited the island of Hoy, and on passing by a farm where extensive draining was going on, I observed that the surface of the ground on each side of the trench was literally lined with fragments of decayed trees that had been thrown out in the process of digging. In the island of Roussay, where I spent a few days in the summer of 1865, there were many traces of ancient forests, not only in the peat mosses towards the centre of the island, but also in two places on the coast much below high-water mark. The trees, for the most part, lay deep in the peat, within a few inches of the clay or rock. Some were prostrate, but the stumps of others appeared quite undisturbed, their root fibres being traceable in all directions through the ground. Many of the smaller branches were flattened by pressure. None of the stems that we saw exceeded 6 or 8 inches in diameter, though we were told that larger pieces are often found by the peat cutters, who dry them in summer, and add them to their winter stock of fuel. It was not easy to determine the different kinds of trees with any certainty. Birch could be distinguished by the peculiar appearance of its silvery bark; other trees had rough thick bark not unlike Pine; that Hazel was one species is evident from the extraordinary abundance of the nuts; leaves also of different shapes are occasionally found wonderfully well preserved. Some of the sites of these trees are curious enough. There is a fresh water lake in the island of Hoy, where trunks and branches of trees are found in abundance under water. I have not myself seen the place, but while exploring with my friend among the hills of Rousay we came upon trees in a somewhat similar place, viz., in a mill dam of 2 or 3 acres in extent, which, owing to the unusual heat of the summer, was perfectly dry, and its black surface was deeply fissured all over. On raising some of the cracked masses of peat, we found that the entire area was full of dead branches and roots of trees, and when we examined the sides of the dam or reservoir, we saw many stems and branches of trees projecting horizontally from the peat. Most of them were about the thickness of a man's leg, but some were a good deal larger; they were all much decayed, and in some instances were so macerated by the water that they were reduced to a pulpy mass of fibres. In the winter of 1838 there was a long-continued gale of north-east wind, which entirely cleared away the shell sand from about 50 acres of the flat surface usually left dry at low water (our rise and fall of tide is 12 feet, and sometimes as much as 15 feet). Going down one day at low tide, I was astonished to see, instead of the white sand, what appeared a wide stretch of black moss covered with fallen trees, lying with their roots sticking up, exactly as I saw trees afterwards in Canada laid prostrate by a hurricane. I went down to the moss, stepped from trunk to trunk of the trees, and found their substance, when cut into by a spade, quite the same as that of the moss in which they lay, just that of our blackest coal peat. The largest of the trees seemed not more than 2 feet in diameter, and all were lying in the same direction, from S.W. to N.E. I secured several specimens with the bark on, but they soon dried and fell into dust. On taking to a boat, I found the same moss surface, mostly denuded of sand, showing itself under the deep clear water, with trees lying along its surface, quite across the bay to Tuftsness, four miles off, where a rupture of the peat had taken place, as all over that ness, under 9 or 10 feet of blowing shifting sand, the same peat moss and tree remains are to be found as under the waters of the bay, although raised above high-water mark some 10 or 12 feet.——2. "On the Lichen Flora of Druidical Stones of Scotland." By Dr. W. Lauder Lindsay.——3. "Notice of some rare British Mosses recently collected near Edinburgh." By Mr. John Sadler.——4. "Notes of an Excursion to the Forest of Fontainebleau." By Mr. George W. R. Hay.——5. "Miscellaneous Communications."

Correspondence.

[*Under this head we shall be glad to insert any letters of general interest.*]

SPIDERS.

SIR,—About the end of February I discovered hidden in a hole in a wall, and enclosed in a thick mass of web, a large garden spider (*Epeira diadema*). It was very dark in colour, but was distinctly marked with those beautiful pencillings which characterise this species. I am unable to ascertain whether as a rule this species hybernates, or whether the individual I found differed from its kind in living through the winter. I have kept a few Geometric spiders in captivity, which have grown to an unusual size; but, although supplied with flies till late in the year, on the approach of the cold weather they all became benumbed, and never again awoke from their torpidity. Moreover, during the spring and earlier part of the summer I have never observed any spiders of this kind of the large size to which they attain in the autumn, so I fancy they die in the winter. At this date, indeed, the weather has been so unusually cold and wet, that I have not found any but very small ones. I find that the Water spider (*Argyroneta aquatica*) lives throughout the winter in its watery nest.

I should be glad if one of your readers would inform me whether spiders in general hybernate or die in the winter, and give me some particulars of this species.

Yours obediently,
ARTHUR G. HARVIE.
London, June 6th.

Short Notes.

THE BEAVER.—The *Cosmos* publishes a paper by M. Hoefer, containing some curious information regarding the beaver. This animal, it appears, was not much known among the ancients; Aristotle and Pliny only mention it from hearsay, whence it may be concluded that it preferred the northern parts of Europe, which were still thinly peopled and uncivilised. About the beginning of the 17th century some might still be seen on the banks of the Danube, on those of the Rhine, and even of the Marne, as also in Switzerland. There is an old cookery-book, entitled *Liber Benedictionum*, by Eccard IV., abbot of St. Gall, in which the flesh of the beaver is considered a delicacy; nay, the good monks of the convent, who were notorious for their strict adherence to the rules of a penitent life, had found out that the beaver was a fish, and might therefore be eaten on Fridays, a very unlucky circumstance for the poor animal, and which must have greatly contributed to diminish its numbers. The *Liber Benedictionum* informs us, by the way, that the peacock, swan, stork, and wild duck formed part occasionally of the bill of fare, as did also the bear; it was, however, admitted on all hands that the latter was not a fish; whether birds were or not, is not stated. To return to the beaver, its real *habitat* is Canada, whence it has spread over all countries down to the 43rd parallel of latitude; only in Europe and Asia it seems gradually to die out. There are still some in Norway, Lapland, and especially in Siberia, on the banks of the Oby. The question arises whether the solitary beaver, which does not congregate with its kin, and has a dull, dirty-looking fur, is the same as the gregarious breed, building dwellings on piles, and having a sleek and shining skin? M. Hoefer replies to the question in the affirmative. In his opinion there is but one species of beaver, the *Castor Americanus*; the Canadian beaver, when brought over to Europe becomes solitary. In support of this opinion he relates the following singular anecdote:—Frederick II. of Prussia had caused a considerable number of beavers to be brought over from America, for the purpose of acclimatising them in the environs of Berlin. But the poor creatures became melancholy, and instead of congregating and building their village, as is their custom in their own native haunts, they separated from each other; their fur, which at first was so glossy, became dull and rough, and, by burrowing in the sand, they rubbed their skins bare so as to assume the appearance of mangy dogs. They did not multiply, and died away one by one.

SAND MARTINS.—I was at Weybridge a few days since and spent a very interesting half-hour in watching the proceedings of a colony of these pretty little summer visitants, who have taken up their quarters in a sand-bank close to the station. They numbered many hundreds, and a porter, more intelligent, I mean more observant, than the general run of porters, assured me that previously to the setting in of the cold winds which have prevailed during the last fortnight, there were twice as many at least. The birds were all in pairs, and busy beyond description in their own pleasant fidgety way, about some process of nidification, but which, for the life of me, I could not discover. Can you or can Mr. Buckland or any other naturalist amongst your readers assist me? The birds, sometimes singly, generally in pairs, after circling in rapid flight high in the air, took the neatest "headers" into their respective holes, (how they distinguished them seems a mystery, for the bank is perforated like a cullender, and each aperture the precise counterpart of the other), remained within for ten or fifteen seconds, and emerging with a smart cheery twitter, renewed their aërial evolutions. I could not detect, though close to them and watching most carefully, anything whatever in their bills, and it is difficult to imagine what building materials they could find in the upper regions of the air, neither did they carry anything out with them so far as I could see. The holes were apparently dug to the usual depth, from two to three feet, and the fine sand extracted was accumulated in a soft heap below; the eggs, I think, are not yet laid, certainly there are neither sitting nor young birds. What, I ask, is their object in perpetually visiting the interior of their future nursery establishments? I got up to a few holes and found them, as I said, some two or three feet in depth, driven horizontally, and as well as I could plummet them, without any turning, into the sand bank. The fleas, as usual, clustered at the mouth, and in return for their board and lodging afforded a most effectual safeguard against impertinent but thin-skinned intruders like myself.—J. R., *Land and Water*, May 25th.

RUMELIAN ROSES.—Mr. Blunt, the British Vice-Consul at Adrianople, in his report to the Foreign Office this year, gives an account of the Rose fields of the vilayet of Adrianople, extending over 12,000 or 14,000 acres, and supplying by far the most important source of wealth in the district. This is the season for picking the Roses—from the latter part of April to the early part of June; and at sunrise the plains look like a vast garden full of life and fragrance, with hundreds of Bulgarian boys and girls gathering the flowers into baskets and sacks, the air impregnated with the delicious scent, and the scene enlivened by songs, dancing, and music. It is estimated that the Rose districts of Adrianople produced in the season of 1866 about 700,000 miscals of attar of Roses (the miscal being 1½ drachm), the price averaging rather more than 3s. per miscal. If the weather is cool in spring, and there are copious falls of dew and occasional showers, the crops prosper, and an abundant yield of oil is secured. The season in 1866 was so favourable that eight okes of petals (less than 23 lb.), and in some cases seven okes yielded a miscal of oil. If the weather is very hot and dry it takes double that quantity of petals. The culture of the Rose does not entail much trouble or expense. Land is cheap and moderately taxed. In a favourable season a donum (40 paces square) well cultivated will produce 1000 okes of petals, or 100 miscals of oil, valued at 1500 piastres; the expenses would be about 540 piastres—management of land, 55; tithe, 150; picking, 75; extraction, 260—leaving a net profit of 960 piastres, or about £8 11s. An average crop generally gives about £5 per donum clear of all expenses. The oil is extracted from the petals by the ordinary process of distillation. The attar is bought up for foreign markets, to which it passes through Constantinople and Smyrna, where it is generally despatched to undergo the process of adulteration with Sandal-wood and other oils. It is said that in London the Adrianople attar finds a readier sale when it is adulterated than when it is genuine.—*Times*.

TOMTIT'S NESTS IN A LETTER-BOX.—A gentleman writing to the *Field*, June 7th, says: I have observed several letters giving instances of this bird's having nested in curious places. Probably the following will interest many of your readers: For four years past a pair of tomtits have built in an unused letter-box in the side-door of my house, and have reared their young. This year they have nine little ones, now nearly ready to fly. There was a tenth, but he has somehow vanished. Mrs. Tomtit is very tame, and never thinks of leaving her eggs or young ones when the box is opened, but will allow herself to be pushed to one side and the family to be inspected, only protesting by hissing, and sometimes—probably after a tiff with her lord, or when the babies have been unusually trying to her temper—by beating with her wings. Mr. Tomtit is rather more shy, popping his head, with a tempting green caterpillar, through the slit of the letter-box, a solace to his spouse attending her sedentary material duties; but Mr. Tomtit himself does not like to be handled. Now that there are nine great hungry mouths to fill, the scene is busy and exciting. Every two minutes one of the old birds enters the nest, with one, two, and sometimes three luscious green caterpillars in its bill. These it breaks up and distributes down the throats of its hungry nestlings, putting its head well down, and giving a good shake, as a preventative to choking; then, taking in its bill any droppings from the young birds, before such droppings can fall to the nest, it flies away with them, showing the greatest care that the nest shall be always clean and wholesome. Should there be no sanitary arrangements to attend to, it takes a crumb of bread for its own delectation, and flies off after more caterpillars. Sometimes both old birds will be in the nest at once, breaking up the crumbs put in for them, and giving their young ones a change of food. The old birds take no notice of the box being wide open, and three or four amused human faces within a yard of them, but proceed with the business of their lives, totally indifferent to our presence.

A BIRD'S PERSEVERANCE.—"About the end of June last (says Mr. Gurney) a spotted fly-catcher began to build a nest over the door of the lodge at the entrance of my grounds. The woman who lives in the lodge, not wishing the bird to build there, destroyed the commencement of the nest. Every day for a week the bird placed new materials on the same ledge over the door, and every day the woman removed them, and at the end of a week placed a stone on the ledge, which effectually baffled the fly-catcher's efforts at that spot; but the bird then began building at the latter end of the ledge, from whence it was also driven, and three stones being then placed on the ledge, the bird relinquished the attempt to build at either end of it, and commenced building a nest on a beech-tree opposite, which it completed, and laid two eggs in it. When the bird was thus apparently established in the beech-tree, the stones over the door were taken away, when the fly-catcher immediately forsook its nest and eggs in the beech, and again commenced building over the door, on the part of the projecting ledge which it had first chosen. The nest was again destroyed, and two slates placed over the spot. The bird contrived to throw down one of the slates from a slanting to a horizontal position, and then began to build upon it. The nest was again destroyed, and the three stones replaced, and kept there a fortnight, after which they were again removed, and directly they were taken away the bird again began building. The nest was subsequently destroyed several times in succession. The bird was twice driven away by a towel being thrown at it. A stone, wrapped in white paper, was placed on the ledge to intimidate it, but the flycatcher still persevered, completed a nest, and laid an egg in it. On hearing the circumstances, I directed that the persecution of the poor bird should cease, after which it laid two more eggs, hatched all three, and successfully brought off its brood."—*Stevenson's Birds of Norfolk.*

NEW USE FOR POTATOES AND OTHER VEGETABLES.—There is at present to be seen at the Paris Exhibition objects apparently formed of meershaum, or of stags' horns, but which, nevertheless, are made of very different substances. The imitation of meershaum is obtained by peeling sound potatoes, macerating them for from twenty-four to thirty-six hours, in water acidulated with eight per cent. sulphuric acid, washing them with fresh water, until they no longer redden litmus paper, wrapping them in blotting paper, then drying them in warm sand, or on plates of chalk or plaster of Paris, which are changed daily for several days, and at the same time compressing them. An excellent imitation of meershaum, which will take colours well, will thus be obtained; but it will not answer for pipes. The result will be harder, whiter, and more elastic if three per cent. caustic soda is used instead of the sulphuric acid. If, after having been macerated for twenty-four hours in the soda solution, the potatoes are boiled with nineteen per cent. soda, a substance resembling stags' horn will be obtained. The acid or the alkali must be carefully washed away. Turnips treated in the same manner as the potatoes afford an excellent imitation of stags' horn, which may be cut into thin plates for veneering, and may be made as flexible as leather, by agitation in glycerine or water. Carrots, treated in the same way, afford a fine imitation of coral, which answers admirably for veneering and other purposes.—*Scientific Review,* June.

ARTESIAN WELLS IN ALGERIA. Twenty-three years ago the French colonists of Algeria made their first attempts to sink artesian wells in their newly-acquired territory; but after boring in two places in the province of Oran to a depth of 98 and 176 mètres without striking water, the attempts were abandoned. In 1856, operations were resumed by the military corps of engineers, and from that date, with two or three exceptions, every boring has succeeded; and at the end of 1864, seventy-five wells were flowing and delivering 4,200,000 litres of water every hour, or 100,000 cubic mètres a day. The water is limped and drinkable, but generally a little brackish. The effect of such a supply on the social life and industry of the country may be imagined. A village and date plantations rise up around every well, and the natives, having something to lose, prefer peace to predacity. Thirty-five of the wells are in the Ouled Rir district, which stretches far to the south. The deepest well is 175 mètres, the shallowest 29 mètres, and the total of all the borings amounts to 6,628 mètres. The entire cost, defrayed by a tax on the natives, was 400,000 francs. Among the material results, we are informed that 150,000 date-trees have been planted in the Ouled Rir district alone, besides fruit-trees of other kinds, and more than 2,000 new gardens have been formed. We may expect that these beneficial operations will be continued, for four boring brigades have been established, all well provided with implements, for the purpose of systematic exploration, and to sink wells in places likely to yield water. Guided by years of experience, their failures are now but few, and year by year their knowledge of the local hydrography, surface and subterranean, becomes more complete.—*Athenæum,* June 1st.

ASSEMBLAGE OF BEETLES.—Walking along the cliff from Ramsgate to Margate, with a strong south-wester blowing, I retired down a gully or "stair" (as they call them in the ordnance maps) to smoke a pipe out of the wind. The tide was up, and I found myself on a small bay of sand, bounded landwise by perpendicular chalk cliffs. The sand to the lower part of the cliffs were covered with thousands of beetles evidently blown down from the fields above by the wind. I counted over thirty genera, most of them represented by four or five species. The insects were mostly on their backs; and, with the exception of some *Bembidia* and a small *Choleva* (*anisotomoides*), they were almost torpid. When put upon their legs they made but feeble efforts to get away, and seemed to be unable to get a footing on the fine sand. I never before saw such a quantity and variety of beetles together in so small a space (about thirty yards), to be got without the least trouble beyond picking them up. It was collecting made easy, as I never saw it before. The exact spot is between Foreness and Whiteness, not far from a cockney erection called Neptune's monument. I subjoin a list of the genera as far as I can recollect:—*Notoiphilus, Calathus, Anchomenus, Pterostichus, Amara, Anisodactylus, Harpalus, Bembidium, Ilybius* (! !), *Homalota, Mycetoporus, Philonthus, Xantholinus, Lithocaris, Silpha, Choleva, Helophorus, Sphæridium, Cercyon, Aphodius, Agriotes, Cneorhinus, Sitones, Alophus, Phytonomus, Trachyphlœus, Cryptorhynchus, Lema, Crepidodera, Coccinella, Coccidula, &c.*—W. C. De Rivaz, 4, Shrewsbury-road, W.—*Entomologist,* June.

HORNS OF THE ROEBUCK.—The first indications of the future horns of the roebuck are two rounded knobs, covered with the well-known "velvet;" these are succeeded by straight simple points, three or four inches long, and in this state the young roe is termed by the German jagers "Spiess bock" (literally, *spear-buck*). In due course these are succeeded by forked horns, having one point or antler directed forwards nearly at right angles with the "beam" or main stem; at this season the bearer is a "gabelbock" (*i.e. fork-buck*, or forker). Another year sees the full complement of three points, the first or lower being directed forwards, the second or upper backwards: after this no further branches are added, although the horns become more heavy and massive as the animal becomes older. But these changes are not always regularly gone through, and although six points, three on each horn, is the full natural complement, heads with seven, eight, and even ten and twelve branches are to be seen in the museums of Germany, where the collecting of deer's horns is a not uncommon mania. Many of these large and magnificent head-gears belonged to roe-deer shot in the last century. The same thing holds good of the red deer (*Cervus elaphus*), so much so that some German naturalists assert that a different variety of the stag, with larger horns ("Brandthirsch"), was then found in Europe; but the fact that many of the old roe heads are equally wonderful in their development, seems to point to the better feeding and greater age of deer of old days as the cause of their superior beauty and size of horn.—*Zoologist*, June.

THE MILKMAN'S PONY AND DOG.— Sir Emerson Tennent's interesting anecdote of the reformed vicious pony, and his now tractable behaviour and proffers of assistance to his master the milkman during his morning rounds, was so highly appreciated and was such a rare instance of gratitude and intelligence in the animal, that I may consider myself fortunate in having it in my power to offer a companion to it in the eccentricity of a dog, whose attachment to both master and pony is shown in the following very singular manner. Mr. Startin, of Richmond, dairyman, now possesses a dog, of the black-and-tan terrier breed, that may be daily seen perched on the back of his stable companion, the horse, whilst making his usual business calls. The affection of the two animals to each other is unequalled in the history of such sympathies. The dog appears perfectly at home in his precarious position, and whether at a walk, trot, canter, or full gallop, is scarcely ever seen to falter in his equilibrium. During Mr. Startin's absence the dog guards, like a faithful servant, both horse and cart, and sticks to his post. So long have the two animals been now allowed to continue in the indulgence of their favourite habit, that it becomes a question of consideration what would be the consequences of a separation. They may still be seen every day at their united labours, to the amusement of the good people of Richmond and the surrounding neighbourhood.—A. H. B.—*Land and Water*, June 15.

A FLIGHT OF LOCUSTS.—At Malta about noon on Saturday, the 9th inst., the sky became filled with locusts, which appeared to be travelling from east to west over the island. The main body preserved a high altitude, but many, perhaps tired by their long flight, settled in different localities along their route. A light breeze was blowing from the westward, so that the insects were proceeding head to wind. The town was quite in a state of excitement. The boys were catching the locusts in their hats, and the sparrows and jackdaws were feasting on them in the air with evident satisfaction. This extraordinary spectacle lasted all the afternoon. During the whole of this time they never ceased passing for a moment, and towards sunset their numbers were considerably augmented. In some parts of the country the fields and gardens were covered with them. Most fortunately, for some unaccountable reason, they made no long stay, and on the following morning, with the exception of a few stragglers, had all disappeared. Nor do we hear of any serious damage having been done by them to the crops, which have already suffered much from the continued absence of rain. A similar visitation occurred at Malta in 1814, the year after the plague; and in 1850 a cloud of these insects appeared on the eastern side of the island and did some injury. —*Malta Times*.

MONKEYS STEALING SPECTACLES.— I am reminded by two communications in your last impression, one on the subject of pickpockets at the Zoo., and the other on the Clifton Zoological Gardens, of a curious incident which I witnessed at the latter place in 1865. The usual stout elderly gentleman of the genus *flâneur* was fixedly regarding the gambols of the monkeys, when an active individual suddenly snatched the spectacles from the old gentleman's nose and made off with them, followed, of course, by the rest of his monkey friends. The antics he played with the spectacles were most amusing to all but the old gentleman, who was scarcely aware of his loss till he saw his barnacles astride the ridgeless nose of the depredator. You can fancy the wild hunt which took place of all the rest of the monkeys after the fortunate thief, and how, when chevied into a corner, he deliberately took off the spectacles and knocked out the glasses, and, failing to break them, rubbed them fiercely against the floor of the cage to spoil their transparency. The old gentleman at last recovered his spectacles minus the glasses, but he will probably keep his nose at a safe distance from the cage for the future. I think a valuable article might be written upon the thievish propensities of animals; perhaps from the habits of the raven, magpie, jackdaw, and monkey, which steal things of no possible use to them, we might obtain some elucidation of the senseless extravagance, and acquisitiveness, and kleptomania of the human species.—C. H., *Land and Water*, June 1st.

EXTRAORDINARY FECUNDITY IN A CAT.—The circumstance I am about to relate occurred at a sheep farm situated about 150 miles from Monte Video. A cat of about ten months old, born on the place, became pregnant, and as the time for kittening drew near was a source of astonishment to every one at the estancia, for the animal swelled almost as broad as it was long, though seemingly it did not experience any pain. On the night of the 7th of October she brought forth four kittens, one of which only was born alive, but died the next morning. On the following night, the 8th, she had three more, also all born dead; but still she appeared very much swollen, and on the evening of the 9th she again brought forth three, which were also born dead—thus making ten kittens at the first litter, which seems to me to be an extraordinary number for so young a cat, and, indeed, for any. However, pussy, although she had lost all her kittens, did not seem at all unhappy, but made friends with a little bitch at the house, who had two pups just born, got into the box in which she was, and now lies all day fondling the pups, which seem quite as contented with her as with their mother, and suck the two—*i.e.*, their mother and the cat—alternately. — L. H. D. (Banda Oriental, South America).—*Field*, June 15.

BEE-KEEPING IN CALIFORNIA.—I have read some very nice articles on bees in *Land and Water*, so you may like to have a little account of bee-keeping in California. The honey made over there is very fine. No doubt the beauty of the various flowers and plants contribute greatly to its sweetness. A friend of mine lately saw an apiary near San José, consisting of a hundred and fifty hives. They were placed in an orchard of nine hundred trees, and all the swarms were produced from forty hives with which the owner had begun the season. The orchards in California are magnificent. The one in question had a hedge of "yoularia," or holly-leaved cherry, grown from seed. Its beauty and symmetry were described as most remarkable. There were two kinds of evergreen cherry, and many Chickasaw plums in full bearing, with delicious peach trees; but the most beautiful and striking object was a circular "driveway" of over a mile in length, leading from the house to the apiary and orchard. This hedge was made of the osage orange, backed by a double row of ornamental trees, with a choice number of Cherokee roses in full perfection. The graceful curves of this serpentine drive, and the rich fragrance of the flowers, combine to make the place in question one of the very loveliest on the Pacific coast. Landscape gardening was thoroughly understood by the man who laid out Colonel Y.'s Californian grounds. There was a mission of San José, but, strange to say, the proprietors of it evidently did not understand horticulture so well as the military man, for all the old fine trees (some thousands of them) were dying away in the grounds, orchard, and vineyard of the mission when Colonel Y. came to the neighbourhood. The vicinity of San José and Santa Clara is called the garden of California, and the Colonel has some large, though young, *Morus multicaulis* trees, and contemplates making no end of silk.—H. E. W., *Land and Water*, May 25th.

THE LARVÆ OF HYDROPTILA.—On Good Friday I selected from a small tributary of the Darenth many cases of *Hydroptila*, concealed in the crevices of the under surface of stones. These contain green larvæ, and apparently pertain to *H. pulchricornis*. A miniature aquarium, consisting of a tumbler and plant of *Callitriche*, has enabled me to watch their habits more narrowly; and I notice a peculiarity not I think hitherto observed in Trichopterous larvæ. It is well-known that the larvæ of most of the larger species, with portable cases, sink rapidly to the bottom when disturbed, but in *Hydroptila* the larvæ remain suspended by a thread in mid-water, in the same manner as many Lepidopterous larvæ are suspended in mid-air; and by this thread they are enabled to regain their lost position without the trouble of commencing *de novo* at the bottom. The little, flattened, seed-shaped cases are very interesting objects; but I almost despair of rearing the imagos, as the conditions afforded by the highly aërated bubbling streamlet in which they were found, are too different from any with which I have the means of supplying them. The cases, while the inmates are yet in the larva state, seemed to be composed entirely of coarse silk, but, before the change, minute sand-granules are worked into the outer surface, thus rendering them much firmer.—R. McLachlan, Forest-hill.—*Entomologist*, June.

THE BURYING BEETLE.—Many years ago, when living in Devonshire, I found a dead rat lying in the shrubbery. Being struck with its *basso relievo* appearance, I examined it more closely, and observed a threadlike border of the finest mould all round it, enclosing even the tip of the tail. Suspecting the cause, I carefully lifted it, and found, as I expected, a pair of burying beetles at work. They were both black, and, as well as I remember, exhibited no peculiarity of shape or appearance; but I did not examine them closely, being unwilling to disturb them, and having an intense antipathy to handling a rat. Last week, while walking across some fields near Highgate, I was surprised at seeing the half-dried mummy of a toad stir, and feeling convinced that it could have no life in it, I turned it over, and found beneath it a solitary beetle, barred with black and yellow like a wasp, and in size between that insect and a hornet. I watched it for some time, and, wishing to give it a safer place for carying out its apparent propensity for an undertaker's work, I moved it a little out of the path, on which the insect made a cast like a hound, and soon found the body. I then moved it a foot, when the beetle, missing it, took wing and soon recovered it. I then moved it away about a yard, but the beetle did not seem equal to re-finding its prey, and ultimately flew off. On returning in the evening I found the toad still undisturbed.—C. C. C. in the *Field*, June 8th.

AN EDIBLE FRUIT.—Mr. Walter Hill, the director of the Botanic Garden at Brisbane, records in the *Queenslander* the existence of an Edible Fruit indigenous to the colony:—"Some years ago," says Mr. Hill, "I discovered in the coast scrubs a small, but rather handsome, tree, the botanic name of which is Macadamia ternifolia; but I was not aware, until recently, that it bore an edible fruit, and, singular to say, the aborigines appear to have been equally ignorant. The tree is now bearing abundantly in the scrubs, both to the southward and northward, and in several localities the children of the Europeans, as well as those of the blacks, are regularly employed in gathering fruit for the purpose of food. The fruit is about the size of a walnut, and contains within a thick pericarp a smooth brown-coloured nut, embracing a kernal of a remarkably rich and agreeable flavour, resembling in some respects that of a filbert, but, to my taste, much superior."

HAIR WORMS.—Several persons have written to the scientific papers during the past few weeks describing the appearance of thousands of these insects; some from Croydon, some from Epsom. The following describes their appearance at Brixton and neighbourhood, sent to the *Gardeners' Chronicle*, June 15th:—The violent thunderstorm, accompanied by a deluge of rain, which burst over the metropolis in the early morning of Monday, the 3rd inst., was followed in the course of a few hours by a curious phenomenon but rarely observed. The rose bushes and other shrubs in various gardens at Kennington, Brixton, and other southern suburbs, were seen to be swarming with small, slender hair worms (about two or three inches long, and not thicker than a lace-pin). These creatures are occasionally found in the earth, but they are parasitic in the bodies of different kinds of insects. A correspondent from the neighbourhood of Carlisle, in a letter also dated the 3rd inst., informs us that he had found a number of these creatures in his garden, stating that "they come out in quantities in our garden on *damp* evenings. They are long, hair-like looking worms, from three to four inches in length, rather pale in colour, and their habit is to wind half of their length round some leaf or stalk, and make a circular sort of motion in the air with the other half." Their history is very obscure, but we believe they are in no wise injurious to plants.

YOUNG CANARIES FED BY AN OLDER NESTLING.—The following appeared in the *Field* (June 8th). I think the following fact will be interesting to many of your readers. I have bred canaries for many years, and have never seen such an example of affection. Early in the season I put up a favourite cock and hen canary, hoping for a fine nest of young birds. Our bitter third or fourth winter nearly killed my birds, and only one young one came to maturity. Since then the hen has laid again, and I have four healthy darlings to cheer me and to watch; and during these watchings—can you believe it?—I see the first young bird, which is a very fine one, feeding its brothers and sisters, and this constantly. The mother is again laying, and the father and son between them (for I fancy it is a young cock) bring up the four little creatures in the old nest. I think it so extraordinary a thing that it is well worth a place in your columns, for the bird is not more than two months old, if it is that.—Henry John Morant (Newnham Rectory, Winchfield, Hants.)

LAGO MAGGIORE.—The Italian papers continue to give very interesting accounts, in a geological sense, of the land convulsions on the borders of the Lago Maggiore. Some time ago a small village on the shores of this water disappeared within the bosom of the lake, its immersion being caused by an extensive land-slip. It now appears that, for several months, the region adjacent to the Tyrolean Alps, to the Lago Maggiore, and the Lago di Guarda, has been subject to a series of convulsions, recurring at periodical intervals, by which the inhabitants have been kept in a state of great apprehension. The shores of the latter lake have been upheaved for a space of ten miles by violent oscillations, and enormous masses of stone and earth continually fall from Monte Balbo, occasioning the utmost consternation among the inhabitants of the valley.—*Athenæum*, May 25.

SILK PLANT.—The Department of State at Washington had received information from the United States Consul at Lambayeque, Peru, says the *Morning Post*, that an important discovery had recently been made in Peru of the silk plant. Preparations were being made to cultivate it upon an extensive scale. The shrub is three feet or four feet in height. The silk is enclosed in a pod, of which each plant gives a great number, and is declared to be superior in fineness and quality to the production of the silkworm. It is a wild perennial, the seed small and easily separated from the fibre. The stems of the plant produce a long and very brilliant fibre, superior in strength and beauty to the finest linen thread. Small quantities have been woven in the rude manner of the Indians, and the texture and brilliancy is said to be unsurpassed.

THE NOVEMBER METEORS.—The *Athenæum* June 1st, says Prof. Adams has determined by elaborate calculation that the periodic time of the November meteors is 33.25 years. In a communication to the Royal Astronomical Society explaining his method, and giving results obtained by other observers, he remarks, "It appears probable that the great comet of 1862 is a part of the same current of matter as that to which the August meteors belong." Should this view receive confirmation, it opens a wide field for speculation, and astronomers will agree with the learned Professor that "it is difficult to believe that the coincidences which have been noticed are merely accidental."

DOUBLE BIRD'S NEST.—Between the upright stems of an oak and two thorns, at the bottom of my garden, a pair of wrens built: whilst they were sitting a pair of flycatchers selected the top of the wren's nest for the foundation of their own, which they completed and occupied before the young wrens had flown, neither pair, so far as I could ascertain, interfering in the least with the other. The wrens have again built in the same situation, so I hope the flycatchers may return to their old home, though I fear the wrens will have left before the others commence operations.—Herbert Greenwood, Sandford Lodge, Hampstead, May 13, 1867.—*Zoologist*, June.

A MOUSE'S STORE.—Mr. J. Dickens, of the Saracen's Head (says the *Zoologist*) near Holbeach, has just discovered a mouse's nest in his garden in which a winter's store of 1329 filbert nuts had been secreted by the industrious little animal. They measured half a peck, and weighed six pounds.

Remarks, Queries, &c.

(*Under this head we shall be happy to insert original Remarks, Queries, &c.*)

AIDS TO EGG-COLLECTING.—In connection with "Kellick's" observations on this subject published in the *Naturalist's Note Book* I venture to make a few remarks:—

In the first place, the practice of inscribing the names on eggs is decidedly to be avoided. Most of our British species have delicate markings which would be marred by any inscription; the point of a pen or pencil is also likely to injure the shell. No careful collector, moreover, would mix or confuse specimens which have cost him time or trouble to procure.

Undoubtedly the best method of blowing is

by means of the blowpipe, of which the end can be inserted in a hole on one side of the egg; the other side and both ends then appear uninjured when mounted on cardboard or laid in wool. This advantage cannot be gained when the old-fashioned method of making a hole at each end is adopted.

It is indispensably necessary that after the egg has been blown it should be washed, and that camphor should be sprinkled all over the cotton wool in which it is laid, to prevent the interior membrane of the shell from decaying, which is often the case if proper attention is not bestowed on this subject. Some collectors recommend rinsing the egg with corrosive sublimate; but as this is extremely poisonous, and requires very great care in use, I have adopted the former method, which has proved successful.

One of the chief points to be considered while endeavouring to obtain birds' eggs is that of not robbing the pretty little nest of one more egg than is required; it may therefore be remembered with regard to our small birds, that generally speaking one or sometimes two more eggs are laid than the mother's wings can cover, and consequently, if old nests are searched for in June or July, one egg will most likely be left when the others are hatched and the young birds flown.

If this "extra egg" can be procured as soon as the usual number are laid, and the collector has patience to wait until an opportunity occurs for him to obtain a pair to it by similar means, a good collection may be formed without destroying any nests, or causing any merry little songsters to forsake their newly-constructed home.

L. H. M.

SPIDERS.—About the middle of August, '66, I noticed a spider had thrown a web from the roof covering the entrance to our yard-door to the garden wall, a distance of about one foot. To keep the frail structure steady in the wind, the spider had suspended at the end of a line of web thrown from the circular network a piece of mortar weighing about thirty grains. Like most, the web was broken; but in the course of a week or so another line was thrown to the wall, and from the centre of the line another piece of mortar was suspended. It was not dropped just over the end of the roof, but had been carried by some ingenious means half way to the wall. Having hung his weight, the spider rapidly "payed out" the circular web and the cross bars. Spiders on the look out for prey usually stand head downwards in the centre of the web. Out of twenty webs one evening I noticed eighteen in the above position. Everyone has seen a fly caught, but all may not have noticed that after it has been wrapped up the spider, still head-downward, commences to pinch his victim in the back, working with its mouth in a horizontal direction—the juices are sucked out and the frame discarded. A spider is not able well or at all to move about in a neighbour's web. Spiders fight fiercely if they have a chance of doing so. For an experiment I put two into one web, when the intruder was savagely attacked, but was too active and strong to be rolled up; and he immediately fastened a line and quickly dropped down to the under part of a leaf, where, fixing a line about the sixteenth of an inch long to support his body, he rested.

Maidstone. T. F., Junior.

DISEASES OF GOLD FISH.—Having read in the *Naturalist's Note Book* for May, 1867, an inquiry by "Aquarian," of some remedy for the film which attaches to gold fish, I have copied from a work called *The Ladies Treasury*, of August, 1861:—"Cure for the film on Gold Fish." Mr. Edward Hewitt, of Speckbrook, Birmingham, writes thus to the *Journal of Horticulture* respecting the film on gold fish:—"That, although his fish in a pond had constant accession of fresh water, yet after a year or two a kind of mouldy looking film came on them in patches, which gradually progressed to the gills, and even extended itself over the eyes, causing partial blindness, and ultimately death. A friend suggested that, as the water was deep, and the bottom muddy, the fish had no shallow scours to clean themselves upon. A place was cut out of the bank at his suggestion, and covered with water only a foot deep. At the bottom was placed sharp grit or drift sand, and small pebbles taken from the turnpike road. The fish immediately commenced cleaning themselves, by rubbing sideways over the bottom, and by this means were completely cured, and the disease never presented itself again." Now, this is the complaint which kills all fish kept in glass globes—therefore it would be well to have a second globe with pebbles and grit and about once a week turn the fish in this.—E. B.

BRITISH SHREWS.—In the article upon British shrews in the number of the *Naturalist's Note Book* it is mentioned that numbers of shrews are found dead in the autumn from some unknown reason. In an early number of *Once a Week*, 1866, it says that an eminent surgeon having dissected a quantity of them found them to be all males, and that each of them had a bite in the jugular vein, evidently from another shrew, and that it was supposed that they were killed fighting for mates for the winter.

SHREW MOUSE.

THE COMMON GREEN ENGLISH LIZARD.—I once kept two common brown lizards in a box of grass (they were captured in heath). After a time some of the scales turned of a green colour, which makes me think that the brown and green English lizards are one and the same animal, as I have always captured the brown in heath, &c., and the other in grass and green localities. I wish to know if any of your subscribers have observed the same thing?

May 29, 1867. "GLOWWORM."

FLEAS IN DOGS.—J. L.—Persian Insect Powder, is recommended by the Editor of the *Naturalist's Note Book*—but I have kept thick-coated Russian and Cuba dogs, and I found washing their backs, especially the lower part, about once a week or so, where the fleas settle most, answers very well. I used a brush and comb, and soap and warm water, and this kept the poor things free from their assailants, and made them quite comfortable.—E. B.

June 11th, 1867.

GOLDEN ORIOLES.—I beg to communicate to you the fact of a pair of Golden Orioles having having taken up their summer residence at Trescoe, one of the Scilly Islands, in the groves at the residence of Mr. Smith, the Lord Proprietor. They are evidently bent on nesting there, as they have all the appearance of birds breeding. This species has been in the habit of visiting Scilly for a long time.

EDWD. HEARLE RODD.

PRESERVATION OF INSECTS.—At p. 170, an alcoholic solution of corrosive sublimate is recommended for the preservation of insects. Let him who uses it beware; I once spoiled a fine lot of *Lepidoptera* with it, for when the spirit evaporated, a white deposit was left on the wings, although they were effectually "preserved." J. W. DOUGLAS.

June 15th.

ENTOMOLOGICAL NOTES FOR JUNE.—Errors at p. 168.—*Rhynchites Bacchus* I once saw taken in Birch Wood, by beating the bushes; there are no *vines* in the wood, and this specimen is the only one known to be British. *Hipparchia Hero* is not a British species, the name was long ago introduced by mistake. J. W. D.

BUTTERFLIES.—I should be obliged if any of your correspondents would inform me of the best way to catch and preserve butterflies, as I have just commenced collecting them and am ignorant on the subject. R. H.

STATE OF THE WEATHER NEAR LONDON.

May and June.	Moon's Age.	BAROMETER.		TEMPERATURE.					Wind	Rain.	REMARKS.
				Of the Air.			of the Earth				
		Max.	Min.	Max	Min	Mean	1 foot deep	2 feet deep			
Thurs. 16	12	30.054	29.977	53	32	42.5	53	52	N.E.	.00	Clouded and cold; densely clouded; overcast.
Friday 17	13	30.124	30.067	60	27	43.5	53	52	S.W.	.00	Fine; overcast; very fine at night.
Satur. 18	○	30.039	29.925	66	42	54.0	53	52	E.	.00	Frost early in morning; fine; very fine at night.
Sunday 19	15	29.867	29.714	67	45	56.0	55	52	E.	.02	Very fine; densely clouded; overcast at night; rain.
Mon. 20	16	29.570	29.529	69	50	59.5	55	51	N.W.	.76	Overcast; constant heavy rain; very wet at night.
Tues. 21	17	29.939	29.560	54	30	42.0	55	51	N.E.	.09	Clear and cold; rain; cold and wet; cloudy; frost at night.
Wed. 22	18	30.046	29.919	48	28	38.0	54	51	N.E.	.12	Clear and cold; snow mixed with hail; overcast; frosty.
Thurs. 23	19	30.101	29.937	51	25	38.0	51	50	N.E.	.00	Very cold and blustrous; heavy clouds; fine; frosty.
Friday 24	20	30.125	30.038	52	25	38.5	50	49	N.E.	.00	Heavy clouds; cloudy; fine; sharp frost at night.
Satur. 25	21	30.044	29.803	56	31	43.5	50	49	E.	.35	Slight dry haze; densely overcast; heavy rain.
Sunday 26	☽	29.640	29.533	71	43	57.0	50	49	S.	.02	Heavy rain; fine; cloudy at night.
Mon. 27	23	29.621	29.557	68	44	56.0	50	49	S.	.00	Heavy clouds; cloudy and fine; very fine at night.
Tues. 28	24	29.807	29.759	70	47	58.5	50	50	S.W.	.00	Densely clouded; fine with clouds; mild at night.
Wed. 29	25	29.929	29.836	74	44	59.0	51	51	S.E.	.04	Densely overcast; showery; cloudy at night.
Thurs. 30	26	30.021	29.929	70	50	60.0	51	51	S.E.	.04	Very fine; overcast and mild; very fine.
Friday 31	27	30.124	30.054	75	40	57.5	52	52	S.E.	.01	Uniform haze; exceedingly fine; fine at night.
Satur. 1	28	30.076	30.055	76	44	60.0	52	52	S.W.	.00	Very fine; very fine throughout.
Sunday 2	●	29.990	29.805	82	56	69.0	53	53	S.W.	.78	Cloudless and hot; very fine; heavy rain at night.
Mon. 3	1	29.819	29.587	63	43	53.0	54	54	W.	.05	Overcast and warm; rain; very fine at night.
Tues. 4	2	29.956	29.899	68	40	54.0	55	54	W.	.00	Cloudy and fine; cloudy; very fine.
Wed. 5	3	29.848	29.737	62	51	56.5	56	54	S.E.	.24	Densely clouded; rather boisterous; rain; cloudy.
Thurs. 6	4	29.730	29.665	68	48	58.0	56	54	S.W.	.02	Cloudy; fine; cloudy at night.
Friday 7	5	29.830	29.662	68	44	56.0	57	56	S.W.	.10	Low white clouds; fine; overcast.
Satur. 8	6	30.037	29.987	72	47	59.5	57	56	S.W.	.00	Fine; cloudy and fine; overcast at night.
Sunday 9	☾	30.198	30.066	75	43	59.0	57	56	W.	.00	Very fine; fine, with clouds; very fine.
Mon. 10	8	30.242	30.227	80	45	62.5	57	56	W.	.00	Exceedingly fine; very fine throughout.
Tues. 11	9	30.268	30.110	82	50	66.0	59	57	S.	.00	Very hot and cloudless; very fine at night.
Wed. 12	10	30.061	29.922	85	50	67.5	60	58	S.W.	.06	Very hot; very fine; cloudy at night.
Thurs. 13	11	30.057	29.901	66	46	56.0	60	56	S.W.	.00	Partially overcast; densely clouded; cloudy at night.
Friday 14	12	29.848	29.790	68	42	55.0	59	57	N.W.	.00	Fine; overcast; very fine at night.
Satur. 15	13	30.024	29.936	62	46	54.0	59	57	N.E.	.12	Fine, with white clouds; cold and overcast; cloudy.
Sunday 16	14	30.090	30.051	62	42	52.0	59	56	N.	.00	Cloudy; cloudy; very fine at night.
Mon. 17	○	30.115	30.092	64	41	52.5	59	56	N.W.	.00	Cloudy; overcast; fine, but cold at night.
Tues. 18	16	30.032	29.978	75	59	67.0	58	56	S.E.	.00	Fine; overcast; overcast and warm.
Wed. 19	17	30.008	29.966	70	40	55.0	60	56	N.E.	.00	Hazy and warm; cloudy; overcast at night.

The Naturalist's Note Book.

Atkinson & Corfield, 18, Cursitor St, Chancery Lane.

IMITATION IN NATURE.

T is in the insect world that the principle of the adaptation of animals to their environment is most fully and strikingly developed. In order to understand how general this is, it is necessary to enter somewhat into details. It seems to be in proportion to their sluggish motions or the absence of other means of defence, that insects possess the protective colouring. In the tropics there are thousands of species of insects which rest during the day clinging to the bark of dead or fallen trees; and the greater portion of these are delicately mottled with gray and brown tints, which though symmetrically disposed and infinitely varied, yet blend so completely with the usual colours of the bark, that at two or three feet distance they are quite undistinguishable. In some cases a species is known to frequent only one species of tree. This is the case with the common South American long-horned beetle (*Onychocerus scorpio*), which Mr. Bates informs us is found only on a rough-barked tree, called Tapiribá, on the Amazon. It is very abundant, but so exactly does it resemble the bark in colour and rugosity, and so closely does it cling to the branches, that until it moves it is absolutely invisible! An allied species (*O. concentricus*), is found only at Para on a distinct species of tree, the bark of which it resembles with equal accuracy. Both these insects are abundant, and we may fairly conclude that the protection they derive from this strange concealment is at least one of the causes that enable the race to flourish.

Many of the species of *Cicindela*, or tiger beetle, will illustrate this mode of protection. Our common *Cicindela campestris* frequents grassy banks, and is of a beautiful green colour, while *C. maritima* which is found only on sandy sea-shores, is of a pale bronzy yellow, so as to be almost invisible. A great number of the species found by Mr. Wallace in the Malay islands are similarly protected. The beautiful *Cicindela gloriosa*, of a very deep velvety green colour, was only taken upon wet mossy stones in the bed of a mountain stream, where it was with the greatest difficulty detected. A large brown species (*C. heros*) was found chiefly on dead leaves in forest paths; and one which was never seen except on the wet mud of salt marshes was of a glossy olive so exactly the colour of the mud as only to be distinguished when the sun shone, by its shadow! Where the sandy beach was coralline and nearly white, he found a very pale *Cicindela;* wherever it was volcanic and black, a dark species of the same genus was sure to be met with.

There are in the East small beetles of the family *Buprestidæ* which generally rest on the midrib of a leaf, and the naturalist often hesitates before picking them off, so closely do they resemble pieces of bird's dung. Kirby and Spence mention the small beetle *Onthophilus sulcatus* as being like the seed of an umbelliferous plant; and another small weevil, which is much persecuted by predatory beetles of the genus *Harpalus*, is of the exact colour of loamy soil, and was found to be particularly abundant in loam pits. Mr. Bates mentions a small beetle (*Chlamys pilula*) which was undistinguishable by the eye from the dung of caterpillars, while some of the *Cassidæ*, from their hemispherical forms and pearly gold colour, resemble glittering dew-drops upon the leaves.

A number of our small brown and speckled weevils at the approach of any object roll off the leaf they are sitting on, at the same time drawing in their legs and antennæ, which fit so perfectly into cavities for their reception that the insect becomes a mere oval brownish lump, which it is hopeless to look for among the similarly coloured little stones and earth pellets among which it lies motionless.

The distribution of colour in butterflies and moths respectively is very instructive from this point of view. The former have all their brilliant colouring on the upper surface of all four wings, while the under surface is almost always soberly coloured, and often very dark and obscure. The moths on the contrary have generally their chief colour on the hind wings only, the upper wings being of dull, sombre, and often imitative tints, and these generally conceal the hind wings when the insects are in repose. This arrangement of the colours is therefore eminently protective, because the butterfly always rests with his wings raised so as to conceal the dangerous brilliancy of his upper surface. It is probable that if we watched their habits sufficiently we should find the under surface of the wings of butterflies very frequently imitative and protective. Mr. T. W. Wood has pointed out that the little orange-tip butterfly often rests in the evening on the green and white flower heads of an umbelliferous plant, and that when observed in this position the beautiful green and white mottling of the under surface completely assimilates with the flower heads and renders the creature very difficult to be seen. It is probable that the rich dark colouring of the under side of our peacock, tortoiseshell, and red-admiral butterflies answers a similar purpose.

Two curious South American butterflies that always settle on the trunks of trees (*Gynecia dirce* and *Callizona acesta*) have the under surface curiously striped and mottled, and when viewed obliquely must closely assimilate with the appearance of the furrowed bark of many kinds of trees. But the most wonderful and undoubted case of protective resemblance in a butterfly which we have ever seen is that of the common Indian *Kallima inachis,* and its Malayan ally, *Kallima paralekta*. The upper surface of these insects is very striking and showy, as they are of a large size, and are adorned with a broad band of rich orange on a deep bluish ground. The under side is very variable in colour, so that out of fifty specimens no two can be found exactly alike, but every one of them will be of some shade of ash or brown or ochre, such as are found among dead, dry, or decaying leaves. The apex of the upper wings is produced into an acute point, a very common form in the leaves of tropical shrubs and trees, and the lower wings are also produced into a short narrow tail. Between these two points runs a dark curved line exactly representing the midrib of a leaf, and from this radiate on each side a few oblique lines, which serve to indicate the lateral veins of a leaf. These marks are more clearly seen on the outer portion of the base of the wings, and on the inner side towards the middle and apex, and it is very curious to observe how the usual marginal and transverse striæ of the group are here modified and strengthened so as to become adapted for an imitation of the venation of a leaf. We come now to a still more extraordinary part of the imitation, for we find representations of leaves in every stage of decay, variously blotched and mildewed and pierced with holes, and in many cases irregularly covered with powdery black dots gathered into patches and spots, so closely resembling the various kinds of minute fungi that grow on dead leaves that it is impossible to avoid thinking at first sight that the butterflies themselves have been attacked by real fungi!

But this resemblance, close as it is, would be of little use if the habits of the insect did not accord with it. If the butterfly sat upon leaves or upon flowers, or opened its wings so as to expose the upper surface, or exposed and moved its head and antennæ as many other butterflies do, its disguise would be of little avail. We might be sure, however, from the analogy of many other cases, that the habits of the insect are such as still further to aid its deceptive garb; but we are not obliged to make any such supposition, since the present writer has himself had the good fortune to observe scores of *Kallima paralekta*, in Sumatra, and to capture many of them, and can vouch for the accuracy of the following details. These butterflies frequent dry forests, and fly very swiftly. They were never seen to settle on a flower or a green leaf, but were many times suddenly lost sight of in a bush or tree of dead leaves. On such occasions they were generally searched for in vain, for while gazing intently at the very spot where one had disappeared, it would often suddenly dart out, and again vanish twenty or fifty yards further on. On one or two occasions the insect was detected reposing, and it could then be seen how completely it assimilates itself to the surrounding leaves. It sits on a nearly upright twig, the wings fitting closely back to back, concealing the antennæ and head, which are drawn up between their bases. The little tails of the hind wing touch the branch, and form a perfect stalk to the leaf, which is supported in its place by the claws of the middle pair of feet, which are slender and inconspicuous. The irregular outline of the wings gives exactly the perspective effect of a shrivelled leaf. We thus have size, colour, form, markings, and habits, all combining to produce a disguise which may be said to be absolutely perfect; and the protection which it affords is sufficiently indicated by the abundance of the individuals that possess it.

The Rev. Joseph Greene has called attention to the striking harmony between the colours of those British moths which are on the wing in autumn and winter, and the prevailing tints of nature at those seasons. In autumn various shades of yellow and brown prevail, and he shows that out of fifty-two species that fly at this season, no less than forty-two are of corresponding colours. *Orgyia antiqua, O. gonostigma,* the genera *Xanthia, Glæa,* and *Ennomos,* are examples. In winter grey and silvery tints prevail, and the genus *Chematobia* and several species of *Hybernia* which fly during this season are of corresponding hues. No doubt if the habits of moths in a state of nature were more closely observed, we should find many cases of special protective resemblance. A few such have already been noticed. *Agriopis aprilina, Acronycta psi,* and many other moths which rest during the day on the north side of the trunks of trees, can with difficulty be distinguished from the grey and green lichens that cover them. The lappet moth (*Gastropacha querci*) closely resembles both in shape and colour a brown dry leaf; and the well-known buff-tip moth when at rest is like the broken end of a lichen-covered branch. There are some of the small moths which exactly resemble the dung of birds dropped on leaves; and there are probably hosts of these resemblances which have not yet been observed, owing to the difficulty of finding many of the species in their stations of natural repose. Caterpillars are also similarly protected. Many exactly resemble in tint the leaves they feed upon; others are like little brown twigs, and many are so strangely marked or humped, that when motionless they can hardly be taken to be living creatures at all. Mr. Andrew Murray has remarked how closely the larva of the peacock moth *(Saturnia pavonia-minor)* harmonizes in its ground colour with that of the young buds of heather on which it feeds, and that the pink spots with which it is decorated correspond with the flowers and flower-buds of the same plant.

The whole order of *Orthoptera*, grasshoppers, locusts, crickets, &c., are protected by their colours harmonizing with that of the vegetation or the soil on which they live, and in no other group have we such striking examples of special resemblance. Most of the tropical *Mantidæ* and *Locustidæ* are of the exact tint of the leaves on which they habitually repose, and many of them in addition have the veining of their wings modified so as exactly to imitate that of a leaf. This is carried to the furthest possible extent in the wonderful genus, *Phyllium*, the "walking leaf," in which not only are the wings perfect imitations of leaves in every detail, but the thorax and legs are flat, dilated, and leaf-like; so that when the living insect is resting among the foliage on which it feeds, the closest observation is often unable to distinguish between the animal and the vegetable.

The whole family of the *Phasmidæ*, or spectres, to which this insect belongs, is more or less imitative, and a great number of the species are called "walking-stick insects," from their singular resemblance to twigs and branches. Some of these are a foot long and as thick as one's finger, and their whole colouring, form, rugosity, and the arrangement of the head, legs, and antennæ are such as to render them absolutely identical in appearance with dead sticks. They hang loosely about shrubs in the forest, and have the extraordinary habit of stretching out their legs unsymmetrically, so as to render the deception more complete. One of these creatures obtained by Mr. Wallace in Borneo *(Ceroxylus laceratus)* was covered over with foliaceous excrescences of a clear olive green colour, so as exactly to resemble a stick grown over by a creeping moss or jungermannia. The Dyak who brought it assured him it was grown over with moss although alive, and it was only after a most minute examination that he could convince himself it was not so.

We need not adduce any more examples to show how important are the details of form and of colouring in animals, and that their very existence may often depend upon their being by these means concealed from their enemies. This kind of protection is found apparently in every class and order, for it has been noticed wherever we can obtain sufficient knowledge of the details of an animal's life-history. It varies in degree, from the mere absence of conspicuous colour or a general harmony with the prevailing tints of nature, up to such a minute and detailed resemblance to inorganic or vegetable structures as to realise the talisman of the fairy tale, and to give its possessor the power of rendering itself invisible.—*Westminster Review*, July, 1867.

BRAZILIAN VEGETATION.

THERE is perhaps no part of the South American continent in which its botanical characteristics are better displayed, or in which more of its peculiar vegetable forms are collected together, than on the great table-land of Brazil. This tract of country, which occupies a great extent of the interior of that vast empire, and includes within it the upper courses of the rivers San Francisco, Tocantins, Araguaya, and Paraná, with their innumerable tributaries, may be described in a very general way as an undulating or moderately hilly region, open, or at least not generally wooded, and diversified by frequent ranges and groups of mountains, of no remarkable height or extent. It comprises the famous diamond district, and all, or nearly all, the gold-producing districts of Brazil. The general elevation of the table-land (at least in its eastern and best known portion, in the province of Minas Geraes) is from 2,000 to 4,000 feet above the level of the sea, and its highest mountains, it would appear, scarcely attain to 6,000 feet. It is strikingly distinguished from the tracts near the sea-coast and along the sides of the great rivers of that country, by the comparative absence of wood. It is, speaking generally, an open country, though there are frequent patches of wood—"islands of wood," as they are expressively called in the language of the country,—nestling in the sheltered hollows and recesses of the hills, and in the ravines of the mountains. These "island" woods are of much less gigantic growth than the forests near the coast, and have not their overpowering luxuriance; often they more remind us, by their general character, of our European woods, but they consist of an astonishing variety of trees. Here and there, principally on the southern parts of the table-land, we meet with groves of a strange and solemn aspect, composed entirely of the Brazilian *Araucaria*, a stately and sombre tree. It grows also, occasionally, intermixed with other trees, in the great forests on the Organ Mountains, near Rio de Janeiro; but on the table-land of Minas Geraes it grows always alone, unmixed with other trees; and its perfectly straight columnar stem, its crown of excessively long branches, spreading like the arms of a chandelier, quite bare except at their ends, which curve upwards, and the dark grey-green tint of its rigid foliage, make it a tree of very striking appearance.

This same Brazilian *Araucaria* might give rise to some curious speculations concerning the dispersion of natural types. It is so nearly akin to the well known *Araucaria imbricata*, that one can hardly help suspecting they must have come originally from the same stock; yet their native regions are now absolutely separated. The one is confined to a narrow tract at a great elevation on the Andes of Southern Chili; the other, though it has a wider latitudinal range, belongs to a lower elevation, as well as to lower latitudes and does not seem anywhere to approach the Andes. Between the regions now inhabited by the one species and the other is interposed the whole extent of the Pampas and the lowlands of Paraguay, in which neither could flourish.

The richest part, botanically, of the great table-land of Brazil is the eastern portion, comprising the diamond district and the principal gold districts of Minas Geraes. It is also the most elevated part. The surface is in general clothed with slender and rather rigid grasses, of many different kinds, growing thinly in separate tufts, not in a dense carpet, and intermixed with a wonderful variety of small slender shrubs with beautiful bright coloured flowers, many of them resembling heaths in general appearance at first sight. In some parts of the *campos* (as the open country is called) the shrubs grow larger, and form a kind of thin brushwood; and some tracts are dotted over with small low trees, standing apart like fruit trees in an orchard, which they a good deal resemble also in size and form. It would be difficult to give an idea, to those not well 'versed in botany,' of the variety, beauty, and interest of the vegetation of this region. Very copious detailed accounts of it are given in "Gardner's Travels," and in some papers by the same author in the "Journal of the Horticultural Society; but mere lists of names would convey little or no information to the generality of readers, and the greater part of the most characteristic forms of this vegetation are little or not at all known in cultivation in Europe. For the most part they belong to the same generic types as those which occur in the great forests in the same latitudes; but instead of appearing as giant trees or lofty climbers, those types of structure are here represented by dwarfish trees, by low slender under-shrubs, or even by herbs; and they branch out into endless minor diversities of form. A large proportion of them are specially and characteristically South American: either peculiar to that continent, or scantily represented elsewhere; others are strange and peculiar forms of widely spread types. For instance, one of the most common herbaceous plants on the *campos* of the gold district, is an *Eryngium*, strictly a congener of our well-known sea side Eryngo, or Sea Holly; but instead of the thistle-like leaves of that and of all the European *Eryngiums*, it has long, narrow, strap-shaped, parallel-veined leaves, forming a rosette at the base of the stem, and fringed throughout their length with sharp slender prickles,—leaves more like those of the pineapple family, than of that to which it belongs. A whole group of species of *Eryngium*, with leaves of this peculiar character, appears to extend through South America, from Mexico to the Rio de la Plata, and I am not aware that any such have been found in other countries.

* * * * * *

The Brazilian uplands lower gradually towards the south, and seem to pass without any abrupt demarcation into the grassy plains of Uruguay and La Plata. And, as in physical geography, there is no strongly marked boundary line between these two regions, so in their vegetable productions the same appears to hold good. The vegetation of the table-land melts or fades by degrees into that of the more southern plains, the distinguishing characteristics of which are perhaps rather negative than positive. The most remarkable and predominant tropical groups thin out and disappear by degrees, as we go southwards, but they are not replaced to any considerable extent by new and local forms. I speak of indigenous plants; for the vegetation of the Pampas and the banks of the Plata has been modified in an extraordinary manner by the introduction of certain plants from Europe, which have naturalized and established themselves so thoroughly, and spread so widely, as to become more predominant and conspicuous than any of the native produce of the soil. The most remarkable instances of this kind are the thistles (*Carduus Marianus* and *Cynara Cardunculus*) and the trefoils (*Trifolium repens* and *Medicago denticulata*), which cover the Pampas to a vast extent, and have been noticed by all travellers. Many other common European weeds of cultivated and waste lands are now among the most common plants on both sides of the Rio de la Plata; and some of them have been introduced within the memory of man.—*Frazer's Mag.*, July 1867.

BRITISH ARVICOLÆ OR VOLES.

THREE tolerable distinct species of these little animals have, for some time past, been known to naturalists, but the actual specific distinctions between the kinds, and the variations in the colour of the fur they assume in various localities have never yet been clearly and accurately determined. The voles are small rodent quadrupeds, nearly allied to the true *Muridæ*, but differing from them in having the head larger and rounder in proportion to their size, the ears being almost hidden in the fur, the tail being also shorter, and in the aquatic species slightly flattened at the sides. Of our British species the water vole (*Arvicola amphibia*), commnoly known as the water rat, is the largest, equalling the common brown rat (*Mus decumanus*) in size.

The fur is reddish-brown above, shading into pinkish-white beneath, and consists of a soft woolly undercoat, well fitted to resist the water, in which the creature is so frequently immersed, mingled with long shining hair, which gives a peculiarly glossy appearance to the back and sides. The incisor teeth are very large and strong, and are covered externally with a layer of hard yellow enamel. Though so thoroughly aquatic an animal in its habits, I am convinced that the water vole is often killed in considerable numbers by colonies of the house rat, which, in the summer months, migrate from the farm buildings and yards, to the banks of streams and ponds, committing great havoc among the younger fish and water-fowl, the blame of which devastation is generally placed to the credit of the poor vegetarian vole. As I have mentioned before, the common rat is as much at home by the waterside as the vole, and I have seen one of the latter pursued by a rat in the water, and vainly endeavouring to rid itself of its enemy by continued diving. The water vole usually selects river-banks or the neighbourhood of large ponds, where its favourite food the *Equisetum* or "mare's tail" grows. In these situations it forms long and winding burrows, which invariably have one outlet above the water and another beneath the surface, so that, in case of danger, it has more than one opportunity for escape. It never enters houses or barns, and shuns the vicinity of man, being a peculiarly shy animal. Its habits, however, are easily watched, and I have frequently observed them on fine balmy evenings in the summer, when the warm breeze gently rustled the waving sedges and water-flags, and bright-coloured dragon-flies hawked on gauze-like wings over the glassy pool in quest of aquatic insects, that were emerging from their pupa state towards sunset, when the moor-hen swam out in security from the tuft of reeds which had concealed her during the hotter hours of the day, followed by her brood, tiny black balls of down, that chased each other in their play, forming little glistening circlets of silvery light on the water. At these times I have seen the water-voles, engaged in foraging for food on the banks, or swimming leisurely about, taking an occasional nibble at some tempting stem, and then diving suddenly and reappearing almost immediately in the same place.

The water-vole, as far as I have observed, never hybernates during the winter months, but remains perfectly lively, laying up, however, a store of food in its burrow, in anticipation of the inclement season it evidently knows is approaching. Besides the common brown kind there is a black variety, found in some parts of England, especially in Hertfordshire and Essex. This has caused considerable difference of opinion as to whether it is a mere local variety, or possesses sufficient claims to be considered a distinct species. I have carefully examined several black and brown specimens taken in various localities, and will proceed to point out what I consider to be the actual distinction between them.

In the first place the black kind is considerably the smaller of the two, a full grown specimen of the common sort averaging thirteen inches in total length, whereas the other rarely exceeds nine; secondly, the tail is, in all cases that have come under my personal notice, considerably longer in the black vole. The head is also smaller, and the eyes larger in proportion to the size of the animal. On dissection, the only distinction I could find was that the principal intestine was considerably larger, when extended, in the black specimens. There was no difference in dentition, but the form of the skull was proportionately more lengthened in the black than the brown individuals. I have seen young specimens of both varieties, but have never met with a black specimen inhabiting the same burrows with the brown ones, but always appearing to form a small colony of their own. Indeed I believe that several species of our smaller mammalia are confounded together or imperfectly known, especially among the bats, shrews, and rodents.

The second species that comes under our notice is the field-vole (*Arvicola campestris*). This species is considerably smaller than the water-vole, seldom exceeding six or seven inches in length. In colour it is light greyish brown above, shading into bluish grey below, and has a tuft of thick hair growing on each side of the jaw, which gives it a peculiarly bluff appearance. It frequents damp pastures and low-lying fields, scarcely if ever being found in hilly localities, its place there being taken by its congener the bank vole (*Arvicola riparia*). It seems to be more prolific than the water vole, generally producing three or four litters in the season, while the others generally only have three or four young ones about the beginning of May. They are also much more destructive in their habits, often peeling the bark from young trees for food, and thus committing considerable damage.

Some years ago a great number of young holly trees were destroyed in the New Forest and in Dean Forest by these voles, the bark being entirely eaten off for a distance of several inches from the ground. Great numbers of young oaks and chestnuts were also found dead, and on being taken up it was found that the roots had been gnawed through below the surface of the ground. The most effectual method of dispersing these marauders it was found was digging a great number of holes in the ground about two feet long, eighteen inches wide, and eighteen inches deep at the bottom; at the top they were only eighteen inches long and nine inches wide, so that when the animals fell into them they were unable to escape. More than 40,000 field-voles were taken in these holes in the space of three months, irrespective of those that were taken out out of the holes by the stoats, weasels, crows, and magpies that had assembled in great numbers to assist in extirpating the little marauders. I have kept both this species and the bank-vole in confinement, and found that they rapidly became tame, allowing themselves to be freely handled, and would frequently take grains of corn from my fingers, though they would resent any liberty from a stranger with a tolerably severe bite. They are perfectly devoid of any unpleasant smell, and make interesting little pets. The third species is the above-mentioned bank-vole. This species is rather smaller than the field-vole, and differs from that animal in having the tail rather longer, and the fur of a bright reddish-brown above, shading into yellowish white beneath. It frequents drier situations than the other species, being found principally in the banks of old hedgerows and among heaps of stones. It is a very active little animal, and moves with great agility. Its habits are identical with those of the last-mentioned species.—*N. L. Austen, in Land and Water*, July 6th, 1867.

THE NATURALIST IN INDIA.

THE streams about Poonah are subject to sudden inundations, owing to the proximity of the mountains. During the hot summer months, when there is no rain, they become dried up, and, excepting small pools here and there, nothing is to be seen but the *debris* of the last storm. Frogs spawn in these situations. One species, a few inches in length, with the belly and throat pure white, is very plentiful; it basks on the sides of the pools, and takes to the water when one approaches, skipping over the pool something in the way a boy *skims* a flat stone. My attention was directed to the surface of the water, which appeared as though large drops of rain were falling on it. Having satisfied myself that this could not be the case, my next supposition was that bubbles of gas were ascending from decomposing matter at the bottom of the pool, which opinion was apparently confirmed by the bubble rising at the time the drop appeared on the surface. I discovered, however, that the water was alive with minute tadpoles. Vast numbers of these little creatures were darting to and from its surface with great rapidity. The frogs I had alarmed were poised upon the water, staring at me intently, and at the margin of the pool were hundreds of tadpoles with the caudal extremity still perfect; others, again, at a distance of some eight or ten feet, had the tail almost separated; whilst a few here and there had lost the appendage altogether, being complete frogs.

About half a mile from my bungalow there were two large hedges of prickly pear, and between them a stagnant pool. I often took up a position under the cool shade of a peepul-tree close by, and watched the habits of the feathered tribe at mid-day. On one occasion, having shot a sun-bird, it fell on the margin of the pool, when some animal jumped from the muddy water, seized it, and instantly disappeared with its prey. A short time afterwards a large green frog appeared on the surface. I shot it, and discovered the bird in its mouth.

The purple honey-sucker of Jerdon, the beautiful blue-wing sun-bird (*Arachnechthra asiatica*, Lath.), is common, and nothing can exceed the grace and elegance of its congener, the Ceylon sun-bird (*Leptocoma zeylonica*). This exquisite little creature sports round the top of the prickly pear, sucking the nectar from its flowers like a humming-bird. Neither species, however, subsists altogether on honey, for flies and minute insects are frequently found in their gizzards. The brilliant green spot on the wing of the male is wanting in the female.

The gaudy lesser crimson-breasted flycatcher (*Pericrocotus peregrinus*) is a tenant of the woods and hedges. Sometimes flocks of males, at other times females only, are observed; the rich and beautiful plumage of the former is very striking; insects and larvæ constitute its favourite food. The shrill, clamorous cry of the koel, or black cuckoo (*Eudynamys orientalis*) was constantly heard in woods and groves; it feeds on fruit. I shot a specimen of a young male European cuckoo (*Cuculus canorus*) on the 16th of October.

At their residence near Poonah the ex-Amirs of Scinde had several fine goshawks, trained for falconry; the species has been shot on the Nepal mountains and Neilgherries. Trained Bhyri falcons (*Falco jugger*) are sold at Poonah by the natives, and fetch high prices. They say these birds inhabit the mountains and woody parts of the district; but there is no more handsome falcon than the teesa (*Poliornis teesa*); its fine, clear, light-coloured eye, and in fact the whole appearance of the bird, indicates grace and strength of wing. In the stomach of a female I found a lizard four inches in length.

Among the many discomforts Europeans have to endure in the East are myriads of fleas, mosquitoes, snakes, centipedes, scorpions, etc., etc., which not only infest gardens, but penetrate into the interior of houses, especially at night. No sooner is the cloth spread than hundreds of beetles, attracted by the light of the candles, dash recklessly into the flame, and fall disabled on the table, intruding themselves into every dish; crickets chirp among the beams overhead, and the whole apartment resounds with the noise and buzz of insect-life. Nor is the scene without very different, though occasionally more attractive; for swarms of fire-flies assemble round the bushes, and with the lucid beam of their tiny lamps illumine the gloom of the tropical night.

On one occasion I was awoke by my servant pursuing a snake across by bedroom floor; he killed it at my bedside. It was a species very common about Poonah, of a greenish-black colour, and about two feet in length, with numerous white spots on its upper surface.

Snake-skins (so entire that even the covering of the eye is retained) were often found under the floor-matting; and a species, white-spotted on the back and sides of the body and about five feet in length, abounds in gardens; on that account one is often obliged to ride on horseback after nightfall, when numbers may be seen crawling about in the roads and gardens, searching for frogs, on which they principally feed. There is a green species, two-and-a-half feet in length, said by the natives to be very venomous. My attention was directed to a circumscribed swelling in the centre of the body of one of these serpents, which on dissection proved to be a frog, fully three times as broad as any other part of the snake's body. Two minute wounds on the frog's back were the only marks of violence discernible.

The cobra di capella is tamed, and taught to dance to the pan-pipe-like sounds of a sort of flageolet. It is said to be plentiful in the cactus hedges, which seem to be a "rendezvous" for all kinds of snakes and vermin. One sultry day, while seated under an acacia tree, I heard a hissing sound behind me, and turning, saw a cobra close by, with raised head and inflated hood, knocking its nose against the stem of a cactus. One of the first injunctions a native servant gives his newly-arrived master is, "*always to shake his boots well before putting them on*," scorpions being apt to take up their abode in the toe!

A green lizard is common in gardens, and on the thatch of bungalows: it preys on scorpions, especially a small black species, abundant beneath stones and the matting of rooms. Centipedes of large size are very plentiful.

The moongus, or grey ichneumon (*Herpestes griseus*), is found in this district, and frequently domesticated. It is exceedingly useful in destroying centipedes and scorpions, but I have never seen it attack serpents; and the story regarding the antidote it obtains for snake-bites in the root of a certain plant called moonguswail, like most Indian tales of that description, is perfectly mythical.

The bandy-coot or hog-rat (*Mus giganteus*) was frequently seen in our houses. This animal is very destructive, and creates much disturbance at night. Sometimes it coursed across the canvas covering of our ceiling—a signal always for "drawn swords," and a *prod* through the "dungaree," together with the pleasing uncertainty as to whether you are transfixing a ghous (as the Mahrattas call it) or a mangur (*Felis bengalensis*), a species of wild cat which prowls about at night, and hides during the day in hedges, or under the thatch of bungalows.

Several species of chameleon are abundant: they frequent bushy places, and are seen basking on the stems of trees; while geckoes are common on the walls of houses. Tigers are found on the mountains and in the jungles. Not far from Kirkee is the village of Maun, where, during midsummer, both the common and jack snipe are abundant in the rice-fields. They arrive about the beginning of November, when also a few painted snipe may be obtained.

Maun is situate close to a range of mountains covered with low dense jungle, extending some distance into the plain, which is studded with villages, rice-fields and gardens, separated by ravines and large tracts of waste and barren country. A dense jungle to the north of the village was said to have been the haunt of a man-eating tiger for some time previous to our visit, and we found the carcase of a bullock lying in a chilli field, not a stone's throw from the village. On both sides of the animal's neck were deep wounds caused by the tiger's teeth, and on the shoulder a long gash, where the claw had ploughed through the skin; the whole of the flesh on the belly and flanks was torn away, the stomach and entrails lying on the ground, where we could see distinct traces of a scuffle, and the footprints of a very large tiger. Pitching our tent within range, we sat up that night, expecting to get a shot at the marauder, as the moon was shining brightly; but after a fruitless vigil, and growing drowsy, I went to bed, and had scarcely been asleep an hour when my servant called me to say the tiger had arrived, and was carrying off the carcase. It was too late, however, as we were just in time to see him disappear in the cover with his prey. The following morning all that remained of the bullock was the skull, and a few pieces of the larger bones. A week afterwards I heard that the same tiger had killed another bullock near a village some ten miles distant.

The kestrel (*Tinnunculus alaudarius*), and also the sparrow hawk (*Accipiter virgatus*), are common. The former may be observed hovering over the plains, and at dusk, not unfrequently in numbers, perched on stones and tufts of grass. Both prey extensively on mice, lizards, and beetles. The latter hawk is trained for quail-hunting. The broad-tailed flycatcher (*Rhipidura fuscoventris*) is plentiful in gardens and wooded localities. It is not shy, and for its size bold and fearless, and will attack birds much larger than itself. The song of the male consists of a few loud and pleasing notes, uttered while the little creature is dancing along the branch with tail and wings expanded like a fan.

The common kingfisher (*Alcedo bengalensis*, Gmel.), the black and white species (*Ceryle rudis*), and the Indian kingfisher (*Halcyon fuscus*, Bodd.), are often observed. The first is common in rice-fields, streams, and river banks; the two latter are not so plentiful; the Indian kingfisher is a tenant of gardens and pools. On the broad tops of peepul, acacia, and mango trees, the lark-heeled cuckoo or Malabar crow (*Centropus rufipennis*, Illig.) perches; grasshoppers and coleopterous insects constitute its favourite food. These birds startle one, while passing under a tree, by the flapping of their large fan-shaped wings; their flight is a sort of sailing motion, which, with the expansive tail, makes them appear much larger than they are in reality. Frequenting like situations may often be seen the beautiful Indian roller (*Coracias indica*), it sports from one tree-top to another with a peculiar zig-zag flight; butterflies and large insects are its favourite food, and are caught on wing. Flocks of the black-headed finch (*Emberiza melanocephala*, Sykes) are common; it is dispersed over the fields during harvest, but disappears soon afterwards. Rock pigeons (*Columba livia*) congregate in the deep wells, in the sides of which they breed. The natives capture them by suddenly throwing a net over the mouth of the well. There is no variety in the wild bird, and although the tame pigeons feed in the fields, the two do not appear to associate. By the sides of hedges, in gardens and way-sides, the Senegal dove (*Columba senegalensis*) is frequently observed. It passes the greater part of the day on the ground, but is often seen likewise on trees. In dissecting and preparing the skins of this species (in fact Columbidæ in general), great care should be taken to remove the fat from the skin of the back and sides, else the feathers will be sure to drop out.

The tailor-bird (*Orthotomus longicauda*), with its curiously-fashioned nest, displaying most marvellous skill and care, is plentiful in groves and gardens, where it may be seen flitting among the dense foliage, emitting its loud cry, resembling that of the mina. The tailor-bird is by no means shy or easily frightened; on the contrary, it is an inquisitive little fellow. I recollect once, when seated under a tree, employed in skinning a bird, one came within a yard of me, and attentively watched the proceeding. It has a droll way of inspecting objects *sideways*, jerking its tail unceasingly when moving. To those familiar with its habits it will not appear surprising that this strange little creature should be the architect of that wonderful nest, formed of cotton, wool, hair, &c., enclosed between leaves, beautifully *sewn* together with vegetable fibre. The young resemble their parents, except in length of tail; also the rufous on the head is not so clear.

Of all rapacious birds the govind-kite is the most useful and abundant; wherever offal exists there this bird is to be found, hovering over the butcher's shop, the kitchen, or the barrack—now leisurely sailing in circles—now darting like an arrow upon its prey, which it devours while on the wing, uttering a clear shrill cry whenever a companion disputes its possession. Its boldness is almost ludicrous. Once, when a servant was bringing mutton-chops from the cook-house to our mess, one of these birds darted upon the dish, and tore away the contents in its talons. The plumage of this species is subject to considerable variety: some are very dark (these I take to be the old birds), others have the under parts light rufous, darkly lined.

The govind-kite, Egyptian vulture, crow, Indian jackdaw, and mina, may justly be termed "*the great scavengers of India.*" What would its large cities be without these useful birds? and lean and degraded as the pariah dog is, abused and cowed by the natives, still he clings to man, and picks up a scanty meal on the dunghill, or feasts with the jackal. From constant ill-treatment he has become the very picture of abject misery, crouching at the sound of the human voice; yet, from some strange instinct, unsolicited he protects the dwelling of the native, and the midnight robber would find it hard indeed to pass his post unchallenged.

The hoopoe (*Upupa epops*) is very common on lawns and in fields. I have been informed that the black-headed bustard (*Otis nigriceps*) was at one time common in this district. It is now seldom met with, having been so much sought after by sportsmen; one specimen was brought to me from the mountains near Poonah with its eyelids sewn together to prevent it running away! The naturalist is likely to be led into error in studying the appearance and habits of the dial-bird (*Copsychus saularis*). The more sombre plumage of the female (which is seldom seen with the male, except during the breeding season) has deceived many. The song of this species is rich and sweet, and frequently imitates the notes of other birds. In habits familiar, it is a common tenant of the gardens, where it pours forth its welcome notes in the afternoon or early morning, and like its rival *redbreast*, sings a bar, and then waits a short time for another individual to reply. This species is the "*nightingale*" of English residents: among flocks of mina birds (*Acridotheres tristis*) may often be seen numbers of the roseate pastor (*Pastor roseus*). The smaller size, peculiar sailing flight, and more pointed wings, will distinguish the latter at a distance.

The rain-quail (*Coturnix coromandelica*) is plentiful during the monsoon. I have shot it in lucerne fields close to my house, and the bush-quail in low jungle near the mountains. We have the Indian golden oriole in woods and groves. It is shy and difficult of approach. The nest, which is placed in the fork of a tree, is formed of dry grass, with a finer description in the interior. The large purse-shaped nest of the weaver-bird (*Ploceus baya*) would fall an easy prey to its enemies, did not the little architect, with surprising intelligence, place it in situations not easily accessible; hence several may be seen suspended from the tips of branches overhanging deep wells, or on the topmost boughs of acacia and thorny trees. The weaver-bird builds in societies, and is docile and familiar in its habits. The common king-crow (*Dicrurus macrocercus*) is often seen on the backs of cattle.

The Egyptian vulture is a native of Eastern Europe, Asia, and Africa. On the temperate regions of the Himalayas it follows man wherever he congregates; and on the plains of India its gaunt forbidding figure is seen stalking among all animal refuse. It is the smallest of the tribe found in the East; its total length seldom exceeding twenty-six inches. In the adult the skin of the head and front of the neck is bare, yellow and shrivelled, giving the animal a melancholy, poverty-stricken appearance. The general colour of the plumage is white, except the quills and their coverts, which are black; the iris is red in the old bird, but brown in the young, which also have the naked part about the head of a leaden colour until the second year. There is great diversity of plumage, from the brownish-black of the young bird to the white of the adult; this latter is attained at the third moult. The habits of this species are strictly domestic. It is usually met with in the filthiest parts of towns and military cantonments. As soon as dinner is announced by the bugle-sound in barracks, Egyptian vultures and kites may be seen hastening towards the scene, which soon assumes a lively aspect from the numbers and activity of the kites, as they dart like arrows on the bones and refuse; while others, with head erect, lifting their legs (much after the manner of rooks), are silently devouring whatever comes in their way. Now and then a vulture in the act of bolting a piece of flesh has to relinquish the morsel to his more nimble companion, whose sharp talons soon tear it off, and he is seen devouring the prize as he sails away. The two species often roost together, and seem to agree very well except at feeding-time. Flocks of both accompany troops for hundreds of miles, and regularly at daybreak, as the new camp is forming, they may be seen approaching from the direction of the previous day's halt.—*Wanderings of a Naturalist in India.* By A. L. Adams, M.D. Edinburgh: Edmondston & Douglas.

AMERICAN PARASITIC PLANTS.

To persons familiar with the principles of cultivation, and with more or less knowledge of our native plants, the fact that there are tribes of plants in other regions of the earth, that, without any attachment whatever to the soil, grow and produce flowers of the most novel form and brilliancy of colours, seems wonderful in the extreme. Such are the Epiphytes, or air-plants of the tropics, whose seeds, lodging on the branches of living or decayed trees, or even upon the very rocks, readily vegetate, and draw from the surrounding atmosphere the constituents of their growth.

This is accomplished chiefly through their roots, as in other plants; and as they are found to increase with much greater luxurance in the recesses of the forest, by the banks of streams, in a sultry, humid atmosphere, we see less difficulty in comprehending the possibilities of their growth and the economy of their being; indeed, their nature is now so well understood, that they are cultivated with ease in our conservatories.

We do not, however, intend to write of air-plants, as our country produces none; but we have, among our native plants, those whose methods of growth are perhaps scarcely less novel and wonderful; such as our parasites, which derive their nourishment from other living plants to which they adhere—depending upon the leaves and roots of such plants for the necessary contact with the atmosphere and the soil.

The name Parasite is of great significance, for such plants are robbers in the fullest sense, and live solely at the expense of their neighbours.

The most marked example in this region of such anomalous plants is the Dodder. Our species, the Cuscuta Gronovii (*C. umbrosa* Torrey, or *C. vulgivaga* Englemann) is as strongly marked, and more widely distributed than either of the other American species.

The genus Cuscuta has generally been appended to the Convolvulaceæ, or the Convolvulus tribe, which consists chiefly of twining plants, and have regular monopetalous pentandrous corollos, and two to four-celled capsules, with large seeds. This order is well represented by the Cypress vine and the Morning-glory.

The cuscutas have no leaves, for these plants need none ; all the necessary functions of leaves, as has been stated, being performed by the leaves of other plants on which they grow. They have, however, a few minute scales in alternate succession, which are in place of leaves, and from their axils spring the branches. Although so anomalous as these plants are supposed to be, yet the right of being perfect plants must be conceded them, and they are properly assigned a place with other Convolvuli.

Eight or nine species grow freely in this country, two of which are found in New England.

C. epilinum, or the Flax Dodder of the old world, mentioned by Gerard and more ancient writers, is naturalized here to some extent. It is said to grow only upon flax, to which it is a great pest, spoiling large quantities. It was noticed by Dr. Cutler as being destructive in his time ; but as that useful plant is now seldom cultivated in this region, the Flax Dodder is but rarely detected. A monograph of the American species, prepared by Dr. George Englemann, of St. Louis, can be found in Silliman's Journal, vols. 43, p. 333, and 45, p. 73.

Under the name of *C. Americana*, the various native species were for a long time confounded. The botanical text-books tells us that the seeds of this strange plant germinate in the earth in the ordinary manner, throwing downward a root into the soil, by which for a short time the tender plantlet is sustained, until it elongates its thread-like stem sufficiently to reach some foster-plant, around which it immediately twines, and into whose tender bark it thrusts aerial roots, which feed upon its juices ; after which, no longer needing attachment to the soil, the primitive root withers away.

After many times plucking the cord-like stems of this plant, and noticing the decisive development of its flowers and seed (for they are as perfect as upon leaf-clad plants), we resolved to prove, with our own eyes, its double nature and singular method of growth. Accordingly we procured some perfect seed of which the wild plant produces an abundance, and of a size by no means diminutive, and planted them in a bed with other seeds, in small rows, each appropriately tallied, and all designed for transplanting, in due time, to suitable places in the border. In a very few days after planting, the Cuscuta-seed uncoiled its feeble embryo, and erected its simple yellow thread into the sunshine and air ; but while we waited for further developments, the spring winds and the warm suns of noon quickly withered them away.

Thus our first attempt at cultivation utterly failed, and solely for the want of some older plants in sufficient proximity for the young seedlings to cling to, but which at the time escaped our reflection. Months elapsed before the experiment was again tried, which was done within doors and in mid-winter with perfect success. The seed readily germinated as before, and when the young plants were about an inch in height, they were taken separately from the earth, and placed here and there on the axils of the leaves of plants near at hand, such as Fuschias, Geraniums, and sundry hanging plants.

With the instincts of their nature (if it be pardonable to use that term), they in a few days attached themselves to these plants, particularly to the Fuschias ; and as the spring advanced, they grew with great luxuriance and flowered freely, but, as might be supposed, to the manifest detriment of the plants about which they twined. This, however, was overlooked in the satisfaction arising from success ; for had their yellow stems been gold, and their clusters of flowers pearls, the satisfaction would hardly have been greater. Those placed on the hanging plants, although they adhered, made but feeble growth. One seedling placed upon a plant of *Dielytra spectabilis* did not twine or extend itself with much freedom, but, taking a turn or two near the extremity of one of the branches, it there expended its strength in perfecting a large conglomerate cluster of one hundred or more bells of unusual size and purity of colour. In the process of transplanting from the earth to their aerial abode, we at first attempted to convey a ball of earth with each seedling, but this was soon found to be worse than useless.—*American Naturalist*, June.

JUPITER.

JUPITER is the largest planet of our system, at the mean distance of 490 millions of miles from the sun. It includes within its orbit all the planets that have yet been described, within its mighty circumference of 3110 millions of miles, around which it travels in 11 years 315 days.

Jupiter revolves on his axis in 9 hours and nearly 57 minutes, hence his day is only about 5 hours long. His diameter is 89,000 miles, hence his circumference is 287,600 miles.

The equatorial portions of Jupiter move round the axis of the planet with a velocity of 28,000 miles an hour, which is 3,000 miles an hour more than our globe moves on its axis. The surface of Jupiter contains 24,884 millions of square miles; and hence, his magnitude is nearly fourteen hundred times that of our earth. His rate of motion in his orbit is about 30,000 miles an hour, carrying along with him a splendid atmosphere, and four moons larger than ours, to adorn his nocturnal firmament; and hence, display a scene of grandeur, wisdom, and omnipotence, worthy of the infinite goodness and perfection of its Creator. We can also see another trait of wisdom in creative intelligence in placing the inclination of Jupiter's axis within little more than three degrees from the perpendicular; and, therefore, there can only be a very slight variation in his seasons; indeed, one might almost term his years a perpetual summer, in which, day by day—

The smiles of morning gild the ponderous globe.

Had Jupiter's axis been inclined as much as that of our earth, his polar regions would have remained alternately in darkness for six years without intermission.

The intensity of solar light on the planet Jupiter is only one twenty-seventh of that of the earth; and hence, the mean apparent diameter of the sun, as seen from Jupiter, is only one-fifth of the size as seen from the earth; but if the intensity of solar light in Jupiter be increased by reflection, by any substances connected with this noble planet, or if the inhabitants have the pupils of their eyes enlarged in proportion to the diminution of solar light, all objects around them may appear even with greater splendour than those do in our earth.

Astronomers have not determined with this planet, as they have done with Mars, that it has an atmosphere of any great extent, yet it may be furnished with an appendage which ministers comfort and happiness to the inhabitants of so august a world, equally as our atmosphere does to the inhabitants of this, our earth; and hence, admitting Jupiter to be a habitable world, and to be clothed with vegetation, after the manner of our earth, ideas which the mind of every rational being cannot fail to entertain, what beauties can we not fancy may adorn so magnificent a globe, enjoying an almost perpetual summer—plants, from the "hyssop on the wall," to others that may far outstrip the cedars of Lebanon in size and grandeur—fruits, whose sweetness may surpass even our ideal nature—and what must be the nature and characteristic of the inhabitants of this noble planet, in majesty and dignity, who are created to dwell in so magnificent an abode? The celestial scenery from Jupiter must be sublimely grand.

As Jupiter reflects to the atmosphere of our earth a combination of the red and the yellow rays of light (oxygen and nitrogen), we find the orange-coloured ray producing, like the red ray, heat; and hence, with Jupiter's aspects, we may safely contemplate increased temperature, fine serene weather, excepting when he is contending with antagonistic influences; then we may look for violent thunder-storms in summer—strong winds, mild air, and very large rocky clouds in spring—large wool-pack clouds in summer and autumn, and mild air, for the season, in winter; but if Jupiter's aspects be combined with those of Saturn or Herschel, in the winter we may have severe frosts. In verification of these facts, we will glance at Jupiter's aspects in the wet year, 1861. Out of twenty-five aspects, solar, lunar, and mutual, the temperature rose in twenty-three of them 115 degrees, and fell on only two aspects 7 degrees, leaving 115—7=108 degrees in favour of Jupiter's calorific properties, making about 4½ degrees rise on the average of his aspects. Rain fell on only five of Jupiter's twenty-five aspects, amounting altogether to three-tenths of an inch during the year, showing that Jupiter is of itself a heatmaking as well as a dry planet. When, therefore, agriculturists see that Jupiter is about to form an aspect, either with the sun, moon, or Mars, he may calculate on fine dry weather for any operations he may have in hand, or would wish to commence. The pleasure-taker may arrange for his pic-nic parties without the fear of being drenched with torrents of rain, except when Jupiter is in aspect with Venus or Saturn, or is passing from an aspect of Mars to one of Venus, Saturn, Herschel, or even the far-distant Neptune, then he may not be surprised if he be suddenly overtaken by a thunder-storm, because opposite currents of electricity will be excited in the earth's atmosphere, on the earth's passing from one angle with Jupiter to a similar angle with Saturn, which may be termed a transition period; so that when the opposite poles of such a celestial battery are brought into contact, either by the lunar rays or some counter current of electricity produced in the upper strata of the atmosphere, which communicating its influence to the lower strata of the clouds, then a storm of considerable magnitude will very probably be the result.

Jupiter's solar aspects, when not connected with any other aspect, are generally attended by tremendous rocky cumulus clouds, highly charged with positive electricity. In the gigantic cumuli being carried off by induction, a grand display of thunder and lightning, with dashing rain, frequently takes place, and sometimes hail.—*The Science of the Weather*. Glasgow: Laidlaw.

The Norwegian Ferns.

Polypodium vulgare.—Is common on stony and rocky places in various parts as far north as East Finmark.

P. phegopteris.—Common in all Norwegian woods. It is to be seen in all the woods round Christiania, and even near Alten and Hammerfest in Finmark.

P. dryopteris.—Is common near Christiania, Bergen, and Trondhjem. It is found in some parts of Finmark.

P. robertianum.—Found in rocky limestone soils from Christiania up to Trondhjem, but no farther north than the last-mentioned town.

P. ræticum.—Common in all mountain regions—up as high as East Finmark. It is found upwards of 4000 feet above the level of the sea.

Woodsia Ilvensis.—Grows in the higher mountain regions from Christiansand up to Finmark. Although scattered over the whole country, it is by no means common, and is always to be met with in the moist crevices of rocks.

W. hyperborea.—The remarks on the preceding are applicable to this species.

L. clavatum.—Is found on mountain morasses in Norway, especially in Finmark. It is said that the Lapps adorn their children's heads with chaplets made from this species, and that the spikes of the plants, projecting on all sides, remind those singular little people of fairies.

L. annotinum.—This rare fern is found in many of the pine forests of Norway.

L. selago.—Is supposed to possess medicinal virtues, and being a powerful irritant, it is used in Sweden and Norway as a decoction wherewith to get rid of vermin in cattle. It is pretty common in this country.

Ophioglossum vulgatum.—This small fern is found in moist places on the shores of some of the Norwegian fjords.

Botrychium rutaceum.—Is by no means common, but we have met with it near Christiania; and a Norwegian friend informs us that he has seen it in Gudbrandsdal.

B. lunaria.—More common than the preceding, and is sparsely scattered throughout this country, even in the extreme north, where the soil is sandy.

Blechnum spicant.—Common in some parts of the west of Norway, and is also found in Finmark.

Cystopteris fragilis.—The brittle bladder fern is pretty common in all damp places in the Norwegian fjelds.

C. montana.—Common in wet places on the Dovre fjeld.

C. crenata.—This rare fern is said to be met with in only one or two places in Gudbrandsdal.

C. regia.—Found in the alpine regions in the south of Norway. We have seen it at Bærum, 7 English miles from Christiania.

Lastrea thelypteris.—Grows in some marshy places. We have seen it near Christiania.

Polystichum filix mas.—Common in shady places in all parts, even in East Finmark.

P. cristatum.—Is not common, but we have found it in sheltered places near Christiania.

P. dilitatum.—Common in all Norwegian forests.

Aspidium lonchitis.—Is to be found in rocky places as high up as the birch grows in the Dovre-fjeld.

A. angulare.—This rare species is to be found near Christiania, Bergen, and Trondhjem. The last mentioned locality seems to be its limit northwards.

A. adiantum-nigrum.—Grows in sandy and rocky spots on the south-west coast of Norway.

A. filix-fœmina.—Common in moist places in the woods in all parts, even in East Finmark.

A. trichomanes.—Common in sheltered places among rocks up to the southern parts of Nordland.

A. viride.—Grows in mountain districts among rocks as far north as the southern parts of Finmark.

A. ruta-muraria.—This diminutive plant grows on old walls, and in the fissures of rocks, near Christiania, Bergen, an Alten in Finmark.

A. septentrionale.—Is common throughout this country in all rocky and stony places.

A. germanicum.—Is a rare plant in Norway. We have found it on Næsodon, a small peninsula running out into the fjord near Christiania. It also grows near Bergen and Trondhjem.

Pteris aquilina.—Is found in rocky places as far north as Nordland.

Adiantum capillus-veneris.—Only to be met with in one or two sheltered places in the extreme south of Norway.

Allosorus crispus.—The mountain parsley grows on all rocky places on the west coast of Norway and in Thelemarken.

Hymenophyllum wilsoni.—Found on moist ground among rocks near Christiansand and Bergen.

Scolopendrium vulgare.—This fern has only been recently discovered in Norway. It grows on old walls.

Equisetum variegatum.—The variegated rough horsetail may be placed among the Norwegian ferns. It is found by some of the rivers and lakes of this country.—*Black's Guide to Norway.*

Indian Spiders and Beetles.

A friend has kindly undertaken to send to your office a small box containing specimens of spiders and beetles. I shall feel obliged if you will name the specimens for me. The spiders are called by the natives "jeramungalum," and are said to be poisonous. They appear during the months of February, March, and April. I have never seen them except at night, when they appear on the walls of the house, or in the verandah. They run at such a pace that it requires the greatest sharpness and activity to secure them. If one comes on the clothes of a native servant, he (the servant, not the spider) rushes away and literally tears the coat off, without waiting to unbutton or untie it. This year I have caught between sixty and eighty, and I have made every one bite me on the soft part of the arm, without any bad effects. The bite is simply painful from the strength of the nippers, but I never could find the trace of any secretion, either on the bitten part or on the nippers, when examined through a Stanhope lens. My friend Captain Mitchell, superintendent of the Madras Museum, having told me of two cases of the bite of this spider slightly poisoning the parties bitten, and one of the gentlemen being a personal friend, I made him give me full particulars. He was at tea in the morning (by candle-light, I think), and felt a bite on his leg. He struck the place with his open hand, and undressing found the remains of the spider which he had "squashed." He described the pain, such as he had no doubt was caused by poison, and not from mere nipping. He left his tea and rode away, not getting rid of the pain for two or three hours. You will doubtless remark peculiar paddle-shaped white appendages, twelve of which are on the last pair of legs next the body. I can form no idea of their probable use. The gold-backed beetles will, I have no doubt, reach you in full beauty. They were found on the leaves of a very common creeper, called in Hindustani bysibalka puttah; in Tamil, oonang yela, and in Telegoo, meendray bukoo. I regret to say I do not know the botanical name. However, I have sent you two leaves of the plant for identification. I have had these beetles for some time in a breeding-cage. A few died. When put in spirits immediately after death they do not change colour; but if dried the golden colour becomes black. Whilst alive they vary in colour from a light bronze to the palest gold. I know very little about beetles, and have not had time since I got the "gold-backs" to examine them minutely with a lens: but, from their very peculiar ladybird-like flight, which is, I suppose, familiar to most, I am inclined to think they belong to that group of beetles. All I have sent you were put into spirit alive.—SMOOTHBORE (Madras, May 10, 1867). [The spiders forwarded belong to a genus now known as Solfuga, but which was formerly described under the name of Galeodes. The particular species forwarded was carefully described by Capt. Thos. Hutton, in the "Journal of the Royal Asiatic Society," under the name of Galeodes vorax. The captain stated that when he spread out on the ground a large white sheet with a lantern in the centre to attract insects, he observed several of these enormous spiders appear and take their stations at a distance from each other, and that the moment an insect, attracted by the light, settled on the sheet, it was snapped up by them and spirited away before he could effect its capture. He described them as having a most voracious appetite, and as often fighting with, and even devouring, one another. In their habits they are nocturnal, being concealed during the day in crevices under stones. They make no web, but secure their prey by darting on it with great rapidity. Capt. Hutton captured one alive, which he placed in a bottle with some earth. In this the spider excavated a cave, in which she deposited fifty ova as large as mustard seeds. These hatched into young that were most tenderly cared for by the parent, who guarded the hole. This animal killed and devoured a lizard whose extreme length was five inches, seizing it behind the shoulder and with her two pairs of jaws rapidly eating her way into its vitals; after eating this meal the spider was lethargic for a fortnight. The same spider seized a young sparrow by the thigh and sawed the limb off, afterwards cutting off the head. The existence of the triangular processes on the hinder legs were noticed by the captain; their use is not known. One singular circumstance was also noticed, that if in the pursuit of their food two came into contact, the one taken at a disadvantage is killed by the other almost without resistance; but that if two approach and grapple, a wrestling match takes place before the weaker "caves in" and resigns himself to his fate. In Egypt there is a still larger species, known as the Solfuga araneoides. The beautiful beetles forwarded are specimens of the family Cassidæ, the particular species being Aspidomorpha crucis. In some parts of India the females string them on thread and use them as ornaments. Some time since Mr. F. Smith exhibited a living specimen at the meeting of the Entomological Society in London. The family is widely distributed, different species being found in various parts of Africa, New Holland, Java, and India.—ED.]—*Field*, July 13.

THE LIMPET.

IN "Edible Molluscs of Great Britain" we read the following:—The shell is oval and conical in shape, apex central, or nearly so, strong sometimes with ribs diverging from the apex to the margin, and sometimes quite smooth. Colours various, pale greyish-yellow or greenish-brown, inside generally, showing the same colour through, and the markings of the ribs distinctly towards the margin; the inside of the apex an opaque bluish-white, and the whole slightly polished.

The common limpet is found distributed all round our coasts, where it is greatly valued as bait by fishermen. At low tide, limpets may be collected in great numbers from the rocks and boulders. Some are seen safely ensconced in holes or depressions made by means of the muscular action of their foot or disk, which is the width of the shell; others are seen creeping about in search of fresh resting-places, or food, with their tentacles slightly protruding beyond the shell, till alarmed by some touch or otherwise; and they adhere with wonderful strength to the rocks.

On the Devonshire coast I have found them very large, and worn quite smooth; some specimens measuring as much as eight inches in circumference.

In many places limpets are used for food, especially on the Continent, where they are oftener eaten than the periwinkle. At Naples they make them into soup, and I am told it is an excellent dish. At Eastbourne we have often seen the Irish reapers come down to the shore and eat the limpets raw, which they had knocked off the rocks with their knives. The poorer classes at Eastbourne also eat them constantly, the children collecting them at low tide from the rocks. At Plymouth they gather great numbers of them, especially from the breakwater, as well as in the Isle of Man, where they are known by the name of "flitters;" and in Scotland the juice of these shellfishes is mixed with oatmeal. In the Feroe Isles they call them "flia;" and in "Life in Normandy" we are told "that limpets are constantly eaten by the poor."

The Patellidæ were also among the shellfish eaten by the ancients. It is a curious fact, and one which is puzzling to archæologists, that limpet shells should be found in such abundance in cromlechs, both in the Channel Islands and in Brittany, surrounding the remains of the dead, often covering the bones, skulls, &c., to the depth of 2 ft. and 3 ft. in thickness. They are found not only in the earliest deposits, but also amongst the more recent. Necklaces of limpets and other shells, strung together on fibre or sinews, are found in early British graves. Limpet shells are also used for mortar.

In the island of Herm, near Guernsey, poultry are fed on Patella vulgata; but it is said that they will not touch Patella athletica, which is also considered too tough for bait.

Sea-birds feed on the Patella, and Mr. Gatcombe, in *The Field*, August, 1863, mentions having once taken from the gullet of an oyster-catcher upwards of thirty limpets. He also adds an account of a curious occurrence which took place on the Plymouth breakwater some time ago: One of the workmen employed on the breakwater observed a sand-piper fluttering in a peculiar manner, and discovered on approaching it that it had been made prisoner by a limpet. It would appear that, in running about in search of food, the bird's toe had accidentally got under a limpet, which, suddenly closing to the rock, held it fast until the man came up, who with his knife removed the limpet, and released the bird.

The French call this shell *Lépas Patelle*, *Jambe*, *Œil de Bouc*, and *Bernicle;* the Germans, *Schüsselmuschel: Napfmuschel*, or *Napfschnecke;* the Spaniards, *Diampa;* the Portuguese, *Lopa;* and the Italians, *Lepade;* and in Cornwall, limpet shells are called *Crogans*.

WOODPECKERS.

Mr. Sterland writing from Sherwood to the *Field*, says:—"The woodpeckers are peculiarly inhabitants of the forest, and that handsome species, the green woodpecker (Picus viridis), is very abundant, our old, decaying oaks being a favourite resort, and furnishing them with an ample supply of food. The light, sandy forest soil is greatly frequented by ants, and here you are sure to meet with the green woodpecker. It is a shy species, and its white eye wears a peculiarly wild expression, with its singular cry, heard in the depths of the woods, has something very unearthly and startling about it. It is generally uttered while it is on the wing, making its odd, festooning flight from tree to tree, but not invariably so, as I have heard it both when clinging to a tree and when on the ground. The latter situation is only frequented where there are anthills, when it willingly leaves its strongholds, the trees, to search for its favourite food.

"Their motions on the trees, for which they are so admirably fitted, are well worth watching. I never saw them by any chance perch on the upper side of a bough, but it is fond of clinging to the under side, where during the day insects chiefly congregate. It is on the perpendicular trunk, however, that it is most at home. Commencing at the base it pursues a spiral course to the top, prying into every chink and crevice, tapping here and there with vigorous and rapid strokes to alarm its insect prey.

"I have remarked previously that nearly all the old oaks in the forest have suffered the loss of their tops by the agency of wind and lightning, aided by natural decay. Sometimes you may see the upper portion of one of these venerable trunks quite denuded of its bark, and riven with many fissures, though the tree is all the while in vigorous growth. On some of these I have often noticed the green woodpecker practise a singular feat. Placing its bill in one of the long cracks I have mentioned, it produces, by an exceedingly rapid vibratory motion, a loud crashing noise, as if the tree was violently rent from top to bottom. I have heard it when the sound was so loud and sudden that the woods rang again. For a long time I was at a loss to know how it was produced, but I one day witnessed the process, and have seen it several times since. It would effectually rouse up all the insects, for it seemed as if the tree quivered from top to bottom.

"Montagu mentions the jarring sound made by this species, but imagines it to be the call of both sexes to each other. With this I do not agree, but think from frequent observation that it is solely for the purpose of procuring food.

"The hole in which the eggs are laid is generally with us hewn through the sound outer portion of the trunk, until at a few inches deep the decaying wood is reached, in which the hollow for the eggs is formed, for nest there is none. I have met with one or two holes where the bird had evidently erred in its calculations. One in particular was about fifty feet from the ground, and had been begun in a tree too sound for the purpose; the hole was chiselled out of the solid wood, and must have cost its maker great labour, having been driven forward in a horizontal direction for about nine inches, but the wood continuing sound the bird had apparently become disheartened in her work, and abandoned it. When I first discovered it it had not been long deserted, for I took the trouble to climb up and carefully examine it, measuring the depth with my stick, and ascertaining by the sound that the wood at the bottom was free from decay. I could not help wondering how the bird, in a hole not larger than the diameter of his own body, could find room to give those violent strokes with its bill which would be necessary to penetrate the solid oak."

Do WOODPECKERS EVER MIGRATE?

The following on this subject we extract from *Land and Water* July 13:—"We may observe that the black woodpeckers (*Picus martius*) which have undoubtedly been observed in the British Islands, however rarely and at distant intervals, can hardly have been other than stragglers from the neighbouring continent. Two much more remarkable instances, however, are upon record (in the 'Zoologist' for 1859), of different species of woodpecker which must have traversed the breadth of the Atlantic! The first relates to the common golden-winged woodpecker (*P. auratus*) of the United States, an example of which was obtained in the county of Wiltshire; the second to a specimen of what appears to have been the downy woodpecker (*P. pubescens*), also a common North American species, which was shot in Dorsetshire. As regards the first, Mr. George S. Marsh, of Chippenham, states—'I have in my collection a specimen of the golden-winged woodpecker, killed in Amesbury Park, in the autumn of 1836. My brother, now member for Salisbury, saw this bird in the flesh before it was preserved; it was brought to him just after it was shot. It was preserved by Mr. Edwards, of Amesbury, and has never been out of my possession.'

The other (*P. pubescens*) 'was shot by Mr. E. P. Cambridge, of Broxworth Rectory, Dorset, in December 1836, from his bedroom window, as it crept among some low shrubs in one of the flower-beds of the lawn.' Full particulars are given, and the bird seems (from the description of it) to be the familiarly known Transatlantic species to which it is referred. Of the well-known *Picus varius* of the United States Mr. Gosse remarks, in his 'Birds of Jamaica,' that four or five specimens of this beautiful woodpecker, all females, occurred to us in the months of December, January, and February, but at no other time was it seen. I have no doubt it is a winter migrant from the northern continent, where, however, Wilson states that it abides all the year.' It is hazardous to argue much from analogy. Reasoning thus, we should indubitably conclude that all woodpeckers were necessarilly tree-frequenting birds, and that no popular appellation could be more thoroughly appropriate ; and yet Mr. Darwin tells us, in the 'Zoology of the Voyage of H.M.S. Beagle,' of a true woodpecker (so far as structure is concerned) which only inhabits treeless territory, and has never been seen upon a tree! In like manner, a species of nuthatch (the *Sitta syriaca*) is only observed creeping about rocks—never upon a tree ; whereas the other nuthatches are as exclusively and emphatically tree-frequenting birds. The hoopoe, to all appearance, is a bird of fluttering and feeble flight, which is performed in undulations like that of a woodpecker or tree-creeper, and nobody would suspect that it could be very long protracted or sustained : yet the hoopoe is a well-known migrant ; and the late Bishop of Norwich (Dr. Stanley) has recorded, in his 'Familiar History of Birds,' that a hoopoe approached a vessel in the middle of the Atlantic, and kept company with it a good way, but did not settle on board, as it probably would have done had it been tired.' No person who had only observed our tiny goldcrests flitting about our conifers chiefly, and other evergreens, would suppose that those diminutive birds could reach our islands from Scandinavia in vast multitudes, as testified from personal observation by the late Mr. Selby and other naturalists. Who, again would suspect from its structure that the short-winged corn-crake, or land rail, was a regular migrant ? And yet people formerly imagined that the powerful winged swifts and swallows were wont to hybernate rather than to cross the sea.—ED."

SCORPION OF TEXAS.

The Scorpions of Middle Texas, so far as I have investigated the subject, do not extend beyond a single species. There may be others, but I have not observed them. The species we have is viviparous, carrying its young, eight in number, on its back, until they are three-fourths of an inch in length. When first seen, clinging to the back of the mother scorpion, they are so small that it requires a microscope to examine them satisfactorily. They are white, and look as if they were very tender. They cling tenaciously, and when by violence they are separated from the mother, she shows manifest signs of distress, running about till she comes in contact with the lost ones, when they immediately climb up and cling again closer than before. At this early period, they seem already to be well versed in scorpion tactics, wielding their nimble tail, and its recurved weapon, with dexterity and swiftness.

Scorpions pass the winter in close quarters, and generally in a torpid state. They are seen early in warm weather coming out at nights, and sometimes during warm damp periods in winter. They are altogether nocturnal in their habits, and are carnivorous, subsisting on insects of various kinds, and even small lizards. As a speciality, they prey largely on crickets. They dwell under old logs, rocks, in old stumps, under the bark of dead trees, under old fences, between the shingles on house-tops, and particularly about the jambs and hearths of fire-places. In temper they are hasty, and will employ their weapons on slight occasions. The pain occasioned by their venom, when injected into one's flesh, is very quickly felt, and quite severe, giving the idea of a burning-hot fluid thrown into the system. It does not last long, nor does it swell much, and is not so painful, nor does it produce so much inconvenience as the sting of the honey-bee. In countries where they abound, people do not regard them with much terror. Chickens are very fond of them, and voraciously devour every one they can find.

I once found a mocking-bird (*Mimus polyglottus*) which by some awkward stroke in his rapid flight, had fractured his right wing. It was running on the ground, and had become quite hungry and light. After dressing and securing the little songster's wing, I turned over some old rails in search of something for him to eat. There were plenty of crickets and scorpions concealed under the rails, for the latter of which he showed the greatest preference. He would peck at them, and by bruising and thus stunning them a little, readily swallow them whole. After he had swallowed seven of them, I thought, as I had volunteered my services as surgeon and physician for him, it would not be prudent for me to suffer him to indulge further at this time ; so I placed him in a large cage with some canary birds, where he remained feasting on nine scorpions a day, until he had recovered the use of his wing, when I set him free.

Scorpions are generally found two or three together, sometimes in large numbers. They shed their skins without a rent, coming out at the mouth, like the snakes. They moult when they are about half-grown, and again when they come to maturity, and I do not know that ever they cast their skin again during the remainder of their life. They live through two winters, as I can testify, and may exist many years. They are not possessed of much intelligence, making no nests or preparation for winter, beyond crawling under rocks and other dry and sheltered places, their principal cerebral developments are amativeness, alimentiveness, and cautiousness.—G. Lincecum, M.D., in *The American Naturalist*, June, 1867.

THE KINGFISHER.

None of our native birds can boast of more beautiful plumage than our little kingfisher (*Alcedo ispida*) ; the glossy metallic blues and greens with which it is adorned seem to belong more to the parrots, trogons, and other species peculiar to warm or tropical countries. Indeed, when I watch the rapid flight of a kingfisher, it always reminds me strongly of some of the Australian parrakeets, especially the *Lathamus discolor*, the metallic colours of whose plumage show most brilliantly during their glancing flight, particularly when the sun is shining.

The kingfisher is constantly to be seen, and yet is not an abundant species with us. The two small streams, the Morn, and the Idle, which intersect our forest district, are very favourable to its habits and requirements; but though it delights to seek its food in secluded spots, it does not confine itself to such, and I have repeatedly seen them glancing up and down the stream which runs past the village, and darting through the arches of the bridge as I stood on it. I have even taken its eggs from a hole in the bank of the stream within a stone-throw of some houses, and of my own garden.

The nest of the kingfisher is another of those questions on which naturalists have greatly differed, and I know not that my own observation has enabled me to throw much light on the matter. Whether a layer of fishbones is *purposely* laid for the reception of the eggs, as Montague asserts, I cannot say, but in every nest I have examined I have never found any other material used, nor have I ever seen the eggs on the bare ground. In every instance they rested on a layer of the castings, which were slightly hollowed for them, though the latter form may have been produced by the mere weight of the parent bird while the eggs were laid. I believe that a deserted hole of the water-rat is usually chosen, and that they rarely excavate for themselves.

The young ones, after they have left the nest, are exceedingly clamorous; so much so, that their loud, shrill twitterings were once the cause of my witnessing the interesting scene of a brood being fed by their parents. They were six in number, and were perched on the boughs of a dead bush overhanging the stream. They seemed very voracious; for though both the parent birds were constantly bringing them food--sometimes a small fish, sometimes what appeared to be like a slug or leach—they apparently failed in satisfying their appetites, and every fresh supply was eagerly competed for, sometimes a sort of scuffle taking place as to which was to receive it. During the absence of the parents the young ones sat very quietly; but their distant approach was quickly perceived, and in a moment their listless attitude was changed into one of animation, they stretched themselves eagerly forward, and with loud twitterings and open mouths showed how expectant they were.—W. J. Sterland, in *Field* June, 22nd.

New Books.

[*Our limited space must of necessity compel us to give but very short notices of new books, but they will perhaps serve as a guide as to what books our readers may ask for at their libraries.*]

Wanderings of a Naturalist in India, the Western Himalayas, and Cashmere. By Andrew Leith Adams, M.D., Edinburgh: Edmonstone and Douglas.

Happy the man, who travelling in a foreign country carries with him some knowledge of natural history. He cannot be at a loss. Though a stranger in the land and ignorant of those he dwells amongst, he is in no want of society; to him the book of nature is opened, and every object animate or inanimate becomes a companion by the way. It is to be regretted that there are so few who possess any adequate knowledge of these subjects; it would surely be better that Natural History should receive more attention, and meet with a more genial recognition at our schools. As it is many of our best students of nature are unable to give to the world the result of their observations. Thrown by chance or necessity in a foreign country, perhaps hundreds of miles away from any of their own countrymen, they naturally take an interest in the ever varying phenomena to be met with, but are unable theoretically to account for or describe such. Those pioneers of civilization in the West, the backwoodsmen and squatters must have far more knowledge of the denizens of the forest and the prairie than any educated and learned man could obtain by a short stay or rapid journey; indeed, how much of the information gathered by these latter has been collected from the rough descriptions of the former. We doubt not that many a bee hunter in the oak openings of the West could have told as good a story of the wild bee's life, instincts, and habits as recent writers have given of the domestic species. Or the hunter tracking the grisly to his den, or scampering over the prairie after the bison, gives us far better accounts of such than my Lord or Right Honorable, who takes a short run and returns to write a glowing account of what he did not see. But want of proper education and training has placed it out of the power of our rougher naturalists to give us the results of their observation. In corroboration of this, we may point to the number of army surgeons, doctors, missionaries, &c., who have given us good and truthful descriptions of the aspects of nature abroad. These are men whose particular professions have compelled them to make a study of such subjects, and being placed at some foreign station, they have turned their knowledge to account, and sent such particulars from time to time as have enabled us to form a pretty good idea of the Flora and Fauna of the world at large. Neither are these the only men, though they form the majority to whom we owe the best works. They gather and transmit the facts from various localities and in small portions, which our more polished writers at home carefully collect and compare, thus producing works by which their respective authors become famous.

It is to an army surgeon that we owe the present entertaining and instructive work. Mr. Adams has taken great pains to present us with a fair description of the Zoology, Botany, and Geology of India. He says, during a sojourn in the East of seven years with frequent change of place, he had many opportunities offered him of making acquaintance with various objects of natural history, the local scenery of Northern India, and the Western Himalayan Mountains; and further on he writes, "In the following reminscences I have aimed at preserving the objects in the order they appeared to me, and attempted to describe the scenes and circumstances with which I was brought in contact, as minutely as the incidents of travel would allow, and in a belief that my jottings by the way would add zest to the drier descriptions of animals. We refrain from making any more quotations here, as we have already done so at some length on another page. We strongly recommend our readers to procure the volume, feeling sure that they will join with us in thanking the author for several hours' most pleasant reading.

A Handy Book to the Collection and Preparation of Freshwater and Marine Algæ, Diatoms, Desonids, Fungi, Lichens, Mosses, and other of the lower Cryptogamia, with instructions for the formation of an Herbarium. By Johann Nave. Translated and edited by the Rev. W. W. Spier, M.A. London: Robert Hardwicke.

We heartily welcome this little work, the want of such a guide having long been felt. Our amateur microscopists are now to be counted by thousands, and it is not in the power of every one to obtain the various works upon the subject issued from time to time, and which are as a rule very expensive. We expect that many have floundered about in the slough of despond, solely through having no adviser; therefore to many, a treatise detailing the necessary instruction, and procurable at a low price, will be invaluable. Mr. Nave aptly points this out in his preface: "the lower Cryptogamia, especially such as the Algæ and Fungi, require a somewhat complicated treatment, so much so that many a beginner is frightened from prosecuting his studies; disgusted by the continued failures which, without a guide to lead him, it was next to impossible for him to escape," and, indeed, we do not think the amateur wise to make such an attempt without the assistance of this little work, or he will most probably find a very great portion of his time thrown away; the principal part of the work treats of the Algæ as being the most extraordinary in variety of form and habit, and requiring many descriptions of methods of preparation. The volume is profusely illustrated, and is in fact all that can be desired.

British Grasses; an Introduction to the Study of the Gramineæ of Great Britain and Ireland. By Margaret Plues. London: Reeve & Co. Crown 8vo. Pp. 307.

This is a very nice little volume, containing sixteen coloured plates drawn from the designs of Mr. Fitch, as well as numerous woodcuts. It comprises descriptions of all the British Grasses, Agricultural, Economic, and Ornamental, and will be found a popular and useful handbook to all who are interested in the subject.

FRENCH AND AMERICAN WORKS.

Mind in Nature: or the Origin of Life, and the Mode of Development of Animals. By Henry James Clark, A.B., B.S., Adjunct Professor of Zoology in Harvard University, Cambridge, Mass.; Member of the American Academy of Arts and Sciences, Boston, Mass., of the Boston Society of Natural History, Corresponding Member of the American Microscopical Society of New York. &c., &c. With over 200 Illustrations. New York: D. Appleton & Co. London: Trübner & Co. 1865.

We have here an elaborate treatise on the organization of animal life. The work is devoted principally to microscopic researches, in which the writer has occupied many years, and from which he appears to have derived some important conclusions. It contains also an account of certain experiments on "spontaneous generation." The object is to prove the existence of a Creative Mind perpetually at work from the plan of the animal creation. The drift of the argument is somewhat obscure, but the value of the physiological inquiries which form the substance of the work is not thereby affected.

Annual of Scientific Discovery; or, Year-book of Facts in Science and Art for 1866 and 1867, exhibiting the most important Discoveries and Improvements in Mechanics, Useful Arts, Natural Philosophy, Chemistry, Astronomy, Geology, Zoology, Botany, Mineralogy, Meteorology, Geography, Antiquities, &c., together with Notes on the Progress of Science during the Years 1865 and 1866; a List of Recent Scientific Publications, Obituaries of Scientific Men, &c. Edited by Samuel Kneeland, A.M., M.D., etc. Boston: Gould & Lincoln. London: Trübner & Co. 1867.

This is a yearly account of all that has been done to forward the progress of science during the year; of mechanical inventions and improvements, of the achievements and discoveries in all the different branches of natural science, of the books published on these and kindred subjects, and memoirs of eminent scientific men who have died during the last twelve months. The volume is small, and the amount of information concentrated in it is wonderful, making it extremely valuable to all lovers of science.

Rapporte sur les Progrès de la Mineralogie. Par G. Delafosse. Paris and London: Hachette & Co.

This is one of a series of reports suggested by the Paris Exhibition, detailing the progress made by France in the various departments of Science, Literature, and Art. In it M. Delafosse, a Member of the Académie des Sciences, discusses the subject of mineralogy, taking it up at the point where the celebrated Abbé Hauy had left it. The learned gentleman gives an account of the principal discoveries, and reviews the leading publications referring to that particular science, and the result shows that for the last twenty years the advance made by French mineralogists and crystallographers has been unprecedented.

New Book of Flowers. By Joseph Breck. Newly Electrotyped and Illustrated. New York: Orange Judd & Co. London: Sampson Low, Son, & Marston.

An interesting Book of Flowers, intended for amateur gardeners, who will find it useful to refer to its pages.

Meetings of Learned Societies.

ZOOLOGICAL SOCIETY.

At a meeting held, Dr. E. Hamilton in the chair, Mr. P. L. Sclater exhibited a specimen, in spirits, of a rare snake, *Siphlopis fitzingeri*, from the coast of Peru. Lord Lilford exhibited a fine nest, with four eggs, of the nutcracker, taken in the Hochanger Alps. Mr. A. D. Bartlett read a paper on the habits and affinities of the lyre-bird. Mr. E. Blyth made some remarks on the deer found in the Indo-Chinese region. Dr. Edwards Crisp read a paper on the comparative form, size, and structure of the viscera of the hippotamus as compared with the same parts in the members of the pachyderm family, and in other animals, and exhibited preparations and casts of the various parts. Mr. St. George Mivart contributed two papers, one on the *Plethodon persimilis* of Gray, and the other on the myology of *Iguana tuberculata*. Dr. H. Burmeister communicated a paper describing a new species of Finner whale (*Balænoptera bonaerensis*) found in the River Plata, near Belgrano, about ten miles from Buenos Ayres. Messrs. P. L. Sclater and O. Salvin read a paper on the birds collected by Mr. E. Bartlett on the river Huallaga, Eastern Peru, with notes and descriptions of the new species. A paper, by Surgeon Francis Day, of the Madras army, was read on some new or imperfectly known fishes obtained from the sea and fresh waters in the neighbourhood of Madras. Dr. J. E. Gray read some notes on the specimens of *Calyptraidæ* in the Cumingian collection. Mr. A. G. Butler communicated some remarks upon the Fabrician species of the *Satyridæ*, genus *Mycalesis*, with descriptions and notes on the named varieties. Dr. J. C. Cox, secretary of the Entomological Society of New South Wales, sent a paper giving descriptions of some new species of Australian land shells. Mr. J. Yate Johnson, C.M.Z.S., gave a description of a new genus of *Spinacidæ*, founded upon a shark obtained at Madeira. Captain R. C. Beavan, C.M.Z.S., read some notes on the Panolia deer (*Cervus eldi*). Professor Lilljeborg, of the University of Upsala, communicated the description of *Halcrosia afrelii*, a new crocodile from Sierra Leone. Dr. J. Murie read a paper describing the anatomy of the pilot whale.

ETHNOLOGICAL SOCIETY.

At a meeting held on June 25th, J. Crawfurd, Esq., president, in the chair, the Lord Colonsay and Sir Basil Maxwell were elected fellows. "Notes on the Tenure and Distribution of Landed Property in Burmah," by Sir A. Phayre. Whatever may originally have been the relative rights of kings and people to the soil in other countries, in Burmah the ancient book of the Dhama-that, or Laws of Menu, represents the people as conferring a share of the produce on their elected king; the right of the King of Burmah, therefore, to a portion of the produce of the land rests on a very different foundation from that of the ancient kings of Egypt. In the former case it is distinctly laid down as springing from the free gifts of the people. In the latter the right was reserved to himself by the King, when he settled cultivators on the land as mere tenants.—"On the Ethnography of the French Exhibition as represented by National Arts," by Mrs. Lynn Linton. This was a most charming paper, as important as interesting to the hearers, from the rich language in which her descriptions of the various products of divers nations were noticed. The history of the development of human ingenuity was capable of being traced from the most primitive efforts at bead stringing to bark ornaments and skin garments, up to the latest invention in telegraphy, steam appliances, and to architecture was reviewed, and the various people who illustrate by their presence in the Exhibition the human race at present existing. The paper was received with loud applause. —"On the Antiquity of Man," by the President. The lowest conceivable primitive state of man was taken as the basis of an argument for the gradual development of civilisation. The main views culminate in the following paragraph:—It may seem to derogate from the value of the evidences now adduced in favour of man's antiquity, that the veritable records which he has left of his own existence are comparatively recent. He had to pass through all the stages enumerated. The dumb and naked savage had to frame a language, to acquire the arts requisite to furnish himself with a permanent supply of food and clothing, to discover the useful metals, to invent the art of writing, to acquire such a knowledge of the heavenly bodies as would enable him to construct a Kalendar, and, in short, to attain that maturity of intellect by which he would be able to make a trustworthy and transmissible record of his own actions. Tracing back to their earliest dates the architectural works of the Egyptians, Chinese, Assyrians, Hindus, and other admittedly ancient peoples, the full date of their monumental histories was shown to be a comparatively recent era, beyond which it was necessary to look back into a much longer vista of previous time, during which those races had progressed from brute barbarism to that degree of civilisation which the earliest of their respective monuments proved each of them had at that epoch actually attained.

GEOGRAPHICAL SOCIETY.

On June 24th, Sir R. I. Murchison in the chair, the list of newly-elected fellows contained the follow-names:—Messrs. C. J. Bayley, F. A. Goodenough, R. Plant, General Sir Moyle Sherer, and the Hon. R. G. Talbot.—The Rev. W. V. Lloyd, R.N., read a paper on the harbours on the East Coast of Manchouria, now being colonised by Russian settlers. He described the rivers as containing great numbers of salmon, bears are very abundant, and tigers are numerous, judging from the skins he saw and the continual depredations they committed. The people were civil, the Russians in charge of the settlement most considerate and courteous to strangers. He heard selections from the operas well played on pianos in private families, and the only drawback to their happiness was a want of white sugar.—Sir Arthur Cotton "On Joining the Rivers Burhampooter, in Assam, with the Yangtse-Kiang in China, by a short route of 200 miles of unexplored country, by which means Calcutta and the cities of China would enjoy the benefit of water-carriage for heavy goods, and Europe would vastly benefit by the more ready introduction of her commerce." This scheme has frequently occupied the minds of all acquainted with enterprise in these countries, and the difficulties which formerly stood in the way of such intercourse being now removed, no time should be lost in opening up this simple route. Sir Roderick said it was a similar idea which induced Peter the Great to join the great Russian rivers, and by their means traffic in that country is carried on most satisfactorily. But in Assam the hill country was almost inaccessible. The snows and ice of winter, the deep gorges in the hills, the basket haunt over rapid torrents, the inhospitable people said to inhabit the locality mentioned by Sir Arthur would, he feared, prevent the project being accomplished. General Balfour said until these high mountains were actually surveyed, until we really knew if the country was what was represented—and he had no idea it was so difficult—he hoped the project would not be given up. Central China would send her articles of trade by this route, emigrants would go down to the tea-gardens of Assam, where there was plenty of work for thousands of her population, and the goods from England could at once pass up from Calcutta to the Eastern Coast of China without interruption. Dr. M'Cosh, who wrote on this subject thirty years ago, pointed out a route by Dacca; General Sir A. Phayre supported this view, and still held that the hills proposed by Sir A. Cotton should be explored. Mr. Crawfurd did not approve of the plan, on the score of the province of China next Assam being poor and only capable of growing rhubarb, of which "a very little went a very long way;" the leeches, too, to say nothing of the savage tribes of the Mishmee Hills, he thought would never permit the transit contemplated; however, he should like, in the interests of geography, that the unknown should be made known, and was convinced that water was the best aid to commerce, but that water way round the Cape of Good Hope. Sir Arthur, in reply to the many speakers, said he was still convinced that the route he contemplated was well worth a trial, and the cost would be insignificant, while the gain would be incalculable.

GEOLOGICAL SOCIETY.

At the meeting held on June 19th, W. W. Smyth, Esq., president, in the chair, Mr. W. T. Lewis was elected a fellow. The following communications were read:—"On Cyclocyathus, a New Genus of the Cyathophyllidea, with remarks on the Genus Aulophyllum," by Mr. P. M. Duncan.—"On the Discovery of a New Pulmonate Mollusk (*Conulus priscus*, P. P. Carpenter) in the Coal Formation of Nova Scotia," by Dr. J. W. Dawson.—"On some Tracks of Pteraspis (?) in the Upper Ludlow Sandstone," by Mr. J. W. Salter.—"On a New Lingulella from the Red Lower Cambrian Rocks of St. David's," by Mr. J. W. Salter and Dr. H. Hicks.—"Observations on certain Points in the Dentition of Fossil Bears, which appear to afford good Diagnostic Characters, and on the Relation of *Ursus priscus*, Goldf., to *U. ferox*," by Mr. G. Busk.—"On the Geology of the Province of Canterbury, New Zealand," by Dr. J. Haast.—"On the Chemical Geology of the Malvern Hills," by the Rev. J. H. Timins.—"On the Relative Distribution of Fossils throughout the North Devon Series," by Mr. T. M. Hall.—"On the Geology of the Princess Islands in the Sea of Marmora," by Mr. W. R. Swan. —"On the Sulphur Springs of Northern Formosa," by Mr. C. Collingwood.—"On the Geology of Benghazi, Barbary, with an Account of the Subsidences in its Vicinity," by Mr. G. B. Stacey.—"Report on the Existence of Large Coalfields in the Province of St. Catherine's, Brazil," by Mr. E. Thornton. —"On the Sources of the Materials composing the White Clays of the Lower Tertiaries," by Mr. G. Maw.—"On the Post-Glacial Structure of the South-East of England," by Mr. S. V. Wood.

ENTOMOLOGICAL SOCIETY.

On July 1, Sir John Lubbock, Bart., president, in the chair, Dr. G. W. Davidson was a elected a member. Mr. Busk mentioned, on the authority of Dr. Cobbold, that the small worm exhibited at the previous meeting was not, as then supposed, *Gordius aquaticus*, but *Mermis nigrescens*. Mr. M'Lachlan exhibited *Ciniflo ferox*, from Folkestone, where that spider had been captured by Dr. Knaggs; and a large spider and a centipede, found in the hold of a ship which had recently brought a mixed cargo, chiefly sugar and hemp, from Manilla. The Secretary exhibited branches of an orange-tree, from the Botanic Gardens, Sydney, New South Wales, infested by two species of Coccus. Mr. Stainton exhibited upwards of thirty species of Micro-lepidoptera, reared from larvæ which he had collected at Cannes and Mentone in February and March. Amongst them were *Depressaria rutana*, *Phibalocera quercana*, bred from Arbutus, two species of Gelechia, which fed on *Silene Nicæensis*, a new Zelleria, bred from the flowers of *Phillyrea angustifolia*, and a Nepticula, bred from the cork-tree. The Hon.

T. De Grey exhibited *Eupœcilia anthemidana* and *rupicola*, from Norfolk; and mentioned the capture in Kent of five specimens of *Hypercallia Christierninana*. The following papers were read:—"A Catalogue of the Cetoniidæ of the Malayan Archipelago, with Descriptions of the New Species," by Mr. A. R. Wallace. 181 species were enumerated, and of these no less than 70 were described as new.—"Observations on Dzierzon's Theory of Reproduction in the Honey-Bee," by Mr. J. Lowe. With a view to test the truth of the theory that "all eggs which come to maturity in the two ovaries of a queen-bee are only of one and the same type, which, when they are laid without coming in contact with the male semen, become developed into male bees, but, on the contrary, when they are fertilised by male semen, produce female bees," from which theory, if true, we might, in the words of Van Siebold, "expect beforehand that by the copulation of a unicolorous blackish-brown German and a reddish-brown Italian bee, the mixture of the two races would only be expressed in the hybrid females or workers, but not in the drones, which, as proceeding from unfecundated eggs, must remain purely German or purely Italian, according as the queen selected for the production of hybrids belonged to the German or Italian race," the writer set to work to obtain hybrids between *Apis mellifica* and *Apis Ligustica*, and also between *Apis mellifica* and *Apis fasciata*, and the result of his experiments was that Ligurian queen-bees fertilised by English drones, and Egyptian queen-bees fertilised by English drones, both produced drones which, as well as the workers, were hybrid in their characters, and bore unmistakable evidence of the influence of the male parent. From this the author drew the conclusion that the eggs of a queen-bee which has been fertilised by a drone of another race, whether they develope into drones or workers, are in some way affected by the act of fecundation, and that both sexes of the progeny partake of the paternal and maternal character or race; from which it followed that Dzierzon's was not the true theory of reproduction in the honey-bee. Specimens of the hybrids were exhibited to the meeting; and Mr. F. Smith (who did not consider *Apis Ligustica* to be specifically distinct from *Apis mellifica*), after an examination of the specimens, corroborated Mr. Lowe's statement that the hybrid drones distinctly showed characters peculiar to *Apis mellifica* in combination with the characters which distinguish *A. Ligustica* and *A. fasciata* respectively.

BOTANIC SOCIETY OF EDINBURGH.

The meeting of this society was held on July 3, W. Gorrie, Esq., V.P., in the chair. The following communications were read:—I. "On the Arctic Cladoniæ." By W. Lauder Lindsay, M.D. In this paper the author commenced by defining the term arctic, applying it only to those parts in Europe, Asia, and America which are situated within or northward of the arctic circle. These regions include vast level, generally treeless, barren tracts of country, whose vegetation is frequently exclusively lichenose, sometimes, indeed, consisting of a single species, the cosmopolite Cladonia rangiferina, or Reindeer Moss. The author enumerated the different species and their forms belonging to the Cladoniæ found in arctic countries, and remarked that, whether these may be regarded as consisting of many or few species, their importance to man cannot be estimated by their mere numerical relations; one species at least (C. rangiferina) is not only superior in economical and even political importance to the better known "orchella weed," but it is in this respect quite on a footing with the valuable grains, timber trees, and other phanerogams of more favoured regions. The author then, in conclusion, considered the economical value and application of the arctic Cladoniæ under the following heads:—1, as fodder or forage to animals, domesticated or wild—*e.g.*, the reindeer and caribou of the European, Asiatic, and American continent, cattle and pigs, &c.; 2, as an ingredient of man's food; 3, as medicines or ingredients thereof, in virtue of their starchy or bitter principles—*e.g.*, tonics, astringents, febrifuges, emetics; 4, in the arts—*e.g.*, perfumery and dyeing.—II. "Recent Regulations regarding the Forest Department of India." By Prof. Balfour.—III. "Recent Botanical Intelligence." By the same gentleman.—IV. "Sexual Organs of Fungi." Dr. Balfour referred to a paper which had been recently published by Dr. Antoine de Bary, in which the author had clearly demonstrated that in the lower class of Fungi the sexual organs greatly resemble those of other Cryptogams. In the former plants the fertilisation takes place by means of the contents of two different cells coming in contact—the one called Antheridia, and the other Oogonia, representing the antheridial and archegonial cells in Ferns, Mosses, &c. Dr. Balfour exhibited and explained coloured drawings illustrating the subject.—V. "On a Supposed New Species of Vellosia, or probably a New Genus in the Order Hæmodoraceæ. By Prof. Balfour. Dr. Balfour stated that he had received from H. Fox Talbot, Esq., Lacock Abbey, Chippenham, the flowers of a plant which he had transmitted to the Royal Botanic Garden last year. It is a native of Natal, and appears to belong to the nat. ord. Hæmodoraceæ. It has not yet flowered in the Botanic Garden, but the following are some of the characters taken from the plant and from the flowers sent by Mr. Talbot:—Stems shortened, triangular, covered with brown scales at the lower part. Leaves with equitant vernation, alternate, distichous, sheathing at the base, lanceolate, about 6 inches long, margins with sharp serratures, apex sometimes split. Flowers solitary, on slender peduncles about 6 inches long; perianth six-leaved, at first delicate lilac, afterwards becoming greenish-white, dry, and persistent, the green colour appearing particularly in the veins, which become prominent; outer leaves of perianth ovate-oblong, and somewhat acuminated; inner leaves bluntish. Stamens six, with very short filaments; anthers, two-celled, narrow, about five times longer than the filaments, opening longitudinally and laterally. Pistil about the length of the stamens. Ovary inferior (one or three-celled), style thick, stigma large, somewhat tongue-shaped, grooved. Ovules, oblong, numerous, attached to a central placenta, anatropal. Vellozias are chiefly natives of Brazil. This plant seems to represent the genus in Africa, and possesses interest on that account. Dr. Balfour proposed to call it Vellozia Talboti. It may turn out to be a new genus; if so, the name Talbotia will be given to it; but the determination of this point must be delayed until the plant flowers at the Botanic Garden.——6. *On the Discovery of Orthotrichum phyllanthum near Edinburgh.* By Mr. John Sadler.

QUEKETT MICROSCOPICAL CLUB.

A monthly meeting was held at University College on the 28th of June, Mr. Ernest Hart, President, in the chair. A paper was read by Dr. Robert Braithwaite on "The Organization of Mosses," which he prefaced with some remarks on the writers on Bryology. He afterwards described the distinctive characters of the spores, stems, leaves, reproductive organs, development of the fruit, sporangia, &c., as well as the habitats of Mosses, mode of collecting, examination, preservation, and uses. At a conversazione which followed, the members had an opportunity of viewing under the microscopes carefully prepared specimens of the spores, prothallia, antheridia of male flowers, leaves showing the chief forms of cell structure, and capsules showing the modifications of the peristome, &c. Four members were elected.

Correspondence.

[*Under this head we shall be glad to insert any letters of general interest.*]

GLACIAL ACTION.

SIR,—An extract from "The Open Polar Sea" occurs at page 66 of the NATURALIST'S NOTE BOOK in which the author states that the exact principle of movement of the ice in glaciers has not yet been determined, and seems to incline to the *plastic* or *viscous* theory of Professor Forbes. Is not that theory now almost universally admitted to be erroneous and inadequate to explain all the phenomena of glacial action? Glaciers do not stretch and accommodate themselves to the irregularities of their bed, as they would do were they formed of a plastic material, but crack and give way under the slightest tension.

Now it has been demonstrated by Professor Tyndall, in a series of beautiful experiments, that ice, after being reduced to powder, can be again consolidated by pressure. This results from the fact that two pieces of ice in a melting state will, if brought into contact, immediately freeze together. Pressure being applied to the pounded ice, by means of a mould filled with a piston as in the Professor's experiments, the particles are brought into close contact, and a solid mass of ice is the result.

The principle of movement in a glacier then is this,—the ice being pressed upon by the superincumbent mass is broken up gradually; the particles roll over each other, as it were, in the direction of the greatest pressure, and are by the same pressure consolidated into a mass. Thus a constant process of pounding and *regelation* (as it is called) goes on along the whole course of the glacier, by which it is continually kept in motion. De la Rive, in his inaugural address for 1865, as President of the Swiss Society of Natural Sciences, thus applies the principle of regelation to glacier action. "Supposing, for example, a graduated series of moulds to exist, each of which differs very little from the one which precedes and that which follows it, and that a mass of ice could be made to pass through all these moulds in succession, the phenomenon would then become continuous. Ice is only plastic under *pressure*, it is not plastic under *tension*, and this is the important point which the vague theory of plasticity was unable to explain."

Hoping I have not trespassed too much on your valuable space,

I remain, Sir,
Yours truly,
GULIELMUS.

Faversham, Kent,
July 10, 1867.

MIGRATION OF INSECTS.

SIR,—It is given as an opinion on page 164 of the *Naturalist's Note Book* that insects migrate, and that the migration of birds of passage is simply their *following* the insects on which they feed.

Now I think it seems improbable that creatures of such poor powers of flight, as most insects have, should undertake so formidable a journey as two or three thousand miles; and supposing they did, the time spent upon the journey would be so great, as to lead to the conclusion that their lives were spent in travelling alone, especially as insects are very short-lived. Is it not more probable that birds of passage themselves are influenced by the changes of the seasons; that they are induced to leave this country by the coldness of the weather, and to return by their affection for the place in which they were born?

Then, again, it is well known that immense quantities of insects survive the winter in holes and crevices, in hedges and ditches, under leaves and mounds of earth, in fact in any place capable of affording them protection from the severity of the weather, where they remain in a torpid state till spring. It is supposed also that large numbers die off every year at the approach of the cold season.

These facts, considering the enormous supplies consumed during the summer might, easily account for the disappearance of insects towards winter, without supposing them to migrate.

If any one of your readers will give me any information on this interesting subject he will greatly oblige

Yours truly,
R. W. B.

Short Notes.

THE GOOD OLD TIMES.—About the year 1809 I was introduced to a residence amidst the beech timber and underwood and commons which abounded on the Chiltern Hills of Buckinghamshire. At this time very many animals and reptiles were denounced as common enemies, and, as such, a price was set upon their heads, decided upon by the vestry and paid by the churchwardens, as shown by the following items as charged in the churchwardens' accounts of the period:—"A viper, a slow or blind worm, 6d. each." These were supposed to sting the sheep while at feed. The tongue of the former was supposed to be its sting, and the latter effected its injury by some other process; and many ailments amongst the domestic farm animals were attributed to the above causes. The general specific was an ointment made by frying the body of either viper, or slow-worm, in lard; and many a good housewife would pay the stipulated reward, thus to become a kind of Lady Bountiful, by a gift she bestowed of the grand specific to anyone requiring it in the neighbourhood. Sixpence was also the price set on the poor hedgehog. He was charged with sucking the milch cows as they lay down during the night, thus producing a disease called "the gargut,"—being no other than an inflammation of the udder, generally then, as now, produced by cold. The grand specific for this was an ointment of hedgehog fat. Another charge was for the destruction of sparrows. In the spring of the year, the price, regulated by the annual March vestry, was, for sparrows' eggs, a halfpenny a dozen, young sparrows a farthing each, hen sparrows, a penny each, cock birds, a halfpenny each. Thus, without taking into consideration the good arising from the destruction by them of innumerable insects, pests of garden and field, they were denounced for injury done to wheat just on the edge of harvest. I am not aware of any kind of parochial reward for foxes, as the slayer of a fox considered himself amply rewarded by carrying it to all the farmers in rotation, a shilling being the expected reward; but a good poultry wife would often make an addition of a bit of victuals and a pint of beer. After having done duty in the neighbourhood of its death, it would be sold by its cunning possessor to some mate in another district, who would pass it off as fresh killed till decomposition would render it past endurance, and the trick was "smelt out." Things are now changed: vipers, whose bite is venomous, and who would rather glide away than attack, are almost extinct. The slow or blind worm neither bites or stings; and the hedgehog, whose small mouth renders it incapable of sucking the mammal of a cow, and whose prickles would soon render its company disagreeable even to a sleeping cow, is now petted by the London bakers for the purpose of devouring the beetles which infest their bakehouses; and is equally useful for the same purpose against those that infest the gardens.—G. in the *Quarterly Magazine of High Wycombe Natural History Society*.

EARTH EATERS.—Many of the miners are natives of the neighbouring republic of Honduras. They are better workmen than the Nicaraguans, but enjoy the reputation of being greater thieves. Amongst them are some who practice the revolting habit of earth-eating. These earth-eaters do not constitute a separate tribe, but are principally negroes and half-castes, seldom Indians, never pure whites. They are easily recognised by their peculiarly livid and sickly colour. Their nickname, "toros" (bulls), must have been given them not on account of their bodily strength, for they are poor, emaciated people, but more probably because they lick the ground as bulls are sometimes wont to do. The earth which they eat is a kind of clay found in the mines. I shall have it properly analyzed when I get home, and it may then be compared with the edible earth of Syria, to which Ehrenberg's researches apply, and with that mentioned some time back by the *Pharmaceutical Journal*. It is called "jabonada," because when moist it has a certain soapiness and causes some foam when brought into contact with the saliva. It is cream-coloured, often tinged with pink, and has a slightly fatty taste. When well selected there is no sand in the pieces, the whole substance dissolving on the tongue; but as tit-bits of this kind are not always obtainable, a slight admixture of sand is not objected to. Earth-eating is a vice which, like any other vice, grows upon people, and when carrried to excess kills its victims without mercy. The same arguments which are applied to the suppression of drunkenness are applied, generally with as little success, to earth-eating. One of the miners in the Javali gave me a full account of the way he used to go on. He was about twelve years old when he took to the habit, and carried it on till he was twenty-five. Commencing little by little, he ultimately ate several pounds a day, and he lived successive days upon nothing but earth, always drinking a good quantity of water and feeling little or no appetite for any other kind of food. At most times he used to eat the earth as it came from the mine, but sometimes he would vary the flavour by an admixture of common brown sugar, or by toasting the clay over the fire. At last he carried earth-eating to such an excess that he became seriously ill, and had to give it up to save his life. More than two years had elapsed since that time, but he retained nevertheless the livid look peculiar to earth-eaters, and thought that he should never regain his natural colour. It is very difficult to say what proportion of the mining population of Chontales are addicted to earth-eating. As the majority regard it as a vice, many practise the habit on the sly; but from my own observation, I should say they amount to about ten per cent.—*Athenæum*, June 22.

WOODLARKS.—Although I cannot pretend to give a naturalist's opinion on the manners and customs of woodlarks, perhaps your correspondent, Mr. Dutton, will allow some weight to the experience of an amateur of some years' standing, who has always considered the woodlark the first of our native songsters, whether in confinement or in its natural haunts. I have seen many taken in nets and horsehair nooses, but I never saw more than ten or twelve in the same flock, and where as many as four dozen were captured at once I should say that some necessity had driven four or five flocks to unite at one point. They are not to be seen in the northern parts of France, except in very severe weather, and they are then taken in the hair meshes that Frenchmen understand laying out so well during the snow. No distinction is made between them and the skylark, unless it is that they sell at one penny apiece, or a halfpenny less than the others, on account of their smaller size, and this at a time when they bring the London bird-dealer from half-a-crown to five shillings apiece. I find that the food our neighbours give the skylarks, blackcaps, and other soft billed birds is better for them than the very doubtful mixture called "German pase." It consists of crushed hempseed, crumbled bread, chopped meat (raw or cooked), and chopped raw cabbage leaf. I am much inclined to think that the habit of omitting a turf in the woodlark's cage is the cause of the brittle nature of their legs after having been some months in confinement. There certainly must be some mistake in the way of keeping them, as few birds seem to survive the year in confinement. They appear to be very fond of chalk, and many persons give them a good supply crumbled in the bottom of their cage. I am not prepared to say it is necessary or healthful, although I can state that they and all larks will eat great quantities if allowed. I seldom see mention made of the crested lark (Alauda cristata), and as it is common throughout the year on the hills of the French coast exactly opposite to our own, I wish any resident on our side would state if they are ever met with. They have no regular song, but a fine clear call of half a dozen notes, frequently repeated. Our naturalists are generally silent on the distinguishing marks of male and female larks, and, notwithstanding some experience, I am compelled to follow their example, except in the case of the skylark, whose spur always overlaps the elbow in the male, if bent backwards. LULO. P.S. I have just found a nest of the crested lark, containing four eggs, near Boulogne. As this nest is not described in the last edition of "Montagu," I can state that it is on the ground in an exposed situation behind a tuft of grass, and composed of fine fibres of the same material. The egg is about the size of the skylark's, but more rotund, of a pale brown, blotched with a darker shade of the same colour.

THE FOOD OF HUMMING-BIRDS.—The following interesting account of the food of humming-birds appeared a short time since in *Wilkes' Spirit*, a New York paper:—"In June I happened to be visiting at a house in Pleasant Valley, Erie county, Pa. One fine morning I was sitting in the doorway, looking out upon a neat flower-garden, when I noticed a number of beautiful humming-birds, flitting from flower to flower busy at their breakfast. Calling my host's attention to them, I remarked that I had seen the question of their food made a disputed point somewhere in print. It was denied that they took honey from the flowers, and asserted that they found in them minute insects, on which they fed. My friend, though a close observer, was not certain on the point, and it was proposed to satisfy ourselves, if possible, by offering them honey. He stated that he had caught humming-birds often, and thought he could do so again. It may be well to observe that the morning was still, and that a heavy dew lay upon the ground. Some honey was taken upon a case-knife, and we walked out upon the boarded paths between the flower-beds. Very soon one of the little fellows, a perfect beauty, one of those with the many-coloured, changeable throat, which sparkles so like a jewel, perched himself upon a board's edge, seeming much fatigued. My friend observed that he was wet and heavy with the dew, and could not fly so long at a time as usual. We neared him once or twice, when he flew away, but at last he suffered us to get near enough to thurst the honey into his face. His bill touched it, but he was apparently perfectly ignorant of the nature of the substance. Again and again did we press our kind attentions; his little eye was seemingly 'on the cost of Greenland,' and a very speculative eye it was too, clear and knowing. His black and shining bill was shaped like a cobbler's pegging-awl. We were about to acknowledge that a humming-bird did not know or care anything about honey, when it occurred to one or the other of us to offer him some on a stick, instead of a knife. We had scarcely done so when his eye changed its far-off look, and running out from his bill something which looked like an exceedingly fine and narrow piece of white tape, he inserted it into the tempting fluid, and sucked away more like a hungry little pig than anything else we could think of. The tongue was put out from the bill nearly, if not quite, the length of the bill itself. It was a pretty sight. The little fellow worked with a will, and seemed perfectly at home. He satisfied himself, and assuming an air of comfort that would have done credit to an alderman, spent a few seconds in composing his thoughts, then away he went without so much as a thank you. We went into the house perfectly convinced that humming-birds do feed on honey."

ON CLEANING DIATOMS.—There is often considerable difficulty in cleaning the diatoms contained in guano sufficiently to render it possible to mount the frustules without the troublesome process of selection. The methods of Bailey and of Edwards are partially successful, but they injure the frustules a good deal, and leave amorphous matter in the slides. The following plan has been found very successful in several instances, and is worthy of further trial :—Take a beaker of six or eight ounces capacity, put into it not more than two teaspoonfuls of guano, and fill it up within an inch of the top with a saturated solution of carbonate of soda. Boil it for half an hour, wash the sediment well, pour off the last water very close, and pour in two ounces of hydrochloric acid. Boil for an hour, wash well, pour off the last water very close, and treat the sediment with an ounce of strong sulphuric acid; let the acid act for about ten minutes, and then add cautiously some bicarbonate of soda, either in solution or suspension in warm water, and shake well during the effervescence, taking care that the fluid does not overflow the edge of the beaker. Wash well, pour in with great caution two ounces of nitric acid, and when the effervescence has subsided add one or two pinches of chlorate of potash, and boil for an hour, or until the sediment has become white. If this does not take place in an hour, it might be well to commence the process anew; but so far as the method has been tried, it has never failed. Then wash, and use the ordinary methods for separating the diatoms according to their specific gravities; that of Okedon, as described in Pritchard, is the simplest and best. This process may seem to occupy a great deal of time, and to be very troublesome; but such is not the case, for if the beaker be placed in a metal bath containing a strong solution of chloride of lime, or of common salt, and then placed over the lamp or fire, it will not require continuous watching, and the vessel need only be examined once or twice.—T. G. Stokes, Aughnacloy.—*Quarterly Journal of Microscopical Science.*

THE STARFISH.—All are familiar with the appearance of the Starfish, though few, even of old oystermen accustomed to annual losses from this five-fingered pest, are acquainted with the manner in which it is so destructive. Even writers upon the oyster, whose general information upon this subject should have taught them better, have fallen into the same error of supposing that the taper fingers are introduced between the valves, and, in some mysterious manner, kill and devour the contents. The Starfish is provided with an extensible mouth, situated in the middle of the underside, and can only injure an oyster of a certain size relative to its own. If the oyster is small enough, it is swallowed shell and all; the body is digested, and the shell ejected. But if its victim is a little too large for this operation, Nature has provided this scourge with the power to turn its stomach inside out, envelope the unhappy oyster, and absorb the dainty flesh within by means of gastric juice. A. Agassiz, in "Seaside Studies," speaks of this peculiarity as follows: "These animals have a singular mode of eating; they place themselves over whatever they mean to feed upon, as a cockle-shell for instance, the back gradually rising as they arch themselves above it; they then turn the digestive sac, or stomach inside out, so as to enclose their prey completely, and proceed leisurely to suck out the animal from its shell." When nothing more within the shell remains to be eaten, the stomach is turned back again, and, gifted with a constant and insatiable appetite; the Starfish is ready to recommence its filthy feeding upon the first oyster within its reach. The countless suckers on the underside of this animal are used only for locomotion, just as the fly walks upon the ceiling by means of a similar contrivance on the feet. The general belief that the Starfish takes its nourishment in some mysterious way by means of the suckers is consequently an erroneous one, as they have no openings at the ends, and do not connect in any way with the stomach.—F. W. Fellowes, *The American Naturalist.*

MUSK RATS.—Sir Emerson Tennant gives the following curious story of a procession of musk shrews in *Land and Water*, July 6, extracted from a letter just received from the Rev. Dr. Boake, Principal of Queen's College, Colombo.—"A curious circumstance connected with the habits of the musk rat, came under my observation some time ago. When going up my avenue at an early hour in the morning, I noticed something gliding along the road, the appearance of which puzzled me. It was of a light bluish-grey colour, and its motion resembled that of a snake of about two feet long; its uniform thickness from end to end, however, as well as a certain knobby or lumpy appearance, satisfied me that it could not be a snake. On coming close enough to distinguish it clearly, I found that it consisted of five musk-rats, each holding on to the hind-quarters of the one before it. Being very near-sighted, I was unable to distinguish the nature of the attachment, but the muzzle of each appeared to be in immediate contact with the buttocks of the one before it. I immediately struck at the leader with an umbrella, which I had in my hand, and killed it, but its death did not break up the remainder of the line, which held together until I had killed the whole of them, one after another. On examination, in which I was assisted by two very intelligent friends, we found that the leader was a full-grown female rat, the state of whose teats proved that she was giving suck; the others were nearly full-grown young ones. We could not discover how they had held on to each other, as they had come asunder in dying, and we could find no marks to show the nature of the attachment by which they had held together. I have not been able to discover that any one else had ever witnessed a family party of rats travelling in a similar manner, and my narrative, recording an isolated fact, can be of little value unless it can hereafter be found to fall in with, so as to explain or be explained by, other facts that may have come under the notice of some one else."

DISTRIBUTION OF ANIMALS.—In "Cosmos" there is an article on the distribution of animals over the face of the earth, in which the writer says that mammalia have at all times, in this respect, been observed with the greatest attention. Prince Charles Bonaparte states their number to be 1,149; Minding fixes them higher, at 1,230; Oken at 1,500; so that, taking the average of all these numbers, we may suppose them to be about 1,300. These species are very unequally distributed; monkeys, for instance, are only to be found under the tropics, with very few exceptions; and kangaroos only in Australia. On the other hand, pachydermata, of which the horse is one, exist all over the globe, except in the arctic regions: it must not be forgotten, however, that there were no horses in America until they were imported. Australia also forms an exception in this, as in many other respects; for instance in the case of certain plants that still thrive there, while in our regions they have been extinct for thousands of years, and are now only to be met with in a fossil state at a depth of hundreds of metres. There are not more than 38 species of pachydermata, forming ten genera, among which we may mention the elephant, hippopotamus, rhinoceros, and tapir. And yet, of all mammalia, this class is most numerously represented in the series of fossil animals we possess; and while at present, as we have said above, pachydermata have disappeared from the Arctic regions, it is there, buried in ice, we find their extinct species. The gradual disappearance of species offers matter for curious comment. Thus, the hippopotamus was very common in the Nile at the time Herodotus visited Egypt, that is, about 450 years before our era. Fifteen centuries later it had become much rarer, and Abdallatif, an Arab physician, who flourished in the 12th century, speaks of it as an animal regarded with terror by the inhabitants. Two of them were shown to this writer at Cairo, where they were kept as curiosities, which proves its rarity at the time. But now the hippopotamus has entirely left the Nile, where the inhabitants do not even know it by name: and it is only in the Niger, the Zaira, and other rivers of Africa it is to be found in our days.

COBRA ATTACKED BY A HEN.—I noticed in the last *Field* an account of the rescue of the egg of a Guinea fowl from the interior of a cobra, which egg subsequently was developed into life. Whether or not there exists a mortal feud between the domestic hen and the cobra I am unable to say; but in 1865, when at Mount Lavinia, in Ceylon, my Malay boy rescued from the bill of a common hen a young cobra about twelve inches in length. The fowl had grasped the little reptile behind the hood, and would have killed it very speedily had not my boy interfered. Perhaps it was her intention to devour it; or may be a presentiment of a raid on her eggs, when the reptile arrived at full cobra estate, impelled her simply to destroy, and not to partake of, the little "varmint." I bottled the cobra alive in arrack, and have it by me now, and one can see very distinctly the mark of the mandible of the hen in rear of the hood. A more perfect creature in every way I never beheld. The spectacles are beautifully marked, and I well remember with what fire and energy the little creature went through the whole performance of raising itself on its tail, expanding its tiny hood, and darting forward at a quill pen held a few inches from it. Was it that the feud between the fowl and the cobra tribes was so great, that even the most juvenile of the progeny of the latter resented the presence of one feather of the wing of the former? Shortly after I left the station an officer was bitten in the wrist by a pet cobra, 5ft. 6in. long. "Satan" was the name of the brute, and its owner used periodically to remove its fangs with a pair of nail-scissors. He did not do this effectually just before the time I refer to; and in taking it up by the neck his hand slipped, and the reptile was able to turn round and strike him on the wrist. He recovered by the aid of cauterisation, brandy, and ammonia.

SYMPATHY AMONG HORSES.—A gentleman writing from Australia to *Land and Water*, July 6th, says:—On a cattle station, where I live, near Ipswich, Queensland, I had often noticed two old mares (very old), the one had a fine foal by her side, the other had none. For many years these aged mares had run together; in winter they sought the ridges for shelter, in summer the banks of creeks were their resort. A deserted shepherd's hut stood by a creek, and on nearing it my attention was arrested by the state of agony and despair the foal seemed to be in; for now he would galop round the hut, making the whole valley ring with his piteous appeals, and then would timidly approach it, peeping in it at an opening, and then, as if in utter despair, scamper back to the creek. When I came to the hut one of the mares was outside, standing still, and seemed to take little or no notice of me, while the mother of the foal was lying down (quite naturally) inside the building; her posture was that of a tired horse trying to rest every limb at once. Her ears inclining forwards gave her the appearance of being asleep. I felt so sure she was asleep that I touched her with my whip—no move; again, no stir. So, on closer inspection, I saw she was dead—a death so easy and free from pain that she must have ceased to breathe while sleeping soundly. Her old companion remained upon the same spot, the foal increasing his speed and the eagerness of his cries just in proportion to his hunger. Well, to make my story short, I came again to the spot three days afterwards with my stockman; we saw only the foal outside the hut, the old faithful friend had herself gone and laid down close alongside her former companion and, strange to say, was quite dead also. Their two frames lay one near the other in the deserted hut, and the foal has joined a herd of bush horses, and seems to have quite forgotten his kind old mother.

SPARROWS IN AMERICA.—We learn that two hundred English sparrows were last year domesticated in Union Park, in New York city, and that they completely destroyed the Canker-worms infesting the shade trees. Forty pairs have just been imported into Newhaven. The English Sparrow also feeds very largely on grain, and may prove troublesome to farmers. The attention of the Boston Society of Natural History has been called to the thieving propensities of this bird. "At a meeting of this Society, held April 18th, Dr. Chas. Pickering called attention to the recent introduction of the house sparrow of Europe into this country. As it threatens great evil, preventive measures should be speedily adopted. Proofs of its destructive habits were cited from standard authors, showing that the bird had been the acknowledged enemy of mankind for more than five thousand years. When writing was invented the sparrow was selected for the hieroglyphic character signifying *enemy*. "Sonnini, in the Dictionnaire d'Histoire Naturelle, published in 1817, says:— 'Sparrows are impudent parasites, living only in society with man and dividing with him his grain, his fruit, and his home; they attack the first fruit that ripens, the grain as it approaches maturity, and even that which has been stored in granaries. Some writers have wrongly supposed that the insects destroyed by them compensated for their ravages on grain; eighty-two grains of wheat were counted in the craw of a sparrow shot by the writer, and Rougier de la Bergerie, to whom we owe excellent memoirs on rural economy, estimates that the sparrows of France consume annually ten million bushels of wheat.'"—*The American Naturalist*.

COAL FIELDS.—The principal coal-fields of the Continent of Europe are those of Belgium, France, Spain (in the Asturias), Germany (on the Rhine and Saar, a theme of such prominent bearing upon the ecent warlike demonstrations of France and Germany), Bohemia, Silesia, and Russia (on the Donnetz). The Belgian field is that which shows the most alarming symptoms of giving out. Twenty years, according to the Report of Mr. Dunn, H.M. Inspector of Collieries, will suffice for the catastrophe of Liège and Hainault. The coal of France, though practically inexhaustible, is of an inferior description, and the consumption of English coal becomes an increasing element in the question of the exhaustion of our home supplies. The richest deposits of all other countries combined are insignificant by the side of the coal deposits of North America. There are four principal areas—the great central coal-field of the Alleghanies, those of Illinois, and the basin of the Ohio, the basin of the Missouri, and the wide fields of Nova Scotia, New Brunswick, and Cape Breton. The total produce of the States of the Union for the year 1864 was returned officially as 16,472,410 tons—less than a fifth, after all, of the total produced by the United Kingdom, and not nearly as much again as we can afford to spare for the exigencies of our neighbours. The production of coal in India forms a marked feature in the industrial progress of our great Eastern dependency. It has more than trebled itself in three years, and reached in 1860 nearly 400,000 tons.—*Saturday Review*, July 13.

REASONING IN A HARE.—The following circumstance was related by a respectable farmer as happening within his own observation; and in illustration of its truth it may be proper to remark, that in the country where it happened—in Cornwall—the hills, which are steep, rise so abruptly and near to each other, that whatever passes on the side of one may be easily discerned on the other. His attention was first drawn to a hare, which he perceived running down a slope, close to the hedge in a field of turnips, and soon afterwards he perceived that in pursuit of her were a couple of dogs. As these dogs entered the field he saw that the hare stopped for a moment and lifted her ears. The pursuers pressed on, but when they had come within little more than a gunshot of their hoped-for prey, the hare stopped, and then ran back for some distance along its former track, when by a sudden spring it threw itself on one side into the midst of the turnips, and there remained crouched and still. The dogs passed onward in their course at a rapid rate; and as soon as they had passed forward on its track, with another bound the hare sprang back to the place it had quitted, and ran upward along the course by which it had come down, with the evident intention of confounding together its upward and downward course. By this time the dogs had come to the lower extent to which the hare had proceeded, and there they stopped, as not knowing what further course to take. It was thus the persecuted creature secured its own safety; and my informant was too generous to help them out of their difficulty.—Video in *Land and Water*, July 13.

WAVES OF LIGHT.—Professor Tyndall states that it requires 39,000 waves of red light placed end to end to form an inch. Multiplying the number of inches in 192,000 miles, viz., 12,165,120,000, by 39,000, gives the tremendous product of 474,439,680,000,000. All these waves enter the eye in a single second of time. To produce the impression of red in the brain, the retina must be hit at this incredible rate. The violet rays being much shorter, it takes 57,000 of them to fill an inch, and the number of shocks required to produce this colour amount to six hundred and ninety-nine millions of millions per second. Sir John Herschel's data differ from these, and show greater disparities of speed between the two ends of the spectrum. Estimating the velocity of white light at 186,000 miles—roughly, one thousand million feet per second, and reckoning 33,866 wave lengths to the inch for the extreme red, 43,197 for the soda yellow, and 70,555 for the extreme violet, the impulses on the retina per second that produce the sensation of these colours reach these numbers:— Extreme red, 399,101,000,000,000; soda yellow 509,069,000,000,000; extreme violet, 831,479,000,000,000. This reveals a difference of more than two to one, while the figures themselves must impress us with the subtlety and inconceivable velocity of the agency with which we have to do.—*Gardeners' Chronicle*, June 29.

AGE OF PARROTS.—A correspondent of the *Field*, July 6, says, there is a green parrot here which was given to my wife in the summer of 1839. The person in Hull from whom she was bought believed her to be about three years old when he parted with her, so that there is no doubt she is now at least thirty-one. She is up to all kind of fun and tricks; at one time laughing, at another crying; now whistling parts of "God save the Queen," and then breaking off with the urgent request, "Fetch the Doctor." She has never been confined in a cage, but lives unchained on a stand, and has not had an hour's illness in her life, which may perhaps be accounted for by the fact that she spends part of every day in the open air. We are old-fashioned people, dining early; and at tea-time, when we have friends with us, both old and young request that Polly may be invited to tea, where she appears to the best advantage, coaxing and wheedling all at the table to give her something, and considering her meal incomplete till she finishes off with a spoonful of cream. She does not seem a year older in respect of constitution than when she came here, twenty-eight years since. Her plumage is as gay and her eyes as bright as ever, and there appears no reason why she should not live as many years as she has already.

RARE BIRDS.—A specimen of that exceedingly beautiful bird, the roller (*Coracias garrula*, Pennant), was recently shot at Howick, in Northumberland, by Mr. C. Lloyd, gamekeeper to Earl Grey. The specimen was about ten inches long—it is now in the possession of Mr. Thomas Gibb, of Alnwick. The roller is a native of the northern parts of Africa. The Rev. F. O. Morris, in his work on "British Birds" records the following instances of its capture in England:—At Skelton Castle, near Redcar, in Yorkshire, July, 1847; at Fixby park, near Huddersfield, in 1824; at Hatfield, near Doncaster, at Halifax, and at Scarborough, in 1832; in Cornwall, in 1844; on the borders of Ashdown Forest in Sussex, and at Oakington, in Cambridgeshire, in 1835; near Newcastle-on-Tyne, North Shields, and Bywell, in 1818; six in Norfolk and Suffolk, the latest in 1838. They have also been twice met with in Ireland and a few in Scotland. The roller is a noisy, clamorous bird. Meyer renders its call by the words "Urah-urah," "Rakker-rakker," and "Crea."—*Land and Water*, June 29th.

NEW VOLCANO IN THE SOUTH SEAS.—The following is an extract from a letter from Mr. J. C. Williams, Her Britannic Majesty's Consul, Navigator's Islands:—"A volcano has broken out at sea, at Manua, about two miles from the island of Olosega. It was preceded by a violent shock of earthquake, which commenced on the 5th of September, and on the 12th dense thick smoke rose out of the sea. Lava was thrown up, discolouring the water for many miles round, and destroying large quantities of fish. Wherever the ashes fell on the adjacent island they destroyed all vegetation. Up to the middle of November dense smoke was still being thrown up, and my informant says that the smoke rose higher than the neighbouring island, which is over 2,000 feet high. We cannot at present ascertain if there is any bank thrown up in the water. Last July we steamed over the place in Her Majesty's ship 'Brisk,' and there were no signs of shoals or anything of the kind."

Remarks, Queries, &c.

(*Under this head we shall be happy to insert original Remarks, Queries, &c.*)

ENTOMOLOGICAL NOTES.—PAPILIO.—This genus attains very large proportions, the colours are varied and brilliant, while a curious feature is often added by the prolongation of the hind wings into two tail-like appendages. The larva is of varied form—sometimes smooth, sometimes covered with fleshy protuberances, sometimes long, and able to throw out at pleasure the first two segments of the body. The genus comprises between two or three hundred known species, among which we find every imaginable tint and gradation of colour, exhibiting occasionally a very bold contrast. In England we have but one specimen, *Papilo Machaon* (Plate, Fig. 2), the beautiful swallow-tailed butterfly; it is the largest of our butterflies, the female occasionally measuring four inches. The base of the upper wing is black, slightly tinged with yellow; the apex of the same colour, with a row of semicircular yellow spots; the margin edged with yellow, spotted with black, forming three large patches, and also broadly marking the nervures; the base of the under wing is yellow, except the inner side, which is black, the nervures being dusky; beyond the yellow portion is a broad black band, marked by faint blue spots and six large yellow crescents; the outer edge is yellow; on the hinder angle is a large round spot of red streaked with blue; the under side resembles the upper. The caterpillar is greenish, with black band on each segment, spotted with red; it feeds on umbelliferous plants. The perfect insect continues until August, and is in some places rather abundant. *Cynthia Cardui*, the Painted Lady (Plate, Fig. 3).—This insect is of large size; it is not very common. The upper wings are tawny brown at the base, ochre-red in the middle, with irregular patch of black; a portion of the apex is also black, with five white spots; near the margin is a series of white crescents and a row of faint yellow spots. Secondary wings the same colour, with three rows of black spots behind—the first composed of five round spots, the second of crescents, and the third of large patches placed on the projecting points; the inner angle has a large black spot, with streak of blue behind. The under side of the primary wing is whitish at the base, and has a large spot, in addition to the corresponding ones on the upper side, tips light brown; the whole tinged with carmine and ochre. The hinder wings variegated with light brown, greyish white, and yellow. The caterpillar is of a brownish-grey colour, with yellow lines on the side, and very spiny; it feeds on the thistle, nettle, and mallow. *Melitæa Euphrosyne*, Pearl-bordered Fritillary.—This butterfly is pretty general, and may be found in August. The wings are yellowish-brown above, blackish at the base, variegated with spots of black, each wing having a row of black spots towards the apex, and a band of the same on the outer margin. The primary wings are yellow underneath, the black spots corresponding with those on the surface, but smaller, tips light yellow. The hind wings have several yellowish spots at the base, the spaces between red, and this colour forms a large spot in the middle; the space between this and the hinder margin is variegated with brown and yellow, and a row of dark spots; the hinder margin has triangular silver spots, forming part of a band of yellowish colour. The caterpillar is black, with lines of orange; it feeds on the violet. *Pieris cratægi*, the Black-veined, White, or Hawthorne Butterfly (Plate, Fig. 1.)—This is a handsome species of a uniform white, with the nervures black; the under side is exactly similar. The caterpillar black when young, but gains a reddish-brown tint, and becomes partially covered with hairs, as its name implies; it feeds on the leaves of the hawthorne, but will attack fruit-trees. It is found principally in the south. *Polyommatus Alexis*, or Common Blue (Plate, Fig. 5).—This is a pretty little insect of a bright lilac blue, the hinder margin edged with black, the anterior edge of upper wing white. The female is brown, powdered with blue at base of wings. The under side in both is brownish ash colour, the upper wings having two ocelli near the body, a slender streak placed transversely, a row of ocelli near the middle, externally a row of crescents edged with reddish-brown; behind these are dark spots on a white ground. The caterpillar is hairy, green in colour, and feeds on grasses. *Lycæna Pheleas*, or Common Copper (Plate, Fig. 6).—The upper wings of this insect are copper-coloured, spotted with black; under pair brownish-black, with copper band dotted with black on its outer edge. The under side of primary wings spotted like the upper, but paler in colour. Secondary wings fawn colour, with indistinct marks. Caterpillar green, with yellow stripe on the back; it feeds on sorrel. Fig. 4 represents the *Audrena nigro ænea*, a species of Bee that makes its nest in banks, excavating a hole of nearly a foot in depth. At the bottom a cell is constructed, which they fill with pollen made into a paste with honey, and in this they deposit their eggs. The colour of the body is black, clothed with tawny-coloured hairs. Antennæ black, wings transparent, legs black and hairy—the hinder pair covered with thick, long, white hair. Fig. 7 is the common May Fly, of greenish-brown colour, with transparent wings, mottled with brown.

BUTTERFLIES.—In answer to R. H., as to the best method of capturing and preserving butterflies, we extract the following from M. E. Catlow's "Popular British Entomology." The entomological net is of various forms and sizes: the one I have used has a pole six feet long, to which is strongly fastened a small hoop of cane to support a green gauze net or bag; by a dexterous turn of the hand, easily acquired by practice, butterflies and other insects may be soon caught on the wing with this simple apparatus. For some of the *Lepidoptera*, such as the Purple Emperor, a much longer rod is necessary, but these will not probably come under the observation of the student until he has acquired some experience, when he will find ways and means for himself. The cane, or hoop, may be about two feet in circumference, and the net half a yard in length. Entomological forceps are also very useful when insects are settled on leaves: these must of course be purchased, so that a description is unnecessary, and they may well be dispensed with for a time; some chip boxes are also useful for putting insects in, when the collector is at a distance from home, that they may not be rubbed by the hand, and the colour injured. The *Lepidoptera* are most easily killed by a slight pressure of the finger and thumb on the thorax, below the wing; this is, at least, generally sufficient; but sometimes, to the great uneasiness of the humane naturalist, they will be found alive some time after; suffocating by means of sulphur is still less certain, and Messrs. Kirby and Spence recommend the following plan:—Fix in the lid of a small tin saucepan filled with boiling water, a tin tube consisting of two pieces, which fit into each other; cover the mouth of the lower one with a piece of gauze, and place your insects upon it, then fix the upper one over it, covering the mouth also with gauze or muslin, and the steam from the boiling water will effectually kill the insects without injuring the plumage. Another more simple apparatus is a piece of elder, or any soft wood with the bark on, placed across the bottom of a mug; stick the insect on this, inverting the mug in a deep basin, into which pour boiling water till it is covered, holding down the mug that it may not be overturned; in two minutes the insect will be dead. This latter plan, however, is objectionable, as the insect can hardly be fixed to the wood by any other means than by running the pin through the thorax when living; and as only experienced naturalists can do this, with the certainty of deadening the feelings of the insect, and at once extinguishing the sense of pain, I would not recommend my readers to practice it. Others advise the head being touched with a strong acid, or that the insect be placed in a covered jar, half filled with bruised laurel-leaves; and beetles may be immediately killed by immersion in boiling water.

This is the only drawback to the study of the delightful science in its perfection, namely, by forming a collection; but it is very evident that insects have not any of the susceptibility to pain that is found in the higher order of animals, for they are frequently seen flying about with apparently the usual sense of enjoyment, when they have been deprived by accident of some of their due proportion of legs or wings; I myself once caught a Tiger-Moth on the wing, which on examination was found to have lost nearly the whole of the lower part of the body. When the insect is killed, it must be prepared for the cabinet: a pin (short whites) should be run into the thorax, and forced sufficiently through to pierce the cork of the box or drawer, and hold the insect firm; it should also be high enough to prevent the legs from touching the bottom. The best method of setting Lepidopterous insects is by having a small board made, with pieces of wood the same length, about three inches wide and half an inch in depth, glued on at intervals of about an inch, or something less; then by sticking the pin with the insect into one of these intervals, the wings rest on the higher parts on each side, and can then be easily fixed with braces in the desired position. The brace is merely a piece of cardboard, long and narrow, fixed with pins into the wood, and bearing gently over the wings so as to keep them steady in their natural attitude; the antennæ and legs should also be extended and kept in their places by pins. When quite stiff and firm, the insects way be removed to their proper place in the cabinet. The best method of arranging insects is in columns, with the generic name at the head of each column, and the specific affixed beneath the insect. A different drawer or box for each order is desirable for the young student, but not indispensable: and these arrangements must depend on means, and increase with his increasing collection. Two of each insect, particularly in *Lepidoptera*, should be procured, if possible, to exhibit both the upper and under side. Should an insect become mouldy, a brush dipped in spirits of wine in which a little camphor is dissolved, will clean it; but the insect must be dried before being replaced in the cabinet. Camphor in the drawers is very necessary to prevent the attacks of other insects, whose presence is easily discovered from the dust under the specimens; when this is seen, they should be taken out, brushed with a camel's hair pencil, then touched with spirits of wine, and placed near the fire till dry. Moths frequently change colour from any oily matter common to all insects; when this is the case, powder some dry chalk on a heated iron, cover it with a fine piece of linen, and apply to it the under part of the insect; the heated iron dissolves the greasy substances, which the chalk then absorbs. Insects, when stiff before being properly placed out, which will sometimes be the case when caught at a distance from home, may be relaxed by being placed on moist sand.

The pupæ are principally found during the first three months of the year, in long grass, on trunks of trees, and felled timber; also in April and May, on pailings. Caterpillars may be discovered in great profusion in May. Butterflies abound in June, July, and August. Moths extend into September.

AN AUDACIOUS MOUSE!—A short time back I was awoke in the middle of the night by some one, as I thought, pulling my hair. I procured a light and looked about, but could perceive nothing, and naturally thought I must have been dreaming. Still I could not get rid of the idea that something had been at my head. I am not superstitious, but certainly felt nervous, so kept the light burning, and lay for some time with my back to the light and face to the wall. I presently fancied I saw the shadow of something move along me from the foot of the bed. I turned quickly round, but could see nothing, so lay on my back with my head raised. I now thought that there might be a rat in the room, but could hear no noise. After several minutes of suspense all ideas were put to flight by what I saw, which was a large mouse climb on the foot of the bed, and, keeping near the wall, stealthily creep up to the pillow; he then made direct, as I fancied, to my face. When quite close I turned sharply round, and he jumped clean over me and fell upon the ground, and I need not say disappeared. Of course it was evident he had got on the bed while I was asleep, and had found the grease on my head so much to his liking that after being frightened away he had made another attempt. I was not over-pleased at the discovery, as you may imagine, so at once removed to another bedroom a story higher, where I slept in peace. But, strange to say, on the following night he, as I presume, found his way up there, for I caught him at the same little game; but in this room he was evidently not so much at home, as after a deal of chasing I captured and consigned him to a pail of water. I know there are plenty of mice in the house, and as I keep a good many birds I am afraid to have a cat, so they multiply and grow fat. But I have never since been troubled in the same way. I have mentioned the circumstance to several persons. No one seems to have ever heard of their coming so close; no doubt the grease was too great a temptation for it to resist. I may mention, as it may be of use to persons troubled with mice, that I lately procured some phosphorous paste to exterminate beetles, and have found four mice dead in the kitchen doubled up, having evidently been feeding off the same. The phosphorus has almost cleared the house of beetles, which was before swarming with them.

Clapham.   H. C.

THE JACKDAW.—This well-known bird is much smaller than the rook (being only fourteen inches in length), from which it is easily distinguished by its hood of hoary grey. It is gregarious, and frequents in large numbers holes in rocks, old towers, &c., where it builds a nest of sticks, lined with wool and hair, which I have often seen it stealing from the backs of cattle quietly resting in the meadows, and seeming rather to like the operation than otherwise. In confinement it is a very amusing bird, but is certainly a better trickster than talker; for, although I have tried several, I have not been able to teach one to speak a word. Jackdaws are so fond of liberty that it is a cruel thing to keep them confined in cages, if it can be helped. I have now four which I reared from the nest, all of which have perfect freedom and are allowed to go in and out of their house at will, which is made in the style of a pigeon-house with two holes. It is generally supposed that only birds of prey cast up indigestible food in the shape of pellets, but this I have frequently observed my jackdaws to do. The pellets are in size and shape very like that of the Kestrel or Sparrowhawk. Jackdaws are very fond of bathing, and in warm weather often bathe two or three times a day; therefore a plentiful supply of water should never be withheld from them.

Mavishbush House.   J. D. S. W.

CURIOUS SNAKE STORY.—Did you ever read or hear of a mouse eating a live snake—eating him by piecemeal I mean? I was lately out collecting specimens of ferns in the neighbourhood of Sheffield when I caught a very fine specimen of the ring-snake. He was about a yard long, very healthy and vigorous. Well, I could get him to eat nothing. I tried the different things that are supposed to be the food of those reptiles—frogs and toads, snails, grubs, &c., &c. —but not a particle would he eat. At length I put a living mouse into the case; but, to my surprise and indignation, instead of the snake eating the mouse the mouse actually eat the snake. I think I have read somewhere of the South Sea Islanders cutting pieces off the bullock while he was alive. They were offering up sacrifices (so the account read), and first took from the living creature as their superstition directed them. The mouse eat and lived on the snake's tail, and both seemed healthy. Mind, there was plenty of bread and meat both raw and cooked in the case when this took place. I make this statement, which was well known to several of my friends here. I say I record this for fear you should think me cruel in hungering the poor little mouse; such was not the case. It was not from necessity, it was from choice.

Droylesdon.   J. POTTS.

[We should like to hear further particulars of this strange story. Has the mouse succeeded in finishing the snake, and is it still alive? Our correspondent will oblige us by sending fuller information.—Ed.]

THE DUCK.—This genus comprises upwards of a hundred species, varying considerable in size and plumage from each other. Its inoffensive and harmless character renders it most pleasant and profitable to keep. The habits of the duck are very curious and interesting; their regular parade to and from the pond is a beautiful country spectacle, to be enjoyed by those who have a liking for the charms. The Rhone duck (imported from France) is generally of a dark colour, and is decidedly preferable to our common English, as its flesh is whiter and of a higher flavour. It will cover from eleven to fifteen eggs, and the time of incubation is thirty days; but I think it much more advisable to put duck's eggs under a hen, which makes a far better mother. It is generally supposed that poultry cannot remain long off their eggs without the young being destroyed. But last month I sat a hen on duck's eggs, and when she had sat half her time I kept her off her eggs for about twelve hours, and then put her back again; at the end of her times she hatched all the eggs with the exception of one, which was barren. The ducklings are quite healthy, and are thriving well. The duck on leaving her nest covers the eggs with leaves, which the hen never does. Ducks will not thrive unless they have free access to a pond or running stream.

Mavisbush House.   J. D. S. W.

OLD BIRDS FEEDING YOUNG.—Seeing the paragraph in this month's NATURALIST'S NOTE BOOK, headed "Young Canaries fed by an older nestling," I thought the following might not be wholly uninteresting to the readers of the NOTE BOOK.

In the early part of last year a cousin of mine got possession of a nest of four young thrushes just fledged, which he brought up by hand, keeping them in a summer-house which had not been renovated for the season, and all four made fine healthy birds. Some month or so afterwards another nest was obtained, containing five thrushes only just stumped, which he also put into the summer house, and I have with other friends many a time seen the elder birds feed the young ones, four of which were also reared.
S. BENNETT.

BRITISH SHREWS.—It is a daily circumstance with me nearly the whole year through to find the common shrew dead, and sometimes in numbers, in my garden. The explanation which I am accustomed to give, and which I am convinced is the true one, is much more simple and reasonable than the suggestion contained in your last (p. 199). It is well known that the shrew has a fœtid smell, distantly resembling musk; and though the cat will kill this animal whenever found, the prey is soon dropped unmangled on account of its ill odour. A fine old bulldog of my acquaintance, which kills mice with evident enjoyment, will not look at a shrew.
THOMAS Q. COUCH.

FLEAS IN DOGS.—J. L.—Experience has taught me that washing dogs once a week with a medicated soap, called "Naldire's Tablet," is much more efficacious in destroying fleas than "Persian Insect Powder." I have used it on both rough and smooth haired dogs, and not only have all fleas been destroyed, but the dogs' coats have at the same time been thoroughly cleansed. Insect powder will not do this.
E. M. W.

BIRDS COUNTERFEITING LAMENESS.—The Partridge is the only bird said to counterfeit lameness and inability to fly in order to lead off a person from the vicinity of its nest; but this is not the case, as I have repeatedly observed other birds (particularly the Blackcap) to act in this manner on their nests being approached.
B. W. B.

A WHITE SWALLOW.—When playing on the Co. Louth Cricket Ground to-day I saw a *white* swallow. The bird flew within a yard of me, so that I cannot be mistaken. It was seen also by all those who were playing. Hearne, who takes care of the ground, tells me that it was flying about all day. The bird was perfectly white, or as Hearne says, "just like a white pigeon."
Milesdown, July 19th.
T. A. H.

SMOKING BIRDS.—I have heard that smoking tobacco under the nostrils of birds newly caught has the effect of rendering them tame and tractable; but, having tried it, I have met with no success. Perhaps some of your readers could inform me on the subject.
J. D. S. W.

STATE OF THE WEATHER NEAR LONDON.

June and July	Moon's Age.	Barometer.		Temperature.					Wind	Rain.	Remarks.
				Of the Air.			of the Earth				
		Max.	Min.	Max	Min	Mean	1 foot deep	2 feet deep			
Thurs. 20	18	30.033	29.994	65	44	54.5	60	57	N.E.	.00	Overcast throughout.
Friday 21	19	30.099	30.076	66	44	55.0	60	57	N.E.	.00	Cloudy; overcast; cloudy at night.
Satur. 22	20	30.124	30.043	72	42	57.0	60	57	N.E.	.00	Fine; Slight dry haze; fine; overcast.
Sunday 23	21	29.987	29.932	75	45	60.0	60	56	N.E.	.00	Very fine; fine; very fine at night.
Mon. 24	22	30.025	29.947	70	44	57.0	61	58	N.W.	.00	Fine; overcast; fine at night.
Tues. 25	☾	30.337	30.179	75	42	58.5	62	58	N.E.	.00	Clear and dry; very fine throughout.
Wed. 26	24	30.486	30.468	74	37	55.5	62	59	N.E.	.00	Cold and dry; very clear; very fine at night.
Thurs. 27	25	30.522	30.419	82	40	61.0	61	59	N.E.	.00	Quite cloudless, and very dry air; clear and dry; very fine
Friday 28	26	30.502	30·474	70	35	52.5	63	59	N.E.	.00	Overcast; scattered low dusky clouds; very fine at night.
Satur. 29	27	30.408	30.273	80	42	61.0	62	60	S.W.	.00	Quite cloudless; very fine; cloudy at night.
Sunday 30	28	30.079	29.860	82	47	64.5	63	60	S.W.	.00	Hot; very fine throughout.
Mon. 1	●	29.819	29.733	83	44	63.5	64	60	E.	.24	Hot, with slight dry haze; hot and dry; cloudy; rain.
Tues. 2	1	29.735	29.654	71	55	63.0	65	61	W.	.04	Close and warm; dull and showery; fine rain.
Wed. 3	2	29.968	29.787	74	55	64.5	64	61	S.	.14	Overcast and warm; rain at night.
Thurs. 4	3	29.856	29.848	72	52	62.0	64	61	S.	.02	Rain; cloudy, with showers; overcast; warm at night.
Friday 5	4	30.072	29.979	71	41	56.0	64	61	S.W.	.00	Fine, with white clouds; very fine throughout.
Satur. 6	5	30.133	30.131	74	42	58.0	64	61	N.W.	.00	Fine; very fine; fine at night.
Sunday 7	6	30.232	30.224	76	42	59.0	64	61	N.	.00	Very fine throughout; rather cold at night.
Mon. 8	☽	30.245	30.158	77	42	59.5	64	61	N.E.	.00	Slight dry haze; very fine at night.
Tues. 9	8	30.305	30.114	77	44	60.5	64	61	N.E.	.00	Very fine throughout.
Wed. 10	9	30.198	30.137	79	41	60.0	64	61	S.E.	.00	Very fine; hot and very fine; cold at night.
Thurs. 11	10	30.122	29.990	73	53	65.0	64	61	E.	.00	Fine; with slight dry haze; very fine; overcast.
Friday 12	11	29.859	29.751	73	46	61.0	64	61	E.	.00	Overcast; fine, with dry haze; fine at night.
Satur. 13	12	29.767	29.688	72	52	62.0	64	61	S.	.26	Overcast; showery at night.
Sunday 14	13	29.769	29.595	71	48	59.5	64	61	S.	.09	Very fine; showery; very fine.
Mon. 15	14	29.589	29.352	65	54	59.5	64	61	S.	.28	Rain; showers and dense dark clouds; boisterous.
Tues. 16	○	29.497	29.487	67	57	62.0	63	60	S.	.27	Showers, and dense clouds; very heavy showers; fine.
Wed. 17	16	29.727	29.623	70	56	63.0	62	60	W.	.32	Boisterous; masses of white clouds in bright blue sky; cloudy.

MIMICRY IN NATURE.

IT is among butterflies that instances of mimicry are most numerous and most striking. There is in South America an extensive family of these insects, the Heliconidæ, which are in many respects very remarkable. They are so abundant and characteristic in all the woody portions of the American tropics, that in almost every locality they will be seen more frequently than any other butterflies. They are distinguished by very elongate wings, body, and antennæ, and are exceedingly beautiful and varied in their colours; spots and patches of yellow red or pure white upon a black, blue, or brown ground, being most general. They frequent the forests chiefly, and all fly slowly and weakly; yet although they are so conspicuous, and could certainly be caught by insectivorous birds more easily than almost any other insects, their great abundance all over the wide region they inhabit shows that they are not so persecuted. It is to be especially remarked also that they possess no adaptive colouring to protect them during repose, for the under side of their wings presents the same, or at least an equally conspicuous colouring as the upper side; and they may be observed after sunset suspended at the end of twigs and leaves where they have taken up their station for the night, fully exposed to the attacks of enemies if they have any. These beautiful insects possess, however, a strong pungent semi-aromatic or medicinal odour, which seems to pervade all the juices of their system. When the entomologist squeezes the breast of one of them between his fingers to kill it, a yellow liquid exudes which stains the skin, and the smell of which can only be got rid of by time and repeated washings. Here we have probably the cause of their immunity from attack, since there is a great deal of evidence to show that certain insects are so disgusting to birds that they will under no circumstances touch them. Mr. Stainton has observed that a brood of young turkeys which greedily eat up all the worthless moths he had amassed in a night's "sugaring," yet one after another seized and rejected a single white moth which happened to be among them. Young pheasants and partridges which eat many kinds of caterpillars seem to have an absolute dread of that of the common currant moth, which they will never touch, and tomtits as well as other small birds appear never to eat the same species. In the case of the Heliconidæ, however, we have some direct evidence to the same effect. In the Brazilian forests there are great numbers of insectivorous birds—as jucamars, trogons, and puffbirds—which catch insects on the wing, and that they destroy many butterflies is indicated by the fact that the wings of these insects are often found on the ground where their bodies have been devoured. But among these there are no wings of Heliconidæ, while those of the large showy Nymphalidæ, which have a much swifter flight, are often met with. Again, a gentleman who has recently returned from Brazil stated at a meeting of the Entomological Society that he once observed a pair of puffbirds catching butterflies, which they brought to their nest to feed their young; yet during half an hour they never brought one of the Heliconidæ, which were flying lazily about in great numbers, and which they could have captured more easily than any other. It was this circumstance that led Mr. Bolt to observe them so long, as he could not understand why the most common insects should be altogether passed by. Mr. Bates also tells us that he never saw them molested by lizards or predacious flies which often pounce on other butterflies.

If, therefore, we accept it as highly probable (if not proved) that the Heliconidæ are very greatly protected from attack by their peculiar odour and taste, we find it much more easy to understand their chief characteristics—their great abundance, their slow flight, their gaudy colours, and the entire absence of protective tints on their under surfaces. This property places them somewhat in the position of those curious wingless birds of oceanic islands, the dodo, the apteryx, and the moas, which are with great reason supposed to have lost the power of flight on account of the absence of carnivorous quadrupeds. Our butterflies have been protected in a different way, but quite as effectually; and the result has been that as there has been nothing to escape from, there has been no weeding out of slow flyers, and as there has been nothing to hide from, there has been no extermination of the bright-coloured varieties, and no preservation of such as tended to assimilate with surrounding objects.

Now let us consider how this kind of protection must act. Tropical insectivorous birds very frequently sit on dead branches of a lofty tree, or on those which overhang forest paths, gazing intently around, and darting off at intervals to seize an insect at a considerable distance, which they generally return to their station to devour. If a bird began by capturing the slow-flying, conspicuous Heliconidæ, and found them always so disagreeable that he could not eat them, he would after a very few trials leave off catching them at all; and their whole appearance, form, colouring, and mode of flight is so peculiar, that there can be little doubt birds would soon learn to distinguish them at a long distance, and never waste any time in pursuit of them. Under these circumstances, it is evident that any other butterfly of a group which birds were accustomed to devour, would be almost equally well protected by closely resembling a Heliconia externally, as if it acquired also the disagreeable odour; always supposing that there were only a few of them among a great number of the Heliconias. If the birds could not distinguish the two kinds externally, and there were on the average only one eatable among fifty uneatable, they would soon give up seeking for the eatable ones, even if they knew them to exist. If, on the other hand, any particular butterfly of an eatable group acquired the disagreeable taste of the Heliconias while it retained the characteristic form and colouring of its own group, this would be really of no use to it whatever; for the birds would go on catching it among its eatable allies (among whom, we suppose, it is comparatively rare), and it would probably be wounded and disabled, even if rejected, and would be as effectually killed as if it were devoured. It is important, therefore, to understand that if any one genus of an extensive family of eatable butterflies were in danger of extermination from insect-eating birds, and if two kinds of variation were going on among them, some individuals possessing a slightly disagreeable taste, others a slight resemblance to the Heliconidæ, this latter quality would be much more valuable than the former. The change in flavour would not at all prevent the variety from being captured as before, and it would almost certainly be thoroughly disabled before being rejected. The approach in colour and form to the Heliconidæ, however, would be at the very first a positive, though perhaps a slight advantage; for although at short distances this variety would be easily distinguished and devoured, yet at a longer distance it might be mistaken for one of the uneatable group, and so be passed by and gain another day's life, which might in many cases be sufficient for it to lay a quantity of eggs and leave a numerous progeny, many of which would inherit the peculiarity which had been the safeguard of their parent.

Now, this hypothetical case is exactly realized in South America. Among the white butterflies forming the family Pieridæ (many of which do not greatly differ in appearance from our own cabbage butterflies) is a genus of rather small size (Leptalis); some species of which are white like their allies, while the larger number exactly resemble the Heliconidæ in the form and colouring of the wings. It must be always remembered that these two families are as absolutely distinguished from each other by structural characters as are the carnivora and the ruminants among quadrupeds, and that an entomologist can always distinguish the one from the other by the structure of the feet, just as certainly as a zoologist can tell a bear from a buffalo by the skull or by a tooth. Yet the resemblance of a species of the one family to another species in the other family was often so great, that both Mr. Bates and Mr. Wallace were many times deceived at the time of capture, and did not discover the distinctness of the two insects till a closer examination detected their essential differences. During his residence of eleven years in the Amazon valley Mr. Bates found a number of species or varieties of Leptalis, each of which was a more or less exact copy of one of the Heliconidæ of the district it inhabited; and the results of his observations are embodied in the paper published in the Linnean Transactions, in which he first explained the phenomena of "mimicry" as the result of natural selection, and showed its identity in cause and purpose with protective resemblance to vegetable or inorganic forms.

The imitation of the Heliconidæ by the Leptalides is carried out to a wonderful degree in form as well as in colouring. The wings have become elongated to the same extent, and the antennæ and abdomen have both become lengthened, to correspond with the unusual condition in which they exist in the former family. In colouration there are several types in the different genera of Heliconidæ. The genus Mechanitis is generally of a rich semi-transparent brown, banded with black and yellow; Methona is of large size, the wings transparent like horn, and with black transverse bands; while the delicate Ithomias are all more or less transparent, with black veins and borders, and often with marginal and transverse bands of orange red. These different forms are all copied by the various species of Leptalis, every band and spot and tint of colour, and the various degrees of transparency, being exactly reproduced. As if to derive all the benefit possible from this protective mimicry, the habits have become so modified that the Leptalides generally frequent the very same spots as their models, and have the same mode of flight; and as they are always very scarce (Mr. Bates estimating their numbers at about one to a thousand of the group they resemble), there is hardly a possibility of their being found out by their enemies. It is also very remarkable that in almost every case the particular Ithomias and other species of Heliconidaæ which they resemble, are noted as being very common species, swarming in individuals, and found over a wide range of country. This indicates antiquity and permanence in the species, and is exactly the condition most essential both to aid in the development and to increase the utility of the resemblance.

But the Leptalides are not the only group

who have prolonged their existence by imitating the great protected group of Heliconidæ;—a genus of quite another family of most lovely small American butterflies, the Erycinidæ, and three genera of diurnal moths, also present species which often mimic the same dominant forms, so that some, as Ithomia ilerdina of St. Paulo, for instance, have flying with them a few individuals of three totally different insects, which are yet disguised with exactly the same form, colour, and markings, so that all four are undistinguishable when on the wing. Again, the Heliconidæ are not the only group that are imitated, although they are the most frequent models. The black and red group of South American Papilios, and the handsome Erycinian genus Stalachtis, have also a few who copy them; but this fact offers no difficulty, since these two groups are almost as dominant as the Heliconidæ. They both fly very slowly, they both are conspicuously coloured, and they both abound in individuals; so that there is every reason to believe that they possess a protection of a similar kind to the Heliconidæ, and that it is therefore equally an advantage to other insects to be mistaken for them. There is also another extraordinary fact that we are not yet in a position clearly to comprehend: some groups of the Heliconidæ themselves mimic other groups. Species of Heliconius mimic Mechanitis, and every species of Napeogenes mimics some other Heliconideous butterfly. This would seem to indicate that the distasteful secretion is not produced alike by all members of the family, and that where it is deficient protective imitation comes into play. It is this, perhaps, that has caused such a general resemblance among the Heliconidæ, such a uniformity of type with great diversity of colouring, since any aberration causing an insect to cease to look like one of the family would inevitably lead to its being attacked, wounded, and exterminated, even although it were not eatable.

In other parts of the world an exactly parallel series of facts have been observed. The Danaidæ and the Acræidæ of the Old World tropics form in fact one great group with the Heliconidæ. They have the same general form, structure, and habits: they possess the same protective odour, and are equally abundant in individuals, although not so varied in colour, blue and white spots on a back ground being the most general pattern. The insects which mimic these are chiefly Papilios and Diademæ, a genus allied to our peacock and tortoiseshell butterflies. In tropical Africa there is a peculiar group of the genus Danais, characterized by dark-brown and bluish-white colours, arranged in bands or stripes. One of these, Danais niavius, is exactly imitated both by Papilio hippocoon and by Diadema anthedon; another, Danais echeria, by Papilio cenea; and in Natal a variety of the Danais is found having a white spot at the tip of wings, accompanied by a variety of the Papilio bearing a corresponding white spot. Acræa timandra is copied in its very peculiar style of colouration by Papilio boisduvalianus and the female of Diadema hirce, while the male of the same insect is like Acræa gea. Acræa euryta of Sierra Leone has a Diadema from the same place which exactly copies it; and in the collections of the British Museum there are six species of Diadema and four of Papilio which in their colour and markings are perfect mimics of species of Danais or Acræa which inhabit the same districts.

Passing on to India, we have Danais tytia, a butterfly with semi-transparent bluish wings and a border of rich reddish brown. This remarkable style of colouring is exactly reproduced in Papilio agestor and in Diadema nama, and all three insects not unfrequently come together in collections made at Darjeeling. In the Philippine Islands the large and curious Idea leuconöe with its semi-transparent white wings, veined and spotted with black, is copied by the rare Papilio idæoides from the same islands.

In the Malay archipelago the very common and beautiful Euplæa midamus is so exactly mimicked by two rare Papilios (P. paradoxa and P. ænigma) that Mr. Wallace generally caught them under the impression that they were the more common species; and the equally common and even more beautiful Euplæa rhadamanthus, with its pure white bands and spots on a ground of glossy blue and black, is reproduced in the Papilio caunus. Here also there are species of Diadema, imitating the same group in two or three instances; but we shall have to adduce these further on in connexion with another branch of the subject.

It has been already mentioned that in South America there is a group of Papilios which have all the characteristics of a protected race, and whose peculiar colours and markings are imitated by other butterflies not so protected. There is just such a group also in the East, having very similar colours and the same habits, and these also are mimicked by other species in the same genus not closely allied to them, and also by a few of other families. Papilio hector, a common Indian butterfly of a rich black colour spotted with crimson, is so closely copied by Papilio romulus, that the latter insect has been thought to be its female. A close examination shows, however, that it is essentially different, and belongs to another section of the genus. Papilio antiphus and P. diphilus, black swallow-tailed butterflies with cream-coloured spots, are so well imitated by varieties of P.

theseus, that several writers have classed them as the same species. Papilio liris, found only in the island of Timor, is accompanied there by P. ænomaus, the female of which so exactly resembles it that they can hardly be separated in the cabinet, and on the wing are quite undistinguishable. But one of the most curious cases is the fine yellow-spotted Papilio cöon, which is unmistakeably imitated by the female tailed form of Papilio memnon. These are both from Sumatra; but in North India P. cöon is replaced by another species, which has been named P. doubledayi, having red spots instead of yellow; and in the same district the corresponding female tailed form of Papilio androgeus, sometimes considered a variety of P. memnon, is similarly red-spotted. Mr. Westwood has described some curious day-flying moths (Epicopeia) from North India, which have the form and colouring of Papilios of this section, and two of these are very good imitations of Papilio polydorus and Papilio varuna, also from North India.—*Westminster Review*, July 1867.

DEW.

WHEN substances exposed to the open air become covered with moisture, at a time when no rain or visible wet is falling, the phenomenon is called *dew*. If a glass of cold water be brought into a warm room, the surface of the glass becomes bedewed. In like manner the windows of a room, especially where many persons are collected and lights are burning, become covered with dew, often in such quantity as to run down in streams of water. So also after sunset, when the sky is clear, the earth cools down more rapidly than the air that rests upon it, and condenses the moisture of the air so as to form dew. If a thermometer be suspended in the air a few feet above the ground under a clear sky by night, it will mark a higher temperature by four, six, or eight degrees, or more, than a thermometer resting on the ground; and what is very remarkable, the difference between the two thermometers will vary with the nature of the surface on which the thermometer is placed. The thermometer resting on long grass will mark a much lower temperature than one placed on garden mould, and this will be much lower than a thermometer placed on gravel; so that at the same moment we may have a copious deposit of dew on grass, where it is most wanted, a smaller deposit on mould, and least of all on the gravel path, where it is but little wanted. Here we have another of those striking instances of design which we have had occasion to point out in other papers.

The formation of dew is intimately connected with the operation of two great natural forces which are in constant activity everywhere around us; namely, the *radiation of heat*, whereby the surface of the earth becomes colder than the surrounding air, and the *condensation of vapour* from the atmosphere by contact with a colder body. Should the temperature of the air be below the freezing point of water, and circumstances be otherwise favourable for the deposition of moisture, *hoar frost* will be formed.

It often happens that after a true theory has been established the incorrect language of an older erroneous theory is retained. This happens in the case of dew. It was formerly supposed that the air dissolved moisture, as water dissolves a salt, sugar, &c. By stirring up the salt or the sugar in water a certain quantity will be dissolved, and when the water will dissolve no more it is said to be saturated. By raising the temperature of the water, we increase, in the majority of cases, its solvent powers, and it again becomes saturated at a higher temperature. By cooling the solution it throws down some of the salt: by reheating it, it takes it up again. Now although the quantity of vapour in the air depends on the temperature, and we speak of the air as being more or less saturated with moisture, yet there is no relation between moisture and the air in the sense that a soluble salt bears to water. Were there no atmosphere, moisture would be formed in greater or less quantities according to the temperature. It would be abundant, highly elastic, and invisible at a high temperature; it would be scanty and have little elasticity at a low temperature. Under any circumstances, whether air be present or not, vapour would be visible only while it was in that state of partial condensation which we recognize as cloud, mist, or fog.

The moisture of the air then, forming as it does an independent atmosphere of itself, can be examined without reference to the other ingredients in the earth's complex gaseous envelope. It is exceedingly sensitive to minute changes in temperature, imparting thereby such wondrous beauty to the sky, softening the air, ministering to the comfort and sustenance of animals and plants, drenching the latter with dew, and thus fulfilling the office of rain, and at lower temperatures covering vegetation with icy feathers of exquisite beauty.

The first thing to be considered in the formation of dew is the source of supply in the invisible vapour of the air. At the freezing point of water the air can contain enough moisture to support two-tenths of an inch of mercury in the barometer. At thirty-nine degrees there can be moisture enough to support about one-fourth of an inch; at fifty-nine degrees half an inch; at seventy-one degrees three quarters of an inch;

at eighty degrees one inch, and so on, the quantity depending strictly on the temperature.

The second point to be considered is the mode in which bodies heated by the sun or otherwise cool down when the source of heat is removed. Bodies may cool by *conduction*, as when a warm body, in contact with a colder one, parts with its heat to the colder one without travelling except from particle to particle until the two bodies are of the same temperature; secondly, by *convection*, as when a fluid body, such as air or a liquid near a hot body has a few of its particles heated, and these ascend while colder particles take their place to be heated, and in like manner to ascend, which process goes on until equilibrium of temperature between the heated body and the fluid is attained; thirdly, by *radiation*, in which the heated body parts with its heat in radial lines which travel into space with the velocity of light, but if they encounter other bodies capable of reflecting them back the process of radiation may be impeded or arrested. The fire warms our rooms by radiation, the candle gives us heat and light by radiation, our bodies cool by radiation, and this process is perpetually going on among all kinds of matter, radiating heat to each other, and tending to establish that equilibrium of temperature which is never attained. If a heated cannon-ball be brought into a room, it will dart its rays in all directions, and raise the temperature of all the objects around it. If a lump of ice be similarly placed the objects in the room will radiate heat to it until it is melted, but in both cases the process is one of interchange. Both the cannon ball and the ice receive heat from the objects in the room, but the one gives out much more and the other much less than it receives. The radiating powers of bodies are however very unequal. If we call the radiating power of long grass 1000, that of hare skin is 1316, raw white wool 1222, raw silk 1107, unwrought white cotton wool 1085, lamp black 961, flannel 871, coloured lamb's wool 832, black lamb's wool 741, snow 657, sheet iron 642, paper 614, slate 573, river sand, 454, stone, 390, brick 372.

The power of condensing moisture from the air will thus, it is evident, depend on the radiating power of the body in question. Some bodies will cool and contract dew more quickly than others; that is, they will cool down sufficiently to condense moisture from the air in the form of dew. The temperature at which the vapour of the air begins to be condensed is called the *dew-point*. One of the earliest methods of finding the dew-point consisted in pouring water, colder than the atmosphere, or made so by the addition of a little nitre or sulphate of soda into a thin glass tumbler and exposing it to the air. If dew appeared immediately and abundantly on its surface the water was poured into another vessel, and allowed to approach nearer the temperature of the air. It was then poured back into the glass, and if the dew still formed abundantly the water was again poured into another vessel, so as to get warmer, until at length that temperature was obtained at which moisture would just be deposited on the surface of the thin glass, but if the water were one degree higher, moisture would not be condensed. Instruments called *hygrometers* have been contrived for ascertaining the dew-point, while those which merely indicate the presence of moisture, more or less, are termed *hygroscopes*. The twisted fibres of hemp, catgut, &c., are thus used, as they shrink and contract by moisture, and open and get longer in dry weather. A hair, an oat beard, Indian grass, &c., are also used. For accurate observation, as well as convenience, the *wet* and *dry-bulb thermometers* are now chiefly used. Two thermometers are mounted in one frame, the bulb of one of which is covered with cambric, and a thread of cotton is led from this into a reservoir of water, which thus keeps the cambric constantly wet; and as the moisture evaporates it produces a depression of temperature in this thermometer as compared with the other, and as the evaporation and consequent depression is greater in a dry air than in a moist, the difference between the two thermometers is constantly varying. In "Glaisher's Meteorological Tables" factors are given for multiplying the excess of the reading of the dry thermometer over that of the wet, and this gives the excess of the temperature of the air above that of the dew-point.—*People's Magazine* for August.

THE GEOLOGY OF HAMPSHIRE.

THE great chalk range which forms the boundary to Northern Hampshire, so far as it concerns the district around St. Mary Bourne, may be said to commence with the Hippenscombe and Buttermere hills westward, and to terminate at Cottington Hill, near Kingsclere, eastward. It comprehends in its course the Inkpen Beacon, which attains to an elevation of about 1,000 feet above the level of the sea, and the more or less continuous hills of Coombe, Walbury, Sidon, and Highclere Beacon. These magnificent hills are interesting from their historical associations, and the remarkable remains in the shape of earthworks, &c., which crown most of their summits, testifying that they must have been strongholds to various tribes of people at different periods in the past history of the county. Most of these entrenchments are of considerable extent, the one on Ladle Hill enclosing an area of about eight acres. On Beacon Hill, within a large enclosed space, there are some peculiar elevations, nearly circular in outline, and rudely pitched with stones. They are considered as hut-circles, possibly the work of the Belgic Britons, who were chiefly located in this part of Hampshire. This hill commands a fine view of the bold and rugged downs around Litchfield, rich in associations if bare in feature, the tumuli dotted about their surface marking the burial places of an early people; while the extended lines of entrenchments, observable on commanding elevations, were used for defensive purposes, probably by the various people who have successively occupied Britain.

Litchfield is stated as signifying "the field of corpses," perhaps from the Saxon *lic*, flesh; the blood of the Saxon having, it is supposed, been freely spilt here in battle. But from the way the word is written in ancient documents, it is quite as likely to be of Celtic origin, and to have nothing to do with the dead. The name has been introduced in order to show the remarkable alterations a word may undergo in the course of a few centuries. Thus, in the Hampshire Doomsday, it appears as Liveselle. In Pope Nicholas's Taxation it is called *Lindeshull*. In the year 1300, it is known as *Lidescelve*. In the Subsidy Roll of Hampshire, A.D. 1327, it assumes the name of *Ludeshulve*. In 1340 it is written *Lideshulve*, and lastly, in 1477, it occurs under the title of *Ludchelfe*. These words are evidently modifications of each other. How it became, subsequently, Litchfield, it is difficult to determine, but, at all events, the transposition appears to have taken place since Saxon times.

Returning to the boundary chain, it may be briefly stated that, on the Hampshire side, the chalk has a gradual dip southwards, the general drainage being consequently in the same direction. On the north of Berkshire side the drainage is in the opposite direction, or towards the Kennet. Here the dip of the chalk is more abrupt than on the south side.

The Upper Test, or Bourne Valley, with its tributaries, are the chief lines of drainage to that portion of the range extending from Walbury to Beacon Hill.

The district consists of Upper and Lower Chalk, the former abounding in flints, the latter being flintless, or containing only occasional nodules. The Upper Chalk is hardly so fine and soft as in some districts, the Sussex Upper Chalk, for instance; and in some cuttings it has a slightly brownish tinge, which is probably due to saturation with water, wet chalk being always more clayey looking than dry. The Upper Chalk of this district would have continued as a sealed book, but for the timely exposure of a portion of it in section by the excavations, now for some time in operation, on the iron-way from London to Exeter. The portion of which my attention in fossil-collecting has been directed, extends for about three miles, from Whitchurch, eastward, to the Devil's Dyke, near Andover, westward. In short, about one mile of chalk on each side of the Test Valley from Chapmansford, at which point the railway crosses the valley. The excavation during this short distance passes through a series of chalk undulations, the depth in the deepest cutting being about 30ft. perpendicular from the surface. The layers of flints follow the same horizontal planes as the chalk, with few exceptions, where the uniformity is broken by the flints being thrown out of their lines of stratification. In these places the chalk has a disturbed, rubbly appearance, for a considerable depth, and is much fissured, the cracks being filled with clay and flint-gravel washed in from the surface. From the clay, water containing iron has infiltrated the chalk, veining it in various directions with reddish-ochreous lines. Fossils taken from these places are usually broken, and very rotten.

With such a favourable opportunity for collecting, the fossils are by no means plentiful, although, as will be seen by the subjoined list, they furnish a tolerable variety of species. It should be remarked that they do not occur indiscriminately mingled in the chalk, but appear to be present in zones, different kinds of remains predominating at different sections; while at intervals there is an almost total absence of organic remains. Following this generalization, the chalk at Whitchurch, which is best observed at a large whiting factory, is peculiar for the abundance of sponge remains, not in the chalk itself, but almost confined to the nodular flints. About a mile from Whitchurch, westward, at the cutting near New-Barn, and occupying the short space of about forty yards in length at the base of the section, Echini of a good many species are abundant. A little further on and *Encrinites* predominate, with small *Zoophytes*. Then follows a blank for a considerable distance, till at one part of the Green-Hill cutting, on the west of the Test Valley, a few sponges, with broken valves of *Inocerami* and *Spondyli* occur. From this point to the Dyke, the chalk again becomes comparatively barren. The chief fossil distinction between the Upper and Lower Chalk is the much greater frequency of *Echinoderms* in the upper, and *Terebratulæ* in the lower cretaceous deposit.

Of the fossils demanding special notice, a few words might be said respecting fossil-wood, of which several good specimens have been met with. A large lump from the New-Barn cutting is *Coniferous*, and its tissues are quite siliceous. It has much the character of the Pine-wood from the older secondary rocks, as the Upper Oolite, from which it is thought that most of the fossil-wood of the chalk is derived. Waterworn specimens of similarly fossilized wood have been found in the white chalk of Sussex.

The *Echinoderms*, commonly known as Shepherds'-crowns—the prickly sea-urchins being their living representatives—are very well typified; but it is rarely that the test and spines are found in contiguity. An unspined sphere of *Syphosoma* is a fine specimen, seven inches in circumference. *Cidaris clavigera* and *sceptrifera* occur more frequently than any other species, and they are occasionally attended with spines. *Micraster gibba, Ananchites hœmispherica*, and *Galerites conica* are fine examples of the commoner Echini.

Representatives of another elegant tribe of fossils, the Star-fishes, are found. Some of these have simply pentagonal bodies, the rays being reduced to mere angles. They are popularly known as "cushion-stars." Remains of such in good form are rare here, although detached angles, with marginal plates, and ossicles of the disk, are not unfrequently distributed in lumps of chalk, and attached to the surface of flints. Tolerably good examples of the commoner species, *uncatus* and *Parkinsoni*, are found. Of the Star-fishes with extended arms, one specimen only has been discovered, and this is quite one in miniature, it being almost a microscopic *Ophiura serrata*. The little fellow, with his flexible rays, lies contorted on a bit of chalk of about the dimensions of a sixpence. It is a very graceful species, the disk being small, and the serrated arms long and whip-like—the serrations being due to the plates of the skeleton overlapping each other like the tiles on a house.

A few detached plates, and portions of a stem of *Pentacrinus*, are all that have been found of this species; but *Apiocrinus* is more abundant, one lump of chalk of great size occurring with a quantity of diffused ossicles, broken stems, heads, and arm-digitations of this interesting sea-lily. The men working on the railway appear to be familiar with this species under the name of "bottle." The ossicles or joints of the Pentacrinite are more beautiful objects than those of the Apiocrinite, or Pear-lily—the former being pentagonal, as its name implies, while in the latter the plates are round or oval.

Fish remains are chiefly represented with teeth, although jaws with maxillary teeth of two species, for which I have no name, have occurred. The teeth of *Corax, Otodus, Lamna*, and *Oxyrhina* are sharp, death-inflicting instruments; the Otodus tooth having lesser teeth at its bass to render its destructive powers more deadly. *Ptychodus* teeth, on the contrary, although equally well adapted for the purposes for which they were made, are flattish, or more or less conical, and fluted, and are in small squarish blocks, with which the mouth and palate of the fish were paved, to enable them to crush shell-fish and sea-urchins.

The *Bryozoa* specified in the list are of almost microscopic minuteness, and are generally found encrusting the surfaces of other shells. From their manner of attaching themselves in irregular clusters to other objects, they have received the name of "sea-mosses," or "mats." Those mentioned under the heads of *Flustra, Escharina*, &c., were found on the tests of sea-urchins, and when examined with a common hand-glass look like lace or crochét work; while *Alecto ramea* spreads itself over shells in the form of delicate sprays, branching out in various directions.

Foraminiferous remains again are very frequently microscopic, and are so minute that millions are required to make up a single cubic inch of chalk. When powerfully magnified they are found to appear in a variety of shapes, some of them having much the appearance of Ammonite shells. Until recently, when their life history was less known, they were placed by naturalists with Gasteropodous and other shells. Many rocks, as well as the deep sea-beds in all parts of the world, are composed of microscopic bodies, of which the *Foraminifera* form a large part. And as chalk is a deep-sea deposit, it is not surprising that the bulk of it should contain a large per-centage of these remains. The ooze, or deep-sea mud brought up on the grapnel, in recovering the Atlantic cable of 1865, in mid-ocean, at a depth of over 2,000 fathoms, was found to contain abundance of foraminiferous shells in a mutilated condition, showing that they were drifted specimens. Of four slides prepared for the microscope, about three fourth of the remains were organic, the remainder amorphous. Of the organic the greater portion was composed of the genera *Rotalia* and *Textularia*, with a small per-centage of the flinty remnants of *Diatomaceæ*, chiefly *Coscinodisci*. This last is a likely form to be present in deep sea mud, inasmuch as it is one which lives freely in the ocean. A few needle-shaped sponge spicules were also observed.

Of the non-microscopic *Foraminifera, Orbitolina globularis* is an interesting example. It is found in both the upper and lower cretaceous deposits of this neighbourhood as well as in flint, but is more common in the Upper Chalk. In size it varies from that of a pea to a large nut, and is sometimes partially bored, and occasionally entirely perforated; and as it makes its way from the chalk-flints into the drift-gravel, it is thought, being occasionally perforated, to have been used by the early flint-working people of the drift-period to form necklaces, and hence it has been named the "fossil-bead." In an article on the Foraminifera, in the "*Annals of Natural History*" for 1860, the following occurs relative to the so-called "beads":—"In some of the figured specimens of *Orbitolini globularis* the not unusual hole in the base is indicated. Occasionally individuals are perforated by a more or less irregular tubular cavity. The roundness of the specimens, and their holes and tubular cavities, appear to have suggested to the old 'flint-folk' of the valley of the Somme that they might be used for beads; for such perforated *Orbitolinæ* are frequent in the gravels that yield the flint axes." I am not aware that there are any reasons for supposing that these little objects ever were adopted as ornaments by the ancient Celts, although, as in the case of other uncivilized races, they doubtless availed themselves of any pretty natural objects for that purpose which came in their way. The more likely suggestion as to the way the holes in the Orbitolinæ occurred is that they grew around the stem of some marine plant.

Chalk fossils have, however, furnished examples of the application made of them by pre-historic tribes, joints of Pentacrinites and a Cidaris having been discovered in tumuli in the neighbourhood of Salisbury. They were found artistically perforated, and had in all probability served as ornaments to the persons in whose tombs they were discovered.—*Flint Implements of St. Mary Bourne*, by J. Stevens. London: Tennant.

TUMBLERS.

THE Rev. E. S. Dixon, in "The Dovecote and the Aviary," in his usually pleasant and lively style, thus describes the habits of the ordinary flying Tumbler:—

"Of all the Doves that cleave the air, give me, *in its unsophisticated and vulgarly bred state*, the pretty little Tumbler. Birds at two or three shillings the pair are better than those at two or three guineas, in spite of the 'Treatise;' the learned author of which we may magnanimously gainsay, without fear of contradiction, as he is long since quiet in his grave. The Tumbler, whether you Frenchify it as the *Pigeon Calbutant*, or Latinize it as the *Columba gyratrix*, is sure to attract notice for its intrinsic excellencies. Do you want a bird to eat? It is as good as any! a merit, though a humble one. It breeds as freely, and with as little trouble; and there is nothing so neat and trim as it is among domestic birds, not even the most perfect of the Sebright Bantams. With its little round head and patting red feet, it is exactly a feathered Goody Two-shoes. And then, its performances in the air! beating all the *Cordes Volantes*, or Tight-rope Diavoli, into disgraceful inferiority. It is decidedly the most accomplished member of the aërial ballet. Pirouettes, capers, *tours de force* and *pas d'agilité*, all come alike in turn. Other pigeons certainly can take any course in the air, from a straight line, that would satisfy Euclid as being the shortest distance between two points, to circles and ellipses, that remind us of the choreal orbits of the planets round the sun; but the Tumbler, while it is rapidly wheeling past some sharp corner in a tightly compressed parabola, seems occasionally to tie a knot in the air through mere fun; and in its descents from aloft, to weave some intricate braid, or whip-lash. This latter performance, I suspect, is quite a *leger-de-vol*, or sleight of wing; the bird does now and then tumble heels over head, and perform somersets, which the best clown at Astley's would be unwilling to risk at the same altitude above *terra firma*—for example, on the tip of a cathedral spire, or in the car of a balloon—but many of these intricate weavings are the result of some trick, best known to the performer, the real solution of which may be suspected to be the non-coincidence of the apparent centre of gravity of the bird with its real one. The Indian jugglers have a similar feat, in throwing a ball in a *spiral* course instead of in an acute parabola, more or less approaching to a vertical straight line; and the laws of motion would assure us that, with a *homogeneous* ball, such a feat is impossible, under the existing circumstances of the universe. But take a large *hollow* spherical shell, heavily loaded internally at *one* point of its circumference with lead, so that the centre of gravity of the mass is by no means in the centre of the hollow sphere, and a clever juggler, by a dexterous twist, will make it play strange freaks. Just so the wings and tail of the Tumbler are made to follow the impulse which themselves have given, and to revolve round the solid body of the bird, in seemingly the most unaccountable fashion.

"Our birds have all been shut up over night, so to-day let us have a morning performance, by special desire. Terpsichore, the saltatory Muse, belongs as much to air as to earth. House-tops, or better, tree-tops, shall be the boards of our rustic opera-stage; clouds shall be the wings; the blue sky, the flies; the rising sun shall do his best to fill the place of the gas in the footlights; the orchestra are selected from the *élite* of Cocks and Hens, Ducks and Geese, with China Geese for the wind instruments and ophicleides, Thrushes and Larks for first fiddles, and the Cow and Pig for a pedal bass,—though the threshing-machine in the distance best represents *that*. The audience is composed of yourself, your wife, three or four boys and girls, the nursemaid with the little one, the woman who is hanging out the week's washing in the orchard, and the gardener who is come with a wheelbarrow to fetch some columbine guano for his melon-bed. This fresh breeze is better than the smell of orange-peel; that hedge of sweet-briar is more fragrant, though less powerful than a leaky gas-pipe. The word is given; *open sesame* falls the trap; the performers appear on their little platform, for all the world like the strolling actors in front of a show at a fair, cooing, bowing, advancing, retiring, in this their *divertissement*. They plunge into their air-bath like truant school-boys into a brook during the dog-days. The respectable aldermanic Pouter swells his portly paunch to the utmost, claps his wings smartly, and sails about in circles: it seems marvellous that *he* should be able to fly at all! But that darling little Cinnamon Tumbler, what a height it is! And now, seven times, I thought I counted, it went over; but whether it was over, or under, or roundabout, it would be difficult to say. Does your neck ache? Pray do not complain of it; greater folks than us, when the Hawk and the Heron were trying to over-reach each other, had to strain their eyes and necks a great deal more to enjoy the sport, and had a chance too of scratching out the one, or breaking the other, by riding into a bramble-bush or a pit —a danger we are not likely to incur on this pleasant grass-plot.

"Tumbling in the air, on the part of good unsophisticated Tumblers, is to themselves an act of pleasure. They never do it unless they are in good health and spirits: their best performances are after being let out from a short confinement. The young Tumbler, as soon as it has gained sufficient strength of wing, finds out by some chance that it *can* tumble; it is delighted at the discovery, and goes on practising, till at last it executes the revolution with satisfaction to itself—a feat the French have not performed of late years. Often and often the young Tumbler may be seen trying to get over, but cannot nicely; the same firmness of muscle and decision of mind are required to execute that *coup*, which empower the leading men at Astley's to throw their fortieth or fiftieth somerset backwards, and enable the *première danseuse* at the opera to drop from the air, and stand for a second or two in an impossible attitude on tiptoe. Beginners are incapable of such excellence."—*Pigeons*, by W. B. Tegetmeier. London: Routledge.

SOMETHING ABOUT JELLY-FISHES.

THE loiterer by the sea-side may have noticed in his rambles on the beach certain gelatinous substances left by the retreating tide. An interest excited by so strange a sight may have prompted a closer examination, and yet recognising nothing tangible or definite in the structure of these shapeless bodies, a desire has been really awakened to know something about them. We will try to satisfy this curiosity by giving a brief account of a few of our more common Jelly-fishes; for these shapeless lumps of jelly, seen stranded on our beaches, are really animals, assuming the most graceful and symmetrical forms in the water.

The Jelly-fishes, or Medusæ, have long excited the attention of naturalists from their singular structure, and the wonderful changes occurring during their growth.

While in the higher expressions of animal life the anatomist may puzzle over the intricacies of a complicated organization of the Jelly-fishes, he is at first more perplexed to find anything like organization in their parts, though they are really highly organized compared with animals still lower in the scale. So transparent are some, that one can hardly detect their presence in the water, and so largely does the sea-water enter into their composition, that certain kinds when dried lose ninety-nine one hundredths of their own weight.

Péron and Lesuer, two distinguished French naturalists, who, in the early part of this century made a voyage around the globe, thus summed up the results of their combined observations on these animals. "The substance of a Medusa is wholly resolved, by a kind of instantaneous fusion, into a fluid analogous to sea-water; and yet the most important functions of life are effected in bodies that seem to be nothing more, as it were, than coagulated water. The multiplication of these animals is prodigious, and we know nothing certain respecting their mode of generation. They may acquire dimensions of many feet in diameter, and weigh, occasionally, from fifty to sixty pounds; and their system of nutrition escapes us. They execute the most rapid and continued motions; and the details of their muscular system are unknown.

"Their secretions seem to be extremely abundant; but we perceive nothing satisfactory as to their origin. They have a kind of very active respiration; its real seat is a mystery. They seem extremely feeble, but fishes of large size are daily their prey. One would imagine their stomachs incapable of any kind of action on these latter animals: in a few moments they are digested. Many of them contain internally considerable quantities of air, but whether they imbibe it from the atmosphere, extract it from the ocean, or secrete it from within their bodies, we are equally ignorant. A great number of these Medusæ are phosphorescent, and glare amidst the gloom of night like globes of fire; yet the nature, the principle, and the agents of this wonderful property remain to be discovered. Some sting and inflame the hand that touches them; but the cause of this power is equally unknown."

Professor Richard Owen quotes these "lively paradoxes" to show the progress made since then in clearing up many points that were obscure at their time, and to show that even the skilful naturalist, with abundant material at hand, may plod on with uncertainty unless aided by the higher powers of the microscope. Recent works published by Professors Agassiz and Clark, and Mr. A. Agassiz, have detailed very fully the anatomy and classification of our native species.

The Jelly-fishes of our coast are represented by numerous globular and disk-like animals of gelatinous texture, more or less transparent, having certain appendages, consisting either of longitudinal bands of vibrating fringes, as in one order; or, as in another order, having appendages surrounding the mouth, and others, thread-like, hanging from the margin of the disk. The parts most conspicuous within the body are the ovaries, or egg-sacks, the stomach, and certain tubes running from the stomach to the periphery of the body.

These animals are apparently radiated in their structure; at all events, it is difficult in certain groups to distinguish a right and left side, and for this reason they are called Radiated animals, and form one of the three classes of the branch RADIATA.

The Jelly-fishes of our coast are common in our harbours and inlets, where the water is fresh and pure from the ocean. A very ready and convenient way to collect them is to moor your boat on the shady side of a wharf where the reflected rays of the sun are avoided, and, as the tide sweeps gently past, to dip them as they are borne along by the current. Some little practice is necessary to discern the smaller kinds, for many species are very minute, and other species, though of good size, are nevertheless hard to distinguish on account of their extreme transparency. They may be dipped from the water with a tin dipper, though a wide-mouthed glass jar is better for this purpose. As they are secured, they may be poured into a wooden pail for assortment and examination at home; or, better, a large glass jar, carried on purpose to hold them, may be filled at once, as too frequent changes destroy them.

Some species are very hardy, and may be kept alive for weeks, while others live only a few hours, gradually diminishing in size till they appear to melt away in the water.

Among the more common forms met with on our coast is the *Pleurobrachia*. Words fail in describing the beauty and singularity of this Jelly-fish. Conceive a globular body the size of a walnut or larger, but perfectly transparent, having eight bands of rapidly vibrating fringes surrounding the body, running from one pole to the other like the ridges on a walnut, and two thread-like appendages, festooned with hundreds of shorter threads, trailing out behind the body like the tail of a comet, and you have a general idea of this Jelly-fish.

The zones of vibrating fringes act like so many little oars, and impel the body through the water. At times, only the fringes on one side are in motion, and then the body rotates in the water like a vital globe. Anon, the different zones alternate in action, and the body describes a spiral course in the water. The most beautiful prismatic hues are exhibited when these fringes are in motion, and these brilliant changing colours often lead to their detection in the water. The long, thread-like appendages, already mentioned, are the most wonderful portion of the structure of this Jelly-fish. They are lined with hundreds of smaller threads, which start at right angles from the main threads, and are all of the extremest tenuity. The distance these appendages can be projected from the body, the instantaneous manner in which they are drawn within the body, and the perfect control the animal manifests in their movements seems incredible, until the movements have been actually witnessed. When contracted, these appendages occupy a space of exceeding minuteness, and when projected from the body seem to run out as a cable runs from a ship. We have sought in vain for any definite solution of the function of these threads, and are compelled to offer one derived from our own observations. Beside the locomotive power derived from the longitudinal zones of fringes, the body will be seen to oscillate to and fro, this motion being produced by the alternate contraction and relaxation of these threads, the resistance offered to the water by the sudden contraction of the expanded threads being sufficient to oscillate the body. The Jellyfish in question, unlike most members of the class, swim with the mouth upward, and the appendages start from the pole opposite the mouth; and since the mouth is unprovided with any organs whereby to grasp food, the mouth has the power of sweeping back and forth in the water by the oscillations of the body, affording greater chances of coming in contact with their food. It has the power of seizing little shrimp-like animals, and a singular sight it is to see this Jelly-fish, with its repast perfectly visible within its transparent body.

There are two other forms of Jelly-fishes not uncommon in our waters, which have the zones of locomotive fringes, but have no trailing appendages, as in the species just described. One of these forms is called Bolina, and is somewhat larger than Pleurobrachia, being pear-shaped, and the larger end divided into two lobes which surround the mouth. These lobes have the power of expanding and contracting, and the contour of the animal is materially altered by their movements. They may sometimes be seen gaping wide, disclosing the mouth, and ready to entrap its food, and again so contracted that the mouth is quite hidden.

Another form called *Idyia* is long and cylindrical like a tube rounded and closed at one end, the other abrupt and open; the open end constitutes the mouth—in fact, it is hardly more than a locomotive stomach. This Jelly-fish has more consistency than those heretofore described, and is quite opaque. At certain seasons of the year they are pinkish in colour. An individual of this species, when confined with Pleurobrachia, soon manifests its carnivorous propensities by attacking, and often swallowing the Pleurobrachia whole. It does not appear daunted if its victim proves larger than itself, but slowly, patiently engulfs its victim; and a curious sight it is to see the Idyia directly after this feat is performed, presenting the appearance of a tight skin drawn around the innermost Jelly-fish, though in a short time its food is digested, and the Idyia resumes its normal shape, and not in the least augmented in size. It probably requires a dozen or more of such game for an ordinary lunch. This statement will not be wondered at, if the experiment is tried of drying a specimen of Pleurobrachia on a white card, and finding nothing left but a few crystals of salt. The vitality of these Jelly-fishes is remarkable; they can be cut in several pieces, and yet they will remain alive for a long time in the water; and one naturalist, after having cut an Idyia in half longitudinally, observed one half to enfold and digest another Jelly-fish.

The three forms thus far described are common representatives of an order of Jelly-fishes called *Ctenophoræ*, or Comb-bearers, the fringes or paddles having been compared by some writers to the teeth of a comb. These fringes form a distinguishing trait of the order. The members of this order are reproduced directly from eggs.

We will now consider another order of Jelly-fishes called *Discophoræ*, or disk-like Jelly-fishes, since the form of many creatures present a disk-like appearance. Members of this order are very conspicuous in the water, owing to their large size, their opacity, and the distinctness of their egg-pouches. They have no zones of locomotive fringes, but hanging below the disk and surrounding the mouth are numerous appendages, and surrounding the border of the disk is seen a delicate fringe of threads interrupted at regular intervals by little dots called eyes. These Jelly-fishes swim in the water by successive expansions and contractions of the disk, making a motion something like the motion made by the partial closing and opening of an umbrella. This motion is very leisurely performed, and the animal appears drifted by the currents and eddies with but little power to direct its course.

Our most common species, the *Aurelia*, occurs abundantly in our bays, sometimes in vast multitudes. When full-grown they measure from twelve to fifteen inches in diameter.

Another form, called *Cyanea*, often attains an immense size. Mr. A. Agassiz gives an account of one that measured seven feet across the disk, and whose appendages stretched out to the length of one hundred and twelve feet; their average size, however, is about one-third the dimensions just given.

The nettling sensation produced by certain Jelly-fishes, when brought in contact with the naked body, has long excited the attention of naturalists. The Cyanea is one of the most formidable in this respect, and Prof. Edward Forbes describes an English species as "the terror of tender-skinned bathers. With its broad, tawny, festooned, and scalloped disk, often a full foot or more across, it flaps its way through the yielding waters, and drags after it a long train of riband-like arms, and seemingly interminable tails, marking its course when the body is far away from us. Once tangled in its trailing 'hair,' the unfortunate, who has recklessly ventured across the graceful monster's path, too soon writhes in prickly torture. Every struggle but binds the poisonous threads more firmly round his body, and then there is no escape; for, when the winder of the fatal net finds his course impeded by the terrified human wrestling in its coils, he, seeking no combat with the mightier biped, casts loose his envenomed arms and swims away. The amputated weapons, severed from their parent body, vent vengeance on the cause of their destruction, and sting as fiercely as if their original proprietor itself gave the word of attack." Peculiar oval cells, each containing a little filament capable of protrusion, have been supposed to be the seat of this nettling sensation. These are called urticating cells, and the whole class of Jelly-fishes are called *Acalephs*, or Sea-nettles, from this peculiar property. These stinging cells cover the surface of the body and appendages, though, strange enough, there are many species possessing these cells that produce no stinging sensation whatever.

The strangest feature in the history of certain Jelly-fishes belonging to the order *Discophoræ*, as the Aurelia, for instance, is their wonderful mode of reproduction. It would require too long a time to detail the successive steps made before the whole truth was known regarding the development of these Jelly-fishes. How the successive stages were described by different zoologists as entirely distinct animals, until at last it was proved that they all represented the different stages of growth of one animal. The Aurelia, for example, gives origin to little locomotive eggs; these, swimming in shoals, finally effect lodgments on the rocks, one end becoming attached, and the other throwing out little tentacles. In this condition they resemble miniature Polyps. Gradually they increase in length, and little transverse seams, or constrictions, appear on the sides of the body, these constrictions deepening, and their edges becoming scalloped. Finally, the seams have deepened to such an extent that their appearance have been compared to a pile of saucers, and at last they become separated one after the other, each turning upside down, and swimming off free Jelly-fishes. In this stage they are called Ephyra, and are entirely unlike their parent in appearance. By the fall they will have obtained their adult form, and a diameter of twelve or more inches.

By far the greater number of our smaller Jelly-fishes belong to another order called *Hydroids*, and pass through phases of growth equally as strange as those above recounted. The limits of our paper will allow only a few words on this group. On the rocks at low water, and on floating weed, little moss-like tufts will be found in abundance. This plant-like growth, when examined under a lens, will be seen active with life. The ends of the little twigs and offshoots appear as little bell-shaped cups, with tentacles studding the free ends like the plates of a flower; these are the fixed individuals, and are the purveyors of the community. In the spring-time little capsules will be noticed on the twigs, within which are to be seen minute globular bodies, to be finally set free by the rupture of the capsule, as free swimming Jelly-fishes. Others bud directly from the twig and drop off singly, as in *Coryne*. These are found by thousands in spring time. Not only do these free Jelly-fishes bud from fixed communities, but in one species young ones bud from the Jelly-fish itself, as in *Lizzia*, and certain others where the young bud from the stomach. All these Hydroid Jelly-fishes produce eggs, which again give rise to plant-like communities.—Edward S. Morse, in the *American Naturalist* for July.

THE DOUBLE COCOA-NUT.

FIFTY-FIVE years ago, on visiting the museum of the College at St. Andrew's, in Fifeshire, amongst other curiosities the keeper took down from a shelf a black lumpy body about a foot in length, and nearly as much in width, and holding it in both hands told me it was a "Pomegranate." I had read of Pomegranates in the Bible when at school, and in dread of the awful words "take him down," had learned to spell the word correctly; but I then had no idea a Pomegranate was like the hulls of two toy boats fastened together by their gunwales, such being the idea to which I compared the object before me. It was not for a number of years after this that I saw or learned anything more about Pomegranates, but on gaining a knowledge of botany I became sceptical of the St. Andrew's Pomegranate being the same as those spoken of in the Bible; and I at length found it was the Double Cocoa-nut.

The principal facts relating to the structure and appearance of this singular palm have frequently been given in your columns, where also the peculiar perforated bowl or socket in which the base of the trunk is immersed has been more than once figured and described. The following observations relating to the mode of germination of the seed may serve in a measure to explain the formation of this bowl.

In a few weeks after a fresh nut is placed in a tan bed, or other warm open material, a white body about the thickness of the finger is seen protruding from between the lobes of the nut, which quickly elongates downwards in a nearly perpendicular direction (in its native country it is said at an angle of 45°), attaining the length of about 2 feet, the end thickening and becoming fusiform. This part contains the true embryo, and may be considered the placenta, and on its bursting on one side, the growth of the embryo commences by the protrusion of the first leaf, which is succeeded by others; roots are at the same time produced. During this process of growth the nut continues to supply nutriment to the young plant through the long cord or funiculus as it may be called, and which it continues to do for several years, the plant gradually increasing in size, and the roots in number and strength, so as ultimately to become sufficient for its support: the funiculus gradually drying up, but not so the point to which the embryo is attached. All Palms germinate in the same manner as above stated, the embryo retaining its connection with the end of the funiculus, which becomes a progressing axis of development of leaves and roots, creeping on the surface of the ground, or burrowing downwards at a more or less acute angle, and becoming analogous to a rhizome. This it continues to do until the plant attains its majority (which is often not before many years), that is, when it has matured its ascending axis, the rhizome remaining in the form of a spur-like stump, even after the plants have attained many years of age. This rhizome structure may assist in explaining the manner of the formation of the socket of the Lodoicea. When I had the opportunity of observing the germination of the nuts, I was not then aware of the bowl appendage, therefore my attention was not directed to that special point, and consequently I cannot speak from direct observation as to how it originates. Seeing that the embryo of Palms continues its connection with the placenta, it would seem that in the case of the Lodoicea the connection of the embryo continues in the lower cavity of the placenta, in which it continues to grow, and through which it receives nutriment, until the seed nut is exhausted, during which time roots have been doing their duty—and the connection of the sac still being continued, it would appear that a reflow of sap from the plant into the sac takes place, which grows with the growth of the plant, and becomes penetrated with the stiff cord-like roots; and thus the holes and tubes are found. Therefore this socket may be viewed as of the same nature of growth as the rhizome of other Palms, differing only in the original growth of the plant being central instead of lateral, and retaining its attachment through life. In the large bowl at Kew the point of attachment is indicated by a few inches of rough surface in the centre at the bottom, and destitute of holes. There is much, however, yet to be learned on this subject, and which can only be obtained by examining plants at different stages of their early growth.

During the last 50 years many nuts of this Palm have come to this country, eight of which germinated at Kew under my own observation, but a want of knowledge of the early nature of the plant, and the circumstances detailed above, must be admitted as an excuse for our not having succeeded in establishing a plant of Lodoicea. This is in a great measure due to the period they take to pass through what may be called their infant state (which may be considered not less than 10 years), and to the want of proper arrangements to keep them in one position, as well as to the fluctuations of heat and moisture during that time. It is impossible, even under the most favourable circumstances, to say what number of years will be required before an ascending trunk can be formed, but certainly it cannot be less than 50.

A plant established in the Mauritius Garden, known to be 30 years old, has still the appearance of a young plant, having numerous healthy leaves rising from the ground, but none of them exceeding 5 feet in height. About 16 years ago a plant growing in a small barrel was sent from the Mauritius, the largest leaf being from 5 to 6 feet in length, but unexpanded. In this state it was forwarded to Kew, but unfortunately it had no protection during the voyage to England, the leaf not even being supported, so that it was twisted with every breeze, and on its arrival the centre of the plant was found to be completely destroyed. A nice plant, properly secured in a large case, was also sent by Mr. Duncan, the late Director of the Mauritius Botanic Garden, but the long voyage proved fatal to it. Had it not been for these untoward events, Kew might by this time have been possessed of Double Cocoa-nut plants. The only plant of it known to me in this country is one lately sprouted in the Botanic Garden, Liverpool, under the skilful management of Mr. Tyerman; and, the nature of the plant being better known, success may now be expected.—J. Smith, Ex-Curator, Royal Botanic Gardens, Kew, in *Gardener's Chronicle*, July 27th.

SNAKES.

IT was, I think, in the summer of 1827 that I first began to collect snakes. I was then stationed with my regiment at Bareilly, and not far from my bungalow was a small *jhil*, or swamp, along the margin of which, defying malarious influences and a burning sun, I have passed hour after hour, continually eyeing every inch of ground in search of the numerous snakes that harboured there. My tackle consisted of a large jar filled with spirits of wine, into which the smaller species were plunged as soon as caught; a good-sized basket, to the top of which was fastened a linen bag without a bottom and the mouth secured by a string, for the larger kind. In my hand I carried a long, thin rod, to the end of which was attached a strong noose or slip-knot. When a snake was discovered basking in the sun, I cautiously and silently approached, until near enough to pass the noose gently over the head, when with a sudden jerk it tightened round the reptile's neck, and from the immediate expansion of the jaws was prevented from slipping off again. A little practice at this kind of fishing soon made me so expert, that I seldom missed the exact spot behind the head, but if this occurred, the reptile would manage to wriggle through the loop and escape among the weeds of the swamp. Once properly secured, however, it would throw its tail over the end of the rod and coil up in a knot, so as to be easily conveyed either into the jar or into the basket. In this manner, at the end of about two years, I had made a very extensive collection, which was afterwards extended to about 200 bottles of beautifully preserved reptiles of different kinds, by the purchase of a large number of specimens from a friend who had once amused himself in a similar manner.

This fine collection was unfortunately destroyed during a long illness, which compelled me to repair to Calcutta, and finally to Europe. On my return to India I found my regiment stationed in Western India, among the Bheels. Here I first fell in with the python, or rock snake, but for a long time I could obtain a sight of none longer than from 6 to 9 feet, while my ambition was to procure one from 25 to 30 feet in length. Time flew on, and I began to think my wishes in this respect would never be gratified, when I unexpectedly fell in with a python under somewhat awkward circumstances. I had gone out among my friends the Bheels for a few days' shooting, coursing, and butterfly-collecting, and had one morning passed several hours much to my satisfaction, when I began to think it high time to recruit exhausted nature by diving among the contents of a large basket of provisions provided for the occasion. A convenient spot was soon found near the foot of some low hills, where there was a small grove of mango-trees, and near them, growing out of the crevices of some enormous outlying masses of green-stone, were two or three large bur or burgut trees (*Ficus indica*), covered with fruit, among which a troop of monkeys (*Inuus rhesus*) were committing tremendous havoc. Selecting the nearest burgut as affording ample shade, the monkeys beat a speedy retreat to the clump of mango-trees hard by, at the edge of which was a narrow strip of tolerably high jungle grass. The tree I had selected sprang up from the crevices of a rock at its base, and here I sat me down, without observing a hole which, passing under the side of the rock, was, as we afterwards found, continued into the hollow trunk of the old burgut from beneath.

There was a space, perhaps of two feet between my back and the rock, and fortunate for me that it was so. My Bheel friends and I had nearly discussed the contents of my provision basket, a task in which they are always ready to assist, when I was startled by feeling something rubbing against my back; and on cautiously looking round, I beheld to my horror the object of my lengthened search, gliding along from the before-mentioned hole between my back and the rock. At the first glance, I candidly confess my blood ran cold from crown to heel, and the impulse was to make a sudden bolt of it, the very worst thing I could have been guilty of; in the next moment my knowledge of the reptile's habits, and a glance at my Bheel guides who were sitting opposite to me, and who on perceiving my consternation had turned their attention to the spot, at once convinced me my only chance of safety lay in remaining stock-still until the reptile had passed on. The eyes of my savage guides were literally starting from their sockets, while at the same time each kept a finger pressed upon his lips enjoining silence and immobility. In a few moments the snake had passed on towards the narrow grassy belt that intervened between the margin of the mango clump and my position; and as soon as his head was fairly concealed by the grass, the Bheels both darted off to an open field; and I, picking up my gun, which perhaps luckily for me had been unloaded, followed their example, and prepared for action. I had loaded one barrel, and was in the act of giving the last home-thrust to the ball in the other, when our ears were suddenly assailed by the most discordant squeaks and screams from the monkeys in the mango clump, the whole troop being in frantic motion and agitated by the greatest alarm, all stretching forward their heads to one particular spot, which said as plainly as words could have done, "There he is." Hastening to the spot where the python had disappeared, I cautiously peered through the long grass to get a sight of him, not knowing whether the clamour was occasioned by his having seized a monkey, or whether he was merely waiting for his prey. We soon perceived him, however, lying at the foot of a large tree, round the lower trunk of which his tail was partially coiled, while the rest of his body (which must have measured between 14 and 15 feet) was coiled, fold upon fold, around the yet convulsively-quivering body of a fine old monkey.

Seeing all was now safe, I called to my syce to bring the horse blankets and halter; the former was quickly spread upon the ground beside the snake, while the syce and I with some difficulty succeeded in removing the coil of the tail from the tree, and then rolled over the snake and his prey together into the blanket, which was speedily folded round them, tying the corners together and making all secure with the halter. I then started off the Bheels to a neighbouring village for some men, a large basket, and some more ropes, hoping almost against hope that they would return before the python relaxed his hold, which I knew well he would not do while a muscle quivered or an atom of life remained in the monkey. The Bheels returned more speedily than I had anticipated, and having procured a large open basket or tokree, the snake in the bundle was rolled into it and the whole well tied up and made secure, as we thought, with the extra ropes. A pole being tied across the basket, five or six men placed the load upon their shoulders and at once started at a jog-trot towards my tent, which was pitched at about half a mile from us. As soon as they were fairly off, I mounted my horse and galloped off to make what preparations I could for the reception of my long-coveted prize; and having cleared out a beer-chest as his temporary abode, I walked to meet my sable companions. I had not gone far, however, when I saw two men tearing over the ground towards me as if for their very lives, jabbering and gesticulating all the while in a most frantic manner; and it soon appeared that the python, on uncoiling from his dead prey, had contrived to push his head out of the blanket and the basket too, which the Bheels behind no sooner perceived than they summarily dropped the basket, and ran back to their village at the top of their speed. Thinking it quite possible, however, that the snake might have pushed his small head out of the blanket without being able to extricate his thick body, I walked on to the spot where the Bheels had dropped him; here we had to proceed with caution, until the trail of the body across the soft earth of a recently ploughed field showed that the monster had actually effected his escape into the long, coarse jungle-grass into which it was not safe to follow him, and although I offered fifty rupees to anyone who would recapture him, I never saw my friend again, and doubt much if the Bheels ever ventured a second time into such an uncanny neighbourhood. Some years after this when I repaired, with a shattered constitution to Mussooree in the Himalaya, after the Afghan campaign, I at length procured a python measuring 18 feet 9 inches in length. It was a magnificent reptile in appearance, but unfortunately had a disease in the gums which is not uncommon with these snakes, and which prevents them from seizing their prey. For six months my specimen ate nothing, and then, being no doubt desperately hungry, it contrived to dispose of a hare. After this, for seven months more it refused to feed, although perfectly active and vigorous. The winter setting in at this time, the reptile in its famished state had no strength to bear up against the cold, and died after having lived more than thirteen months upon a single hare. During the time I possessed this snake it twice escaped from its cage; once, however, it had evidently been let out by a native who had a grudge against me, and as a punishment, when we proceeded to search for the animal I made this man head the column, which he did in dire dismay, as every one assured him the snake would seize and swallow him. At last however, I took the lead myself, and soon discovered the snake basking in the morning sun among some ferns. Ropes and blanket were then brought forward, and a nooze having been cast over his head, and drawn tight, the most desperate struggle began, the animal's streng thactually dragging more than a dozen men after it, until we contrived to bring the end of the rope round the trunk of a tree, which at last brought the monster to a standstill. It then darted furiously at anyone who attemped to pass other ropes around it, and we could do nothing with it until a net was brought and dexterously cast over it, in which it soon entangled itself to such a degree as to become harmless, when we tightened the ropes and, rolling the snake into a stable blanket, carried him with some difficulty to his cage. This species, known as the *Python molurus* of Linnæus, is exceedingly numerous in the Dehra Doon, below Mussooree on the south, but the large ones are not often procurable. Of the smaller individuals, from 6 to 10 feet in length, I have sometimes been offered as many as twenty in the course of a week. The people who catch them are evidently gipseys, living apart as they do elsewhere: after showing these snakes for the purpose of gain, they cook and eat them, as indeed they do most other wild animals. In their hunting expeditions they employ both nets and dogs trained for the purpose; the latter hunt about silently in the tall grass and bamboo jungles skirting the rocky Siwalik range on the south of the Doon, and only "give tongue" when a snake is discovered. The men then advance and secure the reptile in their nets and blankets. The winter is the best hunting season, as the snakes are then found "*chez eux*" under rocks, in tufts of grass or bamboos, etc., while in the rainy summer they are wandering far and wide.—T. H., *Land and Water*, Aug. 10th.

MADREPORES.

THERE are various classes and species of madrepores, but they all possess the same nature, being, as is generally believed, fossilised marine animals, or rather the *fossilised work* of marine animals. The number of years which have elapsed since the skilful artisans performed their work, is uncertain; in all probability it was before the time when "Adam delved and Eve span;" but upon this subject I have neither space nor inclination to enter; it is sufficient for my purpose to say that the marine architects were once endowed with life and breath, and that their work is now literally, as the saying is, "turned into stone."

When in the rough state, madrepores might frequently be passed by unnoticed, and even if picked up, they would possess but few attractions in the eyes of casual observers, and a most valuable specimen might be thrown away; but once let the fossil be cut and polished, its wonders and beauties are then fully displayed, and could scarcely fail to be appreciated, to some extent, even by those who consider themselves, as "Punch" says, "Much above that sort of thing." As I have already mentioned, there are many kinds of madrepores: each class is divided and sub-divided; consequently the varieties are almost innumerable; but those most generally known and sought after are "feathers," "suns," "stars," "sponges," "birds'-eyes," "pin-points," and "honeycombs."

Madrepore-hunting, like most other pursuits and employments, has its drawbacks as well as its delights; very frequently does the collector return home wearied, and perhaps dispirited from a search of many hours, during which time he has found scarcely anything to reward him for his trouble; but patience and perseverance are invaluable companions, and in due course of time may carry all before them.

I believe madrepores are to be found in many parts of the world. I have found them in comparative abundance on the south Devonshire coast; in the "Bradley Woods," situated about eight or nine miles from Teignmouth, there are very extensive quarries of "feather" and "star" madrepore; so manifold are the specimens there displayed, that it is a puzzling matter to decide which to keep and which to throw away, each quarry having its own peculiar sort. The collector feels at first quite bewildered by the mine of valuable pieces around him; his pockets are quickly filled, and as quickly emptied, as fresh wonders meet his view, and at length, finding it totally impossible to keep all, he is obliged to select a few of the best, and to turn his back resolutely on all others.

The "birds'-eye" and "sponge" madrepores are some of the most common kinds; the "honey-comb" and "pin-point" are considered more valuable, and good specimens are much prized by the collector.

Madrepores are shown to great advantage when set in silver or gold, and made into brooches, bracelets, pins, and other ornaments of a similar nature; the art of cutting and polishing these fossils is easily acquired, although lapidaries may say otherwise, and endeavour to impress upon you that it is a very intricate and mysterious business. But of course this is only natural, as, were the secret generally known and applied to a practical use, many an honest, hard-working man would be at a loss to earn his livelihood.

Live madrepores are occasionally dredged up at sea on our own shores. In Rees' Cyclopædia it is stated that "there are about 120 species scattered through the different seas on our globe, some of which are common to our coasts," and that they are "a genus of the class vermes, and order zoophyta—animals resembling a medusa; coral with lamellate star-shaped cavities;" and a little further on, the description of the live madrepore is continued thus:

"In speaking of the animal that fills the cavities of the madrepore, it is said, its feet are numerous, and terminate externally in two conical productions, which, being placed on each side of every one of the lamellæ that give the stellular form to the cavity of the coral, serve to affix the animal to the circumference of its cell, and may with propriety be considered as the instruments by which the little animal forms the lamellæ themselves. . . . . . Admitting that the formation of these corals is the work of the madrepore polype, it may be thus traced through its wonderful labours. It is found that each of the legs of the polype is provided with two processes, which are applied to each side of one of the perpendicular laminæ, while a muscular pyriform body, attached to the other end of the leg, gives to it the power of employing that motion which is necessary for the accomplishment of its task. The young polype may be considered as completing its operation by two distinct processes: the secretion and separation of carbonate of lime from sea-water conveyed through the pyriform body; and its disposition, at the moment of secretion, by the two small processes, where the economy of the animal directs. Proportioned to the number of legs possessed by the infant animal, is probably the number of perpendicular laminæ, or pillars, converging in the centre, which it begins to erect; these, when raised to a certain height, appear to be connected together by a horizontal plate of the same substance; on these the animal erects similar pillars, and places on them a covering similar to that with which he has completed the first compartment.

"Thus seem to proceed the labours of this minute artist; and as the number of its legs or instruments increase, and as they extend in length, so much the number of the perpendicular laminæ and the circumference of the horizontal plates, augment."—*Once a Week*, Aug. 10.

RATS.

THE rat is omnipresent: it is as well known in every quarter of the globe as the common house-fly; wherever food is, there it is certainly to be found. That it performs some useful purpose in the world's economy cannot be doubted—it clears away refuse that would other otherwise create a nuisance; but it is also certain that it destroys a great deal of food, and spoils more. For this reason it has no friends, and it is most remorselessly hunted to death wherever it is to be found. At Bankok, the capital of Siam, they keep rats in the house, thoroughly tame, which act as cats, keeping at a distance any of its kind that may venture to intrude. These tame rats are pretty nearly as big as young cats, and they are so domesticated, that they climb up their masters' knees and are petted, just as though they were some favourite dog. In Germany they sometimes tame a rat, and hang a bell about its neck, a plan that effectively drives away all other rats on the premises, which naturally feel astonished at such a strange ornament upon one of their own kind. By no means should it ever be attempted to get rid of rats by poison, for they creep away to die in the walls or behind wainscotting, and the consequence is that an intolerable smell is the consequence; or they will try to quench their thirst by drinking water or milk, into which, in their agony, they vomit, and the consequence is that they leave the poison behind them, to the destruction of other creatures that come and drink after them.

The ratcatcher is the most effective instrument of extermination when once they have had a lodgment in any house. But prevention is better than cure. Wherever large stores of food are kept it is necessary to place them in a state of defence against this persevering enemy, which is ever on the watch to find an entrance; for, one only fairly in, all the rats of London, or the neighbourhood at least, by some mysterious freemasonry known to rat nature, are speedily informed of the fact, and make for the promised land. The bonded wheat warehouses on the Thames are plated inside the floors with sheet iron; even the doors are covered with a like armour, and the foundations are solidly concreted and filled with pounded glass, for nothing less solid and unpleasant will stay the invading army that is for ever on the watch to sap and mine into the fortress. We have said that the Zoological Gardens is a pleasant land for rats. The quantity of food always on the floors of the animals' dens is a temptation they cannot resist. Rats and mice may be seen any day quietly feeding in the dens of the larger carnivora. The gorged lion lifts up its sleepy eye, but is far too magnanimous to interfere with the tiny partaker of its meal. Who knows? it may fancy, like its brother in the toils, that it is not too little to do it a good turn yet. But night time is the field day, if I may so speak, for the rats. They swim across the canal, and reign here supreme, and in the darkness there are a very much larger number of animals in the gardens than the Society know anything about.

The fecundity of rats is extraordinary; they begin to litter as early as six months old, and they go on for some time having four litters a year, the average number of each litter being eight. A little calculation will show that in a very few years where food is plentiful, and no destructive agency is at work, they would increase to millions; hence we see the necessity for the preventive check, in the shape of the hunting instinct which, from man downward, marks the rat for its prey. But, when driven hard, the little fellow can make a good fight for it, and give as good as it gets. Mr. Jesse tells a tale of a fight between a ferret and a rat, which proves that he can reason and manœuvre for the best fighting ground as well as any general. A gentleman, he tells us, on one occasion turned a ferret and a good-sized rat into an empty room with but one window. "Immediately upon being liberated the rat ran around the room as if searching for an exit. Not finding any means of escape he uttered a piercing shriek, and with the most prompt decision took up his station directly under the light, thus gaining over his adversary (to use the language of the duellist) the advantage of the sun. The ferret now erected its head, sniffed about, and began fearlessly to push its way towards the spot where the scent of the game was the strongest, facing the light in full front, and preparing itself with avidity to seize its prey; no sooner, however, had it approached within two feet of the watchful enemy, than the rat, again uttering a loud cry, rushed at the ferret with violence, and inflicted a severe wound upon the head and neck, which was soon shown by the blood which flowed from it. The ferret seemed astonished at the attack, and retreated with evident discomfiture, while the rat, instead of following up the advantage it had gained, instantly withdrew to its former station under the window. The ferret soon recovered the shock it had sustained, and erecting its head once more took the field. This second rencontre was in all its progress and results an exact repetition of the former—with the exception that in the rush of the rat to the conflict, the ferret appeared to be more collected, and evidently showed an inclination to get a firm hold of its enemy; the strength of the rat, however, was very great, and it again succeeded, not only in avoiding the deadly embrace of the ferret, but also in inflicting another severe wound upon its head and neck." For two hours the attack and defence went on evidently to the advantage of the rat, when the gentleman determined to see what would be the result of turning the latter from its vantage-ground. The consequence was that the rat lost confidence, which the ferret gained, and the latter speedily mastered it, not without being bitten to shreds in the encounter, over the head and muzzle. The conduct of the rat, we are told, was the same in a second encounter, in which it was victorious. This proves that under favourable circumstances it is more than a match for its ancient enemy.

We have said that in France the fur and the skin of this animal are utilised. We are told that if our prejudices were not so great, its flesh might also be used as food. The grain-fed rat is anything but coarse food, and when soldiers and sailors have been in straits for food, rats have been eaten with a relish. We are afraid, however, even if we were to suggest to poor Hodge that he may now and then make a pie out of the varmint in the wheat-rick, he would reply, "Well, maister, suppose thee try it thyself."—*Cassell's Magazine* for August.

Locusts.

There is an article of food which is used by the natives, in its proper season, and does not prepossess a European in its favour. This is the locust, the well-known insect which sweeps in such countless myriads over the land, and which does such harm to the crops and to everything that grows.

The eggs of the locust are laid in the ground, and at the proper season the young make their appearance. They are then very small, but they grow with great rapidity—as, indeed, they ought to do, considering the amount of food which they consume.

Until they have passed a considerable time in the world, they have no wings, and can only crawl and hop. The Kaffirs call these imperfect locusts "boyane," and the Dutch settlers term them "voet-gangers," or "foot-goers," because they cannot fly. Even in this stage they are terribly destructive, and march steadily onwards, consuming every green thing that they can eat.

Nothing stops them in their progress short of death, and, on account of their vast myriads, the numbers that can be killed form but an insignificant proportion of the whole army. A stream of these insects, a mile or more in width, will pass over a country, and scarcely anything short of a river will stop them. Trenches are soon filled up with their bodies, and those in the rear march over the carcases of their dead comrades. Sometimes the trenches have been filled with fire, but to no purpose, as the fire is soon put out by the locusts that come crowding upon it. As for walls, the insects care nothing for them, but surmount them, and even the very houses, without suffering a check.

When they become perfect insects and gain their wings, they proceed, as before, in vast myriads; but this time, they direct their course through the air, and not merely on land, so that not even the broadest river can stop them. They generally start as soon as the sun has dispelled the dews and warmed the air, which, in its nightly chill, paralyses them, and renders them incapable of flight and almost unable even to walk. Towards evening they always descend, and perhaps in the daytime also; and wherever they alight, every green thing vanishes. The sound of their jaws cutting down the leaves and eating them can be heard at a great distance. They eat everything of a vegetable nature. Mr. Moffatt saw a whole field of maize consumed in two hours, and has seen them eat linen, flannel, and even tobacco. When they rise for another flight, the spot which they have left is as bare as if it were desert land, and not a vestige of any kind of verdure is to be seen upon it.

A very excellent description of a flight of locusts is given by Mr. Cole, in his work on South Africa:—

"Next day was warm enough, but the wind was desperately high, and, much to my disgust, right in my face as I rode away on my journey. After travelling some ten miles, having swallowed several ounces of sand meanwhile, and been compelled occasionally to remove the sand-hills that were collecting in my eyes, I began to fall in with some locusts. At first they came on gradually and in small quantities, speckling the earth here and there, and voraciously devouring the herbage.

"They were not altogether pleasant, as they are weak on the wing, and quite at the mercy of the wind, which uncivilly dashed many a one into my face with a force that made my cheeks tingle. By degrees they grew thicker and more frequent. My progress was now most unpleasant, for they flew into my face every instant. Flung against me and my horse by the breeze, they clung to us with the tightness of desperation, till we were literally speckled with locusts. Each moment the clouds of them became denser, till at length —I am guilty of no exaggeration in saying—they were as thick in the air as the flakes of snow during a heavy fall of it; they covered the grass and the road, so that at every step my horse crushed dozens; they were whirled into my eyes and those of my poor nag, till at last the latter refused to face them, and turned tail in spite of whip and spur. They crawled about my face and neck, got down my shirt collar and up my sleeves —in a word, they drove me to despair as completely as they drove my horse to stubbornness, and I was obliged to ride back a mile or two, and claim shelter from them at a house I had passed on my route; fully convinced that a shower of locusts is more unbearable than hail, rain, snow, and sleet combined.

"I found the poor farmer in despair at the dreadful visitation which had come upon him—and well he might be so. To-day he had standing crops, a garden, and wide pasture lands in full verdure; the next day the earth was as bare all round as a macadamised road.

"I afterwards saw millions of these insects driven by the wind into the sea at Algoa Bay, and washed on shore again in such heaps, that the prisoners and coolies in the town were busily employed for a day or two in burying the bodies, to prevent the evil consequence that would arise from the putrefying of them close to the town. No description of these little plagues, or of the destruction they cause, can well be an exaggeration. Fortunately, their visitations are not frequent, as I only remember three during my five years' residence in South Africa. Huge fires are sometimes lighted round corn-lands and gardens to prevent their approach; and this is an effective preventive when they can steer their own course; but when carried away by such a wind as I have described, they can only go where it drives them, and all the bonfires in the world would be useless to stay their progress. The farmer thus eaten out of house and home (most literally) has nothing to do but to move his stock forthwith to some other spot which has escaped them— happy if he can find a route free from their devastation, so that his herds and flocks may not perish by the way."

Fortunately, their bodies being heavy in proportion to their wings, they cannot fly against the wind, and it often happens that, as in the old Scripture narrative, a country is relieved by a change of wind, which drives the insects into the sea, where they are drowned; and, as Mr. Cole observes, they were driven by the wind into his face or upon his clothes, as helplessly as the cockchafers on a windy summer evening.

Still, terrible as are the locusts, they have their uses. In the first place, they afford food to innumerable animals. As they fly, large flocks of birds wait on them, sweep among them and devour them on the wing. While they are on the ground, whether in their winged or imperfect state, they are eaten by various animals; even the lion and other formidable carnivora not disdaining so easily-gained a repast. As the cool air of the night renders the locusts incapable of moving, they can be captured without difficulty.

Even to mankind the locusts are serviceable, being a favourite article of food. It is true that these insects devour whole crops, but it may be doubted whether they do not confer a benefit on the dusky cultivators rather than inflict an injury.

As soon as the shades of evening render the locusts helpless, the natives turn out in a body, with sacks, skins, and everything that can hold the expected prey, those who possess such animals bringing pack oxen in order to bear the loads home. The locusts are swept by millions into the sacks, without any particular exertion on the part of the natives, though not without some danger, as venomous serpents are apt to come for the purpose of feeding on the insects, and are sometimes roughly handled in the darkness.

When the locusts have been brought home, they put them into a large covered pot, such as has already been described, and a little water added to them. The fire is then lighted under the pot, and the locusts are then boiled, or rather steamed, until they are sufficiently cooked. They are then taken out of the pot, and spread out in the sunbeams until they are quite dry; and when this part of the process is completed, they are shaken about in the wind until the legs and wings fall off, and are carried away just as the chaff is carried away by the breeze when corn is winnowed. When they are perfectly dry they are stored away in baskets, or placed in the granaries just as if they were corn.

Sometimes the natives eat them whole, just as we eat shrimps, and, if they can afford such a luxury, add a little salt to them. Usually, however, the locusts are treated much in the same manner as corn or maize. They are ground to powder by the mill until they are reduced to meal, which is then mixed with water, so as to form a kind of porridge. A good locust season is always acceptable to the natives, who can indulge their enormous appetites to an almost unlimited extent, and in consequence become quite fat in comparison with their ordinary appearance. So valuable, indeed, are the locusts, that if a native conjurer can make his companions believe that his incantations have brought the locusts, he is sure to be richly rewarded by them.— *Routledge's Natural History of Man.*

Volcanoes on the Moon.

Assuming the probable, or, at least, the possible, existence of active volcanoes upon the moon, it remains to be seen how the operation of such volcanoes is to be detected from our earth. The colours seen in different parts of the moon's surface are little marked, and grey or neutral-tinted regions are so prevalent that it would be very difficult to note the change of colour, produced by the downfall over large tracts, of matter ejected from erupting volcanoes. Differences of elevation produced by such downfalls afford a much more favourable object of examination. We proceed to show how lunar elevations and depressions are detected. Those of our readers who have watched the phenomenon of sunrise from the summit of a lofty mountain, will have noticed that when the summit of the mountain is in the full glory of the rising sun, the sides of the mountain are still in shadow, and that the neighbouring valleys are plunged in a yet deeper gloom. Corresponding appearances are seen when the sun is setting. Long before the mountain-tops are darkened, the level country around is shadowed over, and the obscurity of night has already settled on ravines and passes. Now, the only respect in which sunrise or sunset on a lunar mountain differs from the corresponding phenomenon on earth, lies in the fact that, owing to the want of an atmosphere, there are no half-lights—nothing but the full blaze of light reflected from parts actually shone upon by the sun, and intense blackness where his rays have not yet penetrated. The black shadows around a lunar mountain are readily seen, and a careful examination of their figure and changes of figure suffices to indicate the shape of the mountain. The approach of sunrise or sunset in the neighbourhood of the larger lunar mountains is an interesting phenomenon, which may be observed with instruments of very moderate power. But slight changes of elevation produced by volcanic agency, to be detected at all (even if observation has been directed to a particular spot), require a powerful telescope, and (which is often forgotten by the inexperienced) skill and practice in the use of the instrument. And although sunrise and sunset are slower processes in the moon than with us (the lunar day being equal in length to our lunar month), yet the time in which it is possible to observe the shadows around small mountains is short; and as favourable opportunities for observation recur only once, or at the most twice, in every lunar month (and bad weather may interfere with observation), the satisfactory observation of delicate features of the moon's surface is a work of time and labour. To detect *changes*, it is necessary, of course, that the moon should be carefully mapped. This has been done by many observers—by Cassini, Riccioli, Schröter, Lohrman, Beer, and Mädler, and others. Photography, at first necessarily limited to minute pictures, but now applied, under the able hands of Delarue, Rutherford, and others, to produce pictures two or three feet in diameter, will one day render effective service in the work we are describing. For a long time, however, the map of the moon now being prepared under the auspices of the British Association, will doubtless be the most complete and satisfactory work of reference. This will largely surpass all other maps in fulness of detail, and also, we may feel certain, in accuracy. But to show that previous labours had been conducted with energy and patience, it is sufficient to note that the elevations of a thousand and ninety-five lunar mountains had been determined, and that in Beer and Mädler's map the positions of no less than twenty thousand craters have been recorded.—*Temple Bar*, August.

Panicum Spectabile and Sorghum.

Dr. Lindley says that the Panicum spectabile grows in Brazil to a height of 6 or 7 feet, "while other equally gigantic species constitute the field crops on the banks of the Amazon." The genus Penicillaria has a wide geographical distribution in tropical countries. P. spicata, Willd., is a very important food plant on the Niger and Gambia rivers, it is in daily household use, and most of the beer of the country is prepared from it. The seeds are said to be even more nutritious than Rice. The fruiting spikes are very close and compact, and average from 18 inches to 2 feet in height; for travelling, a number of these ears are fastened together by their stalks, the ends of the stalks being placed opposite to each other, so as to bring the two opposite spikes parellel, the whole is then readily rolled up and conveyed on the backs of oxen to market. The several species of Sorghum belonging to the tribe Andropogonæ, are perhaps more important than any other Millet-yeilding species. The Sorghums are very imperfectly understood in a botanical sense; those known as S. vulgare, Pers., and S. saccharatum, Mœnch, are the most valuable. These are, however, thought by some authorities to be varieties only of Sorghum halepense, Pers., which grows abundantly in a wild state in the south of Europe, North Africa, &c. The inflorescence of the Sorghums is in large dense panicles; a single fruiting panicle of Sorghum vulgare when ripe frequently weighs 6 or more ounces. The panicle denuded of its seeds make excellent brooms. There are several varieties of this species, the panicles of which are either black, white, reddish, or yellow. This plant has long been cultivated in the south of Europe, Egypt, India, &c.; in Africa it is known as Dawa Corn. Sorghum saccharatum, Mœnch, has lately been brought into notice as a sugar-yeilding Grass. It seems to have been grown in Tuscany, and sugar made from it so far back as the latter part of the last century. Little, however, was known of it in Europe till the French consnl at Shanghai sent some of the seeds to Paris in 1851, labelled "Sugar Cane of North of China." This plant is now largely grown in all quarters of the globe, extending from France to Algeria, Russia, N. America, the East Indies, and Australia. The seeds are much used for soups, puddings, &c. Numerous treatises have been written on the plant, chiefly in France in connection with its sugar-producing qualities. This, as well as S. vulgare, and indeed nearly all the species of Sorghum, appear useful as fodder plants. Cattle and horses are said to be fond of the stems and leaves. There are a whole host of varieties of this as well as of the last species, known only by their native names, given to them in the different districts in which they are cultivated.—*Gardeners' Chronicle*, Aug. 17.

SCIARA.

M. Guérin-Méneville has published a very interesting notice on the migrations of the larva of a particular genus of Tipulæ, known by the name of Sciara. We are indebted to this learned naturalist for the following curious details, which introduce us to one of the most marvellous facts which the history of insects presents to us. The little larvæ of the Sciara are without feet, scarcely five lines in length, and the third of a line in diameter. The body is composed of thirteen segments, and the head is very small and black. In some years, during the month of July, there are met with, in the vicinity of the forests of Norway and of Hanover, immense trains of these larvæ, formed by the union of an innumerable host of little worms, agglomerated together by a glutinous matter. These associations of larvæ resemble some strange kind of animal, having somewhat the form of a serpent. It is, in fact, a living cord, many feet in length, one or two inches in thickness, and formed by the union of little creatures, holding on to each other in myriads, and moving together in one mass. * * M. Guérin-Méneville has observed some of these columns as much as thirty mètres in length. They proceed at a snail's pace, and in a determined course. If the column meets with an obstacle, as a stone for instance, it passes over it, turns round it, or even separates into two portions, which unite after having passed the obstacle. If a portion of the column be taken away, it becomes divided in two, but is speedily re-united by the advance of the hinder portion to the forward one. Finally, if the posterior extremity of this animated ribbon be brought into contact with the anterior, a sort of living circle is formed, which keeps on going round and round, sometimes for a whole day, before it becomes broken and can resume its progress. On touching this serpent of agglutinated larvæ, a sensation of cold is experienced. The phenomenon, so curious, so astonishing, of the union of a prodigious number of apodous larvæ, progressing by a common movement, resulting from the individual motion of thousands of little worms, was first made known, in 1603, by Gaspard Schwenefelt, who adds that the inhabitants of Liberia consider it as a precursor of a bad harvest, if they are found in the mountains; whilst a favourable presage is entertained if they descend to the plains. In 1715, Jonas Ramus speaks of the same phenomenon, and relates another superstitious notion attached to it by the peasants of Norway, who, when they encounter one of these movable columns, throw down in front of it some part of their dress, as their belt or their vest. If the Orme-drag, as they term it, passes over the obstacle, it is considered a favourable sign; whilst, if they pass round it, the result is sinister. * * M. Guérin-Méneville believes that these larvæ, which inhabit certain districts in vast numbers, in some seasons devour all the nutritive matters within their reach. Having thus exhausted their feeding places, they are forced to emigrate from them to seek at a distance new pastures, or probably with the object of undergoing their metamorphosis—*Athenæum*, translated from *Figuiers Les Insectes*.

LASTREA ÆMULA.

This scarce and beautiful fern rarely succeeds under cultivation, and hence we do not often meet with it in cultivation, or in collections of ferns at exhibitions. Numerous as are elegant plants amongst the species of ferns, few equal or surpass this in elegance, whether we note particularly its finely-divided, bright green fronds, or the gracefully half-pendant character of a fine specimen. It is the "hayscented" or "triangular prickly-toothed buckler fern" of the rustic herbarium; but as it is not the only hay-scented or prickly-toothed fern we have, such designations are delusions. In Newman's "History of British Ferns," it is described under the name of *Lastrea recurva*, elsewhere as *Polypodium æmulmu*, and *Lophodium fœnisecii*. It has a stout, tufted caudex, and long, stout, wiry, dark brown roots. The stipes, usually about half the length of the frond, brownish purple, the rachis greenish, and stipes and rachis beset with small spherical glands. Fronds twelve to twenty inches long, rich bright green, drooping, gibbous lance-shaped or elongate triangular. The pinnæ opposite or alternate, the pinnules oblique, oblong, more or less pinnatifid, the margins lobed and toothed, the whole frond having a delicate crispy appearance. The fructification covers the whole of the under surface, and consists of round, brown spore cases, which add much to the beauty of this fern. It is evergreen, widely distributed, but only attains to a luxuriant condition of growth in mild, moist climates ; hence, though occasionally met with in the east of England, it is never so beautiful as in the west. This circumstance gives the key to its cultivation. On the open rockery it rarely thrives, except in districts where it is found wild, in good condition ; but in the cool fernhouse, or the Wardian case, it grows freely, and requires absolutely no care beyond a needful supply of moisture. If never visited with a breath of air, it is none the worse ; and, on the other hand, exposure to wind is decidedly injurious to it. Some years ago, when planting an artificial cave, under glass, with ferns, we inserted a plant of Lastrea æmula in a rather dark and obscure chink, where it could only be seen by looking for it. Now it protrudes beyond the opening, and throws out a graceful tuft of its elegant fronds in a most pleasing manner, and proving that the selection of a damp, shady, sheltered place is a matter of the first necessity in its cultivation. As to soil, light loam, with plenty of silver sand and pounded stone, will suit it exactly. The plant just referred to had not more than a handful of soil to begin life upon, and probably has insinuated its roots amongst the stone and brick of which the cave is constructed, and so has soil enough in what one may call the heart of the rock. The dried fronds emit an agreeable hay-scent for years after the date of gathering them.—S. H., *Floral World*, August, 1867.

THE LYRE-BIRD.

The lyre-birds appear to be more jubilant and active either very early in the morning or late in the evening than at any other periods of the day, and the habits of the different species are very nearly alike. The most singular trait in their character is the extraordinary power they possess of imitating not only the voices of other birds, and the cries and yelpings of different quadrupeds, but sounds produced by man are as readily mocked by the lyre-bird ; and it would appear, from the accounts brought us by those who are familiar with these curious birds in their native haunts, that the far-famed mocking-bird is a mere bungler in his calling when placed in competition with a lyre-bird. Prince Albert's lyre-bird seems to be at the top of his profession. "I once listened to one of these birds that had taken up its quarters within two hundred yards of a sawyer's hut, and it had made itself perfect with all the noises of the sawyer's homestead—the crowing of the cocks, the cackling of the hens, the barking and howling of the dogs, and even the painful screeching of the sharpening or filing of the saw."

Another singular custom they have is that of keeping in pairs, or alone : more than two are never seen together, and most frequently they lead solitary lives, except during the breeding season. They pair early, and commence building their nests in May or June. The solitary egg is laid, and usually in July the young bird is hatched. Their favourite building site is a ledge of rock high up from the ground, so that prowling egg destroyers and devourers of young birds may be defeated, or find it difficult to accomplish their thievish intentions. "The nest is constructed of small sticks, interwoven with moss and root fibres, the inside being lined with the skeleton fronds of the epiphetic fern, resembling horse-hair ; and it is covered in, with the entrance at the sides." The single egg is very dark in colour, and looks as if it had been splashed with ink. During the first month of its life the young bird is covered with down, and it remains in the nest six weeks before it finally departs.

Whether the cock lyre-birds have rows for the sheer love of the thing, or do battle from jealousy, it is not easy to determine ; in any case, they rival in fighting qualifications both game-cocks and the proverbially pugnacious quails.

The following account is copied from an Australian newspaper. The writer observes :—"In one of my rambles I beheld a sight which, to me, was grand in the extreme. In working my way through the tedious scrub, and being upon the brow of a hill, making my way to camp, I heard a din in the valley below which completely astonished me. As I neared it, the noise became abominable, and I wondered what it all meant. Knowing the shyness of bush-scrub animals, I sneaked nearer the scene of the noise, and came in view of as strange a sight as I have witnessed in all my life. About, near as I could guess, a hundred and fifty lyre-cocks were ranged in order of battle, and fighting with indescribable fury.—*Leisure Hour* for August.

COCKROACHES.

To housekeepers, the most interesting information with regard to cockroaches would be couched in a short and simple recipe for effectually getting rid of them. Beetle-traps and poisons never do more than thin their numbers, which increase again with amazing rapidity when such means of repression are discontinued. They may, yet, be thoroughly exterminated, though the methods of accomplishing this desirable end seem to be known only to the professional destroyers of vermin. One of these Nimrods of the kitchen, being once engaged by the writer for this special purpose, took despotic possession of the basement floor for the night, occupied himself there for an hour or so in his murderous preparations before the family retired to rest, locked all up, taking away the keys, and, coming again at daylight next morning, swept up the victims in a mass of several bushels and carried them off. Not a single specimen of *Blatta orientalis* was seen in that house for the five succeeding years during which it continued to be our home.

Cockroaches generally swarm in great abundance on the premises of the baker, where any measure for exterminating them by poisons could not be safely hazarded. Some bakers keep a hedgehog or two for the express purpose of keeping them down, the hedgehog feeding on them greedily, and exhibiting remarkable vivacity, for him, in routing for them. There can be little doubt that rats, who will eat anything, are formidable enemies to cockroaches, and it has been noticed that wherever cockroaches are numerous rats will effect an entrance if they can. We had once a tame jackdaw who would snap up almost any number of cockroaches that could be offered him, but he was of little use in abating them, as he was usually at roost before they came out of their holes. It is probable that in their native East, where they are not compelled to resort to the dwellings of man to shelter them from the cold, these pests of our kitchens form a considerable proportion of the food of birds.

The male cockroach has wings about half the length of his body, though so far as we know he is never seen to make use of them. The female has only rudimentary wings; her young are hatched from eggs, which, however, she does not deposit in any nest, but keeps enclosed in an oblong case attached to her body. The eggs are generally about sixteen in number; the young escape from their oblong cradle by emitting a fluid, which softens a part of it and lets them out. They are active and alert when they leave their mother, though they are much less in bulk than the smallest emmets. Looking to the rapid increase of cockroaches in places favourable to them, it is plain that the female must produce her small broods with astonishing frequency.—*People's Magazine* for August.

New Books.

[*Our limited space must of necessity compel us to give but very short notices of new books, but they will perhaps serve as a guide as to what books our readers may ask for at their libraries.*]

The Practical Poultry Keeper. By L. Wright. London: Cassell, Petter, and Galpin. 1867.

In our number for July we gave a short notice of Mr. Tegetemier's Poultry Book; and we have now before us another work upon the same subject, which if not so elaborate is equally well worthy of attention. Mr. Tegetemier treats the whole subject in a philosophical manner, while the present volume is eminently practical, which cannot fail to make it of more value to one class of readers, and at the same time being much cheaper it will find its way into the hands of many who cannot afford to buy the more expensive one. Mr. Wright's volume will prove to be a valuable vade mecum, containing as it does exact and valuable hints upon profitable feeding and breeding, not forgetting the practical question of profit. We can safely recommend it to such as are in want of a guide, and who as we before observed cannot afford the more expensive Poultry Book; and to those who can afford it we may add that much information may be found in one that is not contained in the other. Both volumes are well worth having.

The Dogs of the British Islands: being a Series of Articles and Letters by various Contributors, Reprinted from the Field *Newspaper.* Edited by "Stonehenge." (Cox.)

A very attractive volume for all who are interested—and who are not—in the Dogs of the British Islands. Well illustrated and well bound, it is a volume fit to grace any drawing room table. It is divided into four sections: Dogs used with the gun, noticing Setters, English Pointers, Field Spaniels, and Retrievers; Companionable dogs, which treats of Terriers, Bull Terriers, Bulldogs, Mastiffs, Sheep and drovers dogs, Hounds and their allies; the third section illustrates the distinctive features of Blood-hounds, Foxhounds, Harriers, Beagles, Fox Terriers, and Truffle Dogs, whilst the fourth treats of Toy Dogs.

An Explanation of the Popular Weather Prognostics of Scotland on Scientific Principles. By the Rev. Charles Clouston. (Routledge & Sons.)

In this little pamphlet is discussed the various weather prognostics of Scotland, which were collected together by Dr. Mitchell, a fellow countryman of the author, who is a meteorologist of considerable experience, and well qualified to write upon this subject. In the book will be found several quaint quotations which add greatly to its interest.

AMERICAN, FRENCH, AND GERMAN WORKS.

Ornithology and Oology of New England: containing full descriptions of the Birds of New England and adjoining States and Provinces, arranged by a long-approved Classification and Nomenclature; together with a complete History of their Habits, Times of Arrival and Departure, their Distribution, Food, Song, Time of Breeding, and a careful and accurate Description of their Nests and Eggs; with Illustrations of many species of the Birds, and accurate Figures of their Eggs. By Edward A. Samuels, Curator of Zoology in the Massachusetts State Cabinet. Boston: Nichols and Noyes. London: Sampson Low, Son, and Marston. 1867.

The volume will be found to command the attentions of all lovers and Students of nature; the subject is somewhat limited but is thoroughly and exhaustively treated—it is well printed and admirably illustrated.

Sorghum and its Products. An Account of recent Investigations concerning the Value of Sorghum in Sugar Production; together with a Description of a new Method of making Sugar and Refined Syrup from this Plant. Adapted to Common Use. By F. S. Stewart. Philadelphia: Lippincott and Co. London: Trübner & Co. 1867.

This is a description of a plant that is now

being largely cultivated in the middle states, and would seem according to the writer likely to become a formidable rival to the sugar cane of Louisiana. The processes of culture as adapted to different varieties, with the result in each case, the soils best suited, the manufacture and use of the products are well described. As a technical treatise it will be most valuable.

Seaside Studies in Natural History: Marine Animals of Massachusetts Bay—Radiates. By Elizabeth C. Agassiz and Alexander Agassiz. Boston: Ticknor and Fields. London: Trübner & Co. 1865

This little volume deals principally with the lower forms of marine life, with especial reference to those found on the shores of Massachusetts.

Essai sur l'unité des Phénomenès Naturels. Par Emile Saigey. Paris: Germer-Baillère.

An essay on the unity of natural phenomena. Most persons are aware that heat and motive force are now considered as equivalent—that is to say, a certain quantity of heat is transformed into a certain sum of force, and *vice versâ*. This law, suggested originally by the application of steam power to locomotion and to manufacturing purposes, has since been more carefully studied, and is found to rule every branch of natural philosophy. It would seem, in fact, that all the forces of nature are susceptible of being transformed the one into the other, according to certain laws which are nothing else than the laws of mechanics. Such is the idea developed by M. Saigey in this interesting treatise.

Etudes et Lectures sur l'Astronomie. Par Camille Flammarion. Paris: Gauthier-Villars.

These essays were originally published in the *Cosmos* and the *Revue Contemporaine*, and are intended to form a series. The sun, the state of astronomy in 1863 and 1864, the position of the planets in 1867, and an appendix of notes bearing upon these subjects, form the materials of which the present volume is composed.

Die Geschichte der Arier in der alten zeit. Von Max Duncker. Leipzig: Duncker & Humblot. London: Williams & Norgate.

This volume, commencing with the dawn of History follows the fortune of the Aryan race in India and Persia to the reorganisation of the Persian Empire by Darius Hystaspes. Especial attention is bestowed on the great religious systems—that of the Vedas and of Zoroaster, Buddhism. The history is, as many of our readers will be aware, a portion of a more comprehensive work. It is, however, complete in itself; and in its present revised condition, enriched by the results of recent investigation, is entitled to rank as a new treatise.

Ueber die Polarländer. Von Dr. Oswald Heer. Zurich: Schulthess. London: Williams and Norgate.

An interesting lecture on the Arctic regions, in which Dr. Heer gives an account of their fossil vegetation. The author is about to publish an extensive work on this subject. These inhospitable climes once enjoyed a temperature nearly analogous to that of Geneva, Dr. Heer rejects all the geological explanations which have been offered for this fact, and thinks we must look for a solution to cosmical changes affecting the entire solar system.

Die Abhangikeit der Insecten von ihrer Umgebung. Von Dr. L. Möller. Leipzig: Englemann. London: Williams and Norton.

Dr. L. Möller has devoted himself to the most minute scrutiny of the insects which have fallen under his notice. He has studied the manner in which they are affected by climate, by weather, by the soil on which they live, by the works of man, or by the modifications of the animal and vegetable life around them. He has observed the influence of various descriptions of food upon the tints of caterpillars, and registered the species of beetles that make themselves at home in ant-hills, the number of which within the sphere of his observation he finds to be precisely one hundred and seventeen.

BOOKS RECENTLY PUBLISHED.

Mushrooms and Toadstools; How to distinguish easily the Difference between Edible and Poisonous Fungi. With two large sheets containing twenty-nine Edible and thirty-one Poisonous Species, drawn the natural size, and coloured from living specimens. By W. G. Smith. 12mo, pp. 74, sewed, 6s. Hardwicke.

British Conchology; or, an Account of the Mollusca which now inhabit the British Isles and the surrounding Seas. Vol. 4: Marine Shells, in continuation of the Gastropoda as far as the Bulla Family. By John Gwyn Jeffreys. Post 8vo, pp. 460, cloth, 12s. Van Voorst.

The Henwife; Her Own Experience in Her Own Poultry Yard. By the Hon. Mrs. Arbuthnot. Pictures by H. Weir. Fifth Edition, price 7s. 6d.; plain Plates, 4s. 6d. Edinburgh: Thomas C. Jack.

Physical and Medical Climate and Meteorology of the West Coast of Africa. With Valuable Hints to Europeans for the Preservation of Health in the Tropics. By James Africanus B. Horton, M.D., Staff Assistant-Surgeon of H.M. Forces in West Africa. Price 10s. John Churchill & Sons.

The Forest and the Field. By H. A. L., "The Old Shekarry," Author of "The Hunting Grounds of the Old World," "The Camp Fire," &c. 1 vol. 8vo. With Portrait and Illustrations, price 21s. London: Samson Low.

Norway; its People, Products, and Institutions. By the Rev. John Bowden, late British Consular Chaplain at Christiania. Post 8vo, 7s. 6d.

Glaucus; or, the Wonders of the Shore. By the Rev. Charles Kingsley. New and Illustrated Edition, containing beautifully coloured Illustrations. Fcap. 8vo, cloth, gilt leaves, 5s. London: Macmillan.

A Handbook for Ladies on Indoor Plants, Flowers for Ornament, and Song Birds. By E. A. Maling. 12mo, cloth. 4s. Smith & Elder.

Letters Home from Spain, Algeria, and Brazil, during past Entomological Rambles. By Rev. Hamlet Clark. 8vo, pp. 162, cloth, 7s. 6d. Van Voorst.

Cattle and Cattle Breeders. By W. McCombie. 12mo, pp. 206, cloth, 5s. Blackwood.

Auvergne; its Thermo-Mineral Springs, Climate, &c. By R. Cross. Post 8vo, cloth, 4s. Hardwicke.

English Cyclopædia. Reissue. Arts and Sciences, Vol. 4. 4to, cloth, 12s. Bradbury.

Stories about Birds. By Mrs. Fairfield. Square 16mo, cloth, 1s. 6d. Hamilton.

Meetings of Learned Societies.

QUEKETT MICROSCOPICAL CLUB.

The second annual general meeting was held in the Library of University College, on Friday, the 26th ult. (July), Mr. Ernest Hart, President, in the chair. The report of the committee showed that the society now numbers 273 members, of whom 130 were elected during the year; that many papers of interest had been read. The treasurer's report gave a satisfactory balance, and in every way the club was in a very prosperous state.

The following officers were elected for the ensuing year:—President, Mr. Arthur E. Durham, F.L.S.; vice-presidents, Mr. Tilbury Fox, M.R.C.P., Mr. Ernest Hart, Mr. William Hislop, F.R.A.S., Mr. John K. Lord, F.Z.S.; treasurer, Mr. Robert Hardwicke, F.L.S.; hon. secretary Mr. Witham M. Bywater, hon. secretary for foreign correspondence, Mr. M. C. Cooke; committee, Mr. W. J. de L. Arnold, Mr. N. Burgess, Mr. S. J. McIntire, Mr. J. Slade.

Correspondence.

[*Under this head we shall be glad to insert any letters of general interest.*]

NAMES OF BIRDS.

SIR,—Would you allow me to say a few words in correction of a common error in the spelling and pronunciation of the name of a very common English bird? I refer to the *yellow-ammer*, which is very frequently written and pronounced *yellow-hammer*. Ammer is the German for bunting. The Germans call the bird the *goldammer*, or Golden Bunting. Yellow being the English equivalent for the German golden, the word, as written and pronounced *yellow-ammer*, has the evident and appropriate meaning of yellow bunting, and the words in both languages are plainly synonymous. Why any bird should be called a hammer I am at a loss to conceive, much more why this particular bird should be so called. What will Macaulay's New Zealander say about the yellow-hammer when he comes to make out its history as recorded in its name? He must either invent a fanciful derivation connecting the bird in some way with a hammer, or place it among his other examples of the capricious folly of the barbarians of the 19th century.

I spoke about this casually in conversation with some friends a day or two ago. One of them said he should not like to call the bird the yellow-ammer for fear of being supposed guilty of the vulgarism of dropping his *h*'s. Another thought that custom fixes pronunciation and spelling, and that to depart from customary pronunciation and spelling, whatever they may be, seems pedantic. If we could persuade educated people to see the absurdity of the wrong and adopt the right method, both these objections would vanish.

Words are said to be the living records of the histories of things, and to preserve this record in its purity as regards one of our very common words, even at the risk of being thought pedantic, is the aim of these few remarks.

I am, &c.,
J. A. H.

Milesdown, Aug. 15.

Short Notes.

THE SWALLOW.—The chimney swallow (*Hirundo rustica*) is almost as much a household bird as the robin; it appeals to our better nature by the fearless confidence with which it seeks our dwellings as the sanctuary where its tender young will be safe; and this, combined with its gentle, pleasing manners, justly makes it a general favourite. Wherever the swallow is found it seems to possess the same instinctive confidence in man, and the same preference for buildings.

In this country a chimney is most generally chosen by the swallow wherein to erect its nest; but in this selection I have never observed it show any particular preference for a shaft in a stack of chimneys more than for an isolated one. I fancy the only condition which seems greatly to influence it in this respect is, that it shall not be one which is in constant use. In my father's house there was an isolated chimney, which certainly was not used more than once or twice a year, and for at least thirty years I never knew this without a nest. It was a short, straight shaft, up which when a boy I have often looked with longing eyes at the prize above; and once or twice I remember an unfortunate young one tumbling down into the empty fireplace when essaying to leave the nest on its first journey. There was a window at a short distance, nearly on a level with the chimney top, and I have spent hours, at various times, in watching the busy labours of the parent birds in constructing and repairing their nest. In some years the winter rain and snow would be so heavy as to demolish the frail structure, when a new one had to be built; in others it merely required a little patching, or a new lining of feathers, to make it habitable; but, with very few exceptions, the same angle of the chimney was always selected for the new nest, and it never varied more than a few inches in its distance from the top.

Though the swallow does not rank high as a songster, yet it has a very pleasing and melodious warble; it chiefly indulges in this early in the morning, even long before sunrise, or towards evening, and it is quite in keeping with the gentle character of the bird.

By what extraordinary instinct does the swallow and its congeners ascertain what weather is prevailing in this country, for such really seems to be the case? In some years, when the season has been backward, I have remarked a few pairs only arrive, and even these have seemed after a day or two to disappear. In the year 1849 the spring was particularly backward; April was cold and bleak, and unfavourable to the development of insect life; and not until the 11th of May did any of the hirundines make their appearance, on which day I first noted a few pairs of the common swallow and the house martin, but the main body did not arrive until three days afterwards. This was no local occurrence, for the same ungenial weather was general throughout England. In 1847 I noticed the same phenomenon, under precisely similar circumstances as regards the weather. A few pairs arrived on the 29th April, but immediately departed, and I saw no more until the 4th May, when I remarked a single pair of swallows; but these were not joined by the main body until the 6th.

By what mysterious system of telegraphy was the intelligence conveyed to the southern voyagers that their journey had better be delayed for a time? We boast of our wisdom and intelligence, but how little able are we to elucidate facts like these.

During the time of building I have often seen the swallows frequent the gutters, or any wet place in the village street, from whence they obtain the mud for their nests; their feet, however, and short legs do not very well fit them for walking, and I never saw one make more than two or perhaps three steps without using its wings. As soon as the young ones can fly they are in the habit of resting altogether on the branch of a tree, generally choosing a withered one, and I have seen the parent bird feed them while thus perching as she passed on the wing.

The swallow is very vigilant to detect the presence of any bird of prey; one or two wild hurried shrieks are uttered by the first who becomes aware of the danger, the call to arms is immediately obeyed, and in a few seconds all within hearing the note of alarm are gathered together, and fly wildly about their enemy. I have noticed that the cuckoo is pursued in this way quite as much as any of the hawks.

How strange it is that the idea that swallows wintered in the mud at the bottom of ponds and rivers should ever have been a matter of belief with intelligent and scientific men, and have been so long and pertinaciously held! A swallow is no more fitted to live under water than any other bird, and a single actual experiment would at once have demonstrated the absurdity of the theory—one which even yet is not entirely exploded. That some swallows have been found during the winter in a dormant condition has often been proved. These are most likely late-hatched birds; but I think it is very questionable if they ever survive the winter in a torpid state, and when such have been accidentally disturbed and roused into temporary activity they almost immediately disappear again, and doubtless perish from want of food. In January, 1842, I knew of an instance in which a pair of chimney swallows fluttered out of the thatch of an old barn which was being pulled down. They seemed in great distress, and after flying about the place during that and the following day, nothing more was seen of them.—*Field*, August 27th.

A RATTLESNAKE AT LARGE.—The following about this appeared in *Land and Water*, August 10th:—A rare bit of penny-a-lining copied from the *Liverpool Daily Mercury*, has been going the round of some of the newspapers under the above heading, which must indeed excite the consternation of our American cousins who dwell in the land of the rattlesnake. Such nonsense is not worth repeating in our columns; but people are, in general, so very ignorant about snakes, that they will believe anything said of them, no matter how absurd the exaggeration. Be it understood that the rattlesnake is a sluggish reptile, by no means rapid in its gait, and most easily disabled by a blow on the spine. It does not spring its rattle when in the act of progression, and one that had really got loose would immediately make for the nearest retreat, and be somewhat difficult to dislodge therefrom. A few weeks ago, a man (one Joel H. Bowkley) brought a large quantity of rattlesnakes to this country, which he has been taking about to the different dealers in live animals for menageries, exhibiting the fangs that had been extracted from them, and handling his fangless rattlesnakes with the utmost *nonchalance*. It seems that eight of these snakes were purchased by Mr. Manders; and the story is, that one of them got loose the other day in his travelling menagerie, then staying at Tunbridge Wells. Not long ago there was a tale about three gorillas (!) having escaped from this proprietor, which alleged gorillas turned out to be three young Cape baboons (*Cynocephalus porcarius*), animals about as dangerous to handle and secure at their age as so many puppies. Something sensational was now, in turn, required as a puff for the rattlesnakes; and, accordingly, with a squad of keepers behind it, armed "with shovels, forks, scrapers, brooms, &c.," we are told that "the reptile leisurely proceeded up the centre of the inclosure, hissing fearfully all the time. On arriving opposite the caravan containing the bonassus, a species of buffalo—an immense animal, weighing upwards of two tons" (the weight of a fine bull of its kind, *i.e.* the American bison, being about 14 cwt.!), "the rattlesnake made a spring, fastened" (!) "on the bonassus, and bit it in the left nostril. The reptile then let go its grip" (grip !), "and, shaking its rattles" (!) "glided through an opening between two of the caravans, where some of Mr. Manders's grooms were filling a cart with straw. To this cart was attached a fine horse. The rattlesnake fastened" (!) "on the off-fetlock of the horse, which immediately plunged and reared to such an extent as to shake the reptile off" (!), "and before it could move away it was crushed to pieces beneath the hoofs of the horse." Of course the two large quadrupeds died in the course of a few minutes, in frightful agonies, "and were buried in a field just outside Tunbridge Wells in the latter part of the same day." It is a curious circumstance that Mr. Manders's bull bison was afterwards seen alive in the possession of Mr. Rice, the dealer, in Ratcliffe-highway, who, it is rumoured, received it in part payment or exchange for three young giraffes ! So many parts of the story are palpably false that we incline to disbelieve the whole of it. It is not true that any snake holds on with a "grip," like a bulldog. The stroke and withdrawal of the fangs are instantaneous ; and that a rattlesnake with its fangs extracted (as we believe in the present instance—will Mr. Manders permit of the mouths of his seven others being examined !) would kill a mature bull bison and a fine horse in succession, may do very well for people who have not the necessary knowledge to criticise, but is quite incredible to the naturalist. The carcase of a fine bull bison, too, we should expect, was considerably too valuable to be buried out of the way. The skeleton would surely be sold for some museum, and the meat would be nought the worse for feeding Mr. Manders's carnivora.—Z.

INDIAN SCENERY.—We could scarcely have chosen a better morning for our excursion. The sun was gilding the snow-covered peaks of the northern Pinjal as we commenced the ascent, and by the time we had gained the temple, his rays, in one flood of golden light, had illuminated half the valley, leaving the southern portion and the slopes of the Peer Pinjal yet intact. Seldom does he shine on more varied and beautiful scenery, for in all my wanderings before and since I have never witnessed its equal. There lay the capital at our feet, half hidden among clusters of poplars, chunars and forest trees—the Dul lake, washing the western base of the Tukt-i-Salaman, stretched westward with all its ever-changing forms. On the placid waters of the lake numerous skiffs shot either rapidly along, or threaded their way through a labyrinth of weeds, diversified by the countless floating gardens, and the Isle of Chunars with its noble plane-trees. The shalimar and pleasure-grounds of the Delhi Emperors, now fading and fast passing into the wild jungle around them, covered portions of the northern bank of the lake. Huri Purbet, like a fortress which had undergone a siege, its walls crumbling into decay, stood on the site of a spur overlooking a scene which for loveliness and grandeur has scarcely an equal. So perfect seemed both the natural and artificial portions of the panorama, so faintly blending with each other, and yet so grand, that the eye in one sweep passed over the most perfect pictures of lake and mountain scenery. Towards the city stretched a noble avenue of poplars, upwards of a mile in length, and straight as arrows ; whilst away towards the east rich pastures and fields teemed with grain ; villages nestled in clusters of trees, which in rows were seen fringing the banks of the classical Hydaspes, that like a huge snake twisted through the plain. Then, last of the many beauties, rose those grand and noble mountains, encircling the whole panorama, and shielding the paradise from the northern blasts, whilst from their rugged sides dashed a thousand rills to fertilize and beautify its soil.—*The Forest and the Field.*

MIGRATORY BIRDS.—It is familiarly known, says a correspondent of *Land and Water*, July 27, that, as a general rule, our feathered summer visitants return year after year to the exact same place, and the young to the site of their nativity in the first instance. It is unnecessary to cite instances of this repeatedly observed fact, which nevertheless seems quite inexplicable. The birds which visit us in winter must, for the most part, necessarily range about more, and of course they proceed further towards the equator, when the temperature renders this needful. Still, the tendency would seem to be for the same individuals to visit the same places year after year, a fact well illustrated by a statement quoted by the late Mr. Yarrell, which I here transcribe. "In the year 1833, a woodcock, with white feathers on the wings, was observed in a cover on the manor of Monkleigh, near Torrington, in the county of Devon. The same bird, or one of exactly similar plumage, reappeared in the same place during the four succeeding seasons, in which period it was so repeatedly shot at by different persons without effect, that it at last acquired among the country people the name of 'the witch.' In 1837 it was killed, and the specimen preserved." In this instance, a peculiarity of plumage rendered the individual bird recognisable ; and perhaps you may know of other instances of the kind, which I shall be glad to learn of. Bewick relates a similar instance of a white woodcock having been observed in the same cover for three successive seasons. Tame gulls, also, that had left the place where they were reared, during the breeding season, have been known to return afterwards, and bring their families with them. Many years ago, we remember that some coots, which had become quite tame upon the water in St. James's-park, left for the breeding season, and made their appearance afterwards.

VULTURES IN INDIA.—Amid all the grandeur of the Himalayas, it is a most attractive sight to the naturalist to behold the vultures and rapacious birds soaring over the vast ravines and around the tops of the mighty mountains. Let him choose a summer evening, with that clear blue sky almost characteristic of the Himalayas, and just as the sun casts its last rays on the snow-clad mountains—when the quiet is only broken by the cry of the eagle, the bleat of the goat, or the shrill pipe of the black partridge—then the vultures, kites, and jackdaws may be seen wheeling in vast circles ; some are gliding along, apparently without an effort, others appear suspended motionless in the vast canopy of heaven ; while, careering in his majesty, the lammergeyer *(gypaëtus barbatus)* gathers up his great wings and stoops downwards, may-hap to rise again and join the medley he has just left, or stretching forth his pinions to their fullest extent, he sails along the mountain brow to the projecting cliff on which his eyrie stands safe, for there who dare assail him? He is usually observed sailing leisurely along the mountain side, now and then flapping his great wings when he wishes to mount higher; but let a govind-kite, or Indian jackdaw annoy him, then, with a rushing noise like that of a fierce wind, he stoops with a grace truly grand and beautiful. Oft when clambering along a rocky precipice, picking every footstep with studious care, and daring not to lift my eyes for fear of making a false step, have my ears been assailed by the furious rush of the lammergeyer, and a feeling that if he only touched me with his pinions I would have rolled into the yawning abyss below.—*The Naturalist in India*.

CINNAMON.—The soil of the cinnamon gardens is a loose white sand: localities near the sea are considered to be the most favourable to the growth of cinnamon. The blossom is of a pale-greenish colour, closely resembling mignionette, and the berry is formed like the acorn, and about the size of a small damson, of a deep purple hue. It ripens at the end of autumn, and is gathered by the natives for the purpose of extracting oil from it. The bark of the branches might be mistaken for that of the hazel, so close is the resemblance; and the young leaves are of a deep crimson, changing gradually to green, having three fibres running lengthwise. When chewed they have the taste of cinnamon. It is not true that the cinnamon groves impart a smell to the air, the spice being contained between the outer bark and the wood. In the process of preparing the cinnamon the peelers select such branches as are sufficiently old, and lop them off with a large pruning knife, the blade being convex on the one side and concave on the other. The convex side is used in loosening the cinnamon from the branch, when it appears in the form of a tube, open at the one side, into which the smaller tubes are inserted, and afterwards spread out to dry in the sun. When dry it is made into bundles, weighing about thirty pounds each, bound up with split bamboo twigs, and carried to the stores, ready for exportation.—*People's Magazine* for August.

FOOD FOR PARROTS.—With respect to food for parrots, I knew one treated and fed by a gentleman for upwards of forty years without the bird ever moulting, and it never shed but one feather at a time. This bird was a very splendid one, and its plumage very much studied by the owner, who was a good judge of birds, and understood the kind of food they ought to eat. He used to say he was certain it was the hemp-seed people principally fed parrots on that caused them to pick off their feathers and spoil their plumage; therefore Polly was not allowed to have but a very small quantity, although most birds are very fond of it. The way this bird was fed was this. Toast crust soaked and squeezed nearly dry again, with about a $\frac{1}{4}$oz. of maw seed sprinkled over it was put into a nice clean washed tin box, with a parting in it; then in the other half about $\frac{1}{4}$ pint of canary, Indian corn, paddy, and a small quantity of sunflower seed, and never more than about one dozen grains of hemp-seed; all this should be thoroughly sifted, as the dust itself is enough to make them itch, particularly the dust from the canary-seed; if you only put your hand down a sack of it, you will find your arm itch for hours. No meat should be given them; they are very fond of the leg-bone of a fowl now and then, to amuse them, but the meat should be cut off very close. They should have a shower-bath every now and then, over cage and all; they are very partial to a bath in summer time. The cage should be wiped and put into a warm room to dry, and be fresh sanded; it should be cleaned out every morning and red bird-sand thrown over the bottom; this was the way the bird was treated, as it was my duty to attend to it, which I did for four years.—H. B. in *Land and Water*, August 3rd.

TOADS.—An old lady of the writer's acquaintance possessed as pets a number of toads, which she kept in some rockwork in her garden, and had tamed by degrees in the following manner. She would catch and imprison the toad she intended making a pet of under a flower pot, and then liberally supply it with different kinds of food such as toads delight in, particularly bread crumbs, which, in the absence of the old lady, the prisoner greedily devoured. It would soon, however, lose its habitual shyness, and upon lifting up the flower-pot the toad would first eat in her presence, and at length take from her hand the food she offered. As soon as this stage in the taming process was reached the old lady would turn out the captive into the society of other toads among the rockwork. Twice a day, during the warmer months of the year, did she approach the abode of her pets, when they would come forth from their hiding places, and eagerly devour whatever she threw to them. They quickly learned to distinguish her footsteps on the gravel walk from those of all other persons, and came fearlessly out of their holes to greet her. It is curious that these reptiles did not become torpid for some weeks after all their untamed kindred had disappeared from view.—*People's Magazine*, August 3rd, 1867.

THE VOLVOX AND ITS PARASITE.—In examining with the microscope some specimens of "Volvox globator," one was found containing one of the Rotifera, a female of *Rotommata Parasitica* (mentioned by Pritchard as sometimes found in such a situation). When first seen it was feeding, picking out the green masses composing the Volvox, and swallowing them, occasionally shifting its position and selecting a fresh spot. Two eggs had been deposited, and another could be seen in the ovary; they were of a reddish tint, and filled with granules. There was no sign yet of organized structure. Twenty-four hours after, the Rotifer was dead, but the young could now be plainly seen moving in the eggs, and cilia were in rapid vibration at two distinct points. While still under examination, one of the young broke through the envelope surrounding him, and, after a few energetic struggles, was freed and swimming rapidly about the interior of his prison, but did not appear to make any attempt to leave it. The egg-shell or membrane left behind was very delicate and transparent, without dots or markings, the aperture broken off by the animal being plainly visible. The other egg would have soon hatched, as the animal was in active motion within it, but unfortunately the water leaking out of the live-box containing it, put an end to the observation. The Volvox did not seem disturbed by its strange occupant, but continued its stately revolutions as though they were not present.—B. WEBB, JUNR. in *The American Naturalist*, July.

MICE IN CORN-BIN.—One day last week (we read in *Land and Water*, July 20th) the coachman of a friend of mine called his attention, and asked him if he could tell what that was, pointing to a moving mass in a corn-bin, which had been cleaned out the day before, and was empty. There being two dogs and three cats always about, he said, "One of your dogs, I suppose." "No, sir, they are mice." The mass was about eighteen or twenty inches long, and about half that in width and height, and was moving and rolling, caused by the under mice trying for air. A cat was put into the bin, but she cut off pretty quickly. A terrier was then put in, and at it he went. There were hundreds in this mass, but none got away. The whole of this lot came there in the night, and what brought them there, and from whence could they have come? He told me he once saw one of his ferrets have a stand-up fight for twenty-five minutes with a rat, a noted old rat that lived under a big stone in a churchyard and had beaten several ferrets off.

THE SENSITIVE PLANT.—The cause of the movements of the Sensitive Plant, says the *London Review*, Aug. 10th, can hardly be considered decided. Some say it is not true contraction, but merely a motion of fluid! Others, that it is accompanied by electric changes, and is, therefore, allied to muscular motion. The observations which M. P. L. Bert publishes, throw hardly any new light on this question; they indicate, however, one important point, viz., that the natural and regular movement of the leaves is produced by a different cause from that of sudden contraction resulting from contact with the fingers. Either seems to have no effect upon the former, but it produces an anæsthetic effort which prevents the latter.

CLIMATE OF LAGOS.—For hundreds of miles the whole line of the adjacent coast is one continuous mangrove swamp, intersected by lagoons, from which fœtid exhalations, caused by the rapid decomposition of animal and vegetable matter, rise and hang over the land like a dense fog. The sun, seen through this noxious vapour, loses none of its power, but looks, even at mid-day, as if it was obscured by ground glass. At such a time, the hot, damp, fœtid air seems to clog and impede the free action of the lungs, and one feels that its impurities are pregnant with disease. Any one who has entered the damp hothouse of Kew Gardens, after it has been shut for some time, may form some slight idea of the atmosphere of this part of the coast.—*The Mountain and the Field*.

A BURNING WELL.—A burning well has just been discovered at Narbonne, by workmen engaged in making borings for an artesian well. The water, which is charged with sulphate of magnesia, gives off in considerable volumes carburetted hydrogen gas, which burns with a reddish smoky flame, but without emitting a smell of either bitumen or sulphuretted hydrogen. The "sinking" for the spring was made on the left branch of the Aude, in a plain situate about two metres above the sea-level, and composed of alluvial mud. The alluvial mud extends to a depth of six metres, then follow tertitary lime-stones and marls, with the remains of marine shells. At the depth of 70 metres, the spring containing the inflammable gas was met with.

NIGHTINGALES.—It is stated by a correspondent of the *Pall Mall Gazette* that "an unusually large number of nightingales assembled during the late spring in the vicinity of Naumburg. They settled about the middle of April in groups of from twenty to thirty in a wood, and remained there eight days. During this time they held a sort of musical tournament, two birds singing solo alternately, and the performance being occasionally varied by a chorus in which all the birds participated. It is positively asserted by ornithologists who were present at this singular concert that there was not a single female bird among the singers. Every now and then the birds moved in a body to another part of the wood, as if to test its acoustic properties."

THE SILKWORM DISEASE.—The continuance of the silkworm disease in France, we read in the *London Review* of Aug. 10th, stimulates scientific men to experiment with a view to the best means of detecting and of curing the malady. The method of detection proposed by M. Pasteur, in which the caterpillars are crushed in a mortar and then examined under the microscope, is crude and expensive. M. Balbiani therefore suggests a better mode of diagnosis. When in the chrysalis state, a very small portion of the projecting process which represent the future wing is snipped off with a pair of scissors, and is placed under the microscope; if now the larva be diseased, the peculiar pebrine corpuscles can be distinctly seen. The advantage of M. Balbiani's method is that it does not involve the death or injury of the silkworm.

SANTORIN.—A letter lately received states that the volcanic disturbances at Santorin have not yet ceased. The new lands which have been raised continue to extend towards the south, and are now within four or five metres of the north of Micra-Kamméni. Formerly the channel was twenty-one inches deep, but it is now not more than three. The island of Aphroessa remains stationary, but Vattia is now divided into two islands. Around the newly-formed lands the sea is of a yellowish-green colour, and has a temperature varying according to the locality, from 25° to 75° centigrade. M. Cigalla, who has studied the volcanic phenomena very carefully, thinks another great eruption will soon occur, and that a true volcanic crater will be formed at the top of the George island.

RODENTIA.—"Cosmos," in an article on "Rodentia," says that the distribution of the rat and the rabbit, which are the two most prominent members of that family, present some remarkable peculiarities. Thus the maximum of these animals is to be found in America, and the minimum in Australia, so that if we take Australia for a unit we have the following scale:—Australia 1, Europe 3, Africa 5, Asia 11, America 18. Polynesia appears to be entirely free from the family. There are at least six times more kinds in the temperate than in the frigid zone; America possesses ten times more than our continent, and there are only 13 kinds which are common to both hemispheres.

SPIDER AND WASP.—Last autumn the writer witnessed a curious combat between a large spider, of the species called in Suffolk the "death's-head" spider, and a fine wasp. The wasp had become entangled in the spider's web, who very cautiously, gradually, and most warily approached its victim, and not without reason, as the sequel shows; for no sooner had the insects closed in mortal combat, than they both fell dead to the ground at the same instant. The sting of the wasp must have entered the body of the spider at the precise moment the latter gave the fatal bite.—*People's Magazine*, August 3rd, 1867.

VITALITY OF SEEDS.—A remarkable instance of the well-known vitality of seeds may be now seen at the Paris Exhibition, a great variety of plants foreign to France having sprung up under the walls and around the buildings in the Park, the seeds of which have been conveyed to Paris in packages from various countries. Especially around the house of "Gustavus Wasa" several plants may be seen which are peculiar to the country of that monarch.—*Athenæum*, July 27.

Remarks, Queries, &c.

(*Under this head we shall be happy to insert original Remarks, Queries, &c.*)

CURIOUS SNAKE STORY.—At the request of Mr. Jowett with Messrs. Brownlow & Stark, naturalists of this town, I have great pleasure in replying to your enquiry respecting the snake and mouse.

I have had the ill luck to lose both. The mouse made his escape and the snake died. The glass front to the box where I kept them was drawn up in slides at the ends it. I appeared to me on first missing the mouse, that the glass had not been put tight down, and the mouse, a half-grown one, got out; this was about ten days after eating the snake. The box that they were kept in was put on a stand in our garden, because the snake smelt so strong in the house. The box was left out all day in the hot sun unknown to me; this, with the snake eating nothing, the poor thing sickened and died fifteen days after he was partly eaten. I give you the names of two parties, both earnest lovers of nature as well as myself, who witnessed what I have stated—John Scott, stone-mason, Sheffield, and Thomas Marsten, joiner, Blackburn.

Yours truly,

JOHN POTTS.

THE RING DOVE, OR CUSHAT.—This beautiful bird is found throughout the whole of Great Britain and Ireland. It frequents mostly the woodland districts, where it does a great deal of mischief by feeding on grain and other agricultural produce; therefore it cannot be considered a friend to the farmer. Its nest is generally found amid the thick branches of the beech or pine, and is composed of a few sticks loosely put together. It lays two eggs, and generally rears two broods in the season. It is easily tamed, but will never breed in confinement, nor has it ever been known to cross with any other variety. I have tamed several, one of which I keep in the same cage with a kestrel. While feeding the hawk, one day last month, with *raw cow's liver*, the pigeon much to my surprise, seized the meat from his very mouth, and before I could remove it had swallowed a large piece. I thought this very strange, as it had formerly been fed on grain, bread, &c., and had never tasted meat of any kind since it left the nest. I have since fed it for days together entirely on flesh, which it likes better than any other food. This proves that it is not entirely granivorous. At feeding time it has to be removed from the cage, or it would not let the hawk eat at all.

Mavisbush House.　　　　　　J. D. S. W.

WOOLHOPE NATURALISTS' FIELD CLUB.—A society was formed in 1851, under this name, for the practical study, in all its branches, of the natural history of Herefordshire and the adjacent district. Meetings of this very useful and flourishing club take place periodically, and one of these was held on the 18th inst., at the Craig-y-pwtt-du Waterfall, in Radnorshire. A goodly number of members and also of ladies attended, and the proceedings were of a very interesting nature. The Bach-howey stream, on which the beautiful waterfall is situate, here divides the lower and upper Ludlow strata, and the spot was peculiarly interesting to the geologist. The oak fern, Polypodium dryopteris, and all the common ferns grew on the side of the deep gorge in abundance. After a picnic luncheon on the grass a paper was read by Dr. Bull, on "Yew-trees and the Church;" and by the Rev. T. W. Weere, on "Recent Astronomical Observations."

SNAKE AND TOAD.—On the 30th of July I surprised a snake on a gravel path in our garden attempting to swallow a toad. The snake measured 18 inches, and the toad was at least twice the size of his mouth. The snake had succeeded in getting the toad half into his mouth, head foremost, although he was struggling violently and evidently not liking the treatment. On seeing me, the snake let go the toad and tried to be off, but the gardener perceiving him killed him. The toad on being released remained for some time stupified, but when placed in a pan of water, speedily revived; he however had lost one leg in the struggle. I cannot think how the snake managed to get the toad into his mouth, as his mouth was very small and the toad nearly full grown.　　　　　　　　　　　　　　　M. L. A.

August 11th, 1867.

THE TALLOW TREE.—In answer to Mr. I. S. asking on page 57 of the "*Naturalist's Note Book*," for any information on the Tallow-tree, I give what I know of it. This tree is a native of China. It grows to the height of the pear-tree, and is very like it in shape. The most singular part of this tree is the fruit, which is enclosed in a husk like that of the chestnut. When this fruit is ripe it opens, showing three white grains which contain the beautiful tallow. The tallow is procured by boiling the seed (after having been bruised) in water, and collecting the oily matter which

floats on the surface. If Mr. I. S. wishes further information on the subject, he can procure it from a book entitled "*Timber, Trees, and Fruits.*"
Mavisbush House. J. D. S. W.

CURIOUS POSITION OF A FLYCATCHER'S NEST.—In the beginning of July, a spotted flycatcher built a nest at the back of a straw target that was daily being used for archery. She laid four eggs and began to sit. Every day the nest was moved to a neighbouring flower bed, as the bird would have been shot through by the arrows if the nest had been allowed to remain at the back of the target, and when the shooting was over it was replaced. The bird never minded it, but always went back to the nest when replaced, although she never sat on it when in the flower bed. I regret to say that a gale of wind blew down the the target and destroyed both nest and eggs. It would have been interesting to see if the bird would have hatched her eggs and reared her young. M. L. A.
August, 11th, 1867.

THE BARN OWL.—Although this owl, as well as the other species in general see far better at night than in the day time; yet when taken young from the nest, they sometimes get so accustomed to the light that they seem to prefer it to the dark. One that I have at present, when shut up in a dark closet during the day, becomes restless and struggles to get free. But when released it is contented and playful, and well deserves the name of "*flying kitten.*" It does not at all object to sunshine. This bird, although some months old, never screeches. A Long-eared owl, too, kept by a friend of mine for three years, was never known to hoot. Perhaps some of your correspondents could inform me whether owls ever utter their notes in confinement, and if it is the male only that does so. R. W. B.

JUVENILE MUSEUMS.—In order to encourage a taste for natural history in the northern counties of Northumberland and Durham, a committee of naturalists at Newcastle-on-Tyne have offered a series of prizes for the best collection of plants, shells, fossils, and other objects. Various conditions of competition are published for the collectors, who must be under seventeen years of age. The late Professor Henslow established similar prizes in his Cambridgeshire parish many years ago. The example deserves to be widely followed, and we hope to see prizes in our public and private schools given for natural history as well as for Latin hexameters, Greek iambics, athletic exercises, and other miscellaneous competitions.

STATE OF THE WEATHER NEAR LONDON.

July and August.	Moon's Age.	BAROMETER.		TEMPERATURE.					Wind	Rain.	REMARKS.
				Of the Air.			of the Earth				
		Max.	Min.	Max	Min	Mean	1 foot deep	2 feet deep			
Thurs. 18	17	29.577	29.487	68	50	59.0	63	60	W.	.06	Rain; low white clouds; fine at night
Friday 19	18	29.745	29.574	65	52	58.5	62	59	W.	.01	Cloudy and boisterous; cloudy throughout.
Satur. 20	19	29.802	29.682	70	52	61.0	62	59	W.	.13	Clear; partially clouded; rain at night.
Sunday 21	20	29.643	29.605	72	51	61.5	63	60	S.W.	.02	Cloudy; partially clouded; cloudy.
Mon. 22	21	29.672	29.651	74	53	63.5	64	60	S.	.20	Rather boisterous; fine, with white clouds; rain.
Tues. 23	☾	29.612	29.598	72	48	60.0	64	60	S.	.02	Cloudy; showery; heavy showers at night.
Wed. 24	23	29.739	29.640	71	43	57.0	64	61	S.	.00	Very fine; cloudy; fine at night.
Thurs. 25	24	29.842	29.695	75	52	63.5	63	60	S.E.	1.48	Very fine; cloudy and fine; rain at night.
Friday 26	25	29.860	29.575	58	47	52.5	64	60	N.E.	.40	Constant heavy rain; boisterous, with rain; rain.
Satur. 27	26	30.047	29.924	64	41	52.5	61	59	W.	.02	Cloudy and cold; densely clouded; very fine.
Sunday 28	27	39.061	29.130	71	40	55.5	61	59	N.	.00	Fine, with low white clouds; fine throughout.
Mon. 29	28	30.064	30.000	65	38	51.5	61	59	N.	.00	Hazy clouds; fine; cold at night.
Tues. 30	29	30.027	29.989	72	44	58.0	61	59	N.	.00	Hoar frost early; rather cloudy; fine at night.
Wed. 31	●	29.973	29.945	72	43	57.5	61	59	N.E.	.00	Fine; dry haze; fine.
Thurs. 1	1	29.982	29.934	62	49	55.5	62	60	N.E.	.00	Dry wind; overcast and cold; overcast.
Friday 2	2	29.992	29.902	57	36	46.5	62	60	N.E.	.00	Overcast; cold; very fine at night.
Satur. 3	3	30.020	30.019	73	48	60.5	60	59	N.	.00	Overcast; fine; cloudy and warm.
Sunday 4	4	29.992	29.936	76	45	60.5	61	58	S.W.	.00	Very fine; fine; cloudy, but fine at night.
Mon. 5	5	29.995	29.897	73	41	57.5	62	59	S.W.	.32	Very fine; fine; densely overcast; rain.
Tues. 6	6	29.935	29.717	66	44	55.5	61	60	S.	.39	Rain; constant rain; fine at night.
Wed. 7	☽	29.762	29.670	70	53	66.5	60	59	W.	.28	Fine; heavy clouds and showers; fine; rain at night.
Thurs. 8	8	29.687	29.670	74	56	65.0	60	59	W.	.03	Densely overcast; cloudy, with showers; fine.
Friday 9	9	29.792	29.748	70	43	56.5	62	59	W.	.00	Fine; very fine throughout.
Satur. 10	10	30.080	29.946	70	45	57.5	64	60	W.	.00	Clear and exceedingly fine; very fine at night.
Sunday 11	11	30.006	29.935	79	53	66.0	64	59	S.W.	.00	Very fine throughout.
Mon. 12	12	30.069	29.958	84	50	67.0	64	59	S.	.00	Very fine; clear and hot throughout.
Tues. 13	13	29.959	29.922	86	54	70.0	65	60	S.E.	.00	Very fine; cloudless and hot; fine at night.
Wed. 14	14	29.948	29.736	91	61	76.0	66	62	S.	.18	Very fine; hot and cloudless; overcast; moonlight, with misty haze.
Thurs. 15	○	30.031	29.887	84	54	69.0	67	63	S.	.27	Rain; showery; slight rain at night.
Friday 16	16	29.800	29.615	75	54	64.5	66	63	W.	.00	Densely overcast; fine throughout.
Satur. 17	17	29.850	29.842	70	54	62.0	66	62	S.W.	.00	Cloudy; partially overcast and fine; cloudy.
Sunday 18	18	30.000	29.986	73	53	63.0	65	61	S.	.00	Overcast; cloudy; very fine at night.
Mon. 19	19	30.071	30.014	80	58	69.0	65	61	S.	.81	Very fine; exceedingly fine and hot; continuous storm of thunder, lightning, and heavy rain.
Tues. 20	20	20.073	29.990	81	51	66.0	66	62	W.	.00	Densely clouded; very fine; clear.
Wed. 21	21	29.985	29.960	82	53	67.5	65	63	W.	.00	Clear and fine; exceedingly fine throughout.

BIRDS OF THE EAST.

EVERYWHERE, the early morning is made beautiful by birds. Refreshed by sleep, they emerge from the bosom of darkness, and hail with rapture the renewal of light. If, then, you take your stand on some lofty slope of Gargarus, and look eastward, you behold the whole mighty level of Asia Minor bathed in purple light, while behind the peaks of Caucasus, the reflection, as of a universe on fire, kindles the whole orient. You then appear to be watching the advent of creation, the tremulous blushing of earth and heaven in the overpowering presence of the Deity, who flings profuse splendour and glory over his nascent works. As you think and meditate, the wail of some solitary jackal awakens the echoes among the hills; the cawing of rooks overhead carries you by association to far western lands, though the force of your imagination is soon checked by the approach of birds of gorgeous plumage from beyond Sahara and the Mountains of the Moon. What balmy freshness then fills the air, what scent of wildflowers, what incense from the young buds, from the pine, from the cedar, from the fir, from the fragrant linden, from the white-blossomed acacia, from the majestic and regal Vallona oak! If you go down by Ephesus or Miletus, you are encountered at certain seasons of the year by large flights of cranes, which, having done their work in Mozambique or Abyssinia, are coming northward to make war upon the frogs in the quagmires of Asia Minor. Yonder, amid the evergreen foliage of the arbutus, with its shining blossoms, or rich red fruit, which scents the air like a heap of strawberries, you perceive the golden-crested hoopoe, preferred by the ancient Greeks before the eagle, as the truest claimant of the bird-sceptre. To see this bird in his real home, you must cross the Ægæan, and take up your stand amid the leafy glades of Parnes or Cithæron, whither of old he retired from the bustle of Athens, to exercise his authority in peace. As a king, he could not but dislike the noise and license of a popular government, where everybody was his own king, and, as our neighbours express it, governed himself *tant bien que mal*. Several of his subjects were suspected of cherishing a hankering after the uplands of Hymettus, for sinister purposes — they were partial, it was thought, to the flavour of honey; and as the bees there piled up their fragrant white combs, scenting the mountain and dripping with pellucid dew, the honey-sucker and several of his companions hovered constantly over the beds of wild thyme and took advantage of every opportunity to dip their little bills in forbidden sweets. The old comic poet of Attica, whose imagination rivalled that of Shakspeare in richness, suggested a very strange project to the birds of his time. The divinities of Olympus, and especially their monarch, Zeus, having grown somewhat exigeant, he counselled the subjects of the hoopoe to erect a vast metropolis in the air, and by spreading out their wings on all sides, to hinder the ascent of the fumes of sacrifices and smoke of incense, on which the Olympians were supposed to live. By this means, he affirmed, the gods would soon be brought to reason, and made to understand that they depended entirely upon man for the supply of their larders. In the development of this grotesque fancy, the Athenian dramatist brings together all the birds of Greece, many of whose characteristic notes are distinctly heard in his verses, twittering, chirping, or pouring forth their liquid voices in song.

It is difficult to connect any idea of happiness with cold. To enjoy life, you must have a genial atmosphere which enables the heart to perform its functions with a thrill of satisfaction, and sends the blood tingling with pleasure through the veins. We talk of the merry month of May, of leafy June, of scorching July, of golden August; but the true type of the North is a man standing in a doubtful attitude, with one eye on the clouds, and the other on his umbrella, which he keeps ready to flap up at any moment against a shower. In many parts of the East, it is quite otherwise. Without fear of coughs or catarrhs, without shivering, without greatcoat, without umbrella, you may sit on rock or fallen tree, or recline at full length on the brown sward, listening to the cicada or the nightingale, while the sweet soft breeze, redolent of a thousand flowers, fans your cheek. Probably, traditions of the past enter largely into your feelings, and steep your fancy in poetry, which may account for the rapt delight inspired by listening even to the twittering of a sparrow amid the ruins of Chilminar, Palmyra, or Karnak. Here, in the highest temple ever reared by mortal hands, you may meditate or dream for many hours in the morning, undisturbed by a single footstep, till you fancy yourself alone with the past, and call up before you generations coeval with Menes. There is in Egypt a white eagle, not, properly speaking, an inhabitant, but a visitor from the interior, far beyond the sources of the Nile. This bird, as you sit on a fallen shaft, often perches himself on the summit of the ruin, and appears to be watching you as intently as you watch him. His whole frame is motionless except the eyes, which roll incessantly in their sockets, and assume at times a fierce expression, as if he meant to fly at your throat. Suddenly, however, his attention is called away by some sound inaudible to you, and off he flies towards the river. If you rise and watch him, you may behold his form disappear among the waters, and soon afterwards emerge again with prey in the beak. He is a fishing eagle, and lives on the mute dwellers in the Nile.

In the distant island of Crete, your eye and your ear are at once delighted by the form and notes of the blue thrush, the rarest bird in the Mediterranean. As you sit and listen on the southern slopes of Olympus, you behold the brilliant songster, seated, perhaps, on the waving bough of some golden willow, its little breast palpitating with music, invoking passionately the coming night—for the thrush never sings so sweetly as at evening's close, so that its latest song is often mistaken for that of the nightingale. Amid the deep gorges of the white mountains, which send their bases sheer out into the sea, you may often hear from the deck the lays of the thrush, which are scarcely terminated ere they are taken up by those of Philomela, so that for a while you almost forget the transition. Soon, however, your ear, if endowed with sensibility, detects the superiority of the queen of night as in throbs and gushes, she commemorates the causes of her sorrow. In those latitudes, all nature seems to be but one instrument of music—everything is in harmony—the calm, deep-blue sky, the rocks, the wood-clad mountains, the streams, the ripple of the waves among white pebbles upon the beach. Suddenly, a sharp, shrill cry is heard far up between the crags—it is the scream of the night-hawk, as it darts upon some prey gliding timidly through the darkness.

The true region of birds, however, is farther east, where Garganus overlooks the plains, where the Mæander winds, where Ephesus and Miletus in ruins, speak of Hellenic civilisation, where the Carduchian shepherd drives his flocks, where the Turk, calm and quiet, mutters: "La illah, ill ullah!" to himself at midnight, or smokes his refreshing pipe, amid the splendours of the dawn.

> Stern winter smiles on that auspicious clime;
> The fields are florid with unfading prime!

Even in December, marigolds and anemones spring from the turf beneath the olive-trees, myrtles are in full blossom, and in the groves the orange-trees display their golden fruit amid the dark-green foliage. Little more than a month later, the almond trees are in flower; hyacinths and daffodils are profuse in the meadows; while the bees in every copse and thicket hum busily at their work. It is then extremely pleasant to sit at midnight on the house-top, and listen to such sounds as greet the ear at such an hour. Among these, one of the most extraordinary is the noise made by the cranes, which, high up in the air, call to each other, apparently that they may not miss their way in the dazzling moonlight. The imagination of the Arabs created a race of beings analogous to humanity, who could share the pleasures of the cranes by flying through the air, and gazing upon the beauty which earth displays in her sleep. This, in fact, was only attributing sense, reason, and the power of observation, to storks, cranes, and other night-wanderers, which must, they imagined, enjoy extreme delight while passing over deserts, broad rivers, lofty mountains, large cities, towers, towns, villages, and hamlets bathed in moonlight, or touched by the mystic glimmer of the stars. A favourite bird with the Muslims is the curlew, to which they attribute a knowledge of religious truth, affirming that, in its solitary flight, it pronounces incessantly one of the orthodox professions of faith: "Lak, lak, lak! la Kharya Kalak fih il mulk"—God alone is king of the world, without second or companion. In the Great Desert, the traveller is often startled by this religious exclamation of the curlew, uttered in a sharp, shrill tone as he wings his way through the air. The belief is common in the East that all birds have a language, which, through incessant study, may be learned by man; and it is certain that these aërial creatures understand each other as well as we do. Upon superficial observation, their notes appear to be few, so that we arrive at the conclusion, that their ideas are so likewise; but this need not be the case, since every inflection of the voice with them, as with us, may convey different shades of meaning, so that their language may be far more copious than appears at first sight. Of course, they have made considerable proficiency in botany, natural history, and meteorology, since they would otherwise be unable to discern, as they do at a glance, the nature of plants, the character of animals, and the changes of the weather. By this knowledge, they preserve themselves from being poisoned, from attacking animals which they are unable to master, and from remaining longer in one climate than suits their health or their provisions. They are likewise extensively acquainted with geography, so that they can traverse vast tracts of country without ever loosing their way, directing their marches no doubt by observing certain mountains, rivers, or coasts, which, from their elevated points of observation, they discover at a great distance. When we ourselves desire to describe the shortest distance between any two places, we say, "As the crow flies," his flight being regulated with mathematical precision in a right line. Notions like these have led the orientals to indulge in wild speculations on the wisdom of the winged creation, which cannot only comprehend the present, but foretell the future; in which opinion several ancient nations concurred, persuading themselves that they might discover the course of coming events by the flight of birds, and the import of those events by the notes they uttered.—*Chambers's Journal*, Sept. 14, 1867.

BURROWING CRABS.

Perhaps the most remarkable of these is the great Cocoa-nut Eating Crab, or "*Ou-Ou*," as it is called by the natives of some of the localities in which it is met with. It is the *Birgous latro* of naturalists. It is found in the Coral Islands dotting the Indian seas and Pacific ocean, and beneath the rustling, waving, cocoa-nut groves, which abound within the torid zone. The *Ou-Ou* forms for himself a home, delving and burrowing, miner-like, beneath the wide-spreading roots of the tropic trees, and excavating deep and cunningly-formed galleries and chambers in the coral sand and broken shells; and one is almost disposed to think that the following lines by Thomson must have been penned in all the fervour of a poet's admiration for the happy lot of our friend of subterranean proclivities :—

"Sheltered amid the orchards of the sun,
Where high palmettos throw their graceful shade,
Give me to drain the cocoa's milky bowl,
And from the pine to drain its fresh'ning wine,
More bounteous far than all the frantic juice
Which Bacchus pours."

Here, like a feudal baron of old, he forms for himself a stronghold, sallying forth like a freebooter, to feast on the spoils of the grove. Curious stories are related of these marauders, and it has been gravely asserted that they have been known to ascend the tall stalks of the cocoa palms for the purpose of detaching and throwing down the nuts. We are not prepared to say that particular palms (when in a more than ordinarily sloping posture) may not have been climbed in the manner stated by certain species. Our own experience, however, strongly disposes us to think that such nuts as from time to time fall to the ground from ordinary causes, constitute the prizes commonly appropriated by *B. latro*. His enormously powerful and ponderous nippers enable him to husk and rend these from their tenacious coatings with surprising speed and facility; and it is only necessary to examine the cocoa-nut husks with the nuts within them, as imported from abroad, to be convinced that our nut-eating friend must be a veritable crustacean Hercules, to be capable of such feats of strength, as the dragging forth of the treasures from their dense fibrous envelopes unquestionably are; and a Hercules he is in his own way, for the tenacious wire-like network of cocoa fibre in which the nut is inclosed, is torn, split, and rent asunder, as though with the iron pincers of a brawny blacksmith, until the coveted dainty is set free. One end of every cocoa-nut has, as most of our readers are aware, three holes in it; these, from their position and quaint resemblance to a face of a living creature, are called the monkey's face. One of these holes is selected as a point of attack, and a succession of adroitly-delivered and heavy raps are rapidly given with the large claw. An opening, or breach, is thus very quickly effected. The narrow pair of nippers now come into operation, and by dexterously inserting them, the whole of the white, sweet, oleaginous contents are deftly scooped and clawed out. *B. latro* has a keen eye to future wants as well as to present enjoyment; he is not only a gourmand, but pretty much of a utilitarian; so he employs his sharp, powerful claws in carding and combing up the bundles of tangled coir, remaining after his husk-splitting operation. This, by dint of much clawing to and fro, at length becomes almost as fine as tow, or the oakum used by shipwrights. When sufficiently manipulated, he gathers together the result of his labours, and transports it to the inmost recesses of his subterranean stronghold beneath the roots; a bed is here made from it, on which our friend reclines; and it helps to form a convenient covering and protection for him when debarred from the pleasures and delights of Crab society during the uncomfortable process of shell-changing. The crafty human inhabitants of these wave-washed isles, are too well versed in the habits of our friend, and too well aware of his provident habits, not to avail themselves of the stores of well-preserved fibre thus laid up; advantage is therefore taken of the buried store, which is unceremoniously dragged forth, collected together, and made use of for caulking the seams of their canoes, and many other useful purposes. During the period of comparative torpidity usually accompanying the shell-shifting process, the wants of nature are wonderfully and wisely provided for. These strange creatures are each furnished with a species of natural magazine, containing fatty matter, which they carry beneath their tails. Some Crabs of large size have been known to yield enough to produce a quart of oil, limpid, of excellent quality, and highly esteemed by the natives. *B. latro* is much given to nocturnal rambling, and frequent visits are by him paid to localities within the cheering influences of the salt-sea wave; but we do not agree with those writers who have accused him of nightly hydropathic journeys. During the breeding season some considerable time is spent by the whole family in exploring the countless rock-pools and lagunes between the coral reefs. Here after the departure of the parents for their homes amongst the roots, the juvenile crabs continue to desport themselves, until grown strong enough to attack the nuts on their own account, when they proceed to join their seniors in the family diggings. The natives, when they set their minds on a Crab-hunting expedition, provide themselves with much the same kind of equipment as a party of English gamekeepers would use when about to extract a secretive badger from his burrow. Digging, and that of the most determined and energetic description, is the favourite method of bringing the game to light, which desirable consummation is rarely arrived at until a very large amount of loud shouting and needless leaping about has been had recourse to. The unfortunate Crabs are very good to eat, and they appear thoroughly aware of it, making use of every effort in their power to avoid capture. They are, nevertheless, ruthlessly overtaken in the subterranean race, dragged forth into the broad sunlight, ignominiously bound with cords twisted from the tough fibre of the cocoa husk (a very requisite precaution by the bye), and lugged off into hopeless captivity.

Some of these nut-feeders grow to a monstrous size (some being over two feet long), are armed with nippers of most formidable dimensions, and make no more of snapping the strong cord with which the Crab-catchers endeavour to secure them, than if they were as many strands of pack-thread. At certain seasons of the year a vegetable diet appears to become unpalatable to our friend. He then asks a change, and levies open and indiscriminate warfare on all the tribe of shell-bearing molluscs he can lay his thievish claws on, not giving even the ghost of a chance of escape. He seizes them forcibly with his nippers, and then extracts them from their snug shell-castles, with a dexterity which an accomplished London shell-fish dealer might look on with envy; and then, not content with devouring the ill-fated tenant, he performs a sort of grotesque, defiant, and triumphal march, with the vacant shell raised like a standard, aloft in his claws, as if for the express purpose of inciting other Crabs more peaceably disposed and less nefarious in their habits, to the perpetration of outrages of a similar character. Take him for all in all, *B. latro* may be considered anything but a well-conducted member of the family to which he belongs. His name denotes the character which he has fully earned and universally maintains.

The countless thousands of islands, reefs, and spots of newly-formed land dotting the South Seas and Indian Ocean, are ever on the increase. The foundations of these are firmly laid at the sea's bottom by legions of that tiny toiler of the deep, the coral insect, and year by year, and age by age, his ceaseless labours progress upward and ever upward towards the light of heaven; layer by layer, and ledge by ledge, are formed, until the pigmy beginning grows to be a strong sea-wall, like the ramparts of some Old World fortress. In time the green wave breaks and feathers on its crest, whilst other walls slowly but surely raise their masses from beneath. Within their circling grasp, a still rock lake at length is formed, round which the angry billows roll and thunder, chafing at the mighty barrier disputing their dominion. Here, within the safe, still pool, collect the thousand and one waifs and strays, ever to be found floating or driven by the tide currents. Fragments of wreck from distant shores, dead fish, empty mollusc shells, echini, sea-weed, and drift-wood cast far out to sea by the floods of the great rivers of the tropics;—all these, and innumerable other objects, find a resting-place on the newly-formed rocks, and in due time are broken up by decay, but are always added to by the same great store, until, wave-borne in their rough, strong, buoyant husks, come cocoa-nuts and other seeds. These quickly germinate, sprout up, and send their roots far out in search of nutriment, and thus bind the loose materials of the new-formed ground together. Watered by the tropic showers and sea spray, the little sea-girt forest grows apace, and the wandering sea-fowl, and migratory birds are not slow in converting it into a haven of rest for their wearied pinions. These last visitors bring in their crops, from far-off continents and islands, the seeds of many shrubs and plants, which, falling amongst elements congenial to their growth, rapidly spring into life, and, like the trees amongst which they find shelter, bear seed in their turn, and in due season die, to afford food for their successors in the kingdom of plants. Man claims some of these realms as his own; others are left to such inhabitants as nature may people them with. The West India Islands, too, are inhabited by many curious and interesting members of the Crab family: one of these known as the Land Crab (*Gecarcinus turicola*), is pretty much of a highlander in his nature. The upland solitudes are most to his taste, and here he forms for himself a snug retreat beneath the earth of the hill-side. As the spawning season approaches, a mighty gathering of the clans takes place, and whole legions, unwarned by fiery cross or blazing beacon, hasten forth to join the living tide flowing onward towards the sea. Through the tangled jungle, down the rock-strewn ravine, over fallen tree-trunks, and among the dense undergrowth of the forest, in ceaseless, creeping, crawling, scuttling thousands; still they come onward, and ever onward, as the bright stars shine out to light them on their way. Banks, hedges, walls, and even houses are passed straight over in this crustacean steeplechase, no flags being needed to keep the mail-clad competitors to the true course—instinct the guide, and the blue sea for a goal, nothing stops the race.

Cuffee and his companions, who have been gossiping and story-telling beneath their cocoa-leaf roofs until half-asleep, appear to become most violent and incurable lunatics, on suddenly becoming aware of the nocturnal exodus: they leap high in the air, shout, scream, and dance like fiends, whilst the most ready-witted of the crew dash off to *de massa* with the startling news. " Hi, golly, sa ; de Crab, de Crab ! he come for sure dis time, sure nuff; plenty catch um bum by ;" and Cuffee keeps his word to the letter, and captures the pilgrims by the basketful, in spite of their claws; and black-faced, woolly-headed Aunt Lilly, the cook, shows her teeth like ivory dominoes in an ebony box, as visions of white, snow-like rice, cocoa-nut milk, capsicum pods, and stewpans pass in pleasing and appetising review before her, and massa himself takes an extra pull at the cold sangaree jug, sleeps pleasantly, and dreams of the Crab feast of the morrow.

At the termination of the spawning season the survivors return to their homes among the hills; and but little notice is taken of them now, as they night by night bend their weary steps on the backward march, poor, low-conditioned, and unfit for human food, like the salmon-kelt on his journey to the sea. A short residence in his earth burrow serves to set our friend the Crab on his legs again, and make even better food of him than can be prepared during the migration. Sugar-cane plantations are his delight, and in them he regales himself like an alderman, nipping through the crisp rind of the sugar-bearing reed, sucking the luscious juices and clawing out the sweet contents, until a rustling sound warns him that Nemesis, in the form of our old friend Cuffee, is not far off, and that active individual, accompanied by a prick-eared cur, and armed with a spike-pointed cane, pounces down on the very spot where *G. ruricola*, Esq. has been so pleasantly regaling himself, and now commences a fierce and relentless action.

Cuffe, Cur, and Spike, v. Crab. Ever on the alert, Crab darts off backwards with astonishing rapidity, keeping a very bright eye on the cur, who rushes pell-mell after him through the canes, cheered on by the shouts and "Ya, ya's" of his sable master, whose aim it is to head back the Crab, or pin him with his spike. This latter feat he all but accomplishes; but the crab darts like lightning a couple of feet backwards, and then shoots off at right angles with the agility of a sprite. One more rapid dart in the opposite direction, the spike is furiously hurled by baffled Cuffee, and is within an inch of transfixing the cur, who sniffs and whines disconsolately at the mouth of a hole, which leads he knows not whither.

When hunting amongst the grass jungles of the Mahratta country, we were greatly amused at the quaint proceedings of a species of Crab which at certain seasons abounds there. These little fellows, members of the genus *Thelphusa*, were, when we saw them, busily engaged in their hay harvest, and actively engaged in mowing the grass. This they did in the most curiously quaint and elfish manner, sitting bolt upright and working their sharp scissors like nippers right and left, until enough to form a bundle had been gathered; then, with this compactly rolled up in sheafs, off they would trot to their holes, and when the load had been safely disposed of, back they would scuttle for others with quite as much bustle, fuss, and excitement as if they had been the owners of a large estate, a hundred acres of meadow hay to get in, and the barometer at change. So we left our funny, clever, energetic little friends with a good speed, hard at it, making hay whilst the sun shone.

These little fellows, we have every reason to think, are purely inland in their habits, and we know of no instance of their being known to travel either singly or in bodies to the sea coast. A member of the same genera, is found in many parts of the south of Europe, forming burrows for itself in the river banks, and from this habit obtains the name of *Thelphusa fluviatilis*. Few specimens reach three inches in length, and the colour is by no means inviting, being of a dingy yellow. Yet it appears to have attracted much attention amongst the ancients: both Aristotle and Hippocrates knew it well, and there are medals that were struck in very early periods bearing representations of this Crab on them. There appear to be some religious associations connected with crustaceans of this description, as we find the monks of the Greek church taking some pains to procure them, and then disposing of the dainty without troubling the cook. In Italy the burrowing Crabs are eaten at Easter, much as we eat hot-cross buns on Good Friday. There are other Crabs which form burrows both in the sands of the sea-shore and the banks and plains of the interior. One of these is the *Sana Crab* (*Ocypoda arenaria*) of naturalists. The wide, open sand-stretches of many tropical countries abound with these remarkable agile little creatures, who excavate holes in the sand close to the borders of the tide. These are the lilliputian pedestrians with whom skylarking midshipmen engage in foot-races along the strand, and meet ignominious defeat in consequence. As autumn approaches, their sea-side retreats are quitted, the inland burrows occupied, and a state of hybernation gone into, until, the winter having passed away and the spring weather come, *Seaward ho!* is the order of the day again.

The *Gelasimus* is in many respects similar in its habits to these fleet-footed gentlemen, but he turns his attention more directly to sapping and mining operations, carrying on his labours in the most cunning and artful manner. Nothing annoys him more than to have prying men or investigating animals, passing their remarks, or taking note of the mouth of his shaft; so he digs away in his deep level, until he has accumulated a goodly quantity of sand and earth, when up he comes stealthily to the opening of his mine, pops out his head, peers sharply and jealously round, and, if the coast appears clear, round he flourishes his claw with all the force and precision of an accomplished round-hand bowler at cricket, and away he casts the proceeds of his excavations, but at the same time taking care that no two clawfuls go in the same direction, less the newly raised sand should betray the secret he is so careful to conceal.

The sands of the reefs and islands of the Eastern seas afford a home for the King Crab (*Limulus*), who, with his odd-looking, shield-shaped body, and long blade-like spike or spear, will be familiar to many of our readers. Some individuals of this species grow to a very large size, and are sought for by the Malays, both on account of the immense number of eggs they sometimes contain, and the natural weapon with which nature has armed them. These lance-shaped spears are often made use of as points for arrows and other warlike implements, mainly because the wounds inflicted with them are more painful and dangerous than those received from instruments of iron or steel. The Malays are by no means an amiable or forgiving race, and take infinitely more pains to poison the blade of the "crease" or serpentine-knife they carry, than to serve a friend or save a life, and we therefore feel far more respect for a Crab who furnishes the point for the arrow, than for the man who fires it. Then there is the *Nut Crab* or *Calappa*, whose queer little legs are so closely tucked away under his odd little shell, that rambling "*Jack Tars*" in search of "*Curios*" not unfrequently gather a few to bring home to their friends, under the idea that when cut and polished they will serve to form elegant brooches and splendid shirt-pins, for the gay promenades of Portsmouth and Plymouth. A dry old salt of a quartermaster, on the Indian station, chanced one day, when on shore for a cruise, to become possessed of a goodly number of these *lucky stones*, as he called them, and by way of securing his treasures placed them in an old silk handkerchief, and stowed them away, with a few dollars and sundry cakes of *cavendish*, in the corner of his chest. It so happened that some piratical ship-mate, not proof against the allurements of *honey dew* and silver, but totally indifferent to natural history, seized his opportunity and spirited off the tobacco and money, but left the *lucky stones* behind. The next day, when our old friend came for his accustomed supply of the weed, he, to his horror, astonishment, and indignation, found the supposed pebbles in active motion, performing foot-races over his best jacket, the handkerchief spread open, and, alas! empty. "Well," exclaimed he, " blow me if this aint too much of the monkey. Why, look ye here, messmates; these here blessed stones have come to life, every man Jack of 'em. *They've chawed all my bacca* and spent every meg of my money; and now I'll heave all the beggars to Davey Jones's locker. Overboard is where I mean to pitch 'em!" and so he did, no doubt to the intense gratification of the falsely accused Crabs.—*Crab, Shrimp, and Lobster Lore*, by W. B. Lord, R.A. Routledge.

ORIGIN OF OCEANIC CURRENTS.

It is generally allowed, and seems to be unquestionably true, that all the currents which agitate the air must be attributed originally to the unequal distribution of the solar heat. The equatorial regions, exposed more directly to the influence of the sun, have a larger amount of warmth communicated to them than that which is received by the Frigid zones, and a portion at least of this warmth is carried by the aerial agencies to the colder regions of the globe. Some of the heat that falls on the intertropical lands passes by radiation into space; but the larger portion of it is communicated by contact to the air which lies above them. The air thus warmed, and consequently rarefied, rises upwards, and flows northward and southward to the poles. In like manner, the air which lies above the intertropical seas receives, from contact with the heated waters, a portion of the heat which they derive from the sun, and warmed and rarefied, this air also ascends and flows toward the colder regions. These aerial currents are modified in their course by various causes which change their direction and their force; but whatever these modifications may be, the ultimate tendency of the currents of heated air is towards the poles, while a counter current of colder air comes to the equator.

As there is nothing to interrupt the currents of air, their influence continues from age to age unchanged. They raise the average temperature of the Arctic and Antarctic circles, but have no particular effect on one locality more than on another.

Those parts of the Torrid zone which are covered with the deep, receive the same amount of solar heat as those that are occupied by the land. Some of the heat which falls on the ocean, like that which falls on the land, is lost by radiation into space. There is also a portion communicated to the air, to which we have already referred; but the larger portion is expended in warming the water at the surface. The water thus heated becomes expanded, and consequently lighter than that which occupies the depths below, and, like the air which has been heated by contact with the intertropical land, it flows northward and southward to the poles. The Gulf Stream on the coast of America is one of the most striking examples of these currents.

If we look on this heating, and consequent expanding of the water in the Torrid zone as the origin of the currents that flow to the colder parts of the globe, it follows as a necessary inference, that the larger the expanse of water that is exposed to the rays of the sun, the larger will be the current that is produced. And, on the other hand, it is equally evident, that the smaller the extent of water surface that is exposed to the solar heat, the smaller will the current be.

This seemingly self-evident inference has not always, however, been adverted to. Sir C. Lyell, in his "Principles of Geology," says:—

"Some have been induced to infer that there never has been any interruption to the agency of the same uniform laws of change. The same assemblage of general causes, they conceive, may have been sufficient to produce, by their various combinations, the endless variety of effects of which the shell of the earth has preserved the memorials. The greater warmth that seems to have prevailed in some former periods of the world's history, is not to be ascribed to a greater degree of heat in the globe itself, but to a different distribution of land and water. If we were to imagine all the land to be collected together in equatorial latitudes, and a few promontories only to project beyond the thirtieth parallel, the mean heat of the earth's crust would augment. A remarkable uniformity of climate would prevail amid the archipelagoes of the temperate and polar oceans, where the tepid waters of equatorial currents would freely circulate. We might expect in the summer of the great year, plants allied to genera now called tropical. Forms now confined to arctic and temperate regions would almost disappear, coral reefs would be prolonged again beyond the arctic circles, and droves of turtle might again begin to wander through regions now tenanted by the walrus and seal."

To this hypothesis Sir Charles refers with evident satisfaction in his "Antiquity of Man," p. 363.

Unfortunately for this theory, it is manifestly impossible that "the tepid waters of equatorial currents could freely circulate" at a time when the Torrid zone is supposed to have been almost entirely occupied by land. In the circumstances conjectured, a larger amount of heat would be raised from the land and carried by the air, and the average temperature of the earth would undergo no change. But it is manifestly impossible that any equatorial current could flow where there was no equatorial ocean out of which it could come.

While these streams, from the sunnier climes, pursue their course toward the colder regions of the globe, counter currents come back again towards the warmer. The cold, and consequently condensed and heavier water around the pole, flows as naturally towards the equator, as that which is heated flows to the poles. When the ocean is very deep, and no land interferes with the movements of the water, the returning stream will flow underneath the other. When the water is comparatively shallow, it must seek a separate channel. Such a return stream as we now speak of, laden with its floating icebergs, comes from the Arctic Ocean through Davis Straits, and passes the coast of Newfoundland.

If there were no continents, or large islands, to interrupt their flow, the natural course of the equatorial streams would be northward and southward, with a deviation to the east, in consequence of the earth's revolution on its axis. But in the northern hemisphere at least, the manner in which the land and water are distributed prevents these currents from flowing in this direction. They consequently occupy those channels which the natural configuration of the globe provides.

These channels are not permanent and continuous; on the contrary, they are liable to great and very remarkable changes. There are evidences, for instance, not to be mistaken, that the State of Massachussetts, and the surrounding parts of the United States of America, had at one time formed the bottom of a stream, which flowed from the north, and carried along with it masses of ice loaded with large pieces of rock. Similar evidences of polar currents are found in Britain, and marks have been discovered on our own hills which show that icebergs had passed over them when they were sunk more than a thousand feet below their present level. By what channels the equatorial waters flowed in those times we cannot tell. These tepid currents carry with them no floating masses, to leave to future ages the traces of their path. We know the course which was pursued by the stream which carried down its treasures of ice to cool the intertropical seas; but we cannot tell in what direction the other currents flowed.—*Papers offered for Discussion at the Meeting of the British Association at Dundee, By Rev. James Brodie, A.M.*

INSTINCT.

What is the true difference between reason and instinct? The question is one that is far more easily asked than satisfactorily answered, since we perceive that while some have gone the length of reducing all the faculties of the human mind to certain instinctive principles of action, others have elevated the animal instincts to a level with rational deliberation. True reasoning, however, would appear to be that faculty of the mind which distinguishes man from, and elevates him above, the brute creation; it is the peculiar privilege of a free and unfettered agent; the faculty, in short, by which that agent is enabled to discern the difference between good and evil.

Instinct, on the other hand, is the innate or natural impulse implanted in all animals, man not even excepted, in order to insure the well-being and safety of the creature. The faculty of reasoning is dependent upon experience and early training; instinct does not proceed from experience, but is a natural and impulsive feeling implanted by the Creator, as when we shrink from danger, or as when a duckling, a water-tortoise, or a young alligator, emerges from the egg to plunge at once into the water; a natural instinct prompting them to do so, although all are hatched upon the dry land.

"Instinct, therefore," it has been truly said, "differs from intellect or reason, by the unerring certainty of the means it employs, the uniformity of its results, and the perfection of its works prior to, and independent of, all instruction or experience; and lastly by the pursuit of nothing beyond what conduces directly either to the continuation of the individual, or the propagation of the kind."

It would appear, then, that reason is founded upon the experiences of the past, no matter whether they are the experiences of the individual reasoner himself, or of others who may have preceded him. And thus is it that children below a certain age are incapable of reasoning, because they possess no experiences of their own as data, nor can they make use of the experiences of others, since to do so must necessarily require some previous training, which would, in fact, amount to experience.

And yet with all our boasted learning and intellectual powers, it is nevertheless a fact that while our reasoning often leads to false conclusions, the instinct of the animal when left to nature, never errs. Why is this? Man may be tempted by the beauty of certain berries to eat thereof and poison himself from not knowing their deadly properties, whereas a monkey or a bird would turn away with the innate assurance that such fruit was noxious! If then our reasonings are thus *fallible*, and animal instincts are *infallible*, it would at first sight appear as if reason were inferior to instinct; yet such is not the case, nor can there be any real comparison between them, because a little reflection must convince us that while reasoning is *a cause*, instinct is, on the other hand, to be regarded as a *mere effect*; or perhaps, it would be more correct to say, that instinct is the means by which the reasoning of another is made, through animal agency, to produce beneficial results. Man's actions, for instance, are, or rather ought to be, the result or effect of his own sound reasoning; the actions of an animal are the instinctive, or mechanical effects of sound reasoning in another. The animal is, consequently, only the machine or instrument, by which the result of sound reasoning is rendered manifest; it gives effect to reasoning, but the cause of its actions does not dwell in, or proceed from it. If I break a pane of glass with my walking-stick, the fracture is no doubt a result produced through the agency of the instrument employed, but the cause of action is centred, not in the stick, but *in my will*. Thus too is it with animal instinct; the animal performs an act at the impelling instigation of another, whose will it cannot resist; and thus man's reasoning is fallible, because it proceeds from a finite and human source, while instinct is infallible because it proceeds from a perfect and Divine source; which is, in other words, to say that an animal performs, or obeys, the benevolent and good-exacting will, of its Creator who reasons for it.

Having thus, somewhat imperfectly perhaps, explained the difference between *reasoning* and *instinct*; namely, that the former is the direct cause of actions springing from the deliberation, experiences, and will of a free agent, while the latter, through the instrumentality of secondary agencies carries into effect or produces the desired results of the reasonings of another, I shall now proceed to notice some of those wonderful and instructive instances of animal instinct which are so well calculated to prove, not only the correctness of the above definition, but likewise the direct and ever watchful agency of a superintending and controlling intelligence that cannot err.

In the southern parts of Afghanistan it is evident that the chief cause of the great sterility that there prevails, arises from the want of permanent supplies of water; and this deficiency is in turn to be attributed to the lowness of the mountain ranges, the elevation being insufficient to insure, as in the loftier regions of the Himalaya, a permanent supply of water from the gradual melting of the snows. The consequence is that when the warmth of the spring sets in, the snow all rapidly melts away, filling the river channels for two or three months nearly to overflowing, but leaving them dry for the rest of the year. The residents in those parts of the country, profiting by experience, have adopted the practice of damming up the river beds at no great distance from the hills for the purpose, when the rush of water begins to decrease, of securing and retaining a supply for the irrigation of their crops throughout the summer. By this means a long deep lake is often formed. Man's reason has, in this instance, enabled him to profit by the experience of the past, and has taught him to supply his wants by preventing the escape of the water.

Very similar to the results of this act of reasoning on the part of man, are the ends obtained by the instinct of the beaver (*Castor fiber*); indeed, so close is the resemblance that we cannot but acknowledge that the effects in either case have proceeded from the free exercise of reason in the ultimate causes from which they have severally sprung.

It is said by those who have narrowly observed them in their native haunts, that the beavers prefer a creek, or river, on account of the advantages they then derive from the current in floating down timber and other materials to the spot selected for their habitation. It sometimes happens that these creeks, and even the smaller rivers, are liable to have their waters drained off during the winter, when the supply from their sources is temporarily cut off, or frozen up by the severity of the frosts. In order to provide against such a ruinous contingency, the animals, with an instinctive wisdom that nothing short of Omnipotence could impart, proceed to construct a dam across the river at some distance below their houses, by which arrangement a body of water is effectually secured. "These beavers' dams," says Herne, "differ in shape according to the nature of the place in which they are built. If the water in the river, or creek, have but little motion, the dam is almost straight; but when the current is more rapid it is always made with considerable curve, convex towards the stream." Herein, then, are at once most conspicuously displayed both reasoning, foresight, and design—the two first in selecting the current as a means of transport, and the latter in constructing a dam for the express purpose of preventing the escape of the water and providing the most suitable form for supplying the strength necessary to resist the current's force. What indeed is more indicative of wisdom and calculation than the form of the dam? Is it not precisely that which of all others man himself would oppose to the current of a stream as being the strongest, and therefore the best adapted to resist the weight and pressure of the water? Man, however, although the most intelligent of created beings, has only ascertained this fact after years of close study and experience, while the very first beaver at once resorted to this method as the most effectual one it could adopt. How did it know, how could it know that winter would ensue? How did it learn that the frost would cut off the supply of water from the sources of the stream and so destroy its habitation? It could know nothing of such things itself, and yet it acted as if it had acquired a perfect knowledge of nature's laws; and why? The answer is obvious, the conclusion, unavoidable, because it was taught of God!

The beaver, then, is compelled to act instinctively, or in obedience to a law of nature, which constrains it to provide for its own safety; and the law thus compelling and controlling its actions is nothing less than the will of God.

Again, there are some species of moths, belonging to the family of the *Bombycidæ*, or silk-spinners, which construct a strong silken cocoon in which the chrysalis, or *pupa*, is destined to pass the winter months; and these not only show that their actions are neither dictated by caprice nor chance, but they actually appear, on the contrary, to evince great powers of reasoning.—Capt. Thos. Hutton, F.G.S., in *Land and Water*, Sep. 7th.

THE DATE PALM.

THE Date Palm (Phœnix dactylifera) is one of the most important of Palms, and if not an article of very great consumption with us, to some nations it affords their chief support. It is difficult to tell why this fruit is not more largely consumed in this country than it is, for it is not only very delicious, but is likewise very nourishing.

The cultivation of the Date Palm extends through Southern Europe and Western Asia, but more especially in Northern Africa, where the tree is a most invaluable one to the desert tribes. In the South of Europe, where it has been introduced, it seldom or never ripens its fruit in perfection. The cultivation of the Date can be traced to a very remote age, and it seems tolerably certain that where the Palm tree is mentioned in Scripture the Date is implied; and from this belief the custom in Roman Catholic countries of carrying branches of the Date Palm on Palm Sunday, and on some other festivals of the Church, has had its origin. In places where the Palm will not ripen its fruits it is largely cultivated solely on account of its leaves, which constitute a regular article of trade. In some parts of the Continent, however, where Palm leaves are not to be had, leaves of Cycads are used in churches instead, these plants being largely grown for that purpose—a better substitute, our readers will say, for a true Palm leaf than the Willow, which in many parts of this country is called "Palm." Besides being a valued symbol amongst Christians of ancient and modern times, the Jews also carried Palm branches in their festivals commemorating the possession of the Promised Land. The Palm tree was a type of Judæa, and as such was represented on the coins of Vespasian and Titus. Valuable, however, as Palm leaves may still be in an ecclesiastical point of view, by far the most important production of the Date Palm is its fruit, which is the chief support of the settled tribes of North Africa, as well as the staple product of many other districts. In the Turkish portion of the district of Bussorah the yearly produce amounts to about 33,000 tons, half of which is consumed in the district, and the other half exported to the Persian Gulf ports, India and England. Nor are Dates consumed by the natives alone in those countries in which they are plentiful. Camels, horses, and other animals are said to be exceedingly fond of them.

Three or four varieties of Dates are known in British commerce. Of these Tafilat is always considered the finest. In their native countries, however, there is scarcely any limit to the kinds known, and their names are derived from their size, shape, quality, &c. These varieties vary considerably in the prices they fetch. In the valleys of the Hedjaz it is said that more than 100 kinds are grown. So large is the value of the Date crops to the different tribes, that the gathering is looked forward to with as much interest as the vintage in the South of Europe, or our own Wheat harvest in England. If the crop fails or is destroyed by locusts, as it sometimes is, a general gloom prevails throughout the entire district. The cultivation of the Date, though so general, is nevertheless an operation requiring some care, as, the plants being diœcious, the female flowers have to be artificially impregnated with the pollen of the male flowers; for this purpose the male flowers are first gathered, and then men climb the female tree and scatter the pollen over the female flowers. About four or five months after this operation the fruits begin to grow, and when they have nearly attained to maturity they are carefully tied up to prevent them from falling, or from injury by the wind. This process of fertilisation appears to have been well known to the ancients, it is mentioned both by Theophrastus and Pliny. In "Delile's Egyptian Flora" a circumstance is related which occurred in the year 1800, when the Date trees in the neighbourhood of Cairo yielded no crop. It would seem that, the land being completely run over by French and Turkish soldiers, a serious check was given to all branches of husbandry and agriculture. The Date Palms flowered, but the artificial fertilisation was omitted, and the result was that no fruit was produced, the pollen of the male flowers, though scattered by the winds, did not reach the female flowers in sufficient quantities to ensure fertilisation.

Dates, as we see them in this country, are the fruits that have been gathered and dried in the sun before becoming quite ripe; for if they are allowed to hang upon the trees till fully ripe they are unfit for keeping, as they soon turn acid or ferment. The Arabs make a kind of Date cake by pressing the fruits in baskets, and this forms their principal subsistence at such times when fresh Dates are not to be obtained; similar cakes are made and cut into slices and sold to travellers by the monks of Mount Sinai. When Dates are fully ripe they contain a large quantity of thick syrup, which the natives express and collect to preserve the Dates themselves and other fruits in; a strong spirit is also distilled from them. Besides these varied uses of the fruits, the trunk, leaves, and indeed the entire plant is valuable for various economic purposes. Baskets, crates, walking-sticks, and a multitude of other articles are made from the petiole. Cordage, and a kind of coarse cloth is made from the sheathing bases of the leaf-stalks, and from the trunks themselves are hewn posts, beams, &c., indeed the huts of the natives are almost entirely composed of parts of this Palm, and even the hard stones or seeds are boiled or ground as food for cattle. Date Palms are not unfrequently objects of exchange or barter, a single tree being often given over from one person to another in payment of a debt. A bridegroom also pays the price of his bride in Date trees to her father. The trees, which grow to a height of 60 or 80 feet live to a good old age; 100 to 200 years is not at all uncommon, and they bear fruit abundantly all that time. The consumption of Dates in this country is, as we have said, very small, the yearly imports upon an average perhaps do not exceed 14 or 15 tons.

Whether the Wild Date (Phœnix sylvestris), which grows abundantly all over India, is a distinct species, is a question on which botanists have disputed. Unlike the cultivated Date its value does not depend on its fruits, but on the quantities of Palm wine, or toddy, and the amount of sagar which are obtained from it. In India large quantities of both are made, and the average yield of a single tree is said to be from 120 to 240 pounds of juice.—J., *Gardener's Chronicle*, Sep. 14th.

THE MOCKING-BIRD OF AMERICA—*MIMUS POLYGLOTTUS*.

THE precise time at which the Mocking-bird begins to build his nest varies according to the latitude in which he resides. In the lower parts of Georgia he commences building early in April, but in Pennsylvania rarely before the 10th of May, and in New York and the States of New England still later. There are particular situations to which he gives the preference. A solitary thorn bush, an almost impenetrable thicket, an orange tree, cedar, or holly bush, are favourite spots, and frequently selected. It is no great objection with him that these happen sometimes to be near the farm or mansion house. Always ready to defend, but never over anxious to conceal his nest, he very often builds within a small distance of the house, and not unfrequently in a pear or apple tree—rarely at a greater height than six or seven feet from the ground. The nest varies a little in different individuals, according to the conveniency of collecting suitable materials. First, a quantity of dry twigs and sticks; then, withered tops of weeds of the preceding year, intermixed with fine straws, hay, pieces of wool, and tow; and lastly, a thick layer of fine fibrous roots of a light-brown colour lines the whole. The eggs are four, sometimes five, of a cenereous-blue, marked with large blotches of brown. The female sits fourteen days, and generally produces two broods in the season, unless robbed of her eggs, in which case she will even build and lay the third time. She is, however, extremely jealous of her nest, and very apt to forsake it if much disturbed. During the period of incubation neither cat, dog, animal, nor man can approach the nest without being attacked. The cats in particular are persecuted whenever they make their appearance, till obliged to retreat. But his whole vengeance is most particularly directed against that mortal enemy of his eggs and young—the black snake. Whenever the insidious approaches of this reptile are discovered, the male darts upon it with the rapidity of an arrow, dexterously eluding its bite, and striking it violently and incessantly about the head, where it is very vulnerable. The snake soon becomes sensible of its danger, and seeks to escape; but the intrepid defender of his young redoubles his exertions, and, unless his antagonist be of great magnitude, often succeeds in destroying him. All its pretended powers of fascination avails it nothing against the vengeance of this noble bird. As the snake's strength begins to flag, the Mocking-bird seizes and lifts it up partly from the ground, beating it with his wings; and, when the business is completed, he returns to the repository of his young, mounts the summit of the bush, and pours out a torrent of song in token of victory.

The plumage of the Mocking-bird, though none of the homeliest, has nothing gaudy or brilliant in it, and, had he nothing else to recommend him, would scarcely entitle him to notice; but his figure is well proportioned, and even handsome. The ease, elegance, and rapidity of his movements, the animation of his eye, and the intelligence he displays in listening and laying up lessons from almost every species of the feathered creation within his hearing, are really surprising, and mark the peculiarity of his genius. To these qualities we may add that of a voice full, strong, and musical, and capable of almost every modulation, from the clear, mellow tones of the woodthrush to the savage scream of the bald eagle. In measure and accent he faithfully follows his originals; in force and sweetness of expression he greatly improves upon them. In his native groves, mounted on the top of a tall bush or half-grown tree, in the dawn of dewy morning, while the woods are already vocal with a multitude of warblers, his admirable song rises pre-eminent over every competition. The ear can listen to his music alone, to which that of all the others seems a mere accompaniment. Neither is this strain altogether imitative. His own native notes, which are easily distinguishable by such as are well acquainted with those of our various song birds, are bold and full, and varied seemingly beyond all limits. They consist of short expressions of two, three, or at the most five or six syllables, generally interspersed with imitations, and all of them uttered with great emphasis and rapidity, and continued with undiminished ardour for half an hour or an hour at a time. His expanded wings and tail, glistening with white, and the buoyant gaiety of his action arresting the eye, as his song most irresistibly does the ear, he sweeps round with enthusiastic ecstacy; he mounts and descends as his song swells or dies away; and, as my friend Mr. Bartram has beautifully expressed it, " he bounds aloft with the celerity of an arrow, as if to recover or recal his very soul, expired in the last elevated strain." While thus exerting himself a bystander destitute of sight would suppose that the whole feathered tribes had assembled together on a trial of skill, each striving to produce his utmost effect, so perfect are his imitations. He many times deceives the sportsman, and sends him in search of birds that perhaps are not within miles of him, but whose notes he exactly imitates; even birds themselves are frequently imposed on by his admirable mimics, and are decoyed by the fancied calls of their mates, or dive with precipitation into the depth of thickness at the scream of what they suppose to be the sparrowhawk.

The Mocking-bird loses little of the power and energy of his song by confinement. In his domesticated state, when he commences his career of song it is impossible to stand by uninterested. He whistles for the dog—Cæsar starts up, wags his tail, and runs to meet his master. He squeaks out like a hurt chicken, and the hen hurries about with hanging wings and bristled feathers, clucking to protect its injured brood. The barking of the dog, the mewing of the cat, the creaking of a passing wheelbarrow, follow with great truth and rapidity. He repeats the tune taught him by his master, though of considerable length, fully and faithfully. He runs over the quiverings of the canary and the clear whistlings of the Virginia nightingale or red-bird with such superior execution and effect, that the mortified songsters feel their own inferiority and become altogether silent, while he seems to triumph in their defeat by redoubling his exertions.

"This excessive fondness for variety, however, in the opinion of some injures his song. His elevated imitations of the brown thrush are frequently interrupted by the crowing of cocks; and the warbling of the blue-bird, which he exquisitely manages, are mingled with the screaming of swallows, or the cackling of hens; amidst the simple melody of the robin we are suddenly surprised by the shrill recitations of the whip-poor-will, while the notes of the kill-deer, blue jay, martin, baltimore, and twenty others, succeeding with such imposing reality that we look round for the originals, and discover with astonishment that the sole performer in this singular concert is the admirable bird now before us. During this exhibition of his powers he spreads his wings, expands his tail, and throws himself around the cage in all the ecstacy of enthusiasm, seeming not only to sing, but to dance, keeping time to the measure of his own music. Both in his native and domesticated state, during the solemn stillness of night, as soon as the moon rises in silent majesty, he begins his delightful solo, and serenades us the livelong night with a full display of his vocal powers, making the whole neighbourhood ring with his inimitable medley."—*Ednore and Samuels' Ornithology and Oology of New England.* London: Trubner.

PROTECTION IN NATURE.

THE slightest observation of the life of animals will show us, that they escape from their enemies and obtain their food in an infinite variety of ways; and that their varied habits and instincts are in every case adapted to the conditions of their existence. The porcupine and the hedgehog have a defensive armour that saves them from the attacks of most animals. The tortoise is not injured by the conspicuous colours of his shell, because that shell is in most cases an effectual protection to him. The skunks of North America find safety in their power of emitting an unbearably offensive odour; the beaver in its aquatic habits and solidly constructed abode. In some cases the chief danger to an animal occurs at one particular period of its existence, and if that is guarded against its numbers can easily be maintained. This is the case with many birds, the eggs and young of which are especially obnoxious to danger, and we find accordingly a variety of curious contrivances to protect them. We have nests carefully concealed, hung from the slender extremities of grass or boughs over water, or placed in the hollow of a tree with a very small opening. When these precautions are successful, so many more individuals will be reared than can possibly find food during the least favourable seasons, that there will always be a number of weakly and inexperienced young birds who will fall a prey to the enemies of the race, and thus render necessary for the stronger and healthier individuals no other safeguard than their strength and activity. The instincts most favourable to the production and rearing of offspring will in these cases be most important, and the survival of the fittest will act so as to keep up and advance those instincts, while other causes which tend to modify colour and marking may continue their action almost unchecked.

It is perhaps in insects that we may best study the varied means by which animals are defended, or concealed. One of the uses of the phosphorescence with which many insects are furnished, is probably to frighten away their enemies; for Kirby and Spence state that a ground beetle (Carabus) has been observed running round and round a luminous centipede as if afraid to attack it. An immense number of insects have stings, and some stingless ants of the genus Polyrachis are armed with strong and sharp spines on the back, which must render them unpalatable to many of the smaller insectivorous birds. Many beetles of the family Curculionidæ have the wing cases and other external parts so excessively hard, that they cannot be pinned without first drilling a hole to receive the pin, and it is probable that all such find a protection in this excessive hardness. Great numbers of insects hide themselves among the petals of flowers, or in the cracks of barks and timber; and finally, extensive groups and even whole orders have a more or less powerful and disgusting smell and taste, which they either possess permanently, or can emit at pleasure. The attitudes of some insects may also protect them, as the habit of turning up the tail by the harmless rove-beetles (Staphylinidæ) no doubt leads other animals besides children to the belief that they can sting. The curious attitude assumed by sphinx caterpillars is probably a safeguard, as well as the blood-red tentacles which can suddenly be thrown out from the neck, by the caterpillars of all the true swallow-tailed butterflies.

It is among the groups that possess some of these varied kinds of protection in a high degree, that we find the greatest amount of conspicuous colour, or at least the most complete absence of protective imitation. The stinging Hymenoptera, wasps, bees, and hornets, are, as a rule, very showy and brilliant insects, and there is not a single instance recorded in which any one of them is coloured so as to resemble a vegetable or inanimate substance. The Chrysididæ, or golden wasps, which do not sting, possess as a substitute the power of rolling themselves up into a ball, which is almost as hard and polished as if really made of metal,—and they are all adorned with the most gorgeous colours. The whole order Hemiptera (comprising the bugs) emit a powerful odour, and they present a very large proportion of gay-coloured and conspicuous insects. The lady-birds (Coccinellidæ) and their allies, the Eumorphidæ, are often brightly spotted, as if to attract attention; but they can both emit fluids of a very disagreeable nature; they are certainly rejected by some birds, and are probably never eaten by any.

The great family of ground beetles (Carabidæ) almost all possess a disagreeable and some a very pungent smell, and a few called bombardier beetles have the peculiar faculty of emitting a jet of very volatile liquid which appears like a puff of smoke, and is accompanied by a distant crepitating explosion. It is probably because these insects are mostly nocturnal and predacious that they do not present more vivid hues. They are chiefly remarkable for brilliant metallic tints or dull red patches when they are not wholly black, and are therefore very conspicuous by day, when insect-eaters are kept off by their bad odour and taste, but are sufficiently invisible at night when it is of importance that their prey should not become aware of their proximity.

It seems probable that in some cases that which would appear at first sight to be a source of danger to its possessor may really be a means of protection. Many showy and weak-flying butterflies have a very broad expanse of wing, as in the brilliant blue Morphos of Brazilian forests, and the large Eastern Papilios; yet these groups are tolerably plentiful. Now, specimens of these butterflies are often captured with pierced and broken wings, as if they had been seized by birds from whom they had escaped; but if the wings had been much smaller in proportion to the body, it seems probable that the insect would be more frequently struck or pierced in a vital part, and thus the increased expanse of the wings may have been indirectly beneficial.

In other cases the capacity of increase in a species is so great that however many of the perfect insect may be destroyed, there is always ample means for the continuance of the race. Many of the flesh-flies, gnats, ants, palm-tree weevils and locusts are in this category. The whole family of Cetoniadæ or rose chafers, so full of gaily-coloured species, are probably saved from attack by a combination of characters. They fly very rapidly with a zigzag or waving course; they hide themselves the moment they alight, either in the corolla of flowers or in rotten wood or in cracks and hollows of trees, and they are generally encased in a very hard and polished coat of mail which may render them unsatisfactory food to such birds as would be able to capture them. The causes which lead to the development of colour have been here able to act unchecked, and we see the result in a large variety of the most gorgeously-coloured insects.—*Westminster Review*, July, 1867.

The Herring.

It is a pity that we do not know more about the natural history of the herring—indeed more knowledge is greatly wanted of the life and habits of all our sea fish. We literally do not know the alphabet, so to speak, of the natural history of our best food fishes. We can only guess at what age the haddock or the herring becomes reproductive, or how long the spawn takes to quicken into life, yet these are the first points that ought to be determined in all animal economy. It is gratifying to find that some of our best writers on natural history are turning their attention to these very material points in the economy of our fish food supplies. So far as the herring is concerned, it is now pretty well determined that it is an animal that breeds and grows in the British seas, and is never absent from the waters that surround our islands. The old story of its annual migration from the arctic seas, the authorship of which, by-the-bye, has been erroneously ascribed to Pennant, has long since been disproved, and the herring is now known to be a very local animal. That is really so, for it has been often shown that the herrings of one locality differ considerably from those of another: the herrings taken in the Frith of Forth, for instance, can be distinguished by fishery experts from those taken in Lochfyne. The food of these fish varies in different places, and is also less abundant in some places than in others; and we have noticed in consequence that the herrings of the inland Scottish lochs are fatter and of better flavour than the fish taken on the open sea-board. We have long been of opinion also that each particular sea or bay has its own particular season so far as the spawning of the fish is concerned; and moreover, that th herrings are arriving at maturity and spawning all the year round, of course at different places of the coast. Some writers on the natural history of the herring are of opinion that these fish spawn at a very early age, that the spawn comes very quickly to maturity, and that the fish arrive at the reproductive stage with great rapidity. But there is no certain information on these points; most of what has been said or written on that part of the natural history of the herring is founded on guesswork, as is also the supposition of some fishery economists that herrings spawn twice a year. Mr. John Cleghorn of Wick, who has studied the natural history of the herring with great care, is of opinion that these fish exist in races, and that, race by race, they come to maturity in the different months of the year; so that we might obtain plentiful supplies of fresh herrings all the year round. Before leaving this part of our subject we may notice, as among the curiosities of fish life and growth, that some persons think whitebait are the young of the herring in a very early stage of its life, and that there are writers who maintain the sprat to be also the young of the herring. It is certainly curious that sprats (*i.e.* fish with a serrated abdomen) are taken along with the young herring in great quantities. We should be very glad to learn that some experiments had been instituted to find out the exact relationship that the sprat bears to the herring, and also to determine the periods of reproduction of all our food fishes.—*People's Magazine*, September.

New Books.

[*Our limited space must of necessity compel us to give but very short notices of new books, but they will perhaps serve as a guide as to what books our readers may ask for at their libraries.*]

Hog-hunting in the East, and Other Sports. By Captain J. T. Newall, Author of "The Eastern Hunters," "John Neville," &c. London: Tinsley Brothers. 1867.

WE have here one of the most pleasant volumes it has been our lot to read for some time. Captain Newall is a sportsman of the right school, combining instructive descriptions of the various animals, with hair breadth escapes and wild encounters sufficient to gratify most people. The district must be the very thing for Englishmen, to judge from his description. He says:—

The entire length of the Province of Cutch is 200 miles, and its greatest breadth, exclusive of the Run, forty-five miles. All kinds of hunting countries are to be found in this space; and a sportsman may according to his taste, or the season of the year, ride a pig either on the open plain of the Run or the level in the neighbourhood of the sea coast, or diversify his sport by a gallop over the stony hills or among the rivers, ravines, and nullahs, of the interior.

As the title indicates, hog-hunting formed the chief amusement, though not the only one, as numerous anecdotes and incidents of other sports will be found scattered through its pages, including one or two bear adventures. Our author has no mean eye for the beauties of nature, as may be seen from the following:—

"I wish I could give you fellows an idea of the glorious scenery of that pass," said Melton. All the lower slopes of the mountains with a southern exposure towards Dhurmsala, were either bare spurs of the most vivid green, varied with the colours of the rocks, or clothed with magnificent forests of oaks and rhododendrons. Those again to the north were clad in the more sombre garments of pine, cedar, and fir. Above the region of the trees, where the widowed mountain rose desolate and grand till it culminated in peaks, precipices, and glaciers, the great seams and clefts of the range were mostly filled with snow, hiding the torrents which somewhat lower broke away and flashed roaring down the mountain. These gorges, however, were but mere intersections of the great upland slopes, which were strewn with huge boulders of granite—the debris from the peaks and precipices above—among which the most beautiful flowers, ferns, lichens, and grapes, in infinite variety, and including many much prized in England, gemmed the rich verdure and mingled with masses of bracken and wild rhubarb, "wasting their sweetness in the desert air."

It is only those who have seen such who can fully appreciate the ruggedness, the desolate, secluded wildness and grandeur of the lone mountain scenery, unstained, uncontaminated by the feeble efforts of man, and showing in its vast and solitary glory the all-powerful impress of the hand of nature in her sternest mood. No sound to break the silence save the dull murmur of some distant cascade, the wild cry of the moonal, some call from the forests below, or the occasional fall of a mass of rock. Such is the great spur of the Himalayas, which separates the Burnaor valley from the Punjaub.

In conclusion, we may say that there are twenty-three illustrations well executed, and of some merit, and that we can confidently recommend the volume to all who are in want of several hours' very pleasant reading.

Mushrooms and Toadstools. By W. G. Smith. Pp. x. and 64; with two large sheets containing figures of Edible and Poisonous Fungi. London: Hardwicke. 1867.

THIS is a very valuable little work, with two sheets of drawings representing the most important edible and poisonous fungi of the British islands. The sheets appear drawn for the purpose of hanging up in schoolrooms and other places, where indeed they will be found of the greatest service, as there are still many we constantly see in the papers who from want of knowledge gather and eat the poisonous kinds.

The Orchard and Fruit Garden. By Elizabeth Watts. London: Warner and Co.

AN excellent little work on fruit-growing; superior to many that have been issued for the purpose of teaching the reader how to procure a good stock of fruit. There are some few faults, but they are of a minor character, and do not in any way detract from the value of the volume; one fault we may mention is giving too many different methods of doing things—though this may possibly be a virtue in the eyes of some who are fond of change and like experimenting.

BOOKS RECENTLY PUBLISHED.

A New Theory of Geology, in which the Truth of the Bible is demonstrated, and Dr. Colenso's Attack refuted, by proving from Facts and Science the Literal Accordance of Geology with the First Chapter of Genesis, and also establishing the Credibility of Noah's Flood, &c. By J. L. Hamilton, Adams and Co.

British Conchology, Vol. IV. Marine Shells in continuation of the Gasteropoda as far as the Bulla family. By John Gwyn Jeffreys, F.R.S. 8vo. Pp. 488, tab. 8, and a coloured frontispiece. Van Voorst. 1867.

The Silkworm Book; or, Silkworms Ancient and Modern, their Food, and Mode of Management. By W. B. Lord, R.A. 8vo. Cox. 1867.

Carolina Sports, by Land and Water; including Incidents of Devil-Fishing, Wild-Cat, Deer and Bear Hunting, &c. By the Hon. William Elliott. Post 8vo. 6s. R. Bentley.

Meetings of Learned Societies.

THE BRITISH ASSOCIATION.
Physical Science.

President, Professor Sir W. Thomson; Vice-Presidents, Prof. Fischer, J. P. Gassiot, Professor Kelland, J. Clerk Maxwell, Rev. C. Pritchard, Prof. Tyndall, Dr. C. Wheatstone; Secretaries, Rev. C. Buckle, Prof. G. C. Foster, Prof. Fuller, Prof. Swan; Committee, Sir E. Belcher, W. R. Birt, Sir D. Brewster, C. Brooke, A. R. Catton, A. Claudet, Dr. Everett, Rev. Dr. J. Forbes, J. Glaisher, Dr. Haan, Rev. R. Harley, A. Herschel, W. P. Hiern, Prof. Hirst, W. H. Hudson, Sir H. James, E. J. Lowe, Prof. Mannheim, C. Meldrum, J. R. Napier, Admiral Ommanney, Prof. Rankine, W. Spottiswoode, Balfour Stewart, Col. Sykes, Prof. Sylvester, G. J. Symons, Dr. F. H. Thomson, Sir A. Scott Waugh, Prof. Williamson.

At the opening of this section on Sept. 5th, the president made a brief verbal address, in which he paid a high tribute to the late Prof. Faraday.

The proceedings then opened with the reading of the report of the Lunar Committee, in which were given the proceedings of the committee, and the results of the investigations of Mr. W. R. Birt in regard to the mapping of the moon, and the changes which were supposed by astronomers to have taken place in the crater Linné. Mr. Glaisher read a paper giving remarks on the original objects and general work of the Lunar Committee. Mr. J. Clerk Maxwell followed with a paper "On a Real Image Stereoscope, with illustrations of Solar Geometry." Mr. Balfour Stewart read a paper "On the behaviour of the Aneroid Barometer at different pressures."

"On Meteorological Observations at Sea," by Mr. F. W. Moffat. This paper was communicated by Dr. Moffatt. For whom the observations were made, for the purpose of ascertaining the quantity of ozone in different degrees of latitude and longitude at sea. The observations extend between lat. 53° N. and 39° S., and long. 83° E. and 25° W. Dr. Moffat had observed that as the wind veered with increasing readings of the barometer from south points of the compass through west to north, ozone disappeared and continued absent while the wind was in points between north and east, and that it re-appeared as the wind veered with decreasing readings of the barometer to south points. The disappearance and re-appearance of ozone with these conditions were so regular that the changes appeared to be the result of an invariable atmospheric law, and Dr. Moffat was induced to examine the law of the rotation of the wind, so clearly developed by Dove, and the results of the examination led him to believe that the polar current is the non-ozoniferous, or that of minimum of ozone, and that the equatorial, or sea-wind, is the ozoniferous, or that of the maximum of ozone. According to the rotation theory, the polar current in the northern hemisphere forms the N.E. "trade," and that in the southern hemisphere forms the S.E. "trade," while the equatorials in the northern and southern hemispheres form the upper or returning "trades." These returning "trades" come to the earth's surface in both hemispheres about the 28th degree (the latitude varies with the season), north and south of the equator. Dr. Moffat stated that if his deductions are trustworthy, the N.E. and S.E. "trades" ought to be the minimum of ozone currents, and the returning "trades" the maximum of ozone currents; that in the northern hemisphere forming the S.W. wind, and the other in the southern hemisphere a N.W. wind; and as these currents consisted of the atmospheres of equatorial latitudes, the quantity of ozone ought to be at least as great at the equator as with the returning currents. Dr. Moffat showed by tabulated results that such was the case, and he expressed a belief that were it not for the modifying effects of the trade-winds, ozone would be a constant quantity at sea.

"Experiments on the Luminosity of Phosphorus," by Dr. J. Moffat. Dr. Moffat gave the results of several interesting experiments which he had made on the luminosity of phosphorus. From these experiments, it was shown that phosphorus in a luminous state produced phosphorus and phosphoric acids and ozone, and that it was non-luminous in a degree of temperature below 39° Fahr., and that it was luminous in a temperature above 45° Fahr. The temperature of luminosity and non-luminosity, however, Dr. Moffat, stated, varied with the pressure of the atmosphere, and also with the direction of the wind. When phosphorus was kept in water, and air in a non-luminous state, the water and air became phosphorated, and they became phosphorescent, on their temperature being increased, and ozone was formed during their phosphorescence. Water reduced to the freezing point also became phosphorated, and it became phosphorescent on being heated. Phosphorus in a non-luminous state did not produce ozone; phosphorated air and water were not ozonized, but they were ozonised when phosphorescent. The author observed that steel needles suspended in phosphorus vapour assumed magnetic properties, and that a stream of vapour arising from phosphorus was attracted by heat and repelled by cold. From results deduced from a series of experiments made upon luminosity of phosphorus in connexion with atmospheric conditions, and extending over a period of four years, it would appear, the author said, that the equatorial or sea-wind is that of phosphorescence and ozone, and that the polar or land-wind is that of non-luminosity and no ozone. From these results, Dr. Moffat is induced to ask, is it not probable, as the sea is the reservoir of ozone, that ocean phosphorescence is the chief source of its development?

On September 6th, Mr. Glaisher was called upon by Sir William Thomson for his report on "Luminous Meteors." The walls of the section-room were hung with several finely-coloured diagrams illustrative of the flights of meteors, and Mr. Glaisher said that the object of the committee was to ascertain more particularly the nature of meteoric flights. Last year there were a vast number of observations. The Committee had arranged for an extensive series of observations of the November meteors, which were very successfully carried out. A large number of meteors had been seen at Greenwich—about 9,000—but these were not included in the present catalogue. One large meteor was observed at Cardiff, and the luminosity remained visible for about 18 minutes. One was also seen above Dundee of extraordinary brilliance, which was ascertained to be about 51 to 57 miles above the earth. A curious detonating fire-ball was then described. This body was seen in broad day-light in France in the month of June last, and was of a very extraordinary character. Another was seen at Glasgow, which passed nearly over St. Andrew's, where it appeared to consist of three parts, each equal to Venus, and it was calculated that this meteor passed at a distance of about 50 miles above the earth. At Aberdeen a brilliant fire-ball was first seen last November, which, it was afterwards found, was seen also over the whole of Scotland, and as far as Nottingham. A remarkable fire-ball, seen near Basle—of which there was a coloured diagram on the wall—had been observed in the Observatory at Basle and also in Paris. A large amount of information was given regarding the reports received from various localities where the meteoric showers of last November were seen—the Cape of Good Hope and other places.

Professor Herschel made a few remarks on the character and quality of the meteoric light. He said that the spectroscope showed a yellow light, but of what this light was composed it was impossible to say. As observers multiplied, however, with telescopes armed with spectroscopes, this difficulty would no doubt be resolved. The connexion between comets and meteors had this year been established without doubt, and that connection gave wide scope for speculation as to the origin and character of meteoric bodies. Mr. Huggins had made an observation of the light of a comet, and although that observation was not perfect, still it was sufficient to identify the light of the nucleus of the comet with that of the meteoric bodies. There were two theories as to these meteors. Leverrier had shown that their orbit extended from that of Uranus to that of the Earth, while an Italian astronomer believed that they came from the utmost fields of space. Fifty-six showers were well established, and it was by the study of these showers that they hoped to continue, and possibly confirm and extend, their researches by the assistance of those zealous observers who had hitherto been their supporters and constant assistants among the members and other observers of this Association.

September 9th.—Mr. Symons read the report of the Rainfall Committee, after which Mr. Glashier, for Mr. Alexander Brown, Arbroath, read a paper giving observations as to the rainfall in that district.

Colonel Sykes, M.P., read a paper on "Storm warnings—their importance and practicability." He calculated that out of 405 warnings given under the system lately in use, the prognostications were correct in 305 cases. Colonel Sykes next read a series of petitions which had been sent praying for the resumption of the storm signals. In speaking of the practicability of working the signals, he said that storms generally came from the westward, and that notice of the advent of these storms could be telegraphed from the west of Ireland to England several hours before the wind actually reached those parts. Indeed, he had been informed by one of the most eminent electricians that as storms generally travelled across the Atlantic to this country they might have a week's warning of them before they reached Britain, by means of the Atlantic cable.

September 10th was taken up with the Pascal and Newton controversy.

September 11th.—The Secretary read a paper from Mr. C. Wheatstone, "On a new Telegraphic Thermometer, and on the Application of the Principle to other Meteorological Indicators." He exhibited the instrument and explained its construction; and concluded by stating the purposes to which it might be applied. If it was desired to ascertain the temperature on the top of Mont Blanc, a portion of the apparatus called the responder might be placed there, and a communication having been established between it and the questioner, observations of the temperature of the mountain might be made hourly in the Vale of Chamouni. Again, the responder might be placed in the bottom of the sea, or at any depth beneath the surface of the earth, and the most accurate observations could be obtained without removing the instrument.

Sir A. Waugh read a paper giving details with regard to the preparations now being made, under the auspices of the Secretary of State for India, for observing the total solar eclipse of August 18, 1868.

A paper was read from R. Russell, "On some deductions by Dr. Tyndall, from his recent experiments regarding the radiant and absorptive properties in the atmosphere."

Geology.

President, Archibald Geikie; Vice-Presidents, The Earl of Enniskillen, Sir P. Egerton, Professor Harkness, Prof. Nicol, Dr. T. Oldham, Professor Ramsay; Secretaries, E. Hull, W. Pengelly, H. Woodward; Committee, Prof. D. T. Ansted, Hilary

Bauerman, Dr. J. Bryce, W. Carruthers, E. W. Cooke, Rev. J. Crompton, Rev. H. W. Crosskey, Dr. D. Dalrymple, Dr. C. Le Neve Foster, Sir Duncan Gibb, J. Gwyn Jeffreys, Col. Sir H. James, Sir C. Lyell, R. Lightbody, Sir J. Lubbock, G. Maw, W. S. Mitchell, Sir R. I. Murchison, G. A. Morton, R. W. Mylne, Dr. H. A. Nicholson, S. R. Pattison, C. W. Peach, J. Powrie, C. B. Rose, S. Sharp, Rev. H. B. Tristram, W. H. S. Westropp, Rev. H. H. Winwood, E. A. Wunsuch, J. Wyatt, E. Wood, Major Woodall.

The business of Section C (Geology) was opened by Mr. Geikie, the president, giving an address on the igneous rocks and the traces of volcanic action in the British Islands. He began by noticing the igneous rocks in the Lower Silurian system, which had been illustrated by Sir Roderick Murchison, Professor Ramsay, and others, and in the Lake district by Professor Sedgwick. In the Lower Silurian in Scotland there had been no great volcanic activity, but in the Upper Silurian it abounded, as was shown in the Ochil and Pentland hills. The volcanic beds in the carboniferous limestone series were frequent, and in the old and new red sandstones. With regard to the basaltic plateau which formed the great feature of the western coast scenery of Scotland, he had at first believed, with Professor Edward Forbes, that it was of the secondary period, but recent examination had now led him to conclude that it belonged to the tertiary. The president noticed the singular persistency of volcanic action from the Lower Silurian upwards, and the various points of difference between the older eruptions and the later. The study of the igneous rocks furnished no proof that volcanic action had been less in the newer than in the older formations. The greatest of these eruptions in Scotland belonged to the Miocene period, which was one of the latest. So far from the activity of volcanic action having decreased, were it now to be resumed, it would be looked upon as but a part of one great system, so near to us geologically were the greatest of the irruptions. Mr. Geikie then spoke of the trap dykes, and concluded by expressing his belief that much remained to be discovered in the field of the igneous rocks.

Professor Phillips complimented Mr. Geikie as one of the greatests geologists in the country of Hutton, Playfair, Jameson, and Maculloch; and he believed that they would receive from his hands some of the best contributions touching the problems which he advanced in his address.

A paper, by Dr. Robert Chambers, was read, giving an account of an "eskar" at St. Fort, near Newport, Fife; and Mr. Milne Holme read a paper on the old sea-cliffs and sub-marine banks of the Firth of Forth. Dr. J. Bryce gave an account of recent researches into the age of the Arran granites. Professor Harkness read a paper by Dr. M. A. Nicholson and himself, "On the Coniston group of the Lake District," which was followed by two papers by Dr. Nicholson, and read by him, the first being "On the Graptolites of the Skiddaw Slates," and the second "On the Nature and Systematic Position of the Graptolitidæ." Professor Phillips, Sir Philip Egerton, and Mr. Carruthers made a few observations on these papers.

The Secretary read a preliminary report, drawn up by Mr. A. H. Scott, of the committee for the exploration of the plant beds of North Greenland, appointed at the Nottingham meeting of the Association. The report stated that Mr. Whymper, having made arrangements to visit Greenland, the Association had voted a grant of £100 to enable him to prosecute this investigation, and that a further grant of £200 had been received from Government. Mr. Whymper started for Copenhagen in April last, taking with him Dr. Robert Brown, and no intelligence of the expedition had been received since it left Copenhagen. The description of the plant remains from North Greenland which had already been brought to these countries had been completed by Professor Oswald Heer, of Zurich, and his work on the flora of the Polar region was now nearly completed, and would be published in a short time.

At the next meeting, Mr. George Maw read a paper on "The Cambrian Rocks of Llanberis, with reference to a break in the conformable succession of the lower beds."

Mr. J. Wyatt read a paper on the "Gradual Alteration of the Coast Line in Norfolk." He began by stating that under the influence of the Atlantic wave villages and many thousand acres of land existing at the Norman survey had disappeared. The changes, however, were not all to the loss of the nation. On the contrary, in West Norfolk there was a continual addition to the area. If they simply regarded the destructive view of the case it would give a very hopeless prospect of the future of Great Britain.

The author proceeded to describe the compensating progress of reconstruction in West Norfolk. At the part of the coast known as the Wash the land was fast gaining on the sea. In the recollection of the author great accumulations of land had taken place, and the ancient port of King's Lynn had been so much affected that navigation had become difficult. The author named especially one part near Nattingham Point, which was at one time deep water, with a safe anchorage, but which was now solid land, and about to be placed under cultivation. It was only a question of time when the whole width of the Wash would be land, except where the channel was conducted and kept secure by the exit of the fresh water and the ebb of the tidal water. Several thousands of acres had been gained, and were now producing fine crops. A secondary object of the paper was to enforce the necessity of an accurate record of the changes of coast lines, and the author suggested that this should be undertaken by a department of the Government.

Professor Oldham, of the Geological Survey of India, read a paper on the geology of that country. He gave a detailed account of the various rock groups, with their fossils, and stated their analogy to those of Europe. With respect to the coal measures, situated in the north of India, and found nowhere else in the country, he said they belonged to the upper coal measures of the south of Europe, and were not of the period of the English formations. Commercially, they were of considerable value. Dr. Oldham remarked on the striking continuity of the great ranges of the system of rocks in India. After some remarks from Colonel Sykes, Sir Charles Lyell said that

Colonel Sykes having exerted himself more than any other to procure the geological survey of India, might well be gratified with the results now brought out in the exceedingly luminous and highly interesting address of Mr. Oldham, which was the first grand general sketch of the geology of India which, he believed, had ever been given.

The President (Mr. Geikie) gave an account of the Geological Survey of Scotland, begun in 1854, under the superintendence of Professor Ramsay. He described on a map the progress of the survey in the various counties in which the work had been entered on, and gave an account of the character of the groups of rocks. The staff, which had been largely increased, were now in Ayrshire. Rather more than 3,000 square miles in Scotland had been surveyed.

The Secretary (Mr. Pengelly) read a letter from the Duke of Argyll to Professor Phillips, giving an account of a discovery which he made the other day at Benmore, in the Island of Mull, where there was the passage of a rock like pure trap into regular granite.

Mr. H. Woodward gave a "Third Report on Fossil Crustacea," and several other papers were read.

At the meeting on Monday, September 9th, Mr. Pengelly read the "Third Report of the Committee for the Exploration of Kent's Cavern, Devonshire." The paper read consisted of a very elaborate account of this richly fossiliferous cave, known as "Kent's Hole," and a number of cases of fossils, containing very many specimens, were produced. The point of interest in the report was the finding of traces of human remains in the old floors of the cavern. One of the discoveries was a marrow bone, which was split longitudinally in a manner impossible to a hyæna, animals whose remains were found in the cave, and which it was impossible to believe could have been split by other means than human agency. To verify his belief in this respect, Mr. Pengelly got the intelligent keeper of the hyænas in the Zoological Gardens, London, to supply the most powerful hyæna in the gardens with marrow-bones for a whole week, and none of these bones were broken in the same way as those found in Kent's Hole. The conclusion from the discoveries which had been made in the cave was that man occupied Devonshire when it was the home of the extinct lion, rhinoceros, mammoth, and hyæna, the remains of which animals had been found in the cavern. In the stalagmite floor of the cave, 20in. thick, below the black mould and the blocks of limestone on the surface, there had been found part of a human jaw containing four teeth, and lower down a great abundance of beautifully-shaped flint implements; more recently burnt bones, and, as now first reported, bone tools had been discovered. Although no part of the human skeleton had been found below the stalagmite floor, that negative evidence could not be regarded as of any weight; on the contrary, they were entitled to hope that as these investigations were prosecuted they would come upon remains of man, as well as of his works, in the lower deposits. Even if they did not, the evidence was irresistible that Kent's Hole was one of the homes of our ancestors, who were contemporary with the extinct animals, the remains of which were found in the cave.

Sir Charles Lyell expressed the thanks of the association to Mr. Pengelly and Mr. Vivian, his colleague, for their report on the cavern, and remarked that there was evidence that man had been contemporaneous with three different kinds of elephants in Europe.

After some remarks by Professor Phillips, Mr. Vivian, Mr. Wyatt, Mr. Brodie, and others,—

Mr. Pengelly said that the three reports of the committee ought to be studied in connection, in order that the full force of the evidence bearing on the antiquity of man might be appreciated. He had only further to say that if man was found contemporaneous with extinct mammals in Devonshire, that did not fix the antiquity of the human race, for it could not be supposed that this ungenial climate was the cradle of man.

A paper by Professor Ansted, "On the conversion of stratified rock into granite in the north of Corsica," led to some discussion, in which the opinion was generally expressed that granite was not an igneous but a stratified rock.

Professor Sir William Thomson read a paper by Dr. Julius Schvarez, "On the Internal Heat of the Earth." It was stated that 370 underground stations had been examined, and only four of them of had shown a decrease of underground temperature. In some remarks on the paper, Sir William Thomson advocated the Association undertaking borings to ascertain the question of underground heat, as mines were uncertain data on which to proceed. He proposed borings of 200ft. under some African desert, and under an old sea-bottom or lake.

Sir Charles Lyell expressed the opinion that it would probably be found when different portions of the earth had been examined that igneous seas and lakes had been formed first in one part and then in another; that the various parts had been successively melted and cooled, and that it was this, and not an internal igneous core of the earth, which explained the appearance of cooling that was obvious in the rocks.

On September 10th, Mr. E. Hull read a paper "On the Structure of the Pendle Range, Lancashire, as illustrating the South-easterly Attenuation of the Carboniferous Sedimentary Rocks of the North of England." Mr. Hull also read a paper entitled "Observations on the relative Geological Ages of the principal Physical Features of the Carboniferous District of Lancashire." Professors Phillips, Ramsay, and Ansted pointed out the importance of the papers as bearing on the question of obtaining coal in countries further to the east. Professor Ramsay, referring to the circumstance that Mr. Hull is an officer on the Geological Survey, remarked that the two papers were calculated to give people some idea of the exceeding pains taken in the preparation of the maps of the Geological Survey. Mr. Peach read a paper on the fossil fishes of the old red sandstone of Caithness and Sutherland. Numerous other papers were read.

Zoology and Botany.

President, Professor Sharpey; Vice-Presidents, Prof. Allman, Professor Balfour, G. Busk, Professor Christison, Dr. J. Davy, J. Gwyn Jeffreys, Sir J. Lubbock, Prof. Allen Thomson, A. R. Wallace; Secretaries, C. Spence Bate, Dr. Spencer Cobbold, Dr. M. Foster, H. T. Stainton, Rev. H. B. Tristram, Prof. W. Turner; Committee, H. W. Bates, Prof. Bennett, Prof. Bentley, Prof. Oswald Bell, H. Buckley, H. B. Brady, C. Brooke, Dr. F. T. Bond, W. Carruthers, Prof. Cleland, Dr. C. Collingwood, Prof. Dickson, Lieut.-Col. Drummond Hay, R. Dawson, Dr. Anton Dohrn, Sir W. Elliot, H. E. Ellis, Dr. A. Gunther, Sir Duncan Gibb, Dr. Hare, Dr. Heaton, Dr. J. Hunt, W. P. Hiern, Rev. C. Kingsley, E. R. Lankester, Prof. Martins, Dr. M'Intosh, Prof. Macdonald, T. Moore, A. Murray, W. T. Mitchell, Prof. Newton, E. Newton, T. Nunneley, Dr. P. O'Callaghan, Col. Playfair, Dr. R. Parnell, C. W. Peach, Dr. W. H. Ransom, Dr. B. W. Richardson.

In Section D (Biology) the proceedings were opened by an address from Professor Sharpey, the President, after which the section was subdivided. In the first department (Zoology and Botany) Mr. Spence Bate read a report on the fauna and flora of the southern coasts of Devon and Cornwall. The exertions of Mr. Bate had been principally directed to the Crustacea, of which he described some new forms, and several interesting larvæ. Full descriptions and drawings of these animals will shortly be published. Mr. Bate also read lists of annelids, molluscs and fish, which had been observed on the Devon coast.

"Fourth Report on Dredging among the Shetland Isles," by Mr. J. G. Jeffreys.—This report was divided into five heads: 1st, the discovery of new species or forms; 2nd, geographical distribution; 3rd, habits of animals, including those supposed to depend on the depth of water; 4th, geological relations; 5th, extraneous incidents. Under the first head were enumerated six species of mollusca new to the British seas, viz., *Terebra tella Spitzbergensis, Rhynchonella psittacea, Ledo pernula, Siphonodentalium Lofotense, Cadulus subfusiformis*, and *Utriculus globosus*. 2nd. The Zetlandic species of mollusca hitherto observed are 383 in all, of which 315 inhabit the north, and 245 the south of Europe. The total number of the British mollusca appears to be 712. Of land and fresh water species 25 only out of 122 inhabit the Shetland Isles. Other particulars were given by way of analysis, and to show the occurrence, for the first time, of southern forms in this district. 3rd. *Natico catena* (a sublittoral species) was dredged alive in from 40 to 50 fathoms. The greatest depth explored by the dredge on the present occasion was 170 fathoms. At this depth, living specimens of 16, and dead specimens of 38, species were procured. The shells dredged from 170 fathoms were of the usual colour; indeed, this was brighter and darker in living specimens of certain species than in average examples of the same species taken in a few fathoms. The notion that colour is absent or fainter in shells from deep water seems to be quite unfounded. 4th. Fossil shells were dredged at depths varying from 80 to 170 fathoms. These belong to species and varieties which inhabit high northern latitudes, and none of them have been discovered living in our seas. 5th. The canine tooth and shoulder-blade of two different quadrupeds were found at a depth of about 85 fathoms, and at the distance of about 25 miles from land. They were unaccompanied by any other terrestrial organisms. The fang of the tooth was corroded. Mr. Jeffreys suspected that this tooth (which Mr. Boyd Dawkins referred to an animal of the weasel tribe) may have been that of a tame ferret which was accidentally killed in 1862, and the carcass of which was then thrown into the sea from his yacht, at a distance of about 35 miles from the place where the tooth was dredged. The bone is supposed by Mr. Dawkins to have been that of a bat; this may have been disgorged or voided by a snowy owl. Dr. Günther added that of the fishes dredged by Mr. Jeffreys two species were new to the British Fauna (although known as Mediterranean), and two other species were new to science. Specimens were exhibited in illustration of the report, including *Spatangus meridionalis*, previously known as Mediterranean, and not as British.

The President drew attention to the importance of Mr. Jeffrey's observation of a bone and a tooth in the dredge. It was a remarkable thing that no bones were dredged up at sea as a rule, and to the palæontologist it was important that the method by which bones are destroyed by the sea should be investigated. —Mr. Jeffreys stated that a gentleman was occupied at the present time in researches on this subject. He also made some additional remarks on the great size of boreal as compared with southern individuals of the same species of mollusc. "Notice of Dredging by the late Dr. Möller off Fair Isle," by Dr. Mörch. "Remarks on Mr. J. G. Jeffreys's Collection of Hebridean Annelids," by Dr. M'Intosh. "On Pelagic Floating Animals observed at Sea," by Dr. C. Collingwood. "Notes on Oceanic Hydrozoa," by Dr. C. Collingwood. "On the Morphology of the Arthropoda," by Dr. A. Dohrn.

At the following meeting on Sept. 6th, Dr. Cobbold read a paper "On the Entozoa of the Common Fowl and of Game Birds in their supposed relation to the Grouse Disease." Dr. Cobbold was very decidedly of opinion that the presence of entozoa had nothing whatever to do with the existence of disease in the bird. The grouse disease had no connexion with any form of entozoa; and the entozoa were, he said, as much in their proper place in the inside of an animal as man was in his proper place on the outside of the globe.

The Rev. H. B. Tristram said he had examined several grouse which he had picked up in the Durham moors, and found that the livers of the birds were reduced to a sort of pulp. He held the disease was peculiarly an epidemic, for the healthiest birds succumbed just as quickly as the weakest. Grouse disease was on the increase, and he attributed this to the slaughter of all the strong and healthy birds by sportsmen and gamekeepers. Gamekeepers were, he said, the most destructive vermin that preyed upon the grouse. A beast of prey when it attacked a covey of birds always struck down the last and weakest of the flock, but the gamekeeper shot the bird that rose first, and thereby the finest and strongest of the covey were taken. In exterminating every animal and bird of prey from our country, we had destroyed the means provided by nature for clearing the land of diseased birds. This was an extremely short-sighted policy, and produced effects the very opposite of those it was intended to produce. Had the buzzard and other birds of prey been left they would have cleared out the diseased birds, and the grouse disease would never have gained a footing. By killing off all the beasts of prey we had exterminated the sanitary police of nature.

After a few remarks from Dr. Cobbold, Professor Busk expressed his concurrence with what Mr. Tristram had said respecting the short-sighted policy of exterminating all the beasts and birds of prey. It was, he said, the opprobrium of the present time, and was producing direful results.

On September 9th, Mr. A. R. Wallace read a paper on birds' nests, in which he sought to show a connexion between the plumage and the nidification of birds, in respect of colour. Some discussion followed as to the causes of the varieties of colour in fish, insects, &c. Dr. McIntosh read a paper on the marine fauna of St. Andrew's, which the president (Mr. Bush) pronounced to be the best contribution to natural history received at this meeting; and several members expressed the hope that Dr. McIntosh would produce a volume on the natural history of St Andrew's.

On September 10th, a preliminary report was read by the Rev. A. Merle Norman, on the Crustacea, Mulluscoida, and Cælenterata, procured by the Shetland Dredging Committee in 1867. Professor Newton read a supplement to a report on the Didine birds of the Mascarene Islands. He also exhibited a large number of bones and drawings to illustrate his paper. The President expressed his regret that so interesting a relic of pre-historic ages should now have become extinct—the dodo having being exterminated by the agency of man. Professor Newton thought that the extirpation of the dodo in the Mauritius was not directly owing to the agency of man, but rather to the fact that great numbers of pigs were turned out loose on the island. These soon decided the fate of the dodo.

Dr. Murie followed with some observations on the service rendered to science by Professor Newton and his brother, Mr. Newton, who had spent a considerable time in the Mauritius, and had thus been enabled to extend his researches into the Didine tribes.

Mr. E. J. Lowe then read a paper on "Abnormal Forms of Ferns." Professor Balfour gave a notice of some rare plants recently collected in Scotland. Dr. Grierson described "The Destruction of Plantations at Drumlanrig by a species of Vole." He exhibited a piece of timber operated on by voles, and also a couple of specimens of the latter species of animals. He accounted for the great increase of voles by the persistent destruction of weasels and similar animals. The voles resembled mice to a very great degree, but were really more closed related to the beaver tribe.

Dr. Spencer Cobbold considered the paper another confirmation of the folly of seeking to contravene the laws of nature, and depriving ourselves of the natural assistance afforded by certain kinds of wild animals.

Professor Newton thought that the whole question was one closely connected with the game laws. The latter would shortly require to be taken up by the section. In every country, republican as well as others, there was a necessity for protecting certain animals by fixed laws. We would require to assimilate our game laws to those of France, by which shooting is altogether prohibited during certain months.

The Rev. Dr. Esdaile spoke in favour of the conservation of moles.

The Rev. H. B. Tristram then read a paper "On the Zoological Aspects of the Grouse Disease." Like his friend Professor Newton he thought that our present game laws should be extended to all birds out of season, and some limit put to the destruction of birds' nests. No class of men had exhibited such gross ignorance on this subject as the members of the House of Commons or country gentlemen in general. Had they studied the moral law of Moses there would not have been so much talk of the grouse disease. In the latter case the destruction of birds of prey was one of the most productive elements of evil. Had there been abundance of birds of prey, all the weaker grouse, all those affected with disease, would have fallen quickly, and thus the "plague" would have been "stamped out."

Sir James Alexander was at one on the subject with Mr. Tristram, as his personal observations had all tended to the belief that birds of prey were the most effectual preventives to disease in birds. In particular he defended the owl as in reality one of the chief protectors of game. As for the weasel it always attacked diseased birds. The balance of nature had been so much disturbed that it was very difficult to set it right. In the Highlands some trout streams had been depopulated by the ravages of rats which were not kept in check by animals of prey.

Dr. Murie thought that the game laws should be altered, so as, by consulting the various habits of game, to close shooting at certain seasons of the year.

Dr. Grierson then replied to some questions which had been put to him in regard to his paper. Voles, he said, seemed pretty generally distributed over the British Isles. They were comparatively harmless, unless allowed to grow to great numbers by the destruction of the natural police of the forest.

The Duke of Buccleuch confirmed Dr. Grierson's observations on the destruction of plantations at Drumlanrig by voles. He agreed with the other speakers in their animadversions against the system of destroying wild animals of prey. Entirely to extirpate the latter would be a great mistake. As for the game laws, what was required was really a law for the general preservation of animals. There was only one wild animal in this country which enjoyed that protection, and that was the noble animal—the fox.

Sir James Alexander next read a paper "On the Preservation of Fishing Streams," which led to some conversation as to the means that ought to be taken for the purification of rivers.

Geography and Ethnology.

President, Sir S. Baker; Vice-Presidents, Sir J. E. Alexander, Admiral Sir E. Belcher, J. Crawfurd, Colonel Sir H. James, Sir J. Lubbock, Sir R. I. Murchison, Admiral E. Ommanney, General Sir A. S. Waugh; Secretaries, H. W. Bates, Cyril C. Graham, Clements R. Markham, S. J. Mackie, R. Sturrock; Committee, Professor D. T. Ansted, J. Arrowsmith, Sir D. Baxter, W. E. Baxter, H. G. Bohn, Sir J. Bowring, Bishop of Brechin, W. Brand,

G. Busk, C. Holt Bracebridge, Dr. P. O'Callaghan, Dr. Cuthbert Collingwood, R. Dunn, Dr. Davie, Sir W. Elliot, General Sir Vincent Eyre, J. Ferguson, Rev. Dr. Ginsburg, H. Gourlay, Dr. J. Hunt, M. N. de Khanikof, Prof. A. Newton, Sir J. Ogilvy, Lieut. S. P. Oliver, Sir A. Phayre, Col. R. L. Playfair, J. Ramsay, J. Sydney Smith, Rev. H. B. Tristram, J. White, J. Yearman.

Thursday.—The President, in opening the business of the Section, said, that Geography was worthy of the high position it occupied in the British Association; as nearly every science was dependent on our accurate knowledge of the earth. Astronomy would afford but meagre results if we were ignorant of the spherical form of our world, and if our observations were confined to our own cloudy shores; but our observations are directed from stations in all positions on the globe, the knowledge of those positions being due to our first explorers. Ethnology was the twin sister of geographical science, as the numerous races of human beings (so diverse and inexplicable) that inhabit the various portions of the earth, from the ice-bound regions of the Arctic circle to the burning deserts of Africa, would have been unknown but for the researches of geographical explorers. Theology was closely interwoven with the study of Geography. The most important events have occurred in certain places that throw intense interest upon the science. The wanderings of certain nomadic tribes, seeking for new pastures for their flocks, have brought to light new countries and have implanted new religions. Far distant lands, tenanted by savage races that knew no God, rescued from a state of barrenness, are smiling with prosperity; the wild beasts and the heathen have retreated before advancing civilization; and the sound of the church bell rings at our very antipodes. The advancement of Christianity is dependent upon the migrations of Christians that shall implant the seed of truth in foreign soils. Those migrations are dependant on geographical discoveries, that bring to light countries and climates favourable to the development of European races. Thus civilization will advance to a higher standard in such latitudes as are conducive to industry and enterprise. The severity of an Arctic region would be as great a barrier to the intellectual progress of the inhabitants as would the burning sun and barren sand of the desert, where Nature has withheld every blessing from mankind. In such localities human energies are overpowered by the oppression of circumstances; and a high standard of civilization can never be attained. The discovery of countries that afford the requisite conditions for a high civilization has been the grandest result of comparatively modern Geography. The voyages of the ancients were generally confined to coasting or to crossing narrow seas by the guidance of the stars, in precisely the same manner as performed at the present day by the Arabs in navigating the Persian Gulf and the Red Sea. Although the enterprise of the Greeks and Phoenicians had overcome the difficulties of the Mediterranean, and had established trading stations on the east coast of Africa, their explorations were bounded by that impassible barrier to the West—the Atlantic ocean. They had visited Zanzibar, and had heard of the existence of the great lakes which Ptolemy long afterwards placed upon his map from the description of ancient merchants as the sources of the Nile; but from the beginning of the world up to the fifteenth century no human eye had pierced the mystery of the Atlantic. At that time there were two great geographical questions to be solved—the Nile and the Atlantic. The fifteenth century was rich in geographical discovery. Marco Polo's travels in Asia had brought renown to Venice, and Vasco de Gama had, by the circumnavigation of Africa, sustained the honour of Portugal, which enterprising country assumed the lead in exploration until Columbus achieved the feat that completely altered the geography of his age—the discovery of America. In the short period of 380 years what vast changes have occurred, not only in geographical discovery, but in its results. America has become a giant. With every variety of climate, from the frigid to the torrid zone, with fertile soil, boundless forests, navigable rivers of prodigious extent, and commodious ports, the future of that wonderful country may be prognosticated by a comparison with the past. If possible, more wonderful in rapid advancement is that extraordinary country at our antipodes, Australia. It is natural to our insular position that geographical science should be more deeply appreciated in England than in other countries. Our strength lies in our commercial enterprise. Our commerce depends on our colonies; these encircle the world. Thus geographical knowledge must be an important element in English education, as hardly a family exists in the United Kingdom that is not represented by one or more of its members either in India or the colonies. Without yielding to exaggerated alarm, we must watch with intense attention the advances of Russia upon the Indian frontier; and beyond all other geographical enterprises, we should devote extreme interest to a new and direct route to India by the Euphrates Valley and the Persian Gulf. Thanks to the untiring zeal of its President, the Royal Geographical Society of London has attained such a position that there is no exploration of importance undertaken in any part of the world without its knowledge and attention. Thus, not only are we in England forewarned of the encroachments of neighbouring powers, should their expeditions be pushed beyond the limits of necessity, but we form a nucleus for all geographical information, should the Government resort to us for that requirement. Free, however, from all jealousy, and above suspicion, the society has this year awarded to the Russian Admiral, Boutakoff, the Founder's Gold Medal, for having been the first to launch a steamer on the Sea of Aral and to conduct his vessel upwards of 500 miles along the course of the river Jaxartes. The attention of geographers has lately been turned to the remarkable journey of M. Gerhard Rohlfs, a young German traveller, who had been expected to visit Dundee, but had been prevented by illness. He had lately returned from an exploration which had led him entirely across northern Africa from north to south. Entering at Tripoli, he had followed an entirely new route, viâ Ghadames to Murzuk; had thence travelled to Kuka, on the shores of Lake Chad, where he had been hospitably received by the Sultan of Bornou, and enabled by his protection and assistance to cross the country southward to the Benuwé, whence he had reached the Niger, and from Rabba crossed the forest country of Yoliba to Lagos in the Bight of Benin. Another recent communication which had been received by the Royal Geographical Society related to the Russian settlements in Manchuria, and gave an account of the great progress made by this advancing power in exploring the difficult country between the frontier of Korea and their Siberian posts on the Amur, viâ Lake Khinka and the Usuri river. With regard to the fate of Livingstone, he (the President) regretted to be forced to the conclusion that the great traveller was dead. The hopes of those who believe the contrary rest on the well-founded belief that the Johanna men who had escaped the slaughter and brought home the news had trumped up the story to excuse their return. It was this very fact of their power of consummate lying that convinced him of the substantial truth of their statement. Natives are scientific liars; they do not lie absurdly, like Europeans, but they concoct their falsehoods with such forethought that the lie itself is an example of profound skill. No native would commit himself to so inartistic a lie as to declare a man to be dead who is still alive, and who might become a witness at a future time against him. Should natives intend to desert their master, they invariably plead excuses that cannot be proved to be false, such as sickness or pretended lameness, that incapacitates them from marching; but the hardihood of the Johanna men in committing themselves, by the confession of their cowardice, is a surprising instance of veracity that could only have been prompted by the urgency of the calamity. The death of Livingstone was a fearful drag on the wheel of African exploration. We know but a portion of those immense lake reservoirs in Central Africa; and geographers will not remain content with the bare fact that the Nile issues from those lakes. England, that has untied the knot, must gather in the extremity of the line.

Lieutenant S. P. Oliver, R.A., F.R.G.S., read a paper descriptive of two routes through Nicaragua, with the view of opening up interoceanic communication through that country between the Atlantic and Pacific.

A paper by Captain Maury, on the "Physical Geography of the Nicaragua route," was read by Mr. Bates. After a description of the phenomena of the equatorial cloud ring, the writer said—To determine the motions of this cloud ring from north to south, and from south to north again, to determine the march of their rains and their rate of travel into the interior from the Caribbean Sea and the Gulf of Mexico on the one side and from the Pacific on the other, is one of the most interesting and suggestive meteorological problems of the day.

On September 6th, Sir Samuel Baker took the chair at a quarter past 11, and stated that the first business would be a report of the Palestine Exploration Fund, which, he mentioned, commenced in a proposal for carrying a water supply to the city of Jerusalem. From that arose the idea of a Palestine exploration, the funds for which were commenced by that benevolent lady, Miss Burdett Coutts, followed by £100 from the Royal Society, £100 from the Royal Geographical Society, and £100 from this association.

Captain Wilson then reported that of the sum of £100 granted last year by the British Association to the Palestine Fund, one moiety had gone towards the costs of Lieutenant Warren's explorations, and the other to the purchase of instruments for meteorological observations in Palestine. Lieutenant Warren's reports and plans had not been completed, but the following results had been already obtained:—The construction of a map on the scale of one inch to the mile of the highland districts of Judea to the north-west and south-west of Jerusalem, of the Jordan valley to about 16 miles north of the Dead Sea, and of a large portion of the plains of Philistia. Those surveys, accompanied by those made by Wilson and Anderson in 1865-6, gave for the first time materials for a correct map of about three-fourths of the Holy Land. At Jerusalem a very important discovery had been made outside the south wall of the sacred enclosure (Haram Esh Shereif)—namely, that the live rock of the hill overlooking Kedron was no less than 53 feet below the present surface, and the great south wall of the Haram has been traced down to that depth, making it in all 130 feet high. In addition, the east wall of the Haram has been found to run on beyond the present south wall, and a second south wall had been discovered 20 feet distant from that already known. At the northern extremity of the city, close to the Damascus gate, foundations of massive walls and of a tower had been uncovered, and Lieutenant Warren was at present engaged in some interesting excavations in the Valley of the Kedron and on the site of the Hospital of the Knights of St. John, near the Church of the Holy Sepulchre. The sum of £50 granted for meteorological purposes had been expended under the superintendence of Mr. Glaisher in the purchase of instruments for the stations of Beyrout, Damascus, Jaffa, and Nazareth, which would enable them, with the observations taken at Jerusalem by Dr. Chaplin, to form an accurate knowledge of the climate of Palestine.

Captain Wilson then read a paper on the recent discoveries in and around the site of the Temple at Jerusalem. "Notes of a Reconnaissance of some portions of Palestine," by Lieut. Anderson, were read by Mr. Bates.

Sir Roderick Murchison made a statement on the subject of the Livingstone search expedition. He stated that Livingstone's object when he set out was to discover whether there was an outlet to the south from Lake Tanganyka, discovered by Burton and Speke, which was a fresh-water lake, and which, but for such an outlet as was supposed to exist, ought to be a saline lake. Livingstone started from the east coast of Africa and reached the north of Lake Nyassa, and had settled the point that there was no communication between Tanganyka and Nyassa, and there was considerable interest now attaching to the question whether Lake Tanganyka might not be in communication with the lake Albert Nyanza, discovered by Sir Samuel Baker, on the north. In order to reach the south end of Tanganyka Livingstone took carpenters to prepare boats, and was prepared to sail to the north end of that lake to determine if there was an opening there either to the Albert Nyanza or to the Victoria Nyanza. If he was alive, he must have passed to the Albert Nyanza, from which he was to descend the Nile. Should he accomplish that object he would then certainly be the most glorious of all explorers in African geography. Having traversed and retraversed Africa several times with black men only, and once before not having been heard of for above a year, there was no occasion for anxiety although he had not been heard of for that time. If he had escaped, they might depend upon it he would go on fearlessly, and on getting to the centre of Africa a long time must elapse before he could be heard of. As to Mousa's testimony of his death, it stood alone, for none of the other Johanna men were present at the alleged murder, and Mousa was not only a liar but a thief, and had, when examined by the Bombay sepoy who had accompanied Livingstone on a part of his journey, given a totally different version from what he had given to Dr. Kirk, having stated to the latter that he was murdered by the blow of a hatchet, and having stated to the sepoy that he was shot to death by arrows. As to Mousa's story that the Johanna men had recovered the body of their leader and buried it, he did not believe that so great a coward as Mousa, who stated that he had concealed himself when his leader was attacked, would have had the heroism to go and make a search for his body. But, whatever the fact, he felt, as President of the Royal Geographical Society, that it was their bounden duty make a search for Livingstone, and he had accordingly urged on Government to send out an expedition to determine the truth of the matter. To the great honour of Her Majesty's Government, this proposal had been most cordially responded to, particularly by Mr. Corry and the authorities of the Admiralty, and the details of the expedition had been most zealously worked out by the Hydrographer of the Admiralty, Captain Richard. As leader of the expedition they had chosen Mr. Young, a warrant officer who had spent two years on the Zambesi river with Livingstone, who knew the natives well, and was perfectly competent to manage them, and who entertained the same hope that he and others did, that Livingstone might be alive. The object of this expedition, which reached the Cape on the 15th of July last, was to get to the north end of Lake Nyassa, about 30 miles from which was the spot of the alleged murder. The party consisted of only three Europeans —namely, Mr. Young, Lieutenant Falconer—a gallant volunteer in the service, and who had been with the 17th Lancers in India—and a seaman who, like Mr. Young, was acclimatized; and though only three men had been accepted, it was to the honour of this country that between 50 and 60 applications had been received from young men in various walks of life to accompany the expedition. They were to be accompanied with a party of Africans and men to sail up the Zambesi, thence up the Scheri, getting the natives to carry their steel boat, which could be taken to pieces, for about 30 miles past the Murchison Falls. After getting past these falls they would again launch their boat and reach Lake Nyassa, and were to explore the east side of that great lake, as Livingstone had done the west. If Livingstone was dead, the expedition party were sure to fall in with memorials of him— his clothes, his apparatus, or, above all, his notes, for to written documents the natives attached immense importance; and all these would be sure to find their way down the lake in the course of native trading. Every article belonging to the German traveller Rocher, who was killed in a quarrel with the natives, had been recovered in this way, and it was impossible that the same traces of Livingstone, if he were dead, could escape the search to be made. The expedition would occupy the party at least till the end of November, and he hoped that by Christmas they would have received such tidings of them as would solve the problem. Sir Roderick concluded by some remarks on the great unexplored regions of Africa, which would probably continue to engage the attention of geographers for centuries to come.

On September 7th, Mr. Crawfurd, President of the Ethnological Society, contributed a paper "On the Antiquity of Man," which was read for him by Mr. Bates. It dealt mainly with the testimony for such antiquity of man as was independent of his own remains, but was prefaced by some observations on the causes which accounted for the paucity of man's own remains. Coming to the subject of this paper, Mr. Crawfurd referred to language, the art of writing, the cultivation of the cereals, and the domestication of animals, many of which had disappeared altogether in their wild state, as so many evidences of man's antiquity. He went on to say. Of all parts of the world the valley of the Nile was most likely to have generated an early civilisation, and to have preserved a record of it, and they might safely believe that Egypt was one of the countries in which arts and letters made their earliest advance. The history of the Jews could pretend to no such antiquity as that of the Egyptians, or even as that of the Chinese. The earliest date which, with any show of authenticity, could be ascribed to the history of Egypt began with the first dynasty of civil rulers, which (taking the dates from the learned work of Leseuer, a pupil of Champollion) corresponded with 8986 B.C., thus making the first dawn of reliable history 10,833 years old. The Pyramids of the first dynasty were built, according to the same authority, B.C. 3460, and the Great Pyramid B.C. 3280, respectively 5,327 and 5,127 years ago. Although the Jews were intellectually greatly superior to both Egyptians and Chinese, still they were a small people, inhabiting a comparatively poor and narrow territory, while they were at least as much a pastoral as an agricultural nation. They had no enduring architectural monuments, for their peculiar religion confined their public architecture to a single temple, a fact which attests the smallness of their numbers and the narrowness of their territory. Even this one temple, which in size did not exceed an ordinary London parish church, was built for the most part of perishable materials, their want of skill obliging them to have recourse to the more advanced commercial States of the Mediterranean coast for artisans, for timber, and for the metals. The early Jews, however, had long passed all the first stages of man's progress; for they possessed an adequate scale of numbers, a calendar, and even the art of writing, almost as soon as we have the first mention of them. All our evidence for the antiquity of the Jews is to be gathered from their sacred writings. There is a general assent among critics in fixing the building of the Temple to the year before Christ 1015—a date which would make it 2,445 years later than the construction of the oldest of the Pyramids. Reckoning backwards, the Exodus preceded the building of the Temple by 480 years, and the bondage in Egypt is given as having lasted 430 years. These united sums give the year B.C. 1925, and beyond this we cannot carry the chronology of the Hebrews, unless it be the arrival of Abraham in Egypt, which is given as B.C. 2499, which would make this event to have happened 789 years posterior to the building of the great Pyramid. After some remarks on the respective antiquity of Assyrian, Hindu, and Chinese civilisation, Mr. Crawfurd concluded with a recapitulation of his argument, maintaining that man was of vast antiquity, and that the portion of his existence which had transpired since he acquired the art of making a durable and authentic record of it was but a very small fraction of it.

Mr. P. N. Compton contributed a paper on the "Coasts of Vancouver's Island and British Columbia," which was read by Mr. Bates.

Mr. J. J. Pratt contributed a paper on the "Colony of New Scotland," in South Africa, which was also read by Mr. Bates.

Mr. Crawfurd contributed another paper, "On the Complexion, Hair, and Eyes as tests of the Races of Man," which was read by Mr. Mackie. He maintained that the hypothesis of climate could no longer be set forth as the cause of colour in the human complexion. If, then, the variety of colour be not the effect of climate, from what cause was it derived? This was one of those inscrutable mysteries of nature which we could not solve any more than we could the varieties of colour in the species of the lower animals. Nature had made colour a distinction of species in the lower animals, and it had done the same, although less definitely, in the races of man, and in both cases they were equally ignorant of the grounds on which it had done so.

Mr. Crawfurd also contributed a paper upon "The supposed Aborigines of India as distinguished from its Civilised Inhabitants." A paper was contributed by Mr. H. H. Howarth, on "Some Changes of Surface affecting Ancient Ethnology," the heads of which were read by Mr. Mackie.

On September the 9th, Sir John Lubbock read a paper on the "Origin of Civilisation and the early condition of man." Sir John said—Many writers have considered that man was first a mere savage, and that our history has on the whole been a steady progress towards civilisation, though at times, and sometimes for centuries, the race has been stationary, or even has retrograded. Other authors of no less eminence have taken a diametrically opposite view. According to them man was from the commencement pretty much what he is at present—if possible, even more ignorant of the arts and sciences than now, but with mental qualities not inferior to our own. Savages they consider to be the degenerate descendants of far superior ancestors. Of the recent supporters of this theory, the late Archbishop of Dublin was among the most eminent. Having briefly considered the arguments brought forward by Archbishop Whateley, Sir John proceeded to state some facts which seemed to militate against the view he advocated. First, said he, I will endeavour to show that there are indications of progress even among savages; secondly, that among the most civilised nations there are traces of original barbarism. It is, I think, improbable that any race of men who had once been agriculturists and herdsmen should entirely abandon pursuits so easy and so advantageous, and it is still more improbable that, if we accept Usher's very limited chronology, all tradition of such a change should be lost. Moreover, even if the present colonists of (say) America or Australia were to fall into such a state of barbarism, we should still find in those countries herds of wild cattle descended from those imported; and even if these were exterminated, still we should find their remains, whereas we know that no trace of a bone either of the ox or of the domestic sheep has been found either in Australia or in the whole extent of America. In the case of the horse the same argument points to Australia but not America. So, again, in the case of plants. We do not know that any of our cultivated cereals would survive in a wild state, though it is highly probable that, in a modified form perhaps they would do so. But there are many other plants which follow in the train of man, and by which the botany of South America, Australia, and New Zealand has been almost as profoundly modified as their ethnology has been by the arrival of the white man. The Maoris have a melancholy proverb that the Maoris disappear before the white man, just as the white man's rat destroys the native rat, the European fly kills the Maori fly, and the clover kills the New Zealand fern. We may, therefore, safely assume that if Australia, New Zealand, or South America had ever been peopled by a race of herdsmen and agriculturists, the fauna and flora of these countries would almost inevitably have given evidence of the fact, and differed much from the condition in which they were discovered. We may also assert on a general proposition that no weapons or instruments of metal have ever been found in any country inhabited by savages wholly ignorant of metallurgy. A still stronger case is afforded by pottery. Pottery is not easily destroyed; when known at all it is always abundant, and it possesses two qualities there—namely, that of being easy to break and yet difficult to destroy, which render it very valuable in an archæological point of view. Moreover, it is in most cases associated with burials. It is, therefore, a very significant fact that no fragment of pottery has ever been found in Australia, New Zealand, or the Polynesian Islands. It seems to me extremely improbable that an art so easy and so useful should ever have been lost by any race of men. Moreover, the art of spinning and the use of the bow are quite unknown to many races of savages, and yet would hardly be likely to have been abandoned when once known. The absence of architectural remains in these countries is another argument. The mental condition of savages seems also to me to speak strongly against the "degrading" theory. I have elsewhere pointed out that, according to the almost universal testimony of all writers on savages—merchants, philosophers, naval men, and missionaries alike—there are many races of men who are altogether destitute of a religion. The cases are, perhaps, less numerous than they are asserted to be, but many of them rest on doubtful evidence. Yet I feel it difficult to believe that any people which had once possessed a religion would ever have entirely lost it. Sir John proceeded to mention cases in which a limited improvement had taken place. After adverting to the unlikelihood of races possessing a knowledge of numbers losing it again, Sir John then referred to various circumstances which seemed to show that even civilised races were once in a state of barbarism. He then briefly adverted to the argument derived from an alleged universality of certain customs. While I do not believe that similar customs in different nations are "inherited from a common source," or are necessarily primitive, I certainly do see in them an argument for the unity of the human race, which, however, be it remarked in parenthesis, is not necessarily the same thing as the descent from a single pair. In conclusion, then, while I do not mean for a moment to deny that there are cases in which nations have retrograded, I regard these as exceptional instances. The facts and arguments I have adduced afford, I think, strong grounds for the following conclusions—namely, that existing savages are not the descendants of civilised ancestors; that the primitive condition of man was one of utter barbarism; that from this condition several races have independently raised themselves. These views follow, I think, from strictly scientific considerations. We shall not, however, be the less inclined to adopt them on account of the cheering prospects which they hold out for the future.

A paper was read, contributed by Messrs. Wallace and Mayne, on the "Peruvian Expedition to the River Ucayali." This expedition was undertaken at the instance of the Peruvian Government with the view of discovering a river route to the eastern slopes of the Andes in Peru, by which the produce of the country might be sent to Europe without crossing the Andes. The vessels penetrated two rivers hitherto almost unknown; and reached towns not far from Lima, thus establishing a navigable route on the Amazon and its tributaries for 3,700 miles, by which goods might be shipped from Peru to Europe or *vice versa*.

Dr. Collingwood read a paper giving an interesting description of a boat journey round the north end of the island of Formosa in the China seas.

Dr. John Davy, the Inspector-General of Hospitals, contributed a paper on the "Character of the Negro, chiefly in relation to industrial habits." Dr. Davy stated that his object was to vindicate the negro from the reproach of being a sluggard or idler, and to show that he was, under continued education, in favourable circumstances, and unenslaved, capable of being civilised, and of making progress in the liberal arts and sciences.

A discussion took place on the subject of the paper. Mr. Crawfurd remarked that the island of Barbadoes, from which the most of Dr. Davy's examples were taken, was in an exceptional condition as regarded the negro race, being so densely populated that the negro must either work or perish. Dr. Hunt said that, as far as regarded bodily strength and the power of resisting heat, the negro was the best adapted of all the dark races for labour in a hot climate, and he really did not understand why he should be so unwilling to work. He hoped some day we might be able to remove the objection the negro entertained to free labour. Speaking of the condition of the freed Americans, he quoted testimony to show that the freedmen were in a most distressing condition in some parts of the States. Mr. Brewin, Cirencester, maintained, on the other hand, that the negro was as willing to work, if fairly treated and regularly paid, as any coloured man on the face of the earth. Having gone to Jamaica to inquire for the Society of Friends as regards the disturbed state of the island, he made a statement highly favourable to the diligence and energy of the negro. Mr. Davis said that Mr. Brewin's description was quite contrary to scientific facts as regarded the negro, and he had quite failed to take into account the percentage of white blood in the negroes of Jamaica. It was that infusion alone which made the Jamaica negro what he was; otherwise he was quite incapable of that continuous labour on which the prosperity of every community was based. Dr. Davy replied, mentioning the names of many negroes possessing great intellectual powers; and Mr. Crawfurd closed the discussion with some remarks to the effect that it was only when in contact with the white man, and through the infusion of white blood, that the negro had ever risen out of savagery. He rejoiced that the negroes had been freed, but he thought the slaveholders' property in negroes should, as in the case of our West Indies, have been compensated, not confiscated.

At the meeting September 10th, Mr. Bates read the abstract of an elaborate paper by M. du Puydt on an exploration of the Isthmus of Darien, with the view of discovering a practicable line for a ship canal. M. de Puydt, in this paper, reported that he had discovered a break in the Andes, which rendered practicable the formation of a ship canal between the two oceans. He made an exploration up the river Tennella, a small stream descending from the eastern slope of the Andes into the Bay of Carthagena. He found little difficulty in making his way to the watershed, which he stated was a low plateau, estimated to be about 140 feet above the level of the sea, this elevation continuing about five miles. He had no instruments for precise measurements, but estimated the height from the rapids in the river. The Indians were, upon the whole, friendly, though they tried hard to deter him by accounts of the difficulties he would encounter. The exploration was only carried to the summit, but from that point the country westward towards the Pacific was described as being perfectly level. No life was lost in the expedition, and sickness was escaped.

Sir R. Murchison, after adverting to the disasters which befel the Scotch colony at Darien nearly two centuries ago, said he did not think Darien would ever hold out any inducements to colonists, nor did he think there was any clear light shed by this paper on the practicability of forming a good and safe ship canal. The project, however, had long been entertained, and Humboldt always said, and, indeed, had said to himself, that if ever a passage was effected through any portion of this isthmus it would be by the route which M. de Puydt had described. An unsuccessful effort had been made seventeen years ago to open this route.

Mr. Crawfurd read a paper on the "Supposed Plurality of the Races of Man." He said it had long been a popular belief among the nations of Europe, but chiefly confined to them, that all the diverse races of man were sprung from a single family, and that wide differences in complexion, features, bodily form, and intellectual qualities, which now existed, were but varieties, the result of long time and the operation of climate and localities. He believed this view to be contrary to nature, unsupported by historical facts, and to be against all probability. What the races of man now were they had been from the earliest dawn of authentic history. The Egyptian and negroes on the Nile monuments were the same as the Egyptian negroes of the present day, and the skeletons found in connection with lacustrian dwellings in Swiss and Belgium were identical with the skeletons of the civilised inhabitants of Switzerland and Belgium of the present day. Mr. Crawfurd went on to speak of the limited knowledge the ancient races had of each other, and of the absence of the means of emigration or dispersion. If the most civilised potent, and enter-prising nations of antiquity had power to acquire but a partial knowledge of the earth and its inhabitants, how could they imagine that feeble savages were able to surmount far greater difficulties than they did? They might, he thought, safely conclude, that when the earth assumed its present form, species of man were distributed over the surface in the same manner as species of the lower animals and of plants. The spread or dispersion of man, according to the popular theory, would have amounted to nothing less than a miracle; but a miracle was a cause inadmissible in science, or at least ought to be restricted to the one great and for ever inscrutable secret, the Creation itself.

Mr. Vivian agreed with the views of Mr. Stuart Poole, of the British Museum, as to different centres of creation, and successive interpositions of creative power in the creation of man, of which the Scriptures recorded the latest. He pointed out the accord between the account of creation in the first chapter of Genesis and the geological testimony as to the order of creation. He felt that those who were most desirous to support the Mosaic record must yet surrender the idea of the earth being only 6,000 years old; and he thought if the Biblical statements were fairly studied it would be seen that there was first a record of the creation of man; male and female, and then a record of the creation of Adam, the progenitor of a later and more intellectual race. The fact that Cain, the son of the first pair in this race, sought divine protection lest any man should slay him for his brother's murder, sufficiently indicated that the earth was populated by other families than that of Adam, as Cain could not have referred to his own brethren, while the fact of his taking wives seemed to lead to the same conclusion. In the lake dwellings and in Kent's cavern they found human remains evidently of a very high antiquity, and who could not have come from the Paradisaic source.

Mr. Wallace supported the views of Mr. Darwin as to unity of origin, and instanced the pigeon as a case of extraordinary variety proceeding from one type. Mr. Crawfurd had said that no barbarous races had the power to spread over the world, yet it was undoubted that the New Zealander originally came from the Friendly Islands, in the Pacific, to which also the Sandwich Islanders were to be traced, and that there was a powerful Malay element even in Madagascar, a distance of 2,000 miles from the Malayan races. Allowing for the great epoch that must have elapsed since the appearance of man, and the great variety of chances that must have occurred to him, he saw no difficulty in supposing that he might gradually spread over the earth from a single centre.

Mr. Crawfurd, in his reply, ridiculed the Darwinian theory, and with respect to savage emigration, said the instances given were comparatively recent, after the races in question had come to be able to build powerful boats, and were expert seamen, so that the facts cited by Mr. Wallace were not to the point. For himself, he had no faith in a monad selecting anything. He did not believe that donkeys ever became horses, pigs, elephants, or monkeys men.

Mr. Cyril Graham then made a statement as to the proposed explorations in Palestine. He said the object of the association he represented was to investigate the ethnology and topography of the Holy Land. The first thing they wanted was a trigonometrical survey. They also wanted to know the geology of the mountains, the fossils they exhibited, the nature of the soil, the trees and flora, the fishes of the sea of Tiberias, and all the phenomena of that wonderful region, the Valley of the Dead Sea. They wanted a catalogue of the beasts, in which the crocodile would appear, and of all the birds, butterflies, moths, and beetles. In fact they wanted to have re-written the great work of Solomon, which had not been handed down, on the natural history and productions of the land. Then beyond the Jordan they found a great field of labour—in the cities of Bashan and Gilead, where many remains of ancient art were to be found. They wanted to examine every point which could throw light upon the cradle of their faith, so that we might read with greater intelligence and more vivid interest the graphic delineations of the Holy Scriptures.

General Lefroy warmly commended the expedition to the support of the public, and Sir Roderick Murchison expressed his sense of the great value of the researches of Mr. Cyril Graham.

Correspondence.

[Under this head we shall be glad to insert any letters of general interest.]

NATURALISTS' MUSEUMS.

SIR,—I see in this month's NATURALIST'S NOTE BOOK that a committee of naturalists have offered a series of prizes for the best collection of plants, shells, fossils, &c., &c. This is at Newcastle-on-Tyne. I have long thought that such a thing might be formed in the neighbourhood of London; in fact, a "Juvenile

Museum and Scientific Institute." I feel that such a thing would be well supported; prizes might be offered for the best collections of shells, fossils, minerals, &c., &c. Surely there are learned scientific gentlemen who would help to form such a thing.

If any of your readers think the idea worth their notice, I should be very glad to correspond with them on the subject.

Trusting you will give publication to this letter,

I remain, Sir, yours obediently,

A JUVENILE MEMBER OF THE RISING GENERATION.

London, S., September 3.

BIRDS OF PASSAGE, AND MIGRATION OF INSECTS.

SIR,—Your correspondent " R. W. B." (page 221) very properly draws attention to the migration theory of birds, propounded by Alfred Leigh Hunt, in page 164 of the NATURALIST'S NOTE BOOK.

This new theory assumes several things which require proof, and the propounder, for brevity's sake I presume, is not too explicit. Would " A. L. H." have us to infer that the whole atmosphere, by land and sea, is crowded with insects? Or do his migratory bands of insects move in columns? Were an atmospheric change, or some meteoric agency to kill the insects, would that occurrence interrupt the migration of birds? Certainly not, is my opinion. But what new theory ever met with a favourable reception? Naturalists tell us, and observations prove, that many birds of passage return to the same place for years. Beranger must have thought so of swallows when he says:—

O swallows, swallows, tell them not,
When back ye fly o'er land and sea.

Now, Sir, sure this periodical return would induce us to suppose that something more than mere epicurean promptings led them to "the old familiar spot." With " R. W. B." I am quite prepared to think that some instinctive love of change induces the birds to migrate, and, with him, I also believe that the short life of insects militates against A. L. Hunt's theory. The very fact of supposing the migration of birds to depend on a continual supply of insects sets out on the hypothesis that insects themselves migrate, and if this migration implies long flights of thousands of miles, it really seems hard, without further and stronger proofs, to accept the theory proposed by A. L. Hunt. But, for the sake of argument, let us for a moment accept the theory under consideration —the birds find insects in abundance; if so, why do they (the birds) come so far, and particularly to *the same places* every year, unless the insects migrate in dense animated zones, simply for the convenience of the birds, and that the birds must, from absolute necessity, follow the insect battalions? But, Sir, in the theory we are trying to examine, the insect migration may not be so great as to extend to thousands of miles, nor even to a hundred miles; but then, in crossing oceans, I fear the new theory must, in order to supply insects for the feathered wanderers, fall back on the much disputed hypothesis of *spontaneous generation*—a thing itself not generally admitted, and still requiring proof. It often happens that swallows, in immense numbers, light on ships, and the testimony of the sailors invariably is that the poor birds are something like skeletons. Sir Charles Wager, Lord of the Admiralty, when in the British Channel, had his deck, rigging, &c., &c., crowded with swallows, and he describes them as *spent and famished and only feathers and bones.* Surely the insects had been scarce by the way. And Adamson, the naturalist, who went to Africa for the express purpose of collecting information regarding the migration of birds, &c., &c., in speaking of the swallow, says:—" These birds pass the seas to get into the countries of the torrid zone at the approach of winter in Europe." This keen observer had missed the insects on their long rambles.

Another writer, in speaking of the swallows at Senegal, says:—" For, as I have elsewhere mentioned, they (the swallows) do not build their nests in this country, but only *come to spend the winter.*" And Sharon Turner, writing in 1829, says:—" The roofs of the houses were covered with thousands of the swallow tribe, which had there assembled preparatory to their annual *migration to a warmer climate.*" A hundred and twenty years ago Klein, a German naturalist, stiffly argued that there was no such thing as the migration of birds; the test of time proves he was wrong. And now, Sir, that Alfred Leigh Hunt proposes and maintains that the migration of birds is but a result of the migration of insects, I for the present leave his new theory to his advocacy, and to the sagacious penetration of the learned correspondents of the NATURALIST'S NOTE BOOK.

I am, Sir, yours, &c.,

H. H. ULIDIA.

Dromore, September 4th, 1867.

Short Notes.

THE CUCKOO.—Every fact illustrative of the peculiarities of the cuckoo is interesting to the lover of nature. An instance has recently occurred which I imagine to be unusual, where a cuckoo's egg was deposited and the young bird reared in the nest of a wagtail, in a conservatory attached to Tidmarsh House, the residence of John Hopkins, Esq. The wagtail's nest was built in the thick foliage of a passion-flower climbing a wall at the back of a conservatory. I saw the overgrown nestling swelling himself out and ruffling his feathers, on the 23rd of June. During the week he shifted his quarters, and took flight on the 30th. It was not likely that the parent cuckoo, which is so shy a bird, entered the conservatory in the daytime, but that she probably took her opportunity very early in the morning; and, as the glasses were then closed, the bird must have entered through two small lights, which were left open in the front of the house. What is remarkable in the above incident is, first that the cuckoo should have become aware of the well-conceived nest of the wagtail, within the conservatory; second, that she should have had the boldness to enter an enclosed building attached to a dwelling-house, from the drawing-room of which it was only separated by glass doors. It is singular in these days when the love and observation of nature so extensively prevail, that we have so little new information regarding disputed and doubtful habits of the cuckoo. We know not with certainty whether she sometimes conveys her egg to the nest of the bird she intends to victimise, in her mouth; for although instances, such as that which is recorded about a wren's nest in the September number of the *Naturalist* for 1854, seem to prove this, the proof is not corroborated. Nor again, do we know certainly whether the cuckoo occasionally assists in feeding her young one, although it seems probable from what has been asserted on this point; nor again are the attempted explanations sufficiently satisfactory wherefore the cuckoo adopts the parasitic method of rearing her young. We may ascribe the singularity to one of the freaks in which nature delights, still these vagaries may usually be traced to some physical cause or necessity, which, as regards the parasite cuckoo, has not become apparent. I cannot but imagine myself, from the mysterious and unobserved way in which the cuckoo manages her operations, and from the seeming passiveness with which the birds she victimizes become reconciled to the intrusion, that the cuckoo may possibly, like some other animals, exercise a certain power of fascination over her victims which induces silence and acquiescence. I further believe that the peculiarly shaped nostril of the bird may be the organ given by nature to assist in the discovery of a foster parent, and a nursery for her future progeny.—*Land and Water*, Sept. 7.

THE THUNDERSTORM OF AUGUST 19th—20th—It is very remarkable that this storm occurred exactly a week behind a spell of deluging rain in the United States, from the Maine frontier to the Rocky Mountains. According to a Washington correspondent to one of the papers, people began to think about furnishing steam arks. Railways were washed away, rivers overflowed their banks, a vast extent of land was inundated; great damage to property and to standing crops ensued everywhere. At Washington six inches of water fell during the 98 hours ending at noon on Sunday, the 18th, the day preceding the occurrence of the storm in England. At Albany, in New York State, and at other places, the showers were attended by various phenomena—small shells and portions of decomposed tropical plants, with gelatinous matter, being found in the pools caused by the rain. In several of the Southern States the crops were very seriously injured. It is obvious that the great Atlantic Telegraph might warn us of many an impending storm by announcing daily the state of the weather in America. The consideration of the following facts will show the utility of this suggestion. Let us suppose, for example, the northerly current to be prevailing in America, and the southerly one in Europe; the latter will have a tendency to swerve from the point of contact, and allow the former to encounter it as a north-west wind. If, on the other hand, the northerly current is in Europe, and the southerly one in America, the latter will have a tendency to impinge on that from the north in a more westerly direction than that of its original course. This effect will be caused by the greater density of the polar current in the upper regions of the atmosphere. If, however, the polar current makes too great a resistance, a whirlwind will be produced in the equatorial current in the direction S., E., N., W. If we knew the weather that prevailed in the rest of the globe—as we may, certainly, by means of all the telegraphs—we might prognosticate that which might be expected. We ought to know, when the barometer is low with us, whether the cold is intense in America or in Asia. If in America, then the west winds will bring rain; if in Asia, the east winds will bring cold. Such a matter-of-fact method would be invaluable to all who are exposed to loss by sudden storms of wind or rain.—A. S. in *Gardener's Chronicle*, Sept. 7.

THE GULF STREAM.—It is undeniable that the influence of the Gulf Stream is felt through a large part of the North Atlantic Ocean, on the western shores of Great Britain, and still further along the northern and north-eastern coasts of Europe. What is the origin of this influence? This practical question has been answered in a variety of ways, by different writers. It seems to have been taken for granted that the Stream rises in the Gulf of Mexico, and hence it is commonly called the Gulf Stream. It is generally supposed that the most, if not all, of its striking peculiarities originate in that quarter of the Atlantic. On the coasts of Cornwall, Ireland, Scotland, Greenland, and yet further north, traces of tropical vegetation are found, which are supposed to be thrown on the beach and lodged among the rocks by the northern and eastern flow of the Gulf Stream. The western slopes of this part of Europe are clothed with moisture and peculiar verdure, in consequence of the steady deposit by the south-west winds from the sea of the fertilizing and warming vapours which abound where the Gulf Stream flows. A similar result is produced off the coasts of

Florida, South Carolina, North Carolina and Georgia, in the southern portion of the United States. It extends, at certain times, along the shores of New Jersey and New York, and is more slightly perceptible all round the extreme maritime regions of New England. We say at certain times, because there are periods on the sea-coasts of Europe as well as America when the course of the Gulf Stream is carried further away from shore than it is at others. During these periods, the effect produced on contiguous vegetation is at once perceptible; a change soon takes place in the surrounding atmosphere; so that all things under its influence are made to feel either the presence or absence of this extraordinary agent of the sea and air.—From *The Broadway*, No. 2.

TREES OF MISSOURI.—Professor Swallow, of the Missouri Geological Survey, gives the following actual measurements of large trees in South-east Missouri:—"The largest is a sycamore in Mississippi County, 65ft. high, which two feet above the ground measures 43ft. in circumference. Another sycamore, in Howard County, is 38½ft. in diameter. A cypress in Cape Girardeau County, at a distance of one foot above the ground, measures 29ft. in circumference. A cottonwood in Mississippi County measures 30ft. round, at a distance of six feet above the ground. A pecan in the same country is 18ft. in circumference. A black walnut in Benton County measures 22ft. in circumference. A white oak in Howard County is 26ft. in circumference. A tulip tree (poplar) in Cape Girardeau County is 30ft. in circumference. There is a tupelo in Stoddard County 30ft. in circumrerence. There is a hackberry in Howard County 11ft. in circumference. A spanish Oak in New Madrid County 26ft. in circumference. A white ash in Mississipi County is 16ft. in circumference. A honey locust in Howard County is 13ft. round. There is a willow in Pemiscot County that has grown to the size of 24ft. in circumference and 100ft. in height. Mississippi County boasts of a sassafras that must be king of that tribe; it measures 9ft. in circumference. There is a persimmon in the same county 9ft. in circumference. In Pemiscot County there is a dogwood 6ft. in circumference. In Mississippi County Papaws grow to a circumference of 3ft., and grapevines and trumpet creepers to a circumference of 18in. to 22in.

THE DEAN IN DIFFICULTIES.—White mice are used to feed the snakes at the Zoological Gardens. When the ladies see a white mouse in a cage with a snake, they say, "Poor little white mouse. How cruel." Sometimes when white mice run short, the snakes are fed with common mice, and then the ladies say, "Oh, its only a common brown mouse, the nasty thing!" I lately heard a capital story of a brown mouse. A certain dignitary of the Church is remarkable for a profusion of snow-white hair, which gives the worthy old man amost venerable aspect. One day, when out for a walk, he fancied he felt something moving in his hair, quite at the back of his head. This object he in vain tried to catch, but was unable so to do until he arrived home; when to the horror of all, it was found that a brown mouse had actually had the audacity to take up his quarters in the decanal hair, and from whence it required some hunting to dislodge the little rascal. What the object was on the part of the mouse in taking up his curious place of abode we know not. Possibly, however, this mouse was deputed by the mice of the adjoining church to go to the Dean and make a formal complaint of their proverbial poverty. The Dean, being a kind-hearted man, they thought might take their case into consideration. We have heard of a "bee in a man's bonnet," but never until a few days since of a "mouse in a Dean's hair.—FRANK BUCKLAND in *Land and Water*, Sep. 14.

BLACK RAIN.—The Rev. Mr. Rust, Slains, Aberdeenshire, writes to a Contemporary regarding this matter as follows:—"It has again turned out, as it did uniformly on all former occasions of known black-rain showers in Slains and Aberdeenshire, or Carluke and Birmingham, that one of the Italian volcanoes has been at work contemporaneously with the last Slains showers. On this occasion, as most usually, it has been Vesuvius. 'Vesuvius,' says a foreign Correspondent, 'which has for the last month been throwing up sheets of flame and smoke, has now subsided into a dormant tranquillity.' As I wrote you last in haste, I had not time to verify another black shower, which fell at Slains, &c., on Thursday, the 27th of September last, at seven p.m., and therefore I did not allude to it in my last communication with you. But it has since been verified; and my general remarks passed on the others are applicable to it. Now do we know of fourteen black showers, and all of them connected by contemporaneousness with Vesuvius or Etna. And what else is it but contemporaneousness that proves the connection between the tides and the moon, the effects and their cause? If we are satisfied with the sufficiency of proof in the one case, we are bound to be so in the other."—*Elgin Courant*.

A WONDERFUL EGG.—The following is from the *Journal de Toulouse*:—"M. Nau, a rich merchant of the island Le Réunton, who has remained 13 years a prisoner among the Hovas, has just brought to Toulouse an egg as remarkable from its size as its extreme rarity. It was found by M. Nau in the recent alluvial deposit of Madagascar at a depth of 4½ feet; it appertains to a bird of the ostrich kind, but of a size much greater, even exceeding that of the *dinornis giganteus* of Australia, which however attained a height of more than 11 feet The egg in question is a perfect oval; it measures one foot in its longest diameter and 10 inches the transversal one; the thickness of the shell is about 3-16ths of an inch; the colour yellowish white. In 1850 M. Abadie brought two similar ones to Paris from Madagascar, which were made the subject of an interesting notice by M. Geoffroy-Saint-Hilaire in the *Comptes-Rendus* of the Institute in 1851. The illustrious academician attributed to the animal, at present extinct, which laid these eggs, the name of *acpyornis* or tall bird. In fact, to judge from some fragments of bones which belonged to it, the *acpyornis* could not be less than 12ft. high. Some scientific men have expressed the opinion that this gigantic bird has perhaps still some living representatives in the interior of Madagascar, but M. Nau, who has traversed the island in every direction, affirms that is not so. The Malgaches themselves regard it as a species entirely destroyed.

CURIOUS CHICKENS.—A favourite hen of the Dorking breed was accustomed to lay its eggs in a pigsty, but day by day the eggs were carefully removed for fear of the pig devouring them. At length the hen began to show the usual signs of incubation, and as she went clucking about the sty, the proper proprietor produced a litter of pigs. Instantly the hen became possessed with a notion that the adoption of this strange progeny would satisfy her maternal craving; consequently she took possession of them, spread her wings over as many of them as she could gather under her, and fluttered about in a state of joyful excitement. This she continued to do for nearly three weeks, until the poor hen was nearly stripped of feathers, from the little pigs poking and rubbing in and out between her wings, and very nearly exhausted. It was a very curious sight to see her hoisted between two of her progeny, or a little later, seated on one of their backs, frantic with apprehension, as they rushed round the sty in the enjoyment of their different gambols, utterly regardless of the frightened clucking of their adopted mother. This occurrence frequently took place in the presence of visitors, who were invited to witness it. The hen was eventually removed.—*People's Magazine*, Sept.

NEWLY IMPORTED SPECIES OF INDIAN POULTRY.—The Peegum Pilly Gaguzes is a species of poultry which Captain Hastings Fraser has brought from Central India, and which he intends to naturalize in Scotland. The cock stands 2ft. 6in. upright, and is a noble bird; his thigh is so big that it can hardly be spanned with one hand; his eagle-like eye and mighty feet are also worthy of remark. The chickens are of extraordinary size and character, and are probably near relations of the Malay and Culm fowl. We understand that, by the last mail, seventeen of these fowl left India, and, with the exception of three chickens, they all arrived safe and in good condition. The great recommendation of this species for breeding is the quantity of flesh which they carry, young birds seven and eight months old weighing as much as 8lb. The Mohammedan Patans of India are very jealous of parting with their breed of poultry, but the native gentlemen or petty chieftain, from whose family these birds take their name, presented a few of them to Captain Fraser, and that officer has brought them to England with the intention of crossing them with Dorkings.—*Illustrated London News*.

GEOLOGICAL CURIOSITY.—A great geological curiosity has just been deposited in the museum of the Hartley Institution, at Southampton, consisting of a piece of flexible stone about 2ft. long, 7in. wide, and more than 1in. in thickness, having the appearance of rough sandstone, which bends with slight pressure like a piece of India-rubber or gutta-percha of the same size. This very interesting specimen of Geology has been placed in a glass case constructed for it, fitted with a lever, by touching the key of which on the outside of the case the flexibility of the stone is shown. It was presented to the Hartley Institution by Mr. Edward Cushen, from his relative, Mr. R. S. Munden, who obtained it from Delhi, in the East Indies. In its natural position the stone is said to run in thin layers in the soil in which it is found, but is so rare in India that it finds a place in the museums at Calcutta. We hear that there is a similar stone, but not so wide as the one under notice, in the British Museum, and another in the museum of the School of Mines, but specimens are very rarely to be met with. Although the stone has a gritty appearance, no grit or dust is thrown off by the motion given to it when under pressure.

THE SENSITIVE PLANT.—In a late number we (*London Review*) alluded to some experiments on the sensitive plant which had been conducted by M. Bert. The subject has now been taken up by M. Ch. Blondeau, who has been experimenting on the leaves with the induced galvanic current of a Rhunkorff's coil. He submitted three plants to the influence of the electric current. The first was operated on for five minutes; the plant when left to itself seemed prostrated, but after a while (a quarter of an hour), the leaves opened, and it seemed to recover itself. The second was acted on for ten minutes. This specimen was prostrate for an hour, after which it slowly recovered. The third specimen was galvanized for twenty-five minutes, but it never recovered, and in twenty-four hours it had the appearance of a plant struck by lightning. A fourth plant was etherized, and then exposed to the current. Strange to say, the latter had not any effect, the leaves remained straight and open; thus proving, says M. Blondeau, that the mode of contraction of the leaves of the sensitive plant is in some way allied to the muscular contraction of animals.

RICE GROWING IN JAPAN.—Two Japanese botanists have communicated a very interesting paper to the Acclimatisation Society; Tanaka and Yekoossina are the names of these gentlemen. In Japan, it appears, they have accustomed rice to grow without remaining swamped in water; by dint of great patience, and by gradually diminishing the supply of water, they have got what they term dry rice, and after a few crops this rice appears to lose its old nature and to be able to get on in dry soil. In the district of Jeddo, the fields that are to be sown with rice are well manured towards the end of March or the beginning of April, and then ploughed. Before sowing, the rice is macerated in water for three days and three nights; it is then exposed to the sun in order to hasten its germination. After picking out the bad grain, the rest is mixed with ashes and the remains of fish, dried, and reduced to powder; the mixture is then strewed along the furrows, which are immediately afterwards filled up with earth. This operation takes place in May. If the weather is very dry, the field must receive liquid manure. In the course of June and July the field must be weeded and the roots earthed up; an abundant crop may then be expected in October or November. This system of tillage is practised in Japan also for wheat and other grain.

CENTAUREA BABYLONICA.—We read in the *Gardener's Chronicle* of Sept. 7th:—No collection of hardy fine-leaved plants—no place where sub-tropical gardening is attempted, should be without this. The flowers are poor and yellow, so much so that they would be better out of sight; but nothing can be more distinctly noble than the great silvery leaves when the plant is in good soil. It is thoroughly hardy. The stem rises to a height of 8 or 10 feet when the plant is in good deep loam, and in any soil it is large. The inflorescence assumes a pyramidial outline, looks like a slender pyramid of yellow, in fact, and those with no objection to comparatively poor-looking yellow flowers may let it flower, but generally it will be found better to pinch out the stems in their earliest infancy, and thus encourage a grand growth of leaves. I have a slight objection to any plant that requires pinching or any other attention to make it assume the character we admire, but this is really so distinct and fine that we must admit it to the front rank of hardy fine-leaved plants. Of course it would prove fine for the group of hardy fine-foliaged plants, its immense silvery leaves contrasting finely with the glistening green ones of the Acanthus and other good green things, which I hope to soon see used in this way.

HOW NATURE PRESERVED A RECORD.—A St. Louis paper mentions an incident which occurred in the surveys of the Iron Mountain Road in the cypress swamps of South-east Missouri. The engineers, having orders to locate their surveys in connection with the United States land surveys, had occasion to search for marks or records made years ago in the swamps. The land surveyors had marked the results of their work by cutting into the body of a tree, levelling off a smooth surface of the trunk, and engrossing their records on the tablets thus prepared. The engineers found the trees of the old survey, and recognised the scars of former cuttings, but to reach the records were compelled to cut into the trees again. New wood had grown up over the old record, completely hiding and protecting it. But, after cutting into the body down to the original tablet, they found the surveyor's record as plain and distinct as when first made.

THE HEN A TACTICIAN.—Hens often display a great deal of cunning and sagacity in the attainment of their objects. A clergyman related the following little anecdote to the writer. During the severe weather last winter he was accustomed to feed the small birds with grain and crumbs of bread; but his success was much marred by the depredations of a hen, whom he had the greatest difficulty in keeping from the food. He tried to effect this by throwing stones at her, till one morning her instinct directed her to try the following expedient. She found that by getting behind a tree, where she could neither be seen by the clergyman nor hit by his missiles, she was able suddenly to shoot forward, pick up a bit, and escape to her hiding-place, before a stone could reach her. This she did for several days, until her hiding-place was discovered and she was driven from her place of security.—*People's Magazine*, September.

STORY OF A DOG.—On Sunday morning, October 28th, the house and outbuildings, with their contents, of Alderman Block, of Fredericton, N.B., were consumed by fire. The *Colonial Farmer*, published in that city, gives the following incident, which is worthy of record, as showing the fidelity of this noble animal :—" It seems that the fire was first detected by a Newfoundland dog, the property of Mr. Block. The noble brute, with almost human instinct, tore his way into the house by means of one of the doors, and aroused the family by his barking, and then ran to the stable door which he endeavoured to open so that the horse, his almost inseparable companion, might escape. There he remained struggling, though every effort was made to entice him away, and when the fire went out he was found lying dead at his post." A correspondent states that the dog effected an entrance to the house by tearing out a panel of the door with his claws, and thus saved the lives of the inmates, who had time to retire, but not time enough to save anything.

THE PHOSPHORESCENCE OF THE SEA.—" An Observer," writing form Strone, says,— On Sunday night last, about ten o'clock, there was one of the finest exhibitions of phosphorescence visible from Strone and the surrounding watering places we have ever witnessed. An east wind produced short, deep waves, and every crest as it broke became vividly illuminated, the surface of the sea gleamed for miles around, and so brilliant was the light that it made the darkness perceptibly less along the coast, like the stars on a clear moonless night. Those who have seen the phosphorescence in this country only were afforded some idea of its appearance in more southern latitudes, where the warmer climate allows the lower forms of marine animals to develop in greater profusion; and as some of our Glasgow naturalists have been lately examining these phosphorescent animals, they have now an excellent opportunity to prosecute their researches further.—*Standard*, Sep. 5.

FUNERAL OF A BEE.—A correspondent of the *Glasgow Herald* transmits the following :—" On Sunday morning last I had the pleasure of witnessing a most interesting ceremony, which I desire to record for the benefit of your readers. Whilst walking with a friend in a garden near Falkirk, we observed two bees issuing from one of the hives, bearing betwixt them the body of a defunct comrade, with which they flew for a distance of ten yards. We followed them closely, and noted the care with which they selected a convenient hole at the side of the gravel walk, the tenderness with which they committed the body, head downwards, to the earth, and the solicitude with which they afterwards pushed against it two little stones, doubtless 'in memoriam.' Their task being ended, they paused for about a minute, perhaps to drop over the grave of their friend a sympathising tear ; and then they flew away."

DISCOVERY OF A CAVE IN A LIMESTONE QUARRY.—As some men were at work blasting in one of the Fulwell quarries, a day or two ago, they discovered about a depth of 60ft. below the top of the limestone bed, a natural cavern, the roof of which subsequently fell in and filled it up. The cave had evidently been at one time a receptacle of water, as its sides were in places worn away by the drip. It had been dome shaped, 30ft. in diameter, and about 20ft. in height, and it is on a level into what is known as the " fish bed," and the locality from which many interesting fossils of extinct fish have been obtained.— *Newcastle Journal*.

Remarks, Queries, &c.

(*Under this head we shall be happy to insert original Remarks, Queries, &c.*)

THE BARK OF TREES.—This subject, I think, has not been sufficiently studied as a character either by naturalists or arboriculturists. Any one possessing only a moderate knowledge of trees could easily determine most of them by a mere glance. I will only mention the birch, beech, oak, and Scotch fir, and your readers can satisfy themselves that it is so. No tree has a more beautiful bark than the birch. When young it is of a silvery white colour. As it grows older it assumes a totally different character. Every bit of silver is gone, and cracked off the lower part of the tree; but upon the upper part it still flourishes as before. The smooth bark of the beech needs little illustration. Unlike the birch, which, although silvery in youth, becomes rugged and deeply corrugated in age, it retains the same appearance to extreme old age, although then the trunk assumes all sorts of humps and protuberances. The bark of the oak has the same character all over, except on the small twigs. It is closely and longitudinally furrowed, and the only difference is, that the smaller the branch the finer the corrugations. The appearance of the bark of the Scotch fir is different in different parts of the tree. At the lower part of the tree it is deeply and longitudinally furrowed, and the spaces between the furrows scale off more or less in large, long, irregularly oblong patches. Higher up, the scales are smaller and not so long. J. D. S. W.

RATS ON THEIR RAMBLES.—A writer (Martin, I think, in his "Tour to the Western Isles"), says that about the year 1700, the ancient race of the Island of Rona was destroyed in the following almost incredible manner:—"First, a swarm of rats, none knew how, came into the island and ate up all the corn. In the next place, some seamen landed and robbed them (the people) of what provisions they had left, and all died before the usual time of the arrival of the boat from Lewis!!" This presumed incursion of rats tries the most elastic credulity. Can any of the correspondents of the NATURALIST'S NOTE BOOK throw any more light on this curious subject?

Dromore, September 5th. H. H. ULIDIA.

HOW TO PRESERVE MILK.—When milk "turns," this effect is caused by the development of an acid in the liquid. This chemical change may be effectually prevented by adding to the milk a small quantity of bi-carbonate of soda. This addition is by no means injurious to health; on the contrary, bi-carbonate of soda aids digestion. One of the great dairies of Paris employs no other method but this for preserving the milk it keeps for sale. J. D. S. W.

HYDROPHOBIA IN DOGS.—Most persons are of opinion that this distemper is caused solely by extreme heat of weather. Others say that this is not the case, but that it is produced by the influence of the "dog-star." This disease is hardly known in tropical countries. Our newspapers, also, record as many cases in winter as in summer. Will any of your scientific readers give their opinion as to its cause?

R. W. B.

FOREST TREES.—Can you, or any of your readers, favour me with a list of "forest trees" which are natives of Britain? and let me know the best book of botany for beginners? R. W. B.

STATE OF THE WEATHER NEAR LONDON.

| August and Sept. | Moon's Age. | Barometer. || Temperature. |||| Wind | Rain. | Remarks. |
| | | | | Of the Air. ||| of the Earth || | | |
		Max.	Min.	Max	Min	Mean	1 foot deep	2 feet deep			
Thurs. 22	☾	30.049	29.998	73	48	60.5	65	62	S.W.	.00	Fine; very fine; clear at night.
Friday 23	23	30.051	30.009	75	49	62.0	64	62	W.	.00	Cloudy; exceedingly fine; clear, with starlight.
Satur. 24	24	30.088	30.038	74	55	64.5	64	62	S.W.	.00	Fine; very fine throughout.
Sunday 25	25	30.027	30.003	75	57	66.0	64	61	S.W.	.00	Cloudy and hot; very fine; overcast at night.
Mon. 26	26	29.971	29.956	69	48	58.5	62	60	N.E.	.14	Overcast; heavy showers; slightly overcast; rain.
Tues. 27	27	30.040	30.000	67	48	58.0	62	60	N.W.	.00	Partially overcast and fine; overcast; cloudy at night.
Wed. 28	28	30.118	30.088	70	51	60.5	62	60	S.W.	.00	Fine; cloudy; clear and fine at night.
Thurs. 29	●	30.150	30.088	72	48	60.0	62	60	S.	.13	Cloudy; very fine; cloudy at night.
Friday 30	1	30.084	29.924	73	49	61.0	63	60	S.	.00	Fine; exceedingly fine; clear at night.
Satur. 31	2	29.858	29.812	78	65	71.5	63	60	S.E.	.00	Fine; exceedingly fine; overcast.
Sunday 1	3	29.919	29.818	80	45	62.5	65	61	S.E.	.00	Overcast; very fine and hot throughout.
Mon. 2	4	30.072	30.041	78	59	68.5	64	61	S.E.	.20	Very fine; clear and fine throughout.
Tues. 3	5	29.982	29.868	74	53	63.5	65	61	S.E.	.22	Violent thunderstorm and heavy rain, 6. A.M., warm and overcast; low fog at night.
Wed. 4	6	29.835	29.807	74	54	64.0	64	61	S.W.	.10	Overcast; cloudy; clear and fine at night.
Thurs. 5	☽	29.821	29.798	73	42	57.5	63	61	W.	.02	Rain; fine; clear, and very fine at night.
Friday 6	8	29.773	29.725	69	52	60.5	62	61	S.W.	.12	Fine; heavy showers; fine.
Satur. 7	9	30.000	29.851	72	40	56.0	63	60	S.W.	.00	Overcast; fine; clear at night.
Sunday 8	10	30.030	29.848	73	40	56.5	62	60	S.	.00	Very fine; cloudy; very fine.
Mon. 9	11	29.856	29.731	74	50	62.0	62	60	S.W.	.82	Very fine; excessively heavy rain.
Tues. 10	12	29.887	29.785	73	41	57.0	62	60	S.W.	.30	Clear; fine; thunder and heavy rain, 5 P.M.; clear.
Wed. 11	13	29.941	29.854	72	56	64.0	62	60	S.	.21	Hazy; cloudy; overcast; rain at night.
Thurs. 12	14	29.877	29.694	73	46	59.5	62	59	S.W.	.00	Rain; fine; very clear and fine at night.
Friday 13	15	29.997	29.903	70	42	56.0	62	60	W.	.00	Slight haze; overcast; very fine.
Satur. 14	○	29.996	29.858	66	40	53.0	62	59	S.W.	.04	Fine; rather boisterous; rain at night.
Sunday 15	17	30.086	29.983	70	40	55.0	61	59	N.W.	.00	Cloudy; fine; clear and very fine.
Mon. 16	18	30.194	30.124	66	36	51.0	60	59	N.W.	.00	Clear; partially clouded; clear at night.
Tues. 17	19	30.317	30.291	61	46	53.5	60	59	N.E.	.08	Overcast and cold; clear and fine; overcast; rain.
Wed. 18	20	30.320	30.209	68	49	58.5	60	58	N.E.	.00	Cloudy; clear, with scattered white clouds; cloudy.

SHARKS.

ROM the equator, east of the Cape, up the Indian Ocean and the Bay of Bengal to where the opaque muddy water marks the region of the "Sand Heads," sharks abound. They are numerous about the Mauritius, off Ceylon, and the Coromandel coast; about the islands in the Bay of Bengal, the Andamans, Cocoas, Narcondam, Nicobar, and all along the Arracan and Burmese coasts, to the S. E. Archipelago, they swarm. In the Calcutta river and the numerous streams and creeks of the Soonderbuns they are perhaps as plentiful; but the turbid waters of the upper parts of the bay conceal them from view. This I saw strikingly illustrated shortly after our entrance into the Hooghly. We had anchored, the tide failing us, off Saugor island, a hideous mud flat, crowned with jungle grass and scattered over with a few wretched buildings; and, while waiting there five weary hours for the flood to make, employed ourselves watching the usual sights that greet the new arrival in Bengal—the gulls, crows, and Braminy kites flying about the ship; the canoes and strange country boats of the natives gliding along by the shore, in the rapid ebb tide; the ghastly bloated corpses, some surmounted by a crow or a vulture, floating down the muddy stream—till, sated with the spectacle, we began to wonder we had seen no crocodiles or sharks, for which the place had an ill fame. Not a living thing appeared to inhabit that filthy water, and, after venting our disappointment thereat, and coming to the conclusion that nothing worth looking at—certainly no sharks—frequented the river, we remained listlessly leaning over the ship's side, smoking our cheroots, and wondering what made the Hooghly so like *café au lait*, when from the gallery forward the butcher threw overboard the entrails of a sheep he had killed and prepared for the cook's functions. We looked at the offal in an idle, uninterested way, as, borne by the ebb, it swept rapidly aft; but hardly had it reached the ship's quarter, just underneath us, when we saw it violently agitated, and then torn and snatched by some six or eight broad shovel heads and grinning jaws, and the water around lashed by angry tails and fins! We started back in amazement. The supposed tenantless stream was absolutely swarming with sharks, prowling close around the ship, but in such thick and foul water as to be invisible till lured to the surface! Strange to say, notwithstanding their numbers, a shark is seldom, if ever, caught in the Hooghly by hook and line.

* * * * * *

There are many species of sharks, some so like each other as only to be distinguished by a close examination of their scales or of their teeth. Some, similar in form, are widely opposed in habits. The ordinary sharks will not go near broken water; but the species found on the Coromandel coast come right into the surf, and have been known to seize men wading little above their knees. The small ones are eaten by the poorer Chittagong Bengalies, Arakanese, Burmese, Talaings, Siamese, and Malays; and immense quantities of their fins are exported to China, to be made into a rich glutinous soup, of which the Celestials are very fond. I have been informed, but I know not if correctly so, that sharks are unknown in the China Seas. At Hongkong, certainly, natives and Europeans bathe anywhere in the harbour without the slightest fear.

It is only the largest sharks, however, which will attack men. Such are mostly the solitary fishes, which keep during the day far out from shore, lurking at the bottom; sometimes in calm weather coming up to look at a fisherman's boat, and during the night approaching the beach.

* * * * * *

The hammer-headed shark (Zygœna) is a common enough species on the eastern side of the Bay of Bengal. They are found in the same haunts as the common shark, but appear to keep more constantly to the bottom. There is nothing peculiar in their habits answering to the singularity of their form, unless we place credence in my old Malay friend's assertion, that in swimming slowly past rocks the zygœna pokes his projecting eye into the crevices, to spy out the crabs which lurk there, and on which it feeds. But a practical objection to this theory is, that such discovery would be in each case useless to the fish, which could not get its mouth in where the eye had penetrated; so that, unless the crab were a fool and waddled out of his retreat, he would be none the worse for his whereabouts being discovered. The hammer-headed sharks haunt the coast; the largest (which range up to 12 or 13 feet) keep furthest out, but never beyond five or six miles from the shore, in 20 or 30 fathoms water.

Vast numbers of sharks, generally of small size, are taken by Bengalese, Burmese, and Malays, in nets, and in what the Burmese call "damains" rows of stakes and mats placed so as to form labyrinths, in which fish of all kinds congregate without finding their way out again. Large sharks are a great nuisance to the fishermen if they get in their nets, as they will bite through several folds, and tear them with the lashes of their tails, before they can be put *hors de combat*. The Arakanese, in their small fishing-boats, go boldly in pursuit of these fishes, which swarm about the bar of Akyab River.

They try for them with a line and hook baited with fish, and when a shark has taken the bait they let him run about as long as he likes, towing the boat after him. When his efforts begin to slacken, another boat joins the first one, and the two are lashed together side by side. The shark is then gradually pulled in, and his head hoisted out of the water, or brought into a convenient position to receive a tremendous blow with a *dá* (a large heavy knife or cleaver). Fresh water is then poured into the wound (a process which the Arakanese say is immediately fatal), and the fish is towed to shore or the nearest market.

I have alluded to the shark's singular companions, the pilot fishes. Their apparently unnatural attachment to the former has never, to my knowledge, been satisfactorily accounted for. The pilot fish (*Naucrates ductor*) is of the mackerel family, and there is nothing in its conformation to explain its eccentric departure from the manners and customs of its kith and kin. It is a widely-spread little fish, being found in all the seas of the temperate and tropical regions. It keeps well out to sea, and only approaches the shore when attracted by ships making for the land, for it has a propensity to follow ships as well as sharks.

The sucking fish (*Echeneis remora*) is also another well known *attaché* (literally speaking) to the shark. It adheres to the latter by the crown of its head, and suffers itself to be thus carried along for immense distances, often being drawn upon deck sticking to the shark's body. It adheres to rocks in the same manner in rapid tideways, and thus preserves its position without effort in the wash of the waves.

* * * * * *

As I said before, none but the largest sharks will attack man, and even the very largest can be frightened away by splashing and making a great hubbub in the water. It is probable also that there must be considerable pressure from hunger before they will act on the offensive; and this may account for the very few casualties which occur, even where these fishes are known to be numerous. I once swam about the harbour at Point de Galle, in Ceylon, for a considerable distance, utterly unaware at the time that it was full of sharks. I need hardly say I did not see the smallest indication of one. In 1843, I was informed by an officer whose acquaintance I made at Singapoor that he and other officers of the regiment stationed at Kyoukphyoo, in Arracan, were in the constant habit of bathing in the harbour there, and that not the least alarm had been caused by a shark within the memory of any one at the station until quite recently, when an officer, who had swum a considerable distance from the beach, was seized by one, and so dreadfully bitten in the thigh that, although he was brought to shore by his comrades (who swam to his assistance in the most gallant manner), he died from loss of blood in a few minutes. In the night these dreadful fishes seem to be bolder, or perhaps are more "on the feed," of which my informant gave me the following proof.

One day during the rainy monsoon of 1842 three men of the Arracan local battalion at Akyab deserted, and smuggled themselves on board a native boat which was about to cross the harbour late in the evening. The weather was dark and stormy, and when the boat reached about half-way across—that is, nearly three miles from either shore—in a tumultuous sea, caused by the race of the tide against a strong wind, the boat capsized. Its occupants got on her bottom, but there being no keel or anything to hold by, were frequently washed off, and helped on again by their companions. All were good swimmers and strong hardy men, and as there was a good chance of the boat being drifted on to some rocks just visible in the darkness, they kept up good heart, till suddenly one of their number (a sepoy), in struggling to regain his place on the boat's bottom, gave a loud shriek and disappeared! Horror seized upon the party, for the Arakanese are all more or less fishermen and boatmen, and long experience in the dangers of those waters at once informed them of the nature of their comrade's fate. They knew the sharks which swarm about that part of the harbour were collecting round the boat, and with this dreadful conviction they lay desperately clinging to the slippery surface of the canoe, fully aware that to slip into the sea was to meet a speedy but frightful death. Not many minutes elapsed before another unfortunate sepoy startled them with a ghastly yell. A few broken words, while he clung to the boat, explained his awful situation; and, with a frantic clutch or two at the slippery bottom, and at his companions, who were powerless to help him, he was swiftly drawn under. The miserable survivors, stupified with terror and bereft of hope, lay still upon their rolling and insecure perch, till they had providentially been carried past the strength of the stream, where the tumbling waves had pitched them incessantly off their seats, and, entering a smoother space of slack water, were enabled to guide the boat to a rock, and there to right her and proceed on their way.

But these horrible occurrences are rare. Fortunate indeed, for those whose avocations call them into tropical seas, is the capricious nature, the timidity, the sluggishness, or whatever it may be, which in nine cases out of ten deters the shark from attacking a man in the water. I have seen at Penang and Singapoor the Clings or Madras fishermen wading up to their necks, dragging their nets along by the shore; and, though they pass many hours of almost every day in the year thus occupied, not a casualty from sharks has ever been known to occur amongst them.

The size attained by sharks has been doubtless much exaggerated, and the accounts we now and then meet with of the capture of a monster out at sea, or in the West Indies, bear too much the semblance of romance, or at least of heated fancy, to be received as a correct record of facts. Moreover, these accounts are generally by unscientific persons.

Of fossil sharks there are teeth to be seen in many cabinets and museums; by which, assuming that the teeth were in the same proportion to the entire bulk as they are in the sharks of the present day, their paleontological (or paleogonous?) owners must have been 50ft. long. In the museum at the Cape of Good Hope I saw a shark's jaw (a donation of no long anterior date, by the captain of a vessel, the name of which I regret not having taken a note of), which measured 21in. from the symphisis of the upper jaw to that of the lower, and 15in. across at the gape. This fish, therefore, allowing him to have been of the usual proportions of the ordinary deepsea shark of the Pacific and Indian Ocean, must have been 19ft. or 20ft. long, and 11ft. in girth at the shoulders.—*Field*, September 28th and October 5th.

NATURALISTS' FIELD CLUBS.

It is manifest that the successful working of a Field Club must depend on the suitability of its plans to the circumstances of its position. Field Clubs commonly belong to one or the other of two distinct classes. 1st. Such as occupy a wide field extending over a large portion of a county, and include amongst their members chiefly professional men, and men of independent position. 2ndly. Such as are established in populous towns.

To the former of these divisions belongs the Cotteswold Naturalists' Field Club, of which we need only say that the intellectual and genial character of its gatherings is such as to induce men of eminence in science, even when residing in London, frequently to attend its meetings. Its publications have not been issued regularly, but are of the highest scientific value.

The Woolhope Naturalists' Field Club has this year issued a volume of transactions, which plainly indicates the Club to be in a thriving and vigorous condition. The speciality of the work, however, mainly consists in that portion of it which contains the Flora of Herefordshire, edited by the Rev. W. H. Purchas. The Flora is accompanied by a map of the county divided into fourteen botanical districts: a schedule follows, pointing out the plants found in each district. The editor modestly disclaims originality in adopting this plan; but we do not know that it has been carried out with the same degree of completeness in any other county. The difficulty of obtaining satisfactory reports from so many districts must have been very great.

We quote from the advertisement:—"It has of late years been felt that a very imperfect view of the botany of any county was given by the plan on which the older Floras were drawn up; that plan being to mention stations for the rarer plants, or those supposed to be such, whilst it was left to be inferred that the remainder were equally common throughout the whole area to which the Flora related. The real truth being that species which, from their frequency in one part of a county, might be expected to prevail equally throughout its whole extent, are found, when specially sought after, to be comparatively local."

Whilst Field Clubs very rightly devote a good deal of attention to the geographical distribution of plants, it may be remarked that the geographical distribution of the Field Clubs themselves is a subject worthy of notice. A map of England marked with the stations of these Clubs would show them to be very unequally distributed. A belt extending from Lancashire along the western side of England to the south coast would include amongst others the following: Bath, Bristol, The Caradoc, The Cotteswold, Cheltenham, Dudley, Exeter, Liverpool, Malvern, Manchester, Oswestry, Preston (1867), Severn Valley, Somersetshire, The Teign, Worcestershire, and The Woolhope. In the rest of England the stations marked would be comparatively few and far between. Are we to apply to the geologists or the ethnologists for an explanation of this?

The list of Herefordshire plants is a large one: some of the districts, particularly that of Ross, have been fortunate in possessing a representative not afraid to attack such formidable botanical problems as the Willows and the Brambles. A list of plants, however, even if it were perfect, would convey but little instruction unless connected with information respecting the physical and geological features of the district to which it belonged. This want has been supplied by the Rev. W. S. Symonds, President of the Malvern Club, who has given an admirable account of the local and geological characters of each of the fourteen subdivisions of the county. It is announced that a future portion of the Flora will consist of a "more detailed mention of the different plants, and will give any further information that may seem needful." The volume contains full reports of the excursions, referring to which Dr. Bull, the President, in his retiring address, remarks, "The published reports of our field days make people wish they had been with us." Not the least doubt of it! Who would not wish to share in such *dies ambrosianæ*, with salmon and the goodly haunch of venison on the board, and such men as Bentham (of the Handbook) and Brodie and Symonds as guests, besides the members of the Club, around it?

Before leaving the Woolhope proceedings we must refer to the series of photographs of remarkable trees in Herefordshire: these are not the only indications that this Club gives more than common attention to the subject of trees, too often almost neglected by botanists.

The Bristol Naturalists' Society differs from most others in having distinct sections for entomology, chemistry and photography, zoology, botany, and geology. A general meeting is held once in the month; the sections also have monthly meetings and excursions, and contribute funds to the library of the Society.

The Liverpool Naturalists' Field Club professedly aims at the extension of a taste for natural science, and seems to have ample scope for its efforts amongst its 720 members. Some peculiarities in its plan are thus noticed by the President:—"As the plan of giving prizes (books on natural history subjects) originated with our own Club, I may state that practically it has been found very successful. Many younger members of the Club, beginning with the prizes (at the excursions) most easily attainable, have been encouraged to proceed zealously with studies which otherwise would not have been entered upon; whilst some of the collections sent in for our annual prizes have far surpassed all our expectations." "Large numbers join our excursions who are not particularly interested in any branch of natural science, and this is just what the chief object of our Club renders a desirable circumstance. The busy appearance of our workers, who often come in when tea is half over, flushed with exercise and animated with success, is a suggestive lesson to others who may be found waiting at the door of our meeting room half-an-hour or even an hour before the appointed time; a lesson on the difference of the amount of pleasure afforded by a walk with a special object, and a walk without one." "Our numerical strength gives to our most valued members facilities for visiting localities at great distances, on terms which could not otherwise be obtained. We are able to engage a special train and make a journey of 160 miles in a day, at a cost, including a substantial dinner-tea, of about seven shillings each, allowing five hours for work at the locality visited."

Naturalists' Societies now in operation in Great Britain have upon their lists probably not fewer than 4,000 members: we may safely add an equal number to represent professors, students, collectors, and others not connected with any society, yet more or less actively engaged in the same pursuit. Such a company should be able to give a good account of the natural history of their own country, yet many interesting branches have been all but wholly neglected, and some are at present without even a moderately useful *Handbook*, *e. g.*, the Fresh-water Algæ, the Annelids, and the Centipedes: but even in the pursuits which are most popular much remains to be done. Members of Naturalists' Societies must be aware that a question is pending which in Zoology and Botany may open a field for investigation, comparatively, as vast as that annexed to astronomy by the invention of the telescope. Yet it is a marvel how few direct their efforts towards the acquisition of evidence for or against the hypothesis of the origin of species by natural selection. Facts well authenticated and chosen with discrimination on either side are equally, and at present pre-eminently, the desiderata of natural science.—*Quarterly Journal of Science*, Oct. London: Churchill.

GEOLOGY AND THE MICROSCOPE.

THE microscope, employed some thirty years back by Ehrenberg in the examination of minute fossil organisms, is now recognised as having already done good service to palæontology, but was quite unknown to the geologist proper until within the last few years, when the admirable labours of Sorby have demonstrated the importance of the microscope as an indispensable instrument of research in the study of physical geology and petrology, as well as indicated how much more may be expected from its more extended application.

The application of the microscope in these enquiries is as yet, however, quite in its infancy, for with the exception of Sorby's invaluable memoirs on some special points of enquiry, literally nothing has as yet been made public which could even serve as an introductory guide to the geologist who might wish to commence the study of the subject. It is therefore with great hesitation, and only after much solicitation, that the author of these remarks has now ventured into print, with the hope that by once breaking the ice, others more capable than himself may be induced to communicate the results of their researches on the same subject.

In the present communication it is not intended

to go into the details of any special microscopic investigation, but, as far as the space at disposal will allow, to attempt a short sketch of some of the results already obtained, in order thereby to illustrate the use of the microscope in similar enquiries, and to place the same before our readers in as plain untechnical language as possible.

When applying the microscope to the examination of rock structure and composition, it is necessary to prepare the specimens previously, in order to be enabled to make full use of transmitted light in their investigation, since a mere inspection of their outer surface, viewed as an opaque object, although sometimes of considerable value, does not, however, give a tithe of the information which their examination by transmitted light will afford.

When in sufficiently thin splinters or laminæ, by far the larger proportion of mineral compounds allow light to pass through them with more or less facility, and amongst these, most silicates, chlorides, fluorides, carbonates, sulphates, borates, and other salts, as well as many oxides, and some few sulphides, sulpharsenides, &c. On the other hand, all native metals, alloys, and most of their combinations with sulphur, arsenic, antimony, &c., along with some few oxides and other compounds, are opaque, even when in the thinnest laminæ, and consequently when present, as they often are, in minute quantity in rocks, although sometimes recognisable by their external crystalline form, are not to be distinguished by their optical properties, as in the case of those bodies which, as before mentioned, are translucent.

When a mineral or rock under examination is entirely in the vitreous state, as, for example, obsidian, it appears when viewed under the microscope, merely as a more or less transparent or coloured glass, presenting, if perfectly in the vitreous condition, no evidence of crystalline or other structure, except perhaps traces of the striæ of viscid fusion. It is usually found on inspection, however, that some part of the mass is sufficiently devitrified to allow of its structure and mineral composition being recognised. In some cases, when the glassy appearance presented to the eye would discourage any hopes of structure being discovered, the microscope proved the reverse most conclusively.

In many cases, however, where the specimens are so perfectly in the vitreous state as to show no trace of structure whatsoever, this may be developed by carefully acting upon the surface by gaseous or liquid hydrofluoric acid.

The rock sections may be prepared for the microscope as follows: a fragment, from one-quarter to three-quarters of an inch square, and of convenient thickness, is chipped off the rock specimen in the direction of the required section, and ground down upon an iron or pewter plate in a lapidary's lathe with emery, until a perfectly flat surface is obtained. This surface is then worked down still finer by hand on a slab of black marble, with less coarse emery, then upon a Water of Ayr stone with water alone, and, lastly, finished by hand with water on a slab of black marble. By these means the surface acquires a sufficient polish without being contaminated with rouge or other polishing powder or oil, as is sometimes the case with purchased sections of rocks. This side of the rock is now cemented by Canada balsam on to a small piece of plate glass about $1\frac{1}{2}$ inch square and $\frac{3}{8}$ thick, which serves as a handle when grinding the other side on the emery plate as before; this grinding is continued until the section is so thin as to be in danger of breaking up from the roughness of the motion, upon which it is completed, by further grinding with emery by hand on marble, and finished first upon Water of Ayr stone with water, and afterwards upon black marble, as before described. The section is now removed from the plate-glass, and mounted in Canada balsam on a slide, covering its upper surface with a thin glass as usual.

The thickness to which such sections need be reduced is, of course, entirely dependent upon the transparency of the rock constituents, and is commonly from $\frac{1}{100}$ to $\frac{1}{1000}$ of an inch.

Thin splinters of rocks and powdered fragments, mounted in Canada balsam, may also be examined with advantage, but cannot replace the above-described sections.

The examination of such a rock section enables a mineralogical analysis to be made, even of the most compact and apparently homogeneous rock, and generally leads to the discovery of other mineral constituents previously unsuspected, from their being invisible to the eye, and also, as Sorby has observed, allows those minerals, formed at the time of solidification of the rock, to be distinguished from such as are the products of subsequent alteration. — *David Forbes, in Popular Science Review, Oct.* 1867.

THE CARPENTER BEE.

The power of boring the most symmetrical tunnels in solid wood reaches its perfection in the large Virginian Carpenter bee (*Xylocopa Virginica*). This bee is as large, and some allied exotic species are often considerably larger than the Humble bee, but not clothed with such dense hairs. We have received from Mr. James Angus, of West Farms, N. Y., a piece of trellis from a grape-vine, made of pine wood, containing the cells and young in various stages of growth, together with the larvæ and chrysalids of *Anthrax sinuosa*, a species of fly parasitic on the larva, which buries its head in its soft body, and feeds on its juices.

Mr. Angus thus writes us regarding its habits under date of July 19: "I asked an intelligent and observing carpenter yesterday, if he knew how long it took the Xylocopa to bore her tunnel. He said he thought she bored about one-quarter of an inch a day. I don't think myself she bores more than one half-inch, if she does that. If I mistake not, it takes her about two days to make her own length at the first start; but this being across the grain of the wood may not be so easily done as the remainder, which runs parallel with it. She always follows the grain of the wood, with the exception of the entrance, which is about her own length. The tunnels run from one to one and a half feet in length. They generally run in opposite directions from the opening, and sometimes other galleries are run one above the other, using the same opening. I think they only make new tunnels when old ones are not to be found, and that the same tunnels are used for many years. Some of the old tunnels are very wide. I have found parts of them about an inch in diameter. I think this is caused by rasping off the sides to procure the necessary material for constructing their cells. The partitions are composed of wood-raspings, and some sticky fluid, probably saliva, to make it adhere.

"The tunnels are sometimes taken possession of by other bees and wasps. I think when this is the case, the Xylocopa prefers making a new cell to cleaning out the mud and rubbish of the other species. I frequently find these bees remaining for a long time on the wing close to the opening, and bobbing their heads against the side, as if fanning air into the opening. I have seen them thus employed for twenty minutes. Whether one bee or more makes the tunnel, that is, whether they take turns in boring, I cannot say at present. In opening the cells, more than one are generally found, even at this season. About two weeks ago, I found as many as seven, I think, in one."

The hole is divided by partitions into cells about seven-tenths of an inch long. These partitions are constructed of the coarse dust or chippings made by the bee in eating out her cells, for our active little carpenter is provided with strong cutting jaws, moved by powerful muscles, and on her legs are stiff brushes of hair for cleaning out the tunnel as she descends into the heart of the solid wood. She must throw out the chips she bites off from the sides of the burrow with her hind legs, passing the load of chips backwards out of the cell with her fore-limbs, which she uses as hands.

The partitions are built most elaborately of a single flattened band of chips, which is rolled up into a coil four layers deep. One side, forming the bottom of the cell, is concave, being beaten down and smoothed off by the bee. The other side of the partition, forming the top of the cell, is flat and rough.

At the time of opening the burrow, July 8th, the cells contained nearly full-grown larvæ, with some half developed. They were feeding on the masses of pollen, which were large as a thick kidney bean, and occupied nearly half the cell. The larvæ resemble those of the Humble bee, but are slenderer, tapering more rapidly towards each end of the body.—*American Naturalist*, September.

WEATHER.

NOTHING is so much calculated to impress ordinary minds with the idea of uncertainty in the weather as the occurrence, during a rainy season, or, indeed, after any spell of wet, of a bright warm day, whose lovely sky inspires the hope that many more will follow in its train, but which is, on the morrow, perhaps sooner, obscured by wild-looking clouds, which presently become dense and dark, and pour down torrents of rain, perhaps accompanied by thunder and lightning. The wind blows up first from the south, then veers to the south-west, and is found in a day or two blowing from the north-west or north, with a great reduction of temperature, and probably, in winter, with some indication of frost in early morn.

Now, every one we meet exclaims, "How changeable and uncertain the weather is!" Strange, however, as it may appear, these various effects, so suggestive of change to our finite minds, have all arisen in their proper order of succession, from one definite cause; they exhibit the different stages of a process wisely designed to bring about a bountiful distribution of rain over the face of the country, to water the numerous productions of the soil, and to replenish our springs and rivers. This process may be described as follows, and the explanation will prove to be an accurate *index to all changes of weather that may be impending*.

First, the *thermometer* indicates the coming change. The atmosphere resting on some limited portion of the globe, within the sphere of our climate, and which, from its position or state at the time is exposed to, or susceptible of external influences, has its temperature thereby considerably raised, a condition so often noticed before storms and heavy rains.

Now, the effect of a rise in temperature is the immediate alteration in the condition of aqueous vapour in the atmosphere; it dissipates all mists and clouds at the time floating in the atmosphere, and causes the temporary suspension of rain, before alluded to; hence the brief interval of fine weather, and the transient clearness before rain comes on again, which renders distant hills and objects unusually visible—another condition frequently observed.

Secondly, this increase of heat also rarefies the atmosphere, which, expanding upwards, overflows from its summit, the excess going off to the surrounding regions; hence the central atmospheric column becomes lighter, and it is rendered mechanically still more so by the larger proportion of aqueous vapour which is now infused into it, and which is lighter than common air. Owing to these causes, the column of air becomes much lighter, as indicated by the rapid fall of the barometer.

The atmosphere now pressing less on the surface than before, evaporation proceeds more rapidly, besides being stimulated by the increased temperature; hence, exposed surfaces dry up more rapidly before rain, a third condition indicating the coming change.

And here must be noticed a wonderful arrangement of Providence. In cold climates, and also in England during the winter season, when evaporation is slow in consequence of the low temperature, a greater reduction of pressure takes place on these occasions, which makes up in a great measure for the more feeble action of heat in evaporating moist surfaces.

But to proceed; the lighter atmospheric column induces an indraught of air at the surface from the surrounding regions, whose atmosphere has become somewhat heavier in consequence of the previous outflowing to their summits; thus we see one cause of winds blowing from opposite quarters, in connection with storms and heavy falls of rain—the rain-drops slanting in various directions, as everybody must have noticed.

The atmosphere at length becomes charged with the aqueous vapour which has been thrown up from the surface, and also brought in from the surrounding districts; and that which has ascended to the higher and colder aerial strata begins to condense into cloud, which gradually increases in density, and descends, assuming those various appearances so highly indicative of approaching rain. We may herein detect the probable cause of one type of cloud so highly ominous of heavy weather at hand. It is well known that there often exist currents in the atmosphere flowing under each other in different directions, and, as it were, brushing each other's surfaces. Now, a sheet of cloud in an upper current will have the motion of such current, and will of course retain it when, through an increase of weight, it descends on the surface of the next current; as this is moving in a different direction, it acts on the under surface of the cloud in the same way as wind acts on the surface of the sea, and gives it a curious wild, wavy appearance. This is the form significantly called "mackerels' scales," and scientifically cirro-stratus, which, with the other form called mares' tails or curl clouds, scientifically cirrus, according to the proverb, "make lofty ships carry low sails."

No ordinary observer need fail in detecting this prognostic of the coming change, as the appearance of the sky on such occasions is sufficiently striking. When the weather has been fine for some time, these curl clouds, like brushes, feathers, wisps, or locks of hair, make their appearance athwart the sky, getting much lower than usual; for their ordinary position is the highest in cloudland, corresponding, in fact, to what is called very high barometer. Their falling, therefore, plainly shows diminishing elasticity in the air, now no longer able to buoy them up in the higher regions of the air. This may be caused either by the passage of air from one region to another where, by some cause it is deficient, or it may be occasioned simply by a warmer wind blowing in the upper strata of the atmosphere. That wind is the south-west; as soon as it begins to blow aloft, the curl-clouds appear and soon cover the sky. Beneath them is formed a stratum of stackencloud (we like our old popular names) or cumulus, as Howard called it, full of protuberances and fleeces curling inwards. The wind turns to the west, the clouds become thicker, and during the night, or certainly within twenty-four hours, rain falls abundantly, and the air becomes colder.

This refrigeration attending summer rains is easily explained. Not only are masses of water precipitated from the high and cold regions of the atmosphere, reducing the temperature by means of their great capacity for heat, but this water, being immediately subjected to evaporation again absorbs a notable quantity of heat, which it takes from the earth and air and in contact with it. Hence arises the cold that is observed after rain storms.

And now another powerful cause of wind comes into operation. We must know that when invisible vapour is condensed into rain, it occupies a space sixteen or seventeen hundred times less than it did before; hence a considerable vacuum or tenuity occurs in the air whenever large quantities of rain descend, and then the air rushes in from the surrounding regions to fill the void thus occasioned, as before explained; and it is probably to this cause, acting in concert with the rarefaction due to heat before mentioned, that we must attribute those terrific hurricanes which sometimes sweep over the surface of the globe. Hence our nautical proverb,

"When rain comes before wind,
Halyards, sheets, and braces mind."

It is just the reverse when rain comes on after it has been blowing hard. A change of wind must follow, from the accession of new air necessitated by the precipitation of water. Hence again, another axiom on board ship,

"When wind comes before rain,
Soon you may make sail again."

If the barometer rises during or immediately after rain, thus showing the influx of air from the surrounding regions to restore the equilibrium, fine weather follows. This is evidence that the cause of the atmospheric disturbance was slight. But it is otherwise if the barometer continues to fall during rain and does not rise after a cessation. This proves that the disturbing cause is extensive and in force, and although a fine day may intervene, we may be sure that the weather continues unsettled.

The temporary cessation of wet may be always safely predicted if (although the barometer shows no tendency to rise) there is *an increase of temperature towards the evening*.

The diminished atmospheric pressure occasioned by heavy downpours in hot regions of the earth, must extend to a considerable distance around where fair weather probably continues, and evaporation is going on, converting a comparatively small quantity of water into a large volume of vapour; in fact, it is not only producing a supply for the heavy precipitation at the centre of the storm, but in a manner supplying the wind for its influx.

Now, as evaporation will proceed more rapidly and produce a larger volume of vapour, in the warmer latitudes, and from the surface of the seas, it follows that the stronger winds will come from that quarter and drive the storm in the opposite direction. Here we see why great storms, first rising in the tropical regions, in consequence of the greater heat and more abundant vapour there, proceed thence towards the Poles, not indeed in a straight course, because the easterly wind of the Torrid Zone first takes them westward, and afterwards the greater prevalence of the west wind with us bends their course to the eastward. The more powerful south-west wind, which at times sweeps across the British Isles, very much alters the character of the storm with us; yet every one will have noticed, even in small storms and gales, the tendency of the wind to shift round from south-east to west and north, during the time they are traversing our island from west to east, and presenting the different parts of the Cyclone to us in succession.

Finally, it cannot be too deeply impressed upon the memory of those who, either on land or sea, should not be surprised by bad weather, that if rain and clouds quickly pass away and are soon followed by warmth and a clear sky, but with the wind between south and west, the change should not be trusted,—it is only the prelude to a speedy return of more rain. If the barometer has risen rapidly after the rain, it will as quickly fall again, introducing more wet and cloudy weather.—*Everybody's Weather Guide.* By A. Steinmetz. London: L. Reeve and Co.

DESTRUCTION OF BIRDS.

In bygone days, thousands of acres of furze and underwood furnished happy homes for many a bird, and the sparrows revelled in the then prevalent thatched buildings, and herein we have something that partly justified, at that time, the war of extermination declared against birds; but now, times are changed. The forest and the common are gone, so are the thatched buildings: while the hedges are grubbed, and the poor birds driven into a very limited space. The parks and shrubberies, the church tower, and the chimney top, are the only places left in which the feathered tribe may build and rear their young: while, on the other hand, their mortal enemy, man, is ever anxious to play the sportsman, and practise on the poor remnant that is left. Hence the very proper cry against the destruction of small birds, and of the good they do in keeping under the insects, whether caterpillar, grub, or fly, which destroy crops of fruit and corn wholesale, and increase as their foes decrease.

When, four years ago, I came to my present residence, the shrubberies teemed with the feathered tribe, in consequence of the encouragements of birds by my predecessor. Wanting fruit, I declared war against the birds; "from early morn to dewy eve," there was I with my gun, till I reduced my supposed enemies so much that my garden was as still as the grave, except when I chanced to walk there: when some sparrow or finch would give the warning to his mates, for birds and beasts can talk to one another as well as my readers can; indeed, the language of bird and beast is now so familiar to me that I can always tell pretty well " what's up;" but more of this anon. The gooseberry trees put forth a goodly promise, and I looked forward with hope: but a few weeks more, and the caterpillars came rapidly; the leaves disappeared from each tree in succession, the fruit shrivelled, and notwithstanding I tried lime, and salt-and-water, the caterpillars finished them off, and then, dropping from them, took up another form of existence. Then came chaffers in their turn, and instead of songs I had plenty of buzz. The cabbages were eaten up by the green caterpillars, and the beans and roses by aphides. I determined to alter my tack for another year, by vowing never willfully destroying another bird about my ground; and I have had my reward. I have not had mischief from the grub and caterpillar tribe for the three last seasons; I have plenty of company and plenty of song. My plan is to procure some of the smallest shot, and with this shoot flying, just as you find the birds have caught the flavour of the fruit you wish to preserve; you will soon find that they can confabulate; and if you pay attention, you may soon understand their language as you slyly attempt to repeat the warning. Like boys, they will try it on a short time, but finding you are in earnest, the fruit will remain unmolested on the trees, and your conscience free from the thought of having destroyed a friend. But leave the fruit unguarded, and a combined attack is sure to follow. This is all settled in a council of birds; for they, like an attacking army, know that scouts are necessary, who give the alarm on the least appearance of danger.

Of the good birds do in the destruction of noxious insects a few anecdotes will suffice. One day seeing a cock sparrow actively employed about fifty yards from me, near a large stone in the road, I was curious to know his business. By the aid of a small telescope I brought him close to my eye; he had a large cockchaffer, and this he took up and dashed with all his might against the stone. I saw part of the chaffer's mailed coat fly off at every blow, and the soft body, when wholly divested, was borne off as a choice morsel for the sparrow's young. I then went and examined the fragments; they consisted of the broken wings and shield of the luckless chaffer.

This summer just opposite a window, a pair of sparrows have hatched successive broods under the shelter of a broken slate: morning and noon are the pair busily engaged in supplying their hungry family with food, and as they pause and carefully look round before they enter, I am enabled to see that their beaks are crammed with what are familiarly called "Daddy long-legs," and other flies. In March last, when the snow lay thick and long on the ground, my attention was directed towards a tapping just outside the room window near where I stood. Peeping through the half-drawn blind I saw a blackbird with a large garden snail, which he was busily engaged in smashing against a large stone. By repeated blows the shell was removed, and the snail soon became a choice feast for the sorely-pressed bird. Just after my park was mown it was found to be unusually full of new colonies of ants, their hills raising great impediments to the operations of my mowers. The hay being carried the rooks came for several days and seemed extremely busy. I was curious to know what they were after; and on searching I found the anthills pecked open and destroyed; the eggs were devoured, except in a few places of long standing, which formed fortresses defying all attacks. Some amateur sportsman, tempted by a good shoot from the road, gave warning to my friends to quit, since which they have not visited me. Partridges are real farmers' friends; their food, when young, consists wholly of insects. Small birds are evidently on the decrease, and many birds formerly known in this district, as the white or screech owl, and the brown owl, are seldom seen; whereas 50 years ago there was not a barn or steeple without its inhabitants, and nightly were they seen flitting silently round the fields in pursuit of mice. The numerous flocks of pigeons that formerly visited the beech woods of this locality each winter have disappeared. One thing is clear,—the unlimited destruction of birds will assuredly hand us over to a worse enemy in the shape of aphides, grubs, and flies. —HENRY GIBBONS in *Quarterly Journal of the High Wycombe Natural History Society*. October, 1867.

A CROCODILE POND.

The crocodile-pond, or "Mugger-peer," as it is called, lies to the north-west of Kurrachee. The journey for the first few miles is of the usual uninteresting description—sandy plains, intersected with deep fissures and ravines, or studded here and there with "scrub"; the oleander-leaved spurge (*Euphorbia nerifolia*), plentiful in all waste and desert parts of Scinde. Emerging from a defile which leads through a low range of hills, the traveller enters on a desert waste, stretching westward towards the mountains of Beloochistan. In the far distance two oases are visible, whose date and cocoa-nut trees are refreshing to the sight after eight miles of the most monotonous scenery. In the vicinity of the nearest grove is an ancient burial-ground, where may be observed several curiously-carved gravestones. I visited the crocodiles (*Crocodilus palustris*) on two occasions at an interval of several years, and although during that time they had been seen by hundreds of Europeans, including a certain class of mischievous young Englishmen (whose chief amusement, we were told, had been to shy stones and sticks down the throats of the gaping monsters as they lay basking on the banks of the pond), yet there seemed no diminution in their numbers, and the wild and unearthy interest of the scene was to us as great as ever. From beneath a little banyan-tree on the verge of the pond, the spectacle, during the steaming heat of a mid-day sun, might call up to the mind of the geologist the sons of the world, when "great monsters" wallowed in the seething waters of the Oolitic ages, when the mighty "Ichthyosaurus," and a host of "fearfully great lizards," dragons, &c., reigned supreme over sea and land. And as the date-palm now waves its shady boughs over the crocodiles of Mugger-peer, so then did the magnificent tree-ferns, gigantic reeds, and club-mosses, shelter their extinct predecessors. The greater pond is about 300 yards in circumference, and contains many little grassy islands, on which the majority of the crocodiles were then basking: some were asleep on its slimy sides, others half submerged in the muddy water, while now and then a huge monster would raise himself upon his diminutive legs, and waddling for a few paces, fall flat on his belly. Young ones, from a foot in length and upwards, ran nimbly along the margin of the pond, disappearing suddenly in the turbid waters as soon as we approached. The largest crocodile lives in a long narrow tank, separate from the others. The Fakirs, and natives who worship in the neighbouring temples, have painted his forehead red,—they venerate the old monster, making a salaam to His Majesty whenever he shows himself above water. A handsome young Beloochee, whose occupation it was to feed the animals, informed us that the said king was upwards of 200 years old! (?) and that, by way of a "tit-bit," he was in the habit of devouring the young crocodiles. During our visit, this enormous brute was asleep on the bank of his dwelling-place, and seemed quite indifferent to our presence, although we came within a foot of him, and even attempted to arouse him by rubbing his nose with a leg of goat's flesh, which, however, a young one greedily seized, and dived under water. Our attendant tried in vain to excite their ferocity, but beyond a feeble attempt to snap their trenchant teeth, the animals showed no disposition to attack us. A pony was wading about in the pond, and feeding on the grassy hillocks, but the crocodiles took no notice of him. The water in the pool felt cold, although fed from two hot springs, the one of which was of so high a temperature that I could not retain my hand in it; yet animal life existed; for I found where the water bubbled up from its sandy bottom, and in the little lade running to the tank, abundance of a species of small black spiral shell, which Mr. Woodward informed me is "very like some in the British Museum, named *Melania pyramis*, an allied species of which frequents the river Jordan." The other spring gushes from under a bed of limestone, containing numbers of fossils, chiefly coral, and other marine zoophites. We had a refreshing bathe in a reservoir close by; the temperature, though not so high as the last, was still warm and pleasant. I should be sorry, however, to repeat the experiment, not from the chances of meeting with a crocodile (for, I believe, the Fakirs of the temple guard well against such accidents), but from the circumstances that (as is generally the case all over the East) lepers, and persons affected with loathsome diseases, repair to such localities. The crocodiles dig deep in the sand under the neighbouring date-trees, and there deposit their eggs. Quantities of deciduous teeth, of various sizes, were strewn along the slimy sides of the pond. Strangers are expected to stand treat, not only by the Fakirs and natives, who gain a livelihood by hanging about the pond and showing the monsters, but even the crocodiles themselves seem to anticipate a feast, and on the arrival of a party come out in unusual numbers. Accordingly we had a goat slaughtered, during which operation the brutes seemed to rouse themselves, as if preparing for a rush. Then our guide, taking piece after piece of the flesh, dashed it on the bank, uttering a low growling sound, at which the whole tank became in motion, and crocodiles, of whose existence we had before been ignorant, splashed through the shallow water, struggling which should seize the prize. The shore was literally covered with scaly monsters, snapping their jaws at one another. They seize their food with the *side* of the mouth, and toss the head backward, in order that it may fall into the throat. A few were observed to bolt their portion on shore after very slight mastication; but the majority, anxious to escape from their greedy companions, made instantly for the water, and disappeared with the piece of flesh sticking between their jaws. Our young Belooch friend informed us that they generally swallow their food at once, and do not, as has been asserted, bury it until it becomes putrid; also that other large individuals besides the old king frequently devour the young soon after they are hatched. Crocodiles wallowing in the mud of the Nile, or gavials in the Indus, are sights which one is prepared to encounter; but the traveller may wander far before he meets with a scene so strange and unexpected as that just described. How these animals found their way inland to this solitary oasis, we could not discover. It can only be surmised that they had probably been introduced by the natives.—*Wanderings of a Naturalist in India.*

SLUGS.

ANNO DOMINI 1867 seems likely to figure in horticultural and agricultural history as the year of slugs. Mr. Mechi has written to the *Times* about them, but still they come. Gardeners have not such a repute for grumbling as farmers; perhaps it is because they have less time for it, or we should have had more written complaints even than have yet appeared concerning the ravages of these slimy creatures amongst plants. Certain is it that they have devoted to their destruction this year much valuable time, which they would gladly have employed in other ways.

It has occurred to me that, before the last slug of the season is crushed under foot or dropped into the jar of salt and water, it might be interesting to some of your readers to know something of the species of slugs which are particularly injurious to gardens, and I therefore propose to give a few remarks about them, without going further into their specific differences than is requisite to enable any one, who has not previously paid any scientific attention to them, readily to put a name upon the particular sort, whose improprieties of conduct he may wish to speak or write about.

The gardener's worst enemy is the common field slug (*Limax agrestis*). It is one of the smallest of our English slugs, and is certainly the most slimy. When walking it is from 1 to 2 inches long, and barely ¼ of an inch thick. When touched it contracts itself into a slimy oval lump ¾ of an inch long by half that thickness, and if turned over two or three times upon the ground is liable to be lost, from the particles of earth which adhere to its sticky exhudation rendering it difficult to distinguish. Its colour varies from creamy brown to grey.

The next to which I shall refer (which in some localities is quite as numerous as the preceding) is *Arion hortensis*. This is the smallest of all the garden slugs, rarely exceeding an inch in length. It may readily be known by its deep black colour, while closer examination will reveal that it is marked longitudinally with indistinct streaks. By many this is erroneously supposed to be the young of that large black slug (*Arion ater*) which is so commonly seen on the grass by the sides of roads and lanes after a shower. As this latter is not often of less size than 3 inches long, and is frequently found as long as 5 inches, it is impossible to confound the two species.

In the gardens around London may be found slugs about 2 inches long, of a chocolate-brown colour, so like the earth upon which they are generally seen crawling, that it requires a tutored eye to detect them. This is the keeled slug (*Limax carinatus*), so named from a slender ridge or keel, which runs down the middle of the back to the tail. This keel is so clearly defined, and of such a distinct amber colour, that it is commonly observed before the outline of the animal is recognised upon the ground. I wish to do justice to all, even in the slug world, and I, therefore, willingly record that the keeled slug is not nearly such a "bull in a china shop" as either *Limax agrestis* or *Arion hortensis* amongst growing plants. Books record that the large *Arion ater* is very destructive amongst cabbages. It may be so, but it has not fallen to my lot to see it; I have often seen its very little brother (*Arion hortensis*) swarming upon cabbage plants; and I also know that the larger species is more fond of dead animal matter, crushed snails and worms, and garbage of all kinds, than of any living plant. I believe of *Arion ater*, that which I am sure of with *Limax carinatus*, namely, that it greatly prefers dead to living vegetable matter, and that if it can find plenty of dead leaves and fallen flowers upon the ground, it will rarely be found climbing a growing plant. Where the keeled slug occurs, it is usually very plentiful. In a small garden, about 40 feet square, on a clay soil on the south side of London, there were destroyed during the first week of last month more than 200 of this species, twice that number of *Limax agrestis* and about 40 of *Arion hortensis*. Children's eyes assisted materially in bringing about this great slaughter; their powers of observation as collectors of natural history objects are greater than many of their seniors are aware of; and when human eyes are within 3 feet of the ground without risk of lumbago—bad luck to the slugs!

I have recorded two dire pests to the horticulturist: I have also referred to two slimy creatures of doubtful character; there remains but one other garden slug to notice, and that is *Testacella haliotidea*. This curious creature feeds solely upon earth-worms, and need, therefore, never be destroyed. It is usually from 2 to 3 inches long, flattish, of a dull yellow colour, and has a small ear-shaped shell near the tail.

Perhaps some may express surprise at learning that there are so few kinds of slugs troublesome to gardeners, and may wish to know what other species have been found in the British islands. A very few words will suffice to give this information. There is a black slug (*Oncidium celticum*) found on rocks washed by the sea waves in a small bay in Cornwall. There is a beautifully spotted slug (*Geomalacus maculosus*) found only near the margins of a lake in the south-west of Ireland. There is a local sea-shore species (*Limax gagates*) found in Ireland, and at South Shields. There is a species occurring in woods, but not often seen (*Limax arborum*), which has the singular habit of letting itself down from a branch by a slimy thread, up which it can crawl again at pleasure. There are also two species (*Limax brunneus* and *Limax tenellus*), recorded as having been found in Northumberland, but both are rarities. Gardeners in the south of England evidently need not be under any anxiety about either of these kinds.

There remain but two more British species, and then all are told. These, like the black beetle and the cricket, are essentially domestic, frequenting cellars, vaults, and damp places, and feeding upon any decaying animal or vegetable matter. I have often found them in places where the only visible means of subsistence was the mildew on the damp walls, and yet they looked as sleek and fat as prize pigs. One is the yellow slug (*Limax flavus*), the other is *Limax maximus*, the largest of all our native species. These two species vary from 4 to 6 inches long, the yellow one rarely exceeding 5 inches. *Limax maximus* is grey or dull black, indistinctly spotted and striped with black; *Limax flavus* is yellowish, and the end of the tail is keeled. Should either of these species be found in sheds or outhouses, their lives may be spared, for there is nothing that I can bring against them as a horticultural crime.

I have now passed briefly in review all the known British slugs, and hope I have succeeded in enabling any one to determine for himself which are the injurious species, and which are not.—*W. T., in Gardeners' Chronicle, Oct. 5th.*

MOSSES.

"Mosses," says a learned botanist, "like the more perfect plants, have roots, stems, branches, and leaves, which may be traced through the whole family, though in some their presence can with difficulty be detected." The roots are (in almost all the species) exceedingly small; indeed, in many of them they are so minute that they cannot be seen without the aid of a microscope. Some of the larger members of the Bryum family have the strongest roots, while in the *Orthotrichum* (or bristle moss), and others that grow upon trees and stones, the root is merely a flattened disc, necessary for attaching the plant to its resting-place. In such cases the nourishment is not, as in other plants, supplied through the root, but is principally derived from the atmosphere; indeed this is the case with all mosses, and on this account they are entirely dependent on the weather—soon withering up under a hot sunshine, and as quickly expanding again into luxuriant freshness after a shower of rain. I have said that the roots of mosses are in most of the species extremely small; but in some, the *Bartramia arcuata* (or curved-stalked apple moss), for instance, their number makes up for their minuteness—indeed, they are so luxuriant that their brown masses almost smother the stems and foilage. Some of the trailing Hypnums and Bryums readily take root from the joints of their stems, while the *Hookeria luscens*, and others, emit rootlets from the edges and surface of their leaves. Let us turn from the roots to the stems and branches of the mosses, which present an immense variety of form. The Hypnums are for the most part trailing, but some of them, such as the *Hypnum dendroides* (or tree-like feather moss), and *Hypnum alopecurum* (or fox-tail feather moss), have strong, upright stems, like miniature palms, with a bunch of foilage at the top; others of the family branch out more or less irregularly, and so quickly spread themselves over the banks, trees, stones, and rivulets. To the mountain torrents the trailing Hypnum, whose feathery masses cover the boulders in some deep ravine, acts as a water-filter, for the stream that has issued muddy and discoloured from the moorlands above, while trickling through its branches, is deprived of many impurities, and leaving its mossy bed it descends, limpid and pure, to sparkle in the sunshine of the valley below. Unlike the Hypnum, the *Orthotrichum* sends out a number of branches from one common centre, while the compact, cushion-like patches of *Funaria*, *Tortula*, and many of the Bryums, are found to be composed of a number of upright plants, each possessing its simple rootlets, stem, and fruit-stalk. The leaves of mosses differ in many particulars from those of other plants. In the first place, always destitute of a foot-stalk, they spring directly from the main stem, to which they are attached by the lower edge; they are always simple and undivided, and never show any hairiness on the surface; for though some of the species have the appearance of a hairy cushion, a close examiner will find that the fine hairs are not on the surface, but at the points of the leaves, and are, in fact, caused by the extension of the midrib to a hairy point. Another peculiarity in the leaves of mosses is that they never fall off in their decay, like those of other plants, and they have a power of reviving again if placed in water, even though months and years may have elapsed since they were gathered and dried. This property is of great advantage to the botanist, who may not have time to look over and examine the specimens he has collected; he can put them by until a more convenient hour, and will then find that, though the mosses may have lost much of their original verdure, their parts and formation will be unchanged. Let us turn from the leaves to examine the last but not least interesting part of the moss—I mean the capsules, or seed-vessels, or in other words, the fruit of the plant, whereby its species is propagated. I have remarked that here we have no gorgeous variety of colour; yet, if we examine some of the *Dicranum* and *Grimmia* families, we shall, on removing the protecting lid, find a scarlet-fringed vessel enclosing the minute seeds. Not for ornament alone is that brilliant scarlet fringe: it is Nature's contrivance for protecting the spores after the lid has fallen off. On a warm, sunny day it expands, to allow the seeds to ripen, and as surely closes up again when the weather is wet or frosty. Though so small as to be in some cases almost microscopic, there is much beauty and variety of form in the capsules of mosses, and chiefly by those capsules are we enabled to distinguish the different species. In *Tortula* they are long and narrow; in *Fu-*

naria, pear-shaped; in *Bartramia*, round, like tiny apples; in *Polytrichum*, they crown the plants like polished urns of a light yellow colour, and quadrangular form; in Hypnum they are smaller, egg-shaped, and generally of an orange colour; while in *Grimmia*, the fruit appears like minute rosebuds, peeping from the foliage of the plants: and so on, there is a difference of form in each of the families, but we cannot enumerate them here. Besides the lid, which is generally of a conical form, the seed-vessels are protected by an outer covering, known as the Calyptra or veil.

When first the young fruit-stalks appear, they are carefully enclosed in the calyptra; as they grow up the membrane is pushed up by them, becomes split at the sides, and assumes whatever form is characteristic of the species. The *Encalyptra* (or extinguisher moss) takes its name from the form of its veil, which resembles the extinguisher of a candle. The *Polytrichum* (or hair moss) is so called from the hairy nature of its external veil; while in the *Hypnum serpens* (or creeping feather moss) the white veils covering the immature capsules are a pretty and remarkable feature in the plant.—*Aunt Judy's Magazine*, Oct.

STONY CORALS.

The Red Coral belongs to the section of zoophytes called Asteroida by Cuvier, in which the surface of the polypidom is fleshy, and each polypus has only eight arms. The polypi which form the massive stony corals of the tropical reefs, are furnished with numerous tentacles, and resemble in their general conformation the Sea Anemones which are so well known now-a-days as inhabitants of aquaria. The coral consists of a deposit of carbonate of lime, and each polypus dwells in a cell which exhibits a number of thin stony rays nearly meeting in the middle. The masses of coral differ exceedingly in size, some consisting of the habitations of only two or three polypi, whilst others are the gradual production of a vast and constantly succeeding population; some form branched trees and shrubs of the most various and elegant forms, others grow in solid masses, but all, when living, present a most beautiful appearance from the charming and often brilliant diversity of colours with which they are adorned.

In the Pacific Ocean several of the coral reefs are extremely beautiful, and the voyager is astonished with the curious and fantastic forms of the various marine productions of which they are composed. Wheat-sheaves, mushrooms, cabbage leaves, with innumerable plants and flowers, are vividly represented by different kinds of Coral, and glow beneath the water in brilliant tints of brown and purple, white or green; each with a peculiar form and shade of colouring, equal in richness and variety to the most beautiful productions of the vegetable world. Corals and fungi start from between the fissures of the rocks; while large portions of the former, in a dead state, connected into a solid mass, of a dull white colour, compose the stone-work of the reef. Solid masses, termed negro heads, of different dusky hues, and generally dry and blackened by exposure to the weather, are also occasionally conspicuous. Even these are not without ornament, for nature delights in the variety of her decorations. They are studded with small shells, and beautifully marked with outlines expressive of their origin. The edges of the reefs, particularly those exposed to the waves, partake of a considerable degree of lightness, and form small coves and caverns, the resort of live corals, sponges, see-eggs, and trefangs, or sea traces, (valued in China, for their invigorating quality,) and enormous cockles, which are scarcely to be distinguished from the rock, excepting when they suddenly close their shells, and discharge living fountains, which rise to the height of four or five feet.

With regard to the formation of coral reefs, it has been conjectured, from the appearance of the low islands in some parts of the South Sea and Indian Ocean (where they occur in rows or groups, while they are totally absent in other parts of the same seas), that Coral animals rear their habitations on marine shoals, or, to speak more properly, at or near the top of sub-marine mountains. As it is known, however, that the polypes can only build their coral within a small distance of the surface of the sea, and the water is often of immense depth close to the coral reefs, it has been supposed that in the Pacific Ocean, where the greater part of the Coral reefs and islands are met with, the bottom of the sea has been gradually undergoing changes, deepening in some places and becoming shallower in others, and by this supposition most of the peculiarities of the Coral reefs and islands may easily be accounted for. Where reefs are formed the bottom is generally sinking; islands indicate that the bottom is stationary or rising. In the latter case, when the corals approach close to the surface, floating substances of every kind are caught by their stony tree-like fabrics, till at length a solid mass of rock is formed, which gradually advances to the surface of the water. The deposits of the ocean no longer tenaciously adhere, but remain in a loose state, and form what is termed by mariners a key upon the summit of the reef; while the sea, by throwing up sand and mud on the top of these animal rocks, progressively raises them above its level. The new island, for such it may now be called, is soon visited by sea-birds; plants successively appear, and carpet the sterile soil with a luxuriant covering. As these decay, vegetable mould is gradually deposited; cocoa-nuts, or some floating seeds, flung on shore by the impetuosity of the waves, take root, and soon begin to grow; land-birds, attracted by the verdant appearance of the bank, fly thither in quest of provisions, and deposit the seeds of shrubs and trees; every high tide and every gale adds some new treasure: the appearance of an island is gradually assumed, and at length man comes to take possession.—*Loudon's Entertaining Naturalist.* London: Bell and Daldy.

MAN IN THE EARLY AGES.

IN a lecture delivered by Professor Huxley at the Birmingham and Midland Institute, October 11, he said—

In approaching the question of the cause which had produced the various modifications of mankind, the first thing to do was to clear the mind of all unnecessary lumber. The first thing was to throw overboard altogether all Hebrew mythology, with its notions about Adam and Noah and the Ark, and all that business; the next thing was to throw over scientific mythology, and get rid of notions about Caucasian man, and a great deal of pestilent nonsense of that sort. And having made the mind a *tabula rasa*, it must be carried back thousands and thousands of years—it would not be an exaggeration to say millions of years—to the time when the great primogenal elephant, rhinoceros, and hyena were roaming this land familiarly. At that time man existed, and there was tolerable trustworthy evidence from recent discoveries that the capacity and conformation of the cranium of the man of that day were as good as the average capacity and conformation of the cranium of the man of the present day. It followed that there was an equal amount of brain; and as there was no reason to suppose that the quality was altered, there was no reason to doubt that the capacities of that man, whether developed or undeveloped, were substantially equal to those of the man of the present day; and reasoning upon the ordinary principles of comparative anatomy, it was justifiable to conclude that the man of that day had the same physical structure in every particular as the man of the present day—that his limbs had the same proportions, his spine the same structure, his arms, hands, and feet the same structure, as the average man of the present day. The implements and weapons relating to that period were of even more value than the remains of man himself, because they showed that he was an intelligent creature, having the same sort of capacity as the man of the present day. Well, then, if going back millions of years, when the physical conformation of the globe was entirely different from what it is now—if this did not help one to get back to any form of man which could be fairly believed to be more degraded than any form of man existing at the present day, how far back was it necessary to go? He believed that if it were possible to look back into the past, to the time when crocodiles haunted the water where the Thames now flows, and palms and tropical fruits grew in the Isle of Sheppy, man as much lower than the Australian as the Australian is to us, would be seen—something which might in some intelligible sense be looked upon as a midway form between ourselves and the lower animals; and he believed that if it were possible to scan the subsequent history of mankind, man would be found living for immeasurable ages in a stationary condition, raising himself but little above the level of the brutes—but still a very important little—gradually spreading over the surface of the globe, finding by slow degrees, and by the process known as natural selection, and the struggle for existence, that his only security lay in intelligence; finding himself weaker than animals, by no means competent to cope with them by claws and tooth, but exceedingly competent to overcome them by sharpness of wit, finding that those who were a little quicker throve better, and multiplied faster than others, and thus by barley corns of progress, mounting step by step to the condition indicated by the recent discoveries in Flanders. But long before this man must have been spread over the habitable world—a habitable world very different from ours, with land where we have water, and water where we have land. This was not language of speculation; it was a physical certainty. Now and then a group of men were shut off for thousands and thousands of years in a limited area, under particular physical conditions. Within the epoch immediately preceding our own—when the fauna and flora were what they are now—the whole of the southern part of Africa was a vast island, like Australia. It was perfectly certain that for untold ages the great sandy desert of Sahara was the bottom of a sea, continuous with the Mediterranean. Imagine in the course of these changes, a stock of men shut off, and mixing with themselves only, for untold ages, and at length hardening down into something like what were called races among animals. Imagine another lot shut off in a different part of the world—in Australia; another in South America; others in Hindostan, and the result would be distinct breeds originating even from one homogeneous kind of men. These breeds were, he believed, what were now known as persistent modifications of mankind. They were persistent because they had persisted so long. They had become what they were in virtue of the selective influences of the different localities in which they were shut up. It was in this way that the truths which lay on the side of those who maintained the diverse origin of mankind and the truths which lay on the side of those who maintained the unity of origin, were reconciled.

A NEW GEOLOGICAL THEORY.

To observe and register facts has hitherto been the chief work of geologists, and right nobly have they laboured in their vocation. The most important facts they have discovered they have, however, hitherto failed to explain : *e.g.* they assign no cause for the recent submersion of the Sahara ; and glacial theories which have been invented to account for the drift and boulders may hereafter be regarded as among the most amazing proofs of human credulity. The purpose of this letter is to present a theory which will account for these and other phenomena, and to exhibit some of the evidence by which that theory is supported.

Prof. Hansen—"probably the most eminent authority among living astronomers upon the lunar theory"—believes that the moon's centres of gravity and magnitude do not coincide; and that, therefore, the hemisphere we see bulges into a mountain too high for water, atmosphere, or life,—the other hemisphere being proportionately depressed. If there be water on the moon, it must be all on the depressed side, where there may be also abundance of life. Moreover, the moon rotates once only while revolving round her primary, the earth, and the light of this world never reaches her farther side. Now, it is quite conceivable that her divided centres should be made to coincide, and that she should be made to rotate in fewer hours than now she requires days for that purpose. And if these changes in her shape and motion were effected, they would roll a large part of the lunar water to the side we see, and would also modify the temperature of the whole of the moon, and invert the temperature of the parts now most depressed. The moon would then be a globe with water on both sides ; but all her newest aqueous formations would be limited to one side, excepting that some portion of detritus borne by the shifting waters would be sprinkled over the surface of the hemisphere into which they rolled. In short, in these and various other ways, if such an alteration as has been supposed were to take place, there would be left evidence of that alteration for the investigation of future lunar geologists, if such geologists should ever be.

I submit that geology has already furnished us with evidence that before our era, and backward to a time remote and at present undefined, but perhaps extending to, though not comprising, the time of the older tertiaries, the earth was shaped as the moon is thought to be, and rotated as the moon does : that is to say, rotated once only while revolving round her primary, the sun. I submit further, that we have evidence that by one of the last mighty changes, this world's previously divided centres were made to coincide, the northern hemisphere rising, and the southern sinking, to the mean level ; and that at the same time the earth received its diurnal rotation. No question is now raised concerning the secondary and primary strata, or the yet more ancient part of the crust of the earth ; nor would I at present start the interesting inquiry whether the rolling of the waters, ofttimes from one hemisphere to the other, be not the normal mode of completing such globes as the earth, the moon, and Mars. My theory is, that the earth was formerly as the moon is now, having all her waters in the northern hemisphere; and that by the last great geological change, she received her present shape and her diurnal rotation.

[Those interested will find the remainder of this letter in the *Athenæum*, Oct. 19th, well worth a perusal, we have not space to quote more.—ED.]

RAINBOWS.

The rainbow presents, when perfect, the appearance of two concentric arches—the inner being called the *primary*, and the outer the *secondary* rainbow. Each is formed of the colours of the solar spectrum ; but the colours are arranged in the reversed order, the red forming the exterior ring of the primary bow, and interior of the secondary. The primary bow is formed by the sun's rays entering the upper part of the falling drops of rain, and undergoing two refractions and one reflection ; and the secondary, by the sun's rays entering the under part of the drops, and undergoing two refractions and two reflections. Hence the colours of the secondary bow are fainter than those of the primary.

Among remarkable rainbows are some which have been almost entirely of a blood-red colour, when the other prismatic tints have formed but an infinitesimal portion of the iris. These, in former times in Europe, and in superstitious countries at the present day, have been supposed to portend some national disaster of war, plague, or pestilence ; which last prediction has been in some measure verified by natural results, where the remarkable rainbow was produced by foggy malaria, arising from the place where it appeared. On the other hand, rainbows, perfectly colourless, have been seen in mists, where the globules of moisture were too minute to refract or reflect the prismatic rays. Distorted rainbows have been seen, where the usual arc or section of a circle lost its line of beauty ; and a rainbow forming a hyperbolic curve on the ground has been witnessed. Another has been seen inverted on the grass, formed by the drops of rain or dew suspended on spiders' webs in the fields. Two rainbows have been also observed at sea, where the secondary one was produced by reflection from the ocean. But the exceptional phenomenon which specially comes under our notice is where supernumerary rainbows have been observed, and which have particularly attracted the notice of meteorologists. A *third* iris between the primary and secondary bows, and *not concentric* with them, has been seen; but only a few cases are recorded. The following account, witnessed by a party of British officers during a cruise among the isles of Greece, and sketched by one of their number, describes one of the few instances on record of this most singular of rainbows :—

"On the 28th December, 1863, I was shooting at a place called Mytica, on the coast of Akernania, Greece. At this spot there is a small plateau, extending along the coast for three or four miles, and running inland for about two miles, surrounded by irregular lofty hills. Opposite lies the Island of Calamos, at a distance from Mytica varying from half a mile to three miles, forming a sort of roadstead, in which our yacht lay. At about 2 p.m., having beaten all the covers, we went on board; and, though there was hardly any wind, we made sail, being anxious to get out where we could find a harbour, or, at least, have sea-room, for the night appeared likely to be squally. After being three hours under way, during which our yacht had barely made as many miles, just about five o'clock we perceived a heavy squall, accompanied with rain, coming down through the gorge of the hills. On this a rainbow made its appearance, of the primary form; and soon afterwards the secondary bow appeared outside, with the prismatic colours inverted, as usual. Immediately this was followed by another distinct rainbow, its colours the same in succession as the primary bow, but the segment visible formed the arc of a circle whose radius was from a perfectly different centre, as it cut both the original bow and its outer arch. It was very bright and distinct, nearly as much so as the primary iris, and more than the secondary bow. The whole phenomenon did not last long, as the sun was near setting at the time; it being mid-winter in these latitudes.

"During that day, and for many days previous, the weather had been very changeable and squally: the gusts coming continually from opposite directions, within a very short space of time, and heavy clouds flying about. Soon after we had seen this strange phenomenon, we found the weather getting so bad, with the prospect of a stormy night, that, by our captain's advice, we ran back for shelter to the place we had left. It was well that we did so; for, although it was not a regular harbour, we anchored close in shore. Here we 'housed' everything, put out two anchors, and managed to hold our ground until morning. Luckily our cables were unusually strong, and the ground good for holding. During the night we had a succession of 'white squalls,' so dangerous in the Mediterranean. From our sheltered position, we were fortunate in escaping their full violence when they swept past at intervals. Even in the darkness of the night, the water, not a hundred yards from us, was lashed into such fury by the tempest that it looked as white as cream. I believe, if we had been anchored at the opposite side of the gorge, our little craft would have suffered severely, if no accident happened to any one on board. As it was, when the wind suddenly veered round, and struck the broad-side, it pitched the yacht on its beam ends, blew in the cabin windows, and our night's rest was completely spoiled. All this time the wind was from N.N.E., and continued, without variation, in that direction until next day—being considered by the sailors altogether a land-breeze, and frequent in that sea. I have sailed a good deal on the coasts of Dalmatia, Albania, and Greece, and have always found these 'white squalls,' come from the land, rushing down the mountain gorges with impetuous fury, and overwhelming the barks of luckless mariners in the Mediterranean.

"I may add that there were three brother officers with me in the yacht, who witnessed this singular rainbow as well as myself—namely, Captain Germon, Lieutenant Forsden, and Lieutenant Dunn. The sketch I made at the time of occurrence, as the yacht was becalmed, and perfectly steady.

A. J. BINGHAM WRIGHT,
"Lt. H.M. 9th Regt. of Infantry."

From the foregoing plain and lucid account, together with the circumstance that the observer was an amateur artist of no mean skill, the circumstances were most favourable for recording this appearance of a rare compound rainbow. While it is interesting to the general reader, it is particularly deserving the attention of meteorologists, who, as far as we know, have not yet satisfactorily accounted for the appearance of eccentric supernumerary rainbows, of which this is an example. In general terms, the appearance of a third iris is considered "probably the result of *reflection*." But we are of opinion that there are other circumstances attending the phenomenon, which lead to the conjecture that the downward force of the white squall, suddenly diverging the rain drops in their descent to a different angle, may have something to do with it. Be this as it may, we leave the solution of the problem an open question for the consideration of meteorologists.—*Leisure Hour*, Oct.

SIGNS OF A HARD WINTER.

Every year about this time the newspapers teem with paragraphs bearing some such heading as we have attached to this. Somebody finds a good crop of berries on his holly or hawthorn-tree, and at once sees therein a presage of a dreadful winter. Another observes that an elder-tree has acquired a deeper tint of red than usual, and he knows thereby that on the 10th of January all the rivers will be covered with three feet depth of ice, and blocks of brandy will be retailed in the taverns by a process of chopping fragments from frozen puncheons. Here is a sample of the prevailing weakness. A correspondent of the *Hants Advertiser*, who dates from Shirley, about two miles from Southampton, states that "he noticed the congregating of swallows the third week in August last, as if preparing to migrate, and now not one is seen. *He attributes* their early departure either to symptoms of an early winter or to the rain-floods, which must almost have drowned them wherever they roosted. *He says* that there are a few martins remaining. *He heard* a nettle-creeper and saw a nightingale on the 12th, but *he has not heard* the blackbird and thrush since the 24th of June; whitethroats have been more numerous than usual this summer, and robins are now in full song and very plentiful. Birds of passage *are said* to have begun their annual migration southwards through Belgium a month earlier this year than usual. Already long lines of storks have taken flight. Bustards have been killed in the neighbourhood of Paris, and wild ducks have passed in such numbers that the eye cannot follow them. This is a presage of a hard winter." This correspondent at Shirley, who illuminates our Hampshire contemporary with a sage presage of a hard winter, is evidently not sage enough to know that birds are governed in their actions by what they feel in the present, and not by what they know of the future. This attribution of prophetic wisdom to animals is as absurd, if not so nasty, as the old priestly process of divining events from the entrails of animals killed for the purpose, or, as sometimes happened, disembowelled without being killed, that the priest might have the entrails extra fresh. There was a migration of birds from northern towards southern parts of Europe a fortnight ago. No wonder, for just at that time there came from the north pole (or some other objectionable place thereabouts) a wave of cold air which pervaded Europe, and made man and beast equally afraid that winter had already come. When the temperature falls suddenly and greatly over a large tract of country, birds, having such perfect command of all climates, invariably make some migrations more or less extensive because they feel uncomfortable, but we do not learn thereby that they know anything of what is to happen six months hence. But the prediction of a hard winter from the appearance of trees is still more ridiculous, and should be expected only from philosophers in the last stage of drivelling and softening of the brain. A holly-tree knows it will be very cold in February, 1868, and so in May, 1867, it forms an extra crop of berries! Sensible doctrine that, to be sure, and very creditable to the free and independent press that gives it currency. We poor darkened horticulturists attribute good crops of fruits, whether holly-berries or grapes or apples, in great part to the temperature and other influences the trees *have been* subjected to, and would be inclined to attribute a large crop of holly-berries in 1867 to a good growth and perfect ripening of the wood in 1866; certainly not to the foresight of the tree in reference to the events of 1868. As to the movements of swallows, we saw millions on the first of this month—that is to say, on Tuesday last—near the village of Walthamstow, in Essex. Perhaps these were the flocks that the Hampshire sage saw congregating in the third week of August last, and which, having anticipated a hard winter, went away, but since then have adopted the opinion that the winter will be a mild one, and so have quietly returned. " Wild ducks have passed in such numbers that the eye cannot follow them." How wonderful, to be sure! Had we not better fly to the tropics to escape the death by frigidity next winter which is thus predicated? We believe we are indebted to our usually sober contemporary, *The Farmer*, for this bit about the wild ducks. If the "Farmer's" eye could not follow them, how intensely intense must be the cold in store for us! Dreadful consideration—"the eye cannot follow them"! Then let every wise man lay in an extra store of coals.—*Gardeners' Magazine*, Oct. 5th.

FOOD OF BIRDS.

During the years 1861—1865 inclusive, I shot a good many of our birds for the purpose of examining their crops, and took notes of the contents, and now thinking it may be interesting to your readers, I have copied out the notes. There are several interesting communications on this subject in the "Zoologist."

Kestrel (*Falco tinnunculus.*)—January, mice, shrews; February, March, mice shrews; April, beetles; May, cockchafers, blindworms; June, insects, mice; July, mice, reptiles; August, September, October, November, December, mice and small birds.

Barn Owl (*Strix flammea*).—January, mice; February, mice and rats; March, moles; April, water-rats; May, young rabbits, beetles; June, mice, insects; July, small birds, bats; August, shrews; September, dormice; October, mice, November and December, shrews, mice.

Missel Thrush (*Turdus viscivorus*).—January, holly berries, misletoe, snails; February, earth-worms, slugs; March, worms; April, snails and caterpillars; May, slugs and gooseberries; June, insects; July and August, garden fruit; September and October, mollusca; November, hips and haws; December, holly berries.

Song Thrush (*Turdus musicus*).—January, February, berries, corn-slugs, and snails; March, berries; April, green food; May, insects, berries; June, currants and snails; July, gooseberries; August, larvæ, berries; September, larvæ and mollusca; October, berries; November and December, rowan berries, hips and haws.

Blackbird (*Turdus merula*).—January, berries and snails; February, snails; March, larvæ and worms; April, larvæ and snails; May, worms; July, currants, gooseberries, cherries, worms, and snails; August, slugs, fruit; September, slugs; October, November, and December, snails, hips and haws, rowan berries.

Hedge Sparrow.—January, February, March, and April, small weed seeds; May, June, larvæ and worms; July, caterpillars; August, insects; September, October, November, December, refuse, small seeds, and larvæ.

Redbreast (*Sylvia rubecula*).—January, larvæ and seeds; February and March, seeds and berries; April and May, earthworms; June and July, currants and larvæ; August, larvæ; September, October, November, December, berries and larvæ.

Blue Titmouse (*P. cœruleus*).—January, insects; February, March, April, they pick insects out of buds and clear trees of leaf-rolling caterpillars; May, insects; June, insects, fruit; July, August, September, berries, insects; October, November, December, berries, hips and haws.

Pied Wagtail (*M. Yarrellii*).—January, February,

March, insects; April, May, insects, caterpillars; June, July, August, insects, slugs; September, insects; October, November, December, mollusca and insects.

Yellow Hammer (*E. citrinella*).—January, corn seeds; February, March, April, corn seeds; May, June, July, insects; August—December, corn.

Chaffinch (*Fringilla Cœlebs.*)—January, seeds; February, seeds, grains; March, April, seeds, insects; May, insects; June, July, August, insects, fruits; September, berries, insects, grain; October, November, December, seeds, grain, berries.

House Sparrow (*Fringilla domestica*).—January, February, March, seeds and refuse; April, May, insects, green tops; June, July, August, seeds, garden fruits; September, October, November, December, grain, refuse, seeds, berries.

Linnet (*T. cannabina*).—January, February, March, seeds of weeds; April, May, June, July, August, insects and seeds; September, October, November, December, seeds of weeds.

Starling (*Sturnus vulgaris*).—January, February, March, April, worms, slugs, insects; May, June, July, worms, fruit, slugs; August, September, October, November, December, grains, slugs, worms.

Rook (*Corvus frugilegus*).—January, February, March, April, May, worms, grubs, larvæ; June, July, young birds, frogs; August, September, mice; October, November, December, carrion.

Ring Dove, Woodpigeon (*Columba palumbus*).—January, cabbage and turnip top; February, March, April, beech-mast acorns; May, June, July, green tops, clover, corn; August, September, October, corn, berries, green tops; November, December, acorns, mast. Woodpigeons seem now to do great harm to the corn. I have shot a good many this summer and have always found a quantity of green wheat in their crops, also turnip tops, and now harvest has begun they eat a good deal of ripe corn.—W.B. in *Land and Water*.

METEORS.

One of my letters received by this morning's post contains the rather puzzling query—"Do you think that there are such hard metallic substances in meteors as to forge a sword blade?" The following answer seems to suggest itself. There is a general tradition among the Tartars that the Siberian iron formerly fell from the heavens. We have a tolerably authentic testimony of a like fall in India. The Right Hon C. Greville, in a communication to the Royal Society (*Phil. Trans.*, 1803, Part 1), gives a very interesting paper, translated from the Emperor Jehangire's Memoirs of his own reign. The Prince relates that in 1620 a violent explosion was heard at a village in the Punjaub, and at the same time a luminous body fell through the air on the earth; that the officer of the district immediately repaired to the spot, and having found the place to be hot he caused it to be dug, and they reached a lump of iron violently hot; that this was sent to court, where the Emperor ordered it to be forged into a sabre, a knife, and a dagger; that, after trial, the workmen reported it was not malleable, but shivered under the hammer; and that it required to be mixed with one-third part of common iron, after which the mass was found to make excellent blades. The Royal historian adds, that on the incident of this iron of lightning being manufactured a poet presented him with a distich that:—"During his reign the earth attained order and regularity; that raw iron fell from lightning, which was, by his world-subduing authority, converted into a dagger, a knife, and two sabres." Other accounts of fallen stones almost exactly resemble this occurrence. The noticeable remark on the unmalleability of the iron tends to make the whole narrative highly credible, and throws additional weight on the inference drawn from internal evidence that the solitary masses of native iron found in different quarters of the globe have the same origin with the meteoric stones analysed by Howard and Vauquelin. Under these circumstances I am of opinion that the forging of sword blades out of meteoric substances harmonises with the historic notice we have concerning such a process.

To return to the general character of meteors. Perhaps the most remarkable meteor of modern times is that which was seen all over England on March 19, 1818—19. It was first observed at 8.15 about the Pleiades, when it moved after the manner of a falling star. The meteor in its way turned pear fashioned. Its colour was whitish, with an eye of blue of most vivid dazzling lustre, which seemed in brightness very nearly to resemble, if not surpass, that of the body of the sun on a clear day. Its height in a perpendicular line was computed to be 69 English miles from the earth's surface. It was about half a minute in passing from its first explosion to its last extinction, and it is said to have travelled at the rate of 300 geographical miles per minute. Some people imagined that they felt the warmth of its beams, others thought they were scalded by it. All accounts agree that there was heard the report of a very great cannon, which was soon followed by a rattling noise like fire-arms; this was attended by an uncommon tremor in the air, windows and doors in houses being sensibly shaken.

Comets never come and go in this fashion; nor can we imagine the possibility of their substance or nucleus being forged into sword blades—therefore, it may be fairly concluded that the periodical shooting stars are quite distinct in their nature, effects, and orbits from comets.

From various writers we collect that ordinary meteors appear—1, in every climate; 2, at every season of the year; 3, at every period of the day; 4, they appear for the most part when the sky is serene; 5, comets are never visible when the sky is cloudy, but meteors being sometimes below the cloud region are visible; 6, they proceed from, as well as towards, all points of the compass; 7, many of them in their course throws up sparks, and divide themselves into several, sometimes larger, sometimes smaller, parts before they entirely disappear—not so with comets; 8, this bursting into pieces is generally accompanied with a rumbling noise like thunder or a sudden report; 9, several after bursting seem to dissolve into smoke. The motion of comets is not sensibly apparent, nor do we ever witness their exploding or vanishing into smoke.—HENRY J. CHURCH, in *Standard*, Sept. 24th.

The Sensitive Plant.

In its native country (Brazil) this singular plant, *Acacia mimosa*, grows to the height of seven or eight feet, and is armed with short recurved thorns; the leaves grow upon long footstalks, which are prickly, each sustaining two pair of wings. From the place where these are inserted come out small branches, having three or four globular heads of pale purplish flowers coming out from the side on short peduncles. "Naturalists," says Dr. Darwin "have not explained the immediate cause of the collapsing of the sensitive plant; the leaves meet and close in the night, during the sleep of the plant, or when exposed to too much cold in the daytime; in the same manner as when they are affected by external violence, folding their upper surfaces together, and in part over each other, like scales or tiles, so as to expose as little of the upper surface as may be to the air. Many of the pinnate acacias close also at night, but are not otherwise sensitive, and do not indeed collapse quite so far, for when touched in the night, during their sleep, they fall still farther, especially when touched on the footstalks between the stem and the leaflets, which seem to be their most sensitive or irritable part. Now, as their situation after being exposed to external violence resembles their sleep, but with a greater degree of collapse, may it not be owing to a numbness or paralysis consequent on too violent irritation, like the fainting of animals from pain or fatigue? A sensitive plant being kept in a dark room till some hours after daybreak, its leaves and leafstalks were collapsed as in its most profound sleep, and on exposing it to the light, above twenty minutes passed before the plant was thoroughly awake and had expanded itself. During the night the upper surface of the leaves are appressed. This would seem to show that the office of this surface of the leaf was to expose the fluids of the plant to the light as well as to the air.

I have kept it in the dark and unexpanded during the entire day. Although easy grown, and required to be treated simply as a tender annual, there is no plant we grow requiring so little trouble, that excites such a lively interest, and yet is cultivated by so few people, as this sensitive plant.—E. S., *in the Floral World*, October.

Rats and Mice in India.

Among small predatory quadrupeds must decidedly be included the common brown rat (*Mus decumanus*), which, as before remarked, is nowhere a more troublesome nuisance than about Calcutta, where it is difficult to keep anything from its ravages, or it numbers within moderate control. About the best plan would be to introduce the breed of ferrets; but then there would be no keeping these from domestic poultry and pigeons, if they were to multiply and become numerous. The common rat especially abounds in the native parts of the town, and a full-grown one is often mistaken for a bandicoot, (*Mus bandicota*) by Europeans. The latter is a much larger and more robust species, with bluff-shaped head, and it is not nearly so carnivorous or omnivorous in its appetite; but it is little known to most people, except by name, and we remember that a reward was long vainly offered for a specimen of a true bandicoot by a gentleman in Calcutta. A full-grown animal of whatever kind is sure to be the very largest that was ever seen! It is also so with a tiger, or with a wild Indian boar, as often with a common rat, which last is tolerably sure to be denominated a bandicoot in India, by people who do not discriminate specific differences. The black rat (*Mus rattus*) is not uncommon among the shipping in the river Hooghly, but we never saw one ashore. The common house mouse of India (*M. urbanus*) is a little different from that of Europe, but has quite similar habits. The writer never saw these mice elsewhere in such extraordinary abundance as at Lucknow, where he has seen them career across the streets in mid-day, and a party of them would be sure to be gamboling about the room when he was sitting at meals. Of other Indian rats and mice there is a small reddish-yellow rat with white under parts (*M. flavescens*) which is common in gardens, and forms its nest in the branches of trees. This kind comes sometimes into and about houses, but does not inhabit them; though we have occasionally known one to retreat during the day, and hide in the interstices of the *jilmils* (or jalousie-blinds) of ground apartments. Another kind of rat, buff-headed and short-tailed (*M. indicus*), not unlike our British water-rat in appearance, abounds wherever there is field cultivation, and sometimes in gardens, together with a diminutive field mouse (*M. terricolor*), and again a species of gerbille (*Gerbillus indicus*), which is a rat-like animal of a fawn colour, with very long and somewhat tufted tail, and with longer hind-limbs and shorter fore-limbs than the true rats have. All these are common species, which a student of natural history is sure to become acquainted with; and there are many more in different parts of the country, varying in their habits, and those which feed solely on grain are much eaten by certain of the lower castes of human inhabitants. Several of these field rats are highly injurious to the cultivator, as they lay up immense stores of provender in their subterranean retreats.—*Leisure Hour*, Oct.

New Books.

Our limited space must of necessity compel us to give but very short notices of new books, but they will perhaps serve as a guide as to what books our readers may ask for at their libraries.]

Mrs. Loudon's Entertaining Naturalist; being Popular Descriptions, Tales, and Anecdotes of more than 500 Animals. A New Edition. By W. S. Dallas, F.L.S. London: Bell and Daldy.

For young persons there is, perhaps, no better introduction to the study of Natural History than this little work. Deservedly popular for its simple and yet instructive description of birds, beasts, and fishes, we may safely recommend it to those who were not previously acquainted with it. It has been revised and enlarged by a gentleman whose knowledge particularly adapts him for the task. Several new illustrations have been added, together with such facts as were required to put it on equality with more recent works.

British Butterflies and Moths: an Introduction to the Study of our Native Lepidoptera. By H. T. Stainton, F.R.S. (Reeve & Co.)

The author of this little work is well known as a popular writer and excellent entomologist, so that it will be a great acquisition to such young people as are about to commence the study of our moths and butterflies. It is just what was required to prepare them for his more learned manual, which should follow the study of the present volume. It is got up with the usual care bestowed by Messrs. Reeve on their works, being illustrated with sixteen coloured plates and many woodcuts.

Letters Home from Spain, Algeria, and Brazil. By the Rev. Hamlet Clark, M.A., F.L.S. Van Voorst. 8vo, pp. 178, tab. 5.

A pleasant record of a trip along the coasts of Spain and Algiers, with occasional excursions inland, with some account of a voyage to Teneriffe, Brazil, &c. The author is an ardent entomologist, and can describe scenes of natural beauty with some force. All lovers of nature will be well pleased with the gossiping and unpretending style of this little volume.

AMERICAN, FRENCH, AND GERMAN WORKS.

Meteoric Astronomy: a Treatise on Shooting-stars, Fire-Balls, and Aerolites. By Daniel Kirkwood, LL.D. (Philadelphia, Lippincott and Co.: London, Trübner and Co.)

This treatise will be found one of great value to many, as the subject is treated with such a breadth that "the place of the meteors in Creation," and not minor points of difference between the rival theories, is everywhere brought home to the mind. Thus we begin with a general view of the solar system, and end with a discussion of the nebular hypothesis, the various facts and observations, and such questions as the meteoric hypothesis of solar heat and Saturn's rings being taken *en route*. There are many points of astronomical interest referred to by Dr. Kirkwood which will make the work of service to a wide circle; while to actual or possible meteor observers it is invaluable, as it contains in a small compass many data necessary for those who work in such an interesting field. The cometic theory of meteorites, so recently established, and so clearly set forth, is the foundation-stone of the science of meteoric astronomy, which, as Dr. Kirkwood has shown, will be second to none in interest, and surpassed by few in the wideness and importance of its field.

L'Eau. Par Gaston Tissandier *Bibliothèques des Mervilles.* Paris and London: L. Hatchette and Co.

The composition, transmutation, distribution, and uses of water.—The ocean forms the subject of the first chapter. The author describes the phenomena of the tides; he then represents the sea in its struggles with the land, and shows what are the productive as well as the destructive effects of the huge mass of waters which occupies so much space on our globe. The system of circulation next engages our attention. Rain, dew, snow, the various modifications of water in the atmosphere, rivers and streams, ice and fogs, are successively examined. The third chapter treats of the physical effects, and the fourth of the chemical properties, of water, and finally, an account of its numerous uses, with reference to the draining of large towns, artesian wells, and mineral springs.

Bibliographia Geographica Palestinæ, Zunächst kritische Uebersicht gedruckter und ungedruckter Beschreibungen der Reisen ins Heilige Land. Von Titus Tobler. Leipsic: Hirzel. London: Williams and Norgate.

This (the bibliography of the geography of Palestine) is a most important contribution to a study of which the abstract interest and the tangible results continue to augment day by day. The number of works extant upon this subject would astonish those who have no acquaintance with it; and the examination, description, and criticism of each by Herr Tobler form, in the aggregate, one of those marvellous monuments of erudition which none would think of looking for out of Germany. An appendix is devoted to maps and views, the latter of which are now almost superseded by photography.

Reisen und Jagden in Nord-Ost-Afrika, 1864-1865. Von Carl Graf Krockow von Wickerode. Th. I. Berlin: Duncker. London: Asher and Co.

A sporting traveller's account of the inhospitable regions between the Nile and the upper part of the Red Sea.

Mineralogy Simplified: a Short Method of Determining and Classifying Minerals, by means of Simple Chemical Experiments in the Dry and Wet Way. Translated from the last German Edition of F. Von Kobell, with an Introduction to Blow-pipe Analysis and other Additions. By Dr. Henri Erni, Chief Chemist, Department of Agriculture. Philadelphia: H. Le Baird. London: Sampson, Low, Son, and Marston. 1867.
A Manual of Blowpipe Analysis and Determinative Mineralogy. By William Elderhosrt, M.D., Professor of Chemistry in the Rensselaer Polytechnic Institute. Third Edition. Philadelphia: T. Ellwood Zell. New York: D. Van Nostrand. London: Trübner and Co. 1867.

Influence of Climate in a Commercial, Social, Sanitary, and Humanizing Point of View.—Being a Paper read before the American Geographical Statistical Society by J. Disturnell, Member of the above Society, etc. Also a Paper on the Influence of Climate in the Equatorial Regions, read before the New York Association for the Advancement of Science and Art, March 1, 1866. Accompanied by a Map of the World, showing the most important Isothermal Lines. London : Trubner and Co. 1866.

The Mines of Colorado. By Ovando T. Hollister. Springfield, Mass. : Samuel Bowles and Co. London, Trubner and Co. 1867.

Meetings of Learned Societies.

[NOTE.—*These Reports should have appeared in our last, but were postponed to make room for the Report of the British Association.*]

QUEKETT MICROSCOPICAL CLUB.

The monthly meeting was held in the Library of University College, on August 23rd, Mr. Arthur E. Durham, President, in the chair.

Mr. R. T. Lewis read a paper on "*Mermis nigrescens,*" in the course of which he gave some interesting particulars of the remarkable appearance of large numbers of these hair-worms, which were found suspended from the leaves of apple trees and shrubs in the morning following a thunderstorm which passed over the southern counties on the night of June 2nd, similar appearances having been noted in the months of June of 1791, 1832, and 1845, on each occasion after a thunderstorm. In length they varied from 2 inches to 4½ inches, but were not more than 1-20th of an inch in width. For the most part they were of a pale yellow colour, except when charged with ova, which gave a brownline. They closely resemble *Gordius aquaticus*, being a genus of the order *Gordiacea*, in the class *Entozoa*, but they differ from *Gordius* in the position of the oviduct, and also in habitat, *Gordius* being generally found in water, whilst *Mermis* inhabits damp earth. The ova in their free condition exhibit two fine filamentous appendages delicately fringed at their free ends.

Numerous specimens were exhibited at the meeting, and their structure demonstrated under the microscope. Twelve new members were elected.

Sept. 27.—This, the monthly meeting, was held at University College, Mr. Arthur E. Durham, president, in the chair. Mr. Slade read a paper on "Snails' Teeth," in which he described those organs of Mollusca known as the tongue, or palate, consisting of a long and narrow strip of membrane on which are arranged, in various patterns, successive series of strong recurved teeth, by the rasping action of which the animal is enabled to obtain its food. By this means the carnivorous mollusca bore through the shells of the animals on which they prey. The number, arrangement, and shape of these teeth afford to naturalists a means of determining species. Dr. Maddox exhibited a collection of beautifully executed microphotographs of deep sea soundings, many of the objects being magnified 3,000 times.

BOTANICAL SOCIETY OF EDINBURGH.

August 14.—This, the last meeting for the session (31st), was held in the Royal Botanic Gardens. Wm. Gorrie, Esq., V.P., in the chair. The following communications were read :—1. *On the Discovery of Buxbaumia indusiata near Aboyne*, by Professor Dickie. Dr. Dickie reported that he picked, on 29th June last, ten specimens of this rare Moss near Aboyne, being the third time it has been met with in Britain. The plants were growing on rotten timber, on the north slope of the hill of Craigendinnie.—2 *Botanical Intelligence.* By Prof. Balfour. 1. *A new Hæmodoraceous Plant.* Dr. Balfour placed on the table a flowering specimen of the plant sent by H. Fox Talbot, Esq., and which was described at the last meeting under the name of Vellozia Talboti. He proposed that it should be made a new genus, and in the meantime he would name it in honour of his friend Mr. Talbot, and designate it Talbotia elegans.—2. *Gases found in Plants.* Messrs. Faivre & Dupré have recently examined the gases found in the Mulberry and Vine, the parts which contain them, and the changes produced in them by the process of growth and development. They have arrived at the following conclusions :—1. The presence of gases in the interior of the root of the stem, and of the branches in the Mulberry and Vine, is a normal and constant fact. 2. The composition of these gases changes with the epochs of vegetation. 3. During the period of inactivity, carbonic acid is in very small proportion, and is scarcely appreciable. Oxygen is present to the same extent as in atmospheric air. During the phase of activity the contrary takes place, and the changes are more marged in proportion as the vegetation is more energetic : with the progress of vegetation, the proportion of oxygen diminishes. 4. In the roots, during the epoch of vegetation, the quantity of oxygen is not so great, while that of carbonic acid is greater than in the branches examined under the same circumstances. 5. In the branches, as in the roots, there is an inverse relation between the oxygen and the carbonic acid ; by adding to the normal oxygen that disengaged under the form of carbonic acid, we obtain a number which is scarcely above the proportion of oxygen in the air. 6. In the Mulberry and the Vine, injections do not penetrate the pith or the bark, whether in the branches or roots. The ligneous layers are alone permeable to mercury. The more the formation of vessels increases, the easier and more complete are the injections. The injections are fuller in the roots than in the branches ; they are also more in the branches than in the young herbaceous shoots. In the old stems of the Mulberry, the central layers cease to be permeable. 7. Microscopic examination proves that the injection specially penetrates the pitted and reticulated vessels, and also the spiral vessels in the young herbaceous shoots. 8. The pittted vessels show distinctly the mercury in the areolæ, as if in so many little pouches formed by thin portions of the wall ; the same observations have been made in regard to the reticulated vessels. 9. The contents of the vessels expelled by the mercury is variable. Sometimes gas only is sent out, this is the case in winter and after dry weather. Sometimes the gas is mixed with sap, which is more or less abundant according to the epoch of vegetation and external temperature. These two latter conditions regulate in a certain degree the contents of the vessels. 10. The contents are so variable that in plants the root vessels of which contain gases and sap, the stem vessels contain only gases, or inversely. 11. The presence in the vessels of animals of oxygen and carbonic acid mixed with the blood, constitutes one of the best established facts in animal physiology; the presence of the same gases mixed with the sap in the vessels of plants, and the modifications which they there undergo, seem to establish an interesting correspondence between these two kingdoms.—3. *Nature and Structure of the Pod of Cruciferæ.* In a paper in the "Liverpool Naturalists' Journal," Dr. J. Birkbeck Nevins gives what he considers a new explanation of the nature and structure of the pod of the Cruciferæ. 4. *On the Palm Trees of Old Calabar.* Extracted from the MS. Journals of the late Mr. W. Grant Milne. By Mr. Sadler. The Ata ukot, Wine Palm or common Mimbo, is apparently an undescribed species of Raphia. It yields a very pleasant beverage, which is much appreciated by all classes of people who have the fortune, or rather misfortune to touch the western shores of Africa. It has been cultivated by the natives for ages for its watery fountain. The trees are generally seven years old before they are tapped. At this age they are from 30 to 40ft. in height. The natives ascend the trees, and pierce a hole to the centre of the stem immediately below the growing point; a small pipe is then inserted into the hole and led into a vessel which is fixed to the tree. In this way it is drained from time to time, which causes the tree to die, and it is then cut down to make room for others. The mimbo thrives best in damp situations, and such localities are generally chosen for its cultivation; at the same time, I have seen avenues of mimbo trees on high sandy places leading to towns. The people employed to tap the mimbo are Ebebo slaves, which are purchased by kings and chiefs at public slave marts. The Calabarians are not a climbing race. The Ebeboes are in practice superior in the art of "speeling." The liquid, when taken from the tree, has somewhat the colour of cream, and has a pleasant sweetish taste. This only lasts a few hours, when it becomes tartish. The natives have certain barks which they bruise and mix with the liquid, which renders it intoxicating. It is sold in the public markets; and in the Ebebo country there are mimbo public-houses, similar to our beer-shops. It is used by the missionaries' wives for making bread, being very subject to fermentation; the bread made with it is excellent. The young leaves of the plant are split up into threads and made into fine bags. 2. The Iya or Bamboo Palm, is another species of the same genus (Raphia). Its petioles are used for house building at Calabar, and all along the coast. These petioles are generally from 20 to 30ft. long. The fruit is used as an article of food, which is not the case with the last-named species. Many of the trees are from 50 to 60ft. high. In the Uwet country the natives do not cultivate the Wine Palm, consequently they tap the Bamboo; but the wine is strong and harsh and unpleasant, and is very intoxicating. I once saw the King of Uwet as tipsy from its effects as any man under the influence of brandy. The inland kings and chiefs indulge themselves to excess in drinking Bamboo wine, and consequently are always in a state of stupidity. The tree is tapped in the same way as the mimbo, at the base of the growing point. In the Qua country, at the foot of the Qua mountains, they use the wine of the Oil Palm (Elais guineensis), which is inferior to that of the Bamboo, being much harsher and stronger. In this case the trees are tapped about 2ft. from the ground, in the same way as already described. I never saw any of the natives intoxicated by this wretched fruit, but I have no doubt that they can supply ingredients to it for this purpose. Another species is the Afea oku ukot, or the white rod mimbo. The petioles of this Palm are white, while that of the Ata ukot are red. Its wine is equal in quality to that of the Ata ukot. The scales of the fruit are, however, much thicker than those of that species and the Bamboo. The Idium ibum is perhaps the most important Palm of all at Calabar. Idim signifies water, and ibum great. It occurs on the banks of the main branch of the Calabar river, but confined to the district of Ikoriofiong. The quantity of wine which this plant produces is astonishing. An ordinary tree will yield a puncheon of a most delicious beverage, which is deservedly a great favourite with the people. In colour it resembles cream, which is sold in large quantities at the mimbo public-houses. When the tree is once tapped it invariably bleeds itself to death. This is not the case with common mimbo; it can be tapped from time to time till the fluid is exhausted, and then it dies. Such is also the case with the Idim ibum, the Iya or Bamboo, the Afea oku ukot, and the Oil Palm. The last of this class of Palms, belonging to Raphia, met with at Calabar, is the Iya asiakia nditto, which signifies children. The base of the fruit is surrounded by numerous scales similar to those produced at the base of bulbiferous plants—these are called by the natives children. This Palm is not common. Another nearly allied species which is plentiful upon the south coast, sends up numerous shoots, similar to the plantain, covering a great space of ground. On the south coast a species of Date is abundant on the sea shore, but not inland. The fruit is small, and of an oval shape. In taste the pulp is similar to that of the Date of commerce. Its foliage also resembles that of the common Date, and might easily be mistaken for it were it not for the fruit. A Fan Palm is plentiful at Citia Camma, but I have not seen the plant, never having been so far south. Captain Kirkwood has two plants raised from seed collected at Citia Camma, where he states it is abundant. 5. *Notice of Two Species of Mosses New to Science.* 6. *On a Fungoid Disease affecting the Human Hair*, by John Bishop, Esq., 7. *Miscellaneous Communications.*—1. Mr. M'Nab laid before the meeting a specimen of a Cratægus which was raised from seed collected during 1828, by the late Mr. Thomas Drummond, in the Rocky Mountain district, during the second land expedition under command of the lamented Captain Franklin, late Sir John. The peculiarity of this tree is that it never flowers before July, and generally about the middle of the month, and during dull moist seasons flowers have been seen as late as the beginning of August. The tree is now about 20ft. high, having a somewhat pendulous head, and bears black fruit. It was many years before it bloomed but now it flowers annually.—2. Mr. M'Nab also placed on the table flowering plants of Goodenia amplexans and Selliera radicans, which were sent to the Botanic Garden last year from Australia by Dr. Mueller.

Correspondence.

[Under this head we shall be glad to insert any letters of general interest.]

BIRDS OF PASSAGE.

Sir,—Although I agree in the main with the opinion of your correspondent, Mr. H. H. Ulidia, in his letter, in your last issue, with respect to the theory proposed by Mr. A. L. Hunt, perhaps you will give me space for a few remarks on this subject.

Your correspondent, after commenting on Mr. Hunt's letter, observes:—"With 'R. W. B.,' I am quite prepared to think that some instinctive love of change induces the birds to migrate," &c.

Now, Sir, if this be so, why should these birds migrate to such far-off lands, incurring considerable weariness and danger, when their love of change might be satisfied by a flight to warmer climates much nearer home, and why should so many of them go and return, year after year, as your correspondent remarks, to the same spot with this love of change implanted in them?

I have no doubt (as "R. W. B." observes) that the temperature of the atmosphere has a great influence on birds of passage; but I am much more inclined to attribute their arrival and departure to the insects on which they feed. It may be observed that when the spring is cold and wet, insects, especially winged ones, are very late in coming forth from their winter haunts; consequently, these birds are late also, for I have remarked that none of our migratory birds arrive in this country, as a general rule, before the insect tribes have made their appearances.

Again, with regard to the reason of the migration, I have no doubt that it is caused merely by the birds instinctively seeking those warmer countries, the mildness of whose climate suffers insects to live throughout the winter. For what can these birds eat during the five or six months they are absent from our island? We have proof that they do not hybernate, and their organism is such as to preclude their eating anything beyond those insects which, in the majority of species, form their ordinary food. I have no doubt, therefore, Sir, that the migration of birds is caused chiefly by their seeking warmer regions where their natural food may be obtained during the period of the cold of our climate, and also, though in a less degree, by the warmth and geniality of the more tropical countries in comparison with our own.

I am, Sir,
Yours obediently,
ARTHUR G. HARVIE.

London, October 7th.

NAMES OF BIRDS.

Sir,—"J. A. H." has been already anticipated in his remarks on the correct spelling and pronunciation of the Yellow Bunting, by Yarrell, who writes the word *yellow-ammer*, and observes:—"I have ventured to restore to this bird what I believe to have been its first English name, *yellow-ammer*, although it appears to have been printed *yellow-ham* and *yellow-hammer* from the days of Dr. Wm. Turner and Merrett to the present time. The word *ammer* is a well-known German term for bunting in very common use. Thus Bechstein employs the names *schnee-ammer*, *grau-ammer*, *rohr-ammer*, *garten-ammer*, and *gold-ammer* for our snow bunting, corn bunting, reed bunting, ortolan or garden bunting, and yellow bunting. Prefixing the letter *h* to the word appears to be unnecessary, and even erroneous, as suggesting a notion which has no reference to any known habit or quality in the bird ("British Birds," 2nd ed., vol. i., p. 493). He is followed by Wood ("Illustrated Natural History," vol. ii., p. 480), who says:—"The reader may have probably remarked that I have called the bird *yellow-ammer*, and not *yellow-hammer*, as is mostly the case. The correction is due to Mr. Yarrell, who well observes," &c.

It certainly would be as well to retain the original pronunciation and spelling of a word where it is possible to do so; though, it must be confessed, that occasionally it would lead to awkward consequences. The common weed "hound's tongue," for instance, must become "hound's dung," a name it has earned for itself from its atrocious odour. In the name "Missel Thrush" we do retain the original pronunciation (*Mistel Drossel*), but in doing this we miss the meaning—Mistletoe.

Occasionally this purism would be of use. The "Reindeer Case," which caused so much scandal a few years ago, and which depended on the spelling of the word (whether with an *a* or an *e*), never could have arisen had the disputants known that reindeer is merely a corruption of the German *renuthier*, meaning literally, "a running animal," and therefore *must* be properly written with an *e*.

The name "Pea-fowl" is, I believe a corruption of the German name "Pfau," itself an abbreviation of the Latin "Pavo," which was intended to represent the bird's harsh cry, "Pāo, Pāo." When two consonants meet in the beginning of a German word the first has a remarkable stress laid upon it. Thus the *p* of "Pfau" (pronounced *fow*) becomes almost as strongly marked, as in our word pea-fowl."

This subject might be carried out to a much greater length; but I will only add, that in nothing more than in pronunciation and spelling does the saying hold good, "Whatever *is*, is right." Both the one and the other are essentially arbitrary, and, in the English language, at least, dependent on no rules.

I remain, &c.,
W. W. SPICER.

Clifton, Sept. 24.

YELLOW-HAMMER *versus* "YELLOW-AMMER."

SIR,—"J. A. H.," in page 254, NATURALIST'S NOTE BOOK, expresses surprise that our common little bird, the *yellow-hammer*, is not written and pronounced *yellow-ammer*. Such authorities as "Webster's Dictionary," by Worcester, 1863, "Sullivan's Dictionary," 1866, "Chambers' Etymological Dictionary," 1867, all agree in spelling and pronouncing the bird in question *yellow-hammer*.

Is "J. A. H." right, and are the modern lexicographers wrong? He is at a loss to conceive why any bird should be called a *hammer*. Perhaps he is; and many of us, too, are equally puzzled when we attempt to account for such words as ninny-*hammer*, *hammer*-cloth, *hammer*-wort, and thousands of others. That a man, a cloth, or an herb should be called *hammer* is quite as strange to me, at least, as that a bird should be called *hammer*. Your correspondent says:— "If we could persuade educated people to see the absurdity of the wrong, and adopt the right method," &c., &c. All right, Sir; but when common consent popularly applied, together with the authority of learned philologists, persist in giving us a word which "J. A. H." rejects, then what are the vulgar or the educated to do?

"What do you read, my Lord?
Words, words, words."

And as they are the representatives of ideas, we must try to understand them.

I am, Sir,
Yours, &c.,
H. H. ULIDIA.

Dromore, Oct. 3, 1867.

JUVENILE MUSEUMS.

SIR,—I am glad to see the remark, in the September number of your NOTE BOOK, respecting Juvenile Museums, and I hope it will be widely carried out. In schools in Oxfordshire prizes are given half-yearly for collections of plants, birds' eggs, and fossils; also in Germany, at the Moravian School, at Newvied, near Coblentz, on the Rhine, every boy, with scarcely one exception, has a collection of old coins or relics found in the old castles on the Rhine, birds' eggs, butterflies, insects, or plants, which engenders in them a taste for natural history, and proves both instructive and interesting through life. Some of the above collections, which I have seen, are most praiseworthy.

I remain, &c.,
W. F.

Sir,—In last month's "*Naturalist's Note Book*," in speaking of a series of prizes offered by a committee of Naturalists at Newcastle-on-Tyne, you expressed a hope that our public and private schools would follow the example. It would perhaps then be interesting to you to know, that the Rev. G. F. Maclear, B.D., Headmaster of King's College School, London, gave two prizes this summer for the best collection of fifty British ferns and wild flowers, and for the best collection of fifty insects. These collections were to be made during the holidays, thereby giving the boys a healthy and instructive occupation and amusement.

This example is worthy of being followed by other schools, and I think you will agree with me, that it is a thousand times better for a midsummer's "holiday task" than the old fashion, so many lines of Latin and Greek translations.

I am, Sir,
Yours obediently,
WALTER WILLIS, A.K.C.

Short Notes.

THE TESTACELLA.—The testacella is by no means rare or uncommon, but is seldom observed or captured, in consequence of its subterranean habits. To find it you must either rise at the dawn of the day, or make nocturnal explorations equipped with a powerful lanthern. It may be discovered, if thus sought for, in most of the market-gardens round about the metropolis, and it is distributed generally throughout all the western counties. It has been taken at Youghal and Bandon, in Ireland, and at Madeira, the Canaries, and in Western Europe. The lingual ribbon of the testacella is extremely large and wide, and made up of over fifty rows of minute teeth, fifty-one in each row. The teeth are conical, evenly curved, and barbed at the point. Each tooth has a projection on the middle from which the posterior end thickens. Imagine any living creature getting into such a trap as this—why, a shark's mouth is a mild kind of painless trap when compared with this slow-moving slug's. If unacquainted with this mollusk's habits, an examination of the mouth would at once lead us to infer the carnivorous propensities of the creature, and a closer insight into its ways and habits would show our judgment to be founded upon correct premises. The testacella is exclusively a destroyer of living things, the earthworm being the game that it hunts with untiring assiduity. It follows out its earthworm through its underground tunnels, as the mole hunts grubs. A very slight inspection of this curious slug will serve to show us how admirably its organization in every way adapts it to follow out its earthworm-hunting propensities. The body is extremely slender, and when stretched to its extreme point of attenuation, becomes so small and wire-like, that progression through tiny holes in the soil is rendered easy in the extreme. It creeps stealthily upon a worm, seizes it with its terrible toothed trap, and slowly swallows it, much after the fashion of a snake when bolting a frog, the victim being sucked, so to speak, by a steady, introversive action of the armed tongue into the gullet. I found the remains of several earthworms in the slug I captured in my garden. Dr. Ball, in describing the habits of the testacella, says: "I first became aware of the testacella preying on worms, by putting some of them in spirits, when they disgorged more of these animals than I thought they could possibly have contained. Each worm was cut, but not divided, at regular intervals. I afterwards caught them in the act of swallowing worms four and five times their own length.

When cold bleak winds and frosty mornings foretell the coming of King Winter, then the testacella, like a wise and prudent slug, mines its way down into the soil until it reaches a depth of more than a third of a fathom from the surface. Having sunk its shaft as deep as desirable, the next thing it has to do is to make a kind of sleeping-room, which is accomplished by working away the surrounding earth. But even this is not a sufficient protection. The slug has no close fitting jacket of fur or feathers to keep it warm, so instead, it secretes from glands provided for the purpose, a thick, glairy mucus, which soon partially hardens, and snugly ensconced in this self-made kind of coffin, the testacella sleeps away the dreary winter months, in utter defiance of Jack Frost, or anything he can do. Woodward thus speaks of the testacella when in winter quarters: "It forms a kind of cocoon in the ground by the exudation of mucus."—J. K. LORD in *Land and Water*, Oct. 5th.

THE PANTHER. — The panther—properly called by the natives the taindwa and borebucha, and erroneously the cheeta—varies in size in different parts of India. The largest I have ever killed was eight feet two inches from tip of nose to end of tail, measured as he lay, and the female measured seven feet six. Their skins are before me—a light yellow or buff colour, with the exception of the belly and chest, where the hair is white and much longer, with distinct black spots from half an inch to an inch and a half in diameter over the spine and towards the extremities, and differently-shaped black marks of larger size on other parts of the body—some of them are black rings, and others almost the shape of a rose. On the generality of skins of the panthers I have killed these black spots were much smaller, and none have been so beautifully marked. Their owners were killed after a desperate fight, in which I was badly wounded, near Chinwarah, in the Nagpore province. Only last year a promising young officer of the name of Shane, of the Artillery, died after three days of wounds received in a fight with a panther, close to the same spot; so that evidently there is a breed of the real fighting panther in that neighbourhood. I entirely agree with Colonel Haly in his account of the immense strength of the panther, which enables him to spring with a goat or sheep in his mouth over high inclosures; such as have been pointed out to me upwards of seven feet high, over which the panther had carried his victim. I know Nursipatam, in the Golconda zemindaree, very well, and remember hearing of the ravages of the panthers. There the jungles are tree jungles, and it is very probable that the animal, in that and in many other parts of India, lives at times in the hollows of trees. In the Deccan and Nagpore countries I have never seen them in trees; there they usually inhabit rocks, in the caves of which they remain, or in the grass and bushes of rocky ravines, the trees in which are comparatively small to what they are in forests. I have never known them in these countries to take to trees when hunted, though their retractile claws and wonderful muscular strength of forearm would enable them to climb any tree. My experience of the felis began in 1836, in the jungles in the neighbourhood of Chunai, on the Ganges, near Seeptresgur. I was lying down, in the heat of the day, when two spotted deer rushed past me, closely pressed by a panther, and I had not time to get my rifle to my shoulder. A day or two after this a tiger passed between myself and shikaree when I had no weapon in my hand. I was very green in those days, and they were the first I had ever seen. A man was struck down near me a short time after this by a tigress, and I began to respect the genus felis. From that time, for twenty years, the blood feud between us has never cooled.—*Field*, Sept. 7.

SMALL BIRDS.—Take the district from which I now write. Around me are many hundred thousands of acres of rich and fertile land, of which a great proportion is arable, and none wood or forest. What is to be done with the hosts of sparrows which swarm in our rickyards, and which devour sometimes one-third of a field of standing corn? The sparrow-hawk, the kestrel, and the merlin find no home with us; and even were they sufficiently numerous to restrain the sparrow tribe I fear that the farmer's chickens and ducklings would be heavy sufferers. Two years since a sparrow-hawk made a nest in a neighbouring tree. When complaints of theft became rife I found, on visiting her nest, the tokens of an awful slaughter of poultry, but of wild birds scarcely a feather. I should not have implicit confidence in the remedy if it were applicable, which it is not. The sparrow is, no doubt, a useful fellow in his place. Where much corn cannot be had he will do good service in thinning the insect tribes; but when too numerous, and when surrounded by corn, his habits become almost entirely graminivorous, and in the spring if he cannot have corn he will eat off every row of growing peas in a parish, to the neglect of caterpillars, aphides, or aught else. I may add that in the case of some of our most destructive insects—as *e. g.*, the larvæ of phalæna grossulariata, and many others—I know of no bird that will feed upon them at all. The robin, of almost saintly reputation, is very useful; but if robins become too numerous they will turn their attention from worm and grub to the strawberry and other fruits. I have seen three or four of these birds destroy or cut in pieces every ripe strawberry on a bed within an hour.

The blue tit is a charming little fellow, and most useful also, but woe betide the small garden in early spring if last year's young family from the crack in the old wall fail to seek new homes. Every bud upon gooseberry tree and flowering shrub will fall a sacrifice to the excessive competition in a useful trade. I might adduce many other instances of the evil of excess in the number of our useful friends, tending to show that man must from time to time interfere to check the superabundance of such tribes as may increase too rapidly. I might also show that in most parts of our island circumstances exceptionally affecting one or more of these tribes must ever exist, rendering the maintenance of a perfect balance impossible, and justifying the interference of man to repress and destroy; that they may also render man's interference needful to cultivate and distribute I am ready to admit.—*Times*, Oct. 2nd.

THE CALIFORNIAN GROUND SQUIRREL.—The common and notorious Californian Ground Squirrel (*S. Beecheyi*) ranges eastward across the Colorado valley, though in Arizona it is by no means so abundant as in California, where it forms colonies approaching those of the prairie dog in extent, and is a great pest to the farmer. In the vicinity of Los Angeles, I had an excellent opportunity of studying its habits. On the flat or slightly rolling dry plains which stretch between that town and the sea-beach, it is exceedingly numerous. The burrows occur usually in clusters, and upon little mounds or hillocks of dirt formed by the soil heaped up during their excavation; but single ones are scattered in every direction. Upon these "earth-works" the animals may be seen at all times, sitting upright, and motionless as statues, their fore-paws drooped, and their eyes intently fixed upon the passer-by; or, when no suspicious object appears, lying and basking in the sun, or playing merrily with each other upon the ramparts of their citadels. I have no doubt that the subterranean passages intercommunicate, and that each animal does not have its own entrance, though he may possess private apartments below. In the vicinity of large encampments, the grass, herbage, and in fact everything green is so closely cropped, that the ground is almost bare; and it becomes a matter for wonder that so many animals can contrive to fill their stomachs. As is the case with those of the prairie dog, the villages are inhabited by a species of burrowing owl, which takes possession of deserted holes. Over the dry plain the graceful mountain plover courses swiftly along; while overhead, or resting upon the ground is the great squirrel hawk, on the look out for its prey. The general manners of these animals call forcibly to mind the prairie dogs. Like them, they hardly venture far from their burrows, to which they hasten precipitately on the first sign of an alarm. Reaching the entrance, they stop a moment in a squat attitude, or rise on their hind-quarters, the better to reconnoitre, venting their displeasure and suspicion by a sharp, chattering bark. They are tough, muscular animals, and must be hard hit to be killed; and even when mortally wounded, will make use of their convulsive death-struggles to reach their burrows, into which they at last drop exhausted, and may be thus lost to the collector.—*American Naturalist*, September.

EXTRAORDINARY DEER HUNT AT SEA.—On Wednesday morning about ten o'clock, a deer was observed running about the sands of Dunnet, within half a mile of Castlehill Harbour, and it was noticed that on reaching the sea the animal leaped in among the breakers, which were pretty heavy, and that after breasting them he swam rapidly seawards. The boat of the schooner Inchbroom, of Thurso, Capt. Sinclair, was speedily manned by him, and by Mr. George Gunn, Castlehill, and two of the vessel's crew, both of whom rowed with a will, Mr. Gunn acting as steersman and Capt. Sinclair as harpooner, standing in the boat's bow with a coil of rope to throw over the animal's horns. On approaching the stag he showed great symptoms of excitement, lashing the sea with his feet, and swimming backwards and forwards with great velocity. The first throw of the line missed the antlers, and as the animal suddenly turned towards the shore, and was approaching the breakers, which would have instantly swamped the boat, Mr. Gunn adroitly "cut him out" by getting the boat slipped in between the stag and the shore, and Capt. Sinclair's next heave of the line was so successful that in a minute or two the deer was in tow of the boat and approaching towards Castlehill Harbour, where hundreds of workmen and others had assembled to witness the extraordinary sight of deer stalking at sea. With a good deal of difficulty and resistance on the part of the deer, which showed capital pluck throughout and made good use of points and feet, he was brought to land and taken to Castlehill stables. He is a fine stag, about five years old, and has seven points. During this season there has been an unusual number of deer seen in that district. In the present case the race of the animal to the sea was probably occasioned by being startled by dogs; but, whatever was the cause, the circumstance of such an animal being caught in Dunnet or any other bay is certainly without a parallel in natural history.—*Northern Ensign*.

A MESSAGE FROM THE STARS.—Pursuing this extraordinary line of enquiry, and obtaining at every step new, confirmatory, and beautiful results, it was resolved to ascertain if the masses of matter obtained from the atmosphere, meteoric stones, and which bear evidence of having been at a very high temperature, gave any indication of the kind of atmosphere in which they were formed. A slice from the meteoric iron of Lenarto, which was analysed by Wehrle, and found to be of sp. gr. 7·79, and to consist of iron 90·883, nickel 8·450, cobalt 0·665, and copper 0·002, was obtained. This was made the subject of careful experiment, and the Lenarto iron yielded 2·85 times its volume of gas, of which 86 per cent. nearly was hydrogen. "Hydrogen has been recognized," says Mr. Graham, "in the spectrum analysis of the fixed stars, by Messrs. Huggins and Miller. The same gas constitutes, according to the wide researches of Father Secchi, the principal element of a numerous class of stars, of which *a* Lyræ is the type. The iron of Lenarto has no doubt come from such an atmosphere, in which hydrogen greatly prevailed. *This meteorite may be looked upon as holding within it, and bearing to us hydrogen of the stars.*" The series of results which are described in this paper, though differing in their general character, have yet a strict relation to each other. When carefully studied, it will be seen that the sponge and the sugar sucking up water are only modified examples of the dense metals absorbing gases. It is by the cautious questioning of nature, and by closely inspecting the phenomena which are constantly occurring around us, that we advance to a knowledge of sublimer truths. Priestley's observation on the porosity of stoneware tubes was the germ of that discovery which may without any poetical exaggeration be described as "a message from the stars."—R. HUNT, F.R.S., in *Popular Science Review*, October.

SUNRISE AND SUNSET.—As is well known to scientific readers, no satisfactory explanation has yet been given of the red glow and splendour of sunrise and sunset. The phenomenon is one of those questions in natural philosophy which wait for a solution. Among the latest attempts at a solution is that by Dr. E. Lommel, in Poggendorff's *Annalen*, in which he shows it to be an effect of diffraction of light ss viewed through a series of dark, or partially dark, screens. He lays it down as an axiom that a point of white light, viewed through a sufficient number of groups of screens, appears not merely reddish of itself, but also appears surrounded by a still more strongly red-coloured aureole of diffracted light. Herein consists the explanation. The lower strata of the atmosphere are full of minute corpuscular bodies—dust, organic and inorganic, particles of carbon in smoke, and watery particles. They serve the purpose of the dark screens, and when the sun is low, the rays traversing a long range of atmosphere undergo diffraction, and by superimposition of adjacent points of light, the effect of redness is deepened. Distant snow-slopes and glaciers, as in the Alps, and clouds near the horizon, come under the influence, and often show a purplish red colour. Aqueous vapour plays an important part in the phenomenon, best seen when the whole morning or evening sky is lit with the brilliant ruddy glow. A mere red glow, without brilliance, is occasioned by the solid particles in the atmosphere. The sun looks red through smoke, and through the clouds of fine sand blown up in the desert.—*Athenæum*, Oct. 5th.

A WISE DOG.—I had the following from an acquaintance, a gentleman who fills the situation of a district registrar in Edinburgh ; at least he did fill that situation so recently as 1862. This gentleman was in the habit of spending his annual holidays with a friend who held a sheep-farm on the southern slope of the Ochil Hills : during his visits he had formed a very friendly acquaintance with one of his host's dogs, and upon the occasion of his visits the dog was aye kindly speered after as soon as the health of the family was inquired about. Mr. Harriott went down to spend his holidays with his Stirlingshire friends in the autumn of 1859, and upon enquiring for his canine friend, the gude-wife informed him that " he was deed an' gane ;" but she observed, by way of consolation, that, "he had left a *sin* jest as gude as himsel'." Mr. H. observed that his death was a great loss, as he was such a wise animal. "Indeed," quoth the gude woman, "ye may say that, we've have money gude tykes sin we cam' ta the farm, but we never had ane like him ; last back end after ye gaed awa hame, Rab left hame ae afternin, an' about the gloaming he brought a sheep doon fra the hill, an' heck, sirs, ye wadna believe it, he gaed nine times ta the hill an' brought a sheep hame wi' him ilka time." "But," said my friend, "why did he bring the sheep home ?" "That's jest whar the whole matter o' the brute's wiseness lies," said she, "every ane o' thae nine sheep was diseased, an' he brought them hame for the dooble purpose of getting cured an' preventin' the rest o' the flock frae be'n smitten."—*Land and Water*, Oct. 5th.

PLANTS AND THEIR LEAVES.—Plants have their idiosyncracies as well as other creatures. There are some which will develop their leaves a fortnight or so earlier than their brothers of the same species, others that will retain their foliage long after it has fallen from other plants of the same specific form. This did not escape the notice of the old Greek naturalists, for Theophrastus, in his work *De Plantis*, mentions a plane-tree in Crete, which never shed its leaves, and he adds, that that was the identical tree beneath whose shade Jupiter carried on his flirtation with Europa. Be that as it may, it is quite certain that, apart from individual peculiarities, such as we have just mentioned, plants of the same species will shed their leaves sooner or later according to the locality in which they grow. In the Canary Islands the vine only sheds its foliage very gradually, so that new leaves often appear before all the old ones are thrown off. The cherry-tree in Ceylon, and the peach in Brazil, are said to become almost completely evergreen. On the other hand, in colder latitudes than ours the leaves fall earlier in consonance with the earlier advent of winter. In the tropics, although there is in general not so well-marked a period of defoliation, yet the dry season seems to act in a similar way to the winter season here. Travellers tell us that there is scarcely a month in the year in which young shoots and leaves may not be seen on the trees, so that the formation of the young leaves, as well as the fall of the old ones, is spread over the whole year, as it were, and is not so much confined to particular periods as in temperate latitudes.—DR. MASTERS, in *Popular Science Review*, Oct.

THE BEECH.—The beech (*Fagus sylvatica*), if it be not the most magnificent of all British trees, certainly rivals the oak itself in size and majestic beauty; a grove of stately well-grown beeches on chalky loam is at once graceful and grand ; the effect on the spectator is thoroughly awe-aspiring ; the massive, smooth, upright fasciculated trunks, and the far-spreading groin-like branches call to mind some huge cathedral nave ; the trunks are pier-like, massive, bossed, and channelled ; the branches like arches interlacing, curving, and entangling ; and the roots, moulded, curved, grotesque, and snaky, help to complete a scene of the most impressive character. The body of the tree is frequently stained of a vivid grass-green, produced by the growth of a parasitic lichen, the beauty of which is enhanced on a summer's day by the bands of pure gold projected on the limbs where the struggling sunbeams find a temporary passage through the dense umbrage above. The value of the wood for building purposes is by no means equal to the beauty of the tree; for whether in a living state and full of sap, felled for use, or dried and made up into furniture, beech-wood is invariably riddled by a parasitic worm; this is one of the principal reasons why the wood is seldom or never used for floors and roofs.—*Builder.*

THE RING-TAILED CIVET CAT.—The Ring-tailed Civet Cat (*Bassaris astuta*) is a queer animal, combining in itself the features of several distinct groups. Thus it has the ringed tail of a racoon, the pointed snout and cunning look of a fox, and the habits, at least in semi-domestication, of a house cat. It is well known to the hunters and miners of California, and by them highly prized as a pet. It is indifferently called "Mountain Cat," "Cat Squirrel," and "Racoon Fox"; is easily tamed, and makes an interesting pet, as well as a useful one, from its dexterity in catching rats and mice. In a state of nature, it is said to be chiefly nocturnal, and to show spirited fight when attacked. It is about as large as a house cat; above, is yellowish or brownish-grey; below, white; and its tail is annulated alternately with black and white.—*American Naturalist*, September.

THE AMERICAN LAKES.—Lake Superior is the largest body of fresh water in the world. It has an area of 32,000 square miles, and a mean depth of 1,000 feet. It is apparently fed by a few insignificant streams, the largest of which are the St. Louis and the Ontonagon. Lake Michigan has an area of 24,000 miles, and a mean depth of 900ft. This lake only receives a few small streams, and yet Lake Michigan furnishes a large proportion of the current that flows over the Niagara and thence down the St. Lawrence into the ocean. These great lakes must get supplied from subterranean sources. It is well known that large rivers on the western plains suddenly disappear through fissures and chasms, never again to reappear on the surface.—*Canadian Paper.*

THE SKYLARK IN AUSTRALIA.—At a recent meeting of the Acclimatization Society of New South Wales, it was stated that the skylarks introduced from England have bred freely, and that numbers are now to be seen in the fields in some parts of the colony. At the same meeting Dr. Bennett stated that Lieutenant Marochetti, of H.I.M. ship Magenta, had presented to the society two Mantchourian pheasants from the north of Pekin—the species known as Swinhoe's eared pheasant (Crossoptilon Mantchuricum), the "Ho-ky" of the Chinese—and it is the first time that this fine kind of pheasant has been introduced into Australia. Three birds arrived alive at Sydney, but one unfortunately died on board.—*Gardeners' Magazine*, Oct. 5th.

A PETRIFIED FOREST.—In the vicinity of Cairo, in a rocky and desolate region, where the mind can scarcely conceive it possible that a forest could ever have existed, countless trees are scattered about in every direction, apparently overthrown by a mighty tempest. The hills and valleys are covered with them; some of them are sixty or seventy feet in length, and upwards of three feet in diameter. There they lie, with their roots and branches perfect, and the very clefts produced by age or heat are visible. But on a closer inspection they will be found to have been changed into a hard stone, which, when cut, shows a fine variety of colour, and is susceptible of a high polish. Nothing is known of the origin of these wonderful trees. The period during which they flourished, and the very place where they grew are matters wrapped in impenetrable mystery.—*Scientific Review*, Oct.

MAGNETIC ATTRACTION.—M. Jaussen, who was sent by the French Minister of Public Instruction to investigate the phenomena accompanying the volcano of Santorin, has made a report to the Paris Academy of Sciences, which contains some interesting particulars. M. Jaussen found that the volcanic deposits and fissures had a powerful magnetic influence on the needle in the direction of the volcanic lines, and that the magnetic dip decreases greatly in localities beyond the volcanic region. An examination of the flames proceeding from the volcano by the spectroscope showed that hydrogen is their chief component; but that they also contain sodium, copper, chlorine and carbon.

GRASS SPONGE.—A new and very important article of commerce has been lately introduced into America, called "New Grass Sponge." It is found in almost exhaustless quantities among the coral reefs of the Bahamas and Coasts of Mexico and Florida. The sponge is washed and freed from grit, passed between india-rubber rollers saturated with glycerine, and then seasoned in ovens. After undergoing this treatment it is fit for use. The purposes to which it can be applied are very various; but it is especially adapted for stuffing beds, sofas, chairs, &c. One pound of this sponge is equal, for these purposes, to one and a half pound of hair.—*Athenæum.*

THE WASP.—There is one curious fact with respect to the wasp worth mentioning, and for which, besides my own observation, I am indebted to the same intelligent naturalist. It is as follows:—If the entrance to a wasp's nest be stopped up in the day time, the numerous wasps which are constantly returning to it, make no attempt to sting the aggressor; but if only one escapes from the inside it attacks him instantly, although, perhaps, not with the same pertinacity as the common bee is known to show.—E. Jesse in *Once a Week.*

LARGE BUNCH OF GRAPES.—An extraordinary bunch of grapes was exhibited at the flower show of Wednesday by Mr. Archibald Fowler, gardener to the Earl of Stair, Castle Kennedy, which weighs 17lb. 2½oz. A 100 years ago report says that a bunch of the white Syrian grape was produced at Welbeck which weighed 19½lb., but many horticulturists have since then doubted its authenticity.—*Glasgow Herald.*

EVAPORATING POWER OF PLANTS.—Some interesting experiments were made by Dr. Hales on the evaporating power of plants. He found that a sunflower plant weighing three pounds perspired about thirty ounces of water in twelve hours during a day in the month of July, but in a warm night it perspired only three ounces, and lost nothing in a cold night; on the contrary, it gained weight by imbibing dew.

New Inventions.

DR. LAWSON'S NEW CLASS AND DEMONSTRATING MICROSCOPE.—In teaching histology to large classes of students, two forms of microscope are required : one for the laboratory, with which the student himself works, and one for the class-room, which the lecturer hands to the nearest student; who passes it to his neighbour, and so on till it travels round the class. The idea of combining these two forms in a single microscope occurred to us as being both economical and convenient. The instrument represented in the adjoining cut was therefore prepared for us by Mr. Collins, of Titchfield Street.

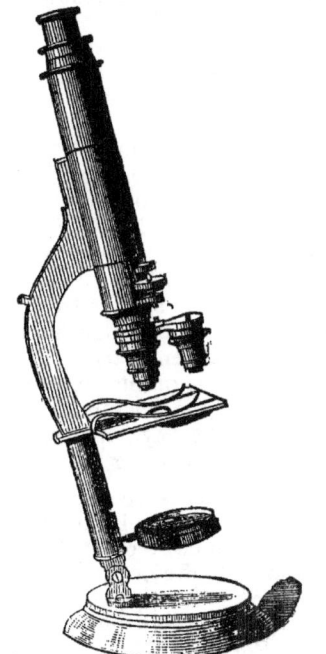

Fig. 1.

Fig 1 represents the microscope as used in the laboratory, with a double nose-piece bearing a 1 inch and ¼ inch object glass.

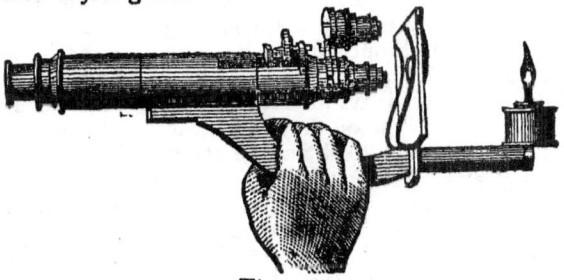

Fig. 2.

Fig. 2 shows the microscope as used in the lecture-room ; the leg is drawn out from the sliding tube, which works in a knuckle-joint in the solid metal foot, and bears the mirror; on this there is fitted a small oil-lamp, and the instrument being grasped by the curved portion between the body and stage, and used like a telescope, transparent objects placed on the stage are seen with the greatest distinctness. It is re- markable, but it is no less true, that no amount of ordinary flickering of the flame is perceptible by the observer. The instrument is provided with a good 1 inch and also with ¼ inch objective, which shows the markings on *Pleurosigma formosum* most satisfactorily. The instrument is intended to meet the want of teachers in medical schools, and public institutions, and has just been selected for the histological laboratory at St. Mary's Hospital.—*Popular Science Review*.

Remarks, Queries, &c.

(*Under this head we shall be happy to insert original Remarks, Queries, &c.*)

THE LAST IRISH WOLF.—In the NATURALIST'S NOTE BOOK, page 128, an extract from *Land and Water*, giving the authority of Thompson's "Natural History of Ireland," says :—"Three places in Ireland are commemorated, each as having the last wolf killed there, viz., one in the South, another near Glenarm, and the third (Wolf hill), three miles from Belfast." As history is but the child of tradition, I might quote you hundreds of other places in Ireland (mountainous districts particularly) all laying claim, strong claim indeed, to the exterminating exploit of killing the last wolf in Ireland. At different times during the last forty years, many very clever men, through the medium of the ablest journals in Ireland, have strenuously laboured to prove the time when, and to point out the place where the last wolf—that once troublesome and dangerous prowler of our fields —was killed ; but the accounts are so conflicting, that the whole affair is still a matter of doubt, each locality I presume, trusting to the validity of its own local tradition. A guide book to the northern coast of Ireland, published in Dublin in 1842, informs us that an Antrim tradition says that in 1712 the last wolf was killed in the neighbourhood of Drumnasole and Nappin.

A "Guide to the Causeway," published in 1822, says :—" Passing the village of Cairnlough, near three miles from Glenarm, the country becomes still more romantic. Tradition says the last wolf killed in Ireland was shot here in 1712."

Cork and Tipperary have their traditions about the last wolf, and those traditions quite agree in pointing out the district of the Galtees mountains as the place where the last wolf was killed in 1715. But a writer in the *Irish Penny Journal*, May 8th, 1841, goes far to nullify, or at least to render premature, the Antrim and Galtees exploits, for he informs us that "there was a presentment for killing wolves granted in Cork in the year 1710."

If so, it would seem that wolves were rather common and dangerous in Cork at that time, and hence it scarcely amounts to a probability that in three or four years they could be totally extirpated; and if the authority at hand is of any value, this view of the subject is still further confirmed by what follows in the *Irish Penny Journal*, which says that in 1739-40 wolves were killed in Co. Wexford, and also that so lately as 1770 a wolf was killed in the Wicklow mountains ! "Who shall decide when doctors disagree ?"

But, again, the *Ulster Journal of Archæology* informs us that a Cork alderman named Howel, writing in 1698, says:—"Wolves, indeed, we have, and foxes, but these are rather game and diversion than noxious or hateful," and, again, says Sir E. D. Burrowes,—"The wolf hunting implied by Howel terminated in 1714 by the death of the last of the race."

At Ballymena, in County Antrim, a very well authenticated tradition states that the last wolf was killed at Wood-hill, near that town, in 1727.

In the *Dublin Penny Journal*, 1832, page 10, we are told that "the last wolf seen in Ireland was killed in Kerry in 1710."

Sir John Ponsonby, in 1662, had a bill brought into Parliament to encourage the killing of wolves in Ireland. In county Louth there is a tradition that in 1718 a wedding party visited Slieve Guillon, raised a wolf on the mountain top, and killed it, but D'Alton, in his "History of Dundalk," published in 1862, does not refer to the matter. Here it may be safely presumed that wolves were killed at many, or indeed, all the places mentioned above, but the chief difficulty is in fixing dates to the transactions. The wolf-killing process was by no means a rare thing, particularly with the old people of the times in question; and 160 years ago we had no flashing telegrams, no iron horse, but few newspapers, posts slow and letters scarce—and hence for years local tradition was the only repository of the wolf-extinguishing engagements, and in the flight of time, as De Quincy says, "Dates may be forgotten, but epochs never."

Dromore.   H. H. ULIDIA.

FOREST TREES.—Your correspondent "R. W. B." in last month's NATURALIST'S NOTE BOOK, asks if any of your readers can favour him with a list of "Forest Trees" which are natives of Britain. I have put down the following, which are natives of Britain, except those which are marked with a (*), and those have become so common that I thought it best to include them.

Acer Pseudo-platanus (the sycamore).
  ,, Campestre (the Maple).
*Æsculus Hippocastanum (the horse chesnut), introduced from Asia in the year 1629.
Alnus glutinosa (the alder).
*Albies exelsa (the spruce fir), introduced from the North of Europe, 1548.
Betula Alba (the white birch).
  ,, glutinosa (the common birch).
Carpinus Betulus (the hornbeam).
Castanea vulgaris (the spanish chesnut).
Cratægus Oxyacantha (the hawthorn).
Fagus sylvatica (the beech).
Fraxinus exelsior (the ash).
Ilex Aquifolium (the holly).
*Juglans regia (the common walnut), introduced from Persia 1562.
Larix Europæa (the larch fir), introduced from Germany 1629.
*Picea pectinata (the common sivel fir), introduced from Germany 1603. There is several large specimens of this fir at Rydal, near Ambleside, Westmoreland.
Pinus sylvestris (the scotch pine or fir).
Populas alba (the white poplar).
  ,, nigra (the black poplar).
  ,, tremula (the aspen or trembling poplar).
* ,, fastigiata (the Lombardy poplar), introduced from Italy 1758.
Prunus Padus (the bird cherry).
  ,, Avium (the wild cherry).
Pyrus communis (the wild pear tree).
  ,, Malus (the crab tree).
  ,, aucuparia (the mountain ash).
  ,, Aria (the white beam tree).
  ,, torminalis (the wild service tree).
Quercus Robur (the oak).
Salix alba (the common white willow).
  ,, Caprea (the goat willow).
Sambucus nigra (the elder).
Taxus baccata (the yew).
Tilia Europæa (the lime tree)
Ulmus campestris (the elm).
  ,, montana (the wych elm).

Besides the above the following shrub may be met with in our woods and forests.

Betula nana (the dwarf birch).
Cornus sanguinea (the dog wood or wild cornel).
Corylus Avellana (the hazel).
Euonymus europœus (the spindle tree).
Juniperus communis (the common juniper).
Mespilus germanica (the medlar).
Prunus spinosa (the sloe or blackthorn).
Rhamnus catharticus (the buckthorn).
Viburnum Lantana (the wayfaring tree).
  ,, Opulus (the guelder rose).

If "R. W. B." wishes to study the structure of plants, I should recommend him to "The School Botany," by Dr. Lindley; or, "The Rudiments of Botany," by Prof. Henfrey.   J. W. W. B.

AN INSECT DESTROYER.—Much the largest number of fleas are brought into our family circles by pet dogs and cats, and the pigsty is generally filled with them at this season of the year, where numbers will hop on you when visiting it for the purpose of feeding or inspection. The oil of pennyroyal will drive these insects off; but a cheaper method, where the herb flourishes, is to throw your dogs and cats into a decoction of it once a week; mow the herb, and scatter it in the beds once a month. I have seen this done for many years in succession. Where the herb cannot be got, the oil may be procured. In this case, saturate strings with it and tie them round the necks of dogs and cats; pour a little on the backs and about the ears of hogs, which you can do while they are feeding, without touching them. By repeating these applications every twelve or fifteen days, the fleas will flee from your quadrupeds to their relief and improvement, and to your relief and comfort in the house. String saturated with the oil of pennyroyal and tied around the neck and tail of horses will drive off lice; the strings should be saturated once a day. Mint, freely cut, and hung round a bedstead, or on the bed furniture, will prevent annoyance from bed insects.—*Gardeners' Magazine.*

The above is a simple and safe method of getting

rid of these pests. Fresh deal shavings are also recommended; the dogs should be allowed to sleep on them. In fact any strong perfume annoys fleas, and they therefore endeavour to get (to them) sweeter quarters.
T. S. G.

NESTS.—Perhaps you may like to be told of a curious place in which I once saw a swallow's nest. In the public room of the Hôtel de Mazagran, at Bouffarik, a few miles south of Algiers, a pair of swallows had built their nest at the top of the chain of one of the lamps which were suspended from the ceiling of the public room. The birds flew in and out most amusingly whilst the room was frequented by the guests, and the waiter told me that they had returned annually for six years. In a corner of the room there was an old, apparently unfinished nest.

Perhaps I may add, that Horace Vernet and his wife were at that time at the hotel. He had property in the neighbourhood, on which he resided much, and he came to bring a sign for the hotel, of the recent taking of some place in Algeria, which he had just painted as a gift to the landlady, and which was to be hung outside by his desire.

On the subject of nests, I remember in my youth that one of the solitary wasps made a nest in the keyhole of a table drawer in the bedroom of my sisters, in Kent, and used occasionally to bring a caterpillar into it. My sisters were much concerned, on my, boylike, one day killing it, taking it for a common wasp.
PETER L. HUSSEY.

LIZARDS.—Do the full-grown English lizards (I am not sure of the species, but I think it is Zootoca Vivipara), ever prey upon the younger ones of the same species?

I have kept a number of lizards, large and small, for some time past in a case closely covered. The disappearance of numbers of the young ones and death of others in an unaccountable way, made me suspect that the larger ones *ate* them. I therefore watched carefully at different times, but saw nothing to confirm my suspicions. One day, however, when feeding them with flies, I saw one of the larger lizards suddenly seize a young one by the head and "worry" it, as lizards are in the habit of doing with flies, worms, &c., &c. I rescued the little reptile as quickly as possible, but it was too late; it was alive, but unable to run about, and died in a short time.
T. SANDELS.

REMARKABLE FECUNDITY IN A DOVE.—I have in my possession a Dove. The Collared Turtle (*Turtur resorius*) which in April last I placed in a cage with a small foreign dove (of what species I do not know). I supposed the turtle dove to be a male, and out of compassion for the little lady whose mate died soon after its arrival in this "cold land," it was given to her companionship. From April until the middle of August it had laid 15 eggs, the other one 5; this is the more remarkable inasmuch as the bird in a state of nature would only have laid 4 eggs (producing two broods) at the most.

I let her sit 14 days on two eggs, thinking that would prevent her laying more, as I feared she might kill herself by exhaustion, but she continued laying until she had completed the number stated. I may mention that with the exception of the two she was allowed to sit, the eggs were taken from her at the end of the second or third day. She is now in as fine condition and as healthy as it is possible for a bird to be.

I should be glad to know if any of your readers can tell me the name and species of the small foreign dove referred to; it is about 7 inches long, slate coloured on the head and back, cream coloured on the under side towards the tail, gradually merging into a deeper shade on the breast, which is beautifully marked with crescent-shaped forms in black; the eyes are black, and the bill long and hooked; the tail black and white; feet red. It was brought from S. Africa, and I have been taught to call it the Madagascar Dove.
T. S. G.

A CURIOUS BEETLE.—In a bottle of spirits from India which I have, there was a curious beetle.

I send a ready-cut block: will you kindly insert it in the "*Note Book*," as some of your subscribers may be able to tell me its name, habits, etc. It is rather imperfect, and as I have drawn it as it is, I cannot of course tell what the missing legs &c., would be like.
A SUBSCRIBER.

MICE AS CANNIBALS.—The common mouse is as well known among animals as the house sparrow is among birds; therefore, I need not give a description of it. It feeds greedily on grain, bread, and the like, but I have never known it to touch *meat* of any kind, (raw or cooked) when left within its reach. In a loft I am in the habit of setting a trap that catches mice by the head and kills them at once. One morning I was surprised to find two mice caught, with their hinder quarters entirely eaten away, the fore parts only being left untouched. At first I thought that this must be the work of some other species of animal, but on examining the mutilated bodies, I found I was mistaken, and that it must have been done by their fellow-mice. It was not from necessity that these mice had become *cannibals*, but from choice, as there was abundance of grain kept within their reach. A few nights later I left another pair of mice on the floor of the same room, and in the morning found them nearly consumed. I should like to hear if any of your readers have noticed this curious fact.

Mavisbush House. J. D. S. W.

FLORA OF BUCKS.—We are requested to remind our readers that Mr. James Britten is still continuing his work of collecting materials for the above, and that he will be extremely thankful for any, even the slightest assistance. Mr. Britten states that the number of Flowering Plants and Ferns which are at present recorded for the county is 771; of these a list will shortly be published, which he will be glad to send to any one interested in the work. Regarding the botany of the entire north of the country he is almost wholly ignorant, so that the work does not yet even approach completeness. Communications should be addressed to him at High Wycombe, Bucks.

HOW TO DISTINGUISH LEPIDOPTERA.—Will some kind reader inform a novice how to distinguish the sexes of lepidopteræ irrespective of wing markings? The sexes of many butterflies, for instance, the Painted Lady, Peacock, and Red Admiral, having no distinctive markings, I am quite at a loss how to arrange them properly in a cabinet. W. F.

THE APPROACHING STAR SHOWER.—As a reader of your valuable and interesting "*Note Book*," my attention has been directed to the articles which have appeared from time to time on the subject of Meteoric Showers. Favoured as we are in this locality with great natural advantages for beholding such phenomena, I am anxious to know your opinion as to the probabilities of a recurrence of such a display as was witnessed in November last.

Kensington, Brecon. T. BUTCHER.

[It is probable that there will be this year an exhibition of the November shooting stars, though it is uncertain whether the phenomenon will be so well seen in Europe as it was last year. As a *display* the shower is not likely to be so splendid as it was in 1866, since on November 14th of the present year the moon will be nearly full. However there can be no doubt that the November meteors will be looked for again with great interest, since the discoveries which have been made respecting the orbit in which they move have presented them to us in a new aspect.—RICHARD A. PROCTOR, B.A., F.R.A.S., in *Intellectual Observer*, October.]

THE ANCIENT IRISH ELK.—I would feel grateful to any of your learned correspondents that would tell me when they (Irish Elk) lived, its size and habits, where skeletons have been found, and where they may be seen, what parts of Ireland it frequented most, and have any petrified remains of the Elk been found, &c?

ATLAS.

FROGS AND THEIR FOOD.—Sir, could any of your numerous correspondents inform me what Frogs feed upon when in the Tadpole condition? FOX.

RINGDOVES.—I have a pair of ringdoves in a cage, and I should feel obliged to any of your correspondents if they could tell me whether I should let them out, and if I did so, whether they would return like pigeons. A. B. P.

STATE OF THE WEATHER NEAR LONDON.

Sept. and Oct.	Moon's Age.	Barometer.		Temperature.					Wind	Rain.	Remarks.
				Of the Air.			of the Earth				
		Max.	Min.	Max	Min	Mean	1 foot deep	2 feet deep			
Thurs. 19	21	30.096	30.014	68	49	58.5	60	58	E.	.00	Fine throughout; overcast at night.
Friday 19	22	30.144	30.122	68	47	57.5	59	59	N.	.00	Fine; low white clouds; clear at night.
Satur. 21	☾	30.137	30.009	66	54	60.0	60	59	S.W.	.13	Uniformly overcast; clear and fine; clear.
Sunday 22	24	30.030	29.857	65	38	51.5	59	58	N.W.	.06	Rain; cloudy and fine; clear at night.
Mon. 23	25	30.014	29.887	66	38	52.0	59	58	S.W.	.01	Rain; cloudy, and rather boisterous; clear.
Tues. 24	26	30.376	29.994	69	31	50.0	58	57	N.	.00	Boisterous; masses of dusky white clouds; clear.
Wed. 25	27	30.434	30.391	63	32	47.5	58	57	N.	.00	Partially overcast; fine; clear.
Thurs. 26	28	30.410	30.381	68	33	50.0	57	57	S.E.	.00	Foggy; very fine; overcast.
Friday 27	●	30.298	30.241	64	44	54.0	57	56	S.W.	.00	Slightly overcast; hoar frost early A.M.; clear and fine.
Satur. 28	1	30.298	30.167	66	47	56.5	58	56	S.W.	.00	Fine; cloudy; clear and fine at night.
Sunday 29	2	30.162	30.131	63	46	54.5	57	57	S.W.	.00	Overcast; cloudy; clear and fine.
Mon. 30	3	30.090	29.895	67	36	51.5	57	57	S.W.	.00	Clear; cloudy; clear and very fine.
Tues. 1	4	30.384	30.290	60	32	46.0	56	56	N.	.00	Clear and fine throughout.
Wed. 2	5	30.070	29.980	59	30	44.5	56	56	S.W.	.00	Overcast; cloudy and boisterous; clear, frosty.
Thurs. 3	6	29.942	29.914	57	31	44.0	55	55	N.W.	.00	Fine; fine, with white clouds; clear.
Friday 4	7	30.098	29.097	52	25	38.5	55	55	N.	.00	Fine, but cold and dry; overcast at night.
Satur. 5	☽	30.044	29.978	54	24	39.0	53	54	N.	.00	Clear; quite cloudless; fine; clear and frosty.
Sunday 6	9	29.932	29.828	51	37	44.0	52	53	N.W.	.15	Foggy; rain; overcast at night.
Mon. 7	10	29.612	29.512	60	31	45.5	52	52	W.	.04	Rain showers; clear and frosty; overcast.
Tues. 8	11	29.675	29.509	57	24	40.5	52	52	N.W.	.01	Clear; masses of white clouds; clear and frosty.
Wed. 9	12	29.828	29.567	48	38	43.0	51	52	S.W.	.30	Hoar frost early A.M.; rain; heavy rain at night.
Thurs. 10	13	30.098	29.670	55	26	40.5	51	51	N.	.00	Cloudy and damp; fine; clear and frosty.
Friday 11	14	30.179	29.924	53	38	45.5	51	51	S.W.	.15	Foggy; rain; heavy rain at night.
Satur. 12	15	29.831	29.753	47	33	40.0	51	51	N.E.	.02	Foggy throughout; cold at night.
Sunday 13	○	29.591	29.513	53	38	45.5	51	51	N.W.	.05	Low fog? dull and cloudy; foggy at night.
Mon. 14	17	29.760	29.629	55	45	50.0	51	51	S.	.04	Foggy; cloudy and fine; clear and fine.
Tues. 15	18	29.750	29.730	58	47	52.5	51	51	S.	.20	Cloudy and damp; fine; heavy rain in evening; clear.
Wed. 16	19	29.834	29.783	64	45	54.5	50	52	S.	.00	Cloudy and damp; fine; overcast at night.

METEORS, AËROLITES, AND SHOOTING STARS.

Early Traditions.

 A CAREFUL observer directing his attention towards any quarter of the sky on a clear night, will see on an average six shooting stars per hour. We may assume therefore that about fifteen appear above the horizon of any place during each hour. More appear after than before midnight, the most favourable time for observation being from one o'clock to three. In tropical climates shooting stars are seen oftener, and shine far more brilliantly than in our northern climates. This peculiarity is due no doubt to the superior purity and serenity of the air within and near the tropics, not to any real superiority in the number of falling stars. Sir Alexander Burnes, speaking of the transparency of the dry atmosphere of Bokhara, a place not farther south than Madrid, but raised 1,200 feet above the sea-level, says—"The stars have uncommon lustre, and the Milky Way shines gloriously in the firmament. There is also a never-ceasing display of the most brilliant meteors, which dart like rockets in the sky; ten or twelve of them are sometimes seen in an hour, assuming every colour; fiery-red, blue, pale, and faint." In our climate about two-thirds of all the shooting stars seen are white; next in frequency come yellow stars, one yellow star being seen for about five white stars; there are about twice as many yellow as orange stars, and more than twice as many orange as green or blue stars.

Meteors or fire-balls are far less common than shooting stars. They are magnificent objects, their brilliancy often exceeding that of the full moon. Some, even, have been so brilliant as to cast a shadow in full daylight. They are generally followed by a brilliant luminous train, which seems to be drawn out of the substance of the fire-ball itself. Their motion is not commonly uniform, but (so to speak) impulsive; they often seem to follow a waved or contorted path; their form changes visibly, and in general they disappear with a loud explosion. Occasionally, however, a meteor will be seen to separate without explosion into a number of distinct globes, accompanying each other in parallel courses, and each followed by a train. "Sometimes," says Kaemtz, "a fire-ball is divided into fragments, each of which forms a luminous globe, which then bursts in its turn; in others the mass, after having given vent to the interior gases, closes in upon itself, and then swells out anew to burst a second time." Meteors which move impulsively, generally burst at each bound, giving forth smoke and vapours, and shining afterwards with a new lustre. In some instances the crash of the explosion is so great that "houses tremble, doors and windows open, and men imagine that there is an earthquake."

Aërolites, or meteoric stones, are bodies which fall from the sky upon the earth. They are less common than meteors, but that they are far from being uncommon is shown by this, that in the British Museum alone there are preserved several hundreds of these bodies. They vary greatly in size and form; some being no larger than a man's fist, while others weigh many hundreds of pounds. Marshal Bazaine has lately brought from Mexico a meteorite weighing more than three-quarters of a ton; but this weight has been far exceeded in several cases. Thus a meteorite was presented to the British Museum in 1865, which weighs no less than three and a half tons. It had been found near Melbourne, and one half of the mass had been promised to the Melbourne Museum. But fortunately it was saved from injury. A meteorite weighing one and a quarter tons, which had been found close to the greater one, was transferred from the British to the Melbourne Museum, and the great meteorite forwarded unbroken to our national collection. A yet larger meteorite lies on the plain of Tucuman in South America; it has not been weighed, but measurement shows that its weight cannot fall short of fourteen or fifteen tons. It is from seven to seven and a half feet in length.

There have been twenty well authenticated instances of stone-falls in the British Isles since 1620. One of these took place in the immediate neighbourhood of London, on May 18th, 1680. Besides these, two meteoric stones, not seen to fall, have been found in Scotland.

The Chinese, who recorded everything, give the most ancient records of stone-falls. Their accounts of these phenomena extend to 644 years before our era, their accounts of shooting stars to 687 B.C. We need not remind our classical readers of the stone which fell at Ægos Potamos, B.C. 465, and which was as large as two millstones. In the year 921, there fell at Narni a mass which projected four feet above the river, into which it was seen to fall. There is a Mongolian tradition that there fell from heaven upon a plain near the source of the Yellow River, in Western China, a black rocky mass forty feet high. In 1620, there fell at Jahlinder a mass of meteoric iron, from which the Emperor Jehanhire had a sword forged.

These traditions had long been known, but men were not very ready to accept, without question, the fact that stones and mineral masses actually fall upon the earth from the sky. In 1803 however, a fall of aërolites occurred which admitted of no cavil. On the 26th of April, in that year, a fiery globe was seen to burst into fragments, nearly over the town of L'Aigle, in

Normandy. By this explosion thousands of stones were scattered over an elliptical area seven or 8 miles long, and about 4 miles broad. The stones were hot (but not red-hot) and smoking; the heaviest weighed about seventeen and a half pounds. The sky had been perfectly clear a few moments before the explosion. With a laudable desire to profit by so favourable an opportunity, the French Government sent M. Biot to the scene of the fall. His systematic inquiries and report sufficed to overcome the unbelief which had prevailed on the subject of stone-showers.

Another very remarkable fall is that which took place on October 1st, 1857, in the department of Yonne. Baron Seguier was with some workmen in an avenue of the grounds of Hautefeuille near Charny, when they were startled by several explosions quite unlike thunder, and by strong atmospheric disturbances. Several windows of the chateau were found to be broken. At the same time a proprietor of Chateau-Renard saw a globe of fire "travelling rapidly through the air towards Vernisson." Baron Seguier heard shortly after that at the same hour a shower of aerolites had fallen a few leagues from Hautefeuille, and in a locality lying precisely in the direction towards which the proprietor of Chateau-Renard had seen the meteor travelling. A mason had seen the fall, and narrowly escaped being struck by one of the fragments. This piece, which was found buried deep in the earth, near the foot of the mason's ladder, was presented to the Academy of Sciences by Baron Seguier.

Aërolites often fall from a clear sky. More commonly, however, a dark cloud is observed to form, and the stony shower is seen to be projected from its bosom. It is probable that what appears as a bright train by night is seen as a cloud by day. Something seems to depend on the position of the observer. The meteor which burst over L'Aigle appeared wholly free from cloud or smoke to those who saw it from Alencon, while to observers in L'Aigle the phenomenon was presented of a dark cloud forming suddenly in a clear sky. In a fall which took place near Kleinwinden (not far from Mühlhausen), on September 16th, 1843, a large aerolite descended with a noise like thunder, in a clear sky, and without the formation of any cloud.

The length of time during which fire-balls, which produce aërolites, are visible, has been variously stated; but we have no evidence which would lead us to accept the story of Daïmachos, that the fiery cloud from which the stone of Ægos Potamos was projected had been visible for seventy days in succession. The story seems to identify the author with a certain Daïmachos of Plataea described by Strabo as a "vendor of lies."

There is another singular fiction respecting fire-balls. It was said that shooting stars and meteors were in reality fibrous gelatinous bodies, and that such bodies had been found where meteors had been seen to fall. Reference is not unfrequently made to this fable by writers ancient and modern. Thus Dryden, in his dedication to *The Spanish Friar* speaking of Chapman's *Bussy d'Ambois* says—"I have sometimes wondered in the reading, what was become of those glaring colours which amazed me in *Bussy d'Ambois* upon the theatre; but when I had taken up what I supposed a fallen star, I found I had been cozened with a jelly; nothing but a cold dull mass, which glittered no longer than it was shooting."

One circumstance remains to be mentioned among the results of casual observation. On certain occasions shooting stars have been observed to fall in much greater numbers than on ordinary nights. Among the earliest records of such a phenomenon is the statement by Theophanes, the Byzantine historian, that in November, 472, at Constantinople, the sky seemed to be alive with flying meteors. In the month of October, 902, again, so many falling stars were seen that the year was afterwards called the "year of stars." Conde relates that the Arabs connected this fall with the death of King Ibrahim Ben-Ahmed, which took place on the night of the star shower. The year 1029 was also remarkable for a great star-fall, and in the annals of Cairo it is related that, "In the year 599, in the last Moharrun (October 19, 1202), the stars appeared like waves upon the sky, towards the east and west; they flew about like locusts, and were dispersed from left to right." A shower of stars, accompanied by the fall of several aerolites, took place over England and France, on April 4th, 1095. This was considered by many as a token of God's displeasure with King William II.: "Therefore the kynge was told by divers of his familiars that God was not content with his lyvying; but he was so wilful and proud of mind that he regarded little their saying."—*Cornhill Magazine*, November.

Lines of Projection.

M. HOEK, a Dutch astronomer, has lately shown that comets are often associated in groups, each group coming from some point of space, following nearly the same course, and appearing about the same time. Thus, the third comet of 1860 and the first and sixth comets of 1863 appear to have formed one group. They came, as it were, from the same point of the heavens, and their orbits, when laid down side by side, coalesce in the far distance, as it were, into a single path, just as the trajectories of several shot, fired from the same gun, would coincide in the portions nearest the gun, even if they had otherwise deviated considerably in their flight. The interval of three years between the appearance of the first and the last of the three is a mere point or instant of time in relation to the enormous periods during which their flight endures. A very slight difference among the original projectile forces, whatever they may have been, or a very small perturbation during their passage, by distant suns or systems, would account for much greater intervals. If, as there is good reason to believe, space itself contains a subtle fluid, a minute difference in the densities of the comets would considerably affect the time of their passage through this resisting medium. M. Hoek, on calculating back from the observed elements of their orbits, has found that for more than a thousand years they had been travelling in company. He had thus traced them back to a distance nearly 2000 times that which separates the earth from the sun. Three years on this period, or a few hundreds of millions of miles on this distance, are a mere nothing. Two comets, which appeared in 1677 and 1683, though 180 years before those above referred to, form, nevertheless, part of the same group, so far as regards coincidence in their lines of projection. During 1000 years, however, those two comets had been some 600 millions of miles in advance of the other three. Even this enormous distance, and two centuries of time, may be as nothing to the length and to the duration of the five trajectories; and, though M. Hoek has confined himself to the correlation of comets appearing within periods of ten years, it is not improbable that many of those whose appearances succeed each other after the lapse of centuries, may have been none the less allied to one another in their birth, and none the less close companions in the early portions of their flight. M. Hoek has concluded from his computations, that comets proceed from some of the fixed stars, and move towards our systems in orbits very much elongated. Such of them as are brought within the range of the attraction of our sun, are drawn from their true orbits and made to wheel round him. Under certain conditions of distance and velocity, their new orbits are so far limited in extent that they continue to move round the sun, like planets, periodically reappearing to us. Under other conditions they pass away from our system, perhaps to be caught by some other sun, and retained within his influence. Of all the comets projected from one common focus, like the five above referred to, many may be entrapped by systems on their way, and may never reach ours. The very star from which a group of comets seems to have been projected may have only served to turn them from a course in another, or even an opposite direction.

M. Schiaparelli, of Milan, while engaged in determining the paths of the August and November meteors, found, to his surprise, that they corresponded with the orbits of two comets, one of 1862, and one of 1866. The coincidence led him to study more carefully the orbits, periods, and peculiarities of those comets. The comet of 1862 approached very near to the earth, having crossed, on the 13th of September, a point in our orbit over which the earth had passed on the preceding 10th of August. Had the comet come a month sooner, it might have formed one of the meteors which were then showered upon the earth. At all events, it moved in their line, and probably in their company; and it presented appearances, varying from day to day, more like a meteor with a trail, shooting now from one side, now from the other, than like an ordinary comet. The period of this body has been computed to be about 108 years, and this appears to correspond with that of the August meteors. It is not, however, very easy to fix a definite period for them, because when they do appear they recur for some twenty or thirty years successively. Moreover, their course through our system must subject them to perturbations, varying in direction and quantity, according to the ever-varying positions of the planets near which they pass.

The meteors of November have a period of thirty-three years, and follow a path which coincides with that of the comet discovered by M. Tempel, at Marseilles, in 1866. And other meteoric showers have been traced to coincidence with other cometic orbits. It has also been observed that comets moving round our sun periodically, undergo a degradation, as if they were continually parting with substance. In 1845, Gambart's comet became divided into two—a large and a small one—which both returned together in 1852, but have not since appeared. Donati's comet evidently shed its substance in a trail along its path; and there are numerous other examples of that degradation and diminution in volume and luminosity which appear to be common to all comets. It is, therefore, by no means improbable that the inter-stellar spaces have comet-dust scattered through them, and that this comet-dust, when it passes through our atmosphere, may form the shooting stars. It might be too bold to affirm that the larger meteors, with their balls and trails, are comets themselves.

M. Schiaparelli supposes that a cloud of matter, cometic or cosmic dust as it were, moves from some distant region of space in a straight line, or at least in a line which is a portion of an orbit so elongated that it may be taken as straight. On approaching our system, this cloud is, by the sun's attraction, drawn out into an extended current, as may be readily understood on considering the superior attractive force exerted upon its front portions. So immense is this dust-cloud, that, when thus wire-drawn, as it were it may take thousands of years in effecting its passage through our system. The form of the current is necessarily that of a comit's orbit; for the law which governs the movements of one particle, governs the movements of all. If this orbit crosses that of the earth once a year, the earth must pass through the torrent, and gather, to itself all such particles as come within the influence of its attraction. Such, probably, are the meteors and shooting-stars of August and November. These, however, do not form parts of torrents coming from distant space, but wheel round the sun with definite periods, like long elliptical rings, through which we pass annually, levying our tribute as we pass. It is, however, extremely difficult to ascertain correctly the elements of these orbits, because the bodies which move in them are subject to extensive perambulations, and are so minute as to escape observation, except when they are almost in contact with the earth.—*Scientific Review*, November.

Principal Star Showers.

IT will probably be interesting if we give brief notices of a few of the principal authentic November star-showers. It is from these data that the first approximation of the period of revolution of this cosmical ring has been obtained. Most writers on this subject have already alluded to these phenomena recorded here and there in old histories. We do not, however, hesitate to reproduce one or two of them once more. The dates of recorded November star-showers are the years 902, 931, 934, 1002, 1101, 1202, 1366, 1533, 1602, 1698, 1799, 1832, 1833, 1866. Conde, in his "History of the Dominion of the Arabs in Spain," mentions that on the death of King Ibrahim bin Ahmad, in the year 902, about the middle of October, O.S., "an infinite number of stars were seen during the night, scattering themselves like rain to the right and left, and that year was known as the year of the stars." An Arab writer relates of the same phenomenon that "in this year there happened in Egypt an earthquake, lasting from the middle of the night until morning; and so-called flaming stars struck one against another violently, while being borne eastward and westward, northward and southward; and none could bear to look towards the heavens." These accounts from Mohammedan sources, though bearing evident marks of superstition and exaggerated observation, are sufficient to show that a probable unusual meteoric display took place in the year indicated.

We have another Mohammedan record that "in the year 599 (A.D. 1202), on the night of Saturday, on the last day of Muharram, stars shot hither and thither in the heavens, eastward and westward, and flew against one another, like a scattered swarm of locusts, to the right and left. This phenomenon lasted until daybreak. People were thrown into consternation, and cried to God the Most High with confused clamour; the like of it never happened except in the year of the mission of the Prophet, and in the year 241."

Any unusual celestial phenomenon was always considered in former ages as some omen portending good or evil to the nation. This superstitious feeling is clearly shown in an extract from a Portuguese work, "Chronicas des Reis de Portugal Reformadas," 1660, relating to an unusual star-shower. "In the year 1366, and xxii days of the month of October (O.S.) being past, there was in the heavens a movement of stars, such as men never before saw or heard of. From midnight onwards, all the stars moved from the east to the west; and after being together, they began to move, some in one direction, and others in another. And afterwards they fell from the sky in such numbers, and so thickly together, that as they descended low in the air they seemed large and fiery, and the sky and the air seemed to be in flames, and even the earth appeared ready to take fire. That portion of the sky where there were no stars seemed to be divided into many parts, and this lasted for a long time. Those that saw it were filled with such great fear and dismay that they were astounded, imagining they were all dead men, and that the end of the world had come." It appears to us that this apparently improbable account may be sensibly true, and that the meteoric display might have been accompanied by a coloured aurora, the streamers of which, with very little imagination, would be suggestive of fire.

It is not necessary to notice any more of these ancient meteoric showers, excepting only to state that the dates have been satisfactorily proved, and that they have done good service as data for modern calculations.

Of modern displays, Humboldt's description of that of November 12, 1799, as seen by him and M. Bonpland at Cumana, South America, is well known. During four hours, thousands of falling stars were noticed. M. Bonpland states that there was not a space in the firmament equal in extent to three diameters of the moon, that was not filled at every instant with bodies and falling stars. The meteors were visible till sunrise. The same phenomena were observed at other places in South America, some distant 700 miles from Cumana.

It must be understood that the small cosmical bodies composing the November ring of meteors move in orbits, which cut the plane of the ecliptic near the point occupied by our earth about the 13th of November, and consequently, can only be seen yearly about that day. And it must also be borne in mind that the smaller showers of meteors which are frequently observed at other periods of the year belong to a collection of meteors moving around the sun in orbits, inclined at different angles to the ecliptic, each system differing from another. In short, it has been found from observation that there are several of these rings or systems crossing the earth's path at different periods of the year, the November and August meteors being the most numerous. From this we may naturally infer that these bodies only become visible on entering the earth's atmosphere, being rendered luminous by the great heat developed by friction, when they burn for a second or two, and are then finally dissipated into smoke or dust.

On account of the apparent rapid motion of meteors, the only satisfactory observations made during great displays are those for the determination of the point in the heavens from which they radiate. This apparent orbital velocity is ascertained to be about thirty-eight miles a second, made up by the compound effect of the movements of the earth and the meteors in their respective orbits, that of the earth being direct, while that of the meteors is retrograde. But when, as in the case of the great shower of last November, the observer is enabled to multiply his observations almost to an indefinite extent, this great velocity does not materially interfere in obtaining a correct determination of the exact position of the radiant point. On the accuracy of our knowledge of the position of this point almost everything depends in the calculation of the dimensions and position in space of the meteoric orbit. It does not, however, require a practised astronomer to notice that, on such a display as that of November last, the majority of the meteors eminated from one spot in the heavens, for that was soon evident to the senses of the most casual observer. It is found, from the average of the observations made by six astronomers, that the exact position of this radiant point of the November meteors is 149° 12' of right ascension, and 23° 1' of north declination. Any person having access to a celestial globe or map can identify for himself this position in a moment. He will see that it is situated between the well-known stars Regulus and Epsilon Leonis. From this accurately-observed radiant point of the November meteors much of our present knowledge of the movement of these bodies is derived. It may be mentioned here that the radiant point of the August meteors is situated in the constellation Perseus. Of meteors in general, about sixty radiant points have been determined with more or less certainty: some of these have, however, been inferred from isolated observations of meteors noticed on the same day in different years.—*Leisure Hour*, November.

Effects of Acid on Meteoric Iron.

SOME interesting particulars concerning aëroliths are given in a series of articles published by the "Cosmos" on the subject. Widmanstætten was the first to discover a singular peculiarity of meteoric iron when treated with acids. We know that if we let fall a drop of one of the latter on a plate of polished terrestrial iron, the polish will be destroyed and replaced by a finely grained surface. This is not the case with meteoric iron; the place where the acid exercises its action will display a variety of complicated figures remarkable for their great regularity. They consist of brilliant lines crossing each other at different angles, and distinctly set off on the dull ground made by the acid on the polished surface. As these lines are in relief they may be printed off on paper. They are owing to the crystallization of the mass, which also contains small and regularly oriented laminæ of a substance insoluble in acids, and which Berzelius has found to be a double phosphuret of iron and nickel containing a proportion of magnesium. This compound is called "Schreibersite;" but the figures it produces are not always regular in all meteorites. This is the case with the iron found at Scriba, in 1814, and at Decotah, U.S., in 1863. That of Caille, on the contrary, discovered in 1828, by Brard, by the side of the church portal, where it had for two centuries past performed the office of a seat, and was called by the people the iron stone, presents these figures with remarkable clearness; the same is the case with the iron found in 1792, at Zacatecas, Mexico. In April last, M. Daubree discovered some new peculiarities in meteoric iron. A polished plate of this substance dipped into an acid may be considered as constituting a voltaic couple. The contact of the liquid with metallic substances which it attacks, unequally developes a current proceeding in the liquid from the impressionable metal to the unimpressionable one, and in the iron mass from the latter to the former. In Widmanstætten's experiments, the existence of this current merely hastens the dissolution of the impressionable metal, but without manifesting its action to the eye of the observer. But the effect is very different when the solution of a metal capable of precipitation is substituted for the acid. The sulphate of bioxide of copper is admirably calculated to reveal the effect, on account of the colour of the copper, which contrasts with that of the iron. No sooner is the polished plate immersed into the saline solution, than the network formed by the needles of the phosphuret of iron and nickel appears in red on the white surface of the pure iron A moment later, a sort of copper ring is deposited round each of the coppered needles; and immediately after, an instantaneous deposit of copper covers the whole surface, which, until then, had remained bare. If this surface be now washed with ammonia, to get rid of the copper, the schreibersite reappears with its long parallel needles, and surrounded with the oblong rings that now appear whiter than the rest of the mass, which has assumed a greyish tint.

Composition of Aërolites.

There is an interesting article on aëroliths by M. Stanislas Meunier, from which the following facts are gleaned. Among the meteorites in which iron is reduced to the state of particles disseminated throughout a silicated mass, the blocks of the Sierra de Chaco, in the desert of Atacami, Chili, deserve particular notice, as being particularly rich in metallic particles. The point where they are to be met with is, according to M. Domeyko, situated at 10 leagues southeast of the silver mines of La Isla, near the copper mines of Taltal. The largest are slightly imbedded in the soil, and are of an irregular spheroidal shape. Their density, according to M. Domeyko, who has devoted much attention to them, is 5·64. They contain three different substances, viz.:—1, a lithoid ash-grey substance, constituting the principal mass: 2, a malleable metal in tuberculous grains; and 3, a vitreous lamellated silicate of great brilliancy. The fracture of the first of these substances has a somewhat shining surface, as if it were resinous. If reduced to powder the magnet will separate from it about 15 per cent. of iron dust, consisting of oxide and pure or carburetted metal. The lithoid mass also contains protosulphuret of iron; acids will partially attack it, the soluble part is a double trisilicate of magnesia and iron, known under the name of "shepardite." The metallic particles disseminated throughout the mass consist of about 89 parts of iron and 11 of nickel, with traces of calcium and phosphorus. As for the lamellated silicate, it is soluble in acids, and contains a little lime and alumina, silica, protoxide of iron, and magnesia, in the proportion constituting peridote. Among the meteorites of our museums there are some bearing a strong analogy to each other; these constitute a separate group, called "the common type." These, when not broken, have a dull and fretted crust or varnish; their fracture, however, is granulated and gray, and the general appearance is that of certain finely grained domites or trachites, although their composition is quite different, the common type of aëroliths consisting chiefly of nickeliferous iron.

Are Comets and Meteors identical.

At the recent meeting of the British Association this new theory was prominently put forth by Professor A. Herschel. The November and August meteors are found to move in orbits coincident with those of well-known comets; therefore it is argued that comets and meteors are the same, or that "the meteoric particles are portions of the comet's tail, shreds of a dismembered mist, torn by the sun's disturbing action from the nucleus of the comet, and left upon its path like embers or smoke-flakes in the track of an expiring flame." All this may be very sublime, but it seems to be rather a jump at a hasty conclusion. There is nothing surprising in the alleged coincidence in the orbit of certain meteoric swarms with that of comets. Both are *erratic* bodies, and therefore it is but reasonable that their courses should be alike. But the nature of the bodies is totally different, if we may believe what we find recorded by the most eminent astronomers. Comets have been described as nothing more than a conglomoration of vapours, of very little density, so little perhaps as to be transparent—stars having been seen even through their nucleus, or most brilliant, and, apparently, solidest part. Such bodies might very possibly be incipient worlds, just passed their gaseous state, and which are to derive solidity from the participation and condensation of the matter surrounding them. But our meteors are manifestly fragmentary bodies, just as indicative of a disruption or breaking into pieces as the fragments of rocks in a quarry. They are described as being composed more or less of silica (flint), oxide of iron, magnesia, oxide of nickel, sulphur, and lime—all which are substances which Professor Tyndall would say have been *dead* long ago—just as the same substances on our earth. Moreover, that wonderful thing, *carbon*, has been detected in them. Now, the presence of carbon anywhere necessarily implies at least *vegetation*; and therefore it is quite reasonable to conclude that the meteoric fragments containing it must have formed part of an earth constituted similarly to our own, but subsequently disrupted, shattered into fragments. Our moon may be only a larger block of such a dismembered world, large enough and endowed with just sufficient velocity to become a companion to our earth in her orbit, without tumbling upon her, like so many of the smaller fragments. Such are a few of the considerations which seem to militate against this new Meteor-Cometic Theory—especially as astronomers seem to agree in considering the hundred asteroids between Mars and Jupiter as "bits of planets blown to pieces," together with the fact, common with the meteors, "that some of them appear not to be round," as other bodies in the firmament.—*People's Magazine*, Nov.

THE FOOD OF THE ROBIN.—*FURDUS MIGRATORIUS.*—LINNÆUS.

AT a meeting of the Boston Society of Natural History (America) a communication was read from Professor Tredwell, of Cambridge, giving a detailed account of the feeding and growth of this bird, during a period of thirty-two days, commencing with the 5th of June. The following is the substance of this report:—

When caught, the two were quite young, their tail feathers being less than an inch in length, and the weight of each about twenty-five pennyweights, less than half the weight of the full-grown birds. Both were plump and vigorous, and had evidently been very recently turned out of the nest.

He began feeding them with earthworms, giving three to each bird that night. The second day he gave them ten worms each, which they ate ravenously. Thinking this beyond what their parents could naturally supply them with, he limited them to this allowance. On the third day he gave them eight worms each in the forenoon, but in the afternoon he found one becoming feeble, and it soon lost its strength, refused food, and died. On opening it he found the provenbriculus, gizzard, and intestines entirely empty, and concluded therefore, that it died from want of sufficient food, the effect of hunger being increased perhaps by the cold, as the thermometer was about sixty degrees.

The other bird, still vigorous, he put in a warmer place, and increased its food, giving it the third day fifteen worms, on the fourth day twenty-four, on the fifth twenty-five, on the sixth thirty, and on the seventh thirty-one worms. They seemed insufficient, and the bird appeared to be losing plumpness and weight. He began to weigh both the bird and its food, and the results were given in a tabular form. On the fifteenth day he tried a small quantity of raw meat, and, finding it readily eaten, increased it gradually, to the exclusion of worms; with it the bird ate a large quantity of earth and gravel, and drank freely after eating. By the table, it appears that though the food was increased to forty worms, weighing twenty pennyweights, on the eleventh day the weight of the bird rather fell off, and it was not until the fourteenth day, when he ate sixty-eight worms, or thirty-four pennyweights, that he began to increase. On this day the weight of the bird was twenty-four pennyweights; he therefore ate forty-one per cent. more than his own weight in twelve hours, weighing after it twenty-nine pennyweights, or fifteen per cent. less than the food he had eaten in that time. The length of these worms, if laid end to end, would be about fourteen feet, or ten times the length of the intestines.

To meet the objection, that the earthworm contains but a small quantity of nutritious matter, on the twenty-seventh day he was fed exclusively on clear beef, in quantity twenty-seven pennyweights. At night, the bird weighed fifty-two pennyweights, but little more than twice the amount of flesh consumed during the day, not taking into account the water and earth swallowed. This presents a wonderful contrast with the amount of food required by the cold-blooded vertebrates, fishes, and reptiles, many of which can live for months without food, and also with that required by mammalia. Man, at this rate, would eat about seventy pounds of flesh a day, and drink five or six gallons of water.

The question immediately presents itself, how can this immense amount of food, required by the young birds, be supplied by the parents? Suppose a pair of old robins, with the usual number of four young ones. These would require, according to the consumption of this bird, two hundred and fifty worms, or their equivalent in insect or other food, daily.

Suppose the parents to work ten hours, or six hundred minutes, to procure this supply; this would be a worm to every two and two-fifths of a minute, or each parent must procure a worm or its equivalent, in less than five minutes during ten hours, in addition to the food required for its own support.

After the thirty-second day, the bird had attained its full size, and was intrusted to the care of another person during his absence of eighteen days. At the end of that period, the bird was strong and healthy, with no increase of weight, though its feathers had grown longer and smoother. Its food had been weighed daily, and averaged fifteen pennyweights of weight, two or three earthworms, and a small quantity of bread, each day, the whole being equal to eighteen pennyweights of meat, or thirty-six pennyweights of earthworms, and it continued up to the time of the presentation of the report. The bird having continued in confinement, with certainly much less exercise than in the wild state, to eat one-third of its weight in clear flesh daily, the Professor concludes that the food it consumed when young was not much more than must always be provided by the parents of wild birds. The food was never passed undigested; the excretions were made up of gravel and dirt, and a small quantity of semi-solid urine.

He thought that every admirer of trees may derive from these facts, a lesson, showing the immense power of birds to destroy the insects by which our trees, especially our apple-trees, elms, and lindens, are every few years stripped of their foliage, and many of them killed.

"The food of the robin," the Professor says, "while with us, consists principally of worms and various insects, their larvæ and eggs, and a few cherries. Of worms and cherries they can procure but few, and those during but a short period, and they are obliged, therefore, to subsist principally upon the great destroyers of leaves—canker-worms, and some other kinds of caterpillars and bugs. If each robin, old and young, requires for its support an amount of these equal to the weight consumed by this bird, it is easy to see what a prodigious havoc a few hundred of these must make upon the insects of an orchard or nursery.—*Edward A. Samuels' Ornithology of New England.*

THE LUMINOSITY OF THE SEA.

I WOULD classify all the cases of luminosity which have come under my observation under the following five heads:—
1. Sparks or points of light.
2. A soft, liquid, phosphorescent effulgence.
3. Moon-shaped patches of steady light.
4. Instantaneous recurrent flashes.
5. Milky sea.

The first of these, or the appearance of points or sparks of light, is by far the most common, and in different degrees may be said to be all but universal. Whether the other forms of luminosity are exhibited or not, sparks of light in greater or less abundance are scarcely ever absent. The sea, more particularly when agitated, sparkles with brilliant points of light, varying in size from that of a pin's head to that of a pea—and of greater or lesser permanency— some being almost instantly extinguished, while others retain their light for an appreciable time. I do not think I ever looked at the sea on a dark night without seeing some few sparks, even though I might enter a remark that the sea was "*not* luminous to-night." But usually these sparks are abundant, and on occasions they present a wonderfully brilliant appearance. On one occasion, when this phenomenon was unusually striking, on the coast of China in lat. 26° N., on drawing up bottles full of water and pouring it out in the dark, the water sparkled brightly as luminous points ran over, but a close inspection revealed nothing in the water but a few minute entomostraca. On another occasion when some water which had been left in a basin exhibited luminosity at night, I got a very brilliant spark upon my finger, and taking it to the light, it proved to be a minute crustacean.

The second form of luminosity to be noticed occurs comparatively rarely. It consists of a soft, usually greenish light, which only makes its appearance when smooth water is disturbed, and is only seen in calm weather. This form appears identical with what we see nearer home, as on the shores of Ostend and in the estuary of the Mersey. This form of luminosity I have observed on only three occasions, and under similar circumstances, and I have reason to believe that the cause is the same on all occasions, whether in the Eastern seas or in the Mersey. On the 5th of July being on the coast of China, in lat. 27°, the weather in the afternoon became dead calm, and after sunset I remarked that the sea was beautifully luminous, but altogether without conspicuous sparks or points of light. Wherever the ripples caused by the advancing ship rolled away, they were crested with bright green light, and the ship's hull appeared to be enveloped in a luminous sheath. On this occasion the effect did not last long, and I did not examine the water microscopically.

The next time I noticed this form of luminosity was in Singapore harbour, on November 6th. The wind was east, thermometer 76°, weather fine. The water was like glass, smooth and beautiful, but exhibited no light except when disturbed; but every oar-stroke of the boat in which I rowed produced eddying circles of light, and a lovely soft green glow crowned every ripple from the bows. A splash in the water produced a shower of a myriad minute sparks, the aggregate of which made up this delicate luminosity, which I never saw so beautifully exhibited as upon this night. The following night the same effect was visible, but scarcely so intense as before (wind N.E., temp. 76°), and on the third night (the wind being E. and temp. 75°), I again observed it. After this I was absent from Singapore two nights, and on my return I no longer noticed the luminous effect.

On each of these three nights I examined the water;—as I filled a bottle, bright sparks of light adhered to my hands, and on bringing it to the light I found that it contained a number of small globular greenish bodies, which floated upon the surface for the most part, but appeared to have the power of freely moving in the water. On closer examination these bodies proved to be *Noctilucæ*; and during the night I observed that the contents of the bottle frequently flashed with bright and rapid coruscations. I had no difficulty therefore in coming to the conclusion that the peculiar luminosity in the harbour was due to the presence of innumerable *Noctilucæ*.

On the 24th of May, lying in Simon's Bay,

Cape of Good Hope, the water was similarly luminous. The weather was fine, wind W.N.W. light, bar. 30·04, thermom. 60°. On examining the water closely I found that, as before, the luminous effect, though soft, subdued, and apparently uniform, was really due to innumerable small sparks, and on bringing the water to the light, I found numerous *Noctilucæ* in it, precisely similar to those observed at Singapore. They were not, however, in sufficient numbers to have produced all the light, for in a wine-glassful of water there were on an average not more than a dozen *Noctilucæ*. But besides these bodies, there were a great number of motes in the water, many of which on closer examination appeared, by their rapid jerking locomotion, to be minute Entomostracous Crustacea. They were so minute, that by the imperfect light on board ship I long tried, in vain, to secure one to place under the microscope. Besides these were some larger species of Entomostraca.

The *Noctilucæ* measured from $\frac{1}{275}$ to $\frac{1}{325}$ of an inch in diameter; they were of a pale greenish colour when seen with the naked eye, closely resembling Volvox in appearance, but with a much less active movement. They had, however, powers of locomotion, though the means were not apparent under the microscope. They had a dark nucleus, usually irregular, but in some cases spherical and well defined. Their circumferential outline was very faint, and their general aspect very variable. A kind of slit appeared to extend through two-thirds of the body, from which faint lines radiated, usually having a double outline, and not reaching the circumference of the sphere, but often terminating in large round granular bodies of various sizes. The whole body was studded with oil globules of various sizes, which strongly refracted the light; but slight movements, which appeared to be taking place in an almost imperceptible manner, soon changed the whole aspect of any individual Noctiluca while under observation, so that the description or drawing of one minute did not answer for the next. Each Noctiluca had a large curved cilium projecting beyond the body, and apparently taking its rise from the nucleus. This form of luminosity, although very striking, appears to be completely extinguished by moonlight, even when the moon is young. It appeared, only less marked, on the two following evenings, and on the third we left the bay. I am informed that Simon's Bay has been remarked as frequently exhibiting this phenomenon.

On the 7th of July, in lat. 28° N., on the coast of China, two days after the occurrence of this form of luminosity, as before noticed, a heavy swell coming in from the S.W. was met by a N.E. wind, and the ship rolled tremendously. The sea was beautifully luminous, every wave breaking into a pale light which was visible at a considerable distance, so that the whole sea was streaked with light, and again that peculiar phenomenon of the ship sailing in a luminous sheath was visible. The night was very dark, and it was lightning vividly and incessantly; the whole scene was eery and weird in the extreme. I mention this case because it was one of the most striking instances of general luminosity which has come under my notice; it appeared to be compounded of the two forms I have already described.

The third form of luminosity to be described consists of moon-shaped patches of steady white light, which I have found to be a very common phenomenon under certain circumstances. Next to the occurrence of sparks and always accompanied by them, this form of luminosity is most frequently seen, and does not appear to be confined to any particular locality. I first observed it in the Mediterranean, on the first night on which the absence of the moon allowed it to be visible, and I have since found it to be no less frequent in the Red Sea, the Indian Ocean, the China Sea, and the Atlantic, north and south of the equator. It is most commonly visible in the wake of the ship, and consists of numerous round patches of light, which might be mistaken for white-hot shot of various sizes beneath the water at different depths. Sometimes, when deep down, they were pale and of a whitish colour, with indistinct outline, and of large size, but when nearer the surface they were smaller and more distinct, and assumed a pale greenish tinge. They usually remained visible for eight or ten seconds, but sometimes less. As these appearances were just such as might be presented by the umbrellas of large *Medusæ*, were such present and luminous, I was strongly inclined at first to attribute them to this cause; and the fact that on one occasion (about a week after I left England) I saw these moonlight patches in the Red Sea on the evening of a day on which the ship had passed through a shoal of *Aureliæ*, led me to attribute them to this cause. I supposed that the *Aureliæ*, struck by the screw, gave out their light under the excitation of the blow, and floated away luminous and dying. But I was forced to abandon this theory afterwards, for I have since many times watched for floating *Medusæ* before the light failed, and not seen one for days and weeks together, and yet the moon-shaped patches have been as bright and as abundant as before; and again, when we have passed through a thick shoal of *Medusæ* towards evening, the luminous appearances have not been more marked than usual, but even less so. Moreover, having secured one of the Acalephs, it has not exhibited any luminosity during the night.

Although, however, I ceased to regard the *Acalephæ* as the source of the luminous appearances in question, there can be no doubt that the great numbers which are always visible immediately under the stern are due to the fact of the eddies of the ship exciting the emission of light in certain animals capable of exhibiting luminosity. Not however that similar appearances are never seen in other situations where they are unmolested, though I must say that in my experience this is rare. Thus in the Indian ocean, in lat. $12\frac{1}{3}°$ N. and long. $55°$ E. (bar $30°$, them. $82°$), among other appearances I noticed now and then a large patch of light with a roundish irregular outline pass by, emitting a pale and steady light, although out of the path of the ship; and on August 17th, being in a small boat on the coast of Borneo in a strong breeze after dark, I observed deep beneath the surface and entirely apart from any influence of the oars, the appearance of large globes of white light, shining persistently and spontaneously.

Although I long and constantly watched for the bodies which produced this remarkable and frequent luminous effect, I did so for a long time in vain. In vain I attempted to penetrate below the surface in search of any animals which could possibly originate the light. Although I could distinctly see the bottom of the ship's rudder, 19 feet deep, I could never detect a trace of any living thing within that depth by day, but no sooner did darkness supervene than they were often in abundance. It was only by accident, on June the 2nd, in lat. $28\frac{1}{2}°$ S., and long. $9°$ E., that I was witness of a circumstance which seemed to elucidate the question. Looking as usual over the stern, there were plenty of moon-shaped patches, accompanied by sparks unusually large and bright. The patches were remarkably persistent, and could be traced for nearly half a minute after the ship had passed. They were evidently a considerable but varying distance below the surface of the water; when far down they appeared large and faint and ill defined, but when nearer the surface they were smaller, brighter, and better defined. As I watched, one of the bright bodies whirled about by the eddy of the rudder came absolutely to the surface and exhibited a nearly rectangular form of great brilliancy, of a pale green colour, and as far as I could judge about six inches long by two broad. It at once occurred to me that it was a Pyrosoma, and that this Ascidian was the usual cause of the phenomenon, the circular form of the patches being produced by the diffusion of the light through a depth of water. I continued watching for a long time in hopes of seeing another, but although so good an opportunity did not occur again, many seemed to come near the surface, diminishing in size, but increasing in brilliancy as they did so; one particularly low down suddenly gave out a dazzling brilliancy, producing a momentary effulgence all around.

I may mention that on a moonlight night when the moon has been dimmed by fleecy clouds, I have been able to see the moonlight patches, but when the moon shone out clearly they were no longer visible.

I have now to describe the fourth form of luminosity exhibited by marine animals, *viz.* momentary recurrent flashes of light. This form is nearly as commonly seen as the moon-shaped patches already described, which it very frequently, although perhaps not always, accompanies. If, however, the latter are well marked, the flashes are almost sure to be visible. I first observed them in the Indian ocean, north of the line, and since then, in the China seas and Atlantic. This appearance is very striking, but can only be seen under favourable circumstances, *i.e.* when the night is dark and the sea smooth. An indistinct transitory patch of light appears in the water, as evanescent as a flash of lightning; so rapidly does it come and go that it is difficult to fix the exact spot where it occurred. The brightness of the flash varies probably according to the depth of the animal producing it below the surface; sometimes it is of considerable brilliancy, and sometimes so pale that it would not have been noticed but for its suddenness. The colour is always whitish, and the form of the flash round, brightest in the middle, and becoming indistinct at the circumference. I have on some occasions seen these flashes occur in such numbers and with such rapidity that it would be impossible to count them, though more commonly they are comparatively few and far between.

But the fact which interested me most in these flashes of light was that they always occurred at a distance from the path of the ship. Although I have seen them accompanying the moon-shaped patches of light in the ship's wake, the places from which I could best observe the flashes were the forecastle or the gangways, when they could be seen in the smooth water several yards distant from the ship's side, and entirely uninterfered with by the ship's motion. This fact proved to me that there were spontaneous emissions of light by some animals below the surface, which voluntarily and at intervals gave out a bright coruscation. Moreover, although rarely, on following with the eye the spot where the flash appeared, it could be seen to reappear further astern, as though the emission was recurrent at different intervals, as is the case with the luminous beetles called fireflies at Singapore. I have also noticed on more than one occasion that the flash, instead of instantly disappearing, was followed by a faint glow which vanished gradually, but whether this was an optical illusion of the retina or not, I cannot be sure.

Whatever may be the animals which produce these luminous appearances, they must habitually swim at a considerable depth. I never was able to make out any definite outline of the light, which always appeared more or less spherical with faint edges, and sometimes the size and faintness of the flashes seemed to prove that the light must have been diffused by its passage through a great depth of water, which would also account for the whitish appearance of what is probably really greenish light. But I am strongly disposed to believe that the sources of the flashes and of the moon-shaped patches are identical; in the one case emitting their light spontaneously, and in the other, under the excitation of the eddies produced by the ship, and especially by the screw-propeller when at work.

Before quitting the subject of these flashes, I must not omit to mention that while at Singapore, having taken some small *Medusæ* in a towing-net in the Straits, I placed them in a glass which stood by my bedside. In the night I observed them flashing brightly with instantaneous flashes, of the same character as those above referred to, although not the slightest shaking was applied to the bottle, or irritation to the animals. So also the *Noctilucæ* of Singapore harbour, which I kept similarly in a bottle, flashed frequently with rapid and bright coruscations; and I am strongly disposed to believe that luminous marine animals in health, and acting spontaneously, without external irritation, always exhibit their luminosity in this manner, and that it is only when strong excitation is applied that they give out a steady but temporary glow.

There remains but one form of luminosity to be noticed, which although I have never been so fortunate as to witness it myself, has been observed by others, who have been longer at sea than I. This is what has been called *milky sea*, an extraordinary phenomenon of rare occurrence. It has been described to me as a general luminous glow, not confined to the crests of ripples or to disturbed water, but occurring in perfectly calm weather, and looking as though the whole sea was composed of a whitish fluid like milk, with no bright spots or sparks. Such an appearance reflecting a faint light upwards illuminates the ship, rendering every part of the rigging plainly visible, and inasmuch as it can only be seen in the absence of the moon, the contrast of the white glowing sea with the black sky produces an effect calculated to strike the observer with a kind of awe. Although I have met with persons who tell me they have not unfrequently seen this phenomenon, I am disposed to believe that it is extremely rare. One who has not really seen it all might erroneously suppose, that such an appearance as I have already alluded to as having twice occurred to me on the coast of China (when the ship seemed to be sailing in a luminous sheath) corresponded to the description of a milky sea, and in a small way it did so, and I considered it at the time as the nearest approach to it I had ever observed. But the milky sea must be something *sui generis*, and I imagine it to be owing rather to a condition of the water under certain peculiar atmospheric or climatic influences than to any extraordinary number of luminous animals in the water. A circumstance which occurred to me seemed to throw some light upon the subject and confirmed me in this opinion. Having put down the towing-net in the Formosa Channel it collected a number of small entomostraca, megalopas, minute medusæ, small porpitæ, pteropods, annelids, globigerinæ, &c., which I placed in a basin of sea water, and not having finished my examination of them they remained upon the table during the night. On stirring the water in the dark the whole became faintly luminous, giving out a general glow as if every particle were phosphorescent, the minute crustacea, &c., appearing as bright spots in the luminous fluid. If the slimy substance, in which in some marine animals at least the luminous property appears to reside, become diffused through the water, as it is probable it may be under certain combinations of conditions and circumstances, a general luminosity of the water may result, similar to that observed in milky sea, while its small sparks, doubtless in great abundance, would remain unnoticed in the universal glow, but would at the same time greatly enhance the general luminous effect.—*The Quarterly Journal of Science*, October. London: Churchill.

THE CLOTHES-MOTH.

FOR over a fortnight we once enjoyed the company of the caterpillar of a common Clothes-moth. It is a little pale delicate worm about the size of a darning needle, not half an inch long, with a pale horn-coloured head, the ring next the head being of the same color, and has sixteen feet, the first six of them well developed and constantly in use to draw the slender body in and out of its case. Its head is armed with a formidable pair of jaws, with which, like a scythe, it mows its way through thick and thin.

But the case is the most remarkable feature in the history of this caterpillar. Hardly has the helpless, tiny worm broken the egg, previously laid in some old garment of fur, or wool, or perhaps in the hair-cloth of a sofa, when it proceeds to make a shelter by cutting the woolly fibres or soft hairs up into bits, which it places at each end in successive layers, and joining them together by silken threads, constructs a cylindrical tube of thick, warm felt, lined within with the finest silk the tiny worm can spin. The case is hardly round, but flattened slightly in the middle, and contracted a little just before each end, both of which are always kept open. The case before us is of a stone-grey color, with a black stripe along the middle, and with rings of the same color round each opening. Had the caterpillar fed on blue or yellow cloth, the case would, of course have been of those colors. Other cases, made by larvæ which had been eating "cotton wool," were quite irregular in form, and covered loosely with bits of cotton thread which the little tailor had not trimmed off.

Days go by. A vigorous course of dieting on its feast of wool has given stature to our hero. His case has grown uncomfortably small. Shall he leave it and make another?—No housewife is more prudent and saving. Out come those scissor-jaws, and, lo! a fearful rent along each side of one end of the case. Two wedge-shaped patches mend the breach,—caterpillar retires for a moment; reappears at the other end; scissors once more pulled out; two rents to be filled up by two more patches or gores, and our caterpillar once more breathes freer, laughs and grows fat upon horse hair and lamb's wool. In this way he enlarges his case till he stops growing.

Our caterpillar seeming to be full-grown, and hence out of employment, we cut the end of his case half off. Two or three days after, he had mended it from the inside, drawing the two edges together by silken threads, and, though he had not touched the outside, yet so neatly were the two parts joined together that we had to search for some time with a lens, to find the scar.

To keep our friend busy during the cold, cheerless weather, for it was in mid-winter, we next cut a third of the case off entirely. Nothing daunted, the little fellow bustled about, drew in a mass of the woolly fibres, filling up the whole mouth of his den, and began to build on afresh, and from the inside, so that the new-made portion was smaller than the rest of the case. The creature worked very slowly, and the addition was left in a rough, unfinished state.

We could easily spare these voracious little worms hairs enough to serve as food, and to afford material for the construction of their paltry cases; but that restless spirit that ever urges on all beings endowed with life and the power of motion, never forsakes the young Clothes-moth for a moment. He will not be forced to drag his heavy case over rough hairs and furzy wool, hence he cuts his way through with those keen jaws. Thus, the more he travels, the more mischief he does.

After taking his fill of this sort of life he changes to a pupa, and soon appears as one of those delicate, tiny, but richly variegated moths that fly in such numbers from early in the spring until the fall.

Very many do not recognize these moths in their perfect stage, so small are they, and vent their wrath on those great millers that fly around lamps in warm summer evenings. It need scarcely be said that these large millers are utterly guiltless of any attempts upon our wardrobes, they expend their attacks in a more open form on our gardens and orchards.

We will give a more careful description of the Clothes-moth which was found in its different stages June 12th in a mass of cotton-wool. The larva is white, with a tolerably plump body, which tapers slightly towards the tail, while the head is much of the color of gum-copal. The rings of the body are thickened above, especially on the thoracic ones, by two transverse thickened folds. It is one-fifth of an inch-long.

The body of the chrysalis, or pupa, is considerably curved, with the head smooth and rounded. The long antennæ, together with the hind legs, which are folded along the breast, reach to the tip of the hind body, on the upper surface of each ring of which is a short transverse row of minute spines, which aid the chrysalis in moving towards the mouth of its case, just before the moth appears. At first the chrysalis is whitish, but just before the exclusion of the moth becomes of the color of varnish.

When about to cast its pupa-skin, the skin splits open on the back, and the perfect insect glides out. The act is so quickly over with, that the observer has to look sharp to observe the different steps in the operation.

Our common Clothes-moth, *Tinea flavifrontella* is of an uniform light-buff color, with a silky iridescent lustre, the hind wings and abdomen being a little paler. The head is thickly tufted with hairs and is a little tawny, and the upper side of the densely hirsute feelers (*palpi*) is dusky. The wings are long and narrow, with the most beautiful and delicate long silken fringe, which increases in length towards the base of the wing.

They begin to fly in May, and last all through the season, fluttering with a noiseless, stealthy flight in our apartments, and laying their eggs in our woollens.

There are several allied species which have much the same habits, except that they do not all construct cases, but eat carpets, clothing, articles of food, grain, etc., and objects of natural history.

Successive broods of the Clothes-moth appear through the summer. In the autumn they cease eating, retire within their cases, and early in the spring assume the chrysalis state.—A. S. Packard, in the *American Naturalist*, October.

EFFECTS OF LIGHTNING.

A LARGE proportion of mankind, and I may say the whole of womankind, regard such thunderstorms as those which raged over many parts of England last August with strong feelings of trepidation and alarm, manifestly betrayed while the tempest wears its most furious aspect, but not always confessed to after it has passed away. There is a wide-spread opinion existing—and one which is doubtless the cause of half the fears that thunder-storms engender—that lightning strokes are always fatal to life; but this is very seldom actually the case. Upon the average not more than twenty persons are killed by lightning in the United Kingdom in the course of a year—a very small proportion of the half million of deaths from all causes that make up the total of our annual bill of mortality, or even of the fifteen thousand violent deaths that are registered during the same period. In France this average is much greater, and in Belgium much less, regard being had in each case to the difference of population. But of victims to lightning strokes not fatal to life there are no statistics; the numbers of such must be very great, for scarcely a thunder-storm occurs without our hearing or reading of some one or more accidents arising from it; the number of reported cases is doubtless but a per-centage of those which are unrecorded, and we may certainly assume that hundreds, and possibly conjecture that thousands of slight injuries are inflicted by these powerful electric shocks in the course of a stormy year.

The injuries which lightning causes to the human body are sometimes very curious, quite sufficiently so, I have thought, to render a few cases worth recounting. The whole subject has at times received great attention from scientific men, and a few months ago an exhaustive work upon the effects of lightning upon all animate and inanimate objects issued from the French press. It represented the life's labour of a physician, M. Sestier, who died before it was fit for publication; to it we are indebted for some of the materials of this article.

The most palpable injuries are those which are external, and leave their marks upon the skin of the victim. It sometimes happens that the surface of the body is marked by a sort of film or plaster, something like the oxide that covers stones and metals that have been affected by the electric discharge, and which arises from the transport of ponderable matter collected by the lightning in its course through the air, and left at the surface of the body penetrated by it. This film is so superficial that it has been removed by slight friction, and it has been proved in some cases to arise from matter gathered from something borne by the person injured. For instance, a lady wearing a gold chain was struck; the chain was melted, and her neck and breast were stained with a purple oxide of gold, while a band or stream of the same dye ran down her body. It has frequently happened, too, that designs and figures of natural objects have been as it were photographed, or more properly electrographed, upon the surface of the skin. A sailor asleep at the prow of a vessel was attacked by the electric fluid, and it was afterwards discovered that the number "44" had been imprinted upon his breast, these figures having been marked upon a sail that the fluid had penetrated before reaching the man. A minister's house was struck, and several persons were injured; the wife received a slight infliction, and strangely enough her right arm was impressed with the image of a red flower that formed the pattern of her dress. Three men were gathering pears when the lightning fell upon them; one was killed, the others stunned; when one of the latter came to himself, he found the branches and leaves of the tree distinctly imprinted upon his body.

The hair of the head and body seems to be frequently subject to destruction. This would not be remarkable, if it was in all cases entirely singed off, for we know that in gas and other explosions, where a man is surrounded by flames, the hair and eyebrows are frequently destroyed; but the lightning is more capricious in its effects. Arago tells of a captain of a frigate who related to him how that his vessel was struck by lightning, and he received several wounds in the head. "Next day," said the captain, "when I wanted to shave myself, I found that the effect of the razor on the beard was to pull it out by the roots, instead of cutting it. . . . The hair on my head, my eyebrows and eyelashes, successively came out in the same way by the roots, and did not grow again." The year after this happened, the captain's finger-nails scaled away. A German physician has recorded a case where a young man had the hair from a space on his head, the size of a five-franc piece, as completely and cleanly shorn as if it had been done with a pair of scissors; and another authority quotes that of a labourer, who had three or four tonsures made by lightning, where the hair was as neatly removed as though it had been shaven by a razor, the skin showing no sign of injury.

Next to the fear of death from lightning, without doubt that of perpetual blindness has the firmest hold upon the popular mind; but here again an examination of actual numbers proves this fear to be exaggerated. Without doubt the sudden flood of intense light into the eye, which only the lightning flash can give rise to, and the strain upon the nerves and muscles of that organ thereby produced, so far paralyses the vision that amaurosis, or temporary blindness, or hemiopsy—partial blindness—is the consequence. There is abundant evidence of this; I myself witnessed a case during the past year. One or two cases in which cataract has resulted from fulguration are likewise on record. But of lasting blindness it is doubtful whether any authenticated instance exists. M. Sestier, in summing up his experiences upon this branch of his researches, and leaving out those cases where the loss of sight has been but momentary, finds only fourteen cases where the blindness has had anything like a notable duration, and of these there are only four instances of its enduring for many days, the longest period in any one case being seven months. He says that he knows of no instance of blindness which has lasted during many years.

Shocks to the nervous system, as may be supposed, are very frequent and of varying violence; they last sometimes but a few minutes, most frequently about a day, and, on very rare occasions, for a longer period, insensibility having lasted even for a week after the shocks occurred. Frights and extravagant actions consequent upon them are too numerous to be dwelt upon; losses of memory are common, and complete changes of disposition and temperament occasional. Paralysis is one of the most frequent consequences. The part of the body affected is generally that which has received the lightning spark, and through which the electric fluid has traversed on its way to the earth, and, as a consequence, the lower members of the body are more frequently afflicted than the upper parts; strangely enough there seems to be a tendency on the part of the left half of the body to become paralysed more often than the right. Is it because there is more life and vigour to resist injury in the right than in the left side? It would appear so. The paralysis, like the nervous affections, is generally of short duration. A telegraph clerk, who was struck in Scotland on the 20th of August last, had both arms paralysed for three hours. In about forty in a hundred of the cases enumerated by M. Sestier, the duration was within twenty-four hours; though it has been known to last for several months. A remarkable case of temporary prostration of a large number of people is offered by a storm which passed over some grounds where a fair was being held, at Springville, Erie, in the United States, on the 27th of June last. One of the exhibition sheds, in which the spectators had taken refuge from the rain, was struck by lightning, and about one hundred persons were stunned and prostrated, in almost every case falling on their faces; some fifty remained insensible for five or ten minutes, a dozen were seriously burned, three or four injured so as to be considered past recovery; but two horses, and these only, were killed outright. It was conjectured at the time that the roof of the building acted as a sort of "distributor" of the electricity, and that each person's head drew off a portion of the charge; but it seems as probable that the poor horses received the full charge, and that the people were influenced by their proximity to the course of the current; for it is proved that it is not necessary to be actually struck to be affected by lightning; many accidents have happened to individuals merely in the neighbourhood of stricken objects. At Borlington, a few years back, two persons were paralysed in the same house in which another two were killed.

Considering what I have said, and what I have still to say, of the evil effects of lightning, it is a pleasant change to have to adduce some instances of its opposite or beneficent influence. The doctrine that "likes cures likes" holds good in the case of maladies to which the destructive element gives birth; whether the fright, or some proper action of the electric fluid works the cure, it is hard to say; but the effect is incontestable. Several cases are reported where individuals, paralysed from their youth, have recovered complete use of their limbs by lightning strokes in after years. A country clergyman, in Kent, was paralysed by apoplexy in 1761, and struck by lightning about a year after, when all traces of the paralysis left him. A man who had lost the use of both arms was guarding some animals in a field; lightning fell upon him, and when he came to his senses, he found that he could use both arms and hands. These are but a few out of many recorded instances. A variety of ailments besides paralysis have been cured or ameliorated by the same agency, even blindness; for one Gardley, some time an actor at the Surrey Theatre, who had been for many years blind of one eye, had his sight quite restored by a lightning-flash.

The question has often arisen whether a lightning-stricken man sees the flash that smites him, or hears the thunder that follows. It may be answered in the negative: so instantaneous is the effect of the sudden shock that the mind must be deprived of the power of receiving any impression concerning the cause of it. Those who have been so far injured as to lose consciousness, and have afterwards recovered, have generally, I may say always, asserted that they saw nothing, heard nothing, and even thought nothing—in fact, that they knew absolutely nothing of what had happened, and have wondered how it came to pass that they found themselves prostrated. This phenomenon accords with the testimony of those experimentalists in electricity who have been occasionally overthrown by powerful shocks. Franklin, for instance, received in his head the discharge of two large Leyden jars. He fell down senseless in an instant; when he became conscious, he wondered how he came to be on the floor, and so innocent was he of what had happened that he actually thought the jars still contained the fluid, and he set about experimenting with them, when his assistants told him that he had himself been the recipient of their contents. In the majority of cases a body lightning-struck falls gently to the ground; the limbs appear to lose their rigidity, and give way beneath the superincumbent weight; there is no violent overthrow. On this account it seldom happens that the victim exhibits any fractures or wounds such as it might be thought would be produced. But this rule has had some marvellous exceptions. On some occasions the body struck has been considerably displaced, and even transported to a distance from the spot where the flash fell upon it. In 1839 two carriers in the neighbourhood of Triel took refuge during a thunderstorm beneath the branches of an oak tree: the tree was struck, and the lightning attacked them; one dropped down on the spot, but the other was lifted and carried to a distance of twenty-five yards, and fell in a thicket of chestnut trees. An analogous case occurred near Chantilly:—A surgeon on horseback, overtaken by a storm, dismounted and took shelter beneath a tree, where a labourer had already located himself. The wind being very high, they huddled together, and held on to the tree. The lightning descended upon them; the labourer was thrown to a distance of six feet, the horse was moved about the same distance; but the doctor was carried up and hurled over a space equal to twenty-five paces. He was seen as a black mass in the air by some boatmen on a moat hard by.—James Carpenter in *Cassell's Magazine* for November.

EXTINCT ANIMALS.

THE saurians, or great pre-Adamite amphibious lizards are found in a fossil state in the English lias, and even in earlier geological formations. They must have abounded at a time when mammalian life was hardly developed. Of these saurians the emperor was the icthyosaurus, a massive monster 30 feet long, with a pendulous stomach, a fish-like tail, a crocodile's hideous head, and four fins like the paddles of a whale. Its skin was that of a whale; its eye was as big as a dinner plate, (18 inches in diameter,) protected by a bony-shield like that of a bird of prey; and its sternum was like the Australian duck rat, that most abnormal and incongruous of creatures. Its teeth were powerful as those of the modern crocodile, only there were about six feet length of them. Its fossilized dung is still often found in large quantities, and always contains remains of fish and reptiles. The icthyosaurus probably fed on its flabbier weaker brother, the plesiosaurus, which was less than 18 feet long, and a feebler and altogether more pot-like creature. It had a vertebral column like a fish, a short rudder tail, and four slender paddles; a long neck, and a small inoffensive head. Professor Owen, who can build up an animal from the bare hint of a single bone, thinks the plesiosaurus lived near the sea shore, and was in the habit of ascending estuaries.

As for the pterosaurus, which is found in the English lias, he was a strange creature, with wings slightly resembling the flying lizard, which has side membranes to support it while leaping from tree to tree. This saurian, found in the English lias, became extinct, it is conjectured, in the time of the chalk formation.

The pliosaurus was another chieftain of the dark and pre-historic ages. He was large as a whale, and had the ferocity and jaws of the crocodile. There were five genera of him. In some of them there were anatomic indications of tendency towards the mammalia structure. Some of these crocodile lizards were more aquatic, others more terrestrial. They are most of them found under the chalk in the wealden, or south-Eastern part of England. The megalosaurus, of from 25 to 35 feet long,—which had an enormous muzzle with strong teeth,—was the most formidable land creature of its age. The iguanodon, another monster of this dynasty of animals, was distinguished by a prehensile tongue. So much for the monsters who passed away as the Pharohs did after them. As the Cæsars went, so went the Saurians.

But let us by no means forget our big friend—that earth-shaker—that great grandfather of all the elephants: we refer to the mammoth. Who would ever have believed in him had not a real specimen been found potted in the ice of Siberia? Remains of fossil elephants are very numerous in what Lyell calls the pliocene period. Bones of elephants are found under the earth in almost all parts of both continents; and the bones and tusks of the mammoth, or gigantic elephant, have always been common throughout Russia, particularly in Eastern Siberia and the Arctic marshes. The tusks, so numerous and so well preserved, long formed an article of commerce; and although considered inferior to modern ivory, were extensively used in Asia and Africa: but still, no complete skeleton—much more a carcase—had been found. In 1799, however, a Tungusian fisherman named Schumachoff, after his sport was over, embarked on the Lake Oncoul, to seek for mammoth tusks round the shores. He came at last to a shapeless mass of ice, the nature of which puzzled him. In 1800, he found the same mass again—by this time divided into two parts, both projecting from the ice, and evidently distinct from it. Towards the end of 1801, it showed itself evidently to be the carcase of a huge animal, for now its one side and one tusk were free. In 1803, the ice between the earth and the mammoth had melted and down it fell on a bank of sand, probably rather overcome with standing for about a thousand years or so. In March, 1804, Schumachoff, steadily following up his big prize, was "down upon him" like a dog or a stag at bay. He now cut off the tusks and bartered them for 50 roubles' worth of goods. In 1806, a traveller visiting the enormous joint, which was, indeed, "cut and come again," found that the Jakutski had much mutilated it, by hewing off its flesh to feed their dogs; white bears, wolves, wolverines, and foxes had also fed upon it, and there were traces of footsteps all round it. The skeleton, now almost bare, was still whole all but the fore leg. The head was covered with dry skin, and one ear was well preserved. The dark grey skin was covered with reddish wool and black hairs. The carcase was 9 feet 4 inches high, and 16 feet 4 inches long from point of nose to end of tail. The tusk measured along its singular curve 9 feet 6 inches, the two tusks weighing together 360lbs.; and the head, with the tusks 414lbs. The skin of one side alone was so heavy that it took 13 men to carry it on shore. Thirty-one pounds of hair that had been torn off by the white bears were collected from the ground. Various other mammoth skeletons were traceable in the same locality, and mammoth's tusks were visible in great numbers in the hollows of the adjacent rocks.

The skeleton of the mammoth (certainly one of the wonders of the world) stands in a room by itself in the Great Museum of the Academy of St. Petersburg, dwarfing the spectators as a Colossus would do. Its great tusks, in whose curve several men could sit, are too much rounded and too much turned upwards to have been useful either for aggression or defence, and we may presume, like giants in story books, the beast was easily overcome by more swift and subtle, though smaller animals. Monster king of the early world, the mammoth must have trampled and munched his way about, enjoying himself after his fashion and biding his time for quiet extinction.

Some mammoth hair and skin given by Mr. Adams and Sir Joseph Banks to the Museum of the Royal College of Surgeons, is still to be seen there. The mammoth seems to have had two sorts of hair—common hair and bristles. That remaining on the skin is of the colour of camel's hair, one inch and a-half long, and very thick-set and curly. It is interspersed with a few bristles almost three inches long, and of a dark reddish colour. Some of these are nearly black, much thicker than horse-hair, and 12 to 18 inches long.

This stupendous creature appears to have existed in England also, and at a time, too, when the temperature was much the same as now, for his colossal remains have been found in the North Cliff, in Yorkshire, in a lacustrite formation, where all the land and water shells can be identified with the existing ones.

The bones of various ruminating animals, many of them allied to the ox and deer tribes, are very abundant in the gravel strata of many parts of England and the Continent. The most gigantic of the extinct deer was the elk, an animal whose skeleton is found in the east of Ireland and in the Isle of Man, embedded in the peat bogs. Owen selected the elk as the representative of a new sub-genus—the megaceros. Perfect skeletons of this huge deer are seldom found, but the detached bones are exceedingly common here and elsewhere. The head of an elk, in the Woodwardian Museum of Geology, in Cambridge, is five feet 6 inches high; from the snout to the tip of the tail measures eleven feet, and between the tips of its horns nearly nine feet. This vast creature, with a forest upon its head, was to deer of the present epoch what the elephant is to the terrier.—*Leader*, Nov. 9.

THE RUBY-THROATED HUMMING BIRD. — *TROCHILUS COLUBRIS*—LINNÆUS.

THIS beautiful little winged gem is distributed throughout New England as a summer visitor. It arrives from the South from about the 15th to the 25th of May, according to latitude, and usually in pairs. The first notice that we have of his arrival, is a humming sound, and now and then a sharp chirp, like that of a large beetle, among the earliest flowers in the garden. We look in the direction of the sound, and perceive our little stranger darting about, and thrusting his bill and little head into the flowers, busily searching for the small insects that inhabit them, and which constitute the principal part of his food. While we are looking at him he suddenly alights on a twig, turns his gorgeous throat towards us, and scans us with his bright little black eyes. While he is perched, he busies himself in arranging his plumage, and cleaning from his feathers the drops of dew that have perhaps fallen upon him, uttering occasionally his merry chirp; presently his mate appears, and alights by his side. The little lovers (for they are still such) then indulge in mutual caresses, and apparently talk over with much earnestness, their plans for future housekeeping. Woe to another humming bird, if he comes in sight, for our little friend is not only jealous of his mate, but is very quarrelsome also, and protects his honour with great courage. As he darts off like a bullet at the intruder, his mate watches with no little interest for the results of the battle that is inevitable. The two males meet in the air, and fierce is the contest; their little wings beat the air with such force that their humming is heard at the distance of several rods: up they mount, rushing against and striking each other with their sharp little bills, until they are both lost to the sight. Presently our acquaintance descends to the twig where his mate is seated, and struts before her with a pride much larger than his body, apparently anxious for her approval of his courage. She caresses him, and, after he has adjusted his plumage, off they shoot for other scenes and pleasures.

About the first week in June, the Humming bird commences building its nest: this is composed of a soft down, that is taken from the stems of some of the ferns; it is covered entirely with lichens, which are glued on with the saliva of the bird, giving it the appearance of a mossy knot. It is usually built on the upper side of a limb, but I have known of cases of its being built in a forked twig. The whole fabric is about an inch and a half in diameter, and about that in depth externally; it is hollowed about half an inch, and is three-fourths of an inch in diameter; it is lined with a soft downy substance detached from flying seeds. The eggs are two in number, white, and nearly elliptical in shape, being of about equal size at both ends. Length of egg, about .45 in., breadth about .31 in. I am inclined to think, that in the latitude of New England, this bird raises only one brood in the season, but further South it undoubtedly rears two. The period of incubation is ten days.

On approaching the nest, the parent bird immediately flies at the intruder, and it was by this means that I have been enabled to find specimens of the nest, when I could not possibly have done so if their locality had not been betrayed by the bird herself. I have heard of young birds being taken from the nest when nearly fledged, kept for several weeks, and fed with nothing but sweetened water, but they always died after a short confinement, and I believe that it is impossible to keep this bird as a pet, from the fact that its actual food is insects, and it cannot live on any other. This little bird is extremely susceptible of cold, and if long deprived of the animating influence of the sunbeams, droops, and soon dies. A very beautiful male was brought me, which I put into a wire cage, and placed in a retired, shaded part of the room. After fluttering about for some time, the weather being uncommonly cool, it clung by the wires, and hung in a seemingly torpid state for a whole afternoon. No emotion whatever of the lungs could be perceived, on the closest inspection, though at other times, this is remarkably observable, the eyes were shut, and when touched by the finger, it gave no signs of life or motion. I carried it out to the open air, and placed it directly in the rays of the sun, in a sheltered situation. In a few seconds respiration became very apparent, the bird breathed faster and faster, opened its eyes, and began to look about with as much seeming vivacity as ever. After it had completely recovered, I restored it to liberty, and it flew off to the withered top of a pear-tree, where it sat for some time, dressing its disordered plumage, and then shot off like a meteor.—*Edward A. Samuels' Ornithology of New England.*

INFLUENCE OF SOUNDS UPON ANIMALS.

The following notes upon this subject have appeared in the three numbers of the *Athenæum*, for October 26, November 2nd and 9th.—Having paid some attention to the physical sympathies of animals for peculiar sounds, I could not read, without interest, the article on "The reasoning power in Animals," which appeared in the *Athenæum* of the 5th of October. It was there mooted that hounds were given to baying when Sunday church bells rang, under the pleasing or displeasing assurance that there was no going a-hunting for them that morning. It may be asserted, with as conclusive proof from experience, that the canine race, especially when civilized by discipline, is capriciously sensative as to sounds, with or without ryhthm. I have again and again known a dog be excited to the most lugubrious howling by a singer or a violent player on an instrument, when quieter music has passed without such demonstration. Surely there can be nothing analogous to "the reasoning power" which makes Tray, Blanche, and Sweetheart express themselves in comment on the chime from the church tower in instances like these. The cause, I suspect, of such manifestations has to be sought elsewhere.

Y. L. Y.

In reading the review of Mr. Watson's "Reasoning Power in Animals," I too, was struck with the passage noticed by Y. L. Y., where the reviewer mentions the howlings of the dogs on hearing the church bells, because they indicated that there would be no sport on that day; but I set it down as a bit of pleasantry on the part of the reviewer, for I do not think that Mr. Watson, or the reviewer, or anybody else, could seriously attribute such an association of ideas to a dog. That musical sounds exercise a remarkable influence upon dogs I have myself seen instances. A house-dog formerly kept at a boys' school would howl in a most peculiar way whenever the school-bell was rung in his presence. As the bell never summoned him to lessons or to meals, to work or to play, he was perfectly innocent of sharing the emotions excited by its sound in the minds of the pupils. I could never satisfy myself whether his howling indicated pain or pleasure; more probably the latter; for if the sound of the bell had been distasteful to him, he would have barked at it; if it had excited alarm, he would have fled; but he invariably stood still, with his eyes fixed on the bell, and continued his lugubrious chant as long as it was rung; the moment it ceased, he silently betook himself to his usual canine occupations as if nothing had happened. Passing out of Oxford Street only a few days since, I observed a reedy barrel-organ sending forth its accustomed hoarse sounds, while at an open doorway on the opposite side of the street stood a dog, uttering the same peculiar continuous howl as noticed above; but the instant the organ ceased, the dog ceased also, and turned to follow the bent of its inclinations. Can this be a canine attempt at *singing?* A collection of carefully observed instances of the effects of sounds upon various animals would not be without interest.

F. L. S.

I have read with much interest the paragraphs which have appeared in the *Athenæum* on this subject, but cannot say I agree with "F. L. S." in thinking that the sound of music produces pleasure in a dog. I myself am musical, and given to much practising; and, moreover, possess two dogs, and am quite sure, that could "F. L. S." see their expression as I go towards the piano, he would not think pleasure stirred them. If the door be open, both dogs get up *at once*, and go straight out of the room; but should it be closed, they both howl with their noses in the air, sitting up at the same time and begging me to leave off; and so accustomed are they to the word "singing," that if I come into the room where one dog is asleep before the fire, and say in a low voice, "Punch, I am going to *sing*," the little creature *instantly* gets up and goes out of the room. Now, I can assure you this is a fact. I have also observed that in playing or singing a scale, the lower notes they do not so much object to, but the higher ones, and particularly certain notes, they howl at in such a way that to try and control them is perfectly useless. When I leave off, I am rewarded by long-continued dancing and springing about me by both dogs. I have often wished to know the cause of it, but no one has ever suggested a reason which satisfied me. My own idea is, that the sound produces an irritating effect on their nerves and brain, and that certain notes stun them.

J. H.

When I was a young man, my elder brother was a dog-fancier, and had a strong bull-terrier, which he sometimes contrived to have introduced to the house. When this happened before our family devotions began, the dog's presence was soon known by his joining in our psalmody; not as if it pained him, but from some impulse that he could not restrain. Some years ago, when part of the service connected with the sacrament in our country parishes was held in the church-yard, the collies belonging to many of the shepherds followed them, and afforded great sport to the youngsters, and gave great annoyance to the preacher and the beadle, by sending forth some inharmonious sounds from the outer circle.

G. T.

I beg the space of a few lines to express my concurrence in the opinions offered on this subject by "Y. L. Y." and "F. L. S." I have a dog of my own, which invariably utters loud cries—a mixture of whine and howl, dismally [protracted—whenever he hears a street organ, or a piano in the house, play any solemn or mournful tune. By lighter airs he is not affected. He is only one out of many who distinguish themselves in the same manner. An accordion, I may add, always moves him. As this matter has nothing to do, as far as I see, with reasoning power, it is not touched upon in my book. The utterances appear to be quite instinctive; nor have I any notion, more than "F. L. S.," whether they are indicative of pain or pleasure; though, as "F. L. S." justly remarks, the probability seems to be in favour of pleasure, as the dog seems to join in the sound from natural inclination, and generally, I believe, manifests annoyance if he is checked in his performance. That the crisis may be canine attempts at singing is, I think, a very reasonable suggestion of "F. L. S."—The author of *The Reasoning Power*.

The Reindeer.

The reindeer, or rane-deer, as some etymologists spell the word, is very widely distributed over the face of the globe. Its varieties are found from the coasts of Sweden and Lapland, through the north of Asia, to Kamschatka; and on the American Continent from the coasts of British Columbia to the north of Newfoundland; its occurrence depends, it would seem, very closely upon considerations of climate.

In earlier times it had apparently a still more extended habitat. Remains of the animal have been found by geologists at the north base of the Pyrenees, and in various parts of France. Immense numbers of its bones have been discovered in the south of France, where they appear to have served as food for the human denizens of the caves. In a cave in the Dordogne, a rudely shaped flint weapon was found in the vertebræ of a reindeer in a similar position. In the bone-caves of Glamorganshire many thousand antlers of the reindeer were discovered some few years since, and the remains of several distinct varieties have been dug up in the west of England, in the bed of the Thames, in Norfolk, in Forfarshire, and also in various parts of Ireland.

An idea at one time prevailed among naturalists that the reindeer existed in the south of Europe as late as the fourteenth century. This belief, which originated with Buffon, was founded on a passage in the printed copies of the works of Gaston de Foix, who, in his "Treatise of Hunting," speaks of the animal as found in Berne and Savoy. Cuvier, however, detected this to be an error, by collating the printed copies of the work in question with the original manuscript in the Imperial Library at Paris. The naturalist Pallas mentions the existence of these deer in the Ural Mountains at the end of the last century; and in the "Encyclopædia Britannica," (ed. 1857), it is stated that "Herds are still found among the pine forests which stretch from the banks of the Oufa under the 55th degree, to those of Kama. They proceed even further south along the woody summits of the prolongation of the Uralian Mountains which stretches between the Don and the Volga as far as 46 degrees." Thus the species approaches almost to the base of the Caucasian Chain, along the banks of the Kouma, where scarcely a winter passes without a few being shot by the Kalmucks.

The Lapland reindeer are found in a wild as well as in a domestic state, and the herds of the latter are sometimes recruited by young ones captured from the former.

When we consider this wide range, it appears strange that all successful efforts for the domestication of the reindeer should have been confined to so small a portion of the old Continent.

The reindeer average in height from nine to ten hands, the wild ones being the largest. Their colour is light, of various shades, and it becomes still lighter in winter. Both males and females of all the varieties of reindeer are provided with antlers, which vary greatly in form, and which are shed at a different period by each sex. During summer, they browse on every kind of green herbage and shrub which they can find; but in winter, their sole food appears to be the lichen known as the "reindeer moss," which they discover by instinct in the snow, digging for it with their tough and pliable muzzles and sharp-pointed fore-feet. It appears to be a well-ascertained fact that they will also eat the "lemming," or field-rat, with avidity.

The writer of a recent work on Lapland says that the reindeer "have nothing of the antlered monarch of the forest about them, but a careworn, nervous look, which" (he adds) "I do not wonder at, considering how they are bullied. There are creatures which sting them all over; and creatures which lay their eggs in their eyes and nostrils, and make themselves comfortable under their skin; and wolves, and gluttons, and dogs, and Laps; in short, barring a rat, I know of no animal that *is* so worried." He admits, however, that their constitutions do not appear to suffer under the treatment they receive, and that, like donkeys, they thrive under it.

It may amuse the reader to contrast with this account the description of a Lap encampment by the learned Von Buch, written at a time when *fine* writing was deemed most essential to a traveller's narrative. We have endeavoured in translating it to preserve the rather florid imagery.

"It is a new and pleasing spectacle to see in the evening the herd assemble round the encampment to be milked; on the hills around everything is in an instant full of life and motion. The busy dogs are everywhere barking and bringing the mass nearer and nearer, and the deer bound and stand still, and then bound again, with an indescribable variety of movements. When the animal, frightened by the dogs while feeding, raises his head and displays aloft his proud antlers, how beautiful and majestic is the sight! and when he courses over the ground, how fleet and light is his carriage! We never hear the foot on the earth; nothing but the incessant cracking of the knee joints, as if it proceeded from a repetition of electric shocks; a singular noise from the number of deer by whom it is at once produced; it is heard at a great distance. When all the herd, consisting of three or four hundred at least, reach the encampment, they stand still and repose or frisk about in confidence, play with their antlers against one another, or in groups browse round a patch of moss. Then the maidens run with their vessels from deer to deer; the brothers and servants throw a bark halter around the antlers of the animal they point out to him, and draw it towards them: the animal generally struggles, unwilling to follow the halter. The maiden laughs and enjoys the labour it occasions, and sometimes wantonly allows it to get loose so that it may be again caught for her, while her father and mother are heard chiding them for their frolic, which has often the effect of scaring the whole flock. On beholding this scene who does not think on Laban and Leah, on Rachel and Jacob? When the herd at last flocks round to the number of many hundreds, we imagine we are beholding a mighty encampment and the commanding mind which presides over the whole stationed in the midst."—*Once a Week*, November Part.

THE WALRUS.

A most distinguished visitor has arrived in London —a beast with whose general appearance most are familiar, by means of stuffed specimens or drawings, but which has been seen alive by few except arctic travellers. The 1st of November, 1867, will ever be memorable in the annals of Natural History as the day on which a living walrus (*Trichechus rosmarus*) arrived at the Regent's Park Zoological Gardens. As it was late in the evening when the van containing the animal arrived, it was determined by Mr. Bartlett to place the huge box in which the beast had travelled alongside the enclosure set apart for his accommodation, and to leave him undisturbed for the night. The next morning a portion of the wire-work of the enclosure was taken down, the box shifted close up to the aperture— a plank carefully removed, and out came the head of the Walrus. The poor beast snuffed and stared about, wondering where he was. We waited quite silent, and then out he came, further and further, till at last, finding the road clear, he waddled right out on to the open. The first thing he did was to put down his great nose and to sniff at the grass—he had, probably, never seen grass before—he then went straight up to a little tree, and examined it with the same sort of curiosity, with which we spectators were examining him. He then made direct to the pond, and pulled himself up on to the edge, first with his chin and then with his flippers. After looking round again, he ducked his head under water with the same kind of eagerness that a two months' absence from a bath would be likely to produce in a water-loving animal. Finding it all right, he slipped into the water with the noiseless glide of an otter; down he went, luxuriating in the bath for which he had pined for two months or more. After a long dive, up came his intelligent head to the surface once more, and he gave a long and anxious look round. At this moment we were much amused to observe the seals in the pond close by. These pretty little things had clambered to the edge of the stone parapet of their pond, and were gazing with all eyes, and with an expression of intense wonder, at the poor walrus, in whom, possibly they recognised an old acquaintance. Jemmy—for that is the name of the walrus—then came out of his pond and up to the railings, so that we had a good look at him. He is just about the same size as the sea bear. I tried to take his measurements, but the moment I put the tape near him he turned round and looked so terribly fierce, that I, of course, instantly desisted. He probably thought the tape was a rope, and knowing from experience that a rope was no friend of his, objected to its coming near him. His head is seal-like, but the eyes are not so large; they remind one much of the eyes of the hippopotamus. Their colour is dark brown, and the pupil exceedingly small. It is, as far as I could make out, not circular, but vertical, like that of a cat. I think that this peculiar structure is given to preserve the retina of the eye from the glare of the sun on the ice, and save the animal from "snow blindness." Again, it doubtless has to do with his being able to see during the semi-darkness of the long arctic winter; possibly it serves both purposes. The colour of Jemmy's coat is tawny, not unlike that of Scotch snuff; his hair is rather short, and throws off the water easily from its surface. When damp, it is apparently divided into diamond-shaped patterns, like a quilted petticoat. In his walk he wriggles much more than the sea bear. His hind flippers are connected together by loose skin; on land they appear awkward, but in the water they give him great facilities of swimming. When displeased he can roar famously. His voice is not at all unlike that of a lion, only, of course, not so loud. He is supposed to be about eight months old, and is certainly not so big as he will be. I make him out to be over seven feet in length. A full grown walrus will measure some sixteen feet long, ten feet girth, and have twenty inches to two feet of tusk, and a weight of over 3000lb. Jemmy's blunt muzzle is the most peculiar part about him. It is full and fleshy, like the "mouffle" of a North American elk. The whole of its anterior surface is covered with strong whalebone-like whiskers; the uppermost rows of these are quite short, the lower are much more developed, being from two to three inches in length. The points of all these whiskers are directed downwards, and somewhat towards the median line of the nose. They look stiff, like wires, but to the touch are soft, like the wetted bristles on a hair-brush. I have now some walrus bristles before me—they are not from Jemmy's nose—when wetted in warm water they become quite soft. Their colour is exactly that of a tortoiseshell comb, and they resemble the teeth of a comb in other ways. They are quite hollow—like a rabbit's tooth—one-third of their length. As in the lion and seal, so also in the walrus, these apparently rude organs of sensation are exceedingly sensitive. The conical cavity of the whisker is filled with nervous pulp; in fact, one might almost say that the whisker is simply a horn cap upon the top of an exceedingly large nerve. In the skull the foramen, through which these nose nerves send their main telegraph wires to the brain is exceedingly large, larger even than in the lion.—Frank Buckland, in *Land and Water*, Nov. 9.

PIGEONS AT SHERWOOD.

Of the family of the Columbidæ, three species are all that I can number, viz., the Ring Dove (C. palumbus), the Stock Dove (C. ænas), and the Turtle Dove (C. turtur).

Amongst our numerous woods and plantations the ring dove is plentifully distributed. It is an indiscriminate feeder on seeds of every kind; and, though well provided with abundance of beechmast and acorns, it levies heavy contributions on the crops of the farmer. In one way or other it is, however, pretty well kept in check, and is not seen in those enormously large flocks which are met with in some parts of the country.

Few of our native birds are shyer in their habits, or more difficult to approach within gunshot. I have often walked to a clump of trees where a pair have been roosting, but they would invariably take flight from the highest part of the trees and as far out of danger as possible, never giving me the possibility of even a long shot, and this I have found to be their general habit. Mr. St. John, in his last interesting work, remarks on the somewhat unusual tameness of these wild and wary birds, that they built in some shrubs close to his house and not above six feet from the ground, where, when sitting, they allowed the members of his family to pass without showing the least alarm. I have recently been told by a friend of a similar instance near his own house.

It would seem almost impossible for any bird to build a frailer nest than the wood pigeon, and I have often wondered that the eggs do not fall or are not blown off by the wind from the slight platform on which they are laid, and through which you may sometimes see them from below. I remember one instance in which a pair had selected a young birch tree as the site for their nursery, the stoutest bough of which was not more than an inch and a half in diameter; but it was on one very much smaller than this, and close to the stem, that this apology for a nest was placed. It was formed of very slender birch twigs; but they had been so sparingly used that it was simply a piece of lattice work, through which the two eggs were distinctly visible from the ground, the distance being about twelve or fourteen feet. One of these eggs was very much larger than the other—a peculiarity I have noticed on several other occasions.

In April, 1861, Mr. Sterling Howard communicated to the Sheffield Literary and Philosophical Society a most remarkable instance of the selection of materials for their nests by a number of domestic pigeons, and these were no other than horsenails! He said: "Over one end of the blacksmith's shop is a rude loft, in which are a number of boxes, the domiciles of the pigeons. The nails, which were abstracted from canvas bags and other receptacles, were of the ordinary kind for horseshoes, of various sizes, some new, others old and crooked. They were, however, laid with some regard to comfort, inasmuch as the points were not allowed to project upwards, but without any admixture of softer materials. This is the more singular as there was abundance of straw, shavings, &c., in the neighbourhood. On these 'iron beds' the birds had laid their eggs, which were just ready for hatching when the discovery was made of the use to which the nails were applied. The nails, when removed, filled a watering-can holding about two gallons, one of the nests containing more than fourteen pounds weight."

The stock dove (C. ænas) is not uncommon, mingling, in the winter more especially, with the small flocks of ring doves. I never found the nest on the ground, where it is stated to be frequently placed; but I knew a very large and almost globular mass of ivy in the fork of an ash tree, in Blythe-corner Woods in the close recesses of which a pair of stock dove, reared their young for several years together. I do not think this species is so numerous with us as the preceding one, but it is still plentiful.

The latter word cannot, however, be applied to the turtle dove (C. turtur), one or two specimens being all I have known in the district, though some have been killed in other parts of the country. I have never known it nest with us, and it can only be considered a rare straggler.—W. J. STERLAND, in *Field*.

ORCHARD HOUSE AVIARIES.

IN addition to the growth of fruit and flowers these houses may be made a great source of gratification and amusement by being converted into what may be called orchard-house aviaries for small birds, a different arrangement of the interior only being requisite; the general elevation or shell of the structure being the same as in ordinary vineries. When an aviary is intended to be combined with a fruit, or flower house, we would erect a close wire trellis on each side the whole length of the house, about 4 feet from the side piers, and arched overhead. Outside of this wire inclosure or cage we would build a 9-inch wall, at about a foot from the piers to support the soil. The piers on which the house stands should be 3 feet high; this will allow a good elevation for the vine border. On the top of the interior walls the hot-water pipes would rest: a single pipe round the house will be sufficient. Against the interior walls we would train peach and nectarine trees to a trellis. The centre walk from the door should descend about a foot or so to the middle of the house, where we would have a shallow glass basin and a small fountain, at which the birds can drink and wash themselves. The vines should be planted outside, one under each sash, and trained inside with wires in the usual way. The interior of the cage should be planted with ornamental shrubs, so as to form thickets in which the birds would build. Flowering creepers should be trained to the wire trellis at intervals, all over the house; these would give, when in bloom, a very gay appearance. Openings in the wire trellis must be made under each ventilator to allow of dressing the vines and gathering the fruit.

It is scarcely necessary to give a list of birds to be kept in such a structure, as all lovers of them have their own especial favourites. Still, where a reference to a work on cage-birds is not at hand, a selection of a few pretty hard-billed species may be of service.

SELECTION OF SMALL HARD-BILLED BIRDS.

Amandava, or Avadavat—an exceedingly pretty bird.	Linnet.
Banded Finch.	Malacca Finch.
Blue Finch—a very beautiful bird.	Mountain Bunting.
Brown cheeked Finch.	Purple Finch.
Canary.	Redbill—a very agreeable little bird.
Cape Finch.	Siskin.
Chaffinch.	The Bullfinch is a most interesting bird in an aviary, but it will disbud the trees in the winter, and thus prevent their fruitfulness when planted inside the cage.
Citril Finch.	
Common Quail.	
Goldfinch.	
Gowry Bird, or Nutmeg Bird.	
Indigo Bird—very beautiful plumage.	Virginian Nightingale, or Cardinal Grosbeak.
Java Sparrow, or Rice Bird.	Waxbill—a small and beautiful little bird.
Lesser Redpole.	

Amongst the fruit trees which might be planted inside the wire inclosure may be mentioned standard apples, pears, plums, raspberries, and many other fruits, and in different portions of the aviary, patches of chickweed, groundsel, and other green food suitable for the health of the birds should be grown; these weeds would be entirely hidden by the judicious planting of ornamental shrubs. Camellias, Roses, Eugenia Ugni, Acacias, Azaleas, Fuchsias, Myrtles, Pomegranates, tender Rhododendrons, Clethra arborea, Eriobotrya japonica, and other ornamental shrubby plants might be grown in such a house.—*Hereman's Handbook of Vine and Fruit Tree Cultivation under Glass.*

SILK WORMS FROM NATAL.

At a recent meeting of the Literary and Philosophical Society, Mr. Latham read the following communication on silk producing worms from Natal:—In the "Natal Herald" of the 8th August last, there are copies of a correspondence between the Chamber of Commerce of this place, and some gentlemen at Natal, regarding certain silk producing worms, as they are termed, found near Graham's Town by Mr. Hiller, feeding on the leaves of the mimosa thorn or acacia. The result of the correspondence was, that some of the cocoons were presented to the Chamber here to have them reported on and their true value ascertained. They came into my hands, and the following remarks on them may be interesting to the Society.

From one of the cocoons the moth now exhibited emerged shortly after its arrival in England, and though much crippled, I have, through the kindness of Mr. Jansen, had it clearly identified with the insect

"Pachypasa effusa," of which there are several specimens in the British Museum collection from Natal. The moth laid about 50 eggs, of which I have mounted two or three, and they are here for examination. The eggs under the microscope exactly resemble in texture those of the ostrich, but each has a small black point, probably of a softer substance than the rest of the egg, and through which the caterpillar may emerge. From one of the cocoons I extracted the chrysalis also exhibited, and further the cast skin of the caterpillar rolled into a small ball as usual; by boiling this for some time in caustic potass, it became so softened that it was possible to get it to its original size, and to show its original form. You have it before you dried, and the series is therefore complete, egg, caterpillar, chrysalis, moth, and cocoon.

The original cocoon is, you will notice, a hard woody-like substance, but, by certain processes, Mr. Hiller states soaking in a solution of soda, the cement agglutinating the silk is dissolved and a soft silky looking bag remains. This consists of a thick outer covering, a loose middle lining, and a thinner internal lining, all of silk, which I hardly think could be wound but might possibly be carded.

As regards the commercial value of the article, an eminent silk broker writes as follows:—It is a carded cocoon, the waste silk is the outer covering of the cocoon and appears of tolerable fine fibre, but is bad in colour and not of a good merchantable appearance, if in quantity worth perhaps 1s. 6d. per lb. all round. Enquiries of a similar nature have been made from time to time by customers in the East, where silk does not form one of the staples of the country, and among other places, from Natal, but we do not find that any good can arise from efforts made to produce silk in any quantity; it is probably the most difficult of all known staples to establish in a new land.—*Mechanics' Mag.*, Nov. 2nd.

The China Pear.

The Pear even in England is generally understood to be a tardy bearing tree, and the old couplet—

> He that plants pears,
> Plants for his heirs,

is an expression of this popular belief; nor is the character entirely undeserved, as with the exception of a few varieties, 10, 12, or even a greater number of years will often times elapse after the trees are planted ere they bear fruit. Such being the case even where it has been long acclimatised, people are naturally backward in planting it here, under new and untried conditions.

But my object just now is not to point out how we shall succeed with European and American varieties (experiments upon which are going on), but to endeavour to direct public attention to the China Pear.

This variety appears to have been in the neighbouring colony of New South Wales for many years. Being struck with the name, as probably denoting that it had been received from China, and knowing how thoroughly all fruits of Chinese origin appreciate our climate, I procured a tree, and as it was late in the season, temporarily planted it between two rows of Grape Vines, on the brow of a schistose slope devoted to Grapes. After remaining there two years it commenced to bear, and has borne regularly and freely ever since; requiring generally a little thinning of the crop, as it has a tendency to overbear.

It has had no doctoring and very little attention, except taking out the leading branch to open the interior of the tree, that it might bear on the inside as well as on the outside of the branches. It is grafted on the common Pear stock of the nurseries—has never been root-pruned nor lifted, and occupies a space of about 6 feet by 6 feet, or 4 square yards of ground. The wood is a dark grey, sprinkled with white dots, robust, long-jointed, of upright habit, and producing a profusion of fruit-spurs.

Unlike other Pears, cuttings readily root, especially if shaded and watered during a dry hot spring, and I feel convinced that it will play an important part both as stock and medium for grafting and double grafting other pears that are shy fruit-producers on the common stock. I have not yet proved its perfect adaptability to the Quince, but am experimenting with some of the best Flemish and French pears on the rooted China cuttings. The Marie Louise shows a stocky, sturdy robustness on this stock that is suggestive of a hopeful future.

This last season a severe thunderstorm most effectually thinned the fruit on the above mentioned tree, besides mutilating the branches to some extent; yet it ripened 50 large fruit, many of which weighed 16 or 17 ounces, a result which is not to be despised from 4 or 5 square yards of ground.

The fruit, when ripe, varies in shape, the breadth being sometimes as great as the length. It has a warm yellowish ground dotted all over with russet; a good-looking and very fragrant fruit. Its flesh is crisp, juicy, and sweet, the skin having something of a musky Pine-apple flavour; and as a cooking fruit, baked, stewed, or in pies, it is unsurpassed by any other Pear, its flesh when cooked having nothing like lumpiness or grittiness about it—in fact, leaving nothing to be desired. I have not said anything about its keeping qualities, as it has not been tested fully—the kitchen demand is so much greater than the supply. But I kept three or four in the summer of 1865-66 for six weeks on a shelf in an ordinary room, and the inference is that if they had been put away in a dry cellar, or some cool, dry, dark place, they would have been preserved much longer. *Fructus, in "Queenslander," Australian Paper.*

New Books.

Our limited space must of necessity compel us to give but very short notices of new books, but they will perhaps serve as a guide as to what books our readers may ask for at their libraries.]

The Nile Tributaries of Abyssinia, and the Sword Hunters of the Hamran Arabs. By Sir Samuel W. Baker, M.A., F.R.G.S., Gold Medalist of the Royal Geographical Society, &c. London: Macmillan and Co. 1867.

Those who take up this volume with the expectation of gathering from it information regarding Abyssinia will be disappointed. Of that country we learn nothing, with the exception of the frontier which is described in a visit paid to Mek Nimmur (The Leopard King), a notorious Brigand, who resided there. Nevertheless, this disappointment will not deprive the reader of any of the enjoyment he will feel on perusing the work. Although published since "The Albert Nyanza," it is really a narrative of Adventures in the Border Countries of Abyssinia, preparatory to the more important undertaking of exploring the Upper Nile.

Beginning with Atbara, accompanied by his brave wife, he visited all the rivers which come from the Highlands of Abyssinia to join the Blue Nile.

From the Atbara valley he journeyed first south, and then west, examining in succession the Settite, Royan, Salaam, Angrab, Rahad, and Dinder rivers, and finishing by a journey northwest along the banks of the Blue Nile from Abou Harraz to Khartoum, where the Blue and White Niles join.

The wonders of the country are well described. As a sample we may give the following extract, which describes the sudden rise of the Atbara, and its change from an almost dry river-bed with pools in the bends to a noble river :—

The cool night arrived, and at about half-past eight I was lying half asleep upon my bed by the margin of the river, when I fancied that I heard a rumbling like distant thunder: I had not heard such a sound for months, but a low uninterrupted roll appeared to increase in volume, although far distant. Hardly had I raised my head to listen more attentively when a confusion of voices arose from the Arabs' camp, with a sound of many feet, and in a few minutes they rushed into my camp, shouting to my men in the darkness, "El Bahr! El Bahr!" (the river! the river!)

We were up in an instant, and my interpreter, Mahomet, in a state of intense confusion, explained that the river was coming down, and that the supposed distant thunder was the roar of approaching water.

Many of the people were asleep on the clean sand on the river's bed; these were quickly awakened by the Arabs, who rushed down the steep bank to save the skulls of my two hippopotami that were exposed to dry. Hardly had they descended, when the sound of the river in the darkness beneath, told us that the water had arrived, and the men, dripping with wet, had just sufficient time to drag their heavy burdens up the bank.

All was darkness and confusion; everybody was talking and no one listening; but the great event had occurred, the river had arrived "like a thief in the night." On the morning of the 24th June, I stood on the banks of the noble Atbara river, at the break of day. The wonder of the desert! yesterday there was a barren sheet of glaring sand, with a fringe of withered bush and trees upon its borders, that cut the yellow expanse of desert. For days we had journeyed along the exhausted bed: all Nature, even in Nature's poverty, was most poor; no bush could boast a leaf; no tree could throw a shade; crisp gums crackled upon the stems of the mimosas, the sap dried upon the burst bark, sprung with the withering heat of the simoom. In one night there was a mysterious change —wonders of the mighty Nile!—an army of water was hastening to the wasted river; there was no drop of rain, no thunder-cloud on the horizon to give hope, all had been dry and sultry; dust and desolation yesterday, to-day a magnificent stream, some 500 yards in width, and from fifteen to twenty feet in depth, flowed through the dreary desert! Bamboos and reeds, with trash of all kinds, were hurried along the muddy waters. Where were all the crowded inhabitants of the pool? The prison doors were broken, the prisoners were released, and rejoiced in the mighty stream of the Atbara.

The 24th June, 1861, was a memorable day. Although this was actually the beginning of my work, I felt that by the experience of this night I had obtained a clue to one portion of the Nile mystery, and that, as "coming events cast their shadows before them," this sudden creation of a river was but the shadow of the great cause.

The rains were pouring in Abyssinia! these were the sources of the Nile!

Of the Sword Hunters of the Hamran Arabs, which gives the second title to the work, and are only to be found described in this Expedition, we have the following account.

I had an audience of a party of hunters whom I had long wished to meet. Before my arrival at Sofi I had heard of a particular tribe of Arabs that inhabited the country south of Cassala, between that town and the Basé country: these were the Hamrans, who were described as the most extraordinary Nimrods, who hunted and killed all wild animals, from the antelope to the elephant, with no other weapon than the sword; the lion and the rhinoceros fell alike before the invincible sabres of these mighty hunters, to whom, as an old elephant-hunter, I wished to make my salaam, and humbly confess my inferiority. From the manner in which their exploits had been hitherto explained to me, I could not understand how it could be possible to kill an elephant with the sword, unless the animal should be mobbed by a crowd of men and hacked to death; but I was assured that the most savage elephant had no chance upon good riding-ground against four aggageers, as the hunters with the sword are designated.

The following is a description of their method of Hunting :—

Their method was to follow the tracks of an elephant, so as to arrive at their game between the hours of 10 a.m. and noon, at which time the animal is either asleep, or extremely listless, and easy to approach. Should they discover the animal asleep, one of the hunters would creep stealthily towards the head, and with one blow sever the trunk while stretched upon the ground: in which case the elephant would start upon his feet, while the hunters escaped in the confusion of the moment. The trunk severed would cause a hæmorrhage sufficient to insure the death of the elephant within about an hour. On the other hand, should the animal be awake upon their arrival, it would be impossible to approach the trunk : in such a case, they would creep up from behind, and give a tremendous cut at the back sinew of the hind leg, about a foot above the heel. Such a blow would disable the elephant at once, and would render comparatively easy a second cut to the remaining leg; the arteries being divided, the animal would quickly bleed to death. These were the methods adopted by poor hunters, until, by the sale of ivory, they could purchase horses for the higher branch of the art. Provided with horses the party of hunters should not exceed four. They start before daybreak, and ride slowly throughout the country in search of elephants, generally keeping along the course of a river until they come upon the tracks where a herd or a single elephant may have drunk during the night. When once upon the tracks, they follow fast towards the retreating game. The elephants may be twenty miles distant ; but it matters little to the aggageers. At length they discover them, and the hunt begins. The first step is to single out the bull with the largest tusks ; this is the commencement of the fight. After a short hunt, the elephant turns upon his pursuers, who scatter and fly from his headlong charge until he gives up the pursuit ; he at length turns to bay when again pressed by the hunters. It is the duty of one man in particular to ride up close to the head of the elephant, and thus to absorb its attention upon himself. This insures a desperate charge. The greatest coolness and dexterity are then required by the hunter, who now, the *hunted*, must so adapt the speed of his horse to the pace of the elephant, that the enraged beast gains in the race until it almost reaches the tail of the horse. In this manner the race continues. In the mean time two hunters gallop up behind the elephant, unseen by the animal, whose attention is completely directed to the horse almost within his grasp. With extreme agility, when close to the heels of the elephant, one of the hunters, while at full speed, springs to the ground with his drawn sword, as his companion seizes the bridle, and with one dexterous two-handed blow he severs the back sinew. He immediately jumps out of the way and remounts his horse ; but if the blow is successful, the elephant becomes disabled by the first pressure of its foot upon the ground ; the enormous weight of the animal dislocates the joint, and it is rendered helpless. The hunter who has hitherto led the elephant immediately turns, and riding to within a few feet of the trunk, he induces the animal to attempt another charge. This, clumsily made, affords an easy opportunity for the aggageers behind to slash the sinew of the remaining leg, and the immense brute is reduced to a stand-still ; it dies of loss of blood in a short time, *thus positively killed by one man with two strokes of the sword.*

There are two maps accompanying the book. The reader will find many useful hints to intending travellers in wild countries. The illustrations might be better, but they do not detract from the reader's enjoyment.

A Handbook of Vine and Fruit Tree Cultivation under Glass. By Samuel Hereman. Published by Hereman and Morton.

We have received this new edition of a good book, and can recommend it to all who are interested in cultivating under glass. Many items of importance have been added, and it is now a very complete and useful treatise. The first chapter treats of Orchard-houses, and will be found interesting ; the second gives the arrangement of Sir Joseph Paxton's Hot-houses, and various Ornamental Conservatories; chapter 3, Hints and directions for Heating; chapter 4, Directions for the Cultivation of various Fruits ; chapter 5, on Orchard and Winter Gardening, and lastly, chapter 6, on Orchard House Aviaries.

AMERICAN, FRENCH, AND GERMAN WORKS.

Influence of Climate in North and South America; showing the Varied Climatic Influences operating in the Equatorial, Tropical, Sub-tropical, Temperate, Cold, and Frigid Regions. Accompanied by an Agricultural and Isothermal Map of North America. Compiled by J. Disturnell, Author of " Influences of Climate relating to the World, &c." New York: D. Van Nostrand. London : Sampson Low, Son, and Marston.

This volume treats only of America, but it contains a tolerably perfect account of American climates from the Arctic sea to Cape Horn. It is interesting and curious to observe how widely the climate of different places in the same latitude varies, as between the Atlantic and the Pacific coasts, the inland and the seaboard, the neighbourhood of the Lakes and the waterless interior of the West. The extremes of American weather are also very noticeable, the thermometer frequently ranging from 125 or 130 degrees in the Northern States, varying from a summer heat of 100 degrees to a winter cold of 30 degrees below zero. It would seem that such a climate must needs be unhealthy, yet the death-rate of the States is far lower than that of England; and that of Canada, with a summer that allows peaches and grapes to ripen in the open air, and a winter almost Arctic in its severity, is one of the healthiest in the world. Not the least valuable portions of Mr. Disturnell's work refer to the soils and products of different parts of the Continent, their actual crops and their potential capabilities.

Geological Survey of Illinois. Vol. I. Geology. Vol. II. Palæontology. A. H. Worthen, Director. Published by Authority of the Legislature of Illinois. London : Trübner. 1867.

We have here before us, in two ponderous volumes, the results of an investigation ordered by the Legislature of Illinois into the geology of that State. The investigation has been most searching and complete, and the work contains a clear and extensive account of the geology of the State at large, and of its mineral wealth.

Rapport sur les Progrès de l'Anthropologie. Par A. de Quatrefages. Paris and London: L. Hachette and Co.

Among the many interesting reports published by the French Government this new volume of M. de Quatrefages will occupy a distinguished place. It is the history of almost a new science. The author begins by defining the province of anthropology, and marking its frontiers. The immense number of data which fall under the head of anthropology accounts for the fact that this science is the newest of all. It was impossible, for instance, to lay down any general conclusion as to the nature and constitution of the human race before the geography of the globe had been thoroughly studied. Yet it is only within a comparatively recent period that both hemispheres have revealed their secrets to travellers, and even now we are very far from having an accurate knowledge of the whole surface of the earth. The first chapter in the book before us reviews the various phases through which anthropological science has passed from the days of Buffon to the Foundation of the Paris Société Ethnologique in 1839. This period comprises only a little more than sixty years, and yet it includes the names of some of the most eminent scientific men—Cuvier, the Schlegels, Blumenbach, &c. The progress of anthropology during the last seventy years forms the subject of the second chapter, which gives us, besides, an interesting and very complete account of the books, periodicals, collections, societies, methods of teaching, and other details bearing upon the science. These two chapters constitute a kind of historical summary or introduction; the book itself is divided into three sections, treating respectively of general questions, the common characteristics of the human race, mixed races and crossings. An appendix gives us the scheme proposed by M. de Quatrefages for the classification of the different branches of the great family of mankind. His style is remarkably simple, and his method is so clear that the book will be interesting even to readers who are comparatively ignorant of natural history.

Les Navigations Françaises et la Révolution Maritime du 14ᵉ au 16ᵉ Siècle, d'après les Documents inédits tirés de France, d'Angleterre, d'Espagne et d'Italie, par Pierre Margry. (Paris, Tross.)

This work is devoted to accounts of various voyages of discovery undertaken by French navigators, compiled for the most part from documents hitherto inedited. M. Margry has been long engaged in searching for documents, which he had reason to believe were in existence, recording the early voyages of Frenchmen, and he has been so successful in his search that if we admit the authenticity of the MSS. now published, it must be conceded that France has stronger claims to the merit of geographical discovery than is generally supposed. The greater portion of the volume is taken up with the voyages of adventurous seamen desirous of reaching India by a shorter route than that round the dreaded Cape of Storms.

Rapport sur les Progrès de l'Astronomie. Par M. Delaunay. Paris and London: L. Hachette and Co.

M. Delaunay's account of astronomical science presents a very complete and accurate description of astronomical discovery. He gives a short survey of the explorations made by astronomers in the planetary system; he then goes on to examine M. Foucault's ingenious method for proving the movement of the earth round the sun, and afterwards describes the most recent charts drawn of the heavens at various latitudes, and, after devoting a few paragraphs to comets and shooting stars, concludes with an explanation of the newest instruments employed by scientific men in their observations.

Beiträge zur Ethnographie and Sprachenkunde Amerika's zumal Braziliens. Von Dr. C. P. F. von Martius. 2 Bde. Leipsic: Fleischer. London: Asher and Co.

Dr. Von Martius has for many years enjoyed celebrity as a traveller in Brazil. This country has never lost its attractions for him, and we are now presented with the results of continual study in two stately octaves, partly compiled from a legion of publications, but largely supplemented by the personal knowledge of the author. The first volume is devoted to ethnology, describing and classifying the various obscure tribes of the Brazilian wilderness as accurately as possible, and also giving an account of their customs, and of the rude traces of civil society among them. The second is philological, and is chiefly a string of vocabularies, bristling with polysyllables of the most formidable appearance. The work is a valuable contribution to an intricate though by no means inviting subject.

Siluria: a History of the Oldest Rocks in the British Isles and Other Countries; with a Sketch of the Origin and Distribution of Native Gold, the General Succession of Geological Formations and Changes of the Earth's Surface. By Sir Roderick I. Murchison, F.R.S., Director-General of the Geological Survey of the British Isles. New edition, price 30s. London: John Murray, Albemarle Street, W.

Meetings of Learned Societies.

ASTRONOMICAL SOCIETY.

A meeting of this society took place on November 8th, the Rev. C. Pritchard, M.A., President, in the chair.—Captain T. Almond, Messrs. S. Courtauld and E. Story were elected Fellows.—The following papers were read:—"Eclipses and Transits of Jupiter's Satellites and Eclipse of the Moon," by Mr. Weston.—"Jupiter without his Satellites," by Mr. Prince.—"Appearance of Jupiter, August 20," by Mr. Hough.—"On the Solar Eclipse, August, 1868," by Mr. Stoney.—"On Jupiter without Satellites exterior to his Disc," by Mr. Burr.—"Annual Parallax of Sirius," by Mr. C. Abbé.—"The Lunar Crater Linné," "Occultations of Stars by the Moon," and "On Lunar Eclipse, September 17, 1867," by Capt. Noble.—"Jupiter without a visible Satellite," and "Account of an Observing Chair," by the Rev. W. R. Dawes.—"The November Meteors of 1867," by the Rev. A. W. Deey.—"On the Newton-Pascal Controversy," by Professor Grant; and "Longitude of Kingston Observatory," by Mr. Kington.

ANTHROPOLOGICAL SOCIETY.

The first meeting of the session was held on Tuesday, November 5th, Dr. Leeman, vice-president, in the chair. Dr. J. Hunt read a report of the last meeting. Mr. Fred Collingwood, the secretary, next read an account of the society's proceedings at Dundee. Mr. John Collinson, F.A.S.L., then read a paper "On the Mosquito Indians," among whom he had resided some years. They consisted of seven distinct tribes, to some of whom the Moravian missionaries had done great good. He said that some of the tribes practised flattening the heads of their children in a manner similar to the Indians of Peru and Columbia. They believe in good and evil spirits, but prefer to supplicate the evil rather than the good. He had compiled a vocabulary of a thousand words of the Wolwa language, and his was the only one which had been formed. The chairman, Dr. Leeman, in speaking of the character of the tribes of the Mosquito shore, said there was a great decline in the civilisation of Central America. He said that there had been a recent discovery of important sculptures in the Mosquito territory. Captain Bedford Pim, R.N., denied the beneficial effects of missionary labours amongst the tribes; and adverting to an account of a disgustingly intoxicating liquor which the native women made for the men of chewed bananas and saliva, he said something similar was used in the Sandwich Islands. Mr. Collinson, in replying to the remarks of the members, said he considered that the pure Indians were superior in moral character to the half-breeds. The king must be a man of pure aboriginal descent. Dr. Charnock, V.P. of the society, objected to the term Indian, as applied to any but an inhabitant of the banks of the Indus, wishing the society to reverse the usages of centuries which originated, however, in the mistake of Columbus, who thought he had reached Hindostan. The society adjourned till Tuesday, November 19th.

BRISTOL NATURALISTS' SOCIETY.

The second meeting of the session took place on October 3rd, Mr. T. Pease, vice-president, in the chair. Mr. F. Fedden read a paper entitled "Observations on the Natural History of Burmah," which described the geographical position of the country, its ruins and minerals, curious mud volcanoes, and also the human inhabitants, amongst whom he had resided seven years. October 10, in the Zoological Section, Mr. Swayne read for Mr. C. O. Groom-Napier, F.G.S., a paper on "The Dodo," which was illustrated with coloured drawings, a set of bones from Mauritius, and Professor Owen's diagram of the skeleton.

GEOLOGICAL SOCIETY.

At the above society, on Wednesday evening, November 6th, W. W. Smyth, Esq., M.A., president, in the chair,—N. Plant, Col. Fox, G. H. F. Ulrich, the Rev. J. J. Bleasdale, D.D., J. Ince, and the Rev. T. S. Wollaston, M.A., were elected Fellows. A paper was read by Mr. Tylor "On the Amiens Gravel and the River Somme." Mr. Tylor came before the society with views entirely differing from those already held. It was his object to prove that the action of the river was the cause of the altered appearance of the formation in the valley, and that the organic remains and flint instruments found at Abbeville and other places were brought down and deposited in their present position by this cause; he instanced the action of the River Lea at the Clapton-terraces as having produced similar results. A careful examination of gravels taken from the highest levels with those of the lower proved that the shells, etc., were common to all. Of the chalk formation itsel some curious conditions were pointed out; in some places fissures were filled in with lias, and in others the very uneven upper surface in places descended in pipes to various depths, and in diameter some of them reached ten feet, containing detritus and flints of various irregular forms; in this *debris* their perfect form and uninjured condition prove that they were deposited in still or slowly moving water. Mr. Prestwich defended his position with his usual ability. He holds that there are two gravels of an older and newer formation lying one over the other. In the older gravel he notices human remains in various forms, and in this rests the differences between the two observers. Sir Charles Lyell went at some length into the inquiry respecting the action of rivers, and pointed out the hundreds of centuries of time requisite to prepare the pebbly gravel composing the debris washed down, and described the condition of river banks after heavy and repeated floods, and the deposition of brick clay, and land and fluviatile shells along the banks; he would have preferred the levels being taken from the river, rather than from the sea, as being more easy for comparison. Sir John Lubbock, Mr. Evans, and several other speakers took part in the discussion. Sixteen new members were elected to the society.

GEOLOGISTS' ASSOCIATION, UNIVERSITY COLLEGE, LONDON.

The session commenced on Friday, November 1st, with a paper by the Rev. Thomas Wiltshire, M.A.,

F.G.S., "On the Chief Groups of the Cephalopoda." The author having given a definition of the forms of life to which the term cephalopoda is restricted, proceeded to divide the class into the two great orders of the *Dibranchiata* and the *Tetrabranchiata*: the common cuttle-fish and the pearly nautilus being taken as types of these orders, various facts in connection with their organisation and habits were mentioned, and allusion was made to some of the other genera now existing in the present seas. These remarks served as an introduction to the description of the fossils belonging to the same class. The belemnites, the ammonites, and the nautili, with their sub-genera, were explained. The old traditions relative to the two former were not forgotten, and the knowledge of more modern times brought to bear upon the subject. The paper closed with some remarks upon the existence of the nautili group in the more ancient deposits, and upon the importance to be attached to the zones of all these fossils in connection with agricultural and mining operations.

GEOGRAPHICAL SOCIETY.

At the meeting held on November 11th, Sir R. I. Murchison, president, in the chair, the Rev. A. A. W. Drew, M.A., W. H. Evans, Sir H. Bartle Frere, and the Rev. J. Graves were elected Fellows.—The President, in opening the session, gave a *résumé* of geographical progress since the last meeting. The latest news received from the Livingstone Search Expedition was dated the 27th July, on which day Commander Gordon, of H.M.S. Petrel, reported that the search party had safely entered the Kongoni mouth of the Zambesi; and having luckily obtained on the spot a negro crew for the steel boat, he had departed at once up stream, before the cruiser's boats recrossed the bar in the evening. No further news was expected till February or March in the coming year. Alluding to Abyssinian geography, he announced that Mr. Markham, the senior secretary of the society, had been appointed geographer to the expedition now on foot, and had departed for that country ten days previously. The other men of science accompanying the expedition had been appointed in Bombay. The geologist was Mr. W. Blandford, the Deputy Superintendent of the Geological Survey of India—as sound and clear-sighted a practical geologist as could have been found at home. The map of Abyssinia recently issued by the Topographical Department of the War Office, and compiled by Colonel Cooke, R.E., was mentioned as the result of a an assiduous sifting and comparison of all previous documents, combined with hitherto unpublished materials. A recent detailed map of the northern parts of Abyssinia had also just been published by Dr. Petermann; and a work had recently appeared from the pen of the learned German traveller, Theod. von Heuglin, containing the narrative of his extensive journeys and researches in Abyssinia in 1861-2. Important papers were expected to be read in the course of the session on different portions of the central American Isthmus, among them one by Mr. Collinson, C.E., on "Nicaragua," and another on "Darien," by M. Lucien de Puydt. An account of his recent explorations in Greenland was also expected from the pen of Mr. Edward Whymper, who had just arrived in England from his arduous journey. Mr. C. R. Markham sent in a paper "On the Portuguese Expedition in the Sixteenth and Seventeenth Centuries," which was read. John II., of Portugal, sent two travellers into the East. One of these men, arriving at the court of King Alexander (Prester John), was detained in Abyssinia during the rest of his life; the other, having penetrated as far as Malabar, returned, and visited Abyssinia. The then king of the country, being in difficulties with his neighbours the Moors, sent letters to Portugal and to Rome asking for help. Portugal sent men and money, and during the short term of their occupancy—from 1526 to 1633, when the Jesuits were expelled—many fortified places were erected. The routes of the Portuguese expeditions were pointed out, and at the conclusion of the paper Sir H. Rawlinson gave a geographical description of the country, aided by a most carefully arranged may by Captain George, R.G.S. Dr. Beke stated that the climate was most salubrious, and pointed out the fact that none of the prisoners were ill or had died. Lord Houghton hoped Government had taken the precaution of consulting former travellers, and Sir R. Murchison stated that such had been the earnest desire of the Foreign Minister, and that no means had been neglected by which information could be obtained. Mr. H. Seymour, M.P., stated that the subject introduced by Lord Houghton had already been fully discussed in Parliament last session, and he had no doubt that the chiefs of the expedition would know how to act when once they had entered upon the campaign. The assemblage was larger than usual, and thirty-six new fellows were elected.

ETHNOLOGICAL SOCIETY.

At this meeting Mr. Crawfurd read Mr. Consul Plowden's notes on Abyssinia and its races, and followed it with a commentary by himself. For the many years this clever traveller dwelt in the country he appeared to enjoy the confidence of the present king, and by his great skill and judgment he succeeded in raising Theodore from a condition little better than that of the rest of his ignorant and sensual fellow-countrymen to a really respectable and praiseworthy monarch. On the death of Plowden the king relapsed into his semi-barbarous condition. In a country so rich in the productions of temperate regions, and where the people are given to none of the vices of their African neighbours, life is most agreeable. Their scrupulous regard to ceremonial in private life, their feasting at the houses of the great and observance of superstitious observances, makes them closely resemble the society of Europe in the middle ages. Their colour is black and nut brown. The Gallas are, according to Dr. Beke (who was present at the meeting) an intruding race, having entered Abyssinia, as the Normans came into England. Building is an art unknown; therefore, there are no antiquities. Mr. Crawfurd stated that with the exception of a few works in the Amharic character they are destitute of literature; but Sir H. Rawlinson, who spoke on the literature as a good ethnological test of the antiquity of races, proceeded at some length into the curious history of the Amharic language and its records. At Axum is an obelisk, and at the sea coast a chair bearing an inscription recorded by the famous Cosmos in the fifth century; and from these early records was traced a language similar, if not identical with that on the inscribed rock in South Arabia, on the opposite coast. These inscriptions were identical in many respects with old inscribed cylinders found in Babylonia, giving dates certainly one, two, and three thousand years B.C. Amongst the guests of the evening were Lady Franklin, Captain Sherard Osborne, and others. A series of photographs of the Nicobar pirates (to whom a melancholy interest attaches just now), taken by Captain Beddingfield, was exhibited.

ENTOMOLOGICAL SOCIETY.

At a meeting on November 4th, Professor Westwood, V.P., in the chair, Mr. Bond exhibited three recent additions to the list of British Lepidoptera, *Psyche crassiorella* of Bruand, *Grapholitha ravulana* of Herrich-Schäffer, and *Coccyx vernana* of Knaggs. Mr. T. W. Wood exhibited variously coloured pupæ of *Papilio Machaon, Pieris brassicæ*, and *P. rapæ*, and read some remarks on the colouration of Chrysalides, with a view to show that their hue was more or less derived from the objects in their immediate vicinity at the time of changing from the larva state. Mr. M'Lachlan exhibited a remarkable species of Mantispidæ from Bahia, which he considered to be the female of the *Trichoscelia notha* of Erichson; also two gynandromorphous insects belonging to Mr. B. Cooke, of Manchester, one a saw-fly, *Dolerus madidus* of Klug, and the other a Trichopterous insect, *Limnephilus striola* of Kolenati; also two monstrosities received from Professor Zeller, a *Hylotoma fasciata*, in which the left posterior tibia was two-jointed, and a *Tenthredo scutellata* with five wings. The following papers were read:—"Descriptions of some new Species of "Diurual Lepidoptera," by Mr. W. C. Hewitson; "A Monograph of the Genus Thais," by the Rev. D. C. Timins; and "A Revision of the Australian Buprestidæ described by the Rev. F. W. Hope," by Mr. E. Saunders.

ROYAL HORTICULTURAL SOCIETY.

At the general meeting held November 5th, Major Trevor Clarke in the chair, five new Fellows were elected and one society affiliated. The Chairman directed attention to a Pelargonium, the result of a cross between one of the quercifolium section called white unique, which was first brought into notice by Mr. Beaton, and Rollisson's unique, as showing how great an improvement may be effected even by a first cross. Major Clarke added that he wished to bring the rough-leaved quercifolium varieties into notice, as they might be much improved. One of their good qualities was their remarkable fitness for button-hole decoration. Mr. Murray directed attention to a piece of a lime tree which had been brought by Mr. Reeves, interesting from the marks which it exhibited, and with which the greater portion of the tree it was taken from was covered. They appeared, however, to be merely the slimy marks of snails. Mr. Reeves having stated that two-thirds of the tree was in a similar condition, Major Clarke said he agreed with Mr. Murray as to the cause, and urged members to bring to the society's meetings anything that appeared to be abnormal, as such specimens frequently proved of much interest in a scientific point of view.

QUEKETT MICROSCOPICAL CLUB.

A monthly meeting of this club was held at University College on the evening of October 25, the President in the chair. Mr. S. J. McIntyre read a paper on "Chelifers," in which he gave some interesting facts with regard to the haunts, habits, and mode of capture of these curious animals, resembling minute scorpions, and having the backward and sideway motions of crabs. Of the fifty-four known species eight are British, and are chiefly found under the bark of trees and in houses, amongst old papers, &c., often rendering good service by feeding on the insects which are usually so destructive in old libraries. Several living specimens were exhibited under the microscopes, where their activity in the pursuit of their prey was conspicuous. A paper by Mr. C. Nicholson, M.A., on "Object Glasses for the Microscope," was read. Nine members were elected.

Correspondence.

[*Under this head we shall be glad to insert any letters of general interest.*]

MIGRATION OF BIRDS AND INSECTS.

SIR,—I do not at all agree with the theory of Mr. Hunt and Harvie (mentioned in the late numbers of the NATURALIST'S NOTE BOOK), in thinking that the migration of birds is caused by the migration of the insects on which they feed. Late in Autumn, after the birds have left for their winter quarters, I have observed on fine days, when the sun shines and warms the surface of the ground, that winged insects come forth and fill the air; this confirms the opinions of Mr. R. W. B., and Mr. Ulidia.

Again, if as Mr. Hunt thinks, birds follow "great hords of insects," they must surely fly at a very slow rate to keep up with the insects, whose powers of flight are well known to be very much less than that of birds.

Again (as stated by Mr. Ulidia) it is very strong on our side, that almost yearly great numbers of migratory birds fall dead from sheer starvation, on the decks of ships bound for distant lands. It is a well-known fact, that a very great proportion of our flying insects are killed by the severe frost of winter. In conclusion, I may add, that I quite agree with "R. W. B." that birds are induced to leave this country by the coldness of the weather, and to return, from their love to the place of their birth,

I am, yours truly,

J. D. S. W.

Mavisbush House, Nov. 9th.

Sir,—I am glad to see more remarks on the migrations of the swallow (*hirundo rustica*) in your valuable columns, it is a subject of great interest to all. Your correspondent "Mr. A. G. Harvie," states in the November number, page 315, we have proof that they (swallows) do not hybernate. Would he (with your permission) insert a few of the most striking proofs in the NOTE BOOK?

Many people laugh at the idea of swallows hybernating, but well authenticated facts have shown that it is not an impossibility: the great White, of Selbourne believed it, so I think the case deserves investigating. Swallows have often been found in a torpid state in winter, but very seldom seen taking their flight across the ocean. How is it that swallows disappear for a week or more, and then return if the weather changes? Do they come back again from the other side of the ocean, or how is it? Hoping I have not trespassed on your pages,

I remain, yours obediently,
T. R. CLEPHAN.

Stockton-on-Tees.

Short Notes.

THE GUINEA FOWL.—The Pintado, or Guinea fowl, is partially known in a domestic state all over Europe, but is most common on the Mediterranean coasts. Africa appears to be its native country, and it was probably introduced into this country from Guinea. It is not only quite hardy, but we find this fowl very profitable to rear, and consider if the mode of rearing it were better known it would be more kept than it is. The first week in June is soon enough to begin sitting common fowls on Guinea fowls' eggs. They come off in July, when plenty of ant eggs can be found for their food. One of our Guinea hens laid 180 eggs from April to October in 1851. Of course we feed them well. We never allow them to sit on their own eggs, but prefer giving them to a turkey, which will bring them up as cautiously as any hen, in fact better. We would recommend turkeys who lose their first brood to be set on the Guinea fowls' eggs to rear them. A turkey can sit on from 20 to 24 eggs, whilst a common hen only upon 15 eggs. They do not like confinement, and if near a good park or grass fields where they can range, will find more than half the food they require. The best way we find to render them tame is to feed them in one particular place, and at one specific time of the day, when they will not fail to come to the accustomed spot. They are fond of roosting in trees, if you are not particular in getting them home to roost early in the evening; but as we are careful of ours in this respect, we can drive them home at an early hour as easily as a flock of sheep. They cannot be put up to fatten, but must be allowed a good range, with plenty of food. We can generally sell them in February for 5s. a couple, and they are as easy to keep as chickens. To rear Guinea fowls, however, a good sitting hen or turkey takes 28 to 29 days to hatch, and as soon as they are hatched they will run about and be very wild, like a partridge. We place the hen and brood under a coop, with a lift similar to that used by keepers in rearing young pheasants, and are careful that there are no apertures through which they can get out, for in that case they would get to a stack of wood, or something of that sort, from which it would be very awkward to get them out again before they starved. Therefore we keep them very close within this coop for ten days, and give them plenty of ant eggs in the left compartment of the coop, and if we can procure sufficient they will require no other food; indeed they will not do well without them. Any one who can rear pheasants or partridges may rear Guinea fowls, as they seem to require the same treatment at first.—Land Steward, in *Gardener's Chronicle*, Oct. 26.

INJURY TO COFFEE PLANTATIONS.—"How many of your readers, I wonder," says the Madras correspondent of the *Times*, October 22nd, "have heard of the 'borer.' I never myself remember to have seen its name in any English newspaper. But here, in Madras, it has long filled the columns of our press, and lorded it over our dinner tables, until just now it had to give place to the Abyssinian expedition. It is a kind of small grub which infests coffee plantations, and which in the coffee districts of this Presidency has done, and is doing, mischief incalculable. A planter told me yesterday that on one of his estates, 320 acres, or about 400,000 trees, had in one season been entirely and irretrievably destroyed by it. He estimated the yearly produce of these trees at £10,000, and considered that of this about half was net profit. The destruction was so sudden as to be inevitable. He had no intimation whatever of danger until he saw the leaves turn yellow and droop, and the trees were then past all hope. This may have been an exceptionally bad case (I mean as regards the extent of the calamity, not as regards the nature, which is almost invariably the same), but there are many more very like. Here and there planters have been positively ruined, and obliged to give up their estates, and leave their homes. There is a report that the Madras Government think of appointing a special commissioner to investigate the subject, and it is, without doubt, well worthy of Governmental notice, for though many doughty champions have entered the list against him, and many schemes have been confidently recommended for his overthrow, the borer does not yet seem to have found his match."

AUTUMN LEAVES.—Wishing to produce something out of the common way in table decoration, the other day the idea occurred to me of using "dead leaves" in lieu of flowers, and the result was so successful that I am induced to give you a short description of the arrangement. The flat part of a Dobson's Dinner Vase was filled with moistened sand, and round the glass stem was twined a slender branch of Lonicera aureo-reticulata, whose pretty green and yellow leaves droop downwards. The outer edge was formed of a fringe of hardy Ferns; next to them a few leaves of Mrs. Pollock, Flower of the Day, or Lady Plymouth Geraniums, their light tints contrasting with the brilliant orange and scarlet of the Sumach Rhus, large and small. Almost black are the curled Perilla leaves, and quite white the tender sprays of Variegated Balm ; the fashionable brown comes from off yon tall Poplar tree that is slowly dying ; and the Virginian Creeper produces the newer shade the French call " *Bismarck en colère.*" A stiff Hart's-tongue supplies the verdant green, and light fronds of Maiden-hair add gracefulness to the group ; stiff and straight are the branches of green and white Periwinkle ; the Amaranthus yields a melancholy red, while in the striped Iresine is seen the colour of Bordeaux wine ; but between these two the ragged Cineraria maritima looks light and downy. Then a few of the sere yellowed leaves of Laburnum, all speckled as they are, a branch of snowy Gnaphalium near the spray of purple Beech, the shaded Liquidambar imberbe, and the pure crimson of the long narrow Cockscomb leaf, need only the shiny Ice plant, a dark olive Camellia or Myrtle leaf, with a spike or two of Juniper and Mountain Heather to om plete as bright a cluster as ever wax lights illumined, though not one flower or berry rises from out our autumn bouquet. And so we find that e'en in withering leaves " a thing of beauty is a joy for ever ;" and in arranging them remember that, at all seasons—

"It is pleasant to note all plants, from the Rush to the spreading Cedar ;
From the giant king of Palms to the Lichen that staineth its stem."

Ariel, in *Gardener's Chronicle*, Nov. 2.

SEA GULLS.—Along our coasts, every summer, during the breeding season, thousands of harmless sea-birds are shot. The fellows who murder them are too clumsy to bag a cormorant, a diver, a scoter, or even a willock who can duck the flash. But the poor honest gull, who follows up the boat, in the hope of the leavings of the luncheon, as a robin might do on land, or a tern who hovers over them with innocent surprise, wondering what they are and mean—they, the most harmless and the most useful of sea-birds, are the special game of cockneys—for there are cockneys elsewhere than in London. The gull is the scavenger of the sea. He does his little best to ward off cholera and typhus from every foul ill-drained harbour. He ought to be preserved—if parliaments were parliaments —as religiously as vultures are in the tropics ; and the fool who shoots a gull ought to be fined a pound.— *Fraser's Magazine* for November.

MONSTER EEL.—On Tuesday an eel of immense size was shown at Mr. Culling's, fishmonger, of Downham Market, which was taken out of the river Ouze, near Denver sluice. It measured in length 5ft. 8in., girth 17¼in., and weighed 36lb. (28lb. after being cleansed). Yarrell, in his "British Fishes" mentions having seen the skins of two at Cambridge which together weighed 50lb. (one 27lb. and the other 23lb.), which were taken within a few miles of the spot where this was captured. The party who secured it left for Cambridge with their prize, and obtained at Ely upwards of £3 by showing it. Ely is said to have obtained its name from rents in the isle being paid in eels. The lords of the manors in the isle were annually entitled to upwards of 100,000 eels—not, we presume, of this size.—*Times.*

Remarks, Queries, &c.

(*Under this head we shall be happy to insert original Remarks, Queries, &c.*)

AMERICAN ASSOCIATION FOR THE ADVANCEMENT OF SCIENCE.—The Sixteenth Annual Meeting was held at Burlington, Vermont, commencing on Wednesday, August 21, and continuing until Monday night, August 26, 1867. The following papers were read in the Natural History Section :—

First Day.

"The Distribution of Precious Metals in the United States," by Col. Chas. Whittlesey.

Second Day.

"The Geological Relations of the Mastodon and Fossil Elephant of North America," by Prof. James Hall. "Considerations drawn from the Study of the Orthoptera of North America," by Samuel H. Scudder. "Traces of Ancient Glaciers in the White Mountains," by G. L. Vose. "The Origin of the so-called Lignilites or Epsomites," by Prof. O. C. Marsh. "The Geographical Distribution of the Sediments and the Fossils of the Hamilton, Portage, and Chemung Groups of New York," by Prof. James Hall. "The Distribution of Limnæa Megasoma and Cognate Genera," by L. E. Chittenden.

Third Day.

"Tellurium a Metal," by Prof. L. Bradley. "Upon some remarkable Fossil Fishes obtained by Rev. H. Herzer from the Devonian Rocks at Delaware, Ohio," by Professor J. S. Newberry. "The Fossil Insects of North America," by S. H. Scudder. "The Winooski Marbles of Colchester, Vt.," by Prof. C. H. Hitchcock. "The Zoological Affinities of the Tabulate Corals," by Prof. A. E. Verrill. "The Coal Measures of Illinois," by Prof. A. H. Worthen. "New Points in the Geology of Nova Scotia and New Brunswick," by Prof. J. W. Dawson.

Fourth Day.

"On some New Fossil Sponges from the Lower Silurian," by Prof. O. C. Marsh. "On the occurrence of Fossil Sponges in the successive Groups of the Palæozoic Series," by Professor James Hall. "The American Beaver," by Lewis H. Morgan. "The Distortion and Metamorphosis of Pebbles in Conglomerates," by C. H. Hitchcock.

Fifth Day.

"On some Fossil Reptiles and Fishes from the Carboniferous Strata of Ohio, Kentucky, and Illinois," by Prof. J. S. Newberry. "Cotta's Law of the Earth's Development," by R. W. Raymond. "On Mountain Masses of Iron Ore in the United States," by Col. Charles Whittlesey. "On the Lower Silurian Brown Hematite Beds of America," by B. S. Lyman. "Explanations of the Geological Map of Maine," by Prof. C. H. Hitchcock. "On the Geographical Distribution of Radiates on the West Coast of America," by Prof. A. E. Verrill. "Considerations relating to the Climate of the Glacial Epoch in North America," by Prof. Edward Hungerford. "Depression of the Sea during the Glacial period," by Col. Chas. Whittlesey. "Ripton Sea Beaches," by Prof. Edward Hungerford.

"On the Cretaceous and Tertiary Flora of North America," by Prof. J. S. Newberry. "On certain Effects produced upon Fossils by Weathering," by Prof. O. C. Marsh. "Geology of Vermont," by Prof. C. H. Hitchcock. "The Insect Fauna of the Summit of Mount Washington as compared with that of Labrador," by Dr. A. S. Packard, jun. "Remarks on the Ichthyological Fauna of Lake Champlain," by F. W. Putnam. "The Embryology of Libellula (Diplax?), with notes on the Morphology of Insects, and the Classification of the Neuroptera," by Dr. A. S. Packard, jun. "On the Flowering of Plants," by James Hyatt.—From *American Naturalist*, October.

THE KESTREL AND SPARROWHAWK.—In an extract from the *Times* on page 317 of this paper, the writer classes the kestrel with the sparrowhawk, and says that if they were allowed to increase he fears the farmers' chickens and ducklings would be heavy sufferers. Now it is a great mistake to think that the kestrel does anything like as much harm as the sparrowhawk. The sparrowhawk is well known to prey greatly on young poultry and game; whilst, on the other hand, the kestrel lives almost entirely on mice, which are the farmers' greatest enemies. Your correspondent "R. W. B.," on page 169 of the NATURALIST'S NOTE BOOK, states that in the year 1866 he found a chicken in a kestrel's nest; but this is quite an exception to the rule. I myself have examined more than one nest daily, for the purpose of finding out what they feed their young on. I have taken as many as a dozen mice and small rats from a nest in one day. During the whole time of incubation I have not found more than two or three small birds of any kind. I hope that what I have said may go in some way to prevent the innocent kestrel from suffering the penalty due to the rapacious sparrowhawk.

Mavisbush House. J. D. S. W.

GROWTH OF FERNS FROM SPORES.—I have been desirous of observing, by means of the microscope, the growth of ferns from spores, and have adopted the plan of scattering the spores on a piece of sandstone which stands in water under a bell glass; but although they germinate quickly, and go on well for a time, the prothallium does not attain its complete growth, so that I have been unable to study the antheridia and archegonia. My sandstone is placed in a cold room where it gets very little sun, and the spores have been germinating for more than two months; perhaps this is too short a time in which to give them up, but I am the more discouraged because they have scarcely made such quick progress as on another occasion when I tried the same experiment, and when they certainly stopped growing before they attained their full development. I may add that I tried cinders, as recommended in your number of last July, but that my spores did not sprout at all upon them. If any of your readers who have studied the growth of ferns scientifically would give me a few hints how to proceed I should be greatly obliged. I am also desirous of ascertaining what book gives the best account of the liverworts, and shall be greatly obliged for any information on that head.

Windermere, Nov. 10, 1867. T.

THE CHELIFER.—I take the liberty of writing to ask if you could give me any account of the Chelifer, or Chilifer, where found, &c.? THOS. S. GUYESS.
Speen Hill, Newberry, Nov. 12, 1867.

[The Book Scorpion (Chélifer Wideri) belongs to the class *Arachnida*. The Rev. J. G. Wood gives the following account of it in his popular Natural History:—"The Chelifer, a little arachnid very much resembling a tiny scorpion without a tail. The body is flattened, and the palpi are much elongated and furnished with a regular claw at the end like that of a true scorpion. The Chelifer is an active little being, running with much speed, and directing its course backward, forward, or sideways with equal ease. It lives in dark places in houses, between books in libraries, and similar localities, preferring however those that are rather damp. It does no harm however to the books, but rather confers a favour on their owner, feeding on woodlice, mites, and other beings that work sad mischief in the library. Its general colour is brownish-red, and it is remarkable that the palpi are twice as long as the whole body. This, as well as an allied genus called Obisium, is found in England. The two genera can be easily distinguished by the cephalathorax—that of Chelifer being parted by a cross groove, and that of Obisium being entire.]

THE HOUSE-SPARROW.—On page 61 of the NATURALIST'S NOTE BOOK, a writer to the *Field* supposes that the benefits conferred by the common sparrow outweigh tenfold the mischief it does in consuming corn and other grain. I think there can be no doubt but that this is far too bold an assertion. In some places it certainly does much more good than harm, but in others it does much more harm than good. As a rule I think the house-sparrow may be considered a friend to the *gardener*, but an enemy to the *farmer*. Where grain and insect food are equally abundant, the common sparrow almost invariably chooses the former to the entire neglect of the latter. The same writer also states that he has found them valuable assistants in clearing his gooseberry and currant trees of caterpillars. But a year or two ago my own gooseberries and currants were nearly all destroyed by small green caterpillars—the shrubs being completely covered with them—and although sparrows flocked in the neighbourhood the insects were left untouched, whilst stacks of grain kept close by suffered considerable damage. A writer to the *Times* (page 317 of NATURALIST'S NOTE BOOK) speaking of the house-sparrow says—"when too numerous, and when surrounded by corn, his habits become almost entirely *graminivorous*." I think the most just conclusion to be arrived at with regard to the common sparrow is, that the evil it does is counterbalanced by the good; and that an indiscriminate slaughter of this bird would be fraught with very serious consequences. This has been already proved by many in various parts of the kingdom. R. W. B.

BIRDS AND THEIR YOUNG.—Having tried the experiment of changing the young of different birds in order to discover their powers of discerning their own from those of strangers, I give the following:—In the spring of 1865 I took an unfledged hedgesparrow and changed it for a young brown linnet of the same size, placing the sparrow in the linnet's nest. On visiting the nest next morning I found that each of the mother birds had discovered the little strangers and shown them no mercy, both of which were lying dead at the bottom of the nests. Last year I put an unfledged jackdaw into the nest of a blackbird, in place of her only young one. Although it was nearly twice the size of the young blackbird the old birds did not perceive the difference, but treated it with the greatest care, and used to make a great uproar when any one approached the nest. The jackdaw throve very well for several days, during which time its foster parents fed it on worms and grubs. One day on examining the nest I found the poor thing quite dead, and being interested in the case I endeavoured to discover the cause, and found that the old birds had treated their young charge to a feast of ivy-berries, which no doubt had poisoned it.

Mavisbush House.   J. D. S. W.

RAIN WATER.—"Pure cold water is the best drink, when it can be received without the dust and other properties, with which it often becomes mixed. As it falls upon the roofs of houses it is soft and pure. 'Hard water,' as it is called, is unwholesome. When no other water can be obtained, as is often the case in cities, 'hard water' may be filtered or distilled, and in this way be rendered perfectly pure and fit for drink."

In the above paragraph, taken from the *Journal of Health* for March, 1855, we are told that *rain water* is preferable to *spring or hard water* for drinking purposes. Is this true?   R. W. B.

ORNITHOLOGY OF BERKS AND BUCKS.—Being engaged in writing a history of the birds of these two counties, I shall be much obliged to any gentlemen who are cognisant of facts connected with the birds of Berks and Bucks, if they will forward notes, anecdotes, &c., to me, at "Messrs. Ingalton and Drake's, High Street, Eton, Bucks (by whom subscribers' names are received).

ALEXANDER CLARK-KENNEDY.

NATURAL HSTORY OF NEW ZEALAND.—As I am contemplating returning to New Zealand I should feel obliged if you or any of the readers of the NATURALIST'S NOTE BOOK would be kind enough to recommend to me any book or books (elementary) on the entomology, conchology, and fish of the above colony.

JAS. R. BURNSIDE.

FROGS AND THEIR FOOD.—Frogs when in a tadpole condition feed on that very common green weed which always collects on the sides of any vessel that has had water in it some time.   W. R. B. GYRINUS.

THE COMMON MOUSE.—The common mouse has a natural appetite for bacon; the common field-mouse eats meat raw or cooked.   J. R. B.

SENSITIVE PLANTS.—Can you or any of your readers inform me which is the best way to raise sensitive plants, the best time to sow them, &c. ? A. de H.

STATE OF THE WEATHER NEAR LONDON.

Oct. and Nov.	Moon's Age.	Barometer.		Temperature.					Wind	Rain.	Remarks.
				Of the Air.			of the Earth				
		Max.	Min.	Max	Min	Mean	1 foot deep	2 feet deep			
Thurs. 17	20	29.705	29.686	62	41	51.5	50	52	S.	.04	Clear; fine; masses of white clouds; rain; clear.
Friday 18	21	29.719	29.665	61	36	48.5	50	52	S.W.	.08	Clear; clear and fine; rain; clear at night.
Satur. 19	22	29.679	29.648	58	32	45.0	50	52	S.W.	.01	Overcast; fine; overcast; low fog; clear.
Sunday 20	☾	29.968	29.812	60	30	45.0	54	53	S.	.00	Foggy; very heavy dew; clear and very fine; clear.
Mon. 21	24	30.040	30.101	58	31	44.5	53	53	S.W.	.00	Overcast; cloudy; overcast at night.
Tues. 22	25	30.177	30.128	62	50	56.0	53	53	S.	.00	Overcast; cloudy; fine; clear at night.
Wed. 23	26	30.044	29.859	57	45	51.0	53	53	S.E.	.00	Overcast & damp; clear & very fine; bright sun; overcast.
Thurs. 24	27	29.942	29.785	61	41	51.0	55	53	S.W.	.00	Overcast; very mild; very fine; clear; low fog.
Friday 25	28	30.130	30.085	62	34	48.0	55	53	E.	.00	Overcast; fine; cloudy and fine.
Satur. 26	29	30.082	29.938	62	45	53.5	51	53	S.	.00	Clear; low fog; clear and fine; clear.
Sunday 27	●	29.502	29.351	51	29	40.0	52	52	N.W.	.17	Overcast; boisterous; very heavy rain; clear and cold.
Mon. 28	1	29.924	29.762	55	30	42.5	51	51	N.W.	.02	Clear; hoar frost; clear and fine; clear and frosty.
Tues. 29	2	29.999	29.738	55	47	51.0	51	51	S.W.	.01	Rain; cloudy and boisterous; cloudy; overcast.
Wed. 30	3	29.982	29.874	54	47	50.5	51	51	S.W.	.06	Overcast and damp; overcast; rain at night.
Thurs. 31	4	29.901	29.877	57	43	50.0	54	52	W.	.06	Overcast and mild; cloudy and fine; overcast.
Friday 1	5	30.010	29.837	65	32	48.5	54	52	W.	.00	Overcast; fine; clear at night.
Satur. 2	6	30.469	30.227	52	24	38.0	51	52	N.	.00	Clear; bright sunshine; clear and frosty.
Sunday 3	7	30.845	30.396	51	32	41.5	50	50	W.	.00	Heavy fog; clear; overcast at night.
Mon. 4	☽	30.190	30.219	53	33	43.0	51	50	W.	.00	Overcast and cold; overcast; fine; overcast.
Tues. 5	9	30.252	30.222	48	24	36.0	49	50	N.E.	.00	Clear and fine; masses of white clouds; clear and frosty.
Wed. 6	10	30.425	30.366	49	25	37.0	48	49	N.E.	.00	Foggy; hoar frost; cloudy; clear and frosty at night.
Thurs. 7	11	30.494	30.471	52	24	38.0	47	48	W.	.00	Heavy fog; very clear, with bright sun; low fog; frosty.
Friday 8	12	30.516	30.493	54	28	41.0	46	47	W.	.00	Low fog; hoar frost; very clear; clear and frosty.
Satur. 9	13	30.518	30.492	49	37	43.0	48	47	W.	.00	Foggy; overcast; densely overcast.
Sunday 10	14	30.471	30.395	51	30	40.5	48	47	N.E.	.00	Overcast; overcast and damp; overcast; mild.
Mon. 11	15	30.309	30.180	41	26	33.5	47	47	W.	.00	Overcast; very mild; heavy fog; foggy at night.
Tues. 12	○	30.277	30.084	44	36	40.0	47	47	N.E.	.00	Overcast and damp; foggy; overcast at night.
Wed. 13	17	30.007	29.852	50	26	38.0	48	47	W.	.00	Overcast; mild; overcast and damp; clear and frosty.
Thurs. 14	18	29.624	29.537	56	40	48.0	49	47	S.	.08	Rain; overcast, showery; overcast and mild.
Friday 15	19	29.603	29.551	61	44	51.5	50	48	S.E.	.00	Foggy, very mild; overcast; fine but overcast.
Satur. 16	20	29.668	29.563	48	38	43.0	48	47	E.	.00	Overcast, boisterous and cold; boisterous, clear and cold.
Sunday 17	21	30.035	29.778	48	30	39.0	47	47	N.E.	.00	Overcast and boisterous; overcast, cold; cloudy.
Mon. 18	☽	30.243	30.162	43	39	41.0	48	47	N.	.00	Overcast, mild; overcast; fine, but overcast.
Tues. 19	23	30.247	30.230	49	26	37.5	46	47	N.W.	.00	Overcast and mild; overcast; clear and frosty.
Wed. 20	24	30.347	30.298	41	36	38.5	45	46	N.	.00	Clear, hoar frost; overcast; overcast and cold.

THE
NATURALIST'S NOTE BOOK.

THE NATURALIST'S NOTE BOOK

FOR

1868.

A MONTHLY RECORD

OF

ANECDOTES, THEORIES, AND FACTS

RELATING TO

NATURAL SCIENCE,

TOGETHER WITH NOTICES OF NEW BOOKS, REPORTS OF
THE MEETINGS OF LEARNED SOCIETIES, ORIGINAL CORRESPONDENCE,
AND DESCRIPTIONS OF NEW INVENTIONS.

Think nought a trifle, though it small appear;
Small sands the mountain, moments make the year,
And trifles life.   YOUNG.

London:
REEVES AND TURNER,
196, STRAND.

INDEX.

ASTRONOMY, METEOROLOGY, and the WEATHER.
Comets and Meteors, 308, 349.
Dew, 365.
Dew of Heaven, the, 7.
Eclipse in August, the, 215, 248.
Eclipse, the Hindu View of the, 377
Electricity and Vegetation, 58.
Electricity, Influence of on Plants, 28.
Lightning, Effects of on Metals, 341.
Lightning Figures, 318.
Lightning, Strange Freaks of, 238.
Lunar Rainbow, 382.
Magnet (Needle), why does it point to the North, 62, 93.
Mars, 140.
Mercury, 375.
Meteors, etc., 381.
Meteor, Killed by a, 375.
Meteors, Luminous, 305.
Meteorological Observations, 374.
Moon, Influence of the, 284, 382.
Moon's Surface, Change on the, 307.
Natal, Meteorology of, 98.
Rainfall, 222, 254, 350.
Rain Water as a beverage, 54.
Rain Water, 29.
Sea and Ice, Colour of the, 17.
Stellar Spectrum extraordinary, 122.
Sun, the, 235.
Sun, the Susceptibility of the, 269.
Sunstrokes, 254.
Telescope, Lord Rosse's, 11.
Thunder, Effects of on Animals, 57.
Venus, 100.
Waterspout, extraordinary, 311.
Water, something about, 359.
Weather, the, 158.
Weather, Signs of the, 184.
Weather of 1868, the Dry Hot, 270.

BOTANY.
Bamboo, Curious use for the, 122.
Baobab, Fruit of the, 214.
Baobab, the Australian, 215.
Bladderworts, 244.
Blossom Time, in, 336.
Botanical Geography, 136.
Boxwood, 199.
Campanula Carpatica, 312.
Cedars of Lebanon, the, 206.
Cranberry Culture, 105.
Cuckoo Flowers, 162.
Desert Plants, 291.
Dodders, 99.
Dragon Tree of Teneriffe, 101.
Dutch Tulips, 184.
Elder Tree, Extraordinary, 246.
Epiphyllum Truncatum, 246.
Fairy Rings, 246.
Flowers, conformation of, 312.
Fraxinella, Luminosity of the, 41.
Fungi as Food, 248.
Grasses, 79.
Grasses, the British, 63.
Hampshire, Botany of, 4.
Hazel, the, 300.
Leaves, Skeleton, 30, 60, 94.
Lilium Auratum, 249.
Lilies, Notes on, 230.
Liverworts, 30.
Maize Cultivation, 237.
Mushroom Cave, a, 330.
Nettles, Sting of, 318.
Oak, the, 280.
Oak Leaves, Skeleton, 190.
Oak, the Cowthorpe, 214.
Oranges and Lemons in California, 326.
Palms of Australia, 214.
Pampas Grass, 350.
Passion Flower, the, 249.
Pear Crop, Profits of a, 249.
Peat Bogs, Botany of, 103
Pines, 67.
Plants, Influence of Electricity on, 28
Plants, Instinct in, 317.
Plants known by their Pollen Grains, 333.
Plants, the sensibility of, 265.
Plants, Uses of, 253, 283, 316, 345.
Potato, more about the, 215.
Rose, the, 303.
Sensitive Plant, a new, 106.
Spiral Vessels, 312.
Shrubs, Australian poisonous, 183.
Stinging Nettles, 158.
Stinging Nettle, the, 285, 349, 380.
Sun-dew as a Fly-trap, the, 176.
Sycamore, 284.
Thymy Wood, 349.
Trees, Growth of, 184.
Vegetable Fibres, 369.
Yew, the, 75.
Yew Poisonous, Is the, 155, 158, 190

ETHNOLOGY.
America, Early Inhabitants of, 310.
Abyssinia, Natives of, 312.
Abyssinia, People of, 39.
Abyssinian Wedding, an, 339.
Abysinian King, an, 68.
American Indians, 323.
Fuegians, 200.
Human Races, 307.
Karens, the, 55.
Man, Antiquity of, 55.
Man's Place in Nature, 207.
Man, Pre-Historic, 71.
Mullatto, peculiar bleaching of a, 277
Namaquas, the, 16.
Negro, Age of the, 222.

GEOGRAPHY.
Abyssinia, 54.
Amazon, the River, 17.
Ascension Island, 142.
Australia, 182.
Borneo, 20.
Brazil, Natural History of, 69.
Cochin China, the Pleasures of, 247.
Country, a Prolific, 184.
Egypt and Ethiopia, Alluvial Plains of, 15.
Killarney, Lake of, 42.
Natal, 94.
Nicaragua and Mosquito, 7.
Ocean, Depth of the, 122.
Orkneys, Summer-time in the, 231.
Palestine Exploration, the, 59.
Seychelles Islands, the, 311.
St. John, the Island of, 313.

GEOLOGY.
Artesian Wells, 184.
Azores, Volcanic Disturbances at the, 18.
Chalcedony, 35.
Deep Sea Dredging, 340.
Diamonds, 312.
Earth, Attraction of the, 253, 282.
Earth's Features, the, 41.
Earth hollow? Is the, 17.
Earth, Temperature of the, 39.
Earthquakes, 351.
Earthquakes, Early, 267.
Flint, 35.

Fossil Gathering, Results of, 334.
Fossil Oysters, Bed of, 213.
Glacis, Great, of New Zealand, 56.
Hyalite, 35.
Ice in deep Mines, 20.
Jaspar, 35.
Opal, 35.
Pit Heaps, 206.
Red Cave Earth, 249.
River Phenomena, 302.
Saurian Remains in the Morayshire Rocks, 56.
Sea and Land, 304.
Siluria, 225.
Vesuvius, 311.
Volcanoes, 175, 203.
Volcanic Activity, 215.
Whisky Springs, 247.

MICROSCOPY.

Agaricus Variabilis, 34.
Diatomaceæ, 12.
Diatomaceæ in the Arctic Seas, 109.
Diatomaceæ, New Species of, 45.
Desmidiaceæ, 43.
Colour, Effects of, produced by Cryptogamic Plants, 82.
Infusoria, Development of, 106.
Plant Life, 81.

MISCELLANEOUS.

Aquarium, Plants for an, 350.
Aquariums, How to construct, 284.
Aquariums, Water for, 284, 317.
Air-tight Boxes, 222.
Albinos, 222.
Ambergris, 182.
Backwoods, In the, 257, 295.
Canadian Sport, 204.
Creation, the Harmony of, 95.
Death in the Box, 190.
Dredging on the Coast of Cornwall, 132.
Earth Eating, 318, 348.
Egg, Curious, 285.
Eggs, Deposit on, 219.
Egg and Nest Collecting, Notes on, 170, 197.
Egg, a Strange, 382.
Folk-Lore, 37.
Game Laws, the, 304.
Hunting in Algeria, 56.
Hydrophobia, 285.
Instinct versus Reason, 378.
Migration viâ Hybernation, 233.
Mimicry in Nature, 238.
Nature Improved, 134.
Notes from Tunbridge Wells, 157.
Pebble Collecting, 348.
Rabbits' Skins, etc., Dressing, 186.
Sea, In the, 175.
Shells, Arrangement of, 94, 124, 156, 187.

Specimens in Natural History, Preservation of, 166, 368.
Tenacity of Life, 184.

ZOOLOGY.

Adders, To cure the Bite of, 350.
Alligators in Mexico, 247.
Animal Sagacity, 273.
Animals, Devices of, 43.
,, Effects of Thunder on, 57.
,, Effects of Sound on, 183.
,, Hair of, 340.
,, Hairless, 252.
,, Language of, 40, 94.
,, Peculiarities of, 28.
,, Taming Wild, 283.
,, Wild, in Captivity, 213.
Ants in Bermuda, 100.
Ant Hill, Large, 254.
Ants in Slavery, 184.
Arachnidæ, 382.
Beaver, the, 240.
Bees, 157.
Bee Hunting, 105.
Bees, Swarming of, 126.
Bee Swarms, 215.
Bird, Curious, 94.
Birds' Diseases, 253.
Birds' Eggs, Colour of, 157, 190, 220, 252.
Birds from India, Arrival of New, 125.
Bird, a Madeira, 350.
Bird Murders, 57.
Bird Murder, British, 245.
Bird, Name of, 62.
Birds in New Zealand, English, 245.
Birds and Reptiles, Affinities between, 92.
Bird, the Secretary, 350.
Birds singing at Night, 252.
Birds, Skeletons of, 124, 157, 189.
Bird Stuffing, 30, 59.
Birds of Switzerland, the, 1.
Bird Tamer, a, 18.
Birds, Taming, 222.
Bird, Unknown, 157.
Birds, Variation in the size and colour, &c., of Eggs of, 223.
Birds, What, to keep in an Aviary, 189.
Bittern, the, 374.
Black Bears, 348.
Blackbird, White, 28.
Blackcap's Nest, 157.
Blackcap, singular nest of a, 126.
Blackbird, White, 313.
Bombycidæ, 289.
Bombyx Gama Mai, Silkworm, 305.
Bunting, Lapland, 222.
Bunting Lapland, 253.
Butterflies, 126, 245, 252, 222, 328.
Butterfly, beautiful, 253.
Butterflies, the first, 157.

Butterflies, our field, 194.
Butterflies, list of, 254.
Butterflies Local, why are? 190.
Butterflies, scales on certain, 198.
Butterflies, Woodland, 227.
Camberwell Beauty, the, 30, 60, 218.
Canaries, 190.
Canaries, curious, 157.
Canine Sagacity, 246.
Cat and a Rat, a, 317.
Caterpillars, Spiny and Hairy, 164.
Cat, Flying, 318.
Cats in the United States, Wild, 248.
Centipedes, extraordinary, 249.
Chaffinch, Nest of, 157.
Chickens Hatched by the Sun, 313.
Chrysalids, 94, 122.
Chrysalids, 154.
Clearwing and Burnet Moths, our, 129.
Cockroach, 126, 308.
Coleoptera at Mickleham, on, 191.
Coleoptera, Notes on, at Darenth Wood, 159.
Colias Edusa, 61, 93, 125.
Colias Hyale, 318.
Cow Superseded, the, 254.
Crab, the Hermit, 237.
Crocodile, the, 57, 181.
Crow, boldness of a, 188.
Cuckoo, Name, 94.
Dodo and its Home, the, 287, 319, 356.
Dog, Anecdote of a, 94, 215, 156.
Dogs, Hair off, 382.
Dogs, King Charles, in Japan, 157.
Dormice devouring flesh, 286.
Dragon Flies, 190, 220, 286.
Eels, 157, 222.
Eggs, Birds, 93, 125,
Egg Collecting, 126.
Eggs, curious colours of, 30, 62, 94.
Eggs of Insects, observations in connection with, 260.
Elephants, 31.
Elephant Hunting, 306.
Elk, the ancient Irish, 28.
Ermine, 155.
Ermine in England, 125.
Filefish on the English Coast, 102.
Fish, a peculiar, 190, 254.
Fish, the Fecundity of, 207.
Fish, Speaking, 92.
Fleas, 298.
Fly, the life destroying of Mexico, 11
Foal, remarkable three-legged, 248.
Fowls Catching Mice, 156.
Fox, Larder of a Provident, 313.
Frogs from Babyhood, &c., 244.
Frogs and their Food, 30, 94.
Gannet, 318.
Glowworms, 157, 222.
Goldfish, Breeding, 78.
Goldfish, Management of, 37.

INDEX.

Goldfinches, 382.
Gooses Egg, size of, 254.
Goshawk, the, 215.
Grasshoppers, a plague of, 311.
Hare and Rabbit, the, 126, 190, 221, 253.
Hare, a Petrified, 248.
Hawk, a bold, 189.
Hawk Moths, on the British, 64.
Hawk, swallowing eggs, 157.
Hedgehog, errors concerning the, 175
Hen Catching Mice, 125.
Hen's Egg, small, 222.
Herring, the British species of, 236.
Heronries, 285.
Horse, a Hairless, 249, 284.
Horse, Sagacity of the, 249.
Ichthyological Curiosity, 92.
Insect Bites, security from, 382.
Insect Bites, remedy for, 247.
Insects at Brighton, 189.
Insects, on Collecting, 360.
Insects, do they feel pain, 188, 219, 250, 313, 341, 379.
Insects, Eggs of, 217.
Insects, on killing, 126, 190, 251.
Insect Medicines, 366.
Insects, Parasites on, 217.
Insects, remarks on several differences on, 127.
Jackdaws casting Pellets, 222.
Japanese Pets, 121.
Kangaroo, White, 313.
Lady Birds, 253.
Landrail, the, 30, 62.
Landrail Swimming, 157.
Larvæ and Caterpillars, 186.
Lepidoptera, Boxes for, 189.
Lepidoptera Hybernating, 321.
Leporides, 104, 277.
Lion, the, 172.
Locusts, 80.
Magpie, 125, 155.
Magpie, Nesting of the, 186.
Martin, Notes on the, 364.
Metra, small, 318, 350.
Mice, 189, 222.
Mice, Carnivorous, 157.
Mites, 221.
Mole, 94.
Mole, Habits of, 124.
Monkeys, 73.
Moths, 157.
Moths, Book of, 318, 349.
Moth, Elephant, Hawk, emergence of, 285.
Moths, Killing, &c., 126, 157, 188.
Moths, on the prominent, 263.
Moth Traps, 221.
Mottled Owl, the, 169.
Mosquitoes, 276, 286.
Mosquitoes, Protection from, 245.
Mouse, Plucky, 377.
Mussells, destruction of, by whelks, 19.

Missel Thrush, pugnacity of the, 30.
Natal Crows, 349.
New Zealand, Zoology of, 30.
Noctuæ, 382.
Nuthatch, the, 57.
Oak Feeding Silkworm, the, 79.
Oology, a curiosity in, 350.
Osprey Shot in Guernsey, 341.
Ostrich and Gazelle Hunting, 104.
Otter, History of a Young, 173.
Owls, 157.
Oysters, 55.
Parrots, Cockatoos, &c., 303.
Parrots, Intelligence of, 237, 251.
Penguin, the, 145.
Pheasant's Nest, amazing site for, 249.
Pholas Dactylas, 188.
Physalia, 129.
Physalia Arethusa, notes on, 249.
Pieris Crataegi, 125.
Pieris Rapiæ, 126.
Pied Sparrow in London, 286.
Piddock, the, 30, 61.
Pigeons, Whistling, 57.
Pigs, Killing Poultry, 157.
Pike Swallowing a Pike, 253.
Plants and Animals, resemblance between, 335.
Pony, anecdote of a, 277.
Portugese Man of War, 286.
Poultry, to Fatten, 57.
Pullett's Egg, extraordinarily small, 190.
Pupæ, 254.
Queen Bee, the, 201.
Rabbits, 382.
Rabbit Keeping, 29, 61.
Racoon, 318.
Rats, 215, 294.
Rat, anecdote of a, 94.
Rat in a Chapel, a, 62.
Rats, sucked by a Cat, 182.
Rats in Sweden, 21.
Ray Pastinaca, 252.
Red Admiral, 286.
Reptiles, 281.
Reptiles of the Mississippi, the, 373.
Ring Doves, 30.
Rock Rabbit, 349.
Robin, the, 183, 240.
Rook, curious, 253.
Rooks in Wet Weather, 190.
Salmon Cultivation, 313.
Saw Fly, 350.
Seal, the, 363.
Serpent found in Malta, a, 316.
Sheep and Rabbits, Appetites of, 249
Shell Fish, 61.
Sphinx Convolvuli, 340.
Shrike, the Red-backed, 154.
Silkworm, Japanese, 318.
Sirex, the Giant, 380.
Slugs, 220.
Snails, Food of, 156.

Snakes, 254, 276.
Sow, Prolific, 382.
Sparrow, White, 62.
Spiders, 20.
Spider, curious, 376.
Spider, extraordinary, 183.
Spider, How the, restores a lost leg, 341.
Spiders, Preserved, 94, 124.
Squirrel, the, 157.
Squirrel Suck Eggs, does the ? 222.
Squirrel, a White, 59.
Stag Beetle, Parasites on a, 214.
Star Fish, the, 146.
Stoat, the, 59.
Sturgeon, large, 157.
Sunfish, the, 221.
Swallow, the, 221.
Thrush, the American Migratory, 251
Tigers, 234.
Tigers, destruction of human life by, 92.
Tiger Hunt, a, 42.
Tigers, Man-eating, 56.
Tomtit, Nest of the, 62.
Trout of North America, 372.
Turtle Dove, the, 183.
Walrus, the, 9.
Wasps, 97.
Watersnake, 190.
Wolf's Flesh as Food, 248.
Wolf Hunting in France, 240.
Wolves, Man-eating, 239.
Woodchat in England, the breeding of the, 187.
Wood Pigeon, Notes on the, 331.
Worms, 182.
Wren's Nest, 189.
Zoological Gardens, 348.
Zoological Gardens, in the, 372.

CORRESPONDENCE.

Alas, poor Otters! A. M. B., 120; T. G. P., 153; A. M. B., 181.
Animals destitute of Hair and Feathers, C. O. Groom Napier, F.G.S., 153.
Birds, a few Remarks on the Sexes of, C. W—d, 309.
Birds Migrate? Why do, H. H. Ulidia, 27; Arthur G. Harvie, 27; H. E. Austen, 54.
Bird Murder, A. M. B., 90; A Lover of Birds, 120, 210.
Common Gallinule, the, A. M. B., 276.
Jack Snipe, Nidification of the, A. M. B., 339.
Magpie, a few Words in defence of, R. B. W., 153.
Nature Improved, A. M. B., 181; James Britten, 212.
Naturalisation of Foreign Birds, J. D. S. W., 121.

Oological Excursions, 212.
Rain Water as a Beverage, R. G. Blunt, 54.
Remarkable Canary, a, F. L. Gibbons, 121.
Solar and Lunar Rainbows, H. H. Ulidia, 89; J. R., 121.
Swallows, Hybernation of, etc., Francis A. Allen, 28; J. B. Waters, 53; T. R. Clephan, 90; H. H. Ulidia, 274; R. B. W. 309; C. W—d, 376.

MEETINGS OF LEARNED SOCIETIES.

Anthropological, 46, 151.
Bath Field Club, 119.
Botanical, 179.
Botanical Society of Edinburgh, 48, 87.
Bristol Microscopical, 52.
Bristol Naturalist's Society, 52, 86, 117, 180.
Entomological, 24, 45, 83, 115, 147, 177, 241.
Ethnological, 23, 47, 115, 151, 241.
Geographical, 22, 47, 85, 112, 149, 176.
Geological, 25, 50, 83, 113, 148, 179, 241.
Geologists' Association, 52.
Horticultural, 88, 115, 148.
Linnean, 25, 50, 86, 114, 147, 178, 241.
Manchester Field Naturalist's Society, 126.
Microscopical, 24, 47, 87.
Quekett, 151, 241.
Royal Physical Society, Edinburgh, 116.
Zoological, 23, 46, 84, 112, 150, 178, 241.

NOTICES OF NEW BOOKS.

Abyssinia described, by John Camden Hotten, 21.
  ,, a Journey to, by M. S. von Heuglin, 209.
Astronomy, Elementary Lessons in, by J. Norman Lockyer, 336.

Baudrimont's (A.) Globe terrestre, 92.
Birds from Nature, by Mrs. H. Blackburn, 90.
Birds, the Food, Use, and Beauty of British, by C. O. G. Napier, 208.
Birds of Berkshire and Buckinghamshire, by A. W. M. C. Kennedy, 210.
Blackburn's (Mrs. Hugh) Birds from Nature, 90.
Boyle's (Frederick) Ride across a Continent, 110.
Burgess's (J. T.) Old English Wild Flowers, 337.
Collingwood's (Cuthbert) Rambles of a Naturalist, 241.
Ferns, Select, etc., by B. S. Williams, 209.
Figuier's (Louis) Ocean World, 208.
Flint's (Austin) Physiology of Man, 91.
Geschite des Golfstroms und seiner Erforschung Von J. G. Kohl, 92.
Glaciers, Les, par Zurcher et Margollé, 92.
Globe terrestre, Théorie de la Formation du, par A. Baudrimont, 92.
Grey's (S. O.) British Seaweeds, 241.
Half Hours with the Telescope, by R. A. Proctor, 109.
Hall's (Townshend) Mineralogist's Directory, 91.
Heuglin's (M. S. Von) Journey to Abyssinia, 209.
Heroes of Discovery, by Samuel Mossman, 22.
Hittell's (John S.) Resources of Calfornia, 91.
Hochstetter's (Dr. Ferdinand Von) New Zealand, 337.
Hotten's (John) Abyssinia described, 21.
Howitt's (Mary) Our Four-Footed Friends, 22.
Iceland, a Summer in, by C. W. Paijkuli, 337.
Kennedy's (A. W. M. C.) Birds of Berkshire, etc., 210.
Kohl's (J. G.) Gerschite, etc., 92.
Lake Victoria, by George C. Swayne, 91.

Lockyer's (J. N.) Elementary Astronomy, 336.
Man, the Natural History of, by Rev. J. G. Wood, 337.
Man, the Physiology of, by Austin Flint, 91.
Man: Where, Whence, and Whither, by David Page, LL.D., 91.
Mineralogist's Directory, the, by Townshend M. Hall, F.G.S., 91.
Mossman's (Samuel) Heroes of Discovery, 22.
Napier's (C. O. G.) Food, Use, and Beauty of British Birds, 208.
Naturalist, the American, 210.
Naturalist, Rambles of a, by Cuthbert Collingwood, 241.
New Zealand, etc., by Dr. Ferdinand von Hochstetter, 337.
Our Four-Footed Friends, by Mary Howitt, 22.
Ocean World, the, by Louis Figuier, 208.
Omerod's (E. L.) British Social Wasps, 110.
Page's (David) Man: Where, Whence, etc., 91.
Paijkuli's (C. W.) A Summer in Iceland, 337.
Pouchet's (F. A.) L'Univers, 22.
Proctor's (R. A.) Half Hours with the Microscope, 109.
Quekett Microscopical Society, Journal of the, 210.
Resources of California, the, by John S. Hittell, 91.
Ride across a Continent, a, by Frederick Boyle, 110.
Seaweeds, British, by S. O. Grey, 241.
Swayne's (George C.) Lake Victoria, 91.
Univers, L', Les Infiniment Grands et Les Infiniment Petits, par F. A. Pouchet, 22.
Wasps, British Social, by Edward Latham Omerod, 110.
Wild Flowers, Old English, by J. T. Burgess, 337.
Williams's (B. S.) Select Ferns, 209.
Wood's (Rev. J. G.) Natural History of Man, 338.
Zucher, etc., Les Glaciers, 92.

Think nought a trifle, though it small appear;
Small sands the mountain, moments make the year,
And trifles life.   YOUNG.

THE BIRDS OF SWITZERLAND.

OUR space will only allow us a brief notice of certain birds, mostly of varieties special to the Alps. Beginning with the birds of prey, or raptores, we must pause to consider the Lammergeier (Falco or Gypaetos barbatus), a formidable animal, called Steingeyer in the Grisons and Bartgeyer in other parts. He is the largest of European birds of prey, and though diminished, occurs still in the cantons of Grisons, Tessin, Valais, and Berne. The females, as with the eagle, are generally larger than the males; a full-grown bird measures $4\frac{1}{2}$ feet in length, 9 to 10 feet from wing to wing (extended), and weighs 12 to 16, and in rare cases 20 lbs. He has a coarse hairy beard over the breast, hence the name Bartgeyer; the young birds are almost black; older, they become a rusty brown on the breast, a gray brown on the lower back, and on the upper back a shining blackish brown. As his usual name implies, he is a fierce enemy of sheep, goats, dogs, hares, &c., and it is an authentic fact that he has carried off young children and destroyed them in some cases.

His visual power is immense. Sailing proudly at great elevations, he sees a victim, pounces upon it with lightning speed, and bears it off. But he only ventures to attack grown men and the larger animals when he sees them in dangerous places, endeavouring in such cases to knock or drive them over the precipices with the blows of his powerful wings. Nothing can compare to the energy of the digestive power of this bird; indeed a course of lammergeier pepsine is strongly recommended to all persons who are dyspeptic sufferers. The lammergeier swallows large pieces of his prey, hair, skin, bones, and all, and is occupied some time in digesting this *crudis indigestaque moles*. Shoulder-blades of large animals and bones 15 inches long, have been found in the stomachs of lammergeiers.

In the spring they inhabit the higher or middle Alpine region, and nestle on summits surrounded by chasms or rocks, inaccessible to man, in places protected from bullets. In the summer they generally fly up to the highest icy summits, near the grazing ground of chamois, sheep, or goats. In winter they are obliged to hunt in the mountain region, but they never go down to the plains. Premiums are offered for their destruction in many cantons.

An equally dangerous enemy of the poultry is the golden eagle (Aquila chrisaetos, Falco aquila) which is found in almost all the Alpine districts, living in the highest and most inaccessible places. This bird is bolder and more lively than the lammergeier, uncommonly sharp-sighted, but yet prudent and shy, 3 to $3\frac{1}{2}$ feet long, and 8 feet across, with extended wings. His clear notes, *plülüf* or *hia hia* sound far and wide through the upper air. A favourite resort of this bird is a rocky fastness above Eblingen (on the Lake of Brienz), the eagle hunters of which village have a high reputation. It is said that the golden eagles fly higher than the lammergeier, and some have been reported to have been seen circling above the Eiger (12,240 feet). Two other species of eagle are found periodically in Switzerland; first, the little white-headed river eagle (Aq. haliætus), a summer bird, found by the rivers and lakes; second, the white-tailed eagle (Aquila albicilla), a winter guest, larger than the golden eagle. The Cathartes perecnopterus occurs on the Saleve, near Geneva.

The Falco tinnunculus, L., is often seen fighting with the crow. He is called Wanner in Berne, is 14 inches long, and one of the most widely diffused of the birds of prey. His cry is *gri, gri, gri*. He is difficult to shoot. The dove-hawk (F. palumbarius, L.) is a desperate destroyer in the farmyard; 2 feet long, emits cries like *giak, giak*, and is distinguished for extraordinary cleverness and cunning in avoiding shots.

The horned owl (Strix bubo, L.) occurs everywhere in wild mountain ravines, and is known by his hollow dismal note, *puhu, puhu, hui*. He grows as large as the golden eagle. The horned owl (Strix otus) is also found everywhere, and known by his cry, *huuk, huuk, hoho*. As in so many cases, it is inconsiderate of man to destroy the owl tribe, which is highly useful as a means of keeping down the number of rats and mice. It is reckoned that each full-grown owl requires yearly 3,000 mice for its support.

Among the crows, we may notice as special Alpine birds the Cornix graculus, L. (stone Crow), a somewhat rare inhabitant of the highest mountains of Grisons and Faucigny, drawing up to the higher regions, and leaving from October to April; for example, near the Hospice of St. Bernard, where it remains a couple of days, and is known as the corneille impériale. The Alpine chough (Pyrrho corax L.) inhabits the mountain districts in large troops, bearing different names in the various cantons, such as Dävi, Fluhtäffi, Däsi; and in Upper Hasli, Chäfi; in the Entlebuch, Ryestare; in Glarus, Alpkray; in Schwyz, Sneetahe; in Appenzell, Bergdulle; in Grisons. Berne; in Fribourg, Tsuvat; in Valais, Chokar. They are found circling round rocky crests, in mountain solitudes, forming with the marmot the only living creatures withing sight. They are regarded by the Sennen as infallible barometers, have been found at 13,000 feet on the Finsteraarhorn, and live upon any thing they can find, especially water-snails and animals frozen on the firn. They have a singular taste for burning coal and smoke, like the genuine Lancashire manufacturer, and they have ever been found swallowing burning wicks. They occupy a high position in the bird world for their cleverness, docility, and liveliness.

Switzerland is exceedingly rich in singing birds. The linnet (F. linaria), called Rebschössli or Blutschössli, appears in troops in autumn and winter, especially in the warmer districts. The Fringilla citronella, L., called Citronli or Schneevögeli, is regarded as the herald of snow, and loves to build its nest in châlets and stables, especially in the Hospenthal. The snow-finch (F. nivalis, L.) is a genuine Alpine bird, found only in the highest inhabited valleys, and on the passes. Yellow buntings (Emberiza citrinella, L.) are numerous in the Grisons and Tessin, in the outfields; chaffinches (F. cœlebs, L.) occur in all woods and bushes, and bullfinches (F. pyrrhula, L.), called Gugger, Bollebiesser, and Bromäs, occupy the uplands in the summer, and the plains in the winter.

The coniferous woods of the mountains are (in summer) one concert of sweet sounds with the notes of the thrush tribe, especially T. musicus, called the Trostle, and Turdus merula, L., appearing first of all the tribe, in winter in the valleys, in summer on the hills. The Turdus cyanus, Gm., and Pastor roseus varieties are rare and confined to the mountain region; but the stone-thrush (T. Saxatilis, L.) occurs frequently in the rocky valleys of the Grisons, Valais, Tessin, and in the Urserenthal.

The Starling (Sturnus varius Wolf.), is so useful in destroying insects that the peasantry build nests for him in many parts. In summer they rise with the cattle to the Alp pastures, sitting on their backs to deliver them from vermin. The common nightingale (Sylvia luscinia) occurs frequently in the lower valleys, as near Sion; but the Sylvia philomela is more rare, confined chiefly to the Lake Leman, Lago Maggiore, and Rhone valley.

The vermivorous birds appear in April, and disappear in the autumn. Sylvia rubecula, the redbreast, called Rothbrustli, Waldrotheli, ascends tolerably high up the mountains; S. Phœnicurus, Baum Rotheli, occurs on the Oberaar glacier.

The singing birds frequenting deciduous woods are numerous, as in Germany, especially the smallest European bird, the golden-crested wren (S. regulus flavidapillus), called Goldhämmarli, Goldhähnli, with its perpetual cry of *zitt, zitt*. Its length is $3\frac{1}{2}$ inches. The water-wagtail (Saxicola œnanthe, M.) is called Berg Nachtigale in the Simmenthal, and lives in swampy mountain meadows. Sax. rubetra, M., the Krautvogeli or Steinfletsch, ascends higher, and Sax. rubicola, M. is rarer.

The Alpine accentor (Accentor Alpinus, M.) is another genuine Alpine bird, called in the in Glarus, Gadenvogel; in other places, Bernese Oberland, Blumtrittli, Blümtvogel; Blumtüteli, Blüttlig, Blümthurlig, because he is fond of eating the hay-seed (called Heüblumt) in winter. This bird builds his nest among Alp roses, and goes up to the névés; he is a cheerful, merry-singing little thing. The different kinds of pipit (Anthus) are summer guests in the Alpine region, the meadow pipit (Anthus pratensis, Buhst,) being useful in freeing the wool of sheep from vermin.

The most common small singing birds are the coal titmouse (Charbonnière), especially Parus Major, L. (called Spiegeli), P. Cœruleus

L., (Blaueli), P. palustris (Kateli, Koberli), and P. cinereus montanus, inhabiting the highest Grisons woods.

Switzerland has seven varieties of the swallow, all of which leave the country in autumn. The kinds peculiar to the mountains are Hirundo rupestris, Scop., found at the Grimsel, Gemmi, Col de Balme, on the Axen, &c., and especially Micropus Alpinus (Wolf), or Cypselus Alpinus, called locally the Bergspyr. These varieties are rare in east Switzerland.

The turtle dove only occurs in south Switzerland and Columba Œneas, the wood-pigeon, is a bird of passage, confined to the lowlands.

The group of gallinaceæ is interesting to sportsmen, presenting especially the Tetrao urogallus, or wood grouse, who live in solitary coniferous districts of the lower Alpine region and Jura. Unfortunately they are not numerous, though latterly increasing. Their average weight is from 9 lbs. to 18 lbs., and their length 3 feet to $3\frac{1}{3}$ feet. The cock has ten to twelve hens; but he lives a hermit life, except in the coupling season, when he makes a deafening noise called Balzen, and this is the only period when he can be easily shot. The hens, which burrow in the grass, are easy to catch. The Tetrao tetrix, or black-cock, is more numerous in the higher mountains. In the winter these birds dig passages of one to two fathoms under the snow, in order to reach the whortle and other berries on which they feed.

The Perdix saxatilis Mayeri, or rock partridge, called Parnissli in the Grisons, is a genuine mountain bird, of variegated plumage, marching about on sunny slopes, among dwarf shrubs and Alpine roses, seldom flying up, and not living in polygamy like most of the gallinaceæ. They are tamer than most Alpine hens, come deep down into the valleys in winter, but do not advance north of the Alps, though they occur in Italy, Africa, Syria, and Persia in large numbers. They are decimated by the birds of prey.

Among other species dear to sportsmen, we may notice the common partridge (Perdix cinerea, Briss), and the quail (P. coturnix, Lath.), but only in the lowlands, and not numerous. The most interesting bird of this class is the ptarmigan (Tetrao lagopus, called in the Grisons Weisshuhn), wandering in couples in summer over the highest snow region, but coming down to the woods in winter. These fowls change their plumage according to the season; in summer and autumn they are variegated, grayish yellow and brownish, with black lines; while in winter they are of a snowy white to the tail, which remains coal black, with a white rim.

They are as large as common pigeons, but heavier and stronger, and their thick feathers protect them against small shot. Numbers are exported from the Grisons.

With unimportant exceptions all the waterfowl of Switzerland are birds of passage. Their number has greatly decreased from what it was in ancient times, partly in consequence of modern improvements in drainage. They are most numerous in the Valais and some parts of Tessin. Considerable confusion has arisen in their classification, owing to the fact that they change feather and colour periodically. Of the subdivision of waders, the different kinds of plovers are most numerous, especially the golden plover (Charadrius auratus or pluvialis, Suck., Ch. morinellus, L.), the King plover (Ch. hiaticula, L.), &c. The ash gray common heron (Ardea cinerea) occurs everywhere by the lakes and rivers, and is very injurious to sport in trout streams, through its voracity. It builds nests on the rocks by the lakes of Uri and Wallenstadt. The silver and purple herons are very rare. The little heron (A. minuta) is easily tamed and a very merry animal. The common white stork (Ciconia alba, Briss.) is universally respected in all the cantons, living on churches, houses, &c., though in certain cases its visits, as in Aargau, are periodical.

The different kinds of snipes occur as birds of passage in March and April, and again in September and October; but some years they are not seen at all. Scolopax, limosa, totanus, tringa, are rare, but Tringa cinclus and ochropus are more frequent; and Tschudi thinks this class of birds more general in the mountains than is commonly supposed. The hooded lapwing (Vanellus cristatus, May), occurs in large flocks from March to October, and the great water crake, (Rallus aquaticus) called Pantalon in the Pays de Vaud, is frequently seen.

Of palmipeds, or swimming birds properly so called, the Swiss lakes contain some species that frequent them most of the year, especially Fulica atra, the black coot or water hen, called locally Belch, Bollene, or Mohre, numerous close to Lucerne, and coming tamely to feed at its bridges; the Podiceps cristatus, known as Grebe, Duchel, and Ruech, on most of the lakes in winter, and shot in large quantities on the Lake of Neuchatel. The P. Minor, or little grebe, is found universally throughout the year, and known as Grundruech on the Boden See, as Tücheli on the Lake of Constance, as Chäferentli in the Grisons, as Müderli and Tünkentli in Berne. The Colymbus Arcticus only appears occasionally on the Swiss waters, but two kinds of tern (the St. nigra, L., and Sterna hirundo), are seen on the lakes throughout the summer, and the gray gull (Larus glaucus) appears in its autumn and winter dress. The L., ridibundus (black-headed gull) is called

Holbrod, Pfaff, and Gyritz, and is a resident throughout the year.

Wild ducks are numerous, especially on certain lakes, as that of Lucerne. The Anas fusca is called Rheinmohr on the Boden See; the Schliefenti of the Lake of Zurich is known as Straussmohr on the Boden See (A. rufina); the Goldaugli (A. clangula), and Tafelente (A. ferina) also Rothmohr, on the Boden See, are numerous during the winter, from November to March.

Snow geese are only temporary visitors on their passage across the Alps, but the merganser pass most of the winter on the great lakes, such as Mergus merganser, called See Kate and See Geiss on the Lake of Constance, and M. albellus, commonly called Nonneli, Eisentli, and Schneegünsli.

BOTANY OF HAMPSHIRE.

Closely connected with the geology of the Forest are its flowers. And though mere geology could not tell us the whole Flora of a district, yet we might always be able, by its help and that of the latitude, to give the typical plants. Close to the chalk, the Forest possesses none of the chalk flowers. No bee-orchis or its congeners, although so common on all the neighbouring Wiltshire downs, bloom. No travellers'-joy trails amongst its thickets, although every hedge in Dorsetshire, just across the Avon, is clothed in the autumn with its white fleece of seeds. No yellow bird's-nest (*Monotropa Hypopitys*) shades itself under its beeches, though growing only a few miles distant on the chalk.

Still, here there are some contradictions. The chalk-loving yew appears to be indigenous. Several plants which we might reasonably expect, as herb-Paris, the bird-nest orchis (*Neottia Nidus-avis*), and the common mezereon (*Dapne Mezereum*), are wanting.

Owing to the want of stiff clay, no hornbeams grow in its woods, except perhaps, a few in one or two cold "bottoms." No Solomon's seal or lillies of the valley whiten its dells. No meadow-geranium waves its blue flowers on the banks of the Avon.

On the other hand, the plants too truly tell the character of the soil. In the spring the little tormentil shows its bright blossoms, and the petty-whin grows side by side with the furze, and the sweet mock-myrtle throws its shadow over the streams. In the summer and autumn the blue sheep's-bit scabious and the golden-rod bloom, with the three heathers. In the bogs the round-leaved sundew is pearled with wet, and not far from it the cotton-grass waves its white down, and the asphodel rears its golden spike.

These are the commonest flowers of the Forest, and grow everywhere over its moors. In its dykes and marshes, the common frog-bit and the marsh-pimpernel spring up in every direction. The buckbean, too, brightens every pool on the south side, and is so common near the Avon that many of the fields are called "the buckbean mead," whilst in the northern parts it is known as "the fringed water-lily."

Very rich is the Forest in all these bog-plants. In Hinchelsea and Wilverley Bottoms grow the water-pimpernel (*Samotus Valerandi*), the lesser bladder-wort, and the bur-reed (*Sparganium natans*) floating on the water. Here, too, perhaps, the easternmost station known for it, blossoms the butterwort (*Pinguicula Lusitanica*), with its pale delicate flowers. In the autumn, also, the open turf grounds round Wootton are blue with the Calathian violet (*Gentiana Pneumonanthe*); whilst its little bright congener (*Cicendia filiformis*) blossoms in all the damp places.

Owing, also, to the presence of iron, the Forest possesses no less than seventeen or eighteen carices. The little thyme-leaved flax, too (*Radiola millegrana*), grows in all the moist, sandy dells.

From this general view it will be seen that the true forest plants are not so much "sylvestral" as "ericetal," and "paludal," and "uliginal." Besides these groups, however, the flora of the district further divides itself into the "littoral plants" along the sea-shores and estuaries, and the "pascual" flowers of the valley of the Avon. In the former division, owing to the want of rocks, no *Statice spathulata* grows on its sea-board. No true samphire (*Crithmum maritimum*) blossoms. The beautiful maiden's-hair fern, once so plentiful on the neighbouring coast of the Isle of Wight, is also from the same cause wanting.

Still, great beauty blooms on the Forest streams and shores. In the latter part of the summer, the mudbanks of the Beaulieu river are perfectly purple with the sea-aster, whilst the sea-lavender waves its bright blue crest among the reed-beds washed over by every tide.

The valley of the Avon is characterized, as may be expected, by the commoner species, which are to be found in such situations. Here, and in the adjoining cultivated parts, which once were more or less a part of the Forest, we find the soap-wort (*Saponaria officinalis*) and the thorn-apple (*Datura Stramonium*), and those colonists which always harbour close to the dwellings of man. Other considerations remain. The situation and climate of the New Forest, of course, have a great effect on its plants. The two myrtles and the sweet-bay grow under the cliffs of Eaglehurst, close to the Solent, unhurt by the hardest frosts. The grapes ripen on the cottage-walls of Beaulieu nearly as early as in Devonshire. I have seen the coltsfoot in full blossom, near Hythe, on the 27th of February; and the blackthorn flowers at Wootton on the 3rd of April.

The area of the New Forest comes under Watson's Sub-province of the Mid-Channel, on the Southern belt of his Inferagrarian zone. Its position lies exactly half-way between his Germanic and Atlantic types. The former shows itself by *Dianthus Armeria* and *Pulicaria vulgaris*, growing near Marchwood and Bisterne. The latter by such examples as *Cotyledon umbilicus*, *Pinguicula Lusitanica*, *Briza minor*, and *Agrostis setacea*. The "British" and "English" types are, of course, plentifully represented.

Looking, too, at the trees and shrubs which are indigenous, we shall find them also eminently characteristic. In spite of what Cæsar says, the beech is certainly a native, pushing out in places even the oak. The holly, too, grows everywhere in massy clumps. In the spring, the wild crab (*Pyrus Malus*) crimsons the thickets of Brockenhurst, in the autumn the maple. The butcher's broom stands at the foot of each beech, and the ivy twines its great coil round each oak, and the mistletoe finds its home on the white poplar.

After all, the trees, and not the flowers, give its character to the New Forest. In the spring, all its woods are dappled with lights and shades, with the amber of the oak and the delicate soft-gleaming green of the birch and beech. In the autumn, the spindle-tree (*Euonymus Europæus*) in the Wootton copses is hung with its rosy gems; and the trenches of Castle Malwood are strewed with the silver leaves of the white-beam.

To return, however, to the plants, let us notice how some particular families seem especially to like the light gravely soil of the Forest district. Take, for instance, the St. John's-worts, of which we have no less than six, if not more varieties. The common perforated (*Hypericum perforatum*) shines on every dry heath, and the square-stalked (*quadrangulum*) in all the damp boggy places. The tutsan (*Androsæmum*) is so common round Wotton that it is known to all the children as "touchen leaves," evidently only a corruption of its name; and its berries are believed throughout the Forest to be stained with the blood of the Danes. The rarer large-flowered (*calycinum*) grows, though not, I am afraid, truly wild, in some of the thickets round Sway. In all the ponds, the marsh (*elodes*) springs up, whilst the creeping (*humisfusum*) trails its blossoms over the turf of the Forest lanes, and the small (*pulchrum*) shows its orange-tipped flowers amongst the brambles and bushes.

Take, again, the large family of the ferns, of which seventeen species are distributed throughout the Forest. First and foremost, of course, stands the royal fern (*Osmunda regalis*), which may be found from the sea-board to Fordingbridge, rearing its stem in some places six feet high, and covering in patches on the southern border, as at Beckley, nearly a quarter of an acre. It grows in Chewton Glen, in all the lanes in the neighbourhood, on Ashley Common, close to the Osmanby Ford River, and rears its golden-brown pannicles in the boggy thickets near Rufus's Stone. But before it, in beauty, stands the lady-fern, with its delicate fronds and its tender green, growing in the open spaces of the beech woods, as at Stonehard and Puckpits, and bending over the Forest streams in large leafy clumps. Then, too, in all the large woods grows the sweet-scented mountain fern (*Lastrea Oreopteris*); and on every bank the hart's-tongue spreads its broad ribbon-like leaves, and the fertile fronds of the hard-fern spring up feathery and light, whilst from the old oaks the common polypody droops with its dark green tresses. The common maiden-hair (*Asplenium Trichomanes*), too, hangs on the walls and Forest banks; and on Alice Lisle's tomb, at Ellingham, the rue-leaved spleenwort is green thoughout the whole year. On Breamore churchyard wall and Ringwood bridges grows the common scale-fern, whilst in the meadows of the Avon springs the adder's-tongue's green spear.

Nor must we forget the brake, common though it be, for this it is which gives the Forest so much of its character, clothing it with green in the spring; and when the heather is withered, and the furze, too, decayed, making every holt and hollow golden.

And now for some other plants, without reference to their species, but simply to their beauty. On Ashley Common and the neighbouring grass-fields grows the moth-mullein (*Verbascum Blattaria*), dropping its yellow flowers, as they one by one expand. In the neighbouring pools, as far as Wootton, the blossoms of the great spearwort (*Ranunculus Lingua*) gleam among the reeds. There, also, the narrow-leaved lungwort (*Pulmonaria angustifolia*), with its leaves both plain and spotted, opens its blue and crimson flowers so bright, that they are known to all the children as the "snake flower," and gathered by handsful mixed with the spotted orchis. And the ladies' tresses, too (*Spiranthes autumnalis*), shows its delicate brown braid on every dry field on the southern border.

Besides these, the feathered pink (*Dianthus plumarius*) blooms on the cloister-walls at Beaulieu; and the Deptford pink (*Dianthus Armeria*) in the valley of the Avon at Hucklebrook, near Ibbesley. The bastard-balm (*Melittis Melissophyllum*) flaunts its white and purple blossoms over the banks of Wootton plantation, whilst at

Oakley and Knyghtwood the red gladiolus crimsons the green beds of fern.

Briefly, let me say that, as is the Forest soil, so are its plants. Nature ever makes some compensations. The barrennest places she ever clothes with beauty. If corn will not grow, she will give man something better. In the great woods the columbines and tutsan shine in the spring with their blue and yellow blossoms, and the wood-sorrel nestles its white flowers among the mossy roots of the oaks. In the more open spaces the foxgloves overtop the brake, and in the grassy spots the eyebright waves its white-grey crest; and not far off are sure to gleam faint crimson patches of the marsh-pimpernel, half hid in moss; whilst the swamps are fringed with the coral of the sundew.

THE DEW OF HEAVEN.

THE insensible vapour, whose birth is in the evaporation from the earth's surface, appears again on the earth in its first and softest way, as dew. Several recent observations on this phenomenon will be full of interest to our readers. We must not forget, as I have often remarked, that the insensible deposition of water from the atmosphere is not confined to the *surface* of the soil. Wherever the atmospheric air can freely penetrate, there the deposition of the dew, under favourable circumstances, takes place. This also often occurs in the interior of the soil, when evaporation is taking place from the surface. The amount of the dew deposited upon the soil has been estimated by Dr. Dalton to be equal to five inches per annum, or about 500 tons of water per acre. Less dew is usually formed during the first than in the second portion of the night. The amount of water deposited in dew varies at different seasons and localities. Autumn, as Mr. Steinmitz observes, is remarkable for its heavy dews, owing to the depression of the temperature during the nights. These are sometimes so abundant as to admit of measurement in the rain-gauge. In one night, towards the end of September, Luke Howard got one-hundredth of an inch of water from the dew, and in the last six days of October eleven-hundredths from copious dews and mists. We must not then forget that dew is only one form in which the aqueous vapour of the atmosphere is deposited on the earth for the service of vegetation. The driest soils contain about 10 per cent. of moisture. We know that when soils are dried in a temperature of 212 deg., and exposed on their surfaces to air saturated with moisture, they absorb very considerable portions of water. Suppose a soil which weighs about 1,000 tons per acre is pulverized so as to be freely permeable by the atmosphere, and that such a soil, after being thoroughly dried, is exposed to the air, then we find from the experiments of Schubler that it will absorb water, in twenty-four hours—

If a sandy clay, equal to	....	26 tons.
If a loamy clay, ,,	....	30 ,,
If a stiff clay, ,,	....	36 ,,
If a garden mould, ,,	....	45 ,,

The inquiry is closely connected with the good effects produced in most soils by deepening and pulverizing them. Well-pulverized soils absorb much more dew than when suffered to remain close. "Sands," observes Mr. Josiah Parkes (*Jour. R. A. S.*, vol. v., p. 132), "appear to be powerful attractors, and in some countries to depend altogether on the nightly deposition of moisture for the support of their vegetation. It is to the copious dews that we have in a great measure to attribute the productiveness of the meadows bordered by rivers. The atmosphere in the neighbourhood of currents of water becomes more highly charged with aqueous vapour than those of the upland. A moisture is deposited from it, in such places on the grasses during the night, in globules of dew; hence the French expression that a river bedews (*arrose*) is more correct than the English one, that it *waters* a country. In India the deposition of dew near to rivulets, when all around is perfectly dry, is very marked." Colonel Sykes (*Trans. Roy. Soc.*, 1850, p. 354), remarks that, "when at Poona in September and October, if there was no deposition of dew anywhere else, it was yet found on the banks of rivulets and the Mota Mola river; but 15 to 20 feet from the water were the limits of the deposition." If, however, the efforts of the husbandman in deepening and pulverizing his soil tend to the increasing their supply of atmospheric moisture, his labours in another direction sometimes diminishes it. "It is evident," says Dove, "that a vigorous vegetation produces rain, which, on the other hand, nourishes again that vegetation, and that the senseless destruction of forests very often has destroyed the fertility of the soil. Previous to 1821, Provence and the department du Var possessed a superfluity of brooks and springs. In that year, the olive trees, which formed almost forests, were killed by frost, and they were cut down to the root in 1822; since which time the springs dried up, and agriculture suffered. In Upper Egypt, the rains, eighty years ago still abundant, have ceased since the Arabs cut down the trees along the Valley of the Nile towards Libya and Arabia. A contrary effect has been produced in Lower Egypt, through the extensive plantation of trees by the Pasha. In Alexandria and Cairo, where rain was formerly a great rarity, it has since that period become much more frequent." "The proportion of forest or woodland required for an agricultural country, in order to ensure a regular and sufficient rainfall without violent storms, has been estimated," observes Mr. Steinmitz (*Sunshine and Showers*), "at 23 per cent. for the interior, and 20 per cent. near the coast. This estimate by Rentzsch related to Germany; but in England the proportion, according to the same authority, is only 5 per cent., and even this is reduced by Sir Henry James, the head of the Ordnance Survey Department, to 2½ per cent. This is certainly a very small proportion, and below that of every other country, the next lowest being Portugal, which has very little woodland." "In Italy the removal of forest," observes Professor Ansted (*Jour. R. A. S.*, vol. iii., N. S., p. 79), "has introduced the sirocco, the effect of which is unfavourable to life of all kinds, and many of the crops have suffered thereby." Near Ravenna a pine forest, extending for about twenty-two English miles, being cut down, the sirocco was introduced, but was got rid of when the wood was allowed to grow again. In other parts of Italy, where the wood was cut down during the time of the French Republic, to enable the manufacture of iron to be carried on, the result was at once seen in an increased severity of climate, the maize no longer ripening. The forests have since been restored, and the climate is restored also. In Belgium favourable results have been obtained by the planting of trees on the right bank of the Scheldt, where large tracts of land, formerly waste, have been rendered fertile. The produce of the plains of Alsace, in the east of France, has suffered since the forests of the Vosges were removed; and the centre and south of France has felt the influence of the *mistral* and other injurious winds only since the forests of the Cevennes have been removed. The cultivation of certain plants and trees has thus become difficult or impossible where it was once easy and natural; and as this has taken place within the period of history, and has followed the disforesting in every case where observation has been made, there can be little doubt as to the cause. Although it is difficult to verify with precision the extent of these changes of climate where accurate and detailed observations are wanting, still the testimony of experience and the comparison of historic accounts point to such a change in Europe within the last thousand years. These conclusions are fully justified and confirmed by such tabular statements as exist, and are not contradicted by any statements, either of fact or opinion. They tend to show that throughout the north temperate zone the summers are cooler, moister, and shorter, than they were formerly; and that, on the other hand, the winters are milder, drier, and longer, than when forests covered a great part of the land, and cultivation was the exception, and not the rule. It is certain that the rivers and streams have also undergone change, and that where their course has not been interfered with, they are more irregular now than formerly, passing more frequently into torrents, becoming dried up more frequently, and carrying off more rapidly the heavy rains."—*Johnson's Farmers' Almanac for* 1868.

NICARAGUA AND MOSQUITO.

Nicaragua and Mosquitia, in spite of their interesting geographical position, have remained until lately almost a *terra incognita*. Nicaragua lies between the 11th and 15th parallels of N. lat., and the 83rd and 88th meridians of W. long. On the north is Honduras, to the south Costa Rica, on the west the Pacific, and on the east the narrow coast line of Mosquito country. In extent it is equal to half the area of Great Britain.

The climate of Nicaragua is varied; on the low coast line of the Atlantic, a tropical heat and humid atmosphere prevail, due, no doubt, to the dense primeval forest which clothes the soil to the water's edge. Inland, however, and on the Pacific side, the open lakes, with savannahs and cultivated country, enjoy a long dry season from December to June.

The scenery of Nicaragua is most beautiful, and perhaps unrivalled in the world. The Atlantic coast line is for the most part of varied character—sometimes rugged, with craggy promontories and points stretching into the sea; at other places verdant, fertile, and watered by magnificent rivers, diversified by noble hills, and forests with trees of such height, that when Columbus discovered this coast, in A.D. 1502, his historiographer, Las Casas, says "they appeared to reach the skies." Inland, towering mountains and volcanoes, level plains, immense lakes, and extensive savannahs, present to the inhabitants the most romantic scenery. The productions of this country are as varied and useful as those furnished by any other part of the globe of the like extent. They include the precious metals, cochineal, cacao, indigo, sarsaparilla, vanilla, caoutchouc, balsams, and dyes, tobacco, hides, timber, such as mahogany, cedar, pitch pine, &c. Half the population are of mixed breeds, and half of Indians; most of them speak Spanish, and are Roman Catholics. Of the Mosquitos there are three distinct races, the aborigines, and the descendants of negroes formerly wrecked on the coast, with settlements of Caribs formerly deported from the Antilles. The aboriginal

Indians are fast disappearing, and consist of about half a dozen tribes—viz., the Valiente, Rama, Cookwra, Woolwa, Tonga, and Poya.

All along the coast there is abundance of the sea fish common to the West Indies and the tropical waters of the Atlantic. The various turtles are taken in great quantities, especially on the small cays in the neighbourhood. They comprise the loggerheaded, green, and hawksbill varieties, of which the green (Chelonia viridis) is the only one worth eating. Both the male and female are taken, whilst at Ascension Island the male turtle is never seen. They commence depositing their eggs in the sand during June, and continue until the middle of October. The young ones are hatched in fifteen days. The eggs of the hawksbill (Caretta imbricata) are eaten, but not the flesh. Its shell, however, is valuable, affording the tortoise shell of commerce. This tortoise shell is obtained by lighting fires of grass upon the back of the animal, properly secured, when thirteen outer scales are skinned off, yielding 6lb. or 7lb. of shell. This is reproduced; but how long the process of reproduction takes is a mystery.

In the shallow water which breaks over the dangerous sand-bar at the entrance of Greytown harbour are swarms of sharks. They may be seen cruising about with their back fins out of the water, in readiness for any prey that they may chance to pick up, and are so ferocious that they will even attack a man in water not much above his knees. Within the lagoon, formerly a fine harbour, are plenty of the American crocodile (Molinia Americana). When not visible, their proximity is made evident to the olfactory sense by a most powerful odour of musk. Although often styled alligators, these are true crocodiles; and Columbus himself declared their identity with the crocodiles of the Nile. The crocodiles like brackish water, whilst alligators are never found except in fresh water. All along the San Juan river, and in the large freshwater lakes of Nicaragua and Managua, there is found a small species of fresh-water turtle, of which both flesh and eggs are eaten, making a good substitute for meat on fast days. The most notable, however, of the denizens of the waters flowing into the Atlantic undoubtedly is that prodigious monster siren the manatee (Manatus Australis), a most queer, paradoxical mammal, something between a pachyderm and a cetacean, half hippopotamus, half seal, and sometimes bearing a grotesque resemblance to the human form. It is unable to keep under water long, and so keeps to shallows and by the banks, feeding on water plants, algæ, &c. It carries its head and shoulders out of the water, and when dried and salted is a standard article of food among the Indians, who are great adepts at harpooning this animal. I have tasted the flesh, and found it not unlike ship's pork.

In the great lakes is also found a large freshwater shark, said to be as dangerous and voracious as its salt-water cousin. The common alligator is also to be seen oftener than is always pleasant to the bather. Perhaps it is owing to the presence of these creatures that the Nicaraguans have such a horror of washing their bodies. Caribs, indeed, and Mosquito Indians are bold swimmers, and like ducks; but the Spanish American half-breeds dread cold water, saying it gives them fever to bathe.

Amongst the fresh-water fish the best, both in lake and river, are the guapote, mojarra, and savallo. They are all good eating, grow to a good size, and take a fly or bait with readiness. The Indians shoot fish cleverly with bow and arrow.

Along the marshy borders of the lakes are plenty of various wild duck, which give good shooting to those who care to follow them over malarious swamps. Up some of the rivers I met with duck very similar to, if not indentical with, the Muscovy. Crowds of other waterfowl are to be seen on the banks, perched on snags, or fishing and diving throughout these waters. Amongst them may be mentioned the herons called "garza," cinereous boat-bills (Cancroma cochlearii), the glossy ibis (Ibis falcinellus), bitterns, egrets, cranes, cormorants, jacanas, a sort of jabiru (Mycteria Americana), darters with snake-like necks (Plotus anhinga), screamers which kill snakes and reptiles, boobies, &c., and seafowl from the Pacific seaboard (as the neck of land between the Pacific and the great lake is only in places some twelve miles across); whilst far overhead soars the marauding frigate bird (Atagen aquila)—called by the Spaniards "tijereta," from its long forked tail resembling a pair of scissors, "tijera" —only descending from its dizzy height to rob some wretched booby or gannet of its prey. Gorgeous kingfishers, too, with highly-coloured plumage, dart along the surface of the deep waters of the rivers.

Several varieties of iguana inhabit the bushes and banks on the margin of lake or river, some reaching a large size. They are much sought after, especially the female (Iguana delicatissima) when heavy with eggs. They are most tenacious of life, as indeed are all of the strobilosaurian family, and easily take alarm. They will take plenty of shot in their bodies without appearing to feel it, and require an arrow or shot right through their brain, which is not large. The Woolwa Indians are great adepts at diving and catching them alive in the water; they must be handled carefully, for they have a good mouthful of teeth, and bite like a

le. Besides the iguanas there are
ards, such as teguexins and ameivas,
 small anolis, with its curious ex-
at or dewlap, which it is able to
ll. Some of them, as Xiphosaurus
change their colour in a manner
chameleon.
t of the terrestrial animals in Cen-
, and one that affords good hunting,
uires much skill in stalking, is the
an tapir (Elasmotherium Bairdii).
"dante" by the Spaniards, and
w by the Caribs. This strange and
ectly known animal is the connec-
ween the elephant and the swine.
wo species known; and probably
s of this animal exist in the dense
jungle, especially on the Atlantic
 highlands. They are harmless
gh, unless wounded, when they will
or charge recklessly. They plunge
thickest woods and apparently
forests without any difficulty, at a
ring trot, crashing through every
thing seems able to bar their way.
id to swim and dive well. They
e to the water kindly, but when
seem to walk at the bottom of the
ne side and up the other, appar-
ess whether it is under water or not.
ember 30th.

RUS AND THE ZOOLOGICAL
GARDENS.

us has some strong points in his
e must in candour admit that he
o certain prejudices to encounter.
place, he scarcely comes up at
he walrus of popular imagination.
, judging from the common engrav-
st with a face so exactly resembling
ountenance as to have given rise to
mermaids. In fact, the only dif-
at a certain diabolic expression is
ed to him by a pair of monstrous
present walrus has a face more like
n on a knocker, and could scarcely
naids unless mermaids are supposed
ge moustaches and to go about
cocoa-nut matting. His tusks are
ble as the imaginary whiskers of a
Moreover, he comes at some disad-
succeeding the sea-bear. That
nimal very judiciously kept a private
is service; and it was a material
magination to see a genuine sailor,
ing with him a smell of salt water;
 hat alone was enough to carry one
Cape Horn. The poor walrus is in
custody of an excellent keeper, who can make
no pretence to an early intimacy with the
monster. Moreover, the walrus, though we are
glad to hear that he is improving in health, has
still the flabby and wrinkly appearance which
is excusable after a compulsory diet upon salt-
pork instead of mollusks, and a residence in a
deal box instead of on an iceberg. As he fills
out, he will probably become more attractive;
his compromise between hind legs and a tail is
well imagined, and produces some very quaint
gestures; his chattering and grunting are decided improvements upon the taciturnity of the
seal; and perhaps the happiest thought was
that of adapting his moustache for the collection
of his food. Gentlemen who dislike razors and
are fond of soup will feel a keen admiration for
this faculty. Finally, his deportment is, on the
whole, creditable; he takes his mussels with
grace and good humour, and, though he refuses
the tributes of nuts and orange-peel offered by an
admiring if rather indiscreet public, it is something to look at a beast who might, if he chose,
insist upon being fed exclusively upon oysters.
We feel grateful for his condescension in putting
up with whelks.

Whatever his success may be as a zoological
star, we feel sure that the walrus will find a
select circle of intelligent admirers. There is an
originality about his whole design which cannot
fail to be attractive. He may not be beautiful,
nor even amiable, but no one can say that he is
commonplace. Moreover, the walrus has in a high
degree one of the merits which give a special
charm to the gardens. We never can look at a
lion or an elephant, or any of the larger beasts,
without a certain sensation of relief. Every lion
necessarily implies a great tract of wild country
to supply him with food. In England, where
there is scarcely room for a cat to pick up a
decent living except as a hanger-on of humanity,
we bear about us a constant sense of oppression,
as if the world were becoming too small for us;
we feel like the American who did not venture to
walk out in England for fear of falling over the
edge; the limits of the habitable world are
growing too narrow. We see a lion, and we
take some comfort by instinctively performing a
rapid piece of mental arithmetic; we roughly
calculate how many leagues of jungle or forest
must be required to fill his larder, and we multiply the area by the presumable number of lions
in existence. Repeating the process at each of
the dens in succession, we feel for the moment
as if we had a little more elbow-room. The
buffaloes we know are disappearing from the
face of America at the rate of so many hundred
or thousand square miles in a year. Luckily
there are other countries where the process of
animal depopulation is not going on so fast. As

we visit beast after beast, we catch a faint whiff of their native haunts, of forest or prairie or swamp, and feel disposed to give thanks that there is a little spare standing room still left, and that a breath from unprofaned wildernesses may be caught by the imagination even in the midst of a London crowd. Perhaps this is the dominant thought which, even in a scarcely conscious form, gives the greatest pleasure to a sight of wild beasts, graceful and interesting as they are in themselves. Certain philosophers may sneer at it, and may long for the time when the world is to be a repetition of Middlesex on a gigantic scale, and when a bit of unenclosed ground will be as great a rarity in Africa or South America as in the most highly cultivated counties of England. Still the longing for some sort of breathing-place naturally strengthens as the world gets more closely packed, and, for instance, gives a great part of their modern charm to the Alps, which once excited emotions of simple horror, as it does to the Zoological Gardens. In this respect the walrus has obvious merits. We cannot look forward to a time when his haunts will be brought under human dominion. Walruses may, as far as we can see, go on tumbling in the Arctic Seas, or crowding each other upon icebergs, till the end of time. There is at least one inviolable preserve which can never be brought under the plough, or subjected to the Constitution of the United States. If our unlucky friend had not been deprived of the company of his species, he might be the progenitor of a long line of walruses, which might flourish their fins and clatter their teeth in defiance of the whole human race until our planet tumbles into the sun, or, after some indefinite lapse of ages, gets too hot for walrusses and icebergs. Some day we may be hard up for lions, but, with due care, we shall never run short of walruses. Meanwhile, we feel some sympathy for the unlucky representatives of their species whose presence suggests so many pleasant associations to their spectators, but who must look at the matter from a rather different point of view. They feel all the inconveniences of overcrowding to a very unpleasant degree. The walrus probably considers even now that he is treated to a rather small allowance of tub, considering the habits of his civilized country of adoption. If he gets to be a few sizes bigger—and we sincerely hope that he may live as long and grow as large as walrus nature permits—he will feel himself unpleasantly cramped even in the largest tank in the gardens. The Zoological Society does its best under unfavourable circumstances, and most of the animals seem to enjoy themselves as much as can be expected. But it is obvious that a little more space would be of immense service. The monkeys have quite redeemed their character under the beneficent influences of an improved habitation. They might have suggested to Mr. Peabody the thought of improving the dwellings of the higher orders of creation. They have room for displaying their humorous vivacity, and indulging in a constant series of practical jokes which might excite the envy of undergraduates. There is a sort of never-ending town and gown row between the monkeys with long tails and the monkeys with short, which testifies to the exuberant spirits of all concerned. It would be pleasant to see the same measures of reform extended to a wider area. If the large carnivora could take a walk rather more than six paces in length, and turn round without scraping the hair off their tails, their attractions would be enormously increased; and at some future time it would be a grand sight to see a walrus as big as a house playing in a real pond, instead of a washtub. But, to give proper play to all the animals concerned, the gardens must be allowed to extend a little further; and considering the way in which most of the park is occupied, we should think that no one would grudge a moderate addition to the most charming show in London.—*Saturday Review*, November 23.

THE LIFE-DESTROYING FLY (*LUCILIA HOMINIVORA*) OF MEXICO.

The *Archives Medicales Belges* contains a paper by Dr. Weber, upon this extraordinary fly, whose ravages lately attracted the attention of Messrs. Morel and Jacob.

It brings forward the chief facts observed by these authors, together with some original information by Dr. Weber himself. We condense the results into as few words as possible:—

The fly *lucilia hominivora* is nine millimetres long; its eyes are situated very near to each other at the back of its head; its palpæ are fawn-coloured; its head very large; cheeks of a golden yellow; thorax dark blue: abdomen of the same colour, but with purple bands: legs black; wings transparent, a little dusky, especially at their bases. It is a dipterous insect. Its *larva* is fifteen millimetres long, cylindrical, narrow at its anterior extremity, its body ending abruptly at the opposite end; it is white and opaque; its body is composed of eleven segments, each of which is provided with a little knob at its inferior border, covered with little spines in the shape of hooks. The chrysalis is cylindrical, and of a dark reddish-brown colour. The fly is oviparous, and in flying through the air produces a strong and continuous buzzing.

It appears that *lucilia hominivora* does not exist upon the high *plateaux* of Mexico, but only in the warm and temperate valleys. At Cordova it is found at a height of 800 metres, at Orizaba, at 1200 metres, and at Monterey, at 500 metres above the level of the sea; but it does not appear to live so high as Anahuac, which is 2000 metres above the ocean. Several cases of disease from this cause called *myiasis* (from the Greek *myia*, fly) have been observed at Acatlan, one of the warmest points in the south of the province of Puebla. The insect has been met with in all the four quarters of Mexico, in the north as well as in the south, on the Atlantic side as well as on the Pacific coast.

The patients feel nothing at first; soon, however, a slight itching of the nose supervenes, followed by headache, and swelling of the olfactory organ; bleeding of the nose is in some cases frequent; pains under the eyes, which the invalids compare to bruises which ache badly, are generally noticed. The nose becomes ulcerated, and from the ulcers issue a certain number of *larvæ*. The general symptoms indicate an inflammatory action more or less intense, followed by erysipelas of the face and head, sometimes this is followed by meningitis and death.

Dr. Weber remarks also that his patients suffered much from want of sleep; one poor fellow suffered so intensely from irritation and want of sleep, that at the period when erysipelas broke out he shot himself. In a case collected by the medical men of French Guiana, 300 *larvæ* were expelled by the aid of injections; but it was impossible to get rid of those which remained, for the injections themselves produce great irritation and pain. The remainder attacked the eye-balls, mouth, and gums, of the unfortunate sufferer in a most dreadful manner, and death followed in the space of seventeen days. Professor Famès attended a lady at Santiago; she is still living, but before all the *larvæ* could be expelled, she lost a portion of the roof of her mouth. A considerable number of cases, more or less distressing, have been collected, but we shall not stay to examine them here.

As for the treatment to be followed, nothing appears so efficacious as injections of chloroform, although this causes more or less pain to the patient. Insecticide medicines, though they kill the *larvæ*, do not expel them, and *cevadilla* (*veratrum sabadilla sem.*) is a somewhat dangerous remedy; though it kills the *larvæ* and expels them by the sneezing which it causes, is apt to produce frequent hemorrhage, and on this account can only be applied at the commencement of the disease. It has also been observed that if the *larvæ* are touched with a solution of sulphate of alumina, they die instantly, and dry up without decomposition, In 1864, a soldier was rapidly cured at Acatlan by injections of lemon juice.

LORD ROSSE'S TELESCOPE.

THE telescope constructed by Herschel, although very wonderful for the day in which it was made, has long since been eclipsed by that belonging to Lord Rosse, and erected by his late father at Birr Castle, near Parsonstown in Ireland. It is superior to Herschel's instrument both in point of size and workmanship. The late Lord Rosse, not fearing that his dignity would be compromised by such an act, went boldly to work, and learned to polish mirrors like an ordinary workman, the consequence of which was that he could bestow unusual pains upon the finishing of the speculum. His Lordship not only learnt the mere handicraft of speculum polishing, but went deeply into the engineering difficulties of the operation, and succeeded in inventing many improvements for diminishing labour and rendering the form of the surface more perfect. The specula ground and polished under Lord Rosse's method are almost entirely free from what is called spherical aberration—that is to say, all rays proceeding from a single point of light, such as a star, are collected into a single point instead of being scattered in a round mass. This freedom from spherical aberration is of course necessary to produce perfectly distinct images. In his *Life of Newton* Sir David Brewster calls it one of the most marvellous combinations of art and science yet seen in the world.

The tube of Lord Rosse's instrument is 55 feet long, and weighs $6\frac{1}{2}$ tons. In form it may be compared to the chimney of a steamboat of enormous size. At one end it terminates in a kind of square box, within which is contained the mirror, whose diameter is 6 feet, and which weighs nearly 4 tons. The weight of the whole apparatus is consequently nearly $10\frac{1}{2}$ tons, or four times as much as Herschel's. It is erected on an oblong mass of masonry, 75 feet in length from north to south, between two solid walls nearly 50 feet high, which serve as supports for the mechanism intended to move this enormous tube in all directions. To the walls are also fixed moveable staircases with platforms that can be brought up to the eye-piece with the greatest facility, no matter in what position the telescope may be placed. This noble instrument has penetrated space to a distance perfectly unattempted before its existence, and has resolved numerous nebulæ into masses of stars that until then were supposed to be mere clouds of luminous matter. The exact forms of other nebulæ have also been accurately determined by this telescope, which fully deserves the glowing eulogium passed upon it by the Duke of Argyle in his presidential address at the meeting of the British Association at Glasgow, in 1855. "This instrument," said his Grace, "in extending the range of astronomical science as it has done, has been the means of throwing certain doubts upon the laws that govern the motions of the heavenly bodies, and render it possible that certain of the far-distant nebulæ are regulated in their movements by other laws than those to which the members of our own system are subjected."

The clearness with which this telescope exhibits every object within its range is so great that the most distant nebulæ are seen with as great distinctness as the nearest planet. On directing it towards the moon, which is only distant from us about 240,000 miles, the surface of our satellite may be explored with a facility almost as great as that with which we examine the details of a landscape with an ordinary telescope.

Maedler, a German astronomer, who has measured nearly every mountain and valley on the moon's surface with the greatest exactitude, stated some years before Lord Rosse's telescope was perfected that if a monument as large as one of the Pyramids existed on the surface of the moon it could have been readily distinguished by the instruments then in use. With Lord Rosse's telescope we can see the surface of our satellite so much enlarged that a space 220 feet long could be readily perceived by a good observer. This enormous eye, measuring 6 feet in diameter, would hardly show us a lunar elephant; but it is certain that if a troop of buffaloes, or animals analogous to them, crossed the field of vision, they would undoubtedly be perceptible. Masses of troops marching backwards and forwards would also be plainly visible, and we may assert with something like absolute certainty that there are neither towns nor villages in the moon, nor any buildings as large as our own St. Paul's, or colossal railway stations.

This telescope, as we have said before, is the largest hitherto constructed, and cost its noble constructor more than £25,000. It must also be recollected that it was not a mere scientific toy belonging to an amateur philosopher, but a real working instrument in the possession of a true man of science, who did work with it that will render his name famous while civilisation lasts. The present Lord Rosse seems worthy in every way of his father's great name, and has already enriched astronomical science with numerous valuable observations.

Under the Microscope.

DIATOMACEÆ.

OF the many beautiful objects that the microscope has revealed to us, there are few so full of interest or so capable of exciting our utmost admiration as Diatoms. Indestructible, they have been brought down to us from the very earliest ages of the world's history, living whenever and wherever a condition of things has been and is found suitable for their development and nourishment. Down in the deep sea, borne on the surface of the rolling river, lying in stagnant ponds and weed-clogged ditches, in rock pools filled with brackish water, in lagoons, lakes, streams, and wells, they are to be found alive; not all alike certainly, but brothers and sisters, aunts, uncles and cousins of the same great family, while their fossil remains cover many acres of ground in all parts of the world. Richmond, U.S., is built upon a marine deposit of them eighteen feet deep, and extending beyond the city over an area the extent of which is not known. A mud bank is found on the flanks of Victoria Land 400 miles long by 120 broad composed of them. In Sweden and Norway they are so plentiful that the inhabitants in times of scarcity mix them (under the name of *Bergh-mehl*) with their flour for bread. In guano they are found in great numbers, having been eaten by shell fish and re-swallowed by sea birds, and in clay deposits left in the beds of dried-up rivers and streams they are very plentiful. Of their size some idea may be formed when we state that one inch of Bilin slate contains some 40,000 millions.

It has long been a disputed point whether they should be classed under the animal or vegetable kingdom. The latest investigators have decided that they are of vegetable nature, although Ehrenberg and many other eminent naturalists seeing some of them endowed with spontaneous motion, slowly moving along, and apparently turning back when they came in contact with any obstacle, and whirling gently about of their own free will, decided that they were animals. It has, however, since been ascertained that this power is shared with many simple plants, such as *Oscillatoria*, *Desmidiaceæ*, *Protococcus*, and others, some of which in certain stages of their development are even more active than DIATOMACEÆ. In spite of this there is still something to be said on the other side, for writes Kützing[*]:—"Comparing the arguments which seem to indicate the vegetable nature of DIATOMACEÆ with those which favour the animal nature, we are of necessity led to the latter opinion. If we suppose them to be plants we must admit every frustule, every *Navicula* to be a cell, we must suppose this cell with walls, penetrated by silica developed within another cell of a different nature, at least in every case where there is a distinct penducle or investing tube. In this silicious wall we must recognise a complication certainly unequalled in the vegetable kingdom. It would still remain to be proved that the eminently nitrogenous internal substance corresponded with the generic substance, and that the oil globules could take the place of starch. The multiplication would be a simple reduplication, but it would remain to be proved that it takes place, as in other vegetable cells, either by the formation of two distinct utricles or by the introreflection or constriction of the wall itself: finally, there would still remain unexplained the external motions and the internal changes, and we must prove the accumulated observations on the exterior organs of motion to be false by a clearer line of argument

---

[*] Dr. Hogg's "History of the Microscope," p. 17.

than has hitherto been adopted by those who are opposed to this view."

DIATOMACEÆ, or brittleworts, so called from the liability of the frustules to separate while being handled, consist of simple cells, the membranes of which are thoroughly impregnated with silex (Flint). These membranes are not destroyed by nitric, hydrochloric, or sulphuric acid, and can withstand the action of red heat, but may easily be dissolved by the use of the caustic alkalies, soda or potash. They consist always of two valves, which are united at the edges like a bivalve, and contain the endochrome-like plant, sometimes oil globules, and a granular substance which has been seen to circulate within. The valves are held together by a kind of frame or hoop, which in many cases under the microscope is out of sight. They are of three kinds. First, those which have an independent existence, moving about by themselves—these are known as free; the second are called stipitated, being attached to other objects, as Algæ, stones, etc.; whilst in the third form numerous frustules are enclosed in and held together by a coating of gelatine. In this state they are said to resemble the frond of a very small seaweed. In colour they vary from a golden yellow to almost chocolate, this latter colour being due to a small quantity of iron in their composition. They are propagated by the production of new cells between the parent frustules, and also by conjugation and further development of the spores. A prismatic or rectangular shape is the typical figure of the family. With any particular genus it is hardly possible to lay down any accurate definition, as great diversity of outline may prevail. Mr. Brightwell thus describes the transition of form produced by a change in the position of *Triceratium*[*]:—"The normal view of the frustule may be represented by a vertical section of a triangular prism. If the frustule be placed upon one of its flat sides, we look down upon its ridge and obtain a front view of its two sloping sides. If it be placed upon one of its ridges we have a front view of one of its flat sides, generally broader than long, and of its smooth or transparent suture or connecting membrane. If the frustule be progressing towards self-division, it is then often considerably longer than broad, and when nearly matured for separation presents the appearance of a double frustule."

In the markings which are found on the valves we have the primary cause which under the microscope place Diatoms amongst the most wonderful of God's creations. These markings are the distinguishing characteristics whereby we are enabled to distinguish the various species, and are consequently, in addition to their beauty, of the greatest importance. The surfaces are beautifully sculptured, and the markings assume the appearance of puncta (dots), striæ (stripes), costæ (ribs), and pinnæ (pinnules) of furrows and lines —longitudinal, transverse, and radiating—of bands, canaliculi (canals), and areolæ (cells.) The markings are chiefly dependent upon the presence of costæ, which are connected with an inner membrane and the striæ: these are not visible until the contents have been removed and the frustule rendered transparent. In many species, under a very high power, these striæ are resolved into puncta; hence their value as test objects, for which purpose they are extensively used. It is by the number and in the difference arising from fineness, approximation, and position of striæ that we are enabled to fix the different species. To observe these markings the student should not be content with any single view, but should roll and turn the specimens on the slide so as to expose other sides, as described by Mr. Brightwell. This will be found a rather difficult operation, requiring time and some patience.

As we have already stated, *Diatoms* are to be found in all parts of the world both alive and in a fossil state. Persons residing near London will find *Diatoma, Surirello, Synedra, Plurosigma, Pinnularia* and others in the Serpentine in Hyde Park, and in the Ornamental Waters in St. James's and Regent's Parks. Many forms have been met with in the Highgate and Hampstead Ponds, in the different docks, in the Surrey Canal, and on Clapham and Wandsworth Commons. Fine specimens of *Gromia* have been found in the marshes at Erith, and at Swanscombe Salt Marsh, half a mile from Northfleet, also in the marshes at North Woolwich. *Pinnularia, Cupidala,* and *Stauroneis* have been obtained on Keston Common, near Bromley, while *Surirella biseriata* and *S splendida*, with many others, have been found in boggy pools on Winter Down, opposite Claremont Park, Esher. Indeed the fresh-water species may be said to be ubiquitous, and may be sought for on brown tufts on sides and bottoms of any ditch and running stream. Johann Nane in his interesting little work says[*]:—"In searching for these minute plants the collector will often be guided by the reddish-brown tint which colours the Algæ on which they are growing, and which betrays their presence. This is especially the case in the bright sunshine, when it often happens that tufts of weed float on the surface of the water, upheld by the gases which have been generated by its ray. The quantity of Diatomaceæ which are sometimes found on the larger Algæ is almost incredible. Species of the genus *Cocconeis* not unfrequently clothe Confervaceæ (for instance Cladophora glomerata) with a deep red brown to such an extent that not a trace is to be seen of the original Cladophora. The Polysiphoniæ and Ceramia are not unfrequently so completely hidden under masses of *Synedra* and *Achnanthes*, that in point of fact they become, not independent plants, but the invisible axis of a coating of Diatomaceæ. Others, however, of the Stipitate species occur more rarely. To secure these the collector must not forget to examine closely the various filamentous Algæ he may chance to come across on his excursions. He must be careful, too, not to overlook those plants whose acquaintance he has already made earlier in the season, for it often happens that a colony of Diatomaceæ will fix themselves on an Alga late in the year, of which not a specimen appeared when the plant was first examined."

The marine forms may be found attached to seaweed and adhering to mooring-posts and piles of wharfs and jettys, also in brackish pools subject to

---

[*] Journal Microscop. Soc., vol. i. p. 248.

[*] A handy book for the collection, etc., of fresh water and and marine Algæ, Diatoms, etc. London: Hardwick. P. 33.

tidal influence. The rarer kinds should be sought for in the stomachs of lobsters, oysters, whelks, and other mollusks. Noctilucea are Diatom feeders, and should be caught in a fine gauze towing-net and preserved. Deep sea soundings are likely to contain some fine specimens. All round the coast, principally during the months of April, May, August, and September, specimens of more or less value are to be found. *Coscinodiscus radiata*, supposed to have been purely exotic, has been found plentifully in a cave attainable only at lowest water in the face of rocks some ten miles south of Aberdeen, while the following have been gathered on Whitley Sands, on the Northumberland coast[*]:—*Amphiprora alata, A. fulva, Actinoptychus undulatus, Biddulphia Baileyii, Epithemia marina, Nitzschia bilobata, N. virgata, Navicula didyma, N. lyra, N. granulata, N. farcipata, N. lineata, N. æstiva, N. retusa, Pleurasigma hippocampus, P. æstuarii, P. marinum, P. lanceolatum, P. arcuatum, Donkinia carinatum, D rectum, D. minutum, Toxonidea insignis*, and occasionally frustules of *Toxonidea Gregariana*.

Deposits of earth and guano are found to contain a great variety of fossil remains. Mr. Kitton, of Norwich, describes[†] nearly two hundred different kinds as having been found in the Monmouth deposit. Amongst others, specimens from the following places will be found worth investigating—Algiers, Mull, Bilin, Italy, Barbadoes, Auvergne, Richmond (U.S.), Bangor (U.S.), New Durham, Kreselguhr, Lapland, Gassa, Obero, Habichtswald, Sullamare, Loch Mourne, Premnay, Wreathum (U.S.), Virginia, Piscataway, Manchester (U.S.), Rappanhanna Schockhoe, Rugen, Slieve Mar Hills, and Bermuda.

Those who wish to obtain a minute account of the different species will do well to consult Dr. Gray's "Handbook of British Algæ," with the "Diatomaceæ" by Mr. W. Carruthers, also "Smith on British Diatomaceæ," and Pritchard's "Infusoria." The following list will be found to contain some of the most important, with a brief description of their chief characteristics:—

NAVICULEÆ—so called from their resemblance to a boat—comprise a very large section. They vary greatly in form and marking, the valves being delicately striated, with or without a central aperture. Some are shaped like the letter S, whilst others are striped longitudinally and transversely; others again are waved.

Navicula is a very large genus, containing some eighty-four British species alone. The valve has delicate moniliform striæ, with central and terminal nodules.

Pinnularia numbers about fifty-three British species. They have central and terminal nodules, with ribs on the valves.

Stauroneis only contains about sixteen British specimens. The central nodule is transversely dilated into a band, free from striæ, which are seen only on the valve.

Pleurosigma.—Of this species Great Britain claims some thirty or forty. This is one that is most commonly used as a test object.

Toxonidea, of which only about two species are natural to this country.

Donkinia.—A front view somewhat resembles the shape of a fiddle. There are about six British species.

Amphiprora numbers about twelve British, while of *Diadesmis* we have but one.

MELOSEIRIA are found on marine Algæ. They are composite, many frustules being joined together by silicious hoops.

M. borreri.—Many beautiful specimens of this are found both in salt and fresh water abundant on marine Algæ. It may readily be mistaken for a mass of Confervæ. Its nature has been misunderstood by several eminent naturalists. Agardh classed it with fresh water Algæ, while Ehrenberg under the name of Gallionella removed it into the animal kingdom.

M. varians are composed of a variable number of segments, are mostly cylindrical, sometimes being disc-shaped or rounded. They are found in fresh water.

M. sub-flescilis is found off Friburg, and another.

M. nummulites is found in the Baltic.

ACHNANTHES LONGIPES.—Of this there are several species, some fossils, others found in fresh water, but it is most common in sea water. In life they are connected by a stem, the upper and lower frustules having different markings. The lower ones have a transverse line, which forms a cross upon the valve. They are very beautiful.

SYNEDRA.—There are about seventy species of this. The frustules are arranged upon a sort of cushion, but in course of time break away. Some species radiate in every direction from the cushion.

S. Ulna is found in great numbers in fresh water ponds and rivers, encrusting confervæ or stones. They keep in groups of golden wands, which in age dilate and have three obtuse teeth visible, with openings between.

BACCILARIA.—So called from their running end to end like a bundle of sticks. They are shorter than *Synedra*, but are otherwise very like them; they also are abundant, covering confervæ like felt. They are found either adhering together in a zigzag manner, or free, gliding about like *Navicula*.

GOMPHONEMA.—Of this there are nearly forty species found in ponds and ditches. It varies in shape, not being unlike a wooden peg with either notched or plain edges. It grows something like a tree, on long filaments, which are attached to confervæ, stones, etc.

LICOMOPHORA is marine, being parasitic on seaweed. It grows on a stalk, but in dense masses, and the stalk widens in process of multiplication, the frustules being spread out like a fan.

RHABDONEMA is marine, and is used as a test object, because in addition to the striæ each frustule has two or four rows of marks, called vittæ. These vittæ are internal silicious folds, and distinguish a large section of Diatoms.

BIDDULPHIA.—This species is chain-like, the frustules adhering to one another by projecting angles. A band of minute cells forms a kind of hoop round the

---

[*] Hardwick's "Science Gossip," vol. ii. p. 162.
[†] Hardwick's "Science Gossip," vol. iii. pp. 133, 156, and 180.

valves; this hoop often becomes detached while multiplication is going on.

AMPHITETRAS.—This is square and cellular, the frustules being frequently piled up one above another. There is a large cell in the corner of each frustule. It is found in a fossil state in Barbadoes deposit and Bermuda earth, alive it is found in the sea off Cuba and the Canary Islands.

ISTHMIA ENEVIS.—This will be found to well repay investigating, being a most beautiful species. It is to be found attached to seaweed on the English coast and in the Channel Islands. It is unlike most others in its mode of increase: two cells form within the valves, and as they increase in size break away; the hoop which once joined the new frustules to the parent ones remains attached to one of them for a time, occasionally altering its shape so as to cause some of them to appear truncated instead of round.

ARACHNOIDISCUS is found attached to seaweed. One species is much used in making soup by the Japanese. In the fossil state it is principally found in guano. The double disc has two inner valves, the outer one being very horney, and having marks upon it not unlike a spider's web. The inner silicious valve supports the upper one.

A. Ornatus is recorded to have been found in a brackish pool of water at Malahide, in the county of Dublin.

HELIOPELTA (The) is found fossil in Bermuda earth. The raised compartments are very beautiful in relief, forming a five or six-rayed star, with lateral spine and striated margin. The number of rays to be seen decide the species.

H. Seuwenhaekii has ten compartments, and a five-rayed star in the centre.

H. euleri has twelve compartments, and a six-rayed star; while

H. metii has eight compartments, and a perfect Maltese cross in centre.

OMPHALOPELLA is found in Bermuda earth and in other guano. It sometimes resembles *Heliopella*, but the rays, although to be seen very plainly, are less raised; the margins also have fewer spines, and the rim is much broader.

OVERSICOLOR.—The rim of this is very radiant. It has a six-rayed star in the centre, and has a beautiful play of colour from tawney to red.

ACTINOCYCLUS.—This species is found alive at Cuxhaven, and in a fossil state in Virginia earth. It has no marginal spines, and from eight to ten divisions.

ASTEROMPHALUS, ASTEROLAMPIA.—In these we have beautiful umbilical rays reaching midway to the margin, from which alternate rays proceed, forming a bright star in the middle, having five cells in each marginal division. They are found fossil in guano in Virginia deposit, Piscataway and Bermuda earth.

COSCINODISCUS are perfectly round, having no rays or division. The structure being wholly cellular, they are to be recognised by the minute regular markings, tubercles, and a variation in the size of Aroelæ. Fossil they are found in the chalk marl of Aran and in Richmond, Virginia, and Bermuda earth, and alive off Cuxhaven.

We have now, we think, said enough to give those of our readers who were not previously acquainted with the subject some idea of what Diatomaceæ are, and where they are to be found. Any one wishing for further information can obtain it, in addition to the works we have already mentioned, from Carpenter's valuable book on the Microscope (Churchill), or Dr. Hogg's useful work on the same subject (Routledge). A great deal remains to be said about cleaning and preparing specimens, for which we have not space; but we cannot do better than recommend for this purpose a little work (which contains every information on the subject) by Thomas Davis (Mr. Hardwick, Piccadilly).

THE ALLUVIAL PLAINS OF EGYPT AND ETHIOPIA.

In Upper Nubia and Egypt, as far south as about 18° N. lat., near Suwákin, an irregular chain of mountains separates the valley of the Nile from the Red Sea. At this point a marked change takes place: the mountain-chain increases in breadth, and acquires the character of a table-land; and it is here that we first meet with the head-streams of the Nile. For it is a singular fact, which cannot be sufficiently dwelt on, that below the point where the Atbara or Astaboras joins the main stream of the Nile, not a drop of water is received by that great river from a single tributary in its course through Nubia and Upper Egypt; so that, whatever may be the magnitude of the Nile of Lower Egypt during the inundations and the extent of country at that time covered by its waters, these waters are only the surplus of those which pass by Mekheirriff in 18° N. lat., after the evaporation and infiltration, as well as the diversion for the purposes of irrigation, to which the river has been exposed and subjected in its winding course through thirteen degrees of latitude, equal probably to a length of 1,300 geographical miles.

Such a phenomenon is exhibited by no other river in the world. Nor is this the only singularity of the Nile. Where that river thus first begins to run in an isolated channel—which, according to our notions of rivers, partakes more of the character of an artificial canal than of a natural stream—it issues from an extensive plain country, formerly known as the island of Meroe, or Ethiopia, consisting of an immensely thick layer of rich alluvial soil, through which the two great Abyssinian streams, the Astaboras, Atbara, or Black River, and the Astapus, Abai, or Blue River, have eaten and still eat their way. The operation of the rivers is evident to the eye, their beds being bounded on either side by a wall of soft clay, from sixteen to twenty feet in height, which is everywhere being undermined, and of which large masses are yearly washed into the current, particularly into that of the Atbara. So enormous is the quantity of soil thus displaced and carried down by the floods, that it is considered amply sufficient to supply the fertilising slime which has formed and is daily adding to the Delta of Lower Egypt.

Before quitting the subject of the physical character

of Abyssinia, I wish to direct special attention to this system of immense deep-cut valleys, in which the rivers of that country flow, as showing the primitive source of the incalculable masses of alluvial soil, which in the course of ages have gone to form the Delta of the Nile, otherwise the country of Lower Egypt. Only in so doing I must remark that the existence of the vast alluvial plains already described, as skirting Abyssinia on the north-west, and the fact that Lower Egypt is now being added to by the erosion and transport of the soil of these alluvial plains, rather than by the direct action of the rivers of Abyssinia on the now (so to say) denuded sides of the valleys in the upper country, point to a time when the detritus from those valleys went to form, not the Lower Delta of Egypt, but the Upper Delta of Ethiopia; and as it was not till after this operation had been completed, and the rivers began to remove their deposits from the upper alluvial plain to a lower level, that the Egyptian Delta could have been formed, it follows that Lower Egypt itself must be of a comparatively recent date. That this should be the case is entirely in accordance with the statements of Herodotus, to which I drew attention many years ago in my "Origines Biblicæ."

That historian writes that, according to the Egyptians themselves, "Menes was the first mortal who reigned over Egypt, and that in his time all Egypt, except the district of Thebes, was a morass, and that no part of the land that now exists below Lake Mœris was then above water:" and again he says, "the Delta, as the Egyptians themselves acknowledge, and as I think, is alluvial, and (if I may so express myself) has lately come to light." And in conclusion he says:—"For my own part I am not of opinion that the Egyptians commenced their existence with the country which the Ionians call Delta; but that they always were since men have been; and that, as the soil gradually increased, many of them remained in their former habitations, and many came lower down. For anciently Thebes [that is to say, the Thebaid] was called Egypt."

I quote these expressions of Herodotus for the purpose of supporting the opinion I have long entertained, that within the historical period material changes have taken place in this alluvial plain country of Meroe, or Ethiopia. And this opinion is corroborated by the fact recorded by the geographer Artemidorus, who flourished about two centuries after Herodotus, that near the city of Ptolemais, on the shores of the Red Sea, which city I have identified with some remarkable remains in 18° 15′ north latitude, a branch of the river Astaboras discharged itself into the sea, of which singular fact a confirmation has been recently found in the travels of Dr. Schweinfürth.

It would seem, indeed, that we have direct evidence of the changes which have taken place in these regions even within the Christian era, in the marked difference which exists between the configuration of the rivers forming the island of Meroe in Ptolemy's map, constructed only seventeen centuries ago, and that of the same rivers in the maps of the present day.—From a Lecture by Charles Beke.—Reprinted in *Athenæum*, Nov. 30th.

Colour of the Sea and of Ice.

The learned Director of the Roman Observatory has printed this year at Florence an extensive memoir, which contains the whole of his observations on Stellar Spectra up to the present date. In offering this interesting little work to the Academy of Sciences at Paris, the author brings forward an interesting observation relating to the colour of the sea. He found some time ago that the spectrum of the colour of the sea lost its red rays at a very slight depth; on going still deeper it lost successively its yellow and its green, at least partially, when the water appeared violet-blue. It was interesting to ascertain whether the same kind of absorption would occur with ice; and Professor Secchi profited by a visit to an artificial grotto excavated in a glacier over Grindelwald, in Switzerland, to determine this point.

The grotto in question is about 100 metres deep, and its sides are transparent and lighted by the sunlight transmitted through the ice. The light thus transmitted was of a beautiful blue tint, in which the red rays were very faint, so that in the interior of the grotto the human countenance had a very ghastly appearance. On looking from the inside towards the entrance, the grotto appeared as if illuminated by a red light, which was doubtless an effect of contrast. The whole effect was quite fairy-like. On analysing the light by means of a spectroscope an almost complete absence of red, and a great diminution of the yellow, were observed. The thickness of the ice was not sufficiently great to produce a more complete effect. This thickness was about 15 metres, or perhaps somewhat less. The texture of the ice was quite compact and continuous, and it was as limpid as crystal, containing only here and there a few bubbles of air.

It appears, then, quite evident, since the ice of the Alps acts exactly as did the water of the sea, and since the former cannot be supposed to contain any extraneous colouring matter, such as might be supposed to occur in the ocean, that the true colour of water is blue mixed with violet, and that this colour increases in strength as the layer of water through which the light passes increases in thickness.

The Country of the Namaquas.

The Namaquas, unlike the Korannas, can be referred to a totally distinct locality, their habitation being a large tract of country on the south-west coast of Africa, lying north of the Orange River, or Gariep, and being called from its inhabitants Great Namaqualand.

It is a wild and strange country—dry, barren, and rugged, and therefore with a very thinly scattered population, always suffering from want of water, and at times seeming as parched as their own land. For several consecutive years it often happens that no rain falls in a large district, and the beds of the streams and rivers are as dry as the plains. Under these circumstances, the natives haunt the dried water-courses, and, by sinking deep holes in their beds, contrive to procure a scanty and precarious supply of water at the cost of very great labour. Sometimes these wells are dug to the depth of twenty feet, and even when the water is obtained at the expense of so much labour, it is in comparatively small quantities, and of very inferior quality. Branches of trees are placed in these pits by way of ladders, and by their means the Namaquas hand up the water in wooden pails, first filling their own water-vessels, and then supplying their cattle by pouring the water into a trough. This scene is always an animated one, the cattle, half mad with thirst, bellowing with impatience, crowding round the trough, and thrusting one another aside to partake of its contents. A similar scene takes place if a water hole is discovered on the march. A strong guard, mostly of women, is placed round the precious spot, or the cattle would certainly rush into it in their eagerness to drink what water they could get, and trample the rest into undrinkable mud.

In this strange country, the only supplies of rain are by thunderstorms, and, much as the natives dread the lightning, they welcome the distant rumble of the thunder, and look anxiously for its increasing loudness. These thunderstorms are of terrific violence when they break over a tract of country, and in a few hours the dry watercourses are converted into rushing torrents, and the whole country for a time rejoices in abundant moisture.

The effect on vegetation is wonderful. Seeds that have been lying in the parched ground waiting in vain for the vivifying moisture spring at once into life, and, aided by the united influence of a burning sun and moist ground, they spring up with marvellous rapidity. These storms are almost invariably very partial, falling only on a limited strip of country, so that the traveller passes almost at a step out of a barren and parched country, with scarcely a blade of grass or a leaf of herbage, into a green tract as luxuriant as an English meadow.

The geological formation is mostly granite, and the glittering quartz crystals are scattered so profusely over the surface, that a traveller who is obliged to pursue his journey at noon can scarcely open his eyes sufficiently to see his way, so dazzling are the rays reflected on every side. In many parts the ground is impregnated with nitre, which forms a salt-like incrustation, and crumbles under the feet, so that vegetation is scarcely possible, even in the vicinity of water. There seem to be few inhabited lands which are more depressing to the traveller, and which cause more wonder that human beings can be found who can endure for their whole lives its manifold discomforts. Yet they appear to be happy enough in their own strange way, and it is very likely that they would not exchange their dry and barren land for the most fertile country in the world.

The euphorbia best flourishes in the ravines, but, from its poisonous nature, adds little to the comfort of the traveller. Even the honey which the wild bees deposit in the rocks is tainted with the poison of the euphorbia flowers, and, if eaten, causes most painful sensations. The throat first begins to feel as if cayenne-pepper had been incautiously swallowed, and the burning heat soon spreads and becomes almost intolerable. Even in a cool country its inward heat would be nearly unendurable, but in such a place as Namaqualand, what the torture must be can scarcely be conceived. Water seems to aggravate instead of allaying the pain, and the symptoms do not go off until after the lapse of several days.—*Routledge's Illustrated History of Man.*

Is the Earth Hollow?

If the earth were a plenary solid body throughout, as mathematicians imagine it to be, or even if its interior were filled with molten rock, as some geologists fancy, there would necessarily be an enormous pressure propagated towards the centre by the weight of the superincumbent strata. Sir John Herschel calculates this pressure to be equal to 300,000 atmospheres; whilst Dr. Young estimates that a block of solid granite, at the centre, would be compressed into half its linear or one-eighth of its cubical dimensions. Now the superficial specific gravity of hard rock is about 2·8, and if this were increased eight-fold at the centre, it would give the earth a mean density of about 12 or 13 times that of water. We know, however, that it is only 5·4 times that amount; consequently, that the central parts are not subjected to this enormous pressure, and therefore, in all probability, that the earth is not a solid body, or composed of ponderable materials throughout its interior. It is, moreover, remarkable that the interior group of primary planets—Mercury, Venus, the Earth, and Mars, which differ but little in size and period of diurnal rotation—have all very nearly the same mean density; whilst the great planets of the external group—Jupiter, Saturn, Uranus, and Neptune—exceeding the Earth some eight or ten times in linear dimensions, rotate about their axes in less than half the time,—the diurnal motion of Jupiter being upwards of 27,000 miles an hour,—whilst their mean density, in the words of Sir John Herschel, is little more than the specific gravity of cork! Now, the laws of philosophy prohibit us from supposing the planets to be composed of imaginary or unknown materials, different from those of which we have actual experience on the earth. Here, then, is a paradox which admits of no solution on the hypothesis of plenary solidity, but which becomes perfectly reconcilable to fact and experience when we conceive the planets to be hollow spheroids, in each of which an extensive vacant nucleus compensates for the denser mass of a more limited solid shell.—*Athenæum,* Nov. 30.

The River Amazon.

The British Consul at Parà, in his report to the Foreign-office on the trade of the past year, remarks, that the opening of the navigation of the Amazon to the shipping of all nations must tend to introduce foreign capital and competition on this great river, and thereby eventually increase the trade, importance, and wealth of the country; but that a considerable time must elapse before any company can be able to compete with the steamers of the Brazilian corporation which receives such large subsidies from the Government. The contract was made in 1852 for 25 years, at an annual subsidy of 720 coutos of reis, or about £80,000.; and the amount has since been increased—first by 60 coutos, and afterwards by 250 milreis per voyage, for running to additional ports. The company had eight steamers in 1866, and carried

10,249 passengers in the year, receiving 111 coutos for passage money and 299 coutos for freights. The total value of produce exported from the Amazon in 1866 amounted to more than 7,384 coutos or (at the exchange of 2s. 2d. to the milreis) £799,983. The imports to Parà amounted to above 4,711 coutos, or £510,429. sterling. The trade with Bolivia by the Madeira river has much increased, and will make considerable further progress whenever steam navigation is re-established. The trade with Venezuela by the river Negro has but little increased, as no steam communication has as yet been re-established. The Amazon river is navigable as far as the frontier port of Tabatinga for vessels of the largest size; but the different tributaries, though of great breadth, are crossed by waterfalls or hidden banks, rendering them impassable by vessels drawing much water. The two provinces of Parà and Amazonas have together a population of about 300,000 souls, without including the wild Indians who infest the dense forests, and many of whose tribes are almost unknown. Large importations are annually made of articles of consumption and luxury from Europe. The cotton goods come chiefly from England; cloth from England, France, and Belgium; metals from England; in hardware the United States compete successfully with England. Rubber is the most important article of export from Parà; the rubber tree grows in great abundance throughout the whole valley of the Amazon. Cacao is also an important export; the quality of the Parà fruit is considered among the best. Brazil nuts are easily collected, but the low price in foreign markets in 1866 decreased the exportation. The valley of the Amazon offers remarkable facilities for raising sugar, but the cultivation is in a most backward state, both owing to the want of field hands and a proper system of culture. No cotton is now grown on the Upper Amazon, where, under the despotic rule of the Marquis of Pombal, in the last century the Indians grew and wove much cotton. The mineral wealth of the Amazon valley is entirely unexplored. Vast quantities of fine cabinet woods, hard woods, and dye woods grow in the forests of Parà and Amazonas; but freight, export duties, and the high price of labour have been too high to encourage exportation. The Government of Brazil have for some years invited foreign immigration into the vast and fertile provinces of the Amazon; and latterly large numbers of "Southerners" have arrived from the United States, and been forwarded up the Tapajos river, where lands are granted them, and in some cases loans of money. It remains to be proved, however, whether the white race can prosper in agricultural pursuits under the tropical sun of Amazonas or Parà.

VOLCANIC DISTURBANCES AT THE AZORES.

MM. Ch. Deville and Fouqué have communicated to the Academy of Sciences the result of their observations at the Azores, where volcanic disturbances have manifested themselves with considerable intensity since December last. On the 25th May 1867, from half-past two in the afternoon until midnight, there were no less than fifty-seven distinct shocks of earthquake! A few days later the ground was in constant motion. On the 1st of June, a very violent earthquake was immediately followed by a volcanic eruption. It commenced by very violent detonations, which lasted all night. The next day the sea was covered with what appeared to be a thin layer of sulphur. At six o'clock in the morning, several jets of water rose into the air, and the sea was boiling. On the 4th some large stones were launched out, but no new land or island was pushed up, as occurred recently near Santorin. During the whole time of the eruption a penetrating and disagreeable odour was diffused through the air; it was evidently that of sulphuretted hydrogen, for it was compared to "rotten eggs." Besides sulphur, certain black, yellow, and red matters floated upon the surface of the ocean. No phenomena of light were observed during the whole time that the observation lasted. It was on the 5th the volcanic intensity appeared to be at its height. On the 7th no more stones were lifted up, and soon afterwards the oscillations of the ground became less frequent and much weaker. However, on the 27th June there was an earthquake, and on the 17th August the ground oscillated, since which date things appear to have settled down to their ordinary state. The gasses evolved during the eruption appear to be principally hydrogen mixed with sulphuretted hydrogen.

A BIRD TAMER.

THE great and distinguishing attainment Mr. Fox has won is in making himself the Rarey of the bird world. It was all an incident to his benevolent disposition, not a premeditated design. It commenced at the time when he was laying out the grounds of his little dell park. While at work upon the walks and flower beds, and turning up the fresh earth with his spade or rake, several of the little birds would come down from the trees, and hop along after him at a little distance picking up the worms and insects. By walking gently and looking and speaking kindly when they were near, they came first to regard his approach without fear, then with confidence. They soon learned the sound of his voice, and seemed to understand the meaning of his simple, set words of caressing. Little by little they ventured nearer and nearer, close to his rake and hoe, and fluttered and wrestled and twittered in the contest for a worm or fly, sometimes hopping upon the head of his rake in the excitement. Day by day they became more trustful and tame. They watched him in the morning from the trees near his door, and followed him to his work. New birds joined the company daily, and they all acted as if he had no other intent in raking the earth than to find them a breakfast. As the number increased, he began to carry crusts of bread in the great outside pocket of his coat, and to sprinkle a few crumbs for them on the ground. When his walks were all finished, and he used the spade and rake less frequently, the birds looked for their daily rations of crumbs; and would gather in the tree-tops in the morning and let him know, with their begging voices, that they were waiting for him. He called them to breakfast with a whistle, and they would come out of the thick, green leaves of the grove and patter, twitter and flutter around and over his feet. Sometimes he would put a piece of bread between his lips, when a bright-eyed little thing would pick it out, like a humming-bird taking honey from a deep flower-bell without alighting. They became his constant companions. As soon as he stepped from his door, they were on the look-out to give him a merry welcome with their happy voices. They have come to know the sound of his step, his walks and recreations. Often when leaning upon his hoe or rake, one of them will alight upon the head of it and turn up a bright eye at his face. Even before he gave up the practice of shooting birds of another feather, one would sometimes hop upon the gilt guard of the lock, and peer around upon the brass trigger with a look of wonder, which he interpreted aright, and left off killing birds susceptible of the same training. He leaves his chamber window open at night, and when he awakes early in the morning, he often finds a robin or goldfinch hopping about on the bed-posts or on the back of a chair close by, trying to say or sing in the best articulation of its speech, " It is time to get up ; come and see the flowers ; a dew of pearl is on their leaves, and the sun is above the sea." And, what is more beautiful still and full of poetry—full of the sweet life of those spontaneous affinities and affections more beautiful than poetry—these birds follow him to the sanctuary on the Sunday, a distance of more than a mile from his house, as a kind of aerial escort singing their Sabbath psalms of gladness and praise on the way. When the indoor service is ended, they meet him on his return, and escort him home with a new set of hymns. Indeed, if they do did not know that he belonged to a denomination that eschew singing in their Sabbath worship on earth, though they pray and hope to sing as loudly and joyfully as any other Christians in heaven, perhaps these little "street musicians of the heavenly city" would follow him into the meeting-house and sing a voluntary over "the ministers' gallery."—*Elihu Burritt's Walk from London to the Land's End.* Sampson Low.

DESTRUCTION OF MUSSELS BY WHELKS.

In autumn last year I first felt the scarcity of mussels, for it was only then, for the last fourteen years, that I had cause for using such commodity in this quarter. Some twenty years and down to fifteen years ago, I recollect there used to come yearly a fleet of East coast luggers for cargoes of mussels for baiting their lines. There were at that time large fields open to them, where they could load without leaving the ground which they anchored at. Glencoe's foreshore, say thirty acres, and Cruart, that shore west of the hotel, say fifteen acres, where so thickly set with mussels that no sand could be seen under them. To-day these places are not called on for mussels by any, except strangers. The shells are in the latter place in large banks huddled together ; in the former, the greater part have been buried under the sand, or taken to deep water by the rolling of the sea. Nothing can give any idea of the numbers destroyed—they were as innumerable as the sand on which they grew. Observing such a great change, and so vast destruction of a very useful commodity, I was induced to examine into the cause. Many were the suppositions of the inhabitants, but an examination of the shell showed the only true cause. Each mussel is drilled through with a fine bore, the size of a darning needle. In some cases several bores are in the one shell, and frequently one is found discontinued, after some other one having got through. From these observations I concluded that the destruction of the mussels was caused by some worm which, after boring through the shell, devoured the contents. In six months more I was in full possession of the secret. The whelk, which is the mussel destroyer, could hardly be supposed fitted for such work. Among our shores the "bucky" is seemingly the most lazy and inactive of animals. The young of the whelk, however, which the ling and cod fishers use for bait, is most active and ferocious. The "gillefinnan," as the Highlanders term it, performs its work as follows : It turns out a portion of its body, which contracts and extends greatly, this giving it a strong sucking power. Inside this sucker there comes out a small tube, about an inch long and of considerable elasticity. The point of the tube is armed all round by a set of teeth like forefinger nails. Their number I have not had as yet proper mode of ascertaining, but they are not many. The smallest opening and contracting of the valve, with the pressure of the sucker, will bore the pearly shell of the strongest mussel through in about an hour's time. After this is finished, the tube is extended all the length and breadth of the mussel, till all is eaten up, unless an accident forces the ferocious creature to let go its hold. They are often, however, found in all stages of consumption. It is amusing to catch them, and force them to let go their hold. Whether these whelks have changed their habits I do not know, but they are not apparently more numerous than they were formerly, at least not to any great extent. I could say much more on the subject, but would rather that the attention of some of our naturalists were drawn to it.—JOHN CAMERON, JUN. (Ballachulish.)

[The above facts, though interesting, are by no means novel. Stevenson, who erected the Bell Rock Lighthouse about sixty years ago, wrote as follows on the subject : " When the workmen first landed upon the Bell Rock, limpets of a very large size were common, but were soon picked up for bait. As the limpets disappeared, we endeavoured to plant a colony of mussels, from beds at the mouth of the River Eden, of a larger kind than those which seem to be natural to the rock. These larger mussels were likely to have been useful to the workmen, and might have been especially so to the lightkeepers, the future inhabitants of the rock, to whom that delicate fish would have afforded a fresh meal, as well as a better bait than the limpet ; but the mussels were soon observed to open and die in great numbers. For some time this was ascribed to the effects of the violent surge of the sea ; but the Buccinum lapillus (Purpura) having greatly increased, it was ascertained that it had proved a successful enemy to the mussel. The Buccinum, being furnished with a broboscis capable of boring, was observed to perforate a small hole in the shell, and thus to suck out the finer parts of the body of the mussel ; the valves of course opened, and the remainder of the fish was washed away by the sea. The perforated hole is generally upon the thinnest part of the shell and is perfectly circular, of a chamfered form, being wider towards the outward side, and so perfectly smooth and regular as to have all the appearance of the most beautiful work of an expert artist. It became a matter extremely desirable to preserve the mussel, and it seemed practicable to extirpate the Buccinum. But after we had picked up and destroyed many barrels of them, their extirpation was at length given up as a hopeless task. The mussels were thus abamdomed as their prey, and in the course of the third year's operations, so successful had the ravages of the Buccinum been, that not a single mussel of a large size was to be found upon the rock; and even the small kind which bred there are now chiefly confined to the extreme points of the rock, where it would seem their enemy cannot so easily follow them." Dr. Harvey, in his "Seaside Book," says: "The proboscis of the whelk consists of two cylinders, one within the other, the outer of which serves for the attachment of the motor muscles, and the general protection of the organ; while the inner, opening near the extremity with a longitudinal mouth, armed with two strong cartilaginous lips, encloses the tongue, and a great part of the œsophagus. The tongue is armed with short spines, and acting in concert with the hard lips, which can be opened or shut, or strongly pressed together, it forms a sort of rasp or augur, by which very hard substances are rapidly perforated; and then the tongue being protruded, the hooked spines with which it is armed are admirably fitted for the collection of food."—ED.]—*Field*, Aug. 24th.

BORNEO.

Borneo, the nurse of pirates, as Africa is "the nurse of lions," was always a place fitted to excite, in a great degree, the fancy of all adventurers. It is the largest island in the world, thinly peopled and only nominally governed by a Malay dynasty residing in the marches and jungles of the northern coast. The southern section of the island has been loosely appropriated by the Dutch, who claim a territory nearly as large as the State of New-York. Borneo, lying under the equator, is a remarkable mixture of mountain ridges and vast lacustrine levels. The ridges run from the centre, at a height varying from 5,000 to near 20,000 feet above the sea, and terminate, towards several points of the compass, in large coast promontaries. They give birth to a great number of rivers, many of which are navigable for a hundred miles into the country. All round the coast—a circuit of 3,000 miles—extends a belt of marshy ground, forty or fifty miles broad on an average, intersected by the outlets of rivers, shaped by channels into deltas and covered over by jungles of reeds and aquatic plants, intermingled with the exuberant growth of shrubs and trees, natural to such a tropical region. A rank, swampy luxuriance, favourable to all modes of life— vegetable, animal, and human—lives over all that region of prahns and pirates—a region that contains nearly one-half the ground of the island. The country has antimony in great quantities, gold, tin, and iron. It has diamonds also, found underneath six or seven stratas of the soil. Its cereals and vegetables are excellent. Almost all our own domestic animals and fowls are found in Borneo, and monkeys of every tribe; but there are no beasts of prey. The island was not spoken of by ancient geographers. It lay beyond the Golden Chersonese—the utmost limit of their knowledge. The Portuguese first visited it in 1526; but its pirates and jungles kept the Europeans aloof. The Dutch subsequently settled upon its southern coast. The English made a few attempts to settle upon it; but they were not successful.— *New York Times*, Nov. 17th.

SPIDERS.

Some very curious observations regarding this insect have lately been communicated to the French Academy of Sciences by Father Babaz, who has been 15 years engaged in these researches. It happened one day, as he was reading in a garden, that a small spider suddenly lighted upon his book, and crawled over the very line he was reading. He tried to blow it away, but instead of letting itself be carried away by the blast, it raised its abdomen, and swung itself up to a leaf overhead. This appeared strange, as there was no thread to be seen. Our observer caught the spider again, put it upon his book, and repeated the experiment, which ended in the same result. He caught it once more, and this time placed himself in the sun, with the insect on a level with his eyes. In this position he at length discovered the evolution performed by the little creature. On receiving the blast, it raised its abdomen, and in so doing projected a thread of inconceivable tenuity to a considerable distance, and, raising itself in the air, disappeared from view. This unexpected discovery induced Father Babaz to examine the question thoroughly; every spider that came in his way had to contribute something towards his researches, and in this way he at length ascertained a fact hitherto unknown to naturalists, viz., that most spiders possess not only the faculty of spinning a thread, but also that of projecting one or several, sometimes of a length of five or six metres, which they use to traverse distances with, and affix their thread to a second point for the support of their web. They even seem to have the power of directing the extremity of the ejaculated thread to a given point; they seem to feel for the place where it is most desirable to fix it. Certain spiders, the Thomisa Bufo, for instance, will eject a bunch of threads which, curling up in the air and shining in the sun with various hues, give the insect the appearance of a peacock displaying its tail. But this is not all; spiders can fly and swim in the air, though they are heavier even than alcohol. To perform this feat they turn their back to the ground, and keep their legs closely folded up on their body, and in this posture sail about with perfect ease. Their flight is often very rapid, especially in the beginning, and they will sometimes escape from the observer's hand quite suddenly, and soar up high in the air.

ICE IN DEEP MINES.

The main entrance to the pits at Dannemora, Persberg, one of the oldest and most celebrated of the Swedish iron mines, is a natural opening or abyss, of so large a circumference as to require some fifteen minutes to walk around its mouth. A scaffold is erected out, so as to overhang this abyss, upon which the hoisting machinery is placed. The observer can look down into this frightful abyss, upward of 500 feet, to which point the light of day extends, and beyond which all is shrouded in darkness, save when feebly illuminated by the dim lights of the miners. One of the most remarkable facts connected with this mine is the large quantity of ice which is always present there. Prof. Von Leonhard, in his *Popular Lectures on Geology*, says: "The deeper you go the more the ice increases. And in order to remove it from the pits it must be raised up in buckets. At some places the ice is 90 feet thick; it forms real glaciers, which are never diminished by any change or external temperature. This fact, however, should not be regarded as contradictory to another, which will hereafter be illustrated, and which is that pits become warmer in proportion to their depth. The phenomenon at Persberg, as we shall see, can be explained on natural principles. When the visitor has reached the bottom he is conducted by his guide into vaulted chambers, through immense regions of ice. Many of these vaults are so large that fifty men can conveniently work in them at the same time." This occurrence of ice in deep mines is not an isolated fact. Ice is found in the pits of Ehrenfriedensdorf, in Saxony. Leopold von Buch tells us that formerly in Norway, mining was prosecuted above the region of eternal snow. Wood, for the timbering, could not be had there, and its want was supplied by filling up a drift with water, and allowing it to freeze; passages were then cut through the ice as they were needed, the balance of the ice being left in lieu of wood for timbers. It is also well known, says the *Mining and Scientific Press*, (U. S.) that the ancient Peruvians obtained ores on the Cordilleras, in places elevated above the perpetual snow line. The mines of Rauris, in Upper Austria, lie entirely within the glacier region, and most of the shafts open in eternal ice, clear as crystal; the miners' huts are surrounded with ice. On what is known as Gold Mountain one of the shafts is sunk 100 feet through pure glacier ice. A gold mine in the deep valley of the Alps, near Salzburg, is the highest in Europe which is now worked. There are two tunnels near this mine entirely surrounded with glacier ice. The miners of this region undergo great hardships from exposure to cold, and to avalanches, which often sweep them to destruction while going to and fro to their work, or while reposing in their cabins on the hill sides. It is stated by one authority that there is a locality deep within one of the iron mines of Dannemora already noted, where the mass of ice is 120 yards thick."—*New York Times*, Nov. 17th.

MUSKRATS.

Muskrats have a curious method of travelling long distances under the ice. In their winter excursions to their feeding grounds, which are frequently at great distances from their abodes, they take in breath at starting and remain under the water as long as they can. Then they rise up to the ice, and breathe out the air in their lungs, which remains in bubbles against the lower surface of the ice. They wait till this air recovers oxygen from the water and the ice, and then take it in again and go on till the operation has to be repeated. In this way they can travel almost any distance, and live any length of time under the ice. The hunter sometimes takes advantage of this habit of the Muskrat, in the following manner: When the marshes and ponds where Muskrats abound are first frozen over and the ice is thin and clear, on striking into their houses with his hatchet for the purpose of setting his traps, he frequently sees a whole family plunge into the water and swim away under the ice. Following one of them for some distance, he sees him come up to renew his breath in the manner above described. After the animal has breathed against the ice, and before he has had time to take his bubble in again, the hunter strikes with his hatchet directly over him and drives him away from his breath. In this case he drowns in swimming a few rods, and the hunter, cutting a hole in the ice, takes him out. Mink, otter, and beaver travel under the ice in the same way; and hunters have frequently told me of taking otter in the manner I have described, when these animals visit the houses of the Muskrat for prey."—*The Trapper's Guide.*

RATS IN SWEDEN.

The black rat becomes every year more scarce in Scandinavia wherever the large brown rat gains a footing. Was once common throughout the whole country. In the days of Linné, the brown rat was unknown in Sweden; about 90 years since the first was seen in Scania. It has now, however, become gradually spread over the land, and is met with in every part to the North Cape. Although at deadly enmity with its smaller brother, it does not interfere with the little mouse. Strange to say, much as this country is overrun with rats, I never saw either a ferret or a rat-trap till I got some over from England. I know no country where a good ratcatcher could make a better living than in this. I once saw the rats drummed out of a house here which was full of them. It was a large wooden building. Two regimental drummers were sent for, who began at the very top of the house, and drummed in every room. The rats bolted very fast, and I had some capital shooting outside. It was long before any came back.—*Ten Years in Sweden.*

New Books.

[*Our limited space must of necessity compel us to give but very short notices of new books, but they will perhaps serve as a guide as to what books our readers may ask for at their libraries.*]

Abyssinia Described; or, The Land of Prester John. Edited by John Camden Hotten. London: J. C. Hotten, Piccadilly.

Mr. Hotten has in his present volume supplied a great want that was felt immediately the Abyssinian question assumed any prominence. Of Abyssinia we know scarcely anything, and yet there have been a succession of travellers who after visiting the country have left accounts of what came under their immediate observation,

It is these that Mr. Hotten has collected and carefully arranged; and with judicious explanatory notes and editorial supervision combined to form in itself a highly interesting book, independently of the value attached to it at the present time as a strictly reliable work on Abyssinia. The editor thus speaks of the arrangement of his book:—

"Part I. takes a cursory view of the results of early and recent travellers in Abyssinia, with such a selection from their works as may serve to give the general reader a very fair idea of life in Abyssinia, from the days of Bruce to the present day.

"Part II. gives one of the best accounts of Abyssinia ever written—that sent home to his superiors in office by Consul Plowden. It really contains everything that it is necessary to know about the country at the present time: its geographical divisions, government, laws, and customs. So closely, indeed, is the information packed in these official despatches, that they very well merit the title of 'literary pemmican,' which a correspondent has given them.

"Part III. contains the story of the British captives, the detention of whom by King Theodore has invested everything relating to Abyssinia with so peculiar an interest at the present moment.

"Part IV. is devoted to those practical suggestions which have recently been made by distinguished travellers to our Government for an armed expedition to Abyssinia to release the captives; the net results, too, of the great French expedition of 1839—43 are here given in the shape of routes to and from every important place in Abyssinia. Major Harris's route has been included, for the reason that it has been recommended by more than one writer that our expedition should land at Tajurrah, and proceed by way of Ankobar to Debra Tabor, or wherever the king and the captives might be situated at the time.

"Part V. will not possess much interest for the general reader, as it is simply a bibliography, as full as the editor could make it, of all the known books published about Abyssinia; to the intending traveller in those parts or to the geographical student it may prove useful."

There are some curious coloured plates, which give an idea of the costume and some of the habits of the natives, and a very good map of the entire country.

L'Univers les Infiniment Grands et les Infiniment Petits. Par F. A. Pouchet. Illustré de 343 Vignettes sur Bois et de 4 Planches en Couleur. Royal 8vo. Paris: Hatchette et Cie.

M. Pouchet has for his object in the present valuable work to diffuse a taste for natural sciences; and though his work is an elementary one, so capitally is it arranged that it is far more likely to attain its end than more pretentious works. The work is divided into four parts, viz., the Animal and Vegetable Kingdoms, Geology, and the Sidereal World. We cannot speak too highly of the illustrations, especially the four coloured plates by M. Faquet. Our readers can judge of their value, the Messrs. Hatchette having kindly lent us one as a specimen—"The Nest of the Tom Tit;" which we have made our frontispiece for the new volume, of which this is the first number.

Our Four-Footed Friends. By Mary Howitt. Illustrated with Engravings from Original Designs by Harrison Weir. Partridge.

Mrs. Howitt's pleasant volume is more in the nature of a gift-book than a work of natural history; but as it is full of anecdotes, many of them illustrating the uses and peculiarities of the domestic quadrupeds, we think it worthy of mention here. It is essentially for the young, but all who read it will rise from the perusal with increased knowledge. The engravings by Weir are entitled to the highest praise.

Heroes of Discovery. By Samuel Mossman. Edinburgh: Edmonston and Douglas.

This is a carefully arranged series of sketches of the lives and discoveries of Magellan, Captain Cook, Mungo Park, Sir John Franklin, and David Livingstone. The history of the great discoveries effected by these worthies deserve to be known by the young, and this volume cannot fail to ensure their attention. The main features of the book are biographical; but there are necessarily numerous incidental notices affecting geographical knowledge, which make it welcome to the young student of geography.

Meetings of Learned Societies.

ROYAL GEOGRAPHICAL.

On Monday, the 25th of November (Sir R. I. Murchison, Bart, President, in the chair), a letter was read from Dr. Kirk, Zanzibar. It stated that a Banian trader of Bagamoyo (on the mainland opposite Zanzibar) had brought to Dr. Kirk a native who had recently returned from the interior in company of a caravan, and who had seen a white man whom there was reason to suppose was Dr. Livingstone. The story of the native, related without questions being put to him, was as follows:—He had left Bagamoyo with the rest of the caravan, and passed along the usual trade route to Wemba and Marungu. When in one of the villages a white man arrived with a party of thirteen blacks, who spoke Suahili. All had firearms, and six carried double-barrelled guns. He was dressed in white, and wore a cloth wrapped round the head. He gave the chief a looking-glass, and was offered ivory, which he declined, saying he was not a trader. He then went northwards. Dr. Kirk added that there was no doubt the white man, of whom he had written formerly, as having been seen on one of the Lakes by an Arab, was a Turk, one of the traders from Gondokoro, who have been met with in Uganda by Zanzibar merchants; the route opened up by Speke had thus been quickly followed by traders, who had now met, some from Egypt and others from Zanzibar, in the centre of Africa. On the second interview with the native of the caravan, Dr. Kirk showed him his albums of photographic portraits. In the second book of 100 portraits, he at once pointed to a staring likeness of Livingstone, which had been kept as a caricature, when he said "That is the man." "But," he added, "come to Bagamoyo, and see my master and the other men; they have seen him also, and will tell you all they know." Mr. Churchill, the consul, and Dr. Kirk intended to proceed to Bagamoyo two days after the despatch of the letter, and glean what further information they could; meantime Dr. Kirk begged of those at home to suspend their opinion. Mr. Churchill, in a despatch to Lord Stanley, further states that Marungu, where the white man was seen, was 650 miles distant from the coast, and that the date of the occurrence was seven months previously (about the end of 1866). Sir Roderick Murchison read a letter from Mr. Price, missionary of Bombay, in which the writer expressed his belief that the nine educated negroes taken from his establishment by Dr. Livingstone would not be likely to desert their master. Mr. Horace Waller, who had been on the Shire, and had had the care of two of these young negroes, also expressed his confident belief that if any diaster had happened to their master in the interior, they would have long ago found their way to the coast, and sought the English Consul. A paper was read on a recent survey through Nicaragua, by J. Collinson, Esq., C.E., made through the untrodden forests of the eastern part of the Nicaragua during the present year. The country near the shores of the lake consisted chiefly of open savannah land; but on crossing the watershed, and touching the streams which flow towards the Atlantic, a dense virgin forest commenced, with a great change in the vegetation. Part of the journey was made on rafts down the Rama River, and two magnificent waterfalls were discovered. The summit-level was found to be only 619·86 feet above the level of the lake, which showed a great break in the Andean ranges in this part of Central America.

ZOOLOGICAL.

The first meeting of the present session was held Nov. 14, G. Busk, Esq., V.P., in the chair. The Secretary read an account of several recent additions to the Society's Menagerie; amongst which were particularly noticed a Penguin (*Spheniscus demersus*) from South Africa, two Great Ant-eaters (*Myrmecophaga jubata*), one from Brazil, presented by Dr. A. Palin, and the other from New Granada, presented by Mr. P. Brandon, and a Walrus, *Trichecus rosmarus*. Mention was made by Dr. Günther of a recent German author who gives a history of the animal, and a fossil skull found near Eley, now in the Cambridge Museum, of great size, but wanting the tusks, was spoken of. The tooth shown to King Alfred as confirmation of a visit paid to the far North by some hardy explorer, must, doubtless, have been a walrus tusk. Additions to our list of birds noticed in Zanzibar, the Pelew Islands, and other places, were recorded by the secretary. Mr. W. H. Flower read the second part of a Memoir on the Osteology of the Cachalot, or Sperm Whale, completing his account of the Osseous Structure of this animal. Mr. Flower came to the conclusion that there was no sufficient evidence of the existence of more than one species of Sperm Whale, for which he was of opinion Linnæus's name, *Physeter macrocephalus*, ought to be retained. Mr. E. Blyth read some notes upon certain Asiatic species of Deer (*Cervus Schomburgki, C. Duvaucelli,* and *C. Eldi*), and their varieties. Communications were read from Dr. G. Hartlaub, containing a report on a collection of Birds, formed on the island of Zanzibar, by Dr. J. Kirk, amongst which were two species new to science,—and on a collection of Birds from some of the less known localities in the Western Pacific,—from Mr. W. T. Blanford, on a new species of Callene from the Pulney Hills in Southern India, proposed to be called *C. albiventris*,—from Prof. J. V. Barboza du Bocage, describing some new species of Batrachians from Western Africa,—from Lieut.-Col. R. L. Playfair, on the Fishes of the Seychelles; the total number of species ascertained to inhabit this group of islands and their shores was stated to be 211. Mr. A. G. Butler read a note on the *Nymphalis Caledonia* of Hewitson. Mr. G. French Angas communicated descriptions of six new species of Helicidæ, from the Salomon Islands. Dr. J. E. Gray communicated some additional observations on the species of Cats (*Felidæ*) in the British Museum; and gave a notice of a new species of American Tapir, proposed to be called *Tapirus Laurillardi*, accompanied by remarks on the other known species of this group. The Rev. H. B Tristram pointed out the characters of three new species of Birds from South Africa. These were *Cypselus Layardi*, a South African representative of *C. melba* ; *G. barbatus*, a South African representative of *C. apus*; and a new Stonechat, proposed to be called *Campicola Livingstonii*.

ETHNOLOGICAL SOCIETY.

At the ordinary meeting of this society Mr. Crauford in the chair, Sir J. Lubbock read a paper on "Origin of Civilization," in which he controverted the theory of Archbishop Whately, that savages were only the degraded representatives of a formerly civilized people, and surveyed at great length the arguments put forward by that philosopher, using as illustrations the many known examples of savage islanders, and others who were found to be destitute of any indication of a former trace of civilization, no remains of pottery, building, or other arts existing amongst them; Australia, the South Sea Islands, and even America being destitute of antiquities or even the bones of domestic animals. Whately maintaining that men at first were keepers of flocks and herds; besides, religion and some social customs, marriage, &c., as they must have existed amongst the supposed ancestors of now degraded races, are in truth, not preserved, or have no indications of being so derived. Mr. Reddy, who holds opposite views, stated that many arguments had been overlooked, that, at least, deserved notice, and criticised the cases of slow but evident emergence from savagedom towards civilization made by some people left to their own development, meeting them with other instances, he thought, equally confirmative of the views he held. Sir J. Nicholson supported Sir John Lubbock's views, and mentioned the fact, that in all the oldest centres of civilization, the cities of Greece and Italy, and even in Sinai and Egypt, rude stone implements were found on the sites of many of the finest monuments of antique civilization, proving the slow and certain progress of human art. He mentioned also, that in the interior of Australia, a rude tribe on first being visited, was found busy in preserving or harvesting the seeds of grasses for a winter store—a fact he laid much stress upon. Professor Busk stated that the possession of flocks and herds might account for a certain tendency towards civilization, but all countries did not possess gregarious animals capable of domestication. Australian kangaroos could not, from their nature, be domesticated, and America had no animal but the llama which was available. Lord Strangford instanced the condition of Europe, and gave an elaborate account of early civilized races, holding the opinion that man slowly emerged from a lower to a higher social scale not always in places where the necessaries of life were easily obtained, but even in localities where natural obstacles had to be overcome with great toil. The President was pleased to think the author so entirely coincided with his views, and Sir John Lubbock reviewed the objections made to portions of his paper. Australia was capable, geographically, of sustaining the present race, who have occupied it for over a hundred years without any evidence of decline. Lord Strangford stated that the next paper was by his friend, Major R. Stuart, on the "Vlakhs of Mount Pindus," related to some nomad people who lived in that little known part of Europe at the head waters of the four rivers of Greece—the Haliacmon, the Peneus, the Achelous, and the Aous. These Wallachians seem to have been Roman soldiers who had been moved from the Danube in the course of some military events of the Empire, and to have been left and forgotten for centuries, until Benjamin of Tudela, who travelled in their country, recorded their existence, thinking them to be Jews. They still continue to preserve their language, and amidst the surrounding people it is strange there should still be preserved a Romaic, perhaps such as was spoken during the reign of the Emperor Aurelian, in Rome. Many words were given as examples of the nearer resemblance to the classic Latin than the equivalents in Italian, &c., and it was in this philologic spirit the speaker viewed the subject. He stated, from the present strides education was making, these Wallack shepherds would, in fifty years at most, have acquired the Greek method of writing, and in that time all trace of the present language would be forgotten or overladen with more modern Romaic. To find a Roman colony whose early history we know, concealed utterly for some centuries, and again so clearly identified, speaking a language doubtless identical with that they possessed when leaving their parent country, was, in Lord Strangford's opinion, a most important discovery in the history of a language. The meeting was an unusually full one.

ROYAL MICROSCOPICAL.

On the 13th of November, J. Glaisher, Esq., F.RS., President, in the chair, a paper was read by John Gorham, Esq., M.R.C.S., " On some peculiarities in the distribution of veins in leaves of the natural order Umbelliferæ." On its conclusion the meeting was made a special general one (due notice having been previously given), to take into consideration a resolution proposed by Mr. E. G. Lobb, and seconded by Major Owen, that the annual subscription of all new fellows elected after the 11th December next shall be two guineas, instead of one guinea, and that the composition fee shall be twenty guineas, instead of ten guineas, as heretofore ; it being distinctly understood that neither the existing annual subscription nor the composition fee of fellows already elected shall be in any way altered or interfered with. A gentleman, who appeared to be unknown to most of the fellows present, but who was evidently bountifully endued with that gift which George Stephenson pronounced to be the greatest ever bestowed by Providence on man, did his best to overthrow the motion, but considerable amusement was manifested when Mr. Slack, in a very clear and able statement of the position of the Society's affairs, showed that the previous speaker had totally misunderstood the matter on which he had been arguing. The president remarked that the question had been carefully and vigorously discussed at several meetings of the council, and that although there was at first considerable difference of opinion amongst its members, they were now unanimously agreed that the proposed increase of subscription was advisable. On the motion being put, it was carried with only three dissentient voices, there being about a hundred fellows present. Several gentlemen were elected fellows, and eighteen others proposed for ballot at the next meeting. We repeat with pleasure the announcement we have once before made—that a room has been rented of the authorities of King's College in which the assistant secretary is in daily attendance, and that the fellows can now use at their leisure, the valuable instruments, objects, books, &c., of the Society.

ENTOMOLOGICAL.

Nov. 18.—Prof. Westwood, V.P., in the chair. Messrs. F. Bates and H. J. S. Pryer were elected Annual Subscribers. Mr. Bond exhibited specimens of *Sterrha sacraria*, recently reared from eggs deposited by two females captured in the middle of August by Mr. Rogers, (of Freshwater) in the Isle of Wight. The females were of a pale yellow colour, but the entire progeny proved to be very dark-coloured, without any of the rich tints of the true type of the species, thus differing from a similar series recently reared by Mr. McLachlan, with which, however they agreed, both in time and food. It was suggested that the late cold and sunless autumn had probably effected this result. Mr. Stainton exhibited a specimen of *Ebulea catalaunalis*, captured at Cheshunt in September last by Mr. Boyd. Mr. Higgins exhibited a fine collection of Butterflies from Borneo and Labuan, containing several grand and rare species. Mr. Trimen exhibited a Grasshopper of the genus Pœcilocerus, of the pupæ of which he had found hundred of pairs *in copulâ* at Natal in the early part of the present year; also a Mantis, with minute fore-legs, very much resembling a Phasma; and a handsome Papilio from Uruguay, allied to *P. Americus* of Kollar. Mr. McLachlan mentioned that *Boreus hyemalis* had recently been taken by Messrs. Douglas and Scott amongst moss near Croydon. Prof. Westwood had received from Dr. Hooker the cocoons of a Saturnia, from which the Chinese manufactured the "gut" employed by fishermen; about twenty-four hours before the time for spinning, the silk reservoir of the larva was taken out, and stretched to the length of twenty to thirty feet. Mr. Stainton mentioned a new habitat for the larva of a Tinea, namely, in the horns of a Kooloo from Natal; and Mr. Trimen had seen the skull of a Hartebeest, the base of which was eaten by what he took to be the larva of a Tinea.

GEOLOGICAL.

Nov. 20.—W. W. Smyth, Esq., President in the Chair. Sir G. W. Denys, Bart., and Mr. S. P. Moore, were elected Fellows. The following communications were read: "On the Glacial and Postglacial Structure of Lincolnshire and South-East Yorkshire," by Mr. S. V. Wood, jun., and the Rev. J. L. Rome. The paper was illustrated with a diagram showing a section by the coast line of Yorkshire south of the wold scarp continued for a distance of 50 miles. The authors in the diagrams defined three different sub-divisions of the boulder clay. On the underlying chalk in certain hollows were gravel beds, containing fossil fresh-water shells, on this was a chalk clay, on this again was a purple clay, and on this, the curious Hezil boulder clay. The clay contains shells peculiarly arctic, and Sir Chas. Lyell pointed out the striking resemblance of the Greenland shells to those found in the beds, showing that in lat. 54 deg. there was at some former time intense cold. "On supposed Glacial Markings in the Valley of the Exe, North Devon," by Mr. N. Whitley, and "On Disturbance of the Level of the Land near Youghal, in the South of Ireland," by Mr. A. B. Wynne.

LINNEAN.

On Nov. 7th., G. Bentham, Esq., President, in the chair. Dr. Campbell exhibited a series of drawings of the Plants of Central India, executed by Mrs. Ashburner. The following papers were read: "Catalogue of the Reptiles of British Birmah, embracing the Provinces of Pegu, Martaban and Tenasserim," by Mr. W. Theobald, jun., and "Descriptions of Fifty New Species of the genus Stigmodera," by Mr. E. Saunders.

Nov. 21.—G. Bentham, Esq., President, in the chair. Mr. W. H. Spencer was elected a Fellow. Mr. Ward exhibited some dried specimens of British Plants, exhibiting the influence of climate and local conditions in altering their character and appearance. Dr. Braithwaite exhibited two Mosses, new to this country, *Amblystegium confervoides* and *Hypnum Bambergeri*, both discovered by Dr. Fraser, of Wolverhampton. Mr. Hanbury exhibited fresh specimens of the Fruit of *Amomum Clusii*, ripened, as he believed, for the first time in Britain. The following papers were read: "On the *Fagus castanea* of Loureiro's *Flora Cochinchinensis*, with descriptions of Two New Chinese Corylaceæ," by Dr. H. F. Hance. "Note on the *Isoëtes capsularis*, Roxb.," by Mr. J. Scott. "Synopsis of the South African Restiaceæ," by Dr. M. T. Masters. "Notes on the Flora of North-East Tasmania," by Mr. W. K. Bissill. "On the Branched Palms in Southern India," by Dr. S. P. Andy, and "Observations on *Thlaspi alpestre* L.," by Mr. J. Windsor.

Correspondence.

[*Under this head we shall be glad to insert any letters of general interest.*]

WHY DO BIRDS MIGRATE?

"What makes thee seek a milder clime?
What makes thee shun the wintry gale?
How knowest thou thy departing time?
Hail! wondrous bird; hail, swallow, hail!"

SIR,—About a hundred years ago, Klein, a German naturalist, argued that swallows and other birds did not migrate, and that their taking to sleep, or their quietly retiring to subaqueous domiciles, sufficiently accounted for their periodical disappearance!

Such eccentric notions are long since completely exploded, so much so, indeed, that the migrant theory is now no longer a disputed subject; but while we all receive this theory as one fully established, there is, perhaps, some room for a diversity of opinions as to *why the birds do migrate*.

That they should have to wander thousands of miles in search of food is but a fanciful assertion, and one that taxes Nature as a niggardly disposed dispensor towards those delightful children of the air. Who will assert that that earnest lover of its native home, the carrier pigeon, when let loose from the hands of the fearless navigator or intrepid traveller will return to its cot in search of food? None; no, some strongly instinctive, some indomitable innate principle of nature prompts it to traverse thousands of miles until it reaches its native home. A search for food cannot be the predisposing principle which stimulates the carrier pigeon, but an unconquerable love of home. Let the eggs of migratory birds be hatched in a cage, confine the young, supply them plentifully with the nourishment they desire, and when the time for migrating arrives the instinct for change of place immediately and wonderfully shows itself by the restlessness of the prisoners and their strong incessant struggles to escape. But *why do birds migrate?*

Evidently the *breeding stimulus* brings them to our shores, and *a decline in our temperature* prompts them to wing their course to other climes. It is admitted beyond dispute that the very same swallows have been known to return to particular houses and gardens for upwards of sixteen years in succession. Accidental wanderings in search of insects never could do this. Never; for there is a *guiding principle* as well as an *erratic impulse*, and if we admit the presence of the one, we cannot well deny the existence of the other. Birds of passage have been confined by naturalists, and with the tenderest care supplied with their favourite food, but the invariable results in all were restlessness, struggles to escape, and in some species (swallows particularly) death to the little migrants when the season for departure came—we need war against nature. That swallows frequently follow ships and eagerly devour the intruding flies which surround the vessel I do not deny, but to conclude from this that such a transitory flight was absolute migration is an untenable process of reasoning. Even at a distance of fifty miles from land I have met with birds of passage; they fed on the flies which rose from the ships; the time was not their season for migrating, and the most experienced on board never imagined that a temporary flight from land amounted to actual migration. Even fish migrate, and many land animals, an immediate result of the same erratic impulse and guiding principle by which birds are stimulated.

Sir Humphrey Davy, in speaking of the salmon, says :—" It is scarcely possible to doubt that the varieties of the salmon which haunt the sea come to the same river to breed in which they were born, or where they have spawned before."

Here, in the north of Ireland, we watch with what certainty the wild geese and other birds migrate from Scotland to the Bog of Allen. They cross the strait from the direction of Portpatrick, and this so invariably, that for many years I have carefully watched their departures. I still find their flight on the same track. No mathematical calculation could be more accurate, and no navigator could steer with the same precision !

Here the erratic impulse and the guiding principle are evidently displayed; but who will tell me that those Highland visitors are in search of food?

But let me call this a partial migration, during the whole course of which there are flies and other insects in abundance, and yet the wild geese condescend not to notice those dwarfish pigmies of the air; the swallow in his sportive gambols may feast on summer flies, but what is he to do in mid-ocean, where the entomologist looks to the air in vain, and where the insects which—

"Creation's grandest miracles proclaim,"

are but aliens, and too scarce for myriad birds to dine on ?

The poet, in contemplating a flight of wild geese in the noon of a late autumn day, beautifully says :—

" I stood abroad, and gazed upon a flight
Of wild geese, thro' the dark blue depth aloft,
Steering their skyey voyage high in heaven ;
As if from some far realm to realm afar."

And again, that the poet considered those birds on a migratory journey is more forcibly enunciated in the following unmistakable language :—

" These fowls, thought I, are last from India,
Or broad Euphrates, and the Persian streams,
And seek the populous empire of the Czar.
Haply the smooth Cayster's song-loved stream,
Or reedy Mincius, last hath laved their plumes ;
Or from the vale where sweet Meander winds,
Or ancient Peneus glides—*they took their way.*"

And Logan, in his well-known and beautiful "Address to the Cuckoo," says :—

" We'd make, with joyful wing,
Our annual visit o'er the globe,
Companions of the spring."

And Mrs. Hemans, in her charming poem on the "Birds of Passage," makes those "joyous birds of the wandering wing" say :—

" We come from the shores of the green old Nile,
From the land where the roses of Sharon smile."

And again :—

" We have swept o'er the cities in song renowned,
We have crossed proud rivers——"

It is thus the poetess furnishes us with an argument in favour of the *erratic impulse* in migratory birds, and immediately after she advocates the presence of that unerring, mysterious instinct, the *guiding principle*, for she again makes the feathered messengers exclaim :—

" And the place is hushed where the children played,
Nought looks the same, *save the nests we made.*"

Yes, the birds annually return to their old nests, not in search of flies, but guided by an irrepressible principle as irrefragable as the law of analogy.

It may, indeed, be said that poets are but questionable authorities on subjects connected with Natural History, but when they are the echoes of the best naturalists, we cannot legitimately reject their opinions, but, on the contrary, receive them as valid, popular teachings.

J. G. Percival, an American poet, in his cheerful poem on an "Escape from Winter," in speaking of his flight and companionship with the swallow, says:—

"We would touch for a while as we traversed the ocean,
At the *islands that echoed to Waller and Moore*,
And winnow our wings with an easier motion,
Through the breath of the cedar that blows from the shore."

And then he proceeds:—

" By *the spirit of home and of infancy led*,
We would hurry again to *the land of our loves*."

At the present advanced stage of Natural History, I think the actual migration of birds admits of no dispute, and while I look on migration as an immediate result of an *erratic impulse* and *guiding principle*, not a desire to feed on insects, still I am open to conviction; and to the learned correspondents of the NATURALIST'S NOTE BOOK, in the words of *Holland's Pliny*, I may truly say :—" For mine owne part, the more I looke into Nature's workes the sooner am I induced to beleeve of her, even those things that seem incredible."

I am, Sir,
Yours, &c.,
H. H. ULIDIA.

Dromore,
December 7th, 1867.

MIGRATION OF BIRDS AND INSECTS.

SIR,—Will you kindly allow me space for a few words in answer to the letters of "J. D. S. W." and Mr. T. R. Clephan in your last issue?

I am sorry that I did not express myself in my last letter with sufficient clearness on this subject, as "J. D. S. W." seems to consider the theory originally started by Mr. Hunt and that which I now support as one and the same. In reality nothing was further from my intention, for, as I stated, I agreed with the objections of Mr. Ulidia and " R. W. B." in answer to Mr. Hunt's theory. What I intended to express was that I believed that swallows do not migrate *only* on account of the cold of our winters, but principally for the sake of those insects which the warmth of Africa (whither most of them migrate) suffers to live throughout the winter; in other words, that on the failure of food here they seek it in warmer countries.

With regard to the proof of the non-hybernation your correspondent asks for, I suppose he as well as myself alludes to their hybernation in the countries to which they migrate, as I presume no one now doubts the fact of their migration. A gentleman who has studied Natural History, and on whose veracity I can depend, has frequently visited different parts of Africa, and assures me that in the winters there he has often seen the swallows flying about as in this country, and chasing the insects that abound during that season. In Goldsmith's "Animated Nature," too, the opinion of Sir H. Davy is cited as implying their not hybernating, and the title of a work reviewed at page 21 of the NATURALIST'S NOTE BOOK (1867), "A Winter with the Swallows," will, I think, convince your correspondent of this fact.

I imagine hybernation to be nothing more than a state of coma and insensibility, and a suspension of the vital functions caused by great cold for a lengthened period; and if this is so, it seems very strange to me that swallows should migrate to much *warmer countries* to hybernate when the same result would take place by their remaining at home. If their instinct would lead them to hybernate, why do not they stay here?

Another conclusion would be that, if heat and cold alone caused the migration of these birds, the means of sustaining life would be secondary to the sensations caused by the variations of the temperature—a reasoning I am unable to follow.

Your correspondent, however, cites Mr. White's opinion that swallows do not migrate at all. In conclusion I submit, with all deference to Mr. T. R. Clephan, that although I have carefully perused the " Natural History of Selborne," written by that celebrated Naturalist, I am unable to find anything stronger than a query on the point, and not a direct opinion.

Apologising for trespassing at such length on your space, but which I trust you will excuse on account of the interest of the subject under discussion.   ARTHUR G. HARVIE.

London, Dec. 17.

THE HYBERNATION OF SWALLOWS.

SIR,—Your correspondent, Mr. Clephan, has anticipated the question which I was going to ask, *i.e.*, how can Mr. A. C. Harvie prove that no swallows hybernate in this country? I know that scientific naturalists, like Professor Owen, Mr. Gould, &c., have set their faces against the idea; but a powerful minority of *working* naturalists are beginning to think that there is something after all in this opinion of the old writers on Natural History. May I refer all your readers who take an interest in the matter to the pages of *"Hardwick's Science Gossip?"* where, in vol. iii., p. 101, I have treated upon the subject at some length, and also to pp. 185

and 214 in the same volume, and pp. 118 and 160 in the preceding volume for additional evidence.

If any of your readers know upon their own, or any other credible testimony, circumstances tending to prove that a portion at least of the *hirundines* winter in England, or to determine the reasons for such a hybernation, will they kindly communicate with you?

I remain,
Your obedient servant,
FRANCIS A. ALLEN.
72, Cambridge-street,
  Belgravia South, S.W.

Short Notes.

INFLUENCE OF ELECTRICITY ON PLANTS
M. Blondeau has sent in to the French Academy a very interesting paper on the "Influence of the electric inductive current on plants." The experiments he describes were made chiefly on fruits and seeds, and were productive of some curious results. The effect of the current on fruits seems to be to cause them to ripen with considerable rapidity. The most unexpected effects were those produced on seeds which were submitted to the current before being sown. Peas and grains of corn which had been electrified were placed in pots of earth, and beside them, and under like conditions, were placed seeds which had not been acted on by the current. It was found that the electrified plants germinated much sooner than the others, and produced better stems and greener and more healthy-looking leaves than the others. A very curious effect was produced in some of the seeds—the stem and leaves grew down into the earth, and the roots came up and took their place.—*London Review.*

PECULIARITIES OF ANIMALS.—The artfulness of animals is a favourite theme with old writers. Of the crayfish, Laurens Andrewe says—"The crenyce eteth the oysters, and geteth them be policye; for whan the oyster gapeth, he throweth lytell stones in him, and geteth his fishe out, for it bydeth than open." Another fish the same writer accuses of unnatural acts:—"Halata is a beste that dothe on-naturall dedys; for whan she feleth her younges quycke, or stere in her body, than she draweth them out and loketh vpon them. Yf she see they be to yonge, thon she putteth them in agayne, and lateth them grow tyll they be bygger."—*Athenæum*, Nov. 20th

WHITE BLACKBIRD.—There is in the garden of a gentleman residing in this parish (Elm, near Wisbeach), (says a gentleman writing to the *Field*, Nov. 23rd a *white* blackbird (Turdus merula). It is a young bird, and, when first hatched, had a patch of black feathers on the top of its head, and some on its breast, but has lately become perfectly white, and is seen daily hopping about the lawn, or feeding with others upon the fallen apples in the orchard.

Remarks, Queries, &c.

(*Under this head we shall be happy to insert original Remarks, Queries, &c.*)

THE ANCIENT IRISH ELK.—
  "Such game, while yet the world was new,
    The mighty Nimrod did pursue."
            —*Waller.*

Your titanic correspondent, "Atlas," in page 324, labours not under the weight of the globe, but struggles under the pressure of a series of formidable queries and perplexing *et cateras* concerning that ancient horned giant of our plains, the Irish elk of other days. "At what time did the Irish elk live?" is the first query proposed by "Atlas." As to the time at which this noble animal roamed our hills, there is no record—even conjecture itself shrinks from the responsibility of fixing a datum. At a meeting of the Geological Society held in the Museum Building, Trinity College, Dublin, in December, 1861, at which Drs. Petrie, Barker, Smith, Stokes, and Professor Jukes, &c., attended, it was shown that early in the fifth century fossil remains of the Irish elk were found, and a lengthened discussion took place as to whether the elk was contemporaneous with man in Ireland. O'Flaherty says that neither history nor tradition can point to the time of the Irish elk, so the curiosity of "Atlas" on this part of the subject is not likely to be soon gratified.

"Atlas" next asks "what size was the Irish elk?" The elk must have been as large as any ox of the present day, and perhaps larger. The horns of an ancient elk dug up at Drogheda, co. Meath, two hundred years ago, are thus described by Dr. Boate, an Englishman, in his "Natural History of Ireland":—"I took their dimensions carefully as follows, from the tip of the right horn to the tip of the left horn, ten feet ten inches, from the tip of the horn to the root where it was fastened to the head, five feet two inches,—the length of the head, two feet, and breadth of the skull one foot."

Waller, when writing of the Irish elk, was so astonished at its size that he soared into an agreeable hyperbole:—

  "What huntsman of our feeble race,
    Or dogs, dare such a monster chase?
  Resembling, at each blow he strikes
    The charge of a whole troop of pikes.
  O fertile head! which every year
    Could such a crop of wonder bear!!
  The teeming earth did never bring
    So soon, so hard, so huge a thing," &c.

If we consider the size of those horns and remember that nature observes a symmetry in the formation of animals, then we must infer that the elk must have been a real monster on four feet. Naturalists have called it *animal magnum, dodonaeus, menabenus,* and Scaliger pronounced it the bison of Pliny. In its general habits, it perhaps differed very little from other animals of the deer kind. I might indeed refer "Atlas" to many places in Ireland where skeletons of the elk have at various times been dug up. At Ballymacward, co. Donegall, in 1691; at Turvey, eight miles from Dublin, in 1684; at Portumna on the Shannon, in county Meath, twenty skeletons were dug up in less than twenty years. Clare, Louth, Fermanagh and Dublin—and indeed almost every county in Ireland—has contributed its skeletons of the Irish elk.

"Atlas" would seem to have some doubt about the tangible existence of the skeletons, for he asks "where may they be seen?"

An elk's head, with all its horns entire, was found in County Clare, and presented to Charles II., who ordered the head to be placed in the horn gallery at Hampton Court, and, if I mistake not, "Atlas" may see this head during the Christmas holidays in the guard-room at Hampton Court. He will easily recognise the horns, as they far exceed in size any of the horns in that magnificent collection.

In the Dublin Museum is a grand specimen of the fossil Irish elk—there stands, very perfect, the skeleton of one of those truly wonderful rovers of our fields in past ages.

The horns extend six feet on each side of the head, that is, a distance of twelve feet. This skeleton was found in a bog near Limerick about forty years ago.

In 1833, an elegant skeleton of the Irish elk was dug up in the vicinity of Dundalk, and presented to a French Marine officer, who brought it to Algiers about the time when the Dey's sovereignty there was declining.

So late as the summer of 1859, a fossil elk was dug up near Slatery and Hollymount, within a mile of Carlow, in the Queen's County; it was deposited in the Museum in Dublin. Several places in Ireland get their names from circumstances connected with traditions of this animal, such as *Lough Damil Deirg*, the *Lake of the Red Ox*, near Dromore, and in Scotland, also, near Fort William, we have *Lough Chaber*, the *Lake of Horns*.

But while I write the NATURALIST'S NOTE BOOK for December has just reached me, and in taking a hurried glance at the article on the *Reindeer*, page 342, I am inclined to think that the horns found in Ireland, to which the writer refers, are not reindeer's horns, but in all probability the horns of the Irish elk. But surely I have said enough, if not fully to satisfy the curiosity of your correspondent "Atlas," at least to merit a portion of his promised gratitude.

H. H. ULIDIA.

Dromore, December 5th, 1867.

RABBIT-KEEPING.—I have for some time kept a fine pair of "Leperoys," a French breed of the large tame grey rabbits. I adopted the German mode of keeping them, viz., I converted a rubbish heap in my garden into a sloping bank. I laid a foundation of bricks (about two dozen) which I placed on the ground in four rows of threes, and on these I fixed my hutch, made of an "egg chest," bought of a pork and egg merchant for 3s. 6d. The rubbish heap was in a corner of my garden. I levelled it at the top, and enclosed it with wire netting at 3d. per yard, cut a hole in the back of the hutch, and jammed it up against the end of the bank—Wire netting (for hares), enclosing bank and side of hutch, into which I placed a pair of "Leperoys" (a cross between hare and wild rabbit originally), who in a few days worked their way out of the hole in the back of the hutch into the back of the bank, and made a hole, through which then came on to the top of the bank. Here they used to feed on the food I threw on to the bank daily over the top of the netting. After a time these rabbits burrowed into the bank again from a hole they made in the angle of the wall, which composed two sides of their bank, and burrowed under the whole bank in a straight line back into their hutch. I have now had three litters of young ones, and my object in writing this letter is to say that the idea that the buck rabbit will devour his young if left with the doe during the time of her littering is fallacious. The first litter my doe had I took the buck from her; the second and third time I left him on the bank. The doe was so fierce he dared not so much as put his nose inside the burrow in which she had made her nest and deposited her young, and the doe keeps him on the top of the bank until the young rabbits are six weeks old. Then, and only then, does the doe allow him to enter the burrow, and she again lives with him.

I have now about twelve or thirteen young rabbits; my doe is about nine months old. She had two young ones only in her first litter, six in her second, and eight in her third. Several of the little ones have been roasted for dinner, and she is now again making her nest. The buck never attempts to kill his offspring, so if any of your readers wish to keep rabbits let them adopt my plan, instead of keeping a lot of miserable captives in solitary confinement in dirty bad smelling hutches. Let the male and female dwell together always on a bank, in unity, as they do in nature; feed them well with vegetables and weeds from the garden, all of which (even nettles) they greedily devour, with a feed of carrots and corn mixed with bran once daily, and they will find they will increase faster than they wish even. At six or eight weeks old I put the young ones on another and similar bank, away from their parents, and thus fatten them up for sale or for our own table. Every six weeks my doe has a litter, and the young ones make their appearance on the top of the bank about twenty-eight days after I have supplied the doe with hay and leaves, with which she makes her nest, either inside the hutch (over the front of which I always have a waterproof curtain) or in the burrows, they have themselves made in several different places on the bank, which is about ten feet square and three or four feet high. ELIZA VACHER.

Regent's Park, London, N.W.

RAIN WATER.—The following is a note on this point by the Rev. J. G. Wood in his edition of "White's Selborne":—"Water obtained from wells is termed 'hard' in contradistinction to rain water, which is termed 'soft.' Hard water is the best for drinking, as rain water is always vapid, and moreover forced to pass over the roof of the house before entering the tub; but it does not answer for washing purposes or tea-making until a little soda has been mixed with it, the carbonic acid of which falls to the bottom as a white sediment. The earthy salts which cause the hardness are very troublesome in steam-engines, as they form an incrustation in the interior which requires to be constantly cleared away. Charcoal, however,

has been found to act as a preservative. It should be made from some hard wood and broken into small pieces—not larger than half an inch cube. This will absorb the salts of lime, alkaline earth, salts of iron, etc., and prevent them from accumulating on the boiler. The charcoal should be renewed monthly."
Dec., 1867.   A. G. H.

CURIOUS COLOURED EGGS.—I heard lately an odd story said to be a fact. Some eggs were opened, and their yolk was of a dark chocolate colour. This was attributed by a farmer to the hens having fed on acorns. Is this true?—and what do you think the chickens would have been like had the eggs been hatched? I hope that you, or some of your correspondents, can answer this question.   L. A. M.

THE PUGNACITY OF THE MISSEL THRUSH.— (*Turdus Viscivorus*).—Last spring, whilst sitting in the summer-house overhanging the rocks of Hawthornden (well-known as the seat of the late Sir Walter Scott), and watching the jackdaws building their nests in the holes and crevices, my attention was called to a kestrel which I saw flying towards his nest on the rocks, and uttering loud cries of distress, followed closely by two missel thrushes, who were endeavouring to take vengeance on him for having chanced to fly in the neighbourhood of their nest (built on the opposite side of the river, in a fir tree).

At another time I saw two sparrow-hawks alight in a neighbouring tree, but they were quickly driven away by the thrushes. The jackdaws themselves well knew the danger of approaching this sacred spot, and therefore always avoided it; but nevertheless they too were sometimes attacked close to their own nesting places.
Mavisbush House.   J. D. S. W.

THE PIDDOCK. — (*Pholas dactylus*).—This fish, well-known among the burrowing molluscs, is very common on our shores. On the coast of Fifeshire, in 1864, I found two very fine specimens of this fish embedded in hard limestone.

How did they make their way into this hard rock with no instrument but their thin shells? Wood, in "Homes without Hands," thinks that their power of boring is so great that they can work themselves into the rock by simply using their shells as we would an awl.

The only proof he gives for this assertion is that they have been seen boring into chalk stone. This might be the case, but I think that it is quite unnatural to suppose that they could do the same in such a hard substance as the above mentioned. At least I can be sure that this was not the case with my specimens, as the entrances to their tunnels are far too small to admit of the fish ever leaving their retreats, which I think proves that the now rock must have been a soft clay when the fish first took up their abode in it.
Mavisbush House.   J. D. S. W.

RING DOVES.—In answer to "A. B. P." in last November's number of the NATURALISTS' NOTE BOOK, asking if he were to release his ring doves whether or not they would remain with him, like domestic pigeons. I have reared several from the nest, but not one, when allowed the use of its wings, has remained many days. The lees seem to have too great an attraction for them.

Last year I tried the experiment of placing wood-pigeon's eggs under a common pigeon; the eggs were hatched, and the young doves lived for about a fortnight, and then died, which was no fault of the foster parents, as they treated them with great kindness, and even after death sat over and endeavoured to warm them. If "A. B. P." wishes to retain his doves, he will have to keep them either confined in a cage or cut their wing twice a year, and keep them in a walled garden.
Mavisbush House.   J. D. S. W.

RING-DOVES.—"A. B. P." asks if ring-doves, when let loose, will return home like common pigeons. They will not, but are sure to fly away; nor will they associate with tame pigeons.   M. L. A.

THE LANDRAIL.—Where does the "landrail" that makes the harsh monotonous cry in the mowing grass go to when all the grass is cut? This mysterious bird is seldom seen, but always heard from field to field as the scythe advances. I believe it is never heard after the mowing grass is gone. Does it change its note, or suppress it?
    S. L. WELLINGTON.

CAMBERWELL BEAUTY.—Will some kind reader inform me when I can find the egg, caterpillar, and chrysalis of the Camberwell Beauty Butterfly (Vanessa Antiopa); and also, when the egg, caterpillar, and pupa of the Spotted Elephant Hawk Moth (Spinx ocellata).   S. R. B.
Dec. 14th.

THE ZOOLOGY OF NEW ZEALAND.—As I am thinking of going to New Zealand in a few months, and as zoology is my favourite study, I should be greatly obliged if you, or any of your readers, would inform me of a book written on this subject.
Mavisbush House.   J. D. S. W.

LIVERWORTS.—On page 355 of the NATURALIST'S NOTE BOOK, "T." asks for information respecting the liverworts. Perhaps the following book may be of use to him:—"British Hepaticæ; or, Scale Mosses and Liverworts." Price fourpence. Publisher, Robt. Hardwicke, 192, Piccadilly.   M. L. A.

BIRD STUFFING.—Could any of your readers inform me how to stuff and preserve birds, as I have frequently tried it, and have been unsuccessful, although I have managed a good many beasts.
    FOX.

FROGS AND THEIR FOOD.—I have noticed your correspondent's answer to my query about frogs and their food; but I beg to state that I kept tadpoles last summer for about a month in an earthenware basin, changing the water every few days, so that none of the green weed could have formed; still they lived, and completed their transformation.   FOX.

SKELETON LEAVES.—I should like to know the best and quickest method of preparing skeleton leaves, and the plants most suitable for that purpose.
    FOX.

ELEPHANTS.

TO write anything new about these well-known beasts is not an easy matter. Our natural-history books have described them till we are in England almost as familiar with the "lordly elephant" as with the "honest ox," or all-enduring Neddy; and if aught had been left unsaid, Sir Emerson Tennant's book on Ceylon has given the subject, one would suppose, an exhaustive ventilation. I have lived so long, however, amongst these animals, in a country where an elephant is as much part of a man's family as the pig is in Pat's shieling, that I may possibly have picked up a few stray facts, and a few little traits, that have escaped the observation of other writers, but are yet not unworthy of note.

It is a remarkable fact that there is hardly an animal in the world whose form has been so ill represented and whose actions so grotesquely caricatured as the elephant. I positively cannot bring to my recollection a painting, drawing, or engraving of this noble creature which could be called correct. On one occasion an illustrated periodical, generally remarkable for the excellence of its woodcuts, gravely published the "view of an elephant race," in which the ponderous competitors were depicted, not only going like greyhounds *ventre à terre* over the plain, but taking flying leaps over five-barred gates like bullfinches! I happened to be behind the scenes as regards the origin and authors of this remarkable *tour d'artiste*, and can affirm that the sketch was sent as a hoax, and that none were so astonished at its publication as the designers. I will not say that all representations I have seen of the animal have been equally travestied; but it is by no means uncommon to see elephants portrayed with hocks like horses, or, on the other hand, legs like stalactites.

The largest elephant known belonged, I believe, to one of the Nawábs of Oude, long before that territory came under British rule, but at what precise epoch I am at this moment unable to state. It is said to have measured 12ft. in height—a monstrous animal certainly. I doubt whether a specimen reaching 10ft. could now be found. The ordinary height is 8ft; and in the Hon. East India Company's Commissariat 7ft. was the minimum height at which these animals were purchased for baggage purposes. In his wild state the full-grown bull elephant is a majestic creature, holding his head above the level of his back, which gives him an air of vigour, soon changed after capture and domestication into a sluggish slouch. With "Sawaree" or riding animals, however, who are never subjected to heavy loads, great pains are taken to retain the erect position of the head. And the mahouts or drivers in the service of native nobles carry this point to an extravagant and ugly extent, just as their "saïses" or grooms make a caricature of the natural and beautiful arch of a horse's neck. When standing quietly, with the top of his skull just a little above the level of the dorsal arch, and his massive forehead nearly perpendicular, the end of the elephant's nose (or trunk) should be a little clear of the ground, which it can be extended to reach by mere elongation of itself, without lowering of the head. The tusks should be thick, white, pointed, curving downwards and forwards, and reaching about half way down the trunk. The forehead and anteal aspect of the trunk is more or less dabbled with whitish and tawny and bluish spots, having a leprous appearance; and the flaps of the ears are also spotted, but to a less degree, with those colours. The ears in the Asiatic elephant do not hang lower than the chin; but the African species has them much larger, extending, in fact, all over the shoulder, and as low down as the elbow. The lower or free edges of the ears—what with incessant flapping, and the friction of thorns and branches—get quickly jagged and torn, and a smooth-edged ear is a very rare point of perfection in a Sawaree elephant. The arms or fore legs are a model of strength and beauty, but the hind legs which are smaller and shorter from the knee downward, are comparatively poor, and look awkward. Heavy, massive skin bulges over the elbows, and overhangs the knees (almost in knickerbocker fashion). The back describes a considerable arch, and the belly slopes downwards with very little curve from the breast to the interfemoral region. The tail is massive at its root, quite straight, and should just touch the ground, the end being fringed round with a single row of bristles as thick as duck's quills. The feet should be large, but not too flat; the fore pair nearly circular, the hind pair oval. Twice round the fore foot should measure the animal's height, and the body (exclusive of the head) should be exactly contained in a square.

The Asiatic elephant is spread over the whole of Hindustan, south of the Himalaya, wherever forest occurs, throughout Arakan, Burma, and Siam, to the Chinese frontier, in the Malay peninsula, and in Ceylon, but not, I believe, in any of the islands of the great Eastern Archipelago. It varies a little in some of these localities, the elephants of Central India being smaller than those of Ceylon and the cis-Himalayan forests, and the race in Burma and Siam being also smaller and shorter in the body. The natives of India recognise varieties or races amongst the elephants of their own country even, the names and distinctive attributes of which I have unfortunately lost my memorandum of; but one race, called "muckna," much prized for its size, gentleness, and fine make, is well known, and remarkable for being sterile and tuskless.

In Tenasserim, the forests of which country border on Siam, the elephant, formerly, abundant, is getting exceedingly scarce. They have become so scared by the Shan or Siamese hunters as to fly the neighbourhood of man for a space, say the Karéns, of half a day's journey. The first sound of the Karén settler's da (or chopping knife) as he commences a clearing in the solitary woods, drives out of the country all the elephants within hearing. During numerous journeys performed in the winter months of six years, in the wildest parts of the Amherst district of Tenasserim, I never once came within sight of a wild elephant. On one occasion I heard them crashing and tearing the jungle far below me, as I stood, shortly after sunrise, on the plateau of Mooleyit, some 6000 feet above the sea; but they were completely hidden by a canopy of forests, and a day's journey off, though apparently so near! More to the northward and westward, however, elephants seem to be commoner; and in some parts of Martaban, on the Pegu frontier, they have been occasionally shot by English sportsmen. In Pavay and Merqui also they are undisturbed, and comparatively plentiful. They prefer the thick forests about the roots of hills, especially on the borders of large plains of elephant grass, which they enter at night to graze. During the rains they ascend the hills a little, where vegetation is then profuse, and in the dry season seek the bottoms near rivulets. In such places they may be found in herds of eight and ten to twenty, composed of females and young males, and always as I was informed by the Shan hunters, led by an old female. The old males live alone, and visit the herds at night. My informants never knew instances of their fighting with one another, nor with the rhinoceros, of which animal the elephant has the greatest dread. The albino or white elephant has never, I am told, been met with in Tenasserim.

The Shans and Karéns employ no devices for capturing these animals in numbers, such as are used in Ceylon, Nepal, and Eastern Bengal; but take them singly, by sheer hunting down and noosing, with prodigious pains and labour. Two men are engaged in this chase, both mounted on one elephant, the strongest and swiftest they can select amongst their tame ones. One man sits on the neck and carries a bamboo about 12 feet long, to one end of which is hitched a noose or running bowline knot at the end of about 30 fathoms of strong 3 inch rope, the standing end of which is made fast to a girth round the elephant's body. The other man sits on the animal's rump, with a goad formed of a yard of line with a lump of lead fastened to the end—an instrument the elephant is much in dread of, and urged by which it will keep up a pace equal to the hand canter of a horse for a considerable time. Thus accoutred, and after having performed some religious ceremonies and been shorn of their hair, the hunters go forth into the vast forest, seeking for the trail of wild elephants, and following them up when found with unwearied perseverance and great sagacity. When a herd is sighted, the men select a suitable subject, one big enough to be of present use, but not so big as to occasion too much trouble in securing—one in fact plainly smaller than the animal they ride. When the choice is made they advance upon the victim without further attempt at concealment. Then commences a chase, the duration of which depends on various circumstances, the density of the forest and the qualities of the tame elephant. If the jungle be very close, or abounding in ratan and other thickets, the quarry generally gets away, as it tears through thorns and branches which would sweep the riders off. But under tolerably favourable circumstances the wild elephant is closed with in four or five hours' run. The foremost rider then holds the bamboo with its noose dangling just in front of its hind leg, and before long the unconscious beast "puts his foot in it." The pursuing elephant is suddenly stopped, the noose instantly tightens, and the third stage of the operation commences in a puny-hauly match, in which no small skill and prudence are called into play. The tame elephant follows for some time longer in tow of the wild one, now yielding to the latter's frightened starts, now giving him severe checks, galling his noosed leg, and eventually tiring him out. The captive is then dragged to the nearest suitable tree, and tied to it. All this while the hunters have been followed by some reserve elephants, which come up by the time the captured one is securely moored. Two of them are driven up, one on each side of the wild elephant, and the riders lash its neck to a tree, so as still further to hamper its struggles to escape. The animal is there kept three or four days without food, when he is unloosed, and forced between tame elephants into an inclosure of four posts strongly planted in the ground. This is the most troublesome part of the business, and the tame elephants have to beat and gore the captured one before he submits to enter within the posts, when he is soon caged in. Here he is hobbled on both fore and hind legs, and kept for a month. At first the animal refuses all food, but hunger masters his wildness in a few days, and by the end of the month he has become sufficiently subdued to be allowed to graze around and outside the inclosure, but of course still strongly hobbled. The teacher then commences a course of hand feeding, standing close by, patting, stroking, fanning and finally mounting the animal, who is taught, by means of a goad, to lift his near fore leg, which serves as a step from whence the rider, holding by the ear, easily gains the neck, and there sits astride. The mode of mounting an elephant in Burma and Siam differs from that practised in India, where the rider puts his foot on the trunk, which the elephant is taught to raise, till, holding by each ear, he scrambles on to the head. When an elephant has been broken in so far as to allow a man to mount him, the rest of his education proceeds rapidly. He soon learns to advance by being nudged behind each ear, by the knees and feet of the driver, and to stop by the pressure of the goad-hook points against his forehead; to turn to the right by the application of the instrument to the left side of the head, and *vice versâ*. He is also taught by constant repetition to obey the various words of command, and is generally fit for use in about three months after his capture. This is in Burma, or the Siamese frontier. In India, where the elephant's training is more elaborate, a longer time is required for his education.

Like the rhinoceros and buffalo, whose skins are bare of hair, the elephant loves to wallow in the mud, and submits with great pleasure to being washed and scrubbed by its keeper. Thick as the hide is, it is very susceptible to mosquito bites, and I have seen an elephant spotted with blood from the probing of a large gadfly which is common in the Tenasserim hills, between 2000 and 5000 feet elevation. It dislikes heat, and on every occasion, during the summer season, seeks the shade. Should this not be available, it blows everything it can pick up on to its head and back, to ward off the rays of the sun; dust, straw, grass, leaves, &c., the accumulation of which gives a ridiculous air to the animal—as if it had gone mad and crowned itself king of Rag Fair. Fatal instances of *coup de soleil* are not uncommon amongst these animals.

In its fondness for water the elephant, notwithstanding its cautious sagacity, sometimes comes to grief. In 1830 one found its way into a deep but small tank at Dinapore, and was unable to get out till they had half filled the pond with large faggots, which the wise beast kept putting under its feet, till it had raised itself sufficiently to step out. In 1833 an elephant at Sonepoor, opposite Patna, met with a worse fate. It had waded into the Gunduck river, near the junction of that stream with the Ganges, till it stepped into a quicksand. Its effort to emerge merely worked it deeper and deeper into the dreadful trap. When its driver and others had cut down branches and plaintain trees, made faggots of them, and cast them within reach of the poor animal's trunk, it had sunk too deeply to avail itself of the assistance. If it could but have disengaged one leg, under which to place a firm substance, all might have been well; but it was not to be. Slowly, slowly, but surely, it settled in its living tomb. It was some hours before they lost sight of the poor eyes staring piteously at the spectators on the shore. It was long before the head itself had sunk under the turbid stream, and when towards sunset I had arrived at the spot, on my way from Hajipoor to Patna, nothing but the end of the trunk was visible, sucking in the last gulps of air the poor creature was able to inhale. The noisy and ostentatious grief of natives has certainly much of humbug in it, and excites our contempt rather than sympathy; but I am convinced the old mahout in this instance was as sincere as loud in his lamentations; and when the dreadful lingering scene of torture came to a close—when the gaping nostrils themselves sunk level with the stream, and the water, pouring, gurgling in, sounded the death knell of the poor patient beast —a chill of horror crept over me, and tears came to my eyes, as I turned, sickened away.

In 1836 an elephant belonging to the commissariat of the late Ramgurh battalion, while picketed in camp, was startled by a native suddenly crossing close in front of him, and with one blow of his trunk broke so many of the man's ribs that the skin over his chest puffed out and collapsed alternately, as he breathed, in a manner frightful to behold. The man continued for a long time in a precarious state. In 1834, when I was a subaltern attached to a party escorting treasure from Bankoora to Burdwan, an elephant, a perfectly quiet beast, belonging to the detachment, which was halted near a village called Indâs, strayed into a paddock where a tattoo (native pony) and its foal were grazing. Whether the little mare was suddenly possessed by an evil spirit, or whether its maternal feelings became excited beyond control at so huge a beast approaching its young one, it is impossible to conjecture; but she attacked the elephant tooth and hoof. The latter tried all in his power to avoid his assailant, but in vain. He retreated, but only to be followed up, pawed, and bitten. He turned round his indiarubber rear to depart, but only to have that portion of his frame saluted with a shower of kicks that sounded like blows on an immense drum; till at last the persecuted animal, loosing all patience, wheeled suddenly round, dashed the tattoo to the ground with one blow of his trunk, and then set off, tail in air, through the bazar, upsetting sheds and stalls, and causing much trouble before he was brought back. The tattoo had been killed on the spot.

The elephant is said to cease growing at forty, and to attain a hundred years of age. At about eighty or ninety it grows thin, and the face wrinkles up and falls in, as much as with the human subject. The only one I have ever seen die a natural death, did so in a sitting posture. She was very old, her keeper said, and had been long declining, and at the last she sat on her elbows and knees for three days and nights before the breath finally left her, which it did without any alteration in her posture. It was in the camp of the old 34th N.I.—now no more—during the Cole campaign of 1833—34. We had been pitched for about a week in a dreary, unhealthy clearing in the jungle, and were rejoiced when the order to move came, which it did the day the elephant died. I was on rearguard the morning of the march, and of necessity the last to leave the ground. By sunrise the tents were struck, loaded, and marched off, and the usual impedimenta of a regiment cleared away. The motley crowd of camp followers and commissariat cattle had departed after the column, and the little plain, lately so teeming with busy life, lay bare and silent as the rearguard marched slowly off, leaving nothing to mark our recent presence but the smouldering embers and broken pots abandoned by the Hindoos; a few vagabond dogs which wandered about, sniffing for the refuse rice that lay scattered here and there; and in the background the dead elephant, sitting like a solemn statue in a Sphinx-like posture. She appeared to be gazing, in her solitary watch, along the path her late companions had passed over. It really struck me as the most dreary scene I remembered to have witnessed. I felt as if we were wronging the old beast in leaving her body to the foul hyænas night would bring forth. I could not help gazing again and again at the motionless form—upright as if still alive. It seemed to attract my eye, look where I would; and, when I turned my horse's head to depart, poor "Choonee" in her stony silence, appeared to reproach us all for our desertion.—*Field*, Dec. 14th, 21st, and 28th.

AGARICUS (CREPIDOTUS) VARIABILIS.

Agaricus (Crepidotus) variabilis, Pers., which for our present research, presents that very favourable condition; one of the earliest known Fungi, which has been many times described and figured, but one whose development-history has been hitherto the same thing as unknown. It was in the mushroom-bed in "Rosenborg" garden that this Fungus had flourished. In the bed prepared for mushrooms it spread its mycelium like a delicate cobweb over the earth, and in the same spot one could find receptacles of all sizes. It was thus easy, by arranging the different stages of development in a descending sequence, to form a series of steps which gradually led from the fully-grown spore-receptacle down to its first rudiments, hardly perceptible as a white point. Under a slight magnifying power this shows itself as a conical felted body. This form is retained by the receptacle until it has attained a size of 1-2mm. The first rudiments of the pileus begin now to be evident as a little globular expansion at the point of the conical stem. At the beginning the pileus grows uniformly at all sides, and the receptacle is therefore at this stage regularly formed, as in Agarics in general. The expanded base of the stem passes quite gradually over into the mycelium-filaments, which radiate towards all sides, so that here the organ designated as a root by the older mycologists is wanting. Only when the receptacle has attained the size of 4—8mm. does the pileus begin to grow more strongly at one side, and thus by degrees the horizontal position is exchanged for the vertical. Since the stem, when the pileus is first commenced, ceases altogether to grow, the fully-grown receptacle is very short-stemmed. The pileus is undulate, wavy at the margin, bulged or lobed, membraneous or half-pellucid. The receptacle is often compound and formed of two receptacles growing together by the stems, or of three or more united by their bases.

For so far the observation of the development of the receptacle offers no difficulties. These begin only when, by the aid of the microscope, we would seek to account for the relations of the earliest developmental stages to the organs of fertilisation, and it was only after many unsuccessful trials that I succeeded in making preparations which would serve to give a distinct conception of these organs. The mycelium-filaments have, indeed, so thin, soft, and gelatinous a membrane, that, when one tries to loose them from the soil, they become, at the slightest contact, confluent into a mucous mass, or a mucous net, with larger or smaller openings. Little better success attends placing some of the soil overgrown by the mycelium under the microscope, for one is not able to apply a sufficiently high magnifying power. However, one can, even by this plan, satisfy oneself of the existence of two organs on the mycelium which cannot be seen by the unassisted eye. There thus present themselves numerous short filaments, which arise up vertically, and bear at their point a globular cell. These filaments are thinner towards the points, and appear to consist of three cells, of which the lowest is only a little longer than broad, the next about twice as long, and the uppermost much longer. Besides these filaments one can discern another organ, much smaller, appearing only just above the mycelium-filaments; but it is seen so indistinctly that one is not at all able to form a conception of its structure. I tried, therefore, placing thin glass plates over the soil, in order to get the mycelium to become spread thereon. This succeeded so far that one could get a very clear view of the growth and ramification of the mycelium. The mycelium grows very quickly, and in the space of a few hours the glass plate, 10mm. long and 6mm. broad, became quite covered over by the delicate filaments, which adhere as closely to the glass as if they were attached with gum. Since the filaments hardly alter their form in drying, these glass plates may be preserved without any further preparation as instructive specimens of the mycelium. The mycelium so formed remained, however, sterile, and I was almost about to give up hope of a successful result, when I hit upon the idea that the mycelium spread upon the soil would, perhaps, after being dried, more readily admit of being separated and brought under the microscope in such a condition that one could get a clear view of the organs seated thereon. This proved itself indeed to be the case, since the soft and mucous mycelium-filaments are prevented by drying from falling together, and can be separated by a fine needle into minute portions, which are quite free from particles of earth, and thus can be examined under the microscope, with the highest magnifying powers. The mycelium is now softened, first with alcohol—when this precaution is not observed, the view is made very indistinct by the quantity of air-bubbles—and, after a drop of water is added, the individual filaments and the organs seated thereon quickly assume the same nature which they had previous to being dried.

It was only by preparations made in this way that I succeeded in getting a clear view of the mycelium-filaments, and of the organs seated thereon, of which I had previously only got an indistinct glimpse, as well as arriving at a knowledge of the organs of fertilisation so long in vain sought after in these fungi.—*Quarterly Journal of Microscopical Science*, January.

JASPAR, FLINT, CHALCEDONY, OPAL, AND HYALITE.

THE states of semi-crystalline silica are so various, and so connected in their variety, that the best recent authorities have been content to group them all with quartz, giving to each only a few words of special notice; even the important chapters of Bischof describe rather their states of decomposition and transition than the minerals themselves. Nevertheless, as central types, five conditions of silica are definable, structurally, if not chemically, distinct; and forming true species: and in entering on any detailed examination of agatescent arangements, it is quite necessary to define with precision these typical substances, and their relation to crystalline quartz.

I. *Jasper.*—Opaque, with dull earthy fracture; and hard enough to take a perfect polish. When the fracture is conchoidal the mineral is not jasper but stained flint. The transitional states are confused in fracture; but true jasper is absolutely separated from flint by two structural characters; on a small scale it is capable of the most delicate pisolitic arrangement; and on a larger scale is continually found in flame-like concretions, beautifully involved and contorted. But flint is never pisolitic, and, in any fine manner, never coiled; nor do either of these structures take place in any transitional specimen, until the conchoidal fracture of the flint has given place to the dull earthy one of jasper; nor is even jasper itself pisolitic on the fracture being too close-grained. The green base of heliotrope, with a perfectly even fracture, may be often seen, where it is speckled with white, to be arranged in exquisitely sharp and minute spherical concretions, cemented by a white paste, of which portions sometimes take a completely brecciated aspect, each fragment being outlined by concave segments of circles. Jasper is eminently retractile, like the clay in septaria, and in agates often breaks into warped fragments, dragging the rest of the stone into distortion. In general, the imbedded fragments in any brecciated agate will be mainly of jasper; the cement, chalcedonic, or quartzose.

II. *Flint.*—Amorphous silica, translucent on the edges, with fine conchoidal fracture. Opaque only when altered, nascent, or stained. Never coiled, never pisolitic, never reniform; these essentially negative characters belonging to it as being usually formed by a slow accumulative secretion, and afterwards remaining unmodified (preserving therefore casts of organic forms with great precision). It is less retractile than jasper; its brecciate conditions being not so much produced by contraction or secession as by true secretion, even when most irregular in shape. But there are innumerable transitions between these two states, affected also by external violence, which we shall have to examine carefully. Within these nodular concretions, flint is capable of a subsequently banded, though not pisolitic arrangement.

III. *Chalcedony.*—Reniform silica, translucent when pure, opaque only when stained, nascent, or passing into quartz. The essential characteristic of chalcedony is its reniform structure, which in the pure mineral is as definite as in wavellite or hæmatite, though when it is rapidly cooled or congealed from its nascent state of fluent jelly it may remain as a mere amorphous coating of other substances; very rarely, however, without some slight evidence of its own reniform crystallization. The study of its different degrees of congelation in agates is of extreme intricacy. As a free mineral in open cavities it is actively stalactitic, not merely pendant or accumulative, but animated by a kind of crystalline spinal energy, which gives to its processes something of the arbitrary arrangement of real crystals, modified always by cohesion, gravity, and (presumably) by fluid and gaseous currents.

There is no transition between chalcedony and flint. They may be intimately mixed at their edges, but the limit is definite. Impure brown and amber-coloured chalcedonies, and those charged with great quantities of foreign matter, may closely resemble flint, but the two substances are entirely distinct. Between jasper and chalcedony the separation is still more definite in mass, jasper being never reniform, and differing greatly in fracture; but the flame-like or spotted crimson stains of chalcedony often approach conditions of jasper; and there is, I suppose, no pisolitic formation of any substance without some inherent radiation, which associates it with reniform groups, so that pisolitic jasper must be considered as partly transitive to chalcedony. On the other hand chalcedony seems to pass into common crystalline quartz through milky stellate quartz, associated in Auvergne with guttate and hemispheircal forms.

IV. *Opal.*—Amorphous translucent silica, with resinous fracture, and essential water. Distinguished from chalcedony by three great structural characteristics: *a*, its resinous fracture; *b*, that it is never pisolitic or reniform; *c*, that when zoned, in cavities or veins, its *zones are always rectilinear*, and transverse to the vein, while those of chalcedony are usually undulating, and parallel to the sides of the vein; level only in lakes at the bottom of cavities.

V. *Hyalite.*—Amorphous transparent silica, with vitreous fracture, and essential water. Never reniform, nor pisolitic, nor banded; but composed of irregularly grouped bosses, generally elliptical or pear-shaped (only accidentally spherical), formed apparently by successive accretion of coats, but not showing banded structure internally. Entirely transparent, with splendid smooth glassy fracture. Sometimes coating lava; sometimes in irregularly isolated patches upon it: apparently connected in structure with the roseate clusters of milky chalcedony of Auvergne. I shall keep the term "guttate" for this particular structure, of which singular varieties also occur among the hornstones of Cornwall.

These five main groups are thus definable without embarrassment; two other conditions of silica, perhaps, ought to be separately named; namely, cacholony, which seems to take a place between chalcedony and opal, but which I have not yet been able satisfactorily to define; the other, the calcareous-looking, usually whitish agate, which often surrounds true translucent agate, as if derived from it by decomposition. I am under the impression that this is chalcedony, more or less charged with carbonate of lime, and that it might be arranged separately as lime-jasper, differing from aluminous jasper, by being capable of reniform structure; but it is certainly in some cases an altered state of chalcedony, which seems in its more opaque zones to get whiter by exposure to light. I shall therefore call it white agate, when it harmoniously follows the translucent zones; reserving the term jasper for granular aggregations. Perhaps ultimately it may be found that nascent chalcedony taking up either oxide of iron, or almuina, or lime, and might relatively be called iron-jasper, clay-jasper, and lime-jasper; but for any present descriptive purpose the simpler arrangement will suffice.—John Ruskin, Esq., F.R.G.S., in *Geological Magazine* for January.

FOLK-LORE.

Perhaps the most amusing, and by no means the least instructive, of the many branches into which the study of local Natural History divides itself, is the one which directs attention to the curious traditions concerning animals and plants which have been handed down from generation to generation, and which still retain their hold in rural districts. Closely connected with this subject is that of the colloquial, or vulgar, names attached to various natural objects, the derivation of which is interesting both to the philologist and the naturalist. We have already expressed our wish to receive and publish all the information obtainable in our own district on these points, and it may be as well to commence with the few notes we have at present collected, in the hope that others may be urged to contribute their quota for the general benefit.

Snakes are ever fruitful subjects of rustic superstition. One of our members had killed a Slow-worm (*Anguis fragilis*), and was carrying it home on a stick. A sagacious peasant, however, warned him to be careful, for the thing couldn't die until the sun set, "no, not if you was to cut it in pieces." Of course, the popular errors regarding snakes are in full force here; although, to his honour let it be recorded, one man confided to us his belief that "common snakes wasn't poisonous, only adders and vipers," which seem to be regarded as two different things. Even the Land Efts do not escape condemnation: there is supposed to be *no cure* for their bite! Report says that a man at Flackwell Heath died from the effects of the bite of a Newt? Further particulars are solicited.

A curious distinction is made between the Common White Butterflies (*Pieris*) and the more brilliantly-coloured species. The former are called Butterflies, but the latter receive the remarkable designation of Hobhowchins!

The following treatment of epilepsy we commend to the medical profession. When other supposed remedies had failed, a travelling packman was consulted. He suggested two methods of cure, both of which were faithfully tried. The first was, that the afflicted person should procure a Jay; every morning, fasting, she was to chew a piece of bread, and then give it the bird to eat; on the death of the poor creature, the fits would cease. To make assurance doubly sure, another remedy was added, viz., a silver ring, to be worn on the ring-finger as an "amberlet" (amulet?), to be subscribed for and presented to the patient without her previous knowledge! The point of the joke lies in the fact that this mode of treatment was announced *by the invalid herself*. We regret that we are unable to state whether a cure was effected.

Among our wild flowers, we find that the name "Cuckoo's Victuals" is applied both to the Wood-sorrel (*Oxalis Acetosella*) and the Herb Robert (*Geranium Robertianum*). The former can trace its claim to the name back to the days of Gerarde, who speaks of it as "Cuckowes meate, because either the Cuckow feedeth thereon, or by reason (that) when it springeth forth and floureth the Cuckow singeth most;" both of these reasons would, however, apply equally well to the Herb Robert. The latter is, indeed, a favourite with our villagers, who also call it "Cuckoo's Eye," "Billy Buttons," and "Ragged Robin." The second of these is applied to the Red Campion (*Lychnis diurna*), in districts where that plant is plentiful: the third is undoubtedly the property of *L. Flos-cuculi*, being admirably descriptive of its jagged, irregular flowers. "Cuckoo's Eye," "Bird's Eye," and "Cat's Eye," are names given to the lovely Germander Speedwell (*Veronica Chamædrys*); and they certainly are by no means inappropriate to the bright blue flowers of the prettiest, though, perhaps, commonest, of our Speedwells. At Buckingham, the Marsh Marigold (*Caltha palustris*) is known by the singular name of "John-Georges;" why, we cannot even conjecture. The name "Devil o' both sides," applied to the Corn Crowfoot (*Ranunculus arvensis*), although inelegant, is at least appropriate, when we consider the sharp spines with which the ripe seed-vessels are beset. "Blackseed" is also well applied to the Nonsuch or Yellow Trefoil (*Medicago lupulina*). A herb in great repute for its healing properties is the Hedge Woundwort (*Stachys sylvatica*); medical skill sinks into insignificance by the side of the ointment prepared from its foliage: it is called "Cows' Weather (or Withy) Wind," the *i* in the last word being pronounced as in *wine*. The Bird's-foot Trefoil (*Lotus corniculatus*) is called "Cats-claws," and "Shoes-and-Stockings." Another spring flower which is connected with the Cuckoo is the Great Stitchwort (*Stellaria Holostea*), which is called "Cuckoo's Meat." The White Campion (*Lychnis vespertina*) claims the names of "Cow-rattle" and "Bull-rattle." The Mealey Guelder Rose (*Viburnum Lantana*) is named "Coventry." The Early Purple Orchis (*Orchis mascula*) is called "Kingfingers."

The Great Mullein (*Verbascum Thapsus*) is vaguely said to be "good for colds," and bears the names "Rag-paper" and "Poor-man's Flannel." Gerarde says that "the root, boiled in water and drunke, prevaileth much against the old cough." The same old writer remarks of the Tutsan (*Hypericum Androsæmum*) that "the leaves laid upon broken shins healeth them, and many other hurts and griefes, whereof it took his name Toute-saine, or Tutsane, of healing all things." Our Buckinghamshire people now call it "Touch-and-Heal," and consider it "a capital thing to put to cuts." It is curious to notice that the Mezereon (*Daphne Mezereum*) still retains a semblance of its proper name in "Mazalum;" there is an idea that it can be budded from the Wood Laurel (*D. Laureola*) "by them as knows how."—*The Quarterly Journal of the High Wycombe Natural History Society*, January.

MANAGEMENT OF GOLD FISH.

THE first difficulty occurs at starting; for, be it known, that gold fish are raised for the market in much the same way as winter cucumbers— that is to say, they are bred in heat—for the gold carp rejoices in a bath of from 80 to near 100 degrees of Fahrenheit; and the fish so produced are known in the market as 'hot water fish.' These hot-water fish are very often queer things; some of them have broken backs, some double tails, many are without the dorsal-fin, and some are "awful about the head;" in fact, hot-water fish are of all shapes and colours—some very lovely, others much deformed. As might be expected, when fish so bred are transferred to water at the ordinary temperature of the season, and left to brave it out, they succumb to the coldness of the climate, and show their silver bellies to the sky. If, therefore, gold fish are to be kept in water not artificially heated, what are known as "cold fish" must be secured; at all events, the others should be bought only in summer time, so that they may suffer a slighter shock, and get used to the climate by degrees, before winter.

Another matter of importance is the water itself. If I had not received so many letters on the subject, I should never have dreamt of folks attempting to keep fish in *rain-water!* It is really absurd; one might as well expect a poor mouse to live its time out under the exhausted receiver of an air-pump. Rain-water is deficient in the first elements of fish life, namely, oxygen— or, rather, its free oxygen is not in a proper form to afford them support; and it also wants earthy matter, such as is always plentiful in river-water. But suppose you have no river-water, then you must turn the rain-water into river-water, and the process is very simple. Fix a filter over a large pan, into the pan throw a handful of old mortar and a spadeful of garden mould that is free from any decayed matter or manure; filter the rain-water on to the earthy mixture, and let it stand a few days, then filter it again into the vessel in which the fish are to be kept, and it will be nearly as good as the purest of river-water for them. To prepare hard spring-water, it is generally only necessary to expose it in an open vessel for a few days, when the salts that cause it to be "hard" will be deposited, the water warmed, and rendered suitable.

Of course we now come to the question about changing the water. If much trouble is necessary to prepare the water for the fishes, who will care to take such trouble daily? Ay! there's the rub. If you want your fishes to live, *you must not change the water at all.* Nature does not change the water, but she plants a number of vegetables in her lakes and streams; and if you wish your golden pets to be healthy and happy, you must do the same. No matter what kind of vessel you may choose to keep gold fish in, and no matter what shells, or blocks of granite, or rock crystal you may use for ornament, the beauty of the scene will be enhanced by the immersion in the lymph of a few appropriate plants. Get a few stems of the common *Anacharis,* or the water starwort (Chard), *Vallisneria, Nitella,* or the noble water soldier— in fact, any of the more elegant aquatics—and fix them at the bottom by means of a pebble attached to their lower stems by means of a strip of bast, and they will soon take root if a few clean pebbles are thrown in, and in a few weeks' time will sprout in all directions, and form a rich green forest under water, giving shade to the fishes and supplying them with oxygen, so that the water never need be changed. Should the glass get coated with a green slime, it will be easy to remove it by means of a sponge; and if the vessel is emptied for alterations, use the same water, unless it is really discoloured. Changing the water kills more gold fish than any other cause, the hardiest fishes cannot stand it; and as to purity, it needs only a little patience at first, and the water will keep pure for years.

The next point is as to feeding. There are some folks who never feed gold fish, "they have been told not to." Remember how the Frenchman's horse broke down, though fed with diminishing rations. No animal can live long if not fed at all. "But they eat the insects in the water!" Eat fiddlesticks! Just consider, here are half-a-dozen fishes, weighing each a quarter of a pound. Where is the food to support them in that bright liquid? In ponds they find a thousand things to eat, which few ladies would like to see in their fish globes; but in such an artificial state they must be fed or perish. Give them the crumb of brown bread, now and then, gentles, flies, or a little millet seed or boiled rice. It is important to give them only as much as they are likely to consume in the course of a few hours, because if food lies about long, it taints the water and spoils its brilliancy. A little observation will soon afford a rule for the quantity, in accordance with the number and size of the fishes. If water snails are kept, the young of the snails will be greedily eaten by the fishes, and afford them a very suitable food— carp of all kinds being very partial to young snails; the snails are useful, too, in keeping down all obnoxious growths on the inner side of the glass. For ornamental purposes the best snails are *Planorbis corneus, nitidus,* and *contortis* and *Paludina vivipara.* Any of the species of fresh water mussels are ornamental, and highly useful in keeping the water pure.

Lastly, do not expose gold fish either to intense sun heat in summer, or frost in winter. They are really tender, but must not be coddled. In their native pools they can escape from the glaring sun to some green, shadowy depth, but in globes there is no escape; and they get blinded, and boiled pretty often, by being exposed in globes that act as lenses, in windows open to the sun for hours together in high summer.—Shirley Hibberd in the *Floral World* for January.

TEMPERATURE OF THE EARTH.

ALTHOUGH the opinions of philosophers regarding the condition of the internal nucleus of the globe are widely different, all are probably agreed as regards an actual increase of temperature from the surface downwards to an unknown depth; and that this is the fact the evidence both of a theoretical and experimental character is probably conclusive. It is no argument against this view that we find strata, in their natural or unaltered state, which on stratigraphical grounds we believe to have been at one time buried beneath newer strata to a depth of several thousand feet; for assuming the increase of heat to be at an average rate of 1° Fahr. for every 60 feet, the boiling point of water would not be reached under 12,720 feet; and while on the one hand it is doubtful whether metamorphism would take place in ordinary strata at this temperature, it is seldom we meet with rocks which we are certain had originally been buried at much greater depths.

Whether this increase of temperature is continuous for any considerable distance in reference to the semi-diameter of the earth, or whether it increases or diminishes according to definite laws, are questions which are probably beyond solution by actual experiment, for, in the words of Humboldt, the question of the internal central heat, as a mathematical problem, "yields rather negative than positive results." The experimental evidences, however, as far as they come within the range of investigation, all point to one conclusion. They are also of several kinds, derived from observations of the temperature of the water springing from different depths through artesian borings—those obtained from testing the temperature of the water issuing from coal-seams and fissures in mines, and those obtained from observations made during the sinking of mining shafts both through wet and dry strata. It is on the experimental evidences we propose here to dwell, and taking some examples from authorities within our reach, to present the reader with a succinct account of what has already been achieved, and afterwards to offer some suggestions as to the best manner, in our opinion, for pursuing further investigations.

One of the most remarkable and carefully-observed cases of artesian borings is that of the Puits de Grenelle, near Paris. The sinking of this bore-hole was watched by Arago till 1840, down to a depth of 1,657 feet, when the borer had left the Chalk formation, and was beginning to penetrate the Gault. The series of observations were completed by Walferdin in 1847. The surface of the basin of the well at Grenelle lies at an elevation of 119 feet above the sea, and the borings extend to a depth of 1794·6 feet from the surface. The water which rises from the Lower Greensand formation is of a temperature of 81·95° Fahr., and the increase is at the rate of 1° Fahr. for every 59 feet.

The next boring we shall describe is that of Neu Saltzwerk, in Westphalia, and situated 231 feet above the level of the sea at Amsterdam. It penetrated to an absolute depth of 2,281 feet from the surface. The salt spring lies, therefore, at a depth of 2,052 feet below the level of the sea, a relative depth which is, perhaps, the greatest that has yet been reached. The temperature of the brine is 91·04° Fahr., and as the mean annual temperature of the air at these works is about 49·3°, we may assume there is an increase of 1° Fahr. for every 54·68 feet. This boring is 487 feet deeper than that of Grenelle, and the temperature of the water is 9.09° Fahr. higher.

An artesian boring in the vicinity of Geneva to a depth of 724 feet, and at an elevation of 1,600 feet above the sea-level, showed the increase to heat at the rate of 1° Fahr. for every 55 feet; while another at Mendorff, in Luxemberg, which penetrated to a depth of 2,394 feet, gave a result of 1° Fahr. for every 57 feet. This boring is particularly interesting and valuable, not only for its depth, but from the fact of its passing through several formations, including the Lias, Keuper, Muschelkalk, Gies bigarré, and entering slaty rocks.—*The Quarterly Journal of Science*, January. London: Churchill.

THE PEOPLE OF ABYSSINIA.

In form and feature the Abyssinians are superior to the most advanced tribes of Central Africa. Of the middle stature, but somewhat slender, they carry themselves very erect; nor are their rounded limbs deficient in muscular power. In complexion, indeed, they vary from light olive brown to jet black; and in the low country the admixture of negro blood is easily discernible. The Amhara women are described by Mr. Stern as plump and well-proportioned, "with high and broad foreheads, aquiline noses, and eyes which, notwithstanding their unpleasing large size and dark brilliancy, are so tempered by a soft dreamy expression, that they rather enhance, than detract from, what Orientals consider the perfection of beauty." Unfortunately they cannot let well alone, but are often tempted to supplement nature by art. It is thus they eradicate their eyebrows, and paint in their place a narrow curved line of bluish tint, at the same time daubing their cheeks with a pigment composed of red ochre and fat. But what an Abyssinian lady most prides herself upon is the luxuriance of her raven hair, though she does her utmost to counteract this natural beauty by dressing it after a hideous and execrable fashion. Sometimes a portion of the head is close shaven and encircled with a narrow greasy fillet, but more frequently the hair is twisted into a multitude of plaits diverging from a common centre, and reminding a European of the statues and monuments of ancient Egypt. Occasionally, in the highest circles, the hair is allowed to fall in natural curls over the neck and shoulders; while countrywomen and domestic servants simply touzle their super-abundant locks into a tangled mass; but all classes alike besmear their heads with rancid butter; disgusting both to sight and smell. To prevent the elaborate plaits from becoming dishevelled by restless movements during sleep, ladies of rank rest their heads at night in a sort of bowl-shaped stool, which they carry with them when leaving home. However particular they may be in the adjustment of their luxuriant hair, the women of Abyssinia are comparatively negligent in the matter of dress. The higher classes attire themselves in a chemise, or under-garment, over which they wear "a loose shirt reaching below the knees, and neatly embroidered in front and on the cuffs." In addition to this simple costume, a *shama*, or toga, with a smart silk border, is on certain occasions wrapped round the form in graceful folds, or a gaudy cloak of European manufacture is thrown over the shoulders. In the humbler grades of society, however, women content themselves with a wide sack of strong coarse calico, with baggy sleeves, girded round the waist with a narrow belt. When going abroad they also wrap themselves in a sort of toga, or winding-sheet, not unlike the Bengali dress, the folds of which envelop their persons from head to foot. The peasant women are satisfied with still less clothing, merely covering their loins with a short petticoat made of coarse cotton or dressed skin. On one point rich and poor are quite in accord. Nothing can exceed their passion for ornaments. Those who can afford it, festoon themselves with chains of silver bells, scent-boxes, rosaries, bangles, and charms against the evil eye; while the less fortunate deck themselves out with strings of amulets sewn in square leather cases, and of beads, the fashion of which varies—as Bruce discovered, to his momentary discomfiture. He had purchased, we are told, "a quantity beautifully flowered with red and green, of the size of a large pea; also some large oval green and yellow ones; whereas the *ton* among the beauties of Tigré required small sky-blue beads, about the size of small lead shot, blue and white bugles, and large yellow glass beads flat on the sides." Tastes, however, seem to have changed since then; for Mr. Stern speaks of large black and yellow beads as being most in vogue five or six years ago. Neither men nor women wear shoes, with the exception of "a few stylish ladies and conceited priests;" but the former sometimes dye both their feet and their hands of a reddish hue. A blue silken cord, called *matteb*, is worn round the neck by every Abyssinian professing Christianity, whether male or female.—*Belgravia.*

Language of Animals.

If, descending in the scale of creation from the quadrupeds and birds that emit sounds which are perfectly audible to themselves and us—whatever those sounds may mean—to that lower world of insect life which emits little and sometimes no sound that our ears can detect, we may still discover reason to believe that they may have some power of speech—possibly by means of sound, possibly by means of touch and signs. Take bees and ants as familiar examples. When the bees in a hive select one particular bee, and station her at the entrance—like a hall-porter at a club in Pall-Mall—and assign to her the duty, which she well performs, of allowing none but members of the hive to pass in, is it not certain that the functionary has been chosen from out the rest, and informed of the wishes of the community? This cannot be done without a language of some sort, whether of the eye, the touch, or the expression of a sound or series of sounds. When black ants make war against red ants, for the purpose of taking the children of the latter into captivity and making slaves of them, is war declared without preliminary consultation? and, if not, must not these belligerent Formicans have some kind of language? The battles of the ants have often been seen, and often described. I was one day strolling on the wild but beautiful shore of Loch Eck, in Argyllshire, when I sat me down to rest by the side of a little rill or burnie that trickled down a bank, when I noticed that a large flat stone or slab, that, ages ago, perhaps, had slidden down from the mountains—a slab that was about five or six feet long by about as many wide—was covered with ants of two species—the one with wings, the other wingless—and that they were fighting a desperate battle, a very Waterloo or Sadowa of carnage. The stone was encumbered with the dead and dying; battalion charged battalion, division assailed division, while episodes of individual bravery—one single combatant against another—spotted the battle-field. There were march and countermarch, assault and defence, retreat and pursuit, and, as far as my unpractised eye could judge, a considerable amount of care and attention to the wounded and disabled. Returning home to my books, I found a description in Leigh Hunt's Companion of a similiar battle, on the authority of a German naturalist, named Hanhart; and a still more interesting description in Episodes of Insect Life, by Acheta Domestica, both confirmatory of what I had seen, and both containing particulars of the mode of battle, which I had been unable to understand. The puzzle was then, as it still is, whether these quarrelsome little Formicans could form themselves into battalions, arrange plans of attack and defence, appoint commanders and captains, and play the parts of Napoleon and Wellington, without some means of intercommunication of idea, equivalent, in its results, to human speech? The question cannot be decided, except inferentially, and by arguing from the known to the unknown. If treated in this manner, there is much more to be said in favour of the proposition that the Formicans can speak to each other than can be said against it—especially if, remembering, with Shakespeare, that there are more things in heaven and earth than are dreamt of in our philosophy, we consider, at the same time, that there may be an infinitude of sounds in nature which our ears are too dull to hear, and of which the vibrations are far too faint and delicate to strike upon the human tympanum.—*All the Year Round*, Jan. 23.

The Earth's Features.

"The true views of the operations of nature in sculpturing the surface of the earth can never be arrived at unless we take into consideration the effects of all possible agencies, and give them their due place in the great work."

Never were truer words spoken than the above,—*Marinists* may rave about what their special agent can do; so may *Subaërialists* proper, *Glacialists*, and every other *ists*, but unprejudiced observers will find that all the different agencies work hand in hand, and that if any of them had been absent, the present features of the earth could not have been formed as we now find them.

Why is it necessary that any new theory should be invented or any *special* theory adopted to account for the present features of the Earth? Why not rather allow the existing forces to do the work nature has assigned each? Let the changes in the earth be considered from "the beginning," and may not a solution for most, if not for all, the apparent difficulties be found? To suit the *special* theories, various forms have been suggested as the first; but is there one of them so simple or better than that given in THE BOOK—"The earth was without form and void, and the Spirit of God moved on the face of the water." From this, the oldest record, it would appear that at "the beginning," the earth was surrounded by an envelope of water. Moreover, this statement agrees with present conditions; for a similar phenomenon might again occur if all the land was sunk in the depths of the ocean. This sea, as proved by Mr. Campbell in "Frost and Fire," must have been motionless, there being no light—when light was created, motion began, and after that, "the dry land appeared,"—since then there has been perpetual motion, during which, parts of the land have been submerged, while other parts have been elevated; and this process has been enacted over and over again. While the land was above the sea, "Frost and Fire," with "Rain and Rivers," have each in their appointed place done their work; neither was the sea idle, as it must have acted on the land as it was appearing above, or disappearing under the waters, carving out the main features afterwards to be remodelled by the other existing forces.

An observer who has seen the sea yearly carrying away a coast may be inclined to believe that it is the great destroyer; while those who live among soft strata that are easily denuded, may pin their faith to "Rain and Rivers," and those accustomed to Alpine or Arctic regions to ice; but an unprejudiced observer will find that "all are right and all are wrong." Moreover, if the advice of the Chameleon—

"When next you talk of what you view,
Think others see as well as you,"

was generally adopted among geologists, it would not be so difficult a task as at present to find "keys to fit all the locks."

The Biblical record may be sneered at because human remains have not been found except among the most recent of the Tertiary deposits. However, in answer to this I may be allowed to put forward Col. Greenwood's suggestion; that there is only negative evidence against the existence of Man and the other land animals from the earliest periods of the earth; for to quote that author's words:—"Where are the fossil remains of *land quadrupeds* found? In cavern deposits, in drift and alluvium 'deposited on dry land,' in filled up lakes, in bogs, or frozen up in polar regions. Now all these land museums are not only modern, but they are superficial and temporary. They are liable to be washed into the sea; and their fossil contents *must be* destroyed before they can be re-deposited in marine strata,"—G. Henry Kinahan, in *Geological Magazine* for January.

Luminosity of the Fraxinella.

When the daughter of Linnæus one evening approached the flowers of Dictamnus albus with a light, a little flame was kindled, without in any way injuring them. The experiment was afterwards frequently repeated, but it never succeeded; and whilst some scientific men regarded the whole as a faulty observation, or simply a delusion, others endeavoured to explain it by various hypotheses. One of them especially, which tried to account for the phenomenon by assuming that the plant developed hydrogen, found much favour. At present, when this hypothesis has become untenable, the inflammability of the plant is mentioned more as a *curiosum*, and accounted for by the presence of etheric oil in the flowers. Being in the habit of visiting a garden in which strong healthy plants of Dictamnus albus were cultivated, I often repeated the experiment, but always without success, and I already began to doubt the correctness of the observation made by the daughter of Linnæus, when, during the dry and hot summer of 1857, I repeated the experiment once more, fancying that the warm weather might possibly have exercised a more than ordinary effect upon the plant. I held a lighted match close to an open flower, but again without result; in bringing, however, the match close to some other blossoms, it approached a nearly faded one, and suddenly was seen a reddish, crackling, strongly shooting flame, which left a powerful aromatic smell, and did not injure the peduncle. Since then I have repeated the experiment during several seasons, and even during wet, cold summers it has always succeeded, thus clearly proving that it is not influenced by the state of the weather. In doing so I observed the following results, which fully explain the phenomenon. On the pedicels and peduncles are a number of minute reddish-brown glands, secreting etheric oil. These glands are but little developed when the flowers begin to open, and they are fully grown shortly after the blossoms begin to fade, shrivelling up when the fruit begins to form. For this reason the experiment can succeed only at that limited period when the flowers are fading. Best adapted for the purpose are those panicles which have done flowering at the base, and still have a few blossoms at the top. The same panicle cannot be lighted twice. The rachis is uninjured by the experiment, being too green to take fire, and because the flame runs along almost as quick as lighting, becoming extinguished at the top, and diffusing a powerful incense-like smell.—Dr. Hahn, in *Floral World* for Jan.

Lake of Killarney.

We rowed first round Innisfallen Island and some way up the Lower Lake. The view was magnificent. We had a slight shower, which alarmed us all, from the mist which overhung the mountains; but it suddenly cleared away and became very fine and very hot. At a quarter to one we landed at the foot of the beautiful hill of Glena, where on a small sloping lawn there is a very pretty little cottage. We walked about though it was overpoweringly hot, to see some of the splendid views. The trees are beautiful,—oak, birch, arbutus, holly, yew,—all growing down to the water's edge, intermixed with heather. The hills, rising abruptly from the lake, are completely wooded, which gives them a different character to those in Scotland, though they often reminded me of the dear Highlands. We returned to the little cottage, where the quantity of midges and the smell of peat made us think of Alt-na-Giuthasach. * * Close to our right as we were going, we stopped under the splendid hill of the Eagle's Nest to hear the echo of a bugle; the sound of which, though blown near by, was not heard. We had to get out near the Weir Bridge to let the empty boats be pulled up by the men. The sun had come out and lit up the really magnificent scenery splendidly; but it was most oppressively hot. We wound along till we entered the Upper Lake, which opened upon us with all its high hills—the highest, The Reeks, 3,400 feet high—and its islands and points covered with splendid trees;—such arbutus (quite large trees) with yews, making a beautiful foreground. We turned into a very small bay or creek, where we got out and walked a short way in the shade, and up to where a tent was placed, just opposite a waterfall called Derryconochy, a lovely spot, but terribly infested by midges. In this tent was tea, fruit, ice, cakes, and everything most tastefully arranged. We just took some tea, which was very refreshing in the great heat of this relaxing climate. The vegetation is quite that of a jungle—ferns of all kinds and shrubs and trees,—all springing up luxuriantly. We entered our boats and went back the same way we came, admiring greatly the beauty of the scenery; and this time went down the rapids in the boat. No boats, except our own, had followed us beyond the rapids. But below them there were a great many, and the scene was very animated and the people very noisy and enthusiastic. The Irish always give that peculiar shrill shriek—unlike anything one ever hears anywhere else.—*Her Majesty's Journal.*

Devices of Animals.

The statement of Mr. Collins is quoted by Mr. E. B. Tylor, in his "Researches into the Early History of Mankind," that a native of Australia will stretch himself upon a rock, as if asleep in the sunshine, holding a piece of fish in his open hand; "The bird, be it hawk or crow, seeing the prey, and not observing any motion in the native, pounces on the fish, and, in the instant of seizing it, is caught by the native, who soon throws it on the fire, and makes a meal of it." Ward, the missionary, in his book on the Hindus, mentions a tame monkey in India, whose food the crows used to plunder while he sat on the top of his pole, to prevent which he would pretend to lie dead within reach of his food, and seize the first crow that came close enough. When he had caught it, the story says, he put it between his knees, deliberately plucked it, and threw it up into the air. The other crows set upon their disabled companion and pecked it to death, but they let the monkey's store alone ever after. This is no uncommon thing for a monkey to do in India, under the circumstances mentioned. I have there seen a monkey attempt the "dodge," but the crows were too knowing to be thus deceived; no doubt they had experienced or witnessed the manœuvre. "One sunshiny day, a walrus," writes Captain Beecher, "of nine or ten feet length, rose in a pool of water not very far from us, and after looking around, drew his greasy carcase upon the ice, where he rolled about for a time, and at length laid himself down to sleep. A bear, which had probably been observing his movements, crawled carefully upon the opposite side of the pool, and began to roll about also, but apparently more with design than for amusement, as he progressively lessened the distance that intervened between him and his prey. The walrus, suspicious of his advances, drew himself up, preparatory to a precipitate retreat into the water, in case of a nearer acquaintance with his playful but treacherous visitor: on which the bear was instantly motionless, as if in the act of sleep: but after a time began to lick his paws, and clean himself, and occasionally to encroach a little upon his intended prey. But even this artifice did not succeed; the wary walrus was far too cunning to allow itself to be cajoled, and suddenly plunged into the pool; which the bear no sooner observed than he threw off all disguise, rushed towards the spot, and followed him in an instant into the water, where I fear that he was as much disappointed in his meal as we were of the pleasure of witnessing a very interesting encounter." We should hardly expect that, even a polar bear would venture to attack a full-grown walrus with fairly-developed tusks; but the young at least appear to be occasionally subject to the depredations of the most formidable beast of prey inhabiting the polar regions. —*Z., in Land and Water.*

A Tiger Hunt.

The jungle was very thick, and we were posted about sixty or seventy yards apart, both of us commanding a hill in front. From it came a nullah which lay between us, and part of this was fully exposed to fire from my tree. Most of you know the anxious excitement with which one generally has to wait for a tiger when being beaten up; but on this occasion we had no opportunity of exercising that commendable quality—patience. The beaters had been taken round to the other side of the hill, and we had barely established ourselves in the mandwas, and the first shout of the distant line announced that the beat had commenced, when the tiger accepted the notice to quit, and came galloping over the hill in splendid style as hard as he could go, and roaring as he came on to the utmost of his ability. There was no sneaking along, or anything in the slightest degree indecisive about the matter. Apparently quite regardless of any hidden danger in front, he galloped straight on to the position held by my friend. L—— would gladly have let him approach closer, but owing to the thickness of the jungle in front and to his right was afraid of loosing sight of him ; so, a favourable opportunity occurring when within about thirty yards, he blazed away sharply right and left. The volley was delivered with such effect that the tiger was knocked clean over into a part of the nullah I have mentioned, and which was commanded from my position, but not so from that of my companion. It was about forty yards distant, and as the tiger recovered himself and tried to scramble out of the nullah, I planted a bullet in his shoulder and dropped him back. Again he got up and made an effort to ascend the bank, and again I dropped him with another bullet placed not far from my first, and so effectually that he needed no third, as he never rose from the last shot. After waiting a while we descended our respective trees, and went down into the nullah, and found him quite dead. He was a fine full-grown male, with enormous whiskers, and had in his death agony driven one of his teeth right through his foot—*Capt. Newall's Hog Hunting.*

Under the Microscope.

DESMIDIACEÆ.

Ranking next in importance, and possessing much in common with Diatomaceæ, the study of Desmidiaceæ will be found full of interest to the microscopical beginner. They inhabit many of the same localities, excepting that they are never found in salt water, not a single specimen having been gathered in the sea. Mr. Thwaites has, indeed, discovered some species in brackish pools, but these have been found identical with fresh water species, and not proving in any way that a single species can lay claim to be considered especially marine. Their whole being and life history is similar to Diatomaceæ, differing only as above and in the universal absence of the silicious coat, but possessing in place of it a hard horny material, which has been found to resist decomposition. They are minute plants consisting of a single cell, of a grass-green colour (with the exception of *Closterium*, which is sometimes brown), encompassed by a transparent structureless membrane, only a few having their integuments coloured : within the cavity is the endochrome. This endochrome is the green colouring matter, and is supposed to be analogous to the chlorophyll, or leaf-green, of the higher plants. Meyen has stated that he has seen the whole interior of *Closterium* granulated, these granules giving with iodine the beautiful blue colour indicative of starch. They are chiefly noticeable for their beautiful bilateral form and the variety of their external markings (assuming the appearance of striæ and puncta), and their appendages consisting of projecting spines or points. "Each cell or frond," says Queckett*, "consists of two symmetrical valves or segments united by a central suture, between which the newly formed portions are interposed."

* Queckett's "Lectures on Histology" (London : Bailliere), vol. ii. page 43.

Like Diatomaceæ much controversy existed with respect to their vegetable nature, until Mr. Ralfs gave us the results of his labours in a painstaking work called "British Desmidieæ," published in 1848, since which time the conclusions he arrived at have been generally accepted by men of science. The result of his researches leaves us little doubt but that their proper place is under the vegetable kingdom. Like M. Meyen he discovered the presence of starch in the cells ; and, what is of even more importance, proved that under the influence of light they give out oxygen, a fact of itself almost convincing. Much stress has been laid upon the fact of some species being endowed with an active motion; but, as we have before observed, a great variety of algæ produce this phenomenon. What may be the cause we are not at present prepared to say, as it is still a debateable point, some contending that it is due to ciliary action, others to a spontaneous movement of the enclosed zoospores.

Their increase takes place by conjugation and multiplication. As we have spoken of conjugation in our previous article we may as well explain the process. Two cells are found to approach each other, when the outer cell wall of each splits and throws a connecting tube out, which thus joins them together ; through this tube the contents of one cell is poured into the other, where, mixing with the endochrome of the receiving cell, it forms a body called sporangium ; and this is afterwards set free by the breaking up of the parent cell. Multiplication has been observed to take place in *Cosmarium, Pediastrum*, and others. By this process the endochrome divides, and a quantity of granular particles are set free, these are called gonidia ; passing through the cell wall they develope into perfect frustules. Mr. Berkeley* in his work on "Cryptogamic Botany" gives an excellent account of the mode of increase, which we cannot do better than quote. He says :—"All agree in their increase by the partition of the mother cell accompanied by the growth of two new half cells; in many cases the division goes no further, but each half with its new lobe grows into a perfect whole and again divides. But this is by no means the case with all, for the two original halves do not always separate, but remain united with their progeny for many generations, thus forming a filiform body, in which the two primary halves are at either extremity and the youngest in the middle of the thread. Nor is the connection always confined to development in a straight line. In those species which divide obliquely an orbicular frond is sometimes found, as in *Pediastrum*, though seldom one of any remarkable size. The fronds, if they may be so called, or cells, differ in almost every conceivable way from a right line, parrallelogram, or curved bow, to a deeply pinnate or strongly serrated thread. They are for the most part strongly constricted, so as to appear like two distinct cells; but this is by no means universal, for in *Closterium* there is no greater constriction than in many species of *Conferva*. They are either smooth, finely granulated, verrucose, or beset with forked spines, insomuch that nothing can be more curious than the varied outlines which they present under the

* "Introduction to Cryptogamic Botany," by the Rev. M. J. Berkeley, M.A., F.L.S. (London : Bailliere), pp. 120-1-2.

microscope. Besides the spines in the genus *Xanthidium*, there is in the centre of each half cell on either side a curious tubercle, the edge of which is sometimes granulated, but whether it has any special function or not is unknown. Mr. Ralfs doubts whether the increase of the fronds by separation can be called propagation; but if it be considered in the following way, it will be clear, I think, that it is properly a propagation, though not a fructification. Supposing the two original lobes to be called A, the second B, the third C, and so on, the mother frond will be represented by A A, the second by A B, B A, the third by A C, C B, B C, C A, of which C B, B C have no part of the original frond, and may therefore be considered as entirely new individuals. Another mode of increase is from the swarming of the grains of the endochrome, which become individualised as in other *algæ*, and so give rise to a new generation. These bodies are figured with filiform appendages by Braun in *Pediastrum granulatum*. But besides these modes of propagation there is another, which consists in the union of two contiguous vesicles, in consequence of which a single spore is formed in the connecting tube. These spores are mostly globular, but like the fronds themselves exhibit great difference of surface, so that apart from the matrix they may be taken for the sporidia of truffles, or other heterogeneous bodies. In many cases they have no resemblance whatever to the parent frond, and though mixed with them would never be suspected to have a common origin, until the union of two vesicles and consequent spore should be observed. These, however, when once formed are propagated by division, exactly after the fashion of the ordinary cells, and in the third generation acquire their normal form, which they may continue to propagate for years without even forming a true spore."

Of their distribution there is little to be said, as we find them almost exclusively confined to Europe, their central point being the South of England, from which point the farther south we go the more the species appear to diminish in number. Some few have been found in the United States, and been described by Bailey, *Anthrodesmus tœnia* being among the number; he has also detected cells of *Closterium* and *Euastrum* in fossil marls of New Hampshire, New York, and in the marl of Scotchtown below the *Mastodon giganteus*. Traces of *Closterium* have been observed in the valuable Himalayan collections of Drs. Hooker and Thompson. We may mention that spores have been found by Mantell in the grey chalk of Folkestone, and a few species have been found in the fossil state preserved in flint and other transparent minerals.

Closterium, Euastrum, Micrasterias, &c., are found as a gelatinous stratum at the bottom on stems of water plants and on stones. *Staurastrum, Pediastrum,* and most of the smaller species float on the top of the water, forming a thin film, or gather like a dirty looking cloud round water plants. They will be found chiefly where there is an admixture of peat and in clear pools better than in running streams, where the water is turbid and muddy. The latter species are rare in limestone countries; but some genera, as *Scenedesmus*, are more common in such districts than elsewhere. A host of forms may be seen by simply exposing a glass of water to the influence of light. Mr. Nave in his little work on "The Collection of Algæ," from which we have before quoted, says:— "They are to be looked for in bogs, ditches, and ponds lying in bleak exposed situations, rarely in shady woods, some as *Closterium* among the filaments of the Oscillatoriæ and Confervæ, others, such as *Palmaglœa macrocca*, on damp moss or the surface of wet rocks and cliffs. Boggy heaths, however, are the spots where they mostly congregate, especially where Sphagnum abounds. Swampy places, and patches of water scattered over the bog, or shallow drains cut through it, all afford a rich supply of *Desmidiaceæ*. They also love ditches and holes in which, though the water itself is pure, the water is of a clayey nature; there they often vegetate in such abundance as to cover the bottom with a dense green film."

A few remarks on some of the chief characteristics of the various species may not be without interest to the reader. Commencing with *Closterium*, which is a large family, we find that they assume a lunate form and are distinguished for their complete outline, which is found to be either straight or arcuate. Many are remarkable for the way in which the cells are marked with a close set longitudinal striæ. In the large round space at the end of the cell and along the concave and convex edges a curious whirling movement of molecules may be seen, but this requires a power of some three hundred diameters. They are found principally on moors and other exposed situations, their little ovals being sometimes joined together. *Euastrum* consists of two notched halves of a bright green colour, having spots of a darker shade. "The compressed and deeply constricted cells," says Dr. Hogg[*], "offer most favourable opportunities for ascertaining the manner of their division, for although the frond is really a single cell, yet this cell in all its stages appears like two, the segments being always distinct even from its commencement. As the connecting portion is so small, and necessarily produces the new segments, which cannot arise from a broader base than its opening, these are at first very minute, though they rapidly increase in size. The segments are separated by the elongation of the connecting tube, which is converted into two roundish hyaline lobules. These lobules increase in size, acquire colour, and gradually put on the appearance of the old portions. Of course as they increase the original segments are pushed further asunder, and at length are disconnected, each taking with it a new segment to supply the place of that from which it is separated. It is curious to trace the progressive development of the new portions. At first they are devoid of colour and have much the appearance of condensed gelatine, but as they increase in size the internal fluid acquires a green tint, which is at first very faint, but soon becomes darker; at length it assumes a granular state. At the same time, the new segments increase in size and obtain their normal figure." *Staurastrum* is of a stellate or cruciform shape, with an excellently defined central division or fissure. It is curiously sup-

---

[*] "The Microscope," by Dr. Jabez Hogg (London: Routledge, 1867), p. 281.

plied with arms, as though for the purpose of seizing its prey. *Pediastrum* is in shape and general appearance like *Staurastrum*, several cells are found united, forming a globular mass. *Anthrodesmus* is also the same shape as the two preceding. *Xanthidium* also stellate or cruciform, but is armed with spines, these spines and processes in their course of formation making their appearance last. *Cosmarium* is seen to glisten as though covered with thousands of minute gems. In *Desmidium* many of the cells are found attached together, giving them the appearance of a long chain, or, as it has been said, resembling a tapeworm. In *Scenedesmus* several cells are united, and the two last halves are furnished with horns. *Micrasterias* is finely cut and toothed, and is of a disc form. On *Syndaridea* Mr. Jenner has found traces of Striæ, and Mr. Bowerbank has also found the same on *Tiercesias*. It has been noticed that *Eutospeira* leads directly to Spirotœmia, a beautiful member of this family.

NEW SPECIES OF DIATOMACEÆ.

Having studied the Diatomaceæ for many years, I am convinced that a large proportion of the new genera and species obtained from dredgings or deposits have no claim to that distinction; no satisfactory generic or specific characters can be deduced from form procured from such sources. It is also a great error to suppose that the locality from whence a dredging is obtained is the habitat of the forms found in it. In the majority of instances the valves only are found, perhaps only one, perhaps only a fragment. The fact that only one valve or frustule is found, is of itself sufficient evidence that we do not know its habitat (it may be a few yards off or a thousand miles away). The living diatom multiplies with great rapidity; if we found its true habitat, it would occur in myriads and not as a rare or unique specimen. The forms found in dredgings, &c., have probably been deposited by the decay of animal and vegetable matter, as Noctilucæ, Ascidians, mollusks, seaweed, &c., and brought there by ocean currents from far distant localities; or it may even happen that they have been washed out of some diatomaceous deposit by river action, and carried forward to the ocean, and at last deposited amongst the *débris* of recent species. I will venture to observe that the publication of isolated and imperfect specimens not only do not advance our knowledge, but on the contrary, are an hindrance to the study of these minute forms, and it would be far better to keep all such in an obscure corner of the cabinet or throw them into the fire, than publish them with crude and imperfect characters. A far greater service would be rendered to the study of minute forms of organic life, if the extent of variation in one single species was made the subject of examination than the publishing a score of rare species.—*Frederick R. Kitton in Quarterly Journal of Microscopical Science.*

Meetings of Learned Societies.

ENTOMOLOGICAL SOCIETY.

At the meeting held December 2—Sir John Lubbock, Bart., President, in the chair—Mr. Pascoe exhibited three preserved species of Longicorn beetles, from India, Java, and Sumatra, but which appeared rather to represent local varieties of the Lamia (Thysia) Wallichii of Hope. Professor Westwood exhibited the unique British specimen of Serropalpus striatus taken some years ago by Mr. Plant at Leicester, also the small globose mud nest of Eumenes coarctata, found near Reigate, being the only British representative of this very numerous genus of solitary wasps. Mr. Smith stated that he had occasionally found the nests in the neighbourhood of Weybridge, the New Forest, etc. He also exhibited a piece of Willow from Mitcham, in which there were not fewer than ten burrows of the leaf-cutter bee, Megachile Willughbiellâ, in close proximity, each burrow containing a number of cells. He had observed that the cells were not uniformly formed of a single kind of leaf, but that sometimes the outer layers of the case were of green Rose leaves, the inner being composed of those of the flowers of Geranium, Poppy, or Centaurea. Mr. Pascoe exhibited and described five new genera of exotic Coleoptera, belonging to different families, natives of Lake N'gami, Ceylon, Sumatra, and Penang. Mr. Truman read a paper "On some Undescribed Species of South African Butterflies, including a New Genus of Lycænidæ," to which the name of Delonura was applied, its nearest ally being the New World genus Eumenia. One of the most interesting of the new species was a Papilio, the male of which resembles the well-known P. Boisduvallianus, whilst the female closely resembles Danais Eucheria. He also suggested that the well-known P. merope, of which males only had been taken in Africa, was the male of the Papilio ceneus, which also resembles a Danais, although it was admitted that in Madagascar the female of P. merope precisely resembles the male, thus exhibiting a curious case of dimorphism in the female sex.

On January 6—Sir J. Lubbock, Bart., President, in the chair—Messrs. S. Barton and G. A. J. Rothney, Professor A. Newton, and Baron Edgar von Harold, were elected Members. The Rev. D. C. Timins exhibited a specimen of *Charaxes Jasius*, bred at Winchelsea, and three varieties of *Argynnis Lathonia*, captured near Boulogne. Mr. F. Smith exhibited two specimens of a wasp captured at Penzance; they belonged to the genus Polistes, and appeared to be intermediate between the North American *P. biguttatus* and the Brazilian *P. versicolor*. Mr. M'Lachlan exhibited a Trichopterous insect new to Britain, *Neuronia clathrata*, of Kolenati, captured at Bishop's Wood, Staffordshire, by Mr. Chappell. The following papers were read:—"Remarks on Mr. A. R. Wallace's Catalogue of Eastern Pieridæ," by Mr. W. C. Hewitson; "On Burmeisteria, a new genus of Melolonthidæ," by Mr. F. Schickendantz; and "On the 'Borer' pest in the Coffee Districts of Southern India," by the Rev. G. Richter. The "borer" was exhibited, and proved to be a species of Clytus.

ZOOLOGICAL SOCIETY.

On the 28th of November—J. Gould, Esq., vice-president, in the chair—Mr. P. L. Sclater read notes upon some recent additions to the Society's Menagerie, and invited particular attention to a specimen of a rare Australian parrot (*Geopsittacus occidentalis*, Gould), forwarded to the society by Dr. F. Mueller, of Melbourne. An extract was read from a letter addressed to the Secretary by Captain J. M. Dow, announcing that he had procured for the society a young living specimen of the newly-discovered Tapir of Panama (*Tapirus Bairdi*), and would shortly forward it to Europe. Prof. Owen communicated two memoirs on the extinct birds of the genus Dinornis of New Zealand, forming the eleventh and twelfth of his series of papers on this subject. These communications contained a description of the integuments of the sole and tendons of a toe of the foot of *Dinornis robustus*, and a description of the femur, tibia, and metatarsus of *Dinornis maximus*. Mr. G. D. Rowley read a paper upon the Eggs of the extinct genus Æpyornis of Madagascar. Dr. W. Baird communicated a monograph of the species of worms belonging to the sub-class Gephyrea; with a notice of such species as are contained in the collection of the British Museum. A communication was read from Mr. S. F. Day on some new or imperfectly known Fishes of the Madras Presidency.—A communication was read from Mr. G. Krefft, containing descriptions of some new Australian fresh-water fishes. A communication was read from Mr. J. Y. Johnson, containing a description of a new genus, and a new species of Macrourous Decapod Crustaceans, belonging to the family Peneidæ, discovered at Madeira. These were proposed to be called *Funchalia Woodwardi* and *Penæus Edwardsianus*. A communication was read from Capt. T. Hutton on the geographical range of *Semnopithecus entellus* in India. Dr. J. S. Bowerbank read a paper on *Hyalonema Lusitanicum*, Bocage. Dr. Bowerbank came to the conclusion from microscopical examination that this species, which had lately been elevated to the rank of a genus by Dr. Gray, and proposed to be called Hyalothrix, was not even specifically distinct from *H. mirabile* of Japan. Mr. G. F. Angas communicated the second part of a list of species of marine mollusca found in Port Jackson Harbour and on the adjacent coast of New South Wales, completing a former paper on this subject; and descriptions of a new genus and some new species of marine mollusca from Port Jackson, New South Wales. A communication was read from Messrs. H. Adams and G. F. Angas, containing the description of a new species of land-shell belonging to the genus Cœliaxis.

On December 12—Dr. J. E. Gray, vice-president, in the chair—an extract was read from a letter received from Dr. J. Kirk, relating to some of the animals of Zanzibar. Dr. Peters communicated a note on the question of the Homology of the quadrate bone in the class Aves, in which he controverted the view recently maintained by Professor Huxley as to its supposed correspondence with the *incus* in the mammalia The Secretary called the attention of the meeting to the fact of an Eland, bred in this country, having been exhibited by Lord Hill at the Show of the Smithfield Club—being the first instance of the introduction of this animal to the meat-markets of Europe. Mr. W. H. Flower read some notes on the anatomy of *Hyomoschus aquaticus*, founded on a specimen of this mammal recently deceased in the Society's Menagerie. Mr. St. George Mivart read some additional notes on the Osteology of the Lemuridæ, in continuation of a former communication on this subject. Dr. J. Hector communicated a notice of the discovery of an egg of the Great Moa (*Dinornis gigantea*), containing an embryo, found in the province of Otago, New Zealand, at a depth of about two feet below the surface. Dr. J. E. Gray read some notes on the mollusks of the genus Catillus, including the description of two new allied genera of this group; he also communicated a description of a new Spider Monkey discovered on the affluents of the Peruvian Amazon, by Mr. E. Bartlett, and proposed to be called *Ateles Bartletti*; and of a new species of Ampullaria from Sierra Leone, proposed to be called *A. ornata*. Messrs. P. L. Sclater and O. Salvin communicated a list of Birds collected at Pebas, Upper Amazon, by Mr. J. Hauxwell, with notes and descriptions of new species. Mr. Hauxwell's collection was stated to have contained 135 species, four of which were considered to have been hitherto undescribed. They also communicated a list of the first collection of Birds formed by Mr. H. Whitely, jun., in South-Western Peru, in the neighbourhood of Lima and Arequipa. The series consisted of upwards of fifty species, many of which were of great interest. Mr. J. Gould read a note on the Australian genus Climacteris, including the description of a new species of the genus proposed to be called *C. pyrrhonota*. Dr. J. E. Gray made some observations upon Dr. Bowerbank's paper on *Hyalonema Lusitanicum*, read at the last meeting, maintaining the accuracy of his own views as to its being generically different from *H. mirabile;* and on the skins and skeletons of the Rhinoceroses in the British Museum. Amongst these Dr. Gray believed that he had detected a skull belonging to a species hitherto undescribed, which he proposed to call *Rhinoceros simocephalus*.

ANTHROPOLOGICAL SOCIETY.

On the 17th December Mr. Wilmot Rose, C.E., read a paper on the "Danish Stone Age." He based his conclusions on those of the Danish professors at Copenhagen. Danish history can be traced 3,000 years at least, when no implements but those of bone, wood, or stone were used. He considered that the trees were felled by alternating incisions in them with stone axes, and the application of fire. The canoes were hollowed out in this way. He expressed a firm belief in the three periods, stone and bone, bronze, and, lastly, iron; and that the rough and polished stones were contemporary, and found at all depths. He said that only three specimens in his collection had been bought of dealers. Colonel Lane Fox next read a paper "On the Resemblance between certain Danish and Irish Flint Weapons." He described the Danish encampments of Sussex, Newhaven, Mount Cabon, and Seaford, which was Roman, describing and exhibiting the worked flints found there. He had not found any near Brighton. The largest of these encampments was Cissbury; there was no foundation for the report that it was a Roman name, but he considered it derived from Cissa, a Saxon general. The pits found here he thought with Camden were huts; but Mr. Turner, in a paper read before the Sussex Archæological Society, said they were used for religious purposes. Colonel Fox had found at Highdown a bronze dagger of peculiar form; ten inches long, accompanied by an oval skull. The discussion of the two papers was taken together. Mr. Higgins referred to the supposed mode of boring the axe-holes, with leather plugs, water and sand; that the so-called shuttles, of which several were exhibited, were not of the Stone Age, and he thought from the universal diffusion of stone weapons that much could not be gathered ethnologically from them. Mr. Peto said he had seen a tree found in a bog, felled with a stone axe, and that the celts were used as charms, being boiled to cure toothache, which other speakers afterwards confirmed. Mr. Dendy, by a curious anachronism, said the Romans adapted the Saxon encampments, on which he was sharply attacked by Mr. Higgins. Mr. Peto said he believed Teutons inhabited England before the Romans. Mr. Rose said that a miller he knew buried his oak chest of celts, which if found two hundred years later might occasion confusion. The Rev. D. Heath had seen bushels of arrowheads on the field of Marathon exactly like the Danish flints exhibited. We are glad to hear that the "Rose collection" will remain on view some weeks longer.

On December 31st, 1867—Dr. Charnock in the chair—the evening was devoted to local Secretaries' reports. Mr. Higgins read a letter from Mr. Alexis Fitz-Jenco, local secretary for Moscow. He had gone to Helingsford and measured the large number of 100 Fins' skulls, &c. Mr. Higgins said that Retsius had always considered Fin crania puzzling. Mr. Fitz-Jenco had remarked the collection of 15,000 stone weapons at Stockholm. Mr. H. next read a letter from Mr. Murray from Australia, who had been struck by the resemblance between Northumbrian inscribed rocks and some aboriginal ones lately discovered in Australia; that he considered the report of the non-fecundity of native half-breeds fallacious, and attributed their infrequency to a custom of murdering them which he had lately discovered. A party of natives had carried away eleven half-breed boys, murdered them and burnt their bodies. This was the first instance he had heard of; notwithstanding which he thought the aborigines mild, gentle, and affectionate. In discussing this letter Mr. Lewis said that these Northumbrian inscriptions had been compared to the tattooing on New Zealanders. Mr. Groom-Napier read his local secretary's report on Anthropological matters recently collected—the first entitled "Notes on two unusually gifted Mulattresses," these had received European education. One was extremely steady, conscientious, highly moral and faithful as a friend, with much prudence and economic talent. The other was rarely gifted in music, drawing, modelling, languages, and science, surpassing even accomplished Europeans. He quoted some facts related to him on the characters of coloured people by a Mr. Kirk. Next a letter from Mr. Walker was read from the Gaboon: he had seen red-haired Negroes, and said that no gold ornaments were made on the Gaboon. Mr. Groom-Napier next made some remarks on the state of Anthropological collections at Bristol, and mentioned some remarkable skulls there. He also gave an account of one of the few survivors.

GEOGRAPHICAL SOCIETY.

December 9—Sir R. I. Murchison, Bart., President, in the chair—the following gentlemen were elected Fellows:—Lieut. F. S. De Carteret Bisson, Messrs. J. Chapman, A. H. Knight, W. M'Arthur, Hon. J. M'Lean, and R. Ramsden, M.A. The President read two letters concerning Dr. Livingstone, which had been received from Dr. Kirk, of Zanzibar, since the last meeting. They were respectively eleven and thirteen days later, and communicated the results of the visit of Dr. Kirk and the Consul to the mainland of Africa, where they went to question other members of the traders' caravan which had fallen in with the white traveller in the interior. The letters confirm fully the impression previously conveyed, that the traveller in the interior is no other than Dr. Livingstone. The following paper was read: "Sketch of a Journey from Canton to Hankow," by Mr. A. S. Bickmore.

ROYAL MICROSCOPICAL SOCIETY.

At the meeting of this society on the 11th December—James Glaisher, Esq., F.R.S., president, in the chair—a very interesting paper "On the Pedicellariæ of the Cidaridæ" was read by Charles Stewart, Esq., M.R.C.S. These singular organs are found in considerable numbers, and in a variety of shapes, amongst the spines of the *Cidaridæ* and *Echinidæ*. They consist of a head composed of three jawlike pieces supported on a long flexible stem, and may be seen waving their heads about in all directions, and snapping their jaws. The author of the paper, like other naturalists, finds it difficult to assign any special function to them. Mr. Hogg mentioned that he had seen them seize food and pass it from one to another to the mouth of the animal. Mr. Stewart did not think that this was the purpose for which they were formed, and thought that although they might grasp an object floating within their reach, they had not been seen by any one but Mr. Hogg to pass food to each other. He instanced the pedicellariæ of the starfishes, which are partially imbedded in the skin, and have no stalks, and could therefore do no more than seize and hold passing prey. It is possible that they may be of use as scavengers to remove offensive matter, or parasitic growth. Papers were also read by H. J. Slack, Esq., F.G.S., "On a Microscopic Ferment found in Red French Wine;" by J. G. Tatem, Esq., "On a New Species of Vorticella," and by Edwin T. Newton, Esq., "On the Anatomical Differences observed in some Species of the Helices and Limaces." Amongst the presents announced was a two-thirds object-glass, by Wray. The Rev. J. B. Reade remarked concerning it that he had carefully examined it with Dr. Millar and Mr. Lee, and that with fifty degrees of angular aperture it gave an admirably flat field, and such excellent definition that it showed distinctly the markings of *Navicula quadratum*, and of the coarser valves of *N. angulatum*. Thirty gentlemen were elected Fellows of the society.

ETHNOLOGICAL SOCIETY.

At this meeting Mr. H. Howorth's paper on the "Origin of the Norsemen" was read. An attempt to answer the inquiry as to who were these relentless invaders of Great Britain and Ireland in the interval between A.D. 760 and 800, is one well worthy the attention of ethnologists, and unassisted by contemporary history, the difficulty is vastly increased of answering such a query. Classical authors mention, however, many people whose history it is possible to trace, who bear a physical resemblance to these red-haired sea rovers, and subsequent Byzantine writers, while they do not offer a direct solution to the inquirer, at least help in some degree to clear up the cloud of mystery connected with the Scandinavian settlers in Northern Europe in the collections of antiquities contained in the several museums of Europe. However, there are of these Danish pirates remains sufficient to warrant us in tracing their starting-point somewhere on the Northern shores of the Caspian sea. The ornaments in metal, the peculiar weapons and the coins bearing cuniform inscriptions everywhere found, together with the well-known pillar records engraved with Runes, enable us to identify this strange race. The paper was reviewed at great length and with considerable ability by Lord Strangford, who brought to bear on this subject much of that skill he has always shown in such investigations as the present. He maintained that philosophical investigations of the relations of language were, after all, of inestimable advantage in the investigation of ethnological questions like that under review; and while he could not agree in many of the arguments put forward by the writer, he congratulated the society in possessing a paper so rich in illustration and so full of learned research.

On Jan. 19th, Mr. Crawfurd, president, in the chair. A paper by Mr. Bickmore, on "The Ainos," was read. The author, during a three years' journey in the Eastern Seas and China, as far as Sumatra, and along the banks of the Amur, fell in with many of these curious people in the northern islands of Japan. Nothing particularly new respecting these people has been added to our knowledge of the Aino race, and the interest attaching to the paper arose from the fact that he had conversed with many individuals, through a Japanese interpreter who accompanied him. He measured many of the Ainos he saw, and found that, although much smaller in person than the generality of the dominant Japanese—the tallest Aino he saw being 5ft. 2in.—yet their open countenances and robust and powerful chests contrasted favourably with the effeminate and subtle-looking Japanese. From their fairer complexion, and the fact of their thick beards, dense hair on their heads, and their generally hairy persons, the author concluded they were not of the Chinese or Japanese race, but were totally distinct. A survey of the history of the people and their country was given, and Sir R. Murchison stated that the author, a pupil of Agassiz, was a keen observer and a man of great promise. Lord Strangford also stated that he had met Mr. Bickmore when in England, and testified to his great ability as an observer. We shall look for the account of his visit to Sumatra with interest.—Mr. Crawfurd read his paper on the plants yielding textile materials, and those contributing colouring matter for staining purposes. From the author's great experience in the languages and knowledge of the productions in Eastern countries, a subject of this nature was sure to be of value; and to those interested in the history of flax, cotton, nettle, and other vegetables producing fibre for weaving, or who desire to know from whence come the various dye stuffs, and their use in ancient times, this paper will be of real value. Dr. R. Brown exhibited and made some remarks on a series of skulls he had brought from Vancouver Island. The first showed the ordinary artificial flattening of the forehead, and partially of the occiput, practised among all the coast tribes of Indians, from 44 deg. N. long. to 53 deg. N. lat. The second was a fine specimen of the conical distortion, practised only by the women of the Koskeemos, a small tribe inhabiting the shore of the Quatseeno Sound, on the north-west coast of the island. The skull exhibited was stated to be that of the woman figured in Mayne's "Four Years in British Columbia" (1863). The next a skull of a Sheshaaht Indian slave woman, whose head, on account of her servile birth, had not been distorted in any way. In answer to queries by Sir R. Murchison and the president, he stated that he was fully of belief that these distortions in no way affected the intellect of the individuals operated on, the brain being merely thrown into another portion of the cranium, but not injured or destroyed. The head of the child was at birth bandaged into this *outre* form, which was likened, not inaptly, though somewhat grimly, to a bony chignon.

BOTANICAL SOCIETY OF EDINBURGH.

The first meeting of the 32nd session was held in the Society's rooms on Thursday, November 14th, Isaac Anderson-Henry, Esq., President, in the chair. The following communications were read:—I. "Observations on New Zealand Plants," by Dr. Lauder Lindsay. In this paper the author refers exclusively to the flowering plants of Otago, which are for the most part illustrative of the variations of the individual from the characters of the species, in relation, more particularly, to the limitation or definition of species. He also gives notes regarding their geographical distribution and economical applications, and their Maori and settlers' names.—II. "Letter from Dr. Robert O. Cunningham, H.M.S. *Nassau*, Rio de Janiero, to Professor Balfour." We reached the Strait of Magellan on the 21st of December, and, with the exception of a short trip to the Falkland Islands to take in provisions and coal, remained there till the 12th of June, when we moved northwards, as the daily increasing severity of the climate necessitated a suspension of surveying operations for the season. Some of the Strait plants were identical with old friends at home. Many of them were species new to me, and a considerable number belonged to genera which I had never a previous opportunity of examining. As examples of British plants that I met with in the Strait, I may instance Sisymbrium Sophia, Serastium arvense, Apium graveolens, Armeria maritima, Galium Aparine

Taraxacum Dens leonis, var. lævigatum, Primula farinosa, var. magellanica, Hippuris vulgaris, Cystopteris fragilis, and Botrychium Lunaria. Most of these plants occur in tolerable abundance, Apium graveolens very copiously indeed. Hippuris vulgaris I have only obtained in one locality as yet—viz., a small stream running into Oazy Harbour on the Patagonian side of the Strait. I believe the only other recorded locality in the Strait is Port Famine, where Captain King procured it. Cystopteris fragilis is common in parts of the woods. Botrychium Lunaria, which Hooker mentions on the authority of Banks and Solander as occurring at Good Success Bay, in the South of Fuegia, I found three specimens of at the entrance of Oazy Harbour. Several of the Algæ are also, I believe, indentical with British species. Thus Codium tomentosum is common. I have found this alga also in abundance in the Harbour of Rio de Janeiro. As some of the plants of the Strait that interested me most, I may mention Calceolaria plantaginea and C. nana, Bolax Glebaria, the Myzodendrons, which are so abundant on the Fagi, Codonorchis Lessonii, Chloræa magellanica, Embothrium coccineum, Sisyrinchium filiforme, Myrtus Nummularia, Fuchsia coccinea, Callixene marginata, Philesia, Cruxifolia and Cyttaria Darwinii. The Myrtus, Callixene, Philesia, and Fuchsia were met with at Port Gallant on our cruise to the westward with the Zealous. I was charmed with the Fuchsia and the Philesia, and realized how much more I valued their exquisite beauty as they occurred in the Strait of Magellan than I would have done had I encountered them at a place like Rio, where there is such a prodigality of splendid flowers. The Callixene is also a lovely little thing, and deliciously sweet. I obtained specimens of it and Myrtus Nummularia, also at the Falkland Islands, where fauna and flora are very much the same as those of the Strait. One thing, however, struck me, and that was, that certain species which I saw at the Falklands I found in the damp woody districts of the Strait, not in the eastern district, which is so much more allied to the Falklands in its general characters. In addition to Cystopteris fragilis and Botrychium Lunaria, I obtained specimens of seven other species of Ferns—to wit, two species of Hymenophyllum, Aspidium mohrioides, Asplenium magellanicum, a Gleichenia (I believe G. acutifolia), Lomaria alpina, and Lomaria magellanica. The latter enjoys a wide range, and appears subject to considerable variation. I have obtained specimens of it at Maldonado, the Falkland Islands, and at Port Gallant, and have seen Brazilian specimens of what I believe to be the same plant. At the Falkland Islands I saw no specimens with a caudex, but some of those at Port Gallant had a straight one about 2 feet high. Among the fungi that occurred to me were species of Agraricus (the common mushroom grows abundantly in many localities, on both sides of the Strait) Polyporous, Tremella, Clavaria, Geastrum, &c. I got a good many fine lichens, and expect to get many more in succeeding seasons. We arrived at Rio on the 1st of July, and expect to leave it in the course of a few days for the Strait, calling at Monte Video on our way. I hope while we are there to get up the river to Buenos Ayres to see Burmeister and the museum. I have enjoyed the three months we have spent here very much, but am very glad at the prospect of our return to the Strait, as the climate here is very enervating. The country is, however, splendid beyond description. As regards plants I have been specially struck with the great variety and profusion of palms and ferns, and my attention was greatly arrested at first by the Lygodia, and other twining ferns, so different in habit from our British Ferns.—III. Notice of Mussana Bark (Albizzia anthelmintica) from Abyssinia, by Henry Hunter Calvert, British Vice-Consul, Alexandria. Communicated by Professor Balfour. The bark has the reputation in Abyssinia and Senaar of being a specific as a tænifuge, for which purpose 2 to 4 oz. powdered are made into an electuary with honey. —IV. Extracts from Botanical Correspondence. Communicated by Mr. Sadler. 1. From Mr. Robert Brown, of the Greenland Scientific Expedition.—I have made, in little more than two months, a collection of Greenland plants amounting to more than 5000 specimens, including a fine lot of mosses (in fruit) lichens, hepaticæ, a few fungi, and algæ, marine and fresh water. In addition to these I made a good collection of skulls, skeletons, &c., of seals and whales and birds, fishes, insects, annelidæ, mollusca, echinodermata, zoophytes, &c., and a large collection of diatomaceous gatherings. We have also brought home about a boat-load of fossil plants, with observations and sections of the deposits. In addition to this I have made several hundred astronomical observations for the latitude and longitude of the places we visited. 2. From Mr. J. F. Robinson, Frodsham.—Mr. R. says :—"This summer at Oakmere, on Delamere Forest, I found the Calamagrostis stricta in tolerable abundance on the part of boggy ground nearest the Abbey Arms Hotel. Two other interesting species were also plentiful, Lycopodium inundatum, and Utricularia minor. This place (I mean the bog adjoining the Mere) is extremely rich in muscological rarities ; amongst others the following occur :—Sphagnum cymbifolium, S. compactum, S. molluscum, S. cuspidatum, Dicranum Schraderi, Campylopus brevipilus, Atrichum crispum, Polytrichum gracile, and Hypnum Schreberi ; near the Abbey Arms, by the roadside, Saponaria officinalis is to be found sparingly, perhaps not truly wild. Claytonia alsinoides will, I think, soon be a naturalised British plant, for this season I found it plentifully in a little wood by the River Mersey, at Ince, Cheshire. I venture no opinion as to how it reached this wood ; it has certainly the appearance of having been there for some years. About two years ago the Anacharis Alsinastrum first made its appearance in our marshes at Frodsham, now it is a sad pest, and will cause much inconvenience to the landholders, if not severe losses. It is in such quantity that in some cases the ditches overflow the roads. In one ditch I have noticed efforts being made to eradicate it, but without the slightest success hitherto. I have of late paid a little attention to Utricularia vulgaris, which is not uncommon in our marsh ditches. In some of the places where it flowered profusely a few years ago, it appeared to be lost, and might be looked for in vain. This was owing, no doubt, to the ditches being partly filled with vegetation. Now that they have been "ditched"—the word used in Cheshire for cleansed—it has again appeared as abundantly as in former years. An interesting question to ask is, how has it lived or existed during these intervening years? as most, if not all, the vegetation in the ditch was in a state of decay—in fact, not unlike a bog or swamp. The beautiful little Ranunculus circinatus, Sibthorp, is also plentiful hereabouts, flowering only at the end of June or beginning of July, long after most of the other Batrachian Ranunculi have flowered. 3. From Mr. Alexander Buchan, enclosing specimens of Centunculus minimus and Radiola Millegrana, both gathered in August last a few yards from high-water mark between the blue rock and the sea, Glen Sannox, Arran. 4. From Mr. Alexander Curle, Abbey Park, Melrose, recording the discovery, by Mr. Alexander Hay, Borthwick, and himself, of Goodyera repens, in a wood near Melrose, in considerable abundance.—"Miscellaneous Communications." 1. Dr. John Lowe sent specimens of double-flowered Calluna vulgaris, collected this autumn by Miss Anna Everard, near Bournemouth. Mr. M'Nab also exhibited specimens of the same collected in Aberdeenshire in 1820. 2. Mr. M'Nab laid before the meeting a longitudinal section of the stem of a Sequoia Wellingtonia, 9 feet in height, raised from seed during the spring of 1857, and which died from being transplanted to an exposed situation during the winter of 1866. The Wellingtonia, he remarked, is easily transplanted during spring, summer, or the early autumn months. The most successful period was during summer. The present specimen, along with many others, was first transplanted on 1st July, 1861. One of the remarkable features of the section now exhibited is the number of apparent woody rings, from five to ten being visible on what is well known to be an annual growth. Several of the known annual growths average, and in some cases exceed, half an inch in breadth, while in a piece of wood, direct from California, not less than twelve distinct prominent rings or markings are visible over half an inch of surface. Their closeness in the native-grown timber, as well as the intermediate rings in the home-grown specimens, is remarkable.

Linnæan Society.

December 5.—G. Bentham, Esq., President, in the chair. C. B Clarke, Esq.; F. E. Kitchener, Esq.; and the Rev. T. Powell, were elected Fellows. J. B. Flower, Esq., exhibited specimens in fruit of Garrya elliptica, ripened in a garden at Bath. F. Currey, Esq., exhibited a remarkable monstrosity of Plantago major, having the flowering spikes very much branched in a pyramidally paniculate manner, the axis and its ramifications being branched. It had been found by Mr. G. B. Wollaston, at Compton, in Sussex. The following papers were read:—"A Contribution to our Knowledge of Lower Annelids," by E. Ray Lankester, Esq.; communicated by G. Busk, Esq. 2. "On the Spiny Lizard, Moloch horridus," by G. A. Wilson, Esq.

On Dec. 19, G. Bentham, Esq., President, in the chair, Dr. Hooker exhibited an extensive series of Japanese Coniferæ, and made some observations thereupon, pointing out the affinity of these with Indian and North American forms. Mr. G. Maw exhibited specimens in flower of Porana racemosa, raised from seeds furnished to him by Dr. Wight. The plant was accompanied by a fossil from the tertiary beds, which was stated to have been identified by Dr. Heer with the genus Porana, but which seemed to accord better with Kydia. Mr. W. G. Smith exhibited a beautiful series of drawings of British Fungi. Mr. Ince exhibited a specimen, in spirit, of the spiny lizard of South Australia, Moloch horridus. J. Robertson, Esq., was elected a Fellow. The following papers were read:— 1. "On the true Fuchsia coccinea of Aiton," by Dr. Hooker. The true F. coccinea was shown to be a totally different species from that which is so extensively cultivated in all regions of the globe under that name. Introduced in 1788, and published in the first edition of the "Hortus Kewensis," it is now only known from living specimens in the Oxford Botanic Garden, and from dried ones taken from the Kew plant, in the Banksian and Smithian Herbaria. The true plant is figured by Salisbury, but both he and subsequent authors have confounded it with the F. magellanica of Lamarck, which is the plant figured as F. coccinea in the *Botanical Magazine*, and everywhere cultivated under that name. This latter is a common Chilian and Fuegian plant, whereas the native country of F. Coccinea is still unknown. This is of the more interest, as it bears on the question of acclimatisation. It has been stated that whereas the Fuchsia was tender, it is now comparatively hardy. The truth seems to be, that the true F. coccinea is as tender as ever it was, while the plant commonly grown under that name (F. magellanica) is much more hardy; hence the statement above referred to. 2. "Note on the Stigmatic Apparatus of Goodenoviæ," by G. Bentham, Esq. The author was led to make observations on the sexual apparatus in this order, from an observation of Mr. Darwin, that fertilisation takes place at the base of the indusium, *on the outside*. This Mr. Bentham could not understand, as in Scævola and Goodenia he had found the exterior of the indusium to be perfectly smooth, without the slightest indication of the papillose structure of stigmatic surfaces. Coming to Leschenaultia, however, a different stigmatic arrangement was found to exist, suggesting an explanation of Mr. Darwin's observation. The whole order had now been examined, and considerable diversity was found to exist in regard to the impediments to impregnation opposed by the structure of the parts, as well as in the contrivances provided for overcoming these obstacles; and the object of the present paper was to describe the differences observed, and to induce others, who may have opportunity to do so, to watch the progress of development in the living plants. 3. Continuation of "Notes on the Structure of Myrtaceæ," by G. Bentham, Esq. An elaborate memoir, passing in review the various genera of this extensive—and by the author much extended—order.

Geological Society.

Dec. 4.—R. Etheridge, Esq., in the chair.—Messrs. H. P. Stephenson, J. D. Orchard, E. Williamson, W. Carruthers, T. Parton, H. Kirkhouse, C. Evans, J. B. Safford, Major E. O. Leggatt, and A. Hamilton, were elected Fellows.—The following communications were read: "On the Graptolites of the Skiddaw Series," by Mr. H. A. Nicholson; and "On the Fossil

Corals (Madreporaria) of the West Indian Islands, Part V., Conclusion," by Mr. P. M. Duncan.

On the 18th December Sir J. Lubbock, Bart., read a paper "On the Parallel Roads of Glen Roy." He described them as extending along the sides of the mountain. He quoted the descriptions of McCulloch and Darwin, and exhibited a large diagram taken from a woodcut of the former, in which the angle of the inclination of the roads was clearly seen. He thought Chambers' account of these roads was more correct than that of McCulloch, but he (Sir John) limited himself to describing their process of formation. Sir C. Lyell said it was a question of great difficulty, and that it was forty years ago since he visited them with Dr. Buckland. Mr. Goodwin Austen, in a somewhat jocose manner, said he was misinformed when he was told that the roads were the result of human action; he thought they were water levels, and he understood Sir John to think the same. Mr. Goodwin Austen next described the formation of a temporary lake in Thibet. Dr. Collingwood next read two papers on the "Geology of Formosa." He described the position and appearance of some remarkable islands called the Tablet, Agincourt, and Pinnacle Rocks; the appearance and the mode of working of a coal mine in Formosa, and exhibited a diagram, as also of the islands named above. It was a low tunnel, a quarter of a mile in length, through which a man could not walk without stooping, and through which issued a stream of dirty water. The Kelung coal burns away very fast, and is an inferior kind of lignite. The Labuan coal was accompanied by a Dammara resin. Petroleum is found in both places. The Douay coal found in the Russian possessions was excellent, but reserved for their own vessels. The President considered it interesting that a large oyster exhibited had been found above the lignite. Mr. Gregory thought Dr. Collingwood wrong in saying that petroleum was found at Kelung, although it existed at Formosa.

January 8, Warrington Smyth, Esq., President, in the chair.—A paper was read for W. W. Stoddart, F.G.S., on "The Lower Lias of Bristol." It was illustrated by good diagrams of sections taken at Ashley Down, Montpelier, Cotham, etc. The resemblance was great between the Bristol and Glamorganshire strata; a strong current had passed through the former in the Liassic sea, of which Cotham was the centre. He described the character of the beds at some length, and thought the "Sutton Stone" series occurred here. Dr. Duncan then read a paper by C. O. Groom Napier, on the "Lower Lias of Cotham, Bedminster, and Keynsham, near Bristol." He had succeeded in obtaining upwards of ninety species at Cotham, which was as many or more as had ever been found in any one locality from the same strata. To obtain these he had broken up many tons of stone into small fragments, examined the surface of thousands of tons in blocks, and spent one hundred days in working at the spot. He described two quarries at Cotham at some length. The strata of the first were in the following descending order:—"A," clay loam, ten to fourteen inches thick. "B," thin limestone, fifteen to twenty, abounds in *Cypris* and *Chondrites*— the first plant bed. "C, D," pale blue limestone, containing a few casts. "E," *Ammonites planorbis* zone—sandy lias, with veins of quartz and sulphate of strontia. The fossils abounding here were *A. planorbis*, *A. tortilis*, *Lima gigantea*, *L. tuberculata*, and twenty-four other species, which Dr. Duncan afterwards said were many more than had been hitherto found in England, being most of the species which had been found at Luxemburgh, the small number hitherto found in England being regarded with some surprise. "F," hard, grey stone, abounding in *Ostrea liassica*. "G," beds of clay. "H," conglomerate, containing casts. "I," pale blue lias, containing eight species of *Lima*, and thirty-one other species. "K," a bed of indurated blue clay, containing *Minotis decussata* and *Perna infraliassica*. "M," the second plant bed, affording *Cypris, Cucullia Nettengiensis*. "N," a bed, like septaria, containing veins of pure sulphate of strontia. "O," the Cotham marble. "P," the Keuper marl. Another quarry, containing strata somewhat differing from the above, by the apparent development of the zone of *Angulatus*, was also described at some length; also fossils. The President spoke of the great value of the elaborate papers they had heard, and particularly of the one by Mr. Napier, and that only those resident on the spot could show that minute knowledge of detail necessary in dealing with the difficult question of the Lower Lias, on which they had heard so much, but knew so little. Perhaps the most important point connected with these two papers was, that the independent researches of the authors at Cotham had led to the conclusion that the Sutton stone was a Liassic, and not of Rhætic formation. The next paper read was by W. B. Dawkins, Esq., on the "Dentition of *Rhinoceros Etruscus*." The paper was an elaborate essay, of minute scientific detail, the dental formula of the whole group of the fossil rhinoceros, with comparative measurements, derived from all the known specimens whose position in the various geological strata to which they belong could be ascertained with sufficient accuracy, their affinities and their range in space and time. Respecting this latter arrangement of Mr. Dawkins's paper, our readers will be most interested. He stated the species *Etruscus* wandered over the Italian portion of the Pleiocene continent, along with *Elephas meridionalis, E. antiquus, Hippopotamus major*, and *R. magarhinus*, passed northwards with the great bulk of the Pleiocine fauna into France, and westwards into Spain, northwards as far as the plain, now the bed of the German Ocean; there it coexisted with the mammoth in the pre-glacial forests of the Norfolk and Suffolk shores, never living with animals fitted for a severe climate, unless the mammoth, which Mr. Falconer considered capable of enduring any climate. During the approach of the glacial period, it retreated northwards, and most probably made its last stand in Spain and Italy. No traces of its existence along with *R. tichorhinus*, or *R. leptorhinus*, of Owen, in the post-glacial period, are recorded. These, favoured by the cold, passed over the Alps as far as Rome. Lately it has been settled by the discoveries of Ceselli that the cave hyæna and cave bear, and the tichorinus and glutton established themselves in the midst of the Pleiocene fauna of Italy. The fossils of the Val d'Arno are of pre-glacial age, since they are portions of animals exclusively of a southern type; and in Italy there is no proof that the

R. Etruscus lived at the time of the irruption of the post-glacial mammals. The interesting discussion on this paper was shared in by Dr. Duncan, Mr. Charlesworth, Mr. Prestwich, and others. Mr. Napier exhibited his fine collection of Lower Lias fossils, and a skull of *Rhinoceros tichorinus*, probably the finest known. The next meeting will be on Jan. 22.

BRISTOL NATURALISTS' SOCIETY.

On Dec. 5th, 1867, Mr. Thomas Pease, V.P., in the chair. Major Austen, F.G.S., read a paper on the "Sowans of Cornwall;" the "Dunes of Norfolk;" the "Sand Hills of Holland," and the "Occurrence of Double Tides." The first three terms are synonymous. The Sowans of Cornwall attain an elevation of 60 feet. Houses are sometimes buried beneath the accumulation of sand drifted by wind, and at some future period owing to the sand shifting again, reappear. Gwithiam and Phillack are partly buried in sand. One accumulation on the baston of Upton is said to have occurred nearly a century ago, and so sudden was the irruption of sand that a large farm was overwhelmed in a moment, and the farmer and his family were obliged to get through the upper chamber window to effect their escape. In 1808 the sand shifting disclosed the farm-house, after being buried for nearly a century. Two fields are now covered to a depth of twelve feet, which a few years since were quite clear. The movement of these sandhills is best arrested by encouraging the growth of plants such as the following:—*Aurmophila arenaria* (sea-reed), *Triticum junceum* (sea wheat grass), *Hippophæ ramnoides* (sand thorn), *Kakile maritima* (sea rocket), *Salsola kali* (saltwort), and *Souchus* (sand thistle). The effect of these plants in checking the progress of the hills is soon apparent. Major Austen mentioned how the Dunes of Norfolk, between Hunstanton and Weybourne protected harbours along the coast which in many parts was yielding to the enroachments of the sea. Here also ancient villages had been overwhelmed with sand—this is brought by the wind which causes the sand to rise in clouds such as are described on the Sahara. Unless recently destroyed, a monument of these sands marks the spot where Eccles once stood; the ruined tower of the old church rears its top above the surrounding dunes, under which lie the houses which were inhabited in 1605. On tides the Major said—The observations made relative to the great tidal wave which approaches our shore twice in the day of twenty-four hours, tend to explain the double tides, by no means unfrequent on the eastern coast of Ireland; thus, when the main portion of the great tidal wave that passes to the westward and on to the North of Ireland has turned its course southward, and its retrograde movement is accelerated by a strong north-west gale, a large body of water is forced into the Irish Sea through the north channel which separates Great Britain from Ireland; but sometimes before this takes place the detached portion which passed up St. George's Channel from the south has marked high water along the eastern shores of Ireland, and has ebbed for some time before the great wave comes down from the north, after completing its boreal course. The consequence of this apparent anomaly is when the St. George's Channel current which entered from the south is nearly at half ebb-tide, the influx of the marine current from an opposite direction through the north channel, causes the tide to rise again along the shore, to the great amazement of those dwelling on the coast, who designate these double tides dead men's waves. Mr. T. G. Pouton next read a paper, "On the Alimentary canal of *Tegenaria civilis*," a house spider; and Mr. J. J. Ranson, on the Anatomy of the Actiniæ." Nov. 8th, in the geological section, Mr. W. Stoddart read a paper "On the Palæontology of the Bristol District."

BRISTOL MICROSCOPICAL SOCIETY.

On December 18th, 1867, W. S. Carpenter, President; Mr. A. E. Praeger read a notice of some points in the microscopic examination of human teeth. Dr. Hudson's paper, read October 16th, "On *Floscularia campanulata*," is only now reported. This species was well described by Dr. Dobie, in the Annals of Natural History, vol. iv., 1849. But he had left several points in its structure undetermined. It had held hitherto the anomalous position of a *Rotifer* whose rotary organ does not rotate. The five lobes of the trochal disc are fringed with fine long hairs, which are generally extended and motionless. They fringe the whole of the circumference of the disc—a fact not hitherto noticed; but as they are set in constantly (though regularly) varying directions, a large portion of them lie out of focus, and are thus by their delicacy rendered invisible when the main outline of the *Rotifer* and its principal tufts of *setæ* are distinctly seen. I have also observed that as the roots of the *setæ* approach nearer and nearer to the bottom of the cavity, between two adjoining lobes, the *setæ* themselves slope further and further away from the trochal disc, until at last those at the bottom of the cavity are actually directed backwards towards the suctorial foot.

GEOLOGISTS' ASSOCIATION, UNIVERSITY COLLEGE, LONDON.

On Thursday, December 12th, 1867, Mr. Henry Woodward delivered a lecture to this association, "On Recent and Fossil Crustacea," in which he pointed out the great interest attaching to this group, not only on account of its wide geographical distribution, but also its early appearance in geological time. He considered that the division *Articulata* was, probably, almost of as great zoological value as the sub-kingdom *Vertebrata*—that, in fact, in palæozoic times, the representatives of the *Articulata* fulfilled the functions afterwards performed by fishes and reptiles—that its members alone, of all the *Invertebrata*, possessed the powers of aërial, terrestrial, and aquatic progression, and in as great perfection as the *Vertebrata*. Mr. Woodward called special attention to those orders and families of crustacea which are of greatest interest to the palæontologist, because they are represented, in some instances, far back in time, their remains being found in lowest Palaeozoic strata. He spoke of those world-wide forms—the bivalve *Entromostraca*, to which Messrs. Parker, Jones, and Brady, have devoted so much attention; which have lived on from

Silurian times to our own—of the *Apus*-like Crustacea, *Ceratiocaris, Pellocaris, Dithyrocaris,* &c., equally persistent ; of the gigantic *Eurypterida* and their modern relatives, the *Limulidæ* (these latter appearing, by recent discoveries, to go back in time to the Upper Silurian)—of the extinct Trilobites and their relationship to *Apus* and *Branchipus*. Mr. Woodward noticed that aberrant group the *Cirripedia*, represented by the "Barnacle" and "Acorn-shell," and their relatives who prefer whales' and turtles' backs to live on, rather than the sides of ships. He mentioned that one fossil, cirripede, had been discovered as low down as the Wenlock limestone, and that the fossil shell of a species parasitic on the whale had been found in the Craig of Suffolk, where such vast quantities of the bones of fossil *Cetacea* are also met with in the Coprolite-diggings in the Crag. He then spoke of the higher forms, the Decapod *Crustacea*, represented by the crab, lobster, and prawn, and showed that the short-tailed crabs have, at present, only been found as far back in time as the Great Oolite, but that the long-tailed type go back to the Coal-measures. In conclusion he strongly recommended this group to the attention of town members, as, from the London clay, some of our finest Tertiary fossil Crustacea had been obtained ; whilst from the chalk of Kent and Sussex and the gault of Folkestone, an equally abundant harvest might be procured. Mr. Woodward's lecture was illustrated with a large series of diagrams and specimens of recent crustacea, serving to show the wonderful diversity of form and modification of the appendages which is displayed in so remarkable degree by this interesting class.

Correspondence.

[*Under this head we shall be glad to insert any letters of general interest.*]

MIGRATION OF SWALLOWS.

SIR,—Will you allow me to offer a few remarks in reply to your correspondent, Mr. S. R. Clephan, concerning the migration and probability of swallows hybernating. He asks for some striking proofs that will show that they do not hybernate.

I would, therefore, suggest that the swallow being unable to exist for any length of time when food is not to be obtained, is sufficient proof as far as my humble opinion is concerned, that they do not assume that torpid state alluded to by Mr. White, of Selbourne.

I have particularly noticed that those animals, reptiles, and insects, that are known to hybernate, if deprived of their usual amount of food even in the summer, they have the power of suiting themselves to such an emergency by immediately returning to some secluded spot, and there sleeping for some time—in some instances for months.

I will mention one. I had a bat brought me in the spring. It flew from my hand, and after flitting round the room several times, ultimately scrambled into a crevice near the ceiling. I found it was impossible to dislodge it, as there was a space between a wooden partition and the wall; but near the end of the summer, to my surprise, the little fellow came out and flew about as lively as ever. Now, had this been a swallow, it could not have survived many days.

Concerning their migration, is it not probable that the few birds that make their appearance on sunny days after the flocks have departed, are either very young or weakly birds that are on their way to the coast from some sheltered place far inland, and taking advantage of the warm sun, and those insects that have been induced by its rays to come from their hiding place to secure a good meal, gain strength, and proceed on their journey; and not as your correspondent suggests, birds returned from the other side of the ocean.

I have watched many flocks of swallows assemble, and seen them start, no doubt, for another land, and on several occasions one or two have left the bulk and returned to the building where they had congregated for some days previously, and here these solitary birds, with now and then another straggler or two, will hover round the projecting roofs, evidently searching for such insects as have been driven by the cold to seek shelter.

These birds I think we shall find are those that are seen on sunny days depending entirely upon the chance of the mild weather continuing, or their strength returning, to enable them to follow the main body. If chance goes against them, I fear they may be numbered amongst the dead which are found nearly every season when the cold suddenly sets in.

Last autumn several swallows made their appearance some time after the remainder had left us, and in localities where they had not been seen during the summer, they were to be seen in small numbers in several of the squares in London; those which I saw being very young, their tails being deficient of the two long feathers; in fact they they were scarcely fledged.

Hoping I have not trespassed inconsistently on the pages of your invaluable NOTE BOOK,

I remain, Sir, yours obediently,
J. B. WATERS.
Crowndale-road, Oakley-square.

WHAT MAKES BIRDS MIGRATE?

SIR,—I am glad to see this question "crop up" in your valuable serial—for it touches one of the most interesting arcana of nature assuredly. The fact of migration is familiar to every one, and we are now acquainted mostly with the winter and summer habitats of all migratory birds; but it is still a moot point with naturalists whether food, temperature, or nidification attract, the swallow genus especially, to Europe, each spring, or whether the tropical rains of Africa repel them thence at that season. As I have observed for many years past that the arrival of the swallows varies yearly, and that such variation is found to tally with the advent of the African rains in the Senegambia country mainly, I am led to infer that repulsion thence, and not attraction hither, causes them in spring to quit their home, Africa—especially as we know that the swallows breed in Africa all the winter, and that the heat there during our summer time is but little below that of Senegambia during that same period; and that, moreover, insect food is over-abundant in that well-wooded and well-watered African district. Want, therefore, cannot drive the swallows thence, but the deluging rains most assuredly do so—just as the cold and snow drive most of the northern migrants southwards for food alone (some sea fowl excepted) as they breed in Norway and Lapland, &c., and thus cold is their expellent thence each winter, as rain is to the warmer blooded birds—if I may so call them—from Africa each spring.

H. E. AUSTEN,
Lieut.-Colonel, and F.M.S.
St. Heliers, Jersey, Jan. 9, 1868.

RAIN WATER AS A BEVERAGE.

Sir,—In reply to the letter of your correspondent "R. W. B." in your issue for December, 1867, the expression "pure cold water" in the passage quoted, must be taken in a limited sense, inasmuch as perfectly pure water is never found in Nature, and can only be obtained by distillation, or by the direct union of its constituent gases, oxygen and hydrogen. Doubtless rain water which has fallen at a distance from human habitations or other sources of contamination approaches more nearly to purity than any other that can be obtained from natural sources, but it is by no means clear that this would be the most wholesome as a constant beverage.

Probably some of the salts contained in ordinary spring water (those, for instance, of lime and soda) are necessary either to the building up of the body or the maintaining it in health, and it is certain that the carbonic acid gas found in such water renders it far more pleasant and palatable as a drink than that which is free from such an admixture, as distilled or rain water.

The most important of the impurities contained in drinking water is organic matter—that is to say, matter which has at one time formed part of an animal or vegetable, and which has subsequently entered the putrescent stage. When this has become dissolved in water, the water may remain perfectly bright, clear, tasteless, and free from colour or smell, and yet be very injurious to drink. The progress of science, however, has discovered a remedy for this evil at once efficacious and simple, so that we are now enabled by the mere process of filtration, to remove not only the visible impurities suspended in water, but also those more dangerous substances which, though unseen, are dissolved in it.
I am, Sir, yours truly,
R. G. BLUNT.
London, December 24, 1867.

Short Notes.

ABYSSINIA.—"The road was very uneven, now ascending a steep mountain-side, now descending into a deep valley. The country was magnificent, far surpassing anything I had previously seen. The high mountains of the Scotch Highlands, covered with the fertility of the Rhine-land, would best represent it; but the vegetation was of a nature quite different from that of the Rhine, characterized as it was by the luxuriance of the tropics. Once the road skirted the side of a mountain the summit of which, raised 1,000 feet above our heads, looked down into a deep valley another thousand below our feet. On the opposite side of the valley the land rose to a similarly steep eminence, which, in one part, was connected to that on which we stood by a low chain of undulating ground, so that a pretty little stream at the bottom, like a silver thread in the dark shadow of the mountains, wound about searching for its channel. Fruitful fields hung over it thick at every curve. The hills, of secondary formation, were broken here and there into rocky chasms, through which leaped innumerable falls of water in their downward course to join the stream; and here I saw for the first time the beautiful Euphorbia, called the Kolquol, whose dark candelabra-shaped branches, tipped with bright yellow flowers, stood out in deep relief from the lighter green around. Bright flowers of every variety, most of which were unknown to me, but amongst others the familiar wild-rose, the honeysuckle, and jessamine, lent their beauty and fragrance to the scene. The whole was a perfect gem of Nature."

* * * * *

"The country through which I passed was similar in its nature to the previous part of my journey. Valleys within valleys, mountains upon mountains, constitute the physical features of Abyssinia. This is admirably shown on the road between Adowa and the eastern frontiers. A few peaks of a height varying between 8,000 and 10,000 feet, form the highest parts of the country, and seem to be a relic of a former condition of the earth. These appear also to correspond with the high masses of Gunna, Debra Tabor, Melza, and Simyen, and probably also with those of the Wolla Galla, Gojam, and other parts. The detritus of these, worn down by continual tropical rains, and perhaps, by glaciers and avalanches, appears, in process of time, to have formed a vast table-land, once covering a greater part of the country. The flat-topped mountains round Wekhni, the Guimb, Magdela, the high plateaus of Bellesa, the hill on which Mahdera Mariam is situated, that in Gojam, which Tadla Gualou has made his retreat, but more especially the portions of Abyssinia I was now traversing, are remains of this second condition of the country. But this in its turn has been abraded by the continual action of rain and atmospheric influence, till its even stratified surface has become indented with deep valleys, and these latter it is which constitute perhaps the greater part of the present Abyssinia."—*Dufton's Abyssinia*.

THE KARENS.—The officers who have been conducting the survey made in British Burmah in 1867, with a view to find the best route for a road or railway from Rangoon to Western China, passed along the Beeling valley, a part of the country occupied by Karens, who seclude themselves in the hills far away from the rest of mankind. Extremely peaceable and quiet, they were in former times much oppressed by more powerful neighbouring tribes, and still adhere to the custom then formed of hiding their villages in dense jungle. The paths to these from the main track are too slight to attract notice, and are jealously concealed; men will say you cannot go in a certain direction, rather than take you near their houses. If a village is approached, there is a general flight of the inhabitants; and on entering it the only things found are, usually, a few cocks and hens, a pig or two, and perhaps a child, who has been forgotten in the hurry of departure. Of the paths which pass near the burial-ground the people are even more careful, as to betray the resting-place of the dead is considered a heinous crime. In passing through their country the usual signs of population are absent, and the only proof of the existence of human beings is the footpaths and the clearings on the hill-sides; it is an extremely rare thing to come across any one at work in the fields. Many of the clearings, indeed, are not under actual cultivation, for ground is abandoned as soon as its fertility begins to decrease, and new jungle is cleared. Rice of an inferior quality and a little tobacco and cotton are the chief produce, grown in quantities sufficient only for local consumption, what export trade there is being confined to the betel nut. The magnificent pyengadow, or iron-wood, occurs on the hill-sides. It is no uncommon thing to see the first branch of these trees at a height of 80ft. from the ground, the stem being perfectly straight up to that point. It is unfortunate that up to the present time no means have been found of making use of this timber, which, from its hardness, effectually resists the attacks of white ants and other insects, and might be procured for any scantling. The Beeling valley is rich, and almost any cultivation would succeed in it.—*The Times*.

ANTIQUITY OF MAN.—A most singular and unexpected discovery has just occurred at Chagny (Saône-et-Loire), by some workmen engaged in digging the foundations of a railway shed. At a depth of about nine metres, in a stratum of sandy clay and ferruginous oxides, remains of proboscidians (elephants, rhinoceroses, &c.), were brought to light, comprising several back-teeth and a formidable tusk in large fragments, which, on being put together, constituted a length of seven feet. The depth at which this was found was still six metres higher than the level of the most considerable inundations of the Dheune, and in an undisturbed stratum. So far there is nothing absolutely extraordinary; but who would have thought of finding, underneath the bed containing these fossil of the tertiary period, an aqueduct of the most primitive kind and of human workmanship! Yet such was the case, the only instance of the kind on record. It is explained by M. Tremaux, who relates the circumstance, by supposing, what seems indeed to have been the fact, that the tertiary fragments above alluded to had been washed into the trench by a violent inundation, and thus filled up the aqueduct. The latter is about 80 centimetres in depth, 60 centimetres broad at the bottom, and only 40 in breadth at the upper surface. It is not easy to account for this principle of making the conduit narrower at the top than at the bottom; at all events the small dimensions of the cavity were evidently caused by the want of proper tools, as to this day the negroes of Africa, in their miserable attempts at what might be termed public works, remove as little earth as possible. However that may be, the discovery of this aqueduct does not by any means authorise us to carry the antiquity of man as far back as the tertiary petiod; for, although the aqueduct lies under a stratum of tertiary materials, this stratum does not belong to the place, but was transported thither later.

OYSTERS.—In a paper addressed to the Société d'Acclimatation M. Delidon makes some interesting remarks on the state of ostreiculture in the commune of Marennes, Charente-Inférieure, and especially on the artificial oyster-beds of the rock of Der. M. Delidon considers the current as the natural vehicle by which the spat of the oyster is carried to those places where it finds suitable materials to fix itself upon. But if no obstacles be put in the way of the current an immense quantity of the spat will be taken out to the open sea and utterly lost, and it is to avoid this that collectors are formed. The ancient Romans used to make them of timber, and this material is used to this day with perfect success, with the single drawback that timber is not very durable. Stone, sea shells, and tiles, therefore, answer much better; but even these are not unattended by annoyance, for as the oyster only travels once in its life—that is, in the state of spat, it becomes necessary, after a certain time, in order not to be at the expense of multiplying the collectors, to detach the young oyster from the stone or tile, and transfer it to the definitive oyster-bed. Now in this preliminary operation at least 25 per cent. of the young oysters are destroyed, because of the thinness of their shells, which break in the attempt of separating them from the tile or stone. This serious loss is partly owing, according to M. Delidon, to the clumsy shape of the knife with which the operation is performed; but, in a great measure, also to the circumstance that the oyster is fixed to the naked tile or stone, whereas, if the latter were coated with some substance that would resist the action of the water, but could be removed without much difficulty by mechanical means, all this loss might be obviated. M. Delidon recommends for this purpose a composition he has tried successfully for the space of two years, and consisting of plaster of Paris made up into a paste with oil.

GREAT GLACIER OF NEW ZEALAND.— The *Westland Observer* has an account of a visit paid recently by the chief officers of the Geological Department to the great glacier on the west side of Mount Cook. The foot of the glacier, which is but 13 miles from the sea, is 1,900 feet wide. Neither the glacier nor the immense field of snow which feeds it is visible from the river until within a quarter of a mile of it, when the stupendous mass of snow and ice at once breaks upon the view. Below the glacier a recent moraine extends for several hundred yards, consisting of *debris* of the rock, 20 feet deep, underlaid by ice and snow, through which considerable streams of water run, which are rendered visible in round holes, caused by the giving way of the ice and by cracks in the surface. On the Southern side there has recently been a great fracture of the ice and breach of the rock, which had fallen in immense masses. The party ascended on the northern side, where the snow or ice formed rounded hills, undisturbed by any cracks or fissures. The glacial matter is porous, and presents tolerable footing; it is of a gray colour, full of small dirt with occasional stones, which had evidently fallen from the surrounding hills. The great peculiarity of this glacier is not only its immense size but the consequent fact of its descending to so low a level—640ft. above the sea level—instead of ending, as is usually the case, at an altitude of some 3,000 or 4,000ft., close to the limit of perpetual snow, among Alpine vegetation. Here the green bush extends some thousands of feet above the glacier, on the steep sides of the range in which the glacier has cut the deep narrow gorge. Not a single Alpine plant rewarded the research of the party, and the temperature on the glacier was scarcely below that on the flat below. With some ceremony the party named it the Victoria Glacier. The height of the peak of Mount Cook is found to be 12,362ft.

MORE SAURIAN REMAINS IN THE MORAYSHIRE ROCKS.— A very interesting addition has just been made to the Elgin Museum, of a portion of a jaw of an extinct crocodile or allied saurian fish, from a sandstone quarry at Alves. It has the double row of teeth of the modern inhabitants of the Nile and Ganges—a large specimen of one of which has been placed beside it for comparison—but the teeth of the one in stone are at least double the size of the recent ones. In other respects they are exactly analogous— the two rows of teeth being similarly placed and striated alike. In the fossil specimen several of the teeth have fallen out, but their deep sockets have been preserved, and are faithfully exhibited in the stone, while the others have been well used, and are rounded on the top by the bones which the creature had crunched in its tremendous jaws when alive. This unique relic was saved by one of the quarrymen while in the act of putting it on a cart to be sent away, and noticing a curious projecting mass at one corner he broke it off, and so saved it for the very valuable collection in which it has now been placed. There can be no doubt of the rock at Alves being of the old red sandstone, and our English scientific friends will find it difficult to assign this fossil to any newer formation as they have done with the other bone beds of Morayshire. This saurian, in fact, will likely establish that the seas of the old red period had shores with large lagoons or estuaries, rich in a tropical vegetation, and abounding in amphibous reptiles.—*Inverness Courier.*

HUNTING IN ALGERIA.— Ostrich hunting then takes place in the hottest season of the year, lasting sometimes forty-five days, from the 26th of June to the 10th of August. "It is the heat even more than the pace which kills the ostrich," say the Arabs, and experience shows that they are right. It is only a select few out of the many nomad tribes who have the privilege of carrying on the noble sport. Previous to the French occupation their only other business was the pillage of the caravans; but now they do it no more, at least in the territory under Gallic jurisdiction. Well made they are, and wonderfully organized for their life of movement and privation; dry and hard, with piercing eye and untiring ankle, possessed of a power of enduring hunger and thirst to their farthest limits. They make much parade of their new-born conversion and uprightness, on the principle, I suppose, of "assuming a virtue if you have it not." Our present goodness must redeem the errors of the past," they say; "we have a few lives upon our conscience, but God alone is perfect!" A "few lives," forsooth! —they are modest, these good Arabs. Toumi, their chief, owned to nineteen murders. "Yes, I killed nineteen individuals in attacking the caravans. Perhaps it is a greater number than is allowed to a good believer; but, after all, we only do as our fathers taught us; nevertheless, I admit that when I think of it I feel puzzled about the Day of Judgment!"— "*Under the Palms in Algeria and Tunis,*" by the Hon. *Lewis Wingfield.*

MAN-EATING TIGERS.— The ravages of man-eating tigers in the Sumbulpore, Baitool, Chindwara, Bhundara, Chandah, and Raipore districts of Central India are so serious that elephants have been placed at the disposal of the district officers to enable them to destroy them. Ordinary tigers do harm only to the cattle, and the sanctioned reward of 50rs. is sufficient to incite native hunters to pursue them. But with man-eaters the case is different. One such brute kills its scores of human beings in a year; and no ordinary native sportsman dare attack it. Captain Fraser, district superintendent of police, Bhundera, reports the destruction of a ferocious man-eater in the neighbourhood of Kampta, which had carried away a young Gondnee woman out of her house at daybreak on the 20th of December. The woman was grinding grain with two others at her side, when the animal sprang into the midst of them and seized the girl. High up in the air ten feet from the ground fragments of the red cords which bound her hair were fluttering on the points of the bamboo fencing. The body was found in a deep ravine; only the head had been eaten away. On his return to the village Captain Fraser was met by all the women, who, accompanied by the village musicians, gave him a hearty welcome. Mothers placed their infants before him, and all vied in expressing their gratitude.—*Friend of India.*

WHISTLING PIGEONS.—Walking in the vicinity of Pekin, one is often surprised to hear a sharp and shrill whistling, which appears to come from a great height, and to proceed from pigeons, which may be seen flying in close bans over head—birds to which one knows nature has denied the power of song. The explanation is, that at Pekin, a large number of vultures and other birds of prey wage a continual war upon the pigeons, and to prevent their destruction, the Chinese have invented a kind of whistle of various forms, manufactured with little gourds, or with small pieces of the rhind of bamboo fastened together, in which they make openings intended to produce long whistling sounds when the wind blows through them. These whistles, which are exceedingly light, are furnished with a small tongue of wood pierced with a hole, by means of which these instruments are attached to the tails of the pigeons. This operation, says a traveller, is performed especially upon those pigeons which in their flight are found at the head of the bands; the rapidity of their course causes the air to strike the whistle, which thus produces a prolonged sound, and drives off the birds of prey, which are frightened by the noise, the cause of which they do not understand. At one of the meetings of the Societé d'Acclimatation, this ingenious whistle was exhibited by M. Champion, one of the members of that society.—*Petite Figaro.*

THE EFFECT OF THUNDER ON ANIMALS. All creatures, (we read in *Land and Water*, Nov. 30th) but more especially the feathered tribe, are sensible of electric influence. Birds, one would imagine, must positively know when a thunderstorm is approaching, for one constantly sees wild birds take refuge in trees, and tame ones evince fear if there is thunder in the air. Surely your correspondent must have noticed on a bright summer's day, when the birds have been singing merrily, how suddenly their wild notes have become hushed on the appearance of an electric cloud. The common expression, "Like a dying duck in a thunderstorm," proves, I should think, that the *Anatidæ* family are peculiarly affected. Dogs seek their kennels, and cattle, ignorant of the law of attraction, leave the open field for the shelter of the woods. Birds have in all ages been considered as weather-wise. Look at the swallows; if they fly high, fine weather is expected, but if they skim the ground it is a sign of rain. This, of course, can be accounted for by the fact of their following the range of atmosphere taken by their insect food. Sea gulls, too, come inland on the approach of a storm. In fact, one might go on quoting examples without limit.

THE CROCODILE.—"Few creatures are so sly and wary as the crocodile. I watch them continually as they attack the dense flocks of small birds that throng the bushes at the water's edge. These birds are perfectly aware of the danger, and they fly from the attack, if possible. The crocodile then quietly and innocently lies upon the surface, as though it had appeared quite by an accident; it thus attracts the attention of the birds, and it slowly sails away to a considerable distance, exposed to their view. The birds, thus beguiled by the deceiver, believe that the danger is removed, and they again flock to the bush, and once more dip their thirsty beaks into the stream. Thus absorbed in slaking their thirst, they do not observe that their enemy is no longer on the surface. A sudden splash, followed by a huge pair of jaws beneath the bush that engulfs some dozens of victims, is the signal unexpectedly given of the crocodile's return, who has thus slily dived, and hastened under cover of water to his victims. I have seen the crocodiles repeat this manœuvre constantly; they deceive by a feigned retreat, and then attack from below"—*Bakers Abyssinia.*

THE NUTHATCH.—(The following interesting note relating to this bird appeared in *Land and Water*. On the 5th of October last, observing a nuthatch upon a piece of slated roofing within ten or twelve feet of my window, I watched it, thinking that it intended to fix the nut it held, in order to break it, but to my surprise, after searching two or three mossy spots where it failed in its attempts to fix the nut, I distinctly saw it fix it in a small crevice of the slates amongst green moss (where it probably now is), and deliberately take two pieces of similar moss and cover over the nut, pressing in each piece of moss with its bill, as if to hide the nut —then, after looking about for half a minute, it hopped to the edge of the slating and flew off; nothing disturbed it. I have often found single nuts in crevices, but supposed that they had been left there by nuthatches which had been disturbed, but as the above was a deliberate intention to hide the nut, and never having heard that it was the habit of this bird to secrete its surplus food, I send you the above account in case you should think it worthy of a notice in your paper.

BIRD MURDERS. — Certain birds annually occur in this country, but not in sufficient numbers to become familiar to everybody. Many of them are conspicuous by their bright plumage, and when they do occur are seen to attract attention. Now the practice is, whenever one of these birds, such as the hoopoe or the golden oriole, is observed, that some person should go and shoot it. The person who does so is never, we may say without exception, a naturalist, and his act is "bird murder" without any extenuating circumstances beyond that of ignorance. The death of that unhappy oriole or hoopoe does nothing to advance the study or the taste for natural history, while thereby the species is prevented from permanently establishing itself as a denizen of this country; for, be it remarked, the hoopoes, orioles, and other birds falling into the category of which we are speaking, almost invariably visit this country in the spring of the year, most usually in pairs, and, if unmolested, would unquestionably build their nests here, lay their eggs, and hatch their young, retire to the sunny south when the summer is ended, and return the following spring.—*Fraser's Magazine.*

TO FATTEN POULTRY.—The following will be found a quick and excellent food for fattening chickens. Set rice over the fire, with skimmed milk; let it boil till the rice is quite swelled out, then add a teaspoonful of sugar. Feed them three times a-day in common pans, giving them only as much as will quite fill them at once. Let the pans be washed and set in spring water, that no sourness may be conveyed to the fowls, as that prevents them from fattening. Give them clean water, or the milk of rice to drink. By this method, the flesh will have a clear whiteness, which no other food gives; and when it is considered how far a pound of rice will go, and how much time is saved by this mode, it will be found to be cheap. It is said that a portion of animal mixed with vegetable food causes poultry to thrive rapidly, but they should be confined to a vegetable diet some time before they are killed. A quantity of charcoal, broken in small pieces, and placed within reach of the poultry, increases their appetite, and promotes digestion.—*Gardener's Chronicle.*

ELECTRICITY AND VEGETATION.—M. Ch. Blondeau states (*Comptes Rendus*, Nov. 1867) that, subjecting fruits—apples, pears, and peaches—to the action of an induced electric current hastens their maturity. Having rendered seeds good conductors by moistening them, he affirms that electrizing them by induced currents causes them to germinate earlier than similar seeds not subjected to such action. He says, "Some haricot beans which were electrized exhibited a singular peculiarity. They germinated head downwards, and root upwards, in the air. That is to say, the gemmule, surrounded by its cotyledons, remained in the ground, while the root, separated by a little stem from the gemmule, erected itself in the air. This fact appears important, as explaining the reason why plants push their roots into the earth and their stems into the air. This tendency is so strong, that efforts to cause them to act otherwise are fruitless; but it may be overcome by the electric shock, in the same way as the poles of a magnet may be reversed. We are tempted to liken the embryo to a small magnet with opposite poles."

THE PALESTINE EXPLORATION.—The Palestine explorers are making large additions to our knowledge of Jerusalem. The cheesemonger's valley—the great hollow separating Zion from Moriah—turns out to have had a shape surprisingly unlike what has been supposed. When the excavations now in progress are complete, we shall have a new map of the Holy City. The present labours are devoted mainly to investigations connected with the sites of the Temple and the Holy Sepulchre. Funds are greatly needed for the completion of these labours, since no public department has yet been established in England which could either take charge of these important works or expect to secure their results for the benefit of the nation. Many a time in past years we have urged the formation of a Semitic department in the British Museum, which, from the nature of the case, would be mainly devoted to biblical illustration. Surely the time has come when this idea might be carried out to the profit of science and religion.—*Athenæum.*

THE STOAT—I once had a very good opportunity of observing one of these animals in West Wycombe Park. It was hunting about some dead leaves very assiduously, and by remaining perfectly quiet I was able to watch it through my glass for a quarter of an hour. On hearing the slightest sound, however distant, it would instantly pause, and rearing itself on its hind legs, peep round in every direction to ascertain the cause. If satisfied, it would resume its search, but if another sound followed immediately, it darted into its hole. Here it would remain a minute or two, and then cautiously emerge, looking about to see if the coast was clear. At last it settled itself down on a bank, and drawing its forelegs underneath its body, it went to sleep. The Stoat is much commoner than is generally supposed, but being very retiring in its habits, and very timid, it is seldom seen. A very fine specimen was taken two or three years ago at West Wycombe, measuring 16 inches in length: it is now in the possession of Dr. Bowstead.—Hy. Ullyett.—*From the Quarterly Magazine of High Wycombe Nat. Hist. Soc.*

A WHITE SQUIRREL.—A white squirrel, we read in the "New York Times," has been killed near Petersburgh, Va. It was about two-thirds grown, and is supposed to be of the grey squirrel species. It had not, however, a grey hair about the body, being perfectly white from the head to the tip of the tail.

Remarks, Queries, &c.

(*Under this head we shall be happy to insert original Remarks, Queries, &c.*)

THE WAY TO STUFF BIRDS—In answer to Mr. Fox (on page 30 of the Nat. Note Book) asking if any of your readers could inform him how to stuff and preserve birds, I have taken the liberty to extract a few notes from Waterton's method, given in the Appendix to his Wanderings in South America.

I have tried other ways of stuffing birds, but have found none so successful as the following:—

Note 1st—In dissecting, three things only are necessary to ensure success; viz., a penknife, a hand not coarse and clumsy, and practice. In stuffing you require cotton, a needle and thread, a little stick, glass eyes, a solution of corrosive sublimate, and any kind of temporary box to hold the specimens. Wire is worse than useless, as it gives a stiff appearance to the object stuffed.

Note 2nd—A very small proportion of the scull-bone, say from the fore part of the eye to the bill is to be left in, part of the wing bones, the jaw bones, and half of the thigh bones remain. Every thing else, flesh, fat, eyes, bones, brains, and tendons, are all to be taken away.

Note 3rd—In taking off the skin from the body it will be well to keep in mind that you must try to shove it in lieu of pulling it, lest you stretch it. Throughout the whole operation, as fast as you detach the skin from the body, you must put cotton immediately betwixt the body and it; this will prevent the plumage getting dirty.

Note 4th—Let us now proceed to dissect a bird. Have close by you a little bottle of corrosive sublimate, also a little stick and a handful or two of cotton. Now fill the mouth and nostrils with cotton, and place it on your knee on its back, with its head pointed to your left shoulder. Take hold of the knife with your two first fingers and thumb, the edge upward, you must not keep the point of the knife perpendicular to the body of the bird, because, were you to hold it so, you would cut the inner skin of the belly, and thus let the bowels out. To avoid this let your knife be parallel to the body, and then you can divide the outer skin with great ease.

Note 5th—Begin on the belly below the breast-bone and cut down the middle, quite to the vent. This done, put the bird in any convenient position, and separate the skin from the body, till you get at the middle joint of the thigh. Cut it through, and do nothing more there at present except introduce cotton all the way on that side, from the vent to the breast bone. Do exactly the same on the opposite side.

Note 6th—Now place the bird perpendicular, its breast resting on your knee, with its back towards you. Separate the skin from the body on each side of the vent, and never mind at present the part at the vent to the root of the tail. Bend the tail gently down to the back, and while your finger and thumb are keeping down the detached parts of the skin on each of the vent, cut quite across and deep, until you see the back-bone near the oil gland at the root of the tail. Sever the back-bone at the joint and then you have all the root of the tail, together with the oil-gland, dissected from the body. Apply plenty of cotton.

Note 7th—After this by shoving and cutting get the skin pushed up until you come to where the wing-joints join the body. Apply cotton and then cut this joint through, and do the same at the other wing, add cotton, and gently push the skin over the head, cut out the roots of the ears, and continue skinning till you reach the middle of the eye; cut the membrane quite through, otherwise you would tear the orbit of the eye.

Note 8th—After this nothing difficult intervenes to prevent your arriving at the root of the bill: when this is effected cut away the body, leaving just a little bit of the skull; clean well the jaw bones, and touch the skull and corresponding parts with the solution. Now all that remains to be removed is the flesh on the middle joints of the wings, one bone of the thighs, and the fleshy root of the tail.

Note 9th—Now fasten thread to the joints of each wing, and then tie them together, leaving exactly the same space betwixt them as your knowledge in anatomy informs you existed there when the bird was entire; hold the skin open with your finger and thumb, and apply the solution to every part of the inside. Neglect the head and neck at present, they will receive it afterwards.

Note 10th—Now fill the body moderately with wool to prevent the feathers on the belly from being injured. You must recollect that half of the thigh, or in other words one joint of the thigh bone, has been cut away. Now as this bone never moved perpendicular to the body, but on the contrary in an oblique direction, of course as soon as it is cut off the remaining part of the thigh and leg, having nothing now to support them obliquely, must naturally fall to their perpendicular. Hence the reason why the legs appear considerably too long. To correct this take your needle and thread, fasten the ends round the bone inside, then push the skin just opposite to it, and then tack up the thigh under the wings with several strong stitches. This will shorten the thigh, and render it quite capable of supporting the body without the aid of wire.

Note 11th—Now is the time to put in the cotton for an artificial body, by means of the little stick, and then sew up the orifice you originally made in the belly, beginning at the vent. Lastly dip your stick into the solution, and put it down the throat three or four times, in order that every part may receive it. When the head and neck are filled with cotton quite to your liking, close the bill as in nature. Bring the feet together by a pin, and then run a thread through the knees, by which you may draw them to each other, as near as you may judge proper. Nothing now remains to be added but the eyes; adjust the orbit to them as in nature, and that requires no other fastener. After this, touch the bill, orbit, feet, and former oil-gland at the root of the tail, with the solution, and then you have given to the bird every thing necessary, except attitude and a proper degree of elasticity.

Note 12th—Procure any common ordinary box, fill one end of it, about three-fourths up to the top, with cotton, forming a sloping plane. Make a moderate hollow to receive it, and place the bird in its right position. If you wish to elevate the wings do so, and support them with cotton. If you wish to have the tail expanded reverse the order of the feathers, beginning from the two middle ones, and when dry place them in their true order, and the tail will preserve for ever the expansion you have given it. In three or four days the feet lose their natural elasticity, and the knees begin to stiffen. When you observe this it is the time to give the legs any angle you wish and to arrange the toes. When the bird is quite dry, pull the thread out of the knees, and take away the needle and all is done."

If Mr. Fox follows the above directions I do not think he will have much difficulty in learning to stuff birds.

Mavisbush House, Jan. 14th   J. D. S. W.

To give "Fox" even a tenth part of the information he needs, would fill pages of the NOTE BOOK, as there are dozens of methods which have their advocates. Some naturalists of my acquaintance adopt the "loose body" system, and others the "made body" method; while the Rev. J. G. Wood has informed me that he stuffs upon Waterton's plan (which I have tried myself with some success, after seeing a beautiful specimen prepared by the former gentleman). I would recommend "Fox" reading the articles upon Taxidermy, in "Maunder's Treasury of Natural History," "Beeton's Book of Birds," or Waterton's works; or better still, procuring a little handbook sold by Gardner, 52, High Holborn, the price of which is sixpence only; it is called "Bird, Animal, and Fish Preserving," and is a very nice little guide for an amateur. "Fox" must, however, bear in mind that the most carefully compiled instructions are of no avail unless he brings to bear upon them the most careful patience, combined with constant practice. A. M. B.

"Fox" will, I think, find the information he requires in Gardner's (52, High Holborn) shilling or sixpenny book on "Taxidermy." It is practical. For position and accessaries consult the plate of "Gould's Birds of Great Britain."
G. O. G. NAPIER.

SKELETON LEAVES.—Mr. Wilkinson says, speaking of the manner of making skeleton leaves:—"Procure the youngest leaves you can find and steep them in urine, or if preferred water, with a little solution of chloride of lime added. The 'pectine' contained in this, together with other acids, has a peculiar effect on the parenchyma, producing such a pure whiteness and tenacity of strength which specimens prepared in any other way never possess. Solutions referred to above (sulphuric acid and water and solutions of caustic potash and chloride of lime) will do for a substitute. After allowing the leaves to macerate for some time, until the fleshy matter is entirely dissolved, remove them into a vessel of clean water and wash them well. Then lay the skeletons between folds of thick blotting paper and press them; then place them before the fire or in the sun, care being taken to scratch the fibres out so that they do not adhere together."

I have never tried this plan myself, but I hope that "Fox" may find it successful. TORTOISE.

The leaves should be gathered when they are in perfection; that is, when some of the earliest leaves begin to fall from the tree. Select perfect leaves, taking care that they are not broken or injured by insects; lay them in pans of rain water, and expose them to the air to undergo decomposition; renew the water once a week, and let it be sufficient to cover them; give them time for their soft parts to become decomposed, and take them out, lay them on a plate with a little water, wash away carefully with a camel hair pencil the green matter that clings to the fibres. When they are thoroughly cleaned, they should be bleached by steeping them for a short time in a weak solution of chloride of lime; then dried and arranged in bouquets, or pressed flat, according to taste.

Another way is to boil the leaves till the green matter separates from the fibres; then clean them in cold water with a camel hair pencil; steep them in a chloride of lime, then dry, and arrange them.
A DE H.

Procure leaves containing the largest amount of woody fibre (such as holly, poplar, or laurel, will do); place them in a large open vessel constantly exposed to sun and air; cover them with rain water, which, as it evaporates, must be renewed; after some weeks the softer portions will decay, and leave the fibres exposed: they must then be laid on a plate, and with delicate touches of a camel hair pencil remove all the pulpy matter, commencing from the mid rib of the leaf. When finished, place the skeletons between blotting paper to dry.

Another method recommended (which, however, I have never tried), is to add a table spoonful of liquid chloride of lime, to a quart of water; soak the leaves, &c., in this for four hours, take them out, wash them well, and treat as before. A. M. B.

"Fox" will find the heads and stems of the white poppy and sage, the stems and calices of the henbane, the hyacinth, and the bell flower, pretty and easily managed. The bearded barley is very beautiful, but somewhat difficult. The best course appears to be to leave the plants to putrify in water for a time, which varies with the season and the plant. They must then be carefully manipulated to remove the adhering tissue, and lastly, bleached with a solution of chloride of lime. Considerable patience and neat handedness are necessary to obtain fine specimens. The plants may be varied almost indefinitely; poplar leaves are about the easiest to a beginner. C. O. G. NAPIER.

In reply to Fox's query concerning "Skeleton Leaves," I subjoin the following remarks. The best leaves for skeletonising are the holly, poplar, ivy, box, fig, and lime; those of the oak, chestnut, elm, and walnut are not so good, as they contain more resin than the others, and do not decay so soon. The following receipt I believe is a good one. Soak the leaves for about four hours in a table-spoonful of liquid chloride of lime, mixed with a quart of water, then wash them in a basin of water, and leave them to dry by exposing them to the air. The larger leaves will require to be left longer in the liquid.
January 6th M. L. A.

CAMBERWELL BEAUTY.—(*Vanessa Antiopa.*)—In answer to "S. R. B." I may state that the egg should be sought for before June, as the larva (which feeds upon willow and various other trees), appears that month, turning to pupa in July, emerging as an imago in August and September. Some few then hybernate and reappear on sunny days from March to May; but it is extremely improbable that "S. R. B." will succeed in procuring this insect in any of its stages, and it is one of our rarest Rhopalocera, and has never appeared in any numbers since 1847. I have seen three living specimens myself, but that was in one of the Greek Isles; they occur, however, in the South of France.

With regard to the second part of "S. R. B.'s" query, the spotted hawk, or spotted elephant hawk moth, as it is sometimes called, is *Seilephila Euphorbiæ*, and the two elephant hawks are *Chærocampa Elpenor* and *C. Porcellus*. I should presume your correspondent intended the eyed hawk, which is *S. Ocellatus*, which appears from the end of May up to July; the larva, August and September (feeding upon willow, &c.); the pupa may be found by searching about those trees in the winter. Should he, however, mean *D. Euphorbiæ*, one of the rarest of the *Sphingidæ*, I can only recommend him where he *ought* to search, which is wherever the sea-spurges grow—the larvæ feeding semi-gregariously upon those plants about August or September, remaining after their change to pupa underground until June, on which month the perfect insect should be sought for at dusk flying over flowers near the coast. Stainton gives Scarborough as a likely habitat, but the remarks upon *V. Antiopa* must also be applicable to this. A. M. B.

"R. W. B." may like to know that Westwood mentions that the Camberwell Beauty (Vanessa Antiopa) is found in the larva state in the beginning of July; therefore, the egg is to be found in June and September, and the pupa in the end of July. He must not expect to find it in England, as Stainton considers it one of our scarcest insects, and it has hardly been seen here since 1847. The caterpillar of S. ocellatæ (or ocellatus, as it is usually called) is, I believe, to be found in August and September, the pupa in October. TORTOISE.

HOW TO KEEP RABBITS. — Having read Mrs. Vacher's note in last month's NATURALIST'S NOTE BOOK, I quite agree with her that rabbits thrive far better when allowed their liberty than when moped up in a small box with only just room to turn.

I think that every one owns that the flesh of wild rabbits is not only more tasty, but also more wholesome than tame.

What is the reason of this? It is principally owing to their having plenty of exercise in the open air, without which no animals will thrive, however well they may be fed; for food will never make up for exercise. Warrens of wild rabbits are now only kept by gentlemen who have a large extent of waste land; but there is no reason why every person who possesses only a few acres should not have as many rabbits as he could wish, either for his own table or the market.

After the first outlay—which need not be great—he would have no further trouble or expense in keeping rabbits.

Let him first fix upon two or three acres of land (any soil) around which he must sink a wall of brick or stone to the depth of three feet, which must be raised above ground about four feet.

Next let him scoop the earth out from the centre, making a wide path to run up the middle and pile the earth up on either side, so as to form banks of a few feet high, in which the rabbits may form their burrows.

Now, all that he has to do is to make two gates, one at each side of the path (these should be covered over with wire netting) as entrances to his preserve, which will then be ready to receive a few pairs of wild rabbits. If you put six pairs of full-grown rabbits in preserve such as this, you may expect to have in one year upwards of sixty young rabbits for your table.

I have often tried keeping rabbits the old way in hutches, but the trouble of keeping them clean, besides being obliged to remove the bucks continually, to prevent them destroying their young, is very great.

By the above mode the rabbits are left entirely to themselves; they never devour their young or give any trouble. I hope that before long we shall see rabbit-keeping as common in the country as poultry rearing is now. J. D. S. W.

Mavisbush House.

SHELL-FISH.—The way in which the various kinds of freshwater shell-fish protect themselves from the frost and cold during the winter, is very curious and interesting. I don't know how they manage in rivers and ponds with strong or gravelly bottoms, but in muddy ponds they burrow into the mud. The common pond-snails (*Lymnœa*), and their allies, cannot burrow in deep water, because, being air breathing animals, they are continually coming to the surface for air. For the same reason they are not able to go very deeply into the mud. They, therefore, seek the shallower water, and crawl under that curious mixture of vegetation and mud which is so common in unfrequented ponds, forming ragged green patches all round the margin. Here they lie warm and comfortable; able, on account of the shallowness of the water, to apply the orifice of their respiratory organs to the surface, to take in a fresh supply of oxygen without the necessity of rising from their bed. Other species whose respiratory apparatus is adapted for breathing under water seem to prefer the deep water, and burrow much more thoroughly than the pond-snails. Thus warmly buried the shell-fish lie in a torpid state I suppose for days, and even weeks, without motion, to all appearance dead. That they are not dead, however, may be seen any fine mild morning, when they come out in abundance to crawl about, and otherwise enjoy themselves, in the warm beams of the sun.

In concluding this note, I ought perhaps to say that not having good opportunities for observation, I have never actually observed what I have been relating in the ponds and ditches themselves, but only in the pans in which I keep shell-fish at home. As, however, I try to keep them as much as possible in a state of nature, I conclude, I think reasonably, that in their native ponds they would guard themselves against the inclemency of the winter weather in the same manner.

J. SANDELS.

THE PIDDOCK.—(*Pholas dactylus*).—I have specimens of this fish, as well as other species, in Devonian limestone, from the Devon coast, and have seen a considerable collection of rocks pierced by it (some very hard) from different localities. The pholas being found all round our coasts, could not get chalk to burrow in everywhere. There are three ways of accounting for this creature's method of boring—the mechanical, the chemical, and the electric; the first being the one generally held. In this case the creature uses its foot as a boring tool. The second presumes on the pholas secreting an acid which corrodes the rock; the third that it possesses a galvanic battery with similar powers. It is possible that all three theories may have a measure of truth; that the foot is used as a borer is clear; and the luminosity of the animal is in favour of an electric current, which is almost always accompanied by chemical decomposition, which would set free the hydrochloric acid of the sea water. The small size of the entrance to the chambers of the pholas is accounted for by the increase of its size during its residence there. Mr. Robertson read an interesting paper some years since before the Brighton Naturalist's Society on this subject which gives much information: it is printed as a sixpenny pamphlet.

C. O. G. NAPIER.

COLIAS EDUSA (CLOUDED YELLOW BUTTERFLY). —This beautiful insect belongs to the family Papilionidœ, and makes its appearance in August, when it

may be seen sporting about in the lucerne and clover fields; it continues in its glory throughout September, and departs about the beginning of October. In some years it is much more plentiful than in others. Its favourite haunts are lucerne and clover fields, open downs and railway banks, especially the latter, if adjoining a clover field. The female does not seem so numerous as the male, so that the collector may capture a number of males before he comes across a single female, which is a much handsomer insect, having the black border of the wings spotted with yellow instead of veined. Among others it may be found in the following localities:—Brighton, Ailesbury, Pershore, Bembridge (Isle of Wight), Bristol, Dorchester, Epping, Lewes, Worthing, Winchester, Truro, Burton-on-Trent. It has very rarely occurred in Scotland. In Ireland, according to Mr. Birchall, it occurs in some seasons on the south and east coast.
H. MEYRICK.

NAME OF BIRD.—Can any of your readers tell me the name of a little bird I have got, which I will try and describe to you. It is the same size as a yellow ammer, the wings and the tail are the same colour, the head and beak are quite white, the throat and upper part of the breast velvety black, mottled with white, the centre of the back and upper tail coverts white; it was shot by a keeper on a common, and though damaged by the dog getting it, I have succeeded in mounting and making a tolerable specimen of it. Your correspondent Fox asks how to stuff birds: tell him to get Gardner's Handbook on Taxidermy, price 1s. 6d., he will find every instruction necessary, at least, I never had any other instruction, and I manage them very well now. B. F. G.
Gainsborough, Jan. 14th, 1868

P.S.—I have a thrush that I have had in a cage 13½ years; how long do they generally live in confinement?

CURIOUS COLOUED EGGS.—I have a duck's egg in my collection, the putamen or inner lining of the shell of which is spotted with black. The yolk itself was dark and bloody, but the egg was quite fresh. The shell of the egg is washed with sooty colour from the bird. I have not been able to account for this, but have surmised that the bird was in an unhealthy state. Another duck's egg, nearly black outside, had no stain on the putamen. Some of these ducks' eggs are laid by a variety of the common duck called the Peruvian var. of Anas boschas—the mallard, and said to be characteristic of it. I have been at the trouble to collect more than one hundred examples of deformities and abnormalities in eggs, and facts, as far as possible, connected with the pedigree of the birds; but I have not been able to hear of any peculiarities connected with birds hatched from these eggs, although they are generally sterile. C. O. G. NAPIER.

A BAT IN A CHAPEL.—Being on a visit last Sunday evening at a village a few miles from here, I went to a small chapel, in which a very hot stove made the atmosphere anything but cool. During the evening a bat flew out of the roof through one of the ventilators in the ceiling near the stove, and after going round the chapel once or twice made its exit the same way. This was repeated a little later on. Of course, I suppose the unusual heat had revived the bat, which had its winter quarters there. Is it usual for bats to be disturbed in winter, or are they usually dormant the whole season? A RAVEN.

LANDRAIL.—(*Galinula Crex.*)—S. L. Wellington is in error in supposing that this bird does not utter its cry after the hay is removed. I have during the past year heard them in clover fields considerably after that time. It also frequents fields of standing corn. Certain it is that it suppresses its note for some two months or so prior to its departure, but that is by no means an exceptional case, as most birds of passage do the same, as evidenced by the cases of the cuckoo, nightingale, nightjar, &c.

In answer to "Fox," I beg to state that, when shooting in Devonshire during September, I have frequently met with landrail, both in clover and barley fields. I have also found them in marshy places where the grass grows high, and by the side of hedges. I have never noticed their cry later than June, after the hay harvest is over. A. G. H.

In the last number of the N. N. B., S. L. Wellington asks what becomes of the Landrail when the hay is cut. Perhaps he does not know that this bird is migratory, arriving here in April and leaving us in October; it also possesses the power of ventriloquism, so that its note is no guide to where it is.
January 6th M. L. A.

THE NEST OF THE TOMTIT—Allow me to point out an error in the title of your frontispiece, "The Nest of the Tomtit."

All who have any practical acquaintance with nests will be at once aware that the nest in question is that of the Reed Warbler (S. amdinaceary) which it faithfully represents, but as the present description may confuse some of your readers, I trust you will excuse this correction; probably the mistake arose in translating from the French.
5th December 1868 J. S., Jun.

WHITE SPARROW—Seeing in your last number a note headed "White Blackbird," I thought perhaps it would interest some of your readers to know that I saw in my garden last summer a white sparrow (*fringilla domestica*). I think that it was quite white, except that its tail had a few dark feathers. It was noticed about the place for a few days and then disappeared, and was never seen again.
July 17th, 1868 A. B.

WHY DOES THE NEEDLE MAGNET POINT TO THE NORTH.—Can you or any of the readers of the NATURALIST'S NOTE BOOK tell me why the needle magnet always points to the north? I know the real reason is not as yet known, but I want to know what people suppose it to be. A. DE H.

COLOUR OF EGGS.—In answer to "L. A. M." acorns have been noticed to turn the yolk of duck eggs to a dark colour, but I believe in no way to alter their taste. The difference in the shade of the yolk would, I think, have no effect on the hatching of the eggs or the young. AQUILA.

THE BRITISH GRASSES.
By C. O. Groom Napier, F.G.S.

HESE plants, although of such vast economic importance, are but little studied by the majority even of botanists; and those, such as the farmers, whose very existence depends on them, have rarely precise and critical knowledge. Yet our British grasses are far more numerous than those of any other country of equal extent. Ireland, noted for its pastures, does not afford so many kinds. One cause of this neglect is the similarity of the species, which, nevertheless, when carefully examined, present points of distinction as absolute as are found in any class of plants. Grasses form a beautiful natural group, which the most common observer will at once acknowledge. The stem or culm is a hollow tube or fistular, strengthened by knots, thus combining lightness and toughness: the bamboo—but a grass magnified, is a striking illustration of this. The knots in our grasses, as in the great bamboo, increase in number as they approach the root. One species, *Molinia cærulea*, is an exception to this in having but one knot; this is near the root. This grass is otherwise peculiar in having a solid stem.

The form and position of the ligule in grasses is a very important means of discriminating species; it is situated between the stem and the sheath of the leaves, adhering closely to the former, and consisting of a thin membraneous substance. It is popularly supposed that grasses are not flowering plants, but this, although an error, yet has botanically a measure of truth. The flower of the grass, although performing all the operations of the most perfect ranunculus, the highest form of plant life as regards the formation of seed and other functions, yet is but a modification of the development of the leaf, although liable to great diversity of form. The florets of the grass are both sessile—without stalks, or on pedicles—with stalks, which last, vary much in length, strength, direction, and multiplication. The envelopes covering the seed, and the seed itself, vary greatly with species. Of these there are about one hundred and fifty which differ greatly in other respects. About twelve species are found in meadows when in good condition, but when the reverse is the case from forty to fifty may be found; these vary much in size with locality and soil. In poor pastures the bad grasses strangle the good ones, in rich the reverse is the case. Different species of grasses thus interweave as they grow. The farmer asks, how shall I turn a bad pasture into a good one? Professor Buckman replies, "Fold sheep on it." The poor grass is killed, but the rich luxuriating in the manure of these animals springs up with a strength hitherto unknown. The food those important tradesmen the butcher, baker, and cheesemonger—the great sustainers of our nation—supply is mainly afforded by cereal and pasture grasses. It therefore becomes a matter of necessity to extend our protecting hand to the good grasses, which fortunately is in most cases easy. The variation of different species of grass in accordance with locality is interesting. Thus many upland grasses whose home may be said to be the dry pasture, when removed to the low and rich meadow cease to yield seed, but propagate by suckers, and subdue those which do not follow their example. Of this, *Agrostis stolonifera* and *A. vulgaris*—the small-clustered and common bents—are examples. Great changes take place in the number of good and bad species of grass by irrigation. Professor Buckman gives an account of some land worth £1 an acre which was irrigated, and remarked the changes in the comparative number and bulk of its grasses attributable to this cause.

The following table of Mr. Buckman's shows the amount of good, middling, and bad grasses from the commencement of the period of his investigations:—

	Commencement.	After 2 Years.	After 4 Years.
Good	7	16	25
Middling	10	6	2
Bad	17	—	—

Professor Buckman qualifies this statement by saying that the bad grasses were not actually extirpated, though they had ceased to be troublesome. Our various grasses are thus distributed: thirty-five in meadow land, fourteen maritime, and twenty-three are weeds in arable land; ten are aquatic, and forty grow in hedges and woods. They are various in their qualities, but such most truly point to the condition of the ground in which they grow.

Although it is a popular error that one species of grass can be turned into another by any treatment, still the practical results of good treatment were seen in the predominance of the desired species. Twelve grasses are of great value as meadow species, although six or eight species predominate. Of these, *Poa pratensis*, *P. trivalis*, *Alopecarus pratensis*, *Dactylis glomerata*, *Phleum pratense*, *Holcus lanatus*, and *Lolium perenne* succeed well in moist meadows; the last (rye grass) especially then attains a large size. The two species of *Agrostis* formerly mentioned are of great value as pasture grasses in high lands. A choice species for lawns is *Festuca ovina*; its leaves are small, and bear frequent cutting. The sweet-scented vernal grass, *Anthoxanthum odoratum*, is the plant which has been supposed to give most of the characteristic odour to hay. This is denied by Knapp, but on gathering a bunch of this grass I was struck by the strength of the haylike smell. It can only, however, give its scent to the earlier hay, as it is withered in June and July. This grass is the only one, except *Bromus diandrus*, which possesses two stamens. Only one species is poisonous, the Bearded darnel (*Lolium temulentum*), of which a few cases of deleterious effects to men and beasts who have eaten it are on record.

The best method of stimulating the growth of good grasses both in pastures and lawns is the subject of many articles in treatises on agriculture and gardening. For pastures a top dressing of old plaster in the winter, to be removed in spring, and a course of liquid manure applied, or instead, bone or hoof chippings, super-phosphate, or other stimulants: for lawns, soot in spring, and the same course of manure as the season advances will be found beneficial, provided always that there is no defect in the soil from drought or drainage; then the auxiliary aid of the drainer or irrigator must be called in.

I have tried the plan so often recommended of endeavouring to uproot weeds by hand. This is a very laborious process, it tears the grass to pieces, and is ineffectual unless the cause which promotes the growth of the weeds—a poor soil—is removed; if it is enriched the weeds dwindle, but the blade covers the ground.

ON THE BRITISH HAWK-MOTHS.

NUMEROUS as are the moths of this country, there are some groups which, for distinct reasons, prove more eminently attractive to the beginner in the study of insects than others. Whilst the peculiar economy of some classes may serve to awaken interest in the thoughtful observer, the size and striking beauty of others will always render *them* universal favourites. And the latter remark applies particularly to that division of our native moths popularly known as the "Hawk-moths," or scientifically as the SPHINGIDÆ. We have thought that a brief summary of these interesting moths, with a commentary on them as we pass, may not prove uninteresting to the readers of the NOTE BOOK. It must be stated, however, that we shall only be able to notice the more striking particulars regarding each species, since space forbids a full or complete history of their separate economies, habits, and structure, which may be found elsewhere.

And, perhaps, before noticing the species, a few general remarks regarding the division SPHINGIDA itself may be desirable. The "Sphingides" are the largest and handsomest of our British moths, if we take them as a whole. Their long narrow wings enable them to fly with inconceivable velocity and force; consequently, in the perfect or *imago* state they are rarely captured, but more frequently taken in the *larval* stage, at which period of their lives many of the separate species are beautifully coloured, and very conspicuous on their food-plants. The "Sphinges" (as these moths are called) have all thick bodies, often pointed at the tail, and in many instances banded with vivid colours. Most of their curious caterpillars are furnished with a horn at the tail, the particular end and purpose of which remains yet to be discovered; but as the caterpillars are in all cases incapable of moving it, it becomes evident that the appendage is not given as a weapon of offence or defence. Most of these caterpillars descend into the earth to assume the chrysalis state, whilst those who do not generally spin their slight cocoons near its surface. And lastly, in regard to the perfect insects, it should be stated that the greater part are possessed of a long tabular apparatus, for the purpose of extracting honey—their sole food—from the flowers.

Amongst the SPHINGIDÆ, the first genus, and perhaps the best known, is that called the *Smerinthi*, easily distinguishable by several marks of characteristics. First, the bodies of these moths are brown, destitute of ornamental spots; secondly, the margin of the wings is waved and irregular; and lastly, the hind wings are not *banded*. A great similarity exists between all the caterpillars of this genus, the chief marked distinction being a difference of tint in the shagreened surface of the body, and a corresponding difference in the colour of the seven side stripes. The Eyed Hawk-moth (*Smerinthus ocellatus*) is the first of this genus, and also the foremost amongst this handsome race of insects, which we call the "Sphinges." Its variety of colouring is indeed beautiful to behold. The English name is derived from the fact that the hinder wings of this grand insect are adorned with two eyelike spots, alone giving a peculiar charm to the species. Midsummer is the time of its appearance in the winged state, but so rapid is its flight that few collectors have an opportunity of observing it in this stage; unless, indeed, by rearing it from the egg onwards. In common with many of its tribe, it has the power of soaring far above our heads, and it often traverses a considerable distance from the locality in which it was developed. The caterpillar is almost as interesting as the perfect insect. The eggs of the present species and also of the two following are very similar; oval, and green, and having a peculiar pearly aspect on the shell. The caterpillar of the Eyed Hawk-moth is rough, and covered with raised points of a white colour. Its shape is very elegant, tapering off to the head, which is triangular, and it is furnished with a blue horn at the tail. In the summer months these interesting caterpillars may be found rather commonly on poplar and willow. In autumn they descend below the earth and become chrysalides, which are glossy, and brown in colour.

The Poplar Hawk-moth (*Smerinthus Populi*) is another very interesting insect. Its history is very similar to that of the last species, but it is more particularly attached to the poplar for food, feeding generally on the well-known Lombardy poplar. The distinction between the caterpillars of this and the last-mentioned is not always so obvious as may be imagined. Although the ground tint of the present species is yellow, and that of the former white, there are often specimens occurring which are of so pale a colour as to be not easily distinguished from specimens of the Eyed. In connection with all the caterpillars of these moths, it may be stated that their attitude when at rest is very imposing and curious, and this it is that has given rise to the appellation "Sphinges" as applied to the family, from a notion that some resemblance existed between the ancient fabulous animal and these caterpillars. The chrysalis of the Poplar Hawk-moth has a very singular aspect, looking very much as though daubed with mud. In regard to the moths themselves, we may just add that they will breed in confinement; a rather unusual thing in this division of our native insects. We have not found the "Eyed" to do so, though the experiment has been repeatedly made by us.

The Lime Hawk-moth (*Smerinthus Tiliæ*), as its name implies, is more confined in the caterpillar stage to the lime for its *pabulum*. It seems to be not quite so common a species as the other two *Smerinthi*, but is certainly equally beautiful, though hardly so gaudy in colouring. Its varied shades of olive-brown and green give it a very attractive aspect. The caterpillar differs from the two former in being greenish, sprinkled with yellow; the oblique stripes being yellowish, margined with red: this latter fact alone will prove sufficient for its identification by the collector. This species was once abundant about London, and even now is occasionally taken in the suburbs. The chrysalis of the Lime Hawk-moth is rough, like the caterpillar, and of a dull red colour.

Leaving this interesting trio, always the first sought by the beginner in entomology, we come next to what perhaps is the most striking, and certainly the largest of our British moths. This is the Death's-head Hawk-moth (*Acherontia Atropos*). This insect measures often as much as five inches across the wings, and is as singular in its markings as it is imposing in aspect. On the thorax we see that remarkable device which gave rise to its name, the skull and cross-bones; and this alone has rendered the insect a source of terror to the superstitious and uneducated mind. But we really must not linger over any of the species we notice. We may remark that in all stages of its history the Death's-head moth is strangely interesting, for it is said that caterpillar, chrysalis, and perfect insect have all the power of emitting a distinct sound resembling the squeak of a mouse. Experiments have been made to ascertain the cause of this, but we believe as yet with little success. The caterpillar of this giant moth feeds on the potato and the deadly nightshade more particularly, though many other plants are given by entomological authors. It is not uncommon in some parts of the country. In colour it is generally yellow, smooth, and sprinkled over with minute black dots. The chrysalis, which is very large and shining, may be found a few inches below the earth, and is often turned up by the rustic labourers, who now send up the specimens to London dealers for sale.

We now come to what is generally considered a rarity in our day. This is the Convolvulus Hawk-moth (*Sphinx Convolvuli*). This insect is very fluctuating as regards its occurrence amongst us. It is scarcely ever seen in the caterpillar stage, which, however, has been described as "green with seven oblique black stripes, the head and horn yellowish." It is said to feed on the bindweed, or the wild convolvulus, hence its name. The perfect insect is delicately marbled and mottled, and in many respects much resembles the next species.

This is the well-known Privet Hawk-moth (*Sphinx Ligustri*). Whilst much commoner than many of this family, it is to us by far the most beautiful of them all. The beautiful marblings and veinings of the upper wings are scarcely excelled by the lovely purple bands on the hind wings, and the delicately marked body. This moth is rarely taken in the perfect state, but its handsome caterpillar is far from rare: indeed it occurs even in the squares and gardens of this great city itself, where privet-bushes—its favourite *pabulum*—skirt the railings enclosing the stunted trees and flowers. Unlike the rough caterpillars of the *Smerinthi*, this is *smooth*, of a delicate apple-green in colour; it has seven purple stripes on each side, and the horn at the tail is hard and glossy black. The chrysalis into which it is transformed has the tubular apparatus before referred to folded up compactly within an exterior case or sheath, giving the insect a truly singular appearance. In confinement the handsome caterpillars of this species are very easy and interesting to rear.

We now come to some rarer species of the SPHINGIDÆ, about which little can be said, as their occurrence in this country is so rare as to render examination and investigation difficult. Some of these are very handsome in colouring, and though scarcely more than visitors here are abundant on the Continent. First amongst these rarities is the Spurge Hawk-moth (*Deilephila Euphorbiæ*). Though so scarce an insect, formerly we read its beautiful caterpillar was very abundant on the sea spurge near Barnstaple. The perfect insect has never been found in this country—at least so says one of our present entomological dignities. The Bedshaw Hawk-moth (*Deilephila Galii*) is another rare species, which has been found near Deal, according to Newman, who says that it requires to be diligently sought after. Then there are the Striped Hawk-moth (*Deilephila livornica*) and the Silver-striped Hawk-moth (*Chærocampa celerio*), the former of which can hardly be considered a British species at all. The latter has occurred at rare intervals, but seems to us to be a very doubtful native of the country.

After this group of rarities, however, we come to some species of this division of moths more generally occurring amongst us. The Small Elephant Hawk-moth (*C. porcellus*) is a very attractively-tinted insect, and not uncommonly met with by the persevering collector. The wings are olive-brown, and patches of pink and rosy red greatly increase the delicacy of its beauty. The caterpillar feeds on the bedshaw, and is either of a uniform brown or green colour, slightly rough, and has no horn at the tail. Some of the segments of the body have black spots, which give a distinctive mark to this species, particularly attached also to a chalky soil. The moth occurs in June, and the caterpillar may be searched for in August on the plant named.

The Large Elephant Hawk-moth (*C. Elpenor*) is somewhat like the former species. The caterpillar, however, from its singularity could not be confounded with that of the former, even were it not different in size. The anterior segments are thickened out, and peculiar eyelike spots on them give the caterpillar a truly striking appearance. It feeds on the willow herb, so common by the sides of ditches, and (so say some) on the bedshaw, like its relative. The chrysalis is yellow-brown, marbled with black. The moth is said to be particularly partial to the flowers of the ragged robin.

The Oleander Hawk-moth (*C. Nerii*) is at the same time a rare and beautiful species; so rare indeed is it that we can hardly call it a British species at all in the present day. The wings are exquisitely varied, and its beauty renders it a very attractive insect to those who speculate in rare species; many of whom are annually deceived by dealers, who pass off as British specimens what in reality have been imported to us from the Continent, where the moth is not uncommon.

Next in order are three very interesting, though small, members of the family SPHINGIDÆ. They are the three representatives of the genus *Macroglossa*. The first of these is the common Humming-bird Hawk-moth (*Macroglossa stellatarum*). This is the merry little creature that we so often see hovering over the flowers at mid-day, unfolding its long tongue and sipping the honey, without even alighting thereupon. Its peculiar humming might and often has led the collector to mistake it for one of the bee tribe, which at first sight it much resembles. Unlike most of this noble tribe of insects, which are called "Twilight-fliers," *this* species flies when the sun is high in the heavens. Its brilliant orange hind wings alone serve to distinguish it from its brethren. The caterpillars of the three *Macroglossas* are not very diverse in general outlines. This one feeds on the bedshaw, and may be found during July and August. It is green or brown, sprinkled with white, and having a palish line along each side. The chrysalis is sometimes found below the surface, but in confinement we have found the caterpillar spin a slight web just *on* the surface within which it is transformed.

The two Bee Hawk-moths are very singular insects. With them we close our brief summary of the *true* SPHINGIDÆ. The Broad-bordered Bee Hawk-moth (*M. fuciformis*) is perhaps the commoner of the two, occurring not unfrequently in the Kentish woods. Its caterpillar feeds on the wood scabious. The moth itself has the wings transparent, similar to those of the bee tribe. This circumstance might lead the inexperienced to overlook these little fellows when collecting, for they much resemble a large humble-bee in flight and appearance. Examination, however, will prove to what family the insect belongs, for the *antennæ*, so peculiarly striped, are not those of a bee or wasp of any kind.

The Narrow-bordered Bee Hawk-moth (*M. bombyliformis*) is rarely seen amongst us now, and is not known in this country in the caterpillar state. The border of the transparent wings being narrower is the chief distinction between this and the last species. This moth has appeared more particularly in the northern counties, and is said to be "not uncommon in the month of May." And thus ends our list. We have gone over these handsome insects as briefly as possible, and in our next shall hope to glance at another group of insects equally interesting. In closing we may remark, that whilst difference of opinion exists regarding the arrangement of some insects formerly considered to be true "Sphinges," all are unanimously agreed now in pronouncing these already enumerated as the *true* "British Hawk-moths," and for this reason we have separated them from others of a doubtful kind.　　　　E. J. S. C.

PINES (*PANDANUS CANDELABRUM, P. ODORATIISSMUS.*)

As many as thirty species of Pandanus have been enumerated. The chandelier tree (*P. candelabrum*), however, is perhaps one of the most striking in appearance of all the species. The branches spread out all round the trunk, bending gracefully downwards, and the ends again inclining upwards, where they are crowned with the tuft of bright green leaves. This species, like some of its fellows of large or tree-like growth, is provided by nature with numerous aërial roots. These roots are thrown out all round the stem, and at irregular intervals from each other—sometimes a group of two or three being so close together as to appear almost united, and at other times a solitary one may be seen branching conspicuously by itself. They are usually most numerous near the ground, and are frequently so thick as to completely obscure the original trunk, but they are by no means confined to the lower part of the trunk. At a distance of some feet from the ground they may be seen either breaking through the epidermis or bark, or hanging down, ready to bury themselves in the soil. A full-grown Pandanus, so supported, has about its lower extremities somewhat the appearance of a mangrove-tree; the aërial roots of the latter, however, branch and curve in a much more irregular manner, which is the nature of dicotyledonous trees to do, while in the families allied to the Screw Pines the contrary is the case. The tips or spongioles of these aërial roots, as they hang from the trunks, are protected by thin woody caps, which fall off or decay when the roots touch the ground. The fruit of *Pandanus candelabrum* is nearly round, and is composed of a series of sub-compressed, ovate, angular, drupaceous nuts or seeds, having an exceedingly hard and bone-like centre, with a stiff fibrous coating, which, when fresh, is covered with pulpy or fleshy matter. The shape and appearance of the fruit is not unlike the bread-fruit; and if it were more elongated, it would much resemble a pine-apple, except in colour, being mostly of a dark green, but yellowish towards the lower part; the apex of each of the drupes is crowned with from four to six brownish sessile stigmas. *Pandanus odoratissimus, L. fil*, is, perhaps, one of the most useful species, in an economic point of view. It is a plant some ten, twelve, or more feet high, with spreading, irregular branches, and closely imbricated leaves, arranged in three spiral rows round the ends of the branches. It grows in the islands of the Pacific Ocean, China, and the East Indies, being common along the banks of the canals and backwaters of Travancore, where it is planted for the purpose of binding the soil. The long leaves are full of tough fibres, which are used for making cordage of various thicknesses, as well as for making hunting-nets, and the drag-ropes of fishing-nets. Matting of all descriptions is likewise made from them. Some of the sleeping-mats, which are dyed or stained various colours, are fine specimens of native plaiting. The leaves are likewise used to make umbrellas, and they are said to furnish an excellent material for paper-making.

The fibre from the leaves is commonly used in Tinnivelley, when mixed with flax, for making ropes. The aërial roots are applied to a variety of purposes in India. Manufactories exist in some localities where hats, baskets, mats, etc., are made from them. On account of their light spongy nature, they make excellent stoppers for bottles in lieu of cork, and the more fibrous part, when beaten out and the pulp removed, is used for brushes for whitewashing, painting, etc. The roots are used medicinally by the native practitioners, and an oil prepared from them has the repute of being a cure for rheumatism. The flowers are odoriferous, as the specific name indicates. Besides the numerous uses already mentioned, the inner or pulpy part of the drupes is eaten as an article of food in times of scarcity. In some parts of N. Australia, indeed, the fleshy drupes of the Pandani are commonly eaten, being held in the mouth and sucked until the fleshy portion is consumed. In the Society Islands the women make very beautiful mats of the leaves, which are first prepared by burying them in the sand near the sea for about a month; this makes them soft, they are then carefully scraped with a shell which removes all irregularities, leaving that portion of the leaf intended for use fine and soft; the more care exercised in this preparation the finer and softer are the mats. After being thus prepared, the leaves are drawn across the edge of a shell previously notched or toothed at regular intervals, by which means they are divided into long narrow strips of equal width and are ready for plaiting.—*The Student and Intellectual Observer*, No. 1.

AN ABYSSINIAN KING.

The capital of Karagué is 1° 40′ south of the equator, within a complete zone of vapour all the year round. Fruitful showers seemed to be continually falling. On the same day, in the absence of marked seasons, sowing, ingathering, and reaping might be seen; and from November to April the rainfall increased or diminished as the sun became more or less vertical. The rain reached its climax about the 10th of April, when it again began to decline. In December, till 7th January, the usual maximum temperature in a hut open to the south was 81°, and the minimum 56°, at an elevation of 5000 feet above the sea-level. They had a great number of English grey days, very few bright ones, and never a perfectly Italian sky. Brushwood was used instead of firewood, which was scarce and dear, otherwise a fire would have been welcome in the mornings and evenings. The hilly nature of the country caused the rains to run off very fast, so that the ground was agreeable to walk on immediately after a shower.

To do honour to the king of this pleasant land, in approaching his palace Speke ordered the men to put down their loads and fire a volley. It immediately produced an invitation to come in. So, leaving the traps outside, Speke and Grant, attended by Bombay and a few of the seniors of the Wanguana, entered the vestibule, and, walking through exterior enclosures studded with huts of royal dimensions, were escorted to a pent-roofed *baraza*, which the Arabs had built as a sort of government office, where the king might conduct his state affairs. Here, as they entered, they saw, sitting cross-legged on the ground, Rumanika and his brother Nnanaji, both men of imposing appearance. The king was plainly dressed in an Arab's black choga, and wore dress stockings of rich-coloured beads and neatly-worked wristlets of copper. His brother, as being a great doctor, which included the pretensions of priest and magician, in addition to the check cloth wrapt round him, was covered with charms. At their sides lay huge pipes of black clay. In their rear, squatting as quiet as mice, were the king's sons, some six or seven lads, who wore leathern coverings about their middles, and little dream-charms tied under their chins. The first greetings of Rumanika, delivered in good Kisuahili, the language of the coast, were warm and affecting; and he heartily shook hands with them in a style common to England and Karagué, so as to make them feel at once they were in the company of men of a far superior order to those of the adjoining districts. They had fine oval faces, large eyes, and high noses, denoting the best blood of Abyssinia. Rumanika was six feet two inches in height; and his towering stature, combined with the simple dignity which stamped him as the shepherd of his people, as well as the pastoral staff, might have suggested a negro Agamemnon. After first asking their opinion of Karagué, which he thought the most beautiful country in the world, he inquired with a sly smile their opinion of Suwarora, and Usui hospitality in general; on which Speke took the opportunity of suggesting to him that it would be in his interest to call Suwarora to order, as his extortions acted as a dam in stopping the stream of traffic which would otherwise flow into Karagué. His curiosity had been excited by a letter which had come for Musa when he was staying with him during Speke's former expedition, and he inquired of Speke how information could be conveyed in that way, and asked, in fact, about all the wonders of the outer world, so that time flew with magic speed till it was time to retire; and the officers went to the spot they had chosen outside the palace for their encampment, with a fine view to the lake. Speke had, however, to return once to show Rumanika how white chiefs sat on their thrones, as one of the young princes had caught a glimpse of him sitting on his iron chair. When he had thoroughly enjoyed the sight, Speke took the opportunity of telling him that they had tasted no milk in Karagué in consequence of the prejudices of the people about their eating forbidden food; so the king gave them a cow for their especial use, and they found on their return that he had thoughtfully sent them another pot of his excellent beer. The Wanguana were in high good-humour now, and goats and fowls were continually brought in from all sides by orders of the king, though beads had still to be expended on the humbler articles of grain and plantains. But the coast-men found the wind very cold, and suspected they must be drawing near to England, which was the only cold place they had ever heard of.

The next day after the introduction, after astonishing Rumanika with the present of a revolving pistol, they were shown into his private hut, which surprised them by its neatness. The roof was supported with numerous clean poles, to which were fastened a large assortment of spears, brass-headed with iron handles, and iron-headed with wooden ones, of excellent workmanship. A large standing-screen of fine straw-plait work in elegant devices partitioned off one part of the room; and on the opposite side, as mere ornaments, were placed a number of brass grapnels, and small models of cows, made in iron for the king's amusement by the Arabs at Kufro. A return visit was paid by Rumanika and his brother the same evening, which was partly prompted by their eagerness to enter with the British officers on some rather delicate business. As they had heard they could find their way all over the world, they thought they would not have much difficulty in prescribing a magic medicine which would kill their brother Rogero, who lived as an outlaw on a hill overlooking the Kitangulé, and was a very sharp thorn in Rumanika's side. As a preliminary to the negotiations, the king had to tell how the case stood. Before their old father Dagara died, he had unwittingly said to the mother of Rogero, although he was the youngest born, what a fine king he would make; and the mother in consequence tutored him to expect to succeed, although primogeniture is the law of the land, subject to the proviso, which was also the rule with the ancient Persians, that the heir must have been born after his father's accession, which condition was here fulfilled in the case of all three brothers. Accordingly, as soon as Dagara had given up the ghost, the three princes fell out, Nnanaji siding with his elder brother, but half of the people siding with Rogero; and a war began, which was of doubtful issue, until Rumanika succeeding in obtaining from the Arabs the assistance of their slaves armed with muskets, and thus forced Rogero into exile, swearing he would have his revenge as soon as the Arabs were gone. Rumanika maintained that Rogero was entirely in the wrong, not only because the law was against him, but the judgment of Heaven also. On the death of the father, the three sons, who only could pretend to the crown, had a small mystic drum placed before them by the officers of state. It was only feather-weight in reality, but being loaded with charms, became too heavy for those not entitled to the crown to move. Neither of the other brothers could move it an inch, while Rumanika easily lifted it with his little finger.

It was of no use for Speke and Grant to deny that they possessed any such charm as Rumanika wanted; so, thinking they were only deterred by scruples, he then promised that, if they would only get his brother into his power, he would not kill him; in fact, he would not touch a hair of his head, but only gouge out his eyes to prevent him seeing to do any more harm. Speke's only alternative, under these circumstances, was to turn the conversation. He told Rumanika that if he would only bridle Suwarora, he would get so powerful through the visits of civilised men, joined with increased trade, that he need not be afraid of anybody; and offered to take one or two of his sons to be instructed in England, since he admired his race, and believed them to have sprung from the Abyssinians, whose king, Sahéla Salassie, had received rich presents from the Queen of England. The Abyssinians, he added, were Christians, and Rumanika would be so now, but that unfortunate accidents had caused his ancestors to forget their traditional faith. A long theological and historical discussion followed, which so pleased the king that he said he should be delighted if two of his sons could be taken to England. To the disappointment of the officers he subsequently drew back, some meddler having told him that there was no milk in England, and milk the young princes must have; and having also hinted that when they got there they might be sold as slaves. Speke finally explained the object of his visit, which was, besides seeing great kings like himself and strange countries, to open a road for commerce to the north, and hoped that Rumanika would assist him. The conference left the king in the best possible humour; he offered to do anything that would please his guests; admired their pictures, beads, boxes, and general outfit, and then took his leave.—George C. Swayne's *Lake Victoria*. London: Blackwood.

THE NATURAL HISTORY OF BRAZIL.

Before this meets the eye of the reader, Messrs. Ticknor and Field, of Boston, will have published a "Journey in Brazil," by Professor and Mrs. Louis Agassiz—an illustrated book of over 500 8vo pages. We have been favoured with advance sheets, from which we are enabled to give the following preliminary notice.

The narrative is interwoven with some of the more general results of Professor Agassiz' scientific observations, especially his inquiries into the distribution of the fishes in the greatest hydrographic basin in the world, and the proof of the former existence of glaciers throughout its extent. The vegetation of the tropics, seen by Professor Agassiz from a palæontological point of view, is drawn in charming pictures by Mrs. Agassiz' pen.

Mr. Agassiz believes that several well-characterised ichthyological faunæ can be distinguished in the Amazons. "The species," he says, "inhabiting the river of Para, from the border of the sea to the mouth of the Tocantins, differ from those which are met in the network of anastomosis which unite the river of Para with the Amazons proper. The species of the Amazons below the Xingu differ from those which occur higher up; those of the lower course of the Xingu differ from those of the lower course of the Tapajos. Those of the numerous igarapés and lakes of Manhaés differ as much from those of the principal course of the Great River and of its great affluents." Even shores, which, from a geographical point of view, must be considered as opposite banks of the same stream, were found to be the abodes each of an essentially different ichthyological population. A few fish, such as the Pirarucu, were found throughout the whole extent of the river, although their migrations were evidently limited to movements from shallow to deeper waters, and back again to shoals.

Even bearing in mind the large number of distinct fanuæ, we are astounded to hear of the multitude of species inhabiting the river: at the close of his explorations, Professor Agassiz writes to the Emperor of Brazil, "it is very difficult for me to familiarise myself with the idea that the Amazons nourishes nearly twice as many species as the Mediterranean, and a more considerable number than the Atlantic, taken from one pole to the other." And again, "All the rivers of Europe united, from the Tagus to the Volga, do not furnish one hundred and fifty species of fresh-water fishes: and yet, in a little lake near Manaos, called Lago Hyanuary, the surface of which covers hardly four or five hundred square yards, we have discovered more than twelve hundred distinct species, the greater part of which have not been observed elsewhere." He estimates the total number as not less than eighteen hundred or two thousand species. His artist made eight hundred drawings of fish.

Professor Agassiz' attention was early arrested by a very peculiar formation near Rio, which he at once suspected to be drift; it was not long before he found, at Tijuca, "a drift-hill with innumerable erratic boulders, as characteristic as any he had seen in New England." The sandy clay of the vicinity which rested immediately upon the partially stratified metamorphic rock frequently contained these boulders. The extensive decomposition of the rock, which often made it very difficult to determine the line of demarcation between the rocks and the drift, had, of course, obliterated every trace of rock-polishing or grooving which might once have been present; yet, even where the disintegration was extensive, it had not destroyed the undulating lines of the *roches moutonnès* upon which the drift rested. Aided by frequent examinations of the geology in the vicinity of Rio, Mr. Agassiz and his assistants were able to trace the same formation throughout every part of Brazil which they explored. Whatever the nature of the underlying rock, they always found at the surface the same homogeneous clayey reddish paste containing quartz pebbles. In the Amazons valley, however, the relations of this sandy clay to the underlying deposits were of a different nature, and have furnished the basis of a remarkable hypothesis presented pretty fully in this work. Throughout the valley, three distinct deposits occur:

1st. Finely laminated clays, resting upon a well-stratified sand-stone, and overtopped by a crust almost resembling a ferruginous quartzite.

2nd. A cross-stratified, highly ferruginous sandstone, with occasional quartz pebbles.

3rd. The ochraceous, unstratified sandy clay already mentioned, spreading over the undulating surface of the sandstone, and filling all its depressions and cracks.

We are not told the extent of the first series of beds; the second sometimes attains a thickness of more than 800 feet, and the third ordinarily varies from 20 to 50 feet.

Notwithstanding the thickness of these deposits, their compact structure, and the fact that the first and second are comformable to each other, while the third lies uncomformably above them, Mr. Agassiz believes that they *all* belong to the glacial epoch. He attributes their position and variable character to the conditions under which they were deposited, and the hardness and compactness of many in the series, to the heat of a tropical sun. This conviction is founded on the correspondence of their materials to those accumulated in glacier bottoms; on the resemblance of the uppermost layer to the Rio drift (the glacial origin of the latter he believes to be unquestionable) and on his views of the physical history of the valley in general. These require the explanation of two phenomena: the filling of the basin of the Amazons with clays and sandstone to the height of more than 800 feet above the sea, with no seaward barrier of rock; and the subsequent denudation of the country to its present level. Mr. Agassiz thought the valley of the Amazons was an immense cretaceous basin filled with recent deposits, and that the history of its formation was briefly this:

1st. The filling of the whole valley with a glacier, which extended from the high lands of Guiana to those of central Brazil. *2nd.* The formation of a vast termal moraine, which, upon the retreat of the glacier, shut out the sea and eventually left an immense fresh-water lake. *3rd.* The partial melting of the glacier, during which time the lower stratified layers were deposited, the coarse materials falling to the bottom, *4th.* The disintegration of the whole body of ice, at which period more or less regular beds of sand were deposited to the depth of 800 feet. *5th.* The breaking through of the morainal barrier and the extensive denudation of the whole country; which was followed by, *6th,* a period of quiet accumulation of ochraceous sandy clay with boulders brought by floating ice at the close of the ice period. *7th.* A second drainage, caused by the total destruction of the seaward barrier and a reduction of the waters to their present level. *8th.* The gradual encroachment of the sea upon the river-bed, destroying all traces of a delta, and causing the former affluents near its mouth to flow into the sea.—*The Journal of Travel and Natural History*, No. 1. London: Williams and Norgate.

PRE-HISTORIC MAN.

When we reflect how very slowly the strata constituting the most superficial crust of the earth were deposited, we may form an idea of the time required for the formation of the alluvia in which the rudely worked flints are found. One of the most distinguished geologists of our day, M. Elie de Beaumont, has remarked in his " Lectures on Practical Geology," that the entrenched camps of the Romans and the megalithic monuments furnish us with proofs of the great age of the surface of the earth. Where rivers drift down slime and stones, where the sea deposits sand and gravel and undermines the cliffs, the movement of uplifting and displacement is more marked; but it still goes on very slowly, as proved by the exploration of the Egyptian Delta. Before the historic period, however, this might not have been the case, and more frequent and powerful revolutions may possibly have caused more rapid accumulations. This possibility does not allow us to approximate with certainty—assuming as a chronological element the actual facts of the deposit—the period from which date the hewn flints, the arms of horn or bone which we disinter. The calculations made on this basis are very arbitrary; as, for instance: a Swiss naturalist, M. Mortol, whilst studying the cone of Torentine deposits of the Tiniére, near Villeneuve, observed that Roman antiquities were found at a depth of 1.30 metres in a stratum of from sixteen to seventeen centimetres in thickness. He assumed this figure as a measure of the uplifting of the cone during a period of time equal to that elapsed since the Roman period—that is sixteen hundred or eighteen hundred years; and he inferred hence, that of the two subjacent layers, the age of the first, in which bronze appears, was three thousand or four thousand years; and that of the lower, in which polished stone instruments were found, was from four thousand to seven thousand years.

Now it is evident that this calculation rests on the hypothesis that the torrent of Tiniére did not drift more alluvia in times anterior to our own than it has done for sixteen hundred or eighteen hundred years—an hypothesis which may be incorrect. When the cold was much more intense than in our day, the climate more severe, and the deep snows swelled the torrents to a greater volume, these deposits may have accumulated more rapidly. It is certain that the quaternary period in which a fauna and climatic condition existed very different from those observed in Gaul at the date of Cæsar's conquest, must have been removed far beyond the historic times; but how many ages elapsed between the age of caves containing hewn stones and that of the dolmens and lacustrine cities?

Without affording us an exact date, the determination of the physical characteristics of the human race is a very important element; for it enables us to ascertain if the tribes which inhabited the caves, the lacustrine cities, or those which deposited their dead under the dolmens, belonged all to the same family, or if they were united by a greater or less affinity with the races of present Europe, whose arrival on that continent dates at least three thousand five hundred or four thousand years ago.

Unfortunately, the number of crania and fragments of skeletons extracted from the deposits of the stone age is very small: and they do not possess identity of shape sufficiently marked to establish the characteristics of a race. A skull was discovered at Neanderthal, near Dusseldorf; another in the plastic clay of a lateral valley of the Arno; a jaw and cranium, presenting a remarkable depression, at Moulin Quignon, near Abbeville; a cranium, indicating a less developed forehead and less elevated stature than those of our race in the cave of Engis near Liege (belonging to the age of hewn stone); and other crania in the turf-pits of Denmark; while human bones have been found in various caves in Belgium and the south of France. All that can be said is, that these skulls, like those from the lacustrine cities, present the well-marked brachycephalic (round head) type which some ethnologists regard as being that of the Ligurian head; the bones of the cranial vault being nearly always very thick, as seen in the ancient Armoricans.

Anatomists have imagined they saw a marked resemblance between the majority of these crania and those discovered in Russia, in the tombs of the Finnish or Tchoudic race; but even if this resemblance were verified, we cannot hence conclude that all the monuments of the stone age were necessarily the work of the same race. A very distinguished Danish antiquary, M. Worsaae, has remarked that as no dolmens or cromlechs are to be found in Finland or in Lapland, their construction must be attributed to another people. On the other hand, M. Alexander Bertrand has shown that the distribution of the dolmens in Europe is but little favourable to the hypothesis that they were made by the Celts; they must belong to a race which spread over the western coast of Europe and penetrated into the interior of the continent by the great water-highways. We may also observe that these megalithic monuments are not found in the Danubian countries, which the Celts crossed before reaching France, nor in

Cisalpine Gaul, whither they immigrated at a later period. The dolmens of the stone age were consequently the work of a people extirpated by the Celts or subjugated and amalgamated with them.

The opinion that the men of the stone age were elder brethren of the Finns, would harmonize with the data of the quaternary fauna. Since the species which inhabited Southern France, Spain, and Italy—the mammoth, rhinoceros, musk-ox, and reindeer—retreated towards the north of Europe and Asia, when the climate moderated, the same may be naturally inferred as regards the human races contemporary with these animals. The Basque or Iberian tribes, the savage Ligurians, who at the time of their subjugation by the Romans, inhabited caves, may, indeed, be the descendants of this primeval people, modified by contact with Asiatic emigrants. Ignorant of the art of cultivating the soil, the autochthonous tribes led a life closely resembling that of the tribes of North America and Arctic Russia, whose ancestors they probably were. Nevertheless, as there is in the beginning an intimate connection between climatic conditions and the social state, we cannot infer from an identity of industrial products an identity of race. The arms and stone utensils made at this day by the savages of Polynesia and some islands in the Indian Ocean, and which are found among the ancient tribes of the New World, present a remarkable similarity to those found in the most ancient deposits and tombs of Europe.

These coincidences warrant us in supposing that the men of the stone age were in a social state, resembling that of the islanders of Andaman and New Caledonia, or rather that of the Greenlanders and Esquimaux. This is strengthened by the fact, that there have been extracted from the caves and ancient deposits of France, Switzerland, and England, oblong hatchets, flat on one side, and convex on the other, having a short handle, and which are identical with those now used by the Esquimaux to scrape the skins of which their garments are made.

Living on the borders of rivers, or in the middle of lakes, these people soon felt the necessity of constructing boats; and those found in the turf-pits and in the beds of certain watercourses resemble in many respects the canoes of the Polynesians and the *kayaks* of the Esquimaux and Greenlanders. They are almost all hollowed out of the trunk of a single tree, and some seem to have carried a mast. One was found in the bed of the Seine, and is now in the museum of Saint Germain; one was buried beneath the grit of the Rhone; another was hidden in the bed of the little river La Loue (Jura), a fourth was discovered in Lake Geneva, near Morges; and lastly and finally, one was exhumed in 1860 from a turf-pit near Abbeville.

The food of the tribes inhabiting the borders of the sea and the rivers was chiefly fish and shell-fish, while those of the interior lived on the flesh of animals, which they killed with their stone weapons. The accumulations of bones found in the caves prove this fact. Some of them are even marked by the instruments used in stripping off the flesh; but the men of that period were not satisfied with devouring the meat: they were fond of the marrow, as indicated by the mode of fracture of the long bones. Another curious peculiarity which assimilates the habits of the stone age with those characterizing savage nations—those of North America, particularly—results from an examination of the human teeth. The greater part of the incisors are much worn and flattened on their upper extremity: this condition of the teeth is also seen among the Greenlanders, and has been remarked in the jaws of several Egyptian mummies. It was produced by the habit of tearing and grinding the meat with the front teeth. The accounts by the ancients of the Troglodytes of Asia and Africa, who continued like the first men, to inhabit caves, agree, in many points, with the facts taught us by the study of the bone-bearing caverns and quaternary deposits. This circumstance is an additional proof of the inequality in the progress of civilization.

Whilst certain nations in Asia had reached, three thousand years before Christ, a social state which excels that of many contemporary peoples, some tribes were, fifteen or eighteen centuries ago, and are even in our day, in the same state of barbarism indicated by the stone age.

Man emerged, probably from the abject and miserable condition in which he grovelled only by the effects of contact with more advanced nations—with those who (history and the comparative study of languages and mythologies teach us) emigrated from the east. Thus without the discovery of Christopher Columbus, the Indian tribes would be, at this moment, what they were four hundred years ago. The primeval autochthonous races of Europe have disappeared or retreated before the influence of emigrants of a superior order: the same is the case with the indigenes of the New World. These races are gradually being extinguished, like the barbarians of Polynesia and Australia.

The tenth chapter of Genesis, which carries us back to a period at least two thousand years before our era, exhibits the greater part of Eastern Asia and the Mediterranean basin overrun by the descendants of nations who had made great advances in civilization. The first period of the stone age in Europe must have preceded this date by a considerable length of time. This datum, which is justified by the Egyptian texts, is again confirmed by the figures represented in the tombs of the fourth and fifth dynasties of the Pharoahs. These figures exhibit a fauna identical with that now found on the shores of the Nile; whence it follows that at the period of the pyramids of Gizeh the zoological distribution in the Mediterranean basin was such as we find it to day. We must therefore go far beyond these times, which preceded our era by three thousand or thirty-five hundred years to find the quaternary fauna. On the other hand the emigration of the Indo-European races, who introduced into our continent the knowledge of agriculture and the manufacture of the metals, cannot be less than three thousand years ago. The close of the polished stone age belongs, therefore, to a period elapsed since that epoch, whilst the age of hewn stone must be fixed at double that number of years in Europe.—*Lippincott's Magazine.*

MONKEYS.

THE ravine down which the brook fell was well wooded, and the trees were filled with the "tota" or "waag," a beautiful little greenish-grey monkey, with black face and white whiskers. I followed a troop of them for a long time, while the porters and servants were resting—not at all with the intention of hurting them, but merely for the pleasure of watching their movements. If you go tolerably carefully towards them they will allow you to approach very near, and you will be much amused with their goings-on, which differ but little from those of the large no-tailed monkeys, "Beni Adam." You may see them quarrelling, making love, mothers taking care of their children, combing their hair, nursing and suckling them; and the passions—jealousy, anger, love—as fully and distinctly marked as in men. They have a language as distinct to them as ours is; and their women are as noisy and fond of disputation as any fish-fag in Billingsgate.

The monkeys, especially the Cynocephali, who are astonishingly clever fellows, have their chiefs, whom they obey implicitly, and a regular system of tactics in war, pillaging expeditions, robbing corn-fields, &c. These monkey-forays are managed with the utmost regularity and precaution. A tribe, coming down to feed from their village on the mountain (usually a cleft in the face of some cliff) brings with it all its members, male and female, old and young. Some, the elders of the tribe, distinguishable by the quantity of mane which covers their shoulders, like the lion's, take the lead, peering cautiously over each precipice before they descend, and climbing to the top of every rock or stone which may afford them a better view of the road before them. Others have their posts as scouts on the flanks or rear; and all fulfil their duties with the utmost vigilance, calling out at times, apparently to keep order among the motley pack which forms the main body, or to give notice of the approach of any real or imagined danger. Their tones of voice on these occasions are so distinctly varied, that a person much accustomed to watch their movements will at length fancy—and perhaps with some truth—that he can understand their signals.

The main body is composed of females, inexperienced males, and the young people of the tribe. Those of the females who have small children carry them on their back. Unlike the dignified march of the leaders, the rabble go along in a most disorderly manner, trotting on and chattering, without taking the least heed of anything, apparently confiding in the vigilance of their scouts. Here a few of the youth linger behind to pick the berries off some tree, but not long, for the rear-guard coming up forces them to regain their places. There a matron pauses for a moment to suckle her offspring, and, not to lose time, dresses its hair while it is taking its meal. Another younger lady, probably excited by jealousy or by some sneering look or word, pulls an ugly mouth at her neighbour, and then uttering a shrill squeal highly expressive of rage, vindictively snatches at her rival's leg or tail with her hand, and gives her perhaps a bite in the hind quarters. This provokes a retort, and a most unladylike quarrel ensues, till a loud bark of command from one of the chiefs calls them to order. A single cry of alarm makes them all halt and remain on the *qui vive*, till another bark in a different tone re-assures them, and they then proceed on their march.

Arrived at the corn-fields, the scouts take their position on the eminences all round, while the remainder of the tribe collect provision with the utmost expedition, filling their cheek-pouches as full as they can hold, and then tucking the heads of corn under their armpits. Now, unless there be a partition of the collected spoil, how do the scouts feed?—for I have watched them several times, and never observed them to quit for a moment their post of duty till it was time for the tribe to return, or till some indication of danger induced them to take to flight. They show also the same sagacity in searching for water, discovering at once the places where it is most readily found in the sand, and then digging for it with their hands just as men would, relieving one another in the work if the quantity of sand to be removed be considerable.

Their dwellings are usually chosen in clefts of rocks, so as to protect them from the rain, and always placed so high that they are inaccessible to most other animals. The leopard is their worst enemy, for, being nearly as good a climber as they, he sometimes attacks them, and then there is a tremendous uproar. I remember one night, when outlying on the frontier, being disturbed in my sleep by the most awful noises I ever heard—at least they appeared as such, exaggerated by my dreams. I started up thinking it was an attack of the negroes, but I soon recognised the voices of my baboon friends from the mountain above. On my return home I related the fact to the natives, who told me that a leopard was probably the cause of all this panic. I am not aware how he succeeds among them. The people say that he sometimes manages to steal a young one, and make off, but that he seldom ventures to attack a full-grown ape. He would doubtless find such a one an awkward customer; for the ape's great strength and activity, and the powerful canine teeth with which he is furnished, would render him a formidable enemy, were he, from desperation, forced to stand and defend his life. It is most fortunate that their courage is only sufficiently great to induce them to act on the defensive. This indeed they only do against a man when driven to it by fear: otherwise they generally prefer prudence to valour. Had their combativeness been proportioned to their physical powers, coming as they do in bodies of two or three hundred, it would be impossible for the natives to go out of the village except in parties, and armed; and, instead of little boys, regiments of armed men would be required to guard the corn-fields.

I have, however, frequently seen them turn on dogs, and have heard of their attacking women whom they may have accidentally met alone in the roads or woods. On one occasion I was told of a woman who was so grievously maltreated by them, that, although she was succoured by the opportune arrival of some passers-by, she died a few days after, from the fright and ill-treatment she had undergone.

To show that their cleverness depends in some measure upon powers of reflection, and not entirely on that instinct with which all animals are endowed, and which serves them only to procure the necessaries of life and to defend themselves against their enemies, I will relate an anecdote to which I can testify as an eye-witness. At 'Khartūm, the capital of the provinces of Upper Nubia, I saw a man showing a large male and two females of this breed, who performed several clever tricks at his command. I entered into conversation with him as to their sagacity, the mode of teaching them, and various other topics relating to them. Speaking of his male monkey, he said that he was the most dexterous thief imaginable, and that every time he was exhibited, he stole dates and other provisions sufficient for his food for the day. In proof of this he begged me to watch him for a few minutes. I did so, and presently the keeper led him to a spot near a date-seller, who was sitting on the ground with his basket beside him. Here his master put him through his evolutions; and, although I could perceive that the monkey had an eye to the fruit, yet so completely did he disguise his intentions, that no careless observer would have noticed it. He did not at first appear to care about approaching the basket; but gradually brought himself nearer and nearer, till at last he got quite close to its owner. In the middle of one of his feats he suddenly started up from the ground on which he was lying stetched like a corpse, and uttering a cry as of pain or rage, fixed his eyes full at the face of the date-seller, and then, without moving the rest of his body, stole as many dates as he could hold in one of his hind hands. (Apes are not quadru*peds*, but quadru*mana*). The date-man being stared out of countenance, and his attention diverted by this extraordinary movement, knew nothing about the theft till a bystander told him of it, and then he joined heartily in the laugh that was raised against him. The monkey, having very adroitly popped the fruit into his cheek-pouches, had moved off a few yards, the crowd following him, when a boy pulled him sharply by the tail. Conscience-stricken, he fancied that it had been done in revenge by the date-seller whom he had robbed; and so, passing close by the true offender and between the legs of one or two others in the circle, he fell on the unfortunate fruiterer, and would no doubt have bitten him severely but for the interference of his master, who came to the rescue.

I have never thought it worth while to teach monkeys of my own any tricks, always preferring to watch their natural actions. I had in Abyssinia a young one of the same breed as the last mentioned. From the first day she was given to me her attachment was remarkable, and nothing would induce her to leave me at any time; in fact her affection was sometimes ludicrously annoying. As she grew up she became more sedate, and was less afraid of being left alone. She would sit and watch whatever I did, with an expression of great intelligence; and the moment I turned my back she would endeavour to imitate what I had been doing. Mr. Rodatz, master of the German brig "Alf," coming up the country for a cargo of animals for Mauritius, gave me a copy of " Peter Simple," the first English book, beside the Bible and Nautical Almanac, that I had seen for more than two years. As soon as I was alone I of course sat down and began greedily to feast on its contents, though I had read it several times before leaving England. "Lemdy" was as usual seated by my side, at times looking quietly at me, occasionally catching a fly, or, jumping on my shoulder, endeavouring to pick out the blue marks tattoed there. At last I got up to light a pipe, and on my return found she had taken my seat with the book on her knee, and with a grave expression of countenance was turning over the leaves page by page, as she had observed me to do—with the difference only that, not been able to read their contents, she turned one after the other as quickly as possible, and that, from her arms being short, and she not yet much used to books, she tore each page from the top nearly to the bottom. She had completed the destruction of half the volume before I returned. During my momentary absences she would often take up my pipe and hold it to her mouth till I came back, when she would restore it to me with the utmost politeness.

These monkeys are caught in various ways. One plan adopted by the Arabs of Tàka has struck me as the most simple, and at the same time as likely to succeed as any other. Large jars of the common country beer, sweetened with dates, and drugged with the juice of the "òscher" (Asclepias arborea), are left near the places where they come to drink. The monkeys, pleased with the sweetness of the liquor, drink largely of it, and soon falling asleep, are taken up senseless by the Arabs, who have been watching from a distance.—*Mansfield Parkyns' Travels in Abyssinia.* London: Murray.

THE YEW.

In strong contrast with all other trees indigenous to the British islands, stands, by reason of its poisonous foliage, the sombre yew. Were not a single example of deleterious properties to exist among our trees, it would at least be in exception to the remarkable and significant rule that everything in nature shall have its dreary side. Thank God, it is left to our own option to turn from the darkness to the light, and to shelter below branches that are not only innocent but liberal. Who would expect that among grasses, the sweet pasture of innumerable kine, and in their larger forms, the source of corn, there is yet one to be found with the taint of poison in it ; and that abreast of the lilies there is a flower freighted with death? Such, however, is the fact, and darnel and colchicum are but illustrations and prefigurements, in their respective provinces, of the mournful truth that comes out so strongly in the consideration of the yew. Not that the berries are poisonous, for these, though viscid, and with no peculiarly fine flavour to recommend them, may be eaten with impunity ; it is in the leaves that the hurtful juices are contained, after the same manner as in the laurel, the little plums produced by which are innocuous, though extract prepared from the leaves is speedily fatal. Probably it is in some measure from this poisonous quality that the yew has been so often associated with death and churchyards ;

Cheerless, unsocial plant, that loves to dwell
'Midst skulls and coffins, epitaphs and tombs.

Remember, however, that it is man who has placed it in such localities. Nature gives the yew a very different abiding-place from the cemetery, and rightly viewed and understood, perhaps the yew may prove after all, notwithstanding its possession of deadly sap, to be a tree that should contribute ideas rather of cheerfulness than of mourning. Upon rugged limestone scars and cliffs, where nothing else, save a little ivy, can establish anchorage, the yew is often seen clinging, as if bound to the rock with clamps of iron. Well-nigh flattened against the perpendicular face of the stone, and with the merest ledge or crevice for its feet, it holds itself unchanged for centuries, and is the most imposing picture nature affords of imperturbable endurance. So, too, upon many a remote hillside, beaten and ravaged by tempests ; exposure to the wrath of the elements seems congenial, and to live in the midst of perils, joy and strength. Being an evergreen too, it contrasts finely with the deciduous trees that ordinarily are not far off, or that circle it as companions ; even with other evergreens it has a contrast such as no other developes, since the young growth which makes its onward push in the spring is of the same unyielding tint as the oldest foliage.

Once a year, at least, we see all other evergreens decked with light and pretty shades of verdure, indicating the flow of their annual tide of life ; the yew, inexorable to the last, gives no register of the seasons, and makes no comment on their lapse. Only for a brief period, when the fruit, looking as if wrought of chalcedony, crimsons before the last sunshine of the autumn, does the yew seem affected by nature's kindnesses and genialities. Instead of an emblem of death and sorrow, it should stand, therefore, as the representative of intrepidity and the impregnable, and I cannot but think that some such view of its true significance must have actuated those who either laid the foundations of their churches and abbeys close to existing yews, or who having raised such buildings, then planted yew-trees close alongside. For what more sublime picture of the endurance of God's kingdom could be selected, or what emblem more exact of the immortality of man? To this day stand the three old yews beneath which the founders of Fountains Abbey sat themselves down in rural council. Ages have passed away since the sound of vespers fell from those beautiful aisles upon the ear of the wayfarer who lingered to gather cowslips in the meads around, or to note the tender blue of the innumerable forget-me-not, or to mark the flow of the tranquil river, and its darting fishes;—everything is gone except the sweet and solemn requiem pronounced by ruin,—everything except those grand old trees, which seem capable of witnessing the rise and fall of just such another fabric, were some architect to tempt them with renewal of the old magnificence.

It may be useful and practically good to deem the yew an emblem of death. We are taught here, as in a thousand other places, that it is better to deem it an emblem of the changeless, that is to say, of Life. Nothing is lost, and everything is gained, by letting nature speak to us, whenever she will, of immortality. The lesson of death and decay is too plainly and too constantly recited to make it needful that we should go out of our way for illustrations; much more should we refrain from converting symbols that are inherently suggestive of good into emblems of what is only too familiar in its reality.

Botanically considered, the yew holds a place in nature shared by only a small company. Plain and palpable as are the great classes and families into which plants are resolvable by men of science, every one of them a solar system as it were, in miniature, certain grand ideas of structure constituting centres round which minor ones are disposed planet-wise,—plain and palpable as are these great classes in regard to their centres, and the mass of their elements, there are located upon the frontiers of all, without exception, certain curious forms which give a hand, so to speak, to either side. Just as whales link mammals to fishes,—living in the ocean, like sharks and dolphins, yet suckling their offspring after the manner of female quadrupeds; just as bats connect mammals again with birds; and just as those comical little creatures, the armadillos, connect, still once more, the mammalia with the reptilian races;—so among plants do certain strange organisms stand midway between the especially great and obvious classes, and constitute the bridges whereby all things are maintained as a unity. The Conifers, to which the members of the yew-tree family stand as a kind of appendix, have for one of their own ennobling functions this very duty of associating forms otherwise unconnected. The stems, the branches, the style of growth, the longevity, the succulent fruit, the beautiful timber of the yew, link it at once, and with applause, to the foresters over which the cedar presides, and which are to oaks and beeches just what opulent islands are to the continents they lie adjacent to; the flowers, on the other hand, point a different way, and when we take that curious Japanese member of the yew-tree group called the *Salisburia*, the leaves are, on a great scale, the leaflets of the maiden-hair fern! No one examining the leaves of this remarkable tree could suppose otherwise than that they belonged to a fern; no one, looking at the substantial woody boughs could have a moment's doubt that the tree conformed, so far, with the oak and walnut! The flowers of the yew itself are inconspicuous in the extreme. They come out early in spring, usually about March, and are so much hidden by the foliage as to be overlooked by any except the curious interrogator. They are difficult, moreover, of dissection, and the two sexes, male and female, are produced upon different trees. Hence it is only upon certain individuals, or those which develop female flowers, that the characteristic red berries are to be discovered. In structure these pretty fruits are not very unlike the acorn of the oak, only that instead of a hard and woody cup, the receptacle is succulent and bright red. That famous fruit of Australia which is described by lovers of the marvellous and by the ignorant as a "cherry with its stone upon the outside," is very nearly the same thing as the yew-tree berry, only produced by a different tree. Botanists call it *Exocarpus*.

The slow growth of the yew, being a part of its life-history, belongs, like the flowers, to the botanical idea of the plant. To this is chiefly owing the hardness and the smoothness of the wood, which for delicacy and beauty of colouring is excelled by few, the box alone, perhaps, presenting a surface of greater evenness and polish. Yew is the most esteemed of all our native woods for high-class turnery-work and for inlaying. It has the recommendation also of being rarely or never attacked by insects, guarded, as it were, like sandal-wood, by some native objectionableness. Sections, both horizontal and vertical, constitute truly beautiful objects for the parlour-museum, and form an excellent nucleus for a collection of such things. When so much time is devoted to "scrap-book" making and to stamp-collecting, useful up to a certain point as such pastimes may be, it seems a pity that as much leisure and activity should not be given to collections of wood-sections, which endure for ever, are beautiful and varied as seashells, and cost little more than the trouble of polishing. In bygone times the wood of the yew-tree was famous among archers, and it is curious to note that no less than three kings of this country have lost their lives through its instrumentality. First, the ill-fated Harold, at the battle of Hastings; then, William Rufus, in the New Forest; thirdly, Richard Cœur de Lion, at Limoges. The battle of Crecy, Poictiers, and Agincourt, were won through the energy of the yew-tree bowmen, and perhaps the milder archery of the present day would be more successful were the competitors to fall back upon the ancient material of their thrice-ancient instrument. The rings indicating age are in general very plainly seen in the yew, and form a striking illustration of the marvellous antiquity the tree is witness to. We often hear of "railway-time" and of "sidereal time;" the yew-tree helps to enforce upon us the grandeur of the idea of "tree-time." The vast age attained by individuals is accompanied, as would be looked for, by commensurate bulk and girth. In the graveyard attached to Bucklaw church, about a mile from Dover, there is, or was until recently, a yew with a trunk of no less than 24 feet in circumference. In Tisbury churchyard, Dorsetshire, there is another, now quite hollow, with an entrance gate on one side, and measuring 37 feet in circumference; while in the churchyard of Fortingal, Perthshire, stand the remains of one which before the trunk fell in, and it became reduced to its present condition of little more than shell, measured round about the incredible number of 56 feet. One of the most picturesque of our ancient yews ornaments the churchyard of Darley Dale, Derbyshire.

No mention of the yew is made in Scripture, though there is reason to believe that it anciently grew upon the mountains of Lebanon, if not there still, since the tree extends far into central Asia. The Hebrew word *eres*, translated "cedar" in the authorised version, would seem to have been, like many other botanical terms occurring in holy writ, of a wide and general sense, including not only the genuine cedar, *Cedrus Libani*, but other species of the conifers suitable for building purposes, and likewise the yew. Among the relics discovered at Nineveh it is said that there are fragments of yew-tree wood, declared to be such by the peculiar structure of the fibre, as seen under the microscope. Truly does this marvellous instrument "cast light into the graves of Time." Virgil uses the name *pinus*, in one place at least, to signify timber-trees in general; and the frugality practised by the ancients in regard to the names of flowers and fruits would seem to give additional weight to the opinion. Scarcely a dozen flowers are mentioned by the ancient poets, including those of the Holy Land. The rose, the lily, the violet, are spoken of; but in all these, and in all the rest, the same kind of collective idea seems to be held. When we read of the yew in the classical poets, it is in the same spirit of dread and disrelish that belongs to modern ones. Ovid, for example, selects this tree to mark the place of descent into Tartarus—"Dismal yew shades the deep declining way that, through labyrinths of shade and horror, leads to Tartarus; languid Styx exhaling continual clouds."—*The Trees of Old England*. By LEO H. GRINDON.

THE TSALTSAL, OR ABYSSINIAN SPEAR-FLY.

In the *Athenæum*, Feb. 8, we read the following from Mr. S. Sharp:—"In all sciences we are much interested in avoiding a variety of names for the same object, and in acting upon the rule that the name by which it is first known shall not without good reason be put aside for a new name. The above-mentioned fly, the dreadful scourge of Abyssinia, was first brought to this country by the traveller Bruce, who called it, as he had there heard it called, the Tzaltzala-fly. It has since been brought here by Dr. Livingstone from South Africa, and it is called in his book the Tsetse-fly. Bruce had very properly conjectured it was the fly mentioned, but without its name, in Isaiah vii. 18, 'The Lord shall hiss, or whistle, for the fly that is in the uttermost parts of the rivers of Egypt.' But it is to Dr. Margoliouth that we are indebted for the remark that it is twice mentioned by name in the Hebrew Scriptures. In Deut. xxviii. 42 we read, 'All thy trees and fruit of thy land shall the Tsaltsal consume;' or, in the Authorised Version, the locust. But it would seem that the writer was not well acquainted with its habits, as it does not destroy vegetables. The next passage is yet more important, because it had hitherto baffled the commentators. Isaiah, in chap. xviii. 1, addresses Abyssinia as 'The land of the winged Tsaltsal, which is beyond the rivers of Ethiopia.' Here, then, we have Bruce's name for this fly supported by the Hebrew writers; and the two together should make the naturalists give up the new name lately introduced by Dr. Livingstone. In Job xli. 7, Tsaltsal is a spear or harpoon with which fish are killed; and hence the formidable little spikes attached to the fly's mouth may have given to it its name. In order to distinguish the insect from the piece of metal, Isaiah calls it 'the winged Tsaltsal,' or the spear-fly."

And in the number for Feb. 22 Mr. Francis Ainsworth writes:—"I would observe that although Tsetse may fairly be looked upon as a corruption of Tzaltzala or Tsaltsal, yet that the two insects (if the Tzalzala of Bruce is, as there is every reason to suppose, the same as the Seroot, or Sirūt, of Sir Samuel Baker), differ specifically, if not generically, certainly as much so as Œstrus from Hippobosca.

"The Tsetse, or *Glossina morsitans*, is figured in Livingstone's 'Missionary Travels,' &c., p. 571, from a drawing made by Dr. J. E. Gray, of the British Museum, and it is described by Livingstone himself (at pp. 80—83) as little larger than the common house-fly, and as being nearly of the same brown colour as the common honey-bee, the afterpart of the body having three or four yellow bars across it.

"The Abyssinian gad-fly, called by Sir Samuel Baker the Seroot-fly, is figured at p. 73 of that distinguished traveller's work on the 'Nile Tributaries of Abyssinia,' and is described as about the size of a wasp, with an orange-coloured body, with black and white rings. There are other differences to be at once detected on comparing the two drawings, but the above are quite sufficient to establish a specific distinction between the two insects. Both, however, have the same formidable spear-like proboscis, from which, Mr. Sharpe so well points out, its Biblical name was derived. Baal Zebub, 'the lord or master of flies' and the 'god of Ekron,' for inquiring after whom the death of Ahaziah was foretold by Elijah (2 Kings, i. 2, *et seq.*), may likewise have been so named from a scourge of a similar kind which afflicted the chief of the five Philistine states.

"Livingstone calls the Tsetse the elephant-fly, from its abounding in districts frequented by that animal, whilst the Seroot-fly appears, from Sir Samuel Baker's notices, to make its appearance with the giraffe in its migrations. It appears probable that as the horse, ox, sheep, reindeer, and even man, in certain low regions of the torrid zone, according to Humboldt, have their especial bot, or gad-flies, so the larger African animals may have theirs; and hence further research may show that the Tzalzala of Bruce differs as much from the gazelle-fly as the gazelle-fly does from the elephant-fly. The Scriptural allusions to the fly as the scourge of 'the uttermost parts of the rivers of Egypt,' and to Abyssinia, as 'the land of the winged Tsaltsal,' would not be affected by such a deduction.

"If these views should prove to be correct, some hopes for the future of such portions of Eastern and Central Africa as are afflicted by the presence of these formidable insects, may be derived from the reasonable supposition that, as the country becomes peopled, the larger animals will withdraw into more remote districts, and with them their fatal scourge of flies."

BREEDING GOLDFISH IN A GLASS SUGAR-BASIN.

The following interesting letters appeared in *The Field* for Feb. 8th.—I beg to inclose Mr. Cary's very interesting account of the breeding of goldfish, which I think will be interesting to the readers of *The Field*. G. Carey, Esq., is the respected hon. curator of the Museum at Ryde, of the Isle of Wight Literary and Philosophical Society.   EDMUND KELL.

Portwood Lawn, Southampton, Jan. 29.

Remy Villa, Monkton-street, Ryde, Isle of Wight.

Dear Sir,—According to promise, I send you an account of my breeding the goldfish in a glass sugar-basin. In the spring of 1866 I put into one of my tanks, two feet long, one foot wide, and six inches deep, with a rustic basket in the centre filled with gravel, and planted with water-cresses and other water plants, three gold fish, two females and one male, as the sequel proved (not knowing at the time or having the least idea of their breeding). Going into the room one day—I remember it was eight days before Whitsunday—I observed the water, which had always been clear, very muddy. I must tell you that at one end of the tank I put in a cigar box filled with earth, in which I planted some roots of a dwarf carex I found growing in a bog, and which the cat is very fond of eating. Seeing the water in such a disturbed state. I thought the said cat had been in the tank. I had not been in the room long before I saw the cause of the commotion, the male chasing one of the females. He drove her up on the basket, which was not an inch under water, being covered with cresses and other roots, &c. She floundered and splashed through, and he did the same in her track. Of course I knew she was spawning. I looked with my watchmaker's eye-glass, and saw a number of little golden balls sticking on the roots of the cresses, &c. The thought struck me that if I removed the ova I could breed them, as I thought, and subsequently proved, that the fish will eat the young.

The first thing at hand was a glass sugar-basin, into which I put a handful of gravel and some weeds. I then with a pair of tweezers picked off the roots, &c., with the ova sticking on them, and put them into the basin; in eight days I had a shoal of little fishes. To watch the development of the ova, I put three or four into a zoophyte trough, which I placed under the microscope and watched daily. On the third day a dark spot made its appearance; on the fifth I could trace the form of a fish curled up, with its tail to its head, exactly as you see the whitings trussed for cooking; this increased in size until the eighth day, when the egg split open, and the little fish wriggled out tail first.

I may add that in a day or so after the first the second female played the same part, the chasing and splashing over the basket continuing the whole day.

Subsequently I removed the fish from the basin into a garden seed pan about one foot diameter and six inches deep, where they are at the present time.

Last spring (1867), within a few days of the same date, exactly the same took place, the same female first, the other a day or so after; but I found out my mistake in placing the 1867 brood with the 1866. I distinctly saw the year-old fish swallowing their brothers and sisters of a few days old. I removed them to a separate pan. The first, eighteen months old, are now about an inch and a quarter long; the second, six months old, about half an inch. I may add that in both broods a number die at about six months old, from as it seems, an enlargement of the bladder and stomach, attended with inflammation.

P.S. I have sent you a simple statement of facts. I leave you to judge whether you think them worth recording.   GEO. CAREY.

Rev. E. Kell, M.A., F.S.A.

AUSTRALIAN TREE VEGETATION.

Statistics of actual measurement of trees compiled in various parts of the globe would be replete with deep interest, not merely to science, but disclose also in copious instances magnitudes of resources but little understood up to the present day. Not merely, however, in their stupendous altitude, but also in their celerity of growth, we have in all probability to accede to Australian trees the prize. Extensive comparisons instituted in the Botanic Gardens of this metropolis prove several species of Eucalyptus, more particularly Eucalyptus globulus and Eucalyptus obliqua, as well as certain Acacias—for instance, Acacia decurrens, or Acacia molissima—far excelling in their ratio of development any extra-Australian trees even on dry and exposed spots, such into which spontaneously our blue Gum-trees would not penetrate. This marvellous quickness of growth, combined with a perfect fitness to resist drought, has rendered many of our trees famed abroad, especially so in countries where the supply of fuel or of hard woods is not readily attainable, or where for raising shelter, like around the Cinchona plantations of India, the early and copious command of tall vegetation is of imperative importance. To us here this ought to be a subject of manifold significance. I scarcely need refer to the fact that for numerous unemployed the gathering of Eucalyptus seeds, of which a pound weight suffices to raise many thousand trees, might be a source of lucrative and extensive employment; but on this I wish to dwell, that in Australian vegetation we probably possess the means of obliterating the rainless zones of the globe, to spread at last woods over our deserts, and thereby to mitigate the distressing drought, and to annihilate perhaps even that occasionally excessive dry heat evolved by the sun's rays from the naked ground throughout extensive regions of the interior, and wafted with the current of air to the east and south, miseries from which the prevalence of sea-breezes renders the more littoral tracts of West and North Australia almost free. But in the economy of nature the trees, beyond affording shade and shelter, and retaining humidity to the soil, serve other great purposes. Trees ever active in sending their roots to the depth draw unceasingly from below the surface-strata those mineral elements of vegetable nutrition on which the life of plants absolutely depends, and which with every dropping leaf is left as a storage of aliment for the subsequent vegetation. How much lasting good could be effected, then, by mere scattering of seeds of our drought-resisting Acacias, and Eucalypts, and Casuarinas at the termination of the hot season along any watercourse, or even along the crevices of rocks, or over bare sands or hard clays, after refreshing showers? Even the rugged escarpments of the rocky, desolate ranges of Tunis, Algiers, and Morocco: even the Sahara itself, if it could not be conquered and rendered habitable, might have the extent of its oases vastly augmented, fertility might be secured again to the Holy Land, and rain to the Asiatic plateau or the desert of Atacama, or timber and fuel be furnished to Natal and La Plata. An experiment instituted on a bare ridge near our metropolis demonstrates what may be done.—*Dr. Mueller's Essay.*

THE OAK-FEEDING SILK WORM.

Dr. Wallace, of Colchester, who wrote the Prize Essay of the Entomological Society on the Japanese Oak-feeding Silkworm, Bombyx Yama Maï, gives the following directions for rearing this insect:—The eggs should be kept, during the winter, in a cool, dry, and well-aërated place, where the temperature does not exceed 40°, at most 50° F., till the Oak trees are breaking into leaf in the hedges. Eggs have been successfully wintered in a perforated zinc box, with double walls, kept in a cool, shaded porch; also outside a north window; in a refrigerator, where the thermometer marked 35°, 40°; or suspended within a dry soda-water bottle, hermetically sealed, and buried in the ground in the shade of a north wall. The temperature must be kept under 50° during the warm sunny days of spring, lest the worms hatch out too soon. They will then keep perhaps better out of doors, in a shady spot, where the cool night air helps to retard the worms. The vicinity of mice, birds, beetles, &c., must be avoided. It is well to plant acorns, or force young Oaklings, in pots, so as to obtain an earlier foliage, in case the worms hatch out prematurely. When the Oaks are breaking into leaf, bring the eggs into a temperature of 60°; expose them freely to light and fresh air; wash them well with water to cleanse away the mould and to moisten the shell, so that the young larvæ may escape more readily; and after a few days let them be exposed to a temperature of 70°, or upwards, and moistened every few days. It is a good plan to place the eggs on blotting-paper covered with a glass funnel, in the early sunshine. The worms will hatch out from 6 to 8 a.m., and crawl up the glass, whence they may readily be removed to their food by means of a stiff camel's hair brush moistened; avoid at all times touching the worms with the finger. Let the food be fresh and moist; admit fresh air freely, but shade the worms from sunshine; avoid the proximity of spiders, tomtits, robins, &c. This silkworm feeds on our English Oak, as well as the Turkey Oak and other kinds. In the same paper for Feb. 8, in speaking of Bombyx Cynthia, he says:—Eggs of the Bombyx Cynthia should be kept in a warm room, on blotting paper, moistened once daily, but not exposed to the sun's rays, lest they should be dried up. They generally hatch out in warm weather the fourteenth morning, about six o'clock. It saves trouble to suspend the eggs, the previous evening, in a muslin bag, to the leaf-stalk of an Ailantus leaf; folding a leaflet within the bag. If it is wished to rear the worms on a tree out of doors, the bag and Ailantus leaf may now both be thrust into a bag of the cheapest black muslin, 2 feet long and 9 inches wide; the mouth of the bag must be fastened up by a string tied round the base of the leaf-stem. The worm will hatch out and feed up therein in safety. To supply fresh food, cut the stalk, untie the string, empty out the dirt, and slip bag and all over another leaf, the first leaf, being undermost. At the third change of leaves, the first leaf, stale and withered, may be withdrawn. When the worms have moulted for the third time, the bags must be discontinued. To feed the worms on Ailantus leaves away from the tree, the stalk must be plunged in water, and it will keep fresh for three or four days. —*Gardener's Chronicle,* Jan. 25.

GRASSES.

It is no doubt the truth that generally speaking grasses are not qualified to take the highest place in the scale of relative beauty among garden plants; but it is true also that they have at least *a* place, and deserve to be much more observed and cultivated than they are at present. To the amateur gardener, whose sole object in cultivating a garden is to derive from it as much physical and intellectual recreation as possible, the grasses offer themselves as admirably adapted for various decorative purposes, both while growing and subsequently when dried for the decoration of the table, or for the formation of vignettes. Some few of the family have indeed acquired a popularity second to none of the favourite plants of the present day; everywhere among the lovers of the picturesque the queenly Pampas grass (*Gynerium argenteum*) is esteemed as one of the grandest of garden decorations, and the universal distribution of this magnificent grass prepares the way at least for a more general appreciation of the beauties of other grasses; and we trust the day is approaching when collections of grasses will be met with in gardens as frequently as we now meet with collections of ferns. Many of the nobler forms are adapted to almost any position in a garden; the Pampas grass is as appropriate in the centre of a lawn as it is on a knoll among rustic scenes, or on a terrace where every detail must be in accordance with the demands of high art. For example, the common Ribbon grass, or Painted Lady (*Phalaris arundinacea variegata*), is known in our gardens as one of the most ornamental plants for the summits of banks and rockeries, and also suitable for the margins of beds, and to form lines of glittering silvery foliage in borders planted on the "ribbon" principle. The Tussack grass makes grand clumps of fountain-like foliage, suitable for the margins of wilderness walks, and among mixtures of plants in the borders. Clumps of the Sugar grass (*Holcus saccharatus*), the Italian Panick (*Panicum Italicum*), the Feather grass (*Stipa pennata*), and others, have a remarkably graceful appearance, and contribute much to the enjoyment of an inspection of the various forms and colours which well-kept borders invariably display. But the place *par excellence* for the display of a collection of grasses is that part of the garden usually denominated "fernery," and where the tasteful cultivator will always have other plants besides ferns, if for no other reason to bring out the distinctive characters of these elegant plants by means of agents which afford contrast and relief.—*The Floral World and Garden Guide*, Feb.

LOCUSTS.

Towards the beginning of the present century, a prodigious body of locusts was precipitated across the Black Sea upon the steppe lying east of Odessa, where it committed the most indescribable devastation. To destroy the invaders, columns of serfs were marched down from the interior; but on arriving at the scene of action, were almost paralysed by the phenomenon they witnessed. For miles, the whole surface of the plain, converted into a black colour, seemed to be alive and in motion, for the scaly bodies of the locusts, closely pressed and locked together, presented the appearance of a huge dusky cuirass reflecting with a strange glitter the rays of the sun. The mass being in motion, advanced inland, slowly but steadily, murmuring like the surges of the ocean, putting the sheep, the cattle, the horses, and the inhabitants on all sides to flight. A stench not to be expressed by words was emitted from the host as it crawled forward, the living devouring the dead, for lack of other provender. Putting their mattocks, spades, pickaxes, and other implements into immediate requisition, the serfs speedily excavated a trench several miles in length across the track of the locusts; but ere they had finished, the enemy was upon them, and soon demonstrated the futility of their device. In the course of a few minutes from their reaching the brink of the excavation, the foremost ranks had been pushed into it by those that followed, and filled it up from edge to edge, so that the multitude continued its march apparently without interruption; then everything combustible was collected, and set on fire in front of the column, with the same result. The whole Black Sea seemed to be transformed into locusts, which, from its low shores, came up in countless myriads, setting at defiance all the arts and industry of man. Several columns of the invaders filed off towards the east, and alighted amid the vineyards of the Crimea, which they soon changed into a waste of apparently dry and sapless twigs. Russia appeared to be on the eve of a calamity like that which fell upon it about the middle of the seventeenth century, when the destruction of the harvests occasioned a famine, which was followed by a plague, so that the population of whole provinces was thinned almost to extermination. In the present instance, the elements came to the deliverance of man. Before a strong west wind, masses of black clouds came pouring up from the Bosphorus, which covered the atmosphere, and ultimately descended in floods of rain. At the touch of descending Jove, the locusts were paralysed, and as the celestial moisture continued to drench them in pitiless fashion, they gave up the ghost, and bequeathed their filthy corpses to the husbandmen for manure; not, however, without sundry fevers and dysenteries.—*Chambers's Journal*, January Part.

Under the Microscope.

PLANT LIFE.

What! were ye born to be
  An hour or half's delight,
  And so to bid good night?
'Twas pity nature brought you forth
Merely to show your worth,
  And lose you quite.

But ye are lovely leaves, where all
  May read how soon things have
  Their end, though ne'er so brave,
And after they have shown their pride,
Like you awhile, they glide
  Into the grave.   ROBERT HERRICK.

IN a description of such objects as are likely to interest those anxious to obtain some knowledge of the wonders revealed by the aid of the microscope, we have endeavoured to follow as closely as possible in the path pursued by the most painstaking and competent authorities, and have devoted the first portion of our little work to a brief consideration of the structure as well as the general characteristics of microscopic plants. Of course it has not been possible in the space at our command to commence at the very beginning, and trace step by step the various changes and modifications to be observed from the first cell formation to the higher orders of vegetation. We have simply taken such genera as are most likely to come under notice, and have given as short an account as possible of their various peculiarities.

In considering the knowledge we already possess of the lower forms of plant life, we think we may venture to say that in no other department of nature has so much been done, so many results been obtained suggestive of success. By the investigations which have been made we have been enabled within certain limits to define where vegetable life ends and animal life begins. We say within certain limits because we are not yet in a position to lay down a rule which shall assure us distinctly that a cell belongs to one or the other, but we are able to distinguish a difference, which, in the majority of cases, enables us to decide to which class the object observed belongs. And it must be remembered that in order to do this we have but one rule for our guidance, and that is that all forms of animal life are dependant upon already formed *organic compounds* for nutriment, whereas a plant obtains its alimentary matter from such *inorganic elements* as it is surrounded by and which it obtains by absorption. Whether the final knowledge (*i.e.*, a distinct boundary line) which many men so ardently desire will ever be obtained we cannot say; perhaps it is not possible that we may with the most energetic study be able to finally settle the question. Even at the present early period of microscopic science, many distinguished men have laboured for years to solve the problem, and have been unsuccessful in reaching the desired goal, and it is quite easy to conceive not one but many men passing the whole of their lives and meeting with the same difficulties. It is the old search after the Philosopher's Stone. But although this may never be accomplished, certain it is that no man works without enriching us with some fruits—without pointing out clearly facts that were previously hidden. And we may well consider

"That which they have done but earnest
Of the things that they shall do."

Equally certain it is that each labourer brings us nearer by at least one step to the primary condition of life, whatever that condition may be. At present the highest powers of the microscope only reveal to us cell formation. Shall we ever get beyond this? Who can tell? Man can but say

For I dipt into the future, far as
Human eye could see.

It may not be wise to strive to see too much, but science must not be trammelled by superstition. The good resulting from investigation more than counterbalances the harm derived therefrom. A thoughtful writer says,

On every herb on which you tread
Are written words, which rightly read,
Will lead you from earth's fragrant sod
To hope, and holiness, and God.

The simple cell, as most of our readers are aware, is the earliest condition of the animal and vegetable kingdom, and a few words of what is known concerning it may not be out of place before proceeding to such objects with the organization of which research has made us somewhat familiar. Quekett tells us, that vegetable cells are divided into two classes, the *celluares* and the *vasculares*, the former containing the lowest and therefore the least complicated forms. In this class, he goes on to say, the Fungi, Algæ and Lichens are composed of single cells alone, occasionally elongated or otherwise modified in shape in the higher forms of each order. The lowest form in each of these orders is a simple globular or ovoid cell. As we proceed two or more cells are united in a definite form, further development occurs in higher groups until we find distinct organs which in the highest of the Algæ and Lichens bear a striking similitude to the leaves and seed vessels of the flowering plants. Further, in describing the vascular class, he remarks that the structure is more complex, the organs numerous, and serving distinct purposes, while their elementary tissues are divided into cells, fibres, and vessels. But this has recently been found to be illusory, the vessels being merely modified cells, and the fibres elongated cells, the walls of which have been thickened, or the entire cavity solidified by subsequent deposits on the internal surface of the cell wall. Mr. Hogg in his recent work on the microscope, in describing the characteristics of cells, says, "the vegetable cell has an extremely fine delicate membrane lining the inner wall, to perceive which we must have recourse to reagents, and then we find the apparently simple cell wall made up of two layers in each, differing in composition and properties. The inner layer has received the name of *primordial utricle*, and its composition has been shown to be albuminous, agreeing in this respect with the *formative substance* of animal tissues, the external cell is regarded as the cell wall, although it takes no part essentially in the formation of the cell, it is composed of cellulin, a material allied to the celluose of vegetable tissues."

Spherical or oval is the typical form of the cell, but in growth, by the action of pressure it takes almost every variety of shape, the walls becoming uniformly or only partially thickened. In many of the lower kinds, as Algæ and Fungi, the original form is retained throughout life, but in most other cases they undergo some alteration, and may become oblong, lobed, square, prismatic, cylindrical, fusiform, muriform, sinuous, stellate, and filamentous; the contents of the cell are colouring matter, starch, oil, raphides, silica, &c.

The principal means we have of distinguishing an animal from a vegetable cell are: first, in the animal cell, a more rapid progress of development, and as it advances a greater variety of form and complexity of structure; secondly, the animal cell is found to develope into tissues when the cellular form entirely disappears, while in the plant, although perhaps modified in form, it still possesses the character of a cell.

We will now pass to the consideration of some few of the many forms with which our microscopic beginner is likely to make acquaintance at first. If those we introduce to his notice excite his interest, and give him a desire to become further and better acquainted with Nature's handiwork, the object we have had in view will have been attained. Imperfect and unsatisfactory we feel he must find it, for space will not allow us to do justice to any one subject (supposing us sufficiently competent), but we may console him by pointing to the many excellent works (a list of which he will find on another page) that go thoroughly into the matter, and will supply him with all that is at present known. And when these in turn have been mastered, there will still remain the great Book of Nature, to the number of pages of which there is no end.

[The above paper was intended to precede the articles which have already appeared on Diatomaceæ and Desmidiaceæ; but owing to the Editor's illness it was omitted. In the next number we shall proceed with the consideration of Confervacea Oscilliatoria and other Algæ.]

On the Effects of Colour produced by Cryptogamic Plants.

We shall find that the variegated colouring of larger tracts of land and water frequently arises from the wide spread growth of excessively small cryptogamic plants, often only to be observed with the aid of a microscope. This is not a rare occurrence in nature. Even in the streets of our European towns we see, during rainy springs, the more shaded bare walls of our houses marked by broad stripes or spots of a yellowish or dark green colour. These are due to the presence of oscillatoræ, or other miscroscopic algæ. In many stagnant waters and slow-running streamlets, even in the reservoirs of the ornamental waters of our gardens, we see appear, in the course of a few days, a velvet-like covering of greyish green, or yellow colour, which, on minute examination, is found to consist of an accumulation of algæ, so small that one drop of water not seldom contains several thousand individuals.

In still more conspicuous and varied phases does this phenomenon force itself on the attention of the wanderer in the damp ravines of Highland valleys and the Alps, where huge rock walls are coloured sometimes sulphur-yellow by the mysterious Lepraricæ, or again are tinted in blood-red circles by the Hæmatococcus; and it is seen in its grandest scale in the so-called red and green snow, which, particularly in polar countries, and in the regions of the Alps, occasionally cover miles with a rose-red or emerald-green hue, an appearance due, as is well known, to the multiplication of a few species of Protococcus.

Not only the mainland and its fresh water shew us such phenomena, produced by algoid vegetation, but also salt waters, nay, even the wide ocean itself, becomes often their birthplace; and in such instances we see with amazement the otherwise dark blue waves glistening with a purple hue, or tinted as with a crimson dye. It is generally understood that the Red Sea owes its name partially to the occasional appearance of immense quantities of a species of Trichodesmium, a microscopic alga which in the early state of its existence is of a deep red colour.

I was not a little surprised in May 1852, whilst crossing the salt waters of the Tagus, from Lisbon to Lavradio, to observe, in approaching the opposite shore, that the ordinary bluish-green waters of that majestic river, had suddenly become of a violet purple colour. A closer examination, however, of the colouring substance soon taught me that this unusual hue had been caused by the presence of a species of Protococcus, which is generated in vast quantities in the extensive neighbouring Salinas.

Several years previously, Messrs. Turrel and Freycinet, whilst sailing round Cabo d'Espichel, on the Portuguese coast, observed the Atlantic ocean glittering with a blood-red colour to the extent of many miles; and the subsequent investigation of this coloured sea water by Montague, proved that myriads and myriads of a red Protococcus had imparted this tint to the ocean.—*The Journal of Travel and Natural History.* London: Williams & Norgate.

Meetings of Learned Societies.

Entomological Society.

January 27th was the anniversary meeting, Sir J. Lubbock, Bart., president, in the chair. An abstract of the treasurer's accounts for 1867 was presented by the auditors. The report of the council for 1867 was read by the secretary. The following were elected Members of the Council for 1868:—Messrs. Bates, Dunning, Grut, Sir J. Lubbock, M'Lachlan, Salvin, G. S. Saunders, W. W. Saunders, F. Smith, Stainton, S. Stevens, Trimen, and Westwood. The following officers for 1868 were afterwards elected:—President, Mr. H. W. Bates; Treasurer, Mr. S. Stevens; Secretaries, Messrs. Dunning and M'Lachlan; Librarian, Mr. E. W. Janson. Sir J. Lubbock read an address.

On February 3, Mr. H. W. Bates, president, in the chair, Mr. Bates returned thanks for his election as president, and nominated as vice-presidents Sir John Lubbock, Bart., and Messrs. W. Wilson Saunders and

H. T. Stainton.—Mr. Bond exhibited the larva of *Drilus flavescens* found by Mr. Harting on the South Downs in a shell of *Helix ericetorum*—skins of the larvæ of a Dermestes, which had not only destroyed the bladder coverings of a number of preserved fruits, but had eaten the jam also—and a gynandromorphous specimen of *Lasiocampa quercus*.—Dr. Wallace exhibited British-born specimens of *Bombyx Yamamai*, and some eggs produced thereby—specimens of *Bombyx Pernyi*, a Chinese oak-feeding species, which he thought there was a good chance of naturalising in this country—the cocoon and imago of *Pachypusa effusa*, an acacia-feeder, from Graham's Town, from which an attempt was being made to obtain silk in South Africa—cocoons of an unknown Bombyx from which the "gut" of fishermen is obtained—and made some observations on the progress of sericiculture in this country, at the Cape of Good Hope, and in Australia.—Dr. Gray communicated a letter received from Dr. G. Bennett, of Sydney, accompanied by extracts from Australian newspapers, respecting a wonderful swarm of the "bugong" moth, *Agrotis spina*.—Mr. Trimen exhibited a specimen of *Apatura Ionia*, a rare butterfly from Asia Minor, placed by some in the genus Vanessa, by others in Pyrameis.—The Hon. T. De Grey exhibited *Hypercallia Christierninana*, captured in Kent; and *Acidalia rubricata* and *Opostega reliquella*, from Norfolk.—The Secretary exhibited a spider sent by Lord Cawdor from Stackpole Court, Pembroke, which proved to be a female of *Pholcus phalangioides* (Blackwall's "Spiders of Great Britain and Ireland," part 2, p. 208).—The President and Mr. Hewitson read communications respecting the date of publication of the second part of Dr. Felder's entomological portion of the "Reise der Novara."—A letter from Dr. Signoret, of Paris, was also read, requesting the communication of specimens of Coccus, or papers or observations thereon; he was particularly desirous to obtain male specimens, which should be placed in tubes in weak spirit, since when dried it was impossible to make drawings of them.—Mr. D. Hanbury communicated some further information respecting his "coffee-borer" in Southern India, supplied to him by Dr. Bidie, who had been appointed by the Madras Government Commissioner for investigating the ravages of the Borer in Madras and Mysore.—The following papers were read: "Observations on the Economy of Brazilian Hymenoptera, from the Notes of Mr. Peckolt, of Cantagallo," by Mr. Frederick Smith; and "A Monograph of the British *Neuroptera Planipennia*," by Mr. R. M'Lachlan.

On Feb. 17.—Mr. W. H. Bates, President, in the chair.—Messrs. L. Cumming and E. P. R. Curzon were elected members.—Mr. M'Lachlan exhibited a living specimen of *Lucanus cervus*, found underground in a cocoon of earthy matter, in which it had been hatched and had probably passed the winter.—Mr. Janson, on behalf of Mr. A. G. Latham, exhibited the nest of a sociable bombyx, from Natal, and the larva-cases of a moth allied to Psyche.—Mr. Pascoe exhibited *Dryocora Howittii*, the type of a new genus of Cucujidæ, from New Zealand.—The following papers were read: "A few Observations on the Synonymy of *Tinea (?) alpicella* and *Zelleria saxifraga*, n. sp.," by Mr. Stainton; and "Remarks upon the Homologies of the Ovipositor," by Mr. A. E. Eaton.

GEOLOGICAL SOCIETY.

At this meeting held January 22—Dr. Duncan, read for the author, John W. Judd, Esq., F.G.S., a paper on "The Speeton Clay." The author gave the various opinions of previous writers on this subject who had differed greatly. Mr. Goodwin-Austen was in favour of the Speeton clay being Neocomian, and quite unconformable with the chalk. Mr. Judd described landslips which had spoiled the section for geological purposes. He exhibited a diagrammatic section of the Yorkshire coast, which was, however, on too small a scale, he said, to show as much as he desired. He considered the Speeton clay as important as the whole English Lias series from the number of beds and variety of species. He criticised Professor Phillips' species, which had been described in his well-known work on the Geology of Yorkshire, speaking of the various beds at great length, and mentioned their continental equivalents. The upper contains septaria, for making cement of great value; it is equivalent to the Guader of Germany. The middle Neocomian of Hilsthon is equivalent to part of the Speeton clay, and the upper part of the Hilsthon strata also. He exhibited a large table on which the various corresponding strata were clearly laid down. He showed that there was a closer relation between the Speeton beds and the Jurassic beds than was formerly supposed—more so than with the Portland. In conclusion, he stated—1st. That the Speeton clay included Filey Bay; 2nd. That it was not Gault; and 3rd. That it consisted of seven clear divisions. Professor Phillips had gone over the ground forty years ago, and had made at the time a large collection of the fossils, but he had too few facts to come to conclusions as clear as Mr. Judd's. In a most interesting speech he spoke of the high value of Mr. Judd's paper. Mr. Etheridge said he had aided Mr. Judd much in determining his fossils, and thought he had done good work in establishing the close correspondence between the British and foreign strata, and in collecting the fine series of fossils exhibited. Mr. Goodwin-Austen said it was a rare treat to see the Oxford professor (Phillips) on his trial, and considered Mr. Judd's paper the most valuable contribution to positive geology the society had received for a long time, and spoke of the complete account which the paper contained of the organic remains found in the beds. Mr. Charlesworth referred to some phosphatic casts which had been mentioned in the paper, and asked if any information could be given about their mode of formation, for shells as well as bones consist mainly of phosphate of lime. Mr. Seeley, of Cambridge, thought the Gault was present in the Speeton clay. Professor Ramsay considered that "Professor Phillips had made a wonderfully good shot about the beds," and asked in reference to a section exhibited, whether there was not a break in the strata. Professor Phillips had never seen a proper account of the chemical processes of the formation of the phosphatic casts which were called by the workmen "cops." Mr. Judd, in reply, said he had not taken Professor Phillips to task so much as some of the speakers supposed, and that from the great assistance he had received in the formation of the paper he was more entitled to the name of editor than author. Professor Phillips' notice of the Hessle drift, as it appeared in section forty years since, was next read by Mr. Evans. Mr. Searles Wood, in discussing it, said the professsor's old notes entirely corresponded with what he had lately seen himself. The discussion was joined in by Messrs. Ramsay, Charlesworth, and Goodwin-Austen.

On Feb. 5 (Mr. Warrington Smythe in the chair) the Duke of Argyle, F.G.S., read a paper entitled, "Notes on a section at Inverary." He reviewed Mr. Geikie's work, published in 1865, on the Geology of the Highlands, in which he held that the formation of the hills and valleys was due to atmospheric agency, and repudiated the older opinion that they were caused by subterranean forces. The Duke entirely differed from Mr. Geikie, and attributed all the leading features of the country to these forces, and ridiculed the notion that denudation—the "gentle rain from heaven" of Shakspeare—could go further than the surface. He considered Mr. Geikie's theory of the formation of the West Highlands purely hypothetical; but at the same time, he said Mr. G. had admitted that until the Highlands are examined by the Geological Survey, the whole would not be known. His grace showed a fine specimen of granite enclosing slate, which bore upon the question of the age of granite, and proved that slate was at least as old, if not older. He exhibited a diagram showing a view of Brander Pass, Ben Cruchan, and Lock Awe, as well as a sketch map of the Highlands from east to west. Mr. G. said that all our hills and valleys are due to erosion, and that time would account for everything. This, his grace ridiculed, and said, without force time could accomplish little. The President commented on the extremely forcible and lucid character of the paper, but advised speakers not to open the vexed question of the origin of granite. Sir Charles Lyell was almost entirely with the Duke in his paper, and mentioned a valley seven miles long, which he himself had seen near Natchez, N. America, and which had been caused by an earthquake in 1815, a few years before he visited it. He considered subterranean forces equally as efficient as running water. (Derisive cheers), Mr. Ramsay thought Sir C. Lyell had run counter to all he had said in his works, and observed, in reply to a previous speaker, that how the Highlands of Scotland were altogether of Silurian date, quite surpassed his comprehension. Sir Roderick Murchison said he stood in a peculiar position; he was expected to defend Mr. Geikie's arguments, but in opposition to him, he thought that the great physical features of the globe were not due to atmospheric agency. His friend, Mr. Geikie, had never examined the country. He spoke of the Duke's fearless manner in dealing with the subject, and thought his facts, so far as he (Sir R.) knew the Highlands, to be unanswerable, and that this question had never been put more philosophically, and thought it must be answered in the same manner. Mr. Carruthers thought the valleys were produced by subterranean agency, aided by denudation. Prof. David Forbes agreed with his Grace. Sir J. Lubbock instanced the denudation of the Weald as an analogue of the process which had gone on in the West Highlands, but was reminded by Sir Roderick that they were talking about the Highlands, and that if they considered the "Weald" he should like to speak for half an hour on it himself. Sir John Lubbock thought the two processes, subterranean and atmospheric, analogous to a vehicle; the horses resembled the atmospheric agency, and the crack of the driver's whip the subterranean. (Derisive cheers). Mr. Evans stood up to advocate the opinions of the younger or atmospheric school of geologists, which had been attacked by his Grace. Prof. Tyndall thought the discussion was so lop-sided, that he was inclined to throw his weight into the scale of Mr. Geikie. The Duke in reply to an expression which had fallen from one of the previous speakers, was quite willing to admit that Mr. Geikie's work was popular in the sense of being un-scientific, but did not think that any indulgence should be shown to it on that account, for it represented the views of a large section of geologists. He concluded his speech by a forcible and brilliant peroration.

ZOOLOGICAL.

At the meeting of this Society held Jan. 9.—Dr. J. E. Gray, V.P., in the chair. Prof. Newton exhibited the humerus of a large species of extinct pelican from the Cambridgeshire Fens. Mr. Sclater exhibited, and made remarks upon, a drawing of a new species of Impeyan, lately named by M. Albert Geoffroy St. Hilaire *Lophophorus l'Huysi*. Mr. W. K. Parker read a Memoir "On the Osteology of the Kagu (*Rhinochetus jubatus*)." A communication was read from Mr. Gerard Krefft, "On Various Points in Australian Natural History." A communication was read from Lieut.-Col. R. L. Playfair, "On a Collection of Fishes made in Madagascar by Mr. Alfred Grandidier," amongst which were two species believed to be new to science, and proposed to be called *Gobius Grandidieri* and *Mugil Smithii*. Mr. H. Adams communicated some descriptions of a new species of shells collected in Mauritius by Geoffry Nevill, Esq. Dr. Gray made some observations "On the Skin of an Otter exhibited by Mr. Bartlett," which he referred to *Baranga Sumatrana*. Dr. Gray also communicated in a synopsis of the pigs (*Suidæ*) found in the specimens in the collection of the British Museum.

On Jan. 23.—J. Gould, Esq., V.P., in the chair.—An extract was read from Mr. G. Krefft, Sydney, stating that, amongst other fossil remains which he was now arranging for the Australian Museum, he had discovered a portion of the humerus of an extinct species of Echidna, from the Darling Downs, indicating the former existence of a gigantic form of this Monotreme in Australia. A letter was read from E. P. Ramsay, giving an account of the habits of the Lyre Bird (*Menura superbæ*), with particular reference to its nesting and eggs. Messrs. Sclater and Salvin communicated descriptions of some new species of birds of the families Dendrocolaptidæ, Strigidæ, and Columbidæ, from various parts of America. Dr. J. E. Gray communicated a description of a new species of Macaque from the province of Szechuen, in the interior of China, which he proposed to term *Macacus lasiotus*, and some notes on the Margined-tailed Otter of Guiana (*Pteronura Sandbachii*). Dr. Murie gave an account of the morbid appearances observed in the Walrus lately living in the Society's Gardens, the death of which appeared to have resulted from extensive ulcerations in the stomach, caused by the presence of numerous entozoa. These notes were accompanied by a description, by Dr. Baird, of the entozoon in question, which was regarded as a new species, and proposed to be called *Ascaris bicolor*.

On Feb. 13.—J. Gould, Esq., V.P., in the chair.— Mr. Sclater made some remarks on a bear recently added to the Society's Menagerie, supposed to have been brought from South America, which appeared to be distinct from any described species. Mr. Gould exhibited two new species of Australian birds, which he proposed to call *Chrysococcyx russata* and *Pitta simillima*. A communication was read from Dr. J. S. Bowerbank, containing observations on Dr. Gray's "Notes on the Arrangement of Sponges," together with descriptions of some new genera of that group. Messrs. Sclater and Salvin read a list of, with notes on, a collection of birds made at Conchitas, Argentine Republic, by Mr. W. H. Hudson, which had been submitted to them for determination by the Smithsonian Institution, Washington. A communication was read from Dr. G. Hartlaub, containing additional notes on the Ornithology of the Pelew Islands, with descriptions of two new species belonging to that group. Dr. J. E. Gray communicated a notice of a new Dolphin transmitted from the Cape by Mr. E. L. Layard, and proposed to be called *Clymene similis*. Mr. Bartlett read some notes on the breeding of several species of birds in the Society's Gardens during the past season.

ROYAL GEOGRAPHICAL SOCIETY.

At the Meeting on January 13th, the President, Sir R. Murchison, read a letter from Dr. Kirk, Zanzibar, October 29th, adding nothing new to our already reported intelligence respecting Livingstone, but yet full of expressions of confidence respecting that worthy traveller's safety. M. Lucien de Puydt's account of his explorations in the Isthmus of Darien was read. The first adventurous journeys of this author were made in 1861, and from the Pacific side of that narrow neck of land, aptly designated the Gate of the World, in his successful efforts to follow up the rivers to their sources, in the mountain range whose ridge serves as a back-bone to the isthmus throughout the district under investigation, he had many opportunities of supplying valuable additions to our already well-stored records of the orography, ethnology, and geography of Darien; and in 1861, having returned from Europe, he landed on the Atlantic side of the Isthmus, secured a small band of Explorers at Carthagena, and sailed into a bay north of the Atrato, where, hidden behind the surf ever breaking over a difficult bar, and completely shrouded with dense woody jungles, he discovered the mouth of the river Tanela. Sailing up this newly-found river in canoes built of mahogany by the intelligent natives, he passed many of their deserted dwellings, and for days (although never far from the natives) he had no opportunity of meeting a single living inhabitant of the region through which he was passing, and from whose hostile feeling towards all strangers he was led to believe he should never escape with his life. On the 24th of August he reached the highest point of what he believed to be the lowest portion of the range, down whose opposite side flowed the waters supplying the rivers of his previous explorations. Not satisfied with the use of ordinary instruments for testing altitudes above the sea level in such a locality, he endeavoured to record by notes made on the rapidity of the stream he had traversed, at certain rapids along its course a series of observations, and from these records certain tables were calculated afterwards, by which method it has been declared that the Tanela river has a fall of 120 feet. The President, while testifying to the importance of a record like this, detailing the discovery of a hitherto unknown river, from its source to its mouth, clearing up the difficulty of a previous impression that it was not, as supposed, a portion of the delta of the Atrato river, yet shared in the discontent of geographers, at the method adopted by the traveller to arrive at an accurate knowledge of its levels, in the total rejection of instruments generally relied on for such results. Mr. Hemmans held this opinion also, and Commander Bedford Pim read an official paper setting forth existing contracts, by which he feared that the region under consideration was excluded from participation in commercial advantages. Mr. S. Cockburn's paper on the physical geography of the Belize river basin, was next read, recording many purely scientific phenomena of the region; and the President announced the arrival of another paper by Lieut. C. Abb, of H.M.S. Doris, containing further particulars of the geography of Belize, to be communicated shortly. The finished water-colour drawings by Mr. P. Skelton, sketches made by Mr. E. Whymper in Greenland, together with some photographic studies of heads of the South Greenlanders, made and coloured by Professor Pink, the famous historian and philologist, are now at the rooms of the Royal Geographical Society.

January 27th.—Admiral Sir G. Back, V.P. in the chair.—The following new Fellows were elected: Joseph Anderson, John Anderson, Geo. F. Angas, Capt. H. Baber, W. E. Blair, R. Davis, Capt. F. J. A. Dunn, C. F. Ellis, W. Falconer, Dr. A. Fyfe, A. Gilliat, J. P. Hunt, R. Jamieson, A. Laybourne, H. Murray, F. M'Clean, B. Newbatt, D. Phillips, T. Plowden, C. S. Price, H. C. Rass-Johnson, Captain G. E. Shelley, A. W. T. G. Thorold, W. Walkinshaw, and F. M. Williams, M.P.—"Report on the Livingstone Search Expedition, by Mr. E. D. Young, R. N. Mr. Young stated that, on arriving at the Kongone mouth of the Zambesi, on the 27th of July, a crew of negroes was at once engaged to man the steel boat and two other smaller boats. Ascending the stream, the party arrived at the Portuguese settlement of Senna, on the 6th of August; but the place, like all others on the south side of the Zambesi, was found abandoned, the Portuguese authorities and settlers having been killed or driven out by the Landeen Caffres. Temporary dwellings had been erected on the northern banks of the river, and Mr. Young was well received and promised assistance in the event of his not being able to obtain hands to convey the boat beyond the cataracts of the Shiré. The expedition reached Chibisa on the 17th of August, and found that the marauding Maziti Zulus had swept down from the north as far as the eastern bank of the Shiré, robbing, burning, and murdering all within reach. The Makololo (whom Livingstone had left at this place on his former expedition) received Mr. Young gladly, and at once agreed to accompany him in search of news of the doctor, with the arrangement that ammunition should be left behind to enable those who remained to repulse the Maziti, should they attempt to cross the river. On the 19th the foot of the cataracts was reached, and the boat taken to pieces. It occupied about 150 men four days and a half to convey the boat, provisions, &c., by land past the long series of cataracts. The boat was then rebuilt, and relaunched on the 30th of August, and the journey continued along the upper waters into Lake Nyassa, the banks of the river being crowded in places by fugitive Ajawa chiefs and their people, flying from the merciless Zulus. Mapunda, on the west side at the entrance to the lake, was passed without being visited, as the Makololo had become alarmed and discontented, and Mr. Young's aim was to push forward as far as possible. Here the first reports were heard of a white man, apparently Livingstone, having been at Mapunda about twelve months previously. Entering the Lake on the 6th of September, a fine breeze carried the party to the eastern side, but a heavy gale of wind succeeded, and the boat narrowly escaped being swamped. Running three hours along the coast, a shelter was at length obtained, and on the shores of the harbour a negro was found, who gave a clear description of the late visit of Dr. Livingstone to the place. Mr. Young followed up the traces hence to the Arab settlement, where he arrived the next day, and was there informed that Livingstone had been there, but, on finding the Arabs could not convey him across the Lake, had departed southward to cross at Mapunda. Mr. Young despatched searching parties by land to make sure of the route Livingstone had followed in coming from the Rovuma, and also the road taken by the Johanna men in returning. He then crossed the Lake to Marenga, where he ascertained that Livingstone had safely passed on at least five days' journey beyond the point where the Johanna men had deserted. The chief Marenga, who was an old friend of Livingstone, assured Mr. Young that if the Doctor had been killed one month's journey beyond his village he (Marenga) would have heard of it. At the question whether he had been attacked by Maziti, Marenga laughed, as it was known that the Maziti had never been seen in this part of the country. At Mapunda Mr. Young found a book with the name "Wakotani" written in it; this being the name of one of Livingstone's educated negro companions, who was stated by Moosa to have deserted, but who, in reality, had been left behind, lame; he was away with the chief at the time of Mr. Young's visit. The expedition then descended the river, and arrived at the mouth of the Zambesi on the 11th of November, the boats being brought safely down and all the party quite well in health.

LINNEAN SOCIETY.

January 16th—G. Bentham, Esq., President in the chair.—Drs. T. C. Cox, M. Foster, R. W. Moon, Messrs. B. D. Jackson, and J. B. Ward were elected Fellows.—Mr. Carruthers exhibited specimens of Cool Plants, preserved in a deposit of volcanic ash, from the Island of Arran, and made some observations upon them.—Mr. Maw exhibited from the lower Bagshot Beds of Studland Bay, impressions of Fossil Leaves, some of which closely resemble those of *Kydia colycina*, and are found in connexion with the flowers of the so-called Porana, exhibited by Mr. Maw at the previous meeting.—Dr. Hooker made some observations upon some remarkable specimens of abnormal Cocoa-nuts, exhibited by him, and read a letter from Dr. E. P. Wright, on a singular monstrosity of the Cocoa-nut from the Seychelles Islands. The following papers were read: "Notes on Mosses, &c., collected by Mr. J. Taylor on the shores of Davis's Straits," by Dr. G. Dickie.—"On a Collection of Fungi from Cuba, Part 2, including those belonging to the Families Gasteromycetes, Coniomycetes, Hyphomycetes, Physomycetes, and Ascomycetes," by the Rev. M. J. Berkeley,—and "A few Additional Particulars regarding *Conchia Edwardsii*," by Mr. T. Edward.

BRISTOL NATURALIST'S SOCIETY.

January 2, S. Swayne, Esq., in the chair.—1st., H. K. Jordan, F.G.S., "On the whelk (*Buccinum undatum*); its development, habits, and distribution." In value it was next to the oyster among British mollusks. Hundreds of hawkers carry it away every morning from Billingsgate to be retailed on countless stalls in the streets of the vast metropolis. It was known to the Romans as *Buccina*—its structure was admirably described by Cuvier. It deposits its 300 or 400 eggs on a stone or oyster; each egg or capsule contains several hundred yelks; but this number is afterwards so greatly reduced that only twenty or thirty come to maturity. Taking 400 as the normal number of capsules, and twenty-five as the average number that arrive at maturity from each capsule, this would give 10,000 young shells as the offspring of a pair of whelks in one season. The mode by which the reduction of the embryo takes place is disputed. Some Scandinavian naturalists assert that they amalgamate with each other; but Sir J. Lubbock states (British Association, 1860), that he has ascertained that the larger embryo swallow the other yelks. Amongst the *Purpuræ* the yelks divide into segments, and the more advanced embryos swallow the segments, one at a time. The whelk requires two or three seasons to attain maturity, and certainly lives six years, for Mr. J. had obtained large specimens outside the Dogger bank, with four-year-old oysters attached to them. The whelks are of distinct sexes, carnivorous and predatory, crawling over the sea bottom in search of dead fish. They attack living bivalves, drilling a hole through the shell and killing and afterwards devouring the inhabitant. A thin shell, like *Mactra stultorum*, would be perforated in four or five hours; a thick cockle in several days. He had examined many perforated bivalves, but never saw a stone or foreign substance bored by the whelk. Dr. Battersby related how the spine of an echinus had been perforated by a whelk; or one of the *Muricidæ*. The whelk does not hybernate, and cold water is its proper habitat. On the coast of Cheshire, a dead dog is covered with stones at low water mark. At the next recess of tide the whelks are found on the stones. The staler the bait the more plentiful they are, hence it is supposed that they possess the faculty of smelling. Whelks extend throughout the Boreal and Arctic seas with a southernmost limit to La Rochelle on the Bay of Biscay; but they lived in the newer Pliocene age of the Mediterranean. He believed that the Romans were fond of whelks, for the shells are found with those of the oyster at Richborough and other Roman stations. Dr. Johnson narrates that when William Wareham was consecrated Archbishop of Canterbury, March 9, 1504, eight hundred whelks at 5s. per thousand were bought for the feast; the best are those from Ramsgate, Grimsby, Harwich, and Whitstable; from the last of which £12,000 worth are yearly captured. (Evidence last year before the House of Commons). Messrs. Baxter, of Billingsgate, had given Mr. J. statistics of the quantity of mollusca yearly sent to the London markets—thus:

1843.	1863.
Whelks....37,000 bushels.	Whelks....37,000 bushels.
Winkles ..46,000 ,,	Winkles ..40,000 ,,
Mussels....26,000 sacks.	Mussels....20,000 sacks.

A sack weighs 200lb. A bushel of whelks weighs 84lb. A bushel of winkles weighs 10lb.

From this it will be seen how important whelks and other mollusks are in the London market. The largest specimen known measured 6½in long, it belongs to Mr. Leckenby, of Scarborough. 2nd., Mr. G. Harding read a paper on the occurrence of the European bee eater, near Bristol. 3rd., Mr. E. Willoughby, on Captain Schultze's white gunpowder.

ROYAL MICROSCOPICAL SOCIETY.

At the meeting held on the 8th of January, James Glaisher, Esq., F.R.S., president, in the chair, a paper was read by Professor Rupert Jones "On Recent and Fossil Bivalve Entomostraca." The Professor said that the word *Entomostraca* (shelled insects), applied to them was a misnomer, for that although they were originally believed to be water insects, and from their jumping motion, some of them were called water-fleas, they are not insects at all, but hold a place amongst the crustacea. He described the structure of different kinds of these small crustacea, especially referring to the various uses of the branchiæ. Nature always makes one part or organ useful, if possible, for more than one purpose, and thus one of these branchiæ may be made to serve as a foot or organ of motion, as a lung or organ of respiration, or as an instrument for holding and retaining the eggs beneath the body. He alluded to the widely-spread distribution over the surface of the earth, not only at the present day, but in ages long gone by. During the whole period of the existence of life on our globe, these little creatures have filled the seas and rivers in immense numbers. They are found in the lowest rocks of the old Silurian, in the strata of the old red sandstone the schists are marked with the little microscopic spots where they have been. In the limestone of Wales they are well preserved; in the coal they are so abundant that they make up whole masses of rocks, and so through all the groups, as plentifully in the marine as in the fresh-water beds. Existing as they did in such vast numbers in the waters and muds of the ancient seas and rivers, it necessarily follows that the acccumulated shells of dead specimens should far outnumber the living; and when we examine our ponds, etc., at the present day, and find them teeming with this form of animal life, we may understand how largely these minute crustacea have contributed to form the carbonate of lime in the various rocks above mentioned. The author explained how new forms had been discovered in the mud of foreign countries, and requested his hearers to induce any of their friends who might be going abroad to bring or send home pill-boxes filled with the dried mud of any of the river banks they might pass in their travels. By keeping these carefully separated, and putting them in distilled water on their arrival in this country, he considered that many new and interesting species might be developed. Amongst the presents announced was a most valuable one from Dr. Wallich of more than two thousand slides, and numerous drawings of microscopic objects; and also a quantity of raw material requiring investigation. This splendid gift, collected by Dr. Wallich with immense labour during many years of his life, has been made to the society without any reserve or restriction whatever. Two gentlemen were elected Fellows, and Chas. Tyler, Esq., and Chas. Stewart, Esq., were chosen auditors of the treasurer's accounts. The names of the officers for the ensuing year, and of those selected to take the place of members of council retiring in accordance with the bye-laws, were announced to the Fellows, and the President mentioned that the Anniversary Meeting would take place on Wednesday, the 12th of February, instead of on the 11th of that month, which, by a clerical error, was the day named in the printed circular.

EDINBURGH BOTANICAL SOCIETY.

Jan. 9.—The President in the Chair. I. "Obituary Notices of Professor Daubeny, Oxford; Rev. Dr. Hamilton, London; and Dr. Schultz, Deidesheim, late Fellows of the Society." By Professor Balfour. —II. "Notice of a New British Moss (Amblystegium confervoides) in Dovedale, Staffordshire." By Dr. John Fraser. Communicated by Mr. Sadler.—III. "Account of a Botanical Trip to the Vosges Mountains, by R. M. Stark, Esq."—IV. "Letter from Mr. Wm. Bell, dated Koslogir, 2d November, 1867, to Professor Balfour." In it we read, I shall endeavour to give, as it were, a bird's-eye view of some of the forests which I passed through in a visit to the hills about two years ago. In doing so, I need not trouble you with any remarks about the vegetation, from the plains upwards—why some spaces are well wooded, and others close to them are quite bare—why those with a western aspect are better wooded than those with an eastern one—why the crests of both the first and second ranges on the side facing the plains have nothing but a scrubby, scanty vegetation, while the back slopes have, as a rule, quite an arborescent one— but proceed to tell you what they are chiefly composed of, and the appearance they present to a stranger. They are chiefly composed of Oak—perhaps four or five species. I have observed one only, perhaps two, on the front range. Next Rhododendrons in point of size and numbers, and a sprinkling of Arbutus, which can scarcely be called a tree; Ilex, Benthamia, a few Horse Chestnuts, and a Cedrela. There is very little underwood, and climbers are entirely wanting. In these respects hill forests contrast strikingly with those of the plains. In the bottom of the deep valleys, Cæsalpinia, Mimosa, Guilandina, Smilax, &c., form most impenetrable thickets, which no animal of any size could possibly make a way through. These, and a few others, such as Vitis, Porana, Lettsomia, Bauhinia, &c., give the Dhoon forests quite a character. It is the entire absence of all such that give the hill forests, where the trees are well grown, a lightsome, pleasant appearance. In rather shady places a wild Solidago is very abundant, in more open drier places two or three species of Gnaphalium are also abundant. On the dryish spaces, where there is but little shade, a small Androsace forms quite a carpet; along the edges of open spots Primula denticulata is most abundant, with magnificent scapes, some of them 20 inches in length; and on damp shady rocks, Primula Stewartii fills every chink, also the Hedysarums and a little Geranium. On the very top of one of the highest peaks of the Tyru range, a spot several acres in extent was covered with a large Potentilla. This plant seemed to have taken almost exclusive possession of the spot, which might easily have been mistaken for a Strawberry field. The decaying foliage formed a contrast to the bright blue flowers of a handsome Aconitum, which was sparingly scattered over the spot. During the rainy season the villagers always graze their cattle on the high ridges; the sheds are generally surrounded with a brushwood defence, and outside that on the lower side there is generally a fine mound of pure manure, not unadulterated with straw or grass. The vegetation around these hills is peculiar. The common Bhang seems as vigorous and healthy there as it does in similar places 9000 or 10,000 feet lower. Nettles of enormous size, most fierce looking, but not nearly so bad as they look; Thistles, Ragweeds, Bedstraws, Chickweeds, Docks, Crowfoots, Shepherd's Purse, and one or two Geraniums, give quite a Scotch look to the district. The Rhododendrons must look gorgeous when in full bloom, as they are both large and numerous, and generally speaking were well furnished with flowerbuds. The largest one I saw measured 17 feet round, but like many other fine trees in that neighbourhood, it was only a shell. It is much more difficult to find a sound tree than an unsound one; enormous numbers have been shelled out to a greater or less extent by fire. The wood of both the Oaks and Rhododendrons—I do not know that any use is made of the last except burning—seems very perishable. Insects go into it very vigorously when slightly decayed, woodpeckers follow after and pick them out. After that process has been repeated a few times, a slaty-headed or the Alexandrian parrot, a barbet, or perhaps a woodpecker, fancies that particular spot for a nest, and does not find it difficult work to gouge or chip out as much half-rotten wood as will make a respectable house for his expected family.

ROYAL HORTICULTURAL SOCIETY.

February 11, was the *Anniversary* meeting.—W. Wilson Saunders, Esq., occupied the chair, on account of the unavoidable absence of the President, the Duke of Buccleuch. Major G. E. Blenkins and Mr. Fortune were appointed scrutineers of the ballot for the election of Council and officers for the ensuing year.

Correspondence.

[*Under this head we shall be glad to insert any letters of general interest.*]

SOLAR AND LUNAR RAINBOWS.

The sky! the sky! I love the sky,
Earth's wondrous, wide-spread canopy,
Doming above us—sight's loftiest bound,
Throwing its brightness on all sides around:
Ever present, though reachless, its splendour on high—
Who loves not to gaze on the beautiful sky?

ANONYMOUS.

SIR,—Of all the meteorological phenomena with which we are acquainted the rainbow is the most delightful. It inspires us with a pleasing sense of the sublime and wonderful; we are astonished at the grand mathematical accuracy it presents, and we are truly amazed at the beauty and variety of the colours it exhibits. From a well ascertained law in nature we find that the drops of rain in falling must assume a globular form, and these globules acting as prisms, decompose the light, and hence the formation of the bow on the cloud.

The rainbow may be caused by the mist of waterfalls, as has been so often experienced at the falls of the Rhine at Schaffhausen, and at the falls of Niagara, etc. Nature, as if to show her power in natural science, sometimes deviates from her ordinary course in producing the rainbow. Sir D. Brewster tells us that many peculiar rainbows have been seen and described; that "On the 10th of August, 1665, a faint rainbow was seen at Chartres, crossing the primary rainbow at its vertex. It was formed by a reflection from the river."

By the reflection of the River Dee, a very curious rainbow was formed at Chester on the 6th of August, 1698. This rainbow was observed and described by Dr. Halley. In *Rozier's Journal*, we are told of "a third rainbow seen between the two common ones, and not concentric with them." This it is supposed, was the rainbow seen by Halley. But we have *lunar rainbows* as well as *solar*, and yet the recorded observations upon those beautiful phenomena of the night, as far as I can ascertain, are by no means as numerous as we would expect. Aristotle, it is said, saw two lunar rainbows. In the county of Derby, according to the Philos. Trans., a well defined and beautifully coloured lunar rainbow was seen in 1711. A very weak lunar rainbow, in which the colours could scarcely be discerned, was seen by M. Weidler in 1719.

M. Muschenbrook saw a white lunar rainbow in 1729, and one of a deep yellow was seen at Isselstein in 1736, and a very well coloured lunar rainbow, only not displaying the same variety of tint as those formed by the sun, was observed at Dijon in 1738.

In October, 1823, a well formed lunar rainbow, of a dull white colour, was seen at Middletown, twelve miles from Edinburgh, and on the 7th of the same month, another was seen at Arras. It is thus described by an observer :—" It was as vivid and distinct in its colours, and as perfect in the segment of the circle which it formed, as any solar rainbow which the writer had ever seen. There was also a second bow, fainter, as if it were the shadow or reflection of the other."

In September, 1832, a lunar rainbow, which lasted two minutes, was seen at Plymouth, and in 1797, from the middle of Durham Down, near Bristol, a grand lunar rainbow, forming a semicircle, was seen. In it the prismatic colours were clearly defined, but not so vivid as in the solar rainbow. In 1834, a gorgeous lunar rainbow, greater than a semicircle, was seen from a ship's mast, in the Bay of Algiers. This beautiful bow of the night, gracing the majesty of Neptune, lasted about a minute and a half, and was, in all respects, like a solar rainbow, except in the faintness of its colours. This is a necessary characteristic of the lunar bow, for as it is formed by light reflected from the moon, it cannot be so vivid in its colour as the solar bow; for, from a well established principle in optics, it is found that the more frequently light is reflected, the fainter it becomes.

It is presumed that even eminent men, such as Sennert, Snellius, Gemma, Trisius, and Dr. Plot, have sometimes mistaken *halos* for lunar rainbows, yet I am inclined to think, that the phenomenon is not quite so rare as is commonly supposed. I can see no reason why the lunar rainbow should not occur quite as often as the solar. From the time of day at which the solar rainbow appears, the weather is prognosticated : " *The rainbow in the morning is a sign of rain ; in the evening, of dry weather.*"

Sir Humphrey Davy thus scientifically accounts for the truth of the proverb :—" A rainbow can only occur when the clouds, containing or decomposing the rain, are opposite to the sun, and in the evening the rainbow is in the east, and in the morning in the west; and as our heavy rains, in this climate, are usually brought by the westerly wind, a rainbow in the west indicates that the bad weather is on the road, by the wind to us ; whereas, the rainbow in the east, proves in these clouds is passing from us."

The subject concerning rainbows, is one particularly interesting, and well worthy of the *Naturalists' Note Book.* I wish your scientific correspondents would direct their attention to this branch of *Natural Science*, and give accounts of the recorded observations upon lunar rainbows. To know when, where, and by whom, observations had been made, would be a great acquisition, and most gratifying to your scientific readers.

That the lunar rainbow appears at night, the faintness of its colours, and its transitory nature, are, I presume, the only characteristics which make it less known than the solar rainbow.

In vol. I., page 307, *Naturalist's Note Book*, there is a very interesting article upon *Rainbows*, and I hope your correspondents will not let the subject drop.

I am, Sir,
Yours etc.,
H. H. ULIDIA.
Dromore, Feb. 1, 1868.

"BIRD MURDER."

SIR,—So much "bosh" has lately been written upon this subject, by parlour Naturalists', whose praiseworthy zeal on behalf of the "feathered choristers of the grove," is only equalled by their evident desire to keep all knowledge bottled up, as an essentially museum article, and to affect that no one ought to collect for themselves, that really I feel tempted, like Artemus Ward's Colonel of the Seventy-onesters, to consign my valuable optics to perdition, and to exclaim, " Its onpossible;" and really it would be " onpossible," for any but men whose studies were not ornithological, to exhibit the amount of rancour which they do, towards anyone fortunate enough to become the possessor of any good bird, without the intervention of the established dealer. In fact, the preconceived idea of some of these nonpareils appears to be, (and no-one has had the courage to dispute it) that you may shoot any bird excepting a rare one, but let *that* go, so that it may be shot by somebody who knows nothing about it, and consigns it in company with that "gay and festive little cuss,"—the sparrow, to the orthodox pudding. Now all this is very well, and far be it from me to uphold the wanton destruction of rare birds ; but this I do maintain, that every man has a perfect and unquestionable right, to shoot a rarity which perhaps he may never see again, and which he requires for purposes of study, as their first discoverer had.

It is not because a bird has been figured and described for us from stuffed specimens or obsolete authors, that we should rest content, and not take the evidence of our own senses when opportunity occurs.

There are some people in this wicked world of ours, who do not hold the theory of everything being correct until found otherwise, and I fancy a disciple of one of these exquisitely humane ornithologists (?) going about exclaiming that he had seen a quantity of birds of some rare species, never before seen in England, but known as an American one, but he forbore shooting one or two, as it was so excessively cruel and he knew all about them. People of atrocious brutality and shockingly deficient of veneration, might possibly question his having the necessary amount of tile on his intellectual roof, while others might be found to dub his new species "Oneythomys" in imitation of a greater authority in a well known case. The poor fellow may have been right or he may have been wrong, but the inevitable bickerings, and ungentlemanly personalities indulged in,—when one person mildly hints to his opponent that he does not consider him to be guilty of an untruth, but should advise him to pour his plaintive tale into the willing ears of the marines—might have been avoided, and science materially served by one timely shot. Supposing Wilson, Waterton, or Gould, had adopted the let-'em-alone style, what should we have known of many beautiful feathered gems which now enrich our collections? A man may be in his way quite as enthusiastic as those true naturalists, and have quite as much right to add to a personal collection, even as they had. Chacun à son gout; and most people are stupid enough to prefer their own to anothers; and depend upon it, that until rare birds are duly licensed by Act of Parliament (which Dii avertite) to wag their tails defiantly in field naturalists' faces,—parlour dittos will constantly have their tender feelings harrowed by some such recital as —"Shocking slaughter of Rara Avis, Esq., in Blankshire, etc., etc."

Apologizing for thus largely trespassing on your valuable space, and assuring those gentlemen now waiting to anoint my devoted head with the anything but essential oils from the numerous vials of their wrath, that I do *not* sanction wanton destruction, but merely assert every man's right to procure specimens.

I remain, Sir,
Yours, etc., etc.,
A. M. B.

MIGRATION OF SWALLOWS.

DEAR SIR,—You will greatly oblige me by inserting the following, which I have extracted from Hardwicke's Science Gossip, page 214, 2nd vol.

"In Jesse's 'Gleanings from Natural History,' are included some of Gilbert White's, of Selbourne, unpublished papers, in one of which is the passage, 'Repeated accounts of swallows in large numbers being seen spring and fall, perched on trees overhanging the water, induce me greatly to suspect that house swallows have some strong attachment to water independent of the matter of food; and, that if they do not retire into that element, they conceal themselves in the banks of pools and rivers during the uncomfortable months of winter.' The hybernation of swallows, either by submersion or concealment in holes and crevices, was a favourite theory of Mr. White's, and a subject he tried to elucidate, but without success." The correspondent of S. G. further adds, had the worthy old naturalist known such a fact as that stated by your correspondent "G. W.," (S. G., page 185, vol. 2nd) his theory would have been much strengthened.

I think your correspondent "Mr. A. G. Harvie," will admit that the forgoing is somewhat stronger than a mere query.

I remain,
Yours obediently,
T. R. CLEPHAN.
Stockton-on-Tees.

New Books.

[*Our limited space must of necessity compel us to give but very short notices of new books, but they will perhaps serve as a guide as to what books our readers may ask for at their libraries.*]

Birds from Nature. By Mrs. Hugh Blackburn. Glasgow: James Maclehose. London: Longman & Co., Hamilton, Adams, & Co., Simpson & Co., Whittaker & Co.

THIS is a reproduction of a work published some few years ago, with the addition of some twenty more drawings of birds, consisting principally of natatores, grallatores, incessores, and raptores. Mrs. Blackburn is widely known as an artist of no mean talent in this particular branch, and the work will be found truthful and of great value to the ornithologist. In an early part of the work we read:

"The drawings, of which a few are here engraved, have been made either from the living bird or from specimens so fresh as to preserve most of the characteristic appearances of life, while the attitude and background have been studied from careful observation of the habits of the wild birds. This has, of course, involved a good deal of trouble, and it is not likely that a single observer will have the opportunity, under these restrictions, of obtaining good drawings of the whole series of British birds. Such considerations have, no doubt, induced most illustrators of the subject, even Bewick himself, to put up with a stuffed skin for a lay figure, and, apparently, to label drawings so made as 'from nature;' but, in the present instance, the artist, without neglecting to refer to stuffed specimens, has refused to be guided by them, in the belief that drawings *really* from nature (and such only) may be made to give a representation of nature more faithful, in most essential points, than the stuffed skin itself. . . . . In order to carry out the same idea of interposing as few interpreters as possible between nature and the actual print, the drawings have been copied on to the stone (or zinc) plate by the same hand as made the original drawings, or, in some instances, the drawing has been made on the stone direct from nature. After what has been said, it will be understood that the choice of subjects has been, to some extent, limited by circumstances. In many cases, however, it was thought better to give several plates illustrating points of interest in the habits and growth of one species, than to occupy the same space with others for a complete history of which the materials have not yet been collected. But an untoward accident which at the eleventh hour has befallen a number of plates we had intended to include has destroyed the links connecting some of our illustrations, and made them even less consecutive than they would otherwise have been. Yet, it is still hoped that this volume may be considered as so far complete in itself, or at all events as a contribution not without some value towards the illustration of the subject, whether or not opportunity be given to the same hand of continuing the series."

Lake Victoria ; a Narrative of Explorations in Search of the Source of the Nile. Compiled from the Memoirs of Captains Speke and Grant. By George C. Swayne, M.A., late Fellow of Corpus Christi College, Oxford. Edinburgh and London : William Blackwood & Sons.

Mr. Swayne has here given a very readable little volume, detailing the chief incidents connected with the explorations of Captains Speke and Grant. Condensed into so small a volume it is a matter of surprise that so large a quantity of matter is contained in it. The mind readily grasps the whole details of the two traveller's journeyings, and becomes even more impressed than by a perusal of the chief works from which the materials are derived. On another page will be found a long extract, and it only remains for us to inform our readers that a more creditable compilation has seldom been made.

Man: Where, Whence, and Whether ; being a Glance at Man in his Natural History Relations. By David Page, LL.D. Edinburgh : Edmonston & Douglas.

Dr. Page having delivered several lectures upon this subject in Edinburgh, has thought it worth while to work the matter up into the present small volume, and the result is perfectly satisfactory. Our readers will find here full particulars of the development hypothesis, written in a mild and temperate manner, and embodying the latest evidence and arguments in support of the theory.

The Mineralogist's Directory ; or, a Guide to the Principal Mineral Localities in the United Kingdom of Great Britain and Ireland. By Townshend M. Hall, F.G.S. London : E. Stanford.

Worked up from the most reliable sources we have here a very valuable guide to the mineral distribution of this country. "The geological formation," the author tells us, "in which each mineral occurs has been inserted, as far as it is possible to do so, and an attempt has been made to diminish the number of superfluous names with which the science of mineralogy is at present encumbered." To those in want of such a guide, (and they are many) the present volume will be found of great service.

AMERICAN, FRENCH, AND GERMAN WORKS.

AMERICAN.

The Resources of California. By John S. Hittell. Third edition. San Francisco : A. Roman & Co. New York : W. H. Widdleton. London : Trübner & Co. 1867.

In this work we have a truthful and compendious account of the resources of California. Gold digging, silver mining, wheat, and cattle, farming, vineyards, and orchards, all receive due attention and are well described. The working of quartz mines receives an extra amount of attention, and the descriptions are graphic and vivid, and will well repay a perusal.

The Physiology of Man ; designed to represent the Existing State of Physiological Science as applied to the Functions of the Human Body. By Austin Flint, Junr., M.D., Professor of Physiology and Microscopy in the Bellevue Hospital Medical College, New York, &c., &c., &c. *Alimentation, Digestion, Absorption ; Lymph, and Chyle.* New York : Appleton and Co. London : Trübner & Co. 1867.

Dr. Austin Flint here gives us an interesting treatise on the Physiology of Man, relating chiefly to the alimentary system ; the functions of the various organs connected therewith, as ascertained by a number of curious and careful experiments ; the nature and value of different sorts of foods, and their effects in nutrition ; the processes of digestion and assimilation, and in fact, the whole natural history of the nutrition of the human body.

FRENCH.

Théorie de la Formation du Globe terrestre. Par A. Baudrimont. Paris: Germer-Baillière.

This volume consists of a series of lectures delivered by M. Baudrimont, on the formation of the earth. In it he says, matter consists of an infinite number of small indivisible particles called "atoms;" these atoms have existed from all eternity, they are indestructible, endowed with motion, and they react upon one another according to certain laws. By this theory M. Baudrimont endeavours to explain the formation of our globe. He believes that all the mathematical and astronomical forces by which the earth is governed will gradually become weaker and weaker. The heat of the sun must diminish in intensity; the earth, consequently, will become cooler in the same proportion, and its inhabitants will dwindle away until life has entirely disappeared.

Les Glaciers. Par Zurcher et Margollé. Paris and London: L. Hachette & Co.

We have here one of the volumes of Messrs. Hachette's Bibliotheques des Merveilles. Taking into consideration the subject of icebergs and glaciers. The authors begin by describing the formation of ice, its use in the ordinary circumstances of domestic economy, and the ever-increasing consumption of it throughout the civilized world. The laws which regulate the formation of glaciers then come under notice; and finally we have an enumeration of the principal ice depôts, including an account of avalanches, floating icebergs, inundations, etc. It is well illustrated by a great number of woodcuts.

GERMAN.

Geschichte des Golfstroms und seiner Erforschung. Von J. G. Kohl. Bremen: Müller. London: Williams & Norgate.

All that is known of the gulf stream will be found collected in this little work. From the days of Columbus to the late researches of Lieut. Maury, the various discoveries connected with it are duly chronicled.

Short Notes.

AFFINITIES BETWEEN BIRDS AND REPTILES.—Prof. Huxley, we read in the *Athenæum*, Feb. 22nd, is working at a subject which is an interesting one for anatomists and Palæontologists, namely, on the affinities between birds and reptiles, or, in other words, on a class of animals which appear to come between birds and reptiles. Few persons on looking at an ostrich and a crocodile would imagine that their skeletons have many points of resemblance, yet, as Prof. Huxley shows, the resemblances are so numerous that it is not difficult to believe that birds and reptiles came originally from a species of animal in which the peculiarities of both were united. As yet there are missing links in the series, but among those which have been found in a fossil state are the pterodactyl, the iguanodon, the archæopteryx, and one or two others. As regards the pterodactyl, Prof. Huxley considers it was this creature that made the footmarks which have been taken for the prints of a bird's-foot in the sandstone of Connecticut. He concludes also that the creature was accustomed at times to walk on its hind legs, in which position its feet would make the tracks now found on fossils, and its tail, dragging on the ground, would form the groove which still exists between the rows of tracks in the slabs, and has long been a puzzle to naturalists. This seems to be a probable solution of the question; but what an amazing spectacle must have been presented by one of those huge creatures walking erect!

SPEAKING FISH.—The following is an extract from an Indian friend's letter. The name and class to which this fish belongs is wished for, which perhaps some of your correspondents will kindly give:—"The river Peyn, a tributary of the Beas, was lowered about three feet by the removal of a weir, and we dragged the river; numbers of fish from half a pound to a pound, and about two dozen from five to ten pounds, were caught. There were no *maheers* [probably mahseers are meant]; they don't grow in the Peyn; but among them were four specimens of a 'speaking fish' ('et mutæ pisces' may be abandoned). All these fish make a sort of grunt, about twice in a minute, from the time they are caught till they die. I was some time before I found out how they did it, but I succeeded. They have large and stout bones, which form the front ray of the fins under the gills, and these are attached to a sort of shoulder bone which is outside the flesh, merely covered by the skin, by a very beautiful and complicated joint. When the fish chooses he can grind the bones forming the joint and socket together, and so makes a noise something like a man does when he grinds his teeth together, only louder and more like a grunt. I watched them so long that I am sure this is the true explanation. I have it with the shoulder blade attached. It is not separable from the blade when every part of the muscles and ligaments are removed, but remains a perfect and beautiful joint. The fish can erect and lock the joint at pleasure."—Glen Nant in the *Field*, Jan. 25th.

ICHTHYOLOGICAL CURIOSITY.—Last week, John Wright, fishmonger, Market-street Brighton, found the claw of a strange looking lobster protruding from the inside of the stomach of a codfish; and on opening the paunch, he found the whole of a claw (six inches in length), and a portion of the body of a shell-fish unknown to him. Proceeding in the task of dissection, to his further surprise, he turned out the perfect body and claws of a lobster, measuring 14 inches in length! He immediately sent this curiosity as a present to Mr. R. Peek, who pronounced it to be a full-sized specimen of the true Norway lobster; the *Nephrops Norvegicus* of Leach, and the *Cancer Norvegicus* of Linnæus. Mr. Peek also stated that these shell-fish are occasionally met with in the Mediterranean, and on some parts of the Scotch and Irish Coasts, and that they have been sometimes taken from the inside of cod fish captured in Dublin Bay. But their proper *habitat* is the rocky shores of Norway. The cod from which these lobsters were taken was in excellent condition, and, as the digestion of fishes is very rapid, it is not unlikely that it had seized the living prey within a few minutes of its capture with the dead bait. It seems that codfish will swallow and digest almost anything: old shoes, pieces of iron, clasp-knives, sharkhooks, and links of chain have been found in them, partially affected by the action of the gastric juice.—*Brighton Observer*, Feb. 21st 1868.

DESTRUCTION OF HUMAN LIFE BY TIGERS.—The following appears in *Land and Water*, Feb. 1st., in the island of Java, according to the latest official statistics published, 148 persons were devoured by tigers in one year, and in another the same fate befell 131 persons. The crocodiles during the same year ate about fifty people a year, and between thirty and forty a year were killed by serpents. The inhabitants, however, do not seem to allow their habitual equanimity to be much disturbed by the fate of so many human beings. The Governor-General some time since offered for every tiger that was killed the sum of 22 guilders (£2), but this did not tempt the Dutchmen to action. *Pall Mall Gazette*.

Remarks, Queries, &c.

THE MAGNETIC NEEDLE.—A. De H. asks "why does a magnetic needle point to the north." If he looks closely, he will observe that it does not point directly north, but rather to the west of the north geographical pole. The theory of magnetism is, that there are two fluids which mutually attract *each other*, but repel *themselves*, and that in a magnet, one is free at one end and the other at the other end of it. It is not positively known why the needle sets itself north and south. Some philosophers suppose the earth to contain a huge magnet, extending from pole to pole, and in this case the north end would attract one end of the needle and the south end the other, thereby causing it to stand north and south. Others imagine that there are two large magnets which cross each other at the centre of the earth, the effect of which, upon the magnet needle, would be nearly similar. Others again believe that the effect upon the needle is caused by currents of electricity traversing the earth from east to west, which would (it has been proved) make the needle set itself at right angles to their direction, or north and south. Barlow explained this by winding a copper wire in parellel coils round a wooden globe, and passing an electric current through it, the two ends of the wire representing the *magnetic* poles. On moving a magnetic needle over it while the current was passing, he found the effect was similar to that produced by the earth. This last theory would, no doubt, be accepted as the right one, if the currents of electricity round the earth could be accounted for: as it is, however, that of the one large magnet is generally preferred, as being the simplest. W. S.

BIRDS' EGGS.—Sir, almost all practical oologists have, at some time or other, experienced great difficulty in the choice of a receptacle for their collection of eggs. The plan most usually adopted is, I believe, to have a box containing trays of different depths, for various sized eggs, but this, besides causing the trouble of lifting up and down, is an expensive affair, as it must be made with great care. At the museum at Brighton is, in my opinion, an admirable arrangement for eggs, being simple, easily constructed, and cheap. It is in shape like an oblique or slanting desk, made of wood (deal) and covered with glass. It is divided into a large number of partitions by means of pieces of wood that go down and across the box. At the top each partition is about two inches deep, and they become smaller and smaller lower down. This box can, of course, be made any size, of any wood, and a wooden lid could be easily constructed to fit it. It is so easily manufactured, that an amateur carpenter could make one for himself. TORTOISE.

SKELETONS OF BIRDS.—Seeing in the February number several answers in reply to "Fox's" query concerning "Skeleton Leaves," I should be greatly obliged if any reader of the NATURALIST'S NOTE BOOK can give me any information as to the best method of preparing the skeletons of small birds and animals, and if there is any book on the subject.

I also see two notes—one in the number for January and one in the number for February—headed "White Blackbird" and "White Sparrow;" I thought, perhaps, it might interest some of your readers to hear that I have in my possession a Stuffed Robin with a white breast, also a Tree Sparrow (*Fringilla Montana*, Lin.) nearly all white. Both were killed about three years since in Huntingdonshire.

An Albino House Sparrow has been in the window of Mr. E. Hawkins, Bear-street, Leicester-square, for some months past; I see it has got a prize at the Crystal Palace Bird Show. G. DEIGHTON.

COLIAS EDUSA.—Being in Cornwall last August and September, I met with that lovely insect the Clouded Yellow Butterfly (*Colias Edusa*) in great profusion in the neighbourhood of Penzance, where it abounded on the cliffs on the sea coast near that town, delighting the naturalist by its nimble and golden flight. I captured a great many specimens, including several females, which are much less rarely taken than the males. Can any of your numerous readers inform me why this butterfly is more plentiful in some years than in others? and also where the Black-Veined White Butterfly (*Pieris Cratægi*) is mostly met with? as in my entomological rambles I have very rarely come across this insect, but captured one when I was in Cumberland a few years ago. A. E. B.

THE CLOUDED YELLOW.—Having seen several letters lately from correspondents in different places concerning the abundance of the clouded yellow (C. Edusa) last summer, I thought it might interest some of your readers to know that I have found them very common in Oxford. Last summer, on a particular hill side (Chilswell Hill), I saw at least twenty specimens in less than two hours one morning. I also saw and caught a few specimens of the brown argus in the same place; but I have never seen either of them before. B. B. SCOT.

COLIAS EDUSA.—In further continuation of the remarks of H. Meyrick upon this fly, I beg to inform him, that I have found the Downs between Farnham and Guildford, (Surrey) a first rate habitat for them during the past autumn. On the 19 and 22 August, I captured a great number, on which latter date, I succeeded, after a severe chase, in taking the rare Colias Hyale. I should be glad if some of your correspondents would inform me of any captures of Hyale during last year, as I am engaged collecting notes upon British butterflies.   A. M. B.

THE COLOUR OF EGGS.—I should like to know the opinion of the naturalists who are readers of the NOTE BOOK as to what is the cause of the colour of eggs. My own opinion is that it is caused by the light or sun acting upon them in the same way as on plants, for it is well-known that all flowers that grow in the dark will become either white or of a very light colour. It has also been marked that eggs which are laid in dark places are of a much lighter colour than those which are exposed to the light. If a bird is disturbed while in the act of laying, the colour of the eggs will not be at all perfect. Last year I found a sparrow's egg which was quite white, without the smallest markings on it.

Mavisbush House.   J. D. S. W.

FROGS AND THEIR FOOD.—Sir, did your correspondent "Fox" carefully count his tadpoles before and after their transformation? Mr. Frank Buckland tells us in his "Curiosities," that the favourite food of tadpoles is the flesh of animals, dead kitten for instance, but that, failing that they are by no means unwilling to make a meal off their weaker brethren, as he proved, by keeping some without food until he found their numbers grow less, the missing ones having been eaten by their comrades. The same author raises a question as to the cause of a lobster changing bright red when boiled. Can any of your correspondents make a suggestion towards a solution of the mystery?

GULIELMUS.

ANECDOTE OF A DOG.—A farmer living close to a railway having made an arrangement with a guard to throw his daily newspaper into his field as the train passed by at full speed, has trained his dog to be on the spot at the appointed time to bring him the paper, which he never fails to do, except on Sundays, when there is no paper or train at the usual time. At first the dog used to wait very patiently, until a train passed some hours later, but not getting his usual packet, has now learnt to know the Sunday from the other days of the week, and quietly stays at home.

Exeter.   SIDNEY STYLE.

CURIOUS BIRD.—I am somewhat puzzled to name the bird which B. F. G. partly describes. At first I was inclined to think it was a Cirl Bunting, but the white head and tail precludes that possibility. I know only two British birds at all like his specimen, one is the Snow Bunting (Emberiza nivalis), a most variable species, especially in the male; and the other, the Mealy Redpole (Linaria canescens), which also varies at different seasons and ages, in its markings. Both these species are however rare, and in some particulars do not accord with B. F. G's. I must, therefore, give it as my opinion that his bird is a variety of one of the Fringillidæ, most probably the Yellow-ammer.

A. M. B.

ANECDOTE OF A RAT.—A neighbour of mine has a cellar which is much infested with rats, a week seldom passing without catching two or three in a wire cage trap which is placed in the middle of the cellar every night. One Monday morning a rat was found snugly covered up in some straw which had evidently been brought to him by his sympathising companions to comfort him during his captivity, the straw being in a corner far away from the trap, so that it could not possibly have gathered it together by itself.

Exeter.   SIDNEY STYLE.

SKELETON LEAVES.—Seeing that one of your subscribers wish for a receipt for skeleton leaves, I beg to send the following:—Dissecting and bleaching leaves; a tablespoonful of chloride of lime in a liquid state mixed with a quart of pure water. The leaves to be soaked in the mixture for about four hours, then taken out and well washed in a bason filled with water, after which, they should be left to dry, with free exposure to light and air.

M. L. R.

NATAL.—For the information of amateur naturalists, who may be desirous of submitting to me specimens of Natural History for examination and identification, I beg to state that as New Zealand is so much inferior to Natal in zoology, I have decided on going there in preference to the latter country. As soon as my residence is fixed I will mention my address.

Mavisbush House.   J. D. S. W.

ARRANGEMENT OF SHELLS.—I shall be very much obliged if some of your correspondents will give me a few hints as to the best manner of arranging a cabinet of land and fresh-water shells, and also tell me where I can get printed labels for the same.

Feb. 6th.   W. F. ATKINS.

CHRYSALIDS.—Would any kind reader of the NATURALIST'S NOTE BOOK tell me what they find the best to keep chrysalids in, as I have kept mine in bran during last year, but have found it very unsuccessful. Also, what they find the best to kill moths with?

ENTOMOLOGIST.

MOLE, &c.—Would any of your readers tell me of a good book in which I should find a full account of the habits, &c., of the mole and field-mouse? Also, if the butterflies are divided into male and female, and if so, how can you distinguish one from the other?

A. B. P.

LANGUAGE OF ANIMALS.—Can any of your readers tell me of a good book, and its price, in which I shall find any account of the Language of Animals? I know there is a very good French work on the subject, but I do not know its name.   A. B. P.

A PERSON living at Henfield, near Bristol, has a cuckoo in a cage. It was caught last summer soon after it left its nest. It eats bread, potatoes, meat, cheese, &c.—*Scotsman.*

PRESERVED SPIDERS.—Can any of your readers tell me how to preserve spiders? I should also like to know the best book on "Coleoptera," and the price.   R. M.

THE HARMONY OF CREATION.

PECIMENS or skeletons of every known animal have been arranged in our museums, or delineated in scientific works, the various features of their structure have been diligently compared, the habits of their possessors carefully noted; the adaptation of their limbs to the performance of their several duties, and of their armature to the purposes of aggression or defence, have afforded interesting subjects of study to the comparative anatomist as well as to the observant traveller.

The value of the information thus accumulated has been in the exact ratio of the number of facts placed at our disposal. In a science so purely investigative as that of natural history, the earliest deductions must necessarily more or less partake of the character of empiricism; and it is only when, from the universality of their application, the surmises of the theorist reveal themselves to be laws imposed upon the animal creation, that the philosopher finds a basis on which to rear a substantial and impregnable edifice.

That such laws do exist is now established beyond the reach of scepticism. The flame first lighted by Cuvier in the damp cellars of the Jardin des Plantes, fanned by a thousand inspirations, has at length burst forth, spreading its beams around with startling radiance, dispersing by their light the monstrous brood of ignorant superstition, and revealing in their real shape the half-seen misshapen progeny of imposture and romance.

It is not without opposition, however, that truths, even of the greatest import, become ultimately established: prejudices, deeply rooted, have to be overthrown; pride and egotism remain obstinately blind to the clearest evidence; and not unfrequently even fraud and deception have to be unmasked before they can be driven from a field whence they have long been in the habit of deriving reputation or profit. In the time of Linnæus, as we are told, one of the most attractive curiosities in a celebrated museum in Holland was a stuffed mermaid, which to the practised eye of the illustrious Swede at once resolved itself into a factitious monstrosity, prepared by patching together the skins of a monkey and a fish. The Dutchmen were furious upon the occasion. The cries of "Great is Diana of the Ephesians" were not louder than those which assailed the adventurous champion of truth; and the philosopher only saved himself by a speedy escape from the scene of so unwelcome a revelation. The strange combinations of parts of heterogeneous animals ingeniously put together by Chinese and Japanese artists, and foisted upon foreigners as specimens of the creatures resident in their respective countries, would, indeed, some of them puzzle Linnæus himself, rivalling as they do the very idols in their joss-houses, in the absurdity of their incongruous appearance, and yet manufactured with so much skill, that the artifice lavished on their construction is not easily discernible.

The existence of the unicorn remained long unquestioned, and its horn, in the ignorance of the Middle Ages, was made the subject of almost incredible deception. This horn was, in fact, the tusk of the narwhal, obtained from the shores of Northern Europe, where, from time immemorial, the whale producing it has formed an object of pursuit for the Norwegian fisherman or the Greenlander. Not only was the tusk in question palmed off upon the ignorant as being the formidable weapon plucked from the brow of a quadruped so terrible in its aspect, that to look upon it when alive was declared fatal to the beholder; but it was thought to be possessed of qualities more nearly allied to magical than to medical potency, being regarded as an antidote to poison, however deadly. A fragment of this precious substance was dipped into the cups of kings before they drank, and the creature which bore it shared with Britain's lion the proud post of guarding from offence our royal arms. It was considered an infallible remedy against pestilence, insomuch, indeed, that the author of the "Loimalogie," a learned treatise on the great Plague of London in the year of our Lord 1666, after bitterly regretting the extreme costliness of this precious alexipharmic, gravely proposes as a valuable substitute the powder of baked toads.

These fables are exploded, and yet, perhaps, the reader will inquire, Why should there not be such an animal as the unicorn? why not a quadruped with a single horn in the middle of its forehead, as well as a rhinoceros with a solitary weapon on the back of its nose?

Simply because such an arrangement is impossible without a violation of those immutable laws, in accordance with which all animals are constructed. The astronomer would not be more startled by the sun's rising in the west than the comparative anatomist would be at the sight of a quadruped so organized. It would be a grand exception to all our experience and a flat contradiction to the established facts on which is raised the superstructure of modern science. In spite, therefore, of the authority of ancient writers, and even of the assertions and surmises of modern travellers, we are well convinced that such a monstrosity can have no existence in creation.

In order to explain to the non-scientific reader how we are enabled to speak thus unhesitatingly upon a subject which apparently depends altogether upon accuracy or falsehood in the assertions of travellers, it will be necessary to premise the data upon which a judgment apparently so hazardous can be pronounced—to explain the law as we find it recorded in the statute-book of nature, before we venture to speak authoritatively upon the probabilities or possibilities of the case.

The fundamental idea, the rock on which all natural science is immoveably based, is the harmony, or rather correspondence between the different organs, invariably conspicuous. No part of any animal is or can be incongruous with the rest of its organization.

Nature abhors incongruity as much as she does a vacuum ; therefore the simple grandeur of the axiom first established by Cuvier, that from the conformation of a tooth it is possible to predicate the configuration of the limbs and the habits of the animal to which the tooth belonged remains the unshaken keystone of natural history.

A second great discovery, which has tended more than any other made in modern times to the advancement of our knowledge, is the universality of plan, in accordance with which all animals have been constructed. The paw of the lion and the wing of the bat, the fin of the porpoise and the flipper of the seal, the pillars that support the colossal bulk of the elephant, and the limbs with which the kangaroo bounds over the herbage, or the mole digs through the soil, are all but modifications of the same instrument, made up of bones homologous in their nature, but varied in their shape, moved by muscles that individually represent each other, and armed with weapons which whether called claws, hoofs, or nails, are obviously but varied shapes of the same organs.

Or, to grapple more closely with our subject, we find the bodies of all vertebrate animals supported by an internal central framework (called, by a *ne plus ultra* of barbarism, the *backbone*), composed of a series of successive pieces, more or less moveably connected with each other, forming the axis or pivot upon which every movement turns. Now, although any one will acknowledge that the vertebral column of a fish represents that of a reptile, and that there is an essential resemblance between the backbone of a bird and that of a quadruped ; it is by no means so obvious that the individual pieces entering into the composition of the spine in these different animals are identical in their nature.—The fish, it is true, being an inhabitant of the water, buoyed upon all sides by the density of the surrounding element, needs not the ball and socket joints that characterize the serpent, and convert its lithe and limbless form into a living rope, adapted equally to wind around the forest bough or bind its victim in its fearful coil. The light, compact, and firmly girded skeleton that bears the eagle through the skies, has its vertebral column arranged in a very different manner from that of the whale, " incumbent on the vasty deep," or the mammiferous quadrupeds only fitted to walk upon the ground. Nay, more, in different regions the vertebræ of the same animal present innumerable diversities of structure: those of the neck are dissimilar to those of the back ; these latter to those of the loins and sacrum, while in the lengthy tail of some animals they vary from the utmost degree of complexity of which they are capable to their simplest possible condition. And yet all these modifications, both of shape and function, are attainable by the suppression or development of a few *elements*, as they are termed, common to the whole vertebrate creation, and so simple, that it will not be difficult to appreciate their importance, so far as is necessary for the explanation of our subject.

Each piece or segment entering into the composition of the spinal column, generally called a vertebra, and regarded as a distinct bone, is in reality made up of parts, each appropriated to a distinct use ; and consequently presents a greater or less degree of complexity in its composition, in proportion as its functions become more numerous and important. In its simplest and primary condition a vertebra may be considered, as its name imports, a mere centre or pivot, upon which, as upon a hinge, the movements of the body are supported. It consists therefore of a single portion or element, to which the name of *centrum* is not inappropriately applicable. Such are the vertebræ situated near the end of the tail in most quadrupeds. More frequently, however, other parts are combined with this central element, the uses of which are of a totally different character.

Along the upper surface of the spine runs that mysterious chain whence issue forth the mandates of the will, the spinal marrow or spinal chord, an apparatus so delicately organized, so impatient of injury, and so incapable of withstanding even the slightest pressure, that in order to insure its safety it is enclosed in a sort of tunnel composed of a succession of arches, each of which is based upon the central element described above ; and this addition increases the complexity of the structure.

A second set of arches, of precisely similar character, may normally be affixed to the under surface of the central element, so as to enclose and defend the main trunks of the vascular system.

And in combination with the above there may or may not be a pair of appendages, derived from the sides spreading out for the insertion of muscles or the attachment of ribs.

All the elements above enumerated are however distinct and independent parts. They may be co-existent in the same vertebra, or any of them may be deficient if their presence is not required. They may be modified in their shape and varied in their dimensions, either relatively or absolutely, until they become adapted to every possible condition under which an animal can exist. But they are always recognisable as the same "elements," easily identifiable by their office and position.

We, moreover, learn from this grand lesson that the osseous skeleton of every vertebrate animal is made up of certain definite combinations of bones, arranged in accordance with a given type from which Nature never departs; insomuch indeed, that by a careful analysis of the skeleton of all known vertebrates it is possible to compare them all with an ideal *archetype* or standard of organization; and thus detect at a glance the aberrations of structure that they individually present.

To these immutable laws, the organisms of the past, as well as those of existing nature, are equally amenable—the mastodon and the megatherium as well as the elephant and the sloth—the saurian monsters of the lias rocks as well as the crocodiles of the Nile and the Ganges—the shattered fragments of the earliest fossiliferous strata, and the last new arrival at the Zoological Gardens.

In like manner it is obvious that in the construction of their limbs all vertebrate animals conform to established laws, the universality of which is now incontrovertibly established. The pectoral fin of a fish, the fore-legs of a reptile, the wings of a bird, the paddle of a whale, the flippers of a seal, the aliform expansions of a bat, are merely modifications of the same elemental parts exaggerated or diminished in their relative proportions, adapted in their shape to the uses they subserve, or even altogether suppressed if their presence is not wanted; but, nevertheless, when present always recognisable and capable of identification.—T. Rymer Jones, F.R.S., in *Golden Hours*, for March.

WASPS.

IF we wish to study the habits of wasps, to become more closely acquainted with them than the mere external examination and the occasional capture of a nest will allow, we must secure a swarm with its nest in active work, remove it to some place more convenient for observation than wasps usually select, and expose the comb freely to view. The most convenient situation is a window ledge, where, under the shelter of a box without a lid, set up on end, the wasps will work as freely as in their more familiar quarters. It is advisable, before establishing the colony there, to see that the sash runs easily and without noise, that we may be able to look with our fingers, as they say, now and then, without irritating the swarm needlessly. It requires a little courage and skill to execute their removal successfully, but, once effected, the spectacle is one of constant varied interest, certainly not surpassed by that of a swarm of honey-bees; while from the smaller number of the insects their proceedings are much more easily intelligible.

Busy as wasps always are, yet a wasp's nest does not present such a scene of universal ceaseless industry as a bee-hive. The stream of life passing in and out is not so strong, and wasps may often be seen, especially in autumn, lying motionless, or slowly crawling over the case of the nest. However, even honey-bees seem indolent and indifferent sometimes, as, for instance, when they are wandering by twos and threes over a new glass which has lately been added to their establishment, and of which they have not yet fairly taken possession.

Supposing the removal of the nest and the exposure of the comb to have been successfully accomplished, the wasps will settle down to their work in a few hours. After watching for a little while we find that the wasps coming into the nest are divisible into two classes, one laden with materials for mending the injuries which the nest has suffered, the other bringing food for the young brood.

Wasps' food is of the most varied kind, they eat fragments of meat, the bodies of insects, fruit, garbage, anything, in short, from which nourishment can be extracted. But it is the nutritive fluid which is extracted from these various bodies that they consume, rather than the solid substance itself. It is true that fragments of the harder parts of insects are sometimes found in their castings, and generally form a large portion of the contents of the intestinal pouch of the larvæ; still, as a rule, wasps live on fluid food.

When a wasp appears with her crop full of fluid, she becomes immediately a centre of attraction. Two or three gather round her, and take up the fluid as she gradually lets it drop out on the upper surface of the comb. Then the larvæ are visited in their cells, and take their food in the most sisterly way, from mouth to mouth, till the supply is exhausted, and the nurse is at liberty to go away and replenish her crop. The solid food which is brought in cannot be so easily distributed, but, however it is portioned out, there is never any quarelling. Strong as the instinct is in wasps to snatch and hold their own against all the rest of the world, yet no feeling of resentment seems to be aroused by the loss of their prey. Once gone, whether to friend or foe, it is lost, and they make no angry attempts to recover it. The distinction of *meum* and *tuum* has no place in a wasp's feelings, any farther than her mandibles can reach. Right and might are to her exactly the same thing, and she who has lost is just as if she had never possessed. Their common nest only excepted.

Wasps' nests are not free from intruders; snails, and the larvæ of different insects, are sometimes found in them. As far as circumstances will allow they are kept scrupulously clean; the tree-nests most particularly so. The excretions are discharged outside the nest; all the dead grubs, and all rejected fragments of food, are carried away to a distance. The refuse of a nest of *V. germanica*, which I kept in a glass case for many weeks, was always removed in this manner, and the grubs were usually stuck up on the panes, at the extreme boundaries of their range, as it were, by the workers. In the same way ground-wasps remove to a distance all they can of the earth and stones which they excavate from their dens. The limits to what they carry away are of course very narrow, as they can only support a very little weight in the air, though they can drag large and heavy bodies along the ground. Probably, it is the smooth, polished margin of the hole which betrays the wasps' nest beneath, the grains of earth and fragments of insects are generally too widely scattered to give any clue to the position either of the tree, or of the ground-nests. But where the ground is stony, the entrance is marked by a heap of pebbles, which the wasps have pushed up from beneath thus far, but could not fly away with.—*British Social Wasps,* by E. L. Omerod, London, Longman's.

METEOROLOGY OF NATAL.

DR. MANN, superintendent of education, whose name is so familiar to meteorologists, has devoted considerable attention to the climatology, races, and productions of Natal. The following are the principal meteorological data which he has collected.

The prevalent wind is a sea breeze, which blows up an incline that lifts it a mile high in the course of seventy miles. This is the broad basis of the colonial climate. The almost constant sea wind is in part a trade wind; but the trade influence is reinforced by a monsoon influence. That Natal, in the parallel of 30° S. lat., is really in the trade wind region at certain seasons of the year, is unquestionable. But in addition to this, the soil of Natal is heated by day under a blazing sun, which so rarefies the atmosphere lying upon it, as to cause the land air to give place constantly before the heavier sea breeze.

During the winter season (from April to September), the normal atmospheric current is gentle and steady; the natural set of the air is rarely interrupted: there is at this season clear sunshine day after day, the temperature rising at Maritzburg to somewhere about 72° Fahr. in the day, and sinking to about 50° Fahr. at night. During the winter season of sunshine, the rainfall is very slight. There are two midwinter months, June and July, in which the monthly fall amounts only to 7-10ths of an inch. Before and after these are two months in which the monthly fall is 1·4-10th inch.

In the summer season (October to March) there are six months in which rain falls on $15\frac{1}{2}$ days for each month, and in which the monthly fall amounts to four inches. The reason for this increase of rainfall in the summer season is that at that period of the year the normal current of the atmosphere is frequently broken for short intervals, as a natural consequence of the increased force of the monsoon influence.

There is a thunderstorm at Maritzburg during the summer season nearly every third day. The rule at this season is that dense clouds collect early in the afternoon, and that rain, generally accompanied by lightning-discharges, pours down for a longer or shorter interval, the sky continuing to be shrouded far into the night.

The range of temperature varies greatly between day and night; it is very steady from day to day during winter; varies little between day and night, but greatly from day to day in summer. About forty-nine days in the year the thermometer exceeds 84° Fahr. and for about twelve days only it exceeds 90° Fahr. The general midsummer range at Maritzburg may be taken at 85° Fahr., when the hot wind is not blowing.

The barometer of Natal is in incessant movement. It makes a small daily wave about eight-tenths of an inch, but in addition to this there are broad undulations continually sweeping along day after day within an extreme range of an inch and a quarter. When the general mass of the air is moving from N.W. to S.E. the glass rises; when the movement is in the opposite direction the barometer falls. When the upper, or N.W., current, attains its fullest development of the surface, it constitutes what is called the *hot wind*. At Natal this wind is a very violent one; it sweeps clouds of dust along the ground, and raises the temperature 86° to 97° Fahr.; the air becomes so dry that vegetation shrivels under its touch. It scarcely ever reaches the coast, but turns up again into the higher regions some thirty miles before reaching the sea.

The hot wind of Natal appears to be intimately connected with the north-west gales of the South Atlantic, occasionally so destructive at the Cape of Good Hope. It is evidently of a cyclonic nature, for it generally begins to blow suddenly from the N.W. in the early morning without any other premonition than the falling of the mercury; towards the middle of the day comes a sudden lull, and a few minutes afterwards a fresh breeze sets in from S.E. This hot wind blows about twenty-five times in a year, on the average, at Maritzburg; its duration is generally restricted to a few hours. Very rarely it blows on two or three days in succession, and then always intermits in the evening.

Rain occurs at Natal with both a high and a low barometer. With a low glass it is the thunderstorm rain of summer; with a high barometer it is the sea rain often associated with gales, and occurs both in summer and winter. Hailstorms of great violence occasionally occur in association with the thunderstorms. The hailstones are angular masses of ice weighing two to three drachms; they destroy vegetation of every kind; a luxuriant garden is thus converted into a bare desert in five minutes. Fortunately, they usually affect only narrow belts of country, so that the same district is rarely visited a second time until after a long interval. Only one destructive hailstorm has been experienced at Maritzburg in eight years.—*Scientific Review*, March.

DODDERS.

WHO among us is not familiar with the pretty Dodder of our heaths and commons? The only wonder is that it has not been brought into cultivation as an ornamental plant in this country before now, or, if not this one, at least some of the handsomer exotic species. In Portugal, we are informed, Cuscuta chrysocoma has long been cultivated for the flower market of Lisbon, where it makes its appearance as regularly as mignonette at Covent Garden. This species was last year introduced by Dr. Welwitsch, who distributed the seeds amongst two or three establishments, but whether it was raised or not I have no means of telling. At any rate, seeds subsequently procured were raised, and plants successfully grown by Mrs. Parsons, of Brighton, who obtained a first-class certificate for it at the Brighton flower show. The three or four pots of this plant exhibited attracted universal admiration, and were, indeed, extremely pretty. It is to be hoped that this novelty will reappear during the coming season, when it will doubtless be eagerly sought after. From my own experiments I can safely say that nothing is much easier of cultivation than the species of Cuscuta. The principal thing to be attended to is the kind of nurse-plant affected—whether herbaceous or woody. This ascertained, there is no other difficulty to encounter; and as most species produce seed in great abundance, there is little danger of losing a species. The excessive productiveness of some of the species is well known to our farmers, to whom the C. Trifolii is a much dreaded pest, destroying acres of its nurse-plant Trifolium. C. Epilinum is no less destructive amongst flax. But this great fecundity is evidently a provision of nature to ensure a perpetuation of the species, for a large proportion of the seeds that germinate are too far removed from the nurse-plant to prey upon it, and consequently perish. These plants are quite leafless, even to the absence of cotyledons, and in germinating throw up a thread-like stemlet, which is sure to incline towards, and eventually seize hold of, any plant near enough to attract it. If the plant be of the right kind, the Cuscuta will soon encircle the branches, pierce the bark or epidermis, and permanently establish itself. At the same time, even if not drawn out of the soil by the nurse-plant, it speedily shrivels, and dies away at the base, thus renouncing all further direct connection with mother earth. When they once get a firm hold they grow with amazing rapidity, and if the nurse-plant is not very strong it soon succumbs.

The safest and surest procedure to raise those species that are parasitical upon herbaceous plants, is to sow the seed of the nurse-plant and Cuscuta together in about equal parts. But to provide against the probable contingency of the Cuscuta choking its nurse, and thereby endangering its own life, it is desirable to have a few pots of the nurse-plant separate, and a little further advanced, and then allow the Cuscuta to run upon them. For those having woody stems a different method must be pursued. The seeds of these may be sown in pots or pans placed immediately beneath the branches of the intended nurse-plant. A little attention is necessary to guide the Cuscuta threads equally over all parts of the nurse-plant.

The species tried grew well on plants belonging to quite different families, provided they were of the same duration. C. chrysocoma succeeds equally well on many Labiatæ, Begonias, &c., but small-leaved densely-branched plants are preferable as nurse-plants, because they admit of a luxuriant growth of the Cuscuta, and render it more effective. These curious and interesting parasites require no other recommendation than their brightly-coloured filiform stems, varying from golden-yellow to crimson, and their dense clusters of small flowers.—*H.*—*Gardener's Chronicle*, Feb. 29.

VENUS.

FOR splendour, no star can bear the least comparison with the planet Venus, which during this month is a most brilliant object in the western evening sky. On the 1st day of the month she will set below the horizon three and a half hours after the sun, this interval of time increasing gradually to more than four hours at the end of March. Universal interest is always created in the popular mind when Venus is in this position, though, when she is a morning star, we have frequently considered her to be a still more magnificent object, owing, perhaps, to the clearer state of the atmosphere in the early morning. At such times the light of Venus is so intense, that a sensible shadow is produced by the interposition of the finger before a piece of white paper. At these epochs of great brilliancy she has frequently been observed with the naked eye within an hour of noon.

Without entering into much detail, a few remarks on the appearance and position of Venus in the solar system will probably be interesting. The order of the planets from the sun, omitting the hypothetical Vulcan, is as follows:—Mercury, Venus, the Earth, Mars, the group of minor planets, Jupiter, Saturn, Uranus, and Neptune. Venus is, therefore, the second planet from the sun, around which she revolves in an almost circular orbit interior to that of the earth. The time occupied in her revolution is about 225 of our days; consequently the inhabitants of Venus enjoy a year about two-thirds as long as ours. The mean or average distance of this planet from the sun is sixty-six millions of miles; and when she is in a direct line between the earth and the sun, or at her least distance, she is about twenty-five millions of miles from us. When near her extreme elongation east or west, she is always seen to the best advantage with the naked eye. She will be in that position, or greatest eastern elongation, on May 7th, 1868. Her greatest apparent brilliancy will, however, take place a month later, when she will be rapidly approaching towards her least distance from the earth. Venus is now truly the evening star, or the Hesperus of the old philosophers. When she is a conspicuous morning star, the ancients have given Venus the name of Lucifer or the harbinger of day. Let us now, in imagination, direct a telescope to this favourite planet on any day in March, 1868. Instead of viewing a globular object similar to the large and distant planets, we find a gibbous one, in form precisely similar to the moon when between the first quarter and the full. This is owing to a considerable portion of the illuminated disk being turned from us. In short, the phases of Venus and the moon are produced by analogous causes, depending entirely on their relative positions with respect to the sun and earth. The telescopic appearance of Venus is therefore like a miniature moon, sometimes round, then gibbous, and finally a crescent, so fine, directly before conjunction, as to appear like an illuminated hair. As a rule, the crescent form takes place at inferior conjunction, the half-illuminated disk at the time of elongation, and full at superior conjunction. The apparent magnitude of Venus varies considerably, according as her distance from the earth increases or diminishes.

The diameter of Venus is 7510 miles, being slightly smaller than that of the earth. She revolves on her axis in about 23h. 21m., thus making the day shorter than ours by a small quantity. Although Venus is now and then comparatively so near us, we know but little of her actual surface, principally owing to her intense brilliancy, which dazzles the eye of the observer. With regard to the two intra-terrestrial planets, Mercury and Venus, it is supposed that they are globes formed similarly to our earth, and illuminated and warmed by the sun. It is believed, also, from special observations of the physical appearance of the surface of Venus, that clouds prevail; if so, there must be water, and probably an atmosphere. This hypothesis would seem to be partially borne out by a phenomenon observed during the transit of Venus across the sun's disk in 1761. While projected on the sun, the planet appeared surrounded by a faint nebulous ring, and at the moment when Venus left the sun, a luminous ring was observed in the same place. These two phenomena could be easily explained, if we suppose the globe of Venus to be surrounded by a very dense atmosphere. Farther than this, the most powerful instrument of the astronomer is unable to add to the little knowledge we possess of the actual formation of these intra-terrestrial planets. Of their peculiar motions in the heavens with respect to the fixed stars, and their effect on each other by their mutual attractions, the results obtained from modern astronomical observations leave but little more for us to learn.—EDWIN DUNKIN, F.R.A.S., in *Leisure Hour*, March.

ANTS IN BERMUDA.

THE Common Ant (*Formica*), of the Bermudas swarms in countless myriads throughout the hot season, and makes sad havoc among the naturalist's specimens, during the drying process; but should a univalve, or crustacean, have to be cleared of its fleshy inhabitant, certain are we that a more sure method could not be resorted to, than to place the specimen within reach of these never weary scavengers; but a short time would elapse ere every particle would be consumed, save and except the shelly covering, which, by this simple process, would be prepared for the cabinet.

The following interesting note, by our friend, Mr. Hurdis, more clearly illustrates the habits of this insect:—

"Every housekeeper, gardener, and all who deal in articles of food, are keenly alive to the destructive habits of the ant, which infests the Bermudas in legions during the greater portion of the year. Nothing appears to escape their active search; and whether it be meat, milk, sugar, honey, cake, or fruit, the ingenuity of the owner has to be exercised, in order to save the same from utter destruction.

"There are two species of ants in the Bermudas, one of which is about the size of the common ant of England, and is supposed to be an importation from the West Indies: the other is a much smaller insect, which I have observed only among the islands in the Sound.

"The ant appears to entertain a natural repugnance to common whale oil, for which reason it is commonly used by the native and other inhabitants as a protection against its annoying depredations. Store-room tables have their legs placed in tin or leaden cups, partly filled with this oil. Shelves made to hang from the ceiling, have their iron supports passing through tin funnels of the same; and meat hooks are guarded in a similar manner. It is only by these means that any article of food can be considered safe from these marauders. The ant is also very destructive to the domestic rabbit, to poultry, and young pigeons, to caged birds, and to all sick animals; and man himself, when in a helpless state, is sometimes attacked by it.

"During the heat of summer, millions of these insects make their appearance upon every road and pathway, and sometimes invade the dwellings of men in such multitudes, as to become an intolerable nuisance. Every tree, and almost every bush then teems with its black columns, ascending and descending in the great occupation of obtaining food.

"Finding the ants, one morning, disposed to attack a bottle of honey (a common wine bottle), I placed the same in a soup plate upon the sideboard, carefully filling the plate with water, as a protection. On returning to the room a short time afterwards, I found the bottle swarming with ants, and on a closer inspection was greatly surprised to find a column of those insects passing and re-passing on the surface of the water, between the rim of the plate and the bottle of honey. This they appeared to do with perfect ease, merely wetting their feet in the operation; in other words, absolutely walking on the water.

"There is another peculiarity in the habits of this insect, which deserves to be mentioned. If a couple of snipe have been killed, and are destined as a present to some friend, they will be suspended by a single thread from the upper part of some cool, open window for the night, to save them from the ants; and yet, notwithstanding this precaution, the birds will be found in the morning covered with ants, while others continue to descend the long and slender passage of communication. Is not this property of discovering food to be ascribed to the power of scent?"

A species of *Myrmicidæ* we found under a stone, in the grounds at Hermitage, in company with another small red ant:—*The Naturalist in Bermuda*, by J. M. Jones, Esq. London: Reeves & Turner.

THE DRAGON TREE OF TENERIFFE.

ONE of the oldest and most interesting vestiges of vegetable life has recently been removed from the spot where it has stood for an almost indefinite number of years, making the place of its growth famous from the fact of its presence. We speak of the celebrated Dragon tree (*Dracæna Draco*) which until recently stood at Oratava, Teneriffe. The removal of this time-honoured tree is due to a furious gale which swept across the island last autumn, but of the effects of which botanists have only just become acquainted. This great loss to the botanical world is the more to be regretted, as it seems that little or no care had been taken by the Spaniards to prop, or otherwise support the tree, which, though living and healthy, from the very fact of its age must have required such aid, being computed by some authorities at six thousand years old.

In July, 1819, the tree was severely injured by a great storm, but it survived, and remained until recently one of the wonders of the vegetable kingdom. The *Dracæna Draco* belongs to the natural order *Liliaceæ*, and is, consequently, a near ally to the asparagus. We have it in cultivation in our hothouses in this country, but of course in a young state. At Kew the plant has attained a height of between twenty and thirty feet, entirely unbranched, the stem marked with the scars of fallen leaves. These tall, straight stems, with a tuft of long leaves at the top, have much the appearance of Yuccas, or rather small palms, and give no idea of the habit of the great tree now destroyed. This young state of the plant has been called the first age, or infancy, and in its native country lasts for a period of twenty-five or thirty years. The second age is that of maturity, or reproduction, and the third age the age of decay. At the second age the leaf scars disappear, and the trunk increases in thickness by the formation of branches; towards the close of this period the plant puts forth its flowers. In the last, or third age, is produced the irregular, or gnarled appearance which the stems of old Dragon trees exhibit. This appearance is produced by the giving-off of aerial roots, and the formation of glandular excrescences on the hollow part of the interior of the trunk. The leaves, which are three feet or more long, and one to two inches wide, are straight and sword-shaped; the flowers are pale yellow or greenish white, and appear in panicles upon the leafy extremities of the branches. The fruit is a yellowish green berry, becoming scarlet when ripe. The introduction of the plant into this country is said to date from about 1640. The great interest of the Oratava tree was its immense size and great age. Baron Humboldt says, when he visited Teneriffe, that the tree was included in the garden of M. Franchi. "In 1799, when we climbed the peak of Teneriffe, we found that the enormous vegetable was forty-five feet in circumference a little above the root. Sir George Staunton affirms that at ten feet high its diameter is twelve feet; its height was reckoned at from seventy to seventy-five feet."

Signor Fenzi, of Florence, who visited the tree in the early part of last year, says it was then in excellent health, "its immense crown covered with innumerable panicles of scarlet fruits, and the huge trunk, although completely decayed in the interior, sustained vigorously the spreading mass of fleshy branches and sword-like foliage. On the west side, where the ground was sloping, a solid wall had been built under about one-third of the trunk, while on the other side two or three half-rotten staves propped the more projecting branches. All around the trunk a dense bush of climbers and other plants clothed its expanded base in a very picturesque confusion. I remember now some bignonias, jasmines, heliotropes, abutilons, etc., and also a flourishing almond tree, covered with blossoms, that had grown quite close to the trunk. Its circumference (as far as I was able to measure it, on account of the inequality of the ground) was not inferior to twenty-six mètres (about seventy-eight English feet), while the total height of the tree did not exceed seventy-five feet. And it was remarkable, that through some crevices in the trunk a small Dracæna was to be seen, growing spontaneously in the decayed substance furnished by the parent tree."—*The Student*, March. GROOMBRIDGE AND SONS.

FILEFISH ON THE ENGLISH COAST.
BY JONATHAN COUCH, F.G.S., M.Z.S.

Although the families or species of Filefishes appear to have been long known in a general way, much ignorance or confusion about them seems to have prevailed among naturalists. Indeed, such may be said to be the case still concerning even those species which are said to be met with in the Mediterranean, one of which, at least, is known to have been taken on our own coasts, and of which a representation is given in my Natural History of the Fishes of the British Islands. It was caught in a crabpot not far from Mevagissey, and its portrait was taken when fresh from the water; after which this example of *Balistes capriscus* was sent to the British Museum, where also there is preserved the only other English specimen, that afforded a somewhat different figure in a wood engraving to my friend Mr. Yarrell. But whether there be not another species, or, as Risso says, two or three, some one of which may be supposed likely to come to us, may be regarded as uncertain; and, therefore, as a subject of interest to the students of nature, it should be looked for with some attention, for it is only with much care and not a little good fortune that some other rare visitors have been saved from destruction. The natural historian Willughby, who travelled in Italy for the special purpose of enquiring into objects of science, was not able to form a decisive opinion as regards the distinction of species in this family; and Linnæus, who copied closely the English author, has confounded together, under the name of *Balistes vetula*, at least two or three species. Nor does it appear that more modern writers have distinguished them with more precision; since Lacépède expresses his belief that one of those of the Mediterranean is the same with the indistinct *Balistes vetula* of Linnæus, while he appears to suppose that another species inhabiting the same sea remained undescribed. Turton had learnt to distinguish his *B. capriscus*, which is our Cornish fish, from the Linnean species *B. vetula*; but even Cuvier seems to leave the matter in the same degree of obscurity in which he found it, since he not only suspects the *B. maculatus* of Bloch to be the same with *B. capriscus*, but he also expresses himself inclined to believe that such is the case also with the *B. buniva* of Lacépède. There are difficulties in assigning these terms, such as I will not, without greater opportunity, attempt to unravel; but as it may be of consequence to observers to be able to distinguish that one which has been met with on our shores from another species that may, not improbably, travel to us, it is my object, in this communication, to provide a description of this latter fish, at the same time believing it to be the same to which Risso has applied the name of *Balistes buniva*, which designation he has derived from the naturalist Lacépède. There is, however, this great inconvenience in the works of Risso, which renders them less valuable than otherwise they would be, that his descriptions of the objects of natural history are slight, and the distinctions are often made to depend on the colour, which is liable to variation according to the season and the extent of wandering. His figures are also far too small to be of use in the critical examination of what he represents; so that, in some cases, a slight variation of form has led him to suppose that what has come under his observation with such casual differences has been of different species. A material point in the distinction between the fishes referred to above, is their relative proportions, in the measurement of which, as regards one of them, as well as in the description, I am greatly assisted by the kindness of my friend W. P. Cocks, Esq., from whom I have been favoured with a sketch of that one which I have concluded to be the *B. buniva* of Risso, and perhaps of Lacépède.

The total length of the example of this *B. buniva*, measured in a straight line to the end of the tail, was $13\frac{3}{4}$ inches, of which the tail measured $2\frac{1}{2}$ inches; depth of body, measured where deepest, which was about the middle of the length, 5 inches; its thickness $2\frac{1}{2}$ inches nearly, while in the example *B. capriscus*, with the same proportion of length, $13\frac{3}{4}$ inches, the depth amounted to $6\frac{1}{2}$ inches. Of the relative extent and shape of the tail I take less account, since there was much difference in this respect between the only two examples which have been taken in England; but the form of the root also differs in the two species, the fleshy part, to which the rays of the tail are attached, being suddenly expanded in the British *B. capriscus*. For the purpose of further distinction between them it is not necessary that we should give a lengthened description, but it is to be observed, further, that in the *B. capriscus* the dorsal fins are much closer together; the vent immediately under the anterior edge of the second of these fins, this second and the anal wider, and less slenderly elevated in the anterior rays, whereas in *B. buniva* the form of these rays is almost triangular, in consequence of the projection of the first rays, from which the others become rapidly shorter, without extending so far towards the most slender portion of the contraction of the body.

It might be wished that some means were devised for securing to the inspection of observers, and, in consequence, to our museums, the examples of very rare fishes and other marine productions, which, not unfrequently, are met with on our coasts. Several of great interest have come under my inspection only by accident, or by the kind assistance of friends, of which of late the instances are foreign.

Botany of Peat Bogs.

The Botany of the peat-bogs, as already said, is remarkable and very interesting. Not that any plants are absolutely peculiar to them; nearly all that they produce may be seen by the waysides among the mountains of Cumberland, seated amid the sphagnum, or upon the swampy margins of some of the lakes, where the soil is peaty; so elegant are they, and in some respects so strange, that the Moss Florula may nevertheless be considered a distinct one. For the lover of wild nature, a glorious spectacle is it at the end of July. Then the Lancashire-asphodel, the sundews, and the blushing-maiden heath hold festival:—then, in the drier parts, the silvery hair-grass and the purple moor-grass contrast their colours; in hollows that the wind has left unscathed, the ermine tassels of the cotton-sedges still swing in the sunshine; while in the wettest parts, where the water forms thin broad lakes, there are aquatic meadows of tender green, formed of the herbage of the *Rhyncospora*, crowded with the little white heads which constitute its bloom. Interspersed with these may also be seen, in less or greater plenty, the speary stalks of the deer's-hair; and in the drier parts, the foliage of the Andromeda, with perchance a flower or two; the tender little cranberry also, reminding us of wild thyme; the dark-green trails of the crowberry, and the stiff and angular branches of the whortleberry. In the drier parts likewise grow copiously the reindeer moss; with now and then a tuft of that other most charming little lichen which borders its gray-green goblets with scarlet beads; or of that pretty moss which protects its capsules with a furry brown cap, and sets us thinking of Robinson Crusoe, and that immortal head-dress he made of the goat's skin. A little later in the season the spectacle transmutes to one of even livelier beauty. When the summer flowers have faded, and the bog seems about to be consigned, like the Arctic regions, to another six months of blackness, for awhile the fate is delayed by the bloom of the heather. Not that its splendour is co-extensive with the area of the morass. Where the swamp-loving plants so much luxuriate, the heather blooms sparingly, or not all; everywhere, on the other hand, where the ground is dry, especially upon the borders, where drainage has taken effect, the purple glow is never forgotten, and these great solitudes, that have never felt the plough in the declining sheen of evening, seem to reflect the sky, and to be themselves the world's flower-set. At the same period, the older of the deep cuttings made for the drainage, teem with ferns, chiefly *Aspidium dilatatum* and *Blechnum boreale*, the latter producing fronds which are often 30 inches long. In many of the peaty and half-dry ditches and sunk fences bordering the mosses, grow also the Osmunda, or Royal-fern, one of the most stately of British plants. Of late years, the original abundance of this plant has been much reduced, through the growth of taste for ferneries, and the transfer to gardens and rockwork of the individuals which previously were the ornament of their native soil. There is nothing novel in this. Scores of species of British plants are now much less frequently found growing in their primitive wild localities than was the case in days gone by, being suitable for the garden, and having, in the course of time, been gradually removed by the cultivator. Take, for instance, the lady's-slipper orchis, the mezereon, the oxlip, and the sweet-brier. As the moss gradually merges into cultivated land, procumbent brambles and many other agrarian plants make their appearance, the belt of vegetation which marks the junction being ordinarily of far greater richness than either of the botanical regions which it separates; at last even the heather disappears, and we step into the meadow or the lane.—From a paper by Mr. Leo H. Grindon in the *Yearly Report of the Manchester Field Naturalist Society*.

OSTRICH AND GAZELLE HUNTING.

The sport popular above all others among the Arabs of the desert is ostrich-hunting, and it presents several points of interest. For a week before the intended expedition, nothing but barley is given to the horses, and water only once a day. They are exercised regularly, and harnessed for actual work in accoutrements much lighter than usual. The hunting parties are composed of from eight to ten persons. Each hunter is accompanied by a servant mounted on a camel, which carries also a portion of the necessary provender for the party, who calculate on an absence of eight days from home quarters. The hunter's only weapon is a club from four to five feet long, terminating in a very heavy knob.

The party, when they observe tracks of their prey, halt and bivouac. The next day, two scouts are sent in pursuit; one, as soon as a flock of ostriches is discovered, returns with the intelligence. The hunters form an extended circle round the quarry, the gaps between each horsemen being filled by the attendants. When every arrangement is made they boldly advance. The ostriches recoil in terror, but are confined within the gradually contracting circle by the rapid evolutions of the horsemen. The strength of the birds fails, and each hunter selects his victim. He pursues it, strikes it a blow on the head with his club, then descends from his horse, and, being careful not to stain the wing feathers, cuts the throat of his prey. If a poor man is celebrated for his skill as a hunter, he has no difficulty in finding a capitalist to furnish him for the chase. A wealthy Arab will lend horse, camel, and equipments, supplying, besides, two-thirds of the necessary provender, in consideration of receiving a similar proportion of the profit resulting from the transaction.

Another mode of destroying the ostrich is to carefully track the bird to the nest. During its absence, two hunters dig a hole and conceal themselves. When the bird returns it is shot. If either of the hidden Arabs should miss his aim at a male ostrich, he is condemned in the value. His companions reason in this manner: "We chose thee," they say, "as the best shot; we placed thee in the good position to do us benefit; and lo! thou workest us such a wrong as this. Thou shalt pay for it."

There is a third way of capturing the ostrich, which is literally by running it down. An ostrich flies in a straight line, and four or five horsemen station themselves at distances of about a league along the road which they know he will choose. The pursuit is taken up by each hunter in succession, until ultimately the bird is exhausted and destroyed.

The next chase in favour with the Arabs is that of the gazelle, which, unlike that of the ostrich, is for pleasure merely. The carcass itself in money is barely worth a franc, yet it has some extraneous value. For instance, the proverbial beauty of the gazelle's eyes, and the whiteness of its teeth, have given rise to a curious practice. Women have one brought to them that they may lick its eyes with their tongue, in the belief that the eyes of their infants will have the same lustrous melancholy. Under a similar idea, they touch its teeth with a finger, which they afterwards put into their own mouth. The horns, shaved thin and mounted with silver, are used by women as instruments to put *kohol* on their eyes, and the skin, after being carefully tanned, is made into *mezoueud*, or cushions, in which they enclose their most valuable articles.

With respect to the Arabs themselves, the education of the desert trains their physical faculties to the highest point. They can distinguish between the appearance of a man and woman at the distance of three leagues. The chief seldom walks, but the ordinary Arab is an indefatigable pedestrian. He makes it indeed a profession, though not a very lucrative one, for he cheerfully accepts four francs for travelling with messages sixty leagues. On such a service he sleeps only two hours out of the twenty-four. When he lies down he fastens a piece of cord of a certain length to his foot and sets fire to the end. By this contrivance he is awakened when the cord is burnt out.—From *The Lamp*, February.

LEPORIDES, OR HARE-RABBITS.

Mr. W. B. Tegetmeier, who has given some attention to this question, has written the following to the *Field*, Feb. 29:—The so-called leporide, or hare-rabbit, has recently been attracting some attention, a pamphlet having been published in Paris by M. Gayot, entitled, "Lièvres, Lapins, et Léporides." The same author has written on the subject in *La Chasse Illustrée*, and *The Farmer* has also been devoting a portion of its columns to the consideration of leporides.

I have read very carefully M. Gayot's article, and that in *The Farmer*, and I fail to see in either any proof of the existence of these animals. The opening paragraphs of the article in *The Farmer*—usually a very carefully edited paper—afford a very good example of the manner in which certain pseudo-scientific views are foisted on the public. They are as follows:—" That there exists a breed of dogs known as the bull-terrier, and exhibiting in combination the characteristics of the two animals from which it derives its name, and that this breed possesses the power of propagating its species without degeneracy, is a fact as well known in France as in this country. One is apt to think that the knowledge of such a fact should have rendered it easy to French naturalists to believe in the existence of another hybrid animal lately brought into notice—the leporide—a cross between the hare and the rabbit."

I will say nothing of the singular assertion that a breed of dogs exists between the *bull* and the terrier, which exhibits the characteristics of these two animals, as I do not believe that a hybrid between a ruminant and a carnivore exists. But, supposing the writer to mean a cross between the bulldog and the terrier, the argument is perfectly worthless as proving the existence of leporides. The cross between two varieties of one species, as are the bulldog and terrier, is not, as is asserted, a species or a hybrid, but a mongrel, which by care can be perpetuated as a distinct breed. These mongrels are perfectly fertile *inter se*, or with either parent, and their existence has no bearing whatever on the production or perpetuation of a hybrid or mule between two distinct species of animal, such as the hare and the rabbit.

That animals so very different in habits and mode of life as the hare and the rabbit should interbreed is not very probable; and if they did, there appears very little doubt that the offspring would be a sterile hybrid. The young hare is born in a comparatively perfect condition, covered with fur, and able to see and move very speedily after birth. The young of rabbits, on the contrary, are much more numerous in each litter; they are born in a very undeveloped condition, perfectly naked and sightless. That animals so diverse should produce fertile hybrids is not to be expected, and I may state that all attempts to cross these two species at the Zoological Gardens have failed. The so-called leporides are nothing more than large brown rabbits, having the same period of gestation, number of young, and undeveloped, sightless condition at birth, that characterise ordinary domestic rabbits. The flesh is white, and totally destitute of the colour or flavor of that of the hare. I have recently examined microscopically, with much care, the fur of the hare, rabbit, and so-called leporide, and find that the fur of the two latter animals is apparently identical, and quite distinct from that of the hare. Unless some evidence very different from what has hitherto been made known is produced respecting the production of the leporide, there is no chance of its existence being recognised by naturalists.

BEE-HUNTING.

From the absence in many parts of the bush of Australia of flowers, the little native bee may be seen busily working on the bark of the trees, and unlike the bee of this country, which is ever on the move from flower to flower, it seems to be unconscious of danger. This may arise from the vastness of the solitudes in Australia, which are seldom or ever disturbed, except by a passing tribe, or by its own wild denizens, which are far from numerous. The bee is therefore easily approached, and the bright clear atmosphere of the climate is peculiarly favourable to the pursuit. A party of two or three natives, armed with a tomahawk, sally forth into the bush, having previously provided themselves with the soft white down from the breast of some bird, which is very light in texture, and at the same time very fluffy. With that wonderful quickness of sight which practice has rendered perfect, they descry the little brownish leaden-coloured insect on the bark, and rolling up an end of the down feather to the finest possible point between their fingers, they dip it into a gummy substance, which a peculiar sort of herb exudes when the stem is broken. They then cautiously approach the bee, and with great delicacy of touch place the gummed point under the hind legs of the bee. It at once adheres. Then comes the result for which all this preparation has been made. The bee, feeling the additional weight, fancies he has done his task and is laden with honey, and flies off the tree on his homeward journey at no great distance from the ground. The small white feather is now all that can be discerned, and the hunt at once commences. Running on foot amid broken branches and stony ground requires, one would think, the aid of one's eyesight; but with the native Australians it is not so. Without for a moment taking their eyes off the object, they follow it, sometimes to the distance of half-a-mile, and rarely, if ever, fail in marking the very branch where they saw the little bit of white down disappear at the entrance of the hive. Here there is a halt, the prize is found, and they sit down to regain their breath before ascending the tree, and to light a pipe, to which old and young men, women and children, are extremely partial. When the rest and smoke are over, with one arm round the tree and the tomahawk in the other, the black man cuts notches in the bark, and placing the big toe in the notches, ascends this hastily constructed stair till he comes to where the branches commence; then, putting the handle of the tomahawk between his teeth, he climbs with the ease and agility of a monkey till he reaches the branch where last he saw the white down disappear; he then carefully sounds the branches with the back of his tomahawk till the dull, as distinct from the hollow sound, tells him where the hive is. A hole is then cut, and he puts his hand in and takes the honey out. If alone, the savage eats when up the tree till he can eat no more, and leaves the rest; but if with others, he cuts a square piece of bark, and after having had the part of the hive as a reward for his exertion, brings down a mass of honey and comb mixed up together, which, though not inviting, is greedily devoured by those below.—*Once a Week*, March part.

[Many of our readers will doubtless recollect a wonderful description of Bee-hunting, similar to the above, in one of Cooper's novels, I think the Oak Openings.—ED.]

CRANBERRY CULTURE.

"To make the desert blossom as the rose" is, or ought to be, the ultimate object of agriculture, and that science does not bound its aim merely to raising fertile lands to their highest point of cultivation, but also devotes itself to conquering those obstacles which opposing nature plants around her waste recesses. Those who are conversant with the cedar swamps of New Jersey can hardly conceive of any spots of earth more unpropitious, or more unlikely to prove valuable to the husbandman; yet these very "dismal swamps," and their threatening, sturdy, obstructive growth of trees, with their "roots set tuskwise," as if in defiance of man's endurance, have been conquered, and promise to yield abundant harvest of one of those luxuries which our increasing civilization is so rapidly changing into the necessaries of life. During the past few years individual exertion has repeatedly shown, beyond the possibility of refutation, but these unconquerable thickets furnish the soil best adapted to the cultivation of the cranberry. A tract of twenty-eight acres of such improved land was purchased less than five years ago by its present owner for eight dollars per acre, and the fortunate experimentalist realised in 1865 a net profit of ten thousand dollars, and from the same plantation, in the following year, a net profit of more than six thousand dollars. Numerous farmers have made a like experiment with uniformly successful results, and more recently companies have been formed for conducting the business on a more extensive scale. Cranberries are in great and growing demand as a most agreeable adjunct to the dinner-tables of this country, and there is a market for them in Europe also for culinary purposes. Four hundred bushels per acre have been raised in repeated instances, but forty is the ordinary average yield. The estimate, and it may be presumed as sufficiently low, upon which calculations of the future profits are based, seem to be as follows:— For the first crop, three years after planting, thirty-five bushels per acre; second crop averaging fifty bushels, and the third crop seventy-five bushels, and the fourth crop, when the plant becomes six years old, one hundred bushels per acre. The large tract of land which has recently been opened for settlement at Fruitland, is in the heart of one of the best cranberry regions of New Jersey, as many of these plants are there found in their native state, and many promising attempts at cranberry culture are now being made in the adjacent districts.—*Philadelphia Press.*

A New Sensitive Plant.

Botanists call sensitive plants those which display a kind of irritability at the approach of some extraneous body; but there is another kind of sensitiveness which consists in spontaneous motions without any apparent cause; and this had hitherto been only exemplified in the *Hedysarum gyrans.* In a paper, addressed to the Academy of Sciences, M. H. Lecoq mentions a second instance, that of the *Colocasia esculenta.* In visiting his hot-house in January last, our author perceived a motion in one of the leaves of this plant; he at first attributed it to a draught, but upon examination remarked the same motion in the four other leaves, there being no more at the time. It was a sort of rhythmical tremor, so long as to affect the plants that stood near. His attention being thus aroused, he continued his observations daily, and found the motions of the colocasia were not regularly periodical. Sometimes its tremor would last the whole day and following night; it usually occurred from nine in the morning until noon, and not unfrequently the plant would remain in a state of perfect rest for days, and even whole weeks. This induced M. Lecoq to attach a few light bells to the plant, in order to be warned of the approach of the paroxysm. On one occasion it began at two o'clock after midnight, and continued nearly the whole morning. The bells tinkled, and the leaves of the colocasia struck the neighbouring plants with sufficient distinctness to enable the author to count the pulsations by a stop-watch; he found them to be between 100 and 120 per minute. On several other occasions the fits were exceedingly violent. On the 2nd of March last, although the temperature of the hothouse had fallen to 7 deg. Cent., the plant seemed to be labouring under a fit of ague, so that the very pot containing the plant, and weighing about 10 kilog., shook so that the hand of a man could not steady it. The rhythmical tremor was likewise communicated to a fine leaf of a *Strelitzia Nicolai,* another of a *Philodendrum pertusum,* and to some fine clusters of flowers of the *Begonia manicata.* M. Lecoq cannot explain the cause of this tremor, but he thinks himself warranted in not attributing it by any means to the temperature; he suggests the possibility of its being the result of a stoppage in the regular perspiration of the plant.

Under the Microscope.

DEVELOPMENT OF INFUSORIA.

ON making a cold or hot infusion of any vegetable or animal substance, covering the vessel with a piece of paper so as to exclude the dust, and then watching it every twelve hours, the first change visible to the eye is a slight opalescence, and the formation of a thin scum or pellicle that floats upon the surface. This appears at times, varying from a few hours to several days, according to the temperature of the atmosphere or the nature of the infusion. On examining the pellicle or film under high magnifying powers, it is seen to be composed of a mass of minute molecules, varying in size from the minutest visible point to that of one thirty-thousandth of an inch in diameter. These molecules are closely aggregated together, and must exist in incalculable numbers. They constitute the primordial mucous layer of Burdach, and the proligerous pellicle of Pouchet. The same pellicle, examined six hours later, shows the molecules to be somewhat enlarged, and these separated by the pressure of the upper glass are already seen here and there to be strongly adhering together in twos and fours, so as to form a little chain. Many twos, also, have apparently melted together so as to form a short staff or filament—*bacterium.* Twelve hours after this, it may be seen that the grouping of the molecules in twos, threes, and fours has become more general, and that several of these form new groups of eight lengthways. Many of them have melted together to produce longer bacteria. At the edges of the molecular mass, and in the fluid surrounding it, may now be seen a vibratile movement in the shorter bacteria and a serpentine movement in the longer ones, whereby they are propelled forwards in the fluid —*vibrio.* From the second or third to the fifth or seventh days, the vibrios are lengthened, evidently by apposition of groups of other molecules, to their ends. These melt together to form a filament, which may extend a third or half, and in a few cases entirely across the field of the microscope.

The movements visible in the molecules and filaments vary according to the amount of development. At first the molecules which float loose in the fluid exhibit gyrations which cannot be distinguished from Brunonian movements. When short bacteria are formed, these exhibit peculiar vibrations,—often turn round on their own axis in various directions, and are slowly changing their place. They rarely dart rapidly through the fluid, or exhibit a serpentine motion. But when the vibrio is formed, the filaments is pushed forward with greater or less velocity, at first presenting a wriggling, but, as it becomes longer, a more decided serpentine motion. A distinct flexure can be seen at certain points in the filaments, between the groups of molecular chains or filaments. Dumas says he has seen the molecules and bacteria uniting endways, a statement the correctness of which Pouchet doubts. On two occasions, however, I was fortunate enough to see this occurrence.

Pouchet thought that the vibriones exuded a mucous matter, whereby one stuck to the other. If so, such exudation can only be poured out at their extremities, as they only unite lengthways, never crossways. I feel satisfied, however, that the reason the actual union has so seldom been seen is 1st, That it only occurs at certain periods of development, and can only be followed by the eye, when the movements are slow ; 2nd, That amidst such a multitude of minute moving bodies it requires a long time before two can be found exactly on one plane, and can be brought so accurately into focus that they can be watched for a sufficient time. Having, however, in the two instances described actually seen the coalescence, I can have no doubt whatever that such is the true method of elongation. Numerous other facts seen among elongated vibriones support this view.

It may frequently be seen, on again examining the fluid in which these bodies have been moving actively, that they are all motionless, evidently dead. This occurs at various periods. They now rapidly disintegrate, and thus a second molecular mass or pellicle is formed. In this, rounded masses may be seen to form, which strongly refract light not unlike pus corpuscles, or the colourless corpuscles of the blood. These soon begin to move with a jerking motion dependent upon a vibratile cilium attached to one of its extremities—*Monas lens*. In a day or two other cilia are produced, the corpuscle enlarges, is nucleated, and swims through the fluid evenly. Varied forms may now occur in the molecular mass, dependent on the temperature, season of the year, exposure to sun-light, and nature of the infusion, all having independent movements. They have been denominated *Amœbæ, Paramecia, Vorticellæ, Kolpoda, Keronæ, Glaucoma, Trachelius, etc., etc.*

Pouchet describes the *Paramecium* as originating in the proligerous pellicle, formed by the breaking down of the primary bacteria and vibriones. It is the secondary histolytic mass of molecules which arrange themselves.

It would occupy too much time to follow the development of all the forms that may arise. They originate always long after the primary vibrios are produced, in the secondary, tertiary, or even later molecular masses, resulting from the disintegration of previous forms.

It frequently happens that soon after some of these higher infusoria are seen, that the pellicle falls to the bottom of the fluid, where it constitutes a dense precipitate, and slowly breaks down ; then another scum forms on the surface, and molecules, bacteria, and vibrios are again produced.

These different forms are spoken of by Ehrenberg and other naturalists as being different species ; but I think it will be found that the laws, not only of a molecular but of alternate generation and parthenogenesis, prevail among them, and one frequently passes into another. Their production is largely dependent on temperature, state of the atmosphere, light—especially the sun's rays,—and other physical conditions.

At other times, it happens that the molecular mass, instead of being transformed into animalcules, gives origin to minute fungi. In this case the molecules form small masses, which soon melt together to constitute a globular body, from which a process juts out on one side. These are *Torulæ*, which give off processes which are soon transformed into jointed tubes of various diameters, terminating in rows of sporules (*Penicillium*), or capsules containing numerous globular seeds (*Aspergillus*). Occasionally filaments are formed from the direct melting together of molecules arranged longways.

Here also I think various so-called plants pass into one another, especially torulæ, which are only embryonic forms of higher fungi. In all these cases no kind of animalcule or fungus is ever seen to originate from pre-existing cells or larger bodies, but always from molecules.

That we should sometimes have animalcules, and at others fungi, is a well-known fact, the exact causes or conditions producing which are not yet explained. The Panspermatists, of course, are of opinion that the germs in the atmosphere are of different kinds, and that as they fall into different infusions they produce different results, in the same manner that varieties in ova or seeds develop themselves in peculiar localities or special soils. This assumption, however, seems to me opposed by the following experiment :—

If an infusion be placed in a deep glass vessel, which again stands in the centre of a shallow vessel containing the same infusion, and the whole covered with a large bell glass, it will be found in eight days that on the surface of the former are numerous ciliated animalcules, while on that of the latter only bacteria and vibrios exist. The experiment may be reversed, for if the shallow vessel be filled to the brim, and the deep vessel has only its bottom covered, then the ciliated microzoa will appear in the former, and the non-ciliated in the latter.

As a result of these experiments, Pouchet has formularized a law to the effect that the production of ciliated animalcules is in an inverse ratio to the square of the surface, and that the production of monads is in a direct ratio to the cube of the mass of the same fluid. To this law I have met with some exceptions, animalcules having been produced in some of our recent experiments in the shallow dish, and vegetations in the deep vessel, and *vice versa*.

It is difficult to explain how germs falling from the air on the same infusion, under identically similar conditions, with the exception that the fluid is in vessels of different forms, can vary the results. Whereas the fact that the higher infusoria are formed secondarily out of the disintegrated mass of the simpler ones, which can only take place where that mass is considerable and floating on the surface of deep fluids, directly confirms the molecular theory of growth, and offers an illustration of how successive disintegrations give origin to different formations.

That the infusoria originate and are developed in the molecular pellicle which floats on the surface of putrefying or fermenting liquids, has been admitted by all who have carefully watched that pellicle with the microscope, more especially by Kutzing, Pineau, Nicolet, Pouchet, Jolly and Musset, Schaafhausen, and Mantegazza. The question therefore is, are the molecules that constitute that pellicle derived from the air or the fluid,—are they precipitated from above, or do they float to the surface from below, like the globules of the milk which produce cream?—From a lecture by John Hughes Bennett, M.D., F.R.S.E., &c., delivered to the Royal College of Surgeons in Edinburgh.—*Edinburgh Medical Journal*.

DIATOMACEA IN THE ARCTIC SEAS.

The following interesting remarks are extracted from a paper by Robert Brown, Esq., F.R.G.S., read before the Botanical Society, Edinburgh, which will be found reported at great length in a recent number of THE FARMER :—

The colour of the Greenland Sea varies from ultra marine blue to olive green, and from the most pure transparency to striking opacity, and these changes are not transitory but permanent. Scoresby, who sailed during his whaling voyages very extensively over the Arctic Sea considered that in the "Greenland Sea" of the Dutch—the "Old Greenland" of the English—this discoloured water formed perhaps one-fourth part of the surface between the parallels of 74° and 80° North latitude. It is liable, he remarked, to alterations in its position from the action of the current, but still it is always renewed near certain localities year after year. Often it constitutes long bands or streams lying north and south, or N.E. and S.W., but of very variable dimensions. "Sometimes I have seen it extend two or three degrees of latitude in length, and from a few miles to ten or fifteen leagues in breadth. It occurs very commonly about the meridian of London in high latitudes. In the year 1817 the sea was found to be of a blue colour and transparent all the way from 12° east, in the parallel of 74° or 75° N.E., to the longitude of 0° 12′ east in the same parallel. It then became green and less transparent; the colour was nearly *grass green*, with a shade of black. Sometimes the transition between the green and blue waters is progressive, passing through the intermediate in the space of three or four leagues; at others it is so sudden that the line of separation is seen like the rippling of a current; and the two qualities of the water keep apparently as distinct as the waters of a large muddy river on first entering the sea." In Davis Straits and Baffin's Bay, wherever the whalers have gone, the same description may hold true—of course making allowances for the differences of geographical position, and the discoloured patches varying in size and locality. I have often observed the vessel in the space of a few hours, or even in shorter periods of time, sail through alternate patches of deep black, green, and cœrulean blue; and at other times, especially in the upper reaches of Davis Straits and Baffin's Bay, it has ploughed its way for 50 or even 100 miles through an almost uninterrupted space of the former colour. The opacity of the water is in some places so great that "tongues" of ice and other objects cannot be seen a few feet beneath the surface.

These patches of discoloured water are frequented by vast swarms of the minute animals upon which the great "Right whale" of commerce (*Balæna mysticetus*, Linn.) alone subsists, the other species of *cetacea* feeding on fishes proper, and other highly-organised tissues. This fact is well known to the whalers, and, accordingly, the "black water" is eagerly sought for by them, knowing that in it is found the food of their chase, and, therefore, more likely the animal itself. From this knowledge, and from observations made with the usual lucidity of that distinguished observer, Captain Scoresby attributed the nature of the discoloration to the presence of immense numbers of *medusæ* in the sea, and his explanation has hitherto met the acceptance of all marine-physical geographers; and for more than forty years his curious estimate of the numbers of individual *medusæ* contained in a square mile of the Greenland sea has become a stand and feature in all popular works on zoology, and a stock illustration with popular lecturers. In 1860, and subsequently, whilst examining microscopically the waters of the Greenland sea, I found, in common with previous observers, that not only were immense swarms of animal life found in these discoloured patches, but that it was almost solely confined to these spaces. In addition, however, I observed that the discoloration was not due to this *medusoid* life, but to the presence of immense numbers of a much more minute object—a beautiful siliceous-moniliform *diatom*, and it is this *diatom* which brings this paper within the ken of botanists. On several cold days, or from no apparent cause, the *medusæ*, great and small, would sink, but still the water retained its usual colour, and on examining it I invariably found it to be swarming with *diatomaceous* life—the vast preponderance of which consisted of the *diatom* in question.

It had the appearance of a minute beaded necklace about 1-400th part of an inch in diameter, of which the articulations are about 1½ or 1¼ times as long as broad. These articulations contain a brownish-green granular matter, giving the colour to the whole plant, and again through it to the sea in which it was found so abundantly. The whole *diatom* varies in length, from a mere point to 1-10th of an inch, and appears to be capable of enlarging itself indefinitely longitudinally by giving off further bead-like articulations. Wherever, in those portions of the sea, I threw over the towing net, the muslin in a few minutes was quite brown with the presence of this alga in its meshes. Again, this summer, I have had occasion to notice the same appearance in similar latitudes on the opposite shores of Davis Straits where I had principally observed it in 1860. This observation holds true of every portion of discoloured water which I have examined in Davis Straits, Baffin's Bay, and the Spitzbergen or Greenland Seas—viz., that wherever the green water occurred, the sea abounded in *diatomaceous* life, the contrary holding true regarding the ordinary blue water. The swarms of *diatoms* do not appear to reach in quantity any very great depth, for in water brought up from 200 fathoms there were few or no *diatoms* in it. They seem also to be affected by physical circumstances, for, sometimes in places where a few hours previously the water on the surface was swarming with them, few or none were to be found, and in a few hours they again rose. But the *diatom* I found plays another part in the economy of the Arctic Seas. In June 1860, whilst the iron-shod bows of the steamer I was on board of crashed its way through among the breaking-up floes of Baffin's Bay, among the Women's Islands, I observed that the ice thrown up on either side was streaked and discoloured brown, and on examining this discolouring matter I found that it was almost entirely composed of the silicious moniliform *diatom* I have described as forming the discolouring matter of the iceless parts of the icy sea. I subsequently made the same observation in Melville Bay, and in other portions of Davis Straits and Baffin's Bay where circumstances admitted of it. During the long winter the *diatomaceæ* had accumulated under the ice in such abundance that when disturbed by the pioneer prow of the early whalers they appeared like brown slimy bands in the sea, causing them to be mistaken more than once for the waving fronds of *Laminaria longicruris* (De la Pylæ) (which, and not *L. saccharina*, as usually stated, is the common tangle of the Arctic Sea). On examining the under surface of the upturned masses of ice, I found the surface honeycombed, and in the base of these cavities vast accumulations of *diatomaceæ*, leading to the almost inevitable conclusion that a certain amount of heat must be generated by the vast accumulations of these minute organisms, which thus mine the giant floes, so fatal in their majesty, into cavernous sheets. These are so decayed in many instances as to be easily dashed on either side by "ice chisels" of the steamers which now form the greater bulk of the Arctic-going vessels, and they get from the seamen, who too frequently mistake cause for effect, the familiar name of "rotten ice." I have since found that, as far as the mere observation concerning the *diatomaceous* character of these slimy masses is concerned, I was forestalled by Dr. Sutherland (Appendix to "Penny's voyage," volume I. pages 91-96). This gives me an opportunity of remarking that though one diatom, as I have remarked, predominates, yet vast multitudes are there of many different species, and even are included; for though Dr. Sutherland expressly states that this brown slimy mass was principally composed of the moniliform *diatom* spoken of, yet Professor Dickie (now of Aberdeen) found in it also *Grammonema, Jurgensii*, Ag. *Pleurosigma, Thuringica*, Kg., *P. fasciola, Triceratium striolatum, Naviculas, Surirellas*, &c. Is it, therefore, carrying the doctrine of final causes too far to say that these diatoms play their part in rendering the frozen north accessible to the bold whalemen, as they do, in furnishing subsistance for the giant *quarry* which leads him thither?

New Books.

[*Our limited space must of necessity compel us to give but very short notices of new books, but they will perhaps serve as a guide as to what books our readers may ask for at their libraries.*]

Half Hours with the Telescope. By Richard A. Proctor, B.A., F.R.A.S. London: Robert Hardwick.

It is with great pleasure we introduce this little work to the notice of our readers. It is an admirable volume, and forms a useful and safe guide to the amateur telescopist. The name of the author is a sufficient guarantee of the truthfulness of the writing. In his preface he says:—"Among the celestial phenomena described or figured in this treatise by far the larger number may be profitably examined with small telescopes, and there are none which are beyond the range of a good three-inch achromatic." The work also treats of the construction of telescopes, the nature and use of star maps, and other subjects connected with the requirements of amateur observers. It is capitally illustrated and altogether reflects the greatest credit upon, both author and publisher. We may mention that it forms a companion volume to half-hours with the microscope, and is published at the same price.

A Ride across a Continent; a Personal Narrative of Wanderings through Nicaragua and Costa Rica. By Frederick Boyle. 2 vols. (Bentley.)

Mr. Boyle has been visiting Nicaragua for the purpose of examining the antiquities of the country, and, as he says, to solve the mystery of the Rio Frio Indians, a fair haired and blue-eyed race, of whom many quaint stories have been told. With regard to his first object, we may say that he succeeded, as he has presented to the British Museum a fine collection of ancient pottery, but with the second he failed utterly, and the wondrous cities really paved with gold, and gardens teeming with nature's choicest fruits and flowers, remain still to be explored. The work is a valuable addition to our very slender stock of knowledge, and those who have read the author's adventures among the Dyaks of Borneo, can well imagine how vivid and enthusiastic he would write about one of the most lovely countries in the world. As a sample, take the following picture of Ometepec, the island mountain that rises to a height of over 6,000 feet from the Lake of Nicaragua :—

I sit by my hut door, in the deep grey shadow of the orange-trees. A carpet of purple-blossoming mimosa is at my feet, spangled with fallen fruit, and the greedy black wasps whiz past me to their meal. Through the twined creepers on the rocks, between palm-stems, and over the flowering brushwood, glitters the golden lake in a changing haze. The hot blue sky is flecked with windy clouds, but we rest in burning calm under the guard of our hanging peak. Each leaf above my head throws a keen, still shadow; but through tiny gaps of foliage long rays quiver down, jewelled with hovering flies. Far off, deep in the thickest wood, the congos howl, and a faint echo of their thunder fitfully strikes the ear—so hot, so still is the noon-day. With noiseless steps the barefoot girls glide past, carrying their loads of water-gourds; a startled lizard rustles through the leaves; sleepily croaking, the parrots flutter overhead, in search of a thicker covert; the insects buzz and dart and hover. Here is more beauty than one can draw—and silence with it.

Could anything by any possibility be more charming. As we have said, Mr. Boyle has rendered us good service, and we heartily recommend his volumes to our readers, confident that they will be thoroughly delighted with them.

British Social Wasps: An Introduction to their Anatomy and Physiology, Architecture, and General Natural History. With Illustrations of the different Species and their Nests. By Edward Latham Omerod, M.D. London: Longmans and Co.

We strongly suspect that there are few of our readers but who at some one period or other of their existence have had cause to regret a too close acquaintance with the subjects of this work. It is in the nature of boys as boys to catch and handle with no tender mercy any living thing, and they are not as a rule to be deterred from trying their hand at a wasp because it possesses a sting. The result of the experiment is not always satisfactory; we have a lively recollection of seeing our own hands so improved as to resemble the boxing gloves of a pugilist more than anything else. We have also derived a certain amount of pleasure in seeing other youths tortured in the same manner. But we think (as far as we are concerned we are certain) from the time when we put off the boy we have cared to have as little to do with wasps as possible, and when by chance we do find ourselves near their habitation move off with as much speed as is consistent with dignity. We never saw much use in a wasp, and certainly never could impress our mind with the fact that he was a social individual. Perhaps we should be wrong in saying we have never admired him, as upon one occasion we remember doing so; but that was when he was dissected, and examined by the aid of a microscope.

In spite of all our objections, we nevertheless are quite willing to hear whatever can be said in their favour, and with this feeling we take up the present volume. Mr. Omerod stands forward their champion. He considers them to be the victims of prejudice, and to be generally disliked because they are not known; so he espouses their cause with a warmth and fervour that does himself much honour and them no scant justice. He commences his work by telling us that wasps have never been found in the fossil state; but, although they have left no prehistoric remains, they found a place in literature very early. Always (he remarks) regarded with the same feelings as at present, Homer, Aristophanes, Aristotle, and many others, are quoted as having said something either to their advantage or disadvantage, while the modern authorities upon the subject are given in a very full and comprehensive manner. Our author then discusses the various methods of taking wasps, always a ticklish operation. From this he proceeds to the classification and distinction of the species, giving their distinctive character and habits. We next come to the anatomy and physiology, a portion we read with the deepest interest, going thoroughly into the matter, and leaving us really nothing whatever to learn. As a specimen of the minute manner in which the work is done, we will quote his description of the legs of a wasp. He says:—

The legs of wasps are formed on the same plan as those of insects generally. The names of the different parts have been adopted from the limbs of Vertebrata. First comes a short flat joint, the coxa or hip, by which the limb is connected to the trunk. The next joint is a still smaller piece, which is let into the articulation, as it were, and thus gives a much greater extent of movement. This is the trochanter, on which the limb turns. The femur or thigh, which is so largely developed in the grasshopper and the flea, succeeds to this. It stands out almost horizontally from the body, and is probably the first in the series which would attract attention. Then comes the shank or tibia, the long straight bone which turns down towards the ground. The tibiæ of the two first pair of legs have only a single spine at the end furthest from the body, the distal end as it is called; while the hind pair have two of these spines: this is important to recollect. Otherwise they are unarmed; contrasting in this particular respect with the corresponding limbs of many of the sand-wasps, which are clothed quite down to the feet with strong hairs or spines.

The articulation between the thigh and shank bones is very strong. The form of the surfaces only allows of movement in one direction, being a hinge joint. The movement by which the limbs are turned backwards or forwards is effected in the articulations between the smaller pieces which connect the thigh to the body; and the extent of this movement is much greater in the fore-legs than in the other limbs. These parts are all comparatively rigid, but the mode of arrangement of the tarsal joints, which come next under consideration, gives the limbs the requisite amount of elasticity.

The tarsi in wasps, as in all other Hymenoptera, are five-jointed. In wasps the first and last joints are longer than the rest; but none are of very disproportionate size. This circumstance, as already noticed, supplies an important distinctive character between wasps and bees, the first or proximal joint in bees, and particularly in the honey-bee, being much enlarged, flattened out and fitted with rows of hairs, called, from their use, pollen-brushes. Poets, into whose dreams the homologies of the insect skeleton never entered, have incorrectly called this over-developed joint of the foot the bee's thigh. Each of the tarsal joints consists of a wedge-shaped piece, the point of which is received between the open horns of the preceding member. The ends of the horns of the last piece are not armed with spines, but rounded off, so as to leave room for the free play of the foot, which forms a kind of sixth tarsal joint in which the limb ends.

The most prominent feature in the foot is a large pair of claws, one on each side. These, it should be particularly noticed, are simple in the Vespidæ, while in the Eumenidæ they are toothed in their concavity. This rule has no exceptions. Between the tarsal hooks we find the pulvilli or cushions on which the insect treads. These are covered on their plantar surface with minute hairs, some of which are hooked at their extremities, and others are bulbous, reminding one of the bulbous suckers with which the arms of the star-fish are provided. It is by means of these bulbs that the foot clings to smooth and polished surfaces; but whether by atmospheric pressure only, or by the aid of a glutinous secretion, does not seem absolutely certain. Though the increased difficulty with which a fly makes its way over a pane of glass damped by the breath seems strongly to favour the first opinion.

The insect sucker consists essentially of a hair, with its extremity dilated into a bulb and hollowed out in the centre. This is seen in the most perfectly developed form on the fore-legs of our great water-beetle, *Dyticus marginalis*; and the same form of instrument, only very much reduced in size, is set over the pulvilli of the fly's foot, where there is no great difficulty in recognising it. It requires, however, a high power of the microscope, and a careful dissection, to display these suckers on the pulvilli of the wasp, which has these parts altogether smaller and much less distinct than many of the Diptera.

Indeed, the bulbed hairs on the wasp's foot, which are meant for suckers to act on smooth surfaces, do not seem to play as important a part in her progression as the little hooked hairs, which are mixed with them, and are as obviously meant for holding to rough surfaces. Wasps do not appear at all at ease on a polished surface: they cannot walk readily up a pane of glass, as their hold is less perfect, and their bodies are heavier in proportion to the area of their feet than those of flies. They walk much better on the rough surface of their own paper nests, where their tarsal hooks and the little hooked hairs of their pulvilli can be of use, than on the window-panes. And they do not seem to take the same quiet monotonous pleasure —happily—as our domestic flies, in walking about the windows; it is a scramble up and a tumble down, and the sash-bar proves an obstruction only to be surmounted by the aid of their wings.

From the consideration of the digestive organs and reproductive system we pass on to the form and mode of construction of nests. Here we learn their method of collecting materials, the building of the outer case, the interior arrangements, extension of the combs, mode of constructing cells and theoretical explanation of their form, and the direction which they take; a full description of wasp paper, and remarks upon the influence of season and position in the mode of construction, finishing with a specific distinction of the various nests. We then have a chapter on the social economy, and another on experimental inquiries, which brings the volume to a close.

The naturalist may well be grateful for the pains Mr. Omerod has taken to make us better acquainted with his clients. His work is a valuable addition to our literature, and will, we are confident, meet with the hearty approval of all his readers. It is highly scientific, and yet exceedingly popular: two results not frequently met with. A casual reader may take the volume up, and will derive as much pleasure from its perusal as any person who is making this branch his particular study. There are some good illustrations depicting the various species, and some showing their nests; the latter done, we believe, by the graphotype process.

Meetings of Learned Societies.

GEOGRAPHICAL SOCIETY.

The sixth meeting of the present session was held on Feb. 10.—Sir R. I. Murchison, Bart., President, in the chair. The following new Fellows were elected: The Rev. T. Coney, E. Cook, H. M. S. Graeme, Major E. Hunter, H. F. Makins, Capt. C. H. Riley, and A. R. C. Strode. Capt. Sherard Osborn read a paper 'On Exploration in the North Polar Region.' He said that he still maintained the desirability, in a national point of view, of keeping open that school of enterprise and adventure, combined with scientific research, which Arctic and Antarctic voyages have ever offered to British seamen in times of peace. For a North Polar expedition there were three routes by which the Polar area could be reached, viz., by Spitzbergen, by Behring's Straits, and by Baffin's Bay: it was well known that he preferred the Baffin's Bay and Smith Sound routes, because the land extended farther north in that direction. The existence of Esquimaux was additional guarantee for health and comfort, and the proximity of the Danish settlement of Uppernavik would ensure communication with England. Dr. Petermann, of Gotha, had communicated to him the pleasant news that a German expedition towards the Pole, viâ the Spitzbergen route, was determined on for 1869, and that M. Rosenthal, of Bremerhaven, had offered for the purpose two screw-steamers, the Albert of 450 tons, and a smaller one named the Bianenkorb. He (Capt. Osborn) fully recognized the importance of ships being sent to follow up the course of the Gulfstream in these high northern seas between Nova Zembla and Greenland, but the result of the three Swedish expeditions since 1861 to Spitzbergen was to show the improbability of an open-sea passage to the north of that land. Messrs. Torrel and Nordenskiöld had ascended, in July and August, mountains 3,000 feet high in the North of Spitzbergen, and had been unable to see trace of open water to the northward. They say, moreover, that all who have had most experience of the northern seas have come to the conclusion that the Polar basin is so completely filled with ice that all attempts to force vessels to the northward have been without success. By the Smith Sound route, on the contrary, it would be possible to travel by sledge or boat along the shores of the land. The French are bent upon trying to reach the Pole viâ Behring's Straits—M. Lambert intending to obtain by public subscription the means to start on this enterprise early next year,—and their attempts have the best wishes of English geographers. During last summer several American whalers had reached a high latitude in this direction, and had sailed along the tract of Polar land which had been discovered by Capt. (now Rear-Admiral) Kellett, in 1849, and had been heard of by the Russian explorer Wrangell, when on the northern coast of Siberia. One of the whalers, Capt. Long, of the Nile, sailed along it for three days, and saw a mountain, resembling an extinct volcano, which he ascertained by rough measurement to be 2,480 feet high. Capt. Bliven, of the Nautilus, reached as far north as 72°, and traced lofty mountains in this new land extending to the north-west. Capt. Raynor, of the Reindeer, determined by astronomical observations the position of a cape on the south-east as 71° 10' N. lat. and 176° 40' W. long. Lastly, Mr. Whitney, of Honolulu, had ascertained that one shipmaster had been as far north as 74°, and could see peaks and mountain ranges extending far to the north-west. During the past summer private enterprise has also been extending our knowledge of the Smith Sound route; Capt. Wells, of the steam-whaler Arctic, of Dundee, having reached latitude 79° (near Kane's furthest point), and sighted Humboldt Glacier. Dr. Hayes brought back from his voyage, in a small schooner, to Smith Sound, the interesting information that during the winter, in heavy north-easterly gales, the temperature rose with the violence of the storm, and fell immediately the gale subsided; and moreover, that the Esquimaux of the east side of the Sound said that if he had gone further northward, on the west side, he would have found natives and good hunting-grounds, with "plenty of musk-oxen." All travellers up Smith Sound have been stopped by water—a sea yielding animal food to support human life or contribute to the health and strength of our seamen. Much has been made of the peril incurred, much of the loss of Franklin and his 100 followers, —alas! he feared, for a purpose. He remembered the sheaves of gallant men he had seen laid in their narrow graves in feverish China; he knew of the thousands thrown to the sharks of the Gulf of Guinea, in order that political capital at home might be made of such services. As to the expense, it has been grossly exaggerated. £686,000 only, out of 115 millions (less than the 164th part) voted to the navy in 1854-64, had been spent in the cause of science, and this includes the maintenance of Greenwich Observatory and surveying operations for charts in all parts of the world. All he asked now was, to explore the shores of Smith Sound; the method of doing it was explained in his paper communicated to the Society three years ago. A committee of the British Association had been formed to promote such an expedition, and he asked the Society to give its President and Council a unanimous vote in favour of it, under Government auspices and encouragement.

On Feb 24.—Sir R. I. Murchison, Bart., President, in the chair. The following new Fellows were elected: Capt. E. Banyton, N. Cork, W. R. Dalziel, A. Gillett, D. Haysman, H. Kingsley, R. L. M. Kitto, J. W. Miers, M. L. Mavrogordato, J. E. C. Pryce, Hon. E. Stirling, and J. W. S. Wyllie.—"On the Geographical Results of the Abyssinian Expedition, to Jan. 22, 1868," by Mr. C. R. Markham. After giving a detailed account of Annesley Bay, and a description of the few fluted columns, broken capitals, and other fragments which mark the site of the ancient Greek emporium of Adulis, he proceeded to describe the ethnological facts he gleaned respecting the Shohos, who inhabit this district—a black, woolly-haired, small-boned race, having regular, and in some cases handsome features, armed with curved swords, worn on the right side, spear, club, and leathern shield, whose garb is a white woollen waist-cloth and mantle, etc. He tells of his progress through the Senafé Pass, whose nearly perpendicular sides are composed of gneiss. He noticed that with horizontal strata there was running water, but where the strata were tilted upwards towards the perpendicular so the water seemed to decrease in abundance. Mr. Markham compared the Komayli Pass to the highlands of Abyssinia with other great mountain passes he had explored. He had been in the Alps and Pyrennees, had ridden or walked up the passes in the Western Ghauts of India from Bombay to Comorin, and knew most of those in the Peruvian Andes. In none of these ranges were there any natural openings so accessible as this one. The table land at an elevation of 8,000 feet, was described with great ability, being full of valleys, ridges, and high peaks. One (not Sowayra) whose summit is 9,100 feet, has a flora of a thoroughly temperate and even English character—juniper trees, lavender, wild thyme, dog-rose, violets, cowslips, and various *Compositæ*. On the sandstone plateaux the vegetation is more Italian in character—maiden-hair fern droops over the clear water pools; lobelias and solanum and a *Myrsine* flourish there. At 5,850 feet there are nothing but acacias and mimosa; 9,000 to 6,000, the temperate flora; at 6,000 to 3,000, the sub-tropical; and from 3,000 to the coast line the dry tropical coast vegetation.

ZOOLOGICAL SOCIETY.

At the meeting held Feb. 27, Dr. J. E. Gray, V.P., in the chair,—Dr. J. Murie exhibited and made remarks on some specimens of young anthropoid apes,—read some notes on a rat, supposed to be from Manilla,—and a paper on the structure of the nocturnal ground parrakeet of Australia (*Geopsittacus occidentalis*), founded upon a specimen of this rare bird which had been presented to the Society's Menagerie by Dr. F. Müller, of Melbourne.—Messrs. Sclater and Salvin read a communication on the Venezuelan Birds collected by Mr. Goering—and on the Peruvian birds collected by Mr. Whitely during a recent excursion on the Tambo Valley south of Arequipa, amongst which were several species of great interest. Mr. E. T. Higgins gave description of six new species of shells of different genera.—Dr. J. E. Gray read a description of a new species of monkey, of the genus Colobus, from Zanzibar. This was proposed to be called *C. Kirki*, after its discoverer, Dr. J. Kirk, who had forwarded the specimen in question to the British Museum from that Island.

GEOLOGICAL SOCIETY.

At the Annual Meeting held Feb 21, W. W. Smyth, Esq., President, in the chair, the Secretary read the Reports of the Council, of the Library and Museum Committee, and of the Auditors.—The continued increase in the numbers of the Society and its general prosperity were stated to be very satisfactory.—The President announced the award of the Wollaston Gold Medal to Dr. Carl Frederich Naumann, Foreign Member of the Geological Society, Professor of Geology and Mineralogy in the University of Leipzig, &c., in recognition of his labours, extending over nearly half a century, in the departments of Geology, Mineralogy, and Crystallography; and especially for the admirable series of Geological Surveys of Saxony and adjoining countries executed by himself and his co-adjutors between the years 1836 and 1843; and for the great Standard work on Geology ('Lehrbuch der Geognosie') which, with the excellent courses of lectures delivered by him at Freiburg and at Leipzig, has exercised a powerful influence on the education of the newer generation of continental geologists. The President stated that the balance of the proceeds of the Wollaston Donation fund had been awarded to M. J. Bosquet, of Maestricht, in aid of the valuable researches on the Tertiary and Cretaceous Mollusca, Entomostraca, and other fossils of Holland and Belgium, on which he has been so long and successfully engaged; and he placed it, together with a diploma to that effect, in the hands of Mr. Godwin-Austen, who undertook to forward it to that eminent palæontologist.—The President read his Anniversary Address, in which he reviewed some of the most important contributions to Field-geology and Mineralogy made during the past year, including especially notices of the progress of the several Geological Surveys.—The ballot for the Council and Officers was taken, and the following were elected for the ensuing year:—*President*, Prof. T. H. Huxley; *Vice-Presidents*, Sir R. I. Murchison, Bart., Prof. A. C. Ramsay, the Earl of Selkirk, and the Rev. T. Wiltshire; *Secretaries*, P. M. Duncan and J. Evans; *Foreign Secretary*, Prof. D. T. Ansted; *Treasurer*, J. G. Jeffreys, Esq.; *Council*, Prof. D. T. Ansted, Duke of Argyll, W. B. Dawkins, P. M. Duncan, Sir P. de M. G. Egerton, Bart., R. Etheridge, J. Evans, D. Forbes, Prof. T. H. Huxley, Sir H. James, J. G. Jeffreys, Prof. T. R. Jones, Sir C. Lyell, Bart., Prof. J. Morris, Sir R. I. Murchison, Bart., R. W. Mylne, Prof. A. C. Ramsay, Earl of Selkirk, W. W. Smyth, A. Tylor, Rev. T. Wiltshire, S. V. Wood, Jun., and H. Woodward.

Feb. 26, Prof. Huxley, the new President, in the chair. 1. Charles Babbage, Esq., F.R.S., "On the Parallel Roads of Glenroy." The author thought they were the result of moraine. The President had restricted the discussion to the question of the "Roads." Sir J. Lubbock wished Mr. Babbage had waited till the appearance of his own paper on the subject in the Quarterly Journal of the Society; for it having been read merely in abstract did not contain all the facts, some of which might have influenced the opinions of Mr. Babbage. He dwelt on the concurrence of his opinions and those of M'Culloch, Darwin, and Lyell. He thought that the "Roads" were formed by a throwing-up process. Mr. Geikie thought Mr. Babbage's paper did not afford a good explanation of their formation. Prof. Huxley said it was clear that the opinions were divided between the tumble-up and the tumble-down theories. Mr. Babbage, in reply, said he had thought it worth while to lay his views before the Society, but many years had passed since he had examined the ground. 2. A paper was read for D. Macintosh, Esq., M.D., entitled a striking instance of lamination in granites. He described some in Dartmoor which had struck him by their close resemblance in appearance to strata deposited from water. 3. A paper by the same author, on cavities in limestone rocks. Prof. Ansted in discussing both, described the changes which he had seen in various walls from the influence of the weather, which he thought analogous to that proposed by the author. Prof. David Forbes differed from M'Culloch, who had been previously quoted, in thinking the action of rain purely mechanical; he thought it chemical in dissolving the constituents of rocks, through the carbonic acid it contained. Prof. Geikie, in defending the author, said rain was very powerful in rounding the edges of granite. Professor Ramsay said he thought Dr. Macintosh had compared the laminated granite with beds of millstone grit; Sir R. Murchison thought that Dr. Macintosh's views were not original; for in one of the earliest papers read before that Society by M'Culloch, the same comparison of some granites with stratified rocks had been made. Prof. Tennant recommended those interested in granite to examine the large slabs now being used for embanking the Thames from Westminster to Waterloo Bridge. Sir R. Murchison mentioned the discovery of a fossil in granite, which one of the speakers said was a calamite, but was corrected by another, who said that it was micaschist that contained the fossil. 3. A paper was also read on the "Changes in the Bristol Channel," by Dr. Macintosh, in which he attributed most of the metamorphoses now actively going on to the influence of the sea.

LINNEAN SOCIETY.

February 6, G. Bentham, Esq., President in the chair.—Messrs. A. W. Bennett, A. G. Butler, and Dr. G. W. Child were elected Fellows.—A letter was read from M. Beccari to Dr. Hooker, dated Sarawak, the 2nd of December, 1867, giving an account of his botanical explorations in Sarawak.—The President informed the Society that the rich Herbarium of M. Gay, containing his celebrated collection of European plants, had been purchased by Dr. Hooker, and presented by him to the Herbarium of the Royal Gardens, Kew.—Mr. W. Rich exhibited a beautiful series of specimens of Unio, from the neighbourhood of London, and Mr. J. G. Jeffreys made some observations upon them.—The following papers were read: "On an undescribed light-giving Coleopterous-Larva, perhaps that of the Fire-fly," by Mr. A. Murray,—and "On the Structure and Fertilization of *Liparis Bowkeri*," by Mrs. M. E. Barber.

At the meeting held, Feb. 20.—G. Bentham, Esq., President, in the chair. Septimus P. Moore, LL.B., and J. Murie, M.D., were elected Fellows. Mr. W. Bull exhibited living plants in fruit of several varities of Aucuba japonica and Aucuba himalaica, together with specimens of the male and hermaphrodite flowers, and made some observations with respect to the very long time during which the pollen of the male plant retains its potency, the female plant having in one instance been fecundated by pollen produced nearly 18 months before. The following paper was read: "On the character and hybrid-like nature of the offspring from the illegitimate unions of Dimorphic and Trimorphic Plants," by C. Darwin, Esq. The author commenced by calling attention to the terms he had previously used—dimorphic and trimorphic. Dimorphic species consist of two forms, which naturally exist in about equal numbers; in the long-styled form the pistil is always longer, and the stamens (excepting in the case of Linum grandiflorum) shorter than in the other form, and conversely. In the long-styled form the pollen grains are almost always of larger size than in the short-styled form. The sexual union of the two distinct forms is necessary for full fertility. Such unions the author had formerly called heteromorphic, but he now regards it as more convenient to speak of them as legitimate, and the offspring thus produced, as ordinarily occurs under nature, as legitimate; while as long or short-styled plants impregnated by their own form pollen are either not fully fertile or absolutely barren, such unions, and the offspring from them, he prefers to call illegitimate. Thus two legitimate and two illegitimate unions can be effected. With trimorphic species the case is more complex. There are three forms which differ greatly in the length of the pistil; and in each form two sets of stamens exist, differing in length, in the size of the pollen grains, and often in colour. The stamens are graduated in length, so that one of the two sets in two of the forms is equal in length to the pistil in the third form; for instance, in the long-styled form the pistil equals in length the longer set of stamens in the mid-styled and short-styled forms. In all these forms the union is fully fertile and legitimate only when the pistil is impregnated with pollen from the stamens which equal it in length; thus the long-styled form can be legitimately fertilised only by the longer stamens of the mid-styled and short-styled forms, and can be illegitimately fertilised by its own two sets of stamens, and by the shorter stamens of both the mid-styled and long-styled forms. So that the long-styled form can be fertilised legitimately in two ways, and illegitimately in four ways. The same holds good with the mid-styled and short-styled forms. Hence, with trimorphic species 18 unions are possible, of which six are legitimate, and produce legitimate offspring, and 12 are illegitimate, and produce illegitimate offspring. The author goes on to describe at great length various observations and experiments with Lythrum Salicaria, Oxalis rosea, Primula sinensis, Primula Auricula, Primula vulgaris, Primula vera, Pulmonaria officinalis, and Pulmonaria angustifolia, and concludes with some general observations. It is remarkable, he observes, in how many points and how closely illegitimate unions between the two or three forms of the same species, together with their illegitimate offspring, resemble hybrid unions between distinct species with their hybrid offspring. Another important point is prepotency. Gærtner has shown that when two species are fertilised with each other's pollen, if they be afterwards fertilised with their own pollen or with that of the same species, this is so prepotent over the foreign pollen that the effect of the latter is entirely destroyed, though placed on the stigma some time previously. Exactly the same thing occurs with illegitimate unions.

ETHNOLOGICAL SOCIETY.

On the 25th instant (J. Crawfurd, Esq., F.R.S., in the chair), Dr. Hyde Clarke read an interesting and very learned paper on the origin of the Varini. The next paper was by Mr. Crawfurd, on the migration of narcotic plants. He mentioned the island of Tobago as often given as the foundation of the name tobacco; others thought it was connected with the Carib word for tobacco-pipe. He quoted at great length King James's "Counterblast to Tobacco," in which he sadly complained that many of the nobility and gentry spent as much as 300l. a year on a vile drug. Mr. Crawfurd considered the effect of tobacco negative on the human frame. He mentioned that the Sikhs proscribed the use of it; that forty million pounds were imported into England; and that the percentage consumed by the population was largely on the increase simultaneously with an improved sanitary condition of our population. He thought that the Greeks were the first Europeans to have a knowledge of opium, which they communicated to the Arabs; and that it was unknown to the Chinese until a comparatively recent period is inferred by the expression applied to it, which signifies foreign smoke.

ENTOMOLOGICAL SOCIETY.

At the meeting held March, 2. Mr. H. W. Bates, President, in the chair. Messrs. G. A. Lebour and A. F. Lendy were elected members.—Mr. E. Saunders exhibited various Buprestidæ, for the purpose of correcting certain errors of nomenclature detected by an examination of the type-specimens in the Fabrician and Banksian collections.—Mr. Pascoe exhibited and read a description of "Eudianodes Swanzii," a new genus of Prionidæ from Cape Coast Castle, and "Oxycorynus Hydnoræ," a new species of Curculionidæ, from South America.—Mr. T. W. Wood exhibited pupæ of various Lepidoptera from Sierra Leone.

ROYAL HORTICULTURAL SOCIETY.

At the meeting held March 3.—W. Wilson Saunders, Esq., in the chair. After the election of eight new Fellows, and some other business of a formal character, the Rev. M. J. Berkeley proceeded to notice some of the more remarkable subjects exhibited. He said at the last meeting he had directed attention to an extremely pretty Gongora, which was unnamed, and which he had since found to be a variety of Gongora maculata, nearly related to one described by Dr. Linley in the "Botanical Register" in 1847, under the name of G. bufonia leucochila, but at the end of the same volume identified as a mere variety of G. maculata. There were also at the same meeting two or three Thujas—viz., T. Zuccariniana, T. falcata, and Juniperus japonica, about which his opinion was asked. In a collection exhibited by Dr. Hooker at the Linnean Society, recently, he could find no trace of such a plant as T. Zuccariniana. Juniperus japonica he believed to be the same as J. chinensis. With reference to a beautiful collection of Cattleyas, which was exhibited by Mr. Marshall, the whole he believed were varieties of C. Warscewiczii. He next directed attention to Dendrochilon glumaceum, with a spike like that of a Grass, and to the fine example of Oncidium macranthum hastiferum, from Lord Londesborough's garden at Grimstone Park. Mr. Pearce, the well-known collector of plants, informed him that he had found the same variety some years ago in the neighbourhood of Quito. A white variety of Cyclamen coum and Iris reticulata, from Mr. Atkins, were then mentioned, also the Crimean Snowdrop, to the beauty of which, however, the specimens sent did not do justice. After noticing the very elegant flowers of Hoteia japonica, plants of which were shown by Messrs. Veitch, Mr. Berkeley remarked of Primula denticulata floribunda, shown by Messrs. E. G. Henderson, that the size of the trusses depended in this case on fusion of the flower-stalks. A plant with very ornamental leaves 14 inches long and 9 inches wide, and supposed to be a Begonia, exhibited by Mr. Wilson Saunders, was then referred to as being one of the most interesting plants in the room, and though nearly allied to the Begonias, probably belonged to a distinct genus. With regard to Skimmia fragrantissima, of which a plant was shown, Mr. Standish had informed him that in raising plants of S. oblata from seed he had found that the male plants were identical with fragrantissima, and the female with oblata; the conclusion, therefore, is that the two are merely different sexes of the same species, as was noticed in our report of the meeting of the Linnean Society of March 7th of last year. Mr. Berkeley then brought under notice some cut Rhododendron flowers, produced in the open air at Coit Coch, the seat of Mr. Lloyd Wynne, in Denbighshire, where on the slate the Rhododendrons were a sheet of flowers, whilst at Abergele, three miles distant, on the mountain limestone, they failed almost entirely. At the last meeting he had read a letter respecting the damage done to the woods at Adare Manor, in Ireland, by Lichens. People naturally wish to know how it is that Lichens do so much injury to trees. Their mycelium does not enter much into the tissues, or when it does, seems to be on extremely good terms with them. In those Cinchonas, for instance, which are so attacked, the medicinal properties of the bark are stronger. The popular opinion was that Lichens injured trees by feeding on their sap, and Shakspeare, in the "Comedy of Errors," has

"Usurping Ivy, Brier, or Idle Moss,
Who, all for want of pruning, with intrusion
Infect thy sap, and live on thy confusion;"

by Idle Moss meaning Lichens. For his own part he believed that though, like some parasites, they obtained certain substances from the bark, the injury which they did was chiefly by their depriving the young buds of access to air and light. Another subject which he wished to mention was that at the last meeting he was shown a piece of wood affected, it was thought, by dry rot. Now, there were two forms of dry rot, the one produced by a fungus—Merulius lacrymans, the other not; in the one case there was a remedy, in the other none. The Fungus could be destroyed, or rather its progress checked for some years by corrosive sublimate although decay, as in the case of kyanised timber and railway sleepers, would ultimately take place. The other form of dry rot was a kind of slow combustion, called eremocausis, in which oxygen combines with the combustible portion of the wood, namely hydrogen and carbon. Taking wood to consist of 36 equivalents of carbon, 22 of hydrogen, and the same of oxygen (C_{36}, H_{22}, O_{22}), the withdrawal of one equivalent of carbon and two equivalents of oxygen for the formation of carbonic acid, and two equivalents of oxygen and two of hydrogen forming water, would reduce the proportion borne by the oxygen and hydrogen to the carbon, as is clearly shown by the chemical formulæ of two varieties of ulmine; and if a similar process could be continued, it was a question whether carbon only in certain cases, as in anthracite, which is nearly pure carbon, might not be left. After referring, in connection with this subject, to the recent discovery of a new acid called xylic acid, in the decayed matter of the trunks of trees, Mr. Berkeley read an account of some trees on a wall covered with a galvanised wire trellis, in which it was stated that the shoots appeared scorched, and were killed where they came in contact with the wire. One explanation of this occurrence consists in the variations in the temperature of the wire at different times; another that galvanised wire being rough would, no doubt, fret the shoots where they touched it, and the expansion and contraction of the wire would be also a constant cause of this fretting. In confirmation of the latter view, it was mentioned that where smooth, painted wired is used, the trees were not injured.

ROYAL PHYSICAL SOCIETY, EDINBURGH.
Session 96th, Meeting 3rd, 1868.

A meeting of the members of the Royal Physical Society, Edinburgh, was held on Wednesday in the Institution Rooms, St. Andrew Square—Professor John Duns, president, in the chair.

Mr. Robert Lawson, was balloted for, and elected a member of the society.

Rev. James Brodie, Monimail, read a paper on the changes that have taken place on the British coast since the time of the Roman occupation. In the course of his paper he said—Three hypotheses have been advanced in regard to the elevation of the British coasts. That which has attracted most attention is the theory of Sir C. Lyell, who supposes that there has been a slow continuous rise of the whole island, or at least of the central parts of Scotland, and then resting his argument on some observations made by Mr. Geikie, which led that gentleman to conclude that the sea shore in the neighbourhood of Edinburgh had risen twenty-five feet since the Roman occupation, endeavours to show that Scotland had been inhabited by man three thousand four hundred years ago at the least. Another hypothesis is that which is advanced by Mr. Geikie, who supposes that there have been a number of partial elevations, one part being elevated at one time, and another at another. A third is indicated by Mr. Chambers, in his Ancient Sea Margins, who, after referring to the opinion of Mr. Darwin, that all upheavals must present inequality, says—"When, looking to actual shifts of relative level in ancient times, we find not inequality but equality, it seems an almost irresistible necessity to speculate on a different explanation. I feel a particular difficulty in admitting partial subsidences of land on the British Islands, when I see such uniform terraces around their coasts. I do not mean to enter into any controversy at present, but propose to bring forward some facts serving to illustrate the changes that have taken place, or may be supposed to have taken place, since the Roman invasion. At a future time I hope to direct attention to the evidences we have of a sudden upheaval of the coast previous to the arrival of the imperial invaders. There has been no change in the relative level of sea and land since the time of the Roman occupation. We begin at the south-western part of England. Mr. Smith of Jordan Hill, some time ago directed attention to the fact that St. Michael's Mount, in Cornwall presented the same peculiar appearance in the days of the Romans that it does at present. Mr. Pengelly, of Torquay, has sent me a copy of a very elaborate paper which he read before the Royal Institution, in which he shows that the place described by Diodorus Siculus, under the name of Ictis, corresponds in all respects with the present appearance of St. Michael's Mount, so that there is every reason for looking on the conclusion of Mr. Smith as correct, and for inferring that there has been no change of relative level since the days of the great historian. When we examine the antiquities of the south-eastern counties, we find that the Romans have left there abundant evidence of a lengthened residence, in the buildings, sculptures, and coins that have been discovered. On the shores of the Firth of Forth, near Edinburgh, we have Roman remains, the position of which afforded Mr. Geikie the foundation on which he rests his argument in support of his supposition of a twenty-five feet rise; but the late Mr. Bryson, and other Edinburgh geologists and antiquarians that I have met with, concur in saying that he was mistaken, and that there has been no change of level since these works were constructed. At Stirling and its neighbourhood we have a greater variety of evidences of Roman occupation than in any other part of Scotland. We have there the remains of a Roman road, which antiquarians have carefully traced. Mr. Nimmo, in his history of Stirlingshire, says—" Nearer Drip its foundations have been lately digged up. The ford hath a firm and solid bottom, and during the summer season little above two feet of water. There was no occasion for a bridge to transport the hardy sons of Rome, whom much more stately rivers did not intimidate from their darling project of subduing and plundering the world." Mr. Bald, in describing the skeleton of the whale found at Airthrie, say—"To the eastward of the place where it was found are the remains of a Roman causeway. . . . It led to the Manor ford. Here was a castellum, which is now destroyed; but which was in good preservation within the last forty years. It appears, therefore, that since the time of the Roman invasion very little change has taken place either upon the bed of the Forth at the place, or upon the adjacent banks." In the country around Stirling there are found in various places roads constructed of trunks of trees. These passed over marshy grounds.

Beside them are found Roman camp kettles, &c. The trees were found in good preservation, in consequence of having been covered over with peat to the depth of several feet. The accounts given of these roads by the different writers in the statistical accounts of Scotland all lead to the conclusion that no change of level has taken place since the imperial legionaries were stationed there. To the north of the Forth we do not find any examples of Roman operations near the sea coast; but we find traces of the native tribes who were contemporary with them. Sir James Y. Simpson describes a cave on the northern shore of the Firth of Forth, in which he found evidences of former occupation, more particularly rude sculptures on the sides of the caverns resembling those on the monumental stones erected by the aborigines in different parts of the country. He therefore concluded that it must have been inhabited by the race to which we refer. The floor of that cave is only a few feet above high water mark. Mounds of shells, the remains of the mollusca used as food by those early settlers of Scotland, are found in various places along the north-east coast. They lie close to the present shore. We may mention, as an instance, the mound that is described by Mr. Jamieson of Ellon, who tells us that at the mouth of the river Ythan he has found a large heap of shells, intermingled with flint implements, indicating the habitation, or encamping ground, of these primitive people. That heap rests on a bed of hardened mud, and is only a few feet above the level of the present high water mark. Other instances of shell mounds close to the level of the sea might be adduced. Those facts seems sufficient to show that the coasts of Britain have undergone no change of level for the last sixteen or eighteen hundred years. I feel, moreover, persuaded that many more facts of a similar kind remain to be discovered. The rev. gentleman then described the inundation of Holland, the Goodwin Sands, &c., finishing up with some remarks relative to submerged mosses, about which he would like further information.

The next paper was read by Mr. Robert Brown, and its subject was a "Synopsis of the Birds of Vancouver Island." In this paper the author gave a summary of the results of four years' occasional investigation of the ornithology of the colony of Vancouver Island, presenting in the form of a synopsis the present state of information regarding the subject. After some introductory remarks, he gave a list, with occasional notes and descriptions of the rarer ones, of 153 species of birds known to inhabit Vancouver Island, belonging to six orders, 37 families and 118 genera. This number, owing to the few collectors, and the little attention paid to the subject, though embracing all that are absolutely known to visit or live within the boundaries named, was small, yet it was considered that the number might be largely increased. Mr. Brown, therefore, concluded by giving a list of 63 species which, though not hitherto found in Vancouver Island, are yet common denizens of the mainland of British Columbia and the territory of Washington, United States, and ought to be looked for by collectors.

Professor Duns, described the *Echinorhinus spinosus*. He said—The shark, whose skin is now before us, was named by Blainville as a sub-genus under *Squalus*, and named by him, from the shape of the muzzle, *Echinorhinus*. Agassiz, looking chiefly at the shape of the teeth, assigns to it a generic character, and takes it as the type of his genus *Goniodus*. Its geographical range is wide, being met with at the coast of Italy, the North Sea, and to the south of the Cape of Good Hope. He believed this was the first specimen which had occurred on the Scottish coast. It is thus of some interest. Dr. Andrew Smith refers in his Zoology of South Africa, to this genus as a deep sea form, "sluggish and unwieldy in his movements, and but seldom observed towards the surface of the water," resembling in this the ground sharks. The first specimen met with in British waters was one taken on the coast of Yorkshire in the summer of 1830. A second was captured shortly after near the Land's End. A third was taken in 1837, and two others in 1838, off the Yorkshire coast likewise. This specimen was floated to the shore on the coast of Bridgeneses, near Bo'ness, Linlithgowshire, on the 10th of January 1867. Though dead when met with, its whole appearance showed that it had been so for a comparatively short time only. Professor Duns had much pleasure in presenting this rare specimen to the Museum of Science and Art.

Dr. John Alexander Smyth exhibited portions of a supposed aerolite, which was picked up a few miles to the west of West Linton, and was supposed to have fallen on the occasion of a severe thunder-storm in July last. The stone was analysed by Dr. Crum Brown, and was found to consist entirely of white iron pyrites, covered with a fine crystallisation of sulphate of iron, formed by the oxidation of the pyrites; and some of the fragments were partially covered with a thick coat of glue, which had been probably applied to keep together the decaying portions of the mass. There was therefore nothing meteoric in its character; and it closely resembled in its history another supposed aerolite which was found near Auchterarder, in 1863, and consisted also of a mass of white iron pyrites.

BRISTOL NATURALISTS' SOCIETY.

General Meeting.

Thursday, February 6th.—Mr. Thomas Pease, F.G.S., one of the Vice Presidents, in the chair. The Hon. Secretary, Mr. A. Leipner, read the minutes of the last meeting, which were confirmed. The Council recommended to the society an alteration of rules 2 and 9, whereby ladies might be admitted into the Society, under the style of Lady Associates. The motion, having been put, was carried unanimously, but subject to being confirmed at the next meeting of the society. Dr. Henry Fripp then read a paper on "The Anatomy of the Retina and the Physiology of Vision," which was illustrated by numerous drawings.

Geological Section.

February 27th, 1868.—The minutes of the preceding meeting having been read and confirmed, Mr. C. F.

Ravis read his paper on "Denudation in the Bristol District," which had been postponed at the last meeting. After some preliminary remarks, the author went on to say—Two chief principles in the theory of denudation have been laid down. The first some years ago by Sir Charles Lyell,—namely, that the amount of waste of previously existing rocks is exactly equal to that of the deposition of new strata. A good illustration of this principle in our own neighbourhood is presented by the condition of things at Aust Cliff. The beach there is strewn with large masses of stone which have fallen from time to time from the cliff. These masses are in process of formation into a bed of conglomerate, which will one day, unless the stones be removed by human agency, constitute a distinct stratum, extending as far into the bed of the Severn as the action of the waves is capable of conveying the stony fragments. Such a conglomerate would be made up of red marle, blocks of the "Bone Bed," masses of the ostrea and other molluscan beds, fragments of gypsum, and the other substances now composing Aust Cliff. In the meantime the cliff is wasting away by the combined action of the sea at its base, and the atmosphere, with its various agencies, on the upper portions, so that the denudation of the old strata keeps pace with the deposition of the new. The other principle of denudation is that which is so clearly and ably laid down by Professor Ramsay in his article on the subject, in "The Memoirs of the Geological Society," vol. I. The object of this principle is to determine the probable *amount* of waste to which the older strata have been subjected, by restoring in section the rocks as they formerly existed above the present surface. After insisting on the necessity of having sections of the existing rocks constructed on a true scale, the professor explains that the depth to which rocks descend below the surface may be determined by continuing the line of dip where strata disappear to the re-appearance of the same strata at a distance in conformity with the curves which are seen in the existing beds. Thus, if strata be seen to dip at a certain angle, and to disappear below the surface, and strata of the same kinds are seen to re-appear in a distant part of the country with a dip in the opposite direction, the surface of the intervening tract being occupied by rocks of a more recent age, the inference is fair that the inclined strata are continuous under ground, and by connecting the beds at the two extremities by an imaginary line, we get a probable section of the strata below the surface. Presuming this inference to be legitimate, it may with propriety be applied to explain the phenomena connected with contorted strata, the upturned edges of which are frequently far apart. Applying this principle to the rocks in our own neighbourhood, I cannot do better than avail myself of one of professor Ramsay's sections. The section is marked by a line drawn through Dundry Hill, crossing the River Avon, and passing by Durdham Down to Blaize Castle, and terminating the flats near the Severn. In this section, the old red sandstone, the carboniferous limestone, and the coal measures are seen to be conformable, and if lines are drawn in accordance with the dips and curves exhibited at the surface, it will be seen that the strata now denuded must have attained a height of nearly 8,000 feet above the existing sea level. The carboniferous strata through which this section passes, is continuous on the surface, by Westbury and Henbury; although interrupted on the line of section by patches of old red sandstone and magnesian conglomerate, the former showing that the whole of the carboniferous limestone has been removed, laying bare the inferior rock, and the latter exhibiting a superficial deposit of new conformable strata, which must have been laid down after the older strata had been removed, the deposit of magnesian conglomerate lying between the two arms of the range of limestone, being probably newer than the carboniferous limestone, (since it is largely made up of the debris of that rock), rests immediately upon the old red sandstone. The new red marl, overlain by the lias and the inferior Oolite, at Dundry, also occupies a similar position with reference to the carboniferous limestone. It is therefore clear that in the one case the carboniferous limestone with the superincumbent coal measures, and in the other the coal measures themselves, have been removed by denudation, prior to the deposition of the overlying secondary rocks. Our own city and suburbs present a most instructive illustration of the effects of denudation in modifying the contour of the ground. The old city stands on low flat land, consisting mainly of new red sandstone; the range of hills on the west and northwest, on which are built the suburbs of Clifton, Redland, Montpelier, Cotham, Kingsdown, &c., consists partly of the older carboniferous strata and partly of lias, which has escaped the denudation to which the foundation of the old city has been subjected. This exemption of the lias from the fate of its once continuous beds, seems to be greatly owing to its being backed by the harder and less yielding rocks of the carboniferous series, and partly to causes dependant upon the direction and comparative violence of currents in the seas, which affected the removal of so much solid matter from our neighbourhood. The great line of the denudation of the lias extends in a north-easterly direction from the city, and has an average breadth of about a mile. Skirting the lias at Ashley, and Montpelier, it forms an extensive bay sweeping around by Horfield, Redland, and White-ladies, to Cotham, there pursues its course in a wider channel, by the east side of the city, and curving round towards the south-west by Bedminster, expands into the great valley running by Ashton and Nailsea, to the moors, bordering the Bristol Channel. In the midst of this line of denudation are numerous masses of lias which have escaped the denuding influences, but which bear on their surface marks of the violent aqueous action to which they have been subjected. The author concluded a long and interesting paper by a short reference to the topics of the Sequence of Geological Phenomena, and the Marks and Agencies of Denudation.

Entomological Section.

February 11th, 1868.—The president of the section, Mr. S. Barton, in the chair. Mr. A. E. Hudd, exhibited a bred specimen of *Cuculia gnaphii*, an insect of extreme rarity in England. This specimen was bred from a larva taken at Tilgate, in 1866, by Mr. E. G. Meek; Mr. Hudd also showed a specimen of *Acidulia rubricata*, a rare species, a few examples of which have occurred from time to time on the South and South-eastern coasts. The president exhibited several splendid species of *Anthophagus* a genus of foreign Coleoptera. Mr. J. W. Clarke (in the absence of the Hon. Secretary on account of indisposition), read a note on *Vanessa levana*, illustrated by specimens, showing the differences between vernal and autumnal broods of this insect, Linnæus described them as distinct species, naming them *V. levana* and *V. prorsa*. Since his time they have always been regarded as distinct, until last year, when their specific identity was placed beyond all doubt, by rearing several individuals from the egg.

Zoological Section.

February 13th, 1868.—The president, Dr. Henry Fripp, in the chair. Mr. A. Leipner occupied the evening with a discussion on the Classification of the Mammalia, with special reference to the several systems proposed by Cuvier, Owen, Huxley, and Dana.

Botanical Section.

Thursday, February 20th.—On this occasion the members were entertained by Mr. W. Sanders, F.R.S., F.G.S., President of the Parent Society, at his residence, Richmond Terrace. Mr. Leipner mentioned a communication from a gentleman relative to a specimen of Wellingtonia, nine years old, which, being transplanted, died. Upon a transverse section being made of the stem it was found that nine concentric rings had been formed in the year, contrary to the theory of only one being formed annually. Mr. Leipner entered into an explanation of the cause of these appearances in the stem, but said that without further information it would be premature to come to a result which would be antagonistic to preconceived theory. Mr. Leipner made a verbal communication on "The Mosses of the Bristol District." He said the locality seemed, so far as it had been worked, to be a very productive one for the study of Muscology, and he had been led to the investigation of it two or three years ago in consequence of having it in contemplation to publish a work on this branch of Botanical science. On one day in January he discovered, in Leigh Woods, thirty-nine species and two varieties, and altogether the district yielded about one hundred species, most of which he had discovered himself, and the remainder had been found by Miss Attwood. There still remained several portions not yet thoroughly investigated, and, as some mosses are extremely local in character, it was thought that more might yet be discovered. The narrow limits of the habitat of Grimmia orbicularis and of some other rare species was noticed. Mr. Leipner accompanied his remarks with a specimen of every species hitherto found in the neighbourhood.

THE BATH FIELD CLUB.

Among the numerous Field Clubs in Great Britain—on the lists of which, it is stated, there are no less than 4,000 members—few have done more or better work than the Field Club at Bath. This is, doubtless, in a great measure due to the energy and scientific learning of the President, the Rev. L. Jenyns, whose labours in connexion with Natural History are well known. At the Anniversary Meeting, which was held last week, the President delivered an interesting address on the proceedings and prospects of the Club. After congratulating the members on their flourishing state, he drew attention to the fact, that by far the greater number of Field Clubs now existing are attached to counties in the West of England. The President stated that, not only have there been weekly walks and periodical excursions devoted to antiquarian and natural history researches, but the club last year published a volume of *Proceedings*, consisting of important and interesting original papers. Mr. Jenyns informed the meeting that a Working Men's Mutual Improvement Association had been formed on the model of the Bath Field Club, and that last summer walks were taken by this body regularly on Saturday evenings, under the direction of one of the members of the Bath Field Club, for the purpose of visiting localities of historical and natural interest, and of becoming acquainted with the wild flowers and plants of the neighbourhood of Bath. The President alluded to the efforts that are being made to establish a local museum at the Literary Institution, and cited the opinion of Mr. Bentham, President of the Linnean Society, to the effect "that local provincial societies cannot better apply their funds and influence than in the establishment of museums aiming at completeness in representing the local district." Two ladies in Bath have made a munificent donation to the Literary Institution in that city for the purpose of founding a local museum, for which Bath is admirably adapted, situated as it is on the confines of three counties. The Literary Institution, already, indeed, possesses the nucleus of such a museum; and the geological collections, illustrating for the most part the geology of the neighbourhood, which are under the superintendence of the eminent geologist, Mr. C. Moore, are among the most interesting out of London. One member of the Club made a collection, during the past year, of the land and freshwater shells about Bath, numbering more than sixty species; while another member has collected many of the birds.

The President further stated, that the editor of Murray's "Handbook of Somerset, Wells, and Dorset"—a new edition of which is in preparation—is desirous of availing himself of the information possessed by the Bath Field Club, with the view of rendering the work trustworthy in the departments of Natural History and Archæology; an example which, we trust, will be followed in the case of the other Handbooks of England.—*Athenæum*, March 7.

Correspondence.

[Under this head we shall be glad to insert any letters of general interest.]

BIRD-MURDER.

Sir,—I was much amused at and pleased with "A. M. B.'s" letter, in the last number of the Note Book, on "Bird-murder." I perfectly agree with him that nothing is more ridiculous than for the man of science to let a rare bird escape so that Giles may eat it in his pie; and I feel assured that "naturalists" who preach such doctrines will find his arguments tolerably unanswerable. My object, however, in writing this is to entreat country gentlemen and others to avoid bird-murder in another sense, or, in other words, to spare some of the most charming winged inhabitants of our country. There seems to be a general idea amongst farmers and gardeners that a certain number of birds must be destroyed, or there would not be a blossom or fruit on a tree in the orchard, and they seem to forget the converse of this proposition, which is as true as their theory is false, viz., that if a certain number of birds did not exist almost every tree would be defoliated by larvæ. Birds, in fact, are invaluable members of society as scavengers*; and if occasionally they so far forget themselves as to attack our fruit, we should recollect that it is owing to them in part that we enjoy that fruit, and should not grudge them their little refreshment. Or if it is really found that they destroy the fruit to a considerable extent, then we should guard our fruit by such devices as nets, &c., but should not be so ungrateful as to shoot our old servants.

If I have not already encroached too far on your valuable space, I should like to say a word to those who shoot birds, especially swallows, only because they are *difficult to hit*. Hundreds of these birds are shot annually by cockney sportsmen. They are not good to eat, in consequence of their being almost entirely flesh-eaters; let anyone who doubts this open a swallow's mouth that has been shot returning to its nest, and the entomological collection contained therein will soon convince him. Similarly gulls are shot at the sea-shore; but for their murder there is *some* excuse, for they are handsome stuffed, and do for our cockney to put over his mantlepiece and look at when "he fights his battles o'er again;" or their feathers, or rather pinions, grace "the girls'" hats. But even these merits when the birds are dead do not half counterbalance their value as scavengers when alive, and, as "Fraser's Magazine" rightly observed, "the fool who shoots a gull ought to be fined a pound."

Obediently yours,
A LOVER OF BIRDS.

March, 1868.

"ALAS! POOR OTTERS!"

Sir,—I see in "Science Gossip" for last month that some kind person has been "taken very ill with pains in his stummick" over the untimely fate of two poor murdered children—no, otters I mean; but this mistake is pardonable, for really the terms in which these "varmint" are spoken of is positively ridiculous—to use no harsher term. After a loud lament, coupled with some untenable arguments, the writer concludes by saying, "Alas! poor otters! peace be to their ashes!" The facts appear to be that two otters bounced out of a rabbit burrow, and were instantly shot by a gamekeeper, as it was his duty to do; for the otter being, perhaps, the worst foe to fish and fishermen which exists, is of course classed in a non-otter hunting country with other vermin, and accordingly destroyed. Thereupon arises this "outcry wild"—Oh! mihi Beati Martine, is it not a horrible tale? &c., &c. —two poor otters murdered in their prime by an unscientific person, who, instead of taking advantage of the proverbial willingness of otters and weasels to allow their domestic arrangements (especially those connected with the dormitory) to be overlooked, and calling upon them with note-book and salt for their tails, actually shoots them—the irrepressible barbarian—that he may have the unexampled audacity to dissect them, if he likes, or the impertinence to have their "poor dead remains" stuffed!

Since the Murder of the Innocents nothing has been half so bad. Racked with the pangs of remorse, I do repent me of the assassination of the stoat, chronicled in these pages. I suppose I shall have some one singing dirges over its "lifeless caricature," and sighing forth—"Eheu! Erminea requiescat in pace."

I remain, Sir, yours, &c., &c.,
A. M. B.

THE NATURALISATION OF FOREIGN BIRDS IN THIS COUNTRY.

Sir,—Our gardens and woods are annually enriched by plants from all climes; and why is there nothing done of the same kind as regards the birds of other countries, some of which would readily become naturalised with us?

From many experiments we know that birds sent to a climate somewhat the same as that

---

* Mr. Haworth says he once noticed a titmouse take five or six large larvæ of Brassicæ (Cabbage White) to its nest in a very few minutes. Swallows are even more useful.

of their native country have thrived remarkably well. Look, for example, to the larks and other birds which have been sent to the other side of the world—viz. Australia—how they have become naturalised to the climate.

Those who now travel in Australia are delighted to see the lark flying up from the plains (far from the haunts of man), while singing its beautiful warbling song. Australia in return ought to supply us with a few of her choice birds, which would thrive as well in our country as ours do there. How many birds could America also supply us with: for instance, there is the Virginian nightingale, a beautiful scarlet bird about the size of a blackbird, and possesses what so few gaudy birds do—an excellent song; and I doubt not that it is quite hardy enough to bear our winters, or if not would soon become so. Why should not these elegant and showy birds be bred in our preserves? I think that all the readers of the NOTE BOOK will agree with me that we want a scarlet bird to enliven our woods. I should like to hear the opinion of naturalists on this subject, and hope that the idea will be followed before long.

I am yours truly,
J. D. S. W.

Mavisbush House, March, 1868.

RAINBOWS.

SIR,—The beautiful subject opened by Mr. Ulidia in last NOTE BOOK is, indeed, not unworthy of its place. He therein wishes his recorded instances multiplied by the readers' personal observations. Accordingly I have much pleasure in forwarding my notice of a lunar rainbow, similar to that described by him as having been seen at Middleton, which I and a number of friends saw from the village of Cove, in Loch Long. It appeared on the opposite shore of the Loch, showing only a small arc of the circle, was of a dusky white complexion, destitute of any of the rainbow colours, and resembled a large streak of light from an open window. Although none of us were scientific men, we all concluded alike; indeed, there were no doubts whatever. It continued for, I think, the space of four minutes, then gradually disappeared in the same manner as an ordinary solar bow. I concur with Mr. Ulidia that this subject may not be allowed to drop for want of communications. Yours truly,

J. R.

A REMARKABLE CANARY.

SIR,—A friend of mine has in his possession a canary which is now four years old, is in perfect health and a beautiful singer, and which, strange to say, is entirely destitute of feathers, with the exception of a thick frill round the neck and upon the shoulders. It has never appeared to suffer from ill-health, and has always presented the same appearance which it does at present. The parent birds were ordinary canaries, with the usual complement of feathers. I should like to know from yourself, or any of your correspondents, whether they have ever heard of a similar case, and shall be happy to show the bird to any one who wishes to see it, on hearing from them through the medium of the NOTE BOOK.

I am yours truly,
F. L. GIBBONS.

Camberwell, S., Feb. 24.

Short Notes.

JAPANESE PETS.—Japanese ladies possess a very choice breed of pet dog, supposed to be the same as that known in Europe as the Charles the Second Spaniel. As some intercourse was still kept up with Japan by England, through the East India Company, during the reign of the Merry Monarch, it is probable that these pets of his court were introduced to this country from the land of the Tycoon. These dogs are small, with beautiful silky hair, fringed paws, and pug nose. So completely is this feature diverted from the purpose it ordinarily serves in dogs as a breathing passage, that it is difficult to believe the effect has not been artificially produced. It was not until we saw some very young puppies quite as deficient in useful noses as their parents, that we could believe the pretty little doggies were not cruelly used in their infancy, by their noses being in some way compressed. They are very delicate little creatures, and the utmost care is bestowed upon them by their mistresses, which they repay by manifesting much satisfaction when in female society, and selecting the long dresses to sleep on. Owing to the peculiar formation of the nose, they snuffle and snort during sleep, and the tongue hangs out from the left side of the mouth. We recollect once going to a dog-fanciers at Nagasaki, where numbers of these little animals were collected for the purposes of sale. They lived in elegant kennels, and at certain times were let out into a small dry courtyard for their morning airing, where they frisked, and barked and snuffled together to their hearts' content, and then these dear little things—dear in more senses than one, for the price ranged from twenty-five to fifty dollars, or from £6 to £12 each—were fed on boiled rice and fish, and replaced in their domiciles. Japanese cats are different from our English tabbies, inasmuch as their tails are merely stumps. In that respect they resemble the Manx cats. Cats are there, as here, the household pets, and are encouraged for the same services which they render to us, viz., that of preying on rats and mice.—*Leisure Hour*, March Part.

DEPTH OF THE OCEAN.—M. Daubrée, in his lecture on the Sea and the Continents, gave his hearers some general information as to the extent and depth of the ocean. In the straits of Dover, he says, the greatest depth is about 30 fathoms, and throughout the English Channel it is under 100 fathoms. Along the west coast of France, the bottom slopes very gradually, so that we must go forty or fifty miles from land to get a depth of 50 fathoms. Thus there is a wide shelf all along the coast at such a level, that if the sea sank some 50 fathoms an enormous tract of plain would be left exposed. In the Mediterranean, on the other hand, there are many places where the depth exceeds 1,500 fathoms. In the Atlantic, as might be supposed, there are places of very great depth, some having been sounded to nearly 2,500 fathoms. But in the Pacific the depths are still greater, for over enormous spaces in that ocean, no bottom has been found by the plumb-line, and the depth has been estimated at more than 4,500 fathoms, say five miles. The whole bulk of the ocean, spread uniformly over its present bed, would probably require an average depth of 2,000 fathoms. Were it spread uniformly over the whole surface of the globe, the average depth would be about 1,400 fathoms. The elevation of the land is very much less than the excavation of the sea, as may be understood from the computation that an average height of 150 fathoms over the existing land surface, or a height of 40 fathoms over the whole surface of the globe, would contain the whole bulk of the elevated land.

CURIOUS USE FOR THE BAMBOO.—The French correspondent of *Land and Water*, Feb. 29, in describing a new work by M. Rambosson on the History of Plants, says:—"The chapter on the bamboo is exceedingly interesting. To the Chinaman the bamboo is nearly everything. After taking a thimbleful of tea, and devouring a small portion of rice with his chopsticks, he may listen dreamily to the wind performing a rather melancholy tune through his favourite avenue. If John Chinaman fails to behave himself, M. Rambosson says that at times a culprit is placed over a growing plant, and such is the vegetable force of the bamboo that it grows through the unfortunate criminal. This custom is peculiar to certain cantons. The victim is placed in position when the sun goes down, and as the growth of the bamboo during the night is extraordinary, the man or woman, as the case may be, is always found impaled next morning. It is a pity that M. Rambosson has not entered into full particulars concerning this barbarous method of training up young bamboos in a way they should not go. We are not even informed in what cantons this system of grafting is exercised. Further on we find that the shoots of the bamboo are delicate and tender, and are eaten like asparagus; but I am inclined to believe that the plant indigenous to our clime would never grow even through an infant. The priests of Buddha, when they fast, eat bamboo tops instead of fish. The bamboo, too, is employed for the yards of ships, for scaffolds for houses, for native pipes, for agricultural instruments, measures, buckets, lance-handles, harrows, hats, baskets, tents, cables, beds, mattresses, chairs, tables, pipes, paper, chopsticks, &c.; and in the Moluccas M. Rambosson says there is a bamboo so hard that sparks fly out of it when it is being cut."

EXTRAORDINARY STELLAR SPECTRUM.—Professor Secchi, we read in the *Scientific Review* for March, after examining several hundred stars whose spectra all correspond to one of the three known types, has at last found a very extraordinary star which gives an exceptional spectrum. It is figured in the catalogue of Lalande (a 4h. 54m. 10s., $\delta \times 0°$ 59′) The red portion of its spectrum is divided into two bands by a wide dark line; the yellow is reduced to a narrow line, very clear and vivid; then comes a wide obscure band and a greenish yellow band, then another dark space followed by a zone of blue.

Remarks, Queries, &c.

(Under this head we shall be happy to insert original Remarks, Queries, &c.)

CHRYSALIDS.—I think "Entomologist" will find that chrysalids keep best in a jar half filled with moist earth, having a tuft of grass on the top. With reference to the killing of moths—and many other kinds of insects—he will find the following plan successful:—Put a few drops of chloroform on a little cotton wool, and slip it into the box containing the specimen; the lid should be kept down to prevent the vapour escaping, and death will result in a few seconds. This, besides being the most merciful way, also prevents them from damaging their plumage, as they die with very little fluttering.
D. R.

In answer to "Entomologist," I have for some time been in the habit of using fine garden mould for keeping chrysalids in, and found it to answer very well. I likewise find that the Rev. Joseph Green, the author of the "Insect Hunters' Companion," also adopted this method, but he says:—"A thin coating of fine sifted garden, or any other mould, to be laid at the bottom of a box, and if you like some moss upon it, and then simply lay the pupæ on the moss, and nothing more. But if moss be used, care must be taken first to *boil* and then *thoroughly* dry it before using.

As to "Entomologist's" second question as to killing moths. I have used many methods, such as hot water, sulphur, and bruised laurel leaves, with strong solution of oxalic acid; but found nothing to answer so effectually as the latter method. Procure leaves of almost any kind of laurel, but if possible the leaves of the laurel from which prussic acid is obtained, known by its broad shining light green leaves; bruise them, place them in a box, then place the moth you wish to kill in the box. In a short time it will become stupified by the fumes of these laurel leaves; then take it in your fingers in such a way as need not be described, as "Entomologist" of course is acquainted with; then pierce it with a pen dipped in strong solution of oxalic acid—the puncture must be made through the thorax under the wings. This method I have used a very great deal, and found it the least difficult of any, and the most merciful way of extinguishing life. G. DAY.

"Entomologist" will, I think, be enabled to rear his pupæ by keeping them under circumstances similar to those in which they are found—that is to say, let him place those species discovered in the ground in a properly drained flower-pot nearly filled with earth (from the place of finding, if possible) covered with a little moss, which will be all the better if it grows. The moss must be kept properly moistened with water—too much damp or too great a degree of dryness must of course be avoided: no one I believe is very successful with bran, as it tends I fancy to dry and harden the pupa-case.

With regard to killing moths, it may be done by enclosing them in a bottle containing either bruised laurel leaves or a piece of blotting paper saturated with chloroform. Both of these plans, especially the first, are open to objection, and the one which I always adopt is to take the insect firmly between the finger and thumb, *underneath* the wings, and stab it in the body at the junction of the fore and hind wings with a steel pen dipped in a strong solution of oxalic acid. The smaller moths, geometrina, &c., may be killed by compression, as in the case of the butterflies. A. M. B.

In answer to "Entomologist" in the March number of the NOTE BOOK, with regard to the best means of killing moths, I would advise him to try chloroform, as that is what I have used, and with great success, to kill lepidoptera. When the insects are enclosed in small boxes, I just drop a very little of the chloroform in and keep them closely shut up for a few minutes, and in the end they are perfectly dead. The larger sort of moths, which are very tenacious of life, will require an *extra* drop. Care, however, must be taken not to let any of the chloroform fall on the wings of the insect. By the use of the above I have killed the large convolvus hawk moth (sphinx convolvuli), and many other kinds. A. E. B.

HOW TO PRESERVE SPIDERS.—In reply to "R. M." we quote the following from a paper read by Dr. Dyce at the Aberdeen Natural History Society on the 21st of January last:—

"All collectors know that, in preserving the smaller and more delicate of the insect tribe, a good deal of care is required, and even with every care, many failures will arise, and it is only after frequent failures and much practice, that anything like perfection can be attained. The great objects generally are to retain the colour and prevent shrivelling. Where there is any degree of firmness in the body of the animal, so much the more easily are these objects attained; but where, as in the *Arachnidæ*, the greater part of the animal is mere pulp, with a very slender covering, more care and much patience is necessary; still I hope to show that all difficulties may be overcome, and that too with an amount of permanence which I confess I was not prepared to find. Before entering into the detail of the method, I may mention a circumstance which, if known, is not attended to, regarding the seat of the colouring matter or pigment, which in many foreign species is very brilliant. This I found to be placed between the outer or external abdominal covering and the pulpy contents within, upon a very delicate membrane, which appeared to enclose the whole contents; upon this inner membrane the pigment is more intimately adherent, so that if the contents of the abdomen are somewhat rudely removed, and without much tearing, the whole mass will be found more or less coloured, while the outer or external covering will be left entirely transparent. To preserve, therefore, the beauty of spiders this must be untouched. In my first attempts, not being aware of this arrangement, I destroyed almost all of them, as here and there only spots of colour remained, the greater part being transparent; but at length I succeeded most perfectly."

After a few further remarks he proceeded to detail his method, which was as follows:—

"First, fix the animal on its back by inserting a pin through the cephalo-thorax. Then cut open the greater part of the belly in a straight line with a very sharp scalpel, or equally sharp pointed scissors, or as much as will enable the pulpy contents to be easily removed. Next, pinch up the pulpy mass with a small forceps, carefully avoiding any dragging out of the contents—this is very essential—then snip away with the scissors, bit by bit, until the whole is nearly removed, or until you can see the colours shining through what remains in the cavity. More than this should not be attempted, and I would recommend it as safer rather to leave a little too much than be too nice in clearing all away. In this way the coloured membrane will be uninjured, and when dry will remain coloured as in life. This is the most troublesome part of the whole. The great requisites are patience and care, for an unwary snip with the scissors may destroy the work of hours. The next point is to distend the empty body. This is to be done by a blow-pipe. It will very soon become firm, and retain its original form, but until it does so, the blowing must be frequently repeated. How long in our cold climate this may be required, I can hardly say, but in the tropics, where the heat of the sun during the day is seldom under 130 deg. or 140 deg., three or four times a day for two or three days was quite sufficient to keep them permanently distended, as well as perfectly to harden any of the contents, which it was thought right to leave within. This was generally all that was required before placing them in their future abode, but sometimes I have coated the interior with a preservative, which I have always employed for the bodies of beetles, moths, and even butterflies, for I empty the bodies of all, and the result is that all my cases of insects are as free from dust arising from the decay of animal matter as when originally put up. Sometimes in the larger bodied *Tarantula*, or moths, I have stuffed them with cotton wetted in the preservative, but generally this is not necessary, the frequent distension by blowing, along with a heated atmosphere, will be perfectly sufficient to prevent future shrivelling. The preservative consists of—Corrosive sublimate, drach. ij.; spirit of wine, a pound; camphor, drach. ss. mixed. This should be applied with a camel's hair brush. No collector in a tropical climate need be informed of the destruction caused by the active little black ant, which infests every house, nay, every foot of ground he treads on. A table with each of its legs in water is not safe from their ravages, for I have known these vermin in the course of a night make a bridge of their bodies across a couple of inches of water, and make a clean sweep of the contents of the table. I once saw a quartern loaf of bread left on purpose on the table, and between mid-day and the following morning so thoroughly eaten that not a vestige remained but the crust, which was left entire. But with the preservative I have now mentioned, and with which the sheets of cork were well saturated, and afterwards dried, I never knew an ant approach or touch an object when placed upon the cork—it was not even necessary to insulate the table for their security. There may, no doubt, be other equally good preservatives against these animals, but having found this after many years so effectual, I never tried another."

[We think our correspondent will find this method perfectly satisfactory, as the learned Doctor relates how he saw some of his specimens in the Museum of the Jardin des Plantes in Paris twenty-five years after they had been prepared, retaining all their colours, in their original brightness, well distended, and in good shape.—ED.]

PRESERVING SPIDERS.—If "R. M." will try the following receipt for preserving spiders, he will find it to answer perfectly:—Dissolve a quarter of an ounce of corrosive sublimate in one ounce of water, and add three ounces of spirits of wine." The spiders should be steeped in this solution for three weeks or a month; when taken out they are quite pliable, and should at once be put into the required position, as they become set in a few hours. D. R.

"R. M." inquires how spiders may be preserved? I beg to say that it would occupy too much space to go into my new method, which is a very difficult one, and requiring great care and anatomical skill; but if "R. M." refers to the January number of the present year, he will there find an interesting paper upon the subject—one which will satisfactorily answer his question. G. DAY.

I know of no better method—in fact, none so good, as that described by R. Dyce, M.D., on page 3 of "Science Gossip" for last January. It requires some dexterity in manipulation, but the results are first-class. A. M. B.

SKELETONS OF BIRDS, &c.—Providing G. Deighton lives in the country, he will find no plan so effective for procuring skeletons of *small* birds or animals as to place the subject in an ant-hill, enclosed in a box profusely perforated with holes. Removing the skin facilitates the work of destruction. A. M. B.

The best way of cleaning these is that pursued by the articulators at the Government Museums. Boil the carcassess, divested of course of their skin and feathers, until the flesh is in rags, and pick the bones with knife and scissors, extracting the brain with a little spoon, and pulling out the tongue and all fleshy parts. The bones with care may be perfectly cleaned in this way. To give them great whiteness they should be bleached in the sun, which is best done in a greenhouse. The plan often pursued of bleaching the bones with a solution of chloride of lime spoils their beautiful ivory surface, unless most sparingly used. I have more than once saved trouble by putting the carcase in an ant's nest, but this will only do part of the work. In high northern latitudes Dr. Scoresby's plan answers. Place the birds in a coarse netting suspended over the ship's side; the *clio borealis* will strip the bones for you. I have the skeleton of a bird anatomized in this way, but it is a rather imperfect one; as also the skull of a snowy owl shot on the Greenland coast. The process of mounting is done with drills and wires, and is a most tedious and troublesome affair. Mr. Deighton's best guide would be a well-mounted skeleton, or engraved plate of the particular species he has in hand.
C. O. G. NAPIER, F.G.S.

HABITS OF MOLE, &c.—In reply to a query by "A. B. P." in the March number of the NOTE BOOK, an account of the habits, &c., of the mole and field mouse will be found in Wood's "Natural History," Vol. I (published by Routledge and Co). Wood again notices them in his "Garden Friends and Foes" and "Common Objects of the Country." He also describes the mole's underground residence in "Homes without Hands," but the first book will no doubt contain what he wants.

In reply to the second question, butterflies are divided into male and female, and generally the sexes are distinctly marked. There is no general rule, and I would recommend "A. B. P." to obtain Coleman's "British Butterflies," an excellent book, published by Routledge and Co., price 2s. 6d. It has an accurate coloured representation of all the species, both male and female (when the latter outwardly vary from the former).

In reply to a query by "Entomologist," I beg to inform him that in the July number of the "Boys' Own Magazine" (6d.) for the year 1863, there is a paper by the Rev. J. G. Wood on "Insect Breeding." It is well worth procuring, and a perusal will satisfy his want.

HOW TO ARRANGE LAND AND FRESH WATER SHELLS.—A cabinet of drawers is the best to begin with; the expense should not be grudged for a good one at once: if purchased second hand, it will not cost more than a rubbishing new one—perhaps 5s. a drawer. The larger shells are best laid out on wadding (pink looks very pretty) in paste-board trays, which can be made at home, or purchased of Cutter, Great Russell-street, or others, at from 2s. 6d. a gross and upwards; the smaller species should be put in glass top boxes, which, however, cost from 1s. 6d. to 4s. a dozen; glass tubes answer very well, and cost about 9d. a dozen. Brice M. Wright, Great Russell-street, will furnish labels. The best catalogue is that by my friend, Mr. J. K. Jordan, F.G.S.: it is compiled from Mr. Gwynne Jeffrey's "British Conchology." If Mr. Atkins wants a general book on conchology, he should purchase the last edition of Woodward's Manual; if a book on British land and fresh water shells only, Mr. Ralph Tate's "Land and Fresh Water Molluscs," price 6s., coloured plates. These will give him many hints on arrangement. It is best to begin by numbering every specimen and entering every number in a catalogue, with date, &c. I warn Mr. Atkins not to be betrayed into adopting the common practice of gumming his specimens on card or wood blocks. I once adopted it, and lost hundreds of beautiful little shells; in many cases from the contraction of the gum breaking them; in others in transit, for it is difficult to pack delicate shells mounted on wood blocks.

C. O. G. NAPIER, F.G.S.

ERMINE IN ENGLAND.—During last month (Feb.) I have heard several persons speak of a perfectly white stoat, which has been seen several times in this vicinity (Ash, Surrey). In one instance it was observed chasing a rabbit through a large field, and this informant stated to me that it was altogether of a white colour, with a black-tipped tail. This one I have not been fortunate enough to see, but on the 17th February I was out very early in the morning, and seeing something moving round the trunk of a pine tree, I fired, and found that I had shot a very beautiful variety of the stoat (*Errustela erminea*). The fur on the back and head was of a very light chocolate colour, thinly interspersed with a few white hairs, the white of the under parts running more up the sides and legs than is usual; the tail, too, differed from most specimens in being white, or yellowish-white, from the root to where it terminated in the black tip (which is never variable, be the colour of the rest of the tail or body what it may). On dissection, I discovered that it had lately killed a field-mouse, as I found two little paws severed at the wrists, a quantity of fur, some bones, and the tail complete, but bitten nearly through at regular intervals, presenting a most curious appearance—something like a snake-pattern chain.

A. M. B.

MAGPIE.—Can you or any of your correspondents kindly inform me whether it is a common occurrence for the magpie (corvas pica) to build its nest in a low bush?—for last season, whilst birds'-nesting in the country adjoining the town of Aylesbury—a place much infested by magpies—I discovered a nest belonging to one of these birds in a low bush by the roadside. The bird left the nest as I approached, but it had not yet laid any eggs. I found a great many more nests of this bird, but they were all built in high trees, and generally quite at the top; one nest which I climbed up to had so small an aperture for the bird's entrance that I found it almost impossible to extract the eggs without the aid of a knife; it contained five eggs, which I believe is about the average number. The nest of the magpie is often usurped by the kestrel and sparrow-hawk, who are only too glad to find such a comfortable, and at the same time so well protected a nest prepared for them without any trouble to themselves.

H. MEYRICK.

ARRIVAL OF NEW BIRDS FROM INDIA.—Mr. Fraser, of 309, Regent-street, has just received, per the last Overland mail, several very interesting specimens of Indian and Chinese birds. The collection includes, amongst others, two pair of Swinhoe's superb pheasant (Euplocamus Swinhoei), one pair of Japanese teal (Querquedula formosa), four specimens of a new species of blue water hens (Porphyrio cœlestis, Swinhoe), from Cochin China, and the first living example of Porphyrio indicus (Horsfall), from Java; several wedge-tailed partridges (Bambusicola thoracica, Temminck), one pearled francolin (Francolinus perlatus) and several doves, &c.

THE MANCHESTER FIELD NATURALIST'S SOCIETY.—We have received the annual report of this Society for 1867, containing an account of various excursions, and also of the soirees held, all of which seem to have been highly successful. We are glad to see the Society numbering some 250 members, without the honorary and corresponding, who number some 50 more. Healthy and satisfactory as this is, we still hope that the next report will show a further increase, for it is in the growth of such societies as this, that we see unmistakeable signs throughout the country, of an increased love of nature and all appertaining thereto.

A HEN CATCHING MICE.—A fact is recorded on page 234, vol. 1, of the NOTE BOOK, of a barn-door fowl being suffocated in consequence of its attempt to swallow a dead mouse. I beg to state that a year or two ago I had a hen that caught and then swallowed a mouse. It was about half grown, but very brisk and lively. When set free in the poultry-yard, it was pursued and seized by this hen, who, after killing it by repeated jerks with her bill, swallowed it whole. It was afterwards observed to catch another mouse in a similar manner. This hen was always very fond of mice, and eagerly eat all that were given her, especially when they were cut into small pieces.

R. B. W.

COLIAS EDUSA.—On visiting the sea-side last year, I was delighted to observe that there was a great prevalence of this most interesting and beautiful species; more particularly so, as I had not previously been able to obtain a single specimen for my cabinet. Last year, however, I succeeded in capturing four or five males, and two or three females. The colour of this butterfly varies in its intensity in different individuals, some being pale saffron, whilst others are of a rich orange. I find C. Edusa extremely difficult to capture; I believe waiting till the insect settles, and then striking rapidly down upon it with the net, is accounted the plan most likely to be successful, and will often save the trouble of a long and most unequally matched chase.

P. G. M.

PIERIS CRATÆGI.—Your correspondent, "A. E. B." desires to know the localities where Pieris Cratægi is to be found. It is pretty common in the localities where it does occur, but is by no means generally distributed. The following are a few of the localities in which it has been found:—Maidstone in Kent, Leominster in Herefordshire, Corsham in Wiltshire, Dorchester, Lewes, Lyndhurst, Peterborough, Worcester, Herne Bay, Cardiff, South Wales, Horsham in Sussex.

H. MEYRICK.

THE COLOUR OF BIRDS' EGGS.—"J. D. S. W." asks a difficult question. No doubt light has much to do with the colouring of birds' eggs, but how is another matter. A writer in the "Annals of Natural History" many years ago gave the result of his analysis of the colouring matter of some eggs; the blue of the thrush, for instance, he attributed to some salt of copper; the black spots on the eggs of the razorbill and quillemot to peroxide of manganese. I tested both these eggs for these substances, and found the author right. C. O. G. NAPIER, F.G.S.

SINGULAR NEST OF A BLACKCAP.—Early in the year 1866, I found the nest of a blackcap (curruca atricapila) made entirely of horse-hair. They usually contain only a thin lining of hair, the rest being composed of dry grass and moss. This nest was beautifully compact and well-finished, but did not contain a particle of any substance but hair. Although great numbers of these birds build in this neighbourhood (Edinburgh), I have not seen any other like it. The nest contained eggs at the time it was found.
R. B. W.

KILLING MOTHS, ETC.—"Entomologist" will find that mould dampened occasionally is the best thing on which to keep naked pupæ, such as the Sphingina, &c., and to allow pupæ that suspend or fix themselves anywhere to remain as they are, or rather *where* they are. His second question is by no means easy to answer satisfactorily. There are a good many methods of killing moths, each of which find their advocates, but they are almost all open to some objection. Some say, pound laurel leaves : put the moth with the leaves into a tightly-closed box, and after a few seconds it will be dead. This plan answers after a fashion, when (1) the box is almost air-tight, (2) the insect to be operated on is small, (3) the leaves were gathered dry and were young and well bruised. A second plan is to get some Prussic acid (nasty stuff to deal with), and get a bone or iron instrument shaped like a pen, but without a nib, and to dip the latter in the former and pierce the moth between the legs. But entomologists who use this or any other dangerous fluid (such as oxalic acid and many others recommended for this plan) beware ! Remember it is better to lose a moth, or let it suffer a good deal, than to endanger your own and others' life. The plan for moth-murder I myself usually adopt is to dip a steel pen in vinegar and stab the insect between the legs, then to pin it down in a box and let it smell strong scent of some kind or another. This usually induces the patient to give up the ghost after a couple of minutes or so. The most difficult cases are females who have not deposited their eggs. They are best killed (*on dit* I never tried it myself) with nitric acid, used as I recommend vinegar to be employed for the assassination.—"A WHOLESALE MURDERER OF BUTTERFLIES AND MOTHS."

ON KILLING INSECTS FOR THE CABINET.—A writer to the "Naturalist" gives the following :— "When I could not procure either laurel leaves or hot water, which I was previously in the habit of using, I thought of employing the vapour of chloroform. I accordingly put about three drops in an eight-ounce bottle in which were three large Lepidoptera, which it killed in about fifteen seconds, or perhaps less. I have since almost always used it with perfect success" Have any of your readers tried this?
Mavisbush House. J. D. S. W.

BUTTERFLIES.—In answer to "A. B." I would say that the sexes of butterflies are generally determined by the markings upon their wings, &c., in many cases very distinct, but experience will teach the young entomologist what nothing else can. It was a matter of some difficulty with myself at first, but close attention and careful comparison enabled me in time to determine (with of course a few exceptions) with tolerable accuracy. G. DAY.

"J. D. S. W." is mistaken in supposing that birds of prey alone cast up pellets of undigested food (see NATURALIST'S NOTE BOOK, Vol. 1). Herons which feed largely upon mice and rats reject the furs, bones, &c., in the form of pellets. I too have observed tame jackdaws to do the same with the husks and other insoluble portions of their food, though I believe it to be of uncommon occurrence. R. B. W.

COCK-ROACH.—A few days ago I caught a cock-roach which was perfectly white, excepting its eyes, which were jet black. Having never seen or heard of one before, I thought it might be a rarity. I should be glad if any of your correspondents would tell me if such is the case. The above specimen turned brown when dry.
Oxford, March 3. SCARABÆUS ALBUS.
[See paper on Cock-roaches in vol. for 1867, page 34.—ED.]

SWARMING OF BEES.—I send you the following extract copied from the *Reading Mercury* of February 29th, 1868, thinking it may interest some of your many readers :—"One of the hives of bees belonging to Mr. Checkley, of White Place Farm, Cookham, Berks, swarmed on the 22nd instant, a circumstance remarkable so early in the season. μέλισσα.

EGG COLLECTING.—Permit me to say for the use of your readers who are egg collectors, that if they happen to have an egg which they cannot blow or clean, the best method is this : Make a small hole in the shell and place it near an ant's nest for a day, or if a large egg longer; and the ants will enter the egg and thoroughly clean it. A. B. P.

In answer to your correspondent, "A. E. B.'s" inquiries about the black-veined white (Pieris Cratægi) I may inform him that this species is met with throughout the South of England. The woods near Maidstone and Leominster are (according to Newmann) favourite localities for it. E. H. WALLAND.

YEW-FRUIT.—Some botanists say that the berries of the yew-tree are poisonous, but blackbirds, thrushes, and robins feed greedily on them : are they injurious to man?
Mavisbush House. J. D. S. W.

PIERIS RAPÆ (var.)—I have in my possession a curious variety of P. Rapæ, with the black spots near the margin of the fore wings wholly obliterated. I am aware of the existence of several varieties, but have never previously seen or heard of one of this description. P. G. M.

THE HARE AND RABBIT.—Could you or any of your readers inform me whether the rabbit and hare ever breed together? Some writers say that they have seen cross-breeds.
Mavisbush House. J. D. S. W.

REMARKS ON SEXUAL DIFFERENCES IN INSECTS.

By E. C. RYE.

HE question "By what characters am I to distinguish males from females?" is often asked by the young entomologist, who has probably seen enough external sexual disparity in certain species to guard him against a too hasty separation of his captures. This question it is impossible, with any degree of practical utility, to answer in a concise manner, further than by enunciating the broad principle that the female, as having the burthen of the future brood, is usually (if not invariably) the larger, and, as being more sedentary (not seeking her mate, but sought by him), is usually proportionately duller in colouration. Of course, a very moderate knowledge of comparative anatomy and but slight manipulative ability are required to distinguish between the generative organs in the sexes of insects; but, as the examination required might possibly slightly injure the specimens, my remarks must be confined to superficial characters. Nevertheless, when the abdomen of a soft bodied insect is distended with eggs, or when (as in many cases) it terminates in a retractile tubular ovipositor, there can be no doubt that that insect is of the female sex.

In the *Lepidoptera* the above-mentioned rule of the larger size (often of the wings, but especially of the bulk of the body) and duller colouring of the female prevails almost generally, well-known examples of it being afforded by the pale female of the orange-tip butterfly (*A. cardamines*), and the "washed out" green of the female "brimstone" (*G. rhamni*). Still, exceptions to the colour test often occur, notably in the "clouded yellows," *Colias Edusa* and *C. Hyale*, whereof the females have more variegated wings; and in the "ghost moth," *Hepialus humuli*, of which the male is plain white above, whilst his partner is variegated with yellow and brick-dust red. A precisely opposite case, however, to that of the ghost moth appears in the "gipsey" (*Hypogymna dispar*), in which the male is entirely dark, and the female almost white. Apparently, also, the size test does not always hold good, the females of certain moths (*Orgyia*, the well-known "vapourer," *Psyche*, *Hibernia*, &c.) being much smaller than their males, owing to their apterous condition: here, however, the corporal bulk is still larger.

This apterous condition seems to be an extreme modification (or, *teste* Darwin, a *result*) of the sedentary habits of the female; and the great activity of the male is well exhibited by the old method of collecting termed "sembling," which consists of breeding a female from the larva state (and, apart from the striking differences between the sexes in that stage in many large species, it appears to be not difficult for an acute observer to acquire the capability of nearly always discriminating between the respective larvae of male and female insects), and taking her to the usual haunts of her species, where she seldom fails to attract numerous suitors for her favour, who lose all fear, and fall an easy prey to the collector. The males of certain species, such as the "Oak Eggar" and "Emperor" moths, may often be seen rapidly scouring heaths in search of their females, who seldom take to the wing. In the active sex, it is worthy of remark that the antennae are often conspicuously pectinated, or otherwise more highly developed than the same organs in the female: this structure is doubtless of assistance to them in their searches, but we have as yet no knowledge of the exact functions of the antennae, and cannot tell in what way intelligence is communicated by them.

In the *Hymenoptera* the female is conspicuously the largest and most powerful in the ordinarily known forms, such as the wasps, bees (hive and humble), &c. And in this order, which contains so great a number of species, of such infinitely varied economy and habits, great sexual disparity often occurs, apart from size, so much so, that the sexes have been often separated as distinct species. The sexes, moreover, here often vary enormously in their relative numerical proportions, a result (or lack of result) probably arising in many cases from our ignorance. The males of certain gall-flies (*Cynipidæ*) are even *unknown* to the present day, although the females abound. A well-known instance of this theoretical widowhood is afforded by the inhabitant of the round, hard, marble-like gall of *Cynips Kollari*, now so abundant all over the South of England, but from which the efforts of our best entomologists have failed to raise a male.

In this order an actual increase of development is often found in the male (omitting reference to mere colour differences), in which sex wings are found, though sometimes wanting in the female; femora are thickened or curved; antennae are increased in length (the male of *Eucera longicornis*, a common burrowing bee, has them exceedingly long), pectinated, furcated, or otherwise varied—processes appear on the head, etc. In the female, excess of development appears to exhibit itself in the varied structure of the ovipositor, which, according to the different habits of the species, is elongated or shortened, or modified into saws, borers, a sting, etc.

In the little studied order of *Hemiptera* some few, but very striking, sexual differences are found, males and females of the same species having been separated as distinct, and the perfect female having even been considered as only in the pupal condition. Amongst others, the genus *Sphyracephalus* exhibits differences in mere colour, *Systellonotus* in the form and development of the elytra, *Harpocera* in the antennæ, and *Globiceps*, *Myrmedobia*, and *Zygonotus* in the entire aspect of the sexes; the males being linear and amply winged, whilst the other sex has but rudiments of wings, and is oval or suddenly inflated behind.

In the *Diptera*, to which order the common house-fly belongs, there are no very striking sexual differences, and such as exist are apparently chiefly confined to the antennæ, which are often pectinated or plumose in the males and more simple in the females. In some the palpi are also more developed in the male, but the proboscis or sucker attains larger dimensions in the other sex. The eyes in this order, also, are often largest in the male, and the sexes (as in *Bibio*) sometimes vary considerably in colour.

In the *Neuroptera*, the *Libellulidæ* or "dragon-flies" are separable sexually from the mere difference in position of the generative organs, which in the female are situated at the apex of the body, and in the male within the eighth abdominal segment, supplemented by other organs at the base of the abdomen beneath. Some few striking colour differences occur here; for instance, the male of the common broad-bodied *Libellula depressa* has its abdomen covered with a light powdery lavender bloom, whilst the female is of a monotonous and dingy yellow tone.

In the Trichopterous section of this order the anal appendages are of so high and complicated an organisation that they are of the greatest possible use in distinguishing the species, which are often exceedingly alike in other respects, and difficult to determine. In certain insects of this order (the *Ephemeridæ*) the males are distinguished by the larger size of their eyes; a character to be sometimes found in other orders.

In the *Coleoptera*, or beetles, superficial sexual characters of great variety and different degrees of development are to be found; the above-mentioned rule of larger or broader size and less shining appearance in the female still however prevailing, in spite of certain conspicuous instances to the contrary, principally among wood-feeding species, and some *Brachelytra* and *Necrophaga*. Perhaps the most general mark of the male is afforded by the greater dilatation of the tarsi, especially of the anterior legs. This widening is carried to an enormous extent in certain *Hydradephaga* (*Dytiscus*, *Acilius*, &c.), wherein the basal joints of the front tarsi in the males form absolutely rounded plates, furnished with suckers beneath. This structure is evidently to ensure the more certain connection of the sexes, and only appears in such excess among the water-beetles, the functions of life in which are necessarily performed in an unstable element. In such species, the females have the upper half of the elytra deeply channelled and roughened, evidently for the purpose of assisting the grasp of the male; and it is to this roughened surface (whether caused by closer and coarser punctuation or by absolute striæ) that the duller appearance of the female is due. The dilatation of the basal joints of the tarsi in the male is modified throughout the order according to the different families, and the clothing of the dilated joints beneath varies also. An absolute difference between the sexes in the number of the joints of the hinder tarsi occurs very rarely in this order (*Cryptophagus*). It is worthy of remark that the females of such insects as exhibit the above-mentioned extremes of difference from the male sometimes (but very rarely) assume the male form;—that is, as regards the absence of channels and more polished surface. I possess a male of *Dytiscus circumcinctus* (in which the female not seldom assumes this male appearance), wherein the elytra exhibit a tendency to the roughened furrows of the other sex.

The head of the male is in very many cases largely increased in bulk, and the mandibles are proportionately (sometimes, as in the "stag-beetle," *Lucanus cervus*, disproportionately) developed. The antennæ also are frequently much lengthened in that sex, especially in the longicorn beetles; and, though exceedingly rarely, even have an increased number of joints. They are also often much increased in other ways, being widened, pectinated, or serrated. The rostrum is, on the contrary, in the *Rhynchophora* much elongated in the female, who doubtless uses it for boring holes in which to lay her eggs. The males of some of this group, however (*Mesites*), have it abnormally developed. But this tendency to an increased development frequently does not stop with an enlargement of the normal organs, but exhibits itself in the presence in many species of tubercles on the front of the head, emarginations and widenings of the clypeus, absolute horns on the head or thorax, or both, etc. The legs also are often much lengthened or thickened, especially the front and hind pair, of which the femora are frequently much incrassated, or even inflated, and armed with a tooth (which in *Colon* sometimes almost equals the tibia in length) beneath, and the tibiæ are elongated, curved and spined, or notched, and sometimes dilated at the extremity. In all species of which the males exhibit these abnormal appearances, certain specimens often occur, intermediate, as it were, between the two sexes: these specimens are males of imperfect development as regards the excessive characters. Superficial male characters are also to be found in other parts of the body, especially on the lower surface of the abdomen, and most usually in the notching out (in an angular or circular way, and more or less deeply) of the hinder margin of the penultimate segments. This is evidently to allow of a freer motion and larger area for the apical segment containing the generative organs; but no satisfactory explanation can be given for other common developments on the abdomen, such as the tubercles and other abnormal structures of the upper surface (usually situated on the penultimate segment), the toothlike elevations and pubescence beneath, etc., so often found in certain *Brachelytra*. In that group the family *Tachyporidæ* exhibit a most marvellous armature of the apical segments, in both sexes (but varying specifically *inter se*, though apparently fashioned on one sexual type), and on both the upper and under side. The *Pæderidæ* and *Stenidæ* also exhibit curious characters, usually on the lower surface of the abdomen; and it may be remarked that a close attention to these sexual differences is often of great use to the student in determining obscure species.

Extravagant instances of external sexual dissimilarity occur also in this order; for instance, the well-known glowworm, *Lampyris noctiluca*, of which the male has wing-cases and ample wings, and the female is a mere flat grub. Its ally, *Drilus flavescens*, a parasite upon snails, exhibits even greater differences between the sexes; but the female is of such excessive rarity that it is not likely to come beneath the notice of the beginner. In the rare *Tomicus dispar*, also, the sexes are widely dissimilar; hence its name. Some *Ptinidæ* and *Anobiadæ* differ considerably in the form of their sexes; and the males and females of certain of the *Elateridæ* are very likely to be specifically separated by beginners.

A great apparent excess of bulk in the female, especially in certain *Meloidæ* and small *Chrysomelidæ*, is owing to the abdomen being distended with eggs. Instances of mere colour difference are too numerous to mention; some species of *Rhynchites*, *Cryptocephalus*, &c., however, are strikingly diverse in that respect.

OUR CLEARWING AND BURNET MOTHS.

These two families of our British moths are to us extremely full of interest. The Clearwings, even if not possessed of so much elegant beauty, would prove attractive to the close and thoughtful observer, from the singularity of their economy; and the dazzling brilliancy of the Burnets, added to their strange time of flying, *must* bring them before the notice of the butterfly collector, since they mingle with these lovely creatures in their midday gambols. In examining these two families briefly, therefore, we feel certain of securing the attention of our entomological readers, and at once proceed.

The "Clearwings," or *Sesidæ*, as they are scientifically termed, are indeed a wonderful tribe of moths. Unlike moths to the ordinary observer, they yet possess those characteristics which have caused them to be enrolled amongst the British *lepidoptera*. In the caterpillar stage of their existence, these insects feed on the solid wood of trees, mining and making galleries in the timber, and by their tunnelling operations often so weakening trees that they die from the effects. Some, however, do not attack the wood itself, but the pith, and of those that do eat only the wood, some prefer one part of the tree or bush to another. Thus we find some feeding in the roots, others in the branches, stems, or even slender twigs of various trees; but all are alike in that their destructive and fatal operations are carried on quite out of sight. They have the appearance of maggots, and the inexperienced would hardly consider them to be caterpillars at all, since their legs are hardly discernible without very close examination. Feeding in this remarkable manner, in due time they form slight (or in some cases compact) cocoons within their galleries, becoming chrysalides, and often leaving an aperture, so that when emerging, they may have no difficulty in coming forth to daylight. It should be stated that these singular *larvæ* are furnished with little hooks at each segment of the body, enabling them to proceed up and down their tunnels in the wood, with the greatest ease and facility.

The Clearwing moths themselves are the very personification of all that is graceful and elegant. How unlike in this, their final stage, to their previous selves! How different this aerial freedom, this beauty of structure, from that life within the stems, roots, or branches of trees passed by the ugly larvæ. Indeed these little creatures are full of intense beauty to the eye which has carefully scrutinized them. Their insignificant size precludes their being noticed by those who are not aware how much of exquisite loveliness God has given to the wings even of our smallest moths. Place a portion of the wing under a microscope; and how wondrous is the revelation! Let us just remark, before leaving these general outlines of the family *Sesidæ*, that all the perfect insects have long and narrow wings, which are transparent, much resembling those of flies or gnats, for which insects these moths may readily be mistaken. The Clearwings are true lovers of the sunshine and the flowers, and fly very rapidly at midday. Their *antennæ* are rather long, and thicker just beyond the middle; in the males they have a row of very short bristles, and thus are called *ciliated antennæ*. Their bodies are long, banded with brilliant colours, and furnished with a tuft or fan of hairs at the tail, greatly adding to the external beauty of these fairy-like creatures when flying. Thus much for the general characteristics of the family.

And now we proceed to notice the species. First on the list is the Red-belted Clearwing (*Sesia myopæformis*. This is indeed a lovely little moth, and by no means uncommon where apple trees abound; for its *larva* mines the slender branches of these fruit trees, and we read that between sixty and seventy have been discovered in a piece of pear-wood about three inches long. The caterpillar feeds throughout the year, and the moth occurs in May, June, and July. The forewings of this, and indeed of nearly all these insects now being considered, have a broad, black tip, and a black bar a little beyond the middle. The hindwings, again, in most instances, have black rays and a black margin. The thorax and body are black in this species, and the body has a bright red belt just about the centre. This it is that gives so striking an appearance to the little insect, and from whence it derives its name.

The Large Red-belted Clearwing (*Sesia culiciformis*), is a much rarer insect than the former. As its name implies, it is larger and handsomer in appearance. Its *larva* feeds on the wood of birch trees, and is said to prefer the stumps of birch trees that have been cut down; it is most perseveringly sought after by collectors in the Kentish woods, where it occurs. In colouring, this species and the last are somewhat alike, but the present insect may be distinguished from the former, by the minute red marks at the bases of the forewings. Next, however, we arrive at the Red-tipped Clearwing (*Sesia formicæformis*) whose *larva* feeds in the shoots of willows, and has been accused of doing much damage amongst the osier beds, by its mining propensities. Feeding throughout the autumn and winter, it becomes a moth about Midsummer. This species, from its possessing red tips to the wings, cannot well be confounded with either of the former. The next two we notice are now considered as rarities. The Fiery Clearwing (*Sesia chrysidiformis*) is a splendid little insect, but unfortunately little is known of its economy in this country. Specimens have occasionally been captured near the coast, for we read of its capture at Folkestone, etc., but it is so rare a visitor amongst us that we can hardly consider it a true "Britisher." The Six-belted Clearwing (*Sesia ichneumoniformis*) is rather a scarcity with us, though formerly taken in the *larval* stage feeding in the hellebore stems, which plant once grew in profusion in a sand-pit at Charlton. The perfect insect has been taken about Margate and Ramsgate, but in very sparing numbers.

Now, however, we come to two species of these delicate insects which occur more commonly amongst us. The first of these is the Yellow-legged Clearwing (*Sesia cynipiformis*). The moth is indeed gaily adorned, and beautiful in exterior, and from these characteristics it has ever been eagerly sought after by collectors, in its peculiar haunts. The male is distinguished from the female by having the tail-fringe black, whilst in the female it is golden yellow. The *larva* lives in the bark of elm and oak trees, and feeds during the winter. The moth is on the wing at Midsummer, occurring in Kensington Gardens and Hyde Park, from which localities, however, we fear that the unwise efforts of collectors will soon cause it to disappear. Early morning is the best time to capture specimens of this moth, and indeed of most of the *Sesidæ*, since they do not assume the gay flight then, which characterises them at midday, and are generally found at rest on the tree trunks or stems, from whence they have emerged. The Currant Clearwing (*Sesia tipuliformis*) next claims our attention. This, perhaps, is the best known of all this interesting family; certainly it is the commonest, since it occurs commonly in many places near London, and even in its precincts, where currant bushes happen to abound. Within the stems of these the little *larva* passes his life, eating away the pith, and often causing the death of the shoots affected. By splitting open the latter in the winter, the little creatures may be found coiled up, and can then be examined at pleasure. They form no regular cocoon, but seem to select joints in the stems for their abodes in the chrysalis stage, working towards an opening before the time for emergence has arrived. The old chrysalis cases may often be seen protruded from the branches in the autumn months. The Currant Clearwing, though the commonest of its tribe, is yet a beauteous little creature. Its flight is rapid, and it is only when settling on the delicious cool leaves of the currant, that one can closely observe its fairy-like beauty and elegance. Its motions, and the fanning of its silken glossy tail-fringe, as it walks over the flowers or leaves, are indeed the perfection of all that is graceful. The glossy black ground colour of the body, and the excessive brightness of the yellow bands, form a delightful and impressive contrast to the eye. June is the month in which this moth flies, and it is generally in the greatest profusion and perfection during the two first weeks of that month.

Four scarce Clearwings next come under our observation, and must be briefly passed over. The Orange-tailed Clearwing (*Sesia andreniformis*), as its name implies, has the tail-fringe of a brilliant orange, very large and conspicuous. The *larva* of this species is entirely unknown, and we only read of one specimen of the moth being taken of late years. The Welsh Clearwing (*Sesia scoliæformis*) has been found near Llangollen, in North Wales. The caterpillar feeds on the wood of birch trees, and the moth appears in June, though so sparingly that we must consider it quite a local species. The White-barred Clearwing (*Sesia sphegiformis*), and the Dusky Clearwing (*Sesia vespiformis*), are both very uncommon in this country, the latter, in the *larval* stage, feeding on the roots of aspen and ash trees. Unlike the rest of this family, Dusky Clearwing has the forewings opaque, and is thus characteristically distinguished from all the others, hence its name. It appears in June, and according to Stainton has occurred at Epping.

The two final representatives of the *Sesidæ* which we are to notice, are the Hornet Clearwings. These, though similar in many respects to the former species enumerated, are much larger, and their bodies have no tuft at the tail. They are banded with brilliant colours. The Willow Hornet Clearwing (*Sesia bembeciformis*) is a fine insect, and as its name implies, resembles much one of the hornet tribe when flying; the forewings are tinged with yellow, and the body, which is yellow, has a brown belt at the base, and another near the centre; the legs are orange-coloured. The fleshy, maggot-like *larva* feeds on the osier wood, spinning a tough, compact cocoon in the twigs. The moth flies at Midsummer. The Poplar Hornet Clearwing (*Sesia apiformis*) is, we think, the commoner of the two—in the perfect state it may be distinguished from the last mentioned species by having a square patch of yellow on each side of the thorax in front, a mark wanting in the Willow Hornet Clearwing; the margin of the wings in this species, also, is wider than in the last named. The *larva* feeds on the solid wood of poplar trees, and sometimes lives concealed for two years. At the end of its caterpillar existence, it spins a cocoon, formed of silk, and chips of poplar wood, near the ground, from which it emerges in the month of June, and may be captured by searching tree trunks in the early morning. It is a very gaily-coloured insect. Cocoons of this Clearwing may be purchased of the London dealers at the proper season, but the speculation is rather a precarious one, since the thickness of the cocoon prevents one ascertaining whether the insect within is dead or alive. Thus, then, ends our list of the Clearwings, or *Sesidæ*. The reader will see that much remains yet to be discovered regarding these interesting moths, since the *larvæ* and *pupæ* of some species are entirely unknown, and the economy, habits, and structure of others has been hardly investigated at all. We would therefore recommend all our entomological readers to study this interesting group of insects carefully.

A few brief remarks, however, on the Burnets, or the *Zygænidæ*, as they are scientifically termed. We have allowed so much space to the Clearwings, that we must now hasten rapidly to a close. The Burnets are remarkable for their beautiful forewings, spotted in so striking a manner, and also for the extreme brilliancy of the red hindwings; they have large and thick *antennæ*, and a tubular apparatus for extracting honey from the flowers; they, like the last mentioned, fly in the sunshine, and are dull and lethargic in cloudy weather; their caterpillars are stout and hairy, and spin silken cocoons on the stems of their food plants. The Transparent Burnet, or the Irish Burnet (*Zygæna minos*) is the first of this family; it *larva* does not seem to be known in this country, since we find it described by a foreign author, Duponchel; it feeds on the birds-foot trefoils. We read that the moths can be captured with the greatest ease after 4 p.m., as they sleep on the flowers, and in some favoured localities crowd together in such numbers, as entirely to change the colour of the blossoms on which they congregate; they occur in the month of June.

The Broad-bordered Burnet (*Zygæna trifolii*) and the Narrow-bordered Burnet (*Zygæna lonicera*) are two species which have *five* spots on the upper wings, distinguishing them from the common species, next to be spoken of. The blackish-green wings of these moths, glittering with the red spots, are full of dazzling beauty, and give a brilliant effect as the insects wing their way over the clover or trefoil meadows, to which they are attached. The last of the Burnets is the common species, known as the Six-spotted Burnet (*Zygæna filipendulæ*). On hot summer days this little insect dashes with inconceivable rapidity across our path, dazzling and bewildering the entomologist, who has scarcely time to look and wonder, before the moth is far beyond the reach either of net or observation. The *larva* of this species is dingy yellow, feeding on the crowfoot trefoil.

But we are compelled to close this paper, which has already extended itself beyond ordinary limits. In doing so, we only stay to remark, that these two interesting families of moths in many characteristics are identical with the "Hawk moths" themselves, with which they and the "Foresters" were originally classed by Linnæus, under the general name of "Sphinges." And we hardly think our entomological dignities right in separating therefrom these families of moths, since they are so much allied in many points of history, structure, and economy. Whether true "Sphinges" or not, however, certain it is that they are most deserving of patient and careful study, and promise a reward to the persevering and careful entomologist who volunteers to work out more fully than has hitherto been done, their separate life histories. And thus we leave our readers for the present.—E. J. S. CLIFFORD.

DREDGING ON THE SOUTH-EAST COAST OF CORNWALL.

By JONATHAN COUCH, F.L.S., C.M.Z.S., &c.

AT the meeting of the British Association of Science of the year 1865, a sum of money was set apart and directions were given for the purpose of encouraging dredging excursions on the coasts of the western counties; and a portion of the sum voted was assigned to the writer, with the condition that an account of whatever of novelty in the department of Natural History might be met with should be communicated to the society. This condition has been complied with; but in addition to this there are some particulars which have fallen in my way under other circumstances that can scarcely be deemed of sufficient interest to claim the attention of that body, but which yet may be judged of sufficient importance to find a place in a communication to a meeting of a more local county society, to the Fauna of which I am thus enabled to make a considerable addition. It is only justice to add, that in pursuing these researches I had the good fortune to be able to enlist the services of Mr. William Laughrin, A.LS., of this place, whose active zeal for this object has long been well known, and who in carrying out the intention has had, from the occasional inclemency of the weather, to encounter no small amount of inconvenience, and even of danger.

As regards the obtaining of fish, the sweep of a dredge is too limited to offer a prospect of much success. At the shallowest depths above named, the Megrim or Scald Fish (Rhombus Arnoglossus) was obtained in abundance, but it was not found between forty and fifty fathoms; where, however, were found an example of the Lancelot and larger Launce which had been buried in the sand: and as regards the latter, it seems remarkable that at the same time the large abundance of its species have changed their quarters to approach the shallow water, while at least in this one instance an example has remained in its winter haunt. A further observation from an observant fisherman seems also deserving of notice. It refers to the habit of some small individuals of several kinds of fish, of seeking shelter within the bell-shaped cavity of some of the larger species of Medusæ. Very small Scads, Bibs, and Whiting Pollacks are often found thus attending on the floating Medusæ; and on the least alarm they have recourse to the protection thus afforded them. Under these circumstances on lifting one of these creatures into the boat, it was seen that there were concealed within its cavity no less than sixty-two young Scads, from which the question arose, that as these Medusæ are generally believed to come to us from a warmer region, is it not probable that in this manner they may convey to us young individuals of some rarer sorts, which otherwise would not have been met with on our coast? The Connemara Sucking Fish was found at 40 fathoms. Among the rarer fishes that have been met with at a recent date, I will mention the Ausonia Cuvieri, and what has been judged a distinct species, although nearly allied—Ausonia Cocksii, a notice of both of which has been already published; and together with these the Scabbard Fish (Lepidopus Argyreus) found floating near Falmouth, for the knowledge of which, with a sketch, I am indebted to the kindness of W. P. Cocks, Esquire; also the Silvery Hairtail (Trichiurus lepturus) taken in a drift-net near Penzance; and of which, in an example caught near Plymouth, I perceived that marks of the dorsal fin were continued to the tail, which is not what is usually represented.

I notice the following crustacean animals as being inhabitants of the deeper water:—Pisa Tetrodon—Stenorhynchus Phalangium—Eurynomè Aspera—Hyas Araneus—Corystes Cassivalaunus — Xantho Tuberculata — Portunus Depurator — Ebalia Bryerii — E. Pennantii — Pagurus Forbesii—P. Hindmanni—P. Cuanensis, a deep-water species first made known as occurring on our coast, by W. P. Cocks, Esq., but which seems to be not exceedingly rare. It was sheltered in a ball of sponge, as is often the case with these smaller hermit crabs, Galathæa Andrewsii.

Dredging.

Shellfish.—Of these we procured Psammobia Vespertina — Crassina Danmonii — Cardium Echinatum—C. Levigatum—Cerithium Lima—Chionè Islandica—Venus Sarniensis—V. Fasciata—Solen Pellucidus—Saxicava Arctica—Lima Hians? or L. Losiconii, a single valve from 35 fathoms. Acmœa Virginea, from a trawl; but it differs from the representation by Forbes, as if from being older—Pectens numerous, and among them S. Tigrinus, but all empty shells.

Dentalium Entalis—D. Tarentinum?—Pelidium Fulvum, on a dead shell of Pinna Ingens-Rostellaria Pes Pelecani, in all its stages of growth. Fusus Propinus, from 60 fathoms. Bulla Lignaria—Turritella Terebra—Trochus Papillosus — Scalaria Clathratulus — Natica Alderi—N. Nitida, from the stomach of Asterias Aurantiaca—Pandora Inœquivalvis—Emarginula Rosea—Marginella Voluta. Two or three examples of a genus which Forbes calls Trophon, but of which he has not given a figure.

Echii and Starfishes.

Echinus Sphœra—E. Miliaris—both of which appear to live at all depths. Echinocyamus Pusillus — Spatangus Purpureus —Amphidotus Roseus — Small examples of Palmipes Membranaceus—Asterias Aurantiaca—A. Glacialis, a migrating species, abundant near the land early in the summer, and afterwards passing into deep water. Luidia Fragilissima, a small example, which did not break into fragments as the larger are accustomed to do. Porania Pulvillea, by far the most beautiful for splendour and variety of colour of all our native starfishes, and the rarest; the colours are liable to variation in different individuals. I have obtained it from a crabpot, but its more usual residence is in deep water. Ophiocoma Filiformis.

There was a time when the flexible species of corals were in abundance on the rather hard, and what fishermen term clean ground, at about the depth now dredged over; but this is now swept clean by trawling, and the shelter formerly afforded to the spawn of fish, by which the parents were led to perform the function of increase near us; as also for a refuge to the young ones, and a nucleus for the hatching of those small creatures which were especially sought after for food is utterly lost. But little, therefore, of these corals was now seen. From a fisherman's hook there was obtained, in rather shallow water, a large example of the newly discovered species, named by Dr. J. E. Gray Rhodophyton Couchii, with branches as long and stout as a finger, and of a lively flesh colour, with the projecting polyps a pale white. It is now in the British Museum. There was also in the deep water an encrusting Alcyonium, apparently a species not known to me, and which took the form of the slender substance that supported it in its contorted windings. Added to these we procured Cellepora Ramulosa, and what I believed to be the rare (Northern) C. Loevigata; but having communicated the specimen to my lamented friend, the late Joseph Alder, he hesitated to decide regarding it. A fisherman informs me that he finds the Alcyonium Digitatum, a common species, to prefer hard and stony ground, as is probably the case with the other members of this family.

Sponges are not the least interesting of the materials obtained in these excursions, and in the study of them I have had the great advantage of the assistance of Dr. Bowerbank, to whom, as being a highly competent authority, specimens of all of them have been submitted for his opinion.

Among the sponges thus examined by Dr. Bowerbank, I have to congratulate myself on the acquisition of two which that gentleman pronounces to be new to science, and the first as such which he has seen since the publication of his book on the subject by the Ray Society. The examples of course remain with Dr. Bowerbank, who has done me the honour to name the first of them Halichondria Couchii. On close examination of another specimen, it was also perceived that although it bore some resemblance to the rare Microciona Fictitia, for which on a cursory view it might be mistaken; yet on dissection, by the help of a microscope it showed itself to be new, and accordingly it is named Microciona Fraudator.

Other sponges are: Halichondria Panicea, crumb of bread sponge dredging a very large specimen. H. Albescens, of Johnston; Hymeniacidon A., of Bowerbank—H. Simulans, Johns Isodictya Boweri—H. Suberosa. In a ball of this I found shut up, but with an orifice, the Crustacean Pagurus Cuanensis, and in one or two similar balls other hermit crabs; but in these instances there was not, as is often the case, a shell on which a sponge had incrusted itself. It is difficult to suppose that the shell had disappeared after having been thus shut up; and it seems equally difficult to imagine how without a solid nucleus the sponge could have formed itself with a cavity as we find it to have done.

H. Incrustans; covering in patches the carapacean and legs of a species of spider crab.

H. Hispida Dictyocylindrus H. Boweri. There is something exceedingly remarkable in the circumstances which have attended the dredging of this species; and which I can explain only by supposing that two species are confounded together, which, on the other hand, I am assured from authority is not the case. Thus in spaces at the depth of about twenty, and again in forty fathoms, there came up examples of this slender branched sponge, measuring perhaps a foot in length, with the surface even roughly hirsute, and which had been fixed to the ground by a well marked and rather broad root. But at other places, and in deeper water, there clearly had never been in any one of the many examples an attachment to the ground; and the branching growth proceeded from both ends, with an intermediate space, not always exactly in the middle, of from one to two or three inches in length, and which appeared to be that middle line from which the branches at each end proceeded; but at no part of this sponge was there even a slight mark of a root. Secondary branches are at least rare in this (variety); and its surface has a finer grain than the rooted examples. Some of them at least appear to have lain along on the ground; but in a single instance one of the ends must have been elevated, since on it was growing, parallel with it, a flexible coral, and two examples of pollicipes scalpellum. In one instance also a fine specimen of Grantia ciliata had fixed itself on a prostrate branch; and of another of small size with three branches at each end of a short middle stem that was scarcely larger than the branches, it was the opinion of Dr. Bowerbank that two examples had lain in contact with each other, and had thus grown into one; but on examination I was not able to discern any mark of such a union, and of a root or footstalk there was none. Other sponges obtained in these dredgings were:—H. Ficus, named by my late friend Joshua Alder, at sixty fathoms; Desmacidon fruticosa, of Bowerbank; Hymeniacidon virgultosa, B., near the land, in Lantivet Bay; Dysidea fragilis, Johnston, Grantia compressa: G. Fistulosa, John.; Leuconia F. B.; G. Ciliata, already mentioned; G. Lacunosa, John., Leucosolinia B., in shallow water, on the carapace of a Corwich crab; Amouracium proliferum and A. Lèvæ, hanging from rocks, in Lantivet Bay.

Of a large variety of worms I am not able to give an account, but they are placed in safe hands; examples having been sent to C. Spence Bate, Esq., and to the British Museum. There was also a species of Polynòè, and what appear to be two species of aphrodyte in addition to the well-known A. Aculeata; Oenus brunneus also, and two or three species of Sipunculus. It may be interesting to add, that having obtained a fleshy substance of a pink colour, of a rather flattened pyramidal form, with a base almost the size of a florin, and which from the structure of its surface I supposed to be a Botryllus; while viewing it with a lens for the purpose of drawing a figure, it went through the process of excluding a young one from the border of its surface. This little one was also pyramidal, and rather more so than the parent; but in other respects much like it.

It is an addition to our natural history to notice that in the spring of the year 1867, an example of the Hawk's Bill Turtle was taken near the French coast, and therefore not to be classed as British; but when brought alive and active to Polperro, there were found closely adhering under the shelter of its tail, two full grown examples of the crab, Planes linnæana; a situation evidently chosen for shelter and support, and from the structure of the hindermost legs, as compared with the more regular swimming crabs, we may conclude that however desirous of keeping near the surface it could not secure this object without extraneous support.

And in addition to these I have now to add the Echinèis remora; of which there is no certain knowledge that it has ever before been obtained in England. Certainly it has never before been obtained in Cornwall, and for the pleasure of being possessed of it, it is proper that I should express my obligation to Mr. Matthias Dunn, of Mevagissey, who had the sagacity to perceive that the example was not of common occurrence, although he was not aware of the interest attached to it. It was obtained from the back of a shark which from its description I suppose to have been different from those that are usually caught on our coast; and which had become entangled in a drift net at the distance of about fourteen miles south of the Dodman. (I have the pleasure of presenting it for inspection at the meeting of the Royal Cornwall Polytechnic Society, after which I wish it to be added to the collection of the Cornish Museum at Truro.) This example of the Remora is rather more slender in its shape than that one from which the figure was taken, as given in my History of the Fishes of the British Islands; and it was also of a darker colour; which last particular may be explained by the circumstance that it came into my possession soon after its capture, whereas the example from which the likeness was taken had been brought from a warmer region, preserved in spirit. The only undoubted example before this that had been obtained in the British Islands, was found in Ireland, attached to the surface of the common Blue Shark.

NATURE IMPROVED.

ONCE upon a time, there lived a painter. His colours were bright, his brushes were good, and he liked to use both. One day, while walking in his garden, his eye was attracted by the pure blossoms of a tall white lily. He fetched his brushes and colours, and daubed the snowy petals with blue and red. Now, *he* admired this: which was more than anybody else did. The flowers were very grand; *but* they were white lilies no longer.

Once upon a time, too, there lived a perfumer. His scents were fragrant and varied. One day, a bouquet of roses was brought to him:—white, and red, and yellow. He sniffed, and sniffed; and at last a bright thought suggested itself. One flower he perfumed with jasmine, another with sandal-wood; one he scented with patchouli, and another with hyacinth: and very sweet they all smelt. *But* "the scent of the roses" was gone.

Some years ago, in Loudon's *Magazine of Natural History*, several communications appeared regarding the practice, then, I believe, first suggested, of disseminating rare or exotic plants in apparently wild situations, where they would be likely to "increase and multiply," and ultimately, permanently establish themselves. It was, in fact, proposed to "paint the lily and add perfume to the rose." The idea, however, met with but little encouragement, and the majority of the writers so decidedly opposed it that the discussion dropped, I had certainly hoped, never again to be brought forward. However, as "J. D. S. W." is anxious to "hear the opinions of naturalists" on the subject, I will offer a few remarks for his consideration.

In the first place, I, as *one* of "the readers of the NOTEBOOK," do not at all think that "we want a scarlet bird to enliven our woods." Even if such a bird were introduced, would it not attract the notice of "A. M. B." and his colleagues, and share the fate which seems hanging over our lovely Kingfisher? Besides, do we really *want* such additions to our Avifauna? Are not our woods already filled with song? and would the occasional appearance of a Virginian bird in our English woods, compensate for the annoyance which it would cause to British ornithologists? Have we not quite as much as, or more than, we can manage, in defending "our feathered friends" from the members of sparrow-clubs, and from pseudo-naturalists?

But it is the opening sentence of "J. D. S. W.'s" letter which most concerns me, as a botanist. "Our woods are annually enriched by plants from all climes." Is this really a fact? and, if so, whom have we to thank for this enrichment? Supposing the statement to be accurate, it appears remarkable, not only that the disseminators have not recorded their work, but that more new plants are not noticed, especially in woods.

It may be urged, by advocates of the improvement movement, that one of our most influential field clubs approves, and even requests the enrichment of the neighbourhood "by a judicious sowing of the seeds of exotic plants." While admitting that such is the case, and venturing my opinion, *par parenthèse*, that, even there, such a practice would be better avoided, it must be borne in mind that this course is to a certain extent, justified by the statement that "the Flora and Fauna of the neighbourhood are now both well known." Granting this with respect to Manchester, of how many other districts could this be truthfully stated?

If we once admit the correctness of this principle, can we guarantee that Naturalisers will confine their operations to such districts as have been well and carefully worked? We must first remember how much is involved in the working out of the Natural History of a district—how easily plants are passed over at some seasons, and how difficult it is to visit several places so frequently and so observantly as to be *quite sure* that not a single plant has escaped notice. An example of this occurs to me: the curious Toothwort (*Lathræa squamaria*) grows in one locality only in our Wycombe district; this is *at the back* of some elm trees, which have a path in front of them. Now unless, as actually happened, some one had gone behind these trees, and that just at the right season, we should have remained in ignorance of the existence of this plant amongst us.

Again, it has been urged that confusion might easily be avoided by the recording of introductions. But how is it to be ensured that occasional visitors or new comers to a neighbourhood, who may wish to investigate its natural features, shall be able to consult such record? Perhaps, too, a plant, when established in one locality, may readily spread to others at some considerable distance, as in the case of *Impatiens fulva*: and should such plant be found some time after in such distant locality by another observer, he would probably announce it as a "new British plant," and add another to the erroneous statements, already far too numerous, which have been commented on by Mr. Watson in his *Cybele Britannica*.

I cannot help recording my earnest opinion, that the day which sees the race of Naturalisers spring into importance will also see the fall of the race of Naturalists. The discoverer of a new or rare plant will lose all pleasure in such discovery, for it will probably have been introduced by some zealous Naturaliser. The local Faunas and Floras, which are now so interesting to their compilers, as well as to their readers, will then of necessity cease to appear. An industrious disciple of the new school may, in a few years, so "paint the lily" that its original features will entirely disappear. We shall lose altogether our *Natural* History; and what shall we gain in its place?

We shall gain a few garden-plants turned loose, which, let us grant, will be ornamental to our fields and banks. We shall gain, perhaps, two or three new birds, which we may hope will engage the attention of collectors. We shall annoy our brother Naturalists of the old school, who like the native flowers and birds of their country, and do not wish them artificially "improved" by newly-introduced companions. We shall mislead the rising generation of Naturalists, perhaps disgust them altogether: and all because we are not satisfied with our own natural treasures.

Perhaps this is not a case for argument. Even this short paper may only by its opposition encourage those against whom it is directed. In conclusion, therefore, let me beg of "J. D. S. W.," and those who think with him, to weigh carefully the following facts in connection with what I have already said :—

1. No Naturalist of note has ever encouraged his view, while many have opposed it.

2. Such improvement as he suggests might please the few, but would certainly offend the many.

3. Our own plants, birds, insects, etc., are not at present so thoroughly known and examined that the excuse of requiring fresh objects for study can be considered of importance. Besides, cultivation would supply these.

If any of my remarks appear harsh, I trust that my interest in my subject may be pleaded in palliation thereof: although I have endeavoured to speak moderately and temperately throughout.

In the words of a brother Naturalist, "The garden, the plantation, and the pleasure-ground, are the proper places for the exhibition of man's improving hand; but let us leave the woods and rocks to their native wildness and magnificence—as long, indeed, as the advance of population allows us to retain any wilds at all!"

JAMES BRITTEN,
Hon. Sec. High Wycombe Nat. Hist. Society.

BOTANICAL GEOGRAPHY.

SCARCELY 1,400 species of plants appear to have been known and described by the Greeks, Romans, and Arabians. At present, more than 3,000 species are enumerated as natives of our own island. In other parts of the world there have been now collected more than 100,000 reputed species, specimens of which are preserved in European herbariums. It was not to be supposed, therefore, that the ancients should have acquired any correct notions respecting what has been called the geography of plants, although the influence of climate on the character of the vegetation could hardly have escaped their observation.

Antecedently to investigation, there was no reason for presuming that the vegetable productions, growing wild in the eastern hemisphere, should be unlike those of the western, in the same latitude; nor that the plants of the Cape of Good Hope should be unlike those of the south of Europe; situations where the climate is little dissimilar. The contrary supposition would have seemed more probable, and we might have anticipated an almost perfect identity in the plants which inhabit corresponding parallels of latitude at equal heights above the sea. The discovery, therefore, that each separate region of the globe, both of the land and water, is occupied, in the vegetable as well as in the animal world, by distinct groups of species, and that most of the exceptions to this general rule are referable to disseminating causes now in operation, is eminently calculated to prepare us to receive with favour any hypothesis respecting the first introduction of species which may be reconcilable with such phenomena.

Botanical regions.—Humboldt was among the first to promulgate philosophical views on the distinctness of the vegetable productions of different regions of the globe. Every hemisphere, he said, is inhabited by different species of plants, and it is not by the diversity of climates that we can attempt to explain why equinoctial Africa has no Laurineæ, and the New World no Heaths; or why the Calceolariæ are found only in the southern hemisphere.

"We can conceive," he adds, "that a small number of the families of plants, for instance, the Musaceæ and the Palms, cannot belong to very cold regions, on account of their internal structure and the importance of certain organs; but we cannot explain why no one of the Melastomas (a family allied to the Myrtles) vegetates north of the parallel of thirty degrees; or why no rose-tree belongs to the southern hemisphere. Analogy of climates is often found in the two continents without identity of productions."

The luminous essay of Auguste de Candolle on "Botanical Geography" (1820) presents us with the fruits of his own researches and those of Humboldt, Brown, and other eminent botanists, so arranged, that the principal phenomena of the distribution of plants are exhibited in connection with the causes to which they are supposed to be referable. "It might not, perhaps, be difficult," observes this writer, "to find two points, in the United States and in Europe, or in equinoctial America and Africa, which present all the same circumstances: as, for example, the same temperature, the same height above the sea, a similar soil, an equal dose of humidity; yet nearly all, *perhaps all*, the plants in these two similar localities shall be distinct. A certain degree of analogy, indeed, of aspect, and even of structure, might very possibly be discoverable between the plants of the two localities in question; but the *species* would in general be different. Circumstances, therefore, different from those which now determine the *stations*, have had an influence on the *habitations* of plants.'

It may be as well to define in this place the technical sense in which the words printed in italics are here used: *station* indicates the peculiar nature of the locality where each species is accustomed to grow, and has reference to climate, soil, humidity, light, elevation above the sea, and other analogous circumstances; whereas, by *habitation* is meant a general indication of the country where a plant grows wild. Thus the *station* of a plant may be a salt-marsh, a hill-side, the bed of the sea, or a stagnant pool. Its *habitation* may be Europe, North America, or New Holland, between the tropics. The study of *stations* has been styled the topography, that of *habitations* the geography of botany. The terms thus defined, express each a distinct class of ideas, which have been often confounded together, and which are equally applicable in zoology.

In farther illustration of the principle above alluded to, that difference of longitude, independently of any influence of temperature, is accompanied by a great, and sometimes a complete, diversity in the species of plants, De Candolle observed, that, out of 2,891 species of phænogamous plants described by Pursh as known in 1820 in the United States, there were only 385 common to northern or temperate Europe.

On comparing New Holland with Europe, Mr. Brown ascertained that, out of 4,100 species, then discovered in Australia, there were only 166 common to Europe, and of this small number there were some few which may have been transported thither by man. Almost all of the 166 species were cryptogamic, and the rest consist, in nearly every case, of phænogamous plants which also inhabit intervening regions.

But it is still more remarkable that there should be an almost equal diversity of species, in distant parts of the ancient continent between which there is an uninterrupted land communication. Thus there is one assemblage of species in China, another in the countries bordering the Black Sea and the Caspian, a third in those surrounding the Mediterranean, a fourth on the great platforms of Siberia and Tartary, and so forth.

The distinctness of the groups of indigenous plants, in the same parallel of latitude, is greatest, as in the case of animals before mentioned, where continents are disjoined by a wide expanse of ocean. In the northern hemisphere, near the pole, where the extremities of Europe, Asia, and America unite or approach near to one another, a considerable number of the same species of plants are found, common to the three continents. But it has been remarked, that these plants, which are thus so widely diffused in the arctic regions, are also found in the chain of the Aleutian islands, which stretch almost across from America to Asia, and which may probably have served as the channel of communication for the partial blending of the floras of the adjoining regions. De Candolle enumerated twenty great botanical provinces, inhabited by indigenous and aboriginal plants; and his son Alphonse, a distinguished living botanist, has made a further subdivision into twenty-seven provinces, between which the lines of demarcation are by no means ill-defined.

There are, however, not a few species which are common to two or more than two of these provinces, and often representative forms which some naturalists would class as mere geographical varieties. The six ornithological divisions of the globe, four of them in the Old World and two in the New, are not on the whole inapplicable to plants, if we wish to take a more large and comprehensive view of the leading features in their geographical distribution, especially as regards genera and families.

This holds true, particularly of the Neoarctic and Neotropical regions, each of which contains a distinct assemblage of peculiar vegetable forms. Those of the table-land of Brazil, which has an elevation of from 2,000 to 4,000 feet, are described by Sir Charles Bunbury, after he had explored the district, as belonging for the most part to generic types, little known except to botanists, for they have not been cultivated in Europe. But when he descended from the Brazilian uplands towards the south, or to the grassy plains of Uruguay and La Plata, he found plants still belonging to the predominant South-American types, though represented by different and local species. Such affinity between the specific forms proper to the more elevated and to the lower stations agrees well with the idea of certain original types having been gradually adapted by variation and natural selection to all the diversified conditions of the surface of the land.

The Pampas and banks of the Plata are also remarkable for the extraordinary manner in which some foreign European plants, especially the thistles and trefoils, have overpowered the indigenous vegetation. The intruders have been introduced by man sometimes unintentionally, and, having naturalised themselves, have become more conspicuous than any of the native products of the soil. They illustrate a principle before laid down, that the organic beings of each great region which man finds in possession of wide areas are not those which are most fitted of all contemporary species to flourish there to the exclusion of all others. They appear to be simply the modified descendants of such an older fauna and flora as happened to preexist under a somewhat different phase of the earth's physical geography, or they are the offspring of colonists which by natural means were able to reach those lands. But the same organisms are powerless to maintain their ground in the struggle for life if brought into competition with species from distant regions which would never without the aid of man have come into contact with them.

Marine plants.—The vegetation of the sea, like that of the land, is divisible into different provinces each inhabited by distinct species, but these provinces are fewer in number because the temperature of the ocean is more uniform than that of the atmosphere, and because the area of land bears a small proportion to that of water, so that the migration of marine plants is not so often stopped by barriers of land as is that of the terrestrial species of the ocean. It is a remarkable fact that Dr. Hooker has been able to indentify no less than a fifth part of the antarctic Algæ, excluding the New Zealand and Tasmanian groups, with British species. Yet there is a much smaller proportion of cosmopolite species among the Algæ than among the terrestrial cellular cryptogams, such as lichens, mosses, and Hepaticæ.

Dispersion of plants.—The fact last alluded to, of the ubiquitous character of cryptogamous plants, deserves special attention. Linnæus observed that, as the germs of plants of this class, such as Mosses, fungi, and lichens, consist of an impalpable powder, the particles of which are scarcely visible to the naked eye, there is no difficulty in accounting for their being dispersed throughout the atmosphere, and carried to every point of the globe, where there is a station fitted for them. Lichens in particular ascend to great elevations, sometimes growing on bare rocks two thousand feet above the line of perpetual snow, where the mean temperature is nearly at the freezing point. This elevated position must contribute greatly to facilitate the dispersion of those buoyant particles of which their fructification consists.

Some have inferred, from the springing up of mushrooms whenever particular soils and decomposed organic matter are mixed together, that the production of fungi is accidental, and not analogous to that of perfect plants. But Fries, whose authority on these questions is entitled to the highest respect, has shown the fallacy of this argument in favour of the old doctrine of equivocal generation. " The sporules of fungi," says this naturalist, " are so infinite, that in a single individual of *Reticularia maxima*, I have counted above ten millions, and so subtile as to be scarcely visible, often resembling thin smoke ; so light that they may be raised perhaps by evaporation into the atmosphere, and dispersed in so many ways by the attraction of the sun, by insects, wind, elasticity, adhesion, &c., that it is difficult to conceive a place from which they may be excluded."

The club-moss called *Lycopodium cernuum* affords a striking example of a cryptogamous plant universally distributed over all equinoctial countries. It scarcely ever passes beyond the northern tropic, except in one instance, where it appears around the hot-springs in the Azores, although it is neither an inhabitant of the Canaries nor of Madeira. Doubtless its microscopic sporules are everywhere present, ready to germinate on any spot where they can enjoy throughout the year the proper quantity of warmth, moisture, light, and other conditions essential to the species.

Almost every lichen brought home from the southern hemisphere by the antarctic expedition under Sir James Ross, amounting to no less than 200 species, was ascertained to be also an inhabitant of the northern hemisphere, and almost all of them European.

When we contrast the cosmopolite character of this class of plants with the comparatively limited range of most of the phænogamous species, we cannot fail to perceive how intimately the geographical distribution of each of is related to their powers of dispersion. But, in order to see a connection between these phenomena, we must first assume that each species has one birthplace, and that it has radiated in all directions in which it is possible for it to spread from the original point or centre where it was first formed.

The most active of the inanimate agents provided by nature for scattering the seeds of plants over the globe, are the movements of the atmosphere and of the ocean, and the constant flow of water from the mountains to the sea. To begin with the winds : a great number of seeds are furnished with downy and feathery appendages, enabling them, when ripe, to float in the air, and to be wafted easily to great distances by the most gentle breeze. Other plants are fitted for dispersion by means of an attached wing, as in the case of the fir-tree, so that they are caught up by the wind as they fall from the cone, and are carried to a distance. Amongst the comparatively small number of plants known to Linnæus, no less than 138 genera are enumerated as having winged seeds.

As winds often prevail for days, weeks, or even months together in the same direction, these means of transportation may sometimes be without limits ; and even the heavier grains may be borne through considerable spaces, in a very short time, during ordinary tempests ; for strong gales, which can sweep along grains of sand, often move at the rate of about forty miles an hour, and if the storm be very violent, at the rate of fifty-six miles. The hurricanes of tropical regions, which root up trees and throw down buildings, sweep along at the rate of ninety miles an hour; so that, for however short a time they prevail, they may carry even the heavier fruits and seeds over friths and seas of considerable width, and doubtless are often the means of introducing into islands the vegetation of adjoining continents. Whirlwinds are also instrumental in bearing along heavy vegetable substances to considerable distances. Slight ones may frequently be observed in our fields, in summer, carrying up haycocks into the air, and then letting fall small tufts of hay far and wide over the country; but they are sometimes so powerful as to dry up lakes and ponds, and to break off the boughs of trees, and carry them up in a whirling column of air.—*Sir Charles Lyell's Principles of Geology*, Vol. 2. London: John Murray.

PHYSALIA.

LET us note among the Liphonophoræ a zoophyte which has attracted great attention, and has been described under many names. Sailors call it the sea-bladder, from its resemblance to that organ; it is also known as the Portuguese man-of-war, from its fancied resemblance to a small ship as it floats along under its tiny sail. Naturalists after Eshscholtz call it Physalia utriculus, from the Greek word φυσαλὶς, a bubble, and utriculus from its stinging powers. It was long thought that the Physalia was an isolated individual. But according to recent researches, they form, an animal republic. Let us imagine a great cylindrical bladder dilated in the middle, attenuated and rounded at its two extremities, of eleven or twelve inches in length, and from one to three broad; its appearance is glossy and transparent, its colour an imperfect purple, passing to a violet, then to an azure; above it is surmounted by a crest limpid and pure as crystal, veined with purple and violet in decreasing tints. Under the vesicle float the fleshy filaments, waving and contorted into a spiral form, which sometimes descend perpendicularly like so many threads of celestial blue. Sailors believe that the crest which surmounts the vesicle performs the office of a sail, and that they tell the navigator "how the wind blows," as they say. With all respect to the sailors, the bladder-like form, with its aerial crest, is only a hydrostatic apparatus, whose office is to lighten the animal, and modify its specific gravity. Mr. Gosse thinks otherwise, however. "This bladder" says Gosse, in his "Year by the Sea-side," "is filled with air, and therefore floats almost wholly on the surface. Along the upper side, nearly from end to end, runs on their edge of membrane, which is capable of being erected at will to a considerable height, fully equal at times to the entire width of the bladder, when it represents an arched fore-and-aft sail, the bladder being the hull. From the bottom of the bladder, near the thickest extremity, where there is a denser portion of the membrane, depends a crowded mass of organs, most of which take the form of very slender highly contractile moveable threads, which hang down into the deep to a depth of many feet, or occasionally of several yards.

"The colours of this curious creature are very vivid; the bladder though in some parts transparent and colourless, and in some specimens almost entirely so, is in general painted with richest blues and purple, mingled with green and crimson to a smaller extent, these all being, not as sometimes described, iridescent or changeable, but positive colours independent of the incidence of light, and, for the most part, possessing great depth and fulness: the sail-like erectile membrane is transparent, tinted towards the edge with a lovely rose-pink hue, the colours arranged in a peculiar fringe-like manner.

When examined anatomically, the bladder is found to be composed of two walls of membrane, which are lined with cilia, and have between them the nutritive food which supplies the place of the blood. Besides this, the double membrane is turned in, or inverted, like a stocking prepared for putting on; and thus, there is a bladder within a bladder, both having double walls; the inner (pneumatocyst) much smaller than the outer (pneumatophone), and contracted at the point, where it is turned in to the almost imperceptible orifice. The inner sends up closed tubular folds into the crest, which, being arrested by the membranous walls of the outer sac, give to the sail that appearance of verticle wrinkles which is so conspicuous. When it is filled with the air the body is almost projected out of the water. In order to descend, it is necessary to compress itself or dispel the air, in part, for the centre of gravity in the animal is displaced, according as the air is in the vesicle, or in the crest. When the last is distended it rises out of the water, and becomes nearly vertical; in short, it then becomes a sort of sail, the floating appendages beneath the body are of divers kinds. Some of these are reproductive individuals; some are nurses, some are tentacles; finally there are organs designated under the name of Surdes by French naturalists; probes or suckers, we may call them, forming offensive and defensive arms truly formidable; for these elegant creatures are terrible antagonists. Dusteste the veracious historian of the Antilles, relates the following:—"This 'galley' (our Physalia), however agreeable to the sight, is most dangerous to the body, for I can assert that it is freighted with the worst merchandise which floats on the sea. I speak as a naturalist, and as having made experiments at my own personal cost. One day when sailing at sea in a small boat, I perceived one of these little 'galleys,' and was curious to see the form of the animal; but I had scarcely seized it, when all its fibres seemed to clasp my hand, covering it as with bird-lime, and scarcely had I felt it in all its freshness (for it was very cold to the touch), when it seemed as if I had plunged my arm up to the shoulder in a cauldron of boiling water. This was accompanied with a pain so strange, that it was only with a violent effort I could restrain myself from crying aloud."

Another voyager, Lablind in his "Voyage aux Antilles," relates as follows:—"One day as I was bathing with some friends in a bay in front of the house where I dwelt, while my friends fished for sardines for breakfast, I amused myself by diving in the manner of the native Carribeans, under the wave about to break; having reached the other side of one great wave I had gained the open sea, and was returning on the top of the next wave towards the shore. My rashness nearly cost me my life:—a Physalia, many of which were stranded upon the beach, fixed itself upon my left shoulder at the moment the wave landed me on the beach. I promptly detached it, but many of its filaments remained glued to my skin, and the pain I experienced immediately was so intense that I nearly fainted. I seized an oil flask which was at hand, and swallowed one half, while I rubbed my arm with the other: this restored me to myself, and I returned to the house, where two hours of repose relieved the pain, which disappeared altogether during the night."

Mr. Bennett who accompanied the exploring expedition under Admiral Fitzroy as naturalist, ventured to test the powers of the Physalia. "On one occasion" he says, "I tried the experiment of its stinging powers upon myself intentionally. When I seized it by the bladder portion, it raised the long cables by muscular contraction of the bands situated at the base of the feelers, and entwining the slender appendages about my hand and finger, inflicting severe and peculiarly pungent pain, it adhered most tenaciously at the same time, so as to be extremely difficult of removal: the stinging continued during the whole time that the minutest portion of the tentacular remained adherent to the skin. I soon found that the effects were not confined to the acute pungency inflicted, but produced a great degree of constitutional irritation; the pain extended upwards along the arm, increasing not only in extent, but in severity, apparently acting along the course of the absorbents, and could only be compared to a severe rheumatic attack. The pulse was accelerated, and a feverish state of the whole system produced, the muscles of the chest even were affected, the same distressing pain being felt on taking a full respiration as obtains in a case of acute rheumatism. The secondary effects were very severe, continuing for nearly three-quarters of an hour; the duration being probably longer in consequence of the time and delay occasioned by removing the tentacula from the skin to which they adhered by the aid of the stinging capsules, with an annoying degree of tenacity. On the whole being removed, the pain began to abate; but during the day a peculiar numbness was felt, accompanied by an increased temperature in the limb on which the sting had been inflicted. For some hours afterwards the skin displayed white elevations, or weals on the parts stung, similar to those resulting from the poison of the stinging nettle. The intensity of the pain depends in some degree upon the size and consequent power of the creature. After it has been removed from the water for some time the stinging property, although still continuing to act, is found to have perceptibly diminished. I have observed also that this irritative power is retained for some weeks after the death of the animal in the vesicles of the cables, and even linen cloth which has been used for wiping off the adhering tentacles when touched, still retained the pungency, although it had not the power of producing such violent constitutional irritation."

The question has been much agitated without being positively resolved, whether the Physalia are venomous or not: if they can kill or make sick the man or animal which swallows them. Listen to the opinions of M. Ricard Madiana, a Physician of Guadalope, who made direct experiments, with a view to settling the question. "Many inhabitants of the Antilles" he says, say that the 'galleys' are poisonous, and that the negroes make use of them, after being dried and powdered, to poison both men and animals. The fishermen of the islands also believe that fish which have swallowed them become deleterious, and poison those who eat them, a prejudice which has been adopted by many travellers, and has even found its way into scientific books. We can state, as the result of direct experiment, that though the 'galley' will burn the ignorant hand which is touched by its tentacles, when dried in the sun and pulverized, it becomes mere grains of dead matter, producing no effect whatever upon the animal economy."—From *The Ocean World*, by Louis Figuier. London: Chapman and Hall.

MARS.

This planet, which is only about twice the size of the Moon, and not much more than half as large as our own globe, is yet peculiarly interesting to us, as presenting the most intelligible features of any object within our reach. In overtaking him about once in two years we find, as he turns to us his round sunny face, that his supposed malignant aspect is changed into that of a miniature Earth, which we might, without much extravagance, imagine to be habitable by man. Not every *opposition*, however, as it is called, admits of an equally near prospect. The orbits of both the Earth and Mars are elliptical, and not fixed with respect to each other, and no two following oppositions happen in the same part of either orbit, so that the most favourable possible juncture, when the Earth is furthest from the Sun and Mars nearest, occurs ordinarily but once in 15 years, when the diameter of Mars, only 13″ in reversed circumstances, expands to 23″·5. Every opposition, however, should set the telescope to work; and we will proceed to describe what we may expect to see.

1. The *Phases*. These are not remarkable: in opposition, a full moon rising through ruddy haze, and, with sufficient power, larger than our Moon to the naked eye: in other situations a dull gibbosity, never sinking to quadrature. Mädler stated at one time that this phasis is always narrower than it should be by calculation; but in a subsequent publication the remark is not repeated. Pastorff thought he saw a phosphorescence on the dark part: but this was probably a deception.

2. The *Dark Spots*. The disc, when well seen, is usually mapped out in a way which gives at once the impression of land and water: the bright part is orange,—according to Secchi, sometimes dotted with red, brown and greenish points; Beers and Mädler think it much less red than to the naked eye: the darker spaces, which vary greatly in depth of tone, are of a dull grey-green, or according to Secchi, bluish, possessing the aspect of a fluid absorbent of the solar rays. If so, the proportion of land to water on the Earth is reversed on Mars: on the Earth every continent is an island; on Mars all seas are lakes; (and those, according to Jacob and Secchi, like our own continents, chiefly confined to one side of the globe; so that the habitable area may possibly be much more alike than the diameter of the planets. From the different distribution of the water (if such it be), long narrow straits are more common than on the Earth: Dawes has observed a singular forked shading, as if of two great contiguous estuaries. The dark spots were early seen, and a long series of drawings is extant from Hooke, Cassini, and Campani, in 1666, to Jacob, Secchi, De La Rue, Lassell, Phillips, Lockyer, Dawes, and others in the present day, with some general correspondence, but a difference of detail; which seems do impart to differences in telescopes, eyes, climates, and skill in delineation: in part to altered projection owing to the inclination of the axis, shewing us sometimes more of N., sometimes of S. hemisphere: and in part also to changes in the planet's atmosphere. The older observers thought the spots variable: Herschel I. perhaps took the lead in supposing them to be permanent, an idea which Kunowsky, as recently as 1822, fancied was due to himself. Schröter's work on Mars, the 'Areographische Fragmente,' which was to have contained 224 figures, was unfortunately left in MS. at his death in 1816, but he has stated that he and Olbers found them vary rapidly. Beers and Mädler took up the subject with great spirit at peculiarly favourable opposition in 1830, recovered some of Kunowsky's spots, and from their further observations in 1832, 1834, and 1837, though the same hemisphere was not always equally visible, inferred their permanence. Mädler, a little shaken as to this in 1839, retrogrades still further at Dorpat in 1841: the drawings, however, of later observers exhibit substantially many of the same forms, and notwithstanding numerous discrepancies, there seems sufficient evidence that most of the spots are really part of the surface. The distant view of the Earth, indeed, might be much of this nature; its outlines at one time distinct, at another confused or distorted by clouds: besides, one affirmative—the re-appearance of a spot—proves more, where there may be hindrances, than can be disproved by many negatives. At present, we could only form an approximate map of Mars; nor shall we ever know the N. so well as the S. hemisphere, as it is turned towards us in the planet's aphelion, even were its markings equally defined, which Beers and Mädler deny. Lockyer too finds them clearer during the summer than the winter of the planet. Under favourable circumstances the dusky spots are not difficult objects; I have repeatedly been able to draw them with my 5½ f. achromatic; a much smaller instrument will sometimes shew the darker ones plainly; while, on other parts of the globe, they are feeble even in large telescopes. Their motion will be very evident, and as the rotation is completed, according to B. and M., in 24^h. 37^m. 24^s. they will not vary greatly from night to night at the same hour.

3. The *Polar Snows*. A circular spot on each hemisphere is so white and luminous as to have occasionally remained visible when a cloud obscured the planet: and frequently to seem, from irradiation, to project beyond the limb, as

I have myself noticed. These zones were figured by Maraldi in 1704, who says they had been occasionally seen for 50 years; in fact they could not long escape the telescope. They were thought to resemble snow before Herschel I.'s time; he gave consistency to the idea by ascertaining that they decreased during the summer, and increased during the winter of Mars, and Beers and Mädler have fully confirmed it, with the addition that the S. polar spot has a greater variety of extent, corresponding with its greater variety of climate from the excentricity of the orbit. Each pole comes alternately into sight, and both are sometimes visible on the edge at once, when the opposition of Mars concurs with his equinox. Herschel I. found they were not (or not always) opposite each other, both being sometimes in or out of the disc at the same time. Mädler and Secchi, with the admirable achromatic at Rome, of $9\frac{6}{10}$ in. aperture and 15 f. focus, bearing ordinarily a power of 1000, found the N. zone concentric with the axis, but the S. considerably excentric. It has been suggested by Beers and Mädler that the poles of cold, like those on the Earth, may not coincide with the poles of rotation;—still they should be diametrically opposite. These observers found in 1837 the N. pole surrounded by a conspicuous dark zone, the only well-marked spot in sight, which they thought might possibly be a marsh at the edge of the melting snow: in 1839 Mädler perceived it had decreased; in 1841 it was no longer visible. About the opposition in 1856 I had interesting views of these zones, which did not seem exactly opposite to each other: the S. was surrounded by a very dark region, never seen by Beers and Mädler; on the intervening limbs were occasionally luminous regions, so bright by contrast as to give an impression of *four* patches of snow, as in one of Cassini's figures in 1666: these were also seen by Secchi at the same time. In 1845 Mitchell with a great achromatic in America noticed a very dark spot in the centre of the snow, which disappeared the next night: at another time he saw some movements in a small bright spot at the edge of the snow. Secchi in 1858 found the appearances at the poles irreconcilable with the idea of circular caps, and was forced to adopt the supposition of complicated and lobate forms.

4. The *Atmosphere*. Such an appendage is implied in the formation of snow, the varying outline or distinctness of the dark spots, and their usual disappearance towards the limb: Beers and Mädler found them also better defined in the summer than the winter of Mars. Maraldi saw and delineated a dusky belt for a considerable time in 1704; something like it also appears in the designs of Schroter, who, from movements in these belts, inferred winds as rapid as our own. Some of Herschel I.'s figures shew white belts, and he says that besides the permanent spots he often noticed occasional changes of partial bright belts, and once a darkish one; we should however, perhaps, have expected that clouds would always reflect a brighter light than land or water. Dawes has at times noticed changeable white spots, as from clouds or snow. The bright 'menisci' or crescents which some observers have seen illuminating the E. and W. borders of the disc may have had an atmospheric cause, as well as the numerous patches of yellowish and bluish light upon the limb described by Mädler, at Dorpat, in 1841. The atmosphere, according to Dawes, is only of moderate density; and seems not to be the cause of the ruddy tinge, as this is most decided in the centre of the disc, while in 1864 he noticed (as indeed I did in 1862) patches of greenish light near the limb. Huggins has also found the planet reddest when its atmosphere was clearest, and remarks that the colour does not affect the snow. The spectroscope shews a vaporous envelope similar to, but probably not identical with, our own. Cassini exceeded all bounds in supposing that the atmosphere could obscure small stars at some distance; this effect, resulting from the contraction of the pupil in a bright light, was imperceptible in the great telescopes of Herschel I., and the idea has been overthrown by the experience of South, who has seen one contact and two occultations of stars without change: in the last, his great achromatic, $11\frac{7}{8}$ inches aperture and nearly 19 feet focus, actually shewed the star neatly dichotomized in emerging. This is not surprising, for the atmosphere, if in proportion to ours, would not extend more than $0''3$ beyond the limb when nearest to the Earth.

It is worthy of notice that Dawes can detect no ellipticity in this planetary globe.

A favourable opposition will occur in 1877.—*From Celestial Objects for Common Telescopes.* By the Rev. S. W. Webb, M.A., F.R.A.S. London: Longmans.

ASCENSION ISLAND.

The volcanic island of Ascension, as approached from the sea, has not so striking an appearance as St. Helena; but owing to its peculiar and predominant rufous colour, and desolate aspect, it is not a little remarkable. Sloping rocks of the roughest lava, broken here and there by sandy bays, stretch along the shore, and the island consists of an irregular series of conical hills of various heights, above which towers Green Mountain, 2800 feet high, whose summit is crowned with trees and green fields, and offers a strong contrast to the other hills, which are reddish or brown, according to the colour of the ashes and cinders of which they are composed. The settlement of George Town is entirely naval in its character, being formed of a number of departmental officers, and of marines, who are all borne on the books of H.M.S. "Flora," 40 guns, which lies off this place, and whose captain is styled the "Captain of the Island." Everything is conducted with the strictest reference to naval discipline, and the island is nothing more nor less than a ship ashore. The landing-place is very indifferent, mere steps cut in the rock, and therefore entirely inaccessible in bad weather. It is well known that the great waves of the Atlantic often set in upon the rock in the form of *rollers*, even in fine weather, and it can never be predicted when they may make their appearance; but whenever they do so all communication between the ships and the shore is cut off, except by signal. It is one of the duties of the master of the "Flora" to direct a flag to be hoisted on the signal-hill when this state of things occurs, and that is pretty frequently.

As our stay was to be limited to one day I was thankful that the weather was calm and the sea permitted us to land; and having done so, I bent my steps in the direction of South-West Bay, with the intention of visiting "Wide-awake Fair," and at the same time exploring some of the geological features of this remarkable island. The whole of Ascension is an erupted mass, the antiquity of which can only be judged of by the worn condition of its surface; but it is entirely the product of a once active, but long since extinct, volcano. Green Mountain, the culminating point, is probably the parent cone, around which a great number of secondary cones and craters are clustered, the rough trachytic lavas of which run sloping to the beach round the greater part of the island.

One or two tolerable roads have been formed, which greatly save the labour of walking in a country where the surface of the ground is heaped with rough and sharp-pointed cinders, which look like the product of a myriad furnaces, and to which the "black country" of Staffordshire is a trifle. From these arise conical hills of a reddish colour, covered with fine ashes, which crackle under the feet, and from out of which peep the rounded overhanging ledges formed by molten lava. Down these hills streams of water have poured during the brief and uncertain wet seasons, forming water-courses which run between the rounded knolls, which look like *roches moutonnées* at the base, and intersect the lava-fields down to the beach. For rain falls occasionally on the island, though unfrequently; and on the day of our arrival it was wet: it rained all night, and next morning Green Mountain was enveloped in cloud. Other hills are hollow and crateriform, the sides formed of loose masses of slag or clinker of various sizes. Up one of these I clambered, and found the interior deep and cup-shaped, but incomplete on one side, the bottom being a small level deposit of mud and sand, produced by the washings of the cinders in wet weather; among these cinders I found several fragments of exploded volcanic bombs, such as are described and figured by Mr. Darwin in his notice of the island.

From this elevation the view was most striking: a deep and broad rocky valley in the foreground, covered with screaming sea-fowl, beyond which rose an irregular series of naked and desolate conical hills piled one above another in chaotic confusion, but surmounted by the verdant and fertile heights of Green Mountain, upon which may be descried trees, meadows and pastures, like the Delectable Mountains seen afar off by the pilgrims.

It must not be supposed, however, that the surface of the island is absolutely without vegetation. The cinders in many places are incrusted with white and gray lichens (Parmelia and Roscella). Some are overgrown with more luxuriant species, as Physcia cæsia, and I also observed a deep-green incrusting lichen on the sea-shore. Many spots, also, in the watercourses, are quite cheerful with patches of bright green, and several flowers spring up here and there which have escaped from the gardens on Green Mountain. I was informed that some person had been in the habit of scattering seeds over various parts of the island. I noticed two species of grasses, a Sonchus, and Aster with scented leaves, &c. The most common plants, however, were the castor-oil (Ricinus), a very handsome yellow poppy with prickly white-veined leaves, and a large-flowered plant (Vinca rosea) which is known on the island as the Madagascar Rose, and is reported to have been imported from thence.

Among this vegetation a few insects occur: large red-winged locusts fly about among the rocks, and a fat black cricket is common—I also saw a pale brown one, but could not catch it. A little moth, very prettily marked, is common wherever a certain succulent plant occurred, and flew about among the rocks, settling for a moment and then taking wing again, unless it happened to get in the shelter of a crevice in the honeycomb of a cinder, where it seemed to consider itself safe. A somewhat larger pale brown moth I also noticed from time to time; but it flew rapidly and was aided by a strong breeze which was blowing, and appears usually to be blowing, over the island.

Besides these insects I saw carrion flies upon the rocks, a hunting spider, and numerous small carrion beetles (Dermestes) in situations to be presently mentioned.

The lava and cinders in the neighbourhood of South-West Bay are whitened here and there by the dung of sea-birds; but the extraordinary scene of the breeding-place of the terns, or wide-awakes, and called "Wide-awake Fair," is a long valley situated about half a mile from the sea in the south-eastern part of the island. The approach to this valley is indicated by an overpowering odour arising from their deposits, which, however, do not accumulate as in some guano islands. Seen from the hill above this valley looks as though a light fall of snow had partially whitened it; but in no place was there any appreciable depth of deposit. The birds, themselves are in immense numbers, hovering over the valley, screaming and making various discordant noises, which, heard at a distance, sound like the murmur of a vast crowd. They are elegant and graceful birds, glossy black above and snowy white beneath, with white foreheads, straight compressed beaks and long forked tails: they measured 2 ft. 6in. from tip to tip of the wings, which are long and pointed. As soon as a visitor makes his appearance among the nests, numberless birds arise screaming in the air, and form a complete canopy over his head; some, bolder than the rest, fly so close that it is the easiest thing in the world to knock them down with a stick, and it is even necessary to strike at them occasionally and give them a slight tap to admonish them not to use their bills against one's face. Meantime crowds of little ones, all ages and sizes, some covered with a grey down and others almost fully fledged, run hither and thither, tumbling over the stones in their hurry to escape from the intruder. Here a chick has but just broken the egg, and the parent bird is nestling over it, and does not leave it until you arrive so close that you could stretch out your arm and take it up. Eggs lay scattered all over the place, deposited in little hollows in the sand, about as large as the palm of the hand, which is all the nest that the "wide-awake" considers necessary; and in several of the rocky crevices in which these eggs were deposited the skeleton or half-decayed body of an adult bird, but more frequently a young one, upon which a number of carrion beetles were busy, showed where it had died and rotted beside the nest.

At the particular season at which I visited this singular spot, the birds were in every stage of growth, from the newly-hatched chick to the bird with first year's plumage, flying with the rest. Eggs also were abundant, but never more than one in the same nest; and although the parent bird was in some cases sitting upon fresh or half-hatched ones, in a great many instances the eggs were cracked, and either rotten or dried up. Many that I picked up felt light and empty, although scarcely injured, and others which I broke contained carrion beetles or their grubs. The eggs were very variously marked, and had not a little variety of form: the common appearance of them was round at one end and pointed at the other, about the size of a plover's egg, and in colour a whitish ground, blotched with faint purplish and distinct rich brown blotches, which often formed a ring round the larger end; but some which I noticed were long and pointed at both ends, and without blotches, but speckled with small purplish and brown spots. There was no other kind of bird, however, visible in the whole valley.

It would be easy for any person to fill a sack with adult birds, although he possessed no other weapon than a stick; and too many of the visitors are not content without maiming a number in mere wantonness; so that the poor birds can hardly be said to dwell unmolested; nevertheless, as long at least as they have nests and eggs to look after, they evince what I should characterize as boldness rather than tameness. I should consider the Solan geese on the Bass Rock as tamer than the "wide-awakes" of Ascension.

Before leaving the island I visited the turtle-ponds, where these animals are kept in store; for Ascension, barren and desolate as it is, has yet one product in which it is not exceeded by any part of the world, viz., turtle. The sandy bays of the island are visited by great numbers of these unwieldy and valuable reptiles, which, entirely marine and oceanic in their habits, visit the shore solely for the deposition of their eggs, and are secured on these occasions by being cut off from their retreat to the sea and turned over on their backs, and then conveyed at leisure to the reservoirs provided for their reception. The sandy shore adjoining George Town, I was informed, is no longer so rich and profitable a beach as it once was, the reason probably being the turtle, like birds of passage return again and again to the same spot to deposit their eggs; and on this beach, as being most accessible, the greatest number of turtle have been turned, so that but few visit it at present. No one but the government authorities is allowed to interfere with this source of emolument, and the turtle form a staple article of food upon the island, being served out twice a week; but the animals are sent to persons in authority in England, and are supplied to merchant ships at the rate of £2 10s. each. The season was just over when I visited Ascension, and the turtle-ponds contained eighty-two animals. These ponds, two in number, were on the sea-beach, each 50 or 60 feet square, and three or four feet deep, and the sea is allowed to wash into them through two grated channels. All the turtle, however, were in one of these enclosures, and could be seen swimming about, ever and anon raising their stupid-looking heads above the surface and snorting out a jet of water. They seemed to crowd together in one corner, where each wave as it broke sent a rush of fresh sea-water into the pond. Numerous small fishes and crabs swam about them unmolested; but on inquiry I learned that they are never fed, although they are not unfrequently kept in the reservoirs for a year or more after capture. They were very variously marked, some with large black spots, others with indistinct radiating streaks upon the plates, and several had a large white patch in the middle of the carapace. One in particular was conspicuous from its very peculiar form. Instead of being gently rounded as usual, the carapace was high and terminated in a ridge, which, as it swam about, was elevated fully six inches above the water— a conformation which it appears occasionally, although rarely, occurs. While I was watching them, preparations were made for getting one out of the pond. A negro walked into the midst of them, and having selected one, he tied a cord round one of the anterior fins, by which it was pulled by several other negroes out of the pond by main force, and laid upon its back on a small four-wheeled carriage prepared for it, in which helpless position it was dragged away without a struggle.

On the lava rock adjacent, where the waves break with great violence, numbers of beautifully coloured crabs (Grapsi, n. s.) ran actively about; the pools abounded with large purple-spined Echini, ensconced in round hollows, and beautiful azure and banded rock fish; but the only seaweed I observed was the cosmopolitan peacock's-tail (Padina pavonia). My exploration, however, was necessarily brief, as I was obliged forthwith to rejoin the ship.—*Collingwood's Rambles of a Naturalist.* London: J. Murray.

THE PENGUIN.

"This singular bird," remarks Mr. E. L. Layard (in his recently published "Birds of South Africa"), "is very common on all our coasts, swimming to great distances out to sea. I once had the pleasure of visiting a breeding-place of this penguin, known as Seal Island, a lonely rock in the centre of False Bay. It can only be approached in certain winds, as the surf breaks on it with great violence. The penguins occupy the lower ledges by hundreds, having dug their holes among the rocks. As we walked over the stones, the birds rushed out at us, snapping at our legs, and drawing blood plentifully from the naked feet of the sailors, in defence of their one solitary large white egg, which is abruptly pointed at the small end, and is laid on the bare ground without any protection from the damp. When not sitting on their eggs, these birds stand upright on the rocks in long rows, balanced by their stiff tails. They feed exclusively on fish, which they overtake beneath the surface by their swiftness in swimming." Mr. Darwin relates in his Journal an encounter with a bird of this very species in one of the Falkland Islands. "One day," he remarks, "having placed myself between a penguin (*Spheniscus demersus*) and the water, I was much amused by watching its habits. It was a brave bird; and, till reaching the sea, it regularly fought and drove me backwards. Nothing less than heavy blows would have stopped him; every inch gained he firmly kept, standing close before me, erect and determined. When thus opposed, he continually rolled his head from side to side, in a very odd manner, as if the power of vision only lay in the anterior and basal part of each eye. This bird is commonly called the "jackass penguin," from its habit, while on shore, of throwing its head backwards, and making a strange noise, very like the braying of that animal; but while at sea and undisturbed, its note is deep and solemn, and is often heard in the night-time. In diving, its little plumeless wings are used as fins, but on the land, as front-legs. When crawling (it may be said on four legs) through the tussocks, or on the side of a grassy cliff, it moved so very quickly that it might readily have been mistaken for a quadruped. When at sea, and fishing, it comes to the surface, for the purpose of breathing, with such a spring, and dives again so instantaneously, that I defy any one at first sight to be sure that it is not a fish leaping for sport."

The late Admiral Fitzroy gave the following interesting account of the mode in which these same penguins feed their young, as observed by him in Noir Island, of the Fuegian group. "Multitudes of penguins were swarming together in some parts of the island, among the bushes and tussac grass near the shore, having gone there for the purpose of moulting and rearing their young. They were very valiant in self-defence, and ran open-mouthed, by dozens, at any one who invaded their territory, little knowing how soon a stick would scatter them on the ground. The young were good eating, but the others proved to be black and tough when cooked. The manner in which they feed their young is curious and rather amusing. The old bird gets on a little eminence, and makes a great noise (between quacking and braying), holding its head up in the air, as if it were haranguing the penguinnary, while the young one stands close to it, but a little lower. The old bird, having continued its clatter for about a minute, puts its head down and opens its mouth widely, into which the young one thrusts its head, and then appears to suck from the throat of its parent for a minute or two, after which the clatter is repeated, and the young one is again fed; this continues for about ten minutes. I observed some which were moulting make the same noise, and then apparently swallow what they had thus supplied themselves with;

so in this way, I suppose, they are furnished with subsistence during the time that they cannot seek it in the water." In other words, we conclude that the moulting birds are fed as the young are fed.

At the north end of Macquarie Island (in lat. 55 deg. south, or in about the corresponding parallel of that of Edinburgh, Copenhagen, and Moscow, in the warmer northern hemisphere—which bleak islet is actually the abode of a peculiar species of parrakeet, the southernmost of any known), Mr. G. Bennett saw a colony of penguins which covered an extent of thirty or forty acres. He describes the number of penguins collected together at this spot as immense, but observes that it would be almost impossible to guess at it with any near approach to truth, as, during the whole of the day and night, 30,000 or 40,000 are continually landing and an equal number going to sea. "They are arranged, when on shore, in as compact a manner and in as regular ranks as a regiment of soldiers; they are classed with the greatest order, the young birds being in one situation, the moulting birds in another, the sitting birds in a third, the clean birds in a fourth, etc., and so strictly do birds in similar conditions congregate, that should a bird that is moulting intrude itself among those which are clean, it is immediately ejected from them. The females hatch the eggs by keeping them close between the thighs, and if approached during the time of incubation, move away, carrying their eggs with them. At this time the male bird goes to sea and collects food for the female, which becomes very fat. [Hence, indeed, the name of penguin, from *pinguis*.] After the young is hatched both parents go to sea, and bring home food for it; it soon becomes so fat as scarcely to be able to walk, the old birds getting very thin. They sit quite upright in their roosting-places, and walk in the erect position until they arrive at the beach, when they throw themselves on their breasts in order to encounter the very heavy sea met with at their landing-place." The same author mentions several instances of the appearance of penguins at a considerable distance from any known land. They generally, however, indicate its neighbourhood.

This very remarkable family of sea-fowl is exclusively austral, and the species have no particular affinity for the awks and puffins of the northern hemisphere. In the condition of their wings they resemble the now probably extinct great awk (*Alca impenhis*), whereas all of the other species of the awk family are capable of flight. As Mr. Gould remarks, the penguins (*Spheniscidæ*) are considerably diversified in form amongst themselves, and have therefore been arranged in as many as six genera, while the species known are perhaps not more than fifteen in number. "The generality of them," as mentioned by that naturalist, "are adorned with many beautifully coloured markings, and in some instances with plumes which hang gracefully behind their heads. The sexes are alike in colour." Weddell remarks of the large king penguin, as observed by him in the island of South Georgia, "In pride these birds are perhaps not surpassed even by the peacock, to which, in beauty of plumage, they are indeed very little inferior. [This, however, is saying rather too much for them.] During the time of moulting they seem to repel each other with disgust on account of the ragged state of their coats; but as they arrive at the maximum of splendour, they reassemble, and no one who has not completed his plumage is allowed to enter the community. Their habit of frequently looking down their front and sides, in order to contemplate the perfection of their exterior brilliancy, and to remove any speck which might sully it, is truly amusing to an observer." The stuffed specimens of this genus, seen generally in museums, are distended so exceedingly out of all shape that they fail to convey even a tolerably correct idea of the appearance of the birds as seen alive—*Land and Water*, March 14.

THE STAR-FISH.—M. Jourdain has just published a splendid memoir on the anatomy of the starfish, *Asteracanthion rubens*. He finds that, as formerly pointed out by Milne Edwards, the general cavity of the body is completely closed. It is filled with a limpid liquid charged with corpuscles of a diameter of about 1-60th of a millimètre. These globules are covered with cilia. He has not been able to discover the wonderful circulatory apparatus which is so frequently described by writers on Echinodermata; and he believes the so-called heart to be nothing more than a glandular body. M. Jourdain's essay deserves the attention of anatomists.—*London Review*.

Meetings of Learned Societies.

LINNÆAN SOCIETY.

March 5.—G. Bentham, Esq., President, in the chair. Worthington G. Smith, Esq., was elected a Fellow. The following paper was read:—1. "On some remarkable Mimetic Analogies among African Butterflies," by R. Trimen, Esq., communicated by Dr. Trimen. It was announced that the first part of Vol. XXVI. of the Society's Transactions was ready for distribution.

March 19.—G. Bentham, President, in the chair. Mr. J. G. Baker, F.L.S., exhibited, from the herbarium of the Royal Gardens, Kew, an extensive series of specimens of the British species of Primula described in Mr. Darwin's paper, and made some observations upon the characters by which they are distinguished. Mr. W. Andrews, M.R.I.A., exhibited drawings, the size of life, of the head of Ziphius Sowerbiensis, a specimen of which rare Cetacean was stranded in Brandon Bay, County Kerry, about three years since. The head was photographed on the spot, and the drawings were enlarged from the photographs. The following paper was read:—1. "On the specific differences between Primula veris *Brit. Fl.* (var. Officinalis, *Linn.*), and P. vulgaris *Brit. Fl.* (var. acaulis, *Linn.*), and P. elatior, *Jacq.*, and on the hybrid nature of the common Oxlip; with Supplementary Remarks on naturally produced Hybrids in the genus Verbascum," by C. Darwin, Esq. The author adopted the view that the Cowslip, Primrose, and Bardfield Oxlip, whose claims to be admitted as species have been discussed at greater length than those of almost any other plants, are really distinct; and that the common Oxlip found in most parts of England is a hybrid between P. veris and P. vulgaris. These views were supported by some rather lengthy observations, amongst which it was noted that the plants emit a different odour; and that while the Cowslip was habitually visited by humble-bees of various kinds, the Primrose was never visited by the larger and very rarely by the smaller kinds of humble-bee, so that the nectar in the two plants must differ much, as nothing in the structure of the flowers could determine the visits of different insects. The Primrose, when legitimately fertilised, produced on an average many more seeds than the Cowslip, in about the proportion of 100 to 55; moreover, the Cowslip and Primrose will not cross either way except with considerable difficulty. A long series of observations and experiments was recorded to show that the common Oxlip is a hybrid between the Cowslip and the Primrose. This case was regarded as extremely interesting, for scarcely any instance is known of a hybrid spontaneously arising in such large numbers over so wide an extent of country as the common Oxlip, which is found almost everywhere throughout England, where the Cowslip and Primrose both grow. Of the Primula elatior, the author observed, that it inhabited districts where neither the Primrose nor Cowslip live, and though in general appearance it differs so much that no one accustomed to see both in a living state would afterwards confound them, yet there is scarcely more than a single character, namely, the linear oblong capsule, equalling the calyx in length, by which they can be distinctly defined. Of this species, plants propagated by seed in a garden during twenty-five years have kept constant, excepting that in some cases the flowers varied a little in tint and size. Although we may feel confident, observed the author, that P. veris, vulgaris, and elatior, as well as the other species of the genus, are all descended from some primordial form, yet, from the facts cited, we may conclude that they are now as fixed in character as very many other forms which are universally ranked as species; consequently they have as good a right to receive distinct specific names as have, for instance, the ass, the quagga, and the zebra. Reverting to the statement that scarcely another instance could be given of a hybrid spontaneously arising in such large numbers over so wide an extent of country as the common Oxlip, the author went on to observe that perhaps the number of well-ascertained cases of naturally-produced hybrid Willows was equally great. Numerous spontaneous hybrids between several species of Cistus have been found near Narbonne, and carefully described by M. Timbal-Lagrave; and some hybrids between an Aceras and Orchis have been observed by Dr. Weddell. The Verbascum hybrids are supposed to have often originated in a state of nature, but the cases require verification. The author had, however, taken in a wild plant for experimental purposes, which, when it flowered, proved to be plainly different from those species of the genus which grew in the neighbourhood, and its subsequent behaviour proved it to be without doubt a hybrid. In the field whence this plant had been removed, thirty-three intermediate plants (between Thapsus and Lychnites) were subsequently discovered, and these proved to be absolutely barren. 2. "Notes on the Discovery of Planaria terrestris in England," by Sir John Lubbock, Bart.

Entomological Society.

At the meeting March 16 Mr. H. W. Bates, President, in the chair, Mr. C. Carrington was elected a Member.—Mr. F. Smith exhibited a larva from Brazil, which was described as forming a large social cocoon, the size of a man's head, within which each individual larva formed a separate cocoon before its change to the pupa. The larva appeared to be that of a butterfly, whilst the formation of the separate cocoons was suggestive of a Bombyx.—Mr. Stainton called attention to the fact that Herr Hartmann, of Munich, had bred a Trochilium, a Grapholitha, and a Gelechia, from twigs of juniper, upon which he had observed some gall-like swellings; an examination of juniper bushes during the spring would probably lead to the discovery in this country of the two last-mentioned insects.—The President announced the proximate publication of the first part of a universal catalogue of Coleoptera by Dr. Gemminger and Baron Edgar von Harold.—Mr. F. Smith read a paper on Ants from the *Guardian* of 1713, and criticised the same, with a view to show that the bulk, if not the whole, of the detailed and circumstantial narration therein contained was not a record of actual observation, but was attributable to the imagination of the writer.

Royal Microscopical Society.

At the meeting on March 11th, the Rev. J. B. Reade, F.R.S., Vice President, in the chair—a paper was read by Dr. Murie, F.L.S., "On the Arrangement of Microscopic Objects in a Cabinet." Every microscopist who possess a large number of slides must have found it difficult to classify them in a satisfactory manner. Experience has shewn us that the method recommended by Dr. Murie is the best that can be adopted. His plan is to arrange them in their zoological order. Separating them first into the broad distinction of mineral, vegetable, or animal, he subdivides these into different organs and structures, and thus each falls into its proper place, and is easily found when wanted. His method of lettering and numbering each slide so as to admit of the indefinite addition of others from time to time without disturbing the order of those already catalogued, is rather too complex for us to describe here; but the paper will no doubt be a valuable one for reference. Dr. Murie, arranged in 1864 the collection of Microscopic objects in the possession of the Royal College of Surgeons (more than 16,000 slides), and is consequently a good authority on the subject. Dr. Cuthbert Collingwood read a paper "On the Coloration of the Sea in various parts of the world." That the increased advantages offered by the society to its fellows since its valuable library and cabinet have been made available during the day in its own rooms are highly appreciated, is becoming apparent in many ways, and in none more so than by the valuable gifts which have been lately made as additions to its collection. We recently noticed the present by Dr. Wallich of more than 2,000 mounted objects, and some volumes of his manuscript notes and drawings; and we have now the pleasure of recording the handsome gift by Mr. Joseph Beck of about 420 slides of bone sections, duplicates of those mentioned in the Histological Catalogue of the College of Surgeons. The president also announced that a gentleman had offered, through Mr. Henry Lee, to present to the society a complete series of any class of objects that might be thought most desirable, to the amount of £20, on condition that four or five others would also contribute perfect series in different departments of natural history, each according to his means. The Rev. Lord Sidney Godolphin Osborne sent for exhibition enlarged models of the gizzard of a rotifer; the paper accompanying them will be discussed at the next meeting. Mr. Crouch exhibited a microscope fitted with a glass stage, like those of M. Nachet, of Paris, so strongly recommended by Dr. Carpenter. Various presents of books were mentioned, and six gentlemen were elected fellows of the society.

GEOLOGICAL SOCIETY.

At the meeting on March 11th, Professor Huxley, F.R.S. in the chair.—An interesting and elaborate paper by Mr. Prestwich, F.R.S., was read "On the structure of the Crag." He exhibited a series of sections in Norfolk and Suffolk, and many fine specimens of fossils. He spoke of the great impulse palæontology had received in 1848 by the discovery in the crag of vast deposits of coprolites by Professor Henslow. He considered the coralline crag at great length with its organic remains, and mentioned the researches of Dr. Falconer amongst its pachyderms. He thought the great mass of the fossils of the coralline crag were extraneous, being derived from older beds. Of the numerous mollusca of the crag (186 species) a large percentage were recent. He proceeded to draw a contrast between the English crag and its foreign equivalents, and considered it well established that the crag *noir* of Antwerp was older than the coralline crag. Mr. Searles Wood, who was called on to open a discussion, thought the crag a deep sea formation, from the entire absence in it of estuarine remains. Sir C. Lyell thought the paper ought not to lead to any important alteration in the views of geologists regarding the climate and age of the crag period. Referring to a piece of porphyry found in the crag which was exhibited on the table, he thought it had been brought from a distance on floating ice, and mentioned how rocks from the Arctic seas were carried on icebergs as far south as the Azores, and instanced some facts of this character which had come to his knowledge. Mr. Henry Woodward read a list of the crustacea of the crag, which were for the greater part identical with recent British species. Mr. Charlesworth spoke of the "crag" as "puzzling," and of a paper that he had read before the Geological Society in 1835 on it, but that many of the sections which he then knew were now closed. The most important point in the paper was the discovery related by Mr. Prestwich of the remains of mammals—as rhinoceros and mastodon at the foot of the coralline crag; this crag might be rich in mammalian remains, but the red crag was incomparably more so. Mr. George Jeffries, who had the pleasure of accompanying Mr. Prestwich on more than one occasion during his examination of the crag, spoke of 70 per cent of the mollusca being still existing. The mollusca of the crag were almost exactly like those of Montimaris: the coralline crag contained 298 species. Professor Ramsay spoke of the variation of the percentage of recent species in the crag, according to different authors which was attributable to the change in men's minds as to the constituents of specific distinctions.

ROYAL HORTICULTURAL SOCIETY.

On March 17th, W. Wilson Saunders, Esq., F.R.S., in the chair—after the election of thirteen new Fellows, and the announcement of several donations of plants and seeds, for which a vote of thanks was passed, the Chairmen of the Fruit and Floral Committees reported the awards made in their respective departments. The Rev. Mr. Berkeley then said that on the last occasion he had directed attention to Oncidium macranthum hastiferum, of which at the present meeting there was a specimen with eleven flowers from Messrs. Veitch, and one with five flowers from Mr. Richards, gardener to Lord Londesborough. Since the last meeting he had been to Kew and examined Dr. Lindley's herbarium, in which he found several specimens of macranthum, which had been met with by a number of travellers in Peru, but none of hastiferum, though there was a pen-and-ink sketch of the flower—which showed a considerable difference in the crest of the lip. The plant exhibited was undoubtedly a variety of O. macranthum, and a very fine thing. An unnamed Oncidium, shown by Mr. Williams, of Holloway, was then stated to be a mere variety of Oncidium obryzatum, which was also shown by the same exhibitor. Zygopetalum crinitum, exhibited by Mr. Wilson Saunders, was next referred to, as exhibiting two extremely distinct varieties in the same plant, one being much more handsome than the other. Whether this difference was the result of a sport, or arose from there being two distinct roots, he did not know. Mr. Berkeley then held up a spike of Dendrobium, of which the flowers were double; the divisions of the corolla were doubled, there were two columns, and two lips. This result he ascribed to a lateral fusion rather than as a case of transformation. He next called attention to a matter of considerable importance in regard to several mushrooms exhibited, of which the gills were paler than he had ever seen before—a circumstance which some might think was due to their having been grown in the dark and not developing their spores; but on close examination he had found that they were being gradually obliterated by a parasitic fungus. It became questionable, therefore, whether mushrooms in this state were wholesome or not. For his own part he should not like to eat them, for, even if they were wholesome, they could scarcely have that fine aroma which good mushrooms ought to possess. The exhibitor was doubtless unaware that the mushrooms in question were diseased; and when we hear, as we occasionally do, of deplorable cases of poisoning by mushrooms, possibly such disasters may not be caused by the mushrooms themselves, but by fungi with which they are attacked. With regard to grapes preserved by placing the stalk in water, according to the French plan, it had been justly remarked that they were certainly not improved in quality by adopting that mode of preservation. In the ordinary way of keeping, grapes became something like raisins; but in this mode water was absorbed to the detriment of the flavour, and even with the addition of charcoal the water might get into a putrid state. The method was originally practised at Thomery, but it was universally acknowledged not to be a success. At the last meeting he had directed attention to two kinds of decay, one being dry rot, the other a process of slow combustion. He had since been informed by a gentleman that he had specimens of wood which singularly illustrated the view of the case which he had advanced, and which showed that if the latter process went on, the wood made a much closer approximation to pure carbon, and which, instead of being brown, as with ulmates and humates, had become almost black. Mr. Berkeley then exhibited several specimens of wood attacked by fungi, and, among others, a curious specimen of Teak from the Madras Museum, in which the medullary rays were being obliterated, and he said it frequently happened that these were completely destroyed in such attacks, while the longitudinal cells remained perfect. Wood was often affected by fungi, although there was no trace of their presence superficially. It might be asked of what interest was all this in a horticultural point of view? he replied that it was of great importance to those about to put up glasshouses. About forty years ago a large range of houses in Northamptonshire had been put up with oak wood, which was in what was known as a "foxy" state, a condition in which no wood would be allowed in the dockyards, and the houses soon became very unsound. The reason of much of the wood in some parts of Northamptonshire being foxy was, that instead of the trees being raised from seed, they were produced from old stools which were generally full of fungus, and the wood from them became affected likewise. It was of great importance to ascertain before buildings were put up that the wood to be used in them was free from the mycelia of fungi. The next subject to which he would advert was a model sent by C. Wykeham Martin, Esq., M.P., of Leeds Castle, Kent, showing a system of heating which was described by him in the first two parts of the Society's Journal. In this mode of warming but a small quantity of fuel was required to heat a large area; and almost any kind of fuel might be used—Mr. Wykeham Martin burnt faggots and even sawdust; and it was extremely cheap, the expense of constructing the foundations and arrangements for heating a house 15 feet by 10 having been only £17 12s.

The Chairman said that those who were at the last meeting would recollect that a medal—the Lindley medal, was voted to Mr. Marshall for his exhibition of Cattleyas; but as it was a rule that members of Council could not take such awards, though Mr. Marshall might have the honour of its being awarded to him, he could not, in consequence of that rule, accept it. With regard to the Zygopetalum crinitum, referred to by Mr. Berkeley as exhibiting two kinds of flowers appearing to come from the same source, his impression was that two seeds had been dropped close together, and had sprung up in close companionship. Now, if the same pod of seed produced the two conditions of the plant in question, he wished to know why we do not import seeds of orchids instead of bulbs. The collection of cattleyas in Mr. Marshall's case were all, he believed, the result of the seed of one species under different conditions, and it would be a great gain to horticulture in this country to import seed and raise plants from it, and in doing this he did not know that there would be any difficulty. Another subject taken up by Mr. Berkeley—dry rot—was of vast importance. He (the Chairman) had seen large portions of ships entirely destroyed by dry rot. Hundreds of thousands of pounds were thus at stake. With reference to Teak, it was one of the most durable and finest of woods for ship-building, and how was it that dry-rot attacked it? He believed that a great deal lay in the Teak wood, when cut, not being properly seasoned; naturally it was full of essential oil, and how dry-rot could penetrate into the pores he did not know. We know that when a lot of timber is put together in an unseasoned state dry-rot is sure to follow, and in ship-building large air-holes are now left to prevent it; but so long as there is any dampness in timber, so long is there a tendency to dry-rot.

Mr. Berkeley remarked that if gate-posts, for instance, were made of unseasoned timber, and painted when full of sap, they were sure to be attacked with dry-rot. He would just add that Prof. Reichenbach had informed him that Dendrobium Bullerianum, shown at a previous meeting, is the same as D. gratiosissimum, a name published by him in *Botanisches Zeitung* in 1865.

GEOGRAPHICAL SOCIETY.

At the Meeting held on March 9th, Sir Roderick Murchison, President in the chair, the following gentlemen were elected Fellows:—C. Anstey, G. Bentley, W. Bull, W. H. Cole, F. Dutton, R. G. E. Dalrymple, Major Goldsworthy, H. Jamieson, the Right Hon. Earl of Kellie, W. W. Lane, Major G. D. Pritchard, W. B. Watson, and W. C. Wentworth.— 'On the Geography and Mountain Passes of British Columbia, with reference to an Overland Route,' by Mr. A. Waddington. Mr. Waddington has devoted many years in exploring, personally or by his agents, the different valleys and passes in order to ascertain which is the most practicable for a waggonroad and railroad from the Pacific across the Rocky Mountains. In explaining the nature of the country, the author said that the two mountain ranges—the Cascade or Coast Range, having an average width of 110 miles,—and the Rocky Mountains a width of 150 miles—nearly meet on the southern frontier of the colony; but diverge further north, and leave a fertile central plain 120 miles wide. In the southern part of the country all attempts to discover practicable passes had been in vain, and no *through* route was possible by way of the mouth of the Frazer River. He had examined the various long inlets or fiords to the northward, and found Bute Inlet to be by far the most suitable as the Pacific terminus of the future overland route. He had discovered a river flowing into the head of the inlet, and had planned a dray-road through the narrow valley thus formed through the whole width of the Coast Range. The road that he had projected ran north-eastwardly across the plain, and struck the Upper Frazer opposite the mouth of the Quesnelle River; the Frazer is here a navigable stream, and affords a route to the Yellow-head Pass of the Rocky Mountains, which leads to the rich level country on the eastern side of the range extending towards the Red River Settlement. The Yellow-head Pass, according to Dr. Rae, is 3,760 feet above the sea-level; the central plain is 2,500 in its southern part; and the Bute Inlet trail runs across it between 51° and 53° north lat.; the pasture is excellent, and the cereals (including wheat) can be grown. Mr. Waddington stated that the Canadian Government had already begun to construct the eastern end of the overland waggon-road between Lake Superior and Red River, but that no arrangement had yet been entered into with regard to the other sections; and he urged the importance of the undertaking on political and commercial grounds.

On March 23rd, Sir R. I. Murchison, Bart., President, in the chair, the following gentlemen were elected Fellows:—Messrs. P. P. Blyth, G. Clarke, C. Cornish-Brown, J. Douglas, J. Lee, J. Moffitt, A. G. Potter, T. F. Quin, Alderman D. H. Stone, H. Unwin, A. Wilson, J. J. Wilkinson, W. Young, and Capt. N. D. C. F. Douglas.—"On a Pundit's Journey to Lhasa and the Source of the Brahmaputra," by Capt. Montgomerie—The Report commenced by detailing the numerous unsuccessful attempts of the two pundits, who had previously been well trained for exploration by Capt. Montgomerie, to advance into Tibet. One of them at length succeeded in eluding the vigilance of frontier governors and guards, and passed from Kathmandu, the capital of Nepaul, viâ Kirong, to Tadum Monastery, north of the Brahmaputra river. From this place, which is on the great Tibetan high road, running east and west, between Gartokh and Lhasa, he travelled in company with a Ladak merchant to Lhasa, reaching the holy city on the 10th of January, 1866. He left Lhasa on his homeward journey on the 21st of April, and, instead of returning to Nepaul, continued along the high road westward, and, crossing the source of the Sutlej in Rakas-tal Lake, re-entered British territory by the Utdhura Pass into Kumaon. By the numerous accurate observations which he took for altitude, it results that the high road between Gartokh and Tibet for a distance of 800 miles lies along a region having an average height above the sea of 14,000 feet; in only one place does it descend so low as 11,000; whilst in several passes it rises to more than 16,000 feet. The road is well kept by the Tibetons, and travelling is facilitated by post-houses (tarjums) being established at intervals of from 20 to 70 miles. Between Mansarowar lake and Tadum glaciers seem always to have been seen on the slopes of the huge mountain masses to the south; and to the north of the road, commencing 80 miles east of Tadum, a very high snowy range was visible, running for 120 miles, and having a very high peak, called Harkiang, at its western extremity. Lhasa proved to be 11,700 feet above the sea-level. Excellent observations for latitude were taken at thirty-one different points, and an elaborate route survey made along a distance of 1,200 miles.

ZOOLOGICAL SOCIETY.

At this Meeting G. Busk, Esq., F.R.S., presided. Dr. Peters, of Berlin, has lately obtained the skull of a rodent (*Lophiomys imhausii*) from Upper Nubia. This animal belongs to a new order of rodentia, is known to exist at Aden, and will doubtless be recorded by observers now with the Abyssinian expedition. The wood block of a figure of the Californian vulture now mature in the society's gardens, was exhibited, taken from a picture made at Panama at the time of the bird's capture when almost a nestling. Dr. Cunningham, in a letter from the Magellan Straits, made copious allusion to the flora and fauna. Mr. W. H. Flower drew attention to the recent work by Mr. Malm on the whale, which that author has recently described under the name *Balænoptera carolinæ*. The work is copiously figured by photographs of its structure, etc., and it is found exactly to resemble the *Physalis Sibbaldi* of Gray in every particular of structure, the only peculiarity of the individual specimen being that externally the skin was slate-colored and spotted in a very unusual manner. Surgeon Day continued his papers on the "Fresh Water Fishes of Madras." Capt. Abbott sent an account of the seals of the Falkland Islands. The trade in the skins and oil of these animals employs a number of twenty or thirty ton boats, which are away on their voyage for five months at a time. The elephant-seal, with prolonged upper lip, though uncommon, is not extinct. The sea-lion (*O. jubata*) is very common; the male is as large as a bullock; the female as small as a calf. Formerly her fur was sought after, now that of the male is secured. The hair is black in youth, brown in mature seals. The fur seal is common up to Berkeley Sound, where they breed. This animal is in size as large as the seals of English seas. Mr. Flower stated that the milk teeth of the *Otaria* are shed so early in life, they have not been noticed after the first month, and as age makes many alterations in external appearance, the bony structure is a more certain means for the recognition of species. A paper on a new species of badger from China, by Dr. Gray, brought he proceedings to a close.

At the following meeting, John Gould, Esq., F.R.S., in the chair.—1. A letter from Sir Rutherford Alcock and M. le Pere David, describing a stag found in the imperial parks of Pekin, *Elaphurus Davidianus*, A. Edwards. It had branching horns, quite unlike those of any other recent species, and a long tail. Several specimens were obtained with some difficulty, with a view of their exportation to France, but the offer was not responded to, but being made to the Zoological Society of London was accepted, and there was a prospect of this species being sent over. This letter likewise mentioned a blue gallinaceous bird, but as the skin had not been obtained, it was not described. Mr. Gould said it was a question whether this deer was exclusively found in parks, like the fallow deer. 2. The Rev. Mr. Hincks on *Cygnus Passmori* as distinct from *C. buccinator*. It being thought by some of the speakers that the first was the young of the second, it was suggested that Mr. Hincks should send some living specimens to the society to settle this point. 3. Dr. Sclater "On the locality of the fine ant-eater now at the Gardens." 4. Mr. Butler "On new or little known species of Lepidoptera." 5. Dr. Gunther, "A report on a collection of fishes made by J. C Mellis, Esq., at St. Helena." Their closest affinities were with West Indian species—one, a horse-mackerel, was likewise found in Japan. Mr. Murray asked if these fish were fresh-water, but was reminded that there was no fresh water in St. Helena. A very interesting discussion followed on the proportionate number of species of Japanese birds and insects. Dr. Gunther mentioned the probability of *Hyalomena* being found at St. Helena; a species had lately been obtained in the Arctic seas. Mr. Blyth asked if many of the St. Helena fish were not of species widely distributed, and not especially characteristic of a particular locality. 6. Dr. Gunther "On twenty-five or twenty-six species of fish from the Amazon." He mentioned Mr. and Mrs. Agassiz' Book, which stated that 900 species of fish had been obtained there. Dr. Gunther said that M. Agassiz differed so much from European naturalists in what he thought constituted specific differences, that this might represent a much smaller number according to his (Dr. Gunther's) diagnosis. 7. Mr. Sclater on the *Marif Hippotragus Bakeri*. 8. Dr. Murie on the supposed arrest of development of the salmon when detained in fresh water. On the authority of Dr. Gunther (Cat. of fish in Brit. Mus.) as to the difficulty of defining certain forms of the *salmonidæ*, he stated that if a specimen which he exhibited could be proved to be a salmon, a physiological law of the highest importance would receive elucidation. A specimen and a drawing of another parr-like fish were exhibited. A detailed description and account of their history was given, the chief point being that they were the produce of some Rhine salmon ova presented to the Zoological Gardens five years previously by Mr. F. Buckland, and had been hatched and the fish retained in a fresh water aquarium in the gardens. Eminent ichthyologists were in doubt whether salmon could be kept alive in a healthy state in fresh water, he adduced the present instance. Dr. Gunther said the specimens in question were not salmon. Mr. Buckland and Mr. Bartlett (Superintendent of the Society's Gardens) said they were. Dr. Murie went on further to show from the migratory habits of salmon, their extraordinary rapid growth after having visited the sea, and the circumstance of irregularity in development, male individuals apparently reaching an adult stage though only parrs in size, that the present instance was but one of arrested development. He was the more inclined to this notion, for while Dr. Gunther negatived its being a true adult salmon, he acknowledged ignorance as to its species. The author called attention to the necessity of further observations on this peculiar physiological phenomenon. Mr. Buckland mentioned an immense number of names by which salmon in different stages were known, and exhibited a large series of specimens. On the subject of the migration of the salmon, he said that the second year they sometimes migrate and sometimes in the third year. Dr. Gunther thought the pedigree of the salmon from the Rhine ova, doubtful; that salmon were very rare at Huntengue, from whence the ova were procured, and that it might be very possible that of some other member of the genus *salmo*. He plainly said that he did not know to what species the specimen belonged, but that it might be a hybrid. 9. J. Gould, Esq., F.R.S., "On five new species of birds, *Brachpterus stellatus*, *Sturnus purpurascens*, *Aulacoramphus lexnotatus*, a small toucan, and a very curious grebe (*Podiceps micropterus*) from Lake Titicaca, South America, with smaller wings than he had even seen in any bird before; it was utterly incapable of flight.

ETHNOLOGICAL SOCIETY.

At the meeting held March 10th. J. Crawfurd, Esq., in the chair. "On the History and Migration of Plants yielding Potables and Oils," by the President. The range of the various plants used in the manufacture of intoxicating beverages was in the main determined by a comparison of their synonyms in different languages. From the results of this system of investigation it would seem to be that the vine came originally from Greece, being thence diffused over Italy, France, Germany, and to England, while Spain owed its introduction to her Mohammedan conquerors. The introduction of hops into England took place from Flanders in the time of Henry the Seventh. Beer, in some form or another, is of great antiquity amongst Teutonic nations. After a notice of the various intoxicating drinks and substitutes for wine or beer in use in various parts of the world, the paper next briefly reviewed the oil-yielding plants in the same manner, being confined, however, to those kinds less perfectly known, or of most recent introduction. "On the Island of Teneriffe, and its Primitive Inhabitants the Guanches," by Miss Haigh. The system of government, manners and religious views of the ancient people were minutely described, evidencing a somewhat advanced scale of civilization, though, as far it was possible to judge, they were ignorant of the uses of metals, and also of boats and navigation. They lived in caverns, often of their own hewing; and similar habitations are at present in use by some of the inhabitants of the island. The whole of the Canary islanders possessed so many features in common, that they might be considered as identical in race, which, in the absence of any proof that they had ever built boats, was a somewhat difficult problem to solve; but inference would point to the conclusion that, by some volcanic convulsion probably, the group of islands had been detached from the mainland, and had also undergone the still further division amongst themselves. Some skulls from the island were exhibited, two of which were those of cavern mummies.

THE ANTHROPOLOGICAL SOCIETY.

March 17.—The President, Dr. Hunt, announced that the annual *soirée* was postponed to May 19 instead of April 14, as originally proposed, and that April 14 would be an ordinary evening meeting. The Rev. J. G. Wood exhibited photographs of Julia Pastrada and her child. She had a long beard, besides an extensive growth of hair on other parts of the body, but was a most accomplished woman in languages, music, and dancing. One photograph represented her alive, and the other as stuffed, in a museum. Mr. Braybrook explained that the council had decided on uniting the committees of historical and physiological anthropology, with Dr. Beigel for president and Mr. Higgins and Mr. C. O. G. Napier as secretaries. Mr. J. M'Grigor Allen's paper, entitled, "Europeans and their Descendants in North America," in the absence of the author was read by Mr. Braybrook. He showed that the North American white population was European in its character, and would remain so, independently of political or climatic conditions. The United States man had never been, never could be, racially independent of the old continent. To effect this, Asiatic, African, and native American blood must predominate. The various distinct European types, so far from being obliterated were exaggerated in the New World. In consequence of the effect of climate in deteriorating the physique of transplanted European races, neither the United States nor any other extra-European settlement could be maintained without a continual influx of fresh blood from Europe. Mr. M'Grigor Allen pointed out the decline of the birth-rate—that the old American stock was fast dying out. The likeness between British and American literature he considered an argument for the unity of race, and that the intellectual aristocracy of America was modelled on the European type. He spoke of the extreme pride of Englishmen as well as of Yankees, but said that the principal difference was that the latter were the more sensitive. He pointed out the distinction which existed between the races composing the United States population, and that they retained their national peculiarities and antipathies. The antagonism shown by the Yankees to the English he compared with that of the Kaffir "brave," whose first proof of manliness was shown in beating his mother. The Rev. Dunbar Heath differed from the author in thinking the national character distinct. Mr. Swinbourne (the poet) considered the literature of America original, and that the writings of Edgar Poe was a proof of this. Dr. Wolff, who had resided twenty-five years in the Southern States, did not fear the extinction of native-born Americans, and mentioned a family in Tennessee where for six generations extraordinary fecundity was shown. On the motion of Dr. Beigel, in consequence of the lateness of the hour and absence of the author of the paper, the discussion was adjourned to March 31, when, in addition to this, Mr. Wake will read a paper on the "Psychological Unity of Man."

On March 31.—1st. The Rev. Dunbar Heath exhibited some Japanese toys. 2nd. Mr. C. O. G. Napier exhibited four earrings of New Zealand greenstone (jade), and corrected some mistakes which had been made with regard to this substance, which was found near Leipzic and the river Amazon, as well as in China and New Zealand. It was said to be so hard that only diamond dust would touch it, whereas it really was softer than quartz; he also showed some specimens of Kawri gum (now largely imported into England by the varnish makers), in a natural state as well as made into ornaments, which vied with those of amber in beauty. Also specimens of the New Zealand flax in the raw and manufactured state; all collected by Mr. J. E. Maphabeck. 3rd. The discussion resumed on Mr. McGrigor Allen's paper. Dr. Hunt explained that the key-note of the paper consisted in the affirmation that races could not be transplanted, and that Europeans in the United States unrecruited from the mother countries would become extinct. Mr. Brookes, the seconder of the motion of adjournment, in the absence of Dr. Beidel the mover, opened the discussion by saying he differed much from Mr. Allen; he thought with Mr. Swinbourne that American writers were very original in literature as well as in mechanics and in diplomacy. He differed principally from Mr. A. in his estimate of the moral characters of the two peoples; thus, the English, though self-confident, were quiet and a little inclined to braggadocio, the Americans the reverse. He thought the last a race created by circumstances, but that the English race having been 2000 years in course of formation and being imperfectly formed, it was premature to base conclusions on European populations who had been but 200 or 300 years resident in America. Mr. Brebner, in following on the same side, thought Mr. Allen had but very cleverly followed Knox. Mr. Bendir thought that Knox should be forgotten, being 20 years old, and that the matter should be settled from fresh facts; he differed from Mr. Swinbourne in thinking the poet Whatman original. Dr. Donovan, who had been some years in America, made a forcible and humourous speech.; he agreed with Mr. Allen that a transplanted race could not survive. He went out to America with the notion that it was the place above all others for man, but soon changed his mind. He thought that the first descendants of Europeans were an improvement for the time as regards temperament; they acquired greater intensity at the expense of physical force. Dr. Hyde Clarke said that the first child born of European parents in America was often called a Yankee, from its constitution, and in Australia an Australian, but that the children afterwards born might resemble the European type. Mr. McArthur, who had been in America, thought the mode of life and not the climate accounted for physical decline. Mr. Higgins called attention to some statistics brought before the Berlin Congress, which showed that the Americans were vastly taller than Englishmen. Among the 25,000 American recruits 12,000 were above 6ft. and in a similar number of English recruits little more than 100. In consequence of the lateness of the hour, the discussion was again adjourned till April 14.

QUEKETT MICROSCOPICAL CLUB.

The annual *soirée* of this club was held on the 13th instant, in the building of the London University, Gower-street. The rooms were filled with an appreciative company, including a large attendance of ladies. Besides the show of instruments by the members, most of the best known metropolitan manufacturers were well represented. The microscopes brought by the members were very numerous and varied in character, from the most costly instruments to the least expensive. An equal variety was observable in the objects shown. The living objects excited, as usual, much interest, and the stands at which the circulation in the foot of the frog, the young trout, &c., were exhibited proved very attractive. The spectroscope in its application to microscopy was shown by Mr. Browning, who illustrated the recent discovery of copper in the red feathers of various birds. A small bottle containing sulphate of copper in solution obtained from the feathers of a single bird excited much interest. Mr. Ross exhibited his new and very useful four-inch objectives, in striking contrast with which was a one-fiftieth shown by Messrs. Powell and Lealand. One of the most attractive exhibitions of the evening was Dr. Madox's marvellously beautiful photographs of microscopic objects mounted on glass for the magic lantern. These were very effectively shown by Mr. How, of Foster Lane, upon a ten feet screen in the dark room. The same gentleman exhibited some very curious kaleidoscopic effects, and a series of photographic views. Besides various optical and electrical exhibitions, including electric discharges in vacuum tubes by Messrs. Horne and Thornthwaite, and polarising apparatus by several persons, there were a few drawings, photographs, minerals, shells, algæ, etc.

Correspondence.

[*Under this head we shall be glad to insert any letters of general interest.*]

ANIMALS DESTITUTE OF HAIR AND FEATHERS.

Sir,—Your correspondent Mr. Gibbon's description of a canary nearly without feathers reminds me of a cock and hen (*Gallus domesticus*) I once saw near Bristol. They were hatched by a farmer from eggs I believe purchased in the market, and were under a year old when I saw them. They were entirely without any rudiments of quills or feathers, and had only half a dozen filaments of down on the sides of the body. The skin was smooth, reddish purple, and varied in colour with every breath of wind from the circulation of blood to the various parts of the body. It was very warm, as one might expect in naked birds in health, which these evidently were, for the temperature of birds is much higher than that of mammals. I have not heard whether these bird s propagated. I have heard of a fish without scales—a perch—but I was surprised the other day to see a horse without hair: it was on view a few weeks ago at the Crystal Palace. It was a well-formed animal, with a skin like india-rubber to the touch, and very warm. At a distance it had the appearance of being carved of some curious marble or serpentine, for its body was mostly dull blue, with large patches of flesh colour; hence it has been called the "blue horse." It had been ridden, I was told, with Lord Stamford's hounds for three parts of a season, but had to be kept carefully clothed. A bath of cold water was necessary every morning, the proprietor assured me, to keep it in health; but it was otherwise strong and hardy.

I remain yours truly,

C. O. GROOM NAPIER, F.G.S.

ALAS! POOR OTTERS!

Sir,—As the author of the paragraph referred to by your correspondent "A. M. B.," will you permit me to make a short answer to his letter?

In the first place, I must say that his remarks are made in such a tone that it would have been simply ordinarily courteous to have published them in the same journal as that in which the paragraph appeared, and have thus given me a fair opportunity of seeing them and replying to them. As it happened, it was by the merest chance I saw his letter.

Notwithstanding "A. M. B.'s" arguments, I must still maintain, as I have done in the paragraph which seems to have so strangely excited him, that it is *barbarous*, *ridiculous*, and *unscientific*, to slay any animal fast becoming rare in the ferile state, and specimens of which are abundant in museums of any repute; especially when, as in this case, there was no reason why an attempt should not have been made to take the animals alive. I am yours faithfully,

Clifton, near Bristol. T. G. P.

A FEW WORDS IN DEFENCE OF THE MAGPIE.

Sir,—The persecution to which this splendid bird is so unremittingly exposed from the prejudice and love of slaughter so inherent in that *indispensable* individual the *gamekeeper*, whose predatory disposition renders him so obnoxious to most Naturalists, will, I fear, too soon compel us to class it among our rare birds. Indeed, were it not that it has a few kind protectors scattered over the country, although "few and far between," it would long ago have been all but extinct.

Even those who aspire to the honourable title of a "lover of Nature," we too often find join in the general persecution this unfortunate bird so little merits.

Your correspondent "H. Meyrick," in the NOTE BOOK for last month, says the magpie *infests* his neighbourhood. Now I maintain that it infests *no* neighbourhood. I only wish it was more common in mine: I would do my best to encourage it, and would be amply repaid by its valuable services in clearing the ground of hosts of noxious insects, alike destructive to the farm and the garden.

It cannot be denied that it destroys a certain amount of eggs and young game; but it should be remembered that this practice is only followed during *two months* in the spring, and that its subsequent usefulness more than compensates for its former thievish propensity. Besides, will not all *true* lovers of Nature rather run the risk of a little pecuniary loss, than see Britain deprived of one of her most beautiful birds—adding a peculiar charm to her woods and forests, and recalling to our minds the grandeur and beauty of a tropical clime, where "Nature reigns supreme?"

These remarks apply as well to many other of our "feathered friends," against whom countless false accusations are rife:—Owls and kestrels—wholesale mice-killers; the gay and cheerful starling; the sprightly jay; the sociable rook; the magnificent heron; the harmless gull, etc., etc. I may conclude this short appeal to the humanity of "generous Britons" by a word on a tame magpie. This bird, which I kept some years ago, could repeat two or three short sentences, such as "Poor Johnny!" (his name) "Go away," "Good morning," etc., with great clearness — more approaching to the human voice than that of many parrots. It used to catch and kill live mice; and if it got more food than it could eat at a time, it used invariably to hide the rest in some corner of its cage to consume at its leisure.

My only excuse for offering these remarks is, that I believe it to be the duty of every admirer of the wonders of Nature to do what he can to protect and encourage all the objects included in that science, whether Animal, Vegetable, or Mineral; and as "small sands" make "the mountain," to withhold not his tribute, however trifling it may seem.

Convinced am I that the TRUE NATURALIST will seldom deem it necessary to destroy *any* of God's creatures, other than is requisite to supply him with food, or to extend the knowledge of his delightful study. I wish more of those who call themselves *Naturalists* would take the following lines as their motto:—

> No birds that haunt my valley free
> To slaughter I condemn;
> Taught by the Power that pities me,
> I learn to pity them.

I am, Sir, yours truly,
Edinburgh, April 10. R. B. W.

Remarks, Queries, &c.

(*Under this head we shall be happy to insert original Remarks, Queries, &c.*)

CHRYSALIDS.—At page 94, March number, an inquiry is made as to the best method of keeping the chrysalids of moths, etc., in order to insure the development of the perfect insect. I will not presume that I can give the very best way of securing this desideratum; but the following suggestion, being from many years' practical attention to the matter, may be found serviceable to the inquirer and perhaps to some others who want to breed moths, etc., from the caterpillar and chrysalis state. I have never tried to preserve them in bran, but should quite agree with your inquirer that the plan would be one of disappointment as a general rule. I should advise as a simple and inexpensive means a trial of the following:—A common flower-pot, say twelve inches over, and as deep as can readily be obtained. This must be filled to one third or not more than half up with clean fresh garden mould, the chrysalids placed thereon covered with a thin laying of coarse moss, which should be occasionally sprinkled with water to keep the whole in a moist state, which I believe is very essential to the successful breeding of the perfect insect. The flower-pot must of course be covered with crape or gauze to prevent the escape of the insects, and should be kept throughout the winter in a cool place, as a cellar or outhouse, as being most in accordance with the nature of the insects, and will doubtless, therefore, be attended with the most satisfactory results.

320, Strand. C. W. D.

Could any of your readers be kind enough to give me a brief account of the treatment of caterpillars—just before and after they become chrysalids—especially with reference to those that burrow? In the first place, ought there always to be under them earth for burrowing; if so, what sort? Again, ought I afterwards to dig the chrysalids up and put them into something else? And also in what sized thing ought I to keep the caterpillars in, and how must I manage about feeding them? If any of your numerous readers could tell me a satisfactory plan that would thoroughly suit the commoner sorts of the Spingidæ, he would greatly oblige A. B.

In answer to a query signed "Entomologist," in the March number, I am happy to inform him that I have kept chrysalids in cotton wool for the last three years, and have always been successful. I have also used prussic acid for killing moths, but I fear that it somewhat changes their colour.

Brighton. J. B.

THE RED-BACKED SHRIKE (Lanius collurio).—This bird makes its appearance in England about the beginning of May, and departs again in September. It is a very local species, but seems plentiful enough where it does occur. I have found it very common in Sussex, especially along the line of coast between the South Downs and the sea. In Sussex it is commonly known by the name of jack-baker. The most peculiar habit of this bird is that of impaling its food upon a sharp thorn; but its reason for so doing has not, I believe, been accounted for: its food consists chiefly of coleopterous insects, but it is asserted by some that it occasionally feeds upon small birds. Jenyns, in his "Observations in Natural History," writes the following respecting its food:—"I have occasionally examined the stomach of this species, but never found it to contain anything beyond the remains of coleopterous insects. From the statement of other observers, however, it would seem that it does undoubtedly sometimes prey on small birds." Last summer, May 6th, I found a redstart (M. Phœnicurus) impaled upon some thorns, and had evidently been placed there by a butcherbird. The male has a chirping note, and occasionally makes a sort of song; they are very conspicuous birds, and delight to perch upon the highest twigs they can find, from which position they are able to dart off, and capture any large insect that may happen to pass, after the manner of flycatchers, to which birds they are very closely allied. They have another habit of hovering for a considerable time over a particular spot, and then suddenly darting away after some insect. The nest of this bird is generally placed in some thick hedge, and is composed of fibrous roots, sprinkled here and there with a little moss, and lined with hair. It lays five or six cream-coloured eggs, with a ring of brown spots round the larger end: two nests, which I found last year, were in very exposed positions. Two other shrikes occur in Great Britain, namely, the great grey shrike (Lanius excubitor), and the woodchat (L. rufus); the former is a winter visitant, and has never been known to breed in this country; and the latter is an African species, and has only very rarely occurred in Great Britain. Some little time ago I saw a woodchat (L. rufus) which had been shot in the neighbourhood of Brighton.

H. MEYRICK.

ERMINE.—Since my note last month upon this subject I have had the pleasure of seeing the "White Stoat." On the 16th March I was standing near a brook, by the side of which were some white ducks pruning their feathers, when suddenly from the opposite bank of the large field through which the brook ran there issued an animal which, even by the uncertain light of the early morning, I could see was white. It crossed the field by doubling backwards and forwards, and then made direct for the lower part towards the ducks. I started in pursuit with a dog and ran it down in the centre of the field, where it sat up looking at me as if bewildered. Being at a few yards distance only when it stopped I would not fire at it, and knowing that they never have their hole in the middle of a meadow I rushed forward with the dog to secure it alive, when what was my horror to see it suddenly disappear—a friendly mole-hill had sheltered the artful little animal, and I was—sold! As if to add to my mortification, I almost fancied I could hear the popular refrain "Not for Joseph!" issuing from the hole, and to all the pressing invitations of myself and dog to "Come out of that!" the fugitive usurper did not incline his ear. As far as I could see, it was quite white as described; but I fear that, should it not be captured soon, it will revert to the usual colour. A. M. B.

MAGPIES.—In answer to H. Meyrick, I beg to say that the magpie often builds in a bush, though not so commonly as in a tree. M. L. A.

On the Downs of Dorset it is very usual for magpies to nest in stunted thorn trees, or bushes, at from seven to ten feet from the ground. I have also often seen them in low apple trees in orchards. A well-grown hedge that has not been plashed for a few years is another favourite position, and indeed some authors, amongst others the late Mr. Jesse, who have sought to establish two species of magpie in this country, have put forward the different localities of the nests (one being in bushes and the other at the top of high trees) as a distinguishing feature between the species. I have taken nests from both positions, but can see no positive variation either in the nests themselves, the eggs, or birds. J. S., JUN.

In answer to H. Meyrick as to whether it is a common occurrence for the magpie to build in a low bush, I may state that cases do now and then occur; in evidence of which, perhaps, I may be allowed to quote an extract from "Beeton's Book of Birds," page 123, which runs thus:—"While travelling between Huntly and Portsay (Scotland) I observed two magpies hopping round a gooseberry-bush in a small garden, near a poor-looking house, in a peculiar manner, and flying out and into the bush. I stepped aside to see what they were doing, and found, from the poor man and his wife, that as there are no trees around for some miles, these magpies during several succeeding years had built their nest and brought up their young in this bush; and that foxes, cats, hawks, and other creatures might not interrupt them, they had barricaded not only their nest, but had encircled the bush with briars and thorns in a formidable manner—nay, so completely, that it would have given the fox, cunning as he is, some days' labour to get into the nest.

A. M. B.

IS THE YEW POISONOUS.—In reply to "J. D. S. W." I quote the following from "Coleman's Woodlands, Heaths and Hedges":—"The poisonous properties of yew foliage when eaten by cattle and horses are well-known; but it appears that, by mixing the leaves in gradually increasing proportions with the ordinary fodder of animals, they can at last be brought to eat it alone, without any apparent ill-consequences. The deleterious effects of yew leaves extend to the human race also, and many melancholy instances are on record in which fatal results have followed their administration, especially to children; for it seems that the leaves have had a considerable repute as a vermifuge. The viscid scarlet berries, however, do not share in the poisonous qualities of the foliage, and are eaten with impunity by children, who generally have a great relish for them." R. M.

In last month's NOTE BOOK, "J. D. S. W." asks if the berries of the yew tree are poisonous. They are generally believed to be so. Perhaps if one were to eat a lot of them they might poison one; but I have eaten them dozens of times, and they have never killed me. They taste bitter and sweet at the same time, and are rather nice—at least I like them.

A. M. H.

The berries of the yew tree are not poisonous, although insipid, but they contain seeds which are highly noxious; they have been known to produce fatal consequences in a few hours after being eaten. A small quantity of the green foliage is not injurious to cattle, but the dried leaves are extremely poisonous; animals that have eaten them dying in a very short time. M. L. A.

In answer to your correspondent "J. D. S. W."

allow me to say that I have frequently seen children eat of the berries without any evil effect.

Uphill, Weston-super-Mare.   O. POOLE.

How to Arrange Land and Fresh Water Shells.—Having had some considerable experience in the arrangement of shells, allow me to add a few hints to my friend Mr. Napier's suggestions in the matter. Drawers I found too expensive for me; they are no doubt the best, but trays, if made with a rim all round, higher at the back and sides than in front, answer the purpose nearly as well, and are cheaper. All my cabinets are made in this manner. They cost, made of well-seasoned deal, with seven trays, each two feet six inches long by one foot six inches wide, and four inches in depth, twenty-five shillings each. The block system is the most economical one for mounting, and in my opinion looks the neatest. It is almost universally adopted in museums and in private collections of any extent. I have used it both for my own collection and for an extensive one in a museum, and cannot say I have experienced the results mentioned by Mr. Napier. As regards packing specimens thus mounted, the only safe plan is to place in deep layer of saw-dust between each layer of blocks. The best cement for fastening specimens to blocks is that known as "Jermyn Street Cement," and is composed of sugar or starch, gum and whitening mixed into a thick paste with alum-water.   T. G. P.

Many thanks to Mr. G. O. Groome Napier for his hints in last number. He advises numbering each specimen, and this is what I should myself wish to do; but do not know how to with the smaller varieties, as bullimi, &c., without completely disfiguring the shell. Will Mr. Napier tell me his plan?   W. T. ATKINS.

Curious Anecdote of a Dog.—I have in my possession a small rough terrier, a regular "vermin" dog, who has, as might be expected, a great antipathy to rabbits. Not long ago, when rabbits were kept near the house, she never rested until she had reached them and succeeded in killing one, so that the hutch had to be removed. A few weeks ago she was prematurely delivered of a litter of puppies; and being without much milk, and at all times a bad mother, I ordered the pups to be destroyed. Some days after their death her milk came, and she appeared uncomfortable. I observed her several times making affectionate advances to the kitten, of whom at other times she took no notice; but as he had long ago left his mother, he was proof against her endearments; and she took to disappearing from home at intervals, being generally brought back by the child of one of our neighbours. At length this boy informed me that he had discovered the reason "Di" went so frequently to his mother's house. There was a half-grown rabbit in a hutch in the garden. The first time the child saw the dog jump into the hutch he thought she was going to destroy his rabbit, when, hastening to the help of the latter, to his surprise he saw "Di" lie down and the rabbit relieve her of her milk. She continued to do this regularly until the milk left her.   EMILIA MARRYAT NORRIS.

Charmouth, April 4th.

Notes from Tunbridge Wells.—I saw and heard the cuckoo (Cuculus canorus) for the first time on April 15th, and the first swallow (Hirundo rustica) made its appearance on the 18th. The golden-crested wren (M. regulus) is very common about here, on account of the numerous fir plantations; for wherever the fir grows in any abundance, there also is sure to be found the golden-crested wren. It is very interesting to watch these pretty little birds busily and actively engaged in searching for their food among the firs, all the time uttering their peculiar little note. They are very fearless birds, but have a peculiar knack of always keeping a branch between themselves and the person who is watching them.

This neighbourhood is rather rich in titmice; the great tit (P. major), the cole tit (P. aten), blue tit (P. cæruleus), and long-tailed tit (P. candatus), are to be found in profusion in every spot where it is possible for them to procure food. On April 17th, I found a viper among a mass of dead ferns, on a hill side, and on opening it, I found it to contain a luyard (Zootoca vivipara), which was quite whole, with the exception of the tail, which had been broken off from the body; the viper was quite a small one, only measuring seven and a half inches. On the afternoon of the same day, a sparrow-hawk (Accipiter nisus) flew over my head, bearing in its claws a small bird, and was closely followed by a starling, for what purpose I do not know. The hawk was uttering loud cries.

Tunbridge Wells.   H. MEYRICK.

Fowls Catching Mice.—I was present at a grand marine battue which occurred on the occasion of the removal of a corn stack to the thrashing-yard. The mice (Arvicola agrestis) congregated in the centre of the stack as the outer portions were removed, so that when the central citadel was stormed there was a terrific scamper of mice. The five men occupied in removing the stack killed all they could, in which they were helped to the utmost extent of their powers by a bull-terrier and a nondescript mongrel—a noted rat-killer—as well as by a lively young cat. The results of killed were as follows:—By men, 35; bull-terrier, 9; mongrel, 12; cat, 7; a Turkey-cock, 2. A number of barn-door fowls and ducks, spectators of the scene, picked up the naked young mice which were thrown on the ground when the mothers were turned out; they came in for the largest share—they must have picked up hundreds. A great many of the mice escaped entirely; but between thirty and forty jumped into a duck pond, and were swimming to the opposite side, when they were pelted and mostly knocked under by some children standing on the opposite side of the pond.   C. O. G. NAPIER.

Food of Snails.—I should like to know if any of your contributors have observed the common snail feeding upon paper, because in July last I planted some flower seeds, and labelled them with yellow glazed paper, stuck in little sticks. In a short time I observed the labels to be nibbled as if by a mouse, and, although annoyed, attached but little importance to that fact, until one night I went out in the garden with an entomological lantern searching for larvæ, and there I discovered *Helix Aspersa* and friend up the stick, like bears at the "Zoo," complacently nibbling away at my labels. A further search revealed more.

And this "little game" continued nightly until the whole of the paper was actually eaten up.

Whether these snails were of a scientific turn, and merely studying botanical terms by a process analogous to swallowing the dictionary, I do not know; but certain it is that they did not appear to consider it as a Latin "imposition," but "digested" it thoroughly, prior no doubt to attacking the "roots." A. M. B.

PIGS KILLING POULTRY.—I have kept several pigs, who take a great delight in devouring fowls. Whenever an unfortunate bird, tempted by the food on which these pigs feed, ventures into the sty in hope of sharing their repast, they make a furious grab at them with their sharp teeth, and happy indeed are the fowls who escape their ravenous jaws. I think that they acquired this habit by having in anger bitten one of the fowls who was stealing their food, and then, having once tasted fowl's blood, they ever after had a craving for it; like the "man-eating lions," who when once they have tasted human blood ever after destroy man when he comes across their path. The pigs after their repast leave no trace of their banquet but a few large wing feathers. Another peculiarity I have noticed in my pigs, which is their love for coals and ashes, which they eat with evident relish. I suppose it aids their digestion, in the same way as gravel does in fowls and other birds.

Mavisbush House. J. D. S. W.

UNKNOWN BIRD.—Can any of your readers tell me the name of a little bird common on the hills round Edinburgh? It is so shy that I have not been able to get near enough to identify it; it seems to be very small, and of a light brown colour. But what struck me most was its song, which is very soft and sweet. Beginning with three or four slow, clear, and rather loud notes, it gradually quickens them until its voice dies away in gentle melody. The chief peculiarity is that it sings, like the lark, on the wing rising and falling in the air; it also sings upon the ground. The bird whose song it most resembles is the gold-crest (Regulus cristatus), which also sings in the air as it floats from one tree to another; but I do not think it can be the same, as I believe this bird (the gold-crest) is confined to fir woods, and is never seen in the open country. I observed it first on the 1st of April: can it be a tit-lark? R. B. W.

KILLING MOTHS.—In using laurel-leaves, it is much better to cut them up with a pair of scissors than to bruise them. Oxalic acid, although a virulent poison truly when swallowed, is not one liable to accident to the entomologist, who need only have a small quantity at a time. A half-drachm bottle containing some crystals of the acid pounded and mixed with water is excellent, and should be applied with a quill pen to the base of the thorax, which should be half pierced through; twice or three times may be necessary. I never heard of an accident from its use for entomological purposes, but it is rather a favourite poison with suicides. Strong liquid ammonia answers well for killing moths and other insects; cotton wool should be saturated with it, and put in a close-fitting tin box or bottle beside them. Chloroform, in my experience, is excellent both for killing insects, reptiles, and other small animals. C. O. G. NAPIER.

OWLS.—Would any of the naturalists who are readers of the NOTE BOOK kindly inform me whether owls migrate; if not, how do they support themselves during severe winters when the ground is frozen hard for weeks together? A supply of their natural food is then not easily obtained, as field-mice, rats, &c., are kept under ground. I would also draw attention to my former query (page 260, vol. 1) as to whether the female of the long-eared owl (Otus vulgaris) ever hoots. I have heard both sexes of the barn owl screech when alarmed for the safety of their young. Also, whether either species utter their notes in a state of captivity; as far as my own experience goes they do not. R. B. W.

LANDRAIL SWIMMING.—I have just seen a stuffed landrail, which was shot in a peculiar manner by Mr. Lees, of Aldershot, from whom I heard the following circumstance. It seems that he was out shooting one day in September, 1866, when his dog stood at point in some low bushes near a wide ditch, and ultimately flushed a bird, which flew plump into the water, dived, came up in the middle of the ditch, swam to the other side, then ran up the bank and again took to flight, when it was stopped by a timely shot. On being retrieved it turned out to be a landrail, much to the astonishment of Mr. Lees, who imagined it to be a water-rail only.

I have never before heard of a similar case, but perhaps some of your correspondents may afford a pendant. A. M. B.

THE FIRST BUTTERFLIES.—Strolling out for a walk on the 3rd of April, I saw the first butterfly this season, and from what I could see of it, as it flew past me, it appeared to be the common yellow butterfly, which is, I believe, the first of its class to make their appearance amongst us. Is it not early for them? The weather here during the last three or four days has been almost like summer, and to-day especially, with scarcely a breath of air, which perhaps accounts for the early appearance of our summer visitant.

Salisbury. BERNARD C. BUSH.

A HAWK SWALLOWING EGGS.—In the *Naturalist* for 1851, page 230, there is a note recording the fact that two lark's eggs were taken uninjured from the stomach of a goshawk; with the query, "How could the hawk have taken up and swallowed such delicate eggs without injury to them." I suppose the writer means to say that they were taken from the crop of the hawk; but is the name stomach ever rightly applied to the crop of a bird? I think it most probable that the hawk, being a large one, swallowed the lark itself whole, at the time it contained the eggs; and not as the writer seems to imagine, devoured the eggs for their own sake. R. B. W.

CURIOUS CANARIES.—F. L. Gibbons saith a friend of his has got a canary entirely destitute of feathers (without the exceptions), which is indeed very alarming, since a friend of mine, strange to say, has in his possession a well-fledged canary (without the exceptions) which entirely deprives it of feathers round the neck. But what is more strange is it being a hen, yet sings like a nightingale. If anybody else should have

in their possession a canary, or canaries, that are inclined to any peculiarities, would they be so kind as to make them become remarkable.
JOHN THOMAS.

BEES.—I have noticed at a building which father is erecting in this place that the plasterer's lime pits seem to be a resort for the hive bee, of which I have seen many on a sunny day, apparently feeding upon the lime. Do they derive any nourishment from it, or what is their object in frequenting such places? I have not observed a single *humble* bee, but only the workers from the hive. Can any of your readers give me any information on this subject?
Smethwick.   GEO. TROBRIDGE, JUN.

SKELETONS OF BIRDS, &c.—The boiling plan is rather ticklish work; it is better to remove all the flesh you can in a fresh state, cut out the brains and tongue, and then soak the partially-cleaned bones in water for a long period, until the whole of the flesh has disappeared by a gradual process of decay. It takes a long time, but the specimens are more satisfactory in the end. Every museum is provided with proper vessels for the purpose, and it is almost the universal mode of procedure, the boiling plan being rarely resorted to.   T. G. P.

CURIOUS NEST OF CHAFFINCH.—Your correspondent "R. B. W." mentions a nest of the Black Cap made entirely of horsehair. This is very singular, and I do not remember hearing of another case: but it is a parallel of a nest of the chaffinch I have in my collection, obtained by my friend G. D. Rowley, Esq., F.Z.S., which was formed entirely of cowhair, instead, as usual, of moss with a lining of cowhair and feathers.   C. O. G. NAPIER.

EELS.—For a few days I kept in a glass aquarium a few small eels; and I wish to know if they were of the same species, or otherwise. I had about two dozen small ones, pure white and clear, about two inches in length, and with small fins at each side of the head. The other two were of a dark brown, with white beneath, and were altogether of a larger size than the first mentioned. They were all got below stones at the side of a river.   FOX.

CARNIVOROUS MICE.—Since my note on "Mice as Cannibals" I have frequently left raw flesh in the way of the common mouse, and it has always been eaten. The other day I left on the table in my bed-room a specimen of the great titmouse, which I intended to have stuffed, but the next day on rising in the morning it was entirely devoured by mice.
Mavishbush House.   J. D. S. W.

KING CHARLES'S DOGS IN JAPAN.—In the extract quoted from the *Leisure Hour* it is said, "It is probable that the pets of his court (Charles the Second's) were introduced to this country from the land of the Tycoon." I should be glad to hear if any of your correspondents can furnish any evidence for this. I think it is just as probable that these dogs were introduced from England into Japan.   C. O. G. NAPIER.

THE COLOUR OF BIRDS' EGGS.—Mr. Napier, in the last number of the NOTE BOOK, suggests that light has an effect in colouring birds' eggs. Yet white eggs are not always laid in a dark place, for the dove tribe lay in an open nest exposed to the light; and so do wild geese, ducks, swans, and greves, yet all these lay white eggs.   M. L. A.

BLACKCAP'S NEST.—Towards the middle of the same year (1866) in which "R. B. W." found this "singular nest," mentioned in the last number of the NOTE BOOK, I found a similar one in a mass of ivy which hung from a tree growing on the bank of a river. The nest was entirely composed of black horse hair, and very neatly built.
Surrey.   C. B. R.

HOW TO CURE SKINS.—Will you or any of your correspondents be so kind as to tell me how to cure hare or rabbit skins, so as to make them soft and pliable, suitable for ladies' muffs or linings, &c.? Also, the best way to cure bird's skins to cut up into feathers for ladies' hats? and you will greatly oblige
B. F. B.

GLOWWORMS.—I noticed a gloworm on Saturday evening, March 21st, as I was walking from Plymouth to Saltash, at about a quarter past ten. Is this not very early for the appearance of this insect? A reply from any of your correspondents in your next publication will oblige
A READER OF THE NATURALIST'S NOTE BOOK.

YEW BERRIES.—In reply to "J. D. S. W.," I would inform him that as a boy I have often eaten handsfull of these berries without any injurious result. I have never heard of cases of poisoning from yew berries, but poisoning from yew leaves is well known.
C. O. G. NAPIER.

THE SQUIRREL.—Can you or any of your correspondents inform me when the squirrel breeds and has young? or (as is the case with mice, rabbits, and other animals) has it no fixed time? I heard of a nest being found with two young on the 20th of March. Is this the usual time?   R. B. W.

LARGE STURGEON.—Having seen an account in several papers of a sturgeon having been caught in the Medway seven and a half feet long, supposed to be the largest ever taken in England, I beg to state that one was caught last year in the Tees, and exhibited in Stockton, upwards of nine and a half feet long.
Stockton-on-Tees.   H. T. A.

STINGING NETTLE.—Can any of your correspondents tell me why it is that if a stinging nettle be tightly grasped no sting is felt?
How long a time usually elapses between the laying and hatching of the eggs of the common water-snail (Paludina)?   TORTOISE.

THE WEATHER.—The scream of the peacock is said to be indicative of rain, but I have frequently heard it screaming before the finest weather. It would be very interesting if some of your correspondents would give a list of the principal "signs of the weather."   R. B. W.

MOTHS.—Could any of your readers inform me of the best method of catching Nocturni, and also if the Deaths Head Hawk Moth (Acherontia atropos) is to be taken in the vicinity of Brighton.
Brighton.   J. B.

NOTES ON COLEOPTERA AT DARENTH WOOD.

By E. C. RYE.

N most, if not all, British works on Entomology, mention is sure to be made of this prolific spot; and, as the present time is about the very best for collecting, I propose to make a few remarks on the *Coleoptera* to be there obtained, in the hope of putting those who have had no experience of the locality in the way of enriching their collections or adding to their knowledge.

Darenth (or, as the natives have it, " Darn ") Wood lies on the south bank of the Thames, between Dartford and Greenhythe, from either of which stations on the North Kent line it can be easily reached, though the *route* from the former is perhaps the better, if rather the longer, one. The wood derives its name from the little village of Darenth, situated on the river Dart (so called from its extreme slowness, apparently), which disembogues itself into the Thames *viâ* Dartford; and is the most westernly of a more or less connected chain of plantations, reaching nearly up to Gravesend, of which Swanscomb and Stone Woods form a part, and are almost equally good for entomological purposes.

Starting, then, from Dartford Station, our path, after turning to the left down the High Street (part of the Roman Road known as Watling Street), and crossing the mill stream just past the church, lies through fields and lanes and across " Dartford Brent " until the direct road leading past the wood to Green Street Green, Betsom, &c., is reached. Almost all this *route* is good collecting ground. In the very first lane (opening on to the aforesaid " Brent,"—an uncultivated grassy common)—the males of the curious *Drilus flavescens* often abound, and are to be obtained by sweeping among the rank vegetation at the sides, where snails (on which the beetle, in its earlier stages, feeds) are plentiful. This species, allied to the glowworm, has in that sex yellow elytra and black pectinated antennæ; but the female, as in *Lampyris*, is a mere grub, of larger size, unsymmetrical outline, and excessive rarity; but one or two British examples being known. In the dry woody stems of the *Clematis vitalba*, " The Traveller's Joy," (*why*, I know not), the little *Læmoplœus clematidis* has been here taken, but very rarely; the little *Tomicus bispinus* occurring commonly in the same situation. The net must be held well under the old wood of the plant, which is then to be thrashed vigorously with a beating stick. The beginner will find plenty of amusement and a bottle full of beetles by sweeping the mallow and other wild plants in this lane, though he will find nothing of peculiar rarity; his net chiefly exhibiting *Apion malvæ, rufirostre* (which differs sexually in colour), &c.;—even the veteran can, however, seldom resist unlimbering his hunting weapons here. Stinging neetles, which abound at the top of the lane, will, if well swept, usually afford the large and handsome *Chrysomela Banksii*; and, as the road becomes more chalky, the rarer and handsomer dark violet *C. göttingensis* may be sometimes found slowly crawling over the paths.

Emerging upon the " Brent," the best course is to keep along an old hedge, dotted with large trees, until the high road is reached. This hedge must be carefully thrashed into the beating net; the best patches being those that *look* the most unprofitable to a casual observer, viz., the dry, withered twigs and branches that are thrust in to fill up gaps. These yield insects not to be found in other places, save as stragglers, and some of which will need a sharp eye, so much do they assimilate in colour, size and contour to bits of broken twigs and dead buds. This likeness, moreover, many of them assist by pertinaciously simulating death. *Acalles misellus*, a small species of the *Cryptorhynchidæ*, may copiously be found by this manner of hunting; but, until the eye becomes accustomed to it, the beginner will run a good chance of often rejecting it, as it contracts its legs together and folds them at right angles to its body—a habit which, added to its dirty brown colour and rough texture, causes it to resemble nothing so much as a rough morsel of bark. With it will occasionally be found the handsome grey and white spotted *Hedobia imperialis*, and the commoner *Anobia* in plenty; whilst our three species of *Rhinosimus* (*Curculio*-like Heteromerous beetles) are not unfrequent, those with a red thorax especially abounding, though usually the rarest. Their smaller and spotted ally, *Lissodema quadriguttata*, often accompanies them. Some Longicorns are also to be found by twig-beating, notably the two Southern *Pogonocheri*, the larger one with wing cases half greyish white, and *Liopus*, and the small brightly marked *Callidium alni*. *Latridius angusticollis* is also thus obtainable here, and (odd locality for such a weevil) the little round rough *Omias hirsutulus*. The pretty little *Apion vernale*, a miniature *malvæ*, not unfrequently will be found in the net, having probably deserted its usual plant habitat. Stray specimens of *Ochina hederæ*, beaten from ivy, and our three southern species of *Magdalinus* (dull blue black weevils) are not unlikely to be thus caught, with (rarely) *Opilus mollis*, a long, slightly hairy frequenter of very dry timber enveloped in spiders webs. The true wood-feeders (such as the *Tomicus* above mentioned) will be probably represented by the minute *Phlœophthorus rhododactylus* (the smaller the beetle, the longer the name), and the rare *Hylesinus obscurus*. Close to the lane leading to the wood, the same method of collecting will produce the spidery-legged *Necydalis umbellatarum*, a *Longicorn*, whose elytra are diminished and gaping, so that the wings are exposed. A very small *Tomicus*, apparently the *T. coryli* of Perris, superficially much like a small female of its companion *T. bispinus*, and not yet recorded as British, is also to be found just here, with (but excessively rarely) *Tropideres niveirostris*. Many stray insects, not properly wood-feeders, will be sure to be found in the net whilst thus engaged.

In a small chalky cutting to the left of the road, where *Dulcamara* grows, the almost circular blue *Psylliodes dulcamaræ* may be beaten into the net,—I do not say *caught*, as its lively jumping habits render it anything but an easy prey; and by generally sweeping wild flowers and young shrubs many good insects will be caught, stragglers on the wing from their metropolis. *Homaloplia ruricola*, a rare and pretty little "chafer," has here occurred, with *Clytus mysticus*, and its common wasp-like congener *arietis*, and the curious *Oömorphus concolor*, difficult to mount. On the return home later in the evening, a rare blue *Harpalus*, *H. punctatulus*, is not uncommonly to be obtained by sweeping long grass. Once I caught the very rare dung beetle, *Odontæus mobilicornis*, here, flying at dusk, after its fashion.

Close to the "Fox" public-house, where entomologists most do congregate, and which lies exactly at the entrance of the lane leading to the wood, are usually some wood stacks, under which the "red-neck," *Stilicus fragilis*, a rare "devil's coach horse," has been taken; and on wild flowers there the still rarer *Leptura revestita* was once found, the commoner cylindrical red and black *Tillus elongatus* being also to be obtained from elder blossom.

Ascending the lane to the wood, through high sandy banks, insects at this time, and on a favourable day, crowd on the collector too fast to be recorded; and the beginner could lay in a large stock of varied material, chiefly plant feeders. It will, therefore, be impossible to do more than indicate the best spots and species. On burdocks, to the right of the lane, I have found *Tanymecus palliatus*, our largest Sitoniform weevil; whereof once, on the Betsom side of Swanscomb Wood, I observed a large number gravely walking in procession over a ploughed field, with no apparent object. In a sandy cutting to the left, stray specimens of the quaint *Orobitis cyaneus* often occur. This weevil (which feeds on a lovely vetch) draws in its limbs when captured, and then exactly resembles the ripe seed of the common wild squill. Its legs are so exceedingly straggly when they are extended, that the contrast is very ludicrous. Crossing the path here, the cumbrous shining black *Molytes coronatus* has often been found.

On reaching the level of the wood, much must be left to the collector's discretion, according to the temporary condition of the plantations. As a rule, old trees, save for fungi growing on them, or for species that frequent rotten wood, are not very productive. For essentially plant insects, cuttings of a year's (or, at most, two years) growth should be looked for. By beating the young plants of oak, hazel, aspen, &c., a great number of species and specimens may be obtained. Perhaps young aspens tempt the beginner the most, being productive of many and beautiful insects. From them he will certainly beat the elegant freckled *Saperda populnea*, which, in its earlier stages, causes knob-like swellings in the stems of the plants; and, with the *Saperda*, *Gonioctena decempunctata* and *G. rufipes* occur commonly; both of which are bright sealing-wax red in colour when alive, with variable black spots—the former to be known by its black legs. The obese *Lina longicollis*, and that little beauty, *Rhynchites populi*, one of our handsomest beetles, with its metallic rich coppery green tint above (deep dark blue beneath), will be nearly sure to reward the collector's toil, accompanied by the wary little *Zeugophora subspinosa*. On the hazel, the larger and equally lovely *Rhynchites betuleti* is sometimes plentifully to be taken. The sexes here are to be known by their difference in colour, the male being bright coppery green both above and below, and the female dark blue. The thorax in the latter sex also is armed with a short sharp spine on each side; but I have specimens of the female assuming the male colour, and *vice versâ*. The female deposits an egg in the young topmost shoots of the hazel, and then half bites through the stem, so as to arrest the growth. Many other species of this interesting genus occur here, chiefly on oak, and mostly of small size. The largest of them, *R. pubescens*, is, as its name implies, slightly hairy. They all have a long rostrum, slightly widened at the tip. A common and conspicuous hazel species is *Apoderus coryli*, bright red, roughly punctured, with a long head, and slightly like its equally common representative on the oak, *Attellabus curculionides*, also bright red, but smooth and more convex and short. On the hazel occur also several species of *Cryptocephalus*, of pretty colours or markings, and usually rare. Chief of these is *C. sexpunctatus*, golden yellow, with black spots; a most wary insect, which requires to be "stalked," as it draws in its limbs and rolls off into impenetrable jungle on the approach of the net.

C. coryli, whose female is uniformly bright red, and male has a black thorax, is found here also, with *C. lineola*, whose deep chestnut red elytra are each streaked with black. Of the smaller species, *C. flavilabris* and *C. punctiger*, both deep blue and shining (the latter the smallest and rarest) are the best; the common little shining black *C. labiatus* abounding on all woody plants, with the narrow *Agrilus angustulus*, one of our very few *Buprestidæ*, a family so numerously peopled in exotic countries. On the hazel also will be found the long-snouted brown "nut weevil" proper, *Balaninus nucum*, whose white grub is so well known to the filbert eater.

On young oaks three other species of *Balaninus* are to be found, viz., *B. turbatus, venosus* (which serves the acorns as *B. nucum* does hazel nuts) and *villosus*. The latter may be recognised by its smaller size and grey colour; but both the former are very much like *B. nucum*, from which *B. turbatus* differs notably in its very long and thin rostrum (the insect has been named *elephas*, from its being *par excellence* a proboscis-bearer), which is not in the least thickened at the base; and *B. venosus* in the lesser breadth of its scutellum. On these trees, too, the spotted *Silpha quadrimaculata* may be found; an unusual habitat for a carrion-feeder, but probably to be accounted for by its searches for larvæ of *Lepidoptera*, which abound on oaks. It is needless to impress on the collector the benefit likely to accrue to him if he be lucky enough to find any dead animals, shot by keepers and nailed to trees or dependent from their branches, or lying in the path. Cats, weasels, hedgehogs, birds, snakes, all are fish (paradoxically) that come to his net. Great will be his plunder in the way of *Necrophaga*. Of other beetles found here on oak, I may particularise *Cistela ceramboides*, *Hypulus quercinus*, a rare narrow Heteromerous species, prettily variegated, occurring in dead wood, and our largest true *Buprestis*, *Agrilus biguttatus*, a dark silky blue metallic insect, slightly spotted with white, which passes its existence in the thick bark of old stumps; not boring into the solid wood, or running galleries between bark and tree, but living between the outer and inner surfaces of the bark itself. Generally sluggish, it flies with great agility in the hot sunshine.

Willows growing near the pond by the "Five Ways," in addition to their usual frequenters, here afford another *Buprestis*, of different shape to the *Agrilus*, being short and squab: this is *Trachys minutus*, darkly metallic, with thin whitish lines. He is a "caution" to set out, owing to his thin, wiry, retractile legs. On these willows also the somewhat uncommon *Corymbites metallicus* is to be sometimes found;—one of the few *Elateridæ* occurring in the wood which are worth bottling—the usual "skip-jacks" being the pest, *Athöus hæmorrhoidalis*, which abounds on every scrap of vegetation, *A. vittatus, Elater balteatus* (chiefly on oak), *Dolopius*, and divers small *Agriotes*.

At the aforesaid pond that very rare *Staphylinus*, *Acrognatha mandibularis*, has been at intervals taken. It frequents the very wettest parts, where dead leaves are in sopping layers, and is absolutely bloated out with moisture. The little active *Bembidium doris*, a local species, is here plentiful; and *Lathrobium quadratum* occasionally occurs.

The black headed "Cardinal," *Pyrochroa coccinea*—scarlet, as its name imports—is not rare in the wood. I once found a whole brood, with their larvæ and pupæ, under bark of a felled tree. It flies strongly, but heavily, in the sunshine.

Of the Longicorn beetles, *Pachyta collaris* is, perhaps, most worthy of remark. It occurs at the skirts of the wood, on white flowers of *Umbelliferæ*, near hops, and probably passes its earlier stages in the poles used for those plants. *Anoplodera sexguttata* is also to be sometimes found, chiefly on the *Viburnum opulus*, or wild guelder-rose. The commoner species of *Rhagium* and *Toxotus*, *Pachyta livida*, *Strangalia melanura* and *armata*, of course abound, with the small species of *Grammoptera;* nor is the little *Tetrops*, with its divided eyes, rare.

Sweeping generally will of course produce many species of plant and flower beetles; the green *Œdemera cærulea*, easily known by the inflated "trunk hose" of its hinder legs in the male, being very common; with, but much more rarely, *Mordellistena abdominalis* and *brunnea*, curious on account of their deep and narrow build. Many species of *Cionus*, small round, convex weevils, all more or less presenting the appearance of having been perforated with a large pin through the back, are to be found on spurge.

Fungoid growth on old trees is inhabited by the bright and spotted *Endomychus coccineus*, *Tritoma bipustulata*, &c.; and in true fungi, *Triphyllus suturalis, Liodes orbicularis, Philonthus succicola*, and many other species exist.

It is obviously impossible in such a limited space as this to make any specific mention of the very numerous small and most interesting beetles with which a close search will be sure to reward the diligent collector, and many of which will thrust themselves upon his observation. I can only indicate here the larger or more conspicuous species, and such as are likely to be of interest, or to be found with ordinary luck. Nor is it necessary for me to dilate upon the delicious scenery, the bounteous flora, and the general gratification felt by the naturalist in the outdoor pursuit of his studies.

CUCKOO-FLOWERS.

It is curious to observe how many of our wild flowers take their names from the Cuckoo; not from the little child's idea that it eats the flowers to clear its voice (although the notion is not more wild and visionary than the conceit of some of the old botanists, who believed that the Hawkweed was so named because hawks and other birds of prey derived their wonderful powers of sight from using the juice of this plant), but because they come into flower about the same time as the Cuckoo makes its appearance in England.

In Greek the same word denotes the Cuckoo and the young fig; a similar reason is assigned for this. The Latin name of the "Ragged Robin" (*Lychnis Flos-cuculi*) would seem to give it a right to be called the Cuckoo-flower; but that is not its common English name, and I believe its old name was the "Flower of St. Felix." It is a meadow blossom, coming up with the grass, and cut down and withering with it; so that it is a suitable flower to be dedicated to the good Roman husbandman, who contemplated the Creator in all His works, and made each the text for some holy thought, believing that "Every creature in the world will raise our hearts to God, if we look upon it with a good eye." "St. Felix's Day" is the 21st of May, and the Lychnis is a May flower. I have heard it called by country people "Robin Wood," which may be a corruption of "Robin Hood."

Shakespeare probably meant by his "cuckoo buds of yellow hue" the various species of Ranunculus—buttercups, lesser celandine, &c.—as he distinguishes them from the "Lady's-Smock" "all silver white," another name for our most commonly known Cuckoo-flower, the *Cardamine pratensis*, of which Gerarde says: "It flowers for the most part in April or May, when the Cuckoo doth begin to sing her pleasant notes without stammering." Its name of "Lady's, smock" is evidently given in honour of the Virgin Mary, to whom all flowers blossoming in "the Blessed Virgin's month" (May) were dedicated. The Cuckoo-buds are also "Mary-buds" and "May-buds."

> "And winking Marybuds begin
> To ope their golden eyes."
> "And 'king-cups' and 'gold-cups.'"

Botanists do not give them half such pretty names. Their generic name of Ranunculus is derived from *rana*, a frog, from the fact of their flourishing best in damp places, the abode of those creatures. An old writer speaks of them as "sundry kind of crow-foote, called ranunculi, or litele frogge's grass." They are too familiar to us to need any particular description; but there are two or three characteristics of the tribe which should be mentioned. They have a great number of stamens springing out beneath the carpels (the little green grains which contain the seed), and these carpels are distinct from each other, instead of forming one seed vessel. Almost all plants possessing these two characteristics are poisonous. Two of the Crow-foot tribe, the *Ranunculus sceleratus* and *Ranunculus acris*, "the wicked" and "the bitter ranunculus," are so named on this account. Cattle will always avoid the stalks of the buttercups growing in the pasture-fields, eating away the grass all round them, and leaving them untouched; the old notion, therefore, of the buttercups making the butter yellow is apparently a mistaken one.

The *Cardamine pratensis* belongs to another great natural order, the Cruciferous tribe, of plants, all of which are very wholesome, and many have very nutritious and strengthening properties. Their name of Cross-bearers comes from the position in which their four petals are placed, so as to resemble a Maltese cross. They have six stamens, of which two are shorter and more spreading than the other four. This is a characteristic of all the Cruciferous plants, which include most of our garden vegetables—cabbages, turnips, radishes, mustard and cress, &c. Some of the Cardamines grow in the Arctic regions, where they are very valuable to travellers and sailors, on account of their antiscorbutic properties. Their botanical name comes from *cardia*, heart, and *damas*, to fortify, from the tonic and invigorating qualities it is believed to possess. Its Shakespearean name has many explanations. Its connection with "Our Lady" comes of course from its being a May flower. The "Smock" may be derived from its whiteness; for its flowers, veined with delicate lilac, look very white among the meadow-grass, and it grows by the river's side and in damp meadows, where, in olden times, webs of linen were laid out to bleach. The country people call it "bread and milk," probably from the whiteness of its flowers; but another reason has been given for this—that it blooms at the beginning of spring, when, from the cows being no longer confined to dry food, their milk becomes plentiful, and they are able to get this luxury for breakfast. The Welsh call it *Hyddyf*, the Germans *Gauchblume*, and the French *Cresson*, or *Chemise de Notre Dame*. It inhabits the greater part of Europe, and is found in the northern countries of Asia and America, near Hudson's Bay, &c. It is sometimes found with double flowers, sometimes with a kind of secondary flower, springing from the centre of the first instead of a seed-vessel. Young plants will occasionally grow upon the old leaves, where they touch the ground, and leaflets will appear on the upper surface of the parent-leaf, and from this a long root-fibre will creep down, and rest itself in the soil below.

This is pre-eminently the Cuckoo-plant, flowering when the Cuckoo sings all day, according to the old rhymes :

"In April—she opens her bill,
In May—she sings all day,
In June—she alters her tune,
In July—away doth fly,
In August—go she must."

The Spotted Purple Orchis (*O. mascula*) is called the Cuckoo-flower in some parts of England. But the *Arum maculatum* and the Wood-sorrel (*Oxalis Acetosella*) are better known as connected with the Cuckoo. The Arum is a favourite with all country children, who delight in searching through its numerous spotted leaves for the closely-folded sheaths which contain the blossoms; the rich crimson columns they call "lords," and the delicate pink ones "ladies." The name is said to have been derived from "our Lord" and "our Lady;" the latter probably came from its being a May flowering plant, and the former to distinguish the dark and the pale blossoms. Pliny calls the Arum *Aris* and *Aron* : the old English name of *Wake Robin* is not easily explained. Its more familiar cognomen of *Cuckoo-pint* has been accounted for by the notion that the spathed leaves would hold about a pint of liquid (an impossibility), or that the moisture lying in them was a reservoir of water for the Cuckoo. But it is much more likely that the name is a corruption of the old Welsh name *pidyn y gög*, or *pidyggw y gög*, "the point or poignard of the Cuckoo," referring to the spade in the centre of the spathe. The French names are *Chou-poivre*, *Pain de lièvre*, *Pied de veau;* the German, *Zehrwurzel*, or *Zehrend Wurzelkraut;* the Italian, *Giaro* (Serpent's bread). Our British species of Arum is not very common in Scotland, but abounds all over England in hedgerows and woods. It is found on the dry, sun-burnt soil of the Holmes, in the British Channel, or Portland Isle.

The Arum possesses a curious property, that of emitting heat. When the column is growing this is evidenced so considerably as to affect a thermometer put into the spathe; and for some hours after it first expands the heat can be felt by putting the hand on the blossom. The fresh juice of the plant is acrid enough to blister the tongue, if tasted; and this is the case with its allies the "Taro" and the "Egyptian Arum;" but its acrimonious, even poisonous, nature may be completely destroyed by exposing it to heat, or by maceration in water: and its roots have been used for the old-fashioned English drink of Saloop, and as a substitute for arrow-root, and in the manufacture of fine starch. It is a powerful stimulant, and the *poudre de Cypre*, used in Paris as a cosmetic, is made from it. The leaves and blossoms contain a saponaceous principle. The Taro roots form the chief food of the Sandwich Islanders, and are boiled to make the thick paste called *poé*.

The Wood-sorrel (*Oxalis Acetosella*) is one of the loveliest of our spring flowers, and has much to interest all lovers of them. There seems no reason for its country name of "Cuckoo's meat," excepting its appearance at the same time; though in France it has the same appellative, *Pain de Cocu*, as well as *Surelle* and *Petite Oseille*, and one of its Welsh names has a similar meaning, "*Susan y gög*." It is also called *Segyr fflug* and *Clychan Fwlylhlêg*, "Fairy Bells," from the notion prevalent among the peasantry that the "good people" use its tiny white bells to ring out their summons to their moonlight revels. The German name is *Sauer Klee*, probably having the same meaning as that which it bears in England of *Wood-sorrel* or *Wood-Sauer*, from the acid taste of its leaves. The Italians and Spanish know it as the "*Alleluia* Flower," and that appears to have been its old title in England; for Gerarde says : "The apothecarys and herbarists call it *Alleluya*, and *Panis Cuculi*, or Cuckowe's meate, because either the Cuckow feedeth thereon, or by reason, when it springeth forth and flowereth, the Cuckow singeth most, at which time also Alleluya was wont to be sung in churches." This must have been between Easter and Whitsuntide. In Buckinghamshire it is called *Cuckoo's Vittles*. It is reckoned amongst our Whitsuntide flowers, though it is more frequently a Trinity flower, being supposed by many botanists to be the Irish Shamrock, about which the beautiful legend is told of St Patrick using it as a symbol of the Holy Trinity, when he found the peasantry unable to comprehend his preaching of that doctrine. The White Clover, which has also a trefoil leaf, and which is supposed by others to be the saint's flower is, I believe, more recently introduced into Ireland; and the Oxalis was reverenced by the Druids, as emblematic of the mysterious Three in One, the object of their secret worship. They honoured it for another reason—because each leaflet of the trefoil leaf is marked by a pale crescent, the emblem of the moon, another of their sacred symbols. Many of the old writers in Ireland speak of "curds and sham roots" as being the spring food of the Irish, and say, "they willingly eat the herb Schamrock, being of a sharp taste, which they snatch out of the ditches." The Four-leaved Shamrock is considered both by the Irish and Welsh peasants as a charm against witches, and the finder of it is supposed to be sure of good fortune all through life. This is rarely to be met with in the Wood-sorrel leaves, and its rarity probably gives it its value. The Welsh bards call this *Segys fflug*, or "Dispeller of illusion."

The Wood-sorrel is an excellent weather-glass; both leaves and flowers close before rain, and the blossoms expand only in full sunshine. If the leaves are roughly handled they will shrink from the touch, droop, and gradually fold up (not suddenly, as is the case with the sensitive plant), and, if carried into a room artificially lighted, they will not re-open. After the flowers have passed away, the seed-pods appear like swollen buds, green and hard, till quite ripe, when they burst open, at right angles, and scatter around their white, pearl-like seeds. The Wood-sorrel possesses another beauty in addition to that of its delicately-veined flowers and emerald-green leaves: its creeping root resembles coral in its hard round knobs or scales of pink and bright red. A variety of the plant, growing in some parts of England, has bright purplish red blossoms, but they are not half so pretty as the little white flowers with their lilac veins.

The Wood-sorrel has utilitarian properties. Gerarde says of it: "It maketh better greene sauce than any other herbe or sorrele whatsoever; and it quencheth thirst, and cooleth mightily an hot pestilentiall fever, especially being made in a syrup with sugar."—C. D.—*Aunt Judy's Magazine* for May.

SPINY AND HAIRY CATERPILLARS.
By E. J. S. Clifford.

THE caterpillars of *Lepidoptera* are indeed a numerous and conspicuous body of insects in the glad summer season. Feeding, as many of them do, in exposed situations, and being, in many species, furnished with striking exterior and brilliant colours, they very naturally attract the attention even of the uninterested bypasser. Those who would hardly take the trouble to search for them cannot but admire the exceeding beauty of their markings, and the variety of forms which exists amongst them. To us one of the most interesting and remarkable adornments with which they are gifted consists in the spines or hairs which clothe so many distinct species. Let us bring a few such kinds before our readers, selecting some of the more conspicuous examples.

It may be difficult to determine the precise end or purpose for which spines or hairs on the bodies of caterpillars are intended. Whilst at first sight they may seem to serve as means of defence from their insect or other foes, we feel certain that such is not the case in all instances. Those, however, which are very densely clothed with hairs may be rendered impregnable to insect enemies (excepting the ichneumon tribes), and disagreeable to feathered foes. This seems more probable in regard to such caterpillars as are furnished with hairs possessing some irritative quality, annoying both to man and animals. Yet we are inclined to think that these appendages are given more for the sake of ornamentation than for any other reason; and it is certain that in many species they form a most graceful addition to the general contour of caterpillars. Besides this, however, many hybernating caterpillars are preserved from the winter's cold by a long covering of hairs, extending down to the very feet.

Amongst the butterflies there are many species whose caterpillars are spiny, or else clothed with hairs of various lengths and numbers. The caterpillar of the Black-veined White (*Aporia Cratægi*) is thickly covered with whitish hairs, which are very beautiful. On the side this caterpillar is leaden-grey, black on the back, and marked with two reddish longitudinal stripes. Then the caterpillars of the two common "Whites" are covered with shortish hairs, though they can scarcely come under the denomination of "hairy caterpillars." Perhaps the most conspicuous examples of spiny caterpillars are those of the handsome "Vanessa" butterflies. They are all very singular in this respect. The caterpillar of the White Admiral butterfly (*Limenitis Sybilla*), feeding on the honeysuckle, is covered with reddish branched or compound spines, and in the ground colour is green. The stripes on the sides are white and brown. The Purple Emperor (*Apatura Iris*) again—that superb insect—is produced from a caterpillar which is furnished with two spine-like appendages on the head, termed tentacles or horns. It is a beautiful creature, and one wishes it were commoner amongst us than at present it is. It feeds on the oak and the broad-leaved sallow, though it has occasionally been found at the poplar.

The caterpillar of the Painted Lady (*Cynthia Cardui*) is spiny, or thorny, as some writers prefer to call it; and feeds on various species of thistle. Singular indeed, it is, that the caterpillars of these insects, when moulting, shed the cases which enclosed their old spines, and come forth entirely renewed in this as in every other respect. Thus the old skin cast off has a singular resemblance to the caterpillar once enclosed within it. The branched spines of all these caterpillars (producing the handsome frequenters of the country which delight us in the summer) are very curious, and well worthy of examination. The Red Admiral butterfly (*Vanessa Atalanta*), the Peacock (*V. Io*) and the two "Tortoiseshells" are all produced from spiny caterpillars, many of them feeding in a social or gregarious manner. The caterpillar of the Red Admiral butterfly is a singular individual, though, for he prefers to seclude himself, like a hermit, away from the gaze of bypassers. These caterpillars feed separately, within two or three leaves of the nettle, which they have spun together; thus they proceed, shifting quarters as soon as their stock of leaves is exhausted. The well-known caterpillar of the Peacock butterfly hardly needs a word of comment from us. In the hot summer months whole hosts of these creatures may be seen feeding amongst the clumps of nettles, and they can be examined at leisure. They are very easy and interesting to rear in confinement, where their spiny covering can be more closely examined. In colour they are black, dotted with white, and their spines are much branched. At the approach of a bypasser we have noticed companies of these caterpillars start back from their feeding simultaneously, as if electrified; nor do they resume operations till the cause of their annoyance has disappeared.

The Large Tortoiseshell (*Vanessa Polychloros*) is a very handsome butterfly; and its caterpillar, feeding upon elm, is rarely found. It is tawny in colour, and thorny, like the rest of the genus. The social caterpillars of the Small Tortoiseshell (*Vanessa urticæ*), on the contrary, can be seen on the patches of nettles that render lively and green the precincts of our great city itself. It is grey in colour, with a black line on the back, and brown and yellow stripes on the sides. Its numerous spines alone render it very interesting, and identify it with the rest of this handsome family. Then the rare caterpillar of the Comma butterfly (*Vanessa C. album*) is spiny, and these are shorter than the spines of those already noticed. There are two ear-like tubercles projecting from the side of the head. It feeds on the sloe, currant, nettle, and hop.

Leaving, however, the "Vanessa" caterpillars, which from their social habits and other characteristics are such striking examples of spiny caterpillars, we come to notice the beautiful caterpillars of the "Fritillary" butterflies. Like those of the last-mentioned class, these are spiny, and their spines, which are compound, are very similar in all the species. Many of them feed on the various species of wild violet which decorate our woodlands, and are difficult to secure. The caterpillar of the Silver-washed Fritillary (*Argynnis Paphia*) has two spines behind the head, which are larger than the rest; a distinguishing mark of this species, which is not common. It is partial to woodland scenery, and is said to feed on the wild raspberry and nettle, as well as on violet leaves. Searching for these caterpillars proves very fatiguing work, since these plants always grow in situations which render examination difficult. The Likeness Fritillary (*Melitæa Athalia*) has the spines rust-coloured on the caterpillar, which feeds on the various species of plantain. Then that of the Greasy Fritillary (*Melitæa Artemis*), perhaps one of the commonest of this group, where occurring, is gregarious, feeding under the protection of a web, spun over the leaves of its foodplant, which is the devil's-bit scabious. In colour the caterpillar is black, with reddish-brown legs. These caterpillars of the true "Fritillaries" are very singular examples of "spiny caterpillars," and we recommend them for examination and study to our readers. The caterpillar of the Duke of Burgundy (*Nemeobius Lucina*) may at once be distinguished from those of the handsome "Fritillaries," already alluded to, although the butterfly itself much resembles them in its markings. It is short and thick, shaped much like a woodlouse. Its colour is reddish-brown, with tufts of hair of the same colour. Like this species, most of the "Blue" caterpillars are woodlouse-shaped, and slightly hairy. Of their economy much remains to be discovered and understood.

Turning to the handsome caterpillars of the "SPHINGIDÆ," we find them nearly all smooth, and destitute of any other appendage than the horn at the tail, and thus they hardly come under the limitation of our title; though the horn may be regarded by some as a large, simple spine. Several, however, of the caterpillars which compose the large and striking group of "BOMBYCINA" are very remarkably adorned with hairs, rendering them especially beautiful. The caterpillars of the "Footman" moths are most of them hairy; covered with a number of little lumps or tubercles, from whence the hairs proceed in little tufts. The best known species of this family is that called the Common Footman (*Lithosia complanula*), whose caterpillar feeds on the lichens which grow on oak, blackthorn, and some writers say on old walls which are covered with lichens. Most of these caterpillars are much alike in the arrangement and quantity of the hairs which adorn their bodies. This, however, is not the case with some others which are to be now noticed. The Crimson Speckled (*Deïopeia pulchella*) is a very rare species, the first of a small family called the "*Eucheliidæ.*" Perhaps not more than one or two specimens occur in all our British cabinets. Its caterpillar feeds (on the Continent) on the forget-me-not, but has never been found in this country. From the descriptions given of it, it must be a beautiful creature. The ground is lead colour, with a covering of black hairs, a broad white stripe down the back, and a double scarlet spot on each segment down the sides. In contrast to this lovely rarity we turn to the common caterpillar of the Pink Underwing (*Euchelia Jacobææ*), which is another of this little group. This is the brilliant little moth that, like a butterfly, is seen busily engaged amongst the flowers of the ragwort at midday. Its caterpillar, which feeds on the above-named plant, is not so hairy as the rest of this family; but its colouring is very striking, being of a deep orange, with black rings at each segment of the body. Singularly beautiful, also, are the hairy caterpillar, of the "Tiger" moths. The caterpillar of the Clouded Buff (*Euthemonia russula*), again, is furnished with red-brown hairs, and a yellow stripe down the middle of the back; it feeds pretty generally on the mouse-ear hawkweed and dandelion, and probably other plants growing on heaths. But the most familiar instance, perhaps, of hairy caterpillars, is given by that of the Large Tiger moth (*Chelonia caja*) itself, the commonest species of this family. Even in the close vicinity of London this handsome creature may be seen taking its rambles in search of a suitable place for spinning its cocoon. It feeds on nettles, and one often sees it crossing the country roads with great rapidity, as if aware that many enemies surrounded it on all sides. The hairs of this caterpillar are very beautiful and silky. In ground colour it is black; the hairs on the back are grey, those of the sides and about the head are brown; the head and legs are black. The loose web it spins is covered over with its hairs, which it sheds before assuming the chrysalis state. Some irritative quality is said to attach to its hairs, but we cannot vouch for the truth of the statement. When touched these caterpillars immediately drop from their foodplant, roll up into a ball, presenting a droll resemblance to the hedgehog. They are probably defended in this manner from many of their enemies.

Others of the division *Bombycina* are possessed of wart-like protuberances, which emit little tufts of hair, or bristles of various natures. But we wish now briefly to speak of some caterpillars of this division which are furnished with hairs so arranged and disposed as to add very materially to their external grace and beauty. One of the commonest caterpillars in the hawthorn hedges in the summer is that producing the Gold-tail Moth (*Liparis auriflua*). It is short and stout, the ground colour black, and it has rows of tubercles on each side from which radiate a number of bristly hairs. The second row of tubercles is ornamented with a tuft of whitish hairs, the third row is coral red. There are two bright red stripes along the back, which give the creature a peculiarly attractive appearance. The common caterpillar of the Pale Tussock (*Orgyia pudibunda*) is another very interesting example of hairy caterpillars. It is of a delicate green colour, with a band of intense black between several segments of the body, and with a tuft of yellow hairs like a brush on the back of each of these segments. The last has a longer and more slender tuft directed backwards. Before changing their skins, these handsome caterpillars spin a little silken house, seeking for retirement from their fellows by bending a leaf over their backs. Lastly amongst these handsome insects called the BOMBYCINA we notice the vivid caterpillar of the Scarce Vapourer (*Orgyia gonostigma*). This is indeed a brilliant creature, for the ground colour is bright orange, and the middle segments of the body have a tuft of brown hairs on the back; there are also two slender tufts of hairs pointing forwards over the head. Delicate pencils of hair also point backwards from the last segment of the body. This caterpillar is a singular instance of the beauty conferred on many insects by the addition of hairy coverings.

Space forbids our noticing the large hairy caterpillars of the "Eggars," and others, of which the "Drinker" is a well-known instance. Suffice it that we have selected some of the most beautiful and conspicuous of this group of our insects. Neither the NOCTUÆ nor the GEOMETRÆ furnish any very striking examples of spiny or hairy caterpillars, hence we pass them over. In conclusion, we remark that these adornments of our native caterpillars form very singular microscopic objects. The variety existing amongst them in so many respects, renders them very full of interest to the thoughtful observer.

PRESERVATION OF SPECIMENS IN NATURAL HISTORY.

BY CAPTAIN OLIVER HALDANE STOKES, LATE ROYAL ENGINEERS, F.R.A.S., F.R.S.M., I.M.S., ETC.

(1) *General Directions.*

(*a*) The specimen when first procured must be wiped dry; and should any blood issue from its beak, or mouth, or wounds, care must be taken lest the feathers or fur, "should the animal be possessed of either," become stained with the blood. Many animals emit blood and fluid matter from their mouths even when several hours after death have elapsed, consequently a pledget of tow or cotton wool should be stuffed into the mouth and throat, and the mouth or beak then closed. A piece of tape or twine will serve as a ligature, and in the case of birds it will be found necessary to pass the twine through the nostrils in order to prevent the ligature from slipping off the beak. The ligature in the case of birds should have its ends left about six inches in length, so that they will form a loop when knotted together by which the bird may be suspended, "as will be explained necessary hereafter." The specimen should, when practicable, be wrapped up by itself in a sheet of strong brown paper, and laid by in a dry, secure place until the next day, or at all events until the blood and animal fluids have become coagulated. In general the specimen should be suspended from the ceiling with its head downwards; a bird can be suspended by a noose of twine fastened round its legs, and a fish by the same round its tail. Quadrupeds can be suspended by the hind legs. In tropical countries especially the suspending twine or string should be saturated with cocoa nut oil, which will prevent ants attacking the specimen; but should the specimens not be hung up, they should be placed on an inclined shelf or stone slab, and a circumscribing line or circle made around it with a small brush full of cocoa nut oil. The ants will not cross a line drawn in cocoa nut or cajeput oil.

(b) The specimen being dead long enough to commence skinning, the following tools and materials will be necessary for general purposes; but should the specimens be large, such as those of a horse, a lion, tiger, whale, shark, ostrich, etc., then larger tools, such as hatchets, saws and knives, nippers and forceps, will be required.

Tools : One straight-bladed knife with straight handle, similar to those in a surgeon's case of pocket instruments; one ditto sharpened on both sides near the point only; one pair straight pocket surgical scissors; one pair small bone nippers; one small bone spatula or paper-cutter; some strong sewing-needles and iron wire; some strong common pins; some strong twine and thread; some small hooks like fishhooks, but without barbs—these should have strings attached to them, and will be found very useful to assist in keeping the skins of specimens from retracting during the progress of the operation of skinning; some fine and coarse brushes like paint brushes, of various sizes.

Materials: Cotton wool and tow, both should be of the finest description. "Powdered chalk." *Solution of corrosive sublimate*—the strength should be about three grains to one ounce of spirits of wine. "Arsenical soap:" this is made as follows:—Take ¼ lb. of common white soap and melt it over a slow fire in an earthenware pot or pipkin; having cut the soap into slices, add ¼ lb. of white arsenic and 1¼ ounces of powdered chalk to the soap when melted, and thoroughly mix the three ingredients together; take an ounce of camphor and dissolve it in a mortar with a little spirits of wine and add it to the soap mixture, having taken the latter off the fire and allowed it to become somewhat cool: the entire must be well blended together and kept closely bottled up—earthenware jars with ground stoppers answer very well, and for travelling about, round tin canisters with well-fitting tops are very useful and not easily damaged.

When the arsenical soap is required for use, a portion of it should be taken out and mixed with water to the consistency of cream; some fatty coarse skins require it to be applied thicker than lighter, delicate skins. The soap is applied with a brush of such a size and coarseness as may be necessary according to the size of the specimen. Care must be taken not to cut one's fingers with the tools in use nor with any sharp particles of bone, or by the claws, teeth, etc., of the specimen; neither should any of the arsenical soap be allowed to get under one's nails, nor should any of the corrosive sublimate of the arsenical soap or of the blood or fluids from the specimen be allowed to get into any cuts or scratches upon the hands of the operator. The hands should never be allowed to touch the eyelids of the operator until they have been well washed, which should frequently be done during skinning and preserving operations in warm water with soap and a nail-brush. The tools should always be put by clean after use.

The operation of skinning any animal should be so conducted as to cause as little extension of the skin and distortion as possible, hence as small an opening as will suffice should be made in the skin. But in many instances the position and extent of the opening must depend upon the nature of the specimen, and also as to what portion of the skin it is more particularly intended to preserve without injury; but as a general rule specimens are opened down the centre of the breast and belly. The greatest care must be taken not to allow the skin to become soiled or stretched, and when possible the operation of skinning a specimen should not be interrupted for more than a few minutes; should, however, such an interruption be unavoidable the specimen should be left surrounded with a dry cloth or towel, and another cloth or towel should be placed outside the dry one and well saturated with water. This precaution will keep the skin moist until the operation can be resumed.

Whilst the skin is being removed from the body the hands should be kept as clean as possible, by means of a coarse towel near at hand, and as the skin gradually leaves the body bits of tow should be placed between the skin and the body, so as to keep all tidy and clean, and prevent the skin reclosing over the body. In separating the bones of the wings or legs of a specimen from the body it is better to dissect out the joints than to cut the bones; in small specimens the joints can be cut through with the scissors.

(2) *Skinning Birds.*

As a general rule birds are skinned by first making a primary incision down the front, which should extend from about the breastbone down to close to the vent; but in some cases the incision may have to extend somewhat higher up on the breast. Again, some birds, such as sea birds, are skinned by a similar longitudinal opening in the back along the spine, and some naturalists make the primary incision under one or both wings.

In cases where the wings are placed very far back, as in some sea birds, it becomes almost necessary to open along the back; but as a general rule the front is the position selected for the opening, unless in cases where the plumage is very light or delicate, when it would be better to open down the back. Again, a second incision sometimes becomes necessary in the case of such birds as ducks, which have the bones of the head so large as to prevent the skull being pushed through the skin of the neck. In these cases an incision must be made at the top or back of the head so as to expose the skull sufficiently.

In some birds it will be found preferable to skin the tail end of the body and legs before the neck end and wings: either method will suffice, and experience alone can enable the operator to choose the preferable mode of procedure.

(3) *General Mode of Skinning Birds.*

Taking as an example a domestic fowl. It should be wiped clean and laid upon its back on a table, with the head away from the operator. The position of the breast-bone should then be felt for and ascertained by the left forefinger. The knife should then be taken in the right hand, the little finger of which as well as the third finger should assist the left hand in exploring in order to find the centre of the breast. An incision must then be made as before mentioned, which should divide the skin only, and cut the roots of as few feathers as possible. The handle of the knife, and fingers, aided by a small spatula, should then be employed to push the skin away from the body so as to lay bare the joints of the wings and legs. The joints to be cut through may be best described as corresponding to that which connects the drumstick to the other half of a leg of fowl at table. The legs and wings being thus cut through by the scissors, or dissected out by the knife, the body should be taken up by the left hand and the skin gently *coaxed* away from it until the finger and thumb can meet behind its back, if it be a small specimen. The junction of the neck with the body should be then laid bare and cut through. The body now remains disconnected from the skin with the exception of the tail end. The body should now be held up in the left hand and the skin cautiously drawn downwards, until the oil glands and base of tail feathers become visible. The root of the tail must then be cut through, but great care must be taken that the tail feathers, or quills, are not cut in the least degree, for if they be they will fall out. The end of the neck is then seized in the left hand and the beak in the right hand, the neck is cut off, and the head is pushed very slowly and cautiously through the skin of the neck until the eyes and ears become visible and the greater part of the bones of the head. When the ears become visible they must be carefully cut across close to the bone of the skull, and the eyes delicately laid bare. During the progress of skinning the head the various muscles and tendons which may appear must be cut across, so as to allow of the separation of the skin. The eyes should then be taken out, but the eyeballs should not be broken, if possible; the tongue should be also cut out. An opening only sufficiently large should be made with the point of the knife in the base of the skull, and the brain extracted by means of the knife and a bit of iron wire with the tip bent, and the cavity of the brain cleaned out with tow. The whole of the interior and exterior of the skull and of the limbs which remain attached to the skin must now be freed from any adhering flesh, and all flesh and fat which may remain attached to the skin must be removed. Great care must be taken in removing the oil glands near the tail. The interior and exterior of the skull, the skin, and bones must next be well brushed over with the arsenical soap—especially over the oil glands. The interior of the skull is then stuffed with tow or cotton wool, and a little tow wrapped around the skull to represent the flesh which has been removed. The legs and wings are wrapped round with tow until they are of their natural size, and a piece of tow of the same size as the neck which has been withdrawn is made into a roll and placed within the skin of the neck. A piece of tow or cotton wool is next taken and formed into an artificial body, "*not larger than that which has been removed,*" and placed inside the skin, which is gently brought so as to nearly close the incision which has been made in it. The legs and wings are then placed in their relative positions, and the neck is drawn out straight in a line from the tail. The interior of the bill and the exterior of the bill and legs should be washed over with the soap solution, and the mandibles of the bill tied together by a piece of thread passing through the nostrils. The legs should then be tied together, and the feathers brushed and arranged. A cone of strong paper is now made and the specimen placed in it head foremost, and the operation becomes complete. With large birds it will be found often convenient to employ two strings with hooks at their ends, by which the body of the bird can be suspended from the ceiling, in preference to laying it on a table whilst skinning.

THE MOTTLED OWL.

On June 15, 1867, I observed some boys around a small owl which was perched on a stick. On closer examination I found that it was a young Mottled Owl (*Scops asio* Bonaparte). It was staring about in a dazed manner and seemed half stupified. I easily persuaded the boys to part with it for a trifle, and took it home. I should judge that it was about two weeks old. It was covered with a grayish down. I put it in a large cage, and gave it some meat, which it ate, but not readily, for it seemed frightened at the sight of my hand, and at my near approach would draw back, snapping its beak after the manner of all owls. It soon grew tamer, however, and would regard me with a wise stare, as if perfectly understanding that I was a friend.

In a short time it would take food from me without fear; I never saw it drink, although water was kept constantly near it. Its food consisted of mice, birds, and butchers' meat, on which it fed readily. I kept the bird caged for about two weeks, during which time it became quite tame, but would not tolerate handling, always threatening me with its beak when my hands approached it. As the wires of its cage broke its feathers when moving about, and as it hardly seemed resigned to confinement, I opened its cage and gave it the freedom of the room, leaving the windows open night and day. About this time I gave it the name of "Scops," to which in a little while it would answer, when called, with a low rattle, which sounded like the distant note of the king-fisher.

One morning Scops was missing; diligent search was made for it, but no owl could be found, and, reluctantly, we gave it up for lost. Once or twice it was seen in the neighbouring woods by different people, and once on the roof of a barn, but was wild and refused to be caught. It had been absent about a week, when, one morning, I was told that my owl was out in the yard. I hastened out and found a half-grown Newfoundland dog playing with my pet. The owl was clinging to his shaggy fur with its claws, snapping its beak, and biting fiercely. I immediately rescued poor Scops and carried it into the house. It was raining hard, and the bird was wet through. On arriving in its old quarters it seemed pleased, chuckling to itself after its manner. It was almost starved, and ate two full-grown blue-birds at the first meal. After this time I gave it the privilege of going and coming when it pleased, but, mindful of its former experience, it never has but once remained away more than two days at a time. It now became more attached to me than ever, and will, at this time, permit me to pat it gently.

When a bird is given it for food, it takes it in its claws, and with its beak invariably pulls out the wing and tail feathers first, then eats the head, then devours the intestines; then, if not satisfied, it eats the remainder of the bird, feathers and all.

That this owl sees tolerably well in the day-time I have proved to my satisfaction. I caught a mouse and put it alive into an open box about two feet square. This I placed upon a bench near Scops who was attentively watching my movements; the moment it saw the mouse, the owl opened its eyes wide, bent forward, moved its head from side to side, then came down with an unerring aim, burying its talons deep in the head and back of the mouse. Looking up into my face, and uttering its rattling note, as if inquiring, "Is'nt that well done?" it flew up to its perch with its struggling prey, grasped firmly in its talons, where it killed the mouse by biting it in the head and back. During the whole act it displayed considerable energy and excitement.

Again, I have seen it pounce on a dragon-fly which was unable to fly, but laid buzzing on the bench; the bird went through the same manœuvres as before, striking the dragon-fly with the greatest precision, and with both feet. I think that these instances prove that the bird can see nearly as well in the day as in the night. In both the above instances the sun was not shining on the objects struck, but they were very near the window, and the light was consequently strong.

Scops will, in taking birds from my hand, almost always look up in my face and utter its subdued rattle. In sleeping, it usually stands on one foot, both eyes shut, but sometimes stretches out at full length, resting on its breast. When sound asleep it awakes instantly on its name being pronounced, and will answer as quickly as when awake. I have heard it utter its peculiar quavering note on one or two occasions, which, notwithstanding its reputed mournfulness, has much that sounds pleasant to my ears. When moving along a plain surface, Scops progresses, with a half walk, half hop, which is certainly not the most graceful gait possible.

When out at night among the trees Scops acts in much the same manner as when in the house, hopping from limb to limb, looking about in a quick, graceful motion of the head, sometimes turning the head around so that the face comes directly behind.

When it returns to the house in the morning, daylight is often long passed, and even sunrise. The alarm note is a kind of low moan; this was often uttered at the sight of a tamed gray squirrel (but with which it has now become better acquainted), and always at the sight of its old enemy, the dog.

While flying, Scops moves through the air with a quick, steady motion, alighting on any object without missing a foothold. I never heard it utter a note when thus moving. When perching, it does not grasp with its claws, but holds them at some distance from the wood, clasping with the soles of the toes. When it has eaten enough of a bird, it hides the remaining portions in any convenient place near by; if its hiding-place is then approached, the owl from its perch watches the intruder jealously, and when its hidden spoils are touched, it lays back its ear-like tufts, snaps its beak once or twice, and drops down on the unlucky hand like an arrow, striking it with its sharp claws until the hand is withdrawn; then, ascertaining that its treasure is safe, Scops resumes its perch, looking at its late disturber with most unfriendly eyes.

Sometimes in the daytime it will take a sudden start, flitting about the room like a spectre, alighting on different objects to peer about, which it does by moving sideways, turning the head in various directions, and going through many curious movements; but it always return to its perch and settles down quietly.

I once placed a stuffed owl of its own species near it, when it ruffled its feathers, gave a series of hisses, moans, and snappings of the beak, and stretched out one wing at full length in front of its head as a shield to repulse what it took to be a stranger invading its own domains. As the stuffed bird was pushed nearer, Scops budged not an inch, but looked fiercer than ever; its ruffled back-feathers were erected high, its eyes sparkled, and its whole attitude was one of war.

Some time since the building in which my pet was kept was torn down, and the bird was absent for two weeks; but a new building has been erected near the site of the old one, and to-day I found Scops in the new cellar, sitting on a projecting stone of the wall, as much at home as in the old place. From this it can be seen that its affection for locality is very strong. Notwithstanding Scops' long absence it is as tame as ever, taking its food from my hand, and behaving in the old manner. Its plumage at this time (Oct. 31, 1867) is perfect, most of the feathers having recently changed. It is mostly *gray*; there are but few marks of red, and but a faint wash of cream-colour on the back, *not red*.—*The American Naturalist*, April.

NOTES ON EGG AND NEST COLLECTING.*

By Mr. C. O. GROOM NAPIER, F.G.S., &c.

PART I.

AT this season, when the birds are busy in the duties of laying and incubation, it is requisite for the collector of eggs now, if ever, to follow them into their haunts. But while he preserves eggs of those species and their varieties, that may be necessary to the formation of a cabinet in illustration of his science, he should remember that he is destroying the embryo of species, and that the number of eggs is limited; although it is well-known that most species will continue to lay several sittings of eggs, after the previous ones have been removed. As the latter sittings of eggs are usually inferior in size and markings to the first, it is reasonable to infer that birds of inferior qualities should be produced, which in process of time might lead to the degeneration of species, and with other assistant circumstances to their extinction. May this not partly account for the increasing scarcity of the roseate tern (*Sterna Dougallii*)?

Most collectors pass through various transformations, the scientific oologist being developed from the embryo who first preserved his specimens on thread. It is for those in this "first stage," that these few lines are written; but those in a more advanced condition may like to hear the latest conclusions of one, whose collection has gone through many stages, having been strung, carded, trayed, and divided.

Specimens illustrating Geology, Botany, and Zoology, should be "authenticated;" that is *accompanied* by information as to locality, formation, date (*year, month, day*), collector's name, and other attendant circumstances. This, so advisable in other sciences, is doubly necessary in oology, where the specimens speak less for themselves than in almost any other branch of natural history. More discrimination is thus necessary in the formation of a cabinet of eggs, than in that of most other branches of science.

As it is desirable to adhere to a uniform system in the authentication of eggs and their preservation in a cabinet, it may be convenient, especially in the case of public museums, to have a copy of good rules, either printed or written, bound up with the volume which contains the catalogue of eggs and nests. It is convenient to devote a page or half a page to each species, leaving an occasional blank for the insertion of

---

* In reply to the great number of enquiries as to the best method of egg collecting, we, by the permission of the author, reprint this article; it originally appeared in *Land and Water* for May 19th and 26th, 1866, but as those numbers have long been out of print we are sure Mr. Napier's twenty years experience will prove new and acceptable to many.—ED.

new species, which may be thus added to the British or other local lists in generic order. It is generally advisable to page the volume and attach a number also to the name of each bird.

The catalogue should contain the fullest information possessed concerning each specimen entered in it. Each individual species should be entered under one number, and each individual egg or set of eggs or nest should be marked with the number and letters, such as A, B, C, &c., to correspond with similar letters in the catalogue. Where the nests are not preserved, it is interesting to record their materials in the catalogue, which should, in addition to the particulars specified, be accompanied by the address of the collector, and in the case of catalogues of public museums, the degree of value attached to his specimens by the scientific world.

Birds' eggs and their nests, be it remembered, are only a portion of the science of ornithology, and their value is in proportion to their degree of identification with the living bird. Eggs are more likely to be mistaken as species than any class of objects that we collect, some even of those genera widely separated in the usual classification of birds, being hardly distinguishable from each other, as for example, those of the wryneck and black redstart. The necessity of connecting the names of the birds with eggs thus becomes emphatic. It is greatly desirable that whenever an egg is taken, it should be indelibly marked. The outside shell should never be touched with water, which more or less tends to wash off the delicate albumenized surface so general on eggs. They should be handled as little as possible, for experience proves that those eggs which have been most handled are most apt to become mildewed. The albumen which gives to eggs their beautiful lustre is one of the most unstable of compounds, which the photographer finds to his cost. Those specimens that are at all stained with the nest require to be kept in an extra dry place, for stains are exceedingly favourable to the growth of mildew.

I mention this particularly, for it is extremely desirable, in a complete collection, to preserve specimens with the artificial stains of the nest, to contrast with the unstained specimens, as laid by the bird. To guard against injury from handling, eggs should be lifted with a spoon, which may be very conveniently made of aluminium or horn. Two sizes should lie in each cabinet; one, about the size of a mustard spoon; the other, somewhat larger than a table-spoon. Let us suppose for a moment that we are in a locality around which birds are breeding, We have found several nests, but have, as yet, not connected them with their individual architects. We sit down and watch in silence their approach, and thus we can obtain a clue to the species in question. Limed twigs are put in the neighbourhood of some nests; horse-hair springes in the vicinity of others, with suitable bait; species are caught, and "assurance is made doubly sure." We watch, with gun in hand, yonder duck scuttle off her nest in the marsh. We fire, and, in obtaining her, alone give scientific value to her eggs. The various eggs are packed up in boxes, with a memorandum written on paper on the spot as to species, situation of nest, date and locality, which, after the eggs are blown, should be inscribed on them with ink in preference to a black-lead pencil. These notes, written on the eggs, should contain as much information as possible, as to situation of nest, number of eggs, locality, date and species, collector's name, and whether the bird has been shot, snared, seen, or identified. Suppose the eggs were those of the dotterell (*Charadrius morinellus*), and were found on Skiddaw, June 12, 1860, 1,800 feet above the level of the sea, and the nest contained four eggs, and the bird was seen by John Smith. We should abbreviate thus :—4 dott., Skiddaw, 6.12.60., 1,8000ft., bd. se.—J.S.

When eggs are very small, and the collector writes a bad and coarse hand, it may be sometimes advisable not to inscribe all these abbreviations on the egg, but it is advisable to mark each egg with the locality, local name and date, and the collector's name, at any rate, in initials. It is desirable to pack each set separately when they are not most carefully marked with full particulars. Having a number of eggs before us which require to be blown, we proceed to drill holes in them, which should be done with conical drills very sharp at the point, and having grooves smoothly and accurately cut with a chisel, all converging towards the point. Those for the largest eggs should be the third of an inch in diameter, those for the smallest the eighth. Some time since I procured drills of various sizes from Mr. J. Everard, 35, Charles Street, Middlesex Hospital, as advised in Mr. Newton's valuable "Suggestions." Eggs may surely be well blown without the aid of instruments, but a great saving of time, fewer breakages, and increase of nicety is secured by the use of good apparatus. The operator is recommended to use a blow-pipe, and to empty the contents by one hole, as nearly as possible at the centre of the surface of the egg, and on that side which is least richly marked. The blow-pipe, of which there are many forms, may be merely a bent tapering tube, or it may be like those of Berzelius or Plattner in shape, figures of which are to be seen in many chemical books. These are more expensive, and in general much too clumsy for egg-blowing, but the form has the advantage of requiring less exertion of wind to produce a steady, continuous stream, which is also less apt to burst the egg. The best material for these blow-pipes, on account of its lightness, is doubtless aluminium bronze, but German silver or aluminium itself answers well. A small syringe is very useful for washing the inside of eggs. A suction-tube with bulb in the centre, which is procurable for 6d., is useful for removing the contents of many eggs. Wire of considerable length for cleaning the mouths of the syringe and blow-pipes should be at hand, and fine scissors, with curved points, for cutting up embryos from eggs that are much incubated. A few hooks made of bent steel wires, such as are used by microscopists, should be carried by the egg-collecting traveller, and a hooked-shaped knife, about the size of a very small penknife, sharply curved at the point, and sharpened inwards, will be found very useful.

THE LION.

There are several varieties of the lion, which may be reduced to two, namely, the African and the Asiatic lion. It is almost certain, however, that these animals really are one and the same species, and that the trifling differences which exist between an African and an Asiatic lion are not sufficient to justify a naturalist in considering them to be distinct species. The habits of both are identical; modified, as is sure to be the case, by the difference of locality. But then such variations in habit are continually seen in animals confessedly of the same species, which happen to be placed in different conditions of climate and locality.

Size for size, the lion is one of the strongest of beasts. Perhaps it is surpassed in point of sheer strength by the mole, but it possesses infinitely more activity than that animal. Moreover, the strength of the mole is concentrated in its forequarters, the hind limbs being comparatively feeble; whereas the strength of the lion is equally distributed over the body and limbs, giving to the animal an easy grace of movement which is rare except with such a structure. A full-grown lion can not only knock down and kill, but can carry away in its mouth an ordinary ox; and one of these terrible animals has been known to pick up a heifer in its mouth, and to leap over a wide ditch still carrying its burden. Another lion carried a two-year old heifer, and was chased for five hours by mounted farmers, so that it must have traversed a very considerable distance. Yet, in the whole of this long journey, the legs of the heifer had only two or three times touched the ground.

It kills man and comparatively small animals, such as deer and antelopes, with a blow of its terrible paw, and often needs to give no second blow to cause the death of its victim. The sharp talons are not needed to cause death, for the weight of the blow is sufficient for that purpose.

When the hunter pursues it with dogs, after the usual fashion, there is often a great slaughter among them, especially among those that are inexperienced in the chase of the lion. Urged by their instinctive antipathy, the dogs rush forward to the spot where the lion awaits them, and old hounds bay at him from a safe distance, while the young and inexperienced among them are apt to convert the sham attack into a real one. Their valour meets with a poor reward, for a few blows from the lion's terrible paws send his assailants flying in all directions, their bodies streaming with blood, and in most cases a fatal damage inflicted, while more than one unfortunate dog lies fairly crushed by the weight of a paw laid with apparent carelessness upon its body. There is before me a lion's skin, a spoil of one of these animals shot by the celebrated sportsman Gordon Cumming. Although the skin lies flat upon the floor, and the paws are nothing but the skin and talons, the weight of each paw is very considerable, and always surprises those who hear it fall on the floor.

There are several Hebrew words which are used for the lion, but that which signifies the animal in its adult state is derived from an Arabic word which signifies strength; and therefore the lion is called the strong one, just as the bat is called the night-flier. No epithet could be better deserved, for the lion seems to be a very incarnation of strength, and, even when dead, gives as vivid an idea of concentrated power as when it was living. And, when the skin is stripped from the body, the tremendous muscular development never fails to create a sensation of awe. The muscles of the limbs, themselves so hard as to blunt the keen-edged knives employed by a dissector, are enveloped in their glittering sheaths, playing upon each other like well oiled machinery, and terminating in tendons seemingly strong as steel, and nearly as impervious to the knife. Not until the skin is removed can any one form a conception of the enormously powerful muscles of the neck, which enable the lion to lift the weighty prey which it kills, and to convey it to a place of security.

Although usually unwilling to attack an armed man, it is one of the most courageous animals in existence when it is driven to fight; and if its anger is excited it cares little for the number of its foes, or the weapons with which they are armed. Even the dreaded fire-arms lose their terrors to an angry lion, while a lioness who fears for the safety of her young is simply the most terrible animal in existence. We know how even a hen will fight for her chickens, and how she has been known to beat off the fox and the hawk by the reckless fury of her attack. It may be easily imagined, therefore, that a lioness, actuated by equal courage, and possessed of the terrible weapons given to her by her Creator, would be an animal almost too formidable for the conception of those who have not actually witnessed the scene of a lioness defending her little ones.

The roar of the lion is another of the characteristics for which it is celebra ed. There is no beast that can produce a sound that could for a moment be mistaken for the roar of the lion. The lion has a habit of stooping his head towards the ground when he roars, so that the terrible sound rolls around like thunder, and reverberates in many an echo in the far distance. Owing to this curious habit the roar can be heard at a very great distance, but its locality is rendered uncertain, and it is often difficult to be quite sure whether the lion is to the right or the left of the hearer. There are few sounds which strike more awe than the lion's roar. Even at the Zoological gardens, where the hearer knows that he is in perfect safety, and where the lion is enclosed in a small cage faced with strong iron bars, the sound of the terrible roar always has a curious effect upon the nerves. It is not exactly fear, because the hearer knows that he is safe; but it is somewhat akin to the feeling of mixed awe and admiration with which one listens to the crashing thunder after the lightning has sped its course. If such be the case when the lion is safely housed in a cage, and is moreover so tame that, even if he did escape, he would be led back by the keeper without doing any harm, the effect of the roar must indeed be terrific when the lion is at liberty, when he is in his own country, and when the shades of evening prevent him from being seen even at a short distance.

In the dark there is no animal so invisible as a lion. Almost every hunter has told a similar story—of the lion's approach at night, of the terror displayed by dogs and cattle as he drew near, and of the utter inability to see him, though he was so close that they could hear his breathing. Sometimes, when he has crept near an encampment, or close to a cattle enclosure, he does not proceed any farther lest he should venture within the radius illumined by the rays of the fiire; so he crouches closely to the ground, and, in the semi-darkness, looks so like a large stone, or a little hillock, that any one might pass close to it without perceiving its real nature. This gives the opportunity for which the lion has been watching, and in a moment he strikes down the careless straggler, and carries off his prey to the den. Sometimes, when very much excited, he accompanies the charge with a roar, but, as a general fact, he secures his prey in silence.

The roar of the lion is very peculiar. It is not a mere outburst of sound, but a curiously graduated performance. No description of the lion's roar is so vivid, so true, and so graphic as that of Gordon Cumming:—" One of the most striking things connected with the lion is his voice, which is extremely grand and peculiarly striking. It consists at times of a low deep moaning, repeated five or six times, ending in faintly audible sighs. At other times he startles the forest with loud, deep-toned, solemn roars, repeated five or six times in quick succession, each increasing in loudness to the third or fourth, when his voice dies away in five or six low, muffled sounds, very much resembling distant thunder. As a general rule lions roar during the night, their sighing moans commencing as the shades of evening envelop the forest, and continuing at intervals throughout the night. In distant and secluded regions, however, I have constantly heard them roaring loudly as late as nine or ten o'clock on a bright sunny morning. In hazy and rainy weather they are to be heard at every hour in the day, but their roar is subdued."

The lion always fixes its residence in the depths of some forest, through which it threads its stealthy way with admirable certainty. No fox knows every hedgerow, ditch, drain, and covert, better than the lion knows the whole country around his den. Each lion seems to have his peculiar district, in which only himself and his family will be found. These animals seem to parcel out the neighbourhood among themselves by a tacit law, like that which the dogs of eastern countries have imposed upon themselves, and which forbids them to go out of the district in which they were born. During the night he traverses his dominions, and, as a rule, he retires to his den as soon as the sun is fairly above the horizon. Sometimes he will be in wait for prey in the broadest daylight, but his ordinary habits are nocturnal, and in the daytime he is usually asleep in his secret dwelling-place.—*Bible Animals.* By Rev. J. G. Wood. London: Longmans.

THE HISTORY OF A YOUNG OTTER.

As an enquiry has lately been made in your columns as to the rearing of a young otter, and the capability of this animal for fishing purposes, I beg to offer you the history of one that I have reared lately, and which has afforded me much amusement. He and his sister were found near a small run of water, in September last, by the gamekeeper, who was attracted to the spot by the whistling of the pair; he soon perceived in the water the mother, who endeavoured to divert his attention from the young, by swimming to and fro near him. Having drawn him off some distance, she made her escape under a temporary bridge of logs. The whistling of the young continuing, he returned near the spot, and discovered them under some brake, a few yards from the stream. There was apparently no nest; so probably the dam was engaged in removing them when his presence disturbed her; however, they were captured, and most obligingly brought to me. From their size, and from their being unable to see for at least ten days after I had them, I presume they were only a few hours old when captured; and a difficult task was before me to rear such helpless ones. I first tried to administer milk with a tea-spoon, but this mode was too fast for their powers of suction. Then I contrived a kind of baby's bottle, by means of a small quill passed through a cork inserted into the neck of a bottle partially filled with milk; with this they were fed five times a day until I had had them five weeks. I had noticed that a cat upon the premises was in an interesting condition, and was anxiously looking forward to her accouchement for a relief, if possible, from my maternal duties. The happy event took place, and four little mousers were born; but, from the irritable nature of the mother, I had grievous doubts as to whether she would obligingly regard those whom I wanted to foster upon her with feelings of affection. By a little manœuvring, however, this was accomplished. I withdrew three of the kittens, and popped one young otter in their place; this she immediately began to fondle, and seemed quite proud of the increased size of her quasi kitten. The other was quickly introduced to share in her caresses; but for the first few hours the athletic powers of the young fishermen astonished her not a little. When I found they had settled down quietly, I removed the fourth kitten, and feeding the cat highly, hoped that all would go on well—as, independently of the trouble I was spared in feeding, she kept them scrupulously clean and dry, which I could not do when they were under my sole charge. From the jealous nature of the cat, they were handled as little as possible. On taking them up about a fortnight after she had had them, I found they had not advanced as much as I had expected, and I resorted again to the bottle; but the remedy came too late for one of them (the female), and she died. I had great fears for the other; however, by extra feeding, both natural (if it may be so termed) and artificially, he was reared. The cat is a half-bred Persian, of a peculiarly savage temper, and generally she had left her kittens to shift for themselves at an early period; but to this foster nursling she was most attached, and suckled him until he was quite as big as herself, following him as he accompanied me for his daily wash in a large pond in the yard, and exhibiting the same solicitude at his aqueous rambles as a hen shows when watching ducklings take the water. He was very wary in his first few essays in the new element, but daily took further dives and swims, and soon began to work among the stones at the bottom and in the mud, instinctively searching for prey. I have omitted to mention that, when about ten weeks old, I got him to eat solid food, such as bread soaked in milk, then a little rabbit, and fish when obtainable. Up to this time he displayed no ferocity, but his muscular strength was prodigious. Having introduced him to a tom cat about three-parts grown, they became excellent friends, and used to delight us through the winter by playing in the breakfast room at high romps and bo-peep, until he became so strong that Master Tom was glad to escape from his playful bites by jumping on the chairs, &c. A singular incident happened during his rearing which I must mention, as indicating the foster-mother's love for her supposed offspring. As they accompanied me one day to the pond, he strayed into a shed where a trained falcon was sitting on her block. She immediately jumped off the block and collared him, rolled him over, and began to rip away at his neck. The cat darting to the rescue, together with myself, upset the hawk, freeing the otter, and then, as I was among them, turned her rage upon me. I had often heard of the fury of a desperate cat, but never experienced an attack before. She bit me through the calf of my leg, and produced a frightful bruise upon my thigh—with her claw, I believe; but the attack was so sudden and instantaneous that I do not know how she made it, or how the blow was given. The triumph with which she walked up the hill, with her furry *protégé* between her fore and hind feet, straddling over him, jealously guarding him from a further attack of her two-legged foes, I could not but admire, bleeding and smarting as I was. For security I have kept him in a small enclosed yard, with a flagged floor, for he was never easy when at liberty unless in the presence of the cats; and, as they began to fight shy of him as his strength increased, they endeavoured to escape by mounting upstairs to the bed rooms, and even upon the roof of the house, whither he would follow them—the first instance, I should think, of an otter taking to such quarters. His foster mother has now quite given him up, and poor Tom, his playfellow, has gone the way of all naughty cats who put their feet once too often into rabbit gins; but I never let the otter loose but he searches everywhere for his old companions, and before Tom's departure he was quite content to lie, without playing, with his forepaws around the cat's neck. I hope as the spring advances to introduce him to the trout in the neighbouring small stream, but I am not very sanguine as to his docility when there; I am afraid he will prove too much of a pothunter to care for his master, and since the fracas with the hawk he has been very shy of being handled. If, however, I am able to do anything with him in the fishing line, I will make it known, with your permission. The large whiskers and nervous structure of the upper lips are of the greatest assistance to the otter in searching among the roots of trees and under banks for its prey, every motion of which is immediately communicated through them. The walrus is provided with the same apparatus on a greatly enlarged scale. It is surprising also what large stones the otter can raise at the bottom of a stream if he can only get his nose as a lever under them: This is thrust in, the flat head follows, and with a twist and jerk of his immensely muscular neck, aided by the loss of gravity of the stone in water, such stones are upturned as at first sight the spectator would think it impossible could be moved by such a creature.—AUCEPS, in *Field*.

VOLCANOES.

Volcanoes are, then, the safety-valves of the earth. Of their number no accurate estimate can be given, but there are nearly 300 active volcanoes known, of which at least 190 occur in the islands or on the sea-coasts of the Pacific Ocean. This includes only the subaërial vents. There are probably double the number beneath the surface of the oceans. They occur all over the world, some singly, others collected in groups, very rarely in the interior of a continent, and for the most part on islands, or on the coast-line, near the sea. There is one remarkable range of volcanoes which, beginning at Tierra del Fuego, passes upwards along the whole coast of southern and northern America, crosses the Pacific by the Aleutian Islands, and then sweeps southward through Kamschatka, Japan, and the Philippine Islands to the Moluccas. It then divides into two branches—one going through Papua, New Zealand, and even to the South Pole in Victoria Land—the other crossing by Borneo and Sumatra, Java, the Andaman Isles, and Burmah. There is probably all along, beneath this immense series of volcanic vents, a large long fissure, through the crust of the earth, which penetrates to a subterranean ocean of lava. Few, however, of the volcanoes of this great arch have been accurately observed and studied, and our knowledge of the phenomena of eruptive action has been chiefly gained from observation of Ætna, Vesuvius, and the burning mountains of the Lipari Islands. All the three phases of eruption have been presented to us by these volcanoes. Stromboli, whose light has served as a beacon since the Homeric ages to the sailor on the Tyrrhenian Sea, has been incessantly active, and is an example of a volcano in a state of "*permanent eruption.*" Vesuvius and Ætna have both had periods of "moderate activity," during which the eruptions were continued, but were also unmarked by any extraordinary violence. This phase of constant but moderate activity exists in different parts of the world. Year after year the sailors who sail the Pacific, see, at certain parts of their course, the "volcano's vapour flag" by day, and its ruddy glare illuminating the sea by night. For the last half century Vesuvius has continued in this state of quiet excitement, sometimes playing at eruption, as it were, for months together, shooting up from its crater, or from cones in its sides, comparatively little jets of ashes, stones, and sand, and now and then bubbling over in a placid rivulet of lava. Now and then, as in 1794 and 1822, after an interval of rest, this moderate activity has been invaded by a fierce eruption, which has absolutely broken up and hurled into the air the whole of the upper part of the mountain, leaving in its place a deep crater, hollow, in the centre of the mountain.—*People's Magazine*, May.

ERRORS CONCERNING THE HEDGEHOG.

Take the case of the hedgehog. It is curious that so much dislike should surround so inoffensive an animal as this; and equally so, that every charge brought against it is erroneous. It is a firmly rooted belief in the minds of farmers—ay, and even of country gentlemen, who ought to know better—that hedgehogs suck the milk from the cows when they are lying at night in the meadows. It is almost inconceivable how so absurd a notion as this should have gained ground, for any person who has ever looked at the mouth of a hedgehog must have seen that it would be physically impossible for the animal to suck a cow. In the first place, the mouth is much too small to enable it to grasp the teat; and in the second, the jaws are armed with a number of sharp, pointed teeth, so that if the hedgehog ever made the attempt, the pain caused would be such that the cow would immediately rise and thus get rid of its tormentor. But I have often found argument in vain, when endeavouring to convince a believer in the hedgehog's sucking propensities of the erroneousness of his belief.

Another equally strange superstition connected with the hedgehog is that it can never be poisoned. What the peculiar condition of the coats of the hedgehog's stomach is which gives it this desirable immunity no one has ventured to state; but the supposed fact is extensively and firmly believed.

A few months ago I kept a hedgehog in my garden. For a short time it appeared perfectly healthy, but one day it showed unmistakeable signs of distress. It became very comatose, vomited considerably, and in less than twenty-four hours died. On examination, the cause of death was explained in the fact of a considerable number of leaves of the aconite, or common monk's-hood, having fallen into the dish of milk from which the little animal had fed during the previous night. The milk had a sensibly bitter taste, having without doubt imbibed the poisonous principle from the leaves of aconite.

My own observations in this respect have been confirmed by a recent writer, who poisoned a hedgehog almost instantaneously by feeding it on a mouse which had been killed with Battle's vermin destroyer—a substance composed, I believe, chiefly of strychnine. So much for the hedgehog's power of resisting poison.—*From "Popular Zoological Errors," by T. G. Penton, in Cassell's Magazine.*

IN THE SEA.

I have a distinct recollection of the creatures that inhabited the sea whilst I was lying along the bottom. I am told there are nothing like them living in the seas of the present day. Even those which approach nearest in resemblance differ in some point or another. The most remarkable of these inhabitants of an extinct ocean were a series of large sponges, called by scientific men *Paramoudræ*, but better known in Norfolk (where I came from) as "Pot Stones." These were originally sponges which grew one within the other, like so many packed drinking-glassses, sometimes to the height of six or seven feet. Through the whole set, however, there was a connecting hollow, which is now filled with hard chalk, the rest being all pure flint. It is very remarkable how these sponges became transformed into their flinty condition. As sponges, they were full of what are called *spiculæ*—that is, flinty, needled-shaped crystals, which act the part of *vertebræ* to the sponge. You may find them in the sponges of the present day. When the "pot stones" existed in this state, as the sponges died and began to decompose, they served as nuclei to all the flinty particles of animalculic shells diffused through the mud. These replaced the decaying matter of the sponge little by little, until the original *Paramoudræ* were turned into " pot stones." That the flint was originally soft may be proved by the fact, that fossil shells are often found imbedded in it. The other creatures I most distinctly remember are now found in a solid state in the chalk, and are commonly known as " Fairy loaves" and " hearts." They belong to an extensive family still living, and known to the fishermen (who often dredge them from the bottom of the present sea) as " Sea-urchins," on account of their spiny covering. The existing sea-urchins crawl along the bottom by means of innumerable suckers. Many a time have the fossil fairy loaves thus crept over where I lay. The hearts were similarly covered with movable spines or bristles.—*Chambers's Journal*, April part.

THE SUN-DEW A FLY-TRAP.

I wish to call the attention of botanists to a very humble little plant, the *Drosera rotundifolia*, or common sun-dew, which not only catches flies but eats them. I was looking early in the spring in a swamp for chrysalids, when I noticed the tiny leaves of the sun-dew, which has beautiful blood-red glandular hairs, each tipped with a glistening dew-drop. The leaves were covered with the wings and legs of gnats. One or two had the hairs gathered into a knot at their centres, and on one a live gnat was struggling hopelessly to escape. I secured two plants and kept them for several weeks by laying the bit of moss on which they grew in a plate supplied every day with water. During this time I fed them with midges, ants, and beefsteak. The tiny drop of dew is glutinous, and any small insect touching them is lost. Every effort to escape but hurries its doom, and in a moment wings and legs are held fast to the tiny bristles.

Now begins the curious part of the affair. All the hairs begin to move towards the insect, but so slowly that their motion is almost imperceptible. In a few hours the hairs touch and cover it with their adhesive points. I placed a piece of raw beefsteak on the centre of a leaf. In twelve hours nearly every hair touched it. They gathered over it in knots and remained so for a day and a half, when they slowly returned to their natural position, leaving the beef a white sodden atom resting on the points of the hairs. I tried it with a bit of paper, but it refused to move for that; then a tiny fly was touched to one of the treacherous dew-drops, smothered, and in a few hours all the ferocious little scarlet hairs had their beaded points upon his body. When the *blossom* bud appeared, the glands no longer secreted the dew, and the leaves lost their brilliant colour.—*American Naturalist*, April.

Meetings of Learned Societies.

ROYAL GEOGRAPHICAL SOCIETY.

Sir Roderick Murchison held his annual reception at Willis's Rooms, which were crowded. The walls of the large room were hung with the Society's maps, but those of most special interest were the splendid diagrams of Africa and North and South America. All the latest discoveries in Africa were faithfully shown, including an accurate tracing of Dr. Livingstone's present journey to the spot from which he communicated his latest intelligence. " South America" should be noticed as affording the best delineation we possess of the vast plains of the Amazons, with which we have been made acquainted by various travellers, but particularly by Mr. Chandless and Mr. Bates.

Mr. Thomas Baines's spirited pictures on Abyssinian subjects attracted much attention. The British Camp at Senafe and the fort of Magdala with the surrounding country were among the principal of Mr. Baines's paintings. His famous views of the Victoria Falls were also proved to have lost none of their original attractiveness.

Mr. Frederick Whymper exhibited a series of sketches and a collection of Indian carvings and skin clothing. Some of the latter, derived from the coast tribes of Northern " Alaska," or Russian America, were of the Esquimaux character: while others, from the great Youkon river, far in the interior, were of the worked buck-skin style, like those commonly found in the Hudson's Bay Territory. Two Co-Youkon pipes showed the infinitesimal amount of tobacco used by these people. They *consume their own smoke* by swallowing it, as do also the Tchuktchis on the opposite Asiatic coast. Mr. Whymper's collection was, perhaps, the most interesting in the room, as it had the advantage of novelty, and related to a people bordering on the Arctic circle, having probably some affinity both to the Esquimaux and the Red Indians. A few of Mr. Whymper's Indian carvings, with a huge Indian mask, were very curious.

A collection of Holy Land specimens and photographs of objects of interest in the country around Sinai, were shown by the Rev. F. W. Holland. Mr. Holland has recently returned from the Holy Land, whither he went under the auspices of the Royal Geographical Society; and an account of his investigations will be read at their meeting next Monday.

Many curious and remarkable specimens of the art of litho-photography were shown. By this system everything photographed from nature, or any given picture, drawing, or print, may be placed on the stone and printed with the lithographic press, thus combining the truth and beauty of the photograph with the brightness, strength, and permanency of the finest litho-drawing. This process will probably become very valuable to the Geographical Society, as it will secure, with marvellous fidelity, the reproduction of old and important maps of which only single copies are extant.

Mr. J. L. Naish again exhibited his Tellurion Globe, the object of which is to teach without mathematics the complete theory of geographical astronomy and to display, by mechanical means alone, the analysis and composition of the total equation of time. This is a very ingenious invention, and elicited the admiration of all and the approbation of the few who could comprehend its apparently complicated mechanism.

One of the smaller rooms was hung round with pictures of Greenland and Arctic scenes, including Mr. Edward Whymper's collection.

The gold medals of the Society will this year be awarded to Dr. Petermann for his great services to geographical science, and to Gerhard Rohlfs for his explorations in Northern Africa.

On May 11.—Sir R. I. Murchison, Bart., President, in the chair.—The following gentlemen were elected Fellows:—M. Blakiston, F. Barlow, W. Busk, Dr. F. C. Cory, A. Ellison, J. T. Fletcher, H. Freeman, J. L. Hart, Rev. W. Hiley, Major T. J. Holland, S. Hoare, S. J. Hobson, W. S. Jones, Lieut.-Col. H. Le Couteu, R. M. Miller, R. Michell, Lieut. C. M. MacGregor, Dr. J. H. Paul, A. Richards, C. W. Roberts, P. J. Rowlands, Rev. C. F. Stovin, G. E. H. Sutton, and Col. R. Wardlaw.—The Rev. F. W. Holland read a paper on his explorations in the peninsula of Sinai during last winter. He stated that it was his third visit to the country on the same errand, and that he adopted the independent mode in his travels, of dispensing with a dragoman and traversing a large portion of the peninsula on foot. In commencing these explorations he had found the best maps extremely incorrect in many parts, and large districts quite unknown. He left Suez, on foot, on the 10th of October last, and on reaching Jebel Musa (Mount Sinai), made the monastery at the foot of the mountain his head-quarters, exploring from this centre, during four months, the numerous wadies and mountains in all directions, south of Jebel Er-Rahar. He occupied a little room at the top of the convent. At sunrise every morning he was awoke by the clanging of the pieces of iron and wooden boards used as bells to call the monks to service, and after making his fire and cooking his breakfast let himself down from a little gate in the garden wall by a rope, and commenced alone his daily explorations, depending on Arab ibex-hunters for his information of mountain paths, the monks and their Arab servants knowing nothing of the country beyond the convent walls. In his more distant excursions he took an Arab to carry his blanket and a bag of provisions, and slept out sometimes for three or four nights. He found, contrary to what he was led to expect, two or three springs of water on every important mountain in the neighbourhood, and considerable vegetation even at the end of a long dry season. He was thus enabled to take the heights of the mountains and measure and map out the endless and sometimes intricate narrow valleys of the country. With regard to the probable route of the Israelites and the sites of events in Sacred History, he had come to the following conclusions. After crossing the Red Sea, somewhere in the neighbourhood of Suez, he thought they took the lower road down the plain along the coast as far as Ain Szouweira, which might possibly mark the locality of Marah. They then turned inland to Elim, which he would place at Ain Howara. Their next encampment was by the sea, possibly near the mouth of Wady Ghwundel, the most fertile place in the peninsula. The Wilderness of Sin he would identify with the plain of Es Seyn, and not with the desert plains of Merkha, as generally believed. From this their route would lay by Dopkhkah and Alusk, and afterwards up the Wady Es Sheikh to the Rephidim, the site of which, after careful examination, he fixed at Mokad Musa,—a narrow gorge in a long unbroken wall of granite, which stretches across the centre of the peninsula and ten miles north of Jebel Musa. With regard to the true Mount Sinai Mr. Holland thought Jebel Um Alowee, possibly a corruption of Eloheem, a previously unknown mountain north-east of Jebel Musa, to be probably the true one. The plain of SennED at the foot of this mountain affords a much larger camping ground than that at the foot of the present Mount Sinai. In conclusion, he entered a protest against the theory that the Sinaitic inscriptions were the work of the Children of Israel; he had copied some hundreds of them, and found not a single point in favour of such a theory.

Entomological Society.

On May 4—H. T. Stainton, Esq., V.P., in the chair—Mr. W. C. Boyd exhibited larvæ of Lepidoptera, admirably preserved by Mr. Davis, of Waltham Cross.—Mr. Trimen exhibited a crippled specimen of *Saturnia pavonia minor*, which (owing probably to the smallness of the box in which it was confined) had emerged from its cocoon tail-foremost.—Mr. Stainton called attention to the history and figure of a small Lepidopterous insect, published in 1750 in the "Mémoires de l'Académie Royale des Sciences de Paris." The habits and transformations were described with great particularity from the observations of M. Godchen de Riville, made in the island of Malta; and though the insect was quite unknown, except from M. de Riville's description, it was clear that it belonged to the genus Antispila. The larva was apodus, and fed upon the leaves of the vine.—Mr. M'Lachlan mentioned that *Anax Mediterraneus*, an African dragonfly, once captured in the island of Sardinia, but which had been rejected from the list of European Libellulidæ, had last year occurred in swarms at Turin, and in other parts of Italy.—Mr. F. Smith exhibited a larva, found by Mr. O. Janson by digging in a sand-bank, which was believed to be that of a Xantholinus, attached to the underside of which were four parasitic pupæ, probably of a Proctotrupes.—Mr. F. Smith also exhibited specimens of a Longicorn beetle, *Cerosterna gladiator*, and of a large Acheta, from India, which had caused great damage to young plantations of Casuarina, along the Madras Railway.—Dr. Cleghorn said that the Acheta appeared suddenly in September last, after some rain at the end of the hot season; during the night the larvæ emerged from the sand and crawled up the young trees, generally biting off the leading shoots; he employed little boys to burrow in the sand, to extract them from the tortuous passages which they made therein, and by this means destroyed bushels of them. The Cerosterna was also very mischievous, but its attacks were principally directed to the bark.—Mr. F. Smith exhibited eight species of larvæ, all of which were described as "borers," and as being very destructive to trees in India; amongst them was the now notorious "coffee-borer," *Xylotrechus quadripes* of Chevrolat.—Captain Taylor, who has been long resident in Coorg, gave his personal experiences of the coffee-borer, and reported that the evil was now on the decrease.—The following papers were read: "Observations on the Duration of Life in the Honey Bee," by Mr. J. G. Desborough, and "Descriptions of Aculeate Hymenoptera, from Australia," by Mr. F. Smith.

On April 6—Mr. H. W. Bates, President, in the chair—Mr. Stainton exhibited larvæ of a new species of Nepticula, found in the leaves of *Euphorbia dendroides*, at Mentone; also, the unique specimen of an insect which was described some years ago as *Nemophora Carteri*, but which Mr. Stainton now believed to be a fabrication composed of the fore wings of a Nemophora and the hind wings of a Cerostoma.—Mr. W. C. Boyd exhibited a strongly marked variety of *Stenopteryx hybridalis*, captured in Herts.—Mr. J. Weir exhibited several interesting varieties of Polyommatus, including a specimen which he believed to be a hybrid between *P. Adonis* and *P. Alexis*.—Mr. H. Druce exhibited a collection of butterflies from Bolivia.—Mr. F. Smith mentioned that for three consecutive seasons a brood of *Clytus arietis* had appeared in one of the cases in the British Museum in which was preserved a pollard oak intended to show the galls of *Cynips Koliari*. Each spring specimens of the Clytus were seen running about the stump for two or three weeks, and then died.

ZOOLOGICAL SOCIETY.

At the meeting held March 26—J. Gould, Esq., V.P., in the chair—letters were read from Sir R. Alcock and M. le Père David relating to their efforts to procure living specimens of the newly-described Chinese stag (*Elaphurus Davidianus*) for the Society's Menagerie.—Mr. A. G. Butler communicated descriptions of some new or little known species of Lepidoptera.—Dr. Günther communicated a report on a collections of fishes made by Mr. J. C. Mellis at St. Helena. The number of species contained in this collection was stated to be thirty-five, six or seven of which appeared to be new to science.—Mr. P. L. Sclater read some notes upon Baker's antelope (*Hippotragus Bakeri*), principally founded upon observations of a living specimen of this rare animal in the Royal Menagerie at Turin, and upon information and a specimen of the head and horns communicated to him by Sir Samuel Baker, its discoverer.—Dr. Murie read a paper on the supposed arrest of development of the salmon (*Salmo salar*) when kept in fresh water. Dr. Murie's remarks were mainly based upon fishes hatched in the Society's Fish-house (from ova presented by Mr. F. Buckland) in January, 1863; one of which had recently died, and another was still living.—Mr. F. Buckland exhibited and made remarks on other specimens of Salmonoids reared in fresh water.—Dr. Günther maintained that there was not sufficient evidence to prove that the ova from which these fishes had been hatched were really those of *Salmo salar*. Judging by the specimens themselves, he believed them to be more probably young of some species of lake trout, or hybrids between two different species of Salmo.—Mr. Gould exhibited and described four new species of birds from different parts of the world. The most interesting of these was a new species of Grebe from Lake Titicaca, in Bolivia, which he proposed to call *Podiceps micropterus*, from its very small wings.

April 23.—W. H. Flower, Esq., in the chair.—A letter was read from Mr. E. L. Layard relating to a specimen of a species of Ribbon Fish (*Gymnetrus*) recently taken near Cape Town.—Dr. J. Murie read a memoir on the anatomy of the Sea Bear (*Otaria*), founded on the animal recently living in the Society's Menagerie.—A communication was read from Mr. C. Spence Bate on a new genus of freshwater Prawns, proposed to be called Macrobrachium.—Mr. St. George Mivart read a note on *Salamandrina perspicillata*, communicated to him by Professor Lessona, of Turin.—Dr. J. E. Gray gave a notice on an interesting species of American Monkey living in the Society's Gardens, for which he proposed the new name of *Mico sericeus*.

The Annual Meeting was held Wednesday, April 29th; Viscount Walden, President, in the chair.—The Report for the past year was read by Mr. P. L. Sclater, Ph. D., F.R.S. The Society now consisted of 2,702 members, being an increase of 243 in the past year. The Society had elected Dr. Ernest Haekel, Professor of Zoology at Jena, and Mr. G. F. Westerman, Director of the Zoological Gardens at Amsterdam, foreign members. The income of the year was £25,041, being an increase of £652. Of this, £21,566 formed the ordinary expenses; but £4,652 had been spent on important new buildings or valuable additions to the live stock. This extraordinary call on the Society's fund had been met by selling £2,000 value in exchequer bills. There was a balance of £2,028 at the beginning of the year at the Society's bankers. The total assets of the Society at the close of last year were £12,950, and the liabilities £2,485. No Society was in so flourishing a condition, for the reserve fund is £10,000. The Society has spent a great deal in printing, having issued a volume of 1,100 pages in octavo, besides three parts of the quarto Transactions, which contain valuable papers by Owen, Flower, Gray, etc. The new deer house, built during the past year, has superseded the old Wapite house, and on its site a large building for the elephants and rhinoceroses is contemplated. 556,214 persons visited the Gardens in 1867, or 28,865 more than in the preceding year. A house for rodents has also been built, the western aviary, the pheasant aviary, and the hippopotamus house, as also a dwelling for the wombats. The Gardens on the 1st of January last contained 2,010 animals—being 531 quadrupeds, 1,320 birds, and 129 reptiles. The most important animals acquired during the year were the walrus, a young female giraffe, and a collection of animals from Calcutta, presented by Baron Rajendro Mullick and Mr. Grote. The following gentlemen were elected on the Council for the ensuing year:—The Hon. T. de Grey, M.P.; Dr. A. Günther, F.R.S.; Robert Hudson, Esq., F.R.S.; H. Pollock, Esq.; Osbert Salvin, Esq., in room of G. Sclater-Booth, Esq., M.P.; Earl de Grey and Ripon, Professor A. Newton, the Bishop of Oxford, and A. J. E. Russell, M.P., retired. Viscount Walden was elected President, R. Drummond, Esq., Treasurer, and P. L. Sclater, Secretary.

LINNÆAN SOCIETY.

April 2.—George Bentham, Esq., President, in the chair.—Messrs. J. E. Harting and T. Howse, jun., were elected Fellows; and Messrs. J. Jackson, W.

Mudd and C. W. Peach Associates. The following papers were read :—"Contributions towards a Monograph of the Species of Annelides belonging to the Amphinomacea, with a list of the known species, and descriptions of several new species belonging to the group contained in the National Collection of the British Museum; to which is appended a short account of two hitherto nondescript Annulose Animals of a larval character," by Dr. W. Baird. "The Effects of Selection in the Cultivation of Plants," by Mr. J. Buckman.

At the meeting held April 16—G. Bentham, Esq., President, in the chair—Messrs. H. Collinson and S. Hurrell were elected Fellows. The following papers were read :—"Note on the Structure of *Genista tinctoria*, as apparently affording facilities for the intercrossing of Distinct Flowers," and "On the Variations of the Angular Divergencies of the Leaves of the Jerusalem Artichoke (*Helianthus tuberosus*)," by the Rev. G. Henslow, M.A.

On May 7—G. Bentham, Esq., President, in the chair—the following papers were read :—"A Brief Account of the Chief Enemies destructive to the Coffee-plant," by Dr. Surgeon Shortt. "On the Silkworm Oaks of Northern China," by Dr. H. F. Hance. "On some New Forms of Trilopterous Insects from New Zealand; with a List of the Species known to inhabit that Colony," by Mr. R. M'Lachlan. "Notes on Jussiæa," by Mr. C. Wright. "Notulæ Capenses," by Mr. P. Mac Owan. "On the Germination of *Orchis Morio*," with some Remarks on the Embryos of the Cryptogams," by Mr. B. Clarke. "Experiments in Pruning, with a View to the Production of Varieties, especially in *Zea Mays*; and Remarks on certain Analogies occurring in the Animal Kingdom, including Notices of Diseases connected with the Growth of Fungi," by Mr. B. Clarke.

Geological Society.

On April 8—Sir R. I. Murchison, Bart., V.P., in the chair—the Rev. J. Carne, Messrs. J. W. Hulke, and L. T. Lewis, were elected Fellows. The following communications were read :—"On the Disposition of Iron in Variegated Strata," by Mr. G. Maw; and "On the Older Rocks of South Devon and East Cornwall," by Dr. H. B. Holl.

On May 6—Professor A. C. Ramsay, V.P., in the chair—the Rev. J. Crombie, C. Judd, Messrs. D. G. F. Macdonald, J. S. Phené, and M. Thomson, were elected Fellows. The following communication was read :—"On the Quaternary Gravels of England," by A. Tayler, Esq., F.G.S. Dr. Buckland was the first who gave attention to this subject among his other extensive researches in the early days of geology. Mr. Tyler thought this epoch was a period of great rainfall, and said that the researches he had lately made in consideration of this paper confirmed the opinions he had expressed in a former paper, lately published in the Journal of the Society. He described a section at Bingley, near Leeds, on the river Aire. This spot had been already rendered famous by the researches of Dr. Buckland. Mr. Tyler described the discovery in the neighbourhood of Bingley of a quantity of cave bones, among which were those of the *Hippopotamus major*. He exhibited a large diagrammatic section of Taff Vale, South Wales; as also of Blaen Rhonda. Speaking of the bone caves he confirmed Buckland's opinion that there were always two holes to a bone cave. Carefully measured sections at Crayford, Erith, Sandgate, and Kemp Town, near Brighton, were also shown. Mr. Prestwich, in opening the discussion, thought the tendency of the paper was to overlook recent discoveries and carry us back to old conclusions, but admitted the existence of a fluviatile period. Mr. Evans, F.R.S., the secretary, thought Mr. Tyler's conclusions not borne out by his facts, and that Mr. Prestwich had gone too far in admitting the existence of a fluviatile period, which answered a good deal to the diluvial period of the older geologists. Mr. Boyd Dawkins considered the author wrong in carrying back operations of denudation, etc., to too early a period, and thought it unfair to go back for causes, when those now in operation were sufficient to account for the geographical features of a country. Sir C. Lyell mentioned the discovery, during the past few days, near Salisbury, of the skeletons of two species of lemmings, one now found in Norway; as also of the Alpine marmot, and some eggs of the wild goose. This was, Sir C. thought, an argument in favour of an Alpine or Arctic climate; for the wild goose now breeds in the far north, and the marmot lives through a well-nigh Arctic winter in the Alps. These belong to the period of the woolly rhinoceros, etc., described in Mr. Tyler's paper. Professor Ansted gave some figures tending to show the impossibility of the excessive rain-fall which Mr. Tyler had urged in his paper as necessary to account for the physical structure of the ground he had described; such, according to Professor Ansted's calculations, would give a body of water larger than the mighty St. Lawrence, the drainage of a whole continent, which certainly could not flow through the smaller valleys of a country like England, even if the water could be obtained there. Mr. Searles Wood and Professor Ramsay likewise spoke at some length, and the meeting adjourned.

Royal Botanic Society, Regent's Park.

At a meeting of the Fellows held Saturday, May 9th, Charles Robert Turner, Esq., in the chair, the following candidates for the fellowship were proposed :—Edward Mappin, Esq.; John Heugh, Esq.; Miss Blundell, Miss Posno, Mrs. George Jessel, William Green, Esq.; G. Wilkinson, Esq., in addition to sixteen elected on the same day. A fine collection of the more curious orchids and other plants, including new varieties of maranta, blandfordia, cypripediums, &c., from the nursery of Messrs. Henderson, of Wellington Road, were exhibited to the meeting. There is now in bloom in the Gardens one of those curious plants so seldom seen in this country, or even in Europe, although common weeds in their native country, Mexico. This class of plants, from the rareness of their flowering, are popularly known as the "aloes which flower only once in a century." The fact is that they flower only once in their lifetime, the act of flowering terminating their existence; and it appears that this final act is advanced or retarded according to the circumstances of warmth, moisture, &c., under which the plant has grown. The common American aloe (*Agave Americana*) the father of the large tribe or family, although flowering in Mexico and other tropical and sub-tropical climes at the age of ten or fifteen years, seldom attains maturity when grown in tubs or pots in England, before eighty or a hundred years; and as in general plants have to pass through so great a variety of vicissitudes before attaining such an advanced age, their flower is very rarely seen. Three, however, have at times flowered at the Botanic Gardens at the ages of eighty-five to ninety years. The plant now in flower, *Fourcroya longæva*, is much more graceful, both in flower and leaf, than the agave. It was raised from seed received from Mexico, where it is said to produce flower-spikes over forty feet in length. It is now about twenty-eight years old, and is most probably the second individual that has flowered in Europe, the first a fellow plant, having also bloomed in the Botanic Gardens in 1864. The flower-stem, which shot up from the crown of flag-like leaves, a few months back, in form exactly like a huge head of asparagus, at first grew very rapidly, and is now over fifteen feet in length; the main stem is thickly studded with drooping branches, bearing stellate flowers of a delicate yellow and white colour. The late warm weather has caused these to expand very rapidly, but as its name implies "long enduring," the plant is expected to continue some time in flower.

BRISTOL NATURALIST'S SOCIETY.

March 1868, Mr. S. H. Swayne in the chair. 1st. "Dr. Beddoe on the method of measuring the human body for Ethnological purposes." Many difficulties lay in the way of establishing satisfactory and uniform systems of measurement, from lack of which much laborious and conscientious work might as well be left undone. Thus the measurement of the girth of the chest of the British recruits are almost useless for scientific purposes, although the directions given by the department appear all that can be wished. In this case the variations depend chiefly on the different degree of tightness with which the measuring tape is applied. The existence of these variations is proved by such facts as these: Equal numbers of men born in the same province and of the same height and weight gave an inch or two more in girth at one recruiting station than at another. Dr. Beddoe in remarking on skull measurements, spoke of Dr. Bush's instrument and process for obtaining radial measures from the *meatus auditorius*, but preferred index callipers and measuring tape, registering the various measurements of length and breadth, taking for the starting point the occipital tuberosity and the *glabella*, which latter he took to be the elevation between the supercilliary ridges. He measured carefully the greatest breadth of the skull as well as the zygoma. He thought the size and weight of brain indications of intellectual capacity. A discussion ensued in which the chairman, Mr. E. Praeger, Mr. Carpenter, Dr. Hudson, and Mr. H. K. Jordan took part. 2nd. "Mr. A. Leipner on *Proteus anguinus*."

Correspondence.

[*Under this head we shall be glad to insert any letters of general interest.*]

"NATURE IMPROVED."

SIR,—Once upon a time, a *few* years ago, there lived a man, a deer-stealer, mayhap, by inclination, a poet by inspiration—I allude to the "divine William;" and he, in one of his immortal plays, enunciated the fact, that to add, by painting, to the beauties of the lily, or to render the violet more odorous, was a work of supererogation. He never said that he himself could be improved: but it has been done, and if you, Sir, will kindly turn to p. 134 of THE NATURALIST'S NOTE BOOK, you will see that a gentleman, by two remarkably elegant parables, has improved, not Nature, but William Shakspeare. After a little botanical horror at introduced Flora, this gentleman, placing himself with an air, *en Grand Monarque*, in the front rank of naturalists, does me the honour to connect my name with a mythical bird which, he rightly says, would attract my notice. I should rather think it would, as well as that of my "colleagues," but not in the spirit he takes it. No doubt I should consider myself perfectly justified in procuring a pair after I had sufficiently studied their habits; beyond that, the "Scarlet Bird" would be at perfect liberty to come or go as it listed. I see that, for the information of Mr. Britten, I must recapitulate that I am neither a sparrow-slaughterer, a battue-shooter, nor do I recklessly destroy more than I require for study, or for a collection which I trust to make one of the most useful in England.

It is rather hard that botanists and conchologists arrogate to themselves the right to guage the requirements of ornithology by their own narrow views, under the guise of an enlarged humanity. I have grave doubts whether Mr. Britten pauses ere he plucks, nay roots up *Myosotis donchutoutshme* to add to his *Hortus siccus*, or whether "T. G. P." (of whom anon) hesitates ere he plunges *Bulimus onowhenevermenshonit* into boiling water to procure a pretty specimen. But, as I have heard some people say, it is only a flower, or a shell; just so, but the inhabitant of the shell has as great a right to sympathy as a bird; while the flower, blooming 'neath a summer sky, delights the eyes and senses of many a wayfarer ere it is "collected" by some botanical destroyer. Do not then, to use a homely vulgarism, let us make fish of one and fowl of the other, for the rule of glass-houses certainly applies in these cases. I am not a conchologist, or a collector of plants, yet I have as great a respect for those individuals as I have for a collector of postage-stamps; but when I see them step out of their groove to do battle with others who do not happen to be in their "line," giving them to understand, at the same time, that they (the Shellites and Plantites) are the "old original naturalists," and all others are "very small pumpkins," why, I think it behoves every *working* student of our English Fauna to combine, rise *en masse*, and with some such war-cry as "a 'J. D. S. W.' 'a Lover of Birds,' to the rescue!" gird at some of these pretentious naturalists (?) and ride them down with "ever-pointed" pens, and let the fatal *grace Dieu* of common sense find its way in at the weak points of their arguments.

No doubt Mr. Britten may be correct in some of his "flowery" statements, and I must say I admire the conservative sentence (which no War-Office official, wedded to routine, could turn more prettily) "We shall annoy our brother naturalists of the old school, who like the native flowers and birds of their own country, and do not wish them artificially improved by newly-introduced companions." So, for the sake of not *annoying* a few octogenarians, Mr. Britten would exclude all foreign or imported beauty. Why then, what a terrible eye-sore Mr. Frank Buckland (a shocking innovator) must be, to say nothing of the Acclimatisation Society. Even the salmon, I see, have a dreadful disregard for the proprieties, and are actually allowing themselves to be "improved" into the Thames. Mr. Beales even, I am certain, never contemplated anything half so bad as this, and if Reform has, as it would appear, infected the Zoological world, why then Mr. Britten, I am afraid, will live to see a great many of his pet theories pushed aside, or "catawampously chawed up."

I remain, Sir, yours, &c.

A. M. B.

OTTERS, OH! OTTERS!!!

Sir,—Not wishing to take up your valuable space unnecessarily, I must say a few words to "T. G. P."

He remarks that I did not give him a fair chance of a reply, by not writing to the journal in which his dirge on vermin was perpetrated, and wails forth that he nearly missed seeing my letter. I am sure I sympathise deeply with him, and *perhaps* I ought to have written to *Science Gossip;* but as I happen to consult my own opinion in such matters, and as I prefer the Note Book to *Science Gossip*, I naturally take my own view of that matter. I have not the slightest wish to be discourteous to T. G. P. as an *individual*, and daresay, as such, he is a very estimable person; but writing as a naturalist, holding some singularly-unhappy views, he, I contend, must put up with a little criticism.

If I am right in supposing him to be the same "T. G. P." whose remarks upon shells appear on page 156, he will take my remarks upon conchologists, in another part of your impression, in the spirit in which they are meant. With regard to his italics, I deny their applicability *in toto*, and, for a further answer, must refer him to "Bird Murder," p. 89.

Yet another word: "T. G. P." says there was no reason why the animals should not have been taken alive. As the original paragraph distinctly represents them making for a pond, independent of the difficulty which would attend their capture, would T. P. G. undertake to stop two full-grown otters in *any* case?

I remain, Sir, yours, &c.

A. M. B.

Short Notes.

CROCODILES.—Geoffroy St. Hilaire, and some other French writers quoted by Milne Edwards, describe the crocodiles of Egypt as seizing fish, and also water birds, by diving after and pursuing them. But this would argue a more active animal than it has always appeared to me to be. I have on several occasions watched them swimming under water. They may be readily observed then, if the stream be clear and the spectator looking down from a high bank. Thus, in many parts of the Koladyn river in Arracan, above the old Koladyn t'hana (police station), and in the Byturnee and the Roro, in Singbhoom, I have seen these animals in their element, but they rarely did more than come slowly across from under some bush to another; and though with their broad powerful tails they readily stemmed a rapid stream, it was seldom the effort was made. They appeared to prefer floating listlessly in the calm eddy of some bay, drawing nearer and nearer to the side, and there lying in the slack water, as we see the efts do in our ponds. When pressed by hunger the crocodile forgoes these lazy pleasures, and betakes himself to his ambuscade. When most to be feared he is most invisible. He then lies either under the drooping boughs of the bushes which shadow the deep water by the bank, or creeps beneath the masses of weeds which choke up the stream near the ordinary watering-place of the village. To understand the danger the villagers are exposed to in obtaining water for domestic use in rivers infested by crocodiles, it is necessary to describe an ordinary "ghât," or watering-place. Down the steep bank a small footpath leads to the river's edge, and here the frequent ingress of feet and dipping of vessels has kept an irregularly triangular space of clear water, through which the bottom may be traced till lost in gloom. This open space is hemmed in by masses of weeds growing close up to the bank, and floating in beds some two or three feet thick. Under this canopy the crocodile glides, and, resting just within the edge, with his muzzle touching the bank, remains motionless and perfectly invisible, till amongst the frequent visitors to the spot one, more heedless than the rest, advances so far into the stream that the crocodile's head is considerably inshore of the unhappy woman's legs. This is the position the animal requires to ensure the capture of his prey. One rapid twist and half turn carries him, with his victim in his jaws, back into the central depths of the river; frequently not a shriek is heard. A floating earthen pot marks the spot where a human being had an instant before stood chatting and laughing, while a few ripples in the water, and a wave or two of the weeds, just indicate where the monster had made his rush. But though this fearful tragedy be repeated perhaps each month, so heedless and apathetic are the natives that they persevere in their rash mode of drawing water. In the upper parts of the Koladyn alone I found the people who lived on the banks prudent enough to inclose the watering places with bamboo palisading.—*Field*.

AMBERGRIS.—Mr. Piesse writing to *Land and Water* says :—Why does Sir Emerson Tennant speak of this (in *Notes and Queries*) as an "ambiguous and equivocal material?" Its origin is known. There is now no doubt about its being the fæces of the sperm whale. Portions of the food of the whale are invariably found in good ambergris, showing its intestinal origin. Among the *débris* may be particularly noticed the beaks of the cuttle fish, so peculiar in their resemblance to a parrot's beak, only that the lower mandible is the larger. This beak appears to be indigestible, and is excreted together with biliary matter. Frank Buckland and other authorities state that the whale feeds on cuttle fish when he can. Permit me to make a "note" on ambergris. Milton is found to speak of this substance in its proper name, at least as *gris*amber, which distinguishes this substance from the transparent resin-amber, but Shakespeare says—

"Gloves perfumed with rose and amber,
Perfume for a lady's chamber."

And the *Times* of February 24, describing the gift of the Golden Rose from the Pope to the Queen of Spain, says, "At every benediction he pronounces upon it, he inserts a few particles of amber and musk, imparting to it the sweetness to which allusion is made in the brief." Now here the word "amber" is mistakingly used for ambergris. Amber has no odour, but the fragrance of ambergris is such that its present market value is eight times that of silver. By the way, at the forthcoming maritime exhibition at Havre, will there be any space allotted for an exhibition of ambergris? its educts and products? If we may judge by the scarcity of ambergris, it would appear that whales, like oysters, have been "over-fished."

RATS SUCKLED BY A CAT.—In a late number of *Land and Water* we read,—I have often known animals to bring up the young of other animals when they had been deprived of their own, but I am about to relate a very curious case in which a cat adopted the animals upon which she preyed! In the autumn of 1864 I was upon a visit at Terregles, the seat of the Hon. Marmaduke Maxwell, near Dumfries. The day after my arrival (my weakness for animals being well known) I was taken to the stables and introduced to a cat in a cage full of hay, out of which three fine sleek half-grown rats very soon made their appearance and played with pussy in the most ridiculous manner. Of course I eagerly sought the history of the case, which was this. Many weeks before some straw was brought to the stables and put into an empty stall, and it would appear that in this straw was a nest of five young rats which had been deserted by their mother upon removing the straw. Hunger made the youngsters squeak for mamma, but she had too great a dread of the cat to put in an appearance, and the poor cat hearing the "rumtitum" and having been robbed of her own little family that morning, made for the young rats, and her parental feelings overcoming her prejudices, she adopted three of them; two having been killed by the fork in removing the straw. In order to keep these rats safe they were placed by the coachman in the cage, and the cat was frequently let into them. It was amusing to observe how completely these rats were regarded by her as her own kittens, for she would frequently bring them mice and seemed astonished at their not eating them.

WORMS.—Every one must have observed the little heaps of stones which are almost always to be seen on garden walks or wherever there is loose gravel. Each of these heaps will be found to surround and cover the hole of an earthworm. Nothing seems to come amiss with earthworms; they will take sticks, paper, bits of slate, anything in short that they can find within reach. Being curious to know how they manage to collect these stones (often of considerable size), in spring, a year or two ago I removed several little mounds, leaving a clear space of several inches round the holes, and in the evening went out with a light to watch. Worms rarely show themselves till evening, and then they always keep their tails fixed in their holes, while feeling around with their heads. One of them, thus lying half out of his hole, soon fastened its mouth on to a stone (about the size of the end of one's thumb) and proceeded to drag it, apparently by the force of suction, quickly back to its hole. This I have since seen repeated several times with small stones, the worm's tail being always kept firmly anchored in the ground. Their strength is surprising. On one occasion I found a stone weighing two ounces drawn over one of the cleared holes, and another weighing one ounce. After two nights some of the holes had eight or nine small stones over them; after four nights one had about 30, another 24 stones. What their object can be in taking all this trouble, and thus covering up their holes, I cannot imagine. Can any of your readers throw any light on the subject?—I. W. in *Gardeners' Chronicle*.

AUSTRALIA.—When we have winter they have summer; when we have day they have night; the compass points to the south, the sun travels along the northern heavens, the mercury of the barometer rises with a southerly and falls with a northerly wind; the animals are disproportionately large in their lower extremities, and carry their young in a pouch; the plumage of the birds is beautiful, their notes are harsh and strange; the swans are black, the eagles are white, the moles lay eggs, the owls screech and howl only in the daytime, the cuckoo's song is heard only in the night; the valleys are cool, the mountain-tops are warm, the north winds are hot, the south winds are cold, the east winds are healthy; the bees are without sting; cherries grow with the stone outside; one of the birds has a broom in his mouth instead of a tongue; another creature (the duck-billed platypus) unites with the body-fur and habits of a mole the webbed foot and bill of a duck. Many of the beautiful flowers are without smell; most of the trees are without shade and shed their bark instead of their leaves; some have no leaves, in others the leaves are vertical. A change has now occurred, what with the advances of cultivation, and the introduction of British birds into the meagre forests, British fish into the rivers, and British plants on the cleared portions of the country. To Mr. Wilson, the proprietor and editor of the *Argus*, this acclimatisation feat is mainly due.—MARQUIS CHISHOLM, in *Greenock Advertiser*.

EFFECT OF SOUND ON ANIMALS.—We possess a cat which is unusually tame, particularly for a "Tom," and with no ear for music, if I may judge by the way in which he and his companions make the short summer night hideous when we go into the country. He is very fond of my daughter, but objects strongly to her repeating French lessons aloud—always jumping on the table beside her, mewing dolefully, and rubbing against her to coax her to stop. A few nights ago she was reading the Psalms of the day in English, and he was lying apparently sound asleep on the back of the chair in which she sat; but she had not finished three verses before he got up, stretched himself and jumped down to the table to coax her, just as he does when she is reading French. Until then, the child thought it was the language to which he objected, although her father (to whom the cat is more attached than to any one in the house) or I may read any language we please without his caring; but since, she has tried him by singing 'The Last Rose of Summer,' and he complained bitterly, and another time she began 'Bedford,' an old tune from Ravenscroft's Psalter, which pleased him no better; and as he takes all her conversation with great amiability, often replying in gentle tones when it is addressed to himself, we must conclude that it is the continuous sound of her voice—and only hers—in reading or singing which distresses him so painfully.—A. A. C., *Athenæum*.

THE ROBIN.—The Rev. F. O. Morris, in a recent number of *Our Own Fireside*, says:—"The late William Thompson, Esq., of Belfast, in his "Natural History of Ireland," will show that there the robin is the same as with us:—In the very mild winter of 1831-32, a redbreast very frequently made one at a breakfast table, helping itself to all that it wanted. In summer it built in one of the outhouses, and visited the kitchen daily, and in the autumn used to sing in the hall. Another was in the habit of entering a house to feed. Another would even go into a lantern to eat the candle in it, and others would alight on the hands of labourers, to eat therefrom. One which used to visit the abode of a tame eagle at feeding time, flew into his perch as soon as he had left it for the ground, and then alighted on the chain by which he was fastened; another visited the same cottage for four or five winters in succession, taking up its abode within doors altogether, until the return of spring. One of a pair, when the days were very fine and bright in October, regularly frequented a stable, and when perched upon the stall, sang without being in any degree disturbed by the general business of the place going forward even within two or three feet of his station. A pair of redbreasts that were assiduously watched during their nidification in a conservatory, were one morning found in great consternation, in consequence of their nest having been taken possession of by a bat, which they eventually compelled to change its quarters.

AUSTRALIAN POISON SHRUBS.—Over some of the healthy tracts of scrub-country towards the south-west coast, poisonous species of Gastrolobium (G. bilobum, G. oxylobioides, G. calycinum, G. callistachys) are dispersed. These plants have in some localities rendered the occupation of country for pastoral pursuits impossible, but these poison-plants are mostly confined to barren spots, and it is not unlikely that, by repeated burnings, and by the raising of perennial fodder-plants, they could be suppressed and finally extirpated. Fortunately, Gastrolobium occurs in no other parts of Australia, except on the inland tract from Attack Creek to the Suttor River, where flocks must be guarded against access to the scrub patches harbouring the only tropical species (Gastrolobium grandiflorum). The deadly effect occasionally produced by Lotus australis, a herb with us of very wide distribution, and extending also to New Caledonia, and the cerebral derangements manifested by pasture animals which feed on the Darling River Pea (Swainsona Greyana), need yet extensive investigation, but may find their explanation in the fact that the organic poisonous principle is only locally, under conditions yet obscure, developed, or in the probable circumstance that, like in a few other leguminous plants, the deleterious properties are strongly concentrated in the seed.—*Dr. Mueller's Essay*.

THE TURTLE DOVE.—We read the following curious fact in the *Field*:—"About two years and a half since I had a pair of wild turtle doves brought up in a cage. They became perfectly tame, but the usual fate of pets attended them; one escaped, and the other died. It is now more than eighteen months ago that it escaped, and I had begun to forget my loss. Within the last ten days a bird of the same species has appeared, joined the companionship of my tumblers, comes at my whistle to be fed, and is as tame as the tamest of them; it even comes upon the tray in front of my dining-room window, where my birds enjoy their morning meal. At first my birds were frightened at the approach of 'the illustrious stranger,' but they are now perfectly reconciled to it. What becomes of it at night I know not, but there it is to be found every morning. It joins the rest in their morning flight, but instead of uniting with them flies in a circle round them, and most interesting it is to observe its elegant motion. Can it be my lost pet?—J. C. M."

EXTRAORDINARY SPIDER.—Rather a singular species of spider, which was unearthed when digging in some ground adjoining the township, was shown us last week. We know of no named species of the *Arachnida* to which it may be mentioned as belonging. The kind to which we allude is about half the size of the common tarantula, and is banded longitudinally with alternate stripes of very dark green and grey. The back is furnished with a kind of shell, to which there are some fifty entrances, and from these the young spiders might be seen leaving the maternal home in great numbers, and again returning after a short stay outside. The creature seemed to possess all the ferocity and courage of its race. It certainly exemplified, at the time it was shown to us, one of the most curious forms of spider we remember to have seen. Perhaps the *savants* of Melbourne would fix the genus. We confess our previous ignorance as to the existence of such a wonder amongst the *Arachnida*.—*Ararat Advertiser.*

DUTCH TULIPS.—The Dutch have long been celebrated for their cultivation of bulbous roots, especially tulips and hyacinths; and from March till June the district around Haarlem is carpeted with a succession of beautiful flowers, beginning with crocuses and ending with ranunculi. The sandy soil of the district, which is derived from the dunes, is highly favourable to bulb culture—indeed, some of the flowers grow on the sand hills, and hundreds of acres of valuable land are, in consequence, devoted to flower farming. In the proper season, as one drives along the roads in the neighbourhood of Haarlem, he is surrounded on all sides by plantations of hyacinths and tulips in full bloom, forming a mass of colour exceedingly varied and rich, while the scent exhaled is most delicious.—*Once a Week.*

ARTESIAN WELLS.—Mr. G. A. Shufeldt, jun., by whom the Chicago Artesian Wells were bored, states, in the *Scientific American*, that the wells are now 711 feet in depth; they commenced filling with water at a distance of 10 feet from the surface, and continued full all the way down; whence he asks—Why did not the centrifugal force throw this water out? and why was no water discharged until the drill had penetrated a particular subterranean stream? Before this point was reached there was plenty of water in the wells, and we could pump out an abundant supply; and this is true of hundreds of other artesian wells scattered throughout the country: they do not discharge the water above the surface, but plenty of it can be obtained by pumping. He adheres to the opinion that water, in flowing wells, comes from a higher source, and is not thrown out by the earth's centrifugal force.

TENACITY OF LIFE.—In the summer of last year I met with a singular instance of tenacity of life in a rabbit. Walking in the wood above Wycombe Park, my attention was attracted to a rabbit which ran out into the open glade pursued by my dog. It doubled again and again in a feeble way, and I hastened to the rescue, believing it to be wounded. I hastily secured it, folded it in my cloak, and carried it home; on producing my prize a piteous spectacle met our view. The little creature had no eyes, and through the empty sockets we could see quite into the head, which appeared hollow and almost in a state of decomposition, while the body was plump and healthy. It appeared to me a singular incident, and worth recording. I should be glad to know if any of your correspondents have met with a similar one, and can explain the cause of it.—E. C.—*From the Quarterly Magazine of High Wycombe Nat. Hist. Soc.*

GROWTH OF TREES.—Some experiments relating to the growth of trees have lately been made by Mr. Thomas Meehan, and recorded in the proceedings of the Academy of Natural Sciences of Philadelphia, from which it appears that "the tree increased in growth only during the three months between the middle of May and the middle of August, and that the ratio of growth is much greater during the month between the middle of June and the middle of July, than during the month preceding and the succeeding month." The special tree, measurements of which are recorded, is Populus monilifera, which was measured weekly from April 12 till August 31, during three different years.—*Gardeners Chronicle,*

A PROLIFIC COUNTRY.—Mr. Catlin, in his "Last Rambles amongst the Indians of the Rocky Mountains and the Andes," says of the Uruguay and the mighty Paraguay, that, "in the course of eighteen hundred miles, they afford a highway and food for more than fifty tribes of Indians, and their waters and shores afford localities for fifty thousand tigers, one hundred and fifty thousand alligators, a million monkeys, five million parrots, tens of thousands of anacondas and rattlesnakes, and now and then a boa-constrictor."

ANTS IN SLAVERY.—It is said that there is a description of ant in Texas, remarkable, not only for keeping other ants in slavery, and employing them on public works for the benefit of the community at large, but also for sowing around their settlement the seeds of a small graminaceous plant, which they afterwards reap and store away in granaries constructed for the purpose. The slaveholding ants are either red or white, whilst the "peculiar institution" is a black or negro ant.

Remarks, Queries, &c.

(*Under this head we shall be happy to insert original Remarks, Queries, &c.*)

SIGNS OF THE WEATHER.—Your correspondent, "R. B. W." is anxious to have "a list of the principal signs of the weather;" but as the prognosticating theories, hypothesis, adages, philosophical observations, etc., etc., of the numerous sages and amateurs in the science of meteorology, from the time of Theophrastus the Greek down to that of Admiral Fitzroy, would be likely to fill the next twenty volumes of the NATURALIST'S NOTE BOOK, I greatly fear there is but little chance of getting even the "principal signs" into a portable form. Seamen, shepherds, and agriculturists are particularly clever in making accurate deductions from "weather signs," and such great writers of antiquity as Aratus, Virgil, Seneca,

Lucan, Pliny, Homer and Hesiod, occasionally lent the charms of their pens to those "signs" which "R. B. W." wishes to possess. The clouds, the rainbow, the sun, the moon, plants, and animals, were the principal data in the meteorological science. But here let me introduce the rules of the shepherd of Banbury:—

If the sun rise red and fiery, wind and rain. If cloudy, and the cloudiness soon decrease, then fair weather certain. Clouds small and round, like a dapple grey with a north wind, then fair weather for two or three days. Large clouds like rocks, forebode great showers. If small clouds increase, much rain. If large clouds decrease, fair weather. Mists, if they rise in low ground and soon vanish, fair weather. If mists rise on the hill tops, rain in a day or two. A general mist before the sun rises near the full moon, then fair weather. If mists in the new moon, rain in the old. If mists in the old, rain in the new.

Lest I intrude I shall quote no more from the weather seer of Banbury. The kite's flying high is a sign of fair weather, and the flying high of herons forebodes wind. Such things puzzled the ingenuity of Lord Bacon. When the seaman sees the petrels take shelter under the wake of his ship, then is he sure of an approaching storm. I have often watched the stormy petrels, and listened to seamen's predictions; they were still true. Sea gulls, when far from land, are sure to take to the masts of vessels before a storm: this every sailor knows. And says the old proverb:—

"An evening red, and a morning gray,
Are certain signs of a charming day;
But the evening gray, and the morning red,
Put on your hat, or you'll wet your head."

And again:—

"When clouds appear like rocks and towers,
The earth's refreshed by frequent showers."

And:—

"In the wane of the moon
A cloudy morning bodes a fair afternoon."

Time presses, for the present I conclude; but should the above prove in any way interesting to "R. B. W." sure I can soon again return to the subject.

Dromore.   H. H. ULIDIA.

"R. B. W." asks (in this month's number of the NOTE BOOK) some of your correspondents to give a list of the principal "signs of the weather." Now to attempt to give even the principal ones would fill up more space than I expect you would care to devote to the subject; but I enclose a copy of a poem entitled "Signs of Rain," written by the celebrated discoverer of vaccination (Dr. Jenner) as an excuse for not accepting the invitation of a friend to join him in an excursion.   A. F. B.

SIGNS OF RAIN.

The hollow winds begin to blow,
The clouds look black, the glass is low,
The soot falls down, the spaniels sleep,
And spiders from their cobwebs peep.
Last night the sun went pale to bed,
The moon in halos hid her head;
The boding shepherd heaves a sigh,
For, see, a rainbow spans the sky.
The walls are damp, the ditches smell,
Closed is the pink-eyed pimpernell,
Hark! how the chairs and tables crack,
Old Betty's joints are on the rack;
Loud quack the ducks, the peacock's cry,
The distant hills are looking nigh.
How restless are the snorting swine,
The busy flies disturb the kine;
Low o'er the grass the swallow wings;
The cricket, too, how sharp he sings.
Puss, on the hearth, with velvet paws,
Sits, wiping o'er his whisker'd jaws.
Through the clear stream the fishes rise,
And nimbly catch th' incautious flies;
The glowworms, numerous and bright,
Illumed the dewy dell last night.
At dusk the squalid toad was seen,
Hopping and crawling o'er the green;
The whirling wind the dust obeys,
And in the rapid eddy plays;
The frog has changed his yellow vest,
And in a russet coat is drest.
Though June, the air is cold and still;
The yellow blackbird's voice is shrill;
My dog, so alter'd in his taste,
Quits mutton bones, on grass to feast.
And see, yon rooks, how odd their flight,
They imitate the gliding kite;
And seem precipitate to fall—
As if they felt the piercing ball.
'Twill surely rain, I see with sorrow,
Our jaunt must be put off to-morrow.

From peculiarity of situation, with the rugged and lofty hills of Dartmoor on the north, and the sea before it, the climate of Plymouth is inclined to moisture, and yet scarcely so much so as the following lines would indicate:—

"The south winds always bring wet weather;
The north wind wet and cold together.
The west wind always brings us rain;
The east wind blows it back again.
If the sun in red should set,
The next day surely will be wet;
If the sun should set in grey,
The next will be a rainy day."

Old experience lays down sundry wise saws. When the stars look larger than ordinary, it is a sign of change of weather. Very bright or double rainbows indicate long-continued rain; the same when the rain smokes as it falls on the ground. Lightning in winter is a sign of coming snow, wind or tempest. Bats flying about in unusual numbers announce that the next day will be warm and fine. Flies bite sharper and tease you more before a tempest. When the gnats dance in the setting sunshine, some hold it a sign of fine weather to-morrow, while sceptics declare it is only a sign of fine weather to-day. If it rains on the 3rd of May, there will be no walnuts, if on the 15th of June, no grapes. Plenty of snow precedes an abundant year; plenty of rain, the contrary. A rainy autumn spoils the wine of that year, and threatens a poor crop of wheat next year. A fine autumn is mostly followed by a windy winter; a wet spring and summer by a fine autumn. On the other hand, when the autumn is fine, the following spring is apt to be rainy.—*London Society.*

LARVA AND CATERPILLARS.—I think that you will agree with me when I remark that the profusion of answers to one or two little inquiries made by the young aspirant to entomology has now brought rather a formidable piece of machinery into motion. I allude now, more especially, to the note signed "A. B." in your last issue, in which a whole series of questions occur; but happily all of them connected with, or tending to, the same object. Some of the said questions may be disposed of in a very few words, while the others will require to be treated upon at some length, in order to make them intelligible and useful to the inquiring mind. However, according to the true English feeling that a civil question deserves a civil answer, and supposing that half-a-score must be met with the same complacency, I hasten to answer the one or two that I imagine require but few words, although, perhaps, not less important in connection with the present inquiry. I would advise any inexperienced breeder of insects to give a supply of earth in every case where larva or caterpillars are confined, as although most of the butterfly larva suspend themselves above ground, and, I believe, most of the Bombyx moths spin cocoons, yet a very great number of species bury themselves in the earth to undergo their change. As to the kind of earth to be used, I have generally preferred earth from a mole-hill when I could conveniently obtain it; but I think this was merely a matter of fancy, as I quite believe that clean fresh garden mould will answer the purpose equally well. As to digging up the chrysalids or removing them in any way, I should strongly urge that they be allowed to remain where they have placed themselves until they are brought out by the natural influence of the season, as I much doubt whether the most observant entomologist could place them again in as good a position as the caterpillar had selected to undergo its changes, or, I may add, its most beautiful and interesting metamorphosis. I had intended to have given a word or two upon cages used for insects, but time fails me at this moment, and I can merely say that I believe they are supplied by most dealers in birds, insects, &c., at a reasonable price. Moreover, "A. B." questions will, no doubt, be met by numerous and varied replies perhaps sufficient to initiate him into the arts and mysteries of breeding entomological specimens. Should this not be the case, I may render him a little aid, from time to time, as opportunity offers. C. W——D.

320, Strand.

NESTING OF THE MAGPIE.—The question put by H. Meyrick with regard to the nesting of the magpie has been well and truthfully responded to by M. L. A., and also by J. S., junr.; but as the latter has alluded to another point in the history of this bird may I be allowed to have a finger in the pie, not to contradict, but rather to confirm the remarks of both your correspondents. Having spent many years among the woods and pastures of this country, animated with a strong desire to become practically acquainted with nature's handy works, I may say that I have frequently met with the nest of the magpie in a holly hedge, which indeed seemed rather a favourite spot with them, and again in a young fir plantation, the nest not more than eight or ten feet from the ground. I have also seen them at the upper part of very lofty trees, not unfrequently leaning over a large pond or lake. The former we used to designate as the bush magpie, while those which selected a more lofty position were most uniformly styled the large or tree magpie. But having taken no small liberties with the nest and eggs in both cases in order to examine and compare, I feel quite convinced that they are one and the same species; at all events, I could find no character either in the birds, nests, or eggs, to justify the idea of two distinct and separate species of birds. True it is that they are more capricious in their nesting operations than many other species, but this in some measure accords with the general character of the bird. The amusing little anecdote forwarded by A. M. B. will further illustrate the peculiarity of character in the magpie: but still I think this circumstance must be understood as an exception rather than part and parcel of the usual habit of the birds. The following solution might possibly explain this particular case—namely, a tame hen magpie kept by the present or a former occupier of the said premises might have prevailed upon a partner to join her in her partial captivity; and if so, I believe that some of the offspring would be likely to revisit the place where they had been reared in security, although such position might differ somewhat from the usual haunts and habits of the bird. Whether such be the case or not, we may conclude from the varied remarks that the nest of the magpie may be found from the gooseberry bush in the garden to the loftiest part of the timber of the forest; and also that, although generally dispersed throughout the country, yet they are less numerous in the northern part than in the woods and plantations of the more southern part of the kingdom. C. W——D.

DRESSING RABBIT SKINS, &C.—The best way of preparing skins, those of the rabbit, hare, cat, &c., is as follows:—In the first place great care must be taken in skinning the animal so as to get the skin as clean as possible, and also a good shape. After it is taken off cut away the fat which remains on the skin and place it in cold water for a short time, then procure some Sicily Shumac, which can be obtained at most oil-shops. Boil it in water for about a quarter of an hour; let it settle, which you can hasten by dashing cold water into it, then, while the liquor is hot, so as you can comfortably bear your hand in, dip the skin three or four times (having previously pressed the cold water out) but be careful not to make the liquor thick; when it is a little cooler, lay the skin in a shallow trough or dish, and pour the clear liquor upon it, and let it remain for a week or ten days; then repeat the process, and continue to do so for a month or six weeks, or longer if necessary, so as to effectually set the hair. After it has lain its allotted time, take it out of the liquor and press all the moisture out; stretch it, nailing it hair downwards on to a board, and, while it is wet, cover the wet side thinly with dubbing (which is a compound of oil and tallow), easily procured at an oil shop in boxes at a penny and twopence each, only do not be persuaded to purchase any but that which is of *a pale yellow colour*, as that of a black colour is often sold instead of the former. But if B. F. B. is able to obtain dubbing from a currier or leather dresser he can there procure the pure article for a few pence, but if the latter is not easily obtained that from the oil shop will do. After the dubbing is lightly spread on with a brush or piece of flannel, the skin must be left to dry gradually; not exposed to artificial heat, as this will cause it to dry hard and horny, but, if left to the influence of the atmosphere, it will dry in a proper manner (but must not be exposed to the sun); after it has thoroughly dried take it off the board, and, with a pumice stone, take off the thin brown skin, which will easily peel off, only care must be taken not to push the stone through the skin thereby making a hole. After all the brown is removed, roll the skin about upon a clean table until it is soft and pliable; trim the edges and it is then fit for use. It of course requires a little practice to turn out the skin well. The above process will do for the skins of cats, dogs, hares, and rabbits, but the skins of mice, rats, moles, &c., require different treatment on account of their more delicate structure.

G.

EGG-COLLECTING.—The misfortune resulting from the use of a solution of corrosive sublimate in the preservation of insects, recorded by J. Douglas on page 200, vol. I. of NATURALIST'S NOTE BOOK has just occurred to me. I dissolved about half an ounce of this substance in alcohol, adding a nearly equal proportion of camphor, and applied the liquid to the surface of about forty eggs in order to preserve them from the attacks of moths and other insects. When dried each specimen showed a white sediment similar to that mentioned by your correspondent, only in this case the objects were not lost as they could be washed clean again. The sediment was seen most distinctly on those shells which were more darkly marked. Can you or any of your readers explain the reason of this? Was it because the solution was too strong? I have constantly used this poison in preparing skins, &c., but have never met with the same effect. Waterton likewise highly recommends it for preserving collections of insects, and seems to have used it with great success in all objects of natural history. He, along with others, recommends its *internal* application to eggs, but if the holes in the shells be stopped with wax, and insects be kept from them by some *external* application, I think this would be hardly necessary.

I should be glad if some one experienced in egg-collecting would give further information as to the management of a cabinet. Is turpentine useful for keeping a collection free from insects? How often is it necessary to remove the specimens in order to clean out the cabinet and change the wool? What is the best means of preventing the shells losing their colour? Isinglass dissolved in gin has been recommended.

R. B. W.

[Read Mr. Napier's article on page 170.—ED.]

Would any botanist kindly inform me what is the cause of the formation of knots in wood? R. B. W.

THE ARRANGEMENT OF SHELLS.—The block plan may answer in a public museum, where the arrangement of specimens is permanent; but with the probability of moving—a contingency which overtakes most collectors sooner or later—I think it increases the risk of injury to the specimens. Sawdust, which "T. G. P." recommends, is not a nice thing to put into one's drawers or small shells. I brought my large collection, 15,000 specimens, packed with cotton wool, tissue paper, and pasteboard in their own drawers a distance of more than 100 miles, travelling per ordinary goods train, mostly in perfect condition. The "Jermyn-street cement" is very firm and useful in its place, but difficult to get off shells, and is a messy smear in a cabinet. At one time I gummed down every thing, but I have given up this; things that have been gummed down are much injured in commercial value, which I have noticed at Stevens' sales. The British Museum cement is much neater and almost equally firm, either for animal, vegetable, or mineral substances; it is composed of three parts of gum tragacanth, one part of gum Arabic, and the two hundredth of a part of corrosive sublimate, the whole dissolved in water. It takes a week to dissolve. In reply to Mr. Atkins, I would say that I put my smaller shells under 1-6th inch long into glass tubes or glass-top boxes, and do not number them; but this might be done with a fine-pointed pen, with very few exceptions, without disfiguring the shell. Finding glass-top boxes rather expensive, I purchased some sheets of talc, which I cut out with a pair of scissors to fit the tops of pill boxes, which shows the small shells beneath very well. Other collectors purchase the larger circular miscroscopic glass covers, which, I believe, cost about 2s. 6d. a hundred. They fit these into the boxes. For young people who have more time than money, this is, no doubt, a good plan, for a little of the gum of which I have been speaking will render these glasses firm in the boxes.

C. O. G. N.

THE BREEDING OF THE WOODCHAT IN ENGLAND.—Mr. Merrick is wrong about this species. We have more than one well-authenticated instance of the woodchat breeding in England. It was, I believe, first discovered by Mr. Bond, in the Isle of Wight. A nest in my collection was taken at Halle, Germany; it is composed of moss, sticks, and grass, and is lined with fine grass, without a particle of hair. It was built in a heather bush (*Calluna vulgaris*). The eggs in this nest are of a pale clear blue, with spots of ash and greenish ochre, but the aspect of the eggs is much more blue than that of the eggs of the red-backed shrike usually is, and they are commonly of a more full shape, and are half 1-16th of an inch greater in diameter. The spots on the eggs of the woodchat are more commonly green, and are larger than are often seen in those of the red-backed shrike. But some eggs, like those of the lesser grey shrike (*L. minor*) are a species which we may quite expect to find some day in Britain. It is common on the Rhine. The woodchat breeds abundantly in many districts in France, Germany, Italy, Switzerland, Spain, Greece, and also in Algeria and Palestine. It lays from five to seven eggs, which vary much, some being of a blue ground, others of a cream colour, a third pale ochre with spots, which sometimes are large, soft, and cloudy, at other times hard and clearly defined. The zone of spots is less characteristic of them than of those of the red-backed shrike. The shrikes are all useful birds, and should be by no means molested in the breeding season especially, for they destroy many of the most troublesome insects, as also the mice and other pests of the farm. I mention these particulars to induce some of your readers to look out for the nest of the woodchat, which in England, if at all, is obtainable in May and June. C. O. G. N.

PHOLAS DACTYLAS.—Having lately began to take in the NOTE BOOK, on procuring the back numbers for this year, I find, in the January number, a notice of the Pholas Dactylus, by "J. D. S. W.," in which he suggests that the hard limestone in which the animals at present live was soft clay when they first took up their abode therein. The locality he gives is Fifeshire, and I am much surprised that no remark on the subject has appeared in any of the four succeeding numbers, as the most recent limestone in Fifeshire is, I believe, of carboniferous age, and consequently was formed and hardened into stone several geological epochs previous to the first appearance of Pholas, which is in the Pliocene period, to say nothing of the individuals existing last year. The fact of the shell being larger than the aperture of the burrow, may readily be accounted for thus :—The Pholas commences its burrow very early in life, and, as it grows, enlarges and deepens it, leaving the aperture only just wide enough for the siphon to pass into the water or mud surrounding the rock. A vertical section of one of these burrows shows them to be subconical, conforming to the form of the animal (vide "Wood's Common Objects of the Seashore"). Further, if the limestone had been soft so recently, that would not account for the entrance being smaller than the bottom of the burrow. W. H. D.
Keighley, May 8th.

KILLING MOTHS.—Seeing that you have frequent applications for the best method of killing moths and butterflies, and having a great abhorrence that unnecessary pain should be inflicted for our pleasure, I venture to give for the benefit of your readers who do not use it, a method I adopted for several years with the utmost success, viz., having secured the insect in a small box (the nearer air tight the better) dip with a pair of forceps a small piece of blotting paper varying from ⅛ to ¼ inch square (according to size of box) into chloroform, and immediately put it into the box with the insect, keeping the lid closed for a short time, and when the insect has ceased to move the pin can be easily run through the throax, and then, by taking the point of the pin with the left hand and steadying the insect with the thumb and finger, prick the under side of the throax with a steel pen dipped in a strong solution of oxalic acid, and life should be extinct. By this method there seems to be no pain inflicted, and the manipulations can be performed with the least injury to the plumage. I strongly deprecate the use of ammonia, as it appears to cause much pain, and I think is not so expeditious or so certain of securing the insect in perfect condition.
Maidstone. R. H. F. G.

DO INSECTS FEEL PAIN?—This is a subject which has engrossed the attention of many entomologists both ancient and of the present day. In fact I can competently assert that no less than three different theories have been advanced by entomologists as to whether the objects of their study feel pain, viz., 1st, That insects do feel pain acutely. 2nd, That they experience no pain. 3rd, and lastly, That they feel pain, but only in proportion to their size. This last is, in my opinion, the most rational theory, and I will state my reasons for so thinking. The anatomy of insects is essentially different to that of the mammalia. With brutes the brains have one particular centre; with insects they are distributed throughout the body; it is therefore rather a difficult matter to kill a stout bodied moth, as we may crush it in one part and yet the vital spark will not be extinguished. I hold that insects having no vital point, a proof that they feel not pain acutely; but I also consider the quiverings and writhings of insects when maltreated sufficient evidence that they must experience some degree of pain.
ENTOMOLOGICUS.

LANDRAILS—Having seen in a few of your late numbers a doubt arising about Landrails craking after the hay being cut, I beg to say that I have in my possession a pair of call bones with which I can bring them into the same field as myself from anywhere within hearing distance. I have a stuffed specimen of a Landrail shot on the 18th August, 1865, which, with the aid of the bones, I shot in a late third crop of aftergrass while responding vigorously to my call. I have noticed this year they were some days later in arriving in this part of the country, having for the last five years arrived on the 25th April. The first I shot this year was on the 3rd May. With the above exception I never heard one call after the hay being cut. If shot immediately on their arrival in a field others will continue to come in their place, 1 having shot eighteen in the season in the same field; but if allowed to remain a few days, begin to get very wary and difficult to flush. Where they disappear to so noiselessly after the end of June, or thereabouts, is a wonder to me. F. W. I.
P.S.—Would any of your readers inform me the exact markings of a good old specimen?

BOLDNESS OF A CROW.—As my informant was driving along the road in a retired place his attention was drawn to a rabbit that had met with the misfortune of being laid hold of by a stoat, in struggling to escape from which it was in its death struggle. His curiosity prompted him to wait and witness the end of this affair; but as he did so, a crow made her appearance. It is probable that this bird had been unsuccessful in looking out for something to satisfy her hunger, or at least she became something more than an uninterested spectator of what was going on; for, unterrified by the hazardous nature of the act, the resolution was presently taken, and down she pounced upon the rabbit, with a powerful effort to carry it off from the formidable jaws of the stoat. If left to themselves it seems uncertain in what manner this contest might have ended; for neither of them appeared disposed to yield the prize; but by this time the third party believed himself warranted to advance his claim; but it was not until he had advanced to lay hold of the prey that the combatants thought it necessary to resign it.   VIDEO.

EELS.—On the 1st of May a few young eels were brought me, which had been found under stones in a brook. They were about three inches long. I placed them in a glass jar of fresh water, and most of them are still alive: but as an experiment, I placed one of them in a marine aquarium, after first keeping it for a time in mixed salt and fresh water, and I was astonished to find that it lived in the salt water as well as in the fresh. It is still alive, and is as lively as ever, though it has been in nearly a fortnight. Can any one tell me whether it is natural to eels to live as well in salt as in fresh water? One of the others accidentally fell into the salt water and was dead in a few minutes. I should also be glad to know what is the food of eels; I suppose in their young state they eat nothing solid. These seem to be of the same kind as the darker species mentioned by your correspondent "Fox," but I am unable to say what species that is.   GULIELMUS.

A BOLD HAWK.—On Saturday afternoon, May 2nd, a curious instance of the ferocity of the hawk occurred at the residence of the Rev. Sackville Cresswell, Posbury House, near Crediton. Two terror-stricken thrushes flew along a passage into the kitchen, closely pursued by a sparrow-hawk. In the presence of the cook the hawk seized one of the thrushes for his prey, and before the poor bird could be rescued inflicted such injuries upon it that it died as soon as it was picked up. The second thrush escaped up the chimney. Frightened, in his turn, by the cook's intervention, the hawk let his victim go, fled into an adjoining apartment, followed by a man-servant, and rushed at a window to get free. He broke a pane of glass by the force of his flight, but then fell, and was captured and killed. Mr. Cresswell has entrusted the bold hawk and his victim to Mr. W. B. Tucker, of Exeter, to be stuffed.

BRIGHTON INSECTS.—During the many years I lived at Brighton, I heard of or saw fresh specimens every season of the Death's-head Moth, and for four successive years I obtained them myself. In 1858 I got 30 larvæ, and conjointly with a friend bred 28 fine moths, and more than 36 cripples. That year also we bred 12 *D. Gallii*, and obtained 3 pupae of *Sphinx convoluli*, and 100 of the perfect moth caught on the wing or brought to us by labourers and children. I found Brighton, true to its reputation, one of the best localities for insects in England, taking personally during seven years diligent collecting the Bath white, Queen of Spain fritillary and Camberwell beauty, besides a host of rare moths and beetles; but I was out almost every day during some summers.
   C. O. G. N.

MICE.—I can fully bear out "J. D. S. W." in his statement concerning mice being carnivorous. This has been proved many times to my annoyance, and I think they prefer recently killed birds to any other flesh. On one occasion I had succeeded in shooting a pair of winchats, and wishing to save them clean for preservation, I placed them in a hedge row, and covered them with grass, intending to remove them upon my return, but was disappointed. On arriving at the place in about two hours after where I had hidden the birds, I found nothing but a heap of feathers to mark the spot. Since then I have had many destroyed by house-mice, and I have noticed particularly that the fattest are chosen for their first meal.   J. B. WATERS.
Crowndale-road, Oakley-square.

BOXES FOR LEPIDOPTERA. — Can any of your readers tell me where I can obtain cheap boxes for preserving specimens of Lepidoptera in? Six or seven years ago I obtained some made of deal, corked top and bottom, 14 inches by 9½ inches, and 2¾ inches in height, for half-a-crown each. Unfortunately I have lost the address of the shop (in London) where I obtained them, and should be glad of any information as to where I could obtain some similar to them in price and size. I should also be glad if any of your readers could tell me what is the best classified list of British Lepidoptera (with synonymes), and where it may be obtained.   E. M.
May, 1868.

WREN'S NEST.—I received an exceedingly pretty nest of the common wren a few days since, composed entirely of fern, and built in the fork of the same plant. The nest is unusually compact—smaller than wrens generally—and contains eight eggs. This being the first that has come under my notice, I think it is worth recording, as all others have been formed of large leaves only, and therefore requiring a much greater thickness of material to allow of the same space in the interior. This bulky appearance has been entirely avoided in the construction of the nest which I possess from the fineness of the leaves selected.
Crowndale-road, Oakley-square.   J. B. WATERS.

WHAT BIRDS TO KEEP IN AN AVIARY.—I have an aviary, or rather have one being made, but how to stock it is a question I must leave to some kind reader. Finches are my favourites, but do all finches agree together? I like all birds, but all birds won't agree with finches, and what I wish to know is what birds will agree with them? If foreign birds, they must be such as can stand an English winter. When I know what birds to stock it with I shall want to know what plants. Which are the best kind of shrubs, weeds, vegetables, &c.
May 6th.   J. R. B.

DEATH IN THE BOX.—I possess a species of tin box excellently manufactured for the purpose of destroying insect life. It is shaped like a cylinder with a top which screws on, and a perforated partition in the middle. The purpose of this is obvious; the insect intended to be killed is placed above the partition, and sulphur, or ammonia, or any stuff employed for insect murder is placed below it. The fumes of the vapour rise upwards through the holes of the partition, and with such deadly effect that, in a few minutes, the enclosed insect is deprived of life.   M.
Tunbridge Wells.

SKELETONS OF BIRDS.—In reply to "T. G. B.," I beg to say the boiling process should not be made to do all the work of cleaning; if it does, it will probably destroy the gelatinised texture of the surface of the bone. The process which succeed best depends on the size of the bones, for those of large animals, as the elephant and the ox, the steeping process is the best, but the operator may have to wait five years for his bones. C. O. G. N.

SKELETON OAK-LEAVES.—I know of a very simple and good method of skeletonising oak-leaves. Procure the leaves quite fresh and uninjured; place them in a book and shut them up to dry. They will dry in a few days or so, according to the atmosphere. Then remove them from the book, and placing them upon some hard flat substance beat them with a brush, when the substantial leaf will all fall out in pieces, leaving only the skeleton remains. FOLIUS.
May 1st 1868.

CANARIES.—In the May number of the NATURALISTS' NOTE-BOOK I see an inquiry for any information about Canaries. My daughter has a hen Canary which sings very sweetly; its notes are something like a linnet's, and not at all loud and shrill like those of the cock canary. Can any of your readers tell me what the name of a large grey moth is which came from a caterpillar, bright green, with deep black spots, and a tuft of magenta-coloured hairs on its tail? It spun a beautifully fine cocoon. P. H. B

KILLING INSECTS, &C.—In answer to "Entomologist" in the March number of "THE NOTE-BOOK," I believe moss is generally considered the best thing to keep pupæ in. Some entomologists consider it ought to be kept dry, others moist. In regard to his second query, How to kill Moths? I may inform him that I have tried sulphur and find it answer the purpose excellently. Some say that it discolours the wings, but I have never found it have that effect. ENTOMOLOGICUS.

A PECULIAR FISH.—I have a very peculiar fish which I purchased of a man hawking them about the streets; it is about four inches long, and its tail, or more properly its two tails joined together, instead of being perpendicular are horizontal, just like the webbed foot of a duck; it seems to swim with difficulty. I purchased it for three shillings, and the man called it a fantail; he had one more with him. The fish is a golden carp. T. R. CLEPHAN.

HARE AND RABBIT.—"J. D. S. W." asks on page 126, if the hare and rabbit ever breed together. I have heard of several instances in which animals *apparently* a cross have been shot. That they will not breed together in confinement is no proof that they will not in a wild state. Mrs. Vacher, on page 29 says, that "Leperoys" (a French breed of large tame grey rabbits) were originally a cross between the hare and wild rabbit. R. B. W.

ROOKS IN WET WEATHER.—Can any of your readers let me know the reason rooks in wet weather, or when the air is damp, have such a propensity to fly low and keep on the ground? They are well-known to have a singular gliding flight peculiar to such weather. Also, I should like to know if there are any marks by which the male can be distinguished from the female. R. B. W.

EXTRAORDINARY SMALL PULLET'S EGGS.—Last month one of my white Dorking pullets laid an egg which measured three quarters of an inch long, and half an inch broad. I have since had three eggs from the same pullet very little larger than the above; of course they contained no yolk. I should be glad to know if any of your correspondents have seen such a small specimen of a hen's egg. M. L. A.

YEW FRUIT.—In answer to "J. D. S. W.," I beg to inform him that, when a schoolboy in the country, I have eaten many hundreds of these berries, and never experienced any ill effects. The stone, however, is very bitter, and I daresay would be injurious, but no one would crack a second from choice after one trial. W. H. T.

WHY ARE BUTTERFLIES LOCAL?—Could you, or any of your numerous correspondents, inform me why some species of butterflies are so very local? Why they abound on particular spots while other places of precisely similar appearance are not favoured by a single individual? This query has, I believe, as yet, never been answered satisfactorily. FOLIUS.
May 1st, 1868.

TO CURE SKINS.—Free them well from blood or fat, and before they are quite dry rub the flesh side over with common alum in fine powder; if they are dry the application of a strong warm solution of alum to the fleshy side of the skin will do. "B. F. B." will find this a "perfect cure" for bird or rabbit skins. C. O. G. N.

A REMARKABLE EGG.—A common duck's egg of the exact size of an *ordinary wood pigeon*, was brought to me on the 19th instant. There was no mistaking its identity, as it had the usual thick rough greenish shell, and was found near a yard in which ducks are kept. It is a very good specimen.
April 22nd. R. B. W.

DRAGONFLIES.—As I am desirous of becoming acquainted with the habits and different species of the "Neuroptera" (Dragonflies), I shall be greatly obliged to any of your correspondents who will inform me of a good work on that subject and its price.
A STOUT-BODIED MOTH.

WATERSNAKE.—In Hamshphire there is a belief entertained that there are two species of snakes besides the viper—one the common ringed snake, and the other a watersnake, which latter is said to be venomous. Can any of your correspondents tell me if this is true, or only a popular error? M. L. A.

BIRDS' EGGS.—I shall feel obliged if any readers of the NOTE BOOK will let me know where I could procure rare British birds eggs, to buy?
Bray, Dublin. F. W. THOMPSON.

TO CORRESPONDENTS.

FRESH SUBSCRIBER.—North London Naturalists' Club, the Cambridge Heath Microscopical Club, and the Queckett Microscopical Club. We know of no others.

R. S., A CONSTANT SUBSCRIBER, and others, who wish for scientific works, will get full information by writing to our publishers (Messrs. Reeves and Turner), who have the largest collection of new and second-hand works in the trade.

ON COLEOPTERA AT MICKLEHAM.

By E. C. Rye.

OPULAR belief, so often founded on erroneous data, usually refers the greatest abundance of insects to the hottest summer months. This, however (putting aside the question of the effect of development of life by increased temperature), is not strictly correct as regards *Coleoptera*; which during the present and ensuing month are very much scarcer than at other times (not excepting the winter, when they may be found in plenty in the perfect state by a diligent collector), as the insects so abundant in spring have mostly died off, their duty of procreation being performed, and their progeny are as yet in their earlier stages of growth. Certain species, however, are to be found at all times; and, in favourable localities, the collector can scarcely fail to make some good captures, though he may have to exercise a greater amount of ingenuity and patience in his hunting than in the spring, when insects seem almost to intrude themselves upon his notice.

Of such favourable localities, combining as it does the united excellencies of chalk, old and young woods, stream and seclusion, and an abundant Flora, the neighbourhood of Mickleham, near Leatherhead, is eminently worthy of notice, and will at all times of the year be sure to repay a visit.

The extension of the rail beyond Leatherhead now renders Mickleham easier of access than of old, when a somewhat long and dusty walk from the former little town was rendered necessary before reaching the collecting ground. That walk, however, was often enlivened by the capture of a good insect, and will doubtless be still adhered to by those who delight in the varied loveliness of the prospects afforded by the adjacent hills and woods. As an instance of the fertility in Coleopterous life of this district, I may note that the casual overturning of a brick in the grounds of Leatherhead Station, not long ago, disclosed to view the somewhat rare wood-feeder, *Phlœotrya rufipes*. Barring incompatibility of size, one would almost as soon have expected to find a hippopotamus under such conditions. The collector will, of course, investigate any plants on the road sides which he may know to be productive: thus, on the *Erysimum*, rustically termed, I believe, "Jack in the Hedge," and known by its faint *onionesque* odour, he will find the pretty *Phyllotreta ochripes*, one of the *Halticidæ*, allied to the "Turnip-fly" or "flea," and divers *Ceuthorhynchi*; of which a recently described species, *C. alliariæ*, Bris., may be known from the common *sulcicollis* by the absence of lateral white shoulder spots, and its light coloured tarsi. On another common hedge-plant, *Sisymbrium officinale* (a peculiarly unsuggestive, wiry, straggling weed, affecting dusty places) many other good *Ceuthorhynchi* are to be found, *tarsalis*, *rapæ*, *constrictus*, *cyanipennis* and *chalybæus* being among them. The road from Leatherhead has afforded the rare, bristly, little *C. setosus*; to get which, many of the common *contractus* must be bottled by the novice.

The beginner, especially at this time, can hardly fail here to make acquaintance with our giant beetle, *Lucanus cervus*, the "Stag;" either females, prostrate, endorsed, and gravely beating the air with sprawling limbs, having dropped from the over-hanging oaks; or males, towards evening, sailing along on strong pinions, and, when struck down, with stiff legs, simulating death. An inspection of common wayside yellow flowers will here often produce the brilliantly green frosted *Cryptocephalus sericeus*; nor is the little yellow-striped *C. bilineatus* rare. Farther on, by beating young birches on the sunny slopes, the amethystine *C. nitidulus* has been copiously found. Soon after leaving Leatherhead the river Mole appears in sight; and it was near here, under a large stone in its dry bed, during a hot summer, that a small congregation of the then excessively rare *Dryops Dumerilii*, a sub-aquatic beetle allied to *Parnus*, was once found.

Continuing the road, and then turning into Norbury Park on the right, so as to cut off a long corner and have a more pleasant path, the village of Mickleham is reached, after twice crossing the circuitous Mole. In this park, famous for its productive ivy blossom, many insects may be taken by the way. The long, active, and delicate *Oncomera femorata*, so rare upon the Continent, has been found here, both at the ivy bloom in autumn, and flying to light like a moth. The grand old elms, especially when infested by *Cossus*, or with exuding sap, harbour good *Brachelytra*, such as *Silusa*, *Ischnoglossa*, &c. And many good things may be found by sweeping as the collector walks along. I have found *Miarus graminis* abundant in the flowers of a small *Campanula* not to be confounded with the true *M. campanularum*, which (though *graminis* varies much in size) is, on the average, smaller, and always considerably less broad. Towards evening I have also swept up the pretty little *Stenus circularis* here, in the meadows near the Mole.

Arrived at Mickleham, the Coleopterist (after duly refreshing himself at the "Running Horses") will soon come to some tempting old palings on his right, drilled by the speckled little *Ptinus lichenum*, which, malgré its name, does *not* feed on the lichen, but in the dry wood. Sweeping the roadside plants, and probably finding *Tychius flavicollis, Lema puncticollis, Galeruca viburni, Bruchus loti, Sibynes primitus, Pria dulcamaræ,* and hosts of others, he will arrive at a sign-post, at the junction of Headly Lane on the left with the main road. If he continue the main road he will come to the foot of Box Hill; and, searching in the shingle at the bed of the Mole there, may find *Tachyusa umbratica,* and the pinched-in little *T. constricta,* with many other good things. Here, also, the exceedingly rare *T. coarctata* and *Ilyobates propinqua* have been taken. Turning over the chalk stones on the hill itself may bring to light both *Licinus depressus* and *silphoides,* the explosive "Bombardier," *Brachinus crepitans,* and perhaps a stray *Callistus,* "the fairest of the fair," with other "*Cretophiles.*"

But it is in Headley Lane and its surrounding woods and fields that the chief harvest is to be found. Immediately on emerging from its stone-walled commencement good beetles are to be found, and there is but little need to particularize localities. A grand old beech tree to the right, besides harbouring under its decaying bark many good *Brachelytra, Cerylon,* and its usual tenant, *Mycetophagus atomarius,* is inhabited by the rare little *Cicones variegatus,* to be obtained by pounding the bark with a heavy flint over the brown paper or net of the collector. At its roots is (or rather *was*) a fine old nest of the black ant, *Formica fuliginosa,* with its satellites, *Myrmedonia funesta, laticollis, lugens,* and *cognata,* the former most abundant, and not readily separable from its multitudinous landlords by the novice. With these, *Oxypoda vittata* occurs in swarms, and the rare *Haploglossa gentilis* has been not seldom found; the flat *Amphotis marginata* being at times tolerably common, and *Homalium pygmæum, Rhizophagus parallelocollis, Cryptophagus affinis,* and *Abræus globosus* frequently seen haunting the entrances of the nest. Once, here, I found the active Acaroid atom, *Leptinus.* The rare *Homæusa* frequents the runs of the ants, and with it a fine species of *Oxypoda* (*O. glabriventris, mihi*) apparently new to science. Lastly, the still Britannically unique *Borboropora Kraatzii,* a quasi mixture of *Tachyusa* and *Scopæus,* was found here by casual sweeping. This casual sweeping will always produce something in Headly Lane; *Ceuthorhynchus urticæ* (very like that pest *Cæliodes didymus,* but narrower, and with no posteriorly well-defined pectoral groove between the middle legs) has been thus taken, and the singly white-spotted *C. quercicola* (or, at least, the insect known usually by that name), *C. cochleariæ, Cryptocephalus morœi, Eusphalerum primulæ, Antherophagus nigricornis,* and *pallens, Crepidodera ventralis, Gymnetron melanarium,*

Epuræa melanocephala (often entirely testaceous) with many other and better species are not unlikely to be found. Turning into the fields to the right of Headly Lane, past the old beech-tree, a variety of productive wild flowers will be observed. On the blue-flowered *Echium vulgare,* the *Ceuthorhynchus* (*echii*) peculiar to that plant may be taken somewhat freely; it is the largest of our species, and looks as if it were covered with cobwebs. On this plant occur also the prettily marked *C. asperifoliarum, Thyamis exoleta,* and *Meligethes seniculus,* easily known from its perplexing brethren by its long ashy pubescence and strongly serrated anterior tibiæ. The woolly leaved *Verbascum* here produces our giant *Haltica, Thyamis tabida,* in profusion; thistles harbour *Psylliodes chalcomera, Ceuthorhynchus trimaculatus,* and the large *C. horridus,* with six jointed funiculus to its antennæ; and, on the common rag-wort (*Senicio Jacobea*) *Thyamis atricapilla* occurs plentifully, with a species allied to *T. ochroleuca,* but having no black mark on the hinder femora, recently described from British examples by Herr Kutschera as *T. gracilis.* In this part, as elsewhere in the neighbourhood, promiscuous sweeping fills the net with varied game; many moderately good species of *Apion, e.g., difforme, varipes, Waltoni, flavimanum, onopordi, ervi, trifolii,* etc., often abounding; and the *Halticidæ* being copiously represented by *Psylliodes cupronitens* (abundant) and *picipes, Aphthona pseudacori, hilaris, herbigradus,* etc., and *Thyamis minuscula, pusilla, lycopi, nasturtii, apicalis,* etc.; and divers *Meligethes, e.g., lumbaris, pedicularius, maurus, difficilis, serripes, lugubris, solidus,* etc. The wild mignonette, *Reseda lutea,* must not be overlooked; on it, early in the season, occurs the rare steel-blue weevil, *Baridius picicornis,* not unaccompanied by *Phyllotreta antennata,* whose male is conspicuous for the sudden widening of the middle of its antennæ. An examination of damp dead sticks will probably produce *Bolitochara lucida, Scaphidium 4-maculatum,* etc., and, perhaps, the rare *Stilicus similis,* which appears to chiefly affect this district, being also found in moss, though always difficult to obtain.

Returning to Headley Lane, and making his way along the slopes on the left hand side of it, the collector may, by sweeping under fir trees, find the lovely red *Eros minutus;* and is pretty sure to get the local *Apion pallipes,* by similarly treating *Mercurialis perennis.* The short Thyme growing on rabbit-hills will afford him *Orchestes pratensis* and *Apion atomarium;* of which latter he may have a score in his net without seeing them. An examination of old tree stumps and felled logs is sure to repay the toil: in the former I have found the little puzzling *Alexia pilifera,* and the fact of *Oxylmæus variolosus* having been also so taken will, of course, induce the bottling of every *Rhizophagoid* beetle. Under bark of felled firs, the usual sub-cortical species of *Tomicus*, *Phlœopora*, *Leptusa*, *Homalata*, *Rhizophagus*, etc., are sure to occur, with *Prognatha* and divers *Hylastes*; and by sweeping under firs I have found *Atomaria fumata*. Wild Celery must be carefully examined for the lovely *Ceuthorhynchideus terminatus*, which is here not uncommon; the droppings of sheep, and, in fact, any stercoraceous deposits, must not deter the collector from their strict examination, as he will then probably be rewarded by *Aphodius Zenkeri* and *A. obliteratus* (the latter being known from the common *A. contaminatus* by its absence of lateral thoracic hairs); any small dead animals that he may find will probably swarm with *Cholevæ*, such as *grandicollis*, *Kirbyi*, etc.; and Fungi will most likely contain *Quedius lateralis*, *Philonthus succicola* and (perhaps) *corvinus*, *Homalium nigriceps*, *Gyrophæna Poweri* (amongst many others), *Homalota intermedia*, *Phlœobium*, *Megarthus hemipterus*, etc. By beating young trees, he may get, amongst others, *Balaninus cerasorum*, *Galeruca sanguinea* and the queer female of *Athöus longicollis*, the linear male of which abounds; and, by shaking dead leaves, *Choleva anisotomoides* and many good *Homalotæ*, *Steni*, *Stilici*, *Scydmæni*, etc., with the inevitable *Ocalea badia*, will be found. Once, in an old elm tree covered with fungus, I took here a dozen of the rare *Quedius truncicola*, evidently preying upon the myriads of smaller beetles and larvæ found in such situations. The brightness of their red abdomens, as they flashed in and out of the wet fungus, will not be soon forgotten by me, and is quite inadequately represented by their appearance when dead. With them, oddly enough, were one or two of that common cellar beetle, *Pristonychus terricola*; rarely seen in such aristocratic company, I should think.

Keeping parallel with the lane, but always remaining on the slopes of the hills to the left, among the trees, very excellent collecting ground will be traversed, until the "Hilly Field" is reached. By sweeping under the trees on these slopes and among dead leaves, especially towards the evening and during the autumnal months, many of those usually rare and always peculiar people, the *Anisotomidæ*, may be occasionally found; indeed, I have seldom come away from this place without more than one representative of certain genera, some of which are also to be taken by sifting dead leaves. The most interesting, and our largest species, is *Anisotoma cinnamomea*, a fine but perplexing insect, whose small and undeveloped males so often suggest the possibility of another species, and which can never be fairly found "at home," in spite of our knowledge that, in its earlier stages at least, it inhabits truffles. Examining fungi has certainly never produced this or any other *Anisotoma*, as far as my experience goes. The commonest (if any be common) in the genus, *A. calcarata*, to be distinguished from all its congeners by the narrow apical joint of its antennæ, and the quadrate apex to its posterior femora in both sexes (strongly toothed in the male), is frequently found in the net during evening sweeping here; and in one spot, among damp dead leaves I have often found the pale (but quite mature) form of the allied *A. litura*, Stephens (*ornata*, Fairm.), which, in our more northernly districts, is very highly coloured, with a dark thorax, suture and sides. Its pallid form may be known from testaceous *calcarata* (which also varies much in colour, as well as size) by the more acute hinder angles to its thorax, its lesser convexity, rounded apex to hind femora in both sexes, &c. With it I have swept the little globose *A. badia*, which, with *Colenis dentipes*, will also probably appear on the paper when leaves are being sifted. The very rare *Agaricophagus* and small *Hydnobius* have been taken here, but no reliable information can be given as to their true habitat. When sweeping for *Anisotomæ*, I have taken such good *Scydmæni* as *angulatus*, *denticornis*, *elongatus*, etc.

On the steep rise of the Hilly Field, the anomalous, eyeless, little *Claviger* is to be found beneath large flints on the chalk, in company with small yellow ants; and the general collecting is so good that the coleopterist *must* get something to please him. Arrived at the top, and emerged upon the brow of the heights partially used for race-horse training grounds, I think the most inveterate beetle-grubber will be compelled to stay awhile; to take in the wide expanse of wood and undulating park; to fill his lungs, deadened by London carbon, with the sharp pure air; to watch the shifting shadows of the clouds;—and, possibly, to think about getting some tea and substantial food at the "Running Horses," to which hostelry he will rapidly descend over springy moss and velvet turf, disturbing multitudinous rabbits on the way, taking his path down the steep side of the hill, at the foot of which stands Mickleham Church. If there be time, he may sweep for *Ceuthorhynchus crux*, or look out for *Phlœopora corticalis* under pine bark; or (at the proper time of year) cut up grass roots for *Trachys nanus* and *Scymnus pygmæus*; or hunt for our loveliest *Haltica*, *Thyamis dorsalis*; or, in fact, continue his labours, with the certainty of getting something, until it is too dark to tell *Odontæus* from a *Chrysomela*.

OUR FIELD BUTTERFLIES.
By E. J. S. Clifford.

Preeminently the favourites of the lepidopterist are those charming creatures—butterflies. When led to give his attention to the insect tribes, they are the first class to which he is attracted, and even in after years, when he is older and wiser in the knowledge of his science, the instinctive love of old returns with renewed force as he wanders through the country in the hot summer forenoon, and sees hundreds of glittering forms disporting in the sunbeams, or hovering over the lovely blossoms that cover the earth. Nor can we wonder that butterflies should thus engross so much of the entomologist's attention, and fill him with such ardour and delight. Though the most inconspicuous of our native *lepidoptera* in number of species, they are by far the most beautiful and elegant. True it is that we have few more than sixty species in all, but how delicate the robes in which they are clothed! Then their time of flight, and their intimate association with the flowers, render them all the more full of interest, and all the more likely to attract notice and observation. They distribute themselves everywhere, for they are not confined to the woodlands or the fields, where floral luxurance abounds, and where the chorus of birds is ever ringing forth, but are our constant visitors in this mighty London, cheering many a lonely spot, where no vegetation is visible, and where bricks and mortar rule supreme. Here too, they look sadly out of place; often seen wandering backwards and forwards amidst the maze of buildings, vainly seeking for more congenial spots wherein to disport themselves in the sunshine.

In this paper, however, we are not to speak of town butterflies, which are but few when compared with those which cluster in the rural scene. Nor are we to take the widest view even of those which are confined to "ruralities." We wish to speak of our "field butterflies," which are indeed a striking and beautiful group. It should be remembered that many other species besides those we shall now name may be occasionally found flying in the fields, but our title is intended to convey that we mean such as are more especially attached to field, meadow, or pasture as the scenes of their joyous gambols at midday. Some of the most striking, then, we shall now introduce to our numerous readers.

First of all we are reminded of our commonest butterflies, the "Whites." We need hardly say that these are the most numerous sporters in the fields on a summer's day. Settling on the flower-heads, or playfully chasing one another through the air, they are ever the most conspicuous of insects when the sun's rays are hottest, mingling with the bees that sportively sip the honey with them from the flowers. The Small White (*Pieris rapæ*) is the most abundant, and its caterpillars, feeding on cabbages, are ever the bane of the country farmer. Not content, either, with the outer leaves of his plants, they actually eat their way right to the very hearts, thus completing the ruin and spoliation they had begun. The eggs, however, of the Small White butterfly are not laid only on the cabbage, since the radish, turnip, and many garden plants are often selected by the female butterflies. It is said that they hatch in twelve or thirteen days after being laid, and it should be remembered that there are two broods during the year, the first in April, and the second in July. This accounts for the fact that we see this commonest of butterflies at all times during the year. Indeed, were it not that both this species and the larger one are subject to the attacks of *Ichneumonidæ* (which may be regarded as minute allies of the farmers), they would speedily become of serious importance, and still more effectually ruin our vegetable crops. It is hardly necessary to describe this commonest of caterpillars, which, however, may be defined as grey-green, and velvety, with a yellow stripe down the back, and another on each side. The chrysalis is attached by the tail, and by a silken belt round the middle: it may be sought and found in almost every imaginable nook and corner, both in the country and the garden. The Green-veined White (*Pieris Napi*) is another common butterfly in our summer fields. It is not so injurious to our vegetables as is the foregoing, and by some it is doubted whether its caterpillar ever feeds on cultivated plants. At any rate it is more particularly attached, we believe, to the rape for food, hence its scientific name. This butterfly differs from the former principally on the underside of the hind wings, whose rays form green veins. The fore wings of the male butterfly can be distinguished from those of the female by the presence of only one black spot instead of two, which are found in the females of this and the last species. The Green-veined White is not so common a denizen of our fields as the last, but may be taken throughout the summer, for there are two broods, one in April and May, the other in July and August.

The next species we notice is that brilliant creature, the Brimstone butterfly, (*Goneptery Rhamni*). This is one of the principal ornaments of our fields in spring. Hybernated specimens come forth at the first warm sunshine that calls forth the primroses and the violets, and it is indeed cheering to behold them after the dreary aspect of winter scenery. The Brimstone butterfly is very peculiarly shaped, in fact we have no other species whose wings are precisely similar in their outline. The male butterfly is distinguishable from the female by the extreme brilliancy of his wings, whilst the pale sulphur colour of the female is by no means devoid of beauty, though of a separate kind from that which attaches to her lord. The silky down which adorns the thorax of the Brimstone is very gracefully disposed, and adds much to its general beauty. We read that abroad this butterfly is liable to great variation in the orange spot which is situated on the hind wings: this has been known to cover nearly all of the wing in specimens which have been captured. The Brimstone butterfly may often be seen hovering around the buckthorn in the month of April, for the purpose of depositing its future progeny. The caterpillar is of a pale green colour, with a whitish stripe on each side. It feeds till the end of June, when it fastens itself by a silken belt, and becomes a chrysalis pointed at both ends. Early in August the new brood of these butterflies enliven our fields, whose floral beauties are then declining, and it continues on the wing the whole year.

Turning to a rarer insect than any yet enumerated, we are reminded of the much prized Clouded yellow (*Colias Edusa*), which is a frequenter of clover and lucerne fields. This butterfly is extremely agile, and it is only by following it amongst the clover that the entomologist can hope to secure any number. Occasionally, it is true, a specimen flies across the field-path to another part of the expanse of purple heads of flowers, but it is rarely that he can be netted in the transit. On a hot day in August it is indeed a beautiful sight to see these butterflies flying, their wings rendered golden by the deep rays of the autumn sun, as they rise one after another from the flowers on which they had settled. Of late years this splendid species has been a more frequent visitor to our fields in the southern counties, and has been very often captured in unnecessary quantities by collectors. Specimens, also, of the pale variety of the female (*Colias helice*) were repeatedly brought to net by insect hunters in the past season. We fear that the numbers taken lessen the probability of this lovely insect increasing amongst us. The eggs of the Clouded yellow are laid on the clover, and the caterpillar may be sought during the summer months on that plant, although it is somewhat difficult to find.

The Orange-tipped (*Anthocharis Cardamines*) is another of our spring butterflies, frequenting the fields in company with the Brimstone already noticed. It is by no means uncommon, occurring even near London, though not in the abundance which it once did. The chief characteristic beauty in the wings of this graceful little butterfly, is the delicate marbling on the under surface of the hind wings. This, when microscopically examined, is found to be caused by the combination of yellow and black scales, which produce the deception. In some parts of France this yellow-winged flutterer is called Aurora, and often in our own country goes by the name of the "lady of the woods." It is more particularly the lady of the fields, however, than of the woods, being emphatically one of our field butterflies.

The wanderer in country fields or meadows in summer must often have been struck by the number of brown butterflies which flutter around his path. These, probably, consist chiefly of "Heaths" and "Meadow Browns." The Large Heath (*Satyrus Tithonus*) is the tawny little butterfly that so restlessly flits from flower to flower, rarely taking any lofty flights in the air. The caterpillar feeds on the common meadow grass, and is of a dull green colour, with a dark line down the back. The butterfly itself is indeed profusely common in the southern counties. Its relative, the Small Heath, (*Cœnonympha (Pamphilus)* is scarcely less so, but is even more attached to fields. Its caterpillar may be swept off the grass by means of the *larva-net*, with which all collectors should be provided. Then the Meadow Brown (*Satyrus Janira*) is another of our dull-coloured, yet beautiful field butterflies, which mixes with those just alluded to in the summer season.

Unlike the foregoing, the handsome Vanessa butterflies are by no means lethargic in flight. Fields more especially yielding a supply of plants of the composite order are resorted to by these handsome creatures. Thus, on wandering through the fields in July or August, we often come upon the vivid Peacock (*Vanessa Io*) resting on a thistle leaf, fanning his gorgeous wings in the sunshine. The flight of this butterfly is very rapid, and the graceful sweeps which it makes through the air are interesting to observe. Then that common butterfly the Small Tortoiseshell (*Vanessa Urticæ*), is to be seen in the summer fields. Throughout the season we shall see this well-known insect mixing with the "Blues," the "Whites," and the "Coppers," of field and pasture land. It seems at home everywhere, however, and we not unfrequently see it dashing along our London streets, where by dexterous turns it manages to elude the caps of excited youngsters in full chase.

Among the lesser butterflies of the field we can only stay to notice four very conspicuous species. The Small Copper (*Chrysophanus Phlœas*) is ever a brilliant little denizen of open scenery. We scarcely ever look at its merry gambols, or see its copper colour displayed when it rests on the blossom of the field, without recurring in thought to its noble relative, now rendered extinct in this country. Beautiful indeed is the lesser species, much more the *Dispar* of thirty years ago, of which only isolated specimens now exist in our cabinets. The Small Copper, however, seems to suffer no diminution in numbers from the annual attacks made on it by juvenile collectors. Its caterpillar is shaped like a woodlouse. It feeds on the various species of sorrel, and is green in colour, with three red-brown stripes. Some are of opinion that from the extreme rapidity with which this little insect passes its transformations, it is probably to be found in all three stages of caterpillar, chrysalis, and butterfly at one time.

We should not omit the sweet little blue butterfly from our list of field butterflies, for this is almost the only one of its tribe common in such scenes. This is the Common Blue (*Lycæna alexis*), a lovely little creature. It is the male alone that possesses the exquisite hue which so charms us. Nothing really can excel the fresh beauty of a "Blue" newly developed from the chrysalis. The silky hair of its little body, the fringe of the wings, as yet not despoiled by contact with the trees or flowers, and the fair lustre of their azure surface, all render it a perfect gem amongst its fellow butterflies. The Blue is a most pugnacious little insect, and contends most earnestly for the possession of a favorite flower-head it has chosen as a resting place, driving away even larger butterflies therefrom. The female Blue is of a dingy colour, but her wings are shaded and reflected with blue, in certain lights looking very beautiful. The dumpy little caterpillar of the Common Blue feeds on the bird's-foot, trefoil, and other plants of the same order.

Lastly, amongst our field butterflies, we notice the "Skippers," brisk little butterflies, some of the species not uncommon. The Large Skipper (*Pamphila Sylvanus*) is the most conspicuous as to size: it is fulvous brown in colour, and very beautiful when just emerged. It flies in July. Then there is that lively little butterfly, the Grizzled Skipper (*Thymele Alveolus*), not nearly so common as the former. The ground colour of the wings is black, the white spots scattered over its surface are square. We believe this species is more particularly partial to damp meadows than other localities. The Grizzled Skipper is said to be uncommon in Scotland, though rather plentiful in some parts of our own country. We have a variety of the species in which the spots on the fore wings are much larger than usual, occupying nearly all of the surface. In conclusion, we add, that to us the "Skippers" are peculiarly interesting, as forming a kind of intermediate link between the butterflies and moths, for they possess the thick bodies, and stout frames of the NOCTUÆ, whilst, in all other particulars, they are essentially butterflies. Thus we must leave "field butterflies" for the present.

NOTES ON EGG AND NEST COLLECTING.

By C. O. GROOM NAPIER, F.G.S., &c.

PART II.

WITH time and patience it is not difficult to cut up an embryo ready for exclusion, and extract it through a relatively small hole in the egg. As the shells of eggs which have been incubated are often very tender, they should be strengthened by means of pieces of paper, which should be gummed round them before they are blown. These pieces of paper may be cut of an oval or circular form, and afterwards removed by damping, with little injury to the eggs; but when put on, they should be allowed to dry before the tedious operation of cutting up an embryo is attempted. It is often advisable when an egg is not very much incubated, and yet a difficulty exists in removing its contents, to wash as much of them out of it as possible with the syringe, and leaving some water in it, put it in a warm place for the contents to decompose, for in this state eggs are much more easily emptied. When an egg is clear it should be put to drain on a cloth bottom downwards for a day or two, if possible, before being packed. It should then be inscribed as before advised. Eggs are packed in many different ways; the most secure is to roll each egg separately in some soft material; those under the size of the redshank in flax or cotton, and those above this size, unless when very brittle, in tow or wool. The eggs should be laid in layers, and the smaller specimens in boxes of pasteboard or chip. It is a very unsafe plan to pack eggs in hay, bran, saw-dust, or sand. I had once a box sent to me containing three hundred eggs of valuable species, of which nearly one hundred and eighty were broken: they were packed in hay and saw-dust. Eggs should not be squeezed into too small a box, neither should they have "room to rattle." Cleanliness and neatness should be especially cultivated by the collectors of eggs and nests; for when either are foul they are especially prone to be attacked by the larvæ of beetles and moths. It is a good plan to gum a piece of tissue paper over the entrance to each egg, having placed within a small quantity of powdered camphor, mixed with a fifth of its weight of bichloride of mercury; this will destroy the eggs or larvæ of insects which are so apt to enter blown eggs for the purpose of devouring the dry yolk or membraneous lining of the shell. Moths and beetles are even more injurious to nests than to eggs, for they eat their supports, and reduce many a fine nest to a mass of crumbling dust. Before nests are placed in the cabinet, it is highly advantageous to transfer them to a tin box for a week or so, and pour over them benzine, containing 2 per cent. of carbolic acid. The benzine should not be too pure; nitro-benzole is the best liquid to use, it does not bleach so much as benzine collas. When the nests are dry, and this may be thoroughly done in a cool oven, they should be transferred to the cabinet. As it is very difficult to preserve nests, even in a well-arranged collection, from the attacks of moths and beetles, it may be advisable to mention a plan which will "once and for ever," scare them away. Let each nest be saturated with a solution of bichloride of mercury, about ten grains to the pint of distilled water, and thoroughly dried. This may be done without injury to the nests, and is very effectual. The cabinet should be made of teak, rosewood, mahogany, walnut, American birch, or other non-resinous wood. Pine, deal, cedar, and sandal-wood, are undesirable, and should be avoided even for the back of the cabinet, bottoms, or sides of the drawers, for they are always accompanied by resinous exudations, which besides staining the specimens, attracts moisture from the air, and induces mildew. As the plan of stringing eggs is generally relinquished on the purchase of a cabinet, I shall say no more about it. Collectors are mostly divided between the *card, tray,* and *division* systems. The "card" has the advantage of showing the markings and shape of the specimens in a most striking manner, but is unnatural, has a glaring artificial appearance, is injurious to the eggs as gumming more or less is, and specimens in this position are much more apt to get broken. The tray system may answer well, if the drawers have a thick sheet of wadding or cotton at the bottom, and if each pasteboard tray has a small quantity of cotton in the bottom of it; the eggs can be changed, removed for comparison with those in other collections, which is not so easy with the card system. Some collectors place their eggs in boxes with glass tops. This plan has the advantage of keeping a specimen or set of specimens separate, of excluding them from dust, and giving great facilities for their close examination without the risk attending their being handled. But the expense of this plan for a large collection is great, as the boxes vary in price from 1s. 6d. to 6s. per dozen, which would involve a considerable outlay for a large collection of about 4,000 eggs and 250 nests such as mine. Most collectors, shrinking from the expense of glass boxes, have adopted divisions for their eggs and nests; these should be made of dry wood, which should not be pine or deal, and may be faced in accordance with the fancy of the collector, with coloured paper. The pieces of wood which form the divisions should fit accurately, so as not to require to be morticed or bradded, so that the divisions may be altered as the collection progresses. Cotton or tow, carefully dried, should be put into these divisions so as to form a good deep bed for the eggs. On the top of the ordinary cotton or tow used for these divisions, it is convenient to put sheets of wadding cut in squares to the size of each space. These may be of pink, green, yellow, or blue, which gives the cabinet a tasteful appearance. It is advantageous in arranging a cabinet for British or European species, to leave vacancies for those species the collector may not at the time possess.

Of British birds, the latest and most extended list is given in my little work, published by Groombridge, "The Food, Use, and Beauty of British Birds." Each division should have a label attached to it, and, in many cases, the locality of the specimens, collector's name, or information as to rarity, or other interesting details connected with the species; these may be engrossed in a large and distinct hand. The additional interest connected with a collection labelled in this way, will amply reward the increase of labour attending such an arrangement, which should, however, be universal in public collections.

Collections of nests are certainly best preserved under glass shades, for each specimen is distinctly isolated, which is highly important, both for the sake of distinction and as a means of keeping the specimens dry. Each nest should be placed on a square or oblong block of non-resinous wood, of an inch thickness at least. This should have a large hole turned in it, into which a circular piece of glass is admitted, which should be cemented there. The glass shade, oval or circular, should have a groove cut for its reception in the block of wood somewhat larger than the glass bottom of the box. The nest, when placed on the block and under the shade, is seen to perfection on all sides, and underneath, without the necessity of its being disturbed. A label, in bold characters, should accompany these nests, giving "fullest particulars" that space permits. The cabinet for nests should contain sliding trays grooved into its sizes, instead of drawers, and on these the blocks, covered with shades and enclosing the nests, should be placed. The above arrangement is somewhat an expensive one, but is the most perfect of which I have heard. It need not cost more than from 1s. 6d. to 1s. 9d. per nest, at wholesale prices; except in the case of very large nests. Specimens of eggs and nests should be kept in a room with a constant fire, summer and winter, far from damp walls, and should be as little as possible exposed to light and dust.

ON CERTAIN BUTTERFLY SCALES CHARACTERISTIC OF SEX.

By T. W. Wonfor.*

NEARLY every one who has worked with the microscope and turned his attention to the scales of insects (especially the Butterfly tribe) has perhaps been struck with the great variety of form to be found not only in different butterflies, but on the under and upper side of the wings of the same insect. If, too, an attempt has been made to find in the "whites" or "blues" the scales described in all works on the Microscope, as found on certain members of each group, he has undoubtedly met with disappointment, especially if he has looked where our standard works tell us they are to be found. Thus, in the case of the azure blue (*Polyommatus argiolus*), we meet with instructions tending to mislead; thus in the 'Micrographic Dictionary,' under "Polyommatus," p. 564, we read—"The scales upon the *under* surface of the wings of *P. argiolus* and *P. argus* have been proposed as test objects. They are of two kinds—one resembling in structure the ordinary scales of insects, the other of a battledore form." Again, under the head of "Pontia," p. 571:—"The form and structure of certain scales existing upon the *under* side of the male is curious." Now, any inquirer looking, in either case, in the situations named, will undoubtedly not find them, for the simple reason that these particular scales are never found on the *under* side.

It was in endeavouring to work out, in 1864, these and a kindred scale that I hit upon certain facts, which perhaps may have been discovered before; but as I have not been able to find any record of them, I thought the subject sufficiently interesting to bring before the microscopic world. One fact has reference to the *position* of the battledore scales; the other tends to the belief that they, and certain other forms to be described, are, in the three families of the Polyommatus, Pontia (or Pieris), and Hipparchia *characteristic marks* of sex—at least I have proved such to be the case, as far as I have been able to obtain specimens for observation. In the "blues" proper there is a marked dissimilarity in the colour of the sexes; for, while the males are of various shades of blue, answering to the names azure, mazarine, &c.,

* Read before the Members of the Brighton and Sussex Natural History Society, Nov. 1867.

the females are of a brownish hue, spotted or dashed with bluish scales. Any person seeing them together for the first time would consider the brown-coloured ones a distinct species; in fact, one often hears the remark made, "Are you sure they are blues?" Now, this difference of colour may have led to the ordinary error that the "battledore" is found on the "blues," for undoubtedly it is found only on the *blue-coloured males*. Curiously enough these "battledore" scales are placed in rows, under the ordinary scales, and at the intervals, so that, if the ordinary scales be removed from the upper portion of the wings, the "battledores" will be found arranged in rows, plentifully on the fore wings, but more sparsely on the hinder wings. I have examined *P. alexis*, (common blue); *P. argiolus* (azure blue); *P. acis* (mazarine blue); *P. Corydon* (Chalk-Hill blue); *P. adonis* (Clifden blue); *P. argus* (silver-studded blue); *P. arion*, (large blue); *P. alsus*, (Bedford, or little blue); and *P. bæticus*, (tailed, or Brighton blue); and in each case found them only on the upper surface of the wings of the males, and arranged, as before mentioned, in rows; in the case of unbattered and well-preserved insects in about equal proportions with ordinary scales. As might, perhaps, be expected, the battledores differ in size, shape, length of blade or handle, according to the particular species, and, perhaps, might be used as adjuncts in determining varieties sometimes met with. I am anxious to obtain an hermaphrodite form of the common blue, *P. alexis*, as figured in 'Humphrey and Westwood's Butterflies,' in which one side is of the character of the ordinary blue male, the other of the brownish female.

Thus far with the "blues" my observations have proved that the "battledore" is characteristic of sex. I had a confirmation of this in the case of the "tailed blue." A collector had supplied me with portions of wings of one of these insects, but was uncertain whether from males or females. I examined all without finding any trace of a battledore; but the next day, obtaining from him an undoubted male, I found at once any number of battledores.

To turn now to the whites, or genus Pontia or Pieris. I had found the two forms of "tasseled" scales, or those having a brush-like termination, figured in the 'Micrographic Dictionary,' on males of the large and small cabbage white (*Pontia* or *Pieris brassicæ*, and *P. rapæ*, and argued that something similar ought to be found on other members of the same family. The first I tried was the green veined *P. napi*. This gave a scale differing slightly from the small white, but somewhat broader and more triangular. The orange tip (*P. cardimines*), for a long time puzzled me, as my specimens were battered;

but having caught insects in good condition, I found the short brush-like scale differing considerably from the other whites. On the Bath white (*Mancipium* or *Pieris daplidice*, I found a scale half-way between the orange tip and small white, that is, the ribbon-like form of the one and triangular brush of the other. All these whites differ also in their modes of attachment to the wing, the stalk being of a different construction from that of the ordinary scale or the battledore of the blues. Though the arrangement of the scales is in rows and at intervals, as in the battledores, they are not so readily made out *in situ*, but from their greater length present the appearance of hairs.

In the case of the Hipparchia family, I happened while at Dorking this summer to come across plenty of the *H. semele* (grayling), and conceived, as there was a well-known scale, brush-like and tapering after the manner of the large white, but differing from it in the markings on the ribbon-like portion, on the *H. janira*, (meadow brown), that there might be something on the grayling. At first I was disappointed, until I discovered my specimens were all females. The next morning I caught some males, when a decidedly shaving-brush like scale was the result. Pursuing the same plan with all the Hipparchiæ I could procure, I have obtained the following results : distinctive scales, differing from each other in *H. tithonus* (large heath, *H. pamphilus* (small heath), *H. ægeria* (wood argus), and *H. megœra* (wall argus). In all these cases the brush-like scales are plentifully arranged in rows, and project considerably beyond the ordinary scales. I have not yet had the opportunity of pursuing my investigations among the other families; but as far as I have gone, I think it is clear there are in the three families of Polyommatus, Pieris or Pontia, and Hipparchia, forms of scales found only on the males. In addition to this, the ordinary scales in males and females are the same, so that these peculiar scales may be taken to be characteristic of sex. What purpose, if any, they serve, I cannot conceive. They seem to me to have their analogues in the beard of man, the mane of the lion, and the plumage of some birds.

In obtaining the scales, I have found the best way to examine a wing is to lay it on a clean slide, place another upon it, and apply a moderate amount of pressure. Upon separating the slips, plenty of scales from either side, in their relative positions, will be found on the glass slides. If required to mount, a ring of varnish may be run round, and when nearly set, a glass cover being laid on the slide, it requires only a finishing coat when dry to make it ready for the cabinet.

BOXWOOD.

IT is certain that if all the wood of the Box trees growing in this country were cut down at one sweep, the quantity would be wholly inadequate to satisfy the insatiable appetite of our wood engravers for any length of time. The size, too, of the trees would not furnish blocks of sufficient diameter for any but small pictures. On this account English-grown Boxwood is oftener used by the turner and mathematical instrument maker, than by the engraver.

Buxus sempervirens has a geographical range through China, Japan, Northern India, Spain, and Italy; but it grows in the greatest abundance and to a larger size than elsewhere, on the shores of the Black Sea. Though Box is still a popular evergreen shrub with us, it was formerly much more so than it is now. The principal, and perhaps only place where it is indigenous at the present time is at Boxhill, in Surrey. As a rule, in this country it seldom attains more than 12 or 15 feet in height, but some varieties in other countries reach 20 or 30 feet. Many of the trees on Boxhill were cut down in 1815, and are said to have realised over £10,000, not for the purposes of the engraver, but chiefly for turnery. That no other wood has et been found equal to Box for wood engraving is conclusive from the immense demand and high price which exists for it. That in greatest repute comes from Odessa and Smyrna, but a valuable kind is imported from Soukoum Kale, in Russia. We are told by the Consul at that port that almost the whole of the quantity exported finds its way into the English market. In one year two British ships took away from that place 373 tons directly to Liverpool, and 1506 tons were shipped in Turkish boats to Constantinople, from which they were re-exported to England. The Boxwood of Abkhasia is reckoned superior to any other growing on the Euxine, and is remarkable for thickness, colour, and for its being free from knots. It grows in the mountain valleys chiefly about Gagri Pitzunda and Diebelda. The trees are cut down into blocks, each weighing from 8 to 100lb. When the wood is shipped in a green state there is five per cent. average loss in the weight on the voyage to England.

In the mountain districts trees may be obtained at the rate of from 40 to 50 copecks per Turkish cantar (14d. to 17d. per cwt.), exclusive of transport expenses. The annual importations of Boxwood into this country from all quarters amounts to between two and three thousand tons, being worth a sum of from £24,000 to £26,000. For the engraver's purposes the logs are cut into transverse pieces about an inch in thickness, and the surface is most carefully smoothed and prepared for drawing upon. When a larger block is required than the natural size of the wood would admit, square blocks are carefully cut of an uniform size, and morticed together with strips of mahogany or other hard wood; but in the case of an extra large plate, numerous pieces are placed side by side to the size required, and are then bolted together behind with brass screws and nuts, the heads of which are deeply sunk into the wood. This is the way in which all blocks for large double-page engravings are prepared.

Before the art of wood engraving became anything like what it now is, the slices of Boxwood were cut longitudinally instead of transversely. It was somewhere about the middle of the last century that the improved system was adopted. By cutting across the grain, a harder and more even surface is obtained, on which an artist can produce finer and more delicate lines and softer shading than could otherwise be done; indeed some of the modern woodcuts are perfect gems of art.

The chief characters of Boxwood are closeness, and exceedingly hard, fine, even grain, to the standard of which no other wood comes up, though many have been tried, such for instance as the Pittosporum undulatum of New South Wales, which was shown in the International Exhibition of 1862. This tree grows to a height of from 50 to 80 feet, and has a diameter of from 18 to 30 inches, though sound transverse sections of more than from 10 to 16 inches are rare. The wood is very even grained, and when carefully seasoned is not liable to split.

Some blocks of it were submitted to Professor de la Motte, of King's College, in 1862, who gave his opinion that it was well adapted to some kinds of wood engraving: he says, however, in his report, that "it is not equal to Turkey Box, but that it is superior to that generally used for posters." The specimens that were prepared for exhibition in 1862 are now in the Museum at Kew, and upon showing them to a practical man—one of the first engravers' block makers in London—he was of opinion that the wood could never come into use, inasmuch as it has a certain degree of roughness when cut, though apparently a very close and solid wood. I next submitted to him the wood of Hunteria zeylanica (Gard.) a small Ceylon tree, upon which he gave a most favourable opinion. This wood has been spoken of by residents in Ceylon as coming nearer to Box than any known wood, both in density and colour; but as it is improbable that this wood will ever be brought from Ceylon to supersede Boxwood from the Black Sea, Box must at present, and will perhaps for some time to come, hold the honourable position which it now occupies in the estimation of artists.—John R. Jackson, Kew, *Gardeners' Chronicle*.

THE FUEGIANS.

AND now let us pass to the other extremity of the great Continent of America—to Cape Horn, and to the Island off it, which projects its desolate rocks into one of the most inhospitable climates in the world. The inhabitants of Tierra del Fuego are perhaps the most degraded among the races of mankind. How could they be otherwise? "Their country," says Mr. Darwin, "is a broken mass of wild rocks, lofty hills, and useless forests; and these are viewed through mists and endless storms. The habitable land is reduced to the stones of the beach. In search of food they are compelled to wander unceasingly from spot to spot, and so steep is the coast that they can only move about in their wretched canoes." They are habitually cannibals, killing and eating their old women before they kill their dogs, for the sufficient reason, as explained by themselves—"Doggies catch otters, old women no." Of some of these people who came round the *Beagle* in their canoes, the same author says—"These were the most wretched and miserable creatures I anywhere beheld. They were quite naked, and even one full-grown woman was absolutely so. It was raining heavily, and the fresh water, together with the spray, trickled down her body. In another harbour not far distant, a woman, who was suckling a new-born child, came one day alongside the vessel, and remained there out of mere curiosity, whilst the sleet fell and thawed on her naked bosom and on the skin of her naked baby. These poor wretches were stunted in their growth, their hideous faces bedaubed with white paint, their skins filthy and greasy, their hair entangled, their voices discordant, and their gestures violent. Viewing such men, one can hardly make oneself believe that they are fellow-creatures and inhabitants of the same world." Well might Darwin add, "Whilst beholding these savages one asks, Whence have they come? What could have tempted, or what change compelled, a tribe of men to leave the fine regions of the North, to travel down the Cordillera, or backbone of America, to invent and build canoes which are not used by the tribes of Chili, Peru, and Brazil, and then to enter on one of the most inhospitable countries within the limits of the globe?" There can be but one explanation. Quarrels and wars between tribe and tribe, induced by the mere increase of numbers and the consequent pressure on the means of subsistence, have been always, ever since Man existed, driving the weaker races farther and farther from the older settlements of mankind. And when the ultimate points of the habitable world are reached, the conditions of existence cause and necessitate a savage and degraded life. Darwin gives the true explanation of their condition when he says, "How little can the higher powers of the mind be brought into play! What is there for imagination to picture, for reason to compare, for judgment to decide upon?" The case of the Fuegians is a case in which there can be no doubt whatever of the causes of their degraded condition. On every side of them, and in proportion as we recede from their wretched country, the surrounding tribes are less wretched and better acquainted with the simpler arts. And it is remarkable that in the case of this people we have proof of another point of great interest and importance, viz., this—that even the most degraded savages have all the perfect attributes of humanity, which can be and are developed, the moment they are placed under favourable conditions. Captain Fitzroy had in 1830 carried off to England some of these people, where they were taught the habits and the arts of civilized life. Of one of these who was taken back to his own country in the *Beagle*, Mr. Darwin tells us that his "intellect was good," and of another that he had a "nice disposition." We see, therefore, that every fact and circumstance connected with the Fuegians agrees with the supposition that their "utter barbarism" was due entirely to the cruel conditions of their life, and the wretched country into which they had been driven.—*Good Words*, June.

THE QUEEN BEE.

THE queen bee, as is known to most, is larger, longer, and tapers more than the working bee. The wings are proportionately shorter, and on the under part of the body she is of a yellowish-brown colour. Like the worker she is armed with a sting. You never see the queen roaming about in search of flowers. Neither the queen nor the drone ever does this. Occasionally, however, the "royal mistress of the hive" flies abroad for an airing, or it may be, according to Huber, for some other equally important purpose.

The prosperity of the hive greatly depends upon the life and health of the queen. There are some circumstances under which even "the busy bee" will not work. Flowers may be scattered thickly over every meadow; trees and bushes may be literally dripping with honey; the bee may have a clean, healthy home, with the wax already made; and yet the bee will not work. How is this? The bees have health, strength, wealth—everything that is needed for bee-life—but the queen is wanting, and they are out of heart. They have no brood-cells to watch, no royal mother to defend, and they completely break down under their discouragements.

Who has not seen a royal cell, the "queen's palace" of the hive? This is not her majesty's residence, but her birth-place. It is unlike the other cells, and hangs down from the edge of some piece of comb. The workers and drones are hatched in cells lying in a horizontal position, but the queen is hatched with her head downwards.

Bee-writers tell us that all the eggs laid in the early part of the season are of the working sort; that the eggs for producing drones or males are laid about two months later; and those for the females immediately afterwards. In the first International Exhibition was exhibited a queen said to have been produced from a larva of the working sort; and the production of a queen in this manner has been pronounced "the most remarkable fact ever brought to light in natural history." My opinion is, *that there never was a queen produced in any other way*, and that all eggs produced by the queen are either male or female. Are not the working bees undeveloped females? Naturalists tell us that they are. And will not the larva of the working bee produce a queen at any part of the season, if treated with the attention and respect due to royalty? I have had abundant proof that such is the fact. Why suppose anything so unnatural as that a queen bee should lay eggs male and female, and *something else*, this something else being the greater part of the eggs produced during the season? Or why suppose anything so unnecessary, when it is known that the eggs of the working bee sort will bring queens whenever a queen is wanted?

In the middle of March, 1856, the queen of a very prosperous hive, of good weight, died. I found her outside the hive, in a very weak state, and placed her within the doorway of the hive; but she died before the following morning. The busy tenants of the bereft home pursued their avocations as if nothing had happened, which convinced me that the deceased mother had been fruitful up to the time of her death. If so, according to my theory the bees could in due time raise another queen, but one that would necessarily be barren, as no drones were in the hive or in the garden. I watched this case with considerable interest, as it might confirm my views, or, on the other hand, set all my calculations at nought. For several weeks the bees worked well, and carried home a good deal of bee-bread—a sure sign that they had found nothing amiss. Now, however, the time had come "to pass the rubicon." The eggs of the late queen had all been used up, and, if no more could be hatched, the bees would become spiritless and sad. I felt persuaded that a queen had been secured, or the bees would not have worked so long. On the 16th of April there were evident signs of mischief. The hitherto industrious creatures ceased to carry in bee-bread. I wanted no further proof that the queen's eggs were not hatching, the cause of which was sufficiently clear. One of my hives having produced drones rather early, I had the opportunity of supplying my failing stock with their one *desideratum*. Therefore, on the 23rd of April I placed in the hive six drones, and prevented their exit by closing the doorway for a short time. If I had put these strangers into a hive where they were not wanted, they would have been expelled or killed without ceremony. Not so here. By the 10th of May a marked improvement had taken place. From this time the tide of prosperity flowed: and I find the following memorandum on June 17th:—"Drones still keep possession, and the population increases very fast." On the 4th of August I took a bell-glass of honey from this hive.—*Leisure Hour*, June.

VOLCANOS.

AT all times, volcanic phenomena possess great interest, and, at this period when the volcanos of the old and new world are in a remarkable state of activity, some account of their phenomena as seen by the most recent lights of science will probably be acceptable.

If earthquakes have always been regarded with awe, volcanoes are even more fearful manifestations of the powers attributed in the fabulous mythology of antiquity to the infernal earth-shaking sovereign "Ennorigæus." An examination of a map of the world showing the volcanic and earthquake districts renders it evident that there is an intimate relation between the two classes of phenomena. Both develop themselves mainly along the same zones, and earthquakes are invariably rarer and more feeble as they recede from the centres of volcanic action. According to the most recent investigations, the known active volcanos or habitual vents of volcanic energy exceed 400. These do not, however, include mud volcanos, the phenomena of which are very distinct from those of true volcanos. Ordinary volcanos are thus classified:

		Now active
Europe	7	4
Atlantic Islands	14	8
Africa	3	1
Continental Asia	25	15
Asiatic Islands	189	110
Indian Ocean	9	5
South Sea	40	26
America	120	56
Antarctic Land	3	3
	410	228

The largest proportion of these volcanos are situated in tropical regions, very few more than $30°$ from the equator. But they are by no means dependent on climate, many in Iceland being on the grandest scale, and others in full blast in the antarctic regions. The loftiest eruptive cones are Sahama in Bolivia, 22,350 feet; and Aconcagua in Chili, 23,004 feet. It is a noteworthy fact with regard to volcanos that the greater number occur either in islands or on coast-lines near the sea. Indeed the proximity of the ocean seems to be a necessary condition for the manifestation of great volcanic phenomena. The sea water probably finds access to the foci of the subterranean fires, and thereby produces enormous volumes of vapour and occasionally water, which frequently accompanies eruptions on a great scale. It was indeed suggested by Sir H. Davy that if the interior of the earth contains large quantities of the un-oxidated metalloids, all the phenomena of volcanos might be occasioned by the penetration of sea-water through deep fissures. Though abandoned by its distinguished author, this hypothesis with some important modifications was entertained by the late Dr. Daubeny and other geologists. It is certain that water plays a most important part in volcanic phenomena, elastic vapours supplying the principal motive force of upheavals. Although upwards of 400 volcanos have been noted it is probable that many more exist. For, independently of the fact that a large portion of the earth's subaërial surface has not yet been explored, the far more extensive subaqueous area doubtless contains several volcanic vents which have not yet raised an eruptive orifice visibly above the surface of the ocean. Graham's Island, which rose out of the sea from a depth of 100 feet in a few days, and attained a height of 200 feet, and a circumference of three miles, is an illustration on a large scale of one of these sea volcanos.

One of the most striking features of volcanos is their remarkable linear distribution. They traverse both hemispheres in a great arched curve, commencing at Terra del Fuego (the land of fire), running up the entire western fringe of that continent, almost to Behring's Straits, crossing the North Pacific through the Aleutian chain of isles, and descending thence southwardly along the peninsula of Kamtschatka, Japan, and the Phillipine Islands, to the Moluccas, from which two lines branch, one enclosing Borneo in a semicircular sweep to the west and north, and continuing through Java and Sumatra to the Andaman Islands, and into Burmah, in which last "wreath of islands" there are no less than 109 lofty fire-emitting mountains—the other threading Papua and the Saloman and New Hebrides Islands to New Zealand, whence it seems continued in Victoria Land almost to the South Pole. Thus not a day passes on our globe without witnessing volcanic phenomena. Heaving volcanos are in full blast throughout Japan; the normal state of that country is indeed that of chronic convulsion, and there is no sign of diminishing vigour in the volcanic centres. The Japanese Islands may be said to rest on treacherous ribs of granite which crust over a mighty sea of molten lava, and so tremendous is the subterranean force in that region that during the eruptions in 1854, men-of-war at anchor were spun round, and the harbours were scoured out to their bottoms. Mr. Scrope, who has made volcanos his special study distinguishes their phenomena by three general phases:

1. That in which the volcano exists incessantly in outward eruption—phase of permanent eruption.

2. That in which eruptions, rarely of any excessive violence continue in a comparatively tranquil manner for a considerable time, and alternate with brief intervals of repose—phase of moderate activity.

3. That in which eruptive paroxysms of intense energy alternate with lengthened periods of complete external inertness—phase of prolonged intermittences.

Very few volcanos are in a state of permanent eruption; the most remarkable example is that of Stromboli, which has been in constant activity since Homeric days. The more common condition of volcanoes is the intermittent, such as is presented by Vesuvius; the most terrible that coming under the phase of prolonged intermittences and paroxysmal eruptions.

When geological research was in its infancy, volcanic action was generally ascribed to some adventitious union of substances, whose combination resulted in the development of intense heat and violent eruptive action. This hypothesis has long been abandoned by those who have carefully studied volcanos. Nor does the upheaval theory of Humboldt and Von Buch now find supporters. This supposed that some upheaving force raised a portion of the earth's crust in a dome-like shape, and that upon this, volcanic products were cast. Far more probable is the theory propounded by Mr. Darwin, who has had peculiar facilities for observing volcanic phenomena. He maintains that volcanos are caused by subterranean forces, and says in his highly interesting work on coral reefs:

It may be considered as almost established that volcanos are often (not necessarily always) present in those areas where the subterranean motive power has lately forced, or is now forcing outwards the crust of the earth, but that they are invariably absent in those where the surface has lately subsided, or is still subsiding.

Sir C. Lyell conceives that aqueous and igneous agents may be regarded as antagonistic forces labouring incessantly to reduce the inequalities, and he adds:

I have come to the conviction that upheaval has nowhere played such a dominant part in the cone and crater-making process, as to warrant the use of the term 'Elevation Craters,' instead of cones and craters of eruption. Such a designation, as well as the theory implied by it, would be alike inappropriate in the case of all the igneous mountains which I have seen, whether in Sicily, or in the volcanic district of Naples, central France, or, lastly, Madeira and the Canaries.

The prodigious quantity of matter ejected from volcanos is amazing. We have only to look at the vast extent and depth of the scoriæ and of lava cast forth by one eruption of magnitude, to realise the formation of cones and craters and the accumulation on volcanic mountains of enormous layers of matter. During the famous eruption of Cotopaxi in 1533, witnessed by the Spaniards under Sebastian de Belelcazar, the plain around the foot of the mountain was strewed through a radius of fifteen miles and more, with great fragments of rock, many of which measured as much as nine feet in diameter; and Humboldt tells us of one rock weighing upwards of 200 tons, as having been launched into the air to a height of several hundred feet during an eruption of this volcano. The force required to produce these results is almost bewildering to our senses; it may be explained however by the power of heat. Bacon long ago cast considerable light on the phenomena of volcanos as connected with heat in his *Novum Organum*, where he says:

Heat is a motion expansive restrained and acting in its strife upon the smaller particles of bodies. But the expansion is thus modified; for while it expands all ways, it has at the same time an inclination upwards. And the struggle in the particles is modified also; it is not sluggish but *hurried* and *with violence.*

Now when we bear in mind that a mere scratch on the surface of our globe, which is nearly 8,000 miles in diameter (for so the depth of only one mile must be considered) brings us to a temperature of 105°, we have only to descend in imagination to the still comparatively slight depth of twenty miles to find the earth's crust red-hot, while if the temperature continues to increase regularly according to the same law, we should come at no very great depth beyond on a liquid sea of fire. But it is probable that this molten mass is at a greater distance from us than this theory would place it. Astronomical calculations tend to prove that the crust of the earth is at least 800 miles thick, and that the coating of our globe must be extremely solid and rigid to enable our planet to preserve its figure. But the further we remove the seat of the subterranean force from us, the more must we be struck by its great power. Earthquakes are indeed terrific evidence of mysterious dynamic laws; but it is only when the subterranean expansive force breaks through the earth's crust, and after violent earth throes a volcano becomes active, that we obtain a just idea of the forces at work in nature's secret laboratory.

A grand example of the tremendous action of this force may be seen in the Monte Nuovo of the Phlegræan fields, which was formed, in September 1538, on the site of the Lucrine Lake, once famous for its oysters. The eruption continued without intermission two days and two nights, and on the third day people climbed to the top of the new hill 440 feet high, and looked into the crater 421 feet deep, within which stones were boiling up. The mountain has remained quiescent ever since that period. On the other hand, the volcano of Izalco in Central America rose suddenly to the height of 1,600 feet on February 23rd, 1770, and has remained since in such constant activity as to serve as a beacon to mariners. The volcano of Tomboro, in Sumbawa, is another amazing evidence of subterranean force. In 1815 it yielded ashes and scoriæ sufficient to form three mountains, each equal in cubic contents to Mont Blanc, or to cover the whole of Germany with scoriæ two feet deep.

But even more tremendous is the volcano of Mauna Loa, a huge domed-shaped mountain in Hawaii, nearly 14,00 feet above the sea, formed chiefly by the repeated outflows of a highly liquid lava boiling up and cascading over the lips of a central vent at its summit. The phenomena of this volcano are on the most stupendous scale. The highest crater, which is circular, 8,000 feet in diameter, and 830 feet deep, is frequently filled by the welling up of the lava from the vents at its bottom. During one of the latest eruptions the lava stream extended sixty-five miles, and averaged four miles in width, and twelve feet in depth. Its discharge was accompanied by columns of fire, scoriæ of filamentous lava (called *Pele's hair*), and dense vapour which towered over the crater to the height of 800 feet for twenty days, darkening the sun and obscuring every object a few yards distant; while from the surface of the lava currents, clouds of steam rolled upwards. On this occasion it is calculated that within ten months 15,400,000,000 cubic feet of molten matter were blown out of the crater, and that the lava overflowed an area of 200,000 acres in the same period of time. The lava in this gigantic crater rarely remains long at the same level. It sometimes rises to the lip of the crater, at other times sinks entirely out of sight. The subsidence leaves irregular shelves or ledges around the walls of the crater. The eruption in 1840 of Kilawea, fifteen miles from Mauna Loa, was if possible, more appalling. The wonderful crater of this volcano is of an irregular elliptical figure, seven miles round, and 1,430 feet deep. It became full in the latter part of 1839 of boiling lava more or less crusted over, and suddenly in 1840, the tremendous caldron was emptied by means of lateral vents. A lava stream four miles wide and thirty miles in length was formed in seventy hours, and for the space of fourteen days it plunged in a vast fiery cataract one mile wide over a precipice fifty feet in height into the sea, where it formed three islands, and killed immense numbers of fish.

Vast, however, as is this crater, it is but a tiny cup compared to those craters with which the moon's surface is crowded. The crater of Copernicus is forty-five miles in diameter, and its depth, according to computations made by aid of the most powerful modern telescopes, is no less than 11,300 feet, while the height of the wall above the general surface of the moon is 2,650 feet. The tremendous energy of the eruptive forces which created such a volcano as this, staggers our senses, and those who have enjoyed a good telescopic survey of this lunar phenomenon doubtless well remember its unearthly grandeur. It is very remarkable, too, how greatly certain areas on the moon's surface resemble terrestrial volcanic regions. The lunar mountain Gassendi is very similar to the extinct volcanic district of Auvergne, and there is even a greater resemblance between the volcanic region of Vesuvius and the Phlegræan fields, and the Mount Maurolycus, with its numerous adjoining craters. The moon indeed, at least as respects the hemisphere which alone we are able to contemplate, presents the appearance of a burnt-out globe once imbued with volcanic life and an intense outward activity, probably with seas and an atmosphere now dried up and extinct. Strange that this orb of whose brilliance poets so sweetly sing, and whose reflected light is the charm of our nights should in reality be a burnt-out globe. Thinking thus, may we not imagine that if our world should not be destroyed in the manner pointed out by the new meteoric theory of the sun's heat, but become a dead planet, it may too, like the moon, shine brilliantly to other worlds, the inhabitants of which will perhaps gaze curiously on the craters and ridges—the bones, so to speak—of our globe, and speculate on what manner of people once lived upon it.—C. R. Weld, in *Fraser's Magazine* for April.

CANADIAN SPORT; OR, MIRAGES OF THE SPORTING WORLD.

THE visions of far-off cities, palaces, gardens, fountains, and lakes that beguile the tired and thirsty pilgrims of the desert are probably but tame and rare illusions compared with those that lure hunters, fishermen, and trappers, or the myriads of men and boys all over the world, that would be such, on and on, year after year, in the pursuit of boundless successes that are always looming in the distance, but are never reached. For one, I confess that ever since I was ten years old I have been seeking from time to time, in all directions and by many wearisome excursions, for that paradise of sportsmen where one can bag the nicest game in any quantities "as fast as he can load and fire," or where he can catch bass or trout of any desirable size "as fast as he can put in his hook;" but I have *never found it!* The exact spot has been pointed out again and again by very credible informants; but always, when I have reached it, there has been some mistake about it. Either I had come a few days too soon, or a few days too late; or the desired region was a few miles further on, or off to the right or left, or even back of where I started; or somebody had got in before me, and had just disappeared with the load of luck that I expected; or the weather was wrong; or the time or day was wrong; or I have not the right kind of tools and tackle. Thus in one way or another, as a sportsman, I have never got much beyond moderate luck, with hard work and hard fare; and I have come to the conclusion that the sporting world is full of mirages, that ought to be exposed and expounded for the benefit of rising generations. I do not believe that my indifferent success is owing altogether to individual bad luck or bad management, but that it is an average sample of general experience. I hear the same story from multitudes of amateurs (told of course in their lucid intervals), and even from old Nimrods. John P. Hutchins said that he "never got through a trapping campaign without wondering at himself that he should be such a fool as to leave a good home and a civilized business to plunge himself into a purgatory of unspeakable hardships for small profits and little sport." And even his father, tough as he is in muscle and story-telling, said nearly the same thing.

The illusions that cover the sporting world comes mostly from the inveterate bragging and exaggerations of sportsmen themselves. The old hunter tells all he can, and more than he can truthfully of his exploits, and says as little as possible of his failures, and the miseries which his successes cost him. Thus the mirage rises, and they who are deceived by it, in their turn, learn to brag of their exploits and conceal their failures; and so the deception passes on from man to man, and from generation to generation.

I mean to step out of this practice, and tell some things about our Canada expedition that will tend to sober the expectations of novices, and put them on their guard against inflated reports and promises of sport.

"We went to Canada in full expectation of being able to get plenty of venison and fish for our winter supplies. When we came away, all hopes of getting these provisions had vanished, and we had found it necessary to borrow meat of our neighbours, the lumberers, and were about to send to Montreal for a barrel of mess-pork.

"Our illusions vanished one after another in this fashion. We were told that at Bass Lake we could catch fine, large bass in any quantities, either by drop-line or trolling. We fished patiently with drop-lines at various times for hours together, and got one nibble! We trolled the lake up and down with two boats, and caught one bass of perhaps a pound weight!

"We were told that at Salmon Lake, during a week or ten days after the 8th of October, we should find myriads of salmon-trout on their spawning beds every evening, and could spear boat-loads of them and salt them down for winter use. We had prepared two excellent spears and a jack; and we worked hard to gather 'fat pine;' and we laid in a store of salt. But we had no success in finding fish, except on one night, and then only in moderate numbers. All we caught were ten trout, averaging perhaps two pounds a piece, and one fine one of over twelve pounds. We had no occasion to salt them, as five of us easily disposed of them otherwise in the course of a week.

"We were told that we could kill all the deer that we should want for the winter. The understanding was that, just before freezing time, we should lay in our stock. I asked how many deer would probably be a fair supply for the party? The answer was 'about twenty.' Such were our expectations. The reality was this: Our party had the opportunity of seeing at a distance the chase and killing of two deer in Bass Lake, by resident hunters. These were all the deer that were taken in Bass Lake or in Salmon Lake within our sight and hearing, or within our knowledge by rumour, during the whole of our twenty days on the hunting grounds. The dogs were laying frequently, and hunters did their best, but no more deer were taken. We had not the slightest chance of killing any in the usual way by running them into the lakes, as our dog was only a puppy that was more likely to lose himself than to find deer. As to the chance of getting venison by the 'still hunt,' that is by shooting deer in the woods, there was little encouragement, as our party only saw one on land during all our journeyings.

"But how about bears? You didn't kill any, of course, but did you see or hear of any? Well, I will tell you all about bears. We expected to have something to do with them, and provided ourselves with a couple of Newhouse's famous bear traps; but we did not set them, and of course did not catch any. We saw scratches on a stump, which Mr. Hutchins pronounced to be the work of a bear's claws made for sport, as a cat airs her hooks sometimes by scratching. One night when we went camping out, Mr. Pitt heard a terrible noise that he thought bad enough to be a bear's growl; but it proved to be the complaint of an owl. And, to conclude, we had a view—in fact, rather too near a view—of a grisly skeleton of a bear, lying by the side of the path leading from our Crusoe shanty to the lake,—a relic left us by some previous hunter and the ravens. That was the nearest we came to seeing a bear.

"To cut the matter short, what did you shoot? I killed a partridge and a pigeon, Mr. Pitt killed several red squirrels (which cooked with some dried beef for want of salt, made an excellent stew). John P. killed some squirrels and a partridge. Mr. Hutchins killed a skunk. Besides these, we hit several paper marks, and some we did not hit. This is a true account of our hunting and fishing down to the time of our 'change of base' and my departure for the States."

A tender conscience and compassion for the unexperienced prompts these confessions. Of course the veterans can do better. They have had their say, and will get more credit than we greenhorns, any way. All ears are open to them. As a counterpoise to their exciting stories, we feel bound to leave it as our last word to amateur hunters, that they should not set their hearts on external success and pleasure, but rather on the benefits to be derived from hard discipline. In that case, we can assure them that they will not be disappointed.—*The Trapper's Guide.* Trübner & Co.

PIT HEAPS.

It almost invariably happens that those things which are most plentiful and easily obtained are least appreciated. Persons living in Newcastle rarely go to see the inside of the fine old Castle, because they can visit it at any time; indeed many of the inhabitants of Newcastle have never been within the Castle, though it is one of the first things that strangers enquire about and are desirous of seeing.

Inhabitants of colliery villages in Northumberland and Durham are so accustomed to see Pit Heaps, that they look upon them merely as collections of rubbish. It is quite true their materials are supposed not to be of any commercial value, but they are of great value to those who study geology and who desire to know something about the conditions of the world, the creatures that lived on it and the plants that grew on it thousands of years ago. The pit heaps, as all your mining readers are aware, consist of inferior coal, portions of stone, and masses of shale or band which are sent up from the mines. There is a black sort of band or shale that lies immediately over the coal of the High Main Seam which contains immense quantities of impressions of ferns and other larger vegetables which flourished when that thick layer of coal was deposited. The shale or band to which I desire at present to draw the special attention of your readers is the *Black Band* that overlies the coal of the *Low Main Seam.* Its colour is a kind of blue-black nearly as dark as coal; it breaks when struck by a hammer or split by a knife into thin leaves or layers, like pieces of slate, and is very easily split. It exists in nearly all the collieries in the North of England, and is found in great abundance at Newsham, Cramlington, Backworth, Gosforth, Dudley, Seaton Burn, Townley Usworth, Pelton, &c. It is of special interest because it contains in great abundance the remains of fishes and reptiles which lived immediately after the Low Main Seam of valuable coal was deposited. The remains which have been found in it consist of teeth, scales, spines, vertebrae, jaws, and sometimes, but very rarely of entire fish. The fish spines vary in length from 2 inches to about 18 inches. The vertebrae, or back bones are generally round like rings and vary in size from $\frac{1}{4}$ inch to 2 inches in diameter. The scales are very bright and polished looking articles and range in size from the $\frac{1}{8}$ of an inch to about 3 inches in diameter. The jaws of fish and reptiles sometimes contain five or six teeth, and sometimes upwards of twenty, and vary in length from a $\frac{1}{4}$ of an inch to 3 or 4 inches. All these things, and even entire fish may be obtained by careful splitting of the shale either at pit heaps or quietly at home, and at every split looking carefully for what may be seen. It requires quick eyes and good light to see the very small and beautiful objects that may be found; and in order to encourage the *young folks in colliery villages* to assist in discovering the wonderful remains that are to be had from the Low Main Coal Shale I offer a series of prizes for the best collections that may be brought or sent to me, viz.:—a neat clasped and gilt-edged pocket bible, and half-a-crown each to the two young persons (either boy or girl) who bring or send me the two best collections of remains of fossil fish and reptiles from the shale of the Low Main Seam; also a copy of Mosley's illustrated Lectures on Astronomy to each of the twelve young folks who send me the next twelve best collections. It will often happen that things which seem of least value to the collectors will be of most value to me, and anything, therefore, that appears at all strange should be sent, and I shall ascertain those portions of most value in a scientific point of view. There are hundreds of young people in the colliery villages of Northumberland and Durham who would be disposed to enter upon this collecting competition if their fathers, mothers, or friends were to encourage them, and any intending collector, or the father or mother of such, calling upon me shall see specimens of the objects I want gathered, as I shall have some here for examination and shall be ready to give any instructions that may be required.—T. P. Barkas, in *Circuit Magazine* for June.

THE CEDARS OF LEBANON.

The far-famed cedars of Lebanon rank amongst the most interesting and awe-inspiring wonders of the Holy Land. The amphitheatre in which they are situated is in itself a magnificent temple of nature, and has its beginning high up in the deep recess of the Kadisha, one of the wildest and grandest of the gorges of the Lebanon. For its grandeur of appearance, the cedar is as much indebted to its peculiar manner of growth as to its gigantic dimensions, the pyramidal form greatly contributing to its natural magnificence. The ancients conceived a very exaggerated idea of the incorruptibility of its timber, imagining that it communicated its durability to whatever it came in contact with, for which reason they not only embalmed the bodies of their dead but sprinkled their manuscripts with its powder, which emits a fragrance destructive to a great variety of insects. The wood of the modern cedar of Lebanon has been proved by experiments to be almost valueless commercially, and only equal to an inferior kind of deal. It was often used by the ancients in the construction of idols; and the reverence with which it was regarded is clearly demonstrated by the various ecclesiastical penalties imposed upon those who should cut or otherwise injure the trees. It is related that when the Moslems where pasturing in the vicinity of Lebanon, they were rash enough to cut some of the older specimens, for which they were immediately punished by the loss of their flocks. In former times, the Maronites were wont to celebrate in the sacred grove the festival of the Transfiguration, when the Patriarch himself would officiate, and perform the ceremonies of mass before a rude altar of stones. The trees, as they stand at present, form a thick forest without underbush, covering an area of forty rods in diameter. The popular fallacy that it was impossible to count them had its origin in the fact, that all travellers disagree as to their number. That they have diminished considerably, admits of no doubt; and while the cedar has been completely naturalised both in England and France, in Lebanon, the ancient land of its glory and abundance, where, in the days of Solomon, there were immense forests, it has almost entirely ceased to exist. At what particular period it was first planted in England, it is now impossible to ascertain. One writer states it was in the "Medico-botanical Garden" at Chelsea in 1683; but this cannot be correct, if the superb specimen which stood at Hendon Palace in Middlesex, and was blown down in the tempest which broke over England on New-year's day 1779, was actually placed there in the presence of Queen Elizabeth. The deodar has been frequently assumed to be identical with the cedar of Holy Writ, as its imposing appearance better accords with the sublime description of Ezekiel. Specimens have been found in the temples of India which have endured for nearly three hundred years without evincing the slightest symptoms of decay.—*Chambers's Journal*, June.

Man's Place in Nature.

Respectfully dedicated to Messrs. Darwin and Huxley.

I.

They told him gently he was made
　Of nicely-tempered mud;
That man no lengthened part had played
　Anterior to the Flood.
'Twas all in vain: he heeded not—
　Referring plant and worm,
Fish, reptile, ape, and Hottentot,
　To one 'primordial germ.'

2.

They asked him whether he could bear
　To think his kind allied
To all those brutal forms which were
　In structure pithecoid;
Whether he thought the apes and us
　Homologous in form:
He said, 'Homo and Pithecus
　Come from one common germ.'

3.

They called him 'atheistical,
　Sceptic, and infidel:'
They swore his doctrines without fail
　Would plunge him into hell:
But he, with proofs in no way lame,
　Made this deduction firm,
That all organic beings came
　From one primordial germ.

4.

That as for the Noachian flood,
　'Twas long ago disproved;
That as for man being made of mud,
　All by whom truth is loved
Accept as fact, what—*malgré* strife,
　Research tends to confirm—
That man and everything with life
　Came from one common germ.
　　　　Tinsley's Magazine for June.

The Fecundity of Fish.

The enormous fecundity of fishes,—some of them yield their eggs in millions, and most of them in tens of thousands—has given anglers and others the idea that it is impossible to affect the supplies by any amount of fishing. The female salmon yields eggs at the rate of one thousand for every pound of her weight. A fish of twenty pounds, as a general rule, yields twenty thousands eggs. As regards the productiveness of a salmon river, the question to be solved is, not how many eggs the fish produces, but how many eggs arrive at the stage of table fish, or in other words, grow to be salmon of say twenty pounds' weight. Well, we have the authority of Sir Humphrey Davy for saying that out of the 17,000 ova which each female salmon on an average annually deposits, only 800 in ordinary circumstances come to perfection. Some fishery economists do not allow that such a large number ever grow to be table fish, and perhaps Sir Humphrey did not mean that the number specified by him became table fish, but merely that they were hatched into life. One writer on this part of the salmon question thinks that only one per cent. of the eggs emitted by the mother fish attain to the point of perpetuating their kind. The destruction of eggs and young fish must therefore be enormous. Large quantities of the eggs, it is known, never come in contact with the milt, and so they perish. Countless numbers of the ova are carried away by the floods into unsuitable places, and they too perish. Then, again, numerous fish-cannibals are waiting at the spawning-beds to feast on the appetising roe; the thousands so eaten cannot be calculated, but so they perish. The young fish, again, are always in danger; and although a river may be positively swarming with young salmon, comparatively speaking, only very few of them ever live to reach the salt-water; all kinds of fresh-water monsters are constantly extorting tribute from the shoal. The smolt slaughter which occurs when the juvenile army reaches the sea is awful. Hordes of large sea-fish are always in waiting in the estuaries at the period of migration, instinctively aware of the feast that is in store for them. That only a very small percentage of the young salmon which go down to the sea as smolts ever return as grilse is obvious. Yet that large quantities of grilse are still left is also obvious from the fact that tens of thousands of these fish are annually killed; indeed, the fishery-lessee is the greatest enemy of the young salmon. It has been shown very conclusively that grilse are young salmon that have not spawned. Then why kill them? It is surely the worst possible economy to kill these virgin fish before they have at least one opportunity of perpetuating their kind.— *Saint Pauls.*

New Books.

[*Our limited space must of necessity compel us to give but very short notices of new books, but they will perhaps serve as a guide as to what books our readers may ask for at their libraries.*]

The Ocean World; being a Descriptive History of the Sea and its Living Inhabitants. Chiefly translated from "*La Vie and les Mœurs des Animaux,*" by Louis Figuier, author of "The World before the Deluge," "The Vegetable World," etc. Illustrated by 427 engravings, chiefly designed under the direction of M. Ch. Bévalet, from specimens in the Museum of Paris. London: Chapman and Hall, 193, Piccadilly. 1868.

We have here a volume well printed, strongly bound, and capitally illustrated, containing a great quantity of information, but nothing that is very new. Shells, Zoophytes, Polyzoa, Medusæ, Echinoderms, and Fishes, are all taken and commented upon, and many anecdotes given, which help to make the volume more attractive. It is essentially popular, and is therefore likely to meet with many admirers. The following anecdote, originally related by M. Cham, is amusing:

"M. R—— was Professor of Botany to the Faculty of Paris, and was, as sometimes happens, more learned than rich; he wished, on the invitations of a stranger, to purchase one of these shells at a very high price, which might be from 3,000 to 6,000 francs. The bargain was made, and the price agreed upon; it was only necessary to pay. The money in the professor's hands made only a small part of the sum the merchant was to receive for his shell, and he would not part with it without payment. M. R——, consulting his desire to possess the shell more than his weak resources, made up secretly a parcel of his modest plate, and went out to sell it. Without consulting his wife, he replaced his silver plate by coverings of tin, and ran to the merchant to secure his coveted Spondylus, which he believed to be *S. regius.*

"The hour of dinner arrived, and we may imagine the astonishment of Madame R——, who could not comprehend the strange metamorphosis of her plate. She delivered herself of a thousand painful conjectures on the subject. M. R——, on his part, returned home happy with his shell, which he had committed to the safe custody of a box placed in his coat pocket. But as he approached the house, he paused, and began for the first time to think of the reception he might meet with. The reproaches which awaited him, however, were compensated when he thought of the treasure he carried home. Finally, he reached home, and Madame R—— in her wrath was worthy of the occasion; the poor man was overwhelmed with the grief he had caused his wife; his courage altogether forsook him. He forgot his shell, and, in his trepidation, seated himself in a chair without the necessary adjustment of his garment. He was only reminded of his treasure by hearing the crushing sound of the broken box which contained it. Fortunately the evil was not very great, two spines only of the shell were broken; but the good man's grief made so great an impression on Madame R——, that she no longer thought of her own loss, but directed all her efforts to console the simple-minded philosopher."

The Food, Use, and Beauty of British Birds. By Chas. Oxley Groom Napier, Fellow of the Geological and other Societies. London: Groombridge and Son.

We have read this little volume with much pleasure, and confidently recommend it to such of our readers as are in want of a good list of the birds that have been, and are met with in the British Isles. Here will be found the localities in which they abound, degree of rarity and food, and an estimate of their comparative value to the agriculturist and society in general. The introductory essay, originally read before the Bristol Naturalists' Society, will be found of great interest to those who have not already made themselves acquainted with it. The following extract on the Ornithological year will serve to show the value of the work:—

If the naturalist rises betimes in midsummer like the French academician, M. Dureau de la Malle, he will find the greenfinch astir at $4\frac{1}{2}$ in the morning; the linnet from 2 to 3; the quail from $2\frac{1}{2}$ to 3; the blackbird from $3\frac{1}{2}$ to 4; the red pole from 3 to $3\frac{1}{2}$; the sparrow from 5 to $5\frac{1}{2}$; the blue tit from 5 to $5\frac{1}{2}$; a strong inducement it is surely to rise early to enjoy the dawning song of the birds. There are few pleasures greater than that of watching our smaller birds, their motions, their nest building, and all their belongings. How tenderly they cherish their young; with all the care and solicitude of a higher class of animals. The shrikes tyrannize over the smaller birds, impalling them on thorns; they are justly called butcher birds. The flycatchers tyrannize over the insect world. The thrushes and blackbirds, whose mellow notes are so delightfully cheering, do not lose their sprightfulness of song when the leaves are fallen. The song of the Robin has this character, cheering us all the year round. It is pleasant to watch the departure of migratory birds; I can imagine few pursuits more soothing to the mind than the study of ornithology, especially in this connexion. The mind wanders with the birds to different shores. In spring it goes north, where there is little night; in autumn it goes south where the weather is milder, thus enjoying perpetual sunshine. But let us pause and examine an ornithological year in the south of England, for there is much to delight all the year at home. The first week in the year the robin begins to sing from the bare hawthorn hedge where it built its nest the preceding March. The larks collect, and when the snow is melted scour the wheat fields. The nuthatch cries gou, dik, dik. The wagtails look lively, and the missel thrush sings its melancholy ditty, which the people of Hampshire consider an indication of stormy weather, tyrannically does it drive the smaller birds from the copse. The hedge accentor or dunnock utters its simple song, which has so little variety. The song thrush joins it in a melodious strain, saluting spring ere it begins. The tits begin to twitter, and the chaffinches are like schools of boys and girls apart, their courting time not having arrived. The second week sees the buntings in numerous flights, and linnets collect from solitary groups of two or three, to large flocks, and the rooks repair their old nests. The third week of the year the blackbird whistles, and the wren utters its feeble twitter. The skylark begins the strain that lasts nearly all the year, only in the end of autumn does it cease; but as the leaves wither and pass away, so dies its song. Long before the leaves are seen, its hopeful song breaks forth in anticipation of spring. The jackdaw preaches from the church top in our third week, the historian of the marriages and funerals of the parish. The brown owl hoots in the first week in February. The barn-door fowl begins to sit. The turkey cock begins to crow, and the yellowhammer utters its tee, tee, tee, teeke. The green woodpecker begins to laugh. The raven builds and croaks over its eggs. The house-pigeon, that frequently nesting bird, has its pair of young. The goldfinch sings and pairs. The missel thrush pairs. The plovers begin to clatter. The cock pheasants crow. The wryneck appears, the forerunner of the cuckoo, that extraordinary of extraordinary birds, of which so little is known, although every one has heard the cuckoo. The goose sits; but the common duck is still laying. The willow-wren is seen, the sand-martin, the swallow, and the black cap begin to sing. Our early birds are gone towards the end of the month. The nightingale arrives about the first week in April and also the cuckoo. The redstart, the tit lark, the wood warbler, the swift, and white throat begin their peculiar notes. Throughout the month the greater number of the small birds build or lay. "The voice of the turtle is heard in the land," but the nightingale and most of the warblers and the cuckoo have not eggs or young till May. April is the richest month in the song of our warblers, particularly the latter part. Many of our birds have second broods in this or the following month, which is much devoted to incubation, and few birds either arrive or leave. The swifts are amongst the first to leave about the end of July. Most of the migratory warblers leave in the month of August, in which month chaffinches, goldfinches, and other birds separate into schools of different sexes. Birds that were silent in the months of June and July begin their autumn song. Many of the purely insectivorous birds have migrated. The snipe in considerable numbers return, the golden plover, and the many ducks and waders that breed within the boundary of the artic circle, which remain from October till February and March, and some even till April; and thus rolls round our year of birds.

A Journey to Abyssinia, the Galla Countries, East Sudán, and Khartum in the Years 1861 *and* 1862. [*Reisne nach Abessinien, &c.*, von M. Th. von Heuglin].

M. von Heuglin was sent by the Gotha committee to ascertain, if possible, the fate of the accomplished African traveller, Dr. Edward Vogel. This volume gives an account of the expedition: the narrative of the journey is not particularly interesting, but the contributions to the natural history of Abyssinia are of great value, being almost exhaustive of the Flora and Fauna of that country.

Among the plants described by M. von Heuglin is one which is deserving of particular notice, namely, the Djibára, or Djibároa—*Rhynchopetalum montanum*.

This peculiar giant of the family of Lobeliaceæ towers above the high grass and *erica* bushes, with a scaly stem, eight or ten feet high, surmounted by a crown of dark-green sword-shaped leaves, which gives it the aspect of a palm. But out of this crown rises a spike, in shape like an enormous taper, to the further height of 10 or 15 feet, which is partially covered with lilac-coloured flowers. The blossoming takes place, slowly and uniformly, from below upwards, and a considerable time elapses before the whole spike of flowers has done blooming; so that, if the stem be struck whilst the plant above shows thousands of flowers still unopened, a shower of perfectly ripe seeds, not larger than those of the poppy, will fall to the ground.

The zone of the Djibároa commences at an elevation of about 11,000 feet, and reaches, where the soil allows it, to the highest summits of the mountains, at first mixed with trees of *Erica arborea* and *Hypericum leucoptychodes*, but afterwards alone, rising by thousands out of the short meadow-grass and numerous small Alpine flowers with which it is interspersed.

Select Ferns and Lycopods, British and Exotic. By B S. Williams, Victoria Nursery, Upper Holloway, N. London.

In this book Mr. Williams, the well-known nurseryman and cultivator of orchids and ferns gives us his experiences of all the more important and beautiful ferns in cultivation, and the result is the best book which has yet appeared on the growth of tender as well as hardy ferns. Nor does it simply deal with the cultivation alone, for each species is described in a full and plain way, while the book is illustrated with good cuts, showing some of the more remarkable species and varieties, and a large one of a scene on Mount Wellington, Tasmania—a fall of snow bearing down the crests of a wood of tree ferns.

The Birds of Berkshire and Buckinghamshire: a Contribution to the Natural History of the Two Counties. By Alexander W. M. Clark Kennedy, "an Eton Boy." Simpkin, Marshall and Co.

Mr. Kennedy has published his Contribution to the Ornithology of Berks and Bucks, and we are confident that our readers will be pleased with the result. The birds are classified as residents, summer, winter, spring, autumn, and rare and accidental visitors. The volume is illustrated with four beautiful coloured photographs, representing the long-eared owl, the hooded crow, the black tern, and the hippoe in their habitation—good specimens of how natural history books might with advantage be illustrated.

The Journal of the Queckett Microscopical Club. No. 2, April. Robert Hardwicke, 192, Piccadilly.

We have received the 2nd part of the Queckett Club Papers, and have been greatly pleased with the contents. The first articles, The Wools of Commerce commercially and Microscopically considered, by N. Burgess, being of great interest and value, as is also the paper on the Hairs of Indian Bats, by M. C. Cooke. The journal is very creditably got up, and is calculated to add to the growing reputation of this excellent society.

The American Naturalist. Vol. II. June, 1868.

The present part contains a very interesting paper by A. S. Packard, Junr., on the Parasites of the Honey Bee, well worthy of attention. There are also articles on the Warblers, and the Goldsmith Beetle, describing their habits, together with a large quantity of other useful information. We are very sorry to see the editors asking for fresh subscribers, without which the magazine must be conducted at a loss. A publication of this admirable character should not require such an urgent appeal, as it is edited with judgment, beautifully printed and well illustrated, and not published at a very ruinous price. We hope yet to see it meeting with the success it deserves.

Correspondence.

[*Under this head we shall be glad to insert any letters of general interest.*]

BIRD MURDER.

SIR,—As various articles have lately come under our notice with this somewhat tragical heading, the following analysis may assist your readers in determining when and where such language may be most properly applied. Many of us have no doubt passed through Leadenhall and other poultry markets and there seen thousands of what appeared to have been specimens of the feathered race, but now stripped of their once beautiful and attractive plumage; while others were to be seen dangling by their necks, merely awaiting the time to undergo a similar manipulation. This of course must be regarded in a business point of view, as many of them were doubtless reared for no other purpose, and must be killed (not murdered) before they can be made ready for the more delicate stomachs of the wealthy, or become an occasional luxury at the table of the middle classes. We must therefore divert our minds of all thoughts of murder in this case, supposing ourselves as willing as our neighbours to partake of a leg or a wing at the forthcoming Festival.

Again, when walking in the fields, or near the shady woods in the autumn of the year, we may have been surprised by a sudden and discordant sound rising from the coverts almost sufficient to paralyse a weak and nervous constitution not quite familiar with a country sporting life. But we soon discover that it is nothing more nor less than what is called beating of the woods for game; and we may soon observe a number of sporting gentlemen stationed in the most likely position to intercept the flight of the birds that are now anxious to make their escape from the intruders, perhaps under some impression of impending danger: at all events they are driven to extremities with the beaters behind them and an array of gunners in the front. Up they must rise, which they do with a truly tremulous fluttering; but it is soon over with them. One, two, three—soon a dozen or more of these beautiful denizens of the woods are prostrate on the ground, while a few others are scrambling away with broken wings, etc., to hide themselves till reported by the markers down, when they are picked by the dogs, the watchers, or the keepers. Now some with the finer feeling of tenderness

"Might learn to pity them."

But we must not confound this with *Bird Murder*, remembering that is duly licensed and gentlemanly sport. We also read of the great havoc made among the grouse kind in the month of August, and the excellent day's sport by one double barrel on the 1st of September to the tune of twenty or thirty brace or from forty to sixty birds killed by one man in one day. But here likewise the licence to kill birds cover and secure the sportsman from the horrible stigma of bird murder. We do not repine at this, as we quite feel that every man should have all the pleasures and comforts of life that he can legally obtain, and we would wish him success in any legitimate pursuit that best meets his own inclination.

But if we still fail in pointing out the culprit to be branded with the foul act of bird murder (supposing it to have any signification), we must advert to another class of beings who do not profess to follow the sports of the field in the general acceptation of that term, but love to range the field and grove for other objects than to acquire the reputation of crack shots. And amongst these there are some who desire no more than to become acquainted with the habits of the animal kingdom in their most natural and lively forms: of course these would not tread upon a worm, much less disturb the harmony of Nature by committing the crime of murder. There are others again who, not content with observing and letting alone, have unfortunately a strong desire to become possessors of a specimen or two of the objects by which they are surrounded; and it is among these I believe that we shall presently drop upon the culprits in question.

When the useful and interesting study of botany be the choice, it may of course be pursued in a very quiet and gentlemanly manner; but if birds and insects are the objects of pursuit, the matter then takes another and a very serious form: these objects are too lively and too timid to suffer the very near approach of man, and generally object to a very close and personal investigation. What, then, is to be done? You may call to them, but they will not stay. The ornithologist may address one bird as Ampelis Garrulus (Waxen Chattern), and another as Oriolus Golbula (Golden Oriole), but they will not be kept waiting. Gentlemen may tell the entomologist that he may take the Meadow Brown or the Garden White in any number he pleases, but on no account to capture the Purple Emperor or the Camberwell Beauty, should these present themselves to his notice: I am inclined to think that the practical entomologist will heed them about as much as the birds alluded to. Nor do I think that the practical ornithologist will value the advice more when told that he may procure specimens of the commoner kind of birds, but must not avail himself of the scarcer species, however great the temptation, or however good the opportunity. A timid collector of birds or their eggs may indeed be induced to withhold the notice of his captures or success from month to month, or from year to year, merely to avoid the aspersion of murderers and ignoramuses, as at page 57; or as a fool, deserving to be heavily fined for the shooting of a sea gull, as at page 120; but assuredly the practical ornithologist will not be so far gulled by such uncharitable and licentious remarks, whether emanating from *Fraser's* or any other magazine, as to refrain from adding a choice specimen to his collection whenever a favourable opportunity occurs for so doing. We must, however, beg that the foregoing remarks are not misconstrued by the young naturalist, as we would by no means give encouragement to shoot and destroy at will, with no especial purpose in view other than mere amusement, remembering that every object was created to fill some important office in the great economy of Nature; therefore, my young friends, learn to use these things as not abusing them. If the extract at page 57 had merely alluded to the ignorance in killing certain birds of the rarer kind I should certainly not have adverted to it again. The remarks are not merely uncourteous, but they are not strictly true: I must contend that there are several extenuating circumstances. If the fact of adding a rare and beautiful specimen to a collection of British birds be not a sufficient apology, allow me to state that much practical knowledge in reference to the sexes of birds, and perhaps more in relation to their varied means of sustenance and support, has been gained by a *post mortem* examination of the bird; and in some cases where nothing short of that would have given so satisfactory and unmistakeable an evidence. The question of how far the various species of birds should be protected by mankind, or to what extent they may be destroyed with advantage, is at present an open question. Many and varied are the opinions that have been advanced upon the subject—some of them doubtless arising from a pure feeling of benevolence. We may also admit that thousands have been destroyed merely from that inherent love of sport which appears to exist among all classes of the community. Upon the whole I believe that much remains to be investigated and considered in relation to the great economy of Nature, before we shall be in a position to censure indiscriminately the overt acts or apparent inconsistencies of our fellow-creatures.

The following extracts from White's "History of Selborne" may not be inappropriate to the foregoing remarks:—

Letter 6. Partridges in vast plenty bred on the verge of the forest, and parties of unreasonable sports men *killed* twenty and sometimes thirty brace in a day.

Letter 11. Three Grossbeaks appeared some years ago in my fields in the winter, one of which *I shot*.

Letter 16. My countrymen talk much of a bird that makes a clatter with its bill against a dead bough or old broken pales, calling it a jarbird. I procured one to be *shot* in the very act, it proved to be the Sitta Uropæ (the Nuthatch).

Letter 15. In the middle of February I discovered in my tall hedges a little bird that raised my curiosity. It was of that yellow green colour that belongs to the Salicaria kind, and I think it was soft billed. It was no Parus, and was too long and too big for the Golden Crowned Wren, appearing most like the largest Willow Wren. *I shot at it*, but it was so desultory that I missed my aim.

The last is an instance where I think every ornithologist would heartily wish that he had *killed his bird*, as the period of the year given in the note would make the circumstance very interesting.

I am yours, &c.,
320, Strand. C. W——D.

"NATURE IMPROVED."

SIR,—I am sure that any one reading "A. M. B.'s" strictures on my paper would imagine that I had been writing in defence of "our feathered friends," and had accused him of wanton destruction of bird-life; whereas I simply made a passing allusion to the subject, urged thereto by one of his own letters in a previous number. I have no wish to "guage the requirements of ornithology" by my own "views." Narrow or otherwise, I am no ornithologist, nor do I profess to be one, although *I* have *more* respect for one than I have for a "collector of postage-stamps;" but I have no hesitation in saying that it is time for every naturalist to put in a word in favour of the preservation of our British Fauna. The manner in which "T. G. P.'s" sympathy for the otters was treated by "A. M. B." does not prevent me from mentioning, in evidence of the above, the boasted destruction of forty-eight kingfishers within the last few years by a person in this neighbourhood: albeit, this statement will probably be met with a letter in which Artemus Ward, comic songs, slang phrases, scraps of French and Latin, and facetious (?) remarks will be ingeniously worked together.

I do not wish to take up your space unnecessarily, but must, in justice to myself, request you to allow me to defend myself against "A. M. B.'s" misrepresentations. In the first place, he accuses me of placing myself, "with an air, in the front rank of naturalists." I have carefully read over my article, but can nowhere find that I have claimed for myself such a position, to which none knows better than myself that I have no right. I did not "step out of my groove" to do battle with others: the opinion of naturalists was asked, and I as a naturalist gave mine; but I quite agree with "A. M. B.," that when botanists and conchologists set themselves up as the only true naturalists, and affect to despise the students of the other branches of Natural History, then it will be time for "every student of our English Fauna to combine" against such a misrepresentation. The only thing is—will such a contingency ever arise?

Again, "A. M. B." wilfully misrepresents me in commenting on what he terms my "conservative sentence;" for he cannot be so ignorant as to suppose that by "naturalists of the old school" I mean "a few octagenarians," any more than painters of the Pre-Raphaelite school would mean painters who lived before Raphael. Neither would I exclude any "foreign or imported beauty;" but I would keep it in its place.

I will not trespass longer on your space, but content myself with observing that, after all, "A. M. B." has left the chief object of my article unattacked.

I remain your's, &c.,
JAMES BRITTEN.
High Wycombe.

OOLOGICAL EXCURSIONS.

SIR,—On going on nesting excursions, the naturalist should take with him a pair of tight-fitting leathern gloves, to prevent his flesh becoming torn, whilst examining thorny bushes, underwood and nettles. He should provide himself with a knapsack, bound firmly on his back, in which to carry a small stock of provisions and a wooden box (those made of wood are preferable to tin, as the eggs are then less likely to be cracked) lined with wool, to contain his specimens. He must also have a small drill to ascertain whether the eggs are unhatched; his dress should be strong, but light, in order to guard against the rays of the sun. It is also necessary that he provide himself with a stout walking-stick—not only to assist him in climbing, etc. (for which it is of great use) but also to destroy snakes and drive away any surly dogs. His boots should be waterproof, and fit tightly. If he is also a collector of skins, he must be possessed of a fowling-piece, and a brace of pistols, besides a game bag.

By taking these precautions, the naturalist may extend his rambles for several days in succession, provided he supplies himself with a sufficiency of cash to defray the small expenses of his board and lodging at the wayside farmhouses. Let him not hesitate to enter any temptingly enclosed plantations and thickets, and never stop to look for those harmless, though universally dreaded phantoms—the "warning boards"—glooming so hideously down from a neighbouring tree or stile. Should he happen to meet with the worthy lord of the domain, or his staunch adherent, the gamekeeper, an excuse is easily framed—such as a short cut to the nearest village, etc., etc.—but should he prefer, let him entrust the worthy gentleman with the secret of his "French leave," as occasioned by that study of studies, "Natural History;" and ten to one he will get a hearty welcome, and many a future invitation to the said estate. Should he, however, unfortunately run foul of a cross-grained old fellow (who neither himself admires Nature nor admires it in others) he will, if he is of the right stamp, cheerfully pay the paltry fine, and console himself with the wise saying, "Nothing venture, nothing gain." But if the excursionist contemplates taking "French leave," let him leave behind his gun and ammunition, otherwise he might be suspected of hostile design against the well-preserved game. But by far the greatest knowledge of Nature can be obtained without the aid of the gun, simply by "observation." Should night overtake him while distant from human habitation, if the weather be dry he can obtain a comfortable nap under a friendly bush wrapt up in his great coat; if wet, however, he should continue his walk, and will probably, by dawn of day, be wiser than before, as Nature can be studied by night as well as by day, and shows then quite a different aspect. He should, however, rest for a few hours the following day.

I think the majority of naturalists' would prefer this rustic pedestrian mode of travelling to the formal visits to fashionable watering places, or railway tours to celebrated ruins, etc., now so much sought after by the "genteel" population.

I am, Sir, yours truly,
R. B. W.

Short Notes.

DISCOVERY OF A BED OF FOSSIL OYSTERS.—Mr. Whittle, of Chorley, is sinking a new shaft down to the Arley seam of coal, at a spot near to the railway, half-way between the Adlington and Horwick stations, on the Lancashire and Yorkshire line, about a couple of miles from the foot of Rivington Pike. Two seams of coal have been passed, and at a depth of 130 yards, the sinkers have cut through a bed of fossil oysters, 2ft. 4in. in thickness. How far the bed extends, it is impossible to say. The oysters are petrified into one solid mass as hard as flint. We have seen two blocks of them which have been brought to Preston as great natural curiosities, by Mr. Dewhurst, coal merchant, who went down the shaft on Thursday, accompanied by Mr. Brindle, flag merchant. The oysters are all perfect in form, and small in size, rather less, perhaps than the London "natives." The conclusion which immediately suggests itself is, that the sea must at a period very remote, have washed the foot of the Rivington range of hills. The whole of West Lancashire is alluvial land; and at one period was covered with a forest of oak. We have a proof of this in the fact that trees are frequently found imbedded in the moss, and also in the bed of the Ribble. Last year we had a paragraph on the large boulder found in the sand hill below St. Mark's Church, which now lies opposite the Wheat Sheaf Inn. To a thoughtful mind the boulder, like the bed of petrified oysters, tells its own tale, and points to the mighty floods which have swept over the district since the sea retired, which bore down the trees and imbedded them in the soil which now overlies them, forming the richest land in the county. The skull and antlers of the gigantic Irish elk, found not long ago in the bend of the Ribble, at the Chain Caul, points to the fact that animals of the mammoth tribe must have roamed through the forest which covered the county at a period since the oysters were imbedded and the upper coal strata formed. Great and mighty changes have occurred, and the small oyster detached from the surface of the block, and handed to us by Mr. Brindle, tells us of the wonders which took place before the earth was made fit for the habitation of man.—*Preston Herald*.

WILD ANIMALS IN CAPTIVITY.—When zoological gardens were first instituted, and it was determined to give wild things a local habitation, we copied too closely the idea of the menagerie. They were collections of dens, dispersed among shrubberies, it is true, but there was no attempt to give the creatures the slightest liberty, or to imitate the conditions surrounding them in a state of nature. We freely admit that with all delicate animals from tropical climates the question of temperature puts limits to these surroundings, excepting in the warm months of the year. Boxed up as they were, the lions and tigers, upon the first establishment of the Regent's Park Gardens, died from exposure to the weather at a terrible rate. Even now, with all the care we take of the monkey tribe, the more delicate among them are continually dying. Notwithstanding their houses are artificially warmed, a hard frost will kill scores of such tender nurslings in the course of a winter's night in this collection. But acknowledging the difficulties thrown in the way of tropical animals in the winter season, it seems to us that with regard to the animals of the colder and more temperate climates we have been backward in surrounding them, as far as possible, with the conditions they are accustomed to, in a state of nature. When we have made the attempt, in nearly every case it has been successful. What information do we get from the beaver, for instance, when we see him in a box? but supply him with a pool of water and a bundle of sticks, and we are at once made acquainted with his habits; indeed we know them more intimately within certain limits than do the Canadian trappers, for there is a keeper watching them all day, when they are at peace and without fear.—*From Cassell's Magazine.*

FRUIT OF THE BAOBAB.—The fruit of the Baobab is an oblong or oval woodly capsule, and hangs from the branches at the end of a long stalk. It frequently measures from twelve to eighteen inches long, and six inches or more across. It is covered with a greenish soft down, and internally it is divided into eight or ten cells. The seeds are numerous, and are imbedded in a pulpy substance, which has a pleasant acid flavour, and when dry is easily pulverized. In Cairo, this is constantly done, and the powder is used for medicinal purposes. In its fresh state the pulp is eaten by the natives, and elephants are said to be very fond of it. In Central Africa, a regular dish is made from it, by beating it up with water to the consistency of a thin paste, which is eaten by dipping in the forefinger, and then sucking it. In some parts, the juice is expressed from the pulp, and is much valued as a medicine in cases of fever. The woody capsules, after the pulp and seeds have been carefully removed, made excellent vessels for holding water, etc. They are also reduced to ashes, which, along with the ashes of the bark, is boiled in palm oil for use as soap. The leaves, which are palmate, giving rise to the specific name, *digitata*, are occasionally used by the natives for covering their huts; while on the eastern coast of Africa, they are carefully dried, and reduced to a powder, which they daily mix with their food, and which has the effect of diminishing the excess of perspiration occasioned by the heat of the climate.—From the *Student* for June.

PARASITES ON A STAG-BEETLE.—I chanced to witness, says a writer to the *Field*, the other day a striking incident connected with a stag-beetle. I found this insect apparently hurt and unable to walk. On taking it up in my hand it suddenly rolled over on its back, apparently dead, and I noticed that about its legs were hanging small red specks of about the size of a pin's head each; but, on closer examination, one of these specks (for I know no other word which I can apply to them) suddenly took to itself wings, and, remaining in the same place for about two seconds, became visibly larger and flew away. Before ten seconds more had elapsed three of the others had done the same thing. By this time the stag-beetle (which I had given up for dead, so profound was the sleep apparently into which it had fallen) rolled slowly over, as though much relieved by its riddance from this parasite (for such I conclude it must have been), and on recovering the use of its legs and wings flew away with a natural "hum." I deeply regret not having had a lens with me at the time, by which I could have inspected them more closely, for their motions were so rapid that it was out of the question to recapture them before they were out of sight, which they of course were almost instantaneously, on account of their extreme minuteness. What these could have been I leave to others to decide from this description.—P. Y.

PALMS OF AUSTRALIA.—Palms cease to exist southwards of the meridian of Gippsland, but their number increases northward along the east coast, while in Victoria these noble plants have their only representative in the tall Cabbage or Fan Palm of the Snowy River, that Palm which, with the equally hardy Areca sapida of New Zealand, ought to be established wherever the Date is planted for embellishment. Rotang Palms (Calami of several species) render some of the northern thickets almost inapproachable, while there also, on a few spots of the coast, the cocoa-nut tree occurs spontaneously. A few peculiar Palms occur in the Cassowary country, near Cape York, and others around the Gulf of Carpentaria as far west as Arnhem's Land. The tallest of all—the lofty Alexandra Palm (Ptychosperma Alexandræ), extends southwards to the tropic of Capricorn, and elevates its majestic crown widely beyond the ordinary trees of the jungle. The products of these entire forests are as varied as the vegetation which constitutes them. As yet, however, their treasures have been but scantily subjected to the test of the physician, the manufacturer, or the artisan.—Dr. Muller's *Essays on Australian Vegetation*.

THE COWTHORPE OAK AND ORIGINAL RIBSTONE PIPPIN.—We have recently, says a writer in the *Field*, visited these two famous Yorkshire trees. The Ribstone pippin at Ribstone Hall is well taken care of, and in no danger of anything save canker. It is not the original tree of this deservedly famous kind, but a sucker from it, and comparatively young and small. The Cowthorpe Oak, one of the most famous and remarkable in existence, is on the other hand, anything but well taken care of. When standing in the hollow interior, and looking up to the sky, it reminds one of an old ruin, and the laureate's lines in "Vivien" may well come to mind:

> Before an oak so hollow, huge, and old,
> It look'd a tower of ruin'd mason work.

Yet this fine old tree, which ought to be a treasure to the county in which it exists, is left quite unprotected, and apparently suffers from mutilation. It used at one time to be fenced in some way to keep off severer ravagers than time; but now it is as much exposed as if it were a common hawthorn bush.

THE ECLIPSE IN AUGUST.—Major Tennant, we read in the *Athenæum*, is going out to India to observe the total eclipse of August 18, with a special view to photography and polarization; the cost of the expedition having been sanctioned by the Secretary of State for India. Major Tennant will be accompanied by three non-commissioned officers of the Royal Engineers, well exercised in photographic manipulation; so that good pictures of all that takes place during this almost unprecedented eclipse may be anticipated. The instruments will be set up at Guntoor or Masulipatam. Thus, with the party under Lieut. Herschel, which we mentioned a fortnight since, there will be two bodies of trained observers on watch for phenomena. The more the better; and it would be a great advantage to science if, along the whole line of the eclipse from Gondar to the New Hebrides, where the totality begins at sunset, parties were stationed to observe the eclipse hour by hour, from its commencement to its close. Such a series of observations would perhaps settle, once for all, the question as to the real nature of the red protuberances seen around the sun.

BEE SWARMS.—Bees swarm at various times and seasons. I have had a swarm as early as the 30th of April, and as late as the 23rd of September. One has left the hive at 7.45 a.m.; another at 4.48 p.m. One swarm has consisted of no more than 5,600 bees; another could boast of an army of colonists, 27,000 strong. Notwithstanding the decision of bee-writers to the contrary, I have had a good swarm two days before the appearance of drones; and I have also had a swarm that did not leave the parent stock till the drones had appeared sixty-five days. Honey-collecting is about as much dependent upon the weather as hay-making. I have known a nice swarm, after having improved every opportunity, starved to death at the end of three months; and I have had a swarm which collected five-and-a-half pounds of honey in one day, and at the end of five days had reached the weight of a good winter's stock.—*Leisure Hour.*

AUSTRALIAN BAOBAB.—By far the most remarkable form in the vegetation of North-West Australia is the Gouty-Stem tree (Adansonia Gregorii); but it is restricted to a limited tract of coast-country. It assumes precisely the bulky form of its only congener, the Monkey-Bread tree or Baobab of tropical Africa (Adansonia digitata), dissimilar mainly in having its nuts not suspended on long fruit-stalks. Evidence, though not conclusive, gained in Australia, when applied to the African Baobab, renders it improbable that the age of any individual tree now in existence dates from remote antiquity. This view is also held by Dr. G. Bennett, of Sydney. The tree is of economic importance. Its stem yields a mucilage indurating to a tragacanth-like gum. It is also one of the few trees which introduces the unwonted sight of deciduous foliage into the evergreen Australian vegetation.—*Dr. Mueller's Essay.*

VOLCANIC ACTIVITY.—The volcanic regions of the globe are in a state of unusual activity. Not long ago Hecla made a tremendous outburst; now Vesuvius is throwing up huge columns of fire, and showers of red-hot stones; eruptions in the West Indies are adding to the disastrous results of the hurricanes; and in Nicaragua blazing vents have opened near the base of the long extinct volcano, Rota, on the western, or Pacific, slope of the highlands. So bright was the blaze that it lit up the towers of the cathedral in the city of Leon, ten miles distant. What does all this mean? Is the fierce impulse travelling westwards, and shall we hear of its breaking out in the islands of the Pacific, and will there be great changes for geologists to record in the configuration of the earth's surface?—*Athenæum.*

ANECDOTE OF A DOG.—A gentleman residing in Birkenhead, having, a few days since, to pay some accounts, placed a very large sum of money in his coat pocket, and in running to catch the 'bus, he, by some unknown means, lost the money from his pocket, and did not discover the fact until he had gone some distance. After returning and using his utmost endeavours to find his lost cash, but in vain, he went home: where to his astonishment, he saw his dog Rover (who must have seen the money fall from his pocket, picked it up, and gone home with it) lying with it in his mouth and awaiting the return of his master, who had been absent for nearly eight hours.—Rev. F. O. Morris, in *Our Own Fireside.*

THE GOSHAWK.—One word about the goshawk. This, as most people know, is a slow, short-winged bird, larger than the peregrine. It is generally got from France or Germany. I have killed many rabbits with the female bird, and one—but only one —hare in my life. Disposition most unquestionably sulky; general conduct, until really in flying order, most temper-trying. But I like the goshawk,—fit as she is only for the slowest flights, stupid and troublesome as she is to train. I can imagine she has an attachment to her master when she knows him, and she can certainly take more rabbits in a day than the peregrine can take grouse.—*Saint Pauls.*

RATS.—These pests may be taken in any or all of the following ways:—1. Set your trap in a pan of meal or bran; cover it with meal and set the pan near the runways of the rats; or, 2, set the trap in a path at the mouth of the rat's hole, with a piece of thin brown paper or cloth spread smoothly over it; or, 3, make a runway for the rats by placing a box, barrel, or board near a wall, leaving room for them to pass, and set the trap in a passage, covered as before. In all cases the trap should be thoroughly smoked over a fire or heated over a stove before it is set, and at every resetting; but care should be taken not to overheat the trap so as to draw the temper of the spring. Also the position of the trap should be frequently changed.—*The Trapper's Guide.*

Remarks, Queries, &c.

(*Under this head we shall be happy to insert original Remarks, Queries, &c.*)

MORE ABOUT THE POTATO.

"*Should old acquaintance be forgot?*"

No sooner had the expeditions of Raleigh brought him into contact with the potato, than the promptings of civilised curiosity snatched it from the depths of American wilds; the agency of commerce brought the botanical stranger to Ireland; its edibleness and general utilitarian properties soon gave a new stimulus to agriculture; the exotic tuber in time became naturalised; and, again, commerce spread it far and wide. With the peasant, the poet, and the philosopher, the potato has been an interesting subject; for, while the great Linneaus was diligently lecturing the Swedes into the necessity of dignifying their agricultural pursuits by introducing the culture of the potato; and while Dr. Anderson in his laboratory was distilling his five quarts of "most agreeable vinous spirits" from seventy-two pounds of potatoes, our rustic poets at home were merrily singing:—

"The potatoes are boiling and that's a fine joke,
The herrings are coming in Dogherty's boat."

And one hundred and forty years ago, Gay, with some knowledge of our national proclivities, writes in rather limping verse:—

"Leek for the Welsh, to Dutchmen butter's dear,
Of hardy Irish swain potato is the cheer."

But the very names by which our favourite tube, the potato, has been known, are numerous and curious; some of them indeed we are half inclined to regard as a little outlandish, and others so profoundly classical that we would imagine our widely spread root had been the ambrosia of old, and had been plentifully cultivated in some sunny locality not far from Olympus centuries before the big ideas of Columbus were conceived. For Peter Cicca, in the year 1553, calls the potato *papas*, and affirms that it was then cultivated and eaten by the people of Quito. In 1598, Clusius calls it *taratoufli*, and he says that in his time it was introduced to Vienna from Flanders.

Thomas Harrist about the year 1586, calls the potato *openawk*, and thus describes it:—"These roots, some as large as a walnut, others much larger, are round; grow in damp soil, many hanging together as if fixed on ropes; they are good food either boiled or roasted."

The celebrated Lord Bacon calls them *potado* roots, and here is his philosophic plan of raising an abundant crop:—"If potado roots be set in a pot filled with earth, and then the pot with earth be set likewise within the ground some two or three inches, the roots will grow much greater than ordinary." What would our farmers of the present day say to this agricultural process?

The Indians of Virginia in Gerard's time called the potato *papus*, and the potato from the Cordilleras was called *arracha*, and *battata* was also a name by which the potato was well known; but when our scientific men take it in hand they call the simple potato *lycopersicon*, and sometimes too they term it *solanum-tuberosum*. And Gerard, that curious old writer, in speaking of the potato, says:—"This plant, which is called *lisarum Peruvianum*, or *skyrrists* of Peru, is generally with us called potatus or potatoes."

And I must not forget to mention the ludicrous derivation of potato given thirty-four years ago by an eccentric writer in the *Dublin Penny Journal*. He says:—"This name is not derived from the Spanish word *batata*, but has been given to it in merry Ireland, and is thus declined pot-eat-o's—that is what the O's—the O'Murphy and the O'Toole—eat out of a pot!" But while speaking of eating potatoes, I may here introduce the old herbalist Gerard's method of cooking them:—"They (the potatoes) are roasted in the ashes, and when they be so roasted infuse them and sop them in wine; and others, to give them the greater grace in eating, do boil them with prunes, and so eat them. And likewise others dresse (being first roasted) with oil, vinegar, and salt, and every man according to his taste and liking." And in old advertisements for cooks it is not uncommon to find that "None need apply who cannot cook a potato well!"

Among the advertisements in the *Pennsylvania Gazette*, published by the renowned Benjamin Franklin in 1756, is the following:—"Just imported, and sold by John Troy, master of the Snow Polly, a parcel of choice Irish potatoes, and a few good servant men and women, at Mr. Sim's wharf, near Market-street."

So late as 1807 Pitman, an agriculturist in Essex, England, sent annually to the market 3000 tons of potatoes, *all washed and ready for sale*. It is by some supposed that the Spaniards brought the potato from Quito at a very early date. Indeed some writers assert that the potato was known in Ireland in 1566, just three hundred years ago; others maintain that Sir Francis Drake, or Sir Walter Raleigh, had the good luck to introduce it.

But, like many other great discoveries, the introduction of the potato is attributed to several men, and accordingly are Sir Thomas Granville, and a man named Lane, who was the first Governor of Virginia, honoured as the earliest importers of the potato. The claims are strongest on the side of Raleigh, because he is best known perhaps; and one of the old Cork street ballads thus records the claims of Sir Walter and the merits of the potato:—

"By Raleigh 'twas planted in Youghal so gay,
And Munster potatoes are famed to this day,
Ballinamona oro,
A laughing red apple for me."

And it is even confidently asserted that the first potatoes introduced to England were accidentally cast on shore from a wrecked vessel at North Meols in Lancashire, a place still famous for its excellent potatoes.

In Sweden, Charles Skytes, in 1747, in order to save corn, proposed to distil brandy from potatoes, but their cultivation in that country was greatly neglected till about the year 1764. Thomas Prentice, in 1728, was the first man in Scotland that had the courage to plant potatoes in the open field. He set them at a place called Kilsyth; but their cultivation had been cautiously and sparingly introduced so early as 1683. In England in 1619, potatoes were an uncommon luxury, even at the Queen's table, and were sold at a shilling a pound. Kirkpatrick, an English agriculturist, and a real epicurean in the potato way, so late as 1796, writes:—"No gentleman who wishes for early potatoes will think the price 'five shillings a pound' too high!" Ireland has long been proverbial for the most excellent potatoes. Even in the time of Dean Swift they were with us common food, for that rollicking divine, in one of his cynical moods, says:—"The families of farmers in Ireland live upon buttermilk and potatoes." Some years ago I saw an honest countryman drain his glass in high humour to the very paradoxical toast of "Here is a speedy downfall to Ireland's best friends!" A fall in the price of potatoes was simply implied in the witty enigmatical toast. In the time of Shakespeare kissing comfits were made of potatoes, for he makes Flastaff say:—

"Let it rain potatoes and hail kissing comfits."

But our own rustic carol is still more expressive and poetic:—

"The sweetest divarshin that's under the sun
Is to sit by the fire till the prates are done."

It is well-known that at one time the people of

Burgandy looked on the potato as poisonous, and in their wisdom interdicted its culture. But let us hear old Gerard on the potato, and look at his queer orthography :—"The potatoes grow in India, Barbarie and Spaine, and other hotte regions, of which I planted divers rootes in my garden, where they flourished until winter, at which time they perished and rotted. The potato roots are among the Spaniards, Italians, and many other nations, common and ordinary meate, which, no doubt, are of mightie nourishing parts, and do strength and comfort nature ; whose nutriment is, as it were, a mean between flesh and fruit. Of these roots may be made conserves no less toothsome, wholesome, and daintie, than of the flesh quinces. And likewise those comfortable and delicate meates called in shops *morselli placentulae*, and divers others such like." H. H. ULIDIA.
Dromore, June 2.

EGGS OF INSECTS.—The eggs of insects are, as a rule, always laid in, on, or near substances upon which the future larvæ may feed, and their minuteness must in a great measure protect them from birds and other enemies, although such is not uniformly the case.

Small as they are, however, they cannot always escape the eyes of certain small ichneumons—*Microgaster ovulorum* in particular, the female of which introduces an egg into them by means of her long ovipositor ; and when the parasitical larva emerges, it feeds upon the other embryo larva.

Insect eggs being so small, and apparently so frail, it might be supposed that their greatest enemy would be the weather, but their nature is such that they are enabled to support with impunity a wonderful amout of extreme heat and extreme cold.

Spallanzani, in experimenting on the eggs of the "silk moth" (*Bombyx mori*), and subjecting them to various degrees of artificial heat, found that they did not quite lose their vitality till 144° Fahrenheit, whilst they bore without injury an artificial cold of 23° below zero.

The eggs are, moreover, generally protected from the inclemency of the weather by the way they are laid, for the parent insects, with an instinct which might easily be confounded with foresight or reason, generally deposits them close to the midrib or on the axil of the leaf, so that the danger of their being destroyed is lessened.

The female of some species—the "gipsy" moth (*Liparis dispar*), for instance, whose eggs have to bear the severe cold of winter—plucks, by means of a kind of tweezers, with which the end of her abdomen is provided, the hair or down from the extremity of her body, and wraps each egg separately in it, and when all are laid, covers the mass with the same down in such a manner that the rain or frost cannot penetrate.

Others, such as the lacky moth (*Bombyx neustria*) and the small egger (*Eriogaster lanestris*), lay their eggs round a twig of hawthorn or other plants, and cover them with a kind of varnish, which effectually protects them from wet and cold.

Very often, also, eggs owe their security to their colour resembling the substances upon or in which they are laid ; and no doubt the way in which the female insect frequently disperses her eggs tends to prevent the extermination of the species.

The eggs of the "cockroaches" (*Blattidæ*) are laid in a very peculiar way, being enclosed altogether, but in separate cells, in a kind of case or capsule, in shape of a kidney, consisting of a tough substance called *chitine* ; this case the female carries at the end of her abdomen until all the eggs are laid, after which it is deposited in some safe place.

The lace-wing fly (*Chrysopa reticulata*), whose larvæ feeds upon aphides, lays her eggs on plants infested with these plant-lice in a curious manner. She attaches a drop of a gummy substance to the stem or branch, and drawing it out to the length of about an inch, deposits an egg at the extremity. In this way the egg is safe from attacks of larvæ of the lady-birds (*Coccinellidæ*) or of the *Syrphi*. The footstalks of the eggs are placed at intervals along the stems.

The care and ingenuity which bees and wasps evince for the safety of their future progeny from the attacks of parasites and other enemies, as well as the solicitude with which the ichneumons provide for the well-being of their offspring, is truly wonderful.

Lastly, I may mention that the eggs of such insects as bees, wasps, &c., which live in community, are so carefully laid and jealously guarded, that there is little danger of their being attacked by parasites and other foes.—*Naturalist's Circular, June.*

PARASITES ON INSECTS, AND OTHER ANIMALS.—For the information of your correspondent, who mentions, page 259, his observations about the house-fly parasite, we observe that this parasite is well known, and described in books on that subject, is even quite common in some localities, and has nothing to do with the transmission of contagious diseases. As far as our present knowledge on the last subject extends, it appears that the organic structures which undoubtedly propagate contagion belong to a much lower stage of organisation than parasites ; one so small as to be only visible with the strongest magnifying powers, and their germs, seeds, or eggs, escape our most careful research altogether, as they appear to be present in the very dust of the air we breathe. The only fact known in relation to flies and cholera morbus is, that it has been observed in many localities that at the time this disease was raging the usual number of flies was either entirely absent, or at least considerably diminished, which is an additional proof that flies are scavengers of the atmosphere. In regard to insect parasites in general, the species which infect the fly is called *Acarus*. The smallest *Acarus* is found on the clothes-moth, the largest on the beetle. They are all very similar to the so-called chicken-louse, and also resemble slightly the cheese-mite. They are usually blind, have two or four suckers or points at their heads, and, like spiders, eight legs, which are commonly arranged two and two, close together. The ticks, lice, fleas, bed-bugs, etc., etc., have to the contrary eyes and only six legs, and belong to a different and higher order. The most curious of these parasites is the one which selects the respiratory orifice of the common garden snail ; it slips through the opening the moment the snail dilates it to respire air, and lays eggs in the interior membrane, where they are developed. The young, after being hatched, feed upon a portion of the snail's body.

The watersnail is tormented by a parasite of the *Distoma*, which attaches itself by a series of hooks to any part of the body or mantle. They sometimes surround the whole animal like tufts of thread. Divers reptiles, like serpents, and even fish, are affected by parasites, who attach themselves to the fins or tail and slowly destroy these parts of the suffering animal. They are often observed among fish captive in an aquarium, and I once found on such a parasite, who had grown large and fat in destroying a small fish in one of the aquariums I used to have in operation, in the Cooper Union in this city, a second parasite who lived on the first. These parasites of parasites are a great curiosity, however, not so very uncommon; they are repeatedly observed by industrious investigators.

In a hygienic point of view the study of this subject is most important, and at the present day undergoes a thorough investigation by observers, aided by the most powerful microscopes. To give the reader an idea of this field of research, I will only name some of the varieties of parasites found on different animals.

Docophorus ictervides, found on every species of ducks; *Neimus obscurus*, found on sand pipers, godwits, etc., etc.; *Neimus rufus*, found on hawks, falcons; *Docophorus lari*, found on gull tribe; *Trichodeites sealaris*, found on oxen, asses; *Tediculus capitis*, found on head of man; *Tediculus vertimenti*, found on clothes of man; *Tediculus tabescentium*, found on bodies of men dying of marasmus; *Tediculus inguinalis*, found on groins, armpits, beards of man; *Acarus scabiei*, the itch insect; *Sarcoptes scabiei*, produce the scab in sheep, and has lately been discovered to be the cause of the mange in dogs. In one pintfull from a dog suffering from this disease as many as thirty or forty of these parasites were found.

I could fill with such lists several columns of this paper, to show how thoroughly the subject is being investigated. I will only add that of all these parasites, and several hundreds more, their habits have been described, their mode of propagation, number of eggs, time and manner of hatching, means of their extermination, etc., etc. They infest most of our articles of food, flour, cheese, sugar, dried figs, and other saccharine fruit; others live on contents of our insect collections, butterflies, etc., etc.; others in the crusts of ulcers, etc., etc.

I refer those who wish to know more on the subject to Rheidi's work, "Treatise de Generatione Insectorum," and Denni's "Monographia Anaplurorum Britanniæ." Bohn: London. — *Scientific American*, May, 1868.

THE CAMBERWELL BEAUTY.—You are no doubt aware of the rapid strides that have taken place in the entomological kingdom during the last half century, or perhaps I shall be more correct and better understood by saying, that a little world of collectors of insects has sprung into existence during the last fifty years. I am unable to give the exact numbe just now; but let it suffice to say that myself may b counted among a small number of those that appeared on the stage at the earliest part of that time with as strong a *penchant* for the capture of insects as ever possessed the mind of an entomological maniac. It must be understood that at the time alluded to the collectors of insects would be about in the same proportion as the Purple Emperor and the Garden Tiger Moth compared with each other at the present day: that is, in the former time rather scarce, and in the latter very numerous; and the real scientific entomologist of course much rarer at all periods of time.

It would occupy too much time and space to give the readers of the NOTE BOOK anything like an account of the journeys that I have made, and the various successes or mishaps that I have experienced, during a period of fifty years collecting of moths and butterflies, and therefore upon this occasion I will confine myself merely to an occurrence in my youthful days, which is as follows :—Some acquaintance knowing my predilection towards the insect tribe introduced me to an old gentleman who had spent much of his life in the same pursuit. I can well remember his showing me a number of his captures, many of which were pinned into frames and hung round the little room as pictures of insects. I was of course much delighted with the sight, and also with the additional knowledge of how many beautiful specimens might be procured by a few walks into the country. My attention was particularly arrested by the beautiful specimens of the Camberwell Beauty with which these pictures were so numerously adorned. I believe I should be within the truth if I were to say that the frames of insects in this little room exhibited from twenty to thirty of these splendid insects (*Vaneses Antropus*). I of course had not arrived at any knowledge about scarcity or common in insect; but being struck over these fine insects, I ventured to ask where I might hope to capture some of the Camberwell Beauties, upon which the old gentleman, with a shake of the head, breathed out, "Ah! I can only tell you, young man, where I used to take them in great plenty some forty or fifty years back, but have not been able to procure them myself since that time. What you see in these cases I collected within a few miles of London, mostly about Camberwell and the Battersea Fields, where I could at that time have soon filled a collecting-box with them in the autumn of the year; but they seem to have passed away now, and I seldom see one on the wing. In fact I have been drawing them from some of these pictures to supply gentlemen who are forming collections in their cabinet drawers; indeed, the insect seems to be going out altogether." And truly I found it so, as I have not seen more than one or two solitary specimens during fifty years' collecting, and but for the circumstance now related should have supposed that they had always been as rare as at the present time; but such I am convinced could not have been the case, as I believe the man I allude to was a truthful and honest collector of British insects. I think his name appears in some entomological work in connection with an insect, where he is mentioned as the discoverer of it in the New Forest. I believe the insect is alluded to by Haworth or Damoville, and the old collector's name, Daniel Bydder.

320, Strand.   C. W——D.

Do Insects Feel Pain?—Since the writing of my last letter I have reconsidered the subject, and will now with your permission cite a few examples in support of and as illustrations to the theory I therein upheld. The portion of my subject on which I shall now advert is "the tenacity wherewith insects cling to life, resulting from the essential difference observable in insect organisation to all human anatomy." A few years ago whilst in the country I captured a fine large specimen of *Arctus Caja* (Tiger Moth) which I took to a chemist's to be killed, but it proved rather a tougher customer than might have been reasonably anticipated. It was dosed with chloroform, and pinned down upon a card. It was apparently dead, but next morning revealed the truth. Far from being dead, the insect was perfectly alive, had disengaged the pin from the card, and was vigorously executing the "dance of death" on its scaffold. Now if this had been instead a human being the dose would I think have affected him *slightly* more. I have lately, however, witnessed a far more forcible example. At Tunbridge Wells a few weeks since I captured an unusually large-sized dragon-fly, as it measured about three inches and a half across the wings. This (there being no general naturalist there) I took, as in the previous case, to a chemist's to be killed, who *successively* but not *successfully* drugged it with vapour of ammonia, chloroform, and finally with that virulent poison prussic acid; but all in vain, the insect was stupified, but not destroyed. Yet the illustrations I have just quoted are only two out of many more equally striking and remarkable.

Dragon-flies are in general, I believe, especially difficult to kill on account of their large size and proportionate great strength. However, the examples which I have just cited prove I think satisfactorily the vitality of insects. But what could those contortions of the "pinned down" insects have implied, so different to any of their movements when free? Possibly they felt uncomfortable. A staunch upholder of the "non-pain-feeling theory" would deny that they could possibly have experienced any feelings of discomfort. But what, then, can be the inducement offered to an insect to fly away at the approach of man, though it may have remained motionless for hours previously? The same individual, or one of the same class, would argue that it is the direction of *instinct* only which yet guides them. I cannot but think that where instinct displays itself thus prominently *pain* must also reside. It is evident that if we deny that insects feel pain, we must also deny that they experience sensations of pleasure, even at the appearance of the bright genial summer which bids *them* also appear. Granting this be true, what gross dissimulators must insects be, apparently possessing feelings which they in reality have not (?), when wherein consists the superiority of insects over inanimate things?

Entomologicus.

This question, asked by your correspondent "Entomologicus," is one which, though worthy of the greatest attention, seems incapable of being decidedly settled either one way or another. We have no means of forming an opinion as to whether insects experience pain at all, except by observing their movements under certain conditions. Most animals have voices whereby to express the sensations of pain or pleasure, but with insects the case is very different; in either event, their only means of signifying their feelings is by their movements. Now, Sir, I apprehend that we cannot, from merely seeing these movements, ascertain what may be the sensations which cause them. How do we know that they are those of pain?

We can only form our ideas of pain from the sensations produced on our own bodies; and seeing, as your correspondent remarks, how essentially different the anatomy of insects is from that of mammalia, I think that our own feelings can be no criterion of theirs, and that with such a difference in view, we have no starting point, which the two classes mammalia and insects have in common whereby to calculate what amount of feeling the latter class has.

Again. Many writers on entomology mention the extraordinary unconcern with which insects receive wounds and loss of members, which if inflicted on ourselves would, if not mortal, at least render us unfit for everything. The instances quoted are so numerous that I will not take up your space with mentioning any. Messrs. Kirby and Spence in their work on "Entomology" have cited many cases, which are well worth perusal. Now, if insects felt any pain under such circumstances would they not show it? Would they eat, drink, and perform their ordinary avocations if suffering any degree of pain? I think that this alone shows that they have extremely little if any feeling.

Lastly. When we consider to what endless persecution, danger, and slaughter, the insect world is subject, does it not seem like attributing *improvidence* to Providence to think that insects could have the same amount of sensation as we have! What endless misery would there be in one of the largest classes of animated Nature! The only conclusion I can arrive at is that insects feel no actual pain at all, at the same time admitting that this and all other theories of the kind can never reach any higher point, but must continue as opinions and theories to the end of time. But whether we think that insects have much or little pain, there would be no excuse for any cruelty practised on them: we know so little, that we cannot afford to injure any living creature because of an opinion founded on mere surmise.

London, June 15.—Arthur G. Harvie.

Deposit on Eggs.—"R. B. W." has himself solved the cause of the deposit on his eggs. The solution of corrosive sublimate was undoubtedly too strong; half an ounce would be enough for a quart or more of spirit, and if the camphor be left out the mixture will be equally efficacious. When applied to the inside of skins it does not matter how strong the solution is, but if used on furs, feathers, or especially insects, care must be taken not to make it too strong. Waterton recommends as a test that a black feather should be dipped in the solution, and then waved for a few minutes in the air, when it quickly dries, and if there be an excess of sublimate white specks appear, in this case more spirit must be added. The inside of eggs may be washed after blowing with the solution; but as Mr. Groom Napier directs in his notes (page 171) no outward application of any kind should be made, or the more delicate colours are sure to suffer.

Isinglass and gin would give a glaze to the surface which, to me at least, is an utter abomination. The only thing to be done is to keep the eggs as much as possible in the dark, especially immediately after blowing, when they are more liable to fade than at a later period. A small circular patch of paper gummed over the hole will exclude all insects, and I do not find any other precaution necessary unless "R. B. W." likes to keep a little musk in his drawers; this is very lasting and effectual. I can confidently recommend the egg drills made by Mr. Everard (whose present address, bye the bye, is 34, Berners-street, Oxford-street); they make very neat and safe holes, especially where large ones are required. On the subject of marking eggs opinions differ very much, and I have known collectors who refused to exchange with specimens which had inscriptions written on them, although neatly done. I certainly must admit that too many details do disfigure an egg, but every specimen should at least have a number, which will at once determine the species, and a date as reference to the collectors' note book; these need only occupy a very small space, as $\frac{2/6/68}{15\ B}$. Many authorities advise that these particulars be marked on the patch of paper, covering the blowing hole; but this does not seem to me to be nearly as satisfactory as if they are placed on the egg itself. J. S., JUNR.

THE COLOURS OF BIRDS' EGGS.—In page 94 of the NOTE BOOK, "J. D. S. W." introduces this exceedingly difficult subject, and as your clever correspondent, Mr. Napier, handles it so briefly, and "M. L. A." feels half inclined to doubt, I venture to give what Darwin said on the subject seventy years since, in his *Zoonomia*:—"It was shown in Section xv. on the Production of Ideas, that the moving organ of sense in some circumstances resembled the object which produced that motion. Hence it may be conceived that the *rete mucosum*, which is the extremity of the nerves of touch, may, by imitating the motions of the retina, become coloured. And thus like the fable of the cameleon, all animals may possess a tendency to be coloured somewhat like the colours they most inspect; and, finally, that colours may be thus given to the egg-shell by the imagination of the female parent; which shell is previously a mucous membrane, indued with irritability, without which it could not circulate its fluids, and increase in its bulk. Nor is this more wonderful than that a single idea of imagination should in an instant colour the whole surface of the body of a bright scarlet, as in the blush of shame, though by a very different process. In this intricate subject nothing but loose analogical conjecture can be had, which may, however, lead to future discoveries; but certain it is that both the change of the colour of animals to white in the winters of snowy countries, and the spots on birds' eggs, must have some efficient cause; since the uniformity of their production shows it cannot rise from a fortuitous concurrence of circumstances; and how is this efficient cause to be detected or explained, but from its analogy to other animal facts?" See with what caution Darwin approaches this very puzzling subject, and how he even reasons hypothetically. Have the progress and researches of seventy years added nothing to clear up this curious inquiry? H. H. ULIDIA.
Dromore.

SLUGS.—In your paper from *The Gardener's Chronicle*, upon Slugs, quoted in the November No. of THE NATURALIST'S NOTE BOOK of last year, it appears to me that a somewhat abundant pest (new to me) finds no place amongst the three mentioned garden slugs; the one I allude to is in form and size precisely the same as *arian ater* (large black slug), this one is of a light cream colour, having a buff caulter; it has no keel like the brown and tawny slug, often found in the gardens at St. John's Wood near London, and which I knew to my cost when leaving there about 12 years ago. There too is to be found 2 species of Testacelli—*T. haliatidea* and *T. Maugii*—the latter is nearly entirely brown, with a gray underside, and in its habits quite distinct from *T. haliatidea*. I could almost be sure, if required, find *T. Maugii* during winter and early spring, as it would bore a tube just large enough for its coffin, in the tubers of pianæ or salvia patens; this hole it would render dry and warm by a thick coating of slime. I have every reason to feel sure the hole was bored by the creature itself, as on October 4, 1844, I found upon taking up a plant of salvia patens a shallow hole begun, and in the surrounding earth a full grown *T. Maugii*. The root and slug I carefully placed in a large pot in the garden house, and upon removing the earth on one side the week following, I had the pleasure of seeing another hole nearly completed; the next week my friend had cased himself in for the winter, closing the mouth with a door in the same manner as the common garden snail (*Helix aspersa*). Should you think this account worth inserting in your "Note Book" I shall feel a pleasure in appearing in one of its pages.
Hale Vicarage LYDIA M. PRATTEN.

DRAGON FLIES (LIBELLULA.)—For the information of a "stout-bodied moth" I extract a few notes from Mudie's *British Naturalist*:—Of the dragon fly there are a great number of specimens, called water nymphs, horse stingers, adder bolts, &c. They vary in length from half an inch to two inches and a quarter. They are all remarkable in their appearance and gaudy in their colours. They are the most vigorous of British winged insects; have four long wings, and make a whizzing noise as they vibrate them in the air. They are usually seen about the margins of rivers, rivulets, and ponds, although they roam to a considerable distance in quest of food. They frequent flowers, not in search of honey, but to prey upon the flies there concealed. The usual way with the dragon fly is to pounce upon his victims while they are sitting, and for that purpose his favourite time for hunting is when the sun is clear. This fly has sometimes been observed to seize butterflies on the wing; but its staple article of food is the moths, which find shelter among the reeds, sedges, and other aquatic plants on the borders of rivers. I greatly fear our "stout-bodied moth," however venturesome, would be able to make but a feeble resistance to this formidable winged inhabitant of the air. He is among insects what the eagle is among birds. The female deposits her eggs in the water, and is then very apt to be captured by fish—particularly the salmon. The eggs fall to the bottom, and are soon hatched in the sand. The larvæ of dragon flies are of a dusky colour, inclining to brown or green. In this state they have six legs, ending in feet armed with claws. They feed voraciously on insects and their larvæ, and are even said to kill when they have no intention of eating. The dragon fly inhabits the water for about two years, changing from the first larva to the ultimate fly.

R. B. W.

MOTH TRAP.—In answer to "J. B." allow me to extract the following letter of mine from *Eyes and No Eyes*:—"A very ingenious moth trap is before me, lately manufactured by an American naturalist. It is a box of which three sides are Japan, and the fourth glass. At one end is a lamp with a powerful reflector; in the glass side opposite is a hole about four inches long and one wide, the glass being composed of four concave and converging pieces. The lamp is lit and the trap placed in the garden. A moth, attracted by the light, flies towards it, and into the hole: it never reaches the lamp, for from the top to the bottom of the trap, a piece of glass extends before it. At the bottom there is a drawer covered with slips of tin, placed at about an inch from one another: into this the moth falls, and as the tin acts like a Venetian blind, it remains quiet in the dark till next morning, when the collector pulls out his drawer and examines his insects. This trap is made in two sizes; the larger costs £2, the smaller £1 10s. It is procurable at Cooke's, in New Oxford-street." "J. B." may also obtain moths by breeding larvæ, digging for pupæ, and by beating bushes and trees, and spreading a cloth below, when he will probably obtain insects both in the imago and larva state. He may, too, *sugar* for Noctui, as described in most manuals of Lepidoptera, and in time may become like yours truly,

A WHOLESALE MURDERER OF BUTTERFLIES AND MOTHS.

THE SWALLOW.—A gentleman happening to know that I was always very fond of learning about the ways of birds and insects belonging to this country, gave me your last year's NOTE BOOK about these things; and I must say that I have been most wonderfully amused at the reading of it, and so I got all the rest that was printed. Now I see that all the gentlemen do not quite agree about the swallows—that is to say, whether they lay by or go away altogether in the cold weather; and, again, if so be they do go away, what do they go away for? Why, if they only look at page 80 in the NOTE BOOK for March last year, from Dumfrieshire, they will find that these creatures are apt to change their ways, according to circumstances: and isn't it likely that the poor little swallows did lay by in former times, as some of your learned men held out in their time. But you know that the earth has been sadly disturbed of late years by the making railroads across the country, by which the old ponds have been filled up and the old banks knocked down or buried in. Then the old pollard trees are made away with, so that perhaps the poor little things do go away now to get peace and rest in another country, just to miss being turned out in the winter, when no insects could be had, or else quite buried in altogether, so that they must remain. I trust that this will serve to throw some light upon the matter.

JEREMIAH SAWCUT.

MITES.—A short time ago, on opening a small collecting-box that had lain unused in a drawer for some time, I there found more insects than I had expected to find, and insects of a different order, viz., mites. After abusing my carelessness in leaving insects in the box without camphor, and congratulating myself that there was nothing of greater value there than a specimen of *Cynthia Cardui*, this question suggested itself —how did these mites get into this box? I turned to my Wood's "Natural History," no answer; and in Colman's "British Butterflies," no query of the sort was mooted. After meditating for some time I arrived at this conclusion—that mites must be ever wandering about, and by marvellous development of the sense of smelling can find out where their food is situated, even if it be in a closed box; and enter the box through some tiny crevice in the same. Against this theory the fact that mites are never (at least so I believe) seen on their rambles might be adduced; still they may travel, perhaps, underneath the surface of wood till they reach their destinations.

I should be much obliged to any entomologist who would give me (through medium of the NATURALIST'S NOTE BOOK) some information of the history of mites besides an answer to my *mighty* question.

"E. M." can get what he desires at Cooke's, 513, New Oxford Street, where he may also obtain Doubleday's "Synonyme *List of Butterflies and Moths*."

June 12, 1868.

A WHOLESALE MURDERER OF BUTTERFLIES AND MOTHS.

HARE AND RABBIT.—In No. 16 of the NOTE BOOK, "J. D. S. W." inquires if the hare and rabbit are ever crossed. They (the hare and rabbit) have been successfully crossed by M. Rouy, of Angoulême, who sends each year to market upwards of a thousand of these Leporides, as he calls them. His object was primarily commercial, not scientific: his experiments, extending from 1847 to the present time, have not only been of great commercial value—introducing a new and valuable breed—but have excited the attention of scientific men, who are now availing themselves of his skill and experience to help them in the solution of minor problems. It is enough to note here that these hybrids of the hare and the rabbit are fertile, not only with either hare or rabbit, but with each other.

T. W. TEMPANY.

"R. B. W." seems not to have noticed the article on this subject (taken from the *Field* of February 29th) on page 104, the April number of the NOTE BOOK.

W. H. D.

THE SUNFISH.—During the fine weather of this month of June sunfishes (*Orthagorisci*) have been several times observed on the coast of Cornwall; but in one instance, reported on the authority of a fisherman worthy of credit, the fish, which is believed to have been the species known as *O. oblongus*, was of a size not before recognised. By the fishermen it was at first supposed to be a floating wreck, as it lay basking on its side; and on approaching it, its length was seen to exceed that of the boat, which measured fifteen feet. They judged it to measure about twenty feet in length, and its eye they compared for breadth to the top of a man's hat. To capture this fish was impossible; but when the attempt was made to kill it, it dashed away with velocity. VIDEO.

SMALL HENS' EGG.—I have the egg of a hen laid last March which only measures an inch and three-eighths in length, and three-quarters of an inch in diameter. Its weight was 223½ grains, and 53½ grains when empty. Both yolk and white were present, the latter proportionally greater in quantity, and very viscid. The poultry wife told me that she had had them only half the size, and without a yolk; also that she once had a goose egg 11 inches by 9, which is preserved in some Museum at Halifax; but I think there must be some exaggeration in the measurement. If any of your readers would like the first-named specimen, I shall be most happy to send it; the first applicant being the fortunate one. Write direct to Keighley. W. H. DALTON.

EELS.—In answer to "Gulielmus," I may state that it is well-known that eels live in salt as well as in fresh water; and when young ascend our rivers in shoals. I took a walk to the mouth of the river Tees on the 31st of May, and in a pool of salt water left by the tide, I saw young eels and sticklebacks. It is thought by some that eels breed at the mouths of rivers. T. R. CLEPHAN.

"Gulielmus" may like to hear that a species of eel inhabits the ponds and ditches of the east coast of Essex, the water of which is constantly varying in saltness. W. H. D.

TAMING BIRDS.—It is stated on page 52, Vol. I., that the Chinese tame wild birds by suddenly immersing them in cold water. Now I have tried this experiment, but as yet without success. If this has been done in China, of course it can be done in this country. Again, on page 230 smoking of birds with tobacco is alluded to. It would be interesting if any of your readers could furnish instances of the above or similar means being used in the art of taming wild animals. R. B. W.

JACKDAWS CASTING "PELLETS."—Not only do domesticated jackdaws reject in the shape of pellets the indigestible portions of their food, but also in a wild state. This I have repeatedly observed both by examining their nesting place, and also by catching and confining the old birds. I have not been able to find out whether the rook has the same habit. R. B. W.

AIR-TIGHT BOXES.—"E. M." can obtain deal store boxes, corked top and bottom and air tight, 16 in. by 11 in., price 5s., or smaller at 2s. 6d. Also Doubleday's synonymic list of Lepidoptera of T. COOKE, Naturalist, 513, New Oxford Street. "F. W. Thompson" can get any bird's eggs at the same place. Can any of your subscribers tell me how to preserve the colour of dried flowers.
June 10th, 1868. R. M.

DOES THE SQUIRREL SUCK EGGS?—The common squirrel is often accused by gamekeepers and others of sucking the eggs of birds. Now, weasels and stoats, as is well known, are able to run up trees in pursuit of birds with great facility. May not such depredations be far more reasonably attributed to these rapacious animals than to the nut-eating squirrel? R. B. W.

THE GLOWWORM.—The *larva* of the common glowworm is luminous, although to a less extent than the perfect insect. I have kept these luminous larvæ until they changed to the pupa state, and ultimately became real shining glowworms. A non-entomological observer might mistake the larva for the imago, as they much resemble each other. GEORGE.

ALBINOS.—White specimens of the following birds have been seen:—Rook, jackdaw, swallow, martin, starling, thrush, blackbird, sky-lark, robin (nearly), house-sparrow; of animals, the common weasel, hare, rat, and shrew-mouse. Rabbits and hares completely black have been shot. Perhaps some of your readers may make additions to the above. R. B. W.

BUTTERFLIES.—On the 19th of May, just before a thunder shower, clouds of a species of white butterfly were noticed to settle on Hartlepool and Coatham Commons, on the east coast. Hundreds could have been caught. Could they have come from over the sea? T. R. CLEPHAN.

AGE OF THE NEGRO.—I have seen it stated that the negro, when free, has forty times as good a chance as the European of attaining the age of 100 years, and thirteen times as good a chance when in slavery. I should like to have the opinions of some of the learned correspondents of the NOTE BOOK on this subject. R. T.

REMARKABLE EGG.—Last summer I picked up in the poultry yard a most remarkable egg. It consisted of two globes, joined together by a small neck of skin. The curious thing was, that the yolk was in one globe, and the white or albumen, in the other; and it was altogether devoid of shell. Can you or any of your correspondents explain the circumstance. FOX.

SMALL EGGS.—In answer to "M. L. A." fowls very often lay their first eggs very small. I have seen a hen's as small as a sparrow's egg, and a pigeon's little larger than a wren's; in both cases it was their first egg. T. R. CLEPHAN.

LAPLAND BUNTING.—Can any of your numerous readers give me a description (however slight) of the colours of the above bird? And also inform me if the crocodile, cirl bunting, and rock pippit migrate or not. C. B. R.

MICE.—Some years ago the fringe of the altar cloth of my father's church was completely destroyed by mice, one of which was taken in the immediate neighbourhood of the table. W. H. D.

RAINFALL.—Have any readers of the NOTE BOOK witnessed the singular phenomenon of rain falling from a serene cloudless sky? R. T.

TO CORRESPONDENTS.

A WHOLESALE MURDERER OF BUTTERFLIES.—Your note on the American moth was never received.

VARIATIONS IN THE COLOUR, FORM, AND SIZE OF THE EGGS OF BIRDS.*

BY C. O. GROOM NAPIER, F.G.S.

Author of "The Food, Use, and Beauty of British Birds."

PART I.

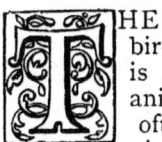HE variation in the appearance of birds' eggs being much greater than is general amongst other portions of animals of assumed species, it is often difficult on these grounds to give them a correct assignment. Much may be done, however, by ascertaining, as far as possible, the limits of variation; but here the student is met by a difficulty, that of the tendency of eggs of different species, or even widely separated genera, to approximate to one another, facts which, at any rate, prove how much is common to birds. The advocates for the origin of species by natural selection will find strong arguments for their theory in the resemblances which the eggs of different species sometimes bear to each other. The eggs and song of the blackbird (*Turdus merula*), usually so different from the song of the thrush (*T. musicus*), sometimes show a very strong resemblance. An egg of the blackbird which I now have, taken by myself, possesses none of the green tint and ochre spots characteristic of the blackbird, but the clear deep-blue green common to the eggs of the song thrush. On another occasion I remember hearing a male blackbird, in a cage, use notes so nearly resembling a song-thrush that I could hardly believe my ears. Could the force of imitation at once influence the song and the colouration of the egg?

The colouration theory advocated in Naumarium by M. Baldamus, supposes that an impression is made on the sensorium of the female cuckoo (*Cuculus canorus*) by the view of the tint of the eggs in the foster-parent's nest, which influences the colour of the eggs laid, and causes the expectant cuckoo's eggs to approximate in hue to the eggs of the foster bird. This is but an application of a popular belief, current in all ages, on which Jacob acted in his dealings with Laban's cattle, and which is even believed to affect the offspring of man. This resemblance, *if it exists*, between the eggs of the cuckoo and of the foster bird, is never such as to render any deception to man's eye at all easy, cuckoos' eggs being amongst the most singular. One object which I have heard brought forward in favour of this theory, is the desire on the part of the female cuckoo to avoid shocking the feelings of the little bird by a glaring intrusion. I have examined about eighty eggs of the cuckoo, which have been taken *in situ* with the eggs of the foster parents, and of these the larger portion, I must confess, do afford some ground for this theory. The influence of an examination of the eggs of a particular species on the female cuckoo might affect the colouring of several of her eggs, which, being dropped in the nests of more than one species, may occasion the apparent flaws in the evidence for the support of this theory. The influence of an empty nest, in which cuckoos sometimes lay, would be null. I will now state my own observations on the subject.

The greater portion of the eggs of the tree-pippit (*Anthus arboreus*), when fresh, have a reddish or grey-brown hue; these are very different colours. The eggs of the cuckoo accompanying them show more variation than is commonly seen with other birds. Four nests of the yellow-bunting (*Emberiza citronella*), containing eggs of this species and of the cuckoo, shewed the light-coloured ground without the tinge of green so common in cuckoo's eggs, and more than a dozen eggs of the cuckoo accompanying eggs of the red warbler shewed the green hue common to the eggs of the first-mentioned bird, and only two others displayed the red tint. The green hue I observed most common in eggs accompanying those of the hedge accentor, which are so eminently blue-green; but with them eggs of a red colour were occasionally found. The egg of the cuckoo in a goldfinch's nest had a light ground and light spots, another had dark spots. An egg of the cuckoo accompanying eggs of the house sparrow was very dark indeed, like the eggs found with it; and a good series of the eggs of the pied wagtail, with the accompanying cuckoo's egg, show, in a most striking manner, the approximation between the different species in colouring. Some of these eggs were fresh; others slightly incubated. My friend, Mr. G. D. Rowley, to whom I am indebted for many of the specimens in my collection, has contributed most interesting papers on this subject to the *Ibis* and *Zoologist*, in which he endeavours to controvert the theory of M. Baldamus. He supposes that the variation in colour, which the learned German attributes to female susceptibility, to be due to the period of incubation, which, however, will not account for one-third of the resemblances which I have observed.

SIZE AND COLOURING OF EGGS, *v.* THE AGE OF PARENTS.—I shall now state a few facts which I have observed with reference to the size and colouring of birds' eggs as apparently influenced by the age of the parents. A correspondent of mine mentioned a pair of golden eagles (*Aquila fulva*) which built on the side of a cliff in Transylvania. The old birds were shot, contrary to his desire, soon after the young could fly, which,

---

* Read before the British Association, 1866.

however, continued to roost on the parental rock. Absence from home prevented him from noticing their movements the next spring, but the year ensuing the birds, which turned out to be a male and female, had paired. They produced two eggs, which were of a very short oval for this species, and half-an-inch shorter than the same pair eventually produced, and wanted the symmetrical shape which the eggs of the same parents afterwards displayed. They were of a blueish-white colour, with a few spots or dots, but no washes of raw umber. The second year the eggs were three in number, and were the eighth of an inch longer. The third year the eggs were more richly marked and spotted with azure and ochre-brown, and were a quarter of an inch longer than the first. The fourth year the eggs were three in number, and, for the first time, richly marked, but did not exceed in size those of the third year. The fifth year the nest was harried by some person unknown, so that the appearance of the eggs could not be ascertained; but on the sixth and tenth years the eggs were two in number and richly marked with raw umber and burnt sienna. On the eleventh year the male was killed, and the female paired three weeks later in the season with one of her young ones of two years old. Her eggs were two in number, and very inferior to those of preceding years, they were somewhat richly marked, but in size did not exceed those of the first year. The eggs of these birds were mostly allowed to hatch, and the young taken from the nest before they were able to fly. The proportion of the sexes was pretty nearly equal, except in the brood last reared, which were females. This is another fact in confirmation of the theory of the effect of the predominance of age in either sex influencing that of offspring, which is so observable amongst domestic animals and man.*

Similar observations may be made with regard to domestic fowls. The little Bantam hen with the Dorking cock produces eggs which are almost too large for her to lay, and the Dorking hen with the Bantam cock produces eggs which are not very much larger than the normal eggs of the Bantam. An egg of the first-named cross was 2 in. 4-16ths long by 1 in. 9-16ths broad, while that of the normal Bantam is 1 in. 13-16ths by 1 in. 6-16ths broad, and the eggs of the Dorking hen and Bantam cock were the eighth of an inch more. The normal size of the eggs of the Dorking are 2 in. 7-16ths long by 1 in. 11-16ths wide.

I obtained a large series, nearly a hundred eggs, of the common buzzard from Ireland, principally from one county. Of these sittings those most richly marked were, with one exception, less in number of eggs than those which, in markings, did got exceed mediocrity. And the same increase in size and richness in markings and decrease in number, as the birds advanced in years, were observed, as related of the golden eagle. The first sitting of four eggs laid by birds of a year old were very faintly marked; the second, the ensuing year, and from the same pair of birds, consisted of five eggs more richly marked and considerably larger; the third year six eggs more richly marked than the preceding, and with a darker shade of brown were laid. I have made similar observations on the eggs of the common kite (*Milvus regalis*) and of the black kite (*M. ater*). One sitting of spotless eggs of the buzzard were of a second nest laid at the end of the season, being from birds of the second year; but another found by a correspondent of mine, of the first year's breeding, were one-half spotless, and the other faintly spotted. Amongst domestic poultry the eggs of very young birds are generally much more slender in shape; this is also very commonly the case with the eggs of birds in a wild state.

EXTREME VARIETIES IN EGGS.—The eggs of the spotted flycatcher (*Muscicapa grisola*) are subject to great variation. A sitting of five eggs most strongly coloured and richly marked were taken May 24th, 1862, by Mr. Dawson Rowley, after which the bird sat two days on the empty nest. This strong manifestation of the brooding instinct is interesting when taken in connection with the extreme richness of the markings in the eggs. How do the blue varieties of the eggs of gulls originate? I received a large series of the eggs of the black-headed gull from Scoulton-Mere, and have compared some thousand others, the dates of which had been carefully marked; the blue eggs were usually laid later in the season, and were more common amongst birds whose eggs had been taken once or twice previously. The dark eggs were mostly produced by birds which had been little disturbed, and were decidedly more abundant in the first sittings of old birds. The extremely dark eggs were fewer in number, being one less than is usual. I have made similar observations, but to a much more limited extent, on the eggs of the greater black-backed gull (*L. marinus*), lesser black-backed gull (*L. fuscus*), the herring gull (*L. argentatus*), and the skuæ (*Lestris caryactactes*).

The eggs of the raven most darkly and richly spotted, appear to be produced by old birds. One I have very green, with few spots, was laid as late as June. Eggs inferior in intensity of markings and thickness of shell are often the produce of unimpregnated birds. Some eggs of the kestrel I now have were laid by a virgin

---
* See the author's paper "On the Proportion of Male to Female Births" in the *Anthropological Journal*, Nos. 18 and 19, 1867.

female in the possession of my friend Mr. G. D. Rowley; they vary in size and richness. The brightness of the colouring is to be attributed to two reasons:—Firstly, its want of thickness, intense colours being more opaque and dark than those thinly distributed; and, secondly, to their not having been incubated, for incubation greatly tends to render dingy bright red, or other vivid colouring in eggs. I have here some specimens of the eggs of the kestrel which have been incubated, and which greatly contrast with the intensely bright red of those I have just mentioned. The eggs of the kestrel (*Falco tinnunculus*) are supposed to be very different from those of the sparrow-hawk (*F. nisus*), for the ground is not blueish-white, or the blotches large, and the egg is free from dark or nearly black points or spots. I have, however, an undoubted egg of the kestrel which has all the marks of that of the sparrow-hawk I have just described. The bright red observed on the eggs of the bearded vulture (*Gypætos barbatus*) by incubation is changed to a yellow hue, and that of the kestrel from a burnt sienna to a sort of olive red. I shall make a few remarks on spotless eggs of birds usually spotted. I have some fragments of the eggs of the kestrel, laid by the same female which I have previously mentioned, which are entirely white, without spots. I have seen eggs of the sparrow-hawk, usually so richly marked, entirely without spots. In these cases the eggs show an approximation to those of their allies—the little red-billed hawk (*Falco gaber*) and the harriers (*Circus*). The sparrow-hawk's eggs, usually so richly marked, contrast most strongly with those of the last-named species, which I have just said are usually spotless. But I lately saw a sitting of eggs of the red-billed hawk, one of which was faintly marked with pale yellow ochre, and was very much like the remarkable variety of the eggs of the sparrow-hawk which I have just described. It is as deficient as they are conspicuous in markings for the species. This is but another proof of generic affinities cropping out which often appear not to be maintained in a small series of eggs, but are so in a larger. The eggs of the missel-thrush (*Turdus viscivorous*) are usually extremely unlike those of the song-thrush, seldom having the clear deep blue-green ground, and being marked with light purple-brown spots; but here I have a variety taken in the neighbourhood of Bristol, in which the colour is bright blue-green, and the spots olive, which is sometimes approached in the eggs of the song-thrush. The eggs of the white-throat and garden-warbler approach each other in markings and colour in the varieties I have before me, although they usually differ so much. The eggs of the robin (*Sylvia rubecula*) and blackcap (*S. atricapilla*), although the types are so unlike, yet they approach in some varieties in my collection. The eggs of the wheat-ear (*Saxicolæ œnanthe*), being usually spotless, appear out of place amongst the chats, which are generally so markedly spotted; but I have two eggs which are distinctly marked like varieties of *S. leucomela*. The eggs of the willow-wren (*S. trochilus*) and those of the chiff-chaff (*S. rufa*) are usually very different; but in the varieties before me the line of demarcation is not strongly drawn, for the eggs are of the same ground colour, and the spots are similarly distributed, the principal difference being that those of the chiff-chaff are of a more violet tinge of colour, but in some other eggs of the chiff-chaff the spots are quite as red as in these eggs of the willow wren. The eggs of the starling (*Sturnus vulgaris*) are of a pale, clear, blue-green, unlike those of their ally, the rose-coloured pastor (*Pastor roseus*), which are nearly white. Mr. G. D. Rowley, however, took two eggs of the starling which could not be told from undoubted specimens of the rose-coloured pastor (*Pastor roseus*). The eggs of the pheasant (*Phasianus colchicus*) are usually of a pale olive green, but are sometimes white, in which they show a resemblance to the eggs of the francolin (*Perdix francolinus*), Hey's sand-partridge (*P. Heyii*), and the silver pheasant (*P. nycthemerus*). The eggs of the red grouse (*Tetrao Scoticus*) are almost always thickly spotted with strong colour; but I have one egg in which the ground is dirty white, without any distinct marking, thus showing an affinity with the unspotted eggs of the partridges and pheasants. The eggs of the stock-dove (*Columba œnas*) and wood-pigeon (*C. palumbus*) are often distinguishable by a cream colour which pervades the interior of the egg of the former when held up to the light; this is much less generally the case with the latter. I have, however, one egg of the wood-pigeon which has a strong yellow tinge in the interior, and one or two eggs of the stock-dove which have it in a less degree. The eggs of the lapwing (*Vanellus cristatus*) are usually pyriform, and very different in size from those of the black tern (*Sterna nigra*). I have, however, one which shews a strong resemblance to some varieties of the former species. It is a singularly marked egg, being of the size and shape of that of the common pratincole. It is greatly covered with large blotches of umber black, having contracted, as it were, within a small surface the colouring of a large egg.

SILURIA.

THE entrance to the Primordial zone is marked by a very apparent quickening of vitality. In the Menævian or lowest distinct formation of the great Silurian base, we mark the introduction of shell-fish,—the first known belonging to the Lingulæ, a family which, if a long pedigree be a proof of respectability, must be very respectable indeed, for it figured among the very earliest in creation, and has held its own, on to the present day. Here, too, comes upon the scene for the first time (though some obscure fossils seem to indicate that they lived in the preceding Longmynd era) the earliest distinct appearance of the Trilobites—beings so entirely unlike anything now existing, and so distinctively peculiar to the primeval ages,—for the whole group had passed away for ever from creation before the close of the Palæozoic period,—that it is impossible not to regard their remains as quite the most interesting relics which the more ancient rocks have preserved.

Perhaps there is no creature we are familiar with that gives us so good an idea of the trilobites as the common woodlouse; and if we imagine his armour-plated back, instead of showing only one arch or lobe from side to side to be tri-lobed, and his legs absent; and further, if we make him capable of assuming a Protean variety of size and shape, now no larger than a house fly, and now as big as a good sized lobster, now bristling all over with spikes and spines, and now as sleek and smooth as a dolphin; in some cases possessing simple, and in other compound eyes of surpassing beauty and mechanism, we shall be able to form a very fair idea of the creatures which filled the place of our present lobsters and crabs in the primeval ocean. The eye of one genus of these crustaceans—the Phacops has long been regarded as one of the wonders of the ancient world, and is often cited as an example of what has been philosophically inferred from a single fossil, as may be gathered from the following well-known words of the late Dr. Buckland:—

"With respect to the waters (of the Palæozoic seas), we conclude that they must have been pure and transparent enough to allow the passage of light to organs of vision, the nature of which is so fully disclosed by the state of perfection in which they are preserved. With regard to the atmosphere, also, we infer that, had it differed materially from its actual condition, it might have so far affected the rays of light, that a corresponding difference from the eyes of existing crustaceans would have been found in the organs on which the impressions of such rays were then received. Regarding light itself, also, we learn from the resemblance of these most ancient organizations to existing eyes, that the mutual relations of light to the eye, and of the eye to light, were the same at the time when crustaceans, endowed with the faculty of vision, were first placed at the bottom of the primeval seas, as at the present moment."

But the basement rocks of the Silurian system not only contain several genera of these fantastic-looking creatures—some of them being the largest and most highly ornamented of any of the family—but likewise shells of the Brachiopod and Pteropod classes, and some sponges, together with the earliest examples of another exclusively Silurian form—the Cystideans—of whose appearance an idea may be gained by imagining a sea-urchin minus its prickles, growing tulip-fashion, on the top of a jointed foot-stalk. As we ascend into the "Upper Lingula flags" we observe an increasing profusion of crustacea—including an extraordinary specimen of the Phyllopod tribe.

It has often surprised us that the Arenig formation should ever have been grouped with the Llandeilo, and still more that it should have been called the *Lower Llandeilo*, seeing that its organisms, as Lyell tells us, are "all differing in *species* from the so-called 'Upper' Llandeilo." If, however, our anticipation should prove correct, that it will be found advisable sooner or later to date the Lower Silurians proper from the latter formation, then these Arenig rocks will fall into a more natural position as constituting the summit of the great "Primordial" base of the Silurian system, which, from the fact of their *genera* being characteristically Silurian, would certainly appear to be their true place. Now for the first time the fauna is joined by the Encrinites or sea-lilies—the feather-flowers of the Nereides' gardens—and the most graceful of all the forms of marine life; and a family, moreover, which has managed to keep its footing, though now in sadly reduced circumstances, up to the present day, being still to be found in the West Indies, while one diminished member of it, the pretty little *Comatula rosacea*, or Rosy Feather-star, has been fished up by Mr. Gosse on the Devonshire coast. Another very curious class of zoophytes begins now to appear, particularly where the sea-bottom shows a muddy rather than a sandy nature, and this is the Graptolites, related, it is surmised, to the existing Sea-pens, Virgularia and Pennatula of our own seas, and showing in their fossil state a wonderful variety of extraordinary forms; some looking more like a delicate saw made of a piece of watch-spring than anything else; sometimes straight with short teeth, and sometimes loosely coiled with long ones. Some species are serrated on one side only, others on both, while some still more eccentric in their appearance, as if anticipating the forms of vegetable life, branch off into two or more arms, or even do their best to look as much as possible like leaves. From the abundance of their remains in certain situations, these zoophytes must have formed quite little forests in the Silurian seas, but they are distinctively Silurian, never appearing beyond the limits of those rocks, while as a rule the branched varieties are confined to the lower division of the system, and the simple ones to the upper.

From this stage the fauna peculiar to the Lower Silurian age appears in all its luxuriance, exhibiting a decided change as it passes from the Llandeilo to the Caradoc, when many new forms, and amongst them the star-fishes, are added ; and the language of the rocks now becomes so distinct as to give us tolerably clear indications as to the aspect our island must have presented at this period, as well as to afford us a vast deal of information concerning the aboriginal inhabitants. The western tracts of England in the Caradoc period were covered by a shallow ocean, with here and there a low island rising out of it, these islands being the tops of the Malverns, the Shropshire and the Welsh mountains, and some of the Cornish hills ; all else was a waste of waters in which no fish ever swam, and whose surf was the only sound to break the eternal silence.

Even what had been divided from the waters showed no sign of vegetation, for God had not yet said, "Let the earth bring forth grass, and herb yielding seed after its kind ;" and the only representatives of the vegetable kingdom were the Thallogens of the tidal waters. Strangely low would have been the aspect of life we should have beheld, could we have bent down and gazed into the transparent depths of that primeval ocean, nothing higher in the scale than creatures corresponding to the crabs and cuttle-fish of our own seas! The waters, indeed, are teeming with lower forms of life ; Trilobites of all shapes and sizes, and especially the pretty little Trinucleus with its dotted fringe and trailing spines, crawl by thousands in the stiller creeks and shallows, now rudely pushing their way amongst the foot-stalks of waving Lingula, and now disturbing colonies of Graptolites, intent on seeking their food amongst the silt, and possibly finding in the sea-worms the prey best suited to their taste. The Molluscs, too, are exceedingly abundant, showing all the five classes whose shells were capable of preservation ; for, of course, the Tunicates would stand no more chance of being immortalized in this way than a sea-anemone. The Conchifera, now so common in modern waters, appear, though sparingly, and the Pteropods, who pass their lives in the open sea, were then, as they always have been, the smallest group of all ; though, if the Tentaculites belong to it, which is uncertain, they make up in individual numbers for a paucity of species. The Brachiopods, so scarce in recent seas, form the prevalent class, and include the Atrypa, Discina, and Lingula, many beautiful species of Orthis, the earliest known Rhynconella, and the newly-introduced genus of Strophomena. Large Gasteropods, both coiled and spiral, exhibit high types of shell beauty, while every now and then a huge Orthoceras drifts by to the consternation of the Trilobites large and small, spine-armed and smooth alike, who well know that for all his looks of flabby inactivity, the embrace of those flexible arms of his is certain death to them, while we are shown that even the primeval seas swarmed with tyrants of the same class, and quite as formidable as M. Victor Hugo's octopus.

A decided change, as we have already pointed out, comes over the Llandovery rocks which overlie the Caradoc. We are now met by many indications that we have left the region of Lower Siluria, and are passing through a group of intermediate or transitional character, preparatory to entering Upper Siluria. This change is seen not only in the composition of the strata, which get more gravelly and sandy and less muddy than they were, but in the appearance of the animal remains entombed in them ; and these, while they still show in the inferior division many Lower Silurian forms (though most of the older Trilobites have disappeared) are, in the superior member of the group, unquestionably more connected with those of Upper Siluria.—*British Quarterly Review*, July.

WOODLAND BUTTERFLIES.
By E. J. S. Clifford.

NUMEROUS and striking as are the butterflies frequenting our fields and pastures, those which are attached to the woodlands are scarcely less so. In our last we brought the more conspicuous of the former before our readers ; in the present paper we intend to change the scene from grassy fields to blooming, flowery woods, where butterfly beauty forms one of the most attractive features that can charm the rural wanderer. It is by no means surprising that butterflies are so plenteous in our woodlands, for they seem of all scenery to be the most congenial to their habits and tastes. Let us glance briefly, therefore, at some of the more interesting and beautiful of our woodland butterflies.

Wandering at early morn through some of the Kentish woods, we may not unlikely come across one of the most elegant and fragile of our native butterflies, the Wood White (*Leucophasia Sinapis*.) This insect varies oftentimes in respect of the black tip of the wings, which in some cases is entirely wanting. Its flight is very lethargic, and it therefore becomes a very easy matter to capture it when once it is seen. The caterpillar producing it is green, striped on each side with yellow. It feeds on the birds-foot trefoil, and some other leguminous plants. May and

August are the months in which to look for the Wood White, which has ere now been taken as near to London as Epping, Brighton, and West Wickham, although it appears to be unknown in Scotland. Another highly interesting species is that called the Marbled White (*Arge Galathea*). Many would be disposed to class this insect with the "Whites," both from its name, and the similarity, in some points, of its colouring, but from them it may be readily distinguished by the possession of only four walking legs, instead of six, and also by the eye-like spots visible on the under side of the wings. The colouring of this handsome frequenter of our woods is creamy white, marbled with black. On the under side, however, the cream colour greatly predominates, and is merely intersected with black lines. The Marbled White is a local species. Many entomologists who have not seen this insect for years, are found coming suddenly upon it in some unlooked-for locality, and are both surprised and delighted by its profusion. And a group of these marbled creatures disporting on a wooded hillside, must indeed be a sight, once seen, not readily forgotten. The caterpillar of the Marbled White feeds on grasses, and, like others of its tribe, it is green, with yellow side stripes, and reddish head and tail. July and August are the months in which to hunt for this most charming of woodland flutterers, partial to wood clearings and the roads adjacent to woods.

A lovely and a common butterfly in the woodlands during this month, is the Speckled Wood (*Lasiommata Ægeria*). In coppiced paths, where the bluebell and the scabious peep forth, and numberless little woodland blossoms send forth their odours on the air, there it is that this speckled flutterer winds in and out amongst the trees, staying anon to sip honey from some charming floweret as he passes. This insect, too, it is, that all who have wandered through such scenery must have observed flying just a little ahead of them, as if wishing to keep them company, and then suddenly mounting over their heads, lost in the windings of the flowery path. This butterfly is also termed the Wood Argus, receiving the latter name Argus, "the many-eyed," from the rich black, eyelike markings that grace its wings. The Speckled Wood is distributed over nearly the whole of England, commonly occurring in wooded country, but it is quite unknown in Scotland. The colouring of the wings consists of deep brown, spotted and speckled with various shades of lighter brown. The eyes on the wings are velvety black, with a pure white centre spot. The caterpillar of this butterfly, like that of the last, is a grass feeder, and the chrysalis may not unfrequently be found under trees, attached to blades of grass. The butterfly itself is on the wing throughout the summer, from April to August. Next we are reminded of the Ringlet butterfly (*Hipparchia Hyperanthus*), one of those species in which the chief adornment of the wings is reserved for the under surface. The wings above are of a sepia brown, surrounded by a greyish-white fringe, and bearing several black spots in paler rings. These rings are not so distinct in the male as in the female butterfly. But the under surface of the Ringlet forms a tableau of extreme beauty. It is adorned with a wreath of the ringlet spots from which the insect derives its name. Much variety exists with regard to these markings in specimens from time to time turning up, and one not very uncommon has no light rings round the black spots on the under side. This butterfly is peculiarly attached to shady recesses in the woods, and the verdant hedgerows around them.

The White Admiral butterfly (*Liminitis Sybilla*) is a rare and a beautiful denizen of our woodlands. It is more usually taken in the shady coppices of Essex, Sussex, Suffolk, Hampshire and Kent than in other counties. This insect is remarkable for its elegant flight and graceful outline. Its colouring, or rather the disposition of its markings, reminds us of its relative, the Red Admiral, only that the bands on the wings are white instead of being red. It seems that this butterfly rather avoids the sunbeams, and frequents more especially the glades of our woodlands, where its beautiful evolutions, and placid sailing through the air, are really delightful to behold. The under surface of the White Admiral is a piece of the most exquisite combination of colours imaginable. It consists of silvery blue and golden brown shaded with a cooler brown and black, and these placed in lively contrast with spots and bands of pure white. The caterpillar of this favourite insect feeds on the honeysuckle, and is a singular creature, with reddish spines, and white and brown side stripes. The favourite resorts of this species are oakwoods in the southern counties, as already intimated. Here, also, we *may* find that most handsome of butterflies, the Purple Emperor (*Apatura Iris*), to which has been rightly accorded the highest place amongst the British RHOPALOCERA. A glimpse of this high-flying species, however, is about all that we can expect to get, in however favourable a locality we may happen to be placed. It is indeed a sight well fitted to inspire the entomologist with ardour and delight, for of all species this is the grandest, both in flight and colour. We read that not unfrequently the Purple Emperor has been lured from his post amidst the tops of the old oak trees, to banquet on some decaying fruits placed on the ground below, and thus entrapped to his destruction. His capture by means of a net seems certainly a hopeless task, since the length of the handle must inevitably render the implement very unwieldy, and consequently difficult to manage. It is the wings of the male alone which possess that glow of rich, imperial purple from which the insect has derived its name and honour. The female butterfly possesses merely a sober garb of brown, but she considerably exceeds her lord in expanse of wing and general dimensions. She, however, is rarely captured, we believe, by collectors, who usually take about ten males to one female. The under side of the Purple Emperor is also very beautiful, consisting of a lively arrangement of orange, brown, grey, and black. The firm muscular wings give promise of great strength in those organs, and this is fully supported by the bird-like flight of these creatures, which have the habit of soaring about midday to vast heights in the air, where they engage in sportive gambols with their brother butterflies. July is the month for this king amongst butterflies, more particularly attached to southern woods.

The "Fritillaries" are especially the butterflies of the woodland scenery. The largest and handsomest is the Silver-washed Fritillary (*Argynnis Paphia*) occurring during the months of July and August. The upper surface of the wings, consisting of black and brown, is so arranged as to produce a most delicate chequered appearance, and the under side is indeed a complication of the most exquisite markings. The harmony of the silvery pencillings, whence the insect derives its name, with the iridescent green, is very beautiful. The two sexes of this species vary considerably on the upper surface, the male being marked with black upon a bright orange brown ground, while the female is destitute of the black borders to the veinings of the front wings, and the ground colour is suffused with olive brown, inclining sometimes to green. Beneath, however, both sexes are pretty much alike, possessing washy streaks of silver, and not spots, like others of this genus. The Dark Green Fritillary (*Argynnis Aglaia*), is a most handsome butterfly, though less in size than the last mentioned. It is somewhat rarer than it, also, but is equally partial to woodland scenery. The under surface of the hind wings is beautifully studded with spots of silver and tawny ground colour. In July and August this species, like the last, wings its superb flight in the *locales* wherein it most delights, and is somewhat difficult, from its rapid movements, to secure. The Pearl-bordered Fritillary (*Argynnis Euphrosyne*) is another instance of this tribe of native butterflies, attaching to our woodlands. This is a comparatively common species, and hence has become a favourite with all young insect collectors. It is considerably less than either of those just noticed, and its wings are rather longer in form than theirs. The caterpillar feeds on the various species of *Viola* occurring in the woods. The Pearl-bordered Fritillary is found in Scotland, though in Ireland we believe it to be unknown. The Small Pearl-bordered Fritillary (*Argynnis Selene*) is the last we can now enumerate of this interesting group. It is very nearly related to the last, and closely resembles it in its markings of the upper side. The distinctive characteristics lie on the under surface of the hind wings, for in addition to the silver border and central spots of *Euphrosyne*, this species has several other silvery or pearly patches distributed over the hind wings; the red colour, also, adjoining the silver border in *Euphrosyne* is supplied by chestnut colour in *Selene*. There is but little difference in the respective sizes of the two insects. This, like the last, is double-brooded, and has a range nearly as extensive.

Next let us look for a while at some of the "Hairstreak" butterflies. First and most striking amongst them we notice the brilliant little Purple Hairstreak (*Thecla Quercus*) which seems like a Purple Emperor in miniature, and which is rather generally diffused in southern woods. It possesses a rich gloss of the imperial colour, which, in certain lights, looks exceedingly beautiful. For, at first sight, the wings appear brown, but, with a change of position, they become illuminated with a purple radiance, extending over nearly the whole surface, excepting a narrow border, which then looks quite black. In the female butterfly, strange to say, the purple, though more vivid, is confined to a small patch extending from the base to the centre of the front wings. The caterpillar of this superb little creature feeds on the oak; it is reddish brown, marked with black. The chrysalis is sometimes found attached to leaves of the oak, at others *under* the surface of the earth at the foot of the tree whereon as caterpillar it had fed, an unusual circumstance in regard to the butterflies. The Purple Hairstreak is a high flier, but occasionally descends within reach of the net, and has not unfrequently been taken gambolling around hedgerows adjacent to woodland country. The Brown Hairstreak (*Thecla Betulæ*) is another beautiful woodland butterfly. This is the largest of its genus. It appears during this month, continuing on the wing during September. It is found in oak woods in company with the Purple Emperor, and was at one time taken in abundance in some parts of Sussex.

Lastly, in this paper, we advert to the "Blues" and the "Skippers," some of which are especially woodland denizens. The sweet little Bedford Blue (*Polyommatus Alsus*) is always found in or near woods. It is the least of all our

British butterflies, and might be readily mistaken by the inexperienced for some other insect. The caterpillar of the Bedford Blue is green, with an orange stripe down the back, and streaks of a similar colour on each side. May and June are the two principal months for this butterfly, although it is sometimes seen much later. The Silver-studded Blue (*Polyommatus Ægon*) is a very exquisite species. Its caterpillar, which is similar in shape to most of its order, feeds on the broom, and other allied plants. July and August are the two months in which to look for this butterfly, which is attached to many of the southern woods.

Finally, then, there are two species of the "Skipper" tribe, which we have observed as partial to the woodlands. The first is the Dingy Skipper (*Thanaos Tages*) a dull gray butterfly, with bands of a darker colour, and possessing a row of white dots near the border. The caterpillar of this species feeds on the bird's-foot trefoil, and is pale green, with yellow lines and black spots. The Small Skipper (*Pamphila Linea*) is perhaps the most common of its family, and is certainly a lively little creature. This insect is widely distributed throughout our woods, occurring plentifully during the present month. With it we take our leave of our woodland butterflies, although many others might have been added to our list. Those, however, which have been selected, seem to have the greatest demand upon our attention, both from beauty and peculiarity of economy. We remark, in conclusion, that of all our *Lepidoptera* the butterflies are the most interesting; and that few though they be, there still remains very much to be discovered of their structure, habits, and economy.

NOTES ON LILIES.

VERY desirable is it that some botanist would do for Lilies what the late Mr. Haworth did for the Narcissi. The genus, indeed, is a good one, and ought not to be broken up, but some of the species are either bad or insufficiently discriminated. This work of revision would be best performed by a botanist-cultivator, as the French call him—a collector resident near the metropolis, and having free access to books, and especially to living plants. Of course, such a student would consult herbaria, and standard books, as Redouté's "Liliaceæ;" but the decisive appeal must be made to living specimens. Some authors, for example, confound the common Orange Lily and the bulb-bearing Orange Lily; but they cannot have compared the plants in a growing state, and certainly have never examined the bulbs. If the reform alluded to does not come soon, the labours of hybridisers will render it extremely difficult, if not impossible, a result which florists probably would not much regret. The following notes are in the florist interest :—

L. pomponium, and its variety *L. pyrenaicum*, are now seldom seen in flower gardens. They do not possess much beauty, their flowers emit an unpleasant odour, and they are mostly relegated to the shrubbery. *L. Martagon* may be allowed to go along with them; being very robust it is well adapted to the wild or semi-wild parts of pleasure grounds. I have seen it growing luxuriantly in the wooded gorge of a deep valley, by the side of a considerable stream, where it propagated itself and sported into a diversity of tints. There is a white variety in cultivation. The scarlet Turk's-cap (*L. chalcedonicum*) is more of a garden plant, and thrives well in any dry sunny nook if left undisturbed, but is impatient of frequent removals. There is a tall, robust variety with a cymose or fastigiate inflorescence. To this group may be added *L. monadelphum superbum*. I give the name which, with the plant, has emanated in Scotland, from the Botanic Garden in Edinburgh. It is certainly monadelphous, as the broad-winged filaments of the stamens cohere at the edges. It may be loosely described as a gigantic *L. pyrenaicum*, only the tops of the petals are less reflected. In the deep moist soil of my garden it multiplies freely, and throws up numerous stems 4 or 5 feet in height, crowned with loose corymbs of from 10 to 16 brilliant canary-coloured flowers. Towards the end of June it is an extremely showy plant.

L. tigrinum is well known, and is valuable as one of the latest of the Lilies. The Poet Laureate speaks of it as a sign of the departing year, asking in winter, "Where is now the Tiger Lily?" The variety introduced by Mr. Fortune being one-half taller, and about 10 days later in flowering, is a most desirable plant.

The American species, *L. superbum, canadense,* and *penduliflorum* are very beautiful, but are difficult to keep in a satisfactory state, at least in the northern districts of the country. It is usually said that they should be grown in a deep peaty border. To this advice I would add, that they should be planted in the full sunshine, and in the warmest nook of the flower garden. What they want in this country is the bright glowing summer of Upper Canada and the Northern States of America. *L. philadephicum*, I believe, belongs to this section, but I have not seen it. *L. colchicum* is a very beautiful species, rare in gardens, and requiring much the same treatment as the preceding. Relays of them all should be kept in pots, and it should be remembered that they sometimes continue dormant for a year. This year I was obliged to bring on my potted superbum by a little bottom heat.

The Orange Lily group is a brilliant one. It is composed of *L. aurantiacum, bulbiferum, umbellatum, kamtschatense, pennsylvanicum,* and, perhaps, some others. The varieties are numerous, and some of them are as intense in colour as the finest Ghent Azaleas. They are for the most part very hardy. *L. pennsylvanicum* is an elegant miniature form of the common Orange Lily, but specifically different. It thrives well in light peaty earth.

L. candidum has been loved as the Lily, *par excellence*, by many generations. It has long been associated with pictures of the Virgin,

"The Lily of Eden's fragrant shade."

For simple statuesque beauty it is, perhaps, unrivalled in the empire of Flora. Only the single variety ought to be cultivated. It thrives perfectly in light and moderately dry soils. To show the capricious effects of situation, I may mention that, to my great regret, I cannot keep this favourite Lily. Being a semi-herbaceous plant, or rather having green leaves above ground, it is regularly killed by damps and frosts in winter. Its congeners, *L. longiflorum* and *japonicum*, with their numerous varieties, which are daily increasing, are surpassingly beautiful plants, but they are rather tender for the general climate of Great Britain. They afford admirable decoration for greenhouses and conservatories; and where there is room a store of them should be kept in cold frames or pits. For several summers I have plunged out *L. longiflorum*, and repotted it in the autumn. It is needful to replace it in the pots before the leaves have withered, for previous to that stage the young shoots for next year start from the bulbs, and then the fibrous roots are injured by the lifting. My success in this matter has not been great. Probably the plan would succeed better in the south.

L. excelsum, or what I got for it from an eminent London nurseryman, has thriven well with me. It is quite hardy. It throws up a stem 4 feet high, which hitherto has been crowned by a single shallow bell of considerable size. The colour is pure white, but the interior of the petals is often soiled in wet weather by the abundant brown pollen, which, I suppose, accounts for the nursery synonymes *L. testaceum, isabellinum,* &c. It is an attractive plant, but not equal to its great Himalayan compatriot, *L. giganteum.* The latter has repeatedly stood the winter and flowered in the open air in the nursery of Messrs. Dickson & Co., Edinburgh, who have also raised many plants from seeds saved in this country. It is a great seed-bearer, and it is to be hoped that in the hands of hybridisers it will yet yield magnificent results.

I say nothing of the gorgeous and well-known *L. auratum*, and the scarcely inferior *L. speciosum*, or *lancifolium* as it is often called. Who will tell us something of *L. carolinianum, concolor, croceum, pumilum, monadelphum* (of the "Botanical Magazine"), *tenuifolium, pseudo-tigrinum, cordifolium, Buschianum, Thompsonianum, Wallichianum,* &c.? Are they extant in this country? Or must some of them be sought aagin in their native habitats?

It will be observed that I have spoken only of the more common hardy species, and probably I have said nothing but what is well known to many. My most important remark, which I put as young ladies do in the postscript, is this, that most Lilies, even those of the hardiest sorts, are weakened by frequent transplantation. *L. chalcedonicum* takes two, sometimes three years to recover the effects of a removal. I suppose the fibrous roots under the scaly bulbs are not merely annual rootlets, as in most other bulbous plants. From this remark a skilful gardener will readily draw his own practical conclusions. It will be perceived that it can be little better than death to Lilies for their scaly bulbs to lie withering on the counters of seed warehouses, where Tulips, Crocuses, &c., may continue for a long time with impunity.—*Dr. Smith, Ecclesmachan, in "Florist and Pomologist."*

SUMMER IN THE ORKNEYS.

MAY-TIME in Orkney resembles April in the Scottish Lowlands, and the fine freshness of the season kindles an irresistible longing to wander forth among the fields and moors, to climb the brown slopes of heathy hills, or to saunter aimlessly along the sea-shore. As we walk abroad the eye is gladdened by the tender green of the grass, the ploughman following his team, the sower with measured tread and swinging arm scattering the seed abroad, and all those familiar accompaniments of rural labour which leave so many pleasant pictures and impressions on the mind. Not less charming and gladsome are the sounds that salute the ear. Like Miriam and her maidens, summer has come with timbrels and with dances, and overhead the blue vault of heaven rings with the rich running raptures of countless larks. The Islands at this season can almost afford to want the woodlands with their vocal verdure when the sky seems to dissolve in drops of liquid melody. The shower of enraptured song falls over the green and furrowed fields, mingles with the murmur of the sea on the shelly shore, and comes wafted to the ear in trembling notes from the far-off heathy slopes of the hills. The skylark—beautifully addressed by the Ettrick Shepherd as the "bird of the wilderness, blithesome and cumberless"—

is the chief songster of Orkney, and he fears no rivals as he sings and soars. Mingling with the minstrelsy of the lark, the mellow note of the cuckoo, soft and low as a dream-voice, may be heard issuing at times from some sheltered patch of stunted copse-wood. From the fields bordering on the moors and low-lying lands, where pools and rushes abound, there comes another pleasant voice of summer—the plaintive cry of lapwings wheeling about in eccentric circles and suddenly swooping to the ground on creaking wings. As the nests of these birds lie exposed on the surface of the soil, and may thus easily be found by marauding farm-boys, Nature has endowed them with a curious and cunning instinct that enables them to feign distress, and so decoy stragglers from their eggs or young brood. It is interesting to watch the evolutions of this strange instinct, and observe how the birds suddenly fall in their flight with shivering wings and plaintive cry, only that they may rise again with graceful curve, and repeat the same beautiful deception. From the abundance of moor-and-marsh land, Orkney is a favourite haunt of the lapwing. It is a migratory bird, spending the winter in the south of England, or across the channel; but it is not unusual for some pairs to remain in the Islands all the year round. There is touching beauty in the plaint of the lapwing as it shrills over the moors in the long summer gloamings. Like the peewit, the ringed plover is a frequenter of marshy places, running rapidly up the grassy hillocks as you approach its retreats, and giving utterance to a soft, whistling cry as it whirls away on the wing. The solitariest nooks and corners touched by wandering foot are also enlivened by the presence of the brown heather linnet, the redshank, with its delicately-pencilled plumage, and the little wheatear, that darts from mound to mound emitting a sharp harsh note. I have noted that the voices of birds have ever something in common with the loneliness or loveliness of their haunts and homes. Seabirds utter a wild, dreary wail that blends harmoniously with the mournful monotone of the deep; the cry of the bittern rises like a natural exhalation from the desolate pool; the plaint of the lapwing accords with the wild brown waste of the moors; and the blackbird's song seems the mellow voice of the luxuriant summer woods.

While song-birds are comparatively few in number, the varieties of sea-fowl and water-fowl impart great interest to the ornithology of Orkney. The fresh-water lochs and marshlands are the favourite haunts of water-hens, coots, teals, widgeons, mallards, shieldrakes, garganeys, grebes and wild ducks. The sea-fowl include, among others, the puffin, cormorant, little auk, and several varieties of divers, guillemots, gulls, and skuas. Many of the fowls are birds of passage, some of them spending the summer and others the winter in the Islands. Wild swans, though fewer now than formerly, come in October from the North. The shieldrake (*anas tadorna*) and the barnacle make their appearance in spring; the eider-duck and brent-goose frequent solitary sounds in winter, while the Iceland gull is seldom seen till the month of May. After midsummer the golden plover, which arrives in large numbers from the north, may be seen haunting the moors and low shores, and sharing the solitudes with curlews and whimbrels and birds of the sandpiper species. Of the land and water birds which remain about the Islands all the season, the most numerous are the dunlin, dotterel, tern, turnstone, redshank, oyster-catcher, and several varieties of the gull and duck tribes. The red-necked phalarope (*tringa hyperborea*) visits the most northerly island of the group about the middle of June, and departs early in September. This bird, which is remarkably graceful in its motions, frequents the lochs, making its nest among the reeds, and laying four eggs of a dingy olive colour with brown spots. A species of sea-fowl, called the horra-goose, from its loud harsh cry, arrives in Deersound, Hoy Sound, and Westray Firth towards the end of December and remains till the close of February.

The local names of aquatic birds are peculiar, some of them being evidently of Norse origin. The cormorant is called the scarff, and a similar name seems to be in use in Faroe. The author of "A Fortnight in Faroe," when alluding to the small tongue of the cormorant, says that Faroese parents frighten a noisy child by asking: "*Qvuj rear skarvur tunguleisur?*" "Why is the scarff tongueless?" and then go on with the answer, "*Tuj han seje Ravenum fra qvear Eavan alti*": "Because he told the raven where the eider-duck's nest was." The black guillemot, which fishes in the firths in all weathers, the common guillemot, the diver, the shieldrake, the long-tailed duck, the razor-bill, and the puffin, are known in Orkney by the names of the *teistie, skout, loon, sly-goose, caloo, baukie,* and *Tammy Norrie*. To Orcadians the scarff, teistie, and common gull may be regarded as supplying the place of the swallow, robin-redbreast, and common crow, which only pay occasional visits to the islands. Foreign birds, of beautiful plumage, driven by stress of weather over leagues of sea, not unfrequently take refuge in the district of Deerness on the East Mainland. Weary with their long storm-driven flight, and bewildered in a strange land, these poor birds almost invariably fall an easy prey to murderous fowlers. After a continuance of north-easterly gales, such rare birds as the goatsucker, the golden-crested wren, and the snowy owl, are occasionally found in the remote island of North Ronaldshay. Four years ago a magnificent Demoiselle crane, belonging to a species which haunts the shores of the Mediterranean, was cruelly slaughtered in the district of Deerness, and the publicity given to the circumstance, originated a discussion in the *Times* on the barbarism of bird-murder. From its position Orkney affords favourable opportunities for observing, at certain seasons, the migratory flights of birds. Seated on a rock by the seashore, or lying outstretched on the heathy hillside, and looking up into the blue expanse, I have often seen the figures of birds fanning the "cold thin atmosphere," in wavering lines or single file. Sometimes a faithful pair may be descried winging their way in company to Norwegian fiords or southern lakes, and sometimes also—sublime, touching, and mysterious sight—the eye catches the form of a solitary water-fowl floating silently and steadily onward, and casting no shadow on land or sea.—*Gorrie's Summers and Winters in the Orkneys.*

MIGRATION *viâ* HYBERNATION.

The migratory habits existing among the feathered race is a feature in their history that has led to a vast number of speculative and curious conjectures, and it is not a little remarkable that the observations recorded from time to time have for the most part been confined to a species or genera of birds that of all others are perhaps the most highly gifted by nature with the powers of locomotion, namely the swallow tribe. It is not easy to imagine what could have induced so great a naturalist as the immortal Linnæus to conclude upon the hybernation of swallows in particular, unless we can comprehend the difficulty under which he laboured for the want of co-operation and faithful assistance in his great and arduous undertaking. But it is by no means remarkable that an opinion embraced or enunciated by so high an authority as Linnæus should at that period have been readily assisted to and adopted by his followers.

The latter position we find most strikingly authenticated in Letter XII. in White's History of Selbourne, where he plainly states that a Swedish Naturalist is so much persuaded of that fact that he talks in his "Calendar of Flora" as familiarly of the swallows going under water in the beginning of September as he would of his poultry going to roost a little before sunset.

It is no wonder that Gilbert White did feel somewhat astonished at the boldness and confidence with which such a theory was supported. Although we are led to conclude from his own writings that he did himself rather cherish the notion of hybernation, at least of some few individuals among the swallow tribe, yet in justice to his memory we must not charge him with trying to enforce a theory upon mankind contrary to his own experience, as no man was more cautious than himself upon that point. Although it may be true from what he had observed that he could scarcely reconcile it with the migration of the swallows in toto, yet he was too discreet to take anything for granted without sufficient reason, and too conscientious to state as a fact that which he was unable to demonstrate. It was doubtless the unseasonable appearance of some of the swallow kind that acted most strongly upon the mind of Gilbert White, namely a bird or two observed on the wing very late in the autumn of the year, and also after the appearance of a few birds rather early in the spring, than their being lost sight of for a few days or a week, and suddenly appearing again as the weather became more congenial to their nature.

These circumstances combined perhaps with the prevailing opinion of that period that the swallows did actually hybernate and pass the cold season under water, did likely bias his mind towards the theory of hybernation. It might not have occurred to him that the birds seen lingering about late in the year and also at times the first comers in the spring would in all probability perish from the inauspicious state of the weather, which is clearly the case at times. This circumstance has been adverted to and well explained by Mr. J. B. Water at page 53 in the NOTE BOOK, observations which I can most fully endorse from my own acquaintance with the habits of the migratory birds while in this country, as I have upon several occasions met with instances where the swallow kind have been picked up in an exhausted condition from the inclemency of the weather; these cases have mostly occurred when the weather in March and the early part of April had been bright and warm, and then suddenly changing to frost and snow, with all the appearance of midwinter for a few days. In such cases, doubtless many of our spring visitors do perish from the cold or the want of insect support, although it would be a matter of chance whether a tithe of these sufferers would come directly under our own notice.

I could if necessary give several remarkable instances of this kind, and also adduce many witnesses to confirm the foregoing statements, but I will now pass on to a few remarks bearing more directly upon the theory of hybernation. At page 27 in the NOTE BOOK for the present year, Mr. F. A. Allen refers the readers interested in the subject to a series of articles appearing in "Hardwick's Science Gossip," written by himself and others in support of the theory of hybernation.

I have availed myself of this advice, and must confess that I am truly indebted to that gentleman for a fund of information, which otherwise it is likely would never have come under my notice or perusal. Although I had spent many years in the country, and bid farewell to the swallows in the autumn, and likewise greeted their return or appearance with much pleasure in the spring, yet I must own that I was rather at a loss to know where these harbingers of spring had been spending their merry Christmasses. From one or two of these articles I now learn that many of the swallows do retire beneath the surface of the water, and there fall into a profound slumber or lethergetic state during the cold and uncomfortable months of winter. Some are described as being found separately with their beaks placed down upon their breast, giving them the happy appearance of a shoemaker's awl, while others are said to be found with beak to beak, wing to wing, and foot to foot, &c.; and one Etmuller, a Professor of Leipzic, asserts that he found more than a bushel measure of swallows closely clustered together under the reeds of a fish pond and under the ice. But we must leave these imaginary swallows to the fate that would I think most likely befall many of them from the predatory foragers of the waters in so apparently insecure a situation.

Again we are informed that dormant swallows have been met with in old dry walls and in sandhills, while some are said to have retired to old hollow trees to pass away the comfortless months of winter. We are also informed that at Whitby in Yorkshire whole bushels of swallows were found in digging out a fox, and others were observed clinging to the shaft of an old lead mine.

But leaving these discoveries, which appear to have been more the habits of the birds of byegone times, we arrive at something of more recent date, and therefore more chance of being confirmed by living witnesses. A Mr. Dobree states that in 1845 while engaged in pulling down an old building he found six swallows in a state of torpidity, that he took them to his residence in his pocket, and placing them near the fire they were all found in the morning perched upon the kitchen grate chirping as in the spring of the year. This must indeed have been a very pleasing and interesting sight, but we must leave them for the present to the amusement of the family where the circumstance occurred, and proceed to notice the case recorded of seven barrow loads of swallows being turned out in excavating for the North Midland line of Railway. We may be allowed as we pass on to remark that this was indeed a most extraordinary occurrence, and could not by any means be reconciled with the few stragglers that have been observed lingering about at a late period of the autumn, as they must have amounted at least to several thousands of birds. And in reading this statement I can only regret that Mr. F. A. Allen or myself was not upon the spot at the time, not merely as eye witnesses to the fact, but that such an opportunity was lost of forwarding at least a few dozen of these dozing swallows to such unbelievers in hybernation as Mr. Gould and Professor Owen. As although they might not believe if even one swallow rose from the dead, yet they could not have remained callous to such an undeniable proof of the hybernation of at least a portion of the Hirundines.

I will now leave these considerations to the more learned Ornithologists—

As no matter what my argument, no matter what my will,
If their nature is to hybernate, they surely do so still.

By way of conclusion I would observe that some gentlemen who appear to take an interest in the hybernation of the swallow tribe asks for some striking proof of their not doing so. I therefore beg to state that from my own experience in habits of the feathered race I should not have thought it, having noticed that when the swallow kind congregate at the latter part of the year nearly three-fourths of them are young birds in their immature and nestling plumage, and the old ones are much worn and soiled. But when they make their appearance in the spring they are I think without exception clothed in a first rate adult and beautiful plumage. I will not contend that this is a decided proof one way or the other; but undergo a moulting, I must think they certainly do somewhere: whether under water, in old banks or underground is the question. But I would venture to ask, at all events, when and where it is probable that this beautiful change in the plumage is effected. C. W.

TIGERS.

THERE appears to be every reason to believe that at least *two* distinct species are now in existence. One found about the N. and NE. extremity of the Great Wall of China and in the Corea, having a rough hairy coat, which was considered by the late Dr. Falconer to be identical with the fossil species *Felis spelæus*; and the other, the well-known Indian 'Bagh' the Royal Tiger as it is often called, from its having been the device of more than one Indian dynasty now counted amongst the things of the past.

Many of the Shikaree, or native hunters of India, assert the existence of two distinct varieties of the latter species; one they describe as being very long in the body and short in the legs, very active, noted for its enormous springs, and extremely ferocious; the other of ordinary make, less fierce, and much more frequently met with.

Tigers, like the generality of wild animals, appear to be much influenced by the nature of the localities they frequent, those of the plains being on the average considerably larger than those of hilly countries; to which circumstance, and to the individual peculiarities of certain animals, we may perhaps trace the belief just referred to, in which, however, some writers still concur.

Tigers are confined to the Asiatic continent; though there their habitat appears to be far more widely extended than is generally supposed. They are said to have been found in the thickly wooded province of Mazanderan, south of the Caspian Sea, and about 1,000 miles west of the Punjaub. Be this as it may, we have the authority of Mr. Layard for asserting, that they have been found as far west as a range of hills running from the Gulf of Cambay towards Delhi. They are met with in most parts of the vast continent which we now include under the general appellation of India; in the wide swampy plains of Burmah and Pegu, where they are especially abundant, as they are also in some of the islands of the Archipelago; while to the eastward they range as far as Siberia and the north-west portions of China. Mr. Atkinson, who vouches for their existence in the last-named localities, in his recently published works, has not, however, furnished us with much information respecting their habits and appearance. An examination of any good physical map will show the wide area, as well as the great differences of altitude, temperature, &c., thus embraced in the habitat of the tiger.

A good many interesting details touching this animal have been published, from which, it would appear, the following deductions may be drawn:—

First, that in confinement these animals are *thinner* than those in a state of nature (our correspondent states that at least one quarter should be added to the weight of the former to give a fair estimate of the latter).

Secondly, so far as can be ascertained, four to six hundredweight may be taken as the average weight of an ordinary sized full-grown tiger in most parts of India.

A consideration of the weight of a full-sized tiger has led some writers to question whether it *ever* springs so as to have all four feet off the ground at once. This, however, appears to admit of no doubt whatever; and although, like the lion, he most frequently carries off great weights by trailing them along the ground, there are cases on trustworthy record where a tiger has cleared a jump of fifteen feet or more with a bullock in his jaws.

This extreme agility, and the adaptability of the animal's structure to withstand the most violent shocks, are only two out of many points in which its affinity to the domestic cat may be noticed.

The voice is another point in which this similarity may be traced, though it has hitherto escaped the observation of naturalists. The deep bass growl, with its many modulations, is known to all who have seen the animal in captivity; but there are two other cat-like noises which we believe are only heard from animals in a wild state, viz. a short fierce snort or grunt, emitted as the tiger springs on his victim, and a terribly harsh raucous '*miiaow*,' which appears to be the call of the male to the female. In the tactics of the two species the same resemblance subsists.

Although instances are occasionally met with when cattle and even men have been carried off by tigers in the open and in broad daylight, they are exceptions to the general rule. Like most of his congeners, the tiger attacks by stealth, crouching under cover near some frequented pool, and springing on his victims as they approach to quench their thirst. He almost invariably springs at the neck, and an examination of the bodies of animals thus killed usually shows that death was caused by a crushing of the vertebræ, and was probably instantaneous.—*The People's Magazine*, for July, 1868.

THE SUN.

The cloud-like nature of the sun's surface follows, moreover, from the nature of the sun's light. This increase of our knowledge we owe to those immortal discovers Kirchhoff and Bunsen, whose wonderful generalization of the results of spectrum analysis has given the present century a new fulcrum wherewith to move the great unknown by the lever of inquiry, and bring it into the light. Their beautiful discovery has happily been described so often and so clearly that the readers of *Macmillan* do not require a detailed notice of it here. Suffice it to remark that not only does it enable us to define the sun as the nearest star and to detect some ten terrestrial elements as existing in a state of vapour in its surrounding, absorbing, and therefore cooler atmosphere; but it enables us to state, as a proved fact, that the light of the sun proceeds from solid or liquid particles in a state of intense incandescence or glowing heat. We shall shortly have occasion to refer again to this method of research: the more recent work regarding the spots demands attention, however, beforehand, in order that we may follow as much as possible the order of time. It has already been stated that the early observers detected that the apparent motion of the spots was due to the real motion of rotation of the sun. But this account of their motion we now know is not all the truth. In addition to this motion they have a motion of their own of such a nature that the nearer a spot is to the sun's equator the faster it travels; in fact the rate of this proper motion depends upon the latitude of the spot. This was one of the chief results deduced by Mr. Carrington from an elaborate daily investigation of the sun extending over six years, a stupendous work unsurpassed in the acumen and patience brought to the task, and rarely equalled in the results achieved. This discovery of the proper motion of the spots at once explained the strange discrepancies in the time of the sun's rotation as given by different observers—discrepancies so great that Delambre declared it was useless to continue observations. Mr. Carrington's work did not stand alone about this time. The great Schwabe had previously determined that if the spotted area were taken at any one time, its amount varied from year to year,—that is, that the spots themselves were periodical; having periods of maximum and periods of minimum, the interval between two maximum or minimum periods being about eleven years. The lamented Dawes and Father Secchi largely increased our knowledge of the solar surface, the latter determining specially that there was less heat radiated from a spot than from the general surface. Some time after Mr. Carrington's book appeared, M. Faye took up the question of solar physics with his usual elaborate treatment, and communicated to the Paris Academy of Sciences two papers of great value, in which, *inter alia*, he broached a new theory to account for the observed phenomena, and especially to explain the dark appearances presented by the spots. M. Faye regards the interior of the sun as consisting of the original nebula from which our whole system has been slowly condensed, in a state of dissociation; that is, at such an intense heat that chemical combinations are impossible; and he looks upon the photosphere as the surface at which this heat is so acted upon by the cold of space as to allow chemical combinations and solid and liquid particles to exist. He goes on to remark that, if the molecular and atomic forces of cohesion and affinity cease to act in the interior of the mass, they come into play on the surface, where in a gaseous mixture of the most varied elements, the operations of these forces will give rise to precipitations (Herschel), clouds (Wilson), and non-gaseous particles capable of incandescence, of which our brilliant terrestrial flames offer so many examples. These particles, obeying the force of gravity, will, in falling, regain the temperature of dissociation, and will be replaced in the superficial layer by ascending gaseous masses, which will act in the same manner. The general equilibrium, therefore, will be disturbed in the vertical direction only by an unceasing exchange going on between the interior and the exterior.—*Macmillan's Magazine.*

THE BRITISH SPECIES OF HERRINGS.

At a recent meeting of the Zoological Society, Dr. A. Günther gave a description of the British species of herring (Clupea) and the distinctions between them. The fish constituting the genus Clupea are distinguished from other closely allied groups by the following characters. The abdomen is serrated, the serrations extending far forward towards the head. All the fins are present in every species; the lower jaw projects beyond the upper, whereas in the anchovy (Engraulis) and other allied forms the snout projects beyond the lower jaw. The teeth, if present, are rudimentary and deciduous, and the scales are very slightly attached.

The only British fishes of this genus recognised by Dr. Günther as being specifically distinct are: 1, the Herring (Clupea harengus); 2, the Sprat (C. sprattus); 3, the Alice Shad (C. alosa); 4, the Twaite Shad (C. finta); 5, the Pilchard (C. pilchardus).

These species are readily distinguished from each other. In the herring a vertical line, drawn down from the front of the dorsal or back fin, is in advance of the ventral fin; and there is a persistent patch of small rudimentary teeth on the vomer or central line of the upper jaw. The scales along the lateral line of the body are less than fifty in number, and, as a remarkably constant character, the number of the vertebræ is fifty-six.

In the sprat the vertical line drawn from the front of the dorsal falls on the ventral fin, both being placed equally forward. There are no teeth on the vomer, as in the herring; the scales are less than fifty along the lateral line, but the number of the vertebræ is reduced to forty-seven. These differences render the distinction between the sprat and the herring remarkably easy.

The two species known as shads were formally confounded. They are easily distinguished from the herring and the sprat by the total absence of teeth, and by the smaller size of the scales, which are more numerous, there being from sixty to seventy along the lateral line. The Alice shad is distinguished from the Twaite shad by the large number of the gill rakers, which are fine and long, and eighty to ninety in number on the outer branchial arch, whereas in the Twaite shad they are short and thick, and from thirty to forty in number on the outer arch.

In the pilchard, which is also known as the sardine, there are no teeth at all. The scales are less than fifty in number, and the gill covers are deeply furrowed. The exotic species of Clupea are very numerous, and, from their close resemblance, it is difficult to arrange them into subgenera or groups. The endeavour to classify them according to the nature and distribution of the teeth was made by Valenciennes and others, but without success, as organs which only exist in a rudimentary condition cannot be regarded as affording a secure basis for the determination of species; hence great confusion has arisen, and numerous supposed species have been admitted into the British fauna.

Thus the whitebait has been regarded as a distinct fish, and named Clupea alba; whereas it is in reality the young fry of the herring.

The facts on which Dr. Günther bases this conclusion are as follows: The dorsal and ventral fins are situated as in the mature herring; the lateral scales are the same in number; there is the same arrangement of teeth on the vomer; the same number of vertebræ—namely 56, a number not found in any other clupeoid; and, finally, whatever may be the size of the whitebait, they are never taken in roe, and an adult or mature fish has never been seen.

These conclusions were generally acquiesced in by the meeting. Henceforth, unless these opinions of Dr.

Günther are proved to be based on insufficient evidence, we must regard the whitebait as herring fry.

Such being the case, the question arises whether or not it is desirable to continue their capture; for it does not follow that because they are young herrings therefore it is a wilful waste of human food to capture them in an immature condition. Of the immense number of young produced by fish, it is obvious that only a minute fraction can arrive at maturity. Nature is prodigal of life, and the balance may possibly be so arranged that we are even increasing the number of adult fish by lessening the teeming myriads of fry, and so leaving more food and a larger scope for those that remain behind.

The Hermit Crab.

We have found the Hermit-crab called by some the Soldier-crab on account of its extreme pugnacity, and receiving the first name, because, like a hermit, it lives alone in its shelly house.

The species belonging to this genus are remarkable for the singular softness of the hinder portion of the body; this is rather long, and is coiled on itself. To protect this soft part, that would otherwise be nipped off by some hungry fish, the crab resorts to some empty shell, and, inserting his tail into the aperture, makes it his home, and carries it about with him in all his perigrinations.

The hermit-crab, like other members of the class Crustacea, increase in size through a process called "moulting." The hardened crust outside does not grow. It is only a hardened skin, as it were. Now as the body within increases in size, the outside shell must be thrown off, to allow the enlargement of the animal. This throwing off of the outside crust is called *moulting*, and takes place at certain times. With the crabs, lobsters, and others, the animal appears to fast for some time, retires to a secluded nook in the rocks, and there awaits the cracking open of its well-worn coat. This crack takes place along the back, and through this opening the animal draws itself. After it comes forth its skin is soft and tender, and some time is required before it is sufficiently hardened to enable it again to successfully battle with its enemies.

Our hermit-crab has still another stage to go through after moulting, for when this process has taken place, it find its coiled shell too small for it, and must go on that tiresome search, called house-hunting. Back and forth it travels on the beach, surveying with critical acumen the tenantless shells on the beach. Here it meets one altogether too large, and an amusing sight it is to see it drag its soft and helpless tail from the shell, to try another one on to see if it fits. Sometimes it meets with a shell that is apparently just the thing, but unluckily it is already occupied by a brother hermit. A freebooter is our hermit, and so without any apologies it proceeds by force to eject the tenant. A fight ensues, and oftentimes ends in the ejectment and mutilation of one or the other. Perhaps the name Soldier-crab is more appropriate, from its belligerent character. Gosse has described one of these fights, from which we subjoin the following: "The Soldiers (as indeed becomes their profession) are well known to be pugnacious and impudent, yet watchful and cautious. Indeed, their manners and disposition, no less than their appearance, bear the strongest resemblance to those of spiders. Two of them can scarcely approach each other without manifestations of hostility; each warily stretches out his long feet and feels the other, just as spiders do, and strives to find an opportunity of seizing his opponent in some tender part with his own strong claws. Generally they are satisfied with the proofs afforded of mutual prowess, and each, finding the other armed at all points, retires; but not unseldom a regular passage of arms ensues; the claws are rapidly thrown about, widely gaping and threatening, and the combatants roll over and over in the tussle. Sometimes, however, the aggressive spirit is more decided and ferocious. One in the aquarium of the Zoological Garden was seen to approach another, who tenanted a shell somewhat larger than his own, and, suddenly seizing his victim's front with his powerful claw, drag him like lightning from his house, into which the aggressor as swiftly inserts his own body, leaving the miserable sufferer struggling in the agonies of death.—*The American Naturalist* for July.

Maize Cultivation.

Maize, or Indian corn, is one of the most important articles of food, and is cultivated far more extensively than any other grain; in the south of Europe, in large regions of Asia and Africa, and almost the whole of North America, it forms the principal food of the inhabitants. Maize was in use in very early times, seeds having been found in the cellars of houses of ancient Greece, and it is also represented in old Chinese pictures. The name "Indian corn" was given it by the early settlers in America, who found the plant cultivated by the Indians. It is a native of tropical America, and is found in its wild state in Paraguay and Chili.

A field of maize is one of the most beautiful and refreshing sights in nature—growing to the height of eight or ten feet, its broad glossy leaves shining in the sunlight, and its feathery flowers gracefully waving with every breath of wind. The cobs or ears, like the common bean, spring from the sides of the plant, they are covered with long tapering leaves, which form a sheath to the ear, and effectually hide it. From the opening, or upper end of this sheath rises a bunch of silver grass, which collects and receives the pollen as it drops from the bloom of the plant produced at the top of the stalk. The seeds are usually of a pale yellow colour; some, however, are white, some blood red, some purple, and some party-coloured. Some ears have beeen known to contain the enormous number of 800 grains. The sheath of the flower is largely used in Southern Europe for packing oranges and lemons; paper of an excellent quality has also been manufactured from this material.

Many and various are the modes of using the maize for food. In America, the green ears are eaten, roasted at the fire, or boiled and shelled like peas, with melted butter. Among the southern planters, homminy is an indispensable dish, morning, noon, and night. The corn is pounded to greater or less fineness, and is then boiled soft like rice, and eaten with meat.

"Indian bread," made of corn meal, is at every table. The meal of maize from Southern Europe is the Polenta of commerce. Having less gluten than wheat flour, it is especially good for biscuit baking.

Attempts have been frequently made to introduce maize as one of the regular crops of this country, but without success; sometimes it will come to perfection, sometimes it will not. In the "Year-Book of Facts" for 1850 is given an account of some seed "sown on the 24th of May, which succeeded very well, and was harvested on the 10th of October, the grain perfectly formed, full and ripe. The amount of crop was at the rate of fifty bushels per acre."

William Cobbett was quite enthusiastic on the merits of Indian corn, probably from his familiar experience of its use in North America. He hoped that at some time, not long distant, the growth of Indian corn, by British farmers and British labourers, might drive out of cultivation what he called the "lazy root," "the demoralising potato." But the refusal of Indian corn to grow in these isles is not such a drawback on our national prosperity as Mr. Cobbett may have imagined. We have come to feel that the fact of one land not been able to grow some particular crop, necessary to human existence or comfort may be directly ordained by the Almighty, to the end of promoting useful commerce and international intercourse, from the increase of which many peaceful and good fruits will yet spring.

The consumption of Indian corn or meal in its natural state for human food is not large in this country. There is, however, an extensive consumption, both at home and abroad, of a preparation from Indian corn introduced by Messrs. Brown and Polson, by the name of Corn Flour.

As a pure starch, Corn Flour is extremely nourishing, and is peculiarly fitted for the diet of children. It is very easily digested, and is essentially a heat-creating food. This is of great importance, for, according to the recent researches of scientific men, there seems to be so intimate and mysterious a connection between heat and life that some have even ventured to suggest their mutual dependence. To most palates Corn Flour is also very agreeable. But "there is no disputing about tastes;" "the proof of the pudding is in the eating." Properly used it makes a most delicious pudding, and is no less acceptable in the shape of pancake, custard, &c.—*The Cottager and Artisan*, July.

STRANGE FREAKS OF LIGHTNING.

Lightning, like light, furnishes another wonderful succession of marvels. How delicate, how subtle! It performs its work sometimes with scarcely a touch. Enumerating a number of instances, the author calls upon us to modify our vulgar notions of thunder and lightning. He says it is a most extravagant idea to compare the causes of thunder and the effects of lightning to the noise and effects of cannon and cannon ball; we are face to face with an essentially superior force. It might be said that it constitutes a transition between this world and a better one: in fact it is really subject to transcendental laws which our weak intelligence cannot grasp. This little volume is a repertory of facts, some of them of the most amusing, some of them of an abundantly terrible character. Illustrating this, he strikingly entitles one of his chapters, "How did the bird get out of the cage?" He derives the expression from Plutarch. When we see animals or men cease moving, thinking, living, suddenly, without any appreciable change in their appearance or the mechanism of their organization, it suggest the image of a cage, the door still closed, no damage done to a single wire, and yet the inhabitant gone. How did it get out? The instances are numerous. Bodies have been killed repeatedly by lightning, and they have not given the slightest trace of any wound or scar, no slight touch of a burn or a contusion, no hint of the way by which the bird sprang from its confinement. Delicate and most subtle, we have said, has often been its work. Think of it melting a bracelet from a lady's wrist, yet leaving the wrist untouched: think of its melting instantly a pair of crystal goblets suddenly, without breaking them. Nay, as we said above, some of its achievements are most humourous. Arago tells how the lightning one day visited the shop of a Suabian cobbler, did not touch the artisan, but magnetised all his tools. One can well imagine the immense dismay of the poor fellow; his hammer, pinchers, and awl attracted all the needles, pins, and tacks and nails, and caused them to adhere firmly to the tools. The amazed shoemaker thought that everything in the shop was suddenly bedeviled, or else that he was dreaming. And there are several well-authenticated cases like this, showing that iron can be rendered magnetic by the electric current. We read of a merchant of Wakefield, who had placed in a corner of his room a box of knives, and forks, and iron tools, destined to be sent to the colonies; in came the lightning, struck open the box, spread all the articles on the floor, and it was found, when they were picked up, that every one had acquired new properties—they had all been affected by the subtle touch of the current. Some remained intact, others were melted, but they had all been rendered more or less magnetic, so that there was not a single nail in the box but might have served the purpose of a mariner's compass. Such anecdotes excite the sense of the marvellous; and in popular science they become windows through which the young inquirer is able to look abroad into the astonishing fields of nature. A great deal of scientific material has of course been reduced to such a matter of routine, that although there is not much scientific education, in any high sense of the word, some of the outer facts are known, and people may be prevented from making very grave mistakes.—*Eclectic and Congregational Review*.

MIMICRY IN NATURE.

You have done me the honour to reprint a few remarks on so-called "Mimicry in Nature," which I introduced in my new work on Central America, and which particularly relate to the predominance of the Willow form on river banks. It is almost unnecessary to say that in the work from which the extract is taken it was undesirable to insert more than a few names in support of my observations, but it might not be difficult to show that most plants bearing leaves of a true

Willow form do grow by running streams. To say nothing of those species of Salix having Willow leaves (or those Salices not having Willow leaves, and not growing by running streams, S. herbacea, &c.) I would remind you of the different species of Nerium (Oleander) our Epilobium augustifolium (*vulgo*, Willow herb), Lythrum Salicaria, &c. That some plants are found by rivers which do not have Willow leaves (as you pointed out) has, in my opinion, nothing to do with the question, how it comes to pass that the Willow form predominates to so great an extent in such localities. The answer may be very simple, but at present it has not come forth. About the term "mimicry" there should be a clear understanding. It is, so far, a thoroughly objectionable one, as by employing it either in zoology or botany the whole question is prejudged; indeed it is assumed—1. That organisms have the power to mimic other organisms; and 2. That they have come in contact with those organisms which they are supposed to mimic. Employ the terms "outer resemblance" instead of mimicry, and we are on neutral, undisputed ground. The subject of these external resemblances of species and whole genera to others having an entirely different organic structure, is a wide and complicated one; and I think that the best way to approach it is to go through the whole vegetable kingdom, and take note of every case where the outer features of one species or genus are reflected in any other. Some years ago my late lamented friend, Dr. Schultz-Bipontinus, read a paper on his favourite order, the Compositæ, in which he pointed out that in this the largest of all Phanerogamous orders, the habit of almost every other order of the vegetable kingdom cropped up again. In Euphorbiaceæ and other large orders, similiar instances are noted. Sometimes this outer resemblance is perfectly startling. I remember finding a Sandwich Island plant, which looked for all the world like Thomasia solanacea of New Holland, a well-known Buettneriacea of our gardens, but which on closer examination turned out to be a variety of Solanum Nelsoni; the resemblance between these two widely separated plants being quite as striking as that pointed out in Bates' "Travels on the Amazon," between a certain moth and a humming bird. This outer resemblance between plants of different genera and orders has played us botanists many a trick, and is one of the many causes of the existence of some almost incomprehensible synonyms in our systematic works. Wendland in his monograph on Acacia described many good species, and thought he knew an Acacia when he saw one; yet one of his new ones (A. dolabriformis) which he referred to the genus from habit alone, turned out to be a Daviesia. Few men had a better knowledge of Ferns than Kunze, yet "mimicry," Puck-like, played him a trick when, relying on the nature of the leaf and venation, he referred Stangeria paradoxa, a Cycad, to true ferns; and Sir W. J. Hooker, good botanist as he was, would never have figured a Veronica as a Conifer, if "mimicry"—using the term for the last time—had not been at play. At present I have no theory to propose on this subject, but whoever has, ought to both bear in mind that it must apply with equal force to the animal and vegetable kingdoms, and that to say that these resemblances are merely accidental, counts for nothing until it shall have been proved that there are such things as "accidents in Nature."—*Berthold Seemann.—Gardeners' Chronicle*, June 27.

Man-eating Wolves.

The Pioneer of Allahabad gives an account of the capture of one of the most destructive of the wolves which have been ravaging the country about the Kutnee Station of the Jubbulpore Railway. Between Novr. 8 and December 19 last no less than eight persons have been killed, and six persons wounded by these wolves. Mr. Olpherts, the resident engineer at the Kutnee Station, thus details the capture of the female wolf and five of her cubs:—"You will be glad to hear that I have got hold of one of the Beroli wolves, the female of the pair that carried off the child near our camp some time ago. With her I have also got five young cubs; the little brutes are all alive, and are now being nursed by a pariah dhaie; their delightful mamma was caught in my trap five nights ago, and as the pit is 13 feet deep, with about four feet of water at the bottom, she had a cold swim of it all night, and was found next morning quite dead. On getting her up out of the pit my man noticed that she was suckling, and with great luck he hit upon the place close at hand. The den was of very elaborate arrangement, having four entrances in opposite directions, and very deep in the interior; it took the men a long time to dig out the interesting family. A year hence these additional pests would have been loose on the wretched villagers, and no doubt their parents would have trained them to live like themselves on little else but human flesh. This wolf having been killed, and her young ones having been found so close to the village of Immilea, leave no doubt in my mind that she and her consort are answerable for the long list of victims which I have inclosed. The death recorded on the 1st December, Immilea village, is that of a poor woman who was torn to pieces and eaten just close to the den. The following list is extracted from the registry at the Thannah:—"November 8th, one wounded; 14th, one killed; 18th, one killed and two wounded; December 1st, one killed; 2nd, one killed; 5th, one killed; 12th, one killed; 17th, one killed and one wounded; 19th, one killed." My readers can form but little idea of the horrible mutilations which the wolves inflict upon those of their victims who are fortunate enough to escape. A little girl has twice been attacked by wolves. On the first occasion she escaped with some severe bites, but when she was seized a second time the wolves succeeded in tearing off and devouring the whole of the muscular portions of both her legs before she was rescued from their jaws —a more pitiable object than this poor little creature presented when brought to the bungalow for surgical aid it is impossible to describe. Mr. Olpherts succeeded in destroying the wolves which injured this child, but not before they had taken many human lives. Very great credit is due to that gentleman for the persevering manner in which he has devoted his leisure time, and no little of his money, to the destruction of these pests. There are still a few pairs of man-eating wolves in the extensive *maidans* of the

Jubbulpore District, but their number has been considerably reduced by the exertions of Mr. Olpherts and his servants.

THE ROBIN (*Erythaca rubecula*),

This household bird is the subject of much rural "folk-lore." He is considered to be under the especial protection of heaven, and is a great favourite of man; even prying, plundering, bird-nesting lads, to whom nothing comes amiss in the shape of either nest or eggs, pass by the nest of the robin, deeming it unlucky to take either. It is firmly believed here, and also in many parts of England, that nothing will eat a robin. I have never known a cat to eat one, although I have frequently known young cats to catch them. A friend of mine who keeps a tame fox, tells me that although Reynard will greedily eat all kinds of birds, mice, rats, and frogs, he will not eat robins; and another correspondent assures me that a tame fox to whom a robin was given, after eating a part of it was sick, and ejected it.

A popular rhyme says—
"The robin and the wren
Are God Almighty's cock and hen."

The robin gets the benefit of the relationship; but few of our little birds, if any, are so subject to be hunted down and cruelly killed as the innocent wren. Wren-hunting with sticks is a popular pursuit of young Rusticus in North Yorkshire, and in Ireland too. That the young robins kill off the old ones every winter is a popular belief here. When I, a few years ago, mentioned this in a contemporary periodical, asking if it was a common belief, I found it was commoner than I had believed. The opinion is entertained in this neighbourhood, not only by the labouring class, but also by the gentlemen farmers; and two or three clergymen to whom I have mentioned it, asking their opinions, although carefully guarding themselves against being classed amongst the "firm believers," expressed themselves as by no means sure that it was not the truth. The robin is also regarded by many as the bird of death, and the visit of one to a house where there is sickness often causes considerable uneasiness. Every church and every old ruin has its robin. The familiarity with which they pick amongst the soil out of a new-made grave, and the old tradition of the "babes in the wood," may, perhaps, have something to do with this opinion. Our literature, especially the old poets, is full of beautiful allusions and addresses to the ruddock, who is often spoken of as a lover of the lowly grass mounds that cover the mouldering tenants of "God's acre."—J. RANSON, *York.—Naturalist's Circular*, July.

THE BEAVER AT THE ZOOLOGICAL GARDENS.

The beaver, as we have said, teaches us his method of constructing his lodge. The power of his incisor-teeth we tested here upon a log of wood eight inches in diameter, which the male animal gnawed nearly through in an hour and a quarter, when it was taken from him, and is now shown as a specimen of his powers. The beaver is not a large animal; it must therefore surprise visitors to notice the size of the branches of trees it has used to construct the covering of its lodge. Some of these pieces are half a hundred weight, and these it managed to drag from one side to the other of its enclosure. The branches having been interlaced together, the interstices we filled up with mud. The old idea that to amused children, that it used its tail to plaster its work, is now proved to be an invention. Its only purpose seems to be to give support to the animal when it sits on its hind quarters, and to serve as a rudder. To all intents and purposes the lodge is made just as it is in the native home of the animal. It has its different entrances and exits, and in the old house there were tunnels which led from the floor of the lodge to a water exit—a most necessary arrangement; but in the new quarters in which it is located, a peep circular wall is built in the inner ring of the pond where the lodge is constructed, which prevents this arrangement. The reason for this interference with the animal's instincts we do not know, unless it is a fear that they should burrow unseen under their lodge and escape as they did before from the Gardens. The cunning of these animals is so extreme, that it amounts to a reasoning power. For instance, every day they heap the sods that are put into the inclosure one upon another by the side of the fence, and if they were not as regularly removed, the animals would be over the wall in no time and off into the canal.

We suppose it would be impossible to give the space for a beaver dam, but if it could be managed it would certainly attract an immense deal of attention. In their native wilds, when located upon a swift stream, they manage to dam up the water on the most ingenious principles. They first fell a large amount of timber with their adze-like teeth, and with these logs they manage to construct a dam on truly scientific engineering principles, namely, with its apex pointed up the stream to resist pressure, and with its two sides gradually sloping towards either bank. By this means they obtain a space of still water to disport in. There was some intention years ago of providing them with the stream of water necessary to incite them to make this dam, but we fancy that a larger number than two beavers would be required to make this very elaborate structure, as, when wild, they always work at it in communities.—*Cassell's Magazine*.

WOLF-HUNTING IN FRANCE.

British sportsmen must often envy France the possession of the wolf. Indeed an undergraduate of Dublin, being called on to enumerate the most regretable events in Irish history, commenced his list with that of the extermination of the last wolf in 1710. No brute in Europe is better adapted than the wolf for being run to death, and none affords the huntsman a better apology for hunting. A bear hunt is most frequently a duel or an assassination. The stag, the roe-buck, and even the wild boar are inoffensive when unmolested; the fox and the badger are too small to be personally dangerous, but the wolf is at once a foe to be respected for his teeth, a brigand accountable for a life of rapine, and a test of strength and mettle for the fleetest dogs. By the term dogs, must, however, be understood the ordinary pack, for the greyhound is often able to attain the wolf on sight, and in such case he invariably mars the sport. In the Aube a couple or two of greyhounds usually accompany the meute both in boar and wolf hunting; the consequence is that most frequently, when the game takes the open country, the greyhounds follow the wolf on sight, and either seize it at once, or so impede its pace, as to enable the pack to arrive and finish the hunt abruptly. In some cases the chances of an exciting run are further diminished by the admission of rifles, and it too often happens that a solitary wolf, the sole hope of the meet, is shot dead in the cover before the dogs give tongue, leaving the huntsmen to disperse for lack of game, or to go in for foxes. Still, occasionally, in spite of guns and greyhounds, a fair run takes place, and in such case the sport, for heat and spirit, is all the most ardent huntsman can desire; the wolf bursts unexpectedly from the cover, and straining for some distant point in possibly another department, bounds straight ahead through all kinds of country, and leads the hounds a chase which often ends in their exhaustion and discomfiture.—*St. Pauls, for July, edited by Anthony Trollope.*

New Books.

[*Our limited space must of necessity compel us to give but very short notices of new books, but they will perhaps serve as a guide as to what books our readers may ask for at their libraries.*]

Rambles of a Naturalist on the Shores and Waters of the China Sea. By Cuthbert Collingwood, M.A. and B.M., Oxon, F.L.S. London: John Murray. 1868.

Mr. Collingwood in this volume describes, in most easy and agreeable style, his travels overland to China, thence to the little-known island of Formosa, to the Chinese coast to Canton, Hong Kong, Singapore, Manilla, and the great island of Borneo; in each of which places topics of interest in the animal and vegetable productions, as well as in the customs and condition of the people, presented themselves to his view in ever-changing novelty, and form a narrative which carries the reader irresistibly from page to page through the whole volume. The author is a great admirer of the sea, and several most graphic passages describe in glowing language its features in storm and in calm, of which those on pages 10 and 11, and the interesting remarks on the colour of the sea at p. 387, are good examples. Indeed, some chapters towards the end of the book are devoted exclusively to observations made upon the open sea; and where an ordinary voyager would have found nothing but weariness and monotony, Dr. Collingwood found materials for the interesting chapters "On the Surface Population of the Ocean," "On the Luminosity of the Sea," as well as the miscellaneous "Observations at Sea" of chapter xxii. The chapter on the luminosity of the sea brings together, from personal observation, the most important facts connected with that curious phenomenon, and groups them in a way which cannot fail to render the subject more comprehensible than it has been hitherto.

The volume forms a most valuable addition to our stock of information, and we are confident our readers will read it with great pleasure and deep interest.

British Seaweeds. By S. O. Grey. London: Reeve and Co.

This is a very useful little manual, convenient in size and moderate in price. The descriptions of the several species are succinct, and yet so characteristic as to render identification easy. The information given as to newly discovered species, remarkable varieties, and the habitats of the various plants described, shows that the author has followed the progress made in this branch of systematic botany. Mr. Gray has evidently studied not only the typical specimens in some of the best herbaria of marine algæ, but also the living plants themselves, and has produced a treatise which is not only handy and popular, but also scientific and exact.

Meetings of Learned Societies.

Ethnological Society.

May 26.—Anniversary Meeting—Prof. Busk in the chair. The following were elected Officers and Council for the ensuing year: *President,* Prof. Huxley; *Vice-Presidents,* R. Dunn, Major-General Balfour, Sir J. Lubbock, Bart., and Dr. H. Tuke; *Treasurer,* F. Hindmarsh; *Hon. Secretaries,* T. Wright and D. W. Nash; *Hon. Librarian,* L. J. Beale; *Council,* W. Blackmore, H. G. Bohn, Prof. Busk, Dr. A. Campbell, Hyde Clarke, Sir A. W. Clavering, Bart., T. F. D. Croker, J. Dickinson, Col. Lane Fox, H. H. Howarth, Dr. R. King, Sir R. I. Murchison, Bart., Sir C. Nicholson, Bart., Capt. S. Osborn, G. Dalhousie Ramsay, Major-General Sir J. Shiel, Lord Strangford, J. Thrupp, and E. B. Tylor.

Zoological Society.

May 14th.—G. Busk, Esq., V.P., in the chair. The Secretary read some notices of the recent additions to the Society's menagerie, amongst which was particularly remarked upon a male lyre-bird, making a pair of these birds now in the Society's gardens. Prof. Huxley read a memoir on the classification and distribution of the birds belonging to his divisions Alectoromorphæ and Heteromorphæ. By the latter term Prof. Huxley, proposed to designate the singular form Opisthocomus, which recent examination had convinced him must be arranged as a distinct group in the vicinity of the Alectoromorphæ. Mr. P. L. Sclater communicated some notes on the pelicans living in the Society's gardens, accompanied by remarks on the other known species of the genus. Two communications were read from Dr. F. Day, the first on a new Gobioid fish from Madras, the second containing observations on some of the fresh-water fishes of India. A communication was read from Mr. H. Adams, containing descriptions of new species of shells, collected in the islands of Mauritius, Bourbon, and the Seychelles, by Mr. G. Nevill.

May 28.—G. Busk, Esq., V.P., in the chair. The Secretary reported that two living examples of Owen's Apteryx (*Apteryx Owenii*) destined for the Society's menagerie, had recently been shipped from Australia, —one by Dr. G. Bennett, of Sydney, and the other by Mr. E. S. Hill, of Wollahra, Sydney,—but they had both unfortunately died on the voyage home. Dr. Günther exhibited specimens of the ova and young of the Axolotl (*Siredon Mexicanum*) which had been deposited and hatched in a fresh-water tank in this country, and made remarks on the strange facts connected with the development of this animal, and on its systematic position. A communication was read from Mr. C. S. Bate, containing a description of a new species of Freshwater Prawn, from South Africa, proposed to be called *Macrobrachium jambonis*. Two communications were read from Dr. J. G. Macdonald, the first contained a description of a supposed new species of Galeocerdo, from the Southern Seas, proposed to be called *Galeocerdo Rayneri*; the second gave additional notes on *Heptranchus Indicus*, chiefly regarding its sexual characters.

June 11.—Dr. J. E. Gray, V.P., in the chair. Mr. P. L. Sclater exhibited a very fine and perfect skin of the Australian Cassowary (*Casuarius Australis*), which had been transmitted to him by Messrs. Scott, Bros., of Queensland, and was believed to be the first example of this species that had reached Europe. Mr. W. H. Flower read a paper "On the Development and Succession of the Teeth in the Armadillos (*Dasypodidæ*)," which have been generally considered as "monophyodont," or animals that generate a single set of teeth. A communication was read from Mr. E. P. Ramsay, containing an account of a collection of birds formed for him by Mr. Spalding, in Rockingham Bay, Queensland, in October, 1867. Amongst these the most noticeable novelty was a new species of the genus Orthonyx, proposed to be called *O. Spaldingi*. Messrs. Sclater and Salvin communicated descriptions of four new species of Birds from Veragua. A communication was read from Dr. Gray, containing notes on the skulls of the different species of Dogs, Wolves, and Foxes (forming the family Canidæ) contained in the British Museum.

June 25.—Dr. E. Hamilton, V.P., in the chair. Mr. P. L. Sclater exhibited two heads of the Spanish Ibex (*Capra Pyrenaica*, Schimper), which had been obtained by Major Howard Irby in Southern Spain, and announced that that gentleman had procured at Gibraltar a young living specimen of this animal, which it was his intention to present to the Society's Menagerie. A communication was read from Prof. R. Owen, containing a description of the sternum of *Dinornis elephantopus* and *D. rheides*, with notes on that bone in *D. crassus* and *D. casuarinus*, and forming the thirteenth part of his series of memoirs on the extinct birds of the genus Dinornis. A communication was read from Mr. R. Brown on the Seals of Greenland. Dr. Günther communicated a report on the species of *Batrachia salientia* added to the collection of the British Museum since the publication of his catalogue of specimens of that order in 1858. A communication was read from Messrs. Sclater and Salvin, entitled "A Synopsis of the American Rails (*Rallidæ*)." The total number of species of this group known to the authors in the New World was stated to be forty-eight, two of which were characterized as new in the present paper. Mr. J. Gould communicated a description of a new species of Kingfisher of the genus Ceyx, from the Phillipines. Dr. J. Murie read a paper on the structure of the gular pouch of the South African and Australian Bustards (*Otis kori* and *O. Australis*) as observed in specimens of these birds now or lately living in the Society's Gardens.

ENTOMOLOGICAL SOCIETY.

June 1.—Mr. H. W. Bates, President, in the chair. —Mr. G. P. Shearwood and Il Cavaliere Francfort were elected Members.—The Secretary announced that an exhibition of useful and destructive insects would be held at Paris in the month of August.— Mr. M'Lachlan exhibited the larva of a Caddis-fly, which was found by Mr. Fletcher, of Worcester, crawling about the bark of willow-trees; he expected that it would produce *Enoicyla pusilla*, the larva of which was well known on the Continent to be non-aquatic. —Mr. Keays exhibited *Psyche crassiorella* from Hornsey Wood.—The Hon. T. De Grey exhibited pupæ of *Hypercallia Christierninana*; the larvæ were found on *Polygala vulgaris* near Shoreham.—Mr. Butler exhibited varieties of *Anthocaris Cardamines* and *Nemeobius Lucina* from Herne Bay.—Mr. Burmeister exhibited drawings of larvæ of Brazilian butterflies, and pupa-skins of many of the species; he also mentioned that he had found the larva of Castnia in the bulbous swellings at the foot of the stem of orchids.—Mr. Sheppard read a letter from Mrs. Russell on the habits of a Meloe.—Mr. Keays exhibited oak-leaves, the outer halves of which were twisted up by *Attelabus curculionoides*.—The Hon. T. De Grey exhibited *Agapanthia cardui*, bred from larvæ in stems of thistles.— Mr. Butler exhibited *Otiorhyncus picipes*, which had been found very destructive to rose-trees at Manchester.—Professor Westwood described the habits of the Sacred Beetle as recently observed by himself at Cannes.—The following paper was read: "Descriptions of New Genera and Species of Heteromera," by Mr. F. Bates. The new genera belonged to the family Tenebrionidæ, and all the species were from Australia.

July 6.—Mr. H. W. Bates, President, in the chair. Mr. Bond exhibited remarkable varieties of *Setina irrorella* and *Arctia villica*; Mr. Pryer, a malformation of *Halias quercana*; Mr. M'Lachlan, bred specimens of *Hypercallia Christierninana*; Mr. Davis, dried skins of the larvæ of numerous species of Lepidoptera; Mr. Wood, various species of Saturniidæ, and made some remarks on their habits; Mr. Butler, a species of Tachina, bred from pupæ of *Halia vanaria*; Mr. Bond, a female of *Drilus flavessens*, which was captured by Mr. Rogers in the Isle of Wight together with two males, which were in simultaneous connection with her; and mentioned that Dr. Knaggs had seen two males of different species of moths, *Tortrix viridana* and *T. heparana*, in simultaneous intercourse with a female of *T. viridana*; Mr. J. Weir, a fine *Monochamus* which had flown into the London Custom House; Mr. Blackmore, a collection of insects of all orders, principally Coleoptera, captured in Tangier during the months of March and April last; the Secretary, the nest of a wasp, probably an Odynerus, placed in the cavity between the limits of a spring letter-clip, and found in an open box on a writing-table in Hampshire; Mr. F. Smith, two specimens of *Ophion macrurus*, bred by Mr. Chapman from cocoons of *Bombyx Cynthia* sent from New York: the specimens reached London alive, and one of them stung Mr. Smith severely in the hand, but the pain was not lasting; and Professor Westwood, two Chalcididæ belonging to the Cleonymus group, which he proposed to describe as the types of new genera. The following papers were read:—"On the larva of *Micropeplus staphylinoides*," by Sir J. Lubbock, Bart.; "Descriptions of New Genera and Species of Heteromera" (continuation), by Mr. F. Bates; "Reports of the Commissioner for investigating the ravages of the Borer (*Xylotrechus quadripes*) in Coffee Plantations of Mysore and Coorg," by Dr. G. Bidie; "A Comparison of some Representative Species of Diurnal Lepidoptera in Europe, India and North America," by Mr. W. F. Kirby; and "On some Points in the Anatomy of the immature *Cœnus macrura* of Stephens," by Mr. A. F. Eaton.

Geological Society.

May 20.—Prof. T. H. Huxley, President, in the chair.—The following communications were read:—"On the Eruption of the Kaimeni of Santorin," by Dr. J. Schmidt.—"On the Structure of the Crag-beds of Norfolk and Suffolk, with some Observations on their Organic Remains. Part II. The Red Crag of Suffolk," by Mr. J. Prestwich.

June 3.—Prof. T. H. Huxley, LL.D., President, in the chair.—M. Gaudry was elected a Foreign Correspondent.—The following communications were read:—"On some Genera of Carboniferous Corals," by Mr. J. Thomson.—"On the Pebble Beds of Middlesex, Essex, and Herts," by Mr. S. V. Wood, jun.,—"On the Cretaceous Rocks of the Bas-Boulonnais," by Mr. W. Topley, and "Note on the Mendip Anticlinal," by Mr. C. H. Weston.

June 17.—Prof. T. H. Huxley, President, in the chair.—Messrs. C. B. Clarke and F. C. J. Spurrell were elected Fellows.—The following communications were read:—"On the Distribution of Stone Implements in Southern India," by Mr. R. B. Foote. "On Worked Flint Flakes from Carrickfergus and Larne," by Mr. G. V. du Noyer. "On the Diminution in the Volume of the Sea during past Geological Epochs," by Mr. A. Murray. "Has the Asiatic Elephant been found in a Fossil State?" by Mr. A. Leith Adams, with a Note by Mr. G. Busk. "On the Characters of some new Fossil Fish from the Lias of Lyme Regis," by Sir Philip de M. Grey Egerton, Bart. "Note on the Geology of Port Santa Cruz, Patagonia," by Capt. T. Baker. "On the Jurassic Deposits in the N. W. Himalaya," by Dr. F. Stoliczka. "On a true Coal-plant (*Lepidodendron*) from Sinai," by Mr. J. W. Salter. "On some Fossils from the Menevian Group," by Messrs. J. W. Salter and H. Hicks. "On Earthquakes in Northern Formosa," by Mr. H. F. Holt. "Memorandum on the Coal Mines of Iwanai, Island of Yesso, Japan," by Mr. A. B. Mitford. "On a New Species of Fossil Deer from Clacton," and "On a New Species of Fossil Deer from the Norwich Crag," by Mr. W. Boyd Dawkins. "Notes to accompany a Section of the Strata from the Chalk to the Bembridge Limestone at Whitecliff Bay, Isle of Wight," by Mr. T. Codrington. "On the Graptolites of the Coniston Flags, with Notes on the British Species of the Genus Graptolites," by Dr. H. A. Nicholson. "On the 'Waterstone Beds" of the Keuper, and on Pseudomorphous Crystals of Chloride of Sodium," by Mr. G. W. Ormerod. "On the Discovery of the Remains of Pteraspidian Fishes in Devonshire and Cornwall, and on the Identity of *Steganodictyum cornubicum* (M'Coy), with *Scaphaspis* (*Archæoteuthis*) *Dunensis* (Roemer)," by Mr. E. Ray Lankester, and "On the Geological Peculiarities of that part of Central Germany known as the Saxon Switzerland, by the late Capt. J. Clark.

Linnean.

June 4.—G. Bentham, Esq., President in the chair.—The President nominated J. J. Bennett, Esq., J. D. Hooker, M.D., Sir J. Lubbock, Bart., and W. W. Saunders, Esq., *Vice-Presidents* for the ensuing year.—The following papers were read: "On the Homologies of certain Muscles connected with the Shoulder-joint," by Dr. G. Rolleston.—"Contributions to the History of *Zamites gigas*," by Mr. W. C. Williamson.—"On the Muscles of the Fore and Hind Limbs in the six-banded Armadillo," by Mr. J. C. Galton.—"The Myology of the Upper and Lower Extremities of the *Oryctopses Capensis*," by the same.

June 18.—G. Bentham, Esq., President, in the chair.—Messrs. E. Story and A. Swanzy were elected Fellows. The following papers were read: "On Branched Palms of South India," by Dr. J. Shortt.—"On the Structure of the Flower in the genus Napoleona, &c.," by Dr. M. T. Masters.—"On the Development of lost Parts in the Nemerteans," by Dr. W. C. M'Intosh.—"Note on the Dimorphism of Flowers of *Cymbidium Tigrinum*," by Mr. C. Parish.—"On the Copal of Zanzibar," by Dr. J. Kirk.—Descriptions of a New Genus and six New Species of Spiders,' by the Rev. C. P. Cambridge.—"Enumeration of the Palms of Sikkim," by Dr. T. Anderson.—"Flora of the Hooshiarpur District of the Panjab," by Dr. I. E. T. Aitchison.—"Observations on the Septum of the Cæcidæ; and Remarks on the Suject of the Suppression of the Genera Brochina and Strebloceras," by the Marquis L. de Folin.—"Enumeratio Muscorum omnium Austro-Americanorum: eorum præcipuè in Terris Amazonicis Andinisque; Ricardo Spruceo lectorum," scripsit Gul. Milten, and "On the Cycadeæ from the Secondary Rocks of Britain," by Mr. W. Carruthers.

QUEKETT MICROSCOPICAL CLUB.

At the ordinary meeting, held at University College on Friday, June 26th, Arthur E. Durham, Esq., F.L.S., President, in the chair, 13 new members were elected, 10 gentlemen were proposed for membership, and numerous presents were announced. Several interesting communications were also received from societies on the Continent and in America. A paper on "Tobacco" was read by Mr. Archer, in which he entered into the particulars of the growth, culture, and preparation of the plant, as well as its structure, constituents, manufacture, and adulterations, the subject being illustrated by a fine specimen of a living plant, numerous dried samples, and some well-executed drawings. At the close of the meeting the president announced that the annual general meeting of the club would be held on July 24, and the proceedings terminated with a *conversazione*, at which a variety of interesting microscopic objects were exhibited.

Short Notes.

BLADDERWORTS.—Three species are described, or perhaps more properly two, with an intermediate one, which may be a variety, or, it may be, a hybrid, between the other two. They are all found in ditches or in deep pools, floating just below the surface of the water. The commonest and largest species, *Utricularia vulgaris*, may be taken as the type of the genus, as regards British kinds. It is of tolerably frequent occurrence, but I think, often overlooked from the fact that sometimes for several years it flowers so sparingly as to escape notice. It consists of slender, very brittle, trailing, branches, one or two feet in length, which are densely clothed with very elegant pectinated leaves. The leaves are, in fact, nothing more than the ribs and veins, for being altogether submerged, the plant has no necessity for breathing pores, nor for the fleshy portion with which the stomata communicate. It is therefore not developed in the ordinary form, but is converted into a number of very elegant little bladders, or *utriculi* (whence the Latin name of the plant), which contain air, and are supposed to be the organs by which the plant is buoyed up to the surface of the water. The little bladders themselves are somewhat flask shaped and flattened, and are very beautiful when seen through a magnifying glass. They are placed upon very short stalks upon the secondary veins of the leaf, close to the mid rib, so that there are two rows of them on each leaf, one row at either side of the midrib. A vein of the leaf passes up the front of each flask, giving rigidity, and branching round the orifice, which it greatly strengthens, terminates at the sides and back of the opening in two or four bristles. The mouth of the flask is closed by an extremely delicate, almost invisible, membrane, having a minute slit in front, through which gases, no doubt, escape.

The flowers are extremely pretty; they are bright yellow, growing four or five together in a raceme, which shoots up with a stalk some five or six inches above the water. In form they are not very unlike the flowers of a calceolaria, being two-lipped and having a short spur.

Utricularia minor is a much smaller species, not by any means so common, and generally found in small pools of water on peat bogs. The flowers are small and pale in colour, and as far as I have been able to observe, the plant is more frequently found in a flowerless state than even *U. vulgaris*.

The third species, or variety, or hybrid, *U. intermedia*, I cannot describe from actual observation. It seems to be rare, and to be characterized by the leaves being tripartite. The vesicles are said to arise from branched stalks and not from the leaves.—*Quarterly Magazine of the High Wycombe Natural History Society*.

FROGS FROM BABYHOOD TO FULL AGE. —What multitudes of frogs are just showing their heads above the water; how earnestly they give out that croak, croak, croak; and their bright eyes show singular excitement for such cold creatures! See what a gluey-like substance, speckled with numerous black spots, floats on the water. Ah! that explains the agitation of the frog kingdom this morning. The race of these creatures is not to perish; provision is now being made for the next generation of these unlovely but interesting reptiles. The black specks in that jelly-looking substance are the eggs, which have just been deposited, and the parents are singing a merry ditty on the happy occasion. By each one of those female frogs above 1,200 eggs will be placed in the water, where the sun will gradually develop the hidden life in each dark speck. Has the reader ever traced the growth of a frog from the egg? The process is worthy of observation. Let us collect some of that substance in which the eggs are embedded, and place it in a vessel, with some of the water and weeds from the pool. We may now be able to watch all the changes. What is the first transformation? The eggs become marked with little furrows, some vital power being clearly at work within. Next we see, in place of the egg, a tiny lump of jelly-like life, which clings to one of the water weeds. How does it hold on? By a small sucker, which it clearly knows how to use. Is this, then, the first form of the frog baby? The reader may call it so, if he please, but it is not a frog at all yet. Mark the third change; our bit of jelly has acquired gills and a tail, and see how swiftly it moves in the water. It is now really a *fish*, though called a tadpole. But what is going to happen? The animal is changing again; a pair of hind legs are forming. This is the fourth state. What next? A pair of front limbs are developed, and it is now evident that the creature does not mean to remain a fish; it has reached the fifth transformation. But what has become of the long tail? Has a part dropped off? Certainly not; it has been *absorbed* into the animal's system, and will soon entirely disappear. We have here reached the sixth stage in a frog's life. The mouth now gradually widens, assuming the form which belongs to the fully developed reptile. Are the transformations complete now? No; the most remarkable change is the last. Hitherto the creature has breathed by gills—a beautiful living machine for obtaining oxygen from water; but now a means must be provided for breathing air. Lungs, therefore, are gradually formed, and the whole series of wonderful transmutations is complete. Thus our frog has passed through eight changes, each bringing him one step nearer to the final shape and condition.—*From "Recreative Natural History," in "Cassell's Popular Educator" for July.*

PROTECTION FROM MOSQUITOES, INSECTS, &c.—If your correspondent "An Edinburgh Subscriber," will refer to the *Times* of May 30, 1868, he will find an article, taken from the *British Medical Journal*, giving the information he requires. The plant alluded to in it—*Pyrethrum roseum*—is spoken of in the garden article of *The Field* of June 6 as the "Insect Killer," and I may add that Keating's so-called Persian Insect Powder is said to be made from it.—STEPHEN GREEN (United Service Club, June 21). [We append the paragraph in question, and shall be obliged if any of our readers who try the recipe will inform us as to its efficacy.—ED.] "A HINT FOR TRAVELLERS.—A well-known German traveller, F. Jager, in his 'Sketches of Travels in Singapore, Malacca, Java,' (Berlin, 1866), describes the powder of the *Pyrethrum roseum* as a specific against all noxious insects, including the troublesome mosquitoes and those which attack collections. He says: 'A tincture prepared by macerating one part of the *Pyrethrum roseum* in four parts of dilute alcohol, and, when diluted with ten times its bulk of water, applied to any part of the body, gives perfect security against all vermin. I often passed the night in my boat on the ill-reputed rivers of Siam without any other cover, even without the netting, and experienced not the slightest inconvenience. The 'buzzing,' at other times so great a disturber of sleep, becomes a harmless tune, and, in the feeling of security, a real cradle song. In the chase, moistening the beard and hands protects the hunter against flies for at least twelve hours, even in spite of the largely-increased transpiration due to the climate. Especially interesting is its action on that plague of all tropical countries, the countless ants. Before the windows and surrounding the whole house where I lived at Albay, on Luzon, was fastened a board six inches in width, on which long caravans of ants were constantly moving in all directions, making it appear an almost uniformly black surface. A track of the powder several inches in width, strewed across the board, or some tincture sprinkled over it, proved an insurmountable barrier to these processions. The first who halted before it were pushed on by the crowds behind them; but, immediately on passing over, showed symptoms of narcosis, and died in a minute or two, and within a short time the rest left the house altogether.—*British Medical Journal.*

BUTTERFLIES.—Catch that large "White Cabbage" lady butterfly (*Pontia Brassicæ*), and ask her a few questions about "auld lang syne," just to illustrate what are called *metamorphoses*. On the 1st of May last year—we like to be particular in dates—her grandmother was a bandaged chrysalis, and about the end of the month became a butterfly. Her elegantly-shaped eggs were carefully laid on the under side of nicely-selected cabbage leaves, without permission of the gardener. Mighty was his rage when, in a few days, his choicest cabbages were sawn into the most intricate patterns by a thriving family of ravenous caterpillars. To kill them all was out of the question. Napoleon's artillery might have failed to accomplish that. Many did perish; the sparrows especially delighted in such delicious morsels. One, however, escaped, in consequence of her exceeding cleverness in feeding on leaves concealed from the birds' eyes. Having formed a chrysalis, she secured the cradle-like bit of work to a sunny wall by a strong but elegant silken band. From this came a butterfly about August, the mother of the one which is supposed to have just been caught by the reader. From her eggs sprang another succession of caterpillars, which changed to chrysalides in September last. Now mark what followed. No butterflies came from these chrysalis forms as usual. They must have died of starvation, as winter yields but very little indeed of the delicate food required by them. This second series of chrysalides were therefore commissioned to keep the undeveloped insects safely wrapped within their folds through the cold and storms of the winter. In the May of this year, each little cradle gives up its brilliant child to sport with the perfumed zephyrs. Thus, in the course of a twelvemonth, the large white butterfly goes through a twofold round of most wonderful changes.—*From "Recreative Natural History," in Cassell's "New Popular Educator" for June.*

ENGLISH BIRDS IN NEW ZEALAND.—The venture of the Acclimatization Society to bring out from London by the *Warrior Queen* an extensive importation of English song birds has proved a complete success, under the careful management of Mr. Edward Bills and his son (says the *New Zealand Examiner*). Out of those shipped there are 524 on board, all of which have arrived in fine health and condition. They comprise 110 starlings, 95 thrushes, 65 blackbirds, 42 chaffinches, 60 linnets, 22 hedge sparrows, 40 goldfinches, eight green linnets, eight yellowhammers, 50 larks, three house sparrows, two mountain sparrows, two reed sparrows, and ten red poll linnets. There are also three white swans, a peacock and peahen. The greatest mortality was among the robins and the sparrows, all the robins having died. Judging by the fine healthy appearance of the birds, and the cleanliness of their several apartments, the society could not have made a better choice in the appointment of a manager, it being apparent that Mr. Bills thoroughly understands the habits of the different kinds. On one occasion, during the passage, a sea broke on board, and left water a foot deep in the deck-house where the birds were caged. Some loss occurred through this. One of the larks had a leg broken, which was amputated by Mr. Bills. It is now healthy, and as sprightly as any of the others. Mr. Bills brings out on his own account, for sale, 60 canaries. eight handsome goldfinch mules, eight song linnets, and three goldfinches. On arrival a number of the members of the Acclimatization Society, including Mr. Clifford, boarded the ship, and were highly pleased with the successful termination of their venture.

BRITISH BIRD MURDER.—If this quotation from the "Journal of a Naturalist" says a writer in the *Gardeners' Magazine*, meets with your approbation, you will perhaps insert it in your journal. Widely circulated newspapers are a medium of often diffusing most useful knowledge, and benefit also the cause of humanity. I can speak most personally interested on the subject of this letter, for I lived twelve years in the south of Italy. I had a house and nine acres of land; the soil was rich and fertile, but, from the extent the birds were destroyed it was impossible to prevent the fearful ravages of the caterpillar and other insects. I think the following reading will attract the farmer and the gardener's eye :—

"DESTROYER OF SNAILS.—The thrush is a bird of great utility in a garden where fruit is grown, owing to the peculiar inclination it has for feeding upon snails. Very many does he dislodge in the course of the day. When the female is sitting, the male bird is particularly assiduous in seeking them out—feeding his mate. After this time the united labours of the pair destroy great numbers of these injurious creatures."—*Journal of a Naturalist.*

I copy the following lines from the book "The Gardener and Practical Florist" :—

"We are inclined to think that the most mischievous bird does a good deal of good as well as harm, for we have killed a chaffinch, believing he was just picking off the buds of a fruit tree, and found a caterpillar in his mouth. From that time we have tried to frighten birds but not to kill them."—A FRIEND TO THE FEATHERED TRIBE, in *Yorkshire Gazette.*

EXTRAORDINARY ELDER TREE.—We have in this neighbourhood an elder tree of such extraordinary dimensions, that a short description of it may perhaps interest your readers. It stands alone, towards the foot of a well-known promontory called "Penpole," and it has the growth of an apple or crab tree, with a single strong but short trunk and spreading branches. The trunk at the smallest part is 19in. in diameter, and the branches cover a surface about 27ft. across in one direction, and 25ft. in another. But the tree is evidently long past its prime. Thirty or forty years ago these dimensions were no doubt exceeded. There has been a pretty fair show of blossoms this year, but the foliage is thin and stunted, except towards the upper part, where there is one of those extraordinary conglomerations of small branches and leaves which we sometimes see on elm and other trees, forming in this case a dense mass of foliage, so thick and almost matted together, that a bird in search of a place of shelter would find it very difficult to penetrate it. Jenny Wren might do so perhaps, but everybody must have observed that Jane frequently creeps about more like a little inquisitive mouse than a bird. Here, then, is my elder tree—which has a right to be called *a tree*—despising the name of a bush or a shrub. And now I wish to know whether any of your readers have ever seen one that can equal it in dimensions, or even come near to it? Also, if any of your kind and courteous correspondents could throw a little light on the cause of the wonderful leafy conglomerations mentioned above, they might confer a favour on other puzzled observers of nature's eccentricities as well as on myself.—George Waring, in *the Field*, June 9.

CANINE SAGACITY.—At Clemecy, on the borders of Switzerland, a wolf towards nightfall entered the village, and immediately gave chase to a small grey terrier belonging to no one in particular. Instead of taking shelter in the nearest cottage, the dog rushed on to the end of the hamlet, and entering a wheelwright's yard, leapt safe and sound into the kennel of a huge mastiff. The wolf had followed too closely to recede, and the mastiff, in spite of a heavy chain that cramped his movements, darted out suddenly and seized the wolf by the skin of the back. The sequel was remarkable. The mastiff, impeded by his chain, began to yield to the struggles of the wolf, which was a full-grown powerful beast, when, just at the right moment, another large dog arrived at full speed, accompanied by the little terrier, who had evidently seen his comrade's need of assistance, and gone off to procure it. This unexpected ally put an end to the conflict, and the wolf was speedily mastered. Madame Bastide,—the wheelwright's wife,—her daughter, and servant—all three witnessed the scene, which they each described as related; and indeed there is nothing in the story incredible, many parallels having occurred to illustrate the intelligence of animals in comprehending a position of urgency, as well as the facilities they possess for making known to each other their wants and wishes.—*Saint Pauls for July*, edited by Anthony Trollope.

EPIPHYLLUM TRUNCATUM.—When well grown, this plant is one of the most showy of the decorative stove plants which flower in the dreary months of November and December. I had a collection of different varieties in flower here, and most beautiful objects they were, mixed with other plants in a warm greenhouse. They range about 3 feet in height, and with the exception of about 6 inches at the top, they are a complete mass of flowers to the bottom of the pot. The young plants were procured from the Messrs. Lee, of Hammersmith, who obtained, I believe, some of the varieties from the Continent. I am not aware what stocks or stock they have been grafted or inarched on, but they seem to grow vigorously. The following varieties are the best and most distinct in colours that have flowered here, namely :—Elegans, Magnificum, Russsellianum, Superbum, Truncatum violaceum, and Ruckerianum. My collection has been managed so as to keep the plants rather dry after they have done flowering, and not to excite them to grow before June or July. At that period they are repotted, the old balls being well reduced. The soil used is richer than what is generally given to succulent plants—namely, some well rotted deer dung, mixed with broken lime rubbish and light sandy loam. They are then kept in a warm moist stove to make their young growths, and generally flower about the middle of November.—W. Tillery, in *Florist and Pomologist.*

FAIRY RINGS.—The origin of every fairy ring is a fungus, and the *agarics* are those which most commonly give rise to them. In the decay of a fungus, we read in the *Gardener's Magazine*, a large amount of phosphates is returned to the earth, and the grass which was originally displaced by it takes possession of the spot, and the phosphates deposited there furnish it with a rich manure, in which it grows more luxuriantly than elsewhere. In the meantime, the fungus has distributed its spores in a circle, and when this circular growth of fungi passes away, the grass takes possession of the first ring so formed, and its vigorous growth gives it the dark rick colour by which it is distinguished from the surrounding herbage. The fungi which formed the first ring decay in their turn, and scatter a fresh ring of spawn outside the first, their growth being always towards the soil on which there have been no fungi; while the grass regularly follows, and thus the ring grows larger year after year. It would occupy many of our pages to follow the explanation into all its details, and we must therefore beg our correspondent to remain content with this brief reply. We may, however, add, that edible fungi are very commonly found on fairy rings, and are associated with them in the minds and experiences of those who hold to the ancient notion of the fairies dancing at night on these, their magic circles. The best champignons we ever gathered were from a fairy ring on Hampstead Heath, some twenty-five years since. There is a chapter on the subject in "Brambles and Bay-leaves."

REMEDY FOR INSECT BITES.—When a mosquito, flea, gnat, or other noxious insect punctures the human skin, it deposits or injects an atom of an aciduous fluid of a poisonous nature. This causes an irritation, a sensation of tickling, itching, or of pain. The tickling of flies we are comparatively indifferent about; but the itch produced by a flea or a gnat, or other noisome insect, disturbs our serenity, and, like the pain of a wasp or a bee-sting, excites us to a "remedy." The best remedies for the sting of insects are those which will instantly neutralise this aciduous poison deposited in the skin. These are either ammonia or borax. The alkaline reaction of borax is scarcely yet sufficiently appreciated. However, a time will come when its good qualities will be known and more universally valued than ammonia, or, as it is commonly termed, "hartshorn." Borax is a salt of that innocent nature that it may be kept in every household; it can be recommended as a domestic and harmless chemical. The solution of borax for insect bites is made thus:—Dissolve one ounce of borax in one pint of water that has been boiled and allowed to cool. Instead of plain water, distilled rose-water, elder or orange flower water, is more pleasant. The bites are to be dabbed with the solution so long as there is any irritation. For bees' or wasps' stings the borax solution may be made of twice the above strength.—Septimus Piesse, F.C.S., *Land and Water*, June 27.

ALLIGATORS IN MEXICO.—On one occasion I discovered an alligator's nest with thirty-nine eggs. It is the custom of the caymans to select some sunny sandy beach, in which they bury their eggs, piling a large heap of sand above them. They then leave their offspring to be hatched by the heat of the sun; although, as the Indians informed me, they keep "a register in their head," and return at the expiration of thirty days, when their newly-produced little ones are ready to be taken on their mother's back and receive their first lessons in swimming. The idea that the alligator devours her young if she can catch them is denied by the Indians, who, on the contrary, declare her to be very kind to them. I should like to have seen in what way the maternal solicitude of one of these horrid creatures is shown, for a nursing alligatress must be a great curiosity. The eggs are about the size of those of our domestic ducks, but bearing a highly-enamelled surface. At each end they are translucent; but an opaque white band encircles the middle, which appears to have a divided membrane across it. The yolk also resembles that of a duck's egg, but has a slight flavour of musk, and the white is nearly of the consistency of jelly.—*Capt. Lyon.*

THE "PLEASURES" OF COCHIN CHINA.—Every morning, on turning my eyes on the beams and rafters of the bungalow, I saw serpents of a large size, creeping and winding over and about them. At first I was horror-struck at the sight, but after a time they had ceased to terrify me, and at length became even familiar to the eye; so that when I awoke I used to look for them as objects of course, and learnt to distinguish my visitants one from another, both by the diversity of their speckles, black and green, and by their size. They twined round and round the rafters and beams, but I never knew one of them to fall upon or molest me. Here, also, the trees and bushes were illumined by swarms of fire-flies, which presented, on a dark night, the grandest sight imaginable. It was my custom to stroll with my friends through the paddy-fields in the interior, and admire the verdure of the country and the majesty of the silent forest; and often has the black scorpion, two or three inches in length, turned towards us his deadly sting, and the wild elephant, the buffalo, or sanguinary tiger, encroached on our path. And here the boa, and other enormous serpents, fatal alike to man and beast, might be seen coiled beneath the bushes, watching eagerly for their prey.—*Voyages in the East.*

WHISKY SPRINGS.—We are horrified to hear of the discovery of a whisky spring near Nodaway, in Missouri. The liquid flows between two rocks, and looks like highly coloured brandy, but it tastes and smells like pure whisky, and has the same intoxicating effect. The local paper in which we find an account of the dreadful discovery says that "Several lawyers, physicians, and newspaper men were preparing to go out yesterday morning to test the discovery, but the aspect of rain deterred them,"—that is to say, they did not wish to mix water with their whisky. The supply from the spring or well is said to be unlimited, and it is believed that other springs will be discovered in the vicinity till they are as abundant as oil wells in Pennsylvania. We almost fear to make these announcements in a New York journal. We fear that our city will be depopulated, and that there will be such a rush to Nodaway that it will become the metropolis of the country, while we lose that commercial supremacy which has long been our boast. We urge Congress to investigate the matter—not too deeply, however—and place a tax of at least ten dollars a gallon on the products of all whisky springs.—*New York Times.*

REMARKABLE THREE-LEGGED FOAL.—
SIR: I send you the enclosed photograph of a foal which was dropped on the 6th instant, and lived until the evening of the 8th. I regret I had not an opportunity of examining it when alive, or when it was being prepared for stuffing. As I only heard of it yesterday, I went to-day to see it, and was conducted to the shed where the creature was "strung up" by an old Frenchman, who told me the only way he could account for it was that the mare "got a fright." He said when the artillery were at big-gun practice she exhibited the greatest horror, and trembled violently the whole time of the practice. When I saw the stuffed animal the parts had dried up considerably, but you will see the arrest of development of the right fore leg; the limb measured only ten inches, and looked like a goat's leg. The other leg was apparently more developed than normal, and terminated in a sort of club foot, with the hoof turned up, which was cloven like the hoof of a bullock. The old man informed me that the right kidney and testicle were absent, as also the bladder. It is looked upon by the natives as a most wonderful animal.—W. G. (Alderney.)

EXPEDITION FOR THE AUGUST ECLIPSE.—The mission sent out to observe the eclipse of the sun on the 18th August, by the Minister of Public Instruction in France, who has granted £2,000 to the purpose, has just left Marseilles for the East. The Academy of Sciences of Paris has also commissioned M. Jassen, known for his spectroscopic researches, to proceed to the East, for the same purpose, and has voted £600 for expenses, to which the Minister of Public Instruction has added £480. The Governor of the French settlement of Cochin China has informed the Minister of Marine that the preliminary preparations for the observations in question are completed. The spot selected is on the coast of the peninsula of Malacca, and it is said that the King of Siam has expressed his desire to be present at the observations. A similar expedition has been organised by the Prussian Government, at the instance of the Berlin Astronomical Society. As each nation selects a spot distant from that to which the English expedition has proceeded, there is every hope that in one place, if not more, the weather will be favourable for observation.

WOLF'S FLESH AS FOOD.—The flesh of the wolf may be taken certainly to be about the rankest carrion in creation, not even excepting that of the common vulture and the turkey-buzzard. Yet all this in reality is less fact than imagination. M. Charles Cauthey, a well-known sportsman in the Côte-d'Or, relates that the landlord of a country inn, himself a sportsman, and wishing to pay the brethren a confraternal trick—or as it is called in French, *leur jour un tour de chasseur*,—had a piece of wolf's flesh cut into small square morsels, and stewed up with veal and mutton cut into pieces of a different shape. The landlord helped the ragoût himself, and being careful to serve each guest with one of the square morsels, was enabled to inform them after dinner that they had all been eating wolf. Two of the guests were thereupon seized with horror, and one to such a degree that he was compelled to retire from the table with precipitation. The others took the joke in good part, and one and all declared they had detected nothing in the dish to excite suspicion in the least degree.—*Saint Pauls for July*, edited by Anthony Trollope.

A PETRIFIED HARE.—A singular fossil was found on Wednesday week by Mr. Jeffry Wilson, of Filey. Having wandered on the sands in search of pebbles, as far as Speeton Cliffs, his attention was arrested by something of a remarkable shape, in what by geologists is called "Speeton Clay," a seam which has for many years and still is, exceedingly rich in fossils of various kinds. On going up to it he found it to be a perfectly-formed petrified hare, sitting in a crouching position, and from one of the ears being laid flat on the head it is presumed that in ages gone by a quantity of earth had fallen upon her, and thus poor "pussy" had become embedded. This distinctly developed specimen, which has caused great interest among the clergy, gentry, &c., who have gone to see it, measures about 16 inches in length, and weighs nearly 14lbs. Mr. Wilson was also fortunate enough in finding near the cliff an immense snake stone of great beauty.—*Leeds Mercury.*

SALE OF FUNGI AS FOOD IN MILAN.—The sale of fungi in Milan is under great restriction, and is only allowed in the public markets, so as to be under the immediate eye of the market inspectors. The sale of all fungi prejudicial to health, as also those but little known, even if not poisonous, is strictly prohibited. The following are the only varieties of fungi which are permitted to be sold in the Milanese markets:—

Name in Milanese dialect.	Italian names.	Botanical names.
Funsg ferrée	Fungo porcino	Boletus edulis
Funsg cocch	Uovolo	Agaricus cæsareus.
Spongignœura	Spugnuola	Phallus esculentus.
Trifola	Tartufo	Lycoperdon tuber.

Any infringement of these regulations is punished by fines and imprisonment.—*H. Soc. of Soc. of Arts.*

WILD CATS IN THE UNITED STATES.—Speaking of wild cats, the *Hartford Times* remarks that these animals are more plentiful in Lichfield county than they were fifty years ago, and adds: "They are probably as bloodthirsty an animal, in proportion to their size, as the tiger. They will often kill sheep and other animals merely to suck their blood, though they commonly devour most of the victim's flesh. Dogs are often charged with ravages upon sheep that are really committed by wild cats. The wild cat, though commonly regarded as a first-cousin of the domestic cat, is really a distinct species —as distinct as the panther. The largest one ever killed in Connecticut was shot ten years ago in East Lyme; it weighed forty-one pounds. These creatures are never inclined to show fight to man, unless wounded, or when pressed by starvation."

RED CAVE EARTH.—The presence of a red earth deposited in caves at some very remote period has long been a puzzle to the geologist. Will the late earthquake in the Sandwich Islands tend to solve the problem? It is stated—"The greatest shock occurred on April 2—a great shower of ashes and pumice. During the great shock, the swinging motion of the earth was dreadful: so violent that no person could stand. In the midst of this tremendous shock, an eruption of red earth poured down the mountain, rushing across the plain three miles in three minutes, and then ceased. Then came the great tidal wave, and then the streams of lava. The earth opened under the sea, and reddened the water," &c. — W. S. A.—*Athenæum.*

EXPERIMENT TO TEST THE COMPARATIVE APPETITES OF SHEEP & RABBITS.—At a recent meeting of the Staindrop Farmers' Club, a paper was read on the comparative appetites of sheep and rabbits. Two hoggett sheep and twelve full-grown rabbits had been put up, and fed for six weeks on oats, cut clover, bran and roots. At the end of that time it was found that nine rabbits in captivity ate as much as two sheep, and of course, when free, they destroy much more than they consume. Some estimate may thus be formed of the injury done to tenant-farmers by rabbits. A farm on which 900 rabbits are shot yearly is taxed far more heavily than if its tenant had to maintain a flock of 200 of his landlord's sheep. The sheep, too, would be useful in fertilising the land, whilst rabbits are of no use at all in that capacity.

A HAIRLESS HORSE.—Considerable interest was excited on Friday week by the appearance of a horse entirely destitute of hair. The animal was yoked in a Freswick cart, and certainly never did man or beast from that district draw such crowds of spectators as did the hairless nag. The huge beast sporting a glossy black skin, presented a singular appearance, more like that of an elephant than an ordinary horse. It appears that he was lately confined in a mill, which was greatly heated, and coming out to the air, immediately rolled himself on a quantity of lime, the result being that in a short time every inch of his body, "from the tip of the nose to the end of the tail," was denuded of its natural covering. There is now little or no chance of vegetation flourishing on his hide again.—*Northern Ensign.*

PROFITS OF A PEAR CROP.—The following statement relates to seven successive years. The account commences when the trees were only eight years old, and one crop failed. They were originally dwarfs on Quince stocks, but are supposed to have now thrown out roots from the pear:—

The 1st registered crop, trees 8 years old					£25	0	0
2nd	,,	,,	,,	9 ,,	30	0	0
3rd	,,	,,	,,	10 ,,	36	10	0
4th	,,	,,	,,	11 ,,	40	0	0
5th	,,	,,	,,	12 ,,	53	10	0
6th	,,	,,	,,	13 ,,	62	0	0
7th	,,	,,	,,	14 (94 bush.)	241	0	0

The distance of the trees asunder is stated to be 10 feet; at the same rate there would be 435 on an acre which, if yielding like the rest, would give a total annual average, in round numbers, of £800 per acre. *Melbourne Weekly Age.*

CENTIPEDES EXTRAORDINARY.—While the workmen were engaged breaking up the condemned barque Charlotte, in Algoa Bay, a number of centipedes, measuring from six to eight inches, were discovered, with fangs of a most formidable description. We hope they won't find their way into any of the habitations here, and would advise those promenading the breakwater of an evening to look out for them. Some of them are nearly as big as lobsters. They are supposed to have got on board among the sugar at Rangoon, where, if people are much troubled with these monsters, they must spend many sleepless nights.—*South African Mail.*

THE PASSION-FLOWER.—The beautiful Passion-flower, now so common in England, is a native of the forests of Central America, where it grows on large stems which hang like festoons from the boughs of forest trees, interleaving them in a network of gorgeous leaves and flowers. The term Passion-flower was applied by the Spaniards, owing to the supposed resemblance presented in various parts of the floral whorls to the accessories of Christ's crucifixion. The conspicuous ray-like appendages, sprinkled with blood-like spots, were compared to the crown of thorns; the stigma is cruciform; nor were the ardent Spaniards slow to discover other fancied resemblances, which eyes less prejudiced than their own in favour of a dominant idea can scarcely recognise.—*"Lessons in Botany," Cassell's.*

SAGACITY OF THE HORSE.—M. de Bouffanelle mentions, in his *Observations Militaires*, that a horse of great spirit and beauty, belonging to his company, having, from great age, his teeth so impaired as to be unable to masticate his food, was supported for two months, and would have been longer, had he been kept, by the two horses who ate with him on his right and left. They took alternately hay and corn from the rack, chewed it, and laid it before the aged animal. This fact, says the author, is fully attested by a whole regiment of cavalry.

AMAZING SITE FOR A PHEASANT'S NEST.—SIR: It is not unusual to hear of very strange places being selected by birds of various kinds for nesting, but the most extraordinary instance of all that have come to my knowledge, and this upon satisfactory evidence, is one of a pheasant laying in a small hollow under the rail upon which trains were passing daily. Even there did she succeed in hatching her brood, and carrying them off in safety.—Z., *Land and Water*, June 25th.

LILIUM AURATUM.—This fine lily is now beginning to put forth its strength, and we seem to be fairly on the road for some extraordinary displays of its blooming powers. At the Edgbaston Nursery of Messrs. Felton and Holiday, there is now in flower the finest specimen of it of which I have yet heard. It has three stems ranging from 6 to 7 feet high, on which are now expanded or in bud 54 blooms.

Remarks, Queries, &c.

(*Under this head we shall be happy to insert original Remarks, Queries, &c.*)

NOTICE OF THE PHYSALIA ARETHUSA (known among sailors and fishermen as the Portuguese man-of-war).—It is amusing, and not a little instructive, to trace the progress of our knowledge of the History of Nature to our own time, from its condition a couple of centuries ago ; when we find in that authentic and respectable publication entitled Miscellanea Curiosa (vol. 3), which derived its authority from the Members of the Royal Society, and was edited by the eminent Doctor Derham ; the following notice of the above-named animal by a clergyman, Mr. John Clayton, in his voyage to Virginia in the year 1688 :—

"In the sea I saw many little things which the seamen called carvels ; they are like a jelly, or starch that is made with a cast of blue in it ; they swim like a small sheep's bladder above the water ; downwards there are long fibrous strings, some whereof I have found nearly half a yard long. This I take to be a sort of sea plant, and the strings its roots growing in the sea, as duckweed does in ponds. It may be reckoned among the potential Cauteries ; for when we were one day becalmed, getting some to make observations thereof, the sportful people rubbed it on one another's hands and faces, and where it touched it would make it look very red, and make it smart worse than a nettle. In my return for England we struck a Hawk's bill Turtle, in whose guts I found many of those carvels, so that it is manifest they feed thereon."

This creature is not uncommon on the coast of Cornwall, in company with Vetellæ of one or two species, conveyed probably by the joint action of the gulf stream and a south-west wind, but its name of carvel is unknown on our coasts. The Portuguese man-of-war has been said to obtain its name from the fact that when a storm arises it is likely to sink to the bottom, which however is not likely to be the case with the ship, and is impossible with the Physalia. Another supposition has been, that whereas the creature is sure to be driven before the wind in whatever direction it may blow the ship referred to will assume the same direction. In the present day no one acquainted with this beautifully coloured animal will be disposed to join in the opinion of the gentleman above mentioned, that the floating bubble like bladder is of a vegetable nature, and that its tendrils are analogous to the roots of duckweed ; but there is something remarkable in the stinging effect that is produced by contact with it, and which is felt also by handling several species of medusæ which, chiefly in summer, are in abundance on our coast. Sailors and fishermen are not generally endowed with great delicacy of skin on the hands, and yet they are often heard to mention the uneasy feeling with which they have been affected from handling these creatures in their native element. But on the other hand the writer has procured Physaliæ while still alive, has closely examined them while floating, without hesitating to turn them about in all directions ; but in no instance has he been sensible of an unpleasant feeling. And as regards Medusæ also, to examine them more effectually, and obtain a correct figure of the species, as it can only be drawn in their freedom of action in the open sea, when he has gone in a boat and handled them at leisure, in no case has he felt the stinging sensation complained of by others : a peculiarity of organization in the skin of the hands not easily to be accounted for.

It may be thought deserving of record that in one instance an example of a Medusa, of a common sort, was weighed at his request, and the weight was found to amount to forty pounds.

JONATHAN COUCH, F.L.S., M.Z.S., &c.

DO INSECTS FEEL PAIN?—Yes, says analogy, and we are too modest to reject the deductions from analogy. Man himself feels pain, the whale, the elephant, and the sparrow, etc., and consequently insects also feel pain. Why not? They have life, and hence we may reasonably presume that that life is susceptible of pain and pleasure. Mr. Harvie argues that insects "have extremely little (if any) feeling," and then, as a matter of course, no pain. Surely Mr. Harvie must be mistaken when he denies insects the sense of feeling. One of the true characteristics of insects is the very delicacy of feeling : take away feeling, take away pain, and what is animal life? Little more than inorganic existence. Mr. Harvie admits that insects eat, drink, and perform avocations, and yet he cannot allow them feeling or pain. Naturalists tell us that "insects, in their instincts, are more remarkable than any other race of beings," and surely this very instinct implies the susceptibility of pain in the possessor. Animal vitality is an active principle, and violence offered to that vitality, whether in a whale or an animalculum, is alike the cause of pain ; for indeed none of us can resist the belief inculcated by the poet that a tortured insect feels as much pain "as when a giant dies." If not, wherein consists the cruelty of killing insects? "But," says Mr. Harvie, "many writers on entomology mention the extraordinary unconcern with which insects receive wounds and loss of members, which, if inflicted on ourselves would, if not mortal, at least render us unfit for anything." I cannot see the analogy here, and hence this reasoning, in my opinion, is quite remote. The physical construction of "ourselves" is quite different from that of insects ; an insect is often provided with six or eight legs—ourselves generally but two ; a man gets a stroke of a sword, a thrust of a spear, or a blow of a stone ; let Mr. Harvie name the kind of weapons and the force of the propelling power that would inflict a similar injury on one of his pain-despising insects. Some of the philosophers of old held that there was no such thing as pain, but I presume Mr. Harvie does not carry his views quite so far. But will your correspondent calmly tell me that if I take this pen with which I write, and amuse myself in mutilating insects, will he I say deny that the insects so mutilated feel no pain, and that I am guilty of no cruelty? Indeed, your correspondent's sympathy for the insects is candidly acknowledged towards the end of his article ; for he says "there would be no excuse for any cruelty practised on them. Admitted, Mr. Harvie, for this very cruelty you condemn implies that it is the cause of pain, and hence its repudiation. Indeed, your able correspondent Mr. Harvie and I quite agree with the poet when he says :—

"And he that *hurts*
Or harms them there is guilty of a wrong ;
Disturbs the economy of Nature's realm."

Without speculating on the organisation of insects, or following too closely the writings of entomologists, it is perfectly safe for us to suppose that insects, in common with other animals even of a higher order, are capable of feeling pain. H. H. ULIDIA.
Dromore.

KILLING OF INSECTS.—I have noticed an inquiry from some of your subscribers, a method to kill insects. I was out amongst the fields, and an accident or incident happened that has been useful to myself since. I record it for the benefit of your readers. I caught a very fine specimen of the *Shrewe*. It was as black as ebony and as smooth as silk or velvet. I put it into my glove, but he soon had his long nose through that. I gave a little girl a penny to bring me a bottle, or anything to put a mouse into; she soon returned with a tin, and I thought it just the thing. Putting a little grass inside, I expected I would be able to get him safe home to place beside my young hedgehog and mole, and other curiosities; but, looking at my treasure a short time after, I found it quite dead. After getting home I set to work to discover the cause, if I could. On examining the inside, I found the tin to be one of Coleman's mustard canisters, with some of the material sticking to the corners. And now to turn the mishap to some useful account. I put *dry* mustard into some of my boxes, where I kill the insects for my cabinet; the article answers beautifully, and I like it for this purpose better than musk or sulphur, or anything else I have ever used. The insects *die soon*, are not at all *discoloured*, and are very *natural in shape*, and appear to die without any struggle, as not a feather or flour on the finest butterflies are at all disturbed. My boxes are made with double bottoms, the inner one perforated with small holes. I put the mustard lowest and the insects above it.

Manchester. JOHN POTTS.

THE AMERICAN MIGRATORY THRUSH (*Turdus migratorius*.)—Perhaps there is no bird in British North America better known to the inhabitants than this somewhat sombre coloured, yet cheerful songster. And this knowledge may be attributed in a great measure to the pleasure its presence gives to the denizens of that northern clime, who, after a long-continued winter—perhaps of great severity—are fully assured of its close, and the speedy return of the thrice welcome summer, by the presence of vast flocks of these birds, which, as an invariable rule, are to be seen on the cultivated grass lands at an early date, even before the snow has gone. In habit, it is very like the English thrush, or still more, the fieldfare, for the common thrush, as a rule, does not move about in flocks. Its breast is of a brick red colour, and from this feature is derived its well-known name among Canadians, of "robin." On some fine morning, about the end of March, when the sun pours forth its warm rays to gladden all nature, those who are blest with children know full well the welcome shout with which they dash into their parents chamber—"the robins! the robins! the robins!" And sure enough it is not only the young to whom the arrival gives pleasure, but to all, old and young, rich and poor, the arrival is considered of sufficient importance to be a general topic of conversation. A short time after their arrival, and generally at the close of the first fine open day of spring, as the sun is shedding its pale and fading rays over the forest, they begin their first attempt at song; and pleasant indeed it is to hear the welcome notes after the long protracted and silent winter, during which the whole country has been as it were icebound, and covered deep with a mantle of crusted snow. There is a circumstance attendant upon the first arrival of the migratory thrush, which, although often repeated by the "old grandmothers" of the country, is nevertheless worthy of attention. It is that a heavy snow storm generally takes place at the very close of winter, and that these thrushes make their appearance in flocks immediately after. The people call it "the robin storm." Now, I have frequently observed this to be the case, and if the snow should melt rapidly the next day, the thrushes are nearly certain to be seen running about the bare patches of ground in cultivated parts. So there is truth even in old women's tales. About the first week in May, they begin to build, generally making their nests on the branch of a tree, against the trunk, not far from the ground. I have, however, known these birds to build in elevated situations, but it is not their usual habit to do so. They lay five eggs of a light blue-green colour in their mud-lined nests, and the observer, looking upon the old birds as they sit close upon them, can see but little difference between the American "robin" and the English thrush. They are found in the summer months high up on the North American continent, even to the confines of the Arctic regions; and I have obtained them in winter time as far south as the Bermudus in latitude 32 deg. N.—J. M. J.

INTELLIGENCE OF PARROTS.—At a dinner party this evening the conversation turned in the direction of Natural History, when the question was asked, "Do parrots ever understand the meaning of words they are taught to pronounce?" A negative answer was indignantly given by some of the ladies, who were evidently shocked at the bare idea; but another, more venturesome than the rest, prepared to justify the affirmative. She had called, that afternoon, with a gentleman on a Captain S——, who kept a grey parrot. The gentleman amused himself with setting his bulldog at the bird, who, far from being in any measure disconcerted, showed unmistakeable signs of resenting the attack; snapping its bill, and exclaiming distinctly, "Go away, go away, get along with you!"

Another of the party told us that she had been visiting some friends lately, where a parrot was kept. The man-servant, named John, had occasion to leave the establishment, and on the day of his departure the bird kept uttering in sorrowful accents, "Poor Pol, poor pol; John gone away, gone away."

But the best story of all was narrated by a clergyman, to the following effect. A friend of his has a parrot, which on one particular occasion made such a chattering noise at family prayers, that it had to be removed. As the servant, who carried the cage, was opening the door, Polly exclaimed with stolid indifference "Sorry I spoke!" Query: Was any one able to conclude his devotions?

These stories, I confess, somewhat startled me, yet as they were related by credible witnesses, we are bound to respect their authenticity. But the matter,

I think, well deserves further notice, and any corroborative evidence to prove a superior intelligence in parrots, will be interesting. COCKEYWAX.

HAIRLESS ANIMALS.—On page 153 of the NOTE BOOK for this year, your clever correspondent (Mr. Groom Napier) gives an account of a hairless horse he saw at the Crystal Palace, but suggests no reason for the anomaly. I, too, saw it, and being much interested in it, consulted several works on Natural History to find what the reason of its nakedness was, or was supposed to be. At length, in an admirable German work, "Thier leben," by Messrs. Brehm and Kretschmer, I discovered this passage, of which I subjoin a translation:—"The naked horse (*Equus Nudus*) is in shape most like the Arabian. It is well built, and of moderate size; but except some hardly visible hairs which are studded at distances on it, it is quite naked. Even the mane and hairs on the tail are absent." Here follows a description of the horse, in which it is stated to be dark grey or brown; the horse at the Palace is probably a variety. "Minute investigations have proved that neither illness or 'doctoring' (German: Fälschung) on the part of the owner are the causes of this nakedness." Is this opinion that the naked horse is a separate species, endorsed by English naturalists? Wood does not mention *Equus Nudus* in his "Illustrated Natural History;" perhaps some of your readers can favour me with further information on the subject. TORTOISE.

ALBINOS.—Your correspondent, "R. B. W." asks or any additional names or specimen of this kind that may have come under the notice of your readers. I therefore beg to submit the following that have come under my own notice. Among the feathered race, namely, the sparrow-hawk, the wood-pigeon, magpie, linnet, goldfinch, chaffinch, and the common whitethroat. I would also observe that I have seen most of the kinds named by "R. B. W.": one white jackdaw, several starlings, one skylark, several swallows, a robin, and many of the sparrow kind; indeed, this curious aberration appears more frequently to occur among the sparrows than with any other kind that has come under my notice. Bewick mentions a white woodcock, and it is not improbable that an instance of this kind does occur at times among every species of the feathered race; nor is this strange phenomenon confined to the feathered race: as several albinos among the human race have been publicly exhibited —a brother and sister, not many years back, with white hair and pink eyes. The man I have seen many times, and learned that the proceeds from his being exhibited did not secure him from poverty in his latter days, as he was assisting the bricklayers some few years back, and having incautiously named to them that he was exhibited in former years as an Albino, they, not knowing or caring about the meaning of such phrase, at once styled him the Duke of Albany, which title I believe he enjoyed, or was rather bored with, till death removed him from further annoyance.

320, Strand. C. W . . . D.

BUTTERFLIES.—Observing the note by T. R. Clephan on page 222 in the July number, I am reminded of a similar circumstance that occurred some twenty or thirty years back. A friend of mine named Alfred Greenwood, of Springfield, Essex, informed me that as he was returning from the Isle of Wight during the warm weather he saw a cloud of butterflies passing over the water towards our shores; they were about the size of our small garden white, and so numerous as to have the appearance of a large cloud of snow flakes. He stated that he saw many of them falling into the water, but not sufficient to remarkably diminish their bulk. I think it likely that the particulars of this circumstance was recorded in the *Zoologist* at the time, as I know that the party named did send occasional notices to that publication. I am not aware whether any instance of the kind has ever been observed or recorded in reference to our indigenous butterflies. If any of your entomological readers know of an instance, I should feel extremely obliged by reference being made thereto, through the medium of the NOTE BOOK. C. W . . . D.

320, Strand.

RAY PASTINACA.—About a fortnight ago, a boy belonging to a tribe of gipsies encamped near the seashore, was amusing himself with catching little fish left in the pools by the tide, at Seasalter, near Whitstable, when he came upon a large flat fish in a pool about a foot deep. Stooping to take hold of its head, the creature whisked its long spring tail round, and drove it quite through the fleshy part of the boy's leg, and on his attempting to release himself, it struck him again on the arm, inflicting a severe wound, though not so bad as the first. The boy was carried to a doctor at Whitstable, who said that he had never seen such peculiarly lacerated wounds. The fish turned out to be a sting ray (*Raia pastinaca*. Linn.), locally known as a fire-slate or sand ray. The tail is armed with a spine, notched on both sides, and the wounds inflicted by its saw-like edges are so dangerous, and difficult to heal, that it is commonly held to be venomous.

GULIELMUS.

BIRDS SINGING AT NIGHT.—Although several birds, such as the Sedge Warbler, Nightingale, &c., sing at night, yet I think the following facts are somewhat out of the usual course. On the 16th of May I was at Ash, in Surrey, and heard a cuckoo give utterance to its note at 11.45 p.m., and this continued with the usual intervals until 12.30 a.m. The night was bright and starlight. This brought to mind that at the same place on 20th February, 1867, I heard a blackbird and several thrushes singing as if it were day at 12.15 a.m. I listened until 1.30 a.m. and found that the thrushes still continued in full song; the weather was fine, but the moon shining through the clouds gave a hazy light something like early morning. On the 27th of June of the same year I recollect hearing a Nightjar "churning" away at 2.10 a.m., and this apparently provoked a lark to burst into full song; however, this was not so singular, as the morning dawned at 2.45 a.m. A. M. B.

COLOUR OF BIRDS' EGGS.—"M. L. A.," on page 158, states—as a fact against the theory proposed by "J. D. S. W.," viz. that the colour of eggs is affected by the light of the sun—that the dove tribe, as well as wild ducks, etc., lay in an "open nest exposed to the light." Now though it is true that these birds make open nests, it is not that they are exposed to the light.

Wild pigeons build amongst the thick foliage of a fir or other tree, generally situated in a dark wood, from which the rays of the sun are effectually excluded. Geese, ducks, etc. usually breed on the banks of rivers, or in marshes, where their nests are pretty well sheltered by the long grass and reeds; their eggs too are often not pure white. R. B. W.

Will any botanist kindly mention the name of that plant, so much like the common rhubarb, which grows in the sand on the borders of rivers? R. B. W.

USE OF PLANTS.—"Plants, besides affording food for animals, perform the almost equally useful function of purifying the air. They possess the property of absorbing the noxious gases, and of giving out oxygen. They therefore withdraw from the atmosphere what animals impart to it, and supply to it what animals consume." In this extract the indirect use of plants to animal health is affirmed. Now if this be true (as no doubt it is) how is it that the vicinity of woods, and those places where vegetation thrives best, and is most abundant, is considered so unfavourable to health, especially in hot climates? Open and clear lands are thought much more healthy than those surrounded with wood, even when the temperature is the same. We likewise find, that where animal life thrives, vegetation declines,—as on the sea coast. Information will much oblige. R. B. W.

REPLIES TO QUERIES.—In answer to P. H. B.'s query in the June number of the "Note Book," I beg to state his moth is the pale tussock, *O. Pudibunda*. He also mentions a hen canary that sings, I knew of a hen bullfinch that whistled. "Entomologicus" says that sulphur does not discolour the wings of moths; I find it does; turpentine generally kills them. "M. L. A." stated in the June number of the "Note Book," that there is a belief in Hampshire that there are two snakes besides the viper in England, the common snake and a water snake, which is venomous, but there is no water snake or poisonous one (except the viper) in England, though there exists one, which is harmless, called the "New Snake." N.B.—The common snake often goes into the water.

May 19th. R. PETRE.

CURIOUS ROOK.—On the 21st of April I was shown a rook which had been shot at Ash in Surrey on the previous day by a man of the name of Hunt. The bird was of the ordinary size and shape, but its upper mandible was protracted downwards some three inches beyond the lower in a regular and graceful curve, channeled inside throughout its entire length, and attenuated to a point somewhat like the bill of a curlew. Upon speaking about this to a person connected with the British Museum, he mentioned having heard of a similar instance, and suggested a new species; but this view I cannot endorse, as in the case I mention it was clearly a deformity, although by its singularity it added, instead of detracting, from the appearance of the bird. A. M. B.

LAPLAND BUNTING.—In answer to "C. B. R." I have extracted the following description of the Lapland Bunting from Johnson's British Birds:— "Crown of the head black, speckled with red; throat and breast black, a broad white band extending from the eye down the sides of the neck; nape bright chestnut; back, wings, and tail variegated with brown, white, and black; under parts white, spotted at the sides with dark brown. Length, six inches and three quarters; eggs pale ochre-yellow, spotted with brown." Neither the cirl bunting nor the rock pippit migrate. M. L. A.

PIKE SWALLOWING A PIKE.—A few days ago, Mr. Martin, miller, Horsebridge, Sussex, happening to see a disturbance in the water of the mill stream, his attention became fixed upon a fish engaged in gorging another almost as big as himself. He fetched his gun and shot the fish, and in taking it from the water, found it to be a pike weighing about a pound. Firmly fixed in its teeth was another pike of about half the length, which it had nearly succeeded in swallowing.

HARE AND RABBIT.—I trust that Mr. T. W. Tempany will give us some authority for the statement made in your last number, p. 221, viz. "that hybrids of the hare and rabbit had been produced fertile with one another." As far as I am able to ascertain, all the best authorities are pretty unanimous in the opinion that there is no authenticated instance of such a cross, or indeed any probability of its being produced. If Mr. Tempany, having the opportunity, will examine the animals sold as leporides in the Paris markets, he will, I am sure, soon see that they are only a large rabbit, and no cross of any kind.

9 July, 1868. J. S., Junr.

ATTRACTION OF THE EARTH.—In M'Cullock's *Course of Reading* we are told that "the reason why a falling stone does not exert any perceptible force on the earth is, not that the earth has any special power which the stone has not, but merely that the earth from its immense bulk has so much greater attraction than the stone, that its *motion towards the stone* is too small to admit of observation or measurement." I would ask, is the earth at all influenced by the stone? Is there mutual attraction between a large body and a small? Is not the attraction confined to the large? R. B. W.

LADY-BIRDS.—I do not know whether any one has observed the partiality which these little insects have for feeding upon dead bird's eyes, for I have noticed that whenever I lay a shot bird by to stuff or dissect I always find one or more lady birds (*Coccinella Bipunctata*), with which we are infested, feeding upon the eyes. It is true that they occasionally attack the parts which are torn by the shot, but the chief and regular banquet appears to be upon the eyes.

A. M. B.

BIRDS' DISEASES.—Two or three of my linnets have been subject to a yellow scab, partly on the beak and partly on the forehead. I was recommended to dab it with sweet oil, which I did, and in a few days the scab left, but the forehead became gradually bare, extending partly round the eyes. One of the linnet's forehead looks very sore. Can any of your readers divine the cause and recommend any better method of treatment?

London, June, 1868. J. T.

BEAUTIFUL BUTTERFLY.—Sir, during my walk before breakfast this morning, I saw a most beautiful butterfly, which had settled on the ground a few feet in

advance of me, but before I had time to examine it, it flew off. What I did see of this beautiful creature, resembled a piece of black velvet tipped with red and orange, and I should think a magnificent specimen. Can any of your readers inform me of its name, and to what class it belongs?
Salisbury.   BERNARD C. BUSH.

THE COW SUPERSEDED!—In *Fowler's Physiology*, published 1857, there is this paragraph:—"Butter may be made from the grass or hay direct, just as good as from the cow, and four or five hundred per cent. more in quantity from the same amount of provender." Not having before heard of this new method of manufacturing this useful article of food, I should feel much obliged, if any of your readers could give me any information about it.   R. B. W.

RAIN FALLING.—In your number of the present month, a correspondent under the signature of "R. T." requests information respecting the phenomenon of rain falling from a serene cloudless sky? I beg to say that I perfectly recollect (and have it recorded in my journal) that in the autumn (1837), one afternoon it rained for a few minutes when apparently it was cloudless.   G. Y.

PUPÆ.—Allow me to record in your NOTE BOOK that, by digging during the winter months for Acronycta Megacephala, I also dug a pupa of Acronycta Alni, which came out in the middle of June, and which is now placed in my collection. Might it not be more freely taken if pupæs found on the barks of poplars, etc., were not put down for A. Megacephala, but brought home and placed in the breeding cage?
    J. LEIGH.

PUPÆ.—Will some reader of "The Note Book" give me a few hints on pupæ digging.   B. S.

SMALL EGGS.—In answer to "M. F. A.," I can state that I was told of a fowl which laid an egg some few weeks ago of a remarkably small size, and a few days after, as if to compensate for such a mistake, she laid one tremendously large, which on being broken was found to contain another small one, both having yolks.   A. M. B.

NATIVE FOREST TREES.—In page 322 of the NOTE BOOK for 1867, "J. W. W. B." has among the list of native trees of Britain, the sycamore and the horse chesnut, which statement he will find contradicted in the "Trees of Old England," by L. H. Grindon (published by F. Pitman), where he says the sycamore was introduced during the later crusades, and the latter in the time of the Romans.
    W. R. L., A LOVER OF TREES.

PECULIAR FISH.—Seeing this in your last reminds me of some gold carp which I saw last year at Portsmouth, two of which had double tails, that is to say an extra tail by the side of their proper one. The person who owned them assured me that one had died lately which possessed *three* tails, a combination entitling it, like the celebrated Pasha, to be called "of many *tails*," I should think.   A. M. B.

LARGE ANT HILL.—Not long ago, I was walking in a wood and found an enormous ant hill, made by the wood ant (*Formica Rufa*); it was chiefly composed of the needles of the Scotch fir. I afterwards came and measured it, and found it was upwards of thirteen yards in circumference and four feet in height. Is not this an uncommonly large ant hill?
    M. L. A.

SUNSTROKES.—Can you or any of your numerous correspondents give instances of the disease called the "sun-stroke" occurring in this country? or is it confined to those which are subject to the vertical influence of the sun? It is supposed that the rays of the moon shining on persons exposed to them for several hours sometimes causes blindness and other evils, called a *coup de lune*; is such the case?   R. B. W.

CURIOUS POSITION OF A NEST.—Last summer I found a nest of the Garden Warbler (Sylvia hortensis) in a bed of coarse over-grown nettles. It was attached to three of the stems in the manner of a Reed Warbler's, and elevated about a foot from the ground. There can be no doubt of the above, as I not only saw the old bird on the nest, but have now two of the eggs in my possession.   C. B. R.

SNAKES.—Will any one inform me about British snakes? How many species have we, and how may the viper be distinguished? Is it the only species that is viviparous? Where do snakes usually deposit their eggs and young? What remedies should be applied in case of bites?   R. B. W.

HYDROPHOBIA.—There is a current opinion that if a person receive the bite of a dog that is not mad, he is in danger of suffering from the disease, if the dog should become so at a *subsequent period*. Has this opinion any foundation? If true, how is it to be accounted for?
    R. B. W.

SIZE OF GOOSE'S EGG.—As your correspondent "W. H. D." thinks there is some exaggeration in the measurement of a goose's egg which measured 11in. by 9in., I beg to state, that I have one in my possession which measures 11½in. by 9½in., and weighed 11 ozs. before it was blown.   T. R. CLEPHAN.

AQUARIUMS.—Sir, will you please to ask in your next number for some method of rendering wood water-tight for the bottom of aquariums, etc.
The College, Epsom.   G. S. BOULGER.

CHENOPODEUM BONUS HENRICUS (Good King Henry). Can any of the readers of the N. N. B. tell me the origin of the above name. I have searched in various books on Botany, etc., but have not been able to ascertain it.   H. F. P.

EXCHANGE.—T. J. D. wishes to state that he is able and willing to make exchanges with the Entomologist, Naturalist, Vocalist, and Novelist. Apply by letter or personally, 15, Russell Street, Covent Garden, W.C.

LIST OF BUTTERFLIES.—Can any reader of "The Note Book" tell me where I can get a list of butterflies and moths, English and Latin, printed on one side only, for labelling.   B. S.

BOXES FOR LEPIDOPTERA.—In answer to "E. M.'s" question in the June number of the "Naturalist's Note Book," he can obtain the boxes he requires at Mr. Thos. Cook's, 513, New Oxford Street.   H. F. P.

VARIATIONS IN THE COLOUR, FORM, AND SIZE OF THE EGGS OF BIRDS.*

By C. O. Groom Napier, F.G.S.

Author of "The Food, Use, and Beauty of British Birds."

PART II.

VARIATIONS IN SIZE.—The aberrations in size between the eggs of birds, even of the same species, are very great. This is more markedly seen in the case of birds in a domestic state, but is hardly less seen in those laid in a wild state. The eggs of the honey-buzzard (*Pernis apivorus*) vary much in size; a sitting in my collection strikingly so, one egg being unusually small. The sitting contained three eggs, which is one more than is usually laid. They were taken at Markash, in the New Forest, from a crow's nest. The first large egg is 2 in. long by 1 in. 12-16ths wide, with a white ground, and was found on the 7th of June. It was taken, but the birds did not forsake, and three days after the second egg was laid, which is somewhat smaller, being 1-16th of an inch less each way, and has a red ground. The third is 1 in. 12-16ths long by 1 in. 7-16ths wide. It was laid on June 13, and was taken, together with the others, by Mr. J. R. Wise. The smaller egg is not much more than half the size of the largest, and its proportion is doubtless due to the exhaustion of albumen induced by laying an extra number of eggs. I have an egg of the barn-owl (*Strix flammea*) which measures 1 in. 3-16ths in length by 1 in. 2-16ths in breadth, the full size being 1 in. 9-16ths by 1 in. 4-16ths 1-2. The eggs of the red-backed shrike (*Lanius collario*) are sometimes very small. I have one 13-16ths in. long by 9-16ths 1-2 broad; the full size is 15-16ths in. long by 11-16ths 1-2 in. wide. The eggs of the blackbird (*Turdus merula*) are sometimes very small. I have one 1 in. 1-16th long by 11-16ths 1-2 in. wide. They are often 1 in. 5-16ths long by 15-16ths in. wide. The eggs of the hedge-accentor (*Accentor modularis*) are sometimes not more than 9-16ths 1-2 in. long by 7-16ths in. wide, which is about quarter the normal size. The eggs of the wheatear are sometimes very diminutive, being not more than 11-16ths 1-2 in. long by 8-16ths in. wide. The eggs of the nightingale (*Sylvia luscinia*) are sometimes nearly double the size of what they are at others, varying from 12-16ths to 15-16ths 1-2 in. long. Eggs of the common sparrow (*Fringilla domestica*) are sometimes very variable in size, from 10-16ths to 15-16ths in. long by 8-16ths to 12-16ths in. wide, or a range of two-thirds. The eggs of the greenfinch (*F. chloris*) also vary much, from 8-16ths long by 6-16ths 1-2 in. wide, to 14-16ths 1-2 long by 9-16ths 1-2 in. wide. Both these eggs were taken from one nest. A double-yolked egg of the yellow-hammer (*Emberiza citronella*) measures 1 in. 1-16th 1-2 long by 10-16ths in. wide. They are usually about 13-16ths in. long. The eggs of the bullfinch (*Fringilla pyrrhula*) are sometimes not more than 10-16ths in. long by 7-16ths in. wide. The full size is 14-16ths 1-2 long by 9-16ths 1-2 in. wide. The green woodpecker (*Picus viridis*) sometimes lays eggs of half the usual size, one egg I have being 1 in. long by 12-16ths in. wide, the full size being 1 in. 4-16ths long by 15-16ths in. wide. The largest specimen I ever saw of the egg of this bird, selected from 400 obtained in the forests of various parts of France, was 1 in. 6-16ths long by 15-16ths in. wide. But this was much larger than any others in the same sitting. I mention this, particularly, because it bears upon the question of the breeding of large species of woodpeckers in England. Mr. J. R. Wise, in his book, "The New Forest," p. 272, mentions the discovery of the breeding of the great black woodpecker (*P. martius*) in Pignel Wood, near Brokenhurst, Hants, by Mr. Farren. "He observed the hen bird," according to Mr. Wise, "in front of a hole, placed about six feet high, in a small oak, from which he had, earlier in the season, taken a green woodpecker's nest. Hiding himself in the brushwood, he, after waiting about half-an-hour, saw the hen return, and had no doubt as to her identity. An endeavour, however, to secure her with a butterfly net proved unsuccessful. He was afraid to leave the eggs." One egg was addled. These eggs are all the full size of those of the great black woodpecker taken from various localities in Lapland and the Alps, being 1 in. 7-16ths long by 1 in. broad, or one full 16th larger than the largest of 400 eggs of the green woodpecker, and is even 1-16th longer than a sitting of authenticated eggs of the great black woodpecker from Norway. The eggs of the rook (*Corvus frugilegus*) are sometimes very small, one I have being 15-16ths in. long by 12-16ths in. broad. This is the smallest I ever saw. The next in size is 1 in. 4-16ths by 14-16ths 1-2 in. wide. A large-sized egg is 1 in. 13-16ths long by 1 in. 3-16ths 1-2 wide. The eggs of the wood-pigeon, usually smooth, have sometimes a rough shell covered with hard lumps. It is very uncommon to find them as small as 1 in. 1-16th long by 11-16ths 1-2 in. wide. The full size is 1 in. 11-16ths by 1 in. 4-16ths wide. The eggs of the house-martin (*Hirundo urbica*) are rarely very small; one, the smallest of a hundred, is 10-16ths 1-4 in. long by

---

* Read before the British Association, 1866.

6-16ths 1-2 in. wide. The normal size is 13-16ths by 9-16ths in. wide. The eggs of the swift (*Cypselus apus*), usually of a slender oval, are sometimes nearly round. I have one 14-16ths in. long by 12-16ths in. wide. The eggs of the green woodpecker are sometimes also nearly round. I have one 1 in. 1-16th 3-4 by 15-16ths in. wide; and I have one of the kestrel 1 in. 7-16ths 1-2 by the same. This is the most perfectly round egg I ever saw of any British bird. The eggs of the pheasant (*Phasianus colchicus*) are sometimes a fifth of the normal size, one being 15-16ths 1-2 long by 12-16ths 1-4 in. wide, another being 1 in. 1-16th by 14-16ths in. wide. The normal egg of the pheasant is 1 in. 14-16ths long by 1 in. 7-16ths 1-2 wide. The eggs of the partridge (*Perdix cinereus*) are much less frequently found of a small size than those of the pheasant. I have one of a white colour 1 in. 1-16th 1-2 long by 15-16ths 1-2 in. wide. The full size of the partridge's egg is 1 in. 8-16ths by 1 in. 2-16ths. The eggs of the moorhen (*Gallinula chloropus*) are seldom found very small, the least I could find out of several thousands was 1 in. 9-16ths long by 1 in. 2-16ths 1-4 wide. The largest moorhen was 1 in. 14-16ths 1-4 long by 1 in. 5-16ths 1-2 in. wide. I have eggs of the moorhen which differ only in size from those of the water-rail, landrail, and coot, which thus harmonises with the arrangement of these birds in one family. The eggs of the Sclavonian grebe are sometimes of a very small size. I have three from Iceland strikingly so, the largest is 1 in. long by 14-16ths 1-2 in. wide. The second is 1 in. long by 12-16ths in. wide. The third is 11-16ths 1-2 in. long by 9-16ths 1-2 in. wide, or about the size of the egg of the sparrow. The full size of this bird's egg is 1 in. 15-16ths long by 1 in. 5-16ths 1-2 wide. The eggs of the common heron (*Ardea cineræ*) are very rarely round. I have one 1 in. 14-16ths by 1 in. 10-16ths, which is much less oval than usual; it is, moreover, of a pale blue colour, which is abnormal in this bird's eggs. The eggs of the black-headed gull (*Larus rudibundus*) are sometimes very small in size, the least out of many thousands is 1 in. 2-16ths long by 13-16ths in. wide. The next largest was 1 in. 1-16th 1-4. The first-mentioned egg was accompanied by one of a somewhat irregular shape and extraordinarily elongated form, being 1 in. 10-16ths 1-2 long by 12-16ths in. wide. The full-sized egg of this species is 2 in. 2-16ths long by 1 in. 9-16ths 1-2 in. wide. The longest I obtained out of some thousands was 2 in. 6-16ths 1-4 long. The eggs of some ducks are found of a diminutive size. I have one of the Iceland golden eye (*Anas Barrovii*) which measures 1 in. 12-16ths by 1 in. 6-16ths 1-4. The smallest of several eggs of the eider (*A. mollissimus*), from Iceland, measures 1 in. 4-16ths long by 1 in. wide. The smallest of several eggs of the scaup (*A. marila*) measures 1 in. 8-16ths long by 1 in. 3-16ths in. wide. These measurements are but fractions of those of the normal eggs of these ducks. The eggs of the terns are more rarely found of small size than those of some wild birds. The smallest of the common tern I ever saw is 1 in. 2-16ths long by 15-16ths in. wide. The full size is 1 in. 13-16ths long by 1 in. 3-16ths wide. I shall now treat of the even greater variations in the eggs of birds in a domestic state, commencing with the common fowl (*Gallus domesticus*). I have been at some pains to gather the largest eggs of the common fowl. My friend Mr. Rowley, also, has examined a vast number of hens' eggs, and I am indebted to him for several of the largest he has ever obtained. The largest measures 2 in. 15-16ths long by 2 in. 3-16ths wide, and weighed $4\frac{1}{4}$ oz., being more than double the normal weight. The largest single-yolked egg I ever obtained is 3 in. long by 2 in. 1-16th wide, and weighed 4 oz. The smallest double-yolked egg is 2 in. 15-16ths 1-2 by 1 in. 11-16ths, and is very abruptly pointed at each end. The largest double-yolked egg was 2 in. 14-16ths 1-2 long by 1 in. 13-16ths wide. It was decidedly shorter, but a little heavier than the last-named; it was laid by a fowl having "a strain" of the Cochin China breed. The smallest egg of the common fowl measured 11-16ths in. long by 9-16ths 1-2 in. wide, and weighed 30 grains when unblown. This is but a fraction of two ounces, which is the normal weight. I have two eggs laid by a hen which has assumed the male plumage, one measures 15-16ths in. long, the other 1 in. 2-16ths in. long. These are the so-called "cock's eggs" which have been for ages talked of, and have, in modern times, been supposed impossibilities. They are produced by a bird whose reproductive organs are in a state of exhaustion, and had, in both the cases I have just mentioned, no yolk. Such a bird, on assuming the male plumage is called a cock: thus is the foundation for the vulgar error. The largest egg I have without a yolk measures 1 in. 1-2 long by 1 in. 2-16ths wide, being the size and shape of a small egg of the rock-dove. But all these very small eggs have a shell abnormal in texture. The smallest hen's egg, with a normal shell I have obtained is 1 in. 2-16ths long by 14-16ths in. wide. The eggs of the Cochin China breed are also liable to great variations in size. The full size is 2 in. 3-16ths 1-2 long by 1 in. 11-16ths wide. The smallest I have seen is 1 in. 5-16ths long by 1 in. wide. All have a smooth and normal texture. The eggs of the bantam, likewise, vary greatly, being, when of full size, 1 in. 13-16ths long by 1 in. 5-16ths 1-2 wide. The smallest I have been able to meet with is 1 in. 6-16ths long by 1 in. 1-16th wide. The eggs of the guinea fowl, when of full size, are 2 in. 2-16ths long by 1 in. 10-16ths 1-4 wide. The smallest is 1 in. 4-16ths 1-2 long by 1 in. 1-16ths 1-2 wide. The eggs of the turkey (*Meleagris gallopava*) are not so often diminutive as those of the common fowl. The smallest I have met with is 2 in. 1-16ths long by 1 in. 9-16ths wide, The most elliptical is 3 in. 1-16th long by 1 in. 11-16ths wide. The normal turkey egg is 2 in. 13-16ths long by 1 in. 15-16ths wide. The eggs of the ducks (*Anatidæ*) vary greatly in size, but are not quite so subject to aberration in texture as those of gallinaceous birds. The normal egg of the common duck (*Anas boschas var domestica*) is 2 in. 6-16ths 1-2 long by 1 in. 13-16ths wide. The smallest I possess, and it is rare to find them less, is 1 in. 14-16ths long by 1 in. 7-16ths 1-2 wide. The largest double-yolked duck's egg I have found measures 3 in. 2-16ths long by 2 in. wide. It had a large folliculus or air bubble at the large end. A large duck's egg, which might have had two yolks, was laid by an Aylesbury bird, and weighed 4 oz. 3-4, or more than double the average weight; it measures 3 in. 3-16ths long by 2 in. 4-16ths wide. The average size of the common goose (*Anser cinereus var domestica*) is 3 in. 1-16th 1-2 long by 2 in. 5-16ths wide; but a double-yolked one measures 4 in. 4-16ths long by 2 in. 11-16ths wide. Eggs of domestic birds are subject to great aberration in form. I have one of a horn shape, laid by a common fowl. A second is of a pear shape. A third is of a natural oval, with a lump at the large end in repetition, apparently, of the "pope's nose" of the bird. A fifth is of a spindle shape, 2 in. 13-16ths long by 1 in. 5-16ths 1-2 wide. A sixth, laid by a Cochin China bird, is flattened on each side, it measures 2 in. 3-16ths 1-2 long by 1 in. 12-16ths broad one way, and 1 in. 8-16ths the other, which is a difference of $\frac{1}{4}$ in. Eggs of fowls, the shells of which resembles, in appearance, crumpled paper, are not uncommon. I have one, however, which is most singularly flattened on one side, and crumpled and puckered all round the edge of the shell, and is otherwise misshapen, it measures 1 in. 15-16ths 1-2 long by 1 in. 9-16ths 1-2 wide on the round, and 1 in. 7-16ths on the flat side. Eggs having a deep crease or bead mark encompassing them are sometimes found. I have in my collection two very remarkable ones.

Almost all eggs have naturally a white putamen. I have two eggs, however, of the common duck in which the putamen is thickly spotted with black; the eggs are likewise singularly washed all over with sooty ash. Another pair of eggs is most curiously washed with sooty olive. The bird has been in the habit of laying similar eggs every spring.

I will state my own observations on the contents of the eggs of the common fowl. The yolk of moderate-sized eggs, of a given breed, are generally as large as those half or three quarters of an ounce heavier. This is not merely found to be the case on comparing the contents of the eggs of such breeds as the Spanish and Cochin China, which differ so much in size, but on contrasting the eggs of a given breed varying in size with each other. The chickens produced from comparatively small eggs are generally equal in size to those from large ones, as the size of the yolk determines their dimensions. It is very large in proportion in the eggs of the Shanghai breed, hence they are popularly termed "rich." The eggs of wild have much larger yolks in proportion than those of tame birds, for the yolk determines the length of the species; and the excess of albumen in the eggs of tame birds is extraneous, like the excess of milk or flesh in domestic animals. The flavour of the contents of eggs, and the proportion of albumen to yolk, has much to do with the character of their food. Hens fed on barley lay eggs with larger yolks, while rye has a contrary effect, probably because barley contains a greater proportion of oil, which tends to increase the quantity of oil of yolk of eggs. The egg of an unimpregnated bird (*hypænum ovum*) is generally inferior in flavour to that of the impregnated, more easily decomposed, and is more apt to have a shell rough in texture or abnormal in form.

As I am still working at the subject of the causes of the variations in eggs, I shall be glad to receive any fresh facts or specimens of an abnormal or curious character, and also when they are for sale or exchange.

IN THE BACKWOODS.*

By J. Matthew Jones, F.L.S.

A FORTNIGHT seems but a brief space, yet much may be done and seen in that time. Some few years ago, on my first arrival from England, I had the good fortune to join an expedition sent to report upon the state of the timber on the admiralty reserves in the western part of this Province, and I was introduced for the first time to the pleasures of a forest life in a snug little camp, pitched in a charming nook beside the limped waters of the ever winding Roseway, a short distance to the northward of Shelburne. It would be useless for me to dilate upon the feelings of one, who fresh from the cultivated vales of old England, finds himself suddenly placed in the midst of the "forest primeval," with no sounds of civilization to mar the sweet

* Read before the Novia Scotian Institute of Natural Science, February 4th, 1867.

stillness which reigns amid these western wilds; and especially upon those of a naturalist, who loves to look upon nature in her pristine garb; to see the land untouched, and the trees and shrubs in every stage of life and decay, just as they have lived and died through succeeding ages; to listen to the unknown sounds and cries proceeding from animals and birds, and participate in the many other events hourly taking place as he journeys on through these trackless solitudes; for it may be truly said that his cup of pleasure is filled to overflowing, and every moment of his time occupied in marking and studying the changing scenes which at every step burst fresh and enchantingly upon his wondering view.

It was on a fine summer's day towards the close of the month of August, a date which will ever remain stamped on memory's pleasant page, that, accompanied by two worthy representatives of Her Majesty's forces, naval and military, I was ushered unto the camp of which I have spoken. We stood upon the bank of a rippling stream, and the first object that caught the eye was the stalwart form of the camp steward, wielding an axe with such power and effect as to make the huge log he was splitting for the night's fire shiver under the strokes, and cause the surrounding forest to ring with their echoes; while near a fire burning briskly between two granite rocks, stood the form of a veritable Indian, reclining in indolent ease over the burning brands, above which hung the stock pot from which the steam was puffing, sending around a goodly smell which made the appetite sharpen as we thought of the eatables within. And then the camp itself; a rough affair it looked—two slender poles some ten feet or so apart, placed upright, a cross pole lashed to them a few feet above the ground, then with their buts resting on this cross pole, and sloping back to the ground, were laid other poles and branches of trees, fern, &c., strewed all over the whole, forming a roof which, although not waterproof, helped to keep off the falling dew at night. The sides were filled in with twigs and brushwood, while the floor of this primitive domicile was covered with a thick layer of spruce branches, the smaller sprays on top to render the couch more comfortable, and then the occupant had to spread his blanket and make himself as much at ease as circumstances would permit. So we commenced our forest life.

From Roseway river camp we journeyed to the northward, and camped again on a small point of land which jutted out into a large lake called "Long island lake," and a prettier spot could scarce be conceived. Before us lay the lake whose mirror-like surface scarce ruffled by the breeze, was dotted over with small islands, clothed with spruce and pine, while the evening sun, hot and powerful, reflected their shadows far down in the depths below, and as the shades of evening drew around, and the orb of day sank in majestic splendour behind the dark mass of forest to the westward, the camp fire began to cast a ruddy gleam of light upon the surrounding objects. The fog now rising from the lake, caused a chilly feeling to creep over us, and more wood heaped upon the burning brands, caused the sparks to fly up like miniature rockets in space, while massy flames poured out from our pile of bulky logs, until bursting up in one grand sheet of blazing light, it dazzled with lurid glare the neighbouring forest, and our company all seated around the seething mass busily consuming the evening meal.

From this camp we one day made an excursion to the eastward, in the neighbourhood of Jordan river, and found the whole district to be densely wooded with hemlock, spruce, and pine. Indeed of these species of *conifers*, the forest in the vicinity of Shelburne appears to be almost wholly composed, and it is not until you arrive some fifteen miles up the country, that groves of maple and oak are seen. The country around Shelburne bears evidence of the ravages of fire several years ago, the present growth of timber being but small.

An island of an acre or two in extent, stands about the centre of Long island lake, and is known as "Indian island," from the fact that in years gone by, the Indians, who had a stationary camp above this lake, buried their dead here. And surely no fitter resting place could have been found for those children of nature, than here beneath the sombre shade of pine or spruce, to take their last long sleep, in the full hope of awaking in the happy, yet visionary hunting grounds they suppose to lie in a brighter and better world beyond the sky. It would appear that the Indians have almost entirely left this part of the Province, for only two or three live in the district, one of whom, named *Peter Paul*, accompanied our party the whole way to Weymouth, and proved himself as generous, noble hearted a fellow as ever smoked the calumet of peace. To the absence of Indians may no doubt be attributed, in a great measure, the large number of bears, and the presence of beaver in the vicinity of the granite hills, mid way across the country, called by some the Blue mountains; but more of these presently. From this camping ground we journeyed along the road which led to the district of Sugar Loaf hill, a fine grove of hardwoods, birch, beech, oak, and maple. It was on the further side of this hill that we bade adieu for a while to civilization. Embarking in a rather frail boat upon a lake, we pulled, not without sundry misgivings as to the probable termination of the voyage, for some low marshy ground on its northern shore, and happily succeeded in reaching the mouth of a small river up which we had to go; but we had not gone very far before we found that our bark must be lightened, and all jumped out and pushed her up the shallows, until we came to a large open savannah of considerable size, on which grew luxuriant grass. Few trees were to be seen about here, and those of a very stunted growth, the most common being the alder. Leaving our boat about mid-way through the plain, we shouldered our packs, which were far too heavy, and made for the north-west end of it, where we entered the thick forest again. Peter Paul having called a halt, addressed us in a very fatherly manner to the effect that we had better look to our weapons, for as he said, "you don't know what be about where we are going." Having complied with his request, we started afresh, and after some pretty bad travelling, arrived about sundown at a small lake at the southern base of the granite plateau. Here we found an old log hut which had been erected some time back by lumberers, and made it our home for two or three days, while we surveyed the country around. This lake from the quantity of small flat stones around its margin, was called "Whetstone lake." The southern shores of this lake are clothed with a heavy growth of timber, which appears to have escaped the extensive fire that raged over the whole extent of the Blue mountain range. The timber is composed of hemlock, spruce, maple, and birch, with an underwood of withrod, and near the water an abundance of fern of two species, the larger being the well known *Osmunda regalis*.

We may here remark in passing that our Provincial maps are in fault in regard to the route we took, for not a lake or river is marked upon any of them in that quarter, whereas the country abounds with lakes and streams, some of good size. We travelled as near as we could north-west from Shelburne, but owing to the swamps and lakes we had to deviate at intervals. The land from the district of Long island lake is very level, and from what I could judge, is capable, when cleared, of extensive cultivation, particularly that portion in which is comprised the open savannah I have mentioned.

Our first excursion from the camp at Whetstone lake led us to the rocky slope of the Blue mountains, which lay in full view before us, and on reaching the elevated ground, one of the Indians sighted a bear which was quietly ambling along among the blueberry bushes, regaling himself on the ripe and luscious fruit. It was at once decided to stalk him true highland fashion, and off we set. The Indian, arriving within range first, sent a bullet through one of his feet, as we afterwards found. Turning round, the fellow made right at C————and myself, standing together some forty yards below. On he came with a growling noise, and when close to us showed a fine array of teeth, which we would have preferred viewing after his decease. There was nothing for it, however, but to stand our ground, when 'crack' went my friend's ponderous Lancaster, and with it the massive conical ball which caused poor bruin to change his course, for with a bound he swerved to the right and was lost in a thicket of birch and alder. Proceeding cautiously along we found him at last stretched out in a little hollow, and a huge beast he was, measuring from tip to tip seven feet two inches. We must here mention a curious fact which we consider worthy of note. On running hurriedly along from boulder to boulder, we slipped and fell through a hole, with the knee cap against a rock. The knee instantly swelled up and gave great pain, and we could barely drag along, when one of the Indians said if rubbed with bear fat it would soon be right again. When skinning the animal he cut off a piece, and we rubbed the part well, and singular enough in a quarter of an hour the swelling subsided almost as quickly as it had risen, and we were enabled to walk back to camp. The Indians have a very ready way of transporting bear meat—cutting it up in small pieces they fold up the bear skin neatly with the pieces within, and then tie the whole with bands of withrod (*viburnum*), and with the same bands secure it across their shoulders as a pack, leaving the arms free for action. Bears were numerous at this spot, and were no doubt attracted by the vast quantities of ripe berries, particularly the huckleberry and blueberry, the (*Gaylussachia resinora*) and (*Vaccinium Canadense*), the former in astonishing abundance. The trees and shrubs which clothe the sides of this rocky range are principally dwarf birch, (*Betula nigra and B. papyracea*) alder, (*Alnus viridis*), interspersed with spruce (*Abies alba and rubra*) and dead pine (*Pinus strobus*). Under stones in Whetstone lake I found several small leeches, (*Hirudo*), one of which was of a white colour. The larvæ cases of a caddis-fly, (*Phryganea*), were abundant, composed of pieces of weed and granite sand. We noticed that the bird droppings which were upon almost every boulder on this range, were of a dark blue colour, caused no doubt by their feeding at this season almost wholly upon the berries of the blueberry and huckleberry. The shores of Whetstone lake were covered with a beautiful granite sand, nearly white.

(*To be continued.*)

OBSERVATIONS IN CONNECTION WITH THE EGGS OF INSECTS.

By E. C. Rye.

THE principal object of by far the greater number of our (so called) "Entomologists" being the mere accumulation of a collection of insects in the *imago* or perfect state, it is not to be wondered at that the less conspicuous (but in reality much more interesting) transitional conditions of the same creatures should receive comparatively little attention. In one Order, however (the *Lepidoptera*), which has of all others the most numerous devotees in this country, the second or larval stage of metamorphosis has long received a considerable amount of attention; excited originally, doubtless, by the superiority for cabinet purposes of bred compared with captured specimens; and at the present day we can boast of many most excellent observers in that Order, who are continually chronicling links in Nature's chain that were previously unknown, and whose labours might with equal interest, and a much greater chance of discovering unrecorded facts, be imitated by the students of other Orders. The pupal condition has also of late, from the same cause, been brought considerably into notice; but unfortunately without much recorded result, on account of the great similarity of allied species in that state.

In the earliest stage of insect life, that of the egg, we seldom find any one interested, save dabblers in microscopy, for whom occasionally the professionals mount certain of the commoner and most sculptured ova of *Lepidoptera* as "objects." I cannot but think, however, that if more attention were given to the eggs of insects, very many additions to our knowledge of their habits and transformations would result. The very varied and elegant forms and sculpture of these eggs ought to be sufficient attraction even for a superficial observer, whose earliest investigations would be sure to profit him by the revelation of a clue to the *habitat* of the parent insects, afforded by the position in which the ova are found, and who would irresistibly be led to study the numerous protective instincts exhibited by those parents. Perhaps, after all, it is only a question of time; and we may be right in imagining the entomologists of 1968 as perfectly capable of teaching us, their great-grandfathers, how to find and name all eggs; for, as science progresses, the larger and more easy objects of study become exhausted, and the worker who desires to distinguish himself is driven back to microscopic forms and the solution of enigmas.

The following superficial remarks may hint to those whose attention has not been turned in this direction (they will, of course, be well known to all others) what a fund of instruction and pleasurable investigation is contained in things of so small a compass.

The eggs of insects differ from those of birds and reptiles, which are never sculptured, and seldom vary from the plain oval; they are of various forms and colours, being round, oval, elliptic, conic, oblong, cylindrical, angular, prismatic, shaped like a pear, flask, lens, boat, barrel, or turban, ribbed, striated, embossed, beaded, reticulated, scaled, or tiled; but more commonly smooth. In colour they are black, white, pearly, yellow, green, reddish, or grey—green and light yellow being perhaps the commonest. Sometimes they are striped or spotted, and either opaque or transparent. With regard to form, there appears little or no connexion in the individual pattern; for species undoubtedly very closely allied may have eggs quite unlike each other, although one particular species will always adhere to its peculiar structure.

They are, of course, usually very small; and it is on account of this that they so often escape observation. The Privet-hawk moth (*Sphinx ligustri*), however, as might be expected from its own bulk, lays very large eggs, of a flat oval shape and greenish tint, which readily admit of the enclosed caterpillar being seen when nearly mature; and on this account, as well as the general abundance of the insect, they will be found easy for the beginner to experiment upon.

Eggs are sometimes deposited singly, but oftener in large quantities, and are either loosely dropped or packed tightly together. In every instance the parent is guided by an unfailing instinct, so that the future larvæ shall come to life in situations adapted to their necessities, and any apparent anomalies or eccentricities of form are sure to be attended by some good result in the œconomy of the species; as Nature does not throw away her labour, though often prodigal of mere ornament. It is in the endeavour to discover uses for peculiarities in structure which we cannot as yet understand, that one of the greatest charms of Natural History exists.

In *Coleoptera* the eggs are usually unornamented, plain, oblong, and somewhat soft, mostly white or dirty yellow; and the females of many species that inhabit bark or wood have long retractile ovipositors, which they insert into chinks and crannies, thus depositing their ova in security.

The perfect insects of certain of the wood-feeders (*Hylastes* and allies, etc.) make burrows in the trees, in which operation the male assists the female; and from the main burrow lateral tracks are eaten, in which the eggs are laid, the young larvæ making separate galleries, which start at right angles from the lateral track, and get larger as the insect increases in size. The peculiar appearance of the wood underneath the bark caused by the regularity of their ravages has given the name of "Typographers" to certain of these beetles. In the larger *Sinodendron* the eggs are placed in spiral curves, each carefully packed in chewed fragments of wood. The large "harmless water-beetle" (*Hydroüs piceus*), often seen in domestic aquaria, envelopes its eggs in a little nest, which floats on the surface, so that the larvæ, when hatched, at once take to their native element. Here it is evident that air and light are necessary, for it has been found that if the nidus be broken up, and the ova allowed to sink to the bottom, decomposition takes place after a submersion of a day or two.

The proceedings of the *Necrophori* and *Coprophaga* are too well known to demand more than a passing note.

In the *Hymenoptera*, the Order containing the bees and wasps, instincts which always strike as most extraordinary, in spite of their familiarity, are shown with regard to provision for the future brood of those insects. It is not necessary here to describe, but I may call attention to the enormous ovipositors of the "Ichneumon" flies, which lay their eggs in the larvæ of other insects. These are so long that hardly any hiding-place can protect their destined prey; but in one instance (*Ophion luteum*) the eggs are attached by a footstalk *on* the skin of the young larva of the Puss-moth (*Dicranura vinula*). In this instance, any one who desires to breed the moth in safety can remove the unwelcome lodger by simply cutting off the footstalk with a pair of scissors; for, oddly enough, the parasite does not commence active operations until its fat friend has built a cocoon and turned to a pupa, having somehow shuffled through the preparatory moultings of its destined food without being dislodged.

The proceedings with regard to oviposition of all the parasitic insects in this Order will most amply repay investigation, as will those of the *Fossores* and Saw-flies, one of which, *Athalia centifoliæ*, places its eggs in little spaces between the outer surface and parenchyma of the leaf of the turnip, having thus secured a safe position with proper exposure to light and air.

In the *Orthoptera*, the Cockroach lays its entire batch of eggs in a leathery little pouch, reminding one of the "Devil's purses" so common on the sea-shore, but without the horns. An account of this peculiar protection will be found in Westwood's "Introduction to Entomology," p. 354. Others of this Order deposit their eggs in cells under ground—the eggs remaining unhatched during the winter.

In the *Neuroptera*, a common pretty green lace-winged fly (*Chrysopa vulgaris*) with golden eyes, of dainty aspect, but of so insufferable an odour as to be disparagingly termed "Stink-fly" by the realistic Dutch, deposits each egg on a foot-stalk, in order to keep it out of the way of other predacious insects; this stalk is like a hair, and is formed by the parent drawing out a drop of gum which dries rapidly. These eggs may often be seen on the garden lilac, the insect being very abundant; the larva feeds on plant-lice. The ova of the *Ephemera* or "Day-fly" are curved, flattish, narrow, and smooth; and Swammerdam was convinced by experiment that this formation materially assisted their rapid diffusion through water, in which the insect naturally abandons them in a mass.

The Dragon-flies also deposit their eggs in the water, immersing their taper bodies so as to reach a secure position on the stems of plants beneath the surface; the larvæ, however, are predacious. In the act of depositing their eggs they may often be seen as mentioned by Westwood, beating their tails rapidly upon the surface of the water, until the eggs form a mass like a bunch of grapes.

In Paterson's "Insects mentioned in Shakespeare" (p. 236) the following interesting passage occurs with reference to a female Dragon-fly after impregnation:—" She deliberately turned her head downwards, descended the stem or leaf of the plant to a depth of some inches below the surface of the water, and there remained for the purpose of depositing her eggs. It was strange to see a creature, who but a few minutes before had been winging her way through the air, thus quietly abiding in a different element, while the great work of providing a suitable situation for her young was about being accomplished. On one occasion my informant, while she was thus engaged, touched her with the extremity of his fishing-rod; she then desisted from her work, crawled up to the surface, and, after remaining there a few minutes, as if to allow the cause of her molestation to pass by, again directed her way downwards, and completed the important task in which she had been interrupted." The same author records the observation of one of the Caddis-flies (*Phryganea*) descending nearly a foot beneath the water, and absolutely swimming at that depth, evidently with the object of depositing its ova, as he found a large bundle of green eggs, closely enveloped in a strong, jelly-like substance, attached to the extremity of the abdomen. This bundle was of an oblong form, bent in the middle, and with the two ends attached to the insect's tail. One is irresistibly reminded of the habits of the "Water Ouzel" by these accounts.

Very many instances of peculiarity in shape and forethought in position of the ova of *Lepidoptera* could be adduced; but it will suffice to mention a few of the more conspicuous—referring the beginner to the excellent chapter thereupon by Dr. Knaggs in the 1st Vol. of the "Entomologist's Monthly Magazine," p. 65 *et seq.* Amongst the butterflies, the yellow packets of eggs of the common large white butterfly (*Pieris brassicæ*) may too often be found on the underside (as usual) of cabbage leaves; but it is among the moths that a much greater care in depositing ova is exhibited. The apterous female of one of these, the "Vapourer" (*Orgyia antiqua*), a very abundant insect, even in the metropolis itself, never strays from the cocoon containing the pupa out of which she came; so she affixes her eggs in a compact single layer on its woolly covering, and, as the caterpillars are brought to outer life in batches (not all at once), there is a constant succession of feeders, the species being visible in all its stages at the same time, which is seldom the case with insects generally. Another moth, almost equally common (the Lackey, *Clisiocampa neustria*), makes with her eggs a broad flat band round the twigs of fruit-trees, etc.; these are often called "Fairy-rings," and it requires a considerable amount of force to detach them; and they are effectually protected from any atmospheric influences by their hard shell and compact array.

The Gipsey moth (*Hypogymna dispar*), which is very much rarer, constructs a cone-like covering with hair from the under-side of her body, thatching it with a sloping roof; the male has not the same quantity of down. The common Gold-tail moth (*Porthesia auriflua*) and another closely allied species, the Brown-tail (*P. chrysorrhæa*), which is much less abundant, also make use of the thick tuft of hairs they bear at the apex of the abdomen, as a protection for their eggs, possessing a minute pair of prehensile hooks in the tail, capable of extensive motion, with which they pull out the down.

Most moths are a long time depositing ova, acting with deliberation and circumspection; indeed, until this urgent duty of Nature is discharged, they are most tenacious of life, and can hardly be killed at all, even mechanically continuing the incomplete task after death. There is, however, one species, the common "Ghost" moth (*Hepialus humuli*), which discharges its little black eggs with great rapidity; possibly, as the larvæ feed on roots of grasses, etc., it may be necessary for the parent to exert a considerable degree of force in laying the eggs in the hope of locating them down some crack in the soil; for, if merely dropped on the surface, the young and weak caterpillar would have less chance of finding its natural food.

The "Wood-leopard" moth (*Zenzera æsculi*), allied to the Ghost-moth, which lives in its preparatory stages in the solid wood of trees, has a long retractile ovipositor—a structure shared by others whose larvæ are internal feeders; and a somewhat similar but lesser development is found in certain species whose eggs are laid deep in flowers or buds.

In the compound Order (*Hemiptera-Heteroptera* and *-Homoptera*) some few curious facts relating to ova are known; for instance, in the former sub-division the egg of the common Water-scorpion (*Nepa cinerea*), which is laid in stems of water-plants, has a crown of bristles presumed to keep a space open for the transmission of air and light; and, in the latter, the *Aphides*, or "Plant-lice," sometimes cover their eggs with down; and the different species of *Coccus*, too abundant on vines and apple-trees, go to the extreme of maternal devotion—actually fastening themselves down as a buckler over their ova, and dying at their post: in some cases they also give out filaments of floccy matter as an additional protection.

In the *Diptera*, the egg of the common yellow *Scatophaga* has two oblique props at one extremity, to prevent its sinking too deeply into the stercoraceous matter on which it is deposited; the common gnat, *Culex pipiens*, has long been described and figured in the act of making its raft or boat of eggs; and the different "Bot-flies" are conspicuous for their instincts in selecting various parts of the bodies of the *Mammalia* in which their larvæ are to feed, so as to secure the safe introduction of their ova.

Lastly, to conclude with a personal matter, in the *Aphaniptera*, each female flea contains about twelve oblong, cylindrical, white eggs: these are deposited close to the ground, especially where dogs are in the habit of lying; and there is no need to remind any one of the eventual destination of their product. Let us in this temperate clime endure the lesser evil when it comes upon us; thanking "geographical distribution" or (other Darwinistic paraphrase for the vulgar "Providence") that we are spared the "Jigger," the female of which in the West Indies burrows in men's toes, swells with an immense number of eggs, bursts, and necessarily produces inflammation, evil speaking, ulceration, and other irritants.

ON THE PROMINENT MOTHS.
By E. Clifford.

AMONGST that important body of our *Lepidoptera* which our modern entomologists have designated the CUSPIDATES, perhaps no class is more peculiar than that containing the "Prominent Moths." We have twelve species in all, some of which are exceedingly rare. They derive their name from a projecting tuft of scales on the inner margin; this, when the wings are in repose, forms a prominence on the outline of the wing; hence the applicability of the term. In the present paper, we wish to direct the attention of our readers to this interesting class of our native moths, noticing each individual species briefly.

In common with others of the CUSPIDATES, the Prominent Moths have very angular caterpillars. In some species the habitual position when the insect is at rest is with the anal part raised, whilst the head is curved backwards. In others, also, the body of the caterpillar is furnished with numerous humps and excrescences, giving it a most grotesque and singular aspect. The first species in order is that known as the Plumed Prominent (*Ptilophora plumigera*), a rare and beautiful moth. It has been recorded as occurring in Buckinghamshire, where Halton and Marlow are given as localities for it. The forewings of this moth are semi-transparent, of a raw sienna colour, with a paler bar beyond the middle. The eggs are laid in November, on the maple, in shady woods and hedges; perhaps more particularly in chalky districts. The caterpillar is pale green, with the back bluish, and a pale yellow line on each side. It is full-fed at the end of June, or beginning of July, when it spins a tight earthen cocoon. The moth emerges therefrom in October, and is the only representative of its genus known in this country. The next species coming under notice is more generally diffused. This is the Pale Prominent (*Ptilodontis palpina*). Its caterpillar feeds on sallow and poplar, and is without hairs or lumps, being rough, with transverse wrinkles. It has a small head, and in colour is green, with six stripes, composed of minute white worts: there is also a yellow line on each side just above the spiracles. It is full-fed at the beginning of October, opening its cocoon on the surface of the ground, and remaining throughout the winter in the chrysalis state. In this stage, we read, it may be occasionally found by the persevering collector at poplars, but more frequently at willows, especially when on the banks of ditches and streams, at the end of September. The moth itself appears in June, and may be found not very uncommonly in this country. Its colour is pale wainscot brown, with three bands of a darker brown, and there are black dots and streaks scattered over the wings, seated always on the rays. The body of the male moth has a split tuft at the extremity.

The Coxcomb Prominent (*Notodonta camelina*) is the first of the genus *Notodonta* itself, and an exceedingly handsome insect. At the end of August its singular caterpillar may be sought on birch, maple and oak, in or about woodland country. Its head is greenish, and is usually raised, and curved backwards, when the caterpillar rests; the body itself is green, paler on the back; the worts on the back are tipped with pink, and armed with short black bristles. On each side is a series of white spots, which, with other spots and connecting lines, constitutes what may be termed a spiracular stripe. The body emits scattered bristles of a black colour from all parts, and the legs and claspers are pinkish in colour. The caterpillar is full-fed in the month of September, and spins a slight cocoon on the surface of the earth, remaining in the chrysalis state throughout the winter, like the foregoing species. The Coxcomb Prominent seems to have no special season, since it has been captured by collectors from May to September. We may remark that it is not unfrequently found sitting on the fronds of fern, and in this position can be readily boxed. It is a common species this, throughout the country, and occurs also in Ireland. The colouring of the moth is rusty-brown, the hind wings being paler than the front ones. The Maple Prominent (*Notodonta cucullina*) is a rarer insect, of which not very much seems to be known. It is said that the caterpillar, feeding on maple, rests with the anal extremity raised, the anal claspers not touching the foodplant. In colour it is dingy white, with a brown stripe down the back, commencing behind the head, and terminating at the hump at the tail. In May the moth is on the wing, and it has been captured at Halton, in Buckinghamshire. The eggs of this moth should be searched for in the month of June.

The Scarce Prominent (*Notodonta carmelita*) is the next on our list of the Prominents. This moth appears on the wing in April, and should be looked for on the trunks of birch trees, and palings near. The forewings of the insect are reddish-grey, darker towards the front edge, where are two pale yellow spots, from which proceed lines and black dots transversely. In the month of June the caterpillar of this insect should be sought for on the birch. It is green, with a rough surface, produced by a number of raised yellow dots, and there is also a yellowish white line along the spiracles. In July it is full-fed, when it descends below the earth, and becomes a chrysalis. The Scarce Prominent has been taken at Birchwood, in Kent, and in the counties of Surrey, Sussex, and Essex. The White Prominent (*Notodonta bicolor*) is a singular and beautiful moth, and a very rare one. It appears on the wing in June, and is said to have been captured in a wood in Staffordshire by an artisan collector. It is recorded from Killarney in Ireland. The wings of this species are white, with black spots and markings; the forewings with the front margin slightly arched. The hind wings are light, and without spots, head, thorax, and body, all of the same colour, although the latter is occasionally tinged with fawn colour. The head and body of the caterpillar are green, adorned with a bright yellow stripe on each side, commencing immediately behind the head.

Two handsome species next claim our attention. The first is the Swallow Prominent (*Notodonta dictæa*). In May and June this moth should be sought, and it occurs throughout England, also occasionally in Scotland. It may be often captured at the bottom of pollard willows, or large poplars. It has been taken in Wicklow, Ireland. The eggs of this species should be looked for on the under side of the leaves of poplars and sallows. The caterpillar is greenish-white, with a yellow stripe on each side. It has rather a large head, notched, and shining, and of a pale green colour. On the twelfth segment, which is humped, is a black, transverse line. In the latter part of September this caterpillar is full-fed, when it spins a thin but large cocoon on the surface of the earth, using the leaf as a roof to its winter domicile. Not unfrequently a variety of this caterpillar, which is pale brown, and destitute of the side stripes, is captured by collectors. The moth itself is beautifully marked. Whitish-brown forms the centre of the wings, with the front margin darker, and a chocolate brown blotch near the tip. Near the inner margin is a rich brown shade, the upper part of which is lost in the centre colour of the wings. The hindwings are very pale, with a compound brown blotch at the anal angle; thorax and body are both greyish-brown. Nearly related in appearance to the last named, as well as in position, is the Lesser Swallow Prominent (*Notodonta dictæoides*). Although rather less, as its name implies, than the last, this would hardly be a sufficiently reliable characteristic without some additional one. This lies in the white mark on the anal angle of the forewings; which in *dictæa* is linear, but in *dictæoides* is decidedly wedge-shaped, and more conspicuous. Otherwise the colouring and markings of both insects are very similar. The caterpillar of this species feeds on the birch, and is usually full-fed in September, when it descends to the ground, forming a slight cocoon between the earth and a fallen leaf; thus protected, it passes the winter in the chrysalis state. In June the moth flies, occurring in most of our English counties, though not abundantly, and also in some parts of Ireland.

The Iron Prominent (*Notodonta dromedarius*) is the next one to which we direct attention. It occurs in the perfect state in June, and is not uncommon in most of our English counties. Its white eggs may be looked for on birch or alder, on both which the caterpillar has been found feeding. It is yellowish-green in colour, with a purple brown stripe on the back from the second to the fourth segments, and the remaining part of the body is covered with small humps. It should be searched for in August; in September it is full-fed, when it descends from the tree whereon it had fed, spinning a slight cocoon on the earth, and, like others of this family, attaching a leaf to the upper surface of it. Several of the chrysalides of this species have been taken in Ireland, and these were found at the roots of alder; they produced the variety which is peculiar to Ireland, known as a distinct species under the name of *perfusca*. These were darker than English specimens of the insect. The colouring of the Iron Prominent is dull purplish-brown, and there is a yellowish patch at the base of the front margin; hindwings greyish-brown. Another rare Prominent is that known as the Three-humped (*Notodonta trilophus*). The forewings of this species are dull brown, with a yellowish tinge and two brown streaks; between the latter is a dull spot; the hindwings are white. It is on the wing through May and August. The eggs are laid on the aspen, poplar, and birch, and the caterpillar may be sought on these plants in July. It is dark green in colour, with humps on several of the segments, and a reddish streak down the back from the head to the fifth segment. Along the spiracles is an interrupted reddish streak. The caterpillar rests with the anal extremity elevated, the anal claspers not touching the foodplant. It was once taken at St. Osyth, in Essex, by a gentleman, who succeeded in rearing the insect to the final state. Although so rare an insect, the Three-humped Prominent is yet widely distributed, for it has been taken in Essex, Gloucestershire, and some parts of Scotland. European specimens are often passed off by dealers as British instances of this beautiful moth.

Next we come to the Pebble Prominent (*Notodonta ziczac*), whose caterpillar presents so striking an appearance. The eggs of this species are laid on the poplar and sallow in June, when the caterpillar may be looked for, as also in September and October. It is certainly one of the most singular creatures imaginable, being covered with humps and protuberances, and resting in a truly odd position on its foodplant. In colour it is generally ashy-grey, with three pale stripes on the sides. At the end of September the caterpillar is full-fed and undergoes its transformation, like others of its genus. The moth flies in May, and occurs in all parts of England. The colour of the wings is ochreous-brown, with a faint rosy tinge towards the front margin; beyond the middle there is a large oval patch of purple and brown. This species derives its name from the peculiarities in the form of its caterpillar; it is perhaps the commonest of this family of moths. Last, though not least important, on our list of these moths is the Great Prominent (*Notodonta hepida*), a truly noble insect. It flies in May and June, and is usually esteemed rare. It has occurred, however, in several of our English counties, and also in Ireland. In colouring it is smoky-brown with an ochreous tinge, and two streaks of a darker brown before the middle. There are also some red-brown spots before the hind margin. The whole surface of the wings has a beautifully marbled appearance. This species is perhaps the finest of the tribe, measuring as much as two and a half inches across the wings. From July to September the large and handsome caterpillar producing it may be looked for on the oak. It is yellowish-green, with two white lines down the back, and an oblique red stripe margined with yellow on the side of each segment. The chrysalis of the Great Prominent should be sought at the roots of oaks in September. In taking leave of this interesting group of moths, we remark that they have a peculiar interest to those who have ever taken the trouble to examine their economy. They seem certainly to be one of the most readily-distinguished classes that exists, the projection alluded to on the forewings serving as an unmistakeable guide to their identification. Much remains yet to be learnt regarding some of the rarer species, and perhaps if tree-trunks were more scrutinised by collectors some of the uncommon "Prominents" might become more general, and light be thrown on their life histories. Altogether the "Prominents" seem to deserve more patient search and study than at present they have received, and we shall rejoice if our brief paper serves to awaken interest in their favour amongst our entomological readers.

THE SENSIBILITY OF PLANTS.

NEWTON discovered why an apple fell to the ground, but no one yet has found anything approaching to an explanation why the seed invariably sends its root downwards and its stalk upwards. All kinds of reasons have been given: the most common is that plants strive towards the sun. Experiments of the most various kinds have proved that no external causes whatever can be found to account for this inveterate tendency. Some of the experiments are very curious. Acorns and beans placed in tubes full of earth, have been turned and turned about, whirled round wheels day and night, till one would have thought they must have lost all ideas of zenith and nadir; but no; in spite of all ingenious attempts which have been made to confuse the vegetable mind it persists in sending its stalk upwards, and its root downwards. One of the most conclusive experiments was made by M. Drouchet: he filled with earth a vase whose bottom was pierced with holes, in the holes he placed bean seeds, so that each plant had every inducement to thrust its roots upwards to get earth, and its stalk downwards to have the light and air; but no again! it remained true to the education which every baby seed must receive on leaving its mother, and which every plant must follow or die—it thrust its root downwards into empty air, and its stalk upwards through the dark thick earth. The first withered, the latter was suffocated, and the infant bean plant perished as a martyr to the law of its nature; but it proved its incorruptible autonomy and invincible constancy.

Another peculiar example of autonomy and constancy in plants is shown in creeping and climbing plants which turn in spirals round any support; they will obstinately persist in climbing in the direction of the first spiral turn, be it to left or right. No surprise—no system of coaxing will make the plant forget or change the direction it first began to climb with its infant shoots. What then is this energy—this invincible desire which exhibits itself in the tender baby milky pulp of the first spiral of the twining plant, and which overcomes any obstacle? Some plants, like the *Ampelopsis hederacea*, may be seen climbing a wall, throwing their delicate arms, like feelers, dying of disappointment where they fail to find a resting-place; but where they do, clinging to the wall with little *discs* like a fly's foot, and so creeping up and up in search of heat and warmth.

As to that strange phenomenon known as the sleep of plants, though it is neither an argument in favour of instinct nor sensibility, it demonstrates a further likeness in their vitality to that of animals. Sleep, indeed, seems an improper expression—it is a sort of vegetable contraction which plants experience at certain times. The leaves in this plant-sleep are drawn together, and become crisp and hard to the touch, and they return to their former state as though extended by a spring. The lotus of the Nile, and the water-lily, as is well known, go to sleep at night, and even withdraw their flowers beneath the surface of the water. Other plants, however, sleep at all hours of the day and night with such regularity and diversity, that Linnæus made a flower-clock, which he called the Dial of Flora, by means of rows of flowers, which expanded in regular succession day and night. But even the flower-clock of Linnæus is not more marvellous than the oscillating movements of the leaflets of the *Hedysarum gyrans* of Bengal, of which two out of every three united on one stem, and forming the leaves of the tree, oscillate one after the other exactly like the pendulum of a clock, and their ascending movements are with jerks precisely like the second hand of a watch.

To return, however, to phenomena denoting sensibility and instinct. We may note that plants may be put to sleep by narcotics, as well as destroyed by poison, and that in the sensitive plant, a drop of sulphuric acid placed on the root of the leaf, not only kills the leaf itself, but when it contracts at the first touch of the poison, all the leaves shut with a sympathetic shudder. The sensitive plant being the most delicate creature in the whole range of vegetable sensibility is necessarily a stranger to none of its symptoms. It goes to sleep regularly in the evening, gathering all its leaves up, and towards midnight it gives them a gentle quiver like a bird or a little lady rousing an instant from sleep, turning over and going to sleep again, and with the first rays of the sun it distends its leaves, and stretches itself out in the sunshine The exquisite sensibility of this delicate creature is so great that a shock, a noise, a too loud voice, and even a strong smell, gives it convulsions. In the West Indies, if you come upon it suddenly, not properly announced, your very shadow is sufficient to give it—not an attack of nerves, for it has been proved to have none, but a fainting fit; but all these isolated symptoms are nothing to the fact that a whole field of them may be thrown into a state of alarm, if their advanced guard discovers an enemy. You may walk up to a bed of them, and by touching the nearest ones with a cane throw the whole republic into a state of terror; from leaf to leaf, from branch to branch, fear takes possession of the whole commonwealth—the enemy is in sight. This proof of sympathetic sensibility, extraordinary as it is, does not, however, surpass the exhibition of sensitiveness made by a plant on a journey in the carriage. When the carriage began to move, it shut itself up in a fright—it was a motion it had not been accustomed to; however, it was gently treated, and getting reconciled to the motion, its confidence returned, it opened its leaves, and seemed quite happy. When the carriage stopped, the courage of the sensitive plant failed again—something dreadful had surely happened; it shrunk itself up in a fright, and so remained until the carriage went on once more. After a few experiments the plant was educated into being a courageous traveller, and it got quite resigned to the little accidents of travel, and never fainted again on any occasion. But what shall we say of the *Dionæa muscipula* of North Carolina, which belongs to the same family, yet is by no means as innocent, since it passes its whole existence in alluring flies into its clutches and putting them to death. Every leaf of the *Dionæa muscipula* is a villanous fly-trap. As soon as the insect alights on the leaf, which the perfidious plant carefully baits with gum to attract it, the leaf, which has a hinge in the centre, doubles up and catches the fly a prisoner; when he is dead the leaf opens, and he is allowed to fall out. The trap is set again, and the *Dionæa muscipula* goes on catching flies to the end of its wicked existence.

But after all, the exceptional sensibilities of particular plants are nothing—nothing in comparison to the miraculous microscopical love-making which goes on between the stamens and the pistils of flowers; how shall we hope to understand their mystery? We cannot do better than borrow M. Michelet's words in his recent delightful book on the "Mountain"—to describe the general method in which the work of fecundation goes on in the flower:—

"This is how it happens. The leaf, some day, is gay and happy with heat and light, and folds itself up, and makes of itself a little home and warm cradle, a soft alcove where a little world shall be born. From its inspired tissue arises a little lady (the pistil) with her virgin dress closely wrapt round the precious treasure she bears within her. All round her, and upwards towards the sun shoot up little jets of life (the stamens.) These are her lovers, her suitors—and they make her a noble court.

"Almost always the little male, springing upwards towards the light goes higher and farther than she. He is subject to two attractions, the splendour of the luscious ray, which tinges him with gold, intoxicates him with life, and the gentle inner warmth of the soft maternal home, which announces to him from within, the propinquity of the object of his passion. There are two different temptations for him: liberty, the unfettered existence in which his light head is waving—the splendour of the luminary who seems the god of flowers. Shall they not prevail? Yes, would say the laws of physics; love says no; and this little flower-lover does as man would do. He bends down towards her, and often with a visible effort, he turns him downwards from the luminous ray towards the shady deep beneath him, seeking for her, and by this single movement, signifying that she is more than the world—love is more than the sun."

This pretty description, when put into plain English, means that the stamens generally bend down towards the pistil to deposit their pollen there, and the work of fecundation is done. But there are numerous and some most wonderful exceptions. In some cases the pistil is, contrary to the general rule, higher than the stamens; so much higher that the stamens must despair of ever laying their fairy offering on the head of their beloved—what is then to be done? Why then, when the hour arrives, and the pistil is aware that her lover has duly prepared his wedding gift, and is dying in desperation at her exalted airs, and the impossibility of getting to the summit of the lady pistil, who rises like a Peak of Teneriffe before him, she descends from her lofty station, stoops down to him, and then, good-natured creature, not to one of her lovers alone; for she goes the whole round of her circle of admirers, takes all they have to bestow, and finally resumes her former state of passionless immobility in the centre of the flower. The passion-flower, the cactus, and the lilly, are all fecundated in this way. But even more wonderful things than this take place; the pistil of one flower separates itself into four parts, and bends each part over like a hook to reach the stamens, so difficult is their position; and in another flower of the bell-shape, when the pistil is too long to be able to bend itself down to the stamens, it tilts its bell right over downside up, and shakes the pollen off from the stamens, so that it drops upon its stigmata, and when it has relieved its lovers of their offerings raises its bell up again to its former position. The poppy and campanula are thus fecundated; and among some aquatic plants a still more wonderful kind of love-making goes on, which would take us into the region of hydrostatics.—*Scottish American Journal*, July 11th.

EARLY EARTHQUAKES.

OF the early disastrous earthquakes, one of the most notable occurred about the year B.C. 285 or or 284, in the island of Niphon, one of the Japanese group. On that occasion, in one of the provinces named Oomi, a large tract of country was ingulfed in a single night, and there was formed, in its place, a lake $72\frac{1}{2}$ miles long by $12\frac{1}{4}$ wide. In an adjoining province named Sourouga there was at the same time upheaved a volcanic mountain, which still continues active. Of the formation of a lake in the place of ground ingulfed during an earthquake, the Lacus Cimini, in central Italy is another example. It is said to occupy the position of a city which was ingulfed about the year B.C. 1450.

The famous Colossus of Rhodes was thrown down by an earthquake in the year B.C. 224. This celebrated statue was of bronze, 105 feet in height, and of similar gigantic proportions throughout. The legs were filled with large masses of stone to give it stability, and there was in the interior of the body a winding staircase, which led to the top of the head, whence a splendid view could be obtained. Its feet were strongly fastened to the two moles, which formed the entrance to the harbour, and ships in full sail passed between its legs. Notwithstanding its great weight, and the strength of its fastenings, it was laid prostrate by the violent undulation of the ground during the earthquake.

About three years after this event, central Italy was much agitated by earthquakes—between fifty and sixty shocks having occurred in one year. Hills were thrown down, the courses of rivers blocked up or turned aside, and many towns were overthrown. About the same time, Libya, on the northern coast of Africa, was greatly shaken, and nearly a hundred towns and villages destroyed.

About the years 85 or 82 B.C., the lake before mentioned, which was formed in the province of Oomi in Japan, was the scene of another convulsion, during which there was thrown up in the middle of it an island, which is now called Tsikou-bo-sima. About twenty-five years after this there was a succession of earthquakes in China, during which whole mountains are said to have fallen down and filled up the valleys. These occurrences were probably landslips on a great scale. From A.D. 107 to 115, parts of China were again much convulsed. In A.D. 262 there were extensive shocks felt over central and southern Italy, Libya, and Asia Minor. In several places, the earth opened and poured forth salt water. These shocks were attended with much noise. A similar discharge of water from fissures opened in the earth occurred during an earthquake in Hungary in A.D. 518, several of the rents were twelve feet wide, and the water which issued from them was boiling hot.

The City of Antioch was, not for the first time, visited with this terrible scourge about the year A.D. 525, on which occasion however the shocks continued at intervals for a whole year, accompanied by excessive heat. Much of the city was destroyed. During the two succeeding years, the citizens rebuilt a considerable portion of the ruined edifices; but they were again overthrown in A.D. 528 by a violent shock, repeated many times in the course of an hour. About thirteen years after this, there was a shock felt throughout nearly the whole of the then known world, during which a large portion of the city of Cyzicus, situated on an island in the Bosphorus, was overthrown. A succession of shocks, which lasted forty days, and were in like manner felt over a large area, including Constantinople and part of Egypt, occurred about ten or twelve years afterwards. These shocks laid in ruins the ancient city Berytus, on the Syrian coast, where Beyrout now stands.

In 557 Antioch was again the centre of a succession of shocks, which extended to several other neighbouring cities. They continued for ten days, and were accompanied not only by loud underground rumblings, but by extraordinary atmospherical phenomena—thunder, lightning, and luminous meteors. Five or six years after this, there was a remarkable occurrence on the banks of the Rhone. A mountain, said to be Dent Du Midi in the Valais, began groaning and grumbling dreadfully for some days, and then a large portion of it, with the houses upon it and their inhabitants, fell into the stream below. This was evidently a landslip, but probably caused by volcanic forces.

The whole empire of Japan was much disturbed by earthquakes in A.D. 600; and eighty-four or eighty-five years thereafter, in the province of Tosa, in the island of Sikokf, one of the Japanese group, there was another dreadful convulsion, during which a tract of land, estimated at half a million of acres, was ingulfed in the sea. Constantinople and its neighbourhood, together with the greater part of Asia Minor, was in 740 again agitated by intermittent shocks, which lasted for about eleven months, causing much damage in the cities, and destroying many of the inhabitants. The coast was in several places elevated, and the sea driven back. Two years afterwards, Egypt and Arabia were similarly agitated, and several landslips of mountains occurred. The turn of Palestine, Syria, and Mesopotamia came next. Between the years 746 and 775 these countries experienced several shocks, attended with much damage to buildings and considerable loss of life. There were several landslips of mountains, and a chasm opened in the earth about 1000 paces in length.

In 794 the celebrated Pharos, the lighthouse of Alexandria in Egypt, was thrown down by a violent shock; and about seven years afterwards the Basilica of St. Paul's at Rome shared a similar fate, along with many other buildings in Italy, during an earthquake which was felt not only in that country, but in France and Germany.

Unfortunate Antioch was again convulsed in 859, when upwards of 1500 houses were reduced to ruins. This same earthquake was accompanied by a great landslip—a part of the mountain Askræos having fallen into the sea. The years 893 and 894 were distinguished by earthquakes very destructive to human life. In the former, 180,000 persons perished in India under the ruins of their dwellings; and in the latter year, 20,000 were in like manner destroyed in Georgia, in the neighbourhood of Lake Erivan.

The Basilica of the Lateran in Rome was overthrown by a shock in 896, and the monastery of Monte Cassino, in the Campania. in 1005. About two years after this, 10,000 persons perished in the district of Irak, in Arabia—partly buried in the ruins of their dwellings, partly ingulfed in fissures of the earth.

In 1021 there was felt, in Germany and Switzerland, a shock attended in the latter country by curious effects. The wells were all troubled, and the water in many of them became red. Great inundations followed the earthquake, and it was accompanied by luminous meteors. Eight years thereafter half the city of Damascus was overthrown by a violent shock, and in 1035 Jerusalem suffered severely. A few years afterwards there was a very fatal shock at Tabriz, in Persia, during which 50,000 persons were buried under the ruins of their houses. In 1052 a violent shock visited Khusestan, also in Persia, during which a large mountain near the city of Ardschan was cleft in twain. Eleven years thereafter the walls of the city of Tripoli, in Syria, were overthrown by a powerful shock. The coast of Syria was in 1069 again violently convulsed, and the sea, after retiring for a considerable distance from the shore, returned with a mighty wave which swept everything before it, with great destruction to life and property.

In 1110 the counties of Salop and Nottingham, in England, experienced a smart shock, and the river Trent was stopped in its course; about a mile in length of its bed was laid dry, and so continued from morning till three in the afternoon.

Persia was again severely visited in 1139. The town of Gausana was destroyed, and black water issued from fissures in the earth. It is computed that 100,000 lives were lost. About nineteen years subsequently there was great loss of life at Antioch, Tripoli, Damascus, Aleppo, and other towns in Syria, through the overthrow of houses, 20,000 persons having perished. In the same year, but whether at precisely the same time is uncertain, a considerable portion of the bed of the Thames was laid dry, as that of the Trent had been before.

Calabria and Sicily were severely agitated in 1169 or 1170; the city of Catania was destroyed, and 15,000 people perished. This earthquake appears to have been connected with an eruption of Mount Etna, which took place about the same time. The whole of England was shaken in 1185. The shock was particularly severe at Lincoln, where the cathedral and several houses were overthrown. The following year there was a severe shock felt nearly all over Europe. It was most powerful in Calabria and Sicily, where many towns were injured or destroyed; while even in England several houses were shaken down.

In 1188 a remarkable convulsion was experienced in the islands of the Indian Archipelago. It is said that on this occasion the islands of Java and Sumatra, which had previously been united, were severed from each other, and the Straits of Sunda formed between them. Sir Stamford Raffles, who found this catastrophe recorded in the Javanese annals, under date of the Javan year 1114, hesitates about accepting the truth of the statement, by reason of the great difference between the geological formations of the two islands. He nevertheless admits that the vast scale of the volcanic convulsions which have occurred in this quarter in modern times tends strongly to corroborate the historical statement. The native annals record other occurrences of the same kind, that took place subsequently. They state that Sumatra, Java, Bali, and Sumbáwa were all at one time connected together; that the detachment of Bali from Java took place about ninety years after the separation between Java and Sumatra, and that seventy-six years later Sumbáwa became a distinct island.

The Chinese Empire began to be much disturbed about 1333, and the convulsions continued for nearly ten years. The capital, Kiang-si, was swallowed up in a great chasm, and the loss of life was immense. Several mountains were either ingulfed in underground cavities, or fell down upon the plains and valleys, blocking up the courses of rivers, and causing great inundations, which proved most destructive to life and property.

In Tuscany, during an earthquake in 1335, a large mass was separated from Monte Falterona, near Florence, and fell down, putting the earth in motion to a distance of four miles. A few years after this event Iceland and Norway were violently shaken, and in the latter country much damage was done. A river was ingulfed, and several days afterwards it reappeared above ground, bringing up with it such quantities of loose materials as to choke up the valley through which its course lay, so producing an inundation. Central Europe was much agitated in 1348—great fissures opening in many places, and discharging pestilential vapours. Two years afterwards a mountain in Switzerland was cleft in twain.

The coast of Syria was in 1402 visited by another disastrous shock, accompanied by a great sea-wave, similar to that which occurred in 1069. It did immense damage. There were also several great landslips among the mountains. In 1456 the kingdom of Naples experienced several violent and destructive shocks, during which 60,000 persons perished. The Grecian Archipelago was greatly agitated in 1491, and in the island of Cos 5000 lives were lost.—*Earthquakes and Volcanoes*, by Mungo Ponton, F.R.S.E. London: Nelson.

THE SUSCEPTIBILITY OF THE SUN.

TWO striking articles on the Sun's relation to the material universe, written in partnership by an eminent astronomer, Mr. Norman Lockyer, and Dr. Balfour Stewart, have appeared in the July and August numbers of *Macmillan's Magazine*. These papers seem to us to have a more than common interest, not only for the general observer of the still unfolding laws of science, but even for the student of those deeper analogies which connect mind and matter. The new point in these articles is the popular exposition of what has only recently been suspected on anything like evidence by astronomers, namely, the exceeding delicacy of the Sun's structure, a delicacy so great that the vast physical changes which go on in that enormous mass which both holds together and warms our whole planetary system, are now all but known to depend on influences exerted over the Sun's mass by planets as insignificant as Venus and as distant as Jupiter,—and very probably also on causes which seem so little adequate to the effect as the magnetic condition of our own tiny planet. When we consider that the Sun is so big that, to use Mr. Lockyer's own illustration in another most attractive little work, it would take *nine years* for a railway train to go round it at the rate of thirty miles an hour (while a train going at the same rate round our earth would only take a month), and that, even in weight, the Sun is 300,000 times the weight of our Earth; in short, that our planet (and still more Venus, which is smaller and lighter) might easily drop into one of the holes or vortices which we call the "spots on the Sun" without adding anything considerable to the Sun's bulk or attractive power,—it seems hardly credible that those gigantic changes in the sun's constitution which we know to be indicated by the appearance of what we term the spots, should be caused by what is called the "approach" of a body so small as Venus, or even, considering its enormous minimum distance, so feeble as Jupiter, to its surface. Yet Messrs. Lockyer and Balfour Stewart evidently hold this to be all but proved. They remind us, that "just as a poker thrust into a hot furnace will create a greater disturbance of the heat than if thrust into a chamber very little hotter than itself. . . . the molecular state of the sun, just as of that of the cannon or of fulminating powder, may be externally sensitive to impressions from without." "We may thus very well suppose," they say, "that an extremely small withdrawal of heat from the sun might cause a copious condensation; and this change of molecular state would, of course, by means of altered reflection, &c., alter, to a considerable extent, the distribution over the various particles of the sun's surface of an enormous quantity of heat, and great mechanical changes might very easily result." These learned men seem convinced that what we call the spots on the sun are really caused by the down-rush of comparatively cold vapour from the surface of the sun's atmosphere into its infinitely hotter interior, and that this formation of comparatively cold vapour on the surface which then rushes down like a falling cloud into the body of the sun, is more or less caused by the approach of Venus and other planets to their minimum distance from the sun. Should any two or three of those planets which are known to affect the sun's spots " be acting together at the same place upon the sun, we may expect," say these writers, " a very large amount of spots, which will attain their maximum at that position of the sun most remote from these planets. When we say that very good evidence has been shown for this statement, we mean that it would have been reckoned conclusive had the statement been of a less wonderful character." In short, it would seem that the centre of our system, the centre not only of its mechanical but of its luminous and heating influence, is a great mass of matter in so highly sensitive and susceptible a state, that even the little satellites, which are nothing in comparison with it, produce what we may almost call gigantic solar *tides* in the atmospheric and vaporous envelope of the Sun's luminous surface. From this our essayists draw the conclusion that " there seems to be great molecular delicacy of construction in the sun, and probably also, to an inferior extent, in the various planets, and the bond between the sun and the various members of our system appears to be a more intimate one than has hitherto been imagined. The result of all this will be that a disturbance from without is very easily communicated to our luminary, and that when it takes place, it communicates a thrill to the very extremity of the system."—*The Spectator*, Aug. 1.

THE DRY HOT WEATHER OF 1868.

The heat and drought during the present season have been very remarkable, and especially the two taken in conjunction. Of course no one can venture to predict what weather the remaining five months of 1868 may bring. The period of heat and drought which has so long continued may or may not be followed by a period equally remarkable for cold and heavy rainfall; for a year which begins with one extreme not unfrequently terminates in the opposite extreme, and taking the average of several successive years, it will be found that heat and cold, sunshine and shadow, wet and drought are very nearly balanced. Putting aside, therefore, as useless all speculation as to the future, let us see what have been hitherto the main features of the year, as regards heat and moisture, near London.

First, as regards heat. The mean maximum temperature of January was 42.90, or not quite a tenth of a degree above an average of 36 years; and the mean minimum temperature was 30.90, or about as much below the average; the mean temperature of the month, therefore, only differed 1-100th of a degree from the average. There were no remarkable extremes either of heat or cold, during the month, the highest temperature attained being 54° on the 15th and 17th, and the lowest 19° on the 2nd.

In February the mean maximum temperature was 51°.07 or 5°.35 above the average; the mean minimum, 34°.41, was likewise above the average, but only 2°.73. The mean temperature of the month was 42°.74, or a little more than 4° above the average. The highest day temperature was 62° on the 25th, a temperature never before reached in February, and on the 1st the temperature was also very high for the time of year, being 59°, a heat but rarely even approached at any time during this month. The lowest point reached during the month was 20° on the 8th, and the thermometer again indicated as low as 22° on the 15th.

In March the mean maximum was 53°.35, or 2°.67 above the average, but with the exception of the 21st and 31st, when the thermometer was at 67° and 60° respectively, in no instance was 60° reached. Although the day temperature was considerably above the average, that of the nights was not in excess to a corresponding amount; for the mean of these was only 33°.74, not quite 4-10ths of a degree more than the average. The lowest night temperature was 23° on the 24th and 29th.

In April, again, the mean maximum temperature was above the average to the extent of 1°.26, being 58°.70; whilst the mean minimum was 36°.90, or 0°.72 above the average. The thermometer stood as high as 69° on the 5th, and on 13 other days was 60° or upwards. The greatest cold registered was 25° on the 12th and 14th, and after the latter date the temperature was never lower than 30°.

Of May the mean maximum temperature was unusually high, being as much as 70°.87, 6¼° above the average, but the mean minimum temperature was 2°.53 below the average. The thermometer registered 87° on the 19th, and again on the 30th, and 82° on the 3rd. The lowest at night was 27° on the 6th, but, with the exception of the 7th, when the temperature was 28°, it never again fell below freezing.

In June the mean maximum temperature was again very high, being 5°.42 above the average, whilst the night temperature, on the contrary, was 3°.31 below the average, being only 45°.33. The warmest day was the 12th, when the thermometer was 86°; and it indicated 85° on the 14th, 17th, and 27th. On 12 days in all the temperature was 80° and upwards. The coldest night was that of the 7th, when the thermometer fell to 35°, and it was 36° on the 2nd and 8th.

In July the mean day temperature was extremely high, being 81°.84, nearly 7¼° above the average. July, 1852, memorable for its extreme heat, had for its mean 81°.16, and July, 1858, 81°90. The heat, therefore, though within a small fraction of a degree of what had been previously recorded, was not without precedent. The highest temperature registered was 93° on the 21st and 22nd. On 19 days in all the temperature was at or above 80°. A thermometer with a black bulb enclosed in a hollow glass sphere placed in the sun indicated 136° on the 21st, and 138° on the 22nd, and only once did its highest reading fall so low as 95°. 119° and 130° were not uncommon readings. High as the day temperature was, that of the nights was not equally so, being only 52°23, or a little more than nine-tenths of a degree above the average. It was marked by no great extremes, 42° was the lowest degree, 66° the highest, but generally it was tolerably uniform.

As regards rainfall, there has been a deficiency in its amount in every month since January, as will be seen from the following statement:—

	Inches.	Inches below the average.
January	1.63	0.00
February	0.93	0.47
March	0.63	0.75
April	0.93	0.59
May	1.05	0.93
June	0.33	1.69
July	1.32	1.04
	6.82	5.47

In January the rainfall was exactly the average amount, but from that time the deficiency has gone on increasing, till at the end of July it amounted to 5.47 inches. An inch of rain in round numbers is equal to 100 tons of water per acre, and the deficiency therefore is equal to 547 tons per acre; in reality it is about 10 tons more. Although in some parts of the country in May, June, and July, there have been long periods without any rain whatever, it has not been so dry near London, for there have been small falls of rain at intervals, so that the longest period without rain was three weeks, from May 29th, when four-tenths of an inch fell, to June 20th, when the amount was six one-hundredths, followed by 0.16, 0.02, and 0.08 inch on the 21st, 22nd, and 23rd. Between the latter date and July 11th, there was only one-hundredth of an inch of rain; but on the 11th and 12th together we had nearly an inch of rainfall, accompanied by heavy thunder; on the 15th it again rained, the measurement being 0.14; then it was dry till the 26th, on which day there was, in all, two-tenths of an inch.

It may be added that 1847 very nearly approached 1868 in the small amount of rain which fell in the first seven months of the year, the rainfall being in that period—January, 1.31; February, 1.34; March, 0.41; April, 0.92; May, 1.59; June, 1.31; July, 0.79—or 7.67 inches in all. In 1857, from February to July, was also very dry.—*Gardener's Chronicle*, August 8.

THE TEMPERATURE.

To the Editor of the Times.

SIR,—Your correspondent in Friday's paper has suggested the utility of a table giving particulars of the summer of 1826. I have for the last 50 years, in my way, made record for every day in the year of the temperature as ascertained by me at regular times from a thermometer never changed in place, and I have extracted from those records the *maximum* of every day of the months of May, June, and July for the years 1822, 1824, 1825, 1826, 1868, as most remarkable years for extreme of heat, which I place at your service.

I remain, Sir, your most obedient servant,
Castlemans, July 27.   A. M. COURT.

	1822. Maximum.	1824. Maximum.	1825. Maximum.	1826. Maximum.	1868. Maximum.
May 1	59	58½	56	52	59
2	81	57	56	54	—
3	59.5	54	56	51	67
4	61.5	54	61	50	62
5	64.5	55	59	50	58.5
6	64	57	63	49	57
7	55	60	60	50	56
8	54	59	59.5	54	62
9	51	59	50	54.5	62
10	51	59	60	58	61
11	55	55.5	59.5	58	59.5
12	51	52	58	54	61
13	50.5	51	56.5	55	61
14	61	50.5	56.5	54.5	62
15	63	49.5	55	55	65
16	60	49	53	58	64
17	61	50	54	60	64
18	65.5	52	56	63.5	68
19	68.5	53	57.5	64	74
20	72	50	58	60.5	66
21	71	52	59	62.5	64½
22	67	51.5	63	—	62R
23	62	52	63	—	61R
24	62	53	61	60	61R
25	62	55	61	60	61.5R
26	58	56	57	61	62
27	58	61	55	60.5	—
28	65	64	54	60	—
29	67	61.3	54½	53	69.5
30	68	60.5	55	57.5	65stm
31	68	61	56	59	66.5
June 1	72	64	55.5	58	69
2	76	64.5	57	58	64
3	75	59.3	57.5	60	61.5
4	76	61	56.5	50.5	61
5	75	58	54.5	64	66
6	76	63	56.5	65	68
7	72	65.3	57.5	65	61
8	74	66	60	64.5	61.5
9	75	68.5	63	65	64
10	69	59	—	67	64
11	69	57	72	68	63
12	68.5	54.5	66	70	68
13	69.5	57	72	71	72
14	72	59	71	—	72
15	63.5	58	69	—	70
16	66.5	58	68	—	70
17	65	59	66	—	70
18	67	58	65	63	72
19	68	57	65	63	69
20	64	53	53	63	72R
21	67	59	58	63	74R
22	73	60	61	64	67R
23	72	59	64	66	68.5R
24	72	57.5	64.5	69	66
25	72	57	64.5	71	69

	26	74	61	62	74.5	70
	27	68½	62	—	75.5	74
	28	65	63.5	—	74	70
	29	63	62.5	61	71	69
	30	67	60.5	—	71	71
July	1	67	—	61	71	67
	2	65	—	64	72	70
	3	—	—	65	74	72
	4	68	—	65	—	65.5
	5	65	—	65	—	68
	6	62	—	62	75	65.5
	7	66	—	60	72	71
	8	64	—	62	72	72
	9	68	—	62	72	72
	10	69	—	62.5	69	73
	11	65	—	65	68	75
	12	64	—	69	70	70stm
	13	65	—	69	68	71.5
	14	69	—	70	68	75
	15	69	—	77	67.5	77.5
	16	66	—	76.5	66	77
	17	66	—	77	70	74
	18	71	—	79.5	63	76
	19	70	—	83.5	66	77
	20	67	—	79.5	65	77
	21	65	—	71	64	79
	22	66	—	68.5	63	81
	23	65	—	64.5	65	71
	24	67	—	65	68	71
	25	65	—	66	68	72
	26	65	—	66	65	72R
	27	67	—	Marked	69	Harvest
	28	65	—	Hot	72	July 7
	29	65	—	Hot	74	—
	30	62	—	Hot	—	—
	31	59	—	—	—	—

The figures 1825 taken at Ripley in Surrey. Haymaking in May; harvest, July 15.

July 19, 1825—hottest day on my record, 83.5.

The figures of 1825, 1826, and 1868—maximum heat of each day, as taken at Castlemans, from thermometer held in the hall of the house in shade, never changing place.

August 1826—hot, dry month; occasional showers. Harvest, July 14.

September 1826—high temperature, with heavy rains and thunderstorms.

November, 1826—coldest month in the year; frost, snow, ice.

The Greatest Droughts in the Present Century.

The longest periods of absence of rain in this climate have occurred generally in the spring and summer, occasionally in the autumn, but seldom in the winter. The following particulars of the greatest droughts, from observations taken in this locality, may be read with some interest at the present time:—The drought in 1817 commenced August 31, and lasted till Nov. 2—63 days. In that time the fall of rain was:—

September	0.33 inch on	4	days.
October	0.42 ,,	8	,,
	0.75 ,,	12	,,

Mean temperature: September, 56°; October, 44.4°. The drought in 1818 commenced May 17, and lasted till September 1—108 days. In that time the fall of rain was:—

May and June	0.87 inch on	7	days.
July	0.78 ,,	4	,,
August	0.30 ,,	4	,,
	1.95 ,,	15	

Mean temperature: May, 50.5°; June, 59.4°; July, 63.2°; August 57.8°. The drought in 1826 commenced February 28, and lasted till July 1—124 days. In that time the fall of rain was:—

March	0.46 inch on	5	days.
April	0.55 ,,	10	,,
May	1.04 ,,	5	,,
June	nil		,,
	2.05 ,,	20	

Mean temperature: March, 42.9°; April, 46.5°; May, 53.1°; June, 64.2°. (The latter month was intensely hot, especially the last week. The bulk of the corn harvest was over by the third week in July.) The drought in 1840 commenced February 25, and lasted till May 4—75 days. In that time the fall of rain was:—

March	0.14 inch on	4	days.
April	0.48 ,,	7	,,
	0.62 ,,	11	

Mean temperature: March 40.5°; April, 51.5°. The drought in 1844 commenced March 26 and lasted till July 1—97 days. In that time the fall of rain was:—

April	0.37 inch on	5	days.
May	0.25 ,,	6	,,
June	0.54 ,,	10	,,
	1.16 ,,	21	,,

Mean temperature: April, 52.9°; May, 53°; June, 59.9°. The drought in 1852 commenced February 15, and lasted till May 6—80 days. In that time the fall of rain was:—

February and March	0.28 inch on	7	days.
April	0.44 ,,	5	,,
	0.72 ,,	12	,,

Mean temperature: February, 37°; March, 41.5°; April, 45.7°. The drought in 1864 commenced June 24, and lasted till August 28—66 days. In that time the fall of rain was:—

June and July	0.82 inch on	13	days.
August	0.21 ,,	5	,,
	1.03 ,,	18	,,

Mean temperature: June, 58°; July, 61.5°; August, 59°. The drought in 1868 commenced May 30, and still continues. Since the 29th of May only 2-5ths of an inch of rain has fallen in Birmingham, and on three days only. The mean temperature of June was 61.5°, or 2.5° above the average. It was the hottest June since 1858, and the driest since 1826. The mean temperature of each of the eight dry seasons in the present century is given because it bears much on this subject, inasmuch as when a long series of dry weather is associated with high temperature, as in 1826, 1844, and the present drought, both circumstances combined have produced more disastrous consequences than any other known meteorological vicissitude in this climate. Many other but less important droughts have occurred in the long range of time we have taken. For example, in 1854 the fall of rain in Birmingham during March and April was only 0·94 inch, and in 1863 the depth for 4 months (February, March, April, and May) was only 3 inches. But the spring of 1852 exceeded them both in dryness. From February 15 to May 6, 1852, the depositions of rain did not reach three-quarters of an inch, and rain fell on 12 days only out of the 80. Part of the autumn of 1865 was very dry. From August 30 to October 7 the depth of rain was only 0·20 inch, but the drought ended on the fortieth day; whereas in 1817 the dry weather began August 31, and continued till November 2. The depth of rain in the 63 days was only three-quarters of an inch, and rain fell on 12 days only. 15 or 20 years are not a sufficient range of time to form conclusions either as regards averages or comparisons of great meteorological events. The springs of 1854 and 1863 were dry, that of 1852 was drier, but all fall into insignificance when compared with the dry springs of 1826 and 1844. The summer of 1864 was remarkably dry, but the summer of 1818 was the driest in the present century. Nothing less than a range of 50 years should be received as a standard of meteorological comparison.—*Birmingham Gazette.*

Animal Sagacity.

The following is from an old newspaper, under date 1816:—"I was exceedingly amused with the article on Animal Sagacity in a late paper; such instances bring the animal very closely to the human species, in reason and good conduct. They are nearly as surprising as that anecdote related by Goldsmith, (I believe) of a venerable dog, who had been brought up and instructed in the family of a strict Roman Catholic, and who, at the close of his life, was sent across the channel into Wales, to finish his days in the family of a Protestant. Such, however, was the force of habit, that nothing, from the moment he entered the Protestant circle, would tempt him to eat meat, either on Wednesdays or Fridays. But the following instance of sagacity in the canine breed is far more astonishing. It was related to me by a Prussian officer, who lately visited this metropolis, as an undeniable fact, and names of persons and places attended the relation of it. A German Count had a very valuable dog, a large and noble-looking animal; in some description of field sports he was reckoned exceedingly useful, and a friend of the Count's applied for the loan of the dog for a few weeks' excursion in the country; it was granted; and, in the course of the rambles, the dog, by a fall, either dislocated or gave a severe fracture to one of his legs. The borrower of the dog was in the greatest alarm, and knowing well how greatly the Count valued him; and, fearing to disclose the fact, brought him secretly to the Count's surgeon, a skilful man, to restore the limb. After some weeks' application, the surgeon succeeded, the dog was returned, and all was well. A month or six weeks after this period, the surgeon was sitting gravely in his closet, pursuing his studies, when he heard a violent scratching at the bottom of the door; he rose, and on opening it, to his surprise, he saw the dog, his late patient, before him, in company with another dog, who had broken his leg, and was thus brought by his friend to be cured in the same manner. I have heard before now a farmer say that he had a horse in his stable who always, on losing his shoe, went of his own accord to a farrier's shop, a mile off; but I never yet heard of a horse taking another horse to a farrier for the purpose. In the case of the dogs there must have been a communication of ideas; they must have come to a conclusion before they set out; they must have reasoned together on the way, discussing the merits of the surgeon, and the nature of the wound.—T. B., Gray's Inn, Dec., 1816.—*Hardwicke's Science Gossip*, August.

Correspondence.

[*Under this head we shall be glad to insert any letters of general interest.*]

HYBERNATION—SWALLOWS UNDER WATER AGAIN!!!

Sir,—Your correspondent "C. W." in quite an agreeable manner enters very freely into the incredible romance of hybernation, and surely the most enthusiastic advocates of the periodical sub-aquatic somnolentia of swallows cannot but begin to wonder at the "bushels" and "barrowloads" of tangible arguments, and particularly the six musical swallows which with such laudable alacrity cast aside their drowsiness and became domestic vocalists on the kitchen grate!! But, Sir, this is the age of expansion, and, "half dead with wonder and surprise," I simply ask, "Is it possible that swallows can live for months under water?"

Absolutely impossible, argues Collison, in combatting the theory advocated by Klein and others. But surely Dr. Hunter's answers were sufficiently clear and argumentative.

In order to test the matter Hunter dissected some swallows. His testimony is, " I dissected several swallows, but found nothing in them different from other birds as to the organs of respiration;" and his inference deduced from this dissection is, "*that swallows could not remain for any time under water without being drowned.*"

Thus spoke Hunter more than one hundred years ago; and still with some natures there are such desires for the regions of improbability, such lingerings after the ludicrous, that even the calm and impartial voice of science in vain appeals to their judgment.

But, Sir, as autumn is fast approaching sure any of your correspondents can easily test the matter: catch a few swallows, submerge them, let them remain until spring, honestly tell the result, and let fanciful theories vanish. Along the Shannon, Blackwater, and Lee, in autumn I have at different times seen thousands of swallows closely congregated, and quite as noisy as the veritable six "upon the kitchen grate;" but, after many minute inquiries, I never was so fortunate as to find a fisherman or any other man that had ever disturbed a swallow in its aqueous chamber: there is not even a remote tradition of anything of the kind. How simple is the theory of migration; but while hybernation sets swallows to sleep under water, credulity shows its powers of expansion, and your correspondents must still see that there is need for the NATURALIST'S NOTE BOOK.

I am, Sir, yours,
H. H. ULIDIA.

Dromore, August, 1868.

THE COMMON GALLINULE (*FORTICA CHLOROPUS.*)

SIR,—I wish to call your attention to a point in Natural History which I believe has been overlooked by most naturalists; while in one or more instances, an incorrect exposition of existing ideas has been made.

Nearly every one living in the country—more especially gamekeepers or the peasantry—will tell you that the male of the Moorhen, or Common Gallinule (*Fortica Chloropus*) is easily distinguishable from the female, by having a bright red bill and forehead, dark coloured plumage, and being altogether a finer bird. The female is described as being grey in plumage, and having a yellowish-green bill tipped only with reddish. Now, I hope to be enabled to prove that the greater part of this impression is wrong, and that most naturalists only confirm this error, and ignore a curious phase in the history of this bird. In proof of this assertion, I will quote a few authors of repute.

Morris, in his beautiful "History of British Birds," gives so good a description of the male bird, that I may be pardoned if I give it at length.

Male—Weight from fourteen to sixteen ounces; length one foot one inch to one foot two; bill greenish yellow; the base bright red, ascending up the forehead, both brightest in the spring; iris dusky reddish. Head small; and on the crown, as is the neck on the back and nape, deep blackish purple grey; throat and breast above, dark slate grey; below, margined with dull greyish white; on the sides streaked with white, and in the spring glossed with a reflection of green; back, very dark blackish brown, with a tinge of olive, brightest in the spring.

The wings have a white edge at the bend; primaries, greyish black. The tail, which is greyish black with a tinge of deep green, is rounded at the tip; upper tail coverts, white, with some black feathers; the former colour is visibly shewn when the bird, as before mentioned, flirts up its tail. There are sometimes a few white feathers on the thighs. The legs, which are placed rather far backwards, are surrounded above the knee with a red band or garter, and are otherwise, as are the toes, which are very long, the hind one considerably produced as well as the others, pale dull green: the latter are fringed out with scales; claws, dark brown.

With regard to the next statement, I shall have some observations to offer, for he says:—

The female is like the male, but is less in size; the red on the bill is deficient. The garter above the knee is also less bright.

Following in the same track, I find in the twenty-second volume of "Cuvier Dictionnaire des Sciences Naturelles," under the heading "Hydrogalline," the statement that—

L'espèce la plus repandue en Europe, et que l'on trouve en Ecosse, en Angleterre, en Hollande, en Prusse, en Suisse, en Espagne, et dans la plupart des départemens de France est l'hydrogalline commune, Hydrogallina chloropus, Lacep.; Gallimula chloropus, Lath.; et Fulica chloropus, Linn.; Poule d'eau, Buff.; pl. eml., No. 877, le mâle; pl. 192 de Lewin. 37 de Graves. Tom II, 110 de Donovan. Cette espèce longue de 12 à 14 ponces, a dans son état parfait la tête la gorge, le con et toutes les parties inférieures d'un bleu ardoisé; le dessus du corps d'un bleu olivâtre foncé; du blanc au bord de l'aile, et des taches de la même couleur sur les flancs et sur les plumes anales, au centre desquelles on voit aussi des taches noires. La base du bec et la plaque frontale sont rouges, et la pointe du bec est jaune; un cercle d'un beau rouge entoure le tibia, et les pieds sont d'un vert faunâtre.

The writer then goes on to correctly describe the colours of the young, after the autumnal moult, pointing out the species which have been created out of their different stages of growth, but says nothing about the female.

Yarrell, in his "British Birds," says:—"The male has the beak yellowish green; the base of it and the naked patch on the forehead, red, irides reddish hazel." He then describes the rest of the plumage, but says nothing about the female, only that "Mr. Gould mentions that he has seen females that were more brightly coloured than the males."

Van der Hœven, in the "Handbook of Zoology," makes no distinction between the sexes of the Gallinule, merely stating "base of the bill, which is yellow at the tip, red."

Macgillivray, in "British Birds," under the heading "Male," writes:—

In the end of autumn, when the moult has been completed, the bill is greenish yellow beyond the nostrils, the basal part and frontal plate crimson red, the latter somewhat paler.

In another part he says—

The frontal plate is of a brighter red than the bill, yellowish at its upper margin. It is larger in the male than in the female. Again, it becomes brighter in spring than at any other season.

Female.—The female differs slightly in size, being somewhat smaller, but the difference in the colours of the plumage is inconsiderable, the head, neck, and especially the sides being merely a little paler, the black beneath the tail less deep, and the abdomen with rather more white. The frontal plate is much smaller.

Gould, on the authority of "Maunder's Treasury of Natural History," is made to say:—

One circumstance respecting this familiar bird appears to have escaped the notice of most ornithologists: we allude to the fact of the female being clothed in a dark and rich plumage, and having the base of the bill and the frontal shield of a bright crimson-red tipped with yellow; her superiority in these respects has caused her to be mistaken for the male, which, contrary to the general rule, is at all times clothed in a duller plumage, and has the upper surface more olive than in the female; the bill is also less richly tinted.

Now, it was this paragraph especially which confirmed my lately aroused suspicion that all was not known with regard to this bird; and, determined to try and find out who was right, I sallied forth, gun on shoulder, to a sedgy swamp frequented by the Gallinules. After floundering through the black mud, which came nearly to the tops of my water boots, I—assisted by the most clever of retrievers—dight "Quail," succeeded in shooting one, apparently a fine male, having a bright red bill and frontal shield. This I dissected on March 26, and although it was much shot about the hinder part, I fortunately discovered the ovarium intact, containing a quantity of eggs, which placed it beyond a doubt that this specimen was a female. Another which I examined on the 28th, though having all the reputed points of the male, yet proved to be a female; as also one brought to me on the 29th. On the 2nd April I shot another, which also proved to be a female, and yet the whole of these birds tallied exactly with the description of the male, as given by Morris, Cuvier, Yarrell, and Macgillivray. "Aha! (I thought) Mr. Gould was right after all;" but yet it struck me as singular that I had seen so many running, and flying, and that *all* were females; for all I saw had richly coloured bills, and plumage. I began then to propound some theory to account for the absence of males, such as that, perhaps, the females drove them away during nidification. Not half satisfied, however, I went again on the 7th April, and shot another female, as I supposed: however, I thought I would dissect it; on doing which, I discovered it to be a male. It was exactly like the others, excepting that perhaps it was a little heavier. Imagine my perplexity! I went again, and shot two, and one of these of more than ordinary size (indeed, the largest I had ever seen), which I had named to a friend as being a male—turned out, on dissection, to be a female! A few days after this, I shot two males; a great difference existed in their relative size, one being much smaller than the other, and not of so rich a colour; it was deficient also of most of the white feathers along the side. On examining several more, I found that *no* outward difference existed between males and females, and that it was impossible to name the sex before dissection.

Knowing that at other seasons I had shot females less gaily attired, I arrived at once at the indubitable fact that *the female moorhen during the breeding season assumes the colours of the male with regard to the bill and legs;* as regards the size or richness of plumage, *no law can be laid down*; for some which I examined were larger, and handsomer, than the males, and *vice versâ*. I have reason to believe, however, that those birds which have a *corrugated* frontal shield are aged, and these specimens I always found to be of a rich olive colour on the back and deep grey on the breast, pointing to the theory that they darken with age, irrespective of sex.

I trust that I have now conclusively proved that the whole of Morris's statement with regard to the female is incorrect. That the editor of the "Dictionnaire des Sciences Naturelles" was ignorant of the change during the season of nidification in the colours of the female; as also on that point, Yarrell and Van der Hœven. Macgillivray, in addition to contradicting his own statement about the colour of the frontal plate (*vide* extract) is clearly wrong when he describes the female as being smaller, paler in colour, and having a lesser frontal plate than the male; while Gould (usually so correct) actually makes "confusion worse confounded" when he states "that at all times" the male is less richly coloured, and has a duller coloured bill than the female.

To account for these various and contradictory statements, I should suppose that the description of the bird has been written at different seasons of the year—the fact of its changes not being known, or being borne in mind. The Rev. J. G. Wood, to whom I have spoken upon the subject, has told me that he considers it an important fact, and worthy of further study, thinking as I do, that it will now be an interesting task to note the exact time at which the adult female doffs her lord's colours, and whether the male participates in the change on the approach of winter. This I hope to be able to determine, and I should be very glad if those of your correspondents interested in the study of ornithology would aid me with further suggestions or observations upon the subject.

I am, Sir, yours, &c.,
A. M. B.

Short Notes.

MOSQUITOS.—My opinion having been requested on the subject of the mosquitos, said to have been introduced into this country from the West Indies during the present hot weather, I am under the necessity of saying that I entirely discredit any such occurrence having taken place. Every year in the hottest part of the summer our common knat, Culex pipieris, is developed very numerously and very rapidly, and no sooner does it make its appearance in the winged state than it (or rather, only the females) immediately wants food, attacking the exposed parts of the body, especially during the night, with the greatest violence. We possess a score of British species of the restricted genus Culex, one of which, with spotted wings, has just been sent to me from Portsmouth as a mosquito; and I fortunately happened to be at the British Museum when a "mosquito" was brought from the neighbourhood of Woolwich, which proved to be nothing but Culex pipieris. The mosquito of the Riviera between Nice and Genoa (which is very venomous, and is guarded against by carefully-stitched mosquito curtains), is certainly only a Culex, which breeds in the open water tanks in the garden or yard of every house, and which is not only never cleared out, but always left open, so that the knats breed in the water perfectly unchecked. There is a minute midge, of quite a different genus, which is called a mosquito in some exotic parts, as in North America, and we have small British species which go under the common name of sand flies (a great misnomer, as they are chiefly found in swampy places only) which draw blood. That the insects are more venomous now than at any other season I do not believe; that the hot weather makes them more energetic I do believe, and that many persons when stung are in an inflammatory condition will, I believe, sufficiently account for the worse effects of the insect's wound. If persons who have water-tanks or open ditches about their houses would be careful shortly after sunset to watch the windows of their bedrooms, they would find the knats beginning to fly about the panes of glass, emitting their hum, and a little pains would enable them to destroy the enemy, and ensure a quiet night's rest.—J. O. Westwood, Oxford, *in Gardener's Magazine*, August 8th.

ENGLISH SNAKES.—Some years ago we witnessed a scene which illustrated in a very plain fashion the hatred shown by most people to all members of the serpent family. Five or six country boys were pelting with flints some creature crawling close to a garden-wall. A glance showed the object of their natural but ignorant wrath, and we could not help saying, "That can't hurt you, it never harmed anybody." They stared, as we proceeded to explain to them that the reptile was as "harmless as a baby." They were silenced, it is true, but doubtless believe to this day in the venomous powers of the *blind-worm*. Thousands of English peasants would, probably, support the boys in their view, and we therefore begin this notice of English snakes with a few remarks on this timid member of the family. Some naturalists might object to class it among serpents at all; but there seems to be no sufficient reason on this occasion for departing from the popular notion. Have any of our readers ever seen a blind-worm? No? Then look out for the first opportunity. They will see an eel-like creature, about twelve inches long, of a greyish colour, somewhat ruddy along the sides, which are marked by small darkish spots. Observe that the tail is not pointed, but blunt, as if a point had been chopped off. Now you may put the worm safely in your pocket, if you please; it cannot hurt you, having no fangs, and the teeth being too small to harm a fly. Marvellous stories and [some fibs indeed have been told of its destructive bite. One ancient writer boldly declares it would poison a full-grown ox. No wonder that the reptile led a sad life, after getting so bad a name. Why is it called the blind-worm? From ignorance at first, and then from custom. It was supposed to be blind; but why, is one of the puzzles constantly presented by popular names. Any one can see two very bright, though small eyes in its head. The popular lines express the common belief on this point—

"If the snake could hear, and the blind-worm could see,
Neither man nor beast should e'er go free."

Well, the creature can see, and man does go free.—*From "Recreative Natural History," in "Cassell's New Popular Educator"* for August.

SUB-TROPICAL GARDEN IN SPAIN.—The finest sub-tropical garden we saw in Spain is that belonging to the Duc de Montpensier, near Los Delicias. It is not scientifically arranged, like a Botanical Garden, though it is called one, and deserves the name better than many others which enjoy that title. Some of the finest Date Palms in Spain are here; one growing near the palace is full 6oft. high, a female plant, which was fruiting abundantly when we saw it. Others, of both sexes, and also of large sizes, are scattered through the grounds. Some other Palms grow freely in the open ground here, among which we noticed fine specimens of Cocos flexuosa, Latania borbonica, and Raphis flabelliformis. Groups of Musas are planted through the garden, and fine examples of Musa Ensete in single plants; also groups of Bamboos and Sugar Canes, which produced a fine effect. Among the rarer plants we noticed Parkinsonia aculeata, 30ft. high, and seeding freely. Sterculia platanifolia and Phytolacca sapota are also fine. It was here we first saw the Erythrinas in their full vigour and beauty; some of them had stems upwards of 3ft. in circumference, and were covered with brilliant scarlet flowers. Lagerstrœmia indica was also covered with its gorgeous flowers, on plants from 12 to 15ft. high. The New Holland trees seemed quite at home in this garden. Araucarias, Grevilleas, and Acacias are growing as freely there as they do in the most favoured parts of their native country. We also observed some very fine specimens of succulent plants planted out in the open ground, such as Cereus multangularis, 20ft. high, and stout in proportion; Cereus monstrosus, 6ft. high, branched into 20 principal stems. Near the latter stood a remarkable plant of Yucca filamentosa, with a stem about 14ft. high, which has sent out ten other stems at that height, each of which is almost 7ft. long. The walks lead through shady groves of Orange trees, Myrtles, &c., to the conservatories, where Pineapples and other fruits are cultivated.—*Gardener's Chronicle*, August 1st.

ZOOLOGICAL GARDENS.—Experiments made at the Zoological Gardens, prove that such places of amusement, may also be turned into most valuable places of instruction in natural history—instruction which Englishmen, colonising every quarter of the globe, will always find more or less valuable. Here, we may realise Lord Bacon's idea in the "Atlantis" of a "a tryal place for beasts and fishes." Here we may learn, as indeed we have done, to acclimatise many creatures, and thus to enlarge the store of food among us. In this sense a zoological garden ranks as a scientific laboratory, if we may so use the word, and not merely as a place of amusement and wonderground for holiday-folk. With this view we hope to see all zoological gardens established in the future take care to surround themselves with ample grounds; for it is this want, we fear, which is hampering the secretary of the Regent's Park Gardens in his labours to exhibit the animals in their natural state as far as possible. Let us take the "great cats," as they are called, the lions and tigers. These, the masters of the brute creation, were the animals that attracted the most attention in the old wild-beast shows, but it is far from being the case now, excepting at feeding time. The reason is obvious: the noble action of the felidæ is utterly unknown as long as they are boxed up in a cage not a dozen feet square. There is a paddock for the rhinoceros, and enclosures for the deer and giraffes, but the lordly lion can only be looked at through iron bars. Surely this is a mistake. Why should not he and the tigers and leopards have an open space, well palisaded, for their exercising ground? The animals would keep their health better, and the king of beasts would be restored to his right position, from which he has been deposed of late. Gordon Cumming tells us he is a sad coward; in other words, he did find any one of them determined to eat him. He had many narrow escapes, nevertheless, and his servant was really munched up. He should, therefore, have been more grateful than to have disparaged the beast when he was at home in safety. We are inclined to indulge in our old faith in the lion, and there can be no manner of doubt as to his majestic appearance when in the open; therefore we trust the secretary of the Gardens will give him a play-ground, that we may see him in all his majesty.—*Cassell's Paper*.

ANIMAL AND VEGETABLE LIFE.—Otherwise well-educated men, who know nothing of the natural sciences (and the number of these is large) often declare that the lowest animal is but little removed from the highest plant. This, however, is a popular error, and the reverse of this is the case. The true statement is that both kingdoms start from the same point. The simplest and lowest forms of both, especially in their immature condition, are almost identical. At this simplest and earliest stage of development, the plant makes quite as decided an approach towards the typical life of an animal as does the animal make a counter-approach towards the typical life of a vegetable. The young spore of a conferva (vegetable) is locomotive, and moves by the same mechanism as a protozoon. Thus the animal and vegetable kingdoms not only meet at their lowest point, but the vegetable, so to speak, travels more than half way to effect the meeting. From this common point of contact the two kingdoms slowly diverge from one another; but the divergence is so gradual, the angle of divergence is so small, that for some distance they move in an almost parallel course. Now, as the vegetable stops far short of the development of the animal kingdom, we must look for the parallel in its higher forms, not in the lowest animals of all, but in those at some little distance up the scale.—*From "Comparative Anatomy," in "Cassell's New Popular Educator"* for August.

ANECDOTE OF A PONY.—The *Scotsman*, on the authority of several trustworthy witnesses, states that an almost unparalleled circumstance was recently noticed at Muirhall, near West-Calder. During the great heat that prevailed in the afternoon, an Iceland pony, the property of Mr. John Waddell, contractor, was for a time left to its own free will during the temporary absence of its driver. The pony, which had been driven for a considerable distance, and was seemingly actuated by a craving for water, was observed by the proprietor of Muirhall, and others who chanced to be in the vicinity, to deliberately walk a distance of fully fifty yards, and with his teeth turn the cock of a water-pipe projecting out of the road embankment, supply itself with a draught of the refreshing beverage, readjust the cock, and return to the position in which it was left.—*Our Own Fireside*, August.

PECULIAR BLEACHING OF A MULATTO. —Dr. B. W. Foster, we read in the *Scientific Review* for August, has recently had occasion to observe a gradual disappearance of the cutaneous pigment in a Mulatto of forty-three years of age. Minute white spots first appeared in the man's back, and, by coalescing, gradually formed large white patches. These constantly extended, until, in the course of six years, the whole of the body became perfectly white, spots of the original colour remaining only on the limbs; the face also remained black. The man was in perfect health during the whole period. Blisters applied to the bleached surface restored the dark colour of the skin in irregular spots. Hence the cause of the singular occurrence has been attributed, with more or less probability, to a sluggish state of the circulation.

LEPORIDES.—The gentleman, writes the Paris correspondent of *Land and Water*, to whom I was referred by the director of the *Jardin d'Acclimatation* has sent me an answer on the vexed question concerning the leporide. M. Gayot writes to me that he cannot communicate the documents at present, as he is busy getting them into a volume, which he hopes to be able to present to the public about the end of the year. But I think that your friend "Rover" may be assured that the leporide is a reality, as M. Gayot states that his book will contain the history of the hare-rabbit, and the fruitful cross between the two races.

Remarks, Queries, &c.

(Under this head we shall be happy to insert original Remarks, Queries, &c.)

DO INSECTS FEEL PAIN?

Your correspondent H. H. Ulidia, at p. 250, confidently answers "Yes;" I take upon myself with equal confidence to answer "No;" and I am convinced, that both theory and well ascertained facts support me in this assertion. When H. H. Ulidia, to fortify his position by a fancied analogy, begins his statement by saying: "Man himself feels pain, the whale, the elephant, the sparrow, etc., and *consequently* insects also feel pain, why not"? he is evidently unconscious of the differences that exist between the structure of the vertebrate frame and that of insects. Now suppose the question had been put in another form, thus: "Have Insects true blood and a brain?" H. H. U. might with equal truth answer, (as he has done, *mutatis mutandis*, to the real question at issue) "Yes, says analogy, and we are too modest to reject the deductions from analogy. Man himself has blood and a brain, the whale, the elephant, and the sparrow, etc., and *consequently* insects also have blood and a brain, why not?" Why not? because anatomy proves that both these organs of life are wanting. If then (as is well ascertained), the nerves proceeding from a brain and blood proceeding from a heart are the seat of feeling, then it is certain that insects are insensible to pain. True, they possess within their bodies a liquid, which flows very slowly, like protoplasur in plant cells, not with the mill race speed of blood discs; and they also possess a form of nerve known as ganglia, but these ganglia, be it remembered, are not analogous to the nerves of the higher animals, inasmuch as they are scattered through the frame, and not concentrated in one great centre, the brain: and Professor Huxley has shown years ago, that the amount of feeling depends in a great measure, if not entirely, on the degree of concentration of nerve matter. But this is theory, so let us come to facts. I presume, that even H. H. U. would hardly assert, that an animal can feel severe pain, without giving some kind of expression to its feelings. But is this the case in regard to the animals in question? Can it be, that "a tortured insect feels as much pain 'as when a giant dies,'" (as H. H. U. believes) and yet that it gives no outward expression of its inner sensations? Is the daddy-longlegs so stoically framed, that when one of its "long legs" is pulled off, with all the assumed accompaniment of crushed fibres and torn nerves, it can nevertheless remain on the window pane, eying the severed member with composure, instead of writhing and rolling in agony? How can a wasp, with half his abdomen gone, calmly eat strawberry jam; how can a beetle or dragon fly, with a pin stuck violently through its breast, in a cabinet, devour the insects near it; how can a crepuscular moth, pinned against a tree, remain quietly in its place, and only begin to flap its wings when the appointed hour arrives for it to take its evening flight; if each one was in an agony of torture, as it ought to be on H. H. U.'s assumption? These cases, and many similar ones have occurred,—not a few within my own knowledge—and I maintain, that such calmness is utterly incompatible with the idea of insects being susceptible of pain. I grant that insects struggle to get free when they are handled, but this is most assuredly due, not to pain, but to the instinct of self-preservation, which is as mercifully imparted to them by an allwise Creator as sensibility to pain is withheld. Moreover, if this shrinking and struggling are to be taken as evidence of positive pain being felt, then the same sensitiveness must be allowed to organisms, to which such an attribute has never been ascribed by even the wildest imagination; such for instance as the Infusoria, the Vorticella, Paramæcuim, etc. If H. H. U. is a microscopist, he must know to his cost, the time and trouble it takes to catch and retain many of these minute creatures; but he would hardly, I think, venture to infer from their motions, that they were suffering agonies from the unavoidable pressure of the bristle on the tweezers. Nay, who shall say, if H. H. U. were able to prove his case, that the Sensitive Plant (*Mimosa pudica*) does not give evidence of pain when a leaflet is snapped across? And this leads me to ask a further question of H. H. U. If sensibility to pain is allowed to *insects*, where are we to stop in the long chain of animated beings? Will he draw the line immediately below the entomological section, and exclude the spiders, crabs, and worms from his favoured region of pain and misery? Or, if he descends that step in the ladder, may not shellfish and starfishes be permitted to feel pain? May not the Hydra be allowed the privilege; although when you cut his stomach in half, each moiety will devour its food as cheerfully as before the little accident, which made "two single gentlemen" out of one. I need scarcely carry the argument further. The *reductio ad absurdum* would only be more complete if we supposed that a volvox or a sponge could feel pain.

But I would look at the matter from another point of view, and assert that the idea of sensibility to pain among the lower animals is scarcely consistent with our notions of God's goodness and mercy, which "are over *all* His works." And, I would ask, is it a proof of goodness to give these delicate feelings to creatures, which are every moment exposed to the loss of limbs, and the crushing of bodies, and similar frightful accidents? Why, on such a supposition as that which H. H. U. hazards, we cannot walk across a garden path without causing agony of the intensest kind, and leaving behind us a train of miserable wretches in the shape of mutilated ants, smashed earwigs, and broken legged beetles. A delicate morsel of old Stilton cheese must become an accusing judge for the sad devastation we have caused among its native population; the cruelties we have inflicted on a host of unoffending mites, young and old!

More than this, we know that the Creator does not waste His gifts, or in other words, endow His creatures with superfluous organs or properties. But this law would be violated if the bulk of the lower animals felt pain. For, for what purpose is this sensation given? Surely that the animal may avoid the dangers which cause it; according to the proverb, "the burnt child dreads the fire." Upon this law the higher animals act; if the "scotched snake" cannot escape the hand that threatens it, by the quickness of its movements it can at least hide itself away, but the power of escape is denied to a large majority of the lower animals. The seven times damaged beetle may shrink with unutterable dread from the falling foot of the passing man,—himself unseen by the biped monster—or from contact with the sweeping train of a damsel's dress, which has often before dragged him relentlessly over the rough pebbles of a gravel path; but of what avail is his experience of previous pain, (or, what is the same thing, his knowledge of the coming evil), if he cannot avoid it! The gift, like that of Apollo to Cassandra, is utterly thrown away upon him.

But an advocate of the "painful" theory may argue, that to give it up is to encourage a recklessness for insect life and to incite children and other thoughtless beings to deeds of mutilation and murder. But surely he does not teach his children, (if he is blessed with any, as I am) to abstain from torturing and killing insects merely because it gives them pain; surely he takes higher ground than this, and tells them that life is valuable for its own sake and because it is a sacred gift from the Almighty, which is not to be wantonly abused, whether the abstraction of it does or does not involve pain. At any rate I am sure he would not argue on that principle in regard to the higher animals, or tell his children, that they must not deprive an unoffending dog of a limb simply because the act of taking it off would cause the poor beast agony and pain.

On the whole I believe we may safely assume, with regard to the lower animals, (*i.e.* the eight orders included under the divisions Arthrozoa and Gastrozoa, and which follow the Vertebrates), (1) that they are endowed with so much feeling, and only so much, as is needful to carry on the work of life; but (2) that they are without that acute form of sensation which we call pain. I am led to this conclusion, (1) because I can find no organs in the lower animals analogous to those, which in vertebrates are acknowledged by the instruments through which the pain acts upon the body; and (2) because I cannot conceive of pain without a corresponding outward expression of it, according to its degree of intensity, and no such outward expression exists in the lower animals. Lastly I believe, that such a property as sensibility to pain is wisely withheld from this class of organisms, because (1) from various causes, the possession of it would in their case prove a curse instead of a blessing; and, (2) because to a very large proportion,—I should say the majority—(those which cannot ordinarily escape threatened dangers) it would be unnecessary and superfluous, and consequently a waste of material.

Clifton. W. W. SPICER.

Your correspondent in page 219 of the *Note Book*, solicits information upon a subject which has frequently occurred to myself, viz: do insects feel pain?

This certainly appears to be a difficult query to solve, as it would be impossible to come to a decided conclusion; but, if we can form an opinion from experiments practised upon them, they seem to feel extremely little, and although Mr. H. H. Ulidia suggests that Mr. Harvie must be mistaken upon this subject, I am certainly of the same opinion as the last named correspondent.

Mr. Ulidia considers that they feel pain as acutely as animals of a much higher order. Now this does not appear to be consistent with nature in general, as insects are exposed to many more dangers of being injured than any other living things, and consequently there must be more killed or maimed in one summer than there are animals existing upon our globe. If we consider that to every furrow made by the plough, we must add thousands of insects that have been deprived of some of their members, or otherwise injured, not even mentioning the spade and many other appliances that unavoidably destroy or cripple immense quantities, this will give some idea of the immense amount of suffering there would exist in the world, if it is to be believed that insects feel the same amount of pain as a giant. The poet evidently is of this opinion according to the quotation introduced by H. H. Ulidia.

That they are susceptible of the slightest amount of inconvenience is quite certain, but I have not been able to distinguish any difference when pinned or otherwise prevented from having their natural freedom.

Take for instance a female wood-leopard, this, I think, is one of the most tenacious of life, press it carefully between the thumb and finger, without using more force than is required to prevent its escape, and the movements and contortions of its body will be found to represent exactly the struggles of one pinned down endeavouring to get free. Now carefully examine one that has been already fastened with a pin, it will seem in great pain, distorting its body in its endeavours to escape: finding this is not to be easily accomplished, it commences to deposit its eggs as far from it as its ovipositar will reach, but if the pin is removed from the cork, still leaving it through the thorax of the victim, it will cease to struggle as before, but creep a short distance, settle down, and appear perfectly happy and not at all inconvenienced by retaining possession of the pin. This does not prove that they are sensitive to a great amount of pain, but would lead us to suppose that they have a great objection to being held stationary by any means, either in the form of a pin or fingers.

I will describe an instance which, I think, proves that insects are not very susceptible of pain in the case of a pin being simply passed through the thorax, if it is not fastened to the box or other substance.

A few days since I received several specimens of the moth referred to, viz. the wood leopard: they had been secured by large pins but not killed. I found one, a male, had disengaged himself from the box, but still carried the pin. I did not fasten it, as I was then preparing to kill them, considering the sooner they were relieved from their misery the better; but upon again looking at the insects I discovered the released moth copulating with one of the largest females, the pins seeming to be of little consequence, and only feeling the necessity of perpetuating its species.

Another instance I will quote that occurred during an entomological excursion, which, I think, will carry out the theory that Mr. Harvie upholds, and also that dragon-flies are extremely difficult to kill.

I accidently struck one of the largest of the family with the stick of my net as I was about to capture it, and divided the body, leaving about a quarter of an inch still attached to the thorax : he immediately fell and made a great buzz in the grass, and only appeared to be suffering from the loss of its balance. I therefore plucked a piece of coarse grass and inserted it where the breakage had occurred ; this done away he flew as if nothing had happened, and continued his usual excursions up and down the lane, and the only difference that appeared in its flight was it seemed to experience a difficulty in turning suddenly, having no joints in its abdomen to act as a rudder.

Crowndale Road, Oakley Sq.   J. B. WATERS.

I am totally unable to follow the conclusions arrived at by your correspondent, Mr. Ulidia, in his letter in your last issue. He says : " Man himself feels pain ; the whale, the elephant, and the sparrow, *and consequently insects also feel pain.*" " Why not ?" Because between the former and the latter class there is an extremely broad line of demarcation drawn. The former are vertebrate, have warm blood, breathe through lungs, have veins, arteries, and nerves in great profusion, and belong to what are generally called the higher animals. The latter, on the other hand, are totally different : they have no warm blood, their bodies are articulate, and their whole organism is far more simple ; in fact, the distinctions between the two classes are so many and patent, that of course your correspondent is aware of them. Now if insects had the same organism as the higher animals have, the reasonable presumption would be that their nervous sensibility would be proportionately great. But when there is such an obvious difference between them, and the inferiority of the latter is so plain, surely we may conclude that their sensibility is proportionately less. I think these reasons are also quite sufficient for disagreeing again with Mr. Ulidia when he asserts that "we cannot resist the belief inculcated by the poet that a tortured insect feels as much ' as when a giant dies.' " For my part I most sincerely resist that belief. Mr. Ulidia must remember that when the " immortal bard " penned the lines on which he founded his belief, entomology was very little studied, and that hardly anything was known of the habits or nature of insects. Besides, we must always allow a margin for a " poet's license."

I give one illustration of my assertion that insects receive the loss of members, or severe wounds, with wonderful unconcern ; I find it in " Coleman's Butterflies :—"A wasp who had been snipped in two by a pair of scissors was seen drinking some syrup which had been spilt close by him. The liquid passing through him, collected in a large ruby bead just behind the wings—where the stomach ought to have been." I think if Mr. Ulidia had met with such a loss, his appetite would be somewhat less, and he would display a greater sense of pain than was shown by the wasp.

Mr. Ulidia has mistaken me in supposing that my repudiation of cruelty towards insects arose from a sort of covert feeling (notwithstanding the statement of my belief to the contrary) that insects do feel pain. On the contrary, it arose from the feeling that—inasmuch as these different opinions and theories can never be settled or confirmed either in one way or another, but must always remain as they are—it is better to keep on the safe side and treat insects well; for, whether possessing much or little feeling, they are a far more beautiful and wonderful work than could ever be made by the hand of man, and for that reason alone should not be abused, even though we may *bonâ fide* believe they have no sensation of pain ; so that, in case they do feel pain, we may be innocent of any charge of cruelty.

London, August 20.   ARTHUR G. HARVIE.

THE OAK.

That the oak has been styled "the father of ships" sufficiently proves its early application in the construction of " wooden walls ;" and with the lingering eye of retrospection we can at once see how the hardy sons of the wave associate the rude trunk of the simple canoe with the robust timbers of the noble ship, and hence, their immediate connection with the commerce, discoveries, and progress of nations.

From the earliest times this majestic tree attracted the attention of the people, whether savage or civilized. The oak is mentioned by Pliny, Theophratus, and other ancient naturalists. Lucan compares Pompey to an oak, and Virgil describes the Italian oak as the monarch of the forest.

That the oak was very common and attracted general attention can be easily inferred when we consider that many places on the Continent, and in these islands, derive their names directly from the oak, or from circumstances immediately connected with it. Pliny calls the Gulf of Engina *Sinus Saronicus*, on account of its being surrounded by a wood of oak trees. Auckland and Oakham, Douro, Duro-magus, etc., etc., all from the oak. The oak must have been very common in Ireland, for the number of places which take their names from the oak is certainly great. We have Derry, which simply means *an oak*, from *duir the oak tree ;* Kildare, *the wood of oaks ;* Derryberry, *the yellow oak ;* Lough Derg, *the lake of oaks,* etc., etc., and the fourth letter of the Irish alphabet, *duir,* or D, simply signifies *the oak tree.*

This fact sufficiently proves the great antiquity of the oak in Ireland, and the early attention it received.

The oak was greatly venerated by the Druids, and the parasitic mistletoe which grew to its majestic stem and lofty branches, was at the proper season cut down with golden sickles by the Druids.

Cæsar, and other ancient writers, tell us that the Druids take their name from the oak, and Pliny asserts that all their places of worship were surrounded by groves of oak, and that they were not permitted to sacrifice but in them.

In the days of the Emperor Domitian we find that the literary victor in the Agon Capitolinus was crowned with branches of oak, the sacred tree of the Druids. It is said that there are at present more than 150 different kinds of oak known, and that America claims more than one half of the number.

The *Quercus ballota,* a beautiful evergreen oak,

grows abundantly in Spain, and at the time of the Peninsular war a French army, ever ready to make the most of circumstances, entered the woods of Salamanca and greatly refreshed themselves by eating the ballota acorns. Indeed the historians and poets of Greece tells us of Balanophagi (acorn eaters) who were remarkably healthy and strong. And many centuries ago the people of England fattened their pigs on acorns. In the British Islands the oak will flourish at the height of 2,200ft.; on the Alps the oak is found so high up as 3,500ft.; on Mount Etna 5,400ft.; on the Himalayas at from 5000 to 9000ft. elevation; on the Mexican Andes at from 3000 to 9000ft.; and on the Andes of Quito the oak is found at an elevation of from 6,400ft. to 9000ft. From a series of observations, extending over sixty years, made by Marsham and Lord Suffield, it was found that at Upsal the leafing of the oak takes place from the 1st to the 8th of May; at Naples from the 1st to the 8th of April; at Paris about the middle of May; and in England about the 26th of April.

The earliest leafing of the oak was on the 31st of March, 1750, and the latest on May 20th, 1799. From those observations it has been shown that at Naples the leafing of the oak takes place about one month earlier than in England. Many oaks are spoken of as incredibly large. It is said that the King's Oak in Dennington Park was 50ft. high before even a knot appeared, and that its base squared 5ft. Chaucer's Oak, planted by the poet it is supposed, was a beautiful tree nearly as large. Dr. Plott tells us of an oak at Norbury 45ft. in circumference, and when it was cut down and lying on the ground, two horsemen, one on each side of the oak, could not see each other. The Babbington Oak in the Gloucester Vale was 54ft. in circumference at the base.

But it seems that the largest oak on record was Damory's oak in Dorsetshire; it was 68ft. in circumference, and within the trunk was a cavity 20ft. high and 16ft. long, and this hollow was taken possession of by an old man, who converted it into an alehouse for the entertainment of travellers. Surely this alehouse was justly entitled to the sign of *The Royal Oak*.

In many of the bogs of Ireland oak trees of immensed imensions have been found, some of them 84ft. long. The Kermes, a species of oak which grows along the Mediterranean, was extensively employed by the people of Barbary in dyeing the scarlet caps worn by the natives of the Levant.

The Romans made buoys of the Cork oak, and when Rome was besieged by the Gauls, the intrepid Camilius, who was sent through the Tiber to the Capitol, had a life preserver made of the Cork-tree under his dress. A decayed oak is thus described by Spencer :—

—— "dry and dead,
Still clad with reliques of its trophies old,
Lifting to heaven its aged, hoary head,
Whose foot on earth hath got but feeble hold."

Another poet in describing a flourishing oak says :—

——"the oak
His lordly head uprears, and branching arms
Extends. Behold in regal solitude
And pastoral magnificence he stands :
So simple ! and so great ! the underwoods
Of meaner rank an awful distance keep."

And in Keats' Hyperion the oaks are styled—" Those green-robed senators of mighty woods." Shakespeare, too, who had an eye to everything, in speaking of the tenacity of the oak calls it the "unwedgeable and gnarled oak." And who has not heard of the "*Shillelah !*" that wonderful specimen of Irish oak ?

But as the genius of mutation is in vigorous action at home and abroad, iron is fast superseding oak, and the "wooden walls" of nations are rapidly disappearing before the iron strongholds of the waves. Surely Scott had been contemplating something like this when he exclaims :—

"All is not oak.——"

And commerce "the golden girdle of the globe" still flourishes, and we all wonder what next our "floating castles" shall be made of.

Dromore, August 1st, 1868.   H. H. ULIDIA.

REPTILES.

I have scarcely met with a question asked in the *Note Book* that I should deem more in place, or more entitled to a reply, than that in reference to our indigenous reptiles. As I believe we have no class of objects in our animal kingdom, (man of course excepted) that has been more grossly misrepresented, at the same time none perhaps more dangerous to deal with, by the tyro in natural history pursuits, than those of the serpent kind. A natural antipathy or prejudice, no doubt, exists amongst the human family connected with the original apple of discord, and hence the offences of any of the species are magnified and multiplied to the fullest extent. Happily the species of the serpent kind indigenous to this country, are but few in number, and even these, I think, may be termed somewhat local in their occurrence. The common snake is perhaps the most general in its distribution, and therefore the most likely one to be met with in our ordinary walks. This species may be most readily identified by the bright yellow markings or patches on each side of the neck; the general colour of its back is greyish olive, rather lighter at the sides, and marked with distinct black spots throughout its entire length, which in full grown snakes will average about 3 feet 6 inches.

This kind I believe to be quite harmless, they are very timid, and will quickly glide out of sight if allowed so to do, but if irritated they will sometimes assume a threatening attitude by elevating the head, hissing fiercely, and with open mouth show two long thread-like retractile appendages as an apology for a tongue, this is very soft and flexible, and when put in motion gives rather a formidable aspect to the whole front. This divided or forked tongue is of course regarded as a sting by the timid, but I believe them to be quite incapable of inflicting injury. Their principle food is frogs and field-mice, both of which they are admirably formed to follow, and in pursuit of the former they will readily take to the water, and hence they are more commonly found in moist places. This species is oviparious, and mostly deposit their eggs in old dunghills, they are not unfrequently turned out by the labourers in removing the soil, but if undisturbed, I believe the young snakes are brought into active life by the natural influence of the season.

The Slow-worm, or Blind-worm as it is sometimes

called, is another creature that suffers much by bearing a bad name among the country people, in fact they are called the viper by some, and said to be more dangerous than an adder; and the woodman feels that he has done a great benefit to his fellow creatures by chopping them up with his shovel or billhook. This species may be easily distinguished by their neat clean appearance, being of a drab colour, with a darkish line down the middle of the back; they average about twelve inches in length and are covered with very fine scales, which have the appearance of being varnished, the head is short and blunt, showing no neck, and the body of nearly the same size throughout, with a very abrupt termination at the tail. I believe the species bring forth their young alive. Their usual haunts are among dead leaves in an open part of the wood, and may frequently be found on an old dry bank in the spring of the year, probably near where they had been at rest during the winter months. They are regarded as rather sluggish in their movements, and are certainly not so agile as the common snake; but as they usually feed upon slugs and earth worms they do not require a hasty movement to secure their prey. I have frequently picked them up and allowed them to twist round my fingers and wrist, and have also examined their mouth, and should conclude that they are quite incapable of inflicting injury upon mankind.

The Adder or Viper is, I believe, the only species of the serpent kind indigenous to this country that we must regard as truly dangerous, and therefore the most important to be readily distinguished from the other two kinds. The usual length of a full grown adder appears to be about twenty-four inches; the general colour of the back is somewhat greyish, but in this they seem to vary at times; as I have met with some with a reddish cast, others more yellow or nearly of a sand colour. However, in every case that has come under my notice, from the smallest size to the largest, and under every shade of ground colour, I have observed one standard mark by which they may most readily be distinguished, namely, a strong zigzag marking down the middle of the back, from the nape of the neck to near the end of the tail. This marking is a kind of chain pattern, and not unlike the teeth of a pit saw, (perhaps to represent the villanous fangs concealed in the head of the reptile). If the ground colour be yellowish or reddish brown the marking will in such case be somewhat of a mahogany colour, but if of an ashy grey the crooked marking will likely be nearly or quite black, and although the creature may be nearly concealed under the herbage, yet two or three inches left exposed is quite sufficient for to determine the species by.

Adders are usually found in warm dry situations, as on a sandy soil among hillocks of short furze and ling, more particularly on slips of rugged waste land on the south side of a wood. They bring forth their young alive, and although I cannot believe that they are quite so aggressive as represented by some, yet I should deem it highly dangerous to disturb one when surrounded by its offspring. We rarely hear of the bite of an adder proving fatal; but a relation of mine nearly lost his life by tampering with one, mistaking it for a snake. I should much advise the young botanist or the gatherer of wild flowers, to bear in mind the plain description here offered, and whenever they are convinced of the presence of an adder to regard it as very bad company and withdraw as quickly as possible.

In case of a bite, I believe that oil of any kind applied to the wound might be of service at the moment, but medical aid should be procured as soon as possible.
320, Strand. C. W . . . D.

ATTRACTION OF GRAVITATION.—THE EARTH AND A FALLING STONE.—Your correspondent "R. B. W.," page 253 *Naturalist's Note Book*, is in a philosophical "fix," and questions the soundness of the following proposition :—" The reason why a falling stone does not exert any perceptible force on the earth is, not that the earth has any special power which the stone has not, but merely that the earth from its immense bulk has so much greater attraction than the stone, that *its motion towards the stone* is too small to admit of observation or measurement."

R. B. W. has, no doubt, heard of the scientific boast made by Archimedes more than 2000 years ago, that the great geometrician was about to pitch the earth out of its orbit by the agency of science, but as he could not find a convenient spot on which to rest his fulcrum, he quietly abandoned the project, and so the earth continues dodging about in its old locality. Your correspondent wi'l readily admits the failure, and admitting this he thinks, that if he in some of his rambles casts a stone from his hand he has not moved the earth. But he has! Yes, in principle the falling stone, no matter how small, has actually moved the earth and quite cast into the shade the contemplated feat of the great Syracusean. I think I see "R. B. W." casting aside the *Note Book*, and hear him half audibly exclaim, "surely this correspondent is indebted to his imagination for his facts."

But let us go on. *Gravitation* is inherent in all matter, and by means of it every particle attracts every other particle, and so far as we at present know it acts at all distances. We lift a pen, an ink-stand, or a stone, and in so doing we exert some strength. Why do we exercise some amount of strength in lifting? To overcome the weight of the body lifted—and it is gravitation which gives weight to all matter. And the attraction existing between every two particles of matter *is mutual*, and the sum of the attractions of two bodies is proportional to the *mass of each*, when the other is constant; and to their product, when both are variable.

The attraction of two bodies being mutual it then follows that if nothing prevents them *they will both move with the same force,* but not *if they are of different sizes*, with the same velocity,—the reason of this is easily understood, for as the same amount of motion will be distributed among a greater number of particles in the one that is larger, each particle of it will have a proportionably smaller quantity. From this principle it evidently follows that when a stone falls to the earth, *the earth moves to meet the stone;* but the distance through which the earth moves is certainly small, just as many times smaller than the distance through which the stone moves as the number of particles in the earth exceeds the number of particles in the stone. Let R. B. W. take a stone, say three inches in diameter, and he lets it fall to the earth through a distance of 100ft., then according to the mutual attraction of of bodies the stone and the earth moved to pass through the distance of 100ft. Let your correspondent not be alarmed, the earth has moved but a short distance to meet the stone. For as the earth is 8,000 miles, or 506,880,000 inches in diameter, and as the stone is but three inches in diameter, then the motion of the stone to meet the earth will be as the cube of 506,880,000 inches is to the cube of three inches, and hence the earth does actually move to meet the stone. A little reflection on the subject, will, I am sure, fully satisfy your correspondent, who will easily see that "science in its ordinary *sense* means *knowledge reduced to a system*; that is, arranged in a regular order so as to be conveniently taught, easily remembered, and readily applied."

Dromore, Aug. 4th, 1868.　　H. H. ULIDIA.

If your correspondent "R. B. W." will consider the great fundamental law of gravitation demonstrated by Sir I. Newton, he will see that the attraction between the earth and the stone must be mutual. This law is: "That all the particles of matter attract one another, directly as their masses, and inversely as the square of their distances." Therefore, although the influence of the stone is too minute to be appreciated, we may be sure that it does exert an influence. As a proof that attraction is not confined to the larger of two bodies, we may instance the earth and moon. The earth is appreciably influenced and drawn out of her course by the moon, so that instead of keeping an exact course round the sun, she is alternately deflected towards and away from him, according as the moon assist that luminary or opposes him.

GULIELMUS.

I should certainly say that the extract from M'Cullock's "Course of Reading" by "R. B. W." is quite correct. It is a universal law in nature that bodies attract each other in proportion to their masses, and according to this the falling stone would attract the earth; although as is stated in the extract, it would produce no perceptible motion of the earth. R. T.

USE OF PLANTS.—R. B. W. asks "How is it that in the vicinity of woods, and those places where vegetation thrives best, and is most abundant, is considered so unfavourable to health, especially in hot climates?"

There is something paradoxical in this question, in fact a sort of contradiction is implied. That the vicinity of large woods should be, in some degree, unhealthy, is evident from the following well-established facts:—Forests detain and condense the passing clouds,—they prevent the free access of sun and wind— forest soil is always covered with long damp grass, rotting leaves, brushwood, etc., etc., and every forest has its hollows and pools of stagnant water. Without going farther into the subject, we all, from obvious reasons, know that such things convenient to a town or village must militate against the sanitary condition of the inhabitants. But, with the latter part of the question, which, with R. B. W., merges into a sort of axiom, I cannot by any means agree, viz: that "those places where vegetation thrives best and is most abundant, are considered so unfavourable to health, especially in hot climates." To be sure we have the frightful jungles of India, and the Valley of Death in Java. In these, decaying vegetables throw off immense quantities of carbonic acid, and as these jungles are too dense for the wind to penetrate, this gas, so destructive to all animal life there remains, and hence the too frequent suffocation of birds, beasts, and men, when they go within the influence of this noxious vapour. The Grotto del Cane in Italy, and Lake Averno, made so celebrated by Virgil, are modified examples of the same principle, although, evidently not by luxuriant vegetation.

Indeed many of the most delightful countries are remarkable for the grandeur of their vegetation. From what I have already said, your correspondent will see that on account of the free access of air, etc., etc., "open and clear lands" are more conducive to health and vigour than if he confines us in his impenetrable woods and forests.

Well, after all, R. B. W. is really a little cynical, for he next says that "where animal life thrives, vegetation declines—as on the sea coast,"—and he wants "information" as to the cause, I presume. R. B. W. is aware that plants, like animals, breathe, that the sea-air is impregnated with spray, that this spray carries with it extraneous substances, such as sulphate of soda, chloride of sodium, chlorides of calcium, magnesium, potassium, and other organic matter, which retard the vegetable respiration, and in other ways prevent the luxuriant vegetation of trees and some other plants on the sea shore. An ordinary man in twenty-four hours spoils 550 cubic feet of air, and a common candle, of six in the pound, produces just the same effect; now if we take the population of a large town, count its inhabitants, its factories, furnaces, gas, common fires, trains, etc., etc., the consumption of oxygen is enormous; but then, vegetables absorb the impure air, (carbonic acid) again, give out the pure air to animals, and thus nature goes on operating for the benefit and preservation of man.

Without more prolixity it is difficult to treat the subject in a satisfactory manner. Still I hope I have said enough, even hurriedly, to satisfy the inquiring mind of your correspondent "R. B. W."

Dromore, Aug. 8th, 1868.　　H. H. ULIDIA.

TAMING WILD ANIMALS.—Although now ransacking the archæology of the ancient village of Slane, during my leisure moments I read the *Naturalists' Note Book*, and recommend it by the way. Well, at p. 222, I find the ubiquitous and indefatigable R. B. W. again; he wants to know how to tame wild beasts, so, I presume, as to "wile the bird off the bush," charm a snake, or beard a lion!

Difficult and dangerous matters, Mr. R. B. W. I never tried them; but, "what I have heard permit me to relate." About the year 1840, the *Times* had an article on the subjugation of animals, and mentioned a Mr. King, a great horse tamer at that time, who said, that by putting his hand into the horse's mouth and pressing the "nerve of susceptibility," the animal became tame immediately. Some men have succeeded in taming horses by biting their ears. Forbes, in his Oriental Memoirs, tells wonderful things about snake charming, but Denon and Abbe Dubois look on the whole charming affair as a cunning bit of consummate knavery. In the year 1791, Don Pedro D'Orbies Y. Vargas published the results of a series of investigations into the nature of serpent charming, and says that a plant, the *quacho-mithy*, is chewed, and the juice rubbed over the bodies of the Indians,—but time presses and I quit Don Pedro. I have often been told that assafœtida will seduce trout, perch, or roach; and here is the secret. "Sprinkle finely powdered assafœtida upon the surface of the water and you will presently see the fish crowding to the spot; and even if you rub your hands well with it and gradually approach the water, gently immersing your hands in it, you will ere long find fish attracted towards you, and losing their natural timidity, actually permit themselves to be taken." I give the above for what it is worth, indeed I never thought of trying the experiment. R. B. W. perhaps may.

Plutarch says, that Cato in his marches took with him many of those people called Psylli, to suck the blood from the wounds of the soldiers who might chance to be bitten by the serpents.
H. H. ULIDIA.
Slane, Co. Meath, August 11th, 1868.

INFLUENCE OF THE MOON.—Various are the evil effects which are or have been attributed to the influence of the moon, but very few of these influences are founded on fact, as "R. B. W." will perceive if he reads the chapter on "Lunar Influences" in "Lardner's Museum of Science and Art." There the popular opinions as to the influences exerted by the moon on diseases, &c., are ably treated upon, and many of them are shown to be absurd. Perhaps one or two extracts will be acceptable to "R. B. W.," so I will give one or two.

"Although the ancient faith in the connexion between the phases of the moon and the phenomena of insanity appeaars in a great degree to be abandoned, yet it is not altogether without its votaries; nor have we been able to ascertain that any series of observations, conducted on scientific principles, has ever been made on the phenomena, with a view to disprove this connexion. We have even met with intelligent and well-educated physicians who still maintain that the paroxysms of insane persons are more violent when the moon is full than at other times." Lardner then gives instances of effects on different persons, which have been ascribed to the influence of the moon. The most remarkable is the fact that Lord Bacon always fainted when lunar eclipses occurred, and he never recovered his senses till the moon recovered her light. Before this can be admitted as a proof of the existence of lunar influence, M. Arago says, "it would be necessary to establish the fact that feebleness and pusillanimity of character are never connected with high qualities of mind."

I believe it is a fact that exposure to the moon's rays is injurious to the sight, and in some cases causes blindness. If I remember rightly, Mr. Gage, the blind inventor, lost his sight through reading in moonlight. If "R. B. W." should desire to read the chapter referred to, he can get vol I. of Lardner's Museum, &c., price 1s. 6d, published by Walton and Maberly.
R. T.

HAIRLESS HORSE (P. 252).—Like your correspondent "Tortoise," I took much interest in the hairless horse at the Crystal Palace, but was obliged to rest contented with the statement of its owner, that it was brought from the Cape of Good Hope, and that there was reason to believe that it was a case of nervous impression on the part of the dam, she having been terribly frightened by an elephant a short time before the birth of the foal. It is a pity that "Tortoise" did not quote Brehm (not Brehm and Kretschmer) more fully, as every patch of evidence helps to throw light on a *vexata quæstio* of this kind. With your permission I will supply the "missing link."

"Fitzinger believes, that we may accept of five original species of horse; and this opinion has at least as much in its favour as that of *savants* who suppose all horses (the Flemish-English cart-horse as well as the Shetland pony) to have sprung from a common source. These five species are—the Tarpan, the Naked, the Light, the Heavy, and the Dwarf. Of the last and the first we have already spoken; of the remainder, the Naked alone needs a short mention. This remarkable animal has been exhibited only within the last few years, and that but rarely; but nothing is known about it: even its native country is a mere matter of conjecture; though a traveller affirms that he has seen whole troops of them in a wild or half-wild state in the interior of Affghanistaun. Those which have found their way to Europe have come through the hands of Gypsies, who state that they have purchased them in the Crimea. Others were taken as booty in Turkey in the wars which occurred towards the end of the last century. The naked horse, &c., &c." (as quoted by your correspondent).

On the same page is a portrait by Zimmermann of a good-looking, rather heavy animal, with a coarseish head, and of a black colour; but otherwise very like the one exhibited at the Crystal Palace. It is labelled "Das nackte Pferd (*Equus Nudus*)."

"Brehm's Illustrirtes Thierleben, 2er Band, S. 352," an admirable work, still in course of publication, which I strongly recommend to students of natural history acquainted with German.
Clifton. W. W. SPICER.

HOW TO CONSTRUCT AN AQUARIUM.—Perhaps the following account of how I constructed an aquarium may be useful to G. S. Boulger. I took a piece of stout planking, and planed it down to the size required for the bottom. At the corners of this I screwed on four upright iron standards (made to order) about two inches wide, bent to fit on to the corners and receive the glass. Round the edges of the board I tacked slips of wood, standing about ¼-inch above the surface. I then had five sheets of glass cut, one the exact size of the bottom, minus the thickness of the glass all round, two of the others of the length of the bottom, minus one thickness of the glass, and the remaining two of the width of the bottom, minus one thickness of the glass. I procured a pound and a half of red putty made up with gold size, spread a little upon the board, and laid the first glass upon it, which of course left a space as wide as the thickness of the glass between it and the edging all round. Having

filled this space with putty and also the inside of the standards, I forced the sides and ends into their places, which of course they just filled. To make all compact, I spread some pieces of tape, on one side only, with the putty, and fitted them into all the corners, horizontal and vertical, so that no putty could touch the water except what might squeeze through the tape, which I found to be little or none. I then finished all off with a good coat of paint on the outside, and after leaving it a few days to dry and set, I filled it with water, and found it to answer admirably. I was not so successful with a large bell glass, fitted into a stand. A day or two after it was filled it cracked across the bottom. Can any one tell me the reason? I am sure it had no rough usage.
GULIELMUS.

WATER FOR AQUARIUMS.—I should feel greatly obliged if you can inform me, through the medium of the NOTE BOOK, whether the water of fresh-water aquariums in which weeds are growing requires changing to preserve the fish in a healthy state; as I have been informed that it does not. Also the best food for a Tortoise. J. WARD.

SYCAMORE, &c.—Be good enough to place the facts before your readers as to the sycamore and chestnut trees. On page 254 of your August No., column 1st, I am made to say that the "horse chestnut," was introduced into England in the time of the Romans. Omit the "horse" and all will be right. It was the sweet or Spanish chestnut, *Castanea vesca*, which was probably brought into this island by the Romans. This noble tree is a native of Thessaly, especially near the banks of the Pereus, where magnificent examples still exist. The time of its being carried into Italy is not recorded. The horse-chestnut, which is a totally different thing, and by botanists called *Æsculus Hippocastanum*, is probably a native of the little known provinces of Northern Persia. It has been abscribed to more northern parts of Asia, to Asia Minor, and to the colder parts of India, but there is no trace of it in Nepal or the Himalayans; and all that can be said with certainty is that it came through Constantinople and Vienna in the beginning of the sixteenth century, and that from the latter place it was dispersed over Western Europe.

The Sycamore, *Acer Pseudo-Plotanus*, is a native of central Europe (Germany, Austria, Switzerland, and Italy) and extends into Asia as far as the lower ranges of the Caucasus. It sows itself so readily as now to be almost naturalized in England. Virgil speaks of it under the name it bears to-day.

Manchester, Aug. 4th. LEO H. GRINDON.

I beg leave to alter a mistake in the last number of the "N. N. B." I stated that "J. W. W. B." had among the list of natives the Horse Chestnut, which should have been the Spanish Chestnut (introduced in the time of the Romans). I may also add that the following among his list are uncertain, viz.:—The Elm, Lime, Aspen, and White Poplar. W. R. L.

DEATH FROM SUNSTROKE.—For the information of one of your correspondents—"R. B. W.," I think—I copy the following from a Dublin paper:—"On Tuesday last (August 4th) Michael Meagher, Esq., coroner for the county Tipperary, held an inquest at Knockanamohily on the body of an old man named William Malone, who died the previous day from an attack of apoplexy *caused by sunstroke*. The jury returned a verdict in accordance with the medical evidence. Until now I was under the impression that death from sunstroke never occurred in Ireland. I wish your correspondents would record any case or cases they hear of.

Melifont, August 13th, 1868. H. H. ULIDIA.

"R. B. W." will have had, by this time, abundant proof that sunstroke occurs in this country, for during the month of July several deaths have resulted from it. In one newspaper it is stated that twenty-nine cases of death from sunstroke occurred in the county of Surrey alone, during the last three weeks of July. R. T.

If "R. B. W." will refer to a file of the *Times*, or any other daily paper issued during the late hot weather, he will find that sunstroke is by no means confined to tropical countries, but is very frequent in England. And in New York, which is far beyond the tropics, hundreds of cases are said to have occurred within the last few weeks. GULIELMUS.

EXTRAORDINARY EMERGENCE OF ELEPHANT HAWK MOTH.—Can any entomologist explain the following *remarkable* circumstance:—A friend of mine had a larva, about an inch long, of the Elephant Hawk Moth (*C. Elpenor*) brought to him about three weeks ago, which was found on some bog-bean, about four miles from here. We went there and found more than twenty, and afterwards three or four on bedstraw. I had 4 pupæ out of those I found, which changed about a fortnight ago.

Fully expecting them to remain in the pupa state until next June, imagine my surprise when, on looking at my pupæ this morning, I found two Imagos emerged. This seems extraordinary, as both the 'Lepidopterist's Calendar" and Mr. Newman's "Moth Nos." say that the Moth is found in June, and the caterpillar in August. Has any other entomologist experienced this unusual occurrence? My friend had a Poplar Hawk Moth (*S. Populi*), apparently fresh from the pupa, given him about a week ago. Could this be from last year's larva? A. MATHEWS.

Oxford, August 5th, 1868.

HERONRIES.—I have traced the existence of a heronry on a river in Cornwall for upwards of forty years with numerous nests to the year 1849, and I believe it continues to the present date. Another heronry began to be formed on another river at the distance of about ten miles in the year 1847; but before the formation of the latter, so far as I have been able to ascertain, the herons that frequented the last-named river for the purpose of fishing were accustomed to make their home at the former for the purpose of breeding. After the first arrival at the latter river for breeding, some of the trees in which the nests had been placed were cut down; but the birds occupied other trees that had been suffered to remain —and so they still continue. However shy and cautious these birds are, they make no difficulty in exposing

their nests to observation; but in winter they leave them, and resort to retired places in cliffs by the sea.
VIDEO.

HYDROPHOBIA.—Your correspondent R. B. W. says, "There is a current opinion that if a person receive the bite of a dog that is not mad, he is in danger of suffering from the disease if the dog should become mad at a subsequent period. Has this opinion any foundation?" Certainly not, and simply because a thing cannot act where it does not exist.

But as hydrophobia has been known to set in even so long as five months after the bite of the dog, this, no doubt, has much to do with the opinion. The infectious matter communicated by the bite does not seem to enter the circulation, yet, by some strange process, which the greatest physicians cannot clearly explain, the disease is communicated from the wound to the throat, so as to produce pain, hydrophobia, with a secretion of infectious saliva of the very same kind as that of the mad dog which inflicted the wound. Another opinion, equally erroneous, and often attended with fatal results, prevails in many localities, viz. kill the dog and a sure remedy against the bite is provided. Surely this opinion, too, is evidently futile.

Bangor, Aug. 10th, 1868.　　H. H. ULIDIA.

DORMICE DEVOURING FLESH.—Some years ago I kept dormice in considerable numbers. A large female, after having been a month in captivity, was delivered of three young, which she almost immediately devoured, though she had plenty of nuts, barley, and soaked bread, hemp seed, and other food. After this I frequently let her out to run about the room. She enlarged an ordinary mouse hole one day and disappeared all but her tail; this, not wishing to lose her, I laid hold of, when she struggled and left the skin of her tail in my hand, but finding she could get no further in the hole she turned round and came out; and I suppose, in anger at the loss of her "brush," seized hold of her tail and continued to eat joint after joint with as much facility as she would have done a radish, until only about an inch was left. This a large male dormouse took a fancy to, for the next day I saw him gnawing away at her stump, having eaten half an inch more; and so ends the tale of the poor dormouse.
C. O. G. NAPIER.

THE STINGING NETTLE.—"Tortoise" sometime ago asked why the venom of the nettle produced no effect when the plant was tightly grasped. There appears to me only one reason for this; the barbed hairs, although sharp, are slender and easily crushed, they can only enter the skin when they have points, and if these are broken by a sharp squeeze they are harmless. The same plan answers with many thorny shrubs. It is all part of the great principles which homeopathists are always urging *Similis similibus curantur*. If the opposing force is greater than the attacking, the last is subdued. Hanneman did not discover this. Hippocrates, the Greek sage, knew it well. From him Shakespeare probably got it, although he was said to know "little Latin and nothing of Greek."

"Tut, man, one fire burns out another's burning,
One's pain is lessened by another's anguish;
Take thou some new infection to thine eye,
And the rank poison of the old will die."

C. O. G. NAPIER.

PORTUGUESE MAN-OF-WAR: PHYSALIA.—In addition to what is said of this creature in No. 20 of the NATURALIST'S NOTE BOOK, p. 249, the following, extracted from Fuller's "Worthies of England," may be of interest. Speaking of the excellency of English ships, he says:—"First, for the Portugal, his *carvils* and caracts, they were the veriest drones on the sea, the rather because their seating was dam'd up with a certain kind of mortar to dead the shot. Of the Spanish the wind hath so much power of them in bad weather that it drives them two leagues for one of ours to leeward." We have here the origin of the word carvel bestowed on the Physalia by Mr. John Clayton.

Polperro, August 13, 1868.　　JONATHAN COUCH.

GOOD KING HENRY, OR MERCURY GOOSEFOOT.—In reply to "H. F. P." concerning the origin of the above name, I give him a quotation from "Thompson's Wild Flowers." It was also called *Tota Bona*. No one can tell after which of our kings it was named, but Henry VI. bore in his own days the name of Good King Henry, and as he founded Eton College he would doubtless be a great favourite with the monks, from whom in all probability our plant received its name.　　W. R. L.

THE RED ADMIRAL.—Bernard C. Bash wishes to know the name of a Butterfly which he saw, and as it is evident this correspondent has not studied entomology, I beg to inform him that the Insect in question was the Red Admiral, *Vanessa Alatanta*, but the colour that appeared orange is only white spots placed near the red on the upper wings; the vibration sometimes giving this appearance if a glance is only obtained, but when quite still the colours are distinct enough.
J. B. WATERS.

PIED SPARROW IN LONDON.—On the 12th of this month (August) I was passing the Horse Guards with a friend, and saw feeding in the road, in company with other sparrows, one of very light hue; a passing omnibus having frightened it up, we could see that the greater part of the plumage was of a light chocolate colour; it had, however, nearly all the wing and tail feathers white, as also part of the head and neck. I have seen one (shot by the gentleman before mentioned in connection with the curious egg) which was very much like this London specimen.　　A. M. B.

CURIOUS EGG.—I possess a most curious egg presented to me by F. Russell, Esq., of Vanbrugh, Blackheath, which he tells me was laid by one of his hens last year. It reminds me of the one described by "Fox," at page 222, excepting that mine is cardiform, with a division down the centre. It was divided inside by a double membrane. The larger part of the heart contained the white, and the other the yolk. The shell, I may add, is of the usual thickness.　　A. M. B.

DRAGON FLIES.—I should be glad to hear of a method of preserving the beautiful colours of dragon flies without gutting them.　　E. H. WALLAND.

MOSQUITO.—Will some kind reader give a description of the Mosquito, stating particularly its size.　　R. T.

EXCHANGE OF EGGS.—A. H. is willing to make exchanges with collectors of eggs of British birds. Apply 114, Ebury Street, London.

THE DODO AND ITS HOME.
BY C. O. GROOM NAPIER, F.G.S.
PART I.

HE islands of Mauritius and Bourbon are generally believed to have been first discovered by the Portuguese voyager, Mascaregnas, who gave his own name to the latter island, while the first he termed Cerne. This name was given from an erroneous belief on his part, that it was the "Cerne" of Pliny (Hist. Nat. vi. 36, and x. 9). The date of the discovery of these islands is very uncertain; Ersch and Gruber call it 1502; Grant 1505; Mr. Broderip in the "Penny Cyclopedia" 1542; and Du Quesne in 1545.

The Dutch admiral, Jacob Cornelius Van Neck, in 1598, was, however, the first who described the natural productions with sufficient distinctness to give us a definite idea of them. Vasco de Gama was thought by some of the early writers, and Mr. Broderip in our own times, to have discovered these islands; but from the account of his voyage, it is not likely he went near this group at all. In the account of the voyage of Van Neck, pigeons and parroquets are enumerated as inhabiting the island now called Mauritius, and a large bird which the Dutch sailors termed *Walchvögel—disgusting birds*, from the unpalatable nature of their flesh; but the flesh of the breast was much better than that of the legs. The island, however, affording an ample quantity of excellent food, such as turtle doves, might greatly account for the contempt with which they treated the flesh of the dodo; it was described as the size of a swan, with a large and hooded head, no wings—meaning probably such as would raise it from the ground. On the wings were three or four black quills, and the tail was ornamented with a bunch of grey curled feathers: it was termed in the French account of the voyage *oiseaux de naussée*, the equivalent of the Dutch. The most striking animals and plants are described—an abundance of birds of different species especially of turtle doves and dodos.

A curious plate illustrates Van Neck's work; it represents the Dutch sailors at their various occupations on this unhabited island, as well as the fauna and flora. Fig. I. is a land tortoise so large that it could carry a man. Fig. II. represents the dodo somewhat distorted, but still recognisable. Fig. III. represents the fan palm, or, as they call it, *Dactier;* from the sap of which they made palm wine. Fig. IV. the *Rabos forçados*, or frigate pelican (*Frigata aquila*); Fig. V. *Corbeau Indienne*, thought to be a species of hornbill. Fig. VI. represents the arms of Holland, Zealand, and Amsterdam fastened to a large tree. Fig. VII. represents a palm Fig. VIII. a large bat. Figs. IX., X., XI. XII. represent blacksmiths at their work; huts built for temporary shelter; a congregation listening to the exhortations of their minister; and fishermen obtaining fish which greatly abounded on the coast by hook, net, and spear. De Bry (1601, p. 105) in his "India Orientalis," mentions this bird, of which he gives two figures in the title-page of his work. It is so carelessly drawn that we cannot accurately determine its species, but it is clearly intended for a bird of this family. De Bry, however, gives an illustration of *Walckuëgels*, which clearly represent cassowaries; he likewise tells us that one of these birds was brought back to Holland by this expedition; but it is not mentioned by any contemporary author.

The Dutch writer Clusius, in his "Exotica" (published in 1605), gives a figure of the dodo which was copied from one of the later editions of Van Neck's work. He describes the beak as marked with black and yellow; the upper mandible much bent down, having a blueish spot in the centre. Its feathers were thin and short, and it was very fat and fleshy in the hinder parts; the feet were yellow, but the legs were black to the knee. The gizzard of these birds contained stones of which he represented one of an inch long.

Willem Van West Zanen, a Dutch voyager, in 1602 visited the Mauritius, and mentions the dodo, of which his men ate many; the birds must have been large indeed, for two in one instance are said to have supplied an abundant meal for his crew. (Strickland and Melville, p. 13). He also describes the island as abounding in birds, and he salted many dodos for ship stores; he appears to have been the first writer who called these birds *dodars*, or *dod-aarsen*, of which dodo is a corruption. Strickland thinks it derived from *dodoor*—the Dutch for *sluggard*—which is very appropriate to a heavy and inactive bird. Sir Thomas Herbert is, however, responsible for the English term "dodo," but he says that its name is derived from a Portuguese word, which means *foolish* or *simple*. The appellation "*dronte*" applied to it by French writers, Strickland suggests (p. 16) may be connected with the German *dronne*, or the English *drone*. Admiral Cornelius Matelief, who visited Mauritius in 1606, and Van der Hagen in 1607, found many dodos, which the latter had salted for consumption on his voyage. In 1611, P. F. Verhuffen describes the dodo under the name of *totersten*, and said they were devoured in large numbers by his men; but that they were formidable in assault, and capable of severely wounding those who carelessly attacked them with their powerful beaks. (Strickland, p. 18).

Pieter Van den Broecke accompanies the account of his voyage by a figure of the dodo, which is more pointed in the bill, and thinner every way than it is usually represented; it might have been another species.

Sir Thomas Herbert visited Mauritius in 1627, but it was still without human residents; he gives an illustration of this bird, which in form of bill is more like Van den Broecke's figure than any other. He published several editions of the history of his travels, in the last of which, entitled "Some years travel to divers parts of Africa and Asia the great," published in London 1677, gives a pretty detailed account of the dodo. "Her body (says he) was round and fat, which occasions a slow pace; a few of them weigh less than fifty pounds—meat it is with some—but better to the eye than stomach, being indeed more pleasurable to look at than feed upon. It is of a melancholy visage as sensible of Nature's injury in framing so massive a body to be directed by complemental wings, such indeed as are unable to hoist her from the ground, serving only to rank her amongst birds. Her head is variously dressed, for one half is dressed with down of a dark colour—the other half naked, and of a white hue, as if lawn were drawn over it. Her bill, hooks and bends downwards; the thrill, or breathing place, is in the midst, from which part to the end the colour is of a light green mixed with pale yellow. Her eyes are round and bright, and, instead of feathers, has a most fine down; her train, like a china beard, is no more than three or four short feathers; her legs are thick and black; her talons great; her stomach fiery, so that she can easily digest stones; in that and shape not a little resembling the ostrich." He also tells us that this bird is covered with fine down, like that on goslings, and that she can digest iron as well as stones.

A bird called "a hen" is figured by Sir Thos. Herbert; it has a long and sharp bill, but the shape of its body is not unlike some representations of the dodo. It may be the same species as a bird represented by Van den Broecke, which, however, reminds us more nearly of the apteryx of New Zealand. Leguat describes such a bird found in the Mauritius by the name of *gelinottes*. Strickland, p. 21, thinks that the *feldhuner* of Verhuffen may also refer to it. Cauche's Voyage (p. 132) mentions birds with the beak of a woodcock, which he says were excellent for eating, and which were attracted by a piece of red cloth, clearly not a dodo.

François Cauche describes the nest of the dodo as made of herbs, heaped together, and that they lay but one egg, the size of a halfpenny roll; but he elsewhere says that it was also that of the egg of the cape pelican (*Pelicanus onocrotalus*), one of which in my collection measures 3 in. 5-16ths long by 2 in. 1-4th wide, or about that of a moderate-sized goose. The size of this egg is in favour of the bird belonging to the pigeon class, for were it raptorial or struthious, it would be most likely double the size. Cauche tells us also that the young birds have a stone in the gizzard, and says "their cry resembles that of a goose, and that their egg is white, and accompanied by a stone the size of a fowl's egg. They build in the forests, and if the young one is killed, a grey stone is found in the gizzard." "The fat," he said, "was excellent for softening the muscles and nerves."

The inhabitants of the British Isles had at least one opportunity of observing this bird in a living state; for Mr. Strickland says that in the Sloane manuscript, preserved in the British Museum, Sir Hammond L'Estrange, the father of Sir Roger, in a commentary on "Brown's Vulgar Errors," narrates as follows:—"About 1638, as I walked London streets, I saw a picture of a strange fowle hong out upon a cloth, and myself with one or two more then in company went in to see it. It was kept in a chamber, and was a great-fowle somewhat bigger than the largest turky cock, and so legged and footed, but stouter and thicker and of a more erect shape, colored before like the breast of a young cock fesan, and on the back of a dunn or deare coulour, the keeper called it a dodo: and in the end of a chymney in the chamber there lay a heap of large pebble stones whereof he gave it many in our sight, some as big as nutmegs, and the keeper told us shee eats them (conducing to digestion), and though I remember not how far the keeper was questioned therein, yet I feel confident that shee afterwards cast them all again." Wilkinson's edition of Sir Thomas Brown's works (v. 1, p. 369, and 11, 173). This notice of Sir Hammond L'Estrange is a solitary record of the existence of this bird in a living state: it was before the Royal Society was formed, or such a remarkable bird would, doubtless, have been laid before that body.

Tradescant's catalogue of his collection of rarities preserved at South Lambeth, near London, in 1656, contains a notice of a "dodar" from the island of Mauritius: this specimen was seen by Willoughby, being mentioned in his Ornithologia printed in 1676. It is mentioned by Llhwyd in the catalogue of the animals in the Ashmolean Museum, 1684; the Tradescant Collection having passed into the possession of Ashmole, who bequeathed it to the University of Oxford. We have now so far the history of this specimen. Was it the same bird seen by Sir Hammond L'Estrange in a living state many years before? It is possible that Sir Thomas Herbert might have brought home a skin of this species; for in one of his letters to Ashmole he says, "South Lambeth, a place I well know, having been sundry times at M. Tredescon's, to whom I gave several things I collected in my travels."

Piso, in his edition of Bontius (1658), gives a figure of the dodo, which is apparently copied from a painting by Savery—several of which I shall hereafter describe.

THE BOMBYCIDÆ.
By E. Clifford.

This is a family of our British moths which does not comprise many species. In them, also, we miss the gay colouring of some preceding; but, whilst the perfect insects are mostly dull-coloured, the caterpillars producing them are often very beautiful; and we have only to quote the common hairy one, called the Drinker, to recall to the minds of our readers an instance of their attractive exteriors. The various species of this family differ much in size, ranging from one inch and a half to three inches across the wings, which is the size of the handsome Oak Eggar. The male moths of some of the Bombycidæ fly at mid-day in the hot sunshine, and there is a curious fact relating to them which we should not pass unnoticed. With certain species, a peculiar attraction exists in the female moths, towards which the collector can attract hundreds of the opposite sex by placing the former in a box in localities where they are known to occur in abundance. With one or two exceptions, the Bombycidæ appear in the perfect state between April and August, having passed the winter in the caterpillar state. Some are comparatively common insects, and the young collector may reasonably expect to secure a fair representation of the family during his first hunting season. Let us in the following, pass over the distinct species, briefly noticing them as we proceed.

The first in order is the Pale Oak Eggar (*Trichiura cratægi*). The forewings of this insect are grey, with an oblique bar of a darker hue, and this is bordered on each side by a waved line, yet deeper in colour. In certain specimens the ground colour is nearly white, and the bar all but black. The hindwings are grey, with a transverse bar about the middle, the body ends in two fanlike tufts of hairs. The caterpillar of this insect is of a dark grey colour, with two red tubercles on each segment, and a row of dots on each side. Its food is whitethorn or blackthorn, and when full-grown it spins a small oblong cocoon. The moth itself flies in August and September. The December moth (*Pœcilocampa populi*) is one of those insects which greet us at the cold wintry season. As a moth it is not particularly beautiful, though varied and mottled. The forewings are smoky brown, with an orange patch at the base, margined outwardly with a pale yellow line, whilst beyond the middle is a pale indented transverse line. The caterpillar of the December moth is very handsome and varied in colouring. It has been seen on the trunks of oak-trees, on the leaves of which trees it feeds, and it is not improbable, that by its similarity to the lichens occurring in such situations, it escapes the notice of birds and other enemies. Its colouring consists of black, grey, and white, and there is a yellowish stripe along each side, and two reddish tubercles on the second segment. When full-fed it spins a very compact cocoon, wherein it changes to a smooth brown chrysalis. It has been known to remain in pupa as long as four or five years. The cocoon should be searched for in various situations and on various trees in August and September.

The Small Eggar (*Eriogaster lanestris*) is a very handsome instance of this interesting family. The forewings are pale chocolate, with white spots at the base and centre, between the latter and the hind margin of the wings is a faint white band. This moth flies in February. The eggs are laid on the sloe and hawthorn, and are covered by the female with a quantity of hair, with which the anal part is furnished. The caterpillar of the Small Eggar is gregarious, feeding in company, and when young spins a web over the hawthorn, on which it most commonly feeds. It is a hairy caterpillar, and nearly black, with three white spots and two red warts on the back of each segment; there is also a white line on each side. It spins a small, compact cocoon at the end of June. The Lackey (*Bombyx neustria*) is, perhaps, the commonest species of this tribe. Its vivid caterpillar occurs on every hawthorn hedge in the country, and throughout the hot months we may find its singular cocoon, powdered with yellow, in all imaginable nooks and corners. The colouring of the perfect insect varies from pale yellow to sandy red; the forewings with two transverse streaks, the intervening space oftentimes darker than the rest of the wings. The Lackey is a very variable insect; one scarcely ever comes across two specimens exactly alike in marking or colouring. The caterpillar is long and slender, and seems to have no power of rolling up, as others of its family do. In its early stage it is gregarious, spinning its web over the leaves and twigs of apple trees, quickly stripping off the bright green leaves. The head of this caterpillar is blue-grey, with four black spots like eyes, the remaining segments are striped throughout with orange, red, black, and blue, beautifully arranged, and giving the creature a parti-coloured aspect. The moth emerges in July. The female lays her eggs in the form of a ring around the twigs of trees. The Ground Lackey (*Bombyx castrensis*) is the next kind we notice. This is a coast species, and is hence sometimes called the Coast Lackey. Like the last, it is a very variable species, and therefore difficult to describe. The caterpillar producing it is hairy and long, its back is blackish in colour, and the sides are blue-grey. The black consists of a broad stripe of equal width from one end of the caterpillar to the other, and is crossed by four orange streaks. The hairs themselves are orange-brown. The food of this caterpillar is the sea wormwood, the wild carrot, and some other plants, and when matured it spins a cocoon amongst the leaves. The moth appears in August.

The Fox moth (*Bombyx rubi*) is one of the larger BOMBYCIDÆ. The male has the forewings reddish-brown, the female dingy-brown, they are adorned by two central pale transverse lines. The moth occurs in June, and in August and September its handsome caterpillar may be looked for. This is a rich, velvety creature, of golden-brown on the back, and with a number of long, silky hairs along the middle. The sides are entirely black. When touched, this caterpillar rolls into a ring, and then displays spaces between the segments of an intense black colour. It feeds on bramble and heath, amongst which its dark cocoon interspersed with hairs may be looked for. It may be, however, that most insect collectors will consider the Oak Eggar (*Bombyx quercus*) as the king of this tribe. It is indeed a noble insect, measuring as much as three inches across the wings sometimes. Its large and striking caterpillar feeds more especially on the hawthorn, and when full grown is a very conspicuous creature. Its ground colour is velvety-black, densely covered with short down of an amber colour, and interspersed with longer hairs. This fine caterpillar spins a brown cocoon, changing therein to a very dark chrysalis. In July the moth appears, and the males fly swiftly during the day. The caterpillar hybernates during the cold winter months. The Grass Eggar (*Bombyx trifolii*) though not so large as the preceding, is yet a very beautiful insect. The colouring of the forewings is dingy-brown, the male being of rather a deeper hue than the female. They have a central spot towards the front margin, a narrow band extends from the tip of the front margin to the middle of the inner margin. The caterpillar of this species is black, with tawny hair on the back, and it is greyish on the sides. There is a bluish stripe on either side of the back, and an orange-red spot on each side on the third and fourth segments. Its food is clover, lucerne, and broom, and it is especially attached to the coast. It is found in autumn and again in spring, living through the winter like the last named. In the month of August the moth itself flies.

The Drinker (*Odonestris potatoria*) is produced from one of the most gaily-tinted caterpillars with which we are familiar. Its food is grasses, and few of those who ramble forth into the country at early morning can fail to come across the brilliant creature as he basks in the early sunlight. The term "Drinker" is applied to this species because the caterpillar has been noticed imbibing a drop of dew from the plant on which it was resting. It is hairy, and when touched, forms itself into a ring. Its colouring is so variegated that it becomes all but impossible to describe it, though it may be said to consist of blue, black, and orange, variously mottled over its body. When full-grown it spins a shuttle-shaped cocoon, which may be found affixed to the stems of various grasses. The moth is on the wing in July, and is one of our most common BOMBYCIDÆ. The Lappet (*Lasiocampa quercifolia*) is a very singular moth. When settled at rest it might be readily mistaken by the inexperienced for a dull and withered leaf. The wings are of a beautiful brown, and possess a purple lustre when the insect has newly emerged. The forewings have a black dot in the centre, and zigzag lines, which are transversely arranged. The singular caterpillar of the Lappet feeds on blackthorn and willow, and the moth appears in June.

The Small Lappet (*Lasiocampa illicifolia*) is generally considered a rare insect, though not uncommon in *some* parts of England, where its caterpillar has been found feeding on the leaves of the whortleberry. The forewings are reddish-brown at the base, and grey towards the hind margin. They have two oblique lines of blackish dots before the middle, and an oblique, whitish band beyond the centre. Cannock Chase and near Sheffield are given as localities for this species. Truly handsome is that large moth, the Kentish Glory (*Endromis versicolora*). Both this and the next species illustrate those species in which the male differs greatly in size from the female, and where the colourings are diverse in each. In the male of the Kentish Glory the ground colour is orange-brown, whilst in the female it is pale smoky-brown, and the wings are nearly transparent. Both sexes, however, are equally adorned with beautiful markings. In April the eggs should be sought on the birch, the *pabulum* of the handsome caterpillar emerging from them in May. The cocoon of this beautiful species is dark brown in colour, and the chrysalis within it is covered with a delicate bloom. The males of the moth, like those of the Oak Eggar, fly swiftly at mid-day, and may be captured by the aid of a female enclosed in a box.

The Emperor moth (*Saturnia carpini*) is the

last of the BOMBYCIDÆ, and is by some considered the grandest in colouring. It is certainly a fine insect, but loses much of its beauty when it has long emerged from the chrysalis. The wings are suffused with a brown bloom, which is exceedingly delicate. The forewings of the male moth are variegated with shades of red, brown, and grey; the hindwings are deep orange, also diversified by brown markings. The female has all the wings of a pearly-grey varied with delicate marbling. Both sexes have an eye-like mark in the centre of each wing, which forms their principal adornment. The Emperor has many other ornamental markings, but those alluded to are sufficient to identify the species. The caterpillar of the Emperor moth is a splendid creature of a delicate green colour; the segments of its body are furnished with pink tubercles, each surrounded by a black ring, emitting a few short bristles. In August and September it feeds on willow, blackthorn, and heath, and before winter spins its singular cocoon, which is so formed as to exclude the entrance of enemies of all kinds. The moth itself appears in April. The group of our Lepidoptera which we have now brought to a close, is perhaps, in respect of the size and beauty of the species contained in it, one of the most conspicuous of all comprised under the general name of BOMBYCES. The extreme beauty of several of the caterpillars producing the different species, renders them to be most eagerly sought, and thus we find many of them becoming rare amongst us which were formerly abundant.

DESERT PLANTS.

A GIFT that came to me from the United States a few weeks ago, pleased me much by its evidence of the wonderful provision made by the All-wise Creator of the universe for the existence and propagation of certain species of plants, and their adaptation in form and habits to the locality destined for them. This gift was a "Californian Rock Rose." When I took it out of the little square card box in which it had travelled by post, it appeared a round mass of dry withered leaves, circling into a close ball, with a root as dry and dead-looking. But after it had been submerged in water for a day or two, what a transformation had taken place! it was then a living, spreading plant, with green leaves, very like one of the Club mosses (*Selaginellas*) in my fern case. The friend who sent it me directed me to place it in a large, deep saucer of water when it had become thoroughly revived, and said it would thrive and grow, and produce seeds, thus treated; but would always dry up whenever I took it out of the water; and would live for years in that condition, always reviving and becoming green again whenever replaced in water. I believe its true name is *Selaginella convoluta*, and it comes from the rocks of California; it is sometimes called the "Resurrection Plant," on account of its resurrection to fresh life after its temporary seasons of death. When it has extracted every particle of nourishment from the rocky locality which is its native home, it dries up into this ball, and is blown away to some more genial soil; a marsh, perhaps, or the margin of some stream, and then it unrolls and spreads itself out, takes root, and is alive again.

The Rose of Jericho, *Anastatica hierochuntica*, another "Resurrection plant," has similar properties. In its dry condition the blossom looks like a little brown seed-pod; but if the stalk is put into water, the little ball on the top of it opens, and expands into a flower, with regular petals. In its dry state it becomes loosened from the soil, and is blown by the wind along the desert till it falls into some pool or moist place, where its seeds can germinate. Many of the *Mesembryanthemums Sempervivums* (ice-plants, stone-crops, and house-leeks), and *Cacti*, known as succulent plants, exhibit wonderful properties adapted to their native localities; they have very few and very small pores in their thick stems, which take the place of leaves, and so they are able to retain the moisture which they suck in during the rainy season, through the long parching drought which follows this, in the desert lands where their native homes are situated. Plants differently constituted would not be able to resist this, neither could these live in wet and cold climates, for the water absorbed by their roots not being evaporated through leaves, would cause the plant to become putrid, and die. In the rainy seasons, in hot countries, where the air is saturated with moisture for several weeks, perhaps once in the year, and the soil is drenched by the violent rains, all the little cells in the tissues of the cactus, and other succulent plants, become filled with liquid nourishment, and these are protected by the tough and thick covering of the outer leathery membrane of their large angular stems; so that they are able to subsist upon the store of food within them till the rains come again. Providence appears to have had two objects in view in creating plants of this conformation for the desert: they are not only able to preserve their own lives, but they are in a great measure the means of preserving the lives of the inhabitants of the arid regions in which they flourish. Many desert plants are furnished with bulbs, and tubers, which growing deep in the earth, out of the reach of the burning rays of the tropical sun, serve as reservoirs of sap for the life of the plant, and furnish the natives with food for themselves and their cattle, as well as the wild animals who have their home in the desert.

The African and American deserts have their distinctive flora. The Cacti are natives of the New World, between 40° N. and 40° S. latitude in America, and are found from the lowest tracts of land along the coast, through the plains, up to the highest regions of the Andes. Many of them have been transported to the Old World, and flourish in the wildest and most barren regions in Africa, in Asia, and in the hot parts of Europe; in Teneriffe, and the Canary isles especially: their fleshy shoots will take root in chasms, and in heaps of stones, where there does not appear to be a particle of vegetable soil. Some species of Cacti grow to a great height; travellers in Cumara speak of their "grand columns, throwing their shadows across the plains." The *Cereus giganteus* grows also in California and Mexico. It is a thick fluted column, the size of man's body, and grows to a height of thirty, forty, or even sixty feet, with three or four branches at the top. This Cactus, which the natives call the *Saguarro*, appears at first in the form of an immense club, standing upright in the ground, the top being twice as large as the bottom. As it grows, the thickness becomes more equal, so that when it is about twenty-five feet high, it looks like a regular pillar, the circumference being the same throughout. Then branches are thrown out; at first in a globe-like form, but as they grow larger they turn upwards, and continue their growth parallel to the trunk at certain distances, so that a Cereus with many branches has exactly the appearance of an immense candelabrum. It has a fig-shaped fruit growing at the side, and nearly at the top of the branches, so that it would be very difficult to reach, but that the old decayed trees split into a number of thin poles, which slant outwards, and with these the fruit can be knocked down. It is eaten fresh by the natives; they boil the sap to a syrup, and make a flour of its seeds. Another Cactus, the *Pitaya* or *Petahaya*, of somewhat lower growth, produces a still better fruit, and the missionaries who visited the country between the Colorado and the Gila, about a hundred years ago, speak of it, and say that the natives often live entirely upon the fruit of this and other Cacti. Most of this tribe of plants have very beautiful flowers as well as fruit, in gorgeous colours. The "Night-blowing Cereus" has a large trumpet-shaped blossom of the most dazzling white, with a tassel of pale yellow stamens in the centre, and a delicious, Vanilla-like scent. Some of the flowers of the *Opuntias*, or "prickly pears," are also very beautiful, and so are the splendid deep red-brown blossoms of the *Peireskias* (the only genus of Cactus which has true leaves) which are found high up on the Andes, and on the shores of Lake Titicaca, 12,700 feet about the sea-level. Nearly all the species of Opuntia have delicious fruit; the *Opuntia vulgaris*, or Indian fig, forms a great part of the food of the natives in the West Indies, in South Europe, Sicily, Greece, &c., where it has long been naturalized. The *Opuntia coccinellifera* takes its name from the cochineal insects which feed upon it; it is cultivated in the West Indian islands, and in Brazil; and the insects exhaust the plants so rapidly that they soon dry up and die, so that the plantations of Opuntia have to be continually renewed. Another species, the *Tuna Cactus*, is grown in fields in the provinces in which the cochineal is most largely carried on—Oaxaca, Tlascala, and Guanaxuato. These Cacti are so valuable on account of the cochineal trade, that they have been introduced into the East Indies and Syria, and of late years into Corsica, Spain, and Teneriffe. They make impenetrable hedges; the boundary line between the English and French possessions in the island of St. Kitts was formed of a triple row of the *Opuntia Tuna*. Stiff-hooked spines take the place of the small succulent leaves which some of these plants have, and they grow so hard and strong as often to lame the creatures that try to get at the sap within their fleshy stems. The wild asses and mules will sometimes injure themselves severely in kicking off the prickly coat of the *Melo-cactus*, which has a very refreshing acid juice, very valuable to travellers and their cattle in time of drought.

Some of the *Euphorbias* living in desert places have the same fleshy angular leafless stems as the Cacti, and the same power of retaining moisture, but they have very different properties: instead of their wholesome watery juice they hold a thick white milky liquid, which in some of the species is poisonous, but in a few harmless, and medicinal. The tree which furnishes india-rubber, which grows, not in the desert, but in the tropical forests of Brazil, belongs to this tribe of plants, and all the Euphorbias have the milky juice in more or less quantities, and probably this helps them to resist the effect of the sun's burning rays. Professor Smyth describes the *Euphorbia Canariensis* as growing ten feet high, in naked, stiff, prismoidal-shaped stems on bare black rocks of lava, where nothing else would grow, on the slopes of Mount Teneriffe. Some of the South African species have beautiful scarlet blossoms, composed of scarlet bracts encircling the stamens and pistils, for, as is the case with our little common spurges, what looks like a corolla is really an involucre. The tall, chandelier Euphorbia, *E. grandidens*, often grows to a height of thirty or forty feet, and its milky juice is used by the savages as poison for their arrows and javelins. I believe it has, however, some useful medicinal properties.

Either this Euphorbia, or one of a similar growth, excited the astonishment of some members of the Abyssinian Expedition, on their arrival in that country. They describe it as growing on some of the mountain slopes in straight stems, fifteen or twenty feet high, thicker than a man's body, branching out into a number of arms, all growing upwards, and all to the same height, like a gigantic candelabrum: with blossoms growing from the extremities of the arms, varying from white, through delicate shades of pink, to deep red. The Abyssinians call it the *Kolquol* tree.

The bulbous and tuberous-rooted plants flourish in the dry karroos of the Cape of Good Hope, in the plains of Barbary, and in the Syrian deserts, and even on the shores of tropical India, buried in sand. Many species of *Iris*, *Ixia*, and *Gladiolus* which have bulbs with their outer leaves, or scales, thickened and fleshy, so as to hold a quantity of nourishment, spring up in great profusion after the rains which pour down in South Africa heavily, during the three months when alone they fall. But the plants with tubers underground are the greatest treasures of the South African deserts. Many of the *Mesembryanthemums* have tubers which the natives eat raw, and the elands, gemsboks, and koodoos live upon many of the plants which have bulbs and tubers for many months, and dig them up with their sharp-pointed hoofs. The *Leroshua*, a small plant with narrow linear leaves, and a stalk not thicker than a crow's quill, has a tuber, sometimes as big as a young child's head, growing twelve or eighteen inches under ground, and this is full of cells containing a watery juice. The *Mokiwa*, or *Mokuri*, a creeping herbaceous plant, has a number of tubers as large as that of the Leroshua, growing in a circle, a yard or more from the stem, which the natives discover by striking the ground with stones, and the sound guides them to the tuber, which is generally about a foot under the soil.

The *Kengwe* or *Keme*, the water-melon of the Caffres, sometimes supplies the Caffres and their cattle with liquid for many weeks. When more rain than is usual falls, the country is covered with these juicy gourds, and all animals feast on them.

On the western coast of South Africa the sandy hillocks are covered with a creeper, which has a prickly gourd about the size of a turnip. The natives call it the *Naras*: it is their chief food for three or four months in the year: it has a delicious flavour, and its seeds, which they dry in the sun, and store away in little bags made of skin, taste and look like peeled almonds. It is greenish-yellow outside, and deep orange inside, when ripe. This plant is one of the greatest treasures in that desert country: its long, spreading roots keep the shifting sands fixed, and where food is so scarce, it affords nutriment equally to man and beast. Every animal, from the ox to the field-mouse, devours it, and birds, especially ostriches, are said also to feed upon it.

Mr. Chapman, in his narrative of his travels in South Africa, exhorts all explorers of these desert lands to become acquainted with their edible plants, which are often their only means of support in seasons of drought.

He says, also, that in the course of his travels he came to a grove of dark-green, glossy-leaved trees, in which the natives found a supply of water—"a pool in the wilderness;" a store of rain-water preserved by the good providence of God, in the cavities of the decayed trunks; which they extracted by means of tubes of bark; and this lesson was most serviceable to him in after-seasons of distress for water.

Near Grahamstown, and in some of the dry plains in the neighbourhood, grow the *Aloes*, great thick-leaved, stiff-looking plants, somewhat like pine-apples in foliage, with great spikes of scarlet blossoms fifteen or sixteen feet high. The *Socotrine Aloe* (the gummy sap of which, dried, is the drug known by that name) is a very beautiful plant, with bright green leaves, and flowers of scarlet tipped with green. Many of the African Aloes yield the same gum in a lesser degree. They are all bulbous plants, and so are the American Aloes, which are not true Aloes but *Agaves;* and although they have many of their characteristics, and the same kind of saw-shaped leaves, they are Amaryllis plants, while the true Aloes are of the Liliaceous tribe. The Agave is cultivated in Mexico for the sake of the sap it produces, from which the wine called *pulque* is made, and the Mexicans make *mezcal*, a strong spirit, from the bulbs, and bake them, taking off the outer skin, when they are sweet and pleasant eating. The *Yuccas* are allied to the Agaves, and have the same kind of stiff, thick leaves, and small, yellowish, bell-shaped flowers. All these plants grow on the desert plains of North America, in the most barren and dry situations, out of the crevices of rocks where scarcely any other shrub would find support.

A species of Acacia, the *Mesquito*, or *Algarobbia*, is often to be met with in dry and barren regions, and, strange to say, it varies in form in the different localities where it is found: in parts of New Mexico it is a shrub with branches and twigs, springing directly from the root and spreading out upon the ground. On the plains between the Gila and the Colorado it is an elegant little tree, with feathery foliage, and roots stretching to an extraordinary depth underground, its thorny branches bearing green or yellowish pods, which do not dry upon them, but fall off at a certain stage of ripeness, sometimes cover the ground an inch deep. The Indians on the Pima eat these pods, and the substance round them has a pleasant acid taste, and will make a cooling drink; the pods when dry are ground into flour. When the grass is scanty they form provender for the horses and mules, who are said to be so fond of them that they can scarcely be kept in order when they get into the Mesquito country.

Very beautiful flowers of the brightest colouring—orange poppies, sunflowers, &c.,—are found in spots in the deserts; indeed, throughout their barren desolation there are often a greater variety of rich and gorgeous flowers found than in the most luxuriant prairie country; even where no grass grows they will spring up in some dry naked waste. Travellers in North America speak of the abundance of *Artemisias* and other odoriferous plants growing up in the sandy soil of the deserts in tough, twisted, wiry clumps, so as to interfere with the progress of their carts, and say that the whole air is sometimes saturated with their turpentine odours. The *Amorpha canescens* (which cover the rolling plains near Kansas with its purple flowers), the *Artemisia absinthe*, or "prairie sage," asters, and sunflowers are everywhere found. Flowers of deep warm colours seem to love the sandy soil. Beauty of the richest character abounds, it would seem, in the barren desert as well as in the verdant plain; and wherever he may bend his steps, over hill or rocky mountain pass, alike in valleys, deserts, and trackless wilds, man may behold and adore the loving and beauteous works of the Great Creator of the universe.—C. E. D.—*Aunt Judy's Magazine*.

RATS.

THE rats, "not to know them, argues ourselves unknown;" for the peasant in his cot, the philosopher in his study, the poet in his airy flights, and the warrior amid the din of battle, must frequently encounter those rambling ubiquitous gnawers.

The rats are not the things of yesterday; for the venerable Father of History, Herodotus, who wrote more than two thousand two hundred years ago, tells us how the Egyptian rats of old, marshalled in immense numbers, like so many volunteers in aid of their country, entered the battle-field, and, in light marching order I presume, stole a nocturnal march into the Assyrian and Arabian camps, and there, with reposing warriors around, devoured the quivers, gnawed to pieces the bow-strings and even the helmet-straps of the slumbering army; so that when the morning sun rose the allied armies fled in disorder, as their weapons, the soldier's hope and indispensible auxiliaries of war, were completely destroyed by the Egyptian rodentia. In commemoration of this national event, a stone statue of Stethon, with a rat in his hand, was erected in the Temple of Vulcan with the following significant and grateful inscription, "On seeing me learn to revere the gods!" A Chinese tradition shows how the rats of the land of tea were equally formidable against the Turks. The kingdom of Khotan was invaded by a powerful Turkish army. The Khotain king, doubting the strength of his men, implored the rats of the desert to come to his assistance, and the night before the battle an overgrown rat appeared to the king in a dream, and thus eloquently spoke to the desponding monarch:—"You have claimed our assistance, prepare your troops to fight a battle to-morrow, and you shall be victorious!"

Early next morning the Chinese quite unexpectedly marched upon the Turks, who were ordered to advance their cavalry, but to the consternation of the troops the harness of their chargers, bows, cuirass-straps, and general equipments, had been half annihilated by the rats, and through this rather curious stratagem of war the Turkish general was slain and his whole army became prisoners. If the rats were heroic among the Egyptians and Chinese, they were formerly a sensitive tribe with us here in Ireland, for we not unfrequently rhymed them to death, or caused them to migrate by the force of rhyme.

To this Irish legend many of the English poets refer. Shakespeare makes Rosalind say:—

I was never so berhymed since Pythagoras' time, when I was an Irish rat.

And Ben Jonson says:—

Rhyme them to death, as they do Irish rats, In drumming tunes.

And Randolph says:—

And my poets
Shall with a satire steeped in vinegar
Rhyme them to death, as they do rats in Ireland.

Dean Swift and Sir Philip Sidney, both refer to the rhyming of rats to death in Ireland. What effect music may have on rats I cannot tell, but it is stated that rats in ships at Calcutta have been lured into traps by music.

Eugene Curry states that ships lying at Limerick were greatly infested by rats, and that there were men brought who by some means lured them into traps. Travellers tell us that white rats are common on the coast of Guinea, and that white rats are met with in many parts of the globe. Upon the authority of Samuel Moss we are told that several white rats were caught at Cheltenham, in England, in 1822. The ferocity of rats is too well known. An American traveller tells me that but a few years ago the town of Chicago, on the Ohio, was so invaded by rats that the inhabitants became alarmed, and the corporation had to offer rewards for the destruction of the prowling depredators. It is a well authenticated fact that many years ago a military gentleman was attacked, and actually devoured, by rats in some of the vaults in Dublin. It is no easy matter to withstand the incursions of rats, or to barricade against their marches. Charles Waterton tells us how they (the rats), on his return to his home in 1813, had gnawed their way through no less than thirty-two doors.

Martin, in his "Tour to the Western Isles," says that about the year 1700 the ancient race of the Island of Rona were all destroyed, partly by an incursion of rats:—"First," he says, "a swarm of rats, none knew how, came into the island and eat up all the corn. In the next place, some seamen landed and robbed them (the people) of what provisions they had left, and all died before the usual time of the arrival of the boat from Lewis."

At the commencement of this paper I designated rats as *ubiquitous*, but I quite forgot that in Tory Island, lying off the coast of Donegal, there is not a rat in the whole island! In the summer of 1864 I spent two days in the island, and the inhabitants told me they never saw a rat in the island, and that their ancestors never saw one. I look on the statements as facts: what would a Buffon say to this? Larwood and Hotten, in their really curious and elaborate "History of Signboards," say:—"We have the RAT and FERRET at Wilson, near Ashby de la Zouch."

Hudibras and Ben Jonson say, "I smell a rat;" Shakespeare says, "But mice, and rats, and such small beer;" Cowper says, "While the rat is on the scout;" and Howitt, still more poetic, writes, "And the water-rat plunging about in his mirth."

That rats frequently commit literary thefts, more annoying to writers than even plagiarism itself, and that they are often guilty of petty larceny in a pecuniary way, are well known, and the injured mortals show their disapprobation by honestly wishing that the whole tribe were "*as dead as a rat.*"

Escaping from ships previous to their sinking, and running from dilapidated houses before their fall, are sagacious movements popularly assigned to rats.

H. H. ULIDIA.

IN THE BACKWOODS.
BY J. MATTHEW JONES, F.L.S.

PART II.

AS we are now in the most famous district in the province for bears, perhaps it will be well to make a few remarks upon the natural history of the black bear (*Ursus Americanus*). The bear comes out of his winter den as soon as the snow disappears, generally about the end of April. The he bear dens by himself. The she bear cubs about the first week in February, and the young are at first about the size of a common squirrel (*Sciurus Hudsonius*). They obtain nourishment from the mother until about the latter end of June, and den with her through the next winter; remaining with her till two years old, and leave her for good when she leaves her den the second spring after birth. Bears are fat when they leave their dens in spring, but soon get poor, finding but little food at that time of year. It is at this time that they are apt to commit forays upon the flocks of the back settlers. These animals are known to sit and watch at the falls of streams for fish passing up in spring. Their principal food, however, consists of the wild fruits of the forest, ants, hornets, wasps, and bees, whose nests they invade for the purpose of securing the larvæ, wax, or honey within. They care nothing for the stings of the infuriated hornets and wasps, but the cubs cry out when stung, but nevertheless keep fast hold of the comb. Cubs will not fight with the mother when she attacks any one, but run up trees. Rutting time is in June, when the he bears are very savage, sometimes going in gangs of twenty or more, and when they come near a she bear they commence fighting among themselves furiously, making the most hideous roarings all the time, and if one gets killed in the fray, the rest fall upon him and eat him. They fight by first rising on their hind legs, and rushing at each other, hugging, biting, and scratching, endeavouring to rip their antagonists' stomachs open with their hind claws. Bears shed their coats about July. They stalk young moose by creeping upon them, and when close to make a great spring. Having killed the moose they skin him just as clean as a man would, and begin to eat the chest first, tearing out the paunch which they throw away. They dislike wet weather, and take shelter where they can keep dry, under rocks, &c., and other places. When the old bears go into dens, in the fall, they take plenty of dead leaves and fern, and make a good bed of them, and the she bear makes no further provision at cubbing time. They always return, if alive, to the same den each fall; but if a porcupine takes possession while they are away in summer, and leaves droppings about, the bear will not return to that den again. A large size bear will weigh over six hundred pounds, and give one hundred pounds of grease, for which one shilling sterling per lb. is given at Shelburne, while at Halifax a wine bottle full sells for four shillings. The meat of the bear is excellent eating, tasting something like mutton. It is best boiled to render it tender, and then fried with pieces of the fat. The tongue is very similar to a calf's tongue when boiled. The Indians cure bear meat by cutting it up into long strips, and placing it on a framework of poles, lighting a fire underneath, so as to dry it in the smoke, which process takes about two days, and if kept dry afterwards in a proper place will keep for a year or more. They never make use of the inside portions of the animal, viz., heart, liver, &c. When they cook fresh meat they cut it up into small pieces, and fry it. The meat, when partially smoked, we found much better boiled than fried, frying making it too hard. The bones of the bear are salted down and used to put into soup. The gall of the bear the Indians use for sprains and wounds.

The Indians appear to be a very superstitious race of beings, and the most trivial events cause anxiety. For instance, one night the light of our fire attracted a little Acadian owl (*Strix Acadica*), which perched on a branch close by, making its curious noise. One of the Indians at once predicted that bad luck would attend our expedition, and begged us to level a gun at the unfortunate bird, whose death alone could cast away the spell that rested upon us.

One day we started with Peter Paul in a westerly direction from the camp, and after travelling about two miles through thick forest and swamps, we arrived on the borders of a good sized lake, with an outlet at its western end. On walking round we came upon a large beaver house, situate on the lake edge, where the water was deep. The house appeared as if two cartloads of faggots had been thrown down in a heap and flattened above. Having no implements to enable us to take it asunder, we were obliged to leave it as it was. Going still further down the lake side we arrived at the outlet, which we found dammed across by the beavers. It was constructed of sticks and mud, overgrown with grass and weeds, the sticks laid over each other in a line of lace work, almost entirely stopping the escape of the lake water down the brook. There was an older dam below this one about fifteen yards lower down the brook. The smaller alders, poplars, and other trees near the dam were cut short off near the ground. This lake on its west side is muddy, with a vigorous growth of rushes, sedges, &c. An island of about half an acre, covered with spruce and pine, divided from the south shore by a narrow passage, has upon its eastern side a very large beaver house upon the shore, extending into the water. The house, or rather stack of sticks, is very large, built of larger sticks than usual. In this great pile there must be several cartloads of sticks and small logs, from the small twig up to pieces four inches in diameter. Some pieces are several feet in length, while others are only three or four inches long. The beaver pups early in spring, having two cubs, but they are sometimes known to have young in August. When the cubs are two years old they pair and go off to another place. Beaver skins sell about Shelburne now for four shillings stirling per pound, whilst some years ago they sold for eighteen shillings per pound. A good skin will weigh four pounds.

About Whetstone Lake the robin (*Turdis Migratorius*) was very common, flocking together in large numbers at sundown on the shore, picking up insect food. The hermit thrush (*T. Solitarius*), well named so from its retired habits, occurred there also, treating us as the shades of evening drew round, to its plaintive note; and the spotted snake (*Coluber sirtalis*) was fond of sunning itself on the granite boulders by the lake side, about mid-day. These boulders had been carried up from the lake to their present position by the action of ice, for the course they have travelled was clearly perceptible in the deep channel which led from each of them to the bed of the lake.

After three days spent in this locality we made a move to the north-west, but had not proceeded far before some of our party shot another bear, and we had to call a halt in order to skin him; we had now arrived on the upper ridge of the granite plateau, from which we had a magnificent view of the country around for many miles on every side, and a wild and curious scene it was. All around us lay a perfect wilderness of granite boulders, from among which rose a dense growth of the blueberry and huckleberry, and interspersed with thickets of dwarf spruce, birch, and alder. The Labrador tea (*Ledum latifolium*) and a species of myrica, were also abundant. Small lakes were seen in every direction, and the shrill cry of the loon (*Colymbus glacialis*) mark the breeding place of that shy and solitary bird. Our camp here was an exceedingly primitive one—a few small poles stuck against the side of an overhanging boulder, and covered with brushwood, was all that gave us shelter, but the day's toil sufficed to send us into a sound sleep, which was only broken by the sharp frost of the early morning. On awaking early I went out to survey the scene, which was indeed lovely in the extreme. The sun was just rising, illuminating the eastern sky with glowing colours;

a flock of wax wings (*Bombycilla Carolinensis*) sat preening their feathers on the bleached branches of a blasted pine hard by, in company with a few migratory thrushes, while a keen north-west wind was blowing, bracing up the nerves, and the whole country round became gradually lit up to the life of another day.

We now travelled still upon the elevated table land, passing here and there through some terribly swampy ground, covered with moss, which sunk at every step, letting us up to the knees. We were freighted with our heavy packs, and above all the heavy green bear skins, and the work told upon all. Sometimes our route lay over spots where in addition to the mossy swamps fallen spruce and pine lay beneath, with their dead sharp-pointed spikes of branches sticking up, on which we occasionally got a painful reminder; but after all our trouble, about noon we gained the summit of a high point of land, on which rested a huge granite boulder, split into two pieces, under which was a large well of delicious water: we gave this the name of "Split Rock Well." Leaving this place, we arrived a little before sundown, near a stream which joined two large lakes. The stream was deep, and about twenty feet wide, and presenting a good site, we camped here. But at dusk three of us started for the upper lake to see the beaver which Peter Paul told us he had seen there some time back, when in company with an old indian he had visited it. We came cautiously upon its banks, and lay down, looking and listening for the animals. In a short time, at some distance we could see in the twilight, ripple marks on the surface, and presently a head or two moving about swimming in the direction of the opposite shore. We watched them carefully, and observed that the beavers coasted along shore, engaged now and then in looking for food, just as we have often seen the water rat of England do in a pond. After watching them for some short time, we heard on our right, where Peter Paul had gone, a loud flap on the water, just as if a paddle had been struck on the lake, and all signs of beaver vanished at once. This we considered came from a sentinel beaver, who, having heard Paul coming in the direction of their head quarters, had sounded this tocsin of alarm. Although we waited for some time after this, not a beaver could be seen.

The next day we travelled also along the table land in a north-west direction, passing over much the same kind of land, the spruce woods getting larger. I chased a porcupine for about a hundred yards, when he took to a spruce tree some twenty feet high and was killed. I noticed that the indians shaved the porcupine of his quills before carrying him. The process is as follows:—taking a sharp knife, they shave from tip of tail to head, and are extremely careful not to get any of the small quills into their hands, as the puncture is very painful. The old woman's tale of a porcupine throwing its quills at a person chasing it, is untrue; the truth of the matter being that if a stick be presented to it, or any one attempts to handle it, it immediately strikes the offender with its tail, driving the smaller quills with such force as even to stick them firmly into a piece of wood. The flesh of the porcupine is delicious, tender, and sweet, the tail when fried nicely being the choicest morsel. We camped this night in dense woods by the side of a stream, and having exhausted all our provisions, began to feel somewhat alarmed that if we did not reach the settlement on the west or Weymouth coast before long, we should fare badly. I may say that we fully expected to have struck some marks of civilization at noon of the first day according to our reckoning, but on sending an indian up the highest trees, during the afternoon, he only gave us the unwelcome intelligence, "no sign clearing, big woods all along." The next morning early, we were determined to try our best to get out of our dilemma, and so it was decided that we should stow away all our goods and chattels, and leave them covered up with branches, so that if we got out all safe we might send in for them afterwards, there being but little fear of robbery in such a situation. We therefore took with us only a blanket and our guns, and being thus lightly burdened we made good way. But after a long and tedious march until mid-day, we could strike no blaze, (*i.e.* the marks placed upon trees by surveyors in the back settlements). And we sat down to rest and devour our last scrap of biscuit and a small tin of chocolate among six, with anxious thoughts as to what would constitute the next meal; off again, we traversed through thick woods, descending all the time, and in a valley first discovered an old blaze, which gave us fresh courage, and we contrived to follow it for some distance, until to our horror we arrived on the shore of a large lake, about mid-way from its extremities, so there was nothing for it but to trudge, wearied as we were, all round its lower end, which having been accomplished, we struck out through the forest again by compass, no blaze being seen. It was getting dark, and we had given up all hope of getting out that night, when Peter Paul, who was some distance ahead, called out, "road, road," and on arriving at the spot, sure enough there lay an old track, which following to the southward till dark we came to an open spot, surrounded by woods, in which was a field of turnips and potatoes. We may be excused when we say that we dispersed at this time with the ordinary courtesies of society, and allowed every one to help himself, and a ludicrous sight it was to see six hungry individuals sitting in the midst of a turnip patch refreshing themselves on the vegetable esculents. An old shed, with large holes in the roof, stood in one corner, and we adjourned to this, and making a fire roasted potatoes and made ourselves as comfortable as we could, but the rain began to pour in torrents, and drenched and lightless we passed a weary night. The morning, however, no sooner dawned than we trudged down the road, and hearing the sound of an axe we directed our course that way, and soon found ourselves in the presence of a worthy settler, whose snug farm-house lay close by on the banks of the Sissiboo river, Digby Co. A forlorn looking group indeed we must have appeared, all tattered and torn as we were, after our hard travel over mountain and swampy barren; but the heart of the worthy Nova Scotian warmed towards us, as he hurried us along to his dwelling, and soon with his table groaning under the weight of good fare, he bade us welcome to civilized life once more, and it is almost needless to add, that while enjoying such welcome hospitality, we soon forgot the weary tramp we had had during that ever memorable "Fortnight in the Backwoods of Shelburne and Weymouth."

FLEAS.

IF the little gentleman has neither beauty of form nor brilliancy of colour to recommend him, nobody at least can deny that he is as fearfully and wonderfully made as man himself. There is no more warlike being to be found among the hundred thousands of the class in which naturalists place him: he prefers six legs to our two, and wears plate-armour to protect himself in his incessant warfare; for the whole body is encased in beautiful dark-brown steel; from the tiny joints start stiff hairs to repel all invasion, and the plump, well-fed body at once suggests his superiority over the tightly-laced, skeleton-shaped figures of distant cousins. Look at him in the solar microscope, where he is a welcome visitor, and always receives, upon his first appearance, an Ah! of delight from one sex, mixed with a concert of low, merry exclamations from the other. How fierce he looks in his knightly armament! How powerful those two arm-like extremities appear, which have only two joints, and move upon flexible pivots in the very cheeks of the strange being! And then those superb hind legs, of such length and marvellous strength, that they enable him to walk with more than seven-league boots, and to leap far beyond the most agile of Turners. Have we not been told, by one of those amiable statisticians who never rest till they have reduced every statement to numbers, that the Londoner who could leap from the Strand at one bound to the top of St. Paul's, would still be second to the young flea who makes his first experiment in jumping?

There is much to be read in his face, even though we do not believe in Lavater nor read the *Phrenological Journal*. An old naturalist established the principle, that the weaker and smaller the animal, the more astute and malicious his features. The face of the little gentleman is small and wrinkled; he looks careworn, as one may well appear who lives, like David, in constant fear of his life, and gets his daily pittance but by stealth and with imminent danger. The eyes, especially, when duly magnified, present an irresistibly ludicrous mixture of reckless wildness with astute cunning, and, were they visible to human sight unaided, would be of endless interest to careful observers.

Nature can hardly be expected to produce such marvellous strength of body and such a decided character all at once; she has to pass him at least through three different stages before she sends him forth, one of the most perfect of her countless creations. He appears first as a pure white egg, all beauty and innocence, though so small that the eye cannot see it; then he assumes the modest form of a sly but harmless maggot, which after a while cunningly wraps itself in its own silken winding sheet, and dies, to all appearance; but lo! before the moon is full again, the magic slumber is broken, death is changed into life, and as the sombre envelope bursts and breaks asunder, the young gentleman, in his glossy garments, leaps forth, armed cap-à-pie, to live and to love as all his wild forefathers have done before him. But he no sooner enters the world, poor little fellow! than he finds it full of strife and struggle, and rare must be his good fortune if he reaches the good old age of six years, and sees grandchildren and great-grandchildren leap and carol around him in the recklessness of his race. Few but fall into the hands of man, generally to be unscrupulously murdered, but at times to be held in sad captivity; for these devoted friends of his must occasionally serve to amuse him in their chains, and he revenges himself on a few, whom he treats with the most refined cruelty, for the wrong-doings of a whole race. Only those who love him in preference to beast or bird are strong and lively enough to stand the severe training; but their strength is remarkable, and it is said that if you fasten a human flea to the end of an unbroken wheat straw, he will be powerful enough to lift it right off the table on which it is placed! The best for public performances are the strongest; they come from Russia, and are sent abroad in pill-boxes, packed in the finest cotton, and with a clear and prominent caution on the top, so as to keep custom-house officers from prying too curiously into the contents of the little parcels. Smaller supplies reach the trainer in the corner of an envelope, packed in tissue-paper, and carefully glued to the left hand, so as to protect them against the blow of the stamp-marker, which would otherwise make a speedy end to the whole colony. The little gentleman in black having actually their market-price, which varies with the season. In the abundance of the summer-months they sell for a few farthings; in winter they rise to a cent a-piece; and a ludicrous story is current of a trainer who, upon unpacking his diminutive performers, found that one had slipped his chains and escaped. Time pressed, and the vacancy had to be filled, or the team of four blacks before the gilt glass coach would not be complete. No one near would acknowledge to own the desired commodity, until an obliging stable-boy was found, who offered to supply the needful animal; but he demanded sixpence for it, and sixpence he got.

Fancy, if you can, the little gentleman used to roam freely through the wild world, and to taste now of the vigour of a young man, and now of the nectar of a fair beauty, suddenly caught and chained! Yes, chained; for as man has discovered the aptness of the horse's mouth to hold the bit, by which he controls the noble animal, so he has found out that the tiny slave, whom he wishes to make useful, has a groove between the neck and the body suitable for his purposes; holding the poor captive by a pair of forceps, he deftly slips a noose of finest floss-silk over his head, passes it round his neck, and ties it with a peculiar knot. The slave is chained! for the silk cannot slip up or down, nor can it be pushed off with the legs; at the same time the refined cruelty of man leaves him at full liberty to use his kangaroo-like springing legs, and keeps him in perfect health, to make him perform well. He is fed well—on the arm of his master; for the little gentleman is dainty, and nothing but the vigorous blood of a healthy man will keep him in good order. Here they have their revenge, in their turn, for it is found that the fastidious creatures will not take supper or breakfast, the only two meals in which they indulge, unless the hand or the arm is perfectly motionless. Moreover, they are regular gourmands, and, with a taste utterly inconceivable to us, they insist upon taking ample time for their meals. How they must chuckle, the little, whimsical beings, when they thus bite and suck to their hearts' delight, while their cruel master has to stand motionless by the hour, fearful lest he should interrupt them in their enjoyment, and find them unable, next day, to perform their task! Still they do not live long in captivity. A patriarch was owned by a famous Italian trainer, well known in this country a few years ago, who had pulled up a bucket from a miniature well for eighteen months. He died apparently from pure old age, being found, one day, dead at his post, with his bucket drawn half-way up the well.

In his freedom he enjoys life as few of his kindred are able to do. A gentle pressure on his steel shanks, and he rises like a rocket, or he leaps sideways from friend to friend. Little heart, bold heart! says Pliny, and the little gentleman in black is no respecter of persons. He finds his victim at the writing table or in the whirl of the dance; he enters the king's palace and the tent of the warrior. We remember the consternation created at a performance of Industrious Fleas, at a royal palace on the Continent. The king and his infirm queen were present, and a small circle of courtiers and ladies crowded round the white marble table, on which the poor little creatures were performing their waltz. A miniature arena had been formed of cardboard on the top of a musical box; at one end sat the orchestra, composed of fleas, each tied to his seat, and having a paper in the shape and colour of some musical instrument attached to his feet. Two little creatures were fastened to opposite ends of a short piece of gold paper, so as to turn their backs to each other, and set down in the middle of the arena. The box was wound up, and commenced to play; the performers, feeling the jarring of the box, or, if you would believe the owner, hearing the music, waved their hands wildly about, as if engaged in an elaborate piece of music, and the two dancers began to whirl round and round as fast as their legs would carry them. The king, a man of great humour, laughed heartily, and asked for a repetition; but behold! when all was arranged again, one of the waltzers had escaped. Thereupon was great consternation and horror; the fugitive must be recaptured, both to enable the performer to obey the royal mandate, and to relieve the unlucky victim. The trainer bares his arm, and sure enough, the fugitive cannot resist the temptation of an early meal. Before he has well commenced, however, he is seized and put into his place. New laughter and universal amusement! All crowd around to see the waltz once more; when suddenly the little rebel kicks, and performs the wildest antics, and the embarrassed trainer has to confess that the captive is not his old pupil—but a new-comer! The king laughed louder than ever, but the performance was ended, and the fee, upon which the unlucky owner had counted, fell far below his expectations.

The animal is not generally so easily captured; his marvellous agility, his almost magic power of disappearance at the critical moment, are no doubt known to all our readers—from books—and his skill in escaping is graphically expressed in the definition of the Frenchman, who heard a flea mentioned, and exclaimed: "Ah, ze flea, ze little animal; you catch him, you put ze finger upon him, and he is not zere!" No wonder that the incessant persecution which he has to endure should, at the end of so many generations, have developed these faculties in the highest degree. If Mr. Darwin's theory is true, that the crane acquired its long neck and long legs by persevering search after fish, the flea may well claim his magnificent legs as the result of the work of ages. It is true, they are lean, and we cannot help admiring the marvellous skill of the tailor whom Goethe has immortalized in his famous song:

> "There was once a king
> Who had a big flea,
> He loved him not a little,
> As much as his son.
> Then called he his tailor,
> The tailor came in;
> There, measure him for a suit,
> And measure him for breeches!"

Those happy days, we fear, are gone; and although he continues, as in the poem, to plague high and low, he no longer can boast that

> "In velvet and in silk
> He was dressed superbly,
> Had ribbons on his coat,
> Had crosses in plenty;
> Was minister at once,
> And had a diamond star,
> Then all his brothers also
> Were great and high at court."

Now, he is, like Cain, a fugitive and a vagabond on the earth, and every one that findeth him slayeth him. And why? Simply, because he does not allow his sword to become rusty, and makes good use of the weapon which he has received from Nature for his support and his defence. Fortunately, there is at least one nation upon earth—a branch of the coming masters of the earth, the Lithuanians—who seem to have a fairer appreciation of the little gentleman in black than other nations boasting of a higher civilization. Their favorite national ballad sings thus:

> "The wolf, the little wolf,
> The son of the forest,
> Steps from the forest,
> Out on the meadow,
> Tears the young calf,
> Tears the little foal—
> That is his labour.

> "The fox, the little fox,
> The son of the forest,
> Glides from the forest
> Out to the farmyard,
> Seizes the gosling,
> Murders the pullet—
> That is his labour.

> "The dog, the little dog,
> The guardian of the house,
> Barks and bites
> The heel of the robber,
> Frightens the thieves,
> Drives away vagrants—
> That is his labour.

> "The flea, the little flea,
> The thirsty, lusting flea,
> Drinks the sweet blood;
> At break of day,
> He wakes the maid-servants
> To milk the rich cows—
> That is his labour.

> "The bee, the little bee,
> The child of the meadow,
> Hums in the heather,
> Stingeth the finger,
> The ear and the face,
> Gives us sweet honey—
> That is her labour.

> "Oh man, oh little man!
> Look at the bee!
> Do you sting like her
> The heart, the little heart?
> Give then sweet comfort
> To the sore wounded heart—
> That is thy labour."

Nor is this the only race of men who value his services and honorably place him by the side of the faithful dog and the industrious bee; for it is well known that pious Hindoos believe him to hold the soul of great and good men, and build him large hospitals, where he is nursed throughout life.—*Putnam's Monthly Magazine*, September.

THE HAZEL.

The Hazel (*Corylus Avellana*) grows, so to speak, everywhere, that is, in nearly all our woods and thickets, the long graceful male catkins and the crimson tips of the female pistils appearing early in the season, to be succeeded at a later date by the well-known nuts which boys and squirrels love to crack. The hazel is so common that few people think of its value, though it is the parent of all our fine dessert filberts, "Kentish Cobs," and other aristocratic offspring.

It has been supposed by some that the hazel

originally came from Asia, the specific name, Avellana, being derived from Abellina, supposed to be the valley of Damascus. Pliny says that the plant was introduced from Pontus into Greece, from which the nuts were called Nux Pontica. The plant is now found growing over a great part of Asia, also in Sweden, Denmark, Holland, Germany, France; and De Candolle says it is to be found wild on the mountains of Sardinia, and suspects it also to be indigenous in the ravines in the vicinity of Algiers. In submerged forests in different parts of England, hazel nuts have frequently been found in a very perfect state, and are also very plentiful in the bogs in Shetland, though the plant itself does not grow there at the present time.

The plant has numerous economic applications, the well-known edible nuts being the most important; these are cultivated to a very large extent in Kent, more especially in the neighbourhood of Maidstone, where the finest sorts are grown. The plants are propagated by suckers, which they produce in great abundance. The soil, a rich loam, is kept well manured and drained. Though the filbert is naturally but a low-growing plant, some care and ingenuity are exercised in these plantations to keep the plants dwarfed, it having been found that by this means a larger crop, as well as a better quality of "fruit," is obtained. These dwarf trees, which are seldom more than 7 feet high, and about 6 feet in diameter, are very uniformly trimmed with an open or cup-like centre, so as to allow plenty of light and air to circulate through the branches; the effect of this cultivation, with a regular system of hoeing and clearing considerably enhances the value of the crops. It is said that one acre of land under such a system of cultivation has been known to yield over 30 cwt. of nuts. Many varieties are known in the market as Kentish Cobs, Red Filberts, White Filberts, Cosford, &c. The name Filberts seems to be derived from Full-beard in reference to the long calyx or husk, which quite envelopes the nut itself.

Hazel nuts are also cultivated to a considerable extent in Spain and Italy; those grown in Spain are known either as Spanish or Barcelona nuts, the latter being so-called from the port whence they are shipped. The whole face of the neighbouring valley of Abelino, in Italy, is covered with nut trees, which yield in good years a profit of 60,000 ducats. Immense quantities of nuts are brought into this country, sometimes amounting in value in one year to £90,000, an enormous sum when we consider that nearly all these nuts are consumed by children, a very small portion being used for the expression of oil.

The nut of the common hazel is perhaps preferable to that of any of the cultivated varieties for the sweetness of its flavour; its small size, however, is the reason why it gives place to the cultivated Filbert, Cob, &c. Two kinds of nut are imported from Smyrna, known in the trade respectively as Turkey nuts, which are small and nearly round, and Turkey filberts, which are long and pointed, similar to our native-grown filberts; these are the produce of Corylus Colurna, and have thinner shells than those of C. Avellana.

The hazel never grows sufficiently large to furnish wood suitable either for furniture or building purposes. The young wood is very tough and elastic, and makes excellent hoops, fishing-rods, walking-sticks, &c.; and the celebrated magic wand or divining-rod is said to have been formed of the young forked twigs. The thicker and more crooked parts of the tree are well adapted for rustic garden work, such as summer houses, seats, &c. The wood makes excellent charcoal, from which drawing-crayons are frequently made.

The hazel has a very straggling habit, forming sometimes a sort of irregular thicket or jungle on banks, where the roots, descending, travel in and out between the irregularities of the stones until they reach the ground below.

The plant, as we have already said, is monoecious, the two sexes being common on every bush, and the nuts produced abundantly; but I recently received at the Kew Museum some hazel nuts from a tree growing among the ruins of Godstow Abbey, which are all perfectly formed, so far as outward appearance goes, but not one of which contains a single "kernel." This at first appears to be a fact scarcely worth noticing, since we can almost always find abortive nuts on any hazel tree, but in this case the produce of the tree has frequently been tested, and last autumn a quantity of the nuts were opened, all of which were abortive. The tree in question is well formed, about 20 feet high, embracing amongst its roots three or four stones several feet in length. The tree, and those surrounding it, all appear in a very flourishing condition. The sterility of this particular tree has become proverbial in the neighbourhood, and is readily accounted for and believed in by the country people from the situation of its growth being over the grave of Fair Rosamond, who was originally buried in the Abbey, but whose body was afterwards removed by order of the Bishop of Lincoln. This explanation is sufficiently satisfactory to the superstitious peasantry.—JOHN R. JACKSON, Kew; in *Gard. Chron.*

River Phenomena.

A phenomenon is noticed as occurring at the mouths of the Mississippi, which Sir C. Lyell says is without parallel, as far as he is aware, in the delta of any other river. The muddy bottom of the sea off the mouths of that river rises up to the height of sometimes ten or eighteen feet above the level of the sea, and from the tops of these new-made islands gush springs of salt or brackish and muddy water, together with a considerable quantity of carburetted hydrogen or inflammable gas, the tubular cavities up which the springs rise being about six inches in diameter, vertical, and as regular in form as if bored by an auger. The following account of the origin of these lumps is interesting :—

"The initiatory moving power may probably be derived from the downward pressure of the gravel, sand, and sediment accumulated during the flood season off the various mouths or passes, upon a yielding bottom of fine mud and sand. This new deposit forms annually a mass of no less than one mile square, having a thickness of twenty-seven feet. It consists of mud, coarse sand, and gravel, which the river lets fall somewhat abruptly when it first comes in contact with the still salt water of the gulf. A cubic mass of such enormous volume and weight thrown down on a foundation of yielding mud, consisting of materials which, as being very fine and impalpable, had long before been carried out farthest from the land, may well be conceived to exert a downward pressure capable of displacing, squeezing, and forcing up laterally some parts of the adjoining bottom of the gulf, so as to give rise to new shoals and islands. Railway engineers are familiar with the swelling up of a peat moss or the bed of a morass, on some adjoining part of which a new embankment has been constructed. I saw an example of this in the year 1839, in the Loch of Rescobie, in Forfarshire, five miles east of the town of Forfar. That lake had been partially drained, and the railway mound was carried over newly exposed, soft, and swampy ground, which gave way so as to let the mound sink down fifteen feet. It then became necessary to pile up additional matter fifteen feet thick in order to obtain the required level. On one side of the embankment, the bog, when I visited the place, had swollen up in a ridge forty feet long, and eight feet high, the upper portion consisting of peaty matter traversed by numerous willow roots. In the highest part of this upraised mass were several irregular cracks about six feet in their greatest width, and open for a depth of two yards or more. On the opposite side of the railway mound, and about 100 yards distant from it, in the middle of what remained of the half-drained loch, a new island or 'mud lump' was seen, which had begun to rise slowly in 1837, and had attained before 1840 a height of several yards, with a length of about 100 feet, and a width of twenty-five feet. It was still strewed over with dead fresh-water mussels and other shells, but many land plants had already sprung up, so that its surface was green. . . . . We need feel no surprise at the quantity of gaseous matter disengaged from cracks in these newly raised islands, when we recollect that almost everywhere in Europe, where a successful Artesian boring has been made, the water at first spouts up to a height far beyond that to which it would be carried by simple hydrostatic pressure. A portion of the propelling force usually consists of atmospheric air and carbonic acid gas, which last is generated by the decomposition of animal and vegetable matter. Of the latter there must be always a great store in the recent deposits of a delta like that of the Mississippi, as they enclose much drift timber at all depths, and the pent-up gaseous matter will be ready to escape wherever the overlying impervious clays are upheaved and rent."—*Spectator*.

The Rose.

How various are the associations of the Rose, once sacred to Venus as the queen of beauty, and afterwards the token of hostile faction, the signal for bloodshed and cruelty, adopted by the contending houses of York and Lancaster; and ever since retained in the royal badge of our United Kingdom, along with Scotland's thistle and the shamrock of Ireland. The diadem of our Queen is a circle on the rim of which figure these three floral emblems, all springing from one stem.

It was at the battle of Tewkesbury, fought in 1471, which brought to an end that great struggle, commonly called "the Wars of the Roses." By the marriage of the victorious Earl of Richmond, Henry VII., with Elizabeth, daughter of Edward IV., the families were reconciled, and the roses which had so long been the badge of war, became also united, and continued the emblem of the house of Tudor.

The rose is acknowledged by all to be the unrivalled queen of flowers, and is one of the few blossoms cherished alike for its loveliness and perfume. It is the favourite flower of all lands, the flower of love and beauty, over which poets of all ages have profusely lavished their loudest and sweetest verses in its praise. It is said to owe its beautiful blush tinge to Venus, who wandering through the woods in despair for the loss of Adonis, trod on its leaves with her bleeding, thorn-wounded feet. It is perhaps the only flower that retains its fragrance after death,—

> "Because its breath
> Is rich beyond the rest, and when it dies,
> It doth bequeath a charm to sweeten death."

And again Shakspeare tells us,—

> "The rose looks fair, but fairer we it deem
> For that sweet odour which doth in it live;
> The canker-blooms have full as deep a dye
> As the perfumed tincture of the roses,
> Hang on such thorns, and play as wantonly,
> When summer's breath their masked buds discloses.
> But, for their virtue only is their show,
> They live unmoved, and unrespected fade;
> Die to themselves, sweet roses do not so;
> Of their sweet deaths are sweetest odours made."

The sweet-brier rose—*rosa rubiginosa*—is the true Eglantine of our poets, and though its flowers possess not the sweet scent of our cultivated varieties, it excels them in the perfume of its leaves.

> "Come, gentle air! and while the thickets bloom,
>   Convey the jasmine's breath divine;
> Convey the woodbine's rich perfume,
>   Nor spare the sweet-leaved eglantine."

But for it we must search in the rich and beautiful hedges that border our sunny green lanes, where its small, deep flushed blossoms and fragrant foliage easily distinguish it from the larger flowers of the common dog-rose—*rosa canina*—that even in winter can boast of beauty.

> "Though of both leaf and flower bereft,
> Some ornaments to me are left—
> Rich store of scarlet hips is mine."

Chaucer calls it,—

> "The swete bramble floure,
> That bereth the red hepe."

There is an old-fashioned cultivated variety of the English rose, beautifully streaked with white and red, called the "York and Lancaster Rose," because considered emblematical of the union. The origin of the moss rose, as explained by a German writer, is full of beauty. He tells us how an angel slept one day beneath a rose tree, and in gratitude for the sweet shade it had afforded, threw over the blossoms a veil of moss, and thus endowed it with an additional grace.— *Golden Hours*, for September.

PARROTS, COCKATOOS, &c.

I have undertaken to tell you a little about the experiment that has been tried here of letting parrots fly wild about the place; but, though it has been a source of great interest and amusement to us, I much fear that there is very little to relate that could be thought worthy of the attention, even in their holiday moments, of an association for the advancement of science. Nor can I honestly say that the attempt to acclimatise these birds—that is to say, to establish them as an addition to our English fauna—has in that respect been attended by success. It is true that they have several times made nests, and on five of these occasions the young ones have been brought to maturity; and, "were it not for those vile guns," the birds would flourish extremely, for illness and death from natural causes would seem to be almost unknown among them. But, unhappily, they share in many of the characteristics of human nature, and in this one above all, that they do not know when they are well off, and every now and then they are seized with a desire to see the world, and take flight to a distance, twelve or fifteen miles perhaps, and sometimes much more; and then they are almost sure to fall a prey to some gamekeeper or lad who is keeping crows off, and who is astonished by seeing these brilliant apparitions among the trees. As regards their breeding, a pair of cockatoos led the way by most unsuccessfully attempting to make a nest in one of the chimneys; but before it was half finished it gave way, and the nest and cockatoos fell to the bottom. It being summer time, they were only discovered after spending a day and a night among the soot. When they were brought out they looked like two dwarf chimney sweeps. They persevered, however, and made another nest in one of the boxes that had been hung against the gables of the house, in hopes of such an event; but though they laid two eggs, and the hen cockatoo sat most perseveringly till September, it was all in vain; the eggs were addled. Afterwards a pair of green parrots—a cock of the Amazonian, and a hen of the Honduras breed—made a nest in one of the boxes, and brought up a young one; but when he was nearly fledged one of the cockatoos thought it right to murder him. The year after, the same pair brought up two children, and it was really a beautiful sight to see the family party flying about, always together, and living on the most loving terms; but the mother and her eldest son both unhappily were shot. Afterwards, one of the common white cockatoos, and the hen Leadbeater (a very large rose-coloured cockatoo), dug out their own nest in the rotten branch of an acacia tree, laid two eggs, and brought up the young birds. These hybrids are very handsome, but do not resemble either of the parents, having very beautiful crests of a red orange colour; otherwise they are perfectly white. The parent birds were so pleased with the success of this experiment, that last year they repeated it, and brought up three young ones, thus making up a flock of seven with the two first born. Unluckily, one of them was shot at in the winter, and came home severely wounded; after which the other birds would not permit him to associate with them, and he always lived in a bush near the house, quite apart from the rest. One day I moved him into the garden, upon which some of the other cockatoos—not, however, his own relations—fell upon him the moment my back was turned, and killed him. One of those traits of character which, as I said just now, these birds, and in fact most wild animals, share with human nature, is their general dislike of cripples. Another of them was also injured, so I took him away to Surrey, where, in spite of his broken wing and broken leg, an old cockatoo befriended him, and treated him as her own son. This year we hoped that the same pair would have nested again; but unluckily a pair of grey parrots anticipated them in the possession of the hollow branch, and, having made a nest in it, brought up two young grey parrots, which are afflicted with the most awful temper. The maternal instinct of another pair of grey parrots took a very absurd form. This year a cat made her lodging in one of the nest boxes, and brought up her kittens in it; and two of the grey parrots, who had not been industrious enough to lay eggs and have a family of their own, were seized with the idea that these kittens were their children. They kept up a constant warfare with the old cat, and whenever she left the box one of them used to get in and sit with the kittens; and they were constantly in close attendance, even when the mother cat was at home. When the cockatoos I have spoken of had their nest in the acacia tree, it was very ridiculous to see the extravagant interest taken in the matter by the others of the same species. They used to sit most of the day on the branches, just above the nest, and whenever the parent bird flew out, she was attended by a troop of the others, screaming horrible acclamations in her honour. There is an immense deal of originality about this race of birds. They have none of the commonplace, humdrum mediocrity. Their curiosity is unbounded, and they evidently look on man and his doings with the keenest interest, mingled with surprise, and with perhaps just a *soupçon* of contempt. There is, moreover, strongly-marked individual character amongst them. No two of them behave in exactly the same manner. I think the large white cockatoo with the broad white crest is the most intelligent of the lot. I had one of them whom I wished to keep chained to a perch, but, though a first-rate London blacksmith tried everything his ingenuity could suggest, the cockatoo beat him utterly. Without breaking it, he contrived to open the ring, or other instrument for holding him, with his beak, though one or two of them must, one would have thought, have required real study to understand.—*From a paper read by Mr. C. Baxter before the British Association.*

The Game Laws.

In the Biological Section of the British Association a paper was read by Mr. A. Newton on the "Zoological Aspect of the Game Laws." Mr. Newton argued that great advantage had arisen from the attention of the public having been called to the question. The most effectual protection to animals was that afforded by public opinion. A most striking instance of its influence was that presented by the fox. Not much more than a century ago the British farmer was only induced to permit the galloping of horses and hounds over his corn by the reflection that they were doing him a great service in ridding him of a pestilent marauder, and he would hear with grim satisfaction that the scourge of his wife's henroost had been run into, or he would willingly at a vestry meeting pass the churchwardens' accounts giving awards for the destruction of a vixen and her cubs among other so-called vermin. Now-a-days the British farmer was generally in the first flight of the horsemen, and the fox had no friend so staunch. A similar change with regard to other wild animals was most desirable. The public should feel that they had an interest in the protection of wild animals, especially during the season of reproduction. The decrease of these animals, however, was often attributed to secondary causes, and not to direct slaughter. Man had no great spite against the bustard or the great copper-fly, but both had been extirpated within living memory, the latter probably owing to the drainage of the fens. Both, however, might possibly have been preserved by a little judicious care. At any rate, if the progress of civilisation unconsciously demanded some few victims, we should abstain from wilfully adding to their number. Mr. Tristram contended, at the last meeting of the Association, that birds of prey were the sanitary police of nature, and that if they had existed in their original strength they would have stamped out the grouse disease, just as the Orders in Council stamped out the cattle plague. The hawk, by preference, made sickly birds its quarry. In Norfolk there was no moor game, and therefore no grouse disease. But he would ask the game preservers of the county whether they really believed that their stock of pheasants and partridges was materially increased by the destruction of everything which they were pleased to call vermin. He believed that the abundance of game had but little to do with the scarcity of birds of prey, and could declare that in some foreign countries the existence of numerous birds of prey was a pledge of the plentifulness of game. Owls were undoubtedly the game preserver's best friend. His most serious foe was the rat, and the owl consumed more rats and mice than any other description of food. So with regard to polecats, stoats, and weasels. With reference to sea-fowl, he confessed a certain amount of sentiment. No animals were so cruelly persecuted. At the breeding season they came to our shores, throwing aside their weary and suspicious habits, and sometimes settling far inland. No one had ever complained of them as injurious, as raising the price of herrings, sprats, or oysters; yet excursion trains conveyed the sportsmen of London to Lancashire, the Isle of Wight, and Flamborough Head for the purpose of destroying these harmless birds. Each bird shot was a parent, and its young were thus exposed to death by starvation. Could men blaze away hour after hour at those wretched birds without being morally the worse for it? We thanked God that we were not as Spaniards, gloating over the brutality of bull-fights, forgetting the agony inflicted on thousands of innocent birds on our coasts, to which that of a dozen horses and bulls in a ring was as nothing. Mr. Newton then referred to the enormous demand for the feathers of the white gull by the modern fashion of ladies' hat-plumes, and almost electrified his fair hearers by informing them that every lady wearing one of these feathers bore upon her forehead the brand of a murderer. He then advocated the legislative appointment of a "close time," to be proclaimed by the local authorities, during which the mere carrying of a gun should be an offence. This plan, he said, had been adopted in several countries, including some of the most democratic. The question was one wholly unconnected with party politics, and it should be so regarded. If the present state of things continued much longer, changes would occur with regard to our *fauna* for which we should receive few thanks from our posterity.

Sea and Land.

There is a theory that the present arrangement of sea and land is the result of glacial action, produced by the procession of the equinoxes, which operates so as to transfer from pole to pole the centre of gravity or attraction by means of vast accumulations of ice and snow at either alternately, through a long period of time called the great year, which is divided into the great summer and winter, each continuing, according to Adhemar, for 10,500 years. "During the whole of this period one of the poles has continually had shorter winters and longer summers than the other. It follows that the pole which submits to the long winter undergoes a gradual and continuous cooling, in consequence of which the quantities of ice and snow, which melt during the summer, are more than compensated by that which is again produced in the winter. The ice and snow go on accumulating from year to year, and finish at the end of the period by forming, at the coldest pole, a sort of mist or cap, voluminous, thick, and heavy enough to modify the spheroidal form of the earth. This modification, as a necessary consequence, produces a notable displacement of the centre of gravity, or—for it amounts to the same thing—of the centre of attraction, round which all the watery masses tend to restore it." The South pole, it is believed, finished its great winter in 1248 B.C., when nearly all the southern hemisphere was covered by the watery masses. About that date, however, began the great winter of the northern hemisphere, and is still progressing. M. Mangin says, "Our pole goes on getting cooler continually; ice is being heaped upon snow, and snow upon ice, and in 7,388 years the centre of gravity of the earth will return to its normal position, which is the geometrical centre of the spheroid. Following the immutable laws of central attraction, the southern waters accruing from the melted ice and snows of the South pole will return to invade and overwhelm once more the continents of the northern hemisphere, giving birth to new continents, in all probability, in the southern hemisphere." The glacial epoch, according to Mr. Wake, consists of several periods, each of which has its maximum point of cold, " but during only one of these periods the accumulation of ice attains so great a height as to result in the change of the earth's centre of gravity, and the consequent submergence and elevation of vast tracts of land." This view extends the range of the glacial changes beyond the time allowed in the original hypothesis of Adhemar, and it is the opinion of Mr. Croll that while "the period of maximum cold must have been somewhere about 200,000 or 210,000 years ago, the eccentricity of the earth's orbit will for more than 100,000 years remain too low to allow of that vast accumulation of ice at the poles which marks a glacial epoch." The connection of the glacial theory of the distribution of sea and land with the presumed antiquity of man on the face of the earth is indicated in the following manner. There is an opinion supported by innumerable facts that man existed in the southern hemisphere previous to the formation of the Indian Ocean about the beginning of the tertiary period. If this opinion be well founded, as it seems to be, Mr. Wake thinks that man cannot have originated less than 200,000 years ago, or previous to the last glacial epoch, during which the continent now occupied by the waters of the Indian Ocean was submerged.—*London Review*, Sept. 12.

THE BOMBYX YAMA-MAI SILKWORM.

"Some of your numerous readers may, perhaps, feel interested in hearing some account of this new silkworm. This remarkably fine and beautiful silk-producing species, imported from Japan, has obtained great favour amongst our entomologists and sericulturists. Its great size and highly attractive beauty, together with the facility with which its food is procurable, at once claim for it the attention of all persons interested in the study of natural history or the cultivation of silk. The larvæ or caterpillars feed wholly upon oak-leaves, preferring the well-matured ones. The eggs are hatched from about the 25th April to the 3rd or 4th of May, just as the leaves are expanding, and with due care are fed to their full size by the beginning of July, when they commence spinning their silken cocoons, almost invariably among the terminal leaves of the projecting twigs. The male moths are larger than the females, the expansion of their wings being generally $6\frac{3}{4}$, those of the females $5\frac{1}{4}$in. They vary in the ground colouring from yellow, salmon, fawn to dun, and the markings upon the wings are very rich and beautiful. The insect is well worth rearing, if only for the sake of its extreme beauty and size, as an object of natural history. As regards the silk, it is much more valuable than that of Bombyx Cynthia, the Ailanthus Glandulosa feeder. Anybody may rear it. It will endure a great degree of cold. Dr. Wallace, the famous Bombyx Cynthia grower, in a letter to me, says: 'It will certainly be a greater boon than Bombyx Cynthia, since the food-plant is more abundant, and the silk more valuable. It is not, however, a tender insect, but hardy as regards cold, and my own experience tells me that it does not succeed in a temperature above 80° or thereabouts. My worms were exposed last spring to 32° and lower for a whole week without effect.' George Gascoyne, Esq., of Newark, says in the 'Entomologist' of October, 1867: 'I have found it so easy to manage, that with such an abundance of food-plant on every hand, there seems no reason why it should not be extensively and profitably cultivated in this country. The temperature, as a rule, varied from 65° to 70°.' This gentleman was very successful in rearing a lot of fine insects last summer. The moths emerged from the cocoons from the 20th to the 30th of August, and produced a number of fertilized eggs, which, without doubt, he will turn to good account this season. Our oak-woods would become very valuable property if this species of silk-worm were properly attended to, for the cultivation of silk; and, in addition thereto, a new field of operation would be opened up for the working classes."

In order to further these objects, Dr. Wallace, Colchester, Essex, has imported large numbers of the eggs from Japan, in order to supply any person disposed to rear the worms, and produce the silk in this country. The doctor has incurred considerable expense, and, therefore expects a remittance when he sends eggs to applicants. Thirteen postage stamps ensure a dozen; twenty-five stamps thirty of these famous eggs. I thought by making this statement persons would be instructed what to do in making their application. I consider that no time should be lost, as the period for hatching is fast approaching. The doctor sends printed instructions with the eggs as regards management, and I shall be happy to advise any person myself respecting their proper treatment.—Yours, &c., ABRAHAM EDMUNDS, Cemetery House, Ashwood Road, in *Berrow's Worcester Journal*.

LUMINOUS METEORS.

At the meeting of the British Association, Mr. A. Glaisher brought up a report on luminous meteors. It stated that the atlas of star showers, of which a few charts were last year exhibited to the association at Dundee, had been completed, and as it might now be obtained by members at a small cost it was hoped that observations of shooting stars would continue to acquire extension and improvement, so that the connection at present shown to exist between shooting stars and comets would be confirmed by the directions and facilities to observers by their use. In addition to the radiant points described in the atlas as first observed in the Northern hemisphere by Dr. Heis and Mr. Gregg, a similar list of radiant points of star showers in the Southern hemisphere is published by Dr. Heis, from the observations of shooting-stars recorded at Melbourne between the years 1858 and 1863 by Dr. Neumayer. A complete meteoric survey of the heavens, with a view to determining the most obvious points of radiation, is thus already terminated, and brought, at least provisionally, to a satisfactory conclusion. With respect to the meteoric shower of November, 1867, the report stated that, although the unfavourable state of the sky prevented observations of the meteors, yet they were well observed in America on the morning of the 14th of November, and they proved to be nearly as abundant as in the previous year. At Hawkhurst, in Kent, a party of observers watched occasionally until midnight, and afterwards with intervals until 6 o'clock a.m. The sky was clear until 10 p.m., and the moon so bright that only one or two stars of the first magnitude could be seen. One meteor only was observed. The atmosphere then became foggy, and drift clouds passed across the moon. At 12.15 the fog had increased so much that the moon could scarcely be seen, and the sky continued to become more overcast until 2 a.m. At about 2h. 5m. a large meteor, comparable to the moon in brilliancy, shot from between Castor and Pollux in a comparatively clear space to the north, under Ursa Major. It left a streak which was perceptible in the space between the clouds. Two or three meteors were observed in gleams among the clouds. At 6 a.m. the clouds became impenetrable, and observations were discontinued. Coming to the meteoric shower of August, 1868, the report stated that at Beeston Observatory, at Nottingham, the paths of 26 meteors were recorded, and some 20 others were counted by Mr. Lowe during two hours 30 minutes—from 9.30 p.m. until midnight—on the evening of the 9th. The meteors were most abundant between 10 and 10.15 p.m., and there were several points of divergence—one in the sword-handle of Perseus, and another slightly north of and above Cassiopœia accounted for the most of the meteors. All were blue (mostly, intensely blue) or colourless, and nearly all left streaks, were very rapid, and vanished instantaneously. One very remarkable meteor in the sword-handle of Perscus appeared and disappeared without moving, like a blue of distant lightning, not more than 40 min. in diameter. The Auguet shower of 1868 surpassed that of previous years in accuracy of radiation (having fewer radiants) and in green, yellow, and orange meteors, making it less confused in appearance, and conspicuously different from that in 1866. The radiant at ϵ Cassiopœia produced nearly the same proportion of meteors as on the 8th and 12th of August, 1867. The proportion of stars of the first and second magnitude was nearly the same as in 1867, while the rate of frequency in 1868 was nearly double that of 1867, and nearly agreed with that in 1866. Some of the largest meteors of the shower were observed soon after midnight of the 10th. Two meteors seen at Cambridge described curves. Attention had been chiefly confined to determining the radiant point from paths of meteors principally close to Cassiopœia. The point appears to be as nearly as possible R.A. 2h. 16m., N.P.D. 36 deg. They always came several at a time, and then a pause. Those that came together were usually in the same part of the heavens.

ELEPHANT HUNTING.

Signalling to the men that I saw the elephants, I descended from my observatory, and, having looked to the guns, took the breech-loader Rigby 10 in my own hands, and gave Moloka the gum-tickler, telling him to keep close to me, and on no account to fire himself. One of the other guns was carried by Chinsoro, and a fourth by one of Maramia's men, who would accompany me, though I asked him and his two companions to remain at the tree.

Taking the lead, I approached the elephants, Moloka at my heels. There was not a breath of air, so I went straight at them. Soon their dusky forms appeared through the long grass, and in a minute or two I was within eight yards of one. Observing that they were standing in a crescent, and that the right-hand one was the one to which I was so close, I went down on my hands and knees, and moved cautiously a few yards to my left. Looking round as I did so, I observed Moloka like a snake in my wake, but Chinsoro and the other man had disappeared. My other two guns were gone! However, there was no room for retreat, I knew Moloka had the infallible gum-tickler, and I felt I could depend on him. Surely the man who but a short time since had said, "If master die Moloka die too," would not desert me now! Slowly raising my head, I at once saw the state of things. Within fourteen yards of my right stood one of the herd, three parts on to me. Another was a few yards on his right, and within the same distance. Two were standing straight on to me, about fifteen yards off, and directly in front, while the fifth was within twelve yards of my left, with its back towards me. Raising myself quickly to my full height, I dropped the elephant on my extreme right with the temple shot, and the second barrel played a similar game with the one next him. In an instant the faithful Moloka thrust the gumtickler into my hands. At that moment the elephant on my extreme left, thunderstruck at the sudden row, turned round to see what was the cause of it. The gumtickler roared, and the huge beast fell, shot in the brain through the forehead, a little below the level of the ear. Moving, as I lowered the gun, to get clear of the smoke from such a large charge, which hung in the still atmosphere, I perceived one of the two elephants which I knew were in front of me, in full charge with coiled trunk. I knew I had but one shot left, and I determined to let him get close before firing. However, I overshot the mark a little, for as I fired, having aimed at the forehead, straight for the brain, I was suddenly sent head over heels, and the gun flew from my hands. For a moment I fancied all was up, but as soon as I could recover myself I sat up, and saw the monster prostrate within a couple of yards of me, his tusks buried deep in the soil.

I often still laugh when I remember how I examined my legs and arms, especially my right arm, to see if there were any broken bones; but, thank goodness! all proved sound. Moloka assisted to lift me on my legs again, having previously picked up the gun; but, alas! the stock of the favourite was smashed in two.

On going up to the animal I found the bullet-hole in the right place, and about two inches above it the gauge of the gumtickler was stamped on his forehead, the hair as well as the skin being fairly cut against the muzzle of the great gun by the force of the blow. I discovered that I had let him come too close, having probably misjudged the impetus of his charge, and that ere I had time to lower the gun he fell, though dead, against it, and thus bowled me over, and broke my favourite weapon.—Faulkener's *Elephant Haunts*.

Change on the Moon's Surface.

Mr. W. R. Birt read a paper "On the Extent of the Evidence of Change on the Moon's Surface." The author remarked that the two opposite questions of fixity of, or change on, the moon's surface must be decided by observation and not assertion. With regard to evidence on the question of fixity, such evidence—resulting from observation and not including theoretical considerations—must, he said, be exceedingly scanty. Indeed, it is difficult to conceive how the unalterable state of the surface of our satellite can be determined by observation; for if, as has been asserted, "all changes on the moon's surface have ceased myriads of ages ago," we are certainly destitute of the records of the observation of the real state of that surface at so remote a period, and even if "fixity" of the more minute details be really established at any one point by a long series of observations, it would be no argument for its universal prevalence, since a state of quiescence might be attained at very different epochs in different regions. The author next proceeded to examine the question of change, and glanced at the attempts to perpetuate a knowledge of the moon's surface by means of maps, drawings, and topographical descriptions, remarking that it is by the study of details that a definite answer must be given. These details are numerous, embracing mountains, valleys, plains, craters, rings apparently nearly filled, bright spots as mountain tops, and others less bright, but presenting phenomena difficult of explanation, dark spots with bright rings or bounded by distinct lines separating them from the surrounding surface. All such subjects must be carefully studied before a conclusion can be drawn as to their unalterable stability or their mutation. The means of obtaining evidence on these points consists in the examination of delineations and topographical notices on the one hand, and comparing them with the moon by personal observation of the objects on the other. Mr. Birt referred to a diagram, giving two aspects of the same spots. One as given—lighter than some surrounding objects—by three authorities, Lohrmann, Beer, and Mädler and Schmidt; the other, as observed by himself at a recent date, in which the spot is darker than all surrounding objects. In connection with these differences of colour, he put the question, "Can we decide for change?" In reply, he pointed out one great disadvantage—namely, the uncertainty of the number of observations on which the earlier records rest, and showed the great importance, not only of increasing our own observations, but also of soliciting the aid of others, that there may be no want of confirmatory evidence to establish the certainty of what is recorded. In the absence of confirmatory observations, Mr. Birt considered that the evidence capable of being brought to bear on questions of change is very limited, especially as former records are more or less open to be regarded as inexact drawings or inaccurate statements when they happen to differ from present observed appearances.

Human Races.

Two schools of anthropologists have laid their views prominently before the world: the physical, and the philological. The first dwell principally on the external form and anatomical peculiarities of man, as affording a true index of the system of classification to be pursued. The second consider physical peculiarity of less importance than language as an indication of the origin and filiation of races.

Man's mind being constituted in harmony with his body, the peculiarities common to each in individuals show an analogy; this renders clear that there is a connecting link between physiological and philologica comparative anthropology. For language as an operation of mind must in its varieties harmonise with physical peculiarities if rightly understood, otherwise the body would not be a type of the mind. Language being only one operation of mind, although the expression or type of many, should not in systems for the classification of races occupy exclusive attention; but it should be most carefully studied as one of the most important products of the action of mind. In systems of classification it is usual to give the first place to those individuals, parts or divisions, which are most highly organised. The mind or director of man should surely receive a higher position than his mere physical portion, for it includes and indicates by its characteristics those of his entire being.

If the human races classed physically are primarily divisible into three grand divisions—the Semitic-Indo-European, the Mongolian, and the Ethiopian—the races viewed mentally may be justly classified as the moral, intellectual, and the passionate; which last division would include the Mongolian and Ethiopian races.

The Semitic-Indo-European is variously subdivisible into branches specially characterised by the predominance of the moral or intellectual faculties, or both. The Greeks, for example, are a highly intellectual race, but are relatively deficient in the moral sentiments. The Arabs, Jews, and the purer branches of the Semitic race, have been in all ages distinguished by the powers and activity of their moral and religious faculties. I shall call them the moral subdivision of the moral-intellectual race. The inhabitants of Western Europe, the Teutonic especially, possess the moral and intellectual faculties in due proportion to each other; they are distinguished as religious yet highly intellectual peoples. I call them the moral-intellectual subdivision of the great moral-intellectual family; yet they possess a large share of the propensities which predominate in the great passionate family: these strengthen their moral and intellectual faculties, and render them the ruling race, for they possess in a larger degree than any the qualities of all races.

The passionate family is divided into two sub-divisions—the motive or mechanical, and avaricious and the domestic. The Mongolic race belongs to the first sub-division, and the Ethiopian to the second.—From *Miscellanea Anthropologica*, 3 Essays by C. O. Groom Napier, F.G.S.

COMETS AND METEORS.

The second discovery to which we allude, and which is scarcely over a year old, is the connection between comets and luminous meteors. It has been found in late years that meteors course through space in swarms or streams, and that these streams circulate in orbits around the sun. Comets, too, as every one knows, move in orbits of various forms and dimensions. Astronomers know comets by the paths they move in. When a comet appears the astronomer observes and calculates its path, and he thus finds whether it is an old or a new visitor. Now about a year ago Professor Schiapperelli, an Italian astronomer, was engaged upon investigating the courses of meteor streams; he had calculated the orbit of that stream which we encounter every tenth of August, and which gives rise to Saint Lawrence's fiery tears; and when he had perfected his calculation, and got out the set of figures that represented the orbit, he found, marvellous to relate, that these agreed precisely with those referring to a comet which visited our skies in the year 1862. It was clear, then, that the meteors and the comet move in the same orbit. Here was a wonderful coincidence; but it might be accidental. Such, however, was not the case. While Schiapperelli was at work upon the August meteor stream, Professor Peters, a German astronomer, was engaged upon that of November, and he found that the orbit of this coincided with that of a comet which appeared at the beginning of the year 1866. Further confirmation came from other quarters. Professor Adams, independently calculating the orbit of the November meteors, corroborated Professor Peters' result, and several other coincidences were established by other astronomers.

No doubt can exist, therefore, that some kind of physical relation exists between comets and meteors. Considering that comets have been known to dissipate or waste away in the course of years, it has been conjectured that meteors are fragments of cometary matter left by the comet upon the track it has passed over; and if this be the case, it is clear that when we have a meteor shower we are penetrating the trail of a comet. We may not unreasonably expect that some day we shall meet a comet itself—perhaps, indeed, we have done so ere this. What will be the result? Superstition would say the collapse of the world; but science knows better. She knows that a comet, formidable as it looks, is, as it were, a sheep in wolf's clothing; she knows that when one once got entangled with Jupiter and his satellites the planet suffered nothing, while the poor comet got bewildered and flew off into another orbit like a frightened child; and she knows that such is the smallness of the mass of a comet that a collision of one with the earth would be but as the collision of a bird with an express train. So she thinks that if we ever do come foul of a comet, we shall experience—a brilliant meteoric shower, and nothing more.—*Cassell's Magazine* for September.

THE COCKROACH.

The cockroach iz a bug at large. He is one ov the luxuries of civilization. He is easy to domestikate, yielding as gracefully to ordinary kindness, and never deserting those who show him acts of courtesy. Let the learned and polite pull hair az much az they please about the ansestral claims ov the cockroach, it iz our bizzness and dooty as bug scrutinizer, to show the critter up az we find him, without caring ho hiz grandfather or grandmother aktually was. Thare iz no mistaking the fakt that he iz one ov a very numerous family, and that hiz late attachment to the home of hiz boyhoyd speaks louder than thunder for his affectionate and unadulterated natur. He don't leave the place he wuz born at upon the slightest provokation like a giddy and vagrant flea, or the ferocious bed-bug, and until death (or sum vile pouder the invenshun of man) knocks at hiz front door, he and his brothers with sisters may be seen with the naked eye, ever and anon calmly climbing the sugar-bowl, or running foot-races between the plates. How strange it iz that man, made out ov dirt, the cheapest material in market, and the most plenty, shud be determined to rid the world of every living bug but himself. I don't doubt if he could hav his own way for six years, every personal cockroach would be knocked off from the bosom ov the footstool, and not even a single pair of them left to repair damages with. Such iz man. The cockroach is born on the fust day of May and the fust of November semi-annually, and iz ready for use in fifteen days. They are born from an egg, four from each egg, and consequently they are all ov them twins. There is no such thing in the annals ov natur as a single cockroach. The maternal bug don't sett upon the egg as the gose doth, but leaves them lie around lose, like a pint ov split mustard-seed, and don't seem to care whether tha ripe or not. But I never nu a cockroach-egg fail tu put in an appearance. They are as sure teu hatch out and run as Kanada thistles or a bad kold. The cockroach is of tew colors, sorrel and black. They are alwus on the move and kan trot, I should say, on a good track, and a good day, cluss to three minutes. Their food seems to consist, not quite so much in what they ate as what they travel; and, often finding them dead in mi coup at the boarding-house; I have already quite cum to the conclusion that the cockroaches can't swim, but they can float. But the most interesting feature of this remarkable bug is the luvliness of thare natures. They kan't bite nor sting, nor skretch, nor even jaw-back. They are so amiable that I have known them to get struck in the butter, and lay there all the day and not holler for help, and then aktually die at last with a broken down heart. To realize the meekness of these uncomplaining little fellers, let the philosophic mind just for one moment compare them to the pesky flea, who lites up man in hiz strength and woman in her weakness like a redd-hot shot, or to the warbling musketo, wild from a Nujersy cat-tail-marsh, with hiz dagger in his mouth ackeing for blood; or, horror of horrors, to the midnight bed-bugg, who creeps out ov a crack az still and az lean az a shadow, and hitches on to the bosom ov buty like a starved leech.—*Josh Billings.*

Correspondence.

[Under this head we shall be glad to insert any letters of general interest.]

A FEW GENERAL REMARKS UPON THE SEXES OF BIRDS, ETC.

Sir,—As your correspondent "A. M. B." asks for assistance from others interested in the study of ornithology, in order to clear up a little discrepancy that has appeared in reference to the common gallinule, or water-hen, I herewith venture a few remarks, which, although not confined to that species in particular, may yet prove useful to some of your junior ornithologists, by preventing too hasty a decision upon the sexes of the feathered race resulting from the size, colour, or general appearance of a specimen. First, I would observe that among the smaller species of birds the nestlings more commonly assume the plumage of the parent hen, irrespective of their own sexes; and where a striking difference in plumage exists between the parent birds this change generally takes place with the first moulting, which in most cases occurs toward the close of the same year that the young are hatched. Again, there are cases where the young birds are so unlike the parent birds, that in earlier times they were regarded as distinct species. Such was the fact with the common starling. The young of these birds were represented as the brown starling, or solitary thrush; and the young of the large spotted woodpecker was described as the *Picus medius*, or middle spotted woodpecker. The common robin is an example where the young birds differ materially from the parent birds, and likewise an instance where the first moulting gives so similar an appearance to both sexes, that it is somewhat difficult to decide which is the male bird; while the song-thrush, nightingale, skylark, etc., undergo but little change in plumage from the nestling state to the end of their lives, and have no very striking feature whereby to determine the sex. As it regards the difference in size found to exist among birds of the same species I believe there is no general rule, as in birds of prey the female is not unfrequently the largest bird, while among the Gallinaceous tribe the reverse is as frequently met with; yet in the greater number of species it is often more the result of age, condition, or plumage, than from any standard or ruling character connected with the species. We will now leave these inhabitants of our fields and woods, and take a hasty glance at the aquatic species, namely, the waders, swimmers, and divers in the watery element. It is obvious that anything like a knowledge of the habits, manners, and changes of plumage in this tribe of birds must of necessity be gathered from various resources, as no man, however favourable his position, could become thoroughly and practically acquainted with all the details in reference to the various birds included under the general term of Water Bird. Of wild fowl we learn that most, if not all, of this order make their first appearance in a clothing of down, and are several years before they attain their full adult plumage; also that many of them are favoured with a summer as well as a winter dress; added to which, some undergo slow and partial moulting to alter or improve their appearance, at various periods of the year: all these circumstances have been somewhat perplexing to the ornithologist when dealing with the aquatic species. However, the great progress made in ornithological researches and investigation during the last half century has removed many of the errors of past times, and will, doubtless, like the plumage of the birds, in a few years become more fully and plainly developed.

With regard to the common gallinule, or water-hen, I may say that a great number of them have come under my notice throughout a series of years, and from the most careful attention to the variety that they present in size and shades of colour, I am led to conclude that both sexes resemble each other very much in quite the adult state; and that a gradual improvement of the plumage takes place for three years from the exclusion from the egg; and at that period the male would be somewhat smaller than the female, but the plumage rather darker, more rich and glossy, particularly about the head and neck. The plate, or bare part above the bill, becomes a bright red from about the middle of March to the middle of April, ruled in some measure by the state of the season; and no doubt but their eyes are a little more bright and sparkling as the pairing time approaches.

320, Strand.   C. W...D.

MIGRATION OF SWALLOWS.

Sir,—Your correspondent "C. W.," on page 234 of the NATURALIST'S NOTE BOOK, asks, when and where the moulting in the plumage of swallows takes place—"whether under water, in old banks, or under ground?" I answer, "Why in any of these places?" The young birds depart from this country in their nesting plumage, the old ones in the "soiled and worn plumage" they had previous to moulting. This process then takes place, we may rightly conclude, in those foreign parts where they pass the winter. Mr. Austen, page 54, says that the swallows breed in Africa all the winter. If this is the case, the theory of the *breeding stimulus* of Mr. Ulidia and others is overthrown. But do swallows, contrary to the habits of other birds, breed both in winter and summer? Two broods are frequently hatched in this country—do they then rear a third in a foreign land? It is more probable that those individuals who nest there are either permanent residents in that country, or at least that their annual migration is not connected with Great Britain, but with some land—perhaps further south—in which they do not breed. Alluding to the periodical rains of Senegambia, Mr. Austen suggests that repulsion thence, and not attraction hither, causes them to visit us in spring. If this is the case, what should induce so many—if not all—of the swallow tribe to return year after year to the exact places occupied by them during the preceding summer, nay, even to the very nest itself, of which we have numerous well-authenticated instances? Why, indeed, should they come so far north at all, if their only object were to escape drowning in the deluging rains of Senegambia? I think there cannot be a doubt that they are influenced by an ardent *love of home;* that *Britain*, and not Africa, is their home, endeared to them by birth, the choice of a mate, and the rearing of their offspring; and that they would continue to remain with us throughout the whole year, were it not that the decline of temperature and deficiency of food compel them to depart. Over and above all these actions, however, we recognise a *guiding providence*, making use of these natural inducements merely as incentives to the creature to do the will of its Creator, and to perform its part in the great field of Nature.

I am, Sir, yours truly,

Sept. 15th, 1868.   R. B. W.

Short Notes.

THE EARLY INHABITANTS OF AMERICA.—At the meeting of the American Association for the Advancement of Science, recently held in the city of Chicago, many of the papers indicated considerable activity in the researches into the character of the early races of men who inhabited America, and some of the investigators are already inclined to claim that the so-called "New" is really the "Old" World. Colonel Charles Whittlesey, in a paper on the "Geological Evidences of Man's Antiquity in the United States," maintained that four American races preceded the red man : first, the mound-builders ; second, a race in territory now called Wisconsin ; third, a warlike race in the region south of Lakes Ontario and Erie ; and, fourth, a religious people in Mexico. Pottery, arrow-heads, &c., have been found in conjunction with and beneath the mastodon and megatherium. A jaw and tooth were pronounced by Agassiz 10,000 years old. Mr. J. W. Foster, in a paper on the same subject, gave an account of the discovery in a deep gold-drift of California of a skeleton covered by five deposits of lava. He exhibited an arrow-head found in the valley of San Joaquin, thirty feet below the surface. The island of Petite Anse is a solid mass of salt at the mouth of the Mississippi, covered with fourteen feet of earth ; embedded in the salt has been found a piece of petrified matting by the side of a fossil elephant. Human remains have also been found during excavations at New Orleans at a depth of sixteen feet. Mr. Foster exhibited a copper knife found in New Orleans, which he believed was a relic of the mound-builders. A water-jug surmounted by a human head and a statuette of a captive with his hands bound behind him, both from Peru, and evidently of extreme antiquity, attracted much attention: It may also be mentioned that the recent explorations of Mr. E. G. Squiers in Peru, and the curious photographs of ancient temples, dolmens, &c., which he has brought back, have renewed some old theories as to a connection in origin between the earliest inhabitants of America and those of the Oriental countries.—*Scotsman.*

EXTRAORDINARY WATERSPOUTS IN THE PAPAL STATES.—The correspondent of the *Morning Post* writes from Rome :—"The first year of Pio Nono's reign was remarkable for one of the greatest inundations ever known in Rome, but it was in the month of November, and in the natural order of the elements. This year has been signalised by an inundation of the Tiber more remarkable still, on account of its having taken place in the usually arid month of August. It was caused by the discharge of a series of waterspouts over the provinces of Umbria and Sabina, which swelled the tributaries of the Tiber into raging torrents, raised the level of that river at Rome nearly twelve feet in a few hours, and swept down corpses of peasants, carcases of cattle and sheep, haystacks, cottages, wood, trees, palings, and enormous quantities of fruit, especially melons, for which the Valley of Rieti is famous, as that of Terni is for hemp, of which also innumerable bundles were hurried down the furious torrent, offering an unexpected harvest to the riverside Romans, who were out in boats and punts all Thursday and Friday hauling the *débris* of Umbrian and Sabine farms ashore. The take of fish was enormous also. Great depôts of lime, washed from the mountain kilns into the streams, killed quantities of their finny inhabitants, who, floating down the Tiber, were netted and even pulled out by hand in such abundance that the price of fish in Rome on Friday, although a *magro* day, was only a *soldo* a pound. The Ancona line of railway was interrupted in the plain of Terni. Some damage was done to the excavations at the Emporium, on the Tiber bank; but the specific gravity of the valuable blocks of ancient marble recently found there prevented them from being washed away, although one of the workmen was nearly drowned while watching the progress of the flood."

NORTH AUSTRALIA.—Mr. T. Baines, artist to the North Australian Expedition under Mr. Gregory in 1855, and subsequently, in 1858, artist to the Zambesi Expedition under Livingstone, read a paper before the British Association on "the Victoria and Albert Rivers, North Australia." The purport of the paper was to show that the mouth of the Victoria river was unfit for settlement, but that on the higher branches of the river, where there was a fine plain of trap, the soil and productions were more favourable. The other rivers ran towards the interior, and are periodically swelled by heavy rains. In some years they are perfectly dry, so that if an explorer visited the country in the dry season he reported that the country was dry; but if he went after the rains he was likely to find rivers five miles broad, extending into very large lakes. Mr. Gregory went in a dry year, but, being a colonial man and acquainted with Australia, he was able to appreciate the signs that showed him how wide these rivers would be if there happened to have been a flood of rain during the previous season. The Victoria flowed into the sea on the north-west coast, in about 15 deg. S. The upper part of the Victoria passed through a fine trap plain; the lower part for about 100 miles passed through a lower level, in which very good grass farms might be found. Still, as a rule, it would be less healthy for Europeans and more liable to fever. Between that and the Albert river is a high table-land of a very healthy character. The Albert makes rather a short course into the Gulf of Carpentaria. A narrow belt of land, probably 100 miles wide, more or less, extended along the sea coast, watered by rivers of moderate length. When Mr. Gregory travelled there it was a dry year, and he was not able to penetrate into the interior. Since that other explorers had found a dry country, and at other times flowing rivers.

A PLAGUE OF GRASSHOPPERS.—Mr. M. Power, of Fort Garry, Red River Settlement, Hudson's Bay Territory, gives in the *Times* an account of the state of destitution which the settlement has been reduced to through an invasion of grasshoppers, and makes an appeal for aid to obtain corn for food and as seed for the next season. He says:—"The grasshoppers came in swarms of countless millions from the north-west on last harvest, and destroyed a great portion of the grain and nearly the whole of the vegetable crops, and deposited their eggs in the ground an inch and a half deep, so that if you were to dig to that depth you would see the earth covered with their eggs. There never were seen finer crops in England or Scotland than were here last harvest, and this year they appeared equally good up to June, and the season continues beautiful up to this time. The grasshoppers began to hatch about the end of May, and to begin their work of destruction in June, and so complete was it, they would begin on a field of wheat, barley, oats, or potatoes, and leave it as though it were newly ploughed and harrowed, scarcely a weed being left or a particle of anything for the use of mankind. The most beautiful part of our settlement is from Fort Garry to the White Horse Plains, and from there to the Portage, a distance of about sixty miles, runs the deep-flowing Assiniboine, with small farmhouses all along its banks, and with large woods and plains all the way, and in all that distance there is not a fruit or a kernel, or a particle of anything left for the use of mankind."

VESUVIUS.—Letters from Naples report that Vesuvius, so far from being tranquil, has been giving indications of life throughout the summer. A fortnight since a party of foreigners, who are too often indisposed to take advice, resolved on ascending to the summit of the new cone. They had no sooner arrived, however, than they were assaulted by an unexpected shower of pumice and fragments of lava. Several of the party were severely wounded, so much so, indeed, that they could scarcely descend the mountain and obtain the assistance which was necessary to enable them to continue their road to Resina. The latest reports state that Vesuvius increases in activity. Those who venture to ascend to the summit of the new cone, we are told, are presented with a magnificent spectacle, nothing less than a vast lake of boiling lava, which at intervals ejects dense columns of smoke, mingled with ashes and red-hot lava. The enjoyment of this spectacle is not, however, without great danger, as we have already described. The thunders are again loud and often repeated, so that the mountain itself trembles. These shocks are not confined to Vesuvius, but extend to the neighbourhood, and as far as Naples, where on Saturday, the 24th of July, one shock was felt which continued fifteen seconds.—*Scotsman*.

THE SEYCHELLES ISLANDS.—Professor E. Percival Wright gives an account of a visit to the Seychelles Islands, a group of islands situate to the south of the equator, in the Indian Ocean. They are twenty-nine in number, and lay about 950 miles from Mauritius, and about 340 miles from the nearest point of Madagascar. They were probably discovered by Vasco de Gama as early as 1502; in 1742 they were taken possession of by the French, and they eventually received the name of Seychelles Islands, in honour of Viscount de Seychelles. They were colonised mostly by French prisoners during the time of the Revolution, who included members of some of the noblest and best families of France. In process of time many of them married blacks, and their descendants now formed the present inhabitants of the islands. Popular belief placed these islands as the head-quarters of the notorious Captain Kidd, and on nights of Creole festivals stories of great hidden treasures are told as they sit round their fires. In 1794 Commodore Newcome captured the islands, and in 1815 they were definitively ceded to Great Britain. De Quincy, the French Governor, who was very popular in the islands, being allowed to retain his post as Governor until his death. Professor Wright proceeded to describe the size and population of the different islands, their climate and productions, and many interesting particulars relating to the inhabitants.—*Report of British Association.*

CAMPANULA CARPATICA.—As a summer bedding plant, the old blue Campanula carpatica is worthy of a much wider recognition. A hardy perennial, it will do well in almost any situation, but it should not occupy a damp and low position during the winter. It commences to bloom by the beginning of June, and will continue to flower through the summer. The seed-pods should be gathered, as they have an unsightly appearance, and their removal tends to induce the production of fresh flowers. The tufts should be lifted in early spring, divided if necessary, and replanted, using some good soil about the roots. It is invaluable for ribbon borders, and when once tried will not be readily abandoned. There is a so-called variety to be met with in some places, under the name of Bowoodiana, said to be much darker in colour and more branching in the habit than the old variety, and said to have been selected at Lord Lansdowne's seat, at Bowood, Chippenham.—*Florist and Pomologist.*

SPIRAL VESSELS.—The functions of spiral vessels, or of vascular tissue in general, have long been a subject of much controversy, and few matters are of more consequence as regards the real history of the distribution of sap in plants. A very able paper on the subject, to which allusion was made by Dr. Hooker in his address, has been published by Mr. Herbert Spencer (than whom few enter more profoundly into questions of physiology), in the "Transactions of the Linnean Society." By a line of close argument and observation he shows, from experiments with coloured fluids capable of entering the tissues without impairing vitality, and that not only in cuttings of plants but in individuals in which the roots were uninjured, that the sap not only ascends by the vascular tissue, but that the same tissue acts in its turn as an absorbent, returning and distributing the sap which has been modified in the leaves. That this tissue acts some important part is clear from the constancy with which it is produced at a very early stage in adventitious buds, establishing a connection between the tissues of the old and new parts. This appears also from the manner in which in true parasites a connection is established between the vascular tissue of the matrix and its parasite, as shown by our President in his masterly treatise on Balanophoræ, and more recently by Solms-Laubach in an elaborate memoir in Pringsheim's Journal. It is curious that in organs so closely analogous to the tracheæ of insects a similar connection should long since have been pointed out by Mr. Newport, in the case of certain insect parasites.—*From Paper read by Rev. J. M. Berkeley before British Association.*

CONFORMATION OF FLOWERS.—With reference to the Unusual Conformation of Flowers, it has been stated that while an habitually inferior ovary may under these exceptional circumstances be found detached from the calyx, and thus be rendered, as botanists say, "superior," the converse change never occurs. M. Carrière, however, in the last number of the "Revue Horticole" (August 15, p. 310), figures and describes such a case in the Cherry. In this fruit, as every one knows, the calyx is inferior, and the ovary consists of a small leafy carpel, which as it ripens into the fruit becomes stony in the interior and fleshy outside. But in the instance cited by M. Carrière the fruit is wholly inferior, and is surmounted by the five lobes of the calyx; in fact the external appearance is precisely that of a Crab Apple. In the interior was a rudimentary kernel (*noyau*) apparently without any hard "stone" surrounding it. Here, then, we have the upper end of the flower-stalk becoming succulent, as in the Apple, and imbedding within it the carpel. The case is a very important one, as showing the nature of the "disc" of the ordinary Cherry flower, which is clearly no calyx-tube, but a dilatation of the axis, and also as showing the relationship between the drupaceous and pomaceous subdivisions of the Rose family. We earnestly hope that M. Carrière will next season have an opportunity of examining the flowers in various stages of development, and we should not think any the worse of him if he put some of the blossoms at our disposal!—*Gardener's Chronicle,* Aug. 29.

NATIVES OF ABYSSINIA.—Dr. H. Blanc, one of the late Abyssinia captives, in a paper on native Abyssinian races, summed up their character in far from flattering terms, observing :—"Taken as a whole, with the exception of the oppressed and hard-working peasants, there is nothing in them to praise or extol. Beggars infest the land, the priests are ignorant and besotted, the soldiers the curse of the country. Abyssinians, I regret to say, are cowardly, adepts at low treachery, lazy, pretentious, and pompous. Naturally drunkards and gluttons, they are very abstemious by necessity, and their festivals are but low and coarse orgies. They have no literature, no means of recreation. Their conversation is a revolting incoherent talk, partly blasphemous, partly lascivious, and when they favoured us with their society, always ending in requests for favours. When we state that cleanliness is a shame, debauchery no disgrace, robbery, treachery, and murder glorious deeds, we have summed up the qualifications most prized by that degraded race; and if their timorous nature made them recoil before the daring act of murdering the white men, their guests, they enjoyed at least, for a while, the idea of their importance, and swaggered full of pride before the few helpless individuals their King detained in captivity and in chains.

CHICKENS HATCHED BY THE SUN.—An inhabitant of Berlin lately, during the great heat, experimented on the hatching of hens' eggs in sand. On the 22nd July he placed six in a cigar-box filled with that material, and exposed the case to the sun on that and the following days. The first chick broke the shell on the 9th August, the second on the 10th, the third and fourth on the 11th, and the other two on the following day. They are all going on well, being fed on boiled eggs cut up small and mixed with millet. The average period of hatching chickens is twenty-one days; in the present case the first was produced in nineteen.—*Scotsman.*

SALMON CULTIVATION.—Mr. Frank Buckland delivered an extemporaneous address on the progress of salmon cultivation in England before the British Association. He said that the measures already adopted had led to a considerable increase in the quantity of salmon brought into the London market during the last few years, and he hoped that a still greater increase would be the result of further improvements. He promised the English public salmon at a shilling a pound, or even less; but added that if they allowed their rivers to be polluted they might expect to pay two shillings, "and serve them right." He concluded by some remarks on oyster culture, in which he ridiculed the popular notion of over-dredging as the cause of the late failure in the favourite bivalve. Oysters, he said, had bred this year, and there was every prospect in five or six years of their being saleable at 1d. each.

DIAMONDS.—Professor Tennant made a communication to the British Association on the recent discovery of diamonds in Cape Colony. This gem, he stated, had been found somewhat abundantly recently in the above district, and he exhibited the casts of some weighing nine carats, worth £500. Some agate, chalcedony, and other precious stones found in the same deposit had been sent him, but he would have preferred some of the sand and mud in which they were deposited. One diamond, found very recently, weighed as much as 15½ carats. He was of opinion that before long we should have a large collection of diamonds from the above country, adding that although we had heard a great deal of diamonds being found in Australia those stones were not worth now so many pence as pounds had been asked for them.

NAME OF NEST AND EGGS.—A nest and eggs came into my possession (writes a subscriber to the *Field*) to-day quite different from any which I have ever seen, and I have seen the eggs of most of our British birds. Will any reader kindly give me any information about them? The following is a description of them: The nest was found near King's Newton, Derbyshire, by two boys, in a hedgerow of a field in the spring. It is composed externally of dried grasses, fine thin roots, mixed with a very little moss and a few partridge feathers. The eggs are remarkable, being the smallest I ever saw, smaller even than those of the willow warbler, and of an uniform dark brown or olive colour. The nest is large for the size of the eggs.

WHITE BLACKBIRD.—About the middle of last March a blackbird's nest (writes a gentleman in *Land and Water*) was taken in my shrubbery, which contained a white bird, the remainder of the brood being of the usual colour. Unfortunately, previously to my becoming aware of its capture, it had been consigned to the cage of some young people, who of course failed to rear it; I have, however, had it preserved.

THE ISLAND OF ST. JOHN.—The Island of St. John in the Red Sea, the *Ophiodes* of Strabo, according to Dr. Beke, is merely an upraised coral reef with a sharp volcanic peak in the centre. It affords neither water nor vegetable productions. The Author found ample evidence, during his journey there a few years ago, that the land on both coasts of the Red Sea was being gradually elevated by subterranean volcanic influence.—*Scientific Review*, August.

THE LARDER OF A PROVIDENT FOX.—The *Perthshire Journal* gives an account of the unearthing of a large litter of young foxes at Grandtully. The den contained 30 white hares, 20 rabbits, 11 grouse, 1 curlew, 1 plover, 4 lambs, 1 kid, 3 water-rats, and, to crown all, 1 mole! More might be in the cairn, but all the above were laid out and exposed to view, all more or less broken.

WHITE KANGAROO.—One of the most beautiful natural curiosities in the colony is in possession of Mr. Hepburn, of Ballarat. It is a milk-white kangaroo, as tame, docile, and harmless as it is possible for any domestic animal to be.—*Australasian.*

Remarks, Queries, &c.

(*Under this head we shall be happy to insert original Remarks, Queries, &c.*)

DO INSECTS FEEL PAIN?

"That, yet of *organs, functions, sense partake*
Equal with animals of larger make,
A world of beauties! that through all their frame
Creation's grandest miracles proclaim."

M. BROWN.

Your learned correspondents, on the negative side, come out in the shape of a formidable triumvirate, armed with "facts," deduced principally from repeatedly wonderful manipulations in the insect world.

Mr. Spicer is purely negative in his remorseless theory; Mr. Waters, with some portion of sympathy afloat, thinks "they feel extremely little" pain; while Mr. Harvie, with all the feelings of a man, and candour of a philosopher, honestly admits that *it is better to keep on the safe side, and treat insects well; so that, in case they do feel pain, we may be innocent of any charge of cruelty.*"

The question at issue is, Do insects feel pain? Mr. Waters admits they feel "*a little,*" and Mr. Harvie even concedes more, for he says, "it is better to *keep on the safe side,*" &c., &c., and hence those two correspondents, although half inclined to argue negatively, have evidently, from absolute conviction, I presume, arrived with me at an *affirmative* conclusion. This conclusion I expected, this conclusion irresistibly forces itself upon the judgment of reflecting men who "feel for all that live;" for although insects are but humble constituents in the mighty chain of animated creation, yet of the very meanest, we cannot but instinctively exclaim—

"There are glorious things even in the dust."

"But," says Mr. Spicer, throwing down his scalpel, and speaking from the dissecting-room, "insects have no brain;" and says that very eminent man, Sir

Everard Home:—"In insects, *the brain* contains, and its principal portion is connected by, nervous chords, with what is usually termed a ganglion, but which, when examined accurately, is found to resemble the brain in texture: among insects the bee has the largest proportion of brain relative to the size of its body," &c. &c.

What does Mr. Spicer say to this direct contradiction about his brainless animals? Again, says Mr. Spicer, *insects have no blood;* and again says Bowerbank, a most successful microscopist (in the *Entomological Magazine*, vol. i. p. 239) *insects have blood*.

And Professor Carus, a great Continental naturalist, confirms the observations of Bowerbank. Even more, Sir, it has been proved that insects have a *circulating* blood. Let Mr. Spicer lift the *Magazine of Natural History*, vol. vii., and direct his attention to p. 236, and there he will read—"The *circulation* in *annulates* is not, as it is in vertebrates, entirely confined to limited and well-defined vessels; but there is a large wide channel, extending the whole length of the animal, through which *the blood* is constantly *rushing* upwards from the posterior towards the anterior extremity.

"This current is kept in motion by the alternate opening and closing of double valves, distributed at regular intervals throughout its extent: this operation causing a motion, as each portion is afresh impelled upwards, which is precisely equivalent to the pulsations of the heart."

Mr. Spicer says insects have no blood, no brains. Bowerbank, Carus, and others, say insects have blood and brains, but I presume your correspondent will "stick to one sound argument, his own."

Do insects feel pain? No such thing as pain, says the redoubtable Mr. Spicer, for they are bloodless, brainless creatures; but the high authorities I have just cited go far to nullify the arguments he advances. But, independent of all these things, we may safely infer that insects do feel pain.

What is life? Mr. Spicer cannot tell, indeed the greatest philosophers cannot tell; they hesitate, and, like Thales of old, can only say, "We will consider." Paley admits that insects feel pleasure, and thus speaks of it:—"In a spring morn, on whichever side I turn my eyes, myriads of happy beings crowd upon my view; the insect youth are on the wing; swarms of new-born flies are trying their pinions in the air," &c., &c. If we admit that insects feel pleasure, surely we cannot but allow that they must have pain also.

But even Mr. Spicer, "that stoic of the woods—a man without a tear," does absolutely admit that insects feel pain, for he is at length forced to say, "*I grant that insects struggle to get free,*" &c., &c. Undoubtedly, Mr. Spicer, "they struggle to get free," and this should teach you to acknowledge that they love their natural freedom, and that you cause pain to them when you hold them in captivity. Don't flinch from this position, and like Mr. Harvie, you will find yourself on the "safe side."

Mr. Spicer, in order that his insects may die without a groan, quite conveniently denies them the right of feeling pain when they come in the way of an "inadvertent step," or are unexpectedly assailed by a whirlwind of crinoline in the street! I should scarcely reply to this, but as we are aware that insects know how to avoid danger, and for the information of your correspondent, I quote the following from *Insect Architecture* (Introduction), p. 17:—"We find herein examples of instinct to parallel those of all the larger animals, whether they are solitary or social; and innumerable others besides, altogether unlike those manifested in the superior departments of animated nature.

"These instincts have various directions, and are developed in a more or less striking manner to our senses, according to the force of the motive by which they are governed. Some of their instincts have for their object *the preservation of insects from external attack;* some have reference to procuring food, and involve many remarkable stratagems," &c., &c. Even against the change of temperature, instinct prompts insects to provide, so that your correspondent need not be alarmed when his imaginary crinoline torpedo sweeps over a solitary insect traveller in the streets.

Just as well might the inventive genius of Mr. Spicer do away with pain in man, so as to make him meet calmly the dangers of the sea, earthquakes, railway accidents, and the other "ills and calamities of life."

But, among a series of curious things, Mr. Spicer asks a most curious question, and here it] is:—"How," says he, in evident triumph, "ean a moth *pinned against a tree* remain quietly in its place?"(!) Now, suppose a giant, like some of the fabled gods of old, pinned the relentless Mr. Spicer to a tree, how could he remain *in his place?* Is Clifton a sort of *terra incognita*, beyond the influence of the Society for Prevention of Cruelty to Animals? But Mr. Spicer will say he is experimenting, and that his "moth pinned against a tree" feels itself quite at home, but "begins to flap its wings" in the evening, when it tries, with all its insect strength, to "take its evening flight." The poor moth, "in its place," (!) feels pain, it feels it is in captivity, it knows it is *not* "in its place," it loves freedom, it in vain flaps its wings, but the cruelty of man, or perhaps I should say, the love of science, keeps it in "its place," its "evening flight" is prevented. Ah, Sir, there is pain there, but unless the moth, in "its place," appeals to the Clifton philosopher in language as unmistakably strong as the ass of old did to the pseudo-prophet, there is no chance of the tortured insect getting free to enjoy its "evening flight."

What is life? We know not; and who can tell how much pain the tortured "moth pinned to the tree" feels; firstly from the absolute torture, and secondly, from the feeling that it is in captivity, that it is not free. Why does it flap its wings? To get free, says Mr. Harvie. Granted: and this, even upon his own admission, is a struggle, a sign of pain. But, Mr. Spicer, "think others see as well as you," for Mr. Waters has had the pleasure of seeing insects pinned to a tree, and his testimony is, that "they are susceptible of the *slightest amount of inconvenience*." This is an indefinite sort of reasoning—this "inconvenience" resolves itself into *actual pain*—but Mr. Waters is so intent upon his "pain-despising" theory, that he forgets his candour amid the chaos of his logic.

But listen to Mr. Waters, and watch his movements. He sticks pins in insects, and for a time he lets the tortured creatures suffer, ultimately he relents, and prepares to kill them, and he tells us the reason in plain English, simply because he considered "*the sooner they were relieved from their misery the better!*" See how admirably Mr. Waters argues in the affirmative. He admits the insects felt rather miserably when transpierced with pins. So do I, indeed. And here, let me remark that, when an antagonist brings into debate his own authority, it is perfectly legitimate to show the inconsistency of that authority with itself, and thus completely counteract its undue preponderance. "Their misery," says Mr. Waters, and that misery is *pain*, just as sure as Mr. Waters is a naturalist. Again, Mr. Waters, with all the dexterity of a practical gladiator, attacks a dragon-fly with the stick of his net; the poor insect evidently gets the worst of the battle, for, according to the victor's account, the vanquished creature had its "body divided;" it fell in the grass, made a "great buzz," and there, as it lay, appeared to be *suffering* from the *loss of its balance.*" (!)

Here Mr. Walters admits that the wounded creature *suffers*, but his candour is again cast aside, and his oblique ingenuity discovers that the dragon-fly suffers "from the *loss of its balance.*"

"The loss of its balance," *nil admirari!* Your correspondents, the advocates of the "painless theory," all admit that insects feel pain, for Mr. Spicer's moth "flaps its wings," and struggles to get free; Mr. Waters' wood-leopard shows "contortions and distortions of the body;" and Mr. Harvie's bisected wasps admittedly felt pain, for your candid correspondent arrives at the conclusion, that "it is better to keep on the safe side, and treat insects well, and be innocent of any charge of cruelty." Permit me, Sir, in the words of the poet to say—

"They are all—the meanest things that are—
As free to live, and to *enjoy* that life,
As God was free to form them at the first,
Who in His sovereign wisdom made them all."

H. H. ULIDIA.

Hillsborough, Sept. 1868.

I have perused with considerable interest and much satisfaction, the several letters penned by various correspondent which appeared on the above-named subject in you issue of the *Naturalists' Note Book* for last month. I perfectly coincide with those correspondents in considering Mr. Ulidia's views wholly untenable, and both his theory and the argument he adduces in its support, alike without foundation. "Yes, says analogy," remarks Ulidia, "and we are too modest to reject the deductions from analogy. Man himself feels pain, the whale, the elephant, and the sparrow, etc., *and consequently insects also feel pain. Why not?*" he asks. Yet in spite of this gentleman's *very remarkable* reasoning on the subject, I must say, that I am most decidedly of the same opinion as W. W. Spicer, when he remarks that Mr. Ulidia "is evidently unconscious of the differences that exist between the structure of the vertebrate frame and that of insects." In the main I agree with the conclusions of your last month's (September) correspondents; but as there are often two (or more) ways by which the same result may be attained, I take the liberty of differing from their arguments in one or two particulars. One instance I subjoin: I find it in Mr. W. W. Spicer's article. The writer (speaking of insects) says he considers "that they are endowed with so much feeling, and *only so much*, as is needful to carry on the work of life; but that they are without that acute form of sensation which we call pain." Whilst I argue that if we deny that insects feel pain we must at the same time deny that they experience sensations of pleasure, or in fact, *any feelings or sensations whatsoever*. I will cite an example in proof of this. Take for instance a moth, hold it gently between your fingers (tight enough however to prevent it effecting its escape), and on gradually, but perceptibly increasing the pressure, you will observe that its struggles and flutterings increase proportionately. Now no one (I fancy) will deny that the moth desires to escape, and as it finds its desires are not complied with, and its position is fast becoming not one of the most enviable, it gives vent to struggling to regain its freedom. Now, I say, if the insect felt incommoded when held gently, as at first, must it not experience *extreme discomfort* when pinched tightly, as at last; and does not *excess of discomfort* amount to *pain*? I agree with your able correspondents Messrs. Harvie and Waters that "Do Insects feel Pain?" is a query "on which it would be impossible to arrive at a decided conclusion either one way or the other;" but are there not, may I ask, other problems equally perplexing now, and always under consideration, concerning which, by carefully investigating details (however trival they may in themselves appear), and by noticing appearances, *we may arrive* and *have arrived*, at tolerably correct conclusions? Besides, "What man *has done* man may *yet do*." Finally I would remark, that although perfectly of the same opinion as such of your correspondents who consider the question at issue "must remain unsolved and decided to the end of time," I sincerely believe, that by patiently observing and giving our most careful consideration to *anything* and *everything* connected with the insect tribe, by persevering studying their anatomy, various habits, and chief characteristics, etc., we may, I say, do *much*; nay, *very much*, towards placing our inquiry on a surer footing. ENTOMOLGICUS.

Now even if we concede (as Ulidia desires) that insects *do* feel pain as acutely as we do—that "man himself feels pain, the whale, the elephant, and the sparrow, etc., and that consequently insects must also feel pain," is in my opinion not correct reasoning, and as U.'s arguments are groundless, so must also be the conclusions he arrives at. Now we all know (or ought to know), that the organization of insects is far different from that of mortals, and consequently, in the words of Mr. Harvie, "we may conclude that their sensibility is proportionately less." There is a law of nature which says that: "The *lower* we go down the scale of animated beings the *less* is the amount of pain experienced." On the highest point stands man; his whole anatomy is more perfect and, consequently, his sensibility to pain is more acute than any of the lower animals; and if this be the case, must not the sensibility to pain of insects compared with that of man be extremely little? I think this is self evident.

P. G. M.

A SERPENT FOUND IN MALTA.

It has been long a subject of traditionary remembrance that no kinds of serpents are to be found natives of the island of Malta; and so well was this known that, in the middle ages, the people of that island were led to make a market of it to their great advantage. A superstitious or fanciful cause was given for this in remote ages; but when heathenism had given place to Christianity a new explanation was advanced, of the well-known exemption of the land from the presence of serpents, and forgetful of the more ancient date of this remarkable fact, imputed to the charms of Circe, it was ascribed to the apostolic authority or benediction of St. Paul, as elicited by the recorded fact of his escape there from the poisonous fangs of a viper; and from which it proceeded, that not only should all such reptiles be banished, but the soil itself should be fatal to them: and such was the power of the earth, at least of a particular cavern in the island, that, wherever it might be conveyed, it would be found effectual, both to protect its purchaser from the venomous bite, and also afford a cure when the injury had been inflicted. That no mistake might exist on the subject, and, no doubt, with the intention of increasing the sale of the article, an address or treatise, written in the common language, was circulated, describing the virtues of this earth, which was formed into lozenges or pellets, of which the smallest, of the weight of a dram, bore the effigy of St. Paul on one side (holding the figure of a serpent twined round a rod), and, on the other, what seems to resemble a cross. Other pieces, in the form of coins, were of larger size, and on their reverse they bore the likeness of a ship. It may be perhaps that this, and a kindred superstition as regards the fossils of the island, may have now passed away, but the fact remains that serpents are not natives of the island; and this has led to another direction of the inquiry in more modern times, and as the island is still naturally free from a brood of these reptiles, it has been the endeavour of a certain class of persons to raise a doubt on the fact of what is stated to have happened to St. Paul when he was thrown by shipwreck on its shores, when a poisonous serpent crept from a bundle of wood, and bit him in the hand, without inflicting an injury. I do not suppose it necessary to speak of the well-known fact that wood, except of some fruit trees, is as scarce in the island as serpents, and yet the people were compelled to obtain fires for important uses. This they procure from distant lands, and it is easy to believe that a serpent may have crept into a bundle of this wood for concealment, and thus be conveyed.

But although it is acknowledged that none of the serpent family are natives of the island, a circumstance I am about to relate will establish the certainty of their occasional occurrence there.

A sailor belonging to one of her Majesty's ships, when in the harbour of Malta, obtained permission to be on shore for a day, and, to amuse himself, he proceeded to take a walk for some distance in the island. For his further amusement he supplied himself with a stick and a bottle of gin, and in the course of his rambles, it happened to him to discover a serpent amidst some rough ground, which, in its endeavour to escape from him, he disabled with a blow, and then seizing it with his hand, he dropped it headlong into his bottle, the mouth of which was conveniently wide for the purpose, and which he carefully closed up. In this condition it was conveyed to his ship, and, on his return to England, it was brought to his home, from whence it was transferred to the custody of the writer.

It is a usual thing with sailors, when on distant stations, to lay aside things they meet with, and, when they return to their homes, to present them to their friends, as examples of what they have seen or obtained in their voyages; and although, in some instances, the supposed curiosities are worthless, except as expressions of the giver's goodwill, they are not unfrequently of much interest to the receiver; and it has often been the good fortune of myself thus to become possessed of materials I have greatly valued. This sailor had not imagined that a snake from Malta would have been more thought of than from any other distant region; but the interest felt in it when presented to me was, for the most part, excited by the bearing it has on the narrative recorded in the Acts of the Apostles, and therefore it became of some importance that the scientific name of the reptile should be ascertained; and to do this with the greater certainty, the bottle with its contents was sent to the British Museum, from whence, through the kindness of the principal naturalist, I am informed that it is the Colubes atrovirens of Cuvier, Zamenis atrovirens of some other naturalists. This example measured in length twenty-three inches, and from the vent to the end of the tail, six inches. It does not possess poisonous teeth, and therefore is not of the same species as that which inflicted the bite on the hand of the apostle. It is a native of the warmer or south portions of the continent of Europe.

Polperro.　　　　　　　　　　JONATHAN COUCH.

USE OF PLANTS.—I beg to thank Mr. Ulidia for his remarks on the "use of plants," but am obliged to confess that he has not yet succeeded in satisfying my "inquiring mind" on this subject. I can perceive nothing paradoxical in the statement that "the vicinity of woods and those places where vegetation thrives best, and is most abundant, is unfavourable to health," because the presence of extensive woods is a proof that vegetation thrives well. On land in which trees of various kinds grow vigorously, I believe almost all plants indigenous to that region flourish equally well. Trees require a highly fertile soil, and are only found there in primeval splendour and abundance. The question is, how can we reconcile the two facts, that plants are conducive to health by absorbing carbon and imparting oxygen; and that where these plants grow in profuse abundance they produce evil effects. Why do we find "many delightfully healthy countries remarkable for the grandeur of their vegetation?" The valleys and plains of India and Ceylon are fruitful in the highest degree; they are indeed remarkable for the grandeur of their vegetation and would be most delightful countries to dwell in

were it not that the climate is unhealthy for Europeans, and apt to cause many fatal diseases. In an extract from the *Galignani*, a M. Caillet is said to have been making experiments on the influence of plants on the atmosphere. He has come to the conclusion that during the night (contrary to what takes place by day) the oxygen of the air is absorbed and carbonic acid found at the expense of the plant. He says that the decomposing action of the leaves requires a temperature of from 10 to 15 deg. Cent., and that rays of dark heat are not sufficient to produce it; that coloured rays act with various intensities—green decomposing no carbonic acid at all. Now if these propositions be granted as true, it would explain the reason why vegetation is languid under the shade of large trees, and also why (if such be the case) habitations surrounded with dense wood are inimical to animal health. I do not believe, however, that these assertions are to be relied upon. Can plants be supposed to be alternately acted upon by gases directly opposite in their effects? Is it probable that night air, which is generally considered only inferior to that which is breathed by day in being slightly damper and colder, is contaminated and rendered unfit for animal respiration by those very agencies which a few hours before purified and imparted direct nourishment to the atmosphere?
R. B. W.

WATER FOR AQUARIUMS.—J. Ward asks, whether the water of fresh water aquariums in which weeds are growing requires changing in order to keep the fish in a healthy state. I beg to inform him that it does not, having once had one in which the water was not changed for months.

The only thing necessary is to get the right proportion of plants, to counteract the deterioration of the water by the absorption of ogygen from it by the fish, which can soon be done with a little care, by increasing or decreasing the amount of vegetation. A few water beetles and other insects should also be kept in the aquarium, in which they act as scavengers, by removing the refuse matter, etc. When once it is properly arranged the result will more than repay the small amount of trouble, as the fish are more healthy than when they are constantly being disturbed by having the water changed; when such a change is required the water is best removed by means of a syphon, which prevents the disarrangement of the contents of the aquarium.
O. R.

Mr. Ward will find that the introduction of water plants into an aqua-rium will obviate the necessity of changing the water. Fish absorb the oxygen contained in the water, and exhale carbonic acid gas. Plants on the contrary live on this carbonic acid gas, (which is composed of carbon and oxygen), and have the power of separating and using the carbon for forming the tissues of which they are composed, and giving off the oxygen in a pure state. If therefore plants are introduced to such an amount as to absorb all the carbonic acid gas evolved by the fish, and to give off sufficient oxygen for them to breathe and live on, the water will remain pure without change. Water plants however require some care; for if the dead leaves and the fungoid growth which always comes with them are not now and then cleared away, the water becomes muddy. A few water snails are very useful in eating any decaying vegetable matter which may accumulate in the course of time. The best plants for aquariums are *Valisneria spiralis*, or *Anacharis alsinastrum*, as neither die in the winter.

Lettuces are the favourite food of the land or garden tortoise, but it will eat any other succulent plants, such as dandelions, or the leaves and twigs of the Virginia creeper; and grass will do for a meal when nothing better is obtainable. I have one which eats bread and milk, which seems to agree with it very well.
Sept. 12.
ARTHUR G. HARVIE.

A CAT AND A RAT—A HARD CHASE.—In the summer of 1859 I was located on the river Lagan, where a number of houses was situated, the fronts just ten yards from the river, and exactly on the opposite side is an ancient graveyard, which for centuries has provided "narrow cells" for "the rude forefathers of the hamlet." The river at this place is fifteen yards wide, and over among the tombs a numerous, bold, and intrusive colony of rats has been long permanently established, and too often prowling companies of the colonists make predatory excursions across the water, to the no small annoyance of the inhabitants of the cottages. As I stood one evening leaning against a tree a large rat crossed the river, passed me quite unceremoniously, but happened to come in contact with a strong and vigilant young cat; and master rat, seeing his position, instantly made for the water, but puss, equally versed in the stratagems of war, cut off his retreat; the rat changed his line of march, ran into one of the cottages, rapidly traversed several rooms, still pursued by the cat; both came to the street again, and the rat finding that "to be or not to be?" was the question of the moment, very sailor-like ascended a beautiful poplar-tree, forty-two feet high, which stood on the bank with a gentle incline above the water. The cat, a real practical climber, as swiftly went up the tree; the rat reached the highest twig, and for a second reconnoitred the advancing foe. Down plunged the rat into the river—down went the cat too—the rat instantly dives; but no sooner had puss touched the water than she dropped her ears and made to the bank; I assisted her to *terra firma*, and for several days she seemed dull and quite dejected at her defeat.
Dromore, September, 1868.
H. H. ULIDIA.

INSTINCT IN PLANTS.—There exists in some vegetables a strong resemblance to that phenomenon which in animal life is called instinct. That this natural tendency to action appears distinctly in plants is evident from the following facts:—When a pole is placed at a considerable distance from an unsupported vine, (the branches of which are proceeding in a contrary direction from the pole), the vine will in a very short time alter its course, and will not stop until it has wound its tendrils firmly round the pole; yet the same vine will carefully avoid attaching itself to low vegetables nearer to it, such as the cabbage. A potatoe left in a corner of a dark cellar has been known to shoot out a runner; which first ran twenty feet along the ground, then crept up the wall, and so through an opening by which the light was admitted. The opening and closing of the petals of flowers according to the temperature of the air, the tendency of the root to grow downwards, etc., etc., also support this view. That which is called instinct in animals is nothing, I believe, but a higher exercise of the same propensity; in plants it is the same in kind though not in degree. The lower animals have no more power than plants to act in opposition to this law of their nature; acting in accordance with instinctive laws is not arbitrary: they must be obeyed, and always are. This is the difference between instinct and reason; man rules his actions, the brute is ruled by them. Let those who would bestow upon beasts that which is only man's prerogative, say whether they are willing to attribute the noble faculty of reflection to a still lower class of organized beings, but equally entitled to it. R. B. W.

STING OF NETTLES.—In the *Naturalists' Note Book* for September, C. O. G. Napier gives a reason to account for the fact, that neetles cause no sting when grasped tightly, which reason, I think, is incorrect. A much more probable reason is the following:—The epidermis, or outer skin (which is insensible to pain), is thicker and harder on the palm of the hand than on the back of it, and other parts of the body. When the nettle is touched with the back of the hand, the hairs of it pass through the epidermis, and affect the true and sensitive skin, thus causing pain. I have found, and I think "Tortoise" and others who like to try the experiment will find, that no sting is felt whether the nettle be grasped tightly or whether it be merely touched with the palm of the hand; and this is simply because the hairs of the nettle are unable to pierce the outer skin of the palm of the hand, and cannot consequently affect the sensitive skin.
August 31st, 1868. R. T.

COLIAS HYALE, &c.—I had the pleasure of taking last month (about the 21st), a fine specimen of Colias Hyale, the locality was Ryde, Isle of Wight. I saw Eduas there, but as I had not my net I could not catch him. The pale-clouded Yellow (Hyale) was sailing slowly along a field, and I easily took it. I took also, "*good*," or rather "*local things*," Polyomnati, Agestis, and Argiolus abundantly, and Stereopus Tages (Dingy Skipper). In this northern locality I have found little, in fact, among the Rhophalacera nothing new but Evebra Plaudrua (Scotch Argus), of which I took two bad specimens yesterday. I have observed that P. Napi (Green Veined White) is far commoner here than P. Rapæ (Small White). In fact I have seen many of the latter and none of the latter.
A WHOLESALE MURDERER OF BUTTERFLIES AND MOTHS.
Oban, Scotland.

FLYING CAT.—The following is extracted from a late paper:—"A nondescript animal, said to be a flying cat, and called by the Bhells *pauca billee*, has just been shot by Mr. Alexander Gibson, in the Punch Mehals. The dried skin was exhibited at the last meeting of the Bombay Asiatic Society. It measured 18 inches in length, and was quite as broad when extended in the air. Mr. Gibson, who is well known as a member of the Asiatic Society and a contributor to its journal, believes the animal to be really a cat, and not a bat or a flying-fox, as some contend. Perhaps some of the readers of the *Naturalists' Note Book* will state their opinions as to the above proving an addition to the known fauna of India. R. B. W.

LIGHTNING FIGURES.—Are the figures that are caused by lightning, real representations of the objects through which the electric fluid passes? Have "designs and figures of natural objects been electrographed upon the surface of the skin" ("N. N. B.," vol 1, page 337), or is this phenomenon to be accounted for merely by the fact that "common electricity in passing between two conducting surfaces actually forms a tree-like figure which can be made visible," as stated on page 40 of the same volume? Perhaps some of your meteorological correspondents may answer these questions. R. B. W.

GANNET.—On Wednesday last a very fine adult specimen of the gannet, or solar goose (*Sula Bassana*), was captured asleep on a piece of fallow ground in this parish; it was in fine condition, but apparently worn out by the length of its journey. I forwarded it to the Zoological Gardens, Regent's Park, where it is doing well. Being very rare to the neighbourhood, I thought you might like to know of its capture for insertion in your NOTE BOOK. G. S. PATEY.

SMALL METRA.—I captured during my walks yesterday morning, an unusually small specimen of P. Metra (Small White variety). It measured with its wings expanded as nearly as possible, but scarcely $1\frac{5}{8}$ inch. Is not the occurrence of so small an individual rather scarce? and I should like to hear if any of your readers have observed previously a specimen or specimens of the above stated small dimensions. P. G. M.

LOCAL NAMES.—It is desired to collect as many as possible of the local names of British plants; and the assistance is requested of all who take an interest in the subject, or who may have the opportunity of ascertaining and recording them. Any lists sent to Mr. James Britten, High Wycombe; or, to Mr. Robert Holland, Mobberley, Knutsford, will be thankfully received and acknowledged.

EARTH EATING.—Can any one inform me whether the edible earth, found in the neighbourhood of Honduras, has been analysed (page 222, vol. 1)? Is not this substance more or less mixed with vegetable matter, and not pure earth? The fact of its dissolving on the tongue, having a fatty taste, and containing sufficient nourishment to support life for above ten years appears to lead to this conclusion. R. B. W.

RACOON.—Where am I likely to procure a female Racoon, and does this animal require any particular care or protection during winter? I have had a fine male given me, and he is perfectly tame and as playful as a kitten. Are they usually so, and is their temper generally good or uncertain? T. C. H.

BOOK OF MOTHS.—Can any of your readers tell me of a good book on Moths, with illustrations, that would be a help to name my collection by; and can any one help me with information for catching butterflies and moths in the lake district? A. B.

JAPANESE SILKWORM.—Will some reader of the "Note Book" tell me where I can get eggs of the New Japanese Silkworm (Bombyx Tamamai).
NATURALIST.

THE DODO AND ITS HOME.
By C. O. Groom Napier, F.G.S.
PART II.

MONGST the catalogues of the older museums a few notices of portions of the dodo may be found. Thus in "a catalogue of part of those rarities collected in thirty years time with a great deal of pains and industry by one of his Majesty's sworn servants, Robert Hubert *alias* Forges, gentleman." A leg of a dodo—a great heavy bird that cannot fly—was mentioned; this was in 1665, or one year before the great fire of London. Grew describes a leg of a dodo in 1681, which afterwards became the property of the Royal Society, and was transferred by them to the British Museum, where it now remains: this specimen may have been the one in Robert Hubert's museum. A dodo's head is mentioned by Olearius in the catalogue of the Gottorf Museum, Copenhagen. The figure of Clusius, of which we have previously spoken, is copied by him, and the head is now highly honoured in the Royal Museum at Copenhagen. Mr. Strickland quotes what he thinks the last notice of the dodo in a living state on the Island of Mauritius. It is extracted from the Sloane Manuscript in the British Museum (Strickland, p. 26). The document he quotes from is entitled "A coppey of Mr. Benj. Harry's journal when he was chief mate of the ship Berkeley, Castle Capt. William Talbot then commander, on a voyage to the coast and bay, 1679, which voyage they wintered at the Maurrisshes. Having a little respite, I will make a little description of the island—first of winged and feathered fowle—the less passant are dodos, whose flesh is very hard."

The dodo had not lived long in its home after the settlement of its enemy—the civilised man; for in 1664 the island was first settled by the Dutch; and in 1693. Leguat, on visiting this island and enumerating its birds, says nothing about the dodo. The dogs, cats, and swine introduced by the European settlers had doubtless a great share in the destruction of this species. Leguat says "these beasts do a great deal of damage, by devouring all the young animals they can catch." He remarks the great change which had taken place amongst the creatures inhabiting the island, for geese and ducks were formerly very abundant, but the water fowl, gelinottes, and sea and land tortoises were now very rare. The Mauritius in 1712 was evacuated by the Dutch, who were replaced by the French. Mr. Strickland, who has made more extensive researches into the bibliography of the dodo than any other writer, can find no trace of it subsequent to the occupation of the French. Baron Grant (he says) resided in the Mauritius from 1740 to 1760, and his son, who compiled the history of the Mauritius from his papers, states (p. 145) that no trace of such a bird was to be found at that time; and M. Morel, a Frenchman, who resided there previous to 1778, and whose attention seems to have been drawn to the subject by the judicious criticisms of Buffon, tells us that the oldest inhabitants had no recollection of these creatures. Bory de St. Vincent, in 1801, was equally unsuccessful in learning anything of the lost dodo.

I have now concluded my brief sketch of the historical evidence for the existence of the dodo, and shall next consider the pictures, which give us a vivid idea of a unique and extraordinary bird. A painting hangs in the British Museum in the centre of which may be noticed a large figure of the dodo. It appears standing on an island in solitary dignity, the monarch of the lower animated world; in the water which surrounds are ducks, and perched high above it, on branches of trees, are macaws, while a dragon fly and several insects float in the air. This bird has a gloomy expression, reminding us of "still life," but it is life, and has not the character of the copy of a stuffed bird. The macaws and the ducks are faithful representatives of living birds, and why should not the dodo be of the ancient inhabitant of a distant isle? But its authenticity does not rest on presumptive evidence. George Edwards, the painter, who presented this picture to the British Museum, said it was drawn in Holland from a *living bird* and that it belonged to Sir Hans Sloane, who gave this information to the artist. This picture, from its resemblance in colour to those painted by Roland and John Savery, distinguished Dutch animal painters, is thought by Mr. Strickland to have been executed by one of them. The dodo must thus have stood between two and three feet high; the head is larger than that of the Oxford or Copenhagen skulls. The colouring of the paintings of the dodo differ considerably, but such would not be incompatible with natural representations taken from one species, or even one specimen, for the plumage of the dodo, like that of many birds, probably varied with age, sex, and season.

Professor Owen, when at the Hague, discovered in the Royal Gallery a representation of the dodo about three inches long, in a large picture of Orpheus, charming the birds and beasts; it is a beautifully executed and highly finished picture, and is considered one of the best works of Roland Savery.

The Royal Gallery at Berlin possesses a picture representing the animals in Paradise, and among them the dodo. Mr. Strickland has represented this figure as his frontispiece; it is dated in 1626

Roland Savery was twenty-three years old, on the arrival of Van Neck from the Mauritius in 1576, who was said to have brought a living dodo; it is, therefore, not improbable that he might have taken his representation from the bird brought home by Van Neck, and as Mr. Strickland suggests, copied it into his later works. Mr. Strickland gives another fine plate of the dodo, in which the bird appears standing on the brink of a pool, watching the movements of an eel; the bird is of a beautiful grey, shaded with olive, and having a dark line at the back of the neck; the hinder part is of a purplish brown, the bunch of tail feathers is yellow, as also the quills, which are marked with black; the legs are yellow, but the beak is purple, with a few yellow stripes. It is the prettiest of Mr. Strickland's illustrations; the attitude reminds us of a living bird, and is as graceful as we can suppose the dodo to be. I have had these plates copied on an enlarged scale for my own museum. The original picture is in the Belvidere Museum at Vienna, and is dated 1628.

W. H. Darby, Esq., presented a large painting to the Ashmolian Museum at Oxford, which represents this bird standing three feet six inches high, but resembling in form and colouring the pictures at the Hague, British, and Berlin Museums. Its size Mr. Strickland considers much exaggerated, for it is nearly double that of the picture in the Brtish Museum, and is larger than we have reason to suppose the bird was from the descriptions of the old writers we have quoted. The Duke of Northumberland and Mr. Broderip are the fortunate owners also of original pictures of this bird.

I will now mention the various remains of the dodo in the different museums. The foot in the British Museum is well preserved, and gives a clear idea of its walking and grasping capacity— it is $9\frac{1}{2}$ inches long, 2 inches across the joints, and $2\frac{3}{4}$ inches at the spread of the strongly formed toes; and the scales on the foot are very large. These dimensions are taken from the fine plate in Strickland's work. The head and foot now at the Ashmolean Museum, at Oxford, which formed part of the Tradescant Collection, and of whose probable history I have spoken, remained attached to the original specimen until 1755, when the Vice Chancellor and trustees of the museum on making their annual visit decided that this specimen, which was in bad condition, should be destroyed. This was surely a grievous error, for the specimen might at least have been put into spirits. The head and foot were cut off, however, yet not in the interest of science, but in conformity with the rules established by Ashmole, by which these portions of the different animals were to be retained in any case, in order that their names might be preserved in the catalogue.* The hooked extremity of the beak is lost, but the eyes are still in a dried state in their original cavity. The skull is $8\frac{1}{2}$ inches long by $4\frac{1}{2}$ inches wide. The foot, the skin of which was decomposed, was carefully prepared by Dr. Kidd, as the skull was dissected by Dr. Ackland. The bone is immensely thick, and the brain-case small. The skull at Copenhagen, which is half an inch shorter than the one at Oxford, is less perfect. These are all that were extant previous to the important discovery by Mr. George Clarke, which has excited so much interest in the scientific world. Strickland thought that the caves and superficial deposits of the island might afford remains of the dodo, and he was not mistaken.

I am indebted to Professor Owen for calling my attention to some interesting points on the osteology of the dodo, and for his valuable and exhaustive paper on the subject in the "Zoological Transactions," for which, and for Mr. Milne Edwards' paper in the "Annales des Sciences Naturelles," I have delayed the publication of the few notes I had made from Strickland and other works. I extract Mr. Clark's statement entire: a garbled account of it has been several times quoted. Mr. George Clark, Master of the Government School at Mahébourg, Island of Mauritius, says:—

"On the estate called Plaisance, about three miles from Mahébourg, in the Island of Mauritius, there is a ravine of no great depth or steepness, which apparently once conveyed to the sea the drainings of a considerable extent of circumjacent land, but which has been stopped to seaward most likely for ages by an accumulation of sand extending all along the shore. The outlet from this ravine having been thus impeded a sort of bog has been formed, called '*La Mare aux Songes,*' in which is a deposit of alluvium, varying in depth on account of the inequalities of the bottom, which is formed of large masses of basalt from three to ten or twelve feet deep. The proprietor of the estate a few weeks ago conceived the idea of employing this alluvium as manure, and shortly after the men began digging in it. When they had got to a depth of three or four feet they found numerous bones of large tortoises, among which were a carapace and a plastron pretty nearly entire, as also several crania.

"When I heard of this, it immediately struck me that the spot was one of the most likely possible to contain bones of the dodo, and I gave directions to the men working there to look out for any bones they might find. Nothing, however, was turned up but a fragment of what I supposed to be the humerus of a large bird. This encouraged me to look further: and my search was rewarded by the discovery of several tibiæ, more or less perfect, two tarsi, one nearly perfect pelvis, and fragments of three others.

"These were found imbedded in a black vegetable mould, the lighter-coloured specimens being near the

---

* Milne Edwards.

springs. My reasons for believing these to be the remains of the dodo are:—the certainty that that bird once existed in Mauritius; the similarity of these bones to what the representations of the dodo which I have seen would lead me to expect, particularly the breadth of the pelvis, the stoutness of the tibiæ and tarsi, and the shortness of the latter; the favourable nature of the spot in which they were found for the haunts of such birds when living—a sheltered hollow with two springs in it; the non-existence, actual, or traditional in Mauritius of any bird to which bones such as these could have belonged; the indubitable antiquity of these bones, proved by the deposit of alluvium which covered them.

"During nearly thirty years that I have inhabited this colony I have made frequent inquiries of old people as to the finding of bones of large birds, and have offered liberal rewards for such; and have consulted with the late Dr. Ayres as to the spots most likely to contain them. We agreed that the floods which sweep the hill-sides and the ravines in the rainy season would be most likely to carry any remains into the sea; and this would doubtless have been the case here, but for the stoppage occasioned by the sand down.*

(Signed) "GEORGE CLARK, 1865."

HYBERNATING LEPIDOPTERA.
By E. CLIFFORD.

In connection with that large division of our insects known as the *Lepidoptera*, there are indeed a variety of interesting and wonderful circumstances, which must ever prove attractive to the true student of nature. Taking merely an external view of them, how full of gorgeous beauty is their apparelling, how intricately lovely their variety of tint and shading! And if we come yet closer to examine them, our wonder and admiration increase with the scrutiny which we exercise. Viewed as regards their structure, habits, economy, instinct, and the many other particulars which are so often alluded to, our native *Lepidoptera* (or butterflies and moths) are indeed strangely and wonderfully productive of intense admiration and interest. Endless is their variety of tint and colouring, endless also their diversity of habits, economy, and flight. And whilst many of these more prominent details are eagerly examined by the entomologist, he is very often apt to pass over one of the less striking peculiarities of this tribe, even that of their hybernation. In the present paper, therefore, we shall briefly remark on the subject, giving such instances as seem most suitable and conspicuous.

The hybernation of insects generally is a remarkable thing, when it is remembered

---

* Owen on the Dodo, in "Zoological Transactions for 1867," page 51.

how delicate are their little frames, and how great the severity of the weather which they outlive. Some of the most tiny little creatures have been found in a state of torpidity, hybernating until the warm spring-time calls them forth to the enjoyment of life, when they reassume the activity that had previously characterised them. Equally astonishing with all such cases is the fact that the delicate forms of caterpillars, or the still more delicate frames and plumage of butterflies and moths, are capable of outliving the winter's frosts and snows, and re-appearing in the next season but little injured by their hybernation. But hybernation of insects, if it be a wonderful thing, is nevertheless a wise and beautiful provision of the Creator, who thus preserves myriads of his tiny creatures that must otherwise perish. Unable to explain the mysteries of the fact, we are nevertheless fully able to appreciate the wisdom that has ordained it. For think what would become of thousands of our lovely species should they be unable to live through the cold months without food! For six months of the year, at least, the caterpillars would look in vain for their accustomed food, since all vegetation has disappeared. So, too, with the winged insects. The flowers that shed their fragrance on the balmy breezes of July are no more, and if our butterflies disported, as was their wont at that time, it would be in the chilly beams of a winter's sun, or else over wide wastes of snow, and under a stormy sky. But to provide for these difficulties, we find that a wise method is contrived, by which means an uninterrupted series of generations is secured to our insect tribes. This is founded on the faculty which insects possess in common with other animals, even that of passing the winter in a torpid state, unaffected by the severity of the weather. It will be interesting to give a few examples of this from our most striking body of insects, the *Lepidoptera* (or scaly-winged tribe). Among the butterflies, several examples of hybernation occur, some in the caterpillar, others in the winged state. The earliest which we notice is that afforded by the well-known Brimstone butterfly (*Gonepteryx Rhamni*), which passes the winter in the perfect state. Often on sunny days in January or February a specimen of this butterfly is seen careering over the fields, as if rejoicing in its emancipation from winter hiding-places. It is probable that the Clouded Yellow butterflies which we so admire in the autumn, also hybernate during the cold of winter. Another, and an exceedingly beautiful example is given by the Painted Lady butterfly (*Vanessa Cardui*), a species which habitually hybernates. During the present summer we have more than once come across specimens that had lived through the winter and were on the wing even till July. Their condition, it is true, was not the best, but their vigorous flight was not in the least abated by the time they had lived. These lay eggs, and produce their new brood of butterflies, which emerge from the chrysalis in August. The *Vanessa* butterflies are all hybernating species, and often cheer us by their flight in the early part of the year. The Red Admiral, with his vivid bands of red; the Peacock (*Vanessa Io*), so richly adorned on the upper side of the wings; the two Tortoiseshells; all these are so well-known as not to need a further comment at our hands. They are amongst those insects with which all must be more or less familiar. These all pass the winter in a winged state; lasting sometimes until the new brood of the year emerges, and mingling with them. It is difficult to explain how, or in what manner these and other butterflies pass the time of their hybernation. Some have been discovered in outhouses, or hid in the crevices afforded by the country barn, with its thatched roof, and many similar nooks and corners have been found to possess their butterfly tenants; but when we consider the number of butterflies which suddenly disappear late in the autumn and hybernate, it is astonishing that they can find housing for the winter, and it becomes somewhat mysterious that more are not found snugly hidden and protected from the cold in the ways we have alluded to. Still, there can be no doubt that in some such way as related butterflies *do* pass the winter. Of course, in the forest or the woodlands, there are so many facilities in the objects around for hybernation, that it must be there, chiefly, that our charming flutterers take up their winter quarters. From the appearance presented by hybernated specimens that have been taken, it has been concluded that they had wintered in damp places, since their brilliant wings had become soiled and mildewed; and we cannot be surprised at the fact when the extreme delicacy of their wings is borne in mind. The only wonder is that so few of them seem at all the worse for their long winter's sleep in out-of-the-way hiding places. Their torpidity, contrasted with their summer exuberance of life, is to us peculiarly impressive, and seems strikingly to illustrate the deadening effect of the winter season on all the activities of motion in the animal creation. The butterflies we have named are the most conspicuous hybernators, although by some it is imagined that certain of the Blues pass the winter in the perfect state. Amongst the large body of our *moths* we find many which hybernate in the winged state. The *Noctuæ* gives many examples, as, for instance, the Red Sword Grass (*C. Vetusta*) and the Sword Grass (*C. Exoleta*), two very handsome species. Then the common Herald moth is a hybernator, re-appearing early in the spring months. A number of others might be named which come to the sallow blossoms in early spring, after having emerged from their winter quarters. Like the butterflies, they are doubtless ensconced in snug corners during the sharp weather, and pass their time in a torpid state. A few of the *Geometræ* also hybernate, but there are not many examples of note. Leaving perfect insects, whose hybernation is indeed wonderful, we come to consider the caterpillars of *Lepidoptera* which hybernate, a still more remarkable circumstance. For to understand that an insect, requiring little or no nourishment, can hybernate without food is not difficult; but it becomes indeed a matter of surprise to find that hundreds of little caterpillars, bereft of their vegetable food, are yet capable of living through the remarkable time of the winter season, and yet re-appearing in the spring uninjured by their fast. To some such let us now allude.

Of the butterfly caterpillars, all those of the handsome Fritillary butterflies hybernate, and feed on the violets that deck the woods in spring. It is not improbable, that these and many other butterfly caterpillars, together with those of other orders, are secreted during the winter amongst dead leaves, moss, &c., around the trunks of trees. The Clear-wing *larvæ*, which feed in so singular a manner, are all carrying on their devastation in the winter months. From their habits of feeding within the stems of trees they are secured from the rough weather, and dwell in safety. Probably they cease to feed during the very intense cold, and become torpid. Such, at least, is the case with the large caterpillar of the Goat moth, that lays low so many of our handsome willow trees. At the approach of winter this singular creature forms itself a nest of the chips of wood which surround it, combined with silk, and ceases from its labours for a while. It is a fair inference that many other mining caterpillars act in the same manner, since they are not found to have increased much in size during the winter, which they naturally would do if their time were employed entirely in eating.

The Lichen-feeding caterpillars of the Footman moths chiefly pass the winter in the state of torpidity so common to all the *Lepidopterous* caterpillars that hybernate in various ways. So also with the singular caterpillars of the brilliant Burnet moths, which live through the winter, and are small in size. Delicate little creatures, it is indeed remarkable that they sustain no injury by their long fast and hybernation! Yet such is the case, for in the gentle springtide, when all nature assumes a green of lovely hue, they awake from their sleep, and set to work at eating as vigorously as before. Truly a marvellous provision of the Creator for the tiniest of His creatures is this selfsame hybernation which we are now considering!

The well-known Drinker caterpillar is one of the hybernating kinds. On warm, sunny days, it is probable that the hairy little fellows take a meal from the grass which is still remaining on the sere earth; others which are hairy are found occasionally feeding on the chickweed and other low plants, even though these are not their appropriate food-plants. This is the case with the handsome caterpillar of the Fox moth (*Bombyx Rubi*), which can be reared through the winter by placing it in a pot planted with chickweed—though bramble is its proper food. And when we take a general glance at the manners and modes of hybernating amongst various species, we are astonished by their diversity. Some are discovered hiding in curled-up dead leaves, which have fallen from their food-plants. The caterpillars of the Broom moth (*Hadena Pisi*), beautifully striped creatures, which feed on the Brake fern, are found amongst the dead leaves of these plants that cluster on the ground. A small species of the *Tinea* family hybernates in the fir cones. The *larvæ* of the Latticed Heath (*S. Clathrata*) hybernates in various situations, and the caterpillar of the Swallow tail moth (*O. Sambucaria*) is found spun up in the crevices of the bark of its food-plant. Singular, indeed, are the situations chosen by several of the little caterpillars of the *Tinea* tribe, a wonderfully delicate group of insects. One makes its winter home in the heads of the thistles, and another is found snugly ensconced in the seeds of the dock. Many of all classes, as we have said, resort to dead leaves, moss, and other decaying substances, amidst which they manage to save their little bodies from harm, or else spin a web to enclose them from the attacks of enemies. One little creature has been found in the seeds of the hollyhock, till these fall to the earth, when they desert them for a more secure resting-place.

The crannies offered by old woodland trees are all eagerly sought by hybernating caterpillars, who are sometimes discovered packed close together, as if for the sake of warmth or companionship. Even old and moss-covered stones or loose bits of stick and bark which the autumn winds have scattered, are each and all found by the persevering collector to hold their insect tenants, or hermits of the Lepidopterous order. In connection with the power possessed by caterpillars to withstand the cold, it should be remembered that many are furnished with long hairs that necessarily aid them in withstanding the influence of the chilly atmosphere. Others, not furnished with protection in the construction of their bodies, are yet furnished with ingenuity, which enables them to overcome the difficulties of hybernation. These provide for themselves little silken homes, which are fastened, not to the leaves, which they instinctively know will be swept away from the stems, but on the latter, which endure throughout the winter, and thus they are in a secure and comfortable lodging. So various, however, are the methods and manners in which the caterpillars of *Lepidoptera* hybernate, that we must forbear to enter further upon an enumeration of them. We have indicated some of the more conspicuous, and this may lead our entomological readers to scrutinize more closely every object they approach in their winter rambles; for the collector should bear in mind that hunting for hybernated insects is a most important department of winter work, which should never be neglected, since many rare specimens by its means may be added to the cabinet. And thus we must close our brief remarks on hybernating *Lepidoptera*. Let our short and cursory glance at the order, as it is thus exhibited, lead our readers to a careful examination of this most interesting topic.

AMERICAN INDIANS.[*]

The red men who are known to us in books are not the red men who are met in their war-paint on the Prairie. They are all red, as the men in Europe are all white; but the interval which separates a Croat from an English gentleman is not wider than the interval which separates a Sioux and a Cheyenne from a Mohican and a Delaware. The red men whom our fathers met on the Atlantic seaboard were of chivalric, though savage race; who showed noble qualities; who were brave, hospitable, magnanimous. They kept their plighted faith. They respected the chastity of women. They had made a great advance from the savage state, for they had ceased to live by the chase only; they had learnt some part of the herdsman's duty and the husbandman's craft. The title of "noble savage" was very properly given to them; and it was not without a certain justice that our poets began to cite them in illustration of some of the simpler and manlier virtues. It is doubtful whether these Mohicans and Delawares belonged to the same stock with the Sioux and the Cheyennes. The Atlantic tribes were tall men, with fine heads and eagle noses; the Prairie tribes are short and squat, with very small skulls, pug noses, and hang-dog looks. The Mohican was clean in person, the Cheyenne

---

[*] Paper read by Mr. Hepworth Dixon before the British Association.

is inexpressibly filthy. A Prairie Indian never cuts his hair; he lets it hang down his back in ropes and coils, matted and greasy, with a few twists and lumps of metal (silver by choice) tied up in it. A delicate woman would not like to stand in the same street with Red Cloud, the Cheyenne chief; at least not until after he had been scraped and boiled. Red Cloud was a very fine gentleman in his way. He had never done a stroke of work in his life. He had never cut down a tree, drawn a skin of water, planted a patch of ground. He would not curry his own horse, or even pitch his own tent. He was a warrior and a gentleman, who could not soil his haughty hands with labour. Yet, the fellow never washed either hands or face. The only cleansing he ever got was a soak of rain or a souse in some river, from both of which he would come shivering and cursing in his quiet Indian way. A redskin's toilet has no connexion with water in any shape. You come upon a lodge—a Comanche tent made of skins, and rudely daubed with figures, the totems of the tribe; a huge fellow is lolling and smoking on the ground, while two or three squaws are puzzling about his head, and combing through their fingers his long and greasy locks. You may see a band of Sioux come riding into a white village, say into Denver or Central City, with a trail of mares and colts behind them, followed by bundles of squaws on foot, fainting under loads of skins and billets. The skins being sold to the white pedlars, the men slip from their horses, seize the coin, rush into the colour-shops (always to be found in a prairie-village, next door to the grog-shops), smear their faces once again with grease, and then patch on, in streaks and daubs, a mass of yellow-acre and blood-red paint. No funnier sight is now to be seen on this planet than a band of these Cheyenne warriors in front of a looking glass.

The squaws, we are sorry to say, are not cleaner than the braves; while they are certainly less picturesque and handsome. These squaws are not allowed to wear long locks,—for flowing hair is a sign of nobleness; and a prairie woman is at best no more than a slave, A man buys her for a blanket, and sells her for a flask of fire-water. He can beat her, cast her off, put her to death.

The prairie women are not attractive. They are short in stature, with squat figures, crooked legs, and very big mouths. Like the men, they tattoo their breasts and faces; but they delight in the coarsest colours and the ugliest lines. A white man must have lived a long time on the Prairie before he can think with any complacency of having to marry a Cheyenne wife.

On the whole, the prairie tribes are probably a thousand years behind those Atlantic Indians who have given so many heroes to our romance and our song.

Some small remnants of the nobler Eastern tribes—Shawnees and Delawares to wit—are still found on the Missouri bluffs: the first near Wyandotte, where the Kansas river flows into the prairie stream; the second some four miles below Fort Leavenworth. These tribes are comparatively civilized. The Shawnees of Wyandotte are very much mixed in blood; some all but white; and the men not only settle on the soil, but keep shops and banks, lend money at 60 per cent. (on the sly), and practise the politer arts. Their chief, who has made money, and taken the name of Armstrong, might hold his own, in bargain and sale, against the smartest trader in New York. These Shawnees have made some progress. They have become nearly white. Armstrong laughs with a knowing chuckle when you tell him the famous story of his ancestor and Count Zinzendorf. The founder of the Moravian missions was one night resting in the Wyoming valley, among Shawnee lodges, on a visit to some Methodist preachers. For some cause, the Indians were annoyed; and in the dark midnight they crept to his lonely hut, meaning to scalp him. The braves stole softly to his canvas lodge, lifted a corner of the hanging, and saw the old man, seated before a fire, with a bible on his knee, and a huge rattlesnake coiled across his feet. Indians believe that a man whom a rattlesnake will not harm is a Manito—a saint, a prophet, a child of God. The desire to kill the count died down in their hearts, they crawled away, and told their wondering fellows of the sight which they had seen. No such charm would work on the modern Shawnees of Wyandotte; but then, as we saw just now, they are almost white; and by a special Act of the Kansas Parliament they have been admitted to the full rights of American citizenship.

The Delawares are a purer race, and they have a certain amount of staying power; but they make bad settlers. These red men have been driven from the Susquehannah, where their noble ancestors made the treaty with William Penn. So long as we have known the Delawares they have been a mild sort of savages; the Five Nations styled them Squaws; but, thanks to their close connexion with the Palefaces, they have now become formidable to their wild brethren in the West. Not liking to settle down they wander through the Prairies, and push their way above the Rocky Mountains; not so much as hunters of buffalo, as in the guise of trappers, guides, and dealers. Armed with good revolvers and sharp bowie-knives, they laugh at the tomahawk and the poisoned arrow; and with the confidence felt by white men, they never hesitate to dash at any number of enemies, however great. We are sorry to say this interesting tribe is slowly but surely dying out.

Among other tribes are the Pawnees, whom the French call Wolves; men far inferior in the scale to Shawnees and Delawares. They are true Western Indians; natives of the country now known as Nebraska. You cannot trust them for a moment. They will dishonour white women, and hack the head off a sleeping guest. These wretches, much broken in battle by the savage Dacotas, are seldom found more than two hundred miles beyond the Missouri bluffs.

The real Prairie Indians are the Cheyennes, the Kiowas, the Arappahoes, the Comanches, and the Sioux. These are all genuine savages, living solely by the chase, and called by the Shawnees and Delawares "the buffalo-eaters." Of these six tribes, the most notable are the Cheyennes, the Comanches, and the Sioux. These powerful tribes are friendly, often allied against other tribes, and latterly against the Palefaces. No one knows their number; we have heard Western trappers say they are a couple of hundred thousand strong. The general opinion is, that they are rather increasing than diminishing in number; but the coming of the two great lines of railway through their hunting grounds—the Nebraska line and the Kansas line—will drive away elk, buffalo, and priarie fowl; and when the supply of wild game is thinned, the Sioux and the Cheyenne will not stay long behind.

A tender heart does not dwell with pleasure on the thought of an original and interesting branch of the human family suddenly dying off the planet; but if any thought could reconcile us to the extinction in a few years of the Comanche, the Sioux, and the Cheyenne, it would be that of their low organization and debased habit of mind.

They are all thieves, cut-throats, and polygamists. An old Comanche chief, called Isa-Keep, told General Marcy that he had four sons; that they were fine lads, and a great comfort to him in his old age—for they could steal more horses than any other young men in his tribe. In French, the name of the Sioux is Cut-throat; and the sacred sign of this tribe is the action of drawing a knife from ear to ear. Every Cheyenne lodge is full of squaws: five or six to a single chief. As one philosopher in black and yellow paint expressed it, " First thing man want on Prairie is plenty wife."

These tribes are all hunters, and the hunting stage is the lowest moral condition in which men exist; yet low as may be the condition of the prairie tribes, one would wish it were possible to save them from destruction. We have seen the Mohican and the Cherokee fade in the white man's presence, though the Mohican and the Cherokee, when our fathers found them on the Atlantic shores, were already dwellers in wigwams and villages, sowers of grain, hewers of wood, and trappers of wild beasts. Compared with a Sioux and a Cheyenne they were almost civilized. Yet they are gone from their old homes; all but gone from the world. And the lower tribes of the West will go; in fact, if the strong white men of the West were not held in check by the New England philanthropists, they would be cut off from the land, root and branch, —warrior, squaw, papoose,—long before the buffalo and elk, the wolf, the rattlesnake, and the coyote.

Boston insists, with noble zeal, that the Indian races shall be saved. How? Up to this time, every attempt to save them has failed. The red man will not work; he is a gentleman, a warrior, a councillor, a hunter. Plant him on the soil, and he will run away. Build him a house, and he will pitch his tent in the parlour. Give him an estate, and he will cut down all the trees. Clothe him with coat and shirt, and he will still daub on the war-paint. Give him a handful of dollars, and he will spend it in one day on whisky and tobacco.

The reason why all these well-meant efforts to save the red men from perishing fails seems to be, that we have tried to save them against the order and law of nature.

The life of man, so far as it comes under observation at all, divides itself into three grand stages. Man is first a hunter of wild game; next, he is a herder of goats and kine; afterwards, he becomes a grower of herbs and corn. A prairie Indian is in the first stage; a Bedaween Arab in the second; a Norfolk farmer in the third. A man cannot pass at will from the first stage into the second; still less can he pass from the first stage into the third. If Rome was not built in a day, neither is a man to be changed in a day—in a generation; hardly in a dozen generations.

A hunter is a wild man. His food is wild game. He lives as the tiger lives; catching his prey by his superior cunning, strength, and pluck. The flesh of that prey is his food, the skin of that prey is his mantle. He is the companion of wild beasts, and his only art is how to seize and kill them. He may not build a house; he may not till the ground; he may not tarry in one place: for the wild game which he pursues is always flying from his poisoned arrow and his plunging knife; and the law of his existence chains him to the buffalo track. His hand is lifted against everything that lives. Such a man is the Cheyenne.

A herdsman is a tame man. His food is milk and cheese, the flesh of goats and of calves. He has to provide for his wants by knowledge, care, and kindness. The cow yields him milk and the goat yields him cloth; yet he wins these requisites from them, not by murderous cunning, but by tender love. He surrounds himself with a world of helpless creatures—goats and horses, sheep and cattle; creatures for whom he has to think by night and watch by day. Where the hunter sharpens his blade, the herdsman has to sharpen his wits, if he would thrive in his art and increase his flocks. Such a man is the Bedaween Arab.

A husbandman is a social man. His food is various and dainty—a mixture of wild game, of domestic animals, of fruit, grain, and green stuffs. He is, in the highest sense, a student and economist of nature; a nursing father to every good and useful thing. Such a man is the Norfolk farmer.

Is it not absurd to fancy that a Cheyenne can be changed in one day from a hunter into a husbandman? The Bedaween who is now a herdsman was once a hunter; and in future ages he may become a husbandman:—but not in one day. The turks are trying to settle one of the Pastoral Desert tribes, the quick-witted and unwarlike Ferdoon branch; but the forcing system fails in Syria as it fails in America. The settlers run away; and the only visible result of this waste of philanthropic power is that the tribe declines. A wise waiting on Nature seems to be our only hope.

A Prairie Indian must first become a herdsman; after he has reached the Bedaween stage, he may advance still further. It is a long course, but we cannot stray from what are seen to be the laws of growth. The first step has been taken in this progress in the introduction of the horse into America. It is through the horse that the Cheyenne's intellectual and moral nature has been reached. The horse has helped him to catch his prey, and the horse has therefore taught him to feel and think. He has come to care for *one* animal, because it is useful to him. That idea may expand. Our duty, clearly, is to encourage it. When a Prairie Indian steals a cow, he kills and eats it, as he would a buffalo. If we could persuade him to keep it for the sake of milk and cheese, a large step would be gained. A cow would make its owner gentle, would be a drag on his wild movements, and would slowly rouse in his heart the desire to possess flocks and herds. The grandson of such a man might grow into an inferior sort of Pastoral Arab; and his descendant of ten generations might even aspire to pass muster as a Norfolk farmer.

It is a slow processs; but growth is slow, and Nature will not be hurried in her work.

The field is vast, and there is room for all. From the Missouri bluffs to the Black Hills there is a country larger than India, which can only be held as grazing land. Crossed by two lines of railway, pierced by a thousand wells, it will afford room for many villages and towns, but the people will be graziers, and the surface will be covered with flocks and herds. In those great pasture lands some remnant of the red race may be saved, living the life of herdsmen and shepherds; while their miserable brethren, kept by a mistaken charity in the Eastern cities, are dying, like dogs in the gutter, at the grog-shop door.

ORANGES AND LEMONS IN CALIFORNIA

AT present, the orange-growing interest centres in Los Angeles county. Ten years ago there were hardly more than twenty-five hundred orange trees in the whole county, and very few of these produced any fruit. Five years afterwards the number of trees had increased to five thousand and upwards. Now, there are upwards of ten thousand trees in bearing condition; and it is estimated that more than a hundred thousand young trees have been started in nurseries and orchards during the past season. "Everybody is planting orange trees," said one of our informants; which, reduced to a sober statement, we take it is that orange culture is fast becoming a leading interest in this beautiful county. One of the oldest orchards contains about 2,000 trees grown from seedlings planted about sixteen years ago. This orchard is in full bearing condition, and the product averages about 1,500 oranges to each tree, although some trees will produce nearly double this number, reaching as high occasionally as 4,000. Another orchard contains upwards of 1,600 trees planted eight years ago, and just coming into bearing condition. These are the largest bearing orchards, although more extensive ones, we believe, have been planted, and the older ones are continually enlarged. At Anaheim, the centre of the German vine-growing interest, the orange does not appear to thrive well; and there are districts at a very little remove from flourishing orchards, where little or nothing can be done in orange culture.

The orange grows moderately well in some of the sheltered valleys of Santa Barbara county, although few successful experiments have as yet been made. But we never saw better oranges than some which were grown near Folsom in Sacramento county. Successful experiments have also been made as far north as Butte county; and more recently it has been ascertained that the orange will do well on a large area in Kern county.

One authority sets down the number of oranges received from Los Angeles, and sold in the market of San Francisco during the past year, at 724,450; lemons, 91,500; limes, 254,000. But during the same time there were imported from Mexico, the Society and Hawaiian Islands, and from other foreign territory, 2,000,000 oranges; 1,000,000 limes; 20,000 pine apples; 30,000 bunches of bananas and plantains, and 350,000 cocoa-nuts; the aggregate value of which was but little short of a quarter of a million of dollars. And not only might every dollar's worth of this fruit have been grown in this State, but as much more for the export trade. There is no danger that tropical fruit-growing will ever be overdone in California. The market demand at home and in the neighbouring States, will always be greater than the supply.

"Is orange-growing a profitable pursuit?" is a common form of enquiry. According to our data, the annual product of each full bearing tree will net about 50 dollars. The number of trees upon an acre ranges from sixty to eighty. Taking the smallest number, you find the total value of fruit from a single acre to be 3,000 dollars. An orange orchard of thirty acres in full bearing, with an average yield, would turn out a crop worth 90,000 dollars. Is there any other kind of fruit culture more promising than this? There are thousands of acres of land which can be had at prices ranging from two to ten dollars an acre, which are probably just as well adapted to orange culture as that now covered by the most promising orchards. There are hundreds of men who have delved in mines only to become poorer year by year. Had these men gone into the southern part of the State ten years ago, and planted orange groves of ten acres each, any reasonable ambition for a fortune would have been satisfied. But ten years is a long time to wait as time is reckoned here. And yet, is there any better place to wait than under genial skies, where the same sun which flushes the orange is a perpetual joy to the weak and the strong—to old men and to children?

There is one other fact to be noted: No oranges which are brought to this market rate so high as to quality, as those brought from the southern counties of this State. The Tahiti orange is sour or insipid, because it must be picked green in order to stand the voyage of not less than forty days, before it can be laid down here. Of half a dozen cargoes examined, we did not find a single lot approaching in quality that of the Los Angeles county orange; although the latter is produced from the same seed as those of the Society Islands. Every winter one may see considerable lots of decayed oranges landed from these islands, which are bought for the purpose of stocking the nurseries in Southern California. The Los Angeles orange is suffered to remain upon the tree until fully ripe, because it is within three days of the market. It begins to ripen in December, and may be considered in its prime in January. It disappears from the market again sometime in March or April, although if allowed to hang upon the tree, it may be kept for some months more in prime condition. But the blossoms begin to appear, and the matured fruit is gathered to make room for the next crop. Neither the Florida orange nor the Havana as they appear in the New York markets, are quite up to the standard of the California orange in freshness and perfect flavor. Much larger fruit, however, is grown in southern Mexico and upon the Isthmus, but not more desirable as to quality. The orange is as certain as any other fruit crop in the State. The gopher sometimes attacks the roots of the tree, and now and then the aphis stings the leaves. But there are no blights and no damage from frosts, save to the young plants, which are extremely sensitive to cold and to heat in the summer solstice. The seedlings hardly attain more than eight or ten inches in height the first year; the more common practice is to graft from well-known bearing trees, as nurserymen graft seedling apple trees. When the full growth is attained, which requires from twelve to fourteen years, the tree is then about twenty-five feet in height, and the top, measured outside of foliage, is from twenty-five to thirty feet in diameter. And whether in June or January, he who would have anything more enchanting than an orange orchard had better start for Paradise at once.

And wherever on this coast the orange tree flourishes, there its tart sister, the lemon tree, will grow also. It is even a more beautiful tree in the matter of foliage, with a leaf of a lighter green, and branches more irregular. It is easily propagated either from seed or cuttings. The tree comes into bearing in eight or nine years, and is probably at perfect maturity at sixteen years. The two varieties best known are the Sicily and the Malaga. Both fruit abundantly, and the net returns are said to be even greater on a given area than from the orange crop. One instance is cited where the yield of five lemon trees twelve years old was sold for 510 dollars. Eighty trees may be set on an acre, and if at maturity the yield were as great as in the instance cited, the product of an acre of lemon trees would exceed 4,000 dollars for a single season. Another species, known as the Chinese lemon, is very prolific, and the fruit grows to a much larger size. It has a very thick rind, and for this reason and because of its rank growth, it does not find favor in the market. The flavor is said to be good; and the acid for drink is not inferior to that of the more popular varieties. It grows on a shrub, never attaining the size of a tree, but a more beautiful hedge never was formed than may be grown from the Chinese lemon shrub; and the fruit will more than pay for all the space occupied in the garden, or elsewhere, as a hedge plant. This variety is also quite hardy, and will probably thrive anywhere in the State, save at elevations where there is much frost and snow.—*The Overland Monthly*, September, 1868.

BUTTERFLIES.

WHAT *is* a butterfly? Well, prosaically speaking, it is a more or less beautiful insect of the lepidopterous order—genus *Papilionidæ*. There are no less than ten thousand species of *lepidoptera*, or scaly-winged insects, of which some eighteen hundred are said to be natives of Britain. Of the *Papilio* (butterfly) group no more than sixty-four can fairly be called British, and, strange as it may seem, the greater number of these are to be found within thirty miles of London. Lepidoptera are divided into three large classes by Cuvier—the *Diurna*, or those which fly by day; the *Crepuscularia*, or those which fly in the evening; and the *Nocturna*, or those which fly by night. The *Nocturna*, or night-flying moths, are identical with the *Phalæna* of Linnæus. A butterfly in its perfect or "imago" state is possessed of four gauze-like wings, covered on both sides with little imbricated scales, which, to the naked eye, look like a quantity of golden and richly-hued farina besprent from the pouncet-box of a fairy. A butterfly proceeds from the chrysalis or aurelia of the caterpillar. A caterpillar is born of an egg laid by a butterfly; it then changes into a chrysalis, which, in course of time, becomes a butterfly that lays eggs and dies.

> So generations in their turn decay,
> So flourish these when those have passed away.

A butterfly may be distinguished from a moth by its club-shaped or knobbed antennæ, and by the beauty and delicate markings of the under as well as of the upper side of its wings, which are usually erect when the insect is dormant or merely resting on some dainty leaf or flower. By the antennæ alone—doubtful though their use is to the insect—the tyro entomologist may distinguish the class to which a lepidopteron belongs. These bamboo-like jointed members are never clubbed at the end in the moth; hence butterflies are grouped as *Rhopaloceræ*, or club-horned, and moths as *Heteroceræ*, or varied-horned.

Butterflies have no mouths, but a long proboscis which they roll up spirally, and by whose aid they sip the nectar from the flowers—their only food. They have lymph instead of blood, and respiration progresses through air vessels along their sides, called spiraculæ, connected with other minute vessels called bronchiæ. But the grandeur of a butterfly is in his wings. These delicate fabrics are amongst Nature's most exquisite mosaics, and it is principally to possess them for cabinets and microscopic objects that entomologists ramble far and near for rare and choice "specimens." Upon first emerging from its silken shroud the wings of the butterfly are moist and wrapped round its body; the air hardens them; under the genial influence of the sun they expand; and, full of life and activity, away starts the fairy shape on its ærial wanderings, when, to use the words of Mr. Joseph Merrin, of Gloucester, "as it flits from flower to flower, it seems an embodiment of pure felicity—happy in what it has, and happier still in searching for something else."

But a short life has the butterfly. The ambient air, the daisy-clad fields, the pathless woods, verdant groves, and cultivated parterres teem with its enemies—the ichneumon fly, the voracious *libellula* or dragon-fly, and the sparrow, among the chief. Gilbert White says the ichneumonidæ deposit their eggs in the aurelia, which of course never then becomes a butterfly. Marwick confirms him; for, writes he, in a note to his *Naturalist's Calendar* for 1795—"Some time ago I put two of the chrysales of a butterfly into a box and covered it with gauze, to discover what species of butterfly they would produce, but, instead of a butterfly, one of them produced a number of small ichneumon flies." Mudie also states that the ichneumon perforates the body of the caterpillar, and devours some of its most vital organs without actually killing it. In due course the caterpillar reaches the chrysalis state, but the parasite has so preyed upon its vitality that no butterfly emerges therefrom. How often have we watched a pretty "Brimstone," avoiding, by its zig-zag mode of flying, its mortal foe, a sparrow. It has been calculated that *one* sparrow destroys on an average two hundred butterflies in a week; while not more than one caterpillar in a thousand becomes a butterfly. The most rare and one of the most beautiful of British Lepidoptera—the Purple Emperor—is from its pugnacity its own destroyer. To the scarcity of females—which number perhaps one in twenty—is attributed the hostility of the males, which fight on the slightest provocation, or no provocation at all, until one or the other is killed. Once we saw a duel between two of these imperial moths, and then we observed, so soon as one had damaged one of the antennæ of the other, the maimed one, utterly helpless and unable to fly, became an easy victim to the wrath of his vanquisher.

In the imago state, by that wonderful provision of nature, instinct, the butterfly lays its eggs on the food necessary to its larvel state, and from a minute egg is born, the following season, a caterpillar, which Mr. Merrin thus faithfully describes: "The caterpillar of each kind varies in shape and colour or marking, but they all have similar cutting jaws; an organ, called a spinneret, near the mouth, for spinning a fine silken thread; a pair of short antennæ; and generally sixteen legs. Each of the first three pairs of legs terminates in a claw; the remainder, called prolegs, are like fleshy stumps; with the inner edge of the bosom fringed with minute hooks, which enable the caterpillar to obtain a firm hold of anything it is crawling over. As the creature goes on feeding it rapidly increases in size, casting off its skin as it becomes too small, until it changes into a chrysalis." This is the third or *pupa* state of the insect; and in it may now be observed most of the parts of the caterpillar, with an addition of other parts in a more or less advanced state, which are peculiar to the perfect insect. While in this tiny tomb it acquires vigour, the perfect *imago* develops, and, the down grown, dyed with every prismatic hue, the butterfly bursts radiantly forth.

While in the *pupa* state respiration is carried on through the thorax, opposite which are apertures purposely formed. "The thorax," says Mr. Merrin, "contains the muscles by which the wings are moved, and other important organs, and is the most vital part. Hence butterflies and many other insects are *easily* killed by being pinched there." We wish we could rely on Mr. Merrin here as implicitly as we do on his other assertions. Butterflies, like all other insects, have the organs of sense. The little insect world that flies, hops, or crawls around us, has as much meaning, as much beauty, as much design, and as much wonder about it as the larger creation. It has instinct, too; and we believe of a far higher order than entomologists are in the habit of giving it credit for. Hear Shakspere—

The beetle that we tread upon
In corporal suffering feels as great a pang
As when a giant dies.

This belief, doubtless, it was that prompted Laurence Sterne's famous Shandean philosophy anent a common fly, and has animated so many of Wordsworth's affectionate allusions to the especial object of this paper, notably his remonstrance with the bird in "The Redbreast and the Butterfly."

What ail'd thee, Robin, that thou could'st pursue
 A beautiful creature
That is gentle by nature?
Beneath the summer sky
From flower to flower let him fly;
'Tis all he wishes to do.
The cheerer thou of our indoor sadness.
He is the friend of our summer gladness,
What hinders thee that ye should be
Playmates in the sunny weather
And fly about in the air together?

Does not Mr. Merrin think that if an ephemera suffers pain and shuns death, a far higher classed insect like a lepidopter does the same? All creation, from Man to the meanest parasite, avoids Death—not, perhaps, because fearing the grisly monster, but instinctively dreading the inevitable last agony caused by the wrenching of life from its frail tenement of clay.

"Fear death?—to feel the fog in my throat
 The mist in my face,
When the snows begin, and the blasts denote
 I am nearing the place,
The power of the night,
 The press of the storm,
 The post of the foe;
 Where he stands, the Arch Fear in a visible form,
Yet the strong man must go!
 For the journey is done and the summit attained,
And the barriers fall,
 Though a battle's to fight ere the guerdon be gained—
The reward of it all."

To return—not *à nos moutons*, but to our butterflies—there is a question we have often thought worthy the consideration of entomologists, viz., the influence of food on larvæ.

The chlorophyllæ in different plants varies in colouring property as well as in density. If the colour of tulips is affected by steeping their bulbous roots in certain dyes, and the texture and colour of silk vary with the different sorts of food given to the silkworm, surely entomologists might cultivate butterflies somewhat after the fashion in which agriculturists improve cattle.

Though *our* butterflying days are over, and we have now more serious work to attend to, we often pleasurably recall bygone sunny days, when, "happy enough in the sport, we saw not the poetical surroundings which a development of the imaginative faculty renders palpable."

Many were the spoils we brought home from rural rambles, impaled on ready pins. Mr. Merrin, we doubt not, makes nocturnal ravages in the haunts of the lepidoptera, armed with a lantern, and a shillelagh with which to beat the hedges, and a jar containing a horrid compound of beer and sugar, to anoint the bushes and flowers.

A naturalist possessing a keen sense of the beautiful must be a happy child of Nature. To him petty professional jealousies, private quarrels, political strifes, are nothing. An European war sinks into insignificance before the discovery of a new insect, reptile, bird, beast, or fish. Who would not envy the raptures of the earnest single-minded Linnæus, who fell on his knees and thanked God at sight of a field of English gorse? Or the complete abstraction of Leuwenhoeck, who was wrapt from mundane cares in such a calculation as would give 17,000 divisions in the cornea of a butterfly, and speculate upon each division being a separate crystalline lens. Truly enviable is the patience of Lyonnet, who dissected a caterpillar, and detected therein 4,041 muscles! And what shall we say of Swammerdam, who devoted ten years to his great work—" The Anatomy of a Day-fly?"—*Victoria Magazine*, Oct.

A MUSHROOM CAVE.

It is pretty generally known that mushrooms are grown in great quantity under Paris and its environs, but it is somewhat difficult to obtain access to these *carrières*, and therefore a few words descriptive of one of them may not be unacceptable. The locality is that of Montrouge, just outside Paris. The surface of ground is cropped with wheat; here and there are heaps of white large cut stones ready to be transported to the buildings of Paris, and which have recently been brought to the surface through the coal-pit like openings. There is nothing like a "quarry," as we understand it, to be seen about, but the stone is extracted as we extract coal, and with no interference whatever with the surface of the ground. We find a "champignoniste" after some trouble, and he accompanies us across some fields to the mouth of his subterranean garden, if we may so call it. It is a circular opening, half of it being covered with planks, and the head of a pole with sticks thrust through it appears a couple of feet above the surface, its base resting in the darkness seventy feet below. We descend by this shaky pole with the sticks thrust through it, and soon reach the bottom of the shaft, from which little passages radiate. A few small lamps fixed at the ends of pointed sticks are placed below, and with one of these we follow our guide. Our passage is narrow, but roomy enough to stand erect, and immediately on entering it mushroom culture begins. On each side of the pathway there is a small bed of moist half-decomposed stable manure, not covered with earth—they are beds which have been made quite recently, and have not yet been spawned. Presently we arrive at beds in which the spawn has been placed, and is "taking" freely. The spawn in this cave is introduced to the little beds by means of flakes taken from an old bed, or, still better, from a heap of stable manure in which it occurs "naturally." Such spawn our guide preferred, and called it virgin spawn, and considered it many times more valuable than that taken from old beds. Of spawn in bricks, as in England, there is none.

Our champignoniste pointed with pride to the way in which the flakes of spawn had begun to spread their influence through the little beds, and passed on, sometimes stooping very low, and cautioning us against the pointed stones in the roof, to where the beds were in a more advanced state. Here we saw, and with much pleasure, little, smooth, pretty-coloured ridges running against all the sides of the passages, and wherever the rocky subway became as wide as a small bedroom, two or three beds were placed parallel to each other. These beds were young, and dotted over on their sides with mushrooms no bigger than sweet pea seeds, but regularly dotted thus, and affording an excellent prospect of a crop. Be it observed that the little beds contain a much smaller body of stuff than is ever the case in our gardens—twenty inches high, and about the same width at base, being about the maximum, and of course these against the sides of the passages have not so much matter as those shaped like little potatoe pits, and placed in the more open spaces. The soil with which they are covered to the depth of about an inch is nearly white—it is simply sifted from the rubbish of the stone cutting above, and the use of this gives the recently made bed the appearance of being covered with whitish putty. Although we are from seventy to eighty feet below the surface of the ground everything looks very neat, in fact very much more so than could have been expected, not a particle of litter or matter out of place being met with the whole time. Some length of bed is made every day in the year, and as they naturally finish one gallery or series of galleries at a time, the beds in each have a like character. As we proceed to these in full bearing, creeping up and down narrow passages, winding always between the two little narrow beds that line the passages, and seeing now and then wider nooks at the side filled with two or three little beds, even if the space be but a few feet long, daylight is again seen, this time coming through another well-like shaft, formerly used for getting up the stone, but now for throwing the requisite materials into the cave. At the bottom lies a large heap of white earth before alluded to, and a barrel of water—for gentle waterings are required in the quiet, cool, mighty stillness of these caves, as well as in the mushroom-houses on the upper crust.

Again we plunge into a passage dark as ink, and are between two lines of little beds in full bearing, the beautiful white button-like mushrooms appearing everywhere in profusion along the sides of the diminutive beds, something like the drills which farmers make for green crops. As the proprietor goes along he removes sundry bunches that are in perfection, and leaves them on the spot, so that they may be gathered with the collection for to-morrow's market. He gathers largely every day, occasionally sending more than 400lb. weight per day, the average being about 300lb. A moment more and we are in an open space, a sort of chamber, say 20 feet by 12, and here the little beds are arranged in parallel lines, a passage of not more than four inches separating them, and the sides of the beds literally blistered over with mushrooms. There is one exception; on half of the bed and for about ten feet long the little mushrooms have appeared and are appearing, but they never get so large as the pea stage, and then shrivel away, "bewitched" as it were. At least such was the inference to be drawn from the cultivator's expressions about it. Generally the mushrooms grow in bunches, and so equally-sized that it is often desirable to gather the whole crop at the same time.—*The Leisure Hour*, October.

NOTES ON THE WOOD PIGEON.

IF the draining of our marshes and the reclaiming of our estuaries have been the means of destroying or driving away many native birds, the progress of agricultural science and the increase in our plantations have tended to the multiplication of others, and of none more than the wood pigeon. No one, I imagine, who knew England and Scotland fifty years ago, but must admit that the entire face of those countries has been greatly altered—high cultivation and the planting of belts of ornamental firs and other trees having effected a remarkable difference in its appearance. If this great change had resulted in the increase of a more useful bird, we might consider ourselves fortunate; but in the case of the wood pigeon this is very questionable, and I therefore take up my pen to write its history with less pleasure than when similarly engaged on the other members of our avifauna. To quote more than a few of the numerous articles which have from time to time appeared in the public papers respecting its destructive propensities would be futile, since they must be well known to all my readers; but I shall attempt to place before them both the sunny and the shady side of the bird's history, and allow them to draw their own conclusions as to whether the pleasing traits in its character do or do not counterbalance the injuries it inflicts. With regard to its distribution a few words will suffice. During winter the wood pigeon is spread over every part of the British Islands, either in small companies or in immense flocks, which betake themselves to the open fields in the daytime, and at sundown retire to roost in woods and plantations of fir and other trees. At this season it is shy, wild, and distrustful; and few birds know better how to keep out of harm's way. It now feeds on cereals, the seeds of wild plants, acorns, beech-mast, and berries, particularly those of the ivy, on the leaves and roots of turnips, their ravages upon which plant often occasion a very great diminution in the value of the crop. In the spring the flocks are broken up, and their members retire in pairs to woods, plantations, shaws, hedgerows, and shrubberies for the purpose of reproduction. A wonderful change in the disposition of the wood pigeon now takes place; for it becomes as tame and confiding as it was formerly shy and distrustful. It no longer fears the approach of man, but, on the contrary, seeks his protection, and courts his intimacy, frequently constructing its nest in his garden, perhaps in the ornamental cedar that overshadows his house, and solacing him with his pleasing *coo-coo-roo* in the morning, and its beautiful aerial evolutions during the other portions of the day. Such is its conduct during the season of reproduction; and all right-minded persons will not, I am sure, allow its confidence to be misplaced, but will permit it to remain unmolested until the period arrives when it will return to the fields and open country, and at once resume its usual craftiness. While writing the above passage, a letter has reached me from the Rev. Edwin Sidney, of Cornard, near Sudbury, in Suffolk, in which he says:—"I have two or three pairs of wood pigeons and turtle doves which breed in the trees round this house. They are never disturbed; and the former have become very saucy and mischievous, plucking up the young peas in the face of the gardener, and provoking him greatly. How well these creatures know that they are safe!"

I now proceed to the cloudy side of the cushat's character, by giving some further details of the immense injuries it inflicts upon our crops, and the baneful effects produced by these birds to any district in which they may take up their abode. To show in what vast numbers the bird is sometimes seen, I extract the following from a letter sent to me by Mr. J. Illsey, dated Daylingworth, in Gloucestershire, February 2, 1866:—"What has astonished me more than anything else is the vast flocks of wood pigeons we have here this winter. I have seen several of fully a mile in length, pass overhead to the beech woods, early in the morning. The people call them 'foresters.'" Now, if the country be suddenly covered with snow, and the favourite beech-mast, acorns, and wild seeds are not to be obtained, the havoc such a flight would make among a field of turnips, to which they would certainly descend, must be immense. On this head a writer in LAND AND WATER says:—"They settle on the turnip fields in hundreds. They begin by eating the young tender leaves from the centre of the turnip; the water lodges, the frost gets in, and it rots. If you shoot a wood pigeon in the winter when returning to roost, his crop generally bursts with the fall, so full is it. Sometimes, if he has been gleaning, there may be some corn or beans; but far oftener there is nothing but a 'gowpen' (a double handful) of turnip-leaves. I have seen part of a turnip-field so punished by wood pigeons that I can compare it to nothing but a gooseberry-garden suffering from caterpillars—merely the strong centre ribs of the leaves left sticking out. Perhaps you will say that this was bad farming, and that the turnips should have been lifted and stored; but on arable farms in Scotland, in the regular rotation of crops, one-seventh of the farm is probably under turnips. If the crop has been good this is more than the farmer requires, and the extra turnips are let to some butcher or sheep-farmer, and consumed by his sheep on the ground."

"During the severe weather of January, 1867," says Mr. Cordeaux, "hundreds of these birds daily frequented the turnip fields in North Lincolnshire, feeding on the green tops of the swedes and common turnips; they appear, however, to give a decided preference to the latter plant. In two contiguous fields, the one swedes, and the other common globe turnip, they invariably congregated in much greater numbers on the white turnips, to the comparative neglect of the swedes. They drilled holes with their bills into the bulbs, which is surprising, considering they were frozen as hard as stones; they thus often do considerable damage to the root. As a general rule I found that the outer skin of the swedes thus operated upon was previously more or less injured, either by the bite of hares or rabbits, or the puncture of some insect."—*Zoologist*, 1867, p. 690.

That the wood pigeon is equally destructive in the corn fields seem certain; for "Scoticus" says:—"In the autumn, when the wheat is just turning yellow, the wood pigeons are very destructive. First, one or two leave the wood and settle, generally in the centre of the field; then ensues a constant stream in the same direction of every pigeon within ken, until some hundreds may be assembled. They don't settle like the partridge, at the foot of the stalk on the ground, but try to alight on the standing stalks of corn; the straw breaks with their weight, and never recovers; it is not merely bent as from heavy rain. Of course they eat some grain, but in this case their actual weight is more destructive than their appetite; the corn lies matted, and, if the weather be warm and damp, begins to sprout. But it is in winter that the wood pigeon is most destructive."

The following instance of the voracity of the wood pigeon appeared in the *Times* of October 22, 1857:—"There was shot lately in the neighbourhood of Inverness, a wood pigeon, in which was found the enormous quantity of 1,100 grains of wheat, barley, and oats (together with 40 peas), the barley-grains predominating. This seems to be no unusual case. In another, killed on a neighbouring farm, was found 70 peas, and a very large quantity of the grains above mentioned, but they were not counted; it was stated, however, that the bird was full to the very bill. The quantity a flock of 100 or 200 of these destructive birds would devour in the course of a harvest season must be very considerable."—*Inverness Courier*.

In the *Field* for January, 1860, a Guildford subscriber writes:—"On the 17th inst. I shot, close to my own house, a fine wood pigeon, and on reaching home, finding it had an immense crop, I took out its contents, which were composed of 690 berries of the ivy, also some portion of the rape leaf, which I suppose was eaten to digest the ivy berries."

As a set-off to all this mischief, St. John remarks:—"Although without doubt a consumer of great quantities of grain, at some seasons the wood pigeon must feed for many months wholly on the seeds of weeds, which, if left to grow, would injure the farmer's crops to a very serious extent."

It is a mooted question whether there be not a great influx of these birds from the Continent during the months of autumn. For my own part, I am inclined to think that there is; for how otherwise are we to account for such streams of them as those described by Mr. Illsey? That their wing power is sufficient to carry them across the German ocean there can be no doubt. That great migratory movements are natural to the pigeon tribe we have abundant evidence; but it will only be necessary to cite the case of the passenger pigeon of America, which excites the astonishment of every one who beholds it during its transit from north to south, or *vice versâ*. Besides England, Scotland, and Ireland, the wood pigeon is found over all the temperate parts of Europe: it also occurs in North Africa, Palestine, and, according to Mr. Jerdon, in Western Asia. The breeding of this familiar species is so well known that it is scarcely necessary to allude to it. Its two oblong white eggs may be seen any day during the spring and summer months on its slight platform of sticks by any person who will seek for it in the woods and shrubberies. The nest is usually placed on the horizontal branch of a fir, or in the middle of a mass of ivy growing on large trees. It rears two, and sometimes three broods in a year. It often commences laying early in April; and its ugly squabs of a later hatching may be seen sitting side by side on their slight and flat platform as late as September and October.—John Gould, F.R.S., &c., in *Land and Water*.

PLANTS KNOWN BY THEIR POLLEN-GRAINS AND OTHER CELLS.

WE have heard it remarked that this subject of the cell-history of species is so immense, that no one man could ever expect to complete it. Just so. And for this very reason we wish to introduce the question to our readers, hoping to enlist recruits into the service of this interesting and important branch of botany. A pleasant service, too; for nature is ever delightful, and, as one of her own poets sings,

"Never did betray the heart that loved her,"

a truth which we must more and more confess, as we extend our researches through her works, especially into this lowly and useful but beautiful and neglected department of the pollen and other plant-cells. Let any one turn his attention to them in some of the most familiar or abject weeds, meeting him in every field and wayside at this season, and the constant size and structure, the numerous resemblances and differences, in the pollen-grains of certain orders will immediately claim his admiration. Many of these forms, as may be seen in the works of Balfour, Fritzsche, Lindley, and Hassell, have been often described and figured; while the specialities of others are either quite unknown or strangely disregarded, though they are amply sufficient to afford novel and curious characters, and even to disclose manifest and constant differences between nearly allied plants, and are, moreover, easily displayed under the microscope. The same remarks apply, as we shall presently see, to the shape, structure, size, and contents of many other cells. In truth, it seems amazing that we have so few appeals, especially concerning species of which sufficient definitions are wanting, to characters of this kind, in our systematic books; and it is to be hoped that the interesting path now only indicated, may soon be candidly examined, if not followed, by the authors of our general and local floras.

The interest of the subject will at once be manifest, if we examine the cells of various common plants, such as are arranged close together in Professor Babington's excellent "Manual of British Botany." For example, of the section with yellow flowers and divided leaves of the order Ranunculaceæ, we shall find the pollen-grains nearly or quite round and smooth, commonly with the usual scars and about $\frac{1}{840}$th of an inch in diameter. Only, extending our observations to Ranunculus arvensis, a curious and remarkable exception will appear in its pollen-grains. These are very rough, have an average diameter of $\frac{1}{470}$th of an inch, being about twice the size of those of its immediate congeners; and thus, both in form and size, we very easily realise a singular difference. In short, here is a plant at once known by its pollen-grains. Then, in other sections of this same order of the Crowfoots, the pollen-grains are neither globular nor rough, but smooth and oval, and with the appearance of a slit or inflection of the membrane, reminding us of the figure of a coffee-berry. This appearance is constant; but in pure water the cell often becomes turgid and globular, when the apparent slit vanishes as if it had been originally due to a linear fold or partial collapse of the cell-wall, as is certainly the case in some other pollen-grains of this shape. But we do not see it in those of Ranunculus arvensis, and some of its near allies, although this coffee-shaped pollen-grain is common to several different orders of plants, and may be well seen, among the Ranunculaceæ, in Ranunculus Ficaria, Caltha palustris, and Trollius Europæa.

Among Leguminosæ, too, this form of pollen is well exemplified in Lotus corniculatus and L. major. Now these are two plants which are regarded by some of our most eminent botanists as nothing but varieties of one and the same species, "Lotus major being only larger in all its parts, from its moister habitat, than L. corniculatus." But our inquiries will show, on the contrary, that the pollen-grains of the smallest of these plants are the largest; for in L. corniculatus their average size is $\frac{1}{1143}$rd of an inch by $\frac{1}{1714}$th, while in L. major, they are about a third smaller, measuring only $\frac{1}{1600}$th of an inch by $\frac{1}{2666}$th. Thus these two interesting plants may be distinguished from each other by the pollen-grains; as we have figured them, with those of some of the Ranunculeæ, in Dr. Seemann's "Journal of Botany," for September, 1866.

The significance of the cell-history, in the present point of view, would be much increased by an exposition of it in the plant-tissues generally. But as we cannot do this now, a few remarkable examples only will be here noticed. Compare e.g., the beautiful radiate or stellate cells of the pith of Juncus conglomeratus, J. effusus, and J. glaucus, with the oval cells of the pith of J. squarrosus and J. bufonius; when the cells of the former three species will be seen as an actinenchyma, and of the latter two as an ovenchyma, a constant and curious difference between these plants, as we have depicted it in the "Ann. Nat. Hist." for December, 1863. Again compare the spores, the tissue-cells of the fronds and involucres of Hymenophyllum Tunbridgense and H. Wilsoni, when they will be found regularly smaller in the former than in the latter fern, as shown by our engravings in Dr. Seemann's "Journal of Botany," for October, 1863. And yet these two plants are often described as mere varieties of one species.

But still more notable illustrations are found

in those beautiful organisms, the raphides and their cells, that we will now only add another remarkable and unexpected proof of the validity of the views there advanced. Premising that the raphidian character is signally fundamental and universal in certain plants, *e.g.* Onagraceæ, as it is present in the seed-leaves, and pervades the greatest part of the tissues from the cradle to the grave of the species, we had long searched in vain for the exception of an ex-raphidian plant in this order, when at last a supposed one was found in Montinia. But further inquiry led to the discovery that this genus, though placed by Lindley and other eminent botanists under the order Onagraceæ, does not truly belong to it, but rather to the Saxifrages, with which its cell-structure better agrees. And thus a seeming exception became a strong proof of the rule.

And this is the only instance in which a plant not familiar to English botanists has been mentioned in this paper. For the examples of microscopical structure have been purposely confined to such as, though not to be found in the books of systematic botany, are abundant in the book of nature, and may be easily verified in the most familiar plants, with the aid only of an achromatic object-glass of half an inch focal length. The pursuit might prove at once delightful and instructive, and could hardly fail to produce useful results; with the conviction, too, that specific details of the pollen and other cells must form an interesting and important part of any future description of the natural characters of our flora.—*The Popular Science Review.*

Results of the Fossil Gathering
from the Northumberland Low Main Coal Shale,

In the June number of the Circuit Magazine I offered a series of prizes for the best collection of fossil fauna, consisting of reptiles, fish, and other animal remains, to be gathered from the shale which overlies the Low Main coal seam in Northumberland and Durham. The result of the offered prizes has exceeded my most sanguine expectations, so far as regards the quantity and quality of the fossils that have been sent to me, but, I am somewhat disappointed that fossils have not been received from other parts of the Northumberland and Durham coal fields where the Low Main Seam is being worked, and where fossils are more or less abundant. The competitors have collected their specimens from the shale heaps of the following collieries: Bedlington, Newsham, New Backworth, West Cramlington, Dudley, and Seaton Burn. The shale which rests upon the Low Main coal varies much in thickness and in the abundance of the fossils it contains.

About ten years ago Mr. T. G. Hurst, the eminent colliery engineer, read an elaborate paper before the members of the Northern Institute of Mining Engineers, on the peculiarities of the Low Main Coal Seam; and the theory he then propounded was that Low Main coal had been drifted by water and deposited on the bottom of a lake or estuary, the coal varying in thickness in consequence of the undulations of the bottom of the lake; and he further expressed his belief that the shale which overlies the coal was originally mud, held in suspension in water, and deposited in varying thicknesses, according to the irregularities of the coal stratum upon which it fell. This theory perhaps most satisfactorily accounts for the facts which have been observed; and it is further evident that during the time the mud which now forms the shale was being deposited, there must have been a gradual deposit of the remains of reptiles, fishes, and entomostraca, as many parts of the Low Main coal shale are crowded with their remains. Fishes, jaws, ribs, vertebrae, spines, fins, and coprolites are deposited in some places in such quantities that there are hundreds of specimens within a superficial area of a square foot. Besides fish remains those of reptiles are occasionally found; they are generally larger in size than those of fish, and the markings on their surfaces are more rough and irregular. Entomostraca, or small fresh water crustaceæ, are present in vast numbers, having apparently been entombed in the mud of the ancient waters when engaged in consuming the softer parts of the fish and reptile remains. The Northumberland Low Main Seam is known in Durham as the Hutton Seam; and it would be interesting to ascertain if animal remains similar to those found in the Northumberland Low Main shale are also to be found in the Durham Hutton Seam. I have not received any specimens from the county of Durham; and with the exception of a few fossils from the shale in Greenside pit, near Ryton, I have not seen any animal fossils from the Durham coal measures. The shale of the High Main coal is characterized by an abundance of plants; principally ferns, calamites, sigillariæ, &c., the shale of the Low Main contains occasional remains of the larger forms of fossil coal plants, but its characteristic fossils are fragments of fish. So far as my experience extends, ferns are absent from the shale of the Low Main. These facts indicate that the coverings of the two seams were deposited under entirely different conditions, and the distance of the two seams from each other, and the variety of fresh water and marine strata which are interposed indicate that the two seams were deposited at wide intervals of time.

The following is the adjudication respecting prizes. First prizes have been awarded to James Laidlaw, Thomas White, and Richard Tootell, of Newsham Colliery; second prizes to G. Walker, W. Scott, J. Cox, W. Darling, A. Scott, G. Bell, M. Waddle, Jos. Forster, Thos. Clough, of Newsham, R. Absolom, J. Reed, Thos. Curley, of West Cramlington, and W. Harrison, New Backworth; and third prizes, John Wilson, Seaton Burn, D. W. Brown, G. Bewick, W. Rule, W. Gledstone, Dudley, J. Calow, Geo. Elliott, Jos. Newton, Christopher Lowther, West Cramlington, W. Yellowley, J. Wardlaw, New Backworth, and to John Short, and — Stafford, of Bedlington Colliery.

The following are the principal fossils that have been found:—

MEGALICHTHYS (*megale*, great, and *ichthys*, fish), has furnished many large, bright, rhomboidal scales; jaws about 3 inches in length, containing large laniary teeth, and numerous small teeth arranged between them; and vertebræ from ¾ inch to 1¼ inch diameter.

CTENODUS (*kteis*, a comb, and *eidos*, form), many palate teeth of this remarkable fish have been found, varying in size from 3¼ inches to 3-8ths of an inch, and with from 5 to 13 ridges or denticulations.

CTENOPTYCHIUS (*ktenos*, a comb *ptyche*, a wrinkle), several scores of the compound crested teeth belonging to this remarkable genus, which is allied to the modern Cestracionts of Australia, have been found.

RHIZODUS (*rhiza*, root, and *odous*, tooth), teeth, scales, and bones of this largest of the carboniferous Saurians have been found, and are of considerable interest to palæontologists as recent researches have indicated that they probably belong to reptiles and not to fishes.

GYRACANTHUS (*gyros*, a circle, and *acantha*, a spine), literally a spiral or twisted spine, several of which, complete or in fragments, have been obtained, varying in length from 5 inches to about 20 inches: the fish to which the larger spines belonged would probably be about 12 feet in length.

RHIZODOPSIS, numerous jaws, teeth, and scales of this beautiful coal measure fish have been found by the collectors; it is a new genus founded by Professor Huxley; about forty maxillary, pre-maxillary, and mandibular bones have been obtained, each containing from 20 to 30 teeth, the average length of each jaw being about 1 inch.

PALAEONISCUS, a few jaws and many scales and teeth have been gathered; this fish is tolerably abundant in the magnesian limestone and marlslate, but its jaws are not frequently found in the coal measures; in size the jaws resemble those of RHIZODOPSIS, but the rugose markings which characterize the jaws of that fish are absent.

PLEURACANTHUS, several beautiful doubly denticulated spines of this genus have been found.

ACANTHODOPSIS. Perfect jaws of this fish have been obtained, and they are the more interesting because the species is new, and only received its name in the annals of Natural History in May last.

DIPLODUS, or double tooth. Specimens of this fossil have been found in great numbers, singly and aggregated in clusters. It has long been a point in dispute among palæontologists whether the fossil was a tooth proper or a dermal tubercle. In the May Annals of Natural History, Messrs. Hancock and Atthey defend the dermal hypothesis; but the matter has been set at rest by the publication of a paper in the Geologist for August, in which the author says he has the mouth and jaws with the teeth attached, and that they are true oral appendages.

STREPSODUS, figured in the Transactions of the Tyneside Naturalists' Field Club, vol. 6, as Holoptychius, has been obtained abundantly, and mounted or unmounted forms a beautiful fossil specimen.

The most prolific field for large specimens of fishes and reptiles is Newsham Colliery. Cramlington and Dudley supply many teeth and a few jaws; Seaton Burn is not rich in specimens, but some of those that are obtained are very excellent; Bedlington Colliery is rich in jaws of fish, and New Backworth furnishes a general assortment of fish and reptile remains, but not in great abundance. The principal fish remains that have been gathered are jaws, ribs, teeth, vertebrae, scales, &c., no whole fishes have been found during the prize collection, and no perfect fishes have at any time been obtained in the Northumberland coal shale.

Great interest in the collection has been taken by the youths connected with various collieries; and special thanks are due to Messrs. Laidlaw and Douglas for the interest they have taken in assisting the youths with their collections. T. P. BARKAS.

RESEMBLANCE BETWEEN PLANTS AND ANIMALS.

Plants, like animals, are endowed with life—strange, mysterious life—of a lower type, perhaps, than that of animals; but on this point, and indeed on many points connected with life, we are very ignorant. One thing is certain, that the life of a plant is subject to very many of the same laws as that of an animal. External circumstances affect it in the same way. A fish that inhabits the water dies if brought into the air, and a land animal is drowned if placed in the water; so, a water plant, if it does not absolutely die when planted in dry ground, cannot thrive, and generally dwindles away, and a land plant cannot bear to be submerged. Nevertheless, plants are capable of adapting themselves to circumstances much more than animals can, and therefore I should suppose that plant-life is of a simpler type than animal-life, and the laws affecting it less intricate.

I once met with an instance, however, that by no means bears out what I have just been saying, and I cannot account for it. A pond containing waterlilies had been drained so nearly dry, that there was only a little soft mud at the bottom; but in this the waterlilies, instead of dying, grew with such luxuriance, sending up such forests of dark green leaves, and such profusion of lovely flowers, that I have never seen the like before or since. Why these waterlilies should have grown better out of their natural element, I cannot say; but, as a rule, plants, like animals, live best in those situations in which nature usually places them.

Another curious point of resemblance been plant and animal life, is that they are said to be affected in the same way by many poisonous substances. If poison is present in the soil or the air in small proportion only, plants become sickly, and we see the effects of the poison in the stunted appearance, the decaying ends of the branches, and the premature fall of leaves. But if poison exists in large quantity, the plants are entirely killed, just as animals would be; and the strangest thing is that poisons act in both in the same way; thus an irritant poison given to an animal would act by destroying the tissues of the body, and it would act in a similar way in a plant; but a narcotic poison, which is supposed to act on the nerves, would take away animal life without destroying any of the tissues, and the same would happen with a plant—life would be destroyed, but the substance of the plant would remain unchanged. No trace of nerves have ever been discovered in plants, as far as I know, but from the effects which narcotic poisons exercise, it certainly would be logical to infer that plants do possess some internal arrangement that is analogous to nerves in an animal. I have heard it said that chloroform will send a plant to sleep, and that a sensitive plant subjected to its influence will droop its leaves ; but I have not tried the experiment.

Plants resemble animals in growing *by the accumulation of matter deposited from food*. It therefore follows, as a matter of course, that plants, like animals, require to eat—though it sounds very strange to put it in that way. We are, however, familiar with the expression "food of plants," which, meaning just the same, does not sound strange at all. A plant *must* have a due supply of food, and that of the proper kind, else it cannot grow. It is quite possible to feed plants, like animals, into different bodily conditions, by giving them different kinds of food. One kind of food will make an animal fat, another thin ; stimulating food will induce a bloated state. It is just the same with plants. One kind of manure will cause an exuberant growth of leaves, another will induce the production of seed, a third the increase of different secretions. But I must now describe to you the way in which plants obtain their supplies of food. It is chiefly by means of their roots, which, though very varied in form in different plants, all agree in one particular, namely, that the very extremities of their fibres are looser in texture, often rather swollen and porous ; and these porous ends of the roots, called by botanists "spongioles," suck up water from the soil, and whatever may be dissolved in the water. This fluid passes up through the substance of the plant into the leaves, where it meets with air (I shall have to tell you directly how this air gets into the leaves) and becomes changed in its nature just as the food of an animal becomes *digested*. The altered sap is then capable of depositing new matter in the plant; so that besides consuming food, plants resemble animals in digesting it.

There is a very beautiful way in which Nature provides for young plants when they first germinate. Most seeds contain a large quantity of starch. This is not soluble in water, but by the action of heat and moisture it becomes converted into sugar, which *is* soluble, and the young plant feeds upon this store of sugar, till its roots are able to draw food from the soil. Very often, just about the time that the store of food in the seed is used up, and the young plant has to begin to forage for itself, it looks yellow and sickly, and our old Cheshire farmers say very expressively that it is "being weaned and is pining for its mother." It is rather remarkable they should speak of it as they would of an animal ; but it is more remarkable still that, in this case, rural Natural History is founded on a strictly scientific fact and not on superstition.

One of the most important of the natural actions performed by animals is that of respiration. Having heard that plants live, grow, eat, and digest like animals, you will not be much surprised to hear that they also breathe. It is true there is none of that regular contraction and expansion of lungs that accompanies the breathing of animals, but every plant that grows requires as constant a supply of the gases that it breathes as an animal does, and it has an apparatus specially formed to enable it to obtain air ; and if through the clogging up of its breathing apparatus it cannot obtain a due supply, it becomes literally suffocated like an animal.

The part of a plant which corresponds to an animal's lungs are its leaves. If you examine a leaf, you will first of all see that it is spread out very flat and think that is in order that a very large amount of surface may be exposed to the air. You will find that the surface of the leaf is covered with a delicate skin, easily separated in some plants, not so easily in others. If you look at this skin through a microscope you will see that it is studded with immense numbers of small green openings. A more careful examination will show that these "stomata," as they are called, are capable of opening and closing to admit the entrance and exit of air and various gases. It is through these openings that air is admitted into the substance of the leaves, where it acts upon the sap that I have already told you found its way to the leaves, and works those changes upon it that can only be compared to the changes that take place in the blood of animals when it comes in contact with air in the lungs.—*From the Quarterly Magazine of the High Wycombe Natural History Society, Oct.*

IN BLOSSOM TIME.

It's O my heart, my heart !
  To be out in the sun and sing ;
To sing and shout in the fields about,
  In the balm and the blossoming.

Sing loud, O bird in the tree,
  O bird, sing loud in the sky ;
And honey-bees, blacken the clover-beds—
  There are none of you glad as I.

The leaves laugh low in the wind,
  Laugh low with the wind at play ;
And the odorous call of the flowers all
  Entices my soul away.

For O but the world is fair, is fair,
  And O but the world is sweet !
I will out in the gold of the blossoming mold
  And sit at the Master's feet.

And the love my heart would speak
  I will fold in the lily's rim,
That the lips of the blossom, more pure and meek,
  May offer it up to Him.

Then sing in the hedgerow green, O Thrush,
  O Skylark, sing in the blue ;
Sing loud, sing clear, that the King may hear,
  And my soul shall sing with you.
    From the Overland Monthly, August, 1868

New Books.

[*Our limited space must of necessity compel us to give but very short notices of new books, but they will perhaps serve as a guide as to what books our readers may ask for at their libraries.*]

Elementary Lessons in Astronomy. By J. Norman Lockyer. Macmillan & Co.

The works of Mr. Lockyer are so eagerly sought after, that we need scarcely call attention to the above. We may, however, remark that it is worthy of the most careful attention, being wonderfully clear and sound in exposition, popular, and at the same time scientific. The illustrations are quite equal to the literary portion, the coloured ones being especially well executed.

A Summer in Iceland. By C. W. Paijkuli. Translated by the Rev. M. R. Barnard. Chapman & Hall.

This work has been translated with considerable care, but although there is much to be gained from a perusal, the book is very heavy. The sketch of the history of Iceland is valuable, as are also the accounts of the eruption of the Great Geyser, and whale fishing on the coasts. The anecdotes about the various animals of the country are also interesting.

The Fresh and Salt Water Aquarium. By the Rev. J. G. Wood, M.A., F.L.S. Fcap. 8vo, 182 pp., and 11 coloured plates. London: Routledge, 1868.

Undoubtedly the best little work upon the subject we have yet seen. Mr. Wood's style of writing is always clear and popular, and the information he gives sound and practical; upon the present occasion he has not departed from his usual careful method, and the result of his work is a Manual that is second to none. Speaking of the formation of aquariums he says:—

There is no need whatever for a complicated glass tank which is so deep that the owner finds great difficulty in getting at the various objects, and which is too heavy to be moved, and occasionally apt to worry its owner by a sudden disposition to leak. Any kind of tub or pan will do for an aquarium, provided that the owner cares more for the inmates than the appearance of their dwelling. I have now at my side a common earthenware pan, eighteen inches wide and three deep, in which are flourishing half-a-dozen sea anemonies, two kinds of sea-weed, and a number of Purpura and other common shells. . . . . An aquarium, which is to fulfil as far as possible the same conditions as the river, the pond, or the sea, ought to be as wide as possible, so as to present a large superfices to the air.

Old English Wild Flowers. By J. T. Burgess. London: Warne & Co.

A very amusing and instructive little volume, rather nicely illustrated with coloured lithographs. The plan adopted by the author has been to take the situations where wild plants grow and describe their inhabitants. The work is more accurately done than the majority of similar works. We may add that the poetry of the subject has been reproduced at length, which will probably make it especially acceptable to young ladies.

New Zealand: its Physical Geography, Geology, and Natural History. With Special Reference to the Results of Government Expeditions in the Provinces of Auckland and Nelson. By Dr. Ferdinand von Hochstetter. Translated from the German original published in 1863, by Edward Sauter, A.M. With additions up to 1866 by the Author. Illustrated with maps, plates, and woodcuts. Stuttgart, Cotta; London, Street.

This work is well worthy the attention of naturalists and those interested in the colony. We extract the following from the chapter on huge wingless birds as being of great interest, and also as a sample of the author's style:—

To the question about the causes of the dying out of those gigantic birds, we must necessarily connect the question about the causes of the final extermination of other large animals of the present period. It is in the 'struggle of life' that we are to seek the clue to the solution of this problem. There are many facts, showing that in the struggle for existence, man acts the main part; that man has already swept quite a number of species from the surface of the earth, and that it is chiefly the largest animals that first succumb. We may even say, that all the larger animals are gradually being exterminated, excepting those which as domestic animals save their existence merely by their absolute dependence on man. The reasons for this are quite obvious. The animal is either useful or noxious to man. If it be a large animal, its useful or noxious qualities are the greater; and in both cases man will strive to kill the beast, either in order to secure to himself the benefits of it, or to avert the great damage. This struggle of extermination will last a longer or shorter time, according to the number of individuals engaged, or—since in the case of large animals, it can be only comparatively small upon a given space,—in proportion to the greater or smaller area of distribution of the animals in question. * * Nor is it to be doubted, that the extermination of the gigantic birds of New Zealand was chiefly accomplished by the hand of man. In briefly retracing the past to the times when New Zealand was not yet trodden by the foot of man, we must assume, that at that time the large Dinornis and Apteryx species, whose bones we find to-day, lived in great numbers upon open fernland, subsisting on the roots of *Pteris esculenta*. Dr. J. Haast notices also the occurrence of bones of the Dinornis in the moraines of the glaciers of South Island, and observes that the present Alpine Flora furnished a large quantity of nutricious food quite capable of sustaining the life even of so large a creature; and as the fruits of these plants seem at present to serve no evident purpose in the economy of nature, he argued the former existence of an adequate amount of animal life, to prevent an excessive development of vegetation. This part was played by the Dinornis. Those huge birds were then the only large animal beings that populated New Zealand; for of indigenous mammalia, except a little rat, there is nothing known. The first immigrants, who throughout the whole length and breadth of the extensive forests found nothing for man to subsist on, except the native rat and some small birds, obtained from the giant-birds the necessary supplies of meat, enabling them to increase in course of time to a whole nation numbering hundreds of thousands. But for those colossal birds, it would be indeed utterly impossible to comprehend how 200,000 or 300,000 human beings could have lived in New Zealand, a country which even in its vegetable world offered nothing for subsistence except fern-roots. That such was really the case is sufficiently proven in the traditions of the natives. Ngahue, one of the discoverers of New Zealand,—so tradition says,—describes the land as the haunt of colossal birds. There are yet some Maori poems extant, in which the father gives his son instructions how to behave in the contests with the Moas, how to hunt and kill them. The feasts are described, which were wont to be instituted after a successful chase. Mr. Cormack as well as Mr. Mantell have found the bones on both the North and the South Islands in great number in the vicinity of camping grounds and fire places of the natives. Mounds were found full of such bones, in which after great feasts the remnants of the meals were promiscuously interred. The flesh and eggs were eaten; the feathers were employed as ornament for the hair; the sculls were used for holding tattooing powder; the bones were converted into fish-hooks, and the colossal eggs were buried with the dead as provision during their long last journey to the lower regions. Consequently those huge birds were in former times the principal game of the natives, and were probably altogether exterminated in the course of a few centuries. They succumbed,—the larger the species, the sooner,—to the same fate that is gradually sweeping the Kiwi, the Kakapo, and the rat Kiore in a similar manner, and before our eyes, from the face of the land. But what next? The Maoris had increased to a very numerous people, the Moas were exterminated; whence were the natives henceforth to get their animal food? This question leads us to the cause and the origin of the terrible cannibalism, that held its sway of terror over New Zealand, when towards the close of the last century the first Europeans landed on its coast. What else is there that could induce a human being to devour his own kindred but want and starvation? There is no other reasonable way of explanation for an act, which is so abhorrent to nature that it occurs even with animals only in exceptional cases when want compels them to take to it as a last resource. It was not barbarity, not savage cruelty, not monstrous heathenism, that drove the uncivilized man of the South Sea so far as to drink his fellow's blood, and eat his flesh; the cannibalism of the South Sea Islanders is to be accounted for in no other way, than the cannibalism of the civilized European, when, shipwrecked, and on the point of starvation, he lays hold of his ill-fated fellow. Cannibalism also is but one of the manifold forms of the struggle of life. It is thus alone that we are able to explain why the history of the past century of New Zealand is but a terrible tale of war and carnage and horrible cannibalism, and why this unnatural state was put an end to within less than twenty years, when by the importation of swine and potatoes on the part of Europeans new means of subsistence had been placed within the natives' reach. Cannibalism has ceased, as it began; but not so the struggle for existence. This has again assumed a new form. From the struggle with the animal world the native, as the stronger, had come out triumphant, but now the tawny South Sea Islander has to wrestle for his existence with the 'pale faces,' and there is no doubt for whom the dooming die is cast in this contest. I am speaking here not only of the open, bloody war between the natives and the English, but of the struggle for existence, as it is carried out between man and man in all those innumerable circumstances which are adduced as reasons why in all parts of the world, in America, in Australia, upon Tasmania, and at the Cape of Good Hope, as well as in New Zealand, the natives are continually growing fewer and gradually dying out."

The Natural History of Man; being an Account of the Manners and Customs of the Uncivilized Races of Men. By the Rev. J. G. Wood, M.A., F.L.S., &c. Africa. London: Routledge & Sons. 1868.

We have here the completion of the first volume of Mr. Wood's work on the Natural History of Man. It comprises the many tribes which people the continent of Africa, and is carefully and truthfully exhaustive of the subject. Should the other continents be as well handled we shall have a most valuable work on the ethnography of the world.

Correspondence.

[*Under this head we shall be glad to insert any letters of general interest.*]

THE NIDIFICATION OF THE JACK SNIPE (*SCOLOPAX GALLINULA*).

Sir,—It has always struck me that a well authenticated instance of the breeding of this little snipe in England would be a desideratum, for although we have the testimony of several writers for, yet we have the positive assurance of a much greater number against the fact of its ever breeding here. It has, indeed, I believe been shot or seen when the summer has been far advanced, although the latest recorded by me is the 3rd of April; and but few people, I fancy, have observed it much later than the middle of April. This being the rule, I hardly know whether I dare venture to assert that I possess a nest and four eggs found in Hampshire this year. The facts are briefly these. Early in August I went down to Aldershot, and while there visited a gentleman who, knowing my fondness for natural history, gave me the nest in question, believing it to be one of the common snipes. Having found this bird's nest myself, I was at once struck by the difference in the materials composing the nest, and the small size and narrowness of the eggs at their tip; the colour also was slightly different (although this is no criterion). On asking my friend, he told me that he saw the bird fly off the nest, that he was sure it was a snipe, but it appeared a *very small one.* (I may mention that he is not a sportsman, and therefore could not tell the difference between the snipes when on flight.) The situation in which he found it was one which the jacks frequent in winter and spring, and the full snipes all the year round.

I have submitted the eggs to several dealers and naturalists; amongst the former, Cooke, of New Oxford-street, and Gardner, of Holborn; and they all appear to consider them veritable Jacks. Mr. G. Gray, of the British Museum, also imagines them to answer the characteristics of that bird's eggs. However, I should like others to see them, especially Mr. C. O. G. Napier, and to that end will leave them at your office for this gentleman or others interested to give their opinion.

I have found that several authors mention the Judcock being found in summer. Thus Yarrell says:—" Mr. C. Girdlestone offered a sovereign to any one who would bring him a bird shot in summer. In 1822 he had one brought to him in June, and in the same month in 1824 he himself saw a pair on Bradwell Common. About two years afterwards another specimen was shot."

Several works mention the Jack procured by Mr. Girdlestone, some giving the exact date, viz., 2nd of June, and the name of the man who got it.

With regard to its building among us several instance are given, the most reliable appearing to be the finding of a nest and four eggs at Garvagh, Londonderry, which was in the possession of Lord Garvagh. Why it should not build with us I know not, as on the authority of Buffon they appear to do so in France; for he says in his " Histoire Naturelle":—" Ces petites bécassines restant presque toute l'année et nichent dans nos marais; leurs œufs de même couleur que ceux de la grande bécassine, sont seulement plus petits à proportion de l'oiseau, qui n'est pas plus gros qu'une aloutte." The " Dictionnaire de Sciences Naturelles " confirms this by saying:—" Elle reste presque toute l'année dans nos marais où elle niche et pond des œufs de la même couleur que ceux de la première " (*i. e.* common snipe).

Mr. Gould, in his superb work " Birds of Great Britain," does not seem to think that it breeds here; he gives no examples, and only instances Hewitson and Wolley.

The eggs which I possess certainly seem to answer the description given by Yarrell, who says that the jacks are smaller and more elliptical than the common snipe, which they otherwise exactly resemble; now on comparison with many eggs in my own, and other collections, I find this to be the case. Meyer's description and figures are also in favour of mine. As for the nest itself, Mr. John Wolley's description of those he found in Lapland, composed of little pieces of grass and equisetum, loosely woven together, interspersed with a few old leaves of the dwarf birch, would seem to be also in favour of mine being a *bonâ fide* jack snipe's. Nevertheless, I cannot give a decided opinion, but will leave that to others.

I remain, Sir, yours, etc., etc.,
A. M. B.

Short Notes.

AN ABYSSINIAN WEDDING.—In Abyssinia, where civil marriages have almost superseded the solemn unions of the church, scarcely one in a hundred will have recourse to a religious ceremony to cement indissolubly the bond between bride and bridegroom. A certain agreement, by which the husband binds himself to pay a stipulated number of cows and shamas (*dresses*) to his wife, is all that is required in that country; and then they may perhaps become attached to each other, and live peaceably in this ever-changing world; or, as not unfrequently happens, they may become disgusted with one another after the lapse of some weeks, or months, and separate. During the period that King Theodore remained in the altered mood which he had chosen, or had been induced by good counsel to follow, many of the chieftains, in order to please their master, sought the church sacrament to confirm, after the example of his Majesty, their matrimonial vow. And did not an ignorant and fanatic priesthood deny this sacred rite to the majority of their applicants, conjugal fidelity and hallowed affection would soon supplant gross sensuality and foul vice. The king's civil marriage being attested by a jubilant nation, nothing else was requisite to make it lasting and secure but the holy communion; and this the happy pair received in grand state, the week following, from the hands of the Abuna Salama, the metropolitan of the church, who had been summoned from Magdala for that purpose. Great feasting is indispensable on grand occasions in Abyssinia, and the amount of raw beef consumed on such a festive day quite exceeds the bounds of credibility. Most guests eat from seven to eight pounds, and absorb, if they can get it, a proportionate quantity of strong intoxicating hydromel. Hundreds of beeves were for about a week sacrificed every day to satisfy hungry visitors, who thronged around the liberal board of royalty; whilst the jars of liquid drained by those thirsty souls exceeded all computation.—*From " Abyssinian Notes," by a late Captive, in " The Quiver."*

AIR-BLADDER OF FISHES.—The contents of the air-bladder of fishes have been analysed by

Humboldt, Biot, and others, and, strange to say, remarkable differences are stated to exist, according as the fish are freshwater or marine. The air consists of a mixture of nitrogen and oxygen, with traces of carbonic acid gas; in fresh-water fishes the largest percentage of nitrogen occurs; in salt-water fishes oxygen is said to occur in the largest proportion. Some, I believe, have maintained that the air of the swim-bladder of carps consists of pure nitrogen. Humboldt, who experimented on the electric eel (*Gymnotus electricus*), found the gas of its air-bladder to consist of 96 deg. of nitrogen and 4 deg. of oxygen. Biot, on the other hand, experimenting on some deep-sea Mediterranean fishes, discovered 87 deg. of oxygen, the rest nitrogen, with a trace of carbonic acid. This, if an undoubted fact, is certainly a singular anomaly, and I confess I share with the late Dr. Davy some doubt as to the accuracy of the experiments. That the same organ should secrete two gases so very different in their nature appears anomalous, and deserving of further inquiry. Indeed, does not the entire subject need more minute inquiry? At present the facts relating to it are few, and seem far from adequate to allow of very satisfactory conclusions being drawn as to the use of the bladder and its secretion in the animal economy; except of a mechanical kind, as effecting the specific gravity of the fish. Were the gas uniformly of one kind, were it constantly azote, it might be easy to assign it a plausible end, the function of the air-bladder might be inferred to be auxiliary to that of the kidneys. The secretion of oxygen is the anomalous fact, so contrary is it to the ordinary course of changes in living animals, in which the general tendency is to the consumption of oxygen—*a priori*, one might almost as much expect oxygen to be exhaled for the lungs, in respiration, as to be separated from the blood by secretion by the air-bladder, and had we not the authority of so accurate an observer as M. Biot, we might be led to suspect that the statement of its being so was founded on error.—*Popular Science Review*, October.

SPHINX CONVOLVULI.—Just at the gloaming in the evening of the 29th of August, I had the pleasure of seeing the beautiful and rare Unicorn Hawk-moth. I was walking in my garden, when suddenly I was aware of the presence of this fine Sphinx, hovering round a large scarlet geranium, against the individual flowers of which it hung in air for about a second over each in succession, its very long sucker inserted into the blossom—so long, indeed, that the head of the insect was fully three inches away as it pumped up the grateful nectar. It shot off from plant to plant along the borders, rifling nearly every blossom on each before it tried another, manifestly preferring the petunias and the zonal geraniums, though many other plants were in flower. The insect remained under my observation for a full quarter of an hour in different quarters of the garden. It was so fearless, or so engaged in its nectar-draughts, that by a little precaution in my movements I could approach quite close to it, and bring down my face to within a foot from it, without at all disturbing it. I believe I could have easily caught it in my hand if I had really wanted it; I did very nearly grasp it, though only half in earnest.

The end of my beauteous visitor was tragi-comic. I was eagerly watching it in the fading light, and admiring the bands of black and red and white on the abdomen, which were beautifully distinct and well-defined, while the wings, from their rapid vibration, were mere shapeless clouds, when I saw that I was not the only admirer. A neighbour's cat was crouching under a bush close by, following the moth with her eyes as eagerly as I. Puss was stealthily creeping, *ventre à terre*, closer and closer to the unsuspecting prey, and though by voice and gesture I sought to frighten her off she pertinaciously returned. At last I ceased, wishing to see the result; and puss made her spring, striking down the moth at my very feet with the utmost ease, closing upon it at the same instant, and carrying it off in her mouth behind the shrubs. I presently pursued; but in the deepening dusk I could find no trace of the moth, while pussy began to purr and to invite caresses, as cats often do when they have caught a mouse, evidently thinking that she had performed a praiseworthy feat. It was a rather ignoble fate for my noble insect visitor.—*P. H. Gosse, F.R.S., Hardwicke's Science-Gossip for October.*

HAIR OF ANIMALS.—Respecting the white furs and hair of animals, the microscope yields us a full explanation of the facts. The difference between colourless and coloured hair is one of pigment or its absence. The appearance of *whiteness* or *darkness* of an object is an optical phenomenon, explicable by material conditions such as are exhibited by the elegant hair and wool structures of mammals when placed under a microscope. In viewing such textures by transmitted light, solid parts which strongly reflect or refract light, will be seen as more or less opaque objects; fluids which are colourless, and transmit light, will be scarcely noticeable; and coloured fluids absorbing all portions of the spectrum but those corresponding to their own colour, reflect and transmit their colour equally whether viewed by reflected or transmitted light. But a colourless part is not *necessarily* transparent, as it may appear with a white tint, which has more or less "body" giving the idea of substance. Thus if we examine a dark coloured hair by transmitted light, it will appear black in proportion to the density and closeness of the pigment—being opaque, it obstructs the passage of light. The same hair seen in reflected light, will exhibit its own proper colour if the cuticle under which the pigmented cortex lies is transparent; but the surface markings of the scale will be distinguishable as fine lines projected over the subjacent pigment. Again, if the pigment disappear and be replaced by fatty molecules, the hair will appear, by reflected light, of a dull white colour, with a considerable body, and by transmitted light, instead of being transparent, it will appear as opaque, and therefore as dark as the pigmented hair, care being taken to exclude all reflected light.—*From Paper read before Bristol Naturalists' Society.*

DEEP SEA DREDGING IN THE GULF STREAM.—At the meeting in August of the United States National Academy of Sciences, a paper was read by Count Pourtales, who has recently been employed by the Coast Survey to dredge the bottom of the ocean along the course of the Gulf Stream, in parallel lines, crossing the current, the lines being about ten miles apart. In starting south-easterly from Florida, he found the bottom for four or five miles made up of the common coral sand of that neighbourhood, with very scanty traces of life. The next area, from 90 to 300 fathoms, and the first part of the way forming a plateau, is a rocky floor made of very hard limestone, derived from living shells. Life was abundant, consisting of lamp-shells, starfishes, crustaceans, and molluscs generally. There were also many bones of the manatee, a dolphin-like animal, usually found living in shallow water. The third area was the regular and common ocean bottom, from 250 to 300 fathoms, covered by the chalky remains of foraminifera—those minute animals found several years since on the telegraphic plateau in the North Atlantic. He also exhibited a map of the bottom of the ocean off the coast, and found, first, extending from the north of Florida to Montauk Point, near Block Island, Rhode Island, a bottom of siliceous sand, perhaps 100 miles wide. Outside of it was a calcareous bottom, occupying the whole area south of Georgia. Between the two off the Carolinas, is a limited deposit of green sand, containing the foraminifera. A letter was read from Professor Agassiz, warmly eulogising Pourtales's papers, and saying that he had solicited the honour of publishing the maps and other results in one of the volumes issued at the Museum of Comparative Zoology in Cambridge, Massachusetts. It opens, he said, an entirely new chapter in natural history. It disclosed what had never been before known, the various fauna at the bottom of the ocean. Among the animals obtained were some that had been extinct since the cretaceous and tertiary periods.—*New York Times.*

EFFECT OF LIGHTNING ON METALS.—The following curious communication has just been made to the Paris Academy of Sciences. A woman was crossing a canal-bridge, near Nantes, when a powerful flash of lightning seemed, according to her own expression, to envelope her; she was not in any way injured, but the contents of her purse underwent an extraordinary change. A ten-franc gold piece was in the small minor pocket of the *portemonnaie*, and two silver coins in the larger division of the same. A certain quantity of the silver was vaporised by the action of the lightning passed through the leather lining of the purse, and was deposited with great uniformity on the gold coin, which had all the appearance of silver, while the surface of the silver coins had assumed the appearance of having been matted or frosted. M. Bobierre, who made the communication, said that he had examined the gold coin with a microscope, and found that the silver was uniformly deposited apparently in the form of globules, without any intervals between them. Having removed a small portion of the silver by means of a weak acid, M. Bobierre found that the surface of the gold coin had been affected, and presented a very different appearance to that produced by the coining press, and was, in fact, nearly in the same condition as the deposited silver; fusion had in fact commenced, but the effect had been instantaneous, and purely superficial.

HOW THE SPIDER RESTORES A LOST LEG.—In one peculiar respect spiders resemble crabs, being compelled repeatedly to change their coats. The first of these moults must be undergone by the young spider before it can even move. The creature is at first bound up like a mummy in a tight covering, confining all the limbs. Some house-spiders obtain nine changes of raiment in a life-time. It is at these seasons that the spider has its only chance of recovering the lost limbs which it often parts with so easily. The loss of a leg is not a trivial matter, as the want of the combing-claw may prevent the proper spinning of the web-threads. Sir Joseph Banks caught a spider having but three legs; he kept it for examination, and in about a month saw the old skin cast off, when the rudiments of five new legs appeared, which in three days grew to half the size of the old ones. In twenty-nine days after there was a second casting off the skin, when the five legs became still larger. It seems, therefore, that lost limbs are not completely restored at one moulting. The feet of most spiders exhibit a complex apparatus, fitted for walking on glass, running over water, along a ceiling, or moving over the fine web lines. The animal may indeed be said to take "hold with her hands." These feet should be carefully examined through a microscope to detect the fine brush, and hooked arrangement by which, according to Mr. Blackwall, the spider clings to the smoothest surfaces.—*From "Recreative Natural History," in "Cassell's New Popular Educator" for October.*

PUFF-BALL.—In a paper read before the Bristol Naturalists' Society, Mr. S. H. Swayne, M.R.C.S., showed an unusually large specimen of the common puff-ball fungus, which he had gathered recently in Herefordshire. He also mentioned that when there he had seen a specimen of the common edible mushroom, which was the largest he had ever met with. It measured about two feet in circumference.

OSPREY SHOT IN GUERNSEY.—On the 30th ult., a fine osprey (female), sometimes called the sea eagle, a rare bird for these parts, was shot in the neighbourhood of Delancey Hill, and may now be seen at the shop of Mr. Couch, taxidermist, Pollet-street. It was 29 inches long, and 69 inches across the wings; weight 3lb. 3oz.—*Local Paper.*

Remarks, Queries, &c.

(*Under this head we shall be happy to insert original Remarks, Queries, &c.*)

DO INSECTS FEEL PAIN?

"Entomologicus" and "P. G. M." do not even attempt to say anything new on the subject, but like a couple of *imaginary quantities* they struggle out.

The production of the first is evidently hypothetically affirmative, and "P. G. M." is equally so if I understand his last sentence, for here it is—"Must not the sensibility to pain of insects compared with that of man be *extremely little?*" Even in this "extremely little" some pain is implied. Thank you, Mr. P. G. M." There is, Sir, this undeniable consistency in the writings of all your correspondents on the negative side, viz., that while they bluntly deny that insects are susceptible of pain, yet they strangely contradict themselves by actually admitting, and even arguing, that insects do feel pain. I am sure the readers and correspondents of the NATURALIST'S NOTE BOOK must have noticed this. But "P. G. M.," in order to be a little original, thus breaks forth from behind his sombre cloud—"The organisation of insects is far different from that of *mortals*." Different from that of *mortals!* Now we are left to infer that insects are *immortals*. I'll say no more to "P. G. M." Anatomise my arguments with animated pens, but save me from such originality.

H. H. ULIDIA.

After the brilliant pyrotechnics of Mr. Ulidia, I suppose a mere schoolboy utterance will find little favour: still, I should greatly like to ask whether you really think the cause of science is advanced by such vicious reasoning as he gives us? Omitting irrelevant matter, the first argument I find is that because Mr. Harvie recommends keeping on the safe side, he therefore has arrived at an "affirmative conclusion." In other words, if Mr. Ulidia refused to draw lots with 10,000 other people, the loser undertaking to emulate Blondin on the tight rope, we should be justified in saying that he felt sure he would be the man chosen. Any honest reasoner would see that Mr. Harvie is morally convinced that insects feel no pain; still, etc., etc. ; and this is plain sense.

Next we come to a few apparently sound sentences. I am not fitted to criticise them, as I have no books here.

Next, "Paley admits that insects feel pleasure." Not much of an argument this.

Next, "They struggle to get free, and this should teach you, etc."

How do we know that in obeying their instinct to struggle and get free, insects do not find just as much fun as in obeying other instincts?

The next few paragraphs I cannot understand.

After this comes such a transparent fallacy that any one can detect it at a glance.

Mr. Spicer asks how the moth remains quietly in its place? Mr. Ulidia answers the question, *only* omitting the most important word, "quietly."

A few lines lower down we have—"and this is a struggle, a sign of pain." This is begging the question. The next paragraph does not affect the argument.

As for the quotation, "Nil admirari," I should very much like to hear your correspondent translate it, with its context:—

"Nil admirari prope res est una . . . quæ possit."

I suppose he would say—"No wonder there is only one thing which can." Let him consult the nearest lexicon, and not repeat his offences to

GOOD TASTE.

The question now under discussion, viz., Do insects feel pain? has already occupied considerable space in the columns of the NATURALIST'S NOTE BOOK, and appears to be of great interest to the readers, as it has brought forth several correspondents upon the subject, all of whom are evidently gifted with inquiring minds, and desirous of assisting us in arriving at a successful issue.

The result I still think will be in opposition to Mr. Ulidia's theory; but should this be the case, let us hope that gentleman will not persist in what appears to be his present opinion, that we are antagonists, and should be opposed in whatever we advance.

I will not accuse Mr. Ulidia with writing that which he well knows there is not the slightest foundation for stating, but must inform him that I really imagine he did on that occasion indulge in a short nap between reading and writing.

Should I be wrong in this conjecture, I am totally unable to account for the extraordinary mistakes has made in his last note concerning statements which he alleges I have forwarded.

Mr. Ulidia commences his attack with—"But, Mr. Spicer, 'I think others see as well as you,' for Mr. Waters has had the pleasure of seeing insects pinned to a tree."

I should feel obliged to Mr. Ulidia if he will inform us from whence he obtained his information, as I have not said so, therefore it must be purely imaginary. And as this correspondent has favoured us with the above extract, I beg to call his attention to the following lines from the same well-known poem:—

"With eyes that hardly served at most
To guard their master 'gainst a post."

And to refer him to what I have actually written:— "Mr. Ulidia again says—'But listen to Mr. Waters, and watch his movements : he sticks pins in insects, and for a time he lets the tortured creatures suffer; ultimately he relents and prepares to kill them."

This has been entirely misrepresented, as the following will prove:—

"A few days since I received several specimens of the moth referred to, viz., the wood leopard. They had been secured with large pins, but not killed. I found one (a male) had disengaged himself from the box, but still carried the pin. I did not fasten it, as I was then preparing to kill them, considering the sooner they were relieved from their misery the better."

Mr. Ulidia now endeavours to show that I placed the pins through these moths, but had he given a second glance at my note he would in all probability have understood that they were pinned when I received them.

Again, Mr. Ulidia says that "misery is pain, just as sure as Mr. Waters is a naturalist." Now I must differ with him in this also, as misery is not necessarily pain.

That I am a naturalist, as suggested, is well known, and therefore I have many opportunities of making observations more than amateur naturalists in general, as thousands of specimens of natural history pass through my hands that cannot be procured by purchase.

But, Mr. Ulidia, I must again refer you to my note, as you have once more arrived at a conclusion that is quite at variance with facts; and as this statement is so much adulterated with sarcasm, I must call attention to the portion of the note to which I refer:—

"Again, Mr. Waters, with all the dexterity of a practical gladiator, attacks a dragon-fly with the stick of his net: the poor insect evidently gets the worst of the battle, for according to the victor's account the vanquished creature had its body divided."

I also give the portion of my note to which he refers, and trust it has been better understood by other readers of the NOTE BOOK than appears to be the case with the above-named correspondent :—

"I accidently struck one of the largest of the family with the stick of my net as I was about to capture it, and divided the body, leaving about a quarter of an inch attached to the thorax."

But in the event of this gentleman not having discovered his error, and as he does not appear to understand in what manner the fly in question became injured, I will inform him that the stick alluded to passes through the centre of the net-hoop, and in striking with the net the stick accidentally came in contact with the body of the fly. This, Mr. Ulidia would have understood had he collected insects for only one season, and probably the same or a similar accident would have occurred to him without acting the part of a practical gladiator as he has represented.

Now, to return to the subject. Is it at all reasonable to suppose that insects were created with that sensibility to pain as compared with man, when we all know (or have opportunities of seeing) numbers of caterpillars every season that have been attacked by parasites, the larvæ of these, varying from one to three hundred, subsisting entirely upon the juices of the body, remaining weeks and even months in the victim, in most cases until the caterpillar undergoes the change into the pupæ state? Now in this instance insects are not subjected to these attacks by accident, therefore I cannot conceive in what manner Mr. Ulidia can account for the same Power that formed these beautiful insects at the same time sending others to torture them during the whole of their lives—which would certainly be the case if they feel pain as acutely as we do.

That it is necessary there should be insects to devour each other and counteract the enormous increase of certain species we can comprehend, but if it is accompanied with as much pain as we should experience were we subjected to the tortures which a number of animals of a proportionate size would inflict, this would be a world of pain indeed. I am therefore of the same opinion, that insects feel extremely little if any pain.

J. B. WATERS.

I have read with much interest your correspondence on this subject, and should like to join the battle under Mr. Ulidia's banner. A raw recruit, indeed; only an undergraduate reading for the School of Natural Science at Oxford; but peradventure I shall not be refused the coloured streamers and the Queen's shilling. It is much to be regretted that our champion has brought a weak point to confront the enemy at the onset: he has, I think, refrained from using some of his more deadly weapons, and has had recourse to the sling and stone. Failing the mark, he has afforded the enemy a strong vantage-ground, of which more than one representative has availed himself. This weak point seized by Messrs. Spicer, Waters, and Harvie, occurs in "H. H. U.'s" remarks (NATURALIST'S NOTE BOOK, page 250) :—
"Man himself feels pain, the whale, the elephant, the sparrow, etc., and consequently insects feel pain." Now there are limits even to the elasticity of analogy, and I fear the boundary line has been a little over-reached in this case. Mr. Ulidia himself must confess he was rash. The point he wished to prove was that vitality involves sensation. This is the great question at issue, but its solution must be sought by a more careful and gradual process : the links in the chain of evidence cannot be so summarily dispensed with ; the chasm between the sparrow and the spider is too wide to be spanned at a single stride. The delicate structure of the insect ; the assumptions, that "deprived of feeling animal life is little more than inorganic existence ;" that "instinct implies susceptibility of pain ;"—these are weighty arguments, and would have been more effective without the preface, "man himself feels pain," etc. Further, I think we can hardly concede that "a tortured insect feels as when a giant dies." Analogy may fairly argue that, even as the physical organism of animals develops in complexity of structure as they rise in the catalogue of animal life, so the physiological powers of sensation increase in the same harmonious proportion. This is a fairer hypothesis than Mr. Spicer's, which maintains that the absence of a nervous system disproves sensation. Insects of course *may* feel : the reasonable inference is that they actually *do* feel in a degree proportionate to the simplicity or complexity of organism. "Can we by searching find out God ? Can we find out the Almighty to perfection ? Who doeth great things past finding out ; yea, and wonders without number."

In his reply to Mr. Spicer's letter of page 278, "H. H. U." satisfactorily settles the main question about the blood and brains of insects, without touching upon the second point. To quote Mr. Spicer's words :—"I would look at the matter from another point of view, and assert that the idea of sensibility to pain among the lower animals is scarcely consistent with our notions of God's goodness and mercy, which are over *all* His works." And I would ask, is it a proof of goodness to give these delicate feelings to creatures which are every moment exposed to the loss of limbs, and similar frightful accidents ? . . . More than this, we know that the Creator does not waste His gifts, or, in other words, endow His creatures with superfluous organs or properties. But this law would be violated if the bulk of the lower animals felt pain." Prove your statement, my dear Sir! "Superfluous organs or properties!" Who, then, is the Creator's Architect? Who dictates the pattern He is to follow in fashioning His creatures? Who decides what organs an insect requires, and what he can dispense with? Who, in fact, laid down "this law" which the Creator is forbidden by Mr. Spicer to violate? And if the sensation of pain is granted to a creature that "he may avoid the dangers that cause it," does it not follow that the instinct of self preservation depends upon sensibility to pain? And do not insects possess this instinct, or are they altogether reckless? Would a gnat as soon fly down a swallow's throat as frisk in the sunshine of heaven? But this is trifling. The passage in Mr. Spicer's article is fatal for other reasons. There is a limit to argument which no human intelligence can pass, and Mr. Spicer has attempted so to do, when he asserts that "the idea of sensibility to pain among lower animals is *inconsistent with our notions* of God's goodness." He might as well say he does not understand why God, who is all holy and merciful, ever permitted sin to exist, seeing He could have prevented it? why, when sin came into the world, He did not wholly instead of partially remove its curse? why, whereas half the infants die before they are responsible, yet God does not cause all to die in infancy who, if they live, He knows will live wickedly? Such questions can be answered neither by Scripture nor philosophy; on such perplexing problems we are *not* to be satisfied, concerning which Milton has described even angelic beings as lost in inextricable difficulty. It is impossible to reason of the Infinite by induction based on the comprehension of finite understanding.

And now I will humbly submit my theory for Mr. Spicer's criticism :—" We know that *the whole* creation groaneth and travaileth in pain together until now : for the creature was made subject to vanity, not willingly, but by reason of him who hath subjected the same in hope ; because *the creature itself also shall be delivered* from the bondage of corruption into the glorious liberty of the children of God." In accordance with St. Paul's words, we see the unsinning brute creation involved in pain and death as the consequence of man's sin. (Perhaps Mr. Spicer may think this "inconsistent with his notions of God's mercy ;" but unfortunately it is a patent fact from which he cannot depart.) We have no authority for exempting the lower animals from their share in the universal curse. It would be presumption in spite of the assurance " the whole creation groaneth and travaileth together in pain." But I firmly believe that they are destined hereafter, in some way according to their nature, to participate in the glorious liberty of God's children. At least I could not presume to believe otherwise when this passage of the Romans distinctly asserts it shall be even so. Wherefore we need not be staggered at the idea that "we cannot walk across a garden path without causing agony" to myriads of insects.

> Oh, yet we trust that somehow good
> Will be the final goal of ill,
> To pangs of nature, sins of will,
> Defects of doubt, and taints of blood.
>
> That nothing walks with aimless feet;
> That not one life shall be destroy'd,
> Or cast as rubbish to the void,
> When God hath made the pile complete.
>
> Behold, we know not anything;
> I can but trust that good shall fall
> At last—far off—at last, to all,
> And every winter change to spring.

C.

Your correspondent, Mr. H. H. Ulidia, must certainly have a curious faculty of seeing (in the letters of other gentlemen) only that which he thinks proper, and of entirely ignoring anything that he finds too difficult to controvert. Besides this, he seems to imagine that the only admissible arguments upon this question are those to be obtained from analogy; although in his last paragraph (of his last letter) he tacitly, though really, denies that idea.

Let us examine his last letter a little. In it he says that Mr. Spicer admits that insects feel pain, in these words—" I grant that insects struggle to get free." This deduction is absurd ; for if you were to hold a goat by its horns, would it not struggle to get free? Yet I should think that no one would be ridiculous enough to hold that it hurt a goat to hold it by its horns.

Mr. H. H. U. then founds an argument for his theory on the fact that insects possess an instinct that leads them to avoid danger. He holds that they avoid danger for the sake of the pain that it would occasion them. Now, may we not more rationally assume that that instinct is given them in order to preserve their species from total extinction ?

Mr. H. H. Ulidia's next objection to Mr. Spicer's letter is a mere quibble. Instead of placing (in the sentence which he quotes) the emphasis upon the word *quietly*, he prefers falsely to put it upon the word *place*. He then asks if *Mr. Spicer* would remain in *his* place if *he* were pinned to a tree ? But in this remarkably sensible question he omits the *quietly*, for obvious reasons.

A little farther on Mr. H. H. U. appears to hold that insects suffer from *mental* pain ! Poor creatures !

Your correspondent then attacks Mr. Waters on the ground of inconsistency, because he (Mr. Waters) says of some moths into which he had stuck pins—" The sooner they were relieved from their misery the better." But this is evidently a mere slip. Do not men talk of being " sick at heart," "heartsore," etc., long after they are quite convinced that the heart has nothing whatever to do with the matter ? Yet you would hardly call a physiologist inconsistent because he said he was heartsore.

It is in his last paragraph, however, that Mr. H. H. U. shows most his contempt of rational argument, for in it he says that "Mr. Harvie's bisected wasp admittedly feels pain, while the wasp in question actually made a meal of some syrup after he had been deprived of half his body.

This, I think, clearly shows the falsity of analogies drawn between the higher classes of animals and the insects. Would a mouse, for instance, eat anything after it had been bisected ? or (to speak more to the purpose) after his *tail* merely had been cut off ?

FRED. J. CROOK.

I wish to let you know that I still keep on reading your books, as I was advised to do last spring ; and I may say, now I have got used to them I look for them every month as regular as I do for my daily food, as I always find something new to be learned from the reading of them. Though I lived most of my time about in the country, and always found a wonderful pleasure at looking on the outside of the trees, and the birds, and the butterflies, and all such kind of things ; but I must say that I did not know so much about the inside, that is, whether they all had hearts, and lungs, and brains, the same as some of us. Now, by reading, I find that some gentlemen who study the matter say that trees, and plants, and such like, have lungs and hearts, and that even these green things regularly breathe through the leaves, while the blood, which is mostly rather whitish, flows from every part of the lowest roots up to the very top leaf of the trees; and I have no reason to doubt that, as I do not for the life of me see how they could grow and get on without something of this kind taking place; but I do not find anybody just yet showing how much pain these things feel when a host of caterpillars are gnawing at their lungs, or eating away into the very hearts of them. Of course I cannot say anything about this matter myself, although I well remember that I once cut a hard branch of a grapevine rather too late in the spring of the year, and I found the juice, as I called it, all running out where I cut the wood off. So I spoke to a gardener about it, and he told me it would likely bleed to death if I let it go on at that rate, but I must put a red-hot poker to the cut if I wished to stop the bleeding, as he called it. Well, I thought this rather sharp work, especially as I had heard this plan spoken of as a great cruelty to live horses. However, I did it by his advice, and as I got a good crop of grapes the same season, why I was glad that I did do it afterwards. Now about the caterpillars and moths, I am told that they really do feel pain at times, though they breathe through the sides, and have no brain in their heads like what they call the warm-blooded animals, but their brains are spread all round their sides and mixed up with the lungs; and the blood, if they have any, is generally rather white and cold, which makes me hope they do not feel so much pain as a horse would with a spear run through, or a red-hot iron put on to a sore place. I certainly did once see some insects like large gnats stand on the pales and shake as if they had got the palsy or the ague; but when I laid hold of one he struggled and kicked so that he kicked some of his legs off, and what was curious the legs kept on kicking after they were off: now whether this was from pain of course I cannot say. And one night I found a large long-legged spider that by some mishap had tumbled into a jar in the bedroom, and as I thought I would take care of him I put some water in, and he crumpled up at the bottom of the jar, and never tried to get out nor even to move about. Well, I let him remain there till the middle of the next day; and then I took him out and laid him on a piece of paper to draw the water out of him, and there I left him for about an hour or so: but when I came back he was up and standing on the wall rubbing one leg at a time, as if he only felt a little chill from the water being cold. Well, I thought then there must be some little difference somewhere between these insect kinds and men and horses, as they would to all intents and purposes have been dead and past recovery in less than one third of that time. As to moths, I am almost satisfied that they do not feel the same amount of pain as a man or a horse. Not that I want to shelter myself in the matter. But I have put a pin through a good many of them in my time, as I did not know how to handle them and fix them without doing so; but I used to carry a little bottle with some aquafortis in it, and I had a piece of quill sharpened up, and pricked them with this underneath after I had dipped it in the stuff, and this very soon put an end to them. To say nothing about the pain, it is best to kill them as soon as you well can, or else they spoil their look by fluttering and kicking about too much. Now a very demure looking man once put a paper in my hand that rather gave me a turn at first, as it was like this:—

"Take not away the life thou can'st not give,
All creatures have an equal right to live."

Well, thinks I, this is a clipper, however. But if we are to follow this up, how for the butchers' meat, mutton and beef; and the fishmongers' salmon, shrimps, and oysters. And then, again, how for the rats and mice, and fleas, bugs, and lice, why they would trouble us wonderfully if we did not keep them under a little: I doubt whether some of these would not get rather roughly handled even by some who uphold such a notion as these lines lead to. But, to finish, I do know that a very clever gardener may make a very nice looking posey by the way he puts things together, though there may not be one real true flower among the whole lot. Lines often read very pretty, but I do not think they amount to much generally by way of argument. And so I hope that the gentlemen who may differ a little in their opinion about the pain in insects, and the like, won't let it lead on to a duel between them, as I should be sorry to know that the editor had lost some of his useful and amusing writers in this sort of way.   JEREMIAH SAWCUT.

THE USE OF PLANTS.

"On pure Maderia's, vine robed, hills of health
In Java's swamps of pestilence and wealth."
—*Montgomery*.

WILL you allow me to endeavour to satisfy the "inquiring mind" of "R. B. W." as to the reason why countries which abound in vegetation are injurious to human health? The fact that the green part of plants when exposed to the light of the sun, decompose carbonic acid, appropriate the carbon to their own growth, and give off the oxygen which it contained, has now been proved by experiments, so as to admit of no ground for doubt; but what takes place during the night is not so clearly understood. Some botanists contend that their action is even then the same, but that they give off a far less quantity of oxygen than during the day; while others think that they then deteriorate the atmosphere by giving off carbonic acid. But even if the latter is true, there can be no doubt that the proportion of the evil is very small, compared with the amount of oxygen which they give off during the day: and therefore a proper proportion of plants and trees are necessary, to purify the air, and keep it fit to sustain human life.

In tropical countries plants perspire considerably, and the amount of moisture thus given out where vegetation is very rank, causes the atmosphere to become humid and deleterious, on account of being overcharged with moisture; while in countries where there are very few plants, the climate is frequently too dry. But probably the principle cause of diseases is the miasma which is constantly arising from the decaying matter; for in hot damp countries, plants spring up and die in a very short space of time, and from the putrifying vegetable mass so formed, various gases arise, all of which are very prejudicial to human life, and laden the air with fevers and other scourges of tropical countries.

The real cause then of such countries being unhealthy, appears to be an undue preponderance of vegetation; and to the proper balance of the two divisions of organised nature we may probably ascribe the healthy and wholesome climate of our own country.

O. R.

I shall indeed feel particularly happy in doing all in my power to satisfy your clever correspondent, "R. B. W.," on this subject. In the NATURALIST'S NOTE BOOK, page 253, he puts the query—"How is it that the vicinity of woods, and those places where vegetation thrives best, and is most abundant, is unfavourable to health?" In p. 273 I hurriedly replied. And again, at p. 316, "R. B. W." tells me he is not quite satisfied that I termed his question a little paradoxical. Now, "R. B. W.," sit down until we again look over your query, and subject it to a bit of simple analysis. Well, your question contains two propositions:—

1st. The vicinity of woods is unfavourable to health.

2nd. Those places where vegetation thrives best are unfavourable to health.

The first proposition I admitted, and endeavoured to assign reasons. The second proposition I do not admit, for as the vegetation mentioned in it may imply not trees alone, but grass, grapes, corn, wheat, potatoes, etc., etc.; and hence the south and many of the central parts of Europe, Madeira Islands, etc., etc., are remarkable for their vegetation and yet quite favourable to health. Again, Sir, taking your second proposition as it stands, we might take the fertility of the ground for the *cause* of being unfavourable to health, whereas I presume you mean that the luxuriant vegetation is the cause; and even the luxuriant vegetation is not directly the cause, but the *decay*, the *decomposition*, of that luxuriant vegetation. Vegetation, instead of being "unfavourable to health," purifies the air, and is absolutely *favourable* to health. We eat, and the most abundant element in our food is carbon; and further, too, we by this means take in more carbon than is really necessary for the supply of our bodies, and again this carbon must be got rid of. And how? Well, it unites in the body with another substance called oxygen, and the union of these two elements produces carbonic acid, this dissolves in the blood, colours it a deep purple, "and escapes from it when by the action of the heart the black blood is exposed to the action of the air on the surface of the lungs." And now, "R. W. B.," if you have quietly followed me so far, you will perceive that it is now the office of the air to again restore this oxygen, which removes the carbon from the blood.

Observe, Sir, that this oxygen must be restored, or we die, for we cannot breathe air that has been deprived of oxygen.

And, Sir, how is the process of restoration carried on? Why, the vegetables come to our assistance—they live and breathe; and as animals in eating take in too much carbon with their food, so the vegetables in eating (with their roots) take in too little carbon; and while animals breathe and give out carbon, the vegetables as eagerly breathe to take it in. The carbon inhaled by the plant forms the *woody* part, and, as a matter of course, becomes *fixed*, and hence the oxygen consumed by the respiration of animals and by combustion is again given out by the plants. But let us hear Sir J. E. Smith on the subject:—"It is agreed that in the daytime plants imbibe from the atmosphere carbonic acid gas (which is a compound of oxygen and carbon), that they decompose it, absorb the carbon, as matter of nourishment, which is added to the sap, and emit the oxygen. The burning of a candle, or the breathing of animals, in a confined space produces so much of this gas, that neither of these operations can go on beyond a certain time; but the air so contaminated serves as food for vegetables, the leaves of which assisted by light soon restore the oxygen, or, in other words, purify the air. This beautiful discovery shows a mutual dependence of the animal and vegetable kingdoms, and adds another to the many proofs we have of the wisdom and wonder-working power of the Creator of all things. In the dark, plants give out carbonic acid, and absorb oxygen; but the proportion of the latter is small, compared to what they exhale by day, as must likewise be the proportion of carbonic acid given out; else the quantity of carbon added to their substance would be but trifling, especially in those climates in which the proportion of day to night is nearly equal, and which, notwithstanding, we know to be excessively luxuriant in vegetation."

Surely, Sir, by this time your correspondent, "R. B. W.," perceives that *plants are conducive to health*—nay, Sir, that they are indispensably necessary to animal life.

But the air is fortunately not pure oxygen. An animal which breathes pure oxygen pants violently, becomes flushed, is soon choked, or dies of inflammation of the lungs, produced by the intense action.

It is well known that if the air were pure oxygen all our little domestic fires would be regular conflagrations; and if in the morning "R. B. W.," while preparing for breakfast, should chance to heat his tongs, poker, or coffee-pot red hot, they would fly off like dangerous bombs or congreve rockets. Whether I have even yet succeeded in satisfying "R. B. W." on the subject I know not; he may feel a difficulty, but in labouring to overcome this difficulty he will have an agreeable exercise.

H. H. ULIDIA.

Being one of those who are inclined to countenance the supposition that the faculty of reason is not entirely confined to man, but enjoyed in a limited degree by the higher families of the vertebrate kingdom, I trust you will allow me to reply briefly to "R. B. W.'s" remarks on "Instinct in Plants." (N. N. B., vol. ii. p. 317.)

He draws attention to the existence of "a natural tendency to action" in some plants, *e.g.* the potato and vine, adding that "it bears a strong resemblance to that phenomenon which in animal life is called instinct." He believes that "animal instinct is nothing but a higher exercise of the same propensity," and paraphrases the difference between reason and instinct thus:—"Man rules his actions, the brute is ruled by them."

Now I have long been searching for a satisfactory definition of instinct, and must confess that "R. B. W.'s" hints are not sufficient to appease further inquiry. In the first place, it is universally admitted that purposive movements are no proof of consciousness or will. Let "R. B. W." satisfy himself on this point by decapitating a frog, and noticing the result. For some considerable time he will see the limbs assume a natural position, and resume it if disturbed. Irritation of the abdomen or back will cause immediate agitation of the feet, with the manifest determination of resenting attack. In this helpless condition a frog has even been known to leap; every action appears influenced by the animal's will. But does this argue that consciousness in a frog is independent of the brain? Certainly not. It teaches rather that many more natural and purposive movements of the body can be performed under the sole influence of the spinal cord in Amphibia than in man: in other words that the spinal cord is a more important nervous centre of reflex and involuntary movements in the lower vertebrata, than in ourselves; even our own respiratory muscles exert purposive movements during sleep, when consciousness is slumbering. Analogy suggests that, if there exists in the frog when thus deprived of the brain (or seat of instinct) the power of purposive movement, there may exist in vegetables the same power quite as absolutely independent of any sensation or consciousness on the part of the individual plant. This at once disproves the necessity of admitting any connection between the instinct of animals, and what "R. B. W." calls instinct in plants.

Nevertheless, "R. B. W." proceeds as if he had positively established this connection, and adds:—"This is the difference between instinct and reason; man rules his action; the brute is ruled by them." His meaning is somewhat ambiguous, but if I understand him aright, he has violated two of the primary rules of logic, (1) by basing his argument on a "Petitio principii;" and (2) by arguing from a particular premise to a universal conclusion. He assumes as proved the identity of the two phenomena, instinct in plants and instinct in animals, and argues of the whole brute creation from what applies only to the lowest families of the invertebrate kingdom; and so arrives at the unsound conclusion, "The brute (*i.e.* all brutes) is ruled by its actions."

But granted that his reasoning is sound. Instinct, then, is a variable phenomenon existing alike in all nature, animal and vegetable; low in plants, a degree higher in the lowest animals, and so on; developing itself in the ascending scale: low therefore in fishes, higher in birds, and highest of all in Mammalia. At the top of the ladder we find man "ruler of his actions," and endowed with reason. And what is this reason? It has been well defined as "the power of combining the intellectual faculties towards the attainment of the object in view"—such faculties comprising memory, understanding, induction, reflection, etc., etc.

Constraining ourselves to adopt for a while the definition of instinct furnished by "R. B. W.", and being forbidden to trespass on the precincts of reason, how are we to account for the sagacity manifested by the brute creation, and especially by dogs? "R. B. W." cannot deny that dogs are endowed with memory: see how they recognise their masters after a separation of many years; Homer acknowledged that, when he sang of Argus and Ulysses. Are dogs then destitute of the faculties of understanding, reflection, and induction? If so, how are we to explain such phenomena as (A) breaking dogs of a bad habit by punishment; (B) their aptitude in learning tricks; (C) their intimate acquaintance with the ways of the household to which they belong, and so forth. The only satisfactory solution must be, that to some extent they are enabled by an effort of the understanding to see that certain actions on their part bring painful results; and, consequently, after repeated punishments attending repeated offences, they learn what to expect. In other words, they generalise from single instances a conclusion that satisfies [the rules of induction. The same explanation may be given in the other examples. A dog is taught to perform a trick by the enticement of food given with a command: the lesson is repeated till the food can be dispensed with; the dog having learnt to expect it, performs the trick: so by constantly observing his master's habits, he knows when to expect his meals, his daily exercise, etc. And as for reflection: under what other process would "R. B. W." explain the pricking of the ears, the wistful attention, the concentrated gaze, the doubtful turn of the head, the short bound forward, the pause, the joyful bark of satisfied recognition and the final rush of welcome, with which a dog receives the distant approach of his master. If reason is the faculty of combining all these mental processes for attaining an object, I do not see how we are to refuse dogs the "prerogative of man;" for it is difficult to conceive how a dog can be thoroughly trained in any branch of field sport, etc., without admitting that he has the power of combining the entire range of his intellectual faculties for comprehending what he is to do, or abstain from doing.

I would not for a moment deny that there is the widest possible distance between the scope of reason in dogs and reason in man—far wider than the gulf separating the so-called instinct in plants and that of animals. Yet I cannot see why we should object to use the title reason with reference to dogs; the only question being whether they have *the power of combining* the operation of those intellectual faculties which daily experience teaches us they possess to a considerable extent. Scripture is not opposed to the idea (Eccles. iii. 18-21.) "I said in mine heart concerning the estate of the sons of men, that God might manifest them, and that they might see that they themselves are beasts. For that which befalleth the sons of men befalleth beasts: even one thing befalleth them; as the one dieth, so dieth the other; yea they have all one breath; so that a man hath no pre-eminence above a beast: for all is vanity. All go unto one place; all are of the dust, and all turn to dust again. Who knoweth the spirit of man that goeth upward, and the spirit of the beast that goeth downward to the earth?" The speculations and theories of science only seem to create new difficulties on the

subject: philosophers hold their own views, but meanwhile no satisfactory conclusion is attained.
C.

ZOOLOGICAL GARDENS.—I fully endorse the wish expressed in the remarks quoted in a previous number, that ampler room may be given to the larger Felidæ, with a view to their more natural appearance, and the better development of their form and structure. Of course such an enclosure as that accorded to the giraffe or rhinoceros in the London Zoological Gardens would be out of the question; because in the case of the carnivera the top must be carefully shut in as well as the sides. But, in point of fact, a much smaller space would be sufficient for the purpose contemplated. I speak from experience, as I am familiar with the gardens at Dresden (Saxony), which, though small, are very well laid out, and where such an arrangement is already made for the benefit of the animals. The "cages" in the Felidæ house are placed in a double row, between which the visitor walks: but *outside*, the whole length of the house is occupied by an enclosure, extending some distance from the wall—I forget the dimensions, but that is a matter of detail only—the floor of which is thickly sanded, while the back is converted into a projecting rockwork by the piling together of large boulders in an irregular manner. Anything more majestic than the appearance of the lion as he clambered up this rocky mound, or stood on its summit gazing about him, a veritable "king of beasts," it is impossible to imagine, at least by those who have not seen him in his native deserts. The animals, too, seem thoroughly to enjoy the privilege of rolling and dusting themselves in the sand. As the outer enclosure opens by doorways into the several dens, the various animals may take their turn of airing at the will of the keeper—one day a tiger, another a jaguar, a third a lion, etc. Or (not so well) the enclosure may be divided, as the deer paddocks are, into as many portions as there are cages, so that the animals may be all out at one time, but each in a circumscribed space. I feel convinced that the proprietors would be well repaid for the outlay by the additional interest the public would take in the larger Felidæ, no longer "cabined, cribbed, confined" in an unnaturally small wooden den; and also by the improved condition of the animals themselves.
W. W. SPICER.

BLACK BEARS.—At p. 295 of this month's NOTE BOOK there is an interesting account of the black bear: but there is one point on which I should be glad of information, for it has always been a puzzle to me:—
The female brings forth her young in January or February, during the period of hybernation: how does she manage to sustain the demands made upon her strength by the bringing forth and suckling of her young, while she eats nothing herself, and then after all comes out fat in the spring? Surely their abstinence is not so complete as is generally supposed. Most animals that hybernate pass the time in a state of torpor, more or less deep, in which the more active functions of the body are suspended, and nutriment is rendered less necessary. But such a state seems incompatible with the constant drain upon the she-bear which must take place during the period of gestation and the suckling of her young. I should be glad to know if any of your correspondents can throw any light upon the subject.—GULIELMUS.

EARTH EATING.—With reference to "R. B. W.'s" query about the edible earth, I quote the following from "Wood's Natural History":—
"Some kinds of clay most probably contain no nourishment, and merely appease hunger for a time, by justifying the old adage, which says 'What wo'nt fatten will fill up;' but other kinds of edible earths or clays really contain nutritious matter. Of this kind is the Luneberg Mountain meal, which being examined by the microscope, is found to contain the dead bodies of animalcules."
This is the Berg Mēhl of the North of Europe. Humboldt found that the clay eaten by the Otomacs of the Orinoco, was composed of silica and alumina, with three or four per cent of lime; the silica and lime of this would most probably be afforded by the shields or shells of diatoms and desmids. It would thus seem that whatever nourishment there may be in edible earth is of animal and vegetable origin.
GULIELMUS.

PEBBLE COLLECTING.—The summer with its pleasures has passed, and cold winter has set in. No more can the "Wholesale Murderer" pursue his vocation, and therefore as "Othello's occupation's gone," he turns his mind to something else—viz., to collecting the pebbles on the sea-shore. After a short time, flints and "sandstones" are easily distinguished from agates and other valuables, and the industrious collector is soon rewarded by the discovery of some pretty pebbles. No sooner, however, is he seen on the beach than he is (unless he is in some unfrequented locality) beset by certain objectionable individuals who pretend to a knowledge of stone love. Selecting as "good 'uns" a few of the collector's treasures, they offer for a certain sum to cut and polish them. The collector agrees, and after a fortnight or so a little bit of stone is given him which he is told is his, which is, I am afraid in most cases not quite true. A wiser and a sadder man, he now takes his stones to the lapidary, who, to be honest (as he is by no means always), certainly does cut and polish them. But the price is large—1s 6d for a small and 2s 6d or more for a big stone. Thus by the time the collector has about twenty stones his pocket has suffered considerably. Can, I want to know, the amateur not cut and polish his stones himself? Will some kind reader of the NOTE BOOK give some concise directions for doing this?

I wish to correct the following mistakes which are in my "notes." In No. 19, page 221, for "of" read "on," and for "synonyme" read "synonymic;" and in No. 22, for "Eduas" read "Edusa;" for "Evebra Plaudrua" read "Erebia Blandina;" and for "many of the latter" read "many of the former." The latter communication was written in August, therefore "last month" means July.
A WHOLESALE MURDERER OF BUTTERFLIES AND MOTHS.

THYMY WOOD.—Among the objections made to the authenticity of the manuscript poem recently discovered by Professor Morley in the British Museum, and attributed by him to Milton, is the one that the term "thymy wood" is an inaccuracy of which Milton could not have been guilty, inasmuch as, say the cavillers, "thyme does not grow in woods:" but this is a mistake. Although thyme does not grow in *all* woods, it may, where circumstances favour its growth, be found in such localities. The soil it affects is either chalk or sand; and it can only exist in spots favoured with fine turf, for tall grass or rank herbage would necessarily choke it. Moreover, it requires a fair allowance of sun and air; so in woods, or those portions of them which have trees standing closely together with intermingling branches, it cannot be found. Still, it is quite permissable to include in the term "wood" those spots in which trees are somewhat sparsely scattered, and in such, by those who seek for it, wild thyme may not unfrequently be met with. In a portion of a wood near Guildford, in Surrey, in which these conditions are fulfilled, I found it growing in close proximity to the trunks of some fir trees whence resin was exuding, so the poet's comparison of the bee

> Who busy in the thymy wood
> Was fettered by the golden flood
> Which, from the amber weeping tree,
> Distilleth down so plenteously;

to Cleopatra in her tomb is not so absurd as adverse critics would imply, but has sufficient foundation on fact to make its employment for such an illustration a perfectly legitimate one. T. W.

NATAL CROWS.—The two principal crows that are found in Natal are the ring-necked crow (*Corvus albicollis*) and the cornland crow (*Corvus legetum*). The former is very common on the coast, and is often seen in the upland country: it is of a jet-black colour, with bronze reflections, and has a broad ring round its neck of snow-white, which greatly improves the look of the bird. When you "outspan" in travelling up the country, you almost always have a visit from one or more of these great birds, which are fully as large as hens of average size. These birds are very courageous, and I have often seen them attack large falcons three times their own size; it is a carrion eater, and is said to assist the vultures in all their feasts. The latter bird is entirely black, with purple reflections—it is generally seen in large flocks, like our crows in England, and keeps more to the cultivated lands than the former; they live almost wholly on grubs, but, when hard pushed, they will not disdain carrion. The length from the point of the bill to the end of the tail is one foot seven inches; they build in trees, and lay from three to five eggs of a light pink, spotted with a darker shade of the same colour.
J. D. S. W.

COMETS AND METEORS.—In the extract from an article entitled "Comets and Meteors," there is the following:—"It is conjectured that meteors are fragments of cometary matter left by the comet upon the track it has passed over." Now, if this be correct, we must take it for granted either that comets are solid bodies and that meteors are fragments detached from them in some way or other; or else that comets consist of streams of meteors. Lardner says that the smallest stars may be seen, without any perceptible diminution of their lustre, through the very heads of comets, and this, of course, would not be the case if comets were solid bodies of the same substance as meteors are; nor could the light of stars be seen through comets if the latter were composed of numbers of opaque bodies. The minute masses of comets, and their enormous volumes, favour the opinion that they must consist of vapour or some such substance, greatly attenuated. I do not presume to say that meteors have no connection with comets, but it seems highly improbable that meteors originate from comets. If any readers of the NATURALIST'S NOTE BOOK will give their opinions on this subject they will greatly oblige R. T.

"STING OF NETTLES."—I find in the NATURALIST'S NOTE BOOK for this month that "R. T." doubts the correctness of the statement of C. O. G. Napier as to the cause of the nettle not stinging when tightly grasped, and is of opinion that it is to be accounted for by the thickness of the epidermis on the inside of the hand; I think, however, that this view is mistaken, for how is it that the ends of the fingers (which are very sensitive) are not stung; and again, if the leaf of a nettle be firmly taken hold of between the sides of the fingers it will not take effect. The sting of a nettle is formed of a single cell, the base of which is expanded into a bulb, which is filled with an irritating fluid, while the apex tapers into an extremely fine point, on which is placed a small cap; on rubbing the gland lightly with the hand the cap is knocked off, and the fine point enters the skin; while at the same time the pressure causes the fluid contained in the bulb to be injected through the tube into the skin, the venomous nature of which fluid causes the irritation. If, however, instead of being lightly touched the sting is firmly pressed, it breaks below the point, and is not sufficiently sharp to enter the skin. O. R.

THE ROCK RABBIT.—This curious animal, although called a rabbit, is not a rabbit proper, but a *coney;* and I have no doubt that it is the same animal which is alluded to in Scripture. It is a very strange looking creature, about the size of the common rabbit, of a grey colour, and looks something like a very large rat. It is very common in Natal, but can rarely be seen in daylight, unless sheltered by a dense bush or wood, as is the case with a large warren situated in the rocks, just in front of my present residence, which is thus screened from the light of the sun. In this place at all hours of the day, on going into the bush, you are almost sure to see several of these creatures sitting on the high ledges of the rocks, just outside of their holes, and looking down upon you, wondering, no doubt, what business you can have in their lonely abode. They will not stir on seeing you raise your gun, and will allow you to take a good aim; but, unless mortally wounded, they will tumble into their holes, and you will never see them again: they are very good eating, and, when taken young, can be easily tamed. J. D. S. W.

BOOK ON MOTHS.—Your correspondent, "A. B." wishes to know of a good book on moths: I can strongly recommend to his notice "Newman's Illustrated Natural History of British Moths," as a most excellent and useful work. It comes out in sixpenny monthly parts, and I have now got twenty-one numbers. The illustrations, which are woodcuts, are first-rate, and every species is represented; and when the sexes differ, each are figured. The scientific names are all given, and also the families to which they belong. The publisher is W. Tweedie, 337, Strand, London. Although I am in the lake district, I am afraid I cannot give him much information with regard to catching lepidoptera in this part; but if he does not happen to possess "British Butterflies," by W. S. Coleman, I would advise him to get it, as it is a cheap and useful little book, and one that contains a great amount of useful information, both as to the modes of catching butterflies, and also names the localities where each species may be found. George Routledge and Sons are the publishers.

Patterdale.   A. E. BUTTEMER.

In answer to "A. B." respecting a good book on moths, I should recommend him to take in "Newman's British Moths," published monthly. I have named *all my moths* by them. There are about twenty numbers out. He can get them at Mr. Tweedie's, 335, Strand, for 6d. each, full of firstclass cuts.

B. SCOTT.

THE SECRETARY BIRD (*Serpentarius reptilivorus*).—This splendid bird frequents the dry and open plains of South Africa, feeding on the snakes and other reptiles which abound there. When erect, it stands three feet in height from the ground to the top of the head, on the back side of which are several long dark-coloured feathers, capable of being erected at pleasure, whence the colonists gave it the name of "Secretary." Its general colour is ash tipped with black; it has very long legs, and can make very good use of them when it pleases. I had a long run after a pair of these birds the other day, but they far out-ran me, and I could not possibly get within gun-shot of them. The young ones are a long time before they can learn to walk, as their legs are unable to bear the weight of their bodies, and snap with the least exertion.

J. D. S. W.

RAIN FROM A CLEAR SKY.—A correspondent in the July number of your publication asks if any of its readers have witnessed the singular phenomenon of rain falling from a serene cloudless sky. On or about the 12th of August, I was sitting on the Boulevards in Paris, when suddenly it began to rain quite fast; the sun was shining most brightly at the time, and the heat was most intense, and there was not a vestige of a cloud to be seen. The fall of rain was unmistakeable, it lasting quite a minute—the pavement was nearly wetted all over. I drew the attention of several strangers to the fact of there being no cloud visible; they all agreed that it was so, which proved I was not in error.   NAPOLEON ARGLES.

SAW FLY.—In the latter end of July, 1867, I caught the large saw fly, about which I have never been able to obtain any information. The scientific name I believe (but am not sure) is *Urocerus gigas*. Can any reader of the valuable NOTE BOOK kindly give me some information as to whether it is a common insect, and also where it is generally to be met with? The locality where I happened to catch the above-named fly, I fancy must have been rather a curious one, as it was on the top of Three Barrow Tor, Dartmoor, an altitude of 1500 feet above the sea. It is the only one I ever captured, nor have I ever seen another since.   A. E. BUTTEMER.

Patterdale.

On the night of October 7th, between 11.30 p.m. and 12 o'clock, a most splendid meteor shot across the sky, illuminating everything with an intense light, which lasted for a few seconds, and then disappeared. I was looking out of a window at the time, and did not see the meteor till the light caused by it had faded away, and then I saw it slowly descending through the constellation Orion towards the eastern horizon. From the *Daily Telegraph*, dated October 9th, I see that this extraordinary meteor was witnessed by several persons residing near London.   R. T.

SMALL METRA.—To the inquiry of "P. G. M." (page 318) I beg to state that I have a specimen of the small garden white (at least, I suppose it to be this species) exactly the size given by your correspondent; and himself, or any friend, may see the same by giving a call. The one that I possess is about the usual size of the wood white, and entirely without markings on the upper side. Some entomologists have been inclined to make it out a distinct species, but I believe it to be no other than a small pale variety of the above-named insect.   C. W...D.

320, Strand.

WEATHER SIGNS.—"A. F. B.," in June number of NATURALIST'S NOTE BOOK, upon "Signs of the Weather," quotes a poem (in question) upon "Signs of Rain," and which he declares "Dr. Jenner" to be its author. So he may be for what I know: but who is "Darwin," who has written a poem nigh word for word the same, and which made its appearance in the "Day of Rest," part 7, November, 1865?

THOS. D.

A CURIOSITY IN OOLOGY.—A friend of mine, when bird-nesting in the South of England in the spring of 1866, found the nest of a song thrush with four eggs in it—three of them of the ordinary size, and the fourth no larger than a pea, but in shape and colour just the same as the other eggs, and therefore he had every reason to suppose that it was laid by the same bird.   J. D. S. W.

TO CURE THE BITE OF ADDERS.—"If you observe the adder's bite soon after it has been given, scraped chalk or soda may be rubbed upon the bite with good effect, as it will absorb the poison not already taken into the circulation." The above I have taken from the "Rural Almanac," as it may be of use to some of your readers.   J. D. S. W.

A MADEIRA BIRD.—Could any of your readers tell me the name of a bird which flew on our ship, as we were passing within thirty miles off the island of Madeira. Its plumage was very much like that of the robin, but rather less in size, and with a curved bill.   J. D. S. W.

PAMPAS GRASS.—I shall be glad if any of your readers can inform me of the best way of preserving and drying pampas grass (*gynerium argenteum*) for the decoration of rooms, &c.   E. M.

EARTHQUAKES.

LTHOUGH as a question of necessity, growing out of experience, scientific minds are agreed upon some of the phenomena of earthquakes, they do not concur upon all of them. While many maintain that the tremblings or concussions of the earth, not unfrequently most disastrous to life and property on its surface, are attributable to expansion caused by intense sweeping and swelling, and rolling in great and continuous fire waves within the heart of the globe, sometimes causing contractions and then expansions of a most fearful character, raising to the exaltation of mountains deeply depressed valleys, and bringing to the level of the lowest depths the aspiring heads of the loftiest ranges of the higher lands, other inquirers in this field of knowledge advocate the theory that the interior of the sphere is stored with fixed or solid gases made so by great pressure, and that when, as fire to gunpowder, intense heat is evolved, explosions follow, and if there be not safety valves through which the suddenly expanded volume may escape, as steam escapes from the overcharged boiler, internal and external violence, often culminating in disasters of the most dreadful character follow.

Either of these theories would be acceptable to the inquirer were there not a third which utterly ignores the doctrines that the heart of this "great round globe" is a laboratory of gases, a region of ever expanding and ever contracting waves of flames which are persistently eating into or retiring from the inner side of the earth's shell. The exponents of this philosophy attempt to explain the causes which find their effects in the earthquake or the volcanic eruption by assuming that the gases and the substances thrown out of the craters of the fire mountains are secondary in character, and have their origin within a short distance from the immediate surface of the globe.

Without attempting to dispute with these theorists, or set up a doctrine as plausible, subject to a like criticism, we may venture to say that while no part of the sphere has been unvisited, the most terrific expressions of nature's anger are invariably in lines running, in a general way, from pole to pole. The lighter earthquakes are usually from the northwest to the southwest, and the "tremblings" are, as a rule, found to run parallel to the equator.

Thus the dreadful earthquake, resulting in the loss (estimated) of upwards of thirty-two thousand lives and 300,000,000 dollars' worth of property, recently experienced on the west coast of South America, which continued through seventy or eighty hours, had its lines longitudinally.

Another peculiarity of the earthquake is that the most dreadful expressions of its character are to be found almost always in certain regions of the earth—along the southern borders of Europe parallel to the Mediterranean and on the southwest coast of South America, while, on the other hand, it is believed that other places are never visited—that is, we have no historical knowledge of the fact—by "earth spasms." Again, there are other regions of the globe where these are unceasing. One of these remarkable spots is in the Atlantic Ocean, near the equator and about midway between Guinea and Brazil. In passing over this track those on sailing and steam ships experience a tremor which is not noticed in other parts of the ocean. Frequent soundings show that there must be a vent or submerged volcano in the spot referred to, for while at times ground is touched at four hundred fathoms, at others no lead line can be found long enough to measure the profoundness of the depth.

This much as to the phenomena of the earthquake, aside from the rapidity of its course. This is illustrated by the fact that the tidal wave, at the time of the greatest violence of the recent terrible visitations in Ecuador, Peru, and Chile, rose on the coast of California—a distance of four thousand miles—some forty feet, and that this rise and fall continued every thirty minutes for the space of a day. It has been ascertained that the shock consequent upon and following the line of the earthquake travels at the rate of ten thousand feet per second, even through the rocky crust of the earth. At this almost electric rapidity of movement it is not to be wondered if thousands of miles are traversed in exceedingly brief periods of time by those movements which may be regarded as reactionary.

Observation has recorded up to the year 1858 some six thousand distinct visitations of earthquake. Of course the number can only be an approximation to those which have really happened.

Among the most noted of these may be mentioned that of

ANTIOCH IN 526 A.D.

This ancient city of Syria has been frequently visited by terrific earthquakes. In the year 115 A.D. it was almost destroyed from this cause. The Emperor Trojan, who was at the time within the city, was seriously hurt while passing a falling building. Three hundred and forty-three years subsequently it was again visited by an earthquake, but in 526 the most disastrous visitation on record occurred in its vicinity. In his "Rise and Fall of the Roman Empire," Gibbon refers at length to this earthquake, and states that upward of a quarter of a million of persons are said to have perished, a conflux of strangers to the festival of the Ascension swelling the multitudes belonging to the city. Commenting upon this dreadful event he says:— "History will distinguish the periods in which these calamitous events have been rare or frequent, and will observe that the fever of the earth raged with uncommon violence during the reign of Justinian. Each year is marked by the repetition of earthquakes of such duration that Constantinople has been shaken above forty days; of such extent that the shock has been communicated to the whole surface of the globe, or at least the Roman empire."

HERCULANEUM AND POMPEII.

In the year 79 A.D. an earthquake of a familiar character visited the northern shore of the Mediterranean, but its most terrible manifestations were in the immediate vicinity of the volcano Vesuvius. The water, while the earth trembled and moved to and fro like the waves of the ocean, belched forth lava, huge stones and ashes, and soon—in a night—the cities of Herculaneum and Pompeii were overwhelmed, as was the surrounding country, with scoria and ashes. Thousands of lives were lost and the cities themselves disappeared, and for centuries existed only in tradition. Sixteen years anterior to this dreadful event both places were visited by an earthquake, without the volcano becoming particularly excited, and seriously injured; indeed, the destruction to the buildings was so severe that it was many years before they presented a perfect appearance, and then only by another calamity to pass away for ever as inhabited towns.

MODERN VISITATIONS.

Passing over the hundreds of visitations which mark the history of the earth previous to the eighteenth century, of which, however, none were so calamitous as those that all but destroyed Antioch, and the cities of Pompeii and Herculaneum, and the villages near them at the foot of Vesuvius, we come to the terrible disasters of

LISBON.

This great earthquake commenced on November 1, 1795. The inhabitants heard a rumbling beneath them just like the roll over hard ground of heavy artillery. This was immediately followed by a shock which threw the greater part of the town to the earth, in vast heaps of debris, burying beneath the ruins thousands of people. The shock, or rather the remnants, lasted about six minutes, and in this brief period of time it is believed sixty thousand persons perished. The sea retired, leaving the harbour dry, and immediately after a great wall of water upward of fifty feet in height rolled with terrific force upon the land. The mountains around were shaken with great violence, and were even rent and thrown in fragments into the valleys below. Multitudes of people sought safety from the falling buildings by crowding upon the marble quay, which had just been constructed at great expense. This quay suddenly sank with the terrified people standing upon it, as founders a ship in mid-ocean while the crew are reposing in fancied security. When the waters closed over the place no fragments of the vast human wreck were to be seen. None of the boats and vessels near by that were drawn into the whirlpool, and not one of the thousands of bodies carried down reappeared upon the surface. Over the spot the water stood six hundred feet deep, and beneath this, locked in the fissured rocks, in chasms of unknown depth, lie the relics of what was the life and wealth of this portion of the earth's surface. When in some future period they are raised again to the surface by a convulsion of the same nature with that which engulfed them the vestiges they contain may reappear converted in part or wholly into stone, like fossils entombed when the strata were deposited. Humboldt, referring to this remarkable convulsion of nature, remarks that an area equal to four times the surface of Europe was affected by it. Not only were the various grand divisions of Europe from the Mediterranean to the Arctic Circle participators in the earth waves, but their effects, like the outer lines of vast concentric circles, were seen on the shores of Barbados, Martinique, and Antigua, where the tide rose twenty feet, the sea putting on the appearance of inky blackness. The waters of distant Ontario were strangely agitated, and the shock was sensibly felt along the coast of Massachusetts.

NEW MADRID, ON THE MISSISSIPPI.

The earthquake which in 1811 visited New Madrid, below St. Louis, is the most important that ever visited North America of which we have any positive knowledge. It is remarkable in that, far from any volcano, there were incessant quakings of the ground for several successive months. During this period the earth, from the mouth of the Ohio to that of the St. Francis—a distance of two hundred miles—rose and fell in great wavelike undulations, and lakes were formed and in turn were drained of their contents. Within this area the surface burst open in great fissures, from which mud and water were thrown many feet. During the continuance of these convulsions the inhabitants, says an encyclopædic writer, distinguished two classes of earthquakes—those in which the movement was vertical and those in which it was horizontal, the latter being regarded as far more desolating than the former. These concussions continued with more or less violence until the destruction of the city of Caracas, which took place March 26, 1812. In its ruins 12,000 inhabitants were buried.

THE CHILEAN EARTHQUAKE OF 1822.

Our readers are not ignorant of the fact that the countries of South America recently and so disastrously visited, are not strangers to earthquakes. In 1822 Chile was visited by one which, between the Andes and the sea, raised an area of land equal to 100,000 square miles to a height of from two to seven feet.

Chile has frequently been visited by terrible earthquakes. Quito, in Eucador, as well as other large towns on the east coast of South America, has more than once been partially destroyed, and in those vast regions which skirt the Andes on the east and the west the earthquake may at any time be anticipated.

MEXICO AND CENTRAL AMERICA

are not unfrequently the scenes of the earth fever, and the north-eastern coast of South America, Venezuela, in which is Caracas, is not less subject to it than are other lines of the southern division of the Continent. In January 19, 1858, Mexico was visited by an earthquake which extended throughout the valley, and, destroying many houses in the city, also the aqueduct which supplied it with water. In all property to the value of several millions of dollars was lost. At the same time the Californias were visited by the wave, as were Guadalajara, Jalapa, San Luis Potosi, Taluca, and other districts. Although many places were seriously damaged, Mexico particularly so, the loss of life was not large.

THE CITY OF QUITO.

On the 22nd of March, 1859, Quito, in Ecuador, was entirely destroyed by an earthquake and many thousands of lives were reported to have been lost. Several small towns in the vicinity were also thrown down at the same time. Not only were thousands of lives lost, but millions of dollars worth of property. Business was utterly prostrated, and this last visitation in August will probably prove its death warrant.

THE EARTHQUAKE OF NAPLES.

On the 16th of December, 1867, the kingdom (now province) of Naples was visited by an earthquake, which continued at intervals through the early part of January. In the city of Naples repeated shocks were felt, greatly alarming the inhabitants, who often left their houses in the middle of the night and sought the more open spaces. The city was more or less injured, but the people were singularly protected. This exception is supposed to be owing to the proximity of Vesuvius, which continued in eruption, discharging clouds of smoke and ashes. From these later dates we have no earthquakes of moment to record until the visitation of

MENDOZA.

On the night of the 20th of March, 1861, a terrible earthquake occurred at Mendoza, in the western section of the Argentine Confederation, entirely destroying the city and killing twelve thousand of the inhabitants. Not a single house or building of any kind was left standing. In proportion to extent and population the city of Mendoza suffered more by this calamity than any other city visited in modern times. In the remarkable earthquakes of Lima, in 1746, Lisbon, 1755, Rio Bamba, in Ecuador, 1797, and Caracas, Venezuela, 1812, not more than a third of the inhabitants were killed, while at Mendoza, out of a population of fifteen thousand, but three thousand escaped destruction. The most remarkable fact connected with this earthquake was that the province of Buenos Ayres, or rather all the country between latitude 25 and 37 and from the Andes to the Atlantic, was shaken for the first time. The streets being narrow and the buildings high, the inhabitants, who were totally unused to such phenomena, were paralysed with terror and neglected to seek refuge in the open courts of their houses until too late. The aspect presented by the city after the first shock was terrific. Hoarse subterranean thunders defeaned the air, animals of all kinds rushed frantically through the open spaces, howling; the earth opened and vomited forth floods of water, while to crown the scene of horror flames burst from the ruins and consumed nearly the entire business portion of the city, with its dead, its dying and its wounded. Out of one hundred inmates of the prison but eight escaped alive. Service was being held in the Jesuit church when the shock came, the walls fell inward with a crash, and priest and penitent together were hurled into eternity. The earth in some places burst open like a bomb-shell, killing hundreds of the fleeing populace; volumes of water gushed forth from the wide fissures and spread to a great distance, and huge rocks were dashed from one mountain to another with great force, making a report like heavy ordnance. San Juan and San Luis, two other populous towns in the Argentine Confederation, shared a like fate; the San Juan river, having left its bed after the first shock, swept over the town, utterly destroying what the earthquake had spared. The wildest terror prevailed in the district visited by the phenomena and the inhabitants suffered terrible privations. Famine prevailed for some time, and bands of desperadoes roamed through the ruined cities, robbing and murdering all whom they encountered. A sickening odor of burning and decomposing bodies filled the air and contributed to the horror of the situation. Profound gloom prevailed throughout the Confederation and in the neighbouring republics for a long time after the survivors of this terrible calamity had begun to rebuild on the sites of their former dwellings.

MANILA.

On the 3d of June, 1863, between seven and eight o'clock in the evening, the city of Manila, in the island of Luzon, was visited by a very destructive earthquake. Without any previous premonition, but instantaneous as the lightning's flash, the city was shaken to its foundation, and in less than a minute, the whole term of its duration, the greater portion of the stone structures of the city and suburbs were in ruins. Such of the houses as were left standing were so shattered by the shock as to be untenable. A large number of people were killed, but the actual loss could never be ascertained. The city presented an awful picture of desolation and ruin. All the principal buildings of the government, all the churches, barracks, etc., were overthrown in the general wreck.

ENGLAND.

A severe shock was felt all over England on the 7th of October in the same year. In some places a low, rumbling noise was heard. The sound at first increased with a gradual crescendo for two or three seconds, until the crash was felt, which lasted for one second and a half and then subsided. Mr. Charles Dickens described the sensation he experienced as if some great beast had been crouching asleep under his bed and was shaking itself and trying to rise.

SHOCKS IN CANADA.

In the same month a severe shock was felt at Montreal, Prescott, and Coburg, Canada, and at Ottawa some buildings were shattered and chimneys thrown down. Three distinct shocks occurred at St. Louis, Mo., on the night of the 28th of September, 1863, each shock continuing six or seven seconds, accompanied by a rumbling noise like distant thunder. Although many houses were badly shaken and the people were greatly frightened, the mysterious visitor descended into the depths without inflicting any further damage.

An exceedingly strong earthquake occurred in Mexico on the 3rd of October, 1864. In Orizaba several persons were killed, and churches and houses were demolished. The oscillations were sometimes from north to south, and as often from east to west. A deep and prolonged subterranean noise was heard, which appeared to take an easterly course, proceeding probably from the volcano of Citalepet. In Acultzingo the atmosphere was filled with a continuous detonation. The shock was felt at Vera Cruz and Mexico city very distinctly for about forty-five seconds.

CALIFORNIA.

The cities of San Francisco and Sacramento, Cal., have long been threatened with destruction by earthquakes. Scarcely a month passes without a shock of greater or less severity being felt in some part of the State. The years 1864—6 were prolific in these appalling phenomena. Two severe shocks were felt all over the State in the month of October, 1864, and again in May of the following year. On the 8th of October San Francisco trembled to its foundation; several buildings were destroyed, large fissures were made in the ground, a bell in a church tower rang, and several lives were lost. The town of Santa Clara, Cal., experienced a slight shock on the 28th of December, and on the 26th of March the usual symptoms of incipient earthquake were felt from San Francisco to Monterey. In July of the same year Sacramento was again visited, but no serious damage was done.

San Francisco was the scene of a very alarming earthquake on the 8th of October, 1865. Most of the public buildings were damaged, and many private houses were shattered by the frequent shocks. The ground opened in some places several feet. The damage done to property amounted to 250,000 dollars. The number of houses levelled to the ground was very small. In other parts of the State severe shocks were felt, out the damage to property was very slight.

ALASKA.

The earthquake current that shook the surface of the earth in so many places in the year 1866, extended to Alaska. The town of Kodiak was visited on the 5th of September. Many houses were thrown down and a few lives were lost. On the 20th of the same month Antioch, Cal., experienced a rather severe shock, but otherwise suffered no serious damage.

At Porto Rico, on the 6th of April, several lives were lost by earthquake and a number of buildings were destroyed. On the 20th of August San Salvador, Central America, was visited by a slight shock, but no material damage was sustained.

A very destructive earthquake occurred in Algeria in the month of January, 1867, which destroyed several villages and many lives.

THE CONVULSIONS IN THE WEST INDIES.

The middle of last November witnessed the inauguration of that terrific series of earthquakes in the West Indies that culminated in the submerging of the island of Tortola, the destruction of ships and stores at St. Thomas, and the perpetration in a greater or less degree of serious damage among the islands of St. Martins, Porto Rico, Antigua, St. Bartholomew, St. Croix, and Jamaica. Jamaica was the first that experienced the perturbation of the troubled earth. About noon of the 11th and 12th of November several severe shocks were felt, resulting in the partial destruction of a house and an estfite. On the 18th of the same month two appalling shocks were felt at Porto Rico, spreading consternation from end to end of the island. At the same time a terrific hurricane swept over this devoted portion of the globe and inundations occurred in numberless places. At St. Domingo the lighthouse was damaged, whole parishes desolated, and many buildings laid in ruins.

St. Johns was visited on the next day, the 19th. Five distinct shocks were felt, the severest known in seventy-seven years. The principal river in the island rose and fell three feet. St. Thomas, St. Croix, St. Peters, Tortola, and Little Saba were struck the same day. The sea was raised fifty feet, and its retrocession swept off human lives and a great deal of valuable property. Little Saba was divided in consequence of the waves, and a volcano at the same moment sprang into active life. St. Thomas was visited by forty-seven almost continuous shocks. The sea rose sixty feet and the city was almost entirely submerged. The United States steamship Monongahela was left high and dry on shore, and the De Soto was badly damaged off the island of Santa Cruz. All the edifices in St. Johns were seriously injured, and St. Martins, for the time being, nearly disappeared from the face of creation.

Competent scientific men on the spot reported the current of undulations to run from north to east. The sky during the prevalence of these earthquakes presented its ordinary appearance. The trade wind clouds hung listlessly overhead; the weather was calm and sultry, and nothing unusual was observed in the vibrations of the compass. A volcanic eruption occurred at St. Bartholomew, but no damage of any moment resulted. St. Kitts was also included in the list of islands that the strangely-troubled disposition of terra firma embraced. The fury of this widely-extended series of earthquakes seemed to expend itself on the unfortunate island of St. Thomas, and the symptoms there exhibited were perhaps more appalling than have been noticed elsewhere.

The sun appeared as if under an eclipse, and only resumed its normal aspect after the lapse of several days. The ocean, which shortly before the first shock receded several hundred feet from the land, rose like one huge wave and moved towards the harbour. It stood up like a huge wall, erect and straight, like solid white masonry, and then advanced on the devoted town, carrying great, heavy ships along with it as though they were mere corks. The 3rd of December more shocks were felt at St. Thomas, unaccompanied by any damage. December 29, one of fifteen seconds' duration was experienced at St. Johns. On the 18th and 19th of the same month St. Domingo city was slightly shaken. Shocks of earthquake continued to be felt at St. Thomas, St. Kitts, and Antigua up to a late period of the present year. St. Kitts and Antigua were visited by a final tremor on the night of the 3rd of April. At the former place lumps of sulphur were thrown upon the island, and as late as the 13th of June three severe shocks were experienced at Porto Rico.

THE UPHEAVING OF THE HAWAIIAN ISLANDS.

The theory of earthquake manifestations travelling in certain well defined lines receives strong colour of support from the eruptions in the Hawaiian islands, almost immediately following the outbreak in the West Indies and in a line west by south from there. In this instance at Hawaii (one of the Sandwich Islands) fearful volcanic eruptions preceded the earthquake. On the 27th of March last the first eruption took place, followed by two thousand shocks of earthquakes. Entire villages were destroyed and hundreds of persons killed. The slope and part of the summit of a mountain fifteen hundred feet high were lifted up bodily by an earthquake and thrown over the tops of trees for a distance of over one thousand feet. The immense tidal waves came rushing in at so great a height that they swept over the tops of the cocoanut trees on the Kona coast. During the severest shock, which occurred on the 2nd of April, no living creature could stand up for a moment. Immense precipices were levelled to the earth. The eruption which accompanied the shocks was of a character terribly grand. Jets of flame rose to a height of one thousand feet. Huge rocks were hurled up among the clouds, and the rivers of lava rushed out into the sea a distance of six miles. Shock after shock convulsed the island. The effects were felt in all the groups, but were most disastrous at Hawaii. The shocks had three distinct characteristics—the undulating, with the motion generally from the north-west to south-east, the sudden, short, sharp, jerking shock occupying hardly two seconds, and lastly, a thumping like a boulder of rock thrown suddenly against the crust of the earth. Each kind was frequently accompanied with a rattling noise like distant thunder of artillery, more or less distinct. The lighter shocks generally had no accompanying noise. At Kapapala, one of the group, the shock was so great as to rend in twain the framework of a mountain side, and hurl down on the plain a portion of its flank. Fissures large enough to engulf a horse and rider were created in the ground. Not a single stone fence was left standing. At the town of Punaluu the moment the first shock took place it seemed as if an immense quantity of lava had been discharged into the sea some distance from the shore, as almost instantly a terrible commotion arose in the sea, the water boiling and tossing furiously. Shortly afterwards a tremendous wave swept in, and when it receded there was nothing left of Punaluu. Every house was washed away, and the number of lives lost was never ascertained. A big chasm opened in the mountain side and admitted the sea. For three days the earth constantly rocked and swayed, and the hills seemed to alternately approach and recede. Most people became sea-sick. Strange roaring and surging noises were heard under the ground, and when the ear was applied to the earth a distinct impression was received, as if a huge subterranean wave had struck the earth's crust.

THE COURSE OF THE EARTHQUAKE CURRENT AROUND THE EARTH.

While St. Thomas and other West Indian islands were still trembling from the earth's convulsions an earthquake took place in that remote region of the globe, Formosa, in the China Sea. The shock was of unprecedented violence, and was attended with a lamentable loss of life. The harbour of Kee-lung was left completely dry for a moment, and the returning wave swept everything before it. A chasm several yards wide opened in the earth's surface, of which no human eye could penetrate the depth. Shocks were also felt at Shanghae, Ningpo, and other places in China. No destruction of property or loss of life occurred there, but the phenomenon was so new to the Chinese that the greatest consternation prevailed.

March 1, a slight shock of earthquake was felt at Augusta, Me., and the same day, at the same hour, a similar shock was experienced on the opposite side of the continent, at Vancouver's Island.

On the 7th of March a serious shock, which destroyed several large public edifices and numerous lives, occurred at Venezuela. On the 31st of the same month a few slight shocks were felt in San Francisco.

Several smart shocks of earthquake were felt at Guatemala on the 8th of April, just a week after the outbreak in the Hawaiian islands.

On May 7, just about the period of the outbreak in the Hawaiian islands, an earthquake made itself understood at Healdsburg, California.

On the 29th of May four heavy shocks occurred at Fort Churchill and Virginia City, Nevada, and extended across to Sacramento City. Several large buildings were shaken and the pumps in the mines stopped working.

EARTHQUAKE MUTTERINGS IN NORTHERN NEW YORK, VERMONT, AND CANADA.

On the morning of the 18th of last December a violent shock of earthquake occurred at Ogdensburg, shaking the firmest buildings and knocking over light articles of furniture. At the same time shocks were felt at Watertown, Rome, Port Leyden, and other places north and west. Auburn and Syracuse also remember the visitation. It was felt throughout Canada, from Belleville to Sackville, N. B. In Montreal people were aroused from bed and made to wonder at what could be transpiring. On the 14th of January a sharp shock occurred near Montreal. No damage was done in any of these instances, except to the nerves of the timid.—*New York Times.*

THE DODO AND ITS HOME.
BY C. O. GROOM NAPIER, F.G.S.

PART III.

In what position should the dodo stand in relation to other birds, is a question which many of the first anatomists have endeavoured to settle. Three families of birds possess genera incapable of flight—the penguins, the auks, and the ostriches. The dodo is certainly most like the last of these families in its feathers, but it differs in the form of its feet and beak. The ostriches are forms allied to the bustards and the plovers, but they differ from them in some very important points of structure. Strickland remarks, p. 36, "If the dodo be then neither an auk, a penguin, or an ostrich, it must either be a unique and entirely independent organisation, representing in its own person a whole order of birds, or (which is far more probable) it must be an exceptional form of some other group to which it stands in the same relation as the ostriches to the bustards, the penguins to the divers, or the *Alca impennis* to the other genera of Alcidæ."

In speaking of the systems which man has chosen to form as a means of arranging his observations of the habits, qualities of organisms or things, he is very apt to use language which implies the subjugation and plasticity of the forms or qualities surrounding him to the systems of his own arrangement. Thus if he finds a new or little known genus or species possessing many points in common with a genus or species perhaps of his own creation, but yet differing considerably from the genus or species in question, he exclaims he has found an "*aberrant form.*" This phraseology, like the idea it is intended to express alike has its birth in error. Systems should shift their ground simultaneously with the knowledge of new forms: to endeavour to bend these forms to suit the shapes of the old systems, is like endeavouring to return the winged butterfly to the chrysalis—it has expanded to such a size in active life that its former place of confinement cannot contain it. Systems of classification founded on dead anatomy bear a similar relation to systems which have their birth in the study of living organisms. Nevertheless the student of Nature in his necessary systems of classification cannot do otherwise than arrange in accordance with diversity and resemblance, and our friend the dodo in accordance with this principle cannot be placed among the penguins, the auks, or the ostriches; and what other division of birds is it more like?

In Vigor's paper on the affinities of birds in the "Linnean Transactions," vol. xiv. p. 484, he held that the dodo was a gallinaceous bird intermediate between the ostriches and the genus *Crax*. For "the head and foot are decidedly gallinaceous, and from the insufficiency of its wings for the purposes of flight it may with equal certainty be pronounced to be of the Struthious structure, but the foot has a strong hind toe, and, with the exception of its being more robust (in which character it still adheres to the *Struthionidæ*), it corresponds with the foot of the Linnæan genus *Crax* that commences the succeeding family." M. de Blainville considers the dodo a raptorial bird from the pointed form of the beak, its strength, and width of the mouth when open, and from the nostrils, which have not an incumbent scale; from the claws being strong and curved, the legs short, the scaly covering of the tarsi, the vulture-like plumage of the head and neck, the *hard* and *bad flavour* of its flesh, and from its not having metatarsal spines. He moreover considers that the head and beak have a strong resemblance to that of *Sarcoramphus*, while the hood reminds him of *Cathartes*. But M. Blainville allows that the feet and toes of the dodo are stronger and shorter than those of any extant vulture, and the latter are not connected, as in these birds of prey, by a membrane. Baron de la Fresnaige, in accordance with De Blainville's views, places the dodo as the lowest sub-family of the *Vulturidæ* ("Revue Zoologique, 1839," p. 193). The dodo he thought frequented the sea-shore to feed on carrion and shell-fish. Mr. Gould formerly adopted similar views to Blainville, but Dr. J. E. Gray thought that "the dodo was altogether an artificial and fictitious bird manufactured by joining the head of a bird of prey approaching the vultures, if not belonging to that family, to the legs of a gallinaceous bird." (Strickland, p. 37.) But the head and foot of the dodo being unlike those of any extant bird, would increase the difficulty; for two species instead of one would require to be accounted for. The head is larger than that of any living bird of prey, and the legs stouter. Mr. Broderip in his excellent paper in the "Penny Cyclopædia" dwells strongly on the slow movements and wingless character of the dodo as being incompatible with a position among the vultures. Professor Owen formerly considered that the dodo had most affinity with vultures, but the recent discoveries of Mr. Clarke have caused him as well as Gould to modify their views in accordance with those previously expressed by Professor Reinhardt, of Copenhagen, Mr. Strickland, Mr. George Gray, and Prince Charles Bonaparte. To Professor Rheinhardt belongs the priority of the theory that the dodo belongs to the pigeons, which was carefully elaborated by Strickland. He, as it were, prepared the certificate of the dodo as a member of the pigeon family, which has been at last attested by these great naturalists. But this great bird differs from the pigeons in many important particulars. The pigeon family are distinguished for their flights, not so the dodo. I cannot conceive why naturalists should be so unwilling to give this anomalous bird the position to which its unique structure entitles it. Had it been more pigeon-like in its habits it would not have been so easily extinguished. Well might the last of the dodos have exclaimed—

"Oh had I the wings of a dove,
I'd make my escape and be gone."

But the dodo has undoubtedly considerable affinity with the pigeon family. The head reminds us slightly of the tooth-billed pigeon (*Didunculus strigirostris*), perhaps more like than that of any other pigeon; but the upper mandible reminds us strongly of that of an aquatic bird; and the ruggedness and strongly marked processes of the skull of the dodo contrast strongly with the smooth and rounded skull of the toothbilled and other pigeons, which indicate gentle and tender dispositions. The whole contour of the dodo, the evident size of the muscles of the head, the strength and stoutness of the feet and legs, the small size of the brain, point to a bird the impersonation of grossness, stupidity, and savage strength: all this is surely not *dove-like*. But the feet of the dodo do certainly approach those of some pigeons in form; for, although a strictly terrestrial bird, it has the toes of a perching bird. The terrestrial parrots and terrestrial cuckoos possess feet similar to those of their perching allies. The arboreal pigeons—*Ptilonopus, Treron,* and *Carpophaga*—have the inner toe shorter than the outer, but in the ground pigeons, *Geophaps* and *Phaps*, it is longer; but the toes are of equal length in the genera *Turtur, Columba,* and *Geopelia*; and in the dodo, who must have lived exclusively on the ground, the inner toe is much longer than the outer. Mr. Strickland thinks that the "head of the dodo agrees most nearly with that of the Trerons," from which he infers "that it fed like those birds on tropical fruits. The dodo, although by no means juicy and tender, was at any rate eatable, and its stomach and breast were its best parts, which would scarcely be compatible with its being a vulture. The flesh of pigeons varies in flavour, that of some species is dry and very tough. The dodo must have had an enormous crop if the painting in the British Museum gives a correct idea of it. The stomach of the dodo must have possessed immense muscular power to enable it to have used the large stones effectually for grinding its food, as is evidently to be inferred from the writings of the early voyagers. The dodo, having a bill that reminds us at once of the vulture's and the albatross's, and feet like those of a scratching pigeon, was probably omnivorous, but perhaps mainly addicted to decaying vegetation.

Some months ago I carefully examined the large series of bones belonging to the British Museum, and received from Professor Owen much interesting information, and a copy of his new memoir on the dodo in the "Zoological Transactions," which may be said to exhaust the subject of the osteology of the dodo. The splendid diagram in his work was in the first instance a tracing of the outline of the dodo as depicted in the well-known painting in the British Museum. On placing the series of bones recently received from the Mauritius in their proper position on this tracing, he was interested to observe their exact conformation in form and size; one of the most interesting of the many analogous instances which have been elucidated by the veteran anatomist, and it illustrates suitably his splendid memoir.

Professor Owen having interested the Bishop of Mauritius in the subject of the dodo, the latter induced Mr. George Clarke, the schoolmaster in the Mauritius, to make researches, which led to the discovery of bones of the dodo* and other interesting species. I have quoted his statement above.

From Professor Owen's own remarks I extract the following :—" The relative size and position of the cervical vertebræ as coadjusted in the position and degree of flexure of the neck, represented in Sir Hans Sloane's painting in the British Museum, are given in plate XV., with the varying proportion, of the pleurapophyses, and other processes. The ribs are of great size: a vertebral one measures nine inches in length, following the outer curve. The pelvis of the dodo is chiefly remarkable for the flatness and great breadth of the posterior half. Corresponding with the characteristic proportions in that part of the body in the old woodcuts of the Dutch *dodærsen;* it includes sixteen coalesced sacral vertebræ. The sternum is deeply hollowed above; correspondingly convex beneath, the keel is low and thick, commencing by a pair of broad obtuse ridges. The head of the humerus is occupied by a fine cancellus structure: the large vacuity below this is crossed in the section (figured plate 23, figure 5) by a transverse slender bar of bone, the small pneumatic foramina at the bottom of the wide and deep fossa for the axillary air cell are open."

The bones of the leg of the dodo are well described in Strickland's work.

The brain case of the dodo is remarkably small in relation to the external size of the skull, which has a honeycombed structure, resembling that of the elephant. The portion of skull, according to Professor Owen, appropriated to the cerebellum was larger in proportion to that encasing the cerebrum than in any other bird. This is in accordance with the feeble intelligence possessed by the bird, and its immense muscular power. It would seem at first sight as if the poorly developed brain of the dodo had needed on some account unusual protection; but the true explanation lies in the size, weight, and power of the bill. Professor Owen now, with Strickland and the others, considers the dodo to have most affinity with the *Didunculus*, or toothed-billed pigeon of the Samoan Islands.

Let us, in conclusion, endeavour to recall for a moment the days when the dodo reigned as the principal animal of the Island of Mauritius. The lovely isle was richly wooded, well watered, and very fertile. The scene of the tale of "Paul and Virginia" has thrown an air of romance around its shores. In the days of the dodo's reign it was uninhabited by man, and his first settlers conquered its kingdom. It is now occupied by a lively and industrious population, who have rendered it one of the most productive spots on earth. The valleys produce abundance of sugar-canes, yarns, manioc, and maize. Various islands of the ocean ruled by wingless birds have undergone similar changes. Where is now the moa of New Zealand, the epiornis of Madagascar, the great auk of Iceland? Dead,

---

* I have a fine series of these bones of the dodo, which have been carefully named by the learned professor.

behind the march of man!—for ever!! In like manner his savage races perish before the advance of the civilised. THE AGE OF GREAT REPTILES IS PASSED, THE AGE OF GREAT QUADRUPEDS, AND THE AGE OF GREAT BIRDS; BUT THE AGE OF MAN IN THE PLENITUDE OF POWER IS COMING.

SOMETHING ABOUT WATER.
By H. H. ULIDIA.

IF Nature so hates a vacuum that such a thing is scarcely to be found, then surely she must love water, for with Coleridge we may indeed truly say:—

Water, water, everywhere;

and, considering this, it is no wonder that water attracted the attention of the ancients, who ranked it as one of the four elements. Indeed, Thales, the Greek philosopher, two thousand five hundred years ago, called water the primal element, and even modern philosophy, with all its wonderful development at the present time, speaks of water as "one of the members most important to the life of the earth." We look at water, and, like the ancients too, we very naturally pronounce it a simple substance; but chemistry, a science of which the greatest minds of antiquity had but little conception, informs us that water is a compound substance, having for its constituents oxygen and hydrogen. The word oxygen is derived from the Greek, and signifies *acid producer;* it is the principle of combustion, and is absolutely necessary for the support of animal life. Hydrogen, too, is also derived from the Greek, and simply means *water producer;* it is the lightest of all bodies.

The metal, potassium, decomposes water when brought into contact with it, for; as oxygen has a great affinity for this metal, the hydrogen, on being freed from the water, instantly combines with the oxygen of the air, and is ignited by the heat generated by the potassium. With delight we view a beautiful lake, and in a sort of poetical language, we call it a "sheet of water," but that "sheet" is an accumulation of distinct aqueous particles, with a space containing air between each particle, and each particle gravitating independently like so many separate masses, each pressing in every possible direction, not only downwards, but laterally, and even upwards; and as an immediate result of this equality of pressure every particle remains at rest in the fluid. Were it not for this lateral pressure, water would not flow from an opening on the side of a vessel; were it not for the upward pressure water would not get up as we see it do at fountains; and were it not for the air that rolls in the spaces between the particles of water our rivers, lakes, and seas would be destitute of fish. Nature, as if to prove this, has formed lakes, and placed them at such elevations that the thin atmosphere but scantily enters the water: the fish cannot breathe in such an element, and must consequently die. Of one of those fish-hating lakes, far up on the Alps, Rogers beautifully says:—

—— in that dreary dale,
A little lake, *where never fish leaped up,*
Lay like a spot of ink amid the snow.

Water, with a wizard-like facility, assumes three forms, the *liquid*, the *solid*, and the *vapour*.

The smooth lake or the convulsed sea, the beautiful snow or the dangerous avalanche, the grey or golden cloud, all but water—we readily acknowledge the sublime transformations, the highly magical, the more noble, and more perfect metamorphoses than the fertile imagination of Ovid ever conceived. When water is heated to 212 deg., it flies off in the form of vapour, cold condenses this vapour, and it again assumes the fluid state, forms water, and this water at a temperature of 32 deg. becomes a solid—ice; and this ice is actually lighter than water, for as the water expands by freezing, the volume is increased, and consequently the gravity must be less. And while old winter in his friged mirth presses the thermometer below the freezing point, laughs and reigns—

—— the stream
Is mute, or faintly gurgles far below
Its frozen ceiling.

It is well known that when sea water is evaporated, the salt is completely left behind, and the vapour has not even the most remote taste of salt; and here science steps in to the great relief of the seaman, so that in the midst of the ocean fresh water is distilled from the briny waves quite as drinkable as the clearest fountain, and our modern sailors, quite unlike Coleridge's "Ancient Mariner," need not exclaim:—

Water, water, everywhere,
But not a drop to drink.

Water exists in the air, and the quantity varies according to the temperature of the place. The atmosphere at 50 deg. Fahrenheit contains about *one fiftieth* of its volume of water in a state of vapour: that is about one *seventy-fifth* of its weight; and at a temperature of 100 deg. the air contains one fourteenth part in volume of water, or about one twentieth in weight.

This vapour diminishes the temperature of the atmosphere and the fertilizing rains gladden the earth; but, says Waller—

Egypt does not on the clouds rely,
But to the Nile owes more than to the sky.

Plants cannot live without water, and in ancient times the overflowing of the Nile was not enough for the Egyptian agriculturists, for we find that they invented machines for raising water from the Nile for agricultural purposes. Many of the properties of water were well-known to the ancients.

Pliny, in his Natural History, says:—"*Aqua in plumbo subit altitudinem exortus sui;*" that is, water ascends in a pipe to the height of the source from which it springs.

Many curious experiments have been made, such as filling hollow globes with water and subjecting them to great pressure, as filling bottles with fresh water, corking them well, and letting them down to great depths in the sea, all in order to prove the compressibility of water. The compressibility of water would now seem to be fully established, for when the bottles were drawn up the water in the bottles had a brackish taste, a thing which could not have happened unless the water inside had *diminished in bulk* and allowed the sea water to enter and mix with it. Suidas tells us that long ago when the Chaldæans imagined that their god was superior to Canopus, one of the votaries of Canopus bored holes in the image of the Chaldæans' god, stopped the holes with wax, filled the image with water, applied fire to the statue, the wax melted, the water rushed out, and thus the inferiority of the Chaldæans' deity was established. But for a while let us turn aside from the philosophers, and hear the poets about water. Shelly finds pleasure in contemplating

—— a crystal *pond*,
Clear as an elemental diamond.

Cowper, at this season of the year, hurries off from "the world without" to the domestic hearth when he talks of

The driving, dashing rain.

But Coleridge, in delightful anticipation, again transports us to all the beauties of summer when he tells us of—

—— a hidden *brook*
In the leafy month of June,
That to the sleeping woods all night
Singeth a quiet tune!

And in spring—

The chiming fall of the early rain

fully compensates for the more violent torrents thus spoken of by Shelly:—

Out of the cups of the heavy flowers,
Emptied *the rain of the thunder showers.*

The poet, while writing the above, was evidently aware, in common with the most accurate of our modern scientific meterologists, that "rain, in almost every instance, is the result of the electrical action of clouds upon each other."

And Sir Egerton Brydges, even in his old age, thus writes of the waters of Geneva:—

Whence comes this grand delight, the bosom's swell,
From this expanse of *waters*, broad and free?
The fresh air blows in current unimpeded,
And the eye dazzles on the surface blue!
Who on its banks of racy breezes dwell,
And the tints of its silvery mirror see,
Are blind and senseless, if they have not heeded
With what a wondrous power it shifts its hue!
Health from its undulating changes flows;
The body braced, the spirits light and strong.
As on a glass the sun upon it glows;
And its sweet murmurs soften into song.
The water nymphs upon its billows play,
Then mourn the shadows of the closing day.

That "water is a good servant but a bad master" is an adage full of truth, and who has not heard that "Adam's ale" was the drink of the gods long before our *usquebaugh water of life* flowed to stagger reason.

But surely the poet had been studying "men and manners" rather than hydrostatics, when he thus cynically exclaims:—

On adamant our wrongs we all engrave,
But write our benefits upon *the wave.*

If Park, in the African wilds, found "consolation" in contemplating a small moss; if Shakespeare discovered "sermons in stones," and Byron "music" in the deep sea, then surely any of us, with a little thought, may at least find a literary or a scientific pleasure in snatching a few hours from useless recreation or the drudgery of toil, to say something about water.

ON COLLECTING INSECTS.
By E. CLIFFORD.

To those whose tastes lead them naturally to the observation of Nature, a variety of paths lies open for research. Oftentimes it becomes difficult, from the very perplexity of these varied branches of science, and their several claims upon attention, for the inquiring student to select such as may prove most congenial to him, and upon which he can more fully exercise his abilities than upon others. The botanist comes to him, it may be, and with impassioned earnestness points him to the flower-spangled earth, asking him what more lovely or interesting objects can claim his study than these? Referring to the structure of plants, their uses and associations, and to their exquisite loveliness, so appealing to human sensibilities in all lands, and at all ages, he certainly comes forward with a weighty force of inducements to the undecided student. But the entomologist, the ornithologist, and others, can separately urge claims as strong, even if they have somewhat less of poetry to connect with the objects they love and study, for they can insist that insects and birds, being animated creatures, must of necessity stand higher in the rank of created things than plants can do. Now, though favouring entomology ourselves, it is far from our intention to cry down any other sister science at its expense. Possibly, nay likely, botany and ornithology, with all other possible "ologies" that can exist, may in many points be far better as studies than entomology; but as far as regards the collection and preservation of their objects, we affirm that the latter science must undoubtedly bear the precedency.

In the present paper, then, we wish to offer a few remarks upon "collecting insects." And first we notice, that, without much doubt, many are deterred from this exciting and instructive pursuit by a sensitive regard to the opinions of others. For entomological pursuits are generally found to meet with little favour in the eyes of those not attached thereto, though such is not so strikingly the case now as formerly, when a lady was reputed insane from her "fondness for collecting insects." Yet, even now, the collector of insects is looked upon either as a person of very doubtful sensibilities, or else as subject to a kind of weakness, not so much deserving blame as pity from those thus viewing his pursuits. Let us briefly inquire into the causes of this treatment, and defend the entomologist as tersely as is possible in our space. The entomologist, we have hinted, is considered by many to be devoting his energy to objects so tiny as not to merit either consideration or notice at the hands of our race. Let us see what grounds there are for these opinions. The animal creation, fresh from the hands of the great Creator, is one great whole, containing forms that range from a considerable size to others not exceeding a grain of sand in magnitude. Now is it, when we come to consider, a reasonable view of animal creation, to look upon the elephant as superior to the humble bee, or the gigantic bird of primæval ages, as far above the lovely butterfly in its claims upon attention and study? Both equally were formed by God himself, both equally show forth His power, and speak to us of His care for the smallest as well as for the greatest of the things He has created. Is it, then, wise, to stigmatise the man who gives his leisure hours to the study of the former, as if he were superior in mind to the individual whose delight is in the intricate formation of the latter, simply because the objects of his research are larger, and consequently more striking in aspect? Surely not. To say the least, such a view must be a very superficial and careless one : for, let us remind the critics of the entomologist that insects display to the attentive observer, in their structure, habits, and economy, a fund of materials such as can never exist in respect of the larger animals for the youthful student. Comforting, indeed, it must be to the insect collector to feel that ignorance is more frequently the ground upon which are based the slights and insults offered to his science by others; and it is possible that if some of those who are loudest in their witticisms or their depreciations at his expense, could be induced seriously to examine some insect wonders, that they might see sufficient in the revelation of interest to silence them for the future. Taking, however, no other ground, the entomologist can plead the highest of reasons for exemption from derision as regards the minute size of his scientific objects. If that Mighty Being, who called them into existence and clothed them with such exquisite beauty, could see fit to surround them with a variety of interesting and wonderful circumstances, surely his human creatures (coming from the same hand) cannot better employ themselves than by carefully and earnestly studying them, showing forth their appreciation of his goodness. But, passing from this, there is another and more important cause operating to hinder the student from collecting insects.

To study insects efficiently, and to collect them for preservation, it is necessary to take away their lives, so that they may be more readily understood, and more easily examined in all the intricacies of circumstantial detail which are connected with them at all stages. But at this point there steps in a host of reproaching critics, who tell us that they are surprised and grieved at the lack of feeling displayed by the entomologist. It must be granted that to the inexperienced there *does* seem an air of plausibility about the accusation of cruelty so often preferred against the collector of insects. But it is only in appearance, and not in fact. Waiving altogether the vexed question whether insects feel pain or no—a question not admitting of solution, and therefore one upon which words seem almost superfluous—it is not difficult to see that no imputation of cruelty to the *humane* entomologist can hold good in regard to the objects he professes to love and study. Insects may, or they may *not*, feel pain; this let us pass on to one side, and ask some of those so excited in their efforts to establish the fact that they *do*, whether they ever devoted as much mental energy to the consideration of the pain *certainly* experienced by thousands of higher animals destroyed for *them*, not as necessary food, but merely as delicacies and luxurious *addenda* to their daily fare? It is one thing to attack the collector of insects with elaborate arguments to prove him guilty of inflicting pain upon God's creatures; but it is another, and a much more arduous one, to clear ourselves from imputations of a similar nature, but infinitely more aggravated by the circumstances attending our actions.

As we have said, however, supposing even that the insect tribes *do* experience painful sensations, still the entomologist is perfectly justified in killing moderate numbers for his own purposes of research and study, and is exonerated entirely from any charge of inhumane feeling in regard to the creatures which thus minister to his intellectual benefit. The animals, we are led to understand, were, as a whole, formed expressly for the benefit of man as an intellectual as well as a sensual being. Whilst he is therefore justified in destroying such as minister to his animal necessities, he is also and equally at liberty to employ such as minister to the nobler part of his being—that satisfy his love for the beautiful, and his passion for acquiring an intimacy with the works of his Creator. If insects had never been destroyed by the entomologist, nothing, comparatively, would have been known of their structure, beauty, uses, and instincts. Again: whilst much knowledge is stored up in books concerning them, the entomologist will learn much more of them by personal inspection and close study of their histories and formation—attainable only by putting a reasonable number to death for this end. Those who rashly and confidently accuse the collector of cruelty, should bear these facts in mind when preferring their charge. And it may well become a subject of wonder that, whilst generally people are so careless of destroying the lives of insects that happen to annoy or vex themselves, or else injure their property in some way, they should so quickly detect what they fancy to be a want of feeling in others. There can be no doubt that the real mistake here, as elsewhere, is the tendency to view the animal part of our beings as more deserving of satisfaction than the intellectual. You are justified, it is said, virtually, in killing animals for food for the body, but not in killing insects as food for the mind—upon which to feast intellectually in after years. This error is a vital one, and one but too commonly fallen into by those who, with an air of innocence, ask us how "we can be so *cruel* as to kill butterflies and moths for the purposes of science?" Such, readers, are the two chief causes deterring the student from pursuing the study and collection of insects as an occupation for the "leisure hour."

Now, however, let us briefly allude to the advantages possessed by the collector of insects. As a first and most important consideration, we remark that the entomologist can preserve his specimens in the most perfect state of pristine beauty from year to year without any difficulty —an advantage not attaching to other animated creatures. Birds and animals, it is true, can be stuffed, but they are far from being images of the lovely creatures that disported on the leafy earth, or poured forth their songs amongst the verdant boughs. So, too, with the botanist and his floral specimens. Readers, have you ever looked into the *herbarium* of a botanist, and contrasted its contents with those of a grassy hill-side in June? If so, you will doubtless have thought that plant preservation was at best but very ineffectual. The *colours* are gone; the natural beauty that lingers on the bud and leaf, all grace and loveliness, have for the most part vanished, and they have left little other than a withered, shrivelled thing behind them. How different is it with insects! For years they can be kept in a state of preservation so nearly approaching to that in which they were caught and killed, that they can hardly be distinguished therefrom: the silky hair remaining intact, and their wings exhibit, with rare exceptions, the whole of their pristine loveliness. Here, then, lies the chief advantage attaching to the collection of insects. But there are others.

The entomologist can follow the objects of his study through a series of stages, than which there is nothing more surprising in Nature. From a tiny egg, not bigger than a pin's head, he can, by rearing, develope the gorgeous butterfly, or the exquisitely tinted moth. Connected with the rearing of specimens, and the care they need, there is interwoven a variety of circumstantial details full of intense interest to the thoughtful mind. In the act of collecting insects is combined a healthful exercise and a fund of interest which is literally inexhaustible. Notwithstanding that for years past the scrutiny of entomologists has been directed to the numerous species which exist, there still remains at the present day much to be unravelled concerning the economy of some of our commonest species. Here, then, is a source of knowledge stimulating alike to the health of body and mind. But we are compelled to leave what to us is a most interesting subject. Suffice it that we have, in however a rambling manner, indicated that whatever may be said by the ignorant to the contrary, entomology is certainly equal in its claims upon the student's attention with any of her sister sciences that engross the time and energies of other men. Whilst not elevating entomology in *all* respects above other branches of study, we still maintain that, in at least one respect—viz., as regards the collection of specimens—it greatly transcends any that can be named.

And here, finally, it occurs to us that after all there is much of poetry connected with the insect tribes. Who can view these sweet little creatures dancing in the summer's sunlight, so full of beauty and of elegance, without feelings of emotion and delight? Who can look upon them in their labours, and see their affectionate solicitude for the young broods, or look on at their perseverance in conquering obstacles, without sensations of profound thanksgiving to the Giver and Disposer of all this world holds? Under the microscope also there are none that can view the *tableaux* of beauty revealed on their wings without seeing an earnest there of still deeper depths of beauty, if we knew only how to reach them with the eye! Thus, then, must we ever consider "insect collecting" as deserving both of the respect of the world generally, and of the attachment of the lover of Nature, who to be a *real* lover, must view Nature in her smallest as well as in her most striking features.

THE SEAL.

THE most vulnerable part of the seal is the nostril, where it is peculiarly sensitive. A blow on the nostril comparatively slight will suffice to stun it, though it is little affected by the heaviest blows on any other portion of its body. To the Greenlander the seal is of inestimable value: of the fur he makes his coat and leggings; with the skin he covers the framework of his frail canoe; of the stomach he makes air-buoys, which he fastens to his lance; and with its teeth he points his long shafted spear. As the seal cannot remain a very long while beneath the water, which is its hunting ground for fish, in frozen climes it bores holes in the ice, and manages to keep them open so as to give it access to its food. It is marvellous the dexterity they display in wriggling up through a funnel of ice as they emerge from the sea. The seal hunter, when he is after his quarry, rears a barricade in the vicinity of an ice hole, and watches his opportunity when the seal has got to some distance. If he can intercept it on its way back to its hole, he is sure of his booty; but if he fail, the whole day is lost, for in a twinkle every seal disappears from the floe.

Seals are predatory in their habits. They hang about fishing grounds and spread death and havoc all around them. They understand nets, which puzzle other fish completely. They sail round them, and in and out, without endangering their liberty. In the west of Ireland there is a belief that seals are supernaturally protected, that bullets will not strike them, that steel will not pierce them, and so the "ould thief" is best let alone. When attacked, the seal faces his foe manfully, and exchanges cuffs with good will, biting when he can, and making an unwieldy but determined use of his forepaws. Scott in his most charming novel has given us a lively description of an actual combat between a seal and Captain McIntyre. With a true sportsman's ardour, the captain intercepts the animal as it makes its escape to the water, undisturbed by the remonstrances of the Antiquary. "Hector, nephew, let alone the *Phoca*, let alone the *Phoca*; they bite, I tell you, like furies. He minds me no more than a post. There, there they are at it—the *Phoca* has the best of it. I am glad to see it," said he in the bitterness of his heart, though really alarmed for his nephew's safety, "I am glad to see it with all my heart and spirit. She has walloped away with all the grace of triumph, and has carried my stick off also by way of *spolia opima*."

Seals are good natural barometers. When an old seal is seen tumbling and rolling along a bank, a storm is sure to follow. They are very fond of music, following boats in which music is heard, and apparently in great delight. Their preference is for Scotch airs played on the Highland pipes, and they are brought into use to assist in their capture. The common seal is capable of attaching itself strongly to his human friends, and develops a gentle and loving nature. Two beautiful stories of tame seals may be read in Maxwell''s "Wild Sports of the West," which are too long for insertion in the narrow limits of this paper. The following account, however, which appeared in the *Field*, touchingly testifies to the strong affectionateness of the seal: we give it at length. "When I was a boy, I was presented by some fishermen with a seal, apparently not more than fourteen days old, which, in a few weeks, became perfectly tame and domesticated, would follow me about, eat from my hand, and showed unmistakeable signs of recognition and attachment, whenever I approached. It was fond of heat, and would lie for hours at the kitchen fire raising its head to look at every new comer, and never attempting to bite, and would nestle close to the dogs, who soon became quite reconciled to their new friend. Unfortunately the winter after I obtained it was unusually rough and stormy. Upon that wild coast boats could seldom put to sea, and the supply of fish became scanty and precarious. We were obliged to give milk as a substitute, of which the seal consumed large quantities; and as the scarcity of other food still continued, it was determined, in a family council, that it should be consigned to its own element, to shift for itself. Accompanied by a clergyman, who took a great interest in my pet, I rowed out a couple of miles to sea, and dropt it quietly overboard. Very much to our astonishment, however, we found it was not quite so easy to shake off. Fast as we pulled away, it swam still faster, crying all the time so loudly that it might easily have been heard a mile away, and so pitifully that we were obliged to take it up again, and bring it home, where, after this new proof of attachment, it lived in clover for several months, and might still be in existence, but for the untimely fate to which most pets are doomed, and to which this was no exception."

Of late years we have had performing seals, and most of us have seen a famous one, which went by the name of the "Talking Fish." They have been taught to bark when bidden, and their bark has been variously interpreted to suit the necessities of the occasion. They will kiss any one who does not, as we should, instinctively shrink from their wet bewhiskered lips, and will execute many similar antics with skill and apparent heartiness.—*The People's Magazine*, November.

NOTES ON THE MARTIN (*HIRUNDO URBICA*).

By Video.

There are circumstances attending the habits of the martin, and not only its instincts, but what we may venture to term its faculty of reason, which appear deserving of record; and it is believed that more would be known if we were more attentive in observing them. Thus it is the custom of these birds to form their nests under the eaves of houses; but on one occasion a crevice in the overhanging stone had caused the rain to drop on the front, which is the usual place of entrance, in consequence of which it became much injured. Under these circumstances it became unpleasant and inconvenient to enter the nest at the accustomed opening; which therefore was closed up by the labours of the birds, and a new entrance was formed on the sheltered side, so that in future the dribbling rain was shifted off in a manner not to injure the fabric.

In building their nest these birds are observed to convey the materials in a little pellet on the top of their bill; and the work is in preference performed in the earlier portion of the day, that by the influence of the sun it may become dried before the approach of night. But in the neighbourhood of a harbour, where the nearest and best place for obtaining the proper materials had become covered with the tide through the forenoon, it was observed that the earlier hours were employed in hawking for food; and that the afternoon was appropriated to the labour of building. On one occasion, however, it happened that the material was too soft to satisfy the builder in regard to the safety of the building. Something of a firmer character was therefore believed to be necessary for security, and a straw was procured, and its ends fastened on the fabric with clay; but the arch thus formed refused to bend itself sufficiently down in contact with the circumference of the edifice. Again and again the attempt was made to cause it to lie along the wall, but all in vain; and repeatedly did the builder stop and look about, as if to consider what could be done to accomplish so necessary an object; without which the nest could not be trusted with the safety of an expected family. At last a sudden thought seemed to have occurred. Instead of labouring to force down the middle of the bow, the end was loosened; the refractory arch fell down, and the beam lay in its place. That these birds retain an attachment to their own individual nests under untoward circumstances appears from a circumstance which was observed in the present year. There were eight nests close together under the eaves of a house; but one of them, and only one, had become much injured at the time when a single pair of the birds arrived in the spring. It was clear that they might have had the choice of the nests, for none others had arrived to dispute it with them. But they set themselves to the task of repairing their own cherished home, which they had accomplished by the time their neighbours had also come. Some particulars of the proceedings of this colony in the past year may be deemed worthy of notice. These eight nests were occupied by eight pairs of birds: and of these, six nests for the first brood produced four young ones in each; in each of the other two nests were three young ones. All the young birds of these first broods were accustomed to resort to their respective nests, not only after they had taken to their wings, but also after the eggs of a second brood were laid; and when an entrance to the nests had become impossible they still continued to cluster about the nests by day, although compelled to seek some other resting-place by night. Of the second brood two of the nests had three young birds in each, and other two only two young ones. Of the others the number was not clearly ascertained; and it was only after a few days from the time when they made their appearance abroad that the whole colony departed to their winter abode. An acquaintance with habits of the martin when away from us might explain why it is that with such abundant broods their numbers increase so little with us.

DEW.

There are few phenomena of common occurrence which have proved more perplexing to philosophers than those which attend the deposition of dew. Every one is familiar with these phenomena, and in very early times observant men had noticed them; yet it is but quite recently that the true theory of dew has been put forward and established. This theory affords a striking evidence of the value of careful and systematic observation applied even to the simplest phenomena of nature.

It was observed, in very early times, that dew is only formed on clear nights, when, therefore, the stars are shining. It was natural, perhaps, though hardly philosophical, to conclude that dew is directly shed down upon the earth from the stars; accordingly, we find the reference of dew to stellar influences among the earliest theories propounded in explanation of the phenomenon.

A theory somewhat less fanciful, but still depending on supposed stellar influences, was shortly put forward. It was observed that dew is only formed when the atmosphere is at a low temperature; or, more correctly, when the air is at a much lower temperature than has prevailed during the daytime. Combining this peculiarity with the former, ancient philosophers reasoned in the following manner:—Cold generates dew, and dew appears only when the skies are clear—that is, when the stars are shining; hence it follows that the stars generate cold, and thus lead indirectly to the formation of dew. Hence arose the singular theory, that as the sun pours down heat upon the earth, so the stars (and also the moon and planets) pour down cold.

Nothing is more common—we may note in passing—than this method of philosophising, especially in all that concerns weather changes; and perhaps it would be impossible to find a more signal instance of the mistakes into which men are likely to fall when they adopt this false method of reasoning; for, so far is it from being true that the stars shed cold upon the earth, that the exact converse is the case. It has been established by astronomers and physicists that an important portion of the earth's heat-supply is derived from the stars.

Following on these bizarre theories came Aristotle's theory of dew—celebrated as one of the most remarkable instances of the approximation which may sometimes be made to the truth by clever reasoning on insufficient observations; for we must not fall into the mistake of supposing, as many have done, that he framed hypotheses without making observations; indeed, there has seldom lived a philosopher who has made more observations than Aristotle. His mistake was that he extended his observations too widely, not making enough on each subject. He imagined that, by a string of syllogisms, he could make a few supply the place of many observations.

Aristotle added two important facts to our knowledge respecting dew—namely, first, that dew is only formed in serene weather; and secondly, that it is not formed on the summits of mountains. Modern observations shew the more correct statement of the case to be, that dew is *seldom* formed either in windy weather or on the tops of mountains. Now, Aristotle reasoned in a subtle and able manner on these two observations. He saw that dew must be the result of processes which are interfered with when the air is agitated, and which do not extend high above the earth's surface; he conjectured, therefore, that dew is simply caused by the discharge of vapour from the air. Vapour is a mixture, he said, of water and heat, and as long as water can get a supply of heat, vapourises. But vapour cannot rise high, or the heat would get detached from it; and vapour cannot exist in windy weather, but becomes dissipated. Hence, in high places, and in windy weather, dew cannot be formed for want of vapour. He derided the notion that the stars and moon cause the precipitation of dew. "On the contrary, the sun," he said, "is the cause; since its heat raises the vapour from which the dew is formed, when that heat is no longer present to keep up the vapour."

Amidst much that is false, there is here a good deal that is sound. The notion that heat is some substance which floats up the vapour, and may become detached from it in high or windy places, is of course incorrect. So also is the supposition that the dew is produced by the *fall* of condensed vapour as the heat passes away. Nor is it correct to say that the absence of the sun causes the condensation of vapour, since, as we shall presently see, the cold which causes the deposition of dew results from more than the mere absence of the sun. But, in pointing out that the discharge of vapour from the air, owing to loss of heat, is the true cause of the deposition of dew, Aristotle expressed an important truth. It was when he attempted to account for the discharge that he failed. It will be observed, also, that his explanation does not account for the observed fact, that dew is only formed in clear weather.

Aristotle's views did not find acceptance among the Greeks or Romans; they preferred to look on the moon, stars, and planets as the agents which cause the deposition of dew. "This notion," says a modern author, "was too beautiful for a Greek to give up, and the Romans could not do better than follow the example of their masters."

In the middle ages, despite the credit attached to Aristotle's name, those who cultivated the physical sciences were unwilling to accept his views; for the alchemists (who alone may be said to have been students of nature) founded their hopes of success in the search for the philosopher's stone, the *elixir vitæ*, and the other objects of their pursuit, on occult influences supposed to be exercised by the celestial bodies. It was unlikely, therefore, that they would willingly reject the ancient theory which ascribed dew to lunar and stellar radiations.

But at length Baptista Porta adduced evidence which justified him in denying positively that the moon or stars exercise any influence on the formation of dew. He discovered that dew is sometimes deposited on the inside of glass panes; and, again, that a bell-glass placed over a plant in cold weather is more copiously covered with dew within than without; nay, he observed that even some opaque substances shew dew on their *under* surface when none appears on the upper. Yet, singularly enough, Baptista Porta rejected that part of Aristotle's theory which was alone correct. He thought his observations justified him in looking on dew as condensed—not from vapour, as Aristotle thought—but from the air itself.

But now a new theory of dew began to be supported. We have seen that not only the believers in stellar influence, but Aristotle also, looked on dew as falling from above. Porta's experiments were opposed to this view. It seemed rather as if dew rose from the earth. Observation also shewed that the amount of dew obtained at different heights from the ground diminishes with the height. Hence, the new theorists looked upon dew as an exhalation from the ground and from plants—a fine steam, as it were rising upwards, and settling principally on the under surfaces of objects.

But this view, like the others, was destined to be overthrown. Muschenbroek, when engaged in a series of observations intended to establish the new view, made a discovery which has a very important bearing on the theory of dew: he found that, instead of being deposited with tolerable uniformity upon different substances—as falling rain is, for instance, and as the rising rain imagined by the new theorists ought to be—dew forms very much more freely on some substances than on others.

Here was a difficulty which long perplexed physicists. It appeared that dew neither fell from the sky nor arose from the earth. The object itself on which the dew was formed seemed to play an important part in determining the amount of deposition.

At length it was suggested that Aristotle's long neglected explanation might, with a slight change account for the observed phenomena. The formation of dew was now looked upon as a discharge of vapour from the air, this discharge not taking place necessarily upwards or downwards, but always from the air next to the object. But it was easy to test this view. It was understood that the coldness of the object, as compared with the air, was a necessary element in the phenomenon. It followed, that if a cold object is suddenly brought into warm air, there ought to be a deposition of moisture upon the object. This was found to be the case. Any one can readily determine this for himself. If a decanter of ice-cold water is brought into a warm room, in which the air is not dry—a crowded room, for example—the deposition of moisture is immediately detected by the clouding of the glass. But there is, in fact, a much simpler experiment. When we exhale, the moisture in the breath generally continues in the form of vapour. But if we breathe upon a window-pane, the vapour is immediately condensed, because the glass is considerably colder than the exhaled air.

But although this is the correct view, and though physicists had made a noteworthy advance in getting rid of erroneous notions, yet a theory of dew still remained to be formed; for it was not yet shewn how the cold, which causes the deposition of dew, is itself occasioned. The remarkable effects of a clear sky and serene weather in encouraging the formation of dew, were also still unaccounted for. On the explanation of these and similar points, the chief interest of the subject depends. Science owes the elucidation of these difficulties to Dr. Wells, a London physician, who studied the subject of dew in the commencement of the present century. His observations were made in a garden three miles from Blackfriars Bridge.—*Chambers's Journal,* November.

INSECT MEDICINES.

THE insect world, notwithstanding its vast extent, plays a very subordinate, though not unimportant part in the modern pharmacopœia. Its most valuable contribution is in the form of *cantharides,* or blistering-flies, an extensive tribe of beetles, of which the common "Spanish fly" (*Lytta vesicatoria*), and one or two species of the genus *Mylabris,* are the most extensively used in medicine. The former insect is abundant in the south of Europe, where it sometimes commits no little havoc among the trees; but it is not common in a living state with us, though it is occasionally met with in the Isle of Wight, and similar mild and sheltered localities. It is a handsome beetle, of a golden green colour and metallic lustre, and is generally about three-quarters of an inch in length. The irritant properties, which chiefly reside in the trunk of the insect, and which render it so valuable to the surgeon, are found to be intensified by warmth of climate; hence foreign samples are more valuable than any which might be found here. The beetles are gathered by shaking the trees on which they swarm, large cloths being spread on the ground beneath; they are then killed by immersion in boiling water or exposure to the vapour of hot vinegar. The dried bodies are generally powdered and mixed with fat or resin, forming ointments and plasters of great value and efficacy.

Besides various species of *Mylabris*, several of the genus *Meloe*, to which our common oil-beetle belongs, are used for blistering purposes; and our native musk-beetle (*Aromia moschata*), a beautiful and fragrant insect, with long antennæ, and which frequents old willow trees, is said to be as powerful a vesicatory as the Spanish fly.

One of the *Mylabris* tribe, a *Meloe*, and the handsome rose-beetle of our gardens (so graphically sketched by the author of "Episodes of Insect Life"), have been severally recommended as remedies for hydrophobia—we wish we could add upon reasonable grounds. In Sweden, however, the oil which exudes from the joints of the *Meloe*, when the insect is handled or otherwise irritated, is highly esteemed as a specific against rheumatic affections. So stag-beetles, infused in oil, were formerly regarded as affording a remedy for earache, while "oil of earwigs" was deemed "good to strengthen the nerves under convulsive motions, by rubbing it on the temples, wrists, and nostrils." Dioscorides recommends for the same troublesome pain, the inside of the *blatta*, bruised or boiled in oil, and dropped into the ears. Blatta is the name given to the two well-known cockroaches of our kitchens; but whether the old botanist alludes to these insects is not certain. We unfortunately have not learnt to turn them to any practical account, but in Jamaica their ashes are used for various medicinal purposes.

Apropos of insects and ears, it may be questioned whether the popular superstition, which has given to the earwig its vernacular name in several modern languages, may not have been too hastily pooh-poohed by scientific writers. That earwigs display no special propensity to enter the human ear may be safely affirmed, yet that insects have found their way into the aural passages, producing no little suffering and alarm, is a fact which does not admit of doubt. The late Captain Speke was thus tormented by a small beetle, which was not completely extracted from the ear for several months. In such a situation any insect would speedily perish, even if left undisturbed; but in most cases the intruder might be easily floated out with a little oil.

The various species of cricket, associated with so many rustic superstitions, were anciently prescribed for colds, swellings of the throat, and other complaints; and Pliny, anticipating the sage counsel of the then unborn Mrs. Glasse, points out the method of catching as well as of cooking. A fly is attached to one end of a hair, and is then introduced into the burrow excavated by the cricket; being eagerly seized by the latter, both are drawn forth together. This description applies to the mole-cricket, an insect, which, though not uncommon in England, is sufficiently grotesque in its appearance to excite astonishment and perhaps some degree of alarm in those who are not acquainted with it. Liniment made from house-crickets was applied to burns and bruises, and the expressed juice of these cheerful little chirpers was prescribed for strengthening impaired eyesight.

Although butterflies and moths have ever been the most admired of the insect tribes, they seem to have contributed very little to the long catalogue of animal remedies, the useful silkworm forming an almost solitary instance. "Silkworms dried," says an American writer, quoting from a curious old medical dictionary, "and reduced to powder, are by some applied to the crown of the head for removing vertigos and convulsions. The silk and case, or coat, are of a due temperature between heat and cold, and can obviate and recruit the vital, natural, and animal spirits. The cocoons," he adds, "are also the basis of *Goddard's Drops*, and enter into several other compositions, such as the *Confectio de Hyacinthe*, when made in the best manner."

The *Hemipterous* order of insects, to which the bed bug belongs, and which is generally regarded as the most repulsive of all, was, however strange it may seem, a somewhat favourite field for remedial agents. Out of it the ancient physicians gathered some of their most unsavoury drugs. Even the disgusting species which English housewives have vainly striven to extirpate for three centuries and a half, but which would seem to have been a rarity in olden times, was prescribed internally for ague and hysteria, and the *odour* thereof was said to give relief in the latter complaint. The same offensive remedy is still administered for fever and ague in some parts of the United States. The plant-feeding species, which are often gaily coloured and sometimes devoid of unpleasant odour, were also formerly used to neutralize the venom of serpents, and for diseases of various (and opposite) kinds.

Long before *formic* acid had been distilled from the bodies of ants, or the name of *chloro-*

form had become dear to suffering humanity, these industrious insects were observed to exhale a powerful smell, and were celebrated for medicinal virtues now unrecognized. The *pupæ*, or chrysalides, were regarded as effectual against deafness, and an infusion of horseants in oil was given in cases of gout and palsy.

That honey should appear on the list of medicines would seem perfectly natural—unless, indeed, its pleasant taste should appear inconsistent. Eight-and-twenty "virtues" were attributed to the luscious compound. But the honey-gatherers were included in the old prescriptions. Powdered bees were applied to bald heads in order to restore its natural covering ; and, for aught we know, they may still play a part, though undisguised, in hair restorers with long prices and longer names. They were also administered for intestinal pains ; and the *apis* of modern homœopathy is said to be a preparation of bee-poison. It does not appear that either wasps or hornets have attained a similar reputation, but the nests of hornets have been employed in veterinary medicine,—just as the earth of ant's nests is (or was) used in some parts of the West Indies.

Spiders and scorpions, unhesitatingly classed with insects until the precision of modern science separated them from their six-footed brethren, held a high position in ancient pharmacy. Not only were they employed to cure the bites or stings of their own species (as the fat of the viper is said to be a remedy for its venom), but in various other ways the old physicians sought to turn these living pests into practical blessings. Scorpions were applied or administered for ague and jaundice ; for pains in the eyes and pains in the gastric regions : for the plague and even for lunacy and demoniacal possession ! Spiders prepared with oil were made into a "sovereign ointment" for diseases of the ears and eyes ; hung round the neck, they prevented or cured ague ; applied to the wrist, they subdued fever ; and (so old Mouffet assures us) if attached to the suffering member, they were able to drive out "that mock of all physicians, the gout." He adds, "For the most part we find those people to be free from the gout in whose houses the spiders breed much," an encouraging piece of intelligence for dirty folks. The webs of various species beside the house spider were administered internally as pills, or externally as styptics. Of all these expedients, there remains but one—the occasional use of cobwebs to arrest the bleeding of the smaller vessels.—*Golden Hours*, November.

PRESERVATION OF SPECIMENS IN NATURAL HISTORY.

By Captain Oliver Haldane Stokes, late Royal Engineers, F.R.A.S., F.R.S.M., I.M.S., etc.

(*Continued from page* 169.)

Fishes.

Specimens of fish may be skinned by one of the following methods :—

(1) When it is intended to preserve the entire skin.

(2) When it is intended merely to exhibit one side only of the fish with the dorsal fin and tail entire, but with only half of the head and *one* of each pair of fins.

As regards No. 1, an incision may be made which will extend along *one* side of the belly of the fish from near the vent to the pectoral fins, or an incision may be made along one side of the dorsal fin, and extending from the head to the tail. Practice and the nature of the fish will determine which line of incision should be preferred. And in the case of flat fish, such as turbot, soles, etc., either side *may* be operated upon ; but generally the side containing the eyes should be left intact.

The skin having been cut through, it must be gently separated from the flesh, and the roots of the several fins cut through with the scissors. Great care must be taken *not* to cut the fins *too close* to the skin. The whole of the bones of the head must be denuded of flesh, and the eyes removed. All flesh adhering to the skin must be scraped and cut away, but *the gills need not be removed.* The tongue if very fleshy must be removed. Arsenical soap should next be applied to the whole of the interior of the head and skin, and to the roots of the fins. The gills, and exterior of the head, skin, and fins, must also be washed over with arsenical soap or corrosive sublimate.

A body of tow or cotton wool should next be inserted, and the skin closed with a needle and thread. When the second method is adopted an incision is made which extends round *one side only* of the fish, and divides the skin into two *unequal* parts.

The head is bisected by the scissors, and the *entire* of the *dorsal fin* and *tail* are preserved, but only *one* of each of the other fins. The preservative solution is then applied, and the skin pinned down over an artificial body of tow or cotton wool.

Skins of fish preserved as described can be mounted similarly to birds, and furnished with glass eyes. The exterior of the skin should be wiped with a wet sponge, and when dry varnished with white or copal varnish.

Preserving Shells.

Shells whether terrestrial or aquatic should be preserved as nearly as possible exactly as they have been found. The *best* way to remove animals from shells (except when the assistance of ants can be obtained) is as follows :—

A room in an outhouse should be furnished with some tin cans of about a gallon content each, arranged in a row, and half filled with water. The newly found shells should be placed in the first can, and allowed to remain there until the animals become decomposed and fall out, partly or wholly, of the shells. As decomposition progresses the contents of the first can should be shifted into the second can, and so on, until when the last can has been reached the shells have become empty and clean. The water in the cans should be stirred up and changed daily. Care should be taken that the operculum of any shell does not become lost or interchanged, nor should the epidermis of any shell be removed. A common toothbrush will suffice to clean the shells. Should the shell have an operculum, a little pledget of tow or cotton wool should be inserted into the shell, and the operculum attached to it by a little glue.

On Catalogues of Specimens.

The best way of forming a catalogue of specimens is to attach to each specimen *a number only*, which will refer to books in which all particulars of locality, date, circumstances, sex, age, etc., should be noted. When the numbers reach say 999, another system of notation should be commenced by lines drawn 93 thus, or $\overline{93}$, or thus $\underline{93}$, or $\underline{\overline{93}}$, or $\overline{\overline{93}}$, or $\underline{\underline{93}}$.

It will be easily seen that with the above seven systems of notation we can readily number 7 × 999 : 6993 specimens.

Preservation of Specimens in Liquids.

Stoneware or glass jars, or bottles with ground stoppers, should be employed, and methylated spirit. All specimens should be injected and thoroughly soaked in a vessel of spirit prior to their being finally bottled. Each specimen should, if possible, be suspended from the stopper by a string and cement, or by a floating buoy of cork. The bottles should be filled with the spirit.

VEGETABLE FIBRES.

LINEN, FLAX.—When we examine with the naked eye a filament of the finest and best flax, we are tempted to suppose it simple and homogeneous. On submitting it to the microscope we find that it is a bundle of slender fibres in juxtaposition and adhering one to another. If we destroy this adhesion by the successive and moderate application of boiling alkalies and alkaline chlorides, and by the mechanical action of a couple of needles under the simple microscope, we at last obtain separate fibres, varying in length from several millimetres to 0·06m, and less. If we place these fibres in an asphalt cell with glycerine or, still better, with one of the liquids employed by M. Bourgogne, and magnify them two hundred or three hundred times, the following characters appear :—

The isolated fibres, or cells composing the flax filaments are seen as transparent tubes, the internal cavity of which is very small as compared with the external diameter. Frequently this cavity is not visible. The surface of the filament is sometimes smooth, sometimes finely striated in the direction of its length. Its diameter is usually pretty uniform, except at the extremities. It is sometimes flattened, but in that case is not twisted upon itself like cotton. The extremities terminate in points, fine, and elongated like needles. This character will be recognized in a collection of the cells, but there are exceptions, though this is the predominant form. Flax filaments seen in very thin transverse section exhibit agglomerations of polygons, with angles always salient, and straight sided, or slightly convex, where the filaments run from the body of the fibre. In the centre of each polygon is a black, or brilliant spot, according as the instrument is arranged, and this indicates the interior canal of the fibre. This canal is usually very small, rounded, and seldom flattened. The filament appears solid and almost full. Sometimes we perceive, though feebly, the layers of cellulose of which it is formed.

HEMP.—Hemp when divided under the simple microscope, exhibits cells similar in length to those of flax, but, on the average, rather stouter. The longitudinal striæ are deeper and more decided. They frequently exhibit very apparent salient sides. Hemp is more frequently flattened than linen, and its diameter is more variable, we never met with spiral striæ, whatever treatment we employed, or whatever might be the age of the plant. When hemp has been strongly bleached, deep well-marked fissures are seen in most fibres ; they are always parallel to their axis, and we never met with them oblique, as in linen.

The points of the cells are generally flattened, the ends rounded, and of very various shapes. Some are like spatulæ, others like lances, but most commonly the points are very irregular. Sometimes we find the ends forked, but this peculiarity belongs chiefly to the foot cells (*cellules du pied*).

Sections exhibit very irregular and varied

shapes. Sometimes polygons with salient angles, at others, and most frequently, they show irregular figures with retreating angles and rounded contours. In masses these figures are seen interlaced. They are in such close contact that it is often impossible to distinguish lines of separation, and the whole appears as a homogeneous mass. The lines of separation can only be recognized by management of the illumination.

In the interior of the sections we notice an aperture representing the central canal. This opening is usually elongated, and conforms to the external form, being usually as irregular.

JUTE.—Jute comes to us from Asia, and is extracted from the bark of a *Corchorus*. When jute filaments are carefully treated with alkalies and alkaline chlorides to destroy the incrusting matter, it exhibits under the lens an agglomeration of thick stout fibres, regular in diameter, and strongly marked with striæ parallel to their axes. The filaments, which at first sight seem simple, can be divided by the needle, and resolved into short stiff cells, terminating in points. Their length varies from 0·0015m to 0·003m, and sometimes they reach 0·005m. The body of these fibres, seen under magnification of from two hundred to three hundred linear, appears flat, and bordered with bright lines, which represent the thickness of the cell walls, which is generally slight when compared with the dimensions of the fibres. The surface is smooth, and shows no trace of fibrous structure, like that of hemp or flax. The margins of the fibres are not always united, but frequently toothed, and showing deep and salient sinuosities. This character is noticed at the points, which are sometimes acute, but more often rounded, or with irregular terminations. The central canal is visible to the extremity of the point.

Sections exhibit agglomerations of polygons with straight sides, closely approximated in groups. In the midst of each polygon a round smooth aperture may be seen, usually very large in proportion to the exterior diameter.—*The Student.*

PLANTS FOR AN AQUARIUM.

THE VALLISNERIA SPIRALIS is a plant peculiarly suited for the Aquarium. It is a native of the sunny climate of Italy, where it is found in the ditches, ponds, lakes, and rivers, and belongs to the order called *Hydrocharidæ*.

A peculiar feature in the economy of this plant is the wise provision of nature for keeping, during the following season, the female flowers upon the surface of the water. These are borne on long spiral-footstalks, which, by means of a coil, rise to and float on the surface. The male flowers, on the contrary, are on straight and short flower-stalks, and when arrived at maturity, and ready to expand, detach themselves from the parent stalk, and, ascending to the surface, float among the female flowers, imparting to them the pollen with which they are loaded. As soon as this process is completed, the female part sinks to the bottom, there to perfect the intention of nature, and lay the foundation of another progeny.

This plant is also propagated by offshots, which is a peculiar feature in this order of plants. This is done by means of a lateral shoot branching from the mother plant. This pushes forward until it finds some place genial to its striking roots, which it speedily does; and in its turn the new plant performs the same functions as the parent plant.

The *Vallisneria Spiralis* is exceedingly prolific. "From six small roots," says Mr. Lloyd, "I procured during the last summer, no less than thirty-two healthy plants; all of which blossomed freely. I measured one of the female flower-stalks, and found its length to be five feet." In this plant, by the aid of the microscope the circulation of the sap can be plainly seen.

The NUPHAR LUTEA, or *Yellow Water Lily*, is another plant well adapted for the Aquarium. It belongs to the order of *Nymphæaceæ*. This plant from the peculiar fragrance of its flowers, is called the *Brandy Bottle*. Its beautiful broad, shining leaves have an ornamental appearance, and form an appropriate resting-place for the amphibia.

The WHITE LILY (*Nymphœa Alba*) is also another variety of this pretty tribe. To this plant, as well as to the Yellow, many medicinal properties were formerly ascribed; and, indeed, it is now much esteemed in some parts of this country.

The *Potamogeton Crispus*, is also a pretty plant. It has a reddish stalk, and brownish green leaves. It adapts itself to any kind of vessel.

The *Potamogeton Densus* is another of this order, and may be taken by the inexperienced for a different family. It is not to be met with in such abundance as the *Natans*. It is a much smaller plant; its leaves are of a transparent green, and attached to the stem opposite to each other.

These plants are well adapted for the Aquarium, and may be cultivated with success. The Molluscs have such a decided preference for them, that they will leave any other plant to feed upon them, and often destroy their beautiful appearance.

The POTAMOGETON NATANS, or, as the words expresses, *sharp-fruited*, is another interesting aquatic plant. It belongs to the order *Potamaceæ*. It is common to all our ponds. The broad leaf of the *Potamogeton Natans* may be seen floating on the surface, similar to a Lily, and for which it might be taken. It is a handsome plant, with brown, ovate leaves, floating on leaf-stalks rooted at the bottom. It makes a good resting-place for the Water Newts and other similar things that require occasional assistance from atmospheric air.

The HYDROCHARIS MORSUS RANÆ, or *Frogbit*, is a useful and interesting plant of the Lily kind in appearance, but belonging to the same order as the Vallisneria; and, like that plant, the circulation may be detected in the leaf-stalks and roots. It has a pretty appearance in the Aquarium, where it will thrive well and bloom freely. The body of the plant, resting on the surface of the water, derives its nourishment from the roots at the bottom of the vessel by means of its long spiral stalks, which descend to it, and, like the female flower of the Vallisneria, its foliage can accommodate itself to the surface. The parent plant dies away in the winter; but during the autumn, a series of small cones are formed attached to stalks proceeding from the parent plant. These in due time are detached, and float on the surface; but on the approach of winter gradually sink. At the return of spring they rise to the surface, when they unfold themselves, and in the course of a few days assume the shape of the perfect plant.

The CHARA VULGARIS, or *Common Chara*, is a plant belonging to the order *Characæ*. It abounds in ponds and sluggish streams, and in those rivers along the shores of which small creeks may be found. It is much sought after for the Aquarium, in which it is a graceful ornament, having a straight stem and whorls of green spiked leaves. Owing to its fast growth, like the Anacharis, it requires looking after and frequent pruning. It is a jointed, leafless plant, with verticillate branches; that is, arranged in a whorl around the stem. These whorls are composed of several tubes, which are encrusted with a calcareous matter.

The ANACHARIS ALSINASTRUM, or *Canadian Water Weed*, is a plant that has obtained notoriety from its rapid growth, and the speedy manner with which it chokes up the stream or river in which it has once taken root. It is very ornamental, and of a bright green colour. It is easily procured, and looks well in the Aquarium; but it must be frequently pruned and kept under.

Mr. J. Hogg, in his work on the microscope, gives the following account of this plant: He says,—"This remarkable plant has recently made its appearance in the rivers Ouse and Cam. It is so unlike any other water plant, that it may be at once recognized by its leaves growing in threes, round a slender, stringy stem. The watermen on the river have already named it *Water Thyme*, from a faint general resemblance it bears to that plant. Most of our water plants require, in order to their increase, to be rooted in the bottom or sides of the river in which they are found; but this flourishes altogether independent of that condition, and actually grows as it travels slowly down the stream, after being detached.

The manner in which this plant was introduced into this country is singular. "One of the Cambridge professors, having received a plant from a friend in Canada, kept it for some time in a glass jar, but not caring about retaining it, threw it away down a drain that emptied into the Cam. The following year a great stir was made about a new weed, which was fast choking up that river; and, upon inspection, the professor was surprised to find it the very plant which he had the year before parted with so unceremoniously."

THE ALISMA PLANTAGO, or, *Great Water Plantain*, is well suited for the Aquarium, as it gives off oxygen in large quantities. This plant is found growing in ditches, and is seen in large quantities about Plumstead, and other parts of Kent.

The NITELLA is another species of the same order as the Chara, and is a most graceful ornament in the Aquarium. The difference between the Chara and Nitella is this—the Nitella has no calcareous matter incrusted upon it, and the stem is but one tube, while the Chara is composed of many.

In this species of plants the circulation of the sap may be seen under the microscope, and, as such, forms an interesting object. The Chara requires preparation, by removing the calcareous matter, before placing it under the microscope; not so the Nitella.

The RANUNCULUS AQUATALIS, or *Water Crowfoot*, is a pretty plant, whether left floating in the Aquarium or rooted to the bottom; in which position it seems to grow best. Some of its leaves, supported on hairlike stalks, are round, and some crenated. The flowers are white, with yellow centres. There are several varieties, but all do well in the Aquarium, and give out a large proportion of Oxygen.

The STRATIOTES ALOIDES, or *Soldier Plant*, grows to perfection in the Aquarium, as it delights in still water. It belongs to the natural order of aquatic plants *Hydrochari daceæ*, of which it is the only species. It is found in the ditches of Surrey and Lincoln, and like the *Hydrocharis*, sends it roots downward to the soil. Soon after being planted, a cluster of leaves, partially formed, exhibits itself on the top of its centre; and, as the vegetation proceeds, the leaves droop over, and form a sort of tent, affording a shelter grateful to the inmates of an Aquarium.

The MYRIOPHYLLUM SPICATUM, or *Water Millfoil*, is a very pretty, bushy plant, and looks exceedingly well in an Aquarium. It belongs to the order *Haloragaceæ*, and is found in ponds, brooks, and streams. It somewhat resembles the fennel, and is very serviceable, as it literally gives off oxygen, so essential to the preservation of animal life.

The ZANNINCHELLIA PALUSTRIS, or *Horn Pond Weed*, is also a pretty delicate plant. It may be found in nearly every pond: it grows rapidly, and the light, delicate green of its verdure forms a striking and beautiful contrast with the dark green of the Chara tribe.

The HOTTONIA PALUSTRIS, or *Water Violet*. This is a beautiful plant for the tank. Its bright green leaves and whorls of light purple flowers have a pretty appearance. It is a British plant of the order *Primulaceæ*, and flowers in June.

The VERONICA BECCABUNGA, or *Brook Lime*, has fibrous roots with straight stalks, branched; the leaves are ovate, crenated, and thick, about an inch in length. The flower-stalks proceed from the joint; they are of a sky-blue, and composed of three petals. It is a beautiful plant for the tank.

To the preceding list of plants many more might be added; but as the fitness of all these for the purpose has been tested, they can be recommended and relied on. As a general rule, any water plant that has a fibrous root, and is not too large, may be had recourse to.

The LEMNA TRISULCA, or *Ivy-leaved Duck-weed*, may be introduced into a fresh-water Aquarium; as may also—CALLITRICHE VERNA, or *Water Starwort*—CALLITRICHE AUTUMNALIS—SAGITTARIA SAGITTIFOLIA, or *Arrow-head*.

The number of plants proper for an Aquarium planted in the shingle, should be about one plant to each gallon of water, and so on for any greater quantity; besides which, a few floating weeds, as the Hydrocharis Morsus Ranæ, or, Frogbit, may be placed in the Aquarium with good effect.—*Handbook for the Aquarium.* Dean.

IN THE ZOOLOGICAL GARDENS.

When we were children, the advent of Wombwell's Menagerie at the neighbouring fair was one of the great events of the year. To behold the actual beasts alive that we had been in the habit of seeing pictured in tales and nursery-books, was indeed a great treat; although we doubt whether the beasts themselves gained in our opinion by this personal verification, from the fact that a child's imagination, especially where the element of terror is concerned, paints pictures much more imposing than the real fact. A roaring lion, in a nursery tale, therefore, somewhat took away from the boy's respect for wild beasts. They got so shockingly tame towards their keepers when they have to depend upon them for their food, that we begin to believe that they were not half so savage as they were made out to be—possibly in order to frighten naughty children. When, outside the caravan, we beheld the mighty boa-constrictor crushing a tiger in his voluminous folds, he was to be respected; but what terror could we feel for the same reptile when we saw his keeper allowing him to fold himself about his neck, and to creep inside his waistcoat? In short, Wombwell took very much of the poetry out of the wild creatures which the youthful mind always associated with scenes of savage life and hair-breadth escapes from peril.

When zoological gardens were first instituted, and it was determined to give wild things a local habitation, we copied too closely the idea of the menagerie. They were collections of dens, dispersed among shrubberies, it is true, but there was no attempt to give the creatures the slightest liberty, or to imitate the conditions surrounding them in a state of nature. We freely admit that with all delicate animals from tropical climates the question of temperature puts limits to these surrouddings, excepting in the warm months of the year. Boxed up as they were, the lions and tigers, upon the first establishment of the Regent's Park Gardens, died from exposure to the weather at a terrible rate. Even now, with all the care we take of the monkey tribe, the more delicate among them are continually dying. Notwithstanding their houses are artificially warmed, a hard frost will kill scores of such tender nurslings in the course of a winter's night in this collection. But acknowledging the difficulties thrown in the way of tropical animals in the winter season, it seems to us that with regard to the animals of the colder and more temperate climates we have been backward in surrounding them, as far as possible, with the conditions they are accustomed to in a state of nature. When we have made the attempt, in nearly every case it has been successful. What information do we get from the beaver, for instance, when we see him in a box? but supply him with a pool of water and a bundle of sticks, and we are at once made acquainted with its habits; indeed, we know them more intimately within certain limits than do the Canadian trappers, for there is a keeper watching them all day, when they are at peace and without fear.

There are two species of lions in the garden—the full-maned African beast from the Cape, and the maneless lion from Goojerat, in India. This is the lion of our heraldic shield, which looks so much like a leopard. Whenever water is an amusement it has been freely supplied. The hippopotami taking their baths were the attractions up to the present time, but the walrus is now the star. This poor beast was captured in Davis Straits, by the crew of a whaler, who, having destroyed the mother, were followed by the young one to the ship's side, where it was captured. Having been fed on salt pork during the voyage, it arrived very much out of condition, but it is now fast getting up its flesh. It would not be possible to give this amphibious animal a field of flat ice to rest upon, but why should its pool be surrounded with a parapet a couple of feet high? The awkwardness it exhibits in getting in and out of its bath, invariably rolling over during the latter process, is a sufficient proof of the inconvenience of the construction. The extreme ungainliness of the creature when walking can scarcely be imagined, especially when viewed from the hind quarters; it looks like a boy with his trousers half down scuffling along on his knees. Possibly, when it is a little fatter, it will not look so ugly; but at present it has anything but an elegant appearance, although it is doubtless excellently adapted for the condition of life in which it is placed. One peculiarity that attracts the visitor's notice, is the singular reticulated net-work of hair hanging from its upper lip, which is used by the animal in sorting its food, and sweeping into his mouth. After it had been in the Gardens three weeks, it already knew its keeper, coming when called, and following him across the seal-paddock to its bed—a large packing-case of open boards, which must be exceedingly draughty in cold weather; but this is an inconvenience which does not disturb him.—*Cassell's Paper.*

TROUT OF NORTH AMERICA.

The brook trout of North America (*S. fontinalis* of Mitchell) is subject to a great diversity in colouring; indeed, so various are its shades and sportlings, that there is seldom any difficulty in recognizing the denizens of particular localities. The nature of its food, habits, and waters it frequents, have seemingly much to do with individual differences in those respects. The lower fins maintain always broad white margins, with more or less of a black lining, whilst the vermillion and golden spots, red hues, and white of the lower parts, are subject to much variety. I believe the dorsal fin and the tail are always spotted, whilst the back varies from a horn to a greenish and blue grey, beautifully spotted and dappled in the denizens of clear sunny brooks, the colouring darkening in accordance with the water. It is not to be wondered at that the more aberrant varieties of the trout have been raised to the rank of species. What can be more perplexing than the following? Into the Lake Utopia I before noticed, flows a small stream from a tarn in the vicinity. In October vast quantities of the true *S. fontinalis* are met with on their way to spawn in the tarn; whilst in Lake Utopia, at the entrance of the brook, is a trout of an average smaller size, of a silver grey, profusely spotted with yellow all over the back and sides, including the dorsal fins; the lower fins are white-margined, but otherwise there is a very decided difference between the two sorts. The former are then heavy with ova, but the light-coloured have neither the ovarium nor milt highly developed; and as to size, individuals of the same dimensions of each sort are plentiful, so that the differences in colouring are not dependent on age. I can find no anatomical distinctions; and as neither can get to the sea, on account of a very precipitous natural fall, and the light-coloured trout seems peculiar to the lake, is not seen in any of its influent or affluent waters, but always apart from the other, the question might fairly be put, is the light-coloured trout a distinct species? If not, what is the cause of the abnormality?

The red-bellied brook trout of De Kay is now believed to be only a regular variety of the brook trout, and by no means an uncommon variety wherever the fish is plentifully distributed.

The most typical specimens of the brook trout are unquestionably those captured on their return from the tideways, where the richness of colouring and flesh cause it to be mistaken for the sea trout, which I observe some authorities erroneously suppose does not proceed above the salt water. Apparently the migration of the brook trout is not regular, even where no obstructions exist. There is, however, a strong disposition in this fish to visit the sea. It is clearly distinct from S. Fario, of Europe. The brook trout averages from 1¼lb. to 2lb., the largest about 5lb., except that now and then a much heavier fish turns up.

In streams much frequented by fishermen and obstructed by mill-dams, although trout may be plentiful, it is seldom the average weight amounts to the above. No doubt the growth of the fish is retarded by its forced restriction to mere tributaries; but it is also likely that the larger trout have been repelled to the lakes and head waters, where we still find them, or in streams not subject to be constantly disturbed. Apparently there are as good trout in these situations as ever came out of American waters; and, provided artificial barriers are removed, and the wholesale destruction is prohibited—when mill and lumber dams contain properly constructed fishways, when all the sawdust and rubbish are excluded, and when the spear and net pass into a tradition—then, but certainly not till then, can it be expected that such splendid salmon rivers as the one on the deserted waters of which I now gaze will be replenished. In this once famous river (the Nashwauk), some thirty years ago, shoal upon shoal of salmon and trout sped their way along its forest-shaded waters unhindered by log or dam. In those days the settler, jaded by toil and wearied out by the long and rigorous winter, could always procure a bounteous supply of fresh fish and flesh to replace the sameness of the buckwheat, potatoes, and salt pork. A patriarch in one of its secluded valleys, remarked to me that his father used to say, "Had it not been for the moose and the salmon, we could not have made our clearings on the banks." Thus, in little more than a quarter of a century, a river upwards of sixty miles in length has been entirely denuded of its salmon, and its forests bid fair, within a further twenty years, to be without a single moose.—*Field.*

The Reptiles of the Mississippi.

The bayous and draining-canals in the rear of the rice lands swarm with the choicest fishes of the Gulf. On the sandy beaches and bosky dunes of the neighbouring islands, the "dagos" hunt great turtles, like those of Cuba. On the Gulf-shore are immense beds of oysters, and near them still more enormous shell-banks, containing millions upon millions of cubic feet of the dead, bivalvular gnathodon. Hundreds of alligators may be seen, any summer day, basking in the sunshine, and rolling lazily into the water at one's approach. In no other part of the world can the habits of this monster saurian be studied to better advantage—its fear of man; its mortal dread when a shoal of porpoises dashes through the water; its curious night-journeys on the land; the ease with which one can call it to the surface by imitating the cry of a dog or the squeal of a pig; the little mound-like elevation of clay, in which the female deposits her eggs in successive layers, to be hatched by the heat of the sun; its bellow, heard most frequently in dark and stormy nights; its skin, impervious, except in a few places, to a musket-ball; the tremendous stroke of its tail in the direction of its huge mouth; the upward movement of its upper jaw; its slow growth, and the great age to which it lives—sometimes, it is said, three hundred years. La Salle and his companions subsisted for a time on alligator-steaks and potatoes. Its hollow tooth makes a good powder-charger, and its skin is prized by tanners. One could locate lots in Plaquemine Parish with enough alligator-spines for rails to fence them. During the high water of spring and early summer, this narrow strip of alluvium fills with water like a sponge. Every acre of cultivated land has then to be drained, with ditches running up almost to the levee on the river bank, and into which the salt water creeps at high tide. Yet these ditches would not suffice to drain off the fresh water, were they not aided by myriads upon myriads of land-crabs, or "fiddlers," as they are commonly called, that everywhere bore into the soil, and honeycomb it with innumerable chambers and passages. At times, the margins of these ditches, as also the banks of the river, are literally covered with these curious creatures, that, without turning round, run in every direction almost as fast as a man can walk. They are armed with a formidable single claw, nearly as long as the rest of the body, sometimes on the right side and sometimes on the left, which they open and raise aloft when alarmed, as a frightened stag throws up his antlers. When they can no longer bore down to the water, they leave the field for the swamp, or the margin of the river. In these bayous, but most abundantly in the Mississippi, may be seen the gar-pike, the lepidosteus of naturalists, now found only in the lakes and rivers of North America, and saved, says Hugh Miller, "amid the wreck of *genera* and species, to serve as a key to unlock the marvels of the ichthyology of those remote periods of geologic history appropriated to the dynasty of the fish." Half fish and half reptile, its wonderful coat-of-mail, covering the entire body with enamelled bony plates, from which a steel will strike fire, as from flint, fitted it for existence in bodies of water dashed about by conflicting tempests and convulsed by sudden upheavals of the earth. The gar-pike has two rows of teeth—one of a fish and one of a reptile—and an air-bladder that almost serves for a lung, and enables it to live out of the water longer than any other fish. He is, as they described him to Lyell, "a happy fellow, and beats all creation; he can hurt everything, and nothing can hurt him." He works his head sideways and upward, like a saurian; his enormous strength and swiftness are surpassed only by his ferocity; he not only lords it over the finny tribes of the Mississippi, but even attacks the mule and the ox when they step into it to drink, and can hardly be torn from its hold.—*Putnam's Magazine.*

The Bittern.

This species appears distributed over most parts of Europe and the southern countries of Asia, and has also been met with in Barbary and the Cape of Good Hope in Africa. It is generally distributed over the British Isles, being apparently of rare occurrence in the more northern parts of Scotland.

The bittern, uncertain in its visits, is abundant in some seasons, and scarcely to be met with during others. In the winter of 1863-4 I remember as many as seventeen individuals being shot in this county. It was formerly a common resident in Norfolk, and in the time of Sir Thomas Browne bred in our fens and broads; but of later years it has become more scarce, its visits being almost exclusively confined to the winter season. Very few are the instances recorded of its occurrence in the summer; in fact, so rare has the nesting of the bittern become in Britain of recent years, that authors such as Yarrell and Morris can give only three authentic instances of its breeding in Great Britain. On two of these occasions the young had been hatched, and in the third instance a single egg was obtained several years ago at Ranworth in this county; and it is from this specimen that the Rev. F. O. Morris in his work on "The Eggs of British Birds," figures his plate. (See vol ii., p. 147). Seeing, then, that the nesting of the bittern is of such rare occurrence in this country, it may prove somewhat interesting to oologists to learn that a nest containing two beautiful fresh-laid eggs were taken on the 30th of March, 1868, in the neighbourhood of one of the Norfolk broads; these I fortunately succeeded in purchasing for my own collection, and while still in the yelk exhibited them at a meeting of the Norwich Naturalists' Society. The old birds were frequently observed for some time previously in the vicinity of the broad by a labouring man residing near the spot, who thinking by their appearance and actions that they had a nest, or were preparing to nest in that locality, therefore watched them, and found his surmises correct, as on the date stated above he found the nest containing the two eggs only. This date is, I believe, unusually early for the breeding of this species; on that point, however, I am not certain, and neither Yarrell nor Morris gives any information of the time of their nesting. The nest, as is usually stated by authors, was composed of reeds and sticks. The eggs are of a uniform pale brownish colour, somewhat resembling the hue of the common pheasant's, but of a shade or two darker; the shell is not of that glossy surface, but of a coarser texture. One egg is a trifle larger than the other, and presents a beautiful oval form; the other tapers rather more at the ends.

The bittern derives its name from its peculiar cry or boom, which is said to resemble the bellowing of a bull.

This species frequents the fens and marsh-lands, subsisting chiefly on the smaller fish and reptiles, and larger aquatic insects. In the stomachs of some individuals I have found roach as much as seven or eight inches in length, quite entire, and in others entire frogs, mice, water-voles, &c.

Although the Rev. Mr. Morris, in his "British Birds," observes that no essential difference appears in the sexes of this species, I am of opinion that, were this subject more fully investigated, we should find certain indications of distinction—*Naturalist's Circular*.

Meteorological Observations.

Those who have not visited a meteorological observatory may perhaps be curious to know what is the kind of work upon which the staff is employed; and for an account, at once concise, accurate, and clear, we cannot do better than refer them to the Report of the Meteorological Committee for 1867. A very few words, however, will suffice to convey a general impression of what these establishments are doing. The main purpose of the observations is to obtain an exact record for every moment of every day, at each of the seven posts of observation, of the temperature and moisture of the air, of the weight of the atmosphere, and of the force and direction of the wind. To effect this a very perfect set of self-recording instruments has been mounted at each observatory, comprising the thermograph, which registers the readings of the wet and dry thermometers; the barograph, to record continuously the pressure of the atmosphere; and the anemograph, to perform a like function for the wind. Of these the two former are worked by means of photography. The thermograph is so arranged that a concentrated pencil of light is made to move up and down in accordance with the rise and fall of the mercury in the thermometer. The light falls upon a cylinder coated with sensitive paper, and slowly rotating by clockwork about a vertical axis. So long as the thermometer remains at the same elevation, the spot of light thrown upon the revolving cylinder will trace out a circle round it, which, when the paper is unrolled from the cylinder, shows itself as a straight line parallel to the upper and lower edges. When the thermometer is rising or falling, the line will incline upwards or downwards; and at the end of forty-eight hours, the period in which the cylinder is made to complete a revolution, the sensitive paper will be photographed from end to end with a line marking, by its elevation above the lower edge, the precise temperature at any moment of the period of observation. These thermograms are all stored away for future reference, and there are now accumulated at Kew actual pictures of every change of temperature, from the first moment when the machinery was set at work. The moisture of the air is recorded in precisely the same way, and in fact upon the same papers, from the indications of a wet-bulb thermometer, and a very similar arrangement records with equal exactness the variations of the barometric columns. A slightly different system, in which mechanical means are substituted for photographic action, supplies an equally continuous account of all the variations in the strength and direction of the wind. With these appliances continually at work, and with a regular flood of returns from all parts of the ocean—including, as they do, observations on the temperature of the sea, the direction and force of currents, and the like—it will readily be understood that an enormous mass of material is rapidly accumulating which cannot but be fruitful in scientific results.—*Saturday Review.*

MERCURY.

It affords a high idea of the watchfulness of the ancient astronomers that they should have detected the existence of the planet Mercury. It is so close to the sun as never to be seen save in the full glare of morning or evening twilight. Laplace says—"A long series of observations was doubtless necessary to recognize the identity of the two bodies which were seen alternately in the morning and evening to recede from and approach the sun; but, at length, as one never presented itself until the other had disappeared, it was concluded that it was the same planet which oscillated on each side of the sun." Yet, as the planet Venus was known by the two names Hesperus and Phosphorus, so Mercury was for a long time recognized by the Greeks under the two names of Apollo the God of Day, and Mercury the God of Thieves, "who profit by the evening," says Arago in explanation, "to commit their misdeeds." Yet it is fully as likely that the name Mercury was assigned to the planet on account of the rapidity of its movements and the difficulty of detecting it. In our latitudes the planet is very seldom visible to the naked eye. It is related that Copernicus who died at the age of seventy, complained towards the end of his life that though he had often tried, he had never been able to detect the planet, "in consequence, probably," says Gassendi, "of the thick vapours which ascend above the horizon on the banks of the Vistula, where the illustrious astronomer resided." The author of this paper has twice seen the planet with the naked eye in the course of this year, and once in 1863. However, Mercury fully deserves the comment of an old writer (named Goad) in 1686, who described the planet as "a squinting lacquey of the sun, seldom showing his head in these parts, as if he were in debt." Yet we learn from Lepsius's *Chronologie der Ægypter* that the Egyptians had watched the planet (which they considered sacred to the God Horus) from the earliest times. The Indians associated Mercury with Buddha: and the tribe of the Asedites, in Western Arabia, directed their worship exclusively to this planet. The astronomer Ptolemy, in the ninth book of the *Almagest* records as many as fourteen accurate observations of Mercury, extending back 261 years before our era, and belonging in part to the systematic labours of the ancient Chaldean astronomers. The earliest of these observations is dated in the year of Nabonasser 494, or sixty years after the death of Alexander the Great, on the morning of the 19th day of the Egyptian month *Thoth*. In the observation, the planet's place was carefully assigned with reference to two fixed stars, neither of which, we feel certain, has ever been visible in our latitudes in such full twilight as always surrounds the planet Mercury.—*From Cornhill Magazine for November.*

KILLED BY A METEOR.

The *Brisbane Courier* of the 25th of August states that several of the vessels just arrived from the southward reported that there was a great deal of electrical atmospheric disturbance on Monday and Tuesday nights, but whether it was the effect, or was simply coincident with the eclipse our informants could not say. In one case it was attended with fatal results, and a man was killed on board the schooner Urania by the explosion of an electric meteor. The vessel was off Crowdy Head on Monday, August 17, about midnight, when a heavy south-westerly squall came on, and all hands were called to shorten sail. A seaman named H. G. Sales was steering, and at 12.30 a.m. on Tuesday the 18th a meteor, like a ball of fire, fell immediately over the vessel's stern, and exploded with a loud report resembling that of a heavy piece of ordnance. Sparks of fire were scattered all about the deck, and the steersman was killed by the shock. Every one on board felt a violent shock like that of a galvanic battery; but none of the crew were injured except Sales, who was at his last gasp picked up. His body showed no marks, but appeared to be blackened, and some six or seven hours after decomposition set in, and the poor fellow was buried over the side. He was a young man, about twenty-three, and a smart seaman. The fire-ball apparently travelled with the wind, which was from the south-west, and when it burst the flash was so intensely brilliant that the steward who was lying in his berth below, declared that he saw the fire through the seams of the deck. The cabin at the same moment was filled with smoke, which blackened papers lying about. Captain Johnstone informs us that the discolouration of the paint was like that produced by "smoking of the ship" with charcoal. A peculiar and indescribable smell was perceived for some time after the explosion, and a quantity of flakes like the soot from a steamer's funnel were scattered about. Captain Milman, of the Lady Young (steamer), informs us that on his last trip to Sydney a fire-ball was observed passing ahead of his ship, about one a.m. on Sunday the 17th. It travelled in a horizontal direction from north-west to south-east. Apparently it was so near the ship that the officer of the watch altered her course to avoid it, when it burst, and for the moment the whole heavens seemed to be in a blaze of light, and at the same time there was terrific thunder. Lightning and thunder continued at intervals throughout the night and next day (Tuesday) until about half-past eight o'clock, when the weather cleared up.

Correspondence.

[*Under this head we shall be glad to insert any letters of general interest.*]

BREEDING AND MOULTING OF THE SWALLOWS.

Sir—I had intended to have made a short reply to the lines of your correspondent, "R. B. W." (page 309, October issue), but other matters prevented at the time. I now beg to offer the following, if space will permit. "R.B.W." appears to have somewhat misunderstood the drift of my question in reference to the moulting of the swallows. It was quite intended as addressed to the supporters of the theory of hybernation, and under such circumstances would be somewhat more difficult to explain or reconcile by the supporters of this unaccountable theory. However, in common courtesy, I beg to thank "R. B. W." for his remarks, and also to state that I am fully in unison with him throughout the whole of his observations, particularly in reference to the swallows breeding during their migration from this country. Mr. Austen's remarks upon their breeding at Senegambia during our winter months must certainly be regarded as an oversight, arising no doubt from mistaking some other species for our British swallows. And I would observe that the same gentleman's remarks upon the swallows being driven away by the heavy rains is also without foundation.

It must be obvious to all who have made the habits of birds their especial study that every species have an appointed time and place to propagate their kind, and that during that process they must of necessity be located and always found within a reasonable distance of their nesting-place, in order to attend upon the unceasing wants of their helpless progeny. And in many cases as soon as the business of incubation is over, and the young ones capable of seeking their own support, those of the gregarious kind unite in flocks, and having no further inducement or necessity to confine themselves to one particular locality, wing their way from place to place in search of food for their own individual support.

We may take as an example of the gregarious kind the common lark. Every superficial observer of the feathered race must have taken notice of the immense flocks of these birds that are flitting about from field to field in the later part of the year, and during the inclement months of the winter season. I will not say that these birds are driven away from their breeding stations by the inclemency of the weather, because I believe that they are influenced and guided by an inward and secret impulse implanted in their nature, which induces them to leave the place where they were nurtured in comfort and security to seek their sustenance elsewhere for a season. And when the winter has passed away, and the snow has vanished from their northern haunts under the genial influence of the spring, and the heath and the moor are exhibiting the wild flowers to enliven the face of nature, the remnant of these feathered songsters return to their native spot, and rejoice in the fulfilment of the laws that were allotted to them by the strict design of an all-wise and beneficent Creator.

I am, Sir, yours respectfully,
320, Strand.   C. W—D.

Short Notes.

CURIOUS SPIDER.—Eperia apoclisa, is remarkable for its interesting habits, which although familiar to arachnologists through the writings of Mr. F. Smith and Mr. Pickard-Cambridge, are not generally known. Mr. Smith in No. 364 of the *Entomologist*, writes: "As I was sitting down by a clump of rushes, my attention was attracted by numerous small dome-shaped nests of white silk. These, I observed, were principally attached to the clusters of seeds which grew towards the tops of the rushes. Numerous sheep were grazing about the spot, and close to the clump of rushes that grew about a yard from where I was sitting, a little heap of dung was deposited. This, of course, attracted a certain species of Diptera. Suddenly I observed a spider drop from one of the dome-shaped nests; down he dropped like a pebble on to the little heap of sheep's dung; the spider had caught a fly. This was a mode of capture I had never before witnessed. I admired it exceedingly; but my astonishment was increased twenty-fold on seeing him, exactly like one of those balls attached to an elastic string with which children amuse themselves, ascend hind-quarters first! The spider had no elastic string? If not, how did he contrive to rebound like a ball? Was the silken thread retracted? I observed no motion in his legs. The circumstances altogether so greatly interested me that I immediately set about laying baits for flies beneath other of the dome-shaped nests. Subsequently I was gratified by witnessing three similar captures and three similar ascents; but I failed to detect any perceptible motion of the spider's legs, which I think I must have done had the creature climbed backwards up the thread; the rapidity with which he ascended appeared to render such a mode of ascent impossible." On this Mr. Pickard-Cambridge observes, in No. 370 of the same periodical: "I have frequently observed the simple, but very striking mode of spiders capturing their prey by dropping upon it like a stone, that Mr. Smith speaks of, but not before in E. apoclisa; in several instances I have seen it in E. inclinata ; in these instances the spider reascended to its original position by running up its thread backwards. I could see a quick motion of the legs, and although unable, from the position I was in, to be quite certain, yet from what I could see I concluded that the slack of the thread was gathered in by the hind legs as the spider ascended. The ascents that I have observed were not so rapid, or instantaneous as those Mr. Smith describes, but I think that a very rapid movement, of the *extremities*, merely, of the legs used in climbing might be difficult to see during so short a time as the operation lasted, but would account for the swiftness with which the ascents were made. Epeira apoclisa is one of our most numerous, as well as most beautiful spiders.—*Field*.

TRUFFLE HUNTING.—The pig was formerly employed in all parts of France in hunting for this precious tuber, which has just appeared in the Paris markets, and in an abundance which has not been equalled for the last sixty years. There is a celebrated caricature of Gavarni's, in which two women of the people are represented as discussing the vintage. "They say there will be plenty of wine this year," says the first lady ; and the other replies, " How we shall get trounced !" Looking at the plentiful supply of truffles, *gourmet* and *gourmand* will probably exclaim, " How we shall suffer from indigestion !" In Provence, the ancient country of the troubadour and ballad, the pig is still employed in searching for the truffle. It is a lean sort of animal, very clever in its way, and is called a *porc de course*, or racing pig, who is duly trained to his business, and for every tuber he discovers he is rewarded with an acorn—he finds a fish, and is offered a serpent. In the department of the Haute-Marne the pig has been replaced by the dog ; the ordinary cur of the country is trained for the pursuit, and readily masters his craft ; his training is neither long nor costly, and his education consists in being kept for a certain time without food, and then set to discover a truffle placed with a piece of bacon in a *sabot* filled with earth. As soon as the dog has found the truffle he is rewarded with a small bit of bread, and the manœuvre recommences. After a few days of this exercise the dog is generally found to be sufficiently trained, and his value reaches as high as £4 at times. There are peasants which make this system of education their trade. A curious fact has lately come to light, which proves that the dog and the pig are not the entire monopoly of finding truffles. The truffle poachers trust to a certain fly to guide them to the beloved tuber. A paper on the subject of this fly has been addressed to the Botanical Society of France by M. Gubler, who reports that the insect is large, that he ever returns to the same spot, and, after numerous circuits, settles, and where he settles a truffle is sure to be found.—*Land and Water*, Nov. 7.

THE HINDU VIEW OF THE ECLIPSE.— What the Great Day of Atonement was to the Jews, the period of an eclipse is to the Hindus. All castes, from the Brahman to the Pariah, keep strict fast. Fearful are the penalties denounced on those who neglect its observance—leprosy, during seven successive transmigrations after this life is over, awaits them. On the other hand, numerous blessings, in the present and future life, will be bestowed on those who meritoriously perform the proper ceremonies ; and one prayer, or *mantra*, repeated during the time of eclipse, has the efficacy of a hundred said at any other time.

The pious Hindu before the eclipse comes on, takes a torch, and begins to search his house, and carefully removes all cooked food, and all water for drinking purposes. Such food and water, by the eclipse, incur *Grahana seshah*—that is, uncleanness, and are rendered unfit for use. Some, with less scruples of conscience, declare that the food may be preserved by placing on it *dharba* or *kusa* grass. This grass is largely used in the ceremonies that follow ; it is known to botanists as *Poa cynosuroides* ; it is esteemed as sacred throughout the length and breadth of India ; and it is thought to be the abode of a benevolent goddess, who secures to man the fruit of his good works.

Women who are near their confinement, when the hour of eclipse approaches, are carefully locked up in a dark room, for it is supposed that, should they see the eclipse, the result would be that the child would be born with some deformity. This is the only exception which the Sastras (*ceremonial laws*) allow : all others, from the infant to the dying man, must go forth to bathe ; and not till the deliverance of the sun is effected, must any one presume to eat. The glorious sun, the source of life and heat, is looked upon as the father of the universe ; and now, in the hour of his adversity, should not his children mourn ?—*Chambers's Journal*.

A PLUCKY MOUSE.—About eighteen months ago a drug clerk in Nashville captured a burly rattlesnake, about four feet long, and sporting eight rattles and a button. He brought it home a prisoner, and prepared a handsome glass case for its reception.

Latterly he had three companions, a chicken-snake, a black and a spotted bush-snake. Some six or eight mice are kept constantly in the case, but for some weeks have been unmolested. A few days ago a fresh mouse was put in. He took a view of the situation, and resolved upon fight. He first "went for" the least of the surrounding "evils." Grasping the least serpent, he severed his head from his body in a few minutes, without injury to himself. He then, after a brief pause, attacked the next larger, cutting off the extremity of its tail. In this case he met with resistance and was several times bitten, but persisted till he killed his enemy.

Going to the chicken-snake, he moved upon its centre—was several times stricken, but continued the contest with remarkable coolness and perseverance. When in very close quarters, he would retreat and take breath. In the midst of this fight the rattlesnake became aroused, and moved excitedly about in the case. The mouse, esteeming this an act of hostility, pounced upon his new foe with desperate courage, biting him about the head, along the sides, and upon the back. He received a fearful warning in the "rattling" of his snakeship, but received no wound from him. Quitting this one, he would turn to the other and renew his persistent assault, and for twenty-four hours he thus continued the struggle.

The poison he had received then began to work ;

he sickened, retired to a corner of the case, and in a few hours expired. This is, perhaps, the most heroic passage to be found anywhere in the "Universal History of the Mouse." He was taken out and buried, like Sir John Moore, "without a drum or funeral note," but amid the silent sorrow of admiring friends.—*From an American Paper.*

Remarks, Queries, &c.

(*Under this head we shall be happy to insert original Remarks, Queries, &c.*)

INSTINCT versus REASON.

"Reasoning at every step he treads
Man yet mistakes his way;
While meaner things whom instinct leads,
Are *rarely known to stray*."

SIR,—Will you allow me a short space in reply to the criticisms of your correspondent "C." upon my note on instinct?

He begins by stating his belief that "reason is enjoyed in a limited degree by the higher families of the vertebrate kingdom." From this I infer he believes that all the invertebrata and the greater portion of the vertebrata do *not* possess the gift of reason. But what does he say to the well-known fact that many tribes of insects display a *far greater* share of intelligence and apparent reason in their actions than the majority of mammalia? And it is probable that if our very limited knowledge of this interesting class of animals were more extended, our surprise and admiration of them would be much increased. Most of those who agree with "C." in classing the lower animals among reasonable beings are wider in their application of this faculty; but none of them, I presume, hold that the lowest forms of animal life (such as the sponge zoophyte, etc.) possess this exalted attribute. What I ask them is, where shall we draw the line between animals that reason and those that do not? Granted that sponges and polypes do not reason: do animalcules, anemonies, and star fishes? If not, do crabs, worms, mollusks, &c.? And so on till we come to the vertebrate kingdom.

Are we then to acknowledge that all the vertebrata have this power, whilst the invertebrata have not? But, as we have seen, many species of the latter class exhibit a decidedly nearer approximation to that faculty of man than the former. The line between man and brutes is so apparent as to preclude the possibility of mistaking it, whilst those who maintain that reasoning is not confined to man are quite unable to draw a line between the beasts that do and do not enjoy this faculty, or even to make a well-founded conjecture on the subject.

I do not positively affirm that dogs and other animals have not some degree of reason; but I say that their seeming reflection, as well as their aptitude in learning tricks, etc., *may* be accounted for by supposing them mere tools or machines in the hands of an over-ruling Providence.

One consideration that inclines to this belief is that brutes, however they vary, their modes of action seldom or never *err*. Now this is the main difference between the intelligence of mankind and that of the brute creation: if beasts could reason in the same way as men, though in a less degree, they would be *much more* liable to fall into mistakes and errors than the "lord of creation."

Your correspondent does not attempt to account for the instinct-like phenomena observed in the vine, potatoe, etc. Of course plants do not reason, but nevertheless they conform their actions (such as habits of growth, etc.) to the circumstances in which they are placed: the same may be the case with animals. "C." next brings forward for my edification a *decapitated frog*, and remarks that "purposive movements are no proof of consciousness or will." I would reply that purposive movements *are* a decided proof of consciousness and will, either in the individual itself or in the *force* exerted over the individual or subject, and to which the subject is a means of accomplishing some end in view.

I would without hesitation say that the movements of the poor frog when in this condition were not *purposive* but *purposeless*; its actions then are not influenced by its will, and therefore can have no purpose; they are both involuntary and unconscious. Even man himself, when beheaded, has been known to make sundry motions with his body though separated from his brain: these are, as every one knows, simply nervous spasms or convulsions of the muscles, such as sometimes take place during dreams, etc.

In the next place we are told that the headless frog if irritated on the abdomen or back, will show a "manifest determination of resenting the attack." This is not true unless the word *apparent* be used in place of manifest. "C." suggests that plants may have this same "power of purposive movement," independent of sensation or consciousness. From this he concludes that the connection between the instinct in animals and plants which I advanced is satisfactorily disproved. If he wishes to maintain this conclusion, he must answer the objections already made as to this "purposive power."

We now come to the two rules of logic which I am said to have violated. The answer to the first is that I did not take as *proved* the identity of the two instincts (in animals and plants), but only gave my opinion, there not being sufficient grounds for certainty in the matter. As to the second, your correspondent has yet to prove that the proposition "the brute is ruled by his actions" (*i.e.* he is under the necessity of obeying his instinctive laws, or he acts without reasoning) is unsound.

In many of the actions of dogs I acknowledge there is evident reason; but as I maintain that the dog, in common with all the lower animals, is "ruled by his actions," it follows that the reasoning is not in formed but in the Former.

Many of the useful engines and machines of civilised man would seem to the barbarous savage, at first sight, to be endowed with life and reason, and if such be the case, why may not the wisest among us make the same mistake with regard to the works of the Creator of the UNIVERSE.

It has not been at all clearly proved that dogs have

the gift of reason; little more so, in fact, than that plants have. Though we can never expect to be certain on this point, we may hope by careful examination to arrive much nearer the truth than we are at present.   R. B. W.
November 12th.

DO INSECTS FEEL PAIN?

What atom forms of insect life appear!
And who can follow Nature's pencil here?
BARBAULD.

Messrs. Crook and "Good Taste," imperfectly armed, enter the arena. Instead of arguments they leave us but "a monument of words," and thus make up the learned heptarchy of the painless theory confederation. "Good Taste," with all his urbanity, indulges in the best taste of not studying the subject. He does not attempt to elucidate, and his laconic sentences require an interpreter. He, however, dreading the "glorious uncertainty" of criticism, in all familiarity treats us to an interesting bit of his autobiography, for in grappling with the arguments of H. H. Ulidia he suddenly comes to a stand-still, and gravely says :—"Next we come to a few apparently sound sentences, but *I am not fitted to criticise them as I have no books here!*" This truly important information from the scribe himself, sounds very like an announcement that "Good Taste" knows nothing concerning the question at issue—so I leave him, and pass on, rather timidly, to encounter Mr. Fred. J. Crook and his goat.

Mr. Crook, in something like *bucolic* language, puts the interrogative, "If you were to hold a goat by the horns would it not struggle to get free?" Undoubtedly, if your goat be very wild your question quite forcibly carries its own affirmative. Then Mr. Crook thus classically and logically proceeds :—"Yet I should think that no one would be ridiculous enough to hold that it hurt a goat to hold it by the horns," and hence it follows that insects are incapable of feeling pain! Beware of the horns, for if "definitions are dangerous," I really dread Mr. Crook's illustration more than I do the horns of a dilemma.

I acknowledge the labours of Mr. Waters as a naturalist; but if his reasoning on our present subject is tinged with even *agreeable faults*, surely I cannot be blamed for showing the soundness of the side I advocate. When I assert that "misery is pain," I associate with it the ideas, misfortune, calamity, unhappiness, wretchedness, suffering from any cause, and Mr. Waters' notion is that "misery is not necessarily pain."

Do insects feel pain? And now a powerful advocate on the affirmative side, your correspondent "C." enters the field just in time to save our colours, and with his well-directed battery of heavy guns so disables the pain-despising veterans that I expect to see their flag of truce soon, so that they may be enabled to carry off their *fallacies*. "C.'s" arguments are numerous and strong, and driven home with logical precision. As the question has attracted more than ordinary attention, I hope the correspondents and general readers of the NATURALIST'S NOTE BOOK will read and *study* the arguments adduced by your talented correspondent "C."

In my last letter, when controverting the assertions of Mr. Spicer concerning the nonexistence of brain in insects, I neglected to add the authority of Linneus, who in speaking of insects says :—"The nervous system, which is ramified from the *brain*, contained in the head," etc., etc.

And, Sir Everard Home, in a lecture "On the internal structure of the human brain, when examined by the microscope, as compared with that of fishes, insects, and worms," says, in the *moth* and caterpillar the *brain* is smaller than in the bee, but similar in structure, as also in the lobster; in the garden snail the *brain* is relatively larger than in the bee.

I am happy to find that the *Victoria Magazine*, in the article on "Butterflies," touches on our subject pretty freely; and I wish the cautions "Jeremiah Sawcut" would come out a little bolder on the question. I now fall back into the reserve, and press forward the advanced column under my spirited and vigorous ally, "C."   H. H. ULIDIA.

Without going into the question of whether or no the lower creatures feel that pain which some assert they do, I am anxious to point out to your correspondent "C." that the passage of Holy Writ he has chosen whereon to found his assertion that they do, does not in fact bear upon the question, but sets forth only the craving of the human race after a better and happier state of existence; and this, in spite of the expression "the whole creation," upon which expression "C." so evidently relies as to lead him to take the verse wherein it occurs and place it (the 22nd) before the 20th. I take it "C." will not deny that verse 18 refers exclusively to a state of actual "*glory*" to be enjoyed by *man only* hereafter. The apostle is evidently cheering *Christians* by placing before them heaven as the termination of their life of travail here, of which lower creatures could and can have no knowledge. But now in verse 19 comes the word "creature," and it is this word I maintain that "C." has misapprehended. The whole question turns upon the meaning of the word κτίσις (creature); that it cannot mean the lower creatures as well as man in this place seems sufficiently evident from the fact that *it* is represented as "waiting for" or expecting or looking forward to a future "manifestation," which cannot be predicted of the lower creatures. *The whole human race* then the apostle declares to be in a waiting state. "For," he goes on to say in verse 18, 'the creature' (ἡ κτίσις again, the whole human race) was made subject to vanity—not willingly—but by reason of him (Adam) who hath subjected the same to death and corruption." *Not willingly*, not of its own accord ! This expression would surely not be used if ἡ κτίσις included the lower creatures.

I further observe that "C." has placed a semicolon after the two last words of this same verse, whereas in the Greek there is only a comma, carrying on these words to the next verse; thus in hope (ὅτι "because" or *that*) that the creature itself also shall be delivered, etc. This seems more evident when in the Greek we find a full stop after the words τὸν ὑποτά ξαντα "him who hath subjected." I would here again remark that the lower creatures cannot have "hope" of their own deliverance, certainly not of attaining "the glorious liberty of the Sons of God."

In the next verse we find κτίσις joined to πᾶσα (the whole creation) and this seems to be "C.'s" strong point. But let us examine this expression. Now πᾶσα κτίσις is used in but few places of the New Testament. In Colossians Christ is said to be the first born πάσης κτίσεως (of the whole creation). And the gospel is announced to be preached "ἐν πάσῃ, τῇ, κτίσει" to all mankind ("every creature under heaven.") Col. i., 23. Again, the Apostles are commanded to preach the gospel πάσῃ τῇ, κτίσει (" to every creature.") In all these places mankind, and mankind *only*, can be intended; and I submit that mankind, and mankind only, are intended by the phrase πᾶσα ἡ κτίσις in the verse under consideration, *that is mankind, including Christian, Jew and Gentile.* For, in the following verse, the Apostle goes on to say, "And not only *they*, but ourselves also who have the first fruits of the Spirit" (that is, are Christians) "even we ourselves groan," etc. Who are *they*, put in antithesis to Christians? Clearly the *rest* of *human kind*, Jews and Gentiles. In short, then, I maintain (with presumption, no doubt, in the eyes of "C.") that the whole passage relates to *mankind only*, mankind longing after, travailing, and groaning after a happier life, in which we are told in verse 6 they are joined by the Spirit above; and that it does not touch at all upon the subject of the condition here of the lower creatures. Whether they feel pain or not I leave to wiser heads than mine to solve; whether "C." has grounds for his theory of *a* happier life for them hereafter I may have hopes to solve; whether they will have a place in another world I may have thoughts and hopes; my only object in writing the above is to endeavour to point out to "C." that in *the* passage of Scripture he quotes, his theory on the subject of the pain felt by the lower creatures fails to find confirmation, or even support.

WINDSOR HAMBROUGH.

C. says:—"We have no authority for exempting the lower animals from their share in the universal curse." "Death passed upon all men, for that all have sinned" through Adam's sin; but where do we find that it passed on *the lower animals as a consequence* of that same transgression? Were animals intended at first to be immortal?

Mr. Ulidia in his lengthy epistles should at least be fair, which in his letter of page 313 he certainly is not. His inability to draw inferences correctly is well known to and commented on by the correspondents of this journal, but I fain would give one instance. Speaking of the moth which Mr. Spicer pinned to a tree (not a most humane action, but not calling for such vehement protestations of horror from Mr. U.), he says that because it flapped its wings at evening and found it was in captivity it felt pain. Now it seems to me that God has given it sufficient instinct to know the hour when it should fly abroad to seek its food, and that this was merely why it struggled. In proof of this Mr. Spicer says it remained quiet until *evening*. I would give one instance of his unfairness, viz., in describing what he terms "the fight" of Mr. Waters with the dragon-fly, in which he evidently wishes us to think Mr. Waters allowed that the creature suffered pain. I have not the last NOTE BOOK before me, but according to my recollection Mr. Waters gave us to understand that the fly was inconvenienced from the loss of balance, and when he had inserted the grass-stalk from being unable to steer itself. W. H. M.

I have been greatly interested in the various letters which have lately appeared on the question, "Do insects feel pain?" and although I do not agree with all the arguments of H. H. Ulidia, yet I hold with that gentleman in maintaining that insects *do* feel pain. "P. G. M." (NATURALIST'S NOTE BOOK, page 318) mentions a law in Nature, viz., that "The lower we go down the scale of animated beings, the less is the amount of pain experienced." Although I firmly believe that such is the case, I did not know that it was ascertained to be a fixed law in nature, neither do I know what reason "P. G. M." has for stating it to be such. Perhaps he will have the goodness to inform me. R. T.

METEORS, ETC.—R. T. wishes to know how we are to reconcile the recent theory that meteors are fragments of cometary matter, with the well-known fact of the extreme tenuity of the substance of comets. He says that if the theory is correct we must take it for granted that comets are either solid bodies, or consist of streams of meteors, and in neither case would their nature agree with their appearance. But may not some comets, at least, consist of a solid nucleus, surrounded by an immense gaseous or vaporous envelope? Sir John Herschel, in his "Familiar Lectures," speaking of the nuclei of comets, says:—"If there be not some little solid mass, it seems impossible to conceive how the observations of a loose bundle of smoke, rolling and careering about, could ever be represented by any calculation. Certain it is, that what appears to be the central point of a comet, *is* that point (and no other is) which conforms rigorously to the laws of solar gravitation, and moves strictly in a parabolic or elliptic orbit." And again, after speaking of the action of the sun upon comets, by which their gaseous parts seem to be subject to a powerful repulsion, while their solid parts are attracted (evidenced by the tail of the comet being always turned *from* the sun), he suggests:—"Might not, under such circumstances, the mere ordinary action of the sun's heat sufficiently weaken their bond of union: and might not the residual mass, losing at every return to the perihelion more and more of its levitating constituents, at length settle down into a quiet, sober, unexcitable denizen of our system?" This seems to me to throw much light on the theory of the connection between meteors and comets; and it is all the more valuable inasmuch as it was written before the discovery of that connection. We may suppose that meteors are the nuclei of old comets. They are *dark comets*, in fact, which having parted with their lighter gaseous constituents revolve in their ancient orbits; although, through their great reduction in size, they have become invisible to us, except when the earth intersects their orbits, and they are brought within the influence of her attraction. And may not the gaseous matter detached from them go towards the formation of that indistinct, nebulous ring round the sun, which is called the Zodiacal Light? GULIELMUS.

STING OF NETTLE. — Notwithstanding what "O. R." says in this month's number of the NATURALIST'S NOTE BOOK, I still doubt the correctness of C. O. G. Napier's statement, and shall continue to do so untill "O. R.," or some one else, gives me better reason than I have at present to make me believe that my opinions respecting the sting of nettles (page 318) are wrong. Has "O. R." touched a nettle leaf lightly with the palm of his hand? If he has not, I ask him to do so now, confidently assuring him that he will not suffer by so doing. When he does so, he will knock off the little caps which he mentions as being at the end of the tubes on the nettle leaf, and will consequently make way for the sharp points of the tubes to enter his skin, which, however, they will not do, at least not so as to cause pain; and why not? Because, as I say again, and as I think "O. R." must admit, they (the tubes) are unable to penetrate the outer skin on the palm of the hand. "O. R." asks why it is that the ends of the fingers (which he affirms to be very sensitive) are not stung. I answer that the ends of the fingers may be very sensitive, and yet may not be so sensitive as the skin on the back of the hand is. Again, "O. R." asks why it is that if the nettle leaf be tightly grasped between the sides of the fingers no sting is felt. Has "O. R." practically tried this? If he has, I cannot possibly see how he arrives at the above conclusion; and if he has not, will he oblige me by doing so, and letting me know the result. When I grasped a nettle firmly between the sides of my fingers, I found, to my cost, that "O. R.'s view of this matter is a mistaken one, for I was severely stung, and the marks caused by the sting remained for hours afterwards. A friend who was with me also experienced a sting when he followed my example. But very likely "O. R." will be more fortunate, which, for his own sake, I hope will be the case, and I should advise him to have some dock leaves, or something by which he can nullify the effects of the sting with him, as I think he will certainly be stung. R. T.

"OLD ENGLISH WILD FLOWERS."—I cannot help expressing my surprise at the terms in which you review the work above named. You say it is "more accurately done than the majority of similar works." Without further comment, will you allow me to submit to your readers a few extracts taken at random from its pages:—

Caltha palustris. "*Like all dark-foliaged flowers,* the plant is poisonous." (P. 46.)

Primula farinosa. "The flower is small, seldom larger than the oxlip." (P. 104.)

Salvia Verbenaca "has always occupied a prominent place in English cookery." (P. 99.)

"Frequent mistakes are made by watercress gatherers in taking the leaves of the water parsnip (*Sium latifolium*) for the watercress." (P. 112.)

"On the borders of the boggy land we may find the marsh mallow (*Althæa officinalis*)." (P. 113.)

Menyanthes trifoliata. "Sometimes rears its tall head by the side of the river. . . . Its flower-stem grows out of a sheath on the top of its stout stalk, and the flowers are scattered down the stem. The leaves are triple, like those of the field bean, and the stalk has a general resemblance to that plant." (P. 114.)

Ranunculus flammula "is distinguished by its silky foliage." (P. 115.)

Trifolium stellatum "is not unfrequent on the south coast." (P. 116.)

Erysimum cheiranthoïdes "frequents the cliffs and fields near the sea, principally in the south-eastern counties." (P. 31.)

Hierochloe borealis "frequents the Scottish glens." (P. 91.)

The words "species" and "variety" are used interchangeably; the Latin names are misprinted in many cases—e. g. *Ruta maria, Festucea, Dactylus, Ulex tianus, Arenaria culora, Hypernicum eloides, Rubra peregrinia.*

Perhaps this "little volume" may be considered "very amusing;" whether it is "instructive" is another matter.

High Wycombe. JAMES BRITTEN.

THE GIANT SIREX.—In the latter end of July, 1867, I happened to catch the giant sirex (*sirex gigas*) about which I have obtained very little information. Can you or any reader of the valuable NOTE BOOK kindly give me some information as to whether it is a common insect, and also where it is generally to be met with? The locality where I captured it I think must have been an uncommon one, as it was on the top of Three Barrow Tor, Dartmoor, an altitude of 1500 feet above the sea. It is a fine insect, of the female sex. A. E. BUTTEMER.

Ambleside.

I find on looking at "Our Garden Friends and Foes," by the Rev. J. G. Wood, that the species of saw-fly I caught is the giant sirex (*sirex gigas*). I see it is there described as being "very plentiful in many parts of England, but is rather local, and apt to be periodical. It is local, because it is only to be found in the neighbourhood of the trees on which the larva feeds," etc. Also he says—"Fir-trees are preferred by the sirex, which drills a small hole in the wood, and lays its egg therein." I am now convinced where I caught the sirex—on Dartmoor, at an elevation of 1,500 feet above the sea—must have been a most uncommon locality for it. When I first captured it I noticed it was rather drowsy, as if out of its element at so great a height. Upon my enclosing it in a small chip-box it revived and became lively. I have it in preservation now, and it is a fine large insect of the female sex. I killed it, like I do almost all insects, by the use of chloroform, as being the most merciful death, and thereby avoiding all chance of giving them *any pain*, if insects "do feel pain," which still appears to be the question at issue with many correspondents of the NOTE BOOK, and which is one they all know, *must* remain undecided in the end, it being impossible to prove for certain whether they experience much, little, or any pain. I think, as Mr. H. H. Ulidia says, "that insects feel pain," but at the same time I say most certainly not to the *same extent* as "man, the elephant, the whale, and the sparrow, &c.," feel it. I myself am of Mr. J. B. Waters' opinion when he says, "that insects feel extremely little if any pain." I shall be glad if you, or any of the numerous correspondents of the NOTE BOOK, will give me further information about the sirex. A. E. BUTTEMER.

LUNAR RAINBOW.—As some of your correspondents have expressed a wish to hear of any recorded instances of *lunar rainbows* occurring in this country, I extract the following from the *Scotsman*:—"A beautiful specimen of the somewhat rare phenomenon a lunar rainbow, was observed on Monday evening (Nov. 2nd) at Dunbar. The bow was first observed about half-past eight o'clock, and was then very clearly defined against a bank of clouds in the west. It extended from nearly north-east to south-west, and remained visible for nearly a quarter of an hour. The colours could be distinctly traced on the south-western portion of the arch, but the north-eastern part was somewhat obscured. The weather at the same time was somewhat boisterous, a stiff breeze blowing, and the clouds in the west were charged with rain, but the moon was shining very bright, so much so that a book of common print could be easily read by its light." R. B. W.

PROLIFIC SOW.—I think one of the most extraordinary cases I have ever heard was related to me by a gentleman residing at Blackheath. Some twenty years ago he purchased an old and rather small sow of the Chinese breed, supposed to be past breeding, in fact ; however, in five consecutive litters which it had after coming into his possession it produced the great number of 108 pigs ; thus—two litters of 19 each, one of 22, one of 23, and the last of 25 ! Sixteen out of the twenty-five were retained, and with these she disappeared in the woods, and did not return until she brought them back weighing eight stone each. She at last fell a victim to the butcher's knife, having been fattened (though of so small a breed) to the respectable weight of sixty stone ! A. M. B.

NOCTUÆ.—Perhaps a description of the method (if method it may be called) by which I captured this year many noctuæ, may not be unacceptable to some of your readers. My bedroom is at the top of a high house surrounded by walnut trees, and has a projecting window. On a table in this window I used to place at dusk a paraffin lamp, and behind it a looking glass adjusted so as to reflect the light out of window. Coming upstairs about 10 p.m., it was usual to find several moths settled on the walls and ceiling, which were easily captured by placing over them a tumbler, or better still, a small wide-mouthed bottle, the cavity in the stopper of which was stuffed full of blotting paper, on which was dropped some chloroform.
W. H. M.

A STRANGE EGG.—In answer to your correspondent, "J. D. S. W." let me inform him that the strange egg he speaks of in the November number of the NOTE BOOK is *rare*, but by no means *unexampled*. For instance, I have in my possession at present a hen's egg, the length of a bantam's egg, but not bigger round than a sparrow's. In an aviary I have seen small birds fly down on the ground for a moment, lay a most remarkable egg (sometimes quite differently shaped and marked from the usual egg of the bird in question) and then fly up again. The egg of which "J. D. S. W." makes mention was probably either the *first* egg laid by a young thrush, or else the bird was terrified or frightened at the time. A. H. M.

RABBITS.—Rabit fanciers may be glad to hear of a cure for the complaint known as the "rot" to which young rabbits are very subject. This disease is generally fatal to them, and is also most contagious : it arises chiefly from their eating *wet* green food. I have lost many fine litters of young rabbits from this complaint (as many as *ten* within a very short time) : at last I resolved to try the effect of half a teaspoonful of raw brandy on one of the rabbits last attacked with the "rot." I administered it with the spoon : in an hour afterwards the little animal seemed quite well again, and ate its food greedily, although it had been almost in the agonies of death when first brought into the house for treatment.

INFLUENCE OF THE MOON.—Since my note on this point, I have been informed that some years ago a person was killed by the rays of the full moon striking upon him as he was sleeping in the open air. If any of your readers could corroborate this statement I should be much obliged. I have read in some work that a certain degree of *heat* is transmitted to our earth from the stars. This seems as probable as that the planet Neptune should receive heat and light from the sun, which to it appears no larger than a "fixed star." R. B. W.

SECURITY FROM INSECT-BITES.—A tincture prepared by macerating one part of *Pyrethrum roseum* in four parts of dilute alcohol, when mixed with ten times its bulk of water and applied to any part of the body, gives perfect security from all attacks of noxious insects. Specimens of natural history should on no account be kept in drawers made of cedar, as this wood, like that of the sandal-tree, distils out its otto and deposits it on the objects near. R. B. W.

HAIR OFF DOGS.—Can you or any of your readers tell me of a remedy to prevent the hair coming off dogs ? I have a litttle pet dog which was born off Cape Horn in August last ; and since I have had it, about a month, the hair has come off very much, the hinder part of its body and legs being quite bare. I may add that its mother came from South Africa.
Salisbury. BERNARD C. BUSH.

ARACHNIDÆ.—Could any of your readers tell me the distinctive marks of the male and female spiders ? There is a prevailing opinion amongst the "old women" that *all* spiders are *females*. This, of course, must be nonsense : it is an established fact that spiders repeatedly change their coats. If so, how many times a year, and at what season ?
"DAS SPINNENGEWEBE."

GOLDFINCHES.—Can any of the readers of the NATURALIST'S NOTE BOOK tell me the best food for goldfinches? H. F. P.

THE NATURALIST'S NOTE BOOK

FOR 1869.

A MONTHLY RECORD

OF

ANECDOTES, THEORIES, AND FACTS

RELATING TO

NATURAL SCIENCE,

TOGETHER WITH NOTICES OF NEW BOOKS, REPORTS OF
THE MEETINGS OF LEARNED SOCIETIES, ORIGINAL
CORRESPONDENCE, ETC., ETC.

Think nought a trifle, though it small appear;
Small sands the mountain, moments make the year,
And trifles life. YOUNG.

London:
REEVES AND TURNER,
196, STRAND.

PREFACE.

THREE years have passed since we first had the pleasure of introducing the "NATURALIST'S NOTE BOOK" to our readers, and the success which has attended our efforts to be useful and amusing, certainly leaves us nothing to regret. Still it is our painful task to inform our many friends that the "NOTE BOOK" in its present shape ceases to exist with this volume; but only that out of its ashes another may rise, which will, we trust, be found more popular and more entertaining. The many letters we have had containing advice and suggestions, all ask the same question—"Why do we not give illustrations?" To this we could only answer, that illustrations are expensive, and our circulation would not admit of extra expenditure. We have again and again been told that with good illustrations our number of admirers would greatly increase. The time has come when we intend to see whether this is so or not. Early in January will be issued the first number of a new series of the "NATURALIST'S NOTE BOOK." It will be an 8vo (size of the "Cornhill"), will contain 48 pp., instead of 32 as hitherto, and two plate illustrations, as well as woodcuts when necessary; the whole printed in better type, upon better paper, and the price will be Sixpence. With these alterations, we think to please all our friends, and gain many more. In conclusion, we can only hope that we shall meet with the same support and assistance that we have hitherto had from our various contributors, and have no hesitation in saying we will do our very best to meet their wishes; and at the same time, make our venture one of the most popular of magazines.

Again reiterating our thanks, we wish all our readers a merry Christmas, and ourselves a prosperous and successful new year.

INDEX.

ASTRONOMY.

Air, the Thin, 156
Asteroids, 199
Astronomical Phenomena, 96
Comets and Meteors, 127
Electricity, 191
Heat, the Source of, 89, 150
Heat of Summer of 1868, 320, 346
Light, &c., 127
Light, some Phenomena, 336
Mars, 17
Mercury, Transit of, 22
Meteors, November, 189
Moon, Mock, 128
Moon Strokes, 128, 158, 188
Moon and Weather, the, 288, 347, 375
Neptune, 94
Neptune, the Planet, 154
Planets: Are they Inhabited? 154, 215
Planets, the three new, 56
Refraction, Effects of, 285
Arrow, 128
Sun the Principal Source of Heat, the, 122
Sun, Heat of the, 376
Sun and Moon larger at rising than setting, 288
Sun spots, 349
Sun's disc, black spots on the, 317
Weather, mildness of the, 128
Winds, east, 127, 158

BOTANY.

Ash tree, 22
Clove, the, 9
Dahlia, the, 191
Fern Culture, 326
Flowers, Colour of, 34
Flowers, to preserve the colour of dried, 101
Flowers, colours of dried, 160, 288
Forest, the Black, 91
Forest Trees, on Submerged, 328
Garden, Round my, 109
Iris, Localities for, 156
Nettles, Sting of, 126, 156, 191, 223
Nutmegs, 55
Pippins, Ribstone, 288
Plants, Fertilization of, 343
Plants, Instinct in, 189
Rice, 253
Trees, 96
Trees, Birch, 160
Trees, among the, 80
Tree, an Australian, 56
Thistle seeds, 95
Tobacco, 171
Vegetable Fibres, 40
Wind Flower, 192

ENTOMOLOGY.

A. Atropos, 191, 376
Ants and their prey, 95
Beetles, 255
Beetles, Book on British, 256
Beetles in Utah, 19
Bombyx Cecropia, 304, 364
Bombyx Quercus, 320
Butterflies, 288
Butterfly, 352
Butterflies (British) List of, 37, 136
Butterflies (British) on the extinction of Species of, 102
Butterflies, Food of, 254
Butterfly, Garden-white, 128
Butterfly, Orange-tip, 128
Butterflies, Peacock, 192
Butterfly, Swallow-tailed, 300
Caterpillars, 192, 320
Caterpillars, Stinging sensation caused by, 351
Chrysalide Keeping, 256
Cockroaches, 319
Cockroaches, Destroying, 319
Colias Hyale, 160
Crickets and Cockroaches, 256
Cricket, Field, 160
Cricket, Green Field, 128, 160
Death Watch, the, 14, 377
Double Broods, 49
Dragon Flies, 256
Entomology, 348
Entomology for the Months, 134, 165, 198, 230, 277
Entomological Apparatus, 160
Entomological Requisites, 190
Erebia Blandina, 352
Erebia Cassiope, 288
Eriogaster Lanestris, 320
Geometræ, on the British, 7, 41, 70, 94, 111, 126, 130, 166, 202, 230, 262, 302, 375
House Flies, 288
Insect, a Curious, 255, 288
Insects, Amount of Pain felt by, 254
Insects, Arrangement of, 156
Insects, Circulation in, 23
Insects, How to form a Cabinet of, 128
Insect Killing, 157
Insect Medicine and Folk Lore, 65, 99
Insects, Physiology of, 269
Insecticide, 21
Ladybirds, 315
Ladybird, to a, 336
Ladybirds, Use of, 351
Lepidoptera, 128
Lepidopterist's Exchange Club, 92
Lepidoptera of Sheppy, the, 141
Lepidoptera, on the killing of, 93, 126
Lepidoptera, Size of, 95
Lithisia Rubicollis, 127
Moth, Death's Head Hawk, 222
Moth Courtship, 158, 192, 222
Moth, Gold-tailed, larva of the, 318
Moth, Puss, 351
Moth, Satin, 126
Moths, Sugaring for, 125
Moths, British, List of, 76, 107, 175, 199, 311, 358

Moths of Buckinghamshire, the Prominent, 274
Oak Eggar Board, 326
Pupæ Digging, 320, 352
Pulex Irritans in a new Light, 205
Red Admirals, Trap for, 320
Silkworms, American, 273, 351
Silkworms and how to rear them, 33, 72, 104, 138
Sirex Gigas, 254, 288, 359, 319
Spider, Habits of the, 255
Spider and Wasp, 318
Vanessidæ, on the Family of, 367
Wasps, Distressing effects of Stings of, 346, 377
Worm, Life Destroying, 95

ETHNOLOOY.

Kaloshes, the, 214

GEOLOGY.

Baltic, Subsidence of the, 215
Barax Lake, California, 135
Coal, 191
Coal Mining in China, 344
Coal, What is, 219
Earth and heavens, beauty of, 376
Earth, Crust of the, 352, 376
Earthquake, Shock of a, 21
Fire, 272, 316
Lava, What is, 215
Lias Beds, on the Lower, at Cotham, &c., 97, 161, 193
Ocean Bottom, the, 19
Salt Mines, Great Polish, 35
Sea Salt, 237
Silver, Pure, and its Properties, 18
Water, 192

GEOGRAPHY.

Continents, Glimpses of Great, 16
Howth, Hills of, 318
Ireland's Eye, 319
Isle of Man, 317
Mexico, New, 343
Shannon, 317
Spitsbergen, 177
Weaver Valley, Botanical Ramble in the, 74

MISCELLANEOUS.

Acclimatization in Australia, 248
Animals, the Reasoning Power of, 27, 83, 120, 169, 184, 216, 250, 284
Aquarium, 320
Aviary, 192, 223
Bottle and Water, 126
Bush Hunt, an African, 179
California, the Naturalist on, 241
Charcoal and Glass, 159, 320
Climate, Influence of, on Colour, 365
Colour, 376
Corfu, Rough Notes on the Natural History of, 234, 257, 289, 321, 353
Cornwall, Rambles in, 363
Country, How to enjoy the, 346
Death before the Fall, 376
Eggs, Shape of, 96
Entomologist's Diary, Extracts from an, 79, 207, 246, 281
Fishing, 376
Folk Lore, 188
Gardener's Soliloquy, 366
Golden Autumn, 299
Hard Words, 43
Human Remains, Latest, 376
Hydrophobia, 313
In Memoriam, 314
Insects, do they feel Pain, 25, 87, 116, 147, 180, 220, 248, 281, 285, 318
Life, Deep Sea, 344
Mesmerism, 376
Mow, the Old Man of, 349
Mummy Peas, 256
Novia Scotia, Notes of a Naturalist in, 13, 110, 375
Planchette, La, 172, 256
Power, the Balance of, 159
Præuscher's Museum, 69
Rare Visitors at Ipswich, 45
Species, Extinction of, 93, 125, 155, 189, 221, 268, 318, 349
Species, Variation of, 46
Sea-side Homes, 306
Skin absorb, Does the, 191
Skins, Preservation of, 351
Sport, a good day's, 319
Spring, Early Morning Rambles in, 178
Spring, 129
Steam, Power of, 376
Summer Time in the Country, 240
Swedish Arctic Expedition, the, 55
Universal Nature, 39
Valley of Death, 376
What is it? 318
Winter, Collecting in, 160
Winter, 369

ZOOLOGY.

Anemones, the best of the cultivated,
Animal, Capture of a curious, 255
Badger, Remarkable habits of the, 48
Beavers, 337
Beetle Stones, 320
Bird Catchers, 201
Bird, Curious, 95, 159
Bird Murder, Sea, 142
Bird Murder, 187
Birds' Nesters, Caution to, 222
Bird's Eggs, 128
British Birds, List of, 297, 324
Birds of Passage, Our Summer, 159
Birds, Protecting Sea, 125
Birds in Norfolk, Rare, 350
Birds, Sea, 160
Birds, Towering, 190
Birds, British, Food of in April, 138
Bitrern, the, 247
Camel Riding in the Desert, 18
Calf, Extraordinary, 96
Cats, Age of, 128
Cat, Notes on the Habits of the, 197
Cat, as sick as a, 23
Crabs, the Battle of the, 23
Crab, Usefulness of the, 248
Cuckoo, the, 192, 224, 256
Cuckoo's Egg, 224
Curlew, the, 225
Cuttle Fish as Food, the, 215
Drivers, the, 330
Duck, Domestic, 223
Duck, Plumage of a, 159
Ducks, 192
Eutyck and Asker, 352
Fish, do Snakes eat, 350, 376
Fish hearing, 288
Fish, New species of Sun, 344
Fish, the Shark and Pilot, 255
Fish, What is a, 288
Fowl, Sea, Preservation of, 157
Fowls Swimming, 124, 157
Frogs, 95
Goldfinch, the, 143
Goshawk and Heathpolt, the, 317
Gray Phalaropes, 352
Guillemots, 190
Gulls, Blackheaded, 127, 159
Hawk, Sparrow, 127
Hawks, 192
Kangaroos, a Plague of, 215
Kestrel, a few words on the, 286
Lamb, Extraordinary, 128
Lark, 160
Lark's Nest in Bank, 192
Lions' and Tigers' flesh as Food, 255
Lizards, Food of,
Magpie's Nest, 160
Martin, Sand, Albino, 320
Martin, Habits of the, 201
Mole, Notes on the, 16
Mollusca, The Distribution of the, 261
Mouse, Fecundity of the, 19
Our Wading Birds, 225, 264, 294, 334
Partridge, the, 132
Peewit, the, 294
Pelicans, 215
Peregrine, 96
Pigeon, Wood, 316, 345
Raven, Notes on the, 78
Rat, Water, Food of the, 351

INDEX.

Rat, Albino Water, 248
Red Squirrel, the, 75
Redshank, the, 225
Reptiles at Zoological Gardens, 361
Reptiles in Ireland, No, and Why? 319, 256
Reptiles of South Africa, 128
Ringed Plover, the, 334
Robin, the American, 93
Sandpipe, the Green, 22
Shrimp, Roes in, 256
Siskin and Mealy Redpole, 127
Snake, a Tale of a, 23
Snake, Water, 160, 191
Snakes, 128
Snakes, English, 189
Snakes, Preserving, 128
Snakes in Spirit, 160
Snipe, the Common, 264
Squirrel, Voracity of a tame, 96
Sponges, 247
Starling, Notes on the, 240
Stoat, the, 10, 124
Stoat, a word for the, 92
Swift, a Visit to the nest of the, 206
Swift, Short Notes on the, 252
Swallow's Nest, a, 22
Thrush, the Missel, 187
Thrush, the Song, 1

Toads inclosed within the substance and roots of Trees, &c., 278
Tortoise, 319, 222, 256
Tortoise, Food of, 160
Tortoise, Water, 94
Turtle Dove, Egg of the, 352
Turtles, 11
Unicorne, the, 94
Wagtail, the yellow, 92
Water Rail, the, 264, 318
Water Rat, 350
Whale, Is the, a Fish, 186, 222, 251
White Mice, 376
Wheat, 376
Wood Pigeon's Nest, 125
Wood Pigeon, the, 288

CORRESPONDENCE.

Bird Murder, 53, 83, 115
Rock Bird Act, 180
Is the Whale a Fish? 208

SOCIETIES.

Halifax Institute of Natural Science, 52
State Microscopical Society of Illinois, 209, 244
Worcestershire Naturalist's Club, 339
Exeter Naturalist's Club, 341

NEW BOOKS.

Ancient Geography for the use of Schools, 20
Brazil, Explorations in the Islands of, 49
Friends in Fur and Feathers, 20
Garden Oracle, the, 51
Japanese Silkworms, Report on the Culture of the, 146
Mineralogy, Rudiments of, 51
Molecular and Microscopic Science, 51
More Light, 146
Naturalist in Norway, the, 113
Plant and Flower Life, Echoes in, 207
Polar World, the, 83
Tellurion Globe, Introduction to the use of the, 21
Travels in the East Indian Archipelago, 20
Tommy Try and what he did for Science, 81
Young Shetlander, the, 145
Weather Facts and Predictions, 208

Think nought a trifle, though it small appear;
Small sands the mountain, moments make the year,
And trifles life.   YOUNG.

THE SONG THRUSH, AND THRUSH SNARES.

HE THRUSH! How suggestive is that little word of the happy country, and of some sequestered woodland dale, whose secret nooks shelter the modest violet which ever seems in very shame to cast down its dew-gemmed petals before the bold and free gaze of its jaunty neighbour—the orange-eyed primrose. Suggestive too is it of the pike haunted pool now seen in its jewelled setting of emerald leaved willows, and topaz-flowered sweet scented sallows, catching the first rays of the early spring sun, which lightly, and as yet coldly, stoops to kiss the vernal water flowers, upturning their fast opening eyes in tender, yet passionate love, toward the charmed source of light and life.

Here in such a scene as this, when the faint grey of the morning makes the old tree-trunks stand out from the surrounding gloom like phantoms of the ancient wood deities, and the dew yet hangs its diamond drops on every nodding wood-sorrel bud and leaf; then you may see the speckled-breasted throstle, or mavis, as our ancestors called him, perched on the topmost spray of an oak or ash, chanting his morning orisons with that wonderful piccolo voice of his, whose every trill is a bold pœan of praise to nature, and to the glorious springtide, which brings with it the joy of the nest building, and all its attendant little happinesses. And then when the partner of his bird-love sits in that beautifully constructed little home of theirs, carefully nursing the four or five black-spotted cerulean eggs, then his rapture knows no bounds, and he sits singing all the morning and evening, as if he were reminding you of the old greenwood ditty which tells—

Oh! merrie it is in ye goode greenwoode
When ye mavis and merle are syngynge.

Lost in song, his throat distended, and eyes half closed in ecstasy, he seems to forget his natural timidity, and at these times you may approach very close to the joyous fellow, who, for all his disregard of self, takes care not to imperil the safety of his partner or their nest by singing too near the bush or low tree in which they are concealed. Tender, as well as bold, he can be, for instances are on record of his feeding his weary mate, as well as singing of love to her, while she was too much occupied with the cares of maternity to trouble herself with such a trifle as dinner. With the enlarged generosity of such a nature, he even extends his aid to the helpless of other species beside his own; for the Rev. F. O. Morris states that Mr. Macgillivray had a male thrush which, when only six weeks old, brought up a brood of young larks, and also fed a young cuckoo with the greatest care. Another one brought up a young blackbird until it could feed itself; and Mr. Knapp mentions that he saw one thrush attend upon, and feed an ailing one of the same species, bringing it worms and snails, which the feeble bird could not otherwise procure. But when the newly-hatched brood are opening their yellow throats in a ceaseless querulous chirp for more, more, then is the time to see his active industry, as in company with the female, or alone, as best suits their domestic arrangements, he works early and late, flitting from copse to meadow and meadow to lawn, prying here, there, and everywhere for the creeping things which are popped into the insatiable little maws in dozens; and when these same youngsters grow up to bird estate, how carefully they are tended by their parents, who teach them what to eat, drink, and avoid to say nothing of the jolly little picnics they have together in the orchard trees, after they have been taught the way to fly up into their branches. Oh! he is a noble fellow, is your bright-eyed thrush, thoroughly English in his manners, yet quite Italian in his capability of singing and loving song; for get up ever so early and you will find the thrush complaining that you were not up soon enough to hear the prelude to his *chanson matinale*. I have heard them often before 2.30 a.m. in the summer mornings, and as late or later than 9 p.m. in the evenings. It is true he goes to rest before you, but his last moments ere he folds his head beneath his wing in slumber, are devoted to song, and when the fragrant cowslip trembles as the field-mouse brushes it in its search for night insects, and the great-eyed owl sails on noiseless pinions over the fields, now dim and indistinct in the waning light: aye, and when even the silver crescent moon rides in the perfumed air, you may hear the mavis challenging the opening notes of the nightingale, while yet there is a streak of light in the western board.

Not always though does he cease, or if ceasing, he sometimes renews his song, for at page 252 of the NOTE BOOK, I have given an instance of thrushes singing between 12.15 and 1.30 a.m. on the 20th February, 1867, the moon shining with a subdued light through the clouds, giving the appearance of early morning; and it was perhaps owing to this that the birds so far deviated from their usual course as to sing in the dead of a winter's night. I remember also in Surrey hearing a cuckoo, thrush, and nightingale singing together when it was quite dark, and the moon shining brightly one summer evening in June. On mild days even in winter, the thrushes will sing, as evidenced by my hearing them in full concert on the morning of the 29th November of the present year in the vicinity of Hyde Vale, Blackheath.

While on the subject of singing it may not be out of place to give an anecdote taken from "Beeton's Management of Home Pets," which shows that the thrush, like some human musical geniuses, sometimes goes out of the regular track and totally alters his style. The author, after vouching for the truth of his informant, says:—

"There lived on the skirts of the city (*i.e.* Manchester) a thriving woodchopper; he had a capital business, employed several hands, and his workshop adjoined his dwelling-house. He was a particularly cheerful man, and from morning till night the din made by his chopper and by the choppers of his boys, was rivalled by his incessant singing and whistling. Well, one day, in spite of his thriving business, in spite of his cheerfulness and singing and whistling, the woodchopper committed suicide. To the surprise and dismay of his wife and his workmen, he was found hanging to a beam.

"The woodchopper's wife was a woman of business; therefore, after having her husband's body removed to the house, and allowing the workpeople an hour or two to discuss the calamity, she set them to work again. It was a sultry summer afternoon, and what with the heat and the sight of the ugly beam, and the thought as to what had so shortly before been hanging there, the choppers rose and fell very languidly indeed, and the men and boys spoke to each other in whispers. Suddenly every mouth was ajar with terror, all the hair in the wood-shed rose on the heads of its owners, for pealing through one place was heard the familiar 'William at the garden gate' in the unmistakeable whistle of the dead woodchopper! The men and boys rushed from the place, and went and told the widow; then they returned all together, and just putting their heads inside the door, listened. With the exception of blocks, and choppers, and billets, the shed was empty; still, from invisible lips issued "William at the garden gate" clear, shrill, unearthly! Neither for love nor money would man or boy venture within the shed to split another billet.

"The place was haunted. Sometimes the most profound silence would reign in the shed for hours, and then would come a sudden burst of the ghostly whistling, scaring away listeners from chinks and keyholes. The widow advertised the business, but no man was found bold enough to buy it. So passed on three months, and the poor woman was fairly on the road to ruin. One day, however, while seated at her window, she saw a bird fly from a neighbouring copse, alight on the roof of the deserted wood-shed, and immediately pipe up the now dreaded tune. Thus the mystery was cleared up. It was a thrush, who attracted by the woodchopper's music, had listened until he had learnt it, and proud of the accomplishment, returned to the same spot every day to publish his scholarship."

This instance certainly shows a vast power of mimicry on the part of the bird, while it also is a warning to those credulous persons who hear in every sound, or see in every gloomy nook, something supernatural, not to always believe the evidence of one sense unless fully supported by the others; and also to thoroughly search the as yet little known book of nature, to reveal mysteries inexplicable to all but her students.

Regarding the nesting of the song thrush, which builds in every hedge and copse in "Merrie Englande," it is a somewhat singular fact that during the years in which I resided in the Ionian Isles, I never could find a single instance either in my own or other people's experience of its ever building there; nor do I ever recollect even seeing them indeed, after the end of March or beginning of April, for with the advent of the bee eaters, orioles, and snails, the exodus of the thrushes, blackbirds, and robins takes place. Can this be a wise provision of Dame Nature for keeping up the balance of demand and supply? It would almost seem so, for I have notes in my possession of the redstart and chiffchaff, which in England appear in the spring, and leave in the *autumn*, being found in Greece —the first in November and the latter in December. No doubt both appear earlier than this, but I can find no distinct memorandum relative to this point, although I see I have noted the arrival of the wryneck in September. While on the subject of migration, I consider it certain that the English or home-bred thrushes receive a large accession to their numbers in the autumn, for I have watched this for some time; and as early as the 5th of last October, I heard them on flight passing over Blackheath between eleven and twelve p.m. Anyone who has heard their migration "cheep" before, will find no difficulty in separating it from the almost similar note of the redwing.

Yarrel, speaking of this, says:—"Towards the end of autumn our native thrushes receive a considerable addition to their numbers from the birds which arrive from the north. Monsieur Nilsson, a Professor of Natural History in Sweden, says 'the thrushes leave that country for the winter and come further south;' and Mr. Selby remarks that 'like many of our autumnal visitants they arrive with a north or north-east wind, plainly indicating the countries from which they hold their progress. After recruiting their strength for a few days, they move onward in a southerly direction.'"

Gould also says:—"It is a question whether some of these, both old and young, do not at this season entirely quit the drier districts for others of a more humid character. They certainly do so in some parts of our island: we also know that in autumn great numbers arrive from foreign parts—probably from Norway and Sweden. On the Continent the thrush is a more regular migrant than with us, and during its passage south, the bird is unmercifully shot, and taken in springes for the purposes of the table."

Very little appears to be known concerning the component parts of the nest, inasmuch as most authors, and indeed country people, will tell you that it is lined with clay; thus Morris says:—"The nest is composed of moss, small twigs, straws, leaves, roots, stems of plants, and grass, compacted together with some tenacious substance with tolerable ingenuity, and is lined with a congeries of *clay* and decayed wood." Now, up to the present, I have never discovered clay to enter into the composition of the interior lining, but have found them plastered with rotten wood in little pieces, cemented by the saliva of the bird upon the under layer of moss, which is (in nine cases out of ten) placed with its rootlets towards the inside of the nest: the reason for this is obvious, though it evinces a most wonderful instinct in the bird; for it will be at once seen that of course the rootlets of moss will in the spring time be almost sure to have a little tenacious damp earth adhering, and this by being placed upside down, forms a sort of receiving base for further and finishing operations. It is just possible that a little horse or cow droppings may enter into the plaster work, but I have been unable to discover it in a nest which now lies before me, and which I have cut up on purpose; I find though, singularly enough, a moth's wing, and a little piece of brass decorating the interior, a fitting accompaniment to the beautiful shining light blue eggs. The eggs vary considerably in colour and size, some being boldly splashed, while others are nearly without the black spots which beautifully relieve their ground colour.

Turning from the poetical theme of song to the prosaic one, concerning the killing and eating of so sweet a musician, we will ignore the well-known springes of the English country boy, and quote a passage from the "Birds of Great Britain," by Mr. Gould, who giving Mr. Boy as on authority, described "La Tenderie," or thrush catching in Belgium, thus:—"The thrush is a great source of amusement to the middle and of profit to the lower classes during its autumnal migration. Many families of Liége, Luxemburg, Luneburg, Narum, parts of Hainault and Brabant, choose this season for their period of relaxation from business, and devote themselves to the taking of this bird with horse-hair springes. The shopkeeper of Liege and Verviers, whose house in the town is the model of comfort and cleanliness, resorts with his wife and children to one or two rooms in a miserable country village, to enjoy the sport he has been preparing for, with their help, during the long evenings of the preceding winter—in the course of which he has made as many as from 5000 to

10,000 horse-hair springes, and prepared as many pieces of flexible wood rather thicker than a swan quill, in and on which to hang them. He hires what he calls his Tenderie, being from four to five acres of underwood about three to five years old, pays some thirty shillings for permission to place his springes, and his greatest ambition is to retain for several years the same Tenderie and the same lodging, which he improves in comfort from year to year. The springes being made, and the season of migration near, he goes for a day to his intended place of sojourn, and cuts as many twigs, about eighteen inches in length, as he intends hanging springes on. There are two methods of hanging them: in one the twig is bent into the form of the figure 6, the tail end running through a slit cut in the upper part of the twig. The other method is to sharpen a twig at both ends, and insert the points into a grower, or stem of underwood, thus forming a bow, of which the stem forms the string below the springe, and hanging from the lower part of the bow is placed a small branch, with three or four berries of the mountain ash (there called sorbier); this is fixed to the bow by inserting the stalk into a slit in the wood. The hirer of a new Tenderie three or four acres in extent is obliged to make zigzag footpaths through it, to cut away the boughs which obstruct them, and even to hoe and keep them clean. Having thus prepared himself, he purchases one or two bushels of the berries of the mountain ash with the stalks to which they grew, and which are picked for the purpose after they are red, but before they are ripe, to prevent their falling off: these he lays out on a table in the loft or attic. The collection of these berries is a regular trade, and the demand for them is so great that, although planted expressly by the side of the roads in the Ardennes, they have been sold as high as £2 the bushel; but the general price is five francs. We will now suppose our thrush-catcher arrived at his lodgings in the country, that he has had his footpath cleared by the aid of a labourer, and that he is off for his first day's sport. He is provided with a basket, one compartment of which holds his twigs, bent or straight, another his berries; his springes being already attached to the twigs, he very rapidly drives his knife into a laternal branch and fixes them, taking care that the springe hangs neatly in the middle of the bow, and that the lower part of the springe is about three fingers breadth from the bottom: by this arrangement the bird, alighting on the lower side of the bow, and bending his neck to reach the berries below him, places his head in the noose, and finding himself obstructed in his movements, attempts to fly away; but the treacherous noose tightens round his throat, and he is found by the sportsman hanging by the neck, a victim of misplaced confidence.

"The workman (who at this season earns a second harvest by this pursuit) carries on his industry in wilder districts, or he frequently obtains permission from his employer to set springs in his master's woods. In this case, he supplies the family with birds, which are highly appreciated as a delicacy, especially when almost covered with butter, with a few juniper berries, and some bacon cut into small dice and baked in a pan; the rest of his take he sells at from 5d. to 10d. per dozen.

No person who has not lived in the country can imagine the excitement among all classes when the Grieves arrive. If the morning be foggy, it is a good day for Grieves; if bright bad Tenderie! The reason is obvious: when the birds arrive in a fog, they settle at once in the woods; if bright, they fly about seeking the most propitious place for food. I may observe a singular feeling of honour is engendered by this pursuit. Nobody will think of injuring his neighbours' Tenderie: a sportsman would carefully avoid deranging the springes. If, when shooting in your own covers, a few are taken for the table, you would hang a franc piece conspicuously in an empty springe for every dozen birds taken. The law is very severe on poachers, who place a springe on the ground to take partridges, woodcocks, or snipes; but if three feet above ground, the law says nothing, and save as a trespasser, the placer of springes in the trees of a wood not his own property, would not be punishable. The number taken is prodigious—as many as 150 thrushes have been found executed in a Tenderie in one morning. The younger members of families of the highest ranks commonly follow this amusement before a gun is placed in their hands.

It may be readily imagined that before 5000 springes are set in a Tenderie of four or five acres, a fortnight, or three weeks, will have elapsed, even should the grocer, linendraper, or publican, be assisted by his wife and children, the amusement is common to all the family—wife, boys, and girls. Many a small tradesman eats little else during his vacation at his Tenderie besides Grieves and Buem. From Liege to Tilf, thence to Ayvale on the rivers Meuse, Outhe, and the Amblere to Chauspritaine on the Vesdre, where the rivers are for miles shut in by precipitous banks, covered with low woods, scarcely an acre is unlet for Tenderie during the months of August, September, October, and November. The first fortnight of August is occupied in preparations, the rest of the time is the harvest of Grieves." It appears that redwings and fieldfares are caught by this method also, as well as a few ring-ousels and blackbirds.

Far different is the course adopted in the Greek Islands, for so soon as the middle of October arrives, may you expect vast flights of thrushes, with which are mingled a few of the missel thrush (called here on the principle of everything large coming from Africa, the Barbary thrush). When it is fully ascertained that these birds have been seen in numbers, which is always the case by the 20th October, then every one is bitten with the desire to go into the olive-groves to "whistle for thrushes." As this is rather a curious proceeding, and opens up a new phase in thrush character, I cannot do better, perhaps, than describe a morning expedition in one of the Ionion Isles, on which occasion I was inducted into the ceremonies attendant on so important a sport as the slaughter of a few dozen deceived and betrayed thrushes. It was towards the end of October that I started for the fern-covered, woodcock-haunted glades of Gorino, in company with a Greek gentleman skilled in "bird murder." As I was a novice at this, besides feeling disgusted at the insignificant game of which we were in search, I had taken the dogs, the peerless "Bella" and the sooty "Moro," under my especial care (which, despite the croakings of my friend as to their spoiling sport, rewarded my confidence by bringing to my bag a fine woodcock and hare). How well I remember how gloriously the morning dawned, the early grew shadows softening the harsh outlines of the forts under whose guns we passed, ere winding up the steep hill upon which the picturesque little village of Potamo is placed. From this elevated spot the view was magnificent; far away below us lay numberless olive groves, over the tops of whose trees could be seen the grey still waters of the Venetian Harbour (unruffled now by the gilded galleys of the famed Republic, which even here asserted its supremacy) and having the shores of the Emarantine Island now gilded here and there with the awakening beams of the sun, which was driving the vapour in clouds from the bosom of the sea. Salvador's high crest yet wreathed in mists; its sombre slopes clothed with the ever verdant holly and ilex, while it seemed yet summer, so calm and warm was the air, its silence unbroken save by the mournful whistle of the curlew on the sand-bars below, or the harsh chattering notes of the wary jay in the thick trees above us; around and about were mossy little dells thickly clothed with high bushes of myrtle and laurel, the velvet sward around luxuriating in the dew, which our hasty passage brushed from off the brown frontage of the *passée* pride of the covert the woodcock concealing form. On we journeyed through ravines, past hill-sides where the crimson fruit of the Arbutus, called here "Frooli di Montagna," or mountain strawberries, tempted us to linger awhile, past vineyards where the sere and rapidly dying leaves augured little as yet for that purple cluster which would depend from every branch when the heat of summer had again clothed them with verdure, past the orange trees and their now small unripe fruit hiding amid glossy dark green leaves, until some miles had been traversed; and we stood at last before the sun had risen high enough to dispel all the night mists on the far off mountains, on the summit of a hill overlooking the sea, from which we expected the thrushes to arrive. We were not the only tenants of the spot we had selected, however, as there were two or three countrymen stationed under the cover of as many trees. My friend now produced his whistle, which was a round hollow piece of silver (though mostly constructed of copper) about one inch in diameter, convex on one side, and concave on the other, with a hole right through the centre. The concave part is placed in the mouth, pressing against the teeth, and by inspiring the breath, and modulating the tones with the closed or open hands, as the case may be a very perfect imitation of the song thrush's note is the result. This the arriving or newly-arrived birds hear, and imagining that it proceeds from the throat of one of their species—who, entirely at his ease, is letting the ornithological world know how excessively overjoyed he is at his safe arrival—alight in the trees which surround and conceal the treacherous imitator, and quickly fell a prey to the ready gun. So infatuated are they, that enormous quantities are killed by this method early in the season; in fact, I know one person who shot one hundred and four, besides other birds, to his own gun in one day.

In this particular instance the effect was wonderful, for the whistles had not been sounding long before high up in the clear air, some half mile away over the sea, some tiny specks appeared. "Thrushes?" queries my friend of another posted a few yards from him. This ascertained, the whistling proceeds more vigorously than ever. The voyagers near us, they appear now to waver in their flight, and hover together in the air; this indecision is, however, overcome by a few persuasive notes from the call, and they descend into the trees with an undulating sweep. Theirs, alas! is no happy welcome to a foreign shore. Bang! bang! go the murderous guns almost simultaneously, and five or six lay bleeding on the velvet turf; the rest take to flight, but are followed and nearly all shot in detail, for while the fatal whistle sounds they may be approached with a moderate degree of caution, and will watch a person with their bright eyes cast down and head on one side to within a few yards of their perch. As Mr. Gould remarks, when speaking of the Belgian system, bright mornings are not considered so good for the sport, for then they are much wilder, and their warning "Thchick" scares everying within hearing. Later in the season the call is of no avail, owing no doubt either to their so constantly singing themselves, or to their being rendered more cunning by experience. Towards the end of December the numbers of thrushes and blackbirds which are to be seen in the more secluded groves surpasses belief, for you may see them bouncing out of every myrtle or briar clump in sixes and sevens, and I have seen days when I really believe enough could have been shot to have filled a bushel-basket; at this time, however, more valuable game is astir, and therefore the precious powder is reserved, and hundreds of the Merulidæ are caught by small fish-hooks baited with a worm and pegged to the ground. Robins, snipes, and various insectivorous birds, suffer in company, and I once had a water-rail brought to me which had been hooked. All is game, and the markets in the winter, and wine-shops they supply, do a large amount of busines in the small-bird line. Very few people, I fancy, are aware how jolly it is after a hard and long morning's fag over rocky dells and around sedgy pools to finish up by a call at some Salvator-Rosa-looking wine-shop, unsling the game bags, heavy perchance with the weight of the green-headed mallard, the rusty-plumaged woodcock, the mountain hare, or partridge, and after a glass of pure (if common) wine, sally out to the coverts surrounding, and knock over a dozen or more thrushes for the stewpan.

Be sure that either Pipi or Cristodulo has brought some maccaroni, and Amastasi some tomato-paste from "La Citta," well knowing that beyond the inevitable dried fish and garlic, little excepting bread, cheese, and wine is to be had in these wild solitudes. Having compounded not a few of these "hunters' feasts" myself, I will, in humble imitation of the great Hawker, who could "pot" his birds first, and also give directions how to consign them to the "aforesaid," afterwards follow suit by giving the recipe for the benefit of the world at large, and such of your readers as are gourmêts in particular. We will therefore imagine that we have returned to the wine-house with a sufficient number of thrushes to satisfy our appetites for the nonce; we have plucked and got them ready, together with a contribution from our bags of an odd snipe or woodcock to give extra flavour. Now take the stewpan, place in a layer of birds, then one of potatoes, cut onions and carrot; add pepper and salt, a few cloves, a blade of mace, and a little lemon-peel, with a dash of tomato sauce or paste; repeat this process until the pan is full, then pour over all just sufficient olive oil to moisten the mass and prevent it from burning. Simmer gently over a slow fire until half done, when cover with red wine (previously heated), and let it stew a little more briskly until done. Some one in the meantime has been boiling the maccaroni in another vessel, and this is turned out as dry as possible in a large dish, some Parmesan cheese grated over it, and the contents of the stewpan poured on the top. "Nasty beggars! to eat such stuff!" I hear some one exclaim. All right! amico mio!—try it once, and all that I am afraid of is that the poor thrushes will have a bad time of it afterwards in consequence. Where oil is objected to (which it would not be if pure), Worcestershire or Harvey's sauce may be substituted in the first stage.

Curiosities of form and colour occasionally occur. I remember once when a boy shooting one which had but one leg, the other, a mere stump, having evidently been accidentally amputated, as there appeared a rounded swelling where the knee-joint had been. White, or partially white thrushes are of far more rare occurrence than in the case of blackbirds, though a charming writer and well-known naturalist writes:—

"Mr. Bix, of Bougate, writes me word of white thrushes found two successive years in that neighbourhood, the one next being within forty yards of the preceding one. The former contained four young—two of them white with red eyes, and the other two of common colour. The latter had also four young—one of them white, and three of them the proper colour; the eyes of the latter, which was kept alive, became afterwards darker. So also Dr. Henry Mosel, of Appleby, Westmoreland, tells me that last year a thrush's nest was found in that neighbourhood with three cream-coloured and two usual coloured young ones, and that this year five were found in a nest all cream-coloured : in one which was taken and kept alive the eyes were scarlet.

"J. W. Lukis, Esq., has forwarded me a curious variety of the young of this species, which is all over of a light yellowish-brown colour, the breast showing incipient marks of the usual spots. There was another of the same colour in the nest, one of which was left with its parents, which were of the ordinary colour, and was brought up by them, the other (the one in question) was kept alive for a month with care. Another, an old bird, was observed at the same time and the same place—Heacham Hall, near Lynn, Norfolk—with white feathers in its tail."

In the British Museum is a pale-brown thrush, whose head, nape, and primaries of wings, are white, throat whitish—and almost wanting the bright brown speckles which usually adorn the throat and breast of the adult male. This specimen was procured in Cambridgeshire.

Having now watched the progress of this most interesting of our native woodland songsters from the cradle to the grave, I will now conclude with a sweet song by Grahame, which tells how and where the nest is placed, although exception must be taken to the incorrect ending of the ninth line :—

> In the hazel-bush or sloe is formed
> The habitation of the wedded pair,
> Sometimes below the never-fading leaves
> Of ivy close, that over-twisting binds
> And richly crowns with clustered fruit of spring,
> Some river, rock, or nodding castle wall,
> Sometimes beneath the jutting root of elm,
> Or oak, among the sprigs that overhang
> A pebble-chiding stream, the loam-lined home
> Is fixed, well hid from ken of hov'ring hawk
> Or lurking beast, or school-boy's prowling eye.

A. M. B.

ON THE BRITISH GEOMETRÆ.
By E. Clifford.

ONE of the most striking divisions of our native *Lepidoptera* is that which comprises the "Geometers," a group of moths deriving its title from the singular manner in which the caterpillars proceed when walking. Unlike the caterpillars of the butterflies, and those of many other moths, these possess four instead of ten claspers, and these are situated at the anal part of the body. Thus, instead of moving in the manner of other caterpillars, the "Geometers" form a loop when walking, taking hold of the twig or leaf with the ordinary six legs and holding tightly therewith, they draw the claspers towards them, and repeat the action till they have reached the desired object. It will be readily understood that by this mode of progression the "looper" caterpillars, as they are termed, can move along much more rapidly than others. Generally the caterpillars of this division are without hairs, and they are often beautifully spotted and banded. The perfect insects offer to the student an endless variety of colouring, and are the most delicate and fragile of our *Lepidoptera*. They possess slender bodies, and in most cases exhibit a similarity of colouring on all wings; thus being distinguished from the fat bodied moths, or *Noctuæ*. Several species fly during the day-time; but the generality, like the great body of our native moths, are night-flying *Lepidoptera*.

In our examination of the *Geometræ*, the first species is one that stands alone as a representative of the family *Europtery̆gidæ*. It is the Swallow-tailed moth (*Europteryx sambucata*). This is a beautiful insect, having wings of a pale delicate sulphur yellow, streaked with olive in a transverse direction. It is not an uncommon moth in the month of July, and often on summer evenings we may see it flitting over the hedge-rows, seeking probably for the elder upon which to deposit its eggs. These, however, are sometimes laid on herbaceous plants, and also on the honeysuckle and several fruit trees. The caterpillar of this moth is humped in so peculiar a manner as to bear a close resemblance to a dried twig, from which it can hardly be distinguished when stretched out at full length. It varies in colour, being of different shades of brown, and striped with a paler colour along the sides. This is one of our hybernating kinds, hence we often meet with it in October; shortly afterwards it betakes itself to winter quarters in crevices of the bark of trees, etc. In June it spins its cocoon of leaves and silk suspended from its food-plant, and becomes transformed into a brown chrysalis, spotted with a darker colour. The Dark-bordered Beauty (*Epione vespertaria*) is a Yorkshire and Hampshire insect, and cannot be considered common. It is an extremely striking species. The wings of the male moth are orange, having a broad border of purple-brown; the wings of the female yellow, and the border nearly similar in colour, but separated by a dark transverse line. The caterpillar of this species is found in August, and feeds on the hazel; the moth appears on the wing in June. Allied closely to this species is the Bordered Beauty (*Epione apiciaria*), similar to it in many points of its history. Its caterpillar is found feeding on willow, hazel, and poplar in the month of September. The Bordered Beauty is not uncommon in the southern counties.

Next in order we come to one of the "Thorn" moths, a group of insects which is highly interesting to the entomologist. They, as many others of the division *Geometræ*, can be captured during the daytime by beating the hedges, herbage, and woodland growth with a walking-stick, netting the insects that fly forth roused by the operation from their resting-places. The Little Thorn (*Epione advenaria*) is or was a common insect in Birch Wood, Kent, at the beginning of July. Its wings are of dingy white, freckled with olive-brown, and having a dark transverse band. The caterpillar is said to feed on the bilberry. Our attention is now claimed by an insect that meets us at almost every step of the rural ramble. Scarcely can we saunter along the woodland paths and brush the underwood growth at our sides without starting forth specimens of the Brimstone moth (*Rumia cratægata*). Its wings are bright yellow in colour, adorned with conspicuous red spots on the fore margin, and dispersed likewise over the wings. The caterpillar is well known to even the youngest of collectors. It has three lumps on the back, and unlike the generality of the loopers possesses eight claspers. It feeds on whitethorn, and when full grown spins its home near or on the ground. Another very pretty little moth in the flowery dell or coppice of the country is the Speckled Yellow (*Venilia maculata*). Perhaps no insect is more liable to variation than this in the disposal of the markings which adorn the deep yellow of its wings. A rare variety occurs which has no spots except four on the coital margin. The caterpillar of this lively little moth feeds on a variety of herbaceous plants almost entirely confined to woods, and found during August and September. Generally we have observed this species rest with its wings over the back, like those of a butterfly. It flies strongly in the month of June.

A beautiful and delicate moth in the woods of June is the Orange moth (*Angerona prunaria*). This species is one in which the sexes exhibit a marked contrast in colouring. The male is of a rich orange colour, shaded and streaked with brown; and the female has the wings of a pale yellow, similarly marked with minute transverse streaks over the surface. The orange moth is, however, a very variable insect. The caterpillar also is subject to variety, but is generally of a grey brown marbled with darker markings. It feeds on beech, blackthorn, and occasionally on broom. Its cocoon is a slight web between the leaves of its food-plant. Next come we to the Light Emerald moth (*Metrocampa margaritata*), a delicate insect, which seems as if it ought to be placed amongst the other Emeralds from which it is separated. The wings are of a pale green, with a transverse white stripe crossing them, which is margined on the inside with a darker green. The caterpillar of this insect is of a dull green colour, with a darker line down the centre of the back. It feeds on broom, and also on elm, hornbeam, birch, and oak. It occurs in the month of September, and the moth flies in our woodlands during July; by no means an uncommon species. The Barred Red (*Ellopia fasciaria*), though a dark-hued insect, is yet very beautiful. The wings are of a brick red, and are ornamented by two transverse lines which are of a clearer and brighter red than the rest of the moth. The caterpillar of the Barred Red feeds on the Scotch fir in September and October, and when full-grown descends to the foot of the tree, making its change amongst the fallen needles there collected. In midsummer the moth itself is on the wing. A somewhat rarer species than the last two named is that known as the Scorched-wing (*Eurymene dolobraria*), a singular species indeed, for its wings look as if burnt by fire. They are of a pale delicate brown, barred with a number of very slender lines of a dark umber colour. The caterpillar has a large lump or wart on the ninth segment; the head is also notched in the middle. Its food is beech and oak, and it forms its chrysalis abode under moss or on the trunks of trees. Therefore by peeling the moss away carefully we may perchance be sufficiently fortunate to light upon some chrysalides of this insect ensconced in the crevices. The moth itself flies in June.

The true Thorn moths are next in order to those just named. The first amongst them is the Lilac Beauty (*Pericallia syringaria*), a splendid moth, occurring in the shady paths of woods in July. The wings of this moth are exquisitely diversified in colouring, and from this cause it is almost impossible to convey by words a correct idea of the markings. The caterpillar is furnished with humps and warts; it feeds during June on elder, privet, and lilac, spinning a slight web on the under side of the leaves when about to become a chrysalis. The Early Thorn (*Selenia illunaria*) is a double-brooded species, appearing in the months of April and July. These two broods are so dissimilar in appearance as to be formerly considered as distinct species, but it is now proved to the contrary. The wings of this moth are all angulated, of a pale brown colour, sprinkled over with small dark dots. The fore-wings have three transverse lines, and the hind-wings are of the same colour as the fore-wings, similarly marked with them. The caterpillar is brown, mottled, and clouded, with two pale streaks along each side; it feeds generally on the willow, and also on various other plants. The Lunar Thorn (*Selenia lunaria*) is so called from a mark shaped like a half-moon which is seen on the fore-wings. These are of a pale wainscot colour, all the wings having sharp angles. The caterpillar has humps, but is by no means constant in colour. It feeds on the blackthorn, and is to be captured during August and September.

Singularly beautiful and striking are the markings of the Purple Thorn (*Selenia illustraria*).

The wings combine markings of purple-brown, pearly grey, and delicate rosy tints, diversified by crescent-shaped spots of white. The body of this moth is very hairy. The caterpillar of the Purple Thorn feeds on birch and oak; when full-grown it forms its web amongst leaves collected on the surface of the ground. The Purple Thorn is a double-brooded species, which two broods differ in colouring, causing a similar error to that made regarding a former species. The Scalloped Hazel (*Odontopera Videntata*) is remarkable from the outline of its wings, whence both its names are derived. These are scalloped, and of a dingy white-brown, while the forewings have two transverse brown lines, which are also scalloped. The caterpillar has eight claspers instead of four, although the first and second pair seem comparatively useless to the caterpillar when walking. The chrysalis of this species is generally found under moss. The moth itself is on the wing in May. Next our attention is claimed by a species common enough in the southern counties during July and August. This is the Scalloped Oak (*Crocallis elinguaria*). The fore-wings are ochreous yellow, with a broad transverse band of pale brown; the hind-wings are paler than the fore-wings, having a central dot. The caterpillar feeds chiefly on the honeysuckle; but also on beech, blackthorn, apple, and pear. It is of a uniform thickness throughout, and much resembles a withered twig in its form. It lives through the winter half-grown, and does not become a chrysalis till the following June, when it should be sought for between the leaves of its food-plant, or amongst the moss at its roots. The Scalloped Oak flies strongly at eventide, and may be taken if watched for where it is known to abound, and struck at quickly as it sweeps along the path. The remainder of this interesting group of the Thorn moths, so partial to gas-lamps, we leave till our next for completion.

THE CLOVE.

THE clove tree (*Carophyllus aromaticus*) belongs to the order of myrtles, which also includes the pomegranate, the guava, and the rose apple. The trunk of the full-grown tree is from eight to twelve inches in diameter, and occasionally much more. Its topmost branches are usually forty or fifty feet from the ground, though I have seen a tree not larger than a cherry tree fully loaded with fruit. It was originally confined to the five islands off the west coast of Gilolo, which then comprised the whole group known as "the Moluccas," a name that has since been extended to Burn, Amboina, and the other islands off the south coast of Ceram, where the clove has been introduced and cultivated within a comparatively late period. On these five islands it begins to bear in its seventh or eighth year, and sometimes continues to yield until it has reached an age of nearly one hundred and fifty years; the trees, therefore, are of very different sizes. Here at Amboina it is not expected to bear fruit before its twelfth or fifteenth year, and to cease yielding when it is seventy-five years old. Its limited distribution has always attracted attention, and Rumphius, who describes it as the most beautiful and most elegant and the most precious of all known trees, remarks:—" Hence it appears that the Great Disposer of things in His wisdom, allotting His gifts to the several regions of the world, placed cloves in the kingdom of the moluccas, beyond which by no human industry can they be propagated or perfectly cultivated." In the last observation, however, he was mistaken, for since his time it has been successfully introduced into the island of Penang, in the Strait of Malacca, and Sumatra, Bourbon, Zanzibar, and the coast of Guiana and the West India Islands. The clove is the flower bud, and grows in clusters at the ends of the twigs. The annual yield of a good tree is about four pounds and a half, and the yearly crop on Amboina, Haruku, Japarna, and Nasalant, the only islands where the tree is now cultivated, is 350,000 Amsterdam pounds. It is, however, extremely variable and uncertain; for example, in 1846 it was 869,727 Amsterdam pounds, but in 1849 it was only 89,923, or little more than one-tenth of what it was before. Pigafetta informs us that when the Spanish first came to the Moluccas there were no restrictions on the culture or sale of the clove. The annual crop at that time (1521) according to the same authority, reached the enormous quantity of 6,000 bahars, 3,540,000 pounds of uncleaned, and 4,000 bahars, 2,360,000 pounds of cleaned cloves—about seventeen times the quantity obtained at the present time. Though this statement at first appears incredible, it is strengthened by the fact that the two ships of Magellan's fleet that reached Fidoro, one of the spice islands, were filled with cloves during a space of only twenty-four days. When the buds are young they are nearly white; afterwards they change to a light green, and finally to a bright red, when they must at once be gathered, which is done by picking them by hand or beating them off with bamboos on to cloths spread beneath the trees. They are then simply dried in the sun, and are ready for the market. In drying their colour is changed from red to black, the condition in which we see them. They are gathered twice a year, at about this time in June, and again in the last of December. The leaves, bark, and young twigs also have some peculiar aroma, and at Zanzibar the stems of the buds are also gathered, and find a ready sale. The favourite locations of this tree are the high hill-sides, and it is said that it does not thrive well on low lands where the loam is fine and heavy. The soil best adapted to it appears to be a loose sandy loam. In its original *habitat* it grows chiefly on volcanic soil, but in Amboina and the other islands where it is now cultivated, it has been found to flourish well on loams formed by the disintegration of recent sandstone and secondary rocks. The native name for this fruit is *Cheuki*, perhaps 'a corruption of the Chinese *Keugi-ki* odoriferous nails. The Dutch name for clove is kruid-nagel herb nail, and for the trees nagelen boomen, nail trees. Our own name clove comes from the Spanish Clavo (Latin Clavus, a nail), which has also been given them on account of the similarity of these buds to nails.

Although cloves form a favourite condiment among all nations, the natives of these islands where they grow never eat them in any form, and we have no reason to suppose they ever did. The only purpose for which the Amboinese use them, so far as I am aware, is to prepare neat models of their praus and bamboo huts by running small wire through the buds before they are dried. The Dutch purchase and send to Europe so many of these models that almost every ethnological museum contains some specimens of this skilful workmanship. The clove probably came into use originally by accident, and I believe the first people who fancied its rich aroma and warm pungent taste were the Chinese. The similarity of the native name to that of the Chinese, and its marked difference according to De Canto from that of the Brahmins or Hindus, lends probability to this view. When the Portugese first came to these islands the Chinese, Arabs, Malays, Javanese, and Macassars were all found here trading in this article. Of the two former nations, the Chinese were probably the first to reach this region, though the Arabs sailed up the China sea and carried on a large trade with the Chinese at Canpu, a port in Hangchau Bay, south of the present city of Shanghai, in the thirteenth century, or fully two hundred years before the Portugese and Spaniards arrived in these seas. —*From Travels in the East Indian Archipeligo.* By Albert S. Bickmore, M.A. London: Murray.

THE STOAT, OR ERMINE (*MUSTELA ARMINEA*).

BY A. H. MALAN.

PERHAPS no animal has so many enemies, and so *few* friends (that is, if it have *any* at all) as the Stoat (or Ermine). And in this case it does not seem to be wholly prejudice that has so universally condemned it; for hawks even destroy numbers of field-mice, whereas the Stoat, being of a more dainty disposition, confines its diet almost exclusively to game, eggs, and rabbits, and does no good whatever in return. People who have ever given a thought to the subject, have a misunderstanding as to what the Ermine is. Some think it is identical with the weasel; but few imagine that muffs and other parts of female apparel are made from the fur of the animal, which they may often see, in company with magpies, nailed up against the walls of barns.

It is generally believed that the Ermine fur is imported from the cold fur countries, but this is not the case. The confusion in supposing that the Ermine and Stoat are two distinct animals seems to have arisen from the fact that this animal in summer, while its coat is brown, is called the *Stoat;* whereas in winter, when *white*, the *Ermine*. Among the chief enemies that this little animal has to contend against, rank the keepers. To tell a keeper that you have just seen a Stoat in one of his covers, is to send him straightway into hysterics. He rushes for his ever-loaded gun, and endeavours to put a speedy termination to the existence of the "*varmint*," as I heard one say this summer, in speaking of the Stoat:—"You may depend upon it, Sir, them Sto-werts be pernicious gentlemen!"

This quadruped is generally distributed over Great Britain, being most frequently met with in thickly-wooded districts. Their holes are made usually in hedge-rows, near some cover or warren, or in walls, but they are also frequently found in woodstacks, etc. In summer the head, neck, and back are brown; the belly a pale yellowish-white; and the tail jet black. In winter it becomes entirely white, except that the tail remains black. Some pretty piebald specimens are sometimes shot when the process of changing its coat is going on. The eyes are large, the ears small and round. These latter seem hardly called into use at all, the animal trusting almost entirely to its *nose* to apprise it of any foe, as well as to shew the whereabouts of its prey. Their food, as has before been mentioned, consists for the most part of young game, eggs, and rabbits; but when these are not forthcoming it does not hesitate to enter farmyards and ravage hen roosts, sucking the eggs, and killing the chickens. Considerable damage is done in a single raid, for the animal only kills the chickens for the sake of their warm blood, and in some cases the bodies of a dozen chickens have been found dead, totally untouched except a small hole in the neck, from which their blood has been deducted. The manner in which this animal catches rabbits, moreover, is worthy of mention. The Stoat saunters from its hole towards sundown, and proceeds at a diminutive canter, with its nose to the ground, until it crosses some rabbit-track, which it persistantly follows until within about two feet of its prey, when it halts, arches its back, and with a spring fixes its fangs just behind the ear, and continues hanging on sucking the blood until completely saturated, when it returns home for a doze, to return in about two hours time to finish its repast. Great havoc is wrought among partridges and young pheasants; because this animal will follow a covey from place to place until it has devoured the last survivor, and in this respect they resemble the glutton of the American wilderness, the pest of the trapper.

Like the rest of their *genus* they are most tenacious of life. I have known a Stoat, after two *buckshot* had passed clean through its back, run on for more than fifty yards, and then, when unable to proceed farther through loss of blood, turn at bay, and bite the finger or nose of its enemy, whether man or dog! They may be frequently shot in winter, where they are plentiful, for their coat being white they are easily seen in the dusk of the evening; and, when following the scent of a rabbit are so absorbed that they can see nothing at all in front of them. The female produces from three to six at a litter, which takes place generally in August, and at this particular period they are doubly fierce.

The *Weasel* (*Mustilla Vulgaris*) is quite another animal, being much smaller, with shorter legs, and never changes its coat like the Ermine.

TURTLES.

THE Tortugas are a group of islands lying about eighty miles from Key West, and the last of those that seem to defend the peninsula of the Floridas. They consist of five or six extremely low uninhabitable banks, formed of shelly sand, and are resorted to principally by that class of men called wreckers and turtlers. Between these islands are deep channels, which although extremely intricate, are well known to those adventurers, as well as to the commanders of the revenue cutters whose duties call them to that dangerous coast. The great coral reef or wall lies about eight miles from these inhospitable isles, in the direction of the Gulf, and on it many an ignorant or careless navigator has suffered shipwreck. The whole ground around them is densely covered with corals, sea fans, and other productions of the deep, amid which crawl innumerable testaceous animals; while shoals of curious and beautiful fishes fill the limpid waters above them. Turtles of different species resort to these banks, to deposit their eggs in the burning sand, and clouds of sea fowl arrive every spring for the same purpose. These are followed by persons called "eggers," who, when their cargoes are completed, sail to distant markets to exchange their ill-gotten ware for a portion of that gold on the acquisition of which all men seem bent.

The Marion having occasion to visit the Tortugas, I gladly embraced the opportunity of seeing those celebrated islets. A few hours before sunset the joyful cry of "land" announced our approach to them, but as the breeze was fresh, and the pilot was well acquainted with all the windings of the channels, we held on, and dropped anchor before twilight. If you have never seen the sun setting in those latitudes, I would recommend you to make a voyage for the purpose, for I much doubt if, in any other portion of the world, the departure of the orb of day is accompanied with such gorgeous appearances. Look at the great red disc, increased to triple its ordinary dimensions. Now it has partially sunk beneath the distant line of waters, and with its still remaining half irradiates the whole heavens with a flood of light, purpling the far-off clouds that hover over the western horizon. A blaze of refulgent glory streams through the portals of the west, and the masses of vapour assume the semblance of mountains of molten gold. But the sun has now disappeared, and from the east slowly advances the grey curtain which night draws over the world. The nighthawk is flapping his noiseless wings in the gentle sea breeze; the terns, safely landed, have settled on their nests; the frigate pelicans are seen wending their way to distant mangroves; and the brown gannet, in search of a resting-place, has perched on the yard of the vessel. Slowly advancing landward, their heads alone above the water, are observed the heavily-laden turtles, anxious to deposit their eggs in the well-known sands. On the surface of the gently rippling stream I dimly see their broad forms as they toil along, while at intervals may be heard their hurried breathings, indicative of suspicion and fear. The moon with her silvery light now illumines the scene, and the turtle having landed, slowly and laboriously drags her heavy body over the sand, her "flappers" being better adapted for motion in water than on the shore. Up the slope, however, she works her way, and see how industriously she removes the sand beneath her, casting it out on either side. Layer after layer she deposits her eggs, arranging them in the most careful manner, and with her hind paddles brings the sand over them. The business is accomplished, the spot is covered over, and with a joyful heart the turtle swiftly retires toward the shore and launches into the deep.

But the Tortugas are not the only breeding-places of the turtle: these animals, on the contrary, frequent many other keys as well as various parts of the coast of the mainland. There are four different species, which are known by the names of the green turtle, the hawk-billed turtle, the logger-head turtle, and the trunk turtle. The first is considered the best as an article of food, in which capacity it is well known to most epicures. It approaches the shores, and enters the bays, inlets, and rivers, early in the month of April, after having spent the winters in the deep waters. It deposits its eggs in convenient places, at two different times, in May, and once again in June. The first deposit is the largest, and the last the least, the total quantity being at an average about two hundred and forty. The hawk-billed turtle, whose shell is so valuable as an article of commerce, being used for various purposes in the arts, is the next with respect to the quality of its flesh. It resorts to the outer keys only, where it deposits its eggs in two sets, first in July and again in August, although it *crawls* the beaches much earlier in the season, as if to look for a safe place. The average number of its eggs is about three hundred. The logger-head visits the Tortugas in April, and lays from that period until late in June three sets of eggs, each set averaging a hundred and seventy. The trunk turtle, which is sometimes of an enormous size, and which has a pouch like a pelican, reaches the shores latest. The shell and fish are so soft that one may push the finger into them almost as into a lump of butter. This species is therefore considered as the least valuable, and indeed is seldom eaten, unless by the Indians, who ever alert when the turtle season commences, first carry off the eggs which it lays in the season, and afterwards catch the turtles themselves. The average number of eggs which it lays at two sets may be three hundred and fifty.

The logger-head and the trunk turtles are the least cautious in choosing the places in which to deposit their eggs, whereas the two other species select the wildest and most secluded spots. The green turtle resorts either to the shores of the Maine, between Cape Sable and Cape Florida, or enters Indian, Halifax, and other large rivers or inlets, from which it makes its retreat as speedily as possible, and betakes itself to the open sea. Great numbers, however, are killed by the turtlers and Indians, as well as by various species of carnivorous animals, as cougars, lynxes, bears, and wolves. The hawk-bill, which is still more wary, and is always the most difficult to surprise, keeps to the sea islands. All the species employ nearly the same method in depositing their eggs in the sand, and as I have several times observed them in the act, I am enabled to present you with a circumstantial account of them.

On first nearing the shores, and mostly on fine calm moonlight nights, the turtle raises her head above the water, being still distant thirty or forty yards from the beach, looks around her, and attentively examines the objects on the shore. Should she observe nothing likely on the shore to disturb her intended operations, she emits a loud hissing sound, by which such of her enemies as are unaccustomed to it are startled, and so are apt to remove to another place, although unseen by her. Should she hear any noise, or perceive indications of danger, she instantly sinks and goes off to a considerable distance; but should everything be quiet, she advances slowly towards the beach, crawls over it, her head raised to the full stretch of her neck, and when she has reached a place fitted for her purpose she gazes all round in silence. Finding "all well," she proceeds to form a hole in the sand, which she effects by removing it from under her body with her hind flappers, scooping it out with so much dexterity that the sides seldom if ever fall in. The sand is raised alternately with each flapper, as with a large ladle, until it has accumulated behind her, when supporting herself with her head and fore part on the ground fronting her body, she, with a spring from each flapper, sends the sand around her, scattering it to the distance of several feet. In this manner the hole is dug to the depth of eighteen inches, or sometimes more than two feet. This labour I have seen performed in the short period of nine minutes. The eggs are then dropped one by one, and disposed in regular layers to the number of a hundred and fifty, or sometimes two hundred. The whole time spent in this part of the operation may be about twenty minutes. She now scrapes the loose sand back over the eggs, and so levels them and smooths the surface, that few persons on seeing the spot could imagine anything had been done to it. This accomplished to her mind, she retreats to the water with all possible despatch, leaving the hatching of the eggs to the heat of the sand. When a turtle, a logger-head for example, is in the act of dropping her egg, she will not move, although one should go up to her, or even seat himself on her back, for it seems that at this moment she finds it necessary to proceed at all events, and is unable to intermit her labour. The moment it is finished, however, off she starts, nor would it then be possible for one, unless he were as strong as Hercules, to turn her over and secure her. To upset a turtle on the shore one is obliged to fall on his knees, and placing his shoulder behind her fore-arm, gradually raise her up by pushing with great force, and then with a jerk throw her over. Sometimes it requires the united strength of several men to accomplish this, and if the turtle should be of very great size, as often happens on that coast, even handspikes are employed. Some turtlers are so daring as to swim up to them while lying asleep on the surface of the water, and turn them over in their own element, when, however, a boat must be at hand to enable them to secure their prize. Few turtles can bite beyond the reach of their fore-legs, and few when they are once turned over, can, without assistance, regain their natural position. But notwithstanding this, their flappers are generally secured by ropes, so as to render their escape impossible. Persons who search for turtle eggs are provided with a light stiff cane or gun-rod, with which they go along the shores, probing the sand near the tracks of the animal, which, however, cannot always be seen on account of the winds and heavy rains that often obliterate them. The nests are discovered not only by men but also by beasts of prey, and the eggs are collected or destroyed on the spot in great numbers.

On certain parts of the shore hundreds of turtles are known to deposit their eggs within the space of a mile. They form a new hole each time they lay, and the second is generally dug near the first, as if the animal were quite unconscious of what had befallen it. It will readily be understood that the numerous eggs seen in a turtle on cutting it up could not be all laid the same season. The whole number deposited by an individual in one summer may amount to four hundred; whereas if the animal be caught on or near her nest, as I have witnessed, the remaining eggs, all small, without shells, and as it were threaded like so many beads, exceed three thousand. In an instance where I found that number, the turtle weighed nearly four hundred pounds.

The young, soon after being hatched, and when yet scarcely larger than a dollar, scratch their way through their sandy covering, and immediately betake themselves to the water. The food of the green turtle consists chiefly of marine plants, more especially the grass-wrack (*Zostera marina*), which they cut near the roots, to procure the most tender and succulent parts. Their feeding-grounds, as I have elsewhere said, are easily discovered by floating masses of these plants on the flats or along the shores to which they resort. The hawk-billed species feeds on seaweeds, crabs, and various kinds of shell-fish and fishes; the logger-head mostly on the fish of conch-shells, of large size, which they are enabled, by means of their powerful beak, to crush to pieces with apparently as much ease as a man cracks a walnut. One which was brought on board the Marion, and placed near the fluke of one of her anchors, made a deep indentation in that hammered piece of iron that quite surprised me. The trunk-turtle feeds on Mollusca, fish, crustacea, sea-urchins, and various marine plants. All the species move through the water with surprising speed; but the green and hawk-billed in particular remind you by their celerity, and the ease of their motions, of the progress of a bird in the air. It is therefore no easy matter to strike one with a spear, and yet this is often done by an accomplished turtler. While at Key West and other islands on the coast, where I made the observations here presented to you, I chanced to have need to purchase some turtles to feed my friends on board the Lady of the Green Mantle—not my friends, her gallant officers, or the brave tars who formed her crew, for all of them had already been satiated with turtle soup; but my friends the herons, of which I had a goodly number in coops, intending to carry them to John Bachman of Charleston, and other persons for whom I felt a sincere regard. So I went to a "crawl," accompanied by Dr. Benjamin Strobel, to inquire about prices, when to my surprise I found the smaller the turtles, "above ten pounds' weight," the dearer they were, and that I could have purchased one of the logger-head kind, that weighed more than seven hundred pounds, for little more money than another of only thirty pounds.—From the *Life of Audubon*. London: Sampson Low.

NOTES OF A NATURALIST IN NOVA SCOTIA.

BY J. MATTHEW JONES, F.L.S.

(Author of "The Naturalist in Bermuda.")

THE BEAVER.

(*Castor Canadensis.*)

IN the days of our fathers, when beaver hats were in vogue, this unfortunate animal became well nigh exterminated in all parts of the inhabited portion of the North American continent. So much was it sought after in this country, that dealers readily gave the trappers eighteen shillings per pound for the skins. This was some thirty or forty years ago. Happily for the beavers that now exist, a much lower price is set upon their felts, and as a matter of course, their persecutors are not numerous, especially in the wild and uninhabited parts of the interior. In the eastern part of this country the animal has totally disappeared, for not a beaver exists in any of the lakes or rivers of that district. In the west, however, the animal is gradually increasing in numbers, and this may be attributed to the absence of Indians in that quarter, and to the barren nature of the central lands, which, from their rocky and sterile nature, can never be cultivated, and will most probably remain in the wilderness state for ages. In this lone region, where the foot of man rarely treads, and the all-prevailing silence is only broken by the melancholy call of the great northern diver, or the hoarse bellow of the moose, animal life reigns in peace ; and it is here, on the margin of lake or rivulet situate in some secluded dell, that the smooth-coated beaver makes its lodge. This lodge, as it is called, looks from without just like a collection of faggots pressed together horizontally, and any one unacquainted with the beaver and its habits might pass it without remark, taking it for a collection of drift wood. It is so entirely different from the singular looking mound we see pictured in some works on Natural History as representing the beaver house, that the Nova Scotian species, in its constructive habits at least, most certainly widely differs from that of Canada, if the following account, published a few years ago, be correct :—" The top of the lodge is formed by placing branches of trees together. The outward coating is entirely of mud or earth, and smoothed off as if plastered with a trowel." No such plastering is found in the Nova Scotian lodges, and I therefore presume that the beaver, like many other animals, changes its constructive habits according to circumstances. On taking off the upper portion of the beaver lodge, the sticks are found more carefully placed beneath, and at the bottom of the heap we find an open hollow space, where the beaver reposes during the day, as it is only after sundown that these animals venture forth in search of food. It is a pleasing sight, when having hid oneself in the bushes close by the shore of a lake inhabited by beavers, to witness the habits of these extraordinary creatures. About half an hour after the sun has descended in the west, and the short twilight of this latitude is merging into darkness, you may perceive here and there about the edges of the lake, ripples on its surface, and the form of the beaver swimming with body nearly submerged ; the head and a portion of its back being only visible. Now and then it stops at a water lilly or horsetail, to bite off the stem and nibble a portion, soon passing on to regale itself upon other aquatic plants. It usually skirts the shore during its nocturnal swim, stopping occasionally to rest upon some accustomed knoll jutting suitably into the water, whereon it can munch its succulent meal in peaceful seclusion, or to search for a grove of the tender barked willow or aspen, which constitute its principal food. It is a very wary animal, and the slightest unnatural sound is sufficient to cause a whole colony of beavers to vanish from sight. As soon as the tocsin of alarm is sounded by the flat tail of a sentinel beaver being clapped upon the water, every member dives, and for a long space not a movement is observable among the inhabitants of the beaver commuuity. It is truly wonderful to see the size of some of the trees felled by beavers. In some cases they have been known to cut with their incisor teeth through a tree nine inches in diameter, but those of two or three inches are generally chosen, and are of course more easily removed for the purpose of constructing the dams and lodges. The Nova Scotian beaver pups early in spring, and has two cubs at a time, and sometimes they have young again in August. When the young arrive at the age of two years, they pair and found a settlement for themselves. The skin of the beaver is used in this country for making winter caps and trimming coats. The fur is always clipped in dressing, as it would appear too shaggy and coarse if the outer hairs were left ; but when properly dressed, it has a very soft short nap, which renders it one of the best looking furs for ornamental purposes, and it is likewise noted for its durable quality.

THE DEATH-WATCH (*ANOBIUM TESSELATUM*).

ENTOMOLOGISTS are not agreed concerning this insect and the noise which is attributed to it. Many conflicting statements appear respecting it; and as an observer, perhaps I may be allowed to communicate my own observations. I have several times devoted my attention to this and other insects, said to be death-watches, in order if possible, to set my mind at rest as to the ticking sound proceeding from them ; and if discovered to ascertain, if possible, how produced. Many times I have failed to discover what I so eagerly sought, and at others I have been somewhat repaid.

One night on retiring to rest, my attention was engaged by a sound resembling the ticking of a watch, or perhaps more correctly described as resembling the tapping the table with the finger nail. I however being tired paid little attention to the sound, but proceeded to undress. I had scarcely done so before the sound was heard again, rather louder than before. I determined to discover the cause, being then much interested in the study of insects, which at that time fully engrossed my attention.

I listened attentively; the sound again ceased, but was soon repeated, and after a little consideration I discovered that it proceeded from a large closet in my bedroom, in which I kept books and papers; I opened the door carefully, but notwithstanding my extreme care, the noise occasioned by the opening of the door put a stop for the time being to the ticking sounds. I waited, and was soon rewarded by the ticking being resumed. I now with care began to remove books and papers one by one, to discover, if possible, the originator of the sounds. For some time I was unsuccessful, inasmuch as the sounds ceased for a few seconds, and then after all was quiet it commenced again; but not until I had removed nearly all the books and papers did I discover the culprit, which I eagerly captured; but alas! my eagerness was not tempered with care, for in my hot haste lest my prize should escape I crushed its fragile form, much to my regret; but however, hastily replacing the papers and books I proceeded to examine the lifeless form; on examining and referring to authorities, comparing their description with the insect before me, I found it was an *Anobium Tesselatum*.

Here is the description from my note book:—
"1864, May, Wednesday 12 a.m. Discovered what afterwards proved to be an *Anobium Tesselatum*, in bed-room closet, from which proceeded a ticking sound resembling somewhat the ticking of a watch, or rather the tapping of the finger nail upon the table, found amongst newspapers and magazines, unfortunately crushed the insect in capturing, but examined it notwithstanding. Body, brown; breast and wing cases spotted, the whole covered with down; legs same colour as body; antennæ of a dull red colour; clubbed with joints of an irregular size, the two or three last being longer than the others."

Now not being favoured with a sight of the insect at work, I can only quote from one who, I suppose, has been thus privileged: "It raises itself upon its hind-legs, and inclining its body beats its head against the wood, paper, &c., with a force sufficient to produce a ticking sound resembling that of a watch." The reason assigned for so doing is as a call to their fellows, or as some say, a love-call to attract the attention of the opposite sex.

I find that Latreille observed *Anobium Striatum F.* produces the sound in question by a stroke of its mandibles upon the wood, which was answered by a similar noise from within. Both the species whose proceedings have been most noticed by British observers is *A. Tessalatum F.* Mr. Carpenter also describes two insects producing this singular noise. One of these is the *A. Tesselatum*, a coleopterous insect of a dark colour, about a quarter of an inch in length. It is chiefly in the latter end of spring that it commences its noise, which may be considered analogous to the call of birds. This is caused by beating on hard substances with the shield, or fore part of the head. The general number of successive distinct strokes is from nine to eleven. These are given out in pretty quick succession and are repeated at uncertain intervals. In old houses where the insects are numerous, they may be heard, if the weather be warm, at every hour of the day. In beating, the insect raises itself upon its hinder legs, and with the body somewhat inclined beats its head with great force and agility against the place upon which it stands. This insect, which is the real death-watch of the vulgar, must not be confounded with a minuter insect, not much unlike a louse, which makes a ticking noise like a watch, but instead of beating at intervals it continues its noise for a considerable length of time without intermission. This latter insect, the *Termes pulsatorium, Lin.*, belongs to a very different tribe (*Neuroptera*). Some affirm that the sound is also produced by the *Atropos*, or wood-louse; but without calling in question the powers of observation possessed by such that affirm it to be the case, as an observer, I do not see that it is possible that the *Atropos* could cause the sound in question. My statement is based upon the knowlege of the insect gained by close observation, and I think that if any entomologist would examine the *Atropos*, he will very soon be of the same opinion as myself. It is stated that the noise proceeds from beating the head in the same way as the *Anobium*. Now an examination of the *Atropos*, and its head in particular, will convince any one that it is impossible on account of its structure, that it should produce the sound, as the integuments of the creature are so fine and tender that the slightest touch is sufficient to rupture them. I am perfectly satisfied in my own mind of the impossibility of such a thing, and cannot but think that it must be patent to the close observer. I am aware the subject is a conflicting one, but the statement I have put forth are the result of close observation, and however much disputed, the appropriate couplet comes as conclusive, "Sir I've seen, and sure I ought to know." GEORGE DAY.

36, Chapel St., Pentonville, N.

NOTES ON THE MOLE.

AMONG the farmer's best friends this little animal is pre-eminent; but it has the misfortune to be judged otherwise, and therefore to be immeasurably persecuted by him. A skilful molecatcher informed me that in one year within the space of two parishes and a limited portion of two others —that is within the six winter months—he had caught one hundred dozen of these creatures, and in another similar season the number killed amounted to one hundred and twenty dozen. Yet the race survives this inordinate slaughter, for in a following year he remarked to me that they were then moderately abundant. But their numbers vary in different seasons; for in very dry seasons they probably die of hunger, when it is not unusual to find them dead on the surface near their heaps. It is certain that potatoes form a portion of their food, although this more frequently consists of worms; and my informant has seen a mole pass along its *creep* with a worm in its mouth, as if carrying it to some retreat. *Dog* moles are believed to be larger than the females. Their nests are always in hedges— such substantial hedges as divide fields in the West of England—except the field be of very large size; and generally the *runs* or passages are found to proceed from the hedge to the middle of the field or to the opposite hedge, although liable to vary. Two moles were procured and placed in a bird-cage with straw, in which they immediately baried themselves by lifting up the straw as they proceeded; and it was observed that the work of digging and heaving was performed chiefly with the arms and hands—a little of the heaving by the back of the head, but not by the nose. When one was compressed by the fingers in the hand the force of its claws was great and painful, almost as if from a bite; but the hind legs used no force in aid; so that in the cage when a wire was removed, and the head and body had been brought through the opening beyond the reach of the opening, it was not able to protrude itself further. In their motions in the cage they often encountered each other, when the aggressor elicits from the other a sharp stridulous squeak; and they were as active as any other might have been for hours together, but they were not able to climb. A single one in a cage made a noise several times. It was handled often with impunity, but at last it became irritated and bit sharply; not by digging into the substance of the flesh, but with a long slender slit. One of the pair died in the cage, and the other escaped from it; which was effected by pulling the wire backwards, and not by pushing it before it. When delivered from its prison it contrived to pass below the floor of the room in which it had been confined, and then it found its way out under the stone of the step, by throwing out much earth before it. It then advanced about two yards in the street; but on a slight alarm it ran back straight to the hole, as if in the possession of perfect sight. When carried to the garden and let loose on a steep slope it searched about over the bare earth, and then began to dig horizontally among the grass, without throwing any earth behind it, so that the passage remained open behind it; at the same time in all its visible actions varying its tail lifted high behind it; but when the opening here referred to was examined at about an hour and a half after the mole had entered it, it was found to be closed up. Its situation, however, does not appear to have been satisfactory, for it soon after quitted the place; and when this is done it is commonly along the surface, and not by digging. The nose of this creature possesses fine sensibility, and is capable of a variety of motions; also the anterior half of the body is possessed of celerity of motion at short angles, and as if the muscular motion were independent of the integument.

VIDEO.

GLIMPSES AT THE GREAT CONTINENTS.

D. Page, Esq., LL.D., Edinburgh, has delivered the first of a series of Lectures, entitled "Glimpses at the great Continents," at the Newcastle Literary and Philosophical Society.

The LECTURER said he proposed, during the course of his three lectures, to give a view of the physical, vital, and industrial aspects of the great subdivisions of the globe; pointing out in respect of each its own contour or shape, its relief or surface condition and climate, according to which the plant and animal life of the globe is distributed, and its mineral and metallic productions, as likewise its fitness or otherwise for human occupation, industry, civilisation, and progress. Having spoken generally of the physical conformation of the globe, the disparity between the surfaces of land and of water, and the various similiarities and analogies between the several continents, and having remarked that unequal distributions of the latter, and the peculiar configuration of the former, no doubt, were so arranged for some beneficial purpose, though the causes remained inexplicable to man. The lecturer said he proposed to deal first with the new world, as representing more clearly-defined and more striking characteristics than the old. Having dwelt upon the physical conformation and relief of the southern portion of the continent in detail, he summed up his observations in the following divisions. First he dealt with the great Pacific sea-board, lying to the west of the Andes, and along which lay the great South American towns, including those recently affected by the volcanic disturbances. Upon this district no rain ever descended, and it was only rendered habitable by the sea fogs, resulting from the intermingling of the cold Arctic Ocean currents with the warmer waters of the Pacific, which overspread the land. Next came the lofty region of the Andes, with a temperate clime on the flanks and a colder region upon the high lands, and at the height of 16,000 or 18,000 feet, perpetual snow. Next they had the region of the Orinoco, a grassy plain scarcely varying in level for 1500 miles; and fourthly, the great forests of the Amazon Plain— a district known as the Pampas Plains, producing vegetation so luxuriantly as to overcome all the efforts of civilized peoples to subdue it, and in consequence uninhabitable. These were the plains to which British commerce and industry were being directed, and from them, in due time, an unlimited cheap meat supply might be expected. Then the table land of Brazil, a district more fitted than any other for the display of human industry; and which, under its present rule, was making rapid progress. The Emperor offered land to immigrants on five years' leases at half-a-crown an acre, and the tempting offer was likely to be largely accepted. Next they had the grassy plains of the La Plata, and lastly the terraced region of Patagonia, the southern portion of which was most bleak and inhospitable. Mr. Page dwelt briefly on the geology of South America, which was extremely simple, noticing its mineral productions and its metals, and alluding to the extensive coalfields of Brazil, and remarking that, though the vegetation was so exuberant, and bird and reptile life so abundant, yet the higher class of mammals was almost altogether absent, only a few of the less important being met with. The horse, ass, camel, ox, lion, tiger, and many others were not indigenous to South America, or was man. The man that found his way there was of the Mongol race of Asia, who had traversed North America and penetrated into the southern division; and, as he found ample food to supply his wants without toil in producing it, or providence in the storing of it, he never passed out of his savage condition, nor attained any degree of civilisation. All the Indians of South America remained in this condition, and so they would so long as there was no incentive to be industrious or provident; and had they been disposed to improve their state, the excess of vegetation would, with their simple implements, have overpowered them. Mr. Page then dealt in a similar manner with North America, speaking of the mountain ranges and the plains under the following classification:—First, the dry seaboard of the Pacific to the west of the Rocky Mountains, rich in metals and fruitful; second, the table lands of the Rocky Mountains, dry, shingly, and sterile, except the tableland of Mexico; next, the great central plain, comprising the great fertile, rolling prairie lands of the southern portion, and the cold, sterile, lake-lands of the northern portion. Then the Atlantic plain—the populous states of America producing every variety of vegetable, minerals, metals, and almost every necessary of civilisation; and lastly, the vast frozen regions of the North. Having spoken of other particulars, the lecturer observed he could say the same of the North American Red Indian as he had done of the South American—that he did not properly belong to America. He had passed from the old world at a comparatively recent period, geologically speaking. He never built towns nor formed social communities, but wandered hither and thither. The only place where civilisation had been to any extent developed was in the tablelands of Mexico (the only place in South America, the plains of Brazil), and for this reason, that they had a temperate climate under a tropical latitude. The people had to lay up food for certain seasons, and take care for the future. Among all the Indian people in America, no trace of civilization was found except in those two spots. All the civilization had gone from the east, as the march of civilisation had always advanced. And the European nations were still advancing westward, across the Atlantic, and settled in the western continent, where they had the choice of all climates, and almost unbounded and most fruitful plains, which held out magnificent hopes as to the future. But while this was going on, centuries must pass before they had a man special to America evolved from the various races who were now occupying the American continent. These must all be fused into one people—into one nationality; and before the heterogeneous peoples could be fused into a homogeneous nationality, generations must pass away; but when that was done, they would have those great plains sustaining the industry of millions; and if the white man was true to his own blood the Red Indian would gradually pass away. The lower race must succumb to the more advanced. There were in America inexhaustible produces in the mineral, animal, and vegetable worlds to sustain a higher degree of civilisation which it was in the power of the present human race to attain; and he looked forward to a white race yet to be evolved from this new world which would outstrip the present race of man in the higher civilisation and attainments which belonged to progressive and advancing humanity.

MARS.

The planet Mars is the only object in the whole heavens which is known to exhibit features similar to those of our own earth, and the accumulated explorations and discoveries of astronomers during the last four hundred years have resulted in the construction of a globe representing the characteristics of this planet as astronomers believe them to exist. At a recent meeting of the Astronomical Society of England a globe of Mars was exhibited, on which lands and seas were depicted as upon an ordinary terrestrial globe. By far the larger part of the lands and seas were laid down as well known entities, respecting which no more doubt is felt among astronomers than is felt by geographers concerning the oceans and continents of our own globe. An interesting description of this globe appears in Fraser's Magazine. To the lands and seas developed in the planet are applied the names of those astronomers whose researches have added to our knowledge on the subject. Each pole of Mars, it seems, is capped with ice, which varies in extent according to the progress of the seasons. Around each cap is a polar sea, the northern sea being termed the Schroter sea; the southern, Phillips sea. The equatorial regions of Mars are mainly occupied by extensive continents, four in number, and named Dawes Continent, Madler Continent, Secchi Continent, Herschel I. (Sir W.) Continent. Between Dawes and Herschel Continents flows a sea shaped like an hour-glass called Kaiser sea, the large southern ocean out of which it flows being denominated Dawes ocean. Between Madler and Dawes continents flows Dawes strait, connecting a large southern ocean and a northern sea, named after Tycho. Herschel continent is separated from Secchi continent by Higgins inlet, flowing from a large southern sea termed Maraldi sea. In like manner Bessel inlet, flowing out of Airey sea (a northern sea) separates the Madler and Secchi continents. Dawes ocean separates into four large seas, and large tracts of land lie between them, but whether they are islands or not is uncertain. In Delarue ocean there is a small island which presents so bright and glittering an aspect as to suggest the probability of its being usually snow-covered. These seas, separated by lands of doubtful extent, reach from Delarue ocean to the South pole.

One of the most singular features of Mars is the prevalence of long and winding inlets and bottle-necked seas. These features are wholly distinct from anything on our earth. For example, Higginson noted a long forked stream, extending over three thousand miles. Bessel inlet is nearly as long, and Nasmyth inlet still more remarkable in its form. On our earth the oceans are sometimes as extensive as the continents. On Mars a very different arrangement prevails. In the first place there is little disparity between the extent of oceans and continents, and even these are mixed up in a most complex manner. A traveller by either land or water could visit almost every quarter of the planet without leaving the element in which he began his journeyings. If he chooses to go by water he could journey for upwards of 30,000 miles always in sight of land, generally with land in view on both sides, in such intricate labyrinthine fashion are the lands and seas of Mars intertwined.—*Boston Journal.*

CAMEL RIDING IN THE DESERT.

The camel told off for my especial riding was a very giant among these beasts; he was muzzled after the manner of a vicious horse, and looked at me in a sour, spiteful manner, that boded anything but amiability of temper. The Arab to whom the brute belonged cautioned me not to go near his mouth, stating that he had an unpleasant habit of biting any Englishman that came within reach. This was by no means cheering at starting, for I did not know how soon I might be abandoned to my fate on the back of this bloodthirsty quadruped. I had in my early days been taught to believe that a dromedary was a beast with only one hump, a very slender body, unnaturally long legs, and possessing the fleetness of the wind; that a camel, on the other hand, was gifted with two humps, and instead of being swift and slender, was of massive proportions, and gentle as a woman. I discover, however, that the term dromedary is applied to any camel that exhibits a little better appearance than its comrades, and for that reason is taken for riding purposes; or, in other words, dromedaries are amongst camels,—I speak of Arabia Petræa—what hunters, hacks, and racehorses are with us amongst horses—simply the better bred animals of a common stock. The ordinary pace of a baggage camel, or one led by a Bedouin, seldom exceeds three miles an hour, but a fast dromedary can, if well ridden, cover from twelve to fourteen. The swinging gait of a fast-going dromedary is by no means unpleasant; indeed, I think it very much more agreeable than the long, monotonous walk, that works the bottom of your back as if it were a hinge, and keeps you continually bowing, in a manner very absurd and ridiculous to a looker-on. Having said thus much about the camel and its saddle, I return to my ill-tempered steed. When I approached him to get on his back, he gave such a yell, compounded of roar and grunt, that I felt fairly scared, and at the same time he turned back his great flexible neck, so as to get a good look at me with his watery lustrous eyes. To mount was not an easy job, for though lying down, as camels always do when they are to be ridden or packed, the height of his saddle was greater than I could well manage to lift my leg over, without springing clean across his back like a circus rider. I made the attempt, succeeded fairly well, and landed in a most undignified manner astride on the "ship of the desert," and to carry out the metaphor, the ship seemed to go first bows under, and then suddenly rising over the wave plunge stern first in the trough, to quickly right, and move away slowly over the sandy sea.—*Land and Water.*

PURE SILVER AND ITS PROPERTIES.

Metals are rarely seen in a state of absolute purity, and as very small amounts of contaminating substances considerably modify their physical properties, and to some extent also their chemical behaviour, the characteristics of pure metals are but little known. Our knowledge of silver has recently been considerably extended by the experiments of Professor Christomanos, of Athens, who has obtained the pure metal by distillation. Silver was well known to be volatile to a slight extent at very high temperatures, but the Professor, by the use of a sort of bullet mould made of well-burned lime, into which he could direct the flame of an oxyhydrogen blowpipe, was enabled to obtain enough of the metal to experiment with. The pure metal he describes as of dazzling whiteness. Its specific gravity is 10·575, which is a trifle higher than that usually given. It is, of course, easily soluble in nitric acid, and in hot concentrated sulphuric acid. In extremely thin layers it shows by transmitted light a bluish green colour; in somewhat thicker, from a yellow to a yellowish brown colour. In the first case, it allows the chemical rays of light to pass, as the Professor proved in an original way. Chemically pure silver he finds is easily soluble in a hot solution of cyanide of potassium. When in such a solution, heated to 60 or 70 deg. C. a glass rod heated to a somewhat higher temperature is immersed, a uniform layer of metalic silver is deposited, which becomes thicker the longer the rod is allowed to remain in the solution.

By filling a test tube with mercury heated to 110 deg. C. and immersing it for a moment or two in the solution, a dull white coating of silver was deposited on the outside, which on the inside was seen as a brilliant silver mirror. The tube was then filled with equal volumes of hydrogen and chlorine, and carried into sunlight, whereupon combination and explosion took place. In the case of a tube left in the solution for a longer time for a thicker layer of the metal, and filled with the same gases, combination only took place slowly, and without explosion. It may be that the mode of silvering glass above described may be utilised for the silvering of glass globes and other ornamental objects, which are now silvered by the somewhat complicated reduction processes.—*Mechanics' Magazine*.

The Ocean Bottom.

Mr. Green, the famous diver, tells singular stories of his adventures when making search in the deep water of the ocean. He gave some new sketches of what he saw at the "Silver Bank," near Hayti :— The banks of coral on which my divings were made are about forty miles in length. On this bank of coral is presented to the diver one of the most beautiful and sublime scenes the eye ever beheld. The water varies from ten to one hundred feet in depth, and is so clear that the diver can see from two to three hundred feet when submerged, with but little obstruction to the sight. The bottom of the ocean in many places is as smooth as a marble floor: in others it is studded with coral columns on dry land. The fish which inhabit this "Silver Bank" I found as different in kind as the scenery was varied. They were of all forms, colors, and sizes—from the insignificant goby to the globe-like sun-fish; from the dullest hue to the changeable dolphin; from the spots of the leopard to the hues of the sunbeam; from the harmless minnow to the voracious shark. One in particular attracted my attention: it resembled a sea fan of immense size, of variegated colours, and the most brilliant hue. Some had heads like squirrels, others like cats and dogs, some of small size resembled the bull terrier. Some darted through the water like meteors, while others could scarcely be seen to move. To enumerate and explain all the various kinds of fish I beheld while diving on these banks would, were I enough of a naturalist so to do, require more than my limits allow, for I am convinced that most of the kinds of fish which inhabit the tropical seas can be found there. The sun-fish, star-fish, white shark, and blue or shovel nose shark were often seen. There were also fish that resembled plants, and remained as fixed in their position as a shrub; the only power they possessed was to open and shut when in danger. Some of them resembled the rose in full bloom, and were of all hues. There were the ribbon-fish, from four or five inches to three feet in length; their eyes are very large, and protrude like those of a frog. Another fish is spotted like a leopard, and from three to ten feet in length. They build their houses like beavers, in which they spawn, and the male or female watches the egg until it hatches. I saw many specimens of the green turtle, some five feet long, which I should think would weigh from 400 to 500 pounds.—*Panama Star and Herald*.

The Beetles in Utah.

The Austin (Nevada) *Reveuie* gives the following description of this formidable plague : "Utah is not only plagued with locusts, but with an insect called 'the elephant beetle.' A reliable person returned from the neighbourhood of Salt Lake last week, saw myriads of them covering the earth with their shining, brownish black bodies, and destroying everything which they met in their path. Even small animals, he was informed by the ill-fated residents, did not escape the voracity of these hordes; their bodies were crowded upon, and worried and wounded cruelly with the powerful antennæ until they fell down exhausted with their struggles and loss of blood, when they were fastened upon by thousands and devoured. The entire carcass of a sheep was eaten and the bones picked in two minutes and a quarter; and it is said that a dead ox would be gobbled up by them in a quarter of an hour. So ferocious are these giant beetles that mothers are afraid to let their children go out unattended by a grown person. In their frequent bloody contests the wounded are devoured on the instant. Our informant says they are about four inches long; their antennæ are stiff, sharp, and full four inches long; they have a short tail formed with a powerful horn, and their shells are so hard that the weight of a man will scarcely crush them. They are very frisky at times, and jump with the agility of fleas. No other species of beetle possesses their faculty of uttering a loud sound, which, made by thousands of them at once, resembles the braying of a band of jackasses. Their noise terrified the horses of our informant and his companion, who could not be kept upon the plain, so great was their fright. On one occasion, while they were riding in a valley that was black with beetles and crushing them under their horses' hoofs, when their hard cases would crack with a report like a rifle, the fierce insects showed a disposition to attack the horses, and fairly drove them from the field. We are informed that a scientific man in Salt Lake was collecting specimens of this formidable elephant beetle for transmission to various institutions of the country."

Fecundity of the Mouse, and a Word for the Weasel.

Mr. T. Hopley sends us the following curious and interesting particulars :—A mouse is able to shift for itself when about a fortnight old; and by the time it is six weeks old frequently, it is said, becomes a parent. Mice have generally between six and ten young ones at a litter—sometimes as many as twelve, and even more. Supposing eight to be the average, and supposing four out of each eight to be females, the capability of increase under the influence of favourable climate, abundant food, &c., and not allowing for any mortality, is as follows :—On the first day of the year 1 mouse about to have young ones. Say by the end of the 1st week 9 mice—*i.e.*, the mother and 8 young ones; end of the 7th week, $(9 \times 5)+4=49$; end of the 13th week, $(49 \times 5)+4=249$; end of the 19th week, $(249 \times 5)+4=1,249$; end of the 25th week, $(1,249 \times 5)+4=6,249$; end of the 31st week, $(6,249 \times 5)+4=31,249$; end of the 37th week,

(31,249 × 5) + 4 = 156,249; end of the 43rd week, (156,249 × 5) + 4 = 781,249; end of the 49th week, (781,249 × 5) + 4 = 3,906,249—nearly 4,000,000 in less than a year! and in 55 weeks, or in less than 13 months no fewer than 19,531,249! When it is considered that the rabbit (so much larger an animal) produces at times seven families in the course of the four seasons, it is probably not too much to suppose, as we have done, that the mouse may produce nine. It is far from uncommon in our country even now to observe half a dozen weasels nailed against a barn-door, while the barn itself and the neighbouring corn-stacks are overrun with the little creatures which should constitute the weasel's principal food.

New Books.

[*Our limited space must of necessity compel us to give but very short notices of new books, but they will perhaps serve as a guide as to what books our readers may ask for at their libraries.*]

Friends in Fur and Feathers. By Gwynfryn. Illustrated by F. W. Keyl, A. W. Cooper, and B. Rice. London: Bell and Daldy.

This little volume is a collection of sketches reprinted from the *Monthly Packet* and *Aunt Judy's Magazine*, being true stories of real pets, as we are told in the preface they are likely to interest and amuse the grown-up reader as well as children, to whom they are principally addressed. They are very nicely written; the story of Korngalle Jack, a pet elephant, being especially amusing, from which we give the following extract. Jack's master was military surgeon at Korngalle, and when he went his rounds was always accompanied by Master Jack, who was warmly welcomed by the soldiers:—

Jack had the air of a grave and anxious medical student as he walked the wards with his master, looking as if he tried to learn and remember what he saw, and he showed one day that he really had thought about it. One of the native orderlies had developed a peculiar talent for giving pills in a short, sharp, and decisive way, that sounds the very perfection of military discipline and smartness. He gave the word of command that mouths were to be open, and then dropped the pills down their throat. The patients, generally Malay soldiers, were very successful in taking their pills and not getting choked, as Englishmen would infallibly have been. But one day a poor fellow was choked, and, coughing violently, the pill fell at the elephant's feet, who at once picked it up, and held it daintily in the finger-like end of his trunk. It struck his master, who saw what he had done, that he could give the pill quite as well as the orderly, whom he had so often watched. So the patient's mouth was ordered to be very wide open, and touching his trunk, his master said to him, "Give it him, Jack, give it him!" The elephant instantly put the end of his trunk to the man's mouth, and, giving a whiff, effectually blew the pill down the soldier's throat.

Travels in the East Indian Archipelago. By Albert S. Bickmore, M.A. London: J. Murray.

The author of this work started to Amboina for the purpose of re-collecting the shells figured in Rumphius's "Rariteit Kamer." Meeting with great kindness from the Governor-general of the Netherland-India, he was enabled to visit the various parts of the Archipelago. The volume is of great interest, and written truthfully and with considerable care. The botanical descriptions are interesting, as are also the manners and customs of the natives. There are some capital illustrations and maps. The volume is got up with Mr. Murray's usual care. We give an extract on "the clove" on another page.

Ancient Geography for the Use of Schools and Private Students. By A. H. Bryce, LL.D. London: Nelson and Sons.

This has the merit of being well adapted for purposes of education. The information is abundant, correct, and well arranged. To awaken the interest and assist the memory of the learner, historical and biographical particulars are connected with names of places, which is a good feature of the work.

An Introduction to the Use of the Tellurion Globe. By J. L. Naish, B.A. London: Wyld.

Contains a description of this globe—which is a simplification of an astronomical instrument exhibited before the Royal Geographical Society and at the Royal Institution—with directions for the solution of astronomical problems by persons possessing no knowledge of mathematics. By a mere mechanical apparatus questions are solved with a degree of accuracy which has astonished persons familiar with mathematical *formulæ*.

Voyage dans le Soudan Occidental. Par M. E. Mage, Lieutenant de Vaisseau. Paris and London: Hachette and Co.

Lieutenant Mage's account of his travels and residence in the tropical regions of Western Africa is an excellent work of its class. This gentleman is of opinion that negroes have been very much calumniated, and that we should not accept altogether the severe judgment pronounced upon them by some modern travellers. The book is written in a highly interesting and instructive manner, and throws new light not only upon the geography, the history, and the natural features of Senegal, but on the political relations of the inhabitants of that country with Europe. It has hitherto been considered impossible for Europeans to influence materially the condition of Western Africa, on account of the supposed difficulties to be encountered by an expedition attempting to sail up the Niger. Lieutenant Mage holds this objection to be futile, and he adds that a sum of between 200,000 and 300,000 francs would be amply sufficient for the purpose. The only means of improving Africa is, in his opinion, to establish colonial centres on each important river, and he would especially discourage the spread of Islamism. His book, handsomely illustrated with maps and woodcuts, is an account of three years (1863—66) honourably spent in the cause of civilisation and science.

Ueber die Berechtigung der Darwinschen Theorie. Von Dr. A. Weismann. Leipzig: Engelmann. London: Williams and Norgate.

Dr. Weismann writes on the development hypothesis, and contributes some interesting illustrations from his especial pursuit, entomology. He surrenders the philosophical basis of his theory, by the admission that vertebrates cannot be held to have originated from invertebrates. If each of the four great natural types has a distinct origin, we must admit at least four creations, and why not four hundred or four thousand? Haeckel is more consistent, and more intrepid. He maintains that the transition from invertebrates to vertebrates may be plainly detected in that interesting animal, the sandeel; to which he naturally attaches extreme importance, esteeming it a species of title-deed, as it were, enabling men and monkeys to establish their common descent from the *cimex lectularius*.

Reise nach den Canarischen Inseln. Mit populärnaturwissenschaftlichen Schilderungen. Von Dr. Richard Greeff. Bonn: Cohen. London: Nutt.

Dr. Greeff's travels in Madeira and the Canaries form an unpretending, but extremely agreeable, volume. The writer is always chatty and cheerful, while his narrative is redeemed from commonplace by a felicitous gift of observation, and an especial attention to the details of natural history, which are not, however, allowed to become too technical for the unlearned reader. The ascent of the Peak of Teneriffe was the principal incident of his travels; he also visited the less known islands of Grand Canary and Lanzarote, and touched at Mogador and Tangier on his way home.

Short Notes.

INSECTICIDE.—A scientific correspondent has supplied the following notes on petroleum as a vermin destroyer:—"As summer is approaching, and 'vermin' (so called) are as usual at this time on the increase, the following extract from a late number of a periodical may be useful to many. Nearly all the animals, &c., mentioned below annoy us at one time or other of the year, and the application of the substance employed is so simple (the only trouble being to obtain it) that it is well worthy of a fair trial, although we cannot for the present use it on an extensive scale:— 'Petroleum oil, especially in the crude state, is found in France to be of great value in destroying insects, slugs, ants, caterpillars, and other mischievous creatures. The petroleum is mixed with water in the proportion of from an ounce to half an ounce to a pint of water in ordinary cases; but when applied to fruit trees or delicate plants the quantity of the oil is still further diminished. A very weak solution, applied to cherry trees with a watering-pot, is said to be completely efficacious against the *ver blanc* or larva of the cockchafer. A strong solution poured into the holes and down walls infested by insects is said to kill them rapidly. Another application of the solution is to rid dogs and other animals of parasites, but the parts must be rubbed with soap a few minutes after the solution has been applied. An agriculturist in the Aube says that the rats and mice with which his cellar had been infested, all quitted it when some petroleum was stored there, and that his garden was cleared of slugs by watering with the rinsings of petroleum casks.' Kerosine, now so largely used amongst us, may also be tried as above: it has been in one or two instances, viz., in infected specimens of natural history, and completely found to succeed.

SHOCK OF EARTHQUAKE.—The newspapers have given some remarkable accounts of an earthquake which has more or less been felt in perhaps every portion of our island, although certainly not in an equal degree in every part. But there is what I believe to be one portion of it that appears to me to demand a record, which has not been mentioned by any observer, perhaps for the obvious reason that few of those who have spoken of it have possessed the opportunity of observing the motions of the sea, and still a less number who might suppose that there were any of the phenomena of the ocean that could be associated with the probable electric actions—as I judge them to be—of the earthquake. The sea had long previously been disturbed with stormy weather, interrupted by an occasional lull, but in all such cases while the waves break high there is a special colour in the water, which, although wanting in transparency, is not absolutely foul. But in the case now referred to the influence of the winds had passed away; there had followed a moderate amount of calm, nor did any high wind, still less a storm, succeed the appearance along our coast, which I especially noticed, and not, in the course of several years, for the first time. The waves sprung up suddenly in a broken and disordered course, not particularly high but turbulent, with an unusual amount of run on the beach, their mudded appearance showing that a disturbed action from the bottom had thrown up the soil that had long been deposited below. This appearance lasted for about twenty-four hours, and then the sea returned to its ordinary condition. It is several years since that Mr. Edmonds, of Penzance, published his observations on phenomena closely resembling the above, and since that time I have noticed it also, as occurring in some instances within a comparatively limited space of the coast, whilst all beyond remained undisturbed, and without any wind to account for it.—*Jonathan Couch, in Land and Water*.

THE GREEN SANDPIPER.—In India the green sandpiper is much commoner than the wood sandpiper, and may be met with in almost every village. Many stay in that country through the whole of the hot weather, but I have never heard of this bird breeding there. Although sometimes shot by the less experienced in mistake for a snipe, it is easily distinguished from that bird when rising at the first glance by its dark plumage, the conspicuously white upper tail coverts, and by its loud whistle, which it always utters when on the wing—"*pleet, pweet, pweet.*" Its flights differs, too, from that of the snipe, being slower and wavering, with more deliberate beats of the wing. It often soars high, circles round, and then returns to the spot it was flushed from, like the wood sandpiper. It is very tame, never concealing itself, and easily to be seen standing by the mud at the water's edge, with its shoulders shrugged up, or taking short runs at the insects, after which it will sometimes wade, swimming back if it outreach its depth. When just alighted it bobs its body and head up and down in a singular manner. In India it is always solitary, or in pairs. Sometimes four or five may be seen by a pool, but they act and move about quite independently of each other. Its European history is much the same as that of the wood sandpiper, but it is evidently not so common or numerous there as the latter bird. The eggs of the two species are very similar, those of the green sandpiper being, perhaps, more thickly and confusedly spotted. A few breed in England.—*Field*.

TRANSIT OF MERCURY.—At the last sitting of the *Academy of Sciences* a letter was read from Father Secchi, of Rome, in which he gave an account of his observation of the transit of Mercury on the 5th instant. Early in the morning the sky was clear, but atmospheric oscillation was strong near the horizon, and prevented micrometric measures from being taken. After sunrise a few clouds made their appearance, and were very near marring the observation, the end of the transit being obtained with much difficulty. Four observers were engaged in the task, each with a different instrument, and the results were nearly alike, except as regards the final emersion, in which there was in one case a discrepancy of 16 seconds; but this was owing to a cloud that was rapidly invading the sun's disc. It was unanimously admitted that the blackness of the planet was four times more intense than that of solar spots; rather an important circumstance.—His Excellency the Minister of Public Instruction sent in a copy of MM. Demogeot and Montucci's report on secondary instruction in England and Scotland. A note was received from M. Gaiffe on the production of electric discharges in the shape of egrets by means of Holtz's machine. He states that if its condenser be suppressed, and the negative conductor terminate in a ball of about 14 millimetres diameter, the positive one ending in a sphere of from five to six centimetres, very short sparks of egrets will be obtained, but so numerous as to produce sound, whereby they may be easily counted. At a distance of 20 millimetres the sounds acquire peculiar purity.—Mr. P. Fischer sent in a paper on certain results obtained by dredging in the Bay of Biscay, near the basin of Arcachon, and at a distance of 36 leagues from the mainland. A quantity of molluscs have thus been obtained which had never before been remarked as inhabiting the French seas Such, for instance, are the *Nexra costellata, Lepton nitidum, Leda tenuis,* &c.—*Galignani*.

A SWALLOWS' NEST.—A correspondent of *Land and Water* sends the following anecdote of the building of a nest by swallows at an inn which stood, and may still stand, near the Sevenoaks railway station. The account refers to an occurrence of rather old date, but the gentleman who relates it speaks of what he actually saw. He says, "Having heard that a pair of swallows had built their nest at an angle of the wall of the inn near the Sevenoaks station, inclosing the wire and crank of the ostler's bell, I took an opportunity of ascertaining the truth of the story. On inquiry I was shown the nest, and so far as I could perceive from the ground, the birds had so continued their nest as to allow of the working of the crank and the wire through it without risk of damage." It seems that the birds had made considerable progress with their mud tenement before they perceived that every time the bell was pulled a portion of it must be destroyed by the action of the crank and wire. That they had thereupon, instead of abandoning the whole of what they had built, adopted the ingenious device of leaving a sufficient opening for the working of the bell, and had subsequently utilised their hut for the purpose for which they had built it, namely, the rearing of a brood of young ones.

PRIMROSE: ASH TREE.—The parishes of Bibury and Sherborne, on the Cotswold Hills, are entirely without wild primroses: indeed, I have never found them truly wild on the Oolite, though where planted, as in the pleasure grounds of Bibury House, they thrive, but do not spread. From Sherborne, I believe I should have to go at least eight miles to find wild primroses. Its place is taken by the cowslip. I believe that if your correspondent would take the trouble to examine, he would find several parishes in Lincolnshire where the primrose does not grow wild, and has never been known to. On Lincoln heath, and the low land lying to the west of it (the valley of the Witham and the Brant), I believe it is very rare. I am very well acquainted especially with the parish of Leadenham, and I never heard of a primrose being found wild anywhere in that neighbourhood, except one which was of a purple colour, and most likely escaped from some garden. The variety known as the cowslip is very abundant; but I suppose your correspondent does not include that in the word *primrose*.—*Notes and Queries.*

A TALE OF A SNAKE.—A most extraordinary incident occurred the other day in the drawing gallery of the Jardin des Plantes, by which death was well nigh caused by the bite of a stuffed serpent. M. Delahaye, the gifted artist, to whose genius we owe the splendid drawings lithographed in the scientific works published by the Sorbonne and the College de France, had completed the drawing of a crotalum, one of the most dangerous of the rattlesnake tribe, and was replacing the stuffed reptile in its glass case, when the jaws, kept open by means of a spring, suddenly snapped on the artist's finger, which bled profusely. M. Delahaye instantly sucked the wound, and rushed to the laboratory for aid. Two doctors, hastily summoned, pronounced the danger imminent. They steeped the finger in a solution of alkali, and then introduced a platina needle into the wound, previously made red hot by the application of electric piles. The patient was next dosed with the usual antidotes for poison. After an hour of this treatment he was sent home. The excitement over, the *savants* inquired among themselves whether M. Delahaye's wound could have proved mortal. To ascertain the fact they sent for a rabbit, and, closing the jaws of the stuffed crotalum on the wretched animal's thigh, inflicted precisely the same wound as M. Delahaye had received. In half an hour the *savants* had the satisfaction of seeing the rabbit die in all the tortures of tetanus.—*Paris Correspondent of Star.*

THE BATTLES OF THE CRABS.—The common edible crabs of the fish-shops are found on rocky parts of our coasts, the smaller animals inhabiting holes in the cliffs, but the larger and more experienced dwelling in deeper waters. When caught and kept *alone* in an aquarium, one of these crabs may become tame and quite familiar; but if placed with others of its race, a series of desperate battles will soon declare the degree to which the ferocity of the crab may extend. In these fights, claws, limbs, and shells are torn, wrenched, and cracked with a fury and energy to which a battle between two game cocks is but play. When a large crab has seized a smaller he tears open the shell, and scoops out the flesh of his living captive. Perhaps, while the conqueror is enjoying his feast, a still stronger crab will tear open the body of the victor, and feed upon him. The most singular fact is, that a crab, while thus being eaten, will actually continue to feed on the victim seized by himself. Here appears a total insensibility to suffering. A crab has been known to loose seven of its limbs in a fight, and immediately after to begin eating a captured mollusk, as if nothing particular had happened.—From "*Recreative Natural History*" in "*Cassell's New Popular Educator*" for December.

CIRCULATION IN INSECTS.—A translation of a paper by M. Jules Künckel appears in the *Annals* for September, confirming the discovery of Blanchard, made in 1847, that the tracheal tubes in insects fulfil the function of arteries, the nutritive fluid being conveyed by them in the interspace between their outer and inner walls. M. Künckel, by dexterous manipulation of the living insect, has succeeded in witnessing the actual course of the blood-globules between the two membranes; and he states that at the point where the tracheæ penetrates the fibres of the muscular tissue the *inner* coat disappears, and the tube terminates cæcally; while the *outer* coat becomes the wall of a system of arterial capillaries. The course of the blood is thus as follows: the fluid is propelled into the tracheal interspaces by the pulsations of the dorsal vessel or heart; it is arterialised by the air which courses through the interior portion of the tracheæ, and reaches the capillary vessels perfectly vivified; thence it is diffused through the tissues (there being no *venous* capillaries) to the lacunæ or vacant spaces therein, and from the lacunæ it is returned to the dorsal vessel again.—*Naturalists' Circular,* October.

THE CHILIAN BEET.—Lately there has been introduced a fine variety of Beta cicla with the above name, and a remarkably good and useful plant it is. When well grown the leaves are often more than a yard long, and present a vivid and most striking coloration. Their midribs reach 4in. or more across, and vary from a dark deep waxy orange to vivid polished crimson. The splendid hue of the lower part of the leaf stalks flows on towards the point, and spreads in smaller streams through the main veins and ramifications of the great soft blades of the leaf, often a foot and even 15in. in diameter, if the plant be in rich ground. The under sides of the leaves are the most richly coloured, and the habit such that these sides are well seen. It requires the treatment of an annual—to be raised in a gently heated frame, and afterwards planted out in very rich ground. It varies a good deal from seed, and the most striking individuals should be selected before the plants are put out. Used sparingly, its effect would perhaps be more telling than if in quantity, and it is well suited for isolation—that is to say, placing singly on the grass near a clump of shrubs. Everybody who values a really distinct object in the flower garden should have it.—*Field,* October 10.

"AS SICK AS A CAT."—No phrase more familiar; but, never having observed that "the smallest of the tribe, of which the lion is chief," is more often sick than its neighbours, the saying always puzzled me, till I lately stumbled upon it with the addition of a second part—

"As sick as cats
With eating rats."

Here the fitness of the illustration comes out; for, however senseless it may seem to compare a sick and suffering Christian to the active wiry little animal popularly supposed to have "nine lives," that same animal is all but invariably "sick" (in every sense of the word) if rashly permitted to *eat* the rat successfully encountered and killed. How strange that this second line should have so entirely disappeared from common speech, when it has not only reason, but the more powerful help of rhyme, to keep it in remembrance!—From *Notes and Queries.*

Remarks, Queries, &c.

(*Under this head we shall be happy to insert original Remarks, Queries, &c.*)

DO INSECTS FEEL PAIN?

"The animal presents, among natural bodies, the most perfect idea of an organism."—Dr. Carus.

"Animals grow, live, and *feel*."—Linnæus.

Although with the philosopher we must admit that "we know but little of the real structure of bodies," still I hold to my original argument, that animal life implies an organism, an active principle; and from these assumptions, which have not been disputed, I conclude that violence offered to that organism, to that active principle, carries pain to the animal assailed.

When I take for granted and assume that man, the whale, and the sparrow feel pain because they are animals, and consequently insects also feel pain because they too are animals, I evidently base my conclusion on the long-established truths, that animal life implies an organism, an active principle, from which I infer that an attack on that organism, on that vitality, must cause pain to the animal assailed; and as insects are animals, well known to be composed of a delicate and wonderful organism, endowed with an astonishingly active principle, and hence that they too if injured must inevitably feel pain. That I might have arrived at my deduction by a more gradual or more circuitous process is evident, but surely the validity of my argument could acquire no new force by a circumlocutionary "beating about the bush." When Linnæus characterises the *animal* world, viz., "Animals grow, live, and *feel*," surely we have a universal proposition; if so insects are animals, and consequently *feel*, and hence that feeling may be a sensation of pleasure or *pain*. The most eccentric reasoner can scarcely have the hardihood to deny that animals grow and live; and, if admitting these two characteristics, why deny that they *feel?* Why, Sir, there is no accounting for taste; and, in order to be "dressed in an opinion," men sometimes *feel no pain* when deviating into the region of scientific blunder. Eliminate *feeling* from the animal world, and a terrible chaos, an awful void is created. What is taste but *feeling?* What is the sense of smelling but *feeling?* What is hearing but a modification of *feeling?* And I run counter to no scientific truth when I call seeing a sublime, mysterious sort of *feeling*. In the wonderful phenomena of life see how early *feeling* manifests its presence, and watch how tenaciously it clings to the last flickerings of vitality. Feeling is a universal sense in the animal world; it is generally diffused, and pervades the whole animal, whereas the other senses are but local, often but imperfectly developed, and some of them even totally absent.

When the great Linnæus was studying the characteristics of the Animal Kingdom he never thought of saying animals grow, live, and see—animals grow, live, and hear—animals grow, live, and taste; no, but he says "Animals grow, live, and *feel*."

Let us now, Sir, turn our attention to the organism of a few insects, but let us first listen to Baron Cuvier when he says:—"With respect to the internal organisation of insects, two or three of these beings which the vulgar treat with contempt might occupy the whole of a man's life."

Then proceeds Cuvier:—"We cannot look without admiration on that work on the anatomy of a single caterpillar to which Lyonnet devoted ten years. A similar examination of the Maybug, recently made by a young naturalist, M. Strauss, is not less calculated to confound the imagination. In this small body, scarcely an inch long, there may be counted 306 hard pieces, serving as an envelope, 494 muscles for moving them, 24 pairs of *nerves for animating* them—all divided into innumerable filaments, 48 pairs of tracheæ not less divided for carrying air and LIFE *into this inextricable tissue*. The *delicacy* and *regularity* of the whole afford a delightful spectacle."

Let us just contemplate the delicacy and perfection of this organism which the greatest of naturalists says "confounds the imagination."

Has this organism any duty to perform? Yes, says Cuvier, it "*carries* air and *life* into this inextricable tissue." Surely, Sir, those admirably constructed organs which *carry* air and life to the insect must also *carry pain* if the insect is injured. In the caterpillar of the Goat-moth Lyonnet counted in the head 220 muscles, in the body 1,647, and round the intestines 2,186, amounting in all to 4,053 muscles in one insect! Well indeed may Professor Owen say that "in insects the highest problem of animal mechanism is solved."

The Myriopoda has 160 legs. In the eye of the ant 50 lenses have been counted; the eye of the house-fly has four thousand lenses, that of the gad-fly seven thousand. The dragon-fly has twenty-four thousand eyes; the butterfly has seventeen thousand lenses in one eye; and the Mordella beetle has more than twenty-five thousand lenses to give it light!

And all this but a small portion of the organism of insect life! Truly indeed is the imagination confounded, and well may the philosopher exclaim:—"We are lost in wonder when we attempt to comprehend either the vastness or minuteness of Creation."

And after all this, what is life? We cannot tell. If we strike a whale with a harpoon, the presumption is that it feels pain; strike a bird with an arrow, and the presumption is that it feels pain; pin a moth to a tree, and surely the presumption is that it feels pain: and such inferences we deduce because they are animals, and because we assume that animals *feel*.

That there is a wide chasm between the whale and the moth I readily admit; still there is a connecting link, both being members of the animal world. That the whale is larger than the moth is true; but still there is an affinity, for surely multiplicity of magnitude is no more a characteristic of feeling in the whale, than that the diminutively formed existence of the living atom is a sign of the non-susceptibility of pain in the insect.

"Nature, enchanting Nature, in whose form
And lineaments divine I trace a hand
That errs not—universal prize!"

Do insects feel pain? Undoubtedly they do, says Shakespeare; and yet some of your correspondents may timidly question what the big, comprehensive mind, the ready perception, the strong judgment, of the great poet had no difficulty in determining, and what his versatile pen as clearly expresses in his characteristic style:—

> "The beetle that we tread upon
> In corporal suffering *feels as great a pang
> As when a giant dies.*"

It is well known that formerly the sense of hearing was denied to insects, and even Bonnet, and Linnæus himself, favoured the heartless opinion; but Shakespeare, with a better knowledge of natural history, or perhaps of *Nature*, says:—

> "I will tell it softly;
> Yon crickets shall not hear me."

Shakespeare was right, as the researches of Brunelli and other naturalists prove.

Insects have brain, muscle, and nerve, a rapidly circulating blood, the sense of taste, touch, smell, hearing, and seeing—a wonderful organism—an organism so complicated and perfect that the examination of a single insect might be the labour of years—an organism that "confounds the imagination;" and if we can impose upon ourselves the idea of the non-existence of pain in such beings, there is no reason why we should not, with some of the ancients, deny the total existence of pain in the whole animal world, man himself included, look on the assumed presence of pain as an ancient hallucination modernised, and calmly reduce all our sensations to the stoic consistency of a piece of granite.

Do insects feel pain? They do, because they have a *nervous system*. And Lewes, in his "Physiology of Common Life," says:—"The nervous system of animals reveals that the mere presence of nerve-fibres and ganglionic substance is all that is requisite for the production of *sensibility* and *volition*, quite irrespective of any arrangements of these elements." The nervous system of insects has been sufficiently proved, and hence the question carries its own affirmative. The structure of insects is even yet but imperfectly understood; so much so, indeed, that what Ray said two hundred years ago, and what the illustrious Cuvier acknowledged in his own time is still applicable, viz.—"There is a greater depth of art and skill in the structure of the meanest insect than thou art able for to fathom or comprehend."

"Tread on a worm and it will turn;" "self-preservation is the first law of nature;" "treat not even the meanest insect with cruelty;" are all but popular breathings of humanity, directly inculcating the idea that insects and the lower animals feel pain. But, Sir, here some of the correspondents of THE NATURALIST'S NOTE BOOK may impatiently ask why do we not at once prove beyond the power of cavil that insects *do* or *do not* feel pain, and by a close and rigid demonstration establish our conclusions, and add so much to the knowledge of Natural History? My answer is that questions of this kind are beyond the reach of mathematical proof: we can only advance such arguments as observation furnishes, and reason from *inductive evidence*.

How did Linnæus know that animals *feel?* Simply by *induction*. How do we know that any man feels? By induction. And how do we know that insects feel pain? Simply by *inductive evidence*. That man, the whale, and the sparrow feel pain are but assumptions deduced from inductive evidence; that insects feel pain is a like conclusion; and as feeling is a thing purely subjective, Linnæus only reasoned from induction when he says animals *feel*. And here, Sir, I wish to notice and correct a mistake into which some of your correspondents have merged. Our present inquiry is not whether insects feel *much* or *little* pain, neither are we wanting to know if they feel as much pain as man, the whale, or the sparrow, etc., etc., but simply *do insects feel pain?* Some of your correspondents too, in something like despair in science, throw down their pens and say the question never can be decided. I cannot take such a limited view of Natural History, for I am confident that future research, patient industry, analogy, induction, and candour, must ultimately establish the fact that insects do feel pain. Nature, as if to prove that she hates violence, even to the smallest of her creatures, is particularly kind to some species of insects in restoring their legs if amputated, for in the "Linnæan transactions," Lansdown Guilding says, "If it (the insect) loses a leg by violence this is reproduced, but of a smaller size, at the next change of skin." It is universally admitted among the scientific that some species of insects (perhaps all) have a language; that this language, this interchange of instinctive sentiment, is carried on by means of feeling; and if this feeling is so fine, so sensitive, so perfect, that the light touch of an antenna is felt and understood, and intelligence telegraphed to little social communities; then, Sir, it is difficult to deny that a heavier touch, amounting to absolute violence, does not carry pain to the insect assailed. I cannot possibly, Sir, see my way to such a contradictory and unnatural conclusion. And as I have in this and previous letters in the NOTE BOOK often referred to the sensibility of insects, and as I would wish to be fairly understood, I give the following extract from Dr. Carus:—"In order to have a clear insight into this fact, it is necessary to fix our idea of the word *sensibility*, as that which we would be understood to convey most correctly, if we say that it consists *in the change operated by outward or inward circumstances in the feelings of a being conscious that it exists as a unity;* consequently if we deny sensibility to the stone or the mineral, it is not because such a body is not subject to the most varied agitations and changes, but because it is merely a member of a higher unity, and in itself is to be considered as an individual, not as a true unity. . . .

"So that this real unity, as we shall hereafter see, *is possible only in the animal*, in which the organs are connected with a unity by means of the vascular and nervous systems."

From his clear and elaborate definition of sensibility by such an eminent scientific writer as Dr. Carus, we find that even insects are susceptible of changes operated by *inward* as well as by outward circumstances in their feelings, and hence it is perfectly fair to deduce as a legitimate conclusion that the sensibility of insects in captivity amounts to actual pain.

Twenty-four lines and no argument from "W. H. M.," who after three months' study discovers, and only now informs us, that pinning a moth to a tree is "not a most humane action," grumbles at my inferences, writes "according to his recollection," but forgets where he left the last number of the NATURALIST'S NOTE BOOK!

Surely the great ideas he enunciates were, as Shakespeare would say, "begot in the ventricle of his memory, nourished, and delivered on the mellowing occasion."

In reference to the views so ably propounded by your clever correspondent "C.," I need only say that he will find some of the greatest interpreters on his side.

Dromore.   H. H. ULIDIA.

I have read with much interest the remarks of your correspondent on this subject, and although I rather incline to the opinion that insects do feel a certain amount of pain, yet I think that hitherto the advocates of the painless theory have had much the best of the argument.

Mr. Waters and his supporters seem to me to have brought forward arguments, while the writers on the other side appear to be more at home in making assertions than in giving any real *reasons* for their opinion.

Mr. Ulidia especially evinces a remarkable capability of misrepresenting the statements of his opponents, and of slurring over in a contemptuous manner those arguments which he is (apparently) unable to answer. I am glad to see from his last letter that he intends to "fall back into the reserve," for until he can write a little more fairly, and a little less conceitedly, he had better not write at all.

As to the "well-directed battery of heavy guns" which "C." brings to Mr. Ulidia's aid, I do not think they will either frighten or hurt the "pain-despising veterans." For my own part, I cannot see any particular force in "C.'s arguments, and they do not seem to have met with much approval from other correspondents of the NOTE BOOK.

Mr. Waters's anecdote about the dragon-fly proves, I think, pretty conclusively that if insects do feel pain, it is in such a slight degree as scarcely to be distinguished from a sensation of mere discomfort or inconvenience; and there are many other incidents recorded by various writers which are quite as striking and convincing. Kirby and Spence tell us in their "Introduction to Entomology," vol. I. chap. ii, of a certain dragon-fly, which on having the end of its abdomen presented to its mouth actually ate off four or five segments, and yet when released it flew away as if nothing were the matter!

Many instances of this kind have come under my own observation. To mention only one of them. I once put two ground-beetles (*Carabus*) in hot water for the purpose of killing them, in order to their preservation in the cabinet. I kept them immersed for some minutes, so as to make sure of their death; and then having pinned them through the right-wing case, and fixed their legs in a natural position, I left them to dry. About five or six hours after, when I took down the setting-board to put some other insect on it, I was astonished to see one of the beetles kicking about, and making most energetic efforts to release itself. I took it off the board, and having withdrawn the pin (an operation of considerable difficulty, for the juices of the insect having dried had as it were glued the pin into the wound), I placed it in a bell-glass partially filled with damp earth, and containing other beetles of the same kind. It immediately began to run about; and when I offered it dead flies it ate them with great apparent relish. The only effect of its wound seemed to consist in a slightly embarrassed movement of the legs on the same side of its body. The hole made by the pin soon healed up, and I kept the beetle for some weeks afterwards in a state of the most perfect health.

Now it seems to me that this insect could not have experienced much pain either from its scalding or transfixion, or it would not have been so lively and so ready to eat as soon as the pin was withdrawn. I fully believe that even had I suffered the pin to remain the beetle would have lived perfectly well, only as that instrument protruded for more than a quarter of an inch below its body, it would not have been able to move about very quickly.

Trusting I have not trespassed too much on your valuable space, I am, &c.   JOHN LANDELS.

The opinions of eminent scientific men, though not, of course, to be accepted as infallible, should nevertheless take precedence of the speculations of those who have not fully studied the question. Professor Huxley, quoted by Mr. Spicer on page 278, says that the amount of feeling depends in a great measure, if not entirely, on the degree of concentration of nerve matter. Consequently creatures which have no nervous tissue can feel no pain, and those which have the nerve matter distributed over a large extent may be only capable of a small amount of feeling, which cannot be termed pain. A patient under chloroform sometimes feels the touch of the lancet, but no pain, the acuteness of feeling being removed by the action of the anæsthetic. The crepuscular moth pinned against a tree, and not fluttering till twilight, feels, no doubt, the presence of the pin in its thorax, just as I feel the presence of the pen in my hand now, but the sensation is not so acute as to be called pain, otherwise the moth would be struggling all the time. Evidently there is no more inconvenience than a man experiences who has been stuck to his seat by a bit of cobbler's wax; when he desires to rise, and finds himself detained, he struggles to get free. As to excessive inconvenience being painful, so is excessive pleasure. Thus, tickling the soles of the feet is at first a pleasant sensation, which if continued becomes intolerable agony. Tungstate of soda when first taken into the mouth is sweet, but the sweetness is rapidly changed to intense bitterness. As to the theological view, I quite agree with "C." in denouncing Mr. Spicer's dictation to the Deity in the matter of superfluous organs, though I can hardly believe that the lower animals will have a future life. "C." founds his hypothesis upon that passage in Romans which "Windsor Hambrough" has clearly shown to refer to mankind only. Certainly death was a law of nature long before the human epoch, as witness the fossils scattered through twenty miles' thickness of strata, and we know that some deaths were violent, by the presence of crustacean remains in the coprolites found *in situ between the ribs* of the great Liassic sauria. At the same time, we find individuals among the lower order of animals (horses, dogs, monkeys, cats, elephants, and *ants*) quite equal to, and often superior to, individuals of our own species in intellect. Dogs have too a low sort of morality, and a conscience, which monkeys also occasionally have, and men occasionally have not. Yet, if all men have souls, we must extend the privilege to many of the lower animals which have not, and cannot have, a divine revelation. Again, there is every gradation from the most powerful intellect to the most utter insensibility, and if the soul be only in the intellect, how much intellect constitutes an immortal soul? If *all* animals have souls, the same must be said of all vegetables, as it is impossible to draw the line between the kingdoms. In conclusion, let me request the gentlemen who take part in this discussion to avoid substituting personalities for arguments, as I already observe a tendency to do so in some of the letters on the subject. W. H. D.

28, Jermyn-street, S.W.

Your correspondents seem to be getting most enthusiastic in the matter of pain felt by insects. I have taken great interest in the several articles that have lately appeared in the columns of your magazine on this subject, and the various *pros* and *cons* thereof. But while the combatants are spending so much time and labour over their theories of analogy, there are many other more important subjects in Natural History at issue, which seem much more deserving of their studies. However much your correspondents may argue, and whatever inferences they may draw from their discussions in their attempt to solve the problem, they can *never* arrive at any positive conclusion, inasmuch as they cannot get metamorphised into an insect, to ascertain whether they experience pain by having their limbs cut off, or being walked over! If they argue for a twelvemonth, they will be *then* no nearer the object of their researches and arguments. Let them rather turn their attention and try to ascertain what becomes of *migratory* birds during the cold season, and especially the *Hirundines*. This is indeed a question that needs answering. One naturalist has suggested one thing by way of explanation, another another. For instance, White imagines the swallow tribe to a great degree remain dormant at the bottom of streams—(to be sure, this theory is nearly exploded now)—another naturalist says in hollow caves, etc. The only *definite* proof that we have of the Hirundine *migrating* is that they are met with both in Africa and England, in the different seasons—and then we *conclude* that they leave us in autumn for the south of Africa, and return therefrom to us again at the beginning of spring. But this is all we know. True, flocks are sometimes met with out at sea, which seem to be then on their passage from one country to another; *they* need not necessarily be migrating, but merely *en route* for some new feeding space. Let Mr. Spicer and Co. turn their thoughts to this subject, and see if they cannot argue it out; and then, perhaps, better success will attend their labours than they can ever hope to have in the matter of whether insects feel pain or not.

I also will ask one question of your correspondents, if you will allow me; and I should be curious to know if your belligerents, *Mr. Ulidia, C.*, etc., etc., can answer it. How is it that the shape of eggs laid in *nests* (such as blackbirds', rooks', etc.) are nearly *oval*, or so elliptical as nearly to be *circular*, whereas those laid on the *bare rock* (such as cormorants, gulls, etc.) are pointed and acute at the smaller end?

The answer to this indeed shows the providence of the Creator in the smallest possible arrangement of the economy of nature. Let your correspondents answer the question about the swallows if they *can!*

A. H. MALAN.

THE REASONING POWERS OF ANIMALS.—The discussion on the above subject has been very spiritedly opened by your correspondents "R. B. W." and "C." In your last issue "R. B. W." makes one very just remark,—"It has not been at all clearly proved that dogs (and he might have added, 'or any class of animals') have the gift of reason ; little more so, in fact, than that plants have." It is always the habit with those who advocate the theory that animals are gifted with reasoning powers, to bring forward an array of anecdotes, of apparent departure from the general line of conduct observed in animals, and asks, "*Are not these* the result of reasoning?" But the question I would now ask is, "*Are they* the result of reasoning?" Amongst the foremost of the cloud of witnesses brought up by our opponents, we find our Canine friends, numerous members of the order Quadrumana, and certain species of birds.

Dogs are said to have "affection for their masters," are very "apt in learning tricks," are "intimately acquainted with the ways of the household," &c., and, *therefore*, are possessed of reason. The mistake into which "C." seems to have fallen results from his giving an imperfect, or at least a too extended meaning to the term reason. If, as he says, the definition of reason is "the power of combining the intellectual faculties towards the attainment of the object in view," but *stops there*, then I grant that we may with some degree of reason give that power to animals. But then there would be no difference between instinct and reason, as the same definition might be given of instinct. I consider reason is "the faculty of the mind by which we draw certain conclusions from certain foregoing premises, by which we determine right and truth, by which we regulate our conduct, and obtain a correct and just view of things." Now, while it is possible for animals to possess the power contained in the first clause of this definition, I deny the possibility of their fulfilling the other three. The position I take is, then, that man alone of all the creatures that God has made upon earth, is endowed with the faculty of reason. The affection of a dog for its master, as well as its aptitude for learning tricks, and even its thorough acquaintance with the ways of the household, may all be attributed to the instinct or sagacity of the animal. They are all things which appeal to the *senses* of the animals, and this appeal to the senses forms the chief characteristic of instinct. Reason is a faculty by which we can produce abstract ideas, or ideas formed in the mind without the intervention of the sensitive medium. Most of the anecdotes related of animals are exceptional cases, in which their instinct is more largely developed, and therefore cannot be related of the whole animal creation. The question is, I presume, whether reason is, or is not, possessed by *animals*. Not whether it is, or is not, possessed by "dogs" or "monkeys." If it is possessed by animals at all, why not by *all* animals? Your correspondent, "C.," "cannot see why we should object to use the term reason with reference to dogs." Well, he may call it reason if he likes, the fact will not make it reason. We shall be only led to ask him "What's in a name." It is vain to talk of gradation in reason; it is nowhere seen in man. One man *displays* more reason than another, because, by a more active use of the faculty, his reason is more highly developed; not because the Creator has been more munificent to the one than to the other. An infant possesses the faculty, as much as the sire of forty; but we cannot perceive it, because it is waiting the fuller development of other faculties which alone can bring the reason into a state of activity. But where do we find the development of reason in animals or birds? As soon as the nestling has attained sufficient power of body to leave its nest it flies away, to seek its own food, to build its own nest, and fulfil its own part in the world of nature; but all without apparent motive whatever. It seeks no knowledge, it strives not to attain a more elevated sphere in life, it interferes not with the proceedings of commerce, science, or government; in one word it possesses no adaptation of means to an end, other than that which is inherent in its nature, and which is attributable to its instinct. The same may be said of animals. The innocent kitten which gambols at our feet, displays no evidence of mental growth. In its acts of petty dishonesty, it shrinks not from the disciplinary measures of law or justice. Its only object in life seems to be a disposition to provide for its own sustenance. It grows older in years, but gains nothing by its experience, and all we can say of it at last, is, "It has grown from a kitten into a cat." Mere anecdotes of extraordinary deeds and actions of animals are far from sufficient to prove the question at issue. All parrots cannot talk, all dogs and horses are not "affectionate," or "apt in learning tricks." Surely if one animal possesses reason, all other animals of the same species possess it too. An anecdote, if anecdotes stand for anything, is related of a gentleman who possessed a monkey, and who was in the habit of taking his glass of *eau-de-vie* after dinner. One day, after taking his usual draught, he replaced the bottle and left the room. The monkey, who had been quietly watching him, stealthily approached the cupboard, took the first bottle that came to hand, and commenced swallowing its contents at a rapid rate; but unfortunately for the animal's *reason*, as well as for the animal itself, it had neglected to examine the bottle, which, by way of caution to reasoning beings, was labelled "poison;" consequently it fell a victim to its own curiosity. Again "R. B. W." rightly observes, "if reason is possessed by animals, why not by plants?" Nay! some species of plants display as much instinct as animals, an instance of which "R. B. W." was kind enough to furnish, in the vine. Look also at the sensitive plant, and the plant familiarly known in America (but whose scientific name I cannot just now call to mind) as the fly-trap, and many others. Lastly, if animals are possessed of reason, in what are they inferior to man? Man is possessed of a soul; Reason is a faculty of the soul. Are animals possessed of a soul? Are they immortal? Reason is not dependent upon the brain, or any other part of the body, for if so it would decay with the body. Instinct is a faculty of the body. *It* depends upon the body for its activity, and ceases when the body dies. Reason is the faculty by which we penetrate the unseen, and draw those thoughts of future happiness, which make this life a seeming paradise. It is the faculty, which enables the philosopher to discover the various component parts which form the vast machinery of the universe. The faculty which carries the astronomer to "worlds unknown," and tells him of suns, stars, and planets, compared with which our earth is but an atom. It is, in fact, the faculty which lifts us above the brute creation, and which constitutes the divine element in our natures.

"And is this all! can reason do no more,
Than bid me shun the deep, or quit the shore;
Fair moralists, afloat on life's rough sea,
The Christian has an art unknown to Thee."

W. NEWBERRY.

THE EXTINCTION OF SPECIES IN OUR LEPIDOPTERA.—I do not think that very much attention has been given to this subject until lately; in fact, not until the last few years, when the circumstance that some of our important species have disappeared, and are now disappearing, brought it forth. Let us trace first the extinction of a few of the most beautiful and prized of our British Rhopalocera since the beginning of this century. Papilio Podalircus was probably found in the fens of Cambridgeshire and of Huntingdonshire at the end of last century, and the beginning of this; but that has become quite extinct. Its near relative (Papilio Machaon) will also, it is to be feared, soon become a creature of the past; for this year (1868) although in many cases a favourable season for insects, has produced both very few imagos and very few larvæ and chrysalides of this species: it has too not been so abundant as it was formerly for several years. Chrysophanus Dispar is another and a celebrated example of the "death of a species;" it was once so abundant in the eastern fen counties that in one case sixteen were taken in half-an-hour in Huntingdonshire. And then again Chrysophanus Chryeis and perhaps also Chryophanus Virgaurve have entirely gone; all these species having become extinct through the draining and the cultivating of the fens which they formerly inhabited, and by the attacks of collectors and dealers upon them. In many cases the disappearance of a species is due to these overpowering attacks which are made not only by their natural enemies, but also by entomologists, upon them; for many collectors are ready to "lay siege to" an insect in the localities where it is well known, but neither energetic nor quick in finding out new localities; thus if a species disappears from *the* place where it was formerly abundant, it is set down as extinct at once—very often without any further investigation. This is the case with Erebia Ligea, and perhaps also with Erebia Hero, both of which—certainly the first—were formerly taken in the Scottish island of Arrand; but it seems are now no longer found there. This being the case, collectors do not think of looking in the neighbouring islands for them, but quietly let the matter rest; the blame here, however, is more to be attributed to the entomologists of the North of England and Scotland, who, by the bye, are usually not so energetic as their southern brethren; but similar instances may be found also in the latter, of this want of activity concerning certain species. When an insect is lost in one locality it may only have shifted its quarters, and may be found in a similar place in the same or in a neighbouring county or island. Thus because Agrophila Sulphuralis has disappeared from Brandon, in Suffolk, where it was discovered by Mr. Dunning several years ago, and for three successive years was taken very abundantly, it may still be existing in other localities in Suffolk or in Norfolk, or in some other county. Even the southern part of England is not all thoroughly explored, but the part that is properly worked, is to a certain extent limited to Sussex, Surrey, Kent, Hampshire, and the Isle of Wight. But Devonshire and Cornwall are not so productive for want of being properly explored. Almost every entomologist must have noticed the comparative fewness of important captures in Wales and in the West of England. Although last season (1868) there have been several insects worthy of note taken in parts of the southern and in the south-eastern portion of Great Britain, there have hardly been any caught in the yet almost entomologically unexplored regions of the west. No doubt if these places were properly searched, we should both find new localities for our regular species, and also some that are now extinct would again be found. We should not give up a good locality entirely if it does not produce for a few years, because it may again prove productive. Of course we cannot expect that we shall find many of the few species that have disappeared except in marshy ground that has not been cultivated; but still I think that by thoroughly searching Great Britain and Ireland (which latter country is almost proverbially said to be neglected) more species would be found; and also if the time of year that foreign insects appeared in was noticed more particularly, and that the same or nearly allied species were looked for in England in the same kind of places that they inhabit in their native country, and in the same time of year as recommended by Mr. Stainton in his "Manual," at page 31; and also if "larva breeding and larva rearing" were more extensively practised than they are now, that it would be of great service in the detection of new species to the English insect fancier. Perhaps if all these ideas were more fully carried out than they have been, we should not have to complain so much of "the extinction of species in our British Lepidoptera." I have given these ideas in a comparatively crude form, hoping that the subject will meet with further investigation; and I shall be very much obliged if any other naturalist will communicate his ideas upon the subject to the NATURALIST'S NOTE BOOK, not only in connection with entomology, but also in other branches of zoology.

ERNEST BELFORT BAX.

GOLDFINCHES.—In reply to the enquiry of your correspondent "H. F. P." as to the best kind of food for goldfinches I would inform him that experience has taught me that the best general food is a mixture of bruised hemp, flax, and canary seeds, added to which I give my birds daily a little maw seed, and watercresses twice or thrice weekly, varying this last named food with groundsel, &c., occasionally. Fresh caught birds require a larger proportion of hemp and maw seeds, also a few thistle heads daily, and if obtainable a teazle head now and then is beneficial. In cases of atrophy or wasting away (very prevalent with fresh-caught birds before they become accustomed to the change of food in confinement) I have found a plentiful supply of watercresses restore them to health. I have at the present time a goldfinch caught in August last, now in full song, but which at one time sickened, crouched in the corner of its cage, and was wasting. I gave it a plentiful supply of watercresses and it recovered. Bechstein relates an instance of a siskin, apparently dying from wasting, but which speedily recovered its song, by being fed only upon watercresses.

MALDON.   RICHARD POOLE.

Your correspondent, "H. F. P." is desirous of knowing what is the best food for goldfinches; and for his information, I extract a few lines from "Cage and Singing Birds," by H. G. Adams. Speaking of goldfinches, he says:—"The full-grown birds may be fed on canary, rape, poppy, and other seeds; some hemp seed may be given when the birds are breeding, and green food occasionally at all times. Lettuce or cabbage leaves, groundsel, and watercresses, are most relished by them." I have kept goldfinches myself, and have always fed them on canary and rape seed, mixed with a little hemp seed, but never found the latter seed suit them so well as either canary or rape. H. G. Adams also says that "if allowed to indulge too freely in hemp seed, stupor and giddiness is sometimes the result; a diet of soaked lettuce and thistle seed will generally remove this. An occasional supply of the latter food will always contribute to the health of this bird, which in old age becomes blind, and loses the bright red and yellow colours of its plumage." Their fondness for the thistle seed in a wild state is well known, and wherever thistles are plentiful, flocks of these pretty species of the finch tribe may be seen assembling in the autumn season. I have found them rather difficult to keep alive in confinement; and I hope that "H. F. P." will have better success with his pet goldfinches than I have had with mine.

A. E. BUTTEMER.

I think "H. F. P." will find no better food for goldfinches than a mixture of canary, rape, and hemp or poppy seeds, favouring them occasionally with a little groundsel.   O. R.

In answer to the query of "H. F. P." as to what is the best food for goldfinches, will you allow me to quote for his information what Bechstein says on the subject:—"They (goldfinches) feed upon all kinds of seeds — groundsel, succory, salad, cabbage, rape, canary, thistle and alder seed; also linseed, dodder grass, &c. In the cage it must be fed upon poppy seed and hemp seed, the first being given as its usual food. He may also have given to him all sorts of green things, such as salad, cabbage lettuce, and watercresses. It contributes much to their health if occasionally supplied with the head of the thistle."

Hampstead.   J. R. ELDRIDGE.

The best food for the goldfinch is canary and hemp seed (mixed), occasionally a lump of sugar as a treat, and *daily* a fresh piece of groundsel will be greatly relished. Fresh water every day, when the cage is cleaned, and for the bottom of the cage, scrape up *some grit from a road*; it will be far better than the usual sand sold for the purpose: it is rougher, and the birds thrive best with it. The person who gives this advice has kept one goldfinch for eleven years.

Freshwater, Isle of Wight.   S. E. P.

"H. F. P." will find the best food for goldfinches to consist of canary and rape seed (mixed). About two or three times a week a few hemp seeds may be given. Green food, sand, and water for drinking and bathing are of course essentials.   C. B. R.

Can any of your readers suggest a remedy for a rather remarkable disease in a caged goldfinch. For some time the poor little bird has been suffering very much, apparently from the growth of the lower mandible. It advances at least a quarter of an inch beyond the upper. The bird is unable to break his seed, and appears to bolt it uncracked. The unnatural growth of the bill has fallen off several times, but begins growing again almost directly. Would it injure the bird to cut the end of the bill when it has attained such an extreme growth? Since this disease has attacked it the goldfinch has entirely left off singing.   A. M. MORRIS.

Charmouth, Dorset.

COLOURS OF DRAGON FLIES.—In answer to E. H. Welland (in the NOTE BOOK for September), I do not believe there is any way of preserving the colours of dragon flies without removing the contents of the abdomen. Not only are the colours lost, but the abdomen shrinks and loses its shape, and crumbles away at the slightest touch after the insects have been kept some time. Gutting a dragon fly by opening the abdomen is a troublesome process, particularly in the smaller ones. I have adopted a plan lately which I believe will prove just as effectual, and which is very simple and expeditious. Perhaps a description may be useful to E. H. Walland. As soon as possible after the insect is killed, cut off with a sharp pair of scissors the abdomen close to its junction with the thorax; place it on a smooth surface, and roll a round lead pencil (or other smooth round body) along the abdomen from the canal extremity to the opening, applying some pressure in doing so. This will squeeze out the whole of the contents, and leave nothing but the chitinous integument in which the colour resides: pass a smooth dried stem of grass, or a reed of suitable size (I always use the reeds out of Trichinopoly cheroots, which are admirably suited to the purpose) into the empty skin, as far as the extremity, and cutting the other end to a proper length, pass it into the thorax. The reed should be of a size to fit the abdomen tightly, and be so far dried as not to shrink afterwards; it should also be sufficiently fibrous and elastic to hold the pin which is passed through it and the thorax. The junction of the parts of the insect can with care be made very neatly; the shape of the insect is thus preserved, and it is not liable to break when dry. I believe that it will preserve the colours, though I have not tried it sufficiently long to answer for it. If the abdomen, instead of being cylindrical in shape, is flattened, a piece of card should be cut of proper size and shape, and used instead of the reed. I should be much obliged if any of your readers who are acquainted with Oriental Lepidoptera, or have access to books on the subject, would give me a little information about Genus Callidryas in general, and the distinctive colour and markings, as well as the sexual distinctions, of the following species in particular: C. Philippina, C. Pyranthe, C. Hilaria, C. Alcmeone, and C. Thisorella.   Q. M. G.

Colombo, Ceylon, Oct. 18.

COMETS AND METEORS.—"R. T." writing on the similarity between the origin of comets and meteors, says:—"Now if this be correcct, we must take it for granted either that comets are solid bodies and that meteors are fragments detached from them in some way or other; or else that comets consist of streams of meteors." Now if every class of meteors consisted of solid bodies, with every meteoric display we should of necessity have a shower of meteoric stones; yet this phenomenon only takes place with what we may term irregular meteors. I have never heard of an instance of a fall of stones taking place with the periodic meteors of August and November. The hypothesis generally received amongst astronomers to account for the periodic meteors is, that they are caused by the earth's approach to two zones or belts of meteoric bodies, which revolve round the sun in elleptical or bits, interior to that of the earth, having their aphilions near that portion of the earth's path which she traverses about the 10th August and 14th November. As regards irregular meteors, it does not always happen that they are followed by a fall of stones; but many instances are on record of such a phenomenon taking place. Dr. Dick, in his "Celestial Scenery," says:—"On the supposition that the bursting of a large planet was the origin of the asteroids, we may trace a source whence meteoric stones probably originate." This opinion appears to have been first broached by Sir David Brewster, and is stated in volume 2 of his edition of "Ferguson's Astronomy." I therefore think it highly probable that the periodic meteors may have some connection with comets; but I think we must look to some other source for the origin of the other class. Sir David Brewster's hypothesis is perhaps the most plausible that has yet been advanced, although it is not alto

gether unattended with difficulties; and I fear we shall have to await the advance of astronomical science and the increase of attentive observers of this phenomenon, for the solution of the problem.
SIDUS.

STING OF NETTLES.—I must again trouble you with a few lines on this subject, in consequence of some remarks from "R. T." which appeared in the December number of the NOTE BOOK. If "R. T." will kindly refer to "Bentley's Manual of Botany," pp. 51 and 52, he will there find the theory I endeavoured to explain fully demonstrated; and I believe the author of that work to be no mean authority. Before writing my last, however, I tried a few experiments, such as I then mentioned, in the presence of some friends, to see whether the aforesaid theory would be borne out in practice, and I certainly think that it was, and can only explain the discrepancy in our accounts by supposing the nettles which "R. T." tried to be of a more vindictive nature, and that or else "R. T." having the misfortune to possess an extremely thin epidermis, must account for his being so "stung." I have now before me some strong, healthy nettles; I took hold of the leaf of one of these firmly between the finger and thumb, and, as I expected, felt none the worse. With dire misgivings I then proceeded to draw it lightly across the open palm of my other hand; need I tell the result to your scientific readers? Scarcely; but for the information of others I will say that I found the dock leaves, which "R. T." with kind forethought, bade me have in readiness, both useful and beneficial; and that it caused me to resolve for the future to leave practical experiments on the sting of nettles to others. In conclusion, I do not wish to be misunderstood. I have no intention of casting the least reflection on the statement of "R. T." but would venture to suggest that his remarks are the result of particularly imperfect observation. O. R.

NEPTUNE.—"R. B. W." seems to doubt that the planet Neptune receives heat and light from the sun, and he says that the latter appears to Neptune no larger than a fixed star. Perhaps, after reading the following extract from "Breen's Planetary Worlds," he will change his opinions on this subject:—"At three hundred times the distance which the sun is from us, or at ten times the distance of Neptune, it has been calculated that the sun is only as bright as the moon is to us. At 20,000 times that distance, the brilliancy of the sun is only equal to that of Venus; and at 250,000 times it sinks to the brilliancy of Sirius." If this be correct, it appears that Neptune receives from the sun at least ten times the amount of light which we receive from the full moon; and we may reasonably conclude that it also receives a considerable degree of heat. It may also be seen that Neptune would have to be removed about 8000 times its present distance from the sun, in order for the latter to appear only as bright as the brighest of the fixed stars. Whether or not we receive any degree of heat from the fixed stars, is a different question, and one not readily decided. It is, however, certain that we receive light from them, and there seems no reason to think it impossible, or even improbable, that a very slight amount of heat may be transmitted to us from the fixed stars. R. T.

KILLED BY A METEOR.—The article under the above heading, which appears in this month's NOTE BOOK, is likely to mislead those who are not versed in meteorology. For, although the term meteor in strict phraseology may be applied to any phenomenon or disturbance occurring in our atmosphere (things in the air), yet in common parlance it is only used to designate those appearances variously called shooting stars, bolides, ærolites, &c., to which class of objects the phenomenon in question did not belong. The man on board the Urania was in fact killed by lightning, of the kind called by Arago globe lightning. This kind, which is much more rare than either forked or sheet lightning, usually appears as a globe of fire, moving at a comparatively slow rate, and appearing to be influenced by the wind, and by objects lying near its path. No satisfactory explanation has been given of it, but it is probably analogous to the globe of fire from the extremity of an insulated conductor, by which Professor Richman, at Petersburg, was struck dead, while making experiments during a thunderstorm. Luminous globes are also frequently seen during volcanic eruptions. Sir William Hamilton observed them in an eruption of Vesuvius. Have they been observed during the late outbreak of that volcano?
GULIELMUS.

UNUSUAL PLACE OF GROWTH OF A SPECIES OF CORAL.—The coral *Eschara Foliaceæ* is of an intertwisted or foliated form, and sometimes acquires so large a bulk as in its convolutions to measure several feet in compass; in which case it can be supported only by some stone or firm foundation. It occurs for the most part in rather deep water, from which it is not unfrequently drawn up by having become entangled with the line of a fisherman. But in its early condition the animal germ floats at liberty; and in some instances it has been known to have fixed its permanent station above the ground on a substance little capable of sustaining any considerable bulk or weight. Thus in one instance an example was brought to me that had fixed its seat on a branch of another species of coral, *Gorgonia Verrucosa*, called by fishermen the Sea Fern, to which it had become attached by throwing what may be termed its root about it in two places, a few inches above that expanded portion by which the *Gorgonia* is supported on its station. In another instance, more strangely still, the *Eschara* was found growing on the stalk of a common fucus or seaweed. VIDEO.

GASLIGHT.—Can any of your readers reconcile the statements made by the late celebrated Dr. Combe and the author of the "Reason why" series, with regard to the merits of *coal gas* now so universally used? The former declares that "a single gas-burner will consume and produce more carbonic acid to deteriorate the atmosphere of a room than six or eight candles." In one of the latter recently published volumes we read:—"Assuming all the lights to be of the same intensity, the degree in which the substances burnt would vitiate the atmosphere may be gathered from the number of minutes each would take to exhaust a given quantity. This has been found to be:—Rape oil 71 minutes; olive oil 72; common tallow 76; sperm oil 76; wax candles 79; spermaceti candles 83; common coal gas 98. Thus it is shown that rape oil is the *most destructive* to the atmosphere, and that coal gas is the *least destructive*." The opinions of your learned correspondents on this subject would much oblige R. B. W.

HAIR OFF DOGS.—A correspondent wishes to know of a remedy to prevent the hair coming off dogs. The following is one which I have recommended to several friends, and have never known it to fail:—As an outward application, he should use a mixture of black sulphur and train oil, and dress the parts with this night and morning; at the same time he should mix with its food twice a day, six drops of Fowler's solution of arsenic, increasing the quantity with caution until the whites of the eyes begin to present a bloodshot appearance, which generally takes place in about a fortnight. He should then leave off, but repeat the treatment after a short interval if necessary.
O. R.

PROLIFIC SOW.—"A. M. B.'s" account in the December number of the NOTE BOOK about that prolific sow a friend of his possessed, is certainly the most extraordinary instance of fecundity in that animal I ever heard of! Her litters far outnumbered even those produced by the celebrated sow the Rev. Gilbert White mentions (vide "Natural History of Selborne," letter lxxv.) which belonged to a neighbour of his, and was killed in about her seventeenth year, when "at a moderate computation she was allowed to have been the fruitful parent of three hundred pigs—a prodigious instance of fecundity in so large a quadruped!" A. E. BUTTEMER.

SNAKES.—On page 281 (vol. 2) of the NOTE BOOK, Mr. C. W. gives it as his opinion that the "blind snake" brings forth its young alive. I have discovered eggs in these creatures on dissecting them, but never young. They may be like the viper *ovoviviporous*, that is, hatch their eggs in their own bodies. In "Wesley's Philosophy," the absurdity of supposing the viper to swallow its young in order to protect them from danger, is proved by the fact that the stomach in all the true serpents reaches to the throat, so that immediately anything is swallowed it is in process of being decomposed. R. B. W.

HARD AND SOFT WATER.—In answer to my former query relating to this subject, Mr. Blunt, on page 54, vol. ii., says, "probably some of the salts contained in ordinary spring water (those, for instance, of lime and soda) are necessary either to the building up of the body or the maintaining it in health." Now I am quite ready to agree with him; but can he or any other of your readers tell me what authority *Miss Nightingale* had for saying that "hard water is a promoter of drunkenness, uncleanliness, and indigestion?" R. B. W.

BOTTLE AND SEA WATER.—This is an extract from a small work on chemical experiments:—"Cork an empty glass bottle very tight, and seal it; then lower it (with a leaden weight attached) a very great depth into the sea, and draw it up quickly, it will become filled with water; the cork and seal both remaining uninjured. No satisfactory explanation has yet been given of this truly astonishing phenomenon." Is it not probable that the pressure of the water upon the bottle breaks or cracks it, so that the water may get in? R. B. W.

WATER-WAGTAIL UNDER BLACKFRIARS' BRIDGE.—On Saturday, the 14th November, when proceeding on a steamboat from Westminster to London Bridge, I was astonished to see on the floating piles underneath Blackfriars' Bridge, a yellow water-wagtail, busily engaged in running up and down the pieces of wood after the usual manner of these birds. It was a cold and raw day, so I conclude the bird had probably been driven there by the severity of the weather.
J. L. VINCENT.

PROTECTION OF SEA FOWL.—An association has at length been formed for the protection of our rock-breeding sea fowl, and some extraordinary statistics published of the annual massacre at Bridlington, Flamborough, and elsewhere. Naturalists desirous of joining, should write to the Rev. H. F. Barnes, The Vicarage, Bridlington. A subscription of five shillings or upwards constitutes membership.
A CONSTANT READER.

MILD CHRISTMAS.—On Saturday last I gathered a cowslip in bloom in the open hedgerow. Owing to the extreme mildness of the present season, many of the spring flowers are to be found; but the cowslip generally blooms only in the latest days of spring, verging upon summer. A. M. MORRIS.
Charmouth, Dorset.

LATE SWALLOWS.—I have several times lately seen a swallow flying about. The last time I saw it was on Saturday, November 14th. I believe, or as Mrs. Brown would say, "have heard tell" that swallows are often seen here nearly as late in the year. Have they been left behind, or are they some of Klein's hybernating swallows? TORTOISE.
Brighton.

WHITE SPARROW.—A pure white sparrow was observed near here last month. Can any of your correspondents tell me if they are common, and what is the reason of their differing so much in colour from the common house sparrow? L. H. M.
Uxbridge.

SWALLOWS.—Can any of your correspondents in localities round London, kindly inform me what was the latest date on which they observed any swallows this season, before their final departure?
Hampstead. J. R. ELDRIDGE.

SISKIN AND MEALY REDPOLE.—Can any of your readers tell me how the females of the above birds differ from the males in plumage? C. B. R.

ILLUSTRATION.

We this month give an illustration from Louis Figuier's "Vegetable World," representing the solitary grandeur of the scenery in South America.

SILKWORMS:

AND HOW TO REAR THEM SUCCESSFULLY.

PART I.

UNDER this head it is my intention to speak more particularly of the *Bombyx Mori*, or Mulberry Silkworm, which still maintains superiority, although of late years other varieties have been introduced; and those most likely to be useful are the *Yama-mai*, or Oak-leaf Worm, and the *Bombyx Cynthia* or *Ailanthus* sorts. I have for some years studied sericulture, both in the South of Europe and England. I can see no reason why silk should not be produced in this country, and with profit too. It may be some time before great quantities of silkworms can be reared, as there are in this country but very few mulberry leaves to feed them on, and it is necessary to begin by planting proper sorts of mulberry trees best adapted for the English climate. I am growing a very excellent variety from Piedmont, introduced by Moretti. This is very hardy, and produces fine leaves on which to feed the worms. I generally obtain seed from Italy as soon as ripe, and sow it immediately; thus I have every year a young stock of plants or seedlings. It requires, however, a certain method to grow them fine: but of this at some future time.

The production of silk I believe sooner or later will become an important profitable industry in this country, but persons must give up feeding silkworms on the leaves of the black mulberry (which is grown for the fruit), lettuce, and other substitutes. Such may be all very well for the amateur's amusement, but to rear silkworms successfully and profitably should be the aim in view.

What is the silkworm?—A variety of caterpillar whose natural food is mulberry leaves, whose natural state of existence is in the open air on the trees themselves.

How is it to be reared in an artificial state?—By adhering to nature as much as possible in the treatment.

Mulberry silkworms' eggs are about the size of a pin's head, more or less, according to the breed. The insect on emerging from the egg is of a dark colour, perhaps derived from its being covered with hairs, for on growing larger it becomes of a creamy white; sometimes with certain spots or dark stripes. Some worms there are naturally dark.

Silkworms have four states of existence, viz., the egg, the larva, the cocoon containing the chrysalis, the moth. In the larva state is the feeding time, and four changes of the skin at intervals of about seven days, preceded by a sleep or torpor of about two days' duration, during which the insect eats nothing. The silkworm has eighteen breathing holes, arranged nine on each side of its body; hence how important must air be to its well-being. Silkworms after spinning their cocoons again shed their skins therein, hidden from human eye, and then the chrysalis state begins. From commencing to spin, the insect never eats again. From the chrysalis and cocoon, which are generally complete in eight or nine days, fifteen or twenty more and out comes the moth, pushing through the silk and spoiling it for reeling. Now the male and female pair. Eggs are then laid, and the moths in a few days die.

Many successful experiments at silkworm rearing in England have been reported at different times, but I believe it is very difficult to produce good eggs in this country without degenerating; but they can be imported yearly from more favoured climes, as is done at the present day by the French and Italians.

The most useful of the mulberry silkworms are those called Common Worms, producing white or yellow silk, especially those cultivated between Turin and Genoa. Very large worms are reared in various districts of Italy, known as Macedonian, and these are several days longer lived, producing more silk, but which is not so fine. There are worms having only three sleeps or change of skins. These are smaller than the common, and give less silk, which is however very fine. They are shorter lived, and eat less food. The smallness of the cocoons, however, is against this variety. The *Trevoltini*, or worms producing three crops in one summer—or at least in Italy, though in England I find it impossible to have more than two crops; and I think it desirable in this country to limit the first to production of eggs for the second crop, to come on in the hottest of the weather, when the mulberry leaves would be more plentiful and good. I do not, however, recommend these worms rather than the before-named. Japanese worms have been introduced into Europe, and and are now much cultivated. They give yellow, white, and green silk. They are small, but very free from disease, and their silk is fine and excellent.

Silkworms are cold-blooded. Their functions are increased by heat and retarded by cold. They gain maturity sooner or later according to the temperature. Before changing their skins, silkworms spin under their feet on the leaves or other things fine webs; and posted thereon, their old skins remain adhering thereto, while the insects walk out of them. While the insect is in this state and shooting its skin a certain humour may be seen as it were exuding from its body between the old and new skins. The worm remains inactive, with its head stationed upward, as it were asleep, or in a torpid state previously to shooting the skin; and during this state it is important not to disturb it. Silkworms mostly have four changes of skins, at intervals of about eight days, growing rapidly after each. After the last change maturity is attained in about ten days, when further food is not required, and the insects commence spinning their cocoons in materials provided for the purpose. The silken balls are finished in from four to six days, and the insects change to the chrysalis state by the eighth, when they are fit to collect for reeling. I think the most congenial temperature for silkworms to do well is about 70° Fah., when supplied by artificial means; but when the natural degree of heat is more it is all the better, if not exceeding 80°, provided plenty of air be admitted to the rearing-room, which indeed must never be entirely excluded. Cold to an extent is not prejudicial, beyond prolonging the life of silkworms, unless at spinning time, and at the changes of skins. Worms cannot spin readily with the temperature below 70°, or 65° at least. Dry warm weather is the most suitable for silkworms. Cold and wet must be counteracted by keeping fires. Smoke is a fatal enemy; as are mice, pigeons, chickens, which would devour them; and flies should be caught, for they are tormentors. The success of silkworm rearing much depends on cleanliness, proper ventilation, and good food administered regularly. Silkworms' eggs have been known to receive no harm from severe frost. The worms themselves have been laid on ice and have survived the treatment.

After these few remarks I shall in my next explain silkworm-rearing more practically, bringing before my readers the daily treatment of the insects, and enumerate those articles and instruments of service, or essential to success.

LEONARD HARMAN, Junr.
Old Catton, Norwich.

COLOUR OF FLOWERS.

COLOUR is light modified by some property of a substance, the nature of which property we know but little.

Light complete and pure coming to the eye is intensely white, but it is weakened by various other tints blending with it, that we never see its full intensity; and well that it is so, as were it otherwise the result would be blindness. Chlorophyle, which causes the green colour of plants, is developed under the action of light, as I have proved by experiments. I placed some geraniums in a shaded place, and the result was that the leaves and stems, which were previously of a dark green, became almost white. Celery also affords a good illustration of the truth of this theory, as the earth is heaped over the young shoots in order that they may be blanched.

The red, yellow, and blue colours of flowers chiefly depend upon a fluid contained in cells, which can be separated from the cuticle. Nourse called this coloured cellular tissue thus lying below the epidermis the Rete. The colour of the leaf owes its origin to chlorophyle, which is a curious substance, granular in form, somewhat resembling wax. The colour of the petals is produced by the cells containing different colouring matters. Professor Balfour says, "by the juxta-position and mechanical mixture of various cells different tints are produced, and the colours are also modified by the nature of the cuticle through which they are seen." In the interior of petals the colour is generally more or less yellow, but it is modified when seen through superficial cells. Along with the colouring matter there is a colourless substance present, the relative quality of which varies, and hence the colour may be deeper or fainter. In flowers as well as leaves the colours depend upon the action of light. It has been said, however, that a powerful action of solar light in some cases tends to discolouring flowers. Hence tulips are screened from the direct rays of the sun.

The petals of some of our red, violet, and beautiful blue flowers if steeped in water give out their colour, but few of them give a blue colour to alcohol; some impart a red and others no colour whatever to that liquid. The juice of some red flowers expressed I have found to be of a blue colour, and it is supposed that the colouring matter in their petals is reddened by an acid, which escapes when the juice is exposed to the air. I have also found that blue and red flowers lose their colour in drying, becoming either a white or a dirty yellow; but I have dried them quickly, excluding air, and more of their colour has been retained. The juice expressed loses its colour very rapidly; hence the reason that, though the colours of flowers may be bright and beautiful, yet they are of no use for dyes. Thomson says, that if the petals of the red rose be triturated with a little water and carbonate of lime a blue liquor is obtained. Alkalies render this blue liquor green, and acids restores its red colour; which experiment I have myself tried, and found the result to be as stated.

The colouring matter in the petals of the blue hyacinth, red clover, tips of the common daisy, lavender, hollyhock, and violet, are found to be the same; and this matter also gives the colour to the petals of the scarlet geranium, and also to the leaves of the red cabbage, which if bruised and steeped in water a blue or violet solution is produced. The acid which causes the reddening is in all probability carbonic, which escapes into the atmosphere on rupturing the vessels containing it. Schubler, in the "Jour de Pharmacie," considers the red, orange, yellowish green colours of flowers to be owing to the absorption of oxygen; the bluish green, blue, violet blue, violet red, and red colours to be owing to disoxygenisement.

The only flower cultivated for the sake of the red colour obtained from its petals is the *Carthamus tinctorius*, or Safflower, grown in Egypt and countries bordering on the Mediterranean. The flowers contain two colouring matters, yellow and red; the last is considered to be an acid. After the yellow colouring matter has been dissolved in vinegar and water what remains is the red, which when properly prepared is a brilliant colour; but though beautiful it is fugitive, removed by washing and destroyed by the sun, and on that account is not of very great use in manufacture.

Red in the petals of many flowers is produced by colouring substances in so small quantities that it escapes on endeavouring to extract it. I have submitted the petals of red flowers to various degrees of pressure, but have generally found the juice extracted to be colourless; but some of the juices obtained from others have borne a crimson hue, and this has been changed to blue by an alkali, and yellow or red by an acid. An authority upon this subject mentions *Papaver rhœas*, the petals of which are a very lively red. These are changed to green by potash, but the carbonate of soda and ammonia, he says, does not alter it. The infusion of these petals in carbonate of soda or ammonia is red, but on the addition of potash it becomes green.

Yellow is a colour more durable in flowers than either blue or red, as will be clearly seen by drying. Yellow flowers give out their colour to both alcohol and water, and are not changed by either acid or alkali as regards the colour, with the exception that it is rendered paler by an acid and deeper by an alkali.

Caventon holds that the flowers of the *Narcissus pseudonarcissus* contain two yellow colouring matters.

If the flowers are digested in ether, we obtain by evaporation a yellow resin, giving out a smell similar to that of the flower, this resin being in a semi-liquid state, but hardens in drying. It is insoluble in water and alcohol, but dissolves in nitric and muriatic acids, and also in alkalies, producing solution of a yellow colour. If these petals previously digested in ether be steeped in alcohol another yellow colouring matter is dissolved, which remains after the evaporation of the alcohol. When in thin crusts it has a fine greenish yellow colour, but when in thick masses a brown. It dissolves readily in water, and when dry absorbs humidity from the atmosphere. It is rendered paler by acids, but brown by alkalies.

The plant so common and abundant upon walls and trees known to botanists as the *Lichen parietinus*, of Linnæus, has a fine yellow colouring matter, soluble in boiling alcohol; when cool the colouring matter crystallises in long brilliant plates.

Many of our British plants have produced yellow colouring matters such as are used as dyes, as dyers' broom, all our native heaths, three-leaved hellebore, and ash, and others we need not mention. Though the yellow colouring matters in the vegetable kingdom are more numerous than blue or red, they have been less studied by those interested in the subject; our knowledge is therefore limited.

The next colour, *green*, which is the paramount colour of the vegetable world, being a compound of yellow and blue, no vegetable product is known which can be used as a green dye. The colour is imparted to cloths by dyeing them first yellow and then blue. We have scarcely a plant bearing green flowers. The last colour is white. White flowers contain a colouring matter. The juice extracted from some white flowers is similar to that of many yellow flowers. Many of them strike green with alkalies, though do not change to red by acids.

GEORGE DAY.

36, Chapel-street, Pentonville.

THE GREAT POLISH SALT MINES.

A CORRESPONDENT, writing, from Cracow, says that the famous salt mine of Wieliczka, which brings a net annual revenue to the Austrian Government of upwards of £600,000, is threatened with total destruction by a stream of water which made its appearance on the 19th of last month, while the workmen were digging in one of the lower shafts in search of potash. All the means hitherto adopted of preventing the water from inundating the mine have been unsuccessful; it flows at the rate of 120 cubic feet a minute, and has already almost filled the lower passages, rapidly dissolving the salt with which it comes in contact. A Government engineer has arrived from Vienna, and a channel is being built under his directions for confining the water and leading it out of the mine; but it is feared that the salt columns which support the transverse shafts may be undermined before the work can be completed.

These salt mines, the most renowned in the world, are situated about eight miles from the city of Cracow, having their mouth or principal entrance in the pleasant village of Wielicksa, which lies on the slope of a wooded hill, and is very picturesque. The opening or square shaft through which the descent is made, is covered by a building or office; and here the visitor is dressed in a long, coarse linen blouse, to protect his clothing while underground. A door is opened, and he goes down by stairs, preceded by boys, who carry lamps only to make the darkness more visible. Or, if he is so disposed, he can descend by the windlass and ropes suspended in the centre of the shaft. More frequently visitors descend by the stairways and come up by the ropes.

No salt is seen for a depth of more than 200 feet; then the veins begin to appear in a bed of clay and limestone; 50 feet further down the stairs terminate, and the salt is everywhere; nothing but salt: overhead, under foot, on every side are dark grey masses of solid salt, whose points and surfaces sparkle in the lamp light. Galleries now branch off in all directions. Lights twinkle, and groups of labourers are seen hacking the floors, or removing in wheel-barrows blocks that have already been cut out. Passing on through one of these galleries, a chapel is reached, which is only the first and oldest of many apartments thus designated, differing only in size and decorations. It is called the chapel of St. Anthony, and is supported by columns of salt left in quarrying the solid rock. It has an altar, crucifix, statues of saints large as life, all of pure salt. The air in this part of the mines, near the surface, is much more moist than that of the deeper excavations, so that the process of dissolving goes on slowly, and in consequence some of these statues of salt are gradually losing their shape. The head of one is nearly gone, the limbs of another, while deeper furrows are observable in many places upon their bodies, making them present a very grotesque appearance when lighted up for exhibition. The smoke of the torches and lamps, added to the dampness of the air, blackens the surface of all objects not recently cut, so that these statues might be mistaken for black marble.

Onward and downward goes the visitor, through halls, chambers, tunnels innumerable. Stairs descend lower and lower, and similar apartments reappear, till he loses all sense of distance or direction; blindly following his conductors, who point out from time to time localities or objects of peculiar interest where all is surpassingly wonderful. Everything is solid salt, except where some insecure roof is supported by huge timbers, or a wooden bridge is thrown over some vast chasm, from which thousands of tons of salt have been quarried and removed. The air grows dryer and purer the deeper you go; the points and faces of the rock more crystalline and brilliant. One enormous hall, out of which has been cut a million hundredweight of salt, has the appearance of a theatre. It is over 100 feet high, and the blocks, taken out in regular layers, represent the seats for the spectators.

In another spacious vault stands two obelisks of salt, which commemorate the visit of the Emperor Francis I. and his Empress. Further on you come to a lake more than 20 feet deep, intensely salt, of course, which is crossed in a heavy square boat. In this you paddle through a tunnel which connects two immense halls. While in the middle of the tunnel the walls behind you and before you are brilliantly lighted up, and a gun is discharged which, with its echoes and reverberations, almost deafens you. Both air and water tremble visibly under the strange and frightful concussion, and you are only too thankful to reach the end of your voyage, and stand once more on solid salt.

Francis Joseph's ball-room is another of the wonders of this subterranean world. It is an immense apartment, both in height and extent, and on some festive occasions is used in dancing. It is lighted by six large chandeliers, which resemble cut glass, but are in reality of crystalline rock salt. Statues of Vulcan and Neptune, sculptured from salt, also adorn this hall, which, well illuminated, exhibits a marvellous splendour, the light being reflected from innumerable brilliant points and angles of the glittering rock.

Down, down, down hundreds of feet further, through labyrinths of shafts, galleries and chambers, crooked passages, vaulted archways, and openings which have no name and seemingly no end. Groups of miners, naked to the hips, are everywhere busy with the implements of their darksome labours; pick, mallet, and wedge are employed incessantly in blocking out and separating the solid mass. Their manner of work is the same simple process in use centuries ago, perhaps by the remotest ancestors of these very men, in these very mines, for they are immensely old. The blocks are marked out on the surface of the rock by grooves. One side is then deepened to the required thickness, and wedges being inserted under the block, it is soon split off. It is then divided into pieces of a hundred pounds each, and in this shape is ready for sale. It is removed in carts or barrows to the shaft, where it is hoisted up, stage after stage, to the surface. Horses and mules are employed, and it is said that some of these animals are born and raised in the mines.

The number of labourers constantly at work is from 1,000 to 2,000. They all live outside the excavations at the present day, although traditions exist of times when the families of some of the miners had their abodes in these fearful depths, and where children were born and reared to the occupation of their parents, seldom or never visiting the outside world. The thing is neither impossible nor incredible, as the air in the lowest part of the mines is considered more salubrious than in their upper regions. But the practice was long ago discontinued, if it ever existed to any extent.

The miners, who are fine muscular and healthy-looking men, are divided into gangs for work, and relieve each other every six hours. A gang will quarry in that time about 1,000lb. weight. The temperature is very even all the year round, and the preservative power of the air is such that wood never decays, but retains its qualities for centuries. People with pulmonary affections are said to have been much benefited by inhaling freely the atmosphere of the mines.

When and how this wonderful deposit of salt was originally discovered is unknown. It was worked in the twelfth century, and how much earlier none can tell.

The extent of the deposit has not yet been fully ascertained. It commences, as we have before stated, about 200 feet below the surface, and has a solid depth of nearly 700 feet, and rests on a bed of compact limestone, such as forms the peaks of the Carpathian Mountains, which it seems to follow. It has already been explored to the continuous length of 2½ miles ; and it is estimated that the aggregate length of all the innumerable excavations of these mines amounts to more than 400 miles.—*Mining Journal.*

LIST OF BRITISH BUTTERFLIES:

TIMES OF THEIR PERFECT APPEARANCE, AND NATURE OF THEIR FOOD.

PAPILIONIDÆ.

SWALLOW TAILED (*Papilo Macaon*). Feeds on carrot, celery, parsley, rue, wormwood, and particularly on cow-parsnip and hog's fennel. Flies early in May, and continues to emerge throughout the summer till the middle of August.

PIERIDÆ.

Wood White (*Leucophasia Luiapis*). Feeds on the tufted vetch (*Vicia cracca*), the bird's foot trefoil (*Lotus corniculatus*), the everlasting pea (*Lathyrus latifolius*), and the bitter vetch (*Orobus tuberosus*). There are two broods. The first flies in May and June, and the second in August.

Black Veined White (*Pieris Cratægi*). Feeds on the plum, blackthorn, whitethorn, and almost all fruit trees. Flies about the middle of June.

Great White Cabbage (*Pieris Brassicæ*). Feeds on all kinds of vegetable greens. There are two broods. The first flies in May, and the second in July.

Small White Cabbage (*Pieris Rapæ.*) Feeds on turnip, radish, and cabbage, and often abundantly on mignionette. There are two broods. The first flies in April, and the second in July.

Small White Cabbage (*Pieris Rapæ*). Feeds on turnip, and radish, especially when going to seed ; also on various kinds of cabbage, and greens cultivated in gardens. There are two broods. The first flies in April and May, the second in July and August.

Green Chequered White (*Pieris Daplidice*). Feeds on various species of radish, turnip, cabbage, and also on wild mignonette. There are two broods. The first flies in April and May, the second in July and August.

Orange Tip (*Anthocharis Cardamines*). Feeds on seed pods of various cruciferous plants, especially on those of the cuckoo flower and the hedge mustard. Flies in May.

RHODOCERIDÆ.

Brimstone (*Gonepteryx Rhamni*). Feeds on the buckthorn. Flies early in August, and continues on wing the whole year.

Clouded Yellow (*Colias Edusa*). Feeds on clover and lucerne when in full blossom. Flies in August, and continues in perfection throughout September.

Pale Clouded Yellow (*Colias Hyale*). Feeds on clover and trefoil. Flies in August.

ARGYNNIDÆ.

Silver Washed Fritillary (*Argynnis Paphia*). Feeds on the dog violet, and other shrubs. It appears about the middle of June, and flies throughout July.

Dark Green Fritillary (*Argynnis Aglaia*). Feeds on the leaves of the dog violet. Flies in July.

High Brown Fritillary (*Argynnis Adippe*). Feeds on the blossom of the blackberry. Flies in July.

Queen of Spain Fritillary (*Argynnis Lathonia*). Feeds on the leaves of the violet. Flies in this country in July and August. On the continent it appears in July, and continues flying till winter.

Pearl Bordered Fritillary (*Argynnis Euphrosyne*). Feeds on violet leaves, but most commonly on the dog violet. Flies in July.

Small Pearl Bordered Fritillary (*Argynnis Selene*). Feeds on the dog violet. Flies in June and July.

Greasy Fritillary (*Melitæa Artemis*). Feeds on the field scabious. Flies in June.

Glanville Fritillary (*Melitæa Cuixia*). Feeds on the narrow-leaved plantain. It appears in May, and flies till the middle of July.

Heath Fritillary (*Melitæa Athalia*). Feeds on common plantain and narrow-leaved plantain. Flies about the middle of June.

VANESSIDÆ.

Comma (*Vanessa C. Album*). Feeds on hop, elm, nettle, and currant; preferring the hop. Flies in September.

Tortoise-shell (*Vanessa Urticæ*). Feeds on common stinging-nettle. There are two broods. The first flies in June, the second at the end of August.

Large Tortoise-shell (*Vanessa Polychloros*). Feeds chiefly on the elm, but also on the cherry, pear, and sallow. Flies from the end of July to the end of August.

Camberwell Beauty (*Vanessa Antiopa*). Feeds on the young leaves of willow, aspen, and birch. Flies about the end of July or beginning of August.

Peacock (*Vanessa Io*). Feeds on common stinging-nettle. Flies in August.

Red Admiral (*Vanessa Atalanta*). Feeds on common stinging-nettle. Flies in July, and throughout August, September, and even October.

Painted Lady (*Vanessa Cardui*). Feeds on various kinds of thistle, on burdock less commonly, and sometimes in gardens on artichokes. Flies in July and August.

White Admiral (*Limenitis Sibylla*). Feeds on the leaves of the common honeysuckle. Flies during July.

NYMPHALIDÆ.

Purple Emperor (*Apatura Iris*). Feeds on the leaves of the sallow. Flies in July.

SATYRIDÆ.

Marbled White (*Arge Galathea*). Feeds on a variety of grasses. Flies in July.

Small Ringlet (*Erebia Cassiope*). Feeds on several grasses, as Poa annua, and Festuca ovina, and very probably on the leaves of young rushes. Flies about the middle of June.

Scotch Argus (*Erebia Blandina*). Feeds on grasses. Flies in July and August.

Speckled Wood (*Satyrus Ægeria*). Feeds on common wild wheat, or couch grass. Flies in April, June, and August.

Wall (*Satyrus Megæra*). Feeds on grasses. Flies in June and August.

Grayling (*Satyrus Semele*). Feeds on grasses found on heaths. Flies in July and August.

Meadow Brown (*Satyrus Janira*). Feeds on different species of grass. Flies about the middle of June.

Gatekeeper (*Satyrus Tithonus*). Feeds on common annual meadow grass. Flies in July.

Ringlet (*Satyrus Hyperanthus*). Feeds on various grasses, and on sorrel. Flies about the middle of June.

Marsh Ringlet (*Chortobius Davus*). Feeds on grasses. Flies in June.

Small Heath (*Chortobius Pamphilus*). Feeds on grasses. Flies throughout the summer.

LYCÆNIDÆ.

Green Hairstreak (*Thecla Rubi*). Feeds on the buds and flowers of the blackberry. Flies in May, June, July, and August.

Purple Hairstreak (*Thecla Quercus*). Feeds on the oak. Flies in July.

Black Hairstreak (*Thecla W. Album*). Feeds on the common elm. Flies in July.

Dark Hairstreak (*Thecla Pruni*). Feeds on blackthorn. Flies about July.

Brown Hairstreak (*Thecla Betulæ*). Feeds on the leaves of the blackthorn. Flies in August and September.

Large Copper (*Polyommatus Hippothæ*). Feeds on two or three species of dock. Flies in July and August.

The Copper (*Polyommatus Phlæas*). Feeds on sour dock or sorrel. Flies in June, July, and August.

Silver Studded Blue (*Lycæna Ægon*). Feeds on the common broom, on clover, and on trefoil. Flies in June and July.

Brown Argus (*Lycæna Agestis*). Feeds on common sun cistus. Flies in July and August.

Common Blue (*Lycæna Alexis*). Feeds on clover, bird's-foot trefoil, and several other plants of the same natural order. Flies throughout the summer.

Clifden Blue (*Lycæna Adonis*). Feeds on clover, bird's-foot trefoil, and other leguminous plants. Flies in May and August.

Chalkhill Blue (*Lycæna Corydon*). Feeds on the bird's-foot trefoil. Flies in July.

Mazarine Blue (*Lycæna Acis*). Feeds on the flowering heads of Armeria Vulgaris. Flies about the middle of June.

Small Blue (*Lycæna Alsus*). I am unable to state the plant that it feeds on. Flies about the middle of June.

Azure Blue (*Lycæna Argiolus*). Feeds on the

blossoms of the holly. Flies in May and August.

Large Blue (*Lycæna Arion*). Feeds on common thyme. Flies about July.

ERYCINIDÆ.

Duke of Burgundy (*Nemeobius Lucina*). Feeds on the leaves of the cowslip. Flies about June.

HESPERIDÆ.

Grizzle (*Syrichthus Alveolus*). Feeds on the leaves of the common silver weed, Potentilla anserina, and P. Alba. Flies in May.

Dingy Skipper (*Thanaos Tages*). Feeds on the bird's-foot trefoil. There are two broods. The first flies in May, and the second in August.

Chequered Skipper (*Hesperia Paniscus*). Feeds on common plantain. Flies in May.

Large Skipper (*Hesperia Sylvanus*). Feeds on the meadow soft grass, and other grasses. Flies in May.

Pearl Skipper (*Hesperia Comma*). Feeds on bird's-foot trefoil. Flies in August.

Small Skipper (*Hesperia Linea*). Feeds on grasses. Flies in May.

Lulworth Skipper (*Hesperia Actæon*). On the continent it feeds on Stipa capillata, a kind of grass not found in England. Flies in the month of August.

T. W. TEMPANY.

UNIVERSAL NATURE.

MAN may observe with pleasure the sun rising in the morning and enjoy its enlivening influence throughout the day; he may regard with interest the various phases of the moon, and be delighted with the sublime grandeur of the heavens on a bright and starlight night, without availing himself of the science of astronomy. He may feel pleasure in observing the swelling bud, and rejoice in the gradual expansion of the green leaf in the spring; he may be delighted with the profusion of blossom in the orchard, and the variety of flowery decorations in the hedgerow; he may partake of the fruit of the garden and enjoy its delicious flavour, without a thought or care for botany or horticulture. He may be charmed by the music of the birds, enchanted with the array of colours, and amused by the sportive movements of the insect tribes, without the study of ornithology or the tediousness of entomological investigations. All these objects and many others may arrest the attention of the superficial observer at various stages of his existence, but still the mind may remain unconscious and uninformed of their connection one with the other, or fail to observe in what manner one part of creation is made subservient to the well-being of the other, and at the same time contribute essentially to the great and glorious system of the universe.

By the philosopher universal nature has commonly been regarded as one continuous and unbroken chain, connected as it were by a series of links which, however diversified in their outward appearance, are each equally necessary to secure the harmony of the wondrous whole; or, in other words, it may be compared to an elaborate piece of mechanism composed of an infinite variety of curiously constructed parts, each of which is so nicely wrought and so wisely adjusted, that notwithstanding every part has its own peculiar functions to fulfil, yet so essential is the co-operation of each with the other to the uniform working of the whole, that the want or failure of the most apparently trivial appurtenance would in some measure destroy the efficiency of the whole stupendous machine. But notwithstanding this axiom is self-evident to the contemplative mind, and most generally admitted by those who have made the works of nature their especial study, yet the relation which the multitude of objects by which we are surrounded bear to each other is a matter which in many cases even in the present day is but imperfectly understood, and will require the united efforts of many elaborate investigations before the great and marvellous combination of nature's laws can become clearly and satisfactorily elucidated. True it is that the ingenuity of man has already done much to facilitate the study of nature. First, by dividing the most prominent and dissimilar objects from each other, and in giving to each division some definite form, created a bias by which the student is enabled more readily to select the class of objects to which he feels most strongly attached; and secondly, by suggesting that a mind chiefly employed in the investigation of one particular group of objects is likely to produce the most satisfactory results. The truth of the first proposition will, I think, be found in the Linnæan system, and the second will be as readily acknowledged in such works as "Kirby and Spence's Entomology," and is still further exemplified in "Huber's History of Bees." However, in bringing these remarks to a close I must observe that, notwithstanding these divisions and subdivisions have been judiciously adopted for the convenience of the student, it must be borne in mind that the objects selected and those rejected are each equally important, and will be found by patient investigation essential adjuncts in completing the great economy of nature. The objects by which we are surrounded are both innumerable and diversified, and each separate object if well worked out would doubtless comprise a history in itself that would in most cases be found useful, instructive, or amusing; and although I would not attempt to influence, and certainly not to dictate to, a fellow-creature in the choice of his labour or amusement, yet I will venture to add, that any individual who may be at a loss in filling up his leisure hours may feel assured that in the study of the works of creation will be found a rational, healthy, and delightful employment. And if none of the usual divisions in nature meet the taste, one of the following suggestions may serve as an agreeable substitute: namely, he may employ them in defining the limit of man's mind; or in drawing the exact line between instinct and reason; or in ascertaining the demarcation between the animal and vegetable kingdom; or amuse himself by pointing out with some precision the most useful and useless among the objects of nature; or, in fine, let him seek out one object in nature that stands alone, disconnected, and independent of every other object in the universe.

320, Strand.   C. W. J.

VEGETABLE FIBRES.

PHORMIUM TENAX.—This fibre is obtained from the vascular bundles of the plant so named, and well known in France for its ornamental character. Seen under the simple microscope, after slight bleaching, it first strikes us on account of the fineness and regularity of its filaments, which separate with great facility. Their length varies from 00·05m to 0·011m. With the compound microscope we see that the diameter of these fibres is of remarkable uniformity all through their length. The central canal is generally very large, and made visible by bright lines at the margins, indicating the thickness of the walls. The points always end alike. They gradually diminish and become circular.

Sections of the raw fibre are most closely allied to those of hemp. They form groups which might be confounded with those of the latter; and the central cavity, large and rounded, has the same appearance. The polygons do not, however appear in such close contact, and their angles are often rounded. When sections are made from a strongly-bleached specimen, the branches are almost always isolated; and in the group the component pieces are slightly separated. In Jute, on the contrary, when submitted to the same treatment, the groups remain entire, and it is rare to see an isolated section.

CHINA GRASS comes to us from China, in tissues known as China Grass Cloth, and made of the fibres of a nettle, *Urtica nivea*, or *Bœhmeria nivea*. This fibre, carefully bleached, divides easily with needles, the filaments separating without effort. This character differentiates it from hemp, the produce of another plant fo the nettle family, and which it somewhat resembles in form, but the fibres of which, when thoroughly bleached, preserve a considerable adhesion to each other. The former are also much larger than the latter; their mean length being double. We have found the length of china grass fibre vary from 0·05m. to 0·12m., whilst those of hemp rarely reach 0·06m.

China grass is, like hemp, often marked with furrows and salient sides. The surface is sometimes uniform, but more frequently garnished with very striking longitudinal canals and fine striæ. In parts near the edges fibrils may be noticed, which seem to detach themselves from the body of the cell. They proceed from the sides or furrows which have been torn, and portions of which still adhere to the surface. We observe, also, a character which this fibre possesses in common with that of flax, in the fissures oblique to the axis, and indicating a spiral disposition in the fibrils. We can also see, in certain very flattened portions, internal striæ, which seem to cross each other. This arrangement is like that in flax. The points are in general lanceolate and less irregular than those of hemp. They begin to thin out at a considerable distance from the termination, and, compared with the body of the filaments to which they belong, they are finer and more elongated than those of hemp.

Sections offer many resemblances to those of hemp. They exhibit themselves in groups when the fibre is raw; their shape is very irregular, with rounded margins; but the filaments are less matted together, and their contact less close. Generally flat and broad, they have some analogy with those of cotton when they are isolated.

COTTON is a hollow fibre, gradually tapering towards the point, which is usually blunt and rounded. It forms a kind of sack, open at one end and shut at the other, and with walls pressed together. Under the microscope the fibres or hairs appear completely isolated. They are flat and twisted. This arrangement, which has been long known, is characteristic of cotton. At the edges of the filaments we see bright lines separated by light shades, which give the appearance of a marginal cushion (*bourrelet*). They mark the thickness of the wall, which is usually very small in comparison with the internal cavity. We have not discovered any trace of fibrous structure in cotton. Its substance appears membraneous. It is often folded in an irregular manner, as might happen to a thin membrane exposed to pressure. The points are usually rounded.

Sections of cotton are perfectly characterized by their rounded outlines, and their elongated forms commonly folded over each other towards the extremities. They often resemble sections of a kidney (*rognon*). The central canal is represented by a black line, which follows the contour of the section. The sections are never in groups but always isolated.

Cotton is easily distinguished from other fibres employed in industry by the shape of its sections, and by the twisted appearance of the fibres seen lengthwise. These two characters enable it to be recognized in all mixtures.—*The Student and Intellectual Observer.*

ON THE BRITISH GEOMETRÆ.
By E. Clifford.
PART II.

THE closing sentences of our last paper referred to a very common moth, but the opening ones of the present will introduce to notice a very rare one. It is singular to observe how many doubtful species there are which have been reputed as really and truly British. As if to eke out the meagre list of our native butterflies, we often see a list of reputed British butterflies given, many of which probably never *did* breed up in our land, and all of which are not *now* naturalised amongst us. This remark applies to the moths as well as to the butterflies, for our list contains many which cannot properly be considered "Britishers." Some of these have been blown at times across the channel, or even introduced in the states of egg, larva, or pupa, but their existence in any number at any part of our islands is a thing not heard of; and thus, if they are talked or written about, naturalists should remember their foreign origin. Now the species next claiming notice amongst our geometers, seems a very doubtful native. We read that "three specimens of this conspicuous French insect have been blown across the channel;" and on this insufficient ground the species has been placed along with native insects of its own family. Its caterpillar has not been found feeding, excepting in Germany and France, where its food is alder, birch, beech, plum, apple, and apricot. We pass, therefore, to the consideration of those which are undoubtedly British.

The Canary-shouldered Thorn, (*Ennomos tiliaria*) is a very beautiful example of the family to which it belongs. Its wings are all slightly scalloped at the margins, and are orange-yellow, marked with minute short streaks of brown. The fore-wings have two very oblique dark lines, and between them is a short central mark of the same colour. The head and thorax are very hairy, and of a beautiful canary yellow; they at once serve to distinguish the species. The caterpillar seems to be unknown to most entomological writers, but there is a description translated from some foreign author in one of our standard works, in which it is said to be "wrinkled and brown, marbled with a darker colour, and possessing humps on the sixth and tenth segments." It feeds on birch and oak. June is the month for the caterpillar, and August for the perfect moth. On the twigs of the ash trees, those graceful vegetable ornaments of the country, we may search for the singular eggs of the Dusky Thorn (*Ennomos fuscantaria*). They are about square, with the angles round; and they are laid very close together. The young caterpillar upon first emerging, is of a dark green colour; but as it grows older, becomes lighter; and at its full size, is of a pale green with little signs of markings. It eats round holes in the ash leaves, and when full-grown suspends itself as a chrysalis within a curled-up leaf; this chrysalis is of a purplish tint just before the moth emerges. The Dusky Thorn is of a dull ochre in colour. This often becomes lead colour towards the hind margins, and the fore-wings have two very oblique transverse lines, gradually approaching one another. The hind-wings have scarcely any indication of marking. The head, thorax, and body, are brownish. This species has been taken at Boxhill, in Surrey. The September Thorn (*Ennomos erosaria*), as its name implies, flies during that month, and also in the previous one. It is partial to gas-lamps, and was formerly common near London, although it has disappeared within the last few years. It still occurs in many parts, however; more particularly in the New Forest, in Hampshire. The caterpillar of the September Thorn is clouded and marbled with brown, and has several humps upon the back, and also on the sides. It feeds on birch, oak, and other trees. The moth itself is variable in colouring, but generally of an ochreous yellow; and the wings possess some delicate transverse lines of darkish brown. The hind-wings are paler than the fore-wings, and have a very indistinct line of brown across the middle.

Another and very familiar species of the Thorn family, equally partial to gas-lights with others that have been noticed, is the August Thorn (*Ennomos angularia*). All the wings of this species are angulated, though not very acutely; they are very variable in colouring. Generally they are of an ochreous yellow, with numerous delicate and very short transverse lines of brown scattered over their surface. This is difficult to distinguish from the preceding species, but the caterpillars are described as decidedly different. The caterpillar of the present moth is red-grey, and is marbled with brown, having on the sixth and seventh segments three warts or humps, besides a large hump on the middle of the back. It feeds on oak, birch, and elm, in June; and the moth flies in August and September. The Feathered Thorn (*Himera pennaria*) is a very beautiful moth. Its wings are pointed at the tip, and the margins of the hind-wings only scalloped; the fore-wings are pale red brown, and sprinkled all over with small brown dots, having also a round white spot near the tip. They have also two oblique transverse lines of a darker brown, between which is a very distinct brown spot. The hind-wings are pale, and have a nearly straight transverse line across the middle. The antennæ of the male moth are beautifully feathered, the shaft being snowy white, and the plumes red-brown; and it is from this fact that the species derives its name. The caterpillar of the Feathered Thorn is of a pale brown, without warts or humps, except two red points just before the tail. It feeds on the oak during May, and the moth emerges from the chrysalis in October.

We now come to a singular class of the geometers—those which possess wingless females. Perhaps no fact is more calculated to excite wonder in the young entomologist than the fact that many of our moths; whilst in the male sex exhibiting the usual wing-appendages, yet in the female, they are found to be entirely destitute of them. Thus, unable to fly, the males are in some way directed to the spots in which they have emerged; and in ordinary cases these wingless females cling to their cocoons, laying their eggs either over or inside the web. The Pale Brindled Beauty (*Phigalia pilosaria*) is a striking example of this singular phenomenon. The female has not the slightest apology for wings. The wings of the male are rounded, and mottled grey in colour, with four transverse bars, which are indicated on the surface. They have altogether a worn or semi-transparent appearance, as though they had been rubbed, and the scales removed in various parts. The antennæ are feathered, and the thorax is very stout and hairy. The caterpillar of this moth feeds on oak, and is described as of a grey-brown, clouded with red-brown, and having warts on several of the segments. This is an early species, flying sometimes in February and March, and it is abundant in the north and west of England. The discovery of the Belted Beauty (*Nyssia zonaria*) is due to the energetic labours of Mr. Newman, who has rendered such valuable assistance to the entomological cause, both by his pen and his personal researches. It is indeed an interesting species, but as yet has not been found save in one locality in Great Britain. Its female, like that of the former, is entirely destitute of wings—and those of the male are small and rounded. The fore-wings dark grey, having two transverse bars parallel to the hind margin. The hind-wings are white, with a dark grey hind margin, a grey bar parallel with the margin, and a second transverse bar across the middle of the wing. The caterpillar of the Belted Beauty is without humps, and of a dingy green colour, marbled with whiter shades, and having a yellowish stripe along each side. It feeds on the common yarrow. The moth occurs in three or four localities in the same neighbourhood, so close together as to be regarded as one, under the names of Birkenhead, Black Rock, and New Brighton, in Cheshire.

The Small Brindled Beauty (*Nyssia hispidaria*) is a very thick-bodied little geometer. The male has small rounded wings of a dark brown colour, with a broad pale band very near the margin. On the dark part of the wing are slight indications of two transverse lines, still darker, which are zigzag. The hind-wings are smoke-coloured, with a darker bar in the middle. The thorax is large in proportion, and square; it is black, powdered with grey. The caterpillar of this moth is described as brown-grey, more or less variegated with delicate orange markings. Its food is the oak. The Small Brindled Beauty was once abundant in Richmond Park, where the collectors dug up its chrysalides around the roots of oak trees; also in the New Forest and in the north of England. Next our notice is claimed by that commonest of insects in the parks and squares of the suburbs of London, the Brindled Beauty (*Biston hirtaria*). Often may we see this rather dull moth clinging to the tree trunks, and seeking to deposit its patches of green eggs among the crevices of the bark. The caterpillar is rather a handsome creature when full-grown, and is much attached to the plum and pear trees of our gardens. It is without humps. The ground colour is of a purple brown and red brown; these colours are arranged in alternate stripes from head to tail, and every two stripes are divided by an irregular black line. On the back of each segment are two small raised spots of a bright yellow; there is a ring of the same colour just behind the head, and a row of seven yellow spots along each side. In June and July we may be sure of meeting with this large 'looper,' feeding on lime, oak, hawthorn, or fruit trees, and often in such numbers as to strip them of their leaves. When full-grown it buries itself in the earth, and changes to a blackish chrysalis; the perfect insect emerging the following April, and crawling up the trunks of trees, as already stated. The colouring is not very attractive, all the wings being smoky brown, sprinkled with dots of yellowish brown. The male moth, however, is rather more lively in its markings than its partner, for his wings have six irregular narrow black bands, crossing in a transverse direction. The antennæ are beautifully feathered also in the male specimens, and the thorax is very hairy.

One of the most handsome and striking of our *Geometræ* is the Oak Beauty (*Amphydasis prodromaria*), a noble insect, both from its size and its marbled markings. The fore-wings are dirty white, with two irregular brown bands, the first of which is short, and near the base of the wing, and its outer edge is bordered with black. The second band is near the hind margin, and its inner edge is bordered with black; the whitish space between these two bands is sprinkled with black dots, and there is a crescent shaped mark near the middle. The hind-wings are paler than the fore-wings, and are transversely waved with black. The antennæ are feathered in the male, threadlike in the female moth. The caterpillar of this handsome moth is described as being brown, marbled with white, and as having two small reddish humps on several of the segments. It feeds in July and August, on oak and birch. The moth emerges in the following March or April, and is far from being a common insect amongst us. Another very handsome geometer follows this grand insect—that known as the Peppered Moth (*Amphydasis betularia*). All the wings are dingy white, sprinkled and streaked with smoky brown. The head is white, and the antennæ of the female are threadlike and black. The thorax is white, and the body dingy white, spotted with black. This is a very variable insect, for some individuals have a decided pattern, others are sprinkled all over with small black dots, and others again are black and unspotted. The caterpillar of the Peppered Moth varies much in the ground colour. It feeds in August on lime, birch, oak, and many other trees. In September it buries itself in the ground, and turns to a rather brown, dumpy chrysalis. The moth itself emerges during the following May. With this handsome moth, not unfrequently turning up even in the suburbs of London, we must close this paper, reserving for our next the interesting family of the *Boarmidæ*.

HARD WORDS.

WHEN people wish to be sarcastic on the subject of Natural History, they usually fall foul of what they consider the unmeaning Latin names by which plants or insects are known to the scientific world. They speak with scorn of those

"Whe *Allium* call their onions and their leeks,"

and ask to be told whether a Peacock Butterfly is any the better for being designated by the high-sounding title of *Vanessa Io*. They will not stop and let you show them that the names—to them unmeaning—are, in many cases, highly significant and appropriate; they ignore the advantage of having an object named in a language which is universally known, and by which a naturalist in one quarter of the world would recognise a plant or an animal found in another, and fall back on the remark that they shall call a Buttercup a Buttercup to the end of their days. Now, it must not be supposed that we have any sympathy with those who pedantically use scientific terms for the purpose of showing off their own knowledge—which is probably very superficial—and of astonishing their listeners. No one but a snob—for there are snobs even among professed naturalists, although Mr. Thackray omitted them from his book on the genus—would speak of natural objects by their scientific names to any but those who were at least as fully able as himself to comprehend them; but we are anxious to show that these "hard words," after all, have a meaning; and to explain this meaning by aid of a few examples is the object of this paper. It will contain nothing new: and those of our readers who already understand the Latin names of plants may pass it over.

Far be it from us to underrate the value, the beauty, or the interest, of our English names. What can be prettier, more appropriate, or more poetical, than the name Daisy, or Daye's eye?—that favourite of Chaucer, who says,

"That above all flowris in the mede
Then love I most these flowris white and rede,
Such that men callin daisies in our towne."

And again,

"That well by reason men callé it maie
The daisie, or els the eie of the daie."

By every principle of good taste and common sense, we are bound to speak of plants or animals by their English names to the many who, without actually studying them, feel an interest in noticing and hearing of the beautiful things around them—an interest which we should encourage by every means in our power, and carefully refrain from checking by any ill-judged display of our own scientific knowledge,

Some persons—we hope but few—are deterred from the study of Natural History by the "hard words" employed. They seem to think it incumbent on them to commence studying botany; for example, by learning scientific names, and shrink from attempting so formidable a task. No mistake could be greater. Those who have not tried it will scarcely believe in how short a space of time one's eye becomes familiarised with the dreaded words. As a further assistance to this end, it is useful to have at one's elbow some books containing both English and Latin names of plants; and then, if we come across a Latin word which conveys no English equivalent to our mind, it is easy to look it out; the chances are that we shall not again forget it.

Before the time of Linnæus, the Latin names of plants were indeed weighty matters; many of them, from their length and copiousness being rather a description of a species than its mere designation. Grateful should we be to that great botanist for having so simplified the matter that the name of a plant can now be expressed in two words: the first word being called the *generic*, the second the *specific*, name. The first is usually common to several plants, closely connected with each other by certain features; the second is applied to but one species of the same genus. Thus—to use a homely illustration—when we say "John Brown"—"Brown" is, so to speak, the genus, of which John and his brothers, William and Thomas, are species. The Latin generic title often denotes some characteristic which is common to all the species comprised under it; or it is derived from the name of some person who is considered by the namer to be worthy of such commemoration. The specific name often refers to some peculiarity in structure of the plant to which it is applied, to its place of growth, or to its likeness to other species, or like the genus is named after its discoverer, or some eminent botanist. Let us now look among our wild flowers for some illustrations of the appropriateness of their Latin names.

First, we may observe that a great many genera are named from a resemblance in their blossoms to some other object. The large, chalice-shaped flowers of the Marsh Marigold suggested the name *Caltha*, from a Greek word signifying a *cup;* and the name *Stellaria* applied to the Stitchworts, was clearly given them on account of their white *star-like* blossoms. The Foxglove earned its more learned title, *Digitalis*, from the resemblance in shape of its handsome flowers to the *finger* of a glove; while the *bells* of the Hairbell and its allies obtained for the genus its name, *Campanula;* the Globe-flower is called *Trollius*, from the German *trolen*, a ball, in reference to the round outline of its blossoms. Sometimes other parts of the plant are selected; the *arrow*-shaped leaves of the Arrow-head gained for it its English name, as well as the Latin *Sagittaria;* the Shepherd's Purse (a translation of its specific name, *Bursa-pastoris,*) owes both these and its generic title, *Capsella*, to its curious seed pouches. The Horse-shoe Vetch is *Hippocrepis*, from the resemblance which the pods present to a *horse-shoe;* the Birdsfoot, *Ornithopus*, from a similar likeness; the Coralwort is *Dentaria*, from its *toothed* root. Other genera were named from diseases for which the species comprised under them were supposed to be remedial; *Scrophularia* is one of these. Of the very many which commemorate distinguished botanists we need only mention *Linnæa, Villarsia, Wahlenbergia, Lobelia, Knappia, Isnardia, Hutchimsia, Teesdalia;* other names, of more ancient, or classical, allusion are, *Daphne, Iris, Narcissus, Euphorbia, Gentiana, Ceutaurea*, &c.

To turn now to specific names, we shall find many which are common to several plants in different genera, and indicate their place of growth. Thus, *palustre* denotes a *marsh*-loving species— *e.g.*, Marsh Willowherb, *Epilobium palustre*, Marsh Bedstraw, *Galium palustre; sylvaticus*, a woodland plant—*e.g.*, the Wood Rush (*Scirpus sylvaticus,*) the Wood Scorpion-Grass (*Myosotis sylvatica*), the Wood Cudweed *Gnaphalium sylvaticum*); *arvensis* or *agrestis* a plant of fields, as the Field Scabious (*Knautia arvensis,*) and the Field Foxtail grass (*Alopecurus agrestis);* two species of Speedwell, growing in similar situations are named respectively *Veronica agrestis* and *V. arvensis*. *Pratensis* denotes a meadow flower; as the Lady's Smock (*Cardamine pratensis*), the Purple Clover (*Trifolium pratense*), and the Meadow Cranesbill (*Geranium pratense);* *aquaticus* and *aquatilis* refer to plants growing in or by water, as the Water Crowfoot (*Ranunculus aquatilis*) and Awlwort (*Subularia aquatica*). *Sativus* points to a cultivated plant or its origin; the Garden Radish is *Raphanus sativus*, the Parsnep, *Pastinaca sativa*, and the Wheat, *Triticum sativum*. *Officinalis* denotes former use, in medicine or otherwise, as the Borage (*Borago officinalis*), common Speedwell (*Veronica officinalis*), &c. *Vulgaris* is applied to very common plants, as the groundsel (*Senecio vulgaris*), Ling (*Calluna vulgaris*), and many more.

Another class of specific names is that which takes its origin in a reference to different parts of the plant. *Bulbosus* shows a plant with bulbous root, as in the Buttercup (*Ranunculus bulbosus*); *repens* denotes creeping roots or stems, as in the Couch-grass (*Triticum repens*). Most names of this class are taken from the leaves; thus we have *Geranium rotundifolium*, the

Round-leaved Cranesbill; *Vicia angustifolia*, the *Narrowleaved* Vetch; *Veronica hederifolia*, the *Ivy-leaved* Speedwell; *Plantago lanceolata* the Ribwort Plantain, with long tapering, or *lanceolate*, leaves; *Tilia parvifolia*, the *small-leaved* Lime; *T. grandifolia*, the *large-leaved* Lime; *Orchis maculata*, an Orchis with *spotted* foliage; Lamium *incisum*, the *Cut*-leaved Dead Nettle; *Chlora perfoliata*, the Yellow-wort, which has *perfoliate* leaves; and so on. Others refer to the colour of the flowers; as *Anagallis cærulea*, the *Blue* Pimpernel; *Helleborus viridis*, the *green* Hellebore; *Centranthus ruber*, the *Red* Valerian; *Gagea lutea*, the *Yellow* Star of Bethlehem; *Lamium album*, the *White* Dead Nettle; others to the size of the flowers, as *Cephalanthera grandiflora*, *Large-flowered* Helleborine; *Ranunculus parviflorus*, *Small-flowered* Crowfoot. The general character of the plant is referred to in such names as *Ranunculus hirsutus*, the *Hairy* Crowfoot; *Geranium molle*, the Dove's-foot Cranesbill, remarkable for its *soft*ness. Some specific names show the likeness of the species which bear them to other plants; thus, *Villarsia nymphæoïdes*, means the *Nymphæa*-(or Water Lily) like Villarsia; *Helmintha echioïdes*, the *Echium* (or Bugloss) like Ox tongue, from the resemblance of its prickly leaves to those of *Echium vulgare*.

Yet another class refers to certain peculiarities in the species themselves. Thus, our Coralwort, which is so curiously propagated by means of little buds, or bulbs, which grow in the axils of leaves, is aptly called *Dentaria bulbifera*, the Bulb-bearing Coralwort. The *Bee*-orchis is *Ophrys apifera*, the *Fly*, *O. muscifera*, in each case the name being taken from the likeness of the flowers to the insects referred to.

Thus, then, we have endeavoured to show that some, at least, the "hard words" of Botany have a meaning. In some cases, the names are misapplied—*pedicularis sylvatica* for example, is by no means a woodland plant—but these are exceptions to the rule. Perhaps this short paper may induce one or two, at least, of our readers to investigate the matter further; in which case its object will have been attained.—*Quarterly Magazine of the High Wycombe Natural History Society*. January.

RARE VISITORS AT IPSWICH.

NOW that the year 1868 has passed away from us, I think we all should do our best to record some of the events of that rare and beautiful summer, which not only brought forth an unusual amount of heat, but an unusual quantity of rare and interesting objects, in almost every branch of Natural History, *Lepidoptera* more especially; at any rate, it has in the above-named locality (which extends about five miles from the outskirts of the town.)

We have had an abundant supply of most of the common insects; of *Hyale* we have had a fair quantity, also several specimens of *Helice*; flying with the latter a nice specimen of *A. Lathonia* was taken by a lamplighter. Not being aware of the rarity of the insect, he sold it to a dealer for the small sum of 6d. Next on my list comes *L. Sibylla*, which were abundant; one dealer captured over a gross; among them were some fine and rare varieties, one (No. 3,) being in my own cabinet. Description. Spec. 1. Upper surface of wings jet black; underside, usual markings. Spec. 2. White upon the upper side in oblong patches; under side a mixture of the ordinary colour, but no order as in common specimens. Spec. 3. Upper surface jet black; hind wings with large round white spot; underside streaked in alternate lines of dirty white and pale brown. Other varieties were equally singular: altogether about 12 were taken. Such an instance I do not think is on record, nor has a variety of *Sibylla* been taken here within the last ten years.

Now for that coveted prize, more frequently seen than captured, *A. Iris* both Emperor and Empress being equally plentiful. At times I saw as many as four sporting together in the sunshine. In one day I took four with a hand-net fixed upon a pole about 30ft. long, and missed twice as many more, to my sorrow, but I cannot say whether they were the same insects or not. They were all drawn to the same *trees*, by that celebrated but secret composition. One fine variety (Exhibited at the Ipswich Fine Arts and Industrial Exhibition) was captured, wanting as in *Silylla*, the white bands upon the wings. Next worthy of notice is a fine Mothydite specimen of *Semele*, taken in the *garden* of Mr. Garrett, Woodbridge Road, more than a mile away from its usual locality. Thus far for *Diurni*.

The Hawk moths were abundant. In some cases there were two broods. By the first of June I had larvæ of *S. Ligustri* down. Some of the larvæ I picked up in the streets of the town, and had others brought me from a similar situation. *Elpenor* put in an appearance as early as the beginning of May. *Fuciformis*, compared with past seasons were scarce. *Testudo* gave plenty of work for sharp eyes. I will here recommend collectors to breed as many larvæ of *C. Caja* as possible, as they are no trouble, greedily devouring any leaf given them, and fine varieties may be obtained. A dealer here obtained two, one a fine black specimen, the other a cream coloured one.

Now for the *Geometræ*. Several varieties of *M. Margaritata* was captured, one entirely wanting the orange upon the wings; others had bands of orange and brown. *A. Prodomaria* were not scarce. I had 8 from one lamplighter. *I. Vernaria* was scarcer than I ever knew it before. I am afraid it is becoming extinct in the locality, where formerly it was abundant; but the wood is now levelled with the ground, and one of the best localities in the district is thus entirely destroyed. *P. Bajulana* was far from uncommon, one dealer capturing a large drawer full. *M. Hartata* were plentiful. I may here express my thoughts why more of this insect are not taken by amateurs. As soon as disturbed by beating they invariably rise and fly over the top of the hop, as the keepers call it; having noticed this in 1867, I went prepared in 1868. In the former year I had only a hand net; last year I took a 10ft. rod with me, and was well rewarded by capturing in one day eighteen, besides other good things. I think collectors will find this a capital plan providing they keep cool, *Hastata* being a sharp flier, seldom letting a second strike succeed in its downfall.

A curious variety of *C. Bilineata* occurred, which has not before been noticed, it differed little from the ordinary type, except a small round *pink* spot in the centre of each fore-wing, the insect is now in the collection of Mr. Newman; another variety I captured myself, having a nearly black band across the fore-wings.

Next comes the *Prominents, &c., Furcula* and *Bifida*, being taken frequently from the lamps. *Dictæ* and *Dictæoides* were brought me by the lamplighters nearly every morning during the seasons, the latter most frequently. I took two *Trepida*, also one *Dodonæ* from the lamps.

Since what I may term the *great capture*, Ipswich has always been a noted place for *D. Orion*. The above-named capture occurred one stormy night, when *one man captured over a gross at sugar*, also one *A. Alni* at the same time. Last year we had a good supply, as many as three and four being picked up upon the grass in one day by a single collector, and such instances were not rare. A friend of mine took two off a tree, which had been sugared the previous evening. I think collectors will be well repaid to examine such trees. I always find it profitable, and I have always thought trees might be sugared with success during the *day-time*. Entomologists all know insects flock to a bleeding tree.

Mr. Last, whom I before mentioned, brushed two rare larvæ in 1867—that of *N. Tritophus* being one, *Alni* the other, and as the Moths appeared in 1868, I think they claim a notice here.

From my old friends the lamplighters I had two *Abjecta* and one *Ashvorthii*, (I take all they catch, thus often getting a good thing) with *Promissa*, which was frequent to diligent sugarers. I will conclude a list which few towns can boast of.

In 1867, we had one *Celerio*; one *Fagi*; two varieties of *Selene*, one with the silver markings in streaks instead of spots, the other with very few black spots upon the wings. A male specimen of *L. Dispar*, with female markings upon the wings. WILLIAM M. COLE.

VARIATION OF SPECIES.

AT present the great question agitating the scientific world is the Origin of Species. The few remarks we now make on this subject are intended to call forth the opinions of those of our readers who have thought it over. At the very outset of the inquiry a great difficulty presents itself—a difficulty partly of a philological character, and partly, perhaps, arising out of the nature of things. What is a species? What constitutes a species has not been pointed out; the term itself has not yet been defined. The truth is, it is difficult to define anything. Few definitions, beyond those of Euclid, are satisfactory. We need hardly say that, until the term "species" has been defined with mathematical accuracy, men will never agree as to the value of specific characters. In this case mathematical precision is out of the question. Could the term be defined with the accuracy of a mathematical definition the controversy would be at an end.

There are specific differences among plants and animals. We all know that; and yet it is surprising how widely divergent the opinions of the best botanists and zoologists are on the subject. Take, for example, the plants indigenous to Great Britain and Ireland. One botanist makes the number of species something like twelve hundred, another botanist, of equal authority, says there are five or six hundred more. Even in such a trifling affair as butterflies, our lepidopterists are by no means agreed as to the number of species.

We come, then, to the question which is not likely to be solved for some time yet—What is the difference between a variety and a species?

Hitherto, it has been found quite impossible to draw a line of demarcation between them. In numerous instances, both in the animal and vegetable kingdom, there exist such slight shades of difference that it is impossible to say where the species ends and the variety begins.

There are differences that can hardly be said to have the value of specific characters. Gardeners are very familiar with multitudes of such differences. The varieties of florists' flowers are endless; yet, surely, there are not as many species as there are varieties? It is quite plain, then, that there are both species and varieties; yet it is on this very point that naturalists are divided. It is agreed on all hands that there are both species and varieties; but what constitutes a species and what a variety? We repeat that this is the great point at issue. All attempts at proving the progressive development of species must fail until we know what a species is.

Yet it must be admitted by every one at all conversant with the subject that the globe gives unmistakable proofs of progression. There were species existing in ages long gone by that do not exist now. We say species, meaning forms of animal and vegetable life different to what now exists. This may or may not favour the theory of development just as we may choose to think. There are certainly higher organisms on the globe now than at one time existed on it. The vegetable forms imbedded in the rocks are all of a low type of organisation; they all appear to be allied to the ferns and horse-tails.

That the whole has progressed in organic forms is certain—that species do vary is also certain. What then? Are we to accept the theory of progressive development as the true theory of life? In other words—Is creation planned in accordance with this theory? The premises hardly warrant this conclusion. There is no authority for saying that living species are the descendants of extinct species. Not a shadow of proof can be adduced in support of the doctrine. Nor does the fact of the variation of species warrant the conclusion that this variation gives rise to higher forms of life. Not a shadow of proof has ever been adduced that variation of species originates higher species. The whole subject remains in the region of mere conjecture. There is not a chain of evidence, there are only a few broken links; for let it be remembered that those who propose such a startling doctrine are bound to support it by irrefragable evidence.

Let us now examine a little more carefully the two points hinted at above. The rocks give infallible testimony that species once existed that do not now exist. Could every link be traced between the beings that now exist on the globe and these extinct species, the controversy would be at an end. But it is not even pretended that the links can ever be traced. It is a mere subterfuge to say that the links are broken and lost for ever. Assertion is not proof. The testimony of the rocks is very meagre and fragmentary indeed. Any attempt at forming a complete system of pre-adamite zoology and botany, and connecting that system in a natural way with the present representatives of the animal and vegetable kingdoms must signally fail. There is an impassable gulf between the present and the past. With our present knowledge, at any rate, no human ingenuity can throw a bridge across the gulf. The gigantic ferns and horse-tails of the coal measures are surely not to be regarded, without any other evidence, as the progenitors of the oak, the elm, and the beech. We are thrown back on the broken links. Let us speak plainly. Give us whole links welded and compacted together, binding like adamant the ancient and modern world in one. When asked to accept a mere theory as veritable truth, we have a right to ask for sufficient facts on which to rely.

But what we have chiefly to do with at present is the variation of species. It is readily admitted that species vary to a wonderful extent. The question is, do they vary so as to give rise to new, distinct, and permanent species? Where is the proof that they do? A farmer is familiar with many varieties of wheat, and many varieties of oats. He understands well what is meant by the term. You may introduce to him a new variety of oats or wheat, but to the farmer it is oats or wheat still. It would be absurd to show a farmer a new variety of wheat and tell him this is a new species. If he understood language he would tell you it is a variety and nothing more. But if you go on to tell him that by-and-by it will become a species; that as soon as its character is fixed it will rise to the dignity of a real species, you might indeed, succeed in muddling his brains, but you would certainly fail in convincing his judgment. The farmer falls back on the logic of facts; he would tell you in effect that, notwithstanding all your fine names, oats are oats and wheat is wheat still. And he would be right. His whole business-life rests on the fact that species are not to be confounded. If he sows wheat he does not expect to reap tares, nor does he ever expect to clip his fleece of wool off his cow's back. There is a broad common sense that, after all, is better than the most brilliant theories of so-called naturalists. There is not a single well-authenticated instance of a species of plant or animal having a parentage inferior in organization to itself. It is only a sophism to tell us that such was at one time the case. If the natural history of the world as it is must be read in the light of other days to be understood, then the other days must afford more light than for some time yet they are likely to do.—*Gardener's Record*, Jan. 2.

REMARKABLE HABITS OF THE BADGER, STOAT, AND WEASEL.

There have been repeated occasions to observe that the habits of the wild animals of the British Islands, as they occur in their intercourse with each other, are but imperfectly known; and this is more especially the case as for the sake of safety to themselves and offspring, they are compelled to seek the cover of the night for any important change of residence, or, as appears to happen not unfrequently when they are driven to seek a supply of food at a distance from their accustomed haunts—to which we may venture to add, when in a joyous spirit even such as in general are accustomed to live in a secluded manner, become instinctively inclined to meet together and indulge in some active and social amusement; and however strange it may appear, observation shows it to be the case with even such of these animals as from what has been commonly noticed of them, we should least of all have supposed to have assembled in a considerable number for any combined purpose. If the impulse had first sprung into existence in a single mind, a consultation must have been held, and a general resolution adopted, before such measures as I have to record could have been carried into effect; and as the circumstances themselves are beyond doubt, the mental impulses of brutal nature become greatly raised in our estimation. The badger in its manner of life is perhaps the most solitary and secluded of all the animals that inhabit the British islands; so that if not sought after, it might be scarcely known to be living among us; and yet at a time within remembrance, when the baiting of a badger with dogs was a frequent amusement, there was found little difficulty in discovering its haunt and obtaining it for the sport; and little difficulty was encountered in replying to any objection that might be raised by those who were judged to be overscrupulous, when they argued against the cruelty of such a proceeding as to expose the animal to the merciless attack of savage dogs for the gratification of scarcely less savage men. The reply was readily made that badgers inflicted injury on the farmer by trampling down the growing corn; and therefore at least their destruction was a public benefit. But since those who felt pleasure in this sort of amusement have ceased among us—although there cannot be a doubt that these animals exist as before—any injury supposed to be inflicted by them has not continued to attract attention. They have, indeed, their favourite haunts, from which it would not be easy to drive them away; but there are times also when observation has shown that they are prepared to change them for others at even remote distances; and when resolved on this migration, it becomes by no means safe for any one to meet them in the way or excite their alarm—it might be said their displeasure—by disturbing their progress. As an instance of this, it was in the time of harvest, at about ten o'clock at night, when the moon was shining brightly, and my intelligent informant was on his way homeward across the fields, so that it became necessary for him to climb over a hedge—such a one as is common in the western counties—all at once he discovered immediately before him a company of badgers, nine or ten in number, of which some were of full size, and others evidently young; the latter, as he judged, marching along in the middle of the company. As soon as the animals perceived what they seemed to have regarded as an unwelcome intruder on their privacy, they raised a grunt, and proceeded to gather round him with what he believed to be an intention to commence an attack. In the dread of such an assault, he speedily begun a retreat through the field, but this seemed only to have encouraged them in their hostile intentions, for they followed him closely until he had reached the gate, over which he was glad to pass; and beyond which they did not continue the pursuit. Nor is this the only instance of which I have received credible information. The individual concerned was passing along a lane at night in a district not much frequented by travellers, when he found himself beset (in a manner he could scarcely explain) by a company of badgers, which assumed towards him a threatening attitude. He was able to count twenty-one of them—some of which were of much less size than others—and the full-grown individuals were in the front and rear; while those which appeared to be the younger were in the middle of the arrangement. In this case as well, the brutes as the man were willing to avoid hostilities, and the badgers pursued their way without molestation. Yet that such an inclination to peace is rather the exception than the rule, will be shown by other instances—which have given occasion to a common opinion among a portion of our country labourers—that this animal will assail any individual it may thus meet with, without having received any provocation. An old man was passing along the road near a wood, attended by his sheep dog, at about midnight, when he met a company of five or six badgers, which he supposed to be the parents, with their young. Immediately as he advanced, they began to attack him, and although he procured a stick from the neighbouring hedge, and was gallantly assisted by his dog, he found himself obliged to seek his safety in flight. On another occasion, the individual found himself compelled to secure himself by retreating to a heap of stones and pelting his opponents. It had been observed of the badger that when it is attacked by a dog it is its habit to defend itself by laying hold of and biting severely the fore leg of its adversary; but aware of this, a dog that had become famous for its success in such conflicts, was always on his guard against this danger by holding back its body and legs from the enemy while its mouth was thrust forward to seize it. The badger was then thrown upward, and as it fell to the ground it was seized by the throat, and soon deprived of life. Nor is this occasional habit of association and attack confined to the badger; for I have received information of repeated occurrences of a similar nature by the common stoat (Mustela Erminea); if indeed at this time these creatures may be termed common, which are fast decreasing in numbers, and may soon become extinct among us. It has been usually by night, when people have had occasion to pass along a rather secluded road, that they have met with a rather numerous company of these animals, which appear to have become associated together for the purpose of proceeding to occupy a perhaps hitherto vacant district. In one instance, as judging from the sounds they uttered, they appeared to my informant to be in very considerable numbers; while the dimness of light was such as to render them only indistinctly visible. But, instead of retreating, as might have been supposed from their ordinary habits by day, they gathered about him in a manner to threaten injury; and it was only with the aid of a trusty staff, that he succeeded in repelling them, with the slaughter of seven of the number—all of which, on examination, appeared to be young ones. In another instance, where the individual found himself compelled to resist the apparently threatened attack of a large number of these animals, they were not driven away until he had killed three of them. Nor is this migratory association of our wild animals always late at night, for my informant was, even in moderate daylight, passing along a public highway in the country, when he found himself beset by a numerous company of stoats, that were not presently dispersed from an apparent intention of attack. Indeed, in the several instances of this nature with which I have been acquainted, the ordinary shyness or timidity of these creatures has been absent; and they, on the contrary, have shown a manifest intention of inflicting injury on the person who has chanced to be a witness of their associated proceedings. And even the little weasel has been seen to associate with others of its race under what we may believe to be a similar impulse. Two officers of the coastguard were on duty together by night in a solitary place near the sea, when they were witnesses to an assemblage of a very large number of the common weasel; although these persons were at a sufficient distance to avoid being molested by them, even if such had been their impulse. These creatures were too numerous to be counted in the imperfect light that prevailed; but it was the opinion of one that their numbers were not less than three score, while the other observer judged that they were not less than a hundred. The circumstances thus related remind us of the accounts reported of the assembling at uncertain intervals of the mighty hosts of lapland lemmings, and their migrations towards the shore; but in our present condition of ignorance as regards the influences which act in the action of animals, and the manner in which they communicate with each other, must remain as merely a matter of vain speculation. VIDEO, F.L.S. & C.M.L.S.

DOUBLE BROODS.

In the summer of 1865 I fed upon the potato the larva of *Macrosila celeus*, G. & R. (*Sphinx 5-maculata*), which came out of the chrysalis in August. I then made record of the fact which to our entomologists was new. The following year I also raised upon the potato *Macrosila carolina*, Clems., a pair of which came out in September. The same year I also raised from larva *Hemileuca maia*, Walk. (*Saturnia maia*, Harr.), part of the brood coming out in October, and one deformed specimen in the following May. Miss C. Guild, of Walpole, Mass., a close and careful observer and a reliable naturalist, informs me that her experience with the last named species is, that of the same brood of larvæ all going into the chrysalis nearly at the same time, part come out in October and others not until the following October, some lying in the chrysalis one year longer than others. I have been puzzled to account for their seeming irregularities, but as instances of the fact increase, conclude it is a provision of nature that our lack of knowledge only makes it strange. In Mr. B. Billings' article in the same number of your paper he enquires if *Melitœa phaeton* may not be double brooded. Mr. Scudder, in his list of butterflies of New England, says, "I have taken the caterpillar just ready to change, upon the barberry in the middle of May; does the larva hibernate?" He also says, "it is very rare in Mass." (1863). I with many others had been in anxious search for this beautiful butterfly up to 1866 without success, except in the extreme southern part of the State, now all of a sudden in this year (1866) they were found in their special localities, low and swampy meadows, quite plentiful, and have continued still more plentiful (from June 17 to July 8) to the present time. Dr. Harris collected in this vicinity from about 1825, and with a few exceptions never had met with it. It is possible that in some instances they may be double brooded, but I have never met with it out of its special season.—*Canadian Entomologist*, December, 1868.

New Books.

[*Our limited space must of necessity compel us to give but very short notices of new books, but they will perhaps serve as a guide as to what books our readers may ask for at their libraries.*]

Explorations of the Highlands of the Brazil, with a full Account of the Gold and Diamond Mines; also Canoeing down 1,500 Miles of the great river Sao Francisco, from Sabará to the Sea. By Captain Richard F. Burton. 2 Vols. Tinsley Brothers.

We strongly recommend all our readers to procure these volumes: sure that a perusal will give much pleasure. The accounts of the journey to Petropolis—of Petropolis itself; of the glens and ravines which interest the prairie land of Muras Geraes; of the interior of the Cachœira gold mine; of the Brazilian forests, and their luxuriance of creepers; of the scenery down the river, and the rapids; and of the great Paulo Affonso, the king of rapids—show what the author can do when inclined.

We see the party winding up almost level zigzags under the shadow of the gigantic trees of a virgin forest, through masses of delicate vegetation, past murmuring waters and Nature's own botanical gardens of ferns and air-plants. The white road glistens in the sun as if powdered with silver. The view is clear, and there are none of those mists which so often seethe up in dense columns from the deep shaggy clefts and valleys. After turning to gaze upon the wide view of the bay of Rio from between mountain shoulders of dense forest rising to cones of granite or jutting into bare knobs of rock, we reach Petropolis itself, with its cheerful streets intersected by brown gravelly streams, which are crossed by black and scarlet bridges, and are surrounded by the greenest grass. The little villas and kiosks, the châlets and cottages, which stand about, are picked out with the most harmonious colours, and round them are gorgeous gardens, yielding in the distance to a maze of forest, "deep with gathered shade, twined and corded, throttled and festooned, with all its llianas, tufted with wonderful epidendra and air-plants, bearded with gigantic mosses of grotesque shape, and rich in every vegetable form, from the orchid to the cardamom, from the simple bamboo and palm to the complicated mimosa, from the delicate little leaves of the myrtle to the monstrous aroids and the quaint, stiff cecropias or candelabra trees." Then, on the journey across the Campos, Captain Burton detaches for us a section of the fissures caused by landslips, and puts upon the paper an exact reproduction of their fantastic variety of form and the vivid hues of their rocky sides, uniting all the colours of the rainbow. The interior of the gold mine which he visited is one of Doré's illustrations of the Inferno.

Except in times of danger the trip seems to have been easy. From Captain Burton's account it must have been pleasant. He tells us of fish being plentiful down the river, some of them weighing over a hundred pounds. But there is not much in the way of game, nor are wild animals to be got at except with difficulty. The various kinds of jaguars are catalogued in one of Captain Burton's notes. Snakes are described in a more telling style. A few facts are given about crocodiles. The vampire bat and sundry kinds of ticks are brought painfully before us. These, indeed, do not belong to the second part of the journey. The most characteristic feature of that is the description of the great rapids of the Paulo Affonso, to which Captain Burton devotes his last chapter. He takes leave of the public in the very spray of the cataract and under the sound of its roar, as if he felt sure that such an ending would atone for all the faults of the preceding volumes. Let us give him a fair hearing:—

The Quebrada, or gorge, is here 260 feet deep, and in the narrowest part it is choked to a minimum breadth of fifty-one feet. It is filled with what seems not water, but the froth of milk, a dashing and dazzling, a whirling and churning surfaceless mass, which gives a wondrous study of fluid in motion. And the marvellous disorder is a well-directed anarchy: the course and sway, the wrestling and writhing, all tend to set free the prisoner from the prison walls. Ces eaux! mais ce sont des âmes: it is the spectacle of a host rushing down in "liquid vastness" to victory, the triumph of motion, of momentum over the immoveable. Here the luminous whiteness of the chaotic foam-crests, hurled in billows and breakers against the blackness of the rock, is burst into flakes and spray, that leap half way up the immuring trough. There the surface reflections dull the dazzling crystal to a thick opaque yellow, and there the shelter of some spur causes a momentary start and recoil to the column, which, at once gathering strength, bounds and springs onwards with a new crush and another roar. The heaped-up centre shows fugitive ovals and progressive circles of a yet more sparkling, glittering, dazzling light, divided by points of comparative repose, like the nodal lines of waves. They struggle and jostle, start asunder, and interlace as they dash with stedfast purpose adown the inclined plane. Now a fierce blast hunts away the thin spray-drift, and puffs it to leeward in rounded clouds, thus enhancing the brilliancy of the gorge-sole. Then the steam boils over and canopies the tremendous scene. Then in the stilly air of dull-warm grey, the mists surge up, deepening still more, by their veil of ever ascending vapour, the dizzy fall that yawns under our feet. * *

Here the Sao Francisco, running swift and smooth out of the north-west, escapes from the labyrinth of islands and islets, rocks and sands, blocks and walls which squeeze it, and receives on the left a smaller branch, separated from the main by a dark ridge. The two, leaping and coursing down a moderate incline of broken bed, burst into ragged, tossing sheets of foam-crested wave, and tumble down the first or upper break, which is about thirty-two feet high. This kind of "Rideau Fall" is known as the "Vai-Vem de Cima"—the "upper go and come." The waters are compressed in the central channel by the stone courses rising thirty to fifty feet above them, and are driven into a little cove on the left bank. The mouth of a branch during the floods, now it is a baylet of the softest sand hemmed in by high japanned walls, and here the little waves curl and flow, and ebb again, with all the movement of a tide in miniature. I timed and felt the pulse of the flux and reflux, but I could detect no regularity in the circulation. The place tempts to a bath, but strangers must bear in mind that it is treacherous, and that cattle drinking here have been entangled in the waters, from which not even Jupiter himself could save them. The waters then dashing against the left or south-eastern boulder-pier, are deflected to the south-west in a vast serpentine of tossing foam, and form, a few paces lower down, a similar feature; called by our guide "half go and come." Here insulated rocks and islands, large and small, disposed in long ridges and in rounded towers, black, toothed, and channelled, and wilder far than the Three Sisters or the Bath and Lunar islands of Niagara, split the hurrying, tossing course into five distinct channels of white surge, topping the yellow, turbid flood. The four to the right topple over at once into the great cauldron. The fifth runs along the left bank in a colossal flume or launders, high raised above the rest; meeting a projection of rock at the south, it is flung round to the west almost at a right angle. Here the parted waters spring over the ledge, and converge in the chaudière which collects them for the great fall. When the sun and moon are at the favourable angle of 35°, they produce admirable arcs and semicircles of rainbows in all their prismatic tintage from white to red. These attract the eye by standing in a thin arch of light over the mighty highway of the rushing "burning" waters; guides to cataracts, however, always make too much of the pretty sight. The third station is reached by a rough, thorny descent, which might easily be improved, and leads to the water's edge, where charred wood shows that travellers have lately nighted in the place. Turning to the north-east we see a furious brown rapid plunging with strange forms down an incline of forty-nine feet in half-a-dozen distinct steps: the flood seems as though it would sweep us away. At the bottom, close to where we stand, it bends westward, pauses for a moment upon the billow-fringed lower lip of the Chaudière that rises snow-white from the straw-coloured break, and then the low, deep thundering roar, shaking the ground and "*sui generis*" as the rumbling of the earthquake and the hoarse sumph of the volcano reveal the position of the Great Cataract.

Rudiments of Mineralogy. By A. Ramsay. London: Virtue.

This is a compact and useful volume. It has been compiled from the standard works of Bischof, Dana, Rammelsberg, and Des Cloiseaux, but it presents one feature, at all events, of novelty and value. Mr. Ramsay appears, so far as we know, to be the first writer on mineralogy who has produced a systematic treatise on this science in which the new chemical notation is regularly followed. Cotta's instructive work on "Rocks," and Dana's new and splendid edition of his "Mineralogy," do not adequately recognise or adopt the advances made in scientific chemistry, although it is evident, even from such use of these advances as has been made in the little book under review, that great advantages will thus accrue to students of the mineral kingdom.

On Molecular and Microscopic Science. By Mary Somerville, author of Physical Geography, etc. 2 Vols. London: John Murray.

Mrs. Somerville has long been a worker in science, and her work has for the most part been in a branch of physical science not often entered upon by females. In consequence of which she has been justly regarded as displaying a degree of mental power decidedly exceptional, and has held a high place in the estimation of the public. In the first volume the subjects of inorganic and vegetable molecules are dealt with. Under these heads there is nothing new to the man of science, but there are many explanations of recent discoveries full of interest to the general reader. The earlier pages are devoted to brief descriptions of the non-metallic elements, and to recent researches on heat and light; which latter are admirable, and display the author's clear style in a marked manner. The second volume deals with molecules as they present themselves in the organised tissues of vegetables. This is not, perhaps, so interesting as the first part, owing probably to its having been done so frequently before; still it is all clearly and ably expressed. Indeed, we can have no hesitation in saying that the author has presented us with the very best compilation expressive of the modern aspects of physics and biology that has been issued for many years.

The Garden Oracle and Horticultural Year Book; an Almanac for 1869. London: Groombridge.

This little work, which Mr. Shirley Hibberd has conducted with singular success for ten years past, is, we are pleased to notice, issued for the eleventh time. It has apparently the freshness of a first appearance, combined with the perfection of planned detail, which only time can give to any serial work. The learned editor offers us this time his own pick and prime of all the thousands of plants that have been introduced to our hothouses from various parts of the world, rejecting wholesale all that are of mediocre merit, and squeezing down the selection to twelve groups adapted to twelve different purposes. Thus, if we want thirty of the noblest plants for a cool conservatory, we may find their names instanter. If we want only half a dozen, to make a blaze of colour at an exhibition, or for a festival day; the very best half-dozen are pointed out to us. In this sort of way all possible wants of plant-growers are anticipated, and some three or four hundred of the choicest greenhouse and conservatory plants are enumerated and described. In addition to this, the *pièce de résistance*, the "Oracle" tells us what work should be done in the garden the whole year through, and it gives descriptions of all the new plants, flowers, and fruits, and selections of the best varieties of garden favourites for all classes of floral amateurs. It is simply astonishing how so much that is valuable and original of Mr. Hibberd's observations can be crammed into so small a compass; but there it is, and to every lover of the garden the "Oracle" is as good as a gold mine—better, indeed, for it is not so likely to drive one mad.

Meetings of Learned Societies.

THE HALIFAX INSTITUTE OF NATURAL SCIENCE.

At the December ordinary meeting of this Institute papers were read by Mr. Haliburton and the President (Mr. Jones).

Mr. Haliburton's paper was upon the geological character of the Pictou coal field; and as might be expected from an author, himself a coal owner, contained much practical information regarding one of the most interesting and valuable products which nature has given to this province.

It appears that there are several varieties of coal found in different parts of the world. *Anthracite*, which is also called a *glance coal* and *stone coal*, is quite compact and hard, and contains some 80 or 90 per cent. of carbon. *Black*, or *Bituminous coal*, and *Lignite*, or brown coal, under which are included many varieties. There is scarcely any substance so useful to mankind as this. It is always found in masses, most frequently in beds, which are usually separated by layers of stone. According to Dana, there is no infallible indication of the presence of coal distinguishable in the mineral nature of rocks, and the geologist usually ascertains the absence of coal from a region by examining the fossils in the rock; these fossils being different in rocks of different ages, they indicate at once whether the beds under investigation, belong to what is called the *coal series*.

There are coal fields in England, France, Spain, Portugal, Belgium, Germany, Austria, Sweden, Poland, and Russia. In the far east also, it is abundant in India, China, Madagascar, Tasmania, Borneo, and other islands of the southern ocean; and it is obtained at Conception, on the coast of Chili. The United States can boast of four extensive areas. One of these commences on the north in Pennsylvania, and south-eastern Ohio, and sweeping south over western Virginia and eastern Kentucky and Tennessee, to the west of the Apalachians, it continues to Alabama, where a bed has been opened. It has been estimated to cover 63,000 square miles. A second coal area, the Illinois, lies adjoining the Mississippi, and covers the greater part of Illinois, the western part of Indiana, and a small north-west part of Kentucky. A third occupies a portion of Missouri, west of the Mississippi. A fourth covers the central portion of Michigan. Besides these, there is a smaller coal region in Rhode Island. The coal of Rhode Island and Eastern Pennsylvania is anthracite. Going west in Pennsylvania, the anthracite becomes more and more bituminous; and at Pittsburg, at its western extremity, as also throughout the Western States, it is wholly of the bituminous kind. The Rhode Island variety is so hard and compact, and free from all volatile ingredients, that for many years it had been deemed unfit for use. The amount of anthracite worked in 1820, in Pennsylvania, was only 380 tons; in 1847, it amounted to more than 3,000,000 tons. In Great Britain the annual amount of coal raised is 35,000,000 tons.

Mr. Haliburton, in the course of his remarks, brought to the notice of the members many facts regarding the run of the coal-seams in the Pictou area, which proved that geologists have hitherto been at fault in their theories concerning the extent of these coal beds. He has proved by actual practice that seams could be struck in certain spots, and also at moderate depths, where, owing to a supposed downthrow fault, it was said no coal could be tapped. By his explorations he certainly has proved, beyond a doubt, that the Pictou coal area is much more extensive, and capable of being more easily worked than has been supposed; and, in future years, when this coal-field becomes, as it must naturally do, the Lancashire of the Dominion, we trust the labour and anxiety attendant upon his investigations, will be repaid him in the flourishing and profitable collieries, which, by that time, will probably be in full work on all parts of the property owned by himself and partners.

Mr. H. pointed out the benefits that would accrue to the coal companies generally by the establishment of a double line of rails to the shipping stage, instead of the single one now in use, which is not equal to the work; and he also pointed out the advantage that would be derived from the deepening of East river—a process which would cost but little in comparison with the gain to the coal traffic.

The paper was supplemented by a shorter one relating to the coal trade of Nova Scotia, in which was pointed out the present state of the market, and the prosperity which awaits the future. The repeal of the Reciprocity Treaty was reviewed, and a mode of overcoming the difficulties which apparently barred the way to a more extensive export of coal from the province suggested. The system of return freights from the Canadian ports, when every vessel could bring her return cargo of flour for Nova Scotia use, could also be carried on with the ports of the United States' seaboard, and amply repay the shipper for the small profit on the carriage of coal. It is thus that English vessels can bring cargoes of coal across the Atlantic to Quebec and other places, and sell it at as low a figure as—or even lower—than American coal, their return freights making up for the loss, if any, of the outward voyage. The removal of canal dues in Canada, and the establishment of a bounty system, Mr. H. considered would allow of Nova Scotia coal being sold at a much low price than it is now.

The President's paper was the record of a series commenced at the opening meeting of the session, upon the Marine Zoology of Nova Scotia, and embraced a view of the Decapodous Crustacea. It was illustrated by specimens of several genera; and, in order to render the subject more attractive, specimens of Bermudian and West Indian crabs were exhibited in order to point out the difference which exists between the members of this widely-spread family.

The *Crustacea* afford interesting objects for the consideration of those who delight in the study of Natural History. They vary in size from microscopic animalcules to those of great size; and it is to the former that the luminosity of the ocean is in a great measure attributable, each minim glowing with phosphoric radiance. Certain crabs are almost exclusively terrestrial, visiting the sea only at given periods. These crabs carry in their gill-chambers sufficient water for the purpose of respiration, live in burrows, and traverse considerable tracts of land in their migratory journeys. One of these, an inhabitant of the Bermudas, was thus described by Mr. Jones:—"These land crabs are very good eating, and it is a favourite sport of the Mudian boys to turn out of an evening after dark, armed with oleander sticks, to cut from the tree that at one end two or three prongs stick out, these prongs being young shoots cut off within three inches of the stem. Each boy, indeed I may say men, for old as well as young occasionally join in the sport, holds in one hand a lantern, while in the other is the oleander stick in question. Thus armed, half a dozen or more rally out to traverse the marsh side, contiguous to the beach in search of coveted *Gelasimi*. Soon the 'tally oh,' is sounded, and away they scamper in full pursuit amid the darkness, tumbling over stumps or stones, or going head first into a cedar bush. Lanterns go out, and legs get well bruised; but the fun grows fast and furious: one crab has been bagged, and lots more are hobbling over the sward; the dim lanterns are seen scattered about, as each owner goes off on his own account, and it is only after an hour's hunt or so, that the tired crab hunters meet to count their spoil. Woe betide the fingers that get a nip from the land crab, for he has such grasping power in his enlarged bifid claw, that the unfortunate hand he grasps will shake with no welcome feeling in it."

Among the Nova Scotian crabs were noticed the common shore crab (*cancer irroratus*), which is extremely abundant on our Atlantic coast, and may be found on all rocky shores beneath the stones at low water mark. The smaller specimens are eagerly devoured by many of the duck tribe, which frequent the coast in winter, but how they manage to digest the stony carapace of the crap appears to be a mystery. The long-legged crab (*Hyas Cocaretata*) of which, however, little is known as regards its habits, as it is an inhabitant of deep water. It must be very common nevertheless on the banks near shore, for the stomachs of cod fish caught during the months of October, November, and December are filled with them. The crabs are swallowed whole by these voracious creatures, although some are of large size, and a specimen exhibited was as perfect in every limb as if it had just been taken from its briny home. A species of soldier crab (*Pagarus*) was also described and its habits of obtaining house accommodation in the harbour, appears to be a very different, and much easier of accomplishment than on shore. When large enough to become a tenant, the soldier crab moves about in search of a suitable home, and having found in some little nook the unoccupied shell of a defunct univalve, inserts his nether extremity in the coil of the chamber within. If he finds it fits easy he is satisfied, but if the shoe pinches he searches about again until he at last finds one suited to his size. He then moves about by means of his strong claws which protrude without the mouth of the shell, and becomes a self-satisfied householder on very easy terms. Should he be attacked by some evil disposed fellow inhabitant of the deep, as he takes his daily walk, he immediately withdraws himself within the shell, closing the mouth by drawing up his pincer claws, and so sets at defiance any attempt to storm his castle. He is never molested by importunate tax gatherers, nor is he troubled with a gas account, for nature gives him a subdued light, sufficient for his purpose; and as to his water rate, he has enough and to spare of that element without having to pay for it, or to live in perpetual fear of its being "turned of in his vicinity." So he leads a happy life, and his only care, if he has such a sense, is having to look for a new house, when he finds the one he occupies too small to contain his increased proportions.

After the reading of this paper on the crustacea, the President brought to the notice of the meeting, a gigantic specimen of the common squid (*ommastrephes*) which had been taken near Cape Sable, the northwest point of the province. It measured over three feet in extent, from the posterior extreme to the tips of the arms, and appeared a perfect giant by the side of a very fine specimen of the same species, taken in Halifax harbour.

Capt. L'Estrange exhibited the head of a cottoid fish, which he had found hanging up on a tree, near Birch Cove Lakes, which may prove a fresh water species, and new to our fauna. It had evidently been left in that situation by some sportsmen, who considered it a curiosity.

In closing the proceedings of the evening, the President congratulated the members upon the present appearance of the Institute Room, which had been recently re-arranged, and the gas and stove fittings placed in more convenient situations. A series of glazed table cases has also been added, in which the typical specimens exhibited by members could be placed, thus forming the commencement of what he hoped would in a few years grow into a well proportioned museum.

Correspondence.

[*Under this head we shall be glad to insert any letters of general interest.*]

BIRD MURDER.

Sir,—A society is, I hear, being formed for the protection of our rock-building sea fowl from indiscriminate slaughter during the breeding season; and to further that purpose it is intended to memorialise Parliament. This, though an excellent thing in its way, is open to grave objections. For instance, though we may deeply deplore the fact of so many birds being killed in mere wantonness (as recorded in the *Field, Science Gossip, &c.*), yet, ere we bring a pseudo game law into effect to bear upon a peculiar section of ari-fauna, we should think upon the evils it will entail, and upon what section of the community it will press the most heavily. Certainly not upon those whom it is intended to thwart—the mere sportsman, or pleasure seeker (who will follow their bent elsewhere)—but upon the real naturalist; not those who rely upon books alone, or upon museums, with their wretchedly caricatured specimens for information, but those who study the great book of Nature, ever open to her lovers in those grand solitudes—where ocean plashes ever on the time and water-worn rocks—where the sea-mew screams its warning note as the white sea-horses rush on the top of the angry billows, when the storm-clouds shut out the view of its seaward mate, hastening homeward with its glistening prey.

Those who have with a sportsman's pride and a naturalist's heart followed the wild birds into their own domain, will know how much is learnt of their habits by the search for, and of their anatomy by the procuration of, specimens. I know myself what were my sensations upon my first invasion on the rock-birds' haunts. It was a cold grey morning in May some few years ago that, getting my crew together at about 3 a.m., I started from Freshwater, Isle of Wight, in an open boat for the Needles. The morning was as yet still. But there was a curious look about the darkened and red flushed horizon, and a hollow sound in the murmur of the short waves as they broke on the shore-lying rocks, or rushed through the hollow "Stag," which foreboded a nasty termination to the morning. The pull-up was pleasant enough. The "Green," which is a spot of verdant sward half-way up the face of the chalk cliff—where an adventurous fowler lost his life some years back by slipping over the edge of the plateau, and being dashed to pieces on the sharp rocks below—was passed, the sea-stocks growing in the crevices above were pointed out, and the "Bench" was arrived at. This, an ugly overhanging rock, framed in by precipitous heights rising hundreds of feet above the water line, was the resort of thousands of guillemots, puffins, and razorbills, which could be seen in rows on ledges of the cliff, standing like sentinels, some at so great a height as to appear no larger than sparrows. I had come expressly for a pair of razorbills; but as these birds prudently kept out of range, a gun was fired to alarm them from their perch, or confuse them, so that they might fly within shot. Hardly had the report re-echoed from the surrounding crags ere a scene followed which I would not have lost for worlds. The air was chequered with black and white, as the birds rushed about in all directions—some to throw themselves for safety into the sea, others to dive still deeper into some far-off cranny, while some which had been concealed to us from below dashed out of the inaccessible fissures which seamed the "Bench" in every direction. Some little puffins who were gravely sitting on some rocks close to the sea scurried off in their grotesque way. The sea gulls screamed defiance, as they poised themselves in mingled fear and rage over our heads. And some cormorants on the adjacent Needles, who were hanging out their wings to dry in that devout style which has no doubt given them the name of "Isle of Wight Parsons," stretched out their long snake-like necks, and launched themselves off to add to the confusion which at that moment reigned paramount in the bird world. The noise of the rapidly agitated wings of so great a number of thoroughly frightened birds was curious in the extreme, and I was too much entranced by the novelty of their various evolutions as they dived, darted, or wheeled in wild dismay to do aught than make a mental study of the scene, although several birds came within gunshot. Some little time was spent in futile endeavours to land; but the rapidly rising wind warned us that it blew dead upon a rockbound, and dangerous leeshore, upon which even in very fine weather it was a difficult task to set foot or hand, therefore I contented myself in observation, vainly wishing that I could procure the egg which I was sure lay concealed beneath the bosom of yonder close-setting sea fowl. Three birds were shot, but in consequence of the danger attendant upon following them to where they drifted were not recovered; I therefore gave up shooting, as this was useless slaughter, and bade adieu to the "Bench." Nearing the "Black Rock" the storm burst upon us, and all our skill was exerted to keep the boat clear of the submerged rocks. Even old B. (a retired man o'war's-man) said, as he shook his head, "If we don't make yonder headland in less than ten minutes we shall have to stand out to sea (which with this Cherbourg wind will be bad enough) or else we shall go on the rocks, or get into the race of the Needles, and that will never do with this 'chop' on." Suffice it to say, that after some hard work the next few anxious minutes passed and we *did* round the headland, where we were in comparatively smooth water, and made Freshwater about two hours after I had calculated—having seen more birds and learnt more of their habits in those few hours, than the contemplation of stuffed specimens in the wretchedly arranged museums of which we boast would teach in a year. The only thing left undone was the actual procuring of the specimens we wanted, which was reserved for another day, and this also taught what books and museums never can teach. For, firstly, you watch a bird's habits in its own sphere, if you are an artist you gain a correct notion of contour, you shoot it, and while yet the body is warm you gain a correct notion of colouring—especially as regards the eyes, the bill, and the feet, which always fade or discolour after death. If you are a taxidermist, you gain a knowledge of attitude, expression, and the thousand and one little things which make a properly mounted specimen something beyond a "stuffed bird." If you are an anatomist you can, in addition to all this, determine many points about the bird you have just shot which would otherwise remain undiscovered were you prevented from shooting it, and which no study of books or museums could always teach. How then to discriminate between the persons who seek by the necessary destruction of a few to materially aid science, or the wholesale bird destroyer, who shoots for pleasure alone, I do not see how it is to be done; and I very much fear that in this case, as in many others, the innocent will suffer more than the guilty.

To be consistent, the prohibition should extend to the shooting of *all* birds during the breeding season; and as some breed two and three times a year, this would make England about as comfortable a place to live in could well be imagined. Fancy a fellow getting penal servitude for shooting a robin in the breeding season; or another one imprisoned or fined by some Justice Shallow for clearing out the sparrows' nests, and destroying their eggs by having his roof-guttering cleaned out. Get this little offspring of the New Game Law introduced into country society, and ornithology as a practical study is *in articulo mortis*, and oology a myth of the past; for many birds only visit us at their breeding season, and can only be procured then, as well of course as eggs of all birds at this time.

I do not for an instant countenance the useless killing of sea birds; but I think that, if we take up this matter on the score of cruelty, we should also turn a pitying eye upon the sufferings of the birds which are brought up (like Dickens's Pirrip) "by hand" in a state of domesticity, turned out while they have no element of wild-bird life about them, and then in a week or so coolly decoyed by the "old familiar feed" into a favourable position where they can be eligibly accommodated in a "battue" by the "sportsmen" who officiate. Perhaps it may be urged in extenuation that the pheasants, etc., are not breeding at that time, and that they belong to the people who shoot them. To this latter argument I should reply as the gentleman did to the costermonger, who, "wallopping" his donkey most unmercifully, was asked what he did it for? "Why," he growled, "'Cos it's my own, and can't I do what I like with my own?" "No," said his questioner. "Certainly not if it involves an act of cruelty. For instance, how do you like this?" added he, laying his stick smartly over his shoulders. "Vot are you a doing on?" roared the fellow. "This is my own stick?" said his tormenter between the blows, "and can't I do as I like with my own?" Now I think "battue" shooting ought to be discouraged, as it really is cruel, unsportsmanlike, and unmanly. For what pleasure can extend to killing birds which are nearly as tame as barn-door fowls, and which require as little healthy exertion to get, as sitting in an easy chair, popping at tame pigeons, and having some one to pick them up, would require. For my part, speaking as a sportsman only, I feel more pride in floundering through a difficult morass and killing a leash of snipes or a mallard cleverly, and having some trouble to get them, than killing any amount of half-wild birds. As a naturalist, I discountenance useless slaughter in any way; but I should be very sorry to see rockbirds or any wild birds under the protection of an Act, which would effectually cut off the ornithologist from the prosecution of those studies which give him such real happiness and healthy recreation.

I am, Sir, yours, &c., &c.,
A. M. B.

Short Notes.

THE SWEDISH ARCTIC EXPEDITION.—In a brief note addressed to the President of the Royal Society, Prof. Nordenskiöld, writing from Kobbe Bay, September 16, communicates a few particulars of the Swedish Arctic Expedition. The highest latitude to which the party were able to navigate their steamer was 81° 9′ where ice stopped them. This was the end of August; but a week later the sea was clear, and from one of the highest peaks of Parry Island "traces only of ice further northward" could be seen. The exploring steamer, after taking in the coal sent out for her use to Kobbe Bay, made again for the north, whether to pass the winter in the ice or not is at present uncertain. Meanwhile, the coal ship returns to Sweden, bringing five of the exploring party, "with the rich geological, zoological, and botanical collections" made during the first part of the voyage. It is probable, therefore, that in a few weeks we shall get full particulars of all that our enterprising rivals have discovered and acquired since they crossed the Arctic Circle in July last.

NUTMEGS.—Nutmegs are the fruit of a beautiful tree which grows in the Molucca Islands, and in other parts of the East. All the parts of the tree are aromatic, but only those portions of the tree called mace and nutmeg are marketable. The entire fruit is of an oval form, about the size of a peach. The nutmeg is the innermost kernel. It is surrounded by a skin, which, peeled off, constitutes the mace of commerce. The tree yields annually three crops. The first one, which is gathered in April, is the best. The others are gathered in August and December. Good nutmegs should be dense and heavy and free from worm holes. When the worm holes have been artificially filled up, the feeling of lightness in the hand is a means of detecting the fraud. An attempt has been made to cultivate nutmegs in the West Indies, but without success.—*New York Mercantile Journal.*

THE THREE NEW PLANETS.—Besides the two planets No. 103 and 104, recently discovered by Mr. Watson, of Ann Arbor, Michigan, U.S., there is now a third recorded by this enterprising astronomer. This planet—105—was discovered by Mr. Watson on the 16th of September and had on this day, at 16h. 3m. 16s. m.t., Ann Arbor, the following position: Right ascension, oh. 13m. 47·42s.; northern declination, 6° 12′ 3·9″. It had the brilliancy of a star of the 11th or 12th magnitude.—*Scientific Opinion.*

AN AUSTRALIAN TREE.—A giant tree, of the Eucalyptus species, was felled lately in the Dandenong Ranges, Australia. At one foot from the ground the circumference was 69 ft.; at 12 ft. from the ground the diameter was 11 ft. 4 in.; at 78 ft., diameter 9 ft.; at 144 ft., diameter 8 ft.; at 210 ft., diameter 5 ft. The tree was 330 ft. high.

Remarks, Queries, &c.

Under this head we shall be happy to insert original Remarks, Queries, &c.)

REASONING POWER OF ANIMALS.

"All nature owns with one accord
The great and universal Lord;
Insect and bird, and tree, and flower,
Bear witness to his wondrous power."

In further confirmation of the theory that the faculty of reason belongs exclusively to man, I am glad to be able to offer the name of the celebrated John Wesley, who unreservedly supports our view. From his able and comprehensive treatise on Natural Philosophy I extract a note or two relating to this subject. He thus writes:—"We must not, however ingenious any creature may appear to be in what it)does, however tractable it may be to our training, or however it may display what we consider profound sagacity in these cases, or in any one of them attribute even the slightest approach in kind to human reason; for the stamp of reason, the capacity of comparing, profiting by experience and teaching one another, so as to establish a growing stock of knowledge, is not in the slightest degree upon even the most apparently wise animal in existence."

The remark expressed by Mr. Newberry in the last number of the NOTE BOOK, that the most sagacious and seemingly reasonable actions of animals are all produced by appeal to their *senses*, quite accords with the opinion of Wesley; for the distinction he makes between instinct and reason is, that "reason is the comparison of what a man purposes to do with the experience of the past; instinct acts from the impulse of present objects on its *organs of sense.*"

The definition of reason furnished by "C." is very imperfect; that supplied by Mr. Newberry is much fairer. A dog that is beaten repeatedly for committing a fault—such as theft—may leave it off not from any knowledge of the goodness or badness of the act, but because from the action of its instinct it is made to avoid the deed, because it is followed by pain. This is precisely similar to the way in which men instinctively are shielded from danger. When any part of our body comes in contact with fire, how instantaneously we start from it! A man lost in deep thought approaches the edge of a precipice, or an uncovered quarry: immediately his foot slips, see how the *instinct* of self-preservation causes him to clutch the nearest twig or root! In such cases as these there is no time for reflection; and all the actions of new-born infants are governed by the same laws of instinct. In this manner may be explained the *ordinary* sagacious conduct of the lower animals. Many of the *extraordinary* deeds related of horses, elephants, dogs, &c., it is probable, are entirely fictitious, and not to be relied upon; those that are well authenticated, I believe to be produced by the arrangement of a *special providence*, such as the instances we have of dogs saving mens' lives, parrots convicting murderers, &c., &c. On page 251, vol. 2nd of the NOTE BOOK, an opinion is expressed *that parrots understand the words they are taught to pronounce.* I would just remark that such an idea is in the highest degree improbable. Why, let that be granted, and you raise them at once to human rank! The utterances of talking birds are made entirely at random, although the curious appropriateness of some of their words have led persons to this absurd supposition. As Mr. Newberry remarks, if reason be possessed by one of the brute creation, it is by all; and I would add if it be possessed by animals, so it is by *plants*, as no line can be drawn between them; and a certain individual belonging to the former class is nothing more than a *tube with sensation*, viz.: the water hydra. To support this opinion—"the motions of plants are as *regular* and *rational* as those of animals; they show as much design and contrivance, and are as necessary and proper to attain their end." After all, I give it as my humble opinion, and I believe it to be that of many others, that the common instances of animal instinct by which we are constantly surrounded, and which cannot escape our observation, are quite as remarkable as those abnormal acts in animal life which excite so much wonder and curiosity. For instance, what induces the young bee, *prior to all experience*, to lay up a store of honey for the winter? Is it reason? No, for reason is the ordering of present conduct by the experience of the past. To take another example—how is it that birds confined in cages, and supplied with plenty of food, nevertheless show a restlessness, and struggle to escape when the time for migration arrives? Is it *reason* that makes birds so act? What *motive* can the bird have for such conduct, when supplied with abundance of food, warmth, and all it requires? Why does it endeavour to free itself only *at that particular time?* Nothing influences it but a law of its being implanted in its nature for wise and beautiful purposes by its all wise Creator, but of which it has no more knowledge than a stone has of the force of gravitation exerted upon it. It is so true that "there is an ever-watchful agency and superintending, and controlling intelligence that cannot err ruling over the actions of animals." And I would here remark, that this ornithological fact is an unanswerable proof that *birds migrate*, notwithstanding "A. H. Malan's" opinion that this has not been sufficiently proved. He also says that the fact of large flocks being met with at sea, far from land, is no proof that they are migrating; that "they may be *en route* for some new feeding-place." Now I take it, that thus meeting birds is a convincing proof that they do migrate; and what, I would ask Mr. Malan, is migration but being "*en route* for a new feeding-place?"

He further remarks, that "the theory of swallows remaining dormant at the bottom of streams *is nearly* exploded." If he has any doubt on this point, he can easily satisfy himself. Let him hold a swallow, or any other bird, under water for half an hour, and then see whether it is dead or alive! With regard to the concluding paragraph in Mr. Malan's letter, I would ask what is *his own* opinion as to the cause of the eggs of birds being differently shaped? I believe that nature has it so only that her beauty may be increased by *variety*. True, some would say that eggs sharp at one end are less likely to roll out of rock-built nests; but eggs are seldom laid in such a position that so slight a difference could produce any effect worthy of note.

Another correspondent "W. H. D." in speaking of the sagacity displayed by animals, far exceeds the bounds of truth when he says that "we find individuals among the lower order of animals quite equal to, and often superior to individuals of our own species in intellect." The fact is that the lowest, most degraded, and least intelligent of the human race, are far exalted above the brutes. The reason which one man actively uses lies dormant, or nearly so in another man, but still he possesses the power of calling it into exercise, and turning it into useful account which no brute can do. The lower animals have not this faculty which renders man so immeasurably above them, and as to being superior to him in intellect, there never has been, or can be such an animal. A little lower down "W. H. D." seems to question the fact that all men have souls. It has been said that "instinct differs from reason by the pursuit of nothing beyond what conduces directly, either to the continuation of the individual, or the propagation of the kind. I think this too limited an application of the term *instinct*, as certainly many of the actions of animals cannot be brought under either of these headings.

With reference to the theory of insects feeling pain, I would ask those of your correspondents who affirm that they *do not*, whether they also deny the sense of pain to fishes and marine animals: for it seems to me that we know about as much of the *feelings* of one tribe as the other. What do those on the *affirmative* side think of the fact that the lobster when alarmed at the report of a cannon *throws off its claws?* It appears to suffer as little inconvenience from the loss of its claws as the spider or fly does when deprived of its legs. To animate naturalists to an unwearied study of these interesting topics, I conclude by quoting the words of the poet:—

"There are still in thee,
Instructive book of nature! many leaves
Which yet no mortal has perused."

Edinburgh. R. B. W.

It is a little difficult to gather from "R. B. W.'s" letter what are his actual views on this subject. He condemns at the outset my impression that "reason is enjoyed in a limited degree by the higher families of the vertebrate kingdom;" and after several paragraphs of well-worded criticism, he condemns his views to the most ignominious defeat by acknowledging "that in many of the actions of dogs there is evident reason." Why should we squabble further? It is evident we are fighting for a shadow; for if dogs exhibit reason in their actions, I presume we are right in supposing reason to exist in dogs—and there the matter ends. Of course its origin must be attributed to God. Yet inasmuch as we are accustomed to say that "many of the useful engines and machines of civilised man" are worked by the steam that is supplied them by the ingenious contrivance of engineer and stoker; so, I think, a discriminating public will pardon us for attributing a dog's actions to his reason, instead of attributing the reason which prompts the actions to the Omnipotent Origin of all Reason: the two statements being expressions of the same thing regarded from two different points of view.

I do not know much about the physiology and anatomy of zoophytes and sponges; nor was I aware of "the well-known fact that many tribes of insects display a far greater share of intelligence and apparent reason in their actions than the majority of mammalia." Is it to the marvellous geometrical exactness shown in the honeycomb that "R. B. W." refers in particular? It is, indeed, a masterpiece of astonishing beauty: and "it would take," says Sidney Smith, "a senior wrangler at Cambridge ten hours a day for three years together to know enough mathematics for the calculation of those problems with which not only every queen bee, but every undergraduate grub, is acquainted the moment it is born." But herein there does not appear to me that wondrous combination of memory, intelligence, and affection, which enables a dog after the lapse of several years to distinguish an old master in a large crowd.

As regards the actions of our headless frog, and my statement that "purposive movements are no proof of consciousness or will," I must refer "R. B. W." to Dr. Kirke's "Handbook of Physiology," pp. 467—470. This is the received text-book for the science school at Oxford, and is considered an authority on such matters; and in the pages mentioned my antagonist will find not only the quotation we allude to, but also further particulars about the movements of frogs, lizards, and eels, that have been decapitated, bisected, and otherwise mutilated by merciless experimentalists.

I beg to thank W. Newberry for his very able remarks on the present subject (N. N. B., Jan. 1869.) They are certainly charged with weighty and convincing argument, and his definition of reason is far more satisfactory than my own, in that it defines the line of demarcation which separates the intellectual capacity of man from that of brutes. But the last few sentences of his excellent note contain a question which human intelligence will probably never be able to answer. "Are animals possessed of a soul? Are they immortal?" "Reason," says "W. N." "is a faculty of the soul; instinct, of the body. It depends upon the body, for its activity ceases when the body dies." Sir, you are somewhat bold in making this statement absolutely, for several philosophers and thinking men who have devoted their lives to the study of psychological investigations, have been led to conclusions which countenance a belief in the immortality of animals. I do not say I include such surmisings in the "symbol" of my creed; yet I am aware that there are stout breastworks and valiant buttresses of argument to defend them against invaders, and I could mention living authors who might not be unwilling to wield a cudgel in defence of the opinion. Is there any force in the following reasoning? Man possesses an immortal soul: but wherein consists the immortality? It consists in the undying existence of the soul's personal identity, memory, affection, and character. (Such was Mr. Liddon's definition of immortality in one of his inimitable sermons preached before the University of Oxford). Now all these mental attributes are more or less observable in lower animals. And if they are said to be immortal in the one phase, can we absolutely deny their immortality in the other? I trow not.   C.

I cannot agree with your correspondent W. Newberry, in denying to animals all reason, and drawing a definite line between *reason* and *instinct*. The latter term is, it seems to me, extremely indefinite, and conveys no meaning whatever; while it has helped to render the consideration of the subject more obscure than it need be. I will state in as few words as possible my ideas on this point, hoping that some of your other readers may give their opinions likewise. I would grant to all animals a certain share of the faculties possessed by man. After observing the analogy which is so evident between the development of *mind* and *body*, I come to the following conclusions:—As we find in the body of an animal that the various organs and limbs are more or less developed as circumstances require their use, so I believe its mental faculties are high or low as outward circumstances require; and further, that as there are some organs or limbs which we find to be only rudimentary, so there are faculties in the mind of the animal which are perfectly dormant, but may be called forth into action if the circumstances requiring their use be incident to a sufficient number of generations of the animal. I think that the intelligence of those animals which have been intimately associated with mankind for a long time, will bear out this view; as also will the case of the lower races of mankind who have retrograded in this respect. I shall be asked how I account for the actions commonly attributed to instinct? I reply that on examining these actions, there is reason to conclude that the conformation of the animal (a cause which has more to do with prompting action than is generally allowed it) together with the force of habit (which we know acts almost mechanically) inherited through an infinite number of ancestors, is alone sufficient to account for most actions, habits, and contrivances of animals. Where it is not sufficient, the very deficiency itself calls forth and develops those latent faculties, previously referred to, until they are adequate for the purpose, *and no longer*. I may mention another power, prompting action, viz., the experience gained by the individual animal. There is no phenomenon in the economy of the animal world which may not be referred to these causes. I will instance the migration of birds. The *habit* recurring at fixed intervals, and inherited as I have said above, is in my opinion quite sufficient to account for it—though this habit was in its origin doubtless, irregular, and caused by the influence of climate, etc., on individuals. To those who partake of the prejudice which has attributed to man only reason, leaving to animals the meaningless property termed "instinct," this may seem an unwarrantable assertion. Those, however, who have in any degree attempted impartially to examine the motives and actions of the animals which are lower than man in the system of nature will, I think, agree that the difference is only in degree; though I readily admit that as we look downward in the scale, this difference increases with greater rapidity—much more so indeed than the differences observable in the physical development of the same animals.

   Cosmos.

DO INSECTS FEEL PAIN?

"Windsor Hambrough" has set forth, very explicitly, one of the two views respecting the passage I quoted from Romans viii. Commentators have always differed as to the genuine interpretation, and although the NATURALIST'S NOTE BOOK is hardly a medium for theological discussion, yet I hope I shall be allowed briefly to state the arguments for my view, that ἡ κτίσις includes the irrational as well as the rational creation.

1. "The manifestation of the sons of God," is a definite Scriptural event, just as much as the second advent of Christ, and it cannot be said of the world of mankind, that they have an earnest desire for its consummation.

2. It cannot be said, in its full and proper force, that mankind were brought into their present state, not by their own act, or "willingly," but by the act and power of God, for which reason it longs for the deliverance promised. "Windsor Hambrough" thinks the "him who hath subjected the same," (v. 20), to be Adam. How can Adam be said to have brought death upon mankind, "in hope," or with the assurance, that at some future time they should be delivered? The "Him" must be none other than God himself.

3. How can it be said of mankind, as a whole, that

they are to be delivered from the bondage of corruption, and made partakers of the glorious liberty of the children of God; and at a time, too, when the sons of God are to be manifested, *i.e.*, at the Resurrection, and Second Advent. This, I think, cannot be maintained with any satisfactory evidence.

4. The context is against W. H.'s interpretation. St. Paul's object is not to show that this state is one of frailty and sorrow, and that Christians must feel it as well as others; on the contrary, he desires to convince his readers that the sufferings of this present state are not to be compared to the future glory of the sons of God; and then to prove how great this glory will be, he describes the whole creation as yearning, with outstretched neck, for the consummation of the Redeemer's kingdom.

And now, it may be asked, can St. Paul's words be better understood with reference to the irrational creation? We think they can.

1. It may with the strictest propriety be said that the irrational creation was subjected to vanity not willingly, but by the authority of God. "Cursed be the earth for thy sake," Gen. viii. 17. "The earth mourneth and fadeth away; the earth is defiled under the inhabitants thereof, because they have transgressed the laws . . . therefore hath the curse devoured the earth," Is. xxiv. "How long shall the land mourn, and the herbs of every field wither, for the wickedness of them that dwell therein," Jer. xii. 4. It is sufficient, then, that the irrational creation was made subject to decay and vanity by the act of God, in punishment for the sins of men.

2. This subjection of the creature to the bondage of corruption, is not final or hopeless, but the whole creation is to share in the glorious liberty of the children of God. "The wilderness and the solitary place shall be glad, and the desert shall rejoice and blossom as the rose." "The wolf shall lie down with the lamb." "Nevertheless, we, according to the promise, look for new heavens and a new earth." These, and numerous similar passages, describe the *palingenesia* of the whole creation that sacred writers tell us shall attend the consummation of the Redeemer's kingdom.

3. This interpretation is supported by the prevalent doctrine of the Jews. Eisenmenger's "Endecktes Judeathum," cap. 15:—"Hereafter the whole creation shall be changed for the better, and return to the perfection and purity which it had in the time of the first man, before sin was."

4. And, after all, it is the common interpretation, and being the obvious sense, is most probably the right one. C.

This question has now been discussed in the columns of the interesting NATURALIST'S NOTE BOOK for the last six months, and the arguments produced for and against their susceptibility of pain, have arisen from "Entomologicus" in the June number asking the query, viz., Do insects feel pain? In reading Mr. H. H. Ulidia's clever article upon the above-named question in the NATURALIST'S NOTE BOOK for this month (January) I come across the following: —"And here, Sir, I wish to notice and correct a mistake into which some of your correspondents have merged. Our present inquiry is not whether insects feel *much* or *little* pain, neither are we wanting to know if they feel as much pain as man, the whale, or the sparrow, etc., etc., but simply *do insects feel pain?* Some of your correspondents, too, in something like despair in science, throw down their pens, and say the question never can be decided." Now I for one must be included among "some of your correspondents," from having made the following remarks when writing to you about the giant sirex. I then said I killed it, like I do almost all insects, by the use of chloroform, as being the most merciful death, and thereby avoiding all chance of giving them *any pain*, if insects "do feel pain," which still appears to be the question at issue with many correspondents of the NOTE BOOK, and which is one they all know *must* remain undecided in the end, it being impossible to prove for certain whether they experience much, little, or any pain. I think, as Mr. H. H. Ulidia says, "that insects feel pain;" but at the same time I say most certainly not to the *same extent* as "man, the elephant, the whale, and the sparrow, etc.," feel it. I write this to show that I certainly "have merged" into a mistake, for I have all along thought from Mr. H. H. Ulidia's former correspondence, that he held insects felt pain to the *same extent* as the higher class of animals feel it. I think, as "Entomologicus" says, "the most rational theory is, that they feel pain, but only in proportion to their size." I have noticed in the writings of the correspondents of the painless theory, that hardly one actually *deny* that insects do feel pain; but, on the contrary, many even admit that they do experience a certain amount of pain. I do not for one moment "in something like despair," throw down my pen, but I certainly think that the question at issue is one which *cannot be positively decided*, although Mr. H. H. Ulidia is "confident that future research, patient industry, analogy, induction, and candour, must ultimately establish the fact that insects do feel pain." In conclusion, I beg to state that I perfectly agree with Mr. H. H. Ulidia in maintaining that insects *do* feel pain; and I wish him every success in establishing "the soundness of the side he advocates." I have no doubt but that in the end he will prove himself to be the conqueror, having in my opinion *by far* the best and most reasonable side of the argument; but when that argument will finally be brought to a close in the NATURALIST'S NOTE BOOK, remains to be seen. In the meantime, I advise him not to "fall back into the reserve," but to press forward vigorously and scatter the enemy—some of whom I think he must have seriously wounded; for what has become of "P. G. M.," Messrs. Crook, and "Good Taste," etc., etc.? A. E. BUTTEMER.
Ambleside.

I have read with much pleasure this interesting and animated controversy which has been carried on for so long by some of your correspondents. It is one of those subjects that requires both a good knowledge of anatomy and careful consideration, in order to settle it satisfactorily. I intend to make a few remarks upon it, which I hope may prove conclusive: but before I do so, I must say that I cannot understand how any persons can disagree about it. Mr. Ulidia and his coadjutors are perfectly correct in what they state, and I only differ from him in two points. The first is, his arguing from analogy; and the second is, in attributing to insects the same perception of pain that we ourselves possess. It is not because man, the whale, elephant, &c., feel pain acutely, that insects should do so; for were we always to argue by analogy in such subjects as these, there would be no end to the blunders and mistakes that we should make. Be it remembered that a grain or two of *fact* is worth a ton of *theory*, and although the latter is never either to be discarded or despised, the former is *always* to be *depended* upon. Hence when we know for certain that *nerves* are the organs through which the *will* operates, and that insects possess *nerves*, we may safely and reasonably affirm that they feel pain. But some direct and indirect experiments that have been made, have proved beyond a doubt that although they feel pain, they do not suffer one quarter as much as any of the Mammalia. Let us suppose, for the sake of argument, that a dog and a butterfly, or any other insect, have one or more of their legs removed. What is the result? The poor dog of course will soon die; but the insect, though showing by its writhings and flutterings that it feels some pain, and considerable inconvenience from the loss of its member, will rapidly recover. I was surprised when I read in one of Mr. Spicer's papers that he was of the contrary side, and still more so when I perceived that he believed that insects not only are devoid of feeling, but also of brain and blood. They certainly do not possess one capital brain, such as we find in the higher orders of animals, but a system of ganglia, which are the *analogues* of the brain, and which extend in a continuous chain from the head to the extreme end of the abdomen, branching out into the large nerves which ramify throughout the whole of the body. A "ganglion" is composed of what is scientifically called "Vesicular and tubular nervine," or, in other words, white and grey nervous matter. The fact of insects having *blood* is, I think, too well-known to admit of doubt. I have seen it circulating pretty freely in the inner side of the abdomen of the blow fly (Musca Vomitoria) under a power of two hundred diameters.

VERITAS.

This is a very important as well as an interesting question to all entomologists, but it is a question which cannot be satisfactorily answered. We can only reason on such a subject by induction and analogy. Mr. Landels says the advocates of the painless theory have hitherto had the best of the argument, but this I think is doubtful. It is scarcely fair to assert that, because a moth or a beetle will pass through certain ordeals without much struggling, or that because they will eat food placed for them immediately after being scalded or pinned; therefore they do not feel pain. We often find that human beings are made almost ravenously hungry by undergoing a surgical operation, but it would not be reasonable to say that the operation was not a very painful one, or they would not be so ready to eat after it. It is well known, also, that extreme pain invariably causes a deadness or numbness to seize the part affected, but which is often felt most acutely afterwards. May it not be so with insects? Have insects a nervous system? Some of your correspondents answer no!—but we know that if they have not an actual system of nerves, branching out from a given centre, and rendered visible by the microscope, they have something analogous to a nervous system. What is it that makes an insect sensible of the touch of a sharp instrument? What is it that enables the insect or the zoophite to secure and enjoy its food but a sense of taste and feeling? There can be no sense either of sight, taste, feeling, or even of existence, without a nervous system or something analogous to it. Surely the Creator who has been so munificent in his provision for the enjoyment of all his creatures, would not deny that enjoyment to insects. But how can there be any enjoyment if the insect possesses no sense of feeling? If it be true that insects are possessed of nervous matter, it follows as a natural inference, that any violent shock upon that nervous matter, causes a sensation throughout the insect, and this sensation we call *feeling*. If an insect then possesses a sense of feeling at all, it must possess a sense of feeling pain as well as pleasure; for to deprive them of one deprives them of all. I cannot see how you can separate one class of organisms from the kingdom of nature, and deny to it one of the most essential elements of existence. W. NEWBERRY.

Mr. Landels, in his first sentence, very candidly tells us that he "inclines to the opinion that insects do feel a *certain* amount of pain. "A certain amount," by which I understand him to mean a *settled, determined* amount of pain. Good. He then introduces us to an insect-boiling transaction in which he blunders; tells us of his astonishment at the rude audacity of a "kicking" beetle after undergoing not only a "scalding," but a "transfixion" operation; and quite fatigued after the Herculean labour of pulling a pin from an insect's wing, he ultimately manages to contradict his first sentence by arriving at the conclusion that "this insect did not experience *much* pain!" But as all these admissions, contradictions, and concessions are but the stereotyped arguments of the correspondents on the negative side, I have only to present my compliments to Mr. Landels. But with me you will acknowledge that *the bit of cobbler's wax experimental philosophy* introduced by the inimitable "W. H. D.," possesses such a formidable amount of learned delicacy that I cannot even by stratagem approach it. Mr. Malan, full of anti-Pythagorean ideas, thinks we cannot metamorphose ourselves into insects so as to prove our arguments: he might just as well tell us that we cannot conveniently get metamorphosed into whales, sparrows, and asses, in order to know if they do or do not feel pain. Is Mr. Malan sure that I am susceptible of pain? Well, I presume he will say he is. Admitted. But how does he know? By what line of argument does he arrive at this conclusion? Just on the same principle as we proceed when we argue that insects feel pain. H. H. ULIDIA.

THE BLACK FOREST.—By this title I do not mean that German Forest, near the Hartz Mountains, so celebrated for its ghostly legends and thrilling romances, but a certain wood in Scotland well known to many naturalists; it is composed of what I consider the most beautiful of all the Conifera, viz., the true Scotch fir, which once extended nearly over the whole of that country; but, owing both to geological occurrences and to the rapid progress of civilisation, has now almost disappeared. Many a time, during my walks and rambles over the moors and mountains in the Highlands of Scotland, have I come across large trunks and branches of this wood, which having been buried for centuries deep in the bogs at length appear by the mutual action of denudation and the hand of man. The situation of this forest is very picturesque, clothing part of one side of the lake with its sombre blackish-green foliage, and then gradually rising for some distance towards the mountains which loom up in grand ranges around and beyond. Fond as I am of wild rocky heights and mountainous views, yet I think that there is nothing so beautiful as, and nothing to surpass, a sylvan scene: it is most pleasant to rest upon the roots of some large forest giant shaded from the burning heat of the mid-day sun, and to see and hear the leaves waving gently in the summer breeze, ever and anon disclosing large masses of light and shade in strong and lovely contrast; those large gnarled trunks resembling in their tortuous bends the vast coils of some gigantic box or python, show well their deep indentations and upraisings covered with moss and lichens. It forms one of the greatest pleasures that a naturalist enjoys to hear the twitterings of the birds and the humming and buzzing of the various insects; and to watch the avocations and gambols of the smaller creatures. Having stayed in that delightful neighbourhood for some time, I have explored it well, and succeeded in capturing many species of rare coleoptera. Among these may be mentioned that most beautiful and local longicorn (Astinomus ædilis). This handsome insect, although only about three quarters of an inch in length, possesses antennæ four or five inches long! I believe that the *great* use of these long mobile appendages remains a mystery, for I have never read anything that has thrown much light upon the subject. Mr. E. C. Rye does not mention where their *true habitat* is, but merely remarks that "they love to settle on felled pine logs." It was only by the merest chance that I discovered it, whilst diligently stripping off the bark of a felled tree. I found several of them in holes with their heads partly out, having their antennæ packed closely around their bodies. I very soon extricated them with my forceps; they proved very fine and perfect specimens. Shortness of space alone prohibits me from writing more upon this interesting subject, but I hope to do so in some future paper.

A. C. E. B.

THE SOURCE OF HEAT.—The above subject has been (perhaps unintentionally) introduced by your correspondents "R. B. W." and "R. T.," in their remarks on the planet Neptune. Whatever may be the opinion of "R. T." as to the amount of heat derived by the planet Neptune from the fixed stars, it may fairly be doubted whether any great amount of heat is derived by the earth either from them or from the sun. It is a well-known fact that heat cannot be generated or transmitted from one body to another without the presence of certain gases to form a conductor. If a room be heated to say 180° to 200°, and then by means of a stream of nitrogen or carbonic acid gas, all air is excluded, the room would in a very few minutes be reduced to a condition below the freezing point. The effect will be better seen if a vessel of water is placed in the room, which would speedily become a frozen mass. Now if we apply this fact to the question at issue, your correspondent "R. T." will find a few rather serious difficulties in maintaining his theory of the source of heat. First, the mean distance of the earth from the sun is 97,000,000 of miles, of which all but a minute fraction is clear space, through which it is impossible for heat to travel, in consequence of the entire absence of air, or any other gaseous conductor of heat. Secondly, hot air is always lighter than cold air, and therefore has a tendency to rise higher; and the more rarefied the atmosphere is, the more rapid is the heated current upwards. So we find that if it were possible for heat to be transmitted from the sun to the atmosphere surrounding our globe, it would float in the upper regions, and never be felt on the earth's surface. The fact presents itself then that the source of heat must be sought for, not in the myriads of fixed stars, or even in the " effulgent orb of day," but in the earth's interior. If "R. T." were fortunate enough to traverse the heights of Mont Blanc, he would find a region of perpetual snow, and if he ascended six miles nearer the sun, according to Professor Glaisher, he would be insensible to cold, the fugidity of the atmosphere at that elevation being so intense as to render the system unsusceptible of its influence. But, on the other hand, if we descend into the "bowels of the earth," we find the temperature increases at the mean rate of one degree Fahrenheit for every forty-five feet. At this rate, water is at a boiling pitch at a depth of six miles; while at a depth of sixty miles the hardest rocks known to the geologist are in a melted state. Besides, what is there in the solid body of the sun to generate and transmit heat to the earth more than there is in the moon, which is sixty-eight times nearer than the sun. Further, the season, when the sun is nearest the earth, and when we should ordinarily expect to feel its influence most, is the coldest season of the year; while the season when the sun is furthest from the earth, is the hottest season of the year, which seems to me a flat contradiction of the theory of celestial heat. Perhaps more of your correspondents will give their opinion on this interesting question.

W. NEWBERRY.

THE PRONG-HORNED ANTELOPE.—Sir,—It is only quite recently that a most peculiar habit of the Prong-horned Antelope (*Antilocapra Americana*), namely, that of shedding its horns, has come under the general notice of Naturalists. In 1865, a young male Prong-horn was added to the Zoological Society's collection, and a short time after its arrival, the keeper discovered that one of its horns was loose, and immediately communicated the fact to Mr. Bartlett, and then it was found that the other horn was also loose, and very soon they both dropped off, much after the manner of the Deer (*Gervidæ*). A communication was made by the Secretary to the *Daily Telegraph*, fully describing the particulars; and there was also a very good account given in the Zoological Society's Proceedings for 1865. The young male was the first specimen that had ever been brought alive to this country.

The doe brings forth its young from the beginning of May to about the middle of June, producing generally two fawns at a birth, but occasionally only one. Eighteen months after birth, the horns drop off, leaving a core which has served to push off the horn, that is the outer shell. The tip of the core is at first quite flexible, and is slightly transparent, but the horn soon begins to harden and grow, generally taking an inward curve; a prong springs from the base, and towards the middle of summer the horns become fully developed, and drop off, to be renewed again in the autumn. The horns in the female are much smaller than in the male. Considering the extensive habitat of the Prong-horn, and also the abundance in which it is found, it is very strange that this habit should not have come under the notice of naturalists before; yet it appears to have been known by the hunters of the Western Plains, for I find the following in Captain Flack's interesting book on the Southern States:— "Hunters for a long time supposed that the Pronghorn, like the common deer, was in the habit of casting its horns every year. They are never seen without horns after they arrive at maturity, and further examination will prove that those ornamental and useful appendages are immovably attached to the skull." Dr. Coues, in the "American Naturalist," also states, like Captain Flack, that the horns are permanently fixed to the skull, but now there is no more doubt upon the subject, which was fully proved by the specimen which lived for some time in the Zoological Gardens. Another peculiar feature of the Prong-horn, is a gland which is placed on the posterior third of the back, and from which is continuously running a liquid which has a musky scent. This antelope has the power of erecting the white patch of hair just above the tail, and which, when brought into action, gives the animal a very peculiar appearance; he especially brings this power into play during the rutting season, when he especially wishes to gain the favour of the does, or when about to meet a rival buck.

H. MEYRICK.
5, Talbot Square, Sussex Gardens.

NEPTUNE.—In a note in the last number of the NATURALIST'S NOTE BOOK, I said that Neptune receives from the sun at least ten times the amount of light which we receive from the full moon, and also a considerable degree of heat: but I now think it quite likely that Neptune, and in fact all the planets, may be quite as warm as, and have as much light as, our earth. Let us see what would be necessary in order for this to be the case. Not long ago I heard a lecturer on the solar system say that although Mercury is so much nearer the sun than the earth is, yet it may receive only the same amount of heat and light as the latter does; and he stated that such would be the case were Mercury protected by a very dense atmosphere. Is not this a wrong conclusion? It is well known that the two elements which combine to form our atmosphere are oxygen and nitrogen, and that the former is a good deal heavier than common air, whereas nitrogen is slightly lighter than the same substance. It therefore appears that one way to make an atmosphere become more dense is to increase the proportion of oxygen to nitrogen; or, which is the same thing, to have a greater amount of oxygen, and a less amount of nitrogen: and since oxygen is the gas by which heat and light are developed, we may conclude that the denser the atmosphere is (of course supposing it to be made dense in the proposed way) the greater will be the amount of heat and light developed by it. It must be remembered that when a small spark, which would be immediately extinguished if introduced into common air, is placed in a bottle of oxygen gas, an intense heat and a dazzling light are the results. Suppose, then, that Mercury were placed at an equal distance from the sun with the earth, and that it was surrounded by a denser atmosphere than that of the latter, is it not right to say that Mercury would be hotter than the earth in proportion as its atmosphere is denser? but since it is much nearer the sun than the earth is, the heat of Mercury would be much greater still. Therefore, Mercury, in order to have the same amount of heat and light as the earth has, would require just the opposite to what the lecturer stated; that is, it would simply need a less dense atmosphere, or, which is the same thing, the proportion of oxygen to nitrogen in its atmosphere would have to be less than it is in the earth's atmosphere. The same may be said with regard to the planet Venus. The superior planets, Mars, Jupiter, Saturn, &c., would, on the contrary, require atmospheres more dense in proportion to their distances from the sun in order for the same amount of heat and light to be developed at their surfaces. This is a very simple way in which the amount of heat and light might be equalised (and perhaps is equalised) on all the planets.

R. T.

COMETS AND METEORS.—I beg to think "Gulielmus" and "Sidus" for their remarks on the connection between comets and meteors. I must confess that I never thought of the matter in the light in which "Gulielmus" puts it. It is quite true, as he says, that many comets lose their tails when in proximity to the sun, but it is quite as true that many comets which, when first seen, have no tails, unaccountably got possession of those appendages; and, in fact, there are changes so frequent and various in the shapes of comets' tails, that I think "Gulielmus" jumps at a very hasty conclusion in saying that the formation of the Zodiacal light may be ascribed to these lost tails of comets. The other day I was surprised to hear, as astronomers were surprised to notice, that a comet proceeded in its course towards the sun tail first! Of course this is only an exceptional case, but it remains to be explained. The observed number of meteors is greatly in excess of the observed number of comets; and, although Arago computed that the number of comets which have visited the solar system is between three and four millions, yet this number, large as it is, could not account for the immense number of meteors, supposing each of the latter to be the head or solid part of a comet. "Sidus" is mistaken when he says

that if meteors are solid bodies we must of necessity have a shower of meteoric stones with every display. Meteors come with such an astounding velocity (varying from eighteen to thirty-six miles a second) that the friction between them and the atmospheric particles being so great, they would be dissolved into gases. The meteor is visible only because the great heat to which it is subjected by friction sets it on fire. I believe that the meteoric masses found on the surface of the earth are simply fragments of such meteors as were too large to be entirely burnt out. There is abundant proof that these stones have been burnt.
R. T.

EXTINCTION OF SPECIES.—In the January number of the NOTE BOOK, Mr. Bax gives an interesting article upon the "Extinction of Species." I perfectly agree with him that the country at large is not properly worked. Most entomologists—I do not say *all*—content themselves with going where they know something is to be obtained worth having rather than explore an unknown district with the prospect of finding only common things. I hope collectors will next summer work over the unknown grounds, and see what is to be had, especially those in Ireland and the North of Scotland, which I am afraid is sadly neglected. Mr. Bax is right in his surmise concerning sulphuralis: it has been captured near Bury St. Edmunds by Dr. Wratislaw, in some quantity, where probably it has been located for years, and no doubt is to be found in other parts if well searched for at the proper season. Mr. Bax thinks P. Podalicus, C. Chryeis, C. Virgaurve, E. Hero, and E. Ligea, have become extinct in England, or rather Britain. I much question whether they were ever here to become extinct. C. Dispar, we all know too well, has gone to the dogs; it used to be taken at Ipswich in a single marshy field, or rather bog; but this has been turned over to the plough, and thus Dispar has perished before civilisation. It used also to be taken in other parts of Suffolk, and I believe it will in some future time appear as plentiful as ever. In Newman's "British Moths," F. Conspicuata is given as single brooded; here it is double, occurring in May and August. Is it so elsewhere? WM. M. COLE.

LOCUSTS.—The destructiveness of these insects is proverbial. Their desolating march is thus described in the Scriptures:—"the land is as a *garden of Eden*, before them and behind them a *desolating wilderness*; yea, and nothing shall escape them." In this country there is a great variety of locusts, from the smallest and scarcely discernable grasshopper, to the largest species nearly three inches long. The coast is visited by the terrible *migratory* locust, but we who live in the uplands are seldom troubled by them, though we are greatly annoyed by the *stationary* one. This species fly by fits and starts, and frequently raise themselves to a considerable height.

I have been planting a great deal of cabbage, parsnips, and other vegetables this year; but as soon as the stalks appeared above ground they were eaten off close to the earth. I find poultry most useful in clearing a garden of these pests. They lay a quantity of eggs which are deposited in masses in the ground.

As I intend making a collection of these insects, would you, or any of your readers, oblige me with a receipt for killing and preserving them.—J. D. S. W. Natal.

SHAPE OF EGGS.—Mr. Malan puzzles me, but I stood on the rocks of Flamborough, and with surprise, I watched the wonderful process of gathering wild birds' eggs, and was amazed. From the bare rocks up came the eggs of razorbills, cormorants, guillemont, etc., in thousands. The eggs, I think, were differently shaped, principally elongated, one end blunt and heavy, the other light and sharp. It occurred to me at the time that had the eggs been globular, or even equally balanced at the ends, they would have rolled down the rocks and been destroyed; whereas the general shape alluded to prevents in a great degree their rolling. This is all I can say at present, but I am sure some of the correspondents can say more. If Mr. Malan turns to the N. N. B., Vol. i., pp. 23, 164, 221, 287, 315, 352, and Vol. ii., pp. 25, 83, 233, 273, he will find something on the *migration* of birds. Anything from your correspondent on the subject will I am sure be acceptable. H. H. ULIDIA.

MILDNESS OF THE SEASON.—On Saturday, the 19th of last December, a warm, sunny day, with the wind from the north-west, while walking on the parade at Brighton, I was surprised to see a large humble-bee fly past. There was no appearance of feebleness in its flight, as if it had just awoke from a long winter's nap, bur it flew with the swiftness and power which are characteristic of these insects. I saw in the papers two or three days ago an account of the capture of a young half-fledged sparrow. I suppose both these strange occurrences were owing to the extraordinary mildness of the weather at such a late season of the year. From the same cause the buds on a lilac bush in our garden are beginning to open and show the green leaves folded up within; and I saw a shrub the other day (of whose name I am ignorant), on which the young leaves were in such an advanced state as to give a green hue to the bush, even when looked at from a considerable distance. J. LANDELS.

SISKIN AND MEALY REDPOLE.—"C. B. R.," in last month's number of the NOTE BOOK, asks, "Can any of your readers tell me how the females of the above birds differ from the males in plumage?" I will inform him that, according to the Rev. C. A. Johns, in "British Birds in their Haunts," the female siskin is described as having "all the colours less bright, and no black on the head." With regard to the mealy redpole—which is not such a very common bird in this country, and visits the British Isles in the winter—I find no difference given between the colours of the male and female; but it is described as being "a northern species of linnet, closely resembling the lesser redpole," the female of which has "all the colours less bright" than the male; and I conclude such to be the case in the plumage of the hen of the mealy redpole. A. E. BUTTEMER.

NETTLES.—After reading "O. R.'s" last letter, I came to the conclusion that further remarks on the disputed subject would be unnecessary, since it seems impossible for either of us to convince the other, all our statements being, as they are, so contradictory.

However, I request the readers of the NOTE BOOK to judge for themselves in this matter, and I am ready to abide by their impartial decision, which I shall await with perfect confidence. What I ask them to do is to draw a nettle leaf lightly over the palm of the hand, and to state whether they experience any sting by so doing; and I hope none will be dissuaded from trying this by thoughts of the "dire misgivings" and the heroic resolve (as to practical experiments) of "O. R." R. T.

THE BAT.—The weather of the present month up to this date (January 11th) has been exceptionally mild, owing to the prevalence of south-westerly winds. From various parts of the country one hears of spring flowers having already been gathered: one proof of the mildness of the season in the North of England is, that I have frequently seen the bat (Pleiotus communis) flying about of an evening in the neighbourhood of Ambleside. According to the Rev. Gilbert White, "bats appear at all seasons through the autumn and spring months, when the thermometer is at fifty, because then phalænæ and moths are stirring." I should be glad if any of your numerous readers could inform me what has been the lowest temperature of the air in the winter months, when they have observed the bat flying about; for I have seen it appear when the thermometer has stood at several degrees below fifty. A. E. BUTTEMER.

CATCHING TORTOISES. — The children in the Southern States of America practice a very curious mode of entrapping the mud-turtles or terrapins (Emys), inhabiting the swamps which abound in those regions. They cover a plant with tar, and having attached a string to it, they float it out on the waters of the swamp. The tar soon softens in the heat of the sun, and by its sudden hardening again in the cool of the evening, the turtles that have crawled on to the plants during the day to bask in the sun's rays, find themselves when they again wish to enter the water so firmly glued to the board as to be utterly incapable of escaping. They are thus retained until the owner of the trap comes to draw them on shore, when they are killed, and I believe eaten. J. LANDELS.

ARCTIA CAJA.—About June or July of this year, I captured a large specimen of the woolly bear, and put it into one of the drawers of my cabinet alive. In a few days it had passed into the pupa state: it had fixed its cocoon to the under side of the drawer, and therefore when the cabinet was shut, it must necessarily have been in total darkness. On going into the country, I left the cabinet in town: when I returned, after a few weeks, what was my surprise to find the chrysalis broken, and a most beautifully-coloured specimen of Arctia caja lying dead in the drawer! I think this rather remarkable, as I was of the opinion that insects owed their brilliant colouring to the light of the sun. FOX.

QUACKING FROGS.—I had heard of frogs in India and other places making very peculiar sounds, but until I came to Natal, I had no idea that there was a frog able to quack just like a duck. When I first arrived, I was surprised to hear by night what I took to be wild ducks quacking in the river, and not to hear or see anything of them in the daytime. But at last I discovered that the noise proceeded from the throats, not of *ducks*, but of *frogs!* The sound they make is so loud as to be heard distinctly half-a-mile off. I have not been able to see any of them yet, and believe that they, as well as other kinds of frog, possess the power of *ventriloquism*.—J. D. S. W.
Natal.

CURIOUS FACT ABOUT AN HARE.—About two years ago, I accompanied two friends of mine—with a brace of greyhounds—in search of a hare. The hare was found, chased, and, after a long run, finally killed by the dogs. While paunching the hare, I observed three large dark looking balls among the intestines, which proved to be three leverets in a mummyfied state. They were covered with hair, and in every respect perfect, but withal hard and dry. The matrix of the dam was remarkably small, and presented a very shrunken and pale aspect. The hare was in good condition.

SINGULAR WHIRLWIND.—Can any explanation be given of a curious whirlwind which was witnessed at the latter end of last summer in a field at Freshwater, Isle of Wight? Some barley still left uncarted was suddenly whirled into the air to the height of thirty or forty feet: it was then carried with great rapidity over the roof of a house near, and finally deposited in a meadow at some distance. The day this occurred was a particularly serene one, and not the slightest breeze moved a single leaf. S. E. P.
Freshwater, Isle of Wight.

BULLFINCH.—Can any of your readers tell me a remedy for a disease from which my bullfinch is now suffering? The feet have a succession of painful lumps upon them, and the poor bird can scarcely move about its cage. It has pecked at one of its toes until it has dropped off. I have been advised to put saffron in the water: is it a good thing? S. E. P.
Freshwater, Isle of Wight.

NEST OF SPOTTED FLYCATCHERS.—On the 11th of last July, while searching for the larva of C. Vinula in an old willow tree on the banks of the Grand Junction Canal a short distance from Willsden, I saw in a cleft of the bark a nest of the spotted flycatcher (M. grisola) containing four eggs; and on visiting it a week afterwards, found three young had been hatched, the fourth egg being addled. Was not this excessively late. V. B. LEWES.

AGE OF CATS.—I lately read in a well-known naturalist's magazine that the extreme age of the cat was fifteen years. On January 2nd, a cat in the possession of an acquaintance, died at the advanced age of twenty-one years. V. B. LEWES.

LEPIDOPTERA.—Have small specimens of lepidoptera been common this season? for I took a specimen of P. Rapæ measuring only sixteen lines, and P. Alexis only ten lines. V. B. LEWES.

BIRDS' EGGS.—Can any of your correspondents give me the address of a good taxidermist from whom I could procure specimens of birds' eggs? H. J. P.

INSECT MEDICINE AND FOLK-LORE.

By William Cole.

Part I.—COLEOPTERA.

BUT few members of the animal tribes are included in the modern "Pharmacopœia" as components in its multitudinous preparations, physicians now preferring, with a few exceptions, the more active and easily obtained principles furnished by the vegetable and mineral kingdoms as aids in battling with

"The thousand natural shocks
That flesh is heir to."

Formerly, however, insects and animals generally held a distinguished position amid the quaint stock of drugs in the stores of the mediæval apothecaries; and the wise-women and wizards of the "good old times" frequently employed animals in their charms and incantations, or (in their more legitimate "practice") administered them both internally and externally, prepared in ways often sufficiently disgusting and quite repugnant to our modern ideas, which demand a certain admixture of *dulce et utile* even in medicine. In perusing the accounts of these formidable remedies one is struck with the prevalence of the notion, "Similia similibus curantur;" and in devising them our forefathers seem to have followed the well-known rule which in the "three bottle" days of the last century gave rise to the proverb of "swallowing a hair of the dog that bit you." A striking illustration of this kind of belief occurred in Bucks some little time back, and was noticed in the daily papers in the report of an inquiry as to the death of a little girl from hydrophobia, resulting from the bite of a mad dog. The child's parents, acting under the advice of some village sage, gave her a slice of the dog's liver nicely grilled before the fire; a meal which they were assured would act as a certain antidote to any bad effects resulting from the bite! It unfortunately failed in this case, and the death of the poor child brought to light a curious instance of an old and absurd superstition still lurking amongst the rural classes in the enlightened nineteenth century.

Passing over toads, lizards, shrew-mice, and such "small deer," of which much that is curious could be told, I must confine myself to an enumeration and brief description of the insects employed in ancient and modern times as curative agents; occasionally enlivening the narrative with some extracts from old natural history and medical works, illustrating the notions formerly entertained respecting them, their habits and virtues. I must also premise that I do not restrict the word "insect" to its true scientific sense, but with the old writers shall include spiders, wood-lice (oniscus), scorpions, etc., in the same category.

Of the very few insects still retaining a place in the "Materia Medica," the most important is the Spanish-fly (Cantharis vesicatoria), which was formerly chiefly obtained from Italy and Spain, but the greater part of the supply is now derived from St. Petersburg and Sicily; the Russian samples being most esteemed. It also occurs in France in some plenty, but is generally very rare in England; although in the summer of 1837 it appeared in such immense numbers on the ash trees in the neighbourhood of Colchester, that it was considered necessary to thresh the trees with poles to free them from the countless swarms of the insects, which threatened to strip them of their foliage. In the same year it was observed near Ipswich, and other parts of Suffolk; also at Southampton, the Isle of Wight, etc.; and a physician of the latter place actually employed some of them as a substitute for foreign cantharides.

In systematic entomology, this insect belongs to a family of the order Coleoptera, or beetles, called Cantharidæ, including a number of allied species more or less useful as vesicatories, and as such have been employed in medicine from very early times. The name "Cantharis," applied to the typical genus, is very ancient; it appears, however, that the old naturalists and pharmacists did not always intend a particular species by the term, but often used it indiscriminately to denote the whole order of Coleopterous insects. The metamorphosis of the various species is still rather obscure. According to Olivier, the young larva of C. vesicatoria is composed of thirteen soft segments, including the head, which is rounded, depressed, and carries two short antennæ. The six front or true legs are short and scaly, and there are two short stiff hairs, or setæ, on the last segment but one of the abdomen. M. Zier says they are of a yellowish-white colour when first hatched, but soon afterwards change to a deep black, with the exception of the two last segments of the thorax and the first segment of the abdomen, which retain the original tint. We now lose the thread of their history, but they are *said* to undergo their subsequent changes in the earth, and to feed on various roots. From recent observations it appears probable that their mode of life may be analogous to that of the larvæ of the genus Meloë, whose history has been so thoroughly investigated by Mr. Newport in his admirable memoirs in the "Linnæan Transactions*," of

---
* Linn. Trans., vol. xx., p. 297.

which I shall presently give some account. The perfect beetles consume the leaves of trees, being particularly fond of lilac and ash, and usually appear, according to Latreille, about the period of the summer solstice. They are of a beautiful golden-green colour, with bluish-black legs and antennæ; their average length is about three-fourths of an inch; but they vary much in this particular, and the females are usually larger than the males. Like many other insects, they feign death, and fall to the ground when touched. They emit a peculiar pungent odour resembling that of mice, and very hurtful to the eyes, causing severe ophthalmia; in consequence of this their collection requires great care, both to guard against accidents, and for their proper preservation. The natives of the places where they occur take advantage of their torpid condition in the morning and evening, and having spread cloths beneath the trees, beat the branches with long poles, their faces and hands being defended by coverings. The beetles are then put into a sieve and exposed to the vapour of vinegar, to kill them; after which they are dried in the shade on hurdles covered with cloth or paper. When dry they are carefully packed up for exportation. Cantharis vesicatoria is sometimes adulterated "with the C. syriaca, and when in powder, with various inert substances and with euphorbium, black pepper, etc."*

The ancients appear to have used several kinds of insects for the same purpose, but their accounts are so vague that it is extremely difficult to identify them. Pliny says:—"Cantharides is produced by a small grub, found more particularly in the spongy excrescences which grow on the stem of the dog-rose, and still more abundantly on the ash."† The former may have been Cetonia aurata (the Common Rose-beetle), which possesses vesicatory properties; and the habits of the latter agree with those of the Spanish-fly described above. The most valued was probably that now known as Mylabris chicorii (Fam. Cantharidæ), which is about half an inch in length, black, with two yellowish bands across each wing-case, and a round spot of the same colour near the base. It is still common in the South of France and the meridional parts of Europe. That this, or a closely allied species‡, was that most prized by the ancients is obvious from the words of Pliny, who says

---

* Phillip's "Pharmacopœia."
† Bostock and Riley's Trans., Book xxix., c. 30.
‡ Burmeister observes:—"The species used by the ancients appears to have been Mylabris Fueslini, Pauz.; it is sometimes found in Germany, and is very abundant in the South of Europe." (Manual of Entomology, Shuckhard's Trans., p. 562.)

"the most active of all in their properties are those which are spotted with yellow streaks running transversely across the wings, and are plump and well filled."* Its blistering properties are quite as strong as those of the true Spanish-fly, and it is still used in Italy and China, either mixed with the latter or even alone.

Many other species of Cantharis and Mylabris possessing vesicating powers are found in different parts of the world. In America Cantharis vittata, Fab. ("the Potato-fly"), has been employed with much success, and is even more esteemed than C. vesicatoria. It is described by Dr. G. S. Schott ["Electric Repertory," Philadelphia, 1812, vol. ii.] as dark brown, with a longitudinal yellow band on each elytron, which are also margined with yellow; thorax nearly round, of a dark colour, sometimes with three longitudinal yellow bands; legs, antennæ, and abdomen, black. It appeared in such numbers during the year 1799 in Philadelphia as to entirely destroy the potato vines in the vicinity of the city. They also feed on beans, peas, mallows, black-snake-root (Actea racunosa), and a number of other plants. They are collected in August and September, and undergo a similar process of drying, etc., to that detailed above. The Americans also use C. cinerea, which is another extremely common and noxious species in many parts of the North. In a paper on Indian drugs in the 11th volume of the "Asiatic Researches," Dr. Fleming mentions a species of Mylabris (first noticed by Lieutenant-Colonel Hardwicke) plentiful in every part of Bengal, Bahar, and Oude, and employed by the natives as a efficacious vesicator under the name of "Telini." It is yellow, with three undulated black bands across the elytra; it is found during the rainy season on the flowers of various species of Hibiscus and Sida. The Indian physicians also use Can. gigas and violaceus, and Mylabris trianthemæ. In the Chinese apothecaries' shops are to be found (in addition to M. chicorii) M. pustulatus, Sidæ, Schæuherri, Fasciata, and the species described by M. Léon Ferrer in the "Revue de Zoologie" for 1859, under the name of Moquinia, which is intermediate in size and position between Chicorii and Pustulatus. C. ruficeps is used in Sumatra and Java; C. atomaria, in Brazil; C. Syriaca in Arabia, Syria, and the south of Europe; Mylabris trimaculatus in the north of Europe, and C. dubia in the southern provinces of France, Italy, and Siberia.

The females of Mylabris are stated by Dr. Gebler to deposit their eggs in the earth, and it

---

* Pliny, Book xxix., c. 30.

is supposed that the larvæ reside in the nests of the various burrowing Hymenoptera (Bees, etc.) found abundantly in places frequented by the beetles.

An insect frequently mentioned by the old writers has given rise to much discussion and many contradictory opinions. By Pliny and the Romans it was called "buprestis," or "vulprestis," and by the Greeks "voupristi." It was described as an insect very similar to the scarabæus, with long legs, and had the habit of concealing itself among the grass in meadows, so that it was liable to be swallowed by cattle while feeding; in which case it caused such a degree of inflammation that death often ensued. This is alluded to by Mouffet in a paraphrase of a passage in Nicander:—

"When cowes or calves are sick, or bellies swell,
They've eat Buprestis, keepers know full well."*

Linnæus applied the name to a family of very brilliant beetles, allied to the Elateridæ (or skipjacks); but these cannot include the "buprestis" of the ancients, as they are wood-feeders in the larval state, and are generally found on trunks of trees, and not amongst grass or low herbage. Mouffet supposed that a member of the great division of the ground-beetles (Carabidæ) was intended; others, including Messrs. Kirby and Spence, thought it was some species of Mylabris, but the opinion of M. Latreille that the "buprestis" may (at least in part) be referred to the modern genus Meloë, seems to carry the greatest amount of probability; their habits agree with the accounts given by Pliny, and they possess vesicatory properties in a high degree. They are sluggish, wingless, dark coloured beetles, with very short oval or triangular wing cases, only partially covering their large bodies, which in the females of some species measure an inch and a half in length, with proportionate breadth. They may be observed in spring in meadows or on heaths, crawling slowly amongst ranunculus, anemonies, violets, and similar plants, on the blossoms and leaves of which they feed. When handled they discharge from the joints of the legs a peculiar yellowish oil, a habit to which they are indebted for their popular name of "oil beetles." This oil has been employed as an embrocation for the cure of rheumatism; and Mr. Drury tells us that it is used in Sweden for the purpose "with the greatest success, by bathing the afflicted part. Of this I have been assured by an ingenious physician who resided there."† Mouffet

* Mouffet's "Theatre," chap. xix.
† See Preface to his "Illustrations of Exotic Entomology."

says in his "Theatre of Insects"* that this "oyly fatness also healeth the chaps of the hands as we have heard of the countreymen about Heildeburg, who have more than once commended its wonderful vertues to us." The worthy old naturalist further extols their medicinal power in cases of dropsy, if compounded in the following manner:—"Take of beetles called Meloë ten drams, radish seed one ounce, make a liquor of it: the dose may be from one ounce to three ounces, as necessity may require." They have also been much praised as a specific for that fearful malady hydrophobia; and Dr. Leach, in his monograph of the British species in the 11th volume of the Linn. Trans., relates the following anecdote communicated to him by Mr. Hunneman:—"The late King of Prussia (Frederick the Great) purchased the nostrum from the discoverer [?] for a valuable consideration as a specific against the bite of a mad dog; and in 1781 it was inserted in the Sect. II. p. 25 of the Disp. Boruss. Brand. According to this publication twenty-five of these animals that have been preserved in honey, are with two drachms of powdered black ebony, one drachm of Virginia snake-root, one ditto of lead filings, and twenty-five of fungus sorbi, to be reduced to a very fine substance; the whole with two ounces of theriaca of Venice (and, if *necessary*, with a little elder-root) to be formed with an electuary." In this instance the Great Frederick seems to have been a little imposed upon, for if the "buprestis" is synonymous with the oil-beetle, the above supposed remedy was well known to the ancients, but has passed into oblivion in company with some other specifics recorded by Pliny, as for example the wonderful curative power of a few maggots from the dead and decomposing body of the rabid animal!

The transformations of the oil-beetle from the egg to the perfect insect are very singular, and were long a great puzzle to entomologists; and indeed even now can scarcely be said to have been traced by actual observation. From the valuable papers by Mr. Newport, before referred to, I glean the following particulars:—The beetles immediately after their exclusion from the chrysalis are shrivelled and weakly, but by

* "The Theatre of Insects or lesser living creatures, as Bees, Flies, Caterpillars, Spiders, Worms, etc. A most elaborate work. By Dr. Mouffet, Doctor in Physick. London. Printed by E. C. 1658." This is an English version of a Latin work left in manuscript by Mouffet, who died about the end of Queen Elizabeth's reign. It is a most curious repository of the entomological and medical learning of the time, and as such is of considerable interest to the naturalist of the present day.

feeding ravenously speedily acquire strength; and the females present a very dropsical appearance from the immense quantity of eggs which are developed, sometimes exceeding 4,000. The female digs a hole about an inch and a half in depth in a dry, sandy situation exposed to the rays of the sun. In this receptacle she lays a mass of eggs, of a bright orange colour, agglutinated together, covering them carefully over with earth to protect them from injury. Each female constructs three or four of these nests before her supply of eggs is exhausted. In due course, the time varying according to the temperature, the eggs burst and active yellow larvæ about one-twelfth of an inch in length make their appearance. They have fourteen segments, including the head, which is short and broad, and carries a pair of five-jointed antennæ. They have three pairs of rather long true legs, and a single pair of pro-legs on the anal segments of the body similar to those possessed by the caterpillars of moths and butterflies. These are used in climbing, the body being arched in the manner of Geometrous larvæ, but in running they employ their true legs only. On each side of the last segment but one there is a long stiff hair or seta. Their movements are extremely rapid, so that in an amusing article in the *Entomological Magazine* by "Delta" (Mr. Edward Doubleday) they are compared to the celebrated "Yanky" pony, which a flash of lightning chased three times round a field, but was obliged to relinquish the pursuit, "not being able to come within a rood of it!" Quickness of motion is doubtless of great utility to them in this early stage of their existence; their habit being to climb the stems and nestle in the flowers of honey-bearing plants, and while "the little busy bees" are engaged in probing the nectaries or rifling the stamens of pollen, they crowd in multitudes upon the thorax, and fix themselves firmly to the underside at the insertion of the legs, abdomen, etc., regardless of the futile attempts of the bees to rid themselves of their evidently unwelcome visitors. It is a remarkable exhibition of instinct that they not only restrict their attacks to those kinds of bees which form their nests in the earth, such as the Andrenidæ, Anthrophoræ, Bombi, etc., but also distinguish from other insects those species of Diptera, or two-winged flies (Volucellæ, etc.), which are themselves parasites of such bees, their object in both cases being to reach the nests of the latter, where they are destined to pass the remainder of their adolescent life. Their habits and development during the earlier larval stages have not been witnessed by naturalists. They are to be found fully grown in August and September as "thick, fat, heavy, inanimate, and almost apodal maggots, of a light orange colour, pent up in their cells in the dry bank of clay or sand, amongst the nests of Anthrophoræ. They have entirely thrown off their caudal appendages setæform antennæ, and their elongated legs. In the place of the latter they retain only six short tubercles on the under-surface of the anterior segments." From evidence afforded by the partially cast-off skin, found still clinging to the full-grown grubs, Mr. Newport was of opinion that the active state continues up to the previous change of skin; and, judging from the hard structure of the mouth and claws, they probably roam from nest to nest in search of food, selecting one at last in which to undergo their final transformations. The exact nature of their food is rather problematical; but as they are not carnivorous, the presumption is that they subsist on the masses of pollen stored up by the bees in the cells for the nourishment of their young.

They exist for a few days in the helpless condition above described, and then change to pupæ, without entirely casting off the larval skin, in which they remain enclosed like a "corpse in its shroud up to the time when they assume the imago state by throwing off a very thin pellicle. This takes place within ten days or a fortnight after the larvæ have become nymphs; but, if the season is unfavourable, the change is retarded. They remain in their cells during the autumn and succeeding winter as perfect insects, in a state of hybernation, until they are roused into activity by the gradually increasing influence of the season," generally appearing in February or March.

I have given this "strange eventful history" at some length, not only on account of the anomalous character of the changes these little hexapods undergo, but also from the various opinions entertained as to their true nature by some of the most eminent entomologists. By Linnæus and Kirby they were regarded as Pediculi (lice); the former describing them as P. apis, and the latter as P. melittæ. Léon Dufour has characterised them as a distinct genus of apterous insects under the name of Triangulus. The specimens examined by him, and also those noticed by Kirby, are described as black in colour, and in this respect seem more nearly related to the larvæ of Cantharis, which are strongly suspected of similar habits, as I have before hinted.

In the "Bulletin de la Société Ento. de France" for 1852, allusion is made by M. Foureau de Bauregard to the use made of the Akis acuminata (a Heteromerous beetle belonging to the family Melastoma) by the natives of Grenada, who administer it to persons suffering from disease of the lungs (phthisis pulmonaria). The collector who furnished him with this information was mistaken for an apothecary by the peasants, who observed him catching beetles, and they taught him their uses.

PRÆUSCHER'S MUSEUM.
By "C."

I WOULD recommend any of your readers who in their summer rambles on the continent may chance to come across " Le Grand Musée, Anatomique, Pathologique, et Ethnologique de Præuscher," to expend the few centimes demanded at the door and to enter. The external appearance of this museum hardly satisfies the anticipations raised by the majestic title assumed in the advertisement : for it bears a striking resemblance to the two-penny shows that invariably swarm into existence at country fairs, wherein you may see the performing pony and the largest woman in the world ; the mighty monsters of savage lands, and a spurious Tom Thumb, all for the small sum of two-pence. The deception about these shows is that the attractions generally resolve themselves into your seeing very little, and having your toes crushed beneath the ponderous tread of stalwart bucolics. But in the present case you will find the arrangements for creature-comfort and agreeable instruction conducted on more scientific principles. Pay, then, your mites, my fellow-aspirants to the laurels of a naturalist, and enter with me. I will be the showman for the nonce, and describe the specimens as we proceed.

Well then, on the right (this I believe to be the starting point generally adopted by brothers of Artemus Ward's persuasion) on the right, we perceive the first division, consisting of natural preparations in spirit illustrating the fœtal state of the human subject. These specimens are admirably preserved, and commence with an embryo of 6 days' formation, another of 10, and a third of 14 days. Some twenty or thirty others show us by a gradual process the various epochs of development, from the first conception to the complete maturity of the perfect infant. They are all clean and in excellent preservation, and each specimen is separately described in the catalogue supplied to visitors, wherein we find more useful information than is generally furnished by such publications. Thus, for example, No. 16 is described as " un embryo de 14 semaines, auquel on voit déjà le developpement des muscles du dos." No. 23, " Enfant de nègre, de 16 semaines ; à cette époque, les nerfs commencent à se développer." Then follows a collection of human "monstra," very interesting and rare, about which our catalogue has much to say. Here we have an infant with no neck (Acephalus spurius) whereof we read, that the fathers of such "lusus" have always been habitual drunkards. The child must at the commencement have had a dropsical head, and as the water kept increasing in the regions of the neck, the delicate sheath of the skull gradually extended itself, and, as it were, absorbed the neck into its interior. No. 35 shows us a very curious monstrum, born at Paris, consisting of twins, nine months old, with one head between their two bodies, which have coalesced into a single trunk ; the four arms and four legs are fully developed, and the general effect of this wonderful specimen might well elicit the exclamation "O gemini !" even from the compound intellect of the notorious brothers of Siam. " Ce jeu de la nature," says our catalogue, " est une des plus grandes rarétes ayant rapport a l'accouchement."

Passing by some examples of rare snakes, toads, and chameleons, we come to a series of osteological preparations, including human skeletons from two months' old and upwards. This collection is very complete, and shows well the period when the scapula begins to be developed, the gradual closing of the cranial fontanelle, &c. The injected preparations that follow are likewise well worth an examination, especially that of a human heart and its great vessels. At a glance the relative position of the aorta and venæ cavæ of the pulmonary arteries and veins, is distinctly shown. Some human specimens preserved and gilded by a mysterious process of galvanism ; the skin of a woman guillotined at Paris ; the skull of a boy, illustrating the fall of the deciduous milk teeth and their replacement by the permanent dentition ; the leg of a man (bearing no small resemblance to a dried herring) and shewing the muscles, blood-vessels, bones, &c., in a shrivelled and "mummified" condition ; such are a few out of the many interesting objects that are before us.

Excellent though these specimens be, I think the gems of the museum must be sought among the artificial preparations in wax, about which pages might be written by any one who allows his love of description and play of imagination to tax the good nature of an editor and the patience of his readers beyond the limits of toleration. Yet it is a great temptation to forget for a moment the oft-repeated question, "Do insects feel pain ?" and the perplexing niceties that separate the reason of a baby from the instinct of a baboon ; and to appear in the pages of the NATURALIST'S NOTE BOOK in other guise than that of a wrangler. Therefore, my friends, accept my apology and be lenient towards my weakness,

"Mais, à nos moutons." once more. And here I have little hesitation in asserting that the "wax statoots" exhibited by Mr. A. Ward, of blessed memory, could bear no comparison with "les préparations artificielles en cire" de M. Præuscher, as far as marvel of execution and subtilty of representation are concerned. The *chef-d'œuvre* of the whole collection is undoubtedly a model from nature of the human head, with its blood-vessels and nerves, the eye and its motor muscles, the lachrymal gland and ducts, the external and internal anatomy of the ear, the nose and its three cavities, the nerves of the neck, consisting of the olfactory, optic, sympathetic, trifacial, facial, auditory, and hypoglossal. All these nerves with their ramifications are beautifully worked out, and contribute towards making this specimen not only of the highest anatomical interest, but also a wonder of plastic skill. Another case contains a series of representations in wax, shewing the origin and daily development of the egg of a common hen. The models are 22 in number, and correspond to the 22 days required for the formation of the perfect chick; thus showing the progress towards maturity that is made day by day until the shell is discarded by the young bird.

Considering that there are nearly seven hundred other specimens all deserving notice, I will briefly say that they include examples of the different races of mankind—of sundry diseases and medical operations, in wax; and a phrenological bust with the situation of the cerebral organs defined according to the views of the celebrated M. G. Combe. There are also some models in wax of subjects which might haply have disturbed the hallowed musings of Saint Antony, and these we will not describe. But before concluding, a few words are due to another "wax-work" which elucidates the progress of the disease known as "le mal des Trichines." The model consists of an enlarged section of the human body, in the intestines of which a great number of trichines are seen moving from side to side in the mucous moisture. These parasites are exaggerated in size in order to show their movements with greater distinctness. Several of them are seen in the act of piercing the intestinal walls and wriggling their way into the abdominal cavities; others are passing into the stomach, and some are seen penetrating into the muscles of the abdomen, where they enclose themselves in transparent capsules. In this manner the whole body of one afflicted may become infested with trichines. The irritation caused by their progress is said to be most agonising, and may pervade every organ, causing the most intense suffering, and eventually resulting in death.

ON THE BRITISH GEOMETRÆ.
By E. CLIFFORD.
PART III.

THERE are not very many members of the division which we are considering that can be said to occur commonly about London; but the next species under notice is certainly one of them. Yet we do not see so many occurring at the present time as was the case a year or two ago. We allude to the Waved Umber, (*Hemerophila abruptaria*) the first in order of the BOARMIDÆ. It is a singularly delicate insect, though not brilliant in colouring, the wings being wainscot brown, the male darker and richer in hue than the female. The fore-wings have a central black dot, on both sides of which is a slender black line, and they are slightly scalloped at the hind margin. There are numerous delicate lines and tints of brown on the surface of both wings. The caterpillar of the Waved Umber is of a dark brown colour, with a whitish ring close behind the head, and feeds on lilac and rose. Hence we so often see the moth in gardens where these shrubs are grown. The caterpillar occurs in June, and spins a silken cocoon on the twigs. The moth is found in May and August, and is considered by some to be double-brooded. The Speckled Beauty (*Cleora viduaria*), is a moth occurring only in Sussex and the New Forest, Hampshire, and its caterpillar is, as yet, totally unknown to entomologists. The insect itself is a beautiful one. The fore-wings are dingy-white, covered with smoky-black markings. The hind-wings are dingy white, with minute black specks, and a black line along the hind margins; the body is indistinctly spotted with black. This moth flies in June. The Dotted Carpet (*Cleora glabraria*), occurs in the Lake district of Westmoreland, as also in the New Forest, Hampshire. The caterpillar is found in May, the moth at the end of July. The wings of the perfect insect are dingy white, sprinkled over with minute black dots, and adorned with other black markings, the most conspicuous of which is a central black spot. The caterpillar of this moth is described as greenish-white, with a black spot on the back of each segment. It feeds on the lichens which grow on fir trees.

The Brussels Lace (*Cleora lichenaria*), is of a singular tint, being green-grey, clouded with darker shades of the same colour; there are two black transverse lines across the fore-wings. The antennæ of the male moth are feathered, of the female thread-like; the head, thorax, and body are green-grey. The caterpillar is of a similar colour with the moth, but is much more beautifully marked; the colours brighter and more distinct. There are two small humps on some of the segments of its body. This caterpillar feeds on the lichens found on park palings, etc.; and is so similar to them in appearance that it is with difficulty distinguished by the collector. It occurs in September and again in May, being in hybernation during the winter. The moth flies in July, and is tolerably common.

A variable species is that known as the Mottled Beauty (*Boarmia repandata*). It is generally of a grey-brown, having a number of waved markings transversely crossing all the wings. These latter vary so much in different specimens that it is almost impossible to describe them in such a manner as would apply to all. The hind margin itself is surrounded by a delicate scalloped black line. The antennæ are feathered in the male, thread-like in the female. The caterpillar of the Mottled Beauty may be found feeding on plum and birch trees in our gardens. In colour it is yellow-grey dotted with black, one line along the back and another on each side of a paler hue. The moth flies in June and July, and is very common.

The Willow Beauty (*Boarmia rhomboidaria*), is a moth with which every entomological reader must be acquainted. The wings are grey-brown, having a dark crescent-shaped spot in the centre of the fore-wings. Several waved lines or bands are more or less plainly marked on all the wings, and the hind margin is surrounded with a delicate zigzag black line just within the fringe. The head, thorax, and body grey-brown. The caterpillar of this well-known geometer is to be found in September, and occurs commonly enough in gardens, feeding on roses, plum, birch, and apple trees. It is dingy grey in colour, but is slightly variegated with darker markings, and has a pale yellow line along each side. The moth itself flies in June and July, and frequents walls, fences, and the trunks of trees, where it may often be seen resting. It is common everywhere. The Satin Carpet (*Boarmia abietaria*), is a local insect, and found only in pine forests, sitting on the trunks of trees in the month of July. Fine specimens of this beautiful moth exhibit a saffron tint over the wings, which are very delicately marked. There is a row of crescent-shaped black marks round the margin of all the wings; and the antennæ of the female are threadlike and very black. The caterpillar is described as reddish-grey, with a yellow line along the spiracles, and often yellowish on the back. It feeds on fir. A singularly pretty moth is the Ringed Carpet (*Boarmia cinctaria*). The wings are very dark brown in colour, with several transverse waved darker lines. The hind wings are paler than the fore wings, especially at the base; the head,

thorax, and body are grey-brown. The caterpillar of this delicate insect is described as having a notched head and a small hump on each side of the fifth segment. It feeds on heath, and is to be found in the month of September. The moth itself is on the wing in May and June.

A large and handsome species next claims our notice. It is called the Great Oak Beauty (*Boarmia roboraria*), and is indeed a striking insect. All its wings are of a grey colour, powdered with minute black spots, and also having numerous dark brown markings. The most conspicuous of these are four black spots on the outer margins of the fore-wings. The hind-wings are very similarly marked with the fore-wings, but rather less distinctly. The caterpiller of this grand insect is very large, and in form much resembles a bit of stick. It has a dark line down the back and a pale line on each side; the space between them is varied with black and white. This caterpillar feeds only on oak. This noble moth was once common in Richmond Park, where collectors have found it spreading its ample wings in June on the trunks. The chrysalides may be found by digging around the roots of oak trees. The species appears to be confined to the south of England. Another species, which is especially attached to the New Forest, Hampshire, is the Pale Oak Beauty (*Boarmia consortaria*). The colouring of this moth is grey, sprinkled with black specks, the base of the fore-wings is dingy yellow-brown; in the centre of the hind-wings is a crescent-shaped mark, grey in the middle. The caterpillar is green-grey, a darkish line along the back, and a pale one on each side; then one or two small humps on the back of the sixth segment, and two small black warts on the twelfth segment. It is an oak feeder and occurs in August. The moth is on the wing in June. The Square Spot (*Tephrosia consonaria*), is an uncommon moth, of which there is little known among entomologists. The male and female are very dissimilar. The male has a grey ground colour, tinged with red-brown, but the colour of the female is grey, without the red-brown tinge; the wings possess many indistinct transverse shades and markings in the male, which in the female are more distinguishable. The caterpillar of this moth is said by foreign authors to be reddish-grey, with several black longitudinal lines, and to have two small humps on the twelfth segment. It is a feeder on birch and occurs in September. The moth flies in May.

On elm, birch, and other trees, during the month of August may be found the caterpillar of the Small Engrailed (*Tephrosia crepuscularia*). This is a beautiful little geometer of a yellow-brown tinge, all of its wings having transverse zig-zag black lines. The antennæ are almost threadlike in the male, quite so in the female. The Engrailed (*Tephrosia biundularia*), is the next species under notice. This is of a grey colour, with a smoky tinge and several transverse black lines on all the wings. The caterpillars of this moth have been found feeding on larch, and it is said that they vary much in colour. This and the last species are very difficult to distinguish the one from the other, and as they are alike in very many points, we shall not linger over a description of them. The Brindled White Spot (*Tephrosia extersaria*), is at the same time a striking and a beautiful moth. The colour is smoky-grey sprinkled over with brown, the fore-wings have four transverse black lines. The hind-wings are not so conspicuously marked as the fore-wings. The caterpillar is grey, clouded with red-brown; it occurs in September, feeding on birch. It remains in the chrysalis state during winter, the moth emerging in June. The caterpillar of the Grey Birch (*Tephrosia punctulata*), occurs on birch in the month of August. The moth itself appears in May, having passed the winter in the chrysalis state. The most conspicuous feature in the perfect insect is the presence of four very dark spots, nearly equally distant, on the outer margin of the fore-wings.

The Annulet (*Gnophos obscurata*), is a very variable moth. It varies in colour from a pearly-grey to a smoky-brown; but the fore-wings have invariably two zigzag black lines and the hind-wings one. Between these lines on each fore-wing is a black ring, or annulet, and on each hind-wing near the middle a similar mark; hence the name of the insect before us. Some very pale specimens have been taken of this moth, and collectors have often been inclined to consider them as belonging to a distinct species. The caterpillar much resembles the moth in colour; and it feeds at night on the salad burnet and the sun cistus, concealing itself under stones or among the roots of grasses by day, and may thus be captured by shaking the latter in some receptacle. The eggs are laid by the female in July and August, and in September the caterpillar is half-grown, when it hybernates, re-appearing in April, when it feeds till May, and is then transformed into a chrysalis. The moth flies in the month of July. We close this paper by a brief notice of three very rare species, which conclude the Boarmidæ. The first is the Scotch Annulet (*Dasydia obfuscata*), a very beautiful moth. The caterpillar is described as of a violet-grey with a white line along the spiracles, and as having two small humps on the twelfth segment. It feeds on the dyer's green weed and the vetch. The moth flies in July and August, and has only been taken among the Scotch mountains. The Black Mountain Moth (*Psodos trepidaria*), is exceedingly rare. It has been taken in the highlands of Scotland in the month of July, but we do not hear of its capture in England, Ireland, and Wales. The Dusky Carpet (*Mniophila cineraria*), closes our list of this interesting family. It is a rather lesser species than the remainder of its fellows; and is a very rare moth. The fore-wings are grey, with three transverse, dark waved lines; the centre of which is rather indistinct. The hind margin of the wing is bordered with a zigzag dark line, and the fringe is slightly spotted. The hind-wings are much paler than the fore-wings, and have an indistinct dark transverse line. The head, thorax, and body are all of a grey colour. It should be stated that it is exceedingly doubtful whether this species be really British; and one of our best entomologists has never seen a British specimen of it, but describes it from a foreign one. Since it has been introduced in our list, however, we just briefly notice it, though at the same time we wish our readers to remember that the grounds upon which it is placed with our native Geometræ are very insufficient.

SILKWORMS:

AND HOW TO REAR THEM SUCCESSFULLY.

PART II.

WHAT implements and instruments are considered necessary in silkworm rearing? This question involves much matter, too long to fully bring before my readers at the present time; and therefore I shall name the most required articles as briefly as possible.

A hatching-box, in which silkworms' eggs are placed in order to be hatched. This can be made of cardboard, or even wood, about six inches square for every ounce of eggs, and having the sides only just above the level of the same; the one-sixteenth of an inch above them, and not more. A square frame half an inch wider each way than the box, to which canvas or fine net is tacked, forming a kind of sieve, with holes about the size of mustard or radish seed. This frame or lid is to lay over the box containing the eggs, the canvas only resting on the sides of the box; the weight of the frame round outside will keep the canvas properly extended without its weighing on the eggs. The little silkworms on immerging from the eggs hasten through the holes of this lid to the leaves placed thereon above, and which when tolerably full of insects can be lifted away and placed on sheets of paper. A more simple plan which I adopt is to double a sheet of stiffish paper in gutter fashion; thus—pasting the two sides to a board, or even the table if a common one, to keep the gutters open at top from half to one inch wide. These gutters may be from half an inch to one inch high. The eggs are to be laid in them nearly a quarter of an inch, or less, in depth—not more. The leaves are to be laid on the top ridges, and the insects running up the sides of the paper soon find the way to them. I have found this an excellent method. It is simple and efficient. The principal advantages are, that the eggs do not lay so much in one lump, and the warm air of the room circulates over and under much better.

A thermometer is necessary in order to maintain the requisite temperature, and a hygrometer to mark the degree of humidity; but a good substitute for the latter is common salt placed on a plate. A room in which salt does not keep dry is improper for silkworms. Stagnant dampness is suicidal to silkworms; a dry room and atmosphere are best. A microscope is also a very useful instrument, and at the present day serves the important use of discovering disease in silkworms and their eggs.

The castle ("Il castello" of the Italians) is the most essential requisite. This is a structure to contain the silkworms, or properly "the silkworms' house." It can be built of any size, to suit the rearing-room or quantity of worms. It is usual for a castle to contain six tables or stages, sufficient for the worms proceeding from half an ounce of eggs. It is constructed by placing four posts of about three inches diameter firmly between the floor and ceiling of the room in pairs at four feet apart, each pair being eight feet distant; thus they stand in a similar way to the posts of a bedstead. Each pair of posts have holes drilled in them an inch in diameter, to connect them like ladders by staves at eighteen inches apart. These staves are to support the stages laid on them, which are four feet wide by twelve feet long, and made thus :—Take two splines two inches by one and a-half inches, and twelve feet long, laying them parallel four feet apart; nail to their bottom edges nine cross splines one inch square, let into the wood half an inch or more; thus connecting them firmly, and dividing the frame into eight equal compartments, each about eighteen inches wide. The ends of this frame, if desired, could be connected with cross pieces of the same depth as the sides, in order to have an edging all round alike, as a protection against the silkworms falling from the stage. The framework constructed must next be covered inside with some material on which to place the insects. Wire netting with two or three inch meshes would be suitable, covering over with stiffish brown paper; or common calico I think better, being more durable, admitting of being washed when dirty. Reeds bedded over the cross pieces and secured to them by tacking over laths, I have found an excellent method. In whatever way silkworm stages are made, they should be of such material that the air can penetrate. Boards must never be used, for they imbibe and retain the moisture when covered with worms and their refuse.

This description of a silkworm house will suffice on a large or small scale, for many such by being placed end to end might form one, ten times the length or more; and if made with only two or three stages for a small quantity of worms, the four posts might be provided with feet, so as to be self-supporting, without the necessity of being so long as to reach the ceiling of the room. Similar stages, but not above two and a-half feet wide, might be built up next the walls of a room if dry, and ventilation was not obstructed.

Sheets of paper or calico the size of the compartments of a stage are required on which to keep the worms. If paper, it is best stout, and without gum or colouring matter. Trays of wood, tin, or cardboard, about fifteen inches wide, will serve to carry the sheets containing the worms when moving them about from one place to another.

To facilitate the removal of worms into clean quarters many persons on the Continent use nets or perforated paper, which being laid over the insects, and leaves distributed over, may be lifted away together, after the worms pass the meshes, or holes. Large silkworm rearers cut the leaves by a machine in the fashion of a chaff-cutter, immediately before wanted to feed the worms; but on a small scale a good large clean knife will answer the purpose.

In order to reach silkworm stages situated too high to get at otherwise, it is necessary to be provided with ladders or steps. Folding steps five or six feet high provided with castors are perhaps the most suitable and convenient. It is usual among noted silkworm rearers to have a stand of wood about one yard square to support the calico or linen on which the silkworms are to lay their eggs. For the purpose a frame could be formed with inch splines, and then half-inch ones could be nailed across at every six inches, not only to give strength, but the better to support the linen. This frame is to be provided with two legs or supports at the back, top part opening and shutting by means of hinges, so that when the stand is placed on a table in a slanting position it is supported thereby. These legs may be about two and a-half feet long, or rather less. This sloping position I think more preferable for the moths than an upright one, which is more generally adopted, by hanging the linen or cloth against a wall. Large baskets or hampers with handles are also convenient into which to put the leaves, when gathered, to convey them home. Sacks and large common sheets would do for the purpose.

It is a general custom in Italy to scrape silk-worms' eggs off the linen on which laid before they are put hatching. This is done with a spoon or bone knife, after having soaked linen and eggs about half an hour in soft water, either in the autumn or early spring. Small brushes or whisks will be found useful when cleaning the litter from the silkworm stages, as well as skeps to carry away refuse, dirt, etc.

Mice, rats, etc., should be trapped, for they are enemies, or they could be prevented from getting up the castle by surrounding the bottoms of the posts with tin.

Some rearers use a dredger, or kind of sieve having holes about a quarter of an inch diameter, to sift the cut leaves over the worms, which does the work more equally than can be done by hand; besides, it avoids the necessity of touching the leaves so much, which I think is a great advantage.

LEONARD HARMANN, Junr.
Old Catton, Norwich.

A BOTANICAL RAMBLE IN THE WEAVER VALLEY.

MOST of the readers of the NATURALIST'S NOTE BOOK will never have heard of the Weaver Valley, yet doubtless they must know, or have heard speak of, the river Weaver in Cheshire; if so, they will know in what point of the compass, or rather in what part of the cheese-making county, to expect to find the Weaver Valley.

We must first introduce our readers to this enchanting place by describing its scenery. England with its hills and dales, lakes and fells, can scarcely boast of a more lovely spot. We imagine ourselves walking on the river's bank, on either side of which is a carpet of the richest green, bedecked with flowers of various hues; rising on both sides of the river on a gentle declivity are woods or trees, clothed with "sheeny verdure;" these, together with the calm, quiet, peaceful waters at our feet, form a beautiful scene, never beheld except with feelings of gratitude. It is true there is no "gushing mountain torrent," no "bold and rugged rocks," admired by many, yet the prospect is sufficient to delight the most enthusiastic lover of rural scenery, and at the same time to carry our thoughts from "nature up to nature's God."

Commencing our walk at a farm-house a little distance from Frodsham, called Cattenhall, we soon reach the botanizing ground, which certainly is not rich in rarities; however, it will well repay us for the exertion. The first flower arresting our attention (supposing our walk to be in May), will be the marsh marigold (Caltha palustris), so called from the Greek "Kalathos," a cup, from the flower having a resemblance to a drinking-cup. It is known in Cheshire by its more familiar name of "May-flowers." In Scotland we often hear it called "gowans":—

We noa have run about the braes
And pu'd the gowans fine.—BURNS.

Although a common flower, we love it for recalling to our memory the happy days of childhood. On the hedge banks we perceive another yellow flower, but much smaller than the marsh marigold, the sweet wood crowfoot (Ranunculus auricomus), a plant which differs from all the other crowfoots, in not having any acrid properties; its specific name is derived from "aureus," gold, and "coma," a lock of hair; hence its Scottish name, Goldilocks. Growing by its side in the richest profusion are the mountain speedwell (Veronica montana), and tuberous-rooted vetchling (Lathyrus macrorrhizus); the first has blue, the latter purple petals, making when commingled a pretty contrast that will almost outvie any splendid flower-beds. The veronica might be supposed from its name to be found only in mountainous places; however, this is not so; it must be searched for, as in the present instance, in shady woods. We frequently hear the speedwell called "forget-me-not," but the true "forget-me-not" is Myosotis palustris, found in ditches and boggy places. The speedwell is still a favourite with country people :—

Thy name alone is like a spell
And whispers love, in speed-the-well.

Looking over a damp, swampy spot by the river's brink we espy a tall plant, with leaves of a delicate green, and white petals enshrouding rather long purple anthers—this is the bitter-cress (Cardamine amara). It is a species much resorted to by some of our native butterflies. Those who study entomology should learn to know all the bitter-cresses. Growing amongst the trees we observe the weasel-snout (Lamium Galeobdolon), a magnificent plant with labiate blossoms, and not by any means common. Sweet woodruffe (Asperula odorata), which makes the air fragrant with a delicious odour: this is more apparent when being dried for the herbarium; its small funnel-shaped petals are very inconspicuous. But whilst we are in the wood, search must be made for two rather rare shrubs, the spindle-tree (Enonymous europæus), and wood daphne (Daphne Laureola); the latter shrub flowers very early, when the surrounding trees are quite leafless; it has a peculiar appearance, its smooth lanceolate leaves and green corolla look very strange, especially at so early a period of the year as February. The wood betony (Betonica officinalis) is very plentiful, and cannot well be overlooked; its virtues are numerous as a remedial agent, so say the country people; in Spain it is so highly esteemed, that they consider it one of the highest compliments to say of a man, "he has as many virtues as the betony." Before emerging from the wood, we shall see a great number of white flowers only a few inches elevated from the ground, these belong to the ramsons (Allium ursinum); the whole of the leaves and flowers have a strong garlic-like smell, thus making it very unpleasant to handle; an infusion of the herb in brandy is reputed to be a specific for the gravel.

Those who are lovers of ferns will find a few "graceful, feathery fronds," namely the common polypody (Polypodium vulgare, a serrate variety), polystichum angulare, and the elegant lady fern (Athyrium Filix-formina).

> Oh then most gracefully they wave
> In the hedges like a sea,
> And dear as they are beautiful
> Are those fern leaves to me.
> TWAMLEY.

After emerging from the wood, and continuing our walk along a pleasant shaded footpath, we shall come across many more of "nature's wildings," two of which are well worthy of our notice—the crosswort (Galium cruciatum), and yellow melilot (Melilotus officinalis); melilot means "honied lotus," so called because when drying it emits a sweet fragrance like that of honey. In damp parts of the meadow, a little distance from the footpath, by looking carefully, we shall not fail to observe the adder's-tongue (Ophioglossum vulgatum), marsh valerian (Valeriana dioica), and the goat's-beard (Tragopogon pratensis); in some parts of the country, the goat's-beard is familiarly known by the name of "John-go-to-bed-at-noon," because of its flowers being closed by twelve o'clock; the roots if boiled when fresh are very wholesome, some say superior to asparagus.

The common burnet (Sanguisorba officinalis), with its large purplish heads of flowers, is rather abundant; however it will well repay the trouble of an examination. The coloured part of the flower is not (as is often supposed by young botanists) the corolla, but the calyx, the corolla is wholly absent; the leaflets are very elegant, and have a taste and smell very similar to the cucumber. About the Valley and at Aston the teasels find a congenial home; both the Dipsacus sylvestris and D. pilosus flourish in great profusion. The meadows are gay all the summer with various species of buttercups, principally ranunculus acris; it is extremely common almost everywhere, but none the less welcome on that account to all who delight in country walks; nor can we look upon its showy golden petals (often very appropriately called "goldcups") without recalling to mind the lines of Strickland:—

> Welcome little buttercups,
> Welcome daisies white,
> Ye are in my spirit
> Visioned a delight,
> Coming o'er the spring time
> Of sunny hours to tell,
> Speaking to our heart of Him,
> Who doeth all things well.

There are many more flowers to be found, such as the beautiful cranes bill (Geranium pratense), giant bell-flower (Campanula latifolia), ladies' mantle (Alchemilla vulgaris), the great horsetail (Equisetum maximum), a pretty tree-like moss (Climacium dendroides), yellow-wort (Chlora perfoliata), spotted orchis (Orchis maculata); and in the early spring months portions of the meadows are resplendent with the cowslip (Primula veris). To conclude our short, but interesting and health-giving ramble, let us recal to mind the words of "Clare," in praise of this "floral gem":—

> Bowing adorers of the gale,
> Ye cowslips delicately pale,
> Upraise your loaded stems,
> Unfold your cups in splendour, speak
> Who deck'd you with that ruddy streak
> And gilt your golden gems?

JAMES F. ROBINSON.

THE RED SQUIRREL.
(*SCIURUS HUDSONIUS.*)

BY J. MATTHEW JONES, F.L.S.

(Author of "The Naturalist in Bermuda.")

A WELL-KNOWN inhabitant of our "forest primeval" is the red squirrel, or chickaree. In those parts where the spruce and pine clothe the country for miles around it is especially numerous, and may be seen jumping from bough to bough, stopping meanwhile to nibble at the cones and scatter their parts over the ground beneath. A merry, sociable little fellow he is too, loving to come near the farmer's house, and even to the very door; now running with a sort of mimic canter along the walk; then, suddenly surprised by the opening of a door, scurrying off to the nearest tree and quickly appearing at its summit. Let the frost be ever so severe, and the snow-storm rage in all its fury, our little friend takes his daily rounds in search of something to please his appetite. It may be a nut, a tasty fungus, or a pine cone; it matters little which, he quietly takes his seat in some quiet nook—generally in the angle formed by the junction of a bough with the trunk. Here, with his back pushed well up against the sheltering tree, and tail held like an umbrella above his head, the red squirrel munches away, heedless of the gale which roars through the forest. He is a fearless and confident creature, for often and often have I tried to get as close as possible to one when thus occupied, and sometimes have succeeded in putting my face within about two or three feet of his, and as long as I remained quiet he would continue his repast as if aware that the eye of one who would not willingly injure was upon him. In summer time it makes a nest in some convenient spot— the hollow of a tree, or outside on the branch. In the latter situation it is made of a rounded form, of sticks, with a small hole for entrance at the side. I have also known one to rear its family of six young ones in an old nail-box left on a beam in a barn a little distance from a house. This squirrel will sometimes change its usual colour to black, and skins of this colour are sometimes obtained from Labrador. It is much more numerous during some years than others, and people account for this by stating that it occasionally migrates from one district to another. During sunny days in early spring these squirrels, amorously inclined, chase each other from tree to tree, uttering a peculiar screaming noise while in pursuit. A more cleanly little creature could scarce be found; and well would it be if the dirty, swarthy Indian who traverses these never ending forest wilds would take a lesson of neatness from this humble denizen of our northern clime.

The red squirrel is found as far north as the limit of trees on this continent. It is common in the northern parts of the United States, and has been observed as far south as Carolina.

LIST OF BRITISH MOTHS:
NATURE OF THEIR FOOD, AND TIMES OF THEIR PERFECT APPEARANCE.
NOCTURNI.
THE SPHINGIDÆ.

EYED HAWK MOTH (*Smerinthus ocellatus*). Feeds on apple trees and willow bushes. Flies in June.

Poplar Hawk Moth (*Smerinthus Populi*). Feeds on the common upright Lombardy poplar, but also in gardens on the common laurel and laurustinus. Flies in June.

Lime Hawk Moth (*Smerinthus Tiliæ*). Feeds on elm trees and lime trees. Flies in June.

Death's Head Hawk Moth (*Acherontia Atropos*). Feeds on the deadly nightshade, potato, and the tea tree. Flies in October.

Convolvulus Hawk Moth (*Sphinx Convolvuli*). Feeds on the bind-weed. Flies in September.

Privet Hawk Moth (*Sphinx Ligustri*). Feeds on lilac, privet, and several other plants. Flies in June.

Spurge Hawk Moth (*Deilephila Euphorbiæ*). Feeds on the sea spurge. The perfect insect has never been found in this country.

Bedstraw Hawk Moth (*Deilephila Galii*). Feeds on the ladies' bedstraw. Flies about midsummer.

Striped Hawk Moth (*Deilephila livornica*). Feeds on the ladies' bedstraw. I am unable to state at what time it flies.

Silver Striped Hawk Moth (*Chærocampa Celerio*). Feeds on the vine. The perfect insect has occurred in England, but can scarcely be regarded as a British insect.

Small Elephant Hawk Moth (*Chærocampa Porcellus*). Feeds on the ladies' bedstraw. Flies in June.

Elephant Hawk Moth (*Chærocampa Elpenor*). Feeds on the large willow herb, and also on ladies' bedstraw. Flies in June.

Oleander Hawk Moth (*Chærocampa Nerii*). Feeds on the oleander. Flies in June and October.

Humming-Bird Hawk Moth (*Macroglossa stellatarum*). Feeds on the ladies' bedstraw. Flies throughout the summer months.

Broad Bordered Bee Hawk Moth (*Macroglossa fuciformis*). Feeds on the common lychnis, the wood scabious, the ladies' bedstraw, and other low herbs. Flies in May.

Narrow Bordered Bee Hawk Moth (*Macroglossa bombyliformis*). Feeds on the field scabious. Flies in May.

THE SESIDÆ.

Red-Belted Clearwing (*Sesia Myopæformis*). Feeds on the solid wood of pear trees, and in the more slender branches of apple trees. Flies in May, June, and July.

Large Red-Belted Clearwing (*Sesia Culiciformis*). Feeds on wood of birch trees, preferring stumps of trees that have been cut down. Flies in May and June.

Red-Tipped Clearwing (*Sesia Formicæformis*). Feeds inside the twigs of osiers. Flies about midsummer.

Fiery Clearwing (*Sesia Chrysidiformis*). I know nothing whatever of this insect.

Six Belted Clearwing (*Sesia Ichneumoniformis*). Feeds on the stems of the stinking Hellebore. Flies in June and July.

Yellow Legged Clearwing (*Sesia Cynipiformis*). Feeds on the bark of elm and oak trees. Flies about midsummer.

Currant Clearwing (*Sesia Tipuliformis*). Feeds on the pith of the twigs of currant bushes. Flies in June.

Orange Tailed Clearwing (*Sesia Andreniformis*). I am unable to give any particulars respecting this insect. One specimen was taken about two years ago at Market Harborough.

Welsh Clearwing (*Sesia Scoliæformis*). Feeds on wood of birch trees. Flies in June.

White-Barred Clearwing (*Sesia Sphegiformis*). Feeds on the stems of the alder. Flies in May and June.

Dusky Clearwing (*Sesia Vespiformis*). Feeds on the roots of ash and aspen trees. Flies in June.

Hornet Clearwing of the Osier (*Sesia Bembeciformis*). Feeds on wood of osier. Flies about midsummer.

Hornet Clearwing of the Poplar (*Sesia Apiformis*). Feeds on the solid woods of the aspen and poplars. Flies about midsummer.

THE ZEUZERIDÆ.

Reed Moth (*Macrogaster Arundinis*). Feeds on the interior of the common weed (*Arundo Phragmites*). Flies in June.

Leopard Moth (*Zeuzera Æsculi*). Feeds on the solid wood of elm, apple, pear, and plum trees. Flies about midsummer.

Goat Moth (*Cossus ligniperda*). Feeds on the solid wood of willows, elms, oak, lilac, and other trees. Flies in June and July.

THE HEPIALIDÆ.

Gold Swift (*Hepialus hectus*). Feeds on the roots of plants in hedges and woods. Flies about midsummer.

Common Swift (*Hepialus lupulinus*). Feeds on the roots of dead nettles (*Ballota fœtida, Lamium album, &c,*). Flies in June.

Wood Swift (*Hepialus sylvinus*). I am unable to state the plant that it feeds on. Flies in July.

Northern Swift (*Hepialus velleda*). Feeds on the subterranean rhizome of the common brake (*Pteris aquilina*). Flies in June.

Ghost Swift (*Hepialus humuli*). Feeds on the roots of burdock (*Arctium Lappa*), stinging-nettle (*Urtica divica*), and dead nettle (*Ballota fœtida*) and (*Lamium album*). Flies about midsummer.

THE COCHLIOPODIDÆ.

Triangle Moth (*Limacodes Asellus*). Feeds on the leaves of the oak. Flies about midsummer.

Festoon Moth (*Limacodes Testudo*). Feeds on the oak. Flies in June.

THE PROCRIDÆ.

Forester (*Procris Statices*). Feeds on the common sorrel. Flies about midsummer.

Scarce Forester (*Procris Globulariæ*). I am unable to state anything about this moth.

THE ZYGÆNIDÆ.

Transparent Burnet (*Zygæna Minos*). Feeds on the *trifolium montanum*, bird's-foot trefoil (*Lotus corniculatus*), and horse-shoe vetch (*Hippocrepis comosa*). Flies in June.

Broad-Bordered Five Spotted Burnet (*Zygæna Trifolii*). Feeds on the horse-shoe vetch (*Hippocrepis comosa*), bird's-foot trefoil (*Lotus corniculatus*), and *trifolium procumbens*. Flies in June.

Narrow Bordered Five Spotted Burnet (*Zygæna Loniceræ*). Feeds on clover and grasses. Flies in June.

Six-Spotted Burnet (*Zygæna Filipendulæ*). Feeds chiefly on crowfoot trefoil. Flies about the beginning of June.

THE NOLIDÆ.

The Short Cloaked Moth (*Nola cucullatella*). Feeds on the blackthorn and on plum trees. Flies about midsummer.

Least Black Arches (*Nola cristulalis*). Feeds on the oak. Flies in June.

Small Black Arches (*Nola Strigula*). Feeds on the oak. Flies in June.

Scarce Black Arches (*Nola centonalis*). I am unable to state the plant that it feeds on. One specimen of this insect was taken on 1st of July, 1858.

THE LITHOSIIDÆ.

Round-winged Muslin (*Nudaria Senex*). Feeds on tree lichens. Flies in August.

Muslin (*Nudaria mundana*). Feeds on tree lichens. Flies in July.

Dew Moth (*Setina irrorella*). Feeds on tree lichens. Flies about midsummer.

Rosy Footman, or Red Arches (*Calligenia miniata*). Feeds on the lichens which grow on the oak. Flies in July.

Four-dotted Footman (*Lithosia mesomella*). Feeds on tree lichens. Flies in June and July.

Dotted Footman (*Lithosia muscerda*). Feeds on lichens. Flies in August.

Orange Footman (*Lithosia aureola*). Feeds on the lichen which grows on the larch-fir. Flies about midsummer.

Pigmy Footman (*Lithosia pygmæola*). Feeds on tree lichens. Flies in August.

Buff Footman (*Lithosia helvola*). Feeds on the lichens of the oak. Flies in June, July, and August.

Common Footman (*Lithosia complanula*). Feeds on the lichens of oaks, blackthorns, and more rarely on larch-firs. Flies in July.

Scarce Footman (*Lithosia complana*). Feeds on the lichens of blackthorns and firs. Flies in July.

Dingy Footman (*Lithosia griseola*). Feeds on tree lichens. Flies soon after midsummer.

Pale Footman (*Lithosia stramineola*). Feeds on tree lichens. Flies soon after midsummer.

Four-spotted Footman (*Lithosia quadra*). It is said by Berge to feed on fir, beech, oak, apple, cherry, damson, roses, horse-chestnut, willow, lime, and various hedgerow plants; but it is most likely the lichen, and not the foliage that it devours. Flies in July and August.

Red-necked Footman (*Lithosia rubricollis*). Feeds on a variety of lichens. Flies in August.

Feathered Footman (*Eulepia grammica*). Feeds on various grasses, on mugwort, on heather, and sometimes on oak leaves. Flies at the end of June. This can hardly be considered a British moth.

Speckled Footman (*Eulepia Cribrum*). Feeds on common heather. Flies in July.

T. W. TEMPANY.

NOTES ON THE RAVEN (*CORVUS COREX*).

By A. E. BUTTEMER.

THIS bird, which belongs to the family of the Corvidæ, is the largest and most powerful of its tribe that is found in any part of the world. Next to it in point of strength and size is the Great-billed Crow found in Abyssinia, which has even a more formidable looking beak than the bird of which I am speaking. In former days the raven was much more frequently seen in the British Isles than it is now, which fact is to be accounted for by the more cultivated state of the country, as it is a bird which loves wild and desolate wastes, far from the dwellings of man; and in such places "the raven reigns supreme, hardly the eagle himself daring to contest the supremacy with so powerful, crafty, and strong-beaked a bird." Owing to its preference to uncultivated districts, it is more frequently met with in Scotland and the adjacent islands than in any other part of Britain, although there are certain localities in England where it is still tolerably common; but the Scottish mountains are the chief resort of this bird, amongst which it builds its nest, and rears its young in more perfect seclusion than it can find in England; for the raven, unlike the jackdaw and the rook, is by no means a sociable bird, not only with man but also among themselves, seldom more than a pair being seen together. I myself have observed it in places on the sea shore of Devonshire, and on the wild rocky coast of Cornwall. In the neighbourhood of the Land's End and the Lizard I have found it not uncommon. During some of my rambles along the magnificent Cornish coast, I have often had the pleasure of seeing a pair of these handsome birds start out of some neighbouring cleft and fly in circles above my head, uttering at intervals their croak, croak, apparently not much liking being intruded upon. There is a particular cave at the Lizard, near to the romantically situated fishing village of Cadgewith, I dare say well known to some readers of the *Naturalist's Note Book*, called the Raven's Hugo. The word "hugo" signifies cave, and it is a dark and sombre-looking cavern, above which is to be seen a raven's nest; but when I visited this cave in August, 1867, the boatman who rowed me to it informed me that the ravens had now deserted it, and the nest had been taken possession of by a pair of hawks. The food which they prefer to any other kind is carrion; but those ravens which frequent the sea coast— and I allude to the shores of Devon and Cornwall —cannot I think find very much of their favorite food there, and consequently I believe they must live upon refuse fish, crabs, &c., and whatever they may happen to come across. Like the carrion crow, ravens are great enemies of game-keepers, as they suck the eggs of pheasants, etc., and prey upon hares. But, in one sense they may be considered their friends, for they are said to consume both rats and mice, and I have no doubt but what they often pounce upon a stoat and other kinds of vermin; for hardly anything comes amiss to the raven, which also devours insects of all sorts, and must have a most wonderful digestion, being able as I well know to swallow a piece of shoe leather, apparently without feeling the least discomfort from it afterwards. Among other parts of England where I have seen the raven, may be mentioned the mountains of Westmorland and Cumberland. In districts like these, carrion no doubt forms their chief food, and they must do some damage to the flocks of sheep which feed upon the rugged slopes of the mountains, for "weakly or ailing sheep are also favorite subjects with the raven, who soon puts an end to their sufferings by the strokes of his long and powerful beak." I was climbing "the dark brow of the mighty

Helvellyn" one day last October, when I surprised a couple of these birds, which kept croaking and flying round the summit of that mountain until I had retired to what they thought to be a respectable distance. The following I extract from "The Illustrated Natural History," by the Rev. J. G. Wood:—"As the bird is so crafty, its capture would seem to be a very difficult business, and the number of tame ravens now existing in England seems to be almost remarkable. The fact is, that while still unfledged the young ravens have a strange habit of falling out of their nests and flapping their wings heavily to the ground. Next morning they are found by the shepherds sitting croaking on the ground beneath their former homes, and are then captured and taken away with comparative ease. Even in this case, however, to secure one of the young ravens is no slight task, for, on seeing that escape is impossible it turns boldly to bay, and makes such fierce attacks with its powerful beak that it must be enveloped in a cloth or a plaid before it can safely be held. It is remarkable that when a raven makes its assault it does not merely peck with its beak, but flings its whole weight upon the blow. The raven is also celebrated for its longevity, many instances being known where it has attained the age of seventy or eighty years, without losing one jot of its activity or the fading of one spark from its eyes. What may be the duration of a raven's life in its wild state, is quite unknown." The peculiar "croak" of the raven can, I think, never be mistaken for the note of any other bird; and although it certainly has nothing of a musical tone in it, yet it is a sound of which I am very fond. Amongst the superstitious and foolish, the raven's croaking has been regarded as an omen of death, misfortune, etc.:

> The sad presaging raven tolls
> The sick man's passport in her hollow beak,
> And in the shadow of the silent night
> Doth shake contagion from her sable wing.
> MARLOWE.

There is certainly an air of great mysteriousness about the whole bird, which possesses a pair of the most cunning and wicked-looking eyes imaginable, and has a peculiar way of rolling them about. Although when in a natural state the raven is so wild and unsociable, yet if taken from the nest when young it is very easily tamed, and becomes a most amusing as well as intelligent pet. Fond as I am of tame ravens, I however give them their true character when I say that, they are most mischievous and destructive birds when in captivity. If kept in confinement it should not be enclosed in too small a space, but allowed the range of a yard. I have had two tame ravens at different times. The first one must have been in the wars, having a broken leg when he came into my posession, from which he must have suffered a great amount of pain, and did not survive very long. My second raven was a young one, when I bought him being only six weeks old, but he, like the other, went the way of most pets, and died much to my sorrow a short time ago. I valued him very much, as he grew up a large and handsome bird, and could talk a little and call the poultry, along with which I kept him. The hens he used to worry, and suck their eggs; but the cock, which was a large game bird, he was afraid to attack openly, but frequently when he was feeding the raven would advance quietly and slyly behind him and pull a feather from his tail, and then would walk triumphantly away. My pet was the cause of his own death, having *too* good an appetite, and was poisoned I believe from eating paint.

EXTRACTS FROM AN ENTOMOLOGIST'S DIARY.

For the last four years I have been in the habit of keeping a diary for registering interesting captures, observations, etc., in entomology, and find it a good plan for reference. I give a few extracts from it, thinking they may be interesting to some of the readers of the N. N. B.; and if you think it worth inserting, I shall be most happy to continue it.

St. Augustine's, Norwich.   R. LADDIMAN.

June 23, 1865.—Weather warm. Went out at 6 a.m. Caught a specimen of the humming-bird hawkmoth (Macroglossa stellatarum) hovering over a bank; had no net with me, but succeeded in capturing it with my hands. Caught two of the small tortoise-shell butterfly (Vanessa urticæ) and a buff ermine moth (Arcta lubricipeda), sitting on a wall.

June 24.—Warm. Caught a humming-bird hawkmoth (M. stellatarum), hovering over a grassy bank.

July 5.—Day very hot; evening mild. Caught a fine specimen of the large elephant hawkmoth (Chærocampa Elpenor), and a pair of the gold-tailed moth (Liparis auriflua).

July 22.—Very hot. Caught two specimens of the humming-bird hawkmoth (M. stellatarum), hovering over a bunch of nettles.

July 27.—Took a pair of the scalloped oakmoth (Crocallis elinguaria), sitting on a bank; caught a peacock butterfly (Vanessa Io). Had a swallow tail (Papilio machaon), a brimstone (Gonepteryx Rhamni), and a privet hawkmoth (Sphinx Ligustri) brought to me.

Sept. 4.—Found larva of the death's head hawkmoth (Acherontia Atropos) feeding on the potato, which was full fed, and changed to a chrysalis on the 7th.

Oct. 13.—Warm. Caught two humming-bird hawkmoths (M. stellatarum).

Nov. 10.—Death's head hawkmoth (A. atropos)

emerged from pupa; a very fine specimen, measuring nearly five inches from tip to tip. Noticed the peculiar squeaking noise produced by this insect when touched, somewhat resembling the squeaking of a mouse. Query.—Has the pupa the power of making this noise, as related by some authors? Note.—The humming-bird hawkmoth (M. stellatarum) seems to have been very abundant this year in all parts of the country. I have frequently observed it flying about the streets of Norwich.

June 11, 1866.—Evening cool and windy. Caught two pairs of the common swift (Hepialus lupulinus), a brimstone moth (Rumia cratægata), and an angle shades (Phlogophora meticulosa).

June 13.—Day rainy, evening mild and damp. Took about twenty larvæ of the gold and brown tailed moth (Liparis auriflua and L. chrysorrhea) feeding on the whitethorn; three pairs of the brimstone moth (R. cratægata); a pair of the garden carpet (Melanippe fluctuata); a common swift (H. lupulinus). Had a pair of the latticed heath (Strenia clathrata) brought to me.

June 21.—Warm. Caught five specimens of the brimstone moth (R. cratægata); a blue-bordered carpet (Melanthia rubriginata). A puss moth (Dicranura vinula) given to me.

June 23.—Went out at 6 a.m. Found a fine specimen of the large elephant hawkmoth (Chærocampa Elpenor) sitting on the grass, and about three dozen larvæ of the small tortoiseshell butterfly (Vanessa urticæ) feeding on the nettles.

June 24.—Day very hot. Saw three large specimens of the privet hawkmoth (Sphinx ligustri) running on a bank in the hot sunshine, two of which I captured; the third escaped.

June 25.—Day hot, evening warm, and moonlight. Caught a fine specimen of the eyed hawkmoth (Smerinthus ocellatus), which proved to be a female, and deposited eight eggs on the following day, but they did not come to perfection; and a privet hawk-moth (Sphinx Ligustri), both of which were flying over a privet hedge.

June 27.—Caught a dozen specimens of the demoiselle dragonfly (Calepteryx); saw a red admiral butterfly (Vanessa atalanta). Evening mild, caught an angle shades moth (P. meticulosa).

June 28.—Windy. Took a buff tip moth (Pygæra bucephala), a grey dagger (Acronycta Psi), and a light emerald (Metrocampa margaritaria).

July 4.—Windy. Took three ghost swift moths (Hepialus humuli) males, on a meadow.

July 6.—Caught a pair of the nut tree tussock (Demas coryli).

July 9.—Evening mild. Caught a large yellow underwing (Tryphæna pronuba), a gamma (Plusia gamma), and a straw belle (Aspilates gilvaria).

July 15.—Hot. Caught a large emerald moth (Geometra papilionaria).

July 17.—Unfavourable. Caught a specimen of the swallow tailed moth (Uropteryx sambucata).

July 18.—Caught a swallow tailed moth (U. sambucata), and a white satin moth (Liparis Salicis).

Aug. 20.—Weather mild, sun at intervals. Caught eight specimens of the peacock butterfly (Vanessa Io), seven of the wall butterfly (Satyrus Megæra), nine large heath (S. Tithonus), and one common blue (Polyomattus Alexis).

Aug. 21.—Rainy. Caught a green field cricket.
(*To be continued.*)

AMONG THE TREES.

Oh ye who love to overhang the springs,
And stand by running waters, ye whose boughs
Make beautiful the rocks o'er which they play,
Who pile with foliage the great hills, and rear
A paradise upon the lonely plain,
Trees of the forest and the open field!
Have ye no sense of being? Does the air,
The pure air, which I breathe with gladness, pass
In gushes o'er your delicate lungs, your leaves
All unenjoyed? When on your winter-sleep
The sun shines warm, have ye no dreams of spring?
And, when the glorious spring-time comes at last,
Have ye no joy of all your bursting buds,
And fragrant blooms, and melody of birds
To which your young leaves shiver? Do ye strive
And wrestle with the winds yet know it not?
Feel ye no glory in your strength when he
The exhausted blusterer, flies beyond the hills,
And leaves you stronger yet? Or have ye not
A sense of loss when he has stripped your leaves,
Yet tender, and has splintered your fair boughs?
Does the loud bolt that smites you from the cloud
And rends you, fall unfelt? Do there not run
Strange shudderings through your fibres when the axe
Is raised against you, and the shining blade
Deals blow on blow, until, with all their boughs,
Your summits waver and ye fall to earth?
Know ye no sadness when the hurricane
Has swept the wood and snapped its sturdy stems
Asunder, or has wrenched, from out the soil,
The mightiest with their circles of strong roots,
And piled the ruin all along his path?

Nay, doubt we not that under the rough rind,
In the green veins of these fair growths of earth,
There dwells a nature that receives delight
From all the gentle processes of life,
And shrinks from loss of being. Dim and faint
May be the sense of pleasure and of pain,
As in our dreams; but, haply, real still.

Our sorrows touch you not. We watch beside
The beds of those who languish or who die,
And minister in sadness, while our hearts
Offer perpetual prayer for life and ease
And health to the belovèd sufferers.
But ye, while anxious fear and fainting hope
Are in our chambers, ye rejoice without.
The funeral goes forth; a silent train
Moves slowly from the desolate home; our hearts
Are breaking as we lay away the loved,
Whom we shall see no more, in their last rest,
Their little cells within the burial-place.
Ye have no part in this distress; for still
The February sunshine steeps your boughs
And tints the buds and swells the leaves within;
While the song-sparrow, warbling from her perch,

Tells you that spring is near. The wind of May
Is sweet with breath of orchards, in whose boughs
The bees and every insect of the air
Make a perpetual murmur of delight,
And by whose flowers the humming bird hangs poised
In air, and draws their sweets and darts away.
The linden, in the fervors of July,
Hums with a louder concert. When the wind
Sweeps the broad forest in its summer prime,
As when some master-hand exulting sweeps
The keys of some great organ, ye give forth
The music of the woodland depths, a hymn
Of gladness and of thanks. The hermit-thrush
Pipes his sweet note to make your arches ring
The faithful robin from the wayside elm,
Carols all day to cheer his sitting mate.
And when the autumn comes, the kings of earth,
In all their majesty, are not arrayed
As ye are, clothing the broad mountain-side,
And spotting the smooth vales with red and gold.
While, swaying to the sudden breeze, ye fling
Your nuts to earth, and the brisk squirrel comes
To gather them, and barks with childish glee,
And scampers with them to his hollow oak.

Thus, as the seasons pass, ye keep alive
The cheerfulness of nature, till in time
The constant misery which wrings the heart
Relents, and we rejoice with you again,
And glory in your beauty ; till once more
We look with pleasure on your vanished leaves,
That gayly glance in sunshine, and can hear
Delighted, the soft answer which your boughs
Utter in whispers to the babbling brook.
—WM. CULLEN BRYANT in *Putnam's Monthly Magazine* for January.

New Books.

Tommy Try, and what he did in Science. By Charles Ottley Groom Napier, (of Merchiston) F.G.S., &c., Author of "the Food, Use, and Beauty of British Birds," and other Works. 1869. London: Chapman and Hall.

Among the numerous books written especially for the young, we are pleased to notice one emanating from the fertile pen of Mr. C. O. G. Napier, a gentleman whose initials appended to various remarks and queries in our columns, may not be unfamiliar to our readers. This work, as its title would intimate, seems rather intended as a book for boys than for the more advanced student of nature, and as such, strictly speaking, hardly comes within the class of books usually noticed by us. However, when we observe the immense amount of trash in the shape of magazines, periodicals, sensational tales, and other works provided for all classes of the youth of this country at the present day, we hail with the more pleasure a work in all material respects calculated to elevate the moral tone, as well as to increase the knowledge and improve the intellectual powers, of the "Boys of the Period," and of which the object is to teach them the advantages and pleasures to be derived from the book of nature ; so at the outset we heartily commend it to the attention to our younger readers.

"Tommy Try," the youthful narrator, gives us an autobiography, commencing from a very early age, when he dates his ardour in the study of natural science, from a visit with his mother and some young friends to the Museum in the city of Exeter, and where his little eyes and mouth were opened wide with astonishment and delight, not unmingled with awe, at the wonderful things he saw there. Being a boy, or rather a child, of remarkable genius, he set to work and endeavoured to form a museum of his own, beginning with a collection of dried plants given him by a lady friend. The book proceeds with his searches after scientific knowledge, the various accidents he met with in his pursuit, his experiments in Chemistry, and studies in Botany, Conchology, Oology, Entomology, and other "ologies," mingled with a good deal of ordinary every-day life. Mr. Napier certainly has well managed a most difficult task —viz., to combine the scientific and non-scientific parts of his work in such a felicitous manner, that the interest is kept up throughout, while the anecdotes and legends told the author by the various persons he met on his rambles, give a pleasant and amusing air to the work. There are one or two passages which appeared to us somewhat out of place, and we must confess to being rather startled by the mention of a certain lady of his acquaintance, somewhat inclined to obesity, whose weight is modestly estimated at 29st the last time she was weighed ! As however we are informed that she was the daughter and widow of an influential firm of brewers, our readers may perhaps consider that she had good reason for being so stout. We must admit having a tolerable share of scepticsm on this point.

Although Mr. "Tommy Try" made the most astounding progress in his studies, he had certainly every facility for indulging in his favorite pursuits. Spending his earlier days in Devonshire, going for a short time to a small country school in that county, and leaving again after the age of ten on account of delicate health, visiting Weymouth, Portland, Honiton, Starcross, Budleigh Salterton, Exmouth, Poole, and many watering places, and spending a great part of his time either in the open country or by the sea shore, it is not to be wondered at that a boy gifted with a taste for the beauties of nature, and having such facilities for learning should have in the course of time a sound practical knowledge of Natural History. Indeed we have no doubt that youngsters having similar tastes, who read this work will sigh with envy at the unusual opportunities enjoyed by him, and long for the same chances of increasing their own knowledge. It will be seen however that most of these advantages were those of his own creation. His instruments and mechanism used in his experiments were nearly all "home-made," and we find him denying himself butter and sugar at his meals in order to lay out their value in the purchase of some scientific work or instrument the price of which was otherwise beyond his reach. We should very much like to know how many of our readers would be inclined to make such a sacrifice *causa scientiæ;* We need say no more as to the rest of the book. The style adopted by the author is pleasant, while with some exceptions the language is plain and choice, and what is of more consequence, will be understood by most of its readers. We give a short extract which seems a fair sample of the rest of the work :—

"In the month of September we settled in the town of Lewes, which is one of the most interesting of neighbourhoods to the Naturalist. It was somewhat late in the season for collecting plants and insects—at least in the superficial way in which I had been accustomed ; for I was not then familiar with the winter haunts of insects, and did not take sufficient interest in the *Cryptogamia* to study or collect them with any spirit ; they are pre-eminently the winter plants. Lewes is situated on ground of varying altitude ; part of the town is very high, and part equally low. The meadows on both sides of the town abound in ditches which afford great varieties of curious objects. In winter there were few flowering plants of interest to be found, but I noticed a good many fresh-water shells, such as *Lemnæa stagnalis, L. Palustris, L. Pereger, Planorbis corneus, P. Marguiatus, P. Vortex,* and *Cyclas Cornea*. Numerous empty cases of the caddis worm, also, which had attracted to themselves a covering of dead shells, consisting of *Limnea, Planorbis,* and other species, together with a few fragments of sticks. During the life of the animal nothing appears but its head and tail ; it thus escapes many attacks from fishes and the larvæ of water-beetles (*Dytiscus*) as it drags its soft and fleshy body along the bottom of its native pool. In the following spring, when I found the animals living in their cases, I noticed how some species appeared to prefer stone and shells, and others sticks, straw, and vegetable substances."

We must observe, however, that there are some faults, which, in order to give an unprejudiced notice, we ought to mention. In the first place, we much object to the character of this youth, and the extraordinary mental powers displayed by him. At first we imagined that the picture as drawn by the Author was a biography of his own youth, but as we proceeded further—although in our imagination we endowed Mr. Napier with the most unbounded genius, perseverance, and industry, together with a no slight share of juvenile precocity—we really could not do otherwise than come to the conclusion that "Tommy Try" was but a creation of the author's brain, and that being fictitious, it was far too overdrawn. We read that at the age of ten this "infant phenomenon" had constructed an electric battery, had given a lecture on Chemistry to a circle of admiring friends—(by the way, he nearly blew them all up) made several chemical experiments, and, before he had attained sixteen, had analysed part of the stomach of a man who had been poisoned by arsenic. But his talent was not in this direction alone. He was gifted with such a genius for music, that a musician hearing him singing an air of his own composition, introduced it into an oratorio he was then composing, and which some time afterwards was much applauded by several crowded audiences. Besides which, he had a considerable taste for painting. It appears to us that had the character of an ordinary boy been drawn, with a somewhat smaller amount of genius, and a larger amount of faults, the interest in the work would have been much increased for to put entire faith in the acts of such a prodigy require a considerable share of credulity. If, however, we are wrong in our supposition, and the author really has given a sketch of his boyhood, we can only say that we humbly apologise for our error, and beg to state our firm conviction that the fame of the Napier (of Merchiston) will one day equal if not eclipse that of the Napier (of Magdala). Another point we deprecate, both in this, and other similar works, is the too common use of the purely scientific names of the shells, insects, plants, chemicals, and other objects mentioned by the author. Those unaccompanied by their English equivalents, will we think be understood by their youthful readers in the same degree with "double Dutch," or North American Indian, and such a use gives an air of pedantry to the book which is wholly foreign to its general tone, and, we hope, to the author's intention. One word more, and we shall have finished this part of our task. Although we much admire the clever introduction of extraneous matter into the general narrative, we must entirely disapprove of the story of the "Lessons in Flirtation" in which a child of ten or eleven gives these lessons to little Tommy. This can have no possible connection with the general object of the work or with the rest of the narrative. By younger boys it would scarcely be understood, by elder ones it may be attempted to be copied, which would make matters worse. These errors, however, are not very grave, and though noticed by us here, do not affect the rest of the book in any marked degree. We need add but little more, except to observe that if a perusal of this work will lead the rising generation to study the works of Creation, and make them love the handiwork of the Almighty, so that they may be brought to look

"From Nature up to Nature's God,"

we feel sure that the labour the author has expended over it will not be lost.

We should only be half doing our work were we to omit mention of the capital engravings with which the book is studded, especially the drawings of shells, which are executed in a very correct style. In fine we need only recommend those of our younger readers who have a taste for the beauties of nature to read this book, which may give them an idea of the way to set about studying some of the "ologies."

The Polar World; a popular description of Man and Nature in the Arctic and Antartic regions of the Globe. By Dr. G. Hartwig. London: Longmans.

Dr. Hartwig in his preface to this work says:—

The object of the following pages is to describe the polar world in its principal natural features, to point out the influence of its long winter nights and fleeting summer on the development of animal and vegetable life, and finally to picture man waging the battle of life against the dreadful climate of the high latitudes of our globe; either as the inhabitant of their gloomy solitudes or as the bold investigator of their mysteries.

We cannot find fault with the learned doctor, for the manner in which he has proceeded to carry out his ideas. If we cannot altogether praise the work on the score of originality, neither can we condemn it as wanting interest. Much of the matter is necessarily worked up from the descriptions of Arctic voyagers, and does not, therefore, come altogether fresh. Yet we certainly must confess that suitable materials have been so well joined and pieced together as to make a whole at once charming and entertaining. We have not space to enumerate the great variety of subjects of which our author treats; so for these particulars must refer the reader to the volume itself, satisfied that he will be as pleased as we ourselves have been with a perusal.

Correspondence.

[*Under this head we shall be glad to insert any letters of general interest.*]

SIR,—I cannot see that a law to protect our rock-breeding sea-fowl would entail any particular evils, but it would effectually stop the systematic slaughter by gentlemen sportsmen and persons in the plume trade, going on at present, in summer.

In spite of what "A. M. B." says I apprehend these *are* the people it will press most heavily upon; ornithologists can collect in winter or go to Scotland (to the Bass rock for instance) or they can prosecute their studies minus the gun.

If the present state of things goes on, in a short time there will be no birds left.

"A CONSTANT READER."

ANSWERS TO CORRESPONDENTS.

HENRY O'CONNELL.—We have forwarded your note with sketch to Mr. Frank Buckland, and await a reply.

T. GARRATT.—1. No: Entomologist, monthly, price 6d; Zoologist, 1s 6d. 2. Cutler, 35, Great Russell-street, Bloomsbury. 3. Yes. No.

W. COLE.—Shall be glad to receive further papers from you.

F. W. TEMPANY.—Please send as you suggest.

S. T. W.—Too late for this Number.

Remarks, Queries, &c.

(*Under this head we shall be happy to insert original Remarks, Queries, &c.*)

REASONING POWER OF ANIMALS.

Allow me a short space in reply to the remarks made by some of your correspondents in the NOTE BOOK for February. After referring to Mr. Lidden's definition of immortality, C. says, "Now all these moral attributes, viz.:—The soul's personal identity, memory, affection, and character, are more or less observable in lower animals." If they are observable in *lower* animals, then, I presume, he will contend they are even more so in *higher* animals. It is certainly the first time I have heard that animals had any idea of the "*soul's personal identity*," or of "*character.*" They may, and undoubtedly do, have memory, and affection, but what idea has a dog or an elephant of vice and virtue, of honesty and dishonesty, of happiness and misery, of right and wrong? Surely this gentleman should pause before he censures other people for making *bold* assertions, when he himself makes assertions *almost* as bold. No doubt there are many authors, both living and dead, who would be willing to wield a cudgel in defence of animal reason, yea, and not only of animal reason, but of vegetable reason too, as is shown by the following lines of Charles Mackay:—

"To everything that lives,
The kind Creator gives
Share of enjoyment; and while musing here,
Amid the high grass laid,
Under your grateful shade,
I deem your branches, rustling low and clear,
May have some means of speech
Lovingly each to each,
Some power to understand, to wonder, to revere."

But perhaps it has not occurred to your correspondent that it is possible for *authors* and authors of the "first magnitude," too, to be mistaken; after all their opinion is but an opinion.

Your correspondent, "Cosmos," would "grant to all animals a share of the faculties possessed by man." What a pity it is he did not occupy the place of the Creator. However, it remains yet to be proved that animals have one faculty which is possessed by man, namely, *reason*. Cosmos says, "As we find in the body of an animal, that the various organs and limbs are more or less developed as circumstances require their use, so I believe its mental faculties are high or low as outward circumstances require; and further, that as there are some organs or limbs which we find to be only rudimentary, so there are faculties in the mind of the animal which are perfectly dormant, but may be called forth into action, if the circumstances requiring their use be incident to a sufficient number of generations of the animal." This is certainly the best part of his reasoning. But whatever dormant faculties there are in an animal which may be called into use when required, there are none which come within the pale of reason. Let there be even the smallest amount of reason in an animal, and we should find a proportionate amount of progress as the result of that reason. Who can look back on the long vista of ages that have passed since man first appeared on the stage of being, and mark his history from the time of Eden's banishment down to the 19th century of the Christian era, without seeing evidences of progress? But where do we look for progress in animals? Take, as an illustration, the means provided for offence and defence, those possessed by animals form a part of their own systems—such are the talons of birds, and the claws and teeth of animals, provided and placed by the Creator in such positions as are best fitted for their use. But in man, being a reasoning creature, there is nothing of the kind. He has to provide his own means of defence; and what progress do we see even in this. At first,

"The ancient arrow-maker
Made his arrow-heads of sandstone,
Arrow-heads of chalcedony;
Arrow-heads of flint and jaspar,
Smoothed and sharpened at the edges,
Hard and polish'd, keen and costly."

But later on,
"The bursting shell, the gateway wrenched asunder,
The rattling musketry, the clashing blade;
And ever and anon, in tones of thunder,
The diapason of the cannonade."

But what progress is made by animals in their means of defence? The bird's talons are the same now as they were on Creation's morn, and the claws of the animal are claws still. In the works of man we see progress *everywhere*, but in the works of animals *nowhere*. All animals are provided with a covering to protect them from cold; man has no such provision made for him, his reason being intended to guide him in supplying the deficiency. One of the most evident results of the active use of reason in man, is the power of absolute control—control over his passions, control to some extent over circumstances, and control over the use of Nature's gifts. But the animal has no control whatever over its actions, and is, in fact, but a living machine in the hands of Providence.

The reference to the habits of animals referred to by your correspondent, is surely no evidence of their possessing reason. The very fact that birds migrate at certain seasons of the year, because of the excess of climate, proves to me that they have no reason by which they might invent some means to provide against such excess of climate. If Cosmos means that the habits of animals, "inherited through an infinite number of ancestors," is a *substitute* for reason in its influence over their actions, then the question is settled at once, and there is no need of further controversy. But until some of your correspondents can discover in the motives and actions of animals, a *proportionate* amount of progress, of inventive genius, and of rational employment, and show that they possess *proportionate* ideas of law and justice, order of society, and other like results of the active use of reason, I must content myself with allowing to *man only* reason, and to animals "the property termed *Instinct*," however "meaningless" it may seem to some.
W. NEWBERRY.

I am very glad to see that this subject is receiving so much attention from the readers of the NOTE BOOK, and I rather think that it will be some time before it is finished. I see that your correspondent "R. B. W." has denied to the lower animals the power of reasoning *in toto*. I would advise him to reflect a little before speaking in such strong terms upon a subject too deep by far to be decided in so sudden and rash a way. I most certainly believe that some animals are capable of reasoning to a certain extent. But do not misunderstand me. My upholding the affirmative side of the question neither derogates from man's high intellectual powers nor imputes to the lower animals immortal souls, but was derived from facts related by Naturalists famed for their learning. These men, like many others of the present day, wrote about what they saw, and what they knew to be perfectly correct, and never credited any assertions unless they were trustworthy.

I will presently relate several anecdotes, together with the names of the authors, who may be implicitly believed; but before I begin I should first like to make a few remarks upon two words, viz:—Reason and Instinct—for many false and foolish ideas prevail, especially among the uneducated, about them. 1st., Reason is an attribute of the mind, or animating principle, and it can be detected and at once separated from Instinct by animals attaining their ends or designs by indirect means ; and which acts also could not otherwise have been accomplished except by careful forethought.

Instinct on the contrary is a fixed and automatic influence which exists in man as well as the lower animals ; it causes the performance of many of those curious and wonderful actions which so often excite our admiration. Infants are good illustrations of Instinct : while being carried up stairs they exhibit no particular uneasiness, but if brought down immediately testify to their possession of the instinctive dread of falling by struggling violently. Another illustration of Instinct, and only that, may be seen in the beautiful and geometrical cells and combs constructed by some families in the order Hymenoptera. For example, the bee, soon after emerging from the pupa condition, is busily engaged in the usual occupations of its tribe in making "propolis," building its cell, and storing it with honey.

The formidable battery of arguments that W. Newberry has thought fit to bring forward in his last paper upon the subject is scarcely fair, for he censures the affirmative side for substantiating their opinion by anecdotes. As I have already stated, unless the anecdotes are perfectly true it is positive waste of paper and ink to relate them ; but if correct they form the best and most convincing arguments that we can employ, since it is only by them and careful observations that this controversy can be decided. He also opines that reason in animals necessitates an immortal soul, and likewise that "Instinct is a faculty of the body." The latter clause I can understand, but I consider the former to be a most improbable and untenable idea. Let us now see what Dionysius Lardner says about "Instinct and Intelligence," in his "Museum of Science and Art," page 115, Vol. VIII. : —" It must not be supposed that Instinct and Intelligence cannot co-exist, or that the animal endowed with either is necessarily deprived of the other. It is certain, on the contrary, that most animals are more or less gifted with both. . . . . Between these powers there is the most complete opposition. All the results of Instinct are blind, necessary, and invariable. All those of Intelligence, on the contrary, are optional, conditional, and susceptible of endless modification.' . . . . .

Such is the opinion of Lardner upon the question we are now discussing.

I will now conclude my argument by relating two anecdotes which I think will clearly prove that the lower creatures can reason. Dr. Darwin says that one day while walking in his garden he saw a Sphinx, which had just seized an insect as big as itself, attempt to carry it off. Failing in this it cut off the head and abdomen, keeping only the thorax with the wings. But finding that the wings hindered its own flight, it alighted upon the ground and deliberately removed first one and then the other, and easily flew off with its burden.

Clarville tells a story of a Sexton Beetle (Necrophorus Mortuorum). He saw a small mouse lying dead upon a piece of hard ground. Shortly afterwards a Sexton Beetle flew towards it and tried to excavate the soil immediately under its body. Finding, however, that it was unable to do so it sought the nearest locality where the ground was soft. Having there dug a hole large enough to contain the mouse, it returned and endeavoured to push the little animal into it. Finding by its unsuccessful trials that it could not accomplish its purpose, it flew off, and presently came back with three or four others, who by their united strength rolled the mouse into its grave.

These will show that it is something more than Instinct which guides and governs the actions of the brutes !

But I do not for one moment suppose or would stultify myself and others with such a belief, that insects and the brutes in general possess reasoning powers equal to our own. But I do maintain that they reason to a certain extent, and I cannot see in what way it is to be disproved. VERITAS.

Leaving to other correspondents to define instinct and reason, I would like to relate a couple of *facts* showing extraordinary sagacity, if not reasoning power. The truth of both I can vouch for, having been witness to one, and the second having occurred to my sisters. About twelve months back I bought several fowls at Stevens', one of which was a black Spanish hen—a tender plaintive kind of bird that looked pitifully melancholy. Upon turning this bird into the run with my other fowls, I found that it was not possible for it to remain there unless I wished it killed, which I certainly did not, so had to fish it out and keep it by itself, until I determined what to do with it. I had too much respect for my garden to allow it full liberty. Having nothing else, I was forced to put it in the round wicker basket in which I had brought it from the sale room. During the day, it was placed at the end of the garden, under a wall, where, with plenty of food, it seemed to pass a happy though lonely kind of life ; at night it was taken into the coal cellar, as security against cats. Now, it used to be frequently a great mystery to me how this bird in its wicker cage came to be at the foot of the coal cellar door about roosting time. I did not think to ask my wife about it ; in fact I supposed she had brought it there, yet thinking to myself she might have gone a little farther and put it inside. Some few days after noticing this, I was looking out upon the garden, where my brother was standing with his hands behind him, contemplating, as I thought, the gravel walk, with the most intensely comical grin on his face, and occasionally breaking out into a loud roar of laughter. So irritable did I get at this as I thought absurd conduct, that I went out to see what possessed him. Why, said he, in answer to my query, I'm laughing at that Spanish fowl of yours ; just look at it.

I did look, and with no little astonishment. It had turned its basket over, and, treading upon the bars like a squirrel in its cage, was slowing making its way to the coal-shed. The mystery was solved ; I no longer wondered how it got to its roosting place at night : certainly if I had not seen the creature going demurely along, treading so carefully on each bar and causing it to revolve over its head, I never should have believed it. Several evenings afterwards I watched it go through the same manœuvre, and showed it to several friends. Was this instinct or reason?

The account of the second I extract from a letter:—"An incident occurred to I and Pet a few days ago that would have amused you greatly... You know the two ugly dogs that live at Arbor's on the Common. You also know it is the usual habit for one of them to come up here and get a meal occasionally; also that I and Pet never go past the cottage without his coming out and greeting us with a welcome bark; and then, trotting perhaps a quarter of a mile down the road. These dogs are now the happy parents of a small puppy—very small and very ugly. We were going over to post, and had got past the cottage some little distance, when we heard our friend barking. We took no notice, thinking he would soon come up to us as usual, but presently hearing him still barking as though to draw our attention, and not apparently gaining upon us as we turned—and you would have laughed as we did—down the road; some distance behind us coming along very slowly was our friend—next him the poor little puppy, and on the other side the mother of the same. It was very apparent that they had brought their offspring out for our particular edification, and probably with a view of discovering our opinions respecting it. We did not stop, as we were in rather a hurry, but looked round from time to time to see the three plodding slowly along; but the father presently getting excited at not being able to reach us, left the other two and came bounding up to us, where, barking with delight and dancing round us and running back a little way and then jumping up to us, he asked as plainly as a dog could that we would wait and see the little one, who was still toiling patiently along by the side of the mother a long way behind. When our friend found we would not stay, he ran back to the others and evidently tried to urge them forward, then he came back and went through the same fuss with us: making a turn in the road we lost sight of them. We were greatly amused, as it seemed quite clear that our approbation was required concerning the little one."

I scarcely can bring myself to believe that in both of these cases instinct is the only motive power. I should like some of your numerous correspondents to send you illustrations of this kind if they have happened to come across any that they know to be true. H. C.

Your correspondent "C." has not quite brought "the matter to an end," nor do I think that we are "fighting for a shadow;" for although I stated that we observe reason in the actions of dogs, I said also that we observe it quite as clearly in plants. So we do, and often much sounder reasoning than many human beings can boast of; and for the good reason that it proceeds much more directly from the Author of all reason. If "C." turns to page 265, vol. 2, he will find an excellent article on the "Sensibility of Plants," which goes far to prove this point.

Would "C." say that the evil designs and machinations of wicked men must be attributed to the "Omnipotent origin of all reason?" Does he ever find that what he calls "reason" in the lower animals ever leads them to do any serious harm to other creatures? He cannot even point to mistakes and blunders in their conduct; so to be candid he must admit that brutes are far superior to man; in that the latter is continually liable to err in all his transactions.

That the insect world display more sagacity than the majority of mammalia is I think a fact beyond dispute. Let "C." inquire of entomologists who have spent their lives in observing the habits of this class of animals, and I think he will be convinced. Take, for instance, the white ants of Africa and the East Indies: these not only rear substantial habitations (often above twelve feet high), and range themselves in order of battle and furiously fight their enemies; but also possess a language by which they can make themselves perfectly understood by their comrades. These ants even build bridges, streets and doors—the soldier ants taking no part in this sort of work. Many curious facts are related of these and other varieties of the ant tribe by Smeathman, Huber, and Gould. The great Linnæus tells us of some ants who keep and feed certain insects called plant lice, or gall insects, and which he named the milch cattle of the ants on account of their supplying the ants with milk. Other ants take prisoners and keep slaves. Now what other class of animals can compete with these insects in their wonderful instincts. "C." will find that Mr. Ulidia is also of this opinion, for on page 250, vol. 2, he says:—"Naturalists tell us that insects in their 'instincts' are more remarkable than any other race of beings."

Notwithstanding your correspondent's quotation from Dr. Kirke, I leave to the readers of the NOTE BOOK to judge whether a decapitated frog can have any "purpose" or motive for its movements when in that condition.

If some of the actions of animals are governed by their reason, all must be; now who would say that their own reason is discernible in the conduct of young animals untaught by experience? That they are not educated by their parents is evident, for if reared by foster parents, or produced by artificial means, their habits remain unaltered.

"Cosmos" appears to imagine that the "ancestors" of the brute creation were to their existing offspring what the most barbarous savages on the face of the globe are to their European brethren!—in short, that they possess the exalted power of gaining knowledge by experience and advancing in civilisation. This is indeed the march of intellect! Such being the case, we need not wonder that some of our friends have concluded that their forefathers were intimately related to certain species of quadrummana. We shall have the brutes rising *en masse*, and by right of superior strength refusing to remain any longer the humble servants of the "lord of creation."

But seriously, does "Cosmos" suppose that animals at the creation were devoid of those beautiful and harmonious habits which render their study so interesting and instructive to mankind? Does our fallen world afford nobler views of nature than at that time when everything was in its pristine perfection, and was pronounced by God himself to be very good?

Unless much stronger arguments than those already

given are brought forward to prove the identity of human reason and the so-called reason in beasts, precedence must be given to the opinion that "man alone of all the creatures that God has made upon earth is endowed with the faculty of reason."
Edinburgh. R. B. W.

"REASONING POWER OF ANIMALS."—A very interesting discussion has been commenced in your columns on the above subject, and if space permit I should like to make a few remarks. The most interesting article I have read upon the subject is in Vol. I of the N. N. B., page 268, which I would recommend your correspondents to read.

The following fact which was told me a short time since by a gentleman who was an eye witness of it, will perhaps assist in explaining the difference between instinct and reason. While walking by the sea side he had frequently noticed the sea birds pick up shell fish, and being too hard for them to break open in the usual manner, they carry them in their bills to a sufficient height, and then drop them on the shingle, which had the desired effect. This certainly looked like reason. At one part of the coast however soft land ran close down to the sea, and a bird was here vainly endeavouring to break open its prey by dropping it upon the soft ground, repeating the attempt time after time, as each proved ineffectual; now, I think it quite clear that if it had been reason which guided the bird in the first place, it would have kept it from the error in the second. Your correspondent, Cosmos, says that the difference of instinct in animals is in degree from man downwards, and that as we descend the scale, the difference increases more rapidly. Now, I think that in insect life we see quite as many acts which look like reason as in the higher classes of creation. The interesting acts of the bee have been already commented on and are now generally known. So, let us take, for instance, the saw fly. Is it reason that causes him to build his snug cocoon before winter approaches? Can it argue that the leaves will soon fall off its favourite blackthorn bushes, and that unless he builds his house before the fall his materials will be gone? Does he know that the frosts of winter would terminate his existence unless he make warm and secure provision for the future? Who taught it to mould such a perfectly finished oval cell, to fasten it firmly to the branch to guard against accidents, and to make it sufficiently hard to defy the hungry bills of its feathered foes from without. In these things I think it shows quite as much, or more apparent intelligence than some creatures which stand much higher in the scale of creation, and yet, if we grant that it has the power of reason in these things where are we to stop? Does it know while performing these labours before sinking into torpidity, that after a few months it is to break from its prison and soar aloft on the wing? I think not, and would rather suppose that it is impelled by a power implanted within it, and that it and other animal life are subservient to man, and were created for his amusement, study, and instruction, for where could we find a more beautiful and striking emblem of the Resurrection than in the case of the interesting little creature I have just mentioned, which after passing a season confined to earth, a picture of misery and helplessness, enshrines itself in a tomb of its own making, and for a season is lost to view; but with the sunny days of spring, that season which brings fresh life to all animate creation, he reappears and flies away on the wing, a very picture of happiness. O. R.

THE REASONING POWERS OF ANIMALS.—R. B. W. accuses me of doubting if all men have souls, because I said that "if all men have souls" many of the lower animals must have the same. I see that, to make my meaning clear to R. B. W. I must add the rest of the syllogism—"But all men have souls; therefore, many, &c." R. B. W. also says that I have exceeded the truth in stating that some of the lower animals are above some men in intellect, and says that all men have the power of reasoning but some only use it; "the lower animals," he adds, "have not this faculty." This is meeting dogmatism by dogmatism. Granted that I am not *quite* sure that some men (idiots apart) have *less* reason than an intelligent dog, I nevertheless believe, that there are some who cannot reason, who cannot grasp the plainest inference, who, in a crisis, where every moment is of the utmost importance (as in a fire, etc.) stand still, bewildered, when one would think instinct would point out the proper course of action: and there are some of the lower animals, whose actions on particular occasions cannot be attributed to instinct, and who evidently reason. But it does not follow that because one dog can reason therefore all dogs can; nor because many men reason therefore all men can: it may be true, but it is not a necessary consequence. Nor is immortality a consequence of reason, or reason of immortality.

R. B. W. and Mr. Newberry hold that, if one animal reason therefore all animals do the same; and consequently all vegetables. The falsity of this hypothesis will be clear, when we reflect that man is an animal which reasons, therefore an oak tree also reasons! And as there is no gradation in reason, (*teste* Mr. Newberry, p. 28) the oak tree and the philosopher are equally intellectual!

May I ask Mr. Newberry if the intellectual powers of, say, Stuart Mill and of the Australian aboriginal are to be considered equal, and would he vote for the latter to sit in the British Parliament and help to rule England? Neither can I agree with R. B. W. that if parrots understand what they say, therefore they are equal to man in intellect; for if that be true, they are equal, as is proved beyond a doubt by the anecdote to which R. B. W. refers, and which, though styled "improbable" by that gentleman, is no more to be disbelieved than are his own observations recorded in these pages.

Mere coincidence will not account for the very numerous similar instances.
28, Jermyn Street, S.W. W. H. DALTON.

DO INSECTS FEEL PAIN?

I wish to offer a few observations on the above subject before the discussion is closed.

1. Some years ago, I tried a number of experiments on one of the lowest forms of animal life (Actima),

and I found that these creatures had the sense of feeling very acute, yet they had no other sense. Therefore, if an animal closely connected with the vegetable kingdom *can feel*, surely insects, which possess a higher organisation, are not destitute of feeling.

2. This morning (Feb. 7th), while I was examining some water out of a small aquarium, in which I keep animalcula, I met with a species of rotifer which had become entangled with a minute fibre, connected, I presume, with some food which had been swallowed. There were perhaps sixty or eighty animalcula of the same kind, but these were evidently enjoying themselves; while the one I have referred to was writhing and turning itself into all kinds of forms. Now, it would roll itself up like a ball; then it would stretch itself out at full length, and then twist itself about like a crushed worm when cut in two by a spade. For an hour or thereabouts, this little creature was writhing about in the water, and by a careful management of the stage, I kept the sufferer in view. No argument was needed to convince me that this *point of life felt pain*. The animalculum in question was about the one-thousandeth part of an inch in length, and about one-six thousandeth part of an inch in breadth: the power used about 450 diameters.

3. When I was feeding some caterpillars in Cornwall a few years ago, I found a number of ichneumon flies cast off in moulting. I paid particular attention to the caterpillars thus infested by the flies. One of the larva, on casting its skin about the third time, became very feeble; its poor body was curled up by the side of the cast off skin, and there it died, having nursed in its body about thirty flies. This caterpillar was evidently a sufferer. It is with me a settled conviction that insects can both feel *pain* and *pleasure*; the degree of pain is no doubt regulated by the nervous system. When animals can be found without nerves they may be found without pain.

I would just call the attention of "C." to "creature" as used by our Saviour in the 16th chap. of Mark and 15th verse. If "C." contends that the term in Romans (in the original) means the whole creation, then it must mean the whole creation in Mark; therefore, on that mode of argument the gospel must be preached to the *whole creation*. J. P. BELLINGHAM.

Hereford.

I fully agree with Mr. Ulidia, that in this, as in any scientific controversy, truth is only to be attained by the exercise of patient industry in research, analogy, induction, and candour. No one should enter upon controversy unprepared to renounce his preconceived opinions, and admit himself mistaken directly he is convinced of his error. We are, or should be, endeavouring, not to overcome our antagonists in argument, but to ascertain the truth, and every argument that is brought forward should be fairly considered by all who are engaged in the controversy. If, for instance, I, holding the painless hypothesis, can detect a fallacy in the arguments of Mr. Spicer, who, as we know, supports the same views, I am as much bound to expose that fallacy as if I agreed with Mr. Ulidia; all party-spirit should be forgotten in the search after truth. Mr. Ulidia has hitherto adduced no argument whatever to show that insects feel pain, nor has he attempted to refute any of the arguments of the negative side, weak and fallacious as some of them are: he has simply seized every opportunity to misrepresent and quibble at the unfortunately chosen expressions of his antagonists, and to load them with ridicule, whilst he passes in silence, or with attempted facetiousness, over those arguments to the terms of which he cannot take exception. Supposing him to be a rational being, and as such, incapable of holding an opinion in the face of evidence and reason to the contrary, I conclude that he has the power to refute those arguments which the negative side have set forth, though he has not yet done so. I trust therefore, that he will do so in the next number of the NOTE BOOK, or if he cannot do so, that he will candidly admit his incapability and let his reason triumph over prejudice, remembering that neither jokes nor declarations of victory are likely to convince the readers of the "N. N. B." I should be glad to see this question settled, but I fear a long time will elapse before we can answer it with any degree of certainty, for the following reason:—

In man there is every gradation of feeling from insensibility to the most acute pain; and pain, I take it, is simply a more or less rapid motion of the nerves; the less rapid the less painful, till it becomes merely a sensation of touch, and then, as in the circulation of the blood, there is lastly no sensation whatever—we do not feel anything.

But, as Huxley says, "the amount of feeling depends on the degree of concentration of nerve-matter," and in man it is far more concentrated than in insects.

Therefore, as the degree of concentration in man is to that in insects, so is the degree of sensibility in the former to that in the latter.

My own impression is that man is so far beyond the insect, that whilst in man the highest point of feeling is intense pain, the highest point in insects is not pain at all. Until, however, we know the exact ratio of concentration of nervine, and have a numerical definition (so to speak) of pain, sensation, and insensibility, both in man and insect, we shall not be in a position to pronounce an opinion on this most interesting subject.

Size cannot be a criterion of feeling, for if it were, the whale, elephant, crocodile, shark, and even some of the mollusca would feel more acutely than man.

To argue that because man feels pain therefore the insect does so, is not strictly logical: but to say "I feel pain, and all men whom I know feel pain, therefore all men do," is quite a lawful conclusion.

Wherein lies the difference? In the fact that the degree of concentration of nervine is the same in all individuals *of the same species*.

It is equally absurd to say insects feel as much as man as to say they do not feel at all, as facts disprove both hypotheses.

28, Jermyn Street, S.W. W. H. DALTON.

So long as Mr. Ulidia continues to mistake sneers for arguments, it would be useless for me to reply to him.

I would like, however, to say a few words to Mr. Newberry, whose letter is, I think, one of the fairest and most able that has been written on the affirmative side of the question. With regard to what he says as to human beings being sometimes made very hungry by undergoing a surgical operation, I am not able to say anything, as I was not aware, until I read his letter, that such was the case, and I have not since had any opportunity for making inquiries about the matter. He says next, "that extreme pain invariably causes a deadness or numbness to seize the part affected, but which is often felt most acutely afterwards." And he asks, "May it not be the same with insects?" Now, in respect to the numbness, I think it is very likely to be as Mr. Newberry suggests ; and in the case before us—that of the scalded and pinned beetle—the embarrassed movement of the legs on the wounded side, which I mentioned in my former letter, rather favours his conjecture. But as regards the subsequent pain, I think that in this case, at any rate, he is mistaken; for although I frequently afterwards not only looked at, but even carefully watched the beetle, I saw nothing at any time which I could in any way construe into a sign of pain. After this question, Mr. Newberry proceeds to argue, that since insects have nerves, they must necessarily have sensation or *feeling*. In this I quite agree with him. He then says, "If an insect, then, possesses a sense of feeling at all, it must possess a sense of feeling pain as well as pleasure." But here I would suggest, that although insects are provided with nerves, and therefore have feeling, yet this feeling may in no case be so acute as to amount to more than a sense of mere discomfort or inconvenience.

In concluding this my second and last letter on this subject, I would like to repeat that which I said clearly enough when I wrote last, but which I think Mr. Newberry has not noticed, or else he has misunderstood me, viz., that animals *do* feel a certain amount of pain. I will add to this, however, that I do not think the amount of pain they feel is anything like equal, even proportionally, to that which the higher animals and men experience. More than this, I do not think that even the higher animals have nearly such an acute and delicate sensation, whether of pain or pleasure, as is that of human beings.   JOHN LANDELS.

The most recent anatomy proves that insects have *digestive organs;* and hence, I conclude, that insects are susceptible of pain. And another argument to which I would appeal, is, that insects are subject to disease, and consequently, from their great sensativeness I must conclude that insects, as animals, are capable of feeling pain. It has been urged by the correspondents on the negative side that as several wounded insects greedily devoured food, they, consequently felt no pain. Now, Sir, it is well known that on the field of Waterloo, and many other battle-fields, the wounded horses (some mortally) did, with great relish, eat the luxuriant grass in which they lay.

Will any man tell me that those horses felt no pain? Some thirty-six years ago when the French were punishing those blots on humanity, the Algerine Pirates, a brave courageous son of the wave was boarding one of their boats: he lost a leg and an arm in the conflict, and when removed to the hospital ship he called for meat ; wine, bread, and grapes, were brought, and the result was he ate twice as much as he ever did at a meal when in ordinary health. "I knew him well, Horatio," and for more than twenty years afterwards, he lived, and often told about his "Algerine hunger." Did this man suffer no pain when terribly mutilated by the pirate's sword ? I could, if necessary, enumerate many other cares to show that excessive pain often produces excessive hunger.

But the correspondents on the negative side are completely retired from our pleasant scientific Champ de Mars. In our combats we ask instruction: we are all strangers to each other, but friends at arms, nothing personal; and why should we retire in offended dignity?

My January article remains unassailed, and without a breach, and I see that many of your clever correspondents strongly advocate my views.

H. H. ULIDIA.

THE SOURCE OF HEAT.

I am glad to see this subject introduced into the NOTE BOOK for discussion: it is one full of interest. With W. Newberry's theory as expressed in the February number, viz., that the source of heat (of course that heat experienced on the earth's surface) is to be sought for in the interior of the earth and not in the sun, 1 cannot agree. How does Mr. Newberry reconcile the changes in the seasons with his opinions : the contrast between summer heat and winter cold ? If his theory were the correct one we might expect an uniform temperature throughout the year. True, the season when the sun is nearest the earth is the coldest in the year, but this is attributable to two causes; first, by the sun's rays falling with greater obliquity, and, secondly, by the excess of the length of nights over that of the days, so that the heat imbibed during the day is wholly parted with during the night. The effect of obliquity in regard to rays will be manifest if a board be held perpendicularly before a fire. It will then receive a body of rays equal to its breadth. But if it be placed obliquely, at an angle of 45 degrees, then only half the rays will fall on its surface and the other half will pass over it. So it is with the surface of the earth in summer and winter. The increased heat in the polar regions is amazingly great during the six months' continued day, which melts, or nearly, the ice and snow produced during the six months' night. In northern countries where the sun is above the horizon for any number of days together, the heat of summer is equal to that of any part of the world. Of course heat cannot be transmitted without the presence of the necessary conducting gases and therefore in absolute space we have reason for believing the most frigid cold exists ; but on the other hand heat may be, and I believe is, generated partially by the passage of the sun's rays through the atmosphere, and partially by their action on the ground and on various bodies. Solar heat is supposed, indeed, to be excited chiefly by the action of the sun's rays on terrestrial bodies, it being found that in the hottest climates, snow and ice lie unthawed all the year on the tops of the mountains (take for instance the South American Andes) and that the heat is in a considerable degree in proportion to the height of the situation or to the warmth imbibed by the surrounding atmosphere from the objects in contact. Thus the presence of perpetual snow on mountain heights is not due to their distance from the earth's interior, and consequently from the source of heat according to Mr. Newberry's hypothesis, but their great elevation above the level surface of the earth, the action of the sun's rays on which, together with their passage, through "the aereal envelope" surrounding the globe is, I think, the cause of heat.

Granted that in the centre of the earth, or even at the depth of 60 miles the hardest rocks are in a melted state, and that in that region a sea of liquid fire alone prevails, it does not follow that its influence extends to any great amount to the earths' crust. Your correspondent says, what is there in the solid body of the sun to generate and transmit heat more than there is in the moon, which is 68 times nearer? (by the way how are these figures arrived at?) In the *body* of the sun, I answer, probably nothing, but in the luminous and phosphoric clouds floating in the sun's atmosphere this property may exist.   W. H. BELL.
Hull.

I have read with considerable interest a letter in this month's NATURALIST'S NOTE BOOK, from W. Newberry, with respect to the source of heat, and with your permission will venture a few remarks on the subject. In endeavouring to prove that the earth cannot receive heat from the sun, your correspondent says that heat cannot be transmitted without a medium to conduct it, which has been proved to be perfectly correct. With light, however, the case is different. This body is supposed to consist of minute rays, which either originate from, or are set in motion by the sun, and travel with the great velocity of nearly 200,000 miles per second. It seems to me not an improbable theory, that these rays become heated by friction in passing through the atmosphere, which heat they convey to the earth's surface, the surrounding lower strata of the air is then gradually heated from the earth by convection. If the above is correct, several of the objections of W. N. will disappear. The extreme cold we experience in ascending to a greater elevation, is accounted for by the fact, that we are then in reality farther from the source of heat, namely, the earth. An objection is also made that the sun is at a greater distance from the earth during summer than winter, and yet the former is the warm, and the latter the cold part of the year. True, but during the summer he is more vertical, and remaining a much longer time above the horizon, enables our portion of the globe to become thoroughly heated before he disappears in the west, and, after allowing night a very short reign, again asserts his power. The reasons why the moon does not give out heat are various: 1st, although its distance from us is so very small compared with the sun, yet we must not forget to take into account her small bulk, being, I suppose, only about 68,000,000th the size of the former body; 2ndly, it does not, I believe, contain heat, except what it receives from the sun, in the same manner as does the earth, and its brightness is only due to the reflection of that luminary cast upon it. Now, if the above is an acceptable theory, we have no proof that the sun contains any heat at all, as light, although generally, yet is not always accompanied by heat, and perhaps this might throw some light on the puzzling questions we so often see asked, viz., the reason why the sun does not consume away? how does he keep up his bulk? &c. In conclusion, I do not think it improbable that some heat may proceed from subterraneous sources, and, as W. N. has shown, there is considerable evidence to support that view; but if we deny that the sun in some way or other is the great source of heat, how are we to account for the high temperature of the equator as compared with the poles, or the heat we experience at midday when standing full in the rays of a summer sun, while within a few hours, when he has hid his face, and a clear night permits the heat he has imparted to be dispersed by radiation, the thermometer will sink to the freezing point.   O. R.

The extraordinary theory of the source of the earth's heat proposed by W. Newberry, is certainly not borne out by facts. In the first place, he says it is impossible for heat to travel the 97,000,000 miles between us and the sun (which, by the way, has been lately proved by Mr. Stone to be only about 92,000,000) because there is no medium to conduct it; but, with or without a conductor, it *does* traverse that space, as Mr. Newberry must himself have experienced during the late hot summer, unless he is like "the man that couldn't get warm." Secondly, it is quite true that hot air rises above cold, but the inference your correspondent draws from it is not by any means true; for the heat of the sun striking through the atmosphere, warms the surface of the earth; that again communicates its heat to the lower strata of the air, and it is kept there and driven down if it attempts to rise by the moisture which is always to be found in the upper strata, and which thus acts like the glass roof of a hothouse. Professor Tyndall has shown that our atmosphere owes its power of keeping in the heat transmitted to it, solely to the moisture which it contains, for *dry* pure air is perfectly transparent to heat. Again, if we were to ascend Mont Blanc, or take a six mile trip with Mr. Glaisher, we should find intense cold, *not* because we had receded from the source of heat, but because we had quitted the more perfect reservoir of heat formed by the lower and denser strata, and entered a rarer region, which suffered the greater part of the sun's heat to penetrate it, without being arrested and retained. In the next place, granting the continuous increase of heat with increase of depth in the earth, and the consequent fluidity at the depth of sixty miles, which is by no means proved, yet what proof have we that this heat is communicated to the surface through the non-conducting crust? Mr. Newberry then asks what there is in the solid body of the sun to generate heat more than in the moon. I answer that there is a great deal more. Astronomers find that light and heat are very intimately connected; indeed, some have gone so far as to say they are identical. Well, we get light from the sun, but none from the moon (except what is reflected from the sun). Is it not reasonable then to suppose that we get heat also from the sun? There are also many phenomena going on in the sun which point to the same conclusion, such as the violent commotion exemplified in the rapid changes of the solar spots, and the metamorphoses observed in the red protuberances, which make their appearance during a total eclipse. With regard to the last difficulty raised by W. Newberry, any schoolboy should be able to tell him that the difference in the seasons is caused not by the difference in the distance of the sun, but by the difference in the inclination of our hemisphere to that luminary. We are turned directly towards him in summer, but inclined from him in winter, and the difference in his *distance* is quite insignificant compared with the difference in the *direction* of his rays.

Faversham, Kent. GULIELMUS.

Your correspondent, W. Newberry, has in the last number of the N. N. B., written a paper upon the "Source of Heat." As there are some remarks in it which I do not comprehend, I write this to inquire their meaning. He commences his article by an assertion that "heat cannot be generated or transmitted from one body to another without the presence of certain gases to form a conductor. Now it is too well-known to admit of doubt that the sun is the true and the only "source of heat" and light that our solar system possesses. Its distance from this globe, according to the most recent investigations, is about 90,000,000 of miles, instead of 97,000,000, as he states; and, with the exception of the atmospheres, both of the sun and of the earth, it is supposed to be empty space between them. He then says that "if it were possible for heat to be transmitted from the sun to the atmosphere surrounding our globe, it would float in the upper regions, and never be felt on the earth's surface." Mr. Newberry is perhaps unacquainted with the fact that the density of our atmosphere near the earth alone causes the hot rays from the sun to be felt; and that it is owing both to the tenuity and to the greater reflective power of the air in the upper regions, that causes the cold to be so intense there. I think that the most decisive proofs that the source of heat is not in our earth are our alternating seasons; for how could the summits of our highest mountains be for ever snow-clad, and how could snow exist at all upon the surface of the ground if the terrestrial heat be so powerful? Moreover, it is known to be a positive and certain fact that the temperature is remarkably equable some short distance below in the soil, and also in the hard rocks. Your correspondent expresses surprise that at our winter season we are nearest the sun, which statement he appears to think is incompatible with the usually received theories of solar heat. It is entirely owing to the peculiar positions that the earth assumes which give the "seasons." The slight elliptic which our globe forms, in revolving around the sun, is caused by the moon and some of the planets, as they alternately impede and help her on by their attraction. Her distance from the sun at the winter solstice is ascertained to be about 3,000,000 of miles nearer than at the summer solstice. As I have mentioned previously, the seasons are caused by her positions. It is supposed by astronomers that the sun possesses a luminous atmosphere, and some very interesting and important discoveries have lately been made by means of an instrument called a "spectroscope." Amongst many others, the rose coloured prominences, which are generally to be discerned upon the periphery of the moon during a total solar eclipse, and which so long puzzled astronomers, are found to be vast masses of hydrogen in a state of vivid incandescence. These examples will I think be sufficient to show that the "effulgent orb of day is the source of heat." A. C. E. B.

From his note on this subject, Mr. Newberry seems to think that the heat we experience is derived from the earth's interior. Now, though the earth contains a vast amount of heat towards its centre, I do not think that we feel any of it whilst on its surface, because the surface of the earth is generally colder than the air which surrounds it. In what way does Mr. Newberry think that the heat is extracted from the earth and made to warm the atmosphere? I am of opinion that the source of heat is not to be looked for in the earth, but in the atmosphere itself, where it remains latent until acted upon by the rays of the sun. According to this view, light makes heat apparent, and in proportion to the amount of light transmitted to a planet is the heat it receives, the density or latent heat of its atmosphere being equal. The immense velocity with which light travels is the probable means by which heat is produced; this is so much greater in low than high grounds. It is well-known that everything in the universe, even snow and ice, contain heat, and that this heat can be made apparent to our senses. It has been ascertained by astronomers that the rays of the sun do not travel through clear space, but that above the earth's atmosphere there is a thin refined kind of air which exerts a perceptible influence on the light of the stars.

R. B. W.

THE BLACK FOREST.—Under this heading, at p. 61, vol iii., of the NATURALIST'S NOTE BOOK, A. C. E. B. states that he has succeeded in capturing many species of rare *Coleoptera*, but only expressly mentions one of them, viz., *Astinomus œdilis*, always found by me in plenty at Rannoch, the place to which he evidently alludes. With reference to the antennæ of that beetle, A. C. E. B. says, "I believe that the *great* use of these long mobile appendages remains a mystery, for I have never read anything that has thrown much light upon the subject. Mr. E. C. Rye does not mention where their *true habitat* is, but merely remarks 'that they love to settle on felled pine logs.' It was only by the merest chance that I discovered it, whilst diligently stripping off the bark of a felled tree." I presume, in spite of the construction of this statement, that A. C. E. B. means to signify an omission on my part, in some unspecified publication, to record the true habitat of the insect, and not of its antennæ. I also presume, though my name is somewhat incoherently brought forward, that the owner of those initials intends to refer to my "British Beetles," p. 208, where the words attributed to me are certainly to be found, but accompanied by a distinct record of the life-history of the species in question; not that there was any necessity for such record, as its habits have long been well known to all Coleopterists.

In papers upon Scotch *Coleoptera*, in the "Entomologist's Monthly Magazine," vol. ii. p. 52, and vol. iii. p. 64, A. C. E. B. will also find accounts by me of the habits of *Astinomus;* and in the "Intellectual Observer," (for 1866 or 1867, I forget at the moment which is the correct year), I have, in a paper on Highland Insects, even *figured* its "true habitat." Apart from these records, A. C. E. B.'s account of his finding the species in holes under the bark of a "felled tree," would not much elucidate the subject. He does not say *what* tree. And there was not much effort required to "discover" the habitat when I was at Rannoch, inasmuch as almost every old pine stump near the Black Wood was riddled by the large holes of *Astinomus*.

I am induced to make these remarks in the hope of persuading contributors to avoid trivial and already copiously recorded facts, and to take a little trouble in looking up subjects before sending to the NATURALIST'S NOTE BOOK, if they wish any scientific value to be attached to their communications.

7, Park Field, Putney, S.W.   E. C. RYE.

A WORD FOR THE STOAT (Mustela Erminea).—If Mr. A. H. Malan, in his article upon the stoat, had given himself some little trouble ere he wrote, he would not have prefaced his article with a misstatement. He says that "the stoat confines its diet almost exclusively to game, eggs, and rabbits, and does no good whatever in return." Now it is a well-known fact that so far from this being the case, the stoat as often kills rats and mice as anything else, only the destruction of these small deer is not noticed as much as the killing of a head or two of game. Of course the fuss made over the loss of a partridge or rabbit taken by a wild animal to satisfy its natural instincts, tends much to bring both stoat and weasel in unenviable notoriety; but I would ask Mr. Malan, ere he makes such a sweeping assertion, to dissect the next few stoats killed, and I have no doubt that in two-thirds of the cases he will find—as I have recorded at page 125 of the NOTE BOOK for '68—mice, small birds, or something analogous, forming the contents of the stomach. To one or two more statements I must take exception; for instance, he twice says the *tail* is black, but it is the *tip* of the tail only which remains black irrespective of any change in the remainder. Then, again, he appears to consider it the rule instead of the exception for the stoat to be white in winter, in England. It is true partially white specimens are often seen, but the English winter is seldom of sufficient duration or severity to cause the stoat to assume the ermine fur entirely. I am willing to acknowledge that the change takes place more frequently in Scotland, but an English killed ermine is a decided rarity. Mr. Malan says, "it is generally believed" (and I should think with some reason too) "that the ermine fur comes from the cold countries" —for I do not think Mr. Malan can mention one firm who depend upon their supply from Great Britain. With regard to their hearing, I have always found it remarkably acute. In explanation of some of these inaccuracies, I should suppose that Mr. Malan had depended upon the observation of some prejudiced gamekeeper instead of his own. It is somewhat singular how little is known of this little animal, for even Mr. St. John, in his clever "Highland Sports," by a remark he lets fall, does not appear to know that the stoat and the ermine are identical!

A. M. B.

THE YELLOW WAGTAIL.—I observed a notice in the January Number of the NOTE BOOK, in reference to a specimen of the Yellow Wagtail being seen at Blackfriars Bridge on the 14th of November last, and had quite expected to find some allusion thereto on the following month, by one or more of your Ornithological readers, but as none appear to have come to hand, I must venture these few lines upon the subject, which I trust will not be unacceptable to your general readers, or offensive to your correspondent. If Mr. Vincent is a practical Ornithologist, he will probably know that we have two species of the Wagtail that somewhat resemble each other, in being yellow underneath. The true Yellow Wagtail (*M. Flava*) makes its appearance in the early part of April, rears its young in our meads (mostly near brooks and rivulets), and then retires southwards rather early in the autumn. The male of this species is olive green on the back, and the whole underpart a uniform bright yellow. The female and young birds are much paler throughout, especially about the neck and breast. The length of these birds is somewhat less than the common Black and White Wagtail. The other species, known as the Dun or Grey Wagtail (*M. Bacrula*), arrives from the North throughout the autumn, and is found with us, at intervals, during the winter months. This species is also yellow underneath, but mostly of a pale colour on the neck and breast, gradually brighter towards the tail, the under covert of which, in some specimens, are of the most lively hue; the plumage on the back is of an ashy grey, shading off to a tint of greenish yellow, to the insertion of the tail, which in these birds are considerably longer than in any other of our British Wagtails. In fact, the agile movements and graceful form of these birds, render them one of the most interesting species among our small British birds.

I must say, in conclusion, that I think it most likely to have been one of the latter species that met the eye of your correspondent at the time specified; but, in either case, I should be much gratified with a reply to these remarks, as it touches upon a point connected with the migratory movement of our feathered race which to myself, with many others, is always interesting.   C. W——D.

320, Strand.

LEPIDOPTERISTS' EXCHANGE CLUB.—An association having for its object the readier distribution by exchange of local species of Macro-Lepidoptera (similar to the London Botanical Exchange Club), was last year inaugurated by Mr. Merrin, author of the "Entomologists' Calendar," &c. Started very late in the autumn, when entomologists in general were badly prepared for such a scheme, from want of duplicates, its success has still been sufficiently encouraging to induce its promoters to continue its working. Some thirty gentlemen, including a few leading entomologists, are now members; but, owing to the causes above stated, only nineteen of these availed themselves of the advantages offered by the club, and from whom about 3000 specimens were received, nearly all of which were redistributed. This number would doubtless have been doubled, or even quadrupled, had the club been earlier announced. The principle of conducting the Exchange is that each member shall receive, as nearly as can be estimated, an exact equivalent for what he sends, or the overplus is returned, or marked in his favour for the next season's distribution. This Exchange being regulated by an uninterested member, and an old entomologist, it is hoped that the club will be the means of saving much ill-feeling consequent on the receipt of bad returns often made in the present system of personal exchange. It is intended for the present to confine the club's operations to Macro Lepidoptera, and to collectors who have pretty well worked their own district, and have local species in duplicate, it offers great facilities for the enrichment of their cabinets; as some members having sent and promised specimens for gratuitous distribution, the return actually made is frequently much greater in relative value than the specimens sent for legitimate exchange would otherwise warrant. An annual subscription of 2s. 6d. has been fixed to defray the expense of conducting the club. Prospectuses, lists of non-desiderater, and full particulars, will be sent on application to either Mr. Joseph Merrin, Glo'ster, President, or Mr. Herbert W. Marsden, Brook Street, Glo'ster, Secretary.

THE EXTINCTION OF SPECIES.—Mr. Cole gives some interesting suggestions on this subject in reply to my article.

It is my opinion, as well as his, that in all probability Podilirius, Chryseis, and Vingtudroe, &c. never did "really exist" in England, but I made allusion to them in my article upon the authority of some of our very good entomologists who think that they did so. For instance, Stainton in his "Manual" introduces Chryseis upon what appears to be very good grounds. And then Stephens introduces nearly all the reputed species, and various other entomological authors do the same. Some are no doubt inserted by mistake, but others frequently find their way, like traditions generally, which have some foundation, but which afterwards get very much exaggerated. Perhaps one or two specimens were taken several years ago, and have subsequently been set down as British without more having been caught; or, some insect closely resembling the "supposed new species" is in roughly labelling a box put down as it were without more scrutiny. And thus an insect that never really bred or "habited" in England is handed down as having done so until it resolves itself into

"Somebody told me that some one said,
That some other person had somewhere read,
In some newspaper you were somehow dead."
(Or we may say "lived.")

I cannot agree with Mr. Cole that Dispar will be again as common as it was before, at any rate in the same places. There is a chance, truly, that it may appear again in some unexplored place in the "west," &c., but until it *does fully appear*, I think that we must regard it as "lost" or extinct. I hope that Scotland is now better "worked" than it was. During the last year several entomologists have been exploring it, and have given accounts of their labours in different magazines, and I hope that more will be done there still, as no doubt much remains to be done; also that other places will be taken into consideration as well, so that we may be able, at some time not very far off, to say that we know perfectly the extent of our English insect fauna.

ON KILLING LEPIDOPTERA.—As one of your correspondents, who signs himself "Entomologist," desires to know the best way to kill moths intended for the cabinet, I thought that I might pen down a concise description of some of the best modes that I am acquainted with. It is known to all students of natural history that insects, in common with other families of the Invertebrata, are very tenacious of life; this is possessed by the lepidoptera to a very high degree. Therefore it is necessary that the entomological beginner should learn the most expeditious means of destroying the lives of his captures. Unlike many others of the insect tribe, butterflies and moths possess soft integuments, downy hairs, and minute and exceedingly delicate scales, which are removed by the slightest touch of any extraneous object; so that in order to keep the detained insects in as good a state of preservation as possible, they should be, if practicable, killed upon the spot. There are many ways employed, some indeed more curious and ingenious than useful; amongst them I will select a few which I think will be most suitable to "Entomologist." If his moth or butterfly is moderately large, it may be instantly deprived of life by a sharp pinch in the thorax; this, although a good deal in vogue with some lepidopterists is, I fancy, inferior to the following. A small moth should be "boxed" at once, and two or three drops of chloroform or naptha put in with it: in a few minutes life is extinct. In lieu of either of these, laurel leaves may be used, but in practice I believe the former are better. There is yet one more way I intend to describe: it is by inoculating either prussic or oxalic acid into the thorax by means of a bone pen. The modus operandi is as follows :— The pen should be dipped into the solution, and then thrust rather sharply into the creature's body: by this means both trachea ganglia are severed, and of course the poison advances, carrying certain death to every part. A. C. E. B.

THE AMERICAN ROBIN.—In the first volume of the NOTE BOOK, page 331, is a paragraph headed "Food for the Robin." It is there stated that at a meeting of the Boston Society of Natural History (America), a communication was read by Professor Tredwell of Cambridge, giving a detailed account of the feeding and growth of this bird during a period of 32 days, commencing on the 5th of June. On the fourteenth day it ate 68 earthworms, or 41 per cent. more than its own weight. The length of these worms, if laid end to end, would be about 14 feet, or ten

times the length of the intestines. Your English readers should know that the American Robin is a very different bird in every respect to its English namesake. The Pilgrim Fathers when they journeyed across the wild Atlantic in the "May Flower" carried none of our feathered songsters with them, but their hearts yearned for home and home associations; and as they did not feel at home without a robin they set to work and found as good a substitute as they could, but the only resemblance is its *red breast*. The American robin is quite as large as our blackbird, and its flute-like notes are very similar to those of the blackbird. It dresses in a chocolate coloured coat, with a long tail, a greyish vest, and a *red shirt* front over a full chest. Its character is also very much to its advantage, as it possesses more amiability than the English robin, which is proverbially fond of fighting with other birds. The American robin is to be met with in all parts of the "States" as well as in Upper and Lower Canada. In the latter provinces I have lived for ten years, and had a tame robin, which was so homely that it would fly from its cage, hop about the room, and *play its flute* on the back of a chair. JNO. S. MARTIN.
Chatham.

THE UNICORNE.—*Place:* In the East and West Indies, and other places. *Meat:* Their meat is not observed. *Names:* Heb., Reem., Arab, Alchercheden. UNICORNEE.—The flesh is bitter and unfit to be eaten, like that of the Indian Asse. The horne being powdered and drunk in water, expelleth poyson, with amber, ivory, leafe gold, and coral, &c. Its much commended against pestilent feavers, and the bitings of mad doggs, and other poysonsome beasts, as also against wormes, and many great sicknesses, and the epilepsy. The horne is sudorifik, alexipharmick, and cardiack, and is therefore good against contagious diseases, &c. The D. is from *gr.* 4 to *scrup. sem.* and more. It's woorne also as an amulet. As for their *description*, in *body* they are not much unlike a horse, but cloven *hoofed*, and have a long horne on their foreheads. They are of a dusty colour, with a maned *neck*, hairy *forehead*, and a white and smooth *horne*, serving to expel and dissolve all poyson, if put into the water after the drinking of any poysonsome beast. It sweateth if venom be nigh. It weigheth thirteen pound. They fight with their mouth and feet. They hate the female except at the time of lust, but love stranger beasts and maids, and are taken by them dressed with sweet herbs.—*From Lovell's Natural History*, Oxford, 1661.

BRITISH GEOMETRÆ.—May I be allowed to ask Mr. E. Clifford to favour the readers of the NOTE BOOK with the names of the very rare, or more especially the doubtful species to which he alludes in the first portion of the list of British Geometræ, p. 41. The omission, I presume, was merely an oversight in getting up the article for the press, as without the name it is rather difficult to know what one is reading about. And I may add, that the first moth named in the list, Canary-shouldered Thorn (*E. tiliaria*), I found not uncommon forty years back, on the Hackney Marsh between Old Ford Lane and Temple Mill, and invariably found them on the trunks of the willow. I have a specimen, at the present time, which I found in a soft or flacid state on a willow in the garden at Temple Mills rather more than forty years back. I believe that most, if not all the Thorn Moths, stand with their wings tip to tip over their back, giving them the appearance of a partly decayed and broken leaf. I do not say that the larvæ will not feed upon the birch and oak, as perhaps they are not particular in their diet, but I merely state this as my own experience in the matter. C. W——D.
320, Strand.

WATER TORTOISE.—I write you a short account of a small water tortoise, which has been in my possession for about three months. It is about two and a half inches long, *i.e.*, its shell is about that length, and its head and neck measure about ¾ of an inch; its tail is about an inch long. The man of whom I bought it, told me to give it raw meat, and I gave it two pieces (about the size of a pea each) which it swallowed. It first went up to them, smelt them I thought, seized its food, and by a jerk of its head seemed to swallow it. It treated the second piece in a similar manner, but would not look at a third I offered it. It eat these when under water, and when it had done rose to the surface. I subsequently tried to feed it when *on land*—it again refused. Two days later it again took a like meal, and then (this was in October) refused all food till about a week ago, when it ate a small bit of an earth-worm. Yesterday I gave it a large worm. When it saw it, it dug its feet into it and seized it by its mouth. It proceeded to tear a large piece out, and by successive jerks of its head this was swallowed. The same process was repeated a good many times, and when it had eaten about two inches of worm, I thought it prudent to take the remainder of its dainty meal away. Thus it ate almost its own length of a large fat earth-worm.
TORTOISE.

NEPTUNE.—For the information of "R. T." I give the authority I had for saying that "the sun appears to the planet Neptune no larger than a fixed star." The following is an extract from "Stellar Worlds," by D. M. Mitchel, A.M., published in 1861 (page 130):—"Leaving this planet (Uranus), we reach the known boundary of the planetary system, at a distance of about 3,000,000,000 of miles from the sun. Here revolves the last discovered planet, Neptune. . . . His diameter is eight times greater than the earth's, and he contains an amount of matter sufficient to form one hundred and twenty-five worlds such as ours. Here we reach the known limit of the planetary worlds, and standing at this remote point and looking back towards the sun, the keenest vision of man could not descry more than one solitary planet along the line we have traversed. The distance is so great that even Saturn and Jupiter are utterly invisible, and the sun himself has shrunk to be *scarcely greater than a fixed star.*" Mitchel is very good authority, as he was an eminent, hard-working astronomer; if his statement be correct, it is difficult to imagine how this planet can obtain heat and light. R. B. W.

CANARY BIRDS.—In the twelfth letter in White's

"Natural History of Selbourne," I find the following "Query: Might not Canary birds be naturalized to this climate, provided their eggs were put in the spring into the nests of their congeners, as goldfinches, greenfinches, etc.? Before winter, perhaps, they might be hardened, and able to shift for themselves." I do not know whether the attempt has ever been made, but I should think if it were, it would be very likely to succeed. I have not the opportunity for trying the experiment myself, but if any of the readers of the NATURALIST'S NOTE BOOK, who have the inclination and the means were to do so, I have no doubt that very interesting results would accrue. As the time of nest-building is just commencing, it will be easy, especially for those who live in the country, to find nests in which to place the eggs. I hope, therefore, that some of your readers will be induced to make the attempt, and that they will communicate the results to the NOTE BOOK, so that those who are unable to make the experiment for themselves, may have the benefit of their observations. J. LANDELS.

CURIOUS BIRD.—I have a young bird of the following description, viz.:—The beak flesh coloured, tinged slightly black; the back of the head black, and forward to the beak red; between the beak and eyes on each side black; the throat and neck red and white; the upper part of the body light brown, and the under part white; the back brown; the tail and wings a mixture of black, white, and yellow; and the legs and feet the usual colour. Its song is that of a Warbler, and is a very lively bird. The gentleman I got the bird from informed me it was a redcap (male) but from the description I find Bechstein does not mention it, nor do any of my works on the natural history of birds, unless it has another name. I shall be much obliged if, from the description above given, any of your numerous correspondents can enlighten me as to this bird. Whether it is a redcap or not, and what species. If so, its habitation, its qualities as a songster, and the best kind of food suitable for it?
Selby. J. B.

A LIFE DESTROYING WORM.—There is a most extraordinary and dangerous insect found here which I have not seen described in any entomological work. I first noticed it when bathing in the river, on the bank; it looked like a very minute cage, composed of small sticks, beautifully plaited together, about half an inch long and a quarter broad. On touching this construction, to my surprise a warm crawled out, emitted a black liquid, and then moved away, carrying the cage with her. I captured it, and showed it to the Kaffirs, who said that several of their cattle had died by eating these insects along with the grass. The Dutch corroborate this statement, and also say that there have been cases of men dying from the effect of their bite. I have since caught several, and kept them together in a glass bottle, feeding them on the leaves of the wild indigo. I have now had them in confinement for more than a month in perfect health. J. D. S. W.
Upper Umkomancy, Natal.

MOTHS.—It would perhaps be interesting to some readers of the "N. N. B." to know of the following curious captures which I have had during the past summer. I have frequently heard say that the Sphingidæ are not to be taken at sugar, but I can vouch to the contrary, as I have captured in that manner one specimen of C. Porcellus and also one of S. Ligustri; the first was not in a quiet position with its wings closed like most moths are when at sugar, but kept them in a continual and rapid motion; however, I am certain it was on the sugar, for as it did not seem at all scared at the little light which I threw upon it I had ample time to examine its movements. As for S. Ligustri it was most decidedly at the sugar, which was spread on a garden pailing, for its trunk was stretched out to its fullest extent, and it seemed to be imbibing the sweets with great relish, but in every other respect it was in the same attitude as when they are found reposing during the day-time.
Brighton. T. B.

CURIOUS BIRD.—I have frequently seen in the columns of the "N. N. B." accounts of the capture of white sparrows, but in no number do I see any mention made about the cinamon sparrow. Now there has been a very fine specimen of the latter captured near Brighton by a birdcatcher during the early part of this month (February). It is now in the possession of Mr. G. Markwick, British and Foreign Bird Dealer, of Queen's Road, Brighton, who has completely tamed it, and intends sending it to the Crystal Palace Bird Show which takes place this month. The specimen is a female, and measures 5 inches from the back to the tail; it coincides with the ordinary sparrow in every respect except the colouring, which is light cinamon throughout, giving it a very curious but charming effect. I should like to know if this is a rare occurrence or whether there are many cases on record of the capture of this bird. T. B.
Brighton.

THISTLE SEEDS.—In the "Gallery of Nature," the author in speaking of the dissemination of thistle seeds, writes or quotes from some author the following. "The brown linnet when feeding on thistle seed, perches on the top of the weeds and tears the downy head asunder in order to reach the seeds which are attached to the receptacle. During this act, many of the grains being loosened, are borne away on their downy wings by the breeze to places far distant from the parent stem, the bird being in this case the indirect disseminator of the thistle. Were the head not torn asunder in this manner, ten to one but it would become soaked with the rains of winter and fall down only a few inches from the original stalk, instead of being transported as it often is across many miles of country. Would the seeds not be blown away by the winds, like the Dandelion and groundsel, when ripe, if never touched by the bird? QUERCUS.

ANTS AND THEIR PREY.—The other day I witnessed, while walking in my garden, a very interesting fight between a centipede and a number of small brown ants, which I will here give for the benefit of your readers. The centipede was crawling lazily along, enjoying the warmth of the sun, and little thinking that a deadly foe was lying in wait for him, but as he passed an ant's nest he was suddenly attacked on all sides. He fought bravely for some time, but at last overcome by numbers was slain, and by the united efforts of his assassins was dragged down into their den. Having safely disposed of him, they returned to look for more; a poor earth worm was their next victim, which they soon dispatched and stowed away in the same place. I do not know if they were satisfied with their day's work or not, for I had to leave the place on the death of the worm. J. D. S. W.

Upper Umkomancy, Natal.

SIZE OF LEPIDOPTERA.—In reply to V. B. Lewes' letter in last month, I can state that I have observed great variation in the size of Lepidoptera during the past season. I saw in a friend's cabinet P. Alexis measuring only 8 lines from tip to tip, with another of 13 lines.

I have in my collection P. Napi only 11 lines across, small specimens of which were formerly considered distinct. I saw last year C. Phlæas, "the small copper," with the rich copper on all the wings, replaced by a milky white. Are such varieties uncommon? J. HENDERSON, Jun.

Reading.

SHAPE OF EGGS.—I have no doubt that the idea which occurred to your correspondent, H. H. Ulidia, with regard to the shape of sea birds' eggs when laid upon a rock, is the correct one. Not only would the shape blunted at one end and sharp at the other prevent in a great degree their rolling, but it would prevent them effectually from rolling off a flat surface, such as that of the rocks upon which the birds lay. If Mr. Ulidia will set one of these eggs rolling, he will find that it will turn round and round, keeping the sharp pointed end towards a centre. I think this fact quite explains the reason of the unusual shape of these birds' eggs. EMILIA MARRYAT NORRIS.

Charmouth.

PEREGRINE.—Last autumn a young peregrine was taken on board a ship on its voyage to the Tyne, and about the same time I got the sternum of an osprey which had flown on board a ship, on to the rigging out at sea, and been taken into Edinburgh. A large hawk, supposed to have been captured on the rigging of a vessel off Flambro' head some years ago, has proved to be a "Jugger Falcon." In Jardine's "Naturalist's Library," vol 1, page 222 (birds) a *Spirjactus* is stated to have been killed on the coast near Aberdeen, also upon the rigging of a ship.

IVY.

EXTRAORDINARY CALF.—A case has just come before my notice, of one of the most singular freaks of nature I have ever heard of. A cow belonging to a gentleman, living at Market Harborough, has given birth to a calf with two heads. I have seen a calf with two heads, and also a lamb with two heads and two tails, and I believe there is a specimen of a calf with two heads in the Museum of Natural History at Birmingham, but in all these instances the heads both sprang from one neck. In the case before us, however, the animal has one head before and the other behind, which gives it a most grotesque appearance.

W. NEWBERRY.

VORACITY OF A TAME SQUIRREL.—Whilst letting my canary out for a fly in our conservatory the foolish little bird managed to get through the wires into my tame squirrel's cage, and before I could extricate the little animal, the squirrel being on the alert, seized it by its spine, and began actually to gnaw the flesh off its backbone. But the singular part is that the bird did not seem to suffer the least pain, but appeared perfectly mesmerized and incapable of action. This seems to disprove the alleged fact that the squirrel will not destroy birds, unless much pressed by hunger.

Saffron Walden, Essex. W. K. D.

ASTRONOMICAL PHENOMENA.—On April 19th, 1863, I witnessed a most extraordinary appearance in the sky, about 8 o'clock in the evening, which has puzzled me ever since to account for, until the thought occurred to me that some of your astronomical correspondents could help me to solve the difficulty. In the western horizon there appeared a fiery-red object resembling the moon.

The moon was shining dimly in the opposite part of the sky; so could this have been a mock-moon as we have all of us heard of, and many have seen mock-suns in more northern localities. P.S.—I may mention that at this time I was staying in Brighton.

FROGS.—"J. D. S. W." mentions a class of frogs in Natal which quack like ducks. It may perhaps be interesting to him if I inform him, that when I was in Queensland in 1866, although the frogs there make the most discordant noises, yet I never heard any that *quacked*, which must indeed sound very peculiar coming from a frog. In the neighbourhood of Brisbane, about sunset, a whole colony of frogs would strike up a chorus of a most disagreeable nature, which more resembled the grunting of pigs than the quacking of ducks! and this lively clamour they would continue throughout the night. A. E. BUTTERMER.

Would any one kindly inform me of any way of attracting moths to any spot. I have read of day-sugaring and night-sugaring, but never saw how to do it or what composition is to be used. In the "N. N. B." for February last Mr. Cole makes mention of some celebrated composition. Would he sell the recipe? I am only a young collector, and should feel greatly obliged for any hints how to collect moths or obtain the larvæ and pupæ. W. W. WALKER.

Margate Street, Swaffham, Norfolk.

TREES.—Last autumn I observed the fruit of many beech trees to be entirely empty, both in its ripe and unripe state. Can any one tell me the reason, as I do not think the dry weather could so affect large trees.

Can any of your readers kindly furnish me with a list of Diœcious British trees.

Is the exact reason known why the mistletoe is found growing so seldom now on the oak-tree, as it appears to have grown much more plentifully on it in the time of the Druids. ARBOR.

CORRECTION.—In my paper, "List of British Butterflies," &c., which appeared in your last number, the following mistake occurs:—Under the family *Pieridæ*, the name of the variety "Small White Cabbage" (*Pieris Rapæ*), is printed twice. In the second instance, this is a misprint for "Green Veined White" (*Pieris Napi*), to which variety my second description applies. T. W. TEMPANY.

ON THE LOWER LIAS BEDS OCCURRING AT COTHAM, BEDMINSTER, AND KEYNSHAM, NEAR BRISTOL.

By C. O. Groom Napier, Esq., F.G.S.

Read before the Geological Society of London. Part I.

HAVING found many of the fossils described in Mr. Tawney's paper on the Sutton stone, read on the fifth of December, 1865 ("Journal of the Geological Society"), at Cotham, Bedminster, and Keynsham, I was induced to pay many visits to quarries in these places, which resulted in my finding *in situ* more than one hundred species of organic remains, ninety of which I have determined with the assistance of Mr. R. Etheridge, F.R.S.E., F.G.S., and of Mr. R. Tate, F.G.S., to whom I offer my acknowledgments: I think with Mr. Stoddart, F.G.S., that the Sutton lias is clearly found at Cotham. Residing five years in the neighbourhood of Cotham, I have been able to make upwards of a hundred visits to the various quarries, have broken up many tons of stone into small fragments, and have examined the surface of perhaps 1,000 tons which have been quarried for building or lime burning. The number of species yet to be discovered here I think is still great, for every visit afforded either fresh species or those showing fresh characters. The bulk of the stone being hard and very tough, the labour in working it is great.

Ammonites angulatus occurs at Cotham in company with Rhynchonella plicatissimus, Pholadomya glabra, Lima gigantea, portions of a Gryphæa irregularis, (?) and the slabs of blue stone contain scales of Pholidophorous.

I have not yet been able to find Avicula contorta in the lower beds; Cardium Philippianum here replaces Cardium Rhæticum of the Rhætic beds.

I will treat the strata occurring at Cotham first, and as these differ considerably at the two quarries I am about to describe, I have adopted in the first instance letters and in the second numbers to distinguish the beds, describing the strata in descending order.

First Quarry.

This is a temporary quarry on land now being prepared for building, situated at the back of a house called Dundry Villa, almost the highest point of what was once Redland Grove.

A. Alluvial soil 10 to 14 inches thick.

B. is a clay loam 10 to 14 inches thick.

C. is a thin belt of limestone, extending to a bed of blue marl, 15 to 20 inches thick. This limestone is in layers, and easily splits into thin slate-like pieces. It abounds in Cypris liassica, and fragments of Chondrites liassinus are also found. Its structure is in fact precisely similar to the plant bed found lower down in the series; but the remains are scarcer, probably owing to the thin slabs of stone, seldom more than from $\frac{3}{4}$ to $\frac{1}{2}$ inch thick.

D. Next follow beds of pale blue limestone, alternating with layers of grey and red marl, the blocks increasing in size with descent. This stratum is six feet thick, and contains casts of Littorina, Lima punctata, and other fossils; but in much smaller numbers than in the succeeding bed.

E. This from the frequent occurrence in it of Ammonites planorbis, may be called the Planorbis bed. It consists of sandy lias interspersed with veins of crystalline quartz; more rarely sulphate of strontia, which is sometimes colourless. Ammonites Johnstoni is much less common here; I examined this bed frequently for two years before I found it. Besides these the bed yields Ammonites tortilis, A. torus, Solarium lenticulare, Turbo-sub-elegans, Cerithium semele, Pleuromya liassina, Cidaris Edwardsi, Pecten Calvus, Ostrea liassica, Lima succincta, L. tuberculata, L. acuticostatus, L. Hettangiensis, L. exaltata, Avicula Sandersii, spec. nov. Unicardium cardoides, fragments of the bones of Ichthyosaurus, Plesiosaurus, and their teeth, rarely Terebratula perforata, Mytilus minimus, and M. Hillanus. This stone sometimes contains a considerable portion of sulphate of strontia, causing it to crumble under the hammer into a whitish powder.

Almost all the remains of Ammonites planorbis have the interior filled with crystals of carbonate of lime, which is less common with specimens of Johnstoni in the beds below.

This bed is highly ferruginous, and contains occasionally minute crystals of galena. This Ammonite bed is enveloped in a thin coating of yellow clay, and is from 3 to 4 feet thick.

F. A hard grey stone containing frequent grains of crystalline quartz. Ostrea liassica is very abundant here. I have not been able to ascertain the precise thickness of this bed.

G. A bed of thick clay succeeds, varying from 9 inches to 1 foot.

H. A conglomerate bed, which is however very friable. In it casts of almost all the shells in the next bed are found; it, properly speaking, adjoins it, for there is no belt of clay or other division between them. It may be regarded as concreted clay from the bed above, mixed with a few casts from the stone below.

I. Consists of pale blue lias in thick beds containing Ammonites Johnstoni, Lima punctata, L. elevata, L. tuberculata, L. gigantea, L. acuticostatus, L. duplum, L. sub-duplicata, L. Terquemi, Pholadomya prima, P. glabra,

Pecten calvus, P. textorius, P. Suttonensis, P. quadricostatus, Perna infraliasina, Perna species, Pleuromya unioides, P. galathea, P. liasina, Unicardia cardioides, Cardinia Listeri, Ceromya gibbosa, Ostrea liassica, O. irregularis, Terquemia arietis, T. Heberti, Plicatula intustriata, Mytilus minimus, M. Hillanus, casts of a species of Gervillia, Cheminizia species, Axinus species, Astarte consobrina, A. thalassina, and Cidaris Edwardsi. Near the bottom of this bed is the bone-bed of this series, about 4 inches thick. It contains scales of Pholodophorus, teeth of Hybodus, scales of Gyrolepis tenuistriatus, and G. Albertii, small coprolites of fish, and Plicatula intustriata. The scales are mostly fragmentary, and badly defined. A lima, which I believe to be L. punctata, is the most characteristic shell of this bed.

J. is a second oyster-bed, abounding in O. liassica and rarely Ammonites Johnstoni. It contains a few ill-preserved Saurian remains, and is under half a foot thick; it lies between layers of unctuous clay.

K. is a bed from 1 to 3 inches thick, somewhat resembling a Rhætic bed. It affords Monotis decussata, Ostrea liassica, Perna infraliassina, Pleuromya unioides, and Cardium Phillippianum, but no Pecten Valeniensis or Avicula contorta, although months were spent in looking for these shells, and many tons of stone were broken.

L. These are beds of argillaceous limestone in thin striata, which readily splits. It is sometimes almost entirely composed of Mytilus minimus, M. Hillanus, Cardinia Listeri, Pholadomya species, and casts of Littorina; this lies immediately on the second plant bed.

M. This is the second plant bed which affords Cypris liassica, Chondrites liasinus, Cardium Phillippianum, Cucullia Hettangiensis, Pleuromya species, and Pecten verminius. This stone frequently has honeycomb-like marks, the impression probably of bubbles of air enclosed in clay, which now indurated forms the stratum. It is, however, so soft and rotten as to be easily broken with the fingers.

N. consists of a bed somewhat resembling the Septaria. It is an indurated clay of a dark grey colour containing veins of colourless crystals of sulphate of strontia in laminæ; crystalline carbonate of lime sometimes accompanies them. I have only once found this and the second plant bed at Cotham, for they are often here entirely omitted, so that "J" stands directly upon the Cotham marble.

O. is the Cotham marble, which, however, has an envelope of clay. It is here found of two varieties, the grey and the brown.

P. The Keuper, or new red sandstone marl, is next found. On its surface I obtained one Pecten (Valoniensis?), and fragments of bones of Ichthyosaurus and Plesiosaurus.

SECOND QUARRY.

A hundred yards or so from the spot of which I have been speaking is a field belonging to Francis Fry, Esq., F.S.A. This has been extensively quarried, and some thousand tons of stones extracted. As the strata are somewhat different from those I have described, they are worth mentioning in some detail. The vegetable soil is rather thicker here (2 feet). The strata are in the following order:—

1. Clay loam 10 to 14 inches thick.
2. Bed of thin limestone from 1 foot to 18 inches thick, somewhat sandy, extending into a bed of blue marl. The stone contains no fossils, but the marl affords numerous examples of Lima gigantea, Pholadomya glabra, Rhynchonella plicatissima, and spines of Cidaris Edwardsi; it is from 9 inches to 1 foot thick.
3. Sandy limestone, passing into the marl; the latter yielding Lima gigantea, Pholadomya glabra, Rhynchonella plicatissima, and spines of Cidaris Edwardsi; the bed being from 9 inches to 1 foot thick.
4. Dark blue compact limestone, containing Ammonites angulatus, Cidaris Edwardsi, Littorina semiornata, Pecten Calvus, Gryphœa (?) species, Terebratula perforata, Ostrea irregularis, Pentacrinus Fisheri, Mytilus minimus, Modiola Hillana, and fish scales, the bed being a foot thick. It is apparently a question whether this is the zone of Ammonites angulatus or not, for many of the above fossils are characteristic of this so-called zone. But it is too thin a stratum to afford a large range of species. The beds above, however, differ slightly from those in the first-named section. The Bucklandi beds are not clearly defined here.
5. Consists of blue limestone alternating with clay, containing Lima gigantea, Ammonites planorbis, A. Johnstoni, Lima punctata, L. tuberculata, L. acuticostatus, L. succincta, L. exaltata, Pecten Suttonensis, P. quadricostatus, Pleuromya unioides, P. galathea, Ceromya gibbosa, Plicatula species, Terebratula perforata, Hemipedium Bechii, Astarte consobrina, fish scales, and traces of Saurian bones.
6. The Oyster-bed, which is separated from No. 5. by a narrow belt of blue clay. It contains Ostrea liassica in great numbers. The conglomerate occurs here with similar fossils to those in the last section.
7. Hard pale blue and cream-coloured limestone, containing most of the fossils in "bed I." of the former section, and also a similar bone bed.

8. Bed of sandy lias, containing an abundance of Ostrea liassica, similar to the "bed J" of the other series.

9. This is "bed K," but "bed L" is omitted.

10. In this bed veins of pure sulphate of strontia run into hard clay of a dark colour.

11. The Cotham marble is next found. I have only obtained in it Ostrea irregularis and Mytilus minutus.

I will now say a few words about Bedminster and Keynsham. The side of a hedge on the left hand side of the road, close to the waterworks on Bedminster Down, affords a good locality for lower lias fossils. The uppermost beds resemble in appearance those first described at Cotham, but the belts of clay are thinner, and the series on the whole more compact. I have not found the Upper plant bed; but "bed D," with its fossils, "bed E" with A. planorbis, etc., but with a less sandy and ferruginous stone.

The fossils I have obtained are much smaller in number than at Cotham, probably because I have worked much less at the spot. The section does not at present afford facilities for examining the lower beds.

Several quarries at Keynsham afford good sections. The first, situated about the eighth of a mile out of the town, affords the Bucklandi series. The second, overlooking the river, and about three-quarters of a mile from the town, affords the Planorbis series and Cypris beds with Lima succincta, L. punctata, L. gigantea, L. tuberculata, casts of Littorina, etc.

Hill's quarry, situated but a short distance from the top of the town, affords a section of the Planorbis series, and numerous belts of lias which have almost the appearance of white satin.

CONCLUSIONS.

That the Sutton stone is a Liassic rather than a Rhætic bed may be gathered, I think, not merely from the fossils which I now exhibit, but from those figured and described by Mr. Tawny. Plicatula intusstriata is most characteristic of the Lima and Pecten beds; but I think, with Mr. R. Tate, that is not exclusively a Rhætic fossil.

"Beds B to K" constitute the typical White lias, being crowned and based by plant beds. I conclude that the Sutton series consists of beds "F, G, H, I, J, K, L;" that "E," abounding in Ammonites planorbis should be called the Planorbis zone or bed. The Planorbis zone and the Sutton series would therefore be but subdivisions of the White lias. Mr. Stoddart, in his paper "On the occurrence of the Sutton lias series near Bristol," read before the Geological section of the Bristol Naturalist's Society, Oct. 24, speaks of the Sutton series as twelve beds of limestone; by this I suppose he includes the whole of which I have been speaking.

The quarry first described by me was 24 feet deep; of this, 22 feet were occupied by the Liassic strata, but there is a difference of several feet in the thickness of the beds in the space of a few yards.

The conglomerate bed, "H," afforded in one case a coral like the mountain limestone species Lithostrotion Martini, as suggested by Mr. Tawney ("Rhætic Beds and Sutton Stone," Geological Journal, page 73, 1867), but Dr. Duncan thinks that it is a species of Montlivaltia; only one or two were found. The stone from some of the beds of which I have been speaking is much used in the neighbourhood of Bristol, and is serviceable for many purposes, as building walls and foundations; inferior builders construct even the entire walls of houses of it. It is quite unfit for sculpture.

From the examination of the strata I have described on land belonging to Francis Fry, Esq., on which Mr. Gay is now prepared to build, I conclude as follows:—That the plant bed which is here omitted is not a necessary accompaniment of the Sutton series or Planorbis zone.

The oyster bed and conglomerate which follow are like those in the first quarry, as also a hard pale blue limestone containing most of the fossils of the bed "I" of the former section. These three last may be considered identical. The equivalents of "K" and "L," the mussel and plant beds, I have not been able to find here; but instead, a thin bed from 1 to 4 inches thick, which I was at first inclined to consider the Rhætic, from its containing Monotis decussata and its lithological character. It also contains Cardium Philippianum, Perna infraliassina, Ostrea liassica, Pleuromya unioides, Ceromya gibbosa, and Mytilus minimus; but never Avicula contorta, or Pecten Valoniensis.

The vein of pure sulphate of strontia running into hard dark clay, such as I have described in a former section, is next found. It is enveloped in clay like what succeeds the Cotham marble, which has hitherto only afforded me Ostrea irregularis and Mytilus minimus. This last rests on the Keuper marl, as in the former section, which affords reptilian remains.

INSECT MEDICINE AND FOLK-LORE.
By William Cole.

Part II.—COLEOPTERA (continued).

CHEMICALLY distinct crystalline substance, first isolated by Robiquet, and named by him Cantharidine, is the active principle of all the insects described in our last paper. It occurs in many other families, and it is probable that most of the Coleoptera which follow owe any medicinal virtue they may possess to the same or an analogous compound.

The pretty Lady-bird beetles (Genus Cocinella), so useful to the gardener and farmer as devourers of the destructive Aphides, the favorites of children, and the theme of many a nursery-rhyme*, were long esteemed as a sovereign remedy for the tooth-ache, and helped to swell the list of the thousand and one cures for dental torments. Cocinella septem-punctata, and bi-punctata, were considered most powerful, and it was sufficient, it was said, to bruise them between the fingers and rub the teeth and gums of the patient. In the "Journal de la Société de Pharmaciens de Paris" the following are also reputed to possess anti-odontological properties, as it is learnedly expressed :—Curculio jaceæ, bacchus, Carabus chrysocephalus, ferrugineous, Chrysomela populi, sanguineolenta; and Gerbi, a learned professor of Pisa, has published a lengthy description of a species of weevil, found amongst thistles, to which he has given the name of Rhinobatus antiodontologicus (a name long enough, as Mr. Kirby observes, to give one the toothache to pronounce), to indicate its remarkable virtue, which he says is so decided that a finger once imbued with its juices will retain the power of banishing the toothache for twelve months!

A singular case or cocoon formed by the larva of another species of weevil (Larinus subrugosus, Chevrolat), found principally on the branches of the Syrian Echinops growing in the desert between Aleppo and Bagdad, is well known in Constantinople and some other parts of the East by the name of Trehala, or Tricula, and in the Persian Pharmacopœias as "Schakar tigal," or "sugar of nests." The beetle which forms these cocoons is thus described by M. A. Moquin-Tandon in his work on "Medical Zoology":— "It is of an oblong form, and of a black colour. It has a projecting snout [rostrum], in the middle of which the antennæ are attached. The elytra cover the whole of the posterior part of the abdomen; they are oblong, and terminate each in a soft and slightly recurved point. Their surface is marked by ten punctuated lines, which commence on the anterior margin, and unite before reaching the opposite extremity." The

---

* Some specimens of these doggerel verses, many of which are of great antiquity, and are found with some variations in most languages of Europe, may not be uninteresting. Children in the North of England on catching a lady-bird, place it upon the hand, and chant the following song until it takes flight :—

"Lady-bird, lady-bird, fly away home,
  Thy house is on fire, thy children all roam;
Except little Nan, who sits in her pan,
  Weaving gold lace as fast as she can."

In Norfolk it is provincially called "Burnie-bee," or Barnabee (or barn-bie, burning or fire-fly, a word said to be of Low Dutch origin), and the following lines are current :—

"Burnie-bee, burnie-Bee,
  Tell me when your wedding be,
If it be to-morrow day,
  Take your wings and fly away."

Mr. Halliwell in his "Popular Rhymes" informs us that they are called in Germany the Virgin Mother's Chafer, or the May-chafer, or the Gold-bird; in Sweden—Gold-hen, Gold-cow, or the Virgin Mary's Maid; and in Denmark—Our Lord's Hen, or Our Lady's Hen. He gives many examples of lady-cow lore in all the above languages; some of them are strikingly similar to our English ones, as will be seen from the second verse of the annexed German song, translated by Taylor :—

"Lady-bird! lady-bird! pretty one! stay!
  Come sit on my finger so happy and gay;
  With me shall no mischief betide thee;
No harm would I do thee, no foeman is near,
I only would gaze on thy beauties so dear,
  Those beautiful winglets beside thee.

Lady-bird! lady-bird! fly away home;
Thy house is a-fire, thy children will roam!
  List! list! to their cry and bewailing!
The pitiless spider is weaving their doom,
Then, lady-bird! lady-bird! fly away home!
  Hark! hark! to thy children's bewailing.

Fly back again, back again, lady-bird dear!
Thy neighbours will merrily welcome thee there;
  With them shall no perils attend thee!
They'll guard thee so safely from danger or care,
They'll gaze on thy beautiful winglets so fair,
  And comfort, and love, and befriend thee!"

The Guernsey children had a curious custom with regard to a beetle they called Pâu (Timarcha lævegata, the "bloody-nose beetle"?), and "never forgot," says a writer in *Notes and Queries*, "whenever they caught this beetle, to place it in the palm of their left hand, when it was invoked as follows :—

"Pâu, Pâu mourtre mé teu sang,
  Et j'te doûrai de bonau vin bleane!"

which means, being interpreted,

"Pâu, Pâu, show me thy blood,
  And I will give the good white wine!"

As he uttered the charm, the juvenile pontiff spat on poor Thammuz, till a torrent of blood, or what seemed such, " 'ran purple' over the urchin's fingers."

The Cornish people have a like "charm" for the same beetles, and when they see one, spit on it and cry :—

"Spit blood, Jew!
Else I'll kill you!"

larva constructs its case of saccharine and amylaceous matter procured from the Echinops; this case is oval in form, and about three-fourths of an inch in length; the exterior surface is very irregular, and of a greyish colour. One side is flattened with a deep grove, where it is fixed lengthwise to the branch. The inside is smooth, white, or reddish; the tissue is thick and cracks beneath the teeth, and has a sweet taste owing to the presence of a peculiar kind of sugar, something like that of the sugar-cane (called by M. Berthelot "trehalose"); the formation of which M. Bourlier thinks may be attributed to the albuminous matter in the saliva with which the insect binds together the starchy materials composing the cocoon. These cocoons are much esteemed in Turkey and Syria as a remedy for bronchitis and diseases of the respiratory organs. They are given in the form of a decoction, half an ounce being coarsely powdered and digested for a quarter of an hour in about a pint and a half of boiling water. They are also eaten as food, and their use in this respect is said to be as universal as that of tapioca and salop in France.

Shakespeare's "shard bourne beetle with its drowsy hums" (Scarabæus stercorarius, the "Dor," "Clock," or "Watchman" of English peasants), and another dung-frequenting beetle with bright red elytra (Aphodius fimetarius), notwithstanding their unsavoury habits, were formerly used in the composition of an ointment called "oyl of beetles," eight ounces of the insects being digested with one pound of laurel oil. The infusion was used for bruises and sprains, and was "good against pains and contractions of the nerves and quartan agues, being outwardly applied." In old Mouffet we read of a "singular oyntment against convulsion made of beetles after this manner. Take of Pepper, Euphorbium Pellitory of Spain, each alike; of the beetles to the weight of all the rest; let them all, being brought to a powder and mixed together in a bath with juyce of spear-wort as much as sufficeth, be macerated and made in the fashion of an oyntment, with which let the pulses of the armes, feet, and temples, etc., be anoynted." But it was not only when dead that they were useful to the physician. With what feelings would ladies now regard these sturdy insects "All alive, O!" and kicking desperately, substituted for their favourite Preston Salts and Eau de Cologne in cases of fainting? Yet our ancestors suffered no such fancies to stand in the way of their use, and would bind them on the skin of the patient confined under half a walnut shell; considering the irritation produced by the beetles' jagged claws, in their efforts to escape, an excellent restorative, particularly if they were placed on the soles of the feet, "because this does wonderfully rouse up one in a lethargy!" A statement which few will disbelieve, when it is remembered that a Scarabæus is able to walk off the table with a brass candlestick on its back! And as prevention is better than cure, perhaps a return to this custom might induce many a fair one to reconsider her resolution to faint; even a Mr. Mantalini could hardly "go off" in the presence of two or three such "dem'd unpleasant monsters."

Closely allied to our native Dor-beetles in structure and habits are the celebrated Sacred Beetles of the Egyptians (Copris sacer, and Ateuchus Ægyptiorum), whose effigies may be seen on so many of the monuments and engraved gems in the British Museum. Besides occupying a conspicuous place in the mystical religion of the ancient people of Egypt, they claim our attention here on account of the medical and magical powers attributed to them in bygone times. Their supposed effects and method of use in the former capacity being nearly the same as the Dor-beetles, I need only mention that they are still eaten by the modern Egyptian women, to promote prolificness, and induce a degree of embonpoint considered necessary for perfect beauty, and proceed to notice their powers as amulets or charms. Pliny advises those afflicted with any kind of ague to wear one of these beetles round the neck wrapped up alive in a piece of scarlet cloth, and in a short time the disease will disappear. Plutarch records that the Egyptian soldiers carried a ring on which was cut the figure of a beetle, to defend them in battle; and a ring with an emerald similarly engraved will effectually preserve its possessor against the machinations of witches and sorcerers. Nor does this exhaust the wonderful powers of such an ornament. Mouffet assures his readers that it is very useful "if anyone be about to go before the King on any occasion; so that the ring ought especially to be worn by them that intend to beg of noblemen some jolly preferment, or some rich province. It keeps away likewise the headache, which truly is no small mischief, especially to great drinkers. Who, then, can despise the beetle whose very image engraven upon stones hath so great vertues?"

The common meal-worm beetle (Tenebrio molita) is mentioned by Pliny as a curative of leprosy; and an oily substance obtained from a dark coloured beetle (Blaps mucronata?) "is marvellously good for affections of the ears;" but he prudently warns the operator that care must be taken speedily to remove the wool with which it is applied, or it will be "transformed into an animal in the shape of a small grub!"

Many of my readers must be acquainted with the handsome "musk beetle," which is common in many places amongst willows about midsummer, betraying its presence even when hidden from the eye by the sweet odour it exhales. Mr. Drury says of it:—"This insect I have been confidently informed by an eminent surgeon (the late Mr. Guy) who tried it, has the same effect as Cantharides, being capable when properly prepared of procuring a strong blister in as short a space of time as the other." Mouffet notices this insect, and his description is curious as a specimen of an entomological diagnosis in "Good Queen Bess's time," although he probably confounded in it two or more species of Longicornes:—"In greatness and colour it resembles broad horn, it hath a little broad head, great ox-eyes, almost three fingers overthwart in length; it hath a forked mouth gaping and terrible, with two very hard crooked teeth; with these whilest he gnaws the wood (I speak by experience) it doth perfectly grunt about like a young pig. May be this is the reason why Hesychius hath related that it being bound to a tree will drive away fig-gnats. The shoulders of it are curiously wrought by nature, they seem to be a hilt made of ebony and polished; it hath six feet, distinguished with three little knees, but they are very weak and faint, and altogether unfit for such a burden. These receive help by two horns that grow above their eyes and are longer than their whole bodies, they are flexible with nine or ten joints; not exactly round, but are rough like goats' horns, which although it can move them every way, yet when it flies it holds them only forth directly, and being wearied with flying she useth them for feet: for knowing that his legs are weak he twists his horns about the branch of a tree, and so he hangs at ease. In that it resembles the bird of Paradise, which wanting feet clings about the boughs with those pendulous nerves, and so being tired with labour takes its ease." With these old writers "the *useful*" only "was the beautiful," the adaptation of the structure of an animal or plant to its mode of life or its value as a link in Nature's chain had little claim on their attention, if unaccompanied by some supposed or real medicinal qualities, so our author concludes with a kind of apology for the absence of these in the present instance, and with a hope that the virtues of the Cerambyx may be unveiled by time:—"I have learned no other use of them in physic, than that taken in the left hand they drive away quartian agues. It may be posterity, being better experienced, will discover more of their vertues, and will not suffer themselves to be perswaded that a creature God hath made so curiously can want rare vertues in Medicaments which He hath bestowed on far baser things (according to his goodness unto mankind)."

The powdered "horns" of the Stag-beetle (Lucanus cervus*) used to be administered to children for various infantile complaints, or pierced with holes and hung round the neck with a ribbon as a defence against the bites of venomous reptiles. Even that poet's favourite, the glowworm, "gilding and glistening in the dew-drop," did not escape our zealous utilitarian forefathers, but was to be given in honey for the cure of stone or gravel, most efficaciously when mixed with oil of roses and earth-worms! With this nostrum, to be found in the "Zoologia Medicinalis Hibernica," by B. Manderville, M.D., published in 1744, I may bring to a close this long list of remedies derived from beetles.

ON THE EXTINCTION OF SPECIES OF BRITISH BUTTERFLIES.

THE subject opened by Mr. Bax in the January Number of the NATURALIST'S NOTE BOOK is worthy of much attention and further study than appears to have been hitherto devoted to it. The question started has never been more than partially answered, and appears to me to be divisable into three heads, viz.:—

1. What species have really become extinct?
2. What have been the real or supposed cause of their extinction?
3. What species appear to be passing away from us?

On all these I have a few remarks to make which, although perhaps of little value in themselves, may yet lead to further discussion, and assist in the elucidation of the subject.

1. Mr. Bax, amongst those species said to have become extinct, includes *P. Podalirius, E. Ligea, C. Chryseis* and *C. Virgaureæ;* but I must support Mr. Cole's views, that these never really were inhabitants of Britain. I have never heard or read of any authentic specimen of *P. Podalirius*, and doubt not but that Mr. Newman is right in his "British Butterflies," where he says, "Perhaps originally placed in a cabinet as a foreign specimen of *Machaon*," although the resemblance between the two species is very superficial. *E. Ligea* is in nearly the same predicament; for although mentioned by many authors as British, no one within my

---

* The belief that this formidable-looking insect is "uncanny" prevails in many places, and the German peasants accuse it of bringing live coals into the houses on its "horns!"

own knowledge has ever even professed to be the happy possessor of a specimen.

The two coppers *E. Chryseis and Virgaureæ* rest on little better foundation, the latter indeed on a worse one than either of the two preceding species. It is true that *Chryseis* is admitted in Stainton's "Manual," who says, "formerly taken near Epping and in Ashdown Forest," which captures, however, according to Coleman, "rest on a tradition," the truth of which I, for one, am much inclined to doubt, especially as the food plant is, according to continental authors, the common Sorrell. As to when or why Virgaureæ was admitted to our lists, I can offer no opinion.

So much for the most likely of our "reputed" species, except Argynnis Dia, which, I think, *may* have been really captured in this country, although the evidence in its favour is very conflicting. Newman says that the number of British butterflies was raised by the exertions of our older entomologists to *one hundred and thirty-nine*, as against the sixty-four now on the list; but the preceding five species are all that appear to have had any plausible foundation laid for their reception.

Turning now to the species still on our lists which *appear to be* or *really are* extinct, they are reduced to two, *E.* Hippothoë and *L. Acis*, for one cannot call *V. antiopa* extinct, though it will certainly never appear alive at Camberwell again. This species has been captured nearly every year, though *very* sparingly, and *P. Daplidice* and *A. Lathonia* seem still as common, or rather as rare, as formerly.

That P. Hippothoë was once tolerably abundant in its particular habitats is undoubted, it having been captured by entomologists still living. That it *may* turn up in some unknown, and hitherto unworked locality, is possible, but barely probable, as when we consider the size and beauty of this insect it appears unlikely it could have been passed unnoticed even by non-entomologists. L. Acis seems to have disappeared in a more mysterious manner, but of this more further on. Mr. Newman says he took it plentifully many years ago, near Leominster; but since then it seems to have gradually decreased in numbers, until the last capture recorded was, as nearly as I can remember, some twenty years ago, of two specimens, at Lower Guiting, on the Cotswold Hills. This brings us to the end of the first division of our subject.

2. The second is of more importance. It is easy to see that years ago certain species existed which do not do so now; but to answer "where or why they have disappeared" is far more difficult. That the drainage of fens and consequent destruction of certain plants on which a given species exclusively feeds, will, with the plant, also destroy the insect, is self-evident, and to this cause alone the death of *P.* Hippothoë is doubtless due; but how are we to account for the disappearance of *L. Acis*, which feeds on a plant (the common Thrift), still widely distributed and tolerably common? I would like to hear the theories of older entomologists on this point. Although there is a great outcry against over-collecting, I do not believe that this alone has had much to do *practically* with the extinction or even material diminution of a species, except possibly in the immediate neighbourhood of large towns (as, for example, *Artaxerxes (var.?)* near Edinburgh, which is, I believe, much scarcer than of yore). Still I am open to conviction as to the truth of the other side of the question when I can see any facts brought to bear it fairly out. That a species of very local habitat *might* be so extinguished I do not for a moment deny, but I hope even the most insatiate of collectors would have sufficient sensibility of feeling not to over-do his part by capturing all he could, day after day, for successive seasons. Although, too, I disagree on the subject of exchange with "C.," in an article entitled "Butterflies to the rescue" in "Science Gossip" of this month, he is quite right in condemning one who "catches a butterfly," I don't care how common, "kills it *without examining* its appearance, and then throws it away because it is rubbed." Such a man may be a "collector," and a very successful one, but certainly he is not a "naturalist." To conclude this division of the subject, it may be better to incorporate with it the third question, "What species are in danger of passing from us?"

These may be said to be eight, viz., *P. Machaon, P. Cratægi, M. Artemis, L. Sibylla, A. Iris, C. Davus, L. Arion,* and *H. Actæon.*

V. C-Album and *Polychloros, T. Pruni,* and *W-Album; H. Paniscus* and *Comma*, still seem to be tolerably abundant at times in their respective localities, and like the clouded yellows, to have no certainty of appearance; and taking one decade with another, I do not see that they are scarcer now than formerly.

P. Machaon has become comparatively much scarcer the past three or four years, and it seems highly probable that the species may die out in a very few more, from exactly the same cause as P. Hippothoë, the reclamation of the fens. *P. Cratægi* is certainly getting rarer year by year, and like L. Acis, without apparent reason: feeding almost indiscriminately on fruit and other trees, it cannot die out from want of food, and the "attacks of collectors," I think, is not a sufficient cause to assign for the disappearance of a species once so common. *M. Artemis* may some day fade away before advancing cultivation, but it will be many years first; for although this species is confined to very restricted localities, these seem to be tolerably abundant and widely separated. We can also understand that the reclamation by draining of the northern and north of Ireland bogs may destroy *C. Davus*, and the extensive felling of oak woods still the habitat of *L. Sibylla* and *A. Iris*, will lead to the extinction of their several inhabitants.

But of all our British butterflies, except *Machaon*, I should imagine *L. Arion* and *H. Actæon* are in the greatest danger of extinction, and both from the same cause, their extremely limited range. It is such species as these the collector should be most careful of, and restrain his desires of getting "a good bag."

H. Actæon being confined to only one or two spots in Britain, although there occurring generally in profusion, would be swept away in a year or two, were the ground it inhabits more easily to be reached; but I believe it is with great difficulty arrived at, and is of too barren a nature to justify agricultural enterprise, which is, after all, the greatest enemy that butterflies have to contend with. So long as this continues, and collecting is not *too* energetically carried on, *Actæon* will be spared to us.

Of *L. Arion* I shall speak more at length, as knowing some little of its habits and habitat. It is, I fear, to be the first doomed of our Diurni; but even here there is room for hope that it may remain on our list for many years, especially as it has been less rare during the past season in the localities known to me (two spots fifteen miles apart on the Cotswolds), than it has for many years. It occurs exclusively on barren broken ground, mostly the slopes of old quarries, and always at a considerable elevation. Here it is very circumscribed in its flight. In 1868 I captured eight specimens in all, four pairs on four different days, and all these were taken within twenty yards of one spot, and this though I carefully worked the neighbouring hill-side; during the past year it was more widely distributed. This species was discovered many years ago on Barnwell Wold, Northamptonshire. The Rev. Mr. Bree, writing in the "Zoologist" in 1852, says that there did not then appear to be any diminution in the number annually observed; but when quoting this in the "Manual" (1857) Stainton adds, "Since the above was written the insect has apparently become really less abundant."

Other localities noted are Brington, Charmouth, Dover, near Glastonbury, near Marlborough, Bideford, near Plymouth, and some others; also "Shortwood and some other spots near Cheltenham," which "other spots" I have good reason to believe are identical with those recorded during the past few years in the "Entomologist," "as Painswick" "near Gloucester," &c.

Now the question I would like to see answered is, "What has been the history of this species for some years past in any of these recorded localities," especially Barnwell Wold, as being the longest and best known? A satisfactory reply would, I think, throw much light on the "Extinction of Species," a subject, the discussion of which I shall watch with much interest, and which will, I hope, be taken up *as it deserves*, by older and abler entomologists than myself.   HERBERT MARSDEN.
Secretary, Lepidopterists'
Exchange Club.
Gloucester, February 13*th*, 1869.

SILKWORMS:

AND HOW TO REAR THEM SUCCESSFULLY.

PART III.

A ROOM to rear silkworms in is best fronting the south, situated on an upper floor, and free from damp, but open to the pure country air if possible. A very small room will suffice in which to hatch silkworms' eggs, and keep the worms during their first and second stages. It should at least have one window of tolerable size, with a door on the north side leading from other rooms behind. A stove should be at one end, and a fireplace, or better, a low hearth at the other; in order to supply such artificial heat as is necessary to hatch the eggs. It is better not to expose silkworms' eggs to the rays of the sun, but they can be placed in the hatching-box on a table or stage in the centre of the room; and should the sun interfere, the window-blind should be dropped. From twelve to fifteen thousand worms could be reared in a room ten feet square, or the number proceeding from about a third of an ounce of eggs. Some rearers in Italy that feed worms from twenty ounces have suitable buildings of proportionate larger size. A cellar of at least half that of the rearing-room is very convenient in which to lay the mulberry leaves, and a shed or other place to dry them in if unavoidably gathered when wet; for they should not be administered to the insects in that state. A room for two of my castles, capable of holding worms from one ounce of eggs, must be twenty feet by twenty, and nearly eleven feet high, with a window opposite each castle. One stove and fireplace will suffice to keep such a room of the requisite temperature. Smoke must not be allowed to escape into a silkworm rearing-room. Heating by means of hot water pipes might be advantageous in rearings on a larger scale, and a room so treated would be managed much better; also for hatching the eggs. Some rearers place the hatching-box and eggs in a common horsehair sieve, placing the same on the two front legs of a chair, laying on its back upon a table, putting under a low oil or spirit lamp, the flame of which is so arranged that it can be turned up or down as more or less heat be required; but about six inches above the flame there should be fixed a sheet of tin or iron a foot square, to distribute the heat, and prevent the flame concentrating too much heat to the danger of the eggs. The sieve may be covered with a mat or blanket. A thermometer should be placed inside to indicate the temperature. The Italian peasant women put the eggs in linen bags, depositing them in their bosoms or between their beds and mattresses; but such a suffocating heat I think is very prejudicial to young silkworms. It would not perhaps be a bad plan with a very few eggs to put them in a strong pill box, the lid pricked full of pin holes, placing the same in one's pocket by day, and on the top of the bed-clothes at night with the garment pinned to the counterpane.

To prepare silkworms' eggs for hatching, it is customary to scrape them from the linen on which laid, by means of a spoon, having previously soaked them about twenty minutes in water, to soften the gum by which they adhere. This operation is best done in the autumn, or very early in spring. The eggs should be washed gently, moving them in the water with one's hands, and after a few minutes the heaviest and best sink to the bottom; and the remnant floating are inferior, and may be poured away with the water. Having spread the good ones out on a napkin to dry in an airy room for a day or two, they should be put away until hatching time. It is not absolutely necessary to detach the eggs from the linen on which they were deposited; but it is more convenient with great numbers, and facilitates the collecting of the worms to have them in less space in a hatching-box. I believe it necessary to import silkworms' eggs from their native source every year or two, for those produced in this country in time degenerate; at least, they might be procured from southern districts of celebrity. Good eggs are somewhat of a violet colour, round, and somewhat indented. This violet colour gradually comes over the eggs, a few days after being laid by the moths; for at first they are of a light yellow.

I would impress on silkworm rearers the advantage of retarding the hatching of the eggs by keeping them as cool as possible, without frost getting to them, in earthen pots or pans, placing the same in dry cellars in warm days of spring. When the mulberry trees have burst into leaf, by about the middle of May, is early enough to hatch the eggs; but it is not always possible to prevent their hatching naturally, even before this, in forward seasons, unless they could be placed in an ice house; which experiment has been successfully practised in Italy to prevent hatching even until the approach of autumn. It is very evident if the hatching could be retarded in this way until June, the leaves would be more plentiful, and better; and the weather more settled. Eggs about to hatch grow lighter coloured, and if a worm or two be immerged there is no alternative, and the hatching must proceed, by increasing the temperature five degrees of Fahrenheit daily, until seventy degrees is reached; which is to be kept up day and night, and the insects will in a few days be all out. I shall proceed to show the management of worms from one ounce in weight of eggs, such quantity being sufficient to fill two of the castles which I have described, supposing they all arrive at maturity; but as this is not always the case, it is usual for every ounce of eggs to allow a further eighth in weight to provide for such loss as may occur. The use of a stove in a hatching room I fancy the best to insure a proper command of the temperature, and the eggs may be placed in the gutter paper, not more than one-eighth of an inch in depth. Of a morning, soon after sunrise, the young worms will be seen running up the sides of the gutters, over which young mulberry leaves are laid for them to crawl on. In an hour or two the leaves will be sufficiently full of worms to be lifted to a sheet of paper, and then placed on the third stage of a castle. Fresh leaves are immediately supplied to them, and to the gutters to continue the collection; and so on, until no more hatching continues before the following morning. Each day's hatching or lot of worms should be kept separately. When the hatching is effected well, in about four days the worms will occupy four sheets of paper. These four lots, consisting together of from forty to fifty thousand worms, by judicious management may frequently be brought to maturity within a day or two of the same time, by placing the later hatched ones in rotation on the higher stages; where the temperature being higher, the insects will feed in proportion quicker than those situated lower, and should have a meal or two more allowed. However, their arriving at maturity on consecutive days rather than otherwise is advantageous, for the work attending them is more divided. In order to make my instructions for rearing these worms the better understood, I shall treat the whole as one lot, and suppose they have left the eggs all on the same day. About 1,700 lbs. more or less in weight of mulberry leaves will be necessary. Silkworms should always have sufficient room to crawl about, and between every two there should be at least the space of a third vacant to allow free circulation of air, so essential for the wellbeing of these insects.

The First Moult.—The first moult of these silkworms begins about the sixth day after they are born, which moult or sleep, lasting two days more, terminates what I term the first period of their life. During this period they will consume nearly 15 lbs. of fresh-cut leaves. On the first day a few ounces will suffice, the quantity gradually increasing until the fourth or fifth day, after which it diminishes as the moult draws near, the insects at last requiring none during their dormant state. In feeding the worms, sprinkle the fine cut leaves gently over them about every five hours, nearly covering them; and when they consume the leaves almost entirely, in less than three hours, give them an intermediate meal. On the fifth day it is well to shift the worms to other papers, dividing each lot into two, thus eight sheets of paper will be occupied by them. This operation of moving silkworms is done by giving them a plentiful meal of whole leaves, on which they soon crawl, and may be lifted away therewith, leaving behind all the refuse and dirt on the old paper. This operation can be repeated until all the worms are collected. During the moult, or dormant state, the insects should not be disturbed by moving or touching them, although the feeding may be continued to those which continue eating; and thus the dormant or sleeping ones remain under the leaves, until they awake and shoot their skins, immediately coming again to the surface, when they begin their second period.

The Second Moult.—This period, like the first, lasts about six days, and 40 or 50 lbs. of leaves are required to bring the insects to their dormant state, two or three days before which they are to be again divided and distributed on fresh papers, so they occupy sixteen sheets, or at least forty or fifty feet of space on the stages; thus they are again perfectly clean before the dormant state comes on. The meals are continued every five hours, or oftener. When the insects consume the leaves faster more should be given.

On the Continent it is customary to feed silkworms up to about ten or eleven o'clock at night, beginning again the next morning at the dawn of day. It is very certain they should have all the leaves they can consume, and always fresh. It often happens that the first worms will be shooting their skins before others have even begun their sleep. The only thing is to continue the feeding with light meals until all are in the sleep under the leaves, when the forwardest may be removed on whole leaves to other papers by themselves, leaving the dormant ones alone until they again show signs of life, when they likewise can be collected and placed on a separate sheet of paper. By attending to this from time to time every paper would contain worms of one age alone. Some people leave the forwardest worms a day or two without feed in order for the others to get up to them; but this is not right. The forwardest are always the best, and ought not to be made to suffer hunger to await the "drones," as I will term them.

Third Moult.—Silkworms having changed or shot their skins the second time, soon begin eating away, and will consume nearly 100 lbs. of leaves cut somewhat larger than before. During this third period the worms require to be cleaned out at least twice, viz., once after the second sleep, and again before the third commences, or on the second and fifth days. To lift the worms from old quarters to new it is a good plan to distribute to them leaves and twigs to crawl on, by which they will be easier lifted than with leaves alone; and these small branches laying at the bottom on the fresh papers will somewhat hold the leaves (afterwards given in feeding) hollowing, admitting the air to circulate more; and thus tend to keep the beds dry, without mouldiness; which latter is very prejudicial to silkworms. Cleanliness is all important. The wooden trays will now become useful for carrying the fresh papers and worms, as also the steps or ladders to reach to the upper stages of the castle. The temperature of the rearing-room should be kept as near seventy degrees Fahrenheit as possible, fresh air being continually more or less admitted. Air must never be entirely shut out under any circumstances, but in fine warm days the windows and doors should be thrown open, especially when the natural temperature admits. It is of service, especially in damp weather, to occasionally burn a little straw or a few shavings in the fireplace, which puts the air of the room in movement.

Fourth Moult.—The fourth period up to the sleep occupies more or less seven days, and over 200 lbs. of leaves if the worms are all alive will be required, which do not want to be cut. The day after the third moult attend to the removal of the insects to clean quarters, always allotting to them double the space they before occupied, for they always fill it by growing. Expel all refuse of the old beds, etc., from the room; and this cleaning out should be done three times before the dormant state arrives. The nets may now be used in order to perform this work quicker. The nets being laid over the worms, and the leaves administered thereon, the insects pass the meshes, and may be lifted away therewith, or raised and hooked to the stage above until the old bed below be removed and fresh papers placed there. The nets with the worms may then be lowered to their previous position. Gathering leaves and attending the worms during this period will occupy the time of two women, one having sufficed up to the present time. The fourth sleep lasts longer than the preceding ones by a day; and while it lasts do not allow the temperature to fall below seventy degrees or rise above seventy-five, unless naturally so, when air must be admitted all the more.

The Fifth Period.—The last moult over, the last period and the most difficult has arrived, in which every care must be used to maintain the worms clean, keeping the place properly ventilated. This period is longer, lasting about ten days more or less, according to the breed of worms, and from 1,500 to 1,600 lbs. or more of leaves must be administered, distributed in abundant meals every five hours, or at shorter intervals when the insects show want of food before. During this period it becomes necessary to clean the worms out at least every three days, using the nets or perforated papers to facilitate expedition. In this period worms in health eat voraciously, grow fast, and therefore cleanliness and ventilation are the more necessary. It is very pleasing now to hear the noise as of a falling shower of hail made by the worms mounting and eating the leaves. When silkworms eat well, and present a clear pearly whiteness, they are doing well, and their maturity becomes evident, for many may be seen crawling over the leaves without eating, directing themselves to the edges of the stages. They appear transparent when looked at against the light. Silk may be seen issuing from their mouths; their bodies contract; their heads become crisp; they evacuate all excrements. The important moment has arrived, viz., "The Mount."

LEONARD HARMANN, Junr.
Old Catton, Norwich.

LIST OF BRITISH MOTHS:
NATURE OF THEIR FOOD,
AND TIMES OF THEIR PERFECT APPEARANCE.
THE EUCHELIIDÆ.

CRIMSON SPECKLED (*Deïopeia pulchella*). Feeds on the forget-me-not (*Myosotis arvensis*). Flies in July.

Cinnabar (*Euchelia Jacobææ*). Feeds on the common ragwort (*Senecio Vulgaris*). Flies in July.

Scarlet Tiger (*Callimorpha Dominula*). Feeds chiefly on hound's-tongue (*Cynoglossum officinale*). Flies about midsummer.

THE CHELONIDÆ.

Clouded Buff (*Euthemonia russula*). Feeds on mouse-ear hawk-weed (*Hieracium pilosella*), dandelion (*Leontodon taraxacum*), heath (*Erica cinerea*), and several other plants growing on heaths. Flies in June.

Wood Tiger (*Chelonia Plantaginis*). Feeds on violets, plantain, and several other plants. Flies in May and June.

Tiger (*Chelonia Caja*). Feeds on almost every plant. Flies in July.

Cream Spot Tiger (*Chelonia villica*). Feeds on chickweed. Flies about the end of June.

Ruby Tiger (*Arctia fuliginosa*). Feeds on dock, plantain, and several grasses. Flies in June.

Muslin Moth (*Arctia mendica*). Feeds on chickweed, dock, etc. Flies in June.

Buff Ermine (*Arctia bibricipeda*). Feeds on docks. Flies about midsummer.

White Ermine (*Arctia Menthastri*). Feeds on almost every plant. Flies in June.

Water Ermine (*Arctia Urticæ*). Feeds on mint, willow herb, and herbs of different kinds. Flies in June.

THE LIPARIDÆ.

Brown-tail Moth (*Liparis chrysorrhœa*). Feeds on whitethorn and blackthorn. Flies in July.

Yellow-tail Moth (*Liparis auriflua*). Feeds on the whitethorn. Flies in July.

Satin Moth (*Liparis Salicis*). Feeds chiefly on the Lombardy poplar. Flies in July and August.

Gipsy (*Liparis dispar*). Feeds on whitethorn, blackthorn, plum, and apple. Flies about midsummer, and continues to fly during the whole of July.

Black Arches (*Liparis monacha*). Feeds on the oak, birch, and other trees. Flies in July and August.

Pale Tussock (*Orgyia pudibunda*). Feeds on oak, lime, hazel, edible chestnut, and many other trees. Flies in May.

Dark Tussock (*Orgyia fascelina*). Feeds on plum, hazel, and other trees, and sometimes on herbaceous plants. Flies about midsummer.

Reed Tussock (*Orgyia cœnosa*). Feeds on the common weed (*Arundo phragmitis*). Flies early in June.

Scarce Vapourer (*Orgyia gonostigma*). Feeds on nut and oaks. Flies in July.

Common Vapourer (*Orgyia antiqua*). Feeds on all trees or shrubs. Flies in July.

Nut-tree Tussock (*Demas Coryli*). Feeds on the nut and beech. Flies in June.

BOMBYCIDÆ.

Pale Oak Eggar (*Trichiura Cratægi*). Feeds on whitethorn and blackthorn. Flies in August and September.

December Moth (*Pæcilocampa Populi*). Feeds on the leaves of the oak. Flies in November and December.

Small Eggar (*Eriogaster Lanestris*). Feeds on the hawthorn, and sometimes on the elm. Flies in February.

Lackey (*Bombyx neustria*). Feeds on apple trees. Flies in July.

Ground Lackey (*Bombyx castrensis*). Feeds on the sea-wormwood, the wild carrot, and some other plants. Flies in August.

Fox Moth (*Bombyx Rubi*). Feeds on bramble and on heath. Flies in June.

Oak Eggar (*Bombyx Quercus*). Feeds on a number of plants and shrubs, particularly on whitethorn. Flies in July.

Grass Eggar (*Bombyx Trifolii*). Feeds on trefoil and clover. Flies in August.

Drinker (*Odonestis potatoria*). Feeds on different grasses. Flies in July.

Lappet (*Lasiocampa quercifolia*). Feeds on blackthorn and willow. Flies in June.

Small Lappet (*Lasiocampa ilicifolia*). Feeds on the leaves of the whortleberry. Flies in April and May.

Kentish Glory (*Endromis versicolor*). Feeds on the birch. Flies in March and April.

Emperor Moth (*Saturnia carpini*). Feeds on willow, blackthorn, heath, and a number of other plants. Flies in April.

GEOMETERS.

URAPTERYDÆ.

Swallow Tailed Moth (*Uropteryx sambucata*). Feeds on honeysuckle, elder, several fruit trees, and on many herbaceous plants, particularly forget-me-not. Flies in June.

ENNOMIDÆ.

Dark-bordered Beauty (*Epione vespertaria*). Feeds on hazel. Flies in June.

Bordered Beauty (*Epione apiciaria*). Feeds on willow, hazel, and poplar. Flies in July.

Little Thorn (*Epione advenaria*). Feeds on the bilberry. Flies in July.

Brimstone Moth (*Rumia cratægata*). Feeds on whitethorn and blackthorn. Flies throughout the summer.

Speckled Yellow (*Venilia maculata*). Feeds on various herbaceous plants. Flies in June.

Orange Moth (*Angerona prunaria*). Feeds on blackthorn, beech, and sometimes on broom. Flies about the end of May or beginning of June.

Light Emerald (*Metrocampa margaritaria*). Feeds on broom. Flies in July.

Barred Red (*Ellopia fasciaria*). Feeds on the Scotch fir. Flies about midsummer.

Scorched Wing (*Eurymene dolobraria*). Feeds on beech and oak. Flies in June.

Lilac Beauty (*Pericallia syringaria*). Feeds on elder, privet, and lilac. Flies about the end of June or beginning of July.

Early Thorn (*Selenia illunaria*). Feeds principally on the willow. There are two broods. The first flies in April, and the second in July.

Lunar Thorn (*Selenia lunaria*). Feeds on blackthorn. Flies in May and June.

Purple Thorn (*Selenia illustraria*). Feeds on birch and oak. There are two broods. The first flies in May, and the second in August.

Scalloped Hazel (*Odontopera bidentata*). I am unable to state the plant that it feeds on. Flies in May.

Scalloped Oak (*Crocallis elinguaria*). Feeds on honeysuckle, birch, blackthorn, apple, and pear. Flies in July and August.

Large Thorn (*Ennomos alniaria*). This insect must not be considered British, though included among British moths. On the Continent it is said to feed on elder, birch, larch, plum, apple, pear, and apricot.

Canary-shouldered Thorn (*Ennomos tiliaria*). Feeds on birch and oak. Flies in August.

Dusky Thorn (*Ennomos fuscantaria*). Feeds on the leaves of the ash. I am unable to state the time of the appearance of the perfect insect.

September Thorn (*Ennomos erosaria*). Feeds on birch, oak, and other trees. Flies in August and September.

August Thorn (*Ennomos Angularia*). Feeds on oak, birch, elm, lilac, etc. Flies in August and September.

Feathered Thorn (*Himera pennaria*). Feeds on oak. Flies in October.

AMPHYDASYDÆ.

Pale Brindled Beauty (*Phigalia pilosaria*). Feeds on oak. Flies in February and March.

Belted Beauty (*Nyssia zonaria*). Feeds on the common yarrow. Flies in September.

Small Brindled Beauty (*Nyssia hispidaria*). Feeds on the oak. I am unable to state the time of appearance of the perfect insect.

Brindled Beauty (*Biston hirtaria*). Feeds on pear, plum, lime, etc. Flies in April.

Oak Beauty (*Amphydasis prodromaria*). Feeds on the oak and birch. Flies in March and April.

Peppered Moth (*Amphydasis betularia*). Feeds on acacia, lime, birch, oak, and many other trees. Flies in May.

BOARMIDÆ.

Waved Umber (*Hemerophila abruptaria*). Feeds on lilac and rose. Flies in May and August.

Speckled Beauty (*Cleora viduaria*). The plant that this insect feeds on is unknown. Flies in June.

Dotted Carpet (*Cleora glabraria*). Feeds on lichens which grow on fir trees. Flies in July.

Brussels Lace (*Cleora lichenaria*). Feeds on lichen. Flies in July.

Mottled Beauty (*Boarmia repandata*). Feeds on plum and birch trees. Flies in June and July.

Willow Beauty (*Boarmia rhomboidaria*). Feeds on roses, plum, birch, etc. Flies in June and July.

Satin Carpet (*Boarmia abietaria*). Feeds on fir. Flies in July.

Ringed Carpet (*Boarmia cinctaria*). Feeds on heath. Flies in May and June.

Great Oak Beauty (*Boarmia roboraria*). Feeds on oak. Flies in June.

Pale Oak Beauty (*Boarmia consortaria*). Feeds on oak. Flies in June.

Square Spot (*Tephrosia consonaria*). Feeds on birch. Flies in May.

Small Engrailed (*Tephrosia crepuscularia*). Feeds on elm, birch, and other trees. Flies in April.

Engrailed (*Tephrosia biundularia*). Feeds on larch. Flies in April.

Brindled White Spot (*Tephrosia extersaria*). Feeds on birch. Flies in June.

Grey Birch (*Tephrosia punctulata*). Feeds on birch. Flies in May.

Annulet (*Gnophos obscurata*). Feeds on the salad burnet, and the sun cistus. Flies in July.

Scotch Annulet (*Dasydia obfuscata*). Feeds on the dyer's greenweed and various species of vetch. Flies in July and August.

Black Mountain Moth (*Psodos trepidaria*). I am unable to state the plant that it feeds on. Specimens of this insect have been taken in Scotland in the month of July.

Dusky Carpet (*Mniophila cineraria*). I am unable to give any particulars respecting this insect. Though introduced in our list of moths, it can hardly be considered a British insect.

T. W. TEMPANY.

ROUND MY GARDEN.

PART I.

WHILE residing in the country the committee of an Horticultural Society offered a prize for the best collection of insects destructive to plants, for which collection my spare time was engaged, and I have every reason to think that had it not been for illness I should have been tolerably successful; and perhaps the little I accomplished might prove interesting to the readers of the NOTE BOOK.

The first thing that attracted my attention was the downy appearance of several apple trees, and these so-called lumps of cotton I made for the time my careful study. The coccus, or American blight, sometimes called the mealy aphis, I found by conversation with nursery men to be a great pest to the apple orchards, and various means were resorted to with a view of exterminating them. You may occasionally perceive the blight floating in the air, looking as though it were a bit of cotton, but if you catch it you will find that it contains the insect so destructive to our fruit trees. These insects appear to live upon the juice flowing between the bark and wood, or on the substance of the envelope itself. It has an appearance similar to the louse which infests our rose trees, but it is of a blood red colour. The female is wingless and viviparous, and when very young is of a pale red, narrow, and flat. When arrived at maturity it is of a dark red, or more inclined to a brown, of an oval shape, covered with filaments and white powder; there are two rows of tubercles along the back. It has short thick legs, four jointed antennæ, setaceous, and about a quarter the length of the body; the rostrum extends to a little beyond the hind coxæ. The male is said to be a small black fly; and though my utmost endeavours were put forth I was unsuccessful in proving whether it was so or no. According to an authority this insect produces eleven broods of young in the course of a single season. The first ten broods are viviparous, and consist entirely of females. These never attain their full development as perfect insects, being only in the larvæ state, they bring forth young, and the virgin aphides thus produced are endowed with similar fecundity. But at the tenth brood this power ceases. The eleventh brood does not consist of active female larvæ alone, but of males and females; these acquire wings, rise into the air, sometimes migrate in countless myriads, and produce eggs, which glued to twigs and leaf stalks retain their vitality through the winter. When the advance of spring again clothes the plants with verdure the eggs are hatched, and the larva, without having to wait for the acquisition of its mature and winged form, as in other insects, forthwith begin to produce a brood as hungry and insatiable and as fertile as themselves. Supposing that one aphis produced 100 at each brood, she would at the tenth brood be the progenitor of one quintillion of descendants

1,000,000,000,000,000,000. They were first discovered in England in 1787, in France in 1812, and in Belgium in 1829.

Another of the most numerous tribes of insects is that of the aphides or plant bugs: they belong to the Hemipteræ, to the group in which is included the Cicadidæ, Cimicidæ, &c. They form a very wide and interesting field for research, as the genus is a very extensive one, the species of which are so little known. In this climate there is hardly a plant but what has its own particular aphis. They assume various colours, but that is somewhat accounted for by the qualities of the juices upon which they live. The aphis infesting the rose tree is green, that on the tansy is red, and the field bean presents us with a black specimen. Now all these and many others are probably the same species, and perhaps the same insect. Their provincial names are collier lice, black shrimps, &c. Gilbert White calls them "smother flies." In the autumn of 1865 they were unusually abundant, causing great havoc among the cauliflower and other greens in the garden: this was the aphis rapæ or vestator.

The bug flies have long and large antennæ, with wings thick where joined to the body, but transparent at the extremities, feet three jointed, and with legs formed for running only. They feed and fatten upon the sap of the plants upon which they live, which sap they procure with a sharp and pointed rostrum. Reamur discovered that the punctures made by these insects when in sufficient quantity not only exhausted the plants but gave rise to nodular swellings and to alteration of the tissues, and it is recorded that the langier plant bug (Lachnus langier) which attacks apple trees, has on more than one occasion destroyed the plantations of Normandy. It was first discovered in England in 1787. One reason of the abundance of these smother flies is that they are produced by animalcular generation, and their fecundity is astonishing. Those most common are to be found on rose trees, and being of a light green colour are hardly discernible from the tender shoots and stalks; they have long wavering and tapering antennæ, with transparent wings, feet with two joints, and legs formed for running.

The turnip fly, or beetle, next took my attention as making havoc among my radishes, cabbages, etc. I found the fly chiefly feeding on the seminal leaves. Very little is known of the economy of this insect, as like other beetles it passes the first three stages of its life below ground, and comes forth as the heat of the summer advances; this is the great pest of the farmer, sometimes devastating his turnip crops, and it is astonishing how soon a field of ten or twelve acres is eaten off; its scientific name is Haltiàca oberàcea.

Another very common insect to be met with in our gardens is the sawfly, specimens of which I found on the cherry and pear trees, which I afterwards discovered to be of the genus Athalia, but had the misfortune to lose my specimens, and so can do nothing but name them.

A beautiful specimen of saw fly I found on a gooseberry tree of a green colour, but of this last I found but one specimen, and have never since met with any others. On the hedge which skirted the garden at the bottom I found the great saw fly (Urocenes gigas), and had splendid opportunity of observing it at its work depositing its eggs; feeling with its beautiful yellow antennæ for the soft spot, and having found it began drilling the desired cavity; the operation took about twenty minutes, during which time it worked almost without cessation, its feet were six jointed, four transparent wings, clear and glittering, a uniform body covered with down, and with its ovipositor it looks quite a formidable insect.

With this notice I must bring these remarks to a close, hoping in my next to continue my excursion round my garden. GEORGE DAY.

36, Chapel Street, Pentonville.

NOTES OF A NATURALIST IN NOVA SCOTIA.

BY J. MATTHEW JONES, F.L.S.

(Author of "The Naturalist in Bermuda.")

THE BLACK FLY AND MOSQUITO.

(*Simulium molestum*) *and* (*Culex pipiens*.)

THROUGH the whole extent of the forests of Nova Scotia, during the months of June, July, August, and September, there are no greater enemies to the comfort of man or beast, than the black-fly and mosquito. The sportsman in quest of trout or salmon, arrives on the bank of some goodly stream, and leisurely draws from the pockets of the cover, each section of his trusty rod. The reel is adjusted, the line run through each ring, and last, the light cast with its gaudy-coloured flies, floats on the breeze. Barely has he time to make a throw over that tempting little pool beneath the grey granite boulder, where the froth is dancing merrily round, than something like a sting on the back of the neck causes one hand to hasten to the spot; but no sooner has the first intruder on the peaceful pleasure of the fisherman been demolished, than every portion of his neck where the hair is not covered by the hat, is attacked and bitten by that terrible little pest the black-fly. Scratch and rub, rub and scratch—"Ah! there's a good rise; one more cast and I have him, bother the black-flies. There he is again, confound the black flies. I've got him, hang the black-flies." Up goes the hand for a scratch, and down goes the rod, and off riggles the crimson-speckled two-pounder, and soon the wearied sportsman follows, leaving his dipterous enemies in full possession of the ground. The scene depicted is no uncommon one, and occurs any day during the summer. Indeed, many a time and oft, has some luckless traveller through the forest, particularly if a few days of damp foggy weather occurs, to travel in haste to reach a settlement, in order to escape being actually driven into a fever by the attacks of thousands of black-flies and mosquitoes, the former by day, and the latter principally by night. Blackflies generally make their appearance in the forest about the first week in May, and should the summer prove a moist one, they become very numerous. If the reverse, however, be the case, and a season of great drought occurs, then the black-fly is not nearly so troublesome. Although fond of heat and moisture, they will survive through eight degrees of frost, and after this degree of cold has been experienced, I have known them to appear again on the first day of November in numbers, when a warm day succeeded the cold spell.

The mosquito also appears about the same time as the black-fly, and frequents the same situations; low, damp spots being evidently preferred to those high and dry. It does not stand the cold as well as the black-fly, and a sharp frost in October generally puts an end to its existence. It is abundant during the warmer months all over the North American Continent, even as far north as latitude 67 deg.

Many have been the antidotes manufactured for the relief of the sportsman and traveller against the attacks of these troublesome creatures. Bottles of nauseous liquids entitled "Angler's Defence," have been concocted from various ingredients; essence of lemon, oil of cloves, essence of peppermint, combined with essential oils of the most pungent odour, have each alike been tried with but partial success; and even the disgusting and peculiarly offensive smelling kerosene and paraffin oils have been smeared over the hands, face, and neck, but to little purpose, for in a few minutes the thirsty suckers, emboldened by the love of blood, come buzzing around again, and commence with renewed vigour.

One half, if not the whole charm of a ramble in the forest in summer time, is lost by the pain produced by the incessant attacks of these two well known insects. In open districts, cleared of timber and under cultivation, they cease to annoy, and, doubtless, as the country becomes more settled and cleared, their numbers will decrease, at least it is to be hoped so.

When encamped in the forest, the only plan to drive them away is to make a large fire close by, and piling on green moss and weeds, to produce smoke sufficient to oust them from the immediate neighbourhood, and as long as this stifling state of existence can be endured, the weary sportsman or naturalist can repose at ease; but no sooner do the fumes cease to fill the camp and its surroundings, than Messrs. Black-fly and Mosquito are at it again.

ON THE BRITISH GEOMETRÆ.

By E. CLIFFORD.

PART IV.

OUR Geometræ exhibit in a wonderful manner that design in Creation which ever strikes the earnest and thoughtful student of Nature. Our readers will, if acquainted with the species that are noticed, have observed how infinitely varied are their markings, and the lines and shades of their colouring. And whilst there are many kinds which might be considered by the careless to be identical, yet there exists some slight variation, which serves to separate species from species, and thus produce an arrangement which is really full of interest and wonder. Well has it been remarked, that no human ingenuity could ever invent such a multitude of patterns as we find upon the wings of these lovely insects, nor could any human taste so dispose colour as to produce similarly harmonious results. God alone could thus form and fashion the most despised of the animal creation; and whilst we remember that He is the artist, and that His power has evoked the beauty of the insect tribes, we may well wonder that they should be regarded with such apathy by the generality of individuals.

Our last paper concluded the family of the BOARMIDÆ, in which were many of our most striking Geometræ. Next we come to a family in which is only one English representative, this is the BOLETOBIDÆ. The only species which we have is the Waved Black (*Boletobia fuliginaria*), and it seems indeed doubtful whether this has any right to be considered a native. The species is named in Doubleday's list; and it is also said that three specimens have been taken in London. The caterpillar feeds on the fungi which grow on timber, and it is probable that these specimens were introduced to our island with some timber that was imported from abroad, in the state of chrysalis. The perfect insect is smoky brown in colour, bordered with a zigzag black line; the head, thorax, and body grey. The GEOMETRIDÆ is the next family under notice, containing the Emerald moths, a truly singular class of insects. The first is the Grass Emerald, in science (*Pseudoterpna cytisaria*). The fore-wings are grey-green, and possess two transverse lines of a darker hue, one straight, and the other zigzag; these are widely separated at the outer margin, but close together at the inner margin. The hind-wings are paler than the fore-wings, and the head, thorax, and body are the same colour as the wings. A singular circumstance connected with this species is, that when it emerges in wet weather from the chrysalis, every part is suffused with a reddish tinge. The caterpillar of the Grass Emerald is of a similar colour with the moth itself, and its head is notched on the crown. It feeds on the common broom, that grows so plentifully on our heathlands; and it is on this account that the moth itself is so common in such places. It flies rather swiftly during daytime, if beaten from its retreat amongst the bushes. June is the month in which to search for the caterpillar, July for the perfect insect.

All of the Emeralds are more or less conspicuous from their green hue, but the next species is particularly so. It is a noble insect, and rightly named the Large Emerald (*Geometra papilionaria*). The wings are all uniformly green, and the fore-wings have two transverse white waved lines, which are rather indistinct. Between these two lines is a crescent-shaped dark green mark, and beyond the second white line is a series of white spots. The hind-wings have a scalloped line passing across the middle, dividing the wing in half. The antennæ of the male are fringed, those of the female threadlike. The caterpillar of this moth is large, of a greenish colour, and possesses numerous humps. It feeds on hazel, and a few other trees, and is found in the month of May. The moth occurs in July, and is still tolerably common in some parts of our old Kentish woods, where it may be seen resting high up amongst the boughs of the oak and birch. Our next species is one that is specially confined to the Essex coast. Hence it has obtained the name of the Essex Emerald (*Geometra smaragdaria*). It has been found in July, and is a beautiful insect. The wings, which are all green, have whitish lines and markings, and the outer margin of the fore-wings is tinged with yellow. The caterpillar occurs in May, but has only been captured in the locality indicated. In June the Small Grass Emerald (*Nemoria viridata*) is on the wing, but chiefly confined to the west and north of England. The colouring is very beautiful. The wings are all of a dingy green, often suffused with a reddish tinge, the fore-wings with a whitish line beyond the middle, and a second shorter one nearer the base, which is frequently wanting. The caterpillar feeds on the whitethorn, and occurs in September, according to some of our entomological writers.

Perhaps the commonest of our Emerald moths in the south is the Small Emerald (*Iodis vernaria*), a singularly delicate insect, with wings of a lovely green hue. The fore-wings have two white transverse lines, the hind-wings one. A peculiar fact connected with this species is the manner in which the female deposits her eggs. Unlike other moths, she does not lay them side by side upon a flat surface; but having fastened one to a twig, she piles one over the other until twelve or fourteen stand out like a thorn or spur from the surface of the stem. The caterpillar of this insect feeds on the traveller's joy, and is of a greenish hue. Equally common with the last named, if not more abundant, is the Little Emerald (*Iodis lactearia*). When first emerged from the chrysalis this moth is of a lovely green hue, but mostly we find the specimens caught to be of a uniform white colour. The wings have two transverse waved lines, which are of a white colour. The caterpillar of this little insect is an oak feeder, hence the moth is particularly abundant in some of our oak woods. It has a long and slender body, and the second segment of this has two sharp-pointed humps very near together on the back. The caterpillar is full-fed about the middle of September; and, after spinning a few threads across the leaves of its food-plant, it becomes a chrysalis in the home thus formed. It remains a chrysalis throughout the winter, and is transformed into a moth a little before midsummer.

The Blotched Emerald (*Phorodesma Cajularia*) is the next species under notice. The wings of this moth, like those of the preceding species, are green, and the fore-wings have two slender white lines; and near the anal angle is a pale blotch of an irregular shape. The hind-wings have a large pale spot at both angles. The head is white, and the body and abdomen whitish-green. We have never seen the caterpillar of this beautiful moth, but some of our authors describe it as of a wainscot-brown colour, with a red head. It feeds on oak, and occurs in May; the moth flying about midsummer. We conclude the Emeralds by noticing the Common Emerald (*Hemithia thymiaria*), which is one of the most beautiful of the tribe. It flies in June and July, and is plentiful in oak woods, upon which tree the caterpillar feeds. The wings of this moth are of a dingy green, and have a dull appearance when compared with those of the lustrous species noticed; yet they are exceedingly beautiful, and their attractiveness is increased by the transverse white line that runs across them. The fringe of the wings is white, spotted with brown, and the thorax and body are both green.

Our next family is a very interesting one. It contains six species, some of which must have come under the notice of most of our insect-collecting readers. The Mochas are all very delicate little moths, occurring principally in our woods, and they may be captured by beating in the daytime. The caterpillars are very singular little creatures, and the chrysalides peculiarly delicate. Little, however, can be said concerning them, for they are not as yet thoroughly understood, even by our best authors, who are unable to distinguish the caterpillar of one kind from that of another, so nearly do they resemble each other. The False Mocha (*Ephyra porata*) is the first on the list. It is a beautiful little creature, of a dullish red colour. In very perfect specimens the red is brick-dust colour in the middle of the wing. A transverse brown line crosses the middle of each wing; and just within this, nearer the base of the wing, is a round white spot with a narrow border. The caterpillar of this species feeds on oak. The chrysalis is either green or buff, with a blunt head; and it is found fastened to a leaf by a belt of silk, in a similar manner to that adopted by some of our butterflies. In autumn we should search for the greenish looper which produces this moth, which occurs in May and June, and is common in the southern counties. The Maiden's Blush (*Ephyra punctaria*) also occurs in May. Its wings are dull red, with a redder tinge about the middle of the wing, across which there is a transverse brown line. The caterpillar of this species, as that of the last, is an oak feeder, and occurs in the autumn months. It should be stated that this moth very closely resembles the preceding; from which, however, it may be readily distinguished by the total absence of a round white spot, present in the other, on each wing.

The Clay Triple-lines (*Ephyra trilinearia*) is the next under notice. All the wings of this little moth are of a fulvous yellow, and have no tinge of red; there are three transverse lines on each wing, and it is from this circumstance that the species derives its name. The caterpillar of this moth is reddish-brown, with yellow markings, and feeds on beech, according to some writers. It is found in autumn, and the moth in May or June. The Common Mocha (*Ephyra omicronaria*) is a beautiful little moth, not uncommon in the woodlands of our southern counties. The wings are whitish fulvous, with a double smoke-coloured line running in a transverse direction across the middle of each. The caterpillar is described as green, with two yellow stripes on each side, and is said to feed on the maple. The Common Mocha occurs in May and June. On the sallow in July we may search for the delicate little caterpillar of the Dingy Mocha (*Ephyra orbicularia*). All the wings of this little insect are smoky grey, mottled, and marbled with darker markings of a similar colour. In the centre of each wing is a round white spot, in a circle of smoky grey. The moth is common in our southern counties in June. The last of this family is the Birch Mocha (*Ephyra pendularia*), a species occurring not unfrequently in Birch Wood, Kent. The colouring of the wings is pale-grey, sprinkled over with specks of smoke colour. In the middle is a round white spot, surrounded by a smoke-coloured cloud, and between this spot and the base of the wing is a transverse row of dots. The antennæ of the Birch Mocha are slightly fringed in the male, threadlike in the female; the head, thorax, and body are of a similar colour with the wings. In June and July the caterpillar may be found feeding on the birch, the moth appearing on the wing in May or June. And thus we conclude our present, reserving for a future paper the large family of "Waves:" delicate little creatures, whose wings are so tender and slight that one rarely can capture them without robbing them of their pristine beauty and elegance.

New Books.

The Naturalist in Norway; or, Notes on the Wild Animals, Birds, Fishes, and Plants of that Country; with some Account of the Principal Salmon Rivers. By Rev. J. Bowden, LL.D., Author of "Norway; its People, Products, and Institutions;" "Guide to Norway," &c. London: L. Reeve and Co.

Were we about to make a tour throughout Europe, at the present time, no country would have for us a greater amount of interest than the Western half of the Great Scandinavian Peninsula. Independently of the pictures raised in the mind's eye of the traveller of the old fierce gods of former years, worshipped by the warlike sea kings, Thor, Odin Friga, and others, and later, ever since the introduction of Christianity, of the sprites and tutelar deities guarding flood and fell, mount and fjord, ready to avenge every fancied insult or neglect, the whole country teems with objects of interest for the artist, tourist, naturalist, or sportsman. Of the two first-named it is not our province to speak. The Norwegian scenery with its snow-capped mountains, calm lakes, and rushing streams, must be seen to be appreciated; no description of ours can sufficiently do it justice. To the naturalist, however, the present work will prove, we believe, extremely welcome, while the sportsman will find many useful hints on the game, water-fowl, and fishing, which are well worthy of attention. Dr. Bowden is a naturalist of no mean pretensions, and, it is evident, is a thorough master of his subject, by the systematic and orderly way in which he treats it. We remember seeing works of a somewhat similar kind, in which all the subjects were mixed together in a heterogeneous mass, and rendered almost unintelligible; we are glad, therefore, to see the scientific way in which our author treats his subjects. After a short summary of the game laws of Norway (which we may remark by the way are very mild,) and its wild animals generally, the brown bear (*U. Arctus*) forms the subject of the first chapter. This animal is still found in considerable numbers in all parts of the country, but more especially in the central districts. The Norwegian peasants have a superstition, when bear hunting, of never alluding to that animal by his usual name, but always speak of him as "the Old Man with the fur coat," "The Wise One," "Uncle Benjamin," and so on, considering it the height of ill luck were any person to mention him by his proper name. This custom, however, Dr. Bowden does not allude to. The next chapter is devoted to the Lynx and Wild Cat; the work then proceeds with descriptions of the Reindeer, Elk, Wolf, Badger, Ermine, and Lemming, with many others *quæ nunc prescribere longum est*. The most remarkable animal described is the Lemming, a little gregarious rodent peculiar to Norway; we can hardly say this, however, with truth, for the only thing that can be said about it, is, that it appears in immense hordes in Norway at stated intervals, coming no one knows exactly whence, most probably from the country of the Lapps, and going no one knows where. From the ravages committed by these little pests during their migration, they are held in the utmost dread by the peasantry; indeed, in former years a solemn fast-day was annually observed and prayers offered that the invasion might be averted, while a long form of exorcism or anathema was thundered forth in Latin by the priest against the offending animals. A copy of this exorcisim is given by the author. In addition, however, to Dr. Bowden's own researches, he has materially added to the amusement of his work by giving us the notes and observations of Ponloppidan, Bishop of Bergen, who wrote and flourished about the middle of the 18th century, and another ancient scribe, Olaus Magnus by name, who lived about the same time or rather earlier. Both of these worthies seem to have been students of nature, though in a rather eccentric manner, and they give the most wondrous anecdotes of the animals of their country. It is curious to observe the immense amount of credulity displayed by these men, though far more educated than their fellows, surrounded by people steeped, so to speak, in superstition and ignorance, sometimes struggling against the popular notions of the day, and often believing in the monstrous inventions and stories that were told them. To be a naturalist in those days, and in a country so imbued with old prejudices and fables handed down through many a long generation, and hitherto faithfully believed in, required no slight strength of mind, and an earnest desire to get at the exact truth. We can hardly judge of these old writings from the few and slight extracts Dr. Bowden has given us, as they are chiefly anecdotes shewing the light in which the Norwegians viewed the character of each animal, they give, however, a very enlivening and pleasant air to the work.

After discussing the animals, we come at length to the birds. As may be almost expected, their great numbers allow but very little space to be devoted to each species; but though small in space as this portion of the book is, it is rich in matter, giving the habitat and distribution of nearly every genus. Beginning with the birds of prey, including eagles, hawks, and owls, which are very numerous, we then come to the feathered game, which has a separate chapter devoted to its description. With the exception of the red grouse the *Tetraonidæ* found in Britain, are common in Norway also. The partridge is not very common, but has been found in the neighbourhood of Christiana. The Capercaillie, Black Grouse, Alpine Grouse, White Grouse, and Hazel Grouse, with one or two hybrids occasionally found, are pretty numerous; but as Dr. Bowden observes, "there is not much shooting here, and the sportsman considers himself fortunate when he bags his ten or fifteen brace of birds in a single day. He will have to go far and fare roughly before he can ever succeed in doing that, but the healthy exercise and fine mountain air to be had in Norway, are so invigorating to the constitution, that no true sportsman will regret the time, trouble, and expense which a sojourn in this country has cost him." The waterfowl next engage our attention; wild geese are numerous, and are hunted and captured in the most primitive manner. We have, however, no time or space to go into the details of the different species and their peculiarities; our readers cannot do better than read it themselves. The fisheries engage numbers of people, and are highly important. We have a capital account of the customs of the inhabitants regarding the consumption of their favourite food. The coarser and larger fish are eaten by the lower classes only, or exported, while in some towns the fish is brought to the door alive; so that the purchaser has no need to make use of the usual olfactory test of its freshness. The author mercilessly sweeps away what remans of the exaggerated powers of the Mahlström. He states that during winter storms, or even when a strong gale in summer is blowing, it is not safe to go into the channel, but with a fair wind, and in fine weather, there is no danger. There is no vortex, although ships caught in the current may be drifted on to the rocks. So little, he goes on to say, is thought of the Mahlström by the hardy northern mariners who are acquainted with it, that the frail barks of the country pass and re-pass at all states of the tide, except under the above circumstances. Small boats actually fish in the centre of the channel, and so far from its drawing in great whales, the fish sport about in the current, and experienced fishermen knowing this, lay down their lines there. The fresh water as well as sea fishing is excellent, and the prices ridiculously small. Last but not least comes a long list of the Alpine Flora of Norway and the places where each species is to be found. The Norwegian ferns also are added to this list, which we are sure will be welcome to many a botanist. We need say but little more respecting this capital little work. Although the actual natural history of the work will not be found new or very original to the reader—and we cannot wonder much at that—the peculiarities and various characteristics of the animals are brought forward pleasantly and agreeably. The anecdotes of the superstitions of the peasantry which, as may be imagined, are pretty numerous, are amusingly told, and mingle well with more sober description; indeed our readers will appreciate our remarks when we say that the style is similar to that of the Rev. J. G. Wood, with whose felicitous descriptions and anecdotes most of our readers are no doubt familiar. We must, however, confess to feeling some disappointment in not finding a single word about the entomology of Norway—we beg pardon—we *are* told that owing to the extent of woodland coleoptera were numerous. But when we consider how completely and entirely the insect world is bound up in the rest of animated nature, and what a vast influence it has on the whole creation, we were surprised that so thorough and earnest a naturalist as our author should have omitted this important part of animal life. Dr. Bowden. however, knows, or ought to know best. We do not find his intention mentioned of saying anything on entomology, and certainly he has stuck to his text, so that perhaps we have no right to complain. Perhaps we are asking too much from one who has given us so much information and amusement already, so we will say no more, merely regretting this important omission, and thinking that a chapter or two devoted to this subject would by no means have been thrown away. The work is adorned with a few lithographs, but with one or two exceptions, the less said about them the better.

Correspondence.

[*Under this head we shall be glad to insert any letters of general interest.*]

BIRD MURDER.

Sir,—A modern Greek proverb tells us "Ena kalon biblion enai o kaleteros filos," it may be that a good book is the best friend, hence I cannot quarrel with your correspondent's signature at page 83 as far as constancy to the N. N. B. extends, the only thing is that it proves that however excellent he may be as a *reader*, he certainly is not a "constant" worker in the fair fields of science, else he would never have made some of the observations he has favoured us with.

As far as the first paragraph is concerned it is entirely a matter of legal interest as to how far any Act will stay the hand of the wrong-doer against whom it is levelled. I opine, therefore, that "gentlemen sportsmen" (having money) and persons in the plume trade (having a living to get) will evade any law, however cleverly worded, by their love of sport or by the exigencies of the situation. As far as gentlemen are concerned, no one deserving that title would willingly be cruel if the pros and cons were pointed out to them of the misery their sport entails upon thousands of unfortunate young birds, whose parents have been shot and have left them to die of horrible starvation. The plumassiers as a body are entirely in the hands of fashion. Direct your act, say I, against the ladies; against those ethereal creations " of the period," who not content with ravaging the Orient for little glittering stones to wear in hair or adorn their white fingers—taking their hair from unknown plebian sources that they may pile it in "chignonatic" profusion on the back of their empty little noddles—despoiling the lowly worm of its intestines to weave into a fabric to enhance their prismatic repertoire of beauty; slaying the savage tiger (through the slight aid of their minion-man) to cover up their delicate claws—no, paws—hang it! no I mean hands and arms, from the severe cold when riding in the "Row," the "Bois," the "Platz," or the thousand and one places where folly shoots time upon the wing; wresting the perfume from flowers and the colour from a species of bug to scent and paint up their persons; killing, maiming, or wounding nature by thefts from the animal, mineral, or vegetable kingdoms, or peering into earth, fire, or water for a "new sensation" in dress or ornament—now press the denizens of the free air into their service to help to cover up the highly cultivated and elevated portion of their anatomy. What rubbish then to threaten vengeance against the plume trade when it is the sweet and tender-hearted ladies, or as some one savagely calls them the "whim-men," who cause all the "Bird Murder" and its attendant cruelties. Appeal to the ladies then to give up wearing plumes for their hats, grebe skins for their necks, and feather fans, and as they are sure not to give up any fashionable idea, why not serve them all with an attachment (a legal one I mean) and make it penal servitude for life (no ticket of leave being allowed) to wear any article made up of birds' feathers. (I expect a handsome testimonial from the great henpecked for this relieving suggestion).

"Constant Reader's" second paragraph is easily answered. In the first place Ornithologists cannot collect in winter for various reasons, one of which is that the very birds which possibly may be required for study are not forthcoming then. Certainly he gets out of this difficulty in an ingenious, if singular, manner, for he says you can "go to Scotland to the Bass Rock for instance" to shoot. I rather like this idea; it is as his satanic majesty observed—speaking of his recherché and pea-green tinted tail—"neat but not gaudy," and opens up the novel supposition that although it may be the height of unnecessary cruelty to slaughter breeding rock-birds off Flamborough Head, Yorkshire, England; yet if you can go to the Bass Rock, Scotland, the same thing there is perfectly justifiable; a sort of reasoning which as they say at dinners,—does equal credit to his head and his heart.

The gay and airy manner in which your contributor casually mentions that ornithologists can prosecute their studies without a gun convinces me at once that "memories of childhood's happy days" tinge his romantic mind with melancholy, and speak to him of those trusting moments when belief in the salt box and its marvellous power over the minds, shall we say tails, of the dicky-birds, had not been shaken by the oft-attempted and never successful trials to ensnare them by its aid. Mythology tells us how Orpheus playing on his lute attracted around and about him all the birds of the air. Alas! we have not that gift now, and as it is an imperative necessity that birds should be procured for study, and as nothing better than the gun has been invented to persuade them to come and be studied, why I cannot at present see any other way (as Mr. Weller says) " of perwailin on em to stop."

I am, Sir,
Yours, etc.,
A. W. B.

ANSWERS TO CORRESPONDENTS.

A. H. MALAN.—Your letter and paper arrived too late for insertion in this Number. All communications should be sent by the 15th of the month; we are put to great inconvenience by receiving letters up to the 23rd. We are anxious to get as many as possible in, and at times it throws us much behind.

A. E. BUTTERMERE.—On protection of sea-fowl. R. S. and A. H. Ramworth: see answer to A. H. Malan.

V. B. LEWIS.—Not room for your list in present Number. Will appear in next.

Remarks, Queries, &c.

(*Under this head we shall be happy to insert original Remarks, Queries, &c.*)

DO INSECTS FEEL PAIN?

"Nothing contributes more to the advancement of science than controversy."

Permit me to examine the portable bundle of small assertions, and still smaller imperatives, so dexterously cast into our forum by the inimitable Mr. W. H. D.

Assertion No. 1. "Ulidia has hitherto adduced no argument whatever to show that insects feel pain."

Assertion No. 2. "Nor has Ulidia attempted to refute any of the arguments of the negative side." Such smooth assertions so politely uttered remind me that some of the ancients sent their heroes through the apertures whence proceed delightfully delusive dreams, and I cannot but surmise that our scientific friend is a recently arrived logician—all poetic—and indulging in the balmy sweets of the enchanting pleasures of imagination. What is on both sides written remains, and to save the tedium of recapitulation, I in all candour submit the whole of the correspondence to the reconsideration of Mr. W. H. D., and with patience await any new assertion he may think fit to make. "Half dead with anger and surprise," I pass rapidly to assertion No. 2, for surely it is a more palpable mistake than even the first assertion, for here he announces that I have "not attempted to refute any of the arguments on the negative side?"

Surely these are some of his own "unfortunately chosen expressions," at which he says I so eagerly grasp. Now, to attempt to refute an argument and to actually refute an argument are two really distinct things, but Mr. W. H. D. asserts that I have not even *attempted* to refute!

If any other correspondent of the "N. N. B." entertain such opinions, then indeed are my arguments, etc., compressed into a real nonentity—a small portion of nothing at all.

Now let us take the "bit of cobbler's-wax experimental philosophy," so argumentatively put by Mr. W. H. D. Who would think of replying to an argument so palpably absurd?

Does he wish us to take it for granted that the constituent parts of our pantaloons are a nervose tissue? To any professor of broad-cloth anatomy I appeal. Or does he wish to deprive us of those *alamode* essentials of civilised life? He does not tell.

Mr. W. H. D. comes out in the imperative, orders me to refute the arguments of my opponents, or instantly say I cannot.

Have patience, Mr. W. H. D., for as you are so charitable as to "suppose me to be a rational being," I know you will assist me in unravelling the following rather knotty argument contained in Mr. John Landel's "*second* and *last*" letter:—"Animals do feel a certain amount of pain. I will add to this, however, that I do not think the amount of pain they feel is anything like equal, even proportionally, to that which the *higher animals* and *men* experience!"

Here I ask the indulgence of Mr. W. H. D. when I candidly confess my total inability to understand this argument: see what a profound jumbling together of animals, higher animals, and men.

How truly, indeed, does Montaigne say, "Everybody is subject to say foolish things; the misfortune is to say them *coriously*."

Mr. W. H. D., with a literary sigh, regrets that I "load with ridicule the unfortunately chosen expressions (absurd arguments) of my antagonists." In order to console your correspondent, I beg to tell him that Mr. Mill says, "ridicule, argument, and acceptance, are the three stages through which doctrine must pass."

So, if the painless theory is right, it must surely survive my "loads of ridicule."

Do insects feel pain? The longer and more attentively I study this interesting problem in natural history, the more truly am I convinced that insects do feel pain. In all my previous letters I have preferred arguing from general principles rather than from particular experiments. The correspondents on the negative side seem to lay great stress on the tenacity of insect life, as that were an argument against their susceptibility of pain, and hence we are in the cause of science treated to a series of minor cruelties, such as the pinning, boiling, scalding, decapitation, and bisection of insects.

Here let us pause, and quietly consider the matter.

Now where a mutilation of parts may seem to cause little or no pain, and where the insect has the power of reproducing those parts, and also when there is great tenacity of life, then, if you will, an obtuseness of feeling so far and for a time may be inferred; but by what parity of reasoning can a total absence of all pain be affirmed? Most certainly I know not; and if the advocates of the painless theory are in possession of the logical secret, I presume they are strongly resolved to keep it. It is well known that many kinds of insects are more difficult to kill in winter than in summer; and Dr. Drummond thinks that a change from a vigorous to a lower vital action may be the cause of superior tenacity of life.

But will any naturalist, will any man, presume to say that in this tenacity of life an absence of pain is implied, that in this strange tenacity of life the presence of pain is extinguished or expelled? Certainly not. Again, Montesquieu, in referring to the obtuse sensibility in the natives of the polar regions, says:— "If you would tickle, you must flay them!"

And again, Vancouver tells us that the natives of some northern countries suffer but little pain even from deep wounds, and that many of them will often amuse themselves in thrusting nails, sharp instruments, etc., into their feet. But surely this obtuseness of feeling in those inhabitants of the far north cannot be used as an argument that they are incapable of feeling pain.

See how the hare continues to run, and the pigeon continue to fly, after being mortally wounded—all only familiar examples of the tenacity of life.

That insects do feel pain, we may indeed draw an argument from the very actions of insects themselves. Ants have been known to inflict corporal punishment on refractory members of their own community, and as a corrective for some misdemeanour. This I argue they never would do if they were not, from experience and instinct, conscious that pain is the result.

Another argument to which I now appeal is—ailment is absolutely necessary for the preservation of animal life. The want or deprivation of this ailment we call hunger, and all must admit this to be anything but a pleasant sensation. The craving after food is common to all animal life from the great leviathan to the smallest insect, and we see all endeavouring to alleviate the pain arising from that most pressing of all burdens—an empty stomach. Surely such an argument is easily understood.

Again, I would respectfully draw the attention of Mr. W. H. D. to the fact that all, or nearly all, the correspondents on the negative side directly or indirectly admit and even argue that insects feel pain; and hence, having such admissions, I cannot see that I am called on to refute their numerous inconsistencies, which he so unthinkingly designates *arguments.*

And now a few words to Mr. W. H. D. He tells me to at once refute the arguments on the negative side, or admit my incapability. Ah! Sir, you are too impatient; you leave but little for future application, nothing for the tedious but ultimately omnipotent agency of study. Examine the sciences, see their slow development, look at inventions and discoveries, and think of the ages of creeping progress through which many of them passed. Science knows no such imperatives as you so dogmatically utter.

The solutions to problems in Natural History seldom start up spontaneously in one mind, they are more generally the aggregate of the application, observations, etc., of many minds, the labour of many pens.

Cast aside your assertions, your imperatives, your strange philosophy, and come out and help us, Mr. W. H. D.   H. H. ULIDIA.

I have been very much interested by the remarks of your numerous correspondents on this subject, and I wish, if you can afford me space, to say a few words on the side of those who take the negative view.

Let us first notice Mr. Bellingham's letter. He commences by telling us that he found, from some experiments he tried on one of the lowest forms of animal life (Actinia), that these creatures had the sense of feeling very acute. By a very active sense of feeling, I presume he means a feeling of pain. Would he kindly favour us with an account of some of his experiments; for though the results seemed so conclusive to him, they might not seem at all so to us.

In the next place he gives an account of a species of rotifer, which, being entangled with a minute fibre, struggled and writhed for about the space of an hour. And he says, "No argument was needed to convince me that this *point of life felt pain.*" It would require a very considerable amount of argument to convince me that the rotifer twisted itself about and writhed so violently because it was in pain. It seems much more reasonable to suppose that it made all these contortions in order to disentangle itself. It strikes me that if Mr. Bellingham were bound with a rope he would make great efforts and struggles to get free; and yet we should not be justified in saying that he felt any pain.

In the third place Mr. Bellingham tells us that a caterpillar, in whose body about thirty ichneumon grubs were being nourished, was very feeble on the occasion of its third moult, and that it died, curled up by the side of its old skin. "This caterpillar," he says, "was evidently a sufferer." Now I have had, among the numerous insects I have kept in captivity, many grub-infested caterpillars, and I have often seen and noticed carefully both the feebleness and also the curling up of the body, of which he speaks so pathetically. But I never considered either of them to be a sign of pain; nor can I now see any reason for so considering them. No one could expect a caterpillar to be anything else but feeble, after having supported, probably for the greater part of its life, a number of voracious grubs, which were continually feasting on the substance and juices of its body. And neither would any one expect such a caterpillar, if it felt any pain, to feed with the same capacity, and apparently find as much enjoyment in life as its more favoured brethren. No human being, I think, would have a very first-rate appetite, or feel very much pleasure in living, who had inside his body twenty or thirty worms constantly gnawing at his flesh, unless he felt no pain therefrom. And neither would a caterpillar. With regard to the curling up of the body of the insect I do not think it is necessary to speak, for I cannot see that it shows anything either in proof or disproof of a feeling of pain.

We come now to Mr. Dalton's letter, which I consider to be by far the best that has been written on the question under consideration. I hope that Mr. Dalton will continue to come forward and help us with his concise and forcible utterances. I entirely concur with him in the opinion, that until we can accurately determine the amount of concentration in the nervous matter which is necessary in order to a determined amount of feeling, and also can agree as to the degree of acuteness of feeling which constitutes that which we call pain, we shall not be able to convince each other satisfactorily, either one way or the other. I believe, however, that by careful observation and study both these things may be determined. I hope, therefore, that those of your correspondents who have facilities for such study and observation will thoroughly investigate the matter.

Mr. Landels' letter, though not very forcible, is, I think, a sufficient answer to Mr. Newberry's, except as regards the ravenous hunger, which Mr. Newberry tells us is sometimes caused in human beings by surgical operations performed on them. Concerning this, Mr. Landels candidly confesses that he is unable to give any opinion. I wish some of your correspondents would tell us what they think of it, especially as Mr. Ulidia gives an account in his letter of some horses at Waterloo and other battle fields, which seemed to be affected by their wounds in a way similar to that in which the human beings were affected by the surgical operations. I can only account for their eating so heartily under such strange circumstances, on the supposition that they experienced that numbness which Mr. Newberry says is invariably caused by extreme pain, and that their hunger was caused by the exhaustion consequent on their wounds in the case of the horses, and in that of the human beings on the operations they had undergone. I suppose, however, that both men and animals showed signs of pain afterwards. If I am right in my conjecture, first as to the numbness, and second as to the signs of pain after the numbness had passed, these stories have no force as disproving Mr. Landels' statement that his beetle must have felt very little or no pain, from all that it underwent; for in his second letter he says, that although he frequently afterwards "carefully watched the beetle, yet he saw nothing at any time which he could in any way construe into a sign of pain."

I agree with Mr. Landels in thinking, that though insects possess nerves, and therefore must also have feeling, yet their feeling may never be so acute as to amount to pain. I go further than he goes, however, for I think that the feeling of insects not only may not, but in reality does not, ever amount to a sense of pain.

Mr. Ulidia commences his letter with a most extraordinary argument. He says, "The most recent anatomy proves that insects have *digestive organs*, and hence, I conclude, that insects are susceptible of pain." I presume that Mr. Ulidia here refers to local pain of a particular kind, for I do not see how his words can possibly apply to pain in general, and if I am right in my conjecture, he might have expressed himself thus: "Insects have stomachs, and, therefore, I conclude that insects sometimes have the stomach-ache!"

I have before noticed what Mr. Ulidia says about the wounded horses, and though I have not specially mentioned the case of the French soldier, what I have said with regard to those who were surgically operated upon will apply equally well here.

I had intended to say something about Mr. Ulidia's January article, which he says remains unassailed, but I think I have already occupied sufficient space, and I will therefore now bring my long letter to a close. Before I do so, however, permit me say, that as Mr. Ulidia has observed, "we are friends at arms," and not enemies, and that in our remarks, however severe they may sometimes appear, we mean nothing personal. I hope, therefore, that in future Mr. Ulidia and others will avoid all personalities. I am sure our discussions will be carried on with greater pleasure and profit if we all observe this rule.

Hampstead.   JUSTITIAE AMOR.

Having seen in a paper by Mr. W. H. Dalton, in the March number of the NATURALIST'S NOTE BOOK, that insects are unable to appreciate pain, I again desire to bring forward my opinions upon this subject more extensively.

A nerve is a tube containing a liquid, or transparent substance, which acts as a conductor, so that when anything presses upon, or comes in contract with, a part of an animal who possesses a "nervous system," it causes a sensation; that is, the contact of the external object is vibrated along the nerve and transmitted to the brain or ganglion, which receives it, and as it were registers it. Mr. Dalton says that feeling or sensation "is simply a more or less rapid motion of the nerves." What he means by this I know not, unless it is that which I have just explained. Having thus seen what sensation is, we will now consider the question "do insects feel pain?"

I have already stated in my last paper upon this subject, that insects possess a nervous system. This is by no means found to be in a rudimentary form in them; and those correspondents who affirm that they feel pain only in proportion to their size are greatly mistaken in their opinion. By this theory they could prove that the whale can feel more pain than a man, merely because it is the larger of the two! But it depends upon the amount of *nerve matter* that creatures possess that determines their sensibility.

Therefore, knowing that insects possess a nervous system, and that pain is simply intensified sensation, consequently insects are capable of feeling pain. This I think, is as fair and logical an argument as can be made. Besides all this, I cannot see why persons should doubt the fact which has been known to scientific men for a long time. How is it possible that an insect which has a well-developed alimentary canal and such great powers of locomotion should be without nerves? Let us suppose an animal (I refer to the higher organic forms) to be deprived of its nervous system, and what is it? Destitute of feeling pleasure or pain, incapable of moving itself, unconscious of hunger, and moreover unable to enjoy any pleasure that it would otherwise have done, did it possess that attribute! We now see in what state an animal would be if it were devoid of nerves. In proof of the *great* sensibility of insects, I will relate a little incident which took place some short time ago. I happened one day to be standing at a window with a pen in my hand, and seeing a small gnat upon the glass, I touched one of its posterior feet with the feathery part, the little creature instantly flew off, thus proving indisputably that it was perfectly cognizant of the contact. To conclude my paper, I will extract a description of ganglia in insects from Rymer Jone's "Animal Kingdom," page 361 article (9 31)...... "As the growth of the larva goes on a change in the arrangement of the nervous system is perpetually in progress. The series of nervous cords connecting the different pairs of ventral ganglia in the larva become flexuous as the insect attains the pupa state; the whole chain becomes shorter; the brain or encepholic ganglion increases in its proportionate dimensions; and moreover, several ganglia originally distinct, coalesce and form larger and more powerful masses. . . . . In the imago, the concentration of the nervous centres is carried to that extent which is adapted to the necessities of the mature state."

This I hope will put an end to this controversy, which has, I think, been thoroughly proved.

VERITAS.

I send you these few lines not that I am desirous of going any further into the discussions of this vexed question, having already stated in former articles I have written my firm conviction that insects most certainly are susceptible of pain; and which, I say, has been the opinion of nearly all those who have taken part in this controversy. My object in writing now, is to ask your correspondents, and also the general readers of the "N. N. B," whether they do not think that it has been a most one-sided argument from the commencement? for such is my opinion, and will be of all, I firmly believe, who read over carefully what has already appeared on this question in the columns of the "N. N. B." All those gentlemen, with the exception perhaps of Mr. Spicer, who incorrectly call themselves belonging to the negative side, and who have written on the subject, have, I say, invariably contradicted themselves in their several letters, and finally have come to the most rational theory that insects *do* feel pain. I think this plainly shows how one-sided the argument has been throughout. If your correspondents want to argue, they should set to work, and "try" and find out whether insects experience much or little pain, for such, already appears to me to be the direction this controversy has tended, viz: not whether insects are susceptible of pain, but if they feel it to a great or little extent. But, here I would call the attention of your correspondents to what Mr. H. H. Ulidia has very justly said in his interesting January article—"Our present inquiry is not whether insects feel 'much' or 'little' pain, neither are we wanting to know if they feel as much pain as man, the whale, or the sparrow, etc., etc., but simply 'do insects feel pain?'" Mr. Landels thinks "that hitherto the advocates of the painless theory have had much the best of the argument." I should be much obliged to him, if he would inform me who these "advocates of the painless theory" are. Most certainly Mr. Landels is not one of them, for he goes on to say, "I rather incline to the opinion that insects do feel a certain amount of pain," therefore, I class him with the numerous band on the affirmative side of the question. In the February number of the "N. N. B.," "Veritas" very wisely says that he "cannot understand how any person can disagree about it." I think, Sir, with me you will agree that the opinions of your numerous correspondents are that "insects do feel pain."

Sidmouth. A. E. BUTTERMER.

This subject, which has been under the discussion of several of your correspondents for some months past, whose different opinions are as opposite as the poles of the earth, seems to verify a doubt on the subject. I for my part am not an advocate of the painless theory; for I suggest that when the Creator has endowed the insect with life, it is very natural that He will have endowed it also with properties fitting to make that life enjoyable. One of the properties which I have to speak of, is the sense of feeling in an insect. Do insects feel pain? I can come to no other conclusion than that pain is prevalent in their system, for when there is a nervous system acting within them, it is probable that when that system is assailed in a rough manner, it will produce pain on the insect in the same way that pain is produced on man, or any other animal. Look how the nervous system is illustrated in the butterfly when it is being chased by a bird. I have seen such a case as that, when a swallow has been in pursuit of a butterfly, how the butterfly has strained every nerve to escape from the clutches of his adversary; how it has flown first to one side of the bird, then to the other, to escape from death.

I maintain that an insect does feel pain, because I am assured by the following incident, which passed under my notice. One blustering summer day, while out for a walk, with the wind blowing strong from the western quarter, with occasional gleams of sunshine, I noticed the rapid approach of a bee borne along by the force of the blast; and, watching the progress of the bee, I saw it blown with violence against the church tower (as I happened to be in the churchyard at that time), and on running to the place, I found the bee so stunned by the force of the blow, as to be hardly capable of crawling about; and it was some moments before it recovered from the sensation, during which time there is no doubt the insect suffered pain.

I think Mr. Ulidia's argument will predominate in the course of time, when fresh facts ooze out from the pens of more skilful observers. J. F.

Mr. Ulidia has satisfactorily shown that pain does not destroy appetite, and consequently that the voracity of the bisected wasp is no proof that it did not feel pain. The argument of the negative side derived from this and similar instances is therefore overthrown. Still I cannot agree with Mr. Ulidia in his assertion that the hunger of which he speaks was due to agony. Was it not rather probably produced by loss of blood? The next argument which Mr. Ulidia has to overthrow is that derived from the anecdote on page 279: can he prove the presence of pain in that case? Next, the crepuscular moth not protesting against transfixion till it wanted to fly, will engage Mr. Ulidia's attention, and the painless detention hypothesis must be overthrown. Next, the unconcern of the cranefly for the loss of its limbs must be accounted for. And if Mr. Ulidia can overthrow all these arguments, he has after all still got to show not only that insects may feel pain, but that it is probable that they do so. The existence in insects of digestive organs, and of disease, has not, as far as I can see, any bearing whatever upon the question of "pain or only sensibility?"

Skipton. W. H. DALTON.

REASONING POWERS OF ANIMALS.

I certainly cannot understand the train of argument that your correspondent, "R. B. W." commences his paper with, for in it he has contradicted his previous opinion of this controversy, and also inclines to the belief that certain plants possess reason. He observes that an article on page 265 of Vol. 2 of the N. N. B. "goes far to prove this point." Now I saw nothing in that paper that in the least hints at reason in plants or anything approaching it; for all the phenomena described there are due to certain irritable tissues which contract under peculiar circumstances, and produce those curious maladies that the writer so naïvely and facetiously mentions. Again "R. B. W.," in advocating this, says, "although I stated that we observe reason in the actions of dogs, I said also that we observe it quite as clearly in plants. So we do, and often much sounder reasoning than many human beings can boast of; and for the good reason that it proceeds much more directly from the author of all reason." What can he mean by this? Does he suppose that because a plant is possessed of certain tissues, which in certain states and under some circumstances move in such a way as to alter the external appearance of the plant, that it reasons?

The reason he gives for this is singular enough. He says that "it is because it proceeds much more directly from the author of all reason." I conclude from this sentence and its context, at once so complex and significant, that "R. B. W." wishes to make out that the vegetable world ought by natural right to be placed above the animal world and even above man. This is evidently his meaning, for he especially draws our attention to it by saying that they often possess "sounder reasoning than many human beings can boast of."

While upon the subject of "Sensibility of Plants," I would advise "R. B. W." to read Structural Botany in "Orr's Circle of the Sciences," part 1, "Organic Nature." With this he will be better able to understand the wonderful and remarkable occurrences which he refers to.

Many persons even go so far as to say that it is impious to apply reason to animals, and that by doing so, it necessitates a soul as well! This is the popular idea, and it has existed for a long time. But it must be remembered that reason is a mental attribute. The word mental does not refer to man alone, but extends to the whole circle of animal life as well.

And what is an animal! It is in fact only a body endued with the divine influence which we denominate life. Therefore it is a most erroneous idea to suppose that man is the only creature endowed with a mind, and also that reason in the "brute" raises it to the same level with man. I will now go on to describe the great and marked difference that exists between reason and instinct, showing at the same time that the latter is not used in a vague sense, as some imagine. First—Any action that animals are not in the habit of performing regularly, and that evidently shows a train of thought is passing through their mind, and therefore an association of ideas, as it is termed, is taking place, may be at once put down as reason. Secondly—But when we see various actions done unhesitatingly and without forethought, with as much ease as if the animal had been in constant practice, then we have not the least doubt of its being instinct! If "R. B. W." will turn back to page 85, and read carefully the anecdote of the sexton beetle, he will clearly see that reason was the cause of its success.

First—Instinct compelled it to go under the mouse and attempt to bury it. Now that instinct was foiled on account of the hard ground; its faculty reason, which had hitherto remained dormant, now comes into play, and causes the beetle to seek for softer soil. Secondly—Having found this, it returns to the mouse, etc. It seems to me that this was as clear a proof of reason in this little creature as it would be in a man placed under similar circumstances. I will again quote that able and clever writer (Lardner) to prove that there is a certain amount of reason in the lower creatures. In Vol. viii. p. 139, of his "Museum of Science and Art," he gives the following anecdote, and appends his own views of it:—

"Gleditsch relates that one of his friends, desiring to dry the body of a toad, stuck it upon the end of a stick planted in the ground to prevent it from being carried away by the sexton beetle, which abounded in the place. This, however, was unavailing. The beetles having assembled round the stick surveyed the object and tried the ground, deliberately applied themselves to make an excavation round the stick; and having undermined it soon brought it to the ground."

"Now," says Lardner, "this proceeding indicates a curious combination of circumstances which it appears impossible to explain without admitting the beetles to possess considerable reasoning power and even foresight. The expedient of undermining the stick can only be explained by their knowledge that it was supported in its upright position by the resistance of the earth in contact with it. They must have known, therefore, that by removing this support, the stick, and with it the toad, would fall. This being accomplished, it may be admitted that instinct would impel them to bury the toad, but surely no instinct could be imagined to compel them to bury the stick; an act which could be prompted by no conceivable motive except that of concealing from those who might attempt to save the body of the toad from the attacks of the beetles, the place where it was deposited."

This is the view that Lardner takes of the subject of reason in animals; and he besides being deeply read in the natural sciences, was a deep thinker as well, and very impartial in his judgments. I am aware that this controversy, like many others of the same nature, is exceedingly difficult to decide, because that each side is perfectly sure that it is right, and the opposite wrong. But I feel almost certain that now the question has been so thoroughly proved and sifted, that very little more can be said on either side, as I hope it is proved beyond a doubt. VERITAS.

Allow me to make a few remarks on the very interesting subject of "the reasoning powers of animals," now under debate in the NATURALIST'S NOTE BOOK. I here start upon the hypothesis that only the vertebrated animals (and possibly not the whole of that large class) have reasoning powers, but that at any rate the mammalia and most likely also the birds are gifted to a certain extent with power of thought and of reason. Now it occurs to me that as man is a mammalian, that it is drawing rather *too* sharp a distinction between him and the other higher animals to say that they are totally devoid of "mind;" for notwithstanding that a great distinction should be made, no doubt, yet there is a medium in all things, and a medium also in this. And it is not at all in accordance with the whole system of nature to make sharp distinctions like this, for every thing in nature is done by the gradual blending of relationships, and not suddenly. So that we see a great difference in mental power between man and the other high vertebrates, and nearly as great a difference between them and the mollusca or other very low orders of animal existence, and another considerable difference between all animals and plants which, in all probability have no reason nor feeling at all. That this rule is not altered in this case (viz: man and the other vertebrated animals) is fully borne out by facts; for not only have dogs been taught a very great number of wonderful tricks, also the ways of the household, but they have also been taught to play at chess and dominoes, (see Wyatt's "The Dog") and jackdaws, magpies, and parrots have been known to do and say what must have been the result of thought. And another thing that goes a considerable way in favour of the affirmative side of this question is, that certain animals can appreciate music, that is if a simple and pathetic air be sung, or played on the flute, clarionet, oboe, etc., or any finely toned stringed instrument, they will at once show their pleasure in different ways. This is especially notable in some lizards, but also in other animals. I do not mean to say that they can understand at all elaborate music, or that any portion of Mendelssohn's "Reformation Symphony" would be anything else to them than what Chinese would be to many of us. But as they do appreciate simple airs in some degree, (and as music is only thought unfettered by words) I therefore conclude that they can think and therefore reason.

As to the story told by "C. R." about the gentleman who saw the birds break their shells on the stones, and one attempted to do so on the sand and found the attempt to be useless, I may say that I think many of the "species humanus" would do the same kind of action if they acted before they thought, and if they were short of common sense at all. I cannot coincide with Mr. W. H. Dalton, that when some members of species reason that it is *not* necessary that they all should do so, for I think that when such appears to be the case, it is because that the thought and reason is latent, and not absent altogether.

EARNEST BELFORT BAX.

THE SUN THE PRINCIPAL SOURCE OF HEAT.

In the N. N. B. for February and March, I notice a discussion between W. Newberry and others upon the interesting subject—"the source of heat." Will you allow me to remark, before stating my views, that, although W. Newberry's hypothesis, that the earth is the source of heat to us, appears to me wrong and contrary to facts, I cannot say that any of the persons who have written against his hypothesis have put the matter in a clear light, or have given any plain statements how the sun is the principal source of heat.

To say Mr. Newberry's ideas are absurd, or to say any schoolboy would have told him this or the other, is no more arguing the question than is saying we do get our heat from the sun, but how we know not.

Mr. Newberry and all his opponents will never see plainly, or understand how we get heat from the sun, until they throw overboard their assumption that a conductor of some kind or other is necessary for heat to be transmitted from the sun to the earth. Here is their grand mistake. Assuming that heat was conducted to the earth by a conductor, is the source of all their errors, and the true reason why they do not fully comprehend that the sun is the principal source of heat.

Let me now as briefly as possible state my views upon the subject. Heat is transmitted from the sun to the earth in rays (not conducted by a conductor) and travels at the same rate as light, viz., about 195,000 miles per second. Here perhaps Mr. W. Newberry, in support of his theory, may say heat rays coming from the sun to the earth, will heat the air through which they pass; therefore the air above, receiving heat before the air below, should be considerably hotter than the air below; but such is not the case, the air close to the earth being hotter than the air above; therefore the sun is not the principal source of heat.

To this I reply I do not think that heat rays from the sun, directly heat our atmosphere in the slightest degree, because there are certain bodies that allow all the rays of heat to pass through them, without retaining or absorbing a single particle.

Now, as one of these bodies is air, and as all persons admit there is more or less air between the sun and the earth, I hope all the writers in the NOTE BOOK on the source of heat will now perceive that the earth can be heated by heat rays from the sun, without the atmosphere being heated directly by heat rays.

But some one may say our atmosphere has a degree of warmth—that it is warmer close to the earth than on the top of a high spire—and warmer on the spire than on the top of a very high mountain. This I admit; but I maintain that heat rays heat the earth, the earth in its turn heating the air by contact. Air close to the earth becomes warmer by contact with the earth; this air rises, and its place is taken by colder air, and so it ever continues. The hotter the earth the hotter the air.

As all Mr. Newberry's opponents have told him why it is warmer in summer than in winter—although we are nearer the sun in winter than in summer—I will just say that all heat rays that fall on a body at an angle are reflected at the same angle, and only those that fall perpendicularly are absorbed: consequently heat rays falling on the earth more perpendicularly in summer than in winter, are more absorbed by the earth in summer than in winter; therefore the earth is hotter in summer than in winter. You cannot have the same amount of heat you otherwise would have, if when you receive a certain amount of heat, you at the same time throw a portion away, any more than you can have twelve pennies in your hand, if at the time you are receiving them three of them rebound and fall to the ground.

I will tell Mr. Newberry what I can do. I can take a burning glass and hold it between the sun and a piece of cotton wool on a clear summer's day, and directly the wool will begin to burn. Now, if Mr. Newberry will stand at the mouth of a coal pit (for this I suppose will be his best place to catch the heat coming from the interior of the earth); if he will stand I say at the mouth of a coal pit burning glass in one hand and cotton wool in the other; if when he holds the burning glass between the pit mouth and the cotton wool, he can by so doing burn that cotton wool, then I will admit that the earth is as great a source of heat to us as the sun.

I do not deny that we do not get a very slight degree of heat from the interior of the earth; but I maintain, and I think Mr. Newberry will admit after reading the above, that the sun is the principal source of heat to us.

Will "R. B. W." kindly give me some information about "the thin refined kind of air," which he says there is above the earth's atmosphere.

THE CALIPH OF BAGDAD.

I shall not attempt to answer the remarks of your correspondents in the "NATURALIST'S NOTE BOOK" for March, singly or in order, as that would take up more of your valuable space than is necessary, but shall at once proceed to offer my remarks on the subject itself. In the first place, your correspondents seem to think that I am advancing an entirely new theory of the source of heat, instead of taking up arms in defence of an old, though, I grant you, not a popular one; and some have fully made up their minds that the popular theory is so infallible, that they deem any dissension from it as only displaying the ignorance of the dissenter; but my own opinion is that there is no branch of science, not even astronomy, that is so perfect in its deductions as to leave little or no room for doubt. The principal objections raised by your correspondents against the theory of terrestrial heat are, the alternation of the seasons, and the excess of heat at the equator. Both these difficulties vanish before a little careful examination of the subject. "How," asks Mr. Bell, do I "reconcile the changes in the seasons" with my theory? I answer by the law of attraction. The same law that "holds the planets in their courses," and that once caused "an apple to fall," also causes the alternation of seasons. What is it that causes the earth to travel in a certain orbit round the sun but the power of attraction, the law of gravity? The same law, then, influences the distribution of heat. The heat after it has been generated in the earth (probably by the electricity which pervades every atom of the universe) is drawn from the earth by the attractive power of the sun, and warms the atmosphere immediately surrounding the earth, but as it rises higher gradually loses its power in the extension of its waves. Thus we find the heat will be much greater, and be drawn from the earth by a much greater force when *the attractive power of the sun* falls perpendicularly than when it falls obliquely, so causing the difference in intensity between summer and winter. The excess of heat at the equator is caused by a combination of the perpendicular action of solar attraction, and the rapid revolution of the earth on its own axis. Every one knows that the earth in revolving on its own axis has farther to travel in the same amount of time at the equator than it has at the poles, which necessitates a more rapid movement, and consequently a greater amount of heat. Your correspondent Gulielmus asks, "What proof have we that heat is communicated to the surface" of the earth "through the nonconducting crust?" Does your correspondent know anything of geology? Has he ever entered "the bowels of the earth and examined for himself the laws, *chemical* as well as *mineralogical*, which govern the properties of matter, and the formation of the earth's crust? If he has, I am surprised that such a question should result in his mind. I am sorry to find your correspondent relies so implicitly in his "school boy" teaching. The presence of perpetual snow on the mountain-tops seems to be a difficulty with Mr. Bell. This is explained, however, by the structure of mountains. Mountains having a direct communication with the earth's interior, such as volcanoes, either active or dormant, are seldom found covered with perpetual snow. But mountains formed by the protrusion of immense masses of granite, and based upon several thousand feet of this solid crystalline substance, are not so susceptible of heat at their surface as the plains formed of thick porous strata. The science of geology furnishes a large amount of evidence in favour of the terrestrial theory. We have only to look at the remains of the carboniferous period to see that a different climate was necessary to produce and sustain the living forms of that period, to that which is experienced by existing races. In fact, beginning at the Silurian period, and tracing the action of climate through every geologic age, we find a gradual cooling down, until we arrive at its present condition. How will the solar advocates explain this? Has the sun been gradually receding from the earth, or was the power in the sun to generate heat greater in past ages than now? W. NEWBERRY.

NOTE.—In my letter on the above subject in the February number I miswrote (through not attending to one thing at a time) 68 for 386 times nearer than the sun. *Vide* "N. N. B." page 61, 43rd line of right hand column. W. N.

Evidently Mr. Newberry must relinquish his theory of heat. The close connection between light and heat, the high temperature under tropical suns, the different temperatures of the seasons, of day and night, and the results produced by the burning glasses of ancient and modern times, all militate against his theory. From numerous experiments made in England and France, concerning the nature of subterranean temperature, the English engineers say that the temperature of boiling water will be reached at a depth of $2\frac{1}{2}$ miles from the surface of the earth, while in France it seems that the same temperature will be reached at a depth of $1\frac{3}{4}$ miles below the surface. So much indeed in favour of Mr. Newberry. In the mining operations of Belgium, experiments show that while at the surface the thermometer stands 33°, and at a depth of 2180 feet the thermometer stands at 50°, at a mine in Montigny, the temperature at surface was 32° to 57°, at a depth of 1843 feet. The greatest depth yet reached by man into the crust of the earth is 3489ft., and there the temperature is nearly 79°, almost equal to the mean temperature at the equator; but still the surface at those mines is comparatively cold. So cold, indeed, that I cannot see any thing to brighten or even favor Mr. Newberry's theory.

Geologists make us rather uneasy, when they tell us that at a depth of twenty-five miles below the earth's surface the heat is so great as to keep in a melted state basalt rocks, etc., and still I am at a loss to perceive any thing turning up to support this theory of heat.

Let us for a time, with some writers, admit, that in the centre of the earth there is "an ocean of fire."

Is this fire increasing or decreasing in intensity, and in what proportion? Is it approaching the surface of the earth, or receding, and according to what ratio?

Is this fire perfectly at rest, or rapidly vibrating? Even with all those questions satisfactorily answered, we look at the sun, we feel the sensation called heat; the sun disappears and the sensation produced by cold is the result. We look at vegetation under the influence of a genial sun, and we say surely there must be heat from the great luminary.

We look at ice, solid water, in the morning, when the oblique rays of the sun strike its surface; again we look, the ice is gone, not by any subterranean heat in disguise, but by the more direct rays of the sun gloriously heating the earth. Is Mr. Newberry out to-day, this terribly cold 13th day of March? What prevents the subterranean heat from acting? But five of your correspondents have so cleverly, and so clearly replied to Mr. Newberry, that I presume he is quite satisfied with their arguments, and their manner of reasoning.

H. H. ULIDIA.

W. Newberry, writing on the above subject, certainly expresses rather novel ideas of our source of heat. He says:—"It may fairly be doubted whether any great amount of heat is derived by the earth from the sun." And produces in support of this argument the following:—"If a room be heated to 180° to 200°, and then by means of a stream of nitrogen or carbonic acid gas all air is excluded, the room would in a very short time be reduced to a condition below the freezing point."

I do not see how the result of this experiment can be made to support W. N.'s argument in the least. He forgets to tell us the temperature of the gas introduced into the room. If the heated air in the room be replaced by cold gas of course the temperature of the room will be lowered. The question which I conceive W. N. wishes to get an answer to, is, can rays of heat be transmitted from one body to another through a vacuum? I answer, it can, and if W. N. doubt it still, let him expose himself to the direct rays of the sun on a bright day, and I think he will feel to his discomfort that we receive a large amount of heat from the sun every day through 95,000,000 of miles of vacuum.

Two other difficulties seem to present themselves to W. N., viz: the decreased temperature of high altitudes, and the fact that when the sun is in aphelion we seem to receive more heat than when he is nearest us. I think both of these may in a great measure be explained away.

The first by the fact that the degree of heat retained in the atmosphere from the sun's rays is altogether dependant on the density of the atmosphere, or in other words, the more dense the atmosphere is, the greater will be the degree of heat retained by it from the rays of the sun.

With regard to the latter difficulty W. N. must remember that, at the time of the year when the sun is in perihelion he is far away to the south; and in high northern latitudes his rays strike the surface of the earth in a slanting direction, and in that manner are spread over a much larger surface than if they fell direct; at the equator the times of greatest heat are at the equinoxes, when the sun is in the zenith.

Barbadoes. T. T.

FOWLS SWIMMING.—My object in addressing you is more to seek than to give information, respecting a circumstance that has lately come under my observation, which, though new to me, may not be so to those who make natural history more of a study than myself. Some poultry are kept in the yard where our business is carried on, which is bounded on one side by the river; and a few days ago, one of the hens, by some unlucky accident, slipped over the quay into the water. I expected that, after some vain splashing and fluttering, she would have disappeared beneath the surface and been drowned; for the water was too far below the quay to reach her, and there was no boat at hand. But instead of this, she was perfectly cool and collected, sat on the water with head erect, and swam about gracefully. I could see her feet moving under the water with exactly the motion of a web-footed bird. A boat was hailed from a quay some way up the river, but it was a ponderous affair, and some time elapsed before it could be got ready and come to her assistance; so that she had been in the water fully a quarter of an hour before she was picked up. All this time she had been gradually getting lower in the water, but continued to swim in a stately manner, till she was taken out, when she appeared much exhausted, but soon revived, on being placed before the office fire. Now I should like to know whether fowls generally swim when they find themselves unexpectedly in the water, or whether it was exceptional in this case; for I was not at all aware that they possessed any power of sustaining themselves in water, or of propelling themselves through it. It has occurred to me that I would mention, at the same time, my encountering an adder, while shooting rabbits on a large tract of sand-hills on the north coast of Cornwall. It was on the 16th of October, 1868, a cold day, with heavy showers and a strong north-west wind. The adder was not torpid, but in a sufficiently lively state to rear his head when he saw me, and coil himself up for a spring. I blew his head off with my gun, and thus had an opportunity of examining his body to see that I was not mistaken. I should be surprised to find an adder, even in summer, where there is nothing but sand and scanty rushes for many miles around; but I cannot account for his appearance at that time of the year, and by no means in a state of torpor. If you think either of these incidents worthy of insertion in your N.N.B., I shall be interested in having the opinions of those more conversant with the subject than myself.

JNO. B. JANIES.

THE STOAT (*Mustela Erminea*).—Mr. A. H. Malan may not perhaps be quite correct in saying that the stoat does no good whatever, but it is well known what a most destructive animal it is to game of all kinds, besides killing no end of rabbits, so that the little good it may do will not nearly compensate for the vast amount of damage this determined little poacher commits. From all I have heard and read about this quadruped, I must own I cannot agree with "A. M. B." when he says, if Mr. Malan was "to dissect the next few stoats killed that in two-thirds of the cases he will find mice, small birds, or something analogous forming the contents of the stomach." He might perhaps find such to be the case in one-third of the instances. The only good that the stoat does do is in destroying numbers both of rats and mice, but this little creature has rather a nice appetite and much prefers either a pheasant, partridge, or a hare, to a rat, etc.

With reference to its changing its coat, is "A. M. B." quite sure it is the "exception" and not the "rule" for the stoat to turn white in the British Isles during the winter season? although, I grant, their coat is not of such a pure white as is the colour of those stoats found in more northern countries.

The Rev. J. G. Wood, in his "Illustrated Natural History," says, "In this country, where the lowest temperature is considerably above that of the ordinary wintry degrees, the stoat is very uncertain in its change of fur, and seems to yield to or to resist the effects of the cold weather according to the individuality of the particular animal. . . . . . Sometimes the animal resists the coldest winters, and retains its dark fur throughout the severest weather, and it sometimes happens that a stoat will change its fur even though the winter should be particularly mild." He goes on to say, after relating some instances in which white stoats were seen during mild and also wet winters,— "It may be presumed that the moisture of the atmosphere and ground may have some connection with the whitening of the hair."

Bewick, speaking of this animal says, "The stoat is likewise found white in the winter time in Great Britain, and is then erroneously called a 'white weasel.' Its fur, however, among us is of little value, having neither the thickness, the closeness, nor the whiteness of those which come from Siberia."

Certainly, ladies' muffs, etc., are made of the fur of those stoats found in colder countries, as the English ermine is not of such a pure white, and even if it was, the animal is not common enough in this country to allow any "firm to depend on their supply from Great Britain." If it was so much sought after, the stoat would soon become extinct in the British Isles.

Sidmouth. A. E. BUTTERMER.

EXTINCTION OF SPECIES.—I have read much in the Naturalist's Note-book about the extinction of English species of butterflies, and especially about the Camberwell Beauty. Now it strikes me that, if this insect has been destroyed in certain localities by reason of drainage, or the destruction of forests, it might easily be planted again in other sections of the country. However, I do not see at all why the Camberwell Beauty should not flourish near London as well as anywhere else. I am told that on the Continent the insect is not rare. In North America it is very common. I myself have caught the C. B. there as late as the beginning of December, and last spring again as early as April, on warm sunny days, in sheltered and sunny spots in the woods. In fact, the animal loves the woods and meadows, skirting the same. If, therefore some naturalists would club together, and import the chrysalis in large numbers, breed them at home, and set them free, I see not the slightest reason why this beautiful object should not be soon very numerous again. Some people may object to this mode of introduction of strangers, as not becoming the collector of British butterflies. Those who do, may let the matter alone, and if they persist in their ideas, they may soon be reduced to catching nothing but cabbage butterflies, or call their collection foreign, if they like that better. I, for one, would not hesitate one moment to call a butterfly English or British, if I succeeded in catching the same here, or found a larva or chrysalis of the Camberwell Beauty on a tree in Great Britain.

Upper Norwood, Feb. 15th, 1869. W. G.

SUGARING FOR MOTHS.—In the March number of the "N. N. B.," your correspondent, W. W. Walker, desires to be informed of a method of attracting moths to a particular spot. I believe the best way is by sugaring. I think the following recipe for making the compound will be of some use to him :—Get one pound of the thickest treacle that can be obtained, add enough ale to make it the consistency of cream, putting in two table spoonfulls of rum, which, after shaking, is fit for use. This composition should be carried in a wide mouthed bottle, so that a painters' brush will go into it; with this brush the composition should be put round the trunks of trees, posts, etc., so that it will run down in long streaks, so as to be more easily sipped by the "greedy" moths. The trees, etc., should be done in this manner about dusk, and visited an hour or two afterwards, approaching cautiously with a bull's-eye lantern, a net, and a plentiful supply of pill boxes of various sizes for the reception of the moths, holding the box underneath the moth and the lid above, carefully closing it; it will be best to hold the net beneath to receive any that may drop. Mild, damp evenings, with little moonlight, will be found best; moonlight nights are generally unproductive. If not successful the first three or four nights, do not abandon it as useless, as a great many moths may be caught in this way, which could not otherwise be obtained. R. LADDIMAN.

St. Augustine's, Norwich.

WOODPIGEON'S NEST.—When a boy, I chanced to find a woodpigeon's nest, in which were two callow young ones. These I carried home, and put them into a basket upon some hay, and then placed them upon the kitchen stove for warmth. Having procured some split peas, I chewed the same into a pulp, and then placing the birds in my left hand, I conveyed their beaks into my mouth. The little fellows greedily sucked the prepared food into their crops, and soon became well grown and full feathered birds; but they could neither stand, walk, nor fly. On close inspection, I found that the bones of their legs and thighs had been broken and reset several times. In short, they were such hopeless cripples that I at once dispatched them by breaking their necks; their remains were put into a pie, which on being cut up was found to be boneless. Immediately I conjectured the cause of the softening of the birds bones, viz., the prepared food which I gave them. In order to test my theory, I procured another brace of young culvers, which I fed upon peas merely saturated with water: they grew rapidly, and soon made good use of both their legs and wings. They too shared the fate of their predecessors, but they proved less profitable, inasmuch as their bones could not be swallowed.

J. B. OWEN.

PROTECTING SEA BIRDS.—I doubt not that in the next number of the "N. N. B." the valiant "A. M. B." will reply to "A Constant Reader" fighting for science *versus* the tender-hearted. But it seems to me that a compromise between the belligerents might be effected, and in this way. Make it, as "A Constant Reader" suggests, a penal offence to kill a sea bird, except in this case: Let a magistrate resident in the town nearest to the place where the havoc ordinarily takes place, have the power of giving a written permission to such persons as he may think fit to shoot one or two gulls; the receiver of this to sign a paper saying that he would not kill any more and that he would kill only for scientific purposes. If he in any way transgressed this let him be punished.

A petition to this effect might, I think, be presented by naturalists to parliament before Mr. Sykes' excellent bill becomes law. It might be drawn up and deposited at some convenient place (say the office of the NATURALIST'S NOTE BOOK) for signature. Hoping that some of your correspondents will let me know through the medium of your pages what they think of this plan, I remain, yours truly, A RADICAL.

ON KILLING LEPIDOPTERA.—Seeing in last number, a correspondent gives several methods for killing moths, I give below one I can recommend, which is adopted by myself and several friends, but I believe is not generally known. Procure a tin canister, of any convenient size, cut out the bottom, and get a lid to fit, so that there are lids both ends; about the middle have a piece of perforated zinc, "cut to fit," soldered inside, this divides the can into two parts. In one division put the bruised laurel leaves, then place the can before a fire, or in the sunshine, the heat will cause a poisonous vapour to rise to the other compartment, into which the moth is then put; it will be immediately stupified without coming in contact with the leaves, which are injurious to its colours. In the case of very large moths this will probably only stupify them, and they would speedily revive when set, but it enables you to operate with the Prussic or Oxalic acid easily, under this treatment a Sphinx Convolvuli was killed by myself last season, and this is the largest British moth except A. atropos.

P.S.—Several S. Convolvuli were taken here last year; I think they must have been unusually plentiful, as I have not heard of their capture before.

Reading. J. HENDERSON, Junr.

BOTTLE AND WATER.—"R. B. W." writing on this phenomenon, says—"Is it not probable that the pressure of the water upon the bottle breaks or cracks it, so that the water may get in." I do not think it at all likely that this is the case. I suppose the experiment has often been tried, and do not think it probable that the cracks in the bottle could have escaped detection in every instance. I think it more probable that the water is forced into the bottle through the cork and seal: this opinion is strengthened by the following quotation from Cassell's "Science Popularly Explained," page 57:—

"*Query.*—Can a cork be sunk so deep that it cannot rise to the surface again?"

"*Answer.*—At a great depth, water forced by pressure into the pores of the cork renders it so heavy that it cannot rise."

Now, if water can thus be forced into a cork by pressure, I do not think it beyond the bounds of probability to suppose the water to be driven through the seal by the same pressure, and thus made to fill the bottle. At any rate I think this a more plausible solution of the mystery than the one suggested by "R. B. W." T. T.

SATIN MOTH.—A friend of mine last summer kept a great number of caterpillars of the satin moth, most of which underwent their transformations into the pupa and imago states in a very satisfactory manner. One of them, however, instead of casting its horny head-piece, as well as the soft skin of its body, as is usually the case with caterpillars on entering the pupa state, only succeeded in throwing off the soft skin, retaining the head, which, being very large and jet black, gave the chrysalis a very peculiar appearance. But, still more remarkable than this, when the perfect moth emerged from the chrysalis, it still carried the head of the caterpillar with it. You may judge how strange the snow-white moth appeared with a gigantic smooth and bare black head stuck on its shoulders, in place of, or rather enclosing as in a case, its own delicate little furry white one, which was scarcely a fourth of the size. My friend killed the insect, intending to keep it as a curiosity; but it was unfortunately crushed before it could be transferred to his store box. J. LANDELS.

THE STING OF NETTLES.—"R. T." is desirous of having the opinions of some of the correspondents of the "N. N. B." with regard to the sting of nettles, and says, "I am ready to abide by their impartial decision, which I shall await with perfect confidence." I shall be most happy to let him know the results of the experiments I have made lately with some nettles. As "R. T." desires, I drew the leaves lightly both over the palm and back of my hand and received no sting whatever. I then grasped them firmly between my fingers and likewise escaped being stung. Afterwards I proceeded to knock the leaves smartly against my hand, and was less fortunate this time, as I was stung rather severely. By the experiments I have made with nettles, I am brought to the conclusion, that they do not sting if either grasped firmly or touched lightly, but if the leaves are hit with a moderate force they then will sting. I should like to know the opinions of other correspondents.

Sidmouth. A. E. BUTTERMER.

BRITISH GEOMETRÆ.—In reply to the query of "C. W." at page 94 of the NOTE BOOK, I may state that the species whose name was inadvertently omitted from my February paper is the Large Thorn (E. almaria). The remarks I there made I intended to be understood generally, as applying to a fact connected with the present arrangement of Lepidoptera; and they were suggested by the conspicuous instance which came in my way of the thing spoken about. Such was the meaning, and such the construction which I imagined most would put upon my words. Whilst not in the least doubting the correctness of "C. W.'s" statement regarding E. litharia, I may observe that the mere fact of a species being found feeding on different trees to that upon which it is ordinarily taken by entomologists does not prove that the latter is incorrectly or doubtfully considered its regular pabulum. The isolated instances of this nature are frequent amongst Lepidopterous larva, but they do not invalidate the rules that have been laid down by repeated observations.   E. CLIFFORD.

LIGHT, &c. — The astronomer mentioned by "R. B. W." may be a very good authority, and, indeed, if he is the one of the same name whom I have heard lecture, I have no doubt of it. But whether his opinion is to be received in preference to that of such astronomers as Lardner and Breen, I cannot say so readily. Even if we admit that the sun appears scarcely greater than a fixed star, it seems almost impossible to conceive that the sun does not act the part of a sun to Neptune, which, like the earth and other planets, revolves round it. Analogy would say at once that Neptune does receive light from the sun. We know that the earth, by rotating on its axis, presents one-half of its surface to the sun, which half is illuminated; and if another body (in many respects like the earth, connected with the same system and revolving round the sun like it) turns on its axis and presents one-half of its surface to the sun, may we not reasonably conclude that it also receives light?   R. T.

COMETS AND METEORS.—Since writing my last letter on "Comets and Meteors," I unexpectedly came upon something which tended to strengthen my opinion that the theory which "Gulielmus" tried to uphold is only a fanciful one, resting on a very unsound foundation. Turning over the pages of an old volume of the *Polytechnic Journal*, my eyes alighted upon a letter written by Sir J. W. Herschel, in which the writer brings several objections against the theory in question. It is true that Herschel wrote more than twenty years ago, and many discoveries have been made since that time; but, in spite of this, I think it would prove very edifying to "Gulielmus" and his supporters to read his objections, and to try and answer them. If any should desire so to do, they must procure the second volume of the *Polytechnic*.   R. T.

BLACK-HEADED GULLS.—While nesting at a loch in the north of Aberdeenshire in the summer of 1866, we got a colony of about seventy black-headed gulls' nests and about three hundred eggs in them. The nests were in an island about one hundred yards in circumference, and were mostly at one end of the island, and there were four coots' nests amongst them. Is it usual for black-headed gulls to build in company? In another island I saw a swan's nest and seven large green eggs, something like a blackbird's in colour. Can any of your correspondents tell me the name of the swan?   A. M. MC. A.
Aberdeen.

SPARROW HAWK.—The following fact may be interesting to some of your readers:—"A cage which had contained a canary had been placed out in the sun in front of a house I was staying at after having been washed, when a sparrowhawk that had been hovering over suddenly made a dash at the bars of the empty cage with such force that it broke its neck against them, and was picked up quite dead." I should be very much pleased to hear a reason for this, in my opinion, curious fact, from any of your correspondents.   "B."
Winchester.

EAST WINDS.—Can any of your readers give me any information in answer to the two following questions? 1. What is the cause of the well-known unhealthiness of east winds? 2. I have heard it said that east winds are usually very prevalent in the spring season, if the preceding winter has been mild. Is this true? If it is, I am afraid that this spring we shall have to endure the unhealthiness and disagreeableness of very many of these winds; for we certainly have not, for a period of many years, experienced so mild a winter as that which is just past.
  J. LANDELS.

SISKIN AND MEALY REDPOLE.—The female Siskin (*F. spinus*) differs from the male in having the crown of the head dusky and grey, mixed, instead of black, and the plumage altogether is much less vivid. The female Mealy Redpole (*F. borealis*) is quite similar to the male in plumage, with the exception of having less white about it. This species is so identical in plumage to the lesser Redpole (*F. linaria*) that by some naturalists they are considered to be of one and the same species.   H. MEYRICK.

EXCHANGE.—A few mornings since I found on the cliff (E) at Ramsgate a remarkably fine specimen of the Robus entronomicus (Linn.). Can you kindly inform me whether this is a common occurrence, as I am inclined to think it presages a very early summer. I have for exchange some very sound specimens of Naufragia Gromnolus, Lentes Capronicus (Niger), Lentes Testudii (Vulgaris), Bensens Scomeotosii (Alba), and many others. I want for them a small collection of mounted objects for the microscope (Diatomaceæ puseri).   VIATOR.

LITHOSIA RUBRICOLLIS.—I shall be much obliged if any of your correspondents would inform me through your paper the way to rear the larva of L. rubricollis and other lichenous feeders. Should they be kept in air-tight bottles or wooden boxes? and what is the month of their appearance in the perfect state, as I find accounts differ considerably. Also what is the best way of setting Lithocolletida, Nepticulidæ, and other micro Lepidoptera. What is a good locality for Selinia Illustraria, the purple thorn moth?
Reading.   J. HENDERSON, Junr.

ASH TREE.—A flourishing young ash tree is now covered with what appeared to be bunches of black or very dark flowers. On close examination, I found them to be composed of woody or barky matter, breaking easily to the touch like old bark. They were exactly of the shape and appearance of thick bunches of flowers attached to the ends of the twigs and branches. Can any one tell me if it is common, or what is the cause of such excrescences?
Middlesbrough.   W. R. L.

CORRECTION.—Allow me to mention a slight error in the printing of my last article on the "Extinction of Species" in your March number, the name of the insect at the beginning of the paper spelt "Vingtudroe" ought really to be "Virgaurae." I also forgot to mention in my "Astronomical" query in your March number that the moon was on the decrease and in its "quarter place" at the time of the "phenomenon." EARNEST BELFORT BAX.

MOON STROKES.—I have heard that moon strokes are not unfrequent in the tropics. A case was related to me by the mate of the "Umjeni" on our voyage out. He said, "that in one of his former voyages, on passing the *line*, a sailor sleeping on deck received a stroke, and that his face was twisted round and distorted in a most frightful manner, from which he never recovered." Do moon strokes ever occur beyond the tropics? J. D. S. W.
Upper Umkomancy, Natal.

REPTILES OF SOUTH AFRICA.—Could any of your numerous correspondents give me a list of the reptiles of South Africa? I believe Dr. Smith, in his "Natural History of South Africa," gives the above; but as I cannot afford to give £15 for any *one* work at present, perhaps some naturalist who has the work, or the use of a library containing it, would send a copy to the NOTE BOOK, and greatly oblige J. D. S. W.
Upper Umkomancy, Natal.

MOCK MOON.—I have read an account of the appearance of a mock moon, and think it quite probable that the phenomena witnessed by one of your correspondents may have been one. I remember that the account I read was very interesting, and when opportunity presents itself, if it should prove acceptable, I will give it for the benefit of those of your readers who may be interested in such matters. R. T.

EXTRAORDINARY LAMB.—Seeing Mr. Newberry's letter on an "Extraordinary Calf," I thought that I would mention what some of your readers may not be aware of, viz: that there is in the anatomical museum, at Cambridge, a specimen of an abnormal lamb, with two bodies, two tails, and six legs, meeting in one head, which has three eyes, one in the middle of the forehead. This was bred on the Sussex Downs.
EARNEST BELFORT BAX.

MILDNESS OF THE WEATHER.—Yesterday I caught a beautiful specimen of the tortoishell butterfly (*Urticæ*), and also a few days back were caught about here an Io (peacock), and several other Urticæ. Owing to the mildness of the present season I should not be surprised in seeing many other kinds of butterflies out. B. R. W.
Petersfield.

Could any of your readers inform me where would be the best place (in the season) to catch Iris, Sinapis, Arion, Cratægi, and Polychorus, and why meadow browns are so much more common than any other butterflies. Also could any one tell me what is the best food forlinnets." B. R. W.
Petersfield.

ORANGE TIP BUTTERFLY.—On the 19th and 20th of the present month I captured four larvæ of the Orange Tip Butterfly (Euchloë Cardamines) at Halvergate, near Norwich, of an unusual size. Thinking it might interest some of your readers I have sent it for insertion (if approved of by you) in the NATURALIST'S NOTE BOOK. W. SEARLES.

GARDEN-WHITE BUTTERFLY.—Yesterday morning (March 5th) my sister saw a small garden-white butterfly (Pieris Rapæ) fly past the window of the room in which she was sitting. The weather was very warm and bright, the wind at the time being from the south-west. Is not this rather an early appearance?
J. LANDELS.

HOW TO FORM A CABINET OF INSECTS?—Will any of your correspondents be so good as to give me a hint about the formation of a cabinet of insects? I have several books on coleoptera, lepidoptera, etc.; but though I can classify each by themselves, I do not know which to put first in a general cabinet.
Aberdeen. A. M. McA.

BIRDS' EGGS.—In reply to the inquiry of H. J. P. relative to birds' eggs, I beg to inform him that I received from T. Dalston, Barnard Castle, Durham, a very fair collection of 50. Although a few got broken in the carriage of them, I found the rest of very good value. I would be glad to exchange a few with H. J. P. F. W. THOMPSON.
Bray.

CORRECTION.—Allow me to point out the following mistake which appeared in last month's number:—For *back* read *beak* in my note concerning the cinnamon sparrow.
Brighton. T. B.

LEPIDOPTERA.—In answer to your correspondent "V. B. Lewes," I have caught some and saw a great many more specimens of *L. Alexis* last summer down at Folkestone about half the general size.
H. F. P.

PRESERVING SNAKES.—I should be much obliged if some of your readers would let me know what they consider the best spirit for preserving snakes, etc.
Upper Umkomancy, Natal. J. D. S. W.

AGE OF CATS.—I saw in last month's NATURALIST'S NOTE BOOK that V. B. L. knew of a cat aged twenty-one years. I know a friend who had a cat at the advanced age of twenty-three, which was quite blind.
B. W. W.

GREEN FIELD CRICKET.—Can any of your readers tell me the scientific name of the green field cricket, as I cannot find it in any of my books?
St. Augustine's, Norwich. ROBT. LADDIMAN.

SNAKES.—My brother put a slowworm into a box with some dry grass, and in a few days a brood of young ones made their appearance. J. R.

SNOW.—Can any kind reader inform me of a way to imitate snow, as I wish to mount a robin in that way? T. B.
Brighton.

Would any of your readers give me a description of the rice plant, and also the plant bearing carraway seeds. QUERCUS.

Where can I obtain a catalogue of entomologists' requisites? W. W WALKER.

SPRING.

SPRING, the youth of the year, is truly a delightful season. It commences, as the calendar informs us, on March 21st, and ends on June 21st, and during these three months, from the time the sun crosses the line till it reaches its highest point in the heavens on June 21st, the summer solstice, the progress of vegetation, and the development of the leaves on the trees rapidly advances. Well may June be termed the "leafy month," for then every tree of the forest is fully out and clad in its richest foliage. At no other period of the year have the trees a brighter hue than during this month. As summer advances they lose their fresh green color, and become more withered, and of a darker tinge, owing to the heat, the dust, alternate rains, and the numerous species of insects which then make their appearance and feed on the leaves of various trees.

I say the spring is a delightful season, as everything in the animal and vegetable kingdom then awakes from its long winter sleep, revived, and endued with new life, under the vivifying and genial influence of the sun, the great source of heat. Although the vernal season in this country is very fickle as regards the weather, and keen blasts from the north and east often occur during the early part of our spring season, and plunge us once again into winter, and such has often been the case at times during the past month, (March) which has proved colder than the average, with frequent bitter winds and occasional snow showers,—as a glance at the daily weather tables published in *The Times* will at once show—yet, I say, in spite of the variableness of our spring climate, whenever clouds give place to sunshine, and warm intervals occur, then swarms of insects may be seen sporting about, glad to come forth from their hibernating quarters, and once more again, if it be even for a short time, enjoy the fresh and genial air of spring. Bees are busy on the wing, sucking the juice from various flowers, and from the blossoms of the apple, pear, peach, plum, cherry, and other fruit trees. The large queen wasp (*vespa vulgaris*) approaching in size to a hornet, may be seen about the middle of April, actively seeking out some suitable place where she may deposit her eggs, and he who kills one of these wasps at that time may be said to destroy thousands, as they are the parents of the future swarms.

During the whole of April, and also into May, our summer birds of passage are arriving. Among the earliest to make their appearance are the wryneck, smallest-willow wren, blackcap, nightingale, and the different kinds of the hirundines. The wryneck, or snake-bird, which makes such a loud and harsh note; and which I heard for the first time this spring on Sunday, April 4th, is also called the "cuckoo's mate," from its appearing yearly just before that bird is heard, for the cuckoo is much more often heard than seen, it being so wild and shy. However, he takes good care to let us know when he has come, by continually sounding forth his peculiar note "cuckoo," which is familiar to all who live in the country, and when his voice is heard, everyone then feels that spring has really come. Before next month's issue of the "N. N. B." is published, the cuckoo will have arrived plentifully. His voice is not heard much after June, and I expect when August comes most of them have emigrated again.

This is one of those birds that builds no nest, but deposits her eggs in the nests of other birds. According to an old Norfolk proverb,

> In April the cuckoo shows his bill,
> In May he sing, night and day,
> In June he changes his tune,
> In July away he fly,
> In August away he must.

The swallow (*hirundo rustica*) usually arrives in England about the 15th of April, though a few stragglers may perhaps be seen before that date. It is soon followed by the house martin, sand martin, and lastly by the swift, which brings up the rear, it being very sensitive of cold, and leaves this country again in August.

The business of nest making is carried on in the middle and latter part of spring, and some broods are even hatched and fly before the end of the season. It is then that the male birds are in full song. Ah! how delightful it is when one awakes early on April and May mornings to hear the joyous singing of our native songsters. It fills us with admiration of the Divine Creator's works when one listens to the rich strains that emanate from the throats of some of our British birds. Let us take a walk in the fields on fine spring days. What a delicious freshness there is in the air. Everything is full of life, lambs skipping about, insects humming on the wing, birds singing and darting out of every hedgerow and bush. Truly, it makes the lover of nature wonder at all around him. What yearnings there are in the breasts of those, both of the old and young, who are cooped up in our large crowded towns, to get away from the turmoil of town life and enjoy a short ramble in the pure country air, and to catch a glimpse of the green fields, which are at this season decked in places with the lovely golden hue of the buttercup. The insects at this period are numerous, and as summer advances become still more abundant.

Those useful birds, the hirundines, destroy infinite numbers of insects, both to feed themselves and their callow young. Here is seen the goodness of Providence, in sending us these birds at a time when the insect life begins to multiply so fast. Birds indeed may be considered our "friends" and not "foes," for the prodigious quantity of insects they destroy must be enormous.

April 6th.   A. E. BUTTEMER.

ON THE BRITISH GEOMETRÆ.
By E. CLIFFORD.
PART V.

THE family next claiming our notice contains many species nearly resembling one another, illustrating the opening remarks of our last paper; for they are yet distinguishable, the one from the other, by the practised entomologist. We begin the family AUDALIDÆ, by noticing the rare little golden-bordered purple (*Hyria auroraria*). This little moth is one of extreme beauty, but is very uncommon in our country, for it has only been seen in Hampshire, Cambridgeshire, and Lancashire. The wings are all of a purple-red colour, with blotches, and a broad border of deep fulvous yellow, which is the distinguishing characteristic of the species. The caterpillar is described as dull grey, and as feeding on the common plantain. It occurs in July; May and June are the months for the perfect insect.

We now come to the true Waves. The small Yellow Wave (*Asthena luteata*, flies at midsummer, and is not uncommon about some of our woods. Its colouring is rich yellow, with zig-zag transverse lines of a deeper hue. The head, thorax, and body are of a similar colour with the wings. Abundant in the country during May and June is the small White Wave (*Asthena candidata*). This delicate little creature has white wings, upon which are numerous waved grey lines. On the hind margin of all the wings are five black dots. The caterpillar feeds on the hornbeam, and is green, with a red stripe on the sides. The Waved Carpet (*Asthena sylvata*) is a beautiful little Geometer. Its wings are pale grey, with zig-zag lines of darker hue. This moth appears about midsummer, and is a widely distributed insect, though not particularly common. Blomer's Rivulet (*Asthena blomeraria*) is the term given to a moth which occurs chiefly in the north of England in the month of June. It has also been taken in South Wales. The wings are all pale grey in colour, the fore wings possessing two bands near the tip, which are of a sienna colour. Both fore and hind wings have numerous delicate markings, which are, however, very obscure. In the month of September we may possibly come upon the caterpillar of the Dingy Shell (*Eupisteria heparata*) feeding on the alder. It occurs abundantly in Hampshire, according to one of our entomological authors. The moth has the wings of a dingy yellow towards the body, but brown towards the hind margin, the colours blending one into the other; the pale portion is marked by transverse waved lines, which are rather indistinct, and a little darker than the general colour. The Dingy Shell flies in the month of June.

A local insect is that known as the Welsh Wave (*Venusia cambricaria*), occurring only in the north and west of England. The wings are of a pale grey, with transverse brown lines differing much in darkness of shade. Near the middle of the wing there is a delicate black mark, crescent shaped; on the hind wings the markings are few and delicate, but the marginal spots are distinct. The antennæ are fringed in the male, thread-like in the female; the head, thorax, and body dark grey. The coasts of Essex and Kent furnish the delicate little Bright Wave (*Acidalia ochrata*), which flies in the month of June. All the wings are dingy yellow, the fore wings with transverse lines of a darker hue. The antennæ are threadlike, and the head, thorax and body of the same colour as the wings. The Tawny Wave (*Acidalia rubricata*) is exceedingly rare, and only two or three specimens have as yet been captured of it, and as these have been taken on the extreme south coast, it is probable they were blown across the Channel from France—hence we pass it over, and proceed to notice the Single-dotted Wave (*Acidalia sentulata*). All the wings of this species are pale wainscot brown, the fore wings with two waved brown lines parallel with the hind margin. The hind wings have a central dark spot, as also the fore wings, and three or four interrupted waved lines, and there is a row of dark brown spots at the base of the fringe. The head, thorax, and body are of a similar colour to the wings. Next come we to the delicate small Fan-footed Wave (*Acidalia bisetata*), whose wings are all pale wainscot brown. The fore wings have two darker transverse waved lines near the hind margin, and a dark central spot: there are also a few small and inconspicuous dots at the base of the fringe round all the wings. The Treble Brown Spot (*Acidalia trigeminata*) bears a close resemblance to the last-named species. Its wings are of a pale brown colour, but the costal margin of the fore wings has a dark mark at the base, extending about a third of its length. This moth is not very uncommon in the north and west of England, though not recognised as yet in the London district. The next species under notice is amongst the least of our Geometræ: it is called the Least Carpet (*Acidalia rusticata*) and is a beautiful little species. All the wings have a whitish ground colour, the fore wings with a central brown bar, which on its outer edge is deeply indented, and in the middle of this is a black spot. The fringe on the hind margin is spotted with black; the hind wings have four indistinct waved lines; the body is variegated with white and brown. The insect visits Darenth Wood in June.

About midsummer the Dark Cream Wave (*Acidalia osseata*) is on the wing. Its markings are very similar to others that have been already described, its wings being yellowish brown, with darker waved lines. The Silky Wave (*Acidalia holosericata*) has only been taken in the neighbourhood of Bristol, and occurs about the beginning of July. Its colouring is wainscot brown, the fore wings sprinkled along the margin with minute dark brown dots, and having five transverse lines. There are no central spots or marginal dots on any of the wings. The small Dusty Wave (*Acidalia incanaria*) is a common moth all over the kingdom in June and July. Its wings are dingy white, sprinkled all over with black specks: these specks or dots are sometimes symmetrically arranged, forming several waved and indistinct lines. Each of the fore wings has also a central black spot. The head, thorax, and body, like the wings, are sprinkled over with black dots. The Obscure Wave (*Acidalia circellata*) is a peculiarly graceful insect, but so rare as hardly to be considered British. It has occurred near Manchester, but is so doubtful a native that we pass briefly over it. On chalky soils the beautiful Lace Border (*Acidalia ornata*) is not by any means uncommon, the caterpillar feeding on the wild thyme. All the wings are silvery white, and have a beautiful broad border parallel to their margin: this border consists of various waved lines, more or less distinct, and of a smoke colour; they include blotches of a brownish colour. The silvery white of the body, and the ground colour, contrasts delicately with these markings. The Mullein Wave (*Acidalia promutata*) has the wings grey, tinged with ochreous yellow, and sprinkled over with minute black specks; the fore wings have four transverse markings; the hind wings are similarly adorned. This is not a very common moth, but yet one generally distributed. The caterpillar is reported to feed on the common millefoil. The Dotted-bordered Cream Wave (*Acidalia straminata*) is a pretty little species, according to the figures given of it, but one of which no description seems current. The name is down in Doubleday's Catalogue, but it appears to be unknown to the generality of our entomologists.

The Satin Wave (*Acidalia subsericata*) has all the wings whitish grey, the fore wings possessing four transverse waved lines, but a shade darker than the ground tint. Between the first and second of these is a central dot on the fore wings, and a very slight indication of the same on the hind wings—there are also a few black dots on the fringe. This delicate little moth is rather uncommon, and occurs principally in the north of England. Another species frequenting the same parts is the Lesser Cream Wave (*Acidalia immutata*). This flies in June. The wings are ochreous grey, speckled with black dots; the fore wings have five, the hind wings four transverse waved lines only a shade darker than the ground colour of the wings. In the centre of each wing is a conspicuous black dot. The Cream Wave (*Acidalia remutata*) is a very common and unattractive-looking moth, for it occurs in almost every part of the kingdom during June. Its colouring is pale dingy brown, speckled with black dots, the fore wings with four, and the hind wings with three waved lines; the hind wings have also a black spot in the centre. Head, body, and thorax are of the same dingy hue as the wings. The Smoky Wave (*Acidalia fumata*), as its name indicates, is of a smoky colour, sprinkled with dots of a darker colour, so small as scarcely to be perceptible to the naked eye. There are on each wing three transverse bars, but no central dots on either of the wings. The female insect is less than the male, and decidedly different—the colour is pale grey, without any tinge of the smoke colour. This species is peculiar to the north of England and to Scotland; the time of flight is said to be midsummer. The caterpillar appears to be unknown. The Subangled Wave (*Acidalia prataria*) is the next under notice. This species occurs every year in small numbers on the sea-coast about Folkestone. The wings are yellowish grey, sprinkled with black dots, and having indistinct transverse lines on all the wings; there is a black spot between the first and second of these lines on the fore wings. The caterpillar of the Subangled Wave is unknown to most entomological authors, and the descriptions of it are generally taken from foreign writers. The Small Blood-vein (*Acidalia imitaria*) is a delicate and beautiful little Geometer. It is not unfrequent in some of our Kentish woods, and may be roused from the hedges by beating during the daytime. The fore wings are much angled, and the whole shape of the insect is peculiarly graceful. The wings are clay coloured, with an oblique brown band, which is continued across both fore and hind wings; this band passes outside a central brown spot, and between it and the hind margin there is a delicate waved line of the same colour. The moth itself is on the wing in July. The Dusky Wave (*Acidalia emutaria*) is yellowish white in colour, with a delicate tinge, as of mother-of-pearl, overspreading its wings. It has several obscure lines and markings of pale grey dispersed over their surface. It occurs occasionally in the south of England, but only on the banks of the Thames. It is a marsh insect, and appears about the middle of summer.

The Riband Wave (*Acidalia aversata*) is one of the best known of the family ACIDALIDÆ. It occurs commonly enough in the south during the months of May, June, and July. The colour is dingy grey, with transverse lines of darker hue. Sometimes varieties occur of this species. One of the most marked of them is that in which a broad band of dark brown fills the space between two of the central lines, hence the term "Riband Wave" is applied to the species. The Plain Wave (*Acidalia inornata*) is of a similar size with the last named, nor are its colours and markings very different, save that it possesses a greater number of transverse lines on the hind wings. The caterpillar of this species feeds on several low plants, and on low shoots of the willow. In May it is full-fed, and spins a web, changing therein to a chrysalis. The moth flies at midsummer, and is said to be rather uncommon.

The Portland Wave (*Acidalia degeneraria*), as its name would lead us to conclude, occurs solely in the Isle of Portland. It flies in July, and is a very beautiful moth of a yellowish grey colour. The Small Scallop (*Acidalia emarginata*) is one of our commonest Geometræ in some parts of the south. It is a very delicate and beautiful little insect. The wings, as the name implies, are scalloped; they are ochreous yellow in colour, and have each a central brown spot; the fore wings have three transverse lines, one on each side of the central spot, and the third on the hind margin. This species is said to occur in nearly all of the English counties. Lastly in the interesting group of fragile little insects is the Bloodvein itself (*Timandra amataria*), a graceful and delicate moth. The fore wings are pointed, the hind wings angled, and all are olive grey in colour, thickly sprinkled with darker dots, and possessing an oblique red stripe passing over them; the hind margins of all the wings are beautifully rose tinted, fading gradually into olive grey. This splendid Geometer is common about midsummer, and occurs in most of our English counties, like its relative, the preceding species. Thus we have gone briefly over the "Waves," comprising some of those insects which are particularly the denizens of our woodland glades in the summer. Our readers will perceive that although much has been done by collectors to elucidate their history, yet much remains for the ardent and earnest student to accomplish concerning them in the states of *larva* and *pupa*.

THE PARTRIDGE (*PERDIX CINEREA*.)

By A. H. MALAN.

MORE is known of this bird than of most of those of similar size which remain with us all the year round, partly because it is a game bird, and partly also, because it is so frequently met with all over Great Britain. Surely there is no need of a description of the partridge? Who has not seen it at one time or another? Who has not either admired it when "working the stubble" and tending its brood, or pitied its fate when seen hanging up in a game-dealer's shop window? The food of the partridge varies according to the season of the year; in the autumn, when the crops are cut, it subsists almost entirely on grain; in the spring and summer, it feeds upon such grain as can be got, and upon insects; amongst the latter, it is extremely fond of ants—in fact these are what the mother bird finds for her young ones as soon as they be hatched: while in winter, when the snow is on the ground, it seeks refuge as well as sustenance in the turnips, the green of which at this time constitutes its only food. These birds pair rather early, but lay their eggs late: the pairing taking place in February, while the incubation does not begin till the middle of May, and sometimes not until the beginning of June. No structure is required by the mother for the process of hatching—a few leaves scraped together furnish a sufficient nest for the accommodation of the eggs. Of these from ten to sixteen are generally laid, though frequently out of the sixteen not more than nine are hatched. The partridge is one of those birds too, which so very shy at other times, throws off all fear of man during the breeding season. We found a nest last summer within *two feet* of the turnpike road, under a bramble bush, where carriages and people were passing almost every hour of the day; and the bird in question hatched ten out of fourteen eggs. Like all fowls, the young are able to run as soon as they are born; and many are the stories told of the mother's mode of drawing away man or dog from her young brood, by feigning a broken wing, and shambling along, half flying, half running, just before the dog's nose or the man's eyes. It would seem strange that the partridge does not increase in numbers, judging by the amount of eggs laid each season; but in reality, if it be a dry season, on the average not more than six out of the twelve young birds, live till they be strong enough to fly; some die from want of water, others fall into cracks in the soil from which they are unable to extricate themselves. Towards dusk the birds that have become separated from the covey during the day, call to their companions, for the purpose of collecting before they roost.

More than one method is adopted for the capture of this bird, though to the real sportsman, the gun and the dog alone are used. And we may here remark that there is a saying—whether it be true or not is another question—that when the partridge is shot it sometimes flies straight upwards for some distance, and then drops to the ground; owing, it is supposed, to the bird having very strong muscles in its wings, which continue to work after life has left the body. Certainly when we shoot partridges they generally fall dead at once, without any such manoeuvres as these. But the peasant (or poacher) supply surer means when the birds are not plentiful, than the gun alone. Often, when the sun is going down, a labourer may be seen coming down the road with a gun-barrel in one pocket, and the stock in the other—the gun cannot actually be *seen*, but there are unmistakable creases on the outside of the coat, which nothing but a fowling-piece could produce: policemen being more severe on this class for carrying a gun along the turnpike road, than on any other.

Let us follow the professional poacher, or perhaps *labourer* would be a more respectful term, after he has passed us. Soon we see him enter a field and proceed cautiously close under the hedge, towards the partridge feeds; as he walks along first out comes the barrel, then the stock, which he carefully fits together, without making any noise in the operation. Having at length reached the place he considers most favourable, (according to the direction of the wind) he conceals himself in the hedge, which joins the stubble or turnips, in a position commanding the whole field, places his gun where it can be used at a moment's notice, and produces a small bird call, with which he imitates the cry, used by separate birds to collect at eve.

Perhaps some single bird is quietly nibbling away at the green of a turnip, when the cry strike upon its ear, suddenly it stops its meal, raises its head to listen; again the cry is repeated, this time the bird notes from what direction the call proceeds, it answers the summons; once more is that cry heard, the poor victim unconscious of its doom, flies towards the supposed companion, but ere it reaches the spot, the poacher has raised his gun and ended the career of the unhappy bird. After this he changes his quarters to another field, for the report of his gun would prevent any more partridges there might be, from calling in that field. Having stationed himself somewhere else, again he calls, and perhaps again with like success, or perhaps he has to call in vain, and he continues this till dark, when with game and gun repocketed, he saunters home by a different road from that which he traversed before, and makes his appearance in the village, looking as innocent as a new born babe.

This "calling" require an immense amount of practice; after we had practised for nine months—though we beg to say for no poaching purposes—our only success was to call up one half grown bird to us. And we would warn our enthusiastic young readers from seriously attempting this pursuit, for perhaps when calling, if they imitate the note accurately, they might be somewhat surprised, in answer to their call, to see not a *bird* flying towards them, but the stalwart form of a *grizzly keeper* rise up before their eyes; and it *might* be hard to persuade him that "they really did not know partridges were game," or "that they did not intend to shoot any," for keepers have got to be too wide awake now to "swallow" such answers.

But inexperienced sportsmen (if they have a license) will find greater sport after a heavy fall of snow or rain than at other times. For when their feathers are wet, the partridge will not rise so quick as when dry, and so allow of a nearer approach being made. They begin feeding as soon as it is light, and continue, off and on, till 11 a.m. at which time they either fly to the stubble or some dry sunny hedge, facing south, and they stay there if unmolested basking in the sun, till about 3 p.m. when they again seek food round the wheatstacks, or in the stubble, or turnips. And it may be noticed that partridges will not feed round ricks in which there are rats, so that it is useless to hope to find them there. They generally roost in the turnips, or near some sheltered nook.

ENTOMOLOGY FOR THE MONTHS.
MAY.

Cheer up ye sad! awake ye dreamers! sloth and sorrow put away,
For summer bright is coming; hark to her herald May!
As with hawthorn branches waving, she calls aloud, "Give ear!"
    The sovereign of the seasons all
    Is coming. Listen to her call,
    And greet her gladly, great and small,
    The queen of all the year!

MAY! is there not music in the very word? the "merrie month," of which poets have sung; it is indeed a merry month. What can be more delightful, on a bright May morn, than a walk in the country, leaving far behind us the "busy haunts" of men, the birds are singing merrily, the trees are fast putting on their green leaves, and the insects are sporting and enjoying themselves in the warm sunshine, indeed resembling living flowers.

    Come then ye youthful seekers of every roving fly,
    With pinions gold-embroidered, or stamped with peacock's eye.

The entomologist who takes a walk on a bright May day will find plenty of employment; for he who keeps his eyes open—as all true entomologists will—cannot go far without meeting with some of the objects of his favourite study, for insects, especially the butterflies, are now appearing in increasing numbers. Many of those which came out last month still continue on the wing, viz., the Orange Tip (*Anthocaris cardamines*), the Whites (*Pieris rapæ, Brassicæ,* and *Napi*), and that lovely butterfly the Brimstone (*Gonopteryx rhamni*), the Wood White (*Leucaphasia sinapsis*), may be observed floating along the lanes; of this butterfly there are two broods, the first appearing in the present month, and the second in August; it is chiefly met with in the south of England. Mr. Newman, in his "History of the British Butterflies," mentions it as having been taken near Epping Forest and in Darenth Wood. I have a specimen in my collection which was taken at the Isle of Wight.

Several of the Hesperidæ are also out, among which we may notice the Dingy Skipper (*Thanaos tages*) the Grizzle (*Syricthus alveolus*), the Chequered Skipper (*Hesperia paniscut*), and the Large Skipper (*H. sylvanus*).

That very beautiful butterfly, the Swallow Tail (*Papilio machaon*), appears early this month, and begins laying its eggs on the milk parsley, hog's fennel, and various umbelliferous plants. The butterflies continue to emerge throughout the summer, so that the caterpillar, chrysalis, and perfect insect may be often taken at the same time. This insect, the largest of our British butterflies, is only to be found in certain localities; it has been taken in large numbers at such places as Whittlesea Mere, Taxley, and Horning in Norfolk. I have myself taken it at Ranworth, a few miles from the place last mentioned.

Several of the Fritillaries are also on the wing, the "Duke of Burgundy" (*Nemeobius lucina*), the Pearl Bordered (*Argynnis euphrosyne*), and the Greasy Fritillary (*Melitæa artemis*), accompanied by the Green Hair-streak (*Thecla rubi*), the Azure Blue (*Lycæna argiolus*), Clifden Blue (*L. adonis*), Small Capped (*Polyomattus phlæas*), Brown Argus (*Lycæna agestis*), and the Common Blue (*L. alexis*).

Amongst the "Nocturnal Lepidoptera" occurring this month we may mention the Broad and Narrow Bordered Bee Hawkmoths (*Macroglossa fuciformis* and *M. bombyliformis*), the Small Elephant (*Chærocampa porcellus*), and the Lime (*Smerinthus tiliæ*), also many of the Clearwings as the Red Belted (*Sesia Myapæformis*), large Red Belted (*S. culiciformis*) White Barred (*S. sphegiformis*), and towards the end of the month the Dusky Clearwing (*S. vespiformis*), which is very rare, the Currant Clearwing (*S. tipuliformis*) and the Six-Belted (*S. ichneumoniformis*), the Common Swift (*Hepialus lupulinus*), may also be observed flying madly along the hedge-rows.

The following geometræ are also on the wing:—the Barred Umber (*Numeria pulveraria*), Latticed Heath (*Strenia elathrata*), Common Heath (*Fidonia atomaria*), Bordered White (*F. piniaria*), False Mocha (*Ephyra porata*), and the Maiden's Blush (*E. punctaria*); the two last mentioned bear a close resemblance to each other. *Porata* has a round white spot on each wing, which is absent in *Punctaria*, and are very scarce insects. Several of the "Carpet" moths also fly this month, the Red Twin-spot (*Coremia ferrugata*), Common Carpet (*Melanippe subtristaria*), Flame Carpet (*Coremia propugnata*), and the Barberry Carpet (*Anticlea barbarata*), which is very uncommon.

Amongst the "Cuspidates" the following may be expected, the Pebble Hooktip (*Platypteryx falcula*), the Oak Hooktip (*P. hamula*), Barred Hooktip (*P. unguicula*). Among the Prominents, the Swallow (*Notodonta dictæa*), the Pebble (*N. ziczag*), and the Great Prominent (*N. trepida*), which is considered a great rarity; the Alder Kitten (*Dicranura bipuscus*), and its near relation the Puss moth (*D. vinula*), are also to be found this month.

A few larvæ may now be looked for, those of

the Oak Eggar (*Bombyx quercus*), Drinker (*Odonestis potatoria*), Lappet (*Luscivcampa quercifolia*), and the Dark Tussock (*Orygia fascelina*).

Norwich.   R. LADDIMAN.

BORAX LAKE, CALIFORNIA.

THIS sheet of water, the Lake "Kaysa" of the Indians, is situated in Lake County, 110 miles from San Francisco, and lies a little east of Clear Lake, about half way between Cache Creek and Hawkin's Arm.

This lake, which is separated from Clear Lake by a low range of hills belonging to the cretaceous period, has, under ordinary circumstances, a length of about a mile and an average width of half-a-mile. Its extent, however, varies considerably at different periods of the year, since its waters cover a larger area in spring than during the autumnal months. No stream of any kind flows into the basin, which derives its supply of water from the drainage of the surrounding hills, as well as, in all probability, from subterraneous springs discharging themselves into the bottom of the lake. In ordinary seasons the depth thus varies from 5 feet in the month of April, to 2 feet at the end of October.

Borax occurs in the form of crystals of various dimensions embedded in the mud of the bottom, which is of an exceedingly unctuous character, and is found to be most productive to a depth of about $3\frac{1}{2}$ feet, although a bore hole, which was sunk near its centre to a depth of 60 feet, afforded a certain proportion of that salt throughout its whole extent.

The crystals thus occurring are most abundant near the centre of the lake, and this rich portion extends over an area equivalent to about one-third of its surface. They are, however, also met with in smaller quantities in the muddy deposit of the other portions of the basin, some of them being, in the richest part before alluded to, over a pound in weight. The largest crystals are generally enclosed in a stiff blue clay, at a depth of between 3 and 4 feet and a short distance above them is a nearly pure stratum of smaller ones, some $2\frac{1}{2}$ inches in thickness, in addition to which crystals of various sizes are disseminated throughout the muddy deposit of which the bottom consists.

Besides the borax thus found in a crystalline form, the mud is itself highly charged with that salt; and according to Oxland, when dried, affords (including the enclosed crystals) 17·73 per cent. Another sample, analysed by Mr. Moore of San Francisco, afforded him 18·86 per cent. of crystallized borax.

In addition to this the deposit at the bottom of the other portions of the basin, although less productive, still contains a large amount of borax, and it has been ascertained by sinking numerous pits on the lake shore, that clay containing a certain portion of this salt exists in all the low ground around it.

The borax at present manufactured is exclusively prepared from the native crystals of crude salt, whilst the mud in which they are found is returned to the lake, after the mechanical separation of the crystals by washing. The extraction of mud from the bottom is effected by the aid of sheet-iron coffer-dams; and dredging machines worked by manual power, the whole of the labourers being Chinese. Until 1866 the only apparatus employed consisted of a raft covered by a shingled roof, with an aperture in its centre, about 15 feet square, and above which were hung, by suitable tackle, four iron coffer-dams each 6 feet square and 9 feet in depth. This raft or barge was moved in parallel lines across the surface of the lake, and at each station the four dams were sunk simultaneously by their own weight into the mud forming the bottom. When they had thus become well embedded, the water was baled out, and the mud removed in buckets to large rectangular washing-vats, into which a continuous stream of water was introduced from the lake by means of Chinese pumps, the contents of the cisterns being at the same time constantly agitated by rakes.

At the present time dredging-machines are employed for bringing up the mud and crystals from the bottom of the lake, and these are introduced into cisterns and washed as above described. In this way the turbid water continually flows off, and a certain amount of crystallized borax is finally collected in the bottom of each tank. This is subsequently re-crystallized, but from the density acquired by the washing water, of which some hundred thousand gallons are daily employed, it is evident that less than one-half the borax existing in the form of crystals is thus obtained, whilst that present in the mud itself is again returned to the lake.

In 1866, when I visited this locality, the crystals of crude borax daily obtained amounted to about 3000lbs., and after being carefully washed, they were dissolved in boiling water and re-crystallized in large lead-lined vessels, from which the crystallized borax was removed into boxes each containing a hundred-weight.

The amount of refined salt daily obtained varied from 2500 to 2600lbs., which was produced, as nearly as I could calculate, at a cost of about £18 per ton.

It is evident from the foregoing description that the system of working employed is exceedingly crude, and by no means calculated for obtaining the best results, and that in order to do so, it would be necessary to adopt some efficient process for the lixiviation of the mud after its removal from the bottom of the lake, and the recrystallization of the borax thus obtained.

The total extent of the muddy deposit considerably exceeds 300 acres, and if we assume that of this area 100 acres, or that portion only now worked for borax crystals, would be sufficiently rich to pay the expenses of treatment by the process at present employed, we shall arrive at the following figures:—

One hundred acres are equivalent to 484,000 square yards, and if the mud were worked only to a depth of $3\frac{1}{2}$ feet, this would represent about 565,000 cubic yards; or, allowing a cubic yard to weigh a ton, which is a very low estimate, the total weight of 100 acres of mud, in its wet state, will be approximately 565,000 tons. If the mud, as extracted from the lake, be now assumed to contain sixty per cent. of water, there will remain 226,000 tons of dry mud, containing, according to the mean of the analyses of Messrs. Oxland and Moore, 18·29 per cent. of borax, but if in practice only twelve per cent. of borax were obtained, this area alone would afford 27,120 tons of crystallized salt.

According to Mr. S. M'Adam, of Edinburgh, to whom a specimen was forwarded for analysis, the crude borax from Borax Lake has the following composition:

Biborate of Soda, dry	51·85
Water of Crystallization	45·44
Insoluble matter	1·42
Sulphate of Soda, dry	0·06
Chloride of Sodium, dry	0·08
Phosphate of Soda, dry	1·15
	100·00

Mr. Moore, of San Francisco, gives the following as the composition of the water of Borax Lake, which has a mean specific gravity of 1·0274:—

In an Imperial gallon.

Chloride of Sodium	1198·66
,, Potassium	9·92
Iodide of Magnesium	·22
Bromide ,,	trace
Bicarbonate of Magnesia	,,
,, Soda	188·28
,, Ammonia	trace
Carbonate of Soda	578·65
Biborate ,,	281·48
Phosphate of alumina	3·52
Sulphate of Lime	trace
Silicic acid	2·37
Matters volatile at a red heat	238·66
	2501·76

In the foregoing analysis all the salts have been calculated as being anhydrous; but crystallized borax contains about 47 per cent. of water, and hence the 281·48 grains found will correspond to 535·08 grains of crystallized salt. Besides the amount of biborate of soda contained in the mud of the lake, its waters are therefore capable of affording at least 6000 additional tons.

LIST OF BRITISH BUTTERFLIES:

WITH THEIR LOCALITIES.

PAPILIONIDÆ.

SWALLOW TAIL (*P. Machaon*). Fens and swampy ground. The fens of Cambridgeshire and Huntingdon. Also taken in Dorset by J. C. Dale, Esq., where in the parish of Glanvilles Wooten he took twelve in three days.

PIERIDÆ.

Wood White (*L. Sinapis*). Woods. Swanscombe and Darenth Woods, Randan Woods in Worcestershire. Woods near Malvern and Sandal Beat, Yorkshire.

Black Veined White (*P. Cratægi*). Heaths and forest lands. Faversham and Herne Bay, Kent. Barnewell and Ashton-wold, Northamptonshire, and the New Forest.

Green Chequered White (*P. Daplidice*). Downs and lucerne fields. Single specimens taken at Dover, Deal, Bristol, &c.

The Small White (*P. Rapæ*), the Large White (*P. Brassicæ*) the Green Veined White (*P. Napi*), and the Orange Tip, may always be found in gardens and lanes during their proper season.

RHODOCERIDÆ.

The Brimstone (*G. Ramni*). Lanes and fields; common in South of England, and taken as far north as Newcastle.

Clouded Yellow (*C. Edusa*). Clover and lucerne fields, sunny banks, and downs on the south coast of England; also taken at Wexford in Ireland.

Light Clouded Yellow (*C. Hyale*). Clover, lucerne fields, and sunny banks. Faversham, and the south coast of England.

ARGYNNIDÆ.

Silver Washed Fritillary (*A. Paphia*). Woods; Darenth, Birch, Swanscombe, and nearly all woods in the south of England. Hainault Forest, Langham Woods, near Stoke Nayland, Suffolk, and woods near Malvern.

Dark Green Fritillary (*A. Aglaia*). Woods and downs, abundant on the downs in south of

England, also on the downs near Arundel, Suffolk, Hainault Forest, and other parts of Essex.

High Brown Fritillary (*A. Adippe*). Woods and heathy places in the southern counties of England, and is taken in plenty as far north as Yorkshire.

Queen of Spain Fritillary (*A. Lathonia*). Woods and downs. Dover, Darenth, and Birch Woods, Kent, Colchester, and at Halvergate, Norfolk.

Pearl Bordered Fritillary (*A. Euphrosyne*). Woods. This is the most abundant of *Argynnidæ*, and may be taken freely in all the southern counties of England, and also in Scotland.

Small Pearl Bordered Fritillary (*A. Selene*). Woods and heaths; nearly as common as *A. Euphrosyne*, and frequents the same localities.

Greasy Fritillary (*M. Artemis*). Marshes and moist meadows. Monkswood and Holm Fen, Huntingdon, and freely throughout the south of England.

Glanville Fritillary (*M. Cinxia*) Grassy slopes; the under cliff, Isle of Wight, is the head quarter of this insect, although single specimens are taken elsewhere.

Heath Fritillary (*M. Athalia*). Woods, marshes, and heaths. Ford Wood and Dartmoor, in Devonshire. Deal, Faversham, Canterbury, most Woods in Essex and Suffolk, and Coombe Wood, Kent.

VANESSIDÆ.

Comma (*G. C. Album*). Fields and commons near Green Hamerton, Yorkshire, and abundantly near Bristol and other parts of Gloucestershire.

Large Tortoise-shell (*V. Polychloros*). Woods and pastures. The Woods of Suffolk and Essex, near Sittingbourne, Herne Bay, and Faversham, Kent, and Woods near Winchester.

Camberwell Beauty (*V. Antiopa*). Since 1819, when it was abundant, only single specimens have occurred near Rotherham, Yorkshire, near Colchester, Essex, the Isle of Wight, Nottingham, &c.

White Admiral (*L. Sibilla*). Woods and forests. Ipswich, Colchester, Black Park, woods near Gravesend, and near Winchester.

The Peacock (*V. Io*), the Small Tortoise-shell (*V. Urticæ*), the Red Admiral (*V. Atalanta*), and the Painted Lady (*V. Cardui*) are to be found commonly during their respective seasons in gardens, lanes, and fields.

NYMPHALIDÆ.

Purple Emperor (*A. Iris*). Woods and forests of oak. Epping Forest, Great and Little Stour Woods. Woods in Essex, Coombe and Darenth Woods, Kent. Dodnash and Raydon Woods, Suffolk, Enborne Copse, Berks, and woods near Ipswich.

SATYRIDÆ.

Marbled White (*A. Galathea*). Cliffs, woods, and moors, and, although local, seems to be distributed over the greater part of England.

Small Ringlet (*E. Cassiope*). Mountainous districts of Cumberland and Westmoreland.

Scotch Argus (*E. Blandina*). Dumfriesshire, near Edinburgh, and in most of the southern counties of Scotland.

Speckled Wood (*S. Ægeria*). Woods and lanes, and occurs from Dover to the north of Scotland.

Grayling (*S. Semele*). Downs and heaths. Newmarket, Gamlingay, and Salisbury Plain. Arthur's seat near Edinburgh, near Durham, and Castle Eden Dene.

Marsh Ringlet (*C. Davus*). Heaths and commons, near Stockport and Ashton. White Moss, Shornmoor, and other places in North.

The Wall (*S. Megæra*), Meadow Brown (*S. Janaira*), Ringlet (*S. Hyperanthus*) and Small Heath (*C. Pamphilus*) abound during their seasons in lanes, meadows, and heaths.

LYCÆNIDÆ.

Green Hairstreak (*T. Rubi*). Waste places near bramble bushes; distributed over the greatest part of England, but only occurs in the south of Scotland.

Purple Hairstreak (*T. Quercus*). In and near woods throughout England.

Black Hairstreak (*T. W. Album*). Woods and wolds, Ripley, near Windsor, near Ipswich, and Bungay, Suffolk, and Southgate, Middlesex.

Dark Hairstreak (*T. Pruni*). Woods and hill sides, Monkswood, Herts, and Barnwell Wold.

Brown Hairstreak (*T. Betulæ*). Coombe, Birch, and Darenth Woods, Raydon Wood near Ipswich, and woods in south.

Large Copper (*C. Dispar*). Used to be found in the fen districts of Cambridge and Huntingdonshire.

The Small Copper (*C. Phlæas*) is to be taken everywhere, and in almost any locality.

Silver studded Blue (*P. Ægon*). Woods, heaths, and downs in the south of England.

Mazarine Blue (*P. Acis*). Chalky districts in Yorkshire, Norfolk, and Hampshire.

Chalkhill Blue (*P. Corydon*). Common on the chalk in south of England.

Clifden Blue (*P. Adonis*). Chalky downs, Croydon, parts of Suffolk and the south coast.

Small Blue (*P. Alsus*). Chalkpits and wood sides in the southern counties of England.

Azure Blue (*P. Argiolus*). About holly bushes and ivy in Epping forest, near Ripley, near Dartford, and various parts of Norfolk, Suffolk, Hants, and Devonshire.

Large Blue (*P. Arion*). Fields and commons, the cliffs near Dover, near Glastonbury, Somersetshire, Barnewell Wold, Northamptonshire, and near Winchester.

The Common Blue (*P. Alexis*), and the Brown Argus (*P. Agestis*) are to be found everywhere in fields, lanes, and on downs.

FOOD OF BRITISH BIRDS IN APRIL.

IT is very important to consider the food of our British birds during the months of the year; for upon this really hangs their economic value, and such should form the basis of legislation for them. I will give the result of some years' examination of the stomachs of a few of our commoner birds during this month.

Kestrel (*Falco tinunculus*, Linn). This is a species of considerable economic value, yet not, however, to be placed in the first rank. Three stomachs, examined in Sussex, contained respectively a lizard, beetles, a field mouse, and a yellow hammer.

Sparrowhawk (*F. nisus*, Linn). Five examined in April in Sussex contained the feathers of a chicken, lizards, some remains of insects, and the head of a small warbler. The sparrowhawk may be placed in nearly the same rank, from an economic point of view, as the kestrel.

The long-eared Owl (*Strix otus*, Linn). The food of this species in April I have ascertained to be beetles, bats, and mice.

Barn Owl (*Strix flammea*, Linn). Two owls contained dormice, water rats, and bats. Three contained field mice and beetles.

Tawney Owl (*S. aluco*, Linn). Two of these birds contained bats, but in one other case a young rabbit and two mice were taken from a stomach.

My correspondent, G. D. Rowley, Esq., has found the white owl rather destructive to the young rabbits of Abbotsleigh Down, Hunts. But we may place all the owls on the whole as A 1 among the farmer's friends.

The Red-backed Shrike (*Lanius collurio*, Linn). I found the food of this species in this month to be beetles, mice, and young birds. It is of the highest economic value as an insect destroyer.

The Spotted Fly-catcher (*Muscicapa grisola*, Linn). The food in April I observed in Sussex to be exclusively insects, principally hymenoptera and diptera. Beekeepers sometimes complain of this bird. A tamed and chained hawk of the Hobby or Merlin species is the best "scarecrow." A kestrel will not do, being liable to eat the bees.

The Dipper, or Water Ouzel (*Cinclus aquaticus*, Bech.), in Devonshine (Dartmoor) feeds on larvæ of caddis flies, pupæ, and larvæ of dragon flies, water beetles, small limnea, planorbis, cyclas, and other aquatic mollusca. It has often been accused of eating the ova of salmon trout and grayling of mountain streams, but this is not in accordance with my experience or that of my correspondents.

Missel Thrush (*Turdus viscivorus*, Linn). The food of this in Sussex I found to be, in April, snails, slugs, and caterpillars.

Song Thrush (*S. musicus*, Linn). The food of this in Sussex and Kent was larvæ and green vegetables. On mentioning this to a friend he said, "Now I shall order all the thrushes to be killed." "Stop," said I, "when you work hard in your garden gathering snails and insects during the winter and early spring months, do you not expect to eat of the green vegetables? be equally liberal to your servant the poor song thrush." "Very well," said he, "but is it so?" I read him my table as follows:—January, February, March, hawthorn berries, slugs, worms, snails. He then began to complain of the injury that the thrushes did to his crops of currants and gooseberries in June, July, and August. "But you have forgotten," said I, "the number of caterpillars and other insects they have given their young in the breeding season." The thrush, like the blackbird, is doubtless extremely useful in moderation when its numbers are in proportion to the extent of farm or garden ground. When they are very numerous, however, they are induced to feed upon fruit, but our own experiences tend to show that they prefer insects and mollusca to fruit. The same remarks which apply to the thrush apply also to the blackbird.

The Ring Ouzel (*T. torquatis*, Linn). Of eight examined during the month of April in Yorkshire all contained small land shells and insect food.

C. O. GROOM NAPIER.

SILKWORMS:
AND HOW TO REAR THEM SUCCESSFULLY.
PART IV.

THE MOUNT AND CROP OF SILK, ETC.

SILKWORMS are "on the Mount" when they are mature, and ready to spin their silk. On the first appearance of maturity silkworms must immediately be provided with the materials necessary on which to spin. As I have before enumerated the different materials serviceable, it is only necessary now to say that such ingredients should be placed in rows across the stages at about eighteen inches apart, which will provide sufficient room to admit the trays between when removing worms to spinning quarters. It is a good plan to arrange the upper stage ready with these materials, having reserved it empty for the purpose, and then place the forwardest worms between the rows, on the papers, using the trays, from which they may be easily slipped into position. If the worms had been arranged some days before in succession according to their ages on the upper stages, the smallest on the lower ones, &c., this work would proceed somewhat with regularity, and the second stage would be left empty, on shifting the insects to the top, and at liberty to have the spinning materials placed thereon, and so on until all the worms are mounted.

When the broom system of arrangement be adopted the brooms used should be sufficiently long and elastic to admit of being bent or curved beneath the ceiling or stage above, forming an arch, the bottom parts of the brooms standing on the stage below from which the insects have to mount. The brooms will stand firmer if placed on the cross pieces of the stage, which is the proper place, unless, indeed, the stages are made somewhat solid with a bedding of reeds. The brooms may be placed so as just to touch each other at their upper parts, and from four to six inches apart on the stage below; but they must not extend beyond the edges of the stages, as then some silkworms might fall to the ground, which would be fatal to them. The insects placed between these rows of materials will soon begin to mount; any ripe ones not finding the way to the foot of the brooms, etc., can be gently taken and placed there; an attention often necessary during the entire mount. It is a good method to lay light twigs of oak, elm, etc., over the silkworms, on which the mature ones will crawl; then by leaning these against the brooms the insects will more readily find their way into them. As the mount may extend over several days, sparing quantities of leaves must frequently be administered to the worms between the rows, in order to push them along, and the temperature should be maintained rather over than under 70 deg. Fahrenheit.

When a great part of the insects have mounted, and are spinning, the remainder should be collected to the centre of each stage, nearer together, otherwise more leaves will be wasted in feeding them than is necessary.

I give 70 deg. Fahrenheit as the heat appropriate for rearing and mounting silkworms, but a variation of five degrees over or under will not produce any mischief; silkworms, however, that are mounting, cannot spin if subject to a much lower temperature, the cold so hardening the silken fluid within them that they cannot eject the silk. All the first worms might be mounted in one castle, and the three or four days later ones in the other. Any remaining to mount after the fifth day in the last castle will be better collected and placed on a temporary stage or two, arranged in a corner of the rearing room, nearer to the stove, or if in a separate room where a temperature of 75 deg. or 80 deg. could be had. Such stages should be first prepared with the spinning materials, and for this purpose shavings, straw, pea haulm, spear grass are very suitable. This kind of loose stuff is also very useful laid round a castle, on the floor, in which any worms that fall will spin their cocoons instead of being killed.

After the insects on a stage are all mounted, all refuse beds, dirt, etc., should be removed, and this can sometimes be done by rolling up the papers, and transporting all from the room. When the little workers become tolerably covered with silk, air must be admitted in greater proportion, especially if the weather is close and sultry, otherwise they may be seized with disease. Silkworms are about five days spinning and converting themselves into the chrysalis state, which, however, is not complete sometimes before the eighth day, when the crop may be gathered, after opening a cocoon, to make sure that the last worms to spin are also in the chrysalis state. The spinning materials containing the cocoons should be taken away from the low stages, first laying them carefully on the clean floor or on tables, stages, etc. The cocoons are then gathered, and the good hard ones should be placed in baskets by themselves, as also the weak ones. Those which are stained or have no consistence should be put aside to serve for spun silk of inferior quality.

The next operation is to remove the floss silk around the cocoons, which is done by turning them round, holding the floss between the finger and thumb.

The cocoons are now fit for sale, or to be reeled. At present I know of no reeling houses in England, and the amateur has to reel his own cocoons as best he can. Of the methods adopted to destroy the chrysalis, reeling the silk so as to be marketable, etc., I cannot now speak, but a few observations on the providing and preserving silkworms' eggs may be useful. I certainly should select all the best cocoons, and generally those first spun, to produce good eggs from, not over large, but hard, especially at their ends, and having a circle round the middle. Wanting yellow, white, or other coloured silk cocoons alone of such sort must be chosen; about 1 lb. of cocoons will produce about 1 oz. of eggs, or about 40 to 50,000 in number. The cocoons must be selected as nearly as can be guessed male and female. The roundest at the ends and large are more generally females, and the smaller and sharper at the ends males. The sex, however, is evident when the moths appear, the females being quiet, larger, and heavier, the contrary being the case with the males. For about fifteen or twenty days from the completion of the cocoons the moths will appear. The cocoons should be made firm to something, either by gluing them to a board, or threading them on twine, and suspending them to nails in a wall.

To string them by means of a needle and thread, only the superfices of the cocoons must be pierced, or the needle might injure the chrysalis. I like gluing them on card-board as well as any way. Silkworms' moths generally push through the ends of the cocoons of a morning soon after sunrise. They afterwards pair, and should so be left about six hours, when they are separated; taking them gently by the wings in each hand, they are pulled by a smart though gentle jerk. The males are placed in a large box in the dark, and the females are put on clean linen suspended on a frame where they will deposit their eggs. A slanting position, and not a perpendicular one, is best for the linen and frame. Two feet square of linen will contain from two to three oz. of eggs. The males will serve again the next day, if more females should be born than males; but they are best not used a second time, for their production is weaker.

The preservation of the eggs after they are obtained, is the most important consideration. The eggs are of a light yellow on being laid, but they soon put on different shades of reddish hue, until at last they remain of a dark violet, and at this juncture the linen containing the eggs should be folded up, put into an earthen pot, and tied down with paper and string, perforating the former full of holes, with a dinner fork. This may be hung up in a cool place, in a cellar, if dry, away from mice or birds.

About October the weather being cooler, the pot might be removed to an upstair cool room, where they can remain until February, only temporarily removing them to a warmer situation whenever there be danger of frost getting to them, which is best prevented, although it might not really injure them.

If mild weather occurs in spring the pot had better again be transferred to a cellar, but particular care must be used to prevent damp getting to the eggs, as they would be injured by it. The object is to keep them dry and cool, which will tend to prevent their hatching too soon in spring, before the mulberry leaves are sufficiently expanded to provide the worms with ample food. The way to detach the eggs from the linen is to soak them first in soft water for thirty minutes. This is best done in October, or not later than February, selecting mild weather. Two persons holding the linen, a third scrapes them from it into the centre by means of a table spoon or bone knife. The eggs are then washed and laid out on blotting paper or a napkin, gently turning them over until partly dry, when they are spread out on another dry napkin for a day or two until quite dry. They must dry in a cool room without artificial heat unless it be very damp weather, when a small fire would do no harm, provided the eggs are not near it, or have more than 40 deg. Fahrenheit of heat.

When washing the eggs they may remain fifteen or twenty minutes in the water, and be stirred about with the hands; by this means the good ones after a time sink to the bottom, and those which float may be poured away as of no use, being light and inferior. In a day or two, when the eggs are dry, they can be put again into the earthen pot, but I think they should not lay in a stratum of more than half an inch thick; therefore, as many pots as are requisite must be employed, for I do not think many eggs laying in a heap take any good. In Italy I have seen them kept in fine wire net kind of baskets a foot high and only about one inch wide. Thus the air plays through. I like the contact of the earthen vessel, which is cool, and tends to preserve the eggs properly until the season for hatching is well advanced; an important point in this country. Indeed, I believe it would answer to make use of an ice house in spring for this purpose. In fact, this is an experiment already effected, viz., preventing by this means the eggs hatching until even the autumn. But suppose we prevent the hatching until June, would not this method be of great service? for the mulberry leaves would then be more plentiful and good, and the weather more settled. Last spring I prevented my eggs hatching in an earthen pot, until the 15th of May, which was more than fifteen days later than would have been the case, had the eggs not have been so preserved. When the eggs are near hatching they gradually grow lighter coloured, and as soon as a worm is seen out, the eggs must be removed from the pot and gradually exposed to the hatching temperature.

Some silkworms' moths lay as many as five hundred eggs, but this is much above the average.

There are lately several other breeds of new silkworms, such as the Bombyx Yamamai or oak leaf; the Ailanthus, and American varieties; and at some future time I shall be happy to pen something about them if interesting to the readers of the NATURALISTS' NOTE BOOK.

LEONARD HARMAN, JUN.
Old Catton, Norwich.

THE LEPIDOPTERA OF SHEPPY.

LITTLE appears to be known about the Isle of Sheppy, as an entomological locality. Several species, as C. Castrensis F. Raticella, etc., have been asserted by more than one authority, to have occurred here; but these are a very few of the curious, and in some instances rare, lepidoptera, to be found in this locality. I propose to mention the more important species I have met with during several years' collecting in the island.

Machaon has been several times seen by different persons, but only once by myself, in 1862. Rhamni was rather scarce in 1868, as also were Atalanta and Io; but the deficiency of these species was amply compensated by the abundance of Hyale, which literally swarmed in lucerne-fields. A friend and myself, on the 8th of August, 1868, took fifty specimens between us, and had we been so disposed, might have taken four times as many. Edusa was plentiful at the same time, but this species occurs almost every year. Galathea is by no means rare in several places, while Hyperantus is abundant. The absence of wood, however, prevents any of the Fritillaries being found here, and Quercus is the only Hair-streak. Corydon and Agestis are both plentiful in spite of the nature of the soil, which is all clay.

The Sphingina include A. Loniceræ, which is plentiful in more than one locality, and the three Smerinthi, of which S. populi is abundant. A. Atropos occurs regularly, though sparingly, every year, and S. Convolvuli was rather frequent in 1868. C. Celerio was also taken in a room last year, probably attracted by the light, and is now in the collection of a friend. M. Stellatarum is abundant.

Among the Bombyces, S. Salicis occurs in immense abundance among poplars in the dockyard; and P. Chrysorrhœa, usually rather scarce here, was plentiful last season. A. Villica is common, and the usually rare S. Papyratia I have taken freely on weedy banks. I have not, however, been able to discover the haunt of C. Castrensis in this locality, though I have one female specimen. Can anyone give me a hint for finding this species?

The Noctuæ include some good species. B. Perla and Glandifera occur abundantly along the dockyard wall, and A. aceris is common, both in the larva and the perfect state. N. Typhæ and Crassicornis occur, the latter at light, which affords H. popularis pretty commonly, also L. Cespitis. The scarce A. pyrophila has been taken here. I beat one from a hay-stack in 1867, and took one on ivy-bloom, 1868. T. Ianthina and interjecta are plentiful in lanes at dusk, and Timbria occurs, Orbona and pronuba being of course pests.—I generally beat these two last from hay-stacks. The ivy bloom yields O. lota, A. pistacina, lunosa, litura, C. vaccinii, spadicea, X. cerago, flavago, and ferruginea in abundance; also more sparingly, O. macilenta and X. citrago. I have taken the rather scarce X. gilvago, and E. ochroleuca is abundant on knapweed (Centaurea nigra). H. chenopodii being plentiful at light, etc. The two Abrostolas occur, and last year small specimens of P. gamma—some not more than an inch in expanse—occurred. C. Nupta is not rare.

The Geometræ are well represented. The pupæ of B. Hirtaria may be obtained by digging round elm trees, and H. abruptaria is no rarity. P. cytisaria occurs freely among furze, and the four Ephyræ—porata, punetaria, trilinearia, and omicronaria—are to be found. The common Acidalias are all present, with the addition of A. trigeminata, osseata, immutata, incanata, emarginata, and above all, Emultaria; this last species is not by any means uncommon, flying at dusk along ditch sides. B. amataria is abundant, as are also S. clathrata and A. citraria. E. unifasciata and the following "Pugs"—E. centaureata, subumbrata, subnotata, (abundant) vulgata, pumilata, and rectangulata—occur in more or less abundance, while C. fluviata appears not to be rare, I having taken several in 1867. P. lignata, S. dubitata, C. mata, dodata, and P. comitata are to be found, and E. cervinata and lipunctaria (another chalk-frequenting species) are abundant.

The Pyrales include H. rostralis, which is plentiful on ivy-bloom, and H. tarsipennalis, not rare in the hedges. P. glaucinalis is frequent in thatch, and A. cuprealis is found in the same situations. C. angustalis is abundant in waste places, and E. flammealis has occurred. P. stratistata is plentiful on more than one pond, and on the canal, near Sheerness, A. nideus occurs in myriads. E. crocealis abounds in wet places, S. cincitalis in clover-fields, S. ferrugalis among weeds and on ivy-bloom, and E. angustea on the dockyard wall. A. colonella is plentiful in places where humble-bees have their nests. H. nimbella occurs along the cliffs, E. elutella freely in old stacks, and E. semirufa has been taken flying at dusk. M. cribrum and pinguis, C. cassentiniellus and falsellus have been taken by me, and C. cerusellas is abundant. C. phragnutellus occurs among rushes.

Of the Tortices and Tiniæ I cannot so confidently speak, having only recently paid attention to these insects. I may, however, enumerate as occurring here, O. scabrana, O. boscana, E. purpurana, A. schrebersiana, A. dipoltella; H. plumbellus, D. granulosella, pimpinellæ, albipunctella, D. badiella, H. geofreella, etc., etc. The species of Micro-lepidoptera appear to be very numerous, and probably some more rarities will occur.

A. Bennettii is not rare on ditch-banks near the shore, and P. acanthodactylus and phæodactylus occur, P. lithodactylus, pterodactylus, Arigonodactylus, and A. polydactyla being plentiful.

In addition to these species, most of the common Lepidoptera are found in more or less abundance. As an entomological locality, the island certainly has its drawbacks, chiefly on account of the absence of wood, the exposed nature of many of the best places, etc., but I think the above list of species will show that it is by no means a bad one.   CIMEX.

SEA BIRD MURDER.

BEFORE discussing the desirability of protecting sea birds from the gradual extermination which threatens them, and the various methods of carrying any project for their preservation into effect, it may be worth while to consider the Bill brought in by Mr. Sykes for this purpose. It has passed through Committee of the Lower House in the same form (with a few verbal alterations) as it was brought in, and will, in all probability, shortly become law. As it may interest all your readers in a greater or less degree, I give a summary of its contents.

As amended in Committee, after reciting that "the sea birds of the United Kingdom have of late years greatly decreased in number, it is expedient therefore to provide for their protection during the breeding season;" it is enacted by

Sect. 1.—The word "sea bird" shall for all the purposes of this Act be deemed to include the different species of gulls, auks, guillemots, puffins, terns, oystercatchers, curlews, skuas, petrels, gannets, divers, razor-bills, shearwaters and grebes, merganser, eider ducks, and shieldrakes.

2.—If any person shall kill, take, or wound, or attempt to kill, etc., or use any boat, gun, net, or other instrument for the purpose of killing, etc., or shall have in his possession, any sea bird recently killed, taken, or wounded, between the 1st April and 1st August, such person, upon conviction, shall forfeit for every bird so killed, etc., or so in his possession, a sum not exceeding one pound, as to the Justices shall seem meet, with costs of conviction.

3.—The Home Office may on application of Justices in Quarter Session vary or extend such prohibited period.

4.—Any person who shall expose or offer for sale, or have in his possession, the eggs of any sea bird during the prohibited period, shall, for every egg so exposed, etc., be fined a sum not exceeding five shillings, and costs, unless it shall be proved to the satisfaction of the Justices, that such eggs were taken before 1st April or after 1st August, or that they were taken solely for the purposes of food.

5.—The offender, if required by any policeman or constable, shall give his name and address, and on refusal and conviction be fined a sum not exceeding two pounds, and costs.

6.—Application of penalty, half to informer and half to overseers of poor.

7.—All offences committed within the Admiralty jurisdiction shall be deemed to be within the United Kingdom.

These are the main points of the Bill for the Protection of Sea Birds, and for my part, I should have been glad to have seen it extended to all our birds, with a few necessary or expedient exceptions. No one, I think, will deny that the Bill will have a most beneficial effect, if, when law, it is stringently enforced. It has been stated by your correspondents that the chief persons interested in the destruction of these birds are sportsmen, (?) naturalists, and the plume trade. The naturalist may easily take another time of the year for prosecuting his studies, and will be able to obtain far better specimens than in spring. The plume trade will (unless its fair customers are attached by "A. M. B.") increase rather than diminish. Young birds in fresh and unspotted plumage are surely preferable to the old birds whose feathers are worn and injured by their arduous parental duties, and in a few years we may hope to find the present decrease changed to an increase. The "so called sportsmen" are hardly worthy of notice; a true sportsman would hardly dream of shooting any harmless bird during the breeding season, much less these inoffensive, and, to their murderers, useless birds, whose parental cares render them tamer than usual. The Bill however, speaks for itself; no argument is really required to point out its advantages, for on every possible ground —reason, common sense, expediency, and humanity,—it seems to be the best means of preventing the extinction of our sea birds.

I think "A. M. B." is rather too hard on "the sex" for enhancing their charms by the adoption of feathers and furs. Our cynic rather overshot the mark in his attack: as the plume trade is to be accused of the wholesale destruction of these birds, if they were restrained from pursuing their nefarious practices and the poor birds allowed to retain their lives and plumage, the fair creatures would soon find something else whereby to gratify their penchant for finery, involving less cruelty and loss of life; but where temptations, and such temptations! in the shape of grebe, swansdown, duck, and all manner of other plumes and feathery "trimmings" (I think that's the word) are displayed before their eyes, who can wonder that they take advantage of the opportunity, and become, at no slight expense, their blissful owners. Who would'nt?

If "A. M. B." can find any objection to make to the Bill under consideration, taken as a whole, without going into mere verbal criticism, I am sure your readers will be delighted to see his facetious remarks on this interesting subject.

London, April 6th. A. G. HARVIE.

THE GOLDFINCH.

THE goldfinch is certainly the handsomest of our small native birds, except perhaps the kingfisher; and when, to such loveliness of plumage, we see united more than loveliness of song, we must indeed own that we are blessed in having such a bird as a native of our island. It is, however, chiefly among the lower classes that the goldfinch is a favourite cage-bird; the rich rather look down upon it, because it is only a native bird, and prefer to patronise "cut-throat sparrows," "Avadavats," and others, which, though beautiful in plumage, have little or no pretensions to song. For my own part, I prefer our little goldy to any one of the gaudily coloured foreign birds, and therefore have I made these few notes, the result of experience of his ways and needs.

In the first place, as to buying the birds. I think the best plan is to buy them when "grey-pates," that is before they have gained the full red-head plumage, the whole head being then a confused blurr of grey. I have got these birds for 2s. the pair, and, in six months after, I have had birds worth 5s. or 6s. each; splendid songsters, and in splendid plumage. The time to purchase "grey pates" is in September or October, and they may be kept in one large cage during the winter, but should be removed to separate abodes in February or March, when they will certainly come out in song.

Many writers recommend that these birds should be kept in a cage covered in at the top; but, as far as my own experience goes, I think the usual round wire cages quite as good, provided the bird be moderately tame. By wire cages I mean those with square wooden floors and round wire upper story—not the tin or "Zollverein" cages—I have no liking for these gaudily coloured, yet cold looking, cages. I think abodes for birds in confinement should be made as natural as possible (though of course no cage is really "natural"), and how such things as these can be liked by the bird, which are made of materials the most un-natural, I cannot tell. I can only say that I find all my birds far happier in the wood and wire cages than in the tin ones.

The best food for goldfinches I have found to be a mixture of canary and rape seed, three parts of the former to one of the latter; a few hemp seeds now and then, as a treat, will be "received with thanks" by our little friend, but this seed should never be used as a general food.

Groundsel and water-cress are his favourite articles of green food, the former especially; and with these he should often be supplied.

Most goldfinches are fond of bathing, and fresh water should therefore be supplied to them for this purpose every day in summer and in winter twice a week if the sun shines; in very cold weather they should not be allowed to bathe at all. Fresh sand should also be given every time after the bird's bath. I should like to hear from "S. E. P." what sort of "grit from a road" he means in his valuable hint on page 30. Eleven years' experience is certainly a high recommendation to follow his plan, and I wish to do so, but am deterred by not knowing what he means by "grit from a road." Is it the dust which is so troublesome on macadamised roads in the summer months?

As goldfinches are the most loving and the easiest tamed of all pets, so also are they generally the most timid and the easiest frightened. One of my own was killed by his cage falling a few feet, by the cord slipping off the pulley; the shock threw him into fits which proved fatal before I could procure any restorative. Another bird, a canary, has performed precisely the same journey more than once, without the slightest shock to his nerves. Great care should, therefore, be taken to treat them with uniform kindness, and never to speak harshly to them, or move them about roughly.

I was much interested in the curious disease mentioned by Mr. A. M. Morris on page 30 of the "N. N. B." as so troublesome to his goldfinch. I have a redpole in which exactly the same thing is apparent, but in a much smaller degree, so that it does not interfere with the bird's eating. I do not think the goldfinch's bill could be cut, after arriving at such a growth as he mentions, without injuring the bird, but I believe it might be pared gradually as it grew, and so kept in some degree under restraint. Could not Mr. Morris grind the seed (which in this instance would have to be hemp and rape, for canary will not grind) and thus save the poor bird the unnecessary trouble of cracking it?

And now, just two words as to the song of the goldfinch. I have noticed that there is a considerable variety of "style," so to speak, in the singing powers of goldfinches. For instance, one little fellow over my head is at this moment warbling away, in almost a wood-lark's softness and delicacy of melody, while a bird in a room at the other end of the house, is making the place ring again with his clear, loud, joyous bursts of song, Every one who hears these birds notices the difference in their song; and yet neither of them, as far as I am aware, has had the benefit of instruction from any other bird. Can any of the readers of the "N. N. B." explain this? A. H. ROWORTH.

HABITS OF THE BURROWING OWL OF CALIFORNIA.

I WISH to state a few facts about the Burrowing Owl (*Athene cunicularia* Molina) that lives in California. I had almost constantly for four years opportunities of observing the habits of this little owl, which is really one of the most notable features in the natural history of California. A colony of these owls lived within one hundred yards of my cabin while I passed a frontier life; and they were very common everywhere in that vicinity. I have seen them every day for years, hundreds and perhaps thousands of them in all. Where I have seen them, they always live in the deserted or unoccupied burrows of the Ground Squirrel (*Spermophilus Beecheyi*.) I came to the conclusion that they were able to drive out the Spermophiles from their habitations, but I am not certain of the fact. It is true that there were, in that region, always a large number of unoccupied burrows wherever there was a colony of Spermophiles; so that there was no lack of unoccupied habitations for the owls to take possession of. But I have noticed that wherever there was a large number of the owls, very few or no Spermophiles lived. *One* or *two* owls would occasionally be seen among a colony of Spermophiles, but they never appear to live in the same hole or burrow with the squirrel; and I have never seen a squirrel enter a burrow that was occupied by owls, however much tempted by fear he might be to enter the first hole he should come to. True, the Spermophile never likes to enter any burrow but his own, and will run past any number of inviting entrances in order that he may at last hide himself in his own domicile. But aside from this, I believe that the squirrels are afraid of the owls, and do not dare to intrude upon them. The notion that the Athene digs its own burrow appears to me apocryphal and unreasonable. I have never seen any evidence of it. Negative evidence proves nothing; but yet the absence of facts is strong presumption against their existence, and it would be strange that I should never have seen any evidences of their digging powers if they have any. After a shower of rain, one sees fresh earth thrown out around the mouths of the burrows of the Spermophiles, but never anything of the kind around the burrows of the owls. They are not constituted for digging, and there is no necessity for it; they can always find any number of holes ready-made for them. That they live in peace and amity with the rattlesnake, I believe to be another error and stretch of the imagination. Rattlesnakes are very abundant where I lived, and I killed one or two almost every time that I rode a mile or more from the house, yet I never saw a rattlesnake near a squirrel's hole but once, and that hole was a deserted one. I once found a large rattlesnake swallowing a squirrel (*Spermophilus Beecheyi*) that it had caught, in the centre of a colony of squirrels, but several yards distant from any "squirrel-hole."

I once took pains to dig out a nest of the *Athene cunicularia*. I found that the burrow was about four feet long, and the nest was only about two feet from the surface of the ground. The nest was made in a cavity in the ground, of about a foot in diameter, well filled in with dry soft horse-dung, bits of an old blanket, and fur of a Coyoté (*Canis latrans*) that I had killed a few days before. One of the parent birds (male or female?) was in the nest, and I captured it. It had no intention of leaving the nest, even when entirely uncovered by the shovel, and exposed to the open air. It fought bravely with beak and claws. I found *seven* young ones, perhaps eight or ten days old, well covered with down, but without any feathers. The whole nest, as well as the birds (old and young), swarmed with fleas. It was the filthiest nest that I ever saw. In the passage leading to the nest there were small scraps of dead animals; such as pieces of the skin of the antelope, half dried and half putrified, the skin of the coyoté, etc.; and near the nest the remains of a snake that I had killed two days before, a large *Coluber?* two feet long. The birds had begun at the snake's head, and had picked off the flesh clean from the vertebræ and ribs for about one-half of its length; the other half of the snake was entire. The material on which the young birds nested was at least three inches in depth. I do not remember the time of the year.

The Burrowing Owls do not migrate. Where I lived they were as numerous in winter as in summer. Perhaps in low, flat plains, that are deluged or inundated by water in the winter, the little owl is obliged to have a far drier location, but I have never seen any such migration. They always remain in or near their burrows through the day, never leaving them to go any distance except when disturbed, when they make a short crooked flight to some other hole near by, and when driven from this last one return to the first again. When the sun sets they sally forth to hunt for food, etc., and are all night on the wing. I had seen them and heard them at all times of the night and early in the morning. They are not strictly nocturnal, for they do not remain in their nests or burrows all day, but their habits, in this respect, are about the same as those of the other owls, as *Strix pratincola*, *Nyctea*, *nivea*, etc., or of the domestic cat. There are very few birds that carry more rubbish into the nest than the *Athene;* and even the Vultures are not much more filthy. I am satisfied that the *Athene canicularia* lays a larger number of eggs than is attributed to it in Dr. Brewer's work. I have frequently seen, late in the season, six, seven or eight, young birds standing around the mouth of a burrow, isolated from others in such a manner that I could not suppose that they belonged to two or more families.—*American Naturalist*.

New Books.

The Young Shetlander; or, Shadow over the Sunshine; being Life and Letters of Thomas Edmonston, Naturalist on board H. M. S. Herald, edited by his Mother. 1868. Edinburgh: Wm. P. Nimmo.

Seldom have we finished the perusal of a Biography with such a mingled feeling of pleasure and regret—pleasure at reading such an interesting and useful work—regret that the subject of it should, by an accident, so sudden and awful in its character, be cut off at the commencement of a career which gave promise of bringing him to a high position among the celebrated scientific men of his day.

Owing to our limited space, we can merely give an outline of his short career, preferring, also, to let our readers peruse his "Life and letters" for themselves; indeed, we should refrain from doing so were it not that our readers may, even from our short sketch, see that Thomas Edmonston was, in character and mind, one of the great men of the time. He was born at Buness, in the isle of Unst, Shetland, on the 20th September, 1825, the son of Dr. Edmonston, a most ardent lover of nature, and especially well versed in ornithology. Thomas, from his earliest childhood, gave promise of more than ordinary intelligence, and his ready observation and retentive memory made him a very precocious child. As may be imagined, the literary resources of his locality were very limited, the chief work on Natural History in the possession of the family being an edition of Bewick, and one or two old works on Botany. Under such a father it was but natural that he should be very well versed in ornithology, especially that portion found in the neighbourhood. This, however, was not the science in which he shone. Botany was his favourite study. At the age of thirteen he had made an admirable collection of the Shetlandic Flora, including a plant hitherto unknown in Britain. From that age he began to make botanical tours through the other islands. Among the distinguished personages who, at distant intervals, visited his island home was Professor Edward Forbes, who became a firm friend of the young naturalist, and, after he left Shetland, maintained a regular correspondence with him. When nearly fifteen, he accompanied his father and mother on a visit to Edinburgh, where he became acquainted with several of the savans of that city. On his return to Shetland he pursued his studies with great vigour, and remained at home nearly twelve months, after which he returned to Edinburgh and studied at the University. His remarkable genius was here recognised, and obtained him the appointment of assistant secretary of the Edinburgh Botanical Society. In the following year he began to give a course of Botanical lectures, in which he was very successful, and which added considerably to his renown; and in 1845—in his 20th year—he was elected Professor of Botany at the Andersonian University of Glasgow, Professor of Natural History, and *ex-officio* Curator of the Museum. Just before he entered on his new duties, he published a work on the Shetland Flora; before, however, three months had elapsed, through the instrumentality of Professor Forbes, he received an offer of appointment as a Naturalist on board H.M.S. *Herald*, on the point of starting on an expedition to the Pacific and California; this offer, with the consent of his parents, he gladly accepted, and set off with his comrades. For about nine months all went well, and Thomas wrote long accounts of the fauna, flora, and general characteristics of the places they visited. In January, 1846—hardly twelve months from his election as Botanical Professor—while landing with a party on the coast of Peru, a rifle, belonging to one of the party, being entangled in the confusion of landing, accidentally discharged, the ball passing through the arm of a clerk and entering the left temple of Edmonston, killing him on the spot. His comrades buried him the next day, on shore, in a spot surrounded with lovely and luxuriant foliage—a spot where he himself would have delighted to wander and study. Thus was ended the career of one who, had he lived, would have been an ornament to science and an example of character, energy, and perseverance. We might of him quote the Poet's words—

"Lives of great men all remind us
We can make our lives sublime,
And departing leave behind us,
Footprints in the sands of time;"

for though he had not attained a sufficient age at the time of his death to reach that point of renown in which he might be called "great" in the popular sense of the word, we can see those elements of character which have in all ages been instrumental in forming "famous men."

As to the work itself, we need say but little. As a rule, we look with a certain degree of suspicion on a Biography of a man, written or published by a relative; and in this case, where a mother's hand describes his childhood, character, and disposition, we opened the work with a great amount of distrust. This, however, has been entirely swept away, both by the unbiassed and open account of his early days, which a mother alone could well depict, and by the letters and remarks of the various strangers, as well as friends, on his character, which fully bear out all that the affection of a fond parent wrote of a loving and much lamented son. We cannot do better than close this short notice by giving the following sketch of Edmonston's character, written by his father, who was in all respects thoroughly competent to appreciate and delineate it.

"No one ever knew him from childhood up who was not charmed with him. Not only were his intellectual faculties wonderful, but his fancy, his affection, his manner were to the last degree captivating. A capacity for the severer sciences, united with the most ardent love for manly sports and gymnastics; the power of indefatigable application, with the most playful imagination and humour; a boundless memory, with a precocious and powerful judgment; a strongly developed power of philosophical generalization, with a perspicuous and fluent style. Meek and gentle as a lamb, he ever shewed the unflinching courage of a lion. He had no hot-bed forcing, everything came to him naturally and spontaneously, I may almost say intuitively. He was as extraordinary as a child as a stripling. Nature did almost all for him—art, or what is called education, little, beyond what he derived from the society of his own family. His deportment was so affectionate and engaging that never in the course of his too short life—no, never! can we recollect a frown, or act of wilful disobedience. All this is saying little of what he was. No wonder we never recovered the blow of the separation. He was the darling of his shipmates. Captain Kellet wrote of him that in all his experience he had never met one whose mental powers and information had so impressed him. Edward Forbes lamented him as a serious loss to science; and all this of a boy of twenty from the solitudes of Unst."

More Light: A Dream in Science. London: Wyman and Sons, Great Queen-street, Lincoln's Inn Fields.

This little work is one of the most singular we have met with for some time. The author, who modestly omits his name, was reading by a fire on a winter evening (probably after a late dinner) and, as is often the case, fell asleep. He dreamed—and this pamphlet is the substance of his dream—that an angel took him somewhere, or rather nowhere, as we are told that he was standing in space. "Sky there was none, nor earth." He is then instructed in metaphysical questions—what is mind? and what is matter? He is shown by ocular demonstration the laws of reflexion, refraction, the critical angle, and the polarising angle. As, however, we are informed that a mathematical demonstration of this work will shortly be published, we refrain from passing any comments, except to observe that we think that instead of one half a dozen angels will be required to work out the figures.

Report on the Culture of the Japanese Silkworm Bombyx Yama-Maï in England in 1867-68. By Alexander Wallace, M.D., M.R.C.P., of Colchester. Colchester: Benham and Harrison.

If any person could rear the delicate Japanese silkworms with success, we think it must be Dr. Wallace, whose essays on the culture of the Ailanthus and the Yama-maï are doubtless known to many of our readers. We hope, however, that the next report on this subject may be somewhat more cheering, as notwithstanding every attention and care, the majority of the worms seem to have died, whether from disease or improper food. It appears to us that the whole question is as to the proper mode of feeding them. At present two of the largest rearers do not agree as to the food the worms ought to receive; one advocating a dry diet, the other maintaining that a few drops of water sprinkled on their leaves is the proper food. However, experience and patience will alone solve the difficulty; we hope to hear again from Dr. Wallace that he has been more successful.

Remarks, Queries, &c.

(*Under this head we shall be happy to insert original Remarks, Queries, &c.*)

DO INSECTS FEEL PAIN?

"Think not that anything HE has created is unworthy thy cognizance, to be slighted by thee."—RAY.

The uncertain gyrations of an erratic pen, too carelessly driven, or the rapid localisation of prankish types, have made me in my last letter put "coriously" for *curiously*, "ailment" instead of *aliment*, and "continue" in the place of *continues*; but as we often find as much transitory relaxation in the welcome variety of a sweeping blunder, as we do of permanent pleasure in the dull monotony of studied correctness, I can now console myself on the superlative legibility of my present MS.

Do insects feel pain? Pain and pleasure are consequences. Pain is the phenomena exhibited after violence done to the animal, and all reason recoils from the idea of excluding insects from the general law. Although I quite prefer arguing from general principles, still any of your correspondents on the negative side (if such there be as well put by Mr. Buttemer) can try the following.

Take a disc of copper the size of a crown piece, and another of zinc somewhat larger; place a disc of paper moistened with sulphuric acid, a little smaller than the copper, between the two discs, and lay them on a table; place a small garden slug (any quietly disposed insect will do) on the copper, as the zinc must be undermost, and note well the results; and if your little subject does not convince you of the painfulness of its position, then submit your own corpus to the influence of a galvanic battery of moderately high intensity, and if you have a friend with you who witnessed the snail or insect-experiment, ask him how you behaved under the shocks of the battery, and I venture to assert that he'll reply, "You behaved very like the snail."

Proof positive that both felt pain. Take a larva of the dragon-fly, put it in a glass vessel, and fill the vessel with the water from which the larva was taken, then drop some crystals of oxalic acid into the vessel, the acid will dissolve on the bottom of the vessel, and now watch the movements of the larva. It darts upwards with a violent spasmodic action, moves about with all signs of evident pain as the solution continues to rise, and at length it dies. On the mind of the experimenter the conclusion must force itself that the creature avoided the solution as long as possible, not from any previous knowledge the poor little fellow had of the deleterious nature of the acid, but to some unpleasant sensation immediately felt, to actual pain evidently experienced.

Here, in a series of experimental proofs I might go on to infinity, and still produce the same rational results, the same convincing proofs that insects feel pain.

But surely, Sir, as Mr. Buttemer justly remarks, "the arguments have all been one-sided from the commencement," for, as I often observed, the amo-negative correspondents are all (with but few exceptions) pro-positive in their admissions and arguments. I wish the correspondents on the negative side would read and consider the letter of "Veritas;" surely the quotation from "Jones's Animal Kingdom" should assist their perception.

I am glad to see our new friend with the noble name, "Justitiæ Amor," enter the field, he at once mounts the critic's tripod, modestly reserves any argument he may have, treats us to the benefit of his heavy "opinions," promises to do something in future, changes imperfect phraseology, and stamps it with the seal of his own perfection, as if he had just finished a treatise on the sublime, and then retires. Now, Sir, we are eagerly searching for information, and we feel happy in having the "N. N. B." in which to meet, in which to converse, and I do hope that "Justitiæ Amor" will abandon his "yes" and "no" recapitulations, and treat us to arguments.

Mr. Dalton contents himself in propounding queries, and pronouncing on the merits or demerits of the answers given. Resign this sinecure place, those judicial functions; come down, labour, and help us. Do insects feel pain?

Even without elaborate argument the question carries its own affirmative—an irresistible affirmative—which speaks to the sympathies, appeals to the judgment, and naturally forces itself upon the whole mind of intelligent man. There is an insect, an organized creature, an animal; there it is, created for purposes wise and good, the formation of that small animal exceeds the educated comprehension of the philosopher; look at its beauty, its activity, its instinct, and shall we in our limited knowledge of that surprising creature, in our admitted ignorance, or culpable humanity, proclaim it an exception to the general law of animal life? Most certainly not. Those myriad insects have their place in creation, their wide sphere of action, and while harmless—

"There they are privileged. And he that *hurts*
Or *harms* them there is *guilty of a wrong;*
Disturbs the economy of Nature's realm."

Those insects have their brain, nerve, circulating blood, all the senses common to animal life, with this difference—that in insects those senses are infinitely finer, in a far higher degree developed, their wonderful instinct, their care for their young, their evident enjoyment under pleasurable sensations, and their pain too when violence is committed on them.

Are we in a position to reasonably deny such a conclusion? No. For as pleasure is but a phenomenon of animal life, so pain is but an antagonistic phenomenon, both acting on the system through the medium of sensation, and that sensation conveyed by the agency of a nervous machinery.

To maintain that insects are alike proof against all pleasure and pain carries with it a sort of stoic consistency that we could possibly respect; but to deny that they are susceptible of pain, and at the same time admit that they are capable of feeling pleasure, are absolute contradictions not easily reconciled.

But, Sir, with Shakespeare let me ask our correspondents of the presumed negative propensities, "Shall these paper bullets of the brain awe them from the career of their humour?" H. H. ULIDIA.
Dromore, 3rd April, 1869.

I perceive this question is being somewhat revived in the March number of the "N. N. B.," though I cannot think with your correspondent, "Justitiæ Amor," that either careful observation or study will *determine* the question at all, inasmuch as we cannot transform ourselves into insects, which it would be absolutely necessary to do if we would determine it satisfactorily. The weightier arguments that have as yet been adduced have been most certainly on the affirmative side. The remarks of the correspondent above mentioned contain a number of assertions, but few arguments. He first attacks Mr. Bellingham on the entangled rotifer. He says, "It would require a very considerable amount of argument to convince me that the rotifer twisted itself about and writhed so violently because it was in pain." The reason is, I presume, because that gentleman has not laid himself open to conviction. Mr. Bellingham considers that because the rotifer writhed and twisted itself about to get free from its entanglements, therefore it felt pain from its contact with the fibre, and a very reasonable conclusion too, but "Justitiæ Amor" does not think so: will he be kind enough to say if he can prove that because the rotifer "twisted itself about and writhed," therefore it *did not* feel pain? Now I have just captured two small flies, and by way of experiment, though much against my feelings, dispatched them by a gradual process. I first amputated two of their legs on one side, and wounded them in the abdomen and thorax with a dissecting instrument. I then placed them under the microscope to witness the result. The insects at first struggled violently, and attempted to walk away; but every instant they fell over on the unwounded side, and showed by their writhings unmistakeable signs of pain, till at length overcome by exhaustion they ceased their struggles, and it could then be plainly seen by a powerful lens that their bodies were agitated by a violent trembling, which continued until death put an end to their sufferings. Now who shall say, or who can *prove* that these flies felt no pain? As I said before, there can be no *certainty* in the matter; but the probability is, and the evidence furnished by their tremblings and contortions goes far to prove, that they did to some extent feel pain. To what extent they felt pain we cannot tell, neither indeed need we wish to know; if they felt pain they felt pain, and there's an end of it. He next defends Mr. Landels' statement, that "his beetle felt very little or no pain from all that it underwent," because Mr. Landels found nothing which he could construe into a sign of pain. To say that a beetle felt no pain because it walked away with the pin fixed in its body, is like saying that a whipped dog felt no pain because it ran away from the person who whipped it. My own opinion is, that the very fact that the beetle attempted to escape from the instrument of torture was, without any difficulty of construction, a sign of pain. Lastly, he criticises rather sarcastically Mr. Ulidia's statement, that because insects have digestive organs he concludes they are susceptible of pain. Perhaps your correspondent may not be aware that the digestive organs not only have a most intimate connection with the nervous system, but are next to the heart itself the most acutely sensible of any of the organs of the body, and therefore I think it is clear proof that the possession of digestive organs indicates a proportionate amount of pain. As Mr. Ulidia says, the "want of sufficient aliment," or what "we call hunger, is anything but a pleasant sensation." Often have I watched the most terrible combats between two insects. If any of your correspondents will take a couple of common crickets, and put them into a glass vessel with a round bottom, and covered over so that they cannot escape, and just shake the glass a little, they will witness a conflict they will not soon forget; in a few minutes the bottom of the glass will be strewn with broken limbs, and in the end one or both of the insects must succumb to their fate. Now in these combats each insect evidently tries to outvie the other in inflicting the most pain. The subject, though extremely interesting, is one which has been thoroughly sifted in the pages of the NOTE BOOK, and one which I think is pretty well settled in the minds of your correspondents; and while I would be the last to advise an abrupt conclusion to any scientific discussion, yet I think the one before us has reached its climax; and if we review the letters from the commencement, we cannot but conclude that the major part of the evidence is in favour of the affirmative side. For my own part, I am more fully convinced than ever that insects have an amount of pain equal to the amount of nervous matter contained in their bodies. W. NEWBERRY.

I think that Mr. Ulidia's arguments are a good example of "great tenacity of life," for after they have been fairly controverted and refuted, and we may say bisected by Mr. W. H. Dalton and others, yet by some unaccountable means they seem to refuse to die, and somehow to find some point upon which to turn and "writhe." This point generally happens to be a slip or slight ambiguity of expression on the part of his opponents. Mr. Ulidia asks what Mr. John Landels meant by a sentence which he quotes, and calls a "great jumble" of words. Here is an exact exemplification of what Mr. W. H. Dalton says as to Mr. H. H. Ulidia taking advantage of "unfortunately chosen expressions;" for it is plain what he means, although this slip has drawn down on him an attempt at irony, but from one whose letters are replete with these feeble efforts—in short, Mr. Ulidia has not answered one of the assertions made by Mr. W. H. Dalton.

Mr. Ulidia confesses afterwards that he thinks that great tenacity of life shows a numbness for the time, and if for the time, why not altogether? In fact, in the natural course of things, we should take the fact as granted that "insects do not feel pain" until our opponents can prove that they do, for the reason that we never prove a negative before an affirmative. However, I will quote a passage occurring in Kirby & Spence's "Introduction to Entomology," which says, "No part of the Creation is subject to so many injuries or to so many disasters." Can it be believed that the beneficent Creator, whose tender mercies are over all his works, would expose these helpless beings to innumerable enemies and disasters, were they endued with the same sensibility of nerve with the higher orders of animals? The head of a wasp will try to bite after it is separated from the rest of the body; and the abdomen, under similar circumstances, will attempt to sting, and what is more extraordinary, the headless trunk of a male mantis has been seen to unite itself to the other sex, and a dragon-fly to bite its own tail, as we learn from J. F. Stephens, Esq., who, while entomologising near Wittleseamere, having directed the tail of one of these insects, which he had caught, to its mouth, to make an experiment whether the known voracity of the tribe would lead it to bite itself, saw to his astonishment that it actually bit off and ate the four terminal segments of its own body, and then, by accident escaping, flew away as briskly as ever. These facts, with hundreds of others which might be adduced, are sufficient, I think, to prove that insects do not experience the same acute sensations of pain with the higher animals, which Providence has endued with more ample means of avoiding them." I think that this is sufficient to prove the negative side of the question. ERNEST BALFONT BAX.

I AM another of those who are deeply interested in this animated discussion, as to whether insects feel pain or not; and I fully agree with those who affirm that they do, but not to such an extent as animals of a higher order; nor can it be argued that every individual of the animal creation is sensible of that amount of pain proportional to its size. Therefore, in my opinion, the amount of pain which insects are susceptible of, ought rather to be determined by the degree of development of their nervous system. According to this theory, then, those insects are the most susceptible of pain whose nervous systems are most fully developed. But to keep strictly to the question in hand, "Do Insects feel Pain?" It seems to me ridiculous to deny it, since it is an established fact, that insects possess a nervous system, or something equivalent to it; and if they possess a nervous system, they also possess feeling, and what else is feeling, but the capability of receiving impressions either of pleasure or pain. Why do butterflies and other insects delight to disport themselves in the sun? Simply because the sensation of warmth conveyed to them by means of their nervous system, which is acted upon by the sun's rays, is pleasing to them. And why poes a caterpillar wince when pierced by the ovipositor of the icheneumon? For no other reason than because it experiences a sensation of pain, though it be but slight. I am convinced that sooner or later it will be universally admitted that insects *do* feel pain to a certain extent, though to what extent I fear will never be accurately determined.

If anyone could put an end to all doubt on this subject, in the cause of which so many have taken up the pen, by bringing forward some undeniable proof on his side, he would have achieved one of the greatest triumphs in the researches of natural history. And though such a thing seems impossible, yet I agree with Ulidia in believing, that the theory that insects do feel pain, will be fully established by indefatigable research, patience, and careful investigation.

Reading. R. S.

This controversy has now dragged its slow length along through eleven numbers of the N. N. B., and at last shows signs of an end. The two assertions of mine which Mr. Ulidia deprecates, were perfectly true when written, and I am ready to accept the verdict of any impartial searcher after truth in this matter. I have taken the whole of the N. N. B. from its commencement, and have consequently seen all the letters that have appeared on this subject, and till the March number appeared I saw nothing but ridicule, without a trace of argument, on the affirmative side.

As to the "cobbler's wax and broadcloth," that was meant as an illustration, not as an argument, though it was not so happy an illustration as the goat held by the horns. I am glad to see that the question has passed the stage of ridicule and entered that of argument.

And now let me tell Mr. Ulidia that his argument of the social penalties among the ants has convinced me that, in the absence of certainty, which can only come by future study, it is highly probable that insects are susceptible to pain, and in my future dealings therewith, I shall take care to give as little pain as possible.

Skipton. W. H. DALTON.

Some remarks made by Mr. Ulidia have drawn my attention to a mistake in the printing of my letter on this question, which appeared in the March number of the NOTE BOOK. In the fifth line of the concluding paragraph I am made to say "that animals *do* feel a certain amount of pain." The word I used was not *animals*, but *insects*. Even Mr. Ulidia might have seen that the word "animals" was a misprint. Allow me, while making this correction, to supply a line which by some oversight I omitted in my manuscript. For the sake of precision the first sentence of the final paragraph should read thus:—"In concluding this my second and last letter on this subject, I would like to repeat what I said clearly enough when I wrote last . . . namely, that, while I see little force in most of the arguments of your correspondents, my opinion is that insects *do* feel a certain amount of pain.

Scuddylaw. JOHN LANDELS.

IN reply to Mr. Ulidia's letter which appeared in the February number of the NOTE BOOK, let me inform him, that though I have racked my brains, I cannot conceive how he imagines that the argument used to prove that insects feel pain, and that Mr. Ulidia himself does, is the same. If I were asked to give my opinion as to the sensitive disposition of Mr. Ulidia, I should immediately reply, that I know by experience that *I* am capable of feeling pain, and since I am of the same *genus*, or (to use a term with hardly so wide a signification), of the same *family* as Mr. Ulidia, I am quite certain that he can feel pain also. If we could *satisfactorily prove* that one spider (for instance) felt pain, then we might fairly say it was indisputable that insects *do* feel pain. But seeing that we are unable to do this, it is absurd to say that the arguments relating to pain felt by the system of man and the insect are identical. A. H. MALAN.

THE SOURCE OF HEAT.

W. Newberry seems dissatisfied with the "popular" ideas, as he terms them, of heat. He seems to think that the usual theories respecting it are erroneous, but I cannot see that any of his hypotheses are as well founded as those that he objects to. For instance, I do not understand how heat is at all influenced by attraction. Now as I will presently show, the gravitation theory will prove the very contrary to that which W. Newberry has set forth. He, I presume, knows the law of gravity? Certainly his statements with regard to the "source of heat" being in the earth, would lead me to the opposite conviction. What is heat? It is supposed, by philosophers, to be matter in motion! I will now apply this to Mr. W. N.'s theory of attraction, and see whether it will prove it or not. One atom of matter attracts another atom, with a force proportioned to the size of each and to the distance between them. Examples of this great law are shown in the revolution of the planets or systems, leaves on a pond, etc., etc.

Your correspondent observes that "the heat . . . . is drawn from the earth by the attractive power of the sun." If he will try that rational and clever experiment proposed by the "Caliph of Bagdad," he will at once perceive how fallacious his own hypothesis is, and for the following reasons:—In the first place, the attractive power of the sun, great as it is, would be insufficient to withdraw anything, however minute, from the surface of the earth, or from below it. In the second place, your correspondent in summing up the different forces, has forgotten one, which will at once dissipate his theories. It is the attraction of the earth. I will now state briefly, how this influences W. N.'s opinions. According to the theory that heat is matter in motion, it will be manifest to all, that although the sun is thousands of times larger than our earth, yet owing to its distance it has no effect upon it in withdrawing any of its constituents permanently. Therefore we see that the earth's distance from the sun compensates for its deficiency in bulk; and consequently the attraction of the former would not permit one atom of its component parts to be taken away. Supposing the theory of W. N. to be correct, and the terrestrial heat to be drawn up into our atmosphere, how is it that the earth is not exhausted? And how is it that the air has not become intolerable if the heat is so constantly being "drawn up?" The radiation of heat at night, which is exemplified in the natural formation of ice in the tropics, would be enough to overthrow W. N.'s theory, which, I cannot help observing, reminds me very forcibly of the story in the "Arabian Nights," of the magician and his loadstone rock. Again there is another weak point in W. N.'s argument which shows it to be unsound. He accounts for the seasons by saying that the heat abstracted from the ground warms the atmosphere, and is greater during summer because the sun is more perpendicular then, and also on account of the "rapid revolution of the earth on its own axis."

The diurnal motion of the earth has nothing to do with either the source or formation of heat; it rather tends to the opposite by forming cool currents of air. But how could the revolution of this globe possibly produce heat? What friction is there to cause it? It takes twenty-four hours to revolve, and where there is no particular impediment there can therefore be no possible reason for the production of heat.

Having thus proved two inconsistencies in your correspondent's paper, I wish now to remark upon the geological statements that he propounds. "Gulielmus," in the March number, very naturally asks whether there is any proof that "heat is communicated to the surface through the non-conducting crust?" To whom Mr. Newberry thus evasively replies:—"Does your correspondent know any thing of geology?" He then speaks of "chemical" and "mineralogical" laws governing matter. I should not have found fault with this if your correspondent had given a definite answer to "Gulielmus," and not contented the readers of the "N. N. B." with a short sentence that had little or nothing to do with the subject. It seems to me that W. N. fancies that I and some others of your readers are ignorant both of the internal fire and also of the supposed primeval conditions of our globe. But while we have direct and everyday testimony to the truth of both doctrines, yet we cannot say decidedly that the internal heat affects the temperature of either ocean, atmosphere, or land, to an extent great enough to produce any marked change. I have been led to speak of this, as the following statement will decidedly show how very low the temperature is in some of the deep mines. Has your correspondent ever read of the vast quantities of ice that are found in many continental mines? If so, how will he reconcile it with his own theory of the "source of heat."

I have now only my last objection to make, and that is to W. N.'s idea of the non-conducting power of the mountains! He observes that many mountains that are "formed by the protrusion of immense masses of granite and based upon several thousand feet of this solid crystalline substance are not so susceptible of heat at their surface as the plains formed of thick porous strata." I said just now, the amount of heat that we receive from the interior of the earth is so small as to have no perceptible effect. And I certainly do not believe that the height of a mountain matters in the least with regard to the passage of heat through it. It has been computed that a grain of sand upon a globe one foot in diameter is as large in comparison as a lofty mountain upon our planet. Besides, I cannot perceive how a short distance like the crust of the earth could at all matter to heat, which we know travels just as fast as light; and which generally radiates from a body, and is not attracted to it. It is not always the most porous bodies that are the best conductors; this is a paradox, and a good example of it is seen in placing a bar of iron and another of wood in a fire, in such a way however as to have one of their ends protruding. The experimentalist should take hold of both, and he will then know practically the truth of my statement.

Lastly a few words upon the "thin refined air" that R. B. W. speaks of. I hope that he will pardon me for explaining his own statement, but as it is necessary to do so in order to show Mr. W. N. more clearly that the sun is the only "source of heat" and light that we receive, I have taken that liberty. It was the opinion of Laplace, Newton, and others, that there is a fine gas which extends throughout space, and which they called ether. Light is supposed to be a wave of ether, and is propagated in a similar way to sound. In conclusion I may remark that it is my opinion that the long established theories that I have adduced in my paper, are far more tenable and sensible than those given by Mr. W. N.; and I should feel obliged to him if he would inform me who are the authorities that he refers to. A. C. E. B.

I have read with deep interest the letters which have appeared in your paper on the sources of heat. I see a great diversity of signatures, but only one appended to letters maintaining that the earth is the principal source of heat, which is Mr. Newberry. He appears to be the only champion of that opinion, and has to put up with a vast amount of ridicule and contradiction, and it seems wonderful to me how he can persist in his opinion, with such convincing proof that he is wrong against him.

The experiments and results with burning-glass ought, in my opinion, to convince him, but he does not seem to think so.

Mr. Newberry says, in his last letter, in effect, that a greater rate of motion of the earth at the equator causes a greater amount of heat there. Why, may I ask, is this? I really cannot see, unless he intends to say that heat is derived from the perspiration of the earth, and that the faster it goes the more heat it gives out!

Really he has found a capital method of evading difficulty, and attempting to throw it in his opponent's way, by asking how solar advocates will explain an assertion which he makes, and does not attempt to explain himself. I refer to the cooling down of the temperature, which he says has been gradually taking place through every geologic age. I think it just as possible that the sun has receded from the earth, or *vice versâ*, as that the fire, which Mr. Newberry assumes to exist under the crust of the earth, is getting cooler and cooler, or that the sun's attractive power is becoming less.

Having attempted to answer Mr. Newberry, I will state my views on the subject.

Heat is transported from the sun to us in the rays. As one of your correspondents has said, no conductor is used. Heat passes through a vacuum, until it comes to within about fifty miles of the earth, when the air begins; when it reaches the earth, the process of absorbing and radiating begins. (I will not encroach upon your space by explaining this, as it is to be hoped that all the correspondents of the "N. N. B." know.) When the earth radiates a portion of the heat received and absorbs the rest, the portion radiated rises into the atmosphere just above the earth, and, as is well known, has a tendency to rise and expand. In rising and expanding, it, of course, by the covering a larger space, gets rarefied, and at last ceases altogether. This will account for the night being colder than the day; *i.e.*, in the night, since the sun is hidden, no more heat can be absorbed, and the rest of what was received in the day is radiated out.

I hope Mr. Newberry will not deny that light bears a great analogy to heat, nor that we get *light* from the sun. Does it not seem much more probable that heat and light are both derived from one and the same source, rather than from two entirely distinct ones? I imagine that, out of one hundred scientific and philosophic men, ninety-nine would, if asked "Which is the principal source of heat, the sun or the earth?" answer, "The sun undoubtedly."

Exeter, April 6. VICTOR VOLANS.

One of the arguments brought forward by Mr. Newberry against the sun being the principal source of heat, was that he is at a greater distance during the warm months than he is during the colder ones; the reasons of this were entirely explained in the "N. B." for March. Now it appears to me that the same argument will bear against his own theory of attraction, for as the sun is at a greater distance, his attraction also will be less during the summer than it is in the winter. If Mr. Newberry has yet any doubt on the above subject I think the following experiment will quite convince him that the heat does not proceed from the earth; let him take a magnifying glass and hold it in such a manner that it will intercept the rays of the sun; these by passing through the lens are concentrated on to one point; on holding a piece of paper at this point or focus the heat is sufficient to set it on fire, and also will cause gunpowder to explode, which requires a heat of 545°. that is if the day is sufficiently clear and warm. If the heat does proceed from beneath us what an absurdity it is for people to carry parasols to shelter themselves from that heat, or to seek the shade for coolness. But still I think T. T. is in error when he states positively that heat can be transmitted without a medium. I had always understood the necessity for some conducting body, to be as Mr. Newberry says a well known fact, and will just mention in support of it that Mr. Faraday in reaching the greatest artificial cold, viz: 166° below zero, by mixing Crystallised Carbonic Acid and Ether performed the experiment in vacuo, I presume so that there should be no conductor by which it could receive heat. Some persons suppose that the earth does not move in a vacuum, but that the interplanitary space is filled with a very rare atmosphere which would be sufficient to act as a conductor; the principal objection to this is that however rare the atmosphere may be it must offer some opposition to the earth's progress, which would surely though slowly retard its movement, and this giving the attraction of the sun greater power, we should finally be drawn into and consumed by that body. This however cannot be the case, if as Mr. Newberry states our seasons are getting colder; some people however, think that they are getting warmer, and if we have many winters like the last they will certainly make many converts.

As such strong objections can be brought forward against both the above theories, it certainly appears to me more reasonable to suppose that the heat is caused by the rays of light becoming heated in their passage through the atmosphere, as I explained in the March No. of the "N. B." Mr. Newberry has supported his views very ably, but I think he must on reflection relinquish the position he has taken up.

O. R.

Mr. Newberry's exposition of his theory in the April Number of the N. N. B. is clearer than that in the previous number, and at first sight his arguments seem to have a good show of reason, but on examination they fail in their object. He ascribes the alternation of the seasons to the law of attraction, and says, "We find the heat will be much greater, and be drawn from the earth by a much greater force when the attractive power of the sun falls perpendicularly, than when it falls obliquely, so causing the difference in the intensity between summer and winter;" but in this he errs. The power of attraction is regulated by the proportionate bulk of bodies and the distance which separates them, and we positively find that when the sun has reached his greatest altitude in midsummer, he is then at his greatest distance from the earth, the earth being then in its aphelion. Now, inasmuch as distance regulates attraction, the influence of the sun is in this respect less in summer than in winter. The velocity with which the earth moves in its orbit is less when in aphelion than it is when in perihelion, and all this I think tends to prove that attraction has neither part nor lot in the matter of the distribution of heat at the surfaces of the planets. What is the cause of the great conflagrations of which we sometimes hear as having taken place on the prairies of North America —the burning of immense tracts of the scorched prairie-grass? Is it caused by the earth's moving with greater rapidity at that particular time, combined with perpendicular action of the solar attraction? I trow not. Are they not of the most frequent occurrence during seasons of long continued drought, when the burning rays of the sun have absorbed every particle of moisture from the parched ground, and the fibres of the tall praire-grass are like so much tinder? Again, what is the cause of the almost roasting heat experienced by those on board a ship becalmed in tropical seas for many weeks together, when it has been torture to tread the deck of the doomed ship? (And I would add that it is not a thing unheard of, for the whole of a ship's crew to succumb to the burning heat). Surely Mr. Newberry does not adduce the same reason for the presence of heat in mid-ocean as on terra-firma. With regard to the science of geology furnishing proofs of the climate of our earth having been much hotter in the early ages of the world than now, we need not suppose that the earth has been receding from the sun, nor that the power in the sun to generate heat was greater in past ages than now; to account for this, many reasons might be brought forward other than those. What is more reasonable than to suppose that our atmosphere was of greater density in former periods, and consequently better able to receive a larger body of rays, and generate a greater amount of heat? W. H. BELL.

Hull.

In his second letter on the "Source of Heat," Mr. Newberry has explained his theory a little more, but he has not produced any arguments which really favour it. The theory certainly is made to appear more plausible by referring the phenomenon of heat to the attraction of the sun upon the heat generated in the earth, for then some of the effects which follow from the established theory will equally follow from this; such as the alternation of the seasons and excess of heat at the equator. But all the recent researches of the most eminent physicists tend to prove that heat is not a ponderable body, and therefore the attraction of gravitation will have no effect upon it. But even if this were not the case, your correspondent's theory does not account for the fact that a lens collects the heat to a focus on the side *opposite* to the sun. It ought to intercept the rays as they rise and bring them to a focus on its upper side. As to the geological bearings of the case, I may say I have studied geology a good deal, but I never met with anything which would countenance the idea that the heat of the interior (if there be such universal heat) could be felt on the surface of the earth.

W. N. says that volcanoes are seldom found covered with perpetual snow. I think he will find, on a careful examination, that the snow-line depends entirely on the height of the mountain and its latitude; its being a volcano or not makes no difference, except, of course, during an eruption. I think it is Humboldt who describes the melting of the snow on Cotopaxi, on the breaking out of an eruption. Then again I should like to know how your correspondent proves that mountains are not so susceptible of heat at their surface as the plains. Some dense substances are better conductors of heat than more porous ones. With regard to the gradual cooling since the earliest geological periods, I quote the following from Sir C. Lyell's Elements:—"It seems to have become a more and more received opinion, that the coal plants do not, on the whole, indicate a climate resembling that now enjoyed in the Equatorial zone. . . A great predominance of ferns and lycopodiums indicates moisture, equability of temperature, and freedom from frost rather than intense heat." And these conditions seem to have been afforded by a different configuration of land and water. I hope these remarks may induce Mr. Newberry to abandon his theory, or at any rate prevent others from espousing it, for nothing is so obstructive to the progress of science as a tenacious adherence to a false theory. Better no theory than a bad one.

For the benefit of "The Caliph of Bagdad," I extract the following from an article by Dr. Richardson in the "Popular Science Review":—"Space inter-stellary, inter-planetary, inter-material, inter-organic, is not a vacuum, but is filled with a subtle fluid or gas, which for want of a better term, we may call still, as the ancients did, Aith-Ur-Solar fire,

ÆTHER. This fluid, unchangeable in composition, indestructible, invisible, pervades everything, and all matter; the pebble in the running brook, the tree overhanging, the man looking on, is charged with this ether in various degree: the pebble less than the tree, the tree less than the man. The ether, whatever its nature, is from the sun, and from the suns; the suns are the generators of it, the store-houses of it, the diffusers of it." GULIELMUS.
Faversham, Kent.

The remarks of some of your correspondents on the source of heat, have only tended to increase the difficulties of the popular theory. We have now three distinct hypotheses introduced:—1st, the popular theory, that the earth is heated by rays from the sun; 2nd, that heat is caused by the friction of light rays passing through the atmosphere; and 3rd, that heat is drawn from the earth by the attractive power of the sun. The Caliph of Bagdad, in the April No. of N. N. B., writing in favour of the first of these theories, says, that "all persons admit there is more or less air between the sun and the earth." Does your correspondent mean that the atmosphere extends from the earth to the sun; that in fact, all space is filled with air, which has neither beginning nor end, but extends from planet to planet, and from sun to sun? It has, I believe, been ascertained that our atmosphere extends but forty-five miles above the earth's surface, if so, I cannot see how it is possible for rays of heat to pass from the sun to the earth. By the by, will your correspondent tell me how he proves that heat is transmitted in rays at all. I think it has been pretty certainly proved that heat is composed of waves, and that the more rapidly the waves succeed each other the intenser becomes the heat. Assuming this to be true, and taking the sun as the nucleus from which the planetary system derives its heat, and considering the lessening of power as the waves extend into space, and the amount of heat felt on the earth's surface, we should find at the sun the heat would be many, many times more intense than would be necessary to keep all known substances of which the sun is composed in a white heat, whereas it is considered highly probable that the sun is a solid body like our earth. The experiment of the burning glass mentioned by your correspondent, and also by Mr. Ulidia, I must confess is not easily explained away; but is it not possible for condensed rays of light passing through the glass to produce a sufficient heat by friction to light the wool? Now I have tried several experiments with the burning glass, and have never failed to light a match by the aid of the sun; but I have tried several lenses of different powers with artificial heat, have held it so close to a fire as to be scarcely able to bear the heat, but have never been able to light even a lucifer match, and yet the heat was much greater from the fire than from the sun. However it is not yet proved that the sun is the source of heat. The subject itself comprises questions which are far from being positively determined by scientific men. Such questions as What is heat? By what process is it generated? and, How does it act upon surrounding objects? must be answered before we can fully determine the question at issue. If the earth derives its heat from the sun, how is it that it is more intense at its centre than at its surface?
W. NEWBERRY.

Most of the correspondents who have opposed Mr. Newberry's theory of the source of heat, appear to maintain the idea that the sun is an immense body of fire, and parts with his rays of heat in the same way as a bar of hot iron. Now it has been calculated by astronomers that if this were the case it would be entirely consumed and burnt to ashes in the course of 4,000 years, and of course meanwhile giving less and less heat. It also seems to me that those who hold the idea that the atmosphere is warmed by connection or contact with the earth, are bound to accept the above theory, viz., of hot rays emanating from the sun.

The view I incline to is that the atmosphere is warmed not by connection but by the action of the rays of light upon the heat which exists in it (as in everything in nature) in a latent state; and that the earth itself and all things on its surface are warmed in like manner, the light making sensible their hidden warmth.

Dr. Dick says, "The rays of the sun produce heat chiefly by exciting an insensible action between caloric and the particles of matter contained in bodies; caloric appears to be a substance universally diffused throughout nature." Great light always develops latent heat; in fact light seems to be the chief source of heat, for although we have heat to a certain point without light, we never have light without a proportionate amount of heat. The burning glass is a good illustration of this, as by concentrating (and so intensifying) the rays of light, it brings out more heat. This theory will likewise easily answer Mr. Newberry's query as to the greater amount of heat experienced on the earth's surface in former ages; namely, that at that time the earth's atmosphere being much more dense (its quality was then very different) contained much more latent heat to be developed.

The cold felt on high mountains and elevated situations may be explained by the fact that the air is rarefied to such a degree that it contains little heat for the sun's light to work upon, and thus the air being so intensely cold keeps everything that comes in contact with it of the same temperature. In the tropics it is warmer, because the rays of light fall perpendicularly, and so act with more power upon the concealed heat, in the same way as the harder a bar of iron is struck the hotter it becomes. For the same reason, summer is warmer than winter. The short nights of summer are warm because the large proportion of heat generated in the atmosphere during the day, has not time to sink again into a latent state, and is prevented from rising and leaving the earth by the vapour of the upper regions.

If the heat we experience be derived from the earth's interior, as Mr. Newberry holds, why does that part of our body which is turned towards the sun feel warmer than the part facing the earth itself? His explanation of the low temperature on the tops of mountains, as having little communication with the interior of the globe will not account for the cold experienced at the same elevation in a balloon.

With reference to the "stellar air," the Rev. Mr.

Purdon, author of "Last Vials," thus remarks:—
"Philosophy has proved that there is a thin and imperceptible fluid which spreads out through the whole region of the stars; so fine that it cannot even absorb the light which travels from the sun to the earth, nearly 100,000,000 of miles, and producing no effect except upon the light of the stars, after a progress of millions of millions of miles. Yet this refined fluid is "air" as strictly as our own atmosphere. It is no more than a kind of atmospheric air infinitely rarefied.
Edinburgh.   R. B. W.

Mr. Newberry evidently considers heat to be a material substance, capable of being attracted by other material bodies, as the sun, &c., and not rather that heat is a vitratory condition of particles. If a red hot ball of iron be suspended, the heat above is greater than below (at equal distance), which is due to the lightness of the hot air. By Mr. N.'s hypothesis there should be more heat below, attracted by the earth.

As to the climate in geological epochs, I must refer Mr. N. to the remarks on glacial action in Devonian, Permian, and Miocene times, in Lyell's Principles of Geology, ch. 9 and 10 in Edit. 10th.
                                                W. H. DALTON.

ARE THE PLANETS INHABITED?—This question of course can never be positively answered with respect to the primary planets; their distance is so great that the highest powers of the mightiest instruments the genius of man may invent, it is probable will never detect evidence of the presence of inhabitants in even the nearest. With our satellite, however, it may prove to be otherwise. As science advances, and new discoveries in optics made, it may some day be announced that traces of the operations of living beings have been found in the moon. However this may be, the future alone will prove. I do not purpose speculating upon the wonders to be unfolded to future generations by the progress of scientific discovery, by means of more perfect instruments of observation, but to advance a few arguments in support of the theory of planetary inhabitability. I wish to show that there are arrangements connected with the planets that are specially adapted to the enjoyment of rational beings.

1. *Mountains.*—Their surfaces are varied with mountain and valley scenery, and in the moon this is especially noticeable. Mountains and valleys add to the grandeur and beauty of our world. Mountains act as barriers to the hurricane in its devastating course. They are depositories of minerals, stones, ores, &c., of the most valuable kind. They are the vast reservoirs from which flow rivers and streams to fertilize and enrich the soil for the produce of grain for man's sustenance.

2. *Light and Heat* are distributed among all the planets. Light is indispensable to every world, and on whatever objects the rays of light fall, colour is produced; it is likely they have the same properties in all parts of the universe, and as light and colour are necessary in a world destined for the habitation of living beings, provision has been made for their extension throughout the system. Heat is also essential to all worlds. Its benign influence is felt from Mercury to Neptune. We must not suppose that because Mercury is in close proximity to the sun, the heat there is insufferable, neither must we conclude that the heat at Neptune is scarcely appreciable on account of his immense distance from that luminary. No doubt wise provision has been made against extreme heat in the one case, and extreme cold in the other. The intensity of heat is in a great measure dependent upon the power of reflection in the objects on which the rays of light fall and the density of the atmosphere through which they pass.

3. *Satellites.*—The principal primary planets are attended by moons; and this fact alone, I think, is sufficient proof of the existence of sentient beings in the planetary worlds. For what purpose in nature could they serve but that of benefiting the inhabitants of their primary by their influence? By adding splendour to its nocturnal skies, and light in the absence of the orb of day. Satellites appear to have been furnished to the planets in number in proportion to their distance from the sun, and although not more than one has been discovered in connection with Neptune, no doubt his moons are even more numerous than those of Saturn, but are invisible through our instruments, owing to the mighty distance intervening.

4. *Atmospheres.*—It may not unreasonably be supposed that *all* the planets are provided with atmospheres more or less dense. The fact that they do exist in some is beyond doubt. The planet Mars, I would refer to as the most conclusive evidence in this respect. Astronomers have long agreed in the opinion that the ruddy appearance of Mars is attributable to the density of his atmosphere. Fixed stars appear to gradually decrease in brilliancy as the disk of Mars approaches them. When a beam of light passes through a dense medium, its colour inclines to red, the other rays being partially reflected or absorbed. The sun when approaching our horizon generally assumes a ruddy aspect, so do the stars, owing to their light having to pass through the lower and denser part of our atmosphere. On the other hand it may be urged that all attempts to discover an atmosphere in our moon have without exception failed. Stars do *not* diminish in brightness previous to occultation by the moon; circumstances, however, attending eclipses of the sun have tended to dispel doubts on this head. During solar eclipses the moon has been observed to be surrounded with a luminous ring, which some have supposed to be caused and produced by its atmosphere, and this with other phenomena furnishes argument in favor of the existence of a lunar atmosphere.

In my own mind there has long been a fixed belief in a plurality of inhabited worlds: there may be, however, some of your correspondents who hold a different opinion. If there be such, I shall be glad to hear their ideas.   W. H. BELL.
Hull.

THE PLANET NEPTUNE.—I beg to offer a few remarks concerning the light of the sun at the planet Neptune.

Your correspondents, R. T. and R. B. W., have been engaged for some months in discussing the principles of this interesting subject, and have each copied extracts from the astronomical books of Breen and

Mitchel to maintain their separate arguments. But when astronomers do not agree in their several opinions concerning the magnitude of the light of the sun at Neptune, it places the argument in a mystery, making it impossible to decide on which side of the question the truth is to be found. In the NOTE BOOK for April, R. T. has mentioned Dr. Lardner in his epistle ; and not having read any extracts in the NOTE BOOK from the last-mentioned astronomer's book, I think it will not be out of place to insert his opinion on the subject. In Dr. Lardner's "Handbook of Astronomy," (concerning the light of the sun at this remote planet) we have the following :—

"The apparent diameter of the sun, as seen from Neptune, being thirty times less than from the earth, is about 60", the sun, therefore, appears of the same magnitude] as Venus seen as a morning or evening star. It would, however, be a great mistake to infer that the light of the sun at Neptune approaches in any degree to the faintness of that of Venus at the earth. If Venus, when that planet appears as a morning or evening star, with the apparent diameter of 60", had a full disk (instead one halved, or nearly so, like the moon at the quarters), and if the actual intensity of light on its surface were equal to that on the surface of the sun, the light of the planet would be exactly that of the sun at Neptune. But the intensity of the light which falls on Venus is less than the intensity of the light on the sun's surface, in the ratio of the square of Venus's distance to that of the sun's semi-diameter, upon the supposition that light is propagated according to the same law as if issued from the sun's centre ; that is, as the square of 37 millions to the square of half a million nearly, or as $27^2 : \frac{1}{4}$, that is, as 5476 to 1.

"If, therefore, the surface of Venus reflected (which it does not) all the light incident upon it, its apparent light at the earth (considering that little more than its illuminated surface is seen) is about 11,000 times less than the light of the sun at Neptune. Small, therefore, as is the apparent magnitude of the sun at Neptune, the intensity of its daylight is probably not less than that which would be produced by about 20,000 stars shining at once in the firmament, each being equal in splendour to Venus, when that planet is brightest."

If, then, the light of the sun at Neptune equals in intensity the intensity of the light which Dr. Lardner has propounded, coupled with the light which it derives from its single satellite, and the numerous other stars which compose the stellar universe, such light is so far from being despicable, that we may reasonably conclude (if such be the case), that the light of the sun at Neptune exceeds by far the light of an Arctic winter on our globe, and may we not expect that heat is transmitted to that planet in like proportion?
J. H.

EXTINCTION OF SPECIES.—I was glad to see the remarks of W. G. in the "N. N. B." on this interesting subject, and I hope that your correspondents will give it the attention it deserves. W. G. has confined his views to the re-establishment of certain members of our extinct insect fauna. But it strikes me that if they were applied to the ornithological branch of natural history, a means might be employed for introducing some beautiful as well as valuable species among the surviving denizens of our heaths and woodlands, whose presence could not fail to be a source of admiration to everybody. The great difficulty we should have to contend with is the ruthless destruction of any rare or conspicuous bird by many of those who carry guns, which habit, I am sorry to say, seldom proceeds from a desire to promote [the advancement] of science by adding a new specimen to the cabinet, but merely from an innate love of slaughter. I have often seen this species of murder committed by those who call themselves sportsmen—men who go for a walk bent on taking the life of every living thing they see, minus the *genus homo*—without the slightest regard to their utility or worth after death ; and failing to satisfy their desire for sport on legitimate objects of the chase, stand by a pond or river endeavouring to show their skill by shooting at every swallow, martin, and any other harmless and useful birds that come within range.

No one enjoys making a varied bag of game more than I, and on many occasions I have procured nine or ten sorts of game birds in the course of a long wild walk, which gave me more pleasure to obtain than killing thrice the number of partridges on a well preserved manor. At the same time I would gladly spare (in common with all true sportsmen) the willow-partridge, bustard, or any birds we were endeavouring to acclimatize or re-instate in their former possessions. Should this meet the views of any of your correspondents I would throw together a few hints for their consideration towards furthering this desirable object.
OTIS.

I see "W. G." in this month's number of the NOTE BOOK, suggests the introduction of foreign pupæ of the Camberwell Beauty. I am personally sufficiently cosmopolitan in my views to admit an European type of this and others of our very rare Diurni into my own collection, until some lucky day when I may be able to replace them with *bona fide* Britishers ; but I nevertheless confess, my mind recoils strongly from the course he proposes, and I feel sure that the entomological world would be all in arms against the plan were it attempted. Certainly "W. G." might call his Camberwell Beauty English when he caught it ; but would other people do so ? especially as under the proposed scheme, the suspicion of its being one of the imported specimens would be so very strongly grounded.

There is also another aspect of the question ; granting the advisability (which I do not), of attempting the re-establishment of this species, what chance of success is there ? and if temporarily established would it not be likely to die off in the same manner as the English species has done ; seeing that whatever adverse influence has effected the diminution of the native breed, would operate still more strongly against the increase of the introduced one ? and I suppose "W. G." does not purpose an annual importation.

How often has the attempt to transplant *Machaon* been made and failed? more than once or twice I fancy. If my memory serves me truly, one gentleman tried many times to introduce it at Matlock, without success; a straggler or two appearing the year after large numbers of Imagos had been set free; but the second year no sign remaining of the breed.

Let "W. G." put this fancy out of his head as soon as he can. If he will look well for them there are lots of butterflies left besides "cabbages," and although these may bear an alarming preponderance as compared with other species, I for one would take more pleasure in the capture of a genuine British *P. Brassicæ*, than in that of a *V. Antiopa*, the land of whose nativity and parentage was open to doubt; and I strongly incline to the belief that all true English entomologists will agree with me in this feeling.

HERBERT MARSDEN,
Secretary, Lepidopterists' Exchange Club.
Gloucester, April 13th.

LOCALITIES FOR IRIS, SINAPIS, &c.—For "B. R. W.'s" information I quote what Newman says regarding the localities where those butterflies "B. R. W." mentions in the April issue of the NOTE BOOK, may be found—"The Purple Emperor (*Aptura Iris*) is a south country insect, occurring every year in the oak woods of Suffolk, Essex, Kent, Surrey, and Hampshire.

The Wood White (*Leucophasia Sinapis*) is not uncommon in woods in the South of England, flying with a light floating movement along the riding paths. I may particularly mention the woods beyond Epping Forest, Darenth Wood, Swanscombe Wood, and Birch Wood, in Kent, as places where I have commonly seen it. It is not so common in the north as in the south of England, and I do not know that it has been seen in Scotland.

The Large Blue (*Lycæna Arion*) is extremely rare, being confined to two or three localities, the principal of which is called Barnwell Wold, near Oundle, in Northamptonshire.

The Black-veined White (*Pieris Cratægi*) in some parts of England is very abundant; it seems partial to the great midsummer moon daisy, on which I sometimes have seen these butterflies sitting by hundreds in cloudy weather. It is very common in the south of England, and I may mention the woods near Maidstone, in Kent, and near Leominster, in Herefordshire, as very favourite localities for it.

The Large Tortoise-shell (*Vanessa Polychloros*) appears from the end of July to the end of August, and then retires for the winter; coming out again in the early spring, and continuing strong on the wing almost until the new brood appears.

This Butterfly is tolerably common in the South of England, being found in woods.

Why the Meadow Brown (*Satyrus Janira*) should be so very common, I know not, unless the reason is that this butterfly, both the perfect insect, and the chrysalis, are so little taken by Entomologists, as compared to some of our rarer species of Lepidoptera, as the Camberwell Beauty (*Vanessa Antiopa*), the Swallow-tail (*Papilio Machaon*), and several other kinds, which are fast becoming very scarce. That splendid insect, the Large Copper (*Polyommatus Hippothoe*), once tolerably common in the fen district, has now, I believe, become quite extinct in this country. I would recommend "B. R. W." to read carefully what Mr. T. W. Tempany has written in the "N. N. B.," on our British Butterflies. He will then see upon what each species feeds, and also when they fly.

"B. R. W." will find no better food to suit Linnets than summer rape seed, mixed with canary seed; but no hemp seed should be given to them. They will relish green food occasionally. Sand and water are of course essentials.

A. E. BUTTERMER.

THE STING OF NETTLES.—In compliance with Mr. Buttermer's desire, I send the following account of some experiment I tried with stinging-nettles. The first nettle on which I experimented was rather an old and faded specimen, the edges of most of the leaves being quite brown. I first drew it lightly across both the palm and back of my hand and felt no sting. I then pressed it between my fingers and still remained unstung. Lastly I struck my hand smartly with it, and was slightly stung on the back of the hand, but not on the palm. I then tried a second nettle, a young one, which had small leaves, with exactly the same results. I then tried a third strong, well-grown specimen, with very large and hairy leaves. I was not so fortunate in escaping stinging with this as with the other two; for, though the palm of my hand still remained unstung, both when the nettle was drawn across it and when struck smartly, the back of the hand was very severely stung when I struck it with the nettle, and was even slightly stung when I merely drew the plant across it. I grasped the nettle between my finger and thumb with the same result as in the case of the other two specimens. There is only one point in which my experience differs from that of Mr. Buttermer, and that is in my hand being stung when I drew the third nettle lightly across it; but I think this was owing to the fact that my hands were chapped with the cold, and their skin therefore rather more tender than ordinarily. I noticed one thing which Mr. Buttermer has not mentioned, namely, that when the nettles are struck with great force against the hand, the sting is not nearly so great as when only a moderate degree of force is used. It may be a mistake, but the poison of nettles seems to me to have much less virulence in cold than in hot weather. Has Mr. Buttermer or any other of your correspondents noticed this?

Scuddylaw. JOHN LANDELS.

THE THIN AIR.—Our newly-arrived oriental friend from Bagdad, as he travels west, has his curiosity laudably excited, and requests our constant and intelligent correspondent, "R. B. W.", to give him some information about "the thin rarefied air," which he says there is above the earth's atmosphere. "The Caliph," if I but rightly understand him, has some doubt concerning the scientific revelation introduced by "R. B. W.," and hence his inquiry about the thin air so far from our revolving atom. Professor Tyndall, in a lecture delivered before the Royal Institution, says:—"Into a vapour thus constituted we have now to pour a beam of light." But what, in the first instance, is a beam of light? It is a train of innumerable waves, excited in, and propagated through, an almost infinitely attenuated and elastic medium which fills all space, and which we name the *aether.* These waves of light are not all of the same size; some of them are much longer and higher than others." And Professor Tyndall quite agrees with "R. B. W." concerning the presence of heat; for, says the learned Professor, "there is no such thing as absolute coldness in our corner of nature." Again, says the Professor, "Space, though traversed by the rays from all suns and all stars, is itself unseen. Not even the *aether* which fills space, and whose motions are the light of the universe, is itself visible." I hope our turbaned correspondent will meet us often, and give us some of his eastern learning, but let him still remember that dame Nature hates a vaccum.

Dromore. H. H. ULIDIA.

"MOON STROKES."—T. D. S. W., in last month's number of the N. N. B., gives an account of a sailor, who while sleeping upon the deck of a ship, received a moon stroke, which had the effect of contorting the poor fellow's countenance. As some of your readers may not quite understand why many persons are affected by moonlight, I shall be happy to give them a short explanation of it, and also to reply to your correspondent's question. It must first be thoroughly comprehended, that we do not receive any *perceptible* heat from our satellite. Experiments have been conducted, with a view of determining, as accurately as possible, whether we do receive any hot rays from it; but as yet philosophers have failed to detect them, even with their most delicate instruments. Having ascertained this point, it will be readily perceived that the phrase "moon stroke" is incorrect; and that therefore we must look for the causes of the "strokes," not in the moon, but on our own planet! It is a self-evident fact, that after a hot day, the heat should radiate from the surface of the ground. Now if any person lies out, in the tropics, on a fine night, he will feel the effect of the radiation of heat from his *eyeballs;* this is carried on so quickly, that the optic nerve is often injured, and blindness thereby produced. Madness was also supposed to have its origin in the effect of the full moon upon certain people, hence the word *lunatic.* And it has, I believe, been noticed, that the insane are very much excited if out in the moonlight. Again, we read in the Scriptures, "The sun shall not smite thee by day, nor the *moon* by night."

T. D. S. W. wishes to know, whether they (moon strokes) ever occur beyond the tropics. I have heard, that people are affected in a similar manner in the Mediterranean. VERITAS.

FOWLS SWIMMING.—I beg to offer the following remarks as a reply to your correspondent at page 124 of last month, in reference to domestic fowls swimming. I believe that they are seldom, if ever, known to venture upon an aquatic excursion as a matter of choice, but if by any chance or accident they find themselves in the position described by Mr. Janies, they generally make the best of it, and swim about to seek for a landing-place; but should they fail in this matter, after repeated efforts they would undoubtedly perish, as I believe that they cannot rise from the water as ducks and most water fowl are wont to do. and their plumage is by no means adapted for a long continuance in the watery element. But with regard to their keeping afloat, I believe that it requires no effort on their part to keep on the surface of the water. The specific gravity of a bird being less than that of water, it follows that they could not go under without a voluntary effort, which does not accord with the habit or inclination of domestic fowls. I have seen fowls that had been reared in a poultry yard adjacent to a river, so much accustomed to the water, that they appeared to have acquired all the confidence of aquatic fowls when on the water, but I have never seen an instance of their actually swimming from the edge of the river. The habit of these fowls was to make an attempt to cover it by flight, which however they seldom accomplished, generally falling short about one third of the distance, and, apparently nothing daunted, they performed the other part with all the ease and agility of ducks, thus proving true the old proverb, that use is second nature.

320, Strand. C. W . . . D.

THE PRESERVATION OF SEA-FOWL.—I am very pleased to see that the protection of sea-fowl is receiving so much attention in Parliament, and that the Bill for their preservation has already been read a second time. I feel sure that every true naturalist must be very glad to have a law established for the purpose of stopping the wanton destruction of the numerous species of our rock-building sea-fowl, both those birds which are resident with us, and also those which come annually to breed on our coasts. I likewise see that the Trinity Board attaches the greatest importance to the protection of the sea-birds, as the safest warning to sailors if near to land in foggy and thick weather. When stopping at Tenby, a few years ago, I visited the Stack Rocks, which are some little distance from that picturesque town, and was much gratified with the sight I saw there. The Pembrokeshire coast, in that part, is very wild and rocky. The day was beautifully fine, with a fresh westerly breeze, which sent the blue billows dashing against the iron-bound coast. These Stack Rocks are situated a little off the mainland, and are yearly visited by myriads of sea-fowl, such as guillimots, razor-bills, puffins, etc., etc., and so great is the concourse of these birds, that they literally cover the rocks. Sportsmen and others, engaged merely in the merciless destruction of our sea-fowl, can, in localities like the above-named, commit endless slaughter in a short space of time. A. E. BUTTERMER.

March 18.

KILLING INSECTS.—As I have not yet seen the following method of killing insects given in answer to "Entomologist's" query, I now give it:—Procure a wide-mouthed stoppered bottle, some cyanide of potassium (to be got at any photographic chemist's) and a little plaster of paris; make a saturated solution of the cyanide, and add enough of it to the plaster of paris to make a thick cream; pour this into the bottle, and when it has hardened and dried it will be ready for use.

An insect put into this will be quite dead in less

than a minute. I have also found it very useful while "sugaring," as moths can be transferred straight from the net into the bottle, and then by the time you reach the next tree the moth is ready to pin into the collecting box. I have found this method much better than boxing them, as they are not so apt to get rubbed. N.B.—While making the bottle breathe the fumes as little as possible.

While sugaring the other evening I took T. Instabilis with a large piece of the chrysalis fastened firmly into its thorax.   V. B. LEWES.

W. W. WALKER enquires about Entomological Apparatus: perhaps the enclosed may be useful to him.
March. T. L.

LIST of Entomological Apparatus, with prices paid about 40 years back.

	£	s.	d.
Net	1	0	0
Forceps	0	7	6
Aquatic Net	0	4	6
Digger	0	2	6
Pins, per packet	0	4	0
Setting Boards in Case	0	15	0
Pliers	0	1	6
Coleoptera Bottles, each	0	1	0
Larva Box	0	1	6
Breeding Cage	0	7	6
Store Boxes, each	0	15	0
Pill Boxes, per gross	0	7	6
Collecting Box	0	5	0
Papilio Net	0	7	6
	£5	0	0

I think the List will be found in Samoulle's Entomology, published somewhat about that time, and that the different articles are described there.
March. T. L., who is *not* an Entomologist.

EAST WINDS.—Mr. J. Landels asks: 1. Why are "East winds" unhealthy? That they are so may be conceded as regards the majority of constitutions; although some are benefitted under their influence. So far as they are unhealthy, it is because they are polar, bringing air from higher and colder latitudes, and consequently such as is colder and drier than the average atmosphere of the place in which they are blowing. The breathing of this cold and dry air tends to irritate the respiratory organs. Further, the coldness of these winds, increased by the rapid evaporation caused by their dryness, acting on the surface of the body, tends to check the healthy action of the skin, depressing the system, and injuriously affecting the internal organs. Possibly, too, there may be causes influencing health, in the peculiar electrical and ozonic conditions of the atmosphere during certain winds. But in the present state of our knowledge, it would be impossible even to specify these conditions. Still further are we from being able to explain them.

2. Are "East winds" unusually very prevalent in the spring after a mild winter? Probably they are. An unusually mild winter implies a more than usual predominance of tropical (S.W.) winds during that season. Now, as on the whole, a certain average of different winds prevails, an excess in one direction during one period renders an excess probable in the opposite direction during a subsequent period; and as, on an average of years, the polar (easterly) winds are more prevalent in the spring months than in others, this is probably the period in which the balance of polar, due to a winter of tropical winds, will be redressed.   CYGNUS.

Those winds which pass over tracts of cold land, or expanses of water, acquire their chilliness. When the air of western districts begins to be warmed, as by the sun of spring it naturally rises by its increased lightness. The vacuum is filled by colder air, and occasions winds. The sun's rays are the prime movers in all aerial currents. Cold north-east winds in western Europe are often occasioned by their passing over icebergs in the North sea; but in Australia north-east winds are warm, especially on the west coast, from their passing over tracts of land heated by the sun's rays. The same is true on the west coast of Africa. The chilliness of spring in northern Europe after mild weather is commonly attributed to a change in the direction of the wind, but this has much to do with icebergs, which loosened from their moorings in the north float down cooling the air for hundreds of miles south of them. The unhealthiness of the east wind in England is to be attributed to its being not an oceanic wind, like the west or south-west, rendered mild by passing over water warmed by the gulf stream. Being mostly a land wind it is parching, and so causes contraction of the vital organs of the human body.
C. O. G. N.

Mr. Landels asks "What is the cause of the unhealthiness of east winds?" It is generally considered that as the east winds comes to us across a large continent, that in their course they are impregnated and charged with unwholesome vapour. In their course, too, the east winds cross uncultivated regions and swampy plains, and no water of any great extent, and hence the dryness of those winds and their readiness to imbibe moisture from our atmosphere. But Forster, and some others who have written and thought much on the subject, are of opinion that east winds in every country of the world are proverbially unhealthy. "Certain *changes* of winds, as well as winds," says Forster, "are known to produce epidemics in many countries where violent atmospherical complaints prevail." He then proceeds:—"But though we admit the influence of atmospheric peculiarities on our health, yet the manner and extent of their operations cannot easily be ascertained." I cannot answer the second question; I never heard the remark before, but I'll keep it in mind.   H. H. ULIDIA.
Dromore.

MOTH COURTSHIP.—I think the following remarkable instance of the attractive power possessed by the females of some moths will be interesting to some of the readers of the "N. N. B," and might, I think, be turned to some account by using the females of certain moths as bait for males. Last summer an ethnological friend of mine had a female of the Oak

Eggar (*Bombyx Quercus*) which had just emerged from the pupa; the breeding cage containing it was placed in a room in front of the house with the door open. "Quercus" had not assumed her perfect state long before she was visited by no less than six "gentlemen" of the same kind, all of which were taken prisoners by my friend, except one, which unfortunately was crushed whilst closing the door; this occurred about four o'clock on a warm summer's afternoon, the six males paying their addresses all in the space of a quarter of an hour, coming in at both back and front of the house. I suppose the attractive power was an aroma given out by the female. I should be glad if any of your readers could enlighten me on the subject.

St. Augustine's, Norwich   R. LADDIMAN.

THE BALANCE OF POWER.—During the past year the swarms of *Pieris Brassicæ* with which we have been infested has been something remarkable. I do not remember any former year at all approaching it. Where there were cabbages cultivated there *Brassicæ* and its *larvæ* were to be found. The cultivation of cabbages has been sadly interfered with, as in most instances they presented the appearance of complete skeletons, in others the leaves have been riddled through and through. I fancy the *ichneumon* flies has been equally numerous, and has had a busy time of it, as upon a garden wall sixty yards in length I counted not less than thirty of those bright yellow patches known as the cocoons of that parasite. We have also been infested with *aphides* in countless myriads, the produce of our gardens being entirely covered with them. I also noticed great numbers of the pretty little ladybird feeding on the *aphides*. I do not recollect having seen them in such numbers previously. Thus it will be seen we have here two of the most common and beautiful examples of the admirable manner in which nature plans her work to maintain the balance of power.   THOS. H. HEDWORTH.

OUR SUMMER BIRDS OF PASSAGE.—As some of our summer birds of passage are making rather an early appearance this season, I think it may perhaps be interesting to the readers of your invaluable NOTE BOOK to know that the Cuckoo was heard in this neighbourhood on April 9th, and again yesterday, the 11th. I saw the first swallow here (Sidmouth) on the 9th, and since then I have seen several more. Blackcaps were observed by me on the 10th.

The weather, during the last few days, has been very warm and sunny, and should it continue so, I have no doubt but that the rest of our summer migratory birds will very soon be making their appearance.

Vegetation is advancing rapidly. Horse-chestnut trees are in leaf, and the buds of the sycamore are unfolding.—I am, &c.   A. E. BUTTERMER.

April 12, 1869.

CURIOUS BIRD.—I see in the March number of the "N. N. B.," a description, by "J. B." of a (so-called) "curious bird," which a friend of his calls a "red-cap." From the description (which is *not* very particular as to details) this bird appears to be nothing more or less than a Goldfinch! If my definition is wrong, I shall be glad to hear a more particular description from "J. B."; he says nothing as to size or shape, length of wings and tail, shape of bill, &c., &c.; nor does he even mention whether it is a "hard billed" or a "soft billed" bird. I send you a short paper on the Goldfinch which perhaps you may think worthy of a place in the "N. N. B."; it is *entirely* the result of experience.

Manchester, March 20th.   A. H. ROWORTH.

WHAT is the usual length of the life of the common Ass? I enclose a paragraph cut from the *Yorkshire Post* of the 15th inst.:—

"BRADFORD.—SALE OF AN ANCIENT DONKEY.—A Bradford auctioneer sold, the other day, on the day of its master's death, a donkey of fifty-three years of age, the faithful companion, during the greater portion of his life, of one Benjamin Keighley, aged eighty."

Surely the donkey therein spoken of, must have far exceeded the usual years of its race!—though I know the case of another also, still living, the owner of which has indisputable evidence that its *fortieth* birthday is not distant.—I am, &c.   T. P. A.

July 18, 1868.

BLACK-HEADED GULLS.—Black-headed gulls I believe invariably build in company. I trust A. M. Mc. A. did not destroy the colony he mentions having met with in Aberdeenshire.

I once heard an instance of a gamekeeper's *braining* all the young gulls in a certain "gullery," because he thought they sucked the grouse's eggs. Deplorable ignorance truly. I sincerely hope his master discharged him.

By far the largest gullery I ever visited is the one at Scoulton in Norfolk, where thousands annually congregate. They literally throng the air.

The Swans named by your correspondent would probably be the Mute Swan, in a state of semi domestication."   "A CONSTANT READER."

PLUMAGE OF A DUCK.—Allow me to call your attention to a very curious feature in the plumage of a duck at present in my possession. Several of the large wing-feathers are turned back, and stand straight out from the bird's sides, giving it a very strange appearance; in other respects the duck is quite an ordinary bird. At moulting time these feathers vanish, but reappear again regularly. The gentleman to whom it formerly belonged, bought it as a "Rhone" duck; perhaps some of your numerous correspondents can inform me whether ducks from the river Rhone possess any peculiarity of plumage.—I remain, &c.

Le Colocubier Manor,   LIZZIE C. GODLEY.
Jersey, March 22.

CHARCOAL AND GLASS.—Can any of your readers explain the following singular occurrence? A short time since, we were mixing with water some charcoal finely powdered, as is usually sold by druggists, in a cut glass tumbler; presently it broke with considerable force, and we saw with dismay the dark contents staining our table cloth and carpet. The next day another lot was mixed in a tumbler as before, but half an hour *after this was emptied*, this also cracked as the other had done. In a visit to some friends soon after, these accidents were mentioned, when some one remarked, "Oh, have you been breaking tumblers; we cracked two through putting in charcoal."

We shall be pleased to know a reason for these things. R. B.

ARRANGEMENTS OF INSECTS IN A CABINET.—I have found it convenient to arrange my insects on an ascending scale primarily, namely:—1st. Aptera (fleas and lice); 2nd. Diptera (gnats, flies, &c.); 3rd. Hemiptera (bugs, &c.); 4th. Himoptera (aphis); 5th. Lepidoptera (butterflies and moths); 6th. Oothoptera (grasshoppers, crickets, &c.); 7th. Hymenoptera (bees, ants, wasps, &c.); 8th. Neuroptera (dragon flies, may flies); 9th. Strepsiptera; 10th. Coleoptera. Your correspondents should consult the works of Latreille, and papers of Lubbock on the classification of insects. C. O. G. N.

COLLECTING IN WINTER.—A. W. B. says "ornithologists cannot collect in winter for various reasons, one of which is that the very birds which possibly may be required for study are not forthcoming then."

But this is not quite correct, for guillemots and gulls (with the exception of the Kittiwake) are found round our coasts all the year.

I mentioned the Bass rock because it was intended that the Act should not extend to Scotland.

"A CONSTANT READER."

WATER-SNAKE.—In answer to M. L. A., in the June number of the "N. N. B.," I can state that there are only *two British species of snake*, viz., the Adder, and the Ringed or Grass Snake, which latter frequently takes to the water, no doubt in search of frogs, newts, etc., which form its principal food. The Ringed Snake is never, I believe, found far from water or damp places. The Adder (our only venomous snake) on the contrary, prefers dry sandy soils. The belief in a venomous water-snake is not confined to Hampshire. J. C.

Chelmsford, June 20.

SEA BIRDS.—I should like to make a little suggestion upon "A Radical's" very excellent idea in your last April number upon the "Sea Birds' Preservation Bill," and that the book for signing names should be left for a few days at different shops in places around London, and in some others of the county towns of England, as it might not be convenient for every one to come up to London, and yet they might wish to put their signatures to the movement. E. B. BAX.

BIRCH TREES.—A great many of the seed vessels or calkins of the birch still hang on the trees unripe, in a hard mass, and have been hanging on the branches since October last, when the other seeds ripened and were blown away by the winds.

Is the flower of the whin-bush and the wind flower identical, if not, what is the difference, or is there such a plant as the wind flower?

Can any reader tell me the specific difference between Betula alba (White Birch) and Betula glutinosa (Common Birch). ARBOR.

LARK.—I was staying in the country, in May, 1868, when one day a boy (I forget the exact day it happened), told me that he found a lark's nest in a hole in a bank, with two eggs in it. He took them. The very next day he went to the same hole, and found another egg. I do not know if this is of rare occurrence. This took place in the county of Worcestershire. C. W. F.

GRAPTA C. ALBUM.—Will any of your Entomological correspondents give me the names of localities where they took G. C. Album, the Comma Butterfly, last season. I had one sent last year from North Wales. Would C. W. describe the breeding-cage for larva he mentioned last number.

Reading. J. HENDERSON, jun.

COLOURS OF DRIED FLOWERS.—I should be greatly obliged if some reader of your interesting Magazine, THE NATURALIST'S NOTE BOOK, would inform me in its pages how to preserve the colours of *dried flowers*, where to obtain a book for the purpose of drying and keeping them, and what its cost would be? FLORA.

Regent's Park, N.W., April 5, 1869.

MAGPIE'S NEST.—Would you mention, in the next number of your paper, the following:—As I was bird-nesting a few years ago in Devonshire, with a companion, we found a magpie's nest with *no covering at all*, out of which we took five fresh eggs. Is this frequent, and when it is most likely to occur?

Exeter. S. B.

SNAKES IN SPIRIT.—White rum, a little under proof, is the best. If there are many in proportion to the spirit it will require strengthening after a few months, so as to bring up the strength to about proof. A hydrometer is necessary to determine this.

C. O. G. N.

COLIAS HYALE.—Last August, a friend of mine took three fine specimens of C. Hyale, the Pale Clouded Yellow, a female and two males, on a patch of Lucerne, on the Great Western Railway Bank, near this town. I saw one alive in the net, and the others afterwards. J. HENDERSON, jun.

Reading.

GREENFIELD CRICKET.—Your correspondent probably means the large green carnivorous grasshopper of our fields, *Gryllus viridissimus* (2 inches long). The field cricket is *G. campestrus*, but it is not green and is about an inch long C. O. G. N.

THE FIELD CRICKET.—I beg to inform Mr. Robt. Laddiman, that the scientific name of the above-named cricket is Gryllus Campestris.

A. E. BUTTEMER.

IN answer to W. W. Walker, I will say, that I believe that he can get the catalogue he desires from T. Cooke, 513, New Oxford Street, London, W.C.

S. B.

FOOD OF TORTOISE.—Can any of your correspondents kindly inform me, what is the best food for Tortoises—how to keep them—and where to buy them? —Yours, etc. A. R. L.

ENTOMOLOGICAL APPARATUS.—Mr. W. W. Walker can obtain a list of entomological apparatus at almost all of the London dealers' establishments.

E. B. BAX.

ON THE LOWEST LIAS BEDS OCCURRING AT COTHAM, BEDMINSTER, AND KEYNSHAM, NEAR BRISTOL.

By C. O. Groom Napier, Esq., F.G.S.

PART II.

HAVING in my first paper described the strata of the Lower Lias, I will now make some remarks on the organic remains which I collected personally in the localities above named, and exhibited before the Geological Society of London. They are now all in my collection. As I said in my first paper, I have found about 100 species of organic remains, of which six are new to science and 76 to the locality, of which a large number are also new to Britain or to the formation.

I propose to call these beds the *Lowest Lias*, as they lie between the Bucklandi beds and the Triassic formation. As I said in the first part of my paper, I have not found the Rhætic bed in the locality of Cotham, where I principally obtained my specimens; and believe, with Mr. W. W. Stoddart, F.G.S., a careful observer of the neighbourhood, that it is wholly absent.—*Vide* his paper, read before the Geological Society last year.

REPTILIA.

The stone and the clay which surround it, forming the lowest lias beds, is but ill suited to the preservation of reptiles. It is but seldom that bones are found in connection. Of this I only found one instance: about eight vertebrata of Icthyosaurus were in conjunction; beside these, there lay, almost in their proper place, about a dozen ribs. The bones were spread on two large slabs of stone, and, consisted almost entirely of phosphate of lime; they were in an exceedingly friable condition.

1. *Icthyosaurus.*—I found about a dozen fragments of vertebratæ of this genus, but scarcely any were worth preserving. Being in a rotten state, they crumbled to pieces on the least attempt to remove them from their natural bed. Had I deemed the specimens of great value, I should have adopted the excellent plan described in the "Field," March 6, 1869, of strengthening the bones, previous to removal, with plaster of Paris. Hot glue is also excellent. I once got out a piece of bone, with its aid, that would have crumbled to dust without it. I obtained three or four very small teeth of Ichthyosaurus from "bed E." The vertebratæ were from the eighth to half-an-inch wide, but none were perfect. The longest tooth was seven-eighths of an inch long by three-sixteenths of an inch wide.

2. *Plesiosaurus* species.—Of this I obtained a humerus, and an alnus somewhat broken, but in good structural condition. The first was about six inches long; the second three inches. They both came from "beds 8" of the second quarry described by me, and were new to the locality.

PISCES.

Mr. Stoddart has been much more fortunate than myself in finding well-preserved fish remains at Cotham. Those found by me consist of a very few, mostly fragments of scales, teeth, and coprolites.

3. *Gyrolepis Alberti, Ag.*—I have rarely found little scales of this, and only in "bed I." They are from the 16th to the 8th of an inch long, somewhat of a lozenge shape, with numerous fine striations, but not so conspicuous as in the next species. New to the locality.

4. *Gyrolepis tenuistriatus, Ag.*—This is also very rare in "bed I." It is about the 8th of an inch long, like a conical pyramid in shape, marked diagonally, from left to right, over the greater part of its surface, with parallel lines. I have found only scales. New to the locality.

5. *Sauricthys.*—This, with the two species mentioned above, are usually supposed to be exclusively Rhætic, and the occurrence of this at Cotham would be used as an argument for the beds I am describing being Rhætic. But the lithological character of these beds is so totally different from the Rhætic series of Gloucestershire or Somersetshire that I cannot consider the occurrence of this genus here of any weight whatever. It is true, I have only found one or two very small teeth, for they are rarer even than the Gyrolepis. The teeth are about a quarter of an inch long, smooth towards the point, but are nearly half their length deeply striated. The root which succeeds presents no marked feature. The locality is "bed T," and it is a new one.

6. *Nemacanthus monilifer, Ag.*—The sole remains of this species I have obtained, is a mammillated portion of a spine, about half-an-inch long, but which is very characteristic of the species. It was found in "bed E."

7. *Hybodus.*—I have found about half-a-dozen very small teeth of this genus in "bed I." They were only a third of an inch long by a quarter broad, and were in the form of a long curved triangle. New to the locality.

8. *Pholidophorus.*—This is the most common and characteristic fish scale of the Cotham beds; but they are rarely found perfect, although sub-

ject to a great variety of form. One is oblong: a quarter of an inch long by the eighth of an inch wide, and has a curious loop springing out of the back, reminding us of the half of a hinge; another, which, I believe, belongs to this genus, is a quarter of an inch long, of a lozenge shape, marked with a number of small lozenges one within another.

MOLLUSCA.

These are much more numerous and better preserved than other organic remains from the same beds. Few persons can visit the localities without finding them; but they may search for days without finding any relics of reptiles or fish.

9. *Ammonites planorbis, Sow.* — This fossil occurs plentifully in "bed E," but it is difficult to extract in good preservation from the hard stone with which it is surrounded, for its thin shell is full of friable crystals of carbonate of lime or sulphate of strontia. It usually preserves its natural form, which is much like that of the Planorbis vortex of our brooks, now found in a living state. Sowerby and others figured this shell from a crushed specimen found higher up in the series. There has been considerable controversy amongst geologists as to the distinction between the Ammonites of the lower lias; Dr. Wright, of Cheltenham, holding the identity of A. Johnstoni, of Sowerby's Conchology, and the two following species.

10. *A torus, Sow.*

11. *A tortilis* is with the above but a variety of Planorbis. Dr. Wright I believe to be partly right and partly wrong. I have obtained about 50 or 60 good specimens of the ammonites mentioned above, in all ages and stages. The true A. planorbis affords in its transverse section, a very peculiar oval in the convolutions; those of Johnstoni and tortilis are different in shape; but the principal distinction lies in the smaller convolutions and in the spire, which sinks in Planorbis much more decidedly than in Johnstoni. I think that Dr. Wright is correct when he says A. torus and A. tortilis are but varieties of Johnstoni. A good typical specimen of torus exists in the collection of the Philosophical Institution, Bristol: it is evidently but a cast of Johnstoni. I found a specimen at Cotham almost exactly like it. Although fragments of Ammonites Johnstoni are very common in several of the beds at Cotham, especially "1" and "5" of the second quarry, yet good specimens are rather rare; they vary from half-an-inch to six inches in diameter. I have got one specimen of large size which I found in "bed E" adhering to another, as two wheels overlap in clockwork.

12. *Ammonites tortilis* appears to present so little difference from Johnstoni that I was at first inclined scarcely to admit it as a variety, but on finding it rather frequently in the Bucklandi beds of Horfield, I was enabled to average the specimens, which contain a greater number of transverse ribs than A. Johnstoni.

The *typical A. planorbis* is without ribs. I have found them nearly perfect from a quarter of an inch up to four inches in diameter. Sulphate of strontia, as I said before, is very abundant in connection with these fossils, but it is mostly in a state of disintegration. I have however before me several little Ammonites planorbis, which are full of little fibrous cotton-like asbestiform crystals radiating from the centre, some of which have a pink color from infiltration of peroxide of iron.

"Bed E" sometimes contains crystals of pyrites, (Bisulphide of iron) but these are usually partially decomposed by some salt of Strontia, which I believe was anciently like the lime surrounding it in a state of carbonate, and that it withdrew the sulphur from the iron by the combined agency of air and water.

13. *Ammonites angulatus, Schloth.*—This is a very well marked species, but is very rare at Cotham. I have not found above half-a-dozen fragments of it altogether, and those in "bed 5" of the second quarry. It derives its characteristic name from a series of sharp curved markings, which in good specimens are almost as sharp as a penknife, and which meet in a peak at that point where the keel is in A. Bucklandi and other keeled Ammonites. It is more common at Keynsham in the Bucklandi series, from which I have several good specimens. New to the locality of Cotham.

I will now speak of the Gasteropoda.

14. *Cheminizia, sp.*—I have found one good specimen of this genus in "bed H" and an inferior one in "bed 8." They were about one inch long by one-third inch broad, but did not present any well defined markings. New to the locality.

15. *Cerithium constrictum, Moore* (query).— I have found a fragment of this very peculiar species, which is so like Mr. Moore's figure illustrating his paper in the journal of the Geological Society, that I ventured to put it down in my list. But my fragments evidently represent a shell three times as large as his. The whorls of the shell are marked by very sharp curved lines following the turn of the spire; one specimen only was found in "bed I." New to Cotham.

16. *Cerithium semele, D'Orb.*—This is a species about half-an-inch long, the size which Mr.

Ralph Tate, F.G.S., has identified amongst my fossils found at Cotham. I have only found one, and that a section; at first sight it might be mistaken for a clausilia, and it was found in the cast bed. It is new to Britain.

17. *Littorina semiornata, Goldf.*—I found one fair specimen of this in "bed 8." It represents a somewhat more elongated species than the common periwinkle of our British coasts, and is rather more than an inch long. My specimen is smooth, without showing any striations. New to the locality.

18. *Turbo sub-elegans, Munst.*—This is a little shell about an inch long, of which I found only one specimen in "bed E." Its whorls are characterised by four principal lines following the course of the whorls which are reticulated. New to the locality.

19. *Solarium lenticulare, Tqm.*—This is less than the 8th of an inch long, small, flat, and smooth. I only found one example in "bed H." I believe this shell to be new to Britain. New, at least to the locality.

20. *Natica.*—I have found one small cast about one-third of an inch long, which Mr. Etheridge thinks to be a species of this genus. Besides these Gasteropods, I have found two other small species of littorina, (in "21 and 22") which I cannot specifically determine.

23. *Turritella; Zenkeni, Dunker.*—Found by me only at Cotham. When perfect it is about one and one-eighth of an inch long by a quarter broad, and rises gradually to the apex. I believe this to be new to the locality, but it is very rare in "bed E."

Conchifera.—This class at Cotham is as usual in the Lower lias much more abundant as regards species than the Gasteropoda. From the numerous species of the genus Lima found in some sections of the Lower lias, some geologists have given them the name of Lima beds, but the researches of which I now speak, were made in strata somewhat lower down in the series than is usually expressed by this term. I found eleven species of Lima at Cotham, which is a larger number than has ever been found in similar strata in any one locality.

24. *Lima gigantea, Sow.*—This is the commonest species at Cotham, and is most widely distributed throughout the lias, stretching in fact up to the inferior oolite, in which I found specimens at Dundry. It is a matter of some difficulty to get a perfect specimen at Cotham, owing to the nature of the stone and clay surrounding them. They are as one in a hundred. The largest specimen found by me, was six inches long, the smallest half an inch; of this size I only obtained two. They are found in the great majority of the beds, "E," frequently in "H," rarely in "Q," abundantly in "6," rarely at Bedminster waterworks, but commonly at the various quarries of Keynsham. Lima gigantea is a most beautiful shell, whether we consider its size, polish, or the delicacy of its markings. It is a rounded triangle. The lines of growth are more defined towards the margin. These are crossed transversely by much finer lines, which become rough and coarse towards the hinge.

25. *Lima punctata, Sow.*, is a much smaller shell than gigantea. It ranges from half-an-inch to three inches long. Coarse, nearly straight lines, cross the shell, about equidistant, and it is much punctured. It is most characteristic of "bed I," but is found in "bed E" and "bed 6," also at Bedminster and the two quarries at Keynsham. I believe I was the first to find it in these localities. Mr. R. Tate, F.G.S., thinks this species distinct from the following, I have not made up my mind fully on the point.

26. *Lima exaltata, Tqm.*—This species differs from the above in having the hinge obliquely placed, and having the longitudinal lines slightly irregular; this is the Lima Dunravenensis of Tawney. I found it tolerably abundant at Cotham; it varies from half an inch, up to three and a half inches long. I am the first who found it in this locality. A named type specimen, was exhibited before the Geological Society on May 22, (see Quarterly Journal of the Geological Society, vol xxiii, p. 310) 1867, at which I exhibited also Ammonites Johnstoni, A. planorbis, Astarte consobrina, L Hettangiensis, L. gigantea, L. punctata, L. succincta, L. tuberculata, Unicardia cardioides, Ostrea irregularis, Terquemia arietis, Pecten calvus, (two species undetermined) Perna infraliassina, Pinna semistriata, Pholadomya glabra, P. prima, Terebratula perforata, Cidaris Edwardsi. I mention these species particularly as they were mostly new to the locality, and I claim priority in discovering many of them. The next species I shall describe is

27. *Lima tuberculata, Tqm.*, which varies from one to three inches long, and at first sight might be taken for a small Pecten maxims shorn of the ears. It is most deeply scalloped with eight ridges, each of which is armed with four more or less clearly defined tubercles, hence its name Tuberculata. It is found in "bed E," more commonly in "bed I," at Bedminster, and at the second quarry at Keynsham. I was the first who found it at Cotham.

28. *Lima acuticostatus, Mart.*—This is a rarer species, six or eight examples are all that I obtained. It has been rightly named, for the costatæ are very sharp, and sixteen or seventeen in number. My specimens vary from the eighth to half

an inch long. I was the first to discover this in the locality, and I believe also in Britain, having found it 7 years ago. I obtained it in "beds E, H, and I."

29. *Lima duplum, Quenst.*—This species was found solitary at Cotham in "bed I." It is a heart-shaped shell about an inch long, with eighteen Costæ of a square form, and very strongly marked.

30. *Lima Hettangiensis, Tqm.* — This is another rare species, it varies from half an inch to one and a half inch long. The Costæ are sharp and rise like a keel. They differ greatly in width, the broad ones are in large specimens the 8th of an inch wide, the small intermediate ones about the 30th. It is found in "beds E and I," and is new to the locality.

31. *Lima subduplicata, Tawney.*—This is very distinct from the last, being intermediate between it and L. tuberculata, or perhaps L. succinta. It is about an inch long and rather rare, I have only found it in "bed E." There are no intermediate Costæ which are very deep and broad. There are four distinct concentric lines of growth, this appears to me to be one of the best defined of Mr. Tawney's species. New to the locality.

32. *Lima succincta, Schloth.*—This varies from one inch to four or five inches long in the Cotham beds, but at Keynsham I found it as much as seven inches long. It is a fine shell. The principal costæ have two or three intermediate ones. Its general outline is most like that of L. exaltata, but it is a clearly defined species. The costæ are most like those of L. Hettangiensis, but they are all more or less rounded, while in the other species they are extremely sharp.

33 *Lima terquemi, Tate.*—I have only found one or two examples of this fine species in "bed I." But one or two fragments I found at Bedminster, at first sight I took to be the Pecten quinqueplicatus of the chalk; but the hinge proves it to be a true Lima. It has six strongly marked costæ raised above the others, but the whole shell is characterised by them. It is about two inches long, and until discovered by me seven years ago, was unknown in Gloucestershire. New to the locality.

34. *Lima valoniensis.*—I found only one example of this shell at Cotham, and a doubtful specimen at Horfield, it is a delicately ribbed species about one and a half inch long, nearly as long as broad. The lines of growth are well defined. New to the locality.

The next most numerous genus to Lima is Pecten, of which the most common is

35. *Pecten calvus, Goldf,* which varies from one to one and a half inch long. The ears are large, the lines of growth towards the margin are two in number, concentric and strongly marked; the Costæ are fine but well defined. There is no other Pecten in the bed that can be mistaken for it. It is nowhere abundant, but I have found it in "beds E, H, 3," and the waterworks quarry at Bedminster. This species is new to the locality.

36. *Pecten textorius, Goldf.*—I found but a single fragment of this shell in "bed I." This species is new to the locality.

37. *Pecten verminius, Sow.*—I found a single imperfect specimen at Cotham. This is a finely ribbed pecten, each rib being crossed by fine lines. The shell is about one and a half or two inches long.

38. *Pecten Suttonensis, Tawn.*—The specimens I found at Cotham are certainly identical with Mr. Tawney's excellent figure and description of this species on his paper on the "Sutton series," in the Journal of the Geological Society. It is very difficult to get a perfect specimen of this pecten, the costæ of which are strongly marked and rise acutely. It is about two inches long by the same broad. It is most nearly allied to P. valoniensis of the Rhætic series, with which Mr. Tate thinks it identical, it is however a coarser ribbed and thicker shell. I found it in "beds H, I, and 3," and at Bedminster waterworks quarry. It was first found by me in this locality.

39. *Pecten valoniensis, De France,* is supposed to be characteristic of the Rhætic bed, but I have not clearly identified it as being found at Cotham, Bedminster, or Keynsham. The first specimens I obtained of P. verminius, I for some time believed to belong to this species.

40. *Pecten Hehlii, D'Orb.*—This is a shell about three-quarters of an inch long, by half an inch broad, having at first sight a smooth surface. On the same slab with this specimen was a very perfect one of Lima valoniensis and another little gem, of a Rhynchonella plicatissimus, but I cannot fix the exact bed where they were found. New to the locality.

41. *Pecten quinqueplicatus(?)*—Several friends and myself assigned some specimens which I found at Cotham and Bedminster to this species; they were in "beds H, I, 3" Cotham, and at the waterworks quarry, Bedminster. They are distinguished by five superior costæ broader and more prominent than the others. The shell is nearly as long as broad, but I have not yet obtained it perfect. New to the locality.

42. *Pecten Etheridgei, Tawney.*—I found a shell at Cotham agreeing precisely in figure and description with Mr. Tawney's. I am inclined,

however, to think it is but the young of Sutton-ensis. New to the locality.

43. *Hinites minutus, Napier.*—This I believe to be new. Shell coarsely striated and round; has seven forked striations; shell, 7-16ths inch long by the same broad. Locality—bed "K," accompanying Monotis decussata.

44. *Avicula cygnipes, Phil.*—I have only found two examples of this shell at Cotham; they were accompanied by Cardium philippianum, Unicardia cardioides, and Ostrea liassica; the beds were "K" and "M." New to the locality of Cotham.

Avicula cygnipes, Phil., varies from one to two inches long by from three-quarters to one and a half inch broad. It has four strongly marked lines of growth and seven radiating ribs, which project beyond the margin of the shell, and give it somewhat the appearance of the webbed foot of a bird. The perfect shell has a long curved ear, but many specimens not showing this, it has been usually figured without it.

45. *Avicula Deshayesi, Tqm.*—I have only found one shell of this species in "bed I;" it is distinguished for the length of its ear, which comes down in a point, and is quite unlike the species mentioned above or the following. New to the locality.

46. *Avicula Saundersi, Napier.* New species.—This shell is 13-16ths in. long by 9-16ths in. broad; thin and flat, with one rib running diagonally across it; surface smooth, sub-ovate, with fine yet very clearly defined concentric lines of growth; umbones slightly curved outwards. Locality—Planorbis bed, Cotham. One specimen only. This I have named after my friend, Mr. William Saunders, F.R.S., F.G.S., whose researches as a geologist and whose map of the Bristol coal fields are so well known.

47. *Perna infraliassina, Quenst.*—This is an uncommon shell which I have found in "beds H, I, K;" it is new to the locality. It is a very flat shell, smooth, yet with decided lines of concentric growth. At first sight a specimen might be mistaken for a distorted mussel. It is however a true Perna.

48. *Perna species.*—Mr. Tate considers a small specimen found at Cotham in "bed I" to represent another species of this genus. New to the locality.

49. *Unicardia Cardioides, Phil.*—This is an uncommon heart-shaped shell found in "beds E, I, and 7;" it is new to the locality, and is about an inch long and broad, by three-quarters of an inch thick. It is marked by very prominent and wrinkled lines of growth, with one longitudinal keel-like ridge, resembling that in Cardium rhæticum.

ENTOMOLOGY FOR THE MONTHS.
JUNE.

" Yes, the summer—the radiant summer's the fairest
  In greenwood and mountains, for meadows and bowers,
For waters and fruits, and for flowers the rarest,
  And for bright shining butterflies, lovely as flowers."

How refreshing, "in the leafy month of June," when the delightful and sweet odours arising from the new-mown hay are wafted abroad by the summer breeze, is a walk in the fields, when the wild rose and the honey-suckle, entwined amongst the hedges mix their fragrance, and load the atmosphere with sweet perfume, or along the grassy banks of some river that—

Through verdant meads and sylvan shades,
Along its winding course swift glides
Murmuring o'er it's pebbly bed,
Or roaring as it splashing falls
O'er Woodnock rocks;

where the brilliant dragon-fly is seen chasing its prey amongst the foliage of the willow trees that overhang the sparkling stream, and gaily-painted butterflies are sipping the sweet nectar from the flowers; such are a few of the many pleasing sights which the reader may enjoy in search of the treasures of June.

The entomologist is now in his glory, and may find plenty to do; to enumerate half the insects he is likely to meet with, would indeed prove a hopeless task, but we will turn our attention to a few of them.

A great many of the butterflies noticed last month still continue to fly, viz., the Swallow Tail (Papilio Machaon), the Wood White (Leucophasia Sinapsis), the Orange Tip (Anthocaris Cardamines), and the Pearl-Bordered Fritillary (Argynnis Euphrosyne); accompanied by the Speckled Wood (Satyrus Ægeria), Wall Brown (S. Megera), Green Hairstreak (Thecla Rubi), Purple Hairstreak (T. Quercus) Small Copper (Polyomattus phlæas), Brown Argus (Lycæna Agestis), Greasy Fritillary (Melitæa Artemis) Glanville Fritillary (M. Cinxia) Silver-Studded Blue (Lycæna Ægon), and the Small Blue (L. Alsus).

A great many of the moths may be mentioned as occurring this month; to enumerate all would occupy too much space, but I will endeavour to notice a few of the chief, beginning with the "Hawkmoths," a great many of which are now to be met with, viz., the Elephant (Chierocampa Elpenor), Small Elephant (C. Porcellus) Bedstraw (Deliphilia Galii) Privet (Sphinx Ligustri), and the Eyed Hawkmoth (Smerinthus Ocellatus); also the Oleander (Choerocampa Nerii), which is exceedingly rare. The Poplar Hawkmoth

(Smerinthus Populi), may now be found sitting on palings and trunks of trees. The Humming Bird Hawkmoth (Macroglossa Stellatarum),—a very pretty object—may also be seen this month, hovering over the Jasmines and Petunias thursting its long trunk into the flowers to sip the sweets; the flight of this beautiful moth is diurnal, and it pursues its flight in the hot noonday sun. The Red Tipped Clearwing (Sesia Formicæformis), the Yellow Legged Clearwing (S. Cynipiformis), and the Currant Clearwing (S. Tipuliformis), a trio of moths nearly related to each other are now on the wing, also the Broad and Narrow Bordered Five spotted Burnets (Zygæna Trifolii and Z. Loniceræ), the Six spotted Burnet (Z. Filipendulæ) Short Cloaked moth (Nola cucullatella), Small Black Arches (N. Strigula), on trunks of trees, Water Ermine (Arctia Urticæ), Gipsy (Liparis Dispar), Dark Tussock (Orgyia fascelina), Nut Tree Tussock (Demas Coryli), Common Vapourer (Orgyia antiqua), Oak Eggar (Bombyx Quercus) Lappet (Lasiocampa quercifolia) and the Fox moth (Bombyx Rubi). The Leopard moth (Zenzera Æsculi) may be found in the early morning on the gas lamps, also by searching the trunks of trees.

The Ghost-Swift (Hepialus humuli) may often be seen at dusk hovering over the long grass in a very spectre-like manner, it is chiefly met with on meadows and damp places.

Several individuals of that interesting tribe of moths, termed the "Footmen" may be met with this month, viz., the Dingy Footman (Lithosia griseola), Four dotted (L. mesomella), the Orange (L. aureola), and the Common Footman (L. complanula); also the Wood Tiger (Chelonia plantiginis), Clouded Buff (Euthemonia russula), Ruby Tiger (Arctia fuliginosa), Scarlet Tiger (Callimorpha Dominula), Muslin moth (Arctia mendica), Buff Ermine (Arctia lubricipeda) and the White Ermine (A. Menthrastri).

Amongst the "Geometræ" occuring this month are the following:—the Brimstone moth (Rumia cratægata), Orange moth (Angerona prunaria), Willow Beauty (Boarmia rhomboidaria) Peppered moth (Amphydasis betularia), Great and Pale Oak Beauty (Boarmia roborariæ and B. consortaria), Peacock moth (Macaria notata), Latticed Heath (Strenia clathrata) Common Heath (Fidonia atomaria), Drab Geometer (Minoa euphorbiata), Phœnix (Cidaria ribesiaria), and the very common Currant moth (Abraxas grossulariata).

Many of the "Cuspidates" are now out, among which may be noticed the Scarce Hooktip (Blatypteryx sicula), Sallow Kitten (Dicranura furcula), Iron Prominent (Notodinta dromedarius) and the rare Lobster moth (Stauropus Fagi). The Buff tip moths (Pygæra bucephala) may frequently be found coupled in pairs on the trunks of elm and other trees, and on the herbage below them.

A great many of the "Noctuas" are now on the wing, among which are the following, viz., the Sycamore (Æcronycta aceris), the Alder (A. Alni), Dark Dagger (A. tridens), Grey Dagger (A. Psi), on trunks of trees, the Figure of Eighty (Cymatophora ocularis), the Miller (Acronycha leporina), Sweet Gale (A. Myricæ), Scarce Marviel-du-Jour (Diphtheria Orion), Common Wainscot (Leucania Pallens), on meadows, the Light and Dark Arches (Xylaphasia lithoxylea and X. polyodon), True Lover's Knot (Agrossis porphyrea), Cabbage moth (Mamestra Brassicæ), Dot moth (M. persicariæ), Large Yellow Underwing (Tryphœna pronuba), Angle Shades (Phlogophora meticulosa) and the Shark moth (Cucullia umbratica).

Amongst larvæ to be found this month may be mentioned those of the Gold and Brown Tailed moths (Liparis auriflua and L. chrysorrhea), which may be taken from the whitethorn in large numbers in company with those of the Figure of Eight moth (Diboba cœruleocephata), and from oak trees the young larvæ of the Pale Tussock (Orgyia pudibunda), called also the "Hop Dog."

The gregarious caterpillars of the Small Eggar (Eriogaster lanestris) may now be found feeding in company under a web on whitethorn and elm. The very common caterpillars of the Garden Tiger (Chelonia caya), well known to everone and called by country folks the "Woolly Bear," may also be found by searching amongst the long grass.

There are two corrections which I should like to make in my article of last month, on page 134, second column, sixth line from top, for "Taxley" read "Yaxley;" in the seventh line of the next paragraph Small "Capped" is inserted, which should have been Small "Copper."

Norwich. R. LADDIMAN.

ON THE BRITISH GEOMETRÆ.

By E. J. S. Clifford.

PART VI.

THE true family of Waves was completed in our last; but we next come to two species bearing that term, which have been placed in a separate family by our entomological dignitaries. The first of these is called the Common White Wave (*Cabera pusaria*), and is one of the commonest *Geometræ* throughout the summer. Along the woodland glades, starting out in numbers from the herbage we tread, now flying strongly in the eventide, or settled quietly on the tree stems, this insect is one of that class with which all must come in contact in the course of a country ramble. It is a delicate little moth, although so common. The wings are all rounded, and sprinkled with grey dots. The fore wings have three transverse grey lines, and the hind wings two. A singular variety of this species occurs, in the which the first and second of these lines are united, and appear as one, so that the fore wings have only two transverse lines on their pearly surface. The caterpillar of the Common White Wave feeds on oak, birch, hazel, and other woodland trees, and is full-grown about September. It rests in nearly a straight posture, and in colour varies from brown to green; it is cylindrical in form, and destitute of humps and protuberances. It spins a cocoon in a loose manner on the surface of the earth. The other species alluded to is the Common Wave (*Cabera exanthemaria*), a species very nearly resembling the last in general appearance. Its wings are yellowish grey, sprinkled over with dark dots, and adorned with indistinct transverse lines. The male has fringed antennæ, the female has them threadlike and white; thorax and body both grey. The caterpillar is uniformly green, and rather slender towards the head; it feeds on sallow and alder. In autumn it is full fed, and then makes a cocoon under fallen leaves, remaining in the pupa state throughout the winter. About midsummer the perfect insects appear to be most abundant.

Next we come to some very beautiful and rare *Geometræ*. The Clouded Silver (*Bapta temerata*) is a most charming little moth, but very little seems known of its transformations. Its colour is white, and the fore wings have a central dark spot. They have also a waved transverse band half way between the central spot and the margin, and a row of very dark crescent-shaped markings on the hind margin. The hind wings have two faint waved lines parallel with the margin, and a series of slender marks on the margin itself. The head, thorax, and body are white. Such are the prominent characteristics of the Clouded Silver, an insect which we cannot describe in detail, since little is known regarding its economy. The White Pinion-spotted (*Corycia taminata*) is a species occurring rather uncommonly in the south of England, and rarely in the north. The caterpillar feeds on the wild cherry, and is green, or purplish brown. It has a broad stripe down the middle of the back, edged with white, and a narrow white stripe encircles the border at the juncture of each segment. The moth itself flies in May, and is very delicate in appearance.

The wings are all white, and the fore wings have two brown markings on the costal margin. The Grey Carpet (*Aleucis pictaria*) is the last of the small group of the CABERIDÆ. This is a rare moth. The fore wings are smoke-coloured, with two transverse darker lines, and a central spot of the same colour. The hind wings are paler, with an indistinct waved line across the centre. The Grey Carpet is not described by most writers in its other states of existence, and very little seems to be known of it.

Our next group of moths is called the MACARIDÆ. It contains some of our most prized native *Geometræ*, deservedly admired both for their beauty and elegance. The first is the Sharp-angled Peacock (*Macaria alternata*), occurring in the south-west of England. The wings of this and the next species are angled in a most singular manner, and have a deep notch just below the tip; the hind wings are also angled. The wings are all grey in the present species, and sprinkled with minute streaks, which are rather darker than the ground colour of the wings, but pale and indistinct to the eye. The hind wings have two broad bands, which correspond with those on the fore wings; between them is a dark central spot. The caterpillar of this species is light green and shining; it has three triangular red marks on the sides of the middle segments; it changes to a uniform reddish brown before entering the ground. Its food is the sallow. This species has not been found in either Scotland, Wales, or Ireland; it is rare in the locality indicated. The Peacock (*Macaria notata*) is the next species under notice. This occurs not unfrequently in many of our woods in the south, and flies strongly in the sunshine when roused from the bushes. The wings are all grey, sprinkled with minute transverse streaks as the last mentioned, and they have three transverse lines of a similar colour. Each of these lines terminates in a dark spot on the costal margin, between which and the outer margin are two very conspicuous blotches, one of which is simple, the other compound, consisting of five small spots crowded together. The moth is extremely delicate and beautiful. The Tawny-barred Angle (*Macaria liturata*) is somewhat generally distributed, though far from being a common insect. Its wings have very slight indications of angles, and are of an ochreous grey colour, with a broad, but indistinct band suffused with orange yellow near the hind margin. The hind wings have two waved transverse lines, and a central brown spot between them. June and July are the months for the insect. Next come we to the last member of the family. Common in our gardens, where its singular caterpillar commits great havoc among our bushes, we all have seen the dingy-coloured V. Moth (*Halia wavaria*) flying at eventide. The hind wings of this moth are slightly scalloped, and grey in colour; they are tinged with a faint purple gloss. The markings on the wings are somewhat disposed in the form of a "V," hence the popular name of the insect before us. The caterpillar rests in a straight posture, with the head erected in a singular manner. When disturbed, it immediately falls from its food and feigns death by remaining motionless. Its colour varies from apple green to lead colour, and it is marked longitudinally with smoke-coloured lines very close together. On all parts of the body are shining black warts, which emit black bristles. The favourite food of this caterpillar is the gooseberry, and when full grown it changes to a chrysalis in a slight web attached to the leaves. July is the month in which the V. moth swarms in our squares and gardens—a somewhat unwelcome visitor.

The group which next comes under notice is called the family *Fidoniidæ*. It contains many very interesting species, some of which are little known, others, again, which are familiar to the youngest collector of insects. First is the well-known Latticed Heath (*Strenia clathrata*), a little moth not unfrequent about some of the clover fields in Kent. It is a beautifully marked insect, its wings looking literally like minute lattice-work. Two colours combine on the wings and produce this effect—smoky brown and dingy white. The dark colour is arranged in five broad transverse bands on the fore wings, and four on the hind wings; these bands are irregular, and vary much in different individuals. The rays are of the dark colour, and, crossing the bands, they divide the white portions into a number of squarish white spots. The fringe of all the wings is a most beautiful object, the brown colour alternating with other square spots of a most lovely whiteness. The body has seven slender belts of delicate white. This moth is chiefly seen on heaths and in clover fields, and is on the wing in May and June. In the south of England a common moth in those months is the Brown Silver-lines (*Panagra petraria*). This insect is of a pale wainscot brown colour, sprinkled with rather darker brown, and having two transverse darker lines, bordered on the outer side with a pale silvery hue. The hind wings are very pale, and have a gloss, as of mother-of-pearl, with a faint line across the middle of them, scarcely perceptible, except on the inner margin. This moth is hardly known in the north and in Scotland. A striking species next comes before us. This is the Barred Umber (*Numeria pulveraria*). The colour of this species is umber brown, sprinkled with darker brown. The fore wings have a broad transverse band of rich brown, which is much broader at the costal than at the inner margin. The hind wings possess no band, but a faint central line.

The Grey Scalloped Bar (*Scodiona Belgiaria*) occurs both in England and in Scotland in the month of June. Its markings are very striking. In the male moth we find all the wings of a pale whitish grey, the fore wings having two very dark scalloped lines. Between these two lines, and equidistant from both, is an oblong spot, almost black. The hind wings have one scalloped transverse line, and a dark spot between this and the base. The head, thorax, and body are almost white. In the female, which is much less than the male, the colouring is much darker; but the markings are the same, except that two of the blotches are somewhat less distinct. The caterpillar of this moth feeds on the common ling, where the eggs are deposited about June. Soon after being developed the little *larvæ* hybernate, and do not resume feeding till the following April, when they grow very rapidly, and are full-fed about the beginning of May. Then they spin slight cocoons on the ground, and change therein to chrysalides. The moth is principally confined to heaths. The Bordered Grey (*Selidosema plumaria*) is a noble insect. The wings are grey in colour, and have a broad band along the hind margin of all the wings of a deeper hue. The fore wings have two transverse bars; the first near the base, and the second near the centre. This species occurs in the south of England, more especially in the New Forest, but is a rare insect. July is the month for it.

A pretty little Geometer is that called the Netted Mountain Moth (*Fidonia carbonaria*), with its little freckled wings. They are all white, speckled with black; and the fore wings have four, the hind wings three, transverse bars. The head, thorax, and body are nearly black, and the body has also six pale grey rings. The moth is found in the mountains of Yorkshire and Scotland in May. After this local insect, we have to describe one that is familiar to most readers. It is the Common Heath (*Fidonia atomaria*), and is confined more especially to such localities as produce heath in abundance. The ground colour of the male is dingy orange brown; but the female is much less in size, and has the ground colour of the wings white. The fore wings in both sexes are traversed by four transverse brown bands, of which the second and third unite at the inner margin. The hind wings have three equidistant bars of brown, and the fringe is alternately brown and pale. Chalky soils are the favourite haunts of this species, abundant in the months of May, June, and July. Lastly, in our present paper, we advert to the beautiful Bordered White (*Fidonia piniaria*). This is a handsome insect, whose markings are most difficult to depict in words. The central parts of the wings are white, or yellow white, blended in a wonderful manner with the broad dark border of the margins. The female moth is orange brown in colour. The under side of the Bordered White forms a tableaux of beauty which it is necessary to see in order to appreciate its loveliness. The caterpillar is whitish green, with a broad line down the back of white, and the segments are very conspicuously marked with pale whitish green. In closing this paper, we would direct our reader's attention to the amount of research which is left open to entomologists who are practical collectors. It becomes the duty of all lovers of nature, and also of those who respect and value our British *Fauna*, to seek to add their contribution of knowledge to the general store of information. If entomologists were more determined in their researches, more willing to undergo the difficulties which attend the discovery of long-hidden facts, we should be able greatly to swell the knowledge stored up regarding our native insects. While so much remains to be discovered respecting our native insects, both in connection with economy and habits, let no entomologist stand still for want of employment. Certain it is that these changes of insects *must* take place, otherwise the perfect insects could never be seen in such abundance; and it cannot be doubted that increased vigilance and more persevering research would succeed in casting much interesting light on what now is dark and obscure respecting so many of our native Geometers.

REASONING IN ANIMALS.

OH for the pen of a ready writer, to transcribe with indisputable eloquence arguments sufficient to establish the doctrine that reason exists in animals below man. Feeling, as I do, convinced that this must be so, I sadly lack the power of analysing and arranging the requisite proof. But there are certain innate convictions that strike root in the mind, spring up, bud forth, and blossom with imperceptible progress, until having thoroughly acclimatised themselves, they refuse to quit the field. The time cannot be recalled when the stray seed first fell—like vibrios and bacteria, their germs seem to exist in the very air we breathe. There may be no admissible foundation for their existence; still less excuse may be found after years of discretion have been attained: nevertheless one might as well attempt to clear an American forest of the impermeable density of its undergrowth, as try to eradicate many of the convictions sown in childhood, fostered unwittingly in thoughtless youth, and matured in the afternoon of life. They are like a growth of ivy that timidly encircles the young tree, harmless at first, but destined at length to sap its nutrient juices and distort its growth. One of these dangerous creepers (is it not so Mr. Newberry?) has seized my mind and developed itself into the conviction that the lower animals REASON. Should any one ask me why I believe this, I doubt if I could find a more substantial reply than that suggested by the feminine logic, "Because I do."

Such were my feelings as on page 346 of the N. N. B. for 1868, I presumed to assert my views; and as might have been expected, they were shortly assailed by R. B. W. and W. Newberry. Yet there were strong auxiliaries in reserve—"Cosmos" and "Veritas" came up in time, and I doubt not, but that their energetic efforts have disconcerted our antagonists for the moment. Meantime, while they are rallying for another onset, I will venture to state my hypothesis more fully.

First of all I am inclined to believe that it is a grand mistake to separate Instinct from Reason, and define them as two distinct endowments. The very fact that reason is supposed by many to exist in the higher animals, and to be deficient in the lowest, seems to argue strongly that it is but a further development of psychical power, rather than a new specialised prerogative conferred upon man alone. Were the line of demarcation broad and evident, so that we could say, man reasons, and stands undeniably alone in enjoying this divine attribute, then truly we should have two great divisions of animated creation—reasoning and non-reasoning beings. But this is not so. On the contrary there is the possibility, nay, a considerable degree of probability, that the dog, the horse, even the beetle and ant, reason as well as man. Avoid it as we will, the startling truth burns on with unsullied brightness, and no one can say that in the cases related by Veritas (p. 84, vol. iii.) the beetles were not prompted by reason. If reason is reason, it must be so to the end of the chapter; and its authenticity must be independent of the grade of life in which it is proved to exist. "There be four things which are little upon the earth, but they are exceeding wise; the ants are a people not strong, yet they prepare their meat in the summer. The conies are but a feeble folk, yet make they their houses in the rocks. The locusts have no king, yet go they forth all of them by bands; the spider taketh hold with her hands, and is in kings' palaces."

To facilitate our enquiry, I shall proceed to divide every animated being, whether Vertebrate or Invertebrate, into two parts, ψυχη and σωμα. Not being accurately acquainted with the writings of Greek philosophers, I can not say whether I am justified in adopting ψυχη to represent the vital and mental faculties as existing in man and all animals severally. If it is unclassical, I apologise: in either case, I beg it to be understood that ψυχη shall include the entire immaterial entity of every creature, whether it be life, soul, instinct, or reason, or all combined. What I wish to maintain is that there may be *degree* in the ψυχη of different animals, just as we find variation in the complexity or simplicity of their physical organisms. Thus the vegetative or vital force may predominate in individuals over the mental and intellectual, as eminently exemplified in the human race; for we see one man by fortitude of constitution shake off the effects of disease or accident which would prove fatal to another less strong, while between the philosopher and the idiot there exists every grade of intellectual ability. In like manner there may be class distinctions of vital and mental phenomena in lower animals. The proverbial cat with her nine lives, the apparent insensibility of some insects to pain, the keen scent of the hound, the cunning of the fox, &c., all point to this. Again consider how the tempers and dispositions of horses and dogs present an endless variety of phases, one is surly or amiable; another vicious or good-tempered. And then remember that probably similar individual varieties may exist in animals of lower standing, modified in a thousand different ways by the characteristic disposition of the class. Thus a maze of permutations and combinations in vital and mental phenomena may exist, as puzzling to comprehend as the manœuvres described by Virgil in his miniature cavalry procession.

I believe Cosmos to be perfectly right in saying that this balance between mental endowment and bodily requirement has been adjusted by the Creator with infinite wisdom and forethought, that to various animals He has dictated special laws, and to man pre-eminently the LAW OF PROGRESS, which is clearly allotted to him alone, and is not, I imagine, in the least a proof that he alone enjoys reason. Those who argue against animals possessing reason lay great stress on the fact that from the beginning of Creation until now, animals below man have made no strides at all towards improving their condition. This is probably true, yet I do not think we can estimate it as of much value in disproving their possessing reason. We would rather suggest that God created man in his own image, bidding him have dominion over the fish of the sea, the fowl of the air, the cattle, the earth, and over every creeping thing that creepeth upon the earth. Here, at the first, God dictated the law which has since been carried out as centuries have rolled on. Each year has added its testimony to the preceding that man is subduing the earth in obedience to God's command, and as a consequence we see progress to be the great feature and watchword of his existence. Now, if God had intended the lower animals to advance in like manner, so that their reason might enable them to contrive (as W. N. suggests) weapons of defence beyond those naturally assigned them, might there not be continued danger of their leaguing against man, and perhaps exterminating our race by the establishment of a dominion of wild beasts? Imagine the lions and tigers conspiring together against us, armed not merely with tooth and claw, but with weapons of their own devising far more formidable. What havoc might be the consequence, it is unnecessary and absurd to consider. But the Creator has imposed upon the lower animals a law which shall not be broken, in accordance with which, though physically stronger than man, they are kept in subjection to him. "Many are the wondrous things, and nought more wondrous than man. He crosses the sea surging with winds of winter, he subdues the earth with plough as the seasons come round in succession, he ensnares with meshy toils the bird, the beast, and the fish, he subjects to his yoke the mountain bull;" and in a word being παντοπόρος, ἄπορος ἐπ᾽οὐδὲν ἔρχεται. Whereas, this might be vastly otherwise if Providence had given the lower animals the power of keeping pace with the lords of creation in the law of progress.

The question of classification is perhaps the most perplexing that has ever arisen in zoology, for although Vertebrata must be admitted by all to stand at the head of animated nature, yet to weigh the respective position of Mollusca, Articulata and Radiata, is a matter of profound difficulty. The inferiority of the last group may seem obvious when contrasted with the two preceding, but it must not be forgotten that the structure of most Echinoderms is far more complicated than that of any Bryozoon or Ascidian, while hardly any two zoologists agree as to the relative standing of Mollusca and Articulata with reference to Vertebrata. This almost obliges us to deny unconditionally the superiority or inferiority of one type over another, each fulfils the object for which it was created far better than could any other. Therefore it seems advisable to say that superiority in special adaptation to a certain end constitutes superiority of standing, rather than to maintain that resemblance to man is the norma for deciding the respective rank of animals in the scale of life. For however much higher Mammals may be than Aves, there are few of us who would challenge a Swift to an aerial race of a hundred miles, for the simple reason that birds are specialized for flight, and consequently fly better than we could. It follows too, that the mind unguided by science and unfettered by her classifications might be inclined to consider the golden eagle higher in the scale than the duckbilled platypus—the vigorous octopus and its gigantic kinsmen of fable, reported to drag down vessels in the China Seas, higher than the delicate semi-transparent amphioxus, the warm-blooded junny higher than the sleepy proteus. Yet science with iron hand lays down her heads of classification, and parcels off the animals of her Noah's Ark by sets. Thus to the uninitiated there appears much that is unsatisfactory and imperfect about classifications, inasmuch as they are all more or less artificial as opposed to natural.

In the midst of all these difficulties we cannot glance around and contemplate nature without falling down in adoration before the Glory of God and the wonders of His work as displayed by the heavens, the earth, and by all things therein. Who can fail to be struck dumb with admiration and awe while considering how He has arranged in the most logical connection the most varied types, while acknowledging that He has knit together in perfection of harmony the most distant families of creation. This "infinite diversity in unity" could proceed only from Him who is perfect in wisdom and power.

Face to face with his Creator stands man, striving incessantly to interpret faithfully the workings of Divine Intelligence, yet at a loss to decide upon the relative position of animated beings as regards their physical organisation. Can he then presume to lay down a law concerning the immaterial essence which causes them to live, breathe, think and feel?

I will conclude this note, which I fear has already transgressed its proper bounds, with a quotation from an essay on classification by Agassiz, on which I fortunately stumbled the other day.

"The principle unquestionably exists, and whether it be called soul, reason, or instinct, it presents in the whole range of organized beings a series of phenomena closely linked together, and upon it are based not only the higher manifestations of the mind, but the very permanence of the specific differences which characterise every organism. Most of the arguments of philosophy in favour of the immortality of man, apply equally to the permanency of this principle in other living beings. May I not add, that a future life in which man would be deprived of that great source of enjoyment and intellectual and moral improvement which results from the contemplation of the harmonies of an organic world, would involve a lamentable loss. And may we not look to a spiritual concert of the combined worlds and all their inhabitants in presence of their Creator, as the highest conception of paradise?"

C.

TOBACCO.

By H. H. ULIDIA.

"*Sublime tobacco!* which from east to west
Cheers the tar's labour or the Turkman's rest."—
BYRON.

THE word "tobacco," and the bitter reality itself, are so familiar to every mouth that it requires but little tact to introduce the subject. Imagine not that I intend writing a dissertation on the presumed merits or demerits of this universal vegetable; and as to whether its use or abuse causes men to live long, or drop rapidly into premature graves, I know not, and while I keep clear of such disputed points:—

On I ramble, now and then narrating,
Now pondering.

In the "Glossographia Anglicana Nova" of 1707, we are informed that "tobacco is a well-known plant, which probably takes its name from Tobago, one of the Caribbee Islands in America, from whence it was brought into England by Sir Francis Drake, Anno 1585." But other authorities, with perhaps a greater degree of geographical accuracy, say that the Spaniards first discovered tobacco in South America, in a province of Yucatan called Tobacco, and not in the island of Tobago, and hence the name "tobacco". It is also stated that Drake brought the tobacco to England so early as 1570, and that it was the Virginian tobacco that was introduced into England by Sir Walter Raleigh in 1585. Hernandez de Toledo in 1560 introduced tobacco into Spain and Portugal; and as a curious production of the new world, M. Jean Nicotius, ambassador from Francis II., procured some tobacco plants and presented them to Catharine de Medicis of France. It would indeed seem that this ambassador was the first to send seeds of the tobacco-plant to the island of Tobago.

According to McCullogh, Humboldt has shown that "tobacco was the term used in the Haytien language to designate 'the pipe,' or instrument made use of by the natives in smoking the herb; and the term, having been transferred by the Spaniards from the pipe to the herb itself, has been adopted by the other nations of the old world."

See what historical difficulties hedge our bit of tobacco. The Massagetae and all the Scythic nations, says Herodotus, were acquainted with herbs which they cast into the flame, and while seated round the blazing pile they eagerly inhaled the ascending smoke—and thus, like the Greeks with their wine, they became really intoxicated. And Strabo asserts that they had a religious order among them who smoked through long tubes.

As to the custom of smoking in Ireland, the distinguished Dr. Petrie says:—"The custom of smoking is of much greater antiquity in Ireland than the introduction of tobacco into Europe. Smoking pipes made of bronze are frequently found in our Irish tumuli of the most remote antiquity, and 'similar pipes of baked clay' are discovered daily in all parts of our island."

The high estimation in which tobacco was held may be inferred from the different names by which it was known, such as *Sacra herba*, *Sancta herba*, *Sana sancta indorum*; while others called it *Hyoscyamus Peruvianus*, or henbane of Peru.

It seems indeed that Nicolaus Monardis was the earliest author that called the popular weed —famous herb, I should say—"tobacco."

Were Monardis alive at present, he would wonder to see the facility with which the mouths of millions snatch at his curious word, and still more would he stare to see the solid reality metamorphosed into miniature fireside cirrocumulus by precocious juveniles scarcely quite into their teens. But, says an antiquated author, in speaking of the native Americans:—"The inchaunters of that hot countrie do take the fume therof vntill they be drunken; that after they haue lien for dead three or fower howers, they may tell the people what woonders, visions, or illusions they haue seene, and so give them a propheticall direction of foretelling (if we may trust the diuell) of the successe of their business!" So much indeed for the power of tobacco among the uncivilised. But the civilised, too, come in for a share of the tobacco, for Valmont Bomare, a French natural historian, tells us that so far back as the year 1750, England received from Maryland and Virginia alone, more than one hundred thousand tons, kept one half for their own use, and handed the other half to their polite neighbours, the French, for the sum of £383,333. And about forty years ago a room which covered nearly six acres of ground was built at the London Docks, as a modest little reception room for the "sublime tobacco!"

In 1754 Holland was famous for the consumption of tobacco, so much so indeed that it was at that time called "one huge pipe!" It was at that time the poet Goldsmith advocated the custom of smoking, and was of opinion that "the healthy and ruddy complexion of the Dutch was owing to their continual smoking."

James I. calls tobacco "the noxious weed," and writes his "Counterblast;" Locke says:— Bread or tobacco may be neglected; but reason at first recommends their trial, and custom makes them pleasant." Some years ago, the Emperor, Napoleon III., issued an edict against smoking in schools and colleges, and as an immediate result, more than thirty pipe factories were extinguished in Paris. "Such and so various are the tastes of men."

Soon after the introduction of tobacco into this country, Gerard says:—"Some people vse to drinke it for wantonnesse, or rather custome, and cannot forbeare it, no, not in the middest of their dinner."

Charles II. forbids the cultivation of tobacco in England.

The smoker has recourse to walnut leaves, etc., etc., and then an Act of one of the Georges prohibits the cutting, selling, or colouring of any leaves for smoking purposes, under a penalty of five shillings a pound.

Lord Bacon, as a philosophical connoiseur in the tobacco line, says:—"The English tobacco hath small credit, as being too dull and earthy: nay, the Virginian tobacco, though that be in a hotter climate, can get no credit for the same cause"

Gerard, from some presumed physical causes, imagined that the people of each country should smoke their own tobacco, but then says "it is not so thought nor received of our tabackians: for, according to the English prouerbe, far fetcht and deere bought is best for ladies."

An article in "Chambers' Journal" (December 16th, 1854), says that tobacco "is the most extensively used of all vegetable productions; and, next to salt, the most generally consumed of all productions whatever—animal, vegetable, or mineral—on the face of the globe." If this be so, then indeed may we truly say of men, whether savage or civilised—

"We see full plainly custom forms us all!"

LA PLANCHETTE.—By C.

A DISCUSSION relating to so interesting and mysterious a subject as Animal Electro-Magnetism, is one which certainly ought to merit the consideration of Corrrespondents to the N. N. B., and in introducing it to their notice I trust that facts and theories of explanation will appear from time to time in subsequent numbers of this magazine. Some of our readers are doubtless acquainted with Planchette, and may be able to furnish striking instances of the extraordinary nature of her manifestations. So that, supplied with an accumulation of substantial and authentic facts, we shall stand a fair chance of being able to deduce some theory for explaining satisfactorily the mysterious agency by which her intimations are prompted. For in every scientific enquiry, as Dr. Whewell says, "it is by a graduated and successive induction alone that the highest and most general truths are to be reached. That when the laws of nature have been caught sight of, much may be done even by ordinary observers (apart from theorists) in verifying and determining them.

For the benefit of those who do not as yet include Planchette within the circle of their acquaintance, I will briefly describe her external appearance. A small oaken board about a foot long and half as wide, skilfully fashioned into the shape of a heart, with rounded edges and polished surface forms the body of our little lady. A hole is drilled through the apex end, in which a pencil is inserted. This limb, together with two others of brass supported on ivory wheels, cunningly made to turn easily in all directions, constitutes her locomotive organs. A large sheet of paper is now securely spread upon a smooth table—Planchette takes her stand in the centre: two persons place their hands lightly on the lobes opposite the apex; and one asks a question of Planchette. In a short time she begins to show signs of movement, and slowly gliding over the paper writes by means of her foreleg, an answer to the question asked. Now this is a simple statement of the fact that I, and probably hundreds of others have seen repeatedly. The explanation must involve abstruse problems of modern teratology, for I am inclined to think that we must classify the agency by which this writing is effected, in the same category with spirit-rapping, table-turning, and electro-biology. What then is the agency? "the spirits," or electricity and magnetism? Probably there are advocates for both sides.

Before venturing to suggest a theory, it will be well for me to relate some further details of personal experience in the matter of these mystical communications. The first questions I asked of Planchette were of a very simple character, involving neither clairvoyance nor prediction to any important degree. The answers were generally written legibly and after a few seconds—sometimes correctly, often incorrectly; at times however, no patience could elicit any response—the table wilfully moving round and round, either in concentric circles or spiral coils. I have sometimes taken Planchette to the houses of friends, to exhibit her before a wondering audience, on which occasions it frequently happened that no answer nor any movement at all could be obtained. But though negative instances are of considerable importance in estimating the validity of induction, yet I think the following affirmative cases will suffice to show that there is something over and beyond (which cannot be attributed solely to animal electricity) prompting and regulating the answers.

In the Christmas Vacation last year, Planchette was a great source of diversion, and being quite a novelty astonished us by her marvellous intimations. Our evening, a French lady, staying on a visit, asked us to convince her that there was no deception in the revelations. She wished to know where her brother was, of whom we knew nothing; Planchette immediately wrote "Tubingen," and she admitted that he was studying at the University there. Another lady requested us by letter to ask Planchette who gave her "her filigree cross," for no one knew save herself and the donor. We did so, and both christian and surname were correctly written with the exception of one letter in the latter. We also learnt the place where the gift was made.

Planchette appears to have been an especial favorite in the neighbourhood and city of Bath for some years past. Having heard several stories similar to the above from persons living there, for whose integrity I can vouch, I will briefly describe one other example. The Misses B—— and friends were gathered round a library table amusing themselves with Planchette, while Mrs. D. wrote letters in another room. After several questions asked and answered it was demanded of Planchette to whom Mrs. D. was writing. "To G." was the reply. Miss B. then went into the other room and asked Mrs. D. the same question. "I am writing to my brother Charles" she answered; and perceiving some doubt and uncertainty in Miss B.'s face, she guessed that the veracity of Planchette was at stake, and continued: "We always call him 'Gorilla,' and for brevity I have substituted 'G' in my letter to him." A common question with youthful members of the fair sex, is "whom will so and so marry"? In one particular case Planchette named a person entirely unknown at the time to the enquirer and the lady alluded to in the question. This is a peculiar and convincing instance of the predictions being fulfilled, for I must add that the marriage has since taken place.

Lord Bacon tells us that "man, the minister and interpreter of nature, does and understands so much as he may have discerned concerning the order of nature, by observing or by meditating on facts . . . The intellect, if left to itself, follows the easiest and most dangerous method of investigating truth, leaping from the senses and particulars to the most general axioms, and from these as first principles, and their unshaken truth, judges on and discovers medial axioms. Whereas the true way should be followed by raising axioms from the senses and particulars, by ascending steadily, step by step, so that at last the most general may be reached."

Now the difficulties attending the search after truth, are many and great. The phantoms that lay siege to human minds are shadowy so as easily to escape detection, and subtle so as to insinuate themselves snake-wise with cunning and deceit; thus causing the intellect to assume the character of an uneven mirror, which, indeed catches the rays of things, but by mingling its own nature with them produces a corrupt and distorted image. "For each man has, (besides the generic aberrations of human nature) some individual cave or den, which breaks and corrupts the light of nature; either by reason of the peculiar and singular nature of each; or by reason of education and conversation of man with man; or by reason of the reading of books, and the authority of those whom each man studies and admires; or by reason of differences of impressions as they occur in a mind pre-occupied and pre-disposed. So that evidently the human spirit (according as it is placed in each individual) is a various thing, and altogether disturbed, and, as it were, the creature of circumstance. Whence Heraclitus hath well said that men seek knowledge in lesser worlds, not in the great and common world."

I may be pardoned for this digression, as caution and clearness in setting forth the scheme for discovering truth, are in themselves important aids to our investigation. But to return to the subject of this paper. The axioms I have been led to deduce from experiments with Planchette are as follows:—

a. The answers are generally given after the lapse of a few minutes.

b. Sometimes they are altogether refused.

c. Often they are true and apparently prophetic.

d. Often very nearly correct, *e.g.*, in the spelling of names, a single letter may be wrong.

e. Often they appear absurd and paradoxical; for example, I once asked Planchette whom a certain lady would marry—The answer declared repeatedly the gentleman's name to be composed of a remarkable jumble of letters defying pronunciation, and that he lived at an equally outlandish place in the neighbourhood of Constantinople—neither the man nor the place could ever have existed.

It may be well to state at the outset, that the universal testimony of Planchette herself, as far my experience extends, attributes in the most straightforward manner her intimations to satanic agency? This is startling on the face of it, and will perhaps deter many from becoming acquainted with so mysterious and dangerous an oracle. But as others will scorn the idea, and be ready with batteries of argument to prove the impossibility of the supposition, I shall also dismiss it without further comment, and proceed to suggest another theory, which will probably be more acceptable as being less supernatural, and independent of the powers of darkness. The substance thereof has been derived principally from an excellent little book "On Force," by Charles Bray. The hypothesis assumes that there is an emanation from all brains, resulting from unconscious as well as conscious cerebration, which forms, not spirits, but a mental and spiritual atmosphere by means of which peculiar constitutions are put *en rapport* with other brains. This "Odylic Vapour" emanates in the highest degree from certain persons of nervous temperament, who appear to have phosphorus in excess in the system; and forms a positively living, thinking and acting body of material vapour, able to move tables, carry on conversations, and declare by mysterious clairvoyance occurrences as yet future or unknown. The odylic vapour feels in common with those from whom it emanates, and possesses the senses of seeing, hearing, and thinking—making up for the absence of muscular organs, either by an electrical power of rapping, by guiding the medium's hand, or by direct writing, as in the case of Planchette with pencil. It is not necessary to suppose that this force is confined to the cerebrations of a few, as for instance to the persons assembled round the room; or that it exists in various degrees, and between those united by friendship and affection. Rather may it be considered an emanation from all brains; and the intelligence new to every person present, that of some brain at a distance, acting through this common source, unconsciously, on the mind of the persons engaged in the enquiry. We may believe that this vapour, acting through the medium of animal electricity which can be made to flow from the human hand at any time by intense action of the will, furnishes answers modified by the affections, sentiments, disposition and religious belief of those through whom it passes; and that the odylic vapour, although drawn from a common universal source, may be concentrated and influenced by individuals. The conciseness and deep thought often evinced by the answers point to the connection between the odylic vapour and a general "thought atmosphere," as all-pervading as electricity, and which possibly in itself is in intimate connection with the principles of causation throughout the universe. "He whose intellectual eye is strong enough to perceive that all things sympathize with all, will be convinced that magic cultivated by ancient philosophers is founded on a theory no less sublime than rational and true;" for there is probably much truth in the explanation of oracles suggested by Dr. Rogers, who describes them as the result of local mundane emanation, acting upon the nervous system of the Pythia, and developing to a wonderful degree the presension or divining power of the brain; standing, as he affirms it did, in relation to all matter. The controlling action of mind being suspended, her brain became entirely subject to a specific mundane influence, which being reflected back on the outer world, resulted in the oracles of Gods.

From formless to formed, from inorganic to organic is the maxim propounded by nature to those who study her; and perhaps the most convincing proof of the infinite power of the creator consists in the conversion of force and heat into sentiency, culminating in the conscious intellect of man. Here is a problem which has staggered some of our modern philosophers who propose to analyse the principle of life into "carbon, nitrogen, and ammonia," who indeed "seem to be wise in this world," forgetting that the wisdom of this world is foolishness with God—who build up vast fabrics of fantastical philosophy based on a foundation shifting as the sand, and consequently unsound—compelled by the pride of intellect to substitute something for the glorious simplicity of the words, "And the Lord God formed man of the dust of the ground, and breathed into his nostrils the *breath of life,* an element which will for ever defy Professor Huxley's attempts at analysis, and remain unknown in the chemical laboratories of our museums.

In conclusion, I hope my readers will take some notice of this paper, and endeavour to throw more light on the interesting topic referred to, bearing in mind Lord Bacon's remarks:—"they who have handled the sciences have been either empirics or dogmatists. The empirics, like the ant, amass only and use: the latter like spiders, spin webs out of themselves; but the course of the bee lies midway: she gathers materials from the flowers of the garden and the field; and then by her own power turns and digests them. Nor is the true labour of philosophy unlike hers: it does not depend entirely or even chiefly on the strength of mind, nor does it store up in the memory the materials provided by experiments unaltered, but changes and digests them by the intellect. And so from the closer and holier league of these faculties (the experimental and the rational), which have not been connected—good hopes are to be entertained."

LIST OF BRITISH MOTHS:
NATURE OF THEIR FOOD, AND TIMES OF THEIR PERFECT APPEARANCE.

THE BOLETOBIDÆ.

Waved Black (*Boletobia fuliginaria*). Feeds on the fungi which grow on timber. Flies in June.

THE GEOMETRIDÆ.

Grass Emerald (*Pseudopterpna cytisaria*). Feeds on the common broom. Flies in July.

Large Emerald (*Geometra papilionaria*). Feeds on hazel and other trees. Flies in July.

Essex Emerald (*Geometra smaragdaria*). The larva of this moth has been found on the coast of Essex, but I am unable to state the plant it feeds on. Flies in July.

Small Grass Emerald (*Nemoria viridata*). Feeds on whitethorn. Flies in June.

Small Emerald (*Iodis vernaria*). Feeds on the traveller's joy (*Clematis vitalba*). Flies in July.

Little Emerald (*Iodis lactearia*). Feeds on the oak. Flies about midsummer.

Blotched Emerald (*Phorodesma bajularia*). Feeds on the oak. Flies about midsummer.

Common Emerald (*Hemithea thymiaria*). Feeds on the oak. Flies in June and July.

THE EPHYRIDÆ.

False Mocha (*Ephyra porata*). Feeds on the oak. Flies in May and June.

Maiden's Blush (*Ephyra punctaria*). Feeds on the oak. Flies in May and June.

Clay Triple-lines (*Ephyra trilinearia*). Feeds on beech. Flies in May and June.

Mocha (*Ephyra omicronaria*). Feeds on maple (*Acer compestris*). Flies in May and June.

Dingy Mocha (*Ephyra orbicularia*). Feeds on sallow. Flies in June.

Birch Mocha (*Ephyra pendularia*). Feeds on birch. Flies in May and June.

ACIDALIDÆ.*

Golden-bordered Purple (*Hyria auroraria*). Feeds on the common plantain. Flies in May and June.

---

* I am unable to state with any degree of certainty the food of several of the species in this family, as I have never succeeded in obtaining the larvæ.

Small Yellow Wave (*Asthena luteata*). Flies about midsummer.

Small White Wave (*Asthena candidata*). Feeds on hornbeam. Flies in May and June.

Waved Carpet (*Asthena sylvata*). Flies about midsummer.

Bloomer's Rivulet (*Asthena blomeraria*). Flies in June.

Dingy Shell (*Eupisteria heparata*). Feeds on alder. Flies in June.

Welsh Wave (*Venusia cambricaria*). Feeds on mountain ash or rowan tree (*Pyrus aucuparia*). Flies about midsummer.

Bright Wave (*Acidalia ochrata*). Flies in June.

Tawny Wave (*Acidalia rubricata*). Flies in June.

Single Dotted Wave (*Acidalia scutulata*). Feeds on the flowers of the burnet saxifrage (*Pimpinella Saxifraga*) and wild chervil (*Anthriscus vestris*). Flies in June.

Small Fan-footed Wave (*Acidalia bisetata*). Flies in June.

Treble Brown Spot (*Acidalia trigeminata*). Flies in July.

Greening's Wave (*Acidalia contiguaria*). Flies in July.

Least Carpet (*Acidalia rusticata*). Feeds on various plants found in hedges. Flies in July.

Dark Cream Wave (*Acidalia osseata*). Flies about midsummer.

Silky Wave (*Acidalia holosericata*). Flies in July.

Small Dusky Wave (*Acidalia incanaria*). Flies in June.

Circellate (*Acidalia circellata*). Flies in June.

Lace Border (*Acidalia ornato*). Feeds on wild thyme. Flies in June and August.

Mullein Wave (*Acidalia promutata*). Feeds on the common millefoil. Flies in June and July.

Dotted-bordered Cream Wave (*Acidalia straminata*). Flies in June.

Satin Wave (*Acidalia subsericeata*). Flies in June.

Lesser Cream Wave (*Acidalia immutata*). Flies in June.

Cream Wave (*Acidalia remutata*). Flies in June.

Smoky Wave (*Acidalia fumata*). Feeds on heath. Flies about midsummer.

Subangle (*Acidalia prataria*). Feeds on the hedge wound-wort (*Stachys sylvatica*). Flies at midsummer.

Small Blood Vein (*Acidalia imitaria*). Feeds on sorrel (*Rumex acetosella*). Flies in August.

Rosy Wave (*Acidalia emutaria*). Feeds on the common knot grass (*Polygonum aviculare*). Flies in June.

Riband Wave (*Acidalia aversata*). Feeds on a number of hedgerow plants, as water avens, common avens (*Geum rivale* and *G. urbanum*), meadow sweet (*Spiræa ulmaria*), etc. Flies about midsummer.

Plain Wave (*Acidalia inornata*). Feeds on several low plants; also on shoots of willow. Flies in June.

Portland Ribband Wave (*Acidalia degeneraria*). Flies in July.

Small Scollop (*Acidalia emarginata*). Flies in June).

Blood Vein (*Timandra amataria*). Feeds on several kinds of dock, sorrel, and knot grass. Flies in June.

CABERIDÆ.

Common White Wave (*Cabera pusaria*). Feeds on oak, birch, hazel, and other trees. Flies in June, July, and August.

Round Winged White Wave (*Cabera rotundaria*). Flies in May.

Common Wave (*Cabera exanthemaria*). Feeds on sallow and alder. Flies in June.

Clouded silver (*Corycia termerata*). Feeds on the blackthorn and the bird-cherry. Flies in May.

White-pinion Spotted (*Corycia taminata*). Feeds on wild cherry. Flies in July.

Sloe Carpet (*Aleucis pictaria*). Feeds on the leaves of the sloe. Flies in July.

MACARIDÆ.

Sharp-angled Peacock (*Macaria alternata*). Feeds on sallow. Flies in July.

Peacock (*Macaria notata*). Feeds on sallow (*Salix capræa*). Flies in June.

Tawny Barred Angle (*Macaria liturata*). Feeds on the needles of the fir. Flies in July.

V. Moth (*Halia wavaria*). Feeds on the gooseberry. Flies in July.

Rest-harrow (*Aplasta ononaria*). Feeds on the rest harrow (*Ononis spinosa*). Flies in May, and again in July and August.

FIDONIDÆ.

Latticed Heath (*Strenia clathrata*). Feeds on various species of trefoil and grasses. Flies in May and June.

Brown Silver Line (*Panagra Petraria*). Feeds on the common brakes (*Pteris aquilina*). Flies in June.

Barred Umber (*Numeria pulveraria*). Feeds on sallow. Flies in May and June.

Gray Scalloped Bar (*Scodiona belgiaria*). Feeds on the common ling. Flies in June.

Bordered Grey (*Selidosema plumaria*). Feeds on sallow. Flies in July.

Netted Mountain Moth (*Fidonia carbonaria*). Feeds on birch and sallow. Flies in May.

Common Heath (*Fidonia atomaria*). Feeds on trefoil, etc. Flies in May, June, and July.

Bordered White (*Fidonia piniaria*). Feeds on the needles of the Scotch fir. Flies in April and May.

Rannoch Geometer (*Fidonia pinetaria*). Feeds on the bilberry. Flies in June and July.

Frosted Yellow (*Fidonia conspicuata*). Feeds on the common broom (*Cytisus scoparius*). Flies in July.

Drab Geometer (*Minoa euphorbiata*). Feeds on the cypress spurge (*Euphorbia cyparissias*). Flies in June.

Black Veined (*Scoria dealbata*). Feeds on knot grass. Flies in June.

Purple-barred Yellow (*Lythria purpuraria*). Feeds on various species of polygonum and dock. Flies in July.

Vestal (*Sterrha sacraria*). Feeds on dock and camomile. Flies in July, August, and October.

Grass Wave (*Aspilates strigillaria*). Feeds on the common ling (*Calluna vulgaris*). Flies in June.

Yellow Belle (*Aspilates citraria*). Feeds on the wild carrot, bird's-foot trefoil, and several other plants. There are two broods. The first flies in May, and the second in August.

Straw Belle (*Aspilates gilvaria*). Feeds on the common yarrow (*Achillea millefolium*). Flies in August.

ZERENIDÆ.

Currant Moth (*Abraxas grossulariata*). Feeds on gooseberry and black currant. Flies about midsummer.

Clouded Magpie (*Abraxas ulmata*). Feeds on elm. Flies in June and July.

Scorched Carpet (*Ligdia adustata*). Feeds on the skewer-wood (*Euonymus europæus*). Flies in June and July.

Clouded Border (*Lomaspilis marginata*). Feeds on the common sallow (*Salix capræa*). Flies from May till August.

LIGIDÆ.

Horse-chestnut (*Pachycnemia hippocastanaria*). Feeds on heath. Flies in May.

HYBERNIDÆ.

Early Moth (*Hybernia rupicapraria*). Feeds on whitethorn, blackthorn, and sometimes on the oak. Flies in January and part of February.

Spring Usher (*Hybernia leucophearia*). Feeds on the oak. Flies in February and March.

Scarce Umber (*Hybernia aurantiaria*). Feeds on whitethorn, and occasionally on birch and oak. Flies in October and November.

Dotted Border (*Hybernia progemmaria*). Feeds on hornbeam. Flies in February and March.

Mottled Umber (*Hybernia defoliaria*). Feeds on hornbeam, whitethorn, blackthorn, hazel, oak and other trees. Flies in October.

March Moth (*Anisopteryx æscularia*). Feeds on the elm, oak, lime, whitethorn, and blackthorn. Flies in April.

London. T. W. TEMPANY.

SPITSBERGEN.

The number of sea birds is truly astonishing. On the ledges of a high rock, at the head of the bay Beechey, I saw the little Auks (*Arctica alle*) extend in an uninterrupted line full three miles in length, and so closely congregated that about thirty fell at a single shot. He estimated their numbers at 4,000,000. When they took flight they darkened the air, and at the distance of four miles their chorus could distinctly be heard.

On a fine summer's day the bellowing of the walruses and the hoarse bark of the seal are mingled with the shrill notes of the auks, divers, and gulls. Although all these tones produce a by no means harmonious concert, yet they have a pleasing effect as denoting the happy feelings of so many creatures. When the sun verges to the pole every animal becomes mute, and a silence broken only by the bursting of a glacier reigns over the whole bay. A remarkable contrast to the tropical regions, where nature enjoys her repose during the noon day heat, and it is only after sunset that life awakens in the forest and the field.

Four glaciers reach down this noble inlet (Magdallena Bay). One called the waggon way is 7,000 feet across at its terminal cliff, which is 300 feet high, presenting a magnificent wall of ice. But the whole scene is constructed on so colossal a scale that it is only on a near approach that the glaciers of Magdalena Bay appear in all their imposing grandeur. In clear weather the joint effect of the ice under the water and the reflection of the glacier wall above causes a remarkable optical illusion. The water assumes a milk white colour. The seals appear to gambol in a thick cream-like liquid, and the error only becomes apparent when, in leaning over the side of the boat the spectator looks down into the transparent depth below.

It is extremely dangerous to approach these cliffs of ice, as every now and then large blocks detach themselves from the mass, and frequently even a concussion of the air is enough to make them fall.

During the busy period of Spitzbergen history, when its bay used to be frequented by whalers who anchored under the glacier walls, these ice-avalanches often had disastrous consequences. Thus in the year 1619 an English ship was driven by a storm into Bell sound. While it was passing under a precipice of ice a prodigious mass came thundering down upon it; broke the masts and threw the ship so violently upon one side that the captain and part of the crew were swept into the sea; the captain escaped unhurt, but two sailors were killed and several others wounded.

One day a gun was fired from a boat of the Trent, when about half-a-mile from one of the glaciers of Magdalena Bay. Immediately after the report of the musket a noise resembling thunder was heard in the direction of the ice stream, and in a few seconds more an enormous mass attached itself from its front and fell into the sea. The men in the boat supposing themselves to be beyond the reach of its influence were tranquilly contemplating the magnificent sight, when suddenly a large wave came sweeping over the bay and cast their little shallop to a distance of ninety-six feet upon the beach.

Another time when Beechey and Franklin had approached one of these ice walls. A huge fragment suddenly slid from its side and fell with a crash into the sea. At first the detached mass entirely disappeared under the waters, casting up clouds of spray, but soon after it shot up again at least 100 feet above the surface, and then kept rocking to and fro. When at length the tumult subsided, the block was found to measure no less than 1,500 feet in circumference. It projected 60 feet above the water, and its weight was calculated at more than 400,000 tons.

Besides the glaciers of Magdalena Bay, Spitzbergen has many others that protrude their crystal walls down to the water's edge, and yet but few icebergs, and the largest not to be compared with the productions of Baffin's Bay, are drifted from the shores of Spitzbergen into the open sea; the reason is that the glaciers usually terminate where the sea is shallow, so that no very large mass, if dislodged, can float away, and they are at the same time so frequently dismembered by heavy swells that they cannot attain any great size.

The interior of Spitzbergen has never been explored. According to the Swedish naturalists who climbed many of the highest mountains in various parts of the coast, all the central regions of the archipelago form a level ice plateau interrupted only here and there by denuded rocks, projecting like islands from the crystal sea in which they are imbedded. The height of this plateau above the level of the ocean is in general from 1,500 to 2,000 feet, and from its frozen solitudes descend the various glaciers above described. During the summer months the radiation of the sun at Spitzbergen is always very intense. The thermometer in some sheltered situations not seldom rising at noon to 62°, 67°, or even 73°. Even at midnight at the very peak of the high mountain ascended by Scoresby, the power of the sun produced a temperature several degrees above the freezing point, and occasioned the discharge of streams of water from the snow capped summit. Hence, though even in the warmest months the temperature of Spitzbergen does not average more than 34½°, yet in the more southern aspects, and particularly where the warmth of the sun is absorbed and radiated by black rock walls, the mountains are not seldom bared; at an elevation nearly equal to that of the snow line of Norway various Alpine plants and grasses frequently flourish, not only in sheltered situations at the foot of the hills but even to a considerable height whenever the disintegrated rocks lodge and form a tolerably good soil.

The flora of Spitzbergen consists of about ninety-three species of flowering or phenogamous plants, which generally grow in isolated tufts or patches, but the mosses which carpet the moist lowlands, and the still more hardy lichens which infest the rocks with their thin crusts or scurfs as far as the last limits of vegetation, are much more numerous. Some of the plants of Spitzbergen are also found on the Alps beyond the snow line at elevations of from 9,000 to 10,000 feet above the level of the sea. According to Mr. Martins nothing can give a better idea of Spitzbergen than the vast circus of uévé in the centre of which rises the triangular rock known to the visitors of Chamouney as the Jardin or the Courtil. Let the tourist, placed on this spot at a time when the sun rises but little above the horizon, or better still when wreathes of mist hang over the neighbouring mountains, fancy the sea bathing the foot of the amphitheatre of which he occupies the centre, and he has a complete Spitzbergen prospect before him. Supposing him to be a botanist the sight of the *Ranunculus glacialis, Cerastium alpanum, Arenaria biflora,* and *Erigeron uniflorus* will still further increase the illusion.

EARLY MORNING'S RAMBLES IN SPRING.

Say, ye that know, ye who have felt and seen,
Spring's morning smiles, and soul-enlivening green,
Say, did you give the thrilling transport way?
Did your eye brighten, when young lambs at play
Leap'd o'er your path with animated pride,
Or gazed in merry clusters by your side?—*Bloomfield.*

Spring is the pleasantest season of the year, the season wherein all the face of Nature gives way to a gradual transformation: from the long dark nights of winter, to the cheerfulness of an opening day; from the cold biting blasts from the northern regions, to the more temperate winds of spring, softened by the rays of the sun as they become more vertical; for every botanical production feels the benefit of such rays, whereby they undergo a gradual transformation. Spring, then, is the season of activity. The trees, the grass, the birds, the insects, in fact everything that hath life, all shake off that monotonous quiet which prevailed over them during the autumn and winter months, and have sprung up anew to revel in the glorious concert which is prevalent in the spring time. If you are abroad among the meadows and pasture-grounds when the dawn of morning spreads across the eastern horizon, then is the time for viewing the richness of spring-time; for the lark, that ever faithful witness of Aurora's first rays, is soaring high up in the cool grey sky to welcome the approach of the orb of day, making the air ring with his melodious notes. The thrush is early astir during this delightful season; for when the shadows of night have barely passed away, you may see him perched upon some neighbouring ash, breaking forth into full song. So fully absorbed is he when singing, that he is inattentive to what is passing around, so that you can get very near him without being observed by him, for he appears to be lost amid the vibrations of his harmony; but when morning advances he becomes silent. Probably he is engaged with his mate in the construction of the nest, or he has gone forth in search of food. The hedge-sparrow is among the first to commence building in this part of the country; and if you know of a nest which is under construction, it is a pleasure to watch these birds, how painful they are in collecting materials suitable for their habitation, for they begin work soon after four in the morning, during which time they are the most actively engaged. Or if your steps should lead you into the interior of a wood during these early ramblings, the least noise (such as the breaking of a rotten twig under your feet) will perhaps arouse the screaming jay from his slumbers, whose discordant cry as he sallies forth spreads alarm to other inmates of the woods, making them fly off in all directions; but the wren, careless of what has been going on overhead, hops about from twig to twig just above your head, narrowly watching your every movement without being the least afraid. Emerging from the wood to investigate the haunts of other birds, which make their nests by the dyke-sides, and other low swampy places, you may perhaps be startled (while passing alongside of a dyke) by the splash of the water-rat, as he disappears below the surface of the water, to reappear at another place where he is more secure. The titlark, not idle in his habits, is astir at this time; taking his flight a little distance up into the air, then descending again in full song, to alight on a neighbouring bush; when he becomes mute and silent. The whitethroat, making as much noise as a dozen birds, is revelling in song in the middle of a bush close by. The solitary crane, standing alone in the middle of a marsh, is attending to the wants of his craving appetite, by catching the fish which abounds in those places; so attentive is he to perform the duties he is engaged in, that he scarcely notices the snipe as it wheels past him, for not a sound does he give utterance to, to fill up the occasional vacuum in the chorus of the birds. The cuckoo, that itinerent bird, comes once more to delight us with his melody, to complete the sounds which greet our ears in the spring-time; for Logan, in his "Ode to the Cuckoo," illustrates the delight of the school-boy to hear him for the first time, in these words:—

"The school-boy wandering through the wood
  To pull the primrose gay,
Starts, the new voice of spring to hear,
  And imitates thy lay."

To the cowboy these morning excursions are his lot (for it is his duty to bring the cows out of the field to be milked), and he feels happy and contented with the lot which has fallen to him, as he scales the silvery dew of early morn, whistling or singing in harmony with the birds; and I must say there is not a more healthful recreation than rising with the lark, and taking to the meadows to study his haunts. In the opening bud there is a suggestion for the poet, and a study for the artist; and it is marvellous what an effect is produced on the bud after the passing of a genial spring shower, how it opens to lick in the precious drops (during which time the song of the blackbird is unrivalled). Edward Jesse, in his opening remarks on country life, makes a forcible impression about such advents of showers when he says—"The return of spring is always delightful, especially when the sun bursts forth after a warm and refreshing shower, reinvigorating the earth, and causing it to smile, if the expression may be used, with opening buds and flowers." Such, then, are the pleasures to be derived from early ramblings in spring; the delight and study of the naturalist, and a field wherein all the lovers of nature may increase their knowledge; adding at the same time pleasure to the eye and satisfaction to the mind. J. H.
North Lancashire, May 3.

AN AFRICAN BUSH HUNT.
By J. D. S. W.

THINKING that it might interest your readers to know the Kaffirs' mode of hunting a bush, I give the following:—

It was in September last that we received a message from one of the chiefs that they were going to hunt a large bush in our neighbourhood and wanted to know if we would join them, saying as an inducement that there were several tigers in it. We were very glad to go, and agreed to meet them as early as possible the next day.

Accordingly, the following morning we started, taking our guns with us, in hopes of shooting some game, and after a ride of about five miles we arrived at the bush.

Several hundreds of Kaffirs had already collected with a great number of dogs, each man armed with two or three Assagais (short spears) and Iwizas (knobbed sticks, or, as they are generally called in the colony, "knob carries"). The Kaffirs then form themselves into a line, stretching right across the bush, and all together move forward, the dogs going before and searching the underwood for game, which, when once driven out, had very little chance of escape.

The blue buck (a beautiful little animal, about the size of a hare) started up in every direction, and one blow from a "knob carrie" generally laid the little creature flat; but when a bush buck (a large brown antelope) made its appearance, it received a shower of assazais. The woods rang with the barking of dogs, and the screams of the natives, who, whenever they had knocked down a large buck, remained on the spot, disputing who had killed it, and it was very difficult to keep the game which we ourselves shot, the Kaffirs always claiming it, and saying it was their dogs that killed it.

How different was the noise and excitement of this day, to the almost painful silence which I have experienced while walking alone in these wilds "where Nature reigns supreme," and where one's thoughts are instinctively raised from nature to nature's God. I can truly say with Pollock:—

"Pleasant were many scenes,—but most to me
  The solitudes of vast extent untouched
  By hand of art, where Nature sowed herself,
  And reaped her crops, whose garments were the
    clouds."

One of our number having gone in another direction by himself, shot a leopard lying across a branch of a tree, with a large charge of shot; it was a splendid full-grown male, beautifully marked, and was by far the best part of that day's booty. After the hunt, the Kaffirs had great feasts on buck's flesh, which, like all other meat they eat, nearly raw, just singing it in the fire.

It must not be supposed by my giving a description of this mode of hunting, that I approve of it—far from it. I think that if it is not put a stop to by Government there will soon be no game in the colony. What is the use of the game laws prohibiting "white men" to shoot at certain seasons of the year, while the "natives" are allowed to hunt them in this merciless way all the year round.

Upper Umkomancy, Natal, February, 1869.

Correspondence.

[*Under this head we shall be glad to insert any letters of general interest.*]

ROCK BIRD ACT.

SIR,—I think the suggestion of a "Radical" is one that should be acted on. Let a magistrate, as he says, be allowed to grant a permit to any one wishing to get a pair of birds, or their eggs, for any particular purpose, and let any infringement of the terms of the permit be visited by double penalties, or imprisonment. This I think would put a stop to the slaughter, and yet allow the necessary number to be procured for science. This, the middle course will, however, I am sure find no favour in the eyes of the extremists, who will have the "entire animal" and nothing else. However, if "Radical" will kindly draw up the countercheck, I am sure hundreds would sign as he suggests; I would say *thousands*, only I know that the effeminate spirit of the age is all for twaddle and mock tender-heartedness; and so, heaven save the mark! the timid are afraid of being out of fashion, and would as soon sign their death-warrant, as anything which would bring them into such cruelly bad company as that of a "Radical," and Yours, &c.,

A. M. B.

Remarks, Queries, &c.

Under this head we shall be happy to insert original Remarks, Queries, &c.)

DO INSECTS FEEL PAIN?

Creatures, that, by a rule in Nature, teach
The act of order to a peopled kingdom.—*Shakespeare.*

Ye, therefore, who love mercy, teach your sons
To love it too.—*Cowper.*

Mr. Ernest Balfour Bax lies twelve months in reserve, then throws down his ultimatum, enters our literary campaign, and takes up a chosen position just in time to be rendered *hors de combat* by a strong, direct counterpoise from the lance of his own right hand man, Mr. Dalton!

Mr. Dalton openly and honestly admits the validity, the conclusiveness of my arguments, acknowledges his conviction, throws up the negative side, which he for a time so strenuously advocated, and at once boldly comes over to the affirmative. Surely this is science, and a simple proof that "men should know why they write, and for what end;" but at the same time it affords us another and a less pleasing proof of the great truth, that what is a demonstration to one man is to another an absurdity.

Do insects feel pain? "Yes," says Mr. Dalton, "because I see arguments strong and conclusive in support of the affirmative." "No," says Mr. Bax, "nothing but floods of 'irony,' no argument." Well indeed may Mr. Bax to Mr. Dalton say—

"You shot your arrow o'er the house
And hurt my big opinions."

And, Sir, I have Mr. Landels also, for he, too, in plain and very unmistakeable language says, his "opinion is that insects *do* feel a certain amount of pain." This is quite candid; and although Mr. Bax talks of the trisection and "bisection" of my arguments, still he never ventures to maintain the non-existence of pain in insects, but reasons hypothetically, and after cautiously wading through a series of his own mental incongruities, arrives at the conclusion that "insects do not experience *the same* acute sensation of pain with the higher animals." If this admission does not evidently imply the presence of *some pain* in insects, I resign all pretension to understand plain English.

But, Sir, listen to the strange logic of your correspondent—"insects do not experience the same acute sensations of pain with the higher animals;" and hence he thinks "this is sufficient to prove the negative side" (!)

But why do I dwell on this? Surely Mr. Dalton's candid letter is the best reply to the curious production of Mr. Ernest Balfour Bax.

I assure you, Sir, it is now evident that the inconsistencies, self-contradictions, and want of earnestness in the advocates of the painless theory are conspicuously degenerating quite below the status of ordinary argument, where science, a theory or a principle, demands an advocacy. Mr. Newberry's reply to "Justitiæ Amor," concerning the digestive organs and nervous system in insects, is so ably to the point that he leaves me not a word to say. Mr. Malan, after a repose of three months—not indeed a repose, for he has been all the time "racking his brains"—starts up mentally confused, and all dim perception concerning the agency of inductive evidence as referred to in my February letter.

Your correspondent tells us that from real experience he is convinced that he is capable of feeling pain himself, and that as he is of the same "family" as H. H. Ulidia, the King of Dahomey, and the Caliph of Bagdad, he is quite certain that those respectable gentlemen are, as a matter of course, also susceptible of pain. All right, Sir; a fair specimen of inductive evidence; but this "family" affair staggers me a little. Well, let us take another example. How does Mr. Malan know that the ass, the crocodile, gorilla, or goose, is capable of feeling pain? Your correspondent will at once reply, "simply because I am of the same 'family'" (!) Here I pause, while I advise Mr. Malan to *consider*.

The great law of gravitation is an inductive law; and here family, genus, race and order, are no longer connecting strongholds for the mental agility of Mr. Malan.

Believe me, Sir, when I briefly assure you that it is by inductive evidence we know that men and other animals feel pain. Consider the matter, study the subject, be in earnest, and your clear intellect, your "racked brains," must ultimately illuminate your now confused ideas, your unwilling perception.

The correspondents on the negative side seem not to consider the necessity of studying the question before us, and hence they appear, blunder, drop the pen, and conveniently evaporate. What a wide and noble field is the mighty range of animated nature, how diversified, how wonderful! And the insect, as a part of animated nature, as a lasting wonder of creative skill, we cannot overlook or despise; even its very smallness attracts attention, for, says the greatest of ancient naturalists, the nature of things is best seen in its smallest portions. In all creation, small as well as great—

"Man may read
The Maker's hand; intelligence supreme,
Unbounded power, on all his works imprest."

Insects have life, pleasure, disease, and *death*, and who can reasonably say they are *incapable of feeling pain*? None. Look at insect life, study it, consider the voracious appetites of those Lilliputians of the animal world, and we cannot but pronounce much of their life as one gigantic, one continual struggle for food. Deprive them of this food and they become dull and stupid, they linger and die, and in this transition surely " the *hunger pain* is gnawing there," so as to be acutely felt. Are we prepared to deny the existence of " hunger pain " in man, and the higher animals of the brute creation?

Your correspondents will, I presume, unanimously exclaim, "Certainly not!" And, this conceded, surely hungry insects must feel pain. But, Sir, the correspondents on the negative side are all imaginary opponents—they are gone. Still we are ready friends at arms. And while we read and appreciate the NATURALIST'S NOTE BOOK, let us not neglect to

"Go forth under the open sky, and list
To Nature's teachings."

There we receive and store up lasting instruction; there we see "forms unfashioned fresh from Nature's hand;" there they speak to us; there we must attentively listen; there we cannot but study and think; there we collect facts innumerable; and there we have real pleasure in the elevating and delightful pursuits of Natural History.

Dromore, May 27. H. H. ULIDIA.

I think that this discussion ought to have ended long ere this, it being now just a year since it was commenced, yet here I am, Sir, again troubling you with a little further correspondence upon this disputed subject. Seven letters appear in the May issue of the "N. N. B." on this question; and I perceive amongst them the letter of one correspondent of the so-called negative side, who, like all the rest belonging to that side, blunders, and writes in the same inconsistent manner, when he tries to prove that insects do not feel pain, by not actually denying, *in toto*, the absence of pain to them. I allude, Sir, to the letter of Mr. Ernest Balfour Bax. In perusing that gentleman's communication, no one can fail to notice how palpably he contradicts himself. After running down Mr. Ulidia's arguments, which he says "seem to refuse to die" (its a pity but that Mr. Bax's arguments were not dead and buried long before this), he thus proceeds:—"In fact, in the natural course of things, we should take the fact as granted that 'insects do not feel pain' . . . ." Now observe, he becomes rather more rational towards the end, for after giving an extract from Kirby and Spence's "Introduction to Entomology," and relating how wasps try to bite after having their heads severed from their bodies, and several other instances, which he thinks shows that insects are incapable of feeling pain, he goes on to say, "these facts, with hundreds of others which might be adduced, are sufficient, I think, to prove that insects do not experience the same acute sensations of pain with the higher animals, which Providence has endued with more ample means of avoiding them." Now here I will ask Mr. Bax, who said that they do feel pain as acutely as the higher class of animals experience it? Here again, Sir, allow me to point out to your correspondent that he does *not* deny the feeling of pain in insects; for, to quote Mr. Bax's words, their not being sensible to "the same acute sensations of pain with the higher animals," does by no means prove that they therefore are not susceptible of pain! No such thing. I myself perfectly coincide with Mr. Bax that the myriads of insects, as I have before said, do not experience pain to the same extent as man, etc.; for nothing will convince me that when a fly, or a gnat, etc., has a leg cut off, they feel this painful operation as much as human beings do. No. Yet again, on the other hand, I *will not* deny the total absence of pain in insects. Most certainly not. Do insects feel pain? You, Mr. Bax, and all your followers—which by-the-bye are becoming rather scarce, some having retired altogether from this controversy—have not as yet done anything like sufficient, either by your weak arguments or by your quotations, to *prove* the negative side, or to convince those on the affirmative side that insects do not feel pain, since hardly one of you will absolutely *deny* pain to them. This discussion has now, as I said in the beginning of this letter, lasted just a year. Who, after perusing what has appeared in the pages of the "N. N. B." on this question, can, after having read the letters produced by Mr. Ulidia, "Veritas," and others on the affirmative side, doubt but that "insects do feel pain," especially after those clever correspondents have thoroughly proved, either by their own careful investigations and experiments, or by their extracts from scientific works, that insects possess a nervous system? And, consequently, can any reasonable persons have but one opinion on this question?—and surely that opinion must be that "insects can and do feel pain." I strongly advise all those of the so-called negative side to try the experiments given by Mr. Ulidia in his last clever and forcible letter, which, together with others that gentleman has written, all containing so much rationality and convincing proofs, ought to remove all doubt, and fully establish the fact, viz., that "insects do feel pain."

Sidmouth, May 6th.   A. E. BUTTEMER.

I have been much interested in the controversy on this subject, which has occupied so much space in the "N. N. B.," and, although it has already assumed a great length, I venture to hope that you will allow me a little space to state my views on the subject. I shall not stay to remark upon the unsound and unjust arguments of Mr. Ulidia, or any one else, but merely to offer a few general remarks upon the subject. What we seek after is the truth, and whichever party may be the victors, such victory thould not be made a subject for exultation over the adversaries, but rather both sides should rejoice that the truth has been found.

I think none of the parties on the negative side wish now to assert that insects do not feel *any* pain, even if such were their opinion at first, as such an assertion it is impossible *to prove*. Therefore the question seems to resolve itself into this, whether insects feel great or little pain? I hold the latter view.

Some years ago, when I first read, "Colman's British Butterflies," I confess I was somewhat startled at the assertion that *insects do not feel pain;* since then, however, I have given some attention to the subject, and am more than ever convinced of the truth of this statement, or, at any rate, that the amount of pain they feel *is very small*.

Insects, all must own, are more exposed to injuries and dangers than all other animated beings,—birds, beasts, fishes, and even their brother-insects preying upon and destroying them, while man keeps up a never-ceasing war, intentional or unintentional, against these apparently doomed creatures. But over all this hangs an overruling Providence, which directs and equalizes all things; and would it not be blasphemy to suppose that the Great Creator should place some of his creatures in such a position, without means of defence, or something to alleviate their sufferings? Of means of defence, few insects are possessed, except in so far as they resemble other natural objects, such as leaves, twigs, etc., therefore I conclude that there must be something to neutralize the amount of feeling and pain in this lower order of nature. This something, then, I believe to be insensibility to pain. Let us see whether these statements can be proved.

It is a fact that all men are not equally sensible to pain, but according to their condition and circumstances feeling is modified. Mr. Wood in his "Natural History of Man" (now publishing), in treating of the Bosjesmans, relates an anecdote which illustrates almost total insensibility to pain, even in human beings. Having lent the number containing this anecdote to a friend, I cannot now quote it, but the substance is as follows:—A Bosjesman was engaged in carting firewood, and was driving a heavily laden wagon, when by some means he got under the wheels, which passed over him. It was expected, of course, that he would be killed on the spot; but what must have been the surprise of the Europeans present to see the man get up disconcerted and proceed to urge forward his team! Upon being asked if he were not badly hurt, he complained most of the little stones having been pressed into his flesh! I think this looks surprisingly like insensibility to pain. What does Mr. Ulidia think?

Again, as one of your correspondents mention, many savage nations are given to cutting themselves severely, and inflicting injuries which, if not mortal, would produce permanent injuries to Europeans. A Kaffir can stand a blow on the skull with apparent unconcern, which would stun if not kill an Englishman; and throughout the whole races of the world, the more the people are exposed to dangers and pain, the more power have they to resist the one and insensibility to feel the other. Surely this is Providence.

If, then, we see that man's power of feeling is accommodated to his state, it is but reasonable to suppose that it is the same throughout the animal world. For instance, it seems to me evident that a sheep would feel more pain on being wounded than a hippopotamus or a bison, simply because their states are different—the one being inured to hardship and pain, and the other not.

I might bring forward many more arguments in favour of the painless theory; but as my paper is already too long, let one anecdote suffice. Some few years ago I found a humble bee with the whole of the abdomen gone (apparently eaten by a bird), but yet this insect was alive. Neither does this instance stand alone, for other naturalists have noted similar occurrences. If Mr. Ulidia or any one else were forcibly deprived of their stomach, would not the pain alone be sufficient to kill him? I think it would.

From these and other arguments I can bring forward I am led strongly to believe that the amount of pain felt by insects is extremely small, amounting almost to nothing; and that a feeling of pain is not necessary to allow them to feel pleasure, as some correspondents have stated.

In conclusion I will say that it would afford me (and doubtless others too) much pleasure to hear the matured opinions of the correspondents on both sides.

Smethwick.   GEORGE TROBRIDGE, junr.

Though, as I said in my last, I agree with Mr. Ulidia in the affirmative view of this question, I cannot help protesting against his method of supporting that view. The "general principles" upon which he bases his "arguments" appear to consist chiefly of quotations from poetical and theological authors, with a few conclusions of anything but a logical nature drawn from well-known facts. Actual experiment is the only sure ground of argument. The question is, is the degree of concentration of nervine in insects above or below that point where the concentration enables the vibration of the nerves to be sufficiently rapid to produce pain. Common sense without facts cannot answer this, and to lay down that pain is a law of all animal life is clearly an assumption, for all animals have not nerves. The argument of the galvanized slug does not bear on the question, for the mollusca have a considerably higher degree of concentration of nervine than the insecta. The dragon-fly larva in oxalic acid evidently felt pain, and that experiment is a ground for argument.

Mr. Ulidia asks me to come and work: I regret that my roving life (on the geological survey) prevents me from doing so to any extent, as I am always moving from town to town. All I can do, therefore, is to take the facts recorded by actual observers and reason from them: parlour and field naturalists, working in concert, are equally useful to science, as the organ-blower and organist in producing music, each is necessary to the other, though the observer, like the organist, has the more important share in the work. As pleasurable sensation does not require so rapid a vibration of the nerves as pain, it is not necessary that all animals that can appreciate the former are capable of the latter.

Why Mr. Newberry thinks Mr. Bellingham's Rotifer felt pain puzzles me. "Justitia Amor," and Mr. N. hold opposite views on this question, and each thinks his view is that of common sense. Mr. N.'s statement about the digestive organs I must beg to deny: the stomach is the *least* sensitive of the important organs.

With creatures possessing so little feeling as insects, it is not improbable that the nervous vibration ceases more rapidly than in the higher animals, and therefore the moth pinned to a tree would feel no pain after the first few moments, which might not be long enough to wake it from sleep. When it wanted to fly, the least motion of its body would set the nerves round the pin vibrating and produce pain, which it would intensify and prolong by fluttering. For a similar reason crane flies and lobsters lose or cast off their limbs with apparent unconcern: the wound heals almost immediately.

The instinct of reproduction is with the lower animals almost as strong as that of the conservation of life, the former being more important: consequently the slight pain caused by mutilation, even if lasting, would not prevent union. W. H. DALTON.

Long Preston, Leeds.

This interesting discussion shows at last some signs of drawing to a close, as the majority of those who argued against the probability of insects feeling pain appear to have left the field, some wearied by the perseverance of Mr. Ulidia, and more perhaps who are afraid of his satirical remarks, I cannot say replies. But his own party appear to be divided, and it is difficult to tell whether they are arguing that insects feel the same degree of pain as the higher animals, or that they only feel it in a modified degree, which dwindles into nothing in the more minute insects; but we are now told that rotifers experience acute pain. Now, if this is the case, where are we to stop? These creatures, which are all but invisible to the naked eye, are next to infusoria the simplest form of animal life, and border so closely upon the vegetable kingdom that if we allow the feeling of pain to one, we can scarcely deny it to the other. Plants may be poisoned by the same poisons which prove fatal to animals; they may be rendered insensible by chloroform, and from the manner in which tendrils are put forth by climbing plants, and grasp at the surrounding supports, they might seem to be gifted with both eyes and reason, and from these and other instances I could mention, there would be quite as good grounds for arguing that they can feel pain as there is to suppose that rotifers do so, simply because they describe certain motions under certain circumstances. There is proof on every side that in nature there is no waste, and that mercy is over all the works of creation; but if pain is felt by these minute creatures, there would certainly appear to be both waste and cruelty—waste, because so far as we can see it would be of no use to them, and cruelty on account of the constant disasters to which they are subject. If it were proved that insects of this class feel pain, a man of feeling would be afraid to take a country stroll, because he must unavoidably tread upon, kill, or mutilate, and so cause misery to some of these creatures, which had both right and power to enjoy life equal with himself. Surely those gentlemen who defend the pain-feeling side of the question must reflect with regret on the time when they partook of that much-prized old Stilton, which abounds in animal life, and consider the destruction and misery they must have caused. O. R.

Though agreeing with much that Mr. Ulida says respecting this question, still I think his arguments anything but convincing, and unless better ones can be procured by the correspondents on the affirmative side, the question may never be settled. The first experiment he mentions is open to the following objection:—If Mr. Ulidia were to replace the living man by one recently dead, he would find the actions of the two subjects, while under treatment, somewhat similar. Would he then add, "proof positive that both felt pain?"

As for the larva of the dragon fly, might not its instinct tell it that the water was in an unnatural state, and consequently a place whence it ought to escape? With regard to the "entangled rotifer," I fully concur in the opinion of "Justitiæ Amor." Movement is no proof of pain. A man in an epileptic fit might by his struggles be thought to suffer intensely, but this is not the case. I am of opinion that the "writhings," &c., of the flies in Mr. Newberry's experiment were not produced by a sensation of pain, but by their endeavours to escape. Every reader may judge for himself how far these endeavours could be successful, with a minus quantity of legs, wounded abdomen, and injured thorax.

Southampton. LIBRA.

REASONING POWER OF ANIMALS.

"Reason," says Locke, "is that faculty which discovers the proofs of ideas, and rightly applies them." Dr. Reid identifies the power of reason with the faculty of judgment, and considers judgment to be "an act of the mind by which one thing is affirmed or denied of another;" and it is defined by Stewart as "that power by which we distinguish truth from falsehood, and combine means for the attainment of certain ends." Will any of the advocates of animal reason assert that a dog or an ape can distinguish truth from falsehood? or combine means for the attainment of certain ends, knowing to a certainty that certain means used in a certain manner will of necessity produce a certain result? Is it possible, I ask, for any class of animals to attribute certain effects to the operation of certain causes? *e.g.* the fact that a mountain exists in any given locality proves to a reasoning being that there must have been an elevation of the earth on the one hand, or a depression of the earth on the other, or perhaps a combination of those two causes, or else such a result could not have been attained. Again: if I plant a seed in the ground, I know that unless something disturbs that seed it will germinate, and grow up into a tree; moreover, I know that it will grow up into a particular kind of tree, according to the kind of seed planted. Will any of your correspondents show me out of all the vast Creation any living creature, be it beast, bird, reptile, fish, or insect, to whom the same deduction shall appear, and by whom the same method of reasoning shall be understood? Or, to go a step further, will any one show me an animal that is perfectly acquainted with, and can easily work out the simplest rule in mathematics? When this has been done I will at once give up my ground, and confess that animals are possessed of reason.

I must confess that I was somewhat staggered when I read your correspondent Mr. Bax's statement that dogs can be taught to play at chess and dominoes. I am entirely unacquainted with the work from which he appears to quote the fact, but I certainly must beg to be allowed to express my doubt as to the authenticity of Mr. Wyatt's information.

I cannot agree with your correspondent, "Veritas," in separating reason from the soul, and making it simply a "mental attribute." That reason is a faculty of the soul is fully proved by its coexistence with the soul after death, and that it is something superior to mind is fully proved by the fact that a lunatic, though possessed of a mind, is for the time being destitute of the active powers of reason. Anecdotes without number might be told to show that animals have not the power of reason. A monkey will patiently watch the traveller desert his camp fire in the lonely forest, and as soon as it feels itself safe will quietly approach the fire and sit down to enjoy its warmth; and when the embers die away will rejoin its companions in the woods, never thinking that by adding more fuel the fire might be made to burn for a longer time. Many authors, too, might be quoted whose unwavering opinion is that animals are not possessed of reason.

Monboddo says:—"As yet no animal has been discovered in the possession of language" (and consequently not of reason), "not even the beaver, who of all animals we know, that are not of our own species, comes nearest to us in sagacity." Locke says:—"The power of abstracting is not at all in brutes, and the having of general ideas is that which puts a perfect distinction between man and brutes." Perhaps some of your correspondents will contend that animals have both reason and language too; but this I absolutely deny, for where language exists under the influence of reason, we have evidences of its progression in the literature which emanates from it. Look at the productions of Milton, of Shakespeare, of Locke, Bacon, and Macaulay. Now, if we had *the least* remains of animal literature it would be indisputable evidence of their possessing reason, but we have not, and so the probability is that they have neither *reason* nor its resultant *language*.

Whilst speaking of language, I am reminded of a question asked me by W. H. Dalton, viz., "if the intellectual powers of say Stuart Mill and the Australian aboriginal are to be considered equal," and if I "would vote for the latter to sit in the British parliament and help to rule England?" I answer, "Certainly not!" But, at the same time, I do not hesitate to say, that if the Australian aboriginal had been brought up under the same influences as Stuart Mill, had lived from his childhood in the same society as Stuart Mill, and his "intellectual powers" had been brought out by the same educational course as those of Stuart Mill, he would have been in every respect equal to Stuart Mill, and no respectable borough need be ashamed of making him their representative in Parliament.

The great mistake lies in making reason to depend on the condition of the brain.

W. NEWBERRY.

"See then the acting and comparing powers
One in their nature, which are two in ours;
And reason raise o'er instinct as you can,
In this '*tis God that acts*, in that 'tis man."
—*Pope's Essay.*

"Veritas" commences his article in your last issue by accusing me of contradicting my "previous opinion of this controversy." If your correspondent had duly considered the arguments he wishes to refute, he would not have fallen into such a palpable error. I must inform "Veritas" that there is a vast difference between the two statements: "animals and plants possess reason," and "reason is observed in the actions of animals and plants." The last is the opinion I expressed from the first, and to which I still adhere. I further remarked that these two classes of organised beings afford instances of sounder reason than do many individuals of the human race.

Of this the uniform regularity and unerring precision observable in their general conduct is an undeniable proof. The reason I gave for this belief, and which your correspondent calls "singular," was that their actions proceed "much more directly from the author of all reason," and *i.e.* they are under the direct control and influence of the Almighty. Were this not the case, the lower animals would be as accountable for their deeds as man himself, and man, if he were so governed, would cease to be an accountable agent.

Thus "Veritas" will perceive that I do not wish to place the vegetable or animal world above man, any more than the mineral because stones always obey the law of gravitation.

I should be much obliged to "Veritas" if he would inform me in what way "certain irritable tissues" cause the vine so constantly to direct its course towards the upright pole; the strawberry runner to cross a gravel walk in search of proper soil in which to deposit its young shoots; the roots of all plants to persist in growing downwards even when their earth is uppermost; the *Dionæa muscipula* to catch flies, and keep them entrapped until completely *digested*.

The movements of the *Hedyearum gyrans* appear to be quite spontaneous. Alluding to it Chambers says:—" Generally all its leaflets twist and whirl themselves about in an extraordinary manner, though the air of the house in which they grow is perfectly still; sometimes only a single leaflet will move or all will become motionless together. . . Sometimes in a moment as if from the pure love of mischief, the leaflets will begin to move again. M. Dutrochet describes all these movements to an interior and vital excitation." This writer further remarks:—" Although plants may not feel as the higher animals do, which have a regular nervous structure and a brain, yet they may possess an irritability analogous to, or even identical with, that possessed by polyps and sponges. It is a beautiful and exalting idea certainly, to believe in the sensation and enjoyment of vegetable life." Another has justly declared that "the motions of plants are as regular and *rational* as those of animals."

"Veritas" next gives us his definition of an animal —"it is in fact only a body endued with the divine influence which denominate life." This definition might with equal propriety be applied to a plant unless your correspondent holds them to be creatures without life! I quite agree with him that it is a "most erroneous idea to suppose that man is the only creature endowed with a mind," but I also consider it quite as erroneous to imagine that the term *mind* necessarily implies reason. It is much more clear that the lower animals possess memory and affection, than that they enjoy reasoning powers. If the brute really possesses reason of the same kind as man, in what respect is the one inferior to the other? If any one says, "In the amount allotted to it," I answer, why then are not animals much more prone to blunder in their transactions than mankind, instead of, as is the case, much less?

There is no doubt a difference between the constant and regular actions of animals, and those which vary according to circumstances: but I do not see why both of these classes of animal performances (which may be called primary and secondary instinct) may not be attributed to a superintending Providence; that animals receive special guidance in special circumstances. This was the opinion of the great Sir Isaac Newton— certainly a very weighty authority on any subject of controversy. In his famous thirty-first query, or General Scholium to the optics, he says:—"The instinct of brutes and insects can be the effect or nothing else than the wisdom and skill of a powerful, ever-living Agent, who being in all places, is more able by his will to move the bodies within his boundless, uniform sensorium, and thereby to form and reform the parts of the universe, than we are by our will to move the parts of our bodies."

That the Deity is thus constantly acting through existing animals was also the opinion of Addison. Alluding to some remarkable instances of sagacity he says, "they can no more be explained than gravitation can; and come not from any law of mechanism, but are an immediate impression from the first mover, and the *Divine energy acting in the creature.*"

Now if, as your correspondent holds, some of the actions of the inferior animals are directed by their reason, it necessarily follows that all must be; for, as Lord Brougham says, "the supposition that instinct is to cease and reason to begin in a certain event, implies that the animal acting by instinct all the while was reasonable and intelligent, else how could he know when to lay down his instinct and take up his reason." He thus explains the occasional errors and imperfections of instinct, "as in the majority of cases the design is perfect and the wisdom complete, it is probable that further knowledge would remove all apparent anomalies, and reduce everything to order and to a consistency with perfect wisdom and skill." It ought to be distinctly understood that the word *mind* does not imply reason, and therefore anything influenced solely by contact with their senses (such as tricks, music, etc.) does not affect our subject.

The scriptures tells us that God at the creation "breathed into man the breath of life," *i.e.*, gave him power to act, independently of every other creature, to do either right or wrong. Nothing makes man superior to other creatures but the absolute possession of reason; otherwise there would be no such difference: the highest brute (the ape) would simply be a man with a lesser development of intellect, and these intellectual powers would gradually become less perceptible as we descended the scale of animal life. Progress is one of the chief characteristics, and a never absent trait of reason; and where do we observe it but in man?

Another thing that militates against this theory is that brutes fail to imitate some of the simplest operations of man. For instance, why does the ape, which learns from men, to sit beside a fire and appears to enjoy the warmth, not go a step further and keep up the fire by heaping on fuel?

The anecdote "Veritas" tells us about the beetle has not much force, for if instinct (or a superintending power) "compelled it to go under the mouse and attempt to bury it, why should not the same power instruct it as to its further proceedings, viz., that of "making an excavation round the stick."

To conclude, I cannot allow with Mr. "Veritas" that this question has been "thoroughly proved and sifted," unless he is able to answer clearly and intelligibly the objections proposed in this paper.

Edinburgh.   R. B. W.

IS THE WHALE A FISH?

I am induced to ask this question because many sensible, though unscientific men, with whom I have spoken on the subject, have held the opinion that the whale *is* a fish.

Perhaps some of your readers will say that no one, except he be a scientific naturalist, is able to argue or rightly to decide this question; and therefore, that the opinion of those who are not naturalists can have no weight in it. Before I have finished my letter, however, I think they will feel themselves constrained if not entirely to agree in the opinion that the whale *is* a fish, at least to admit that, although their opponents are neither naturalists nor men of science, yet they are quite as competent to argue the question as those who hold the contrary opinion, and, moreover, that they have a considerable amount of reason to show in support of their belief.

The question, it should be said, is not whether or not the whale is a fish, according to the classification of naturalists, but whether the classification of naturalists can be justified.

Only two or three weeks ago a friend of mine, who had just been reading some account of the whale, said to me, "It's all very well for you naturalists to pretend that the whale isn't a fish, and then to pull us up if we venture to speak of it as such. The whale is a fish all the world over, whatever you may say to the contrary." I set to work there and then to convince him of his error; but although I brought forward all the reasons which are usually given by naturalists in support of their opinion, to my surprise and chagrin those arguments which I thought so convincing were soon all knocked on the head, and I was eventually compelled, though much against my will, not only to confess myself beaten, but even to come right round to the opinion of my opponent.

I shall now proceed to lay before you the arguments on both sides of the question, giving first those made use of by naturalists, and secondly, those which are used in support of the opinion that the whale is a fish.

I. The following are the chief reasons which are given by naturalists for their decision that the whale is *not* a fish—

1. "Fishes breathe by gills, which require the air to be conveyed to them through the medium of the water. On the other hand, whales breathe by lungs, to which the atmosphere must be directly admitted. From this cause a fish dies if it be kept long out of the water, and the whale would be drowned if it were kept very long immersed in it."

2. "The fish has 'cold blood,' a heart with only two chambers or cavities, and what is termed 'a single circulation.' The whale is a 'warm-blooded animal,' has a heart with four cavities, as in man, and has a 'double circulation.' In the fish, therefore, the blood which is sent from the heart passes to the gills, and, after receiving the small amount of aeration it requires, continues its course onwards to nourish all parts of the body. In the whale the blood is first propelled from the *right* side of the heart, through the capillaries of the lungs, to be thoroughly aerated, or arterialized, and then it returns to the *left* side of the heart, whence it is propelled to circulate generally, and nourish the body."

3. "Fishes have no external ear-openings; whales have them, and hear well in the water."

4. Lastly, fishes multiply by spawning. They lay eggs, sometimes in places which they have specially prepared for their reception. After this their care for their young ceases, except in some exceptional cases, as that of the stickleback for instance, and they leave them to shift for themselves. Whales, on the contrary, give birth to living young, which they tend and protect with the greatest assiduity and tenderness, and which they suckle and nourish with their own milk.

These arguments are quite conclusive as to the whale not being a fish according to the classification of naturalists, but they prove nothing as to the correctness of the classification itself.

II. The argument which I take to prove beyond all possibility of contention or doubt that the whale is a fish is as follows—

"Fish" is a popular term applied to all those animals, whether vertebrate or invertebrate, which constantly reside in the water, and which could not exist for any length of time if they were removed from that element.

Thus, for instance, the dolphin is ordinarily called a fish, because its natural habitation is the sea, which it never leaves. But the seal or the walrus is never so called, for although it is true that it seems to be most at home when in the water, yet it very often leaves that element, and, moreover, spends almost perhaps quite as much time out of it as in it.

Take another example. The common jellyfish is called a fish, because its whole existence is passed in the water, and it would speedily die if it were kept out of it. But the great water-beetle (*Dybiscus*) is never so designated, although, as its name implies, it spends far more time in the water than out of it. And why is this? Simply because it has the habit of leaving the pond or stream which it inhabits at the time of dusk, sometimes as often as every evening, to take long flights over the surrounding country, or to hover about over the surface of the water. And the beetle appears to be quite as much at home when performing its airy evolutions as when it is cleaving its way through the waters of the pond; whereas the jellyfish, when removed from its native element, is in the uncomfortable and anomalous position of "a fish out of water."

I think that from what I have now said you will have a clear understanding of the popular definition of a "fish."

Of course the popular classification is quite as liable to error as that of naturalists, and I have no doubt that many animals are placed by it in the class of fishes, which, even according to the popular definition of the term "fish," ought not to be there. But this is owing to ignorance of the habits and mode of life of such animals.

Therefore, notwithstanding these occasional errors, since the word "fish" has from the remotest times been used with the meaning above stated, and is so universally used in the same signification now; and since there is nothing in the word itself which is at all opposed to such a meaning, I hold that naturalists have no right arbitrarily to restrict its meaning as they do. Let naturalists fix on some other term if they will, expressing, if they think it desirable, some characteristic or characteristics, exclusively belonging to that class, which at present they call "fishes," and then there will no longer be any difficulty or disagreement; but let them not, to suit their own convenience, restrict a popular term, and then tell the public they are wrong if they do not also restrict it, instead of continuing to use it in that more wide signification which it has hitherto borne.

I do not expect that many—perhaps none of your correspondents will agree with me in the views to which I have given expression in this letter, but at least they must admit that though I may not have satisfactorily proved my case, yet I, and those who think with me, have not a little reason on our side.

Trusting that my letter will meet with a favourable reception from you, I am,
JOHN LANDELS.
Scuddylaw, near Berwick-on-Tweed.

BIRD MURDER.—Since this subject was introduced, I have been expecting that some of your correspondents would come out more fully, and soften at least the horror that humanity must feel at the idea of murdering the unoffending little birds. As killing, when unaccompanied by *malice prepense*, is denominated homicide, I humbly submit, on behalf of ornithologists and young sportsmen, that bird-killing is, at the very worst, nothing more than simple *avicide*.

The greater number of those who advocated the painless theory being now converted, I may be permitted to assert that more individual deaths, and consequently a greater amount of suffering, is inflicted in a few moments by the evaporation of a few drops of putrid water, than by all the horrible bird murder committed on the shores of Great Britain in the course of a year.

The seasons are made up of calms and storms, of clouds and sunshine; universal life, of pain and pleasure, of sorrow and enjoyment. Through the whole range of animated nature one class of beings become subservient, in destruction, to the existence of another. Yet, on reflection, it will be found that the sum of enjoyment in the individual far exceeds the amount of pain, for the latter is for the most part of short duration.

Animals are deprived of life to gratify the appetite and sustain the body, without giving the slightest twinge to the conscience, or offending the most delicate feeling. The poet is not false to his mission who dines on mutton, and afterwards, with true feeling, sings of

"The lamb that crops the flowery mead."

Deer and hares are bred and carefully preserved, often to the extermination of human beings, provided with dainty pasture, and not suffered to be disturbed by the bark of plebian colley,; and is it unfair to demand that they should in return give a spurt of running, and shorten what will soon be a life of decay for the gratification of their owner? A few moments' pain for a life of enjoyment? Surely not. The balance is in their favour.

If it be conceded that this fair earth and all it contains were called into existence to show the wisdom and the power of the Creator, and to minister to the wants and comforts of man whom He has made next to the angels, it follows that man has a right to exercise his power in exacting their services, so far as he can do so without materially disturbing the economy of Nature. If prompted by a longing for excitement, a desire for adventure or an inclination to engage in arduous pursuits, he has every right to do so, if he encroach not on the rights of his fellowman. Let him hunt, shoot, and fish, not with the intention of inflicting pain, but for the sake of healthful recreation, pleasure, or gain: he commits no deed of cruelty, violates no law, yet there is a limit he must not pass.

Where the animals are not numerous, and the locality confined, moderation must be kept in view, or the economy of nature will be disturbed, and the rights of others violated.

In the case of sea-birds, such a danger can hardly ensue. They are very numerous and widely distributed, so that if considerable numbers be destroyed at particular periods, their place will soon be replenished. Suppose their average life be only five years, at the lowest calculation they would increase tenfold in the same time, and as many of their breeding places are never approached, this will allow a large margin for both use and sport.

As for the poor little starvlings deprived of their feeders, the chance is their number is small in proportion to the number of full-grown birds killed, and these can be left to the commiseration of the young lady who wept lest her lapdog should grow sick after inserting its white teeth in the leg of the butler

The amount of pain caused will be infinitessimally small, compared with that naturally taking place under a few yards of sea surface. NERO.

THE MISSEL-THRUSH (TURDUS VISCIVORUS).—This bird is considerably larger than the song-thrush, which it resembles in general appearance. It builds early, generally in the beginning of April. The nest is formed on the outside of moss and small sticks, bound round with rushes, or other materials; next to this comes a layer of mud; and the lining is like the blackbird's, of dried grass. I have also seen wool employed. It lays four or five eggs of a whitish ground-colour, which sometimes gives place to a light cream colour, spotted with dark red-brown spots, chiefly towards the larger end. The eggs vary much in size and shape. Those in my collection were taken out of the same nest. One of them is very long and pointed, the other the bluntest egg I ever saw. The spots on the former (which is the largest of the two) are much more numerous, though smaller, than those on the latter. The crow seems to be exceedingly fond of the missel-thrush's eggs, perhaps because it builds earlier than other birds, and so no other eggs are to be got. At any rate I have often seen battles between the two birds. One I watched, though I did not get near the combatants till just at the end of the fight, on the 6th of last month (April), though with what event unfortunately I could not discover; there was a pair of crows engaged. On another occasion I found a nest about three feet from the ground in the fork of an apple-tree, the four eggs of which, from the evolutions of a crow near, I feel convinced were devoured by him. The nest of the missel-thrush is very frequently placed in the fork of an apple-tree near a house, from which no doubt it tries to obtain protection from its foes. The forks of other trees are often chosen to receive the nest, especially if covered with ivy. The nest is often well concealed. That out of which I took the eggs I have at present was placed at the joining of a small branch of an oak with the trunk, that was in the hedge on the side of a turnpike road. The bird sat unmoved through all the noise of the carriages until the eggs were taken. As I ascended the tree the birds kept up their angry shriek that is so often heard; but as I blew the eggs at the foot of the tree they uttered a low, dismal, plaintive note, all the time sitting not more than ten yards off me. This nest, notwithstanding its open position, was by some means rendered rather difficult to see until we knew where it was, and then, like many other things, appeared perfectly plain. I have heard it said that the missel-thrush sometimes associates with the fieldfare; but this I do not believe to be true—at least I never saw it. On the contrary, I believe that the former bird is very much given to fighting with others of the same kind, and I should not be much surprised if it sometimes carries off their eggs, being the largest of the genus. The note of the missel-thrush (at least that with which he generally favours us) is not very musical, though perhaps he sings oftener than is suspected. I have heard a curious misconstruction of the word *Holm-screech*—people have talked to me about it as if it were spelt *Home-screech*, referring to the boldness it assumes in the breeding-season. Although when the missel-thrush is mentioned it always puts the idea of a familiar bird into my head, it is decreasing in some places, I believe, rather rapidly. Here for instance it is seldom heard, and whenever my collection of eggs is looked at, some one will say, "You did not take those here," pointing to the missel-thrush's eggs. Nor did I; nor have I ever found its nest here. Perhaps the scarcity of orchards, which furnish the forks of apple-trees, is the cause of this in Hampshire; as in Devonshire, where orchards abound, and where there is hardly a house of any size which has not apples to make the cider from, this bird abounds. I will now conclude by signing myself (though some of your classical readers may think the Latin rather canine)

OVORUM COLLECTOR.

MOON STROKES.—Your correspondent, "Veritas," has indeed given "J. D. S. W." and your readers a very "short explanation" why persons are affected by moonlight so as to have their countenances distorted by its influence, and he must allow me to add, not to my mind a very satisfactory one. I must first quarrel with his assertion that "as yet philosophers have failed to detect" heat rays from the moon, "even with their most delicate instruments." In a book of reference now before me I find it stated in a letter from Melloni to Arago, that he (Melloni) "concentrated the rays (moons) "with a lens, over three feet diameter, upon his thermoscopic pile, when the needle was found to deviate from 0° 6′ to 4° 8′, according to the phase of the moon." However, I admit that this degree of heat would not probably affect a person exposed to the moon's rays whilst sleeping, but still it does not follow that "we must look for the causes of the strokes not in the moon, but on our own planet." The very quotation from Scripture given by "Veritas" would lead us to look for them in the former: "The Sun shall not smite thee by day nor the moon by night." It may be very possible that a person lying asleep in the moonbeams may experience some bad effects from radiation; but that the countenance is liable to distortion from that cause I for one cannot admit. That the moon has *a* certain decided influence upon animal matter appears from the fact often recorded, and which I believe many a naval man can attest, that in the tropics fresh meat hung out for coolness over the stern of a ship will, if the moon shines brightly, become ere long unfit for food; in fact putrescent. For this effect earth radiation will certainly not account. Has there then never been discovered any influence, any force exerted by the moon upon animal matter which can by some possibility account for or rather induce both these phenomena? I think any one who without prejudice reads Baron Von Reichenbach's "Researches on Magnetism," will come to the conclusion that there is. It is impossible here to enumerate or follow his numerous experiments undertaken to demonstrate the existence of what he calls "Chrystallini," or elsewhere "odylic force," which he found to be exerted by the sun, but I will just quote his words at the conclusion of his experiments with the moon's rays. (P. 105, sec. 120). "From all this it follows that the moon's light is not mere moonshine; that although it yields us no heat (?) yet along with its light it possesses a powerful force, which exhibits the same properties as that residing in Crystals, &c. The moon is therefore a fifth source of this influence." May not this discovery of Reichenbach's throw some light on the matter in question, viz., the peculiar influence of the moon on those long exposed to the action of its rays?

WINDSOR HAMBROUGH.

FOLK-LORE.—The curious names which the country people give to the animals, plants, etc., amongst which they live, and combined with the superstitions, &c., are very interesting to the naturalist, I therefore send you these few, which may be acceptable to some of your readers. There is here the usual prejudice against the weasel (Mustela vulgaris) which they call the "futrit," and will tell you that it will spring at your throat, and suck your blood, and its teeth, when once fastened in your throat, cannot be got out again, being like screws. The popular belief about the frog is that it cannot be killed, and even though you was to cut one in pieces, it would come and sit at the back of your head all night.

The lizard, land eft, and newt, are believed to be very poisonous.

"Pop-hole" is the name applied to the willow wren (Sylvia trochilus), on account of the shape of the doorway of its nest. It is also called the "muffety."

The hedge-sparrow (Accentor modularis) is known as "birrety," but I cannot tell the reason.

The magpie (Pica caudata) is always the subject of much superstition. A peasant once told me that he would eat the egg of any bird except the piets, which, he said, "had a drap o' deil's bleed in them."

The lesser tern (Sterna minuta) is called the "sang liverock" (sand lark), while the common tern (Sterna hirundo), and the black-headed gull (Larus ridibundus) are known as "picktirl" and "picktirk :" the latter is supposed to be an adult of the former. On account of the ring round the neck of the black-headed bunting (Emberiza schoeniclus), it is called the "ring fool" (fowl), and "water babby" is applied to the dipper (Cinclus aquaticus).

The meadow brown butterfly (Hipparchia janira), because of its dark colour, is called the "deevil's butterfly."

The dragon fly is believed to be the locust over all this county, in spite of all I could say to the contrary.

There is a good deal of superstition about the snail. If you can catch it by the horn, and throw it over your left shoulder, you will be sure to find something. You will likewise hear the children going along singing—

"Snail, snail, sheet oot your horn,
An' I'll gie you milk and breed the morn."

The following story was afloat in a parish in this neighbourhood :—One of the farmers had a cow which was delivered of a most extraordinary looking calf—in fact, so curious was it that the farmer ordered it to be killed, but was overruled by his sons, who wished to see what it would grow to. A day or two after, one of the sons went into the barn, where it was kept, when it rushed up the barn at him, barking with all its might. A. M. M'A.

INSTINCT IN PLANTS.—I think "R. B. W." will be much interested to see what Professor Carpenter says on this interesting subject :—"There are evident limits to the supply of alimentary materials to the roots of plants, so long as they remain in the same spot; and some change must take place to ensure its continuance. As the plant cannot remove itself to a new situation, its wants are provided for by the simple elongation of its radical fibres ; and their extension takes place, not by increase throughout their whole length, but by addition of fresh tissue to their points. This addition, being made in the direction of least resistance, enables the fibrils to insinuate themselves into the firmest soil, and even to overcome the obstacle presented by solid masonry ; for however narrow the crevice may be into which the filaments enter, the subsequent expansion of the tissues by the infiltration of fluid is so great, as to enlarge the opening considerably, and even to rupture masses of stone. This tendency to increase in the direction of least resistance, will also evidently cause the root to grow towards a moist situation ; and by keeping this in view, many of the facts regarding the so-called *instinct* of plants, which at first sight appears so remarkable, may be satisfactorily explained." Here follows a series of very extraordinary cases, *e.g.* when the water of the New River was conveyed to a distance by wooden pipes, the roots of trees thirty yards off "found" the joints, and insinuating themselves into the pipes, caused an obstruction to the water's course. The "dispersion of vapour" through the atmosphere in a particular direction also appears to exercise some influence on the direction of the radicles of plants, *e.g.* "Here is a peculiar case, in which one tree grew upon the trunk of another, having originated from a seed deposited at about twelve feet from the ground. One of the large roots which it sent down subdivided about two feet above the surface of the ground, instead of proceeding directly down to it, as did all the rest. Now this subdivision took place above a large stone, on the centre of which the root would have impinged, if it had continued to grow directly downwards : and it would appear as if its division, half proceeding to one side and half to the other, was due to the direction given to its growth by the ascent of vapour, from the sore beneath."—*Carpenter's Comparative Zoology, p.* 195. I confess this latter explanation does not seem very satisfactory ; it requires considerable elasticity of imagination to believe in the "fissle" properties of vapour, acting too on so fine a surface as the extremity of a radicle. But we are not responsible for professors' theories. C.

NOVEMBER METEORS.—During the great shower of meteors which took place in November, 1866, I stationed myself, with a telescope, for the purpose of taking a view of the train of one of the meteors, and after many attempts, at length succeeded in sighting one left by a very fine meteor, and I was astonished at what I saw. The train, instead of remaining, as they all appeared to do to the unaided eye, a mere line of light, formed itself into waves and convolutions, increasing in breadth, but gradually dissolving as it spread and twisted about. It became precisely similar in appearance to a line of yellow smoke, which, after issuing from a chimney, is acted upon by a gentle breeze. Upon removing my eye from the telescope, it still seemed a straight line, which gradually faded, and was at length lost, but upon again referring to the glass, it was visible, though much attenuated and altered in form. I saw it for at least two minutes after it became invisible to the naked eye, still spreading and assuming new forms. This fact has quite convinced me that the trains left by meteors is caused by the combustion of the matter constituting the body, and continues to be produced until either the body is wholly consumed or until the meteor leaves the atmosphere. In all the accounts of that grand display, I have never read of any one succeeding in obtaining the view I saw, and I mention this as it doubtless will be interesting to some of your readers ; and I shall be glad if any of your correspondents can confirm my statement from actual observation.

FELIX.

ENGLISH SNAKES.—Your correspondent, "J. C.," does not seem to be aware that a third English snake has been added to our list of reptilia, viz., "Coronella lævis," found about six or seven years ago in Hampshire, where it had probably been previously confounded with the viper, which it somewhat resembles. In the *Intellectual Observer* for April, 1863, there is a beautifully coloured plate of the snake, with description. In case "J. C." should not have access to that work, I transcribe for his information a few lines from it:—"In general appearance it much more closely resembles the viper than the common ringed snake (Natrix torquata), but may at once be known from the viper by the imperfect V on the top of the head, and instead of a single dark zig-zag line down the centre of the back, as in the viper, there are two rows of dark spots down the back; the head is also much shorter, smaller, and rounder than the head of the viper." I may add that unlike the viper it is *not* poisonous.

Allow me also to inform your correspondent, "Arbor," that the "wind-flower" is the Anemone; the French call it "Herbe au Veut." Greek *anemos* wind.

"The coy anemone, that ne'er uncloses
Her lips until they're blown on by the wind."
—*Horace Smith.*
W. HAMBROUGH.

EXTINCTION OF SPECIES.—Your correspondent, "W. G.," proposes a plan which I have long wished to see carried out, viz., that some naturalists should club together, and import the pupæ of Antiopa in large numbers, with a view to acclimatizing this insect. W. G. says, "I am told that on the Continent this insect is not rare." During the spring and autumn of 1866 I was staying at Heidelberg, and can testify to the accuracy of the above statement. Breeding such lepidoptera as the one in question would, to me at least, be far more interesting than rearing silk worms year after year. One great obstacle is, that it would be next to impossible to bring over enough pupæ of this butterfly in one season to give the plan a fair chance of success. Were there only a few set at liberty, the chances are that no two would ever meet, and the Camberwell Beauty would remain as great a rarity as it now is. Again, if the climate has anything to do with its scarcity, which I fancy is the case, the winter that must be passed would thin the ranks of the few introduced. On the whole I would suggest that this insect be bred by collectors throughout England (I am sure that numbers would undertake the pleasant task), and kept by them for consecutive seasons, until a large number could be set at liberty during a certain year to live or die, as the case might be. If anything is to be done, let it be done directly. Would any person—say W. G.—be kind enough to come forward, and direct our first steps with regard to obtaining the pupæ, and distributing them to collectors? I am afraid there would be great difficulty in getting the insect to breed while in confinement; but why not make the experiment?
Southampton. W. JOHNSTON.

ENTOMOLOGICAL REQUISITES.—I think that W. W. Walker might easily obtain the requisites for insect collecting on a much smaller and less expensive scale than that of the list given in the last number of the N. N. B. by "T. L." To begin with, the following may very well suffice W. W. Walker:—Lepidoptera net from 1s. 6d. to about 2s. 6d.; insect pins 1s. per ounce; pocket collecting boxes for the field from 6d.; setting boxes, without case, about 9d. or 1s. each (about three sizes would be required); permanent collecting boxes from about 3s. 9d. The best place to buy them is at a regular cork manufacturer's. To kill insects air tight tin or wooden boxes containing wool, or blotting paper saturated with such poison as the "naturalist dealer" may recommend, are necessary. If used with caution chloroform, laudanum, prussic acid and ether are all efficacious. Instead of a regular store box, W. W. Walker may buy cork in sheets and line a suitable box with it himself. An expensive breeding cage is not absolutely necessary: a good sized dry and well-ventilated box, or even shade, may serve the same purpose. W. W. Walker should take care to provide himself with an ounce of camphor to preserve his collection from numerous insect pests which would destroy his specimens. Insect cabinets may be had from 25s. upwards, all ready lined. IMAGO.

BIRDS' "TOWERING."—Mr. A. H. Malan appears to consider it doubtful that partridges sometimes rise in the air before falling, when shot. That this is a fact, however, I as well as many other sportsmen are witnesses to. It is called "towering," and is believed only to occur when the bird is hit either in the head or near the heart. I have seen them rise up suddenly, as if blown up by some explosive agent to a great height, and then suddenly drop as dead as "a door nail," always dying in the air. Other birds will do the same; the last I noticed, "tower," was a turtle dove (Columba turtur), which I shot, and this one rose higher than I ever remembered one to do before, coming down with such force (from an altitude of perhaps ninety yards) as to cause its feathers to fly in all directions on reaching the ground. Ducks and some other birds also I have noticed, if shot in the head while swimming, will spin round and round on their own axis, with remarkable velocity, before they finally succumb to death. A. M. B.

GUILLEMOTS.—A reference was made by Mr. Buttemer (whose statement I can confirm) in the Number of the "N. N. B." for May to the myriads of guillemots (*Uria*) frequenting the southern coast of Pembrokeshire. The rock (which he mentions) not very far from Tenby is inhabited by these birds in such numbers as to take its name from them. It is called Eligug Stack, Eligug being the local name for this guillemot. This rock rises abruptly from the sea. Every ledge is occupied by long rows of birds in a constant state of restless activity, while on the top they stand as thickly as they can be placed, keeping up the most jabbering noise. The sea below is at the same time—if the weather is fine—thickly dotted over with myriads of these little birds, either floating on the water or diving for their food. They may also be seen in great numbers on the island of Shomar, off the coast of Pembrokeshire. I may add that the coast of Pembrokeshire offers a wide field for the chonchologist, not less than one half of the British collection of 600 varieties of shells being found on it, besides various others usually met with only on foreign shores.

A FORMER RESIDENT IN TENBY.
Gravesend, May 10.

To Preserve the Colours of Dried Flowers.—Your correspondent, "Flora," wishes to know of a mode of preserving the colours of dried flowers. I have a receipt by me which I think will answer the question, which I will take the liberty of copying, hoping it will be of some use. The process is as follows:—After having gathered the plants—which should be done in dry weather—place each between several sheets of blotting-paper and iron it with a large smooth iron heater, pretty strongly warmed, until all the moisture is gone out of them. Colours may thus be *fixed*, when otherwise the plants become pale, or nearly white. In compound flowers, with those also of stubborn and solid forms, some little art is required in cutting away the under part, by which the profile and forms of the flowers will be more distinctly exhibited. After completing the above process, care should be taken to keep them in a dry place. A book for their final reception may be obtained of any stationer for a trifling cost, or made to order, and of any size.   R. LADDIMAN.
St. Augustine's, Norwich.

Does the Skin Absorb?—I read in a late paper that a certain continental physician had proved to his satisfaction that the skin of the human body had no power of absorption; so much so that he expressed his willingness to be immersed in a bath prepared with any poisonous ingredients, provided they were not of a corrosive nature. I have not heard the result of his experiments. I believe until now the opinion was universal, that the skin both absorbs and perspires. We are told that some persons on the point of dying from thirst have prolonged their lives by standing up to the neck in the sea; and that others have been nourished without food by taking milk baths. On the other hand, can perspiration, which we are informed is continually passing from us, take place at the same time that the skin is absorbing? I should like to hear the opinions of some of your readers on this subject.
R. B. W.

Water Snake.—"J. C.," in answer to "M. L. A." erroneously gives him the information that "there are only *two* British specimens of snakes." Allow me to correct this: our British snakes are *three* in number, viz., common snake (Coluber Natrix), smooth snake (Coluber Austriacus), and viper or adder (Pelias Berus). All of these are ophidians belonging (if we exclude the crocodiles not represented by any English species) to the third order of the reptilia. The slowworm (Anguis fragilis), though often called a snake, is not properly recognised as one, as belongs to the second order, or Saurians. The common snake *is* a water-loving species, and I have caught dozens at various times while in the act of swimming. They swim easily, carrying their head in a most graceful manner out of water and dive with equal facility when alarmed. With country people *all* snakes are venomous, and the sight of "Natrix" taking a bath would be quite sufficient to establish a new species, in their eyes.
A. M. B.

The Sting of Nettles.—I will inform Mr Landels that I have again made some further experiments with nettles, and after drawing the leaves of a few strong specimens lightly both across the palm and back of my hand, I met with the same results as before, totally escaping being stung. I may perhaps be fortunate in possessing a thick epidermis; but I certainly think that Mr. Landel's hands being "chapped with the cold," made his skin "more tender than ordinarily." When the leaves are hit with a great force, some of the barbed hairs on them, which are very slender, are crushed, making the sting felt less severe than if knocked moderately hard. With regard to the poison of nettles being less virulent in cold than in hot weather I have never noticed; but the venomous effects experienced must in a great measure depend upon the condition of the blood and health of the particular person.   A. E. BUTTEMER.

A. Atropos.—I find that in nearly every entomological work I have consulted, atropos is mentioned as emerging from the pupa only in October. Is it not a rule for many to pass the winter in the pupa state? On August 17, 1868, I had a larva of this insect brought home by a friend; it was nearly full grown. On the 20th it went down, and from that time till April 8, 1869, I saw nothing of it. On the last mentioned date I emptied part of the soil from the box it was kept in, and found a living pupa. I am daily expecting its transformation. Am I right in supposing that this is a common occurrence, and that it should be mentioned in natural histories of British moths?
W. JOHNSTON.

The Dahlia.—Being a subscriber of only a few months, I trust you will excuse me if I ask too much. I wish for some information on the experiment or attempt to darken the dahlia. Please inform me, if you can, the name of a book expressly on the subject, or please give me the name of the darkest seed of dahlia, the most suitable soil, and the best time for setting the seed; if you cannot, perhaps some kind contributor to the NOTE BOOK might.
E. S. KING.

Asteroids.—I should be glad if some of your correspondents will inform me what the views of modern astronomers are with regard to the asteroids—whether they are still supposed to be fragments of one large planet which has burst, and whether the orbits of those which have been more recently discovered intersect in the same point; I should also like to know any discoveries which modern research have made in this subject.   O. R.

Coal.—Is it certainly known what coal is? I know it is usually considered to be wood that has lain for ages deep beneath the soil, and caused by vast forests being engulfed by the earth during its changes and transformations. But one obstacle to this belief is, that trees have been found in a *petrified* state, converted by their long burial not into coal but into *stone*. Can any of your correspondents throw light on this matter?   R. B. W.

Electricity.—Has any specific difference been discovered between the nervous and electric fluids? That they are identical would seem from the fact that in great fear the hair stands on end and sparks are observed in the dark, as well as from various other phenomena. How is the electricity from the positive

substance excited by the action of the acids in a Galvanic battery? in a common machine this is produced by friction. Answers to these queries, or preference to a work on the subject, will much oblige,
R. B. W.

WATER.—Must not all water have been originally formed by the burning or ignition of oxygen with hydrogen? The capacity for conducting heat is said to be in proportion to the closeness of the particles in a body; how, then, is water a better conductor than wood since the particles of the former can be much more easily separated than those of the latter? In drinking water, is not some of the oxygen and hydrogen absorbed by the system?   R. B. W.

DUCKS.—I should feel obliged if through the pages of your NOTE BOOK you could afford me some information in regard to ducks. I have two ducks and a drake at Aylesbury. They were hatched March, 1868. Up to this time they have not laid. I fed them during the autumn and winter on bruised acorns; has this food been the cause of their not laying? Any information on this subject would greatly oblige
NETLEY COTTAGE.

ERRATUM.—On perusing my last letter on the light of the sun at Neptune, I found I had made two mistakes in extracting from "Dr. Lardner's Astronomy." The first is, or as $27^2 : \frac{1}{4}$, instead of $37^2 : \frac{1}{4}$. The second mistake is a little lower down, and is put down (considering that little more than its illuminated surface is seen) instead of considering that little more than half its illuminated surface is seen.   J. H.

MOTH COURTSHIP.—The instance R. Laddiman quotes relative to Lasiocampa (or Bombyx) Quercus is one well-known to entomologists, who constantly practice it for the capture of the males; it will only answer, however, in the case of a virgin female. The "Glory of Kent" (Endromis Versicolora) will, I believe, "assemble" in like manner; and possibly a few of the tiger moths.   A. M. B.

WIND FLOWER.—"Arbor" is informed that the whin-bush is the common gorse or furze (Ulex Europæus), and that the name wind flower, though poetically applied to more than one flower, is properly applicable only to the wood anemone (Anemone Nemorosa); anemone I may remark coming from the Greek "anemos" (wind).   A. M. B.

"Arbor" asks on page 160—(1) "Is there such a plant as the wind flower, and is it identical with the robin?" The "windflower" is the anemone, a word derived from the Greek word for wind. Its downy seeds have caused it to bear that name. (2) What is the difference between Betula alba (White Birch), and Betula glutinosa (Common Birch)?" What he calls Betula glutinosa is probably Alnus glutinosa (Alder), which belongs to the order Betulaceæ.
RUSTICUS.

LARK'S NEST IN BANK.—I very much doubt the probability of this occurring, and fancy that the boy must have been having a "lark" with your correspondent, "C. W. F." I never knew or heard of such a case, unless "C. W. F." means that they were the eggs of the titlark (Anthus pratensis), which would be found in the situation described.   A. M. B.

HAWKS.—On the 13th of last March a hawk, while in pursuit of a small bird, darted through the glass of the greenhouse at Pare Bracket, Camborne, scattering it many feet. The hawk was stunned by the blow, and captured, and I am sorry to say killed. My informant does not state whether it was a sparrowhawk or kestrel.   H. BUDGE.

AVIARY.—Would some of the readers of the NOTE BOOK kindly inform me what size you would need an aviary to be to hold about twenty small birds, and what is the best material for its construction, as I am thinking of getting one up here, which I would keep always in the open air. Would not fine wire netting do?   J. D. S. W.
Upper Umkomancy, Natal.

PEACOCK BUTTERFLIES.—On the 22nd April last I saw a fine specimen of the peacock butterfly (Vanessa Io) in the vicinity of Caterham Junction, Surrey; but the wind being high I failed to capture it. Thinking it rather an early appearance, and that it might interest some of our readers, I send this for insertion (if approved of by you) in the N. N. B.
WHATELY W. JUGALL.

CATERPILLARS.—I would be obliged if any one would tell me of any way to preserve these insects, so that they would keep their colour out of spirits, as there are some most beautiful ones here; and I am thinking of making a collection.   J. D. S. W.
Upper Umkomancy, Natal.

"RHONE" DUCK.—Miss Lizzie Godley is informed that no special breed of ducks inhabit the banks of the "Rhone." Hers is a "Rouen" duck—a celebrated breed—and the fact of the feathers of the wing being recurred (though singular) is not without a parallel.   A. M. B.

AN ENQUIRY.—What is the name of the tree that grows in India bearing poisonous blossoms, to which bees and other insects are attracted, and then perish?
R. B. W.

ERRATUM.—In my note on the "Source of Heat," a misprint occurs: for connection read *convection*.
R. B. W.

CORRECTION.—In my letter on "Preservation of Sea Fowl," in last month's NOTE BOOK, a misprint occurs in the eighth line from the top. For "rock-building" read "rock-breeding."
A. E. BUTTEMER.

Can any of the readers of the "N. N. B." inform me why the sun when setting, and the moon when rising appears larger than at any other time.
Gravesend, May 10.   G. O. Howell.

CUCKOO.—Very lately in this neighbourhood a cuckoo was heard singing at intervals throughout the whole night. Is this usual or not? I do not recollect having noticed it before.   B.
Halstead.

CUCKOO.—I heard the cuckoo on the 19th of April. Is not this early?   H. F. P.,

ON THE LOWEST LIAS BEDS OCCURRING AT COTHAM, BEDMINSTER, AND KEYNSHAM, NEAR BRISTOL.

By C. O. Groom Napier, Esq., F.G.S.

PART III.

50. *Pholadomya glabra, Ag.*—The Bristol geologists considered the bad specimens I at first found of this to belong to the genus Anatina, but Mr. Tate identified them with P. glabra. I latterly found good specimens, which vary from $1\frac{1}{2}$ to 2 inches long by $1\frac{1}{4}$ to $1\frac{3}{4}$ in. broad. The characteristic obliquely transverse lines seven in number are strongly marked. It is found in "bed H," in stone, so hard that it is difficult to extract the specimens in anything like perfect condition. In "bed 2," however, they are imbedded in clay, and consequently easy to extract; but here they are little better than casts. It was new to the locality until found by me.

51. *Pholadomya prima, Ag.*—This is a small species about 1 inch long, which is marked by three or four diagonally transverse lines, each the eighth of an inch apart at the margin of the shell. As it is one of the oldest species of its genus, it has not been inappropriately named "prima." I have only found one or two examples of it in "bed I." I believe it to be new to the locality.

52. *Pholadomya species.*—I have found another example of this genus, which clearly differs from the preceding: my two specimens are too imperfect for description. New to the locality.

53. *Pleuromya unioides.*—This is a common shell in "beds E and K," and is less abundant in "H, I, 3, 6, and 11." Casts are very abundant at Bedminster. It varies from $1\frac{1}{4}$ to $1\frac{3}{4}$ in. long by half to one in. broad. The general outline of the shell is like that of Unio pictorum; it is, however, marked on about half its longitudinal diameter by clearly defined lines which have their origin in the hinge. The stone of the bed in which these shells are found is so intensely hard and unfavourable for their preservation, that it is but rarely we can obtain a good specimen, although casts are not uncommon. I was the first to identify this in the Bristol beds.

54. *Pleuromya galathea, Ag.*—This also in form resembles a Unio, but has not the concentric lines of the last species. I was also the first to obtain this species in the locality. It is sparingly distributed at Cotham in "beds I, 6, and 7."

55. *Pleuromya liassina, Schubler.*—This is uncommon in "beds E, H, I, and 3," and I believe is new to the locality. The shell is marked by very coarse, concentric lines of growth, and is from $1\frac{1}{4}$ inch to $1\frac{1}{2}$ inch long. The casts are common on the floor of the quarries of Bedminster.

56. *Pleuromya musculoides.*—This is a peculiar species, nearly as long as broad, marked by fine concentric lines of growth. It is most like P. unioides, but is a much broader shell. I think it may safely be considered distinct from it. It is almost destitute of the concentric lines pointing to the hinge, and is new to the locality.

57. *Cardinia Listeri, Sow.*—This is found in "bed 4," but is not abundant, and is new to the locality.

58. *Ceromya gibbosa, Etheridge.*—This shell is about an inch long, and somewhat triangular. I have only found casts, singly in "bed I" and "bed 3," and is new to the locality.

59. *Ostrea liassica.*—This is the commonest shell of formation, and might I think be obtained by the bushel. They are seldom more than $1\frac{1}{2}$ inch long; but good specimens having both valves are rare so low down as the beds of which I have been speaking. The most curious specimen I found among them was a lower valve containing two small pearls, and the remains of a third. They are each about the eighth of an inch long, but the pearly lustre has long since scaled away. O. liassica varies so very much that it may be worth while to describe a few of its principal forms. Var. *a* consists of a smooth shell almost as thick as broad, which is however found to be composed of scaly, overlapping plates. Var. *b* has a very smooth shell composed of parallel plates. Var. *c* shews a very close approximation to O. irregularis. All these varieties vary very much in thickness, and like the oysters of the present seas, take the form of other shells or objects they come near. I have one very fine specimen of Lima succincta, with three of Ostrea liassica adhering to it, one of which has all the marks of this coarsely ribbed lima. Large slabs are found at Cotham studded with this species. It occurs in "beds E, G, H, I, 5, 7, 9, 11," frequently, and less abundantly in several of the others.

60. *Ostrea irregularis, Schloth.*—True to its name, this oyster is of a most irregular form. It is sometimes very like a Gryphæa. I have one valve in particular not to be distinguished from G. incurva. Some eminent paleontologists to whom I have shown it declare it to be G. incurva; while others decline to decide the point; a third party is positive it is only O. irregularis. I have consulted about twenty of my brother F.G.S.'s on this point, as it is one on which the geological historians of the lias lay much stress; that is to say, on the question of

the limits of the distribution of that very common shell G. incurva, which has given the name Gryphite limestone to a large portion of the lias. The typical Ostrea irregularis is not found in all the beds at Cotham; it is most abundant in "bed 2," but is also found in "bed E." Those in "bed 2" are accompanied by Ammonites angulatus, and Cidaris Edwardsi. The shells are beautifully preserved; they vary from half an inch to three inches, by three-eighths to $2\frac{3}{4}$ in. broad. Some are almost round, others oval; some are shaped like a toe-nail, and others like a snuff-box. The blue clay, from the large size of the shells found in it, and the Cidaris, represents, I think, deeper water than some of the other formations. Those beds, however, which afford Pinna and Ammonites planorbis, I believe must have been of considerable depth, although the wide distribution of the Ammonites in these series is certainly in accordance with the theory of their floating considerable distances, like their living congener the nautilus, into water of varying depth. Questions like these, however, should always be *sub judice*, for the analogy which the animals of our present seas afford us is of very limited value, even where the habits of the recent animals are sufficiently known to enable us to found an opinion on them.

At Cotham I found two species of the new and little known genus Terquemia, which has been called after M. Terquem, the old and distinguished historian of the lias. Only five species are known.

61. *Terquemia Heberti, Tqm.*—I only found one shell of this attached to a slab—a Pinna semistriata in "bed 6." At first sight it appeared like a deformed oyster—I consider it a remarkably fine specimen of T. Heberti. It is nearly round in shape, thin, but convex; and strongly, but most irregularly ribbed. It is new to the locality.

62. *Terquemia arietis, Quenst.*—Resembles the last; but the ribs are sharper and much more numerous. I have one with two valves free from the matrix. They are very uncommon at Cotham. I found them in "beds I and 7," adhering also to Pinna semistriata. It is new to the locality.

63. *Plicatula intusstriata, Emmerich.*—This little bivalve I found in "beds I and 7," and at Bedminster in the waterworks quarry. At Cotham they accompanied the teeth of Hybodus, the scales of Pholidophorus and Gyrolepis; many feet above the beds affording Ammonites Johnstoni. Therefore it seems unwarrantable to restrict this fossil, as some geologists do to the Rhætic series, for Ammonites are not held to be Rhætic. This Plicatula, however, is very rare at Cotham, and not common at Bedminster. It varies from one-eighth to half an inch long, and is of an oval form; the upper valve having a concave disc, curiously marked with intersecting branch-like veins. It is new to the locality.

64. *Plicatula Stoddarti, Napier, N.S.*—This is about an inch long by $\frac{7}{8}$ths wide, being a nearly circular shell. There are three principal and about seven minor lines of growth. The shell has six broad and prominent ribs. The inside of the valve is tolerably smooth, but is marked by concentric lines of growth. I have only been able to find it in "bed I" and the "cast bed." I have dedicated it to Mr. W. W. Stoddart, F.G.S., in acknowledgment of the value of his labours as a practical geologist in the west of England, and particularly in the strata in which it was found. It is new to the locality.

65. *Rhynchonella plicatissimus, Quenst.*—The specimens found at Cotham of this were not more than a quarter of an inch long. It is finely plicated, differing considerably from the next. My specimens were attached to the same slab which contained Lima valoniensis and Pecten Hehlii. This Rhynconella is a perforated species. It is new to Cotham.

66. *Rhynchonella variabilis.*—Of this I obtained several specimens in the blue clay of "bed 2," but they were extremely rare. It is a coarsely plicated species.

67. *Terebratula perforata, Piette.*—This was not uncommon in "bed 2," but extended to "bed 4," also in "beds E and I." But except in "bed 2," it is rare to find a good specimen; it varies from a half to one inch long, and is of an oval form.

68. *Anomia pellucida, Tqm.*—This is a pretty little circular species, about one-third of an inch across, with a smooth shell. I have only found one example of it in "bed I" at Cotham. It is new to the locality.

69. *Anomia socialis, Tawney.*—This an oyster-like Anomia; Mr. Tate thinks it but the young of O. liassica. The upper valve is marked by no very distinct feature, except a deep crease (line of growth) near the margin. The inside of the valve is flat, and marked by concentric lines of growth; it is about the same size as the last. I have only found two specimens in "beds I and J," and a doubtful one in E;" but it is also found in the waterworks quarry at Bedminster. It is new to Cotham.

70. *Mytilus minimus.*—This is widely distributed in the beds of Cotham, being found frequently in "E, I, and K," and abundantly in "L," which may be named from its abundance the mussel bed. It is also found in "beds H and 9;" in the second quarry at Bedminster,

and also in Hill's quarry at Keynsham. It is shaped much like the recent M. edulis, and varies from ½ to 1½ inch long. The shells are beautifully preserved in several of the beds, from which I have both valves *in situ*. When freshly extracted from the stone they have a peculiarly beautiful purple tinge about them, and the lines of growth, as is usual in this genus, are concentric.

71. *Mytilus Hillanus, Sow.*—Differs principally from the preceding by a ridge which rises diagonally in the shell. Its general outline reminds me strongly of the recent Mytilus modiolus; it is equally abundant as the preceding in "bed L," but is rather less common in "beds E, I, K," etc.

72. *Protocardia Philippianum.*—This is a small species, which reminds one much of C. rhæticum; the diagonal ridge is, however, strongly marked. It is very common in "bed K," but the specimens are destitute of shell. I have found one with the shell in "bed I." It is found also in "beds H, L," and very frequently in "9;" it varies from one quarter to three quarters of an inch long, by a little less broad. It is new to the locality.

73. *Cucullæa Hettangiensis, Tqm.*—This is but rarely found in "bed L," and is new to the locality; it is one inch long by one-third broad, by as much deep, and has one very long diagonal ridge towards the hinge. The external margin of the shell is slightly intersected. It is new to the localities.

74. *Cucullæa Austenii, Napier, N.S.*—This is a somewhat smaller species, which I have dedicated to my friend Fort Major Austen, F.G.S. It is marked by very prominent lines of growth. It is destitute of the diagonal line, mentioned as characteristic of the above. It is found at Bedminster in the second quarry, and also in "bed L." It is new to the localities.

75. *Lucina species.*—This has very strongly marked circular lines of growth. It is a little round shell ⅓rd of an inch long, which Mr. Tate has identified amongst my Cotham fossils. They are principally found in "bed K," but generally as casts. It is new to Cotham.

76. *Astarte consobrina, Chap. and Dew.*—This is new to the locality, and is found in "beds E and I." It is characterised by numerous prominent lines of growth, extending about one-third of the diameter of the shell. The margin is slightly intersected; it is a round, oval shell, seven-eighths of an inch long by as much broad. This is new to the locality, and very rare; found in "beds E and I" only.

77. *Astarte thalassina, Quenst.*—This is marked by prominent concentric lines of growth extending all over the shell, and is about the same size and shape as the preceding; it however wants the marginal intersections. It is new to the locality and unique in "bed I." New to Cotham.

78. *Astarte species.*—Besides the two preceding I have found another distinct species, which I cannot at present describe. It is found in "bed I," and is new to the locality.

79. *Monotis decussata, Munster.*—This is a very rare shell at Cotham. I have only found four specimens—two in "bed K," one in "bed E," and one in "bed 10,"—in fact in the Cotham marble. This shell is supposed to indicate the Rhætic bed, which here however it does not. It is a Liassic fossil, although a rare one. At Cotham it is found about one-third of an inch across. It is a circular shell. I have found it very common in the "Rhætic beds" of Aust, etc., but is new at Cotham.

80. *Gervillia species.*—I have found a couple of casts in "beds E and I" at Cotham of a shell of this genus. They are about two inches long by one inch, and resemble in form the bent rudder of a small boat. They are new to the locality.

81. *Cypricardia species.*—This is a small species, about one-third of an inch long by a quarter of an inch broad, and as much thick. Its principal characteristic is a very prominent diagonal ridge. It is new to Cotham.

82. *Axinus*, or *Cypricardia.*—This is very different from the preceding. It is a larger and more oblong shell. It is new to Cotham.

83. *Pleurophorus angulatus, Moore.*—I have found one example in "bed K." This is somewhat shaped like a solen, only it has a very prominent diagonal ridge. It is new to the locality.

84. *Pleurophorus elongatus, Moore.*—Unique in "beds I and K." New to the locality. This is also very like a solen, but wants the ridge. It is 1½ inch long by one-third of an inch wide, and has rather a smooth shell. It is new to Cotham.

85. *Pinna semistriata, Tqm.*—This is one of the finest shells found at Cotham. It varies from two to six inches long. Fragments are not uncommon, but perfect shells are yet to be found. The casts are marked by deep striations, extending over a part of the shell. The inside of the shell is marked by little thorn-like tubercles, which I have not seen mentioned by any author. Fort Major Austen, F.G.S., was the first who called my attention to a large Pinna being found at Cotham, but he did not identify the species with the above. I obtained in all about ten good specimens after some weeks' hunting.

86. *Anatina Cothamensis, Napier, Sp. Nov.*—This shell is oval and pointed, half an inch long

by one-quarter broad; surface marked by fine curved striations, granulated at the posterior edge. I have found this solitary specimen in the Planorbis bed, Cotham.

ENTOMOSTRACA.

Of these little crustaceans I have found two species at Cotham. The first is just visible to the naked eye, being about the size of a point of a pin.

87. *Cypris Liassica, Brodie.*—I was the first to find this in the "plant bed L" at Cotham, where it is seen adhering to the little shells and plant remains. It is more abundant at Horfield. I have good examples attached to a slab, containing Ammonites angulatus.

88. *Estheria minuta, Alberti.*—This is common enough at Bedminster, but I have not yet found it at Cotham.

ECHINODERMATA.

89. *Hemipidinum Beechi, Wright.*—This was for a long time supposed to be a bivalve, but most paleontologists now consider it as part of the jaws of a sea egg. It is found in "beds E, I, and 7," and also at both quarries at Bedminster.

90. *Pentacrinus Fisheri, M.S., Edward Forbes.*—Major Austen, F.G.S., perhaps the greatest living authority on the Crinoids, has kindly named this species for me. Small sections of the stem and branches are all that I have obtained at Cotham. It is apparently a long and slender species, the diameter of the stems being three feet long. The section of the stems resembles a five cornered star. I have only once found the bed of it, but it is almost composed of it. It is No. 6. of the second quarry at Cotham. I also found this species sparingly in "beds E and 4."

91. *Cidaris Edwardsi, Wright.*—Of this I have found both spines and plates. I believe they are new to the locality. The spines are rarely perfect. I found one *in situ* on a plate, but this specimen was unfortunately broken; the spines vary from $1\frac{1}{2}$ to $1\frac{1}{4}$ inch long, deeply fluted, or rough and thorny. They were found in "beds E, H, and I," and abundantly in "bed 2."

92. *Uraster species.*—I found an ossicle of a species of this genus in "bed E." It resembles a knot tied in white string and flattened. It is new to the locality.

ZOOPHYTUM.

93. *Montlivaltia species.*—New to Cotham. I found one specimen in the cast bed at Cotham. It much resembles Lithostrotion Martini of the mountain limestone, is circular, and about $\frac{1}{3}$rd of an inch in diameter.

94. *Montlivaltia species.*—This is distinct from the above; the septum is rather coarse, and it is double the size. It was found in the first quarry at Bedminster. I will not venture to describe it, as the specimen is imperfect.

95. *Spunge.*—I have found a small specimen in "bed 2," which belongs apparently to some member of this family. It is something like a worn cast of a brain stone, but is only the quarter of an inch in diameter. New to Cotham.

PLANTA.

96. *Chondrites liassinus, Quenst.*—This is a beautiful seaweed-like little plant, perhaps allied to the recent Hymenophyllum; it is very rare at Cotham. The fronds are about three inches long, but they fork very much. The leaflets are about the eighth of an inch long, and of a pointed oval shape. I only found it in the upper and lower "plant beds C and L." New to Cotham.

97. *Naidita.*—I have found traces of this both in "beds C and L," but they are scanty and imperfect. New to Cotham.

98. *Cardiocarpon species.*—I found a scale-like substance in the lower "plant bed L," which appears to belong to this genus of the coal measures. It may be the scale of a cone. New to Cotham.

99. I found some distinct traces of wood in several of the lower beds of Cotham.

100. *Otopteris obtusa var. densa, Major Austen.*—This was found by the Major many years ago at Cotham, and has been described by him in the Reports of the Proceedings of the Bristol Naturalist's Society. I mention this as it is probably the only true fern in the Ammonites planorbis zone of the West of England.

ADDENDA.

101. *Beetle.*—This is the Elytra of a small species of about $\frac{3}{8}$ths of an inch long. New to Cotham.

102. I take this opportunity of describing a new and peculiar little species of Vermicularia, which I believe I am the first to obtain. It is in blue clay of the Bucklandi bed at Keynsham. It is about $\frac{1}{4}$ inch long, and rises in a spire like a Spirorbis. It is a tube about the 20th of an inch in diameter, crenated towards the inner margin. At first sight it might be taken for a Solarium. I propose for it the name Vermicularia convolutus.

NOTES ON THE HABITS OF THE CAT.

By Video.

THE intrinsic character of the domestic cat appears to have been little studied, and all that is generally understood of it is that it is an animal which is tolerated on account of its usefulness, but which is little capable of attachment to the people of the house, and always shy and suspicious of a stranger; if indulged with freedom it will take liberties, whilst in regard to improved habits it will be very little indebted to education, so that self will still constitute a distinguished portion of its character. But although this may be the general nature of the cat, there will occasionally be found a variation as well of temper as feeling; and when these are seen to spring up into existence spontaneously, or from the influence of passing circumstances, they become deserving of notice as descriptive of character in the individual, perhaps different from what is usual in its race. The first, apparently trivial, instance that I have to relate has a tendency to show that a desire to give pleasure to a protector, or perhaps obtain approbation for the performance of an acknowledged duty in one from whom it had been little expected. Whatever had been the exciting motive in the feline mind it certainly went far to prove in the household that the principal actor was of some use in a case where a suspicion had been felt and expressed of the contrary.

In places where, from special circumstances, rats have shown a particular interest in a house, it is not always easy to drive them away, even with the dread of a prowling cat hanging over them. Such appears to have been the case in an instance referred to, and which was felt to be a reproach to the mistress of the house, and even in the estimation of the cat herself, if we may form an opinion by what followed. After many efforts she succeeded in pouncing upon an unwary rat, and then nothing must satisfy her but that the mistress must become a witness of her success. The presence of a servant was not sufficient, and it was not until with wandering and crying she had obtained access to the superior authority and displayed the proof of her zeal and success to her inspection, that she showed herself satisfied and silent. It may have been from the success of this exploit and the caresses that followed, that afterwards it became a distinguished trait in the habits of this puss, to demand applause for successful proceedings similar to the one now related; for a colony of mice having succeeded to the rats, she made a prize of one of them late at night, and then with prey in her mouth she made her way into the servant's bed-room, and there with crying made such a clamour as to excite the wonder what could be the cause. A light was procured, and then, satisfied with the applause which followed, and which she seemed to feel was her due, she laid the mouse at the maid's feet and quietly retired.

But in proportion to this desire of approbation or applause, there appears also to have existed a feeling of jealousy to a rival; which may indeed display itself in the larger portion of our domestic animals, but appears the more remarkable in one that appeared to manifest an unusually unsociable temper, even for a cat; and which our narrative will show to have been so deeply engraved in its nature as to drive it to desperation. It may even be said to have died finally of a broken heart.

She was the only one that survived of a little brood, and therefore received the whole amount of the attention of a parent, but without the appearance of replying to it with affection or playfulness; nor could she be induced to join in or tolerate the amusements of a family of little children. Ever sullen and solitary she grew up to maturity, and on the death of the mother succeeded to the privileges and duties of the inheritance; and at last she became the parent of a solitary kitten, which in its earliest infancy she nourished in a satisfactory manner. But when this young one had become capable of joining in and enjoying the sports and caresses of the children of the house, a change was observed to have come over the spirit of the parent. This was shown at first in the manner in which she discountenanced her kitten when she entered on her gambols, and especially when she received attention or protection from her human playmates, who were then compelled to interfere and protect the innocent and frolicsome little one from the persecution of its ill-tempered and jealous parent. In proportion as the younger individual advanced in growth, and correspondingly in the favour, from her good humour, of the various branches of the family, so also was this persecution increased, with the well understood intention on the part of the parent, to compel what now appeared to be a rival, to seek a habitation in some other district. This, however, was not permitted; the rival had become what the parent had not been —a favourite, and although she had never been illtreated, the older cat appeared at last to have adopted the resolution of no longer remaining in the situation she had so long occupied. She suddenly disappeared, and when after a time she was sought for she was discerned to have retired to a recess in a dilapidated house, beyond which she could never afterwards be traced.

ENTOMOLOGY FOR THE MONTHS.

JULY.

Who loves not the gay butterfly, who flits
Before him in the ardent noon, array'd
In crimson, azure, emerald and gold;
With more magnificence upon his wing—
His little wing—than ever graced the robe
Gorgeous of royalty; is like the kine
That wanders 'mid the flowers that gem the mead
Unconscious of their beauty.
CARRINGTON.

IN the month of July, summer is in the height of its splendour; the orchards are now laden with fruit, the fields and gardens are full of flowers, the trees are in their fullest leaf, and all things have put on their gayest dress. Richly attired butterflies are fluttering from flower to flower, sipping the sweet nectar, and displaying their lovely tints, while their wings "expand and shut in silent ecstacy." The monarch of all British butterflies, the Purple Emperor (Apatura Iris),

"A gem of purest ray serene,"

is now pursuing its stately flight, high over the tops of the oak trees, in the South of England; the rare Silver-washed Fritillary (Argynnis paphia) is also on the wing, in company with its near relations, the Small Pearl-Bordered (A. Selene), the High Brown (A. Adippe), and the Dark-Green Fritillary (A. Aglaia); the Red Admiral (Vanessa Atalanta) and the Painted Lady (V. Cardui), are displaying their colours by the road-side; also the Marbled White (Arge Galathea), Scotch Argus (Erebia Blandina) Grayling (Satyrus Semele), Gate-Keeper (S. Tithonus), Small Copper (Polyommatus phleas), Green Hairstreak (Thecla rubi), Purple Hairstreak (T. quercus), and the Black Hairstreak (T. W. Album). Several of the "Blues" are now to be observed, among which are Chalkhill (Lycæna Corydon), Silver-studded (L. Ægon), and the Common Blue (L. Alexis), and, towards the end of the month, the Large Tortoiseshell (Vanessa polychloros).

A great number of moths were out last month, but a still greater number are now to be met with. It would be useless to attempt to enumerate half that we are likely to find. A great many of those mentioned in my last are still on the wing, accompanied by an infinite number of others, a few of which I will endeavour to name, leaving the remainder for the Entomologist to find out for himself. We may still observe the Humming-Bird Hawkmoth (Macroglossa stellatarum), pursuing its diurnal flight over our Jasmines and Petunias; also many of the "Sphingidæ" mentioned last month.

Six individuals of the family of the "Footmen" are also now out; viz., the Speckled (Eulepia Cribrum), Four-spotted Footman (Lithosia quadra), Buff Footman (L. helvola), Rosy Footman (Calligenia munata) Common Footman (L. complanula), and the Scarce Footman (L. complana). The Ghost Moth, mentioned in my last, may still be seen careering madly along the hedge-rows.

The following may also be expected; viz., the Red-Belted Clearwing (Sesia Myopæformis), Six-Belted Clearwing (S. Ichneumoniformis), Wood Swift (Hepialus sylvinus), Short Cloaked Moth (Nola cucullatella), Muslin Moth (Arctia mendica), Cinnibar (Euchelia Jacobææ), Garden Tiger (Chelonia caja), Cream-Spot Tiger (C. villica), Brown and Yellow Tailed Moths (Liparis chrysorrhea and L. auriflua), Satin Moth (L. salicis), Gipsy (L. dispar), Black Arches (L. monaca), Dark Tussock (Orgyia fascelina), Reed Tussock (O. cœnosa), Lackey (Bombyx neustria), and the Oak Eggar (B. Quercus).

The Swallow-tailed Moth (Uropteryx sambucata), comes out about the middle of this month, and may often be seen in the evening flying about our hedges and gardens. It has a very peculiar flight, and may easily be captured when seen, as it invariably flies in a straight line. Others of the "Geometræ" may also be taken, among which are the following; viz., the Bordered Beauty (Epione apiciaria), Little Thorn (E. advenaria), Early Thorn (Selenia illunaria), Dotted Carpet (Cleora glabraria), Mottled Beauty (Boarmia repandata), Common Wave (Cabera exanthemaria), Tawny Barred Angle (Macaria liturata) Common White Wave (Cabera pusaria), Rest Harrow (Aplasta ononaria), Bordered Gray (Selidosema plumaria), Clouded Magpie (Abraxas ulmata), July Highflier (Ypsipetes elulata), Common Carpet (Melanippe subtristata), Light Emerald (Metrocampa margaritaria), Grass Emerald (Pseudoterpna cytisaria), Large Emerald (Geometra papilionaria), Essex Emerald (G. smaragdaria), Small Emerald (Iodis vernaria), Common Emerald (Hermithea thymiaria), and the Scalloped Oak (Crocallis elinguaria), which may frequently be found sitting on banks, &c., in the day time.

The following "Noctuas" also fly this month; viz., the Buff Arches (Gonophora dedrasa), Peach Blossom (Thyatira batis), Marbled Beauty (Bryophila Perla), Brown-line Bright-eye (Leucania conigera), Clay (L. lithargyria), Cosmopolitan (L. loreyi), Smoky Wainscot (L. impura), Common Wainscot (L. pallens), Twin-spotted Wainscot (Nonagria geminipuncta), Dark Arches (Xylophasia polyodon), Bordered Gothic (Neuria Saponariæ), Straw Underwing (Cerigo Cytherea), Dot Moth (Mamestra persicariæ), Garden Dart

(Agrotis nigricans), Gray Arches (Aplecta nebulosa), Marbled Clover (Heliothis dipsaceus), Plain Golden Y. (Plusia Iota), Burnished Brass (P. chrysitis), Broad Bordered Yellow Underwing (Tryphœna fimbria), Large Yellow Underwing (T. pronuba), and the Old Lady (Mania maura). R. LADDIMAN.
Norwich.

LIST OF BRITISH MOTHS:

NATURE OF THEIR FOOD,
AND TIMES OF THEIR PERFECT APPEARANCE.

LARENTIDÆ.

INTER MOTH (*Cheimatobia brumata*). Feeds on plums, quinces, medlars, and on the leaves of many other trees. Flies in October, November, and December.

Northern Winter Moth (*Cheimatobia boreata*). Feeds on birch. Flies in October.

November Moth (*Oporabia dilutata*). Feeds on blackthorn, hornbeam, sloe, oak, and many other trees. Flies in November.

Autumnal Moth (*Oporabia filigrammaria*). Feeds on sallow. Flies in August and September.

Twin Spot Carpet (*Larentia didymata*). Feeds on the common chervil (*Anthriscus sylvestris*). Flies in June.

Mottled Gray (*Larentia multistrigata*). Feeds on lady's bedstraw. Flies in April.

Gray Mountain Moth (*Larentia cæsiata*). Feeds on the wort, whortleberry, or bilberry. Flies in June, July, and August.

Yellow Ringed Carpet (*Larentia ruficinctata*). Feeds on the white meadow saxifrage. Flies in July.

Striped Twin Spot Carpet (*Larentia salicata*). Feeds on bedstraw. Flies in June.

Beech Green Carpet (*Larentia olivata*). Feeds on a species of bedstraw (*Galium mollugo*). Flies in June.

Green Carpet (*Larentia pectinitaria*). Feeds on G. mollugo and G. saxatile. Flies in June and July.

Rivulet (*Emmelesia affinitata*). Feeds on the seeds of various plants. Flies in June.

Small Rivulet (*Emmelesia alchemillata*). Feeds on Galeopsis tetrahit and G. ladanum. Flies in June.

Grass Rivulet (*Emmelesia albulata*). Feeds on the seeds of the yellow rattle (*Rhinanthus Cristagalli*). Flies in June.

Sandy Carpet (*Emmelesia decolorata*). Flies in June.

Barred Carpet (*Emmelesia tæniata*). Feeds on holly trees (*Ilex aquifolium*). **Flies in June and July.**

Haworth's Carpet (*Emmelesia unifasciata*). Flies in July.

Heath Rivulet (*Emmelesia ericetata*). **Feeds** on heath. Flies in June and July.

Pretty Pinion (*Emmelesia blandiata*). **Feeds** on eyebright (*Euphrasia officinalis*). Flies in May, June, July, and August.

Netted Pug (*Eupithecia venosata*). **Feeds** inside the seed capsules of the bladder campion (*Silene inflata*) and the red lychnis (*Lychnis dioica*). Flies in May and June.

Pinion Spotted Pug (*Eupithecia consignata*). Feeds on fruit trees. Flies in May and June.

Toadflax Pug (*Eupithecia linariata*). Feeds on the seeds and flowers of the wild snapdragon or yellow toadflax (*Linaria vulgaris*). Flies in June.

Foxglove Pug (*Eupithecia pulchellata*). Feeds on the flowers of the Digitalis purpurea. Flies in May and June.

Lime Speck (*Eupithecia centaureata*). Feeds on the flowers of Senecio jacobæa, S. erucifolius, Achillæa millefolium, Pimpinella magna, P. saxifraga, Lilaus pratensis, Campanula glomerata, Solidago virgaurea, Eupatorium cannabianum, and Scabiosa columbaria. Flies throughout the summer months.

Bordered Lime Speck (*Eupithecia succenturiata*). Feeds on the mugwort (*Artemisia vulgaris*). Flies in July.

Shaded Pug (*Eupithecia subumbrata*). Feeds on Apargia hispida and Crepis taraxicifolia, and numerous other trees. Flies in June.

Guenée's Pug (*Eupithecia pernotata*). Feeds on the flowers of the golden rod (*S. virgaurea*).

Lead Coloured Pug (*Eupithecia plumbeolata*). Feeds on the flowers of the common cow wheat (*Melampyrum pratense*). Flies in May.

Haworth's Pug (*Eupithecia isogrammata*). Feeds on the flower buds of Clematis vitalba. Flies in June and July.

March Pug (*Eupithecia pygmæata*). **Flies in June.**

Edinburgh Pug (*Eupithecia helveticata*). Feeds on common juniper (*Juniperus communis*). Flies in May.

Freyer's Pug (*Eupithecia arceuthata*). **Feeds** on I. communis. Flies in May.

Satyr Pug (*Eupithecia satyrata*). **Feeds on** the petals of nearly every flower; among others, Knautia arvensis, Galium mollugo, and Centaurea nigra. Flies in June.

Pauper Pug (*Eupithecia egenaria*). **Flies** about midsummer.

Gray Pug (*Eupithecia castigata*). **Feeds on** nearly every tree. Flies in May.

Golden Rod Pug (*Eupithecia virgaureata*).

Feeds on the flowers of the golden rod (*S. virgaurea*).

White Spotted Pug (*Eupithecia albipunctata*). Feeds on the common hogweed (*Heracleum sphondylium*), and wild angelica (*Angelica sylvestris*). Flies in May and June.

Valerian Pug (*Eupithecia valerianata*). Feeds on the seeds and flowers of the common valerian (*V. officinalis*). Flies in May.

Larch Pug (*Eupithecia lariciata*). Feeds on larch and spruce fir. Flies in May.

Triple Spot Pug (*Eupithecia trisignata*). Feeds on the flowers of A. sylvestris. Flies in June and July.

Dwarf Pug (*Eupithecia pusillata*). Feeds on spruce fir (*Pinus abies*). Flies in May.

Marbled Pug (*Eupithecia irriguata*). Flies in April and June.

Pimpinel Pug (*Eupithecia pimpinellata*). Feeds on the Pimpinella saxifraga. Flies in April, and again in August.

Ash Tree Pug (*Eupithecia fraxinata*). Feeds on the ash. Flies in June and July.

Ochreous Pug (*Eupithecia indigata*). Feeds on the cypress and wild juniper. There are two broods. The first flies in May, and the second in August.

Wild Thyme Pug (*Eupithecia constrictata*). Feeds on Thymus serpyllum. Flies in July and August.

Campanula Pug (*Eupithecia campanulata*). Feeds on the seed capsules of the Campanula trachelium. Flies in July.

Narrow Winged Pug (*Eupithecia nanata*). Feeds on the flowers of the common ling (*Calluna vulgaris*). Flies in May.

Plain Pug (*Eupithecia subnotata*). Feeds on flowers and seeds of various species of Chenopodium and Atriplex. Flies in June and July.

Common Pug (*Eupithecia vulgata*). Feeds on whitethorn (*Cratægus oxyacantha*). Flies in May and June.

Bleached Pug (*Eupithecia expallidata*). Feeds on the flowers of S. virgaurea. Flies in July and August.

Wormwood Pug (*Eupithecia Absynthiata*). Feeds on the flowers of the E. cannabinum, S. jacobæa, S. erucifolius, A. millefolium, and S. virgaurea, and other plants. Flies in June and July.

Ling Pug (*Eupithecia minutata*). Feeds on the common ling (*C. vulgaris*). Flies in June.

Currant Pug (*Eupithecia assimilata*). Feeds on the leaves of the black currant. Flies in May, and again in August.

Slender Pug (*Eupithecia tenuiata*). Feeds on the sallow. Flies in June.

Maple Pug (*Eupithecia subciliata*). Feeds on the maple (*Acer compestris*). Flies in June.

Oak Tree Pug (*Eupithecia dodoneata*). Feeds on the oak. Flies in May and June.

Brindled Pug (*Eupithecia abbreviata*). Feeds on the oak. Flies in March and April.

Mottled Pug (*Eupithecia exiguata*). Feeds on the black currant, alder, barberry, whitethorn, ash, and sallow. Flies in May and June.

Juniper Pug (*Eupithecia sobrinata*). Feeds on the needles of I. communis. Flies in July.

Cloaked Pug (*Eupithecia togata*). Flies in June.

Double Striped Pug (*Eupithecia pumilata*). Feeds on the flowers of Anthriscus sylvestris. Flies in April and May, and again in July and August.

V. Pug (*Eupithecia coronata*). Feeds on C. vitalba, E. cannabinum, A. sylvestris, and S. virgaurea. There are two broods. The first flies in April and May, and the second in August.

Green Pug (*Eupithecia rectangulata*). Feeds on the blossoms of the apple, wild crab, and pear. Flies in June.

Bilberry Pug (*Eupithecia debiliata*). Feeds on the leaves of the whortleberry (*Vaccinium myrtillus*). Flies in June.

Dentaled Pug (*Collix sparsata*). Feeds on Lepimachia vulgaris. Flies in June.

Small Seraphim (*Lobophora sexalisata*). Feeds on Salix capræa. Flies in May and June.

Seraphim (*Lobophora hexapterata*). Feeds on S. capræa and Populus tremula. Flies in June.

Yellow Barred Brindle (*Lobophora viretata*). Feeds on the privet (*Ligustrum vulgare*). Flies in May and June.

Early Tooth-striped (*Lobophora lobulata*). Feeds on sallow (*S. capræa*) and honeysuckle (*Lonicera periclymenum*). Flies in April.

Barred Tooth-striped (*Lobophora polycommata*). Feeds on ash and honeysuckle. Flies in April.

Juniper Carpet (*Thera juniperata*). Feeds on I. communis. Flies in October.

Chestnut Coloured Carpet (*Thera simulata*). Feeds on I. communis. There are two broods. The first flies in April and May, and the second in August.

Shaded Broad Bar (*Thera obeliscata*). Feeds on the needles of the Scotch fir (*Pinus sylvestris*). Flies throughout the summer months.

Pine Carpet (*Thera firmata*). Feeds on common fir. Flies in July.

Ruddy Highflyer (*Ypsipetes ruberata*). Flies in May.

May Highflyer (*Ypsipites impluviata*). Feeds on the alder (*Alnus glutinosa*). Flies in May.

July Highflyer (*Ypsipetes elutata*). Feeds on several species of sallow; among others, S. capræa and S. cinerea. Flies in July.

Blue Bordered Carpet (*Melanthia rubiginata*). Feeds on the blackthorn and bullace. Flies in July.

Purple Bar (*Melanthia ocellata*). Feeds on lady's bedstraw (*G. verum*). Flies in June.

Beautiful Carpet (*Melanthia albicillata*). Feeds on bramble and raspberry. Flies in June.

Argent and Sable (*Melanippe hastata*). Feeds on sweet gale (*Myrica gale*) and birch (*B. alba*). Flies in June.

Small Argent and Sable (*Melanippe tristata*). Feeds on hedge bedstraw. Flies in June.

Chalk Carpet (*Melanippe procellata*). Feeds on C. vitalba. Flies in May, June, and July.

Sharp Angled Carpet (*Melanippe unangulata*). Feeds on common chickweed (*Alsine media*). Flies in June.

Wood Carpet (*Melanippe rivata*). Feeds on G. mollugo. Flies in July.

Common Carpet (*Melanippe subtristata*). Feeds on G. mollugo. Flies in May and July.

Silver Ground Carpet (*Melanippe montanata*). Feeds on the leaves of the primrose (*P. vulgaris*). Flies throughout the summer.

Galium Carpet (*Melanippe galiata*). Feeds on two species of bedstraw (*G. verum* and *G. mollugo*). Flies in June.

Garden Carpet (*Melanippe fluctuata*). Feeds on nasturtium (*Tropæolum majus*), cabbage (*Brassica*), and other garden plants. Flies throughout the summer.

London.   T. W. TEMPANY.

HABITS OF THE MARTIN (*HIRUNDO URBICA*).

MANY are the traits of character of our native birds that pass among us with little observation, but which are of interest when we seek to trace them in reference to their inward feelings, as exerted among themselves, and to each other. Some remarks of this sort are recorded in the volume of NATURALIST'S NOTE BOOK for the Year 1868, p. 364, of the common Martin; and, as a continuance of the same, the following records have been made of the actions of what may be supposed the same birds at the time of their first coming in the present season. Of the several nests that were left, when the birds forsook them on their departure in the autumn, only one survived the winter, so that when the first pair arrived in the spring, as they did about a week before their old companions and next neighbours, no choice was left to them; they might enter the only remaining nest which continued perfect, or they must exert themselves, and be at the pains of collecting materials, and building another dwelling. But it would appear that the existing nest was not their own original property, and a point of ornithological honesty forbade their taking possession; or we may suppose that they feared a quarrel with the original proprietors, who probably would soon arrive and put in their claim. Be this as it may, this pair of birds set themselves about the erection of a new nest, and presently afterwards the former inhabitants of the still remaining nest made their appearance, together with those which also had occupied the lost retreats, which they found themselves compelled to rebuild, if they would wish themselves well accommodated. But then comes the interesting portion of my narrative. The new structure which had been begun by the pair of birds that first arrived, was only half erected, when the female martin found herself compelled to give up the labour, and enter it and deposit her egg. It was an apparently sudden and unexpected act of parturition, and she found herself exposed to danger, and the unpleasant gaze of passers by, from which, however, she was soon relieved by the sympathy of her kind-hearted companions of the neighbourhood. Dropping their own inferior cares, the whole of them set to work; the requisite materials were soon collected, and with their united labour the unfinished portion was built up, while the female inhabitant remained within it. Who shall deny to these innocent birds a feeling of generous sympathy with a neighbour in distress? That they also discern and reason on surrounding circumstances, the writer has had occasion to notice. Thus, in fine weather, when building their nests, the work is carried on in the early portion of the day, and afterwards left to dry, while the builders are in search of food; but when the neighbouring situation, that supplied the materials was covered with the tide, knowing from experience that the mortar could be had in the afternoon, the morning was devoted to flight, and the labour of building deferred to the more convenient season.

VIDEO.

BIRD-CATCHERS.

IN the suburbs of all our thriving towns every possible encouragement is given, intentionally and unintentionally, to songbirds. The love of townsmen for rurality causes them to plant trees in plenty near their suburban residences; and hence the villages that encircle every great centre of trade and manufacture are peculiarly the resort of nightingales and other warblers, that not only render immense service to the cultivators of the land, but give such a charm to the scenery and the peaceableness of the country, that we should be justified in protecting them at almost any price. Now it so happens that bird-catchers, professional and amateur, are perpetually prowling about the fields and gardens in the vicinity of towns, and that they succeed in trapping the birds to an extent which threatens their utter extirpation. Long before the month of May was out, the nightingales were apparently extinguished. Whether the cold killed them or merely stopped their song it may be difficult to prove, but it can be proved that tens of thousands were caught in traps; and as to the London birds, a large proportion of them may be found at this moment in cages in St. Giles's and Spitalfields. Very few of our readers propably have any idea of the extent to which bird-catching is followed as a recreation by the rougher part of the labouring population. Pale attenuated lads that are shut up all the week in workshops, and gigantic navvies with terrific muscles and daring sunburnt faces, sally forth together in boisterous companies on Sunday mornings with traps, decoys, and pockets filled with refreshments, to snare singing birds for amusement. All the roads that open on green suburbs swarm with parties of amateur bird-catchers all the forenoon on Sundays. The result is not only a painful and injurious destruction of birds, but a vast amount of trespass and damage to property, with a little riotous drinking at roadside houses, which, as we have often said, are as much open on Sunday mornings in the suburbs as they are on week days, a man posted at the door being the only peculiar feature of the Sunday morning traffic.

Now we have no ambition to maunder about the trapping of singing birds, though the subject might be made available that way. To prohibit trapping or shooting them would be of little use; they would be caught and shot in spite of the law, simply because we could not enforce it. We must do the best possible to preserve them as public benefactors in the most material sense; as they are benefactors, indeed, spiritually considered, for a merry song gushing from the bosky woodland affords a joy to all who hear it, which cannot be surpassed amongst all the rest of the pleasures that belong to the summer and the country. We may, perhaps, do much in this way without doing wrong to the bird-catchers, professional and amateur. To both the trapping of birds is a source of healthy occupation and amusement; and the rough parts of the population cannot be compelled to follow in the footsteps of respectability. But comparatively harmless and certainly amusing as the pursuit is to those who follow it, to place it under some restrictions would not be a great hardship. So at least we believe will be the opinion of those who have witnessed the operations of the bird-catchers, and shuddered at their cold-blooded way of twisting the neck of every bird they catch which they do not value, rather than give it its liberty. The wrong involved in the restriction is this—that it is a restriction upon amusement presumed to be innocent at least by those who indulge in it, but which we believe to be hurtful to the public interests to an extent far exceeding the benefit derived from it by its votaries. Those who know the bird-catching class, will not fear that if we make their traps and nets useless by an act of legislation, they will not be long in finding another recreation to replace it; and the wrong done will be infinitesimal and shadowy. The question then arises, how shall we accomplish the object we have in view? We think all that need or should be done is the imposition of a tax of small amount; say to legalize the act of snaring small birds there must be an Excise license, renewable yearly at a cost of five shillings. Bird-catchers who live by the art would be immensely benefited, for it would sweep out of their way tens of thousands of competitors, who, when successful, thin the flocks the others feed upon; and, when unsuccessful, act as scares to drive the birds away. The license would serve as a serious check to trespassing and damage of trees and fences, and by restricting the practice of the art to men who understand it, the wants of the public as to caged singing birds would be supplied as heretofore, and the destruction of bird-life would, no doubt, be beneficially lessened. What would be the result to the revenue is, perhaps, scarcely worth speculating upon; yet we may reasonably assume that the tax would add something to the public exchequer.—*City Press.*

ON THE BRITISH GEOMETRÆ.

By E. J. S. CLIFFORD.

PART VII.

ONE of the most local of our *Geometræ* is our next species, the Rannoch Looper (*Fidonia pinitaria*). We read that it is taken on heath, amongst the pine trees in Blackwood, near the shores of Loch Rannoch, but we do not hear of its capture in any other part of our country. It is a beautiful little moth, with rusty wings, displaying four faint waved stripes, one of which only runs across part of the wing. There is a spot between the two middle stripes, and the hind wings possess three of the latter on their surface. In the female moth all the stripes are broader and darker in colour. July is the month for this little *geometer* in the perfect state; and the caterpillar is found in May, feeding on the bilberry. The Frosted Yellow (*Fidonia conspicuata*) seems to be a very abundant species in certain localities. Its front wings are yellow, dusted with brown at the margins. The hind and costal margins are broad and black. The hind wings are thickly speckled with gray, and the female is more marked in this particular. The hind wings have white stripes from the root of the wing. It is interesting to observe the habits of this lively little moth. When at rest its wings are erect, in the same way as those of a butterfly; and similar to the latter tribe of insects, it often flies in the hot sunshine. June and September seem to be the months for it, as it is a double-brooded species. The caterpillar of the Frosted Yellow is thin and smooth, it is of a greenish brown, and has a yellow stripe down the side. It feeds on the common broom, and has a peculiar way of lying at full length along the branch. The pupa state is assumed about October, according to most entomologists.

Among those delicate little moths found in the neighbourhood of London is the Drab Looper (*Minsa euphorbiata*). It has no markings whatever on its wings, being drab, without spot or stripe of any kind. Still it is particularly beautiful as it flits over our garden trees and bushes, and we love it because of its attachment to our homes. Like our last-named insect, this too flies in the daytime. June is the month in which we may expect to see it abroad. The caterpillar producing it is of a yellowish green, with dots of black and white. It has also a black line on the back, and a black spot on the last division or segment of the body. Its food consists of the several kinds of spurges, and hence its name. Next come we to the somewhat rare Black-veined (*Scoria dealbata*) which has occurred in Kent, and also on the Cotswold Hills. The wings of this moth are all white, and have no spots, but are adorned by black lines, and branch off in different directions. The black nerve lines on the under side also serve to distinguish this insect, which is on the wing in the month of June. It is a singular instance of the extreme folly of some entomologists when hunting for rare or local insects, to read that some few years back two gentlemen "succeeded in capturing over one hundred specimens of the above-named rare *geometer* in the most beautiful condition." There can be no doubt that it is owing to these ridiculous onslaughts upon rare species in their confined places of resort for flying and propagating, that so many of our valued British insects are dropping away from amongst us. If the entomologists thus distinguishing themselves could view their act in the right light, they would scarcely have thought it a matter to boast about that "they had succeeded in capturing over a hundred specimens" of one moth. It is to be regretted that so many scientific men thus lower themselves to the level of the mere "specimen collector." Passing, however, from this *not* unnecessary digression, it is interesting to read that the caterpillar of this beautiful moth feeds in confinement on the dock leaves, so easily procured in the country. The colour of it is ochreous, the line down the back dark grey, and only distinct on some of the segments of the body. On the under side there is a whitish central line between two dark grey ones. Also on each side there is a brownish streak just above the legs.

The only notes to be gathered regarding our next species are very few and far between. This is the Pink Stripe (*Sterrha sacraria*). From what can be gleaned it seems to be a lovely little moth. The front wings are of a light straw colour, with a pink oblique stripe from the top to the margin. The hind wings are lighter, and have no mark upon their surface. The antennæ are long and hair-like. It seems that only isolated specimens of this insect have been taken by entomologists. Amongst other localities, it has been captured at Clapham Common, Croydon, Plymouth, Barnstable, Peckham, and Torquay. Our next *geometer* is more likely to come before the personal notice of many entomological readers of this journal. It is the Grass Wave (*Aspilates strigillaria*) a moth flying in June and July, or even occasionally as late as August. The colouring is soft and very delicate. The wings are all of a pale stone colour, dusted with brown, and possessing brown stripes. There are four stripes on the fore wings, and three on the hind wings, two of which are parallel to one another. The caterpillar of the Grass Wave is well worth seeking and rearing to the winged state. It is green or grey, or even brown in some specimens taken, and has a pale line on the back. Its food is the oak, broom, and blackthorn, upon which it feeds in September and October, and again in spring. This caterpillar has a habit of feigning death directly it is touched. When full fed, it spins a web amongst the twigs of its food-plant, and therein changes to a pupa, in which state it remains about three weeks. In clover fields, we may not unlikely meet with the Yellow Belle (*Aspilates citraria*) a day-flying moth. This is a species that varies much in size and colour, also in regard to its markings, which in some cases are altogether wanting. The fore wings are pale yellow, merging into a brighter colour on the outside, with a slight sprinkling of brown or grey. The hind wings have a spot, and outside this a peculiar mark resembling the two wings of a bird when represented flying in the distance. The Straw Belle (*Aspilates gilvaria*) is the last included in the *Fidonidæ*, a very interesting group of moths. This is at once a beautiful and rare insect. It is said to fly in the month of August. The caterpillar is green, and striped with rust colour. Its food is the common millefoil or yarrow, upon which it may be found in June. The perfect insect has the fore wings pale sulphur colour, sprinkled with a brownish tinge, and possessing a spot and a stripe. The spot is near the front of the wings, and the stripe stretches from the point to the inner margin of the wing. The hind wings are paler, and also possess a spot and a stripe. This in some cases is nearly indistinct, and in others very much broader than as seen in the ordinary type specimens of the insect.

There is, perhaps, scarcely a commoner insect in our gardens than that now to be described, the Large Magpie (*Abraxas grossulariata*), sometimes termed the gooseberry moth, though its caterpillar is more frequently found on currant than among gooseberry bushes. This is one of those insects with which nearly all are acquainted, and it is also one of those kinds that our well-meaning friends who wish to swell our collections are for ever bringing before us a great prize. From its heavy flight the Magpie is easily made a captive, and we have before now known it to stand quietly to be taken between the thumb and finger of a delighted youngster. The wings are of orange, white and black, disposed in spots and blotches, with bands connecting them together. There are fewer spots on the hind wings. The body of this moth is buff, yellow, or orange, spotted with black. This, however, is a species which is extremely variable, and in some specimens taken the various colours each have the predominance. It is more abundant in the Midland Counties than elsewhere. The caterpillar exhibits the same colours as the perfect insect. It makes its appearance in May, and feeds to the great annoyance of gardeners on the gooseberry, currant, and other garden bushes. The chrysalis is very curious; marked with rings, and having the ground colour black and shining. It is enclosed in a slight web which the caterpillar spins upon the under side of leaves, or in some convenient crevice in palings or walls. The Clouded Magpie (*Abraxas ulmata*) though not so common as the last named insect, is yet very abundant where it occurs. It is really a handsome moth. The fore wings are white, with the base brown, and striped with yellow. Near the front of the wings is a lead-coloured eye-like spot. The body is yellowish, with black spots. The moth flies in the month of June, and is said to be extremely variable in colouring; for sometimes the lead colour prevails over nearly the whole surface of the wings, the stripes being very diffused and obscure. The caterpillar feeds on the elm, and occurs in September. It is of a green tinge, and has a yellow line on the side, with the head and tail black. When it is touched it drops immediately, suspending itself by a thread. It is said by an observant entomologist, that wherever the caterpillar occurs it is generally in boundless profusion, according to his own experience relating to it. He also tells us that the creature seems to have the power of producing an almost unlimited supply of silk.

In chalky districts a very beautiful little *geometer* occurs, called the Scorched Carpet (*Ligdia adustata*). This little species has the ground colour of the wings creamy white, brown or purple brown at the base. There is a broad curved band across the wings, all of which have a dot in the middle. The wings have just the appearance of being scorched, hence the term applied. June to August we may meet with this beautiful little insect in the southern counties. The caterpillar producing it is green, with a white spot on the side, dotted with red. It may be found feeding on the spindle tree during May. The Clouded Border (*Lomaspilis marginata*) is one of those little insects that so delight us in the woodland scenery of the summer time. It seems partial to chalk, and may be often seen flitting restlessly along the still and silent woodland glades that are sheltered from the noonday sun. The wings are whitish, and deeply bordered with brown. The border in the front wings is deeply indented and interrupted. In some specimens there is a band of brown across the hind wings; this is so interrupted in others as to assume the appearance of distinct spots. In fact, the insect is altogether very variable, both as regards markings and tint, for the brown is much deeper in some than in others that have been captured. This moth occurs from May to July. The caterpillar is said to be dark green, and to feed on the sallow in June and September.

In closing this paper, we allude to the solitary English representative of the Family *Ligidæ*. This is the Horse-chestnut (*Pachycnemia hippicastanaria*). We read of its being taken at Haslemere in Surrey, by an entomologist, who says that it was excessively abundant on heaths, and we also find it recorded as occurring in the New Forest in great numbers, but with these exceptions no localities are given for it. The caterpillar is as yet undescribed. The wings of this species are of a peculiar shape, long and narrow, and of a dark brown grey colour, with a silvery tinge. The hind wings are white, with a reddish shade. The female moth is said to be much less in size than the male. Leaving this species, so remarkable as filling up a blank, and suggesting a link between species and species, we remark that there can be little doubt that increased energy on the part of entomologists would serve to elucidate more of its history. If entomologists would forego the specimen mania to which we have alluded, and apply themselves to the less agreeable but more useful study of insects in their earlier stages, we should esteem it a great thing gained. We do not want an increased number of insect collectors merely for the sake of transferring insects from their native haunts to glass drawers; this is not particularly desirable, or beneficial to the science generally. What is required is an additional number of such men as Kirby and Spence—practical entomologists, who gave their earnest and determined assistance to the science by energetically working out the history of various species, and who, unassisted, have cleared up so many difficult and obscure problems relative to our native insects, both as regards structure and economy. It is our earnest desire that some of our degenerate "specimen collectors" may be transformed into the likeness of such entomologists as these; then, and then alone can we expect to fill up the blanks in our entomological knowledge.

PULEX IRRITANS IN A NEW LIGHT.

IF any enquiring reader wishes to know whether that little tormenter scientifically known as Pulex irritans, and vulgarly as the flea, has ever been found of any use in the economy of nature's realm, we are happy to inform him that we can answer his question in the affirmative. It must not be imagined that we are going to discuss the question whether it is desirable that the human form divine should be subject to sundry little aggravating bites, which are liable to make one's angry passions rise, or whether the ordinary avocations of flea-ish life are at all beneficial to humanity at large. Our object is to place him before our readers as we have seen him, in a new light, earning an honest livelihood (mirabile dictu!) by the sweat of his brow, and affording a subsistence to the individual whose philanthropic ingenuity helped him to such a desirable end.

"From information received," (to use police parlance) we went to an exhibition opened by Mr. Kitchingman, in order to view the performances of his stud of trained fleas, or, as worded in his announcements, "of trained apterous insects, the only specimens of the articulata in the world ever taught to perform." These apterous labourers were harnessed by means of an extremely fine hair or fibre of silk, which was tied round their bodies having the two ends rising perpendicularly above their backs and fastened to a split in a tiny straw, which formed the pole of the carriage they were engaged in drawing. We must confess that at first we entered the room with some feelings of alarm, suggested by the thought that some of the menagerie might escape, but this was soon dissipated at the sight of their burdens, which at once set our minds at rest.

The performances were highly interesting and considerably varied. One flea was engaged in a swing, his motion being caused by his kicking violently against one side of a well in which he was placed, which exertion bumped him against the other side and made him indignantly jump away again, so that the unfortunate creature was in a perpetual state of kicking. Another hauled up a little ivory bucket from a well, while a third drew a ship along a tight rope, walking upside down. A third was occupied in turning a cardboard cylinder after the manner of a treadmill, but two others still more unhappy, were occupied in a compulsory see-saw worked by each in turn giving a vigorous spring into the air, thus bringing the other at the opposite end of the balance to the ground. The largest, and consequently we presume the laziest, declined to jump at all, but remained sitting quietly down, leaving his comrade miserably suspended from the beam, and frantically clutching at the air in a vain attempt to reach the ground. A military pulex was engaged in firing off a miniature cannon, but on a former occasion the shock had been too much for his nervous system, so that when we were present he was unable to perform. The exhibitor kindly gave us a good deal of information about his collection which was very interesting. The fleas are generally imported from Russia and Belgium as being larger and more docile than the English ones, and are set to work immediately, the training beginning with a starvation of two days. At first they are very refractory, persisting in progressing by a series of violent jumps instead of a proper jog trot; but after a week or so they sober down and draw their burdens steadily unless stirred up to violent exertion, when they will gallop vigorously for a few inches, but sit down to rest and regain their breath directly afterwards. After they once learn to walk steadily, we were told, it is difficult to persuade them to leap again. At night all the performers are unharnessed and fed on the back of the employer's hand, after which repast they repose in a box enveloped in cotton wool. If at night any performer does not feed heartily, and with a good appetite, his progress is proportionately languid and slow the next day; but when any member of the establishment declines to eat for three or four days, his end is expected in a short time. About a hundred others are usually kept in stock and training, as they are comparatively short lived, three or four months being supposed to be the allotted period of their days. Perhaps confinement and hard labour affects their spirits. The workman engaged in drawing up the bucket had however reached the hoary age of 9 months, and his demise therefore will not be unexpected. The immense muscular power possessed by these creatures is here fully demonstrated. No doubt many of our readers have experienced the difficulty of holding a wild pulex for a minute or two, before consigning it to perdition. The flea Hercules drews a model of a ship estimated to be 500 times his own weight in a very easy manner. It seems that the English fleas are the most stubborn and difficult to train, but when once properly subdued they work better and last longer than the others, but the Englishman we saw, was anything but steady, tugging and straining at his collar in a frantic manner.

One of the most interesting features of the exhibition is the beautiful form of the models employed for the work. They are carved in ivory and exquisitely finished, and of course of the minutest size possible, being adapted to the fleas in a most ingenious manner, and manufactured by the exhibitor himself. The delicacy of touch and sight attainable after practice is surprising, as each performer is harnessed without the aid of a glass, merely being taken between the operator's finger and thumb. Mr. Kitchingman told us also that he knows every individual performer by sight, so that he has no difficulty in selecting each member of his troupe for his own work.

Altogether the exhibition was most amusing and edifying, and we certainly must confess that for once these little torments, have been turned to some account. If any enterprising reader takes a fancy to experimentalize for himself, we only hope he will train his troupe in some out of the way spot, where if they should escape, the consequences will be visited on himself alone.

A VISIT TO THE NESTS OF THE SWIFT.—By Video.

In the month of September I took the opportunity, by means of a long ladder, of examining two nests of the Swift (hirundo opus) that were in the stone-wall of a moderately high dwelling house. It was apparent that the birds had taken the opportunity of favourable circumstances to form their nests in crevices between the stones; but they must have also excavated the mortar that united them, and which was formed of lime and earth, not of very firm consistency. One of these nests had scarcely penetrated more than six inches, and the passage was so narrow and crooked, that it would not be easy for a single bird to inhabit it, still less a pair of them. I came to the conclusion therefore that it had been occupied as a residence by the male only. The nest itself was formed of straws and bits of weeds, cut into small pieces of an inch or less in length. The larger nest was a foot or more in depth, and wider, but still crooked in its passage, and within it a straw or two, some pieces of the stalks of groundsell, another stalk of a plant with the roots, the stem six inches long, and about the thickness of a crow-quill, some stiff roots like those of grass, jointed, of some inches in length and twisted, a piece of common moss, of the length of a finger, with a good quantity of vegetable materials, which must have been gathered from the ground when in the natural condition; but there was not a feather in either of these nests. These materials lay loosely in both nests, without being interwoven; and in the larger nest remained one egg, which appeared as if fresh, although it had been forsaken by the birds at least since the beginning of August. In proportion to the size of the bird it appeared large, the form a long oval, white, with a tinge of flesh appearing through it. This egg was presented to a distinguished ornithologist. The larger nest might hold a parent bird with two young ones; but the smaller nest's cavity could not hold them; from which it is concluded that it harboured the male only; a supposition corroborated by the fact that a kindred species, the Osculent Swallow has a smaller nest for the male, distinct from the female. In the year following that in which these observations were made, among others in the neighbourhood, three individuals of this species appeared, and proceeded to occupy the crevices already described; which number I account for in the supposition that one of them was the solitary young bird hatched in the last season, and which had accompanied the parents both in their retreat and return.

A curious fact noticed of the Swift in a former season is, that shortly after its arrival in wildness of flight one flew into a house through an open window, and alighted on the head of a boy; and another entered a chapel through a single open pane of glass. It was caught and brought to the writer, who set it at liberty.

EXTRACTS FROM AN ENTOMOLOGIST'S DIARY.

(*Continued from page* 80.)

March 24, 1867.—Day very mild. Saw the red admiral (Vanessa atalanta), and tortoiseshell (V. urticæ) on the wing.

May 5.—Day warm. Saw a red admiral (V. atalanta). Took a pair of the tortoiseshell butterfly (V. urticæ), and two seven spotted ladybirds (Coccinella septempunctata).

May 11.—Day warm, evening cool. Took a gamma moth (Plusia gamma). By exchange;—Brimstone butterfly (Gonopteryx rhamni), wood white (Leucophasia sinapsis), marbled white (Arge galathea).

May 16, 1867.—Took two larvæ of the oak eggar (Bombyx Quercus) from the whitethorn.

May 24.—Took a nest of the larvæ of the small eggar (Eriogaster lanestris) whitethorn.

June 1.—Privet hawkmoth (Sphinx Ligustri) emerged from the pupa state.

June 7.—Privet hawkmoth (S. Ligustri) from pupa state.

June 12.—Caught two orange tips (Anthocharis Cardamines).

June 22.—Took buff and white ermine (Arctia lubricipeda and A. Menthastri) and a Cinnibar moth (C. Jacobœæ).

July 6.—Took a common footman (Lithosia complanula) and a white ermine (A. Menthastri).

July 10.—Oak eggar (Bombyx Quercus) male, emerged from the pupa state.

July 13.—Garden tiger (Arctia caja), and oak eggar (B. Quercus) male, emerged from pupa.

June 16.—Small eggar (E. lanestris) began the chrysalis state.

Aug. 17.—Very hot. Took several specimens of the wall butterfly (S. Megæra).

Aug. 20.—Warm. Took painted lady (Vanessa Cardui).

Aug. 22.—Warm. Caught a specimen of the peacock butterfly (V. Io), and a large cabbage (Pieris Brassicæ).

Aug. 23.—Very hot. Took three clouded yellow (Colias Edusa) males, a peacock (V. Io), and a small copper (Polyommatus phlæas). Hellesdon, near Norwich.

Aug. 24.—Very hot. Took four fine specimens of the clouded yellow (C. Edusa) males, a peacock, (V. Io), and three red admirals (V. Atalanta), also a pair of the yellow underwing moth (Tryphæna pronuba.) Hellesdon.

Aug. 26.—Weather hot. Took three clouded yellow (C. Edusa) males, and a small copper (P. phleas) on a clover field. Hellesdon.

Sept. 8.—Warm. Saw red admiral (Vanessa Atalanta), and clouded yellow (C. Edusa). South Walsham. Caught a gold spot moth (Plusia Festucæ).

Note.—The clouded yellow (Colias Edusa) has been very abundant in Norfolk during the past season. Those captured here were chiefly males. I know of only one female being taken, by a "brother Entomologist," which is now in my possession.

R. LADDIMAN.

St. Augustine's, Norwich.

New Books.

Echoes in Plant and Flower Life. By Leo. H. Grindon, Lecturer on Botany at the Royal School of Medicine, Manchester. Author of "Life, its Nature," &c.; "The Trees of Old England;" "British and Garden Botany," &c., &c. London: F. Pitman, 20, Paternoster Row.

In this little work the author gathers together a number of observations and memoranda respecting the similarity, or rather unity and harmony, that exist between different species of plants and flowers, "from a poet's point of view." As he says in his preface, they do not pretend to be more than mere memoranda which science may some day find it worth while to detach, but which have not hitherto been collected. We extract as a specimen of Mr. Grindon's style a paragraph on the language of flowers:—

"The truth, as we have said, is that these sweet things, these flowers and trees, lotus and honey-suckle, scabious, and agrimony, and silver plantain, exist in the world as intimations of what in mankind is realized and fulfilled. Therefore they must needs seem to sympathise, also to have their ways, their manners and customs, all in turn anticipating something human. This is the source of the picturesque science called the 'Language of Flowers,' which, rightly viewed and understood, is no capricious and arbitrary association of certain sentiments with certain herbs, but the philosophy of the harmonies that were instituted in the beginning, between vegetable nature on the one hand, and our own souls on the other. How exquisite are these supplementary enrichments of creation ! We thank God, as we ought, for our daily bread, and for prosperity in the undertakings to which we address ourselves, and for our physical health, and for the return of fine weather ; how slow are we to remember that a right and consistent piety thanks Him as reverently, and as gratefully, and as constantly for all such excellent additions to the beauty of the world—since, if there were no such concords of flowers and plants with our thoughts and feelings, the green and blossomy earth would be to us like voiceless birds. Here at least it is scarcely true that it is the lover who makes the beauty; for though nature opens her stores in proportion to the amount of seeing eye that we carry with us, it is not *men* who in soul, but God who does it for the watchful and the earnest. The Language of Flowers was not contrived as some think, by the Orientals ; nor is its extension among the Saxon races owing to the industry and ingenuity of certain ladies. In its integrity it is a part of the very method and order of nature ; and, although much misconceived and misrepresented, the day will come when it will take its rightful place among the sciences . .

He who stays among the forms and surfaces is only a vegetable anatomist—expert and learned it may be, as to externals, but he is no botanist till he asks 'What do these things signify ?' Both occupations are good ;

let neither observer look with disparagement on the other : one is Lucretius, enumerating the phenomena ; the other is Virgil, extracting and portraying the loveliness."

Weather Facts and Predictions. By G. F. Chambers, F.R.A.S. (Reprinted from *The Churchman* Newspaper, February, 1868.)

This pamphlet is devoted to a collection of facts and predictions concerning the weather, partly founded on the author's observation, and partly drawn from the writings of Admiral Fitzroy and other Meteorologists and Weather Guides. There are observations deduced from the barometer, thermometer, hygrometer, winds, ozone, clouds, mists, fogs, dew, and hoar frost, rain, thunder, and lightning, sunrise and set, moon, in fact everything which has the slightest influence on the variations of the weather. Persons who wish to study the weather will find this little work very useful.

Correspondence.

[*Under this head we shall be glad to insert any letters of general interest.*]

IS THE WHALE A FISH?

Sir,—I think that your readers will agree with me that Mr. Landels' arguments on this subject are by no means convincing as he would have us so believe ; indeed I shall endeavour to prove to them that his premises, and therefore his arguments, are bad from beginning to end. In the first place, I beg totally to dissent from his opinion that "though their opponents (*i.e.*, the opponents of the theory usually received by naturalists) are neither naturalists or men of science, yet they are quite as competent to argue the question as those who hold a contrary opinion. It appears to me that the persons who are most competent to argue a question like the present one, are those who have made these and other kindred subjects their study, and who consequently know most about them ; and it is generally admitted that a popular definition or idea of anything, as opposed to that of science, is frequently the wrong one. Indeed your correspondent stultifies himself on this point, as he goes on to say :—" of course the popular classification is quite as liable to error as that of naturalists, and I have no doubt that many animals are placed by it in the class of fishes, which even according to the popular definition of the word 'fish' ought not to be there. *But this is owing to ignorance of the habits and mode of life of such animals!*" Exactly so. Yet this popular classification, of which Mr. Landels elects himself the mouthpiece, presumes to deny the correctness of the classification of men, who by their very knowledge of the subject are denominated naturalists ! How on earth can people argue and attempt to decide a question of which they are confessedly ignorant? So much for the respective merits of the two parties.

I will now go back a little to review the "popular definition" of your correspondent, remarking by the way, that he evidently forgot the old maxim, "omnis definito est periculosa." "'Fish' is a popular term applied to all those animals, whether vertebrate or invertebrate, which constantly reside in the water, and which could not exist for any length of time if they were removed from that element." According to this popular definition therefore, tadpoles, the larvæ of ephemeræ, libellulidæ, and other insects, water snails, and numerous annelids—in fact all living creatures which live in the water, are fish ! Verily Sir, the sooner this definition is amended, the better. Perhaps, however, these creatures are some of those which the ignorance of the *populus* has erroneously termed fish. From this point of view therefore, and considering this definition as it stands, to be the "popular" one, the question simply becomes one between ignorance on the one hand, and science on the other. But I maintain, with all deference to your correspondent, that this is not, and cannot be, the true *popular* definition. The *populus* would never (to quote the language of Mr. Bumble) make such a hass of itself as to say for a moment that insects, snails, &c., are fishes, and as a matter of fact, people in general give the term 'fish' a far narrower meaning than Mr. Landels evidently imagines. The smallest charity boy in London would laugh at your correspondent if he asked him whether certain insects were fishes or not. Mr. Landels clearly forgot that although fish are animals that live in the water, everything that lives in the water is not necessarily a fish. "A rook is a black bird, but every black bird is not a rook." The question *now* is whether the definition of your correspondent is a correct one, and of its correctness your readers can judge for themselves. I apprehend therefore, that until Mr. Landels draws a new definition of the term (a difficult job I imagine) that can be called "popular," with some reason, it is useless to touch upon the merits of the question itself.

I will only draw your readers' attention to one more passage in this singular letter. Mr. Landels says that popularly a *dyticus* is not designated a fish, "*simply because it has the habit of leaving the pond or stream which it inhabits, at the time of dusk,* sometimes as often as every evening, *to take long flights over the surrounding country,* or to hover about over the surface of the water." Your readers will therefore be good enough to remember that this water beetle is not a fish, simply because of this habit of leaving the water; to follow out the same argument—that if it could not fly, but lived all its days in the water, it would be a fish. Surely Sir, if your correspondent had given a little more consideration to the subject he would not have made such an egregious statement.

I have only one other observation to make on this subject which I hope Mr. Landels will not take particularly to himself as some of your correspondents will see that I allude to them as well. If your readers actrally wish to contribute to the success of this magazine they should write on some subject which is really interesting and scientific. I think some of your correspondents forget that the NATURALIST'S NOTE BOOK is not issued to enable anybody to appear in print, or for only a few persons to exchange ideas, but that when any letter appears in these columns it is in a certain sense dedicated to the public at large, and can be read by any person. The present question, although perhaps made the most of, has been settled long ago, and cannot seriously be discussed again. I think that if Mr. Landels had given this subject the thought he shews in some of his former letters he would not have sent such a production to the columns of a public magazine, for it must be apparent to any person not directly interested, that if your correspondents are reduced to the necessity of discussing a question similar to this one, their scientific knowledge and literary powers must be at a very low ebb.

I hope, Sir, these observations will be taken, as they are written, in good part; they are made in no unfriendly spirit to your correspondents, but merely in a sincere desire to see this NOTE BOOK become really scientific, and that it may gradually improve, so that in time it may become one of the leading scientific journals of the day. If any reader thinks these remarks out of place he may attribute them to the irritability of an

OLD FOGEY.

Meetings of Learned Societies.

THE STATE MICROSCOPICAL SOCIETY OF ILLINOIS.

Lexicographers define the word microscope as meaning an optical instrument in which the smallest objects are discerned. It is of Greek derivation, being a combination of the two words mikros, *small,* and skopoe *to view.* Like that of all nations and of arts, the history of the microscope has had its brilliant periods, in which it shone with uncommon splendor, and was cultivated with uncommon ardour, and these have been succeeded by intervals marked with no discovery, yet, in recent years, there is probably no branch of practical science which has undergone such essential and rapid improvements as that which relates to the microscope. Though dating far back into antiquity, it has become quite a new instrument in modern times, and has already accomplished much in disclosing the structure and laws of matter, and in making as important discoveries in the infinitely minute world as the telescope has done in that which is infinitely distant.

The exact degree of proficiency in its use attained by the ancients must doubtless be numbered among the lost arts, over which moderns mourn so eloquently but in vain. There is abundant evidence, however, that it was known to the ancient world, single microscopes, in the form of glass globes containing water, being the first instruments employed; an idea perhaps borrowed from the crystalline lens of small fishes, which may be taken out of the eye in such a state of perfection as to give a very perfect image of minute objects.

A magnifying lens of rock-crystal was found by the indefatigable explorer, Mr. Layard, among a number of glass bowls in the northwest palace of Nimroud.

Hemispheres of glass and afterwards lenses were subsequently used, so that no person has pretended to claim the invention of the single microscope.

Methods of producing microscopic globules of glass are given by Butterfield, in the philosophical transactions, 1678; by Father di Torre, of Naples, in the same transactions for 1765 and 1766; by Sivright, in the Edinburgh *Philosophical Journal* for 1829; and by Dr. Hooke, in his *Micrographia;* but these methods in their perfection are of no value compared with lenses of glass when ground and polished to the same focal length.

Mr. Stephen Gray long ago proposed to construct single microscopes with drops of water which he lifted up with a pin and deposited in a small hole made in a piece of brass. The drop retained a sort of imperfect sphericity, and showed objects with some distinctness. The weight of the drop, however, destroyed its spherical form, causing minute irregularities in the circumference of the aperture in which it was placed.

To avoid these, Sir David Brewster placed minute drops of pure turpentine varnish on plates of thin parallel glass, forming plano-convex lenses of any focal length; and, by dropping the varnish on both sides, he formed double convex lenses, with their convexities in any required proportion.

The same eminent savan was the first to propose the use of the diamond and other precious stones for the construction of single lenses, many of which were executed from the diamond, the sapphire, garnet, and spinelle ruby, by Pritchard, Hill, and others, as far back as 1824.

The diamond, it is believed, produces the most superior lenses, having less aberration and greater magnifying power with a given focus than lenses of a like construction from glass. But the great cost and labor involved, coupled with the perfection attained in the manufacture of glass lenses at the present day, makes the use of the diamond and other precious stones very rare, if, indeed they are now used at all.

With this brief and necessarily imperfect sketch of the origin of the single microscope, we proceed to take a hasty glance at the history and merits of

THE COMPOUND MICROSCOPE,

an instrument which, whether we consider the beauty and perfection of its construction, its ready adaptability to recreative and educational as well as purely scientific purposes, or the invaluable services it has rendered, and continues to render to the store of human knowledge, is every way worthy of a high niche among the monuments of the remarkable age in which we live, and few departments of science there are but must confess their obligations to it; few there are to which it is not absolutely indispensable. To its demonstrations must be conceded the origin of professorships of histology in our medical schools, since, in the first place, it was owing to the importance of the facts brought to light that, in 1841, the council of the Royal College of Surgeons, London, were led to establish a chair of histology, which is now an important branch of the education of the medical student throughout the world.

But while priding ourselves upon the progress which has been made in the construction of the compound microscope, until it has reached a degree of perfection which has earned for it the reputation of being the only instrument in science which works fully up to the theory of its construction,—we are not unmindful,—without any double entendre being intended,—that, like everything of human invention, it also has seen the day of small things.

The compound achromatic microscope consists, essentially, of two parts : An object-glass and an eye-piece; so called because they are respectively near the object and the eye when the instrument is in use. The earliest of which it is believed there is any record was invented by Zacharias Zansz, or his father, Hans Zansz, spectacle-makers at Middleberg, in Holland, about the year 1590. One of their microscopes which they presented to Prince Maurice, was, in the year 1617, in the possession of Cornelius Drebell, of Alkmaar, who then resided in London as mathematician to King James. From that time to the present, the attention of the learned in such matters has been given to the perfecting of the capabilities of the instrument, until, as already stated, there seems nothing left to improve. It is, however, within the last 25 years that the microscope has made its greatest advancement,—a fact to be attributed, no doubt, to the encouragement and stimulus given to scientific instrument-makers by the establishment of

MICROSCOPICAL SOCIETIES.

The first of these, the Microscopical society of London, was established in 1839, or just 30 years ago. It owes its existence to a handful of gentlemen engaged in scientific pursuits, who aimed at affording assistance and encouragement to microscopical investigations. Among the first promoters of the society may be found the honoured names of Bowerbank, Carpenter, and Quekett, and from the seed then planted has arisen a great and powerful society, invested with special privileges by royal charter, and now taking the lead as the Royal Microscopical society of London, the most influential, as it is also the most ancient of all such societies.

The example thus set has been followed throughout Europe, until scarcely a city, town, or village of importance can be named that does not possess its own society, or club for the cultivation of microscopical pursuits. Nor is the example confined to this special object. It has been the means of establishing other associations for the promulgation of whatever may be interesting, advantageous, or new in botany, chemistry, geology, entomology, or zoology, until there is not a specialite in science that does not possess its representative society.

It is needless to descant upon the benefit conferred thereby upon the observer, the student, and the world at large. Nor has the example been without its influence upon the serial literature of the day. Indeed, it may be claimed that it has created a press of its own, as may be seen in the increasing number of scientific journals ably edited and abundantly supported. Add to these the published "Transactions" of the various learned societies, several hundreds in number, all of which are admirably printed, and the majority accompanied with costly illustrations. The influence of such a tidal wave on the interests of science must be at once apparent. Nor did the usefulness of the parent society (for such the London society may justly be called) end here. From its formation it has given such an impetus to the opticians' art as to have produced a keen, but friendly, competition, which has resulted in a degree of perfection deemed impossible a few years ago,—a competition which is year by year producing the most marked benefits to science, and, therefore, to the world.

Photography, too, has been brought within the range of its operations with signal success, as evidenced by a page of *The Times newspaper*, containing 12,500 words in the space of the eighth of an inch square; 200 kings and queens of England; the whole of the Sermon on the Mount; the play scene in Hamlet; Wilkie's village school in an uproar; Rosa Bonheur's horse fair; the charter of the State Microscopical society of Illinois,—each of these within the space mentioned, and only a gleaning from hundreds which are exhibited under the microscope with a marvellous beauty, accuracy, and fidelity of execution incredible to believe until witnessed.

The time-honoured saying of good Bishop Berkeley, "Westward the star of empire takes its way," is as true in science as in material things. Thirty years ago, when the founders of the London society met together, the city in which we live was little better than a swamp. Ten years later, when the writer first saw it, it was despised even by the cranes, who preferred the limped waters of Calumet to the terra-aqueous soup afforded them at the spot where Haddock, Peck, Burton, *et id omne genus*, then paddled to their stores; where, if perchance accompanied by their wives, they offered them a rail to cross the quaking bog, instead of offering them an arm, the rail being the most useful implement of the two. The only decent tavern where the traveller could find "native rye" with a strong smack of "fusil" was the old Sherman house, opposite which, in a wooden erection 10 by 12, presided the Hon. Hugh T. Dickey, as judge of the circuit court of Cook county, surrounded by such an aborigines bar as would lead the more civilized spectator to doubt whether they were the exponents or the examples of the criminal code of the state. But "The good old times—the good old times," have fled,

"And, like the baseless fabric
Of a vision, left not a
Wrack behind."

A new "Sherman," with less "fusil," and a trifle more costly; a new court-house; a new judge, with a bar cleaner and better dressed, if not otherwise improved, have usurped the old landmarks, whose places will know them no more for ever. *Tempora mutantur;* and we are willing they should be. And so, on this 30th day of May, 1869, we are able to note that just 30 years from the foundation of the first microscopical society of which we can find any record, we have with us, in all the pomp and pride of circumstance,

THE STATE MICROSCOPICAL SOCIETY OF ILLINOIS.

The charter of the society was procured at the last session of the legislature, and has already been published in extenso in *The Times* of April 12.

A brief statement of the society's inception will be found in the president's address, as given below.

The following are its officers:

President—Dr. W. W. Allport.
Vice Presidents—Hosmer A. Johnson, M.D., George F. Rumsey, James V. Z. Blaney, M.D., J. F. Beaty.
Treasurer—George M. Higginson.
Secretary I. Hankey.
Secretary Foreign Correspondence—Samuel A. Briggs.
Council—S. A. Briggs, Joseph T. Ryerson, N. S. Davis, M.D., I. Hankey, W. C. Hunt, M.D., W. E. Doggett, J. H. Hollister, M.D., J. F. Beaty, Walter Hay, M.D., R. Ludlam, M.D., Samuel J. Jones, M.D., George M. Higginson.
Curator—H. F. Munroe.
Librarian—John Robson.
Photomicrographer to the Society—John Carbutt.

The society now numbers fifty-six resident members, one associate member, and as

Corresponding Members—Lieut. Col. J. J. Woodward, war department, Washington; Christopher Johnson, M.D., professor of principles and practice of surgery, University of Maryland, Baltimore; Prof. H. L Smith, Hobart college, Geneva, N. Y.; J. H. McQuillen, M.D., Philadelphia.

Honorary Members—W. S. Sullivant, Columbus, O.; W. H. Walmsley, Philadelphia, Pa.; Rev. R. H. Walker, late of Wadham college, Oxford, England.

The objects of the society are the promotion and extension of microscopical knowledge in the west, and more particularly in our own state, by associating those together engaged in such pursuits, whether for purely scientific purposes or for recreative or educational purposes.

The society extends the right hand of fellowship to the geologist, the chemist, the mineralogist, the anatomist, and the botanist,—all of whom find the miscroscope a useful companion and indispensable aid in their interesting researches.

To the first of these it reveals, among a multiplicity of other facts, "that our large coal beds are the ruins of a gigantic vegetation ; and the vast limestone rocks, which are so abundant on the earth's surface, are the catacombs of myriads of animal tribes, too minute to be perceived by unaided vision."

To the mind of all, it opens out an extended and vast tract, opulent in wonders, rich in beauties, and boundless in extent.

As aids to the proper cultivation of the society's work, there have been formed committees or sections on

Floral structure,
Cryptogamous plants,
Vegetable histology,
Animal histology,
Crystallography,
Vegetable parasites,
Animal parasites,
Pathology of vegetable structure,
The adulteration of food.

These will give the reader a fair general idea of the scope of the society's work.

But it is by no means solely to the student and votary of science that the society holds forth its inducements. To the business man, the artisan, and the lover of knowledge, whoever he may be, the society throws wide its doors, for there are no circumstances or conditions of life which need be altogether cut off from these sources of interest and improvement.

If there be one class more than another which especially needs to have its attention thus awakened to such objects of interest as by drawing its better nature into exercise shall keep it free from the grovelling sensuality in which it too frequently loses itself, it is our hard working population, for which we build our schools, and whose educational advancement is one of the great social problems of the day.

"A walk without an object," says Mr. Kingsley, of muscular Christianity fame, "unless in the most lovely and novel scenery, is a poor exercise, and, as a recreation, utterly nil. If we wish rural walks to do our children good, we must give them a love for rural sights, an object in every walk. We must teach them—and we can teach them—to find wonder in every insect, sublimity in every hedge-row, the records of past worlds in every pebble, and boundless fertility upon the barren shore." To attempt to inspire a love of nature by books and pictures, in those who have never felt her influence, is almost hopeless. Once more : "I have seen," says the same gifted author, "the cultivated man craving for travel, and succss in life, pent up in the drudgery of London work, and yet keeping his spirit calm and his morals perhaps all the more righteous, by spending over his microscope evenings which would too probably have been gradually wasted at the theatre." Such is the testimony of one of the ablest pens of the present day.

But there is yet another class to whom the society extends an invitation ; those who are at once our joy and our pride, without whom life would be a blank, a mere caravansary, with none to care for or entertain. If the man of culture can find relief from the cares and drudgery of his daily life in microscopic pursuits, what may not the cultivated woman find in the same direction ? With such gifted nanes before as Agnes Catlow, the Hon. Mrs. Ward, and a host of others as examples, surely she need not slight the possession of that which can be made the most delightful of her many accomplishments.

With her microscope by her side, she is all the better prepared to enjoy the beauties of her favourite poets,—Thomson, Cowper, Wordsworth, and Bryant.

To the mother, especially, does the microscope recommend itself, as the most beautiful and interesting aid to the education of her children— which is, or ought to be, her first care. A child may be interested by the account of nature's wonders, as by any other instructive narrative, but they have little of *life* or *reality* in his mind ; far less than has the story of adventure which appeals to his sympathies, or even than the fairy tale which charms and fixes his imagination. And yet, all the stories, rich with eastern imagery, cannot vie with the least of the brilliant revelations of the brazen tube. With the microscope, a single rural or even suburban walk will afford a store of pleasurable occupation for weeks in the examination of its collected treasures. A large glass jar may be easily made to teem with life, in almost as many and varied forms as could be found by the unaided eye in long and toilsome voyages over the wide ocean, and a never-ending source of amusement is afforded by the observation of their growth, their changes, their movements, their habits. The schoolboy, thus trained by an affectionate and careful mother, looks forward to the holiday which shall enable him to search afresh in some favourite pool, or to explore the wonders of some stagnant waters, with as much zest as the keenest sportsman longs for a day's shooting or a day's fishing, and with this advantage over him, that his excursion is only the beginning of a fresh stock of enjoyment, instead of being in itself the whole.

Such are a few, and a few only, of the various objects which this society holds forth as worthy of labour and co-operation on the part of all who are interested—as who is not?—in the diffusion of knowledge useful to the individual, the community, and the entire race. As a meeting of social scientific interest the Conversazione of Friday evening may well challenge comparison with any heretofore attempted, while in many of its features it is entirely new, not only in our own city and state, but in the United States.

Despite the attractions of the oratorio, and the forbidding aspect of the weather, the visitors began to arrive promptly at the hour indicated in the card of invitation. The spacious halls were beautifully decorated with flowers, while various objects of vertu were tastefully distributed about the rooms, in one of which was placed a valuable melegioscopio, with six portfolios of drawings, kindly loaned for the occasion by George E. Stanton, Esq. This attracted much attention during by the entire evening, and most deservedly so, the views being the most costly and exquisite productions of the photographic art, while their size, as pictured through the magnificent lenses of the instrument, contributed an impression of being verily and indeed transplanted as if by enchantment, to the distant and remarkable scenes they so wonderfully portrayed.

Upon entering the drawing room, the guests were received by Mr. and Mrs. Ryerson, and then introduced to the president. The members mustered in strong force, each wearing a neat badge of ribbon with the society's monogram.

THE PRESIDENT'S ADDRESS.

The President then delivered the following address:

Ladies and Gentlemen: The *character*, as well as the large *number* present this evening, indicates an interest felt by the most *respectable* and influential portion of our citizens in "The State Microscopical Society of Illinois," hardly hoped for by its *projectors* and those who were the most instrumental in its organization.

In view of the manifest interest felt in this society, I have been requested to state to you its origin, present condition, and objects, as well as *some* of the uses of the microscope.

In the early part of the past winter a circular was issued from "The Chicago Academy of Natural Sciences," inviting all those in the city who took an interest in microscopical investigations to meet at their rooms, for the purpose of organizing a microscopical section to the academy.

Agreeably to this invitation quite a respectable number of gentlemen met. At this meeting a diversity of opinion existed. Some were in favour of a society that should work in connection with the academy, whilst *others* wished a separate organization. A committee was appointed to take the matter under consideration, and to report their conclusions, and a plan for organization, at a subsequent meeting. After holding several meetings, at which the report of the committee, and the views of the various gentlemen present were freely discussed, it was thought that an independent society could be more easily managed, and that more good could be accomplished by it than by working as an adjunct to any other society. As a result of this conclusion, a temporary organization, which has been known as "The Chicago Microscopical Club," was formed. A bill was immediately prepared and sent to our state legislature, and a law was passed incorporating "The State Microscopical Society of Illinois," under which act of incorporation we are now organized and acting, and into which the Chicago Microscopical Club has been merged.

From the statement I have made you will see that our society is but a few months old, and yet I am pleased to state that we have some sixty resident members, among whom are some of the leading members of the medical profession and the best amateur microscopists of the city and state. Hardly a meeting has passed recently at which we have not received donations to our cabinet, either from our own members or from microscopists residing in different parts of the country, some of which, as you will see, are exceedingly rare, beautifully prepared, and artistically mounted.

We are also receiving offers of exchanges and donations from prominent microscopists and the officers of kindred associations not only at home but abroad. The proceedings of some of our meetings have been published in the scientific journals of Europe, aswell as of our own country.

From the past, the society has every reason to be encouraged and to look with hope to the future; expecting, as it does, that its list of resident working members will be largely increased at our next meeting, which, in accordance with the provisions of our by-laws, will not occur until the first Friday in October.

In addition to resident membership, the by-laws of the society provide for honorary, associate, and corresponding memberships. And, while we intend to be somewhat liberal in the admission of resident members, care will be exercised to admit none to the other memberships whose names would not be an honour to the society, or whose contributions will not increase the interest of its meetings, and the usefulness of the society.

The leading object of the society will be the cultivation of microscopy in the investigation and demonstration of the views that propose scientific subjects, and special committees have been appointed for the special systematic investigation of Floral structures, Infusoria, Cryptogamous Plants, Vegetable and Animal Histology, Vegetable and Animal Pathology, Vegetable and Animal Parasites, Crystallography, and kindred branches, during the ensuing year. Besides which it is desired to make the microscope useful in social and commercial interests, by detecting adulteration in food and fraud in fabrics, and to exhibit from time to time, so far as may be possible, to such of our citizens as may appreciate it, the minute handiwork of our Creator as it can be seen in no other way than through the almost infinite vision of the microscope.

In all His works, however we may enlarge or refine our vision, we find nothing common or unworthy of our careful notice. The eager traveller crosses oceans and continents, climbs rocks and mountains, that he may gaze upon the beauties and wonders of the landscape; unmindful, too often, of the not less wonderful creations that surround his path and are crushed beneath his feet.

The wayside flower, the springing leaf, the tuft of moss, the blade of grass, or tiniest insect often reveals, under the microscope, colours that contest in brilliancy and beauty with the rainbow and sunset, and form more subtle grace and delicate tracery than sculptors have ever chiselled or artists' pencil can hope to rival.

There are few things about which the public have a more erroneous impression than the use of the microscope. The popular notion that microscopy is one of those abstruse sciences the acquisition of which requires years of study and patient practice, is an error, as it is a simple art easily acquired. The microscope is merely an instrument of observation. It sharpens the eye, and peers into everything. No invention of man has a wider range of application in its uses. It should be the companion, not only of the scientific, but it might with profit be found in every counting-room, workshop, and household. As an instrument of education it has no equal, and no school-room should be without it.

From the fact that the microscope has been so extensively used by scientific men, let no one suppose that it is for the exclusive use of gentlemen. The ladies, with their quick perceptions, refined organism, and delicacy of touch, are peculiarly adapted to manipulate both instrument and objects, and there is no reason why practice would not render them skilful microscopists. Besides the instruction and personal pleasure, there would be derived from the use of this instrument, ladies would find it to be an easy and agreeable way of entertaining their friends. They would also find many valuable hints in the delicate tracery of minute organisms visible only under the microscope, which would suggest beautiful designs for their embroidery and fancy work, and its skilful management by them might with propriety be regarded as a refined accomplishment.

As a teacher of theology this brazen tube has no rival. No doctor of divinity, however learned and eloquent, can so successfully urge the fallacy and utter absurdity of atheism, and rout with shame and confusion the advocates of infidelity. For it reveals in every atom of the universe that "the hand that made us is divine."

So "he that hath eyes to see let him see," and, in the beautiful lines of Young, so appropriately placed on the programme of the evening by our efficient committee of arrangements,

"Think naught a trifle, though it small appear:
Small sands the mountain, moments make a year;
And trifles life."

It was listened to with marked attention by the brilliant assemblage, and at its close received unmistakable marks of approbation.

On motion, the president was unanimously requested to furnish a copy to each of the city papers for publication.

(To be contained.)

Short Notes.

THE KALOSHES.—These people dwell in a long line of rude houses outside the settlement. Their dwellings are shanties on a large scale, with a small entrance, often circular in shape, and a hole in the roof to let the smoke out. The idea of these constructions must have been derived from the Russians; in some cases the very unusual circumstance of the sleeping-rooms being apart from the main chamber was to be observed. The Kaloshes are by no means a prepossessing people, and have a bad reputation. Their dress is commonly a blanket, at least in summer time; they frequently black their faces all over, and sometimes paint themselves in red, black and blue stripes and patches. They wear a pin of bone or metal stuck in their lower lip; this is said to denote maturity; it is at least never worn by the young. They appear to be more than usually lazy natives, probably from the fact that Nature has been so kind to them; salmon is abundant, deer and bear meat are to be had for the hunting, and the berries are innumerable. Their canoes are much inferior to those of the lower coast, whilst their skin "baidarkies" (kyacks) are not equal to those of Norton Sound and the northern coast. Their grave-boxes, or tombs, are interesting; they contain only the ashes of the dead. These people invariably burn the deceased. On one of the boxes I saw a number of faces painted, long tresses of human hair depending therefrom. Each head represented a victim of the (happily) deceased one's ferocity. In this day he was, doubtless, more esteemed than if he had never harmed a fly. All their graves are much ornamented with carved and painted faces and other devices.—*From Wymper's Travels in Alaska.*

THE CUTTLE-FISH AS FOOD.—We now come to a class of animals which, but for the unreasonable prejudice of our fishermen and the poor generally, might, in the absence of better diet, afford them a large supply of cheap and nourishing food. I refer to cuttle-fish. Cuttle-fish of various kinds form the staple diet of the fishermen of France and Italy, and very wholesome and nourishing food they are. But the denizens of our own coasts, from silly prejudice, would rather starve than eat them, and, in sinful waste, leave many tons' weight yearly to rot upon the shore, or to be carted away as manure,—and this sometimes in the face of the dire necessity which so often overtakes the poor fishermen in bad wintry weather. The main thing upon which their foolish antipathy to these animals is founded, is the presence of the wonderful ink-bag with which they are endowed, as a mode of defence against their enemies. Quite as rational would it be to object to eat the flesh of oxen or sheep because they possess a gall-bladder, or that of the cod because the fish has an oily liver.—*Scientific Opinion.*

PELICANS.—The striking feature in these birds is the large pouch connected with the lower jaw. It is formed by an expansion of the lax unfeathered skin of the throat, is calculated to contain ten quarts of water, and when empty can be contracted so as to be hardly visible. In a state of nature the pouch is used as a store bag for fish, its usual food. The pelicans build broad heavy nests in trees, constructed like those of the swan, of large sticks. From this habit the pelican was, of old, known in the Hebrew language as *kaath*, the vomiter; hence, also has arisen the fable of this bird tearing open her bosom to feed her young with her own blood, the snowy plumage of the breast being ruffled and reddened during the operation. The pelicans are active and powerful birds both in the air and in the water. The pelican is a tameable and friendly bird. It has been proposed to teach it to fish for others besides itself, in the same way as the Chinese have trained the cormorant—a ring round its throat removing the temptation, which otherwise might prove irresistible, of swallowing its capture.

SUBSIDENCE OF THE BALTIC.—The Cronstadt journals mention an extraordinary subsidence of the waters of the Baltic in that locality. It began in the evening, the wind being S.W. and rather fresh. At ten at night the level of the sea was a foot lower than ordinary, and continued still to sink. The following morning at six it was two feet below its normal point, the wind having veered round to N.E.; and at two in the afternoon the greatest depression was arrived at, namely, three feet two inches. The water then began to mount rapidly, and during the night exceeded its ordinary level by a foot. Nearly all the steamers plying between Csonstadt and St. Petersburgh were aground, a circumstance almost unprecedented. As to the cause of this phenomenon nothing is known; but the supposition is that a strong north-east wind drove the waters towards the Swedish, Danish, and Prussian coasts.

WHAT IS LAVA?—A telegram in the morning papers states that "the eruption of Mount Vesuvius is increasing in intensity; the flow of lava is more copious, and the dynamic action of the cone more vigorous." But what is lava? Coming no one knows whence, it might be suspected to be formed of, or at least to contain, unusual substances; but such apparently is not the case. Here is an analysis, by M. Silvestri, of lava recently thrown out of Vesuvius:—Silica, 39; lime 18; alumina, 14; magnesia, 3; protoxide of iron, 13; potash 1; soda, 10; water, 2; which means that the specimen closely resembled common wine-bottle glass. In short, lava, though varying considerably in colour and solidity or friability, and occasionally containing little groups of crystalline minerals, would seem to be a sort of rough natural glass or earthenware mainly produced from sand, chalk, clay, and similar common earthy substances.—*Express.*

A PLAGUE OF KANGAROOS IN AUSTRALIA.—Kangaroos have increased to such an extent in the south-east of South Australia as to become a serious injury to the colony, as they starve out the sheep. The increase of the kangaroo has arisen from the destruction of the native dog and the decrease of the aborigines. A kangaroo league has been projected for the purpose of extirpating the kangaroos, or to endeavour to make their skins a marketable commodity, so that it may be profitable to hunt the animals down and thus keep their numbers within bounds.

Remarks, Queries, &c.

Under this head we shall be happy to insert original Remarks, Queries, &c.)

"ARE THE PLANETS INHABITED?"

Having seen discussed, in the current number of the N.N.B., the question of the plurality of inhabited worlds, I hazard a few remarks on this very interesting but very speculative subject. With regard to the possibility and even probability of our satellite and the primary planets being the abodes of sentient beings, I quite agree with Mr. Bell; and, moreover, admit the value of the arguments he has advanced in support of this hypothesis; but, at the same time, consider them, *per se*, of scarcely sufficient stability on which to build a theory of such magnitude and weight. My views do not so entirely depend on the apparent adaptability to life, with regard to physical characters, such as hills, vales, atmospheres, &c., which our moon and the planets all, more or less, possess (for this may be only in accordance with the unity of design displayed throughout material creation), as on the recent revelations of spectrum analysis, which seem to prove the elementary material constituting the earth to be essentially the same as that entering into the formation of the sun and fixed stars.

Doubtless most of the readers of the N.N.B. are aware that the process of spectrum analysis consists in the splitting up of a ray of light, by means of a prism, into its component rays. A ray of pure white light, submitted to this treatment, presents a spectrum of seven coloured bands (ranging from red to violet) being differentially refrangible; but the spectra resulting from the light evolved from various chemical substances in combustion exhibit certain characteristic bars, by means of which the presence of the particular metal or substance, from which the ray emanates, may be accurately detected. This test is so delicate, that, in a mixed flame, the existence of an infinitesimal fraction of the metal sodium produces on the spectrum its indicative line. Unfortunately, the test admits of being applied only to the light of self-luminous bodies; for the spectra of our satellite and the planets, shining with reflected light, are found to be precisely similar to that of the sun. However, on the results of spectrum analysis a system of solar and stellar chemistry has been based; a science, which, at present, is quite in its infancy, but which, seeing the significant deductions it has already made, promises to establish as a fact, that the chemical constitution of these heavenly bodies (viz., the sun and fixed stars) is similar to that of the earth we inhabit.

Admitting, then, the sun to possess terrestrial elements, we are led by analogy to infer, that the chemical composition of the other members of the solar system corresponds with that of the earth and the great central luminary; which analogy is strengthened by the discovery, that such a correspondence actually exists between the two latter and the far-distant fixed stars. This inference is, in some measure, confirmed by a comparatively recent astronomical surmise, concerning the primary formation of the solar system, according to which the planets are the broken rings of plastic matter, thrown off by centrifugal force from the surface of a rotating molten sphere. This sphere subsequently became the sun; and the several portions of each ring, obeying the natural law of gravitation, coalesced into a single globular body, which, in some instances, threw off secondary rings, forming, in like manner, the planet's satellites. If this theory, which is not without reason for its support, be true, we may safely conclude, that throughout the solar system an uniformity of composition exists, since its parts were originally derived from a single homogeneous mass. And this view, it may be added, receives supplementary confirmation from the analysis of meteorites, which occasionally having fallen upon the earth have never presented any element in their composition with which we were previously unacquainted.

It is, then, extremely probable, that a chemistry is common to the sun and his surrounding planets. Hence, on the latter, as on the earth, we should find water and carbonic acid for the support of the plant, and oxygen and vegetable matter for the maintenance of animal life. And, admitting the existence of chemical elements, and consequently of chemical force, it would follow that the other great powers of nature, viz., electricity, magnetism, &c., were also present; for these, by scientific experiment, are found to be mutually convertible with chemical affinity and with one another. Accordingly, there are on the planets the essential conditions of life—chemical material, and physical force. Why, then, does not life exist? Because, it may be argued, life radically depends, not on physical conditions, but on a peculiar vital principle, entirely distinct from any physical power.

This objection is more apparent than real; for the vital force, seeing the difficulty of drawing any clear line of separation between the higher chemical and lower vital processes, partakes, in all probability, of the same essential nature, and is a correlative of the properly so-called physical powers.

Planetary organisms, owing to the diverse conditions under which they exist, may certainly be very different from terrestrial. They may have arrived at a state of immense intellectual development; or be represented by creatures of even a more degraded type than that of our polypus or anemone; or what, perhaps, is more probable, considering the infinite variety of organized forms peopling the earth, may partake of a nature so entirely unlike that of terrestrial existences, as not to admit of comparison with any form of life with which we are acquainted. Still, that vital organization of some kind does exist on the planets, I think highly probable; but whether science will ever arrive at such a state of perfection as to investigate the character of these planetary beings, is a question which, with our present partial knowledge, it would be morally impossible to decide. J. WILLCOCKS.
London.

REASONING POWER OF ANIMALS.

Your correspondent "R. B. W." wishes to show that I have fallen into a "palpable error" by stating that he had "contradicted his previous opinion of this controversy." In order to show the readers of the N. N. B., as well as your correspondent, that the "error" is on his side, and not on mine, I refer them to the March number of the N. N. B. On page 86, and at the thirteenth and fourteenth lines from the bottom of the left hand column, they will read *one* of R. B. W.'s opinions concerning reason in animals. It runs thus—"Although I stated that we observe reason in the actions of dogs, I said also that we observe it quite as clearly in plants." It is the first clause in this sentence that I am about to speak of, the latter will be mentioned presently. We have here a genuine admission that reason is observed in the actions of dogs; hence I conclude, as my colleague "C." very correctly observed, that "if dogs exhibit reason in their actions, I presume we are right in supposing reason to exist in dogs—and there the matter ends." But Mr. "R. B. W." had declared plainly, some short time previously, and in his last paper also, his firm conviction that *man possessed reason exclusively*, and in order to strengthen his assertion, quoted Wesley!

This, then, is the contradiction that I referred to in my paper, and I think that all impartial readers will understand that *my* remark was naturally one of surprise at so sudden an alteration of opinion. With regard to your correspondent's remarks upon plants reasoning, I have little to say, and I cannot really see much difference between the two statements, "animals and plants reason," and "reason is observed in the actions of animals and plants;" for in the former we have a very positive assertion, and in the latter a sentence with exactly the same meaning, but expressed a little differently. It is a matter of course, that if reason be observed in the actions of an animal, consequently we are justified in saying that it reasons.

Your correspondent in his last article says that "Veritas" will perceive that I do not wish to place the vegetable or animal world above man," &c. If Mr. "R. B. W." had recollected what he wrote in the March number, he surely would not have informed me that I had not duly considered the subject: for he there stated that we observe *much sounder* reasoning in some animals and plants than in *many human beings*.

It was this rash statement that called forth my remark, which Mr. "R. B. W." now impugns. In short, it is one of two things, either your correspondent *has* contradicted himself, or he has rendered his paper so ambiguous that it is unintelligible. For it is self-evident, that if we observe sounder reasoning in animals and plants than in some men, surely we may say, with equal propriety, that those creatures rank above those people. At least, it seems so to me, and until "R. B. W." satisfactorily explains its meaning, I must still adhere to my original construction of it.

Your correspondent appears not to understand what I said about "irritable tissues." Many of the tissues composing certain vegetables are capable of expanding and contracting. Barberry and Dionæa muscipula are excellent examples. In the former plant the stamens contract suddenly and with force, even when touched by a thorn.

"R. B. W." finds fault with my definition of an animal, but he perhaps is not aware that it is correct. The only difference between an animal and a vegetable is, that in the former we find that besides the Divine influence, or "vital force," as it is sometimes called, it possesses attributes which raise it at once far above the vegetables. I firmly believe that the *life* in both kingdoms is the *same;* but while the vegetables have "vital force" sufficient to grow and flourish, animals have many gifts (if I may so term it), viz., reason, memory, thought, &c., which of course raise the one above the other.

"R. B. W." allows that animals, besides having minds, are capable of affection, and have *memory*. If your correspondent had reflected a little before passing judgment upon the anecdote of the Sexton beetle, he would at once have perceived that it was an uncommon occurrence. Although burying beetles are engaged daily in the summer time in removing small dead animals and putrid matter from the surface of the ground, yet such a peculiar circumstance as the one narrated would not happen twice in a beetle's life. It was related by the naturalist as being wonderful. So it is; and I think that every one who reads it with attention will be struck with the *evident reason* that the little creature showed. In fact, I *could* not "explain it away" without granting the beetle both foresight, forethought, and reason. I will try to show this. An irresistible instinct compels many of the Necrophaga to bury all the dead creatures that it may come across. Agreeably to this *law*, or rather cogent influence, our little friend goes under the mouse, but owing to the hard ground, it was foiled in its design. What was it to do? Instinct being but a fixed principle, and only acting in the occupations of procuring food, &c., could not possibly have anything to do with the next movements of our industrious beetle. Its seeking for softer soil, finding it, excavating it, returning to the beetle, endeavouring to push it into its grave, its failure, and therefore perception of its own incapability of accomplishing it without assistance, its deduction, intention, and lastly, success. The result would teach us, however unwilling we may be to receive it, that there was undoubtedly a train of thought passing through the beetle's mind. It is quite evident that there is a perfect syllogism in that anecdote. But in spite of your correspondent's protestations, I feel sure that in his own mind he believes the lower animals do reason, or he would never have contradicted himself as he has done.

Lastly, I will say a little more about "Reason" as an attribute, for Mr. "R. B. W." appears to think that it alone separates man from the lower animals. This I believe is the reason why the correspondents on the negative side contest the point so obstinately. But it is man's great intellectual powers that marks the difference. It is, by the way, worthy of a remark, that while your correspondent denies reason to the brutes, he allows them several of man's attributes, as memory, affection, &c. Now, I argue that if an animal has memory, it necessarily *must* think, and therefore draws conclusions; but I go no further. I still feel positive that animals reason to a *certain extent*, but of course not in the least approximating that power that it is man's privilege and happiness to enjoy. If your correspondent is satisfied with my answers to his objections, I hope that he will inform me, and not write in such an ambiguous style, for while he does so, his arguments are invalid, and we know not whether to meet him as a friend or a foe.

VERITAS.

As "Veritas" was not behindhand in coming to my assistance at a former period of our contest on this subject, I again ask your forbearance, and taking up the gauntlet in his behalf which "R. B. W." threw down in your last impression, I venture to criticise the clauses of "R. B. W.'s" note, beginning with the last, and taking them backwards in order.

a. I confess myself again at a loss to fathom the depths of my opponent's reasoning and scholarship. If it is true that beetles excavated the earth to get at the impaled mouse, we *must* admit that the action gave evidence of reason. Means for an end thus unquestionably employed fulfil all the requisite conditions of a rational act, however much the notion may militate against our sentiments. Am I to suppose that the beetles went to work blindly, being unable to resist the force of "instinct or the superintending power," which was *turned on* like gas at the discretion of some higher power controlling the stop-cock? The idea seems strangely unnatural; nor can I imagine for a moment that any animal was ever compelled directly by Providence to perform such an act without divining the object or anticipating the result.

b. By what elasticity of translation does "R. B. W." paraphrase the words "breathed into his nostrils the breath of life" to mean "gave him power to act independently of every other creature, to do either right or wrong?" If "R. B. W." will refer to his Septuagint (Gen. i. 20, and ii. 7) and Greek Testament (Acts xvii. 25) he will see that the same words for "breath and life" are applied to the denizens of air and water, to the creeping things of earth, as well as to man. In fact the literal meaning of the Septuagint in the verse "Let the waters bring forth abundantly *the moving creature that hath life*" may be more faithfully rendered by "creeping things of living souls"— words which might form the basis of reasoning as unsound and delusive as our opponent's paraphrase. So "R. B. W." must abandon this outpost without further struggle, and the remainder of the paragraph depending thereon must likewise be seceded. How often must we remind ourselves that in a question of this kind, which will probably always be open to debate, one side cannot lay down such unqualified assertions as "Nothing makes man superior to other creatures but the absolute possession of reason." The very essence of our dispute is, whether man is, or is not, the sole possessor of that useful and much-coveted commodity: and it is laughable to refute us by a *petitio principii*.

c. Lord Brougham may say much, and was doubtless well qualified to say more—yet no men are infallible, and Lord Brougham being a man —— &c.; but we will not insult his lordship's memory by concluding the syllogism. So with little hesitation, and due respect for rank and learning, I maintain that *it need not follow* that "if some of the actions of inferior animals are directed by their reason, all must be." Even as the sun, which shines so brilliantly to-day, may be dimmed by clouds to-morrow, so I presume may be the case with reason. There are other motives in man at any rate which influence his actions besides reason. Do men never do anything unreasonable when angry, starving, tipsy, or in love? For aught we know, animals may at times be influenced by similar motives.

d. While staying at Geneva last winter I went into a watchmaker's shop to see some mechanical marvels. There were watches as small as a sixpence, which the jeweller confessed were not warranted proof against getting out of order. If "R. B. W." were wrecked on a savage island, would he sooner be left with Farmer Wurtzle's honest old turnip, never known to lose or gain a minute, or have to depend on one of those delicate little finniking toys for regulating his dinner-hour and bed-time? If he should prefer the former (key of course included), my unscientific parallel illustrates a fact—that the more delicate and complicated an organism the greater its liability to be deranged. In other words, it is not very surprising that man is more prone to blunder in his transactions than lower animals. For man's superior powers of reasoning admit an infinity of modifying influences which cannot be recognised by the intellect of other animals; and like our tiny watch, man's reason is far more liable to blunder than the coarser and less complicated machinery of a brute's intellect.

e. With reference to the first part of "R. B. W.'s" note, I humbly and sincerely trust there may be truth in William Bryant's lines (quoted "N. N. B.," p. 80):—

"Nay, doubt we not that under the rough rind
In the green veins of these fair growths of earth,
There dwells a nature that receives delight
From all the gentle processes of life,
And shrinks from loss of being. Dim and faint
May be the sense of pleasure and of pain,
As in our dreams; but haply real still."

In conclusion, may I express the hope that Mr. Ulidia will contribute something decisive towards settling this discussion.   C.
Oriel College, Oxford.

Now that the insects are settled, will Mr. Ulidia lend his aid in this discussion and endeavour to annihilate by his biting sarcasm the miserable attempts at logic adduced by both writers on this question, in the last number of the N. N. B.? Let Mr. Newberry advance with kind and winning words (and a whip in his pocket) towards a dog that has been caught stealing, and see whether the irritated brute will trust him; he will find that the dog will detect the hypocrisy and run away. Perhaps Mr. N will say the fear was due to consciousness of merited punishment; if so, here is conscience, so either way "I have thee on the hip." Mr. U's example of cause and effect is unfortunately chosen, for a mountain may be due neither to elevation nor depression, but to denudation. The faith of the agriculturist finds an exact parallel in the agricultural ant of Texas, which sows and reaps a particular sort of barley, erects cities, constructs roads, and has a regular civil and military force, goes to war, etc., and is as much civilised as many human tribes (*Science Gossip*, January, 1868). Language and reason both exist without literature in savage tribes, and as certainly do they exist in the lower animals. Whether Mr. U. believes it or not, intellectual power depends upon the brain, and the lower races of men are inferior in this respect to the Caucasian. R. B. W. in a letter of a very "circular" nature, asks "If the brutes really possess reason of the same kind as man, in what respect are they inferior?" I reply, in extent of reasoning power; the brute cannot conceive of anything not material, of any abstract ideas. I am at a loss to know what R. B. W. really thinks, for he seems to me to hold that the lower animals and vegetables both have and have not reason, and to give his support alternately to either view. Will he oblige us by being a little more explicit in the enunciation of his views, and his reasons for holding them? W. H. DALTON.

WHAT IS COAL?

Above the fine-grained sandstones and coarse conglomerates of the Devonian period, and reposing on the coralline deposits of the mountain limestone, lie a series of bituminous shales and beds of coal. Your correspondent, R. B. W. asks "Is it certainly known what this coal is?" By the tone of his letter he seems to have some doubt as to its vegetable origin, because all fossilised vegetation is not found in the form of coal. The difficulty, however, is only imaginary. First, let us consider the character of the carboniferous vegetation, and the conditions under which it existed; and then, compare it with the remains of "trees found in a petrified state," and "converted not into coal but into stone." Most of the vegetation of the coal measures was of an endogenous character; and as a rule all endogenous plants are softer and more succulent than the exogens, and consequently more likely to succumb to the action of intense heat and pressure. The gigantic forms of club-mosses, equsitums, beds of reeds, and tree-ferns, the dense foliage of the araucaria, palm trees, and other kindred forms, as well as the coarse, rank, prairie-like grasses and peat bogs, form the chief beds of coal; and when we consider that not one forest or jungle merely, but forest after forest of these succulent plants sprang up and decayed, each one as it died promoting the growth of its successor, and considering too that this process was carried on for ages past human calculation, we cannot be surprised that we should now find such beds of mineralised vegetation as those of the coal period. Again, the conditions and climate of this period were such as to produce such a result. Botanists tell us that carbon forms the chief nourishment of plants. Now in the carboniferous strata we have evidence of an atmosphere highly charged with carbon, added to which the waters contained an excess of carbonate of lime in solution. Thus we see that the character of the plants, as well as the condition and climate, tended to produce such a deposit as that we find in the shape of coal. But this was not all; had the great drama stopped here we should still have been without the treasures of "black diamonds" with which our land is so highly favoured. Again, the land disappears beneath the surging waters, and deposits of sand and limestone are found upon it, until in the lapse of ages, what with pressure combined with intense heat from beneath, the beds of decayed vegetable matter became mineralised and formed into coal. The evidences that coal is fossilised vegetation are too numerous to admit of a doubt. The lignite beds of the oolite, and the peat bogs of the later tertiary and alluvial foundations are but coal beds in different stages of development. A short time ago coal, as pure as that of the carboniferous period, was found in the chalk beds of Kent. But then says R. B. W., "How do we account for the trees converted into stone, not coal." One cause may be, that the harder and more woody trees, existing under less favourable conditions, sometimes became partially crystallised before they had had time to become thoroughly decayed. Often we find that those trees or plants which appear to be converted into stone are only coated by a mineral deposit, which afterwards becomes crystallised; and such plants as stigmaria and sigillaria, occurring largely in the coal beds, are generally coated in this manner, and their hollow, reed-like stalks filled up with mineral matter. An example of this deposition may be witnessed in the petrifying wells of Derbyshire, or indeed may be artificially produced in the laboratory. Take a vessel containing water, in which a block of limestone has been placed, and having bored a small hole in the bottom, fix a sponge in it so as to allow the water to flow out drop by drop; you will find that any object you may place under it will receive a coating of carbonate of lime. If R. B. W. requires more definite and certain evidence of the vegetable origin of coal, let him collect a quantity of dead leaves, moss, and other partly decayed vegetation, and compress it as closely as possible between two layers of clay, then subject it to heavy pressure accompanied by a medium intensity of heat for a few weeks, and he will not only have a seam of coal of his own production, but will have an illustration of the natural process by which the coal beds are formed. W. NEWBERRY.

There is not the least doubt that coal has been formed from the remains of vast forests, chiefly composed of gigantic tree ferns, club mosses, and "horsetails," submerged by the sea, or by large rivers, and subjected to great pressure under the earth. The difficulty mentioned by R. B. W., that some trees are found turned into stone instead of coal, may be explained thus: these petrified trees are generally found upright, or nearly so, and their roots almost always terminate in or under a bed of coal. Now it is found that the soft parts of the trees are most easily converted into coal, such as the leaves, bark, and small branches. Therefore, when the forest was submerged, the soft, peaty mass of accumulated leaves and branches of which the soil was composed, and the soft parts of the standing trees, were converted into coal; while the hard trunks resisted longer the action of the water, and gave time for the slower accumulation of stony matter in their interior. In proof of this it is found that the bark of all the petrified trees appears as a coating of friable coal, which crumbles away on being touched. In a wood near here, I have been able to thrust a walking stick two or three feet down into the peaty soil, which would form a good bed of coal if laid under water, and then buried under an accumulation of sediment. GULIELMUS.

COAL.—If a tree in a fresh condition be buried in clayey soil, and that soil be subsequently, by the

weight of superincumbent beds, compressed into stone, the tree would become coal in process of time; if, however, it be buried in sand which permits the percolation of water, it decays and passes off as carbonic acid, &c., being replaced, if the percolating water be charged with lime, silica, or iron, by mineral matter, atom for atom. It often happens that the bark (of coal measure tree-ferns) remains as coal, whilst the trunk is converted into sandstone of a different colour from that enveloping the whole; this may be accounted for by supposing a hollow tree, buried in situ in sand, and afterwards filled from above, with sand of a different colour. If rotten wood be soaked in ferruginous or calcareous water and then dried, and after two or three repetitions of this treatment be heated to expel the remaining organic matter, the structure will be found to be assumed by the mineral matter. Sulphate of iron, "green vitriol," is the best for the purpose. W. H. DALTON.
Malham, Skipton.

DO INSECTS FEEL PAIN?

It appears to me that this question has at length resolved itself into the following conclusion, "that all insects do feel pain in some proportion or intensity yet to be determined"; and I would suggest the following theory. Granting that all animate nature does feel pain, and taking man as the most elaborately formed specimen of sensibility, or appreciation of the most minute pain, as the one extreme; and the zoophytes, which even will reproduce their kind from the mangled atoms of one of themselves, and therefore representing an almost entire insensibility to pain or feeling, or the other extreme; we have therefore two extremes, between which, it is manifestly fair to suppose, ranges sensibility in its various degrees, differing in intensity according as the subject occupies either a high or low position in the scale of animated creation. So, I take it that insects do feel pain though but in a small proportion; and as a proof of this it must strike all your readers who have any knowledge of entomology that the appreciation of pain or its effect on the nervous system of some of the Lepidoptera, as V. Io, or Urticæ, which in common with the ordinary home fly very frequently hybernate, and even after our severest winters are to be seen again resuming their little life of endless activity, when the rays and warmth of the sun have gained sufficient influence to call them forth from the nooks and crannies which have served them as snug winter homes. Now from this I argue that these insects have an extremely dull or insensible nervous organisation, or else the effect of the cold would be to kill them. Another thing which has occurred to my mind during this question is, "Whether the pain which is felt by insects is not universal, but local;" that is, I mean in one part of their body only—that part which is affected. As there exists in insects no one centre of nervous organs to and from which all sensations of feeling must go and come, but a number of small bunches which might be called, if it be lawful to coin a word, "brainlets," I think that perhaps the pain is felt only in the nearest centre or else distributed over the whole, so that in the equal distribution the intensity of the shock must be much lessened, if not indeed altogether lost. But I will not, Sir, take up more of your valuable space, but hope that these two points may be examined by some others of your subscribers, so that we may arrive at some just conclusion.
J. A. FOWLER.

I certainly expected that after Mr. Ulidia's formidable attack upon my article that he was about really to drive my arguments "as chaff before a mighty tempest," or that he would at all events attempt to do so. But I was much surprized upon finding that he merely referred me to Mr. Dalton's letter, and I really cannot find anything much in that gentleman's May effusion which has to do with my paper. He certainly there comes over to the affirmative side (although he moderates his opinions in the June number), but from an argument, of which I myself cannot see the validity, until it can be proved that what are supposed to be "social penalties among the ants" are really so. Mr. Ulidia says that "*Ernest Balfour* Bax" (which allow me to say is *Belfort*) "lies twelve months in reserve," &c., and he seems to blame me for so doing. I, myself, must say that I think it was nothing more than judicious caution on my part to avoid entering the field with such formidable antagonists as Messrs. Ulidia, Buttemer, and Co., until I saw the direction the arguments of the affirmative side took; but finding that hardly any of them were at all valid, and *none* of them were convincing, I therefore wished to state my arguments for the negative side, and also to try and refute some of those of my opponents. Mr. Ulidia seems to think that if insects feel pleasure, that they therefore feel pain. Now in the first place, it is not proved that they do feel pleasure at all; and in the second place, Mr. Ulidia does not state whether he means animal or intellectual pleasure: either way I do not see how Mr. Ulidia makes pleasure to have anything to do with bodily pain, such as a cut, or an undue degree of pressure; also how does your correspondent argue from the fact that insects have disease and death, that they also feel pain; for plants grow sickly and die, and yet he would not wish to intimate that they feel pain, I presume. Mr. Ulidia also says that because insects feel hunger, that they therefore feel pain; but how does he prove that they do hunger, for butterflies, moths, and many other insects eat hardly anything after they have arrived at their perfect state; it is only as larvæ that they feed, and certainly in that state they do not show any signs of pain when deprived of food. Lastly, allow me to suggest that if Mr. Ulidia would moderate the number of his "quotations from poetical and theological authors," and (to use his own favourite expression) "would come out and help us" more fully, that it would be of great advantage to this controversy and to science generally. ERNEST BELFORT BAX.

As this has been a question of more than ordinary interest, and seems now likely soon to terminate, I should like, before its conclusion, to say a few words on the subject. In the first place, I hold it an absurdity to suppose that any creature possessing life and animation should not possess also a nervous system; but that all insects possess it in an equal degree I deny. My opinion is this:—The greater power insects have of self-defence, and the less they are exposed to danger, the greater amount of nervous system are they endowed with. Does not this coincide with the wondrous disposition of Providence which in the world of nature we are constantly experiencing? Mr. Bax mentions in proof of the non-pain feeling theory the fact of a wasp "endeavouring to bite after having its head severed from its body." May not the working of its jaws have been that agonised movement which invariably accompanies intense pain? I say "yes." Thus I draw my inference. The wasp is an insect which is exposed to few dangers, and has ample means of self-defence; consequently is more acutely sensible to pain than those insects which are more exposed. That the movement of its jaws is not an attempt to bite is proved by a corresponding motion of the legs; it cannot be in this case an endeavour to escape: there is only another cause for it, viz., the writhing of agony. The fact of a moth pinned to a tree remaining quietly in its place until its usual time for evening exercise goes on to prove my theory. The moth is exposed to many dangers, and has no means of defence beyond that of flight (and what avails this against the wing and beak of the swallow and fern-owl), therefore has little susceptibility to pain. Mr. Waters also mentions the fact of a moth following up the bent of its inclinations and ideas of pleasure with a pin through its body! Does this or does it not uphold me? To save time I shall venture to anticipate a question from your correspondent, viz., what do you say (Mr. J. F. S.) to the fact of a wasp feasting on syrup after having its abdomen taken away? To this I reply by other queries: do the nerves extend to the abdomen, or if so, may not the nerves have been deadened by the operation the bee had passed through, and upon their resuming vitality the insect died of pain, combined with the loss of an important organ.

J. F. SUTTON.

EXTINCTION OF SPECIES.

In last month's issue Mr. W. Johnston, of Southampton, addresses me with regard to the best way of obtaining pupæ of the extinct Antiopa. I wrote a letter to Mr. J., but had it returned by the Post-office. I now take again the liberty to send you a few lines for insertion in your valued paper. As I advised before, it would be necessary to start a society with subscriptions; and for money, I think, you will find plenty country people in Germany to collect certain species of butterflies, cocoons, crysalisses, caterpillars and all. I am not sufficiently acquainted with German or Continental Lepidopteræ, but am to leave here on the 24th of June to settle in Stuttgart. If Mr. W. Johnston will move in the matter, I shall be glad to help him, and I think that the best way would be to import the caterpillars by post, which takes only forty-eight hours, to London. As to the possibility of introducing V. Antiopa, I have not the least doubt. All depends upon the management; and if eggs, caterpillars, &c., are set free, this ought not to be done in one locality, but different parts of the country. V. Antiopa is an essentially wood-loving insect, likes underbrush and outskirts of forests. I think the Isle of Wight, Bath, &c., would be excellent places. As to the winter season, I may add that the winters in America are much severer than here—besides, V. A. has two broods a year. One comes out in America in April, as soon as the sun is warm enough; another brood appears in September, and until severe frost sets in, I have seen and caught them. Of course, no attempt of setting the insect or caterpillars free ought to be made except you can command several thousand of the latter. These ought to be distributed among such members who are faithful to the cause and are sure to take care of them, and as the caterpillar of V. A. lives on food which is abundantly obtained in Great Britain, there can be no doubt of success. Only no half measures. A very large per centage will for certain go to destruction through a number of causes, among which the collector will be one. If you had a thousand good caterpillars turn to crysalisses, you might have a good chance of seeing the perfect insect pair and let them start on their errand to distribute their eggs. This is my opinion as a stranger, and I shall be happy to hear others give their experience.

WOLDEMAR GEFFCKEN

Mr. Marsden, in reply to my advice to plant the Camberwell Beauty again in this country, thinks that the experience has been tried with Machaon, but in vain. I am of opinion that the attempt to plant the insect has been executed with too little care. The large number of pupæ or imagos set free does not ensure success.

First of all is the question, what and where is the best locality for this insect, and what may be the reason of the total destruction of the original large number of these butterflies (V. Antiopa). My opinion is that one reason may be found in the heavy smoky air in the neighbourhood of London, where the insect used to roam some sixty years ago. At that period the number of factories, railroads, etc., which now crowd every part, were next to nothing. Such localities ought not to be tried.

Next comes the question, did the gentleman who tried the experiment set fifty, one hundred, or two hundred insects free at one time? I doubt it. From my own experience I know how difficult it is to get even in twenty pupæ one pair out at a time, and how else can anybody expect success? Pairs at the very least ought to be set free. If the matter is not taken in hand by a regular breeder, and tried season after season, and in vast numbers, of course failure only is the end of the trouble. Collect two hundred pupæ, and you are sure that only ten in a hundred is good for anything: this would be twenty. Now tell me if you have tried it, how many will come out at one time, and how many pairs, and then calculate the smallness or nothingness of the attempt. That the trial with Machaon did not succeed is certainly no reason to give up Antiopa nor to leave Machaon, or others out of the question. Let somebody start an Acclimatisation Society with subscriptions, put the trial in the hands of men who understand, and you will see success.

As for the horror you depict against introduction of foreigners, I must candidly confess I cannot see it. You have other foreigners among the Lepidoptera, and do not object to them. Why this exclusiveness? Is Great Britain a Continent or only a part of Europe? Has Great Britain any particular, beautiful, or rare specimens which are not to be found on the Continent, or are you losing only the beauties which you once had in common with other countries?

Of course I do not wish to persuade anybody's fancy to keep aloof from collecting insects on British soil, which he otherwise can only obtain by purchase; but I think that Great Britain, being a less favoured country as to collecting butterflies than the Continent, might well afford herself the pleasure to plant as many fine Lepidoptera on her soil as possible. The very destructive kinds are abundantly represented; the rare ones cannot possibly do much more harm, if this question should be taken into account by some frightened persons.

Taking everything into account, it remains still an open question whether anybody wishes to keep singularly British butterflies and moths for himself, or have the pleasure to collect others with his own hands. As for representing an importation as genuine British, depends on the veracity of the owner. I for one would feel as if I cheated myself, if I let anybody suppose I did possess what was not true. But if certain Lepidoptera are once planted here with success, I suppose after a few years you may take out objectionable specimens from among your collection and put British subjects in their places. Call them then descendants of foreigners, as we all are more or less in whatever country we may be born. As most of British collectors will have no chance to collect on the Continent, and yet are Europeans by birth, I think my suggestions are not quite so small as "Mr. Herbert Marsden, Secretary, Lepidopterists' Exchange Club" thinks; and I hope soon to see his name mentioned as "Secretary of Lepidoptera Acclimatisation Society," thus affording the British collectors a large field for researches.

Upper Norwood. W. G.

ACHERONTIA ATROPOS, OR DEATH'S HEAD HAWK MOTH.—As your correspondent Mr. W. Johnston, at page 191, seeks information respecting the above-named moth, if space will permit, I beg to offer the following as the result of my experience in rearing or breeding this species. Whether Atropos is considered by entomologists generally as double-brooded, I am not at present aware; but I have procured the larva quite full grown as early as July in some years, and in others as late as the first week in October. I would have it distinctly understood that it has never occurred with me in the larva state in both the months named during one and the same season. I have procured them in July and August one year, and in another year I have seen no full grown larva till September or the early part of October. With regard to their appearance in the winged, or perfect state, I have found that the moths from the larva procured in July and August generally made their appearance from the chrysalis in October of the same year, whilst those procured as late as September seldom, if ever, emerged from the chrysalis state till the middle of July of the following year. It has been asserted that this insect emits a peculiar plaintive note in the larva and pupa state, as well as in the perfect, or moth state; but although I have handled upwards of twenty from time to time, in all the various changes, yet I have failed to obtain a sound from any but those in their winged and perfect state of existence. C. W . . D.

320, Strand.

TORTOISE.—In the April number of the N. N. B. some inquiries were made concerning the food and mode of keeping the tortoise, and as nobody appears to have given any answer to them, I will endeavour to do so in a few words. A few years ago I happened to become possessed of one of these animals, and it was very curious to notice its habits. About the middle of November it burrowed underground, and did not appear again till the middle of the following April. During the remainder of the spring it scarcely touched any food, which consisted of dandelions, lettuces, sow thistles, and some other milky plants; but as soon as the summer came it began to eat voraciously. As the autumn advanced its appetite decreased in avidity, and for the last eight weeks it scarcely touched anything at all. What seemed most wonderful was the timidity it showed when a shower of rain happened to fall. It used to scuttle away as fast as possible into some corner where the rain did not penetrate. During the spring and summer it used to sleep about sixteen hours a day. In the beginning of June it showed an unusual amount of exertion, and was up by five in the morning, traversing the garden, and examining every fence and gate. This happened probably from an amorous cause. It showed remarkable sagacity in recognising those who had been kind to it. It was always allowed to run free in the garden, and used to find its own food. If these few words prove at all useful to "A. R. L.," it will be very gratifying to M. E. E.

MOTH COURTSHIP.—I can only corroborate Mr. Laddiman's statement in your May number. Many a night I used to stay up till twelve o'clock when I lived in the United States, and collected the males attracted by the female Cecropia and Polyphemus. I had no opportunity to try the experiment with other moths, but am told by other collectors that they made their principal collections this way, it being besides the easiest opportunity for pairing and obtaining good eggs. My house and garden lay less favourable, being too near the sea, yet I caught every night from nine to fourteen large moths measuring from 4 to 6½ inches from tip to tip; and my cat used to kill many during the night, being undoubtedly attracted by the flutter of the animals. If I kept my window open and had a female exposed in the room, the males were sure to enter; and my friend told me that at one time in the heat of the summer, having all the windows open and several female Cecropias about the house, the males came in such swarms that he killed between sixty and seventy in one evening; and finally had to shut himself up in his house to avoid further destruction. So much for moth courtship! These large moths have a peculiar, but not unpleasant scent, which undoubtedly attracts the males. Yet these beautiful insects are little known, notwithstanding their abundance. I myself lived sixteen years in the United States, and fifteen of these in the country, without seeing any at all. Not until my time allowed me to pursue again entomological studies did I become aware of the existence of these large and many other moths. W. G.

CAUTION TO BIRDS'-NESTERS.—Whilst chatting to a countryman one day, I chanced to notice two black spots on his thumb, and made the remark, "One would think you had been bitten by a large snake." He then related the following anecdote: "When I was a boy, and strolling through the woods hunting for birds' eggs, I discovered a crow's nest high up in an oak tree, and climbing to it, I was just able to put my hand in to take the eggs, when something gave me a dreadful bite. I pulled back my arm, but the enemy, a large fitch, kept his hold on my thumb, with his teeth to the bone. I grasped the brute by the throat and scrambled down the tree till I got to a fork where I could rest my back, when I beat the head of the stinking creature against the tree until he was dead." I never forgot to act upon his experience, and became doubly cautious, when a lady related to me how one day she found a wren's nest, and inserted her finger to ascertain what was in it. Not liking the feel of the contents, she had scarcely withdrawn her hand when an adder came gliding out of the mossy ball, which he had made a bed of, after having probably devoured the young wrens.

P.S.—Why fill your columns with such abstruse subjects? Instinct v. Reason; Measurement of Pain; Squaring the Circle; or Perpetual Motion, we may hammer away at to threescore and ten,

"Casting buckets into empty wells
And growing old in drawing nothing up."

If every one of your subscribers would but furnish the facts of interest from his own note book, how much more charming than such dry-as-dust speculations.
Camberwell. J. ROWE.

IS THE WHALE A FISH?—On this question I think your correspondent John Landels is wrong to argue in favour of the popular error that the whale is a fish. The point is, Are we to lower the scientific standard to the popular level, by putting such a loose construction on the word fish, or are we to endeavour to raise the popular standard by shewing what a fish really is, and that a whale is merely a mammal, adapted for continual life in the water? I believe the reason why people call all inhabitants of the water fishes, is because they are not familiar with any other name for them; whereas if they were shewn the difference between a fish, a crustacean, a mollusc, and a mammal, they would never think of calling them by the same name merely because they all live in the water. We might as well call bats and insects birds because they fly in the air. The difference between popular and scientific knowledge ought to be one of degree only, not of kind; and therefore I think the proposal of Mr. Landels to find another scientfiic name for fishes a step in the wrong direction. Rather keep the popular name, but shew the people what it really means, and make them familiar with the terms mollusca, crustacea, etc., to be applied to other aquatic animals. I give your correspondent credit for good intentions, but I hope he will see that he is going backwards instead of forwards. GULIELMUS.

DOMESTIC DUCK.—A Duck belonging to a friend of mine was given eight eggs to hatch. A few days afterwards another duck was observed always sitting close beside it on the same nest. Nothing particular was thought of it for a while, but at last curiosity was aroused and the nest examined, when it was found to contain no less than twenty one eggs. Which of the ducks the after-laying belonged to is still a mystery, for, unfortunately, within a day or two of the discovery, this nest (together with several others containing sitting birds) was robbed of its eggs by some wandering vagrant. In the interests of Natural History one cannot but regret this untimely ending to the incubation of these "Siamese" mothers; it would have been so exceedingly curious to see to which of them the young would take, or whether, each having taken an equal share in the hatching, they would divide the young equally between them. This very curious circumstance occurred at Bourne Hall, near Fleetwood, during last month. A. H. ROWORTH.
Manchester, June 13th.

THE STING OF NETTLES.—I think that the stinging propensities of nettles act very differently on some of your correspondents and on myself. A short time since, seeing a large bed of nettles on a sheltered hedge-bank, I tried experiments with some of the healthiest and strongest I could find, drawing one lightly across my hand without feeling any pain, then striking it smartly with just the same result. I at once concluded that this was one of the red dead nettles (Lamium purpureum), which have not the venomous power of stinging. However, I made use of another, the "great nettle" (Urtica disica), first seizing it with a firm grasp receiving no pain whatever, and then drawing it gently over my hand receiving a smart sensation for my trouble. From experience, therefore, I quite agree with the following lines:—

"Soft and gently press a nettle,
It will sting you for your pains,
Seize it with a hand of metal,
And it soft as silk remains."

Gravesend, June 11th. G. O. HOWELL.

AVIARY.—In answer to J. D. S. W., I will give a description of my own aviary. It is 22ft. long by 11ft. wide, and 9 ft. high, and made of 22 pieces, 18 of these, which form the sides, are 9ft. long, and 3ft. 8in. wide, the remaining 4, which form part of the top, are 11ft. long, and 3ft. 8in. wide; the remainder of the top is a wooden roof, which occupies the width of 2 pieces, viz.: 7ft. 4in. The 18 side pieces are wooden frames, with a support across the middle, covered with fine wire netting; the top pieces are the same without any support across the centre. Were I to have another made, I should have the sides under the roof boarded as it is I have been obliged to have shutters made to protect the birds from the weather.

I have about 60 birds in this, mostly of the finch tribe, they do well, and appear very contented. The advantage of having it in so many pieces, is, that it can be easily removed.   J. R. B.
Southgate, N.

CUCKOO'S EGG.—When at Chiselhurst, Kent, on the 18th of May last, I saw a cuckoo shot by Mr. Howlett, gamekeeper to Lord Sydney, which, being a clean shot bird, came into my possession. On skinning it the next day I noticed a swelling in the body, and working carefully, succeeded in taking out uninjured a perfectly formed egg, which, with the bird, is now in my collection. I find the cuckoo's egg very difficult to properly authenticate, but in this case there is fortunately no doubt. Another bird was flying in company, possibly the male, and most likely the shot bird was at the time in search of a nest to deposit her egg.   A. M. B.

Allow me to inform Mr. W. Newberry that although I do not vouch for the statement that dogs were ever taught to play at chess and dominoes, yet the work from which I quoted the fact, is I believe an authentic one in many respects; but as the book was lent to me, and is now returned, I can neither quote the fact word for word, nor can I give the name of the publisher, but I believe that the author of it has since gone out as naturalist to the "Palestine Exploration Expedition." I hope that this will in some way satisfy Mr. W. Newberry.   ERNEST BELFORT BAX.

V. IO AND A. ATROPOS.—In last month's number of the N. N. B., mention is made by W. W. Ingall of having seen a specimen of Vinessa Io on the 22nd April last. If W. W. I. will look in Stainton's "Manual of Butterflies and Moths," he will see that Peacock Butterflies that have hybernated are to be found even in March. W. Johnston too cannot have consulted the above mentioned work, or he would have seen that A. Atropos (Death's Head) is found in the perfect state from August to October, but the occurrence that he mentions is an uncommon one.
   W. E.

GRAPTA C. ALBUM.—This butterfly is very rarely found in the Eastern, Metropolitan, and South Eastern English Counties, and never in Scotland. It is moderately common at Worcester and York, and is also found at the Lakes, Burton-on-Trent, Peterborough, and near Newport Pagnell. The comma has quite disappeared from the neighbourhood of London, where, according to some writers and living entomologists it was very abundant. Last season a good many specimens of this butterfly were taken in the neighbourhood of Bristol.   W. E.

THE CUCKOO.—Your Halstead correspondent "B" asks in the June number of the "N. N. B." whether it is usual for the cuckoo to sing during the night. I think it is not unusual, for they are heard very frequently, at intervals during the night, in the neighbourhood of Gravesend. On the 3rd of June, at nearly 10 o'clock, p.m., several were heard by myself and others, near the village of Chalk, a short distance from Gravesend.   G. O. HOWELL.
Gravesend, June 7th.

BOMBYX QUERCUS.—I should feel greatly obliged if any of the readers of the N. N. B. could inform me the reason why the above named moth is called the Oak Eggar, and in what way it is connected with the oak; I have always found the larvæ on the whitethorn, and have never heard of its having been found on the oak. Is it because the cocoon is shaped somewhat like an acorn?   R. LADDIMAN.
St. Augustine's, Norwich.

SUN AND MOON LARGER AT RISING AND SETTING.—If G. O. Howell will refer to Dr. Brewer's "Guide to Science," p. 395, he will find the question he asks, also the following answer: "the appearance is an illusion, in consequence of terrestrial objects being placed in close comparison with them at one time and not at the other."   YORICK.

CATERPILLARS.—Can any of your readers inform me how, when I have found some of these insects, to find out of what lepidopterum they are the larvæ? I should also feel much obliged if some one will recommend a good and cheap work on British Beetles (Coleoptera), cost say two or three shillings. W. E.

I beg to inform Mr. G. O. Howell, that the reason the sun appears larger when rising and setting than at other times, is owing to the refraction of its rays, which when it rises or sets, fall upon our eyes at a greater angle than they do when it is situated more vertically or obliquely with regard to us.
   ERNEST BELFORT BAX.

BEETLES.—Will any reader of the N. N. B. kindly inform me of a new work on beetles, if possible with coloured plates, and state the price?   B. B. NOEL.

CORRECTION.—In my note of 7th May last about Peacock Butterflies, my name was spelt wrong. It should be Ingall not Jugall. By kindly correcting this you will greatly oblige
June 10th.   WHATELY W. INGALL.

QUERY.—Could you or any of your correspondents inform me of some simple method of preventing the teeth from falling out of dried skulls?   C. R. M.

I shall feel much obliged if you will inform me what the British butterflies feed on in their perfect state.   A. M. B.

FOOD OF LIZARDS.—Can any of the readers of the N. N. B. give me some information about the habits of the lizard, the food it eats, &c.   T. SMITH.
Iping House, Sussex.

PEACOCK BUTTERFLY.—A correspondent mentions having seen a peacock butterfly on the 22nd of April. I saw one much earlier—on the 9th.   T SMITH.
Iping House, Sussex.

LA PLANCHETTE.—Will "C." kindly inform me where "La Planchette" may be obtained, and how much her wonderful ladyship costs?   T. SMITH.
Iping House, Sussex.

CHRYLISADES.—Will some of the readers of the N. N. B. tell me the best method for keeping chrysalides.   H. F. P.

OUR WADING BIRDS.
No. I.—THE REDSHANK.
BY ALEXANDER CLARK KENNEDY.

THIS handsome wader, the Redshank, so termed from the rufous colour of its legs and feet, whose habits and life history we are now about to consider, is, although partially local, generally distributed over the sea-board counties of Great Britain. It appears to occur in most parts of Scotland, and is particularly numerous in Shetland; and is found more or less abundantly in many of the northern parts of England. We have paid a visit to one of its breeding haunts in Northumberland many miles from the sea, but this is unusual, as it generally selects fens or water-meadows not far from the coast, or some large river.

In the celebrated fens of Lincoln and Cambridgeshire, which a century ago harboured during the summer months many a bird which now never visits us, and afforded shelter to the wildfowl in winter, and such sport to the duck-shooter as never can be obtained again, the redshank still manages to hold his own, although species after species have been totally exterminated; and Montague, were he alive now, certainly would not recognise the spots he visited where men lived by the trade of snaring Ruffs and Reeves, and might well say, with the poet—

"Tempora mutantur, et nos mutamur in illis."

The redshank breeds in Kent and Norfolk, and in the fens of Essex, and many other counties, too numerous to mention, which offer attractions to the wading birds. It has been in the county of Suffolk, however, that we have had the best opportunities of observing the habits of this interesting species, not only in the breeding season, but at all times of the year.

In the early part of the spring but few redshanks are to be seen, and it is not until the end of March or beginning of April that the first large flocks arrive at their summer quarters, which consist merely of extensive marshes by the side of a large tidal river, at the distance of about five miles from the sea coast. We are now speaking of the particular breeding ground with which we are best acquainted, but all of their haunts are much alike; with this difference, that some are many miles inland, others at a moderate distance from the sea, and others again are within a few yards of the ocean itself. The migrations of this species are carried on chiefly at night, when they fly in small parties, consisting of three or four members, and seldom more. When they first reach their breeding ground of the previous year, they become very restless, continually fly round and round one after another, uttering all the time their curious shrill note "twee-twee," which is repeated faster and faster until it is emitted from the throat of the bird as quickly as is possible for it to be, and lengthens into a single note, which the bird generally utters while in the act of hovering, previous to alighting on the ground. After getting accustomed to their old haunts, which they seem to do in about a week, the redshanks pair, and now begins the laborious undertaking of nidification.

In the case of this bird, in common with many of the waders, the nest is a mere nothing, being composed of the stalks of grass or reeds stamped down, so as to form a hollow to receive the eggs. Sometimes these are deposited on the wet mud without any apology for a nest; but in this case they are usually protected from being washed away by the tide, which daily covers the entire marshes by having the benefit of a rough kind of canopy of reeds woven together by the old bird. We have often wondered why the eggs do not get bad from their daily bath, but in no case have we seen an addled egg; and it is also a curious thing that many of the young ones do not meet a watery grave, but we believe that such a fate is very unusual. The eggs are always four in number, and when the female commences to sit, she arranges them with their smaller ends pointing to the centre of the nest: they are not unlike those of the common peewit or green plover, but are rather smaller and generally more pointed; they are browner than the eggs of the plover, and have not so much olive in their colouring and are spotted and blotched with brownish-black; but they differ very much in general markings, and two are scarcely ever found alike. It is a noticeable fact that the eggs of almost all water birds differ far more than those of land birds. The redshank is easily tamed, and does good service in a garden. The young of this species are very quaint little fellows, and are able to run as soon as they leave the egg, but we have noticed that they do not endeavour to seek safety by this means, but merely crouch down on the ground and try to become as small as possible, and can scarcely be compelled to quit this position even by the close proximity of a dog's nose. It is next to impossible to find these little fellows without a good retriever or setter, as their brown coloured bodies and small persons enable them often to escape being noticed by a man when almost trodden upon. It is wonderful, too, what a capital ventriloquist a young redshank is; for a bird within a yard of a person can make its tiny voice appear to proceed from a long distance, or first on one side, then on another, now behind you, now in front.

The eggs are laid towards the end of April or early in May, but we think that this species generally produces a second brood, as we have found fresh eggs as late as the 9th of June, and young birds had been hatched in the second week in May. At night the redshank seems to need no rest, if we may judge from the continuous choruses which are performed during the time when all men sleep. Early in the morning, as soon as the first streak of dawn appears, these birds are awake and are off to the "mud-flats" to secure their breakfast, which consists in small worms and insects, for which they probe with their long red bills deep into the ooze, sometimes advancing into the water knee-deep, and allowing the little ripples of the advancing tide to besprinkle the lower parts of their plumage. After their meals they enjoy a bath vastly, and run backwards and forwards, hither and thither in the mimic waves, splashing the water about, and apparently playing one with another like children. We must confess that we have often shot this pretty wader, both for a natural history collection and in order to ascertain the nature of its food; a wounded bird will swim well and rapidly, but never dives; nor will the redshank take the water from choice, but if winged, the art of swimming sometimes enables it to escape its pursuers. The flight of this bird is very graceful, and it is really a lovely sight to see several of them hovering in mid-air previously to touching the ground, when they show the white parts of the wings to perfection; and many a hot summer's afternoon have we passed pleasantly, while concealed among the rough-tangled grass which grows on the dilapidated old banks of the Suffolk river, and watched the redshanks feeding and washing themselves, and listened with pleasure to their plaintive cries, which are varied at intervals by the lonely scream of the solitary curlew, or the hoarse croak of a venerable heron as he flaps lazily high overhead in the bright blue sky; and anon the well-known "pee-wit-a-wit" of a green plover, or the chorus of a flock of dunlins flying past, would relieve the monotony of sounds.

We could say much more of the habits of this interesting bird, but we may have wearied our readers already; so will merely add a few remarks to complete its history. It is not generally known that, in a state of nature, many of this class of birds are accustomed to perch; we have often observed a redshank on a gate post or uttering his "twee-twee" from the summit of a pollard oak or willow, and we have seen the woodcock on a tree; and the snipe and greenshank are recorded as occasionally perching; also the curlew. We must mention the great fondness felt by the redshank for its young; for when a stranger approaches the spot where its little ones are concealed, both the old birds will dash around the intruder in circles, making a deafening noise the while, and should he be accompanied by a dog, they even dare to swoop down at it. In the winter months few redshanks remain near their breeding places; but what few stragglers are left, associate together in considerable flocks, and become extremely wild and unapproachable.

The geographical distribution of a bird is usually thought a "dry" subject; so I will suppose that those who wish to find out for themselves this fact, and the various changes of plumage which this species undergoes, can refer to the works of Yarrell, Jenyns, or Gould.

There is one other species of redshank which is found in Great Britain, named the spotted redshank (*Totanus fuscus*), but this bird is far from common; and we have been informed that in its habits it much resembles the bird we have been considering—*Totanus calidris*.

No. 2.—THE CURLEW.

MANY a time and oft we can remember that, when seated, enveloped in great coats behind a river's bank or in a tiny ambuscade made of peat and concealed from view among the rank herbage which borders small pieces of water, shivering with the chill blast of winter, and trying to warm our benumbed feet under the shaggy coat of the retriever which always was our companion, we have been enlivened by the mournful cry of the curlew as he flew overhead, looming large against the pale moonlit sky; and although sometimes he may have scared away the wild fowl for which we were impatiently waiting, we will readily forgive him this, for we love to listen to the plaintive note of the long-billed bird, who if he only knew how close we were to him, would not have ventured so near our retreat.

Often, too, when taking a solitary walk over the moorland wastes of the north, where few living things are to be met with except grouse and blue hares and an occasional plover or hawk, the curlew has arrested our steps and we have sat down on the purple heather and watched with infinite pleasure his circling flight; and when tired of reconnoitering the intruder on his domains, he alights on a crag beyond the dyke, we have crept up to within twenty yards of him, and cautiously peeping through an aperture in the stones, have seen him, in company with his mate, walking hither and thither with stately tread in search of incautious insects, which his sharp eye soon detects.

By the sea shore also this bird has been one

of our familiar companions; and although he will not suffer such a near approach now as he would on the mountain side or the mud flats of a tidal river, yet he allows himself to be admired from a respectful distance; but should you advance towards him, with or without hostile intentions, you will see him open his big wings and hear his warning cry as the sea breeze carries him far out of shot above your head, and perhaps deposits him on the sand some miles away, where he may be safe from man's prying eye, and enjoy awhile the solitude he so dearly loves.

Curlew shooting is a sport much carried on upon some of the more retired coasts of England, but the species is not found in such numbers as it used to be, which indeed may be said of almost every water bird; for, as improvements in agriculture by draining and reclaiming waste lands are progressing, the poor birds suffer severely, being driven from one stronghold to another, until in a few years but few sea fowl will delight the eye and ear of those who love nature. Towards the end of the autumn and throughout the whole of the winter months, the curlews join together and form immense flocks, sometimes comprising two or three thousand individuals. While in this state they are extremely wild, and it is very hard to obtain a shot at them, although various ambushes are resorted to by fishermen and gunners, of which the most usual is to sink a barrel large enough to conceal a man, in the mud, near the spot to which the birds come to feed, and as they wheel overhead, unconscious of danger, a couple of barrels or a heavy single duck gun can do good execution. They often resort to grass and stubble-fields to feed, and we have often managed to get near a flock in a meadow while they were too engrossed with their dinners to keep a good look out; and we remember our disgust, when on a hot day in April we got ourselves well hidden in a deserted quarry within thirty yards of about the same number of curlews, and felt sure of bagging at least three or four; as we suddenly rose the whole flock flew up and made towards us, and so taken by surprise were we that both barrels missed, and the birds flew by within a few feet of our face. The food of the curlew consists of various insects, both land and water; shell fish, cockles, and particularly small crabs are its favourite delicacies; and blades of grass and berries are occasionally eaten, but we have found by dissection that the little green crabs which are so common on our coast are its most usual food. It is an energetic feeder, and is fond of splashing about in the water and washing itself; it thrusts its bill up to the base in the soft mud, and its plunges are seldom made in vain, for it seems to know by some wondrous instinct the exact spot where its food lies concealed. These birds often stand in long lines, like a company of soldiers; some on one leg in order to rest themselves, and others making use of both for support, and now and then turning their heads gravely from side to side, and one of them will sometimes leave the line and wash himself, returning again after the operation to his old position. A company of curlews will seldom allow themselves to be led into danger, but single birds may be tempted to alight near a skilful imitator of their cries; few men, however, are adapts at this art, which is, we believe, very difficult to acquire, and can only be learnt by those who are really well acquainted with birds and know their various call notes. A dog is a good assistant to the man who shoots wild birds, for by its means curlews, plovers, and others of the same species may be tempted within reach of the gun.

The curlews betake themselves—towards the end of March—from their haunts by the sea shore to the moors in the North of England and Scotland, where they breed. During this time of migration, these birds are met with at great distances inland, for they get weary with their long flights and are compelled to rest before continuing their journey. Many, however, nest in the south, and we have known them breeding in Hampshire, Wilts, Cornwall, and other counties. The nest is generally placed in heather or rough grass upon the slope of a hill, and does not give the old birds much trouble in building, for it is but a few reeds or bits of grass trodden down on the ground and surrounded by heather. In this rude nest the female lays three or four eggs, and although these are said to be always arranged with the smaller ends pointing to the common centre, we have not found it to be the rule. A nest which we found in Northumberland on the 27th of April, last year, contained four eggs, which the old bird had just left, arranged by no means well, for they seemed to point each in a different direction. They are large for the size of the bird which lays them, and are of a dark dull green tint, blotched and spotted with light and dark brown, but they vary considerably in markings. The young are funny creatures to look at—all legs and no body—and until about a fortnight old are covered with a brown soft coat, which they change after a while for their proper plumage. They run very quickly, and conceal themselves from sight in a moment if pursued; it is hard to find them without a dog, for they squeeze themselves into the smallest crevices and become invisible to the unpractised eye. The curlew, when taken young, will live well in confinement, and does the gardener good service by ridding him of many noxious grubs and insects; but it should be kept pinioned in a walled garden, or it may take it into its head to run off. This species varies much in size; the females are larger than the males, but do not differ materially from the latter in plumage. Mr. Lubbock, in his "fauna" of the county of Norfolk, speaking of the variety in size of this bird, says, " small parties of curlews of the very largest size arrive in our marshes about harvest time, and are known to gunners as the great harvest curlews—probably old females collected together after the breeding season. The difference in the size of the birds, composing two flocks feeding on the same island and not far asunder, might be seen at the distance of a hundred and fifty yards : in one party were seven very large curlews; in the other about twenty, so much smaller that a hasty conclusion might be drawn that they were in reality whimbrels; but to remove doubt, on two being shot, they proved genuine curlews." Curlews differ also to a great degree in the lengths of their bills.

This bird has ever been associated with wild scenes and lonely haunts, and is held in fear by the peasantry in some parts of England and Scotland, and much superstitious feeling has arisen on the subject. In the latter country it is called the "whoup," and this name is also given to a long-nosed goblin supposed to be peculiar to the north; Sir Walter Scott talks, in the "Black Dwarf," of "norricouz and lang-nebbit things aboot the land." Fishermen, too, have been known to refuse to start when the scream of a curlew has been heard, supposing that a storm will certainly arise.

The curlew does not take to the water unless compelled to do so, but when winged he can swim remarkably well. The weight of the curlew is from twenty to thirty ounces, and its length about twenty-four inches : a full description of its plumage may be found by reference to Yarrell or Gould, but we do not think it necessary to detail it here. Although this bird is esteemed by fishermen and poor people, its flesh has a decidedly rank and fishy flavour; but this is partly removed if it is shot on the moors or anywhere far from the sea. The scientific name of this species is *Numenius Arquata;* the first of these words means the new moon, and applies to the curlew's bill.

LIST OF BRITISH BIRDS:
By W. NEWBERRY.

CLASS I.—ACCIPITRES.
ORDER I.—RAPTRICES (PLUNDERERS).
Family I.—VULTURINÆ.
Genus I.—NEOPHRON.*

Species I.—*Neophron percnopterus* (*White Vulture*).
Migratory.
Size †: Length, 27 inches; extent of wings, 18 in.; bill, $2\frac{4}{6}$ in.
Colour: White, with end of wings dark brown.
Food: Carrion, small animals, etc.

Family II.—FALCONIDÆ.
Genus I.—BUTEO (BUZZARDS).

Species I.—*Buteo Fuscus* (*Brown Buzzard*).
Permanently resident.
Size: Length, 19 in.; extent of wings, 49 in.; bill, $1\frac{7}{12}$ in.
Colour: Brown; lower parts cream colour; breast spotted, and streaked with white.
Food: Small animals, birds, larvæ, and the larger insects.
Builds in trees in the depths of thick woods.
Lays 4 eggs, $2\frac{1}{2}$ in. $\times 1\frac{5}{8}$ in.; grey, with large brown spots.

Species II.—*Buteo Lagopus* (*Rough-legged Buzzard*).
Migratory winter visitor.
Size: Length, 21 in.; extent of wings, 51 in.; bill, $1\frac{2}{6}$ in.
Colour: Brown; head streaked with white; anterior part of the tail white.
Food: Small quadrupeds, birds, etc.

Genus II.—AQUILLA (EAGLE).
Species I.—*Aquilla Chrysætus* (*Golden Eagle*).
Permanently resident in Scotland.
Size: Length, 33 in.; extent of wings, 72 in.; bill, $2\frac{4}{6}$ in.
Colour: Yellowish brown; tail, dark brown.
Food: Hares, fawns, lambs, and all kinds of small animals.
Builds in inaccessible cliffs and mountain crags.
Lays 2 eggs, 3 in. $\times 2\frac{1}{3}$ in.; white, with brown spots.

---

* Only two individuals of this species have been seen in Britain, both of which were observed in the county of Somerset. One of them was shot, and has been described by Mr. Selby.

† In all cases the size of the bird given is that of the *male*, and the size of the egg is the *diameter* of its length and breadth.

Genus III.—HALIÆTUS (SEA EAGLE).

Species I.—*Haliætus Albicilla* (*White Tailed Eagle*).

Permanently resident in Scotland and Ireland.

Size: Length, 36 in.; extent of wings, 72 in.; bill, $3\frac{5}{12}$ in.

Colour: Dark grey; under parts greyish-brown, under part of the tail white.

Food: Fish, birds, small animals, and carrion.

Builds on rocky cliffs generally near the shore, though nests are often found in the interior.

Lays 2 eggs, 3 in. × $2\frac{1}{6}$ in.; white, with fine reddish spots.

Genus IV.—PANDION (OSPREY).

Species I.—*Pandion Haliætus* (*Fishing Osprey*).

Migratory, though often breeds in Scotland.

Size: Length, 24 in.; extent of wings, 64 in.; bill, $1\frac{5}{8}$ in.

Colour: Dark brown, approaching a bluish cast; head and neck white, streaked with brown.

Food: Exclusively fishes.

Builds in reed or rush beds on the lakes and rivers of unfrequented districts.

Lays 4 eggs, $2\frac{2}{6}$ in. × $1\frac{5}{6}$ in.; white, patched with brown.

Genus V.—PEMIS.

Species I.—*Pemis Avipora* (*Bee Hawk*).

Migratory.

Size: Length, $24\frac{1}{2}$ in.; extent of wings, 52 in.; bill, $1\frac{2}{6}$ in.

Colour: Male—brown, with dark streaks; throat and under part white, streaked with brown. Female—head bluish grey, upper parts dark brown, lower parts light brown.

Food: Chiefly honey, and the larvæ of bees, wasps, etc.

Builds in woods and secluded spots.

Lays 3 eggs, $2\frac{1}{2}$ in. × $1\frac{2}{6}$ in.; white, with large brown spots.

Genus VI.—MILVUS.

Species I.—*Milvus Regalis* (*Kite*).

Permanently resident.

Size: Length, 25 in.; extent of wings, 61 in.; bill, $1\frac{1}{2}$ in.

Colour: Male—reddish-brown, with dark streaks. Female—Greyish-white, with dark streaks.

Food: Birds, small animals, and insects.

Builds in trees, generally in thick woods.

Lays 3 eggs, $2\frac{1}{6}$ in. × $1\frac{9}{12}$ in.; white, finely spotted with brown.

Genus VII.—NAUCLERUS.

Species I.—*Nauclerus Furcatus* (*Swallow Kite*).

Migratory; only two have been killed in Britain.

Size: Length, 22 in.; extent of wings, 47 in.; bill, $1\frac{1}{6}$ in.

Colour: Back, wings, and tail black; head and lower parts white.

Food: Insects, lizards, and even snakes.

Genus VIII.—FALCO (FALCONIDÆ).

Species I.—*Falco Gyrfalco* (*Jerkin*).

Migratory.

Size: Length, 21 in.; extent of wings, 49 in.; bill, $2\frac{1}{2}$ in.

Colour: Greyish-white; under parts yellow.

Food: Small animals and birds.

Species II.—*Falco Perigrinus* (*Perigrine Falcon*).

Permanently resident.

Size: Length, $16\frac{1}{2}$ in.; extent of wings, $36\frac{1}{2}$ in.; bill, $1\frac{1}{12}$ in.

Colour: Male—dark grey, streaked and spotted with black; under parts light grey. Female—dark brown; under parts light red.

Food: Rabbits, hares, partridges, and all kinds of birds.

Builds on cliffs and mountain peaks.

Lays 4 eggs, 2 in. × $1\frac{7}{12}$ in.; red, spotted with dark red.

Species III.—*Falco Subbute* (*Hobby Falcon*).

Permanently resident, though very scarce.

Size: Length, 12 in.; extent of wings, 26 in.; bill, $\frac{9}{12}$ in.

Colour: Male—dark grey; under parts cream colour, cheeks black. Female—upper parts dark brown, lower parts yellowish-red.

Food: Insects and small birds.

Builds in trees, generally in wild desolate spots.

Lays 4 eggs, $1\frac{4}{6}$ in. × $1\frac{1}{6}$ in.; bluish, with greenish-brown patches.

Species IV.—*Falco Vespertinus* (*Red-legged Falcon*).

Migratory; according to Yarrel, only nine individuals found in Britain.

Size: Length, 12 in.; extent of wings, 24 in.; bill, $\frac{9}{12}$ in.

Colour: Male—upper parts bluish-grey, lower parts orange colour. Female—with head of yellowish-red.

Food: Small birds, insects, field-mice, etc.

Species V.—*Falco Æsalon* (*Rock Hawk*).

Permanently resident.

Size: Length, 11 in.; extent of wings, 26 in.; bill, $\tfrac{9}{12}$ in.

Colour: Male—upper parts greyish-blue, with dark bars; lower parts dark yellow. Female—Greyish-brown; lower parts orange, with dark markings.

Food: Chiefly small birds, mice, etc.

Builds amongst the high grass and heather in wild districts.

Lays 4 eggs, $1\tfrac{7}{12}$ in. × $1\tfrac{1}{6}$ in.; light red, spotted and patched with dark red.

Species VI.—*Falco Tinnuculus (Kestrel)*.
Permanently resident.
Size: Length, $13\tfrac{1}{2}$ in.; extent of wings, 25 in.; bill, $\tfrac{9}{12}$ in.

Colour: Male—bluish grey, under parts yellowish-red, tail striped black. Female—reddish-brown, with dark streaks.

Food: Field-mice, shrews, birds, and insects.

Builds in trees, often in deserted nests of other birds.

Lays 5 eggs, $1\tfrac{2}{8}$ in. × $1\tfrac{1}{4}$ in.; orange colour, patched with reddish-brown.

Genus IX.—ACCIPITER.

Species I.—*Accipiter palumbarius (Goss Hawk)*.
Very rare in Britain.
Size: Length, 20 in.; extent of wings, 43 in.; bill, $1\tfrac{1}{2}$ in.

Colour: Male—dark grey; upper part of head black, cheeks white. Female—upper parts light brown, lower parts greyish.

Food: Rabbits, hares, and smaller animals.

Species II.—*Accipiter Nisus (Sparrow Hawk)*.
Permanently resident.
Size: Length, 13 in.; extent of wings, 23 in.; bill, $\tfrac{9}{12}$ in.

Colour: Male—bluish-grey; under parts light red, barred and striped. Female—upper parts greyish-brown, lower parts light grey.

Food: Birds, and small animals.

Builds generally in trees, though sometimes on rocks or in other nests.

Lays 5 eggs, $1\tfrac{7}{12}$ in. × $1\tfrac{1}{4}$ in.; bluish, spotted and patched with brown.

Genus X.—CIRCUS (HARRIER).

Species I.—*Circus Cyaneus (Common Harrier)*.
Permanently resident.
Size: Length, $18\tfrac{1}{4}$ in.; extent of wings, $39\tfrac{1}{2}$ in.; bill, $1\tfrac{1}{12}$ in.

Colour: Male—bluish-grey. Female—brown, with orange stripes.

Food: Birds, small animals, lizards, snakes, and insects.

Builds on the ground in lonely spots.

Lays 5 eggs, $1\tfrac{3}{4}$ in. × $1\tfrac{1}{3}$ in.; of a light blue colour.

Species II.—*Circus Cinneraceus (Ash Coloured Harrier)*.
Permanently resident.
Size: Length, 17 in.; extent of wings, 34 in.; bill, 1 in.

Colour: Male—bluish-grey, with white-tail coverts. Female—upper parts dark brown, lower parts reddish yellow.

Food: Small animals, lizards, and birds.

Builds on the ground, similar to C. Cyaneus.

Lays 5 eggs, $1\tfrac{1}{4}$ in. × 1 in.; bluish-white.

Species III.—*Circus Eruginosus (Marsh Harrier)*.
Permanently resident.
Size: Length, $21\tfrac{1}{2}$ in.; extent of wings, 37 in.; bill, $1\tfrac{5}{12}$ in.

Colour: Male and female both dark brown, tinged with grey; head white.

Food: Water-fowl, frogs, lizards, and insects.

Builds generally on the ground, though sometimes in the fork of a tree in marshy situations.

Lays 4 eggs, $1\tfrac{9}{12}$ in. × $1\tfrac{1}{4}$ in.; of a whitish colour.

ON THE BRITISH GEOMETRÆ.
BY E. J. S. CLIFFORD.
PART VIII.

THE *Hybernidæ* are a class of geometers peculiar and interesting in economy. Many of the separate species have females whose wing appendages are so imperfectly developed as to give them a very singular appearance. The wings of the male moths are mostly very delicate in texture, and dull in colouring. The first species is the well-known Early Moth (*Hybernia rupicapraria*), a moth which appears on the wing as early as January or February—hence its name. It braves the coldest weather, and greets the wanderer in England, Scotland, and Ireland. The wings are of a dark brown hue in the male, and they possess two transverse lines still deeper in colour. Between these lines is seen a conspicuous spot. The wings of the female are very short and small; they are pale brown, with a dark band across the centre. The eggs of this species may be looked for on hawthorn or oak in the month of February; they will be found either on the trunks or twigs of those trees. The caterpillars are usually full-fed by the beginning of June, and then descend to the ground, and become chrysalides in slight webs which they form on the surface of the earth. Perhaps less common than this, but certainly more gaily attired, is the Spring Usher (*Hybernia leucophearia*). In this species the female is almost destitute of wings, and looks as unlike a moth as may well be imagined. The male moth is subject to much variation, sometimes being dark brown, with a central pale bar, and occasionally pale in hue, with dark transverse lines. At the end of April the young caterpillars of the Spring Usher may be found feeding in concealment between the leaves of oak, which they draw together by silk for a domicile. In June they are full-grown, and then change to chrysalides on the surface of the ground. The moth itself first appears in February or March, being one of those heralds of spring which we are so glad to welcome at the opening of the vernal season.

Our next species, the Scarce Umber (*Hybernia aurantiaria*), is said to be very common in Ireland, but is not so generally distributed as are the two last named. Its caterpillar feeds on the whitethorn, and generally at night. Occasionally it has been taken on the birch and oak. Its colour is dusky black, with a pale brown stripe down the back. When arrived at maturity, it spins a slight cocoon on the surface of the earth, and changes to a reddish-brown chrysalis. The moth flies in October and November, and occurs in several of our English counties. The female has mere rudiments of wings, of a dark brown colour. The Dotted Border (*Hybernia progemmaria*) is another moth of spring, appearing in February and March, and occurring commonly throughout the country. In appearance this is a somewhat striking geometer. The ample fore wings of the male moth are reddish-brown, with three transverse dark lines; the hind wings pale with central spots, and waved lines outside the spots. The wings of the female are very short, and quite incapable of flight. The caterpillar of this species should be searched for in May, feeding on the hornbeam. In colour it is brown, with a pale stripe along the back, and one on each side. At the beginning of June it is full-grown, and turns to a chrysalis just below the surface of the ground. This is brown, and shining in appearance. The Mottled Umber (*Hybernia defoliaria*) is a beautiful geometer, and well worthy of a search. The wings of the male—pale wainscot-brown, with two dark bands—have a very lively aspect. The wings of the female are nearly invisible. The body is of a pale brown colour, with two very conspicuous dark spots on the back of each segment. A variety of the male occurs which has the wings all reddish-brown, and freckled over with minute dots. The caterpillar of the Mottled Umber is without humps or protuberances, and is brown on the back, with black lines on each side, below which the body is bright yellow. It is a very beautiful and abundant creature, and has a curious habit of swinging in mid-air suspended on a thread. An entomologist tells us that he has seen thousands thus hanging suspended, and not unfrequently they swung with the motion of the breeze into his mouth and eyes—a rather unpleasant mode of becoming acquainted with an entomological fact, one would imagine. The food of this caterpillar is hornbeam, hazel, oak, or whitethorn, besides other trees, on which it occurs more or less commonly. At the middle of June it is full-fed, and then changes to a pupa on the surface of the ground among the leaves. The moth appears on the wing in October, lingering amongst us till the cold of winter drives it to hybernating quarters. It is common throughout our country.

When March winds have given way before April's sunny showers, the March moth (*Anisopteryx Æscularia*) occurs on the wing. The caterpillar of this species feeds on elm, oak, lime, and hawthorn. The head and body are pale green, with a white stripe on each side, and one more distinct at the spiracles. The moth itself is very varied in colour, but not brilliant in appearance. The fore wings are long and pointed, dingy brown in colour, with a pale transverse line beyond the middle. The hind wings are pale, with a dark central spot, and a faint zigzag line just beyond it. The female is wingless; she has a conspicuous tuft at the extremity of the abdomen.

Next in order is the Winter Moth (*Cheimatobia brumata*), a species whose power has been felt by many agriculturists and landowners, in respect to the ravages it commits in pear and apple orchards. Its wingless female deposits her eggs in the crevices of the bark of various trees and shrubs during November and December. They give forth the enclosed *larvæ* about the beginning of April. Extremely small at first, these little caterpillars might appear insignificant to the farmer, but no sooner have the rough winds subsided, and genial breezes called forth buds and leaves, than their destructive career is unmistakably realised. They eat into the half-expanded buds, which thus wither and die; and were it not for the sparrows, bullfinches, and other birds, who render such an important service to us by eating multitudes of these, they must become a serious nuisance. This caterpillar varies, being sometimes green and sometimes smoky brown. There is scarcely a tree which we can name that is not subject to the ravages of this insect. The moth into which it is transformed is grey-brown in colour, and has several narrow bars, which are waved. The hind wings are pale, with scarcely any markings. The female has very short wings, and her powers of motion seem to be limited to *running* about on fences and trunks of trees. Thus she has more of the manner of a spider than a moth about her, and often deceives the collector by this simulation. In October and November this moth appears, and not unfrequently lingers amongst us till the last month of the year.

Somewhat similar to that of the last-named is the caterpillar of the Northern Winter Moth (*Cheimatobia boreata*), feeding on the birch. This species is not so abundant as the last. Though not uncommon in some of the English counties, it has not been recorded as appearing in Scotland or Ireland. The moth is grey-brown in colour, with an ochreous tint over the fore wings. The female has very small, undeveloped wings, which are quite incapable of flight. The November Moth (*Oporabia dilutata*), as its name would imply, may be found on the wing in that month, and is commonly distributed throughout the country. It is a species liable to much variation, and therefore difficult to describe. The caterpillar is apple-green in colour, but, like the perfect insect, liable to great variations in marking. It feeds on hawthorn, hornbeam, oak, and sloe; in fact, almost every forest tree will furnish specimens of it. It is full-fed in June. The Autumnal Moth (*Oporabia filigrammaria*) is very delicately marked. The fore wings are grey, with numerous darker waved lines. The caterpillar, it appears, feeds on the sallow, and is rich velvety-green above and whitish below, having also pale yellow stripes on each side. In April these caterpillars bury in the earth in order to undergo their transformations. The perfect insect flies in August and September, and has only been taken in the north of England and in Scotland. In our next moth we see one of those numerous instances afforded by the *geometræ* of a most delicious and striking variety of marking and colouring, blended with wondrous power. The Twin-spot Carpet (*Larentia didymata*) is at once a beautiful and common insect. The fore wings are brown, varied and mottled with grey bars, and shaded with a variety of tints. Near the margin of the wing is a double dark spot, from which the insect derives its name. The hind wings are pale, with several transverse waved markings. The female is altogether paler in hue, and does not look so striking as her lord. The caterpillar may be found feeding on the chervil, and is best taken by beating the leaves of that plant into an umbrella in April or May. In colouring it is pale green, with a narrow dark stripe on each side. At midsummer the moth flies, and occurs commonly throughout the three kingdoms. In most parts of England the Mottled Grey (*Larentia multistrigata*) may be found in early spring. It is pale grey in colour, barred with a darker tinge, and having transverse markings, which are irregular and interrupted, almost like a series of dots. In April the egg is laid in various species of bedstraw. It is stated that the caterpillar will feed freely on the sweet woodruff in confinement— with what truth we are unable to say. Lastly, in this paper, we advert to the Grey Mountain Carpet (*Larentia cæsiata*), a really beautiful little insect. The fore wings, which are grey, are mottled and varied with a variety of shades, and spots of a darker colour are spread over their surface. The markings are zigzag, and produce a very lively effect. In July the eggs may be searched for; they are laid on the bilberry, and the young larvæ emerge about twelve days after they are deposited. After feeding a short time, the caterpillar hybernates at the surface of the earth around the roots of the foodplant, and does not resume feeding until April of the following year. About the middle of May it is full-fed, and spins a cocoon amongst the leaves of its foodplant. From this it emerges as a moth at midsummer, and is particularly abundant in our northern counties. It is also generally found in Ireland. From its habits of flight it is probably rarely met with, for it needs active entomologists to hunt for these mountain species of our native insects.

ENTOMOLOGY FOR THE MONTHS.
AUGUST.

Behold again, with saffron wings superb,
The giddy butterfly. Released at length
From his warm cell, he mounts on high,
No longer reptile, but endowed with plumes,
And through the blue air wanders; pert, alights,
And seems to sleep, but from the treacherous hand
Snatches his beauties suddenly away,
And zigzag dances o'er the flowery dell.
HURDIS.

BY now taking a walk into the country how many pleasant sights and sounds our eyes and ears may feast upon; the corn fields, whose golden fruit may be seen waving to and fro like the rolling waves of a mighty ocean, the golden grain bending more and more to the earth as if inviting the hand of the reaper; the rippling of the brook, the busy hum of the insects, and all the pleasant sights and sounds which tend to make up the charms of the country. The harvest is indeed a merry time; can there be a more picturesque or lovelier sight than that of a group of busy reapers, plying their cheerful task in the hot noonday sun? And when the sun has set in its grandeur behind the western hills and the last trace of day has gradually vanished, the stars appear, and a pleasant shade spreads over the face of the earth, then the harvest moon appears majestically in the opposite quarter, and shedding her silver light, which is softly reflected from mountain and tree to sleep in the silent valley below and to enlighten the merry labourers of the harvest field.

Let us pay a visit to the clover field this month and see what pleasant sights await us there. Amongst the multitude of butterflies we may observe the beautiful Clouded Yellow (Colias Edusa) dancing over the flowery carpet, looking like a living flower, perhaps in company with its first cousin the no less lovely Pale Clouded Yellow (Colias Hyale); the flight of these beautiful butterflies is very strong and rapid, and their chase is one of great excitement; they are both very uncertain insects and will be found abundantly one season, and perhaps no more will be seen in the same locality for several years. I may just add that Edusa was very plentiful in various localities round about Norwich in the year 1867. Hyale also occurred abundantly in 1868.

Besides those butterflies just noticed a great many more may be expected, among which may be mentioned the Brimstone (Gonopteryx Rhamni) and the Swallow-Tailed (Papilio Machaon), which may be observed in company with the foregoing, also the Tortoiseshell (Vanessa Urticæ), Peacock (V. Io), Red Admiral (V. Atalanta), Painted Lady (Cynthia Cardui), Scotch Argus (Erebia Blandina), Grayling (Satyrus Semele), Meadow Brown (S. Janira), Wall (S. Megæra), Gate Keeper (S. Tithonus), Small Heath (Chortobius pamphilus), Green Hairstreak (Thecla Rubi), Black Hairstreak (T. W. Album), Small Copper (Polyommatus phleas), Brown Argus (Lycæna Agestis), Common Blue (L. Alexis), Clifden Blue (L. Adonis), Azure Blue (L. Argiolus) and the Pearl Skipper (Hesperia Comma).

Amongst moths appearing this month we may expect the Gipsy (Liparis Dispar), Satin Moth (L. Salicis), Pale Oak Eggar (Trichiura Cratrægi), Lackey (Bombyx neustria), and the Grass Eggar (B. Trifolii), also the following "Geometræ":—Purple Thorn (Selenia illustraria), Scalloped Oak (Crocallis elinguaria), Canary-shouldered Thorn (Ennomos tiliaria), August Thorn (E. angularia), Feathered Thorn (Himera pennaria), Waved Umber (Hemerophila abruptaria), Dotted Carpet (Cleora glabraria), Small Blood-vein (Acidula imitaria), and the Belle (Eulobia palumbaria), and amongst the "Cuspidatæ," the Oak Hooktip (Platypteryx hamula) and the Barred Hooktip (P. unguicula).

The Old Lady (Mania maura) may be found this month sitting about in out-houses, boathouses, and various other places. A great many more might have been mentioned, but I am compelled to leave them out. A great many larvæ may also be found feeding this month, among which may be named those of the following moths:—

Eyed Hawk-Moth (Smerinthus Ocellatus). The caterpillar of this moth is very beautiful. the ground colour is green, sprinkled with white, and having on each side seven oblique white stripes; the horn at the tail is blue. It may be found feeding in gardens on apple trees, and also on willow bushes.

Privet Hawk-Moth (Sphinx Ligustri). This is quite as pretty a caterpillar as the foregoing, and is so well known as to require no description. It feeds on the Privet (Ligustrum vulgare), also on lilac bushes.

Poplar Hawk-Moth (Smerinthus Populi). Found feeding on the poplar, and in gardens on the common laurel and laurustinus.

Death's-Head Hawk-Moth (Acherontia Atropos). The caterpillar is very large and smooth, the ground colour is yellow, and is sprinkled over with small black dots, and having seven blue stripes on each side, the horn at the tail bends downwards, again turning up at the tip. It feeds on the potato, also on the Deadly Nightshade (Atropa belladonna) and tea tree.

Bedstraw Hawk-Moth (Deilephila Galii) feeds on the Ladies' Bedstraw (Galium verum).

Small and Large Elephant Hawk-Moths (Chœrocampa Porcellus and C. Elpenor). Both these caterpillars also feed on the Ladies' Bedstraw (G. verum); the latter also on the Willow Herb.

Ruby Tiger (Arctia fuliginosa). The caterpillar may be found feeding on grasses, also on dock and plantain, and is common everywhere.

Pale Tussock (Orgyia pudibunda), called also "Hop Dog." This very beautiful caterpillar is common everywhere, and may be taken in great numbers from the oak, on which it feeds.

Fox Moth (Bombyx Rubi). The caterpillar feeds on brambles and heath.

We must not omit to notice this month the Grasshoppers and Crickets. The Green Field Cricket (Gryllus viridissimus), a merry little fellow, and one of the largest, may be heard in the evening, *fizzing* away in the hedges and corn fields; it is no easy matter to capture them, as they are very shy, and directly they become aware of your presence their performance ceases.

I will conclude with the following beautiful little sonnet addressed to these insects by the poet Keats:

The poetry of earth is never dead:
  When all the birds are faint with the hot sun,
  And hide in cooling trees, a voice will run

From hedge to hedge about the new-mown mead :
That is the grasshopper's—he takes the lead
  In summer luxury,—he has never done
  With his delights, for when tired out with fun
He rests at ease beneath some pleasant weed.
The poetry of earth is ceasing never :
  On a lone winter evening when the frost
  Has wrought a silence, from the stove there thrills
The cricket's song, in warmth increasing ever ;
  And seems to one in drowsiness half lost,
  The grasshopper's among some grassy hills.
Norwich.   R. LADDIMAN.

ROUGH NOTES ON THE NATURAL HISTORY OF CORFÚ.

MR. Rowe, in the last number of the N. N. B., while asking a question, seems to think it would be interesting if all were to furnish facts from their own Note Books. Acting upon his idea, and willing to show the example, I have referred to my notes, and after brushing away some of the overlying cobwebs of the "memories of the past," have gone back ten years, and raked up some facts bearing on the Natural History of Corfú, one of the Ionian Isles. Some little preface is however desirable, for the double purpose of not plunging at once without method into the subject, and for the purpose of collecting my thoughts as I go on ; I therefore preface my "rough notes" with the incidents of the voyage, which like most voyages is as the nigger said of the twins " Dey am berry much alike, specially dis one." Be this as it may, it was in the month of May 1859, that I had occasion to leave England for the Ionian Isles ; accordingly I embarked on board the good old tub "Melbourne," lying off Portsmouth Dockyard. As in most troop ships of her age and converted capabilities, there was not much room to move about in at any time ; and now this was made doubly apparent by the inevitable confusion of shipping and finding places for passengers, ladies, and the officers and men of the detachments of various regiments, who were going to join or relieve their comrades at Gibraltar or Corfú. It was a most amusing scene however, for everything and every one seemed to be just where they were least wanted ; and the cackling of poultry, yells of pet dogs, who had unfortunately forgotten to put their toes in their pockets, or anywhere but exactly under some other toes of heavier calibre ; the complaining grunts of the doomed porkers, and the presence of a considerable amount of heavy swear (not included in the bill of lading) formed the sum total of a scene which would have delighted Hogarth. The day, as most days, however, as I have observed, came to an end about evening, and as the ship's gong sounded eight bells, the soldiers and sailors bustled about preparing their too long delayed tea, and rigging their hammocks for the night. So far as the rigging up was concerned this was easy enough, but the getting into them was quite a different affair, at least for the landsmen, for many a poor fellow gave himself a severe headache in the attempt, for it is one of the exasperating peculiarities of the hammock, that as soon as you catch hold of the side which coyly objects if possible to be seized at all, and balance yourself on the tips of your toes to make your spring, so sure does it glide with a crab-like motion from your fingers, and the performance has to be again repeated ; another attempt, and you find yourself by a prodigious effort with one leg in at the side, while the other leg and rest of your body is underneath ; then comes the tug to get yourself in altogether, the hammock meanwhile swaying from side to side with a most graceful but fatiguing motion, positively refusing to be entered under any pretext whatever. You feel you ought to swear, but it really is too great a luxury to indulge in when you require all your energies for the task before you : you feel that you can't hold on much longer, so you make another supreme gymnastic attempt, getting your legs and arms twisted in so complex a form that you are utterly unrecognisable even to yourself. Ah! what was that ? a nasty sensation as if the deck had suddenly leaped up violently flourishing an iron ring bolt, and hit you a most cowardly blow on the back of the head. On communing privately with yourself, as soon as you have done with the nightmare you appear to have been nursing for the last few moments, you find that part of your impression is correct ; the only thing is that you went to the deck by getting your fingers twisted and so letting go your hold of the vile things they call hammock lashings, and not that the deck came up to you. Sitting up a little dazed and confused at the turn affairs appear to be taking, you muse upon the dangers of those who venture upon the Sea! the Sea! (vide Barry Cornwall) and think that you will go upstairs as you call it, much to the disgust of the blue-water sailors, and have a turn or two on the roof. Being now a pretty good sailor, and familiar with nautical terms I can afford to laugh at the blunders of others and call any one a land-lubber who fails to get into his hammock properly ; but in those days it was anything but a laughing matter, I can assure you, for we never can ourselves see the joke in the pain which gives pleasure to others. To sailors, landsmen and soldiers are fair game, and many a joke I saw perpetrated that night, the old soldiers not one whit behind the tars in their tricks upon the greenhorns. "I say, Bill!" said one salt to another, "you should ha' seen one o' them lobsters! such a go! my eye! he fell out of his hammock in the curous way which them poor lubberly chaps has got, and there he was a standin on his ed, with his feet hitched into the lashins and he could'nt get em out no how till I went and cut him adrift and clapped him right way up—I thought I should have died a laffin tho', for as soon as he was righted he says, says he! can't I have never a bedstead to sleep in— I ain't used to sleepin in a bag, I ain't! and the last time I see him, he was along with the pannikins and swabs having made hisself comfortable under his mess-table and said as how that sooted his fireplace a good lump better."

At eleven o'clock the next morning we sailed away from old England, giving and receiving a hearty cheer, and we stood out clear of the forts. It was the day upon which the Queen's birthday was appointed to be kept, and as we steered slowly towards the "Spit" we could see the troops drawn up in grand divisions on South-sea Common and hear the salvos of Artillery and Infantry feux-de-joie as they saluted the Royal Standard precisely at twelve, the ships in the harbour answering and shrouding the fast receding land from our sight. Our ship now wore a more orderly appearance under the magical fingers of discipline; and as the dinner bugle sounded everything was taut and trim, even the soldiers had brushed up and presented a smart and clean appearance as dressed in white duck trousers and slops, a black silk handkerchief confining their throats, and a knife slung sailor-fashion round their waists, they attended with the tars for their grog.

By 5 p.m. on the 20th, we were out of sight of land, and fairly in the Bay of Biscay. The wind which had bowled us along fairly under sail, was here rather inconvenient, and the long swells—I don't mean of the period but of the Atlantic,—crossed our bows and made the vessel pitch, and the young sailors heave until naught was heard but plaintive cries from sundry plaintiffs to be at once thrown overboard or suffered to die in a manner best befitting their several ranks. The next day was a more severe repetition of this, the vessel appearing as if it had determined upon standing up on its hind legs and then after a little thought about it, coming down with a dreadful crash (in your stomach) upon its nose, the impish spirits of the storm, the sooty-coloured little stormy petrels actually dancing over the tremendous waves with the most don't-I-like-it sort of expression in the world, doubly annoying to one who like myself felt so terribly ill at ease. However about midnight we left the bay, and after that the change was wonderful, the sea left off ill-using us, and people who before were the most determined to die, began to take notice of the headlands which we passed and thought that after all they would live a little longer just to oblige. We passed the Berlingas—ugly looking crags well out to sea, upon the largest of which is a lighthouse round which were wheeling the Skua Gulls or pirate birds (Lestris Cataractes), from *Lestris*, a pirate vessel, and *Katarasso* to dash down upon, so-named from the habit they have of despoiling more peaceful gulls of their finny prey; and by the 24th, five days and a half after leaving England, steamed in, fired our signal gun, and cast anchor off the Mole of Gibraltar, in the middle watch. My first impression of Gib., which I believe owes its name to the Moor Tarik, who conquering it in the time of Roderic the Visigoth gave it the name of Geber el Tarik (the rock of Tarik) corrupted by lapse of time into Gibraltar, did not carry out my preconceived idea, most pictures making it appear too barren-looking, I fancy, perhaps from being sketched from the north front, which has a more forbidding look than the rest of the rock. From the sea as you look to the town on your right is the New Mole, with several batteries near it, commanding the harbour and forming a line of defence, apparently along the whole length of the town which consists of a regular olla podrida of yellow tiled houses, white towered churches, and nondescript buildings, half mansion, half store; some very handsome residences are a little higher up, standing in the midst of pleasant gardens, with walks here and there bordered by various trees— in fact the rock for about half way up seems a constant succession of gardens and trees, seemingly citron and orange, an oleander with its thousands of rose coloured flowers, occurring here and there, and adding fresh colour to the glowing beauty of the scene. At the extreme summit of the "Lion of the Mediterranean" is the signal staff, looking down hundreds of feet on the precipitous rocks, which are here clothed with but scanty vegetation, hardly serving to mask the loop-holed galleries and approaches, cut in their sombre depths. The sea wall, as indeed all the place itself, was bristling with guns in casemates, embrasures, or mounted "en barbette," which latter style is simply a traversing wooden carriage, under cover of the walls upon which is placed a gun carriage and gun, so managed that while both carriages are protected the muzzle of the cannon plays freely over the top of the parapet without any embrasure whatever; the advantage of this is that it commands a much greater circle of range than if its line of fire were stopped by the cheeks of embrasures or casemates. A curious effect is produced by the apparently odd mixture of churches, guns, yellow tiled houses, and blossoming flowers and trees. The Mediterranean zebecques with their strange "fore and aft" or "wing and wing" sails, were gliding about the Strait, attended closely by the white gulls foraging for offal thrown over from these fishing boats, or making dashes at the fish which the clear water plainly revealed in shoals about our bows; they were something like a whiting, but would not bite at any bait, although they sometimes nibbled lazily at some very beautifully formed seaweed which was floating about; I also saw two Clouded Yellow Butterflies (Colias Edusa) fly near the ship. The provision boats by this time had swarmed around, and I saw several things sold very cheap, albeit they are cheaper on shore. Oranges, fine large ones six for a penny; a bundle of twenty-five common cigars for six-pence; a loaf of bread, double the size of those sold us on board at ninepence was only three half-pence; a singular looking cave (St. Michael's Cave) which is said to lead from Gibraltar to Tangiers on the opposite African coast, was pointed out to me, through this supposed passage, which indubitably leads under the rock to a great depth, the monkeys are popularly believed to have come; be this as it may, it is a well known fact that the Gibraltar apes, and those on the opposite shore are identical. We remained but a few hours for mails, and got our anchor apeak and steamed away, so that I had no opportunity to land; but on a subsequent occasion, five years after, I did land. The main street of the town is a fine wide thoroughfare, with shops and houses in a good style on each side, several picturesque "majos" and swarthy moors were stalking about, the never failing cigarillo tucked daintily in at the corner of the lips, for your true Spaniard never holds his cigar or cigarette between his teeth. At one of the shops I bought a very pretty scented sandal-wood fan, for a dollar and a half, which would be worth treble the money in England. Behind the jealously closed jalousies peeped many a dark eyed doña, wondering if the Englishmen were such terrible monsters after all, and half disposed to slight the counsel of "Padre Angelo," and bestow one heart-quaking glance in return for the covert kiss of the hand. Ay de mi, the havoc Las niñas cause, by a look, a sigh, the flutter of a fan, or the waft of a handkerchief when we are young and well,—tender. The market at the Waterpool Gate, is a marvel; fruit, fish, and game in artistic confusion; here on one stall tended by a good-looking man, are the half tropical fruits of which Spain with her Moorish associations can boast. Dates, gourds, golden, white, and purple grapes, pomegranates, figs, nectarines, melons, olives, blood and golden oranges, and heaps of other beautiful things. On the fish stalls see the huge tunny, the gilthead, the iridescent and opaline red mullet, and that calm and peaceful Diogenes of the deep, the oyster. From here take a caleche, a gay sort of tent upon wheels drawn by a swift bell-betinkled and most unmulish-like looking mule, a perfect picture of symmetry. "Click, clack, my coast is clear, for I am a muleteer," you would sing, only that the grave looking driver might object to your arrogating to yourself such a rank: however it is a click and a crack, and off we go, bound for the North Front, which is a bold scarp of the rock mined, countermined, and galleried at every available point. The embrasures of "St. George's Hall," a concealed sort of cave chamber, being just discernible; thousands of rock doves (Columba Livia) were flying in, and about the fissures which seamed the stupendous mass towering in stern grandeur above us, filled the air with the sound of their rapidly agitated pinions, as we shouted to scare them from their inaccessible haunts. Not far from this is the Neutral Ground. The line of demarcation between English and Spanish interests, regularly guarded by a cordon of the sentinels of both nations, the white Spanish sentry towers alternating with, and contrasting prettily with the dark sentry boxes of the English. Our caleche now took us to a fonda or hotel in the town: where for a moderate sum we procured very good wine and a good dinner, the only drawback being that for my Peruvian dollar's value in the country from whence I came 4s. 4d. I only got 4s., and all English shillings shared a similar fate, 11d. being the rate of exchange. English gold however was not subject to any amercement. The Alamader is worthy of a special visit; it is the public place of resort in the evenings, a sort of square with statues, rows of trees and flowers, avenues leading to nowhere only to other avenues: it really is a most beautiful place, and when I saw it was enlivened by the evolutions of a smart company of those soldier artificers, the Royal Engineers. The remainder of the voyage out was very pleasant. Being now in the blue and tideless Mediterranean we had nothing to fear but a white squall, which fortunately did not beset us. Coasting Algeria which lay on our starboard bow or right hand, we felt the heat greatly, and at night the dew fell like rain when there was the slightest haze; on very clear nights, the sky was a study, so gloriously shone the stars, the milky way being plainly visible in its entirety, while the sea flashed and glittered in emulation with the phosphoric gleam from the unseen bodies of millions of microscopic medusae;

sometimes a great fish would dash along, plainly discernible by the lambent gleam of weird sea-fire, which lit up its track; and the porpoises which had been in attendance on us the greater part of the day, would sometimes return in the night, and gambol, and rush before the bows as playful as kittens, every action as plainly visible as by day. It has often struck me, that however fast a ship may be going, and I have scudded at 18½ knots, the porpoises always seem to keep ahead and cross the ship's counter, with the greatest ease when she is at full speed, dash off suddenly and wait until it gains on them. I believe they thoroughly enjoy the lark and laugh to themselves at the slow thing man calls a ship; looking at these animals, for they are cetaceans, *not fish*, as many suppose, you will at once see the meaning of the term "Porpoise," for the little eyes, swinish snout, and "pale countenance," certainly warrants the name given them by the Italians, and from which the English is derived "Porco pesce," *i.e.* Pig fish. I think it was about this spot, or else off Tunis, that some years after I first saw the Mediterranean flying fish (Exocetus Exiliens) on flight; I was lazily looking out of the lower deck ports when something rose under the port gangway, right out of the sea, looking at first like a large dragon-fly or magnified grasshopper, and after giving me a full view for about two hundred yards, popped back into its more congenial element with the same suddenness that had characterised its exit. On the 27th May, some little commotion was caused on board by the accidental poisoning of a little child by chloride of lime. Fortunately one of the surgeons succeeded in saving its life: not so however with another poor little thing, a few days after, which died with Hydrocephalus, and was consigned to the deep with that service peculiar to those buried at sea. I know nothing more solemn than the last words of this service; and the upright plunge of the weighted body as the sea moodily closes over the corpse for ever, and the vessel forges ahead and effaces the last ripple which is the only evidence that below it is sinking to unknown depths a creature once instinct with life and power. How the grim fishes upon which man wages a ceaseless war, must grind their savage teeth in anticipation of the Ghoul-like revenge they will take when tearing the heavily shotted death-hammock open, they gash and tear the flesh of their pale enemy, now no longer able to bring science and reason to bear to fend off their savage attacks. Alas! let us not seek to pierce the dread mystery which enshrouds the fate of the ocean-buried or drowned seamen; let us leave them at rest in their sea-tangled graves, and thank Heaven that the beautiful world of Nature still leaves us something to live for, something to hope for.

A. M. B.

(*To be continued.*)

SEA-SALT. By C.

AT this season of the year, when John Bull migrates with his family to the sea-side, we cannot do better than recommend to his notice "The Ocean World," by Louis Figuier (English translation) as a pleasant source of instruction and amusement. Armed with this book, the morning paper, and a pipe, he may banish to the winds all anxiety and bother, and pass many an enviable hour under the shade of that dis-used lugger; secure from importunate appeals to have a boat, or try a brandy-ball. There are few things perhaps more enjoyable, than dreaming away a tranquil hour in this way, provided your bones are not very prominent, and the shingle not unusually rough. For beside the delights of shade and sea-breeze, you may rely upon immunity from gnats and such-like insect pests, that trouble the siestas of the inland idler. It may be too, that J. B.'s memory has been slightly addled by the heavy business of the last six months. He may have forgotten a few little elementary details respecting the vague immensity of ocean; if so, the "Ocean World" (which has suggested and considerably assisted this paper) will be found doubly edifying to the worthy gentleman. The implication may be presumptive, but we were rather amused the other day, while walking on the sands, to see that cherub Alicia, tired of erecting sand-castles, and pebble-fortifications, throw aside her spade, and prompted by a sudden desire for imformation, assail Paterfamilias with the very natural question: "Papa, please why is the sea salt?" Now this enquiry took Mr. B. entirely by surprise: he dropped the *Times*, and lifted an astonished glance over his spectacles, replying with evident displeasure, "my dear, dont you see I'm reading, and can't be bothered; run away." So Miss A. walked moodily back to her sand-hills, staring vacantly at the big ships that fringed the horizon; and pondered like the Homeric heroes in her dear heart, whether, as nurse said, they were actually employed by the nation in precipitating sacks of salt into ocean's bosom, to prevent the brine from losing its savour. There might have been some excuse for J. B.; for when a man is intensely occupied with the state of the money market or the Irish Church, he cannot be expected at a moment's notice to turn the current of his thoughts into so totally different a channel as that of natural laws. The tax upon the complicated junctions and branch-lines of the nervous railway is too great ; and on the whole we have no scruples in overlooking the momentary peevishness of Alicia's papa. At any other time he might have explained to her how in its earliest infancy our earth was a mass of incandescent matter, before the atmosphere had learned to condense its watery vapours, and shed them upon the world in grateful showers or tempestuous storms. When rain fell on the burning surface for the first time, it became charged with all the soluble mineral substances contained in the earth's crust. The waters thus medicated began to accumulate in the natural basins of the primeval world, afte. levying their tribute on its mineral wealth. The produce of this tribute is jealously guarded by Father Neptune from the pilfering attempts of his powerful neighbour Phœbus ; and is constantly being doled out to his subjects who honestly trade with it, and prevent its becoming a drug in the market. For although the sun may exert his utmost strength in evaporating the sea's water, yet the water that thus rises to the sky is pure and fresh, containing scarcely the slightest traces of salt. "Falling as rain upon the land it washes the soil, percolates through the rocky layers, and becomes charged again with saline substances which are borne sea-wards by the returning currents. The ocean therefore is the great depository of all substances which the waters can dissolve and carry down from the surface of the continents, and as there is no channel for their escape, they would constantly accumulate were it not for the creatures which inhabit the seas, and utilize the material thus brought within their reach."

We will now consider in what way this utilization of salts is carried on in nature's marine laboratories.

The Molluscs that inhabit the infinite and elegant varieties of shells with which we are all familiar, constitute the most important detachment of workmen found in the vast manufactories of ocean's depths. Beautiful indeed are the outlines, endless the varities of size and shape ; and complete the gradations of shade and colour among shells, from the brilliant crimson and yellow of the Mitra and Purpuræ, to the sombre black of the common mussel, and dingy stone-grey of the appetising oyster. And yet they are all elaborated by the same secreting process which abstracts the arbonate of lime dissolved in sea water and converts it into substantial homes for busy workmen. So inexhaustible are the resources of nature ; so infinite her varieties of combination and design as displayed in this single branch of her operations.

If we assign to Molluscs the foremost ranks in the sea's army of Elaborators, Crustaceans may fairly claim to succeed them. Strong, hardy, and destructive, these marauders appropriate no small portion of the sea salts in fabricating their cuirasses, gauntlets, and greaves of calcified mail. Well may they be compared to the heavily armed knights of the middle ages, at once audacious and cruel ; barbed in steel from head to foot, with visor and corselet, arm-pieces and thigh-pieces, nothing in fact is wanting to complete the resemblance. Thus equipped they pursue their nocturnal expeditions of plunder far away in the depths of ocean, or among the shallower pools of their rocky homes. They fight *à l'outrance* not only with their enemies, but even among themselves. Often their battles rage with fury scarcely to be believed : nor are their limbs proof against the savage onslaughts that ensue : feet, tail, and above all antennæ, suffer fearful mutilation ; yet happily for the vanquished, a few months' repose suffices for the regeneration of a lost limb ; and in consequence we often see crustaceans with talons of very unequal size ; the smaller being those lost in battle and re-placed. "We have seen lobsters," says Moquin-Tandon, "which have in an unfortunate encounter lost a limb, sick and debilitated, reappear at the end of a few months with a perfect limb, vigorous and ready for service. O nature, how thou fillest our souls with astonishment and wonder !".

We will not linger any time over the ubiquitous tribes of fishes, or the Acalephæ and Echinoderms, though all these classes undoubtedly perform an important share in appropriating the sea salts to purposes of private economy. The result of their labours, however, is not so apparent to the casual observer, and this must be our excuse for passing them by.

There is no spectacle in nature more worthy of admiration, and more extraordinary than that which we will now consider, viz—Coral Islands. The zoophytes which construct them, are but lowly organised beings, gifted with a half latent life only, small and fragile animalcules, yet silently and incessantly they labour in their ocean home, and as they exist in innumerable aggregated masses, their cells finish by producing enormous masses of calcareous matter. These increase and multiply with such incalculable rapidity, that they form reefs and even islands. "What a singular combination is here presented ; trees, one half of which are animated, growing at the bottom of the sea ; polyps, one half of which is imprisoned and riveted to their person; their stomachs in the bark, their arms in the branch, their movements perfect repose !"

"Omnipotence wrought in them, with them, by them,
Hence what Omnipotence alone could do
Worms did.—I saw the living pile ascend,
The Mausoleum of its Architects,

Still dying upwards as their labour closed:
Slime the material, but the slime was turned
To adamant, by their petrific touch;
Frail were their frames, ephemeral their lives,
Their masonry imperishable."

And even as the work progresses in its several branches for ever in silent and undiscoverable majesty, the surface of ocean raises the diapason of its deep-mouthed harmony, blending with the winds in soft modulation or the wildest roar, to remind us of the burden of creation's hymn :—
" O Lord, how manifold are thy works! in wisdom hast thou made them all: the earth is full of thy riches. So is this great and wide sea, wherein are things creeping innumerable, both small and great beasts."

———The finer sense perceives
Celestial and perpetual harmonies!
The purer soul, that trembles and believes,
Hears the archangel's trumpet in the breeze,
And where the forest rolls, or ocean heaves,
Cecilia's organ sounding in the seas,
And tongues of prophets speaking in the leaves.

NOTES ON THE STARLING.
(Sturnus Vulgaris).

THE love for communion with other birds exhibits a marked peculiarity in the habits of the Starling. So rare is the occurrence, and to such a few tribes of birds are these oddities extended, that such a case hardly passes unnoticed; hence the marked peculiarity. I have sometimes seen starlings fly over along with rooks, and jackdaws; and it appeared to me to be rather a strange sight, but I find the Rev. Gilbert White, has noticed such an occurrence, and he suggests that they fly along with rooks, on the motive of interest, as the rooks (according to the conclusions which anatomists have arrived at) have by reason of two large nerves which run down between the eyes, into the upper mandible, a more delicate feeling in their beaks than other round billed birds, and can grope for their meat when out of sight. Relying on such a statement, we can but say that such congregating of birds exhibits a strange peculiarity, different from the majority of the tribes of birds, which are never seen intermingled in flocks one with another. As far as my observations have led me to witness, I find that during hard frosty winters, the presence of the starling is found wanting, and also if the winters have been mild, I have seldom if ever seen this bird, so that it appears to me to be of a migratory nature, but where it passes such winters I have never learnt, but I suggest that it will seek out the warm recesses of the woods in the midland and southern counties in England, as the weather is very cold here, with the breezes blowing off the waters of Morecombe-bay. As a singer I must confess that he is remarkably good, but has very low notes; and while in the habit of uttering such low notes, he makes occasion to use his wings at the same time. This bird has also a remarkable imitative power, for I recollect being once deceived by him, for thinking that some one was whistling to call my attention, I found out that it proceeded from this bird. Starlings do not indulge in song when they first make their appearance, being then collected together in large flocks, but when the time of separation arrives, or in other words, when the birds have paired together, then his song commences, and continues throughout the period of building the nest and hatching the eggs, till the young make their appearance; then his spare time is taken up in helping his mate to provide for them, making his song is less frequent, which continues to die away till the young can fly, when he is scarcely ever heard afterwards. The church is very near the house where I reside, and every year there are numbers of these birds build their nests in the ivy which almost encircles the same, and the old stagers (if I may term them so) occupy some holes in the building under the spout. Now these birds are subject to a great deal of annoyance from the neighbouring boys, who commit depredations on the birds' nests and rob them of their eggs, yet nevertheless, a second lot of eggs are deposited, and sometimes they manage to rear a nest of young birds. The nest of the starling is a carelessly constructed affair, very much like the nest of the water-hen for untidyness, but differing in the choice of the material, as the starling builds with straw, and dried grass, interwoven with a few feathers stuck here and there, while the water-hen only uses dried reeds, and rushes of a year or more's growth. The majority of starlings about here lay six eggs of a blue green colour, but I have occasionally found eight in some of their nests. The ivy mantled vicarage, in close proximity to the church, is also a favourite haunt for the starlings, and a few years ago I was an eye-witness of a fight for the rights of building, between a few of these birds and some house-sparrows. The sparrows at that time were very numerous, consequently they drove off the starlings to some neighbouring trees, only to be incessantly troubled with the birds flying back again, for the din which the sparrows made when fighting, arrested my attention. But since that time the starlings have become more numerous, and now there is a more settled amity between them. This year a white starling has been observed among them. I cannot do better than conclude with the following anecdote, which

I think ought to convince your non-reasoning advocates of their error, for if reason or instinct is manifested in birds, it is manifested in a still greater degree in animals. I have extracted it from Miller's "Country Life," as related by the Rev. Mr. Slader, in the Zoologist. He states that one was built under the eves of a roof, in the basin of a drain pipe, and that the young in their eagerness to obtain food, fell out of the nest; one was killed; the remaining two he picked up and placed in a basket covered with netting, which he hung up near to the nest. The next morning one of them disappeared, the last one he carefully watched, and saw the old bird approach it with food, but instead of feeding the little prisoner, she tempted it by hunger; the sight of the food, and its attempts to reach her by struggling, and forcing its way through the netting prevailed, when it fell to the ground unhurt. She then enticed it into a corner of the shrubbery, to the very spot where she had also concealed the other young one, which had be-before been missed.   J. H.

North Lancashire.

SUMMER TIME IN THE COUNTRY.

WHAT a glorious unison of words! It makes one feel, after being an eye-witness of such enchanting scenery, like those beautiful poets of old, whose musings transported them into the land of fairies, where they beheld those spirit forms, gliding amidst labyrinths of roses, and sporting through fragrant bowers, where the heat of their everlasting day cannot penetrate. What a pleasure it is, after toiling along the dusty roads of civilization, with almost the heat of a tropical sun shedding his rays down upon you perpendicularly, making the perspiration teem from you, and being constantly annoyed by gnats, and other stinging insects preying upon your face and hands; I say what a pleasure it is, after being tormented so, to plunge into the thick shady wood, whose cool recesses brings back renewed energy to your tired limbs, and to there ramble about looking at the beautiful revealings of universal nature in the shady parts; or to wander along the banks of a meandering stream, as it sports along over the loose pebbles, keeping in harmony with the notes of the feathered songsters in the trees overhead. Summer is now in the prime of beauty, for we cannot tread our foot down without disfiguring the features of some pretty flower, and the fragrance which fills the air spreads such a sweet aroma around, as to make quite an agreeable sensation to the smell. Dame Nature has now laid her green carpet on the country lanes, which are trodden only by the foot and team of the farmer, as he wanders to his work in the fields, or perhaps some inquisitive tourist has discovered such bye-paths, on which he walks with caution, fearing lest he should tear his coat or trousers with some wild bramble, as it grows unheeded in its careless way.

There is a charming aspect about such rough uncivilized roads, when the hedges nearly meet on either side, and the scents which pervade these hedges, from the wild rose and honey-suckle, complete the loveliness of the scene. In the green pastures may be seen a lot of newly weaned lambs, walking hither and thither not knowing where to go, and keeping in companies like a batallion of soldiers under drill. The dull drone of the heavy laden bee puts a languid feeling on our nerves, and not till we have taken a nap under the shade of some spreading beech tree, and made another tour through the land of muses, have we become as active as ever. Nearly all our feathered tribes are still in full song, and the incessant harmony produced by them is pleasing in the extreme. The death-knell of spring has been sent forth in the departing voice of the cuckoo, as she wings her flight to far off shores. Are we not reminded of pious Bishop Hooker (when engrossed among such sylvan beauties) who after having done active duty in the thronged city till old age came on, thought it expedient to retire to the country to study and pray. We cannot but admire the beauties shown forth in sweet summer time, in such places where the artist seems captivated as to which scene is the loveliest to impress on his canvass; till tired and weary with his day's work, he wanders to his temporal home, as night cometh on apace, and the orb of day has sunk in golden splendour in the north-west. What sublime meditations! what exultant pleasures! are to be derived from these rustic rambles. The passage of the various coloured butterflies strikes the eye as they fly from one flower to another, and whose stay with us is very brief; do they not remind us of the frailty of human life? To the citizen whose concupiscent ideas lead him hither and thither, when in the country cannot fail to find something pleasing whichever way he turns. Again, what a delight it is to sniff the pleasant odour of the new mown hay, and watch the rustics engaged in haymaking, and to hear the merry laugh which breaks upon the ear as the jokes are passed to and fro. In the distance, the sturdy mowers are engaged in cutting down more of the crop, and the heat of the mid-day sun with his burning rays will take a great effect on them; but according to Bloomfield the heat is ineffectual on their bodies, when he says—

Hark! where the sweeping scythe now rips along;
Each sturdy mower emulous and strong;
Whose writhing form meridian heat defies,
Bends to his work, and every sinew tries.

While pondering o'er such happy scenes, our thoughts recall the days of the olden time which we have read of, when after the hay and wheat harvest is finished and the last load has been safely housed, then commences the rejoicings of the harvest home feast, when the young men and maidens dance on the light fantastic toe to the strains of an old fiddle. The sweet note of the swallow (*hirundo garrula*) is heard as it passes overhead among the numerous insects which sustain it and its young. The haunts of the landrail (*orityigometra*) are now laid bare by the scythe of the mower, and his loud harsh note is missing. The month of October is put down in the volume entitled "Country life," by Thomas Miller, as the month for the migration of this bird, and he mentions hearing it in autumn. I for my part must say that I have never heard his note after hay-time in this part of the country. Or if we take an evening walk, whether along the hedgerows in the fields or through the interior of a wood, we hear the low notes of the birds as they retire to rest, mingled with the dull moan of the cows in the fields, foretells the approaching stillness of night. Occasionally may be heard the scream of the owl as he sallies forth in the twilight out of his retreat in quest of prey, his greatest favourite being the field mouse. The dull bat may now be seen winging his flight under the shade of some spreading sycamore, or circling round some sombre massive tower. So we find, as the seasons advance, the peculiarities of birds are every year the same; for the same power who orders the ebb and flow of the ocean is manifested in the migratory birds also, for when the time of departure arrives the main body of the same are missing. So much then for the beauties of summer scenery and the pleasures to be derived therefrom; for if we meditate on such a rich display it very naturally leads our thoughts to a higher sphere, viz., from the works of Creation to the God who created them.

North Lancashire. B. C.

THE NATURALIST IN CALIFORNIA.

IN December, 1860, I found myself at Los Angelos, under orders to report at Fort Mojave, Colorado Valley, as soon as practicable. I therefore started on the fourth, in company with a train of wagons going with supplies to the Fort, mounted on a mule, and well supplied with material for collecting in that little known region.

The southern part of California, even near the coast, was still brown and barren looking from the effects of the long dry season, although some rain had fallen for a month past. There is very little tree growth except along the streams, and most of these sink in the dry season before reaching the sea, so that the nearly level plain bordering the coast for a width of twenty-five miles has a desolate appearance, though it is densely covered with herbage, and in spring puts on a garb of the most beautiful green, varied with myriads of pretty flowers. Already the lower grounds along the river bed are commencing to revive, and flocks of geese (*Anser hyperboreus* and *Bernicla Gambelii*) begin to enliven the scene; the Kill-deer (*Ægialitis vociferus*), a constant resident where water is permanent, and occasionally flocks of other waders are seen.

But the route leads away from the haunts of these semi-aquatic migrants, over the driest part of the plain towards Cajon Pass, and although animals of all kinds are less abundant there now than in the moist spots, they are more distinct from those of the Atlantic States. Ground Squirrels (*Spermophilus Beecheyi*) abound, their villages occupying every little elevation, and the squirrels themselves, which do not hibernate here, may be seen running in all directions or sitting erect near their burrows, and allowing a very near approach, confident that they can escape under ground from any enemy. But occasionally a Squirrel Hawk (*Archibuteo ferrugineus*) is seen sitting on the ground devouring one of these audacious burrowers. The White-headed Eagle and various smaller hawks, are also on the watch for these and any other small animals they can catch, such as Gophers (*Thomomys umbrinus*), Jumping-mice (*Dypodomys agilis* and *Perognathus parvus*), Wood-mice (*Hesperomys Sonoriensis*), Hares (*Lepus Californicus* and *Audubonii*), besides such birds as fall in their way.

About the gardens are the omnipresent House Finch (*Carpodacus frontalis*), the Black Pewee (*Sayornis nigricans*), Raven and Western Crow (*Corvus carnivorus* and *caurinus*). The Western Flicker (*Colaptes Mexicanus*) was the only one of its tribe observed in this nearly woodless plain. Large flocks of Gambel's Finch (*Zonotrichia Gambelii*), and other species, flitted among the hedges, while the Golden-crowned Wren and Audubon's Warbler were the only insectivorous species that could glean a subsistance at this season among the dry willows. The Song Sparrow (*Melospiza Heermannii*) like its eastern representative, enlivens the early morning with an occasional song, while the Rock Wren (*Salpinctes obsoletus*) and Cactus Wren (*Campylorhynchus brunneicapillus*) chirrup loudly from the tiled roof or dense thickets. Flocks of Quails (*Lophortyx Californicus*) become common as we get farther from the town, and the little Burrowing Owl (*Athene cunicularia*) is often seen sitting sleepily at the mouth of an old squirrel burrow. Meadow Larks and Horned Larks, as well as the little Pipit, are so numerous in places on the bare plains as to almost darken the air when they fly, and the curious Mountain Plover (*Podasocys montanus*) run in scattered flocks over the driest tracts, or wheel in swift columns around the sportsman, their white underparts sometimes shining like snow-flakes as they turn like their more aquatic cousins of the seashore.

Thus it will appear that these plains have a great variety of animals, even as seen in a hasty journey and at a bad season, but nothing very peculiar to this part of the State occurred. Two fine specimens of the Red-tailed Black Hawk (*Buteo calurus*) would not allow of a very near approach, and the first specimen collected was a Cassin's Kingbird (*Tyrannus vociferans*), which I could scarcely believe a winter resident, although I have since found it to be so, even as far north as Santa Cruz, whilst its closely allied relative, the *T. verticalis*, leaves the State entirely in winter.

Approaching the mountains at Cajon Pass, extensive thickets of shrubbery, with occasional low trees, give promise of a new and more varied fauna in the spring, but at this season few animals were seen besides those mentioned. A Coyote (*Canis latrans*) dogged our steps in hopes of some scraps to be left at camp, and at night the dismal barking howl of these animals was our constant serenade. Nests of the Woodrat (*Neotoma Mexicana*) were common, consisting of twigs, bark, etc., piled up three or four feet high among the bushes.

Hares became so numerous that I saw more than twenty during the day while riding along the road, and a new bird appeared in pairs, or small families, running on the ground with much the appearance of Snow-birds. This was Bell's Finch (*Poospiza Bellii*), one of the more southern group. I also shot a black-tailed Gnat Catcher (*Polioptila melanura*), the most peculiar of the three allied species found in this State, which was hopping among the low bushes, scolding like a wren.

The weather here was warm and pleasant by day, but frosty at night. Insects were scarce, and I searched in vain for mollusca, though several fine snails are found on the neighbouring mountains where limestone abounds. As I am, however, only giving my observations on that particular journey, I omit for the present to mention these and many higher animals, which I have since found to be inhabitants of the same region.

Large groups of Live Oak (*Quercus agrifolia*), seen at a distance only, surrounding San Gabriel and San Bernardino, would no doubt yield many birds and other animals not observed along the route traversed.

Cajon Pass. — The pass is entered quite abruptly from the plains by a picturesque cañon, usually narrow and rocky, through which flows a dashing mountain stream, clear and cold, but not observed to contain fish. Along its banks grow Live Oaks, Buttonwoods (*Platanus Mexicanus*), and various Willows, while a few Pines (*Pinus Sabiniana?*), Firs (*Abies Douglassii*) and Nut Pines (*P. monophyllus*) straggle down from the neighbouring mountains. The slopes of the nearest mountains are, however, covered chiefly with low shrubs. Among these the loud ringing trill of the Wren Titmouse (*Chamæa fasciata*) was the chief bird-music at this season. Other birds observed were a flock of Pigeons (*Columba fasciata?*), Lawrence's Goldfinch (*Chrysomitris Lawrencii*), and the Western Bluebird (*Sialia Mexicana*), none of which frequent the bare plains below. Just below the summit, where we camped December 7th, I shot the first seen of the Shining Flycatcher (*Phainopepla nitens*, a species rare west of these mountains, and peculiar enough to attract attention from its habit of flying upward from a bush to a great height, in a zigzag manner, in pursuit of insects, somewhat like Pewees, which it much resembles otherwise. I have heard of the Mountain Quail (*Oreortyx pictus*) as occurring in this spot. The Pass being only about 4000 feet above the sea, and the mountains around it low and nearly treeless, does not offer so good a field for a collector as would be the San Bernardino range, which rises over 8600 feet forty miles south-east of here, and is covered high up with heavy coniferous and oak timber. The light coating of snow which greeted our eyes on the summit the morning of December 8th, is an index of the greatest cold ever experienced here, though the summits of the highest mountains in sight are often white in patches the entire summer.

As we are now about to enter on a new natural region, that of the interior deserts, I may as well digress a little from the line of travel to mention some other land animals I have observed west of this range, and north of latitude 34° 30′, a region which I have called the "Southern coast-slope" of California, extending north-east and south-west for about one hundred and forty miles, and fifty in breadth. Besides the mammalia mentioned, the Coast Fox (*Vulpes littoralis*), if really distinct from the Gray, does not occur northward. Deer (*Cervus Columbianus* and *C. Mexicanus?*) are not uncommon, and some small feline animals (*Felis eyra?*) with long tails, are said to occur. The Jaguar (*F. onca*) has been reported, but all other mammals except Skunks (*Mephitis occidentalis* and *M. bicolor*) are rare.

The Couguar (*Felis Concolor*), Grissly Bear (*Ursus horibilis*), Raccoon (*Procyon Hernandezii*), Badger (*Taxidea Americana*), Wild Cat (*Lynx rufus*), Gray Squirrel (*Sciurus leporinus*), Antelope (*Antilocapra Americana*) and Mountain Sheep (*Ovis montana*) occur more or less abundantly in various stations on the mountains or plains, but most of them are limited to particular spots, and are more abundant in other parts of the State.

The most peculiar birds not yet mentioned are the Contraband Hawk (*Buteo zonocercus*), which I found but once near San Diego, in February; the Rock Swift (*Panyptila melanoleuca*), a few of which breed in some cliffs near the same place; the Texan Nighthawk (*Chordeiles Texensis*), a summer visitor, the Little Vireo (*Vireo pucillus*) and Hooded Oriole (*Icterus cucullatus*), also migratory; the Long-tailed Mocking-bird (*Mimus caudatus*) and Long-billed Sparrow (*Ammodromus rostratus*), the latter confined to the sea-shore. These, as well as the White-bellied Auk (*Brachyramphus hypoleucus*), have not been found farther north, though the land species mostly occur farther east. Altogether I have noticed forty-eight species of mammals, and two hundred and forty-eight of birds, in this region. Of the birds thirty-two are summer visitors, thirty-two winter, and the rest resident.

Of reptiles I found twenty-eight species and six of batrachians, a few of the former are not known northward, viz., Hallowell's Rattlesnake (*Crotalus Hallowelli* nom. prov.), the Coppery Whipsnake (*Drymobius testaceus*), and Couch's Gartersnake (*Eutainia Couchii*). Two species of Gerrhonotus (*G. Webbii* and *G. olivaceus*) are also reported as only from these mountains, and I found two other undetermined lizards on the seacoast and Claueute Island. The fishes are few in the fresh water, and as yet undetermined.

On my return to the coast, just six months later, I found the summer fauna of this region in full development. The Rock Swifts flew high over the mountains with harsh croaking notes; the Vireos and Orioles sung sweetly in the high trees; the Mocking Bird, and many others, enlivened the shrubbery or chaparel, and at evening the nighthawks flew swiftly about our camps. Humming Birds of various species had nests on the trees, of which I unfortunately upset one and broke the eggs before I saw it. Brilliant flowers abounded, and though the dry season was commencing in the plains, the mountains were so inviting that I much regretted my inability to spend a month or two there before going to the military post at San Diego.

The Desert.—The whole country between the mountains and the Colorado Valley may be called desert, although only that part near the mouth of the river is called so on the maps, being nearly level and almost as barren of vegetation as the sea-beach. The route to Fort Mojave passes over an undulating country, destitute of trees except on the summit of the San Francisco Mountains, where it rises over 5000 feet above the sea. The lower tracts consist of salt or alkaline flats, sand-hills or bare rocks, while the higher support only a scanty and useless vegetation. Junipers (*J. occidentalis*) and Nut-pines cover a few of the highest points, while a little lower the Yucca tree (*Y. baccata*) forms extensive groves. Many species of Cactaceæ, and other desert plants, form the most characteristic vegetation elsewhere.

In such a region the higher animals cannot be expected to abound, and those found are chiefly stragglers from more favoured tracts, but still there are some of much interest. Descending the eastern slope we find Harris's Squirrel (*Spermophilus Harrisii*) scarce at this cold season, but common on our return in June. This little animal has much the appearance and habits of Tamias, but is nearly white. I saw also tracks of the Sage Fowl (*Centrocercus urophasianus*) corresponding in color with the granite rocks among which it lives, and have seen a specimen killed near here.

The only peculiar bird known is Leconte's Mock-thrush (*Harporhynchus Lecontei*), which is also of a pale grayish brown, like a fadad specimen of the coast species (*H. redivivus*), but is admirably colored for concealment among the thorny bushes growing on the sand-hills it inhabits. Both of these animals having dark colored representatives in less barren regions, offer excellent instances of the influence of "natural selection," but have some peculiarities not to be explained by the influence of the climate and country they inhabit.

The road for nearly one hundred miles eastward follows the Mojave River, which, being permanent for half that distance, and supplying moisture to a narrow tract of bottom-land, forms a sort of oasis in the desert, cultivable, and with its upper parts lined with trees and shrubs.

Some of the common Californian birds were rather frequent here, but I found none of interest at that season. On returning in June I found here the Purple-throat Humming Bird, the Little Vireo, and various other summer species. Fresh water shells of the genera *Lymnea, Physa* and *Planorbis* occurred, also two species of *Succinea*, in the more elevated cool parts of the valley.

It is in the class of reptiles, and especially lizards, that the fauna of the desert excels. Although none were visible in December, and I had not time to collect many on my return in June, I have ascertained that seventeen species have been obtained chiefly in this region by various naturalists, principally those of the Mexican Boundary and Pacific Railroad Surveys. One which they seem to have overlooked, although the most remarkable, perhaps, because inhabiting such a desert region, I described, after my return, as Agassiz's Land-tortoise (*Xerobates Agassizii*). In size it is about equal to the species of the Gulf Coast, but differs in color and other particulars. The Indians hunt for them on the mountains among cacti and other fleshy-leaved plants, on which they probably feed, rarely or never descending to the valleys. A Water-turtle (*Actinemys marmorata*) also lives in the Mojave River. One small Cyprinoid fish (*Algansea formosa*) has been found by Dr. Heermann in this stream.

Towards the sink, or "Soda Lake," which rarely contains water, the sand becomes very dry and almost bare of vegetation. A few trees (*Chilopsis linearis*) of small size grow there, and among them I saw a flock of the Arctic Bluebird (*Sialia arctica*). The only other bird of interest seen east of this was the pretty Black-throated Finch (*Poospiza bilineata*), which is pretty common in the shrubby tracts.—J. G. Cooper, in *The American Naturalist*. June.

Meetings of Learned Societies.

THE STATE MICROSCOPICAL SOCIETY OF ILLINOIS.

(Continued from page 214.)

THE COMMITTEES.

The following committees were then announced by the president:—

Floral Structure.—Dr. J. H. Ranch, George M. Higginson.

Infusoria.—Samuel A. Briggs, James Hankey, George F. Rumsey.

Cryptogamous Plants.—Henry F. Monroe, Joseph T. Ryerson.

Vegetable Histology.—Dr. R. M. Ludlam, Dr. John Davies, Dr. H. N. Small.

Animal Histology.—Dr. J. W. Freer, Dr. W. C. Lyman, Dr. Isaac Danforth.

Vegetable Pathology.—Dr. Hosmer A. Johnson, Dr. Benjamin Durham.

Animal Pathology.—Dr. J. H. Holister, Dr. W. C. Hunt, Dr. John F. Beaty.

Vegetable Parasites.—Dr. N. S. Davis, Dr. Samuel J. Jones, Dr. J. Crouse.

Animal Parasites.—Dr. Charles G. Smith, Dr. William C. Stimpson.

Crystallography and Mineralogy.—Dr. J. V. Z. Blaney.

Food and its Adulterations.—Dr. Walter Hay, E. H. Sargent, Albert E. Ebert, J. Hankey.

There being nothing more of a business character, the president declared the meeting adjourned until the first Friday in October next, and the chair being vacated, the company proceeded to an inspection of the interesting objects so profusely displayed for their instruction and delight. This, of course, was that portion of the evening upon which centered the chief interest of the occasion.

THE EXHIBITION.

It was truly a beautiful scene. The spacious drawing-rooms were filled to repletion with a brilliant company, but only intent upon seeing and enjoying the objects of interest by which they found themselves surrounded and tempted. Wherever the eye rested, whether upon the walls which were graced with superb paintings by Paul Weber and other eminent artists, or upon the great table, where was displayed the perfection of the optical art, from the hands of Ross, Powell and Leland, Beck and Beck, Nachet *et fils*—names which have become historic in the annals of optical progress—or upon the company, each for himself and herself, busy in searching out the unspeakable riches of the microscope field so bounteously spread before them, it was at once apparent that the occasion was one of no ordinary interest, and justify the remark of a lady well known here for her activity in everything which tends to the promotion and diffusion of sound and useful knowledge: "It is really the most delightful and instructive meeting I ever attended. I did not think it possible that science could array herself in such an attractive and social form, or that a scientific meeting could be conducted so easily and informally, yet withal so interestingly to others than its own members."

Upon the great table in the rear drawing-room, was arranged thirty microscopes, with their glittering and beautiful apparatus.

Each instrument had attached to it a card, with the name of the exhibitor, and the object exhibited. Down the centre of the table was arranged, by Mr. H. M. Wilmarth, a suitable apparatus for the due distribution of light to the instruments.

As a guide to others who may contemplate a similar exhibition, it may be briefly described as a bronzed pipe laying upon and running the length of the table, supported upon small brackets; attached to the pipe by rubber tubes were eleven lamps with argand burners and porcelain shades, affording a flood of deliciously soft light, and entirely free from glare.

Upon this table some of the wags of the society had displayed the garden ant, labelled "A lady of the period," "Our a(u)nt." In another place, a female mosquito, labelled "The first arrival of the season," "Lady Mosquito."

The marvel of this table, as a work of art, was the Lord's Prayer, written with a diamond in a space the hundredth part of an inch in diameter, exhibited by vice-president Rumsey.

The following is a catalogue of the exhibitors, the instrument, and the object exhibited :—

No. 1. J. T. Ryerson, Esq., Dallmeyer, London, proboscis of the house fly.

No. 2. F. V. Wadskier, I. P. Cutts, London, corpuscles in human blood, T. L.

No. 3. George F. Rumsey, Pike, New York, the Lord's prayer written with a diamond in a space the 100th part of an inch in diameter.

No. 4. I. G. Langguth, Jr., French, eye of cockchafer.

No. 5. Dr. H. Webster Jones, Grunow, New Haven, trichina in pork, T. L.

No. 6. The secretary, Smith and Beck, London, arachnoidiscus, T. L.

No. 7. A. A. Munger, Baker, London, polycystina, T. L.

No. 8. M. Polacheck, French, spiral vessels from rhubarb.

No. 9. E. S. Pike, Boston Optical Works, accidium grossularia.

No. 10. W. Henri Adams, Bulloch, Chicago, diatoms from the Sandwich Islands.

No. 11. The president, books and plates, synapta dignitata, Buffam, Lake Co., Ill.

No. 12. The secretary, Society of Arts, prize microscope, the first mosquito of the season.

No. 13. M. Polachek, Nachet, Paris, clematis vitalba.

No. 14. Dr. Benjamin Durham, J. W. Queen and Co., Philadelphia, pampas grass.

No. 15. Dr. Daniel T. Nelson, W. H. Bulloch, Chicago, trichina spiralis, from human muscles, T. L.

No. 16. John B. Gerard, McAlister, Philadelphia, spiracle of the drone fly.

No. 17. Dr. George H. Cushing, J. Tentmayer, Philadelphia, cricket's gizzard, T. L.

No. 18. Samuel Johnson, W. H. Bulloch, Chicago, trachea (breathing apparatus) of the silk worm, T. L.

No. 19. M. Polochek, elytron of beetle (opaque) light reflected.

No. 20. Secretary of the Chicago Academy of Sciences, Powell & Leland, London, bones of the starfish (opaque.)

No. 21. Dr. C. H. Hollister.

No. 22. The secretary, Smith & Beck, London, weissa viridula, illuminated with parabola, with Ross' new four-inch objective.

No. 23. William C. Hunt, Nachet et Fils, Paris, lung of frog (opaque.)

No. 24. George H. Hathaway, Dresden, "Lady of the Period," Our aunt, T. L.

No. 25. Dr. R. Ludlam, Buffam, Lake county, Ill., marine-algæ callithamnion hookier, T. L.

No. 26. Dr. H. A. Small, Buffam, Lake county, Ill., tongue of snail, L. T.

No. 27. H. F. Monroe, arachnoidiscus, T. L.

No. 28. Geo. M. Higginson, W. H. Bulloch, Chicago, fresh flowers—Arbutelar, cinneraria, cuphea, verbena and geranium, and polariscope.

No. 29. Foster & Boerlin, human flea.

No. 30. Foster & Boerlin, fossil earth from Nottingham, Md.

No. 31. Foster & Boerlin, probocis of butterfly.

No. 32. Foster & Boerlin, dust from miller's wing.

No. 33. Foster & Boerlin, feet and legs of dytiscus.

No. 34. Foster & Boerlin, leg of flea.

No. 35. W. H. Bulloch, human hair.

No. 36. Foster & Boerlin, hair of mouse.

No. 37. Foster & Boerlin, photograph Declaration of Independence.

No. 38. J. G. Langguth, Jr., spicules of sponge.

No. 39. John Corbutt, diatoms from guano.

No. 40. Foster & Boerlin, photograph of Trafalgar square, London.

No. 41. J. Horace Tracy, W. H. Bulloch, Chicago, circulation of blood in foot of frog.

No. 42. S. A. Briggs, W. H. Bulloch, Chicago, monen plate.

Nine others not entered in time for catalogue.

Upon the table in the library were displayed 16 instruments, exhibiting the following objects:

By Foster & Boerlin—Photograph of Trafalgar Square, London.

By John Carbutt—Diatoms in guano.

By J. G. Langguth, Jr.—Spicules of sponge.

By Foster & Boerlin—Photograph of the Declaration of Independence, with photographs of prominent men of the time surrounding it.

By Same—Hair of the mouse.

By W. H. Bulloch—Human hair.

By M. Polachek—Elytron of beetle, opaque, light reflected.

By Foster & Boerlin—Leg of a flea.

By Same—Feet and legs of dytiscus.

By Same—Dust from a miller's wing.

By Same—Proboscis of butterfly, light transmitted.

By Same—Fossil earth from Nottingham, Md.

By Same—Human flea.—Binocular.

By Same—Simple microscope, with object.

By the secretary society of arts, simple microscope,

The exhibition of objects in the floral department was conducted by George M. Higginson, Esq., with a first-class instrument made by Walter H. Bulloch, of this city, with one of William Wale's one-and-one-half inch object glasses. It consisted mainly of parts of fresh flowers, selected more particularly with reference to beauty of colouring and form, grouped artistically to show the same to the best advantage. These were exhibited as opaque objects, the light being concentrated by a large convex lens upon the slide. Parts of the geranium, verbena, cineraria, cuphea, and pansy were shown in this way, the colours of which were exceedingly rich, and the forms as beautiful as could be conceived. Mr. Higginson also exhibited the silicious star crystals in the caly of the deutzia scabra, and also one of the older leaves of the same plant. Salicene was also shown with this microscope, under transmitted light polarized.

The exhibition, by Samuel A. Briggs, Esq., of Moller's datomaceen typen platte, drew crowds of visitors throughout the entire evening.

The same remark applies to the display of beautiful objects given by the photomicographer to the society, Mr. John Carbutt, with the oxyhydrogen microscope.

The circulation of the blood, as exhibited in the web of the foot of the frog, and ably exhibited by Mr. J. Horace Tracy, of St. Luke's Hospital, was a constant source of pleasure to the company.

Refreshments were most bountifully supplied throughout the evening by the very liberal host, who, with his 'fayre ladye," was actively engaged in dispensing the hospitalities of the evening. Visitors continued to arrive up to eleven o'clock, many having previously attended the oratorio; and it was not until the hour of twelve had struck, that the last of the guests took their departure.

There seemed to be only one opinion upon the interest and pleasure afforded during the evening—that the whole affair was creditable alike to the host and hostess, the entertainers and the entertained, and an example worthy of emulation.

That it is creditable to a youthful community like this is beyond question,—a community which everybody says and believes has no parallel the world over in its eager and unscrupulous pursuit of mere money-making. The conversazione on Friday demonstrated this to be a libel. No community in this country or elsewhere more readily seizes every opportunity for the advancement of knowledge which is properly presented to its notice, than the community in which we live.

At the recent conversazione of the Royal Microscopical Society of London, there were 200 instruments on exhibition, and 1,500 people in attendance.

Parva componere magna. The State Society, on Friday evening, exhibited 51 instruments to an assembly of not less than 300 persons. London has a population of nearly 4,000,000; we claim 300,000; the Society's exhibition, in extent and interest manifested may therefore be favourably compared with that of the most influential society of the day.

The instruments, apparatus, and objects exhibited on Friday evening represent a money value of not less than $6,000, and when to this sum is added at least $1,000 more for libraries in this connection, a total of $7,000 is exhibited as devoted to this special and delightful pursuit,—a remarkable showing for a city of pork and breadstuffs; and yet not remarkable, for it is a part of history—and no uninteresting part either—that literature and the arts have always received their greatest strength and greatest impulse from just such commercial centres as our own.

CONCLUSION.

The Society is under many and great obligations to Mr. and Mrs. Ryerson, in the extensive and admirable preparations (not microscopic) and exertions made in behalf of the Society, its members, and friends; to George E. Stanton, Esq., for the use of the melegioscopio, with its accompanying drawings in six folios; to H. M. Wilmarth, for the use of lamps and other apparatus for illumination; to Drs. Nelson, Ware, and Cushing for the use of their microscopes and apparatus; to Gov. Bross, T. V. Wadskier, and others, for like instruments; and to Messrs. Foster and Boerlin, Polachek, and Langguth for like favours, which contributed so much to the success of the evening; and, lastly, to Mr. John Corbutt, for his services and aid rendered to the Society by the use and exhibition of the oxyhydrogen microscope, at the cost to himself of much valuable time and trouble.

EXTRACTS FROM AN ENTOMOLOGIST'S DIARY.

(*Continued from page* 207.)

March 13, 1868.—Small eggar (Eriogaster lanestris) emerged from pupa state.

March 15.—Warm. Saw four specimens of the Brimstone butterfly (Gonopteryx Rhamni), males, on the wing, also a small Tortoiseshell (Vanessa Urticæ).

April 23.—Took four larvæ of the Oak eggar (Bombyx quercus) and six of the Dark tussock (Orgyia fascelina) from the Whitethorn, also three of the drinker moth (O. potatoria) feeding on grasses.

May 1.—Took four larvæ of the oak eggar (B. quercus) and one of the dark tussock (O. fascelina).

May 27.—Weather mild. Captured a specimen of the common swift (Hepialus lupulinus); found also larva of the garden tiger (Chelonia caja).

May 28.—Warm. Took a privet hawkmoth (Sphinx Ligustri) and a ghost (Hepialus humuli), male.

June 3.—Evening cool, moonlight. Captured two females of the ghost (H. humuli). Found some larvæ of small tortoiseshell (V. urticæ) feeding gregariously on the nettles.

June 5.—Evening cool. Took a pair of the privet hawkmoth (S. Ligustri, and an angle shades (Phlogophora meticulosa).

June 7.—Took a quantity of the gregarious larvæ of small eggar (E. lanestris) from a whitethorn hedge. Found also a privet hawkmoth (S. ligustri) sitting on pailings, with wings scarcely expanded, having not long escaped from the chrysalis.

June 9.—Favourable. Captured the following moths, viz: Common yellow underwing (Tryphæna pronuba), angle shades (P. meticulosa), cabbage (Mamestra brassicæ) and five of the brimstone (Rumia cratægata). Saw a swallow-tailed moth (Uropteryx sambucata).

June 12.—Warm. Dark tussock (O. fascelina) and five tortoiseshell butterflies (V. urticæ) emerged from pupæ state.

June 13.—Captured specimens of the nut tree tussock (Demas Coryli), a common yellow underwing (T. pronuba). Three of the dark tussock (O. fascelina) emerged from pupa state.

June 29.—Warm. Captured three specimens of the swallow-tailed moth (U. sambucata), a golden Y. moth (Plusia iota), a willow beauty (Boarmia rhomboidaria) and five pairs of the burnished brass (Plusia chrysitis).

July 6.—Cool evening. Captured specimens of the following moths: Gray dagger (Acronycta psi), sitting on the trunk of an oak tree; dark arches (Xylophasia polyodon), light arches (X. lithoxylia) and common yellow underwing (T. pronuba).

July 7.—Took a swallow-tailed moth (U. sambucata), a pair of the burnished brass (P. Chrysitis), and a common yellow underwing (T. pronuba).

July 10.—Captured a female of the drinker moth (O. potatoria).

July 17.—Very hot. Captured two pairs of the meadow brown (Hipparchia janira), three pairs of the wall butterfly (Satyrus megæra), four pairs of the large heath (S. tithonus), and a peacock (Vanessa Io.) Saw a painted lady (Cynthia cardui).

July 18.—Weather hot. Captured specimens of the peacock (V. Io.), large cabbage (Pieris brassicæ), green veined (P. napi), wall (S. megæra), small copper (Polyommatus phleas), and the great dragon fly (Ictinus pugnax).

July 20.—Very hot. Took a fine specimen of the painted lady (Cynthia cardui).

July 22.—Weather very hot. Captured a fine specimen of the swallow-tailed butterfly (Papilio machaon), female, a pair of the painted lady (C. Cardui), three pairs of the large cabbage (P. brassicæ), and a brimstone butterfly (Gonopteryx Rhamni), male. (The above were taken at Ranworth in Norfolk.)

July 23.—Weather very hot. Captured a pair of the swallow-tailed butterfly (P. machaon), flying over a clover field, also three specimens of the brimstone (G. Rhamni), a male and two females, and three of the small copper (Polyommatus phleas). (Ranworth and South Walsham.)

July 25.—Very hot. Captured a small ringlet (Erebia cassiope) two pairs of the painted lady (C. cardui) and a pair of the peacock (V. Io). Pupa of the eyed hawkmoth (Smerinthus ocellatus) brought to me.

Sept. 5.—Warm, sun at intervals. Caught a pair of the pale clouded yellow (Colias hyale).

Dec. 24. Found a specimen of the herald moth (Gonoptera labatrix).

R. LADDIMAN.

St. Augustine's, Norwich.

Short Notes.

THE BITTERN.—In England it is said to breed only in Lincolnshire, Cambridgeshire, and Norfolk. In old times the bittern was held in high esteem for the sport it afforded when pursued by trained falcons. Both birds would mount in spirals, oftentimes out of sight; the bittern straining every nerve to keep above the hawk, the hawk doing his best to rise above the bittern so as to make the fatal pounce. The bittern, being of weaker flight, rarely escaped, but often in his death involved his enemy's; for as the cruel falcon came down with rushing wings, exulting in his fierce soul, the bittern, in his dire extremity, thrusting up his sharp beak, empaled the triumphant savage, and both came tumbling from the clouds together, striking the earth with a thump which drove the last breath from both. A lesson to tyrants not to push the weak to despair. On account of its furnishing such excellent sport to the humane of former times, rigorous laws for its protection were passed in the reigns of Henry VIII. and of Edward VI., which imposed a fine of eight pence and a year's imprisonment for every egg taken or destroyed. There was something like protection. The long hind claw was a most excellent toothpick, for, besides its functions as such, it had, if the wisdom of our ancestors was infallible, the highly meritorious property of preserving the teeth from decay. It appears, moreover, that the fowl had then the power of displaying a brilliant light from the centre of its breast, which attracted fish to it in great shoals, so that the satisfying of its hunger took but a small part of the night, and much time was left for other pursuits.

SPONGES.—Until of late years the animal nature of the sponge was disputed. Then it was referred to the Amœba forms, creatures which are mere sprawling drops of jelly, without mouths or stomachs, but which, however, manage to move about, and even in some species build up most elaborate internal structures resembling minute shells. Now, through the investigations of Professor H. J. Clark, we know that they are colonies of such comparatively highly organised beings as those I have described, and we are also able to state, upon the same authority, that their young are free, roving globules, resembling an isolated individual of the parent stock.

THE USEFULNESS OF THE CRAB.—All crabs discharge a most useful duty, being in fact the scavengers of the sea, consuming the dead animal matter which would otherwise do much to corrupt the waters along the coasts. Thus even the voracity of the crab promotes the well-being of the natural world, and consequently benefits the human race.—*Cassell's New Popular Educator.*

ALBINO WATER RAT.—A writer in the *Field* says:—I am not aware whether a white, or rather a sort of creamy pink, water rat, with pink eyes, has been often seen before; I certainly never saw or heard of one until I caught the one I now have ten days ago. One of the gardeners saw an odd animal run out of the grass, and threw his hoe at it, which cut off about two inches of the tail. A cage trap was set near the hole it ran into. In less than half-an-hour the rat walked quietly into it, and was caught alive. It seems quite contented in a cage, and eats cabbage leaves in your presence, when you give them to it; in fact, it seems quite at home.

ACCLIMATISATION IN AUSTRALIA.—About a dozen rabbits were let loose in Barwon Park, belonging to a gentleman named Austin, in South Australia, some few years ago, and recently in one year, 15,000 rabbits were killed on the estate. The partridges let loose failed to increase in numbers. The pheasants multiplied very of cover; hares, likewise, did not do well, they do slightly, owing to a want not appear to like the native grass. The rabbits are not only very numerous, but very large.

Remarks, Queries, &c.

(Under this head we shall be happy to insert original Remarks, Queries, &c.)

DO INSECTS FEEL PAIN?

"Behold the impaled and helpless fly
Who bleeds a victim to the optician's eye;
Before his glass spins in repeated round,
And strives to flutter from the deadly wound.
Firm and unmoved the speculative sage,
Eyes the vain efforts of its insect rage."

The "rare fertility of fancy," the studied inconsistencies, the dull series of permanent blunders, and the calm monotony of periodical exit, still continue to characterize the "advance backwards" of the imaginary advocates of the painless theory. But, Sir, when I speak of the "advocates" of the painless theory, or rather of their arguments and advocacy, the terms are absolutely indefinite, or convey an idea referring to glaring contradictions and luxuriant incongruities, so ludicrously jumbled together as to constitute a sort of illogical conglomerate, a heterogeneous phenomenon, wonderfully constituted for immediate analysis. Inconsistent as are many of the arguments propounded upon any interesting topic, it must be admitted that upon this lengthened discussion there have been many specimens of unskilful reasoning since it was first broached. It is apparent that amongst those who have relinquished the contest, at least some are more clearly convinced upon the subject than formerly. But here, Sir, a new correspondent enters the field, and in quite a novel capacity, fresh, and all vigour, as if justed started from *dormer entranse*, he assumes the functions of plenopotentiary extraordinary and veritable interpreter general for the whole negative camp! Your name, Sir, "George Trobridge, jun.," deliver your message. Then Mr. Trobridge, after announcing his own opinion, viz.: that "insects feel *a little pain*," thus speaks, thus interprets for the negatives: "I think none of the parties on the negative side wish now to assert that insects do not feel any pain, even if such were their opinion at first." Hear this, Messrs. Buttemer, Newberry, Veritas, &c., &c., who so ably supported the affirmative. Thus speaks the interpreter general of all the negatives, Mr. George Trobridge, jun.; but as contradictions and inconsistencies are the very elements in which the correspondents of the painless theory approach us, we must expect something new after all this. Here is Mr. Trobridge's first proposition, "none of the parties on the negative side wish now to assert that insects do not feel any pain;" or, in less complicated language, all the correspondents on the negative side now assert that *insects feel pain.* Then proceeds Mr. Trobridge hypothetically, "even if they held the negative opinion at first" they, now, *una voce,* cast it aside and rationally exclaim *insects do feel pain.* I wish the seer of the interpreting faculties had made his appearance sooner. I expected him, or something like him, long ago; but, "better late than never," even now, he is welcome; and I hope "the parties on the negative side," for whom he is spokesman and interpreter, will so appreciate his interpretation as to make a present of the N. N. B. to Mr. George Trobridge, jun. Mr. Trobridge very candidly leads us to believe that the correspondents, *en masse,* on the negative side, have by some means been convinced that insects feel pain, if ever they believed the contrary, a thing something doubtful; and surely Messrs. Buttemer, Newberry, Veritas, and myself, are presumptious enough to suppose that in our long and earnest advocacy of the affirmative, we had something to do in dragging the negatives to conviction. But stop! Sure Mr. George Trobridge, jun., wants to change the subject into *do insects feel much or little pain?* and thus magician-like imitate that capricious hag of old—

"Circe, the saffron-robed witch,"

with which the indefatigable Ulysses and his men had to contend, but our arguments must be to Mr. Trobridge what the herb *moly* was to the enchantress of antiquity.

And here, Sir, I again meet with my old friend Mr. W. H. Dalton, quite as philosophic as when we first met, and quite as dexterous in swinging his ponderous baton of self inconsistencies. I respectfully ask the correspondents on both sides to hear Mr. Dalton, and judge accordingly.

In the May N. N. B., just one month ago, when replying to my arguments, Mr. Dalton says:—"And now let me tell Mr. Ulidia that his argument of the social penalties of the ants has convinced me that, in the absence of certainty, which can only come by future study, it is highly probable that insects are susceptible to pain, and in my future dealings therewith I shall take care to give as little pain as possible." This is plain English, publicly admitting the force of my argument, and even proclaiming that he was "convinced" by its validity, and even promising to give "as little pain as possible to insects in future;" but with a tergiversation, a self-contradiction, to me totally unaccountable, Mr. Dalton in the June N. N. B. says:—"Though, as I said in my last, I agree with Mr. Ulidia in the affirmative view of the question, I cannot help protesting against his method of supporting that view"!! Gentlemen, what say you to this sort of logical progress in a month? It is perhaps expecting too much to ask Mr. Dalton to be even consistent with himself on this question.

"To what inconsistencies are we not dragged, Horatio!

Hem! Shakespeare. Mr. Dalton grumbles at the authorities I introduce to prove my case, but does not attempt to refute them, simply mentions the quotations I so profusely hurl against the negative arguments; but to the utter danger of his inconsistencies he forgets that he was "convinced" (according to his own admission) not by "quotations," but by a simple original argument of my own, and one which has often I presume, attracted our attention, a common argument with which we are all familiar. Shall I proceed? No. For Mr. Dalton's arguments appear

"———In such questionable shapes
That I will———"

just leave them so.

And now appears "O. R.," a sort of breathing disjunctive, enveloped in a dense hypothetical element, well understanding that there is "much virtue in if," and seems to be some fractional part of a special negative, for he thinks that *if* insects feel pain, his "man of feeling," cannot take a country stroll, lest he tread on insects and cause pain; that he cannot alleviate his "hunger-pain" on a bit of cheese lest he should be *g*uilty of cruelty to myriad inhabitants of "Old Stilton." Let "O. R." be at ease, and in his refined humanity remember that—

"The sum is this; if man's convenience, health,
Or safety interfere, his rights and claims
Are paramount, and must extinguish theirs."

Surely "O. R." should know that

"A necessary act incurs no blame."

As "Libra" says he agrees with much I have said, as he is another fanciful neutral, I just leave him to contemplate the sublime arguments likely to emanate from his favourite, philosophic, "dead man."

Mr. Ernest Belfort Bax, although he "really cannot find anything much," again, with "judicious caution," ventures out, foil in hand, and audibly grumbles at the number of my quotations. If my quotations are erroneous, or not to the point, there they are, Sir, refute them—if they are to the point, if they bear strongly upon the subject don't grumble, but appreciate.

Surely, Sir, Ernest Belfort Bax cannot be so shallow as to suppose that in reasoning we are denied the right of introducing authorities to prove our arguments. But as Mr. Bax "really cannot find anything much," he perhaps finds everything nothing.

Do insects feel pain? They do, most assuredly, as it is agreed on all sides that they have feeling. For, as has been argued by Buffon and others, and as it is so well expressed in ANIMATED NATURE, "Feeling is the guardian, the judge and examiner of all the rest of the senses. It establishes their information, and detects their errors. All the other senses are altered by time and contradict their former evidence; but the touch still continues the same and is never found to deceive."

Here, Sir, the power, the supremacy, the relative perfection of feeling, are forcibly set forth; insects possess this feeling, this supreme sense, and as a logical, as a natural sequence, they are capable of feeling pain. To deny this is to deny a self-evident truth, and so strongly, so powerfully has this truth flung itself into the moral perception of the correspondents on the negative side that they all invariably admit that insects are susceptible to some degree of pain. When rational conviction becomes dominant the unworthy agency of subterfuge is at once paralysed and abandoned, candour occupies its proper position, and truth and argument receive the welcome of honest antagonists. But Sir, while some of the speculative sages of the painless theory, cynic like, cannot condescend to see the force of arguments from the poets, they can conveniently stoop to exhibit their own inconsistencies with admirable docility.

Yet the promptings and the unconquerable instincts of humanity, the dictates of reason and common sense, so over-rule even the most strenuous advocates of the painless theory, that they cannot quite do away with the idea of pain in insects, and through all their writings, various as they are, one single mind, one grand unity of thought conspicuously struggle for rational ascendancy through the confused debris of special contradictions, and clearly proclaim that insects do feel pain when injured. Scientific inquiry evidently implies the presence of reason, application, labour, candour, earnestness, and other indispensable auxiliaries, the ultimate object being truth, and as truth is always consistent with itself, we must in such investigations patiently examine arguments, reject fallacies, cast aside inconsistencies, and work with all zeal and impartiality to arrive at the truth. And again I have to call the attention of the correspondents on the negative side to the subject under consideration, viz., *Do insects feel pain?* Their want of earnestness, their inattention or carelessness, cannot excuse their erratic logic.

Kirby and Spence, in speaking of the language of ants, say:—"In communicating their *fear*, or expressing their anger, they run from one to another in a semicircle, and strike with their head or jaws the trunk of the ant to which they mean to give the alarm." This *fear* evidently implies that they dread pain.

See that spider at the flame of the candle, does he seem to suffer pain? Surely the advocates of the painless theory must reply, he does—*a little*.

How often have we, on a summer day, such as this is, in early boyhood, cap in hand, wantonly captured and thoughtlessly killed the nimble, many-coloured butterfly, forgetful of the philosophy inculcated by Gisborne—

> Let them enjoy their little day,
> Their humble bliss receive;
> Oh! do not lightly take away
> The life thou canst not give.

But where are the amateurs of the negative side to read this? They are not here; they are retired, NOTE BOOK in hand, calmly soliloquising that insects do feel *a little pain*.

Do insects feel pain? They do or they do not. But that they do, must ultimately become an axiom in natural history.

Cast aside the "toils of office," leave the town one of those beautiful days, take the country—don't fear a little journey on foot—make use of your eyes, your ears, your reason, your judgment; look at insect life in its myriad forms, not too presumptiously—see its activity, its beauty, its diversity—try to convince yourself that that insect life is one of the connecting links of animated nature, a great phenomenon which you do not fully comprehend. Repeat your journeys, study natural history in the field and pool as you would astronomy in the heavens; be in earnest, love the science or stay at home, look at things, collect facts, compare theories, and give us a candid answer to the interesting question—*Do insects feel pain?*

Your correspondents, C. and Mr. Dalton, express a hope that I will now take up the subject, "Reasoning Power of Animals." I greatly regret that at present I cannot, as I am just slowly recovering from, in the words of my physician, "a serious illness," so that absolute rest, physical and intellectual, is strictly enjoined. I hope, in a short time, to be able to comply with the request of your clever correspondents, should the subject not be settled. The above article on pain in insects was nearly all prepared for the July number of the N. N. B., when I took suddenly ill.

Dromore.   H. H. ULIDIA.

REASONING POWER OF ANIMALS.

In making a few additional remarks on this subject, let me at the outset endeavour, if possible, to put in plainer language my own impressions with regard to it. Reason is observed in the beaver's dam, in the bees' hive, and the ants' storehouse: reason is observed in the growth, maturing, and decay of trees and the various phenomena of other plants; reason is observed in the falling stone, the rising vapour, and the ebbing tide; in short, all the objects and laws of the universe establish the fact that a great all-intelligent MIND superintends, directs, and animates all the features and phases of nature, animate or inanimate. Now I am inclined to think that as every inanimate object blindly follows the law of its Creator, so the animate portion of creation may be influenced by Divine superintendence, but moderated according to the degree of the development of *individual will*.

As this is a subject of such an abstruse nature, I dare say my last letter expressed too decided an opinion; but I think also that the *triumveri* who figured in your last in favour of the affirmative side of the question, would do well to render their position a little firmer before challenging their opponents. I should be sorry to declare absolutely that the lower animals have no share of individual reason, but think that the objections to such an opinion cannot be so lightly dispensed with. A few I jot down.

In circumstances in which man's reason would fail to direct him, the instinct of brutes occasions them not to err.

Young animals, untaught by experience, act reasonably.

If we allow reason to animals, must we not also to plants, as no line can be drawn between them, and this faculty does not descend in gradation.

There is nothing in the shape of progress or increase in knowledge observable in the lower animals, and this is the most distinguishing feature of reason.

If a superintending Providence directs the animal in those actions which go under the name of instinct, why may not the same control what are called their reasonable actions?

I confess I was surprised at the contemptuous way in which your correspondent, C., treats the ideas of such great men as I quoted. He contents himself with the simple remark that "no men are infallible." Can he bring forward as great an authority as Sir Isaac Newton to support the affirmative side? I will make use of one of C.'s own statements to further my views. On page 169 he says "I am inclined to believe that it is a grand mistake to separate instinct from reason, and define them as two distinct endowments," and so on. Now Sir I. Newton believed that the faculty in brutes and insects was exerted by the divine influence *acting immediately* in the same way as we move the parts of our bodies; therefore, according to C.'s own idea, that instinct and reason are one and the same faculty, it follows that the same influence which prompted the beetles (to quote the example of Veritas) to attempt to bury the mouse, further directed it to excavate the stick on which the animal was fixed.

That brutes appear to act intelligently is no *proof* that they do so; they may, for all that, act mechanically, and yet receive pleasure and enjoyment in their actions. Though your correspondent may consider the promptings or instinct like the "turning on of gas from a stopcock," will he deny that birds feel any sense of pleasure in building their nests and laying in them their eggs, although they know nothing of their future brood?

Lastly, I trust that this *third* "miserable attempt at logic" (a science I do not profess to be much versed

in) will not be entirely lost amidst the rays proceeding from the brilliant compositions of Mr. W. H. Dalton which appeared during his staunch advocacy of the *painless theory*, and from which the "biting sarcasm" of Mr. Ulidia drove him as "chaff before the mighty tempest." R. B. W.
Edinburgh.

Food of Lizards.—T. Smith, in the N. N. B. for July asks for information concerning the habits and food of the lizard. The following observations are what I have gleaned in my experience of this interesting little creature, the most elegant and agile of the reptilia. To begin with, we must supply our little scaly friend with a suitable habitation in the form of a Wardian case or glass shade, where he may disport himself among the ferns and mosses in the company, perhaps, of the slothful salamander, the grass-loving tree frog, and the toad, whom our nursery legends endow with such formidable qualities. The domicile selected for these reptile pets should be sufficiently ventilated to maintain a temperature suitable alike for lizards and ferns, taking care to keep up a certain degree of moisture requisite to both. The Jersey, or green lizard (Lacerta viridis), is perhaps the handsomest of his family, and with care will thrive well in captivity. In price he varies from 1s. or 1s. 6d. to, say, 3s. or 4s., according to size and the condition of the "naturalist market." The sand lizard (L. Agilis), who, though of a more sober hue than his Jersey cousin, is no less sprightly, is also a pretty pet for the fern case, though perhaps not quite so hardy. Zootoca vivipara, differing from the latter in his smaller size and orange belly spotted with black (his summer livery), and some slight variation in marking, is another of the lizards who, by his grace and agility, no less than by his hardiness, is a great acquisition to the fern case. I can only speak from experience of these three, but I should fancy that many others may successfully be reared in captivity. The favourite food of all lizards is the common house fly—this, and all other flies, they will swallow with avidity, seldom refusing them when placed in contact with their hungry jaws. The Jersey lizard, like the salamander, also enjoys occasionally a black beetle, which, if too large to swallow at once, he will make two or three bites of, rejecting the legs: lizards generally leave the wings of flies untouched. The common earth worm, the meal worm, and gentles, also form a part of our friends' bill of fare. In seizing his prey the lizard is as swift as an eagle; for flies he will climb as high as you give him the means of doing. (N.B.—Your fern case should be stocked with plants capable of supporting him, or else with miniature trees, such as the reptilia in the Zoological Gardens are provided with.) When a lizard catches his prey, he will give it a few vigorous shakes before disposing of it. Lizards, like all reptiles, will sometimes despatch worms as long as themselves. When baulked of his prey the impotent rage of our little friend is very amusing. Sometimes his hungry mouth, gaping for its prey, will close on a stone or piece of earthenware with which the mould is interspersed, and once in my experience a sprightly green young gentleman was laid low in the pride of his greediness and plumpness by a mouthful of mould, which he must have swallowed instead of his prey, and which, choking his windpipe, soon reduced this luckless example to gourmands to a stiff corpse. Sometimes, I regret to state, Mr. Lizard covets that which is his neighbour's; for not unfrequently, when one of the community catches a fine bluebottle, the greed of another causes a struggle to ensue, in which case might makes right, and the mutilated bluebottle becomes the spoil of "he of the strongest jaws." Twice or three times a week is considered enough for the creatures to be fed, yet the safest plan is to put a few flies or worms, &c., into the shade where they are kept, daily—this ensures all your pets getting a share, whereas if you feed them only twice or thrice a week, some of them who are not lucky enough to catch any of the insects may go a longer period unfed than would be desirable. Of course T. Smith knows that as the lizard, like other reptiles, hybernates in winter, it does not require food at that season. I have heard from a good authority of baby lizards being successfully reared on milk. They were put to swim in saucers containing it, which caused them involuntarily to swallow some. T. Smith may perhaps succeed in catching the sand lizard, as, though extremely swift, it is so numerous in sandy districts, such as Bournemouth, Hants., and Poole, in Dorset, that during a long walk one is almost sure of securing one of the graceful little creatures if he really try. Imago.

P.S. Can you inform me in your next what is the price of the "Lepidopterist's Guide?" also what kind of beetle it is the larva of which burrows in the bark of the ash tree? I should also be greatly obliged could you inform me how to preserve the colours of dried flowers.

Is the Whale a Fish?—Your correspondent, "Old Fogey," in his letter on this subject, entirely ignores the statement I made near the commencement of my letter, "that the question is not whether or not the whale is a fish according to the classification of naturalists, but whether the classification of naturalists can be justified." As I have before said, I do not think that it can. I still hold that naturalists ought not arbitrarily to restrict a popular term to suit their own convenience, as they have done in this case. If there were any restrictive meaning in the word itself, there would be some reason for using it in a restricted sense; but there is no such restrictive meaning, and therefore I think that naturalists should find some other name for that class of animals which at present they call Fishes. There are two classifications—the popular classification and the classification of naturalists. In the popular classification the word "fish" has always been used in a wide sense, and naturalists are not justified in appropriating that word and using it in a restricted sense, and they certainly are not justified in telling the "*populus*" it is wrong because it prefers to understand the word in its popular sense rather than in the sense which they have chosen to give to it.

Your correspondent, Gulielmus, thinks my proposal that naturalists should find a new scientific name for the class they call fishes, is "a step in the wrong direction." "Rather," he says, "keep the popular name, but show the people what it really means." I would ask your correspondent who are to be the judges of what it really means? As I have before said, there is nothing in the word itself by which we can fix its meaning, and therefore the next best thing we can do is to accept the meaning which it most generally bears.

Both your correspondents object to my definition of the word "fish," because, according to it, aquatic larvæ, tadpoles, whales, &c., are fish. And, I ask, why not? There is nothing more unreasonable in their being so called than in rotifers and insects being included under the common appellation of Articulata. Your correspondents should remember that the scientific and popular classifications are based on entirely different foundations, the former being based chiefly, if not wholly, on the structure of animals, whereas the latter is based on the habits, mode of life, &c., of the animals classified—and keeping this in view, they must admit, that under the popular classification, aquatic larvæ, tadpoles, whales, and *pisces*, have as many, if not more, points in common than *rotifers* and *insects* have under the scientific classification.

Your correspondent, Old Fogey, accuses me, as the mouthpiece of the "*populus*," of denying the *correctness* of the scientific classification. But this I never did. On the contrary; I consider that naturalists are quite correct in excluding the whale from their class of fishes, and I am sure that any one of the "*populus*" who know anything of the structure of the whale, would agree with me in so thinking; but it does not therefore follow that naturalists are right in restricting the word "fish" to the class of animals to which they apply it.

Your correspondent appears to have allowed his "irritability" at my heterodoxy to get the better of his judgment, or he would not have given utterance to such remarks as are contained in the last paragraph but one of his letter.

I now leave this question to the consideration of your readers, and hope in your next impression to see some letters in support of, as well as in opposition to, my views.   JOHN LANDELS.
Scuddylaw, Berwick-on-Tweed.

Mr. J. Landels, in his attempts to prove that the whale is a fish, says, "'Fish' is a popular term applied to all animals, whether vertebrate or invertebrate, which constantly reside in the water, and which could not exist for any length of time if they were removed from that element." Now if this was the case water snails and many insects, as well as tadpoles, would be fishes; therefore, it is very evident that his arguments for the affirmative side of this question are unfounded, and consequently the conclusions which, through those arguments, he arrives at, must be erroneous.

What reason have we for supposing that the whale is a fish? Simply its fish-like mode of progression in the water and its similarity of appearance. These are all the reasons I can see, and if these are really all it seems curious why a person should attempt to wield them against the formidable arguments of some of his opponents. A bat moves through the air like a bird, and when flying somewhat resembles a bird, but still I hope you don't intend to say a bat is a bird; because bats belongs to the class mammalia, and birds do not. Now, allow me to tell you, Mr. J. L., there is a far greater difference between a whale and a fish than there is between a bat and a bird.

Fishes are produced from spawn, whilst whales are born alive: this circumstance alone is sufficient to show that the whale cannot be a fish; but I will mention a few other differences to show you there is less reason to call a whale a fish than there is to suppose a bat is a bird. Fish are cold blooded, their circulating fluid being only exposed to the water in the gills: but the whale has no gills, nor anything resembling them; on the contrary, it has true lungs in a great bony chest, into which the air is freely admitted, not by the mouth, but by a peculiar apparatus through which the animal breathes the pure air of heaven, like other mammalia, and is thus enabled to maintain the warm temperature of its body even in the icy seas. Again: fish if removed from the water and brought into the air in a short time die, whereas the Cetacea if deprived of air and confined under water are speedily drowned.

Added to all this, there is the slight difference in the tail of the whale, which, unlike that of fishes, is horizontal; and also the vast difference in the formation of the heart.   J. F. SUTTON.

SHORT NOTES ON THE SWIFT (CYPSELUS APUS). —There are few persons, either residents in the country or even in our large towns, who are not familiar with the sight of the swift, or can have failed when seeing it to have been struck at its vast power of flight as it dashes through the summer air. This bird belongs to the family of the Hirundinidæ, and in colour is the least handsome of the swallow tribe. Indeed, it has no pretensions to beauty of plumage, being of a uniform sooty brown, with a small greyish patch beneath its beak. Owing to its rather dingy appearance the swift is also called the black martin, by which name it is often known, although the former is much the most appropriate one, as it is the swiftest flyer, I believe, of all birds found in any regions of the globe. The muscles of its wings must be wonderfully strong, for on account of its small and weak feet it rarely, if ever, perches, so that during the long summer days it is fully sixteen hours on the wing, it being an early riser, and retiring again to roost late. But although the swift is not able to walk well, its feet are admirably adapted for clinging, and hangs by its sharp claws to walls and houses.

The swift, which is a lover of sunny regions, does not usually arrive in England till the last week of April, the twenty-seventh of that month being the first day I observed it this spring. It is a bird which is most impatient of cold, and many are the stories told of benumbed swifts being picked up should any sudden decrease in the temperature occur. Its sojourn with us lasts for about thirteen weeks, departing again in the middle of August, although I have noticed them linger on till the beginning of September. Why the swift should leave us at that lovely season of the year is a mystery, and a great puzzle, I believe, to all ornithologists, and is, as the Rev. Gilbert White has said, "one of those incidents in natural history that not only baffles our researches, but almost eludes our guesses." Their early retirement cannot be on account of any deficiency of heat, the temperature at that period being much higher than it is on their first arrival in this country. It may perhaps be owing to the failure of certain insects that they feed on. I should be most happy to hear from correspondents of the NATURALIST'S NOTE BOOK what their opinion is upon this interesting subject, if they would kindly inform me through its pages.

Unlike the rest of its tribe, the swift is no songster, and does not even twitter like the swallow and martin, but has only one harsh note, which is nothing more than a scream. During fine summer days, or in hot thundery weather, several will collect together and dart through the air screaming as loudly as they can. From its peculiar screeching note the rural population of our island have given it the name of "squeaker."

The swift is indeed a bird of the air, and both eats, drinks, and collects materials for its nest when on the wing; and in the middle of the day it may be seen, looking like a black speck in the sky, actively seeking for insects at a great height from the ground.

This bird builds its nests under the eaves of churches and houses, and only lays two pure white eggs at a time, and breeds twice in the summer.

A. E. BUTTEMER.

ANSWERS TO ENQUIRERS.—In your last month's issue of the N.N.B. are several inquiries from what I suppose to be young aspirants to entomological pursuits; should the following replies meet your approval they are at your service for the coming month :—
"A. M. B." asks what kind of food our butterflies feed upon in the perfect state. I believe that butterflies take no other food or sustenance beyond what they are capable of drawing up through that fine and wonderfully formed instrument which is when at rest closely curled up and mostly hidden from sight by the palpi or projecting part of the face of the insect. This instrument is known by the entomologist as the proboscis, tongue, or trunk, and is not only found to exist in most of the butterfly kind, but is even more fully developed in several of the sphinx moths, being most particularly conspicuous in the species known as the Convolvuli or Unicon Hawk moth; this appendage can be inserted into the petals or cup of a flower in an instant to extract the nectar therefrom; upon which alone they appear to subsist.

"H. F. P." enquires the best method for keeping chrysalides. I would advise that this enquirer avail himself of the last year's volume of the N.N.B., where he will find the same question responded to in various forms from page 94 to 190; likewise numerous means used to destroy the vitality of the insect, and to preserve it uninjured in its beauties for the cabinet, with many other little matters appertaining to entomology.

"W. E." asks how he may determine, from the appearance of the larva, to what species of fly they belong or will likely produce. I must reply that this knowledge is a work of time, and cannot be acquired in one season, but may be greatly facilitated by an acquaintance with an experienced and friendly entomologist. There are books with plates of larva, food, and perfect insects, which are beautifully executed, and will in many cases show all required at a glance; but good works of this kind are very expensive, and cheap or low priced ones, with coloured plates, are more amusing then really useful.

However, as I have already observed, this and many other little difficulties may be cleared up, and a good fund of information obtained, in reference to entomology, by perusing the papers, &c., kindly contributed from month to month by Messrs. Clifford, Tempany, &c., to the N.N.B. C. W . . d.
320, Strand.

RICE.—In response to "Quercus," who asks in the April number of the N.N.B. for information respecting the rice plant, I send the following :—Rice is the seed or grain of a kind of corn, and grows in a spike similar to oats. It is very abundantly grown in China, the East and West Indies, and America. It is also cultivated in the south of Europe, at Piedmont, from which place Switzerland draws its supply. It cannot thrive without much moisture, and, therefore comes to the greatest perfection in marshy lands. The method of cultivation varies according to the climate and local circumstances. The cultivators of rice always inundate their grounds, and the higher the water rises the higher the plant grows, the ear always appearing above water; it requires as much heat to mature the seed as it does moisture to nourish the plant in its growth. The following method is adopted in China, where the numerous rivers, the excellent irrigation, and the great extent of marsh land, especially in the S.E., afford abundant facilities. The low lands of the middle and southern parts of the Chinese dominions are annually inundated by the Kiang and the Yellow rivers, which overflow their banks, owing to the heavy rains that fall near their sources. When the waters have receded the earth is covered with a thick coating of slime and mud, which fertilizes the fields as perfectly as the richest manure. The ground is then carefully harrowed; in the meantime the rice intended for seed has been soaked in water, in which a quantity of manure has been stirred, and this has forwarded its growth so much that the young plants appear above the ground in two days after they have been deposited in the earth. When the plants are about six or seven inches in height they are taken up, the tops cut off, and the roots washed carefully. They are then planted in rows about a foot apart, and harvested twice in the year, there being two crops, the first about May or June, and the second in October or November. The instrument employed for the purpose of reaping is similar to the European sickle, only that the edge instead of being smooth is notched like that of a saw. This useful grain is the universal food of the Chinese, who pity Europeans because they have not the rice plant. In India the women thrash and prepare the rice, which is a very laborious employment, and the Brahmins live almost entirely upon it; indeed, it has been said, that rice sustains one-third of the human family.

Gravesend.   G. O. HOWELL.

FOOD OF BUTTERFLIES.—A. M. B., in answer to A. M. B., begs to inform him that butterflies, as a rule, feed upon the nectar contained in the cups of various flowers, some few confining themselves, however, to one particular plant. To give a list of all these would, I fear, take up the whole of the N. N. B.; some few, however, which occur to my mind at the present moment, I may mention as a guide. *P. Machaon* feeds on scabious; *G. Rhamni* appears to haunt the red geranium; *C. Edusa* and *Hyale*, lucerne and saint-foin; *H. Semele*, the flowers of the common ling, or heath; *A. Iris* has been known to feed on fallen fruit, or still worse, on half putrid animals or birds, and I have seen the *Vanessidi*, *Atalanta*, and *Polychlorus* eagerly imbibing the sweet sap which exudes from wounded trees; *A. Paphia* has a great passion for bramble blossoms, as also most of the genus thecla; *P. Argiolis* is fond of the flowers of the holly, and *P. Sylvanus* of those of thistles. It must not be imagined that this is all which the butterflies named feed on, as an hour's observation on the part of A. M. B. would show. Let him take up his station at this season of the year in some wood, and watch such flowers as those of the scabious, bramble, honey-suckle, bedstraw, and others, and note the various butterflies which alight to rifle their sweets, and he will gain a clearer idea of the nature of their food than anything but a very exhaustive list could give him. As I have endeavoured to give him the key to the knowledge he seeks, would he do me the favour in future (as I am the " old original A. M. B.") to sign himself A. M. B. No. 2?   A. M. B.

DOES THE SKIN ABSORB?—This is still to some extent an open question in physiology, although the balance of proof, as well as of authority, is greatly in favour of an affirmative answer. The difficulty of determining the point is increased by the circumstance that the skin is also constantly exhaling fluid by the sudariporous glands.

In the practice of physic it is a common custom, where the introduction of medicines into the system by the stomach is inadmissible, to make use of the lymphatics of the skin for the purpose. By the inunction of mercury into the surface the specific effects of that substance are as surely though less rapidly produced. Tartar emetic also administered in this way is often observed to produce vomiting, or the other results of its being taken by mouth. It has been objected to the many proofs of this kind that the friction used may make a breach in the epithelial covering, and force the medicament into the lymphatics of the *cutis vera*. But it is a well-ascertained fact that mere immersion of the body in water soothes thirst. Frogs and lizards that have been kept for a time in a dry atmosphere gain weight rapidly when the tail and trunk only are immersed in water. Dr. Madden found by experiment that a man put in a warm bath increased in weight, which, considering that exhalation from the lungs and skin were actively going on at the time, could only be accounted for by cutaneous absorption.

Dr. S. Smith instances a case where a man who had lost nearly three pounds in weight in an hour and a quarter's active work in a very hot and dry atmosphere, regained eight ounces by immersion in warm water for half an hour. There is no doubt of the fact which "R. B. W." adduces, that patients have been kept alive by baths of nutrient fluids.

THOMAS Q. COUCH.

THE MOSQUITO.—In reply to R. T.'s note, asking for a description of the mosquito, I give the following:—In all hot climates this insect takes the place of the common gnat in the cold and temperate. It is not quite so large, but is a much worse enemy. The people in America are terribly tormented by mosquitoes. Humboldt, in speaking of them, says that there are three different species; some sting from an early hour in the morning, all day long, until five in the afternoon, when they disappear, and a second set "mount guard." These have their hours of attack and then retire, and are followed by the night army, the most dreadful and venomous of all. During the intervals of the disappearance of one host and the appearance of the next, a brief and delightful repose is given to the tortured Indians. An old missionary, in accents of grief and despair, said "he had spent his twenty years of mosquitoes in America." The Indians say that there are more mosquitoes than air. Sometimes they are compelled to bury themselves in the sand, only leaving their heads, covered by a handkerchief. In India mosquito curtains are in common use, and many people use veils during the day. We also have a good share of these little torments out here in Natal—there are two varieties, the black and the white. Some people, when bitten, retain the marks of the wounds, their countenances being disfigured by large red blotches for several days; while others (myself among the number) hardly feel their bite, which only lasts for a few seconds. You can always tell when the mosquitoes are coming by their peculiar buzz, quite different from that of any other insect. A solution of ammonia is said to alleviate the pain of the bite.   J. D. S. W.

Upper Umkomancy, Natal.

SIREX GIGAS.—Two of the above during the past week have been captured in this town (Saffron Walden), the specimens of which I have now before me. The insect somewhat resembles a hornet. It has four wings, which are transparent, and of a brownish colour. They have the antennæ jointed, of a yellow colour. The head is black, with two yellow spots above the eyes; the thorax black. The body is yellow, with a broad band of black in the centre. The abdomen is prolonged into a horn, and the ovipositor is about a half an inch in length, is black, something like the sting of a wasp, which when not in use is sheathed, and projects out under the abdomen. I should like to hear if any captures have been made in any other parts of the country, as I find it is a native of cold and mountainous countries.

S. REGELOUS.

THE AMOUNT OF PAIN FELT BY INSECTS.—You will pardon me again "harrowing up the feelings" of insects, but the subject is of such interest that I can hardly refrain from pursuing it. It seems to be a generally acknowledged fact now amongst your readers, that insects have a certain amount of feeling, and I certainly think that this amount can be determined scientifically. Pain, undoubtedly, has its seat in the nerves, and it therefore depends on the development of the nervous system what degree of pain is felt by any animal. In man, as in the other vertebratæ, the brain is the chief centre of the nerves, and consequently the most vital organ. This, then, is undoubtedly the reason that many savages are almost insensible to pain, the development of the brain being deficient. Insects, according to the limited knowledge I have derived from the writings of others, are not possessed of brains, the centre of the nervous system being in the thorax. I therefore conclude that the amount of feeling in insects is small. A paper on the internal anatomy of insects, with more especial relation to their nervous system, from some kind scientific friend, would throw a great light upon the subject, and be a source of much pleasure and benefit to Smethwick. GEO. TROBRIDGE, Junr.

HABITS OF SPIDER.—My attention was called the other evening to the actions of a garden spider, which at first sight seemed to be repairing a broken web. Such, however, was not the case, as it might have been seen pulling the web to pieces in a most systematic manner. From subsequent observations it seems that the web is destroyed every day, and replaced by a new one. The manner in which he set to work was most interesting; he collected the threads in his fore legs as he went, and every now and then might have been seen to throw away a little ball of refuse matter, taking it between its two hind claws and using some force in the ejectment. Last night, he being still in the same position, the old web was destroyed but no new one made, as the spider, which is a small one, had managed to secure a large fly, and since then has been busily engaged trying to devour it, not having left it, apparently, during the whole of the night. I have not studied spiders particularly, and possibly these remarks may be superfluous; I leave it, therefore, to your judgment as to whether they are worth insertion in the N. N. B. GEO. TROBRIDGE, Jun. Smethwick.

BEETLES.—In reply to Mr. Noel's query respecting a recently published work on coleoptera, I think that I can recommend to him E. C. Rye's "British Beetles." This book is very well written, containing the best classification of coleoptera, a concise and clear description of very many species of every "section," and ninety-six beautifully coloured figures, besides some woodcuts. I think also that he should procure Stephens's "Manual of British Beetles." This work, price 5s., has been considered to be rather confused in nomenclature; but I cannot say that there is any great fault in it. Certainly, there are two or three "sections" in the wrong places, but with Mr. Rye's book as well, this defect in Stephens's will matter little. I perhaps ought to have mentioned that this work is not illustrated. If Mr. Noel would like to know of another book, there is Curtis's "British Beetles," which is, I believe, half a guinea in price. I cannot speak of it from experience; but the coloured engravings in it are said to be unrivalled for beauty.
VERITAS.

A CURIOUS INSECT.—Suspended from a hawthorn hedge by a fine thread, I, the other day, found a most curious insect. I have seen it before, and since then have found it in immense numbers on oaks and other trees in Sutton Park near Birmingham. It is about three-eights of an inch long and in general appearance closely resembles a caddis worm, being enveloped in a case like a rolled up dead leaf, and protruding only its head and six claspers. When at rest it adheres to a leaf or the trunk of a tree by suction, and so fast dies it hold on that it is difficult to pull it off without tearing it in pieces. I kept one and gave it hawthorn for food, but it almost immediately fastened itself to a leaf and has not moved since, which is now several weeks. Can one of your correspondents inform me what the creature is? GEO. TROBRIDGE, Jun. Smethwick.

CAPTURE OF A CURIOUS ANIMAL IN A RABBIT SNARE.—An animal which baffles the skill of those who have seen it to define, was a few days ago found in a snare set for rabbits in the demesne of the Marquis Conyngham, at Slane, County Meath. It is thus described by the gamekeeper:—The size of a good cat, with a tail about a foot and a quarter in length, covered with strong wiry hair. The snout is sharp and pointed, something like a weazel's. In the mouth there are four large tusks, two pointing upwards and two downwards. A small mane or dark brown hair runs down the whole length of the back; but the strangest thing of all is that it has twelve toes or claws on each foot, in two rows—seven on the outside row, which are exceedingly sharp, and five on the inside. In general it is more stoutly built than animals of the cat kind. Still, the body is lithe and supple. The colour throughout is dark brown, and white on the breast.—*Saunders's News-letter.*

THE SHARK AND PILOT FISH.—I was greatly interested on our voyage out by watching the habits of the shark and pilot fish. It is generally believed that the pilot fish follows the shark to share in its repast, but I do not think that this is the case. We frequently threw pieces of flesh into the water to them. The pilot fish first came up and smelt the meat, and then went away and led the shark to it, who always swallowed the whole, and left none for his little companions. On a dark night you can see the entire shape of the shark in the water below shining all over with phosphorus. Now this phosphorus is considered by most naturalists to be animalcules, and if so it may reasonably be presumed that the pilot fish live on these, for they are frequently seen clinging to the sides of the shark. J. D. S. W.
Upper Umkomancy, Natal.

LION AND TIGER'S FLESH AS FOOD.—It will surprise some of your readers to hear that the flesh of these carnivorous beasts is eaten, and liked by those who have tried it. Captain Kennedy, in his journey through Algeria and Tunis, says, "the flesh (of lions) is eaten, and contrary to our expectations, we found it excellent, and made a capital supper upon the end of the ribs, stewed, with a little salt and red pepper. It tasted like very young beef, and was neither tough nor strong flavoured." Some of the Dutch boors out here are very fond of tiger's flesh, which they say is "first rate," but the strong smell that they have after death would prevent me, and I think most of the readers of the N. N. B. from touching it.

Upper Umkomancy, Natal. J. D. S. W.

Whatever Mr. Ernest Belfort Bax may think of the authenticity of the work from which he quotes the fact of dogs playing at chess or dominoes, I must confess to an incredibility which I cannot shake off as to the authenticity of the particular fact referred to. The mere moving about of the chessmen is not playing at chess any more than drawing my pen a number of times across a sheet of paper is writing a letter. If dogs could play at chess they would be far superior in intellect to the majority of the human race.

W. NEWBERRY.

KEEPING CHRYSALIDES.—Your correspondent H. F. P. desires to know of a mode of keeping chrysalides. I use long trays of cardboard filled with bran or sawdust, in which I lay the chrysalides; these trays are fixed up inside the breeding cage. Of course, where a cocoon is provided, neither bran nor sawdust will be required. I have long adopted the above plan, and should advise H. F. P. to try it too, and hope he will be as successful as

ONE OF THE "BRETHREN" OF THE "NET AND PIN."

THE CUCKOO.—In the June number of the N.N.B., B., from Halstead, asks if it is usual for the cuckoo to sing during the night; and in the July number G. O. Howell does not seem certain on that point. Whatever may be the habits of the bird at Halstead and Gravesend, here in Hampshire it sings all through the night at intervals. At whatever hour one may wake, the cuckoos are always heard singing, rivalling the nightingale, at least in continuous song, if not in melody. M. L. A.

In my paper, "List of British Moths," which appeared in your July number, the following typographical errors occur. Under the description of "Foxglove Pug," read *Digitatis* for *Digitalis*; under "Lime Speck," read *Silaus* instead of *Lilaus*; for *Dentaled Pug* read *Dentated Pug*; and also under "May and July Highflyers," read *Ypsipetes* instead of *Ypsipites*.

T. W. TEMPANY.

I should recommend B. B. Noel to get Mr. E. C. Rye's book on "British Beetles." It is a recent work, and contains sixteen coloured plates, and six different species are figured on each plate. The price is half a guinea. This information may also be useful to your correspondent W. E. I do not know of any good work on British coleoptera published at so moderate a price as two or three shillings,

A. E. BUTTEMER.

A NORTHERN NOTE.—This morning, June 16th, High Street and Kirkstone, vale of Troutbeck, were deeply covered with snow. Coniston and range were also covered, but not so deeply. Wind easterly. Can we imagine that we are only five days off Midsummer's day! FILIX.

ROES IN A SHRIMP.—No doubt many of your readers are not aware of the quantity of roe that is in a shrimp. Having counted the contents of three, I am able to inform your readers that the first contained 1,362, the second 1,498, and the third 1,608; making a total of 4,468 in the three shrimps, or an average of 1,489 in each. HENRY O'CONNELL.

Mr. T. Smith asks for information respecting the lizard and its food. It subsists chiefly on insects, and is found in dry situations, particularly in heaths. Like the slowworm, it breaks off its tail when captured. It remains under the roots of trees in a state of torpor during the winter, but emerges from its retreat in the beginning of spring. M. L. A.

MUMMY PEAS.—At the Rectory, Wrotham, about ten miles from Gravesend, are some peas in full bloom, the seed of which were taken from the hand of a mummy, a few years ago, by the rector's nephew. The mummy was supposed to have been from 1800 to 2,500 years old. G. O. HOWELL.
Gravesend.

BOOK ON BRITISH BEETLES.—In answer to W. E. and B. B. Noel, a book on British Beetles, with plates plain or coloured, is published by R. Hardwicke, 192, Piccadilly. The price is, plain 2s. 6d.; coloured 4s.

St. Augustine's, Norwich. R. LADDIMAN.

REPTILES IN IRELAND.—Would Mr. Ulidia, or any other Irish correspondent, kindly inform me whether it is true that there are no reptiles, with the exception of a small lizard, found in Ireland, and if so, what is the reason? J. D. S. W.
Upper Umkomancy, Natal.

ERRATUM.—Allow me to correct a little mistake in my paper on "Reasoning in Animals." At the sixteenth line of the right hand column on the 217th page, read *they* instead of *it*. VERITAS.

CRICKETS AND COCKROACHES.—Can any of the readers of the N. N. B. kindly inform me of a way of getting rid of crickets and cockroaches?

HAWKMOTH.

DRAGON FLIES.—I should feel greatly obliged if any of the readers of the N. N. B. could inform me of a method of preserving the colours of dragon flies.
St. Augustine's, Norwich. R. LADDIMAN.

TORTOISES.—Could you kindly inform me through your valuable paper as to whether Tortoises will breed in England, and the time of year, also the best way of propagating them. S. DRUMMING.

PLANCHETTE may be obtained from Cremer, Bond Street. Price half-a-guinea. C.

LA PLANCHETTE.—Will you kindly inform me in your next number where "La Planchette" is to be obtained, and at what cost. O. C.

In my note on the composition of coal, page 219, first column, bottom line, the word *foundations* should be *formations*. W. NEWBERRY.

ROUGH NOTES ON THE NATURAL HISTORY OF CORFU.

(Continued from page 237.)

THE next day we coasted Tunis, being sometimes within two or three miles of land, so that the ruggedly beautiful rocks which appeared to tower steeply from the sea as well as the higher cloud-shrouded mountains far beyond, were plainly distinguishable. Later in the day it rained heavily, and a pretty little Turtle Dove (Columba Turtur) sought our vessel for safety, and as a matter of course, was caught by one of the men while clinging to the rattlins; it was in a most exhausted condition, having, perhaps, flown hundreds of miles from the interior of the country in its passage to more congenial regions. Sunday, the 29th May was our last on board, and in the morning the Church Service was read by the captain of the vessel to the men mustered beneath a large awning, now rendered necessary by the increased heat. On board a man-of-war this ceremony is far more imposing. For instance, I remember when on board the magnificent Galatea (now commanded by H.R.H. the Duke of Edinburgh) the men were beat to quarters as if going into action, and soldiers and sailors mustered on the gun-deck, lining the sides, the chaplain standing between them, while the darling frigate herself was as spick and span from truck to keel, as the finest lady in the land when about to be presented at court. On one occasion while the chaplain was reading Service, a handsome little canary, which had escaped from the land (we were then lying off Malta) perched itself directly over his head on one of the yards, and began singing with so much *abandon* and shrillness, that the service could not proceed until the feathered psalmist had been driven away, and—but I must "clew up" these yarns, or in my unravelled threads of discourse about things not bearing on the subject-matter, I shall lose the skein of my argument.

At 3 p.m. we passed a large island, rising to an enormous altitude in the centre, until lost in the enveloping mists which canopied its highest peak; at the foot lay nestled the town, and several large houses gleaming in the rays of the fierce sun which beat upon their walls. Part of this island, which lies midway between North Africa and Sicily, and is called Pantelaria, appeared to be in a high state of cultivation, judging from the ploughed lands and vineyards near the town, which the clear air plainly revealed. About midnight a breeze sprung up abaft our beam, and aided by this we steamed and sailed at about 14 knots, until the engines were obliged to be stopped through over-heating. The next day—our course having hitherto been southerly, we took a sharp turn as it were to the north-east, leaving Malta behind us, and kept near the coast of Sicily, which was now on our port-bow; at no time were we very close to land, therefore we had but a dim view of the volcano Etna, which gleamed through the hazy distance a yellowish white; whether caused by sulphur ashes or by the natural colour of its rock formation we could not determine.

By five the next afternoon land hove in sight, as two islands lying off both bows; farther ahead were some high mountains, appearing by a deceptive trick of the distance to connect the two. Three hours after we passed in between them, and then saw that one only—that on the port, was an island, sweeping round like a half moon to within a few miles of the mainland of Greece, on our starboard. The reason we had not seen this before was, that we had been in the narrow neck of the gulf, and some promontories which were thought the ends of the two islands, had hidden some bays which widened the passage, and allowed us on coming up to see that beyond them the land still continued on one side, and on the other, swept round in high mountains as before described.

The vessel now was going very slowly, stopping every now and then to allow soundings to be taken, a man being stationed in the chains for that purpose with lead and line; poising himself and making two or three preliminary casts, the leadsman would at last let the hissing coil of line fly from his hand, and hardly ere it was buried by the waters, it would be rapidly hauled up again, the result being given in a deep sonorous chaunt, "By the deep, nine;" "By the mark, ten," and so on, as the knots revealed the fathomed depth of the sea under our bows. Going farther up the inlet, and passing some beautifully wooded and fertile land sloping quite to the water's edge, we saw at midnight a bright light on our port. Sometimes going half speed, and sometimes stopping altogether for fresh soundings, we at length neared the light, and then saw that it was a beacon on the summit of a high rock at the entrance to a harbour; off here we hardly steamed at all; the soundings, which were now taken by two men at rapid intervals, betraying our close and anything but pleasant proximity to submerged rocks. At last we slowly steamed into position just off the lights of a town; a gun previously cast loose and loaded, was fired, the anchor let go, and by 2.30 a.m. on the 1st June, 1859, the good old Melbourne was at her journey's end in the splendid harbour of Corfú.

I turned in for an hour's sleep, and as morning dawned, came up on deck again, while the land wind was still blowing, bringing with it the perfume of countless flowers, in which I thought I distinguished the never-to-be-forgotten odour of the orange blossom, chaste emblem of love and wedded happiness. As I leaned over the bulwarks drinking in all the glories of this fair scene so greyly beautiful in the coming glory of the light, I could but think how pure, how redolent of maiden loveliness is the morning when the grey mantle of the summer night's mists are cast from her rosy brow, and reveal the smiles with which she greets the still sea; the song of birds, and the dewy flowers fainting through all the chill night for the anticipated kiss from her balmy lips. As the fleecy clouds rolled upward from the lower land and piled themselves in little bright masses on the higher slopes of the mountains, the town and country emerged from its concealment, and the first thing which struck me was the citadel, built on two high rocks, with a break or valley occurring between them. Of great natural strength, this part is further aided by scientifically built fortifications, and a garrison of several thousand soldiers of various branches of the British Infantry. Seen from the sea on the extreme left is Capo Sidero saluting battery, from which is fired the morning and evening gun; above this on the summit of a high rock, almost hidden by wild olive, fig, and prickly pear trees, are the square built towers of the grand powder magazine of Castellamare; just below on the right and between the two peaks mentioned before, is the Garrison Hospital, a long low building, with trees in front, and a nice garden at the side; below this again, on a wall just above the sea, is a range of white buildings running almost the entire length of the citadel, forming the barracks for officers and men. Rising steeply above this is the right peak, the highest point for some distance around, on which is situated the lighthouse and signal staff, from which on clear days a view of places distant eighty miles can be obtained. Here is the "Half Moon Battery," commanding the whole of the town and district; below the rock is the clock tower and a few scattered houses, residences of the General and staff. Just before you come to the Cunette, or Citadel Ditch, separating the Citadel from the town, is a bastion, on the right flank of which is cut a Venetian inscription under a bas-relief, in Pentelic marble, of the Lion of St. Mark, perpetuating the memory of the brave Schulemberg, who in July, 1715, after several bloody engagements, forced the Turks to raise the siege of Corfú. Looking towards the town, now well to your right, you notice that it rises slightly in the centre, and consists of the usual assortment of large and small houses, yellow tiled roofs, green jalousies, white walls, and church towers, which go to make up the sum total of Mediterranean towns; the two most striking edifices being the Palace of the Lord High Commissioner (the only slated house in Corfú) standing in pleasant gardens, and the bell-shaped tower of the Cathedral of San Spiridione, dedicated to the patron Saint; behind the town are the mountains of Casturi, Benizza, and the wooded slopes of San Pantaleone, and the Kardacchio. At the fag end of the town is the Waterport, a collection of shops, lanes, and market places, in which is sold everything, from a bunch of garlic to a knife, the latter eminently qualified either to prune vines with, or to introduce into the stomach of a friend with whom you may have a difference of opinion. Above this very dirty and distinctly odoriferous quarter, frowns the almost impregnable fortalice of Fort Neuf; very strong and majestic, too it looked in the early morning. Further to the left the land describes a curve, ending in hills thickly clothed with olive groves and vineyards, shutting from the sight the inlet of the "Venetian Harbour" and the island of the Lazzaretto, or Quarantine Station. Now turning our back to the town we see the mountain of San Salvador, the highest point of which is 2,591 feet above the level of the sea. A monastery is built on this peak, and a little village seems to hang in mid air upon the side; this is all of Corfú that we can see. The North Passage, leading to Venice and Trieste, washes the foot of the mountain to its right, and separates the island from the mainland of Albania, a wild and grandly mountainous region, the home of the wild boar, wolf, and other fauna, whose haunts are among the snows which perpetually hide the crests of the highest rocks. Two or three small islands lie in the harbour, which is about six miles across, the largest of which is Vido, a strongly fortified place belonging exclusively to the English, who use it as a rifle range. It is about a mile from Corfú and exactly opposite it, commanding the entrance to the harbour by strong forts heavily mounted.

If I have not tired the patience of my readers too greatly by all this dry detail, I should like to give a brief synopsis of its extraordinary history ere I break into the perhaps more interesting detail of its *Natural* History. Craving indulgence, I must premise that Corfú ("Non Piú," as it is called in allusion to its fertility) is the most northern of the Ionian Isles, or group composing the Septinsular Republic, and is about 32 miles long, by from 12 to 18 broad, lying in latitude 39°.37′ N. long. 19°.55′ E. It is (I am speaking now of 1859) under the Protectorate of Great Britain, and governed by a

"Voulè," or Parliament of native gentlemen, subject to, and somewhat influenced by, the decree or ruling of an English representative of the Sovereign, the Lord High Commissioner.) Its products are wines, oils, tobacco, olives, and various other things; it has, however, no commerce worth mentioning. There are one or two small rivers, and two or three lakes; the country is mountainous, well wooded, and fruitful, abounding in wildfowl and game, and though hot, is generally considered very healthy. Its history, ancient and modern, is most remarkable and noteworthy, it having been both by conquest and treaty, at one time or another, in the hands of nearly every nation under the sun.

Almost the first tidings we can glean of its existence is, perhaps, as far back as two thousand years before Christ, and in the Heroic period, when Ulysses coming from the island home of the nymph Calypso, sighted Corfú (then the ancient Scheria, the home of the Phæacians) lying like a shield on the horizon.

It was supposed from its great fertility to have been the abode of Ceres, and according to Diodorus Siculus,—Kerkyra, one of the daughters of Oceanus, and Tethys was abducted by Poseidon, and carried into the Island to which she gave her name—Corfú being called to the present day *Kurkera*, by the modern Greeks. There are, however, various other learned derivations for this name, as also speculations as to the origin of the Phæacians, the primeval settlers, but as all this would be too abstruse for an article of this sort, the enquiry into mythology need not be carried further; but pretty nearly authentic records carry us as far back as 703 B.C., when some Corinthians under Chersicrates, driven from their country by civil dissensions, emigrated to Corcyra (Corfú) and formed a settlement in the sheltered bay of the Calikropulo, now Paleopolis. Some years after (variously fixed as about 672 or 664 B.C. and by some as 582 B.C., after the death of Periander, the Tyrant of Corinth) the Corcyreans determined upon shaking off all allegiance to Corinth, which brought about the most ancient sea-fight on record, and in which the Corcyreans carried themselves so valiantly, and proved themselves so dangerously skilled in maritime warfare, that on repulsing the Corinthian fleet, with great loss, they founded the present crest of the Island, a War Galley proper, Or, on a field Azure, and by 490 B.C., had become the first sea-power of Greece.

For the next two hundred years this unfortunate island was a prey to civil war, anarchy, rapine, and bloodshed, caused by the struggles between the Democratic and Oligarchic parties for supremacy. Of course, as usually happens in such cases, inimical nations stepped in, to add their quantum of discord to their own advantage; and we find, therefore, a miserable record of fluctuations between Athenian, Corinthian, and Macedonian influence until 229 B.C., when the Illyrian pirates under their queen, Teuta, took the island by storm, and were in turn forced to disgorge their prey to the Roman Republic, by Caius Fulvius.

Some years after Christ, upon the decline of the Roman Empire, numerous hordes of Barbarians ravaged Corfú (among them, Attila the Hun) followed by the Goths and Saracens. In the eleventh century it was taken by a Norman adventurer, Bohemond (afterwards Prince of Antioch) grandson of Tancrede de Hauteville, and cousin of the famous Knight Tancred; by the year 1146, we find it in the hands of the Sicilians, and in 1152, subject to the Venetians, under Manuel Comnenus, and as far as I can discover from the vague chronicles of the day, vacillating between Venetian dominion, and a sort of self-government, until a Sea-Rover, one Henry Count of Malta, mastered the garrison, leaving his representative Leone Vetrano, to be hanged by Reneiri Dandolo the Venetian, who retook the island. (Prior to this, I should have mentioned as an interesting fact, that in November, 1192, our Lion Heart, the Great Richard of England, touched here on his return from the Crusades.) The Venetians ultimately lost the place, however, to a powerful despot of Epirus, but the exact date of this is shrouded in the mysteries of the past. It would appear that after a variety of misfortunes, it passed by treaty to the French king, Charles of Anjou, about 1267, remaining in the hands of the French, or Sicilians, until the Venetian Admiral, John Miani, besieged and took the place in 1386. After no very peaceful interval, during which the Turks had twice laid waste the country, without it being in the power of the now enervated Venetians to repel them, they, the Turks, in 1715, after more three hundred years of Venetian rule, laid siege in proper form to Corfú. Then it was that the glory of the age, the illustrious Schulemberg, destroyed the last hope of the loathed Ottoman, in his splendid defence and ultimate destruction of the foe. The Turkish fleet was signalled on the 5th July, and after a bloody and obstinate resistance on the part of the besieged who endeavoured to bring the fleets into action, the outworks of Saint Saviour, and Monte Abram, succumbed to the Turks. This allowed them to concentrate their forces on the weak points of the Citadel; but the brave garrison by superhuman efforts, and desperate sorties, repulsed every assault with severe loss. On the night of the 17th of August, the Seraskier (having previously received information, which compelled him to at once raise the siege, or carry the place), led the whole of his army to the assault. It was now that the patriotism of the people shewed itself—the garrison outnumbered, weakened by all the ills attendant on a protracted siege, suddenly found at their greatest need unexpected (if unskilled) assistance; for the townspeople rallied to arms, and men, women, and children, nay even the priests, fought side by side with the defenders. The carnage was frightful — besiegers and besieged fought behind heaps of slain, and at the end of six hours' continuous hand to hand conflict, the Turks seemed still to be paramount. At last Schulemberg threw himself with but a few followers, on the right flank of the enemy, and succeeded by brilliant and daring charges, in entirely breaking up and routing an army three times his own in point of numbers; a fearful tempest (ascribed to the kind intervention of the Patron Saint,) followed and completed their discomfiture, and hurridly embarking the remnant of the Ottoman forces fled, pursued by the Venetian admiral, and by the thought that in this disastrous attempt they had lost fifteen thousand men. Mementoes of this great battle are constantly occurring in the shape of leg and arm bones, coins, pieces of various arms of warfare, and skulls, of which I have turned up quantities myself at the chief points of assault.

After the treaty of Campio Formio, the Ionian Isles passed into the power of France until the 17th March, 1799, when the garrisons capitulated to the combined Russian and Turkish forces. For several years from this date it was in a dreadful state of anarchy, until Napoleon again secured the island, which surrendered soon after, May, 1814, to the British, under whose protection it remained until formally ceded to Greece, by the wishes of the Ionian people in 1864.

This, then, is a brief account of the history of Corfú itself, gathered from my own notes, and various authorities, condensed so as not to take up any unnecessary space in the "NOTE BOOK." The other six islands composing the Ionian group have a nearly distinct history of their own; it will therefore be sufficient to mention their names. The second island nearest Corfu, therefore is Paxo, the smallest of all, whose crest is a fish-spear, in allusion to its fisheries. Third, Santa Maura, anciently Leucadia, notable as the scene of the death of the inspired poetess of Greece, the immortal Sappho, who—

"With heart upon her lips and soul within her eyes,"

and in spite of the teachings of her magnificent Ode to the Goddess of Love, flung herself from the promontory called the "Lover's Leap" on to the cruel rocks below, in the agonizing pangs of her unrequited love, for the handsome Phaon. Fourth, Ithaca, or Theaki, the kingdom of Ulysses, and scene of his culminating triumph, when he slew the suitors for Penelope's hand, with the magic bow, after his absence of thirty years. Fifth— Cephalonia, called by Homer, Samos, the largest island of the Mare Ionicum. Sixth—Zante, "Bella fior di Levant," as it is called by an old poetical expression, deriving its ancient name Zacynthus, from a son of Dardanus, who colonized the island from Psophis in Arcadia. Seventh and last—Cerigo, the most southerly of the group, and about 250 miles from Corfú, famed under the name Cythera, as being the birthplace of the Ocean-born Goddess of Love, Venus Aphrodite, who rose from the sea-foam off this island. Bulwer in his "Last Days of Pompeii," makes Glaucus sing to Ione, "The birth of Love," in which beautiful poem, he evidently favours the supposition, that the sea-foam Venus rose from off the island of Cyprus; but I think there are as many, if not more ancient authorities for Cythera, than not; ancient coins, and the present crest of Cerigo show Venus in a shell, on the waves of the sea, with her arms raised above her head in the manner of the Syrens.

Here I am again wandering away into mythology, that fascinating and profitless study, all the while totally ignoring the fact, that I am still on the vessel's deck in the harbour of Corfú, looking at the scenery, the Greek boats, and fish playing around our bows. (These fish were I found out afterwards, smelts.) To return therefore, I landed about noon, and being very fatigued, gave but a passing glance to the boquet of gigantic geraniums, which fringed the Esplanade, and around which were fluttering dozens of the Brimstone butterfly (Gonepteryx Rhamni) and its variety G. Cleopatra. About this latter I am very dubious, I am told that it is a variety having been bred from the same brood as the common Brimstone, and yet though believing this, I cannot reconcile in my mind the fact of its being so *constant* a variety abroad, and so exceedingly rare at home. I have taken in Corfú perhaps twenty in the course of one day, and have always found them constant in their markings, the magnificent orange-flame coloured suffusion of the wings, being as distinctly defined in one, as in the other—a regularity of marking which you seldom find in *varieties*. Not having bred from the egg, I cannot however go against the testimony of those who profess to have done so; I merely record my observations as far as they extend.

A. M. B.

To be continued.

THE DISTRIBUTION OF THE MOLLUSCA.

THE different genera of the organic world are peculiar to, or most frequent in, certain localities, and even species and varieties have their limits. This habit pervades the entire range of organisms, from the lowest plants to man, whose qualities are, to a very great extent, the type of the locality he inhabits. The geography of the Mollusca is perhaps the best known to science. The labours of Mr. Louis Agassiz, Dr. Sclater, and Professor Edward Forbes, have done much towards giving us a clear idea of zoological geography. Climate alone is insufficient to account for the distribution of animals—some higher cause rules here. But while we admit this, still we must acknowledge that climate exerts considerable influence in modifying the qualities of species.

The distribution of the Mollusca may be considered from three points of view. First, as regards *geography;* second as regards *depth;* and third, as regards *time:* the last belongs to Geology.

We shall now survey the principal divisions of the ocean, the line of demarcation being drawn, not by latitude or longitude, but by genera and species.

The Mollusca of the arctic seas are well known to show considerable analogy with those of the later tertiary periods of Europe. Hence the great interest connected with their comparison, as it affords—provided we are satisfied with this line of argument—a proof that an arctic climate formerly existed in temperate regions: it is the northern drift of which we are speaking. Even when species are found living in Britain, identical with those of the arctic regions, still there is often a difference in the form or size of British and arctic specimens; certain species, such as Cyprina Islandica, being comparatively small in the south of Britain, larger in Scotland, and attaining their greatest size in Iceland.

The countries included in the arctic molluscan province are Lapland, Iceland, Greenland, the west coast of Davis's Strait, and Behring's Straits. About two hundred species are enumerated by the various arctic voyagers, as found in these seas. Of these about one half are peculiar to these seas, and the other half are either found living in the temperate regions of Europe, or in their so-called glacial strata.

The Boreal-province includes the North Atlantic from Nova Scotia to Iceland, and from thence to Feroe, Shetland, and the Norway coast. The number of species is very large, and more than one half are common both to Scandinavia and the North American coast, while a great number also are found on the British coast. The province called Celtic by Professor Edward Forbes, embraces the coasts of Britain, Sweden, and Denmark.

Our British Mollusca are about seven hundred in number; those bearing shells are above five hundred. Of these about thirty are peculiar to Britain. The shells of the Baltic are identical with those of this province.

The Lusitanian province stretches from Madeira and the Canaries to the coasts of Spain and Portugal, and includes also the Mediterranean; but as one might expect, on close examination, the Mollusca in so large an area differ so widely that we are forced to admit the existence of minor divisions. The number of species found on the coast of Madeira by Mr. McAndrew, was 156, of which forty-four per cent. were identical with British species, and eighty-three found near the Canaries. The shells of the Mediterranean are six hundred in number, but it is probable that more extensive dredging will result in great accessions being made to this list. A very small number of species only are identical with those now found in the West Indies. Nine genera are peculiar to the Mediterranean. In the character of its shells the Black Sea resembles the Mediterranean, but does not contain much more than a tenth of the number of its species. The number of shells found on the Spanish and Portuguese coasts is much smaller than one would expect, and can only be attributed to the scanty explorations that have been made. As we might expect, the number of species identical with those of Northern Europe is much greater on the Atlantic, than on the Mediterranean coast of Spain.

The Sea of Aral, and the Caspian, contain a few peculiar species, but they have been so little explored that it is premature, we think, to form them into a province. The proportion of salt contained in these seas is much less than in the ocean.

The West of Africa affords a considerable number of fine shells, the species most numerous being those of Murex, Conus, and Clavatula. The South African province contains four hundred species; the characteristic genera are Terebretella, Chiton, Patella, Trochus, Fissurella, Cypræa, and Conus. A large number of these species are not found elsewhere.

The Indo-Pacific province stretches from Australia to Japan, the greater part of the east coast of Africa, the Red Sea, Persian Gulf, the Asiatic coast, and the islands of the Indian Archipelago. The Molluscs of the Red Sea remind us of those of India, the per centage of those found also in the Mediterranean being much less. The shells of the Persian Gulf are but little known. One species, the Brindled Cowry (*Cypræa princeps*), has been sold for £50.

The seas of New Zealand and Australia have been formed into a province. As might be anticipated, their Mollusca have little in common with those of the rest of the globe.

The Japonic province includes the coast of Japan and the Corea.

The Aleutian province, the centre of which may be taken to be the Aleutian Islands, shows great analogy with the Boreal province of the West, a considerable number of the shells being identical, a fact especially interesting when we consider that very few species are found common to both the south-eastern and south-western coasts of America.

The Californian province is very distinct from that of Panama ; the most numerous genera found there are Chiton, Acmæa, Fissurella, Trochus, and Purpura.

The marine shells of Panama are upwards of 1300. The region included stretches from the Gulf of California to Peru. For our knowledge of this province we are much indebted to the researches of Dr. P. P. Carpenter, who has catalogued 654 species as found at Mazattan.

The Peruvian province contains a long list of species, and extends from Callao to Valparaiso.

The Magellanic province includes the extreme south of America and the Falkland Islands. Many genera, the species of which are usually small, here reach an enormous size, and afford, in many cases, the chief animal food consumed by the quadrupeds and human population of that wild and desolate coast.

The Patagonian-province extends from St. Catherina to Point Melo, on the east coast.

The number of species found also in the Falkland Islands is very small, but a large number are identical with Brazilian species, yet the majority are peculiar.

The Caribbean-province extends from Brazil to the West Indies, and includes also the northern coast of South America and the Gulf of Mexico. A total of 1500 species is enumerated by Professor Adams as belonging to the province.

The Trans-Atlantic-province, or that on the coast of the United States, does not afford a large number of species, only 230 being known, of these only fifteen are found in Europe.

The study of the terrestrial and fresh water Mollusca affords even better grounds for their division into provinces ; but we shall not enter into it here, as it belongs to the land world.

We shall now say a few words on the depth of the sea or ocean in which Mollusca are found.

The observations of Milne Edwards, Audouin, and Professor Edward Forbes, have led to the division of the sea into four zones :—the deep sea coral zone from fifty to one hundred fathoms ; the coralline zone from fifteen to fifty fathoms ; the Laminarian zone, which stretches from fifteen fathoms to low water ; and the Littoral zone, between high and low water marks. The great stronghold of Crania, Thetis, Neæra, Yoldia, Dentalium, and Scissurella, is in the deep sea coral zone, while Buccinum, Fusus, Pleurotoma, Natica, Aporrhais, Philine, and Velutina, which are among the most ravenous and predatory of Molluscs, are found in the coralline zone. They attack the bivalves, whose shells, among the relics of former seas, as in those of the present, show evidence of an assault and a murder.

The principal genera of the Laminarian zone are the Nudibranchiata, Aplysia, Trochus, Nacella, Rissoa, and Lacuna, which feed so much on the seaweed of this region.

The Littoral-zone, which being accessible as the tide recedes, is best known, affords Cardium, Mytilus, Tellina, Solen, Trochus, Patella, Littorina, and Purpura, or in plain English, cockles, mussels, razor-fish, limpets, periwinkles, and tingles, species which are the first to attract our attention, and which are so much used for food.—From the new edition of the *Ocean World*, edited by C. O. G. NAPIER.

ON THE BRITISH GEOMETRÆ.

BY E. J. S. CLIFFORD.

PART IX.

PERHAPS there are few arguments stronger in favour of the practice of exchange, than the fact that insects are many of them so extremely local as to be entirely confined to certain parts of the country. Those who from time to time have declaimed against this mode of enriching the cabinet of the entomologist, as mean and unworthy of the science, are undoubtedly greatly in error. Nothing can be more natural and easy, and nothing more equal and just, than that collectors whose homes are in widely different parts should, by the practice of exchanging their native insects, oblige each other, and add to one another's knowledge. Now these remarks are illustrated by the species upon which we are now engaged. In our last we described one of those northern *Geometræ* that few southern collectors have an opportunity of obtaining except by exchange. And the plan of which we speak becomes one of which none need be ashamed, for it is beneficial to both parties concerned in such cases. Another such insect recommences our description of our native *Geometræ*. It is called the Yellow-ringed Carpet (*Larentia ruficinctata*), and is peculiarly beautiful. The fore wings are greyish lead-colour, with five yellowish bars, and numerous dotted lines. The hind wings are of a similar colour, but paler, with obscure darker bars towards the hind margin. The caterpillar of this insect feeds on the meadow saxifrage in May, and is of an olive-green colour, with a series of red spots down the back. The perfect moth itself is generally on the wing in the month of July, and its principal localities are Lancashire, Westmoreland, Cumberland, and Perthshire. Another northern species is the Twin-spot Carpet (*Larentia salicata*), common in Scotland, and in some parts of Ireland. The colouring of this moth is varied and attractive. The fore wings are lead colour, with many zigzag markings, some of which unite so as to form a bar; the hind wings are pale, with dark waved markings near the hind margin. The caterpillar is said to feed on several species of bedstraw in a state of nature, and in confinement on the sweet woodruff, upon which it thrives exceedingly well. In fact we may note, for the benefit of insect-rearers, that most of those caterpillars whose food is the bedstraw will feed in a state of confinement on this plant with great readiness. June and August are the months in which this moth appears, and it is confined to the localities indicated.

We now come to the consideration of some of our most lovely native insects. At midsummer, the Beech-green Carpet (*Larentia olivata*) may be looked for, since it is an insect generally distributed, though not to be termed common. Its fore wings are delicate olive-green, with a triangular blotch at the base, and a central serrated bar of a darker colour. Beyond this is a double zigzag white line, and a series of three dark spots near the angle of the wing. The hind wings are brownish lead colour, without any conspicuous markings. The Beech-green Carpet lays its eggs at the end of August on a species of bedstraw, and the caterpillars when first hatched are red, soon becoming, however, of a dingy hue, and hybernating early at the roots of the bedstraw. A commoner geometer than this last is the Green Carpet (*Larentia pectinitaria*), occurring throughout the British Isles in June and July. The caterpillar of this species is said to be a very sluggish creature, and fond of hiding at the roots of its foodplant, so that entomologists rarely secure specimens for want of knowing this peculiarity. When first hatched from the egg they are of a bright red colour, but when full-grown they are olive-brown, with a dark line down the back. The food is two species of our bedstraw plants. The Rivulet (*Emmelesia affinitata*) is not an uncommon species in several of our counties, but has not been taken in Scotland or Ireland. Its caterpillar is said to be enclosed in the seed capsules of several plants, and is of a dirty white colour, with a black head, and a black plate on the second segment. June is the time for the moth, which is beautifully varied in colour and markings. The fore wings are dark grey, with a number of transverse lines both darker and lighter; just beyond the middle of the wing is a distinct rivulet line of a pure white colour. The hind wings are paler, and have a lighter bar across the middle.

Starting up from the woody copse, or else beaten out of the leafy hedge by the searching entomologist, perhaps no moth is more full of delicate, fragile beauty than the Small Rivulet (*Emmelesia alchemillata*). This species flies in June, and occurs wherever its foodplants are found in England, Ireland, or Scotland, according to our best authorities. Its fore wings are dusky grey, with numerous transverse lines; and, like the last-named, this insect has a pure white rivulet line just beyond the middle of the wings. The hind wings are much paler, having a bar across the centre, which is not very constant. The caterpillar of the Small Rivulet is short, stout, and stumpy in appearance; its colour is dull red, suffused with yellowish-green; the line down the back is broad, and also of a yellowish-green colour, with a slender dark line in the centre. The chrysalis of this insect is enclosed in a tightly-spun earthen cocoon; it is yellowish-green, tinged with red. The Grass Rivulet (*Emmelesia albulata*) is another interesting species. It is pale grey in colour, inclining even to white, with many transverse lines quite white; the hind wings are almost without markings. The caterpillar of the Grass Rivulet has been described as dingy white, tinged with green, and having a broad stripe down the back of a darker colour. When full-grown it spins together the sepals of the yellow rattle, feeding on the seeds till it has reached its change, when it becomes a chrysalis within the home it had previously formed. In June following the August in which it has been transformed it appears as a moth, and is generally distributed throughout Great Britain.

The Sandy Carpet (*Emmelesia decolorata*) next comes under notice. This moth is of general occurrence, but not by any means common. Its colour is pale wainscot, with numerous irregular waved lines of white, the most conspicuous of which are a pair almost close together across the middle of the wing. The hind wings are dingy white, with few and inconspicuous markings. The caterpillar of this species is undescribed by our writers in the science. By beating holly-bushes about the neighbourhood of Killarney some of our enterprising collectors succeeded in capturing several of a very beautiful little moth, the Barred Carpet (*Emmelesia tæniata*). It is supposed that this insect resorts to the hollies for concealment, not in order to deposit its eggs. The colouring of this moth is very beautiful. Its fore wings have a triangular blotch at the base, and a broad transverse bar of a deep brown colour. The hind wings are pale in colour, with a waved transverse line below the middle, and a black spot above it. Haworth's Carpet (*Emmelesia unifasciata*), as its name implies, is so called from having been first made known by that collector. The fore wings are dull brown in colour, with many transverse lines which are waved, and a rivulet line just beyond the centre. The hind wings are pale brown, with a few darker lines, and a central darker spot. Haworth's Carpet has been taken at the Lake district, north of England, and at Epping and Forest Hill, in the neighbourhood of London.

Two very delicate little *Geometræ* must close our present paper. One is the Heath Rivulet (*Emmelesia ericetata*), which, as its name implies, is confined to heaths, occurring in the Lake district, and at Edinburgh and Glasgow, in Scotland. It flies in June and July. The fore wings of this moth are smoke-coloured, and traversed by white bars, the first of which is very near the base, and generally single. The second and third are always double. The hind wings are of a paler hue, with transverse lines faintly indicated. The Pretty Pinion (*Emmelesia blandiata*) is the other insect to which we allude. The caterpillar is stated to be green in colour, with a row of reddish triangles down the back, and a line above the spiracles of yellowish-green. It feeds on the eyebright. The moth itself is whitish-grey, with a triangular blotch at the base of the wings, and a band across the middle. The hind wings are lighter, with a dark spot, and several waved lines below it. In May and June the moth is flying, and has been taken chiefly in Scotland and the north of England, where it occurs abundantly in certain localities. And with this species we close our present paper, bringing to an end that great body of our *Geometræ* which precedes the genus *Eupithecia*, or the "Pug moths." This division, from the fact that very many of the species are nearly alike, and others have been doubtfully classified, we shall pass over. In our next we shall resume our enumeration of the British *Geometræ*, commencing that section which follows immediately after the genus *Eupithecia*. Let us hope that our readers will still follow with interest the descriptions we shall then bring before them, and be incited to study for themselves this wonderful family of our native insects—the British *Geometræ*.

OUR WADING BIRDS.

No. 3.—THE COMMON SNIPE.

By ALEXANDER CLARK KENNEDY.

SNIPE shooting we have always thought is the most enjoyable sport to be obtained in this country, and we are far more pleased with bagging five or six couple of longbills than twenty brace of partridges or pheasants; and we are not certain that we should not prefer a good day in an Irish bog above a morning spent in slaying hetacombs of woodcock and hares on a strictly preserved estate.

How pleasant it is on a bright morning in winter to sally forth, after an early breakfast, accompanied by your retriever or setter, to the marshes; and if you are a true lover of the sport the road will seem short, for it is surprising at what a rate you can get over the ground when you have visions of snipe and wild ducks before you; so, at least, we have generally found it. And the sharp wind, which brings the bright colour to your cheeks, although very pleasant, will not allow you to dawdle on your way, and hurries you on to the bog, over whose heaving bosom you will soon be trudging, the frost-tipped grass crackling under your feet; and the loud report of your gun, as every now and then you lay low a snipe, will be re-echoed from the sides of the cloud-capped mountains which so often surround an Irish or Scotch marsh.

The variety of this charming sport has ever been so enchanting to us, for you can scarcely tell what may turn up; perhaps as the smoke of your second barrel clears away, you will be chagrined to see a cunning old duck and mallard rising from a rushy pool within a few yards of your setter, whose motions you had not been observing when you knocked over that worthless jack snipe; or maybe a teal will suddenly spring up just behind you, and as you bring him to bag and "Nep" rushes off to fetch him, his companion silently quits the ditch in which she had been hiding, and you do not catch a glimpse of her until she scuds away high over head, at a safe distance from your destroying shot. Hares, too, occasionally come to the bogs, to feed and you will often fall in with rabbits on the dryer portions of a piece of marshy ground; and sometimes you may manage to bring down a couple of woodcock to top the bag, or perhaps a widgeon or golden plover.

The common or "full" snipe (*Scolopax gallinago*) for the most part arrives in this country towards the close of September, or during the early part of October, but a small proportion remain throughout the year and breed in suitable localities, chiefly in the north of England; and throughout Ireland and Scotland this bird is found during the summer months. This species, the delicate flavour of whose flesh is probably familiar to most of our readers, is about eleven inches in length, and weighs four ounces, and is of sombre although very prettily marked plumage. The bill of the snipe is a beautiful object, and when examined under a powerful microscope each of the numberless indentations on the upper mandible may be seen to advantage. When the bird is young its bill is very tender, but hardens as it grows older, and reaches the length of three inches; although we have killed snipe with a bill of three inches and a quarter, it is unusual for it to extend beyond the previously-mentioned length. Its food, which it procures principally during the night, consists of minute shells, insects and their larvæ, and small portions of various grasses; and a little gravel is usually swallowed in order to digest the food better.

During the winter, and as late as the middle of April, these birds associate together in flocks, sometimes composed of forty or more individuals, and called "wisps." When in this state they are very hard to approach, as they seem to be far more watchful than if they were scattered in pairs or singly. On certain days also snipe will allow you almost to tread upon them, while on others they rise from all sides before you are within a couple of hundred yards of their marsh. Quaint old Colonel Hawker, when speaking of these birds, says that snipe shooting is like fly-fishing, and that you should not fix a particular day for it; and he advises us, if much rain has fallen, to wait until the wind may have had time to dry the rushes, or the birds will not lie well. These birds, when flushed, almost invariably fly against the wind, and we have found it a good plan to walk down wind, as a succession of satisfactory shots may thus be obtained; and afterwards to return over your ground up wind, and allow the dogs to point any snipe which you may have passed; and by acting thus we have often picked up several birds, which the dogs must almost have walked over when going down the wind.

The snipe chooses wild moorland wastes and rushy pools for its summer haunts, and generally places its nest upon the top of a small tuft of long grass or reeds; but occasionally the rough structure is found almost on the bare ground, away from any rushes or water among the heather. The young of this species are covered, similarly to the young of most of the *grallatores*, with a soft brownish down, when first hatched: they can get over the ground very fast soon after they leave the nest, but cannot fly for a long time. The eggs, which are four in number, are of a green, or more properly speaking greenish-brown, ground, spotted and irregularly blotched with dark brown and ochre; they vary much in markings; but a "clutch" of eggs, that is those taken from the same nest, are usually alike. The cry of the snipe, although perhaps rather harsh, is nevertheless pleasing; to us it has always been so, because it brings back to our recollection many a pleasant day spent on the mountains of the north, in Erin's marshes, and by the wild sea coast in many parts of this country. This bird has been our companion by night as well as by day; for, while watching in the darkness for wild ducks by the side of the lake or stream, we have been surrounded by snipe flying within a few yards of our ambush, and with loud cries looking for a suitable feeding-place for their evening meal. On a still moonlight night these birds look very ghostlike as they fly slowly around, for their flight during the night is very different from the swift jerking motion given to the wings by day. It is a very delightful occupation for a naturalist-sportsman to observe the habits of the various species of water birds which frequent marshes and lakes during night; for they seem far less shy, and, unsuspecting danger from man, feed on in fancied security, and shew their various peculiarities to perfection. Seldom can one approach the home of the duck and teal during daytime, as they soon catch sight of a man's figure, however great an adept he may be at stalking, and with "quacks" of warning to their friends on neighbouring ponds make off to a more secure retreat. Not so, however, at night, although even then they keep a sharp look out; and many an evening have we passed by the side of the marsh watching the birds arriving for the night, sometimes with a gun, but as often without, for the ornithologist proper is not a mere collector of specimens. Let us give a rough sketch of an evening spent in this way:—Taking up our position, on a still autumn evening, when, although not cold, the nights are apt to be chilly, under the shelter of a small clump of trees near an extensive lake, we are soon comfortably settled, and ready to see what is to be seen; but the moon has not shewn itself at present, and what little daylight remains soon fades away into darkness. For a time no noises disturb the stillness of this home of water-fowl; but a faint whistling of wings presently makes itself heard, and betokens the arrival of some of the tenants of the pond, and in less than a minute a loud splash at the further end of the water shows that several ducks have alighted. Soon after a "coil" of teal make their appearance, and we can hear their curious cries as they fly around overhead, reconnoitering before trusting themselves on the pond, for doubtless they have met danger here ere now, and are determined not to risk encountering it a second time. Suddenly a splash among the rushes close to the bank on which we are seated shows that a moorhen has left her retreat, and in a few seconds the well-known notes which proceed from all parts of the water testify that her example is being speedily followed by others of the same species. The moon breaks forth from a bank of clouds behind which she has been hiding, and as her bright rays fall upon the pond we are enabled to see the arrival of a flock of mallards and duck, quickly followed by a hoarse croak, which betokens the approach of a pair of noble herons, and we are delighted to see them coming towards our bank; and the moon before again disappearing just gives us time to watch the long-legged fellows alight among the small fishes, which are always to be found in large numbers in the lake. We know that we must not move in the least now, for any motion, however slight, would be sufficient to send away the herons, who would probably scare most of the other inhabitants of the marsh. So we determine to remain patiently where we are, and are soon rewarded by hearing the cries of a host of curlews in the neighbouring "mere," and a loud "too whit-too-woo" close above our head tells that the owl is not idle during the darkness, whatever he may be when the sun shines. As we know that the herons will not stay much longer, but will be going home to their trees for the night, we cautiously rise from the ground, and, in order to see the effect of a shout on the denizens of the water, give a loud yell. Great is the noise and confusion that follows; we see the ducks and mallards scuttling off, while the moorhens and coots seek safety under the thick tangled reeds, and all the snipe in the vicinity are dashing about overhead; and a pair of peewits, rudely awoke from sleep, add their voices to the general din, which is not lessened by the cries of numerous teal as they take their departure, or by the noisy curlews in the adjoining marshes, and all the redshanks of the county seem to have left their beds to do honour to the occasion by making as much noise as they possibly can. Having succeeded in observing to our satisfaction the result of a sudden noise on these various birds, we leave them to return to their homes in peace, while we return towards our own!

During the breeding season the snipe make a most peculiar noise called "drumming," which is performed by the male bird when on the wing, generally at a great altitude, and is effected by the birds suddenly descending towards the ground, and allowing his wings to make a whistling sound, which may be heard at a long distance. In the summer, or rather spring months, these birds make a noise termed "bleating," from the resemblance which the cry has to the bleating of a goat. Hard winters sometimes tell severely on the snipe, emaciating their bodies, and often rendering them very tame. In the winter of 1866-67, these birds were so much affected by the frost and snow in the neighbourhood of Windsor and Eton that they became tame enough to sit upon the door-steps of cottages, and when disturbed they would only fly for a short way.* We have known the snipe to be killed by flying against telegraph-wires; and blackcocks, larks, landrails, and other birds, sometimes meet their death in this way. During the winter before last we were shown one which had received a deep gash upon the head, and the wing was cut clean off, which testifies to the rapidity with which the bird must have been flying, when it came in contact with the wires. When wounded, this bird, if it happens to fall on dry land, will spread out its tail in the shape of a fan, and throw itself back into a defensive attitude, and will even offer a feeble resistance with its bill to the hand put forward to capture it; but we have never observed a snipe act thus if a dog attempts to catch it, in which case the poor bird usually appears completely cowed.

The Latin name of the Common Snipe is *Scolopax gallinago;* and the pretty little Jack Snipe, *S. gallinula*, its near relation, remains to be considered in a future paper. This species perches occasionally, but is seldom seen to do so, nor is often observed upon the ground, owing to its retiring habits.

No. 4.—THE WATER RAIL.

AMONG the more comparatively common of our native wading birds may be included the little water rail (*Rallus aquaticus*), but it is not often noticed by the ordinary observer of animal life in the

---

* "Birds of Berkshire and Buckinghamshire," page 116.

country, for it takes delight in hiding itself in the thickest and most impenetrable reed-beds it can find, and it requires an extremely well trained dog to make it leave the retreat it may have chosen. But, though not often seen, the impression of a foot somewhat smaller than a moorhen's may be sometimes noticed in the soft mud, and which is generally to be attributed to the rail; for the spotted crake, one of its near relations, and whose foot-prints are very similar, is but seldom met with in any numbers in Great Britain, whereas the water rail remains throughout the entire year, but perhaps there is a partial migration in the winter months.

It is, although not very numerous, a fairly well known bird; but is not often met with on open streams or large rivers, being much more partial to retired swamps and lakes, which possess an abundance of rushy covert around their margins. Amongst the dense reeds and thick undergrowth of tangled water-plants, which are its chief haunts, it can make its way with wonderful rapidity; but if it thinks that its movements are being watched, it immediately dives out of sight, and the ripple of the water alone indicates the spot where the bird disappeared, which, on coming up again, only allows the tip of its pink bill to show above the surface; and even this is usually concealed by the foliage of the reeds, to the stalks of which it will cling for a great length of time with its feet. Besides being an adept at diving, the water rail can swim well, and many a time have we watched these birds making their way, apparently almost motionlessly, from one side of a lake to the other; however, we think that they seldom leave the rushes, except in order to enjoy a bath, for they never remain long upon the water. Sometimes one may be seen standing upon the bank of a stream, engaged in preening its feathers with its long pink bill; and we have had the good luck to watch the rail while seeking its food; but this sight is a rare one, and opportunities seldom offer, for the bird generally feeds among the rushes, where its proceedings cannot be noticed. The food of this rail consists chiefly of water-weeds and various grasses, which is occasionally varied by small insects, and mice have been found in the stomachs of dissected individuals. The rail very seldom takes to its wings, and if compelled to fly by a dog, will take a short flight, soon dropping again into as thick cover as it can find. Its flight is slow, and peculiarly straight, even more so than the moor-hen's, thus rendering it an easy bird to shoot. This species appears to be extremely erratic in its habits, sometimes being found on furze-commons, also in meadows, and we have killed water rails in turnip fields, near a river. This bird does not shew much fear when captured, and will in time, we believe, become quite tame. That exquisite writer on natural history, the late Mr. Charles St. John, relates that one of these birds, which his retriever caught in a hedge, was taken to his house, in order to be shown to the children. It had remained for two hours in the pocket of a shooting coat, and when released from this prison, the little creature shewed fight at everything that came near it, and when it was finally turned loose in a stream of running water, it went off quite quietly, jerking its tail, and not seeming to care in the least to hurry away from its persecutors.

Although the rail appears to be a remarkably lean bird, such is not generally the case; all we have ever shot have proved very fat, and this bird will be found excellent on the table. It is, however, not a large morsel, only weighing about five and a half ounces, large individuals weighing six. The feathers upon the back and wings of the water rail are brownish, and the lower portions of the body leaden-black, with streaks of white on the flanks, and the same color underneath the tail, which is very short, and is jerked up and down as the bird moves along. The beak is red at the extremity, gradually assuming a darker tint towards the base. The irides are red; and the legs and feet of a lovely coral hue, but are in some specimens almost flesh-colored, and vary much according to the age of the individual. The legs of the water rail are placed very far back, and enable it to run with great swiftness; so much so, indeed, that we have been beaten in a race over an expanse of open marsh-land by one of these birds, which nothing could induce to trust to its wings. The rail feeds principally at night, and towards evening it is occasionally to be seen moving from one spot to another; and during the daytime, especially on hot summer mornings, it remains concealed amongst the rushes and will not venture forth. The rail, when winged, or even mortally wounded, always attempts to make its escape; and if it should happen to fall in the water, it dives to the bottom and seeks refuge in a hole under the bank, if such is to be found; and unless this bird is killed dead, the sportsman generally will have great trouble in securing it. This species seldom varies in plumage, but an exceedingly rare example was shot in Berkshire, during the year 1832; it was a pure albino, and the rich red beak and pink eyes, must have formed a lovely contrast with the white hue of its plumage.

The nest of this bird, which is always artfully concealed, is generally placed on the ground under a small alder bush, or in the midst of thickly growing rushes, and sometimes possesses a rough canopy of water plants, which so effectually hide the structure that a bird's nester must have very sharp eyes to enable him to detect it. We have never found a nest ourselves, but have inspected one, *in situ*, the day following that on which it had been discovered: it was placed beneath a low alder, and had only been found by a boy happening to see the old bird leave the clump of bushes one evening and fly to a neighbouring pond. This nest contained, if we remember rightly, nine eggs, and the number laid is generally from eight to ten. They are considerably smaller than those of the common water-hen, and are of a greenish-buff ground colour, spotted and blotched with pale ash and brown, reddish marks appearing on parts of the shell, and rendering them extremely pretty eggs. The young birds soon take to the water, and in a very short time become as expert as their parents in swimming and diving. The old birds take great care of their offspring, and will sometimes attack a dog who is hunting in the neighbourhood of the nest; and it is related by Mr. St. John * that his retriever, on coming up to him with a young rail of a few days' old in his mouth, was pursued by the affectionate mother in a great state of excitement, and uttering loud cries of alarm. We have been informed that the little birds, before they are old enough to take care of themselves, are liable to become the prey of one of the most loathsome of animals, the water-rat; and moor-hens, young wild ducks, teal, and other water fowl of tender age, suffer severely from this pest. Nor is this the only enemy they have to contend with, for stoats, weasles, and even foxes, are fond of resorting to lakes during the night, to prey upon incautious youngsters and wounded birds which may venture to trust themselves on dry land. Hawks do not trouble them much, nor do the owls, partly because these birds are getting scarcer every year; and the food of the commoner kinds, such as the kestrel and barn owl, consists more of mice, rats, and moles than birds; and partly owing to the snug, quiet retreats which the rail selects, and to its shy retiring habits. This bird occasionally alights on small trees, such as willows, and we have observed it sitting upon a gate post more than once.

THE EXTINCTION OF SPECIES.

WHEN Mr. Bax introduced this subject in the January number of the N. N. B., I was in hopes that his paper would have been the means of introducing its discussion, and of elucidating some *facts* relative to the causes real or supposed of the diminution or apparent extinction of certain species of British butterflies. In this hope I have been—perhaps in common with some other of your readers—to a great extent disappointed; as, excepting Mr. Cole's and my own communications, nothing has yet been said on the subject; although much has been written about a proposed reintroduction of the Camberwell Beauty.

Since the appearance of my own paper in April, an able article has adorned the pages of "The Entomologist"—[*vide* "Newman's Entomologist," No. 66, page 276]—on the relative scarcity or commonness of a given species from year to year; and it strikes me that the theory therein expounded, need only be somewhat further extended to account, to a great extent at least, for their extinction, as well as occasional rarity.

Further than this, I have seen nothing bearing on the subject; and were it not that M. Woldemar Geffcken has referred to me personally in his articles in the July number of the N. N. B., I should not again enter the arena of discussion. But there are some points in those articles I must beg "W. G." to reconsider. Write what he may, I shall never be able to see the desirability of attempting the re-introduction of any wild denizen of the land, be it mammal, bird, insect, or flower. I would do all that lay in my power to preserve those we have by fair means, by which I mean protection from such evils as advancing civilization will permit of; but further than this I think it is unadvisable to go. This much is certain; that the knowledge of any country's native flora or fauna cannot be increased by the introduction of fresh species; and if the study of Natural History has for its object the advancement of such knowledge, then all the energy and time devoted to the rearing, etc. (as is proposed), of such foreign introductions, is merely lost by being diverted from its more legitimate channel of studying and investigating the economy of native inhabitants.

Mr. Johnson laments having to rear silkworms year after year, which is doubtless tame work enough; but surely he can breed some of the two thousand species of lepidoptera known to us as British, without having to go abroad in search of novelties.

Quitting, however, the desirability or otherwise of the re-introduction of the Camberwell Beauty (as this species has been taken in hand *par excellence*), as being a matter on which we never are likely to agree, I wish to point out one or two errors into which I think "W. G." has fallen.

Firstly, he says *V. Antiopa* has two broods a year. Is he sure of this?—as in this country at least *all* the *Vanessæ* hybernate. If *V. Antiopa*

---

* "Natural History and Sport in Moray," page 189.

appears in America in autumn and up to the time of severe frost setting in, and again on the earliest warm days of spring, and these two appearances are distinct broods, what do the larvæ of the autumnal brood feed on, and how do they contrive to live and feed up during the winter?

In his second paragraph he expresses an opinion that the attempt to transplant *P. Machaon* has been attempted with too little care. Perhaps so; but that he may judge for himself I now give my authority, viz., Merrin's "Lepidopterist's Calendar" (p. 56), where, speaking of this insect, he says:—"The late Mr. John Wolley turned out a large number of the perfect insects in the neighbourhood of Matlock, and in the autumn of the same year the larvæ were found feeding on the common fennel; but only an occasional straggler of the perfect insect was seen the following season. A similar experiment has been tried in Devonshire, etc." Here at least is the fact that the enlarged butterflies paired and produced fertile ovæ.

Another error M. Geffcken falls into; or if it be not an error, he is singularly unfortunate, is the proportion of pupæ which in careful hands produce imagos. He says ten in a hundred, but my own experience has been nearer ninety. Of course if reared from the egg, a much larger proportion would fail, and I here speak of pupæ only. In refutation of his theory of imagos emerging at long intervals, I will only state one fact which has happened to myself within the last few weeks. On July 3rd, I brought home part of a brood of *V. Io*, about two-thirds fed; some of these I sent or gave away, keeping about sixty. After they got settled in their cage, I did not find one dead body, although, as I never counted them, I cannot say positively that none died. They began to go into pupa on July 12th, and three days later all (61) were duly hung up. These 61 emerged, July 20th (7), 21st (40), 22nd (7), 23rd (6), leaving one which would have assumed the perfect state next day had I not purposely killed it for examination. *V. Urticæ* has appeared with me in much the same proportion in former years. We have here the immediate precursor and successor of *V. Antiopa* in classification; to which species they bear the strongest apparent structural resemblance, and I believe an almost exact similitude of habits in those countries where they occur in common; so that what we *know* of the two species would appear fairly applicable to the third. Yet *V. Antiopa* continues amongst our greatest rarities, although one can hardly imagine the capture of some dozen examples of the species during the same season without supposing that they had a fair chance of pairing and depositing ovæ.

Moreover, *C. Hyale* has been some years as scarce in England as *V. Antiopa;* and a year or two later it will be almost swarming, as last season, while *Antiopa* continues as rare as ever. Still we must suppose that the *Vanessa* has as good a chance of meeting its mate, and so of re-establishing itself, as the *Colias;* better indeed, as it is of gregarious habits; and, if this be so, there must be some as yet unexplained reason for its continued scarcity; doubtless identical with that which caused its diminution in the first place, and analogous to that which has foiled the attempts to transplant Machaon, and which can only be explained by supposing some physiological inadaptability to resist adverse influences of soil or climate.

A matter more concerning "W. G." personally is, whether he would call the introduced "beauties" British or Foreign; but on this point I will only ask him to compare his own remarks on pp. 125 and 222, and tell us how he reconciles the two statements.

One word more and I have finished, having I fear already occupied too much space. He expresses a hope of some day seeing my name with another secretaryship attached thereto; but I fear he must forego this hope, as were I as friendly to his scheme of introduction as I am antagonistic to it, I find one amateur post of this kind quite as much as, or rather more, than my limited time will allow me to attend to.

HERBERT MARSDEN,
Secretary, Lepidopterists' Exchange Club.
Gloucester, August 12th, 1869.

PHYSIOLOGY OF INSECTS.

By Veritas.

IN compliance to the desire of Mr. Trowbridge, for some correspondent to write a paper on the internal anatomy of insects, I have ventured to make these following remarks, which I hope may prove of some little service and interest to other readers of the N.N.B, as well as to your correspondent. In order, therefore, to make a careful selection, it will be advisable to take a "model insect," as it is called, for our type. Out of so many orders this is often a difficult matter to accomplish, so I propose to take no insect in particular, but only describe the characteristics of the class, which I think will answer our purpose very well. The following may be given as a good definition of an insect. The body is divided into three parts, viz., the head, thorax, and abdomen. The head is the seat of the oral and optical organs; the thorax contains part of the œsophagus, and the dorsal vessel and the stomach, and possesses the locomotive organs, which consist of four, sometimes two, wings, and two or three pairs of legs. These latter form one great characteristic of insects, for they sufficiently distinguish them from their nearest neighbours, the Arachnida. The leg is divided into four parts—1st, femur, or thigh; 2nd, tibia, or shank; 3rd, metatarsus, or ankle; 4th, tarsus, or foot.

The abdomen contains the remaining portion of the digestive organs, which is the intestines or viscera, their auxiliary vessels, surrounded by fatty tissue, and the generative organs. By this short dissertation upon the general distinguishing points of the class, I intended merely to show their various organs in a cursory way, as a sort of preface to my explanations, which I have now to make in a more lengthened manner. The internal anatomy of our "model insect" may be divided into six systems:—

    1st. The Digestive System.
    2nd. The Muscular System.
    3rd. The Nervous System.
    4th. The Respiratory System.
    5th. The Circulation of the Blood.
    6th. The Generative Organs.

1st. The Digestive System. Collectively speaking this is always denominated the alimentary canal; and for the purpose of observing its manifest analogy to many classes of animals, it will be best to watch, in imagination, the food as it passes through the insect's body. The mouth being either provided with transverse mandibles, or a tongue only suited for sucking, of course there are no molars, but the food, after being softened by the saliva, passes down the gullet into the stomach, where it is mixed with the gastric juice, which soon reduces it to a pulp, similar to the "chyme" in ourselves.

There is at this stage a slight difference in some insects. For instance, both Acheta Domestica, Acheta Campestris, and Blatta Domestica, possess veritable gizzards. These organs are also possessed by several families in the coleoptera. All these gizzards are found below, or rather, beyond the stomach proper, and are usually like a minute pea in shape. Within them are rows of teeth, which by the movement of the muscular walls triturate the food. From this second stomach the aliment, now wrought into a soft condition, is conveyed into the intestines, after undergoing a slight change by the admixture of certain fluids. By the peculiar movement of the intestinal canal, scientifically called the "peristaltic" motion, the pulpy mass, which by degrees loses much of its fluid condition and nutritive properties by absorbtion, is moved slowly on, and at length ejected. This brief description even shows what highly organised creatures insects are.

2nd. The Muscular System now claims our attention. How wonderful are the evolutions of insect life! What rapidity and yet facility of movements they have! It is indeed enjoyable to watch those active beautiful beings, whether running or flying, leaping or swimming, accomplish surprising feats of strength without apparent effort. But then compare them to ourselves, or to any large animals however powerful, and we feel insignificant, comparatively speaking, in bodily energy.

The common Mole Cricket (Gryllotalpa Vulgaris) can raise a weight of more than two ounces from off its leg! And many other instances of a similar nature are on record. But let us now examine the vast muscles that give this creature and others their immense strength. Muscles may be divided into two classes, viz., voluntary, such as those which are under the direct control of the animal, like the muscles which move the legs, &c.; and involuntary, those that are not under the will of their possessor, as those about the dorsal vessel, stomach, etc. Physiologists have separated these into two other classes, which is most convenient and simple. They are the striped and unstriped. The former belong to the voluntary, and the latter to the involuntary muscles. The difference that exists between the two is easily understood, and more easily described. The striped muscle is composed of a series of parallel muscular fibres, which again are crossed by parallel bands at right angles, whereas the unstriped, as their name implies, are destitute of parallel markings. A muscular fibre has three properties: irritability, extensibility, and contractibility. Mr. Ulidia, in his January article on "Do Insects feel Pain?" has there extracted a description of muscles, &c., that would be sufficient without anything else to prove the great powers that these interesting animals are endowed with.

3rd. The Nervous System. I have at last arrived at the nervous system that has indirectly caused and kept up that great and wearysome argument on pain in insects that seems never to show a sign of ending. In reviewing the different articles that have appeared on both sides of the argument, I can say with truth that I have not seen *one* valid argument produced by those who have been, and are now, defending the negative. This is not fancy, and I am sure that all who have read both sides with attention will, or have come, to the same conclusion.

The Nervous System in insects commences in the head, where it is much broader, and contains more vesicular nervine than other points, and proceeds horizontally in a line from the Eucephalic ganglion, or brain, to the apex of the abdomen. The ganglionic matter composing the nerves and smaller filaments is called tubular nervine, and branches out of the vesicular matter. Here, then, we find that our "model insect" is not only the possessor of a *brain*, but of a nervous cord, and set of nerves ramifying over the whole of the body as well. Every external point of an insect (beetles excepted) is susceptible, and that in a high degree to external impressions; and, therefore, may we not say that if an insect be trodden upon, or otherwise injured, it feels pain?

I suppose that of all the external organs of insects the antennæ present the most remarkable; for they are the most delicately sentient. Indeed, some Naturalists, from a protracted study of insects, have come to the conclusion that they possess some sense that we know nothing about. How far this is correct we cannot say, and as this paper is devoted only to the material portion of insects, it would be unsuitable to introduce mere hypotheses relating to their spiritual nature. As we all know, the antennæ vary considerably in size, shape, and construction in the various orders. Now, upon almost all antennæ are numerous depressions, and minute nerve filaments have been observed to rise to the under surface of these cup-like marks. If I might hazard an opinion as to the great use of the antennæ, I should say that they are the principal seat of the sense of smelling. This idea I have long entertained, and subsequent study and observation have in a great measure strengthened it. Whether it be correct or not future research alone can decide, but I think that it is near the truth. However, the nervous system is of all the organs the most difficult to explain, for it is the only one that connects the material body with the spiritual nature. After analysing the nerves physiology has done its work; here comes that mysterious life which dwells in all animated bodies, and which defeats every attempt that human wisdom and genius makes to find out its true nature. Perhaps the most curious of all the things connected with the nervous system is its admirable application to the optical organs of insects. The number of eyes, or, more correctly, "facets," in insects, ranges from fifty to twenty-four thousand! The full force of this statement may not at once strike the reader, but after a little further explanation it will be more apparent. Two nerves, called optic nerves, branch out one on each side of the brain, and spread out into thousands of branches, each one of which is connected with a facet. Many persons might be surprised at the number of facets, and inquire their use. I will attempt to explain it. Insects are not capable of moving their eyes as we are, so in order to give them as extensive a view as is necessary, they receive thousands of little views, which by the arrangement of the nervous filaments are presented to the insect's mind as one uninterrupted picture. We have still one more point to examine before we leave this interesting branch of insect anatomy. It is the manner in which the muscular system obeys the *will*. The nervous filaments spread, as I remarked before, over the whole body, and one or more branch nerves accompany every muscle. And although the individual creature is not aware of it, yet there is not a single movement, however trivial, such as the raising of a leg, contraction of a claw, &c., that the "will," as it is termed, has not ordered! We cannot tell how it is, but we only know that the nerves cause the muscular fibres either to extend or contract by irritation.

4th. The Respiratory System. Insects, unlike the vertebrata, do not possess lungs, but the organs which are substituted for them are truly very wonderful in arrangement. Along the sides of the insect's body, at least from the thorax to the apical extremity of the abdomen, are small holes, called spiracles, which of course vary much in size in different insects. These spiracles are crossed by minute fibres placed upon a delicate membrane, which is fine enough to admit the air but strong enough to exclude anything else. At the back of the spiracle is a tube called a "trachea," which branches out in all directions, conveying oxygen to the remotest parts of the creature. Both the spiracles and trachea are beautiful objects for microscopic examination. In order, however, to make my description more lucid, I think that it would be well to mention the usual situations of the spiracles before speaking more of the tracheæ. In the coleoptera the spiracles are generally found on the abdomen, two on every "ring," one on each side. In the water beetles they increase in size as they approach the anal extremity, and are of a considerable magnitude in Dytiscus Marginalis, "the great water beetle." Now, on the contrary, in Musca Vomitoria, the blowfly, the spiracles are largest on the thorax, and diminish in size on the abdomen. The general appearance and shape of the spiracles is often preserved in many species of the same order. We will lastly turn our attention to the construction of the tracheæ. They are tubular, and within them is a continuous fibre, which being as it were wound round like the iron spring in a child's pop-gun preserves the cylinder in its position. As the membrane itself is strong it is not liable to be crushed, and with this double barrier it is quite secure from harm.

5th. The Circulation of the Blood. This is not quite such an interesting part of insect anatomy as those which we have already examined, but it is just as necessary to the creature as any other organ, and therefore claims our attention. It cannot be said an insect possesses a heart, for this is not strictly the case, but there is a large sort of artery called the dorsal vessel, which by its pulsations drives the blood up and down the body through several channels. The blood is nourished by the absorbtion of all the nutritious portion of the food, and renovated by the oxygen of the air in a way very analogous to that in mammals. Any person can satisfy himself as to the existence of blood in insects by cutting open the abdomen of a fly, removing the intestines and fat carefully, and placing it under a microscope magnifying 150 diameters.

6th. The Organs of Reproduction. This again is a great characteristic in animal life, and in insects there is as great an analogy in these organs to those in creatures of higher classes as any other parts. The sexual organs are situated in the last and smallest joint of the abdomen. The male possesses a seminary tube and auxiliary glands. These latter secrete certain fluids, which by mixing with the "semen" serve to render it more fluid in order to facilitate its expulsion. The female possesses the ovaries, or egg-bags, and when the ova are in a perfect state the sexual instincts, operating in both, lead to their function, and of course to the deposition of semen in the body of the female. Here, according to some authors, is a curious arrangement. Within the body and some little distance from the ovaries is a small bag or "sac" in which the seminary fluid is deposited. When the period for the laying of the eggs has arrived the ova come down one by one towards the natural outlet, and in doing so become fecundated by coming in contact with the semen in the bag.

This, then, ends my paper on the Physiology of Insects ; and if it proves of interest to your correspondent I shall feel that it has accomplished what I desired. I do not think that insect anatomy is studied enough by many entomologists, for they are too often only content with making a large collection, and seldom think of dissecting the lovely creatures that they so eagerly pursue.

FIRE.

By H. H. Ulidia.

FIRE, which literally signifies a "purifer," must have been known to men from the earliest times; and, although when, where, or by whom it was first discovered, are things beyond the grasp of history, still we have good reasons for believing that the discovery and use of fire are nearly coeval with the very existence of man. The "flaming sword" of the cherubim gives us early indication of fire; and that Tubal Cain, five thousand seven hundred years ago, was "an instructor of every artificer in brass and iron," evidently proves an acquaintance with the application of fire, even in the arts. Erebus and the Cyclops of Grecian mythology, and the rude natural philosophy of the ancients, all imply the existence and their knowledge of fire.

Nearly three thousand years ago iron was discovered in Mount Ida, in Greece, by the Idæi Dactyli, who accompanied those early adventures—the Phœnicians. The Dactyli immediately set to work and "forge" iron tools and armour.

The application of bellows to the fire is mentioned in Isaiah nearly two thousand years since:—"Behold I have created the smith that bloweth the coals in the fire," and "I will purify your scoria and take away all your tin." The invention of the axe, saw, and wimble by Dædalus, is more than two thousand years old —all clearly showing the use of fire in the hands of the ancient artisans. Then we have the begrimed and sweating Cyclops, hammer in hand, before the scorching fire, forging the heavy thunderbolts of Jupiter; and the cunning Prometheus snatches "fire" from the chariot of the sun even in defiance of Jupiter himself. Seeing the agency of fire no wonder indeed that the ancients were at a loss to tell what it was.

Heraclitus looked on fire as the great principle of every thing ; and Hippocrates, the celebrated physician, of Cos, freed Athens from a destructive plague by kindling fires in every town, and thus purified the contaminated air by burning aromatics.

The sun, according to Anaxagoras, is but a terrestrial mass in a state of inflammation; and Empedocles, the Pythagorean, considered light to be a body emanating perpetually from luminous bodies ; and he maintained that fire is the principle of life. And now comes the philosophic Plato with his hypothesis : life, says the Grecian sage, consists of spirit and fire, and the heat of the blood is the source of the fire. Fire (says he) in its elementary figure, is that of a pyramid ; let us look at the *pyr*, or flame of our burning candles, gas, &c., &c., and acknowledge the justness of the primitive idea of the Athenian philosopher. The ancients, according to Aristophanes, were in the habit of obtaining their "mundane fire" from "celestial fire" by the instrumentality of burning glasses.

In accordance with this opinion we find that Archimedas, with his hexagonal mirrors, reduced to ashes the Roman fleet under Marcellus in the bay of Syracuse; and Procless, too, by his burning glasses, completely destroyed the navy of Vitellius.

Lord Napier, in his "Secret Inventions," June, 1569, speaks of having invented "another mirror, which, receiving the dispersed beams of any material 'fire' or 'flame' yieldeth also the former effect;" that is, "the burning of the enemies' ships at whatever distance appointed;" and with the same facility and destructive results as if the rays of the sun were concentrated by the glass. Buffon, even on a day in March, set beech boards on fire at a distance of 150 feet, and melted tin and lead at a distance of 120 feet, with his burning glasses.

As with the Hindus, fire was considered the first, greatest, and most powerful of all the elements, it readily became the visible symbol of their God, and hence we have the fire-worshippers, who build their temples over subterraneous fires, and who from their "shrines of flame," behold—

"—— the mighty flame burn on,
Through chance and change, through good and ill,
Deep, constant, bright, unquenchable!"

Turn we now to the chemists, or alchemists perhaps, of mediæval times, selfish, or science-loving, studying the structure of matter, and searching for the philosopher's stone. Here they are as described by Paracelsus:—"They are not given to idleness, nor go in a proud habit, or plush and velvet garments, often showing their rings upon their fingers, or wearing swords with silver hilts by their sides, or fine and gay gloves upon their hands, but diligently follow their labours, sweating whole days and nights by their furnaces. They do not spend their time abroad for recreation, but take delight in their laboratory. They wear leather garments with a pouch, and an apron wherewith they wipe their hands. They put their fingers amongst coals, into clay and ordure, not into gold rings. They are sooty and black like smiths or colliers, and do not pride themselves upon clean and beautiful faces." All this is labour, hard labour before the fire.

Fire, says Epicurus, is an intense heat; the light and heat of the sun, says Lucretius, are the results of the rapid motion of "primary particles;" Cardanus asserts that fire, on account of its motion, penetrates everything; but Fludd is of opinion that heat is not the essence of light. Bacon affirms that fire "is merely compounded of the conjunction of light and heat in any substance." Telesius assures us that heat is the cause of motion; Athanasius Kircher teaches that common fire is simply air made to glow by the violent collision of bodies; and Lemery hypothetically exclaims, "it seems probable that fire is only a very violent motion of minute bodies round their centre."

See how fire—that active spark of "visible nature and the common world"—kept the Cyclops and the philosophers alike busy.

Fire and its agency come to the assistance of the geologist; upon them he starts his hypothesis and builds his theories.

Fire, the *materia ignis* of some of the ancients, is everywhere around us—in the very air, as proved by actual demonstration, in the earth by well-supported hypothesis. And see that electric spark which Thales, two thousand four hundred years ago, looked on with wonder and pronounced it animated, now no longer dumb, but a real talking meteor in the hands of science; a winged messenger, before which, even Mercury, the once docile errand-boy of the gods would be but a dormant mythological agent. Fire, everywhere.

There is spontaneous combustion in the vegetable world; and science, with her proofs in store, points to many cases where members of the human family have been entirely consumed by spontaneous combustion. We look around us, we silently contemplate, and in wonder exclaim "fire, everywhere."

AMERICAN SILKWORMS.

SEEING an article in your July number at page 222, on moth-courtship, by my friend Woldemar Giffcken, I am induced to address a few words to your readers relative to the American silkworms and their introduction into England.

As a silkworm rearer I feel myself greatly indebted to the above gentleman, and his name will ever be gratefully remembered by me. He sent to me American cocoons of Bombyx, "Cecropia, "Promethia," and "Polyphemus" on no other terms than doing the best I could to produce eggs; and forward some of those I succeeded in getting, to him at Stuttgart.

In one of the last letters written to me by Woldemar Geffken he says,—I have a twelve months' experience (relating to me) because I had cocoons' larvæ, eggs and moths of B. Cecropia at one and the same time.

I have succeeded in getting fertile eggs in sufficient numbers of Cecropia. Of "Promethia" two moths only at present have laid, but others I daily expect to do so. The Polyphemus disappoints me, for which I am sorry. I had only eight cocoons, about half were bad. The moths came out of the others at different times, and too many days intervening between the exit of a male and female to be of any use at pairing—thus, only unfertile eggs. The

Cecropia moth is decidedly the most beautiful creature I ever saw. Many of the cocoons are nearly as large as hens' eggs, plentiful in silk; although not of fine texture, it doubtless would produce a durable article when spun. I have some Cecropia silkworms now in third age (18th July) and I am so pleased with them, not only for their most beautiful changes of colour from mourning ("jet black") to yellow, then dark, green, blue, red,—but at their little trouble, for they never wander from the spray of plum leaves on which they are. All that seems necessary is to supply a fresh sprig of leaves every four days or so, plunging the foot stalk in water in order to keep the leaves fresh; not to touch the insects, but when removing them to the fresh food to do so on the old sprays or leaves, depositing the same on the fresh bough secured from falling. My last Cecropia eggs laid only a few days back will not hatch much before the end of July, therefore the rearing will take place during hot weather. I shall try some in the open air, some in an airy room, some in the sun, and shade, &c. I shall be glad if any of your readers could make any suggestions to me the better to insure success with this most beautiful silkworm, which I really believe is one day to become of great public or domestic usefulness. One thing is certain, and that is, "Crecopia" is an acquisition of sterling worth to lovers of entomology!

I think the Polyphemus cocoon also good; indeed it is large and compact, and I should say preferable to Promethea in point of use, here in England. The Promethea much resembles the Ailanthus variety of cocoon from Japan, and may in some way be allied therewith, but I should call it inferior to the latter.

I shall reserve to make further report on my experiments to a future time, and hope these few lines may to some extent interest the readers of the NATURALIST'S NOTE BOOK to know more of American silkworms.

LEONARD HARMAN, Jun.
Old Catton, Norwich.

THE PROMINENT MOTHS OF BUCKINGHAMSHIRE.*

By the REV. H. HARPUR-CREWE.

THIS most beautiful family of moths may well be styled the *crême de la crême* of the British Lepidoptera. There is an indescribable softness and beauty of colouring in the caterpillar, and a refined loveliness in the perfect insects; they are, with few exceptions, so rare and difficult to obtain that they may most classically be called the aristocracy of the Scale-winged moths.

The name of Prominent Moths is, I may remark, given to this family from the very sharp and prominent ridge which the edges of the anterior wings of the perfect insect present as it sits at rest; and more especially from the fact that in most of the species which form this group there is on the lower edge of each anterior wing a small pyramidal appendage which, when the insect sits at rest with closed roof-like wings, forms a very remarkable prominence towards the centre of the ridge. Our own county of Buckingham is singularly rich in this very beautiful group of moths. With two or three exceptions they are all found in the shire, and that, too, in our own immediate neighbourhood. No less than fifteen species have been taken in Buckinghamshire; I have taken thirteen myself. I propose to take them in order and tell you how, and where, and when to take them.

1. *Stauropus Fagi* (the Lobster Moth)—This insect is one of the largest in the group, and also one of the rarest. It derives its name from its very singular caterpillar, a most remarkable creature, of a reddish-brown colour, with numerous long thin sprawling legs, in appearance strongly resembling the crustacean whose name it bears. It feeds, as far as my own experience goes, exclusively on the beech in August and September. I have several times beaten it into an umbrella from the overhanging boughs of beech trees in the rides of the woods at Buckland Common and St. Leonards. It is difficult to rear, as it often refuses to feed in confinement. The perfect insect, which is pale reddish-brown, clouded with a darker colour, appears in May and June, and may be found by searching the stems of the large detached beech trees. It has been taken several times at Velvet Lawn. The pupa, in common with that of all the rest of this group, is enclosed in a strong earthern cocoon just below the surface of the ground at the foot of the tree on which the larva has fed.

2. *Petassia cassinea* (the Sprawler Moth).—If you have chanced to look up at the gas-lamps on the outskirts of the town on a warm, dark, still night in October, you may probably have observed some largish moths dashing wildly about them, or seated at rest on their sides; and if you have taken the trouble to catch one of them, the chances are ten to one that you have captured the pretty soft-looking pale brown moth streaked with black, which, why or wherefore I know not, goes by the name of the Sprawler. The caterpillar is a beautiful glossy yellowish-green, striped with white. It feeds on various trees in May, *e.g.*, beech, hazel, lime, and oak;

---
* Read before the Society at the Sixth Evening Meeting of the Fourth Winter Session, April 27th, 1869.

and is particularly partial to the wych elm, from which tree I have beaten it in some numbers in Suffolk. I used to spread a large sheet under the tree and beat the boughs with a long pole. I have taken the perfect insect at lamp-light when sitting reading in my room at Drayton-Beauchamp.

3. *Gluphisia crenata* (the Dusky Marbled-Brown Moth).—This insect is so rare that I believe only four have ever been taken in Great Britain; one of these was beaten, in the caterpillar state, from a poplar tree at Halton a few years since by my excellent friend the Rev. Joseph Greene, in whose collection I have frequently seen the perfect insect. There is little doubt that the insect occurs all over the county, and only requires to be looked for to be found. The moth is a dull-coloured insect of little beauty. The larva is pale green, with a yellow line on each side, and some conspicuous rusty-red spots on the back.

4. *Ptilophora plumigera* (the Plumed Prominent.)—The males of all the Prominent family are prettily feathered and plumed, but the plumes of this species are so singularly large and beautiful that it has been styled, *par excellence*, the Plumed Prominent. When almost all nature is asleep in the gloomy month of November this beautiful and delicate moth is busy and alive. It generally makes its appearance with Guy Fawkes, about Nov. 5. It is of a uniform reddish-brown; the wings semi-transparent and indistinctly marked with yellowish streaks. It lays its eggs, which are of the same colour as the bark, on the twigs of the maple; and in May and June the caterpillar, which is long and slender, whitish or bluish-green with white lines on the back, may be beaten full fed from the maple bushes at the edges of the woods. I have frequently taken it in the woods at Drayton-Beauchamp. It is uncertain in its appearance.

5. *Ptilophora palpina* (the Pale Prominent).—This pale ashy-grey insect proclaims its own name. It is one of the common species of the family. The colour of its wings may best be described as oak-wainscoat-brown. It appears in June and July, and in the two following months its curious powdery greenish-white caterpillar may be found feeding on various species of willow and poplar, especially the aspen and the abele. It has a rough wrinkled back and a conspicuous yellow stripe on the sides. The little white conspicuous eggs of this moth may be found on the backs of the poplar leaves in July and August, and the little larvæ are easily reared. It is found throughout the county.

6. *Notodonta Camelina* (the Coxcomb Prominent).—This moth, which from its red colour and large wing protuberance, has been named the Coxcomb, is the only one of the Prominents which can really be called common. It is extremely abundant in the caterpillar state in the months of August, September, and October, and may be beaten from ash, beech, hazel, lime, elm, maple, sallow, apple, and birch. It is whitish—or bluish-green, with two conspicuous red warts near near the tail, by which it may always be distinguished from the rest of the genus. The moth is mostly red with darker shadings. It appears from May to September, and occurs everywhere.

7. *Notodonta cucullina* (the Maple Prominent).—This rare and beautiful Prominent may be said to have its head quarters in Buckinghamshire. I once took two larvæ in Suffolk, and a friend during many years collecting took four of the perfect insect in the same county. I once beat two larvæ from a maple bush in Herts. It has been taken a few times in Norfolk and Kent, but until about sixteen years ago it was one of the very rarest of our British Lepidoptera, and lucky was the collector who possessed a specimen in his cabinet. It so happened that one midsummer day about that time I was entomologising in a wood in this parish (Drayton-Beauchamp), when at the back of some maple leaves I found a number of delicate white eggs, which I at once saw to be the eggs of a species of Prominent Moth closely allied to the Coxcomb, but undoubtedly distinct. I watched these eggs with the greatest care: in due time the little larvæ hatched, and when full fed I found to my intense delight that I had reared the caterpillar of that beautiful rarity—the Maple Prominent. During the same season my friend Mr. Greene took a number of the larvæ in the woods at Halton, and he and I subsequently took a large number in the woods in this neighbourhood. The Rev. Bernard Smith has also taken it plentifully in the neighbourhood of Marlow, and there is little doubt that it occurs in most parts of the county. The moth appears about midsummer; the larva—which is pale whitish-green, slightly hairy, with a hump in the middle of the back, and always rests with its tail in the air—feeds exclusively on the maple, and prefers those bushes which are in the middle of the beech woods. It is full fed in September. It feeds on the underside of the leaf and may easily be seen by turning the branches back one by one, or it may be beaten into an umbrella. The moth in shape and form most closely resembles the preceding species, the Coxcomb, but differs widely in the colouring of the upper wings, which are conspicuously variegated with buff and white.

8. *Notodonta Carmelita* (the Carmelite Prominent).—This beautiful moth, one of the rarest

of its class, has for many years past been taken sparingly in Black Park, a wood belonging to Sir Robert Bateson Honey, Bart., of Langley Park. It may at once be distinguished from the rest of its family by the almost uniform purplish-red colour of the wings, relieved only by a conspicuous white or yellowish spot on the upper edge of the anterior pair. The caterpillar, which is bright apple-green marked with yellow on the back, and a white yellow and pink stripe on the sides, feeds exclusively on the birch in July; and on the trunks of this tree the moth may be found sitting in May.

9. *Notodonta dictæa* (the Swallow Prominent). This moth and its neighbour the "Lesser Swallow" may at once be distinguished from all the rest of their fellows by their long, slender shape, when at rest, much resembling that of a swallow with its wings closed, and by their uniform whitish-grey colour, with a conspicuous dark stripe at the base and tip of the anterior wings. In the present species these stripes are chocolate brown. If any one will take the trouble to turn up a number of branches of the black, Italian, or Lombardy poplar in August and September, the chances are that he will find various small very white eggs, or a very long, thin, glossy, whitish-green caterpillar with a yellow stripe on the sides and a red hump at the tail. These are the eggs and the larva of the Swallow Prominent moth. It feeds upon all kinds of poplar, and sometimes, upon sallow and willow. There is a variety of the caterpillar which when full fed is of a uniform pale brown. The moth appears at the end of May and in June and July.

10. *Notodonta dictæoïdes* (the Lesser Swallow Prominent).—This moth in form and marking almost precisely resembles the preceding species, but the dark lines in the upper wings are always a beautiful rich *purplish*-brown, whilst the intervening portions of the wing are much whiter than in *dictæa*. The larva too, is totally different, being of a uniform deep purple with a conspicuous yellow stripe on the side. It feeds invariably on the birch and is full fed in September and October. I have taken both this and the preceding species in this parish (Drayton-Beauchamp) and believe that, though they are nowhere common, they occur wherever poplar and birch trees are to be found.

11. *Notodonta dromedarius* (the Iron-coloured or Dromedary Prominent), the latter appellation being derived from the wonderfully humpy appearance of the caterpillar,—resembles the Carmelite Prominent in colour, but is of a much darker shade. The upper wings (the rusty brown tint of which varies a good deal in intensity) are more or less marbled with yellow. The caterpillar, which is one of the most singular looking creatures in the insect creation, is bright yellowish-green, more or less saddled on the back with purplish-brown. It has no less than five humps on its back, and rests like the larva of the Maple Prominent with its tail in the air. It feeds in September on birch and alder, and occasionally on hazel. I have several times taken it in this parish. The moth appears in May, June, and July.

12. *Notodonta ziczac* (the Pebble Prominent) is at once distinguished by the conspicuous markings at the tip of the anterior wings, resembling the polished eye of an onyx or some other pebble—whence its name. It is not a very uncommon species. Its singular brown and purple larva resembles the larva of *dromedarius* in form but has two humps less. It feeds upon all kinds of poplar and sallow in September and October. The moth appears in May and June. It occurs all over the county.

13. *Notodonta trepida* (the Great Prominent). —The larva of this magnificent moth, the king of the Prominents, I have several times beaten from oak trees in this neighbourhood in July. It is as gorgeously bright as the moth is softly beautiful. The ground colour is the brightest apple-green, with yellow lines on the back and large yellow and red stripes on the side. I know nothing more exciting to an entomologist when he has spread his sheet under the spreading boughs of a large oak and given one of the branches a sharp tap with his pole, than to hear a loud thud on the sheet, and to see a large fat larva of *trepida* lying sprawling on its surface. This caterpillar feeds exclusively on the oak and is full fed in July. The moth, which appears in May, has the upper wings of a uniform soft dusty green, more or less suffused with saffron and marbled with dark olive. It may be found sitting not far from the ground on the trunks of large oaks. When touched it moves its wings in a peculiar tremulous manner, whence its Latin name *trepida*. The Essex and Suffolk collectors have a curious and ingenious way of catching the males of this insect. When they breed a female moth they take her out into the vicinity of the woods before dark, and fetter her by a horse-hair or piece of fine silk (tied round the junction of the thorax and abdomen) to the stem of a large oak. As soon as it is dark, various male suitors make their appearance, anxious to woo and win. Having secured a specimen or two for his cabinet the collector permits the wedding to take place, and is thus sure of a set of fertile eggs to breed them for the following year.

14. *Notodonta chaonia* (the Lunar Marbled Brown).—This pretty Prominent may, with the

next and last species, easily be distinguished from its compeers by the conspicuous, broad, whitish bar in the centre of the soft ashy-brown upper wings. It is altogether a paler and brighter looking insect than the next species *N. dodonæa*, and appears a month earlier. I have several times beaten the larva, which is full fed at the end of June or beginning of July, from tall oaks in this neighbourhood. It is a uniform glaucous sickly green, with two yellow stripes on the back and one on the sides; and feeds exclusively on oak. The moth appears in May.

14. *Notodonta dodonæa* (the Marbled Brown).—This pretty little Prominent, altogether a smaller, narrower, and darker insect than the preceding species, has its upper wings conspicuously marbled and bound with white, thence its name. It appears a month later than its congener *chaonia*. I once beat the larva from oak, on which it exclusively feeds, in this neighbourhood; and Mr. Greene met with it sparingly at Halton. It is exceedingly like the caterpillar of the Carmelite Prominent in shape and colour, yellowish-green, and wrinkled with two slender yellow dotted lines on the back and a yellow and pink stripe on the side. It is full fed in August. I can assure my readers that if these few disjointed remarks of mine should induce them to employ their spare moments in trying, during the next few years, to breed and make a collection of the Buckinghamshire Prominents, they will find it a source of unflagging interest and unceasing delight. I have now almost given up entomology for my flower garden, but I reckon amongst the happiest days of my life those in which I used to shoulder my sheet and pole to thrash the oaks in the sunny glades for the gorgeous larva of the regal *trepida;* or hunt the maple bushes in the deeper shades for the smaller but no less rare and beautiful caterpillar of *cucullina*.

ENTOMOLOGY FOR THE MONTHS.

SEPTEMBER.

VERY few insects are to be found this month. Most of those who have enraptured and gladdened the eyes of the entomologist are fast disappearing, many of them perishing, and others selecting a snug nook where undisturbed they may pass their long winter's sleep. Amongst those which hybernate are the Brimstone (Gonopteryx Rhamni), Red Admiral (Vanessa Atalanta), and Tortoiseshell (V. Urticæ).

Should the weather be favourable the Clouded Yellow (Colias Edusa) and the Pale Clouded Yellow (Colias Hyale) may be still observed on the wing, also the Humming-Bird Hawk-Moth (Macroglossa Stellatarum).

We may also expect the Figure of Eight (Diloba cæruleocephala), Pale Oak Eggar (Trichiura Cratægi), Autumnal Rustic (Noctua glareosa), Marveil-du-Jour (Agriopis Aprilina), Flounced Chestnut (A. pistacina), Lunar Underwing (A. lunosa), Green Brindled Crescent (Miselia Oxyacanthæ), Red Line Quaker (Orthosia lota), Black Rustic (Epunda nigra), Centre-Barred Sallow (Cirrhædia xerampelina), Sallow (Xanthia cerago), Pink-Barred Sallow (X. silago), Orange Sallow (X. citrago), Dusky Lemon Sallow (X. gilvago), and the Brick (X. ferruginea).

Many of those on the wing last month are also now to be found, viz., Lesser Lute-string (Cymatophora diluta), Rosy Rustic (Hydræcia micacea), Bullrush (Nonagria Typhæ), Silver Y. (Plusia gamma), and the rare Convolvulus Hawk-Moth (Sphinx Convolvuli).

Should the entomologist be unsuccessful in hunting above the surface of the earth, let him try below the surface for some of those who have not yet attained the perfect state. Pupæ digging is rather trying work; but let his motto be "*Nil desperandum!*" and if not successful at first, let him try, try, and try again. Perhaps it may be as well to mention a few of the trees whose roots are worth searching; those generally considered productive are the ash, elm, oak, and beech.

The following is a brief list of pupæ to be found at the roots of the trees above mentioned:—

Ash.—December Moth (Pæcilocampa Populi), Coronet (Acronycta Ligustri), etc.

Elm.—Lime Hawk Moth (Smerinthus Tiliæ), Scarce Umber (Hybernia aurantiaria), Spring Usher (H. leucophearia), March Moth (Anisopteryx æscularia), Sprawler (Petasia cassinea), White Spotted Pinion (Cosmia diffinis), and Gray Shoulder Knot (Xylina rhizolitha).

Oak.—Oak Beauty (Amphydasis prodromaria), Great Prominent (Notodonta trepida), Lunar Marbled Brown (N. chaonia), Marbled Brown (N. dodonæa), etc.

Beech.—Coxcomb Prominent (Notodonta camelina), Square Spot (Tephrosia consonaria), Nut-Tree Tussock (Demas Coryli), Red Necked Footman (Lithosia rubricollis), etc.

We may also find by digging at the roots of privet the pupæ of the Privet Hawk-Moth (Sphinx Ligustri).

And now I have arrived at the conclusion of "Entomology for the Months;" and I hope if any *abler* entomologists than myself have discovered any errors, they will kindly overlook them. My chief object in writing these from month to month has been for the use of the *juvenile* entomologist, and I believe in every instance the common as well as the scientific names have been given.

Norwich. R. LADDIMAN.

TOADS ENCLOSED WITHIN THE SUBSTANCE OF THE ROOTS AND BODIES OF TREES.

MANY are the accounts that have been given of the discovery of toads within the substance of the roots and bodies of trees, as also within solid stones or rock, and in blocks of coal at a considerable depth from the surface of the ground; but it has been the practice of the generality of the students of nature to raise doubts as regards the truth of the narratives that have been given of such occurrences, or even to reject them altogether from the hastiness or imperfection of the observations themselves, as by ignorant people, or from the alleged impossibility of creatures of any kind continuing to live under the circumstances implied in so long and close an imprisonment. And in truth, on no theory that we are able to form can such a supposition be accounted for. But it still remains that facts are stubborn things; and although philosophers by not employing themselves in cleaving wood, nor working in the depths of a coal mine, have not met with an opportunity of being witnesses of the occurrence of such remarkable appearances, yet on such repeated evidence as has been produced, and where there cannot have been any imaginable motive for deception, some degree of credit at least may be assigned to the relations of these matters, as they lie before the public. I have indeed, nothing to add to what has been told us of living cold blooded animals within solid rocks or blocks of coal, but as regards the somewhat less wonderful fact of the discovery of a toad in an apparently solid root of a tree, I can with confidence depend on the truth of the account given me by an acquaintance, of whose correctness of observation and general veracity I have no doubt, and the circumstances attending it were written down at the time when the particulars of the case were fresh in the memory. It is general in Cornwall that the hedges are high and wide, while in many places the roads are so limited as to be inconvenient for the passage of carts and waggons, which indeed were little in use when these hedges were first made. Formed for the most part of earth only, these hedges are liable to decay as well as injury, so that not unfrequently the lower portion as it faces the road will fall away, and thus lay bare the roots of trees that crown the summit. From this cause it happened that a stout portion of the root of an oak tree was left projecting from the lower part of the side of a hedge, in such a manner as to be inconvenient in the passage of vehicles, and in consequence it was removed with a saw, after which it was conveyed to the house of my informant, in the open court of which it lay for the space of about three months, when it appeared to have become dry, and during which it had been used as a block on which to chop wood for the fire. Its diameter was about five or six inches, and over the whole of the surface it was sound, without any appearance of a flaw. But at last its fate was to be prepared for the fire, and my informant himself, who was the national schoolmaster of the village, proceeded to cut it into the requisite lengths, after which it was split so as to be separated into sections; in the cleaving of which, close below a knot, he discovered a cavity, that was shut up on all sides, and within which he found a living toad—which he closely examined and described to me. One noticed that it completely filled the hole in which it was contained, but he judged it to be somewhat less than the ordinary size of the generality of its race; its colour all over, as well the sides and belly as the back, very dark, while the eyes appeared bright, and its active powers were shown in moving about; tubercles were well marked on the skin. The creature thus suddenly produced to day was carried to the house and shewn to his wife, and then to several persons who chanced to be in the way, after which it was set at liberty.

It was particularly observed in this case, that externally there was no mark on the surface of the wood, of a wound or opening through which this creature could have passed into the cavity in which it was found, but no doubt was felt that at some time, probably long ago, there had been an open cavity into which the toad had crept at a time when it was about to enter upon its season of torpidity, in which it continued until the orifice had become closed by the advancing growth of the wood, and finally of the bark, after which it had continued in its unconscious state, until perhaps the violent chopping of the wood for the fire, or the influx of air by the laying open of its retreat had awakened it to life.

That such an explanation as is offered in the present case may also be applied in other instances, in which a toad has been found enclosed within the stock of a living tree, will appear from cases that have been recorded, although the attending circumstances have not been so minutely noted as in that of which an account has been here given. Thus, in the Memoirs of the Academy of Sciences for 1719, we are informed that a toad was found alive in the heart of an oak, without any visible means of entrance to the cavity, and from the size of the tree it was thought that the creature might have been confined in that place for eighty, or even a hundred years. That no creatures which are incapable of long continued torpidity could survive such a long confinement without the access of air may be readily admitted; but that others may be met with preserved within enclosed cavities of trees appears beyond doubt. There is a distinct remembrance of the discovery of the nest of a small bird, containing eggs, within the substance of a stout branch of a tree that had been cut down and become dry, and when the cavity had not become entirely closed, so that a small orifice remained, but it was easy to suppose from the attending circumstances that the growth of another year might have altogether shut up the nest and obliterated every mark of an entrance; On the other hand, while the common woodpecker is accustomed to form its nest within the body of an aged tree, observation shows that its place of entrance cannot be effectually closed, for in an instance where this was attempted by filling it with solid materials, the industrious operator set to work, and soon succeeded in excavating another passage.

JONATHAN COUCH, F.L.S., C.M.Z.S., &c.

LIST OF BRITISH BIRDS.

BY W. NEWBERRY.

Family III.—STRIGINÆ (OWLS).

Genus I.—SYRNIA (DAY OWL).

Species I.—*Syrnia Funerea (Hawk Day Owl).*

Migratory; only one shot in England, and described by Thompson.
Size: Length, 15 in.; extent of wings, 29 in.; bill, $1\frac{3}{12}$.
Colour: Upper parts dark brown, spotted with white; lower parts white, with brown bars.
Food: Small animals, birds, &c.

Species II.—*Syrnia Nyctea (Snowy Owl).*

Permanently resident in the Shetland Isles.
Size: Length, 23 in.; extent of wings, 56 in.; bill, $1\frac{9}{12}$ in.
Colour: White, with head spotted and lower parts barred with very light brown.
Food: Small animals, birds, &c.

Species III.—*Syrnia Psilodactyla (Little Owl).*

Permanently resident, but very scarce.
Size: Length, $10\frac{1}{2}$ in.; extent of wings, 17 in.; bill, $\frac{5}{6}$ in.
Colour: Upper parts brown, lower parts yellowish.
Food: Insects, mice, small birds, and quadrupeds.

Genus II.—SCOPS (OWLETS).

Species I.—*Scops Aldrovande (Little Horned Owl).*

Migratory.
Size: Length, $7\frac{1}{2}$ in.; extent of wings, 14 in.; bill, $\frac{9}{12}$ in.
Colour: Light grey or brown, with white spots and dark brown undulating lines.
Food: Chiefly insects, small birds, lizards, etc.

Genus III.—BUBO (EAGLE OWL).

Species I.—*Bubo Maximus.*

Migratory.
Size: Length, 24 in.; extent of wings, 58 in.; bill, $2\frac{1}{2}$ in.
Colour: Upper parts dark brown and orange, lower parts reddish yellow, with brown spots; throat white.
Food: Birds, Animals, lizards, etc.

Genus IV.—ULULA (HOOTING OWL).

Species I.—*Ulula Aluco (Brown Hooting Owl).*

Permanently resident.
Size: Length, 14 in.; extent of wings, 31 in.; bill, $1\frac{6}{12}$ in.
Colour: Tawny brown, marked with darker brown.
Food: Leveretts, rats, mice, birds, and sometimes insects.
Builds in holes of trees and rocks, in wild districts.
Lays 4 eggs, $1\frac{11}{12}$ in. × $1\frac{1}{2}$ in.; pure white.

Species II.—*Ulula Tengmalmi.*

Migratory.
Size: Length, $10\frac{1}{2}$ in.; extent of wings, 21 in.; bill, 1 in.
Colour: Upper parts chocolate, spotted with white, lower parts light brown, marked with dark brown.
Food: Small birds and animals.

Genus V.—ASIO.

Species I.—*Asio Otus (Mottled Horned Owl).*

Permanently resident.
Size: Length, $14\frac{1}{2}$ in.; extent of wings, 36 in.; bill, $1\frac{6}{12}$ in.

Colour: Light yellowish brown, mottled and striped with greyish brown.
Food: Birds, moles, field mice, moths, and all nocturnal insects.
Builds in deep woods, often in old, rook's nests.
Lays 5 eggs, $1\frac{9}{12}$ in. × $1\frac{2}{6}$ in.; pure white.

Species II.—*Asio Brachyotus* (*Short Horned Owl*).
Permanently resident.
Size: Length, 15 in.; extent of wings, 38 in.; bill, $1\frac{3}{12}$ in.
Colour: Yellowish brown, with broad dark streaks above, and narrow streaks beneath, and has a dark ring round the eye.
Food: small animals, birds, etc.
Builds on the ground.
Lays 5 eggs, $1\frac{2}{3}$ × $1\frac{3}{12}$ in., white.

Genus VI.—Strix (Screech Owl).

Species I.—*Strix Hammea* (*Barn Owl*).
Permanently resident.
Size: Length, 14 in.; extent of wings, 35 in.; bill, $1\frac{1}{3}$ in.
Colour: Upper parts yellowish, longitudinally marked with black and white chain-like markings; face and lower parts white.
Food: Mice, birds, moles, and rabbits.
Builds in barns and outbuildings, or holes of trees.
Lays 5 eggs, $1\frac{1}{2}$ in. × $1\frac{1}{4}$ in.; pure white and highly glazed.

Order II.—Vagatricis (Wanderers).

Family I.—Corvinæ (Crows).

Genus I.—Corvus.

Species I.—*Corvus Corax* (*Black Raven*).
Permanently resident.
Size: Length, 26 in.; extent of wings, 52 in.; bill, $2\frac{3}{4}$ in.
Colour: Glossy black, reflecting purple and green tinges.
Food: All kinds of carrion, dead fish, worms, insects, and birds.
Builds sometimes on rocks, but generally on tall trees.
Lays 7 eggs, 2 in. × $1\frac{1}{3}$ in.; light green, patched with brown and grey.

Species II.—*Corvus Leucopheus* (*Pied Raven*).
Migratory; only one individual seen in the Isle of Harris.
Size: Length, 25 in.; extent of wings, 49 in.; bill, $3\frac{1}{3}$ in.
Colour: Black and white, variously distributed.

Food: Same as Corvus Corax, with which it is often identified.

Species III.—*Corvus Corone* (*Carrion Crow*).
Permanently resident.
Size: Length, 22 in.; extent of wings, $41\frac{1}{4}$ in.; bill, $2\frac{1}{4}$ in.
Colour: Black, reflecting green and blue.
Food: Chiefly carrion, also mollusca, worms, insects, and birds.
Builds on rocks or in trees.
Lays 6 eggs, $1\frac{3}{4}$ in. × $1\frac{1}{6}$ in.; grey, spotted and patched with dark brown.

Species IV.—*Corvus Cornix* (*Hooded Crow*).
Permanently resident.
Size: Length, $10\frac{1}{4}$ in.; extent of wings, 39 in.; bill, $2\frac{1}{4}$ in.
Colour: Head, wings, and tail black, back and lower parts grey.
Food: Fish, worms, larvæ, insects, mollusca, lizards, &c.
Builds on rocks and in trees.
Lays 6 eggs, $1\frac{7}{12}$ in. × $1\frac{1}{12}$ in.; bluish, spotted grey and greenish brown.

Species V.—*Corvus Frugilegus* (*Rook*).
Permanently resident.
Size: Length, $19\frac{1}{2}$ in.; extent of wings, $38\frac{1}{4}$ in.; bill, $2\frac{1}{4}$ in.
Colour: Black; reflecting purple, blue and green.
Food: Larvæ, insects, worms, seeds, &c.
Builds in tall trees, often in vast numbers.
Lays 5 eggs, $1\frac{5}{6}$ in. × $1\frac{1}{4}$ in.; light blue, thickly spotted and blotched with reddish brown and grey.

Species VI.—*Corvus Monedula* (*Jackdaw*).
Permanently resident.
Size: Length, $14\frac{1}{2}$ in.; extent of wings, 30 in.; bill, $1\frac{1}{4}$ in.
Colour: Black, tinged with dark grey.
Food: Larvæ, worms, insects, and vegetable matter.
Builds in high towers and ruined buildings.
Lays 7 eggs, $1\frac{5}{12}$ × 1 in.; bluish, with brown and purple spots.

Genus II.—Pica.

Species I.—*Pica Melansleuca* (*Magpie*).
Permanently resident.
Size: Length, 18 in.; extent of wings, 24 in.; bill, $1\frac{1}{3}$ in.
Colour: Head, neck, breast, and part of wings black, the rest white.
Food: Larvæ, worms, insects, lizards, and sometimes eggs.
Builds in trees.

Lays 5 eggs, $1\frac{5}{12} \times 1\frac{1}{12}$; greenish, freckled with brown and reddish grey.

Genus III.—GARRULUS.

Species I.—*Garrulus Glandarius (Jay).*

Permanently resident.

Size: Length, $14\frac{1}{2}$ in; extent of wings, 23 in.; bill, $1\frac{1}{12}$ in.

Colour: Reddish brown, head grey, with black spots, primary coverts blue.

Food: Larvæ, insects, gasteropods, worms, seeds, &c.

Builds in high or thick hedge rows, or bushes.

Lays 7 eggs, $1\frac{1}{4}$ in. $\times$ 1 in.; grey, with fine brown and purple spots.

Genus IV.—NUCIFRAGA.

Species I.—*Nucifraga Caryocactes (Nutcracker.)*

Migratory.

Size: Length, $12\frac{1}{2}$ in.; extent of wings, 21 in.; bill, $1\frac{3}{4}$ in.

Colour: Reddish brown, top of head, wing coverts, and tail dark, tipped with long white spots.

Food: Nuts, fruits, and sometimes, though seldom, insects, larvæ, &c.

Genus V.—FREGILUS.

Species I.—*Fregilus Graculus (Chough)*

Permanently resident.

Size: Length, 17 in.; extent of wings, 34 in.; bill, $2\frac{1}{4}$ in.

Colour: Glossy black, with blue and green reflections.

Food: Worms, larvæ, snails, insects, and seeds.

Builds in holes in the sea cliffs and often in caverns.

Lays 5 eggs, $1\frac{3}{4}$ in. $\times 1\frac{1}{6}$; dull white, with light brown spots.

Note.—In my list of British Birds, page 229, Genus V., for *Pemis* read *Pernis*.

EXTRACTS FROM AN ENTOMOLOGIST'S DIARY.

(Continued from page 247).

March 7, 1869.—Mild. Saw peacock butterfly (Vanessa Io), on the wing.

April 7.—Pale tussock (Orgyia pudibunda) emerged from pupa state imperfectly developed.

April 11.—Very warm. Saw specimens of the peacock butterfly (Vanessa Io) and small tortoiseshell (V. urticæ) on the wing, also about a dozen of the brimstone (Gonopteryx Rhamni) one of which I captured.

April 13.—Pale tussock (O. pudibunda) emerged from the chrysalis state.

April 15—Took three larvæ of the oak eggar (Bombyx quercus) and one of the dark tussock (Orgyia fascelina) from the whitethorn.

May 2.—Took six larvæ of the oak eggar (B. quercus) from a whitethorn hedge.

May 13.—Took a nest of larvæ of the small eggar (Eriogaster lanestris) from the whitethorn.

May 16.—Took some larvæ of the figure of 8 moth (Diloba cœruleocephala) from the whitethorn, also one of the drinker (Odonestis potatoria) feeding on grasses.

May 18.—Took a fine specimen of the poplar hawkmoth (Smerinthus populi) sitting on a bank.

May 30.—Eyed hawkmoth (Smerinthus ocellatus) emerged from the chrysalis state.

June 3.—Buff tip moth (Pygæra bucephala) emerged from the pupa state, imperfectly developed.

June 6.—Warm. Took a pair of the orange tip (Anthocharis cardamines), ailanthus moth (Bombyx Cynthia), and eyed hawkmoth (Smerinthus ocellatus) emerged from the chrysalis state.

June 14.—Took an orange swift (Hepialus sylvinus) flying over a bank of nettles, also some larvæ of the dark tussock (O. fascelina) and small eggar (E. lanestris).

June 19.—Took a buff tip moth (P. bucephala) sitting.

June 20.—Mild. Took an eyed hawkmoth (S. ocellatus), a pair of the privet moth (Sphinx ligustri), a belle (Eulobia palumbaria), and a female of the orange tip butterfly (A. cardamines), also a quantity of the larvæ of the small eggar (Eriogaster lanestris), lackey (Bombyx neustria, and garden tiger (A. caja).

June 21.—Took a quantity of larvæ of the lackey (B. neustria), and an eyed hawkmoth (S. ocellatus). Ailanthus moth (Bombyx Cynthia) from the pupa state.

June 28.—Day very hot. Took a specimen of the swallow tailed butterfly (Papilio Machaon), brimstone (Gonopteryx Rhamni) male, orange tip (A. cardamines) female, and buff tip (P. bucephala). (Horning, in Norfolk).

July 10.—Weather warm. Oak eggar (Bombyx quercus) female, and satin moth (Liparis salicis) emerged from the chrysalis state.

July 16.—Warm. Four specimens of the lackey (B. neustria) emerged from the pupa state.

July 19.—Warm. Ailanthus moth (Bombyx Cynthia) and a dozen specimens of the lackey (B. neustria) from the chrysalis state. Took two specimens of the swallow tail (P. Machaon) and five of the ringlet (Erebia cassiope). (Ranworth, in Norfolk).

July 25.—Took a goat moth (Cossus ligniperda) sitting on a bank.

July 27.—Took a pair of the dark arches (Xylophasia polyodon).

July 31.—Took a pair of the humming bird hawk-moth (Macroglossa stellatarum) hovering over some larkspurs.

Aug. 1.—Warm. Took six larvæ of the swallow tailed butterfly (Papilio Machaon) feeding on the wild carrot, and one of the elephant hawkmoth (Chærocampa Elpenor) from the willow herb. (The above were taken from the marshes at Ranworth.)

St. Augustine's, Norwich, R. LADDIMAN.

Remarks, Queries, &c.

(*Under this head we shall be happy to insert original Remarks, Queries, &c.*)

REASONING POWER OF ANIMALS.

Until R. B. W. is kind enough to inform us explicitly what his views actually are on this subject, we, his opponents, must labour under a disadvantage; for the discussion appears to be making its progress much after the manner of a mill-wheel or a cluster of gnats repeating their mazy evolutions in a sunbeam. It goes round and round, twisting about month after month, each fresh number of the N. N. B. producing from R. B. W. some fresh modification of his views, until from the labyrinth of his contradictory statements, it is impossible to disentangle his real opinion. At one time he denies *in toto* that animals reason. At another time he says, "dogs certainly do reason." Correcting himself again, he says a dog's reasoning "is produced by an arrangement of a special providence." And in his last note, disregarding all former scruples, he flings reason broadcast through beavers' dams, ants' storehouses, growing trees, decaying plants, falling stones, rising vapours, and ebbing tides.

It is not within the province of the present controversy to consider the possibility of reason extending to the vegetable creation. The question is—do *animals below man* reason? So, had R. B. W. contented himself with the beavers and ants, he would have been saved from the egregiously ridiculous mistake of confusing the obedience of matter to natural laws with the power that organised and enforces those laws. "Reason observed in a falling stone!" and also, may be, in the course pursued by the butcher's knife when thrust into a sheep's throat. We must picture, then, to ourselves, a stone thrown into the air, and hesitating in its ascent whether or not it shall prove the absurdity of the laws of gravity by continuing to rise *ad infinitum*. Gradually its good sense gets the better of its rash indecision. No, it were heartless to shatter in one moment a paltry axiom that has cost the world and its philosophers centuries to deduce! Reason prevails—the stone drops. Where could a more palpable use of an "ambiguous term" be found? Truly, Sir, logic is a science to which your attention may justly be recommended. The phenomena of falling stones and ebbing tides certainly establish the fact that God superintends and directs nature, binding her by immutable laws; but to say that reason is observed in these phenomena, surpasses the widest boundary of rational talk. "Will not the spectator now cry out that we are endeavouring to be mad with some method and consideration!"

You admit that "the Divine superintendence influencing animals may be moderated according to the degree of the development of *individual will*." How then is this to be reconciled with a former statement, that "the actions of animals are under the *direct control* and influence of the Almighty?" which evidently is intended to exclude the supposition that animals are allowed to use *their own discretion* in performing actions which appear to indicate the possession of reason. If you admit the active energy of individual will, I cannot see how you will exclude a certain amount of reason consequent thereon.

With reference to your other objections, p. 250—

(*a*) I do not know what "cases" are referred to. Are they such as are common to men and animals? If so, it would be hard to show that human reason, *per se*, fails where animal instinct prevails. And as you do not allude to my argument based on the unscientific parallel of a Geneva watch and an honest old English lever, I will not repeat it here, as it must obviously be irrelevant—and yet I think it will hold water.

(*b*) "Young animals, untaught by experience, act reasonably." I think this statement a little bold, unless reason and instinct are considered identical in species, though differing in degree. We cannot say how much experience may suffice to bring a young animal to reason, *e.g.*, how often a puppy must be whipped before he learns to cure a fault—yet I should certainly say there must be *some* experience required.

(*c*) Though the vegetable and animal kingdoms undoubtedly approach each other very intimately, so that the border-land is constantly being disputed, yet it need not follow that reason, if assigned to the one, must be claimed by the other. No one, I believe, would maintain that reason descended to the uttermost root-fibrils of the animal tree (whereof man forms the "corona"), and few would rashly attempt to draw the line of demarcation where reason ends in descending to the lower branches. The sum total of my opinion on this matter may be thus expressed: If reason is evidently discerned in many actions of lower animals, may we not justly infer that they reason to a certain extent? You say that "the faculty of reason does not descend *in gradation*." Another arbitrary assertion, which cannot at present be proved by any ingenuity of ratiocination or argument.

(*d*) The "progress or increase in knowledge," though a mark of the greatness of human reason, is no proof against the existence of animal reason. My views on this point have already appeared (N. N. B., p. 170). I will only add that I cannot see the slightest necessity for supposing reason and progress to be inseparable; and even if there were, this might haply be a source of fallacy. "The same disposition to suppose that what is true of our ideas of things must be true of the things themselves, exhibits itself in many of the most accredited modes of philosophical investigation, both on physical and on metaphysical subjects. In one of its most undisguised manifestations, it embodies itself in two maxims, which lay claim to axiomatic truth—Things which we cannot think of together cannot co-exist, and things which we cannot help thinking of together, must co-exist" (quoted from "Mill's Logic").

(e) If the "reasonable actions" of animals are absolutely controlled by Providence, where does the *individual will* come in, by which, we are given to understand, such actions may be moderated?

(f) "Contempt for great men" is a failing to which I will never plead guilty. My remarks upon the infallibility of Lord Brougham, " or any other man," are made with all due respect to rank, learning, and every other attribute of masculine excellence. *Quot homines, tot sententiæ*. Why, then, may I not be permitted to dissect out the tissue of my opinions, even though they may not conform to those of others greater than myself? The instruments employed are the scalpels of study, the callipers of collateral reading, the scissors of a smattering acquaintance with scientific authors, quick and dead. And there is no very considerable amount of youthful bumptiousness in such conduct. Before the invention of compasses, a certain clod from Bœotia challenged a learned citizen of Athens to draw a circle free-hand for five drachmas a side. They met on a day, judges were chosen, papyrus and style were allotted to the combatants. Rank before rusticry. The citizen drew, with great precision, a figure not altogether unlike an apple dumpling; the other regarded it with a knowing grin—scratched his head, and by a clumsy adaptation of the little finger, to serve as a pivot, contrived to produce a figure that came far nearer the mark. The mighty man fails, with all his strength, to move the mass of rock—the weak man, assisted by a crowbar, displaces it with one hand. The eagle drops the tortoise on the rocky shore, and feasts at leisure upon the impregnable meal. Considerable are the triumphs of a mind furnished with proper and suitable instruments, and " since the subtilty of nature far exceeds the subtilty of sense and intellect, the fair reasonings and speculations of men are a kind of insanity, only there is no one standing by to notice it." So says Lord Bacon. Armed as they are with the scientific weapons of modern invention, and the results of untiring experiment and constant research, it must indeed be a reproach to men if their progress in the interpretation of nature has stood still since the days of Sir Isaac Newton.

Rather more than a century and a half ago, it was deemed an axiom that " a thing cannot act where it is not." Even R. B. W.'s champion, Newton, was so positively convinced of this, that he was compelled to draw upon his ingenuity before he could convince himself that the sun acted upon the earth, not being there. To escape the Scylla of impossibility, he plunged headlong into the Charybdis of hypothetical surmises, and " imagined a subtle ether which filled up the space between the sun and the earth, and by its intermediate agency was the proximate cause of the phenomena of gravitation."

" It is inconceivable," said Newton, in one of his letters to Dr. Bentley, " that inanimate brute matter should, without the mediation of something else which is not material, operate upon and affect other matter *without mutual contact*. That gravity should be innate, inherent, and essential to matter, so that one body may act on another at a distance, through a vacuum, without the mediation of anything else, by and through which their action and force may be conveyed from one to another, is to me so great an absurdity, that I believe no man, who in philosophical matters has a competent faculty of thinking, can ever fall into it." Commenting on this passage, Mr. Mill writes: " To us it is not more wonderful that bodies should act upon one another ' without mutual contact,' than that they should do so when in contact. We are familiar with both these facts, and we find them equally inexplicable, but equally easy to believe. To Newton, the one, because his imagination was familiar with it, appeared natural and a matter of course, while the other, for a contrary reason, seemed too absurd to be credited."

I cannot at the moment oblige R. B. W. by suggesting any weighty authority for my views as a counterpoise for the opposite scale; still the foregoing remarks must rescue me from the charge of unfounded contempt for the imaginary fallibility of Sir Isaac Newton. Since there is nothing new under the sun, the opinions here advocated have probably appeared ere this in far more forcible guise, untarnished perhaps by sundry cobwebs they may have caught while stowed away in the dusty corners of my cerebral lumber room.

Renounce conceptions and make acquaintance with facts, is a maxim of genuine value. In searching for truth it will not do to rely implicitly on the doctrines of any man, however great, if experience militates against them. For " the human intellect is not of the nature of dry light, but receives a tincture from the will and affections which generates knowledge *ad quod vult*." And Truth is the daughter of Time, not of Antiquity—golden saying, and worthy of constant remembrance! " All the earth calleth upon the truth, and the heaven blesseth it: all works shake and tremble at it, and with it is no unrighteous thing. As for the truth it endureth, and is always strong; it liveth and conquereth for evermore. With here there is no accepting of persons or rewards; but she doeth the things that are just, and refraineth from all unjust and wicked things; and all men do like her works. Neither in her judgment is any unrighteousness, and she is the strength, kingdom, power, and majesty of all ages."

We must not anticipate nature, but rather endeavour to interpret and unravel her mysteries, following neither the ant, who amasses only and uses, or the spider, who spins a web out of herself, but rather the bee, who collects materials from field and garden, and then by her own power turns and digests them.

The editor's patience must be getting exhausted at the chameleon-like aspect which this controversy has gradually assumed, and as we seem to have convinced one another no more than when we began, that one side is right and the other wrong, I, as having commenced the struggle, beg humbly to suggest that we desist shortly from it, leaving the space for more profitable talk. If R. B. W. wishes to have the last word, by all means let him answer this (I hope my last) letter, and unless he sweeps my views into the back ground very decidedly, I will refrain from answering his replies. I am aware that I shall never convince him, and equally certain that he will never

return the compliment by convincing me, so I give my vote for retiring from a fruitless contest. C.
Oriel Coll., Oxford.

I am glad to see that R. B. W. is *a little* coming round to the most sensible idea that the higher animals (at all events) can reason; for in his last letter he says, "I should be sorry to declare, absolutely, that the lower animals have no share of individual reason," thus seeming to have some doubts upon the negative side, and when a man has doubts upon the side he has upheld for a long time, there is some hope of converting him, particularly as R. B. W. states some of the reasons for not quite agreeing with us, reasons which I do not think the affirmative side will have much difficulty in disposing of.

I will now endeavour to answer some of them myself. R. B. W.'s first reason is this: "In circumstances in which man's reason would fail to direct him, the instinct of brutes occasions them not to err." I think that if R. B. W. would look a little closer into Natural History, he would find that this is not always the case. Let him read C. R.'s letter in the March number, and he will find that the instinct of the birds did err in this case. I could also adduce many other instances of a similar nature.

But even if this were the case, as R. B. W. says, it would not argue anything; for some men, although they have greater intellect than others, still, in common occurrences very frequently do not act so well as others of less intellect, but of quicker perception. I think, also, that what many people call instinct in brutes is identical with what is called "acuteness," and "sharpness" in man, and that the reason why men of deep thought very often do not appear to have this so much as others, is owing to their being so much absorbed in great problems as not to be able to allow their minds to fall back directly into ordinary events of life. Women, too, whose minds, it is generally admitted, are not so capable of deep thought as those of men, have this quality frequently highly developed. In the same way, but in a lesser degree, animals have it, and for this reason, no doubt, they have not got inventive faculties, which, by the bye, are quite distinct from reason, which would not be so useful to them as the qualities of perception, and thence we do not find traces of progress as we do in man.

R. B. W. next says that "Young animals untaught by experience act reasonably." If this is the case, why is it that young birds and animals have to be so carefully tended by their parents?

The idea seems still to be running in R. B. W.'s mind about plants reasoning, although it has been refuted so well by Veritas in the April number. I never could myself understand the connection animals have with plants. It seems to be easy enough to argue that because man (an animal) reasons, therefore other animals do; but to say because animals reason, therefore plants do, is perfectly illogical, as there is an immense and impassable barrier between the animal and vegetable kingdoms. We might as well say that the mineral kingdom reasoned, as to say that the vegetable one did, as we have as much proof of the one as of the other.

Again, allow me to ask R. B. W. how he proves that reason "does not descend in gradation," as we have unmistakeable proof that it "does descend in gradation," for we see the highest reason in man, the next in the other mammalia, and the next in the birds, and so on, until we come to molluscs and insects, who in all probability have next to none at all. I may also say in passing that I think that the degree of bodily pain felt by animals is in a great degree influenced by the amount of brain as well as of nerve, so that it descends in gradation in the same way that reason does.

R. B. W.'s fourth reason I think I have already answered at the same time as the first.

With regard to the fifth reason, I have only to ask R. B. W. to prove first that a "superintending providence" does guide any of the actions of brutes, and if it does, why the reason of animals should be so guided more than that of man; but it is not for an antagonist in argument to put the question "Why not?" as it leads to the affirmative "Why?" and *we never prove the negative before the affirmative.*

I beg now to inform R. B. W. that we have the great Darwin on our side, not to speak of Bishop Butler, and other still older authorities.

Lastly, I wish to make known a fact which I think some of your correspondents must overlook, namely, that there is as much external and analogical evidence that animals have immortal souls, as that men have them, and that attempting to prove that the former have none, also to a certain extent involves the latter in the proof.

In conclusion, allow me to state, that if stronger reasons than those of R. B. W.'s cannot be brought forward, it is evident that the question must be settled.

ERNEST BELFORT BAX.

REASON IN BRUTES.

Before offering any remarks upon "R. B. W.'s" article, I must apologise for the somewhat discourteous remark with which I began my last, and at which "R. B. W." appears justly hurt. I must also refer him to my May letter, paragraph 3, in which he will notice that Mr. Ulidia's sarcasms had nothing to do with my change of views.

I would define reason and instinct thus:—

Reason—An act of the intellect notified by the action of the brain which accompanies it.

Instinct—An action of the brain independently of the intellect.

In man the domination of the intellect is so nearly complete that instinct is seldom observed except in children.

In the lower animals, it sometimes though rarely happens that intellect makes its appearance, and though more apparent in some races than others it is not a faculty extended to all individuals of the same species.

Animals that feed on the flesh of others are, as a rule, more intelligent than vegetable feeders.

Language certainly exists in many races of the lower animals. As to "R. B. W.'s" objections, I grant the truth of the first two statements, but do not think they bear on the question. The third I deny in toto. Man is an animal, but that does not prove that all animals reason; so it does not follow that if a dog reason, all dogs, still less all the lower animals, reason.

As to reason having no gradation, I must say that the idea seems absurd. I think there is every gradation from the highest intellect to its utter absence. Progress and accumulation of knowledge are concomitant only with higher intelligences than as yet exist in the lower animals.

Why should a train of thought in man be called "reason," whilst in the Sexton Beetle a similar phenomenon is classed as intellect? W. H. DALTON.

DO INSECTS FEEL PAIN?

I am "presumptuous" enough (to use Mr. Ulidia's somewhat peculiar orthography) to believe that the readers of the N.N.B. will see anything inconsistent in my statement, that, though convinced by one of the only two arguments Mr. Ulidia has brought forward in the whole of this controversy, I felt impelled to protest against his usual method of supporting the affirmative side by quotations, quibbles, and false logic. If we are to consider poets, in general, as scientific authorities, we must believe in the production of bees from the putrescent carcase of a calf (teste Virgil); and Shakespeare tells us that "The poor beetle feels as great a pang as when a giant dies;" also, "The toad wears a precious jewel in its head." Both these statements are palpably false.

And now, I think, the insect question had better be dropped; all arguments have been put forward that can be, and personalities are becoming the order of the day. I, for one, shall write no more; and if Mr. Ulidia continues to indulge in his discourteous sarcasms, I shall treat them and him with well-deserved contempt, and be silent. W. H. DALTON.

I think now that every candid reader of the N.N.B. must come to the conclusion, after perusing Mr. H. H. Ulidia's August article, that he is utterly incapable of answering the arguments propounded by the negative side, for his last communication does not contain an answer to a single argument, but is filled up with nearly three columns of vain efforts at satire upon certain gentlemen's letters which he feels but too surely shake his theory to the very foundation.

Mr. Ulidia asks me to refute his "poetical allusions." Now, Sir, would your correspondent kindly inform me what there is in them *to* refute? What is there, for instance, in such passages as

"Behold the impaled and helpless fly?"

and what is there in any other of the quotations that he brings forward, either in his last, or in any other article, which has anything in it to argue from either one way or the other? Mr. Ulidia confesses that in *one* case the arguments of the negative side appeared in such "a questionable shape," that he thought it better not to "tackle" them at all, but more judicious to leave them out altogether from his letter, thus plainly intimating that he was *rather* frightened of them, and evidently remembering that

"He that fights and runs away
Lives to fight another day."

"Libræ," he, in like manner, "fights shy of."

Then he comes to my letter, wrests a part of a sentence without giving the context, tells me to appreciate his articles more than I do, and then closes the satirical (?) part of his article.

We now come to his arguments. The first argument he adduces is this: "Do insects feel pain? They do most assuredly." We must confess that this strongly partakes of what has been termed the woman's argument—"because it is so."

He then, in despair, falls back upon Buffon (a rather antiquated authority, by-the-bye), because he can find but few scientific men of modern times who will agree with him in his opinions in this respect.

It is needless for me to go through the number of assertions which he makes, the axioms which he lays down without any arguments to prove them, and the theories that he builds upon them being quite incompatible with all ordinary ideas of logic.

Lastly, may I request Mr. Ulidia to condescend to answer, if he can, the objections that I have made in my last letter to his theory, and may I remind him that "virulent abuse" is not at all convincing, and that it generally looks like "a bad case," and that it is unworthy of a scientific man; and may I hope that next month, your clever correspondent Justitiæ Amor, will again come forward and annihilate Mr. Ulidia's weak attempts at satire, and still weaker attempts at argument. ERNEST BELFORT BAX.

This argument has now I think about ended, after dragging its way through a great many numbers of the N.N.B., and most of those who have taken part in this discussion on the negative side, have at length come to the inevitable conclusion that insects are capable of experiencing *pain;* and to what extent they feel it has had nothing to do the whole time with the real question that has been so long at issue, viz.: for fourteen months. Some of those who came out at first so boldly and rashly, retired early in the day, and even those who kept up their persistent weak arguments, were, like their coadjutors either obliged to retire from the field or else admit that insects feel a *certain amount of pain,* which is all those on the negative side desired to prove. They were mainly brought to this conclusion, Sir, by the writings of your clever correspondent Mr. H. H. Ulidia. In conclusion I trust that gentleman will take part in any other arguments that may arise in the columns of your interesting "Note Book," and hope long ere this Mr. Ulidia has quite recovered from his "serious illness" and become perfectly well again.

Sydenham, S.E. A. E. BUTTEMER.

EFFECTS OF REFRACTION.

The information which G. O. Howell desires to obtain, concerning the increase of magnitude in the disks of the sun and moon when rising and setting, and which has only been slightly answered by two of your correspondents, has made me desirous of giving him fuller information.

The perceptible increase of size in the sun and moon, while passing from the zenith to the horizon, is not the only eccentricity which is manifested, but according to the principles of hydrostatics and optics their apparent position in the heavens is affected.

We have the following from Dr. Lardner's account, concerning this point. The ocean of air which surrounds, rests upon, and extends to a certain limited height above the surface of the solid and liquid matter composing the globe, decreases gradually in density in rising from the surface (H. 223); that when a ray of light passes from a rarer into a denser transparent medium, it is deflected towards the perpendicular to their common surface; and that the amount of such deflection increases with the difference of densities and the angle of incidence (0.92). These properties which the air has in common with all transparent media, produce important effects on the apparent position of celestial objects. Then further on, he gives the effects on rising and setting in these words. "Its mean quantity in the horizon is 33' (that is, the mean quantity of refraction) which being a little more than the mean apparent diameters of the sun and moon, it follows that these objects, at the moment of rising and setting, are visible above the horizon, the lower edge of their disks just touching it, when in reality they are below it, the upper edge of the disk just touching it. The moments of rising of all objects are therefore accelerated, and those of setting retarded, by refraction. The sun and moon appear to rise before they have really risen, and to set after they have really set, and the same is true of all other objects."

Then again, he briefly remarks on the oval form of the disks of the sun and moon when rising and setting, and which I have no doubt but G. O. Howell will have particularly noticed, that is, he will have perceived the orb of the sun longer than broad, the perpendicular diameter being longer than the horizontal diameter.

Thus G. O. Howell will observe that the atmosphere which encompasses the surface of our globe increases in density the nearer the planet approaches the liquid or solid matter composing the earth, and so causes the visible increase of the orb, which is entirely the work of refraction. I think Dr. Brewer's Guide to Science exhibits the appearance of a very poor one, when he says, the appearance is an illusion (which I must confess is true) in consequence of terrestial objects being placed in close comparison with them at one time and not at the other, but he ought to have stated the case in a clearer light; for if there is no refraction in the atmosphere, it follows that the orb of neither sun nor moon would not in any way be enlarged, as their distances is precisely the same in both parts of the heavens. J. H.

A FEW WORDS ON THE KESTREL (*FALCO TINNUNCULUS*).

By Oologist.

Acting on Mr. Rowe's advice, and following Mr. A. M. B.'s example, I humbly offer to the readers of the N.N.B. a paper on the Kestrel. My reasons for choosing this bird are twofold; 1st, because I think that I may be able to find something to say about it; and 2nd, beause it is the first bird, according to scientific classification, of those whose eggs figure in my collection; which, from various unlucky reasons, has been reduced to the scanty spoils of this year. With this preface I will begin, with the best of my ability, to describe the bird I have selected, with his habits, breeding haunts, &c.

The kestrel is a beautiful bird, as all who know him will testify. I do not intend to enter into accurate description of its size, since a better authority than I, no doubt, has done it for me in the July number of the N.N.B., to whom I will also refer the readers of this magazine for a description of the colour of the bird. The wings of the kestrel are longer and more bent than those of the sparrow-hawk; this makes a distinction by which one may readily be known from the other when on the wing at a long distance off. The female of this bird is larger than the male, as is the case with most, if not all, of the *Falconidæ*.

The kestrel may often be seen hovering over a field at a great height, and while we watch it it sinks gracefully down for some distance, hovers again, and, perhaps after having repeated the performance again, finally swoops down to the ground on to its prey; or else after hovering for some time, perhaps having lost sight of its mouse, in wide circles, flies up, up, until the eye can see it no longer. In the event of a mouse being captured, the kestrel either flies away with it to some distant tree, or to its nest if it have one, or remains to eat it on the spot. In the latter case, how often have I pursued it from field to field with a gun, cautiously creeping behind the hedges trying to get a shot at it, but always failing. I have no doubt, from its so constantly dropping in fields, that it chiefly feeds on mice, though most probably large insects also are devoured by it; and it is thus a friend to the farmer, who, however, in mistake for his zeal for the sparrow-hawk, often kills it, and nails it up to the barn-doors among rooks, &c. It also, I should think unjustly, suffers the same fate at the hands of the gamekeeper, who also intends to slay its mischievous relation.

The cry of the kestrel is described by a certain author on Natural History as "a sharp, ringing, half-laughing cry," which expresses it very well. It is very much the same as the sparrowhawk's, judging from the sound uttered by some young specimens of the latter, with whom I lately had the pleasure of an acquaintance. It seems to be uttered generally, if not always, when the bird is in a wood, or near its nest.

The kestrel seldom begins the labours of nidification until the middle of May. It builds a loosely constructed nest of large sticks, often with no interior lining of softer material; the nest is placed on a high tree in a thick wood, or in a piece of rock, or old quarry in a wood. I have heard too of kestrels breeding in company on the cliffs by the sea shore.

I will give an account of the nest, out of which, on the 20th of May last, I took the eggs that I have in my possession now. It was built about half way up a moderately high fir tree; it was composed of rotting moss, &c., and was one of those hybrid, rotten, old-as-Adam nests that everyone who enters a wood and looks about him can always see about him in plenty; the bulk of this model nest was in a slanting position, and a small portion of it had tumbled down on to a branch just below that on which the nest had originally rested, and formed a small flat platform, in which were laid four fresh kestrel's eggs. These differed much in colour and size; two being smaller than the other two. One of them was very dark, being of a dark red ground-colour, marked (how can I express it?) with much darker red, while here and there patches of colour like the ground colour, yet somehow quite different, were to be seen. The larger ones (which I have given away, and so cannot describe accurately) were lighter than the former, but darker than the remaining one, which was of a white ground colour, the large end being very dark red, and the rest of the eggs spotted with dark red.

LA PLANCHETTE.—The agent named Planchette, which your correspondent "C." has made the subject of a communication to the N.N.B., appears to be one of many methods of obtaining real or fancied communications from the unseen world. The most ancient mention we have of such an agency is probably the divining cup of Joseph, Gen. xliv. 5, &c., and the enchantments used by the magicians of Egypt, Ex. vii. 11, &c. Thirty years ago such things were considered either too childish or too antiquated to claim more than a passing attention from the educated, but no we have returned to divination or sorcery. These matters were, however, continuously practised in some form or other in bye places, even in the United Kingdom, and it is well known that they have even been so in Egypt, India, Africa, the West Indies, &c. Yet some persons seem to consider them the discoveries of modern science. But it is incontrovertible that the most ignorant nations have practised such things from time immemorial; true, under various names. It is probably of small moment what are the circumstances under which such consultations are made. A planchette, a table, an obeah stick, a piece of rag, a ball of crystal, will answer; for the success seems to depend on the belief and expectancy of the operators or enquirers. Those who are materialistic in their views will likely fall most easily into these delusions. I venture to call them such, for supposing Planchette, &c., to be speaking the truth when she avows herself the mouth-piece of Satan, is it not a delusion of a solemn kind for a man to put himself under the teaching of the great enemy of his race? Again, if the devil has nothing to do with these manifestations, should there be any confidence placed in a system claiming such a source, and thus proceeding from a false basis? There is an old proverb, "Speak of the devil and he will appear." Let us take care that we do not insure the fulfilment of what we do not desire, unless we are prepared to treat the whole existence of this being as a myth. A. G.

In the N.N.B. for last month, "S. Regelous" asks for information concerning the capture of *Sirex Gigas*. I have several fine female specimens of this insect in my collection, which were taken in Chatham Dockyard; these I have no doubt were brought in the pupa state from Northern Europe or North America, in the pine logs, which are so largely used in H.M. dockyards for shipbuilding purposes. I may also state, that I have several species of foreign Longicorn Beetles taken in the same dockyard, which owe their introduction into this country to the same means, viz.: importation. *Cerambyx Heros* is one of these: of this fine beetle, a native of Southern Europe, I have six or eight specimens, and have seen others. This insect arrives either in the larva or pupa state in logs of Italian oak timber, from which the imago emerges about midsummer, and either crawls along, or flies briskly, according to the temperature of the weather, much to the discomfiture of any workmen who may happen to see the long-horned black stranger. When handled, it produces a sound by the friction of the thorax, almost similar to that of the Death's Head moth. *Morimus lugubris* is another of this family, also a native of Southern Europe. I have but one representative of this species. I have also another species, of which I do not know the name; but the specimen I have is as large as *C. Heros*, but not quite so rugose, and is of a chocolate brown colour. Another importaton is that of the European Scorpion (*Scorpio Europeus*), which no doubt secretes itself in the shakes or cracks so common in the Italian oak timber. I have had several of these creatures, and have kept them alive for several months, feeding them on flies, young cockroaches, &c., until the cold weather killed them.

W. CHANEY.

EXTINCTION OF SPECIES.—Owing to my absence from home. I have been unable to answer "Mr. Geffcken" earlier. I have to express my regret that this gentleman met with such non-success in his recent attempt to correspond with me. My address is 8, Onslow Road, and it will give me great pleasure to receive any letters on this subject. In the mean time could Mr. G. reconnoitre, and let us know with what feeling the country people (Germans) have received his plan? The season is now too far advanced for anything to be done beyond forming some Society to consider how we ought to proceed next year. However, I should much like to hear the opinions of other readers, and now solicit them to come forward and lend their aid. It is evident that a society *must* be formed, if the project is to be carried out with any chance of success. If Mr. G. would be kind enough to make inquiries concerning V. Antiopa, of the country people surrounding Stuttgart, no doubt many readers would be much obliged, and with me look forward with pleasure to his letter on the subject.

W. JOHNSTON.

ANSWERS TO ENQUIRERS.—In answer to you correspondent "Hawkmoth," I have to inform him that I was once told that the dried root of the Valerian (perhaps obtainable at a druggists) placed about the haunts of cockroaches, &c., would, upon their eating it, destroy them. (Query), will they eat it? Allow me also to inform "R. Laddiman" that the contents of the bodies of dragon-flies should be carefully pressed out through a slit made along the under side of the abdomen and hot sand introduced. But the colours of dragon-flies are certainly not "fast." I should suggest to "Geo. Trobridge" that his curious insect may be the larva of a small moth, Porrectaria (?) (Haworth); perhaps Leucopenella, a specimen of which I reared from an odd-looking caddis-like case which was walking about on a whitethorn leaf in the early part of this year. Allow me also to record the capture (at Worthing) of Camptogramma Gemmaria in my drawing-room early this month.

Worthing. W. HAMBROUGH.

WHAT IS A FISH?—Naturalists tell us that "a fish is an animal without legs; it has a jointed backbone, and it breathes under the water by means of gills." And, says Milne Edwards, the French naturalist, "fish breathe by gills and never by lungs at any period of their lives. Their heart is composed of two cavities, the auricle and ventricle, containing only dark blood; this blood is sent to the gills, and returns from these, after being exposed to the oxygen, to be distributed to the various parts of the body, no heart being interposed between the gills and the other organs of the body; their blood is cold, and their skin naked, covered only by scales; they lay eggs, that being their mode of reproduction, and finally, their limbs have the form of fins." When we look at many of the prominent characteristics of the whale, and see how widely they differ from the received definition of a fish, I am sure Mr. Landels will have great difficulty in inducing naturalists to concede to his arguments.

Dundrum. H. H. ULIDIA.

SUN AND MOON LARGER AT RISING AND SETTING.—Your correspondent G. O. Howell has received two answers to his question in the June number. As these answers are quite different from each other, perhaps he doesn't know which to rely upon. The first answer given by "Yorick" is the same as that given in Herschel's Astronomy. The second given by "Ernest Belfort Bax" does not account for the difference in size. It is true that refraction does produce an effect upon the appearance of the sun and moon when near the horizon; it simply makes the vertical diameter of the sun or moon appear shorter than the horizontal one. It is well known that as the horizon is approached, the degree of refraction increases very rapidly, and in consequence of this the lower part of the sun is more highly refracted than the upper, and therefore the vertical diameter will appear shorter than it really is, while the horizontal diameter, all parts of which are equally distant from the horizon will appear the same. R. T.

CURIOUS INSECT.—Can any of the readers of the N. N. B. kindly inform me of the name of the following insect, new to me, if the description is sufficiently accurate. The body consists of seven rings covered over, as seen under the microscope, with stiff bristles of a dark hue. The thorax is horny, smooth, and dark, and on its head are fixed a most remarkable pair of pincers, resembling with much closeness those of a scorpion, which reptile the whole insect much resembles. It was taken off a recently cut frame cucumber, and when under the microscope, with some pieces of the rind, was seen to nip off small portions and convey them to its mouth. These instruments consist of four joints, the upper one being of the size and formation of those of lobsters, &c. J. A. FOWLER.

Brighton.

DOES RAPIDITY OF PHYSICAL INJURY PREVENT THE SENSATION OF PAIN?—A "painless knife," which, when in operation, makes twenty-five revolutions in a second, has recently been offered to humanity, upon, I presume, the principle that rapidity of injury prevents the sensation of pain. What are the opinions of the correspondents of the N.N.B. concerning this theory? H. H. ULIDIA.

Strangford.

RIBSTONE PIPPINS.—I have very frequently heard Ribstone Pippins called *Ripstone Pippins*. I have also seen them in fruiterers' and greengrocers' shops marked as such. Now, I think this most decidedly wrong. Ribstone Pippins are so called because the pips were brought from Holland, and planted at Ribstone Hall, near Knaresboro', in Yorkshire.

Gravesend. G. O. HOWELL.

FISH HEARING.—I have read that fish have no external organs of hearing, yet I think that some fish absolutely do hear, as carps in fish-ponds have been trained to assemble at the sound of a bell. I should like to have the opinion of some of your correspondents on this subject. G. O. HOWELL.

Gravesend.

QUERY.—Can any one of your readers kindly inform me in the N.N.B. the best method of determining the genus species, &c., of any moth that has been caught. I should also be glad if anyone could tell me how long insects ought to remain set before being finally placed in the cabinet. W. M.

BUTTERFLIES.—Is it known what becomes of these insects in the night time, or in wet weather? and what is the greatest duration of life in an insect in its perfect condition. Can anyone inform me by means of your "Note Book" the best kind of weather to go in search of specimens? W. M.

THE MOON AND THE WEATHER.—Some people believe that the moon has an influence upon the weather in the same way as it has upon the tides. I suppose that this idea is erroneous; but if so, how did it originate, and is it of long standing?

ERNEST BELFORT BAX.

SIREX GIGAS.—In reply to Mr. S. Regelous I may say that Sirex Gigas is not at all an uncommon insect in most parts of England, especially in the Midland Counties. It is taken not unfrequently near Leicester, as well as other places. ERNEST BELFORT BAX.

THE WOOD-PIGEON.—Will any reader of the N.N.B., through the medium of its pages, kindly furnish me with a few notes descriptive of the wood-pigeon, its habits, &c. G. O. HOWELL.

Gravesend.

EREBIA CASSIOPE.—Would Mr. R. Laddiman kindly mention the locality and particulars of his capture of Erebia Cassiope last year, as it is rarely taken so far south as Norwich. ERNEST BELFORT BAX.

HOUSE FLIES.—Would any one kindly inform me whether all the house flies die before the approach of winter, or whether any of them hybernate?

ERNEST BELFORT BAX.

COLOURS OF DRIED FLOWERS.—In answer to Imago in your last issue, he will find by referring to one of the latter numbers of the N.N.B. an answer to his query. YORICK.

ROUGH NOTES ON THE NATURAL HISTORY OF CORFU.

(Continued from page 260.)

THE day after landing I got up with the intention of going about the town and viewing the various objects of interest which would be sure to divert one on landing in a strange country, but I was stopped in this purpose by the fact that it was Ascension Day, and that a Festa, or "Paniarè," was held in a grove a few miles out of the town. There were two ways of going to it, one by water, and the other by land, and as I thought that I should see more of the country and people if I went by land, I chose the longest way round to the "One Gun Battery," as it is called, from the fact of there being at one time a gun mounted at that point, by the French, when they held the island. Starting early in the afternoon, so that I might saunter along and observe all the curious things incidental to first impressions of a new country, I passed along the front of the University, a large and ancient building, and wended my way, in company with a young Englishman who acted as my guide, through the clean looking suburb of Kastrades, by the side of the sea, and up the road which passes the "Casino" or country seat of the Commissioner. Looking back from here you saw the Bay of Kastrades, deserted by the fishermen, whose boats with furled sails lay idly at anchor, while their owners were on shore taking part in what was the greatest and most holy festival of the Greek Church for the year; not only the crews of these boats, but indeed every person who could crawl, were hastening up the ascent, eager for the opportunity of making a devotional pilgrimage to the shrine of "Isa Elia," which was in a little church in the grove of the Kardacchio. The road up which we were now toiling was fringed on both sides by olive trees, whose gnarled, split, and aged trunks yet afforded sufficient nourishment to support the vigorous shoots of the spring and the fruit-bearing branches of the autumn. Aloes, prickly-pears, and cacti formed the hedges and protected the cottage gardens of the Maltese peasants: the only people, I believe, in this island who make gardening a profitable success. One cottage ornee which I passed, evidently the residence of some high class native, was shut in by a stone wall, on and over which was growing a high hedge of rose bushes, the blossoms of the sweet scented roses, nearly hidden by the trailing luxuriance of the purple and white of the elegant passion flower, among which revelled the wild bees, and dozens of curious little beetles.

The air was inexpressibly silently hot; not a breeze ruffled the leaves of the Carob trees overhead, on which rested the ear-piercing cicadæ, the curious stridulous hum of these insects almost drowning the far off din of the fair. No one who has not heard their shrill vibrating chirp can form the least idea of the effect produced, when thousands, nay, tens of thousands, are acting in concert, for then you actually have to speak very loudly in order to be heard. The noise made by one alone is equal to that produced if you hold a knife by its blade on a table and rapidly vibrate the handle, then letting it go suddenly; and fancy if you can the united attempts of a few thousands of these "going ahead" at one and the same time. These little demons of discord are, I believe, the same as those described by the ancients as "Tettigonia," or "Earthborn," and various reasons from the earliest days have been given as to the cause of their persistent vibratory hissing; the most generally received opinion, however, appears to be that it is caused by the rapid motion of the wings over a sort of cavity or drum in the back. Often have I watched these large-eyed, transparent, winged flies as sitting on the bark or leaf of a tree, they drummed away with "promptitude and despatch," until fancying themselves observed, they suddenly stopped, gave one decided distinct "fizz," and "darted away with themselves" as quick as thought, to give another tree the benefit of their exasperating *melody*. On the principle of the eels soon getting accustomed to be skinned, I suppose, you hardly notice them in time, in fact look forward to them as a cheerful unit in the grand sum total of nature.

Near here the road suddenly widened and exposed a vista of surpassing loveliness; below us lay the Lake Calikiopulo (about which anon) its clear glittering bosom silently reflecting the image of the majestic mountain of Santa Decka, or the "Ten Saints," the tranquil sheet of water only broken by the sudden leap and plash of some large Mullet (*Mugil Capito*) jumping in very wantonness, and shaking the sparkling drops of one element into the glorious light of the other. That great hawk, wheeling in seemingly purposeless circles above, is evidently lazily enjoying the beautifully pure and cooler air above the lake, and has no interest here save his own pleasure, unless, indeed, he may be watching that little group of dab-chicks swimming about. Ah! An arrow from a bow, a shooting star, flying downwards through the void, could hardly descend more quickly to the surface of the water. A ruffle of the silver, a dash, a plunge, and a brief struggle, an upward flutter of the strong wings, and before the poor little dab-chick knows what is the matter, it is seized in the relentless talons of its enemy, who proudly emerges with its victim, turns his stern eye from side to side, arches his barred tail, gives all his plumage a shake in mid-air to free it of the water drops, and with a few strong strokes of the sturdy pinions, sails away to some inaccessible rock, to tear in undisturbed solitude its prey. The rest of the group, more fortunate, and perhaps more alert, have dived or flown, and now reappear again at a considerable distance.

Now we cut into another and more frequented road, and here the carriages, horsemen, and wayfarers, like ourselves, are crowding the way; they are mostly townspeople, however, with a pretty considerable sprinkling of soldiers and sailors, dark-eyed Maltese, and darkly handsome Italians, who are going merely for the fun, and not for religious reasons; the country people, who are our chief study, are not in great force along this road, but we shall find them at the fair.

A greater press of people, more dust, more noise, and the curiously confused sound of laughter, violins, guitars, songs, shouts, and scraps of nearly every known European language, betray our proximity to the Festa, even had we ignored the fact that sundry odours of cheese, wood fires, wine, and the "parlous savoury" scent of roast lamb had saluted our noses ere this. Here we are at last in a scene which by its beauty and diversity of colouring and association, is positively bewildering. Picture to yourself a grove of grand old olive trees, through the interstices of whose grotesquely gnarled trunks you catch glimpses of the blue Mediterranean on three sides. Feasting, dancing, singing, al fresco on every hand; sheep roasting whole at wood fires, outside tents, decorated with flags of all nations, and booths for the sale of wine, bread, cheese, and mysterious confectionery: their enterprising owners standing near and bawling out in a perplexingly polyglot style, "Ela edo, kallo krasi;" "Venez ici Messieurs;" "Buon vino;" "Vera goot vhine, koom along Johnny, koom along; eaty the vhine, an strinky the laäm, makey yourself similar my brother," and similar fraternal, and "jolly companion" invitations.

What a magnificent study for a colourist some of these gay groups of peasants would make; the men fine stalwart fellows most of them, clothed in a neat and becoming costume, consisting of a short black cloth jacket (sometimes trimmed up the front with gold) large convex silver buttons up the sides, the jacket thrown open to display the elaborately "got up" white shirt of fine material confined at the throat with a black silk handkerchief; blue zouave "bags" of rather coarse material, admirably contrasted by white stockings. A sash gorgeously banded in crimson and amber, and of expensive Italian silk, confines the waist, and serves to hold the cigarette pouch or the more dangerous knife. The feet are cased in shoes of undressed leather, turned up in a peak at the toes, and fastened with thongs of leather, or sometimes neat black shoes of English manufacture, fastened with silver buckles, take their place; the head is covered with a red fez, or skull cap, with blue silken tassel, or else by a hat of fine straw; put this costume on any one with a soldier-like bearing, having short black hair, and a heavy moustache curled at the ends, in the peculiar sardonic style they affect, place a cigarette between his lips, and you have then the portrait of the Greek peasant as he should be complete. Candour, however, compels me to add that the model should persistently and conscientiously *stink* (rude word, but the only one which will do) of garlic, and that above all he must not be *too* clean.

The women are, however, the centre of attraction, not as regards their beauty, for the men beat them in that, but on account of their dazzling and studied toilet. These poor things toiling like slaves (which indeed they are to their lords and masters) all the week in the fields and vineyards, hoeing up ground, cutting wood, and all sorts of hard work, and dressed in the most primitive costume, now come out on these gala days in silks, velvets, and satins, literally blazing with gold and gems, the latter often of antique workmanship, being handed down from generation to generation, some of the ornaments in fact being of the most curiously beautiful and recherche designs; their hair now is braided with gay silks, gold coins, real and false pearls, and their breast is a perfect repository of jewelery.

The general dress is a skirt of violet or crimson shot silk, just short enough to reveal their gay shoes of black or purple velvet, confined by silver or silver-gilt buckles, a bodice of rich velvet, laced up the front with ribands, confines the bust, covered with a chemisette of fine lawn, frilled at the throat with valuable lace, a short jacket of rich crimson, black, or purple velvet, with loose large sleeves open at half arm to display the armlets and laced under-linen, covers this. These jackets are really marvels of workmanship and expense, for in addition to being made of silk velvet, they are embroidered in the most magnificent manner on the seams, back, and arms with real gold thread, and lace, and variously coloured silk in beautifully figured scrolls, arabesques, and dragon-like looking birds or serpents. A sash much narrower and shorter than worn by the men, but of equally rich material and colour, confines the waist of the skirt under the jacket, and is clasped by a silver or golden buckle. Immense rings of massive gold literally cover the fingers, often being large enough to fill up the space between the knuckle and the next joint. Some have an ornamented gold signet plate, others a roughly cut garnet or topaz inserted. The breast is covered with medals, and pictures of saints engraved on as large a gold plate as they can afford, ornamented at the edges sometimes with stars in filagre work, as are the earrings. The head is surmounted by a sort of coronet of hair, often plaited with ribands, covering which, yet not entirely hiding it, is a white linen kerchief, which hangs in not ungraceful folds down the back.

The more jewellery they can heap on their persons the better they like it, and having no idea of taste, yet they cannot help being picturesque. One redeeming point, which we cannot apply to the ladies of this country or time is, that the Greek women never think of adorning themselves by tricky imitations of gold ornaments. Oh dear no! your contadina will wear nothing but silver or " oro fino," sometimes above, never below, 18-carat.

Various villages have their own peculiar style of dress; the women of Karusades, for instance, wearing long paletot jackets reaching nearly to the heels, and the women of Potamo invariably contrasting their fine black hair with a coronet tastefully tied with scarlet ribands.

A Greek lady from the mainland whom I noticed, had on a crimson and blue shot silk dress, crimson velvet long jacket, stiff with gold embroidery, beautiful lace and muslin, under a black velvet bodice, and a low fez cap worked with gold and silk to represent gems; depending from the crown was a double gold tassel, tossing saucily over her shoulder. She looked *distingué*, but was not pretty. In attendance on her was a warlike-looking Albanian, who was stalking along with that martial, yet careless step, which so greatly distinguishes these people. As he was dressed in the national costume. I cannot do better than describe him as a guide for the future. His head, then, was covered by a large red Phrygian cap, with an immense blue silk tassel hanging by a gold cord from the centre, a fine white shirt, the arms of which came through the upper and under jackets, which were of fine green cloth and crimson velvet respectively laced, slashed, and embroidered with gold on back, edges, sides, and hanging sleeves. A gay silk sash, as usual, confined the waist and supported the "fustanella," a tunic of white linen pleated in countless folds, which caused it to widen above the knees, and which fell over drawers of fine white linen reaching below the knees, where they were met by the leggings of richly laced cloth falling over the shoes, and thus completing a costume, perhaps the handsomest of any in Europe.

Here, under the shade of those ancient olive trees, which have perhaps beheld Kerkyra, the lovely sea-queen of this charmed isle, and her two dark-haired, stately sisters—have waved their sad, evergreen leaves over the fair head of the Princess Nausicaa, as she discovered Ulysses in these very groves, when, after leaving Ogygia, the home of his deserted love, Calypso, he was finally wrecked in sight of the famed gardens of the luxurious city of the Phæacian king, Alcinoüs, and the lost ship of the storm-tossed hero himself, turned by the malice of Neptune into yon rocky island, lies but a stone's throw from the land. Here, then, in these classic shades, where once the Dryads roamed, and chased the long-eared bat, and the wise staring owl, from their flower-cups of night dew, when the moon shone brightly, and these robbers of their treasure were abroad—are the descendants of the ancient Phæacians celebrating a religious festival with the Romaika, that relic of the Phyrric dance, and with songs whose antiquity is vouched for by the fact that the unlearned cannot translate some of the words found in them. In the shade of these fig trees, growing on the ruins of the ancient temple of Nemesis, whose grey fluted columns still crop out of the ground in places, are seated a group of fierce-looking men, their fierceness redeemed by a certain nobility of mien and manner. They are gazing over the sea—that marvellous azure sea, calm and smiling now, like a handsome woman, and like the beau sexe, hiding a stormy depth which oft rises to the surface in quick sudden bursts of passion, wrecking happiness or life—these men, so fiercely moustachioed, with, no doubt, a pretty little bright knife hidden away in the folds of their voluminous sashes, are singing. Is it about love? Ah, no! these are the "palikaria," the lineal descendants, may be, of the old sea kings—well, pirates, if you will. They are singing a song of the sea, about a noted buccaneer who drew down destruction and retribution on the head of the hated Turk. Note well the leader, who sings in a deep, full voice; mark how he hisses his words out when he has to name the loathed Ottoman; see how his eyes sparkle with a wild joy when he comes to the battle-scene, as if he could feel the hot blood of his foes rushing over his poignard hilt, like Johannes of Statha. The others, who accompany him with voices and guitars, are hardly less moved, their earnest attitudes, and war-lighted faces, bespeak their thoughts.

Hist! What, Byron's name here? Yes. A group of younger men than those who have just finished singing, are talking of 31, and as they warm with the subject, you hear Lord Byron's name associated with that of Riga, Marco Botzaris, and other patriots, who have fought, bled, and starved, to free their country from the thrall of the accursed followers of the Prophet, who, they say, caused the death of the noble Capo' d'Istrias, assassinated though he was by the knife of a Santa Mauriot—a wretched traitor to his country's cause. Leaving this spot, let us stray yet nearer the sea, to that patch of verdant sward on the edge of yon orange grove, whose delicately scented flowers even thus late in the season, imbue the air with their subtle aroma, breathing perhaps of love and wedding favours, to some of those dark-eyed beauties, who, guarded with all a mother's, or jealous duenna's care, are sitting in close proximity to a ring of young men of the middle class. All these youths are well educated, so that, perhaps, some beautiful ode will be sung, to convey the passionate love of one of their number to some one of the maidens sitting near, whose cheek will burn, and whose heart will throb, as the "flower words" fall upon her anxious ear, but who will betray no other consciousness, that those sweet words are intended for her only; for did she betray the locked secret of her heart, there would be no more festas for her where she would have the opportunity of exchanging a sly glance or token with Anastasi, who is now touching his guitar with a skilful hand, at one moment making it wail like the cry of the seabird in a storm, then softly gliding his fingers over the quivering strings, making them sigh as the nightingale sighs, when a dark cloud overshadows the moon, until louder and louder grows the wild strain, until it ends in a sparkling ronda, whose every note bespeaks the ecstatic joy which leaps and laughs in the player's veins. That was, however, but the prelude,—it now abruptly changes to the accompaniment, which bold, yet sweet, admirably suits his voice as he sings with deep feeling the following song, which, though lacking the magic fire of the Romaic, is yet as nearly a literal translation as is compatible with the peculiar rythm.

THE DREAM.

("To Oneiro.")

List! Soul* of mine, to a dream of delight,
  Which in fancy fulfilled all desire:
Methought in sweet gardens I was roaming with thee,
  And of kisses we ne'er seemed to tire.

---

* "Psyche mou"—term of endearment.

All nature seemed dark, save the spot where we stood;
  Not a star twinkled over the sea;
All their splendour united, above us was shining,
  And their rays were concentred on thee.

As in homage they flashed and hailed thee as Queen,
  I addressed them with greatest surprise,
And scornfully asked, "Who among you above
  Dares to rival my lady's bright eyes?"

"Tell me! has it e'er been your fortune to shine
  O'er such tresses of beautiful hair;
Such hands, such a foot, such adorable lips,
  Or a figure like that of my Fair?"

The stars shrank abashed at my passionate words,
  And, soft as the nightingale sings,
They murmured "Ah yes! 'tis a goddess on earth,
  More lovely than those who have wings."

Their lights now had paled—by thy beauty outshone,
  And as kisses we interchanged sweet,
Every kiss that you gave me a rosebud became,
  And fell on the ground at our feet.

Some formed a carpet of living perfume,
  And lay piled in odorous beds;
While others upsprung with leaves and with flowers,
  And arched themselves over our heads.

* * *

This, then, was my dream, darling girl!
  Now doth it rest with thee,
To mature to full bloom these rosebuds of sleep,
  By giving thy love to me.

See! the stars are peeping forth timidly, as if ashamed to spoil the pleasures of the day by warning all these gay throngs that night approaches swiftly in these latitudes, driving away her half-sister eve, who toys here with the lover-like twilight but for a brief period. The first rays of the moon are glinting over those tiny wavelets, and the night-bird's soft note is heard as the festa ends; and standing alone, after all have departed, you may watch the last boat's load of gay friends disappear in the gathering gloom, and may yet hear floating on the wings of the ocean zephyrs the last sweet strains of the farewell songs.

This being one of the months—June, which is close time for birds in the island—(not so much on account of themselves and any young families they may have, but to put a stop to sportsmen and others going through the vineyards and knocking off the fruitful blossoms of the vines.) I did not see any birds in the markets, and indeed, at this time there are very few to be seen in the country, for most of the birds found are migratory, coming in April; leaving the end of May, and not reappearing again until August, at which season they remain only for a few days; these are what I feel disposed to call the Eastern birds, such as the Oriole, Bee Eater, Roller, and several others; for the Northern birds, such as the Redwing,

Woodcock, and so on, have a migration of their own (as in England) to the island in October, and remain the winter, departing as the summer birds come in—even to the Thrushes and Robins. This and some other curious facts relating to the different times of appearance and departure of the migratory birds, I must reserve for another time, and go on with the natural history and memorabilia for

JUNE.

Some time in this month, hearing of a good habitat for Lepidoptera, I made a trip to the Racecourse, which is part of the sandy flat, which forms the shore of the lagoon—Calikiopulo, the ancient harbour of the Paleopolis; this place lies about a mile from the town-gate of Porta Reale.

Leaving Kastrades on the left, and the suburb of San Rocque on the right, I struck the main road between them, past the Greek Hospital, and after a few minutes walking on a dusty road, fringed with vines and fruit trees, arrived at the Racecourse, which lies to the left of the road.

Standing on a hillock and turning your back on the road, the view is superb—the plain stretches before in undulating grassy and sandy belts intersected by ditches with little rushy nooks near the margin of the water, which sweeps in a large curve before you; this lagoon, or salt-water lake, is so shallow in places that you may see the grey mullet (*Mugil Capito*) as they dash madly along near the shore, is an inlet from the sea, so narrow at its entering neck that palisades or hurdles formed of reeds are stretched across to confine the fish to the shallower parts, and being gradually brought nearer the land from either shore, force the fish to seek safety in the curve of the horse-shoe shaped lake, where, of course (owing to the sand which has silted up this ancient harbour for ages), they flounder about in water barely sufficient to cover them, and fall an easy prey to the seine or cast-net.

As I shall have frequent occasion to refer to this spot, I should premise that "to Limne," as the peasants call it, is about a mile broad in its widest part, and extends about half that distance seaward; on the left it is bounded by the neck of land running from Kastrades to the "One Gun Battery"—the groves of the Kardacchio, the scene of the Ascension Fair. From here that part appears as a succession of gardens with alternating terraces of vines growing in the scanty earth on the rocky plateaux, and owing to the numerous olives, presenting a generally well-wooded and fertile aspect. Guarding the entrance of the channel from the sea is the "Rock of Ulysses" ("Podicanesi," or "Rats' Island," the natives call it), on which is built a monastery surrounded by cypress and orange trees; this is backed to seaward by the rugged scarps of the mountains of Casturi and Benizza, which trend round in a wide bay until they completely shut out the view beyond.

Opposite the "One Gun," on the right shore, are the beautifully-timbered rocks of Peramà, where is situated the chief water reservoir of Corfu.

Above, and seeming to overhang the lake, though in reality far beyond, is the grand outline of Sancta Decka, sombrely imposing in its changing features of bold rock, grassy slope, and deep gorge; half way up the mountain, beneath some precipitous crags, lies the village of the same name, only distinguishable as a rather large mass of white houses and cottages.

Below is sleeping in the mid-day heat a rich and strikingly coloured landscape, the blueish green olives easily picked out from the deeper green zones of the orange trees; again, the brighter leaves of the vines showing almost yellow against the black, gloomy cypresses which started up here and there, like unhappy thoughts in the still regions of the heart; bush, hill, and valley, in which lay the orchard-gardens all aglow with ripening plums, mulberries and cherries; then marshland bordering the lake, adown which sped swiftly and silently a purely bright stream of clear cold water—so cold, indeed, even in the hottest months, that it is the only water in the island which sportsmen debar their dogs from entering to bathe when hot or thirsty. Close to this, at its embouchere into salt water, are sand-banks on which various wading-birds collect, in their season; between this and the spot where we now stand is an olive grove called Catacalu; and having now cursorily surveyed the landscape, from left to right, we will wend our way thither.

In passing over the intervening strip of sun-baked saline soil, the residuum of the winter floods, I observed a great number of the Yellow wagtail (*Motacilla Flava*) uttering their tremulous chirp, and jumping up at the flies which hovered about the surface of the ground. These little birds are most indefatigable insect destroyers, and I have seen them tamed and kept in rooms and shops abroad, to clear the place of flies; and I remember seeing one whose master had fastened, by some means or another, a cock's crest made of red cloth to its head, and the little thing, as it peered curiously about and took little, short running jumps at its prey, presented a most comical appearance, which I did not forget for days. A few larks started up lazily as I went along, as also a bird which puzzled me exceedingly at the time, but whi

I now conjecture to have been the Pallas sandgrouse (*Syrrhaptes Paradoxus*), which my readers will recollect, have established themselves as English birds in our lists by having visited Norfolk and other places in packs.

A few Alpine Swifts (*Cypselus Alpinus*) were circling overhead, in company with swallows, and over the placid waters of the glittering lake a great Heron (*Ardea Cinerea*) flapped heavily, slowly enunciating his frog-like croak, in utter defiance of harmony, or any other heron.

Skirting this, to the land side, were some vines, about which was flitting a peculiar and elegant little bird belonging to the insectivorous order, and whose ruddy plumage and white tipped ruddier tail, which it constantly flirted and expanded, much in the manner of a robin when it "ducks," at once marked it out as being the Rufous Sedge Warbler (*Salicaria Galactotes*), "Cochinora" of the Greeks. According to the Rev. F. O. Morris, it has been shot in England, and as I think it one of the species likely to occur in the spring, it may not be unwise to give a short description, for the benefit of my readers, from the pen of that distinguished naturalist. After stating that it was shot at Brighton by Mr. Swaysland, he writes:—"Male; length, seven inches. The bill is slightly curved, the upper mandible is brown above, the sides pale yellowish brown, of which colour is the lower mandible; from the base of the bill there is a dark streak going back to the eye. Iris reddish brown; over and under the eye, and passing backwards, is a short cream-white streak. Head, crown, neck, and nape, fawn colour; chin, throat, and breast dull white; back, fawn colour. The wings have the first quill feather short, the second and sixth of nearly equal length, the third, fourth, and fifth equal in length, and at the same time the longest in the wing. Greater and lesser wing coverts fawn colour; primaries and secondaries brown, the outer edges reddish buff, greater and lesser under wing coverts, delicate fawn colour. The tail, which is much cuneated, and consists of twelve feathers, has the two long middle ones reddish buff, the others reddish buff over two-thirds of their length, each gradually shortening, then crossed by a broad band of black, the remainder white, the outside paler on each side, with the largest portion of white. Underneath the tail is marked as on the upper surface, but is not so bright. Upper tail-coverts reddish buff; legs, toes, and claws, pale brown."

Around the blossoms of the Scabious or Greater Knapweed (*Centaurea Scabiosa*), which grew on the grassy knolls in profusion, the Clouded Yellow (*Colias Edusa*), and Painted Lady (*Cynthia Cardui*), were flitting in great numbers, alighting, as is their wont, on the sweet petals to take a sip of butterfly nectar, and then gaily passing on their way to another favourite flower. A few Marbled Whites (*Arge Galatea*), were pursuing their devious flight over the tops of the long grasses, the beautiful half mourning wings in strong contrast to the azure of the Blue (*Polyommatus Alexis*), who pugnaciously followed, and teased its more sober companion among the flowers. Here it was that I saw, for the first time, a butterfly which, in my noviciate to natural history, fairly took away my breath, I mean the magnificent Swallow Tail (*Papilio Podalirius*), the zebra-like markings, and superior size of the pale yellow wings, distinguishing it at once from its congener, the hardly less splendid *P. Machaon*. How I chased, panted, and perspired under a sun 95 deg. in the shade, ere I captured my valued prize, I need not remind any one who has studied in the field as well as in the cabinet.

In a sun-crack in the ground, just before reaching the olive trees, I saw a small frog going through a variety of gymnastic feats, and struggling in a very curious and ornamental manner. I thought, from his style and evident respectability, that he could hardly be in training for a circus, so was on the point of concluding that he was having a little jocular exercise, on some unknown principles of his own, when I happened to look more minutely into the crack, and saw at once the reason which induced him to go on "thusly;" a large snake (*Coluber Natrix*), was sluggishly lying at the bottom, and coolly persuading the unfortunate Batrachian down his capacious throat. He had one hind leg in his jaws, and was slowly gulping "Froggy" down. This process being naturally a slow one, I watched the snake for some time, (which did not attempt to move), ere I interfered with his digestion, and despatched his snakeship with a sound blow from a stick, and had the satisfaction of seeing poor Mr. "Rana Temporaria," jun., hop off to his afflicted "Pa," a *little* the worse for wear. A. M. B.

(*To be continued.*)

OUR WADING BIRDS.

No. 5.—THE PEEWIT.

BY ALEXANDER CLARK KENNEDY.

WHO does not know the peewit by sight, and who is not familiar with its slow, laboured flight, as it twirls around one's head, or tumbles downwards towards the ground, always recovering itself before reaching it, and again darting upwards and circling above us? And who has not, at some time or other, been struck with the plaintive scream of the lapwing, who accompanies you as you take your morning walk over the moorland waste, or by the river's side? There is something so inexpressibly soothing in that wild cry, when heard on a dreary moor, where there are perhaps no habitations for miles around, except a lone shepherd's cottage; and when the loud notes of the peewit mingle with the mournful shriek of the curlew, and the harsh cry, or (in spring) the monotonous "drumming" of the snipe, there are few more pleasing sounds to the true lover of nature in all her wild beauty.

In many, and indeed most parts of England, this species remains throughout the year, but in others it only stays to breed, or perhaps is a mere passing winter visitant. In some localities the provincial name of lapwing* is bestowed on this bird, on account of the tardy and laboured manner in which it flaps its long rounded wings; while in Scotland it is generally termed the "pease-weep;" and in the fens of Norfolk and other counties it is known by the name of "pywipe." Another title for this species is the "horned-pie," which name we have never heard used except in the county of Suffolk, but it is by no means an inappropriate one, for the long crest which surmounts the head of the green plover somewhat assumes the shape of a cow's horn.

These birds pair toward the end of February, and begin to build their nests in the following month, and by the middle of April the first brood of young are hatched, although the second laying do not hatch out until the end of May, and we have often seen young peewits in June. The eggs of this common species, well known to most juvenile collectors, are greatly esteemed for their fine flavour, and consequently many thousands are taken annually and forwarded from all parts of the kingdom to the London markets. It is recorded that, during the spring of 1839, no less than two hundred dozen of these eggs were taken from Romney marsh; and the numbers sent from Norfolk, Cambridgeshire, and Lincoln, a few years back, were immense. Mr. Lubbock states that, about the year 1820, it was no uncommon occurrence for a couple of men to collect nearly a bushel of these eggs in any of the Norfolk fens in a single morning. The nest of the peewit is usually merely a slight hollow in the ground, lined with a few bents or pieces of withered grass, but sometimes no lining whatever is used. It is placed most often on a small tussock of grass, or in the midst of a patch of low-growing reeds, and not at all rarely in a ploughed or grass field. The eggs are always four in number, and are arranged in the nest with all their smaller ends meeting in the middle; but, until the old bird commences to sit upon them, they are placed carelessly. Their colour is a deep olive brown, streaked and blotched with blackish brown and dark ochre; and if laid in a ploughed field it is by no means an easy task to discover them, so nearly do they approach the line of the earth by which they are surrounded. We have often seen dogs find these bird's nests of their own accord, and in some places they are especially trained to do so by the "eggers," who collect eggs to send to large cities as articles of luxury. Mr. Lubbock mentions the fact of a dog who was quite unused to this pursuit, after seeing two or three nests found, began to search for them, and not only found, but brought several to his master the same day, without breaking a single egg. There is, we believe, a particular breed of dogs who are better than all others for finding the eggs of such birds as plovers, terns, and dunlins, and this kind consists, as we have been informed, of some small terrier breed; and these dogs, on finding eggs, will bark until they succeed in calling their master's attention to the spot. The peewit will often make an attack on dogs who approach too near its nest, and even almost strikes men as it dashes around them when they are encroaching on its breeding domains. It is, of course, at "drawn daggers" with hawks of all kinds, magpies, jays, and particularly crows, for the latter birds are worse robbers than any of the others, and will even occasionally carry off a young plover, when eggs are not procurable. We remember reading a note in a newspaper not long ago, in which the writer stated that he saw a carrion crow attack and eventually succeed in carrying away a young peewit, whilst the two bereaved old birds flew around the cruel murderer with pitiful cries, but they availed nothing, and the sable robber escaped with his booty.

The peewit is not held in much estimation for the table now-a-days, but in ancient times it was greatly valued, as we may see by reference to Wade's "Chronological History of Great Britain," where it is stated that in the year 1633 the regular market price for one of these birds was tenpence, while twelve tame pigeons were only worth sixpence. This plover feeds principally on slugs, caterpillars, beetles, worms, and various kinds of grubs. We have often remarked that the peewit employs a very peculiar device

---

* The greater part of the present paper was originally published in the "Naturalist's Circular," a now defunct periodical; but it has been considerably altered and revised since its first appearance.

in order to procure earth-worms, for which its slender bill is not sufficiently strong to pierce deeply into the soil. When the bird wishes to take a meal, it takes its stand upon a sod of earth under which it knows that worms are concealed by reason of their casts, and then, resting upon one leg, beats the ground with the other. The unfortunate worms, fearing that the vibrations of the earth are caused by their unrelenting enemy, the mole, immediately make their way to the surface, and fall an easy prey to the cunning plover. The young of this species are able to run immediately after being hatched, and they can get along at a great rate, bobbing their little brown heads up and down as they go: they are not fully feathered, however, for some days, and they hide under tufts of grass or reeds when pursued, until they are better able to take care of themselves by learning to fly.

This plover is much disliked in some parts of Scotland, for it is said that flocks of these birds used to hover over the fleeing Covenanters, by which means their pursuers were enabled to discover their whereabouts. But it is also related that an ancestor of the Lincolnshire family of Tyrwhitt was saved by his retainers, as he lay helpless and badly wounded after a skirmish, by the same means. The peewit is extremely useful in a garden, as it entirely subists upon noxious grubs and insects. Besides its usefulness to the gardener, the bird is very ornamental, and its light weight enables it to walk over beds of flowers without injuring them in the least. Their wings may either be pinioned in order to prevent their escaping by flight, or the extreme joint of one wing may be amputated, or the wing itself simply clipped. From a walled garden they cannot escape if properly pinioned, as they are unable to perch by reason of the formation of their feet. They will soon become very tame, and will readily come to the call of their master, or of anyone who is accustomed to feed them, and often become familiar enough to eat corn or soaked bread from the hand, and feed with the barn-door fowls. If taken while still young, the peewit of course becomes tame in less time than one captured after it had enjoyed some months of liberty would do; but even old birds are not long in resigning themselves to their fate.

Variations in the plumage of this bird sometimes occur. In the year 1862 a white variety was shot in Ireland; and pied and dun-coloured specimens have occasionally been obtained in this country. These plovers collect in vast flocks during the winter months, and are very difficult to approach while in this state, as they keep an extremely sharp look-out; and one may generally notice sentinels upon every available rising ground and hillock around a flock which is feeding; and they seem to perform their duty well, if one may judge from their restlessness, for they are continually running backwards and forwards, looking first in one direction, then in another, taking short flights, and occasionally rising high into the air so as to spy out the movements of any enemy who may be in the neighbourhood, and warning their companions by their wild cry, if the danger is too imminent. The peewit is unable to bear a long continuation of snow and frost, and soon becomes emaciated, and in hard winters are sometimes sufficiently tamed by the cruel season to allow themselves to be caught by dogs, and are even taken up in the hand. Sometimes, too, they are starved to death by reason of the absence of their proper food, and we have known these birds frozen to the ground and unable to move on our approach. Young woodcocks are reported to have been observed in the act of being carried by their parent, and we have known several instances in which the eye-witnesses were perfectly trustworthy, but we rather doubt a fact related by a gentleman in a late periodical, which states that an old peewit, on being disturbed from her nest, made off with an egg under her wing for the distance of a couple of hundred yards!

The green plover is common throughout the European continent, and is met with in Siberia and other parts of Asia. In Egypt, too, it is observed, and occurs in Japan, China, and Persia, besides other localities which we need not mention here. The weight of the male bird is about seven ounces and a half, and the length rather more than a foot. The length, weight, and general appearance of the female is similar to that of the male, but the crest of the latter is usually the longest, and the colours are perhaps rather brighter upon the back and wings, which are large and rounded.

Its Latin name, Vanellus, probably means a fan, being given to this plover on account of the fanning motion made by its wings, which is audible for a long distance. Its usual note may be rendered by the words "peese-weet-a-weet, a-weet," uttered very shrilly; and it has also a shorter cry, which cannot well be described in words. The peewit is called "dixhuit" in France, from its peculiar note. A green plover in confinement will often attach itself to domestic animals; and Bewick mentions that one of these birds, when winter deprived it of its accustomed meal of worms and grubs, approached the house, and by degrees became tamer and tamer until it took up its permanent abode in the kitchen, and became a fast friend of a dog which lived there; and it often washed itself in the bowl of water set apart for the dog, much to the annoyance of the latter, but which, nevertheless, never quarrelled with the impudent bird.

LIST OF BRITISH BIRDS.
By W. Newberry.

Family II.—Graculinæ (Grakles).
Genus I.—Thremmaphilus.
Species I.—*Thremmaphilus Roseus (Cow Bird)*.
Migratory.
Size: Length, 9 in.; extent of wings, 14 in; bill, $\frac{9}{12}$ in.
Colour: Head and neck black, body rose colour, tail dark brown; the male has a dark crest.
Food: Icsects, seeds, and larvæ.

Genus II.—Sturnus.
Species I.—*Sturnus Grittatus (Starling)*.
Permanently resident.
Size: Length, $9\frac{1}{4}$ in.; extent of wings, $15\frac{1}{2}$ in.; bill, $1\frac{1}{4}$ in.
Colour: Black, with all the feathers, except those on the head, tipped with white and brown.
Food: Worms, larvæ, and insects.
Builds in ruined buildings, hollow trees, and holes in rocks.
Lays 6 eggs, $1\frac{1}{4} \times \frac{5}{6}$; pale blue.

Order III.—Cuculinæ.
Family I.—Cuculæ (Cuckoos).
Genus I.—Cuculus.
Species I.—*Cuculus Canorus (Common Cuckoo)*.
Migratory.
Size: Length, 14 in.; extent of wings, 23 in.; bill, $\frac{5}{6}$ in.
Colour: Bluish grey, marked with dark brown, white and light grey.
Food: Eggs, insects, caterpillars, &c.
Lays 2 or 3 eggs, $\frac{1}{6}$ in. $\times \frac{2}{3}$ in.; grey, speckled with brown, which are deposited in the nest of the pipit, &c.

Species II.—*Cuculus Americanus*.
Migratory; only 2 seen in Britain, and 2 in Ireland.
Size: Length, 12 in.; extent of wings, 16 in.; bill, 1 in.
Colour: Upper part grey, lower parts white, tail dark, tipped with white.
Food: Insects, larvæ, &c.

Order IV.—Volitatrices.
Family I.—Cypselinæ (Swifts).
Genus I.—Cypselus.
Species I.—*Cypselus Melba (Alpine Swift)*.
Migratory; only 3 seen in England and 1 in Ireland.
Size: Length, 9 in.; extent of wings, 21 in.; bill, $\frac{5}{12}$ in.
Colour: Upper parts and wings dark grey, lower parts white.
Food: Insects.

Species II.—*Cypselus Apus (Black Swift)*.
Migratory.
Size: Length, $7\frac{1}{2}$ in.; extent of wings, $16\frac{1}{2}$ in.; bill, $\frac{1}{4}$ in.
Colour: Glossy black, with greyish throat.
Food: Insects.
Builds in towns and ruins.
Lays 3 eggs, 1 in. $\times \frac{5}{6}$ in.; pure white.

Family II.—Hirundinæ (Swallows).
Genus I.—Hirundo.
Speeies I.—*Hirundo Rustica (Chimney Swallow)*.
Migratory.
Size: Length, $8\frac{3}{4}$ in.; extent of wings, 14 in.; bill, $\frac{1}{3}$ in.
Colour: Upper parts dark blue, throat and breast reddish white.
Food: Insects.
Builds in chimneys, under eaves, and in outhouses.
Lays 5 eggs, $\frac{5}{6}$ in. $\times \frac{7}{12}$ in.; white, with fine red spots.

Species II.—*Hirundo Urbica (Martin)*.
Migratory.
Size: Length, $5\frac{2}{3}$ in.; extent of wings, 12 in.; bill, $\frac{1}{3}$ in.
Colour: Head, back, wings, and tail black, posterior and lower parts white.
Food: Insects.
Builds in the corners of windows, under eaves or rocks.
Lays 5 eggs, $\frac{9}{12}$ in. $\times \frac{3}{6}$ in.; pure white.

Species III.—*Hirundo Riparia (Sand Martin)*.
Migratory (an Albino was captured at Leicester in July last).
Size: Length, $5\frac{1}{3}$ in.; extent of wings, 11 in.; bill, $\frac{3}{12}$ in.
Colour: Upper parts brown, lower parts white, with a brown band across the breast.
Food: Insects, &c.
Builds in sand banks, &c.
Lays 3 eggs, $\frac{3}{6}$ in. $\times \frac{5}{12}$ in.; pure white.

Species IV.—*Hirundo Purpurea (Purple Martin)*.
Migratory.
Size: Length, $7\frac{1}{2}$ in.; extent of wings, 16 in.; bill, $\frac{1}{4}$ in.
Colour: Dark purple, with brownish wings and tail.
Food: Insects, &c.

Only one, according to Yarrell, has been seen in Britain, and is now in the Museum of the Royal Dublin Society.

Family III.—CAPRIMULGINÆ (GOATSUCKERS).

Genus I.—CAPRIMULGUS.

Species I.—*Caprimulgus Europeus.*
Migratory.
Size: Length, 11 in.; extent of wings, 23 in.; bill, $\frac{1}{3}$ in.
Colour: Dusky grey, with yellowish red markings.
Food: Insects.
Builds under the branches of trees, or on the ground among the fern and heather.
Lays 2 eggs, $1\frac{1}{6}$ in. × $\frac{5}{6}$ in.; white, shaded with brown.

ORDER V.—EXCURTRICES.

Family I.—LANIIDÆ (SHRIKES).

Genus I.—LANIUS.

Species I.—*Lanius Excubitor* (*Cinerius Shrike*).
Migratory.
Size: Length, $10\frac{1}{2}$ in.; extent of wings, $14\frac{1}{2}$ in.; bill, $\frac{9}{12}$ in.
Colour: Upper parts light grey, lower parts white, a broad black band on the cheek, tail black. Female, with breast waved with grey.
Food: Insects, reptiles, birds, &c.

Species II.—*Lanius Rutilus* (*Woodchat Shrike*).
Migratory; very few ever seen in Britain.
Size: Length, $7\frac{2}{3}$ in.; extent of wings, $12\frac{1}{2}$ in.; bill, $\frac{7}{12}$ in.
Colour: Upper part and wings black, lower parts white, tail and cheeks black, posterior grey, head and neck reddish.
Food: Small animals, birds, and insects.

Species III.—*Lanius Collurio* (*Flusher*).
Permanently resident in the South of England.
Size: Length, $7\frac{1}{4}$ in.; extent of wings, 12 in.; bill, $\frac{1}{2}$ in.
Colour: Back reddish, head, neck, and posterior grey, breast and cheek bright red, with black band across, tail white.
Food: Insects, and sometimes lizards and young birds.
Builds in bushes and hedgerows.
Lays 6 eggs, $\frac{5}{6}$ in. × $\frac{3}{12}$ in.; cream colour, spotted and patched with red and grey.

Family II.—MYIOTHERINÆ (FLYCHASERS).

Genus I.—MUSCIPA.

Species I.—*Muscipa Grisola* (*Grey Flychaser*).
Migratory.
Size: Length, $6\frac{1}{6}$ in.; extent of wings, $10\frac{1}{4}$ in.; bill, $\frac{1}{12}$ in.
Colour: Upper parts brownish grey, lower parts grey, wing coverts reddish brown.
Food: Insects.
Builds in holes of trees and old buildings.
Lays 5 eggs, $\frac{9}{12}$ in. × $\frac{2}{3}$ in.; bluish white, spotted with brown, red, and grey.

Species II.—*Muscicapa Atricapilla* (*Pied Flychaser*).
Migratory.
Size: Length, $5\frac{1}{4}$ in; extent of wings, 8 in.; bill, $\frac{5}{12}$ in.
Colour: Male—Upper parts black, wings and forehead patched white, tail tipped with white. Female—Upper parts brownish grey, lower parts light grey.
Foods: Insects, etc.
Builds in holes or on the forks of trees.
Lays 6 eggs, $\frac{2}{3}$ in. × $\frac{1}{2}$ in., pale blue.

Family III.—CORACIIDÆ.

Genus I.—CORACIAS (ROLLERS).

Species I.—*Coracias Garrula* (*Garrulus Roller*).
Migratory, now rarely seen in Britain.
Size: Length, 13 in.; extent of wings, 18 in.; bill, $1\frac{1}{3}$ in.
Colour: Head, neck, and back bluish-green, breast light brown, smaller wing coverts, quills and tail blue, tinged with green.
Food: Insects, etc.
Builds in hollow trees, or in holes near the banks of a stream.
Lays 5 eggs, $1\frac{1}{12}$ in. × 1 in.; glossy white.

ORDER VI.—JACULATRICES (DARTERS).

Family I.—ALCEDIDÆ.

Genus I.—ALCEDO (KINGFISHERS).

Species I.—*Alcedo Ispida.*
Permanently resident.
Size: Length, $7\frac{1}{4}$ in.; extent of wings, $10\frac{1}{4}$ in.; bill, $1\frac{1}{2}$ in.
Colour: Upper parts, including head, wings, and posterior, green or blue, spotted with blue and yellow, lower parts and throat reddish and orange colour.
Food: Small fishes.
Builds in holes in the banks of streams or ponds.
Lays 6 eggs, 1 in. × $\frac{9}{12}$ in.; pure white.

Genus II.—MEROPS (BEE-EATER).

Species I.—*Merops Apiaster.*
Migratory.
Size: Length, $10\frac{3}{4}$ in.; extent of wings, $16\frac{1}{4}$ in.; bill, $\frac{1}{2}$ in.
Colour: Top of head, neck, and back reddish, posterior yellow, forehead light blue, throat

yellow, lower parts green.
Food: Bees and other insects.

ERRATA.—Page 280, Genus VI, Species I, for "Strix Hammea" read *Strix Flammea*; page 280, Order II, for "Vagatricis" read *Vagatrices*; page 280, second column, Genus II, Species I, for "Pica Melansleuca" read *Pica Melanaleuca*.

GOLDEN AUTUMN.

SUCH is the appellation awarded for this quarter of the year by Thomas Miller in his country life, and a more truthful word could not be uttered; for in it are emblazoned the various beauties of the skies, so common during this season, mingled with the tone of the harvest fields, and the tints of the decaying foliage, all share in the selfsame glorious colour, unsurpassed only when the setting sun gives a more heightened illumination to the scene. Amongst the many avocations which the farmer has to indulge in throughout the year, there is none of them, I believe, brings more pride to his heart than to witness a heavy crop of grain, and to see the straws hanging listlessly downwards with the weight of the full ears. The busy harvest is now in its prime, and the reapers are bending to the task with a will both earnest and effective. To illustrate the earnestness of their endeavours we have only to witness them work by the light of the September moon, at such times when the crop is being housed; then it is that the aspect of the countenances of those engaged betokens a strong proof of my assertion. The spring and summer holidays of the swallow are now drawing to a close, and we may now see them collected in vast numbers on the roofs of houses, &c., contemplating their return journey. The short stay of the swift is ended, he has taken his flight to his winter station, and his scream is heard no more. What a wide contrast is displayed betwixt the seasons of summer and autumn in the music of the choristers of the grove. I have now watched the progress of nature in the songs of the birds, and have perceived the gradual lessening of such music, which every week is portrayed in wide proportions from the longest day. A great many birds cease singing in the decline of summer, and when the presence of autumn is announced the list of birds which continue in song is very small. The sweet note of the robin, which a few months ago was scarcely distinguishable, is now heard amidst complete silence, and every low turn of notes is now thundered forth upon the ear, re-echoing again and again as they are sent forth. The notes of the thrush and blackbird are heard during prolonged intervals, when the warm rays of the sun predominate. The wren is another of those birds which help to cheer the dull monotony of the country in the autumn season. Amongst the arrivals of birds, which take place towards the end of autumn, I may mention the snipe, redwing, and fieldfare, which stay with us throughout the winter and then proceed to their breeding grounds, on the moors, in spring. Nutting is a favourite occupation in the country during this season, and it is one which is much adhered to while there is fruit on the hazel boughs.

The character of the scene in autumn is widely different from the scenes of either spring or summer, in respect to the trees alone. Take the beech tree for example; there you will perceive a great change in the colour of the foliage, from the fresh light green of spring, and the still darker green of summer, to a bright tone of lemon yellow, and a tint of brown intermingled, in autumn. In reference to a great many other trees we may decidedly say the same, excluding the ivy, laurel, fir, &c., which retain their colours throughout the year. What solemn thoughts are brought home to the mind while we wander through the leafy woods in autumn, when after a slight frost the night previous the effects are displayed on those leaves which have been nipped as they come tumbling down from aloft by the action of the winds. At first they drop singly and silently, but when the season of autumn advances, and the cold foreboding winds of winter approaches, then they may be seen descending in showers to the earth. How happily are such thoughts illustrated in the following verses, which I have cut from an old Penrith paper: they are to this effect—

AUTUMN.

O beautiful season! how fair is the scene!
When bright tints of autumn are mix'd with the green!
The woods all the shades of the artist unfold,
From dark foliag'd pines to the ash leaf'd with gold.

The fruit trees bend down 'neath their luscious store,
More rich than the blossom that deck'd them before;
The cornfields deserted, the sportsmen may roam;
The farmhouse resounds with the glad harvest home.

But short are these pleasures, and transient their stay;
Those beautiful tints are but signs of decay,
The trees which are now dress'd in colours so fair,
Will soon be left leafless, unshelter'd, and bare.

'Tis pleasant, in quiet October, to see
The leaves, gently quivering, fall from the tree,
Not hasten'd by tempests, but faded and brown,
They let go their hold and drop noiselessly down.

O! thus may we be in the autumn of life,
Not tost by the tempests of sorrow or strife,
But ripen'd and ready, with friends standing round,
May we fall as the leaves gently fall to the ground.

St. John's Vale. J. R.

In early mornings in October and November may be seen the effects of the dew in the night shown forth on the spider's webs among the trees, for there on the thin delicate threads are arranged in wonderful precision vast numbers of dew drops sparkling like jets of silver in the glittering sunshine. Slight mists predominate on the low grounds and rivers during October mornings, and the appearance of the landscape under such effects assume a weird aspect, the more so when we view the tops of the naked trees above the mist in the far distance. What changes are wrought by the hand of the Creator in the short space of twelve months, and in such strict accordance and harmony are the laws of nature alike in every year that passes. As far as the present year is concerned I may state in regard to the trees alone, and the various transformations in their appearance up to the season of autumn, and which will conclude my remarks on the trees, that to every beholder of nature there is a striking impression stamped up on his mind of the wonderful and mighty works of the Creator. Commencing with the new year you will observe the trees naked and bare, but on nearer observation you will perceive the buds are all formed and all made ready for the acting propensities of the sap in the spring. As the year rolls on so does the appearance of the trees change; the buds begin to swell with the virtue of the sap (as it wends its way through the intricacies in the branches) and continue to do so till they burst in green leaf, being then clothed in the verdure of spring. Leaving spring and entering on the summer quarter, you will now see that the leaves which once wore the clear sparkling hues of spring have begun to be tinged with a dark green hue, and to look dull with the burning rays of the summer sun and other effects. The same power who keeps in check the many planetary bodies which are scattered over the face of the universe, and whose power over them is so great that each one of them moves not an atom of space out of its former course, is manifested also in the workings of the sap in the trees, for there is such a time for it to rise and such a time for it to fall, and I suggest that when the longest day arrives its course is no longer upwards, but it must gradually descend again to its winter station in the roots, which is quite obvious when we observe the gradually decaying foliage after that date. My observations on the aspect of trees in autumn I have given previously; suffice it to say that when the death of autumn is announced we leave the trees as we began with them, that is, naked and bare. Autumn is the season and joy of the sportsman, for early in the morning, not early by the time, but the light, he is out among the field spreading destruction among the partridge, rabbit, hare, and other game. We are now immersed in the decline of light, for the sun is now traversing his southern journey, which every week is manifested in the shortening day. To the observer of nature there is a charm in every season, and a scene which is never obliterated from his memory. J. H.

North Lancashire.

THE SWALLOW-TAILED BUTTERFLY (*PAPILIO MACHAON*).

By R. LADDIMAN.

UNDER this head I intend writing a few words on the largest of British butterflies, the Swallow-tailed (*Papilio machaon*), which I trust will prove interesting to some of the readers of the N. N. B. Doubtless there are many who read that valuable little periodical who have not witnessed the "fine sight" of a swallow-tailed butterfly on the wing—to those especially this may be interesting; should this be the case, I shall consider myself amply repaid for my trouble in writing this.

No doubt most of my readers are aware that this butterfly frequents chiefly fens and marshy places—

Where the dragon-flies dart 'mid the rustling reeds,
And the great sleek water-rat builds and breeds;
Where the moor-hen glides through the waving sedge,
And leads her young to the marshes' edge;
Where the stagnant pool is with duckweed green,
And gnats rise in clouds when the air's serene;
And the alder grey, like a sentry, stands
To warn men's feet from the swampy lands.

Amongst places frequented by this butterfly are Wicken Fen in Cambridgeshire, Yaxley, Horning, and Ranworth* marshes in Norfolk, but it has been taken very near Norwich. A few years ago an "old entomological friend" of mine captured a fine female of this butterfly within a mile of Norwich, and accounts for its appearance as having been conveyed here with some timber whilst in the chrysalis state.

I shall not easily forget the first Swallow-tail I saw and captured. It was a sultry day in the July of 1868, that I was returning, with a friend, from an entomological excursion. We were riding along a road leading from Ranworth, and passing a field of clover in full bloom, I happened to cast my eye across it, when I saw in the distance something fluttering over the flowers: what it was I knew not, but suffice it to say we stopped, and I was over the gate in

---

* I believe not mentioned as a locality for this butterfly.

very little time, and net in hand was soon "in clover." Wending my way across the field, I soon reached the object. Imagine my surprise on seeing that it was a Swallow-tail. I was in ecstasy—one good sweep and the prize was mine, and fluttering in my ring net; but, better still, before I had time to transfer my capture from the net to my collecting box, another "gentleman," very welcome, I assure you, favoured me with his company. I as quickly despatched him, and again mounted the gate, rich with two beautiful specimens of *Machaon*, which were soon safely pinned down in my collecting box. So much for my first "Swallow-tail adventure."

The caterpillar of this butterfly is very beautiful. It is smooth, and of a lovely green, each segment is encircled with a black ring, containing six spots of an orange-red colour; the head is also provided with a forked appendage, which is retractile, and from which it emits a strong-scented fluid when alarmed. It feeds on hog's fennel, milk parsley, wild carrot, and various other umbelliferous plants, the latter constituting its chief food in Norfolk, and from which all mine have been taken. It has also been found feeding on celery, wormwood, and rue. The "rustics" round about Horning and Ranworth collect these caterpillars and sell them at a penny each to various entomologists visiting these localities. Some of the country folk have queer notions as to the metamorphoses of insects. One of them we came across asserted that after Swallow-tails (in his own words) had done being butterflies, they changed to "chrysalises" again.

I was rather amused a few weeks ago. Whilst at Ranworth entomologising, I came across a "small boy" who had about a dozen of these caterpillars in a box, and offered him a fair price for them. "Not for Joe," says the "young hopeful." I then inquired what he intended doing with them? He said he should keep them and feed them on carrot tops till they turned to "christians" (chrysalids) and get threepence (?) each for them, and off he sallied. These caterpillars are little or no trouble to rear, and will eat the cultivated as well as the wild carrot readily, seldom or ever wandering from their food—they will invariably keep to a leaf till it is completely devoured, and are very pretty objects whilst feeding. When the caterpillar is full fed, it wanders about in search of a place where it may pass the chrysalis state, generally selecting the stalks of grasses, &c. It then commences operations by fastening its tail firmly by a tough silken thread, fastening another thread round the middle of its body; it hangs in this manner for two or three days, sometimes longer, and turns to a chrysalis of a bright yellowish-green colour, and in this state remains throughout the winter.

Mr. Butler, in "Nature and Art," gives a very nice description of the emergence of the butterfly, which I cannot refrain from copying. He says, "When the butterfly is nearly ready to emerge, the pattern and colouring of the upper wings may be distinctly seen through the thin shell-like covering. The wings are then always very small and thick. At the time of transformation the chrysalis first splits longitudinally from the head to the end of the thorax. The hairs of the back are first seen to appear through the narrow opening, and gradually the head begins to rise, encumbered by its imprisoned antennæ, which in the chrysalis lie along the edges of the wings. Then the thin envelope cracks at the sides, the under anterior portion is forced away from the upper part, the legs begin to appear two at a time, the antennæ are released and brought forward, the proboscis is uncoiled, the opening gradually enlarges, and the insect, bringing its legs into action, soon draws itself from its place of confinement, and, can we add? 'flies away to enjoy the pleasures of sunshine and nectar.' Not so: there is much to do yet ere it can attain to such aërial joys. Its wings are now small, shrivelled, thick, and heavy with moisture, therefore our butterfly runs up the nearest wall or stem, and, hanging its wings downwards, sits quietly for several minutes; and now those beautiful organs of locomotion begin to increase so rapidly, that a sharp eye may even detect their growth. If closely examined at this stage, it will be seen that the nerves or veins of the wings are filled with a liquid which, being forced into them, radiates through exceedingly minute nervelets over the entire surface of the wing, which, being formed of two delicate and distinct tissues, is at this time slightly swollen, balloon fashion, and thus, in about twenty minutes, the wings attain the required dimensions. When they are nearly full grown the insect commences to open and shut them, which prevents them from clinging together, after which it remains perfectly quiet until they are firm and ready for flight. The butterfly then commences to flutter (some moths will do this for many minutes), and, after taking a wheel in the air, as if to satisfy itself of the reality of its newly acquired powers, it flies away to the enjoyment of life and pleasure."

ON THE BRITISH GEOMETRÆ.
By E. J. S. Clifford.
Part X.

IN resuming our remarks upon this most interesting section of our native moths, we observe that the species to which we have come are indeed full of beauty and delicacy. The Dentated Pug (*Collix sparsata*), illustrates this fact, for it is one of the most lovely little moths imaginable. The fore-wings are grey, with a distinct spot, and a dark margin almost forming a costal stripe; there are various other spots and transverse lines, most wonderfully disposed, and giving intense beauty to the insect. The caterpillar of this species is pale green, with five white lines down the back, and a broad yellow line along the spiracles. June is the time for the perfect insect, which is said to occur about Cambridge, but is not reported from Ireland or Scotland.

Next we come to the Small Seraphim (*Lobophora sexalisata*), a delicate little geometer, which is said to occur in some of our English counties, Northern and Southern. The fore-wings of this moth are grey-brown, with four pale transverse lines, the first of which is short and indistinct, and is situated near the base of the wing. The hind-wings are grey, with an indistinct darker bar across the middle, and a dark hind margin. The caterpillar of the Small Seraphim is uniformly cylindrical in form, without humps or excrescences, but a good deal wrinkled, and the thirteenth segment terminates in two points directed backwards. It is a caterpillar usually resting at full length on the midrib of a leaf of its food-plant, with the head tucked in out of sight. The colour of the body is apple-green, with three whitish stripes down the back. Its food is the common sallow, upon which it may be found feeding early in September. In the middle of the month it spins a slight oval cocoon among the fallen leaves. The chrysalis is short and brown, it remains throughout the winter within the cocoon referred to.

The Seraphim (*Lobophora hexapterota*), is a very singular moth. Its caterpillar is described as of a most beautiful green colour, with a sulphur line on each side. It feeds on sallow and aspen in the month of June, and is the most common species of the genus to which it belongs. The moth itself is very beautifully marked. The fore-wings, which are broad and ample, are of a pale grey colour, with a slight ochreous tinge; they have numerous transverse markings, many of which are too irregular to describe. The Yellow-barred Brindle is the next species in order (*Lobophora viritata*). The fore-wings of a delicate green colour, traversed by slender waved white lines, and ornamented by a series of black spots, several of which combine, and form a broad band across the middle of the wing; beyond this band is a double series of black spots. The hind-wings are pale brown, with a slight trace of a spot, and a transverse line below it. The caterpillar of this insect is beautifully varied in colour with purple-brown and apple-green, disposed on the back and abdomen. It is destitute of humps or warts, but the thirteenth segment possesses two points, each of which emits a slender bristle. The caterpillar feeds on the privet, and in July it connects the leaves of that shrub together by silk, becoming a pupa in the home thus formed. May and June are the months for the moth, which is said to occur very commonly at Killarney in Ireland.

Early in the spring we may search the honeysuckles for the eggs of the Early Tooth-striped (*Lobophora lobulata*), a moth peculiarly marked and coloured. This insect has the fore-wings long and rather pointed, and of a pale grey colour, with five transverse markings of a smoky tinge. The hind-wings are grey, with a series of obscure spots, and an interrupted marginal line. Occasionally, we read, this species is of a beautiful light green colour when first emerged from the chrysalis. It is not improbable that the eggs of this moth are laid also on the sallow, for the caterpillar feeds both on this and willow in confinement according to some entomologists. Towards the end of June the caterpillar is full-fed, and it then rests in a nearly straight position, the middle of the back slightly arched. It spins a slight web on the surface of the ground, and changing to a chrysalis remains in that condition throughout the winter. In April the moth appears; it occurs in England as well as Scotland, but is not recorded as appearing in Ireland. The Barred Tooth-stripe (*Lobophora polycommata*), is still more striking an insect even than our last. The fore-wings are long and narrow; they are pale wainscot brown, with various darker markings. The eggs of this species seem to be laid on honeysuckle or ash, on both of which the caterpillar will feed in a state of confinement. About June it is full-fed, and rests in nearly a straight position. The body is dull green on the back, with a still darker line or stripe down the very centre. April is the month for this moth, which has been taken both North and South, but more particularly about Windermere. Like our last, the caterpillar of this species changes to a chrysalis just below the surface of the earth, and remains such through the cold months. The Juniper Carpet (*Thera juniperata*), is a very abundant moth on the downs about Croydon and Mickleham, and may be obtained by searching the stems of the juniper bushes with a lantern. The fore-wings are narrow and pointed, and of a most delicate grey, with a blotch on the base, and a band rather darker. The hind-wings are pale, with a very slight indication of two darker transverse bars. The caterpillar of the Juniper Carpet is green, with a stripe on each side, of lemon yellow. Its food is the common juniper, and is sometimes very abundant where that shrub occurs. The chrysalis into which it is transformed is green, and either suspended amongst the twigs, or else found on the surface of the earth. October is the month for the perfect insect, whose localities we have already indicated. A striking insect is the Chesnut-colored Carpet (*Thera simulata*). It has rich brown fore-wings, with a band and blotch of a darker hue, both of which markings are bordered by very deep margins, and contrast beautifully with the lighter parts of the wings. The hind-wings are smoky grey. The caterpillar of this moth has been described as short and stumpy, of a grass-green colour. The line down the back is broad, and pure bluish white, bordered on each side by a slender stripe of the same colour. The spiracular line is the same. There are no dots or marks upon this caterpillar, which is said to be of a very sluggish habit. The Chesnut Carpet is double-brooded, appearing on the wing in April and May, and again in August. It has been taken near Newcastle, Darlington, and Glasgow, and is reported as common in Ireland. The Shaded Broad Bar (*Thela obeliscata*), appears on the wing during the summer months, and is said to be common in many English counties, though not so in Ireland. The fore-wings are brown grey, with a blotch at the base, and a median band darker and brighter, with a decided tinge of chesnut. These markings are not bounded by dark margins, but have several dark wing-rays, and a dark inner margin. The hind-wings are pale in colour, with a smoky tinge on the hind margin. The caterpillar of this species is attached to the needles of the Scotch fir, on which it feeds. Its colour is dull green, with three white stripes down the back, each of which is somewhat double. Many recent writers seem to consider this is but a variety of a continental species, but as this latter has not been proved to occur in this country, we doubt the assertion, and consider the two species to be distinct.

The Pine Carpet (*Thera firmata*), is perhaps more especially attached to Scotland than to our own country. The caterpillar feeds upon the fir, and is often found resting in a nearly straight position upon the needles of this tree. The head of the caterpillar is red, the back of the body is dull green, with a darker stripe, and on each side there is a slender stripe of dingy white. The moth has the fore-wings chesnut grey, but of a very pale hue. There is a blotch at the base, and a median band of a rather brighter colour, but these are hardly distinguishable from the general ground colour of the wings. The hind-wings are pale wainscot brown, without markings. The Ruddy Highflyer (*Ypsipetes ruberata*), is a moth which seems to have a very wide range in England, but does not appear to occur in Scotland. The fore-wings are grey marbled, with numerous transverse markings. At the base of the wing there is usually a triangular space, rather pale in colour, which is followed by a broad darker band. The hind-wings are pale grey, with a faint spot and two transverse bars. The caterpillar of this beautiful insect has been described as rather hairy, of a dirty-white colour. It is stated that it becomes transformed to a shining black chrysalis in the autumn, remaining such through the winter. May is the month in which the Ruddy Highflyer should be sought; it is one of those geometers that are difficult to catch, but when secured it is indeed a prize. We next come to another Highflyer, that termed the May Highflyer (*Ypsipetes impluviata*). The fore-wings of this insect are greyish-green, with a broad band of pale grey, which band contains a spot, long, narrow, and black, and rather indistinct. Between the medium band and the hind margin there are different tints transversely arranged, each tint bordered by zig-zag lines. The caterpillar of the May Highflyer is stout and obese; it conceals itself during the day in a rolled up leaf of the alder, on which tree it feeds only by night. In colour it is dingy yellow, with lines of a dull green colour. The moth itself is said to appear in May, and again in July and August. It is by no means common, but has been captured in various English counties, as also in Ireland and Scotland.

We must close this paper by a reference to one of our most variable geometers, that called the July Highflyer (*Ypsipetes elutata*). This insect has the fore-wings of a dull olive green, with a small blotch at the base, and five transverse bars of smoke colour. In July the eggs are laid on various species of sallow. The young caterpillars come forth in twelve days, and feed on sallow leaves, until half-grown, when they hybernate. In the spring they feed again, as soon as the buds expand. About the beginning of June they are usually full-fed. It is said that the caterpillar of the July Highflyer has a singular habit of secreting itself among the seed down of the sallow, and coming forth only at night to feed. It is certainly a very lethargic creature. When touched, however, it doubles up, and falls from the food-plant. It constructs a cell in the down of the sallow, and changes therein to a brown chrysalis. In July this very variable insect occurs; it seems to be very much attached to woodland scenery in the south. We have frequently found it in abundance about the Kentish woods, and have been much surprized at the amount of variety existing between diverse specimens. Perhaps there is no moth that varies to a greater extent than does the July Highflyer. Its name is certainly very appropriate, for it is undoubtedly a high-flying insect, and is with difficulty captured by the collector. When started from the hedges, this moth has a habit of soaring away into the air to a great elevation, but it usually returns to the hedge from whence it was roused by the insect-hunter. The wings are very delicate, and suggest to us that we may, not unprofitably, advise all young entomologists in this place to be extremely careful in the way they handle these fragile moths, the geometers, since a touch oftentimes denudes them of the delicate scale covering of the wings—which constitutes the beauty that so charms our eyes.

BOMBYX "CECROPIA."

AMONG the various breeds of silkworms none have pleased me more than the American "Cecropia," or plum-leaf variety, and therefore, as I have now brought a successful experiment therewith to its conclusion, I will, according to my promise in my last, report thereon. I send with this to the editor of the N. N. B. cocoons for inspection, which he will kindly return to me at a future time, after having examined or shown them to interested friends. The imported ones sent me in the spring by Woldemar Geffcken, Esq., certainly were more substantial and better covered with silk, but the worms from them have not yet spun, and this first experiment I am about to give is carried out with eggs received from America through Dr. Wallace. It strikes me forcibly that there is more than one variety of "Cecropia silkworm," from a difference perceivable in the colour of the silk. Be this as it may, this first experiment is sufficiently satisfactory, being ocular demonstration, that this variety can be reared in England; and I have but little doubt, with proper management, cocoons equal to imported ones can be produced. Time and experience must teach a way to perfection.

I received five hundred eggs in a hatching state on 15th June. I collected about one hundred young worms, putting them on twigs of plum, apple, and cherry, with their stems plunged in a bottle of water together. On the 16th I found the insects had been feeding in preference on the plum leaves and a little on apple, but the cherry was hardly touched. To day their bodies presented a deep mourning cast. They continued feeding up to the 20th, when I provided fresh sprigs of plum, and again on the 27th. They were now becoming lighter coloured in their bodies. Occasionally I found one or two dead, dried up, having fallen after being placed on the sprigs. This shows the necessity of placing them securely, with the old leaves on the fresh. I tried laying leaves, grass, &c., round the bottle, on which now and then one or two fell, and could then easily be replaced in position. On 1st July the worms were mostly in their first sleep. The tubercles covering their bodies now presented a coppery colour. I moved them from a kitchen where hatched to a keeping-room without fire. On the 3rd I observed five worms had changed their skins. I saw one push it off, leaving it sticking in a lump on the plum leaf. The insect was now yellow, slightly touched with black at the tubercles. The tubercles are arranged in twelve segments of six, or about 172 in number; they stand out erect from the insects' bodies like so many towers. This yellow colour after shooting the skin, soon goes off, and becomes replaced by the former jet black. Fresh food supplied on the 5th, removing the worms to it on the old sprays without touching or disturbing them. Some were still in first sleep—all looked healthy. The weather had been cool, seldom over 60° and often down to 50° Fahr. To-day the temperature rose to 65°, and on the 6th reached 70° I continued changing to fresh food as required, and on the 12th the second sleep began, and by the 16th most of the worms had changed their skins.

The insects daily became more interesting, varying as they did in different tints of blue, yellow, green, black, and red.

20th. Third sleep beginning. Two rows of tubercles along top of back appear surmounted each with a transparent yellow crystalline drop; two rows on each side of belly more or less blue.

23rd. Several had changed the skins. Their sides, legs, and heads of light green, and the tubercles erect as windmills, stiff, and surmounted with pointed hairs; the top of backs now of blueish cast.

27th. Found one dead, hanging down from the branch putrified. I counted fifty-five worms alive and doing well. The others I sent out, excepting five or six lost. Now growing rapidly, several over two inches in length.

31st. Fourth sleep, or moult, commenced; some of the insects were three inches long.

4th Aug. This morning on changing the sprig I counted fifty-four worms—one was gone.

I observed that several had changed their skins. They present a beautiful appearance : six tubercles above the head are larger, and red, resembling crowns; behind these are yellow ones, the rest being blue, and all of crystalline look; the eight breathing holes on each side are well defined between the blue carbuncles.

7th. Many still in fourth sleep, and some half dozen yet to sleep.

9th. Some of the worms now growing rapidly. I put all on six branches eighteen inches long, stuck in a large jar covered with muslin; previous to this I had used a large glass pickle jar. I saw a worm eating its old skin.

12th. Removed fifteen backward worms on fresh twigs by themselves. I noticed two of the forwardest nearly four inches long; these were getting lighter in colour. The carbuncles during this stage do not increase in size with the insect. I put mulberry and ailanthus leaves to them, which were eaten.

13th. Found leaves consumed. Filled a large flower-pot, a 15-inch one, with water, and fitted a perforated board thereto, through which I stuck up fresh branches for the worms. This I placed on a dresser in kitchen, and brought the worms to it. Fresh branches were added as wanted, and the old ones withdrawn.

20th. Changed water in flower-pot, as I did at least every other time when using bottles. To-day I counted the worms and found only forty-eight, or six deficient; one I found dead, the other five I cannot account for being lost, but I fear they were seized upon by some hens during my absence in Yarmouth, otherwise they must have got away. I had found one or two occasionally running about when foliage was deficient, as several did again on the 22nd, and on the 23rd I stamped on one, poor thing, on the floor. I transferred ten of the backward worms to a plum-tree branch in garden, protected with open muslin, and calico on top to throw off rain.

24th. A worm began cocoon this morning, and another about noon. By 1st September all were spinning but four, and these I put by themselves.

On the 9th of September I collected the cocoons, which should remain in the dormant state until next summer, when I hope to produce plenty of eggs from them.

Of the worms I placed on the plum-tree in the garden, I must say a few words at a future time, when I will also make a few remarks on the general management of this very interesting silkworm, which I think will throw out some further light or guide to the amateur silkworm rearer. I have endeavoured to study the habits of this silkworm, and there are several points to which I would allude, and which I doubt not will materially assist to greater success; in the meantime, I think if others would give accounts of their practice, a great assistance to the progress of silk culture would result; for it will be the means of arriving at some desirable and more expert method of rearing large quantities of these silkworms, suitable in a profitable point of view, and adapted for the English Climate.

LEONARD HARMAN, Jun.
Old Catton, Norwich.

THE BEST OF THE CULTIVATED ANEMONES.

EVERYONE who knows the bright flowers of the variously coloured varieties of the common Hepatica, the very bravest of our early spring flowers, will welcome this species, (*Anemone Angulosa*) fully twice the size of the common Hepatica in all its parts, with flowers of a fine sky-blue, as large as a crown piece, and distinguished from the common kind by its five lobed and toothed leaves. It is a native of Transylvania, and is hardy everywhere throughout these islands. Obviously, the only thing to determine about such a valuable addition is how to best grow and enjoy it. It is naturally more an inhabitant of the elevated copse than of the crest of the Alps; it is not able to flourish thoroughly exposed to the fiercest blasts like the little alpine plants that cushion down their stout if diminutive leaves, shorter than the very moss, so that injury from the fiercest gale is out of the question. I have seen it in sandy soil in a thin shubbery attain a height of more than a foot when not in flower, and the shelter and slight shade received from surrounding objects is decidedly favourable to its development. On all properly formed rockworks, or in their immediate vicinity, it will be possible to give it a suitable position, while in spaces between American plants and choice dwarf shrubs in beds it will succeed to perfection. When plentiful enough it may be used as an edging to beds of choice spring flowering shrubs and for naturalisation in open spots in shrubberies, or in open rather bare and unmown spots along the margins of wood walks.

Anemone Hepatica (Hepatica triloba; common Hepatica.)—To add perfume to the violet, paint the lily, or gild the yellow crocus, would seem to be no more wasteful excess than to praise this exquisite little flower. Let Philip Miller speak, and tell us how much esteemed it was in his day :—" These plants are some of the greatest beauties of the spring; the flowers are produced in February and March in great plenty before the green leaves appear, and make a very beautiful figure in the borders of the pleasure-garden, especially the double sorts, which commonly continue a fortnight longer than the single kinds, and the flowers are much fairer." And these plants have half disappeared, with many others, since that time. There is a cheerfulness and a courage about them on warm sunny borders in spring which no other flowers possess; they are hardy everywhere, are not fastidious as to soil, though they love a deep loam, and present a charming diversity. The principal varieties are the single blue, double blue, single white, single red, double red, single pink (carnea,) single mauve purple (Barlowi), crimson (splendens), and lilacina. Every variety of the common Hepatica is worthy of care and culture. Is it possible to imagine a more beautiful feature than we may produce by planting a mixed edging of the various colours round, say a bed of dwarf American plants, occupying space that perhaps would otherwise be naked? It is but one of many ways in which we may tastefully use them. The plant is a native of many hilly parts of Europe, usually frequenting half shady positions, which will be found to suit it best in a cultivated state also. It is readily increased by division or by seeds, the double kinds by division only.

Anemone thalictroides (Meadow Rue-like Wind-flower).—A delicate, diminutive, and interesting species, with the "habit and frondescence of Isopyrum, the inflorescence of Anemone, and the fruit of Thalictrum." These qualities, in addition to its dwarf habit, usually only a few inches high, make it worthy of cultivation. The flowers are white, nearly an inch in diameter, open in April and May, the flower stem bearing a few leaves near the summit, so as to form a sort of whorl round the flowers. It is a native of many parts of North America, and is increased by seed or by the division of its tuberous roots. There is a pretty double variety, A. thalictroides fl.-pl., with the flowers somewhat smaller than the single ones, and very neat. Being small and fragile in its parts it requires a little more care than most of its brethren, should have a light peaty and moist soil, in association with other delicate growers, or be placed in a position where it is not liable to be overrun by coarse neighbours. It is, perhaps, more correctly known as Thalictrum anemonoides.

Anemone narcissiflora (Narcissus-flowered Wind-flower).—I did not intend including this species, not thinking it sufficiently ornamental, but Mr. J. Duncan, of the Royal Gardens at Kew, has favoured me with the following note respecting it:—"This is a very striking and handsome sort, and distinct from any of its relatives. In cultivation its average height is about a foot. The petals are pure white above, and purple below, but they vary somewhat as regards colour. Proceeding inward, next in order are the yellow anthers which, contrasting with the corolla, justify the specific name. The scape is about twice the length of the foliage, and bears at its summit a considerable tuft of flowers, each of which is about an inch across. The leaves are stalked, and the blades have a soft feel. All the green parts of the plant are hairy. I notice this kind is mentioned in only a single English nurseryman's catalogue, although it deserves more prominence, and is adapted for the rockery, the border, or for pot treatment. It can be increased by division or by seed sown when ripe. It blooms in spring, and is a native of Germany, and does well in sandy soil."

Apart from the fine Anemone japonica and its varieties, there are a few dwarf Anemones in the country unworthy of cultivation, insufficiently distinct, difficult to obtain, and of the last, probably, Anemone Halleri is the best.—*Gardeners' Chronicle*.

SEA-SIDE HOMES: AND WHAT LIVED IN THEM.

MILE after mile of sloping sea-beach occupies the front of a low island on the Carolina coast, and contends, along a foamy line, against waves that ceaselessly advance, to be continually repulsed; a sea-front flanked with sand-works blown by the wind into tumuli over the trenches, where lie buried countless shells that will only come to light again as fossils, when the books of to-day, and those who wrote them, have become indistinguishable dust; beyond which there is a vast bed of oozy mire hidden by the rank growth of reeds that rustle and surge with every breath of wind. Among the sand-mounds, defended by these buttresses alike from the open violence of the sea and the insidious approach of the marsh, are sequestered spots, bestrewn with shells, carpeted with slender grasses whose nodding spears trace curious circles in the sand about their roots, with here and there a half-buried vertebra of a stranded whale, or the rib of some ill-fated vessel, telling a tale of disaster by sea,—spots so secluded that the measured cadence of the wave-beats, confused by this and that avenue of approach, only enters with an inarticulate murmur. Here is the chosen home of two beautiful birds that come and pass the summer months together; a peaceful home, secure, it would seem, from danger of any sort; a house that falls not when the rain descends; and the floods come, and the winds blow, though it is built upon the sand. Alas! that even were it founded upon a rock, the gates of ornithology should prevail against it.

It is late in May—the last week of a month that is not, in this warm climate, "a pious fraud of the almanac," as it is in New England—and the birds are busy now. Six weeks ago they came from their winter retreat in the far South, to this well-remembered spot. The Least Terns came dashing along high in the air overhead, their pearly white forms wavering between the blue water and the bluer sky, ruling both and uncertain which to choose; and saw, with cries of exultation, the end of their long journey. As swiftly, yet more secretly, the Wilson's Plovers flitted along the shore, half concealed by colours that repeat the hue of the sand, from one headland to another, across gulf and river's mouth in succession, till they too greet their homes with joyous notes. Separated for a long interval, or at most little heeding each other, the Terns and the Plovers are to come together again, and rear their young under the shadow of each other's wing. While they are flashing through the clear air, or skimming lightly over the mirrored beach, and occupied, after mutual recognition, each in their own way with the preliminaries of the great event of their lives, let us see what manner of birds they are. Then, when we come to look in upon their homes we shall not be visiting strangers.

The Least Tern is, as its name implies, the smallest bird of its kind in our country; but it has several near relatives in other parts of the world; cousins so nearly alike that they have often been mistaken for each other. They form a race, or "subgenus," as the naturalists call it, that is distinguished from other Terns by diminutive size and dainty form, even among a class of birds all of which have exquisitely moulded shapes, and by a crescent of pure white on the forehead, sharply defined in the jetty black of the rest of the crown. They are delicate pearly-blue above, with snowy-white underplumage, that has an indescribably soft and silky lustre; the long-pointed outer primaries, that cleave the air so deftly, are black, silvered with a hoary gloss of exceeding delicacy; the bill is bright yellow, tipped with black; the feet are of the same colour, and are likewise tipped with the black claws. The little bird of our country answering to this description, has a variety of names in and out of the books. In many places it is called "Striker," from the way it has—after hovering in the air, its slender bill pointed straight downward, its clear eyes intently surveying the water below, and at length fixing upon some unlucky shrimp or minnow—of dashing impetuously down to secure its prey beneath the water; and just possibly, its scientific name, *Sterna*, as well as the English derivative, *Stern*, or *Tern*, may be traced to a classic root (seen in *sterno*, "to strew or scatter," and also "to throw down") and have its origin in this same habit. A more apt and elegant designation is that of "Sea-swallow," by which this and other species are universally known. They are all, indeed, swallows of the sea, replacing over the waters those familiar birds of the land, and having many features in common. Popular language has, as usual, caught the idea of these striking points of resemblance, and caged it in an expressive word. Even the written history of this bird's names is not devoid of interest; for a study of the various words unfolds a story of human thought. Thus our forefathers in ornithology called the bird the Least Tern (*Sterna minuta*), because they did not know it was different from the European species of that name; but it is, nevertheless, for the pearl-blue extends over the tail instead of being confined to the back and wings, and the size of the bill, and of the white crescent, are not the same in the two species. Nuttall gives it as the Silvery Tern (*S. argentea*); a pretty name, and one very suitable, but founded upon the wrong premise, that our species is the same as one that lives in South America. When Dr. Gambel found out that it was different from both these species, he bestowed upon it the title of the Bridled Tern (*S. frenata*), another very distinctive name, that would be well applied, were it not for the fact that M. Lesson, a French ornithologist, had previously called it the Antillean Tern (*Santillarum*), because it is found in those islands in the winter. So we have no choice in the matter of a scientific name, in which there is not the same license as in the case of our common designations. But let the latter be as various as they may the little bird is always the same. It spends the winter in Central America and about its islands; when spring opens it courses northward to visit us; a few extend along the Pacific coast, some up the Mississippi and its tributaries, almost to their very sources; and more along the shores of the Atlantic. Some of the latter go as far as New England, but there are attractions all along, and detachments drop off by the way, stopping here and there, till the ranks are fairly decimated before the most adventurous birds make their final halt. But "their tricks and their manners" are pretty much the same under all circumstances, and what these are we shall presently see.

A very different bird is Wilson's Plover; a wader, not a swimmer; as they say, in words as long as the bird's legs, a grallatorial, not a natatorial, species; which simply means that the little bird is content to run along the sand and dabble with bill and feet, in the wavelets, instead of boldly dashing in among the breakers, like a Tern, for instance. It belongs to a genus well-named *Ægialitis*, which signifies a "dweller by the sea," and has never been known to forfeit its right to the name. We have several other species of the same group. The commonest and most widely diffused of these is the "Killdeer," that everybody knows throughout the length and breadth of the land; the Ring Plover and Piping Plover are two others, familiar to all New Englanders. Wilson's is characteristic of the South Atlantic coast; it only incidentally, as it were, strays northward as far as Massachusetts, and is, consequently, the least generally known of the four kinds; but once seen it can never be mistaken afterward. It is smaller than the Killdeer, but larger than either the Ring-necked or the Piping Plover, to which it is very similar in coloration, if not in the precise tint. The under parts of all three are white; the upper parts of Wilson's are much darker than those of the Piping, and yet a trifle lighter than those of the Ring Plover. A collar of pure black crosses the white of the breast; a crescent of black occupies the crown between the eyes, separated from the bill by the white forehead; on the nape and sides of the head the grayish brown merges into a clear warm buff. This, it must be remembered, is only the nuptial plumage, and of the male bird; the latter, at other seasons, and the female at all times, have these black bands replaced by buffy brown; and this is the plumage in which the bird is oftenest described. But the greatest peculiarity remains to be noticed. Wilson's Plover has a very large entirely black bill, while both the Ring and the Piping have a very small bill, orange-yellow at the base, tipped with black. For the rest it wants the bright-coloured circle around the eyes, formed by the margin of the lids, that the other species display during the breeding season. Its eyes are clear brown; its legs livid flesh coloured, and longer than those of the others; it is not half-webbed like the Ring Plover—only about as much so as the Piping. Its large black bill gives it a singular expression, and undoubtedly corresponds to some difference in the nature of its food, if we could only find out exactly what. Such is the bird that hurries along the coast from the South in April. Upon their arrival they gather in small flocks, of from half a dozen to a score or more, and ramble over both the clean sea-beach and the muddy flats in search of food, sometimes straying into the adjoining salt-meadows if the grass be short and scanty enough not to impede their way. They are naturally gentle and confiding birds, thinking no evil, and prone to take others to be as peaceable and harmless as themselves; but they have only too often to learn wisdom by saddest experience of broken limbs and maimed bodies, and to oppose treachery by wariness and caution. In the spring, if not at other times, they have a note that is half a whistle, half a chirrup, and sounds very different from the clear mellow piping of either of their nearest relatives. After a little while spent in recuperating their energies after their long flight, in putting on their perfect dress, in sham fights and ardent pursuits along the strand, more pressing duties call them from the water's edge to the recesses of the sand-hills. There we shall find them "at home," no longer in flocks but in pairs, and keeping house with the Sea-swallows.

The spot is indicated by the fleecy cloud of the Terns flecking the air overhead. We toil on over beds of loose dry sand, in which our feet sink and slip backward, and gain the recess among the mounds. The ground is here more firm and even; the wind has swept it clean of superfluous sand, and piled up the sweepings here and there in odd nooks; the rains have packed it tight and washed every shell and pebble clean. The most careful housekeeper in the world could make her home no more tidy than the wind and rain have made this shelly dwelling-place of the Terns and Plovers. As we walk on, we see that other visitors have been before us, each one leaving its "card" engraven on the fine sand. Here goes a curious track straight up and over a sand hillock, as if half a dozen little animals had ran a race one after the other, on stilts, the points of which pricked into the sand and formed a band of indentations four or five inches broad. These are the footprints of only one creature, however—the sand-crab, a curious little fellow, with a square body, and eyes upon the ends of two poles that stick straight out when wanted for use, and shut into the shell like the blades of a pocket-knife, when their owner goes to sleep—a singular crab indeed, mounted upon a wonderfully long set of eight legs (to say nothing of two claw-nippers), all of which he contrives to move at just the right moment, as if he were playing a tune upon piano keys, and so plays himself sidewise over the sand with marvellous ease and celerity, the only wonder is that he does not forget a leg in his haste. He is a very grallatorial crab, and lives in the holes in the sand we see all about, just like a prairie-dog. There is a tortuous trail along the sand, where a water-snake, perhaps a *Nerodia sipedon*, crawled out of his pool in the marsh beyond, to enjoy the sun's rays, or possibly on an egging expedition like ourselves. Here is a fainter line, straight as an arrow, looking just as if a pencil had been drawn along a ruler's edge; it is the mark left by the long slender tail of the little striped lizard, and if we look closely we shall see it bounded on either side by a succession of faint dots where the creature's toes barely disturbed the grains of sand. There again is a curious track, a pair of rounded depressions, side by side, and hardly more than an inch apart, outside of which, in the intermediate distances, are another pair, wider apart, and much longer. It is clear that a Marsh Rabbit has passed this way, planting his forefeet straight downward, and drawing his hinder ones leisurely after, half squatting at each step, as he loped out of his home in the bushes to nip the beach grass for a change of diet. And so we might go on reading signs as plain as print; but the birds are by this time alarmed as they never were by former visitors. They know by intuition that we are not one of them, though among them, and that our coming bodes no good, however much we may affect to care for them in an abstract way. So in a moment all is changed, and confusion reigns where were peace and quiet. The quick-witted Terns were the first to sound the alarm; they had watched our approach, and straightway changed their heedless and joyous cries to notes of anger and fear; at the signal the sitting birds had arisen from their eggs and joined those already overhead. The male Plovers, off foraging for insects and minute sea-creatures, surprised at the noise, had come hurrying home, only to have their worst fears confirmed, and be met half-way by their terrified mates, who had stolen quietly from their nests when the Terns deserted theirs, instinctively looking for comfort and protection where it had never been denied before. It is a strange sight, and a mournful one, already too painful to be wholly interesting, and the tragical end has not come yet. The Terns seem not to know what fear is; they dash about our heads, plunge as though to strike us, recede a little, approach again, always keeping in a cloud above us; and from every throat come notes of anger and fear and beseeching combined; a very Babel of tongues. The Plovers are more timorous; they are flitting to and fro, low over the sand, at a little distance, in anxious groups of three or four, with indescribably touching appeals for mercy to spare their homes; now alighting and squatting in hopes they are still undiscovered, and again running swiftly along, too frightened for a moment's rest. A dark day indeed for the poor birds! Bird's-nesting is a sad business, at best; it makes little difference to the birds, it is to be feared, whether their eggs are stolen by school-boys, to be played with and forgotten before the Saturday afternoon is over, or by grown-up people to make books with, and be kept thereafter in cabinet drawers. What difference there is, seems to be that the boys let the old birds off altogether, and are satisfied with robbing the nests; while the larger children rob and then shoot the parent birds, to "authenticate the specimens."

Where are the eggs? Here, then, and everywhere about the sand lie the Tern's, till we are in danger of treading on them unawares. There are not so many of the Plover's, though still plenty for our purpose; but both kinds are nearly of the same colour as the sand, and their markings conform to the unvarying variegation of colour of the shelly strand, so that it is an easy matter not to see them, even when looking straight at them. Here is a set of Plovers' eggs, and there, not a yard off, one of Terns'; we may sit down and examine both together. It may be best, however, after noticing carefully the nests and their surroundings, to gather a lot of each kind of egg, and carry them home with us for more particular examination.

Properly speaking there are really no "nests" in either case. Neither the Tern nor the Plover has any architectural instinct, because none is needed. Both lay their eggs in a slight hollow in the sand, about four inches in diameter; but even this hollowing is sometimes scarcely appreciable, and the eggs seem as if dropped by accident on the ground. It is probable that at first no hollow, or only the slightest one, is made; and that subsequently the depression becomes better defined by the movements to which the eggs may be subjected, and the weight and motions of the parent birds or young. In some instances there is a difference between the two kinds of nesting-spots, happening thus: the Plovers sometimes lay in a scanty tuft of slender straggling grass, which was not done by any of the Terns, at this breeding-place; and again, the Terns frequently line the depression with little flat bits of shell, which the Plovers have not been observed to do. Sometimes the pieces of shell seem to have been lying there before, and thus only to have been used as a nest-lining by accident as it were; in other cases the regular disposition of the fragments in a circle, leaves no doubt that they were carefully arranged by the birds. This method of making a shell-nest is just like that of the Auks and Guillemots, that breed in cracks in the rocks, and raise a little platform of pebbles to keep their eggs from the wet; and is, doubtless, for the same purpose,—to defend the eggs from whatever moisture might be in the sand. Still, of two Terns' nests, side by side, one may have the shells, and the other be without them, or at least not have them specially arranged. Neither bird uses any dried grasses, sea-weed, or other soft pliable substances, in this particular locality at least.

The number of eggs deposited must next claim our attention; and in this matter, as seeing is believing, we must differ with some very respectable authorities. It is a common belief, circulated from one writer's book to another's, that Terns generally lay three eggs, and the little Sand-pipers and Plovers always four. The belief is true enough, as a general rule; but every rule has its exceptions, and here are two notable ones. The Least Tern, breeding in North Carolina, generally lays *two* eggs; sometimes only *one;* rarely (if ever) three; and never four; at any rate, we have not found more than two in any instance, and our experience may count for something, seeing that we have just explored a tolerably extensive breeding place. Still it would be injudicious for us to proclaim that the bird may not lay three in other localities. But as for four eggs from one Least Tern at a single laying we flatly refuse to believe it till we see it. If any one is inclined to object to the assertion that the *one* egg, found in some instances, would have been succeeded by another, we can discountenance the assumption by replying that the solitary eggs in question were nearly hatched when found. Again, Wilson's Plover lays three eggs,—no more, no less, as far as our observations have gone, with respect to nests actually found. The suggestion that the fourth one would have been laid in due time is combatted by what has just been advanced in the other case, namely, the mature condition of the embryos. Yet we know the bird sometimes lays four, because we have killed females just going to lay, finding one egg in the oviduct, almost ready to be expelled, and the three others in a highly developed state, still attached to the ovary. The time of laying varies a great deal, in the cases of both the birds. They may deposit eggs at any time between the second week in May and the first in June; the greatest number lay about May 20th. Some of the Terns may even commence earlier, as young birds, already quite strong of wing, are to be seen flying about by the 20th of June. Early in the latter month, nearly fresh eggs, eggs nearly hatched, and newly fledged young, of the Plover, may all be observed. These little nestlings are very pretty and very curious specimens of early birdhood; they can run quite cleverly over the sand as soon as fairly dry from the egg, if not " with half a shell on their backs," as is popularly supposed to be the case with young partridges; and are rather difficult to find, from their knack of hiding, like their parents, by squatting closely on the sand. Their legs seem disproportionately long, like a young colt's. They have black bills, like their parents, from the moment of birth. They are covered all over, except a little space on the neck, with woolly down, that is white below, and beautifully variegated with black and buffy brown on the upper parts. The newly fledged Terns are very different from the old ones, being curiously mottled above with different colours, in which the pearl-blue scarcely shows; without a black cap, the head being white, except some slaty feathers over the ears and nape; the bill blackish, and the feet dull-coloured, and the tail much less forked. They cannot be mistaken for any other species, however, for there are none so small as they.

We have now only to examine the eggs we have collected; and here again we must give the specimens themselves precedence over authorities. If Nuttall, for example, had had ours before him when he wrote of the Least Tern, we should not now read in his Manual, that the " eggs, three or four in number . . . . . are about one and a half inches, by three-quarters of an inch in breadth." Ours, we see, are considerably smaller than this, and of a different shape from that implied by these dimensions, averaging only 1.25 inches long, by just 1.00 in breadth. The longest and most pointed one is 1.300 by 1.0, the shortest and roundest 1.20 by .98; these measurements probably representing very nearly the extremes of variation. The ground colour varies decidedly; the differences may be reduced to two kinds, in one of which the colour is very pale clear greenish-white, and in the other pale-dull drab or olive whitish, the latter apparently due to the mixture of a little brownish in the green. These colours are speckled all over with small splashes, irregular spots, and dots, of clear brown of several shades; and others of a paler, ill-defined, somewhat lilac, hue, appearing as if it were brown *in* the shell, instead of on the surface. The markings are often very evenly distributed over the whole egg, but more frequently, perhaps, tend to form a circle, at or around the larger end, particularly in those cases where they are large and splashed. The point of the egg is often free from markings, or with only a few small dots.

The plover's eggs are of the same general pattern of coloration as the Terns', but are larger, and otherwise conspicuously different. The variation, both in size and shape, is very considerable; thus one measures 1.45 by 1.05, and another only 1.22 by 1.00; a variation not only of absolute size but also of relative length of the long and short axes, resulting in a very decided difference of shape. All agree in having the greatest number short diameter the large end, as usual among birds of the order, and the difference is mainly due to a greater or less elongation and pointedness of the smaller end. The shorter axis varies only within narrow limits; but even in eggs taken from the same nest a difference of .15 may be observed in the lengths of the long axes, with, of course, a corresponding discrepancy in contour. The ground colour is difficult to name; it may be called pale olive-drab, more decidedly inclining to a greenish hue in some, and to a brownish in others. The eggs are thickly marked all over with brown so dark as to be almost black; the markings are in irregular, sharply defined spots, small splashes, and fine dots. In some specimens the markings show a tendency to run into fine lines, and in these are smallest, darkest, most numerous and most sharply outlined; but ordinarily the distinctive splashed character is maintained. Commonly the markings are rather larger, and consequently more thickly set on the larger part of the egg, where there is also some tendency to run together, though scarcely to form a ring around the butt; but in none of the specimens examined was the pointed end free from spots. Here and there may usually be observed a few pale obsolete spots, as noticed in the Terns' eggs, but they are fewer and much less conspicuous, and in fact are hardly to be detected without close scrutiny.—*American Naturalist*, September.

LIST OF BRITISH MOTHS:
NATURE OF THEIR FOOD,
AND TIMES OF THEIR PERFECT APPEARANCE.

ROYAL MANTLE (*Anticlea sinuata*). Feeds on lady's bedstraw (*G. verum*). Flies in June.

The Flame (*Anticlea rubidata*). Feeds on the great hedge bedstraw (*G. mollugo*). Flies in June.

Shoulder Stripe (*Anticlea badiata*). Feeds on the leaves of dog-rose (*Rosa canina*). Flies in April.

Streamer (*Anticlea derivata*). Feeds on the leaves of R. canina. Flies in April.

Barberry Carpet (*Anticlea berberata*). Feeds on the common barberry (*Berberis vulgaris*). There are two broods, the first flies in May and the second in August.

Red Carpet (*Coremia munitata*). Feeds on groundsel. Flies in June and July.

Flame Carpet (*Coremia propugnata*). Feeds on Brissica. Flies in May and June.

Red Twin-spot Carpet (*Coremia ferrugata*). Feeds on the leaves of the ground ivy (*Glechoma hederacea*). Flies in May.

Dark-barred Twin Spot Carpet (*Coremia unidentata*). Feeds on lady's bedstraw (*Galium verum*) and sweet woodroffe (*Asperula odorata*). Flies in May and June.

Large Twin-spot Carpet (*Coremia quadrifasciata*). Feeds on low plants, hawthorn, &c. Flies in June.

Yellow Shell (*Camptogramma bilineata*). Feeds on grasses. Flies in June and July.

The Gem (*Camptogramma fluviata*). Feeds on the leaves of the Polygonum persicaria. Flies throughout the summer.

The Fern (*Philbalapteryx tersata*). Feeds on C. vitalba. Flies in June.

Slender-striped Rufous (*Philbalapteryx lapidata*). Flies in August.

Oblique Carpet (*Philbalapteryx liguata*). Flies in June.

Many-lined (*Philbalapteryx conjunctaria*). Flies in March and September.

Small Waved Umber (*Philbalapteryx vitabata*). Feeds on C. vitalba. Flies in June and August.

The Tissue (*Scotosia dubitata*). Feeds on common buckthorn (*Rhamnus catharticus*). Flies in August.

Brown Scallop (*Scotosia vetulata*). Feeds on R. catharticus. Flies about the end of June.

Dark Umber (*Scotosia rhamnata*). Feeds on R. catharticus. Flies in August.

Scarce Tissue (*Scotosia certata*). Feeds on the leaves of Berberis vulgaris. Flies in May and June.

Scallop Shell (*Eucosmia undulata*). Feeds on sallow. Flies in June.

Red-green Carpet (*Cidaria psittacata*). Feeds on the Oak (*Q. robur*). Flies in October and November.

Autumn Green Carpet (*Cidaria miata*). Feeds on oak, birch, and alder. Flies in October.

Short-cloak Carpet (*Cidaria picata*). Feeds on alsine media. Flies in June.

Hazel Carpet (*Cidaria corylata*). Feeds on the small leafed sloe. Flies in June.

Marsh Carpet (*Cidaria sagittata*). Feeds on the seeds of the meadow rue (*Thalictrum flavum*). Flies in July.

Common Marbled Carpet (*Cidaria russata*). Feeds on the leaves of wild strawberry (*Fragaria vesca*), also on whitethorn (*Crataegus oxyacantha*), birch (*Betula alba*), and on sallow (*Salix caprœa*). Flies in May and August.

Marbled Carpet (*Cidaria immanata*). Feeds on F. vesca. Flies in July.

Warter Carpet (*Cidaria suffumata*). Feeds on G. mollugo. Flies in April.

Wetted Carpet (*Cidaria reticulata*). Flies in July.

Small Phœnix Moth (*Cidaria silaceata*). Feeds on enchanter's night shade (*Circœa lutetiana*),

There are two broods, the first flies in May and the second in August.

The Phœnix (*Cidaria ribesiaria*). Feeds on the leaves of the currant and goosberry. Flies in June and July.

The Chevron (*Cidaria testata*). Feeds on B. alba and S. capræa. Flies in July.

Northern Spinach Moth (*Cidaria populata*). Feeds on the wortleberry (*Varcinium vitis-idœa*), and on sallow (*S. capræa*). Flies in July.

Barred Yellow (*Cidaria fulvata*). Feeds on R. canina. Flies in July.

Barred Straw (*Cidaria pyraliata*). Feeds on G. mollugo and G. aparine. Flies in July.

The Spinach (*Cidaria dotata*). Feeds on the black currant (*Ribes nigrum*). Flies in June.

Dark Spinach (*Pelurga comitata*). Feeds on various species of goose-foot (*Chenapodium*). Flies in July.

EUBOLIDÆ.

The Mallow (*Eubolia cervinaria*). Feeds on the common mallow (*Malva sylvestris*). Flies in September.

Fortified Carpet (*Eubolia mœniata*). Feeds on broom. Flies in June and August.

Small Mallow (*Eubolia mensuraria*). Flies in June and July.

The Belle (*Eubolia palumbaria*). Feeds on needle green-weed (*Genista Anglica*), and on the common broom (*Spartium scoparium*) Flies in June.

Chalk Carpet (*Eubolia bipunctata*). Feeds on L. corniculatus. Flies in July.

Oblique Striped (*Eubolia lineolata*). Feeds on G. verum. Flies in May and June.

Manchester Treble-bar (*Carsia imbutata*). Feeds on the cranberry (*Vaccinium oxycoccos*). Flies in July.

Treble-bar (*Anaitis plagiata*). Feeds on the leaves and flowers of the perforated St. John's Wort (*Hypericum perforatum*). There are two broods, the first flies in May and June, and the second in August and September.

Pale Gray Carpet (*Lithostege griseata*). Feeds on the seed pods of Sisymbrium Sophia. Flies in June.

The Streak (*Chesias spartiata*). Feeds on S. scoparium. Flies in September.

Broom Tip (*Chesias obliquaria*). Feeds on S. scoparium. Flies in May, June, and July.

SIONIDÆ.

Chimney Sweeper (*Tanagra chærophyllata*). Feeds on the blossoms of the common earth nut (*Bunium flexuosum*). Flies about the end of June.

DREPANULÆ.
DREPANULIDÆ.

Scalloped Hook-tip (*Platypteryx lacertula*). Feeds on the leaves of B. alba. Flies in June and September.

Scarce Hook-tip (*Platypteryx sicula*). Flies in May and June.

Pebble Hook-tip (*Platypteryx falcula*). Feeds on B. alba. Flies in May and August.

Oak Hook-tip (*Platypteryx hamula*). Feeds on Q. robur and B. alba. Flies in May and August.

Barred Hook-tip (*Platypteryx unguicula*). Feeds on the leaves of the beech (*Fagus sylvatica*). There are two broods. The first flies in May and the second in August.

Chinese Character (*Cilix spinula*). Feeds on C. oxyacantha. There are two broods. The first flies in May and the second in August.

PSEUDO-BOMBYCES.
DICRANURIDÆ.

Alder Kitten (*Dicranura bicuspis*). Feeds on A. glutinosa. Flies in May.

Sallow Kitten (*Dicranura furcula*). Feeds on S. capræa and S. cinerea. Flies in June.

Poplar Kitten (*Dicranura bifida*). Feeds on the leaves of tacamahac (*Populus balsamifera*), and aspen (*P. tremula*). Flies in June.

Puss Moth (*Dicranura vinula*). Feeds on several varieties of narrow-leaved willow (*Salix*). Flies in May and June.

The Lobster (*Stauropos fagi*). Feeds on Q. robur and B. alba. Flies in June.

The Sprawler (*Petasia cassinea*). Feeds on Q. robur. Flies in October.

Rannoch Sprawler (*Petasia nubeculosa*). Feeds on B. alba. Flies in March and April.

PYGÆRIDÆ.

Buff-tip (*Pygæra bucephala*). Feeds on hazel (*Corylus avellana*), elm (*Ulmus campestris*), lime (*Tilia europœa*), and other trees. Flies in June.

Chocolate-tip (*Clostera curtula*). Feeds on Populus tremula. Flies in April and July.

Scarce Chocolate-tip (*Clostera anachoreta*). Feeds on Populus nigra and Salix capræa. Flies in August.

Small Chocolate-tip (*Clostera reclusa*). Feeds on S. capræa and S. cinerea. Flies in May and and August.

NOTODONTIDÆ.

Dusky-marbled Brown (*Gluphisia crenata*). Feeds on P. nigra. Flies in June.

Plumed Prominent (*Ptilophora plumigera*). Feeds on Acer campestris. Flies in October.

Pale Prominent (*Ptilodontis palpina*). Feeds on the poplar (*Populus*), also on several varieties of willow and sallow (*Salix*). Flies in June.

Coxcomb Prominent (*Notodonta camelina*). Feeds on Q. robur, B. alba, and A. campestris. Flies throughout the summer months.

Maple Prominent (*Notodonta cuculina*). Feeds on A. campestris. Flies in May.

Scarce Prominent (*Notodonta carmelita*) Feeds on B. alba. Flies in April.

White Prominent (*Notodonta bicolor*). Flies in June.

Swallow Prominent (*Notodonta dictœa*). Feeds on P. nigra and S. capræa. Flies in May and June.

Lesser Swallow Prominent (*Notodonta dictœoides*). Feeds on B. alba. Flies in June.

Iron Prominent (*Notodonta dromedarius*). Feeds on B. alba. Flies in June.

Three Humped (*Notodonta trilophus*). Feeds on B. alba and P. nigra. Flies in May and August.

Pebble Prominent (*Notodonta ziczac*). Feeds on sallow (*Salix*) and poplar (*Populus*). Flies in June, July, and August.

Great Prominent (*Notodonta trepida*). Feeds Q. robur. Flies in May and June.

Lunar Marbled Brown (*Notodonta chaonia*). Feeds on Q. robur. Flies in May.

Marbled Brown (*Notodonta dodonœa*). Feeds on Q. robur. Flies in May.

Figure of Eight Moth (*Diloba cœruleocephala*). Feeds on whitethorn (*C. oxyacantha*). Flies in September. T. W. TEMPANY.

HYDROPHOBIA.

"But soon the truth was brought to light,
To show the rogues they lied,
The man recovered of the bite,
The dog it was that died."

GRATIFYING would it be if we could confirm the truth of these lines in all cases, besides the one quoted above from Oliver Goldsmith's "Death of a Mad Dog." Of all the ills that flesh is heir to, none is so terrible in its deadly effect, or so dreadful in its course, as this disease—Hydrophobia. And it is not a little surprising that, notwithstanding the rapid progress made by the healing art within the last few years, no cure has even been discovered, at least, no decided and authentic case of a cure, except at its earliest stages. Indeed, the bite of the deadly cobra, puff adder, or rattlesnake, is not to be dreaded nearly as much as a snap from one of our little pampered favorites, if he happens to be "going mad." If in future ages, some happy and illustrious savant should discover a cure for this malady, we think it will be the man who can give a correct answer to the questions, "Under what circumstances is rabies developed, and *what is it?*" The animals most subject to it are the wolf, dog, and cat, but we need only be concerned with the dog. From very early times there have been various delusions with regard to rabies, (as we prefer to call the disease in the animal,) the chief of which was that the afflicted beast was seized with madness at the sight of water, and rushed away from it; whence the name of the disease hydro-phobia or fear of water. This idea is now shown to be incorrect, as rabid dogs have been known to drink very freely during the first stage of the disorder, and as it proceeds, to plunge their heads up to their eyes in the stream, in their eagerness to cool their burning throats. Another notion was, that it was caused by a want of water; but several wretched animals having been condemned to a lingering death by being deprived of it, without exhibiting any signs of rabies, by some cruel experimentalist; this idea also falls through. In fact, as time advances, the only thing gained is to expose the absurdity of the different theories, without coming to a solution of the question *what is it!* This much is known from the symptoms attending its progress—that it is a poison permeating the system, and developed chiefly in the saliva, which as it increases, becomes so clogged and thick, as to stop the air passages, causing death by suffocation; and this is most probably the reason of the desire shewn by rabid animals to bite everything that they can lay hold of, as if to clear the poisonous saliva from their mouths. As Mr. Wood in his Natural History suggest, when we consider that dogs perspire through their tongues, if any violent sudorific could be administered so as to enable them to get rid of the poison, perhaps such a remedy might be successful; and the motions of the animal in its violent rushings about and delirous howlings as if to clear the poison from its throat, seem to bear out this idea. As to the cause of rabies, except through innoculation, next to nothing is known. Spontaneous generation has been suggested, but there is no reason for giving it any prominent place among the numerous propositions regarding it. Disease unchecked, starvation, and illusage, are among the causes which would most probably promote it, but when we hear of a wretched lap dog, fed up to its very eyes, being attacked, we must conclude that something else is the cause. We candidly confess we dont know.

Some writers on this subject have applied the specific term Hydrophobia to the disease both in the canine and human subject; and no doubt there are some good reasons for this, as the same poison which affects the dog, also destroys the man. But there is this important difference, that in the *dog* the poison is generated, which at once takes effect when introduced into the human system. For the sake of clearness, therefore, if for no other reason, we prefer distinguishing the disease, considering it as rabies, in the animal, and hydrophobia in the human being.

Unlike rabies, hydrophobia is caused by innoculation only, being usually introduced through the poisonous saliva of a rabid animal, into a wound caused by a bite, or by the virus touching a raw spot. In some cases it has been caused by a dog licking an unhealed sore, and we have heard of another case, (though its truth appears doubtful) caused by a dog licking a person's face, by which the saliva was absorbed by the skin. There are numerous other cases, most of which shew that at the time of the bite, or licking, or whatever it was that introduced the disease into the system, the animal exhibited no symptoms of rabies. We have a report of a case taken from a Newspaper before us at this moment, in which a dog bit a little girl, who died from the poison within a month, but the animal had no appearance of rabies up to the time when it was killed; so that it seems many months may elapse before an infected animal may be seized with the active disease. When a person has been bitten, the usual method is to destroy every particle of the saliva, by cauterizing the wound with nitrate of silver, or to burn it out with a red hot iron. The other method that of excision, is not considered as safe, as the blood running from the cut might mingle with the poison, and be again conveyed to the system in a more liquid and transmittable form; for the same reasons washing the wound is dangerous. Of course every bite from a rabid animal is not attended with fatal results, or even with any danger at all, for, as frequently happens, when the bite is given through thick clothing, the animal's teeth are wiped dry or clean in piercing the outer fabric; consequently wounds on the face and hands are by far the most dangerous. In the disease itself the main features are similar to those of rabies, the saliva appearing to become envenomed, and affecting the throat and lungs. The spasmodic convulsions of the throat at the sight or even the idea of water, which increase so as to seize the whole system, are not apparent in rabies, except perhaps in the final convulsion, but in both the primary cause of death is the working of this subtle poison. The delirous howlings and noises made by persons in the last stages of the disease, and supposed to be imitative of a dog's bark, are most probably, caused by the sufferer's endeavour to clear his throat from the mucous saliva which closes the air passages. Fortunately the attack, when most severe, is the shortest, death often relieving the victim within 24 hours of the first appearance of the malady, but sometimes it last for four or five days. It has been remarked, that in the case of wounds from tiger and cat bites, the old scars periodically become inflamed and sore, and this takes place annually from the time the wound was received. In the same way persons who have recovered from the bite of a rabid animal, feel the scar painful at times, especially at the annual recurrence of the event, although the wound may have healed quickly; indeed, a bite of a mad dog generally heals in a perfectly healthy manner, although the person afterwards may die from its effects.

Certainly in the whole category of diseases, nothing seems to approach hydrophobia in its terrible certainty, or in the fearful agony experienced in its attacks. Fortunately for us, however, it is of comparatively rare occurrence, though that is not owing to any preventive measures of our own. The senseless practice of muzzling dogs during the "Dog Days," which was ordered in the Metropolis last year is, we are glad to find discontinued, but some better method of prevention must yet be found, ere we can hope to stamp the disease entirely out. The immediate destruction, or a strict quarantine for twelve months, of all dogs who shew the slightest symptoms of rabies, as well as those who are known to have been bitten, together with the merciful slaughter of all diseased, homeless, wandering curs would, we think, do a great deal of good; and, whatever the doctors may say to the contrary, prevention is better than cure, any day, specially if that cure consists in nitrate of silver being rubbed on a raw wound.

IN MEMORIAM.

SOME months ago a friend presented me with rather a peculiar dog, bearing a very striking resemblance to a fox, especially about the head and tail. His general colour was tawny-red, varied by the most perfect white upon the chest and under part of the body. His feet also and legs were white, and always kept scrupulously clean. The tail might have done duty for a fox's brush in any squire's hall, though contrary to the custom with foxes it was usually carried upright, and curled slightly over the back. Perhaps he might be more fitly compared to a gigantic squirrel; yet, as "fox-dog" was the title usually bestowed upon him by observant street-boys, I will not gainsay its applicability. Whatever the physical resemblance might have been, it was testified morally by certain distinct qualities of a vulpine nature—*e.g.*, while passionately fond of ducks and chickens as articles of diet, he could never be induced to eat beef; and though addicted to lamb, he generally refused mutton altogether. He showed a surly disinclination to fraternise with other dogs until the acquaintance had continued for some time. Furthermore he delighted in hunting toads about the garden; and could not bear buzzing insects, especially moths and cockchafers. These two last features of character (so rustic naturalists tell me) are particularly observable in foxes—but the authority for this statement may be open to suspicion. Though unacquainted with his pedigree, I understand that my dog was born and bred upon the Welch mountains, whence he was subsequently exiled for chasing sheep. Friends gave different verdicts concerning his ancestry—some declaring he was a high-born Collie, others denouncing him as a degraded mongrel—while a certain dog-dealer assured me that undoubtedly there flowed in his veins the vulpine blood.

It is now my painful duty to record the tragic end of my beloved nondescript. On Sunday last (Aug. 8th), disregarding any possible relationship with Renard, he essayed to avenge the many murders of his cousins by attacking an old horse on the establishment. No entreaties or execrations would deter him. The chase waxed hotter and hotter: horse gallopping wildly, dog close at his heels; frightful flingings out of hind-legs from the one, subtle evolutions to avoid them from the other; neighs of desperate indignation, barks of bullying bravado; and so forth round and round the meadow. At last the fatal kick caught him full in the temples, and laid him insensible on the field of battle. Dead? No. A minute afterwards he recovered: we carried him off and washed the wound, which formed a crimson crescent between the eyes. On further inspection it seemed only skin-deep; the frontal bone was sound, the eyes unhurt. Next day all appeared well, the scar soon healed, and the dog seemed none the worse. On the second and third days after the accident he ate very little, and drank moderately. A dreamy lassitude appeared to oppress him—his gait was at times undecided, and his usually restless activity gave place to a desire for sleep. These symptoms seemed strange; we did not connect them with the kick, for the wound had healed so quickly that any apprehensions of serious results were never entertained. Yesterday, the fourth day after the affair, he had recovered his appetite, though the same dull stupor seemed to overpower him. In the evening, however, having been enticed into a run across country, he regained his old spirits for the time, under the influence of breeze and sunshine—scampering after rabbits through furze and bramble, chasing heifers on the hills and thoroughly enjoying himself. This morning he appeared worse again, and about 11 a.m. he was seized with a species of fit—foaming profusely at the mouth and rolling his blood-shot eyes, while standing on three legs, the left foreleg being bent upwards and affected with spasmodic movements. He scarcely seemed to recognise us; and the symptoms so evidently indicated madness in some form or other, that unanimous sentence of death was passed.

Now I have not had much experience in canine disorders, and never knew a dog go mad before from a similar cause. A gardener more versed in such phenomena said to me the day after the accident—"That dog will go mad, Sir; mark my word." And it was principally at his instigation that the execution took place. He described the case as an instance of "sullen madness," distinguished from "raving madness." Maternal horrors of hydrophobia prevented my dissecting the dog, and being consequently debarred from obtaining information by examining the brain, &c., I should be grateful to any correspondent who would answer the following questions:—Is it a common occurrence for animals to sicken with mania after concussion of the brain? Do the symptoms generally resemble those recorded in this case? Might the disease possibly have been a temporary seizure or must the brain have continued affected until the dog died? Are there several species of madness in dogs? If so, what may their characters and causes be? Lastly, are there any authentic cases of interbreeding between foxes and dogs in the wild state?

August 13th, 1869.   C.

Remarks, Queries, &c.

(*Under this head we shall be happy to insert original Remarks, Queries, &c.*)

LADYBIRDS.—The subject of the vast swarms of the very pretty beetle Coccinella septem-punctata having been discussed so freely in the leading daily and weekly newspapers, I was rather disappointed to find not a single paragraph concerning them in the N. N. B. Mid-Somerset appears to have been liberally patronised by the welcome little invaders, and wherever I prosecute my inquiries I hear wonderful accounts of their abundance. My first business is to make my friends understand what a ladybird is. The other day I asked six adult persons in succession, and not one of them knew what I meant by a ladybird! On introducing a specimen to one of these rustics, he exclaimed, "O! that be a God A'mighty's cow!" Another said, "We used to call they things lady's cows up the country." The common name for them in the neighbourhood of Birmingham is lady-cows, which I presume is merely a corruption of the above. In other countries it is called by similar names, as the Virgin Mother's Chafer, in Germany; the Virgin's Cow, in France; Virgin Mary's Maid, in Sweden; and Our Lady's Hen, in Denmark. Why should the insect take its name from the Virgin in so many countries? Even when the Virgin does not give it a name, we find a determination to invest it with a sacred title; as, for instance, God's Cow, in France; Our Lord's Hen, in Denmark; and God Almighty's Cow, in Mid-Somerset. A gardener informed me that he saw them on a lawn recently "as thick as the blades of grass;" but, although I have seen vast numbers of them, I have witnessed nothing like that. My own observations only date from the 2nd of September, but I daresay they made their appearance here much earlier. On that day I noticed they were particularly abundant, even on the foot-roads; and on looking in the same places a week later they seemed quite as numerous, although large numbers had been killed by pedestrians—the dead bodies of the slain evidently not scaring away their comrades. From this fact I infer that these insects do not intend to leave us; but I shall be glad to learn how far the swarms have pushed their way into the north. "F. R. S.," in the *Times*, gave an interesting account of their appearance on the coasts of Kent and Sussex, on the 14th, 15th, and 16th of August. The largest assemblages are said to have been on the points of the coast nearest the Continent, and "a Fellow of the Royal Society, when working on Dover pier, observed an enormous multitude of these insects like a cloud coming over the sea, as if from Calais. They were flying from east to west." One account I have read speaks of a similar invasion on the shore at Brighton in 1807, and another publication refers to an invasion on the South Kentish coast in 1847. I have not seen any account which speaks of *two* previous invasions, so possibly one of the above dates is incorrect. Any further information will be acceptable.

Castle Cary.   W. MACMILLAN.

FIRE.—On taking up the last number of the NOTE BOOK, and observing from the list of contents that there was an article on "Fire," I turned to it, expecting to find a treatise upon the nature of fire, concerning which many people have now, as formerly, very vague notions. Finding, however, that the article in question was only an interesting summary of the opinions of the ancients, and a history of the use of fire, I venture to supplement the same by a chapter on the nature of fire, as ascertained by modern researches in science. Fire may be spoken of under two heads —either as denoting a red-hot or white-hot condition of matter, when a body is luminous through heat; or as flame, when two gases combine at high temperatures. The heat of the electric spark passing through the air heats the particles of oxygen and nitrogen to the extent that they become luminous. Air powerfully compressed, shows its latent heat by becoming for an instant red-hot. Iron may be made red-hot by friction; and if fire be interpreted to signify any perceptible amount of heat, the hammering of a piece of lead on an anvil will produce fire, by the conversion of force into heat. Flame, again, is the combination of two gases at a high temperature. Both substances must be gaseous, and if the temperature be not sufficient to vaporize the least fusible substance there is no flame; chemical action there may be, as in a red-hot cinder, but no flame. In a candle, the heat first applied from a burning body decomposes the wick and the tallow, making various hydrocarbon gases, which combining with the oxygen of the air produce flame; or, to speak more correctly, produce a flame of hydrogen and oxygen, holding in its current numerous particles of red-hot carbon, some of which are passing off as smoke; whilst the rest, meeting the oxygen of the air, are converted into carbonic acid whilst red-hot. But it is not necessary for oxygen to appear upon the scene. A mixture of hydrogen and chlorine heated to the temperature of combination combines with a flash, producing hydrochloric acid gas, which, dissolved in water, forms the "spirits of salt" of the chemist. Anaxagoras' theory, that the sun was a terrestrial mass in an incandescent state, was very near the truth, as discovered by modern physicists. The sun is proved to be a mass of the same elements as the earth, but not incandescent, its light coming from an intensely heated atmosphere, through apertures in which the dark body of the central orb may be occasionally seen.   W. H. DALTON.

THE WOOD PIGEON (COLUMBA PALUMBUS).—This pretty bird, which is about the same size as the well-known jackdaw, is common in most of the English counties, and I have found them very plentiful in Devon. In colour, it is of a dark bluish grey, with green and purple reflections about the neck. This bird is the largest British species of pigeons, the other kinds being found in England are the stock dove (Columba ænas), the rock dove (Columba livia), and the turtle dove (Columba turtur); the last-named bird is not a resident in this country, but is found in Southern Europe, some parts of Asia, etc., and visits England in the spring, taking its departure again southwards in the autumn months. The wood pigeon resorts to woods and copses bordering on fields, and is a wild shy bird, and appears, from the localities it frequents, to like to have some thicket close at hand wherein to retreat should it be suddenly surprised— which is not often the case, it being so wary. It has a rapid and powerful flight, and makes a particularly loud flapping noise with its wings, which can be heard at a considerable distance. The note of the wood-pigeon, like all its species, is plaintive and monotonous. They are by no means classed among the farmer's best friends, and indeed are ranked by most of them as enemies, feeding on grain of all kinds, and are particularly partial to young turnips, which they are said to destroy in great numbers and pull up by the roots; but notwithstanding all the harm they commit to the corn, turnips, etc., on the other hand they do some good, though few farmers will allow such to be the case, and shoot them as often as they get an opportunity of so doing. Like all birds, the wood-pigeon pairs in the spring; and at the approach of autumn collect together, and during the winter season fly in large flocks, which increase in size during severe weather. Perhaps these few notes, from my own observation of the wood-pigeon, may prove interesting to your correspondent, G. O Howell, as well as to other readers of the NATURALIST'S NOTE BOOK. A. E. BUTTEMER.

ANSWERS TO QUERIES.—In your last issue are several questions put by "W. M."—who I should suppose to be a tyro in the study of entomology—which I think might soon be solved with a little observation, and interchange with some friendly entomologist, or by carefully studying such works as Edward Newman's "British Butterflies," or his work on "British Moths." In the first place, your correspondent asks the best method of determining the genus, species, etc., of any moth that has been caught? He cannot do better than study such books as the above, and carefully compare his captures with them: in this way he may soon familiarise himself with them. He also asks, in the second place, how long insects should remain "set" before being placed in the cabinet? Now there is no fixed time for them to remain so; they may be placed in the cabinet as soon as the wings are quite dry and stiff. In the third place he inquires, what become of these insects in the night-time, or in wet weather? They no doubt select some snug spot at such times, and remain quiet, and reappear as soon as the sun shines. Again, he asks, what is the longest duration of life in an insect in its perfect condition? Most butterflies "give up the ghost" soon after depositing their eggs; some live longer; some "more fortunate ones" hybernate throughout the winter, and reappear the first fine day in spring. Lastly, he asks the best kind of weather to go in search of specimens? Any *warm sunny* day either in spring, summer, or autumn, by taking a walk he is sure to meet with some of the insect fraternity. These and many other little matters may soon be cleared up if your correspondent will read, mark, learn, and inwardly digest the valuable articles contributed to this work by Messrs. Clifford, Laddiman, Tempany, etc., from month to month.

THE SHANNON.—Here I write from "Sweet Auburn, loveliest village of the plain, "the birthplace of Oliver Goldsmith, hallowed, and I may say universalized by his pen. Here are Lough Ree and the river Inny, where Goldsmith so thoughtlessly wandered in youth.—" The village statesmen are gone," the "hawthorn bush" has long since disappeared, and the black and ruined walls of the "Three Pigeons," with a melancholy grin tell us of the march of mutation. The Falls of the Shannon are truly magnificent. The Falls, or rather the rapids, are about 1,500 feet in length, 1,000 feet broad, and immediately above them the river is 40 feet deep. And here a passing word on the instinct of birds. In passing through Lough Ree in the steam ship immense flocks of birds are seen quietly resting on the waters, and scarcely leave the way of the floating castle, but as soon as a small boat attempts to approach the winged children of the lake, off they go with a speed prompted by something like a reasoning process. It would indeed seem that experience has taught the birds to look on the big ship with confidence—they seem to know that the ship's mission is not that of stopping to kill birds, that she must go on; and they also seem to know that the pigmy boats are but pirates among the birds. We are here a little confounded at those immediate results of brute observations. Are those things instinct of some high order, or are they derived from some mysterious mental process, which men would willingly venture to call absolute reasoning? I honestly admit that I know not. H. H. ULIDIA.

Lough Ree.

THE GOSHAWK AND HEATHPOLT.—"And here I take it worth remembrance that Sir Frances Basset, Knight, aforesaid, in the beginning of the reign of King Charles II., in the morning about ten o'clock, on Tyhyddy (Tehidy) Downs, himself or his falconer let fly a goshawk or tassell to a heathpolt or heathcock, which they had there sprung or started on the wing, which birds of game and prey in a short while flew eastwards, over St. Agnes parish, and quite out of sight, so that they despaired of ever finding them again; but the next day, before twelve o'clock, to their wonder and amazement, a person sent from the Mayor of Camelford brought both to Tyhyddy to Sir Francis—the hawk well and alive, with his varnells on his legs, whereon his owner's name aforesaid was inscribed, but the heathpolt was dead; which messenger gave this further account of this rare accident, that the day before, as near as could be computed, about a quarter or half an hour after ten o'clock in the morning, the said hawk, in the midst of Camelford-town, struck down his game dead upon the spot; so that by computation their flight straightforward, only in half an hour's space, was at least thirty-two Cornish miles."—*Hals (died* 1739), *quoted in Davies Gilbert's "Parochial History of Cornwall,* 1838."

BLACK SPOTS ON THE SUN'S DISC.—On the evening of the 20th of August I observed through a telescope of moderate power no less than twenty-eight dark spots on the sun's disc, scattered over different portions of his surface; the majority of them were of very small proportions, as to be scarcely discernible, while a few of them were almost the size of a pin's head. Two of them were of large dimensions, and on closer scrutiny I observed that the centre of these large spots were of an uniform blackness, while the outside of them wore a less opaque darkness; and I suggest that, if I had had a telescope of a higher power, I should have seen that this transparent darkness would have transformed itself into a multitude of smaller spots which my telescope would not bring to light. The sun was setting through a slight haze at the time, which moderated his power, so that I could look on him without affecting my eyesight. I hope some of your more scientific correspondents will inform me what is the true cause arrived at by astronomers concerning these non-luminous spots. J. H.

ISLE OF MAN.—The Isle of Man has many things to interest the Naturalist—the island itself seems to have derived its name from Manannan, a celebrated seaman, of whom it has been said that he was the greatest mariner of the western part of the world, and he was able to presage good and bad weather from his observations of the heavens, and from the changes of the moon; wherefore the Scotii, and the Britons gave him the title of "God of the Sea;" they also styled him Mac Lir, that is, "Son of the Sea." The

island was also called Eubonia Insula, and we are told that a migration from Ulster to the Isle of Man, took place in the year 254. Of the Isle of Man, Ninnius says :—"it has a strand without a sea, a ford far from the sea, and which fills when the tide flows, and decreases when the tide ebbs." Ninnius also says the peninsula of Peel was once an island quite separated from Man—this we can fully understand when we bring geology to our aid. H. H. ULIDIA.
Peel.

EXTINCTION OF SPECIES.—Several correspondents of the N. N. B. are for forming a "Lepidoptera Acclimitisation Society." Now what would be the advantage of forming such a society? If Britain has not sufficient butterflies to please all entomologists, she has as many as she wants. If entomologists want foreign specimens in their collections, let them go abroad and collect them ; that is if they are desirous of catching them in their own nests—if not, let them obtain them by purchase or exchange. Surely they wouldn't call the imported insects British, any more than foreign animals born in the Zoological Gardens. If a species has become extinct, I say let it no longer be considered a native of Britain ; and also, let it not be expected to form part of a British entomological collection that has been collected since the extinction thereof. J. R. B.
Southgate.

HILL OF HOWTH.—Here the geologist has a subject. Howth is a peninsula with many small peninsulas jutting from its sides—the bold rocks facing the sea greatly resemble the northern coast of Antrim, but Howth presents no appearance of basalt. Clay slate enters largely into the composition of the pile, there is also much limestone ; lead and gold are found in small quantities, and in 1451 a search for tin was made, but with what result I cannot tell. The highest point of the hill is 563 feet above the sea, and from this elevated spot the Mourne Mountains in Down, and the Mountains in Wales can be distinctly seen. The Scandinavian Sea Kings called the hill "Hofda." It was subsequently called Houeth, and then Howth—"Hofud" meaning hoved. At present I cannot say more. I may return to the subject at a future time. H. H. ULIDIA.
Fin's Quoit.

SPIDER AND WASP.—Several species of spiders are found in gardens, one in particular which spin those large geometrical webs is plentiful in the autumn. A large specimen of this kind, dark green with white stripes, had spun its web between two branches of a rose bush, in the meshes of which a worker bee got entangled ; he was immediately seized by the spider and wound round with numerous threads: however, before he was quite killed a large wasp dashed at him, and fought with the spider for several seconds; the spider had the worst of it, and retreated with the loss of a few legs, and a sting of which it afterwards died. The wasp then seized the bee, and put an end to its struggles by severing the head and body from the abdomen; it flew away with the latter, and alighting on a neighbouring plum tree, made a meal of the contents of the honey-bag. J. H.

LARVA OF THE GOLD-TAILED MOTH (LIPARIS AURIFLUA).—During the month of June while out collecting larva I came across some of the above, which I took with my hand. Afterwards I was attacked with a stinging sensation about the neck and face resembling the sting of nettles, which for a time baffled me as to its cause. I took no notice that time to find out the cause; but another day, taking some more larva of the same moth, the old sensation came on again : then I remembered reading of a gentleman dissecting some of this larva and being attacked in the same manner, but he attributed the cause to hot sand he filled the larva with after dissection. Perhaps some of the readers of the N.N.B. have been affected in the same way, and could explain the cause.
S. REGELOUS.

THE WATER-RAIL.—In the interesting article on the water rail in last month's N. N. B. is the following passage :—"We have been informed that the little birds, before they are old enough to take care of themselves, are liable to become the prey of one of the most loathsome of animals, the water-rat; and moorhens, young wild ducks, teal, and other waterfowl of tender age, suffer severely from this pest." Now I have (very likely wrongly) always thought that the water-rat was a very harmless creature, and fed almost, if not entirely, on vegetables. The sight of one swimming across a clear stream or pool is to me a pretty object. Perhaps some of your readers who live in the country will kindly inform me through your pages what is the diet of this little creature.
H. BUDGE.

DO INSECTS FEEL PAIN ?—In the N. N. B. for May Mr. Malan said—" If it could be satisfactorily proved that one spider felt pain, then it might fairly be said it was indisputable that insects do feel pain." I think that I can prove by the following example that a spider does feel pain :—The other day I saw a wasp get entangled in a spider's web, and when the spider saw what it was he ran away as fast as his legs would carry him, showing I think that the spider must have been susceptible of pain ; for if not, why should he run away ? It must have been that he was frightened of being stung by the wasp and so caused pain.
JOS. LAING.

Can any of the subscribers of the N. N. B. tell me of any preparation for the preservation of the skins of animals, birds, etc. ? JOS. LAING.

WHAT IS IT ?—On the 15th of June I captured a moth belonging to the family of the Swifts (Hepialidæ) which is quite different to any figured or described in Mr. Newman's History of the British Moths. The fore wings measure $1\frac{1}{4}$ inches from tip to tip, the prevailing colour being orange, with two indistinct whitish lines beginning at the base and extending to the middle of the wings, one inclining towards the costal and the other towards the inner margin ; the hinder wings and abdomen are smoke-coloured, with an orange fringe, the thorax orange and very hairy. I have submitted it to several of the " Brethren of the net and pin," but none of them can determine what it is. I should feel obliged if any of the entomological readers of the N.N.B. could help me.
Norwich. R. LADDIMAN.

DESTROYING COCKROACHES.—"Hawkmoth" desires to know a way to destroy cockroaches. One way is to cut four or five pieces of pasteboard, or strips of wood, and lay them slanting against the sides of an ordinary basin; pour into the basin (taking care not to soil the sides) a mixture of treacle and water, or beer and sugar. The cockroaches will be attracted by the syrup, and walking up the roadways made for them fall headlong into the basin. Another plan, which may be pursued simultaneously with the above, is to place a few lumps of quicklime where the cockroaches frequent; care must be taken, lest children might burn their fingers with it. H. F. P.
Canterbury.

ENQUIRERS.—Would it not be better for the numerous incipient Haworths, Stephens, and Kirbys, who ask about keeping pupæ, killing moths, &c., &c., so many times over through the pages of the N.N.B., to get some such book as the newly published "Lepidopterist's Guide," by Dr. Knaggs. This would give them all the information they require on such points, and so serve space which might otherwise be devoted to subjects of more general interest; as it contains reliable information on nearly everything pertaining to Lepidopterology, from the laying and searching for ovæ to the arranging of the cabinet. M.

SIREX GIGAS.—Your correspondent "S. Regelous" mentions two of the above having been captured at Saffron Walden. I did not know that it was so particularly a native of cold and mountainous countries, and should be much obliged to him if he would inform me where he got the information from. The sirex, according to the Rev. J. G. Wood, is very plentiful in some parts of England, and is common wherever fir trees abound. If he will turn to the volume of the N.N.B. for 1868, page 381, he will see that a very fine specimen of the sirex was caught by me, about two years ago when in Devonshire, on Dartmoor.
Sydenham, S.E. A. E. BUTTEMER.

SIREX GIGAS.—In answer to S. Regelous, I beg to say that during the month of July I captured two specimens of S. Gigas in Leicestershire. One of them appeared to have been injured, as it could only fly a few inches without resting on the ground; its colour was dark brown, with yellow rings round its abdomen; its thorax was brown, as also its head and antennæ, without any yellow whatever. Specimen No. 2 was mostly yellow, with brown rings and dark patched thorax, the antennæ with broad yellow and brown bands alternate, the head brown, and the wings a beautiful transparent brown. W. NEWBERRY.

NO REPTILES IN IRELAND, AND WHY?—Our eminent foreign correspondent, J. D. S. W., from a luminous spot in Africa, where tigers are as unceremoniously devoured as chickens, asks me why we have no reptiles in Ireland. He might just as well ask me why the monkey, boa-constrictor, and his half intellectual neighbour, the gorilla, are strangers to our land. That we have no reptiles in Ireland (the harmless little lizard excepted) is a fact, but to give the reason why is rather a bar to naturalists. I wish our inquiring friend, in Africa, good health, and leisure to still speak to us in the N.N.B. H. H. ULIDIA.

IRELAND'S EYE.—The island is almost all a rock, but I found a few men reaping in it some of the finest corn. The island contains 53 acres. Natural caves, dark and gloomy, into which I entered, but not liking the sad music of the surging waves as they dashed against rocky sides I reluctantly returned. The highest point of this dreary island is 350 feet above the sea. On the highest point I found *sea pinks* and *mountain hare-grass*. But as the Thulla rocks are rather a primitive writing desk, as night is approaching, and a storm at hand, I'll close up and retreat from *Occulus Hiberniæ*. H. H. ULIDIA.

COCKROACHES.—One of the most effectual methods of getting rid of these animals is by keeping a hedgehog and allowing it to run free about the house. I have tried this experiment twice, and the house became perfectly free from these pests as long as the hedgehog remained in it. Another but less effectual method is by laying plates, full of beer, on the floor where the cockroaches are most abundant, as they are partial to it. The beetle poison sold by T. Chase, of 14, Holborn, W.C., is of great use. It is sold in shilling boxes. W. M.

A GOOD DAY'S SPORT.—On the morning of the 12th of August, about three quarters of a mile from this town, I captured specimens of C. Edusa, P. Brassicæ, Rapæ-Napi, L. Magæra, H. Janira, Sithonis, C. Pamphilus, C. Cardui, V. Atalanta, Io, Urticæ, C. Phlæas, P. Argiolus, P. Alsus, P. Corydon, P. Adonis, and Agestis, and also saw A. Paphia and P. Comma, or nearly one-fourth of our British species, near a large town, and in a very small space both of country and time. J. A. FOWLER.
Brighton.

On Sunday, August 25th, an extraordinary quantity of these insects visited Norwich, everything being covered with them. I have read reports of their appearance at Ramsgate, Walton-on-the-Naze, Southend, and other places, even more plentiful than here. Have any of your readers noticed them? Those seen here were chiefly the seven-spotted (Coccinella septempunctata). By the bye, does any one know the origin of the name, "Bisha-barny-bee," given to this insect in Norfolk?
Norwich. R. LADDIMAN.

—Early in July I found on the side of a rather steep bank about 15 feet high, on a large moor in Derbyshire, two white eggs, they were in a hole at the top of the bank, which extended about one foot underneath the ground; there was no nest, only a slight shallow hole in which the eggs were placed. They were laid by one of the Doves, but I cannot find out which, and I should feel much obliged if any of your readers could inform me by what bird they were laid. AN OOLOGIST.

TORTOISE.—In reply to Mr. S. Dunning, I can inform him that the tortoise does sometimes breed in this country. In the autumn of 1862 the gardener of W. William, Esq., of Tregullow, Cornwall, observed the female of a pair of tortoises kept in the garden laying some eggs, and removed them to the hot house, where two of them were afterwards hatched. About

the same time the following year one more was reared, the previous two at that time being healthy and active.
H. BUDGE.

ALBINO SAND MARTIN.—The other week a beautiful specimen of the Sand Martin was captured in the neighbourhood of Leicester, and was, I believe, the only individual of the pure Albino type on record. Its colour was snowy white, except the bill, eyes, tarsi, and feet, which were of a delicate pink. The bird was first noticed through its being most unmercifully attacked by a number of martins and swallows.
W. NEWBERRY.

BEETLE STONES.—In the quarries on Giltar Point, about three miles from Tenby, are found some very curious stones called "beetle stones." They are oval-shaped, varying in size from a blackbird's to a hen's egg, and are of deep black colour, containing the white outline of a beetle. They take a fine polish, and are cut into thin squares and ovals by the Tenby jewellers, who set them in brooches, etc. Are they not antediluvian beetles?
G. O. HOWELL.
Gravesend.

ERRATA.—I desire to correct one or two errors which, I am sorry to find, have crept into my "Diary." On the second column of page 247, tenth line from top, for *Small* Ringlet (Erebia Cassiope) *read* Ringlet (Satyrus Hyperanthus); and on p. 281, second column, tenth line from bottom, for Erebia Cassiope *read* Satyrus Hyperanthus. I am sorry the above should have tended to mislead your correspondent, Mr. Ernest Belfort Bax.
ROBT. LADDIMAN.
St. Augustine's, Norwich.

HEAT OF SUMMER OF 1868.—I have heard it stated that the great heat of the summer of 1868, also the great mildness of the following winter, was partly owing to the fact that the Gulf Stream was diverted in its course, and also that the disturbed state of the interior of the earth during last year had an influence on the temperature. Is there any truth in either of these statements?
ERNEST BELFORT BAX.

CHARCOAL AND GLASS.—In the May number of this periodical, is a notice relating to a curious experiment tried by R. B., I myself have also tried it both with hot and cold water, and find it will not answer. I think R. B. must have had something else beside charcoal in the glass, unknown to him. I have shewn the paragraph to several of my friends, who have also tried it unsuccessfully.
Bath.
W. P. R.

BOMBYX QUERCUS.—Will any of your readers kindly inform me through the medium of this work the reason why the above moth is called the Oak Eggar, and in what way it is associated with the oak? I have never heard or read of the caterpillar feeding on that tree; all I have found have been taken from whitethorn. Is it because the cocoon is shaped somewhat like an acorn?
R. LADDIMAN.
St. Augustine's, Norwich.

ERIOGASTER LANESTRIS.—Can any of your readers account for the "mortality" of the larvæ of Eriogaster Lanestris (Small Eggar)? I have had hundreds of these larvæ, and have always found that the greater part of them die off before reaching the chrysalis state. Have any of your readers been as unfortunate with the caterpillars of this moth?
St. Augustine's, Norwich.
R. LADDIMAN.

TRAP FOR RED ADMIRALS.—It may be of some service to the readers of the N. N. B. to know that a small heap of rotten fruit in gardens will form a most effective trap for Red Admirals (V. Atalanta), and it was in this way that some specimens of Camberwell Beauty (V. Antiopa) were caught at Lewes, near this place
J. A. FOWLER.
Brighton.

It is only now, having just reached Dublin, that I have an opportunity of seeing the NOTE BOOK. Surely none of the correspondents on the negative side can feel offended. We want information, we read the NOTE BOOK, and all, all, whether negatives or affirmatives, are simply literary combatants, permanent friends at arms.
H. H. ULIDIA.

ERRATUM.—Will you kindly in next month's issue of the N. N. B. kindly correct a ludicrous error, typographical I suppose, which occurs on page 288, in my note on a curious insect, which should read—"These instruments consist of four joints, the upper one being of similar construction to that of a lobster."
J. A. FOWLER.

PUPÆ-DIGGING.—Could any of your correspondents give me any information about pupæ-digging, or refer me to any pamphlet on the subject? I do not know whether Mr. Hambrough is aware that Camptogramma Gemmaria is the female of C. fluviata. He will find this proved in "Newman's British Moths," page 172.
Dulwich.
ARTHUR W. OWEN.

CORRECTION.—In my letter to you on "Do insects feel pain?" in the September issue of the N. N. B., the following mistake occurs:—For "which is all those on the *negative* side desired to prove," *read* "which is all those on the *affirmative* side desired to prove."
A. E. BUTTEMER.

CATERPILLARS.—As I am desirous of making a collection of caterpillars, I should feel obliged if any of your readers would kindly inform me, in your next issue, the best method of preserving them, so as to keep their colours.
R. LADDIMAN.
St. Augustine's, Norwich.

AQUARIUM.—Can any of your readers inform me the best method of setting up and stocking a fresh water aquarium. Do they require fresh water every day.
H. S. A.
Stockton-on-Tees.

CATERPILLARS.—Can any of your readers kindly inform me in the N. N. B. the best way of preserving caterpillars so as not to shrivel up, as I think of making a collection?
YORICK.

NOTICE.—British Lepidoptera in exchange for foreign shells, fossils, or minerals. Address—B. A., Post Office, Faversham.

QUERY.—Could any of the readers of the N. N. B. tell me what is the origin of the word "butterfly?"
Gravesend.
G. O. HOWELL.

ROUGH NOTES ON THE NATURAL HISTORY OF CORFU.

(Continued from page 294.)

ON reaching the olive-grove, the first thing which arrested my attention was a little hill thickly covered with the luxuriant frondage of the common fern, or brake, called by the modern Greeks "Vrakla;" and if we bear in mind that this word would be written with the "Beta," as pronounced by Anglo-Greek scholars, why we have then a most curious resemblance or query-derivative of the Scottish, "Bracken." Rising above the fern, and assuming the proportions of large bushes, the Myrtle (*Myrtus Communis*) was growing, and filling the air with the perfume exhaling from its fragrant blossoms, whose purely white petals formed an agreeable contrast to the shining green of its leaves. Some Hairstreaks (*Thecla Rubi*) and (*Thecla W. Album*) were "twinkling" their wings around them, and the adjacent bramble blossoms, soaring off to the tops of the trees, having a little playful tournament among themselves, and then returning for another sip, and frolic over the bushes. Resting on the leaves or flowers in the sluggish quietude peculiar to the genus were several Forester Moths (*Geryon Statices*), who hardly deigned to open their splendid metallic-green wings even when brushed off the foliage. Here, indeed, were to be seen butterflies of all hues sporting in the sunshine, or resting awhile on the blossoms of the many beautiful flowers around. The Silver-washed Fritillary (*Argynnis Paphia*) dashing in wild strong flight to its favourite resting-places, the various bramble blossoms, and then as wildly dashing off at our approach; the pugnacious little Blue (*Polyommatis Alexis*) chasing and teasing everything that came in its way, even to the gorgeous Swallow-tail (*Papilio Machaon*), which passed in swift flight before our admiring gaze. On the top of this hill the vegetation was scantier, the limestone rock cropping out in places, their hot flat surfaces affording a most convenient basking-place for the beautiful green lizards, who would peer at you with their bright eyes from a safe distance, and then with a rapid whisk of the tail would disappear so suddenly, as to induce the belief that you must have been mistaken in thinking that you saw them there at all. Some of the larger ones of this species, which haunt the recesses of old ruinous walls or secluded briar-tangled rocks, are formidable from their size and ludicrous ferocity, for when fairly brought to bay and "cornered," without a possibility of escape, they will actually run open-mouthed at anything you present to them, be it stick or finger, and fasten on it with such bull-dog determination that it is a hard matter to make them quit their hold; owing, however, to the smallness of their teeth and jaws, they cannot inflict a serious wound, in fact cannot draw blood from the finger; they pinch though very hard, and their tenacity is astonishing, inasmuch as I have more than once carried them hanging by my finger without any other support for the distance of a half mile or more. Of course they are perfectly harmless; and one of about eighteen inches or longer is a really pretty creature, for in addition to an elegant shape, the colour of the back is so vividly green, and the sides are so beautifully jewelled with rough turquoise and emerald-looking little knobs, that if we take into consideration the bright yellow of the under parts, we must pronounce it as being (to say nothing more) the least repulsive of reptiles.

Some other little bright-eyed fellows, with brown bodies and red throats (an allied species to our Lacerta Agilis), peered anxiously round the tree trunks for sundry unfortunate beetles or flies.

On looking back over the ground I had just traversed, from the top of this little hill, the whole of the intervening ground was plainly distinguishable, backed by the towering height of the Citadel and the Albanian mountains beyond, their white snow-line gleaming purely brilliant against the background of bright blue sky.

Descending the slope on the other side, I stood in a little dell or woody glade, carpeted by springy turf more verdant than any around, by reason I conjecture of the superior dampness of the slightly hollow ground retaining the dew for a longer period, even if it were not more than usually shaded by thick trees.

The sunnier parts of this glade were thronged by the upright stems and thickly clustered flowers of the Golden Rod (*Solidago Virgaurea*), whose really pleasant honey-like fragrance was rendered quite aromatic, as also the perfume from the Sweet Marjorem and the Wild Thyme, by the increased heat of the atmosphere, which seemed to almost beat upon the earth and then be refracted in quivering waves above, until it almost obscured the view of those objects seen through its heated undulating haze. The insect world reigned here triumphant: the slumbrous hum of the bees—each singing its self-satisfied song, as a part-atonement to the flower it was despoiling—rising and falling in a measured cadence as the soft breezes brought it to or took it away from our ears. The curious rustle (like rapidly crumpled paper) of the wings of the dragon flies (*Libellina*) as they turned in their darting flight, or rustled off from their point of observation on some leafless twig, the shrill chorus of the dancing gnats, all spoke of Nature. Nor were the Lepidoptera wanting to complete the *beau monde*, for with numbers of species observed before appeared the Pearl-bordered Fritillary (*Melitea Euphrosyne*), and the fragile and chaste little Wood White (*Leucophasia Sinapis*), the very embodiment of graceful elegance, and yet there is something about this little insect which speaks ever to me of sadder scenes than those it haunts, for as it wavers in its laboured flight over the beautiful flowers, the pale and ethereal white wings hardly seeming to support the delicately formed body, it seems always to remind me of some fair girl, wan and wasted, yet still sadly beautiful, slowly and surely fading away in the fell clutches of the wierd foe consumption, which, ere it closes its venomed and relentless fingers on the tender form of its youthful prey, seems to take a ghoul-like delight in making its hapless victim appear as an embodied spirit to suit its dainty appetite, ere the dread time arrives when the voice is dumb, and the vase of life lies a shattered wreck indeed at the feet of its destroyer.

Ay di me! this digression leads me in fancy far from my subject—far from the joyous life around this delightful scene—far from the sunny air—far from the deep blue skies—to the cold shudder of the dank, dark tomb; so true is it, I suppose, that even in the brightest, happiest thoughts there lies a world concealed of grim skeleton mysteries, which a false or careless note struck jars to its inner depths.

To return. About the various species of Erica, which lay sparsely scattered around, the Rock-eyed Underwing (*Hipparchia Semele*) was playing, its strong flight when aroused so unlike that of the Wood White. A favourite habit of the Rock-eyed Underwing appears to be to alight on ground similar to its colouring, at least I have always noticed this to be the case in England; but here they invariably alighted on the trunks of the olive trees when startled, and getting into some crevice of the bark, or under some knot, their wings folded over their back in the manner of the Rhopolocera, it really was a most difficult matter to distinguish their under surface with its varied markings of mottled and waved umber, greyish-white, and yellowish-brown, from the grey and brown wrinkled bark of true old olives, this—one of the numerous disguises of insects, say what the opponents of the disguise theory may—is only an exemplification of what is constantly occurring. Not many months ago I was entomologising in the Bois Jacques, at Enghien, near Paris (a most delightful spot, by-the-bye), and on my way thither came to an old wall. On this, and closely assimilating to its grey and broken mortar, I found by the merest chance a Red Underwing Moth (*Catocala Nugota*) so like its surroundings, that those to whom I pointed it out imagined it to be only another broken spot in the plaster. In the wood, and resting on the trunk of a chesnut tree, I found another, and this also was most difficult to any but a trained eye to distinguish from the bark; there were many more (what we should suppose) congenial resting-places around, and the fact of these not being chosen shows I think clearly that design, and not accident, was the motive power at work.

From this flower and insect tenanted dell I disturbed a little owl who was hiding in the recesses of an old tree; he disappeared, however, as suddenly as he came, so that I could not determine the species. Hundreds of bright green Beetles (*Cassida Viridis*) were crawling over the fern or marjorem tops disputing their possession with the bees, and upon the stalks of a lilaceous flower which grew here in profusion were to be seen multitudes of Tree Frogs (*Rana Arborea*), the beautiful green of their bodies as seen when resting on fern, or other bright green plants, seeming now of a blueish cast: whether this was a fancy of mine or not I leave others to determine, but I am almost inclined to think that they, like the chameleon, have the power of slightly changing their colour to suit various situations; be this as it may, they are certainly handsome little creatures, with yet an air of comicality perfectly irresistible, as they sit squatting with their feet doubled up under them, winking their bright golden eyes as you look at them, with a most knowing expression. When captured they express their annoyance by ejecting a considerable quantity of clear water, collected mayhap in the pores of the skin.

Swallows were circling overhead, and these, with the exception of a few insectivorous birds, chiefly warblers, were all the species observed. From here I struck a footpath past fields of flax and Indian corn to the road, opposite a place called Scalia, and from thence returned to the town; not, however, without calling in at a roadside "Krasipuleon," to get a glass of the claret-like country wine. In payment I tendered a gold piece, the only money I had; and after the till had been ransacked, and "Pipi," and "Andrea," and various others had been appealed to for change, I was told by the landlady—a handsome dark-eyed woman of an uncertain age—that it was "No force by, by, you give." The next time I went that way I took silver, and, curiously enough, met the same answer, so that, not wishing to keep this confiding dame out of her money, I left a sum over and above, and used to draw on my account whenever I called. From this interchange of courtesy we became quite friendly, and any Englishman who happened to call was always asked (whether he knew me or not) after the health of the "Signore Inglese." Anyone who has seen a French cabaret can form a good idea of a Greek wine-shop, for there is the same bench-like counter, the same proportion of square-shaped bottles, with the same varied contents, and the picture of the patron saint judiciously placed, with a little lighted taper in front, as if to keep a sharp look out, from the only eye which doesn't squint, after the liqueurs. This I always think a kind intention on the part of the shopkeeper, for we know that some of the saints—that is to say when they were only friars—*could* manage to drink just a little, perhaps about enough to kill two or three gentlemen of the old school; and so I say that it is very thoughtful to place their images where they can see the fun. One thing I cannot bear, and that is to see the Virgin (albeit, we do not worship her in the same way as southern nations) meekly looking out from some little niche in these places. The whole thing seems so horridly *mal-apropos*—about as much so as decorating a church with clippings from *Punch* or choice plates from the *Newgate Calendar*, or putting Bill Sykes into the pulpit to preach a sermon to his "Dearly beloved Pals."

On the roadside in a dry ditch fringed with various flowers I made capture of the pride of the Lepidopterist's heart, the rare and lovely Bath White (*Pieris Saplidice*), the "Greenish Half Mourner" of Vernon. They were flitting about in hundreds, quite as common as the Cabbage Whites in England, and as easily caught. These were the last objects of interest I saw before the sun went down, and I returned to town delighted with my walk, and with my mind stored with new materials for study.

Later in the month I took a fishing in the sea from a place called the Mandrachio, a sort of dockyard harbour, protected by a mole constructed of large stones. Standing on this you throw out a line, made of twisted horsehair, baited with the sea-worm, and by this method I caught several curious little hump-backed fish of iridescent hue, large-eyed and Perch-finned; these fish, which varied much in size, belonged to the Sparidæ, and eagerly took the bait offered to them, so that I and another fishing one evening for about an hour and a half caught over six dozen.

One little fish which I occasionally caught was of an olive-green colour, with the exception of a dark spot on each side of its neck, encircled by a narrow waved line of most vivid scarlet, and another of just as bright a blue. The name of this one is unknown to me, as also that of another of a most vivid light green found among the rocks.

The Bogue (*Boöps Vulgaris*) was another fish which was caught from here, a most handsome one also this—white of so dazzling a lustre that it rivalled silver, in which seemed inserted five or six longitudinal bars of gold; the shape, too, was exceedingly elegant. The Rock Goby (*Gobius Niger*) haunted the stones of the inner basin of the Mandrachio, lurking under them like some ugly black little demon of the deep, and occasionally poking out its malign and deformed-looking head in search of its food, and then scuttling off in high haste, as if greatly enraged, to some other crevice.

Another way of fishing was with the rod and line for mullet, and in this situation, or in the Citadel ditch, a still better resort for them, they would refuse everything excepting bread-paste. They require the roach stroke, and as fine tackle as is used for roach. Coming from England, I had of course the correct touch, and my first essay brought sixteen to bank. After this, for the whole five years I remained, I never caught another, save one quite by accident; this I attribute to fishing with worms afterwards for coarser biting fish, and thus losing the delicate turn of the wrist required. The natives considered them very difficult to catch; and the only one who seemed to always be successful was a Creole of the name of Domenico, and he certainly was as clever an angler as he was a shot. I think in this ditch, which was not more than perhaps fifteen feet across, or a hundred yards long, that you might at this period of the year see the mullet playing or basking near the surface a thousand strong, and of all sizes, from that of a sprat to the respectable length of sixteen or eighteen inches. Many species of Rock fish inhabited this water, which was in direct communication with the sea; and among these was a curious little thing which at first you could hardly imagine to be a fish, as it waggled its flat newt-like tail and corkscrewed itself up from the bottom, poking its nose into the Algæ growing on the sides, and retaining its hold while feeding by the action of a sucker; it is, however, a fish, the Sea Snail (*Liparis Vulgaris*), though its vernacular appellation is one admirably calculated to point to its peculiarities.

I saw one or two Cuttle Fish (*Sepia*) about the Mandrachio, appearing like the curious things one dreams of, more than a reality; for perhaps you may be looking at nothing particular in the water, when suddenly a no-shaped sort of a myth passes across your field of vision. Just as you are petrified with horror under the cold stare of two large glassy eyes, situated you hardly know where, and which make you feel as if you would like to call out "Murder!" or "Fire!" or something equally insane, the dreadful thing disappears like a flash (of blue and sulphurous flame, you think); and then you give a great gulp of relief, and remember, to your own inward satisfaction, that after all it must have been a cuttle! A. M. B.

(*To be continued.*)

LIST OF BRITISH BIRDS.
By W. Newberry.

CLASS II.—PASSERES.
ORDER I.—CANTATRICES (SONGSTERS).
Family I.—ORIOLINÆ (ORIOLES).

Genus I.—ORIOLUS.

Species I.—*Oriolus Galbula.*

Migratory, and scarce in England.
Size: Length, $9\frac{1}{2}$ in.; extent of wings, 17 in.; bill, $1\frac{1}{12}$ in.
Colour: Male—yellow, wings black, tipped with yellow, tail black and yellow; female—upper parts greenish yellow, lower parts light yellow, wings and tail brown, tipped with yellow.
Food: Seeds, berries, and insects.

Family II.—MYRMOTHERINE.

Genus I.—CINCLUS.

Species I.—*Cinclus Aquaticus* (*Water Ouzel*).

Permanently resident.
Size: Length, $7\frac{3}{4}$ in.; extent of wings, $12\frac{1}{4}$ in.; bill, $\frac{9}{12}$ in.
Colour: Upper parts grey, except head and neck, which are dark brown, throat white, breast reddish, tail and quills dark brown; has a white spot on each eyelid.
Food: Seeds, mollusca, and small fishes.
Builds in banks near a stream; the nest very large and arched over.
Lays 6 eggs, 1 in $\times \frac{9}{12}$ in.; pure white.

Family III.—TURDINÆ (THRUSHES).

Genus I.—TURDUS.

Species I.—*Turdus Merula* (*Blackbird*).

Permanently resident.
Size: Length, $10\frac{3}{4}$ in.; extent of wings, 16 in.; bill, $\frac{5}{6}$ in.
Colour: Male—black, with tarsi and feet dark brown, and bill yellow; female—dark brown, bill, throat, and lower parts brown.
Food: Berries, seeds, worms, snails, and larvæ.
Builds in hedgerows and bushes.
Lays 5 eggs, $1\frac{1}{12}$ in. $\times \frac{5}{6}$ in.; bluish, spotted and speckled with brown.

Species II.—*Turdus Torquatus* (*Ring Ouzel*).

Migratory.
Size: Length, $11\frac{1}{2}$ in.; extent of wings, 19 in.; bill, $1\frac{1}{12}$ in.
Colour: Dark brown, freckled with grey, a broad crescent of white on breast, bill yellow; female rather lighter.
Food: Worms, snails, seeds, &c.
Builds in bushes and hedges.
Lays 6 eggs, $1\frac{1}{12}$ in. $\times \frac{9}{12}$ in.; bluish, freckled with brown.

Species III.—*Turdus pilaris* (*Fieldfare*).

Migratory.
Size: Length, $10\frac{3}{4}$ in.; extent of wings, $19\frac{1}{2}$ in.; bill, $\frac{9}{12}$ in.
Colour: Head, neck, and posteriors grey, back and lore brown, throat and breast reddish yellow, lower wing coverts white.
Food: Berries, seeds, worms, snails, and larvæ.

Species IV.—*Turdus Viscivorus* (*Missel Thrush*)

Permanently resident.
Size: Length, $11\frac{1}{2}$ in.; extent of wings, $19\frac{1}{2}$ in.; bill, $\frac{5}{6}$ in.
Colour: Upper parts greyish brown, lower parts light yellow, tail tipped with white, has a yellow band over the eyes.
Food: Seeds, worms, larvæ, &c.
Builds in bushes or thick branches of trees.
Lays 4 eggs, $1\frac{3}{12} \times \frac{5}{6}$ in.; reddish, with brown, red, and purple spots.

Species V.—*Turdus Musicus* (*Song Thrush*).

Permanently resident.
Size: Length, 9 in.; extent of wings, 14 in.; bill, $\frac{9}{12}$ in.
Colour: Upper parts light brown, head and neck reddish-brown, breast yellowish, each feather tipped with black, wing coverts reddish yellow.
Food: Seeds, berries, snails, worms, &c.
Builds in hedges and bushes; nest lined with mud.
Lays 5 eggs, 13 in. $\times \frac{9}{12}$ in.; bluish, with scattered black dots.

Species VI.—*Turdus Illiacus* (*Redwing*).

Migratory.

Size: Length, $8\frac{3}{4}$ in; extent of wings, 14 in.; bill, $\frac{9}{12}$ in.

Colour: Upper parts dark brown, with black spot before the eye, and a white bar across it; breast white with brown streaks, secondary coverts tipped with white, sides and wing coverts red.

Food: Worms, larvæ, and seeds.

Species VII.—*Turdus Varius.*

Migratory, one shot in Hampshire, and 1 near Christchurch.

Size: Length, $10\frac{3}{4}$ in.; extent of wings, $14\frac{1}{2}$ in.; bill, $1\frac{1}{12}$ in.

Colour: Upper parts yellowish, linulated with dark brown, lore and throat white, sides, breast, and neck light yellow, linulated with dark brown.

Food: Worms, larvæ, caterpillars, and seeds.

Species VIII.—*Turdus Aurigaster.*

Migratory; very few obtained in Britain.

Size: Length, 8 in.; extent of wings, $11\frac{1}{4}$ in.; bill, $\frac{1}{6}$ in.

Colour: Head dark brown, neck, back, wings, and tail umber (the tail yellow underneath) throat and foreneck brown, passing into a dull white, bill, toes, and claws black.

Food: Seeds, berries, insects, &c.

Species IX.—*Turdus Saxatilis.*

Migratory; only one shot in Hertfordshire.

Size: Length, 8 in.; extent of wings, 13 in.; bill, $\frac{2}{3}$ in.

Colour: Male—head, neck, and fore part of back greyish blue, scapulars brownish, back white, upper tail coverts dark brown, wings and middle tail feathers dark brown, outer tail feathers and lower part of body chestnut red; female—upper parts brown, spotted with white, lower parts reddish, throat white, tail brown and reddish brown.

Food: Berries and insects.

Family IV.—SAXICOLINÆ.

Genus I.—ACCENTOR (CHANTERS).

Species I.—*Alcentor Alpinus* (*Alpine Chanter*).

Migratory; three shot in England.

Size: Length, 7 in.; extent of wings, 9 in.; bill, $1\frac{5}{12}$ in.

Colour: Brownish grey, throat white, with triangular black spots, sides brownish red, wing coverts tipped white.

Food: Seeds and insects.

Species II.—*Accentor Modularis* (*Hedge Sparrow*).

Permanently resident.

Size: Length, $6\frac{1}{4}$ in.; extent of wings, $8\frac{3}{4}$ in.; bill, $\frac{7}{12}$ in.

Colour: Brown, head, neck, and breast grey, streaked with brown.

Food: Seeds and insects.

Builds in hedgerows.

Lays 5 eggs, $\frac{5}{6}$ in. × $\frac{7}{12}$ in.; bluish.

Genus II.—ERITHACUS.

Species I.—*Erithacus Rubecula* (*Redbreast*).

Permanently resident.

Size: Length, $5\frac{2}{3}$ in.; extent of wings, 9 in; bill, $\frac{5}{12}$ in.

Colour: Upper parts dark olive, wing and tail feathers brown, face and breast red.

Food: Seeds, berries, and insects.

Builds in mossy banks, &c.

Lays 5 eggs, $\frac{9}{12}$ in. × $\frac{7}{12}$ in.; reddish white, spotted and freckled purple.

Genus III.—FRUTICICOLA.

Species I.—*Fruticicola Rubetra* (*Whinchat*).

Migratory.

Size: Length, $5\frac{1}{4}$ in.; extent of wings, $9\frac{1}{4}$ in.; bill, $\frac{5}{12}$ in.

Colour: Upper parts yellowish red, lower parts reddish, a yellowish band over the eye, bar of white down each side of neck, base of tail and patch on wing white.

Food: Seeds and insects.

Builds in low shrubs and tufts of grass (breeds twice in a season).

Lays 5 eggs, $\frac{2}{3}$ in. × $\frac{3}{6}$ in.; light blue.

Species II.—*Fruticicola Rubicola.*

Permanently resident.

Size: Length, $5\frac{1}{2}$ in.; extent of wings, 9 in.; bill, $\frac{5}{12}$ in.

Colour: Head and throat black, breast and lower parts brownish red, side of neck, tail coverts, and spot on wings white; upper parts dark brown, tipped with brownish red. Female—with a yellowish grey throat.

Food: Insects and seeds.

Builds in low shrubs and high grass.

Lays 5 eggs, $\frac{2}{3}$ in. × $\frac{7}{12}$ in.; bluish, with fine brown dots.

ERRATA.—Page 297, Genus II, Species I, for "Sturnus Grittatus" read *Sturnus Guttatus*; page 297, right hand column, line 12, for "towns" read *towers*; page 298, Family II, Genus I, and Species I, for "Muscipa" read *Muscicapa.*

THE OAK EGGAR MOTH (*BOMBYX QUERCUS*).

By R. LADDIMAN.

DOUBTLESS the majority of the entomological perusers of our "old friend," the "Naturalist's Note Book," are well acquainted with this common moth; but I take the liberty of writing a few notes on it, trusting they will be of some use to those who are less familiar with it. When I began the "fascinating" study of entomology, the Oak Eggar was one of the first moths that took my attention, and is therefore one of my most esteemed "moth friends." As soon as the leaves of the whitethorn begin to shoot, the "juvenile" caterpillars of *Bombyx Quercus* make their appearance. At this period of existence their prevailing colour is brown, with bright yellow markings along the middle of the back. It feeds, and grows very rapidly, changing its skin several times. When full-grown it is a very pretty object, and has—like many other larvæ—the power of rolling itself into a ring when touched; then its colour is velvety black, thickly covered with short hairs of an amber brown colour, interspersed with longer ones, so that the back of the creature is almost invisible, except when it rolls itself up, then a black ring is distinctly seen between every alternate segment, with an interrupted white line along each side. When it has reached its full size (which is to the length of about three or four inches) it ceases feeding, and commences preparations for the next stage of its existence, by spinning a very tough and compact cocoon, somewhat like an egg in shape (hence its name), varying from an inch to an inch and a half in length, into which small space our caterpillar of three inches manages to push itself. The cocoon when dry is very tough, and is interwoven with very short hairs from the body of the caterpillar; it then changes to a chrysalis of a dark brown colour. The cocoon is generally fixed on the faded branches of the whitethorn, or to the stems of grasses, etc. I should strongly advise my readers to handle the cocoons as little as possible, as the short hairs on the surface are extremely irritating to the skin, causing an unpleasant itching for hours afterwards.

From about the end of June to the beginning of July the perfect insect makes its appearance. The whole four wings of the male are deep mahogany brown in colour, each wing having a broad transverse bar of bright fulvous; the margin of the bar nearest the body is clear, the outer margin shading off gradually to a very dark brown; between this bar and the base of the fore wing is a spot of the purest white. The head, thorax, and body are of a deep mahogany brown above, and fulvous beneath. As is the case with most moths, the female is the largest in size, the colour of fulvous, the bar being narrower, and not so distinct as in the male; it has also a white spot on each of the fore wings.

The females of this moth possess an aroma which proves very attractive to the males. Many instances are on record of the attractive power of the females of *Quercus*, as well as other individuals of the family *Bombycidæ*.* I should advise my readers who may be in want of males to try an experiment or two with a female—it should be one fresh from the chrysalis, if possible. Having obtained one put it into a box, placing a piece of gauze over it to prevent its escape; take it into a field or lane where whitethorn hedges "reign supreme," and carefully watch it, and I think they will be rewarded with as many males as they require. In this way they have been taken by scores. The most wholesale instance I have heard of is recorded by a correspondent in the October number of "Science Gossip," who mentions having taken over fifty in this manner in one day.

The caterpillar of this moth seems to be very liable to the attacks of the ichneumons. Perhaps "Oak Eggar flesh" is a "dainty morsel" with them; I have lost a great many through this "tyrant" to the entomologist. I have had a great number of these larvæ, but have never been able to bring a fifth part of them to their perfect state; but it must not be all laid to the "ichneumon's door," for I have found a great many of the caterpillars dead in the cocoon. In 1867 I had four caterpillars; two of them came to perfection. In 1868 I had ten caterpillars, but none of them reached the perfect state. This year I have had thirteen larvæ and obtained only two females. Other of my entomological friends have been quite as unfortunate as myself. I should be glad to hear the experience of the readers of the "N. N. B." on this subject.

FERN CULTURE.

FERNS are the plants for the million. They are not confined to any particular country: they have a wide geographical distribution. Indigenous Ferns provide a treat of no common character to all who choose to collect them, and tend them with care afterwards, a much greater one than any other tribe of native plants, barring of course, a few of the choicer alpines. Beautiful as the majority of our native plants are, and particularly suited for ar-

---

* See "Moth Courtship," pp. 158, 192, and 222, of the N. N. B.

tificial cairns of rock-work, collectors and growers generally who have means at their disposal cannot rest contented with the possession of them alone. The love of plants and flowers in some natures is true and deep. Once the affection is grounded, its extension laterally follows intuitively, and the Fern collector, after he has explored and secured all that are good in the British Islands, longs to accommodate the more beautiful and interesting of the exotic species. The mason, the carpenter, the glazier, and the engineer are all consulted, and the upshot is that the house is reared—probably the beginning of a collection hereafter to be famous, possibly the whole thing ending in defeat. Unfortunately some people are defeated by having or allowing things of first importance to be done upon a wrong principle; and it is because of this, and because we occasionally see a good principle carried out, and corresponding success following it, that I beg to trouble your readers as a matter of interest to them, with the following line of success in a remarkably short period of time.

A very enthusiastic admirer of trees and plants, and one holding a fine collection of Coniferæ, of Roses, of Rhododendrons, of Hollies, and of border-flower plants generally, latterly took to Ferns. He had, after battling a little with indigenous plants—having with the aid of an excellent wife and grown up-family, collected much with his own hands—indulged in the very praiseworthy idea of having a house, not of the princely Mendelian character, which can only be imitated by the few, but of such a kind as thousands can well afford to rear. It was a simple span-roof, so erected as that the plants could never be more than a yard from the glass. This could not be filled at once with fine species, for it would be a too extravagant entrenchment upon the nice little sums that are apportioned out of a year's income for detached projects outside the household concerns altogether. It was made to do duty, therefore, for a collection of Coleuses, some Dracænas, and such-like plants, that put in a respectable appearance, and are come-at-able at a small figure. The one side was reserved for Ferns, and by extraordinary attention they have grown up wonderfully fine, getting up in the space of 18 months from the common nursery stock to be nice half specimen plants.

The house is 40 feet long, and about 12 feet wide, with a path up the centre. It is heated by water-pipes. On either side the path is a brick partition about 4 feet high. Within this enclosure is a bed of cocoanut fibre, which forms capital groundwork for the plants to rest upon, the finer particles at the top being especially fitted for rearing the thousands of spores that are shed indiscriminately over the surface. The heating is effected by hot water, a flow and return pipe round the house being sufficient to provide heat at all times. The atmosphere, nicely moderated in point of heat and moisture, is striking to the senses on entrance; and the health of the collection amply testifies to the good and simple mode planned and carried out for the successful cultivation of a tribe that is wonderfully beautiful at all times.

Prominent among the lot stood out Adiantum farleyense, than which a more beautiful species does not exist, especially seen under the influence of what might be called the semi-Wardian case culture adopted by Mr. Giar and his gardener Mr. Crombie, in the suburbs of Falkirk. It evidently delights at times to be bathed in a profusion of atmospheric moisture, for the quadripinnate fronds, that are handsome at all times, seem to grow with exuberance in a climate of the kind. The grand pendulous fronds in their varying shades of green, and the elegant pendulous habit with which they are invested, single this out as a plant suitable to be placed in company with any of flora's subjects. Without the case, in the ordinary atmosphere of the house, the following kinds were particularly noteworthy: The superb forms of Gymnogramma Laucheana, and the more beautiful G. Parsonsii, as if dipped in gold, contrast well with the tassal-like silvery G. Wettenhalliana; then G. Pearcei has very fine pinnæ, so multitudinous and so nicely cut as to look more beautiful in its relation, as a work of nature, than the finest piece of lace as a work of art.

Then the Maiden-Hairs (Adiantum) are quite captivating, and have probably more admirers than all the other races put together. Their fitness for intermixing with a variety of flowering plants is beyond question, and the wonder is why this sort of garnishing is not more common. A. concinnum latum, grown on cleverly, is a grand form, and well repays liberal treatment. A. curvatum, a plant not often seen in good condition is unusually promising, as it is decidedly beautiful, from the form and curvature of its pinnæ and generally good looking fronds. A glaucophyllum is an acquisition to the dwarf forms of the family. A. pubescens is another fine dwarf species, the fronds growing closely together, and the pinnules and pinnæ being invested with interest from the distinct pink tinge that adorns the normal green. A. cardiochlæna is a noble looking plant among some of its tiny compeers, and was here in fine style; the pinnæ lie very flat, and look very lustrous. A. cristatum and A. velutinum were both noticeable species in the collection, and well done.

Among other genera are Phegopteris (Polypodium) sancta, like a dwarf Trichomanes, elegant among others, and well adapted for a choice position. Polypodium appendiculatum had long and depending fronds with brown and crimson stipes and rachis, and contrasted well with the dark green pinnæ, being a capital plant for Acrophorus chærophyllus, at all events as grown in the collection in question, the light green fronds reaching to a good size, and the colour fine toned in proportion. Davallia aculeata is one of the most distinct of Ferns for contrasting with its fellows, the rachis being adorned with prickles, and the pinnæ of a bright shade of green. Pteris ternifolia has fine fronds with almost entire pinnæ of a distinct glaucous hue, and would strike a superficial observer. Others too numerous to particularize are doing equally well in the low-house of an intermediate temperature. The beauty of the groups is very much enhanced by a proper system of culture at work, and they all provide a feast to every onlooker, no matter what his plant proclivities may be. Add to this the no very great cost incurred from beginning to end, and the wonder is why their cultivation is not far more general. A real enjoyable hour could be spent daily amongst them, and the writer is indebted to Mr. Gair for giving him an opportunity of seeing so much upon so small and economical a scale. After all, there is some virtue yet in Cocoa-nut refuse, all other conditions being equal. The field of seedlings was apparently a fruitful one, for it yielded enough for reinforcing "our own collection," and supplying quantities to friends and acquaintances to try their "'prentice hand" upon. A.—*Gardener's Chronicle*, October.

ON SUBMERGED FOREST TREES IN CUMBERLAND BASIN.

NEAR the margins of the head waters of the Bay of Fundy are found, in several places, certain accumulations which geologists have distinguished by the name of "submerged forests." One of the most extensive and most plainly visible of these is to be found near the head of Cumberland Basin, and has been carefully examined and geographically described by Prof. Dawson in his "Acadian Geology," page 32; but similar appearances may be seen elsewhere on the shores of Chiegnecto Bay, and also of Cobequid Bay, and of some estuaries of streams emptying into Minas Basin. At the several places referred to, on the extensive slope of the flats between high water and low water mark, there are found embedded in the marine alluvium portions of trunks and also stumps of trees, the latter often remaining in their original position and resting upon the remains of upland soil, upon which they are supposed to have originally grown.

Great importance has been attached to these remains as evidences of a subsidence of the land generally in that section of the country where they are found. Dr. Dawson, with apparently no hesitation, utters the opinion that there has been a change of sea level here, the cause of which he says must be assigned to "either the rupture of a barrier previously excluding the sea water, or an actual sinking or subsidence of the whole western part of the Province." He believes that "a subsidence has taken place over a considerable area, and to a depth of about forty feet;" and this subsidence he supposes to have been gradual. Entertaining, as I most certainly do, a profound respect for so eminent an authority, I must nevertheless take the liberty of at least questioning this conclusion, and of expressing the opinion that too much importance has been attached to the appearance of these submerged tree stumps. I shall briefly give my reasons for doing so in this paper.

I am not aware that any evidences of a subsidence of the land in the Western or Northern part of Nova Scotia, have been discovered, except these appearances at Cumberland Basin, and a few other similar localities. If these appearances can be sufficiently accounted for through other causes of a distinctly local character—causes which we may now see in daily operation, we may reasonably conclude that the subsidence is *not proven*. The action of the tides about the heads of the Bay of Fundy may easily be imagined even by those who have never witnessed them. Wherever a vertical surface, whether of rock or earth, is presented to the tidal current, the bank so exposed is rapidly worn away by the great force of the current. The matter thus swallowed up by the water and held in suspension by it for a time, is eventually deposited upon the flats, or gentle slopes, over which the tides flow. It sometimes happens that the alluvial deposits thus made again undergo the same process. If we examine any of the channels intersecting the marshes formed by the Bay of Fundy tides, we shall find that, throughout a large proportion of their length, there, is a gradual change going on in the *locus* of the channel itself. On one side of it we shall usually find an abrupt bank of alluvial soil; on the other, a broad expanse of recently deposited mud, sloping gradually from high-water down to low-water mark. This bank is being constantly sapped, and its component materials carried away by the tide which, on the other hand, is as constantly depositing a corresponding quantity on the opposite slope. Thus, where artificial means are not taken to prevent it, the older marsh land is being daily engulphed whilst new marsh is being made; but, as of course, the upland banks and sandstone cliffs bordering the Bay and its estuaries are constantly being subjected to this same sapping process, the whole area of marine alluvial deposits is steadily and rapidly enlarging. As might be supposed from the great abrading force of the tides of the Bay of Fundy, combined with the effect of winter frosts in this climate, the work of disintegration and removal goes on rapidly among even the firmest materials, which go to form the shores of the head waters of the Bay; these are the new red sandstone of Colchester, Hants, and Kings, and the soft carboniferous sandstones and shales of Cumberland Counties. Still more rapidly does this process go on where the shore happens to consist of a deep gravelly upland soil. To the existence of such soils at several localities on the margin of the channels of the Bay and to their rapid washing away by the tides may, I think, be attributed the appearances at Cumberland Basin and elsewhere, which are supposed to be the remains of extensive submerged forests.

We find all the broader expanses of marine alluvium, or marsh land, about both arms of the Bay of Fundy, dotted with isolated patches of upland. These are called islands, even where they are not bathed by the water on any side; because of their island-like appearance as they uprear themselves above the sea-like level of the marsh. Some of these on the shores of Cobequid Bay and Minas Basin show, where sections of them have been made by the action of the tides, beds of new red sandstone covered with a deep layer of soil; but, for the most part, both there and elsewhere, after going beneath the surface soil, we find them to consist merely of beds of gravel. Where not denuded of their growing timber, its prevalent varieties, especially where the gravelly sub-soil is found, are usually pine, oak, and birch, and often differ from those of the neighbouring main upland. These so-called islands vary in area from a few roods up to several hundred acres; and in elevation from 10 or 15, up to 60 feet above the level of the surrounding alluvium. They abound in the marshes of Truro and Onslow. Long Island and Boot Island, on the seaward margin of the Grand Pre are notable examples of them; and others are to be seen of smaller dimensions in the marshes skirting the rivers of Kings County. We find numbers of them again in the broad alluvial plains of Cumberland and Westmoreland. In the midst of the great Tintamarr there is one which comprises several farm steadings; and there is another of comparatively large area near the mouth of the Missiquash, and but a short distance from the site of the submerged stumps described by Dr. Dawson. It is no part of my present purpose to discuss the question of how these islands were formed. I think, however, that the supposed subsidence of the western coast of Nova Scotia may be accounted for by the disappearance of one of them in the vicinity of Fort Lawrence ridge in Cumberland County.

I have already referred to the abrading force of the tides upon the banks of their containing channels. The rapidity with which the tidal current saps and removes the material forming those banks is very remarkable. Cobequid Bay forms in part the boundary between the townships of Truro and Onslow. Farmers now mow grass and make hay in Onslow on the identical spot where, within the memory of many persons still living, the same processes were carried on in Truro, the Bay having changed its bed to the extent of its whole width within so brief a period. This is unmistakeably proved at one particular spot by the fact that the remains of a breakwater formerly built in Truro have gradually become "annexed" to Onslow. It is possible that in other localities the tides have made equally great encroachments on the Onslow shore. Such being the case, where the shore of the Bay consists of a compact, clayey alluvium, it may easily be conceived that the abrading effect of the tide certainly could not be much less where the enclosing banks consist of a loose upland soil resting upon beds of gravel. If a proof of this were required, it might be found at Savage's Island, in Truro. This is one of those many isolated patches of upland already referred to, which lies upon the immediate southern margin of Cobequid Bay. In the old times of the French dominion in Acadia, the northeastern and most elevated part of this island was consecrated and used as a burial-ground; and it is still so used by the Micmac Indians in that part of the Province. We may reasonably suppose that the old Acadian French would not bury their dead very near the brow of what must have been, even then, a steep, but no doubt wooded bank, exposed to the destructive action of the tides. At all events, that destructive action has been so great that so long ago as five-and-twenty years since, or more, many of the graves on Savage's Island had been opened at the bottom, and human bones were occasionally to be seen strewn down the steep bank where the undermining tide had produced land-slides.

Now, let us suppose that, some centuries since, there existed one of these gravelly and then wooded mounds, similar to others now to be seen in that vicinity, on the margin of the Cumberland Basin, at the most western extremity of the marsh which extends from the mouth of the Missiquash to the mouth of the La Planche. A glance at the map will show that on no other part of the shores of Chiegnecto Bay is the tidal current likely to strike with greater force than on this very spot. What would take place? The tide would gradually undermine the upland bank opposed to it. All the finer particles of earth would be carried away by the water. The coarser and more ponderous pebbles and boulders, if any, would sink to a lower level. Meanwhile the surface soil, being above the immediate action of the water, would still remain like a closely woven mat, held together by the intertwined roots of growing trees and the rootlets of grasses and other vegetable productions. Eventually this undermined and mat-like surface would slide, or drop, into the water in large flakes. The submerged turf would almost immediately collect a coating of mud from the overflowing tide; whilst the trunks of the still standing trees would be broken or ground off by the action of floating ice, the stumps and roots remaining embedded in the bottom of the Basin. This process, which may be witnessed on a small scale on the banks of any stream, would be continued until the whole hillock or island disappeared.

I believe that, in fact, this is what has taken place at the spot, off Fort Lawrence ridge, so particularly described by Dr. Dawson. This is only a conjecture, it is true: but it is one which seems to be favored by more facts than that other conjecture that there has been a recent subsidence of the whole western or northern coast of Nova Scotia. There are no evidences in confirmation of the latter view—at least none that I am aware of—except the appearance of these submerged tree-stumps and turf in Cumberland Basin, and in some other spots about the Bay of Fundy, where their presence can be still more easily accounted for upon the former hypothesis. These vegetable remains cannot be of very great age. We have continuous records of the history of Nova Scotia for over two hundred years. We may fairly assume that these forest fragments became submerged within that period. Had there been, within that period, any sudden subsidence of a large tract of country to the depth of forty feet, it would almost unquestionably have been attended with some very striking phenomena, which the inhabitants of the country could not have failed to observe, and of which they would have handed down to us some written testimony. Had there been, within that period, any subsidence, either sudden or gradual, to such an extent, we should surely find upon the coasts of the country numerous evidences of it which could not be explained away upon any other hypothesis than that of there having been such a subsidence. We have no such additional evidences. I therefore think that, for the present, we are justified in concluding that there has been no such subsidence, and that the instances of the submergence of forest trees, herein referred to, are local and exceptional, and are attributable simply to the action of the tidal currents in the Bay of Fundy.—*Nova Scotian Institute of Natural Science.*

THE DRIVERS.

A VERY few hours' residence in the tropical regions of Africa brings one into a very undesirable familiarity with that extensive tribe of insects, the ants, some species of which are found in all parts of the world, but which are greatly multiplied in the tropical regions of the globe. Africa, it is believed, can boast of a greater variety than any other land. Their name here is legion. They are everywhere; out of doors and in doors; in your food and in your bed, determined to share both. They are of all sizes; some so small that they pass easily between the threads of common muslin, and even insinuate themselves into your watch as it hangs in your chamber; others measure nearly an inch in length. The habits and food of the different species differ greatly. Some, as the Termites, called white ants (which, however, are not true ants, but Neuropterous insects), eat vegetable matter exclusively, destroying our houses, furniture, and clothing; others are carnivorous; others feed upon sugar or the sweet juices of plants. Any one of the many species found in so great abundance would furnish sufficient material for months of study for the enthusiastic naturalist.

It is of one species only that I propose to speak, the Drivers (*Anomma arcens* of Westwood?); an insect whose life-history is yet very imperfectly known, but of whose habits the dweller in the tropical regions of West Africa cannot long remain ignorant.

The Driver ants vary in size from ¾ in. to 1 in. in length, the soldiers being the largest. They are of a glossy jet-black colour, with a large head armed with exceedingly sharp, branching forceps, or mandibles, with which they seize and cut up their prey. They do not appear to have any fixed habitations, as do the Termites, but excavate the earth from between the roots of trees, and in the cavity thus formed lay their eggs and rear their young, and from which they issue in incredible numbers (literally millions of millions) to go upon their raids.

The night is chosen for their foraging expeditions. In the midst of social enjoyment the stirring announcement is made, "Here are the drivers!" and instantly, as by an electric shock, all are on the alert to escape a personal attack. Lanterns and bamboo torches are lighted, and a search made about the house to learn the direction taken by the assailants; and if in their usual numbers the house is often left to them entirely for hours. And still more unwelcome at the hour of midnight is the bleating of sheep, and cackling of hens, in the enclosure. "All hands" are awakened from their slumbers, and the whole yard lighted; the animals are released from confinement and left to take care of themselves; the fowls removed to a place of safety, if one is to be found; but if neglected and left without the chance of escape their destruction is sure.

The Drivers are alike the enemy of man and beast, though there are times when their visits are most welcome. On their approach every kind of vermin is seized with consternation, and seeks safety in flight. Centipedes, cockroaches, scorpions, &c., &c., leave their hiding-places, and are seeking places of greater security, only to fall at last into the clutches of their relentless foe, from whom there is no escape.

An invading army could not exhibit a higher state of discipline than is seen in the movements of these insects. They enter a house usually at one point, where a strong guard is stationed to defend the pass; they then branch off right and left, and again divide, and subdivide, till the whole ground is completely covered; not an inch is left unexplored, and every crack and cranny is entered, giving but little hope of escape to any creature that may be found secreted there. Attacking their prey they plunge their forceps into it, regardless of the size or strength of their antagonist. Nothing will cause them to relax their hold. The animal or insect writhes and twists under the pain, but his case is rendered more hopeless every moment by additions to the number of his assailants; at length, when completely exhausted by struggling, he yields to his fate, and is despatched at the victors' leisure.

The attack goes on simultaneously, in different parts of the house. Animal substance being almost exclusively the food of the Drivers an immense number of the smaller vermin that infest our dwellings are consumed by them, and some of the larger animals when confined are also destroyed by them. They have been known to attack a human being, when rendered helpless by disease, and cause his death in a few hours. It is interesting to see a band of these midnight marauders returning home from the scene of plunder on the approach of day. Issuing from the same place they entered they are each seen bearing away some trophy with them; a joint of a cockroach's leg, the body of a spider, or the larvæ of some insects, &c., are the various spoils. As the labourers pass on with their loads they are guarded by a large body of soldiers which are stationed along the sides of their path; or, if they are to pass through a place of uncommon exposure, these soldiers form a covered passage, by standing upon each other's back and hooking their forceps together: through this arch thus formed the labourers pass in safety.

When they leave a house it must be from some signal from the leaders, as some of them are seen running from one to another evidently giving command. The retreat is made in good order; not one individual is ever left behind. They often bridge narrow streams of water when these come across their path, by going in large numbers upon a flexible plant on one side of the stream until their weight causes it to bend to the other side. For courage and activity the soldiers have no equal; they know no fear, and when on duty they stand with their shining black heads erect and forceps open, ready to seize on any passing animal. No horse, donkey, or dog can be induced to cross their path, seeming to have an instinctive dread of them; and woe be to the individual, man or beast, who gets among them at night. If a twig is drawn through their ranks they instantly close their forceps upon it; and others in turn close upon their bodies and legs, till a mass of them is seen at the end of the stick looking like a bunch of curled hair.

These insects have no eyes, but their sense of smell is very acute, for if the breath be blown on them from the distance of some feet they are instantly in motion, running to and fro with the greatest speed, evidently aware of the approach of some living being. Though at times they are of great service in ridding our houses of cockroaches and other vermin, yet, when their haunt is near, their visits are much too frequent to be tolerated. Various methods are used to get rid of them, though often with but little success. When they are in large numbers in a small space, scalding water is perhaps the best method. By throwing straw or other combustible material upon them, and suffering them to overrun it (which they quickly do), they may then be destroyed by applying a match to the mass. Gunpowder, also, is sometimes used in their holes; hot ashes, spirits of turpentine, and other articles of the same kind, are useful to turn them from their course. When a live coal is dropped in their way they immediately attack it, though hundreds may perish in doing so. They are very sensitive to the light of the sun, which is fatal to them. They seldom move during the day, and then only during cloudy days, choosing then the dark woods or thick grass. Their rate of progression is about two yards in a minute, and in their journeys from place to place they go from four to eight abreast. I have seen a stream of Drivers crossing an open path at six o'clock in the morning, and at six at night their number was undiminished. How long they had been passing before I saw them, or how long it continued, I am unable to say. Their path, from constant travel, became quite worn and smooth. The natives are very careful to remove all grass from the vicinity of their houses, as a means of keeping off these pests.—By Dr. C. A. Perkins, in *American Naturalist*.

ON THE BRITISH GEOMETRÆ.
By E. J. S. CLIFFORD.
PART XI.

IN several of our English counties, and in many Scotch localities, the Blue-bordered Carpet (*Melanthia rubiginata*) occurs pretty frequently. It is a beautiful little geometer, and one of that class which seems to stand out conspicuously as possessing different characteristics from most of this family of our moths. The fore wings are white; they have a dark and almost triangular blotch at the base, and another somewhat larger on the costal margin. These are of a smoky black colour. The head and thorax are brown, with small white markings. The caterpillar of this insect appears to be full grown about the beginning of June, and then rests tightly attached to its food-plant. The colouring of the body is apple-green, and there is a dark stripe or band down the back. On each side there occurs a yellowish or greenish stripe. The food of this caterpillar is blackthorn and bullace: it is stated that it occasionally is found feeding upon damson as cultivated in gardens. It spins a loose web, and changes therein to a smooth brown chrysalis. There is a variety of this species in which the blue colour of the hind margin is more or less spread over the wing, and another in which the wings are entirely of this colour—a most curious circumstance. Next in our descriptions we come to the Purple Bar (*Melanthia ocellata*), a striking species occurring in England, Ireland, and Scotland. The eggs of this moth are deposited on the lady's bedstraw in the month of June. The caterpillar is full-fed by the middle of July, when its appearance is as follows:—Colour of the head and body yellow-brown, tinged with olive-green; the head has three parallel longitudinal stripes, almost white; and the body has numerous and distinct white markings. At the end of July the caterpillar spins together little stems of the bedstraw close to the ground, and forming the slightest covering; they change to brown and shining chrysalides. The Purple Bar has the wings creamy white, with a triangular blotch at the base, and a broad band in the middle, both of which are of a rich dark brown colour. The hind wings are white, with a single spot, called the discoidal spot, in the centre of the wings.

A very striking insect is that called the Beautiful Carpet (*Melanthia albicillata*), which occurs in various parts of England, in some Irish counties, but not, according to Newman, in Scotland. The ground colour of the fore wings is a creamy white, with two large brown blotches, one at the base, the other near the tip; there are a number of smoke-coloured markings running across the wings; the hind margin and fringe are smoke-coloured also. The hind wings are creamy white, with two delicate lines extending across them. The larvæ have been reared from the eggs by Mr. Beauchamp, who found that they fed by preference on bramble. They are velvety-green, with a few hairs, and a brownish head; a series of yellowish-brown spots along the back, the under side green, marked with whitish lines. The perfect insect appears in June and July. The young collector is usually much gratified when he can add to his collection the Argent and Sable (*Melanippe hastata*), which does not appear to occur at all commonly, though it has been taken in various parts of the three kingdoms. All the wings are white, chequered with a number of spots and markings of black; the fringe is alternately black and white; the antennæ are black, with white rings, the thorax black, and the body grayish. The caterpillar is rather singular; the segments wrinkled, with a leathery appearance, the colour black or brownish black; on each segment is a white spot, and above it a minute black dot. The birch and the sweet gale furnish it with food; and it prefers to spin the leaves together, when it feeds under cover. About the end of August it is mature, and becomes a chrysalis, appearing in the moth state the following June. Nearly allied to the last, and somewhat resembling it, is the Small Argent and Sable (*Melanippe tristata*), but this seems to occur principally in the North of

England and in Scotland. In Ireland, Mr Birchall reports that it is common. The caterpillar, which may be found in the hedge bed-straw in July and August, rests in nearly a straight posture, but when disturbed rolls partly round. It is slightly attenuated in front, of a brown colour, striped with black, with two white dots on each segment. The species passes the winter in the chrysalis state, and the moth appears in June. The fore wings are smoky black, with two white bars: one near the base of the wing is narrow; the second is angled, and interrupted by black dots; the hind margin is tinged with brown, and marbled with grey. The hind wings have the same ground-colour as the fore wings, with a broad white bar, also interrupted, and with two white lines at the base; the head, thorax, and body are smoky-gray.

The Chalk Carpet (*Melanippe procellata*) is at once a handsome and imposing moth. Its fore wings are white: they have various dark markings; the ground-colour is smoky brown, varied with rusty-brown. The hind wings are of the same colour as the fore wings, with a few transverse dark lines, which are parallel to the hind margin. The head and thorax are dark brown, the body white. Towards the end of July the young caterpillars appear. The full-grown appearance of this species in the caterpillar state is cylindrical in form, and of a dark wainscot-brown colour. The head is small, dotted with black. On the back of each segment are two or four black dots; the spiracles are all of a black colour. The food of this caterpillar is the traveller's-joy; when full-fed it spins a slight web, remaining in the chrysalis state throughout the winter. In May, June, and July, the moth itself appears. It is common in the southern counties of England, but is not reported from Ireland and Scotland.

In June also the Sharp Angled Carpet (*Melanippe unangulata*) flies in the woods of several English counties. This moth has the fore wings smoky brown at the base, marbled with pale brown and grey, and bounded by a zigzag white line. The middle of the wings is occupied by a broad dark band, which is sharply angled on its outer margin. Beyond this is a white zigzag band. The head, thorax, and body are marbled with grey and brown. The caterpillar of the Sharp Angled Carpet is stout, and rather attenuated at both ends. The head is brown, beautifully dotted and marked with black. The body is smoky brown, delicately veined and mottled. Its food is the common chickweed, and it is full-grown about the beginning of August. At this time it spins a cocoon on or just below the surface of the ground, remaining in the chrysalis state during the winter months. The species is occasionally double-brooded in confinement in captivity, but not in a state of nature. June is the month in which the perfect insect should be looked after.

Beautifully varied are the wings of the Wood Carpet (*Melanippe rivata*), a not uncommon species in our southern counties. This moth has the basal portion of the fore wings smoky grey, bounded by a slender white line. Beyond this is a slender grey bar. The hind wings are pale grey, rather darker at the base, and having three darker waved lines before the middle of the wing. Head and thorax are both brown grey, the body grey, with two black spots placed on the back of each segment. The caterpillar of this moth is of a dingy brown colour, variegated and mottled most beautifully with darker lines. The food is the common great bedstraw occurring in hedges. About the end of July the species is full-fed, when it spins a cocoon on the surface of the earth. In July the moth is on the wing. Its favourite localities have been already indicated.

A very common geometer in nearly all parts of the United Kingdom is that called the Common Carpet (*Melanippe subtristata*). The basal part of its fore wings is of a smoky gray colour, bounded by a white line. Beyond this is a gray-brown bar, then a double white bar, and then a smoke-coloured band, which is traversed by darker and whiter slender lines. The caterpillar of the Common Carpet feeds on the same plant as our last-named species. The body is brown, variegated, and mottled, several of the segments having a black line down the back, while others are adorned with white markings. About the end of June it is full-fed, when it spins a cocoon on the earth, changing therein to a chrysalis with no particular markings. The Common Carpet is a double-brooded species; it appears first in May, and then again in July, towards the end of the month. Some entomologists are of opinion that this species and *M. rivata* are one and the same in kind, only varying considerably in appearance. Newman, however, seems to look upon them as indisputably separate and distinct for elaborate reasons, which he assigns at length in one of his works. Several columns are consumed in the pointing out the differences between the two; with these, however, we shall not now delay our readers. Now to one or two other kinds before we close this paper.

The Silver ground Carpet (*Melanippe montanata*) is a very pale geometer, so pale indeed that it looks almost like a "Small White" while on the wing. It is a beautifully delicate little moth, with the fore wings creamy white, and an ochreous blotch at the base. The costal margin has several transverse brown spots; the hind margin has a broad but pale band of smoky brown, intersected throughout by a scallopped white line. The hind wings are nearly white, with a few indistinct markings, and the discoidal spot. The caterpillar of this moth is of a pale brown colour, with a number of various markings, differing in colour and shape; there is a narrow stripe down the back of nearly all the segments of a blood-red tint, intersected with black and smoke-colour. It feeds on the primrose, on which it also hybernates, being full-fed about the end of March. Throughout the summer the moth may be seen on the wing. It is common in England, Ireland, and Scotland. Lastly, we allude to the Galium Carpet (*Melanippe galiata*). This species has the fore wings white, with a smoky blotch at the base; the costal margin has a black cloud marking half-way between the median band and the tip; and there is also another in the middle of the hind margin. The caterpillar feeds on two kinds of the bedstraw. It is double-brooded, the second brood occurring early in September. The markings of this species vary very much in the caterpillar state. In June the moth appears on the wing. It is more particularly attached to the chalk districts of Kent and Surrey, where it is often very abundant.

OUR WADING BIRDS.

No. 6.—THE RINGED PLOVER.

BY ALEXANDER CLARK KENNEDY.

HAPPY the man who takes a delight, however small it may be, in the works of the Almighty! Time need never hang heavily on his hands; there is no cause for him to complain that he can find nothing to do; he need never spend an idle or unprofitable hour, for the study of nature is, as all know, the work of a lifetime; and when we think we know a great deal, experience will quickly shew us that our knowledge is a mere smattering, and that it is impossible to learn too much of the beautiful creatures which surround us. However much time we devote to this absorbing pursuit, however unflagging our application, whatever the means of gaining fresh information at our disposal, we shall very often find ourselves ignorant of the *minutiæ*; and the lines of the poet Young are especially applicable to the study of natural history:—

Think naught a trifle, though it small appear,
Small sands the mountain, moments make the year.

A hot afternoon in June or July has often found us stretched at full length among the smooth, round stones, and short, wiry grass, behind a bank of shingle; far away from our fellow men, with the cloudless sky above our head, and the deep green ocean rolling majestically a few hundred yards from us, and breaking with pleasant murmurs on the pebbly beach. Yes! we have ever loved to be alone with nature; the turmoil of business o'er, and the world and its doings cast behind our back for awhile, we are always happy in the innocent occupation of observing the seemingly insignificant habits and apparently uninteresting forms of animal life. Let us return in thought to an hour thus pleasantly passed, and abandon ourselves for a short time to the contemplation of the scene before our eyes. Carefully raising our head above the shingly bank which hides us from view, and which stretches for several miles on either side, for it is the high water mark, we cautiously peer through the rough grass which waves gently in the warm wind, and gaze upon the sea. Far out on its bosom glide the trim merchantmen, with their white sails glancing in the sun, bound perhaps for the tropics, or returning, may be, from the distant north; and the brown canvass of the little fishing boats, which venture much nearer shore than the large craft, contrasts well with the background of blue sky, as they rise and fall with the slight swell. To our right lies a vast expanse of open marsh land; behind is a small tract of alternate sand, shingle and patches of stunted grass; and to the left hand, at the distance of about two miles, rise majestic cliffs, on whose beetling ledges we can see by the aid of a field glass, the shining white plumage of the kittiwakes, and the pied guillemots can be descried standing soberly in long lines, while many a queer little puffin is diving among the surf below; and numerous detachments of sombre cormorants have just left their nests—in more than one of which we can see the gaping mouths of the youngsters—and are winging their way with their swift, strong flight, through the air, to yonder shallows, where they will doubtless find a plentiful supply of sand-dabs to appease their craving appetites. The tide is slowly retreating, and tiny islets of gleaming sand by degrees make themselves visible above the water, and are soon taken possession of by flocks of dunlins. In that still pool, close to the beach, a pair of oyster-catchers are washing themselves, and sending into the air little clouds of silver spray as they chase each other hither and thither; and not far from them a single young bird of the same species is endeavouring to open a mussle with its yet tender bill. Several pairs of kittiwakes are feeding on a detached bank of sand; and upon yon dark rock, covered with green shiny seaweed, a couple of hundred yards distant from the shore, and over which the waves now and then dash with violence, a magnificent great black-backed fellow—a king of gulls—has taken his stand; while his mate is floating motionlessly with the tide at a little distance from the spot on which her lord and master has thought fit to alight.

While we are looking at a small party of redshanks which have just arrived from the distant marshes, a loud chorus of discordant cries betokens the coming of a flock of curlews, who are generally among the earliest to reach the feast which the exposed sands offer them. Looking above into the fathomless sky, to-day bright enough for Italy, we perceive a score or more of silken plumaged terns sailing around on outspread pinions. Now and then one leaves its companions, and gradually lowering its graceful flight as it passes over the spot where we are lying, reaches the retiring waves, when suddenly dropping downwards almost perpendicularly, it dips its bright carmine bill beneath the surface, hardly touching the water with its pink feet, and seizing the luckless sand-eel just behind the head, returns with swiftly beating wings to the young "sea-swallows," who are patiently awaiting the return of their parent far up upon the beach behind. We have noticed only a single pair of herring gulls to-day, although usually plenty are to be found along the shore, and none of the dear little terns (*Sterna minuta*) have made their appearance, so we conclude that they must have gone off upon a distant fishing expedition. Several long-winged swifts are skimming about overhead, and numberless sand martins are chasing the tiny insects which swarm in the warm sunlight. But what are those small black and white birds, with long, yellowless, and well-shaped round heads, who seem so restless, and who are ever and anon flitting from one spot to another, and often approaching within a few yards of us? They are the ringed dotterel; dear little creatures, whose confiding nature and picturesque appearance have made us their firm friend, and seldom do we take the life of these tiny sea birds when shooting on the shore, sparing them in remembrance of the pleasure they have afforded us in days gone by. They are, indeed, trustful little fellows; one old bird discovered our retreat just now, and at this moment seven plovers are looking at the intruder on their domain with wonder expressed in their bright eyes, as they run along the shingly bank towards us; but as the dog, on whose shaggy back our head is resting, pushes his large black nose through the grass to see what is going on, an old gull as she flies overhead catches sight of him and utters a hoarse warning cry, on which the entire body of dotterel take themselves off and join a larger company on a distant bank. Looking at our watch, we find that the time has slipped rapidly away, and we have stayed much longer than we had intended among the sea birds, so we hurry homewards as fast as our limbs, which have become quite stiff from the effects of remaining so long in the same cramped position, will allow. The ringed plovers accompany us the whole way along the shore, flitting anxiously round and round in pairs, and sometimes swooping at the old retriever, who has been amusing himself by hunting among the stones for their eggs.

If we visit the same beach on a winter's morning, we find the scene vastly changed. The bitter wind pierces us through and through, and the sand is dashed in our face mercilessly by the blast, which sweeps towards us over the cold grey sea, whose waves are foaming with fury as they break with a dull roar upon the shore. The redshanks are off with a wild clamour as soon as their sentinels catch sight of our form in the distance, and the terns have long since left their pleasant summer quarters; and but few of the numerous gulls which we noticed then are now remaining. The continued frost seems to have emaciated the curlews cruelly; and even the hardy cormorants are compelled to quit their natural element and seek shelter from the chilling blasts in the inmost recesses and cosiest nooks of the gaunt, dreary cliffs. A few wigeon may be occasionally seen swimming in the quieter pools somewhat sheltered by the rocks; and you will probably meet a company of hooded crows gorging themselves on some stinking sheep, or large fish, which has been cast up by the tide. Everything wears a dreary aspect. But the little ringed dotterel is still a companion for you, and the cold apparently does not affect his constitution to any great degree, for he seems lively enough as he flits on in front of you, cheering your spirits with his plaintive cry, and charming your eyes with his pretty piebald plumage.

In some parts of England the ringed plover (*Charadrius hiaticula*) is to a degree migratory; but on most of the coasts of the United Kingdom some are to be seen throughout the year. They form immense flocks during cold weather, and often keep company with the dunlins which frequent the great tidal rivers in the winter months. During the spring and autumn small parties may be met with by river sides and near large reservoirs many miles inland. The flight of this species is pretty, and is generally only taken for short distances, as the bird seems of a particularly restless disposition, continually hovering around an intruder; and if its eggs are in the immediate vicinity, it is by no means an uncommon thing for the old bird to swoop at a dog. The ringed plovers pair towards the end of February, or beginning of March, and nidification commences in April. The nest in which the eggs are deposited scarcely deserves such a name, for it consists merely of a slight depression in the loose sand, or among pebbles and small stones; and the colour of the surrounding ground is generally so admirably adapted to that of the eggs, that constant practice and a good pair of eyes are necessary to enable one to discover them without the aid of a four-footed companion. The eggs, which are invariably four in number, are of a pale brown or buff ground, with ash and black spots and blotches of darker brown; they vary, however, to a considerable extent. They are sought for by fishermen on many parts of our coasts, and are by no means bad eating; many being sent to London, where they are disposed of to the public as plover's eggs, and fetch a high price.

The adult bird has a broad black gorget on its breast, narrower at the back of the neck; the forehead is black, and a white streak passes through the eye, under which a black line extends along the cheek from the bill, which is yellow at the extremity and brown at the base. The lower portions of the plumage are pure white, and the back and crown of the head have a pale ashen tint. Young birds are covered with the fluffy down peculiar to all the little members of the British wading birds.

TO A LADYBIRD.

(From *Fun*.)

Ladybird, ladybird, fly upon me,
  Although it is whispered, it's true,
That when you're matured you begin with a B,
  And the letter that follows is U.
You won't find a poet your praises to sing,
  If you happen to end with a G;
But in the meantime you're a beautiful thing,
  So, ladybird, fly upon me!

Ladybird, ladybird, fly upon me,
  And do me the favour to sip
The delicate nectar you happen to see
  On the bud of my roseate lip.
If, when you're developed, you happen to cling
  To my drapery, squashed you will be;
But in the meantime you're a beautiful thing,
  So, ladybird, fly upon me!

"YORICK."

SOME PHENOMENA OF LIGHT.

LIGHT takes eight minutes to travel from the sun to the earth. When it reaches the earth its properties may be tested by experiment, and it is found that light may be made to turn wheels and to lift weights, for it possesses inseparable heating powers, and heating force can always be made to do work. Light, therefore, is motion of some kind, or it could not impart motion to solids. At one time it was supposed that luminous bodies emitted particles with enormous velocity, which particles, impinging on the retina of the human eye, caused the sensation of light. This view was held by Newton. The emission theory, however, has been proved to be untenable, and now no doubt remains that light is the wave motion of an almost infinitely elastic fluid, which fills all space from star to star, and is believed to bathe the atoms of all solid, liquid, and gaseous bodies. This fluid is known as the "interstellar ether."

Waves of sunlight are of different lengths, all mixed together. But these waves may be separated from each other, and spread out upon a white screen, with the shortest waves at one end and the longest at the other, all the intermediate gradations being orderly arranged between the two extremes. From this power of separating, measuring, and examining the waves, have resulted all the modern discoveries in spectrum analysis, phosphorescence, and florescence. A simple method of separating the waves, is to take a glass prism and hold it horizontally where the sunlight is streaming in through a window. The waves, passing through the prism, will be bent out of their course, and some of them will be thrown upon the wall at the other end of the room. The rays thus thrown will be coloured, with the red at one end and the blue and violet at the other, with yellow and green in between. Colour, in fact, is nothing but a phenomenon of wave-length, a short wave producing the sensation of blue, longer wave producing the idea of yellow, and a still longer giving the sensation of red. There are a vast number of invisible waves coming to us from the sun, some of them too short and others too long to produce any sensation upon the retina or nerves of the human eye. In fact, the invisible waves of the sun are far hotter and do about nine times more towards warming the earth than those waves which excite the sensation of vision.

On examining the colours, or "spectrum," thrown upon the wall by the prism, it will be seen that the blue waves are most bent from the original direction of the sunbeam, and the red rays least bent from that direction. In other words, red and blue rays have different refrangibilities. At one time it was believed that the refrangibility of any particular ray could not be made to vary, but the discovery of fluorescence has shown that under certain conditions the refrangibility of light does vary. To show this, a good supply of blue and violet light is necessary, such light consisting of short waves, and the experiments are very beautiful.

Choose a room where the sun shines in through the window, and then block out all the light, by means of a shutter or otherwise, taking care that all cracks are stopped. Then cut a hole about six inches square in the shutter, and stop the hole with two or three thicknesses of rich deep blue or bluish purple glass. A broad beam of deep blue or purple light from the sun will thus stream down into the otherwise dark room. Then hold in the deep-blue light a bottle or other article made of uranium glass.

Ornamental bottles made of this glass, which is sometimes called "canary" glass, because of its light-yellow colour, are commonly on sale in chemists' shops. They are plentifully made to hold smelling-salts, and may cost from sixpence to three shillings each. The blue light should be very deep and not very not brilliant. When the uranium glass bottle is held in it, the bottle will appear to glow with great beauty, with all the brilliancy of a glow-worm, or as if white hot. Here, then, the short, dark-blue waves have fallen upon glass, and that glass has taken them up, and lengthened them out into yellow, or much longer, waves.

Instead of the uranium glass just mentioned, a solution of freshly-dissolved pure sulphate of quinine may be held in the blue rays to show fluorescent phenomena, but the result is not quite so striking as with uranium glass. White rags, wetted and dripping with the solution, will shine like the moon, when held in the blue rays. Any rich blue glass will do for the window, about three thicknesses of the common cobalt blue glass of the shops being usually sufficient when sunlight is used. Violet glass, not too red, gives still more beautiful effects, the richest of the whole being produced by manganese glass. In lecture experiments on fluorescence, the electric lamps are used, with disks of manganese glass in front of the condensing lenses. A very good ghost has been made, by clothing a man in a dress covered with beads of uranium glass, with a mask on his face, covered with sulphate of quinine. When such a man is illuminated with scarcely visible violet rays of low brilliancy, he glows out like the full moon in a dark room, and has a hot appearance, as if newly arrived from an unpleasant place, the road to which is paved with good intentions—at least, so we are taught by those who profess to know the locality.

Fluorescent bodies lengthen out the short invisible waves beyond the blue end of the spectrum, so as to render them visible; at least, this is the opinion of Professor Stokes, who has written one hundred quarto pages in the "Philosophical Transactions" of the Royal Society (1852), in order to demonstrate it; but since then the still more curious phenomena of phosphorescence have been studied by very able writers both at home and abroad, and appear in many cases to be very intimately connected with those of fluorescence.—*Scientific Review*.

BEAVERS.

I HAVE been for three years almost constantly engaged in trapping beavers, so that what remarks I may have to make on their habits and history, though somewhat at variance with the stereotyped notions prevalent in compilations, are yet the result of my own independent observations.

About January their tracks may be seen in the snow near the outlet of the lakes where young fir trees grow. At this time they prefer young fir trees as food to any other kind of tree, the reason, doubtless, being that at this period the sap has not risen in the willow or alder (*Alnus oregana*). It is not often that females are caught in the spring; and the males seem to travel about, as the runs are not used so regularly as they are when the beavers are living near.

Some of the beavers become torpid during January, especially those living near lakes, swamps, or large sheets of water which are frozen. They do not lay in a store of sticks for winter use, as stated by Capt. Bonville (Washington Irving's 'Adventures of Capt. Bonville'), as one day's supply of sticks for a single beaver would fill a house—and if a stick were cut in the autumn, before the winter was over it would have lost its sap, and would not be eaten by the beaver. A beaver never eats the bark of a tree that is dead, though he may gnaw a hard piece of wood to keep his teeth down. A little grass is generally found in the houses, but is used as a bed and not for food.

If February is an open month, the beavers begin to come out of their retreats, and frequent any running water near them; but it is generally March before the bulk of them come out of winter-quarters. When they come out they are lean; but their furs are still good, and continue so till the middle of May—though if a trapper thought of revisiting the place, he would not trap after April, so as to allow them to breed quietly.

About the end of March the beaver begins to "call." Both males and females "call" and answer one another. Sometimes on one "calling," half-a-dozen will answer from different parts of the lake. I have known beavers to "call" as late as August. Males fight during the rutting-season most fiercely. Hardly a skin is without scars; and large pieces are often bitten out of their tails. The beaver holds like a bull-dog, but does not snap. It shakes its head so as to tear. When trapped, it will face a man, dodge a stick, and then seize it, taking chips out of it at every bite. It seems to attack from behind.

The period of gestation is known with little certainty, as they are never trapped in summer. The female brings forth sometime about the end of June; and it is a year before a beaver is full-grown; and even then it has not the *embonpoint* of an elderly beaver.

I have read that the beaver breeds at any time during the year; but this cannot be, or all the kittens that are trapped in the fall would not be of the same size. It produces from three to four at a birth. The teats are placed between the fore legs. The young (called kittens) wimper like young puppies when suckling, even when two months old. The females prefer deep sedgy lakes to bring their young up in, and they feed on grass about that time of the year (July or August). They feed on willow about April, May, and June. I cannot say whether they are born blind or not, but suspect so. They are very fond of water-lillies (*Nuphar advena*, Ait.) in the spring. It is with me a matter of uncertainty whether the female litters in a house, under the ground, or in the dry sedges; but I should think, under ground or in the houses. In the autumn more females are caught than males. Trapping commences in September and continues to May; after that the trappers leave them alone, so that I do not know much about their doings in the summer.

They begin to build their dams about July or August, as soon as the summer floods begin to subside. For this purpose they generally choose a bend in the stream, with high and clayey banks, and commence by felling a large tree that will reach across the water; or they fell a tree on each side of the water so as to meet in the centre. They then float sticks from 6 to 4 feet long down to the dam, and lay them horizontally, filling in the spaces with roots, tufts of grass, leaves, and clay or mud. The branches of the first tree are the perpendicular supports, almost all the remaining sticks being placed horizontally and crosswise. The last six or eight inches in height is very insecurely constructed, being nothing but mud and leaves.

The highest dam I ever saw was only about 4 feet 6 inches; but the generality of them are not above 2 or 3 feet. The action of the water by bringing down mud, gravel, or fallen leaves, strengthens the dam by making a sloping bank against it; and, the willow sticks of which it is composed sending forth their roots and shoots, the dam in course of time becomes a fixture bound together as strongly as well could be. The winter floods almost invariably destroy the upper part of the dam, which is reconstructed afresh every year. The shape of the dam is almost always semicircular, with the crown of the arch down stream, thus reversing the order of things; but I have no doubt this is in consequence of the heads of the first or principal trees being floated down stream when they are first thrown. The body of water raised by these dams varies, of course, according to the fall of the original stream, from a small hole of 20 feet diameter to a lake of miles in length. In the former case the beaver builds his house close to the dam, so as to get depth of water, and there saves himself from any hungry panther (*Felis concolor*, L.) or wolf who might feel inclined to indulge in beaver-meat. The beaver also burrows into the banks of streams, always taking care to have two entrances, one under (or close to) the water, and a smaller air-hole on land. With a good dog, capital sport may be had on some of the smaller rivulets leading into or out of a lake. The houses are formed of water-logged sticks placed horizontally in the water. They have always two or more entrances, and a small chamber with a little grass for the beaver to lie on. The top of the house is constructed very thick, to guard against attacks by animals. Mud and roots are used to make the house solid; but no mud is seen from the outside, as the top is covered with loose sticks left there by the beaver after taking the bark off. The houses are generally about 4 feet in height, and about 6 in diameter on the outside, and would hold about four beavers, though I have known small houses to hold two only.

The traps generally used in securing the beaver are large steel traps with a strong spring at each end, and fastened with a chain, from 4 to 6 feet long, to a pole, which is stuck in the bottom of the water as far out as the chain will allow, so that the beaver, when he feels the trap, may run into deep water; and as he gets tired, the weight of trap taking him down, he drowns. A beaver, when trapped never tries to get to land, but makes a dive for the deepest water; and should the water be shallower than 4 feet, he will, in a short time, amputate his foot so as to relieve himself. He always takes his foot off at a joint, and draws the sinews out of his shoulder instead of biting them through. The stump heals up ; and I think the beaver is none the worse for it, though he gets shy, and, perhaps, tells the other beavers to beware of traps. A beaver is generally caught by his fore foot ; and should the trap be set too deep below water, his toe-nail only gets caught. The trap is set in the beaver-run, or just where it springs into a hole in the bank. It must not be set in too shallow water, for then he amputates his foot,—or in too deep, for in that case he does not get caught at all, but swims over the trap. The proper depth to set a trap is 5 inches. The beaver is then caught by his fore foot. Sometimes the teeth of a beaver are found to have grown beyond their proper length. I once saw one with the lower teeth $3\frac{1}{2}$ inches beyond the gums. He was caught in a trap, and was miserably thin ; but, singularly enough, he had about the finest fur I ever saw. He was an aged animal. It is rare to see a beaver which has been trapped with its teeth whole, as they are often broken in trying to get out of the trap. A full-grown beaver weighs about 34 lbs. I am not an anatomist ; but still I do not think there is anything very peculiar about its internal structure*, except that the heart weighs a mere nothing—the cavities being so very large. An old beaver when shot sinks, a kitten floats. A good skin will weigh $2\frac{1}{2}$ lbs. ; but it is very rarely that one weighing that amount is caught in Vancouver Island. The Hudson's Bay Company give only from 75 to 85 cents. per lb. at Victoria for peltries, so that a trapper now-a-days cannot get very fat at the work. There are at present very few beavers on either Vancouver Island or the mainland, compared with what there must have been some years ago ; but they have been increasing for the last six years ; and no doubt by the time beaver-skins come into fashion again there will be a plentiful supply.

WORCESTERSHIRE NATURALIST'S CLUB.

The fifth field meeting of this band of scientific observers was held on Tuesday last, at Cleobury Mortimer, just beyond the north-western border of the county. The route taken was by the Severn Valley line to Bewdley, and thence by Tenbury line to the Cleobury station, which is, however, more than two miles from the town. The last-named rail is carried through the heart of Wyre Forest, disclosing scenes of sylvan beauty that the traveller would fain pause to revel in if it were possible, but the inexorable iron horse will not admit of a moment's delay when once its snort has been given. At the Cleobury station the party dismounted, and, joined by other members from Bewdley, proceeded under the conduct of Mr. Davison, who here awaited them, to explore the ground and park surrounding Mawley-hall, the residence of Sir Edward Blount, Bart., the worthy proprietor and representative of a very ancient family, who had kindly placed his grounds at the disposal of the club. The scenery is here of a very interesting character, the landscape being thrown into many picturesque dells effected by denudations of the Old Red Sandstone and the upthrow of the Upper Silurian Rocks. Here was a fine opportunity for woodland researches—

"Wandering in uncertain ways,
Through wilderness and woods of mossed oaks."

Some fine sylvan effects were in the course of this ramble presented to view, among which may be mentioned an avenue of beech-trees simulating a gothic aisle, while in various places grand old beeches, aged and lofty pines and larches, as well as majestic oaks towering straight upwards to nearly the height of a hundred feet, besides others of venerable age and large dimensions commanded due admiration. The botanists were on the alert in these shady coverts, and as De Lille remarks in one of his poems—

"Active they rise, and o'er the fields anew,
From wood to mead or hill their search pursue ;
At night the herbal on its ready leaves
Each captured plant triumphantly receives."

But on this occasion, save the blue-flowered Devils—bit Scabious, the Agrimony, and *Lycopus Europæus*, few captures were made, except of *Fungi*, including specimens of the genera *Aganicus* and *Baletus*. On the old oaks some monstrous specimens of *Polyporus Dryadeus* were seen, almost too weighty to carry off, but some enthusiasts of the party would not be denied their prize.

The naturalists after wandering for some time through these inciting scenes came in front of Mawley-hall, which is a large brick mansion of the Georgian period (18th century), and its interior is fitted up according to the fashion prevalent at that date. The hall is noble and spacious, the walls ornamented in stucco, with trophies and numerous fanciful devices, and there are also various glass cases enclosing curious specimens in natural history, as otters killed on the estate, a white rock, &c. The staircase of polished wood leading from the hall is wide, and its balustrade represents the quaint aspect of a wriggling serpent—

"Like Ophiucus huge i' the Northern sky,"

its dragon-like head being at the bottom of the stairs, and its turned-up tail at the top. The housekeeper led the party into various rooms adorned with family portraits, and mostly wainscotted in a fashion now gone by, with carved wood. In the ante-room, whence the gallery of the chapel is entered, some ecclesiastical robes were shown, and a richly embroidered chasuble, was said to have been preserved above four hundred years, having been used in the

---

* *Vide* Cleland, Edin. New Phil. Journal, new series, vol. xiii. (1860) pp. 14—20.

church of Mamble, by the officiating priest, long previous to the Reformation. But it did not appear to have the rust of antiquity upon it. From the back windows of the hall is a fine wooded landscape view, bounded by the vast bulk of the Titterstone Clee Hill.

Having taken a cursory prospect of the gardens of the mansion the party passed on to "the Old Forge," a name that commemorates the time when iron ore was here brought to be smelted with the wood abounding in the vicinity. The mode of manufacturing iron has changed, and smelting by wood no longer takes place at this spot. Still the picturesque scenery remains of a broken stony weir across the river Rea, down which the water gushes sonorously, while below is a one-planked rustic foot-bridge, which is of old construction and shakes, as if it was one day destined to fall, and inspires fear as we cross it.

From the Old Forge a walk of about two miles brought the party to the little town of Cleobury, and the church, which is a plain structure with a shingled spire rather out of the perpendicular, was next visited. Here the curate, the Rev. E. Spencer Lowndes, met the naturalists, and explained its history and architecture. He supposed it to have been founded by some of the great family of the Mortimers, who owned the land around, and founded Wigmore Abbey, but only a single Mortimer is here buried, and that was owing to the accident of one of the Lady Mortimers being suddenly confined when passing through the place, and the infant dying was buried in the church. There is little of interest about the building except the chancel arch, which is Early English, but the chancel is of a later date, and in debased style. Mr. Lowndes stated that our Queen was descended in the female line from the Mortimer family, the Earl of Cambridge, grandfather of Edward the Fourth, having married a Mortimer.

From the church the naturalists proceeded to the house of William Weaver Jones, Esq., for this gentleman, who is an old member of the club, had kindly invited his associates and their friends to visit him and inspect his extensive museum of fossils and minerals. He had also most hospitably invited the club to take luncheon at his house, and the members were well prepared from a long walk to enjoy the hospitality of Mr. Jones. The company at first proceeded into his garden, where an array of fossils and various curiosities are laid out upon ascending terraces in a most singular and curious manner. The winding walks are lined with masses of rocks and fossils belonging to all the formations of the vicinity, and many of these are of extraordinary size and remarkable aspect. The scene is in fact unique, and must be seen to be fully understood in its imaginary character. Numerous shrubs and evergreens are dispersed among the fossils, their verdancy contrasting with the whitened stones; and many of the shrubs and trees, especially the cypresses and *Wellingtonias*, are of great beauty. The assembled gentlemen dispersed themselves among the walks, admiring the fossils and the general *tout ensemble*, and among the guests of Mr. Weaver Jones we observed Captain Bartleet, J.P., president of the club; Edwin Lees, F.L.S., vice-president; G. H. Griffiths, M.D., hon. sec.; J. S. Haywood, treasurer; Revds. J. H. Thompson, T. L. Wheeler, jun., E. S. Lowndes, and — Purton; Capt. Jervis, R.N., Capt. Addey, and Capt. Harrison; Dr. Grindrod, Messrs. Ald. Firkins, J. D. Jeffery, B. Pow, E. Baugh (Bewdley), Hilary Hill, J. Smith (Droitwich), J. L. Bozward, J. Gabb (Bewdley), J. Andrews, H. Rowe, Sclatter (Redditch), J. Wood, F. R. Jeffery, E. Smith, Danks (Bewdley), Tart, Davison, Price (Birmingham), Lamb, Boughton, R. Bartleet, jun., &c., &c.

An excellent and substantial collation had been prepared by Mr. Jones for his expected guests, which was partaken of with the hearty appetite always engendered by field excursions; and from the numerous guests that crowded the tables of so enjoyable a repast, it was some time before all could be again mustered in the garden to go on with scientific study. Here might be contemplated in detail the relics of systems of animated life existing ages ago, but now passed away from this Tellurian scene, and a volume would be required only to make a catalogue of them. A few of the more local specimens may be referred to, as the palatal teeth and spines of the Cestracient fishes of the Mountain Limestone, including *Ctenacanthus* and *Hybodus*, also fine specimens of *Conularia*, &c. The collection has also some unique specimens of fish remains from the yellow sandstone at Farlow, near the Clee Hills, among which *Pterichys oblongus* may be mentioned, a species allied to the *P. macrocephalus*, discovered in the same deposit by Mr. T. Baxter, of Worcester. There are also numerous Trilobites, with other fossils and corals of the Silurian System, besides many coal plants, and grand specimens of chrystalized coal. It was impossible in the short time allowed adequately to examine so multifarious a collection; and at last the party were called off by the president to hear a paper by Dr. Griffiths, on the antiquities of Abdon Borf, upon the Brown Clee Hill, and on the geology of the district around. The paper entered into a general view of the geology of past geological periods, and was full of lucid details and eloquent illustrations. It was received with much applause, and Capt. Bartlett moved a vote of thanks to Dr. Griffiths for his excellent paper, which was warmly accorded.

The Rev. J. H. Thompson next produced some rare plants that he had recently gathered, describing them in his usual pleasant manner, and distributing specimens to the botanists around. Among these plants, gathered at Coleshill Bog, and in the northern part of Worcestershire, was *Viola palustris*, which had been supposed lost to the country, and *Rapistrum rugosum*, new to England, which he had recently received from Surrey.

The Rev. E. S. Lowndes then read some curious extracts that he had made from the parish books of Cleobury, which related to old times and manners, and especially to the numerous things that had formerly to pay tithe, with anecdotes of the difficulty that clergyman had in collecting such petty imposts. Mr. Lowndes also exhibited a brass medal of ancient date, which was found in the year 1863, in pulling down the front of the Old Lion Inn, at Cleobury. It was about the size of a shilling, and had upon it the head of Cardinal Cajetan on one side, with the legend San Caietanus JHIEN. L.C.R.; and on the reverse the Virgin seated on a throne crowned, with the legend PROV. EJUS GUBER. Mr. Lowndes suggested that the amulet had been worn by some Roman Catholic, and secreted at the inn at a time when penal laws against the Roman Catholics were strictly enforced, and it might have been dangerous to have been found with such an emblem. Mr. Lowndes pointed out that both the Virgin and Child were crowned, the former represented in a richly embroidered robe, but the latter unclothed, holding in his hand a globe. The legend might signify that the wearer of the amulet was under the care of his mother —*Providentiâ ejus gubernatricis*. He could not explain the legend round the cardinal's head, but it was suggestive that Cardinal Cajetan, here represented as a canonized saint, with the nimbus, was a great defender of the Papacy in the sixteenth century, and a determined opponent of Luther.

Mr. E. Lees said they were all much indebted to Mr. Lowndes for the kindness and attention he had shown them that day, and he would move a vote of thanks to him. He himself had once before visited Mr. Weaver Jones in company with a talented associate now lost to them and the world by a too early death (Mr. G. E. Roberts), and he was pleased to revive old memories by the sight of a collection unequalled in its way, and of which he might safely assert to his comrades of the club that, take it for all in all, they would never look upon its like again. (Applause.) Mr. Lowndes had aided Mr. Jones in their entertainment that day, and well deserved their thanks.

The Rev. E. S. Lowndes acknowledged the compliment paid him, and said that his friend Mr. Jones had long looked forward to this visit of the club with great delight, and he had wished to assist him in every way within his power.

Captain Bartleet then announced that at the next meeting of the club, the last of this year, a presentation to Mr. E. Lees of the portrait so ably painted by Mr. S. Cole, and which was now on view to subscribers to the fund at Mr. Haywood's, the treasurer, Broad-street, Worcester, would be made.

The President observed that they had enjoyed a day long to be remembered in the annals of the club, and their best thanks were due to Mr. Weaver Jones for the opportunity of inspecting a most remarkable and unequalled collection, which had been the work and pride of his life. It had given him much satisfaction to inspect it, and they were all highly pleased. They also had to thank him for his warm-hearted hospitality, and he would ask them to show their appreciation of Mr. Jones by giving three hearty cheers in his honour. This was done with enthusiasm and effect.

Mr. Weaver Jones replied with some emotion, and said he was most happy to see the club, and his collection would be open to the inspection of any member at any time he might please to come. (Cheers.)

The party were then invited to partake of wine and cake in the drawing-room, where Mr. and Mrs. Jones received another expression of thanks and good wishes. The day was wound up by a walk to the railway station, the naturalists exciting much attention by their invasion of the quietude of Cleobury and its peaceful precincts.

At this meeting the Rev. J. Crosskey, of Edgbaston, and Capt. Jervis, R.N., of Malvern, were proposed and duly elected members of the club.

EXETER NATURALISTS' CLUB.

The last Field Meeting was held at Teignmouth, on Saturday, September 18th, but owing to the unpropitious state of the weather but few members attended. Mr. D'Urban exhibited some specimens of the scarlet ibis from South America, in various stages, showing the changes that they undergo in the colour of their plumage, from the young to the adult. He also exhibited specimens of peat from Dartmoor, and of mill-board manufactured from it. Mr. Parfitt exhibited specimens of two rare insects he had taken on Haldon, in August, viz., *Neides Tipularies* and *Coreus Nirticornis*, two plant bugs; the former is extremely rare. Mr. Parfitt also exhibited drawings he had prepared showing the circulation of the fluid in the cells, and stems of plants in illustration of what is termed the circulation of "Protoplasm":—

WHAT IS PROTOPLASM?

Mr. PARFITT read the following paper:—Many of you, I have no doubt, saw exhibited at the soirées given at the Albert Museum, a microscope, having on its stage a glass trough, in which was a fragment of an aquatic plant, showing the circulation through the thin transparent epidermis, and reflected light. In front of this instrument was placed a card, stating that this exhibited the circulation of protoplasm. This statement evidently made some impression, as I heard it quoted at the Mayor's banquet given at the Public Rooms. Protoplasm is a substance that has made a great noise in the world of late, having been brought prominently forward by many investigators, and particularly those who have spent much time in searching into the development of life, or, as it is termed by some, "Spontaneous Generation." Protoplasm is a term that has been given to a certain nitrogenous substance. At the present time there is great confusion amongst both writers and investigators, as to what the substance really is. Thus Dr. Carpenter says, in one place, that it is a thin viscous mass, and in another that it is granular; and in speaking of the circulation of Protoplasm in plants, he says, "But if after the removal of this layer, a deeper stratum be sliced off, this will be found to consist of larger cells, some of which greatly elongated with particles of chlorophyll, in are smaller number, but carried along in active rotation by the current of Protoplasm." Here it will be observed, Dr. Carpenter means by the word Protoplasm, the fluid contained in the vegetable cells, and the only evidence of its motion is the movement of the grains of chlorophyll, so that you do not see the Protoplasm in motion, but the chlorophyll which is floating in it. "It will often be noticed that the rotation takes place in contiguous cells in opposite directions." Dr. Lindley says it is "the same as is found in the propagation, by sporidia, such as by division into cells, or a gelatinous substance which organizes itself into cells." And again, in his glossary, under the word Protoplasm, Dr. Lindley says it is "The matter which is deposited over the inside walls of a cell subsequently to the formation of the cell itself," or, in other words, each individual cell is lined, or coated on the inside with this peculiar substance, in which, so far as we know, the earliest, or beginning of life resides, so that the vitality of a plant is kept up by its whole cellular structure being coated with this protoplasmic film. If we are to place any reliance on this meaning of the word Protoplasm, this should certainly precede all other formative matter. Instead of succeeding it, as stated by Dr. Lindley, it should be the first out of which the animal or plant is formed. Professor Huxley adopts the same definition of Protoplasm as given by Dr. Lindley, and he illustrates his views by taking, as an example, the hair of a common nettle, which is only another form of vegetable cell, but it has the advantage of a transparent skin, so as to show the circulation within, and it is this the Professor points to us as an example of Protoplasm. Now, if we look at this circulating medium as the blood of the plant, out of which its whole structure is built up, that each part selects for itself the necessary ingredients from the flowing stream, similar to that of the blood flowing in our veins, the whole subject becomes simple enough, instead of viewing this Protoplasm as a distinct mysterious something, the chemical basis of the elementary organs of plants has been found to be oxygen, hydrogen, carbon, and nitrogen. Albumen and Fibrin also occur in plants, and more especially in the seed. These substances also abound in the animal kingdom. The two latter, in particular, play a very important part in the animal economy. "The albuminoid principles furnish those essential ingredients of the blood which are concerned in repairing the soft azotised portions of the body, such as the muscular and nervous tissues. Hence the albuminoid principles have been termed the plastic materials of nutrition." Albumin is the characteristic ingredient of the white of eggs, and of the serous portion of blood, indeed it constitutes about 7 per cent. of the entire mass of the blood. Professor Owen says, "Vertebrates, like lower animals, begin in a semifluid, nitrogenous substance, called 'plasma,' which primarily differentiates into albumen, fibrin, and lemma, or basement membrane." This corresponds in a most remarkable manner with the formative process as seen going on in the colloidal and molecular aggregations of the disentegrated portions of the fish, flesh, and fowl, that Pouchet, Hughes, Bennet and myself have been investigating. The laws which govern these primates appear to act in the same way even when exposed to very different conditions. From this you will observe that it is impossible to separate the vegetable from the animal kingdom, either chemically or otherwise. It was believed for a long time that the two kingdoms could be separated by a chemical test. That is to say it was believed that starch was an ingredient of the vegetable kingdom only. But now starch is found abundantly in all the lower forms of what are recognized as animal life; and the lower in the scale, or the nearer the one kingdom approaches the other, the more abundant does this appear to be, so that in fact we know not where one begins and the other ends. Dr. Lionel Beal has written two very able articles on this vexed question, what is Protoplasm. He reviews all the works of the principal writers who have used this word, and it appears to me, after reading these, that the subject is more involved than ever, for there is such a contradiction of ideas, that I feel convinced it would be impossible, in the present state, to define the true properties of the substance, either chemically or otherwise. Max Schultz included under this head the active matter forming the sarcode of the Rhizopods, as well as the substance circulating in the cells of Vallisneria, or what we see circulating in the stems of Charas, as well as the white blood-corpuscles that are floating in our veins, the mucus and pus-corpuscle, and other contractile bodies widely distributed. Kühne considered all contractile material to be Protoplasm, and consequently includes the different forms of muscular tissue. This somewhat corresponds with what Professor Huxley said in an article in the *Fortnightly Review*, that when we are eating meat we are eating Protoplasm. In this he is partly right, but we are also eating many other substances besides Protoplasm. His assertion then is involved, and it does not convey the meaning intended. Nearly all observers have agreed in opinion that the cell or elementary part of a fully formed organism consists of different kinds of matter, and I think this can be easily proved by chemical tests, for if you will observe in these cells (from the stem of a water-lily leaf), you will see that the lining membrane is coloured purple, while the rest of the cell walls remain untouched, and these other cells show you the cell membrane more or less shrunk up, carrying with it the grains of what appear to be chlorophyll, the same as we have seen floating in the stems of the Chara. This, when acted on with dilute nitric acid, loses its colour, and the cells or granules become broken down, leaving a white trace on the glass. The same test applied to what Prof. Huxley calls the best example of Protoplasm—white of egg—rendering it of a white opalescent appearance, and causing it to swell up into a larger volume. If a portion of this be pressed between plates of thin glass and examined with a high microscopic power, it will be seen to have assumed a minute, granular or molecular form, having just the appearance of highly disintegrated flesh, whereas the same power applied to the albumen before the acid is applied gives no structure at all. It will be seen then, I think, from the action of the acid on these two substances, that they are not the same. Dr. Beal draws a line between living and dead matter called Protoplasm, and he says:—"It must be obvious that the chemistry of the complex matter now termed Protoplasm, embraces the chemistry of formed matter, and the chemistry of the active living, growing matter of the organism. By chemical analysis we can ascertain the composition of the first, and can learn many facts concerning its elementary chemical characters, but it is obvious that chemistry can teach us little with regard to the composition of living matter, for we kill it when we attempt to analyze it; and, in truth, we analyze not living matter, but the substances resulting from its death." In this it will be seen that it is a matter of impossibility to ascertain what Protoplasm really is, for the instant that the matter so termed is deprived of life its constituents are changed, it is Protoplasm no longer. It will not be necessary for me to impress upon you the desirability of using extreme caution in the use of this word, which has of late become so common in almost everybody's mouth, and of which few appear to know the meaning.

Short Notes.

NEW MEXICO.—In 1867 a surveying expedition was arranged by the Kansas Pacific Railway Company to discover the better route for a line of railway to the Pacific Coast, to pass through Kansas, Colorado, New Mexico, and the more southerly part of California. To this expedition Mr. Bell was attached first of all as photographer, but the physician to the expedition left it to return home, and our author filled his place. A doctor, it seems, has a kind of perpetual holiday in "them parts," for the climate is so healthful, that physic is literally a drug in the market. The distance I travelled, writes Mr. Bell, beyond the pale of civilization and railways, was about 5000 miles. We cannot possibly follow the author through all his wanderings, but can only briefly direct attention to a few amongst the very many subjects of interest to be found in the pages of the volumes before us. We can form some idea of the canon through which the Colorado flows for a long way, when we read that for 300 miles the cut edges of the table lands rise abruptly, and often like a wall, to a height of 3000 feet, and sometimes a mile, from the surface of the water. This wonderful gorge is, we are told, entirely due to the erosive action of water. The plateau of the Colorado has been raised to an average elevation of 7000 feet; "over this plateau the Colorado formerly flowed for at least 500 miles of its course; but in the lapse of ages its rapid current has cut its bed down through all the sedimentary strata, and several hundred feet into the granite base on which they rest." Canons are, it seems, in every case due to the action of water, and not volcanic force; a groove once formed, the physical conditions of the strata being favourable, and a regular water channel fairly established, it matters not what may be the structure and density of the underlying rocks, the attrition of ages does its work, and strange as it may seem, the water has "succeeded in cutting through 1000 feet of the hardest granite." It is impossible for a country to be anything but useless and sterile where canons abound, simply because these natural drains carry away all the rainfall, so that vegetation has no chance to live. A terrible adventure is recorded in the second volume, the scene of which is the Canon of Colorado; the story is too long to give in extenso, but the gist of it is as follows:—A party of three, gold miners, on the 24th of August, in the year 1867, were pounced upon, near the Colorado, by a band of Redskins, and one of the three was killed, the other two contrived to escape, and sought concealment in a narrow slip of land on the margin of the stream. To recross a wilderness of 300 miles with the Indians on their trail, was hopeless. In every other direction their route was intercepted by the deep canons of the Colorado, impassable for them and their mules. The only chance left them was to descend the Colorado. They made a raft, and shoving off at midnight trusting to the chances of the stream. Day by day they drifted on, the lofty walls of the canon rising pitilessly above them, and with only an occasional gap where a tributary entered the main stream. They were unable to escape by these, the stream being too rapid to permit of their making head against it. At night they fastened their raft to a rock. On the fourth day they heard a noise of falling water, and before they had time to prepare, the raft dashed into a foaming rapid. One of the two navigators tried to shove the raft away from the rocks, but slipped, and disappeared at once in the stream. The survivor clung to his raft, but, worst of all, his provisions had been carried away. He now floated onwards in despair, sometimes whirling over rapids which threatened immediate destruction, and finally was caught in a whirlpool, round which he was carried for hours, and from which, as he stated, and clearly believed, he was rescued in direct answer to his prayers. Six days passed, and White had no food beyond a few green pods of mesquit bushes. But the worst of the stream was behind him. At the end of this time he came to a place where the gorge opened, and a few friendly Indians lived at the bottom of the canon. They gave him half a dog and some beans in exchange for a revolver, and he proceeded on his journey. Three days afterwards, fourteen days from the start, he arrived at a Mormon settlement, where he was kindly welcomed. His body was blistered from the heat of the sun; his reason was almost gone, his form stooped, and his eyes were so hollow and dreary that he looked like an old and imbecile man.—*North Tracks.*

FERTILIZATION OF PLANTS.—That in the majority of highly-developed plants the presence of pistil and stamen in the same flower is, as it were, a kind of safety-engine kept in reserve in case of the failure of the ordinary modes of fecundation, was a fact unsuspected before Mr. Darwin's patient and laborious researches established the fact, that as a rule the pistil is not fertilized by the pollen from the stamens of the same flower, but by pollen carried from other flowers through the agency of the wind, and especially of insects. The American traveller, Spruce, has indeed come to the conclusion, from his investigations of the palms of the Equator, that the hermaphrodite structure of plants is an earlier development, which has gradually advanced to the higher type of unisexuality. On the Continent, Professor Hildebrand of Bonn has contributed several articles to the *Botanische Zeitung*, and other botanical magazines, containing the result of observations which fully bear out Darwin's principle of cross-fertilization, and which show that many hermaphrodite plants are so constructed either that the pollen cannot fall on the stigma of its own flower, or that the stigma is not in a receptive state at the time that the pollen is discharged. Our own *Parnassia palustris*, or "Grass of

Parnassus," a common plant in damp mountainous situations, has been shown to be an illustration of a similar structure; the anthers, at the period of maturity, completely covering and enclosing the pistil, and discharging their pollen outwardly. The stigmatic surfaces are also not developed till a later period, and absorb the pollen-grains conveyed to them from other flowers by insects while seeking the honey attached to their peculiar nectaries. Any careful observer may detect similar phenomena in the case of our common "London Pride" and other saxifrages. More recent observations have been made by several observers on the fertilization of the genus *Salvia*, several species of which are furnished with remarkable appliances for cross-fertilization. Each anther consists of two cells at opposite ends of a long and very versatile connecting thread. One of these anther-cells only contains pollen, and this is attached to the longer arm of the thread, and is concealed in the throat of the corolla; the barren cell attached to the shorter arm projecting into its mouth. When a bee enters the flower in search of the honey abundantly contained at the bottom of the tube of the corolla, it strikes against the shorter arm, causes the structure to rotate, and brings the fertile anther-cell in contact with the back of the bee, where it necessarily deposits some of its pollen, which the insect carries away, and leaves on the stigma of the next flower it enters. The French botanist, M. Bidard, has, on the other hand, paid attention to the fertilization of grasses, and finds a set of phenomena with a different signification. He states that the pollen of *Gramineæ* does not exhibit any trace of pollen tubes, and that self-fertilization takes place before the anthers are extruded beyond the scales of the flower. The heat of the breath or a ray of sunshine is sufficient to bring about the phenomena of fecundation; and the natural hybridization of grasses is impossible, owing to the exact closing of the chamber containing the fecundating organ.

DEEP SEA LIFE.—Dr. Carpenter has returned in safety from the third trip in deep sea dredgings. His results quite bear out the conclusions drawn from the two previous ones. Some new facts, however, of extreme interest, have been discovered, the publication of which we may expect shortly. It is hardly possible to exaggerate the importance of these investigations, in their bearings on the most important general problems of biology, physical geography, and geology. They teach us that the bottom of the deep ocean is the home of many creatures, who live there in the absence of light, under great pressure, in water often excessively cold—just above freezing point—abounding in carbonic acid and in organic matter. Of these influences the one which makes itself most felt is that of cold. It is this, and not the pressure, not the want of bright sunlight, that stunts the creatures, and makes them reproduce at the bottom of equatorial seas the fauna of arctic surface regions. Nor is the life at these depths confined to low-born Foraminifera, or to that wonderful protoplasmic Bathybius, which Prof. Huxley told the British Association at Exeter, he had now found in soundings from many quarters of the globe, and which therefore seems to be a *vast thin sheet of living matter enveloping the whole earth beneath the seas*. Where, as in certain regions, the deep waters are warm, highly organised beings, of bright colours and well-appointed eyes, are brought up by the dredge. These researches press upon us the question,—Is it possible for living matter to be born and nourished in the absence of light, in the presence of carbonic acid, and in the absence of any heat higher than the temperature of about 32° F., in the absence, that is, of almost any force which can be transmuted into vital force? At these great depths there is no vegetation properly so called, and Professor Wyville Thomson, who is associated with Dr. Carpenter in these researches, is of opinion that here the lowest living beings feed on the lifeless organic matter which exists in so large a quantity in the water. We seem here to be near the transition from complex lifeless proteid matter and living protoplasm. The exact condition and nature of this organic matter is of extreme importance, and we understand a distinguished chemist is about to make it the subject of an enquiry. There is another point of no less interest. These organisms, which are thus building up chalk strata (for this deep Atlantic ooze is nothing but incipient chalk) at the bottom of the ocean are to a very large extent identical with many of the remains found in the chalk formations. This is so much the case that we may speak of races of animals building the old hills of millions of years ago, and laying now the foundation of the chalk hills of times to come, themselves remaining unchanged all the time between.

COAL-MINING IN CHINA.—Professor Bickmore, in a lecture on the Minerals of China, at the American Association for the Advancement of Science, said that coal was used for fuel ages before its properties were known to Europeans. Marco Polo, the great Venetian traveller who visited Pekin more than 600 years ago, found it in common use. The only mode of transporting this mineral in the northern parts of China is on the backs of camels, mules, and donkeys. The Professor described a mine in Pekin, which he descended for a mile, being obliged to crawl on his hands and knees, as the height of the adit or tube was only 4 or 5 ft. The coal is drawn up in baskets on sleds, each basket holding from a peck to half a bushel. The only covering of those who drag it up is a thick layer of coal dust. The slow and laborious mode of taking the coal to the surface is the only one Professor Bickmore saw in the mines he visited; neither are there any adits or tunnels for the admission of pure air. Accidents from the explosion of fire-damp rarely or never occur, however, probably because the Chinese are unable to dig lower than the water level for want of proper pumping apparatus. For the same reason the best coal in China remains as yet undisturbed, and awaits the enterprise and improved apparatus of Western nations. Coal occurs from place to place over the whole empire. It is overlaid with a red sandstone, and the Chinese commence their operations where the strata chance to outcrop, and follow them down at whatever angle they chance to lead. Professor Bickmore also showed, by extracts from ancient works, that petroleum was not only known, but "used for lamps," more than 160 years ago. The Chinese name for it is "Oil of stone," which, as is well known, is identical with our name petroleum.

NEW SPECIES OF SUN FISH.—Mr. M. Dunn, of Mevagissey, writing to the *Western Morning News*, says:—"A short time since a large specimen of that occasional summer visitor to our coasts from the deep sea, the sun fish (*Cephalus brevis*, Cuvier), was found by Thomas Pollard, fisherman, of Mevagissey, sleeping on the surface of the water within the circuit of our bay. After a long contest for the fish, which was over 200lb. in weight, it was captured. On its being landed a strange-looking parasite animal was found clinging to its side. Not knowing its name or genus, I forwarded it to Mr. J. Couch, of Polperro, who, after much research and consultation, and with the authority of Dr. J. E. Gray, of the British Museum, pronounces it to belong to a genus hitherto unknown to science. The name assigned to the creature is *Penelus Pilfena*."

Remarks, Queries, &c.

(*Under this head we shall be happy to insert original Remarks, Queries, &c.*)

THE WOOD PIGEON.

At the request of Mr. G. O. Howell I will endeavour to give a pretty clear description of the habits of the above bird, which however is very well known, being widely distributed throughout this country, but whether it is found as plentifully in Scotland and Wales I am not able to say. It is a great favourite with myself and most who are fond of the feathered tribes, playing no small part in rural sights and sounds; for who has not listened with pleasure to its soothing and melodious notes on a still summer's eve. There is a peculiarity about its cooing which I have observed on several occasions, namely, that although the bird itself may be in a tree close at hand, yet its notes seem to proceed from a considerably distance, owing I presume to the peculiar nature of the sound. The Wood Pigeon is much sought after for the sake of its flesh, and indeed it is a plump bird, and well worth the eating, but it is no easy matter to get within gunshot, for it is extremely shy, especially in the winter, when these birds congregate in large flocks, and coming down from the woods commit sad havoc with the farmer's newly-sown grain. In the summer time they may be shot by lying in wait for them early in the morning, as they come to feed upon the peas, beans, or oats, in recently cut fields; the sportsman must take care to conceal himself from view, by hiding beneath a bower constructed with branches of trees, etc, and he must wait until they approach rather near if he wishes to kill them on the spot, they are so well protected by their plentiful and stout feathers. The Wood Pigeon is an early breeder; the eggs may be found as early as March, and as late as July. The favourite place for building is in a hawthorn tree or bush, perhaps because the thorns afford the security lacked by the conspicuity of the nest itself; but almost any place does, as it may be frequently found in the fork of a tree, on an old pollard, in a bushy fir, or in the ivy surrounding it, or in a prickly holly, and numerous other places. The nest is a poor concern as compared with those of many other birds, being a simple platform of dry sticks, having no lining beyond occasionally a few root fibres, yet it is so constructed that one can often remove the whole affair without its falling to pieces as one would imagine. On account of the paucity of materials used in its structure, the eggs, which never exceed two in number, and being white, may sometimes be seen from beneath; but in this one is liable to be deceived by a white feather, which is often left in the nest by the old bird. No doubt many of the readers of this article have been startled by the sudden exit and loud flapping of wings of the female pigeon as she leaves her nest, thus discovering its whereabouts. By reason of this many a nest has been robbed which would otherwise have remained unnoticed. The young are able to fly in about three weeks from the time when they were hatched, during which time they are most unsightly little creatures being the very picture of helplessness; nevertheless they are very good eating at this period (if I may be allowed this cruel suggestion). The food which the old birds supply to their unfledged, consists chiefly of seeds and grains, as may be ascertained by opening the crop of one of these young ones. In conclusion, I may as well add that there are four distinct varieties of Wild Pigeon found in England, viz.:—the Ring Dove, the Stock Dove, the Rock Dove, and the Turtle Dove, of which the first is the one usually denominated Wood Pigeon, although the Stock and Turtle Doves are very similar in habits, choice of haunts, etc, and are frequently confounded with the Ring Dove. I hope that this humble attempt at a description will meet the requirement of Mr. G. O. Howell with respect to this familiar bird; if it does not, I will resign to the pen of one who is better qualified than myself to perform this agreable task.

Reading.   A. TOMES.

HEAT OF THE SUMMER OF 1868.

I, in all willingness, at once make an effort to free my literary antagonist, Mr. Ernest Belfort Bax, from his present meteorological difficulty. He, in common with all the correspondents of the NATURALIST'S NOTE BOOK, remembers that the summer of 1868 was unusually hot, and the winter uncommonly mild, and he has heard it asserted that the following were the causes:—

1st. That the gulf stream was diverted in its course.

2nd. The disturbed state of the interior of the earth.

Mr. Bax then very justly asks, is there *any truth* in either of these statements? Not a particle, so far as the test of science goes. That the gulf stream should deviate from its course, and the interior of the earth become refractory, in order to produce a hot summer and a mild winter, are but fanciful creations of the contriving brain of inventive theorists.

Simpler causes are quite at hand. We all know that in these islands a north wind brings cold, and a south wind heat. June and July of 1868 were the hot months, and we had a continual south wind during those months. Discarding all invention and elastic theories, surely this would sufficiently account for our hot summer, and as the south wind returned after autumn, the same cause simply applies to our mild winter. Burns, at his plough, had some idea of the north wind when he says, "Cald and black does the north won' bla."

Meteorologists, as the result of long and careful observations, lay it down as an axiom, that, "in our climate, the temperature of the air depends upon *the direction of the wind*, quite as much as upon *the season of the year*, that is, the position of the earth with regard to the sun."*

It is well known that the gulf stream is but, perhaps, 8° warmer than its adjacent water of the Atlantic, while many days of July, 1868, were 20° above the ordinary temperature. Earthquakes in the Sandwich Islands, new comets, Vesuvius in action, as well as the presumed wanderings of the gulf stream, and hypothetical commotions in the interior of the earth, have all been pushed forward as plausible causes of our torrid summer and mild winter of 1868. Admit the gulf stream driven from its general course (a thing altogether doubtful) by some preponderating force, then the probability is, that the cold water at the bottom was partially driven up, cooled the great ocean current, and consequently lowered the surrounding temperature.

That the agency, virtues and vices of the gulf stream, have often been exaggerated there cannot be a doubt.

That somewhere in the interior of the earth some sort of fire exists, is an hypothesis, and that this hypothetical fire should by some hypothetical agency suddenly start into action and communicate its presumed influence to our summer of 1868, are but still weaker hypotheses springing from the first; and in this chain of conjecture, we must remember the axiom in mechanics, that "*no chain is stronger than its weakest link.*"

From the days of that old grim historian, Herodotus, and perhaps long before his time, down to the present, men have in vain attempted to discover the causes which produce earthquakes, so, for the present, their influence upon climate is but imperfectly understood. As I am sure other correspondents of the NATURALIST'S NOTE BOOK are just now writing to free Mr. Bax from his meteorological mists, I must be brief, cease abruptly, fold up, and despatch my MS.

Dundalk, Oct. 1869. H. H. ULIDIA.

HOW TO ENJOY THE COUNTRY.

A NOTE, BY "YORICK."

IT is not all half-shut-eyed indolence in the country, reposing beneath mighty oaks and chesnuts, watching the motions of their great outspread arms, and listening to the whistling of the winds that causes them.

---

* "Scientific Review."

It is delicious, we grant, to hear these, and see the dancing lights and shades around, and the fleets of sailing clouds above, bearing all sorts of pennons, while the mower is swinging his scythe in the meadow below, or on the hillside opposite, with as much grace and rhythm as Jullien does his *bâton*. Ah! there is music in harmonious labour as well as in the operas (works) of Rossini. There is utility, too, in both, though one is immediately productive, the other not. We acknowledge it here amidst the ploughmen and cultivators, sons of the sickle and the scythe. Rural enjoyments are not all thus somnolent, passive, and sensuous. Do you hear that brook, now quiet, now brawling? It is denominated a trout-stream, and the noise made is said to be a conversation between that shy creature and his neighbour—the Naiad. You have seen the elegant fishing-tackle, which nothing that has fins, it would seem, could ever escape? Well, that is made for this very rivulet. It was invented for this very trout brook. Now throw it in, and troll and travel, troll and travel, half-an-hour. Have you caught anything in all that weary tramp? "Why, no, nothing but happiness and health; I have been expecting every minute to lay the glittering prize upon the green bank, but have not had a bite as yet—perhaps I shall." It has frequently been mooted whether fishing for amusement is right—is it Christian? There is no difficulty in replying. It is perfectly moral, in our opinion, for every city gentleman to buy fishing-tackle of great price and murderous look, and use it also with all his skill, in as many trout streams as he pleases. From our own experience in such matters we are willing to say, "The blood of all the trout which they may catch be upon us and on our children!" We will be responsible for all the misery they will cause the fish. But though the pretty tenants of the water may be missed, the mark the sportsman aimed at has been hit. He may carry home no exquisitely sweet trout for breakfast, yet he will thus have a keener relish for his codfish balls and mutton chop.—*Autumn Leaves.*

DISTRESSING EFFECTS OF THE STINGS OF WASPS.—At about 5 o'clock in the afternoon of Monday, the 16th of August, 1869, I was searching among the loose stones of a small embankment in my garden for the entrance to a wasp's nest. I struck my spade unwittingly into what proved to be the heart of the nest, from which there issued immediately a vast number of wasps in great excitement, one of which, before I could make good my retreat, stung me on the left eyebrow, and, presently afterwards, another drove his tiny weapon into my left wrist. For the moment I felt only a sharp smarting, and as I had frequently been stung by wasps before and felt little inconvenience, always suffering a great deal more in pain as well as swelling, from the sting of a bee than from that of a wasp (and having been a beemaster for some 35 years I have had many opportunities of judging between them). I thought but little of it, and having rubbed in some oil, expected the anguish would soon abate, as in former cases. I was, however, to learn a lesson to the contrary. After a few minutes I experienced violent and distressing heat and pain all over my head, especially about the ears; I was then slightly sick, and immediately afterwards felt faint and dizzy, till I seemed to spin round like a top, lost my balance but not my consciousness, and fell into a currant-bush, which I broke down in my fall. I managed to get upon my legs again and to reach the house staggering like a drunken man; then I fell into, rather than set down on, a chair, and having been assisted by my wife and daughter, I got up stairs to my dressing-room, where, attempting to sit down, I became faint again, and trying to stand and draw off my shoes, I staggered forward falling on my knees in a state of semi-unconsciousness, from which I was only recovered by cold water being copiously dashed into my face. After this I was enabled, with assistance, to lie down on my bed, where I experienced a complication of most strange and distressing symptoms. My hands, my feet, and my chest became as red as though I had the scarlet fever, and the heat and itching of them, one and all, was something such as I never felt before and hope never to feel again. This was allayed by sponging frequently with soda and water. I quaked, trembled, and my teeth chattered as if I were in an ague-fit, and I was tremendously sick, throwing off the stomach, which was in severe pain, nearly a wash-hand bason full of a fluid intensely acid and bitter. This continued at intervals till late at night, during the whole of which I remained in a state of the utmost uneasiness, utterly unable to sleep. Next day I was much relieved, the feeling more or less giddy and uncomfortable, while the swelling of the face and wrist was considerable. I should observe, however, that the swelling was at no time very great, nothing at all equal to what I have experienced from the sting of a bee. Perhaps if the swelling had been greater the other symptoms might not have been so severe. At one time I felt quite as if I was about to die, and I suppose a little more would really have put an end to my life. How true it is that "there is but a step between us and death," while "we know not what a day may bring forth."

I may add that though somewhat invalided for some time past, I was as well as usual when this occurred, and I am unconscious of anything in my system which could predispose for such violent and unusual effects. The wasp which stung me on the eyebrows seemed to me to be *straight from the nest*, not one of those which had been flying about while I was searching for the nest, and which certainly shewed no anger or disposition to attack me. Is it not probable that the state of rage it was in, on its castle being assailed, may have caused the venom to be more violent in its action and more virulent in its effects? Some suggest the creature might have been feeding on some putrid substance, but that, I think, is not the habit of wasps; nor do I understand how the diet should communicate its poisonous qualities to the virus; if it were a *bite*, not a *sting*, one would understand how it might act in the same way as the deadly puncture of the dissecting-room.

CHARLES H. BINGHAM,
Vicar of Ramsey, Huntingdonshire.

P.S. How is the venom in these creatures supposed to be generated or secreted? And what is the connexion between their food and the venom?

THE MOON AND THE WEATHER.—In reply to the inquiry of Mr. Ernest Belfort Bax, I may briefly say, that, to be really "weather wise" has long been the desire and the study of navigators, shepherds, and agriculturists. When the island of Rhodes, 3,000 years ago, was sovereign of the sea, we find that her hardy sailors were in the habit of *presaging* the weather from observations of the moon and other heavenly bodies; the early shepherds of the east, and the agriculturists of all nations, ancient and modern, all looked to the moon in order to form some idea of the approaching weather. Many of the great classical writers, poets of antiquity (but sure Mr. Bax puts an embargo on the authority of poets in general) speak of the influence of the moon on the weather. We learn from Hesiod, Virgil, and others, that many of the farming operations of other times were commenced on certain days of the moon. And just at home with us, more than 2,000 years since, it was asserted of the great seaman, Man-an-nan McLir,* that he could presage good and bad weather from his observations of the heavens and the *changes of the moon*. So much indeed for the stern antiquity of the opinions concerning the moon's influence on the weather, and in accordance with those popular and stereotyped notions of the ancients, many wise weather saws have been briefly and *poetically* embodied, such as—

> I saw the *new moon* yester'een,
> With *the old moon in her arms*,
> And if you go to sea master
> *I fear you'll come to harm!*

Again we have—

> The sun last night went pale to bed,
> The *moon in haloes hid her head*.

And—

> In the wane of the moon
> A cloudy morning bodes a fair afternoon.

And, again, of the moon we have the beautiful old adage—

> Pallida *luna* pluit, rubicunda flat, alba serenat.

These, and thousands of other proverbs concerning the prognostication of the weather, from observations of the moon, are known to everybody. But here, a question naturally forces itself, as implied in the inquiry propounded by Mr. Bax. Is there any truth in those old yarns of the sea, any reliance to be placed in those poetic scholiums of the ancients, any solid knowledge blended in those often unpolished rustic brevities of "the days o' a lang syne?" I at once, unhesitatingly, say yes. For, I am of opinion, that the rude, but matured deductions drawn from their ever repeatedly keen observations of the heavens, did, perhaps, as much for the safety of the Lydians, who, even 500 years before the Rhodians, monopolized maritime commerce, as meteorological science now does for our ships and seamen. The results of long observation prove to us that the times of new and full moon generally bring changes in the weather—that baro-

---

* The names "McLir," and McLure, the discoverer of the North-West passage, are the same in meaning, a remarkable fact.—H. H. U.

metric changes, atmospheric disturbances, are caused by the influence of the moon, science attests, and hence, we, without being "minions of the moon," may safely conclude, that now, as from the greatest antiquity, the influence of the moon in a greater or less degree acts upon the weather.

But at a time like the present when Luna, the pale luminary of the night, frowningly threatens, according to the mathematical calculation of some of our scientifics, to toss old Ocean's waves into our very domiciles, but then doesn't, proving by the very modesty of her pranks that philosophers are but men, perhaps the less we say, or presume to predict, about the influence of the moon on our little world and its physical affair, the better.

Dromore, Oct. 1869. H. H. ULIDIA.

ENTOMOLOGY.—I see by the questions asked by your correspondent, W. M., in the N. N. B. for last month, that he is quite a beginner in entomology, for there are scarcely any of them to which a direct answer might be given. However, if the following information can be of any use to him I am only too happy to give it. In the first place he asks for the best method of determining the genus or species of moths, &c., when captured. Now all I can say to this is, that such a knowledge can only be acquired by practice, as there are so many species which differ but slightly from each other that it often requires an experienced head to determine to which they really belong; but if he were to read some good work on the subject, such as Newman's "British Moths," &c., he would find it a great help. He then asks how long can an insect remain set before being placed in the cabinet. Now this is a fault into which I find most beginners invariably fall, for they are always in such a hurry to see their specimens in the cabinet (which by the way is not an article of necessity at first) that they do not give them time to get quite set, but take them off the board as soon as their wings begin to get stiff, while the body still contains a large quantity of moisture: the consequence is that in course of time this moisture diffuses itself throughout the wings, causing them to droop, and thereby deteriorate the value of the specimen. My own plan is to leave all insects on the board in a dry and dustproof place until I require it for fresh ones—in most cases not for many weeks—as I always keep a large stock of boards by me. He also wishes to know where butterflies resort at night or during the rain. Now if W. M. would take the trouble to go out during a shower he will find that most of them try to conceal themselves in a wonderful manner by alighting upon such flowers as they most resemble in colour: for instance, the Brimstone Butterfly (G. Rhamni) will invariably settle on the underside of a yellow plant, while most of the blues will disguise themselves by closing their wings and reposing under some tufts of grass, or other plant which has gone to seed, and to which they most resemble by their prettily speckled undersides. Then again as to the age of insects, this is a question which is utterly impossible to answer; for while some only live a few weeks, or at the most a month, there are others which, after enjoying the pleasures of summer, retire to some old cranny, and there pass the winter, appearing again in the spring, and making upon the whole an existence of nearly a year; to these latter belong most of the Vanessæ, i. e., the Tortoisshell (V. Urticæ), the Painted Lady (V. Cardui), &c. The Brimstone Butterfly (G. Rhamni), and several others, also pass the winter in this state, which is termed hybernating. The last question which he asks is with regard to the best kind of weather for capturing them. Now as for butterflies, the best time is of course a bright sunshiny day, with as little wind as possible; but moths are very fastidious about the weather, and seem to appear only when they like, for I have often taken some very good ones on a dark and damp night, such as was but little tempting for a four mile walk over Brighton Downs, so that W. M. will have to determine this last item by his own observations.

J. W. B.

SIR,—Some months ago, your correspondent O. R. made an inquiry as to the origin of the planetoids. The following remarks, collected from various sources, may assist him in forming an opinion on this subject.

The theory that these small bodies are fragments of a large planet once existing between the orbits of Mars and Jupiter, originated with Dr. Olbers, the discoverer of Pallas. There are many facts which seem to support this theory, a few of which may be mentioned.

1. The mean distance of the planetoids would place them between the orbits of Mars and Jupiter, at a point almost coinciding with that at which, according to Bode's law of distances, the original planet would have revolved.

2. At a point near the descending of Pallas, the orbits of Ceres and Pallas were found by Dr. Olbers to coincide, and this peculiarity has been noticed with regard to several other planetoids.

3. Although astronomers give very varied estimates of their size, there is no doubt they are all very small; in fact most of them are so minute that all attempts to measure them, with the use of the most powerful instruments, have been ineffectual. The largest of them does not exceed 500 miles in diameter. Many of the planetoids are not spherical, but present most irregular aspects to the earth.

4. An American astronomer calculated that the destroyed planet had a diameter exceeding that of the planet Mars. Chambers, in his "Astronomy," says that the hypothesis of Olbers is the most satisfactory yet propounded.

Arago, although objecting to this theory, agrees with most astronomers in saying that there must be some intimate connection between them. Another foreign astronomer, named D'Arrest, writes as follows:—"One fact seems above all to confirm the intimate relation between all the minor planets: it is that if their orbits are figured under the form of material rings, these rings will be found so entangled that it would be possible by means of one among them, taken at hazard, to lift up all the rest."

Some persons affirm the planet (if such existed) must have been burst by some internal explosion; and Lagrange "has calculated that an explosive force, equal to twenty times that of a cannon ball, would cause such an explosion."

Others affirm that the planet must have been destroyed by contact with a comet, and in maintaining this theory call attention to the fact that Ceres is surrounded by a very large atmosphere (calculated by Schraeber to be 686 miles in altitude), stating that this may have been caused by the fragments becoming enveloped with the comet's tail. On the other hand, it should be remembered that many of the planetoids seem to have no atmospheres at all. Vesta, for instance, has not afforded any undisputed traces of an atmosphere. R. T.

EXTINCTION OF SPECIES.—I observe that Mr. Marsden addresses me again in your valuable paper of this month, and as he seems to have read in my articles on the "Extinction of Species" what I never wrote, I must needs come to an explanation of the subject. As to my experience of obtaining only about 10 per cent. of good pupæ, I beg to observe that I did not mention to have raised them myself, but said very plainly, "collect two hundred pupæ," etc. If Mr. Marsden confounds the word "collect" with "breeding," it is not my fault. If he collects pupæ, he is naturally exposed to more risk than if he breeds from a collection of young caterpillars which are healthy. Next to this I will only mention that while some larvæ are exposed to a great many dangers, others go comparatively harmless to their final development. Mr. Marsden's question, "how I can reconcile my two statements," is incomprehensible to me. What he has read that I have not written, I cannot tell. My ideas of collecting is beyond his simple British view of the matter. If he has a British collection strictly speaking, there are many lepidoptera which ought to be left out of it, because they are not originally British, though nobody can tell with anything like exactitude when they made their first appearance in England. Does he call those British, and why?—and where will he draw the line when it is known that clouds of some kind of lepidoptera have migrated from the Continent to England? Now all those in the least doubtful ought to be carefully weeded out from his collection. If he continues to keep them among his strictly British insects, he is not true to his word when he speaks of "a British collection." It would be mixed or foreign. I know I shall never agree with Mr. M. on the subject, and thus it is better we drop a controversy which might become as lengthy as the venerable discussion on "Do insects feel pain?" —a bore to a number of readers of the N. N. B., and only an amusement to the combatants. The last point I have to raise is a question of Mr. M.'s, "whether I am sure of the two broods of V. Antiopa!" I can assure him that I am. But to rear two broods it is by no means necessary to suppose that larvæ must feed through the winter when snow covers the ground, especially in America. Whether there are two broods of V. Antiopa on the Continent—I mean annually—I do not know. In America I caught perfect specimens, only smaller than the summer broods in April, when snow still covered the ground; but the sun shone warm in sheltered spots of woods. Had they wintered in the imago they would undoubtedly have shown the symptoms of wear and tear. Although it is well known—but perhaps not to Mr. Marsden—that the bear and tiger moths caterpillars, hybernate in America, and are the first out on sunny days in spring. This is not necessarily the case with the larvæ of V. Antiopa. Of the latter, the pupa hybernates, and the first brood of larvæ comes from those first imagos in spring; be they fresh ones, or those that did pass the winter in a torpor, which latter is known to be the case. Should Mr. Marsden wish to consult a higher authority than my simple experience, I can refer him to Harris's Treatise, "Insects injurious to vegetation," Boston, New York, 1863, page 298, viz., "the butterflies come forth in July. A second brood of caterpillars is produced in August, and they pass through all their changes before winter." In the same way a number of pupæ hybernate without a question of food for their caterpillars, to produce the imago for due time in spring. I am sure Mr. M. knows this as well as the first beginner of a collection. Where the distinct broods are to commence I leave to his own choice. W. GEFFCKEN.
Stuttgart.

THE OLD MAN OF MOW.—Mow Cop, or as it is more commonly called Mow, is a small village built on the side of a very steep hill in Staffordshire. The chief attraction to this bleak spot is an immense piece of rock, which stands in a slanting direction, and which I should think stands about two or three hundred feet above the level of the ground on which it stands; though only about one hundred feet or so appear above the level ground (if level it may be called), on account of it standing in an immense hollow at the summit of the hill. There are some curious traditions of how it has got there: one of them is that his Satanic Majesty was flying away with it over the hill in his apron, when his apron-strings broke and down it fell, so making the hollow in which it stands. It seems to me very much like as if the stone had been quarried all round it, and that it had been left standing there by itself. I have been told that on a clear day it may be seen from the sea with a powerful telescope; and I should think that very probably it may be, as it can be seen for a very considerable distance even with the naked eye. There is a splendid view from the top of this hill on a fine summer's day; for even when I was up, I could see over several counties, and it was a very wet, misty day. Two or three hundred yards from the Old Man are the remains of an old castle, of which only the keep and part of the castle-wall now remain.
Congleton. JOS. LAING.

SUN SPOTS.—Sun spots are generally composed of three parts, viz., the *nucleus*, which is in the centre, and is very dark; the *umbra*, next to that, which is not of so dark an appearance; and the *penumbra*, at the outside, which is comparatively light. This will, I think, satisfy "J. H." as to the cause of the less opaque darkness noticed at the outside. Norman Lockyer, F.R.A.S., says, "Sun spots are cavities or hollows eaten into the photosphere (the luminous envelope surrounding the sun), and the different shades represent different depths." The opinion of most astronomers with regard to the sun spots seems to be that they are openings in the sun's photosphere, through which we see less brilliant parts of the sun's envelope, forming the penumbra and umbra; and farther down still the dark body of the sun is exposed to view, forming what we call the nucleus of the sun spot. Some astronomers think there is a connection between the sun spots and the aurora borealis, and were bold enough to affirm that on account of numerous sun spots visible during the summer months, we might expect to see magnificent displays of the aurora borealis during the autumn. I have already noticed accounts of its appearance at London and Worcester. At the latter place the display lasted half an hour, and was very brilliant. If any of your readers should notice any displays of this interesting phenomena, will they kindly favour us with an account? R. T.

EXTINCTION OF SPECIES.—I notice another letter on this subject in the October number of this paper from a correspondent, "J. R. B." He wishes to know what would be the advantage of forming a Society for the Acclimitization of certain Lepidoptera. Should entomologists really make up their minds to attempt what has been proposed, the advantage of such a society is obvious. It might insure success, when otherwise nothing could progress satisfactorily. In the first place, "J. R. B." seems to think that it is proposed to introduce insects now extinct. No such thing: it is proposed to increase the number of certain insects, particularly Antiopa, by means already laid before the readers of the N. N. B.; in fact, to preserve insects which are feared to be becoming extinct, but which have not yet quite disappeared from Great Britain. I quite disagree with "J. R. B.'s" assertion, that Britain has as many butterflies as she wants. Doubtless many entomologists join me in a wish for greater variety, and yet we should never dream of attempting the introduction of a really foreign insect. Even were anyone to propose acclimitizing such an insect, I should not oppose his scheme; on the other hand, I should do all I could to favour it, if there were a chance of success. W. J.
Southampton.

In last month's NOTE BOOK A. E. Buttermer asks me where I obtained my information respecting Sirex Gigas, as to its being a native of cold and mountainous countries. The work from which I gained my information was "Maunder's Treasury of Natural History," which I should be happy to quote if, Mr. Editor, your valuable space will admit. "Sirex Gigas is a genus and family of hymenopterous insects, of which the Sirex Gigas may be taken as a type. They have the antennæ jointed, and inserted near the forehead, the mandibles inserted internally, the maxillary palpe very small, nearly conical, and two-jointed, with the extremity of the abdomen prolonged into a horn, and the ovipositor exserted and formed of three threads. These insects are of large size, and generally inhabit pine forests in cold and mountainous countries, and produce during flight a buzzing noise like that of humble bees. In those countries they appear in great abundance, so that they become objects of popular dread. The larva have six feet, with the posterior extremity of the body terminated in a point. They live in wood, where they spin a cacoon and undergo their transformation. The Sirex Gigas has sometimes, though rarely, occurred in this country, and is as large as a hornet." (Query). Has the larva been found in this country?
S. REGELOUS.

WATER RAT OR WATER VOLE.—"There are many animals which have been saddled with a bad reputation merely on account of an unfortunate resemblance to another animal of really evil character. Among these misused innocents the Water Vole is very conspicuous, as the poor creature has been commonly supposed to be guilty of various poaching exploits which were really achieved by the ordinary brown rat. It is quite true that rats are often seen on the river banks in the act of eating captured fish, but these culprits are only the brown rats which have migrated from the farmyards for the summer months and intend to return as soon as autumn sets in. The food of the true Water Rat, or Water Vole, as it is more correctly named, is chiefly of a vegetable nature, and consists almost entirely of various aquatic plants and roots. . . . . . My own testimony coincides precisely with those of other observers, for I never yet saw the true snub-nosed, short-eared, yellow-toothed Vole engaged in eating animal food, although the brown rat may be often detected in such an act. . . . It will sometimes leave the water side and travel some little distance across the country in search of cultivated vegetables."—Rev. J. E. Wood, in *Routledge's Illustrated Natural History*.

DO SNAKES EAT FISH?—Before the slate quarry at Penn Recca near here was drained, a person told me that he saw a "long cripple" glide into the water and swim some way, but it did not stay long, and when it came out again he killed it, and wishing to see what it had eaten, opened it, and found it full of small minnows, of which there were plenty in the pool.

When my brother was at Holne Chase a short time ago he saw a snake, which on being disturbed went into an ornamental pond near, and coiled itself round the bottom of a pot of lilies, which was standing there: more than an hour and a half afterwards he saw it in the same position, and apparently watching for some small fish or whatever else should come in its way. The owner said he was unable to keep any fish in the pond, and he could not tell how they disappeared. Did the snakes eat them?

Perhaps some of the numerous readers of the N. N. B. may be able to give me some information of the subject. J. S. A.
Ashburton.

RARE BIRDS IN NORFOLK.—On the 19th of August, being at Yarmouth, I had the pleasure of seeing a pair of the Wood Sandpiper (*Totanus Glareola*) on a marshy place at the north end of the town, called the "Allotment."* They were most elegant birds on the wing, and uttered notes something between those of the Ringed Plover and the Redshank: one of them (a young female) I saw cleverly shot by Mr. James Nudd, junior, a resident of Yarmouth, and this one is now in my possession; the other one escaped. The next morning (20th August) I saw a bird feeding on the shore of the North River, and I cautiously crept up and watched it running and feeding for some time, until, not feeling at all convinced that it was a Dunlin, I shot it, and then found that it was a fine specimen of the Curlew Sandpiper (*Tringa Subarquata*) in transition between summer and winter plumage. This also was a female. — A. M. B.

Does rapidity of physical injury prevent the sensation of pain?—I don't think that rapidity of injury does *prevent* pain, but I do believe it *defers* the sensation. You may accidentally cut your finger with a sharp knife and not be aware of the fact until some time afterwards. A person may be able to endure any reasonable amount of pain after an operation though he cannot bear up against the operation itself. For instance, many persons would rather bear the most excruciating tortures than go to a dentist to have a tooth drawn, simply because they dread the operation. Some people, a little bolder than the last, take chloroform to deprive them of consciousness during the dreaded operation. The new knife, however, entirely supersedes the use of chloroform, because the patient does not feel any pain until the operation is over. — J. F. SUTTON.

STINGING SENSATION CAUSED BY CATERPILLARS.—In the last number of the N. N. B. there is a note made by Mr. Regelous on the above subject. The following fact may be of some interest to your correspondent:—On the 3rd of this month I found a large velvety-looking caterpillar feeding on the bramble, and having no collecting-box with me, I carried the insect carefully in my hand. After some little time I found a stinging sensation between my fingers similar to that described in the note above referred to, and for a while I was unable to trace its cause. On a close examination, I found that some minute hairs had become detached from the caterpillar, and were acting nettle-like on my fingers whenever I permitted them to meet. Had I lifted my hand to my neck and face, I should doubtless have felt the same sensation in those parts as Mr. Regelous did.
Castle Cary. — W. MACMILLAN.

AMERICAN SILKWORMS.—I am very much obliged to Mr. Leonard Harman to mention my name in connection with the introduction of these undoubtedly valuable breeds. If the Cecropia was taken in hand and bred by poor people, I am sure this might prove in time a benefit to that class. Little trouble, with a large return in silk. No want of food, as apple, plum, and cherry grow plentifully in England; and, finally, the Cocoon can stand the coldest temperature. What more is necessary, if otherwise the silk proves good enough to be used for coarser fabrics? The matter now rests in competent hands with Mr. L. Harman, and if anything can be done, he will prove it soon enough. — W. GEFFCKEN.
Stuttgart.

PRESERVATION OF SKINS FOR THE CABINET.—In answer to J. Laing I beg to offer two methods for the preservation of the skins of birds and animals. 1. A paste composed of four pounds of white curd soap, sliced and dissolved by boiling in one pint of water, to which is afterwards added one pound of arsenic and one ounce of camphor, then to be boiled again until it is of the consistency of paste. 2. A powder, composed of four pounds of alum, one pound of arsenic, and two ounces of flour of sulphur, well mixed and ground fine in a mortar. Both the above preparations are exceedingly useful, but care must be taken with them in consequence of their poisonous nature. For this reason I only use the paste, as it is less liable to come in contact with the air than a fine powder. — W. NEWBERRY.

An Oologist asks to what species of Dove two eggs belong which he found in a hole on a Devonshire moor. We give it up. If he had given a description of the eggs, *i.e.*, of their size and shape, we might perhaps be able to form some idea to what bird they belonged. How does your correspondent know they belonged to one of the doves? No British species of Columba habitually deposit their eggs in such a place. The Rock Dove (*Columba Livia*) builds in the sheltered and secluded parts of rocks but not in ground holes. A gentleman writing on the Stock Dove (*Columba Enas*) says he has found them in Norfolk building in rabbit warrens, but whether true or not I cannot say. No such instances have come under my own observation. Their general place of resort being the hole of a tree or in ivy covered ruins. — W. NEWBERRY.

ERRATA.—In my paper "List of British Moths," which appeared in your last number of the N. N. B., the following mistakes occur:—Under the head of "Flame Carpet," for "Brissica" read Brassica; under "Oblique Carpet," for "P. liguata" read P. Lignata; under "Small Waved Umber," for "P. vitabata" read P. vitalbata; for "Warter Carpet," read Water Carpet; and, under the same head, for "G. mollogo" read G. mollugo; for "Wetted Carpet" read Netted Carpet; under "Dark Spinach," for "Chenapodium" read Chenopodium; and under "Maple Prominent," for "N. cuculina" read N. cucullina.
— T. W. TEMPANY.
[Kindly forward your address.—ED.]

PUSS MOTH.—Could any correspondent of the N. N. B. tell me how to prevent grease in moths? I had some Tiger Moths (*C. Caja*) last year which were quite spoilt by an oily substance which spread over the wings and body. Last August I reared some larvæ of the Puss Moth, which I have now in the pupa state; and as these moths are very liable to become greasy, I should like to know a remedy for it. The larvæ were found feeding upon willow by the river-side; they formed their curious cocoons of small pieces of wood, glued or cemented together; they are quite hard, and firmly fixed to the sides of the breeding-cage. The moths will emerge in June. — J. H.

FOOD OF THE WATER-RAT.—Until a few weeks ago, I like many others believed that the food of the water-rat consisted of the young of water-fowl, etc.; but whilst taking a walk the other week I watched a water-rat feeding, and to my surprise found it was eating grass. The question then naturally came in my head—Where do all the young birds go? and I rather more than suspected that the pike must have a hand, or rather a mouth, in it. When I got home, looking at Mr. Wood's "Natural History," I found my suspicions were true. JOS. LAING.

Mr. Budge is decidedly mistaken in supposing that the water-rat feeds entirely on vegetables, if it does so at all. I once found a blackbird's nest, with eggs in it, about six feet high, in a bush near a river; about half an hour afterwards I passed the spot, and, to my surprise, saw a water-rat jump out of the nest, and dive into the water. On looking into the nest, I found a few fragments of eggs only. A friend informs me that he has seen a water-rat devouring a young waterhen. RUSTICUS.

THE USE OF LADY-BIRDS.—Lady-birds are exceedingly useful in gardens and greenhouses, as they live chiefly on the *Aphis*, a species of insect which crowds the trees in millions. From the bodies of these insects, which inhabit the under side of leaves, a thick sweet liquid called honey-dew drops upon the upper surface of the leaves below. This liquid injures plants by stopping up the pores of their leaves, and soon makes them look yellow. Lady-birds, therefore, are very serviceable to us, by removing the *Aphis*.
Gravesend. G. O. HOWELL.

BUTTERFLY.—ORIGIN OF THE WORD.—Two Saxon words—*buter*, butter, and *fleoge*, fly, make up our common English word butterfly. Naturalists tell us that from the yellow species, resembling the colour of butter, the name butterfly became a general appellation for the papilio; but as to when the word, in its present form, made its way into natural history, I am unable to inform Mr. Howell. H. H. ULIDIA.
Lurgan.

GRAY PHALAROPES.—It may interest some of the readers of the N. N. B. to know that three Gray Phalaropes (*Phalaropus lobatus*) were shot in this neighbourhood during the month of September. One on the 24th, another on the 25th, at Bopeep, and the third on the 27th at Bexhill. These are the only occurrences of the Gray Phalarope in this locality, since the autumn of 1866. F. PERSHOUSE, Junr
St. Leonards-on-Sea.

EREBIA BLANDINA.—I beg to mention the Isle of Man as a good locality for E. Blandina (the Scotch Argus). I took several in July and August on the hills in the direction of Laxey and Onchan. I also caught a specimen of the Yellow Ringed Carpet (*Larentia ruficinctata*), and some Five-spot Burnet Moths.
September 2nd. J. H.

Will "R. B. W.," or any other of your correspondents, give me a definition of the soul? Say whether it is in any way connected with the mind? And also whether the mind is not that calculative faculty commonly denominated the power of reasoning? J. F. SUTTON.

Can any of the readers of the N. N. B. tell me how to make a good butterfly net (portable), one that can be carried in the pocket and fixed on the end of a walking-stick; also where I can obtain any caterpillars of the privet hawk moth, or any common species. If preserved in spirits would be preferred.—Address R. T. W., office of the N. N. B.

AQUARIUM.—"The Handbook of Plain Instructions for the Management of Fresh Water Aquaria," edited by James Bishop, and published by Dean and Son, 65, Ludgate-hill, E.C., will furnish "H. S. A.," with all the information he requires. The price is 1s.
St. Leonards-on-Sea. F. P., Junr.

PUPÆ-DIGGING.—I would recommend Mr. Arthur W. Owen to get an admirable little work on "Pupa-digging" by the Rev. Mr. Greene, price 2d. It is published by Edward Newman, 9, Devonshire-street, Bishopsgate, N.E. G. O. HOWELL.
Gravesend.

PUPÆ DIGGING.—I should recommend Arthur W. Owen to get "The Insect Hunter's Companion," published by John Van Voorst, 1, Paternoster Row, which contains "An Essay on Pupæ Digging," by the Rev. Joseph Greene, M.A.
St. Leonards-on-Sea. F. P., Junr.

EGG OF THE TURTLE DOVE.—I think that "An Oologist" will find that the eggs of which he speaks belong to the Stock Dove (*Columba Ænas*), which sometimes lays its eggs in deserted rabbit warrens.
JOS. LAING.

Can any of your correspondents tell me if it is a usual thing for kittens to be born with their eyes open, because I have just seen a family of six which were born in that condition. L. K.

CRUST OF THE EARTH.—Was the matter forming the crust of the earth in its earliest stage of existence, in a state of fluidity? G. O. HOWELL.
Gravesend.

In answer to S. Regelous, I beg to say that I have a specimen of *Sirex Gigas* taken by a friend in the neighbourhood of Chelsea on August 12, 1869.
West End, Esher. Yours respectfully, C. M.

BUTTERFLY.—G. O. Howell will find an answer to his query on the origin of the word "butterfly," in *Notes and Queries*, 3rd Series, vol. II., p. 29.
Bath. W. P. R.

I suggest to W. Newberry that his "List of British Birds" would be greatly improved by affixing the average date of arrival and departure of each of our migratory birds. J. F. SUTTON.

Will any reader inform me whether I can obtain a list or a book of all the British Insects properly classed and with both English and scientific name?
B. B. NOEL.

EUTYCK AND ASKER.—Can any of the readers of the N.N.B. kindly tell me what bird is meant by the Eutych, Eutick, or Eutyck? and what lizard is meant by the Asker? JOS. LAING.

Will any of the numerous readers of the N. N. B. kindly inform me the best way of dying grass and moss green for trimmings, etc. JOHN BROWN.
Birmingham.

H. S. A. will find all the information he requires in a small pamphlet on the Aquarium, published by Dean and Son, London, price 1s. W. NEWBERRY.

ROUGH NOTES ON THE NATURAL HISTORY OF CORFU.

(*Continued from page* 324.)

JULY.

HEAT everywhere!—no escape save at the early morn or the darkening eve from the rays of the fiery sun, which blazes and flames in the sky until the deep and beautiful azure seems only a powerful reflector, serving to enhance, by its cloudless brilliancy, the beams of the solar god of day, which savagely floats at the last timid cloud of the morning, hurrying to escape to the colder regions of the north ere dissipated by the dry breath of its pursuer. See the snow on the far-off mountains shudders and falls dead from the rocks it covers, or short mosses it protects, and the dews spring to the air, and are lost in the bright presence. Noontide comes and the air affords no food for the insatiable sun; so he turns his attention to the earth, and the things animate and inanimate thereon; the ground cracks and opens before him, the pools dry up and the salt sea even grows tepid beneath his touch, shrinks in its bed, and leaves the seaweed to die upon the rocks it once covered; the flowers gasp in the open nooks and long for the night and its starlit dews, and the birds cease their song and hide in the cooler glades. Have you a fancy for touching things as you saunter along in the little shade there is, dreading the time when you must cross that open space which brazen-like glows before you?—if so, pray touch that rail by your side, or this cannon peeping over the ramparts. Ma foi! you will not try it again, I fancy, for if you are not burnt at the tips of your fingers you are so nearly singed that it is a miracle you escaped. You quicken your pace to escape as soon as possible from "Glorious Apollo." Vain confidence in your own cleverness!—you but hasten the catastrophe; that is the third time you will have to change your linen to-day, and you begin to seriously question the advisability of having three warm baths of perspiration and uncomfortableness per diem. Well, you have been warned, and it is your own fault; everybody is taking a siesta now, and no one goes out in the day, so the natives assert, but those patient animals (which never die, but as legends run are translated) and—(oh, my country)—Englishmen. Do you doubt me? Come down the main street, let us struggle on together, making tracks to avoid the cross currents of sun, and judiciously pausing near the damp fountain places to get a breathe. Do you see anyone in the street save those beggars, and porters asleep under the piazza? Yes, yes, all very well but the shopkeepers? Well, here is a jeweller's—" orefice " in gold letters above the window—see here is one of the Ionian rings you admired on my finger the other day, just like it! There is the shield for your initials set in the middle of a chain of little gold medallions, seven in all, which go round the finger. One you see has the Galley of Corfu engraved on it, the other the fish spear of Paxo; then Venus for Cerigo, Ulysses for Ithaca, Tripod for Zante — Figure bearing wand for Cephalonia, and Sappho's harp for Santa Maura in succession. Here also is a bracelet in fine filagree gold, the motto "Elpizo" (hope) upon it; what a nice and also suggestive present for the little Rosina. You will buy it; let us go in then. Halloo, no one about, and all these cases of rich jewellery. He "Bottega," "Maestro," "Diavolo," "Mr. Thingamy," and you exhaust your limited stock of Italian; you ran through a still smaller catalogue of modern Greek, and then commence the language understood all over the world—namely, an imperative stamp of the foot. Just as the cases quiver and the glasses rattle, a snore and a snort is heard; the inner door opens hurriedly, and out comes a little fat man—bald as to the head—smilingly and sleepily confused as to countenance, perspiringly oleaginous as to general appearance. Evidently this elderly party has been to sleep! A nice thing this would be in London, say you; why the shop if in the Strand would be moved to Cornhill, jeweller and all, by some expert thief or other. Poor beggars, there they don't know any better! none of these foreigners do. How much for this bracelet? "Si Sighore, this is the finest work of Malta—no, Genova I do mean;" and after blundering through several sleepy mistakes, you purchase it for ten Peruvian dollars or Colonni. Hardly have you been bowed out ere you hear the inner door click, and the worthy shopkeeper resume the thread of his repose.

This is curious, but then perhaps he is a well-to-do man, and can afford to perseveringly apply himself with zeal and fortitude to the study of sleep. Now just below us I can see a fruit stall standing out, the melons and tomatoes gleaming in the soft light which the awning throws over them; the poor man who keeps that is looking out for a customer I'll be bound. What a lovely sight; Lance must have painted one of his fruit studies from this very stall. Cherries, like ladies lips, side by side with golden oranges. Grapes of all shapes and colours, even to the little Zante or Corinth grape, which we call grocers' currants, straying over the sides of huge panniers, their velvet skins splendidly contrasting the blushes of the peaches kissed by the sweet young figs, gourds, melons, and apples confused with tomatoes and the purple egg fruit. In the shop from the outer wall, of which springs the striped awning hovering over these glories of the sunny isles, we shall find the merchant at work on the vegetables. Let us go in—empty! Hark, the voices of the night, thus early two distinct snores, a grunt, and a long enduring sigh. Well I'm!—no don't swear he is asleep too, so shy a punkin at his head, and let us go.

The fact is all the town at this hour is asleep, and as this fact slowly dawns on your bewildered sense, you say to yourself, with the superciliousness peculiar to your nation, ah, well thank goodness, I am English, and not like these poor devils, not able to face a little sun or fatigue. I was cast in a different mould, and my physique is a *little* different, I flatter myself, from that of these rascally thin-blooded foreigners. In good truth, if you have a thoroughly strong and sound constitution, and keep all your pores open, you *may* do almost anything, and face a sun which in England would kill you. The air is so pure and the climate so constant, that you know what you have to expect, and you will never, as in England, find a hot day succeeded by a bitter cold one, or *vice versâ*. Do not sleep or dawdle about in the sun, for it would be far better to work as hard as you could in the noontide heat than do that; drink all the water you like, even if you are as hot as a furnace; if in good health it will never hurt you: nor will wine either if exposed to much fatigue; eschew, however, spirits, save a glass now and then of "rake" (a first cousin of absinthe); this in moderation, say a thimbleful to a half glass of water, acts as an excellent tonic, and is (so the Greeks say) good for the chest and voice.

Some time about the middle of the month—I think the 18th—I went on an entomological expedition, with two other English people, to a place called Benezza, about eight miles to the eastward of the town of Corfu. We passed through Kastrades at about six in the morning, chatting merrily of the prizes we hoped to make; the air at that hour was cool and redolent of sweet odours, and, after a little walking, we reached the point of the Calikiopulo, opposite Perama: here we hailed the ferry boat, and while being carried over, noticed that the water was so clear that at no time did we lose sight of the bottom, and yet in places it must have been two or three fathoms deep. On landing, we struck through the olive groves by the sea, and had not gone far before we came to an open spot, on the borders of which the myrtle bushes clustered with their sweet flowers. Flying low from an ilex (*Ilex quercus*) I caught the white hawstreak, and hovering above the myrtle the lovely white admiral *Limenites camilla*). With this beautiful butterfly I was enraptured, for such is the elegant contrast of colour, that catch it when or as often as you may, it never seems to pall upon the sense. Near this I caught some more, and then entered on a road lined with white stone columns, below which were rocky dells, and above thick high bushes of various sorts. These Colonni, placed as gudies for the traveller along this rocky way, are I believe of ancient date: about here I captured dozens of the Fritillary (*Argynnis paphia*), and as we journeyed on in the lovely woods by the side of the Ionian sea, still as the lake we had just left, the dense foliage opened, and disclosed the mighty rocks of Casturi and Benizza towering ruggedly hundreds of feet above us, and clothed with dark pines on their summits—from one of which issues the stream which supplies the town with water. A tributary of this mountain torrent —a tiny threadlike little streamlet, dripped from a rock in the shade hard by; concentrating its forces by the aid of a stick, we managed to fill our water cups, and thus dilute a bottle of honey-like Orgeat, and rising refreshed proceeded on our way, and soon reached Benizza, which we found a very pretty clean little place; the houses as usual having a trellis work covered with muscatel grape vines in the front acting as a porch, under which the women sat spinning or making fishing nets. Without stopping, we passed right through the village to a spot reported great in insects: here we caught *A. paphia*, *Goneptyrix rhamni*, and the two swallow tails (*Papilio machaon* and *Podalirius*). By the side of an orchard under the slope of a hill, we were gratified by a sight of the glorious Camberwell Beauty (*Vanessa antiopa*); it vanished, however, from our despairing sight, and we saw no more of the famous stranger. A scarlet tiger moth (*Hypercompa dominula*) fell to our share, and this was all we got before we returned to the village gardens, where we feasted upon figs, for which we were not allowed to pay by reason of the good proprietor knowing a friend of mine very intimately. Outside the village wine shop I saw a remarkably handsome young man standing—he was short and rather stout proportioned; but he had gold coloured hair, fresh complexion, and bright blue eyes. So astonished was I that I spoke to him in English, but as he did not understand and returned some answer in Greek, I was forced to conclude that he was "Rara Avis in terris;" certainly not "nigroque," however.

Quite a sensation was caused by the attempt of a daring fellow of one of the regiments stationed in Corfu to escape to Patras in Independent Greece two hundred and fifty miles distant. Had he reached there, it seems that he would have been free; so, tired of a military life, he formed the project to get away one dark night by stealing a yacht, which lay in the Mandrachio; and was actually well away on the coast of Albania, ere a gunboat started in pursuit the next morning, and brought him back. He had but just completed a term of imprisonment for a similar offence. He was again placed in confinement in the main guard-room, the only egress from which, besides the door, was by a skylight in the roof some forty feet above the floor. Strange to say, in the morning he was again missing, and a rope over the battery adjacent told the tale of another attempt on the sea. Boats were sent in pursuit off the coast, men searched for the runaway without avail, and after two days every one concluded that he had this time indeed escaped. On the afternoon of the third day after this, some rumours were afloat in the garrison that he had been seen in one of the subterranean passages of the citadel. The place was scoured, ever nook and hiding place searched, and after the lapse of an hour, actually found him in a dark hole cold, wet, and half starved, being all that time without food. Poor wretch, I pitied him, for he looked miserable, and yet quietly determined. He was subsequently tried by court martial I heard, and sentenced to four years' penal servitude. At that period I believe such a sentence exempted from future military service. *A propos* of military affairs and courts martial, I heard a good thing (too good to be true I am afraid) about a prisoner tried by one of these courts. The case (one of those frivolous charges too often investigated and too frequently punished by these quasi-judicial assemblies) was going against the man with a shameless disregard to all fairness, and with an evident bias to the stronger side; when all at once the prisoner, who had been uneasily fidgetting for some time between his escort, and had thereby drawn on himself the severe censure of the martinet of an adjutant, stooped, and looked about as if in search of something under the table, which formed the "bench." "Steady, sir, how dare you, stand to attention. What are you doing?" said the president of the court, too angry to be coherent. "I am looking, sir," said the prisoner, calmly, "for justice. I have not found it yet above the board. I thought possibly it might be hiding under the table!" Some young "subs" tittered at this, but at once composed their features into the proper degree of vacuity under the freezing glances of offended martinetdom; and the poor fellow got some addition to his punishment for his irrepressible witticism. Not but what wit is thoroughly appreciated in its proper place in the "service," for I have been to amateur theatrical representations in the fine opera house of Corfu, in which the performers, both officers and men, have convulsed the audience by their clever assumption of character. One of the most thoroughly humorous fellows I ever met was one whom I will call Captain Sanghthed; and if not bearing exactly upon the subject of Natural History, yet perhaps I may be pardoned if I give a precis of the conversation I had with him, touching the development of his histrionic abilities. After I had bothered him for some time to (as the snake said to the bird he was crushing) unfold a smooth unvarnished ta(i)l(e), he, in as nearly these words as I can recollect, launched into

AMATEUR THEATRICALS.

It is now some years (said he) that I was quartered in a place, which shall be nameless; but to give you a faint idea of the style of thing I may state that, beyond a little snipe shooting and fox hunting in winter, a vast quantity of drill and wind in summer, and a little quiet lady-killing and cub hunting in autumn, the place afforded no society or fun, excepting what you made for yourselves. It was in this delectable retreat that I first officiated as prompter in a Noah's Ark sort of an arrangement; a cross, as one of ours said, between the military dead-house and the red barn.

I will remember the piece, the loved one of all amateurs—"The Charcoal Burner." The piece was apparently very well cast, and I thought, as I sat shivering in my nook, with bill, pistol, and the book before me, that I had never seen a better got up Matthew Esdaile. Contrary to the general rule, a sergeant took the part of the Charcoal Burner, and looked his part to perfection I must say; but when the curtain rose to a miserably thin house, I could see that all the performers were not at their ease; for instance, one would forget his part and suddenly ejaculate "Ah!" in a tone of deep and thrilling mystery as if it were in the part, walk across to my side, and with the vain idea that the audience could not see through this very shallow manoeuvre, audibly whisper "Quick! what's the cue." All, however, went pretty well, until the scene where old Matthew, in gloating over his ill-gotten wealth, is shot in the back by the Charcoal Burner. At the proper cue the Charcoal Burner duly fired. Click! went the pistol (I am afraid I spilled some of the brandy and water I had been drinking into the cap bag when it was in my nook). Another attempt, with the same result! when, to my horror and the amusement of the "house," the old man distinctly muttered, "Hang it man! do something, stab me, can't you?"

Thus appealed to, the unfortunate Charcoal Burner lost his head, and forgetting what he had in his hand, took a step forward, and buried the muzzle of his pistol to the hilt as it were in the heart of old Matthew, who immediately died *secundum artem*. The roars of laughter which shook the building at the sight of a man stabbed with a pistol, threatened at one time to stop the progress of the piece. Order being once again restored, the play was resumed, with some unimportant hitches, until the end of the second scene in the second act, after which the Charcoal Burner is not required for some time. On the cue being given for his reappearance, he was nowhere to be found, and the back scenes, entrances, and green-room resounded with the shouts for Smuggins. These cries were soon taken up by the delighted audience, and a perfect Babel ensued. In the midst of this pandemomium, some of the amateurs came to me with the pleasing news that I should have to go and read the part, as there was no one else to do it. In vain I protested that I had no histrionic powers, could never face an audience, felt ill, had a sudden attack of asiatic cholera, and a host of other evils. At last I summoned up courage to go on the stage, presented to the public by the sometime defunct Matthew Esdaile as Ensign Sanghthed, who has kindly consented, owing to the severe indisposition of Sergeant Smuggins, to read the remainder of the part. A storm of hisses, cat-calls, and other soul enlivening strains, greeted this, my first appearance in public, and you may depend did not add to my self-possession. However, I commenced, and blundered on, and with the trifling mistake of continuing to read into another actor's part (while the poor fellow stood staring at me, wondering when I *should* leave off) got on pretty well, and warming to the work, actually got a pitying clap for my spirited rendering of one passage. All the more difficult (as the Weekly Ribunations said in its critique upon our acting, as Ensign Sanghthed had to retain a jujube in his mouth during the reading). Yes, you may laugh, but I had a severe sore throat at the time. Well, we finished the charcoal business, and I must say I think some of its blackness was infused into the character of one of its members at least, for subsequent events proved that when Sergeant Smuggins took leave of us that evening, he also took with him about £150 of his captain's money, as well as all the available cash belonging to the Blager's Amateur Society—he being unfortunately both pay sergeant and theatrical treasurer. Up to the date of my exchange he had not been heard of. There was an after piece, but as he had to perform a jig, and as the whole fun of the piece hinged upon the assumption of the Irish brogue, I certainly did not feel competent to undertake that, and therefore the curtain was dropped and the money returned at the doors. You may think after this that I should never attempt the stage, but I suppose the inherent vanity of man is such that he only sees in the failures of others the opportunity to show the world that he is the one destined to make it acknowledge his unquestionable superiority to the old style, or mayhap I was influenced by the glorious contemplations of the fact that I had read before an audience of some hundred or more persons without being actually hissed off the stage. Be this as it may, a month or two after we were ordered abroad, and we had not been settled in our new quarters long, before I had the felicity of seeing my name in print as Marquis de Rotondo in "Don Cæsar de Bazan." I remember the flutter of excitement I was in when I first saw the elaborately got up bill lying upon the ante-room table, half fearing before I looked at it that the printer had made some mistake and had not inserted my name; but there it was, and as I heard my brother officers comments upon the cast, how hard I tried to look unconcerned when they came to my name; but it would not do, sleeping or walking that splendid line, more beautiful than any I had read before even in Shakespeare or Milton, would ever fairy-like float before my vision! I can recall it now! Marquis de Rotondo (Mr. A. Sanghthed).

This was about a week before the performance was to take place, so I had plenty of time to admire my name and to lead the conversation at every available opportunity to the piece. I ordered fifty of the bills to be struck off for my own private use, and sent them to every one of my friends, and as some of them were in India and some in the Colonies, it cost me a nice little sum for postage. Let me say I was perfect in my part, which was that of an old man—a rather curious thing for me to be cast for, you will think; but you know I was called "old Sanghthed" when quite a boy. When I say I was perfect in my part, I mean of course in the words, for I knew as much of the stage walk and appropriate gestures then, as a donkey is likely to know of the parentage of his father. I presume I must have appeared a little "wooden."

I should have stated before that, being now in a foreign country, we could not get professional ladies to assist us, and therefore had to fall back upon the youngsters of our corps to represent the divine sex. Two were found of our own rank, but by far the best of our "women," as we called them, was a young private of the name of B——h, and this fellow I would pit against any actress I every saw; his tone of voice was all that could be desired, his action admirable, and his get-up irreproachable. I have known him to make the acquaintance of women, or follow them in the street, solely for the purpose of studying a certain toss of the head, peculiar carriage, or some new fashion in dress. My Countess was one of the junior Ensigns: an awful scamp, however, she (I mean he) was, and we used to rehearse together until we knew every word of each other's parts, and decided that we should make a great hit (which we certainly did) in the opera-house now hired for the occasion. To be brief, the eventful night came; and after the usual confusion of some one having got the sword intended for another, and finding the richest part of your dress as well as your wig had been appropriated by some "super," who had to come in once about the middle of the piece, and was then comfortably seated in one of the boxes waiting his turn to come on, solacing himself meanwhile with some dark-eyed donna. After all these *desagrémens* had been comfortably squared, as well as a serious fracas between Don Cæsar and Don Jose for the possession of the Order of St. Garlico, a tinsel star of the most comet-like effulgence, we mustered behind the great curtain as handsomely dressed and proper a lot of dare devils as you would wish to see. The band in front was playing a lively set of quadrilles; and though the first bell had rang, we formed three sets on the stage, and wigged, powdered, and armed as we were, did ladies' chain, balancez, set and turn partners, with more than exuberant jollity: we were actively engaged in the performance of one figure, and I knew the Marchioness (who was my partner) was performing some highly improper steps for a lady, when to the confusion of all, by some mistake on the part of the scene-shifters, up went the curtain so rapidly that the audience had a full view of the King Don Cæsar, soldiers of the guard, the Judge, and Alguezil, performing the most extraordinary capers that it is possible to conceive. The confusion was terrific, for in trying to rush off the stage the swords entangled themselves in the ladies' dresses, and more than one whom it would take something to send to grass made a closer acquaintance with the boards than was conducive to the comfort of his elongated nasal prolongation, as some one calls it. Unfortunately at this instant, while yet the tear of mirth stood in every eye, the great man of the garrison took his seat in his box, and quickly learned from his aides the cause of the laughter, which was still echoing, and drowning the saluting strains of "God save the Queen." The curtain was lowered again, and quickly rose on the set piece; and I think this episode made the people more genial, and disposed to look over our blunders. All went very smoothly until it was my turn. I can remember coming on in a sort of nightmare state of existence. I ought to have said, "Where on earth can we be?" But my tongue clave to the roof of my mouth, and I mentally applied those words to myself. I saw hundreds of eyes staring at me, nodded insanely to one or two I recognised in the stage boxes, took a walk round the stage, the prompter almost shouting my cue; but I was deaf to all save the smothered roar of disappointment, for I had that dreadful malady "stage fright" in its severest form. Howls of "Stage to let!" "Off! off!" only drove the cue farther from memory; when I was recalled to my senses by the behaviour of the Marchioness, who giving me a tremendous kick shouted out, "Take that, you lunatic duffer—come out of it!" By "it" I suppose he meant the state of coma I was in. Strange to say, I found my voice almost directly; and instead of resenting such a really painful insult, I went on with my part as soon as the screams of laughter had sobered down a little. I need hardly say that the spectacle of a lovely and distinguished lady, dressed in the height of Spanish fashion, bestowing a kick and curse at the same time upon her bosom lord was ludicrous in the extreme; and this was not the worst treatment I received at her hands (very white they were too, as well as her arms, for both had been covered with a sort of flour paste, in lieu of violet powder, to hide the ravages committed by the sun in the cricket-field). It had been arranged between us that when I came to a certain part I should half draw my sword from the sheath, to add due effect to my words, so that when my Marchioness gave me the cue I commenced very valiantly—"Your honour! Let any one dare to attack your honour, and this good sword now rusting in honourable repose will leap from its scabbard." Here I essayed to draw; but to no purpose did I try, swear, and pull—the sword would *not* come, it was immovable. To add to my vexation, I could see my brute of a Marchioness shaking with suppressed laughter, the perspiration running down in streams at his efforts to control himself, and forming little puddles of paste in sundry nooks of his features. I also was in a dreadful state, for I was stopping the progress of the piece by my efforts to subdue my refractory sword, until warned by the voice of the prompter to proceed. How happy I was when the piece came to a finish! I found out subsequently that that beast Jokely (my Marchioness) had poured some melted shellac into my sword sheath, and thus for the nonce rendered my good sword immovable. To my delight, however—I suppose on the principle of one fool making many—I was not the only sufferer by this night's business. It seems the Judge, a very jolly fellow of ours, had come dressed in a pair of white stockings. All voted, of course, that this was not *en règle* for a Judge's costume. But what was to be done? There was no time to lose. At last some bright wit suggested the stockings could be painted black, which was accordingly done while they were on poor Ned's legs by the aid of some lamp-black and oil, which was standing handy in the scene-painter's den. After the performance the Judge wined pretty deeply, and throwing himself upon his bed slept in nearly all his clothes, forgetting all about the stockings. Of course with the morning came the inevitable bath; but it was useless scrubbing, the paint had been mixed with some diabolical compound, had penetrated the stockings, and poor Ned S.'s legs remained for about three weeks in a suit of most melancholy mourning. We had a nice life in the garrison you may suppose after this, constant inquiries being made for the gallant Marquis, and the Judicial Blackleg—a name which poor Ned retained to his death, which happened in '66. I intended to drop the drama after this; but several of my chums persuaded me to try again, and I, willing to believe I should one day be a celebrity, was nothing loth to be decided by their opinions (expressed, I believe, solely with a view to their own amusement). Be this as it may, at our next performance some six months later, I had so much improved, thanks to the counsel of our leading tragedian, that it was voted that I should soon be fit to play in sixth-rate parts. That was a proud moment for me when I read in the *Mediterranean Buster*, that amongst the talented amateurs of the 201st Blazers we could not fail to perceive that more than one of their number had greatly improved since the last representation. In particular, the assumption of the waiting man's character by Mr. A. Sanghthed was remarkably fine; seldom, indeed, have we seen a subject so excellently handled by an amateur. The cool and collected way in which he brought in the wine goblets when ordered by the King, and the graceful tone of voice in which he noticed those memorable words, "It is, my Liege," stamp Mr. Sanghthed as an actor of great talent. It is much to be regretted that the plot of the piece allowed Mr. Sanghthed to appear but once, and that upon the occasion quoted above; yet we are fully convinced, had his part been twice as long, Mr. Sanghthed would have been eminently qualified for the task. Such dulcet paragraphs as this were an immense incentive to exertion, and after some years I had become quite a respectable delineator of character, and had attained to playing second or third-rate parts. I remember about this time a circumstance occurring which caused a great stir. We were about going on the stage to play "Othello," when we discovered that our chief performer who was to play the noble Moor was decidedly "screwed;" however, he seemed pretty quiet, and by the aid of cold water plentifully applied we freshened him up sufficiently to go on, telling him at the same time to look to the prompter if he should lose himself. He got on pretty well for some time, and being darkened for the character the audience did not perceive his state. He certainly now and then addressed me as Iago (I was playing Cassio), and when I corrected him once in a whisper, said—"Orr ri, Sanghed, ol booy!" But beyond a few in the immediate vicinity of the stage no one heard this, and his faltering and uncertain delivery was only looked upon by some of his admirers as a proof of his genius in coming the "darkie business;" many in the house (it was crammed with soldiers and sailors) looking upon the illustrious Moor as little better than a full-blooded buck nigger.

LIST OF BRITISH MOTHS:

NATURE OF THEIR FOOD,

AND TIMES OF THEIR PERFECT APPEARANCE.

NOCTUÆ.

TRIFIDÆ.

BOMBYCIFORMES.

BUFF ARCHES (*Thyatira derasa*). Feeds on the common bramble (R. fruticosus). Flies in July.

Peach Blossom (*Thyatira batis*). Feeds on R. fruticosus. Flies in June and July.

Lesser Satin Moth (*Cymatophora duplaris*). Feeds on B. Alba. Flies about Midsummer.

Satin Carpet (*Cymatophora fluctuosa*). Feeds on B. Alba. Flies in June.

Lesser Lutestring (*Cymatophora diluta*). Feeds on Q. robur or B. Alba. Flies in June and July.

Poplar Lutestring (*Cymatophora Or.*) Feeds on P. tremula and P. nigra. Flies in June and July.

Figure of Eighty (*Cymatophora ocularis*). Feeds on P. tremula. Flies in June.

Yellow Horned (*Cymatophora flavicornis*.) Feeds on B. Alba. Flies in March.

Frosted Green (*Cymatophora ridens*). Feeds on Q. Robur. Flies in April.)

BRYOPHILIDÆ.

Marbled Green (*Bryophila glandifera*.) Feeds on lichens. Flies in July and August.

Marbled Beauty *Bryophila Perla*). Feeds on lichens. Flies in July, August, and September.

Tree Lichen Beauty (*Bryophila Algæ*). Feeds on lichens. Flies in July.

BOMBYCOIDÆ.

Scarce Marveil-du-Jour (*Depthera Orion*). Feeds on B. alba and Q. robur. Flies in June.

Dark Dagger (*Acronycta tridens*.) Feed on P. spinosa and C. oxyacantha. Flies in June.

Gray Dagger (*Acronycta Psi*). Feeds on C. oxyacantha, P. communes, and other trees. Flies in June.

Miller (*Acronycta leporina*). Feeds on B. alba. Flies in June.

Sycamore (*Acroncyta Aceris*). Feeds on Quercus rober, Acer pseudoplatanus, and Æsculus hippocastanum. Flies in June.

Poplar Gray (*Acronycta megacephala*). Feeds on several species of poplar, among others balsamifera. Flies in June.

Grisette (*Acronycta strigosa*). Feeds on C. oxyacantha. Flies in June and July.

Alder (*Acronycta Alni*). Feeds on A. glutinosa and C. oxyacantha. Flies in June.

Coronet (*Acronycta Ligustri*). Feeds on privet(*L. vulgare*), and ash (*Fraxinus excelsior*). Flies in June and July.

Knot Grass (*Acronycta Rumicis*). Feeds on H. vesca, P. aviculare, dock, and other plants. Flies in May and June.

Scarce Dagger (*Acronycta auricoma*). Feeds on R. fruticosus. Flies in May and July.

Light Knot Grass (*Acronycta Menyanthidis*). Feeds on M gale. Flies in June.

Sweet-gale Moth (*Acronycta myricæ*.) Flies in May and June.

Powdered Wainscot (*Symira venosa*.) Feeds on Arundo Phragmites. Flies in June.

LEUCANIDÆ.

Brown-line Bright-eye (*Leucania conigera*). Feeds on Triticum repens, and several other kinds of grass. Flies in July.

Delicate (*Leucania vitellina*). Feeds on grasses.

Double-line (*Leucania turca*). Feeds on the spring wood rush (Luzula vernalis.) Flies in June.

Clay (*Leucania lithargyria*). Feeds on various kinds of grass. Flies in July.

American Wainscot (*Leucania extranea*). Flies in September.

Obscure Wainscot (*Leucania absoleta*). Feeds on A. Phragmites. Flies in June.

Cosmopolitan (*Leucania Loreyi*). Flies in July.

Shore Wainscot (*Leucania littoralis*). Feeds on Ammophila arundinacea. Flies in June and July.

Striped Wainscot (*Leucania pudorina*). Feeds on A. Phragmites. Flies in July.

Shoulder-Striped Wainscot (*Leucania comma*) Feeds on Dactylis glomerata and other grasses. Flies in June.

Devonshire Wainscot (*Leucania putrescens*). Feeds on grass. Flies in July.

Southern Wainscot (*Leucania straminea*). Feeds on grasses. Flies in June.

Smoky Wainscot (*Leucania impura*). Feeds on grass. Flies in July.

Common Wainscot (*Leucania palleus*). Feeds on grass. Flies in June, July, and August.

Flame Wainscot (*Meliana flammea*). Flies in June.

Silky Wainscot (*Senta ulvæ*). Feeds on A. Phragmites. Flies in June.

Small Rufous (*Cœnobia rufa*). Flies in July.

Reed Wainscot (*Nonagria Cannæ*). Feeds on reed mace (typha latifolia). Flies in August.

Bull Rush (*Nonagria Typhæ*). Feeds on T. latifolia. Flies in September.

Twin Spotted Wainscot (*Nonagria geminipuncta*). A. phragmites flies in July.

Brown Veined Wainscot (*Nonagria arundineti*). Feeds on A. phragmites. Flies in July.

Fenn's Nonagria (*Nonagria brevilinea*). Feeds on T. latifolia. Flies in August.

Large Wainscot (*Calamia lutosa*). Feeds on A. phragmites. Flies in August.

Fen Wainscot (*Calamia Phragmitidis*). Feeds on A. phragmites. Flies in June.

Brighton Wainscot (*Synia musculosa*). Flies in August.

Small Wainscot (*Tapinostola fulva*). Feeds on sedge (carex), also on stems of grass (poa aquatica). Flies in September.

Concolorous (*Tapinostola concolor*). Flies in June.

Mere Wainscot (*Tapinostola hellmanni*). Flies in June.

Lyme Grass (*Tapinostola elymi*). This insect is very rare; one or two specimens only have been taken in England.

Bonds Wainscot (*Chortodes bondii*). Flies in June and July.

Small Dotted-Buff (*Chortodes arcuosa*). Feeds on the turfy hair grass (*aira cæspitosa*). Flies in June and July.

Brindled Ochre (*Dasypolia templi*). Feeds on cow parsley (heracleum sphondylium. Flies in October.

AMPAMIDÆ.

Frosted Orange (*Gortyna flavago*). Feeds on

C. palustris, E. canabium, D. europæa, S. nigra, A. lappa, V. thapsus. Flies in June.

Ear Moth (*Hydræcia nictitans*). Feeds on grasses. Flies in July.

Butter-bur (*Pelasites vulgaris*). Flies in October.

Rosy Rustic (*Hydræcia micacea*). Feeds on Cyperus, Carex, etc. Flies in August.

Flame (*Axylia putris*). Feeds on various low plants. Flies in June.

Clouded-bordered Brindle (*Xylophasia nurea*). Feeds on species of Rumex, Primula, and several grasses. Flies in June.

Light Arches (*Xylophasia lithoxylea*). Feeds on grasses. Flies in June.

Reddish Light Arches (*Xylophasia sublustris*). Flies in June.

Dark Arches (*Xylophasia polyodon*). Feeds on grasses. Flies in June and July.

Clouded Brindle (*Xylophasia hepatica*). Feeds on S. media, grass, etc. Flies in June.

Slender Clouded Brindle (*Xylophasia scolopacina*). Feeds on a species of wood rush (*Luzula*), and also on coarse grasses.

Birds-wing (*Dipterygia Pinastri*). Feeds on different species of block (*Rumex*). Flies in June.

Silver Cloud (*Xylomiges conspicillaris*). Feeds on L. corniculatus. Flies in May.

Feathered Brindle (*Aporophyla australis*) On the continent this insect feeds on Asphodelus, microcarpus, and cichorium. Flies in August.

Small-mottled Willow (*Laphygma exigua*). Feeds on plantain. Flies in October.

Bordered Gothic (*Neuria saponariæ*). Feeds on silene and other low plants. Flies in July.

Feathered Gothic *Heliophobus popularis*). Feeds on grasses. Flies in September.

Beautiful Gothic (*Heliophobus hispidus*). Feeds on grass. Flies in September.

Autler (*Charæas graminis*). Feeds on grasses. Flies in August.

Feathered Ear (*Pachetra leucophæa*). Feeds on grass. Flies in June and July.

Straw Under-wing (*Cerigo cytherea*). Feeds on grasses. Flies in July.

Flounced Rustic (*Luperina testacea*). Feeds on grass. Flies in August and September.

Dumeril's Luperina (*Luperina dumerilii*). This moth is very rare; two specimens only are said to have been taken.

Guenee's Luperina (*Luperina Guenéei*) Flies in August.

Hedge Rustic (*Luperina cespitis*). Feeds on grasses. Flies in August.

Crescent-striped (*Mamestra abjecta*). Flies in July.

Large Nutmeg (*Mamestra anceps*). Flies in June.

White Colon (*Mamestra albicolon*). Feeds on various species of chenopodium and Atriplex. Flies in May and June.

Confused (*Mamestra furva*). Feeds on grasses. Flies in July.

Cabbage Moth (*Mamestra brassicæ*). Feeds on various species of rumex and chenopodium, and also on cultivated varieties of brissica.

Dot (*Mamestra persicarie*). Feeds on elder (*S. nigra*), and a variety of other plants. Flies in June.

Rustic Shoulder-Knot (*Apamea basilinea*). Feeds on wheat. Flies in May and June.

Union Rustic (*Apamea connexa*). Flies in June and July.

Dusky Brocade (*Apamea gemina*). Feeds on various species of grass. Flies in June and July.

Small Clouded Brindle (*Apamea unanimis*). Feeds on grass. Flies in July.

Doubled-lobed (*Apamea ophiogramma*). Flies in June.

Crescent (*Apamea fibrosa*). Feeds on the common yellow flag (*Iris pseudacocus*). Flies in July.

Common Rustic (*Apamea oculea*). Feeds on grass. Flies in July.

Marbled Minor (*Miana strigilis*). Feeds on grass. Flies in June and July.

Middle-barred Minor (*Miana fasciuncula*). Flies in June.

Rosy Minor (*Miana literosa*). Flies in June and July.

Cloaked Minor (*Miana furuncula*). Flies in July.

Least Minor (*Photedes captiuncula*). Flies in July.

Haworth's Minor (*Celæna Haworthii*). Feeds on cotton grass (*Eriophorium*). Flies in July and August.

CARADRINIDÆ.

Treble Lines (*Crammesia trilinea*). Feeds on plantago major. Flies in June.

Marsh Moth (*Hydrilla palustris*). Feeds on plantago and other low plants. Flies in May and July.

Reddish Buff (*Acosmetia caliginosa*). Flies in June.

Mottled Rustic (*Caradrina morpheus*). Feeds on Docks and other low plants. Flies in June. July, and August.

Uncertain (*Caradrina alsines*). Feeds on A. media. Flies in July.

Rustic (*Caradrina clauda*). Feeds on A. media. Flies in June and July.

Pale Mottled Willow (*Caradrina cubicularis*). Feeds on wheat, peas, etc. Flies in June.

T. W. TEMPANY.

THE REPTILES AT THE ZOOLOGICAL GARDENS.

THE reptile-house in the Gardens at Regent's Park is apt somewhat to disappoint the ordinary observer. Its occupants in many instances are stowed away comfortably beneath the blankets with which they are generally provided; and those which are visible are lying motionless on the gravel, or reposing in the branches of a tree. Very little motion is to be seen, unless it be among the lizards, which are more active than the serpents; but of whom the larger kinds are in the habit of standing in apparently the most uneasy attitudes for a considerable time. In this, and many other respects, they resemble the serpents, and there are indeed species which seem to form connecting links between the two Orders.

The *Ophidia* are, however, seen to much greater advantage at their feeding-time, which occurs once a week; not that they are all fed so often, for many will take sufficient food at a meal for several weeks, and some (in particular the pythons) have been known to fast for months together. Having been present lately on the occasion of these creatures receiving their usual allowance, we purpose to give a short account, from careful observation, of the manner in which they seized and killed their prey.

If we disregard the scientific divisions of the Order which comprises these animals, we may divide them into three classes: firstly, those which seize their prey with their teeth, and crush it in their folds; secondly, those which seize and swallow it alive, after the manner of lizards; and thirdly, those which bite, or rather strike it with poisonous fangs. Of the first, the finest examples are the pythons and boas, besides which there are the yellow snakes of the West Indies, and others. Those of the second are fewer in number; they include the rat snake of Bengal, viperine snake, English snake, etc. The present specimens of the third class include rattlesnakes, and Indian and Egyptian cobras, water vipers, etc.

These divisions are not strictly scientific, as some of the poisonous serpents have a structure closely resembling that of the boas, and are classed with them, but they will serve our present purpose better.

The constricting serpents, as we may term them, are kept in large cases, the entrance to which is either by a glass door in the front, which opens by sliding up, or by a similar contrivance at the back, in the wooden partition. The colubrine snakes are in some of these cases generally, and indeed are so harmless that little precaution is needed. The venomous serpents have no opening but a small one on the lid of the case, about two or three inches square. Through this their food is introduced; and all necessary operations for the cleanliness and order of the interior are performed with a rod of stout wire, to the evident disgust of the occupants, who, if new comers, strike at it vigorously with their fangs. The first to be fed were the yellow snakes, and other species in the same case. The keeper, having unceremoniously removed the blanket, beneath which most of the occupants of the compartment were huddled together, as usual, quickly introduced under the glass door about a dozen sparrows and one or two Guinea pigs. The former immediately retired to the darkest corners, seeming however to be quite unconcerned as to the presence of the snakes, as in some cases they stood on the bodies of the latter, which for the most part remained motionless. The Guinea pigs were more restless, moving slowly about as if in search of food. They seemed to be preferred by the snakes to the sparrows; and presently one of the reptiles, waiting his opportunity, seized a Guinea pig by the neck, and jerking it nearer threw two or three folds round it, killing it in a few seconds.

The other snakes rapidly despatched the sparrows in the same way, when seized; but they were apparently in no hurry, as there was a number of the birds in one corner for more than an hour, which had not been touched during that time. It may be well to remark that there is nothing revolting in the spectacle of a serpent taking its food. Its victim suffers neither the mental or bodily torture ordinarily supposed. When seized, it is killed without delay, especially if it struggles to escape; and before its seizure it is never conscious of danger. Not only is this well known to those in charge of the creatures, but we can verify it from actual and careful observation. A rabbit will approach a snake out of mere curiosity, and after sniffing at its head, and even being touched by its tongue, will start to another part of the enclosure, and resume its composure, returning again in the course of its explorations to the same snake without the least uneasiness, except what arises from a want of cabbage leaves, and the indigestibility of the gravel flooring. Guinea pigs show even less concern, and are not so easily startled by any moving object. We are induced to make these remarks because a well-meaning but injudicious individual wrote to the *Times* some time since upon what he considered the cruelty of giving live animals to be tortured slowly to death. It was, however, shown during the discussion which ensued, that facts were in direct opposition to the suggestions of sentimental imaginations upon the subject.

The snakes which had seized the sparrows, etc., waited till their prey was quite dead before they uncoiled and began slowly to prepare for swallowing it. The pythons, which occupy an adjoining case, and are the largest serpents in the collection, were next supplied with two or three ducks. The largest python instantly seized one, and threw one fold round it. He then remained perfectly motionless, appearing to be satisfied with having secured the bird, and did not at once kill it. The duck did not seem at first much concerned at such unusual treatment, but soon became restless, on which the python tightened the fold, and in about a minute had quite destroyed it. Having waited for some minutes, as if to make sure that life was extinct, he slowly unwound his coil from the body, and touched it with his muzzle, moving it about till he had found the head. The idea of lubrication with saliva, now quite exploded, evidently arose from this habit of feeling over the body with the mouth. Having taking the head into his mouth, he began to swallow the carcase, his jaws stretching to an mmense extent to allow of its passage. When he found any difficulty, he used the part of his body which lay nearest to it to push it gently, and considering the apparent difficulty, was not long in completing his meal. The supply of food is never stinted, and we believe that it is not uncommon for a python to devour six or eight ducks and rabbits on one day. Of course a full meal takes a long period to digest, as is the case in all reptiles.

The colubrine snakes might with propriety be termed legless lizards, as, with the exception of the want of limbs, they are in most respects similar in structure to the saurians. A fine lively specimen of the Bengal rat snake was fed with half a dozen frogs, which he pursued with great speed round the enclosure, and, driving them one by one into a corner, seized and swallowed them, in spite of their struggles. We will now turn to the venomous serpents, and in particular the rattlesnakes. The keeper having put two young Guinea pigs into the case, one of the snakes instantly struck at that nearest to him. The action of a venomous serpent in wounding an animal cannot strictly be called a bite, as, though the fangs undoubtedly represent teeth, the jaws are not closed upon the object struck, which is simply punctured, the snake in most cases retiring immediately. The Guinea pig almost immediately showed signs of giddiness, but its body did not appear to swell; it seemed to be thrown into violent convulsions, and in about a minute fell helplessly on its side, with no other sign of life than an occasional spasmodic motion of the jaws. A larger animal would not have been so soon killed; but as the snakes, being confined, have not often occasion to use their venom, it is probably more powerful than when they are in a wild state. There are a large number of puff-adders in one case; and a Guinea pig being introduced began sniffing about as usual; but though he was touching one of the reptiles, it did not seem disposed to strike, when suddenly another puff-adder darted at full length from an opposite corner, and striking the creature, remained with its fangs apparently buried in its flesh, contrary, we believe, to the usual habit of the reptile. His intention was perhaps to prevent any of the others from devouring it. There are specimens of the two species of cobras, the Indian and Egyptian; perhaps the most interesting of all serpents: but, on account of their excitable nature, it has been found necessary to hide them partially from view by filling the lower half of the case-front with ground-glass, so that it is not easy to observe them.

The appearance of the cobra when about to give the fatal stroke is graceful, and yet terrible to see. The inflated hood, the waving motion of the head, and the peculiar expression of the eye, combine to impress the observer of its consciousness of the deadly power which it possesses, and with which it threatens any living creature that dares approach it. Venomous serpents can generally be distinguished by the broad head and stumpy tail which they possess; but this rule does not always hold good, some of them, for example the cobras, having a structure closely resembling that of the colubrines, with the exception of the fangs and organs pertaining to them. There are in this house some young alligators, which are kept with the water-tortoises. They seem to pass their time generally in sleep, but when feeding-time comes are extremely alert. On some mice being thrown into the water, the alligators pursued them, swimming with the mouth raised out of the water. Having seized the unfortunate mice, they held them under the surface till drowned, and then tossing them into the gullet bolted them whole. The tortoises are not fed with live animals, but with raw meat, which they tear in mouthfuls under the water. Considering the number of species which exist, the collection seems deficient in the *Chelonia;* but with regard to the *Sauria* and *Ophidia*, it is probably unequalled.

RAMBLES IN CORNWALL.

DOUBTLESS there are few readers of the N.N.B. who have not, at one time or another in their lives, visited Cornwall; and it is not superfluous to suppose that many who peruse its pages from month to month are residents in that interesting county; and both to those who have, and likewise to those who have not, wandered along its iron-bound coast, where the huge billows of the clear blue Atlantic are seen rolling in and dashing against the shore in their fullest grandeur, these lines may perhaps prove of interest. From its being of so narrow an extent with the ocean surrounding it on three sides, Cornwall possesses the most equable climate of any of the English counties, even surpassing Devonshire in that respect. Both the coolness of its summer and the mildness of its winter are proverbial, which is proved by numerous exotic trees and plants flourishing out of doors all the year round in certain sheltered localities in this western district of old England. Thus the climate is particularly favourable to persons of delicate constitution, and if there are any subscribers of the N.N.B. (but I trust there may not be) who are afflicted with any pulmonary disease, I would strongly recommend all such who are able to pass the winter in some sheltered place on the southern shores, as Falmouth, Penzance, &c.

When stopping at Penzance, in the year 1867, I was told that snow was very seldom seen, and when it fell it did not lie long; thus showing how salubrious a climate this populous old town enjoys. It is beautifully situated, having about a south-south-east aspect, and is in a great measure protected from the cold polar winds by high ground to the north. It overlooks the far-famed Mounts Bay; and unless the weather is thick a fine sweep of coast is seen, extending to the Lizard Point, some twenty miles distant. St. Michael's Mount is situated about three miles eastward off the town of Marazion, or Market Jew. It is an island at high tide, but may easily be approached on foot at low water. From the tower of the chapel in the castle on the summit of the Mount there is as may be imagined a fine prospect all round of both ocean and land, and the sea in the neighbourhood of St. Ives is visible. Numerous and pretty are the excursions to be made in the vicinity of Penzance, which any visitor arriving there will ere very long discover; but, not having space here, I cannot now enumerate all the picturesque rambles I have made, both on foot and in vehicles, when stopping at "salubrious" Penzance, which I will leave to all my readers to find out for themselves on their arrival there; at least those who have not visited this town.

To the entomologist the neighbourhood of Penzance is of interest, for I have captured on the cliffs near to the town several fine and rarer species of our butterflies and moths, amongst which may be named that lovely insect the Clouded Yellow (*Colias Edusa*), and the beautiful Oak Eggar Moth (*Bombyx Quercus*), &c. So, should the visitor be an entomologist, he will find ample scope for pursuing his delightful study, both on the cliffs and in the secluded little valleys around Penzance. If he is a good pedestrian and requires an exhilarating walk, he should approach Penzance (as I have done) by walking along the coast from the Lizard Point; many objects of interest being worth seeing on the way, such as Kynance Cove, etc. To the ornithologist the cries of the numerous kinds of gulls and other sea-fowl will sound pleasing to the ear, and at intervals a raven or two may fly by, whose approach is announced by their peculiar and ominous croak. Perhaps in some wild and secluded spot he will have the good luck (though I have never seen them) of beholding that beautiful though scarce species of British corvidæ, viz., the Cornish Chough; once common, as its name denotes, in this part of England; but now, I am sorry to say, rarely seen, even among what was formerly their favourite haunts. The note of the Chough (*Fregilus Graculus*) is very similar in sound to that of the Jackdaw (*Corvus Monedula*), which latter bird is everywhere common enough; but of all the British Corvidæ found most abundantly in Cornwall is the Magpie (*Pica Caudata*) and hence they are frequently termed "Cornish pheasants." Rare birds sometimes occur in Cornwall, and amongst others may be mentioned the little Bustard (*Otis Tetrax*) which has been shot in the Lizard district. Owing to the denuded and somewhat bare character of the inland country of Cornwall, many birds abundant in other parts of England are not so often found in this westerly district of Great Britain.

Many species of Falconinæ, Accipitrinæ, and Milvinæ are common enough. Likewise the ornithologist may observe in his rambles along the coast numerous and different kinds of the Natatores, or web-footed birds. Both the Guillemot (*Uria Troile*) and the Razor-bill (*Alca Torda*) are found plentifully in many parts, from the spring till the later summer months. Both these birds are known in Cornwall by the name of "Murrs."

To the entomologist this county does not present generally, excepting certain localities, a wide field for the capture of what may be termed a "good" insect, which may be in a great measure accounted for by the comparative bleakness of the country and the absence of trees, which do not flourish well, owing to the heavy gales and storms which sweep in great violence over this portion of England. The wind during the winter months is frequently terrific, and as an instance of the great force with which it blows, I may mention that the tombstones in the churchyards, in exposed situations, are supported by stone work; thus my readers may learn for themselves how severe these gales must be, and that it is no "gentle zephyr" which blows over this westerly county. During the last fortnight I have visited and rambled along what was quite a new district to me, viz., the northern coast of Cornwall. Grand as the slate cliffs in this part are I yet give my preference to the beautiful serpentine ones of the Lizard, and the still sublimer and more massive ones around the Land's End, in which latter district is situated the celebrated Logan Rock. Starting from the small romantically situated town of Boscastle, and having explored the cliffs and country in its vicinity, and seeing the different objects of interest about there, not leaving out Tintagel or King Arthur's Castle, I wended my way down to Newquay, from which place I am writing these lines, in a comfortable little lodging, overlooking the small harbour and the bay, where just at present numerous boats are coming in laden with pilchards. To the stranger entering Newquay, especially if it be on a dull misty day in November, the town does not present a very lively appearance. The situation of it is bleak, having for the most part a northerly aspect, and so is exposed to the full force of the polar winds. I fear all those of my readers who are not particularly lovers of nature, but prefer more lively and fashionable towns, would turn up their noses at this place, and perhaps imagine one a fool for stopping more than a single day here; but all those having a less artificial taste, and who prefer the beauties of rock, sand, and sea to bricks and mortar, will think very differently. Everyone to his own opinion; but I feel sure all readers of our "friend," the N.N.B., will agree with me in preferring the quiet retreat of a small country place, where Nature can be seen in all her beauty, to the confusion, noise, and business of large commercial cities. The country around Newquay, though undulating, is decidedly uninteresting, and there is really scarcely a tree to be seen. The sands here are good, and one can walk a considerable distance along them at low water under the rocky slate cliffs, the beauty of the scenery being enhanced by the cries of the sea-fowl, and the solitude by the croakings of a pair of ravens. How grand the clear blue billows look rolling in one after another over the sand. On yonder rock may be seen sitting that long necked glossy bird, the Cormorant (*Phalacrocorax Barbo*), or its smaller and less beautiful neighbour the Shag (*Phalacrocorax Graculus*) may be observed flying over the crested waves. I will conclude my paper by advising all those of my readers who have both got the time and means, and have not yet visited Cornwall, to do so and take some rambles in this far westerly and interesting county of England, and thus I will leave all to judge of its beauties for themselves, resting assured that very few will be disappointed with its magnificent coast scenery, which is unrivalled by any other similar scenes in England—so says Murray in his "Handbook to Devon and Cornwall."

A. E. BUTTEMER.

"BOMBYX CECROPIA."

IN the October Number of this Book I reported my experiment with the above silkworm, and now will make a few remarks according to promise.

I note what W. Geffcken, Esq., says relative to this new insect at page 351 of the November issue, and perfectly agree with him, while thanking him for his kindly remarks on my management. I mentioned having placed ten of the above silkworms on a plum tree in my garden; I got eight good cocoons from them, which I collected on 3rd. October. Two either died or got away; I never saw them since, dead or alive. In spite of the past intemperate season, this out-door experiment was, if anything, more successful than my indoor one, for the occason were more substantial. Doubtless, this is the most natural way of feeding this silkworm, especially on a large scale. It would be impossible indoors, on cut branches, for decapitating the trees so much would soon entirely consume them. As to gathering the leaves and feeding the insects, as is done with B. Mari, even if successful, would be too expensive a method, considering the long life of this worm. A means of operating with little cost and trouble is requisite. At present I see no better way than employing a hedge of plum protected from enemies by a kind of moveable tent provided with proper ventilation.

This last summer has been much against silkworm rearing generally, by reason of so much prevailing cold, and my late-hatched silkworms have done badly. I should propose in a backward Spring the use of artificial heat in May, in order to bring the moths from the cocoons. A temperature of 65° to 70° Faht., I should say, was appropriate during the pairing, depositing of the eggs, hatching them, and feeding the young larvæ. I put the eggs in paper gutters half an inch deep, or thimble papers, which I place among the boughs and leaves, but I think plants in pots or boxes would be better. I sprinkle them of an evening, when near hatching, with tepid water to soften the shells. The insects leave the eggs in twelve or fifteen days after being laid, according to the temperature, and soon distribute themselves over the leaves. Some hay strewed round would serve to receive any worms which fall or come down; this would preserve them from being injured, and they could the easier be lifted again in position on the boughs without touching them. This method might do also out-doors.

"The Cecropia" appears to me to delight in drinking or sucking moisture from the leaves. I always washed them by shaking in a pail of water (the boughs) before changing the food. The insects on a hedge, perhaps, might be syringed lightly over by a garden apparatus imitating a natural shower. If such a hedge was uncovered at night, the "natural dews" would supply this moisture. I am not prepared to say that it is necessary, but another year I will prove further on this point.

I think neither apple or cherry leaves constitute good food for this silkworm. "The plum" is its natural food, or the Canadian wild forest variety; but most descriptions seem equally relished. I cannot recommend substitutes, for I hold each variety of silkworm should have its "natural food" destined for it. "B. Cynthia" feeds on various leaves, but I find nothing answers so well as the Ailanthus, the native or natural food of this silkworm, and my experiments therewith I shall report at a future time. I trust these few remarks will be acceptable and prove of use to sikworm rearers.

LEONARD HARMAN, Jun.
Old Catton, Norwich.

THE INFLUENCE OF CLIMATE ON THE COLOUR OF THE HUMAN RACE.

MANY theories have been advanced within the last few years to show that the human race are not all of the same species. Some of these theories were so flimsy and devoid of anything approaching sound argument, that they vanished into nothing, and the theorists themselves were glad to fall back and hide themselves behind the scenes, to screen themselves from the biting darts of scientific ridicule. But others were of such a nature as to stand out and defy the monospecie advocates to do their worst, and even now they remain an unsolved problem in the minds of scientific men.

The question of the origin of the human race must of necessity be to a certain extent speculative, as nothing definite can be ascertained in regard to it; still, this should not prevent us from searching as far as the limits of possibility will allow us, and the fact that the question still remains doubtful is a valid reason for our persevering efforts.

The human race are divided into five distinct varieties, or *species*, we will call them (if our opponents will not object to us borrowing the expression for the occasion), according to the colour of their skin, viz.:—the Caucasian, Indian, Malayan, Negro, and Mongolian types, or the white, red, brown, black, and yellow races. Now, the question remains to be answered. What is the cause of the different colours if all men sprang from the same pair? It is of no use to beg the question by attributing it to the influence of climate consequent upon their early migration; a great deal more is laid to the charge of that agency than it can be proved to be guilty of. Would it be possible for Europeans ever to become Negroes by emigrating to Africa? or would it be possible for Negroes to become white by a prolonged residence in Europe? Nay, if you will, we will allow generations to pass, and then say by what climatal action can we account for five distinct colours of the skin? It will perhaps be objected that the colours of the various races are so blended into each other, that it is impossible to show the exact line of difference between the European and the Mongolian, or the Mongolian and the Indian, or the Indian and the Malayan, and so on; but it must be remembered that the ojection applies equally to the climatal theory. Will our opponents shew the exact degree of heat required to produce a Negro, a Malayan, or an Indian? There *is* a difference between these races, and all men know that yellow is not brown, and that brown is not black. It cannot be doubted that climate has *some* influence upon the skin, for many people will be quite sallow in the heat of summer, but quite fair again when submitted to a lower temperature; but this action is not permanent, and is quite different in its character from that which is observed in the Negro. But it will be asked, if we deny that climatal action does produce the effects in point of colour which the different races show, what proofs can we advance in support of our theory? First, then, we have geographical evidence to prove that climate has no permanent effect upon the skin. The natives of Van Dieman's Land are darker than the aborigines of Northern Australia; the native Mexicans are much darker than the Indians of Equatorial Brazil; the Spaniards of Guyaquil near the equator (although living in a much hotter climate), are most of them lighter in complexion than are the Spaniards in their own country (as are also those of Chili), the Guicas of South America are much lighter than the Indians living in the same country; and the Bosnian soldiers who settled in Nubia in the year 1420, were distinctly recognised by Burkhardt after a lapse of nearly 400 years. Surely, four centuries were sufficient to alter the colour of the race, if it were possible for climate to do it.

It is an established law of nature that the equator is the hottest part of the earth, and that the heat gradually decreases in intensity as we near the poles ; if, then, climate were the cause of variation in colour, we should find that the people would be darkest at the equator, and would gradually become lighter as we receded from the equator and neared the poles, where they would be lightest of all. But this is not in accordance with actual facts. The natives of Borneo, immediately on the equator, are lighter than those of the volcano islands. Again, the people of England are lighter than those of Northern Russia, or the Indians of Labrador, which, although it is in the same degree of latitude, is very much colder. Moreover, there are tribes on both the East and West coasts of Africa that are blacker than other tribes further inland, yet living in the same degree of latitude.

Secondly, we have evidence in the physical constitution of the different races, that the color of the skin is not attributable to the action of climate. If a negro intermarries with a European, the offspring would be a mulatto, and if that mulatto were united to a European the result would be a quadroon, and so the colour of the skin assumes a lighter hue as the blood of the white race predominates ; but, on the other hand, if a quadroon intermarries with a negro, the the result is a mulatto, and so the colour of the skin becomes darker as the negro blood predominates. All this may take place, and has taken place, in the same climate and in the same state of society, as is revealed to us in the annals of American slavery, thus showing that *race*, and not *climate*, determines the colour of the skin. The colouring matter, whatever it is, is evidently a port of the system, as if it were not, the children of negroes would be born white, and could not become black until climate had acted upon the cuticle. It is very possible that in the case of only one existing colour besides the original tint, it might in the first instance be caused by some external or internal disease which would affect the skin, and the appearance be hereditarily transmitted from one generation to another; but this is evidently not the case with the five different races. It is generally believed that our first parents were red, and any one who has eyes to see with, and possesses any knowledge of the human frame, can see that the white, fair, and soft skin of the Caucassian is not the *result of*, or an hereditary appearance *left by*, the primary action of any disease whatever. What, then, is the cause of the difference in colour ? What, in fact, is the colour itself? Many explanations have been offered; but none which meets the requirements of the case. Foissac says, that " the blackness of the negro is owing to the predominence of carbon in his vegetable diet ;" but this cannot be, as there is quite as much carbon in the blubber eaten by the Esquimaux as in any of the vegetables that ever graced the table of an African prince. Again, I believe it is Berthold that attributes it to an excess of carbon deposited, by means of perspiration, under the skin. This is equally impossible, for if it were so, the same effect would follow in the case of animals, and instead of beholding the vast *variety* which adds to the beauty of creation, we should have all African animals black as the negro, European animals white, American animals red, and so on. Even if we could account for the Malayan and the negro being a gradual darkening of the European, we are still at a loss to account for the original colour, red, or the Mongolian yellow. What degree of heat is required to produce a red or yellow appearance of the skin?

I am aware that there are many difficulties in either theories—difficulties, too, that have puzzled the brains of the most learned ; I am also aware that there many who will stand in direct opposition to the theory of a plurality of species, and it is to elicit the opinions of the friends of the N. N. B. that I venture to open the discussion. I am at present unable to see the plausibility of the climatal argument in accounting for the colour of the skin: if, therefore, your numerous and able correspondents are ready to furnish proofs (from facts) that climate is the cause of colour, I am ready to cast aside my present opinions and receive the truth.

W. NEWBERRY.

THE GARDENER'S SOLILOQUY.

To sow? or not to sow? That is the question?
Whether 'tis nobler in the mind to suffer
The greatest torment of a gardener's life
In poring yearly through " fat catalogues,"
Or to take means by poping them, when sent,
In the waste-basket,—to be looked to

No more ; and, by doing so, to say we end
The thirst for new and special novelties
That flesh is heir to. 'Tis a consummation
Devoutly to be wished. To grow ? to sow ?
To grow ?—perchance to cram our beds and
    borders
With useless rubbish. Ay ! there's the rub !
For to pick out the best of the trade-lists
Full of " ennobled roots," and " improved seeds,"
Must give us pause. There's the respect
That raisers have for their own progeny ;
For who would bear to look o'er all the lists
Now daily sent to gardeners or employers,
" Descriptive guides," " *Vade mecums*," little
    books
For teaching when to sow, transplant, and reap,
When he himself might the commotion end
By never reading them ? Who would yearly
    bear
To sow the good old seeds of former lists ?
But that the thought of something after seed-
    time—
That the " ringleaders," " gems," and " first
    crop " peas,
New brocolis, French beans, and cauliflowers,
Might not turn out so profitable or early
As the well-tried old sorts, puzzles the will,
And makes us rather grow the seeds we have
Than order others we know not of.
An Aged Gardener.

ON THE FAMILY "VANESSIDÆ."

By R. Laddiman.

THE fifth family of diurnal lepidoptera, called the *Vanessidæ*, or " angle wings," contain some of the most conspicuous of our British butterflies, from their vividness in colour. The caterpillars of chief of the individuals of this family feed on nettles, are spiny and of a uniform thickness ; the chrysalis is angled, having the head divided into two points, resembling ears, and hang suspended by a silken thread attached to its tail. In the perfect insect the wings are angled, and are richly embellished with vivid and showy colours.

This family contains eight British individuals, viz.,—the Comma (*Vanessa C-album*) ; Camberwell Beauty (*V. Antiopa*) ; Tortoiseshell (*V. Urticæ*) ; Large Tortoiseshell (*V. polychloros*) ; Red Admiral (*V. Atalanta*) ; Peacock (*V. Io*) ; Painted Lady (*Vanessa* or *Cynthia Cardui*) ; and the White Admiral (*Limenitis Sibylla*).

The Comma or white C butterfly (*Vanessa C. album*) has all its wings deeply indented, more so than any other British butterfly ; the fore wings are raw sienna-brown in colour, having a broad band of reddish-brown along the hind margin containing seven darker brown spots ; the hind wings are of the same colour as the fore ones, having also a band of reddish brown along the hind margin, and three brown spots near the bottom, also a row of red-brown spots parallel with the marginal band. The under side is marbled, and has in the middle of each of the hind wings a pure white mark in the form of the letter C, which have been compared by some to a comma; hence the two names : white C butterfly, and comma butterfly.

The caterpillar feeds on elm, hop, and nettle, more frequently on the hop, and keeps on the underside of the leaves ; when full grown it changes to a chrysalis, which hangs suspended with its head downwards, in which state it remains about a fortnight. The butterfly makes its appearance about September ; it is very fond of nettles and blackberries, and is comparatively rare.

The Camberwell Beauty (*V. Antiopa*). This butterfly is sometimes called the " White Border " and " Grand Surprise ; " it would be indeed a *surprise* to an entomologist to meet with a living specimen of this butterfly. Years ago it was very plentiful at Camberwell, but is now, it is to be regretted, almost extinct. It is one of the largest of this family ; the colour of all the wings is of a rich puce-brown, having a broad white band on the hind margin, and a row of blue dots within this margin, with two whitish spots on the costal margin of the fore wings.

The Tortoiseshell (*V. Urticæ*) is the commonest, and is to be met with almost everywhere from early spring to autumn ; and in Norfolk it is called by persons ignorant of the science the " King George."

The caterpillars are to be found in June and July feeding on the stinging nettle in great abundance ; the young larvæ are gregarious, feeding under a web, but after changing their skin the second time they wander about more freely over the food plant ; when full fed, which is to the length of about an inch and a quarter, they crawl away and select a spot suitable to pass the chrysalis state, which is generally under the coping of a wall or shed, but more often they hang suspended from the under part of the leaves of the nettle, by a silken thread : it hangs with its head downwards and remains in this state for twelve or fourteen days. Many of these butterflies hybernate during the winter and re-appear the first fine day in the early spring, and continue to fly until the next brood make their appearance.

The Large Tortoiseshell (*V. polychloros*), or

elm butterfly, so called from the caterpillar feeding on the elm. This insect is far from being so plentiful as the last, the only specimen I have heard of in this locality is one seen by a friend—and brother entomologist—a few years ago within a mile of Norwich, who was unsuccessful in capturing it. This butterfly bears a close resemblance to the last; the prevailing colour of the wings is dull fulvous-brown, the fore ones having three large square spots of black on the costal margin, and two round spots situated near the middle of the wings, also two larger ones below these; the hind wings also have a black spot on the costal margin.

The Red Admiral or Alderman butterfly (*V. Atalanta*) is one of the most vivid in colour, and is perhaps the nearest approach of any British butterfly to the splendour of the tropical ones. We are told that Atalanta was a young lady so swift of foot that she could run over the sea on the "light fantastic toe" without splashing her ankles, or over the corn fields without bending an ear of corn with her *weight*. She must have been light indeed, as light as the butterfly who is named after her. I do not imagine an ear of corn would bend much under the weight of our "Atalanta of red;" about running over the sea we will leave, for I do not much think our "winged friend" will be likely to attempt that.

Vanessa Atalanta is certainly a grand insect, but the brilliancy of the colours are only to be found on the upper surface of the wings; the deep velvety-blackground, the white spots, red bands, and blue edges together form a beautiful and very lively contrast; the creature itself seems to be aware of its own loveliness, as it sits perched on the head of a thistle, expanding its gorgeous wings and displaying its rainbow colours: after tasting the flowers of the field by way of a change, he often pays a visit to our gardens, then he

"Round about doth flie,
From bed to bed, from one to t'other border;
And takes survey, with curious busy eye,
Of every flower and herbe there set in order;
Now this, now that, he tasteth tenderly,
Yet none of them he rudely doth disorder.
Ne with his feete their silken leaves deface,
But pastures on the pleasures of each place.

"And evermore, with most varietc,
And change of sweetness (for all change *is* sweet),
He casts his glutton sense to satisfie,
Now sucking of the sap of herbe most meet,
Or of the dew, which yet on them doth lie;
Now in the same bathing his tender feet:
And then he percheth on some branch thereby,
To neatten him, and his moist wings to dry."

* * * * *

"And whatso' else of vertue good or ill
Grew in the garden, fetched from far away
Of every one he takes and tastes at will,
And on their pleasures greedily doth prey.
That when he hath both plaied, and fed at fill,
In the warm sunne he doth himself embay,
And there him rests in riotous suffisaunce
Of all his gladfulness, and kingly joyaunce."

"What more felicitie can fall to creature,
Than to enjoy delight with libertie,
And to be lord of all the works of Nature?
To reign in the aire from th'earth to highest skie.
To feed on flowers, and weedes of glorious feature?
To take whatever thing doth please the eye?
Who rests not pleased with such happiness,
Well worthy he to taste of wretchedness."

(SPENSER).

The Red Admiral is also very fond of the sap which issues from trees after the bark has been cut away; they will sometimes collect by scores around one of these trees. I once saw a miscellaneous collection of sugar tubs, etc., round which dozens of this butterfly were flying.

The caterpillar of the Red Admiral is spiny, and feeds on the stinging nettle; its colour is grayish-black, the head and tail being slightly darker, and the body is speckled with dirty white, with a yellow line on each side; as soon as it is hatched it spins itself a silken house, interweaving with it the leaves of the food-plant, and feeds under cover, removing to another place when provision is exhausted; when full-fed it wanders about in search of some spot in which to pass the chrysalis state of its existence. Having selected a spot suitable to its mind, it fastens a silken thread to its tail, and hanging head downwards it passes into the chrysalis state. The chrysalis is red brown, beautifully variegated with gold. The perfect insect emerges in July and continues on the wing to the end of September, or even to the middle of October, providing the weather is favourable. Many of these butterflies hybernate during the winter months, and reappear in early spring.

The Peacock (*V. Io.*). This is another elegant butterfly, rather more common than the last, but similar in habits; the larvæ of this butterfly also feed on the nettle, they are gregarious, and continue so till almost fed; it is of a beautiful black colour, studded with white dots, forming three distinct lines on each of the segments, it is also covered with long spines, each one being studded with shorter ones, the chrysalis like the foregoing also hangs by its tail, and remains in this state about three weeks. The perfect insect is very beautiful, the lower half of the fore wings are of a deep red-brown colour, the base of the costal margin is black, delicately barred with yellow, beneath this are two spots of a black colour, beyond the second black spot is a beautiful large eyelike mark, containing a number of colours, below this eye are two whitish spots. The hind wings are smoky-brown towards the hind margin, and towards the inner margin red-brown; it has also a beautiful eye-like mark at the apexical angle of the wing; the underside of all the wings are jet black.

This beautiful butterfly is common everywhere in July and August, and abounds in clover fields; it is also very fond of alighting on the heads of the various kinds of thistles. I have sometimes captured as many as a dozen or two of these butterflies on a single clover field.

The Painted Lady (*Vanessa*, or *Cynthia cardui*), another very beautiful butterfly, much less common than the last; its caterpillar feeds upon thistles, the colour is black, with stripes of a yellowish grey, it is also covered over with spines; the chrysalis is angled, and hangs suspended by its tail with its head downwards to the leaves of the thistle on which it feeds. The eggs are deposited in May and June, and the perfect insect appears about a month afterwards; the fore wings are intermixed with black and carmine, at the tip of the wing is a black spot, and five white spots situate near the black one, the bottom of the wings are delicately powdered with scales of an orange red colour, the hind wings resemble the fore ones in colour, but the white spots are absent; it has also three rows of whity spots of various shapes parallel with the hind margin.

This butterfly is also a frequenter of our fields and lanes, and is not very abundant; it is very fond of thistles, and is a frequent visitor of our garden, and is particularly fond of verbenas. This butterfly also hybernates throughout the winter months and reappears in spring; it is rather an uncertain insect, and occurs more plentiful some years than others.

The White Admiral (*L. Sibylla*, or *Camilla*) is a very graceful insect, and chiefly occurs in the south, but is only taken in certain localities, such as Sussex, Surrey, Hampshire, and Dorsetshire. Woods and lanes are the spots where

"Fair *Camilla* wings her flight serene."

The elegant flight of this butterfly cannot fail to excite admiration; we are told of an old entomologist who was so fascinated with the graceful flight of *Camilla*, that long after he was unable to pursue her, he would be conveyed to the woods and content himself by sitting down and feasting his eyes on the flight of this lovely insect.

The caterpillar of this beautiful butterfly feeds on the leaves of the honeysuckle; it is pale green, having reddish-brown head and legs, and a pale white streak on each side. The chrysalis hangs suspended by its tail to the leaves of the food-plant. The perfect insect pursues its flight in July.

WINTER.

WINTER is now nigh at hand; autumn with its golden tinted skies and thick fogs has almost passed away, and we must now be preparing to face the many cold biting breezes of winter. All our migratory birds have long since fled to their ever temperate home, leaving behind them the cold icy winds and the dismal solitude of a dreary landscape. The incessant hum of the insect world is no longer heard; their silence is perhaps occasioned by the same cause which is exhibited in the case of the swallow and other migratory birds; for the soft winds of autumn may perhaps have wafted them gently to those sunny climes where the swallow occupies his time in the winter season, at the same time when those summer visitants are pursuing their backward journey; or like some of those unlucky birds which have been left behind, they have to undergo an ordeal of starvation, and so droop and die around us. Although the winters for the past two years have been unusually mild, and devoid of frosts, yet the character of such winters are accompanied with long intervals of rain.

During the brief spaces of time which occur between the long continuous times of rain, when the thick masses of watery clouds make way for sunshine as it produces a slightly perceptible warmth on the face of the watery earth, then it is that the presence of winter is forgot, and woodland music again greets the ear, and fancifully leads the mind to an idea which verges strongly on spring. Perched on the naked boughs of the skeleton trees, the thrush, unmindful of the icy blast which might occur within a few hours' notice, breaks forth into melody which reverberates, strangely, yet pleasantly, through the dreary vacuum of winter solitude. If the rain in the winter season has come chiefly out of the southern quarter, it very often happens that should the weather moderate and disperse the rainy clouds for awhile, the wind during that period has gone over to the north-western quarter, then, again, thick clouds accumulate together in heavy masses in that quarter, and as they begin slowly to move upwards, the winds begin to blow stronger, till at last we are greeted with a heavy shower of hailstones. Such wild stormy weather had always a soothing charm to the ever memorable poet Burns, when he says:—

The sweeping blast, the sky o'ercast,
    The joyless winter day;

> Let others fear ; to me more dear
>   Than all the pride of May.
>
> The tempest's howl, it soothes my soul,
>   My griefs it seems to join ;
> The leafless trees my fancy please,
>   Their fate resembles mine.

It is not about such mild drizzling winters that I have to refer, but about such winters when king frost reigns supreme. When long frosts sets in, and the sky has not a cloud to dim its colour, then it is that the atmosphere produces a chilling effect, as the gentle breeze wafts its icy breath over the gradually drying earth, when along the western and northern horizon is seen at the close of day a blue band of vapour, extending to a very even altitude towards the zenith, along the whole length of the mass. The stars during such nights as these give a more dazzling brightness, and the countless numbers of these small bright orbs shine in splendour through the clear rarified frosty nights. The different constellations are now seen to perfection, and the planetary worlds move on their respective courses with increased lustre ; in fact we may take in at a glance the whole host of heaven, from the largest planetary body in sight to the star of the highest magnitude discernable with the naked eye, coupling with them that thin delicate streak of light, the milky way. Sometimes the aurora borealis is seen to perfection, with its moving spires of various coloured lights reflecting on all around. It is on such cold starry nights as these that I wish to linger, and recall to memory the many stirring scenes that arise to my mind's eye, when pressing along with cautious and noiseless steps over the rough uneven stones of a solitary skeer, a mile from the main land, on Morecambe sands, and fearing lest some unexpected flounder would spread alarm to a flock of wild ducks which are feeding by the river close a-head, and so lose the chance of a lucky shot. These species of ducks, called blue bills, in common here, visit us in winter, and the latter part of autumn seasons, leaving us again in spring to proceed, I suppose, to their breeding grounds in Norway and other high latitudes bordering on the Arctic circle. Many a duck shooting tale have I listened to from the fishermen, and longed to have been with them on their exploits ; when (while crouching down undiscernible behind the huge boulders which characterise the lonely skeer above mentioned) they have heard the whirring of the wings of a solitary wild duck rapidly approaching, but could not see it (owing to its flying too low under the glare of the moon) till the tip of its wing has flapped them on the shoulder as they have noiselessly peered from behind their hiding place to try to get a glimpse of it, and then seeing it fly rapidly from them, but dare not shoot, as its course is in a straight line with some other companions, but have had the satisfaction to hear their companion's gun sealing its death warrant, as with a splash its dying body is immersed in the river below, to be soon in the hands of its destroyer. There is another method adopted for catching the wild ducks on the sands, that is, by setting nets for them composed of one cord of the strongest hemp. It will be as well to observe here that these ducks, which sometimes number thousands, come up with the flow of the tide in large flocks, diving for shell-fish as they advance. It is well known by the fishermen that these birds come up the same track several times in succession ; and taking particular notice of the track they have gone over, their next business is to place their nets right across that track when the tide is out, and when the next tide has come and gone they proceed again to their nets, and very often one or more ducks which have fallen victims to the snare are found entangled in the net, and drowned. During winter mornings we find the rippling brook sparkling along under a slight mist, and the wagtail evidently in search of food is seen fluttering along over its surface, alighting occasionally on the few stones which are seen above the water line.

Such clear frosty weather as I have been speaking of only continues for a stated time ; the dreary landscape is still uncovered of snow, without which a wintry scene is incomplete. Let us now be prepared to witness a scene altogether the reverse. The once clear sky has now a thick leaden covering, and the sun has set below the western board with a pale sickly light as the clock strikes the hour of 4 p.m., reconciling us to short days and long nights. The southern wind sighs in fitful gusts through the naked trees, or in the words of the poet Thomson to this effect :

> Along the woods, along the moorish fens,
> Sighs the sad genius of the coming storm ;
> And up among the loose disjointed cliffs,
> And fractured mountains wild, the brawling brook
> And cave presageful, send a hollow moan
> Resounding long in list'ning fancy's ear.

Thick darkness now prevails, and not a star is visible to beautify the face of the cloudy universe. Rude Boreas now begins to show more of his devastating power as he roars through the branches of the trees ; and we may now say with Bloomfield—

> For, hark ! it blows ; a dark and dismal night :
> Heaven guide the traveller's fearful steps aright !

When we arise in the morning we hear no

more of the rushing wind, but we see the snow coming down in thick flakes in a perpendicular line. The appearance of the trees covered with snow has a chill but pleasing effect. The robin has now made his appearance out of his snug retreat, uttering his plaintive note in close proximity to the house door, demanding as it were a few crumbs for breakfast. No more do we hear the merry tune of the lark, nor yet the shrill note of the thrush, for there is such a death-like stillness prevails as to make it both monotonous and depressing. Everything, both animate and inanimate, seems to be wrapt in this unnatural stillness, for the sound of the horse and cart as they pass over the snow is scarcely heard, and the figure of the pedestrian moves on in silence.

If the snow continues to lie for a lengthened period of time on the surface of the earth, then it is that such weather proves disastrous to the birds, for many of them die from hunger and starvation, while others are reduced to such a weak helpless state as to be easily caught. The thrush, redwing, and blackbird appease their hunger by eating the still lingering haws on the hawthorn trees, and the fieldfare searches for food in those places in the fields uncovered of snow by the sheep and cows. Chaffinches, yellow-hammers, hedge-sparrows, wrens, and other birds may now be seen in the vicinity of farmhouses, picking up the few scattered grains in the farmyard along with the noisy house sparrows. As we take our walks through the snowy fields we sometimes come across a lot of bird's feathers lying on the snow by the hedge sides; mostly the feathers of the robin are found with their red tinge, showing the doings of the destroying hawk. But apart from these silent scenes we have the merry festivities of Christmas and the New Year to cheer the dull monotony; and while engrossed among such merry assemblies, when the toasts and sentiments are drunk with enthusiasm, may we not forget to drink success to the NATURALIST'S NOTE BOOK, which has been so ably penned and conducted from its commencement. And while we bid adieu to the eventful year of 1869, may I be permitted to hope that the same spirit which has animated the pens of those whose able compositions have appeared from time to time in the past numbers of the N.N.B. will be continued with the same earnestness in the numbers of the future; so that together with a determination on the part of us all to still continue to give our support to that glorious banner THE NATURALIST'S NOTE BOOK, which has flown so nobly through the breeze to its many destinations for the past three years, we may rest assured that success will crown our efforts.
J. H.
North Lancashire.

ON THE BRITISH GEOMETRÆ.
By E. J. S. CLIFFORD.
PART XII.

IT has been well said that the commonest things by which we are surrounded challenge and satisfy our innate love of the beautiful, if we did but examine and study them as they deserve. Specially is this truth illustrated by the insect world, where there exist forms of the most exquisite beauty, only to be appreciated by a close and careful scrutiny. Now there can be little doubt that the insect collector himself errs much in regard to this. We mean to say that far too many of our regular collectors of insects get into the habit of admiring a species, not so much in accordance with any recognised standard of beauty or elegance, but more in proportion with its scarcity or extreme rarity. This is an error, for some of our commonest moths and butterflies are yet endowed so magnificently in respect of colour and form, that they outvie many rarer kinds. These remarks find an apt illustration in the species of this family to which we are now arrived. It is called the garden carpet (*Melanippe fluctuata*), and well indeed does it merit the title, for it is one of our most abundant garden insects at the proper season. And yet, though so frequent a sight, it is none the less a very beautiful one, when we happen to get a glimpse of the delicate moth at rest, or skimming gracefully among the flowers at eventide. Its fore wings are grey, with a darkish blotch at the base, and another larger one on the costal margin. The hind wings are clouded and barred by smoky brown, and the head, thorax, and body are grey; the latter with two spots placed in a transverse manner on each segment. The caterpillar of the garden carpet is very variable in colour, being either brown-grey or green. Its food is the several varieties of the cultivated cabbage, or it consists of other garden plants; for this insect is not confined to one special kind of food. It is double-brooded, and the second brood of caterpillars is full fed at the beginning of September. Throughout the summer the moth itself is on the wing, and it may be said to occur throughout England, Scotland, and Ireland.

Amongst the many "good things" said to occur in birch wood, the royal mantle (*Anticlea sinuata*), has been mentioned. This is one of the most beautifully marked geometers we are acquainted with; its fore wings are particoloured, and there is a large triangular blotch at the base of a leaden colour. The remainder of the wings consists of creamy-white and black, so mixed and varied as to present a most striking effect. There is a narrow spot on all of the wings; the head and thorax are almost black. The older collectors gave this moth a somewhat fitting title when they called it the "royal mantle." The caterpillar is uniformly cylindrical, without humps or warts; the head is yellow-green, marked with black—the body is bright green, with two stripes down the back. All parts of the body emit fine short black hairs: its food is the lady's bedstraw, and it is full fed by the end of August, at which time it spins a slight web amongst the leaves and flowers, and changes to a short chrysalis of a reddish-brown colour. The moth is on the wing in the month of June. In that month also, we may keep a look-out for the not very common geometer called the flame (*Anticlea rubidata*), a species occurring in several of our English counties, though not reported from Ireland or Scotland. The eggs are laid at the end of June on the great hedge bedstraw, and other kinds of the same genus, and they give forth the enclosed caterpillars in ten or twelve days. In August these latter become full fed, and rest in a nearly straight position. Their colour varies, being either red-brown or grey, but in either case delicately varied, and marked in the most exquisite manner. When full-grown, this species goes into the ground to assume its change, where it forms a small earthen cocoon. The flame moth has the fore wings with a small dark blotch at the base, edged with white, and then a rust-coloured band. After this we find a brown bar delicately edged on both sides with white, and other bands shaded off in various ways, which blended, form a most imposing aspect on the wings of this fragile little moth.

In the month of March, when the trees and bushes are just budding forth, we should search on the buds or the stems of the dog-rose for the eggs of the shoulder stripe (*Anticlea badiata*). On this plant the caterpillar feeds, and it is full-fed at the end of May, when it rests in a straight position, and, singular to say, only attached by the claspers. At the early part of their existence, the caterpillars of this moth are green, afterwards they vary slightly, and in mature life are shaded by purple, and marked by paler lines on the body. When about to assume the pupa state they descend to the ground, and become chrysalides on the top of the earth in a slight cocoon. In April the moth appears, and it is said to be common in some of our English counties, as also it is in Ireland, according to one entomologist. Similar to our last in some of the particulars of its economy is the streamer (*Anticlea derivata*). Its eggs are laid on the same plant about the same time. But our streamer moth is a more conspicuous insect than our last; its fore wings, which are purple brown, have a delicate gloss over the whole surface. They possess also two dark bars—the first near the base is short and narrow; the second, before the middle of the wing, is very strongly pronounced. There is a dark blotch on the costal margin. In the month of May the caterpillar of this species is full fed, and is of a delicate green colour, with various red blotches. When about to change, this insect descends from its native bush, and, penetrating the earth, becomes a chrysalis therein. The month of April brings forth the beautiful imago of the streamer, which is not of frequent occurrence in this country now, whatever it may have been in the past.

Beautifully mottled and varied is the barberry carpet (*Anticlea berberata*). Its fore wings are grey, with numerous markings of umber-brown, too complicated and diverse to render palpable by any amount of explanation. This is one of those moths which must be seen in order to its beauty being appreciated; its hind wings are of a pale grey, with several darker zigzag lines parallel to the hind margins. The head, thorax, and body have the same shades of colour disposed in a transverse direction. The caterpillar of the barberry carpet is said to be very slow in its habits, and so disinclined is it to move that when touched it generally drops from its food plant suspended by a thread. In colour it varies from a sienna brown to a very pale grey tint: its food is the common barberry, on which it may be found during the summer. The species is double-brooded, the moth appearing in May and August. It has been taken in Essex and Suffolk, but not in the North of England, or in Scotland or Ireland.

One of our noted northern geometræ is that called the red carpet (*Coremia munitata*, a very delicate little moth. The fore wings have a reddish blotch at the base, then a narrow band, and lastly, a broad reddish band, with dark margins. The hind wings are dingy grey, with waved transverse markings both lighter and darker. The eggs of this species are hatched in June; the young caterpillars feed on the groundsel during the autumn, which they leave before the winter commences. At spring they eat again, and are full fed before the end of March. When full fed, the caterpillar of the red carpet is about an inch in length, and is of a dull green or brown colour. The body is slightly sprinkled with black dots, and has two distinct blotches on the sixth and seventh segments: it spins up in moss, and becomes therein a brown pupa. In June and July the moth is on the wing in those localities to which it seems confined. In Orkney it is very abundant. We read with somewhat of indignation of a collector who was seen to box (*i.e.* kill) hundreds of the moths in this locality, which were in such bad condition as to render it difficult to select a dozen worth preserving!

Here, if you like, is an instance of that foolish—nay, culpable cruelty to our rare insects without any end in view whatever! And yet we are monthly reading grave articles, composed and sent to our scientific periodicals, either wondering at, or trying to explain, the extinction of species! Is it at all a matter of mystery, at least in relation to the lepidoptera, when we are constantly seeing our collectors misconduct themselves, and cast a shadow of reproach on the science? Think, readers, how many broods of caterpillars may have been prevented from appearing by this slaughter of hundreds of the species now before us! Little wonder, grave scientific friends, that we are now discovering by degrees an "extinction of species!" Let us see to it that we are moderate in our captures, then we may expect that insects generally will be more abundant, the rare species equally with the common will be in less danger of dying entirely out from us. We do not say that many other causes do not operate in addition to the one named, to render some butterflies and moths more scarce than others; yet we do say that a great measure of this exceeding rareness, or absolute extinction, must be referred solely to the unwise conduct of collectors, whose "zeal is not according to knowledge," who catch and kill more specimens than they can possibly require for their cabinets.

NOTES OF A NATURALIST IN NOVA SCOTIA.

THE SNOW BUNTING (*Emberiza nivalis*).

BY J. MATTHEW JONES, F.S.A.

ONE of the familiar birds of our severe winter is the snow bunting. It arrives in flocks about the beginning of December; never failing to show itself when the first good snow storm clothes the country with the white mantle of winter. It generally frequents the more open and elevated spots, particularly commons, and other like places devoid of trees. No degree of cold that we have, say 20 deg. below zero, appears to be too intense for the frame of this pretty little sparrow. Often have I been cheered when driving through the blinding snow drift, some bitter midwinter's day, to see flock after flock rise before me, the only living creatures to be seen on my dreary way. Where they rest, and how they procure food during heavy storms, I have never been able to ascertain, and an ornithological friend, whose observations have extended over a period of thirty years, makes the same remark. Certain it is that the snow bunting is always to be seen busy at such times, either on the wing, or settling on some bare patch of ground which the wind in its fury keeps clear of snow. Insect life is not abroad at such times, and one would imagine that grass, and other reeds, would not be sufficiently abundant in spots where vegetation even in summer but sparingly clothes the ground. Seeds, however, it must be, that this bird exists upon, and therefore we may presume that its microscopic eye can discern such minute atoms even amidst the white powdery snow. When shot, they are generally found to be in a fat condition, which satisfactorily proves that whatever food it feeds upon, it must find it in abundance. When once winter sets in with severity earlier than is usual, the snow bunting appears sometimes as early as the middle of November, but, as I observed before, its general date may be set down as the first week in December. Throughout the winter months it continues to reside here, although should a spell of open weather occur, which frequently takes place in the month of January, owing to a succession of warm revolving gales reaching our ice-bound land from the region of the Gulf Stream; then you will lose sight of the bird for several days, for it has gone probably to the northern parts of the province, which are not affected by these southerly winds. It immediately returns with the northerly snow storm, and may be seen in a few hours after it has commenced. This circumstance makes me think that the snow bunting's life is to a great extent dependent upon snow, for the bird appears in its true element only when hurried along on the driving gale, and half hid from view by the frozen particles which whirl and eddy around. It departs from Nova Scotia about the end of March, sometimes earlier, according to the season, but I have never known them to stay until April came in. They doubtless follow the snow northward, and as it melts in each succeeding latitude as the warm rays of the springtide sun proclaim the coming summer, so they pass onwards until they reach near the parallel of 60 deg., to form their nests in the crannies of rocks, and line them with the down-like hair of the arctic fox.

THE CRUST OF THE EARTH.

YOUR correspondent, Mr. Howell, now turns his attention to geology, and asks, "Was the matter forming the crust of the earth in its earliest stage of existence in a state of fluidity?" This is an old question, and one which Pythagoras no doubt asked and studied 2,400 years ago; for the great philosopher of Samos was, I am sure, a geologist, if we are to judge from his writings. I am rather unwilling to tell your correspondent what Strabo, Fracastoro, Burnet, Whiston, Leibnitz, Vallisneri, Moro, Generelli, Hutton, Mantell, Beche, and a formidable array of others said about the crust of the earth, and the philosophical rows they instituted in tearing theories to pieces.

But, let us suppose that your correspondent is out on a ramble, or in some of the museums, and that he meets with a piece of rock, that in that rock he sees clearly a petrified plant, shell, fish, reptile, &c., &c., quite as solid as the rock in which it is embedded; surely he would begin to think, to wonder a little, to reason, to speculate a good deal, to act the geologist in full. He would wonder how the plant or animal got into the rock, and he would evidently start a hypothesis as to *the state* of the rock when the plant or animal tumbled into it. Now, sir, what would he naturally think? If he is anything of a cosmogonist I, in silence, can easily anticipate his reply. He would then dive into the crust of the earth itself, he would read Laplace, Lyell, and Liebig, become a regular geologist; still his wonder would increase, but his clear conceptions would still have to struggle with a dense impenetrable penumbra in the distance.

He would be told that our earth was, at some indefinite time, suppose 40,000,000 of years ago, a respectable ball, no less than 482,000 miles in diameter, instead of a miserable 8,000 miles, as at present! His brother geologists (some at least) will demonstrate to him that our earth was at one time a "fire-mist," a sort of mythical little *ignis fatuus*, to the philosophers at least, a mere gas bubble, floating through space.

Almost any work on geology will give your correspondent the opinions, the theories, of geologists concerning the crust of the earth, but, through all, I would advise Mr. Howell to remember that our speculative giants are, even yet, only hammering geology into something like a science, and, like the sweating Cyclops of old, forging the ponderous thunderbolts. There is still a considerable amount of noise attending the gigantic operation.

H. H. ULIDIA.

Dromore, Nov., 1869.

Remarks, Queries, &c.

The earth is full of beauty,
The flower, the shrub, the tree,
The river, with its ceaseless song,
The wild birds' melody;
The green meads, where the oxen low,
The upland, vale and lea:
The seasons, as they come and go,
Are beautiful to me.

The sea is full of beauty;
I know not charms me most,
The rippling of its peaceful wave,
Or foam, when tempest tost.
I've stood, on many a summer e'en
Entranced upon the shore,
And spell-bound oft have listened to
Its wild terrific roar.

The heavens are full of beauty,
Viewed from our earthly home,
When Sol mounts on his golden car,
Or star-gems stud the dome;
But thousand-fold more beautiful
Will those blest realms appear,
When God shall raise us to his side,
And wipe away each tear.

AARON SMITH.

DO SNAKES EAT FISH?—I have searched in several works on Natural History for an answer to this enquiry, and for the information of "J. S. A." I will jot down the result of my investigation. M. C. Cooke in his work on "British Reptiles," speaking of the common snake (Tropidonotus natrix), says:—"The snake is very fond of the water, and may often be surprised coiled up in sunny weather with its head out enjoying the luxury of a bath. It will dive after the water-newts, especially when rather hungry, bringing them to the shore in its mouth, and devouring them upon dry land. Some kinds of snake have been detected catching fish; but whether this was merely an idiosyncracy on the part of one or two individuals, or whether it is a confirmed habit, we are not in possession of sufficient evidence to determine. Such a predilection on the part of the common snake we have not yet heard of. This reptile is generally found in wet situations, or not far from water, whilst the viper evidently prefers a drier locality. We have heard of vipers being found on marshes, but are doubtful whether the creatures so called were not common snakes;" and again Sir William Jardine in his notes to Bohn's edition of "White's Selborne," writes—"that the common snake often takes to the water and swims well and boldly. Not only do they swim across the wide parts of the river Ouse, but they have been seen to swim to the Isle of Wight from the Hampshire coast, and have occasionally been seen swimming in Portsmouth Harbour. As a proof of the accuracy of Mr. White's observation, that snakes probably go into the water to procure food, I may mention that a gentlemen lately saw one of these reptiles in a stream and under some weeds, consequently under water, watching for prey. Having

observed it for some minutes he took it out of the water, when it not only emitted a most unpleasant stench, but struck at him several times like a viper." The foregoing may help to throw some light on the nature of the snakes' food, and if any of your numerous correspondents could bring forward facts bearing on the question from their own personal observations it would prove most interesting, and might tend to clear up any remaining doubts on the subject.
JOHN R. ELDRIDGE.

THE MOON'S INFLUENCE UPON THE WEATHER.—I should like to make one or two remarks upon the two interesting articles which Mr. Ulidia was kind enough to furnish us with in reply to my meteorological queries. Mr. Ulidia seems to think that the observations of the ancients lead us to the conclusion that the moon has some (at all events) amount of influence upon the weather ; he also says that the changes of the moon generally betoken a change in the weather. I must confess, that although I have heard some people say that they have noticed it to be so, that neither myself nor several of my friends have found the weather to change more at this time than any other; and I always thought that scientific men of modern times were unanimous in believing this to be a delusion—perhaps the "ancients" might have noticed more particularly "sublunary" appearances, such as the mist commonly called a "halo," that we frequently see surrounds the moon (and which we all know generally indicates wet weather) more than the direct phases of the moon itself; besides if the moon had an influence on the atmosphere, such for instance as it has upon the tides, it would be invariable, such as it is in the latter case, and if the influence were not similar how is it to be explained ; anyhow, this action of the moon on the weather remains to be explained. The idea also presents this difficulty, viz., that the moon is continually changing ; therefore, the weather would have to be continually changing also, if this theory were adopted, and we frequently have months of hot weather in the summer time, *vide* 1868. With regard to Mr. Ulidia's other article respecting the heat of the summer before last, and mildness of last winter, he seems to think that the south wind would be sufficient to cause the great heat of 1868 without any other reason ; but do we not frequently have a south wind blow in the summer without the same effects ? besides the south was not universal, but in some places a west wind ; and in the south and south-west of England an east wind prevailed during the whole of July and August, and the heat was the same there as in all other places ; so that while the south wind very probably had a great deal to do with it, especially in some places, still I think that we must not altogether attribute the heat to this cause, for the reasons that I have before stated. Hoping Mr. Ulidia will kindly favour me with a further answer to those questions, I will conclude by thanking him for his information. E. BELFORT BAX.

EFFECTS FROM A WASP'S STING.—I observed a paper in last month's issue of the NATURALIST'S NOTE BOOK, describing some very serious symptoms which followed the sting of a wasp that the writer received. That gentleman was evidently in a weak state of health at the time, or he would never have experienced the bad result, which I do not hesitate to say might have ended in death, if he had been wounded by a greater number. It is a more grave affair than people imagine to be stung by a wasp, although both the wound and the pain are inconsiderable ; yet if the health be bad, or a constitutional defect exist, this apparent trifle may close the earthly days of a man very prematurely. Only a few months ago, I read in a newspaper an account of a Scotchwoman who lived near Loch Laggan in Inverness-shire. This person kept bees, and one day, while watching them, a bee flew upon her nose, inserting its sting at the same time ; she was soon taken very ill, and shortly afterwards died. These instances show, I think, that a previous weak state of the health renders a person far more liable to occurrences of this kind, than he would be if in *sound* bodily health. Your correspondent asks how the venom is secreted ? This is accomplished in much the same way as other animal fluids. The viruent liquid is contained in a membraneous sac, of somewhat oval form, which, in *Vespa Tenesties*, is about one-eighth of an inch in length. The lower end of this poison-bag ends somewhat abruptly in a tube, and leads to the sting, which is a beautiful little instrument. It, or to speak correctly, they, for there are *two*, are nicely packed in a hollow sheath. It is the latter that is popularly supposed to be the *sting ;* but this is not the case, as a little careful dissection will clearly show. With fine needles, this is by no means a difficult operation, and success depends more upon a knowledge of anatomy, than upon manual dexterity. The sting will be seen to consist of three parts, the sheath and its two barbs, which are arranged admirably, so as to combine thinness with strength and celerity of movement. The manner in which the insect stings is the following :—Having flown upon the face, or other exposed part, it projects the sheath slightly into the skin, by strong muscular action. The serrated barbs being guided by the sheath, dart deeply and repeatedly into the flesh, while the poison is freely poured into the lacerated wound from the gland, which is contracted by the same action of the muscles. If Mr. Bingham possess a microscope, he will be surprised and pleased with the wonders of insect structure that it will reveal to him, and he may there view with delight those terrible weapons of the Ground Wasp, which, but for Providence, had so nearly proved fatal to him. Should such a circumstance occur to any of your readers, I would suggest that they should rub either a little olive oil or ammonia on the wound. VERITAS.

THE DEATH WATCH.—I gather, from Mr. Day's article, in page 14, that there is considerable doubt as to what insect causes the strange ticking which secures for the performer the above name. In that article, Mr. Day records the capture of *Anobium Tesselatum*, when searching for the mysterious insect. The Death Watch has also been described as a small brown beetle, in the answers to correspondents in various magazines. One evening recently, while sitting quietly in a house in this town, I had the pleasure of hearing the distant watch-like sound which is so alarming to some weak and ignorant persons. I had previously heard the sounds, but had been unsuccessful in my search for the cause of them. An intelligent companion enquired if I knew what caused the ticking. "Certainly," I replied; "it is a small brown beetle." To this my friend objected, urging that the sounds proceeded from a spider. I then produced Mr. Day's articles, and a paragraph by Miss Watney, to show that I was right. Nothing daunted, my friend challenged me to a search for the insect itself. Of course I was only too happy to avail myself of this best of plans for clearing up a disputed point, for personal observation is better than articles or paragraphs guaranteed by the best authorities. After a patient search, we traced the sounds to proceed from a picture-frame which hung upon one of the walls. The frame was thereupon carefully removed to the centre of the table, and, to be quite certain that we had not lost the insect in shifting, we halted in our operations till we heard the insect in its new position; then, removing the paper which was pasted on the back of the picture, we sought diligently, and found a small spider. I was still incredulous, and examined every corner and crevice, but without result. Of course my friend was more confirmed than ever, and I was left in a state of doubt. Since that evening, I have asked nearly a score of persons about the Death-Watch, and have been told, in every case, that the ticking was caused by spiders. Yesterday I was in a neighbouring town, and asked a friend there on the subject. He instantly replied, that the Death-Watch was a spider, for he had looked for the insect, and found it. Will some entomologist kindly give me his opinion on the subject.

Castle Cary. W. MACMILLAN.

DEATH BEFORE THE FALL.—What is the opinion of your readers as to the occurrence of death in the animal world prior to the fall of man? We can hardly imagine the peaceful serenity of the first garden disturbed by the roar of the enraged lion feasting on the mangled remains of the playful fawn, or the shrill screams of the songster, borne aloft in the bloody talons of the rapacious hawk, nor yet that the language of scripture relating to the millennial age is entirely figurative. Still it is unlikely that their bodily structures were so suddenly changed after that event. Death must have occurred in the insect creation, and geology assures us that animals preyed upon one another ages before man became an inhabitant of the globe. R. B. W.

FISHING (An Anecdote).—Alphonso was fishing. He had flung over the parapet of a bridge his slender line armed with a hook, and fitted with a quill float, and he waited patiently upon fortune. To him there arrived the sprightly Theodore: "Alphonso, friend of my soul!" remarked the latter, "what sport have you had?" "Not even," said Alphonso, with a deep sigh, as he sent his float yet once again down its swim, "not even a celebrated Carthaginian General!" "Indeed!" said Theodore. "Are there many of that sort of fish in these waters?" "I did not," said Alphonso, with a grave smile, "mean a fish: I meant *An-nibble!*" YORICK.

HEAT OF THE SUN.—Can any correspondent give us anything new as to the origin of the sun's heat? Is it not entirely fabulous to suppose that the sun is a vast body of fire, with heat-rays constantly rushing from it to the earth, or that it throws off heat-rays from an incandescent atmosphere? As light cannot exist without a proportionate amount of heat, is there any better theory than that of friction, or chemical action of the rays of light with the earth's atmosphere? R. B. W.

ACHERONTIA ATROPOS.—Can any of your readers tell me the best method of keeping the pupæ of *A. Atropos* (Death's Head Hawk-moth) so as to bring them to their perfect state? I have heard that they will not come to perfection after the cell is broken; is there any truth in this statement? I have several larvæ which were dug out of the ground, an exit of which I am anxiously awaiting. HAWK-MOTH.

Having heard it remarked in several instances of the plentifulness of the pupæ of the Death's Head Moth (*A. Atropos*) in several parts of the country, I wish to inform your readers it has been as plentiful in Norfolk, I having myself obtained 30 very fine specimens, and shall be most happy to make exchanges with any friends for pupæ of any other Hawk-moths, excepting *S. Ocellatus*, *S. Papuli*, *S. Filiæ*, and *S. Ligustri*, or chrysalis of *P. Machaon*.

Ivory Street, Norwich. W. SEARLES.

LATEST HUMAN REMAINS.—Can any geologist inform me whether any of the bones of the antediluvians, or other traces of the existence of man before the Flood, have been discovered? When were the last human remains disinterred, and to what age were they supposed to belong? R. B. W.

POWER OF STEAM.—Is the force of compressed *steam*, or *hot air*, unlimited? Could they burst any vessel in which they were confined, without a means of escape? R. B. W.

WHEAT.—Will any correspondent kindly inform me whether the most useful of our cerials is a native of this country, or where does it grow wild, and when was it introduced into England? R. B. W.

MESMERISM.—Will any reader give his opinion as to what Mesmerism, or Animal Magnetism, is? Who was Mesner, and what was his theory of the "odic force"? R. B. W.

"VALLEY OF DEATH."—Will some reader of the NOTE BOOK favour us with a short account of the "Valley of Death" in the island of Java—where situated—when last visited—and the cause of the accumulation of carbonic acid? R. B. W.

WHITE MICE.—Can anyone oblige me with information concerning the habits and localities of white mice and rats, dormice, and Guinea-pigs? R. B. W.

Will any of your readers oblige me with the name of a work on zoology which gives an account, or reference, to all the known species of mammalia and birds on the globe? Also, which is the best *educational* manual in this science. R. B. W.

COLOUR.—As it is generally believed that colour can only be produced by the action of rays of light on solid bodies, must not all precious stones and metals, as well as marine plants, shells, &c., be colourless, unless exposed to the light of day? R. B. W.

www.ingramcontent.com/pod-product-compliance
Lightning Source LLC
Chambersburg PA
CBHW060234240426
43663CB00040B/2611